Map 3 Europe After the Congress of Vienna, 1815

The major European powers re-drew the map of Europe with the Congress of Vienna in 1815 after the defeat of Napoleon. This map shows the dismantlement of the massive empire France had acquired under his leadership.

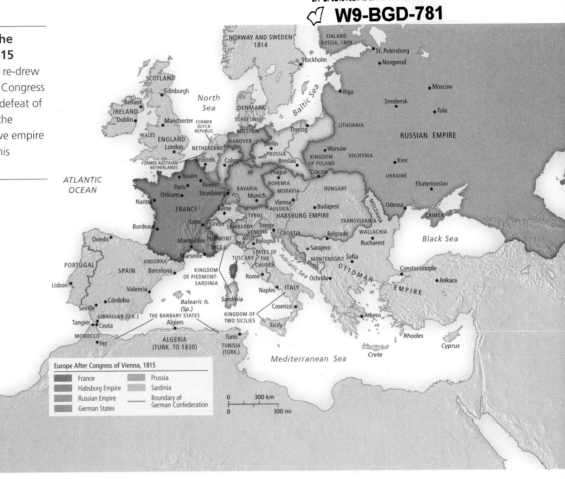

Map 4 Europe After World War I

The map of Europe changed dramatically after World War I with the collapse of the old authoritarian empires and the creation of independent nation-states in eastern Europe. What neither Map 3 nor Map 4 can show, however, is the expansion of "the West" beyond European borders to embrace cultures on other continents, including Australia, Africa, and North America.

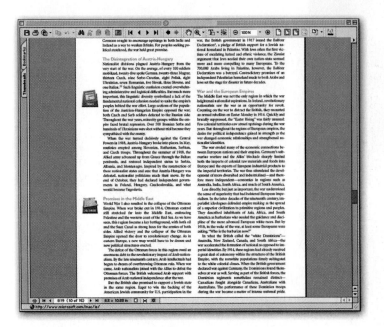

Would your life be easier if you had an electronic version of your textbook?

MyHistoryLab contains the complete text with icons that link to selected sources. You can print sections of the text to read anytime, anywhere.

Are you overwhelmed by the time it takes to find primary source documents, images, and maps for your research papers?

MyHistoryLab contains over 1,100 documents, images, maps, and video clips—all in one place—to help make writing your research paper easier and more effective and to help you better understand the course material.

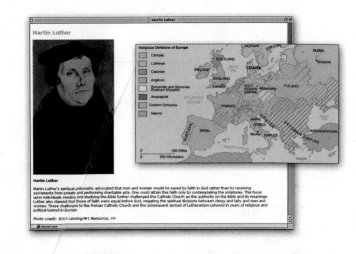

Are you sometimes overwhelmed when you study for exams?

MyHistoryLab provides an integrated quizzing and testing program that includes chapter pre-tests, post-tests, and exams. A customized study plan, generated from the chapter pre-tests and post-tests, shows what you've mastered as well as where you need more work. Look for these icons in MyHistoryLab.

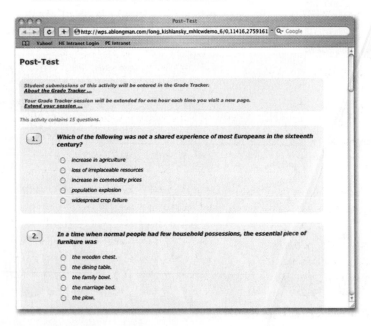

THE WEST

The Tutor Center
Addison-Wesley • Allyn & Bacon • Benjamin Cummings • Longman

Need extra help during evening hours?

Get help from The Tutor Center when your instructor is often unavailable—5 pm to midnight, Sunday through Thursday, spring and fall terms (Sunday through Wednesday, summer term). Tutors can help you navigate MyHistoryLab or review your paper for organization, grammar, and mechanics.

Did your professor assign other books to read?

MyHistoryLab allows you to read, download, or print over fifty of the most commonly assigned works for this course—all at no additional cost! The following titles are all available on History Bookshelf.

1. *Aesop's Fables* (c. 500 BCE)
2. *Histories*, Herodotus (c. 450 BCE)
3. *Lysistrata*, Aristophanes (c. 448 BCE)
4. *The Oedipus Trilogy*, Sophocles (c. 425 BCE)
5. *The Republic*, Plato (360 BCE)
6. *The Ethics of Aristotle* (c. 350 BCE)
7. *The Bhagavad-Gita* (c. 100 CE)
8. *The Iliad*, Homer (c. 800 BCE)
9. *The Upanishads* (c. 600 BCE)
10. *Letters of Marcus Tullius Cicero* (c. 45 CE)
11. *De Agricultura*, Marcus Cato (141 CE)
12. *The Lives of Plutarch* (c. 200 CE)
13. *The Confessions of St. Augustine* (401 CE)
14. *The Secret History of the Court of Justinian*, Procopius (558 CE)
15. *The Arabian Nights* (c. 800 CE)
16. *Beowulf* (c. 1000 CE)
17. *Four Arthurian Romances*, De Troyes, (c. 1170)

18. *The Song of Roland* (c. 1200 CE)
19. *The Prince*, Machiavelli *(1505)*
20. *95 Theses,* Martin Luther (1517)
21. *Romeo and Juliet*, Shakespeare (c. 1590)
22. *The Essays of Francis Bacon* (1601)
23. *Leviathan*, Thomas Hobbes (1651)
24. *When London Burned*, G.A. Henty (1665)
25. *Captivity and Restoration*, Mary Rowlandson (1682)
26. *Treatise on Government*, John Locke (1690)
27. *Gulliver's Travels*, Jonathan Swift (1726)
28. *Three Sermons*, Jonathan Swift (1750)
29. *An Inquiry into the Slave Trade*, Anthony Benezet (1771)
30. *Wealth of Nations*, Adam Smith (1776)
31. *Pilgrim's Progress*, John Bunyan (1794)
32. *Sense and Sensibility*, Jane Austen (1811)
33. *The Napoleon of the People*, Honore Balzac (1812)
34. *The Afghan Wars*, Forbes (1839)
35. *The Communist Manifesto*, Karl Marx (1848)

36. *Origin of Species*, Charles Darwin (1859)
37. *Narrative of the Overland Expedition to Northern Queensland*, Fredrick Byerley (1867)
38. *Japanese Manners and Customs*, J. Silver (1867)
39. *20,000 Leagues Under the Sea*, Jules Verne (1870)
40. *To the Gold Coast for Gold*, Sir Richard Burton (1883)
41. *The Jungle Book*, Rudyard Kipling (1894)
42. *Heart of Darkness*, Joseph Conrad (1899)
43. *Moorish Literature*, Rene Basset (1901)
44. *River Wars of the Sudan*, Winston Churchill (1902)
45. *The Woman Who Toils*, Vorst (1903)
46. *Congo Free State*, Marcus Dorman (1905)
47. *The Beginnings of Israeli History*, Kent & Jenks (1912)
48. *Clairvoyance*, Swami Panchadasi (1916)
49. *The Psychology of Dreams*, Sigmund Freud (1920)
50. *A Biography of Simon Bolivar*, Sherwell, (1921)

Now, flip through *The West: Encounters & Transformations*. You will find the icons shown on the opposite page. Each icon will direct you to a place in MyHistoryLab to help you better understand the material. For example, when reading about 19th-century European politics, you may find an icon that links you to an original source document by Martin Luther or Karl Marx.

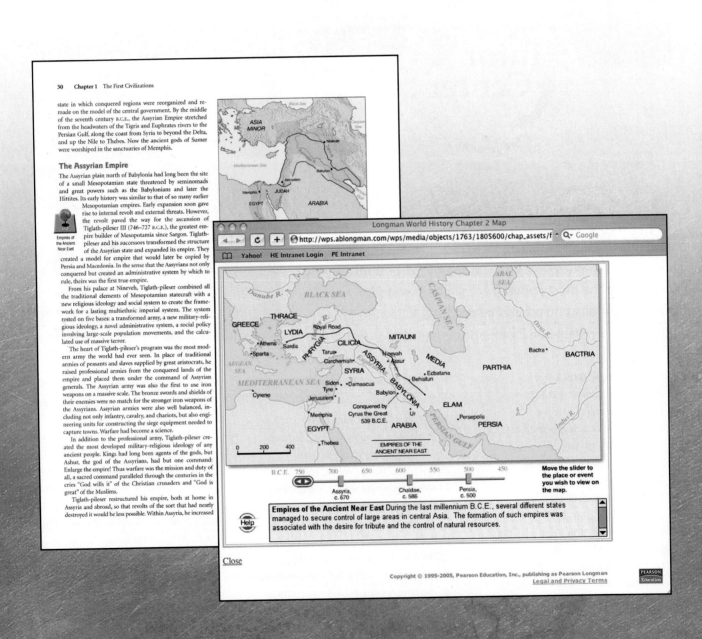

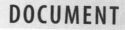

DOCUMENT

This icon directs students to primary source documents that support the material they are reading. In addition, the documents offer headnotes and analysis questions to focus students' reading.

IMAGE

Photos, cartoons, and artwork offer students opportunities to learn the course content in a more visual way. Each image includes a headnote and analysis questions.

MAP

Interactive maps with headnotes and questions help students visualize the material they are studying. Atlas maps and printable map activities from a Longman workbook give students hands-on experience.

VIDEO CLIP

Historical video clips are included, along with headnotes and thoughtful questions.

THE WEST

Encounters & Transformations

Second Edition

Brian Levack
University of Texas at Austin

Edward Muir
Northwestern University

Meredith Veldman
Louisiana State University

Michael Maas
Rice University

PEARSON

Longman

New York   San Francisco   Boston
London   Toronto   Sydney   Tokyo   Singapore   Madrid
Mexico City   Munich   Paris   Cape Town   Hong Kong   Montreal

Senior Acquisitions Editor: Janet Lanphier
Senior Development Editor: David B. Kear
Executive Marketing Manager: Sue Westmoreland
Supplements Editor: Kristi Olson
Media Editor: Melissa Edwards
Production Manager: Donna DeBenedictis
Project Coordination, Text Design, and Electronic Page Makeup:
    Elm Street Publishing Services, Inc.
Cover Designer/Manager: John Callahan
Cover and Frontispiece Art: Moors and Christians play chess, alterpiece of San Nicolas,
    14th c., Mallorca, Spain. © Ancient Art and Architecture Collection, Ltd.
Cartography: Maps.com
Photo Researcher: Photosearch, Inc.
Manufacturing Buyer: Roy L. Pickering, Jr.
Printer and Binder: Quebecor World Versailles
Cover Printer: Coral Graphic Services, Inc.

Library of Congress Cataloging-in-Publication Data

The West : encounters & transformations / Brian Levack . . . [et al.].
    2nd ed.
        p. cm.
    Includes bibliographical references and index.
    ISBN 0-321-36404-X
    1. Civilization, Western—History—Textbooks.   I. Levack, Brian P.

CB245.W456 2007
909'.09821—dc22
                                                    2005032587

Please visit us at http://www.ablongman.com/levack2e

ISBN 0-321-36404-X (single-volume edition)
ISBN 0-321-36405-8 (volume I)
ISBN 0-321-38413-X (volume II)
ISBN 0-321-38414-8 (volume A)
ISBN 0-321-38415-6 (volume B)
ISBN 0-321-36403-1 (volume C)

1 2 3 4 5 6 7 8 9 10—QWV—09 08 07 06

Brief Contents

Detailed Contents

11 The Italian Renaissance and Beyond: The Politics of Culture   342

12 The West and the World: The Significance of Global Encounters, 1450–1650   376

23 The West and the World: Cultural Crisis and the New Imperialism, 1870–1914   742

24 The First World War   776

Documents

Maps

Features

Chronologies

Preface

We wrote this textbook to answer questions about the identity of the civilization in which we live. Journalists, politicians, and scholars often refer to our civilization, its political ideologies, its economic systems, and its cultures as "Western" without fully considering what that label means and why it might be appropriate. The classification of our civilization as Western has become particularly problematic in the age of globalization. The creation of international markets, the rapid dissemination of ideas on a global scale, and the transmission of popular culture from one country to another often make it difficult to distinguish what is Western from what is not. *The West: Encounters & Transformations* offers students a history of Western civilization in which these issues of Western identity are given prominence. Our goal is neither to idealize nor to indict that civilization but to describe its main characteristics in different historical periods.

The West: Encounters & Transformations gives careful consideration to two basic questions. The first is, how did the definition of the West change over time? In what ways did its boundaries shift and how did the distinguishing characteristics of its cultures change? The second question is, by what means did the West—and the idea of the West—develop? We argue that the West is the product of a series of cultural encounters that occurred both outside and within its geographical boundaries. We explore these encounters and the transformations they produced by detailing the political, social, religious, and cultural history of the regions that have been, at one time or another, a part of the West.

Defining the West

What is the West? How did it come into being? How has it developed throughout history? Many textbooks take for granted which regions or peoples of the globe constitute the West. They treat the history of the West as a somewhat expanded version of European history. While not disputing the centrality of Europe to any definition of the West, we contend that the West is not only a geographical realm with ever-shifting boundaries but also a cultural realm, an area of cultural influence extending beyond the geographical and political boundaries of Europe. We so strongly believe in this notion that we have written the essay "What Is the West?" to encourage students to think about their understanding of Western civilization and to guide their understanding of each chapter. Many of the features of what we call Western civilization originated in regions that are not geographically part of Europe (such as northern Africa and the Middle East), while ever since the fifteenth century various social, ethnic, and political groups from non-European regions (such as North and South America, eastern Russia, Australia, New Zealand, and South Africa) have identified themselves, in one way or another, with the West. Throughout the text, we devote considerable attention to the boundaries of the West and show how borderlines between cultures have been created, especially in eastern and southeastern Europe.

Considered as a geographical and cultural realm, "the West" is a term of recent origin, and the civilization to which it refers did not become clearly defined until the eleventh century, especially during the Crusades, when western European Christians developed a distinct cultural identity. Before that time we can only talk about the powerful forces that created the West, especially the dynamic interaction of the civilizations of western Europe, the Byzantine Empire, and the Muslim world.

Over the centuries Western civilization has acquired many salient characteristics. These include two of the world's great legal systems (civil law and common law), three of the world's monotheistic religions (Judaism, Christianity, and Islam), certain political and social philosophies, forms of political organization (such as the modern bureaucratic state and democracy), methods of scientific inquiry, systems of economic organization (such as industrial capitalism), and distinctive styles of art, architecture, and music. At times one or more of these characteristics has served as a primary source of Western identity: Christianity in the Middle Ages, science and rationalism during the Enlightenment, industrialization in the nineteenth and twentieth centuries, and a defense of individual liberty and democracy in the late twentieth century. These sources of Western identity, however, have always been challenged and contested, both when they were coming into prominence and when they appeared to be most triumphant. Western culture has never been monolithic, and even today references to the West imply a wide range of meanings.

Cultural Encounters

The definition of the West is closely related to the central theme of our book, which is the process of cultural encounters. Throughout *The West: Encounters & Transformations,* we examine the West as a product of a series of cultural encounters both outside the West and within it. We show that the West originated and developed through a continuous process of inclusion and exclusion resulting from a series of encounters among and within different groups. These encounters can be described in a general sense as external, internal, or ideological.

External Encounters

External encounters took place between peoples of different civilizations. Before the emergence of the West as a clearly defined entity, external encounters occurred between such diverse peoples as Greeks and Phoenicians, Macedonians and Egyptians, and Romans and Celts. After the eleventh century, external encounters between Western and non-Western peoples occurred mainly during periods of European exploration, expansion, and imperialism. In the sixteenth and seventeenth centuries, for example, a series of external encounters took place between Europeans on the one hand and Africans, Asians, and the indigenous people of the Americas on the other. Two chapters of *The West: Encounters & Transformations* (Chapters 12 and 17) and a large section of a third (Chapter 23) explore these external encounters in depth and discuss how they affected Western and non-Western civilizations alike.

Internal Encounters

Our discussion of encounters also includes similar interactions between different social groups *within* Western countries. These internal encounters often took place between dominant and subordinate groups, such as between lords and peasants, rulers and subjects, men and women, factory owners and workers, masters and slaves. Encounters between those who were educated and those who were illiterate, which recur frequently throughout Western history, also fall into this category. Encounters just as often took place between different religious and political groups, such as between Christians and Jews, Catholics and Protestants, and royal absolutists and republicans.

Ideological Encounters

Ideological encounters involve interaction between comprehensive systems of thought, most notably religious doctrines, political philosophies, and scientific theories about the nature of the world. These ideological conflicts usually arose out of internal encounters, when various groups within Western societies subscribed to different theories of government or rival religious faiths. The encounters between Christianity and polytheism in the early Middle Ages, between liberalism and conservatism in the nineteenth century, and between fascism and communism in the twentieth century were ideological encounters. Some ideological encounters had an external dimension, such as when the forces of Islam and Christianity came into conflict during the Crusades and when the Cold War developed between Soviet communism and Western democracy in the second half of the twentieth century.

* * *

The West: Encounters & Transformations illuminates the variety of these encounters and clarifies their effects. By their very nature encounters are interactive, but they have taken different forms: they have been violent or peaceful, coercive or cooperative. Some have resulted in the imposition of Western ideas on areas outside the geographical boundaries of the West or the perpetuation of the dominant culture within Western societies. More often than not, however, encounters have resulted in a more reciprocal process of exchange in which both Western and non-Western cultures or the values of both dominant and subordinate groups have undergone significant transformation. Our book not only identifies these encounters but also discusses their significance by returning periodically to the issue of Western identity.

Coverage

The West: Encounters & Transformations offers both balanced coverage of political, social, and culture history and a broader coverage of the West and the world.

Balanced Coverage

Our goal throughout the text has been to provide balanced coverage of political, social, and cultural history and to include significant coverage of religious and military history as well. Political history defines the basic structure of the book, and some chapters, such as those on the Hellenistic world, the age of confessional divisions, absolutism and state building, the French Revolution, and the coming of mass politics, include sustained political narratives. Because we understand the West to be a cultural as well as a geographical realm, we give a prominent position to cultural history. Thus we include rich sections on Hellenistic philosophy and literature, the cultural environment of the Italian Renaissance, the creation of a new political culture at the time of the French Revolution, and the atmosphere of cultural despair and desire that prevailed in Europe after World War I. We also devote special attention to religious history, including the history of Islam as well as that of Christianity and Judaism. Unlike many other textbooks, our coverage of religion continues into the modern period.

The West: Encounters & Transformations also provides extensive coverage of the history of women and gender. Wherever possible the history of women is integrated into the broader social, cultural, and political history of the period. But there are also separate sections on women in our chapters on classical Greece, the Renaissance, the Reformation, the Enlightenment, the Industrial Revolution, World War I, World War II, and the postwar era.

The West and the World

Our book provides broad geographical coverage. Because the West is the product of a series of encounters, the external areas with which the West interacted are of major importance. Three chapters deal specifically with the West and the world.

- Chapter 12, "The West and the World: The Significance of Global Encounters, 1450–1650"
- Chapter 17, "The West and the World: Empire, Trade, and War, 1650–1815"
- Chapter 23, "The West and the World: Cultural Crisis and the New Imperialism, 1870–1914"

These chapters present substantial material on sub-Saharan Africa, Latin America, the Middle East, India, and East Asia. Our text is also distinctive in its coverage of eastern Europe and the Muslim world, areas that have often been considered outside the boundaries of the West. These regions were arenas within which significant cultural encounters took place. Finally we include material on the United States and Australia, both of which have become part of the West. We recognize that most American college and university students have the opportunity to study American history as a separate subject, but treatment of the United States as a Western nation provides a different perspective from that usually given in courses on American history. For example, this book treats America's revolution as one of four Atlantic revolutions, its national unification in the nineteenth century as part of a broader western European development, its pattern of industrialization as related to that of Britain, and its central role in the Cold War as part of an ideological encounter that was global in scope.

Organization

The chronological and thematic organization of our book conforms in its broad outline to the way in which Western civilization courses are generally taught. We have limited the number of chapters to twenty-eight, in an effort to make the book more compatible with the traditional American semester calendar and to solve the frequent complaint that there is not enough time to cover all the material in the course. However, our organization differs from other books in some significant ways:

- Chapter 2, which covers the period from ca. 1600 to 550 B.C.E., is the first in a Western civilization textbook to examine the International Bronze Age and its aftermath as a period important in its own right because it saw the creation of expansionist, multi-ethnic empires linked by trade and diplomacy.
- In Chapter 4 the Roman Republic, in keeping with contemporary scholarship, has been incorporated into a discussion of the Hellenistic world, dethroned slightly to emphasize how it was one of many competing Mediterranean civilizations.
- Chapter 12 covers the first period of European expansion, from 1450 to 1650. It examines the new European encounters with the civilizations of sub-Saharan Africa, the Americas, and East Asia. By paying careful attention to the characteristics of these civilizations before the arrival of the Europeans, we show how this encounter affected indigenous peoples as well as Europeans.
- Chapter 16 is devoted entirely to the Scientific Revolution of the seventeenth century in order to emphasize the central importance of this development in the creation of Western identity.
- Chapter 17, which covers the second period of European expansion, from 1650 to 1815, studies the growth of European empires, the beginning of global warfare, and encounters between Europeans and the peoples of Asia and Africa. It treats the Atlantic revolutions of the late eighteenth and early nineteenth centuries, including

the American Revolution, as episodes in the history of European empires rather than as revolts inspired mainly by national sentiment.

- Chapter 26 not only offers a comprehensive examination of World War II, but also explores the moral fissure in the history of the West created, in very different ways, by the Holocaust and the aerial bombings of civilian centers that culminated in the use of the atomic bomb in August 1945.

- Chapter 28, "The West in the Contemporary Era: New Encounters and Transformations," includes an extended discussion of the emergence of European Islamic communities and the resulting transformations in both European and Islamic identities.

What's New in this Edition?

In preparing the second edition of *The West: Encounters & Transformations* we have focused on two goals: to make the textbook more teachable and to strengthen our emphasis on the encounters that have transformed the West.

Organization

We have reduced the number of chapters from twenty-nine to twenty-eight, in order to make the book even more compatible with the typical fifteen-week semester. In a number of chapters, moreover, we have made significant rearrangements of material:

- In Chapter 3, we have discussed the Persian Empire before beginning our study of Hebrew and Greek civilizations to emphasize the argument that the latter two civilizations emerged in a political world dominated by Persia.

- Chapters 6 through 9, which deal with the period from about 300 to 1300 C.E., have been rearranged along more thematic, less chronological lines. We have adopted this strategy to emphasize the importance of the interactions among different religious communities during a period that was crucial to the development of Christianity and Islam.

- Chapter 17, "The West and the World: Empire, Trade, and War, 1650–1815," which appeared as Chapter 19 in the first edition, has been placed earlier in the book because it is concerned mainly with eighteenth-century developments. It now precedes the discussion of eighteenth-century society and culture.

- In Chapter 22, "The Coming of Mass Politics: Industrialization, Emancipation, and Instability, 1870–1914," we have replaced the "nation-by-nation" narrative with a thematic approach that more effectively conveys the processes by which European elites sought both to capitalize on and control the new forces of popular nationalism.

- Our treatment of both the Holocaust and the decision to use atomic bombs against Japan, which appeared as a separate chapter in the first edition, is now embedded in Chapter 26, "World War II." This volume still includes a far more extensive and in-depth exploration of these developments than any other Western civilization textbook.

- New sections on "Postwar Nationalism, Westernization, and the Islamic Challenge" in Chapter 25, and "Islam, Terrorism, and European Identity" in Chapter 28 are the most striking examples of our decision to give more coverage to Islam throughout the book.

New Feature: "Encounters & Transformations"

We have introduced a new feature, "Encounters & Transformations," in about half the chapters. These essays reinforce the main theme of the book by giving specific examples of the ways in which cultural encounters changed the perception and identity of the West.

Features and Pedagogical Aids

In writing this textbook we have endeavored to keep both the student reader and the classroom instructor in mind at all times. The text includes the following features and pedagogical aids, all of which are intended to support the themes of the book.

What Is the West?

MANY OF THE PEOPLE WHO INFLUENCE PUBLIC OPINION—POLITI- cians, teachers, clergy, journalists, and television commenta- tors—refer to "Western values," "the West," and "Western civilization." They often use these terms as if they do not re- quire explanation. But what *do* these terms mean? The West has always been an arena within which different cultures, religions, values, and philosophies have interacted, and any definition of the West will inevitably arouse controversy.

The most basic definition of the West is of a place. Western civilization is now typically thought to comprise the regions of Europe, the Americas, Australia, and New Zealand. However, this is a contemporary definition of the West. The inclusion of these places in the West is the result of a long history of European expansion through colonization. In addition to being a place, Western civilization also encompasses a cultural history—a tradition stretching back thousands of years to the ancient world. Over this long period the civilization we now identify as Western gradually took shape. The

"What Is the West?"

The West: Encounters & Transformations begins with an essay to en- gage students in the task of defining the West and to introduce them to the notion of cultural encounters. "What Is the West?" guides stu- dents through the text by providing a framework for understanding how the West was shaped. Structured around the six questions of What? When? Where? Who? How? and Why?, this framework en- courages students to think about their understanding of Western civilization. The essay serves as a blueprint for using this textbook.

New! "Encounters & Transformations"

These features, which appear in about half the chapters, illustrate the main theme of the book by identifying specific encounters and showing how they led to significant transformations in the culture of the West. These features show, for example, how encounters among nomadic tribes of Arabia led to the rapid spread of Islam; how the Mayas' interpretation of Christian symbols transformed European Christianity into a hybrid religion; how the importation of chocolate from the New World to Europe changed Western consumption patterns and the rhythms of the Atlantic econ- omy; and how Picasso's encounter with African art led to the transformation of modernism. Each of these essays concludes with a question for discus- sion.

Encounters & Transformations

Ships of the Desert: Camels from Morocco to Central Asia

A remarkable thing happened when the Arab followers of the dynamic new religion of Islam encountered the humble beast of burden the camel. The camel helped make Arab armies lethal in battle, which meant that the mes- sage of Islam spread rapidly through conquest. In addition the caravan trade that transported goods on the backs of camels brought the Arabs into contact with a vast stretch of the world from Spain to China. In the ex- changes that took place along the caravan routes, Islamic religious ideas were widely disseminated, and Arab merchants gained access to a lucrative trade that enriched Muslim cities. The success of the caravan trade changed the very appearance of large parts of the West by making obsolete the old Roman roads and the shipping lanes that had unified the Mediterranean, Europe, and North Africa in the ancient world. Narrow camel tracks replaced roads; oases and cities along the caravan routes supplanted ports in economic significance.

Before Muhammad began to re- cite, the camel had already trans- formed the life of Arabia. Camels were highly efficient beasts of bur- den, especially in arid regions, be- cause of their bodies' capacity to conserve water. Able to drink as much as twenty-eight gallons at a time, camels can last four to nine days without water and travel great distances in this period. The fat in their humps allows camels to survive for even longer without food. As pack animals, camels are more efficient than carts pulled by animals because they can traverse roadless rough terrain and cross

rivers without bridges. They re- quire fewer people to manage them on a journey than do wheeled vehicles.

Arab fighters were especially menacing because they developed the "North Arabian saddle" that let them ride the one-humped Arabian camel with comfort in battle. The new saddle required only one rider who could grasp the camel's reins with one hand while slashing downward at enemy troops with a sword in his other hand. Warriors on camels could attack infantry with speed and crushing force. By 300 C.E., camel-breeding Arab tribesmen, empowered by their new military technology, inaugu- rated the "Caravan Age." The Arabs seized control of the lucrative spice trade routes and became an eco- nomic, military, and political force by exploiting and guarding the wealth of the caravans.

After Muhammad established his community in Mecca, Islam literally "took off" on camelback. Tribes- men on camels proved an unstop- pable force as they spread Islam first throughout Arabia and the Middle East, and then with light- ning speed across North Africa into Spain and Central Asia. Camels played a significant role in the expanding Islamic economy be- cause they made long-distance trade extremely profitable. The transformations the camel brought were most evident in the former

Roman provinces wh mous Roman roads h primary conduit of la Thousands of miles c nected the provinces Empire and let troop: from one front to and ever, camels changec Because these "ships do not need paved r routes did not have t Roman road systems, chants bypassed then New trade routes acr and other harsh terra to camels quickly de Morocco to Central A astonishing consequc 700 paved roads start pear. Because camels walk on narrow path streets and wide mar carts and wagons tha Greek and Roman cit use. Bazaars with nar lanes appropriate to (sprung up to replace and wheeled vehicles peared in these lands just roads and the sh; that changed. There consequences as wel caravan traffic reache China, bringing Chin; Chinese ideas to the

Question for I How might the history have differed had not c replaced the system of

The Camel Caravan
This modern photograph shows a string of camels cross-

Focus Questions

The introduction to each chapter includes a state- ment of the main question that the entire chapter addresses. It also includes a set of questions that the individual sections of the chapter seek to answer. Each of these questions is then repeated at the begin- ning of the relevant section of the chapter. The reason for this strategy is to remind the student that the purpose of studying history is not only to learn what happened in the past but also to explain and in- terpret the course of events. This pedagogical strat- egy reinforces the approach that the essay, "What is the West?," introduces at the beginning of the book.

"Justice in History"

Found in every chapter, this feature presents a his- torically significant trial or episode in which different notions of justice (or injustice) were debated and resolved. The "Justice in History" features illustrate cultural encounters within communities as they try to determine the fate of individuals from all walks of life. Many famous trials dealt with conflicts over basic religious, philosophical, or political values, such as those of Socrates, Jesus, Joan of Arc, Charles I, Galileo, and Adolf Eichmann. Other "Justice in History" features show how judicial institutions, such as the ordeal, the Inquisition, and revolutionary tribunals, handled adversarial situations in different societies. These essays, therefore, illustrate the way in which the basic values of the West have evolved through attempts to resolve disputes, contention, and conflict.

Each "Justice in History" feature includes two pedagogical aids. "Questions of Justice" helps students explore the historical significance of the episode just examined. These questions can also be used in classroom discussion or as student essay topics. "Taking It Further" provides the student with a few references that can be consulted in connection with a research project.

"The Human Body in History"

Found in about half of the chapters, these features show that the human body, which many people tend to understand solely as a product of biology, also has a history. These essays reveal that the ways in which various religious and political groups have represented the body in art and literature, clothed it, treated it medically, and abused it tell a great deal about the history of Western culture. These features include essays on the classical nude male body, the signs of disease during the Black Death, bathing the body in the East and the West, and the contraceptive pill. Concluding each essay is a single question for discussion that directs students back to the broader issues with which the chapter deals.

Primary Source Documents

In each chapter we have presented a number of excerpts from primary source documents—from "Tales of the Flood" to "Darwin's 'Descent of Man'"—in order to reinforce or expand upon the points made in the text and to introduce students to the basic materials of historical research.

Maps and Illustrations

Artwork is a key component of our book. We recognize that many students often lack a strong familiarity with geography, and so we have taken great care to develop maps that help sharpen their geographic skills. Complementing the book's standard map program,

Justice in History

The Trial of Joan of Arc

After only fifteen months as the inspiration of the French army, Joan of Arc fell into the hands of the English, who brought her to trial for witchcraft. The English needed to stage a kind of show trial to demonstrate to their own demoralized forces that Joan's remarkable victories had been the result not of military superiority but rather of witchcraft. In the English trial, conducted at Rouen in 1431, Joan testified that her mission to save France was in response to voices she heard that commanded her to wear men's clothing. On the basis of this evidence of a confused or double gender identity, the ecclesiastical tribunal declared her a witch and a relapsed heretic. The court sentenced her to be burned at the stake.

Political motivations governed the 1431 English trial for witchcraft, but Joan's [...] vides some clues [...] tity conflicts. The [...] evidence against [...] resulted in her c[...] spiritual "voices" [...] hear and her cro[...] men's clothing.

From the begi[...] emergence onto [...] Joan's voices intr[...] came into contac[...] claimed that she [...] voices of St. Cath[...] and the Archang[...] Joan, these voice[...] of divine comma[...] the English judge[...] demonstrate that [...] not from God bu[...] they could prove[...] had evidence of [...] cery. Following s[...] ial guidelines, the[...] authentic messag[...] would always co[...] dogma. Any devi[...] doctrines would [...] dence of demoni[...]

distinctions that were alien to her. When they wanted to know if the voices were those of angels or saints, Joan seemed perplexed and responded, "This voice comes from God . . . I am more afraid of failing the voices by saying what is displeasing to them than answering you."⁷ The judges kept pushing, asking if the saints or angels had heads, eyes, and hair. Exasperated, Joan simply replied, "I have told you often enough, believe me if you will."

The judges reformulated Joan's words to reflect their own rigid scholastic categories and concluded that her "veneration of the saints seems to partake of idolatry and to proceed from a pact made with devils. These are less divine revelations than lies invented by Joan, suggested or shown to her by the demon in illusive appari-

to prove bad behavi[...] ing that a young ma[...] to marry her on acc[...] moral life. They asse[...] godmother was a no[...] who had taught her [...] of these ploys work[...] because Joan consist[...] these charges. She d[...] admit to one allegati[...] dressed as a man.

Some of the charg[...] and many of the que[...] asked concerned hov[...]

The said Joan put [...] tirely abandoned [...] clothes, with her l[...] short and round [...] of young men, she[...] breeches, doublet, [...] joined together, lo[...] tened to the said [...] twenty points, lon[...] laced on the outsi[...]

The Human Body in History

The Ecstasy of Teresa of Avila: The Body and the Soul

Teresa of Avila (1515–1582, canonized St. Teresa in 1622) eloquently expressed the intimate connection between physical and spiritual experiences that was a common feature of Catholic mysticism. She was a Spanish Carmelite nun whose accounts of her own mystical experiences made her a model for other nuns throughout the world. Filled with religious ardor, she devoted herself to an ascetic regime of self-deprivations so intense that she fell ill and suffered paralysis.

Often afflicted by an intense pain in her side, Teresa reported that an angel had stuck a lance tipped with fire into her heart. This "seraphic vision," which became the subject of Gianlorenzo Bernini's famous sculpture in Santa Maria della Vittoria in Rome (1645–1652), epitomized the Catholic Reformation sensibility of understanding spiritual states through physical feelings. In Teresa's case, her extreme bodily deprivations, paralysis, and intense pain conditioned how she experienced the spiritual side of her nature. Many have seen an erotic character to the vision, which may be true, but the vision best demonstrates a profound psychological awareness that body and spiritual sensations cannot be precisely distinguished. As Teresa put it, "it is not bodily pain, but spiritual, though the body has a share in it—indeed, a great share." She described the paralysis of her soul and her body as interconnected: "The soul is unable to do either this or anything else. The entire body contracts and neither arm nor foot can be moved." She then described, in remarkably graphic terms, her repeated vision:

It pleased the Lord that I should

sion. I would see beside me, on my left hand, an angel in bodily form—a type of vision which I am not in the habit of seeing, except very rarely. . . . I pleased the Lord that I should see this angel in the following way. He was not tall, but short, and very beautiful, his face so aflame that he appeared to be one of the highest types of angel who seem to be all afire. . . . In his hands I saw a long golden spear and at the end of the iron tip I seemed to see a point of fire. With this he seemed to pierce my heart several times so that it penetrated to my entrails. When he drew it out, I thought he was drawing them out with it and he left me completely afire with a great love for God. The pain was so sharp that it made me utter several moans; and so excessive was the sweetness caused me by this intense pain that one can never wish to lose it, nor will one's soul be content with anything less than God. . . . So sweet are the colloquies of love which pass between the soul and God that if anyone thinks I am lying I be-

seech God, in His give him the same

Visions such as th[...] difficult to interpret. was going on in thos[...] quies between Teres[...] God? Teresa associat[...] as if she had to suffe[...] receive divine illumi[...] she described as a sv[...] Her sensibility about [...] relationship between [...] and spiritual experie[...] especially pronounc[...] sixteenth-century Ca[...] and suffering were u[...] a form of penance, a[...] body could play a p[...] redemptive role in e[...] tuality. The best way [...] this world was in bo[...] because through pai[...] escaped the temptati[...] flesh and renounced [...] tions of the world.

For Discussion

How was pain underst[...] religious value? What v[...] around Teresa that mig[...] preoccupation with pai[...]

An angel is about to pierce her side with an arrow.

St. Teresa lies su[...] the air in a swo[...] a vision.

At that point Oliver Cromwell (1599–1658), the commander in chief of the army and the most prominent member of the Council of State after 1649, had himself proclaimed Protector of England, Scotland, and Ireland. Cromwell had been a leader of the revolution, a zealous Puritan who had provided crucial support for the execution of the king and the establishment of the republic. At the same time, however, Cromwell feared that the Levellers and now the radical Puritans of the Barebones Parliament would destroy the social order. The establishment of the Protectorate, in which Cromwell shared legislative

litical achievement of their cousin, Louis XIV of[...] the same time, however, they realized that they c[...] return to the policies of their father, much less a[...] of Louis. Neither of them attempted to rule i[...] without Parliament, as Charles I had. Their mai[...] was to destroy the independence of Parliament [...] it with their own supporters and use the pre[...] weaken the force of the parliamentary statute[...] they objected.

The main political crisis of Charles II's rei[...] attempt by a group of members of Parliament, [...] the Earl of Shaftesbury (1621–1683) and know[...]

Allegorical View of Cromwell as Savior of England

DOCUMENT

John Locke Justifies the Glorious Revolution

John Locke wrote Two Treatises of Government between 1679 and 1682, during the reign of Charles II. The main purpose of the book was to justify armed resistance against Charles, who was pursuing absolutist policies, including attacks on the freedom of the English Parliament. Locke did not publish the Two Treatises, however, until after the Glorious Revolution of 1688. In order to justify that revolution, Locke wrote two new paragraphs, claiming that when a king abandons his responsibility to enforce the law, as James II had when he fled to France in December 1688, the government was dissolved and the people had the right to form a new one, as they had when they offered the crown to William and Mary in February 1689.

There is one more way whereby such a government may be dissolved, and that is when he who has the supreme executive power neglects and abandons that charge, so that the laws already made can no longer be put in execution. This is demonstrably to reduce all to anarchy, and so effectually to dissolve the government. For laws not being made for themselves, but to be by their execution the

bonds of the society, to keep every part of the body in its due place and function, when that totally cea[...] government visibly ceases, and the people become fused multitude, without order or connection. Wh[...] is no longer the administration of justice, for the s[...] of men's rights, nor any remaining power within t[...] munity to direct the force, or provide for the nece[...] the public, there is certainly no government left. W[...] laws cannot be executed, it is all one as if there wer[...] and a government without laws is, I suppose, a my[...] politics, inconceivable to human capacity, and inc[...] with human society.

In these and in the like cases, when the govern[...] dissolved, the people are at liberty to provide for th[...] selves, by erecting a new legislative, differing from [...] by the change of persons or form, or both, as they[...] it most for their safety and good. For the society ca[...] by the fault of another, lose the native and original[...] has to preserve itself, which can only be done by a [...] legislative and a fair and impartial execution of the [...] made by it.

Source: From Two Treatises of Government by John Lock[...]

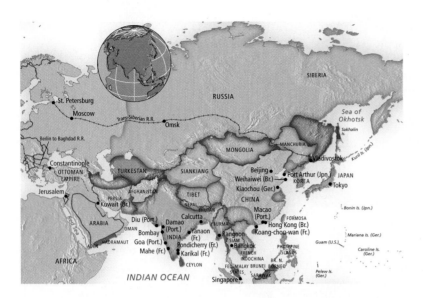

we include maps focusing on areas outside the borders of Western civilization. These maps include a small thumbnail globe that highlights the geographic area under discussion in the context of the larger world. Fine art and photos also tell the story of Western civilization, and we have included more than 350 images to help students visualize the past: the way people lived, the events that shaped their lives, and how they viewed the world around them.

Chronologies and Suggested Readings

Each chapter includes chronological charts and suggested readings. Chronologies outline significant events, such as "The End of World War II," and serve as convenient references for students. Each chapter concludes with an annotated list of suggested readings. These are not scholarly bibliographies aimed at the professor, but suggestions for students who wish to explore a topic in greater depth or to write a research paper. A comprehensive list of suggested readings is available on our book-specific website, www.ablongman.com/levack2e.

Glossary

We have sought to create a work that is accessible to students with little prior knowledge of the basic facts of Western history or geography. Throughout the book we have explained difficult concepts at length. For example, we present in-depth explanations of the concepts of Zoroastrianism, Neoplatonism, Renaissance humanism, the various Protestant denominations of the sixteenth century, capitalism, seventeenth-century absolutism, nineteenth-century liberalism and nationalism, fascism, and modernism. Key concepts such as these are identified in the chapters with a degree symbol (°) and defined as well in the end-of-text Glossary.

MyHistoryLab Icons

Throughout the text, you will see icons that will lead students to additional resources found on MyHistoryLab.com. These resources fall into four categories:

The **document** icon directs students to primary source documents that support the material they are reading in the textbook. In addition, most documents offer headnotes and analysis questions that focus students' reading.

The **image** icon leads students to photos, cartoons, and artwork that relate to the topic they are reading. Most images include a descriptive, contextualized headnote and analysis questions.

The **map** icon refers to maps, many of which are interactive and contain headnotes and questions designed to help students visualize the material they are learning. Printable map activities from Longman's outstanding geography workbooks allow students to interact with maps.

The **video** icon leads students to video clips that focus on the regions, people, or events discussed in the text.

A Note About Dates and Transliterations

In keeping with current academic practice, *The West: Encounters & Transformations* uses B.C.E. (before the common era) and C.E. (common era) to designate dates. We also follow the most current and widely accepted English transliterations of Arabic. *Qur'an,* for example, is used for *Koran; Muslim* is used for *Moslem.* Chinese words appearing in the text for the first time are written in pinyin, followed by the older Wade-Giles system in parentheses.

Supplements

For Qualified College Instructors

Instructor's Resource Manual

0-321-42735-1

In this manual written by Sharon Arnoult, Midwestern State University, each chapter contains a chapter outline, significant themes, learning objectives, lesson enrichment ideas, discussion suggestions, and questions for discussing the primary source documents in the text.

Test Bank

0-321-42731-9

Written by Susan Carrafiello, Wright State University, this supplement contains more than 1,200 multiple-choice and essay questions. All questions are referenced by topic and text page number.

TestGen-EQ Computerized Testing System

0-321-42573-1

This flexible, easy-to-master computerized test bank on a dual-platform CD includes all of the items in the printed test bank and allows instructors to select specific questions, edit existing questions, and add their own items to create exams. Tests can be printed in several different fonts and formats and can include figures, such as graphs and tables.

Companion Website (www.ablongman.com/levack2e)

Instructors can take advantage of the Companion Website that supports this text. The instructor section includes teaching links, downloadable maps, tables, and graphs from the text for use in PowerPoint, PowerPoint lecture outlines, and a link to the Instructor Resource Center.

Instructor Resource Center (IRC) (www.ablongman.com/irc)

Through the Instructor Resource Center, instructors can log into premium online products, browse and download book-specific instructor resources, and receive immediate access and instructions to installing course management content. Instructors who already have access to CourseCompass or Supplements Central can log in to the IRC immediately using their existing login and password. First-time users can register at the Instructor Resource Center welcome page at www.ablongman.com/irc.

MyHistoryLab (www.myhistorylab.com)

MyHistoryLab provides students with an online package complete with the entire electronic textbook and numerous study aids. With several hundred primary sources, many of which are assignable and link to a gradebook, pre- and post-tests that link to a gradebook and result in individualized study plans, videos and images, as well as map workbook activities with gradable quizzes, the site offers students a unique, interactive experience that brings history to life. The comprehensive site also includes a History Bookshelf with fifty of the most commonly assigned books in history classes and a History Toolkit with tutorials and helpful links. Other features include gradable assignments and chapter review materials; a Test Bank; and Research Navigator.

Delivered in CourseCompass, Blackboard, or WebCT, as well as in a non-course-management version, MyHistoryLab is easy to use and flexible. MyHistoryLab is organized according to the table of contents of this textbook. With the course management version, instructors can create a further customized product by adding their own syllabus, content, and assignments, or they can use the materials as presented.

PowerPoint Presentations

These presentations contain PowerPoint slides for each chapter and may include key points and terms for a lecture on the chapter, as well as full-color images of important maps, graphs, and charts. The presentations are available for download from www.ablongman.com/levack2e and www.ablongman.com/irc.

Text-Specific Transparency Set
0-321-42732-7

Instructors can download files with which to make full-color transparency map acetates taken from the text at www.ablongman.com/irc.

History Video Program

Longman offers more than one hundred videos from which qualified adopters can choose. Restrictions apply.

History Digital Media Archive CD-ROM
0-321-14976-9

This CD-ROM contains electronic images, interactive and static maps, and media elements such as video. It is fully customizable and ready for classroom presentation. All images and maps are available in PowerPoint as well.

Discovering Western Civilization Through Maps and Views
0-673-53596-7

Created by Gerald Danzer, University of Illinois at Chicago, and David Buissert, this unique set of 140 full-color acetates contains an introduction to teaching history through maps and a detailed commentary on each transparency. The collection includes cartographic and pictorial maps, views and photos, urban plans, building diagrams, and works of art. Available to qualified college adopters on Longman's Instructor Resource Center (IRC) at www.ablongman.com/irc.

For Students

Study Guide
Volume I: 0-321-42733-5
Volume II: 0-321-42734-3

Containing activities and study aids for every chapter in the text, each chapter of the *Study Guide* written by Carron Fillingim, Louisiana State University, includes a thorough chapter outline; timeline; map exercises; identification, multiple-choice and thought questions; and critical-thinking questions based on primary source documents from the text.

Companion Website (www.ablongman.com/levack2e)

Providing a wealth of resources for students using *The West: Encounters & Transformations,* Second Edition, this Companion Website contains chapter summaries, interactive practice test questions, and Web links for every chapter in the text.

Research Navigator and Research Navigator Guide

0-205-40838-9

Research Navigator is a comprehensive Website comprising four exclusive databases of credible and reliable source material for research and for student assignments: EBSCO's ContentSelect Academic Journal & Abstract Database, the *New York Times* Search-by-Subject Archive, *Financial Times* Article Archive and Company Financials, and "Best of the Web" Link Library. The site also includes an extensive help section. The Research Navigator Guide provides your students with access to the Research Navigator website and includes reference material and hints about conducting online research. Available to qualified college adopters when packaged with the text.

Mapping Western Civilization: Student Activities

0-673-53774-9

Created by Gerald Danzer, University of Illinois at Chicago, this FREE map workbook for students is designed as an accompaniment to *Discovering Western Civilization Through Maps and Views.* It features exercises designed to teach students to interpret and analyze cartographic materials such as historical documents. Available to qualified college adopters when packaged with the text.

Western Civilization Map Workbook

Volume I: 0-321-01878-8
Volume II: 0-321-01877-X

The map exercises in these volumes, created by Glee Wilson at Kent State University, test and reinforce basic geography literacy while building critical-thinking skills. Available to qualified college adopters when packaged with the text.

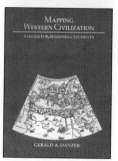

Study Card for Western Civilization

0-321-29233-2

Colorful, affordable, and packed with useful information, Longman's Study Cards make studying easier, more efficient, and more enjoyable. Course information is distilled down to the basics, helping students quickly master the fundamentals, review a subject for understanding, or prepare for an exam. Because they're laminated for durability, they can be kept for years to come and used whenever necessary for a quick review. Available to qualified college adopters when packaged with the text.

MyHistoryLab (www.myhistorylab.com)

MyHistoryLab provides students with an online package complete with the entire electronic textbook, numerous study aids, primary sources, and chapter exams. With several hundred primary sources and images, as well as map workbook activities with gradable quizzes, the site offers students a unique, interactive experience that brings history to life. The comprehensive site also includes a History Bookshelf with fifty of the most commonly assigned books in history classes and a History Toolkit with tutorials and helpful links.

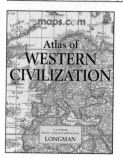

Longman Atlas of Western Civilization

0-321-21626-1

This fifty-two-page atlas features carefully selected historical maps that provide comprehensive coverage for the major historical periods. Each map has been designed to be colorful, easy to read, and informative, without sacrificing detailed accuracy. This atlas makes history—and geography—more comprehensible.

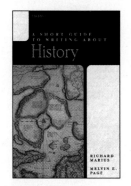

A Short Guide to Writing About History, Fifth Edition
0-321-22716-6
Written by Richard A. Marius, late of Harvard University, and Melvin E. Page, Eastern Tennessee State University, this engaging and practical text helps students get beyond merely compiling dates and facts; it teaches them how to incorporate their own ideas into their papers and to tell a story about history that interests them and their peers. Covering both brief essays and the documented resource paper, the text explores the writing and researching processes; identifies different modes of historical writing, including argument; and concludes with guidelines for improving style.

Penguin-Longman Partnership

The partnership between Penguin Books and Longman Publishers offers a discount on the following titles when bundled with any Longman history survey textbook. Visit www.ablongman.com/penguin for more information.

Available Titles

Peter Abelard, *The Letters of Abelard and Heloise*
Dante Alighieri, *Divine Comedy: Inferno*
Dante Alighieri, *The Portable Dante*
Anonymous, *Early Irish Myths & Sagas*
Anonymous, *The Epic of Gilgamesh*
Anonymous, *The Song of Roland*
Anonymous, *Vinland Sagas*
Hannah Arendt, *On Revolution*
Aristophanes, *The Birds and Other Plays*
Aristotle, *The Politics*
Louis Auchincloss, *Woodrow Wilson* (Penguin Lives Series)
St. Augustine, *The Confessions of St. Augustine*
Jane Austen, *Emma*
Jane Austen, *Persuasion*
Jane Austen, *Pride and Prejudice*
Jane Austen, *Sense and Sensibility*
Edward Bellamy, *Looking Backward*
Richard Bowring, *Diary of Lady Murasaki*
Charlotte Brontë, *Jane Eyre*
Charlotte Brontë, *Villette*
Emily Brontë, *Wuthering Heights*
Edmund Burke, *Reflection on the Revolution in France and on the Proceedings in Certain Societies in London Relative to that Event*
Benvenuto Cellini, *The Autobiography of Benvenuto Cellini*
Geoffrey Chaucer, *The Canterbury Tales*

Marcus Tullius Cicero, *Cicero: Selected Political Speeches*
Miguel de Cervantes, *The Adventures of Don Quixote*
Bartolome de las Casas, *A Short Account of the Destruction of the West Indies*
René Descartes, *Discourse on Method and Related Writings*
Charles Dickens, *Great Expectations*
Charles Dickens, *Hard Times*
John Dos Passos, *Three Soldiers*
Einhard, *Two Lives of Charlemagne*
Olaudah Equiano, *The Interesting Narrative and Other Writings*
M. Finley (ed.), *The Portable Greek Historians*
Benjamin Franklin, *The Autobiography and Other Writings*
Jeffrey Gantz (tr.), *Early Irish Myths and Sagas*
Peter Gay, *Mozart* (Penguin Lives Series)
William Golding, *Lord of the Flies*
Grimm & Grimm, *Grimms' Fairy Tales*
Thomas Hardy, *Jude the Obscure*
Herodotus, *The Histories*
Thomas Hobbes, *Leviathan*
Homer, *The Iliad*
Homer, *The Iliad* (Deluxe)
Homer, *Odyssey Deluxe*
Homer, *Odyssey: Revised Prose Translation*
The Koran

Deborah Lipstadt, *Denying the Holocaust*
Machiavelli, *The Prince*
Bill Manley, *The Penguin Historical Atlas of Ancient Egypt*
Karl Marx, *The Communist Manifesto*
Colin McEvedy, *The New Penguin Atlas of Ancient History*
Colin McEvedy, *The New Penguin Atlas of Medieval History*
John Stuart Mill, *On Liberty*
Jean-Baptiste Molière, *Tartuffe and Other Plays*
Sir Thomas More, *Utopia and Other Essential Writings*
Robert Morkot, *The Penguin Historical Atlas of Ancient Greece*
Sherwin Nuland, *Leonardo Da Vinci*
George Orwell, *1984*
George Orwell, *Animal Farm*
Plato, *Great Dialogues of Plato*
Plato, *The Last Days of Socrates*
Plato, *The Republic*
Plutarch, *Fall of the Roman Republic*
Marco Polo, *The Travels*
Procopius, *The Secret History*
Jean-Jacques Rousseau, *The Social Contract*
Sallust, *The Jugurthine Wars, The Conspiracy of Cataline*
Chris Scarre, *The Penguin Historical Atlas of Ancient Rome*
Desmond Seward, *The Hundred Years' War*
William Shakespeare, *Four Great Comedies: The Taming of the Shrew, A Midsummer's Night Dream, Twelfth Night, The Tempest*

William Shakespeare, *Four Great Tragedies: Hamlet, Macbeth, King Lear, Othello*
William Shakespeare, *Four Histories: Richard II, Henry IV: Part I, Henry IV: Part II, Henry V*
William Shakespeare, *Hamlet*
William Shakespeare, *King Lear*
William Shakespeare, *Macbeth*
William Shakespeare, *The Merchant of Venice*
William Shakespeare, *Othello*
William Shakespeare, *The Taming of the Shrew*
William Shakespeare, *The Tempest*
William Shakespeare, *Twelfth Night*
Mary Shelley, *Frankenstein*
Aleksandr Solzhenitsyn, *One Day in the Life of Ivan Denisovich*
Sophocles, *The Three Theban Plays*
Robert Louis Stevenson, *The Strange Case of Dr. Jekyll and Mr. Hyde*
Suetonius, *The Twelve Caesars*
Jonathan Swift, *Gulliver's Travels*
Tacitus, *The Histories*
Various, *The Penguin Book of Historical Speeches*
Voltaire, *Candide, Zadig and Selected Stories*
Carl von Clausewitz, *On War*
von Goethe, *Faust, Part 1*
von Goethe, *Faust, Part 2*
Edith Wharton, *Ethan Frome*
Willet, *The Signet World Atlas*
Gary Wills, *Saint Augustine* (Penguin Lives Series)
Virginia Woolf, *Jacob's Room*

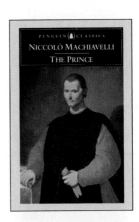

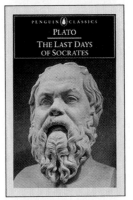

Longman Library of World Biography Series

Each interpretive biography in the new Library of World Biography series focuses on a figure whose actions and ideas significantly influenced the course of world history. Pocket-sized and brief, each book relates the life of its subject to the broader themes and developments of the time. Longman Publishers offers your students a discount on the titles below when instructors request that they be bundled with any Longman history survey textbook. Series titles include:

Ahmad al-Mansur: Islamic Visionary by Richard Smith (Ferrum College)
Alexander the Great: Legacy of a Conqueror by Winthrop Lindsay Adams (University of Utah)
Benito Mussolini: The First Fascist by Anthony L. Cardoza (Loyola University)
Fukuzawa Yûkichi: From Samurai to Capitalist by Helen M. Hopper (University of Pittsburgh)
Ignatius of Loyola: Founder of the Jesuits by John Patrick Donnelly (Marquette University)

Jacques Coeur: Entrepreneur and King's Bursar by Kathryn L. Reyerson
   (University of Minnesota)
Katô Shidzue: A Japanese Feminist by Helen M. Hopper (University of Pittsburgh)
Simón Bolívar: Liberation and Disappointment by David Bushnell (University of Florida)
Vasco da Gama: Renaissance Crusader by Glenn J. Ames (University of Toledo)
Zheng He: China and the Oceans in the Early Ming, 1405–1433 by Edward Dreyer
   (University of Miami)

Acknowledgments

In writing this book we have benefited from the guidance of many members of the superb editorial staff at Longman. We would like to thank our acquisitions editor Janet Lanphier for helping us refine and develop this second edition. David Kear, our development editor, gave us valuable criticisms and helped us keep our audience in mind. Heather Johnson superintended the copyediting and proofreading with skill and efficiency, while Christine Buese helped us locate the most appropriate illustrations. Sue Westmoreland, the executive marketing manager for history, offered many creative ideas for promoting the book.

The authors wish to thank the following friends and colleagues for their assistance: Kenneth Alder, Joseph Alehermes, Karl Appuhn, Sharon Arnoult, Nicholas Baker, Paula Baskovits, Paul-Alain Beaulieu, Kamilia Bergen, Timothy Breen, Peter Brown, Peter Carroll, Shawn Clybor, Jauabeth Condie-Pugh, Patricia Crone, Tracey Cullen, Arthur Eckstein, Susanna Elm, Benjamin Frommer, Cynthia Gladstone, Dena Goodman, Stefka Hadjiandonova, Matthias Henze, Stanley Hilton, Kenneth Holum, Mark Jurdjevic, Werner Kelber, Cathleen Keller, Anne Kilmer, Jacob Lassner, Robert Lerner, Nancy Levack, Richard Lim, David Lindenfeld, Brian Maxson, Sarah Maza, Peter Mazur, Laura McGough, Roderick McIntosh, Susan K. McIntosh, Glenn Markoe, William Monter, Randy Nichols, Scott Noegel, Monique O'Connell, Carl Petry, Michael Rogers, Karl Roider, Sarah Ross, Michele Salzman, Paula Sanders, Regina Schwartz, Ethan Shagan, Julia M. H. Smith, James Sidbury, and Rachel Wahlig.

We would also like to thank the many historians who gave generously of their time to review during the various stages of development of our second edition. Their comments and suggestions helped to improve the book. Thank you:

Melanie A. Bailey, *South Dakota State University*
Brett Berliner, *Morgan State University*
Alfred S. Bradford, *University of Oklahoma*
Linda Charmaine Powell, *Amarillo College*
Daniel Christensen, *California State University, Fullerton*
William L. Cumiford, *Chapman University*
Rebecca Durrer, *Columbia College*
Steven Fanning, *University of Illinois at Chicago*
Sean Farrell, *Northern Illinois University*
Judy E. Gaughan, *Colorado State University*
Jennifer Hedda, *Simpson College*
David Hudson, *California State University, Fresno*
Rebecca Huston, *Hinds Community College*
Barbara A. Klemm, *Broward Community College*
Molly McClain, *University of San Diego*
Randall McGowen, *University of Oregon*

John A. Nichols, *Slippery Rock University*
James T. Owens, *Oakton Community College*
Elizabeth Propes, *Mesa State College*
Miriam Raub Vivian, *California State University, Bakersfield*
Anne Rodrick, *Wofford College*
Jarbel Rodriguez, *San Francisco State University*
Jacquelyn A. Royal, *Lee University*
Jutta Scott, *South Carolina University*
Susan O. Shapiro, *Utah State University*
Steven E. Sidebotham, *University of Delaware*
David Stone, *Kansas State University*
Charles R. Sullivan, *University of Dallas*
Mary C. Swilling, *University of Mississippi*
Larissa Juliet Taylor, *Colby College*
Jonathan Ziskind, *University of Louisville*

We would also like to thank the historians whose careful reviews and comments on the first edition helped us revise the book for its second edition. Our thanks for your contributions:

Henry Abramson, *Florida Atlantic University*

Patricia Ali, *Morris College*

Joseph Appiah, *J. Sergeant Reynolds Community College*

Sharon L. Arnoult, *Midwestern State University*

Arthur H. Auten, *University of Hartford*

Clifford Backman, *Boston University*

Suzanne Balch-Lindsay, *Eastern New Mexico University*

Wayne C. Bartee, *Southwest Miami State University*

Brandon Beck, *Shenandoah University*

James R. Belpedio, *Becker College*

Richard Berthold, *University of New Mexico*

Cynthia S. Bisson, *Belmont University*

Richard Bodek, *College of Charleston*

Melissa Bokovoy, *University of New Mexico*

William H. Brennan, *University of the Pacific*

Morgan R. Broadhead, *Jefferson Community College*

Theodore Bromund, *Yale University*

April A. Brooks, *South Dakota State University*

Nathan M. Brooks, *New Mexico State University*

Michael Burger, *Mississippi University for Women*

Susan Carrafiello, *Wright State University*

Kathleen S. Carter, *High Point University*

William L. Combs, *Western Illinois University*

Joseph Coohill, *Pennsylvania State University–New Kensington*

Richard A. Cosgrove, *University of Arizona*

Leonard Curtis, *Mississippi College*

Miriam Davis, *Delta State University*

Alexander DeGrand, *North Carolina State University*

Marion Deshmukh, *George Mason University*

Janusz Duzinkiewicz, *Purdue University, North Central*

Mary Beth Emmerichs, *University of Wisconsin, Sheboygan*

Steven Fanning, *University of Illinois at Chicago*

Bryan Ganaway, *University of Illinois at Urbana–Champaign*

Frank Garosi, *California State University–Sacramento*

Christina Gold, *Loyola Marymount University*

Ignacio Götz, *Hofstra University*

Louis Haas, *Duquesne University*

Linda Jones Hall, *Saint Mary's College of Maryland*

Paul Halsall, *University of North Florida*

Donald J. Harreld, *Brigham Young University*

Carmen V. Harris, *University of South Carolina at Spartanburg*

James C. Harrison, *Siena College*

Mark C. Herman, *Edison Community College*

Curry A. Herring, *University of Southern Alabama*

Patrick Holt, *Fordham University*

W. Robert Houston, *University of South Alabama*

Lester Hutton, *Westfield State College*

Jeffrey Hyson, *Saint Joseph's University*

Paul Jankowski, *Brandeis University*

Padraic Kennedy, *McNeese State University*

Joanne Klein, *Boise State University*

Theodore Kluz, *Troy State University*

Skip Knox, *Boise State University*

Cynthia Kosso, *Northern Arizona University*

Ann Kuzdale, *Chicago State University*

Lawrence Langer, *University of Connecticut*

Oscar E. Lansen, *University of North Carolina at Charlotte*

Michael V. Leggiere, *Louisiana State University at Shreveport*

Rhett Leverett, *Marymount University*

Alison Williams Lewin, *Saint Joseph's University*

Wendy Liu, *Miami University, Middletown*

Elizabeth Makowski, *Southwest Texas State University*

Daniel Meissner, *Marquette University*

Isabel Moreira, *University of Utah*

Kenneth Moure, *University of California–Santa Barbara*

Melva E. Newsom, *Clark State Community College*

John A. Nichols, *Slippery Rock University*

Susannah R. Ottaway, *Carleton College*

James H. Overfield, *University of Vermont*

Brian L. Peterson, *Florida International University*

Hugh Phillips, *Western Kentucky University*

Jeff Plaks, *University of Central Oklahoma*

Thomas L. Powers, *University of South Carolina, Sumter*

Carole Putko, *San Diego State University*

Barbara Ranieri, *University of Alabama at Birmingham*

Elsa M. E. Rapp, *Montgomery County Community College*

Marlette Rebhorn, *Austin Community College*

Roger Reese, *Texas A&M University*

Travis Ricketts, *Bryan College*

Thomas Robisheaux, *Duke University*

Bill Robison, *Southeastern Louisiana University*

Mark Ruff, *Concordia University*

Frank Russell, *Transylvania University*

Marylou Ruud, *The University of West Florida*

Michael Saler, *University of California–Davis*

Timothy D. Saxon, *Charleston Southern University*

Daniel A. Scalberg, *Multnomah Bible College*

Ronald Schechter, *College of William and Mary*

Philip Skaggs, *Grand Valley State University*

Helmut Walser Smith, *Vanderbilt University*

Eileen Solwedel, *Edmonds Community College*

Sister Maria Consuelo Sparks, *Immaculata University*

Ilicia J. Sprey, *Saint Joseph's College*

Charles R. Sullivan, *University of Dallas*

Frederick Suppe, *Ball State University*

Frank W. Thackery, *Indiana University Southeast*
Frances B. Titchener, *Utah State University*
Katherine Tosa, *Muskegon Community College*
Lawrence A. Tritle, *Loyola Marymount University*

Clifford F. Wargelin, *Georgetown College*
Theodore R. Weeks, *Southern Illinois University*
Elizabeth A. Williams, *Oklahoma State University*
Mary E. Zamon, *Marymount University*

BRIAN LEVACK
EDWARD MUIR
MEREDITH VELDMAN
MICHAEL MAAS

Meet the Authors

Brian Levack grew up in a family of teachers in the New York metropolitan area. From his father, a professor of French history, he acquired a love for studying the past, and he knew from an early age that he too would become a historian. He received his B.A. from Fordham University in 1965 and his Ph.D. from Yale in 1970. In graduate school he became fascinated by the history of the law and the interaction between law and politics, interests that he has maintained throughout his career. In 1969 he joined the history department of the University of Texas at Austin, where he is now the John Green Regents Professor in History. The winner of several teaching awards, Levack teaches a wide variety of courses on British and European history, legal history, and the history of witchcraft. For eight years he served as the chair of his department, a rewarding but challenging assignment that made it difficult for him to devote as much time as he wished to his teaching and scholarship. His books include *The Civil Lawyers in England, 1603–1641: A Political Study* (1973), *The Formation of the British State: England, Scotland and the Union, 1603–1707* (1987), and *The Witch-Hunt in Early Modern Europe* (1987 and 1995), which has been translated into eight languages.

His study of the development of beliefs about witchcraft in Europe over the course of many centuries gave him the idea of writing a textbook on Western civilization that would illustrate a broader set of encounters between different cultures, societies, and ideologies. While writing the book, Levack and his two sons built a house on property that he and his wife, Nancy, own in the Texas hill country. He found that the two projects presented similar challenges: It was easy to draw up the design, but far more difficult to execute it. When not teaching, writing, or doing carpentry work, Levack runs along the jogging trails of Austin, and he has recently discovered the pleasures of scuba diving.

Edward Muir grew up in the foothills of the Wasatch Mountains in Utah, close to the Emigration Trail along which wagon trains of Mormon pioneers and California-bound settlers made their way westward. As a child he loved to explore the broken-down wagons and abandoned household goods left at the side of the trail and from that acquired a fascination with the past. Besides the material remains of the past, he grew up with stories of his Mormon pioneer ancestors and an appreciation for how the past continued to influence the present. During the turbulent 1960s, he became interested in Renaissance Italy as a period and a place that had been formative for Western civilization. His biggest challenge is finding the time to explore yet another new corner of Italy and its restaurants.

Muir received his Ph.D. from Rutgers University, where he specialized in the Italian Renaissance and did archival research in Venice and Florence, Italy. He is now the Clarence L. Ver Steeg Professor in the Arts and Sciences at Northwestern University and former chair of the history department. At Northwestern he has won several teaching awards. His books include *Civic Ritual in Renaissance Venice* (1981), *Mad Blood Stirring: Vendetta in Renaissance Italy* (1993 and 1998), and *Ritual in Early Modern Europe* (1997 and 2005).

Some years ago Muir began to experiment with the use of historical trials in teaching and discovered that students loved them. From that experience he decided to write this textbook, which employs trials as a central feature. He lives beside Lake Michigan in Evanston, Illinois. His twin passions are skiing in the Rocky Mountains and rooting for the Chicago Cubs, who manage every summer to demonstrate that winning isn't everything.

Meredith Veldman grew up in the western suburbs of Chicago in a close-knit, closed-in Dutch Calvinist community. In this immigrant society, history mattered: the "Reformed tradition" structured not only religious beliefs but also social identity and political practice. This influence certainly played some role in shaping Veldman's early fascination with history. But probably just as important were the countless World War II re-enactment games she played with her five older brothers. Whatever the cause, Veldman majored in history at Calvin College in Grand Rapids, Michigan, and then earned a Ph.D. in modern European history, with a concentration in nineteenth- and twentieth-century Britain, from Northwestern University in 1988.

As associate professor of history at Louisiana State University, Veldman teaches courses in nineteenth- and twentieth-century British history and twentieth-century Europe, as well as the second half of "Western Civ." In her many semesters in the Western Civ. classroom, Veldman tried a number of different textbooks but found herself increasingly dissatisfied. She wanted a text that would convey to beginning students at least some of the complexities and ambiguities of historical interpretation, introduce them to the exciting work being done now in cultural history, and, most important, tell a good story. The search for this textbook led her to accept the offer made by Levack, Maas, and Muir to join them in writing *The West: Encounters & Transformations*.

The author of *Fantasy, the Bomb, and the Greening of Britain: Romantic Protest, 1945–1980* (1994), Veldman is also the wife of a Methodist minister and the mother of two young sons. They reside in Baton Rouge, Louisiana, where Veldman finds coping with the steamy climate a constant challenge. She and her family recently returned from Manchester, England, where they lived for three years and astonished the natives by their enthusiastic appreciation of English weather.

Michael Maas was born in the Ohio River Valley, in a community that had been a frontier outpost during the late eighteenth century. He grew up reading the stories of the early settlers and their struggles with the native peoples, and seeing in the urban fabric how the city had subsequently developed into a prosperous coal and steel town with immigrants from all over the world. As a boy he developed a lifetime interest in the archaeology and history of the ancient Mediterranean world and began to study Latin. At Cornell University he combined his interests in cultural history and the classical world by majoring in classics and anthropology. A semester in Rome clinched his commitment to these fields—and to Italian cooking. Maas went on to get his Ph.D. in the graduate program in ancient history and Mediterranean archaeology at the University of California at Berkeley.

He has traveled widely in the Mediterranean and the Middle East and participated in several archaeological excavations, including an underwater dig in Greece. Since 1985 he has taught ancient history at Rice University in Houston, Texas, where he founded and directs the interdisciplinary B.A. program in ancient Mediterranean civilizations. He has won several teaching awards.

Maas's special area of research is late antiquity, the period of transition from the classical to the medieval worlds, which saw the collapse of the Roman Empire in western Europe and the development of the Byzantine state in the East. During his last sabbatical, he was a member of the Institute for Advanced Study in Princeton, New Jersey, where he worked on his current book, *The Conqueror's Gift: Ethnography, Identity, and Imperial Power at the End of Antiquity* (forthcoming). His other books include *John Lydus and the Roman Past: Antiquarianism and Politics in the Age of Justinian* (1992), *Readings in Late Antiquity: A Sourcebook* (2000), and *Exegesis and Empire in the Early Byzantine Mediterranean* (2003).

Maas has always been interested in interdisciplinary teaching and the encounters among different cultures. He sees *The West: Encounters & Transformations* as an opportunity to explain how the modern civilization that we call "the West" had its origins in the diverse interactions among many peoples of antiquity.

THE WEST

What Is the West?

MANY OF THE PEOPLE WHO INFLUENCE PUBLIC OPINION—POLITICIANS, teachers, clergy, journalists, and television commentators—refer to "Western values," "the West," and "Western civilization." They often use these terms as if they do not require explanation. But what *do* these terms mean? The West has always been an arena within which different cultures, religions, values, and philosophies have interacted, and any definition of the West will inevitably arouse controversy.

The most basic definition of the West is of a place. Western civilization is now typically thought to comprise the regions of Europe, the Americas, Australia, and New Zealand. However, this is a contemporary definition of the West. The inclusion of these places in the West is the result of a long history of European expansion through colonization. In addition to being a place, Western civilization also encompasses a cultural history—a tradition stretching back thousands of years to the ancient world. Over this long period the civilization we now identify as Western gradually took shape. The many characteristics that identify any civilization emerged over this time: forms of government, economic systems, and methods of scientific inquiry, as well as religions, languages, literature, and art.

Throughout the development of Western civilization, the ways in which people identified themselves changed as well. People in the ancient world had no such idea of the common identity of the West, only of being members of a tribe, citizens of a town, or subjects of an empire. But with the spread of Christianity and Islam between the first and seventh centuries, the notion of a distinct civilization in these "Western" lands subtly changed. People came to identify themselves less as subjects of a particular empire and more as members of a community of faith—whether that community comprised followers of Christianity, Judaism, or Islam. These communities of faith drew lines of inclusion and exclusion that still exist today. Starting

The Temple of Hera at Paestum, Italy Greek colonists in Italy built this temple in the sixth century B.C.E. Greek ideas and artistic styles spread throughout the ancient world both from Greek colonists, such as those at Paestum, and from other peoples who imitated the Greeks.

about 1,600 years ago, Christian monarchs and clergy began to obliterate polytheism (the worship of many gods) and marginalize Jews. From a thousand to 500 years ago, Christian authorities strove to expel Muslims from Europe. Europeans developed definitions of the West that did not include Islamic communities, even though Muslims continued to live in Europe and Europeans traded and interacted with the Muslim world. The Islamic countries themselves erected their own barriers, seeing themselves in opposition to the Christian West, even as they continued to look back to the common cultural origins in the ancient world that they shared with Jews and Christians. During the Renaissance in the fifteenth century, these ancient cultural origins became an alternative to religious affiliation for thinking about the identity of the West. From this Renaissance historical perspective Jews, Christians, and Muslims descended from the cultures of the ancient Hebrews, Greeks, and Romans. Despite all their differences, the followers of these religions shared a history. In fact, in the late Renaissance a number of thinkers imagined the possibility of rediscovering the single universal religion that they thought must have once been practiced in the ancient world. If they could just recapture that religion they could restore the unity they imagined had once prevailed in the West.

The definition of the West has also changed as a result of European colonialism, which began about 500 years ago. When European powers assembled large overseas empires, they introduced Western languages, religions, technology, and culture to many distant places in the world, making Western identity a transportable concept. In some of these colonized areas—such as North America, Argentina, Australia, and New Zealand—the European newcomers so outnumbered the indigenous people that these regions became as much a part of the West as Britain, France, and Spain. In other European colonies, especially in European trading outposts on the Asian continent, Western culture failed to exercise similar levels of influence.

As a result of colonialism Western culture sometimes merged with other cultures, and in the process both were changed. Brazil, a South American country inhabited by large numbers of indigenous peoples, the descendants of African slaves, and European settlers, epitomizes the complexity of what defines the West. In Brazil, almost everyone speaks a Western language (Portuguese), practices a Western religion (Christianity), and participates in Western political and economic institutions (democracy and capitalism). Yet in Brazil all of these features of Western civilization have become part of a distinctive culture, in which in-

A Satellite View of Europe
What is the West? Western civilization has undergone numerous transformations throughout history, but it has always included Europe.

digenous, African, and European elements have been blended. During Carnival, for example, Brazilians dressed in indigenous costumes dance in African rhythms to the accompaniment of music played on European instruments.

For many people today, the most important definition of the West involves adherence to a certain set of values, the "Western" values. The values typically identified as Western today include universal human rights, toleration of religious diversity, equality before the law, democracy, and freedom of inquiry and expression. However, these values have not always been part of Western civilization. They came to be fully appreciated only very recently as the consequence of a long and bloody history. In fact, there is nothing inevitable about these values, and Western history at various stages exhibited quite different ones. For example, the rulers of ancient Rome did not extend the privileges of citizenship to all the inhabitants of the empire until a century after it had reached its greatest size. The extent to which women could participate in public life was limited by law. Rich and powerful people enjoyed more protection under the law than did slaves or humble people. Most medieval Christians were completely convinced that their greatest contribution to society would be to make war against Muslims and heretics and to curtail as much as possible the actions of Jews. Western societies seldom valued equality until quite recently. Before the end of the eighteenth century, few Westerners questioned the practice of slavery; a social hierarchy of birth remained powerful in the West through the entire nineteenth century; most Western women were excluded from equal economic and educational opportunities until well into the twentieth century. Swiss women did not get the vote until 1971 (and in one canton not until 1990). Also in the twentieth century, Nazi Germany and the Soviet Union demonstrated that history could have turned out very differently in the West. These totalitarian regimes in Europe rejected most of the Western values so prized today and terrorized their own populations and millions of others beyond their borders through massive abuses of human rights. The history of the West is riddled with examples of leaders who stifled free inquiry and who censored authors and journalists. These examples testify to the fact that the values of Western societies have always been contended, disputed, and fought over. In other words, they have a history. This text highlights and examines that history, demonstrating how hard values were to formulate in the first place and how difficult they have been to preserve.

The Shifting Borders of the West

The geographical setting of the West also has a history. This textbook begins about 10,000 years ago in what is now Iraq and it ends in Iraq, but in the meantime the Mesopotamian region is only occasionally a concern for Western history. The West begins with the domestication of animals, the cultivation of the first crops, and the establishment of long-distance trading networks in the Tigris, Euphrates, and Nile River valleys. Cities, kingdoms, and empires in those valleys gave birth to the first civilizations. By about 500 B.C.E., the civilizations that are the cultural ancestors of the modern West had spread from southwestern Asia and North Africa to include the entire Mediterranean basin—areas influenced by Egyptian, Hebrew, Greek, and Roman thought, art, law, and religion. By the first century C.E. the Roman Empire drew the map of what historians consider the heartland of the West: most of western and southern Europe, the coastlands of the Mediterranean Sea, and the Middle East.

The West is now usually thought to include Europe and the Americas. However, the borders of the West have in recent decades come to be less about geography than culture, identity, and technology. When Japan, an Asian country, accepted human rights, democracy, and industrial capitalism after World War II, did it become part of the West? Most Japanese might not think they have adopted "Western" values, but the industrial power and stable democracy of a traditional Asian country that had never been colonized by a European power complicates the idea of what is the West. Or consider the Republic of South Africa, which until 1994 was ruled by the white minority, people descended from European immigrants. The oppressive regime violated human rights, rejected full legal equality for all citizens, and jailed or murdered those who questioned the government. Only when that government was replaced through democratic elections and a black man became president did South Africa fully embrace what the rest of the West would consider Western values. To what degree was South Africa part of the West before and after these developments?

Russia long saw itself as a Christian country with a tradition of cultural, economic, and political ties with the rest of Europe. The Russians have intermittently identified with their Western neighbors, but their neighbors were not always sure about the Russians. After the Mongol invasions of the thirteenth and fourteenth centuries much of Russia was isolated from the rest of the West; during the Cold War from 1949 to 1989, Russian communism and the Western democracies were polarized. When was Russia "Western" and when not?

Thus, when we talk about where the West is, we are almost always talking about the Mediterranean basin and much of Europe (and later, the Americas). But we will also show that countries that border "the West," and even countries far from it, might be considered Western in many aspects as well.

The Astrolabe

The mariner's astrolabe was a navigational device intended for use primarily at sea. The astrolabe originated in the Islamic world and was adopted by Europeans in the twelfth century—a cultural encounter that enabled Europeans to embark on long ocean voyages around the world.

Asking the Right Questions

So how can we make sense of the West as a place and an identity, the shifting borders of the West, and Western civilization in general? In short, what has Western civilization been over the course of its long history—and what is it today?

Answering these questions is the challenge this book poses. There are no simple answers to any of these questions, but there is a method for finding answers. The method is straightforward. Always ask the *what, when, where, who, how,* and *why* questions of the text.

The *What* Question

What is Western civilization? The answer to this question will vary according to time and place. In fact, for much of the early history covered in this book, Western civilization as we know it today did not exist as a single cultural entity. Rather, a number of distinctive civilizations were taking shape in the Middle East, northern Africa, and Europe, each of which contributed to what later became Western civilization. But throughout time the idea of Western civilization slowly began to form. Thus the understanding of Western civilization will change from chapter to chapter. The most extensive change in the place of the West was through the colonial expansion of the European nations between the fifteenth and twentieth centuries. Perhaps the most significant cultural change in the West came with acceptance of the values of scientific inquiry for solving human and philosophical problems, an approach that did not exist before the seventeenth century but became one of the distinguishing characteristics of Western civilization. During the late eighteenth and nineteenth centuries, industrialization became the engine that drove economic development in the West, and during the twentieth century industrialization in both its capitalist and communist forms dramatically gave the West a level of economic prosperity unmatched in the non-industrialized parts of the world.

The *When* Question

When did the defining characteristics of Western civilization first emerge, and for how long did they prevail? Dates frame and organize each chapter, and there are numerous short chronologies offered. These resources make it possible to keep track of what happened when. Dates have no meaning by themselves, but the connections *between* them can be very revealing. For example, dates show that the agricultural revolution that permitted the birth of the first civiliza-

tions unfolded over a span of about 10,000 years—which is more time than was taken by all the other events and developments covered in this textbook. Wars of religion plagued Europe for nearly 200 years before Enlightenment thinkers articulated the ideals of religious toleration. The American Civil War—the war to preserve the union, as President Abraham Lincoln termed it—took place at exactly the same time as other wars were being fought to achieve national unity in Germany and Italy. In other words, by paying attention to other contemporaneous wars for national unity the American experience seems less peculiarly an American event.

By learning when things happened, one can identify the major causes and consequences of events and thus see the transformations of Western civilization. For instance, the ability to produce a surplus of food through agriculture and the domestication of animals was a prerequisite for the emergence of civilizations. The violent collapse of religious unity after the Protestant Reformation in the sixteenth century led some Europeans to propose the separation of church and state two centuries later. And during the nineteenth century many Western states—in response to the enormous diversity among their own peoples—became preoccupied with maintaining or establishing national unity.

The *Where* Question

Where has Western civilization been located? Geography, of course, does not change very rapidly, but the idea of where the West is does. The location of the West is not so much a matter of changing borders but of how people identify themselves. The key to understanding the shifting borders of the West is to study how the peoples within the West thought of themselves. These groups include Muslims and the peoples of eastern Europe (such as the Soviet Union during the Cold War), which some people have wanted to exclude from the West. In addition, the chapters trace the relationships between the West (as it was constituted in different periods) and other, more distant civilizations with which it interacted. Those civilizations include not only those of East Asia and South Asia but also the indigenous peoples of sub-Saharan Africa, the Americas, and the Pacific islands.

The *Who* Question

Who were the people responsible for making Western civilization? Sometimes they were anonymous, such as the unknown geniuses who invented the mathematical systems of ancient Mesopotamia. At other times the makers of the

West were famous—saints such as Joan of Arc, creative thinkers such as Galileo Galilei, or generals such as Napoleon. But history is not made only by great and famous people. Humble people, such as the many millions who migrated from Europe to North America or the unfortunate millions who suffered and died in the trenches of World War I, can also influence the course of events.

Perhaps most often this book encounters people who were less the shapers of their own destinies than the subjects of forces that conditioned the kinds of choices they could make, often with unanticipated results. When during the eleventh century farmers throughout Europe began to employ a new kind of plow to till their fields, they were merely trying to do their work more efficiently. They certainly did not recognize that the increase in food they produced would stimulate the enormous population growth that made possible the medieval civilization of thriving cities and magnificent cathedrals. Answering the who question requires an evaluation of how much individuals and groups of people were in control of events and how much events controlled them.

The *How* Question

How did Western civilization develop? This is a question about processes—about how things change or stay the same over time. This book identifies these processes in several ways. First, the theme of encounters and transformations has been woven throughout the story. What is meant by encounters? When the Spanish *conquistadores* arrived in the Americas some 500 years ago, they came into contact with the cultures of the Caribs, the Aztecs, the Incas, and other peoples who had lived in the Americas for thousands of years. As the Spanish fought, traded with, and intermarried with the natives, each culture changed. The Spanish, for their part, borrowed from the Americas new plants for cultivation and responded to what they considered serious threats to their worldview. Many native Americans, in turn, adopted European religious practices and learned to speak European languages. At the same time, they were decimated by European diseases to which they had never before been exposed. They also witnessed the destruction of their own civilizations and governments at the hands of the colonial

Map 1   Core Lands of the West
The geographical borders of the West have changed substantially throughout history.

Cortés Meets Montezuma
As the Spanish fought, traded, and intermarried with the native peoples of the Americas during the fifteenth and sixteenth centuries, each culture changed.

Tenochtitlan.

powers. Through centuries of interaction and mutual influence, both sides became something other than what they had been.

The European encounter with the Americas is an obvious example of what was, in fact, a continuous process of encounters with other cultures. These encounters often occurred between peoples from different civilizations, such as the struggles between Greeks and Persians in the ancient world or between Europeans and Chinese in the nineteenth century. Other encounters took place among people living in the same civilization. These include interactions between lords and peasants, men and women, Christians and Jews, Catholics and Protestants, factory owners and workers, and capitalists and communists. Western civilization developed and changed through a series of external and internal encounters.

Second, features in the chapters formulate answers to the question of how Western civilization developed. For example, each chapter contains an essay titled "Justice in History." These essays discuss a trial or some other episode involving questions of justice. Some "Justice in History" essays illustrate how Western civilization was forged in struggles over conflicting values, such as the discussion of the trial of Galileo, which examines the conflict between religious and scientific concepts of truth. Others show how efforts to resolve internal cultural, political, and religious tensions helped shape Western ideas about justice, such as the

essay on the *auto-da-fé*, which illustrates how authorities attempted to enforce religious conformity. At the end of each "Justice in History" feature are several questions tying that essay to the theme of the chapter.

Some chapters include two other features as well. Essays titled "The Human Body in History" demonstrate that even the body, which is typically understood as a product of genetics and biology, has a history. These essays show that the ways in which Western people understand their bodies, how they cure them, how they cover and uncover them, and how they adorn them tell us a great deal about the history of Western culture. For example, the book explores how the bodies of World War I soldiers afflicted with shell shock were treated differently from women experiencing similar symptoms of hysteria. Shell-shocked soldiers gave people a sense of the horrors of war and stimulated powerful movements in Europe to outlaw war as an instrument of government policy.

The "Encounters and Transformations" features show how encounters between different groups of people, technologies, and ideas were not abstract historical processes but events that brought people together in a way that transformed history. For example, when the Arabs encountered the camel as an instrument of war, they adopted it for their own purposes and were able to conquer their neighbors very quickly and spread Islam far beyond its original home in Arabia.

The *Why* Question

Why did things happen in the way they did in history? This is the hardest question of all, one that engenders the most debate among historians. To take one persistent example, why did Hitler initiate a plan to exterminate the Jews of Europe? Can it be explained by something that happened to him in his childhood? Was he full of self-loathing that he projected onto the Jews? Was it a way of creating an enemy so that he could better unify Germany? Did he really believe that the Jews were the cause of all of Germany's problems? Did he merely act on the deeply seated anti-Semitic tendencies of the German people? Historians still debate the answers to these questions. These questions raise issues about human motivation and the role of human agency in historical events. Can historians ever really know what motivated a particular individual in the past, especially when it is so notoriously difficult to understand what motivates other people in the present? Can any individual determine the course of history? The *what, when, where, who,* and *how* questions are much easier to answer, but the *why* question, of course, is the most interesting one, the one that cries out for an answer.

This book does not always offer definitive answers to the *why* question, but it attempts to lay out the most likely possibilities. For example, historians do not really know what disease caused the Black Death in the fourteenth century, which killed about one-third of the population in a matter of months. But they can answer many questions about the consequences of that great catastrophe. Why were there so many new universities in the fourteenth and fifteenth centuries? It was because so many priests had died in the Black Death, creating a huge demand for replacements. The answers to the *why* questions are not always obvious, but they are always intriguing, and finding them is the joy of studying history.

The Beginnings of Civilization, 10,000–2000 B.C.E.

I N 1991 HIKERS TOILING ACROSS A GLACIER IN THE ALPS BETWEEN AUSTRIA AND Italy made a startling discovery: a man's body stuck in the ice. They alerted the police, who soon turned the corpse over to archaeologists. The scientists determined that the middle-aged man had frozen to death about 5,300 years ago. Ötzi the Ice Man (his name comes from the Ötztal Valley where he perished) quickly became an international celebrity as the world's oldest freeze-dried human. The scientists who examined Ötzi believe that he was a shepherd herding flocks of sheep and goats to mountain pastures when he died. A few grains of wheat on his clothing suggested that he lived in a farming community. Copper dust in his hair hinted that Ötzi may also have been a metalworker, perhaps looking for ores during his journey. An arrowhead lodged in his back indicated a violent cause of death, but the exact circumstances remain mysterious.

Ötzi's gear was state-of-the-art for his time. His possessions showed deep knowledge of the natural world. He wore leather boots insulated with dense grasses chosen for protection against the cold. The pouch around his waist contained stone tools and fire-lighting equipment. The wood selected for his bow offered special strength and flexibility. In his light wooden backpack Ötzi carried containers to hold burning embers, as well as dried meat and nutritious seeds to eat on the trail. The arrows in his quiver featured a natural adhesive that tightly bound bone and wooden points to the shafts. The most noteworthy find among Ötzi's possessions was his axe. Its handle was made of wood but its head was copper—a remarkable innovation at a time when most tools were made of stone. Ötzi was ready for almost anything—except the person who shot him in the back.

Ötzi lived at a transitional moment, at the very end of what archaeologists call the Neolithic Age, or "New Stone Age," when people made refinements in tool-making techniques over those of previous ages. For example, Neolithic artisans carved remarkably delicate arrowheads and blades that

Papyrus Harvest This painted wall sculpture from the Tomb of Nefer and Kahay in Saqqara Egypt dates to the fifth dynasty, 2494–2345 B.C.E. It shows farmers harvesting papyrus, the plant that grows along the banks of the Nile. Records were kept on papyrus, making it an essential element of Egyptian society and government.

Ötzi the Ice Man
This artist's recreation shows Ötzi in his waterproof poncho carrying his state-of-the-art tools.

imals. The growth of civilization also depended on constant interaction among communities that lived far apart. Once people were settled in a region, they began trading for commodities that were not available in their homelands. As trade routes extended over long distances and interactions among diverse peoples proliferated, ideas and technology spread.

How did the encounters between these early human societies create the world's first civilizations? To answer this question, this chapter asks the following questions:

- What is the link between the food-producing revolution of the Neolithic era and the emergence of civilizations?
- What transformed the earliest settled communities in Southwest Asia into the first cities, kingdoms, and empires in history?
- How did civilization take shape along the Nile River in Egypt?
- How and why did food production and the use of metals transform the lives of the men and women who populated Europe in the Neolithic Age?

Culture, Agriculture, and Civilization

- **What is the link between the food-producing revolution of the Neolithic era and the emergence of civilizations?**

Anthropologists use the term culture° to describe all the different ways that humans collectively adjust to their environment, and organize and transmit their experiences and knowledge to future generations. We can understand a people's culture as a web of interconnected meanings that enable them to understand themselves and their place in the world. Each culture is distinctive; thus we use labels—"Greek culture" or "American culture." Yet all cultures constantly borrow from their neighbors and change over time.

We often use *culture* and *civilization* interchangeably, yet in the history of human development, civilization has a specific definition. Archaeologists define civilization° as a society differentiated by levels of wealth and occupation in which people lived in cities. With cities, human populations achieved the critical mass necessary to develop specialized occupations, as well as a level of economic production high enough to sustain complex religious and cultural practices. As villages evolved into cities, their social organization grew more complicated. The labor of most people supported a small group of political and religious leaders. A city's leaders controlled the mechanisms of not only government and warfare but also the distribution of food and wealth. They

could be used for a variety of tasks, from hunting to sewing. The Neolithic Age was a long period of revolutionary change lasting from about 10,000 to about 3000 B.C.E. that altered human existence on Earth forever. Even the most advanced technological developments of the twentieth century did not reshape human life as profoundly as did those of the Neolithic era.

This chapter traces humanity's first steps toward the civilizations that developed in Southwest Asia, Egypt, and Europe—regions that made crucial contributions to the development of Western civilization. First we will consider the most fundamental encounter of all—the relationship between humans and the natural world. Many thousands of years of human interaction with nature led to food production through agriculture and the domestication of animals. This revolutionary achievement let humans develop new, settled forms of communities: first villages, then cities, and eventually kingdoms and empires. Civilizations grew from the foundations of agriculture and the domestication of an-augmented their authority by building temples to the gods and participating in religious rituals that linked divinity with kingship. Thus, in early civilizations three kinds of power—economic, political, and religious—converged.

The Food-Producing Revolution

Food production made civilization possible. For the first thousands of millennia of their existence, modern humans, known as *Homo sapiens sapiens*° ("most intelligent people"), did not produce food. Between 200,000 and 100,000 years ago, *Homo sapiens sapiens* first appeared in Africa and began to spread to other continents. Scientists refer to this stage of human history as the Paleolithic Age, or Old Stone Age, because people made tools by cracking rocks and using their sharp edges to cut and chop. *Homo sapiens sapiens'* use of tools demonstrated adaptation to new environments and practical needs. They scavenged for wild food and became shrewd observers of the natural environment. They followed migrating herds of animals, hunting with increasing efficiency as their weapons improved. They also created beautiful works of art by carving bone and painting on cave walls. By

Cave Drawings

45,000 years ago, these humans had reached most of Earth's habitable regions, except for Australia, the islands of the South Pacific, and North and South America.

The end of the last Ice Age about 15,000 years ago ushered in an era of momentous change: the food-producing revolution. As the Earth's climate became warmer, causing changes in vegetation, humans began to interact with the natural environment in new ways. The warmer climate allowed cereal grasses to spread quickly over large areas; hunter-gatherers learned to collect these wild grains and grind them up for food. Some groups of hunter-gatherers settled in semipermanent camps near rivers and wetlands, where wild grains grew. When people learned that the seeds of wild grasses could be transplanted and grown in new areas, the domestication of plants was under way (see Map 1.1).

At the same time that people discovered the benefits of planting seeds, they also began domesticating pigs, sheep, goats, and cattle, which eventually replaced wild game as the main source of meat. Domestication° occurs when humans manipulate the breeding of animals in order to serve their own purposes—for example, making wool (lacking on wild sheep), laying extra eggs (not done by undomesticated chickens), and producing extra milk

Map 1.1 The Beginnings of Food Production

This map shows early farming sites discovered by archaeologists where the first known production of food occurred in ancient Southwest Asia.

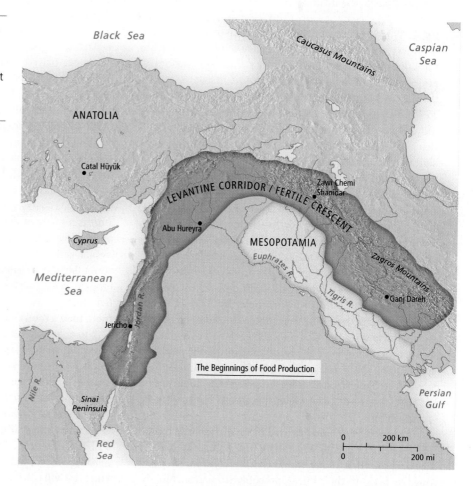

(wild cows produce only enough milk for their offspring). The first signs of goat domestication occurred about 8900 B.C.E. in the Zagros Mountains in Southwest Asia. Pigs, which adapt very well to human settlements because they eat garbage, were first domesticated around 7000 B.C.E. By around 6500 B.C.E. domesticated cattle, goats, and sheep had become widespread.

Farming and herding required hard work, but the payoff was enormous. Even simple agricultural methods could produce about fifty times more food than hunting and gathering. Thanks to the increased food supply, more newborns survived past infancy. Populations expanded, and so did human settlements. With the mastery of food production, human societies developed the mechanisms not only to feed themselves, but also to produce a surplus, which could then be traded for other resources. Such economic activity allowed for economic specialization and fostered the growth of social, political, and religious hierarchies.

The First Food-Producing Communities

In Southwest Asia, where sufficient annual rainfall enabled crops to grow without irrigation, people began cultivating food in three separate areas. Archaeologists have named the first area the Levantine Corridor° (also known as the Fertile Crescent°)—a twenty-five-mile-wide strip of land that runs from Jericho in the Jordan River valley of modern Israel to the Euphrates River valley in today's Iraq. The second region was the hilly land north of Mesopotamia at the base of the Zagros Mountains in the western part of modern Iran. The third was Anatolia, or what is now the central region of Turkey. In each of these three regions, archaeological evidence reveals how human societies made the revolutionary shift to food production.

The small settlement of Abu Hureyra near the center of the Levantine Corridor illustrates how agriculture developed over a long period at a single site. Humans first settled here around 9500 B.C.E. They fed themselves primarily by hunting gazelles and gathering wild cereals. But sometime between 8000 and 7700 B.C.E., they began to plant and harvest a small number of grains. Eventually they discovered that crop rotation—planting different crops in a field each year—resulted in a much higher yield. By 7000 B.C.E. Abu Hureyra had grown into a farming community, covering nearly thirty acres that sustained a population of about 400. A few generations later, the inhabitants of Abu Hureyra began herding sheep and goats to supplement their meat supply. These domesticated animals became the community's primary source of meat when the gazelle herds were depleted about 6500 B.C.E.

Families in Abu Hureyra lived in small dwellings built of mud brick containing several rooms. Archaeological evidence shows that many women in the community developed arthritis in their knees, probably from crouching for hours on end as they ground grains. Thus we assume that while men hunted and harvested, women performed the labor of grinding grains and preparing food. The division of labor along gender lines indicates a growing complexity of social relations within communities.

To the south of Abu Hureyra, at the southwestern end of the Levantine Corridor, the farming village of Jericho offers a second example of the way the food-producing revolution led to greater social complexity. Jericho began to develop rapidly after 8500 B.C.E. Located at an old hunting-gathering site along a stream in the Jordan River valley near modern Jerusalem, Jericho expanded to encompass nearly ten acres after its inhabitants started cultivating crops, including wheat, barley, lentils, and peas. They soon learned that if they let a field lie fallow for a season, the soil would be richer and more productive the following year. Archaeological evidence shows how Jericho's growing wealth enabled the community to evolve. The inhabitants developed more elaborate political, religious, and economic structures. Fairly sophisticated engineering projects, such as the digging of a nine-foot-deep ditch around the village as a flood control device and the erection of a massive stone wall to protect against attackers, indicate the emergence of some form of political organization. Other findings hint at religious beliefs. Jericho's people buried their dead within the settlement, sometimes under the floors of their houses. They placed plastered skulls of their deceased on the walls, a practice that may suggest worship of the family's ancestors.

Archaeological evidence also reveals that long-distance commerce played a part in the lives of these villagers. They exchanged agricultural goods for turquoise from the Sinai Peninsula, shells from the Mediterranean and Red Seas, and most important of all, obsidian from Anatolia. This volcanic stone was the most important commodity in the Neolithic Age because it could be used for making sharp-edged tools such as arrowheads, spear points, and sickles for harvesting crops.

The second region of village settlement, the lands at the foot of the Zagros Mountains north of Mesopotamia, reveals a different sort of development pattern from that exhibited in the Levantine Corridor. Archaeologists have unearthed a hunter-gatherer camp at Sawi Chemi Shanidar, dating to about 9000 B.C.E. In this settlement, the domestication of animals long predated the development of agriculture. The settlers herded animals, but they did not cultivate crops for more than a thousand years.

The third region of early settled communities, Anatolia, followed patterns more like those of the Levantine Corridor. Around 8500 B.C.E. a few simple settlements appeared. The villagers raised pigs and traded obsidian for materials from far away, such as the highly prized blue lapis lazuli stones from northeastern Afghanistan. A thousand years later, about 7400 B.C.E., Anatolians began cultivating a variety of crops, including wheat and lentils. They started herding sheep at roughly the same time as the Abu Hureyra villagers, and domesticated dogs for hunting, herding, and protection. Many new villages sprang up in this region during the next millennium. The farmers lived in rectangular houses. More than mere huts, these houses featured plastered walls, hearths, courtyards, and ovens for baking breads.

Sometime after 6000 B.C.E. Anatolian communities grew more complex, with the emergence of religious beliefs and social hierarchies. For example, the Anatolian town of Çatal Hüyük consisted of thirty-two acres of tightly packed houses that the townspeople rebuilt more than a dozen times as their population expanded. Çatal Hüyük controlled the obsidian trade from Anatolia to the Levantine Corridor. The wealth from this trade fostered the emergence of social differences. The townspeople buried some of their dead with jewelry and other riches, a practice that indicates distinctions between wealthy and poor members of the society.

The long-distance obsidian trade sped up the development of communities in the Levantine Corridor, the Zagros Mountains, and Anatolia. These trade networks of the Neolithic Age laid the foundation for commercial and cultural encounters that would shape the development of civilizations for the next 5,000 years.

The Birth of Civilization in Southwest Asia

■ What transformed the earliest settled communities in Southwest Asia into the first cities, kingdoms, and empires in history?

By 6000 B.C.E., settled communities that depended on farming and herding had become the norm throughout Southwest Asia. With better and more plentiful food, such communities expanded steadily. Prosperity further stimulated commerce, and merchants from different regions began traveling regularly to one another's villages to trade. Mesopotamia, the dry floodplain bounded by the Tigris and Euphrates Rivers, became the meeting place of peoples and ideas from across an enormous geographical area. Over time, these Mesopotamian village communities began to resemble one another and a more uniform culture developed. The development of this more uniform culture set the stage for the emergence of civilization in Southwest Asia.

Sumer: A Constellation of Cities in Southern Mesopotamia

About 5300 B.C.E. the villages in Sumer, an ancient name for southern Mesopotamia, began a dynamic civilization that would flourish for 3,000 years. At the height of this civiliza-

tion, Sumerians (who called themselves "the black-headed people" because of their characteristic dark hair) lived in thriving cities governed by leaders who controlled agricultural production, regulated long-distance trade, and presided over the worship of the gods.

Sumerian civilization was linked to water. Over centuries, the Sumerians learned to control the unpredictable waters of the Tigris and Euphrates Rivers. Sumerians first dug their own small channels to divert floodwaters from the two great rivers to irrigate their dry lands. Then they discovered that by combining the labor force of several villages, they could build and maintain irrigation channels on a large scale. The lands irrigated by river water provided rich yields of crops that fed Sumer's growing population. Villages blossomed into cities that became the foundation of Sumerian civilization.

By 2500 B.C.E., about twelve major cities in Sumer had emerged that controlled the Mesopotamian floodplain in an organized fashion. Some cities achieved impressive dimensions. Uruk, for example, covered about two square miles by 2500 B.C.E. and had a population estimated at between 10,000 and 50,000 people, including the peasants living in the countryside, many of whom labored to provide food for the urban populations as well as for themselves.

These cities served as the economic centers of southern Mesopotamia. Craft specialists such as potters, toolmakers, and weavers gathered in these urban settings to purchase food, swap information, and sell their goods. By providing markets for outlying towns, the cities spun a web of economic interdependence. Long-distance trade, made easier by the introduction of wheeled carts drawn by oxen, enabled merchants to bring timber, ores, building stone, and luxury items unavailable in Mesopotamia from Anatolia, the Levantine Corridor, Afghanistan, and Iran. With the introduction of the potter's wheel, Sumerian artisans could mass-produce containers for trade and storage of grain and other commodities.

Within the cities, an elite, headed by a king, controlled all economic resources. Centralized authorities directed the necessary labor for irrigation and water control, maintained warehouses for storing surplus grains, and distributed food to workers who labored on building projects for the king. Archaeological excavations reveal that the elite—priests, aristocrats, important civil administrators, and wealthy merchants—lived in luxurious houses near the temples, while everyone else crowded into small mud-brick houses with few comforts. Control over the economic resources of their cities enabled kings to supply armies and lead them into battle. Sumerian kings frequently waged war against one another in an effort to increase their territory and power. This rivalry prevented Sumerian cities from uniting politically, but the kings maintained diplomatic relations with one another as well as with rulers throughout Southwest Asia and Egypt, primarily to protect their trading networks. Safe trade links helped tie the Sumerian cities together and fostered a common Sumerian culture.

Through trade and warfare and from the many diplomats, soldiers, travelers, and slaves who passed through Mesopotamia's cities, the Sumerians knew much about the natural resources, economic organization, and customs that characterized the foreign peoples around them. The world known to them extended from India to the east to the Caucasus Mountains to the north; to Egypt and Ethiopia to the south; and to the Mediterranean Sea to the west. Sumerians strongly believed that the gods favored them over all other peoples, and they developed intense prejudices against their neighbors, accusing them of cowardice, stupidity, and treachery.

Religion—powerfully influenced by Mesopotamia's volatile climate—played a central role in daily life. Sumerians knew firsthand the famine and destruction that could result from sudden floods, storms, and winds. They envisioned each of these natural forces as a god who, like a human king or queen, had to be pleased and appeased. The all-powerful king Anu, the father of the gods, ruled the sky. Enlil was master of the wind and guided humans in the proper use of force. Enki ruled the Earth and rivers and guided human creativity and inventions. Inanna was the goddess of love, sex, fertility, and warfare. Sumerians believed that in order to survive they must continually demonstrate their subservience to the gods, and their practice of constantly feeding these deities with sacrifices was one way of doing so.

The Sumerian worldview revolved around religious belief. Each Sumerian city was protected by one god or goddess. The deity's temples served as the center of the city and the focus of religious life. In Uruk, for example, two enormous temples dominated the community: the Ziggurat of Anu (the supreme sky god) and the Temple of Heaven Precinct. This latter complex of buildings contained a colonnaded courtyard and a large limestone temple dedicated to Inanna (also known as Ishtar), the goddess of love and war and the city's special guardian. All Sumerian cities had similar temples that towered over the city, reminding all the inhabitants of the omnipresent gods who controlled their destiny.

Sumerians told exciting stories about their gods and heroes. One of the most popular figures in Sumerian ballads was the legendary king Gilgamesh of Uruk. Part god and part man, Gilgamesh—accompanied by his stalwart companion, Enkidu—embarked on many adventures that delighted Mesopotamian audiences for thousands of years.

DOCUMENT

The Clash Between Civilization and Nature: The Taming of Enkidu

The Sumerians saw their civilization as tightly linked to nature, as this passage from the tale of Gilgamesh suggests. This excerpt tells how Enkidu, Gilgamesh's companion, first became civilized. Originally living like a wild animal, Enkidu prevents hunters from trapping game. But city officials send him a prostitute who tames him by having sex with him for a week, and introducing him to cooked food, beer, and clothing. As a result of this epic sexual encounter, Enkidu loses his ability to talk to the animals. The episode teaches that civilization imposes control on natural forces, transforming them in the process. In the figure of the prostitute we see nature controlled and regulated by the city—a metaphor for the Sumerians' civilization.

In the wilderness the goddess Aruru created valiant
    Enkidu . . .
He knew neither people nor settled living . . .
He ate grasses like gazelles,
And jostled at the watering hole with the animals . . .
Then Shamhat [the prostitute] saw him—a primitive,
A savage fellow from the depths of the wilderness! . . .
Shamhat unclutched her bosom, exposed her sex,
And Enkidu took in her voluptuousness.
She was not restrained, but took his energy . . .

For six days and seven nights Enkidu stayed aroused,
And had intercourse with the prostitute,
Until he was sated with her charms.
But when he turned his attention to the animals,
The gazelles saw Enkidu and darted off,
The wild animals distanced themselves from his body . . .
Enkidu knew nothing about eating bread for food,
[nor] of drinking beer he had not been taught to.
The prostitute spoke to Enkidu, saying:
"Eat the food, Enkidu, it is the way one lives.
Drink the beer, as it is the custom of our land."
Enkidu ate the food until he was sated,
He drank the beer—seven jugs!—and became expansive
    and sang with joy!
He was elated and his face glowed.
He splashed his shaggy body with water,
And rubbed himself with oil and turned into a human.
He put on some clothing and became like a warrior.
He took up weapons and chased lions so shepherds could
    rest at night.
With Enkidu as their guard, the herders could lie down.

Source: Excerpts from Kovacs, Maureen Gallery, translator, *The Epic of Gilgamesh*, with an Introduction and Notes. Copyright © 1985, 1989 by the Board of Trustees of the Leland Stanford Junior University. With the permission of Stanford University Press, www.sup.org.

The tale describes how the gods created Enkidu to be Gilgamesh's companion and balance the king's rash disposition. Together the two men battled monsters and set out on long journeys in search of adventure. As a result of his travels, Gilgamesh became a wiser king and his subjects benefited from his new wisdom.

Sumerian culture exerted an enormous impact on the peoples of ancient Southwest Asia. Sumerians devised the potter's wheel, and also the wagon and the chariot, which proved essential for daily transportation and warfare. The Sumerians were skilled architects, as their ziggurats and city walls reveal. Their irrigation systems show their mastery of hydraulic engineering. They also developed detailed knowledge about the movement of the stars, planets, and the moon—especially as these movements pertained to agricultural cycles.

The Sumerians also made impressive innovations in mathematics. The first numerals (symbols for numbers) emerged around the same time as writing. Archaeologists have found many Sumerian tablets that show multiplication tables, square and cube roots, and exponents, as well as other practical information such as how to calculate compound interest on loans. Sumerian numeracy has left a lasting imprint on Western culture. The Sumerians divided the circle into 360 degrees, and developed a counting system based on sixty in multiples of ten—a system still in use in the way we tell time.

Perhaps the Sumerians' most important cultural innovation was their development of writing. The Sumerians devised a unique script used to record their language. Historians call the symbols that were pressed onto clay tablets with sharp objects cuneiform°, or wedge-shaped, writing. The earliest known documents written in this language come from Uruk about 3200 B.C.E. Researchers believe, however, that the roots of cuneiform writing date back 10,000 years, when people began to cultivate crops and domesticate animals in Southwest Asia. To keep track of quantities of produce and numbers of livestock, villagers began using small clay tokens of different shapes to represent and record these quantities. The tokens took the uncertainty out of transactions, reducing conflict because parties to a transaction no longer had to rely simply on memory or spoken agreements. After several centuries, people stopped using tokens and simply impressed the shapes directly on a flat piece of clay or tablet with a pointed stick.

As commodities and trading became more complex, the number of symbols multiplied. By 3000 B.C.E. the number of symbols had been streamlined from about a thousand to approximately 500, but learning even 500 signs required intensive study. The scribes, the people who mastered these signs, became valued members of the community. Sumerian cuneiform writing spread, and other peoples of Mesopotamia and Southwest Asia began adapting it to record information in their own languages.

Cuneiform Texts

This clay tablet, written on in cuneiform, or "wedge-shaped" letters, is early in the development of the script. Dating from about 3000 B.C.E., it lists what are probably temple offerings under the categories day one, day two, and day three.

From Akkad to the Amorite Invasions

The political independence of Sumer's cities ended around 2340 B.C.E. Conquered by a warrior who took the name Sargon ("true king"), Sumer's cities found themselves swallowed up by Mesopotamia's first great empire. Sargon came from Akkad, a region in Mesopotamia north of Sumer. Sargon's people, the Akkadians, had lived in Mesopotamia for more than a thousand years. The Akkadians began to migrate into Mesopotamia from their original homes somewhere in the Levantine Corridor during the late fourth millennium B.C.E. Their settlements grew in size, and although they intermingled with the native Sumerian population they preserved their own language and customs.

By bringing cities with very different languages, culture, and traditions under his rule, Sargon (r. ca. 2340–ca. 2305 B.C.E.) created a dynamic empire that endured for more than a century. The term empire° identifies a kingdom or any other type of state that controls foreign territories, either on the same continent or overseas. The realm that Sargon had established reached its greatest extent about 2220 B.C.E. Controlling a large empire posed new challenges for Akkadian rulers. To surmount them, Sargon and his successors imitated and expanded on the governing methods they observed in individual Sumerian cities. For example, to secure the loyalty of their many subjects, Akkadian kings presented themselves as symbols of unity in the form of semidivine figures. After a king's death, his subjects worshiped him as a god. Some monarchs claimed to be gods while they were alive.

Raising the revenues to meet the costs of running their enormous empire presented another problem for Akkadian kings. The king paid for all the public buildings, irrigation projects, and temples throughout his realm, as well as for the immense army required to defend, control, and expand it. Monarchs generated revenues in several ways. One key source of revenue was the leasing out of the vast farmlands that belonged to the king. Kings also required conquered peoples to pay regular tribute in the form of trade goods, produce, and gold and silver. In addition, Akkadian kings depended on the revenue generated by commerce. They placed heavy taxes on raw materials imported from foreign lands.

In fact, most Akkadian kings made long-distance trade the central objective of their foreign policy. They signed treaties with foreign kings and sent military expeditions as far as Anatolia and Iran to obtain timber, metals, luxury goods, and construction materials. Akkadian troops protected these international trade routes and managed the maritime trade in the Persian Gulf, where merchants brought goods by ship from India and southern Arabia.

The cities of Mesopotamia prospered under Akkadian rule. Even so, Akkadian rulers could not hold their empire together for reasons that historians do not completely understand. One cause was marauding tribes from the Zagros Mountains, who repeatedly infiltrated the kingdom and caused tremendous damage. Akkadian kings lost control of their lands and a period of anarchy began about 2103 B.C.E. "Who was king? Who was not king?" lamented a writer during this time of troubles. The kingdom finally collapsed about 2100 B.C.E.

With the fall of Akkad, the cities of Sumer regained their independence, but they were quickly reunited under Ur-Nammu (r. ca. 2112–ca. 2095 B.C.E.), king of the Sumerian city of Ur. Ur-Nammu established a powerful dynasty that lasted for more than a century. The kings of Ur strengthened the central government by turning formerly independent cities and their territories into provinces and appointing administrators to govern them.

Ur's kings also centralized economic production in their empire. The royal administration controlled most long-distance trade and developed a vigorous industry in woolen garments and leather goods. Ur's rulers supported thousands of artisans and laborers who were paid in beer and various agricultural products. The materials the artisans produced were traded throughout Southwest Asia. Wealth also flowed to the kings of Ur from farming and herding. The kings owned huge herds of livestock that grazed on royal estates, but ordinary people were not permitted to possess agricultural lands. Most of Ur's citizens worked either as tenant farmers on estates owned by the king and the political leaders, or as slaves. Each year government officials collected tens of thousands of cattle and hundreds of

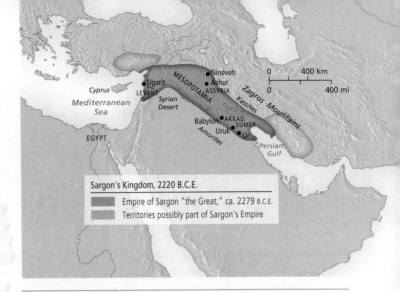

Map 1.2 Sargon's Empire, 2220 B.C.E.
Sargon of Akkad created an empire that included many distinct ethnic groups. For the first time in history, rulers had to struggle with the resistance of diverse subject peoples.

DOCUMENT

The Legend of King Sargon

The Akkadian king Sargon inspired many legends. The following story tells how his mother, a priestess, bore him in secret and put him in a basket in the river, from which a water bearer rescued him. The document explains how Sargon eventually became king of the Mesopotamians through the favor of the goddess Ishtar. The tale of a baby found in the bulrushes who achieves greatness was a Sumerian story already old in Sargon's day. A similar tale about the prophet Moses would be recorded in the Hebrew Bible more than a thousand years later. The recurrence of such literary motifs over a period of more than 3,000 years indicates the pervasive influence of Sumerian culture on subsequent civilizations of Southwest Asia.

Sargon, the mighty king, king of Agade, am I.
My mother was a high priestess, my father I knew not . . .
My mother, the high priestess, conceived me, in secret she
  bore me.
She set me in a basket of rushes, with bitumen she sealed
  my lid.
She cast me into the river which rose not over me.
The river bore me up and carried me to Akki, the drawer of
  water. . . .
Akki, the drawer of water, took me as his son and reared me.
Akki, the drawer of water, appointed me as his gardener.
While I was a gardener, Ishtar granted me her love.
And for four and [. . .] years I exercised kingship.
The black-headed people I ruled, I governed. . . .

Source: From *Chronicles Concerning Early Babylonian Kings*, by
L. W. King. London: British Museum, 1907.

thousands of sheep and redistributed them to temples throughout the kingdom for use in sacrifices.

The most important innovation in Ur occurred in the realm of the law. Ur-Nammu compiled the first known collection of laws in ancient Mesopotamia. His laws reveal his determination to provide social justice for his subjects. The custom of writing down laws so that citizens and later generations could refer to them became a strong tradition in Western civilization.

The kings of Ur used political innovations, economic centralization, and legal codification to strengthen their hold over Sumer's cities; they did not, however, challenge or change the key facets of Sumerian culture. Ur's monarchs continued the long Mesopotamian tradition of building elaborate temple complexes featuring ziggurats, palaces, and tombs to demonstrate their piety. Like earlier Mesopotamian rulers, Ur's kings considered themselves gods. They placed their tombs in the temple complex of the moon god Nanna, Ur's special protector.

Despite their sophisticated government, the kings of Ur could not stave off political fragmentation. About 2000 B.C.E., seminomadic peoples known as Amorites began invading Mesopotamia from the steppes to the west and north. They seized fortified towns, taking food and supplies and causing widespread destruction. Their invasions destabilized the economy of Mesopotamia as well as of other regions of Southwest Asia. Peasants fled from the fields, and with no food or revenues, inflation and famine overcame the empire. Ur collapsed, and Mesopotamia shattered once again into a scattering of squabbling cities. Taking advantage of the political turmoil and attracted by the abundant food supplies, tribes of Amorites settled in Mesopotamian lands.

New Mesopotamian Kingdoms: Assyria and Babylonia

Within a few generations, the Amorites absorbed the culture of the Mesopotamian urban communities they had conquered. Two new kingdoms, Babylonia and Assyria, emerged in the lands once controlled by Sumer and Akkad and coexisted for more than two centuries. The phenomenon of invaders absorbing the culture of sophisticated communities they conquered and then creating something new would often be repeated as Western civilization evolved.

Ashur, the major city in Assyria, began as a trading hub on the upper Tigris River some time before 2000 B.C.E. The discovery of bronze making may be one reason that Assyria's power began to expand. Bronze, an easily worked but very hard metal, became highly valued for both military and ornamental uses. By 1900 B.C.E. the Assyrians had

Ziggurat of Ur
Built of mud-brick, the Ziggurat of Ur was the focal point of religious life. This vast temple was built by King Ur-Nammu of the Third Dynasty (2112–2095 B.C.E.) and restored by the British archaeologist Sir Leonard Woolley in the 1930s.

established an extensive trading network in metals as well as agricultural products such as barley and wool that reached as far as Anatolia and Syria. They also controlled and operated about a dozen trading colonies throughout these regions.

By 1762 B.C.E., however, Assyria and all of Mesopotamia fell under the rule of King Hammurabi of Babylon, one of humanity's first great empire builders. The kingdom of Babylonia, a mixture of Sumerian and Amorite cultures, emerged about 1800 B.C.E. as the dominant power in southern Mesopotamia. To secure their rule and enrich their coffers, Babylonian kings embarked on the conquest of neighboring lands. Their capital city, Babylon, grew wealthy. Under the leadership of Hammurabi (r. 1792–1750 B.C.E.), Babylonia gained control of all of Mesopotamia, including the Assyrian realm. Impressed by his own victories, Hammurabi called himself "King of the Four Quarters of the World."

Hammurabi also called himself the "King of Justice," a well-deserved title because his historical legacy is a rigorous system of justice codified in law. The 282 civil, commercial, and criminal laws contained in the Law Code of Hammurabi unveil the social values and everyday concerns of Babylonia's rulers. For example, the irrigation system on which Babylonian agriculture depended is a frequent focus of the code. Many laws related specifically to damages and personal responsibility with regard to irrigation. Similarly, the code buttressed Babylon's social hierarchy by drawing legal distinctions between classes of people. The crimes of aristocrats were treated more leniently than were the offenses

DOCUMENT
Hammurabi's Law Code

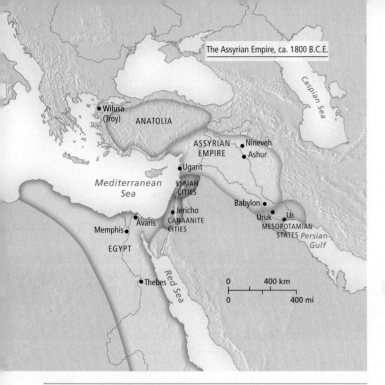

Map 1.3 Assyrian Empire, ca. 1800 B.C.E.
The Assyrians combined warfare and commerce to create their empire in Mesopotamia.

of common people, while slaves were given no rights at all. At the same time, however, Hammurabi's Code introduced one of the fundamentals of Western jurisprudence: the idea that the punishment must suit the crime. One law reads: "If a man has opened his channel for irrigation and has been negligent and allowed the water to wash away a neighbor's field, he shall pay grain equivalent to the crops of his neighbors."[1] Through its introduction of such abstract principles as "an eye for an eye," Hammurabi's Code helped shape legal thought in Southwest Asia for a millennium. It is possible that it later influenced the laws of the Hebrews, and thus through the Hebrew Bible continues to mold ideas about justice to this day.

Babylonian society contained a private sector of merchants, craftspeople, farmers, and sailors. With no ties to the temples or the king, these free people grew prosperous. Merchants traveling by land and sea brought textiles and metals as well as luxury items such as gold and silver jewelry and gems from Anatolia, Egypt, Iran, Afghanistan, and lands along the Persian Gulf and Red Sea. This private sector enjoyed a degree of personal freedom unique in ancient Mesopotamia.

Nevertheless, Hammurabi and his successors imposed increasingly heavy taxes on their subjects. These financial demands provoked great resentment, and when Hammurabi died, many Babylonian provinces successfully revolted. The loss of revenue weakened the Babylonian imperial government. Successive kings tried to maintain their control by increasing the number of bureaucrats to enforce laws and to collect taxes, but such measures only made the government top-heavy. By 1500 B.C.E. it collapsed.

The Emergence of Egyptian Civilization

■ How did civilization take shape along the Nile River in Egypt?

As the civilizations of Mesopotamia rose and fell, another emerged far to the south: Egypt. A long and narrow strip of land in the northeast corner of the African continent, Egypt depended for its survival on the Nile, the world's longest river, which flows north into the Mediterranean Sea from one of its points of origin in eastern Africa 4,000 miles away. The northernmost part of Egypt, where the Nile enters the Mediterranean, is a broad and fertile delta. In ancient times, Egypt controlled an 850-mile strip of land along the Nile. The river flooded annually from mid-July to mid-October, leaving behind rich deposits of silt ideal for planting crops. In its ancient days, the Nile abounded with fish, water birds, and game on the shore. The rich banks of the Nile provided an ideal setting for agriculture and settled communities.

Historians organize the long span of ancient Egyptian history into four main periods: Predynastic (10,000–3000 B.C.E.), the Old Kingdom (3000–2200 B.C.E.), the Middle Kingdom (2040–1785 B.C.E.), and the New Kingdom (1600–1100 B.C.E., discussed in Chapter 2). Times of political disruption between the kingdoms are called intermediate periods. Despite these periods of disruption, the Egyptians maintained a remarkably stable civilization for several millennia.

The Old Kingdom, ca. 3500–2200 B.C.E.

Like the peoples of Mesopotamia, the Egyptians were originally hunter-gatherers who slowly turned to growing crops and domesticating animals. Small villages, in which people could coordinate their labor most easily, appeared along the banks of the Nile between 5000 and 4000 B.C.E. By 3500 B.C.E., Egyptians could survive comfortably through agriculture and herding. With the transition to settled life complete, Egyptian society began to develop in many new ways. Small towns grew quickly in number along the Nile, and market centers connected by roads emerged as hubs where artisans and merchants exchanged their wares.

Towards the end of the Predynastic period, between 3500 and 3000 B.C.E., energetic trade along the Nile River resulted in a shared culture and unified way of life. Towns along the Nile grew into small kingdoms, whose rulers constantly warred with one another, attempting to grab more land and extend their power. The big consumed the small, and by 3000 B.C.E., the towns had been absorbed into just two kingdoms: Upper Egypt in the south and

Lower Egypt in the north. These two then united, forming what historians term the Old Kingdom.

With the unification of Egypt under one king, a new era dawned for this civilization. In the newly built capital city of Memphis, the Egyptian kings established themselves as the focal points of religious, social, and political life. Under the kings' careful supervision, the Old Kingdom stabilized and took on many of the characteristics of early civilizations we have seen in Mesopotamia, such as semi-divine kingship, literate bureaucracies, a centralized economy, and strong support of long-distance trade.

Egyptian monarchs considered themselves gods as well as kings and believed that Ra, the sun god and creator of the universe, had chosen them to rule as his representatives on Earth. In their role as religious leaders, kings claimed to control even the Nile and its life-giving floods. To the Egyptians, the presence of the kings meant that cosmic order reigned, and that the kingdom was protected against forces of disorder and destruction. The rulers steadily amassed more power, and by 2600 B.C.E. they owned the largest and richest agricultural lands.

DOCUMENT

Elders' Advice to Their Successors

The power of the kings was highly centralized. Authority began with the king and passed to his court officials and then to provincial governors who delegated power to the mayors of cities and villages. Administrators collected Egypt's surplus produce—coinage would not be used in Egypt for another 2,000 years—and then the kings' officials redistributed it throughout the kingdom. Surplus crops fed the armies that protected Egyptian territories and long-distance trade as well as the peasants who labored on public works such as temples, roads, and irrigation projects.

The job of keeping records of the kings' possessions and supervising food production fell to the scribes, who were trained in hieroglyph writing. This form of writing involved a set of several thousand signs called *hieroglyphs,* literally "sacred carvings." Hieroglyphs represent both sounds (as in our alphabet) and objects (as in a pictorial system). The hieroglyph system was very complex, all the more so because it diverged from the spoken Egyptian language. Consequently, learning hieroglyphs for literary or administrative purposes meant acquiring a second language and took years of schooling to master. It was worth the effort, however, for knowledge of hieroglyphs gave scribes great power. For 3,000 years, these royal bureaucrats kept the machinery of Egyptian government running despite the rise and fall of dynasties.

Narmer the Unifier of Egypt

Carved pieces of stone called *palettes* were originally crafted in the Predynastic period as holders for cosmetics, but they evolved into objects with important religious and symbolic functions. This sample shows King Narmer of Hierakonpolis, who lived about 3100 B.C.E. With his right hand he holds a mace and is about to smash the skull of an enemy. He stands on two dead enemies, as a servant behind him carries his sandals. A falcon god, Horus (*Hierakonpolis* means "City of the Falcon"), sits in a papyrus plant holding an enemy's severed head. Narmer wears the White Crown of Upper Egypt and a bull's tail, symbolizing his virility. On the other side, he wears the Red Crown of Lower Egypt, which he has conquered.

Like bureaucrats, priests in the king's service grew powerful. Priests came from elite families, often the king's, and their positions passed from father to son. They owned vast estates, including the temples to the god they served, and they became enormously wealthy. In addition, they often played a major role in political life. Kings sought their advice to ensure that in their leadership they were implementing the will of the gods.

Religious Beliefs in the Old Kingdom

Egypt's religion was polytheistic°. Egyptians believed that many gods controlled their destinies. Ra, the sun god, was one of the most important Egyptian deities. Embodying the power of Heaven over Earth, Ra had created the universe and everything in it. He journeyed across the sky every day in a boat, rested at night, and returned in the morning to resume his eternal journey. By endlessly repeating the cycle of rising and setting, the sun symbolized the harmonious order of the universe that Ra established. The sun's reappearance at dawn every day gave Egyptians the hope of life after death.

Evil, however, constantly threatened the order of the universe in the form of Apopis, a serpent god whose coils could trap Ra's boat like a reef in the Nile. Ra's cosmic journey could continue only if proper worship and justice existed among humans. To make this possible, Ra created Egypt's kings, who shared in his divine nature and who ruled as his representatives on Earth.

Gods and Kings in Mesopotamian Justice

Mesopotamian kings placed a high priority on ruling their subjects justly. Shamash, the sun god and protector of justice, named two of his children Truth and Fairness. In the preface to his law code, Hammurabi explained the relationship between his rule and divine justice:

> At that time, Anu and Enlil [two of the greatest gods], for the well-being of the people, called me by name, Hammurabi, the pious, god-fearing prince, and appointed me to make justice appear in the land [and] to destroy the evil and wicked, so that the strong might not oppress the weak, [and] to rise like Shamash over the black-headed people [the people of Mesopotamia].[2]

Courts in Mesopotamian cities handled cases involving property, inheritance, boundaries, sale, and theft. A special panel of royal judges and officials handled cases involving the death penalty, such as treason, murder, sorcery, theft of temple goods, or adultery. Mesopotamians kept records of trials and legal decisions on clay tablets so that others might learn from them and avoid additional lawsuits.

A lawsuit began when an individual brought a dispute before a court for trial and judgment. The court consisted of three to six judges chosen from among the town's leading men, who typically included merchants, scribes, and officials in the town assembly. The judges could speak with authority about the community's principles of justice.

Individuals involved in the dispute spoke on their own behalf and presented testimony through witnesses, written documents, or statements made by leading officials. Witnesses took strict oaths to tell the truth in a temple before the statue of a god. Once the parties presented all the evidence, the judges made their decision and pronounced the verdict and punishment.

Sometimes the judges asked the defendants to clear themselves by letting the god in whose name the oath was taken make the judgment. The accused person would then undergo an ordeal or test in which he or she had to jump into a river and swim a certain distance underwater. Individuals who survived were considered innocent. Drowning constituted proof of guilt and a just punishment rendered by the gods.

The following account of one such ordeal comes from the city of Mari, about 1770 B.C.E. In this case a queen was accused of casting spells on her husband. The maid whom she forced to undergo the ordeal on her behalf drowned, and we do not know whether the queen received further punishment:

> Concerning Amat-Sakkanim . . . whom the river god overwhelmed . . . : "We made her undertake her plunge, saying to her, 'Swear that your mistress did not perform any act of sorcery against Yarkab-Addad her lord; that she did not reveal any palace secret nor did another person open the missive of her mistress; that your mistress did not commit a transgression against her lord.' In connection with these oaths they had her take her plunge; the river god overwhelmed her, and she did not come up alive."[3]

This account illustrates the Mesopotamian belief that sometimes only the gods could make decisions about right and wrong. Kings willingly allowed the gods to administer justice in their kingdoms. In this way, divine justice and royal justice became part of the same system.

By contrast, the following trial excerpts come from a homicide case in which humans, not gods, made the final judgment. About 1850 B.C.E., three men murdered a temple official named Lu-Inanna. For unknown reasons they told the victim's wife, Nin-dada, what they had done. King Ur-Ninurta of the city of Isin sent the case to be tried in the city of Nippur, the site of an important court. When the case came to trial, nine accusers asked that the three murderers be executed. They also requested that Nin-dada should be put to death because she had not reported the murder to the authorities. The accusers said:

> They who have killed a man are not worthy of life. Those three males and that woman should be killed in front of the chair of Lu-Inanna, the son of Lugal-apindu, the religious official.

In her defense, two of Nin-dada's supporters pointed out that she had not been involved in the murder and therefore should be released:

> Granted that the husband of Nin-dada, the daughter of Lu-Ninurta, has been killed, but what had the woman done that she should be killed?

The court agreed with this latter argument on the grounds that Nin-dada was justified in keeping silent because her husband had not provided for her properly. Then the members of the Assembly of Nippur faced the three murderers and said:

> A woman whose husband did not support her . . . why should she not remain silent about him? Is it she who killed her husband? The punishment of those who actually killed him should suffice.

Hammurabi stands because his status is lower than Shamash's. He raises his hand in a gesture of respect and speaks directly to the god.

The god, seated on a throne, wears a crown of horns, a scepter, and a ring. Flames rise from his shoulders.

Hammurabi's code was written in Babylonian cuneiform script. This stone copy stands taller than seven feet.

In accordance with the decision of the court, the defendants were executed.

This approach to justice—using witnesses, evaluating evidence, and rendering a verdict in a court protected by the king—demonstrates the Mesopotamians' desire for fairness. This court decision became an important precedent that later judges frequently cited.

Questions of Justice

1. How would a city benefit by letting a panel of royal officials make judgments about life-and-death issues? How would the king benefit?

2. These trials demonstrate that the enforcement of justice in Mesopotamia depended on the interaction of religious, social, and political beliefs. How does this interaction help us understand Mesopotamian civilization?

Taking It Further

Greengus, Samuel. "Legal and Social Institutions of Ancient Near Mesopotamia," in *Civilizations of the Ancient Middle East,* ed. Jack M. Sasson, vol. 1, pp. 469–484. 1995. Describes basic principles of law and administration of justice, with a bibliography of ancient legal texts.

Kuhrt, Amélie. *The Ancient Middle East: ca. 3000–330 B.C.,* vol. 1. 1995. An authoritative survey combining archaeological and textual evidence.

The Law Code of Hammurabi
This copy of Hammurabi's Code shows Hammurabi receiving the law directly from the sun god, Shamash.

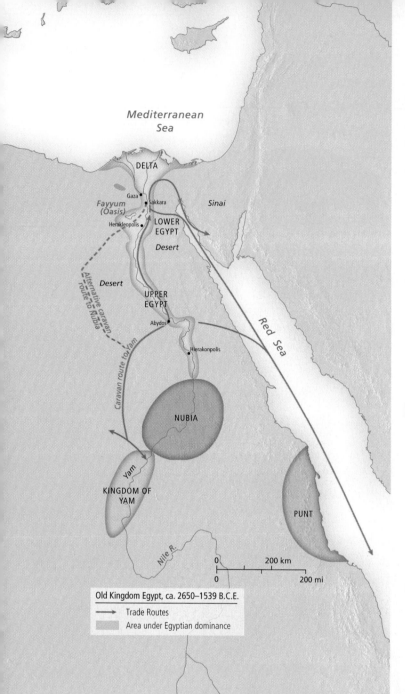

Map showing Old Kingdom Egypt with labels: Mediterranean Sea, DELTA, Gaza, Sakkara, Fayyum (Oasis), Herakleopolis, LOWER EGYPT, Sinai, Desert, Desert, Alternative caravan route to Nubia, UPPER EGYPT, Caravan route to Yam, Abydos, Hierakonpolis, Red Sea, NUBIA, Yam, KINGDOM OF YAM, PUNT, Nile R.

0 — 200 km
0 — 200 mi

Old Kingdom Egypt, ca. 2650–1539 B.C.E.
→ Trade Routes
▢ Area under Egyptian dominance

Map 1.4   Old Kingdom Egypt, ca. 3000–2200 B.C.E.
During the Old Kingdom, Egyptians traded with the kingdom of Yam, Nubia, and the land of Punt (modern Somalia). Egyptian rulers built pyramids in Lower (northern) Egypt.

The Pyramids

With their emphasis on the afterlife, Egyptians took great pains to provide proper housing for the dead. Many tombs were built as monuments to the dead person's wealth and social status. These structures provided not only a resting place for the corpse but a symbolic entryway to the next life. Members of the elite were buried in expensive tombs filled with ivory furniture and other luxurious goods, but kings had the grandest tombs of all.

Burial customs in the Old Kingdom grew ever more elaborate. For the first several centuries of the Old Kingdom, kings built their tombs in the city of Abydos, the homeland of the first kings. The tombs consisted of an underground room with a special compartment for the royal corpse. The king's treasures filled nearby underground rooms. Above the ground sat a small palace featuring courtyards and halls suitable for a royal afterlife. The earliest of these tombs, dating to about 2800 B.C.E., contains the bones of animals and people sacrificed to accompany the ruler into the next world.

About 2680 B.C.E., architects began building a new kind of royal tomb. The defining feature was a great four-sided monument of stone in the shape of a pyramid. Elaborate temples in which priests worshiped statues of the king surrounded the monument. The structure also included compartments where the king could dwell in the afterlife in the same luxury he enjoyed during his life on Earth. King Djoser, the founder of the Old Kingdom, built the first pyramid complex at Saqqara near Memphis. Known today as the Step Pyramid, this structure rests above Djoser's burial place and rises high into the air in six steps, which represent a ladder to Heaven.

For the next 2,000 years, kings continued building pyramids for themselves and smaller ones for their queens, with each tomb becoming more architecturally sophisticated. The walls grew taller and steeper and contained hidden burial chambers and treasure rooms. The Great Pyramid at Giza, built around 2600 B.C.E. by King Khufu (or Cheops), stood as the largest human-made structure in the ancient world. It consists of more than two million stones that weigh an average of two and a half tons each. Covering thirteen acres, it reaches over 480 feet into the sky.

Building the pyramid complexes was a long and enormously costly task. In addition to the architects, painters,

IMAGE

The Pyramids at Giza

Egyptians also worshiped Osiris, the son of the sky and the Earth, as god of the dead. According to Egyptian belief, Osiris was murdered by his brother Seth, god of chaos, after Osiris married their sister Isis, goddess of fertility. Seth cut Osiris into pieces and scattered them over the Earth, but Isis gathered the pieces and restored Osiris to life. The death and resurrection of Osiris symbolized the natural cycles of regeneration and rebirth that the Egyptians witnessed each spring as their fields bore new crops. After his regeneration, Osiris became king of the underworld, where he judged the dead. Egyptians associated this powerful deity with mummification, by which they tried to preserve bodies after death. Representations of Osiris appeared in pyramids, where the mummies of kings rested for eternity.

sculptors, carpenters, and other specialists employed on the site throughout the year, stone masons supervised the quarrying and transportation of the colossal building blocks. Peasants, who were organized into work gangs and paid and fed by the king, provided the heavy labor when the Nile flooded their fields every year. As many as 70,000 workers out of a total population estimated at 1.5 million sweated on the pyramids every day. Entire cities sprang up around pyramid building sites to house the workmen, artisans, and farmers. The construction of enormous pyramids stopped after 2400 B.C.E., probably because of the expense, but smaller burial structures continued to be built for many centuries.

The Middle Kingdom, ca. 2040–1785 B.C.E.

Around 2200 B.C.E. the Old Kingdom collapsed, due to economic decline, the deterioration of royal authority, and a cycle of terrible droughts that triggered a breakdown of law and order. For 200 years, anarchy and civil war raged in Egypt during what historians call the First Intermediate Period. Finally, the governors of Thebes, a city in Upper Egypt, set out to reunify the kingdom. In 2040 B.C.E., Mentuhotep II consolidated his rule and established a vigorous new monarchy, initiating the Middle Kingdom (see Map 1.5).

Rulers in the Middle Kingdom defined a new role for themselves. They still viewed themselves as gods, but their rule became less despotic. Although they continued building large temple complexes to house themselves in the afterlife, these structures were not as grandiose as the Old Kingdom pyramids. The highly centralized bureaucracy opened to men of any social standing, as long as they could read and write hieroglyphs. Wealth spread more widely. The kings launched many public-works projects for the benefit of their subjects. Amenemhet I (r. 1991–1962 B.C.E.) and his successors transformed the marshy Fayyum Oasis, fifty miles southwest of Memphis, into a well-irrigated agricultural community that yielded abundant crops even in dry years.

Greater concern for the lives and needs of ordinary people also characterized the religious life of the Middle Kingdom. Because it stressed moral conduct more than the performance of rituals open only to the wealthy, the religion of the Middle Kingdom comforted more people with the hope of a satisfying afterlife.

DOCUMENT

Hymns of Praise to a Victorious King

These passages come from a collection of hymns of praise to King Sesostris III of the Middle Kingdom. Written on a papyrus scroll, the hymns were probably read aloud in an elaborate ritual when Sesostris, who lived in the northern city of Memphis, visited a town in southern (Upper) Egypt. References to "Two Lands" and his "double crown" refer to the symbolic unity of all of Egypt that this king represents. The Bowmen are raiders from Nubia, evidently a considerable problem during Sesostris's reign. The praise includes more general allusions to other enemies as well. Needless to say, the king triumphs over all of them and wins the universal devotion of his subjects.

I.

Hail to you, Son of Re [the sun god], our Horus,
    Divine of Form!
Land's protector who widens its borders,
Who smites foreign countries with his crown;
Who holds the Two Lands in his arms' embrace;
Who subdues foreign lands by a motion of his hands;
Who slays Bowmen without a blow of the club;

Who shoots the arrow without drawing the string;
Whose terror strikes the Bowmen in their land,
Fear of whom smites the Nine Bows.
Whose slaughter brought death to thousands of Bowmen,
Who had come to invade his borders. . . .
His majesty's tongue restrains Nubia.
His utterances make Asiatics flee. . . .

II.

How the gods rejoice:
You have strengthened their offerings!
How the people rejoice:
You have made safe their frontiers!
How your forbears rejoice:
You have enriched their portions!
How Egypt rejoices in your strength:
You have protected its customs!
How the people rejoice in your guidance:
Your might has won increase for them! . . .

Source: From Miriam Lichtheim, *Ancient Egyptian Literature: The Old and Middle Kingdoms,* Volume 1. Copyright © 1973 by The Regents of the University of California. Reprinted by permission.

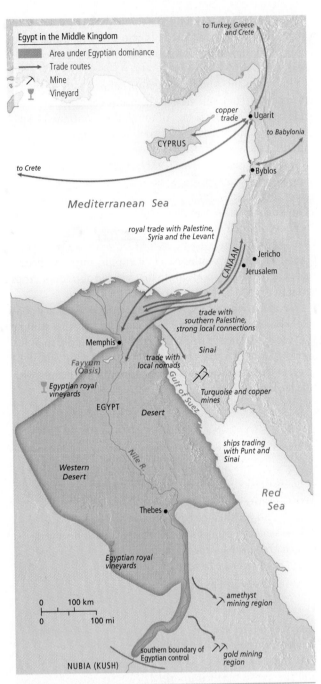

Egypt in the Middle Kingdom
- Area under Egyptian dominance
- Trade routes
- Mine
- Vineyard

to Turkey, Greece and Crete

copper trade

Ugarit

CYPRUS

to Babylonia

to Crete

Byblos

Mediterranean Sea

royal trade with Palestine, Syria and the Levant

CANAAN

Jericho

Jerusalem

trade with southern Palestine, strong local connections

Memphis

Sinai

trade with local nomads

Fayyum (Oasis)

Egyptian royal vineyards

Turquoise and copper mines

EGYPT

Gulf of Suez

Desert

ships trading with Punt and Sinai

Western Desert

Nile R.

Red Sea

Thebes

Egyptian royal vineyards

amethyst mining region

0   100 km
0   100 mi

southern boundary of Egyptian control

gold mining region

NUBIA (KUSH)

Map 1.5   Egypt in the Middle Kingdom

During the Middle Kingdom, Egyptian merchants traded extensively with Southwest Asia and the cities of the eastern Mediterranean. Turquoise and copper mines in the Sinai were heavily exploited.

Egyptian Encounters with Other Civilizations

During both the Old and Middle Kingdoms, Egypt's kings sought to protect the trade routes along which raw materi-

als and luxury goods were imported. Rulers did not hesitate to use force when necessary to protect their commercial interests. Some of them sent their armies to make punitive attacks in the western desert and in Sinai to stop raiders from robbing trade caravans. Other kings tried to maintain good relations with the chief trading cities of Syria and Palestine in order to stimulate trade.

From the earliest years of the Old Kingdom, Egypt cultivated friendly ties with the Mediterranean port city of Byblos, north of Beirut in modern Lebanon. Exchanges between Byblos and Egypt benefited both sides. Egyptians imported timber from Byblos for the construction of tombs and learned many shipbuilding techniques. The people of Byblos gained technical skills, especially in masonry and engineering, from the Egyptians, and also adopted some of the Egyptian gods. Thoth, the god of writing, became Taut in Byblos.

During the Old and Middle Kingdoms, Egyptian interactions with Nubia, the territory to the south, proved economically important. Egyptian merchants systematically exploited its natural resources of gold, timber, and animal skins. They enslaved many Nubians and transported them for labor in Egypt. Agents of Egyptian rulers, called Keepers of the Gateway of the South, tried to protect the merchants by keeping the peace with the warlike Nubian tribes. Slowly, Egyptian monarchs made their presence more permanent. About 1900 B.C.E., king Amenemhet built ten forts at strategic locations where trade routes from the interior of Africa reached the Nile River. Egyptian merchants placed the gold, ivory, and other natural resources that reached these forts into boats, which they sailed northward along the Nile to Egypt. Egyptians came to depend on these vast resources of Nubia.

Commercial connections between Egypt and other African lands were less important. Egyptian merchants traded with the land of Punt (modern Somalia) for spices and rare woods, and they opened turquoise mines in the Sinai. During the Old Kingdom, some merchants traded for skins, ivory, incense, and slaves among the peoples living in the Kingdom of Yam, located at the tributaries of the Nile River in the interior of eastern Africa, but the Egyptians abandoned trade with Africa south of Nubia during the Middle Kingdom.

With the desert on both sides of the Nile Valley protecting Egypt from invasion by foreign enemies, the Egyptians developed a distinctive culture characterized not only by economic prosperity but also by a powerful sense of self-confidence and optimism. Attracted by Egypt's stability and prosperity, peoples from different lands sought to settle in the Nile Valley. They took Egyptian names and assimilated into Egyptian culture. The government settled these immigrants, as well as war captives, throughout the kingdom where they could mix quickly with the local inhabitants. This willingness to accept newcomers into their kingdom lent Egyptian civilization even more vibrancy. During the last years of the Middle Kingdom, many merchants and large numbers of settlers moved into Egypt from Syria and Palestine. Around 1750 B.C.E., one such group from Syria, called the Hyksos, took control of Egypt and changed the direction of Egyptian history. As we shall see in Chapter 2, the Second Intermediate Period was marked by both foreign invasion and internal division.

The Transformation of Europe

■ How and why did food production and the use of metals transform the lives of the men and women who populated Europe in the Neolithic Age?

The elements that produced civilization in Mesopotamia and Egypt began to appear about 10,000 years ago. Western history claims the cultures that developed in these regions as remote ancestors. But in Europe, the core territory of Western civilization today, civilization developed later than in the floodplains of Mesopotamia and the Levantine Corridor. Because the climate was colder and forests had to be cleared, food production was more difficult in Europe. Consequently Europeans made the transition from hunting and gathering to food production much more slowly. The food-producing revolution that had begun in Southwest Asia around 8000 B.C.E. spread to Europe a thousand years later when farmers, probably from Anatolia, ventured to northern Greece and the Balkans. It took another 4,000 years for the inhabitants of Europe to clear forests and to establish farms and grazing lands. By 2500 B.C.E., most of Europe's hunting and gathering cultures had given way to farming societies. New patterns of wealth, prestige, and inheritance had begun reshaping some communities but Europeans did not yet live in cities. Without the critical mass of people and possessions that accompanied city life, Europeans could not yet develop the specialized religious, economic, and political classes that characterize a "civilization." The transition to food production, however, laid the economic foundations of subsequent European cultures (see Map 1.6).

As farmers and herders spread across Europe, people adapted to different climates and terrain. A variety of cultures evolved from these differences. Archaeologists have named the different cultures of Neolithic Europe after some distinguishing feature of their pottery, tools, methods of constructing houses, or burial customs.

The Linear Pottery Culture

By 5000 B.C.E. one of the most important of these cultures, the Linear Pottery culture, had spread across Europe from

CHRONOLOGY	
The Beginnings of Civilization	
150,000 years ago	Modern humans first appear in Africa
45,000 years ago	Modern humans spread through Africa, Asia, and Europe
15,000 years ago	Ice Age ends
10,000 years ago	Food production begins
9,500–3,000 years ago	Settled villages, domesticated plants and animals, and long-distance trade appear in Mesopotamia, Anatolia, and Egypt
7000–2500 B.C.E.	Agriculture spreads through Europe
3000 B.C.E.	Sumerian civilization develops in Mesopotamia
3000–2200 B.C.E.	Old Kingdom in Egypt
3200 B.C.E.	First known written documents in cuneiform appear
2040–1785 B.C.E.	Middle Kingdom in Egypt
1900 B.C.E.	Assyria grows powerful through trade and conquest
1800 B.C.E.	Babylonian civilization emerges; Hammurabi's law code prepared
1750–1560 B.C.E.	Hyksos rule in Egypt

modern-day Netherlands to Russia. Archaeologists call it the Linear Pottery culture because its people decorated their pottery with parallel lines. Their customs varied slightly in different regions, but they shared many similarities as well. For example, the Linear Pottery farmers lived in small villages of about sixty people. They built clusters of permanent family farmsteads made of timber and thatch, and rebuilt them over many generations. These farm families cultivated barley and other grains and kept sheep, goats, dogs, and, most important, cattle, which provided wealth and prestige. From gifts of jewelry and other luxury goods left in graves, archaeologists theorize that women were held in high esteem, perhaps because the people in these communities traced ancestry through them.

After about 4500 B.C.E., villages consisting of several hundred people began to appear in northern Europe, and the trend toward cultural diversity accelerated. In different regions, people used different kinds of pottery and probably spoke distinct languages.

As Linear Pottery settlements slowly spread, competition for farmlands and grazing lands stiffened. Archaeologists believe that men who controlled the livestock—the source of wealth and prestige—developed political authority. These early European elites tried to increase their influence by seizing the lands and herds of others. Conflicts broke out among groups, and people fortified their villages with defensive works. These struggles marked the beginnings of warfare in Europe.

During this era, the peoples of the Linear Pottery communities began building communal tombs with huge stones called *megaliths*. Megaliths survive in regions from Scandinavia to Spain and on islands in the western Mediterranean. The best-known example of a megalithic structure is Stonehenge, a monument in England. People began to build Stonehenge about 3000 B.C.E. as a ring of pits. Later generations reconstructed it several times, adding large stones. Stonehenge took its final form about 1600 B.C.E., when builders positioned immense stones, each weighing several tons, in standing positions. Stonehenge possibly measured the movement of stars, the sun, and the planets, and perhaps served as a place for religious ceremonies.

Around the same time early Europeans began experimenting with metallurgy, the art of using fire to shape metals such as copper into items such as tools or jewelry. Knowledge of metallurgy spread slowly across Europe from the Balkans, where people started to mine copper about 4500 B.C.E. Metallurgy would eventually prove as revolutionary as food production, but its beginnings were very modest. At first, people worked with copper only part of the year. Ötzi the Ice Man, for example, may have been both a shepherd and a coppersmith. Gradually, as copper tools and ornaments became more widely used, metalworkers became specialists. As villages became larger, wealthier inhabitants demonstrated their social status by wearing precious copper jewelry. Trade in metals flourished, changing Europe's economy by creating long-distance trading networks. In turn, these networks provided the basis for the meeting and blending of different cultural assumptions and ideas.

The Battle Axe Cultures

Between 3500 B.C.E. and 2000 B.C.E. the Battle Axe cultures gradually replaced the Linear Pottery cultures across Europe. Named for the stone and copper battle axes used in warfare, Battle Axe peoples cultivated many different types of crops and lived in rectangular single-family thatched dwellings. They may also have been the first peoples to domesticate the horse.

One of the better understood Battle Axe cultures is that of the Kurgan peoples, who made their homes on the edges of the Russian steppes beginning about 3000 B.C.E. A warrior culture, the Kurgan people had to cross long distances to trade for the copper they needed for their weapons. They began to migrate from southern Russia about 3500 B.C.E. As they traveled, their culture spread far to the west and south.

Scholars theorize that the Kurgan peoples brought with them a language that became the ancestor of the tongues spoken by half the world's population today. The majority of the languages spoken in Europe, the Americas, and other lands colonized by Europeans, as well as Persian and Armenian spoken in Southwest Asia, share similarities in vocabulary and grammar inherited from an Indo-European parent language. Most historians argue that the Kurgan peoples spoke this parent language, which then spread throughout Europe in the course of their migrations. The development of the Indo-European languages represents a foundation of Western civilization: the languages we speak.

Technology and Social Change

As the peoples of Europe developed their diverse cultures, their societies became socially stratified. One important tool that helped alter human relationships in early Europe was the plow, which became widely used around 2600 B.C.E. Once plow technology took hold, agricultural life in Europe underwent substantial changes over the course of a mere 200 years. The use of plows meant that fewer people were needed to cultivate Europe's heavy soils. With more people available to clear forest lands, new settlements sprang up and farming communities spread. The expansion of land

---

Map 1.6 Neolithic Cultures in Europe

During the Neolithic period, most of the peoples of Europe changed their way of life from hunting and gathering to food production. In the process, many new cultures developed.

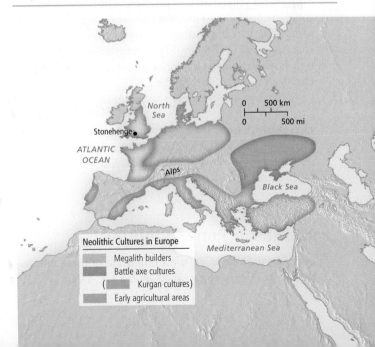

Neolithic Cultures in Europe
- Megalith builders
- Battle axe cultures
- (Kurgan cultures)
- Early agricultural areas

Stonehenge

This megalithic monument consists of two circles of standing stones with large blocks capping the circles. It was built without the aid of wheeled vehicles or metal tools, and the stones were dragged from many miles away.

under cultivation enabled farmers to move out from old family-controlled lands and start new homes. As a result, opportunities for individual initiative and the accumulation of wealth increased. Some farmers could afford trade goods of high prestige, and they passed their lands and possessions to their descendants, who used their inherited resources to acquire even more wealth. By exchanging these expensive and prestigious objects, men cultivated friendships and loyalty, established political and military ties, and formalized mutual obligations. Growing divisions resulted between rich and poor, the powerful and the weak.

Such changes were evident in western Europe between about 2600 and 2400 B.C.E. For the first time, individual graves played a prominent role in burial customs, which may indicate the emergence of new forms of authority based on the preeminence of individual men in the community, particularly those who controlled land and inheritances. The tombs contain weapons and luxury goods, suggesting not only that these individuals were wealthy and powerful men who could afford expensive symbols of their prestige and power, but also that they were warriors as well as or instead of farmers.

As warriors gained power, wealth, and influence in their communities, they emerged as political leaders, and they passed their wealth, political power, and social status down to their sons. These families came to dominate their societies. Historians call these elite groups nobles or aristocrats. The presence of male-dominated groups, designated by birth, that controlled the greatest wealth and enjoyed the greatest privileges in society remained unchallenged in Europe and a defining characteristic of Western civilization until the eighteenth century.

Conclusion

Civilization and the West

This chapter has described the change in human patterns of life from nomadic hunting and gathering to living in settled communities in which food was produced through agriculture and domestication of animals. This transformation took more than 8,000 years. The changes in food production led to the development of village settlements. Powerful elites emerged, and an individual's social status and gender defined what kind of work he or she performed. Soon human communities took on new characteristics. In Southwest Asia and Egypt, civilizations arose by about 3000 B.C.E. that were based on cities and devoted their resources to irrigation, warfare, and worship. The invention of writing enabled communities to record their laws and traditions. It also reinforced the long-distance trade that linked communities throughout Southwest Asia and beyond. Trade among these cities led to the encounters of different peoples. They exchanged new food production technologies, advances in crafts, new approaches to government and administration, and stories and religious ideas.

These changes unfolded over many centuries and did not happen everywhere at the same time. Europe lagged behind Southwest Asia and Egypt in the development of cities and the emergence of civilization. By the end of the Neolithic Age, "the West" did not yet exist, but from the civilizations of Egypt and Southwest Asia, Western civilization would inherit such crucial components as systems of writing and numeracy, the idea of a law code based on abstract principles, and gender-based divisions of labor and power.

By 3000 B.C.E., the rulers of Egypt and Mesopotamia had spun a web of interrelated economies and shared political interests. Over the next millennium, cities such as Ur and Ashur grew powerful under the watchful eyes of ambitious kings who constantly fought with one another. But these kings did not yet possess the skills needed to rule vast empires for an extended period of time. As we will see in the next chapter, they would soon learn.

Suggestions for Further Reading

For a comprehensive list of suggested readings, please go to www.ablongman.com/levack2e/chapter1

Andrews, Anthony P. *First Cities.* 1995. An excellent introduction to the development of urbanism in Southwest Asia, Egypt, India, China, and the Americas.

Bogucki, Peter. *Forest Farmers and Stockherders: Early Agriculture and Its Consequences.* 1988. A clear synthesis of archaeological evidence from northern Europe.

Cunliffe, Barry, ed. *The Oxford Illustrated Prehistory of Europe.* 1994. An important synthesis of recent research by leading archaeologists.

Fagan, Brian. *People of the Earth: An Introduction to World Prehistory.* 1998. A comprehensive textbook that introduces basic issues with a wealth of illustrations and explanatory materials.

Harris, David R., ed. *The Origins and Spread of Agriculture and Pastoralism in Eurasia.* 1996. A collection of detailed essays by noted experts that draw on the latest research.

Kemp, Barry J. "Unification and Urbanization of Ancient Egypt," in *Civilizations of the Ancient Middle East,* ed. Jack M. Sasson, vol. 2, pp. 679–690. 1995. Describes the emergence of towns and political unification of the early phases of Egyptian history.

Kuhrt, Amélie. *The Ancient Middle East: ca. 3000–330 B.C.,* vol. 1. 1995. An authoritative and up-to-date survey that combines archaeological and textual evidence in a lucid narrative with rich documentation.

Murnane, William J. "The History of Ancient Egypt: An Overview," in *Civilizations of the Ancient Middle East,* ed. Jack M. Sasson, vol. 2, pp. 691–718. 1995. A good place to start for a "big picture" of ancient Egyptian history.

Quirke, Stephen. *Ancient Egyptian Religion.* 1992. A brilliant synthesis and explanation of basic Egyptian beliefs and practices.

Redford, Donald B. *Egypt, Canaan, and Israel in Ancient Times.* 1993. A distinguished Egyptologist discusses 3,000 years of uninterrupted contact between Egypt and southwestern Asia.

Schmandt-Besserat, Denise. *How Writing Came About.* 1996. A highly readable and groundbreaking argument that cuneiform writing developed from a method of counting with tokens.

Shaw, I., ed. *The Oxford History of Ancient Egypt.* 2001. Provides excellent discussions of all aspects of Egyptian life.

Spindler, Konrad. *The Man in the Ice: The Discovery of a 5,000-Year-Old Body Reveals the Secrets of the Stone Age.* 1994. A leader of the international team of experts interprets the corpse of a Neolithic hunter found in the Austrian Alps.

Trigger, Bruce G. *Early Civilizations: Ancient Egypt in Context.* 1995. A leading cultural anthropologist examines Old and Middle Kingdom Egypt through comparison with the early civilizations of China, Peru, Mexico, Mesopotamia, and Africa.

Notes

1. *Code of Hammurabi,* trans. J. N. Postgate, 55–56. Cited in Postgate, *Early Mesopotamia: Society and Economy at the Dawn of History* (1992), 160.

2. Samuel Greengus, "Legal and Social Institutions of Ancient Near Mesopotamia," in *Civilizations of the Ancient Middle East,* ed. Jack M. Sasson, vol. 1 (1995), 471.

3. Ibid., 474.

The International Bronze Age and Its Aftermath: Trade, Empire, and Diplomacy, 1600–550 B.C.E.

2

I N 1984, SCUBA-DIVING ARCHAEOLOGISTS BEGAN TO EXCAVATE THE WRECK OF A rich merchant ship that sank about 1300 B.C.E. at Uluburun, off the southern coast of Turkey. Its cargo of raw materials and exotic luxury objects revealed a prosperous world of international trade and cultural exchange. A partial inventory includes ebony logs, ostrich eggshells, elephant tusks, and a trumpet carved from a hippopotamus tooth from Egypt. From Southwest Asia came exquisitely worked gold jewelry as well as nearly a ton of scented resin, perhaps intended for use as incense in religious worship. Finely painted storage jars from the island of Cyprus held pomegranates and probably olive oil. The archaeologists also recovered swords, daggers, and arrowheads, as well as hinged wooden writing boards with a thick wax surface on which business accounts could be recorded.

The most valuable portion of the cargo that the divers lifted from the ocean floor, however, consisted of 354 flat copper bars, each weighing about fifty pounds, and several bars of tin. When melted and mixed together, these metals produce bronze°. This alloy, which is much tougher than copper or tin by themselves, lends itself to the making of dishes, jewelry, tools, and especially weapons. The use of bronze ushered in a new era in the ancient world.

About 3200 B.C.E. people living in northern Syria and Iraq began making bronze. The technology spread slowly throughout Southwest Asia and into Egypt and Europe. Because deposits of tin and copper are not always present in the same areas, merchants traded over long distances to obtain the ores

House of the Admiral This lively wall painting, which may depict a religious celebration, comes from the so-called House of the Admiral on the island of Thera, midway between Crete and Greece. The painting is about twenty-two feet long and a foot and a half high. Created about 1500 B.C.E., before a volcanic explosion destroyed the settlement on Thera, this painting shows scenes of busy maritime activity outside a harbor town.

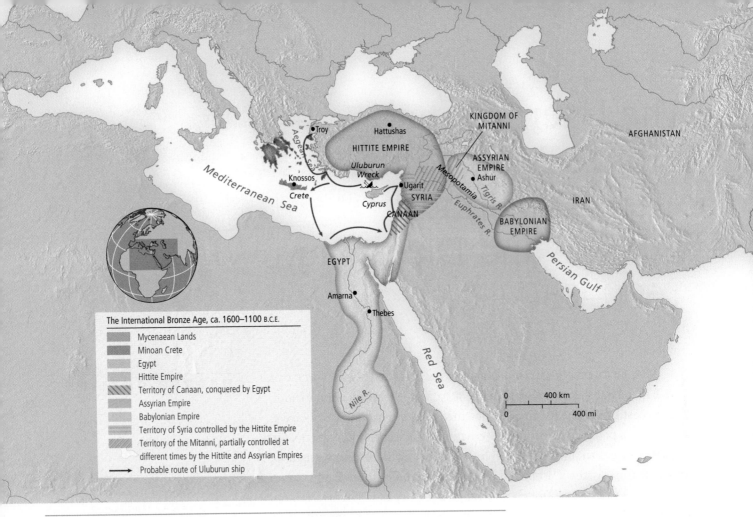

Map 2.1   The International Bronze Age, ca. 1600–1100 B.C.E.

For 500 years, networks of commerce and diplomacy tied together the distinct cultures of Egypt, Greece, Anatolia, and Southwest Asia.

with which to forge the prized alloy. As they traded, they spread knowledge about bronze technology among diverse peoples. By 1600 B.C.E., when peoples throughout Southwest Asia, Egypt, and Europe had mastered bronze making, the International Bronze Age began (see Map 2.1).

The new international trade in bronze provides the key to understanding how four separate regions became linked in a large area of political and cultural influence and thus began to lay the foundations of Western civilization. Egyptians controlled the first region, which consisted of their territories along the Nile in northeastern Africa and lands under their control in Southwest Asia. To the north, the Hittites dominated a second region in Anatolia (modern Turkey). To the east, Mesopotamia, the third region, contained the kingdoms of the Assyrians and the Babylonians. In the west, the fourth major region lay in the eastern Mediterranean where the Minoans on Crete and the Myceneans on mainland Greece developed maritime kingdoms. Several small mercantile kingdoms developed on the eastern edge of the Mediterranean region, serving as buffers between the great powers. These different cultures depended on an international trade network

to obtain the metals and other goods they needed for everyday life.

The continued quest for new sources of wealth spurred rulers in Egypt, the Hittite kingdom, Assyria, and Babylonia to conquer large realms and construct enormous, multiethnic empires. Yet these same rulers recognized that constant warfare interrupted trade and interfered with the successful management of territories. Discovering the advantages of international cooperation for the first time, rulers during this period developed a system of diplomacy that produced long periods of peace—an unprecedented achievement. That the Uluburun cargo ship could stop at so many ports and take on board merchandise from so many different kingdoms illustrates the benefit of these peaceful times.

This chapter examines how the peoples of the International Bronze Age and its aftermath engaged in a series of commercial, technological, and cultural exchanges. How, in other words, did the varied encounters between Bronze Age societies transform both international relations and these societies themselves? To understand these transformations, we shall consider the following questions:

- How did Egypt during the New Kingdom use warfare and diplomacy to develop an empire that reached from Nubia to Mesopotamia?
- What were the political, religious, and cultural traditions of the Hittite Empire in Anatolia and the Assyrian and Babylonian Empires in Mesopotamia?
- What were the characteristics of the Mediterranean civilizations of Minoan Crete, Mycenaean Greece, Ugarit, and Troy, and what roles did they play in international trade and politics?
- What forces brought the International Bronze Age to a close and how did the Phoenicians, Assyrians, and Babylonians build new kingdoms and empires in its wake?

Civilization of the Nile: The Egyptian Empire

- How did Egypt during the New Kingdom use warfare and diplomacy to develop an empire that reached from Nubia to Mesopotamia?

Egypt played a central role in the economic, diplomatic, and cultural networks that shaped the International Bronze Age. A prosperous new phase of Egyptian history began when the Middle Kingdom ended about 1650 B.C.E. During the next 500-year period, Egyptians created a vast multiethnic empire stretching from Africa to Southwest Asia. Under the direction of talented and aggressive rulers, Egyptian imperial civilization reached its greatest height.

From the Hyksos Era to the New Kingdom

Egyptian history changed course abruptly at the end of the Middle Kingdom when the Hyksos, a people from northern Palestine whose name meant "peoples of foreign lands" in Egyptian, invaded Egypt and established a new regime in the northern delta region. The Hyksos introduced to Egypt an advanced military technology that was revolutionizing warfare throughout Southwest Asia, Anatolia, and Greece. This technological innovation consisted of a chariot with wheels of bronze spokes. Two young men wearing bronze chain-mail armor rode into battle on each chariot, one driving the horses, the other shooting bronze-tipped arrows at the enemy. Troops of trained charioteers and bowmen easily outmaneuvered the traditional massed infantry forces and inflicted terrible ca-

sualties from a distance. Chariot warfare reshaped the economic policies and foreign relations of Egypt and all the other kingdoms and empires of the International Bronze Age. To meet the enormous expenses of training and supplying armies of charioteers, rulers carefully organized domestic resources and tried to acquire more wealth through trade and conquest.

About 1550 B.C.E. King Ahmose I (r. ca. 1569–ca. 1545 B.C.E.) mastered the new military tactics and technology and expelled the Hyksos from Egypt. Historians call the period of renewed Egyptian self-rule that began with Ahmose the New Kingdom (ca. 1550–1150 B.C.E.). Ahmose's new dynasty continued the highly centralized system of government that had been developed in the Middle Kingdom, but also added a powerful new force: a permanent, or standing, army. For the first time in Egyptian history, a ruler could count on the readiness of highly trained regiments of charioteers and infantrymen to go to war whenever he wished. Troops would also remain as garrisons in conquered lands. The standing army thus extended the ruler's reach and influence abroad. In this era, Egypt pushed its territorial boundaries into Asia, reaching as far as the Euphrates River (see Map 2.2).

During the New Kingdom, Egypt's kings first took the title *pharaoh,* which means "great house"—or master of all Egyptians. Pharaohs exercised wide-ranging and unrivaled political power. Egyptians believed that the gods entrusted their safekeeping to the pharaoh's care and that he had the final authority in matters of government, law, religion, and warfare. In return for the authority granted him by the gods, the pharaoh had the duty of maintaining peace and order in Egypt and bringing this order to the entire world. He did this by caring for the temples and cults of the gods, conquering Egypt's enemies, and ruling wisely.

Egypt during the New Kingdom developed a highly organized bureaucracy that helped the pharaoh maintain order. Egypt was divided into two major administrative regions: Upper Egypt in the south, governed from the city of Thebes, and Lower Egypt in the north, ruled from the city of Memphis. Regional administrators raised taxes and drafted men to work on the pharaoh's building projects. The chief minister of state, the vizier, superintended the administration of the entire kingdom. Every year the vizier decided when to open the canal locks on the Nile so that farmers' fields could be irrigated. He supervised the Egyptian treasury and the warehouses into which produce was paid as taxes.

Temples also played an essential part in the government of Egypt. Priests collected taxes, organized building projects, and administered justice among the thousands of peasants who labored in the vast estates attached to the temples. The temple of Amun at Karnak, for example, controlled a workforce of nearly 100,000 people.

VIDEO
The Temple of Karnak

The Mummy

The burial practices of the ancient Egyptians provide a window into their society. They reveal Egyptian attitudes about life, death, and the afterlife. Egyptians believed that a person could have an afterlife only if the person's body remained in recognizable form after death.

The Egyptians also thought that every human possessed three spirits active after death: the Ka, Ba, and Akh. The Ka was a person's life force, created at birth but set free at death to live in his or her tomb, where the spirit inhabited the deceased's statue and cared for the body. The Ba could take many shapes and travel outside the tomb, and it accompanied the corpse to final judgment. The Ba comprised all the qualities that made a person unique; without a body to return to, the Ba and the deceased's personality would vanish forever. The Akh represented a person's immortality and lived among the stars. These three spirits could survive only if the body did not decay, and so preserving the corpse became a central issue in burial practice.

Egyptians began experimenting with embalming or mummification between 3000 and 2600 B.C.E. and continued to develop the art for the next 3,000 years. The rise of Christianity in Egypt in the second and third centuries C.E. ended the practice of preserving corpses. Ancient records and modern scientific investigation have uncovered the secrets of mummification. Embalming took place within seventy days after death. By means of a metal hook, highly trained experts extracted the brains through the nostrils and discarded

them. Sometimes they filled the skull with linen cloth and resin. Through an incision below the ribs the embalmers removed all the organs except for the heart. (That organ represented a person's life and would be examined by the gods on Judgment Day.) The embalmers wrapped the liver, lungs, stomach, and intestines individually and placed them in separate containers within a chest carved from alabaster. Next the embalmers thoroughly dried the corpse by packing it with natrun, a natural compound of sodium carbonate and bicarbonate. After drying for forty days, the skin shriveled and the embalmers padded the body with aromatic packing materials to re-create as lifelike an appearance as possible. The priests then added hairpieces and artificial eyes. They applied a layer of resin over the face and body followed by a coat of paint—red for men and yellow for women.

Customarily, embalmers placed magical amulets on the corpse to protect the deceased in the next

world. They also decorated the body with expensive jewelry and insignia of rank. Then they tightly wrapped the corpse in long strips of linen. Before placing the corpse in a shroud, they fitted the face with a painted linen mask. The masks of royalty were made of gold.

Finally the corpse was placed in its coffin, which was painted with a stylized portrait of the deceased. The dead person's family and friends carried the coffin to the tomb. After the proper prayers, the priest conducting the burial ceremony touched the eyes, ears, nose, and mouth painted on the coffin to enable the dead person to see, hear, smell, and breathe for eternity. Then the priest and family sealed the tomb. When prepared in such a fashion, a body could last forever.

For Discussion

What does the practice of mummification reveal about Egyptian attitudes toward death and the boundaries between life and death?

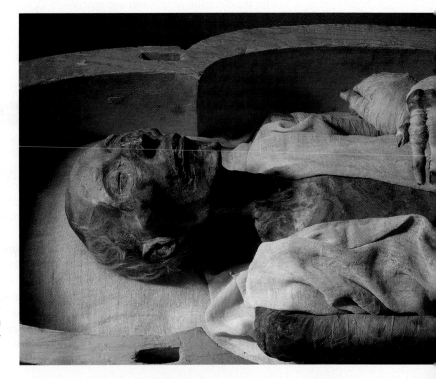

Mummy of Ramesses II
Both a science and an art, mummification preserved the body of King Ramesses II (r. 1279–1213 B.C.E.) for more than 3,000 years. This near-perfect example of a mummy is the product of an Egyptian tradition of preserving the body after death that began at the beginning of Egyptian history.

In the New Kingdom, women played an important role. Under Egyptian law, women and men had complete equality in matters of property, business, and inheritance. In addition to preparing foods, weaving cloth, and caring for livestock and children, women arranged burials and worshiped at tombs to ensure an afterlife for departed family members. Some women held priesthoods. The most powerful, the "God's Wife of Amun," was often a member of the royal family. This priestess had administrative responsibilities as well as the obligation to perform religious rituals. The wives of priests and officials formed musical groups called "Singers of Amun" that sang, clapped, and danced to the accompaniment of stringed instruments during religious rituals.

Military Expansion and Diplomatic Networks: Building an Empire in Canaan and Nubia

During the New Kingdom, pharaohs conquered territories far beyond the borders of Egypt. The military power that came from chariot warfare technology, and the ability of the pharaoh to use the great wealth of the country to support a large army, made these conquests possible. A well-developed logistical system also contributed to Egypt's military strength. With food and supplies carefully prepared in advance by government administrators, the Egyptian army regularly waged war far from home.

Egyptian attitudes toward non-Egyptians also encouraged the imperial expansion of the New Kingdom. Egyptians divided the world into two groups: themselves (whom they referred to as "The People") and everyone else. Egyptians were people who lived in the Nile Valley and spoke Egyptian. The other peoples known to the Egyptians were the Nubians, Libyans, and the inhabitants of Southwest Asia. Egyptians believed that forces of chaos resided in foreign lands where the pharaoh had not yet imposed his will. Thus it was the pharaoh's responsibility to crush all foreign peoples and bring order to the world.

In their drive to establish order in the world, Egyptian rulers in the New Kingdom clashed with kingdoms in

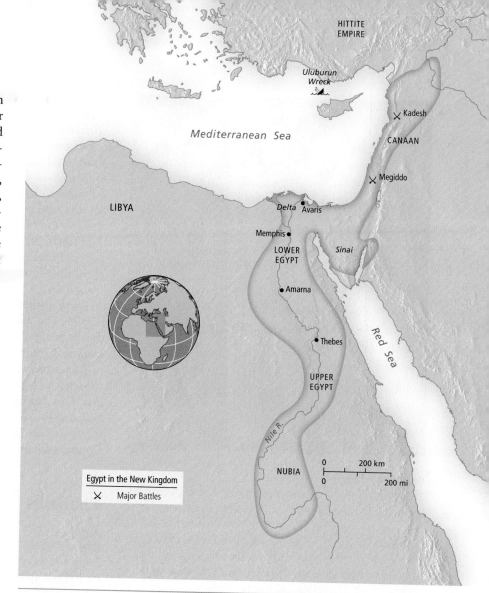

Map 2.2 Egypt in the New Kingdom
During the New Kingdom, Egyptians conquered Nubia, Canaan, and parts of Southwest Asia as far as the Euphrates River. They created a prosperous, multiethnic empire.

Anatolia, Syria, and Mesopotamia. Under the dynamic leadership of Thutmose I (r. 1504–1492 B.C.E.), the armies of Egypt conquered southern Palestine. A coalition of Syrian cities slowed further advance, but by the end of the reign of the great conqueror Thutmose III (r. 1458–1425 B.C.E.), Egypt had extended its control over all the lands between the Orontes River in Syria and the Euphrates in Mesopotamia. The western portion of this region, called Canaan (modern-day Lebanon, Israel, and parts of Jordan and Syria), provided the Egyptians with additional wealth, both because of Canaan's own natural resources and because Canaan was a vital trading center with ties to Mesopotamia and beyond.

The New Kingdom also expanded its territorial grip southward, seizing the populous and prosperous African land known in antiquity as Nubia or Kush (modern

Enemies of Egypt

These tiles found at the mortuary temple of Pharaoh Ramesses III were made around 1170 B.C.E. They depict Egypt's enemies with such great attention to details of clothing, hairstyle, and stereotyped physical features that we can know the ethnicity of the men. From left to right: a Libyan with tattooed arms, a Nubian with black skin, and a bearded Syrian. All wear handcuffs, a sign of their defeat and Egypt's triumph.

Sudan). Nubia was extremely rich in gold and other natural resources, while trade routes from central and eastern Africa that converged in Nubia further augmented its wealth. In order to gain control of these riches, Egyptian forces conquered Nubia about 1500 B.C.E. An Egyptian governor, called the King's Son of Kush, ruled the vast region in the pharaoh's name, but Egyptian control depended on the cooperation of Nubian princes who organized local labor and guaranteed the regular delivery of tribute. In return for this collaboration, the princes were permitted to govern their communities. To strengthen further their grip on Nubia, pharaohs encouraged Egyptians to migrate to Nubia and establish communities along the Nile River. These Egyptian colonies increased the population of Nubia and exploited the fertile river lands for the benefit of the pharaoh.

Although willing to use war to further their imperial interests, the pharaohs grew to prefer diplomatic means. Evidence of their diplomacy comes from an archive of documents discovered at Tell el-Amarna in 1887 C.E. Written in Akkadian, the Mesopotamian language used for international communication, these letters show that Egyptian pharaohs were in regular contact with the rulers of neighboring peoples, as well as with their own officials in Canaan and Syria. In their correspondence, the monarchs referred to themselves as "Great Kings" and addressed one another as "brother," despite their constant rivalry. By using these titles, the rulers recognized each other's authority and created a sense of international community. They cemented their ties by arranging marriages among the royal families and exchanging lavish gifts. By these means they could guard their frontiers and protect the merchants who crisscrossed their territories.

Egypt gained more than enormous wealth from its empire. The cultural encounter between Egyptians and the people they conquered resulted in an exchange of ideas and traditions. Egyptian speech adopted hundreds of Canaanite words. Many fairy tales about exotic lands modeled on Southwest Asia made their way into Egyptian literature. Numerous gods of conquered peoples entered Egyptian life as well. For example, Baal and Astarte, who were worshiped widely in Southwest Asia, became popular Egyptian divinities.

Pharaohs: Egypt's Dynamic Leaders

Egypt's success during the New Kingdom hinged in large part on the talents of its pharaohs. These rulers defined all aspects of Egyptian life, from empire building and trade to agriculture and worship.

Hatshepsut the Female Pharaoh and Thutmose III the Conqueror

One of the most remarkable rulers of the New Kingdom was Hatshepsut (1479–1458 B.C.E.), the first female pharaoh. With the aid of trusted advisers, Hatshepsut pursued policies of peace, though her armies waged war when necessary to secure Egypt's possessions in Southwest Asia.

Because pharaohs had always been men, all of the images of kingly power were male and the elaborate rituals of ruling presumed a male ruler. Hatshepsut carefully adapted her image to these expectations. For example, in the inscriptions and paintings of the great funerary temple that she built near Thebes, Hatshepsut is represented as a man, the son of the god Amun-Re. In more private contexts, she referred to herself as a woman. Several decades after Hatshepsut's death, her name was systematically removed from monuments throughout Egypt, probably to inform the gods that Egypt had returned to "proper" male kingship.

Thutmose III (r. 1458–1425 B.C.E.) succeeded his mother Hatshepsut and began a reign marked by military glory. He led his armies into Canaan seventeen times during his reign. In one of his greatest victories at Megiddo (in mod-

Hatshepsut as a Bearded Pharaoh
Although she was a woman, tradition required that Hatshepsut be depicted as a man.

ern Israel) Thutmose captured more than 900 war chariots from his enemies. To maintain Egyptian authority throughout his empire, Thutmose established permanent garrisons in conquered territories, just as Ahmose had done when the territory had first been conquered. Thutmose cultivated a triumphant military atmosphere at court that was quite different from that of Hatshepsut, yet he also wrote literary works and pursued an interest in science. From Syria he brought back samples of the region's flowers and plants and had them painted on temple walls. Under his influence, Egyptian artists perfected their ability to capture detail, movement, and emotion in painting and sculpture.

The Amarna Period: The Beginnings of Diplomacy

Four decades after Thutmose III's reign, Egypt experienced a religious revolution, begun when Pharaoh Amenhotep III (r. 1388–1351 B.C.E.) turned away from traditional beliefs and practices. Amenhotep called the sun Aten and worshipped his physical form, the sun seen in the sky. The pharaoh's son, Amenhotep IV (r. 1351–1334 B.C.E.), changed his own name to Akhenaten ("one useful to Aten") and with his religious advisers took the revolutionary step of declaring that Aten was the only god. Thus the Egyptians in the Amarna Period first developed monotheism°, the idea of a single, all-powerful god.

Full of religious enthusiasm, Akhenaten and his queen, Nefertiti, abandoned the capital of Thebes and built a new city where no temple had ever stood. Left open to the sun, the city received the first rays of light as each day dawned. Because the modern name for this site is Tell el-Amarna, historians refer to this period of religious ferment as the Amarna Period. Akhenaten attacked the worship of other gods, closed down many temples, and appropriated their wealth and lands for himself. Paintings and sculptures no longer depicted Aten in the traditional way, as a falcon-

headed god, but instead represented the deity as a simple disc with radiating beams of light. Akhenaten forbade the celebration of ancient public festivals to the other gods and even the mention of their names. His agents chiseled their names from monuments and buildings across the land.

Akhenaten gradually lost the support of the general population as well as that of the priests who administered the temples of other gods. The people of Egypt were unwilling to abandon the many traditional gods who played such an important role in their daily lives. After Akhenaten's death, the royal court returned to Memphis and then to Thebes. Akhenaten's monotheistic religion thus did not survive him.

The Battle of Kadesh and the Age of Ramesses

After Akhenaten's death, rule of Egypt passed through the hands of several men before Ramesses I took the throne in 1292 B.C.E. and established a new dynasty, the nineteenth in Egyptian history. The greatest king of the nineteenth dynasty was Ramesses II (r. 1279–1213 B.C.E.), who ruled

---

DOCUMENT

A Hymn to Aten Sung by the Pharaoh

The following Egyptian hymn was sung to Aten, the sun god, by the pharaoh. It describes a single god who created the universe:

Splendid you rise, O living Aten, eternal lord!
You are radiant, beauteous, mighty,
Your love is great, immense.
Your rays light up all faces,
Your bright hue gives life to hearts,
When you fill the Two Lands with your love.
August God who fashioned himself,
Who made every land, created what is in it,
All peoples, herds, and flocks,
All trees that grow from soil; they live when you dawn
    for them,
You are mother and father of all that you made.
I am your son who serves you, who exalts your name,
Your power, your strength, are firm in my heart;
You are the living Aten whose image endures,
You have made the far sky to shine in it,
To observe all that you made . . .

Source: From Miriam Lichtheim, *Ancient Egyptian Literature: The Old and Middle Kingdoms, Volume II.* Copyright © 1976 by the Regents of the University of California. Reprinted by permission.

Egyptian Tomb Robbers on Trial

In New Kingdom Egypt a council called a *kenbet,* composed of the local governor and temple priests, combined the functions of prosecutor, judge, and jury. There was no counsel for the defendants. At the village level people might bring lawsuits against one another at the *kenbet,* and women and men alike represented themselves at trial. Another court, the Great Kenbet, handled all cases of property and taxation affecting state revenues as well as all offenses against the pharaoh and the government. This court consisted of high officials of the government and was headed by the pharaoh's chief administrator, the vizier.

One of the most serious crimes in Egypt was robbing tombs. People accused of this crime were interrogated by the authorities, who routinely used beatings and torture to extract confessions. The Great Kenbet then delivered a verdict. Conviction of tomb robbing carried the death penalty. Lesser crimes not related to tomb robbing could result in confiscation of property, beatings, forced labor, and body mutilation.

The following document comes from the trial record of tomb robbers in the Great Tombs of the pharaohs in the Valley of the Kings.[1] These tombs were situated a few miles from the Nile River at Thebes, where most of the New Kingdom pharaohs and their families were buried. The trials were conducted over a period of several summer days during the reign of Ramesses IX (r. 1125–1107 B.C.E.). The vizier, assisted by the overseer of the granary and treasury and two royal stewards, conducted the proceedings, which were written on a papyrus scroll unearthed in 1872 C.E. The account shows how justice was carried out in the New Kingdom.

Examination. The herdsman Bukhaaf of the temple of Amun was brought. The Vizier said to him, "When you were about that business in which you engaged and the god caught you and brought and placed you in the hand of pharaoh, tell me all the men who were with you in the Great Tombs." Bukhaaf replied, "As for me, I am a field worker of the temple of Amun. The woman came to the place where I was and she said to me, 'some men have found something that can be sold for bread; let's go so you may eat it with them.'" [Bukhaaf gives some misleading testimony that does not deceive the Kenbet.] Bukhaaf was examined with the stick [i.e., beaten]. "Stop, I will tell," he said. The Vizier said to him, "Tell the story of your going to attack the Great and Noble Tombs." Bukhaaf said, "It was Pewer, a workman of the City of the Dead [the Tombs] who showed us the tomb of Queen Hebrezet." The Vizier and the others said to him, "In what condition was the tomb that you went to?" Bukhaaf said, "I found it already open." He was examined with the stick again. "Stop," he said, "I will tell." The Vizier said to him, "Tell what you did." He said, "I brought away the inner coffin of silver and a shroud of gold and silver together with the men who were with me. And we broke them up and divided them among ourselves."

[Bukhaaf's punishment is not recorded, but it was in all likelihood death.]

On the third day of the trial of thieves, a carpenter Thewenani was examined for a different robbery. He proclaimed his innocence and swore a great oath, "If I speak untruth may I be mutilated and sent to Ethiopia."

Despite several beatings and torture, Thewenani would not confess, and the vizier let him off with the warning that if he was accused again, he would be sentenced to death. Later that day, Ese, the wife of the gardener Ker who had been implicated in stealing silver from the Great Tombs in still another case, was brought before the Kenbet. She swore an oath to be truthful or be mutilated and placed on a stake. She denied any connection with the robbery, but one of the officials at the trial asked her how she had suddenly gotten rich enough to buy several slaves. Her answer that she had saved the money from selling the produce of her garden did not convince the Kenbet, which brought in her slave to give testimony against her. Her fate is not recorded.

Why did Egyptian officials prosecute tomb robbers with such energy? They considered tomb robbing a serious crime for both religious and economic reasons. Egyptians were deeply concerned about the afterlife and stressed the proper treatment of the dead. They believed that when people died they were judged by the god Osiris. If they had lived good lives, their bodies would live again. The families of the deceased had the obligation to provide food and water at the graveside for the dead to eat. They also were required to remember the name of the dead. "Provide water for your father and mother who rest in the desert valley. . . . Let the people know that you are doing it and then your son will do the same for you," advised one religious text.[2] In Egyptian

The jackal-headed god Anubis leads Hunefer into the courtroom, where his heart is weighed against a feather on giant scales.

Because the feather and the heart weigh the same, it means that the court decides that Hunefer has led a just life.

The god of wisdom, Thoth, stands by the scale, and records the result of weighing.

Horus leads Hunefer to the great god Osiris who judges and rules the dead. Hunefer can look forward to a peaceful eternity.

Osiris

Judgment Day
Painted about 1285 B.C.E., this papyrus scroll shows the trial of a man called Hunefer on the day of judgment.

eyes, robbing a tomb violated basic principles of religious behavior. It was a monstrous sacrilege.

The many gifts placed in a grave with the dead person were intended to make the deceased person's afterlife as comfortable as possible. Pharaohs and the wealthy elite of Egypt filled their tombs with luxury items of incalculable value—an irresistible lure for thieves. In addition to their profound desire to prevent sacrilege, Egyptian officials worried that plundering this treasure and putting it back into circulation would cause prices to fall and thereby derail the economy. From the point of view of Egyptian officials, tomb robbers deserved nothing less than death. Only this way would justice be served.

Questions of Justice

1. To what extent do both the living and the dead play a part in this trial?
2. The "International Bronze Age" witnessed the rise of strong, highly centralized states. What do these tomb raiders' trials reveal about the links between law, religion, and central state power?

Taking It Further

Goelet, Ogden. "Tomb Robbery Papyri," in *The Oxford Encyclopedia of Ancient Egypt,* ed. Donald B. Redford, vol. 3, pp. 417–418. 2001. Provides the latest analysis of the documents relating to the trials of tomb robbers as well as further bibliography.

Kruchten, Jean-Marie. "Law," in *The Oxford Encyclopedia of Ancient Egypt,* ed. Donald B. Redford, vol. 2, pp. 277–282. 2001. An excellent overview of Egyptian law with helpful suggestions for further reading.

for sixty-six years. Ramesses's efforts to restore Egyptian authority in Syria brought him into conflict with the king of the Hittites, Muwatallis, who wanted to conquer some of Egypt's possessions for himself. In 1274 B.C.E. the armies of Ramesses and Muwatallis clashed in a battle at the city of Kadesh in northern Syria. Muwatallis's huge Hittite army, with about 3,500 chariots and 37,000 infantry, caught the Egyptians by surprise, but in a last-minute counterattack led by the pharaoh himself, Egyptian troops rallied and pushed their enemy back. The battle ended in a stalemate, with heavy losses on both sides.

The Battle of Kadesh°, perhaps because of its indecisive outcome, resulted in a treaty between the two kings. Writing in Akkadian, the Egyptian and Hittite monarchs signed a treaty of friendship and cooperation in 1269 B.C.E. Ramesses formally abandoned Egyptian claims to the city of Kadesh and northern Syria. In return, the Hittite monarch acknowledged Egypt's right to control Canaan, establishing a boundary between the two states. The two powers also agreed to give one another aid and military assistance in case of invasion by a third party or in the event of internal rebellions. The Battle of Kadesh thus yielded nearly a century of peace between the Hittites and the Egyptians. During this period commerce flourished, benefiting both realms. With peace established with the Hittites, Egypt enjoyed many decades of prosperity under Ramesses II's rule.

VIDEO

Abu
Simbel

Civilizations of Anatolia and Mesopotamia: The Hittite, Assyrian, and Babylonian Empires

■ What were the political, religious, and cultural traditions of the Hittite Empire in Anatolia and the Assyrian and Babylonian Empires in Mesopotamia?

Egypt was only one of several large, highly centralized empires that developed during the International Bronze Age. As we can see on Map 2.1, Egypt's main rivals were the Hittite Empire in Anatolia and the Assyrian and Babylonian Empires in Mesopotamia.

The Growth of Hittite Power: Conquest and Diversity

By about 1650 B.C.E., the Hittites had established control over the rich plateau of Anatolia (modern Turkey). Like the Egyptians, the warlike Hittites were among the first people to use the new chariot warfare technology. For two cen-

turies Hittite power gradually expanded across Anatolia and into western Mesopotamia, as well as southward into Syria where the Hittites stood face to face with the Egyptian Empire. Within a century Hittite conflict with Egypt led to the Battle of Kadesh, as we saw earlier. The expanding Hittite Empire played a prominent role in the network of trade and communication of the International Bronze Age. From the carefully kept inventory tablets that have survived, historians know that the Hittites made great profits by trading textiles, grains, and metals to markets as far away as Cyprus and the Aegean, Syria, and Mesopotamia in return for metals and luxury goods.

At the top of the Hittite Empire was the Great King, who ruled in the name of the supreme God of Storms. Like Egyptian rulers, the Great King owned the land of all his subjects, and he gave agricultural estates to the noblemen who served as his officials. In return they supplied the soldiers and charioteers he demanded for the army. The Great King also strengthened ties of allegiance throughout his empire by requiring his officials and subordinate monarchs to swear oaths of loyalty to the main Hittite gods. The Great King gave further unity to the empire by playing the role of chief priest of all the gods who were worshiped by the many different communities under his control.

Hittite kings worked hard to provide uniform justice throughout their realm for rich and poor, male and female alike. This proved a complex undertaking because as the Hittite Empire expanded, it grew increasingly multiethnic, absorbing many smaller kingdoms with their own languages and cultural traditions. The many different peoples who made up the Hittite Empire were permitted to follow their own customs and laws. Administering justice thus required close cooperation between subject peoples' local authorities and the Great King's legal officials. The Hittite tongue served as the official language of law and government, but the empire's cultural diversity and ties abroad forced the Hittites to keep records in other languages as well. The Hittites' use of cuneiform script, borrowed from nearby Mesopotamia, provides evidence of extensive cultural interaction with that region.

The Hittites spoke of their "thousand gods" because their religion drew from the empire's many subjects as well as from neighboring regions. The imperial government deliberately brought the statues of the gods of its subjects to its capital city of Hattushas and built many temples for them in an effort to promote the unity of all the people under the Great King's rule. Hittites believed that their gods were present in the form of their statues and that the gods wished to communicate with their human worshipers. Priests appointed by the Great King managed this "conversation" by making appropriate offerings to the deities at fixed intervals in an elaborate calendar of festivals and holy days. According to Hittite belief, properly worshiped gods would protect the empire as well as any individuals who might pray to them privately. In the Hittite afterlife, the souls of the deceased lived in a huge palace ruled by the Goddess of Death in the Underworld, located far below the Earth's surface.

The Mesopotamian Empires

The kingdoms of Mesopotamia, which rivaled the Hittite Empire in wealth and power, had an equally vital place in the political, commercial, and cultural networks of the International Bronze Age. During this period, two powerful empires emerged in Mesopotamia: Babylonia in the south and Assyria in the north.

The Kingdom of Babylonia

By about 1600 B.C.E. people known as Kassites infiltrated Mesopotamia as raiders, soldiers, and laborers. Their language and precise place of origin are unknown, but by 1400 B.C.E. they had gradually gained control of most of southern Mesopotamia. For the next 250 years, until about 1150 B.C.E., Kassite monarchs maintained order and prosperity in Babylonia, establishing the longest-ruling dynasty in ancient Southwest Asian history.

During these centuries, Babylonia enjoyed a golden age. Kassite kings politically unified Babylonia's many cities through a highly centralized administration that closely controlled both urban centers and countryside. These skilled monarchs won the loyalty of individuals of all ranks and temple priesthoods by giving them tracts of land. The Kassite kings gained a reputation for fair rule and for that reason were popular with their subjects. The government spent lavishly on temples, public buildings, and projects such as canals throughout the kingdom.

Under Kassite rule, Babylonia became renowned as a center of trade, culture, and learning. Science, medicine, and literature flourished during this period. With encouragement from the Kassite kings, who wished to demonstrate their full integration into Babylonian society, scribes systematically copied the works of earlier Mesopotamian cultures to preserve their intellectual legacy. Treatises on omens, astrology, and medicine gathered an enormous body of knowledge. Babylonian doctors earned fame throughout Southwest Asia. Gula, the goddess of healing known as the Great Physician, was the divine patron of a religious center where doctors received their training.

In literature, the Babylonian creation epic *Enuma Elish* tells the story of the origin of the world by Marduk, the god of Babylon and sole lord of the universe. The order that Marduk creates reflects the organized rule that the Kassite kings provided for Babylonia. Babylonian authors also wrote versions of the *Epic of Gilgamesh,* the Sumerian story about the establishment of civilization that we discussed in Chapter 1. These two great works were translated into many languages and entertained people throughout Southwest Asia for more than a thousand years.

DOCUMENT

Hittite Military Rituals

Religious rituals and magic played an important role in every aspect of Hittite life, including warfare. Hittite warriors believed that the gods were usually on their side in battle. They thought that if the gods saw them as impure, they would suffer defeat in combat. After a purification ritual, defeated Hittite soldiers could return to soldiering with renewed morale and vigor. The following document explains the ritual of purification that soldiers performed after a military defeat:

If our troops are defeated by the enemy, they perform the Far-Side-Of-The-River-Ritual. On the far side of the river, they cut in half a person, a billy goat, a puppy, and a piglet. Half of each they place on this side and half on that side (of the river). In front they build a gate of hawthorn. . . . Over the top they draw a rope. In front, on either side, they light a fire. The troops go through the middle. When they reach the river, they sprinkle them with water. Afterward they perform the Ritual-Of-The-Battlefield for them in the usual way [and can return to battle].

Source: From Richard H. Beal, "Hittite Military Organization" in *Civilizations of the Ancient Near East 4V*, edited by Jack Sasson, Charles Scribner's Sons, © 1995 by Charles Scribner's Sons. Reprinted by permission of The Gale Group.

The Kingdom of Assyria

Babylonia's chief rival for dominance in the Mesopotamian region during the International Bronze Age lay to the north: Assyria. Around 1350 B.C.E. Assyria recovered from more than a century of submission to the neighboring kingdom of Mittani in Syria. Under the skillful rule of Ashur-Uballit (ca. 1365–1330 B.C.E.) the Assyrian kingdom began a new phase of expansion. Like the rulers of the Egyptians and the Hittites, Ashur-Uballit and his successors understood the value of close diplomatic ties with other great powers. As a letter found in Egypt reveals, he tried to win the favor of the pharaoh:

Thus speaks Ashur-Uballit, king of Assyria. May everything be well with you, your house, your land, your chariots and your troops. . . . I am sending you a beautiful chariot, two horses, and a bead of authentic lapis-lazuli [a valuable gemstone] as your greeting gift . . . My messenger will see how you are and how your country is, and then may he come back to me.[3]

Like their rivals, however, Ashur-Uballit and other Assyrian kings were also quite willing to go to war to safeguard their economic interests. To that end, Assyrian kings pushed westward, clashing with the Hittites over trade, metal ores, and timber. The Assyrians built a string of garrisons on their border with the Hittite kingdom and seized territories in northern Syria that had come under Hittite control. Assyrian kings also competed with Babylonia for control of copper, tin, horses, and other prized natural resources in the hilly lands to Mesopotamia's north and east. The mighty ruler Tukulti-Ninurta I (r. 1244–1208 B.C.E.) led his armies to victory over Babylonia and by the time of his death Assyria controlled all the lands extending from northern Syria to southern Iraq—the greatest reach Assyria would ever attain. Even though Babylonia would reassert its independence within the next twenty years, Assyria dominated Mesopotamian affairs for the next two centuries.

Civilizations of the Mediterranean: The Minoans and Mycenaeans

■ What were the characteristics of the Mediterranean civilizations of Minoan Crete, Mycenaean Greece, Ugarit, and Troy, and what roles did they play in international trade and politics?

The Egyptian, Babylonian, and Assyrian Empires of the International Bronze Age were each rooted in civilizations that had emerged thousands of years before. In Europe, however, the cold climate and extensive forests slowed the development of city life and therefore of civilization. It was not until the International Bronze Age that two vigorous and distinctive civilizations developed in the eastern Mediterranean: the Minoan civilization of Crete and the Mycenaean civilization on mainland Greece.

Several smaller coastal cities and kingdoms situated on the eastern Mediterranean participated in the brisk trade that so characterized the International Bronze Age. These coastal kingdoms served as buffer states between Egypt, Mycenaean Greece, and the Hittite Empire. The two most prosperous, the mercantile kingdoms of Ugarit and Troy, played a "middleman" role in the trading and diplomatic networks that developed during these centuries.

Minoan Crete

About 2000 B.C.E. small urban communities on the island of Crete began to import copper and tin from the eastern Mediterranean. Sir Arthur Evans, the late-nineteenth-century British archaeologist who first discovered the remains of these communities, named them "Minoan," after the Cretan king Minos in Greek mythology. In the course of the second millennium B.C.E., the Minoans developed a busy merchant navy that traded with Greece, Egypt, and the coastal communities of the eastern Mediterranean. Crete became a thriving center of long-distance trade. Minoan

Snake Goddess
One of the most important divinities of Minoan civilization was the Snake Goddess. Here she (or her priestess) is captured in typical pose and dress: She grasps a snake in each outstretched hand and wears a tight-fitting, layered dress that exposes her breasts. A sacred cat perches on her head.

civilization was the most brilliant in the Mediterranean until the sixteenth century B.C.E., when it was surpassed by that of the Mycenaeans.

Despite the rich array of artifacts and sites unearthed by archaeologists, the basic beliefs of Minoan religion remain a mystery. Historians do know that Minoans worshiped the powerful Mistress of Animals at some mountaintop shrines, and that in their homes they prayed to a goddess whom they always depicted as holding a snake. Statues show this Snake Goddess (or her priestess) wearing a many-tiered skirt, with breasts exposed and snakes coiled around her outstretched arms.

The Minoan economy revolved around four major urban administrative centers, called palaces, at Knossos,

Phaistos, Mallia, and Zakros. The Knossos palace alone occupied three acres. At its center stood a courtyard surrounded by hundreds of rooms intended as living quarters for the governing and religious elite, administrative headquarters, shrines for religious worship, and warehouses for storing crops and wine. These warehouses, which could hold more than a quarter of a million gallons of wine or olive oil, show the Minoan rulers' tight control over the production of wealth on Crete. Palace administrators told farmers how much to grow and collected the produce from them, then gave back sufficient food for their subsistence. Palace officials also controlled the specialized artists who produced the crafts that were traded abroad.

The Toreador Fresco

The Minoan elites lived in great luxury in palaces connected to warehouses. Vivid frescoes (plaster painted while it is still wet) of sea creatures, flowers, court officials and acrobats in bright garments, and scenes of daily life adorned their walls. The residents enjoyed indoor plumbing and running water, comforts that most people in the West would not enjoy until the nineteenth century C.E. The palaces had no fortifications, suggesting that the Minoans felt quite safe on their island.

Like other monarchs, Minoan rulers carefully kept precise records of their wealth and possessions on clay tablets. Accountants recorded long lists of the livestock, produce, raw materials, and merchandise brought to the palace warehouses, as well as land holdings, debts, and payments made to the palace. These administrators used a form of writing known as Linear A, a simplified hieroglyphic script that developed on Crete around 1700 B.C.E., probably influenced by Egyptian writing. Linguists have not entirely deciphered the script.

Minoan mercantile documents found in ports along the eastern coast of the Mediterranean as well as the excavation of Minoan trading posts on the islands of the central Aegean Sea, on the island of Rhodes, and in other locations along the eastern Mediterranean coast reveal the international reach of Minoan travel and commerce. Minoan merchants sold their wares on the Greek mainland, and Minoan delegations brought rich gifts to the courts of Egyptian pharaohs. Exporting luxury goods—jewelry of precious metals and stones, painted vases, and delicate figures carved in the deep blue gemstone called lapis lazuli°—to eager foreign buyers made the Minoans wealthy.

Minoan prosperity and power came to a sudden and unexplained end around 1450 B.C.E. At that time all of the Cretan towns and palaces were destroyed except for Knossos, which fell about seventy-five years later. Excavations reveal that immediately after the destruction of the Minoan palaces, artifacts from mainland Greece appeared on Crete and throughout the Aegean. Graves on Crete began to contain Greek-style weapons and armor. Archaeologists do not know whether Mycenaean Greeks from the mainland caused the collapse of Minoan power or merely took advantage of it, but it is certain that invaders from Greece took control of Crete and its trade networks around this time. The international economy and the balance of maritime power in the eastern Mediterranean shifted from the island of Minoan Crete to the mainland of Mycenaean Greece.

Mycenaean Greece

A German archaeologist, Heinrich Schliemann, first brought the Bronze Age civilization of mainland Greece to light in 1876 C.E. Determined to prove that the epic poems of the Greek poet Homer about the Trojan War were based in fact, Schliemann first dug at Troy (see next section) and then at the fortress of Mycenae, the home of the Greek king Agamemnon in Homer's *Iliad*. He made spectacular finds of golden treasures and sophisticated architecture at Mycenae, which archaeologists today believe was only one of perhaps six kingdoms on the Greek mainland. The name *Mycenaean* refers both to the kingdom of Mycenae and, more generally, to the culture of Greece during the International Bronze Age. Mycenaean civilization lasted from around 1600 to 1100 B.C.E.

By 1400 B.C.E. a uniform Mycenaean civilization had reached its apex throughout southern Greece and in Mycenaean settlements abroad. The larger Mycenaean communities consisted of heavily fortified palaces with outlying agricultural lands. As on Crete, the Mycenaean palaces functioned as administrative centers of food collection and distribution. They also served as manufacturing centers that produced pottery, jewelry, tapestries, and other trade goods. Literate bureaucrats living in the palaces were essential in governing the Mycenaean kingdoms. Like their counterparts in Crete and Southwest Asia, they recorded long lists of livestock, slaves, farm produce, land holdings, taxes, and tribute taken from peasants and slaves. They also kept detailed records of imported and exported luxury goods and raw materials. These administrative records were written on clay tablets in a script known as Linear B, an early form of the Greek language spoken today.

The most influential kingdom in southern Greece during this period was located at Mycenae, where kings governed from a citadel looking down on a broad agricultural plain. This center of power reveals much about life in Bronze Age Greece. Thirty royal burials consisting of deep shafts arranged in two circles on the citadel and dating from 1600 to 1450 B.C.E. suggest a highly warlike people. The graves contain bronze swords, daggers, spearheads, and stone arrowheads and blades. The skeletons of the rulers buried in these graves stood nearly six feet tall, which made them tower over the general population. Apparently they enjoyed better nutrition than their subjects, whose graves reveal more diminutive skeletons. The many gold and silver drinking vessels and pieces of jewelry found in the graves further demonstrate that the Mycenaean leaders enjoyed tremendous luxury.

The Mycenaean kings also relied on aristocratic warriors, who enforced the monarchs' decisions and served as military officers during wartime. As in Egypt, Anatolia, and Southwest Asia, elite warriors used light, fast-moving chariots pulled by horses. They also took their favorite weapons of war with them to the grave, suggesting that they valued military prowess very highly.

The Mycenaeans took advantage of the peaceful conditions in the eastern Mediterranean that diplomatic ties between Egypt and the Hittite Empire had helped create. With the collapse of Minoan Crete, they assumed control of commerce across the Aegean Sea and the eastern Mediterranean. During the fourteenth and thirteenth centuries B.C.E., Mycenaean merchants extended Minoan commercial routes, establishing strong links with Egyptians and the inhabitants of Ugarit and other coastal towns. Ships carried Mycenaean commodities in large clay vessels painted with distinctive designs as far west as Spain and northern Italy.

Mycenaean rulers also forged diplomatic ties with Egyptian monarchs. Ambassadors of Pharaoh Amenhotep III visited Crete and the Greek mainland, including Mycenae, where they presented ceremonial plaques bearing the pharaoh's name. In the interest of maintaining good relations and brisk commerce, Egyptian and Mycenaean rulers avoided war with each other during this period, but Mycenaean relations with the Hittites were not quite so cordial. To extend and protect their trade routes, some Mycenaean Greeks settled on the coast of Asia Minor, a sphere of Hittite influence. There they engaged in trade, piracy, and warfare with surrounding communities. Hittite documents dating to the fourteenth century B.C.E. tell of meddling Mycenaean kings who slipped away to sea in their ships, out of the reach of landbound Hittite forces.

Two Coastal Kingdoms: Ugarit and Troy

Many independent cities existed along the border regions between Egypt, Mycenaean Greece, and the Hittite Empire. A string of these small communities stretched along the seacoast from the Aegean Sea to the Gaza Strip and served as a buffer between the three major powers. The two most notable of these cities were Ugarit and Troy.

Ugarit: A Mercantile Kingdom

Directly east of Cyprus on the Syrian coast lay the port city of Ugarit, which controlled a small but influential kingdom of about 2,000 square miles. Ugarit became a highly cultured city with international connections because of its rich natural resources. The fertile plain offered arable land for grape vines, olive trees, and grains, while the heavily forested surrounding hills provided timber for shipbuilding and construction. Perhaps Ugarit's greatest asset was a fine natural harbor that made the city a hub of international trade. Merchant ships like the one that sank at Uluburun sailed to Ugarit from Cyprus and the Aegean, the coast of

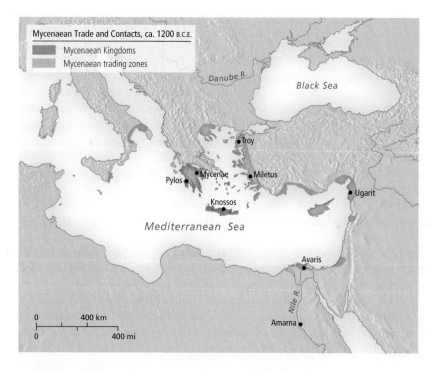

Mycenaean Trade and Contacts, ca. 1200 B.C.E.
■ Mycenaean Kingdoms
■ Mycenaean trading zones

Danube R.

Black Sea

Troy

Pylos · Mycenae · Miletus

Knossos

Ugarit

Mediterranean Sea

Avaris

Nile R.

0   400 km
0   400 mi

Amarna

Map 2.3 Mycenaean Trade and Contacts, ca. 1200 B.C.E.
The Mycenaean Greeks traded extensively with communities throughout the eastern Mediterranean world, including Egypt, the coastal towns of Asia Minor, and Canaan. Sometimes their commerce was little more than raiding and piracy.

DOCUMENT

The Millawanda Letter

About 1300 B.C.E., a Hittite king wrote the following letter to an unknown Mycenaean king, complaining of the behavior of a lesser ruler on the Aegean coast of Asia Minor who had defied the Hittite king's commands. Millawanda was the Hittite name for the coastal town in Asia Minor where the Mycenaeans had established a stronghold.

The author's insistence on the formalities of diplomatic communication is striking. The letter indicates the significant role of international diplomatic relations among the great powers, but it leaves some questions unanswered: Was the Mycenaean kingdom of Ahhijawa on Rhodes, on Cyprus, or in Greece? What was the previous trouble over the city of Wilusa (another name for Troy)? And what was the fate of the messengers?

I have to complain of the insolent and treacherous conduct of . . . Tawagalawas. We came into contact in the land of Luqqa [in southwest Asia Minor]; and he offered to become a vassal of the Hittite Emperor. . . . I order him, if he desires to become a vassal of mine, to make sure that no troops of his are to be found in Ijalanda [an unknown location] when I arrive there. And what do I find when I arrive at Ijalanda? The troops of Tawagalawas fighting on the side of my enemies. I defeat them, take many prisoners, devastate the district, scrupulously keeping the fortress of Atrija intact out of respect for my treaty with you. Now comes a Hittite subject, Pijamaradus, . . . who steals my 7000 prisoners, and makes off to your city Millawanda (Miletus). I command him to return to me: he disobeys. I write to you:

you send a surly message, unaccompanied by gift or greeting. . . . So I go to fetch him. I enter your city Millawanda, for I have something to say to Pijamaradus, and it would be well that your subjects there should hear me say it. But my visit is not a success. I ask for Tawagalawas: he is not at home. I should like to see Pijamaradus: he has gone to sea. . . . Are you aware, and is it with your blessing, that Pijamaradus is going around saying that he intends to leave his wife and family, and incidentally my 7000 prisoners, under your protection, while he makes continual inroads into my territory? Kindly tell him either to settle down peacefully in your country, or to return to my country. Do not let him use Ahhijawa as a base for operations against me. You and I are friends. There has been no quarrel between us since we came to terms in the matter of Wilusa [Troy]: the trouble there was all my fault, and I promise you that it shall not happen again. As for my military occupation of your city Millawanda, please consider it a friendly visit. I am sorry that in the past you have had occasion to accuse me of being aggressive and of sending impolite messages: I was young then and carried away in the heat of action. I may add that I also have had harsh words from you, and I suggest that the fault may not lie with ourselves but with our messengers. Let us bring them to trial, cut off their heads, mutilate their bodies, and live henceforward in perfect friendship.

Source: From Denys L. Page, *History and the Homeric Iliad,* Copyright © 1959 by The Regents of the University of California. Reprinted by permission.

---

western Anatolia, and Egypt. Caravans laden with goods arrived from Mesopotamia, the Hittite lands, and Canaan. People from all these places settled in Ugarit, whose population is estimated at 10,000 inhabitants. Another 25,000 people lived as farmers in the Ugarit countryside.

In Ugarit's spacious houses archaeologists have excavated numerous baked clay tablets containing legal, financial, literary, diplomatic, and religious texts written in Ugaritic, the local Semitic language. The tablets demonstrate the literacy of the Ugaritic elite. Young people studied their own language in school while also mastering foreign languages useful in trade and diplomacy. The tablets show an innovative alphabet. In it, each spoken sound was represented by just one letter or sign. This Ugaritic alphabet was the ancestor of all modern alphabets that follow the same principle of one sign per spoken sound.

Ugarit was always overshadowed by mighty Egypt to the south and the combative Hittite Empire to the north. To

maintain Ugarit's independence, the port city's rulers had to be clever diplomats. Archaeologists have unearthed records of treaties made between the kings of Ugarit and Hittite, Assyrian, and other rulers in Southwest Asia. These treaties show that Ugarit played an influential role in international diplomacy.

Troy: A City of Legend

Troy, the best known and yet most mysterious of all Bronze Age cities, has captured the popular imagination for 3,000 years, but archaeology cannot explain the origins of the people who lived there, or even their language. Historians do know that like Ugarit, Troy was a city embedded in the intricate web of trade, diplomacy, and warfare that linked the societies of the International Bronze Age.

Situated in northwest Asia Minor on a promontory overlooking a bay about six miles from the Aegean Sea, this city has become immortal as the site of the Trojan War in

Homer's epic poems the *Iliad* and the *Odyssey*. Composed about 750 B.C.E., these stories were legends, not history. Still, they formed part of an enduring oral tradition that began in the International Bronze Age and reflect social conditions and perhaps even events that actually occurred.

Archaeologists have unearthed numerous distinct layers of occupation and construction in Troy, as generations of inhabitants rebuilt their city from about 3000 to 1200 B.C.E. Around 1700 B.C.E. the inhabitants of Troy VI (meaning the sixth major layer of occupation) constructed huge gateways and a royal palace consisting of many spacious mansions. A fortified citadel, Troy VI was built with monumental blocks of masonry similar to that used by the Hittites and the Mycenaeans, suggesting that techniques of military engineering had spread among these kingdoms. The Trojans prospered in the fifteenth and fourteenth centuries B.C.E. by trading with Mycenaean Greeks, Hittites, Cypriots, and merchants from Ugarit. But around 1270 B.C.E., an earthquake tumbled the mighty walls of Troy VI and the city went up in flames. The Trojans' prosperity and influence ended.

Heinrich Schliemann, the first archaeologist to excavate Troy, erroneously concluded that Troy VI was the city destroyed by Mycenaean Greeks in Homer's *Iliad*. Later archaeologists proved that Greeks had nothing to do with the city's collapse. Most archaeologists believe that if there is even a kernel of truth in Homer's stories about the Greek destruction of Troy, it must lie in the violent end of Troy VIIa, the modest city built within the rubble of Troy VI's fortress walls by the survivors of the earthquake. This new version of the city also fell to ruin about 1190 B.C.E., probably as the result of warfare. Hittite royal documents indicate that at this time Mycenaeans were raiding the coastlands of Asia Minor in search of slaves and booty, and Linear B tablets from the Greek mainland list slaves captured on the Asia Minor coast. These records suggest that Troy VIIa may well have fallen prey to a Mycenaean attack. Some historians believe that in the centuries following Troy VIIa's destruction, the story of a Mycenaean raid slowly took on epic proportions as generations of Greek bards told and retold it. Older tales recounting the glory of Troy VI may have augmented the legend of the Trojan War.

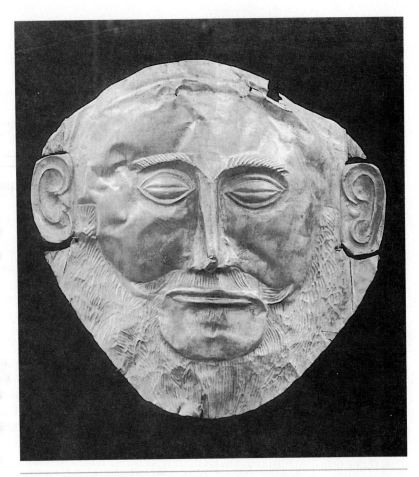

The "Death Mask of Agamemnon"
This thin gold mask, about eleven inches long, was found at the citadel of Mycenae in the tomb of a ruler who died about 1550 B.C.E. Heinrich Schliemann, who excavated the tomb, mistakenly jumped to the conclusion that it was the death mask of King Agamemnon, who led the Greek forces during the Trojan War, as told in Homer's *Iliad*. Later archaeologists have discovered that this king died several centuries before the period that Homer described.

The End of the International Bronze Age and Its Aftermath

■ What forces brought the International Bronze Age to a close, and how did the Phoenicians, Assyrians, and Babylonians build new kingdoms and empires in its wake?

The intricate diplomatic, cultural, and economic interconnections between Egypt, Southwest Asia, Anatolia, and Greece broke between 1200 and 1100 B.C.E. These formerly vibrant civilizations plummeted into a dark age marked by invasions, migrations, and the collapse of stable governments. The era of prosperity and international cooperation ended abruptly. In the aftermath of these turbulent events, however, the people of Southwest Asia from the Mediterranean coast to Mesopotamia gradually developed new and powerful kingdoms with distinctive cultures.

The Raiders of the Land and Sea

Developments in Mycenaean Greece and the Hittite Empire were pivotal in bringing the International Bronze Age to an end. The collapse of Hittite and Mycenaean power contributed to migrations throughout the eastern Mediterranean. People fled their homes in search of new lands to settle. Overcoming all resistance, these displaced groups plundered cities and brought destruction to the entire eastern Mediterranean as they moved southward.

Warfare among the many competitive kingdoms of Mycenaean Greece probably began this chain of disasters. These conflicts resulted in the breakdown of the palace-centered economic system about 1150 B.C.E. When the Mycenaean kingdoms collapsed, the economy disintegrated as well. Literacy disappeared because without palace inventories to record, there was no need for scribes to learn Linear B. Trade and population declined rapidly, and many Greeks migrated to the coast of Asia Minor. The Greek language and some religious beliefs survived, but the crafts, artistic styles, and architectural traditions of Mycenaean life were forgotten. In contrast to the brilliance of Mycenaean civilization, the poverty and hardship of the era that followed merit the name "dark age."

For the Hittite Empire, a deadly combination of economic decline and invasions early in the twelfth century B.C.E. triggered the government's collapse. The subject kingdoms in the western regions of the Hittite Empire began to rebel, and peasants fled their lands. The Hittites became ever more dependent on foreign sources of grain, forcing their rulers to import larger supplies from Egypt and Syria. Rebellions occasionally blocked these shipments, worsening the Hittites' plight. By the first decade of the twelfth century B.C.E. an enemy force of uncertain origin stormed through the Hittite Empire and burned the capital city of Hattushas. With no effective leadership, Hittite power soon crumbled.

As Hittite and Mycenaean power collapsed, migrating peoples surged across the eastern Mediterranean. In Egyptian documents these people are referred to as Raiders of the Land and Sea°. They came from many places, impelled not only by political instability and economic decline, but also by earthquakes, plague, and climate change. The raiders included pirates and mercenaries, as well as migrating groups that traveled with their families and livestock in search of new lands. The raiders' movements destabilized all the regions linked together by the trading and diplomatic networks of the International Bronze Age. Moving south through Syria and Palestine, the raiders de-

stroyed Ugarit and other coastal cities. Bound together in a loose confederation, the raiders moved further south toward Egypt in search of land and food. By 1170 B.C.E., the Egyptian Empire had lost control of Syria and Canaan. Ugarit fell at the same time. Groups of raiders settled on the Mediterranean coast and extended their power inland. Organized political life in Canaan disintegrated and the last of the Bronze Age cities collapsed by about 1100 B.C.E. One group of raiders, the Peleset People, who settled on the coast of Canaan, are known to us as the Philistines, a name that survives in the modern word *Palestine.*

Egypt was able to marshal its military might and avoid total destruction at the hands of the Raiders of the Land and Sea, but it slipped into a long economic and military decline. Drought, poor harvests, and inflation ruined the Egyptian economy, while weak rulers struggled unsuccessfully to hold Egypt together. The bonds between Upper and Lower Egypt were severed, and the land of Egypt split once again into separate kingdoms.

In Mesopotamia, the kingdoms of Babylonia and Assyria also experienced an economic and political breakdown. Historians attribute this decline primarily to invasions by seminomadic peoples originating in Syria and the Iranian Plateau. Their monarchs lost power and political influence, but the Assyrians and Babylonians nevertheless maintained their identity as distinct peoples throughout these troubled centuries.

After the International Bronze Age ended about 1100 B.C.E., two regions acquired special importance: the eastern coast of the Mediterranean, where the Phoenicians established a maritime culture, and Mesopotamia, where the kingdoms of Assyria and Babylonia revived. (We will examine the civilization of the Hebrews, which also emerged in the aftermath of the International Bronze Age, in Chapter 3.)

The Phoenicians: Merchants of the Mediterranean

Two hundred years after the International Bronze Age drew to a close, a dynamic maritime civilization took shape in the independent port cities that stretched along the eastern Mediterranean seaboard. Byblos, Tyre, and Sidon were the most powerful of these cities. These seafaring people, whom historians call Phoenicians, continued the commercial traditions of Ugarit and other small Bronze Age kingdoms. By following old Minoan and Mycenaean trade routes of the International Bronze Age, they created a large commercial sphere of influence. Hundreds of their ships crisscrossed the Mediterranean and ventured into the Atlantic Ocean in search of trade. By 950 B.C.E. they had established extensive trade and political connections with peoples of the Levant and spread their civilization into the

Mediterranean world as far as North Africa, Italy, and Spain.

The search for metal ores motivated much of Phoenician commerce. Phoenician metal prospectors located deposits of precious ores in North Africa, Spain, Italy, Britain, and France. They traded with the local inhabitants in these regions who had been working the mines for centuries. In this way Phoenician traders established economic connections with lands that would later become the center of Western civilization (see Map 2.4). The enterprising Phoenicians also learned techniques of smelting metals for weapons, tools, and jewelry that had been developing in European lands since the International Bronze Age, and they transmitted this knowledge to Southwest Asian peoples. In return, they brought back Asian and Egyptian artistic styles to western Mediterranean lands.

By 800 B.C.E., Carthage ("New City"), a colony located on the northern coast of modern Tunisia, had become the chief Phoenician city in the west. For this reason, Phoenician culture in the western Mediterranean is called Carthaginian. With its magnificent harbor and strategic location midway between the Levant and the straits of Gibraltar, Carthage controlled trade between the eastern and western Mediterranean. Its inhabitants developed a land-based empire on the North African coast and in Spain. Phoenicians were more interested in trading than settling, however. Their approach to trade facilitated good relations with the southern Mediterranean's native inhabitants, especially in Sicily and Italy.

Phoenician religion showed remarkable continuity through time and across the Mediterranean. Many of their gods and goddesses had also been worshiped by Southwest Asian peoples during the International Bronze Age. Even though the deities' names differed among many Phoenician cities, their roles as protectors and warriors remained the same. The chief gods were Baalat ("Lady of the Heavens") and her husband Baal ("Lord of the Heavens"), who represented the order of the natural world and protected the Phoenicians from danger. Many parents killed their first-born son as an offering to the Lord and Lady of the Heavens at moments of crisis or as an offering for the fulfillment of a personal vow. Child sacrifice continued at Carthaginian settlements, often secretly, as late as 200 C.E. In the western Mediterranean, the Lady of the Heavens became associated

---

Map 2.4   Phoenician Expansion, ca. 600 B.C.E.

Several centuries after the collapse of the International Bronze Age, adventurous merchants from the eastern Mediterranean coast developed a commercial empire across the Mediterranean Sea. By 600 B.C.E. Carthage had become the chief Phoenician city in the western Mediterranean. It controlled the resources of North Africa and parts of Spain.

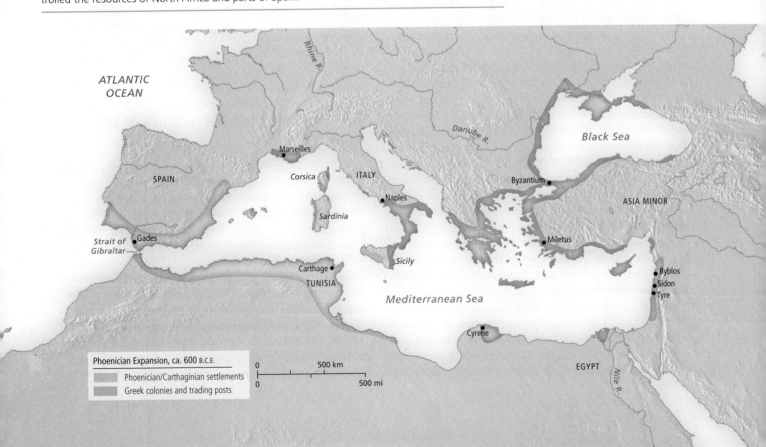

Phoenician Expansion, ca. 600 B.C.E.
  Phoenician/Carthaginian settlements
  Greek colonies and trading posts

with the practice of sacred prostitution, in which every sexual union between a priestess and a male believer symbolized the fertility and regenerative power of the Lady of the Heavens.

The Phoenicians' most lasting cultural contribution to the peoples of the Mediterranean world was the alphabet. The Phoenicians developed a system of writing based on that of Ugarit in which each letter represented a single sound. Thus the alphabet could be used to record the sounds of any language. The Phoenician alphabet spread throughout the Mediterranean world, where the Greeks and then the Romans adopted it. In this way it became the source of all alphabets and writing in the West.

Known mainly as accomplished sailors and merchants, the Phoenicians did not develop a large, centralized state. Their cities, therefore, became vulnerable to attack by larger empires and lost their independence in the fifth century B.C.E. Their strong mercantile and seafaring culture, however, lasted into Roman times. As we will see in Chapter 4, Carthage grew into a vast Mediterranean empire and became Rome's greatest enemy.

Mesopotamian Kingdoms: Assyria and Babylon, 1050–550 B.C.E.

The decline of both Assyria and Babylonia at the end of the International Bronze Age did not result in their outright disappearance as kingdoms. Torn apart by invasions, they nevertheless managed to survive. Beginning in about 1050 B.C.E., the Assyrian and then the Babylonian imperial regimes began to regain effective control over their territories, reestablish their commercial power, and reconquer neighboring lands.

Neo-Assyrian Imperialism

After 1000 B.C.E., the Assyrian kings slowly reasserted their dominance in northern Mesopotamia. In 745 B.C.E., Tiglath-Pileser III (r. 745–727 B.C.E.) ascended the Assyrian throne and ushered in a century of rapid expansion. This Neo-Assyrian Empire was the first in history to control the Tigris, Euphrates, and Nile River valleys, where civilization had first emerged two millennia before (see Map 2.5). By 500 B.C.E., Nineveh, the Neo-Assyrian capital city, boasted at least 500,000 inhabitants.

Neo-Assyrian rulers, who called themselves "Kings of the Universe," developed a highly militarized empire. To terrify their victims and aid their conquests, they cultivated a reputation for extreme cruelty. Assyrian armies tortured, butchered, and enslaved the inhabitants of defeated cities. Then, after carting off everything of value, they burned the cities to the ground. News of their atrocities spread to neighboring areas, which quickly and understandably surrendered.

CHRONOLOGY	
ca. 3200 B.C.E.	Bronze making begins in Northern Syria and Iraq
ca. 2000 B.C.E.	Minoans build first palaces built on Crete
ca. 1650–1600 B.C.E.	International Bronze Age begins; Hittite Kingdom emerges
ca. 1550 B.C.E.	New Kingdom begins in Egypt
ca. 1450 B.C.E.	First palaces built at Mycenae in Greece; Linear B script develops
ca. 1400 B.C.E.	Kassites gain control of Babylonia
ca. 1351–1334 B.C.E.	Amenhotep IV (Akhenaten) rules in Egypt; Amarna Period
ca. 1190 B.C.E.	Troy VIIa falls
ca. 1244–1208 B.C.E.	Tukulti-Ninurta I conquers Babylonia
ca. 1200–1150 B.C.E.	International Bronze Age ends
ca. 1000 B.C.E.	Aramaeans invade Assyria
ca. 900 B.C.E.	Phoenician civilization develops
ca. 750 B.C.E.	Phoenician alphabet reaches Greece
721 B.C.E.	Assyria conquers Northern Kingdom of Israel
603 B.C.E.	Neo-Assyrian Empire falls
612–539 B.C.E.	Neo-Babylonian Empire emerges; astronomy flourishes

Like their predecessors during the International Bronze Age, the Neo-Assyrian rulers grew wealthy from agriculture and trade. They also exploited their subjects more harshly than previously. Provincial administrators imposed crippling taxes and systematically drained away their subjects' resources. With these revenues, the kings could maintain armies of more than 100,000 men. At the same time, the government strengthened the economy by rebuilding cities, increasing the amount of land under cultivation, and building roads to improve trade and communications throughout the empire.

As the Assyrians conquered more and more peoples, they faced problems that have troubled empires ever since: How can subject peoples be controlled and what degree of cultural independence should they be permitted to retain? Assyrian solutions were thoughtful yet violent. Assyrian rulers permitted their subjects to continue their traditions and religious practices without interference. If they rebelled

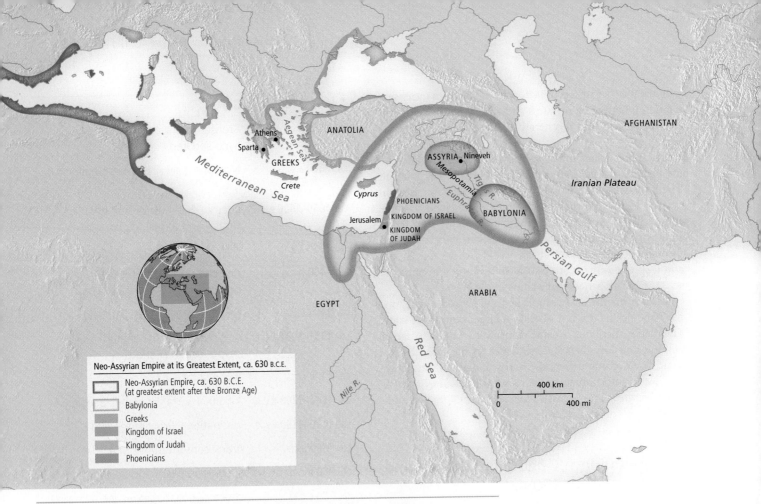

Map 2.5   The Neo-Assyrian Empire at Its Greatest Extent, ca. 630 B.C.E.
By 630 B.C.E., the Assyrians had recovered their strength and established the Neo-Assyrian Empire.
This huge realm included Mesopotamia, the Israelite kingdoms, Phoenicia, and parts of Egypt.

against Assyrian authority, however, the army would crush them and deport entire populations to distant corners of the empire. Some Assyrian rulers depopulated entire regions. Perhaps as many as a million and a half people were forced from their homes by Assyrian deportation policies.

Ashurbanipal (r. 669–626 B.C.E.), the last strong ruler of the Neo-Assyrian Empire, attempted to create a uniform culture throughout his vast realm. At his command, scholars collected subject peoples' written knowledge, translated it into Akkadian, and distributed copies on clay tablets throughout Assyrian lands. Ashurbanipal did not succeed in imposing a standardized culture on the empire, but he was the first monarch to try to organize the diverse cultural inheritances of his many subject peoples.

Despite its prosperity and efficient administration, the Neo-Assyrian model of imperial rule failed to bring lasting unity to its peoples. Subject peoples who had endured brutal treatment at the hands of Assyrian administrators nursed a bitter resentment and revolted as soon as possible. The most significant of these rebels was the Babylonian king Nabopolassar in southern Mesopotamia (r. 625–605 B.C.E.). He allied himself with Persian kings and began a successful

revolt against Assyrian rule. By 603 B.C.E., the Assyrian Empire collapsed again, this time for good.

The Neo-Babylonian Empire

After Nabopolassar acquired Assyrian territory, he built the Neo-Babylonian (or Chaldean) Empire into the most powerful in Southwest Asia, which lasted until 539 B.C.E. His son, the brilliant general Nebuchadnezzar II (r. 604–562 B.C.E.), conquered lands that had broken free when Assyrian rule collapsed (see Map 2.6). Babylonian armies seized Egypt, Syria, Phoenicia, and the kingdom of Judah, where they destroyed the city of Jerusalem and exiled many Jews to Babylon. (We will learn more about this exile in Chapter 3.)

With the wealth acquired from these conquests, Nebuchadnezzar made his capital city, Babylon, one of the most luxurious in the ancient world. A moat flooded with waters from the Euphrates River surrounded Babylon's eight miles of walls. The Ishtar Gate, which opened onto a grand avenue leading to the temple of Marduk, Babylon's greatest god, was decorated with glazed, brightly colored tiles. According to tradition, Nebuchadnezzar built the "Hanging Gardens of Babylon" for a favorite wife who

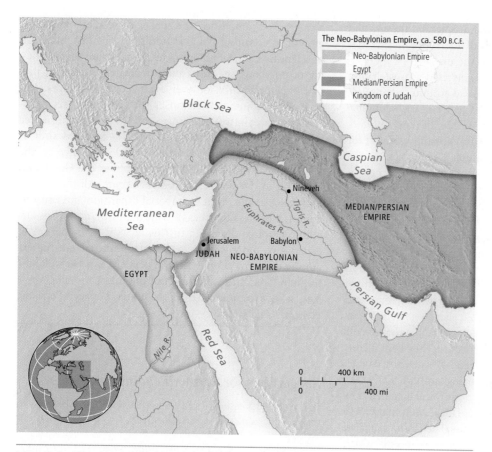

Map 2.6   The Neo-Babylonian Empire, ca. 580 B.C.E.
By ca. 580 B.C.E., the Neo-Babylonian Empire had replaced the Neo-Assyrian Empire as the dominant power in the Middle East.

Ishtar Gate

The magnificently tiled Ishtar Gate, right, provided a dramatic entrance to Babylon, the capital city of the Neo-Babylonian Empire. Babylonian artists used brightly colored tiles to create complicated three-dimensional depictions of animals, including lions, which represented royal power. The gate now rests in a museum in Berlin.

missed her mountainous homeland. Splendid flowers and plants cascaded down the slopes of a terraced hillside that from a distance seemed to float in the air.

The Neo-Babylonian Empire comprised a constellation of wealthy cities in which life revolved around the uninterrupted worship of Marduk. At the center of each community stood a magnificent temple to the all-powerful god. The Babylonians considered proper worship essential for the prosperity of their communities. They looked to the king to provide the peaceful conditions in which they could worship their gods without interruption. The king, for his part, expected his subjects to obey his commands, and he counted on the priests to bolster his authority.

Religion not only gave the Babylonians a profound sense of spiritual security, it also expanded their scientific knowledge. The Babylonians believed that proper interpretation of the celestial bodies through astronomy could help them understand the will of the gods. Building on the Sumerians' mathematical and astronomical legacy, Babylonian astronomers patiently observed and recorded the movements of the stars, the planets, and the moon. They kept a continuous log of observations between 747 B.C.E. and 61 C.E., an astonishing achievement. Starting around 500 B.C.E., they had accumulated so much astronomical data that they could perform complicated mathematical computations to predict eclipses of the moon and sun. They also calculated the first appearance of the new moon every month, which enabled them to devise a calendar. These brilliant astronomers' calculations, which Persians and Greeks would later adopt, helped lay the foundation of Western science. From these able scientists, the West inherited the names of many constellations, the zodiac, and many complex mathematical models of astronomical phenomena.

Conclusion

The International Bronze Age and the Emergence of the West

The International Bronze Age and its aftermath marked two early but crucial phases in the formation of Western civilization. Within a large geographical area centered on the eastern Mediterranean but stretching far beyond its shores, an intricate network of political, commercial, and cultural ties was established among cities and kingdoms that had previously lived in relative isolation from each other. The forces that exposed the cultures of these areas to each other were the expansion of international trade; the development of a new military technology; the growth of large, multiethnic empires; and the establishment of diplomatic relations among rulers. Long before it was possible to identify what we now call the West, the ex-

change of commodities, the spread of religious ideas, the growth of common political traditions, the dissemination of scientific and technological techniques, and the borrowing of one language from another created a complex pattern of cultural diffusion over a vast geographical area.

During subsequent centuries the content of such cultural interaction would change, and the geographical area within which these exchanges took place would shift as well, first to the lands controlled by Persia, then to the Hellenistic world conquered by Alexander the Great, and later still to the sprawling Roman Empire. All these shifts took place as the result of imperial expansion and consolidation, a process that began with the formation of multiethnic empires discussed in this chapter. Each period of expansion, moreover, involved new cultural encounters among different peoples. In the next chapter we will continue to look at the aftermath of the International Bronze Age, as we explore a series of encounters between Persians, Hebrews, and Greeks.

Suggestions for Further Reading

For a comprehensive list of suggested readings, please go to www.ablongman.com/levack2e/chapter2

Bryce, Trevor. *The Kingdom of the Hittites*. 1998. The latest synthesis of Hittite history and culture.

Cline, Eric H., and Diane Harris-Cline, eds. *The Aegean and the Orient in the Second Millennium: Proceedings of the 50th Anniversary Symposium, Cincinnati, 18–20 April 1997, Aegaeum 18*. 1998. A collection of papers by experts providing state-of-the-art discussions of all aspects of the connections among Bronze Age civilizations of the eastern Mediterranean and Middle East.

Dickinson, Oliver. *The Aegean Bronze Age*. 1994. Now the standard treatment of the complex archaeological data.

Dothan, Trude, and Moshe Dothan. *People of the Sea: The Search for the Philistines*. 1992. A recent, highly popularized survey of the archaeological material.

Drews, Robert. *The End of the Bronze Age: Changes in Warfare and the Catastrophe ca. 1200 B.C.* 1993. A controversial but well-argued analysis that offers new solutions to the question of why the Bronze Age ended.

Fitton, J. Lesley. *The Discovery of the Greek Bronze Age*. 1996. A lucid and well-illustrated study of the archaeologists who brought the Greek Bronze Age to light in the nineteenth and early twentieth centuries.

Harding, A. F. *The Mycenaeans in Europe*. 1984. Exploration of the trade and cultural connections between Mycenaeans and the rest of Europe.

Hornung, Erik. *History of Ancient Egypt: An Introduction*, trans. David Lorton. 1999. A concise and lucid overview of Egyptian history and life.

Knapp, A. Bernard. *The History and Culture of Ancient Western Asia and Egypt*. 1988. A reliable archaeological and historical overview without excessive detail.

Kuhrt, Amélie. *The Ancient Middle East, ca. 3000–330 B.C.,* 2 vols. 1995. A magisterial, up-to-date overview, with an excellent bibliography. The place to start for a continuous historical narrative of the region.

Macqueen, James G. *The Hittites and Their Contemporaries in Asia Minor.* 1986. This account stresses the interconnections of Hittites and other peoples.

Markoe, Glenn. *Phoenicians.* 2000. The best and most up-to-date treatment of Phoenician society by a noted expert.

Page, Denys. *History and the Homeric Iliad.* 1959. An entertaining and provocative examination of the historical context of the events described in Homer's *Iliad.*

Redford, Donald B. *Egypt, Canaan and Israel in Ancient Times.* 1992. An excellent, detailed synthesis of textual and archaeological evidence that emphasizes interconnections among cultures.

Schulz, Regine, and Matthias Seidel, eds. *Egypt: The World of the Pharaohs.* 1999. A sumptuously illustrated collection of essays on all aspects of Egyptian society and life by leading experts.

Traill, David. *Schliemann of Troy: Treasure and Deceit.* 1995. A fascinating discussion of the motivations and methods of the archaeologist who discovered the Bronze Age.

Walker, Christopher, ed. *Astronomy Before the Telescope.* 1996. A fascinating collection of essays about astronomy in the premodern period, which makes clear Western civilization's enormous debt to the Babylonians.

Wood, Michael. *In Search of the Trojan War.* 1985. A valuable introductory discussion of the archaeological and historical problems of placing Homer's Trojan War in its Bronze Age context.

Notes

1. T. Eric Peet, *The Great Tomb Robberies of the Twentieth Egyptian Dynasty,* 2 vols. (1930; reprinted in one volume, 1977). Contains texts and translations of this and other trials.

2. Regina Schulz and Matthias Seidel, eds., *Egypt: The World of the Pharaohs* (1998), 485.

3. Translated in Amélie Kuhrt, *The Ancient Middle East,* vol. 1 (1995), 350–351.

Persians, Hebrews, and Greeks: The Foundations of Western Culture, 1100–336 B.C.E.

3

I N THE SECOND HALF OF THE SIXTH CENTURY B.C.E., CYRUS THE GREAT, A Persian king from southern Iran, created the largest empire the world had ever seen, with territories in Asia, the Middle East, Africa, and Europe. According to one of the many legends surrounding this celebrated ruler, Cyrus grew restless as a young man under the rule of another king. He summoned the Persian tribal leaders who owed him allegiance and instructed them to spend a day clearing land with sickles. When they finally stopped their backbreaking labor, he invited them to a magnificent banquet. After the men had devoured the last delicacy, Cyrus asked them which they enjoyed more, tasting the wonderful food or sweating in the fields. The chieftains shouted in unison that they preferred the wine and fine foods. Cyrus then proclaimed:

> *Men of Persia, follow me and I promise that you will enjoy this sort of luxury for the rest of your lives, but if you do not, your lives will be full of painful toil with no such rewards from your present masters.*[1]

Without hesitation the men joined Cyrus in his successful revolt. Under his able leadership the Persians conquered more than twenty-three different peoples in territories ranging from the eastern Mediterranean coast to central Asia. Cyrus's successors added Egypt and parts of Greece and India to the Persian Empire. With its huge expanse and the stable government it provided to an enormous mix of cultures, the Persian Empire marked a turning point in the history of the ancient world.

This chapter examines the civilizations that developed during the six centuries following the collapse of the International Bronze Age around

Persian Art Persian artists drew freely from the artistic traditions of their subject peoples. This illustration shows how they put their own stamp on the Babylonian art of ceramic tile. The tiles show two members of the elite imperial guard, known as the Immortals. The details of their uniforms appear in vivid color. Soldiers like these in Xerxes' army attacked the Greeks in the fifth century B.C.E.

1100 B.C.E. When long-distance trade in copper and tin broke down, iron became the preferred metal for making tools and weapons throughout the ancient world. As a result of the widespread use of iron, archaeologists refer to the new period as the Iron Age. Its most significant features, however, were not its metal products but its distinctive religious, political, and cultural innovations. These innovations, which became fundamental to Western civilization, originated in a series of encounters between Persians and other peoples, particularly the Hebrews and Greeks.

For two centuries after Cyrus's death in 530 B.C.E., the Persian Empire prospered as its leaders methodically expanded their territory abroad and shrewdly managed their many subject peoples. The interaction of local cultures with that of Persia made an indelible impression on the history of the West. From their Assyrian and Babylonian subjects, the Persians inherited—and improved on—a political legacy of ruling a multiethnic empire. They also benefited from a scientific tradition that stretched back to the Sumerians. The Persians' capacity to borrow and adapt the most useful features of other cultures strengthened their own highly organized and justly administered empire.

Two peoples who established their own political identities during this era of Persian imperial dominance made even more important contributions to Western culture. From the Hebrews, who benefited from Persian rule and eventually were granted a measure of religious autonomy within the empire, came a tradition of monotheism, the worship of only one god. Monotheism became the main characteristic of the Hebrews' religion, Judaism, and it later became central to Christianity and Islam as well. Thus the three great religions of the West, which traced their origins back to the same roots, all professed a belief in only one god.

The other people who developed their cultural traditions in a world dominated by Persia were the Greeks. The most distinctive contribution of the Greeks to the West was the political tradition of democracy°, the conviction that people should share equally in the government of their communities, devise their own political institutions, and select their own leaders. Democratic institutions originated in the Greek city-state of Athens, which never succumbed to Persian military power, in the sixth century B.C.E. Following their victories over the Persians in the following century, Athenians were free to develop their democratic institutions in an atmosphere of great economic stability and security.

Victories over the Persians also made it possible for Athenian artists and thinkers to flourish. During what is known as the Classical Age of Greece, Athenians established philosophical schools that laid the foundations of Western philosophy, wrote dramas that grappled with fundamental moral questions, and created a distinctive Greek classical style in sculpture and architecture that has continued to be a source of inspiration in the West up to the present day.

This chapter addresses the major question of how the cultural traditions of the peoples of the Persian Empire, the Hebrews, and the Greeks laid the foundations of Western culture. More specifically, the major sections of this chapter will ask the following questions:

- How did the Persian Empire bring the peoples of the Middle East together in a stable realm, and what elements of Persian religion and government have influenced Western thought?
- What political and religious beliefs and institutions gave Hebrew civilization its unique character, and what consequences came of its interactions with the Assyrians, Babylonians, and Persians?
- How did Greek city-states develop in the framework of a larger world dominated by Persia?
- What were the intellectual, social, and political innovations of Greece in the Classical Age?

Persia: An Empire on Three Continents

- How did the Persian Empire bring the peoples of the Middle East together in a stable realm, and what elements of Persian religion and government have influenced Western thought?

Persian history began about 1400 B.C.E., when small groups of people started migrating with their herds and flocks into western Iran from areas north of the Caspian Sea. Over five centuries these settlers slowly coalesced into two closely related groups, the Medes and the Persians.

The Medes organized a loose confederation of tribes in western Iran and began to expand their territory. By about 900 B.C.E., they established mastery over all the peoples of the Iranian Plateau, including the Persians. In 612 B.C.E., with the assistance of the Babylonians, the Medes conquered the Assyrians. Then they pushed into central Asia Minor (modern Turkey), Afghanistan, and possibly farther into central Asia. In the sixth century, under the leadership of Cyrus the Great (r. 550–530 B.C.E.), Persia broke away from Medean rule and soon conquered the kingdom of the Medes. Under the guidance of this brilliant monarch and his successors, the Persians acquired a vast empire. They followed a monotheistic religion, Zoroastrianism, and governed their subjects with a combination of tolerance and firmness.

Cyrus the Great and Persian Expansion

After ascending the Persian throne about 550 B.C.E., Cyrus embarked on a dazzling twenty-year career of conquering neighboring peoples. His military genius and organizational skills transformed the small kingdom near the Persian Gulf into a giant multiethnic empire that stretched from India to the Mediterranean Sea. Cyrus's swift victory over the Medes put Persia at the center of the Middle East and thrust it into face-to-face encounters with a diverse array of peoples.

Cyrus expanded his empire beyond Persia in several stages. In 546 B.C.E. he conquered Asia Minor, where he first came into contact with Greeks living on the westernmost coast and islands, a region called Ionia. Cyrus conquered these Ionian Greek cities and installed loyal Greek administrators. Next he defeated the kingdom of Babylonia in 539 B.C.E., thus gaining control of the entire Mesopotamian region. After that he brought Afghanistan under his control and fortified it against the raids of the Scythian nomads who lived on the steppe lands to the north of his realm. These fierce warriors posed a perpetual threat to the settled territories of Persia.

With his borders expanded and secured, Cyrus turned his attention to the welfare of his Persian homeland. Dissatisfied with his capital city of Susa, he founded a spacious new capital city called Pasargadae. Builders, craftsmen, artists, and merchants flocked to it from Asia Minor, Egypt, Mesopotamia, and Greece. Inspired by Cyrus's leadership, these artisans turned the new capital into a cosmopolitan city of great ethnic diversity.

After Cyrus died in 530 B.C.E. while fighting against steppe nomads north of Persia, his son Cambyses II (r. 529–522 B.C.E.) continued his father's policy of expansion by subduing Egypt and the wealthy Phoenician port cities. The capture of Phoenicia gave the Persians a new strategic advantage. With control of Phoenician naval resources, the Persian Empire could reach overseas in a way that the landlocked Hittites could not during the International Bronze Age. Phoenician fleets became an integral part in Persia's invasion of Greece, as we will see later in this chapter. By the time of Cambyses's death in 522 B.C.E., Persia had become the mightiest empire in the world, with territorial possessions spanning Europe, Asia, the Middle East, and Africa (see Map 3.1).

To ensure that they could easily communicate with their subjects, the Great Kings of Persia established an elaborate system of roads to link their provinces. Special officials maintained supply stations at regular intervals along these roads. The chief branch of this system, called the Royal Road, stretched between Asia Minor and the Persian homeland. Persian road building was an indication of the sophistication of the Great Kings in managing an empire. These roads not only facilitated the transportation of soldiers and commercial goods from one part of the empire to another, but they also made possible the flow of ideas and the transmission of cultural traditions.

A Government of Tolerance

The key to maintaining power in such a diverse empire lay in the Persian government's treatment of its many ethnic groups. The highly centralized Persian government wielded absolute power, but it rejected the brutal model of the Assyrian and Babylonian imperial system in favor of a more tolerant approach.

After conquering Babylonia Cyrus began a popular policy of allowing peoples exiled by the Babylonians to return to their homelands. Though Cyrus was Zoroastrian, he made a proclamation to the Babylonians presenting himself as an agent of their chief god, Marduk:

> *I am Cyrus, the king of the world. Marduk, the great god, rejoices at my pious acts . . . I gathered all their peoples and led them back to their abodes . . . and at the order of Marduk . . . I had all the gods [of exiled peoples] installed in their sanctuaries . . . May all the gods whom I have led back to their cities pray daily for the length of my days.[2]*

Subject peoples were permitted to worship freely if they acknowledged the political supremacy of the Great King. In this way the Persians won the loyalty and gratitude of their ethnically diverse subjects throughout the empire.

The firm but tolerant methods of governing developed by the Persian government provided a legacy for Western civilization. As we will see in Chapter 4, Macedonian rulers continued to permit subjects to worship as they wished in the Hellenistic period following Alexander the Great's conquest of Persia.

Zoroastrianism: An Imperial Religion

The Great Kings of Persia and the Persian people followed Zoroastrianism°, a monotheistic religion that still exists today. Its founder, the prophet Zarathustra, known more commonly by his Greek name Zoroaster, lived and preached sometime between 1500 and 1200 B.C.E. His message spread widely throughout Iran for a thousand years before it became Persia's chief faith.

Persians transmitted Zoroaster's teachings, known collectively as the *Avesta*, through oral tradition until scribes recorded them in the sixth century C.E. According to Zoroaster, Ahura Mazda (Lord Wisdom), the one and only god of all Creation, is the cause of all good things in the universe. He represents wisdom, justice, and proper order among all created things. Another eternal being, Angra Mainyu (or Ahriman), opposes him. This spirit of destruction and disorder threatens Ahura Mazda's benevolent arrangement of creation.

CHRONOLOGY

Persia

550 B.C.E.	Cyrus starts the Persian Empire; Zoroastrianism becomes the empire's religion
546 B.C.E.	The Persians conquer Asia Minor
539 B.C.E.	The Persians capture Babylon
530 B.C.E.	Cyrus dies fighting Scythian steppe nomads
525 B.C.E.	Persian troops conquer Egypt
522 B.C.E.	Darius becomes king; the Achaemenid dynasty begins
490 B.C.E.	Greeks stop Persian invasion of Greece at Marathon
480–479 B.C.E.	Xerxes' invasion of Greece fails

In Zoroastrian belief, Ahura Mazda will eventually triumph in this struggle with the forces of evil, leaving all creation to enjoy a blissful eternity. Until then, the cosmic fight between Ahura Mazda's forces of light and Angra Mainyu's forces of darkness gives meaning to human existence and lays the foundation for a profoundly ethical way of life. Ahura Mazda requires humans to contribute to the well-being of the world. Everyone has the responsibility of choosing between right and wrong actions.

At the last Day of Judgment, sinners who have not listened to Ahura Mazda's instructions, such as those succumbing to the "filth of intoxication," will suffer eternal torment in a deep pit of terrible darkness. Those who have lived ethical lives will live eternally in a world purged of evil. In a period of transformation called "the Making Wonderful," the dead will be resurrected, and all will live together in the worship of Ahura Mazda.

The Great Kings of Persia believed themselves to be Ahura Mazda's earthly representatives. They committed their energies to fighting the forces of disorder active in their world. In this way, Zoroastrianism provided an ideological support for the Persian Empire's wars of conquest and consolidation at home. The Great Kings lavishly supported the Zoroastrian church, and its priests, called magi, established the faith as the empire's official religion. They built grand temples with sacred fires throughout Persian lands. Because Zoroastrian worship at fire altars occurred wherever Persian power expressed itself, the religion became a reminder to subject peoples of an enduring imperial presence around them. Although the Persian Empire tolerated other religions, Zoroastrianism became the official religion that supported the emperor.

Zoroastrian beliefs have played an important role in shaping the three great Western religions: Judaism, Christianity, and Islam. The Zoroastrian belief that God was opposed by an powerful spirit of evil contributed to the gradual development of the Jewish belief in Satan, who appears in the later books of the Hebrew Bible, into a demon with a distinct personality. Early Christians developed the concept of Satan, later known as the Devil, more clearly during the first century C.E., when they transformed him into a cosmic force of evil against whom Christians must engage in combat. The prophecy of a final struggle against the Devil, followed by the establishment of the kingdom of God on Earth, was incorporated into Revelation, the last book of the New Testament. The Zoroastrian idea of a final

Darius the Great Giving an Audience

In this carved panel from the Treasury of the Palace at Persepolis, the Great King Darius (r. 522–486 B.C.E.) is shown receiving a dignitary who has come to speak with him. Darius is seated on his throne and holds a staff of office. Subject kings from all over the Persian Empire also came to court to pay their respects and bring tribute.

judgment, followed by an afterlife in Heaven or Hell, became a central concept in Christianity and Islam.

The Achaemenid Dynasty

In 522 B.C.E., a Persian nobleman, Darius, seized the imperial throne by murdering one of the sons of Cyrus the Great and initiated the Achaemenid dynasty. Named for a legendary ancestor, Achaemenes, the new dynasty inaugurated an epoch of territorial expansion and cultural activity that lasted until the Macedonian conqueror Alexander the Great overwhelmed Persia in 330 B.C.E. Darius built a new capital city at Persepolis. Like Cyrus before him, Darius drew workmen, artists, and material resources from among the many peoples of his vast empire. Greeks, Egyptians, Babylonians, and Scythians, among others, made the imperial capital a glittering city crowded with luxurious palaces where people of many cultures came together in the service of the Great King.

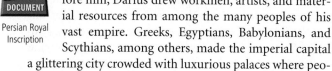

DOCUMENT

Persian Royal
Inscription

From this power center, Darius controlled an efficient administration. He expanded and improved Persia's roads, set up a postal system, and standardized measures and coinage. He also reorganized Cyrus's system of provincial government, dividing the empire into twenty provinces called *satrapies*. Each province paid an annual sum to the central government based on its productivity. The provincial governors, Persian noblemen called *satraps,* collected these taxes and gathered military recruits. In addition, the provincial capitals imitated Persepolis, maintaining administrative archives and serving as local centers of tax collection and bureaucracy. As we will see in the next chapter, this system of administration served as a model for later empires, particularly that of Alexander the Great.

By 513 B.C.E. Darius had greatly expanded his empire. On his northeastern frontier he annexed portions of India as far as the Indus River. He built a canal in Egypt that linked the Mediterranean and Red Seas. But his conquests on the northwestern frontier of the Persian Empire had the greatest impact on Western civilization because they brought Persia into direct contact with the Greeks. Eager to

Map 3.1   The Persian Empire at Its Greatest Extent

The Persian Empire begun by Cyrus about 550 B.C.E. grew to include all of the Middle East as far as India, Egypt, and northern Greece. This multiethnic, multireligious empire governed its many peoples firmly but tolerantly.

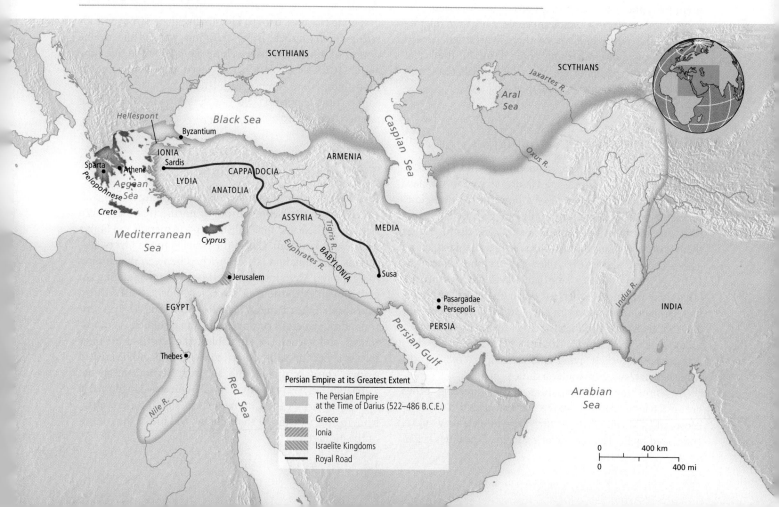

Persian Empire at its Greatest Extent

- The Persian Empire at the Time of Darius (522–486 B.C.E.)
- Greece
- Ionia
- Israelite Kingdoms
- Royal Road

conquer Greece, Darius sent troops across the Hellespont, the channel of water that separates Europe from Asia, in order to establish military bases in the north of Greece. Such incursions along the Greek frontier were only a small part of Darius's grand imperial strategy, but to the Greeks the growing Persian presence caused profound anxiety. The stage was now set for the confrontation between the Persians and the Greeks, a confrontation that demonstrated the limits of Persian imperialism.

Hebrew Civilization and Religion

■ What political and religious beliefs and institutions gave Hebrew civilization its unique character, and what consequences came of its interactions with the Assyrians, Babylonians, and Persians?

One of the most influential civilizations in the West has been that of the Jews, a people who originated in the Middle East during the International Bronze Age. As we saw in Chapter 2, the Raiders of the Land and Sea destroyed many Canaanite cities around 1100 B.C.E. and caused great upheaval among the local populations. At about the same time, different groups of seminomadic pastoralists, called *Hapiru* ("landless people"), began to migrate into the hill country of Canaan, where they settled, herded their flocks, and began farming. Some historians think that this settlement was the origin of the biblical Hebrews, who gradually cohered into tribes and then kingdoms.

The Settlement in Canaan

If these historians are correct, sometime around 1100 B.C.E. one small group of wandering Hapiru arrived in Canaan, bringing with them the seeds of a powerful new religious belief. They gave allegiance to only one god. Belief in this deity gave them a strong sense of identity and distinguished them from the Canaanite peoples, who worshiped many gods. These followers of one god became known as Hebrews, then Israelites, and later Jews. Many centuries later, their traditions explained that a leader called Moses had led them from slavery in Egypt to freedom in Canaan, and that he had communicated God's law to them. Known today as the Ten Commandments, these laws forbid such acts as murder, theft, lying, and worshiping other gods. Later biblical laws were built on these principles.

By absorbing new members and conquering other groups, a loose confederation of tribes gained control of most of Canaan during the eleventh century B.C.E. Impressed by the Hebrew victories, many Canaanites began

to worship the Hebrew God and joined the Hebrew tribes. Gradually these various tribes came to believe that they all shared a common history and a common ancestor, Abraham, who had traveled to Canaan from his home in Mesopotamia long before Moses. According to biblical tradition, Abraham was the first person to worship only one god. For this reason, he is considered the first Hebrew monotheist and the ancestor of the Jews.

The Hebrew tribes built shrines to their God throughout Canaan. The most important religious site was the shrine in the town of Shiloh, where they celebrated their allegiance to their God and settled disputes about property, inheritance, and crime. They kept their most sacred object, the Ark of the Covenant, in this shrine. The Ark of the Covenant was a gold-covered box that reputedly contained a divine and mysterious power. Concealed from the sight of everyone but the priests who organized God's worship, the Ark symbolized the connection between God and his followers as well as the unity of all the Hebrew tribes.

The confederation of Hebrew tribes faced many enemies in Canaan. The most serious threat came from the Philistines, who were descendants of a group of Raiders of the Land and Sea called the Peleset. They controlled the Mediterranean coastal plain in Canaan and pushed relentlessly at the Hebrews living in the inland hills. Around 1050 B.C.E., a Philistine army defeated the Hebrew tribes in battle, captured the Ark of the Covenant, and destroyed Shiloh. According to traditions recorded in the Bible, the desperate Hebrews chose a king to give them stronger leadership, even though tribal tradition was hostile to the notion of kings. The tribes chose Saul to be the first king about 1020 B.C.E., and he retrieved the Ark from the Philistines. Some twenty years later, a popular warrior in Saul's court named David succeeded Saul as king and reigned from approximately 1000 to 962 B.C.E.

The Israelite Kingdoms

David was a talented monarch. By establishing a strong alliance among the Hebrew tribes of northern and southern Canaan, he defeated the Philistines permanently and built a prosperous kingdom. Called the Israelite monarchy by historians, this kingdom lay sandwiched between the empires in Egypt and Mesopotamia (see Map 3.2). By imitating the government institutions of these neighboring states, David transformed the nature of Israelite society. He set up a centralized bureaucracy run by professional soldiers, administrators, and scribes. David established a census as the basis for tax collection and military conscription, and he created a royal court complete with a harem. Jerusalem, an old Canaanite city, served as the capital of his new kingdom. He moved the Ark of the Covenant from Shiloh to Jerusalem, bringing the worship of the Hebrew God under the control of the monarchy.

During the reign of David's son Solomon (ca. 962–922 B.C.E.), the kingdom of Israel enjoyed peace and prosperity. One of Solomon's greatest achievements was the construction of a grand temple in Jerusalem to serve as the house of God and a resting place for the Ark of the Covenant. Constructed with the technical assistance of architects and artisans from the neighboring Phoenician kingdom of Tyre and the forced labor of Solomon's subjects, the Jerusalem temple became the focal point of religious worship in his kingdom.

VIDEO
The Old City
of Jerusalem

Solomon pursued an ambitious foreign policy devoted to developing long-distance commerce. He controlled the major trade routes running from Egypt and Arabia to Syria, and under his supervision Israelite merchants prospered as middlemen in an expanding system of international commerce. Under his leadership, the kingdom enjoyed substantial control over the trade of horses sent south from Asia Minor and chariots sent north from Egypt. Solomon developed his own corps of charioteers to protect these trade routes from bandits.

With the assistance of Phoenician shipbuilders, Solomon constructed a merchant fleet for trade in the Red Sea. His merchants sailed as far south as Somalia, the portion of the African coast that touches the Arabian Sea, from where they brought jewels, gold, ivory, and other items of luxury. In addition, Solomon also developed overland trade with Arabia and established economic ties with the kingdom of Sabaea (Sheba) in Yemen. According to tradition, the Queen of Sheba visited Solomon, bringing delightful gifts, including spices from East Asia. What Solomon's merchants traded in return is uncertain. Solomon developed diplomatic relations with Egypt, as well as the seafaring Phoenicians, and other kingdoms in Africa and Middle East. He married foreign princesses in order to cement diplomatic ties, and he permitted his wives to build shrines in Jerusalem to gods of their homelands.

When Solomon died in 922 B.C.E., his heirs' inability to placate the northern Israelite tribes, who felt that Solomon had favored his own tribe of Judah at their expense, caused the Israelite kingdom to break into two parts. The kingdom of Israel, in the northern region of the former kingdom, established its capital at Shechem and remained reasonably stable in comparison to its southern rival. In the southern kingdom of Judah, Solomon's successors retained Jerusalem as its capital, but political stability remained elusive for them due to dynastic instability and quarrels among the leaders. Only for two brief periods did the kingdom of Judah enjoy stable government. During the two centuries after 922 B.C.E., however, both of the two successor kingdoms struggled to survive under the shadow of the far more powerful neighboring empires of Assyria and Babylonia. The gap between the rich and the poor in both kingdoms widened in the course of these tumultuous centuries. The upper classes grew extremely wealthy from trade and the accumulation of land, which they acquired from the indebted poor. In their anguish the poor called out for social justice, a cry heard by the prophets.

The Hebrew Prophets

As kings and aristocrats became more rapacious, and as taxes increased, more and more debt-ridden peasants lost their farms to rich landholders. The poor found champions in the Hebrew prophets. These men spoke out on behalf of the downtrodden with words they believed to be inspired by God. These social critics strongly censured what they saw as religious and moral decay among the landowners and kings, such as the worship of Canaanite gods, a practice that remained widespread. They urged the

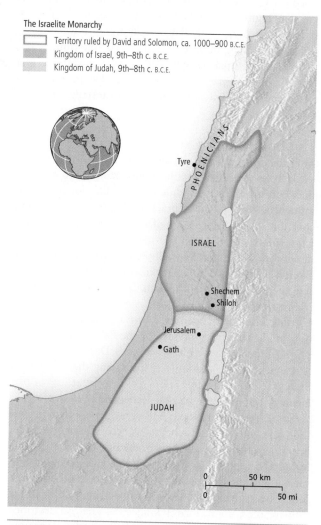

The Israelite Monarchy

☐ Territory ruled by David and Solomon, ca. 1000–900 B.C.E.
▨ Kingdom of Israel, 9th–8th c. B.C.E.
▨ Kingdom of Judah, 9th–8th c. B.C.E.

PHOENICIANS

Tyre

ISRAEL

Shechem
Shiloh

Jerusalem
Gath

JUDAH

0   50 km
0   50 mi

Map 3.2   The Israelite Monarchy

The kingdom established by David (ca. 1000–962 B.C.E.) and expanded by his son Solomon (ca. 962–922 B.C.E.) unified the Hebrew tribes of Canaan. At Solomon's death, the realm split into two smaller kingdoms. Assyrian armies destroyed the northern kingdom of Israel in 722 B.C.E., and Babylonian forces destroyed the southern kingdom of Judah in 586 B.C.E.

entire population toward moral reform and spiritual consciousness. The prophet Elijah, who lived in the ninth century B.C.E., proclaimed that kings should not break the laws with impunity but should conform to the same laws as everyone else. The principle that kings and rulers are not above the law remained as a basic political idea in what eventually became the West. In the next century, another champion of social justice named Amos mocked the irony and hypocrisy of the royal court's celebrating lavish religious ceremonies in God's name while the poor starved. Isaiah, a prophet who lived in Jerusalem, demanded that people attempt to establish a just society in order to avert divine punishment. He had no patience for religious observance empty of personal commitment. According to Isaiah, God said:

> What need have I of all your sacrifices? . . . I am sated with burnt offerings of sacrificial rams . . . Incense is offensive to me. . . . Though you pray at length, I will not listen. Your hands are stained with crime. Wash yourselves clean; Put your evil doings away from my sight. Cease to do evil; learn to do good; devote yourself to justice; aid the wronged. Uphold the rights of the orphan. Defend the cause of the widow. (Isaiah 1:11–17)

Preoccupied with internal problems, the Israelites failed to note the growing power of the neighboring Assyrian Empire. As we saw in Chapter 2, Assyrian armies under the command of King Tiglath-Pileser conquered the Israelite kingdom in 733 B.C.E. Eleven years later, when the Israelite ruler refused to pay tribute, the Assyrians destroyed the kingdom and deported nearly 30,000 Israelites to Mesopotamia, a standard Assyrian practice with defeated enemies. The deported Israelites, who became known as the Lost Ten Tribes, eventually forgot their cultural identity in their new homes and disappeared from the historical record. The kingdom of Israel had come to an undignified end.

The kingdom of Judah, however, survived. By accepting the overlordship of the Assyrians and later the Babylonians, who had replaced the Assyrians as the dominant power in the Middle East by the late seventh century B.C.E., Judah escaped Israel's fate. After the destruction of the northern kingdom, a mood of religious reform spread throughout Judah. People began to believe that God had destroyed the kingdom of Israel in anger, though they disagreed about the causes of his rage and how to appease him.

To regain God's favor, some of Judah's leaders insisted on the absolute primacy of the temple in Jerusalem as the place for religious worship on the assumption that God disapproved of his followers' worshiping him at many shrines instead of only one. By insisting on Jerusalem as the sole place of worship, the priests of Jerusalem increased their power. With the help of the king's soldiers, the temple priests in Jerusalem violently suppressed all other shrines to God scattered across the land. The consequences were greater uniformity of worship among the Hebrews and a centralized religious authority. These developments enhanced a sense of Hebrew identity.

Some Hebrew prophets, however, sought to appease God by countering this trend. They challenged the supremacy of the Jerusalem priests and emphasized the need for personal reform and the creation of a just society. One of these prophets was Jeremiah, who began preaching in 627 B.C.E. In the tradition of Isaiah, he placed little value on the strength of the temple priesthood's prayers on Judah's behalf. He predicted that God would cause the Babylonians to destroy Judah because its people were corrupt. Jeremiah's predictions proved correct. When Judah revolted against the Babylonians in 598 B.C.E., the Babylonian king Nebuchadnezzar sent a large army to crush the rebellion. The next year he captured Jerusalem and deported Judah's king and high priests to Babylonia. Ten years later, when another revolt broke out, Babylonian forces burned Jerusalem to the ground and demolished Solomon's temple, the spiritual and political center of the kingdom of Judah. Perhaps as many as 20,000 people were deported to Babylonia, an event historians call the Babylonian Exile°.

The Wailing Wall

The Babylonian Exile

After the destruction of the Jerusalem temple in 587 B.C.E., the Hebrew exiles living in Babylonia struggled to maintain their cultural and religious identity. But Babylonian culture influenced their religious practice. Babylonian astronomy contributed to the institution of a seven-day week (and perhaps sabbath worship on the seventh day). The Hebrews developed a calendar that adopted Babylonian names of months. For example, the Babylonian month Nissanu is the same as the Hebrew month Nisan. Like the Babylonians, the Hebrew exiles structured their calendar around seasonal festivals. The exiles added their own new religious celebrations to the structure provided by the Babylonian calendar. The Hebrews observed a New Year's Day and a Day of Atonement in the autumn. In the spring they celebrated Passover, the commemoration of the departure of the Hebrews from Egypt under the leadership of Moses.

Sometime after the year 538 B.C.E., an anonymous author, known to biblical scholars as Second Isaiah (because he wrote some of the chapters of the Book of Isaiah), comforted the dispirited Hebrews in Babylonia. Trying to find meaning in the destruction of the kingdoms of Israel and Judah, he explained that God's primary interest lay in the human spirit, not in earthly kingdoms. The god described by Second Isaiah was a truly universal god who alone governs all creation and shapes the lives of all the peoples of the world. This vision of a single, universal deity not bound by time or place was perhaps the greatest legacy of Hebrew civilization to the West.

Second Isaiah promised that God would return his people to Jerusalem and that Cyrus the Great King of Persia would serve as God's agent in this task. The reference to the

Persian king suggests that Second Isaiah wrote sometime around 538 B.C.E., when Cyrus instituted his policy permitting all peoples exiled by the Babylonians to return to their homelands. Many of the Hebrew exiles in Babylonia returned to their old homes, now governed by Persia, and attempted to revive traditional religious life in Jerusalem.

The Second Temple and Jewish Religious Practice

Nearly two generations passed before the Hebrews, with Persian assistance, finished building a new temple in Jerusalem, called the Second Temple. In 458 B.C.E., with the authority of the Persian king, a leader called Ezra the Scribe began to organize and regulate religious practices. He instituted regular sabbath worship and began a program of teaching religious law to the population. For the next 500 years this restored temple worship was the center of religious life. Historians call the Hebrews who lived after the completion of the Second Temple Jews. Henceforth, the people are known as Jews and their religion is called Judaism.

Ezra and other religious thinkers believed that God had destroyed the kingdoms of Israel and Judah before the Babylonian Exile because the people had failed to observe religious law properly. For this reason, knowledge of the law (or Torah) through study and observance now became all-important for the preservation of the Jewish community and Jewish identity. In particular, the priesthood in Jerusalem, which controlled secular and religious affairs, insisted on very strict observance of laws concerning temple sacrifice and ritual. The priests also made a decision that determined the status of women in Jewish society. By deciding that descent through the mother determined Jewish identity, they assigned women a crucial role in determining membership in the Jewish community. In this one respect the priests enhanced the status of Jewish wives.

Despite these reforms, the public role of women in organized worship grew quite restricted. Prior to the Babylonian Exile, women participated in worship as priestesses, singers, and dancers. Canaanite religion gave a high status to female goddesses of fertility, and Israelite women sometimes participated in their cults. In the Second Temple period, however, the Jews worshiped only one male god and denied all other deities. Women could not enter the most sacred portions of the temple where the main sacrifices were performed because according to religious law the blood of menstruation and childbirth made them ritually unclean. Many of these ancient attitudes regarding the place of women in religious and family life have survived to the present day, especially in the exclusion of women from the most sacred rituals and responsibilities in some forms of Judaism and Christianity.

The Hebrew Bible

After the Second Temple was built in 515 B.C.E., the Hebrew Bible (called the Old Testament by Christians)

CHRONOLOGY

The Israelite Kingdom

ca. 1100 B.C.E.	The International Bronze Age ends; Hapiru arrive in Canaan
ca. 1000–922 B.C.E.	David and Solomon rule the Israelite kingdom
922 B.C.E.	The Israelite kingdom splits into Judah (southern kingdom) and Israel (northern kingdom)
ca. 800 B.C.E.	Prophets begin to preach moral reform
721 B.C.E.	Assyrians destroy northern kingdom (Israel)
587 B.C.E.	Babylonians defeat southern kingdom (Judah) and destroy Jerusalem and Solomon's temple
538 B.C.E.	Cyrus of Persia permits Israelites to return to Palestine and rebuild the temple

slowly took the shape it has today. Like many other peoples in the ancient Middle East, the Jews believed that their God had chosen them to serve him. They believed that historical events described in the Bible illustrate and interpret that relationship. As a historical document, the Bible provides a chronology of the world from the moment of its creation and gives an account of the early development of the Hebrew people. Drawn from a variety of oral and written sources, and composed many centuries after the events they describe, the biblical accounts condense and simplify a very complex process of migration, settlement, and religious development.

Many details in the Bible have been confirmed by non-Hebrew sources, but the Bible must be understood primarily as an expression of religious meaning through historical traditions of different sorts. It combines highly detailed narratives with folklore, prophecies, parables, stories, and poems. The Bible provides far more than the narration of events. It explains God's presence in human lives and establishes a moral vision of human existence. As a result no book has had more influence on the religious thought of the West.

For many people, the significance of the Hebrew Bible lies in the religious principles that its stories illustrate. The book describes a single God who protects the Earth and his chosen people, the Hebrews. Historical events demonstrate his concern for them, for he punishes and rewards his people in accordance with their actions. In the Hebrew Bible, events such as the restoration of the temple in Jerusalem by

Isaiah Scroll

Discovered in a cave near the Dead Sea in 1947 and now housed in the Shrine of the Book in Jerusalem, this text of the biblical book of Isaiah was written between about 300 and 100 B.C.E., making it nearly a thousand years older than the next surviving manuscript of Isaiah. The two copies of the book of Isaiah differ in only a few minor details, demonstrating the care with which biblical texts were copied and passed on by generations of scribes.

Cyrus have significance in terms of a divine plan and the fulfillment of prophecy. As part of this divine plan, God expects his followers to follow a strict code of compassionate, ethical behavior toward their fellow human beings. As a religious work the Hebrew Bible provides the basis of Judaism. In conjunction with the New Testament, written in the first century C.E., it is the core text of Christianity. Muslims also recognize both the Hebrew and Christian texts as holy writings, superseded only by the Qur'an.

Greece Rebuilds, 1100–479 B.C.E.

■ How did Greek city-states develop in the framework of a larger world dominated by Persia?

As we saw in Chapter 2, at the end of the International Bronze Age Greek civilization entered a period of bitter poverty and political instability. This period, known as the Dark Age, lasted until about 750 B.C.E., when a period designated by historians as the Archaic Age began. The Archaic Age was marked by economic growth at home and many Greek encounters with Phoenicians and Persians abroad (see Map 3.3). This period of revival set the stage for Greece's Classical Age, a time of great cultural achievement.

The Dark Age, ca. 1100–750 B.C.E.

Compared with the wealth and splendor of Mycenaean communities in the Bronze Age, Greek life in the Dark Age was quite gloomy. Few new settlements were established on the mainland, and urban life disappeared. Maritime trade declined precipitously and the economies controlled by the

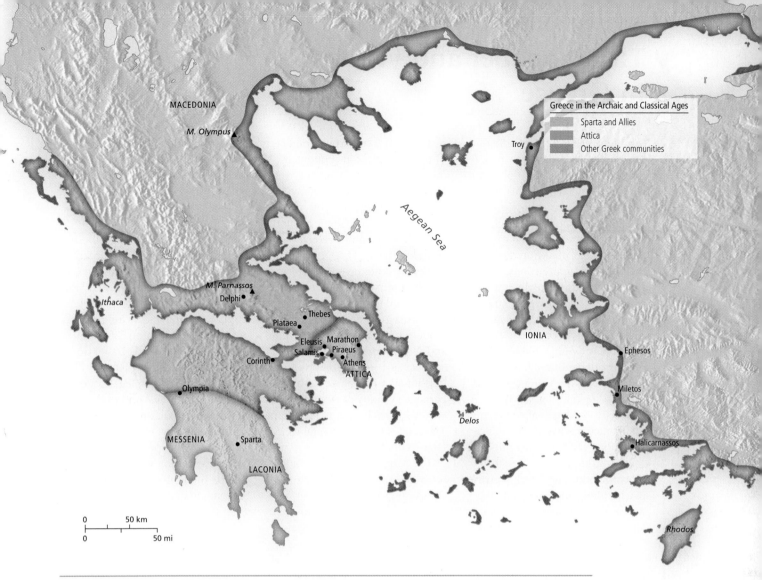

Map 3.3 Greece in the Archaic and Classical Ages

During the Archaic and Classical Ages, Greek cities spread from Greece to the shores of the Black Sea and as far west as Italy and southern France. This map shows the Greek heartland: the mainland, the islands of the Aegean Sea, and Ionia. Although never unified politically in the Archaic and Classical Ages, the people in these cities spoke Greek, worshiped the same gods, and shared a similar culture.

palaces broke down. Because there was no longer a need for scribes to record inventories, Linear B writing dropped out of use entirely. A serious decline in agriculture led to a steep decrease in food production and population.

A slow economic recovery began in the Greek world about 850 B.C.E., when the population began to grow again and when trade became brisker. Because of the harsh living conditions on the mainland during the Dark Age, many Greeks had abandoned their homes and moved to a region called Ionia that encompassed the coasts and islands of western Asia Minor. Relatively isolated from other Greek communities, these pioneers developed their own distinctive Ionian variation of the Greek language. By 800 B.C.E. the Ionian Greeks were regularly interacting with the Phoenicians in the eastern Mediterranean. These seafarers forged a connection between Greeks and the cultures of the

Middle East that exerted a lasting impact on Greek society because it marked the end of Greek isolation (see Map 2.5).

The Archaic Age, ca. 750–479 B.C.E.

Between about 750 and 650 B.C.E., many fresh ideas poured into Greece from the Middle East through contact with the Phoenicians and other peoples. Historians call this exciting period the Archaic Age. Encounters with Middle Eastern poets, merchants, artisans, refugees, doctors, slaves, and spouses brought innovations to Greece: new words such as *tyrant* and *gold;* new economic practices such as the use of coinage and charging interest on loans; new myths and literary themes (such as the story of the Great Flood; see document on page 69); new ritual procedures for sacrificing

The Alphabet and Writing in Greece

Sometime around the middle of the eighth century B.C.E., Greek merchants brought the alphabet to Greece. They adopted this system of letters from seafaring Phoenicians whom they encountered while trading in the eastern Mediterranean. To write down their business transactions, Phoenicians used an alphabet of twenty-two letters derived from the one invented in the Bronze Age at Ugarit. Recognizing the potential of writing, the Greeks quickly adapted the Phoenician script to the Greek language and began to read and write. By 650 B.C.E. the Greek alphabet and the literacy that went with it spread widely, following trade routes throughout the Mediterranean world. The Greek alphabet reached Italy and eventually the Romans, whose adaptation of the alphabet is the one we use today.

The adoption of the alphabet deeply affected Greek society because it let information of all sorts be preserved in written form—and widely shared. The alphabet is easy to learn because each letter represents one sound, and therefore many people in the Greek world began to exploit the potential of reading and writing.

Unlike the cultures of Mesopotamia and Egypt, in which writing was the specialized expertise of an elite scribal class, the more open Greek culture never limited writing to a particular group. People of all sorts employed it. For example, government officials began to write down laws, which for the first time became available for all members of the community to see. Having written laws posted in public helped to undercut the ancient privileges of the aristocracy to interpret the oral law, something they often did arbitrarily and unjustly. Thus written laws

contributed to the development of fairer political institutions in the Greek poleis. Merchants kept track of shipments, payments, loans, and debts, thereby helping the economies of Greek communities to thrive and become more complex.

Perhaps the most significant development of all, however, was the beginning of written literature. The first works of literature to be rendered in writing were the *Iliad* and the *Odyssey* of Homer, the product of a long tradition of oral transmission combined with the particular genius of Homer, who gave them their final written form. These tales became central to Greek culture.

But soon writers were not just recording oral poetry, they were composing original poetry to be read and recited. Tragedians composed the intense dramas that explored fundamental questions of human psychology. Mythological tales were set down and considered critically, leading eventually to the development of scientific thought (see text on Ionian philosophers). As soon as historians could read the accounts of

earlier historians, they began to criticize them in different ways, and the Western tradition of critical history took root.

Thus the adoption of the alphabet transformed Greek society. Reading and writing—which depend on the alphabet—helped shape the Greek intellectual legacy that we value so highly today. But the importance of the alphabet and of reading and writing in the West is still far more profound: Western civilization is based on the writing and interpretation of texts. Sacred books, legal codes, scientific inquiries, and the rich and varied traditions of literature are fundamental to who we are and how we experience the world. And they were made possible by the alphabet and the advent of reading and writing.

Question for Discussion

Why was the alphabet essential to the development of Greek literature?

Chart of the Development of the Alphabet
This chart shows how the first five letters of the Phoenician alphabet developed into the first five letters of the English alphabet.

DOCUMENT

Tales of the Flood

In one of the most popular tales of the Classical Age, a god destroys the Earth in a great flood but permits some humans to survive on a boat and repopulate the Earth once the waters subside. Here we see excerpts from three versions of the flood story composed by Babylonians, Hebrews, and Greeks. The similarities among the texts suggest that the story may have originated in an earlier Mesopotamian culture and then spread to these three cultural traditions.

The Epic of Gilgamesh: How the Gods Spared Uta-napishti

[Everything I owned] I loaded aboard:
all the silver I owned I loaded aboard,
all the gold I owned I loaded aboard,
all the living creatures I had I loaded aboard.
I sent on board all my kith and kin,
the beasts of the field, the creatures of the wild, and
    members of every skill and craft . . .
. . . For six days and [seven] nights,
there blew the wind, the downpour,
the gale, the Deluge, it flattened land.
But the seventh day when it came,
the gale relented, the Deluge ended.
The ocean grew calm, that had thrashed like a woman in
    labour,
the tempest grew still, the Deluge ended . . .
Enlil [a powerful god] came up inside the boat,
[and blessed Uta-napishti and his wife, saying:]
In the past Uta-napishti was a mortal man,
but now he and his wife shall become like us gods!

The Hebrew Bible: The Story of Noah and the Ark

Then the Lord said to Noah, "Go into the ark with all your household, for you alone have I found righteous before Me in this generation. Of every clean animal you shall take seven pairs, males and their mates, and of every animal that is not clean, two, a male and its mate. Of the birds of the sky, also. . . . For in seven days I will make it rain upon the earth, forty days and forty nights, and I will blot out from the earth all existence that I created. And Noah did just as the Lord commanded him. . . . And on the seventh day the waters of the Flood came upon the earth. . . . [When the Flood had ended] God spoke to Noah, saying, come out of the ark, together with your wife, your sons, and your sons' wives. Bring out with you every living thing of all flesh that is there with you: birds, animals, and everything that creeps on earth; and let them swarm on the earth and be fertile and increase on earth.

Greek Mythology: Deucalion's Story

In this Greek tale, King Deucalion survives because his father, the god Prometheus, warns him.

When Zeus, the king of the gods, decided to destroy humankind . . . Deucalion by the advice of Prometheus constructed a chest, and having stored it with provisions he embarked in it with Pyrrha, his wife. But Zeus, by pouring heavy rain from Heaven flooded the greater part of Greece, so that all men were destroyed, except for a few who fled to high mountains in the neighborhood. . . . But Deucalion, floating in the chest over the sea for nine days and as many nights, drifted to Mount Parnassus, and there, when the rain ceased, he landed and sacrificed to Zeus . . . And Zeus . . . allowed Deucalion to choose whatever he wished, and he chose to create men. At the bidding of Zeus, he picked up stones and threw them over his head, and the stones became men, and the stones that Pyrrha threw became women. . . .

Sources: From *The Epic of Gilgamesh: The Babylonian Epic Poem and Other Texts in Akkadian and Sumerian,* translated by Andrew George (Allen Lane The Penguin Press, 1999). Translation copyright © 1999 by Andrew George. Reproduced by permission of Penguin Books Ltd.; from *Tanakh, A New Translation of The Holy Scriptures According to the Traditional Hebrew Text,* 1985, Exodus 7–8. Published by the Jewish Publication Society; and reprinted by permission of the publishers and the Trustees of the Loeb Classical Library from *Apollodorus: Volume I,* Loeb Classical Library Volume L 121, translated by J. G. Frazer, Cambridge, Mass.: Harvard University Press, 1921. The Loeb Classical Library® is a registered trademark of the President and Fellows of Harvard College.

---

animals; new gods and goddesses (such as Dionysus, the god of wine); and new inventions of convenience (such as parasols to provide shade).

By far the most valuable import from the Phoenicians was the alphabet. As we saw in Chapter 2, the Phoenicians, who had been using an alphabet of twenty-two letters for at least three centuries, introduced the system to Greece sometime just before 750 B.C.E. The adoption of the alphabet, to which the Greeks added vowels, was one of the developments that marked the beginning of the Archaic Age. Because an alphabet records sounds, not words, it can be adjusted easily for any language. Greeks quickly recognized the potential of the new system, and quickly adopted it throughout their communities. Greeks learned to write and read, first for business purposes and then for pleasure. They began to record their oral traditions, legends, and songs. At the same time, they began to compose an entirely new literature and write down their laws.

Homer's Epic Poems

Two of the greatest works of literature ever composed, the *Iliad* and the *Odyssey,* were soon written down in the new alphabet. A Greek poet named Homer, who probably lived around 750 B.C.E., is credited with composing these poems, but they were certainly not entirely his personal invention. The stories of the *Iliad* and the *Odyssey* drew from a large and widely recited cycle of tales about the legendary Trojan War that wandering poets had recited for centuries. The poets had elaborated on the stories so much over time that all historical accuracy was lost. Nevertheless, many details in the poems, especially about weapons and armor no longer used in Homer's day, suggest that the earliest versions of the poems were first recited in the International Bronze Age and may be very loosely based on events of that time.

The body of poems of which the *Iliad* and the *Odyssey* were a part tells how an army of Greek warriors sailed to Troy, a wealthy city on the northwest coast of Asia Minor, to recover a beautiful Greek princess, Helen, who had been stolen by a Trojan prince. After ten years of savage fighting, the Greeks finally stormed Troy and won the war, though their greatest fighters had died in battle. When the surviving heroes returned to Greece, they were met with treachery and bloodshed.

The genius of Homer lay in his retelling of these old stories. He did not relate the entire saga of the Trojan War because he knew that his audiences were familiar with it. Instead, he selected certain episodes in which he emphasized aspects of human character and emotion in the midst of violent conflict in fresh ways. In the *Iliad,* for example, he describes how the hero Achilles, the mightiest of all the Greeks fighting at Troy, grows angry when his commander-in-chief Agamemnon steals his favorite concubine. In a rage, Achilles withdraws from the battle and returns to fight only to avenge his best friend who had been killed by Hector, the mainstay of the Trojan defense. Achilles eventually slays Hector, but does not relinquish his fury until Hector's father, Priam, the king of Troy, begs him to return his son's corpse for proper burial. "Honor the Gods, Achilles, and take pity upon me, remembering your own father," implores King Priam. "Yet I am still more pitiful than he. I have endured more than any other mortal: I kiss the hand of the man who has killed my sons." Achilles relents and weeps, his humanity finally restored after so much killing. In Homer's hands, the story of Achilles' anger becomes a profound investigation into human alienation and redemption.

The *Odyssey* tells a different kind of story. The hero of this poem, the Greek king Odysseus, wants nothing more than to return to his wife after the fall of Troy. His trek takes ten years, full of suspenseful adventures as he sails about in the Mediterranean Sea. Odysseus's endless patience, relentless cunning, intellectual curiosity, and deep love for his family finally brings him home. Due to their very human strengths and weaknesses, Achilles and Odysseus are two of the most finely drawn characters in Western literature.

The Polis

In addition to telling epic tales that glorified heroes of the past, Greeks in the Archaic Age experimented with new forms of social and political life. They developed a new style of community called the polis° (plural *poleis*), or city-state. A polis was a self-governing community consisting of an urban center with a defensible hilltop called an acropolis° and all the surrounding land farmed by citizens of the polis. Greek cities varied in size from a few square miles to several hundred. All contained similar institutions: an assembly in which the men of the community gathered to discuss and make decisions about public business; a council of male elders who offered advice on public matters; temples to gods who protected the polis and whose goodwill was necessary for the community's prosperity; and an open area in the center of town called an *agora,* which served as a market and a place for informal discussions.

Living in a polis provided an extremely strong sense of community. A person could be a citizen of only one polis, and every citizen was expected to place the community's interests above all other concerns. Even the women, who were citizens but not permitted to play a role in public life, felt powerful ties to their polis. While only citizens had full membership in a polis, enjoying the greatest rights and bearing the greatest responsibilities, every city had noncitizens from other communities. Some of these noncitizens had limited rights and obligations, whereas slaves had no rights at all.

Colonization and the Settlement of New Lands

A population boom during the Archaic Age forced Greeks to emigrate because the rocky soil of the mainland could not provide enough food. From about 750 to 550 B.C.E., cities such as Corinth and Megara on the mainland and Miletos in Ionia established more than 200 colonies overseas.

Greek emigrants traveled by boat to foreign shores. Many colonists settled on the Aegean coast north into the Black Sea region, which offered plentiful farmlands. The important settlement at Byzantium controlled access to the agricultural wealth of these Black Sea colonies. Greeks established many new cities in Sicily and southern Italy, as well as on the southern coast of France and the eastern coast of Spain. By 600 B.C.E. Greeks had founded colonies in North Africa in the region of modern Libya and on the islands of Cyprus and Crete. Greek merchants also set up a trading community on the Syrian coast and another in the Egyptian delta, with the pharaoh's permission.

New Greek cities such as Syracuse and Tarentum in Italy, Massilia (Marseilles) in France, and Neapolis (Naples) in Italy gave land-hungry settlers the opportunity to prosper

Athenian

(front)   (back)

Jewish Second Temple Period

(front)   (back)

Athenian Coinage

The coins made in Athens displayed the head of Athena on one side, and her sacred bird, the owl, on the other side. The coin shown at the top dates to the height of the Athenian Empire, about 450 B.C.E. On the bottom, another coin of similar weight and appearance is called a Jehud (from the Persian name of the province of Judah). Minted near Jerusalem, its front shows a face based on Athena. Its back shows an owl and Hebrew writing. The similarities of these coins reveal the international influence of Athenian coinage and the importance of standard weights in long-distance trade.

through farming, manufacturing, and trade. The colonists obtained metal ores, timber, and slaves from the regions they settled and began growing wheat, olives, and wine for export. Merchants carried the goods to markets all over the Mediterranean. The overseas world of the Greeks prospered, and a vibrant Greek culture with common language, gods, and social institutions spread throughout the Mediterranean and into the Black Sea.

Although all of the Greek colonies maintained some formal religious ties with their mother city-states, or *metropoleis,* they were self-governing and independent. Some colonies failed, but others grew rich and populous enough to send out their own colonies. Because the Greek colonists seized territory by force and sometimes slaughtered the local inhabitants, relations with the people already living in these lands were often quite tense.

The Greek adoption of coinage spurred commercial activity among many Greek communities. Coinage first replaced barter as a medium of exchange in western Asia Minor about 630 B.C.E. as a form of portable wealth that could be used to buy goods and services. Minted from pre-

cious metals and uniform in weight, coins helped people standardize the value of goods, a development that revolutionized commerce. By 600 B.C.E. Greeks living in Ionia and on the Greek mainland began to mint their own coins. Each city-state used a distinctive emblem to mark its currency. When Athens became the dominant economic power in the Aegean during the second half of the fifth century B.C.E., Athenian coinage became the standard throughout the Greek world and far beyond.

Greek colonization played a critical role in shaping Western civilization by creating wealthy centers of Greek culture in Italy and the western Mediterranean. Sometimes overshadowed in the historical record by city-states of the Greek mainland, such as Athens, Sparta, and Corinth, the impressive new poleis spread Greek civilization, language, literature, religion, and art far beyond Greece itself. The colony of Syracuse in Sicily, for example, grew to be larger than any city in Greece. Greek communities deeply influenced local cultures and would make a tremendous impact on Etruscan and Roman civilization in Italy, as we will see in Chapter 4. Overseas colonies also prepared the way for the rapid explosion of Greek culture that followed the conquests of Alexander the Great.

Elite Athletic Competition in Greek Poleis

Athletic contests called panhellenic° games, because they drew participants from the entire Greek world, were a mainstay of aristocratic Greek culture in the Archaic Age. As many as 150 cities regularly offered aristocratic men the chance to win glory through competition in chariot racing, discus throwing, wrestling, foot racing, and other field events. Through sports the Greeks found a common culture that allowed them to express their Greek identity and honor the gods at the same time.

The Olympic Games, which originated in 776 B.C.E., carried the most prestige. Every four years Greek athletes from southern Italy to the Black Sea gathered in the sacred grove of Olympia in central Greece to take part in games dedicated to Zeus, the chief Greek god. The rules required the poleis to call truces to any wars, even if they were in the middle of battle, and allow safe passage to all athletes traveling to Olympia. Records show the naming of champions at Olympia from 776 B.C.E to 217 C.E. The Roman emperor Theodosius I, who was a Christian, abolished the games in 393 C.E. because they involved the worship of Greek gods.

The Hoplite Revolution

The new wealth flowing through the Greek world transformed everyday life. For the first time, men who were not aristocrats could afford to purchase weapons of war. Called hoplites°, these heavily armed infantry used their own funds to purchase helmets, shields, swords, shin guards, and thrusting spears. Hoplites entered the battlefield in massed ranks, four to eight deep, a formation called a phalanx°. Each man relied for protection on the man to his right, whose shield protected his own sword arm. Cooperation was all-important, for if the line broke, the individual soldier became more vulnerable. Fighting in massed units like this replaced the combat between individual aristocrats and their retinues that had characterized Greek warfare in earlier periods.

Greeks glorified battling in this close-knit manner. Hoplite fighting generated a sense of pride and common purpose that had political consequences, as hoplites demanded a political voice in the communities for which they fought. Their growing confidence directly challenged aristocratic families who traditionally held tight control over community decision making.

In many poleis, new political leaders arose to champion the cause of the hoplite citizenry. These political leaders were known as tyrants°, a word borrowed from the Middle East that originally did not have the negative connotation it carries today. Tyrants typically came from the ruling classes, but they found their political support among the hoplites and the poor who felt otherwise left out of the political life of the community. When tyrants seized power in a polis, they served the interests of the community as a whole, not just the aristocrats. They promoted overseas trade, built harbors, protected farmers, and began public-works projects to employ citizen workers and to beautify their cities. They also cultivated alliances with other tyrants in other poleis to establish peace and prosperity. Most important, the tyrants' authority enabled a broad range of Greek citizens to participate in government for the first time.

But tyrannies contained a fatal flaw. The power of the tyrant was handed down from father to son, and the successors rarely inherited their fathers' qualities of leadership. As a result, the tyrannies often became oppressive and unpopular, especially among the hoplites and poor who had sup-

---

DOCUMENT

Tyrtaeus: The Glory of Hoplite Warfare

During the mid-seventh century B.C.E., the Spartan poet Tyrtaeus wrote many poems glorifying warfare on behalf of the polis. Spartan troops sang his poems as they marched into combat. This poem explains why young men should seek glory and avoid shame by fighting in the front ranks.

It is a noble thing for a good man to die fighting in the front
    lines for his country;
but to abandon his city and fertile fields, to be reduced to
    poverty,
this is most grievous of all things, for then a man wanders
    from place to place
with his beloved mother and elderly father, his small
    children and lawful wife. . . .
And so, since a wanderer receives no recognition, neither
    honor nor respect nor mercy,
let us fight with all our might for this land, and die for our
    children,
never caring to spare our lives.
Stand together and fight, then, O young men; take no step
    in shameful flight.
Be not overcome by fear, but let the heart be great and
    strong in your breast,
never flinching when you face the enemy. . . .
So let every man bite his lip, and, with both feet firmly on
    the ground,
take his place for battle.

Source: From *Ancient Greece: Documentary Perspectives, Second Edition* by Stylianos V. Spyridakis and Bradley P. Nystrom. Copyright © 1997 by Kendall/Hunt Publishing Co. Used with permission.

ported the tyrants in the first place. Few of them lasted more than two generations.

Two of the most important poleis on the Greek mainland, Sparta and Athens, both experienced hoplite revolutions, but the two poleis developed very different political and social systems. In Sparta, the hoplite class formed an egalitarian elite that had consistently opposed the rule of tyrants but ruled the rest of the population in an authoritarian manner. Athenians, on the other hand, developed into a democracy, including the entire population in the political process.

Sparta: A Militarized Society

Cut off from the rest of Greece by high mountain ranges to the west and north, Sparta dominated the Peloponnese, the southernmost part of Greece. Until about 700 B.C.E. Spartans lived very much like other Greeks except that their hoplite forces achieved political power without the aid of tyrants, whom they despised. Rapid expansion in the Peloponnese prompted Spartans to develop a highly militarized way of life among the Greeks. All political power rested with a corps of warrior hoplites that comprised the entire population of male citizens. The Spartan hoplites, who called themselves "the Equals," controlled all the polis's land and spent their time in military training.

The Spartan military system grew more elaborate after 700 B.C.E. when the Spartans conquered Messenia, a fertile region in the western Peloponnese. To maintain control over the Messenians, who vastly outnumbered them, the Spartans brutally reduced the Messenians to the status of helots°, a level barely higher than beasts of burden. Technically free, helots were nevertheless bound to the land and forced to farm. If a Spartan master sold the land to another Spartan, the helots stayed with the land. Helots paid half of their produce to their Spartan masters and could be murdered with impunity. Controlling the helots through terror became the Spartans' preoccupation.

In Sparta's social hierarchy free subjects stood one level above the helots. These individuals included merchants, manufacturers, and other businessmen who lived in communities throughout Spartan territories. Free subjects paid taxes and served in the army when necessary, but they were not Spartan citizens.

The male and female citizens of Sparta stood at the top of the social pyramid. They devoted themselves completely to a military way of life. The greatest responsibility of all Spartan citizens was to fulfill the needs of the polis. From early childhood, boys trained to become soldiers and girls trained to become the mothers of soldiers. Boys left home at age 7 to live in barracks, where they mastered the skills of battle. They learned that their comrades-in-arms played a more important role in their lives than their own families. Young married Spartan men were not permitted to live with their wives, but had to sneak away from their barracks at night to visit them.

DOCUMENT

Greek Versus Barbarian

In the following excerpt Hippocrates of Kos (d. ca. 400 B.C.E.), known as the Father of Medicine, explains the forms of government of the Near East and the character of the people, whom he calls Asiatics. Like other Greeks of his time, Hippocrates believed in the superiority of Greek civilization. In this passage, he explains that the climatic zones in which people live determine the characteristics of their culture.

The small variations of climate to which the Asiatics are subject, extremes of both heat and of cold being avoided, account for their mental flabbiness and cowardice . . . They are less warlike than Europeans and tamer of spirit, for they are not subject to those physical changes and the mental stimulation that sharpen tempers and induce recklessness and hot-headedness . . . Such things appear to me to be the cause of the feebleness of the Asiatic race, but a contributory cause also lies in their customs; for the greater part is under monarchical rule . . . Even if a man be born brave and of stout heart, his character is ruined by this form of government.

Source: From Paul Cartledge, *The Greeks: A Portrait of Self and Others*, 1993. Reprinted by permission of Oxford University Press.

Contempt for pain and hardship, blind obedience to orders, simplicity in word and deed, and unabashed courage were the chief Spartan virtues. Cowardice had no place in this society. Before sending their men to war, wives and mothers warned, "Come home with your shield—or on it!" Sparta's splendidly trained armies won a reputation as the most ferocious force in all of Greece.

After its conquest of Messenia, Sparta strengthened its presence further by organizing the Peloponnesian League, an informal alliance of most of the poleis in the Peloponnese. Spartans avoided wars far from home, but they and their allies joined with the Athenians and other Greeks in resisting Persia's aggression against Greece, as we will see shortly.

Athens: Toward Democracy

Athens, the best known polis of ancient Greece, made an incalculably rich contribution to the political, philosophical, artistic, and literary traditions of Western civilization. The first democracy in the ancient world, Athens developed principles of government that remain alive today. Athens's innovative form of government and the flowering of its intellectual life stemmed directly from its response to tyranny and Persian aggression.

In the eighth and seventh centuries B.C.E., the Athenians settled Attica, the territory surrounding their city, rather than sending colonists abroad. In this way, Athens gained more land and a larger population than any other polis on the Greek mainland. By the beginning of the sixth century, aristocrats controlled most of the wealth of Attica, and many of the Athenian peasants became heavily indebted to them, pledging their bodies as collateral on loans. They risked being sold into slavery abroad if they could not repay the debt.

With civil war between the debt-ridden peasantry and the aristocracy on the horizon, both segments of the population of Attica agreed to let Solon, an Athenian statesman known for his practical wisdom, reform the political system. In 594 B.C.E. Solon (ca. 650–570 B.C.E.) enacted several reforms that limited the authority of the aristocracy and enabled all male citizens to participate more fully in Athenian public life. These reforms created the institutions of public political life from which democracy eventually developed. Solon cancelled debts, eliminated debt-slavery, and raised enough funds to buy back enslaved Athenians. Then he took additional steps to give all Athenian men a greater voice in governing their city. Taking advantage of a rise in literacy, Solon directed scribes to record his new laws on wooden panels for the whole community to see. This diminished aristocratic control of the interpretation of Athenian law and ensured that the laws would be enforced fairly for all Athenian citizens, regardless of their status.

Solon next organized the population into four classes based on wealth. Only men in the two richest classes could hold the highest administrative office of *archon* and be elected to the highest court, traditionally a base of aristocratic authority. From the third class, Solon created the *boule*, a council of 400 men who prepared the agenda for the general citizen assembly. Men from the fourth and poorest class, who could not afford hoplite weapons, could vote in the citizen assembly, though they could not be elected to any office. Finally, men of any class could serve on a new court that Solon established. Women and slaves had no voice in government at all. These changes provided a temporary solution to Athens's problems.

After a generation of internal peace, Athenian aristocrats began to chafe at their loss of power and rebelled against Solon's system. In ca. 560 B.C.E. a nobleman named Peisistratus (ca. 590–528 B.C.E.) seized power and ruled Athens as a tyrant. Like other tyrannies in Greece, Peisistratus's regime initially enjoyed widespread support. He sponsored building projects, supported religious festivals, encouraged trade and economic development, and supported the arts. He initiated a vigorous tradition of Athenian intellectual life by inviting artists and poets to come to Athens from all over Greece. His sons, however, abused their power, and jealous aristocrats assisted by Sparta toppled the family's rule in 510. Peisistratus's surviving son fled to Persia.

Two years later, the assembly selected a nobleman named Cleisthenes to reorganize Athens. By cleverly rearranging the basic political units of Attica, Cleisthenes unified Attica and made Athens the center of all important political activity. Building upon Solon's reforms, he set the basic institutions of democracy in place with a new council of 500 male citizens drawn from throughout Attica, which made decisions for the community. He ensured that every male citizen had a permanent voice in government, broke the power of aristocratic families, and set up the lasting, fundamental structures of Athenian democracy. The strength of Cleisthenes' new system would be tested in the face of invasions by Persia in the fifth century B.C.E.

The Persian Wars, 490–479 B.C.E.

Around 510 B.C.E. the Persian king Darius conquered the Ionian Greek poleis. The Persians ruled their new subjects fairly, but the Ionian Greeks nevertheless revolted in 499 B.C.E. Ionian Greek rebels traveled to Sparta and Athens to ask for assistance against the Persians. The Spartans refused to send any troops when they learned how far away Ionia was. The Athenians, however, sent an expeditionary force that helped the rebels burn Sardis, a Persian provincial capital. The Persians crushed the rebellion in 494 B.C.E., but they did not forget the role of Athens in it.

The Marathon Campaign

In 490 B.C.E., after four years of meticulous planning, a Persian army crossed the Aegean Sea in the ships of their Phoenician subjects. They landed at the beach of Marathon, some twenty-six miles from Athens. The vicinity around Marathon was the traditional stronghold of Peisistratus, the former Athenian tyrant. The Persians brought Peisistratus's son Hippias with them, planning to install him as the new tyrant of Athens.

To save their city, the Athenians marched to Marathon, and with the aid of troops from a neighboring polis (Spartan reinforcements arrived too late), the outnumbered Greek army overcame the Persian forces. Their surprising victory at Marathon demonstrated that a well-trained hoplite force could defeat a far more numerous foe. It also showed that Cleisthenes' democratic reforms had unified Attica so firmly that its citizens had no interest in helping the Persians restore tyranny. Democracy worked.

Athenian Naval Power and the Salamis Campaign

After Marathon, Athens embraced even more dramatic reforms. A new political leader named Themistocles persuaded his fellow citizens to spend the proceeds from a rich silver mine in Attica on a new navy and port. By 480 B.C.E. Athens possessed nearly 200 battleships, called triremes°. With three banks of oars manned by the poorest citizens of the polis, the triremes transformed Athens into a naval powerhouse. The entire male citizen body of Athens, not just the aristocrats and hoplites, could now be called to arms. The Athenian navy embodied Athenian democracy in action in which every male citizen had an obligation to defend his homeland.

The battle of Marathon dealt a shameful blow to the Persians' pride that they resolved to avenge, but a major revolt in Egypt and Darius's death in 486 B.C.E. prevented them from invading Greece again for nearly a decade. In 480 B.C.E., Xerxes I, the new Persian Great King, launched a massive invasion of Greece. He brought an overwhelming force of some 150,000 soldiers, a navy of nearly 700 mostly Phoenician vessels, and ample supplies. His troops crossed from Asia into Europe by means of a bridge of boats over the Hellespont, while the navy followed a parallel path by sea in order to supply the troops. They intended to smash Athens.

Terrified by the magnitude of the Persian army, fewer than 40 of the more than 700 Greek poleis joined the defensive coalition that had formed in anticipation of the invasion. Under the leadership of Sparta, the Greek allies planned to hold back the Persian land force in the north, while the Athenian navy sailed north to attack the invaders at sea. The Spartan king Leonidas led the coalition. Under his command, a Greek force stopped the Persians at the pass of Thermopylae until a traitor revealed an alternate path through the mountains. On the last day of the battle, Leonidas, his entire force of 300 valiant Spartans, and several thousand allies died fighting.

Their sacrifice was not in vain. The disaster at Thermopylae gave the Athenians precious time to evacuate their city and to station their highly maneuverable fleet in the narrow straits of Salamis, just off the Athenian coast. In a stunning display of naval skill, the Athenian triremes defeated the Persian navy in a single day of heavy fighting. Xerxes returned to Persia and withdrew most of his forces to Asia Minor, but he left a large army in northern Greece.

Early in 479 B.C.E., a combined Greek army once again stopped the Persians at the battle of Plataea, north of Attica.

Warfare at Sea

In the classical world navies relied on long rowed vessels with bronze battering rams. This painting of a war galley was made about 550 B.C.E. and shows soldiers, oarsmen, and a man at the helm. Athenians perfected the war galley. Their ships could reach a speed of more than nine nautical miles per hour for short distances.

In this battle a large contingent of Spartans led a decisive final charge. That same year, the combined naval forces of Greece defeated the Persian navy off the Ionian coast. Without a single substantial military success, Xerxes gave up the attempt to conquer Greece.

The Classical Age of Greece, 479–336 B.C.E.

■ What were the intellectual, social, and political innovations of Greece in the Classical Age?

The defeat of mighty Persia by a handful of Greek cities shocked the Mediterranean world. Xerxes' failure did not seriously weaken Persian society, but it greatly strengthened the Greeks, not only by boosting their economy and by enhancing their own position in the Mediterranean but also for what we would now call their self-image. After the defeat of the Persians, the Greeks exhibited immense confidence in their ability to shape their political institutions and to describe and analyze their society and the world around them. In the political realm, the emboldened Athenians created a powerful empire that made them the dominant power in the Greek world. During this time democratic institutions flourished in Athens. Yet the very success of Athens sowed the seeds of its demise. After alienating many of the other Greek poleis, Athens lost the long and bitter Peloponnesian War with Sparta.

The distinguishing feature of the Classical Age was its remarkable level of creativity, especially in drama, science, history writing, philosophy, and the visual arts. Despite the turmoil of the Persian and Peloponnesian Wars, Greek society remained rigidly hierarchic with strictly defined gender roles and a large class of slaves who performed much of the heavy labor. The structures of Greek society provided many male citizens with the leisure time for debating public affairs in a democratic fashion, for attending plays, and for speculating about philosophical issues. The many deities of the Greek pantheon were the subject of much Greek art. Greeks worshiped these gods in temples that established the Classical style, which was imitated by Romans and other peoples throughout subsequent centuries. None of the Greek cities produced as many creative men as Athens, which makes its experience as an empire and a democracy particularly revealing.

The Rise and Fall of the Athenian Empire

With the Persian threat to Greece nearly eliminated, Athens began a period of rapid imperial expansion. This aggressive foreign policy backfired. It set off waves of discord among the other Greek city-states that led to war and the eventual collapse of the Athenian Empire.

From Defensive Alliance to Athenian Empire

After the battle of Plataea, the Greek defensive alliance set out to clear the Persians once and for all from the Ionian coast. The Spartans soon grew disillusioned with the effort and withdrew their troops, leaving Athenians in charge. In the winter of 478 B.C.E., Athens reorganized the alliance, creating the Delian League°, named for the small island of Delos where the members met. Athens contributed approximately 200 warships to continue attacks against the Persians, while the other members supplied ships or funds to pay for them. The league ultimately gathered a naval force of 300 ships. By 469 B.C.E. it drove the last Persians from the Aegean.

With the Persians ousted, several poleis tried to leave the league, but the Athenians forced them to remain. The Athenians were rapidly turning the Delian League into an Athenian Empire organized for their own benefit. In subsequent decades the Athenians established military garrisons and intervened in the political life of many cities of the league by imposing heavy taxes and establishing many rules and financial regulations. Several open revolts broke out, but no polis in the empire could overcome Athens's might. In 460 B.C.E. Athens sent approximately 4,000 men and 200 warships to assist in an Egyptian revolt against Persia, but Persian troops destroyed the entire expeditionary force. Sobered by this fiasco, the Athenians moved the treasury of the Delian League from Delos to Athens, claiming that they were protecting it from Persian retaliation. In fact, the Athenians spent the league treasury on public buildings in Athens, including the Parthenon. Athenian policy had become indifferent to the original purpose of the league, but the revenues generated by the league's exploitation simultaneously enabled democracy to flourish at home.

Democracy in the Age of Pericles

The chief designer of the Athenian Empire was Pericles, an aristocrat who dominated Athenian politics from 461 B.C.E. until his death in 429 B.C.E. During the so-called "Age of Pericles," Athenian democracy at home and empire abroad reached their peak.

During the Age of Pericles, about 40,000 citizen men lived in Athens. Only men over age 18 could participate in the city's political life. Women, foreigners, slaves, and other imperial subjects had no voice in public life.

The representative council of 500 men established by Cleisthenes continued to administer public business. The citizen assembly met every ten days and probably never had more than 5,000 citizens in attendance, except for the most important occasions. The assembly made final decisions on issues of war, peace, and public policy by majority vote. Because men gained political power through debate in the assembly, a politician's rhetorical skills played an all-important role in convincing voters.

Ten officials called *generals* were elected every year by popular vote to handle high affairs of state and to direct Athens's military forces. Generals typically were aristocrats who had proven their expertise. Pericles, for example, was reelected almost continually for more than twenty years.

The vast increase in public business multiplied the number of public administrators running the empire. By the middle of the fifth century, Athens had about 1,500 officials in its bureaucracy. Now responsible for administrating the Delian League, boards of assessors determined the amount of money its members would pay. Many legal disputes arose among cities in the league, forcing Athens to increase the number of its courts. Because of the constant need for jurors and other office holders, Pericles began paying wages for public service, the first such policy in history. Jurors were chosen by lot, and trials lasted no more than a day to expedite cases, save money, and prevent jury tampering.

Athenians took steps to ensure honesty in public affairs. Every official who spent public revenues had his account books examined at the beginning and at the end of his term in office. Citizens meeting in the assembly had regular opportunities to write down the name of any other citizen they disliked or distrusted on a broken piece of pottery called an *ostrakon*. If a sufficient number of citizens singled out the same person, he would be expelled from Athenian lands for ten years, though his property would remain intact for his return. This procedure, called ostracism°, provided a way to get rid of corrupt or overly ambitious politicians. A strong sense of shared identity and common purpose resulted from these democratic institutions and attracted men of all social classes to public service.

Additional reforms by Pericles gave women a more important role in Athenian society. Before 451 B.C.E., children born to Athenian men and their foreign wives attained full citizenship. Pericles' new law allowed citizenship only if both parents were Athenian citizens. As a result, Athenian citizen women took pride in giving birth to the polis's only legitimate citizens. Nevertheless, citizen women continued to be denied full freedom of action in public life.

Conflict with Sparta: The Peloponnesian War

Sparta and its allies felt threatened by growing Athenian power. Between 460 and 431 B.C.E., Athens and a few allies fought intermittently with Sparta and the Peloponnesian League. War broke out between the two sides in 431 B.C.E., dragging on until 404 B.C.E. (see Map 3.4). In the beginning of the conflict, called the Peloponnesian War, the Spartans repeatedly raided Attica in the hope of defeating Athenian forces in open battle.

Thanks to Athens's fortifications and the two parallel five-mile-long walls connecting the city to its main port of Piraeus, the Athenians endured the devastating Spartan in-

CHRONOLOGY

Classical Greece

490 B.C.E.	Battle of Marathon; first Persian invasion stopped
480–479 B.C.E.	Xerxes invades Greece and is defeated
478 B.C.E.	Delian League formed; expansion of Athenian democracy and imperialism
450s B.C.E.	Pericles ascendant in Athens; Herodotus writes his *Investigations* (*Histories*)
477–432 B.C.E.	Parthenon built in Athens; sophists active
431–404 B.C.E.	Peloponnesian War; Thucydides writes his *History*
429 B.C.E.	Death of Pericles; Euripides and Sophocles active
415–413 B.C.E.	Athens's campaign in Sicily fails
405 B.C.E.	Sparta defeats Athens at Aegospotami
399 B.C.E.	Trial and death of Socrates
399–347 B.C.E.	Plato writes *Dialogues* and founds Academy

vasions. Safe behind their fortifications, they relied on their navy to deliver food and supplies from cities of the Athenian Empire that Spartan armies could not reach. The Athenians also launched attacks from the sea against Spartan territory almost at will. With the hope that their greater resources would sustain them until victory, the Athenians fought on. Although plague struck the overcrowded city in 430 B.C.E., killing almost one-third of the population including Pericles, Athens and Sparta continued to fight.

In 421 B.C.E., Spartan and Athenian generals agreed to a fifty-year truce, but a mere six years later war broke out again. The reckless policies of Alcibiades, an Athenian general, started a new round of warfare. A nephew of Pericles, Alcibiades lacked his uncle's wisdom. In 415 B.C.E. he persuaded the Athenians to send an expeditionary force of 5,000 hoplites to invade Sicily and take its resources for the war effort. Just as the fleet was about to sail, Alcibiades' enemies accused him of profaning a religious festival, and he fled to Sparta. After two years of heavy fighting, the Athenian expedition ended in utter disaster. Syracusan soldiers captured every Athenian ship and either slaughtered the Athenian soldiers or sold them into slavery.

The Collapse of Athenian Power

The Peloponnesian War dragged on for another ten years, but Athens never fully recovered from the catastrophic loss of men and ships in Sicily. At the suggestion of Alcibiades,

Map 3.4   The Peloponnesian War

During this long conflict that lasted from 431 to 404 B.C.E., the forces of Athens and its allies struggled with Sparta and its allies for control of mainland Greece. Though Sparta defeated the Athenian Empire, Athens survived as an influential force in Greek social, political, and economic life.

the Spartans established a permanent military base within sight of Athens, which enabled them to control Attica. When 20,000 slaves in the Athenian silver mines escaped to freedom under the Spartans, Athens lost its main source of revenue. The final blow came when Lysander, the Spartan commander in chief, obtained money from Persia, which continued to maintain an active interest in Greek affairs and built a navy strong enough to challenge Athenian sea power. At the battle of Aegospotami on the Hellespont, Lysander's navy sank every Athenian ship. Athens surrendered in 404 B.C.E.

The victorious Spartan forces pulled down Athens's long walls stretching to Piraeus, but they refused to burn the city to the ground as some enemies of Athens demanded, because Athens had been Sparta's valiant ally in the Persian Wars. Instead, the Spartans set up an oligarchy°, or government by a few. Led by the "Thirty Tyrants," a violent and conservative political faction, the oligarchy soon earned the hatred of Athenian citizens. Within a year they overthrew the tyrants and restored democracy.

Sparta's victory did not bring peace to the Greek world. Following the defeat of the Athenian Empire, the Spartans began a shortsighted attack on Persian provinces in Asia Minor. Angered by Sparta's aggression, the Persians retaliated by financing Athens and other poleis to fight Sparta. Bitter war raged among the Greek poleis, but finally agents of the Persian Great King negotiated the King's Peace in 386 B.C.E. With this treaty the Persians promised not to intervene again in Greek affairs. In return the Greek cities of Asia Minor would remain under Persian control. The war-weary Greek states eagerly agreed. For the next two decades, the Greek city of Thebes dominated Greek affairs after defeating Sparta in 371 B.C.E., but wars among different poleis continued on a small scale. When not fighting other Greeks, many Greek hoplites fought as mercenaries for Persian kings in the period after the Peloponnesian War. These Greek soldiers learned that well-trained, highly disciplined hoplite troops were more than a match for the Persian army. In the next chapter we will see how the kingdom of Macedonia to the north of Greece benefited from this important lesson.

The Social and Religious Foundations of Classical Greece

Amid the violence of the Classical Age, the Greek poleis developed a vibrant way of life in which men and women had distinct roles to play, one that freed men for involvement in public affairs. Greek men and women lived very different lives, guided by strict rules of behavior. A hierarchy of gender roles determined individuals' access to public space, legal rights, and opportunities to work. In this emphatically patriarchal society, only men held positions of public authority, controlled wealth and inheritance, and enjoyed the right to participate in political life. Women were expected to engage in domestic activities, out of sight of non-family members. At the bottom of society slaves of both genders were completely subject to their masters.

Gender Roles

Greek women were expected to marry early in puberty, typically to men at least ten years older. Through marriage legal control of women passed from father to husband. In the case of divorce, which only men could instigate, the husband had to return his wife's dowry to her father. Greek houses were small and usually

divided into two parts. In the brighter front rooms husbands entertained their male friends at dinner and enjoyed active conversation and social interaction with other males. Wives spent the majority of their time in the more secluded portions of the home, supervising the household slaves, raising children, dealing with their mothers-in-law, and weaving cloth.

Greek men feared that their wives would commit adultery, which carried the risk of illegitimate offspring and implied that husbands could not control their possessions or access to their homes. Consequently, Greek men strictly monitored and closely controlled women's sexual activity. Because men considered females powerless to resist seduction, respectable women rarely ventured out in public without a chaperone. Slaves went to market and ran errands. To the typical Greek husband, the ideal wife

(a)

Male Views of Women: Subservient or Out of Control?

In male-dominated Greek communities, men idealized passive women and had great anxiety about losing control over them. (a) This Athenian vase of the fifth century B.C.E. reflects Greek men's view of a properly subordinate woman. In the image, the wife bids goodbye to her young husband, who is going off to war. Her place is at home, tending to chores until his return. (b) This vase depicts male fears about females freed from social constraints. It depicts women as wild, drunken, and potentially murderous followers of Dionysus, god of wine. (c) Greek men's worst nightmare was women fighting back. This vase portrays an Amazon, a mythological female warrior, fighting on horseback. According to myth, Amazons fought in battle like men and ruled themselves.

(b)

(c)

stayed out of public sight, dutifully obeyed him, and was satisfied by sexual relations with him three times a month. She was not supposed to mind if he had relations with prostitutes or adolescent boys. Above all, she was expected to produce legitimate children, preferably sons, who would continue the family line and honorably serve the polis.

Women who worked outside the home did so primarily in three capacities: as vendors of farm produce or cloth in the marketplace, as priestesses, and as prostitutes. Female vendors in the marketplace came from the lower classes. Their skills in weaving cloth and making garments, as well as in growing vegetables in their gardens, gave them the opportunity to supplement the family income.

Priestesses served the temples of goddesses such as Hera in Argos and Athena in Athens. In classical Athens, more than forty publicly sponsored religious cults had female priests. These women gained high prestige in their communities. Greeks believed that some women possessed a special spirituality that made them excellent mediums through whom divinities often spoke. Such women served as oracles, as in the temple of Apollo at Delphi. They attracted visitors from all over the Mediterranean world who wanted to discern the gods' wishes or learn what the future might bring.

Prostitutes lived in all Greek cities, but unlike priestesses, their profession was considered shameful. In Athens, most prostitutes were slaves from abroad. Some women worked as elite courtesans called *hetairai*°. Because Greek men did not think it possible to have intellectual exchanges with their spouses, they hired hetairai to accompany them to social gatherings and to participate in stimulating conversations about politics, philosophy, and the arts. Like ordinary prostitutes, hetairai also were expected to be sexually available for pay.

The most famous of all hetairai was Aspasia, who came to Athens from the Ionian city of Miletus. She became Pericles' companion, and their son gained Athenian citizenship by special vote of the assembly. Aspasia participated fully in the circle of scientists, artists, and intellectuals who surrounded Pericles and made Athens "the school of Greece." According to legend, she taught rhetoric and regularly conversed with the philosopher Socrates.

The Athenian orator Demosthenes famously summed up Greek attitudes toward women with these words: "We have hetairai for the sake of pleasure, regular prostitutes to

Male Homosexuality
This painted vase displays a common homoerotic scene, the courting of an unbearded youth by an older man. The youth holds a garland that suggests athletic victory.

care for our physical needs, and wives to bear legitimate children and be loyal custodians of our households."[3]

In classical Greece, where men considered women intellectually and emotionally inferior, some men believed that the best sort of friendship was found in male relationships. It was not uncommon for Greek men, especially prominent members of society, to have adolescent boys as lovers. In these relationships the older man often assumed the role of mentor to his younger companion. Some poleis institutionalized such relationships. In the city of Thebes, for example, the elite "Sacred Band" of 150 male couples led the city's hoplites into battle during the fourth century B.C.E. These men were considered the best warriors because they would not endure the shame of showing cowardice to their lovers. The Sacred Band could defeat even Spartan warriors.

Slavery: The Source of Greek Prosperity

Unlike free citizens of a polis, slaves were totally under the control of other people and had no political or legal rights. Masters could kill them without serious penalty and could demand sexual favors at any time. Slavery existed in every polis at every social level. The slave population expanded in the period after 600 B.C.E. as poleis prospered and demands for labor increased.

Most information about Greek slavery comes from Athens, which was the first major slave society that is well documented. Between about 450 and 320 B.C.E., the thriving polis had a total population of perhaps a quarter of a million people, one-third of whom were enslaved. The proportion of slaves to free people was similar in other poleis. In the Archaic Age the Athenian aristocracy began to rely on slave labor to work their large landed estates. Most of these slaves had fallen into bondage for debt, but after Solon made the enslavement of Athenian citizens illegal in 594 B.C.E., the wealthy turned to sources outside Attica. Many slaves were captured during the Persian Wars, but most

DOCUMENT

Aristotle on Slavery

slaves were either the children of slaves or purchased from the thriving slave trade in non-Greek peoples from around the Aegean.

Athenians and other Greeks relied on slaves to perform an enormous variety of tasks. The city of Athens owned slaves who served as a police force, as public executioners, as clerks in court, and in other public capacities. Most slaves, however, were privately owned. Some labored as highly skilled artisans and businessmen who lived apart from their owners but were required to pay them a high percentage of their profits. Every Greek household had male and female slaves who performed menial tasks. Some rich landowners owned gangs of slaves who worked in the fields. Others rented slaves to the polis to labor in the silver mines, where they were worked to death under hideous conditions.

Slavery did not necessarily last until a person's death. A few slaves won their freedom through the generosity of their owners. Others saved enough money from their trades to buy their freedom. Freed slaves could not become citizens. Instead, they lived as resident foreigners in the polis of their former masters and often maintained close ties of loyalty and obligation to them.

Slavery was so widespread in Athens because it was extremely profitable. The Athenian political system evolved to permit and support the exploitation of noncitizen slaves to benefit the citizen class. The slaves were primarily responsible for the prosperity of Athens and gave the aristocrats the leisure to engage in intellectual pursuits and to create the rich culture that became part of the core of Western civilization.

Religion and the Gods

Religion permeated Greek life. It provided a structured way for Greeks to interact with the deities who exercised considerable influence over their lives. Greeks worshiped many gods, whom they asked for favors and advice. Every city kept a calendar of religious observances established for certain days. Festivals marked phases in the agricultural year, such as the harvest or sowing seasons, and initiation ceremonies marked an individual's transition from childhood to adulthood.

Above all, Greeks gave their devotion to the gods who protected the city. For instance, during the annual Panathenaea festival in Athens, the entire population, citizens and noncitizens alike, honored the city's patron goddess Athena with a grand procession and numerous sacrifices. Every fourth year, the celebration was expanded to include major athletic and musical competitions. In a joyous parade, the citizens would convey a robe embroidered with mythological scenes to the statue of Athena in her temple, called the Parthenon, or House of the Virgin Goddess, that stood on the Acropolis hill in the center of the city.

The Acropolis and the Parthenon

The Acropolis of Athens, crowned by the Parthenon, stood as a symbol of Athenian imperial culture.

Although every polis had its own set of religious practices, people throughout the Greek world shared many ideas about the gods. Like the Greek language, these shared religious beliefs gave a common identity to Greeks. They also distinguished them from so-called barbarians who worshiped strange gods in ways the Greeks considered uncivilized.

Most Greeks believed that immortal and enormously powerful gods and goddesses were all around them. These deities often embodied natural phenomena such as the sun and moon, but Greeks attributed very human personalities and desires to them. Because these divine forces touched every aspect of daily life, human interactions with them were unavoidable and risky, for the gods could be as harmful as they were helpful to humans.

The Greeks believed that the twelve greatest gods lived on Mount Olympus in northern Greece as a large and quite dysfunctional family. Zeus was the father and king; Hera was his sister and wife; and Aphrodite was the goddess of sex and love. The jealous clan also included Apollo, god of the sun, prophecy, and medicine; Ares, the god of war; and Athena, the goddess of wisdom. Greek mythology developed a set of stories about the Olympian gods that have passed into Western literature and art.

In addition to their home on Mount Olympus, the gods also maintained residences in cities. Temples served as the gods' living quarters. They displayed the wealth and piety of every polis, for Greek cities spared no expense to employ the finest architects and best materials. Rows of carved marble columns surrounded the central room and supported the temple's roof. Sculptural decorations on the temple walls that told stories about the gods were painted with bright colors, but today they have been bleached white by centuries of sunlight and weathering. The god's likeness, typically a large statue, stood at the center of these rectangular marble structures, facing an altar in front of the building.

Worship at Greek temples consisted of offerings and sacrifices. Outside in the open air, worshipers offered the gods small gifts, such as a small bouquet of flowers, a pinch of incense, or a small grain cake. On especially important festivals the Greeks sacrificed live animals to their gods. Priests and priestesses supervised these rituals. The god inside the temple watched the priests prepare the sacrifice, heard the sacrificial animals bleat as their throats were slit, and listened to women howl as blood poured from the beasts. Finally, the god smelled the aroma of burning meat as the victim was cooked over the flames. Satisfied, the god awaited the next sacrifice.

In addition, Greeks took pains to discern the future. They hired religious experts to analyze their dreams and to predict the future based on the examination of the internal organs of specially sacrificed birds. Greeks and non-Greeks alike traveled to consult the priestess of Apollo, the so-called Oracle of Delphi, at a shrine in central Greece. If the god chose to reply to a particular query, he spoke through the mouth of his oracle, a priestess who would lapse into a trance. Priests stood nearby to record and explain the oracle's utterances, which often could have more than one interpretation. When King Croesus of Lydia asked the oracle what would happen if he went to war with the Persians, Apollo told him that "a great kingdom will fall." Croesus never dreamed it would be his own.

Intellectual Life

In the Classical Age, Greeks investigated the natural world and explored the human condition with astonishing freshness and vigor. Their legacy in drama, science, philosophy, and the arts continued to inspire people in many subsequent periods of history. The term *Renaissance*, which is applied to several cultural movements in later periods, refers to attempts to recapture the intellectual vitality of the Greek Classical Age as well as that of the Romans, which drew heavily from it.

Greek Drama

Greek men examined their society's values through public dramatic performances. Peisistratus, the tyrant of Athens, introduced plays around 550 B.C.E. Initially, plays were performed in annual festivals dedicated to Dionysus, the god of wine, and authors entered their plays in competition. Dramatic productions soon became a mainstay of Greek life. In their plays set in the mythical past, the playwrights explored issues relevant to contemporary society. Above all, Greeks who attended the plays (only men were allowed) could expect to be educated and entertained. Fewer than fifty plays from the Greek classical period have survived, but they count among the most powerful examples of literature in the Western tradition.

In tragedies Athenian men watched stories about the terrible suffering underlying human society. In many of these plays an important aristocrat or ruler is destroyed by a fatal personal flaw beyond his or her ability to control. With an unflinching gaze, playwrights examined conflicts between violent passion and reason and between the laws of the gods and those of human communities. Their dramas depicted the terrible consequences of vengeance, the brutality of war, and the relationship of the individual to the polis. In the plays of the three great Athenian tragedians—Aeschylus, Sophocles, and Euripides—characters learn vital lessons through their suffering, and the audience learns them, too.

Aeschylus (525–456 B.C.E.) believed that the gods were just and that human suffering stemmed directly from human error. His most powerful works include a trilogy called the *Oresteia*. This collection of three plays expresses the notion that a polis can survive only when courts made up of citizens settle matters of murder, rather than leaving justice to family vendettas. The cycle of retaliation that tormented the family of King Agamemnon of Mycenae for generations finally ends when Athena and her citizens provide the hideous deities of violent revenge an honorable resting place in Athens.

Another of Aeschylus's plays, *The Persians,* reflected the triumphal mood of Athenians after the defeat of the Persians at Salamis and the Persian withdrawal from Greece. This play shows the tragic consequences of Xerxes' limitless arrogance and ambition. Aeschylus also makes a sharp distinction, for the first time in Greek literature, between Greek civilization and foreign barbarism. This distinction developed into a major theme in Greek thought, and it still is used to categorize cultures today.

In the plays of Sophocles (ca. 496–406 B.C.E.), humans are free to act, but they are trapped by their own weaknesses, their history, and the will of the gods. In *Antigone,* a young woman buries her outlaw brother in accordance with divine principles but in defiance of her city's laws, knowing that she will be executed for her brave act. The misguided king who wrote the law and ordered her death realizes too late that a polis will prosper only if human and divine laws come into proper balance. In *Oedipus the King,* Oedipus unknowingly kills his father and marries his mother. When he learns what he has done, Oedipus blinds himself. Although he knows that fate caused his tragedy, he understands that he was the one who committed the immoral acts.

Like Sophocles' works, the plays of Euripides (ca. 484–406 B.C.E.) portray humans struggling against their fates. In these works, the gods have no human feeling and are capable of bestial action against humans. Unlike other writers of his day, Euripides showed remarkable sympathy for women, who often fall victim to war and male deceit in his plays. At the end of *The Trojan Women,* the despairing Trojan queen Hecuba stands amid the smoldering ruins of her vanquished city, lamenting the cruel life as a slave that awaits her: "Lead me, who walked soft-footed once in Troy, lead me a slave where earth falls sheer away by rocky edges, let me drop and die withered away with tears."[4]

In addition to the tragedies, Greeks delighted in irreverent comedies. Performances of comedy probably began in the seventh century B.C.E. as lewd sketches associated with Dionysus, the god of wine and fertility. The playwright Aristophanes of Athens (ca. 450–388 B.C.E.) proved a master at presenting comedy as social commentary. No person, god, or institution escaped his mockery. Although fully committed to Athenian democracy, Aristophanes had no patience for hypocritical politicians or self-important intellectuals. His comic plays are full of raunchy sex and allusions to the day's issues, containing withering sarcasm, silly puns, and outrageous insults. Audiences howled at the fun, but these plays always carried a thought-provoking message as well. *The Birds* is an apt example. In this satire, Aristophanes tells the story of two down-on-their-luck Athenians who flee the city looking for peace and quiet. On their trek they have to deal with an endless stream of Athenian bureaucrats and frauds, whom Aristophanes mercilessly skewers. Finally the travelers seize power over the Kingdom of the Birds—and then transform it into a replica of Athens. This satire of Athenian imperialism shows Athenians helpless to avoid their own worst instincts.

Scientific Thought in Ionia

Greek science began about 600 B.C.E. in the cities of Ionia, when a handful of men began to ask new questions about the natural world. Living on the border between Greek and Persian civilizations, these Greek thinkers encountered the vigorous Babylonian scientific and mathematical traditions that still flourished in the Persian Empire. Following the method of carefully observing the natural world and systematically recording data, these men began to reconsider traditional Greek explanations for natural phenomena. They rejected notions of gods who arbitrarily inflicted floods, earthquakes, and other disasters on humanity. Instead, they looked for general principles that could explain each natural phenomenon. To these investigators, the natural world was orderly, knowable by means of careful inquiry, and therefore ultimately predictable. These scientists inquired about the physical composition of the natural world, tried to formulate the principles of why change occurs, and began to think about proving their theories logically.

Thales of Miletus (ca. 625–547 B.C.E.), the first of these investigators, theorized that the Earth was a disk floating on water. When the Earth rocked in the water, he proposed, the motion caused earthquakes. Thales traveled to Egypt to study geometry and established the pyramids' height by calculating the length of their shadows. Perhaps influenced by Egyptian and Babylonian teachings, he believed that water gave rise to everything else. His greatest success as an astronomer came when he predicted a solar eclipse in 585 B.C.E.

One of Thales' students, Anaximander (ca. 610–547 B.C.E.), wrote a pioneering essay about natural science called *On the Nature of Things.* Anaximander became the first Greek to create a map of the inhabited world. He also argued that the universe was rational and symmetrical. In his view, it consisted of Earth as a flat disk at its center, held in place by the perfect balance of the limitless space around it. Anaximander also believed that change occurred on Earth through the tension between opposites, such as hot versus cold and dry versus wet.

A third great thinker from Miletus, Anaximenes (ca. 545–525 B.C.E.), suggested that air is the fundamental substance of the universe. Through different processes, air could become fire, wind, water, earth, or even stone. His conclusions, along with those of Thales and Anaximander, may seem odd and unsatisfactory today, but these men were pioneers in the scientific exploration of the natural world.

Dragons and Serpents
Current archaeological research suggests that the dragons and serpents appearing in Greek mythology represent ancient attempts to explain dinosaur fossils. Greek vase painters illustrated these stories with such accuracy that paleontologists today can identify the dinosaur. This vase, painted about 550 B.C.E., shows the hero Hercules and the princess Hesione fighting the sea monster that had been holding her captive. Scientists believe that the monster's head might have been modeled on the skull of *Samotherium,* a giant giraffe that lived about eight million years ago. Many fossils of this creature have been found in Greece and Turkey.

Their brave willingness to remove the gods from explanations of natural phenomena, and their effort to provide arguments in defense of their theories, established the foundations of modern scientific inquiry and observation.

These Milesian thinkers sparked inquiry in other parts of the classical Greek world as well. Soon other investigators developed their own theories. Heraclitus of Ephesus (ca. 500 B.C.E.) argued that fire, not gods, provided the true origin of the world. Leucippus of Miletus (fifth century B.C.E.) and Democritus of Abdera (ca. 460–370 B.C.E.) proposed that the universe consisted entirely of an endless number of material atoms. Too small to be seen, these particles floated everywhere. When the atoms collided or stuck together, they produced the elements of the world we live in, including life itself. These atomists had no need for gods in their explanations of the natural world.

The Origins of Writing History
The Western tradition of writing history has its roots in the work of Herodotus (ca. 484–420 B.C.E.), who grew to adulthood in the Ionian city of Halicarnassus. This Greek author concerned himself with finding the general causes of human events, not natural phenomena. He called his work *Investigations* (the original Greek meaning of the word *history*), and he attempted to explain the Persian Wars. He believed this conflict deserved to be analyzed and remembered because it had been the greatest war ever fought. For Herodotus, "the war between the Greeks and the non-Greeks" was just one episode in an unending cycle of violence between barbarian and civilized, between oppressed and free.

Gods appear in Herodotus's narrative but do not play a causal role in events. Instead, Herodotus attempted to show that humans always act in accordance with the general principle of reciprocity; that is, people predictably respond in equal measure to what befalls them. He described reciprocal violence in legends, such as that of the Trojan War, and recounted the conquest of Lydia by Cyrus the Great in the sixth century. He tells how the Greeks became involved in Persian affairs and finally triumphed over Persian aggression.

DOCUMENT

Herodotus, Histories

Herodotus traveled widely. He frequently visited Athens, where he read portions of his analysis of the Persian War to appreciative audiences. He also made voyages to Egypt, Babylonia, and other foreign lands, gathering information about local religions and customs. Herodotus relished the differences among cultures, and his narrative brims with vivid descriptions of exotic habits in far-off lands.

Although he considered Greeks superior to other peoples, Herodotus raised basic questions about cultural encounters that still engage us today. How can we judge whether one culture's customs are better than another's? Is it possible to evaluate a foreign culture on its own terms or are we doomed to view things through our own eyes and experiences only? Herodotus made description and analysis of foreign cultures an integral part of his "investigations." Today historians justly refer to him as the "Father of History."

Western civilization also owes an incalculable debt to Thucydides of Athens (d. ca. 400 B.C.E.), who further advanced the science of writing history. His brilliant *History of the Peloponnesian War* stands as perhaps the single most influential work of history in the Western tradition because it provides a model for analyzing the causes of human events and the outcomes of individual decisions. In it he combines meticulous attention to accuracy and detail with a broad moral vision. To Thucydides, the Peloponnesian War represented a profound tragedy. At one time under the wise leadership of Pericles, Athens epitomized all that was good about a human community. In this "school of Greece," culture flourished and creativity and political accomplishment had no limits. Unfortunately, Athenians, like all humans, possessed a fatal flaw, the unrelenting desire to possess more. Never satisfied, they followed unprincipled leaders after Pericles' death, embarking on foolhardy adventures that eventually destroyed them.

In Thucydides' analysis, humans, not the gods, are entirely responsible for their own triumphs and defeats. As an analyst of the destructive impact of uncontrolled power on a society, Thucydides has no match. Even more than Herodotus, he set the standard for historical analysis in the West.

Nature Versus Custom and the Origins of Philosophical Thought

The Greeks believed that their communities could prosper only when governed by just political institutions and fair laws. They questioned whether the political and moral standards of the day were rooted in nature or whether humans had invented them and preserved them as customs. They wondered whether absolute standards should guide polis life or whether humans are the measure of all things. No one has answered these questions satisfactorily to this day, but one of the legacies of classical Greece is that they were asked at all.

During the fifth century B.C.E., a group of teachers known as sophists°, or wise men, traveled throughout the Greek-speaking world. They shared no common doctrines, and they taught everything from mathematics to political theory with the hope of instructing individuals in the best ways to lead better lives. The best-known among them was Protagoras (ca. 485–440 B.C.E.), who questioned the existence of gods and absolute standards of truth. All human institutions, Protagoras argued, were created through human custom or law and not through nature. Thus, because truth is relative, an individual should be able to defend either side of an argument persuasively.

Socrates (469–399 B.C.E.), an Athenian citizen, challenged the sophists' notion that there were no absolutes to guide human life. He spent his days trying to help his fellow Athenians understand the basic moral concepts that governed their lives by relentlessly asking them questions. Because Socrates wrote nothing himself, we know of his ideas chiefly through the accounts of his student Plato of Athens (ca. 428–347 B.C.E.), who made his teacher the central figure in his own philosophical essays.

Plato established a center called the Academy in Athens for the purpose of teaching and discussion, and earned a towering reputation among Greek philosophers. Like Socrates, he rejected the notion that truth and morality are relative concepts. Plato taught that absolute virtues such as goodness, justice, and beauty do exist, but on a higher level of reality than human existence. He called these eternal, unchanging absolutes Forms°. In fact, in Platonic thought, the Forms represent true reality. Like shadows that provide only an outline of an object, what we experience in daily life is merely an approximation of this true reality. Plato's theories about the existence of absolute truths and how humans can discover them continue to shape Western thought. In particular, Platonic theory emphasizes how the senses deceive us and how the truth is often hidden. Truth

Symposium

At drinking parties called *symposia,* men would gather to enjoy an evening meal, complete with dancing girls, musicians, and wine. After dinner they often discussed serious issues, including matters of philosophy and ethics. This cup was painted in Athens about 480 B.C.E. It shows a young man reclining on a couch while a young woman dances for his pleasure.

The Trial and Execution of Socrates the Questioner

In 399 B.C.E. the people of Athens tried and executed Socrates, their fellow citizen, for three crimes: for not believing in Athenian gods, for introducing new gods, and for corrupting the city's young men. The charges were paradoxical, for Socrates had devoted his life to investigating how to live ethically and morally. Although Socrates could have escaped, he chose to die rather than betray his most fundamental beliefs. Socrates wrote nothing down, yet his ideas and the example that he set by his life and death make him one of the most influential figures in the history of Western thought.

Born in Athens in 469 B.C.E., Socrates fought bravely during the Peloponnesian War. Afterward he openly defied the antidemocratic Thirty Tyrants whom the Spartans had installed in Athens. Socrates did not seek a career in politics or business. Instead he spent his time thinking and talking, which earned him a reputation as an eccentric. His friends, however, loved and deeply respected him.

Socrates did not give lectures. Instead, he questioned people who believed they knew the truth. By asking them such questions as "What is justice? Beauty? Courage?" and "What is the best way to lead a good life?" Socrates revealed that they—and most people—do not truly understand their most basic assumptions. Socrates did not claim to know the answers, but he did believe in the relentless application of rational argument in the pursuit of answers. This style of questioning, known as the Socratic method, infuriated complacent men because it made them seem foolish. But Socrates' method delighted people interested in taking a hard look at their most cherished beliefs.

Socrates attracted many followers. His brightest student was the philosopher Plato, to whom Socrates was not only a mentor, but a hero. Plato wrote a number of dialogues, or dramatized conversations, in which Socrates appears as a questioner, pursuing the truth about an important topic. Four of his dialogues—*Euthyphro, Apology, Crito,* and *Phaedo*—involve Socrates' trial and death.

The trial began when three citizens named Lycon, Meletus, and Anytus accused Socrates before a jury of 501 men. After hearing the charges, Socrates spoke in his own defense, but instead of showing any remorse, he boldly defended his method of questioning. Annoyed by Socrates' stubbornness, the jury convicted him.

Athenian law permitted accusers as well as defendants to suggest alternative penalties. When the accusers asked for death, Socrates responded with astonishing arrogance. He suggested instead that Athens pay him upkeep for making the city a better place. Outraged by this response from Socrates, the jury chose death by an even wider margin. Socrates accepted their verdict calmly.

While Socrates sat in prison waiting for his execution, a friend named Crito offered to help him escape. Socrates refused to flee. He told Crito that only a man who did not respect the law would break it, and that such a man would indeed be a corrupting influence on the young. Socrates pointed out that he had lived his life as an obedient Athenian citizen and would certainly not break the law now. Human laws may be imperfect, he admitted, but they permit a society to function. Private individuals should never

disregard them. To the end he remained a loyal citizen.

On his final day, with his closest friends around him, Socrates drank a cup of poison and died bravely. Plato wrote, "This is the way our dear friend perished. It is fair to say that he was the bravest, the wisest, and the most honorable man of all those we have ever known."[5]

Historians and philosophers have discussed Socrates' case since Plato's time. Were the accusations fair? What precisely was his crime? In the matter of corrupting Athens's youth, there is no doubt that at least two of his most fervent young followers, Alcibiades and Critias, had earned terrible reputations. Alcibiades had betrayed his city in the Peloponnesian War. Critias was one of the most violent of the Thirty Tyrants. Many Athenians suspected Socrates of influencing them, even though these men represented everything he opposed.

Charges of impiety were harder to substantiate, but Athenians took them seriously. His fellow citizens knew that Socrates always participated in Athenian religious life. But during his defense Socrates admitted that his views were not exactly the same as those of his prosecutors. His claim to have a divine *daimon* or "sign" who sat on his shoulder and gave him advice was eccentric though not actually sacrilegious. Many Athenians thought this daimon was a foreign god rather than Socrates' metaphor for his own mental processes.

The reasons for Socrates' prosecution lie much deeper than the official charges. His trial and execution emerged from an anti-intellectual backlash bred in the frustrations of Athens's defeat in

Socrates on Trial
Many sculptors made portraits of Socrates in the centuries after his death. Though Socrates was viewed as a hero who died for his beliefs, this sculptor did nothing to glamorize him in this portrait. Socrates was famous for the beauty of his thoughts—and the ugliness of his face.

the Peloponnesian War and in the Thirty Tyrants' rule. Even though Athenians had restored democracy, deep-seated resentments sealed Socrates' fate. In many societies throughout history, especially democratic ones like that of Athens that grant freedom to explore new ideas, people who fear change and creativity often strike out at artists, intellectuals, and innovators in times of stress. Athenians resented Socrates because he challenged them to think. He wanted them to live better lives, and they killed him.

Questions of Justice

1. What does this trial reveal about the nature of Athenian justice?
2. What does this trial tell us about the attitude of Athenians toward philosophy?

Taking It Further

Brickhouse, Thomas C., and Nicholas D. Smith. *Socrates on Trial*. 1989. A thorough analysis of Socrates' trial.

Stokes, Michael. *Plato: Apology, with Introduction, Translation, and Commentary*. 1997. The best translation, with important commentary.

can be discovered only through careful, critical questioning rather than through observation of the physical world. As a result, Platonic thought emphasizes the superiority of theory over scientific investigation.

According to Plato, humans can gain knowledge of the Forms. This is possible because we have souls that are small bits of a larger eternal Soul that enters our bodies at birth, bringing knowledge of the Forms with it. Our individual bits of Soul always seek to return to their source, but they must fight the constraints of the body and physical existence that stand in the way of their return. Mortals can aid the Soul in its struggle to overcome the material world by using reason to seek knowledge of the Forms. This rational quest for absolutes, Plato argued, is the particular responsibility of the philosophers, but all of us should do our best to embark on this search.

In his great political work, *The Republic,* Plato described how people might construct an ideal community based on the principles he had established. In this ideal state, educated men and women called the Guardians would lead the polis because they were capable of comprehending the Forms. They would supervise the brave Auxiliaries who defended the city. At the bottom of society were the Workers who produced the basic requirements of life. Workers were the least capable of abstract thought.

Plato and his student Aristotle (384–322 B.C.E.) stand as the two greatest thinkers of classical Greece. Aristotle founded his own school in Athens, called the Lyceum. Unlike his teacher, Aristotle did not envision the Forms as separate from matter. In his view, form and matter are completely bound together. For this reason, we can acquire knowledge of the Forms by carefully observing the world around us and classifying what we find. Following this theory, Aristotle rigorously investigated a large range of subjects, including animal and plant biology, aesthetics, psychology, and physics. His theories regarding mechanics (the study of motion) and his argument that the sun and planets revolve around the Earth acquired great authority among medieval thinkers and were not effectively challenged until the Scientific Revolution of the late sixteenth and seventeenth centuries.

Aristotle's idea regarding politics had an equally important impact on Western thought. In contrast to Plato, who described an ideal state, Aristotle analyzed the political communities that actually existed in his day, the Greek poleis. This empirical approach to politics, which paralleled his approach to studying the natural world, led him to conclude that human beings were by nature "political animals" who had a natural tendency to form political communities. By living in such societies they learned about jus-

tice, which was essential to the state and which was its guiding principle. Aristotle's view that the people themselves, not the gods, formed the state proved immensely important in the history of Western thought. It has survived in modern democracies, especially in the United States, where the Constitution proclaims that the people themselves established the government and determined how it should be structured.

The Arts: Sculpture, Painting, and Architecture

Like philosophers and dramatists during the Classical Age, Greek sculptors, painters, and architects pursued ideal beauty and truth. Classical artists believed the human body was beautiful and an appropriate subject of their attention. They also valued the human capacity to represent in art the ideals of beauty, harmony, and proportion found in nature.

Myron, The Discus Thrower

Classical Greek men celebrated their ability to make rational judgments about what was beautiful and pleasing to the eye—and to create art that embodied those judgments. To create a statue that was an image of physical perfection, sculptors copied the best features of several human models while ignoring their flaws. They strove to depict the muscles, movement, and balance of the human figure in a way that was both lifelike in its imitation of nature and yet idealized in the harmony and symmetry of the torso and limbs. This balance between realism and idealism, as well as the belief that the human male body came closest to perfection and that men embodied the most admirable virtues, ex-

The Male Nude in Greek Sculpture: Polyclitus's Spear-Carrier

This Roman replica of a bronze statue of a warrior, probably Achilles, by the Greek sculptor Polyclitus of Argos, reflects the desire of Greek artists to depict the ideal man. The spear-carrier's anatomy is perfectly proportioned, and his muscles indicate the discipline and preparation for battle. He is the perfect male citizen, balanced and controlled yet poised to fight. The original statue has not survived.

plains the proliferation of male statues—many of them nude—throughout the Greek world.

Greek painters explored movement of the human body as well as colors and the optical illusion of depth. The figures that they depicted on vases and on walls became increasingly lively and realistic as the Classical Age unfolded. Artists portrayed every sort of activity from religious worship to erotic fun, but regardless of the subject, they shared a similar goal: to create a lifelike depiction of the human figure.

In a similar effort to capture ideals of perfection, Greek architects designed their buildings, especially temples, to be symmetrical and proportional. They used mathematical ratios that they observed in nature to shape their designs. The buildings they created show a grace, balance, and harmony that have inspired architects for more than two millennia.

The temple of Athena in Athens, called the Parthenon or "House of the Virgin Goddess," stood as the greatest triumph of classical Greek architecture (see illustration on page 81). Built on the Acropolis of Athens, the temple symbolized Athens's imperial glory. Using funds appropriated from the Delian League, Athenians built the huge temple between 447 and 432 B.C.E. and dedicated it to their divine protector. The architects Ictinus and Callicrates achieved a superb example of structural harmony, perfectly balancing all the building's elements according to mathematical proportions copied from nature. For the Parthenon's sacred inner room, Phidias, a friend of Pericles, sculpted a statue of Athena made of gold and ivory over a wooden core and decorated it with gems and other precious metals. The temple also displayed an elaborate series of carved and brightly painted marble panels depicting the mythology of Athena. The Parthenon remained nearly intact until 1687 C.E., when powder kegs stored inside exploded, causing irreparable damage.

Conclusion

The Cultural Foundations of the West

During the period from 1100 to 336 B.C.E., several of the elements of what would later be considered Western culture came into being. The peoples responsible for this legacy—Persians, Hebrews, and Greeks—did not have a conception of "the West" as a distinct cultural realm, but their religious, philosophical, and political traditions later became essential components of the Western cultural tradition. These traditions arose in a world dominated by Persia. Some of them came directly from Persia itself. Persians preserved and transmitted older Middle Eastern traditions of science, mathematics, astronomy, and navigation, which they bequeathed to the Greeks

and then to the people of the western Mediterranean, North Africa, and eventually Europe. At the same time the official religion of Persia, Zoroastrianism, had a demonstrable impact on Judaism and subsequently on two other great monotheistic religions of the West—Christianity and Islam.

Other Western cultural traditions developed among the people who either were permitted a degree of religious autonomy within the Persian Empire or who successfully resisted conquest by Persian armies. The Persian policy of tolerating other religions allowed the Hebrews to develop their distinctive version of monotheism and the ethical teachings encapsulated in the Bible. These beliefs entered into the mainstream of Western religious culture. In Greece, where Persian expansion met its limits, the democratic institutions of the Athenian polis became well established. Under the political and cultural leadership of Athens, Greek civilization thrived, producing the most enduring artistic and philosophical contributions of the ancient world to Western culture. Many of these traditions were transmitted to a broader geographical area by the Macedonian king, Alexander the Great, who conquered the Greeks and destroyed the Persian Empire. To these military achievements, and the cultural effects of his victories, we now turn.

Suggestions for Further Reading

For a comprehensive list of suggested readings, please go to www.ablongman.com/levack2e/chapter3

Boardman, John. *Persia and the West: An Archaeological Investigation of the Genesis of Achaemenid Art.* 2000. A brilliantly illustrated study that stresses intercultural influences in every aspect of Persian art.

Boyce, Mary. *A History of Zoroastrianism.* Vol. 2. 1975. This authoritative examination provides a masterful overview of the religion of the Persian Empire.

Burkert, Walter. *The Orientalizing Revolution: Near Eastern Influence on Greek Culture in the Early Archaic Age,* trans. Margaret Pinder and Walter Burkert. 1993. Explains how the Semitic East influenced the development of Greek society in the Archaic Age.

Cohn, Norman. *Cosmos, Chaos, and the World to Come: The Ancient Roots of Apocalyptic Faith.* 1993. Expert critical analysis of apocalyptic religions in the West, including Zoroastrianism, ancient Judaism, Christianity, and other faiths.

Finkelstein, Israel, and Neil Asher Silberman. *The Bible Unearthed: Archaeology's New Vision of Ancient Israel and the Origin of the Sacred Texts.* 2001. An important archaeological interpretation that challenges the narrative of the Hebrew Bible and offers a reconsideration of biblical history.

Gottwald, Norman K. *The Hebrew Bible: A Socio-Literary Introduction.* 1985. Combines a close reading of the Hebrew Bible with the latest archaeological and historical evidence.

Just, Roger. *Women in Athenian Law and Life.* 1989. Provides an overview of the social context of women in Athens.

Kuhrt, Amélie. *The Ancient Near East, ca. 3000–330 B.C.* Vol. 2. 1995. This rich and comprehensive bibliography is a remarkably concise and readable account of Persian history with excellent discussion of ancient textual evidence. Many important passages appear in fluent translation.

Lindberg, David C. *The Beginnings of Western Science: The European Scientific Tradition in Philosophical, Religious, and Institutional Context, 600 B.C. to A.D. 1450.* 1992. This highly readable study provides an exciting survey of the main developments in Western science.

Markoe, Glenn. *Phoenicians.* 2000. The best and most up-to-date treatment of Phoenician society by a noted expert.

Murray, Oswyn. *Early Greece.* 1983. A brilliant study of all aspects of the emergence of Greek society between the Dark Age and the end of the Persian Wars.

Osborne, Robin. *Greece in the Making, 1200–479 B.C.* 1996. An excellent narrative of the development of Greek society with special regard to the archaeological evidence.

Stewart, Andrew. *Art, Desire, and the Body in Ancient Greece.* 1997. A provocative study that examines Greek attitudes toward sexuality and art.

Walker, Christopher, ed. *Astronomy Before the Telescope.* 1996. A fascinating collection of essays about astronomy in the pre-modern period, which makes clear our enormous debt to the Babylonians.

Wieshöfer, Josef. *Ancient Persia from 550 B.C. to A.D. 650,* trans. Azizeh Azodi. 1996. A fresh and comprehensive overview of Persian cultural, social, and political history that relies on Persian evidence more heavily than on biased Greek and Roman sources.

Notes

1. Based on Herodotus, *History,* vol. 1, trans. Rex Warner (2000), 125–126.

2. James B. Pritchard, *Ancient Near Eastern Texts Relating to the Old Testament.* 3rd ed. with supplement (1969), 315–316.

3. Demosthenes, *Orations,* 59.122.

4. From Euripides, *The Trojan Women,* trans. Peter Levi, in John Boardman, Jasper Griffith, and Oswyn Murray, eds., *The Oxford History of the Classical World* (1986), 169.

5. Plato, *Phaedo,* 1.118.

The Hellenistic World and the Roman Republic, 336–31 B.C.E.

4

O NE EVENING AFTER DINNER IN 193 B.C.E., AT THE PALACE OF A GREEK king in Asia Minor, two battle-hardened generals from different lands debated the identity of the greatest military commander of all time. Both generals came from aristocratic backgrounds. One had grown up in Rome, the other in Carthage, an imperial city on the coast of North Africa. They conversed in Greek, the language of diplomacy and culture that was used throughout the Mediterranean and the Middle East. The Carthaginian was Hannibal, a military genius who had led the armies of Carthage in a savage war against Rome between 218 and 201 B.C.E. and who now lived in exile. The Roman, who was visiting Asia Minor as part of a diplomatic mission, was Publius Cornelius Scipio Africanus. This equally brilliant general had defeated Hannibal and ended the bloodiest war in Rome's history. When Scipio asked Hannibal who he thought was the world's greatest general, Hannibal named the legendary Macedonian conqueror Alexander the Great. With a smile Scipio then asked his former foe, "What if *you* had defeated *me?*" "In that case," replied the Carthaginian in a flattering tone, "I would be the greatest general of them all."

This anecdote illuminates some fundamental elements of a period that historians call the Hellenistic Age. First, it reveals a cosmopolitan, Greek-based culture in which a Carthaginian general, whose native tongue was a Semitic language, and a Latin-speaking Roman aristocrat could easily communicate. Second, these two warriors shared knowledge of the history of Mediterranean lands, politics, and diplomatic etiquette. Most of all, both admired Alexander the Great, who had made their cosmopolitan world possible. Scipio, Hannibal, and doubtless their host sought to imitate the Macedonian king. Alexander and the civilization he had inaugurated had set the standard for success in the minds of men from very different cultural backgrounds.

Celt and Wife This dramatic statue epitomizes the mixing of cultures in the Hellenistic Age. The statue is a Roman copy in marble of a bronze original made at Pergamum in Asia Minor by a Greek sculptor. The artist tells the tragic story of a defeated Celt. Rather than be captured alive, he has just killed his wife and is at the precise moment of taking his own life. In typically Hellenistic style, the artist combines anatomical accuracy with psychological agony.

The Hellenistic period began when Alexander (r. 336–323 B.C.E.) conquered the Persian Empire, extending Greek culture as far east as Afghanistan and India. Greeks called themselves *Hellenes,* and thus historians use the terms *Hellenism* and *Hellenistic* to describe the complex cosmopolitan civilization that developed in the wake of Alexander's conquests. This civilization offered a rich variety of goods, technologies, and ideas to anyone who knew or was willing to learn Greek. Just as people throughout the world today study English because it is the primary language used in science and technology, global business, and international politics, Greek became the common tongue used in trade, politics, and intellectual life.

Political borders did not limit Hellenistic civilization. After Alexander died, the empire he had built fragmented into smaller kingdoms that often fought one another. Despite the instability and warfare, however, Hellenistic culture thrived within Alexander's successor kingdoms. It also spread far beyond the lands conquered by Alexander, mainly in the western Mediterranean, where it had a profound effect on the civilizations of North Africa, Europe, and especially Rome. Romans, Jews, Persians, Celts, Carthaginians, and other peoples all absorbed elements of Greek culture—its philosophy, religion, literature, and art. Hellenism gave a common language of science and learning to diverse peoples speaking different languages and worshiping different gods. Hellenism thus gave a cultural unity to a vast area stretching from Europe in the west to Afghanistan in the east. Large portions of this cultural realm ultimately became what historians call the West.

The spread of Hellenistic culture over this vast area involved a series of cultural exchanges. Greek culture offered great prestige and possessed a powerful intellectual appeal to non-Greek peoples, but it also posed a threat to their local, traditional identities. Instead of simply accepting Greek culture, these non-Greek peoples engaged in a process of cultural adaptation and synthesis. In this way Hellenism, which throughout this period remained open to outside influences, absorbed foreign scientific knowledge, religious ideas, and many other elements of culture. These elements then entered the mainstream of Hellenistic culture and were transmitted to the greater Hellenistic world. Some of the basic components of Western civilization originated in these cultural encounters between Greek and non-Greek peoples. These include the seven-day week, beliefs in Hell and Judgment Day, the study of astrology and astronomy, and technologies of metallurgy, agriculture, and navigation.

The Hellenistic era and the age of independent Hellenistic kingdoms came to a close in 31 B.C.E., when the Roman politician and military commander Octavian (later known as Augustus) won control of the Mediterranean world, the Middle East, Egypt, and parts of Europe. This political development did not, however, put an end to the influence of Hellenistic culture. By forging a new, more resilient civilization in which Greeks, Romans, and many other peoples intermingled in peace, the Romans created their own version of Hellenism and introduced it to western Europe.

The main question this chapter seeks to answer is how the encounter between Greeks and the many peoples of the Middle East and Europe, especially the Romans, laid the foundation of Western civilization. In order to answer this main question, the individual sections of the chapter ask the following more specific questions:

- How did Alexander the Great create an empire in which Greek civilization flourished in the midst of many diverse cultures?
- What were the distinguishing features of Hellenistic society and culture, and what was the result of encounters between Greeks and non-Greeks?
- How did the Roman Republic come to dominate the Mediterranean world during the Hellenistic Age, and how did Roman rule over the Hellenistic East affect Rome's development?
- What political and social changes brought the Roman Republic to an end?

The Warlike Kingdom of Macedon

- How did Alexander the Great create an empire in which Greek civilization flourished in the midst of many diverse cultures?

The Hellenistic Age had its roots in Macedon, a kingdom to the north of Greece that was rich in timber, grain, horses, and fighting men. Most Macedonians lived in scattered villages and made a living by engaging in small-scale farming, raiding their neighbors, and trading over short distances. Relentless warfare against wild Thracian and Illyrian tribes to the north and west kept Macedonians constantly ready for battle.

Macedonians spoke a dialect of Greek, but their customs and political organization differed from those of the urbanized Greek communities that lay to their south. Unlike democratic Athens, Macedon had a hereditary monarchy. Cutthroat struggles for ascendancy in the royal family trained Macedonian kings to select the best moment to deliver a lethal blow to any enemy. Maintaining centralized political control over their territory proved a constant problem for Macedon's kings because independent-minded nobles resented their rule. Only the army of free citizens could

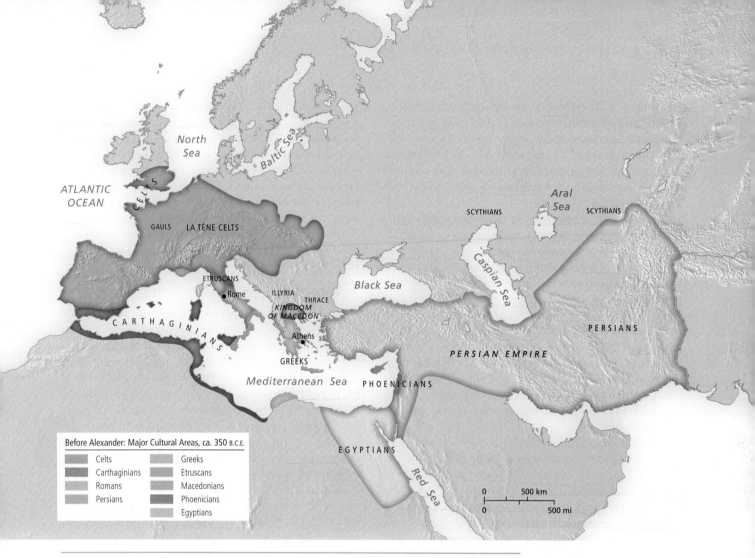

North
Sea

Baltic Sea

ATLANTIC
OCEAN

CELTS

GAULS   LA TÈNE CELTS

ETRUSCANS
• Rome
ILLYRIA
THRACE
KINGDOM
OF MACEDON

CARTHAGINIANS

Athens •

GREEKS

Mediterranean Sea

PHOENICIANS

Black Sea

Aral
Sea

SCYTHIANS

SCYTHIANS

Caspian Sea

PERSIANS

PERSIAN EMPIRE

EGYPTIANS

Red Sea

Before Alexander: Major Cultural Areas, ca. 350 B.C.E.

- Celts
- Carthaginians
- Romans
- Persians
- Greeks
- Etruscans
- Macedonians
- Phoenicians
- Egyptians

| 0 | 500 km |
| 0 | 500 mi |

Map 4.1   Before Alexander: Major Cultural Areas, ca. 350 B.C.E.

During the Hellenistic Age, Greek culture influenced many cultures. This map shows the realms of the Persians, Celts, Romans, Carthaginians, and Phoenicians, whose societies would participate in the Hellenistic Age.

legitimize a king's reign. In return for their support, the soldiers demanded the spoils of war. As a result, Macedonian kings had to wage war continually to obtain that wealth and keep their precarious position on the throne.

Unity and Expansion Under King Philip

Throughout most of the Classical Age of Greece these fierce Macedonian highlanders knew little of city life and seemed like savages to sophisticated Greeks. When cities started to appear in Macedon in the fifth century B.C.E., Macedonian aristocrats began to emulate the culture of classical Greece. The members of the royal family, for example, claimed the Greek hero Hercules as their ancestor. This move won them the right to compete in the Olympic Games, which were open only to Greeks. Macedonian aristocrats also offered

rich stipends to Greek playwrights and scholars to lure them to their capital city of Pella.

In the political realm, however, Macedon shrewdly avoided Greek affairs. During the Persian Wars (490 B.C.E. and 480–479 B.C.E.), Macedonian kings pursued a cautious and profitable policy of friendship with the Persian invaders. During the convulsions of the Peloponnesian War (431–404 B.C.E.) and its turbulent aftermath, Macedon refrained from exploiting Athens, Sparta, and the other Greek cities as they bled to exhaustion. The lack of Greek entanglements, however, could not ease the tensions between kings and nobles. In 399 B.C.E., Macedon slipped into a forty-year period of anarchy. Just as Macedon was on the verge of disintegration, King Philip II (382–336 B.C.E.) stepped forward and transformed the Macedonian kingdom.

A ruthless opportunist with a gift for military organization, Philip consolidated his power by eliminating his rivals, killing many of them in battle. He unified the unruly nobles who controlled different regions of Macedon by demonstrating the advantages of cooperation under his leadership. As Philip led the nobles to victory after victory over hostile frontier tribes and shared his plunder with them and with the common soldiers, the Macedonians embraced his leadership (see Map 4.1).

Philip created a new army in which the nobles had a special role as cavalry armed with heavy lances. Called the Companions, they formed elite regiments bound to their king by oaths of loyalty. Philip reorganized the infantry, or foot soldiers, who were recruited mainly from the rural peasantry, into phalanxes. The main function of these phalanxes, unlike those of the hoplites, was to use long lances to hold off the enemy while the cavalry galloped in to strike a fatal blow. This new strategy gave Philip's armies an enormous tactical advantage over traditional Greek hoplite formations. After seizing the gold and silver mines of the north Aegean coast of Greece, Philip had ample funds to hire additional armies of mercenaries to augment his Macedonian troops.

With Macedon firmly under his control, its borders secure and his army eager for loot, Philip stood poised to strike at Greece. In 349 B.C.E. he seized several cities in northern and central Greece, inaugurating a decade of diplomacy, bribery, and threats as he maneuvered for power over the rest of the Greek poleis.

Recognizing that Philip represented a threat to Greek liberty, the brilliant Athenian orator Demosthenes organized resistance among the city-states. In 340 B.C.E., when Philip attempted to seize the Bosporus, the link to Athens's vital Black Sea trade routes, the poleis took action. Demosthenes delivered a series of blistering speeches against Philip known as "the Philippics" and assembled an alliance of cities. In 338 B.C.E., however, Philip crushed the allied armies at the battle of Chaeronea in central Greece. In this confrontation Philip's 18-year-old son Alexander led the Companions in a charge that won the day for the Macedonians.

Philip imposed Macedonian rule over Greece by establishing a coalition of Greek cities called the League of Corinth, of which he was the leader. He also established Macedonian garrisons at strategic sites and forbade Greek cities to change their form of government without his approval. For the Greek poleis, the age of autonomy had passed forever.

Philip next cast his eyes on the Persian Empire. In 337 B.C.E. he cloaked himself in the mantle of Greek culture and announced that he would lead his armies and the forces of Greece against the empire to the east. His reason? To avenge Persia's invasion of Greece in the previous century. Philip's shrewd linking of classical Greek civilization with Macedonian force now became a rallying cry for imperialist expansion under Philip's direction. But as Philip laid plans for his assault on Persia in 336 B.C.E., an assassin murdered him. Philip's son Alexander replaced him and continued his plans to invade the East.

The Conquests of Alexander

A man of immense personal charisma and political craftiness, Alexander won the support of his soldiers by demonstrating fearlessness in combat and displaying military genius on the battlefield. He combined a predatory instinct for conquest and glory with utter ruthlessness in the pursuit of power. These traits proved to be the key to his success. By the time of his death, at the age of just 33, Alexander had won military victories as far east as India, creating a vast empire. Alexander's successes made him a legend during his lifetime, and millions of his subjects worshiped him as a god. Historians consider him a pivotal figure in the history of Western civilization because his conquests led to the dissemination of Hellenistic culture in lands that were to become important components of the West.

VIDEO
Greek Heritage in Turkey

Alexander the Great
This silver coin minted about 315 B.C.E. shows Alexander wearing an elephant scalp, which refers to his battles in India; a diadem, which was a symbol of kingship; and ram's horns, which alludes to a connection with Zeus, king of the gods.

After brutally consolidating power in Macedonia and Greece following his father's death, Alexander launched an invasion of Persia. With no more than 40,000 infantry and 5,000 cavalry, Alexander crossed the Hellespont—the narrow strait dividing Europe from Asia where the Black Sea meets the Aegean Sea—and marched into Persian territory in 334 B.C.E. Darius III, the Great King of Persia who had ascended the throne two years earlier, proved no match for Alexander's tactical brilliance. The young Macedonian king won his first great victory in battle over Persian forces at the Granicus River, giving him control over Asia Minor with its rich Greek coastal cities and fleets. He then marched into Syria, where he broke the main Persian army near the town of Issus in 333 B.C.E. Just as he had done at the battle of the Granicus River, Alexander led the Macedonian cavalry's victorious charge into the teeth of the enemy. From this victory Alexander gained control of the entire eastern coast of the Mediterranean Sea and the Persian naval bases located there.

When the maritime city of Tyre succumbed to Alexander's siege in 332 B.C.E., Darius panicked and offered the young Macedonian his daughter and all of his empire west of the Euphrates River in return for peace. Alexander rejected the offer and marched into Egypt, where the inhabitants welcomed him as a liberator from their Persian masters. From Egypt he advanced into Mesopotamia, where he crushed Darius once again on the battlefield at Gaugamela near the Tigris River.

When Alexander entered Babylon in triumph he once again received an enthusiastic welcome as a liberator. From Babylon his forces ventured southeast to Persepolis, the Persian capital, which Alexander captured in January 330 B.C.E. He plundered the city and burned it to the ground. The enormous wealth he acquired from Persepolis paid for all of his military activities for the next dozen years and invigorated the entire Macedonian economy. Darius escaped the destruction of his capital but was soon murdered by his own nobles. The once-powerful Persian Empire lay in ruins.

Alexander had fulfilled his father's pledge to gain vengeance against Persia, but he had no intention of slowing down his march of conquest (see Map 4.2). He pushed past the tribesmen of the harsh Afghan mountain ranges to penetrate Central Asia. Then in 327 B.C.E. he entered the

Map 4.2 Macedon and the Conquests of Alexander the Great

Alexander led troops from his Macedonian homeland as far east as the Indus Valley. He defeated the Persian Empire and incorporated it into his kingdom. This map shows the route of Alexander's march of conquest and the sites of his most important victories.

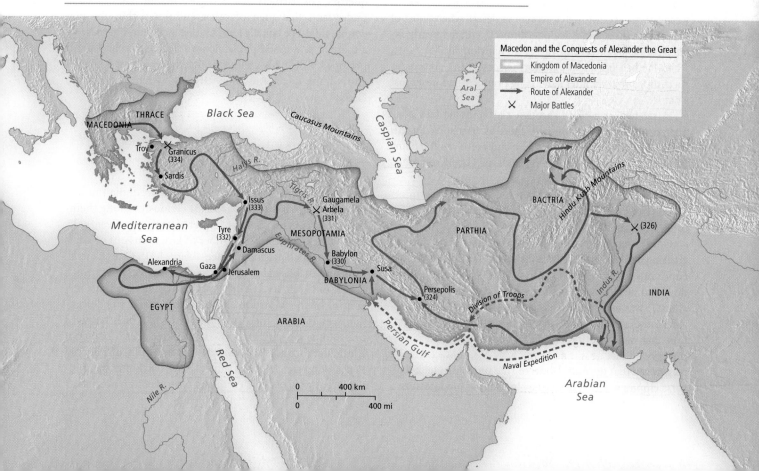

CHRONOLOGY

Alexander the Great and the Greek East

359–336 B.C.E.	Philip II rules Macedon
338 B.C.E.	Philip II conquers Greece (Battle of Chaeronea)
336–323 B.C.E.	Alexander the Great reigns
334 B.C.E.	Battle of Granicus River fought
333 B.C.E.	Battle of Issus fought
331 B.C.E.	Battle of Gaugamela fought; Alexander founds Alexandria in Egypt
330 B.C.E.	Alexander destroys Persepolis, capital of Persia
327 B.C.E.	Alexander reaches India
323 B.C.E.	Alexander dies at Babylon
323–ca. 300 B.C.E.	Successors to Alexander establish kingdoms

territory that is modern Pakistan through the Khyber Pass. There he defeated Poros, an Indian king, but then the tide of fortune slowly turned against him. After crossing the Indus River and advancing into India, his exhausted armies refused to go any farther. The route he chose for his return westward passed through a scorching desert, where most of his soldiers died, and Alexander himself suffered nearly fatal wounds. While recuperating at Babylon in 323 B.C.E., where he had begun to plan further conquests, Alexander succumbed to fever after a drinking bout. He had never lost a battle.

In strategic locations through the lands he had conquered, Alexander established cities as garrisons for his troops. More than a dozen of these cities received the name Alexandria in his honor. Thousands of Greeks migrated east to settle in the new cities to take advantage of the expanded economic opportunities for trade and farming. These Greek settlers became the cultural and political elite of the new cities.

Governing an empire of this size proved to be a difficult challenge. It was much easier for Alexander to conquer an enormous empire than to rule it. The Macedonian kingdom that he led was geared to seizing land and plundering cities. It was another task entirely to create the infrastructure and discipline necessary for ruling an immense territory that had little linguistic or cultural unity. Alexander understood that he was no longer king of just Macedon. He recognized that the only model of rule suitable to such a diverse empire was that devised by his Persian predecessors: a

Great King presiding over a hierarchy of nobles who governed Persian territory, and subject kings who ruled non-Persian regions.

Necessity thus forced Alexander to bring his Macedonian troops and his new Persian subjects together in an uneasy balance. To that end, Alexander persuaded his army to proclaim him "King of Asia"—that is, the new Great King. With his Companions he simply took over the government of the former Persian Empire from the top. He included a handful of loyal Persians in his administration by making them regional governors or satraps, while offering other Persians minor roles in his regime.

These practical steps promised to bring order to the empire. By adopting the elaborate Persian role of the Great King, Alexander demonstrated to his foreign subjects that his regime stood for security and continuity of orderly rule. His proud Macedonian soldiers, however, ultimately stymied his efforts. They refused to grovel before him as Persian royal ceremony dictated. And though Alexander may well have thought of himself as a god, they refused to worship him while he lived. Instead, they saw Alexander's recruitment of 30,000 Persian troops into their army as a threat to the traditional relationship between Macedonian soldiers and their king. They also resented the marriages with the daughters of Persian noblemen that Alexander forced on them in order to unite Macedonians and Persians—although no Persian nobles received Greek wives. The Macedonian troops expected to keep all the spoils of victory for themselves. They wanted to be conquerors, not partners in a new government. They failed to understand that men of other cultures within the new empire might be equally loyal to Alexander and thus deserve a share of power and public honor. Alexander's charismatic personality held his conquests together, but his death destroyed any dreams of cooperation between Persians and Greeks.

Successor Kingdoms: Distributing the Spoils

Alexander left no adult heir, and the Macedonian nobles who served as his generals fought viciously among themselves for control of his conquered territory. Eventually these generals created a number of kingdoms out of lands Alexander had acquired (see Map 4.3). One general, Ptolemy, established the Ptolemaic dynasty in Egypt, which lasted until 30 B.C.E. Antigonus "the One-Eyed" gained control of the Macedonian homeland, where his descendants established the Antigonid dynasty, which survived until Rome defeated it in 167 B.C.E. The largest portion of Alexander's conquests, comprising the bulk of the old Persian Empire, fell to his general Seleucus. But in the mid-third century B.C.E., the Parthians, a people from northeast-

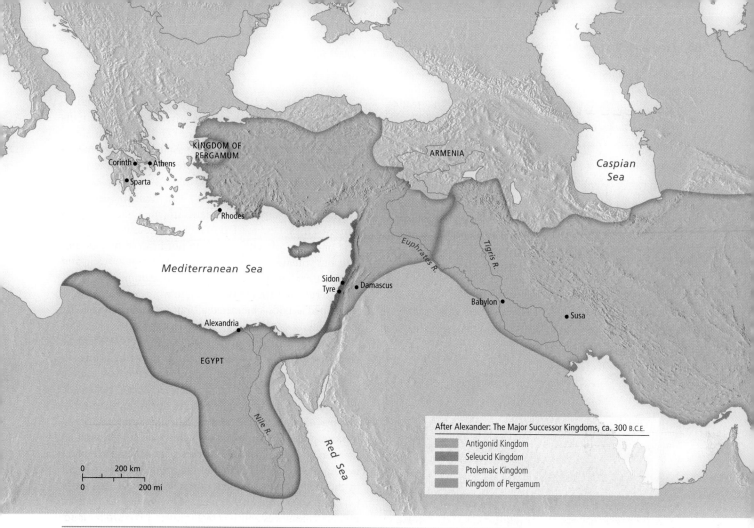

Map 4.3 After Alexander: Major Successor Kingdoms, ca. 300 B.C.E.
After Alexander's death, his generals quarreled and broke the empire into several smaller kingdoms.

ern Persia, shook off Seleucid rule and created a vigorous state. By 150 B.C.E. the Seleucids ruled only Syria.

Smaller kingdoms were also carved out of the areas Alexander had conquered. Bactria (in northern Afghanistan) came under the rule of a Greek-speaking government that would control it well into the second century B.C.E. In 303 B.C.E. the Indian king Chandragupta Maurya conquered the easternmost Indian territories and incorporated them into his own non-Greek kingdom in India. Another lesser successor kingdom emerged in Asia Minor. Centered on the city of Pergamum, a buffer between the Seleucid and Antigonid kingdoms, it was ruled by the Attalid dynasty.

Following the example of Macedon itself, the Hellenistic successor states all maintained a monarchical form of government, in which a king ruled the people with the support of the army and highly regimented bureaucracies. The members of the administrative hierarchy were all Greeks and Macedonians; indigenous people were not recruited into the ruling elite. Greek was the language of rule in the successor kingdoms. The talented queen Cleopatra (69–30 B.C.E.), who was the last descendant of Ptolemy to rule in

Egypt, was the first of her line ever to speak Egyptian. Greek-speaking monarchs were nonetheless aware that they needed to cultivate the goodwill of their non-Greek-speaking subjects. As one monarch asked in a Hellenistic political dialogue, "How can I accommodate myself to all the different races in my kingdom?" A subject answered: "By adopting the appropriate attitude to each, making justice one's guide."

The king towered over Hellenistic society, holding authority over all his subjects and bearing ultimate responsibility for their welfare. Following the example of Alexander, Hellenistic monarchs earned legitimacy by leading their troops into wars of conquest. A king embodied the entire community that he ruled. He was at once the ruler, father, protector, savior, source of law, and god of all his subjects. His garb reinforced his elevated position—kings arrayed themselves in battle gear with a helmet or Macedonian sombrero, crowns, purple robes, scepters, and special seal rings. Monarchs earned the loyalty of their subjects and glorified their own rule by establishing cities, constructing public buildings, and rewarding their inner circle.

Ptolemaic King of Egypt

This golden ring depicts Ptolemy VI, who ruled Egypt from 176 to 145 B.C.E. Although he and his court spoke only Greek, he is depicted as a pharaoh wearing a double crown, the age-old symbol of Egyptian monarchy. The image on the ring demonstrated the integration of old and new political symbols in Egypt during the Hellenistic Age.

This worship of Hellenistic monarchs drew from indigenous traditions throughout the Middle East, but in its Hellenistic form it had a political rather than a spiritual significance. People worshiped their kings as a spontaneous expression of gratitude for the protection and the peace that good government made possible. For example, when the Antigonid king Demetrius "the Besieger" captured Athens in 308 B.C.E., the pragmatic Athenians sang a song in honor of their new master: "The other gods either do not exist or are far off, either they do not hear, or they do not care; but you are here and we can see you, not in wood and stone but in living truth."[1] Deification legitimized a king's right to rule. In turn the ruler cult, in which monarchs were worshiped as gods, channeled all-important loyalty directly to the king.

In addition to the loyalty of their subjects, Hellenistic kings also depended on permanent professional armies to wage the military campaigns so essential to maintaining their authority and to defending their territories. Hellenistic kings fought wars over much larger territories than those that had led to squabbles among Greek city-states in previous centuries. The conquest of such territories required an increase in the size of field armies. The Athenian hoplites had numbered about 10,000 in the fifth century B.C.E., but in the Hellenistic Age kings routinely mustered armies of between 60,000 and 80,000 men. Many soldiers came from military colonies established by the kings. In return for land, the men of these Greek-speaking colonies were obliged to serve generation after generation in the king's army and to police the native, non-Greek populations.

Hellenistic Society and Culture

■ What were the distinguishing features of Hellenistic society and culture, and what was the result of encounters between Greeks and non-Greeks?

Chronic warfare among Hellenistic monarchs made political unity among the Hellenistic kingdoms impossible. Nevertheless, the social institutions and cultural orientation of Greek-speaking people in all these kingdoms gave them a unity that their monarchs could not achieve.

Cities: The Heart of Hellenistic Life

Alexander and his successors seized dozens of Greek city-states scattered across the eastern Mediterranean and founded dozens of new glittering urban communities in all the territories they conquered. Hellenistic cities were much more than garrisons put in place to enforce the conquerors'

DOCUMENT

Descriptions of Alexandria

Ptolemy II, who ruled in Egypt from 283 to 246 B.C.E., exemplifies these notions of Hellenistic kingship. Ptolemy expanded his dominions by conquering parts of Asia Minor and Syria from rival monarchs. He also expanded the bureaucracy, refined the taxation system, and funded many new military settlements. With his support, merchants established new trading posts on the Red Sea, where they engaged in commerce with merchants from India and other eastern lands. Ptolemy patronized the arts and sciences by building impressive research institutes and libraries. He transformed Egypt's capital city of Alexandria, founded by Alexander in Egypt in 331 B.C.E., into the leading center of Greek culture and learning in the Hellenistic world. To reinforce his authority and majesty, he encouraged his subjects to worship him as a god.

power. They continued traditions of learning, art, and architecture, as well as traditions of citizen participation in public life that had flourished in the classical poleis. Most important, people in cities throughout the Hellenistic world spoke a standard version of Greek called Koine° that gave them a sense of common identity. Greek city life defined Hellenistic civilization.

On the surface, many of the institutions of the classical poleis remained the same: magistrates, councils, and popular assemblies ran the cities' affairs, and some form of democracy remained the ideal in local government. Yet beneath the surface, the poleis had undergone radical changes. Because kings wielded absolute power, once-independent cities such as Athens and Corinth lost their freedom to make peace or wage war. They now served as the bureaucratic centers that administered their rulers' huge kingdoms.

Hellenistic kings preferred to maintain the illusion of the cities' independence and rarely intervened in urban affairs, permitting considerable freedom in local government. Nonetheless, Hellenistic methods and those of classical Greece differed in one important way. Democracies had developed in Greece during the Archaic and Classical Ages to protect the interests of the poor as well as the rich. Now, in the Hellenistic Age, the wealthy dominated society and government while the condition of the poor deteriorated. Rich men appointed by the king controlled all the courts, held all the magistracies, and represented all the cities at the court of the kings, who in return showered these civic leaders with honors. Through land grants, tax immunities, and other favors, the monarchs developed networks of personal ties that bound civic leaders to them. In return, these urban elites did more than serve their king. They spent their vast fortunes on behalf of their cities, building magnificent temples, gymnasiums, and other structures for their fellow citizens.

Hellenistic kings and aristocrats spent fortunes turning their cities into showcases of art and design. Distinctive styles of building and ornamentation quickly spread from the east to Carthage, Rome, and other communities in the western Mediterranean. Laying out streets on a grid plan became standard in the Mediterranean world, lending a sense of order to urban space. Stone theaters for plays and spectacles, council halls, and roofed colonnades called *stoas* sprang up everywhere, as did baths with heated pools and gymnasium complexes with sports facilities and classrooms.

In all the major Greek cities of the Hellenistic world, architects built on a monumental scale, integrating sculpture with surrounding buildings and the natural landscape. Temple precincts reveal designers' delight in sweeping vistas across carefully planned terraces and grand stairways. Redefined by these features, the natural setting served as a backdrop for the temple and its processions and rituals.

The freestanding sculpture that decorated public spaces in Hellenistic cities took classical Greek forms in new directions. Turning away from representations of ideal perfection, Hellenistic artists delighted in exploring the movement of the human body and varieties of facial expression. Their subjects ranged from alluring love goddesses to drunks and haggard old boxers. Artists enjoyed portraying the play of fabrics across the human body to accentuate the contours of male and female flesh. Sometimes painted in

Greek Athletics and Culture

This model of the Greek city of Priene in modern Turkey depicts it as it looked in the fourth century B.C.E. The gymnasium complex, with its exercise fields and long colonnade, can be seen at the bottom of the picture. Athletic competition was a significant part of Greek culture. Every self-respecting Greek city had at least one gymnasium. More than just sports centers, gymnasiums served as centers of education and social life for Greek-speaking communities. In these clusters of colonnaded porticoes, wealthy young men of the city learned the basics of Greek literature, rhetoric, science, and music from teachers paid with public funds. For centuries gymnasiums produced leaders and carriers of Hellenistic culture. Here lies the paradox of Hellenism: At the same time that gymnasiums created a shared culture and sense of unity over an enormous geographical extent, they also established a sense of exclusivity and distance from people who did not speak Greek.

Aphrodite of Melos: The Hellenistic Portrayal of the Perfect Female

Perhaps the best-known female statue surviving from antiquity is that of Aphrodite of Melos, popularly known as the Venus di Milo (her Italian name). Sculpted from marble in the second century B.C.E., the goddess is half-nude. She rests on her right foot and seems to step forward toward the viewer. Though her arms are missing today, originally one arm was probably raised to cover her breasts in a gesture of modesty. Her facial expression is serene. The garment draped loosely around her hips gave an artist the opportunity to explore the play of thin cloth over her thighs, expressing his delight in movement and physicality. Somewhat more sedate than other voluptuous representations of Aphrodite, the goddess of love, this statue portrays a male vision of a perfect woman, highly sexual but also charmingly modest.

Nude statues of Aphrodite meant to be erotic and provoke sexual feelings in men became popular in the Hellenistic Age as the result of changing male attitudes about women. Greek women in the Classical Age led secluded lives at home, with no role to play in warfare, politics, debate, or intellectual pursuits. Men appreciated women primarily as mothers and maintainers of the household, not as objects of sexual desire. Statues of women in the Classical Age generally presented them as heavily draped to protect their bodies from the stares of men. In this misogynistic environment, homoeroticism flourished, and men idealized young men as suitable objects of their love and sexual desire.

In the Hellenistic Age, Greek women achieved more social freedom. Although still excluded from politics, women won greater legal rights and participated more fully in activities outside the home. One consequence of women's changed status in the polis was that men began to appreciate them more fully as objects of sexual desire. Male intellectuals debated whether sex with young men or with young women was better for men, and male artists began portraying women as an erotic ideal. Men created nudes like Aphrodite of Melos for other men to enjoy. It is not known what Hellenistic women thought of these statues.

Aphrodite of Melos
Aphrodite, the goddess of sexual love, displayed the perfection of the female form. This marble statue found on the Greek island of Melos was carved in the second century B.C.E.

For Discussion

What does this work of art tell us about attitudes toward sexuality and the status of women in the Hellenistic Age?

In order to appreciate the beauty of a work of art, is it necessary to understand the values of the society in which it was made? Is it possible for a work of art to be meaningful or beautiful at another time or place but not today?

bright colors, these statues explored human frailty and homeliness as often as they celebrated beauty and lofty emotions.

As we saw in Chapter 3, citizenship in the city-states of classical Greece was a carefully limited commodity that gave people a sense of identity, guaranteed desirable rights and privileges, and demanded certain responsibilities. The territories controlled by any city-state were relatively small, yet even Athens at the height of its empire never considered giving Athenian citizenship to all of the people it ruled outside Attica. In contrast, during the Hellenistic Age, large kingdoms containing many cities were the basic political units. People were subjects of a king and citizens of their particular cities. To be sure, some philosophers played with the idea of a universal citizenship of all humankind, but there was no notion of a citizenship shared by all the people in one kingdom. Citizenship lost its political force because individual cities had lost their political autonomy. In a sharp break with earlier practice, important individuals sometimes gained the honor of citizenship in more than one city, something that Greeks in the Classical Age would have found inconceivable.

Hellenistic cities contained more diverse populations than had classical poleis. Alexandria, in Egypt, the largest and most cosmopolitan of Greek cities, boasted large communities of Macedonians, Greeks, Jews, Syrians, and Egyptians. Although these groups lived in different areas of the city and often fought violently with one another, they all participated to varying degrees in the Hellenistic culture of the city. For example, Alexandrian Jews who spoke Greek translated the Hebrew Bible into Greek, a version called the Septuagint°, so that they could more easily read and understand it.

In some older cities such as Babylon and Jerusalem, deep-seated cultural and religious traditions prevented the complete penetration of Greek civilization. Many traditional customs and forms of religious worship, such as the Babylonian worship of the great god Marduk, continued untouched by the Greek way of life. Even the Greek language found limited use in local government. In Mesopotamian cities, for example, local administrators continued to use Aramaic, the local language. The leading families of these cities learned Greek, however, so they could communicate with the members of the king's government and gain political influence.

New Opportunities for Women

One measure of the status of women in a society is the level of female infanticide. Greek parents in the Classical Age routinely abandoned unwanted female babies, leaving them to die. In Hellenistic families, however, particularly those of the Ptolemaic nobility, baby girls were raised in greater numbers than before. Greek women in Egypt, as well as many other Hellenized lands, enjoyed full citizenship and held religious offices. Many owned land and property, paying taxes as men did, but they could enter into business contracts only of minimal value.

Women in the upper levels of Hellenistic society had the opportunity to wield considerably more power than was conceivable for aristocratic women in the classical Greek period. The wives of Hellenistic kings emerged as models of the new, more powerful Hellenistic woman. Inscriptions engraved in stone praise Hellenistic queens for demonstrating such traditional female virtues as piety and for producing sons. As public benefactors, these women built sanctuaries and public works, sponsored charioteers at the Olympic Games, and provided dowries for poor brides. Queens sometimes exerted real authority, supporting and commanding armies. For example, in Egypt the Ptolemaic queen Arsinoë II (r. 276–270 B.C.E.), sister and wife of Ptolemy II of Egypt, directed the armies and navies of the Ptolemaic kingdom in their conquest of Phoenicia and much of the coast of Asia Minor. Egyptian sources refer to her as Pharaoh, a royal title usually reserved for men. The reverence paid to her was also related to the worship of the goddess Isis, with whom she was often identified.

To a lesser extent, opportunities for nonaristocratic Greek women also increased during the Hellenistic Age. In Alexandria young women received education in dancing, music, rudimentary reading and writing, and scholarship and philosophy. Often the daughters of scholars became scholars in their own right. Although their work is lost, we know that women wrote about astronomy, musical theory, and literature, and many female poets competed for honors. A few Hellenistic women distinguished themselves as portrait painters, architects, and harpists. Despite these accomplishments, women still had fewer rights and opportunities than men, and they remained under the supervision of their male relatives. In Egypt, a woman still could not travel overnight without her husband's permission.

Hellenistic Literature, Philosophy, and Science

The Hellenistic Age witnessed the continuation of some trends in classical Greek scholarship while promoting some striking innovations in literature, philosophy, and science.

Literature: Poetry and History Writing

Much Hellenistic literature has vanished, but some surviving works give a glimpse of creativity and originality, which often combined urbanity and thoughtful scholarship. Hellenistic poets turned to frivolous themes because the repressive political climate discouraged questioning of authority. Light comedy became immensely popular, especially in the hands of the playwright Menander of Athens (ca. 300 B.C.E.). This clever author delighted audiences with escapist, frothy tales of temporarily frustrated love and happy endings. These plays, known now as New Comedy, developed from the risqué satires of classical Athens. They featured vivid street language and a cast of stock characters: crotchety parents, naive young men and silly young women, tricky slaves, and wicked pimps.

Theocritus (ca. 300–ca. 260 B.C.E.), who came from Syracuse but wrote in Alexandria in the 270s B.C.E., invented a new genre called pastoral poetry. His verses described idyllic life in the countryside, but his coarse herdsmen reflect the sadness and tensions of city life. Of all the Hellenistic poets, Theocritus has had the most wide-ranging and enduring influence, providing a model for pastoral verse in Rome, Shakespeare's England, and even nineteenth-century Russia. The other great poet from Alexandria, Callimachus (ca. 305–240 B.C.E.), combined playfulness with extraordinary learning in works ranging from *Collections of Wonders of the World* to his moving love poems, the *Elegies*. His poetry provides the best example of the erudite style known as Alexandrianism, which demonstrated a command of meter and language and appealed more to the intellect than to the emotions.

Powerful Hellenistic monarchs influenced the writing of history. Kings wanted flattering accounts of their deeds, not the probing, critical independence of mind that Thucydides had offered in the classical period. Some writers resisted these pressures, however. Hieronymous of Cardia, a professional administrator who lived to age 104, described nearly three generations of political intrigue that followed Alexander's death. His conclusion? Fortune, not the efforts of mighty kings, determines the affairs of men.

Philosophy: The Quest for Peace of Mind

The study of philosophy continued to flourish in the Hellenistic world. Plato's Academy and Aristotle's Lyceum remained in operation in Athens, drawing intellectually curious men from around the Mediterranean. In this environment several new schools of philosophy arose. Three of them in particular—the Epicureans, the Stoics, and the Cynics—shared the common goal of overcoming what they called disturbance, thereby acquiring an inner tranquility or peace of mind. According to Xenocrates (d. 314 B.C.E.), the head of the Platonic Academy, the purpose of studying philosophy "is to allay what causes disturbance in life."

The first of these philosophical schools, the Epicureans°, was founded by Epicurus of Samos (341–271 B.C.E.). Known by its meeting place, the Garden, this school was open to women and slaves as well as free men. Because Epicurus believed that "the entire world lives in pain," he urged people to gain tranquility in their troubled souls through the rational choice of pleasure. The word *epicurean* today denotes a person of discriminating taste who takes pleasure in eating and drinking, but the pleasure Epicurus sought was intellectual, a perfect harmony of body and mind. To achieve this harmony Epicurus recommended a

DOCUMENT

Honoring a Famous Woman Poet

In the third century B.C.E., a distinguished female poet named Aristodama visited the city of Lamia in Thessaly, where she recited from her work. The Lamians enjoyed her performances so much that they made her a citizen of their town and gave her several honorific titles to show their appreciation. The remarkable inscription on a marble plaque from Lamia recording the town's decision to honor Aristodama reveals that in the Hellenistic Age a person's citizenship was not confined to one city. It also shows the greater freedom and status available to women in the Hellenistic Age. It would have been almost unthinkable in Classical Greece for a woman to become a famous poet.

. . . Resolved by the city of the Lamians. Since Aristodama, daughter of Amyntas, a citizen of Smyrna in Ionia, epic poetess, while she was in our city gave several public recitations of her poems in which [our] ancestors were worthily commemorated and since the performance was done with great enthusiasm, she shall be a Special Friend of the city and a Benefactress, and she shall be given citizenship and the right to possess land and a house and the right of pasture and inviolability and security on land and sea in war and peace for herself and her descendants and their property for all time together with all other privileges that are given to other foreign guests and benefactors.

Source: From *The Hellenistic Age: From the Battle of Ipsos to the Death of Kleopatra VII*, edited and translated by Stanley M. Burstein. Copyright © 1985 by Cambridge University Press. Reprinted by permission.

virtuous and simple life, characterized by plain living and withdrawal from the stressful world of politics and social competition. Epicurus also reassured his students that they should fear neither death nor the gods. There was no reason to fear death because the soul was material; hence there was no afterlife. Nor was there any reason to fear the gods, who lived in a happy condition far from Earth, unconcerned with human activity. With these fears assuaged, humans could find inner peace.

The main rival to Epicureanism was Stoicism°, the school established by Zeno of Cition (ca. 335–ca. 263 B.C.E.) at Athens in 300 B.C.E. Taking its name from the Stoa Poikile (the Painted Portico) where Zeno and his successors taught, Stoicism remained influential well into the time of the Roman Empire. Stoics believed that all human beings have an element of divinity in them and therefore participate in one single indissoluble cosmic process. They could find peace of mind by submitting to that cosmic order, which Stoics identified with nature or fate. Thus the word *stoic* today carries the meaning of a person who responds to pain or misfortune without showing passion or feeling. Stoics believed that wise men did not allow the vicissitudes of life to distract them. Rather than calling for withdrawal from the world, like the Epicureans, Stoicism encouraged people to participate actively in public life. Because Stoicism accepted the status quo, many kings and aristocrats embraced it. They wanted to believe that their success formed part of a cosmic, divine plan.

Cynics° took a different approach to gaining peace of mind. Inspired by Antisthenes (ca. 445–360 B.C.E.), a devoted follower of Socrates, the Cynics taught that the key to happiness was the rejection of all needs and desires. To achieve this goal, Cynics rejected all pleasures and possessions, leading a life of asceticism. Diogenes (ca. 412–324 B.C.E.), the chief representative of this philosophy, made his home in an empty barrel. Cynics manifested contempt for the customs and conventions of society, including wealth, social position, and prevailing standards of morality. One prominent Cynic, Crates of Thebes (ca. 328 B.C.E.), caused a public scandal when he did the unthinkable: He took his wife, the philosopher Hipparchia, out for a meal in public instead of leaving her at home where respectable women belonged. The word *cynic* today usually refers to a person who sneeringly denies the sincerity of human motives and actions. Some Cynics took the doctrine of Diogenes to extremes by satisfying, rather than denying, their simplest natural needs. Their behavior, which included public masturbation and defecation, repelled so many people that their philosophy failed to have a lasting impact.

Comedy Mosaic from Pompeii
Brilliant decorative mosaics have survived in great numbers from the Hellenistic world. Often derived from Greek paintings, which have entirely disappeared, these scenes give a vivid glimpse into everyday life. This mosaic is based on a scene from a comedy performed in a theater. We can almost hear the music as street entertainers play and dance in front of a rich man's house.

Explaining the Natural World: Scientific Investigation

While Athens remained the hub of philosophy in the Hellenistic Age, the Ptolemaic kings made Alexandria the preeminent center of scientific learning. These monarchs sponsored scientific research and lectures on the natural world by professional scholars at an institution called the Museum. Nearby, the Library housed hundreds of thousands of texts that attempted to organize the knowledge of the world. In addition to summarizing the work of previous scholars, Hellenistic scientists sought to depict the world as

it actually was. This emphasis on realism involved the rejection of some of the more speculative notions that had characterized classical Greek science.

In mathematics, Euclid (ca. 300 B.C.E.) produced a masterful synthesis of the knowledge of geometry in his great work, the *Elements*, which remained the standard geometry textbook until the twentieth century. Euclid demonstrated how one could attain knowledge by rational methods alone—by mathematical reasoning through the use of deductive proofs and theorems. Equally famous as a theorist and engineer was Archimedes of Syracuse (ca. 287–212 B.C.E.), who calculated the value of pi (the ratio of a circle's circumference to its diameter) and measured the diameter of the sun. A sophisticated mechanical engineer, Archimedes reputedly said: "Give me a fulcrum and I will move the world." Archimedes put his scientific knowledge to work in wartime. During the Roman siege of Syracuse in 212 B.C.E., he built a huge reflecting mirror that focused the

CHRONOLOGY

Hellenistic Literature, Science, and Philosophy

ca. 445–360 B.C.E.	Antisthenes founds the Cynic School at Athens
390–320 B.C.E.	Heraclides of Pontus notes that some planets orbit the sun
ca. 350 B.C.E.	First books on human anatomy are written
310–230 B.C.E.	Aristarchus of Samos establishes heliocentric theory
ca. 310–230 B.C.E.	Pytheas of Marseilles explores coasts of the North Sea
ca. 295 B.C.E.	Ptolemy I founds Museum and Library in Alexandria in Egypt; Menander of Athens writes New Comedy; Zeno of Cition teaches Stoicism at Athens; Euclid writes *Elements of Geometry*
287–212 B.C.E.	Archimedes of Syracuse calculates the value of pi
276–194 B.C.E.	Eratosthenes of Cyrene calculates the Earth's circumference
ca. 190–127 B.C.E.	Hipparchus of Nicaea argues that the Earth is the center of the universe
140s B.C.E.	Polybius writes history of Rome's rise to world power
60s–40s B.C.E.	Cicero writes on rhetoric and philosophy at Rome
129–199 C.E.	Galen codifies Hellenistic medical knowledge

bright Sicilian sun on Roman warships, burning holes in their decks.

Astronomy advanced as well during the Hellenistic Age. In their research, Hellenistic investigators borrowed from the long tradition of precisely recorded observation of the heavens that Babylonian and Egyptian scholars had established. This intersection of Middle Eastern and Greek astronomical work produced one of the richest new areas of knowledge in the Hellenistic world. For example, Heraclides of Pontus (ca. 388–312 B.C.E.) anticipated a heliocentric (sun-centered) theory of the universe when he observed that Venus and Mercury orbit the sun, not Earth. Aristarchus of Samos (ca. 310–230 B.C.E.) established the idea that the planets revolve around the sun while spinning on their own axes. Eratosthenes of Cyrene (ca. 276–194 B.C.E.) made a calculation of the Earth's circumference that came within 200 miles of the actual figure.

The sun-centered view never caught on because of fierce opposition from the followers of Aristotle, whose geocentric (Earth-centered) theories had become canonical. Instead, Hipparchus of Nicaea (ca. 190–127 B.C.E.), who produced the first catalog of stars, insisted that the Earth was the center of the universe. The geocentric view of the universe prevailed until the sixteenth century C.E., when the Polish astronomer Nicholas Copernicus, who had read the

work of Heraclides and Aristarchus, provided mathematical data to support the heliocentric theory (see Chapter 16).

Medical theory and research also flourished in the great Hellenistic cities. Diocles, a Greek doctor of the fourth century B.C.E. who combined theory and practice, wrote the first handbook on human anatomy and invented a spoonlike tool for removing arrowheads from the human body that physicians used on King Philip of Macedon. Doctors during this period believed that human behavior as well as disease were products of the interactions of fluids in the body, called humors. They argued about whether to categorize the humors as hot, cold, wet, and dry; as earth, water, fire, and air; or as blood, phlegm, yellow bile, and black bile. Praxagoras of Cos (late fourth century B.C.E.) argued that the body contained more than a dozen kinds of humors. He also studied the relation of the brain to the spinal cord. Other doctors, such as Herophilus and Erasistratus, who lived in Alexandria in the fourth century B.C.E., systematically dissected human cadavers. They also may have practiced vivisection, operating on living subjects to study their organs. There is some evidence that with the king's permission they conducted experiments on condemned criminals who had not yet been executed, a practice that is outlawed today. Through dissection these physicians learned a great deal about the human nervous system, the structure of the eye, and reproductive physiology.

The Hellenistic medical tradition continued long after the Hellenistic age came to an end. Galen (129–199 C.E.), the greatest doctor of antiquity, organized Hellenistic medical knowledge, producing accurate, realistic descriptions of human anatomy, and formulated a theory regarding the motion of the blood from the liver to the veins that was not replaced until William Harvey discovered the circulation of the blood in the seventeenth century (see Chapter 16). Galen's theories, like many other aspects of Hellenistic culture, had a profound impact on Western scholarship during the Middle Ages.

Encounters with Foreign Peoples

During the Hellenistic Age, Greeks encountered large numbers of foreign peoples, and the effects of these interactions laid some of the foundations of the West. The encounters took place when Greeks explored the unknown regions in Africa and Europe; when Hellenistic culture met with resistance from Babylonians, Egyptians, and Hebrews; and when Celtic peoples migrated to the boundaries of the Hellenistic world.

Exploring the Hellenistic World

A spirit of inquiry—combined with hunger for trade and profit—drove men to explore and map the unknown world during the Hellenistic Age (see Map 4.4). Explorers supported by monarchs ventured into the Caspian, Aral, and Red Seas. By the second century B.C.E., Greeks had established trading posts along the coasts of modern Eritrea and Somalia, where merchants bought goods, particularly ivory, transported from the interior of Africa. Hellenistic people also craved pepper, cinnamon, and other spices and luxury goods from India, but Arab middlemen made direct trade nearly impossible. One intrepid navigator named Eudoxus made an unsuccessful attempt to find a sea route to India by sailing down both the east and west coasts of Africa, but he never got farther than Morocco.

The most ambitious and successful of all Hellenistic explorers was Pytheas of Marseilles (ca. 380–306 B.C.E.). Setting out from the Greek city of Gades (the modern Spanish port of Cadiz) in about 310 B.C.E., he sailed around Britain and reported the existence of either Iceland or Norway. He may even have reached the Vistula River in Poland. Throughout his journeys Pytheas contributed much to navigational knowledge by recording astronomical bearings and natural wonders such as the northern lights.

As these explorers expanded geographical horizons, Greeks developed a lively though condescending interest in the different peoples of the world. Greeks considered themselves culturally superior to non-Greek-speaking peoples,

Map 4.4   Hellenistic Trade and Exploration

During the Hellenistic Age, merchants traveled widely across the breadth of the Mediterranean and throughout the Near East. They sailed into the Persian Gulf and Indian Ocean on commercial ventures. Some explorers sailed along the east and west coasts of Africa as well as Europe's Atlantic coast, reaching Britain and the North Sea.

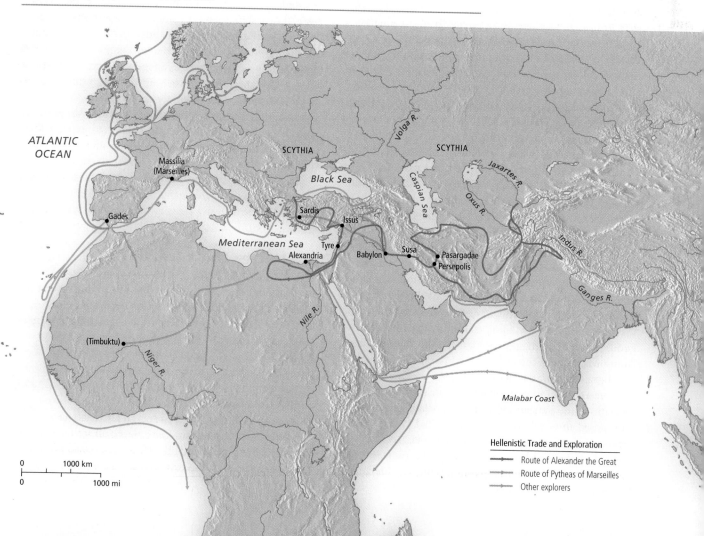

including Jews, Babylonians, Celts, steppe nomads, and sub-Saharan Africans who lived beyond the borders of Hellenistic kingdoms. Greeks considered all of these peoples barbarians. Despite this prejudice, educated men and women throughout the Hellenistic world enjoyed reading accounts in Greek of foreign peoples' customs, myths, natural history, and forms of government.

Knowledge about different peoples often came from non-Greek intellectuals who translated their accounts into Greek. For example, Berosus, a Babylonian priest, wrote a history of his people that provided Greek readers with extensive astronomical knowledge as well. Manetho, an Egyptian priest, composed a history of his land. Hecataeus of Abdera, a Greek, wrote a popular history arguing that Egypt was the site of the origin of civilization. Most of what was known in the West about India until the Middle Ages derived from the reports of Megasthenes, a Seleucid diplomat. Information about the histories and belief systems of their neighbors entertained intellectuals and helped Hellenistic rulers govern their conquered peoples.

Resistance to Hellenistic Culture

Despite this curiosity among educated Greeks about foreign customs, a great barrier of mutual incomprehension and suspicious resentment separated Greeks and their subjects. Language was one such barrier. In most kingdoms, administrators conducted official business only in Greek. Few Greek settlers in the cities or even in far-flung, isolated military colonies ever bothered to learn the local languages, and only a small percentage of the local populations learned Greek. Many communities preferred to ignore their Greek rulers completely. In Babylonia, for example, age-old patterns of urban life centering on temple worship continued outside the influence of Greek culture. Some non-Greeks, however, hoped to rise in the service of their Greek masters. They made an effort to learn Greek and to assimilate into Hellenistic culture. Their collaboration with Greek rulers alienated them from their own people and provoked divisions within native societies.

Many people conquered by the Greeks continued to practice their traditional religions. Still stunned by the loss of their empire, some aristocratic Persians found solace in practicing Zoroastrianism, the traditional Persian religion. As we have seen in Chapter 3, Zoroastrianism teaches that the world is in the grip of an eternal struggle between the good forces of light, represented by the divine creator, Ahura Mazda, and the evil forces of darkness, represented by Angra Mainyu, the demonic destroyer. These Persians interpreted Alexander as Angra Mainyu's agent. In the aftermath of the Persian defeat an important religious text (composed in Greek, ironically) predicted that a military messiah would soon restore Persia's true religion and rulers. In Babylon a book known as the *Dynastic Prophecy* (ca. 300 B.C.E.) expressed similar hopes for Babylonians.

Resentful voices also rang out in Egypt. The *Demotic Chronicle* (ca. 250 B.C.E.) and *The Oracle of the Potter* (ca. 250 B.C.E.) maintained that the Ptolemies had brought the punishment of the gods to Egypt by displacing the pharaohs and interfering with religious customs. One day, the book assured readers, a mighty king would expel the conquerors. Not coincidentally, a series of open rebellions erupted in Egypt about the same time that these works gained popularity.

The Jewish response to Hellenism produced the best-known account of resistance, preserved in the Hebrew Bible as the First and Second Book of Maccabees. After Alexander's death in 323 B.C.E., Jerusalem and Jewish Palestine passed to the control of the Ptolemies and then the Seleucids. The Ptolemaic monarchs at first tolerated Jewish religion and welcomed the rapid assimilation of Jerusalem's priestly aristocracy into Greek culture. Under the rule of these Hellenized priests, a gymnasium and other elements of Greek culture first appeared in Jerusalem. At the same time, however, traditional Jewish worship at the temple in Jerusalem continued.

The situation changed in 167 B.C.E., when the Seleucid king Antiochus IV Epiphanes tried to demonstrate his authority by further Hellenizing the city; when the Jews resisted, his soldiers desecrated the temple by introducing foreign worship there, an abomination in Jewish eyes. Initially, Antiochus intended to advertise his own strength, not to suppress Jewish practice, but his plan backfired. A family of Jewish priests, the Maccabees, began a religious war of liberation. They drove Antiochus's armies out of Palestine, purified the Temple in Jerusalem, and established an independent Jewish kingdom under their rulership. Later, when Jewish writers sought to explain their actions to the Greek-speaking Jews of Alexandria, they described their struggle in terms of resistance to Hellenism. However, the Maccabean dynasty that had led the victorious struggle against Hellenism soon adopted many Greek customs, causing deep rifts within Jewish society.

Celts on the Fringes of the Hellenistic World

In addition to the Greek culture that spread throughout the Mediterranean and Near East, Celtic civilization flourished in Europe during the Hellenistic Age. Celtic peoples emerged in continental Europe north of the Alps about 750 B.C.E. The Celts, who lived in tribes that were never politically unified on a large scale, shared common dialects, metal- and pottery-making techniques, and agricultural and home-building methods. They are the ancestors of many peoples of northern and central Europe today.

Through trade and war, Celts played an influential role on the northern margins of the Hellenistic world from Asia Minor to Spain. Trading routes were established as early as the eighth century B.C.E., but commerce was often interrupted by war. The military activities of Celtic tribes restricted the expansion of Hellenistic kingdoms, thereby pressuring them to strengthen their military capacities.

Archaeologists call the first Celtic civilization in central Europe Hallstatt° culture, because of excavations in Hallstatt, Austria. Around 750 B.C.E., Hallstatt Celts started to spread from their homeland into Italy, the Balkans, Ireland, Spain, and Asia Minor, conquering local peoples on the way. These people left no written records, so we know little of their political practices. The luxury goods and weapons left in their graves, however, indicate a stratified society led by a warrior elite. Hallstatt sites were heavily fortified, suggesting frequent warfare among communities. Men gained status through competitive exchange of gifts, raiding, and valor in battle. In southern France, Celts encountered Hellenistic civilization at the Greek city of Massilia (modern Marseilles). There they participated in lively trade along the Rhône River for Greek luxury goods, including wine and drinking goblets.

In the middle of the fifth century B.C.E. a new phase in Celtic civilization began, called La Tène° culture, which takes its name from a site in modern Switzerland. More weapons appeared in tombs than in the Hallstatt period, indicating intensified warfare. La Tène Celts developed new

centers of wealth and power, especially in the valleys of the Rhine and Danube Rivers. They also founded large, fortified settlements in these regions as well as in present-day France and England.

La Tène craftsmen benefited from new trade routes across the Alps to northern Italy, the home of Etruscan merchants and artisans. Etruscans traded bronze statuettes to the Celtic north, and they may have also introduced the two-wheeled fighting chariots found in aristocratic Celtic tombs. Greek styles in art reached the Celts through these Etruscan intermediaries, but Celtic artists developed their own distinctive style of metalwork and sculpture. Many Celtic communities began to use coinage, which they adopted from the Greeks.

For about a century relations between the Celtic and Mediterranean peoples centered on trade, but around 400 B.C.E. overpopulation in central Europe instigated massive migrations of Celtic tribes. In 387 B.C.E. one migrating group of Celts sacked the city of Rome. Their invasion had an unexpected effect on Roman military technology: The Romans began to use the highly effective Celtic short sword, which became the standard weapon of the Roman legions.

This period of hostile migrations lasted until 200 B.C.E. Some Celts traveled to lands that are Slavic today (Slovakia

---

DOCUMENT

A Jewish Martyr for a Hellenistic Audience

This excerpt from the narrative of II Maccabees in the Greek version of the Hebrew Bible tells the tragic tale of an old Jew who endured martyrdom for his refusal to compromise with Hellenistic life. Written for a Greek-speaking Jewish audience in Alexandria, the story is told with many allusions to Plato's account of the death of Socrates, demonstrating how Greek ideas had influenced even the enemies of Hellenism.

Eleazar, one of the foremost teachers of the Law, a man already advanced in years and of most noble appearance, had his mouth forced open, to make him eat a piece of pork. But he, resolving to die with honour rather than to live disgraced, walked of his own accord to the torture of the wheel. . . . The people supervising the ritual meal, forbidden by the law, because of the time for which they had known him, took him aside and privately urged him to have meat brought of a kind he could properly use, prepared by himself, and only pretend to eat the portions of sacrificial meat as prescribed by the king; this action would enable him to escape death, by availing himself of an

act of kindness prompted by their long friendship. But having taken a noble decision worthy of his years and the dignity of his great age and the well-earned distinction of his grey hairs, worthy too of his impeccable conduct from boyhood and about all of the holy legislation established by God himself, he answered accordingly, telling them to send him at once to Hades. "Pretence, he said, does not befit our time of life. Many young people would suppose that Eleazar at the age of ninety had conformed to the foreigners' way of life and because I had played this part for the sake of a paltry brief spell of my life, might themselves be led astray on my account; I should only bring defilement and disgrace on my old age. Even though for the moment I avoid execution by man, I can never elude the grasp of the Almighty. Therefore if I am man enough to quit this life here and now, I shall have left the young a noble example of how to make a good death, eagerly and generously, for the venerable and holy laws." So saying he walked straight to the wheel . . .

Source: Excerpt from *The New Jerusalem Bible*, copyright © 1985 by Darton, Longman & Todd, Ltd. and Doubleday, a division of Random House, Inc. Reprinted by permission.

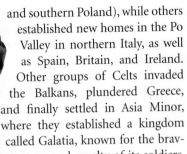

and southern Poland), while others established new homes in the Po Valley in northern Italy, as well as Spain, Britain, and Ireland. Other groups of Celts invaded the Balkans, plundered Greece, and finally settled in Asia Minor, where they established a kingdom called Galatia, known for the bravery and cruelty of its soldiers. These fighters played an important role as mercenaries in the constant wars among the Hellenistic successor kingdoms. Ultimately the Celts were absorbed, together with the peoples in the Hellenistic kingdoms in the eastern Mediterranean, into the Roman Empire.

Celtic Warriors

These two Celtic statuettes of fighting men reveal the impact of Hellenistic art on native traditions. The first warrior, who stands stiffly and without a well-articulated anatomy, is the product of Celtic artistic traditions untouched by Greek art. The second figure shows the influence of Greek styles. He is well-balanced to throw a spear. His muscles are clearly understood and he turns convincingly in space.

Rome's Rise to Power

■ How did the Roman Republic come to dominate the Mediterranean world during the Hellenistic Age, and how did Roman rule over the Hellenistic East affect Rome's development?

From Rome's Capitoline Hill a tourist today can look down on the Roman Forum and see a large field of broken buildings and monuments. These remains lie at the heart of what was once an enormous empire extending from northern England to Iraq and from Morocco to the Black Sea. On the western slope of the neighboring Palatine Hill, archaeologists have uncovered hut foundations from the city's earliest occupants in the tenth century B.C.E. How the Roman Empire emerged from this crude village above a swamp remains one of the most remarkable stories in the history of the West.

During the Hellenistic Age, Rome expanded from being a relatively small city-state with a republican form of government into a vast and powerful empire. As it conquered the peoples who ringed the Mediterranean—the Carthaginians, the Celts, and the Hellenistic kingdoms of Alexander's successors—Rome incorporated these newcomers into the political structure of the republic. Trying to govern these sprawling territories with institutions and social traditions suited for a city-state overwhelmed the Roman Republic° and led to the establishment of a new form of government, the Roman Empire, by the end of the first century B.C.E.

Roman Origins and Etruscan Influences

Interaction with outsiders shaped the story of Rome from its very beginning. Resting on low but easily defensible hills covering a few hundred acres above the Tiber River, Rome lies at the intersection of north-south and east-west trade routes that had been used in Italy since the Neolithic Age. Romans used these same routes to develop a thriving commerce with other peoples, many of whom they eventually conquered and absorbed into their Roman polity.

Settlements began in Rome about 1000 B.C.E., but we know little about the lives of these first inhabitants. So small was the scale of village life that clusters of huts on the different hills may have constituted entirely different communities. What would one day be the Forum°—the place of assembly for judicial and other public business—was an undrained marsh, which villagers used as protection and burial grounds.

Control of the Tiber River crossing and trade allowed Rome to grow quickly. Excavated graves from the eighth century B.C.E. reveal that a wealthy elite or aristocracy had already emerged. Women evidently shared the benefits of increased prosperity. One grave contained a woman buried with her chariot, a symbol of authority and status. In the course of the seventh century the Roman population in-

creased rapidly. Extended families or clans emerged as a force in Roman life. Throughout this early period of Roman history, according to Roman legend, kings exercised political authority.

Historians think that Latin, the Roman language, was only one of at least 140 distinct languages and dialects spoken by Italy's frequently warring communities during the first four centuries of Rome's existence. During this period, Romans developed their military skills in order to defend themselves against their neighbors. Nevertheless, the Romans had amicable relations with some neighbors—particularly the Etruscans, who lived northwest of Rome.

In the sixth and seventh centuries B.C.E., Etruscan culture strongly influenced that of Rome. Like the Romans, the Etruscans° descended from indigenous prehistoric Italian peoples. By 800 B.C.E., they were firmly established in Etruria (modern Tuscany), a region in central Italy between the Arno and Tiber rivers. By the sixth century B.C.E. they controlled territory as far south as the Bay of Naples and

Map 4.5   Celtic Expansion, Fifth to Third Century B.C.E.

During the Hellenistic Age, Celtic peoples migrated into many parts of Europe and Asia Minor. This map shows their routes.

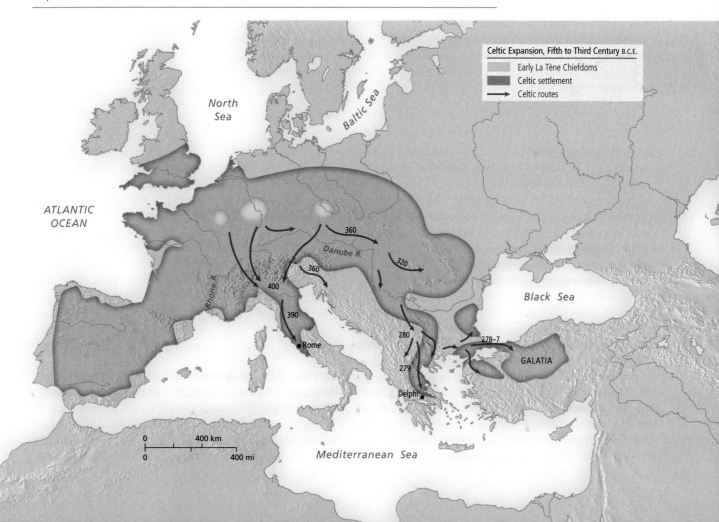

View of the Forum from Capitoline Hill
This view down into the Forum valley was taken from the site of the temple of Jupiter, Rome's mightiest god. All victory processions after a successful war would have ended at this temple, where sacrifices were made. Now tourists visit the remains of buildings from which Rome ruled an international empire.

east to the Adriatic Sea. The Etruscans maintained a loose confederation of independent cities that often waged war against other Italian peoples.

Etruscans carried on a lively trade with Greek merchants, exchanging native iron ore and other resources for Greek vases and other luxury goods. Commerce became the conduit through which Etruscans and later Romans absorbed many aspects of Greek culture. The Etruscans, for example, adopted the Greek alphabet and subscribed to many Greek myths, which they later transmitted to the Romans.

During the sixth century B.C.E., the Etruscans ruled Rome, influencing its religion and temple architecture. Although the Etruscans and Romans spoke different languages, a common culture deriving from native Italian, Etruscan, and Greek communities gradually evolved, especially in religious practice. The three main gods of Rome—Jupiter, Minerva, and Juno—were first worshiped in Etruria. (The Greek equivalents were Zeus, Athena, and Hera.) In addition, Romans learned from Etruscan seers how to in-

terpret omens, especially how to learn the will of the gods by examining the entrails of sacrificed animals. Etruscans also gave the Romans a distinctive temple architecture that differed from that of the Greeks. While people could walk around a Greek temple and see it from all sides, Etruscan and eventually Roman temples featured deep porches and were placed on a high platform at the back of a long sacred enclosure. This positioning directed the worshipers' attention to the god's temple and the altar in front of it rather than the building's placement in the landscape.

The Beginnings of the Roman State

By about 600 B.C.E. Romans had prospered sufficiently to drain the marsh that lay at the center of their city, which they came to call the Forum. At the same time they began to construct temples and public buildings, including the first senate house, where the elders met to discuss community affairs. Under the rule of its kings, some of whom were of

Etruscan origin, Rome became an important military power in Italy. Only free male inhabitants of the city who could afford their own weapons voted in the citizen assembly, which made public decisions with the advice of the senate. Poor men could fight but not vote. Thus began the struggle between rich and poor that would plague Roman life for centuries.

About 500 B.C.E., when Rome had become a powerful city with perhaps as many as 35,000 inhabitants, the Romans put an end to kingship and began a new system of government that historians call the Roman Republic. According to legend, in 509 B.C.E. a courageous aristocrat named Brutus overthrew the tyrannical Etruscan king, Tarquin the Arrogant. After the coup, Roman aristocrats established several new institutions in place of the kingship that structured political life for 500 years. An assembly comprising Rome's male citizens, called the Centuriate Assembly because of the units of 100 into which the population was divided, managed the city's legislative, judicial, and administrative affairs. As in the Greek poleis, only men participated in battle and public life. Each year, the assembly elected two chief executives called consuls, who could apply the law but whose decisions could be appealed. As time went on, the assembly also selected additional officers to deal with legal and financial responsibilities. A body of elders, called the Senate, comprising about 300 Romans who had held administrative offices, advised the consuls, though they had no formal authority. Priests performed religious ceremonies on behalf of the city.

Hatred of kings, which became a staple of Roman political thought, prevented any one man from becoming too prominent. A relatively small group of influential families held real power within the political community, by both holding offices and working behind the scenes. This kind of government is known as an oligarchy, or "the rule of the few."

To celebrate the end of the monarchy, the people of Rome built a grand new temple to Jupiter on the Capitoline Hill, looking down on the Forum. Probably at the same time the Romans also established the community of Vestal Virgins as caretakers of the sacred fire and hearth in the Temple of Vesta, one of Rome's most ancient religious sites. In such ways the welfare of Rome became a shared public concern.

Tensions between the rich and the poor shaped political and social life at Rome during the Republic. At the top of the social hierarchy stood the patricians°, aristocratic clans whose high status extended to the days of the kings. These men, including the legendary Brutus, had been responsible for toppling the monarchy. Because they monopolized the magistracies and the priesthoods, they occupied most of the seats in the Senate. Other rich landowners and senators with lesser pedigrees, as well as the prosperous farmers who made up the army's phalanxes, joined the patricians in resisting the plebeians°, the poorest segments of society. The

plebeians demanded more political rights, such as a fair share of distributed public land and freedom from debt bondage. These efforts of poor Romans to acquire a political voice, called the Struggle of the Orders°, accelerated during the fifth century B.C.E., when Rome experienced a severe economic recession.

A victory in the plebeians' struggle came in 494 B.C.E., when they won the right to elect two tribunes each year as their spokesmen. Tribunes could veto magistrates' decisions and so block arbitrary judicial actions by the patricians. Then, in 471 B.C.E., a new Plebeian Assembly gave plebeians the opportunity to express their political views in a formal setting, although without the formal authority to enact actual legislation. About 450 B.C.E., the plebeians took another major step forward with the publication of the Law of the Twelve Tables. Until that time, Romans did not write down their laws, and aristocrats often arbitrarily interpreted and applied laws to the disadvantage of the poor. The plebeians pressed for codification and public display of the law to ensure that the rights of all free Romans would be recognized and respected. The Twelve Tables covered all aspects of life from the proper protection of women ("Women shall remain under the guardianship [of a man] even when they have reached legal adulthood") and debt bondage ("Unless he pays his debt or someone stands surety for him in court, bind him in a harness, or in chains . . . ") to religious matters. Even when cruel, the law could now be applied uniformly.

The plebeians continued to make their presence felt in Roman life. In 445 B.C.E., a new law permitted marriage between plebeians and patricians. This enabled wealthy plebeians to marry into aristocratic families. A high point came in 367 B.C.E., when politicians agreed that one of each year's two consuls should come from the plebeian class. The plebeians now were fully integrated within the Roman government. Moreover, around the same time Romans limited the amount of public land that could be distributed to any citizen. The new arrangement prevented aristocrats from seizing the lion's share of conquered territories and permitted poor citizen soldiers to receive a share of captured land. The last concession to the plebeians came in 287 B.C.E., when the decisions of the Plebeian Assembly became binding on the whole state. The plebeians acquired their political strength and full acceptance in the political arena by simple extortion: They threatened to leave the army if the aristocratic elite failed to meet their demands. Without the plebeians, who constituted the bulk of the Roman army, the Republic could not protect itself from invaders or conquer new lands.

The political success of the plebeians resulted in the formation of a new upper class in Rome, consisting of wealthy patrician and plebeian families. At the same time a new underclass of slaves emerged as the result of military expansion in Italy. Poor Roman farmers eagerly settled in newly conquered territories. These farmers in turn served as soldiers in further wars of expansion in which Romans enslaved other conquered peoples. Thus a self-perpetuating cycle of conquest, settlement, and enslavement began to take shape, reaching full development after 200 B.C.E.

Roman Territorial Expansion

During the period of the Republic, Rome conquered and incorporated all of Italy, the vast Carthaginian Empire in northern Africa, and Spain, and many of the lands inhabited by Celtic people to the north and west of Italy (see Map 4.6). As a result of these conquests, the Roman state found it necessary to change the methods of government established in the fifth century B.C.E.

Winning Control of Italy

The new political and military institutions that developed in Rome enabled the Romans to conquer the entire Italian peninsula by 263 B.C.E. In the process the Romans learned the fundamental lessons necessary for ruling much larger territories abroad. Romans began to expand their realm by allying with neighboring cities in Italy. For centuries, Rome and the other Latin-speaking peoples of Latium (the region of central Italy where Rome was situated) had belonged to a loose coalition of cities called the Latin League. Citizens of these cities shared close commercial and legal ties and could intermarry without losing citizenship rights in their native cities. More important, they forged close military alliances with one another.

In 493 B.C.E. Rome successfully led the Latin cities in battle against fierce hill tribes who coveted Latium's rich farmlands. From the success of this venture, Rome learned the value of political alliances with neighbors. Rome and its allies next confronted the Etruscans. In 396 B.C.E. they overcame the Etruscan city of Veii through a combination of military might and shrewd political maneuvering. From this experience, the Romans discovered the uses of careful diplomacy.

A temporary setback to Rome's expansion occurred in 387 B.C.E., when a raiding band of Celts from the Po Valley in the north of Italy defeated a Roman army and plundered the city of Rome before returning home. Only after a generation did Romans recover from this disaster and reassert their preeminence among their allies. Still, they had learned that tenacity and discipline enabled them to endure even a serious military reversal.

The next major step in Rome's expansion came in 338 B.C.E., when Roman troops smashed a three-year revolt of its Latin allies, who had come to resent Rome's overlordship. The peace settlement set the precedent for Rome's future expansion: Rome permitted defeated peoples to become citizens, giving them either partial or full citizenship depending on the treaty it struck with each community. The conquered allies were permitted to continue their own customs, and were not forced to pay tribute. Rome asked for only two things in return: loyalty and troops. All allied communities had to contribute soldiers to the Roman army in wartime. With the huge new pool of troops, Rome became the strongest power in Italy.

In return for their military service and support of Rome, the newly incorporated citizens, especially aristocrats from the allied communities, received a share of the profits of war. They also received the guarantee of Roman protection from internal dissension or outside threats. Those communities not granted full Roman citizenship rights could hope to earn it if they served Roman interests faithfully. Some communities joined the Roman state willingly. Others, particularly the Samnites of south central Italy, resisted bitterly, but to no avail.

Romans continued their march through Italy, becoming embroiled in the affairs of Greek cities of the "toe" and "heel" of the boot-shaped Italian peninsula. Some of these Greek cities invited King Pyrrhus of Epirus, a Hellenistic adventurer, to wage war against Rome on their behalf. Pyrrhus invaded southern Italy with 25,000 men and twenty elephants. Though he defeated Roman armies in two great battles in 280 B.C.E., he lost nearly two-thirds of his own troops and withdrew from Italy. "Another victory like this and I'm finished for good!" he said to a comrade,

CHRONOLOGY

Rome's Rise to Power

ca. 509 B.C.E.	Roman Republic is created
508 B.C.E.	Romans sign treaty with Carthage
494 B.C.E.	Tribunes of the Plebeians created
474 B.C.E.	Plebeian Assembly is created
ca. 450 B.C.E.	Twelve Tables of Law is published
387 B.C.E.	Celts sack Rome
287 B.C.E.	Laws of Plebeian Assembly become binding on all Romans
280 B.C.E.	Pyrrhus of Epirus is defeated
264–241 B.C.E.	First Punic War
218–201 B.C.E.	Second Punic War
215–168 B.C.E.	Wars with Macedon
149–146 B.C.E.	Third Punic War
148–146 B.C.E.	Macedon and Greece become a Roman province
67–62 B.C.E.	Pompey establishes Roman control over Asia Minor, Syria, and Palestine

giving rise to the expression "a Pyrrhic victory," which is a win so costly that it is ruinous. Without Pyrrhus's protection, the Greeks in southern Italy could not withstand Rome's legions, and by 263 B.C.E. Rome ruled all of Italy.

The Struggle with Carthage

By the third century B.C.E., imperial Carthage dominated the western Mediterranean region. From the capital city of Carthage located on the north African coast near modern Tunis, Carthaginians held rich lands along the African coast from modern Algeria to Morocco, controlled the natural resources of southern Spain, and dominated the sea lanes of the entire region. Phoenician traders had founded Carthage in the eighth century B.C.E., and the city's energetic merchants carried on business with Greeks, Etruscans, Celts, and eventually Romans.

Hellenistic culture deeply affected Carthage as it did other Mediterranean and Middle Eastern cities. During the Classical Age, Carthaginian trade with the Greek cities in Sicily, and likely with Greek artisans in north Africa, introduced many elements of Greek culture to Carthage. For example, Carthaginians worshiped the Greek goddess of agriculture, Demeter, and her daughter, Kore (also called Persephone), in an elegant temple served by Carthaginian priests and priestesses. By the fourth century B.C.E. the Carthaginian Empire was playing an integral role in the economy of the Hellenistic world by exporting agricultural products, raw materials, metal goods, and pottery.

Rome and Carthage were old acquaintances. Eager for widespread recognition at the beginning of the Republic, Roman leaders signed a commercial treaty with Carthage. Several centuries of wary respect and increasing trade followed. In 264 B.C.E., just as Rome established power throughout the Italian peninsula, a complicated war between Greek cities in Sicily drew Rome and Carthage into conflict. When a Carthaginian fleet went to help a Greek city in Sicily, another city asked Rome for assistance in dislodging them. The aristocratic Senate refused, but the Plebeian Assembly, eager for the spoils of war, voted to intercede. Rome invaded Sicily, setting off the First Punic War, so called because the word *Punic* comes from the Latin word for *Phoenician*.

The First Punic War between Rome and Carthage for control of Sicily lasted from 264 to 241 B.C.E. During this time the Romans learned how to fight at sea, cutting off the Carthaginian supply lines to Sicily. In 241 B.C.E. Carthage signed a treaty in which it agreed to surrender Sicily and the surrounding islands and to pay a war indemnity over the course of a decade. Roman treachery, however, wrecked the agreement. While the Carthaginians struggled to suppress a revolt of mercenary soldiers, Rome seized Corsica and Sardinia, over which Carthage had lost effective control,

CHRONOLOGY	
Imperial Carthage	
ca. 850 B.C.E.	Phoenicians found Carthage
600s B.C.E.	Carthage expands in North Africa, Sardinia, southern Spain, and Sicily
508 B.C.E.	Carthage makes treaty with Rome
500–200 B.C.E.	Conflicts with Greeks in Sicily
264–241 B.C.E.	Carthage fights First Punic War against Rome
218–203 B.C.E.	Hannibal fights in Italy
218–201 B.C.E.	Carthage fights Second Punic War against Rome
202 B.C.E.	Battle of Zama; Hannibal is defeated near Carthage
149–146 B.C.E.	Carthage fights Third Punic War against Rome; end of Carthaginian Empire
146 B.C.E.	Destruction of the city of Carthage

and demanded larger reparations. Roman bad faith stoked Carthaginian hatred and desire for revenge.

War did not resume for another two decades. Under the able leadership of Hamilcar Barca (r. 238–229 B.C.E.), Carthage put its energy into developing resources in Spain, while Rome campaigned against Celts living in the Po Valley and fierce tribes on the Adriatic coast. During these years trade between Rome and Carthage continued, reaching new heights. Soon, however, the rapid growth of Carthaginian power in Spain led to renewed conflict with Rome. The Second Punic War (218–201 B.C.E.) erupted when Hamilcar's son, Hannibal, 25 years old and eager for vengeance, ignored a Roman warning and captured Saguntum, a Spanish town with which Rome had formal ties of friendship. In an imaginative and daring move, Hannibal then launched a surprise attack on Italy by crossing the Alps and invading from the north. With an army of nearly 25,000 men and eighteen elephants, he crushed the Roman armies sent against him. In the first major battle, at the Trebia River in the Po Valley, 20,000 Romans died. At Lake Trasimene in Etruria in 216 B.C.E., another 25,000 Romans fell. In the same year at Cannae, 50,000 men perished in Rome's worst defeat ever.

Despite these staggering losses, the Romans persevered and eventually defeated the Carthaginian general. They succeeded, first of all, because Hannibal lacked sufficient logistical support from Carthage to capitalize on his early victories and take the city of Rome. Second, most of Rome's allies in Italy proved loyal. They had often seen Romans prevail in the past and knew that the Romans took fierce revenge on disloyal friends. Thus the Roman policy of including and

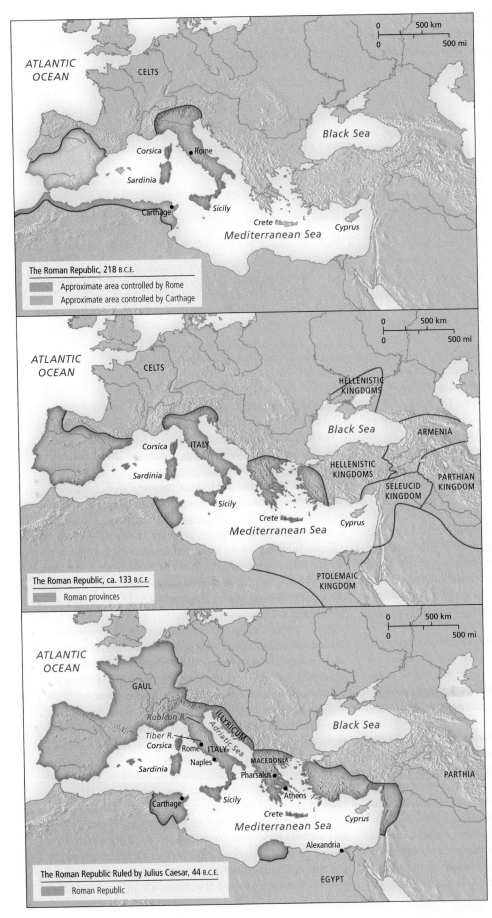

Map 4.6   The Roman Conquest of the Mediterranean During the Republic

Armies of the Roman Republic conquered the Mediterranean world during the Hellenistic Age, overcoming the Carthaginian Empire, the Hellenistic successor kingdoms, and many Celtic peoples in Spain and Gaul.

protecting allies paid off. A third reason for Hannibal's defeat was the indomitable Roman spirit. The Romans simply refused to stop fighting, even after suffering devastating casualties.

The turning point in the war came when Roman commanders adopted a new strategy. After incurring so many defeats, the army dared not face Hannibal in open battle. Instead, Fabius, the Roman commander in Italy, avoided open battle and used guerilla tactics to pin down Hannibal in Italy, thus earning the nickname "the Delayer," while Publius Cornelius Scipio Africanus, the Roman general introduced at the beginning of this chapter, took command of Roman forces in Spain. Within a few years he defeated Carthaginian forces there, cutting completely the thin lines of logistical support to Hannibal. In 204 B.C.E., Scipio led Roman legions into Africa, forcing Carthage to recall Hannibal from Italy in order to protect the city.

In one last effort Hannibal confronted Scipio on Carthaginian soil. At the battle of Zama near Carthage in 202 B.C.E., fortune finally deserted Hannibal. Scipio put an end to his string of victories, forcing him into exile. Hannibal had won every battle but his last. Though Scipio spared Hannibal's life and did not destroy Carthage, the peace treaty transferred all of Carthage's overseas territories to Roman control.

Because the war against Hannibal had claimed so many Roman lives, many vengeful Romans agitated for the total destruction of Carthage. In particular, the statesman Marcus Porcius Cato (234–149 B.C.E.), who ended every public utterance with the demand "Carthage must be destroyed!" goaded Romans to violate the peace treaty and resume war with its old adversary. The Third Punic War (149–146 B.C.E.) resulted in the destruction of Carthage. Survivors were enslaved, and the city was burned to the ground and plowed under with salt. Its territories were reorganized as the Roman provinces of Africa.

Plutarch, *The Life of Cato the Elder*

Conflict with the Celts

Celtic peoples in western Europe fiercely resisted Roman military expansion. After Carthaginian power ended in the Iberian peninsula (modern Spain and Portugal) following the Punic Wars, Romans struggled for more than a century to establish their control over the region's natural resources, particularly its metals and rich farmlands. Not until the reign of Augustus (31 B.C.E.–14 C.E.) did the Romans bring the Iberian peninsula under complete control. The constant fighting drained Rome's manpower and contributed to severe economic and political turmoil in the Republic during the second century B.C.E.

Relations with the Celts had not always been acrimonious. The Roman colonies along the Mediterranean coast that formed an administrative unit called "the Province" (modern Provence) traded peacefully and actively with their Gallic Celtic neighbors. By the late second century B.C.E., Rome made military alliances with the Aedui, a Celtic

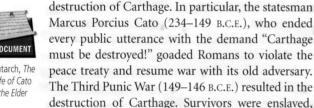

CHRONOLOGY

The World of the Celts

ca. 400 B.C.E.	Celts expand from central Europe
ca. 390–386 B.C.E.	Celts invade Italy and plunder Rome
281 B.C.E.	Celts kill Macedonian king in battle
279 B.C.E.	Celts invade Greece
270s B.C.E.	Celts establish kingdom in Asia Minor
100s B.C.E.	Romans campaign against Celts in Spain
58–50 B.C.E.	Julius Caesar fights Celts in Gaul

tribe that lived further inland. Peace with the Celts, however, ended in 58 B.C.E., when the Roman general Julius Caesar invaded the part of Gaul that lies across the Alps. There he found numerous Celtic tribes with sophisticated political systems dominated by warrior aristocrats. After eight years of bloody conquest and massacre, Caesar conquered Gaul, turning the region into several Roman provinces that within a century became an integral part of the Roman Empire.

From the sack of Rome by Celts in the fourth century B.C.E. to the incorporation of some Celtic lands into the Roman state at the end of the Republic, the Celts were a significant factor in Roman life. In his *History*, Polybius suggested that the constant threat of Celtic invasion contributed to the growth of Roman military force. The Roman Republic was geared for constant warfare, and the Celts frequently were the enemy. Thus the Celts shaped Roman foreign policy as well as the Roman allocation of military resources.

Rome and the Hellenistic World

By the end of the Punic Wars, Rome had become involved in the affairs of the vigorous Hellenistic kingdoms of the East. Initially reluctant to take direct control of these regions, Roman leaders gradually changed their policies. They assumed responsibility for maintaining order and gradually established absolute control over the entire eastern Mediterranean region.

The Macedonian Wars

Rome waged three wars against Macedon between 215 and 168 B.C.E. that resulted in mastery of Macedon and Greece. The First Macedonian War (215–205 B.C.E.) began when the Macedonian king, Philip V (221–179 B.C.E.), had made an alliance with Hannibal after the Roman defeat at the battle of Cannae. The results of the conflict were inconclusive.

Rome entered a second war with Macedon (205–197 B.C.E.) because Philip and the Seleucid king Antiochus III of

Syria had agreed to split the eastern Mediterranean between them. The poleis of Greece begged Rome for help, and Rome responded by ordering Philip to cease meddling in Greek affairs. Philip refused, and Roman forces easily defeated him with the support of Greek cities. In 196 B.C.E. the Roman general Titus Quinctius Flamininus declared the cities of Greece free and withdrew his forces.

These cities were not truly free, however. Rome installed oligarchic governments on whose support the Romans could rely. These unpopular regimes perpetuated the class distinctions of Rome. When Antiochus III sent an army to Greece to free it of Roman control, Rome struck back again, defeating him in 189 B.C.E. Rome imposed heavy reparations but claimed no territory, preferring to protect the newly freed Greek cities of Asia Minor and Greece from a distance.

Rome's policy of control from a distance changed after a third war with Macedon (172–168 B.C.E.). A harsher attitude took hold in Rome when a new Macedonian king tried to supplant Rome as protector of Greece. After a smashing victory, Rome imposed crippling terms of surrender on Macedon. Rome chopped Macedon into four separate republics and strictly forbade marriage and trade across the new borders. Roman troops ruthlessly stamped out all opposition, destroying seventy cities that objected to Rome's presence and selling 150,000 people into slavery.

When some Greek cities tried to pull away from Roman control and assert their independence, the heel of Rome came down hard. To set an example of the danger of resistance, the Roman commander Mummius burned the opulent city of Corinth to the ground and enslaved its inhabitants. For weeks afterward, ships carrying plunder and slaves from the fallen city docked in Italy.

The Encounter Between Greek and Roman Culture

Romans had interacted with Greek culture to some degree for centuries, first indirectly through Etruscan intermediaries, and then through direct contact with Greek communities in southern Italy and Sicily. During the second century B.C.E., when Rome acquired the eastern Mediterranean through its wars with Macedon, the pace of Hellenism's intellectual influence on Rome accelerated. In addition to fine statues and paintings, Greek ideas about literature, art, philosophy, rhetoric, and education poured into Rome after the Macedonian wars.

This Hellenistic legacy challenged many Roman assumptions about the world. But there was a paradox in the reaction of Roman aristocrats to Hellenism. Many noblemen in Rome felt threatened by the novelty of Hellenistic ideas. They preferred to maintain their conservative traditions of public life and thought. They also wanted to present to the world the image of a strong and independent Roman culture, untainted by traditions from other cultures. Thus during the second century B.C.E., Romans occasionally tried to expel Greek philosophers from their city because they worried that Greek culture might corrupt traditional Roman values. At the same time, many Romans truly admired the sophistication of Greek political thought, art, and literature, and they wished to participate in the Hellenistic community.

Consequently many aristocrats learned Greek but refused to speak it while on official business in the East. While Latin remained the language spoken in the Senate house, senators hired Greek tutors to instruct their sons at home in philosophy, literature, science and the arts, and Greek intellectuals found a warm welcome from Rome's upper class. Cato the Censor, the senator who had insisted that Rome destroy Carthage, embodied the paradox of maintaining public distance from Greek culture while privately cherishing it. He cultivated an appearance of forthrightness and honesty, traditional Roman values that he claimed were threatened by Greek culture. He publicly denounced Greek oratory as unmanly, while drawing upon his deep knowledge of Greek rhetoric and literature to write his speeches praising Roman culture.

Before their exposure to the Hellenistic world in the second century B.C.E., Romans had little interest in literature. Their written efforts consisted mainly of inscriptions of laws and treaties on bronze plaques hung from the outer walls of public buildings. Families kept records of the funeral eulogies of their ancestors, while priests maintained simple lists of events and religious festivals. By ca. 240 B.C.E., Livius Andronicus, a former Greek slave, began to translate Greek dramas into Latin. In 220 B.C.E., a Roman senator, Quintus Fabius Pictor, wrote a history of Rome in the Greek language—the first major Roman prose work. In the next century, Polybius, a Greek historian who stood watching with Scipio Aemilianus while Carthage burned, made a major contribution to the writing of Roman history. Taken to Rome from Greece as a hostage in the 160s B.C.E., Polybius came to realize the futility of opposing Roman force. His *History,* written in the analytical tradition of the Greek historian Thucydides, traces Rome's astounding rise to world dominance in a mere fifty-three years and includes moralizing attacks on the abuse of power.

Hellenistic culture also had a major impact on Roman drama. Two Roman playwrights, Plautus (ca. 250–184 B.C.E.) and Terence (ca. 190–159 B.C.E.), took their inspiration from Hellenistic New Comedy and injected some fun into Roman literature. Their surviving works offer entertaining glimpses into the pitfalls of everyday life while also reinforcing the aristocratic values of the rulers of Rome's vast new domains.

Many educated Romans found Greek philosophy extremely attractive. The theory of matter advanced by the Hellenistic philosopher Epicurus, whose ethical philosophy we have already discussed, gained wide acceptance among Romans. Epicurus believed that everything has a natural cause: that "nothing comes from nothing." Romans learned about Epicurus's theories of matter and the infinity of the universe from the poem *On the Nature of the Universe* by the Roman poet Lucretius (d. ca. 51 B.C.E.), who wrote in Latin. The Hellenistic ethical philosophy that held the greatest appeal to Romans was Stoicism, because it encouraged an active public life. Stoic emphasis on the mastery of human difficulties appealed to aristocratic Romans' sense of duty and dignity. The great Roman orator and politician Marcus Tullius Cicero (106–43 B.C.E.), in particular, combined Stoic ideas in a highly personal yet fully Roman way. Cicero stressed moral behavior in political life while urging the attainment of a broad education. Cicero's high-minded devotion to the Republic won him the enmity of unscrupulous politicians. He was murdered in 43 B.C.E. because he made a series of public speeches accusing Antony of being a threat to Republican freedom.

Despite their openness to Greek philosophy, many members of the Roman ruling elite objected to foreign religious practices. In 186 B.C.E., for example, the Senate suppressed the popular orgiastic cult of the wine god Bacchus, not simply to protect public morals, as they claimed, but to demonstrate and extend their authority over religious worship. Nevertheless, at crucial moments Rome welcomed foreign gods. In 204 B.C.E., two years before the end of the war with Hannibal, the Senate imported the image of the nature goddess Cybele, called the Great Mother, to Rome in order to inspire and unify the city. The cult of Cybele flourished in the Hellenistic kingdom of Pergamum, where devotees worshiped her in the form of an ancient and holy rock. A committee of leading citizens brought this sacred boulder to a new temple on the Palatine Hill amid wild rejoicing. When the ship carrying the rock got stuck in the Tiber River, legend has it that a noble lady, Claudia Quinta, towed the ship with her sash. Not only did Rome defeat Hannibal soon after the arrival of Cybele's sacred stone, but the move cemented Roman relations with Pergamum.

The massive infusion of Hellenistic art following the Macedonian wars inevitably affected public taste. The most prestigious works of art decorated public shrines and spaces throughout the city. Many treasures went to private collectors. Greek artists soon moved to Rome to enjoy the patronage of wealthy Romans. Although copyists made replicas of Greek masterpieces, distinctively Roman artistic styles also emerged, just as they did in rhetoric, literature, philosophy, and history writing. In portrait sculpture, especially, a style developed that unflinchingly depicted all the wrinkles of experience on a person's face. In this way the venerable Roman tradition of carving ancestral busts merged with Greek art.

Circular Temple

This circular temple from the city of Rome near the Tiber River dates to the late second century B.C.E. It is the earliest surviving marble temple in Rome. The plan of the temple as well as the original marble of the columns and much of the rest of the building came from Greece.

In architecture, the magnificent temple of Fortune at Praeneste (first century B.C.E.), a town near Rome, combined Italian and Hellenistic concepts to produce the first great monument demonstrating a genuinely Greco-Roman style. By the end of the Republic, Romans had gained enough confidence to adopt the intellectual heritage of Greece and put it to their own ends without fear of seeming "too Greek."

Life in the Roman Republic

During the Hellenistic Age, Rome prospered from the acquisition of new territories. A small number of influential families dominated political life, sometimes making decisions about war from which they could win wealth and prestige. The Roman Republic remained strong because these ruling families took pains to limit the amount of power any one man or extended political family might attain.

Patrons and Clients

The ruling families of Rome established political networks that extended their influence through all levels of Roman society. These relationships depended on the traditional Roman institution of patrons and clients°. By exercising

A Corrupt Roman Governor Is Convicted of Extortion

Governors sent by the Roman Senate to rule the provinces wielded absolute power, which often corrupted them. One such man was Gaius Verres, who was convicted in 70 B.C.E. in a court in Rome for his flagrant abuse of power while governor of Sicily. The courtroom drama in which Verres was found guilty reveals one of the deepest flaws of the Roman Republic: the unprincipled exploitation of lands under Roman control. It also reveals one of Rome's greatest strengths: the presence of men of high ethical standards who believed in honest government and fair treatment of Roman subjects. The trial and its result reveals Republican Rome at its best and worst.

While governor from 73 to 71 B.C.E., Verres had looted Sicily with shocking thoroughness. In his pursuit of gold and Greek art, Verres tortured and sometimes killed Roman citizens. His outraged victims employed the young and ambitious lawyer Marcus Tullius Cicero (106–43 B.C.E.) to prosecute Verres. They could not have chosen a better advocate.

The prosecution of Verres marks the beginning of Cicero's illustrious career as one of the most active politicians and certainly the greatest orator of the Republic. Cicero also stands as one of the most influential political philosophers of Western civilization, one who hated the corruption of political life and opposed tyranny in any form. His many works have influenced political thinkers from antiquity to the present.

In the Roman Republic, only senators and equestrians between ages 30 and 60 could serve on juries for civil crimes such as those committed by Verres. All adult male citizens had the right to bring a case to court, but women had less freedom to do so. After swearing oaths of good faith, accusers read the charges in the presence of the accused, who in turn agreed to accept the decision of the court.

When trials began, the prosecutor was expected to be present, but the accused could decline to attend. The prosecution and the defense both produced evidence, then cross-examined witnesses. Since a Roman lawyer could discuss any aspect of the defendant's personal or public life, character assassination became an important—and amusing—rhetorical tool.

After deliberating, the jury delivered its verdict and the judge gave the penalty required by law, generally fines or periods of exile. No provisions for appeal existed, but pardon could be obtained by a legislative act.

Cicero worked this system to his advantage in his prosecution of Verres. He nimbly quashed an attempt to delay the trial until 69 B.C.E., when the president of the court would be a crony of Verres. Then, with a combination of ringing oratory and irrefutable evidence of Verres's crimes, Cicero made his case. The following excerpt from his speech shows Cicero's mastery of persuasive rhetoric:

> Judges: at this grave crisis in the history of our country, you have been offered a peculiarly desirable gift . . . For you have been given a unique chance to make your Senatorial Order less unpopular, and to set right the damaged reputation of these courts. A belief has taken root which is having a fatal effect on our nation—and which to us who are senators, in particular, threatens grave peril. This belief is on everyone's tongue, at Rome and even in foreign countries. It is this: that in these courts, with their present membership, even the worst criminal will never be convicted provided that he has money. . . . And at this very juncture Gaius Verres has been brought to trial. Here is a man whose life and actions the world has already condemned—yet whose enormous fortune, according to his own loudly expressed hopes, has already brought him acquittal! Pronounce a just and scrupulous verdict against Verres and you will keep the good name which ought always to be yours. . . . I spent fifty days on a careful investigation of the entire island of Sicily; I got to know every document, every wrong suffered either by a community or an individual. . . .
>
> For three long years he so thoroughly despoiled and pillaged the province that its restoration to its previous state is out of the question. . . . All the property that anyone in Sicily still has for his own today is merely what happened to escape the attention of this avaricious lecher, or survived his glutted appetites. . . . It was an appalling disgrace for our country.
>
> . . . In the first stage of the trial, then, my charge is this. I accuse Gaius Verres of committing acts of lechery and brutality against the citizens and allies of Rome, and many crimes against God and man. I claim that he has illegally taken from Sicily sums amounting to forty million sesterces. By the witnesses and documents, public and private, which I am going to cite, I shall convince you that these charges are true.[2]

Republican Portrait of Cicero

This portrait of Cicero captures his uncompromising personality. The style of depicting every wrinkle conforms both to Hellenistic interest in psychological portraiture and traditional Roman directness. In the Republican period this type of portraiture was enormously popular.

Cicero's speech was persuasive, and the jury found Verres guilty. Verres went into exile in Marseilles to avoid his sentence, but he did not avoid punishment altogether. Justice—relentless and ironic—caught up with him some years later during the civil wars that followed Julius Caesar's death. Mark Antony, who was also a connoisseur of other people's wealth, wanted Verres's art collection for himself and so put Verres's name on a death list to obtain it. The former governor of Sicily was murdered in 43 B.C.E.

In his prosecution of Verres, Cicero delivered more than an indictment of one corrupt man; for a brief moment he revealed some of the deepest, fatal flaws of the Roman Republic. The trial inspired some short-term reforms, but not until the reforms of the emperor Augustus did the relationship between Roman administrators and provincial populations become more fair.

Questions of Justice

1. What does Verres's trial reveal about weaknesses in the Roman Republic?
2. Cicero's speech illustrates his disdain for corruption and tyranny. What are the tensions between personal morality and the requirements of governing a large empire?

Taking It Further

Gruen, Erich S. *The Last Generation of the Roman Republic.* 1974. A magisterial analysis of the Republic's decline, with emphasis on legal affairs.

Rawson, Elizabeth. *Cicero, A Portrait.* 1975. This book gives a balanced account of Cicero's life.

influence on behalf of a social subordinate, a powerful man (the patron) would bind that man (the client) to him in anticipation of future support. In this way complex webs of personal interdependency influenced the entire Roman social system. The patron-client system operated at every level of society, and it was customary for a man of influence to receive his clients on matters of business at his home the first thing in the morning. In a modest household the discussion might involve everyday business such as shipping fish, arranging a marriage, or making a loan. But in the mansion of a Roman aristocrat a patron might be more interested in forging a political alliance. When several patron-client groups joined forces, they became significant political factions under the leadership of one patron.

Pyramids of Wealth and Power

Like its political organization, Rome's social organization demonstrated a well-defined hierarchy. By the first century B.C.E., a new, elite class of political leaders had emerged in Rome, composed of both the original patrician families and wealthy plebeians who had been able to attain membership in the Senate through their service in the various public offices. The men of this leadership class dominated the Senate and formed the inner circle of government. From their ranks came most of the consuls. They set foreign and domestic policy, led armies to war, held the main magistracies, and siphoned off the lion's share of the Republic's resources.

Beneath this elite group came the equestrian class. Equestrians normally abstained from public office, but were often tied to political leaders by personal obligation. They were primarily businessmen who prospered from the financial opportunities that Rome's expansion provided. For example, during the Republic, equestrian businessmen could bid on contracts to collect taxes in different areas. The man awarded the contract was permitted to collect taxes—with few restraints on his methods. After paying the Senate the amount agreed upon in the contract, he could keep any other tax funds that he had gathered. Many equestrians accumulated fortunes in this way.

Next in rank came the mass of citizens who were known as plebeians. As we have seen, this group had acquired political representation and influence, but the Plebeian Assembly had gradually come under the control of politicians who were the clients of aristocratic patrons. These wealthy plebeian politicians, who had become members of a new ruling class, had little interest in the condition of the large body of poor plebeians, which now had no direct means to express its political will. The demands of army service kept many plebeians who had small farms away from their land for long periods of time. Rich investors seized this opportunity to create huge estates by grabbing the bankrupt farms and replacing the free farmers with slaves captured in war. Sometimes impoverished plebeians became dependent tenant farmers on land they had once

owned themselves. As a result, these plebeians turned more and more to leaders who would protect them and give them land.

Rome's Italian allies had even fewer rights than the plebeians, despite their service in the Roman armies. Although millions of allies inhabited lands controlled by Rome, only a privileged few of the local elites received Roman citizenship. The rest could only hope for the goodwill of Roman officials.

At the bottom of the Roman hierarchy were slaves. By the first century B.C.E., about two million slaves captured in war or born in captivity lived in Italy and Sicily, amounting to about one-third of the population. Romans considered the slaves to be pieces of property, "talking tools," whom their owners could exploit at will. Freed slaves owed legal obligations to their former masters and were their clients. The brutal inequities of this system led to violence. The slave gangs who farmed vast estates in Sicily revolted first. In 135 B.C.E. they began an ill-fated struggle for freedom that lasted three years and involved more than 200,000 slaves.

Thirty years later another unsuccessful outburst began in southern Italy and Sicily because slave owners refused to comply with a senatorial decree to release any slaves who once had been free allies of Rome. 30,000 slaves took up arms between 104 and 101 B.C.E. The most destructive revolt occurred in Italy during the years from 73 to 71 B.C.E. An army of more than 100,000 slaves led by the Thracian gladiator Spartacus (gladiators were slaves who fought for public entertainment) battled eight Roman legions totaling about 50,000 men before being crushed by the superior Roman military organization.

The Roman Family

A Roman *familia* typically included not just the husband, wife, and unmarried children, but also their slaves and often freedmen and others who were dependent on the household. Legitimate marriages required the agreement of both husband and wife. Women usually married at puberty, and men did so in their twenties. In most families only two or three children survived infancy. Although Roman men could have only one wife at a time, men frequently cohabited with women to whom they were not married (concubines). Having a concubine was perfectly acceptable, but doing so was legal only if both parties involved had no living spouse.

The Roman family mirrored the patterns of authority and dependency found in the political arena. Just as a patron commanded the support of his clients regardless of their status in public life, so the male head of the household directed the destiny of all his subordinates within the *familia*. A man ruled his *familia* with full authority over the purse strings and all of his descendants until he died. The head of the family, or *paterfamilias*, held power of life and death over his wife, children, and slaves, though few men exercised this power. In practice, women and grown children often had a great deal of independence, and aristocratic women often exerted a strong influence in political life, though always from behind the scenes.

Upper-class Romans placed great value on the continuity of the family name, family traditions, and control of family property through the generations. For these reasons they often adopted males, even of adult age, to be heirs, especially if they had no legitimate sons of their own. Legitimate offspring always took the name of their father, and in case of divorce, which could be easily obtained, continued to live with him. Illegitimate offspring stayed with the mother.

With very few exceptions Roman women remained legally dependent on a male relative. In the most common form of marriage, a wife remained under the formal control of the *paterfamilias* to whom she belonged before her marriage—in most cases, her father. In practice this meant that the wife retained control of her own property and the inheritance she had received from her father. A husband in this sort of marriage would have to be careful to avoid the anger of his wife's father or brothers, and so he might be inclined to treat his wife more justly. Another form of marriage brought the wife under the full control of her husband after the wedding. She had to worship the family gods of her husband's household and accept his ancestors as her own. If her husband died, one of his male relatives became the woman's legal protector.

The stability of family life through the generations desired by free Romans was impossible for slaves to attain. Former female slaves (freedwomen) remained tied to their former masters with bonds of dependency and obligation. Roman law did not recognize marriage between slaves. Some Roman handbooks explaining how to use slaves to maximum advantage advocated letting slaves establish conjugal arrangements. Owners could, however, shatter such alliances by selling the enslaved partners or their offspring.

Beginnings of the Roman Revolution

■ **What political and social changes brought the Roman Republic to an end?**

The inequalities of wealth and power in Roman society led to the disintegration of the Republic. The rapid acquisition of territories and enormous wealth overseas heightened those differences. Roman reformers' attempts to face the new economic realities met with fierce resistance from those who profited the most from imperial rule: politicians, governors, high military personnel, and businessmen. These men sought personal glory and political advantage even if it came at the Republic's expense. Their quest for political prominence through military adventure, coupled with deep-seated flaws of political institutions, eventually overwhelmed the Republic's political structure and brought about a revolution—a decisive, fundamental change in the political system.

The Gracchi

During the second century B.C.E., more and more citizen farmers in Italy lost their fields to powerful landholders, who replaced them with slaves on their estates. As a result, the slave population of Italy increased dramatically. Some members of the political elite feared the danger inherent in these developments. If citizen farmers failed to meet the property requirements for military service and pay for their own weapons, as they traditionally had done, Rome would lose its supply of recruits for its legions.

Two young brothers, Tiberius and Gaius Gracchus, attempted some reforms. Although their mother was an aristocrat (the daughter of Scipio Africanus), she had married a wealthy plebeian. Thus, the brothers were legally plebeian, and they sought influence through the tribunate, an office limited to plebeians. As a tribune, Tiberius Gracchus (162–133 B.C.E.) convinced the Plebeian Assembly to pass a bill limiting the amount of public land that one man could possess. The new law required that the excess land from wealthy landholders be redistributed in small lots to poor citizens. While the land redistribution was in progress, conservative senators ignited a firestorm of opposition to Tiberius Gracchus. He responded by running for a second term as tribune, which was a break with precedent. Fearing revolution, a clique of senators in 133 B.C.E. arranged for assassins to club Tiberius to death. Land redistribution did not cease, but a terrible precedent of public violence had been set.

A decade later, when Tiberius's brother Gaius Gracchus became tribune in 123 B.C.E., he turned his attention to the problem of extortion in the provinces. With no checks on their authority, many corrupt governors forced provincials to give them money, valuable goods, and crops. Gaius Gracchus attempted to stop these abuses. In an attempt to dilute the power of corrupt provincial administrators chosen from the Senate and to win the political support of equestrians in Rome, he permitted equestrian tax collectors to operate in the provinces and to serve on juries that tried extortion cases. Gaius also tried to speed up land redistribution. But when he attempted to give citizenship to Rome's Italian allies in order to protect them from having their land confiscated by Romans, he lost the support of the Roman people, who did not wish to share the benefits of citizenship with non-Romans. In 121 B.C.E. Gaius committed suicide rather than allow himself to be murdered by a mob sent by his senatorial foes.

The ruthless suppression of the Gracchi (the Latin plural form of *Gracchus*) and their supporters lit the fuse of political and social revolution at Rome. By attempting to effect change through the Plebeian Assembly, the Gracchi unwittingly paved the way for less scrupulous aristocrats to seek power by falsely claiming to represent the interests of the poor. The introduction of assassinations into the public debate signaled the end of political consensus among the oligarchy. Rivalry among the elite combined with the desperation of the poor in an explosive blend, with the army as the wild card. If an unscrupulous politician were to join forces with poverty-stricken soldiers, the Republic would be in peril.

Gaius Marius (157–86 B.C.E.) became the first Roman general to play this wild card. He rose to power when the angry Roman poor made him their champion. Despite his equestrian origins, this experienced general won the consulship in 107 B.C.E. A special law of the Plebeian Assembly put him in command of the legions fighting King Jugurtha in Numidia in North Africa, and he brought the war to a quick and successful conclusion. Then in response to a new threat from Germanic tribes seeking to invade Italy, Marius trained a new army and trounced the invaders.

In organizing his army Marius made some radical changes. He eliminated the property requirement for enlistment, thereby opening the ranks to the very poorest citizens in the countryside and in Rome. These soldiers swore an oath of loyalty to their commander in chief, who in return promised them farms after a victorious campaign. Marius's reforms put generals in the crossfire of the long-running political struggle between the Senate and the Plebeian Assembly, the two institutions authorized to allocate lands won in war.

Marius achieved great personal power, but he did not use it against the institutions of the Republic. When he left public life in old age, the Roman Republic lurched ahead to its next major crisis: a revolt of the Italian allies.

War in Italy and Abroad

In 90 B.C.E. Rome's loyal allies in Italy could no longer endure being treated as inferiors when it came to distribution of land and booty. They launched a revolt against Rome known as the Social War (from the Latin word *socii*, which means "allies"). The confederation of allies demanded not independence but participation in the Roman Republic. They wanted full citizenship rights because they had been partners in all of Rome's wars and thus felt entitled to share in the fruits of victory. The allies lost the war, but soon afterward Rome granted citizenship to all Italians. Rome's new citizens quickly became a potent force in Roman political life. Their presence in the political arena tilted the political scales away from the wealthy in Rome toward the population of Italy in general.

DOCUMENT

The Ruinous Effects of Conquest

Roman conquests in Italy damaged the economy of newly captured rural areas. The following excerpt from the work of the Roman historian Appian, written in the second century C.E., describes the process of Roman settlement in newly taken territories in Italy, and the consequences of that settlement. The reforms of the Gracchi were intended to correct some of these problems.

The Romans, as they subdued the Italian peoples successively in war, seized a part of their lands and built towns there, or established their own colonies in already existing towns, using them as garrisons. Of the land thus acquired by war they assigned the cultivated part forthwith to settlers, or leased or sold it. Since they had no leisure as yet to allot the part which then lay desolated by war (this was generally the greater part), they proclaimed that in the meantime those who were willing to work it might do so for a share of the yearly crops—a tenth of the grain and a fifth of the fruit. From those who kept flocks, a tax was fixed for the animals, both oxen and small cattle. This they did in order to multiply the Italian race, which they considered to be the most laborious of peoples, so that that they might have plenty of allies at home. But the very opposite happened; for the rich, getting possession of the greater part of the undistributed lands, and being emboldened by the lapse of time to believe that they would never be dispossessed, and adding to their holding the small farms of their poor neighbors, partly by purchase and partly by force, came to cultivate vast tracts instead of single estates, using for this purpose slaves as laborers and herdsmen, lest free laborers be drawn from agriculture into the army.... Thus the governing class became enormously rich and the number of slaves multiplied throughout the country, while the Italian peoples dwindled in numbers and strength...

Source: From *A History of Rome through the Fifth Century, Volume 1, The Republic*, edited by A. H. M. Jones (New York: Walker and Company, 1968), p. 104.

The Social War in Italy was followed by wars abroad. The aristocrat Lucius Cornelius Sulla (138–78 B.C.E.), consul in 88 B.C.E., was setting out with an army to put down a serious provincial revolt in Asia Minor when the Plebeian Assembly turned command of his troops over to Marius, whose military reforms had aided the poor. In response, Sulla marched from southern Italy to Rome and reestablished his control by placing his own supporters into positions of authority in the Senate, the Plebeian Assembly, and various administrative offices.

However, only a year later, when Sulla returned to Asia Minor to resume command of the war against King Mithradates of Pontus, Marius and the other consul, Cinna, won back political control of Rome. They declared Sulla an outlaw and slaughtered his supporters. When Sulla returned to Italy in 82 B.C.E., at the head of a triumphant and loyal army, he seized Rome after a battle in which about 60,000 Roman soldiers died, and then murdered 3,000 of his political opponents. The Senate named him dictator, which gave him complete power. With the support of the aristocratic Senate, whose power he hoped to restore, Sulla crippled the political power of the plebeians. In particular, he restricted the powers of tribunes to propose legislation because they had stirred up so much political instability for fifty years. After restoring the peace and the institutions of the state, Sulla surprised many people by resigning as dictator in 80 B.C.E. Like Marius, Sulla was unwilling to destroy the Republic's institutions for the sake of his own ambition. It was enough for him to have restored peace and the pre-eminence of the Senate. Nevertheless, he had set a precedent for using armies in political rivalries. In the next fifty years the Senate conspicuously failed to restrain generals backed by public armies, thereby contributing to the collapse of the Republic.

The First Triumvirate

The Roman Republic's final downward spiral of social turmoil was provoked by three men: Pompey (Gnaeus Pompeius, 106–48 B.C.E.), Marcus Licinius Crassus (ca. 115–53 B.C.E.), and Gaius Julius Caesar (100–44 B.C.E.). Pompey, the general who suppressed a revolt in Spain, and Crassus, the wealthiest man in Rome who had been one of Sulla's lieutenants, joined forces to crush the slave revolt of Spartacus in 71 B.C.E. Backed by their armies, they then coerced the Centuriate Assembly into naming them consuls for 70 B.C.E., even though Pompey was legally too young and had not yet held the prerequisite junior offices.

During their consulship, Pompey and Crassus made modest changes to Sulla's reforms. They permitted the tribunes to propose laws again and let equestrians serve on juries. After their year in office they retired without making further demands. Pompey continued his military career. He received a special command in 67 B.C.E. to clear pirates from the Mediterranean in order to protect Roman trade. The following year Pompey crushed another rebellion in Asia Minor. He reorganized Asia Minor and territories in the Middle East, creating new provinces and more client kingdoms subservient to Rome.

When Pompey returned to Rome he asked the Senate to grant land to his victorious troops. The Senate, jealous of his success and afraid of the power he would gain as the patron of so many troops, would not comply. To gain land for his soldiers and have his political arrangements in Asia

CHRONOLOGY

Social Conflict in Rome and Italy

133 B.C.E.	Tiberius Gracchus initiates reforms
123–122 B.C.E.	Gaius Gracchus initiates reforms
107 B.C.E.	Marius serves his first consulship
104–100 B.C.E.	Marius holds consecutive consulships
90–88 B.C.E.	Rome fights "Social War" with Italian allies
88 B.C.E.	Sulla takes Rome
82–80 B.C.E.	Sulla serves as dictator
77–71 B.C.E.	Pompey fights Celts in Spain
73–71 B.C.E.	Spartacus's slave revolt
70 B.C.E.	Cicero prosecutes Verres in court

Minor and the Middle East ratified, Pompey made an alliance with two men even more ambitious and less scrupulous than he: his old ally Crassus and Gaius Julius Caesar, the ambitious descendant of an ancient patrician family. The three formed an informal alliance historians call the First Triumvirate°. With their influence now combined, no man or institution could oppose them. Caesar obtained the consulship in 59 B.C.E., despite the objections of many senators. By using illegal means that would return to haunt him, he directed the Senate to ratify Pompey's arrangements in the Middle East and Asia Minor and to grant land to his troops. He arranged for Crassus's clients, the equestrian tax collectors, to have their financial problems resolved at public expense.

As a reward for his efforts on behalf of the triumvirate, the perpetually debt-ridden Caesar arranged to receive the governorship of the Po Valley and the Illyrian coast for five years after his consulship ended. Later he extended that term for ten years. During this time, he planned to enrich himself at the expense of the provincials. As he set out for his governorship, he assumed command of Transalpine Gaul (northwest of the Alps) when its governor died. This put Caesar in a position to operate militarily in all of Gaul—and ultimately to conquer it.

Julius Caesar and the End of the Republic

Caesar's determination to conquer Gaul lay in pursuing personal advantage. He knew that he would win glory, wealth, and prestige in Rome by conquering new lands, and so he promptly began a war (58–50 B.C.E.) against the

Celtic tribes of Transalpine Gaul. A military genius, Caesar chronicled his ruthless tactics and military successes in his *Commentaries on the Gallic War,* as famous today for its elegant Latin as for its unflinching glimpse of

The Career of Julius Caesar

Roman methods and justifications of conquest. In eight years Caesar conquered the area of modern France and Belgium, turning these territories into Roman provinces. He even briefly invaded Britain. His intrusion into Celtic lands led to their eventual Romanization. The French language developed from the Latin spoken by Roman soldiers. Similarly Spanish, Italian, Portuguese, and Romanian also derived from the tongue of Roman conquerors and are called "Romance" languages.

Meanwhile, the other members of the triumvirate, Crassus and Pompey, also sought military glory. The wealthy Crassus raised an army out of his own pocket, reputedly asserting, "If you can't afford to pay for an army, you shouldn't command it!" His attempt to conquer the Parthians, the successors to the Persian Empire, ended in disaster in 53 B.C.E. in Syria. The Parthians killed Crassus, destroyed his army, and captured the military insignia (metal eagles on staffs, called standards) that each legion proudly carried into battle. Pompey again assumed the governorship of Spain, but stayed in Rome while subordinates waged war there against Spain's Celtic inhabitants.

In Rome, a group of senators grew fearful of Caesar's power, ambitions, and arrogance. They appealed to Pompey for assistance, and he brought the armies loyal to him to the aid of the Senate against Caesar. The Senate then asked Caesar to lay down his command in Gaul and return to Rome. Caesar knew that if he complied with this request he would be indicted on charges of improper conduct or corruption as soon as he returned to Rome. Facing certain conviction, Caesar refused to return for a trial. In 49 B.C.E. he left Gaul and marched south with his loyal troops against the forces of the Senate in Rome. Recognizing the enormity of his gamble ("I've thrown the dice!" he said when he crossed the Rubicon River, the boundary of land under direct control of the Senate), he deliberately plunged Rome into civil war. Because of his victories in Gaul and his generosity to the people of Rome, Caesar could pose as the people's champion while seeking absolute power for himself. Intimidated by Caesar's forces and public support, Pompey hastily withdrew to Greece, but Caesar overtook and defeated him at Pharsalus, a town in Thessaly, in 48 B.C.E. When Pompey fled to Egypt high officials of the Ptolemaic pharaoh's court immediately murdered him to win Caesar's favor.

It took Caesar more than two years to complete his victory over the Senate and return to Italy in 45 B.C.E. Back in Rome, he had himself proclaimed dictator for life and assumed complete control over all aspects of government, flagrantly disregarding the traditions of the Republic. Because

he did not live to fully implement his plan, his long-term goals for the Roman state remain unclear, but he probably intended to establish some version of Hellenistic monarchy.

Once in power, Caesar permanently ended the autonomy of the Senate. He enlarged the Senate from 600 (its size at the time of Sulla) to 900 men, and then filled it with his supporters. He also established military colonies in Spain, North Africa, and Gaul to provide land for his veterans and to secure those territories. He adjusted the chaotic Republican calendar by adding one day every fourth year, creating a year of 365.25 days. The resulting "Julian" calendar lasted until the sixteenth century C.E. He regularized gold coinage and urban administration and planned a vast public library. At his death, plans for a major campaign against Parthia were underway, suggesting that conquest would have remained a basic feature of his rule.

Caesar seriously miscalculated by assuming he could win the support of his enemies by showing clemency to them and by making administrative changes that disregarded Republican precedent. These changes earned Caesar the resentment of traditionalist senators who failed to recognize that the Republic could never be restored. On March 15, 44 B.C.E., a group of idealistic senators, led by Cassius and Brutus, stabbed Caesar to death at a Senate meeting. The assassins claimed that they wanted to restore the Republic, but in reality they had only unleashed another brutal civil war.

Marcus Antonius (Mark Antony), who had been Caesar's right-hand man, stepped forward to oppose the conspirators. He was soon joined by Octavian, Caesar's grand-nephew and legal heir. Though Octavian was only 19, he gained control of some of Caesar's legions and compelled the Senate to name him consul. Marcus Lepidus, commander of Caesar's cavalry, joined Mark Antony and Octavian to form the Second Triumvirate°. The new trio coerced the Senate into granting them power to rule Rome legally.

At the battle of Philippi, a town in Macedonia, in 42 B.C.E., forces of the Second Triumvirate crushed the army of the senators who had assassinated Caesar. But soon Antony, Octavian, and Lepidus began to struggle among themselves for absolute authority. Lepidus soon dropped out of the contest, while Antony and Octavian maneuvered for control of Rome. Reluctant to begin open warfare, they agreed to separate spheres of influence. Octavian took Italy and Rome's western provinces, while Antony took the eastern provinces.

In Egypt, Antony joined forces with Cleopatra VII, the last descendant of the Hellenistic monarch Ptolemy. Both stood to gain from this alliance: Antony would gain the resources of Egypt in his quest to gain complete power over the eastern provinces, while Cleopatra would strengthen her rule in Egypt. In response to this alliance, Octavian launched a vicious propaganda campaign. Posing as the conservative protector of Roman tradition, he accused

Antony of surrendering Roman values and territory to an evil foreign seductress. The inevitable war broke out in 31 B.C.E. At the battle of Actium, in Greece, Octavian's troops defeated Antony and Cleopatra's land and naval forces. The couple fled to Alexandria, in Egypt, where they committed suicide a year later.

The 31-year-old Octavian now stood as absolute master of the Roman world. He had a clear vision of the problems that had destroyed the Republic, and from its ashes he planned to rebuild the Roman state. Under the leadership of Octavian, who came to be known as the emperor Augustus, Rome created a new political system, the Roman Empire, in which Octavian had unprecedented power over a vast geographical area.

The new world order that Octavian created brought an end to the Hellenistic Age. Rome now ruled all the lands that Alexander the Great had conquered, except for Persia and the territories farther to the east, and Hellenistic culture would now have to accommodate the realities of Roman rule. As we will see in the next chapter, Octavian succeeded where Alexander had failed: He created a world empire that had the infrastructure it needed to endure, and the peaceful conditions that enabled its culture to flourish and spread.

CHRONOLOGY

The Collapse of the Roman Republic

60 B.C.E.	The First Triumvirate is established
58–50 B.C.E.	Julius Caesar conquers northern and central Gaul
53 B.C.E.	Crassus is killed in the Parthian War
49 B.C.E.	Caesar crosses Rubicon River and begins civil war
48 B.C.E.	Battle of Pharsalus; Pompey is killed in Egypt
45 B.C.E.	Caesar wins civil war
47–44 B.C.E.	Caesar serves as dictator
44 B.C.E.	Caesar is murdered; civil war breaks out
43 B.C.E.	The Second Triumvirate is formed; Cicero is murdered
42 B.C.E.	Battle of Philippi; Caesar's assassins are defeated
31 B.C.E.	Octavian defeats Antony and Cleopatra and gains absolute power

Conclusion

Defining the West in the Hellenistic Age

During the Hellenistic Age the cultural and geographical boundaries of what would later be called the West began to take shape. These boundaries encompassed the regions where Hellenistic culture penetrated and had a lasting influence. The lands within the empire of Alexander the Great, all of which lay to the east of Greece and Egypt, formed the core of this cultural realm, but the Hellenistic world also extended westward across the Mediterranean, embracing the lands ruled by Carthage from North Africa to Spain. Hellenism also reached the edges of the lands inhabited by Celtic peoples. Most of all, Hellenistic culture left a distinctive mark on Roman civilization in Italy. In all these locations Greek culture interacted with those of the areas it penetrated, and the synthesis that resulted became one of the main foundations of Western civilization.

During the period of the Roman Empire, which will be the subject of the next chapter, a new blend of Hellenistic and Latin cultures, in which Hellenism was an important but not the dominant component, took shape. The geographical arena within which this culture flourished was that of the vast Roman Empire, covering a large part of Europe, North Africa, and the Middle East. The culture that characterized this empire gave a new definition to what we now call the West.

Suggestions for Further Reading

For a comprehensive list of suggested readings, please go to www.ablongman.com/levack2e/chapter4

Boardman, John, Jasper Griffin, and Oswyn Murray, eds. *Greece and the Hellenistic World.* [*The Oxford History of the Classical World.*] 1988. A synthesis of all aspects of Hellenistic life, with excellent illustrations and bibliography.

Cohn, Norman. *Cosmos, Chaos, and the World to Come: The Ancient Roots of Apocalyptic Faith.* 1993. This brilliant study explains the development of ideas about the end of the world in the cultures of the ancient world.

Cornell, T. J. *The Beginnings of Rome: Italy and Rome from the Bronze Age to the Punic Wars (ca. 1000–264 B.C.).* 1996. A synthesis of the latest evidence with many important new interpretations.

Crawford, Michael. *The Roman Republic,* 2nd ed. 1992. This overview by a leading scholar lays a strong foundation for further study.

Cunliffe, Barry. *The Ancient Celts.* 1997. This source analyzes the archaeological evidence for the Celtic Iron Age, with many illustrations and maps.

Cunliffe, Barry, ed. *The Oxford Illustrated Prehistory of Europe.* 1996. A collection of well-illustrated essays on the development of European cultures from the end of the Ice Age to the Classical period.

Gardner, Jane F. *Women in Roman Law and Society.* 1986. Explains the legal position of women in the Roman world.

Green, Peter. *Alexander to Actium: The Historical Evolution of the Hellenistic Age.* 1990. A vivid interpretation of the world created by Alexander until the victory of Augustus.

Gruen, Erich S. *The Hellenistic World and the Coming of Rome.* 1984. An extremely important study of how Rome entered the eastern Mediterranean world.

Kuhrt, Amélie, and Susan Sherwin-White, eds. *Hellenism in the East: The Interaction of Greek and Non-Greek Civilizations from Syria to Central Asia After Alexander.* 1987. These studies help us understand the complexities of the interaction of Greeks and non-Greeks in the Hellenistic world.

Pollitt, J. J. *Art in the Hellenistic Age.* 1986. A brilliant interpretation of the development of Hellenistic art.

Notes

1. Athenaios, 253 D; cited and translated in J. J. Pollitt, *Art in the Hellenistic Age* (1986), 271.

2. From *Selected Works* by Cicero, translated by Michael Grant (Penguin Classics 1960, second revised edition 1971). Copyright © Michael Grant 1960, 1965, 1971. Reproduced by permission of Penguin Books Ltd.

Enclosing the West: The Early Roman Empire and Its Neighbors, 31 B.C.E.–235 C.E.

5

I N THE MIDDLE OF THE SECOND CENTURY C.E., AELIUS ARISTIDES, AN ARISTO-cratic Greek writer who held Roman citizenship, visited Rome, where he gave a long public oration in honor of the imperial capital. His words reveal what the Roman Empire meant to a wealthy, highly educated man from Rome's eastern provinces: "Rome is to the whole world what an ordinary city is to its suburbs and surrounding countryside . . . you have given up the division of nation from nation . . . you have separated the human race into Roman and non-Romans."

Aristides' description of the empire as one grand city with a unified culture set off from the "barbarian" peoples in the world is an exaggeration. Nevertheless it points to the key element of the Romans' success—a willingness to share their culture with their subjects and to assimilate them into the political and social life of the empire. Aristides understood that Roman culture flourished primarily in cities, and he believed that Roman urban life was the mark of civilization. He dismissed with a contemptuous sniff those not fortunate enough to live as Romans. In Aristides' opinion, Rome's destiny was to bring civilization to the rest of the world. His satisfied view of the Roman Empire demonstrates how successfully Rome had created a sense of common purpose among its elite citizens.

During its first two and a half centuries of existence, the Roman Empire brought cultural unity and political stability to an astonishingly diverse area stretching from the Atlantic Ocean to the Persian Gulf. Imperial rule disseminated Roman culture throughout not only the Mediterranean region and the Middle East, but also much of northwestern Europe. Within imperial Rome's parameters—intellectual, religious, political, and geographic—the basic outlines of what we call the West today were drawn.

Marcus Aurelius This magnificent bronze statue shows the emperor Marcus Aurelius (r. 161–180 C.E.) raising his right hand in a gesture of command, compelling the viewer to obey. A triumph of the art of bronze casting, this statue conveys the majesty of the Roman Empire.

This chapter examines the Roman Empire at the height of its power (ca. 31 B.C.E.–235 C.E.). We will see how its encounters with far-flung subject populations helped shape its development. Autocratic and exploitative, the Roman imperial system nonetheless provided the climate for rich developments in social, religious, and political life. Military force maintained the imperial system, but the peace and prosperity that accompanied Roman rule persuaded many subject peoples of its benefits. The new regime established a stable governing system that brought a nearly unbroken peace to the Mediterranean world for more than two centuries. Historians call this era the *Pax Romana°*, the Roman Peace. In these centuries Roman culture slowly took root across western Europe, North Africa, and the Middle East, transforming the lives of local populations. In the eyes of millions of people during these years, Rome ceased to be an unfamiliar and predatory occupying power. They came to regard Rome as a civilizing agent that provided unity and common culture. But others, particularly the slaves whose labor fueled the Roman economy and the small farmers whose taxes supported the Roman state, experienced Rome as an oppressive ruler.

This chapter analyzes imperial Rome's constantly evolving political and cultural community as three concentric circles of power—the imperial center, the provinces, and the frontiers and beyond. In the imperial center stood not only the emperor but also the Roman senate, the chief legal and administrative institutions, and the city of Rome itself, an important model of the Roman way of life. In the second circle, provincial populations struggled with the challenges raised by the imposition of Roman culture and politics and in the process contributed to the construction of a new imperial culture. The outermost circle of the empire, its frontier zones and the lands beyond, included Romans living within the empire's borders as well as the peoples who lived on the other side, but who nonetheless interacted with Rome through trading and warfare. Throughout the chapter we will explore what it meant to be a Roman in each of these concentric circles.

How did the encounters between the Romans and the peoples they conquered transform the Mediterranean world and create a Roman imperial culture? Four questions guide this exploration:

- How did the Roman imperial system develop and what roles did the emperor, senate, army, and Rome itself play in this process?
- How did provincial peoples assimilate to or resist Roman rule?
- How did Romans interact with peoples living beyond the imperial borders?
- What was the social and cultural response to the emergence and consolidation of empire?

The Imperial Center

- How did the Roman imperial system develop and what roles did the emperor, senate, army, and Rome itself play in this process?

After civil wars left the Roman Republic in ruins, a new political system emerged from its ashes. Rome continued to acquire and rule huge territories far from Italy. Its form of government, however, changed from a republic, in which members of an oligarchy competed for power that they shared by serving in elected offices, to an empire, in which one man, the emperor, held absolute power for life. Roman culture, with its strict social divisions and political structures, its distinctive forms of architecture and art, its shared intellectual and religious life, and its legal system defining the rights of citizens and subjects, was now securely anchored by an imperial system based on force (see Map 5.1).

Imperial Authority: Augustus and After

As we saw in Chapter 4, Julius Caesar's heir, Octavian, destroyed the Republic while pretending to preserve it. Octavian wrenched the state from the spiral of civil war and claimed that he had restored normal life to the Republic. In his own eyes, as well as those of a people weary of bitter civil war, Octavian was the savior of Republican Rome. In public affairs, however, nothing could have been further from the truth. Behind a carefully crafted façade of restored Republican tradition, Octavian created a Roman version of a Hellenistic monarchy, like those of Alexander the Great's successors in the eastern Mediterranean. By neutralizing all of his political enemies in the Roman Senate; vanquishing his military rivals, such as Antony and Cleopatra; and establishing an iron grip on every visible mechanism of power, Octavian succeeded where Julius Caesar and other less able Republican politicians had failed: He achieved total mastery of the political arena at Rome. No one successfully challenged his authority.

To mask his tyranny, Octavian never wore a crown and modestly referred to himself as *Princeps*, or First Citizen. He took several steps to create a political position in Rome that was all-powerful and at the same time unobtrusive. In 27 B.C.E., as he boasted in the official account of his reign, Octavian "transferred the Republic from his power into that of the Senate and the Roman people." This abdication was a carefully organized sham. In reality, he maintained absolute political control over Rome. Following his instructions, the powerless Senate showered honors on him, including the title "Augustus" (which is how we will refer to him throughout the rest of this chapter). This invented title illustrates well the political cleverness of Rome's absolute master. "Augustus" implied a uniquely exalted, god-like authority in the community, but the word had no previous associations with kingship. Augustus "accepted" the Senate's plea to remain consul and agreed to exercise control over the frontier provinces where the most troops were stationed, including Spain, Gaul, and Syria. The senators rejoiced, calling Augustus "sole savior of the entire empire."

In 23 B.C.E. Augustus took further steps to establish his paramount position. He had held the consulship every year since the end of the civil war in 31 B.C.E., but he recognized that holding the power of a consul year after year was inconsistent with his claim to have restored the Republic. So in 23 B.C.E. he renounced the consulship and shrewdly arranged for the Senate to grant him unprecedented power, but disguised by Republican trappings. He assumed the powers of a tribune, which included the right to conduct business in the Senate, the right to veto, and immunity from arrest and punishment. He could now legally intercede in all government activities and military affairs by virtue of "greater authority" granted to him by the Senate. Other generals continued to lead the legions into battle, but always in his name. Other magistrates continued to administer the state in accordance with the traditional responsibilities of their office, but no one was chosen without his approval.

Augustus selected or approved all his provincial governors. He assumed direct control over particularly rich provinces, such as Egypt, and those, such as Germany, that required a strong military presence to ward off invaders and control the recently conquered population. The Roman Senate maintained authority over peaceful provinces such as Greece and Sicily. Yet even in these provinces, Augustus intervened whenever he wished.

Map 5.1 The Roman Empire at Its Greatest Extent

The Roman Empire reached its greatest extent during the reign of Trajan (r. 98–117 C.E.). Stretching from the north of Britain to the Euphrates River, the empire brought together hundreds of distinct ethnic groups.

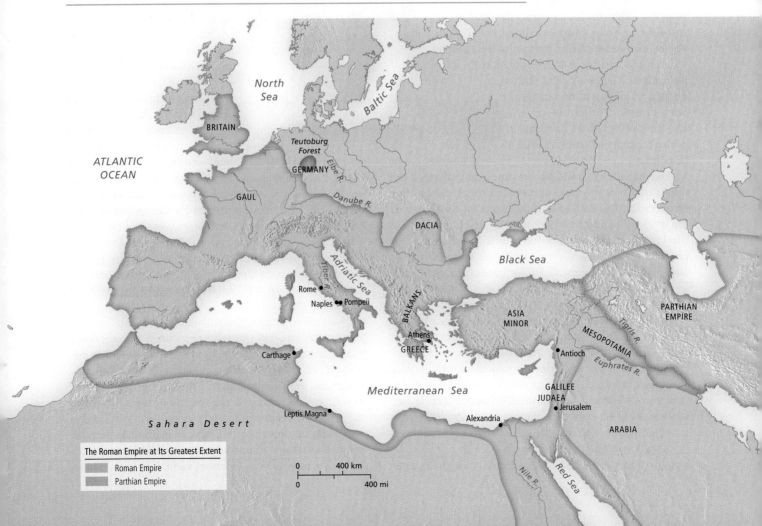

Augustus: A Commanding Presence

This imposing statue of Augustus dating to 19 B.C.E. depicts him as a warrior making a gesture of command. His face is ageless, the carving on his armor celebrates peace and prosperity, and his posture is balanced and forceful.

Later rulers, accepting the trappings of monarchy more openly than Augustus, used the title *imperator,* or emperor. Despite this change, the imperial system established by Augustus long survived his death, even when the throne was occupied by men such as Caligula (r. 37–41 C.E.), who tried to have his favorite horse elected to the Senate, or Nero (r. 54–68 C.E.), who murdered both his wife and his mother.

The Problem of Succession

Augustus, following the example of the Hellenistic world, hoped to establish a hereditary monarchy, in which power passed down through his family. When he died in 14 C.E., his stepson Tiberius (r. 14–37 C.E.) took control of the empire without opposition. A hereditary monarchy was now in place. Some senators muttered occasionally about restoring the Republic, but this remained an idle—and very dangerous—dream. Neither the army nor the people would have supported a Senate-led anti-imperial rebellion.

The hereditary principle remained unchallenged for centuries, in part because it staved off the instability that would have come with open competition for the throne. In the dynasty inaugurated by Augustus, which is known as the Julio-Claudian dynasty and which lasted almost 100 years, every ruler came from Augustus's extended family. Nero, the last of Augustus's family line, committed suicide in 68 C.E. He left no heirs and so no obvious successors to the throne. Four men contended for the throne.

During this "Year of the Four Emperors," Rome learned what the historian Tacitus later called the "secret of empire"—that troops far from the imperial city could choose emperors. Four different emperors took the throne in quick succession, as different Roman armies competed to put their commanders on the throne. The winner of this contest was the general Titus Flavius Vespasianus, or Vespasian (r. 69–79 C.E.), who learned of Nero's death while in Palestine breaking the back of a great Jewish rebellion. By the end of 69 C.E. Vespasian defeated his rivals and became

the first emperor who did not come from the Roman nobility. Born into the equestrian class, he built his reputation on his military prowess.

The Flavian dynasty that Vespasian established lasted twenty-five years until the death of his last son, Domitian (r. 81–96 C.E.). A conscientious and able monarch, Domitian nevertheless ruled with an openly autocratic style. He executed many aristocratic senators, creating a reign of terror among Rome's elite. Fittingly, a group of senators murdered him.

To avoid the chaos of another succession crisis, the Senate cooperated with the army in choosing a new emperor, the elderly Nerva (r. 96–98 C.E.). They hoped that this highly respected man who had no sons would ensure a smooth transition to the next regime, and so he did. Under pressure from the restless military establishment, Nerva adopted the vigorous and experienced general Trajan (r. 98–117 C.E.) as his son and heir. He thus inaugurated the era historians call the Antonine Age. For almost a century, Rome enjoyed competent rule, to a large degree because Nerva's practice of adopting highly qualified successors continued. After Trajan adopted Hadrian (r. 117–138 C.E.), Hadrian in turn adopted Antoninus Pius (r. 138–161 C.E.). Antoninus adopted Marcus Aurelius (r. 161–180 C.E.) to succeed him. Historians consider the Antonine age a high point of Roman peace and prosperity. The Roman historian Tacitus, who survived Domitian's tyranny to live during Nerva's and Trajan's reigns, praised these latter emperors for establishing "the rare happiness of times, when we may think what we please, and express what we think."

This time of peace ended with another imperial murder. Marcus Aurelius unfortunately abandoned the custom of picking a highly qualified successor, and instead was followed to the throne by his incompetent, cruel, and eventually insane son Commodus (r. 180–192 C.E.). In 192 C.E., several senators arranged to have Commodus strangled, triggering another civil war.

A senator from North Africa, Septimius Severus, emerged victorious from this conflict and assumed the imperial throne in 193 C.E. Fluent in Latin, Greek, and Punic,

DOCUMENT

The Accomplishments of Augustus

In 14 C.E., the 76-year-old Augustus composed a text detailing his achievements. He ordered that the text be engraved on bronze tablets and erected outside his mausoleum after his death. As the following excerpts show, Augustus presented himself as the savior rather than the destroyer of Republican traditions.

At the age of nineteen, on my own initiative and at my own expense, I raised an army by means of which I liberated the Republic, which was oppressed by the tyranny of a faction [Antony and his supporters] . . . Those who assassinated my father* I drove into exile, avenging their crime by due process of law; and afterwards when they waged war against the state, I conquered them twice on the battlefield [at Philippi in 42 B.C.E.].

I waged many wars throughout the whole world by land and by sea, both civil and foreign, and when victorious I spared all citizens who sought pardon. Foreign peoples who could safely be pardoned I preferred to spare rather than to extirpate. About 500,000 Roman citizens were under military oath to me. Of these, when their terms of service were ended, I settled in colonies or sent back to their own municipalities a little more than 300,000, and to all of these I allotted lands or granted money as rewards for military service. . . .

The dictatorship offered to me [in 22 B.C.E.] by the people and by the senate, both in my absence and in my presence, I refused to accept. . . . The consulship, too, which was offered to me at that time as an annual office for life, I refused to accept. In [19, 18, and 11 B.C.E.], though the Roman senate and people unitedly agreed that I should be elected sole guardian of the laws and morals with supreme authority, I refused to accept any office offered me which was contrary to the traditions of our ancestors. . . .

I repaired the Capitol and the theater of Pompey with enormous expenditures on both works, without having my name inscribed on them. I repaired the conduits of the aqueducts which were falling into ruin in many places because of age . . . I completed the Julian Forum and the basilica which was between the temple of Castor and the temple of Saturn, . . . and when the same basilica was destroyed by fire, I enlarged its site and began rebuilding the structure, which is to be inscribed with the names of my sons. . . .

I gave a gladiatorial show three times in my own name, and five times in the names of my sons or grandsons; at these shows about 10,000 fought. Twice I presented to the people in my own name an exhibition of athletes invited from all parts of the world, and a third time in the name of my grandson. I presented games in my own name four times, and in addition twenty-three times in the place of other magistrates. . . . Twenty-six times I provided for the people in my own name or in the names of my sons or grandsons, hunting spectacles of African wild beasts in the circus or in the Forum or in the amphitheaters; in these exhibitions about 3,500 animals were killed. . . .

I brought peace to the sea by suppressing the pirates. In that war I turned over to their masters for punishment nearly 30,000 slaves who had run away from their owners and taken up arms against the state. The whole of Italy voluntarily took an oath of allegiance to me and demanded me as its leader in the war in which I was victorious at Actium [in 31 B.C.E.]. . . . I extended the frontiers of all the provinces of the Roman people . . . I restored peace. . . .

---

*Augustus refers here to his adoptive father, Julius Caesar.

Source: Augustus, *The Accomplishments of Augustus* (14 C.E.). From Naphtali Lewis and Meyer Reinhold (eds.), Roman *Civilization: Selected Readings*, 3rd ed., Vol. 1 (New York: Columbia University Press, 1990), pp. 561–572.

---

the Phoenician language still widely spoken in North Africa, Septimius Severus exemplified the ascent of provincial aristocrats to the highest levels of the empire. The Severan dynasty he established lasted until 235 C.E. Septimius Severus could afford to ignore the Senate because he was popular with the army—he raised its pay for the first time in more than 100 years. But when the last emperor of his dynasty, Severus Alexander (r. 222–235 C.E.), attempted to negotiate with the German tribes by offering them bribes, his own troops killed him because they wanted the cash for themselves. Once again, the murder of an emperor provoked civil war. Fifty years of political and economic crises followed the end of the Severan dynasty. As we

will see in the next chapter, the imperial structure that emerged after this time of crisis differed significantly from the Augustan model.

The Emperor's Role: The Nature of Imperial Power

Under the Augustan imperial system, four main responsibilities defined the emperor's role. First, the emperor both protected and expanded imperial territory. Only the emperor determined foreign policy and made treaties with other nations. Only the emperor waged war—both defensive wars to protect the empire from its enemies and aggressive campaigns of conquest. Generals fighting under

Augustus's orders conquered huge tracts of Spain, Germany, and the Balkans. The emperor Trajan won great glory by conquering the rich Dacian kingdom north of the Danube River between 101 and 106 C.E. Other emperors smashed internal revolts or fought long border wars. From Augustus's reign onward, the northern frontier along the Rhine and Danube Rivers saw occasional, bitter warfare with various Germanic peoples. Marcus Aurelius had to pawn palace treasures to finance campaigns against confederations of Germanic tribes along the Danube frontier.

The emperor's second responsibility was to administer justice and to provide good government throughout his dominions. In theory all citizens could appeal to the emperor directly for justice. In addition, the emperor and his staff responded to questions on points of law and administration from provincial governors and other officials who ruled in the emperor's name. Emperors provided emergency relief after natural disasters, looked after the roads and infrastructure of the empire, and financed some public buildings in many provincial cities.

The emperor's third responsibility stemmed from his religious role. As *Pontifex Maximus,* or High Priest, the emperor supervised the public worship of the great gods of Rome, particularly Jupiter, as well as the goddess Roma. Emperors and subjects alike believed that in order to fulfill Rome's destiny to rule the world, they must make regular sacrifices to the gods.

Finally, the emperor gradually became a symbol of unity for all the peoples of the empire. He embodied the empire and served as the focal point around which all life in the empire revolved. Inevitably, the emperor seemed more than human, even worthy of worship, for he was the guarantor of peace, prosperity, and victory for Rome, and he had infinitely more power than anyone else alive.

Worship of the emperor began with Augustus. He was reluctant to call himself a god because Roman tradition opposed such an idea, but he permitted his spirit to be worshiped in a paternal way, as a sort of *paterfamilias* or head of a universal family of peoples of the empire. He also referred to himself as the "son of a god"—in this case Julius Caesar, whom the Senate had declared divine. After Augustus, imperial worship became more pronounced, although only a few emperors, such as Domitian, emphasized their divinity during their lifetimes. Most were content to be worshiped after death, assuming that the Senate would declare them gods after their funerals. On his deathbed, Vespasian managed to joke, "I guess I'm becoming a god now."

In Rome's eastern provinces such as Egypt and Syria, where people for thousands of years had considered their kings divine, the worship of the emperor spread quickly. Each city's official calendar marked the emperor's day of accession to the throne. Soon, cities across the empire worshiped the emperor on special occasions through games, speeches, sacrifices, and free public feasts in which people ate the flesh of the animals sacrificed in the emperor's honor. At magnificent temples, priests conducted elaborate public rituals to venerate the emperor.

This cult of the emperor provided a focus of allegiance for the diverse peoples of the empire and so served as a unifying force. Although most people would never see their ruler, he was in their prayers and their public spaces every day. In addition to encouraging worship or veneration in public ceremonies throughout the empire, emperors made their presence felt by building and restoring roads, temples, harbors, aqueducts, and fortifications. These public works demonstrated the emperor's unparalleled patronage and concern for the public welfare. In turn, local leaders emulated his generosity in their own cities.

Other elements of material culture also made the imperial presence real for the emperor's subjects. Coins, for example, provided a glimpse of the emperor's face and a phrase that characterized some aspect of his reign. Slogans such as "Restorer of the World," "Concord with the Gods," and "The Best Ruler—Sustenance for Italy" brought the ruler's message into every person's pocket. Statues of the emperor served a similar purpose. (One statue of an emperor found in Carthage had a removable head, so that when a new ruler ascended the throne, the town leaders could save money by replacing only the head.) In his own portraits, Augustus tended toward the conventions of classical Greek portraiture that presented him as remote and ageless. In contrast, his successors placed portraits of their faces on their coins and statues, making them easily identifiable in surviving sculpture.

Emperors also used military and sporting victories to make their presence felt throughout the empire. In the Republic, conquest had brought wealth and glory to its many generals. In contrast, in the new imperial system, only the emperor could take credit for victory in war. Imperial propaganda described the emperor as eternally triumphant. Sporting events, too, glorified the emperor. At the Circus Maximus in Rome, a chariot racetrack where a quarter of a million people could gather to cheer their favorite charioteer, as well as in racetracks throughout the empire, enthusiastic crowds shared the pleasure of the competition with the emperor or his representatives.

Aqueducts: The Pont du Gard

This graceful aqueduct, now known as the Pont du Gard, was built about 14 C.E. to carry water to the city of Nîmes, in the south of France, from its surrounding hills. Romans were highly sophisticated hydraulic engineers, and waterworks like this aqueduct were a common feature of all the large cities of the empire.

The City of Rome

The city of Rome stood as a monument to the paramount authority of the emperor. Augustus boasted that he had found Rome built of brick and left it built of marble. Though an exaggeration, this claim nevertheless reveals the effect of monarchy on Rome's urban fabric. Every emperor wanted to leave his mark on the city of Rome as a testimony to his generosity and power. As Rome grew, it became the model for cities throughout the empire. Its public spaces and buildings provided a stage for the acting out of basic activities of imperial rule (see Map 5.2).

The center of political and public life in the city of Rome was the Forum, an area filled with many imposing buildings—administrative headquarters such as the treasury and records office, law courts, and the Senate House. Roman laws were inscribed on gleaming bronze tablets and placed on the outer walls of these buildings, testimony to the principles of justice and order that formed the framework of the Roman state. Basilicas, colossal colonnaded halls in which Romans conducted public business ranging from finance to legal trials, crowded against the sides of the Forum.

Because public and religious life were intertwined, the Forum also contained many grand temples of the gods who controlled Rome's destiny. For example, the goddess Concordia, who represented political agreement among Romans, had a gleaming shrine. Jupiter, Rome's chief god, had a huge marble temple on the Capitoline Hill looking down on the Forum. An altar to the goddess Victory stood in the Senate, where generals took oaths of allegiance to the emperor before marching to war.

The Forum particularly highlighted the emperor's power within the imperial system. Emperors built huge arches in the Roman Forum to celebrate their triumphs. After a victorious military campaign, emperors paraded through the Forum on the Sacred Way, passed under the arches, and finished at the temple of Jupiter. Delighted crowds watched defeated kings pass by in chains and marveled at huge floats piled high with loot. In the victory

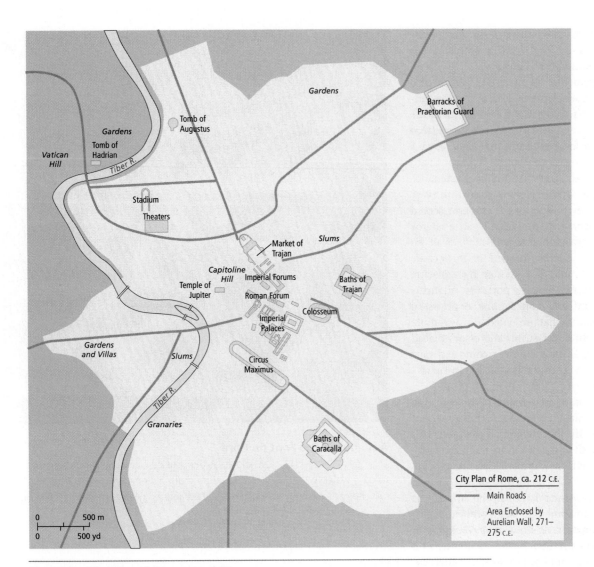

Map 5.2 The City of Rome, ca. 212 C.E.
This diagram shows the main public buildings of the imperial capital. Most cities elsewhere in the empire imitated this urban plan.

parade, slaves carried grandiose paintings that depicted important battles and other scenes of the war.

The might of the emperor was on display not only in the Forum but throughout the city of Rome. Emperors spent gigantic sums on baths, stadiums, and additional forums. Trajan's Forum, by far the biggest, included libraries of Greek and Latin texts, an enormous basilica for public business, a multistoried marketplace not unlike a modern mall, shops, and a marble column thirty-eight meters high on which was carved the story of Trajan's victorious Dacian Wars. The emperor Caracalla was renowned for constructing the biggest and most expensive bathing complex. The Colosseum, built by Vespasian and Titus, replaced Nero's private pleasure pond and provided a spot in the very heart of the city where as

The Colosseum

many as 50,000 happy spectators could watch the slaughter of men and animals at the emperor's expense. Romans could also go to the Circus Maximus to see horse-drawn chariots compete for victory under the emperor's auspices. Emperors also built and maintained theaters, libraries, parks, and markets for the public's enjoyment.

Other impressive monuments dotted the city's landscape. The tombs of Augustus and his family stood in the Field of Mars, a region of the city full of public buildings. Hadrian's mausoleum was just across the Tiber River. A great map of the empire built by Augustus delighted viewers while at the same time asserting imperial claims to control of the world. Emperors built their palaces on the Palatine Hill, which looked down on the Forum from the east, and great men's mansions covered nearby hills.

To erect these monumental buildings, the Romans pioneered certain architectural techniques and styles. They were the first to build extensively in concrete, which allowed them to develop new methods of construction. The concrete vault, for example, made possible the enormous baths and public buildings that graced the streets of Rome. The Pantheon, built by Hadrian, is the largest ancient roofed building still standing today. With a diameter of 142 feet, its dome has no interior supports.

Dome of the Pantheon

The wealthy of Rome lived in luxury that would not be equaled in the West for centuries. By the time of Trajan's reign, eleven aqueducts provided Rome with 300 million gallons of water every day. Prosperous Romans could have fresh water for drinking and bathing pumped directly into their homes. The aqueducts also supplied the enormous demands of the imperial bath complexes built for the entire population.

In stark contrast to the gleaming homes and public buildings were the filthy slums of the poor. Unlike wealthy Romans, the impoverished majority of Rome's inhabitants lived in the valleys between Rome's seven hills or by the Tiber River, where they crowded into apartment buildings up to six stories high. Each building contained several apartments, consisting of small rooms without plumbing, fireplaces, or proper ventilation. Lacking proper foundations, apartment buildings often collapsed and could easily become firetraps. (Perhaps it is not a surprise, then, that Augustus established the first professional fire department in Western history.)

The Agents of Control

The emperor stood at the heart of the imperial system devised by Augustus. But the imperial center also included other agents of control. The Roman Senate continued to play a significant administrative role in the new system. As it grew to represent not just the aristocracy of the city of Rome, but a new ruling elite drawn from the provinces, the Senate solidified networks of power and communications that tied the imperial center to its outlying regions. The army, too, constituted an important element of the imperial center. It not only conquered new territories and ensured the emperor's rule throughout the empire, it also served as a force of Romanization°, bringing Roman cultural and political practices to distant regions.

Baths of Caracalla
The gigantic bath complex built by Caracalla in 212–216 C.E. (seen here in an architect's reconstruction) covers more than fifty acres in central Rome. It contained numerous pools heated to different temperatures, exercise grounds, and rooms for reading and relaxation. With walls covered in colored marble, statues, and works of art prominently displayed, the baths were a visual treat for the public. The building's structure demonstrates Roman architectural planning and hydraulic engineering at their finest. One of the bathing pools has been converted to a stage where today theater productions are performed.

The Roman Senate: From Autonomy to Administration

In the imperial system fashioned by Augustus, the Senate continued to function, but with a more restricted role. To maintain the illusion that he had saved rather than destroyed the Republic, Augustus took pains to show respect for the Senate. He allowed its members to compete among themselves for promotion and honor in his service. He permitted the old Republican offices such as tribune and consul to remain in place, and encouraged ambitious men in Rome to compete for them. Augustus also emphasized integrity in the service of the state and sent able senators to govern provinces, thereby reducing corruption.

In these ways the basic machinery of government inherited from the Republic continued to operate—but in conformity with the emperor's wishes. In the new imperial system, the emperor, not the Senate, controlled military, financial, and diplomatic policy. Free political debate was silenced. Because he wanted to avoid the ruthless competition for power that had destroyed the Republic, Augustus eliminated his opponents and filled the Senate with loyal supporters.

Deprived of its autonomy, the Senate became an administrative arm of imperial rule. Senators served as provincial governors, army commanders, judges, and financial officers. They managed the water and grain supplies of the city of Rome, and some of them served on the emperor's advisory council. Aristocratic senators learned to serve the empire faithfully even if they disliked the emperor.

Emperors often brought new men into the Senate from the provinces as a reward for their support, with the belief that Rome grew strong through admitting the best of its provincials to the highest levels of government. Broadening Senate membership in this way enabled more and more of the Romanized elites of the empire to feel they had a stake in the imperial enterprise. Some Roman-born senators, however, balked at such inclusiveness. The emperor Claudius (r. 41–54 C.E.) caused considerable dismay among the snobbish Roman senators when he admitted a few new members from Gaul. Nevertheless, the numbers of provincials in the Roman Senate increased in the first two centuries. By the end of the third century C.E. more than half of Rome's senators came from outside Italy.

While the emperor's relationship with the Senate was of primary importance, other social ranks also played crucial roles in imperial administration. Many members of the equestrian class served in government positions. In addition, many emperors employed freedmen (former slaves) on their administrative staffs and benefited from their loyalty and competence. During Claudius's reign, some senators complained that the freedmen in his administration possessed more influence and easier access to the emperor than did the senators themselves.

The Roman Army and the Power of the Emperor

Like the Senate and administration, the Roman army was a crucial component of imperial rule. The army could make or break an emperor—something that every ruler understood. Without the army's support, Augustus would never have succeeded in transforming the Republic into his imperial system. In 41 C.E., after the death of Caligula, soldiers of the palace guard dragged the lame, stammering Claudius from behind a curtain and forced him to take the throne, as a means of ensuring imperial continuity—and their own livelihoods. When Vespasian took the throne in 69 C.E. with the support of his troops, no one in Rome, least of all the emperors, could doubt the power of the army to influence political affairs. After 235 C.E., many emperors, including Aurelian (r. 270–275 C.E.) and Diocletian (r. 284–305 C.E.), rose through the ranks and became emperor due to the support of their fellow soldiers.

Augustus created a highly efficient professional army that would be the bulwark of the empire for nearly two and a half centuries. His first step was to reduce the army from 60 to 28 legions, so that the troops now totaled 150,000 citizens. (Trajan later added two more legions.) To solidify the loyalty of these legions, Augustus established regular terms of service as well as an ample retirement benefit. He also violated Roman tradition with the creation of the elite Praetorian Guard, which consisted of one and a half legions stationed in Rome to serve as a ceremonial escort for the emperor, maintain order in the city, and enforce the emperor's will throughout Italy.

The strength of the army was augmented by subject peoples who were not citizens. These subjects served as auxiliary troops. After completing their years of service, auxiliaries received Roman citizenship—an important incentive for recruitment. The combined legions and auxiliaries brought the military strength of the Roman army to 300,000 men.

Legionaries enlisted for twenty-five years but only about half survived this term of service. Short life expectancy rather than death in battle kept the figure low, although regular rations and medical care may have helped soldiers live longer than civilians. A soldier with special skills, such as literacy, could rise through the ranks to have significant responsibilities and perhaps become an officer. For those who survived their period of enlistment, Augustus established military colonies in Italy and the provinces of Africa, Spain, and Asia. He rewarded more than 100,000 veterans with grants of land in return for their military service. Later emperors continued the same practice.

The imperial army epitomized many of the values central to Roman imperial culture. It maintained a very high degree of organization, discipline, and training—characteristics on which Romans prided themselves. To the Romans, strict military discipline distinguished their soldiery from disorganized barbarians. Military punishments were notoriously ferocious. For example, if a soldier fell asleep during sentry duty, his barrackmates were required to beat him to death. But tight discipline and vigorous training did produce highly professional fighters. To keep in fighting trim, troops constantly drilled in weaponry, camp building, and battle formations. A Roman soldier was expected to march twenty miles in four hours—while carrying his forty-pound pack and swimming across any rivers encountered along the way.

Life in the Roman Provinces: Assimilation, Resistance, and Romanization

■ How did provincial peoples assimilate to or resist Roman rule?

Beyond the city of Rome and the imperial center lay the second concentric circle of power, the Roman Empire's provinces. In these diverse regions some people assimilated readily to Roman ways, while others fiercely resisted. Unlike the Greeks of the Classical Age,

Romans in the imperial era were willing to include their subjects in the political and cultural life of the empire. Anyone could adopt the practices of Roman daily life, while formal grants of Roman citizenship gave many people the legal rights and privileges that Roman citizens enjoyed.

The Roman way of life manifested itself most noticeably in cities. Modeling themselves on an idealized version of the imperial capital, provincial cities became "little Romes." They served the empire's purposes by funneling wealth from its massive hinterland into imperial coffers. As Roman culture came to predominate in urban centers, however, the division between city and countryside widened. Provincial urban elites benefited from government that was more efficient and orderly than it had been during the Republic. In contrast, rural inhabitants, who formed the majority of the empire's population, faced economic exploitation and threats to their traditional ways of life. Social unrest always boiled beneath the surface of the Roman peace. Yet of the many revolts against Roman authority, only one ever succeeded. Roman military brutality kept most subject peoples in check, but so, too, did the more positive aspects of imperial rule. Many provincial people came to think of themselves as beneficiaries rather than as victims of the Roman Empire.

The Army: A Romanizing Force

More than any other institution, the army mirrored the growth of the Roman Empire from a diverse collection of conquered territories to a well-organized state with a common culture. During the Republic, soldiers tended to be drawn from the city of Rome and surrounding regions—a natural consequence of the fact that Roman soldiers were required to be Roman citizens. In the course of the first two and a half centuries of imperial rule, however, the number of troops from Italy steadily diminished as territories under Roman rule increased.

The army was a significant Romanizing force throughout the imperial era. Army bases in far-flung regions provided the first taste of Roman culture and language to provincial peoples. The army introduced provincial recruits to the Latin language, Roman religion, social organization, and values. Oaths of loyalty bound soldiers to the emperor and Rome, neither of which most legionaries would ever see. Latin, the language of command and army administration, provided another common bond to men whose mother tongues reflected the empire's ethnic diversity. Many inscriptions on soldiers' tombstones reveal that a simplified version of Latin developed in the army. (This language became the ancestor of French, Spanish, and other Romance languages.)

Roman soldiers who settled in the provinces also served as a Romanizing force. Soldiers could not legally marry during their military service but many men reared families anyway with local women. Septimius Severus pragmatically abandoned the restriction against marriage in the army at the end of the second century C.E. At retirement, most soldiers stayed near the bases in which they had been stationed. Many towns arose full of former military personnel and their friends, families, and small businesses. These towns helped transmit Roman culture and values to provincial peoples.

Sports Riot!

In 59 C.E. a riot broke at the amphitheater of Pompeii between the Pompeians and spectators from the neighboring town of Nuceria who had come to see the gladiatorial games. Badly outnumbered, many Nucerians were killed and many others badly wounded. As punishment, the amphitheater was closed for ten years.

Each of the legions with a contingent of auxiliary troops was stationed as a permanent garrison in a province with an elaborate logistical infrastructure to provide weapons, food, and housing. Legions had a standard chain of command to organize officers and men. The architecture of camps and fortification, as well as weapons, armor, and tactics, followed the same conventions across the empire, thus reinforcing the army's role as a Romanizing force. Generals and staff officers often had postings in different provinces during their careers, so there developed a strong sense of shared enterprise.

After conquering new territories and peoples, Roman armies remained in place as occupying forces. Initial relations tended to be hostile. The Romans spoke a different language from that of their subjects, worshiped different gods, and enforced strange and unwelcome rules. The tension between Roman armies and provincial populations never entirely went away, but gradually the conquered peoples became Romanized. As the occupying Roman forces settled in and raised families with local women, defeated peoples started to assimilate into Roman culture. They adopted Roman customs and language, and provincial elites began to enter Roman politics. Romanization transformed the provinces from occupied zones where shattered communities obeyed foreign masters to well-integrated territories in which Roman culture flourished.

Administration and Commerce

Conquered lands were quickly organized into provinces. One of the chief accomplishments of the Augustan state was establishing a well-managed and prosperous provincial system that lasted until the late third century C.E. A governor ruled over each province: He administered justice, supervised tax collection, and orchestrated the flow of slaves, timber, metals, horses, spices, and other treasures back to Rome. Although the Roman Empire at its height had about 50 million inhabitants, only a few thousand men participated directly in imperial administration in the provinces. Most administrative work was performed at the local level by city councilors, who in turn were loosely supervised by imperial governors and their staffs. The governors' responsibilities included protecting the frontiers, collecting taxes, administering justice, and suppressing rebellions.

This structure of government gave rise to an administrative-military class that drew its members from both the senatorial and the equestrian orders. In the service of the emperor, these men enjoyed splendid careers, climbing the ladder of success through appointments in different provinces. As a group, they provided a cadre of officials with empire-wide experience. Gnaeus Julius Agricola is an apt example. The father-in-law of the historian Tacitus, Agricola had a brilliant military career under the Flavian emperors. During his five years as governor of Britain, he

DOCUMENT

Agricola the General

The historian Tacitus wrote a biography of his father-in-law, the general and administrator Gnaeus Julius Agricola (49–93 C.E.). Agricola had a glittering military career under the Flavian emperors. As commander in chief of Roman forces in Britain from 78 to 83 C.E., he subdued most of the island and advanced deep into Scotland. Agricola encouraged urbanization and Mediterranean customs such as public bathing and chariot racing. In the following selection, Tacitus considers the implications of deliberate Romanization.

The following winter passed without disturbance, and was employed in salutary measures. For, to accustom to rest and repose through the charms of luxury a population scattered and barbarous and therefore inclined to war, Agricola gave private encouragement and public aid to the building of temples, courts of justice and dwelling houses, praising the energetic and reproving the indolent. Thus an honourable rivalry took the place of compulsion. He likewise provided a liberal education for the sons of the chiefs, and showed such a preference for the natural powers of the Britons over the industry of the Gauls that they who lately disdained the tongue of Rome now coveted its eloquence. Hence, too, a liking sprang up for our style of dress and the toga became fashionable. Step by step they were led to things which dispose to vice, the lounge, the bath, the elegant banquet. All this in their ignorance they called civilization, when it was but a part of their servitude.

Source: From Tacitus, "Agricola 21" in *Complete Works of Tacitus*, edited by Moses Hadas, translated by Alfred John Church and William Jackson Brodribb (New York: The Modern Library, 1942).

brought that distant province firmly under Roman control. Agricola epitomized loyalty to the state, experience in military affairs, and a thoughtful approach to drawing the elites of defeated enemies into the imperial way of life.

Extensive transport and commercial networks also helped both to connect the many provinces of the vast Roman Empire and to spread the Roman way of life. More than 40,000 miles of roads crisscrossed the empire. These roads, however, were built to move troops, not goods; throughout the Roman era transporting goods by land remained far more expensive than moving them by water. Rivers and the Mediterranean Sea were the primary conduits of trade. With pirates quelled by the Roman navy, shipping flourished. Improvements in harbors, ports, and linking canal systems further encouraged the growth of long-distance trade around the Mediterranean.

The Cities

The empire's territory consisted of a honeycomb of cities. Each "cell" in the structure constituted one administrative unit comprising the main urban center as well as the surrounding lands and villages. The Romans called each of these cells a *civitas*°, or city. Without the cities, Rome could not have held together the huge territories conquered by its armies. As centers for tax collection and law courts, cities were the locations where the imperial administrators interacted with provincial aristocrats, who had influence over the local population. Through cities, the empire's vast territories were linked to the imperial center.

More than a thousand cities dotted the imperial map (see Map 5.3). In regions where Roman urban traditions were little-known, the Romans created new urban centers. Cities such as Lugdunum (Lyons) in France or Eburacum (York) in Britain were created in the first years of conquest as centers of Roman culture and authority. In contrast, in regions throughout the Mediterranean where urban culture had deep roots, provincial cities such as Athens or Jerusalem had long been centers of learning or religion.

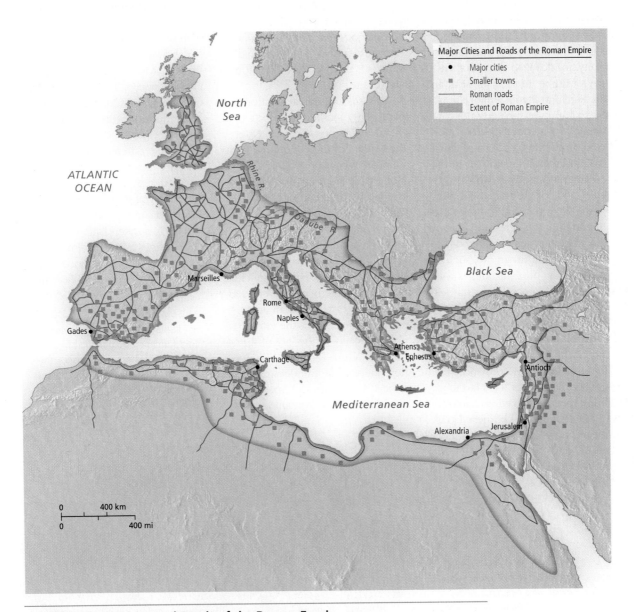

Map 5.3   Major Cities and Roads of the Roman Empire

Thousands of miles of roads linked the cities of the Roman Empire. Used primarily as military highways, the roads also helped merchants travel with their wares. When they crossed imperial frontiers, merchants traded with many peoples eager for Roman goods, especially wine and luxury objects.

The Roman City: Agent of Cultural Transformation

Between the second century B.C.E. and the first century C.E., Roman armies conquered much of western Europe. The Celtic peoples who inhabited these regions did not dwell in cities like those in Italy and the Mediterranean world. They lived in small villages scattered over the landscape. But as soon as the bloodshed of conquest was over, the Roman conquerors began to establish cities. These new urban foundations imitated Mediterranean cities, and especially an idealized notion of the city of Rome, in their physical and architectural layout. All of them had a forum in the center of town, flanked by a council house (modeled on the Roman Senate), basilicas, and temples—temples to the community's gods as well as the chief gods of the Roman Empire, to the emperor, and to Rome itself. In addition, the cities provided all the amenities and requirements of Mediterranean urban life, such as bathhouses, brothels, arenas for gladiatorial combat and wild beast hunts, and slave markets. Two main streets intersected in the heart of the town, connecting the city to the larger Roman road system that linked the provinces together and that let local farmers bring their produce into market.

The emergence of these cities meant more than political or economic development. Through their architecture and layout, as well as the lifestyle they promoted, provincial cities became agencies of cultural change, the stages on which the Roman way of life was acted out. In these cities, provincial peoples encountered Rome not just as a military conqueror but also as a cultural force. Thus the cities played an essential role in the process known as Romanization, in which local populations slowly acquired the characteristics of Roman life: They started to speak Latin, worship Roman gods, employ Roman architecture and styles of art, and habituate themselves to the Roman way of life.

This cultural transformation was particularly marked in the ranks of the local aristocratic elites. Often the leaders of the conquered communities who were willing to go along with the Romans were rewarded with Roman citizenship. They took a leading role in their city's senate, administering the city and its agricultural lands and collecting taxes. They paid for public buildings out of their own pockets to demonstrate their civic-minded generosity, just as Roman aristocrats did throughout the empire and especially in the city of Rome itself. In return for their cooperation, these local grandees could expect rewards from Rome. Some even entered the Roman Senate.

For Romans, the cities symbolized a transformation from the old way of life of conquered peoples to the Roman style of living, a transformation from barbarism to civilization. Romanization was a two-way street, however. Just as much as the local populations assimilated the notion of Roman cultural superiority, adopting aspects of Roman life and benefiting materially from their encounter with Roman culture, Rome took something in return. By drawing these provincial peoples into the imperial matrix, Rome grew more cosmopolitan. Roman art and literature reflected images and themes drawn from provincial cultures. Roman life differed subtly from one province to another as local cultures made their presence felt on the dominant Roman forms. These differences ranged from provincial accents in spoken Latin to specialized cuisines and agricultural techniques. Yet all the provinces—and the cities in them—were Roman.

Question for Discussion

For Romans, the cities symbolized a transformation from barbarism to civilization. What characteristics, then, defined "civilization" to the Romans? What alternative definitions of "civilization" were available?

Little Romes

The amphitheater at the Tunisian town of El-Djem (the ancient city of Thysdrus) was built in the early third century C.E. and was one of the largest in the empire. Like the Colosseum in Rome, which it imitated, this arena could seat more than 20,000 spectators at gladiatorial fights and other entertainments. These public activities were popular throughout the empire.

Some urban hubs, such as Carthage and Alexandria, teemed with several hundred thousand people.

Certain common patterns characterized urban life throughout the empire. All cities governed themselves. A city council modeled on the Roman Senate presided over each city's affairs. Only a handful of the community's wealthiest men served in the city council and held the various magistracies and priesthoods. Council membership passed from father to son. Wealthy women held no administrative office and had no role in public decision making, though they sometimes presided as priestesses in civic religious observances. The male citizens of each city voted on local issues and elected town officials. City councils managed the grain supply, arranged for army recruitment, supervised the marketplaces, administered justice in local law courts, and most important of all, collected taxes for the central government. Councilors paid out of their own pockets for the upkeep of public works, aqueducts, and baths, and funded religious festivals and public amusements. As provincial officials performed their public responsibilities on behalf of their hometowns, they imitated the efforts of that greatest patron of all, the emperor himself. The city councilors were the "mouthpiece of Rome."

The Countryside

Control of the countryside was the key to the prosperity of the imperial system. The wealthiest men owned the most land. Landholdings, however, varied greatly in size and distribution. The emperor was the greatest property owner, controlling millions of acres of land throughout the empire. Augustus, for example, personally owned the entire province of Egypt. Like Augustus, wealthy Roman investors owned properties in many different regions of the empire. Some of these landed magnates chose to enter a life of public service either in Rome or in their home cities. Others preferred to enjoy the benefits of their enormous wealth away from the risks of political life.

At the bottom of the pyramid toiled the peasants, who lived in the countryside and performed the agricultural labor that made local landowners rich. The circumstances of peasant life varied greatly throughout the empire. Some peasants owned small farms sufficient to maintain their families, perhaps with the assistance of seasonal wage laborers or a few slaves. Others rented their lands from landlords to whom they owed payment in the form of produce, money, or labor. Degrees of dependency on landlords varied as well. Extremely fierce penalties for inability to pay rents ranged from enslavement to other forms of bondage.

All landowning peasants faced one constant threat—the possibility that a more powerful landowner might seize their fields by force. When this happened, peasants had little hope of getting their land back. The imperial system favored the property rights of the wealthy and worked to the disadvantage of the rural poor. Cities gobbled up the peasants' crops; government officials extorted taxes from them; and landlords and soldiers bullied them. Rabbi Hanina ben Hama, who lived in Palestine about 240 C.E., stated bluntly that the empire established cities "in order to impose upon the people forced labor, extortion and oppression." In addition to this relentless exploitation, famine, natural disasters, and debt constantly threatened the peasants' very survival.

Despite these hardships, the peasantry during the empire's first three centuries managed to produce enough surplus crops to maintain the imperial system, especially the army with its ravenous demands for supplies and foods. Indeed, agricultural productivity during this era was remarkable, considering the low yields of farms, the difficulty and expense of transportation, and the rudimentary farming technology of the time. Some historians estimate that Europe did not see a comparable level of agricultural productivity again until the seventeenth century.

Food staples in the Mediterranean region included olives, grains, and wines. Dates were a coveted sweet, because the Romans did not have sugar. In more northern regions butter replaced oil and beer substituted for wine. Large flocks of sheep and herds of cattle provided necessary wool and leather.

Terrain and climate as much as investment and local farming custom determined the methods of agricultural exploitation. In Sicily and parts of southern Italy, chain gangs of slaves predominated, working on vast estates. Migrant workers labored in the olive groves of North Africa, while seasonal movement of grazing animals predominated in hilly regions of Italy and the Balkans. In Egypt, the annual flooding of the Nile determined the rhythms of agricultural life and made the Nile Valley one of the empire's chief producers of grain.

Revolts Against Rome

Conquest by Roman armies could be a long and brutal ordeal. After the shock of military defeat and surrender to Roman generals came the imposition of the administrative structures of Roman rule and the mechanisms of economic exploitation. Not surprisingly, resentment simmered among conquered peoples. Revolts against Roman authority often followed soon after a subject people's initial defeat, while freedom was still a living memory. The stories of several revolts illustrate that subject peoples rarely adjusted smoothly to Roman rule and that Roman force usually—but not always—proved overwhelming.

Arminius and the Revolt in Germany

In 9 C.E. Arminius, chieftain of a Germanic tribe called the Cherusci, led the only successful military revolt against Roman rule. As a young man serving in an auxiliary

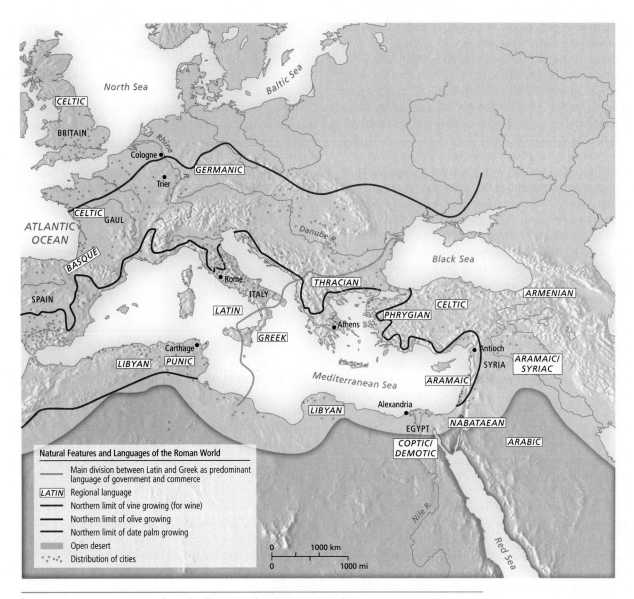

Map 5.4 Languages and Agriculture in the Roman Empire

The 50 million inhabitants of the Roman Empire spoke many different languages, but the two most dominant were Greek in the eastern regions and Latin in the west. Another important division was that between the wine-drinking regions in the south and the beer-drinking territories in the north.

regiment in the Roman army, Arminius earned Roman citizenship, learned to speak Latin, and gained the rank of equestrian. Arminius seemed to be a real friend of Rome, but the Cherusci had a history of belligerence and resistance. Arminius's tribal ties proved stronger than his loyalty to the empire. The Romans underestimated the pugnacity of their new Germanic subjects and sent the wrong man, Lucius Varus, to be their governor. Varus was a peacetime administrator, not a general. His previous experience in Syria and North Africa had not prepared him for the challenges he encountered east of the Rhine River. He imposed economic exploitation and taxation—the hallmarks of the

Roman peace—on the Cherusci too quickly. Not used to a monetary economy, debt, and foreign control, the tribe and its allies rose in revolt, led by Arminius.

Arminius lured the unsuspecting Varus into a trap in the Teutoburg Forest, slaughtering Varus and three entire Roman legions. A relief army under the command of the future emperor Tiberius contained the disaster, but nevertheless, when Augustus died in 14 C.E., all of Rome's legions were on the west side of the Rhine. No emperor ever again attempted to conquer Germany. One lasting result of Arminius's successful revolt is the linguistic distinction that still cuts across Europe. Whereas French and Italian derive from Latin, German does not because the tribes living between the Rhine and Elbe Rivers managed to throw off the Roman yoke in 9 C.E.

Boudica's Revolt in Britain

Fifty years after Arminius's victory, another major uprising broke out in Britain, led by Boudica, the queen of the people known as the Iceni. The revolt had a long, complex history. In the decades following the initial conquest of the island by the emperor Claudius in 43 C.E., the Romans consolidated their power by playing favorites among the local tribes. They encouraged tribes not under Roman control to ally themselves with Rome as client states. Under King Prasutagus, the Iceni were one of these client states that supplied troops to the Roman army in return for Roman protection. Before King Prasutagus died in 60 C.E., he named the Roman emperor his co-heir with his wife, Boudica, and his daughters. Within a few years the emperor Nero pushed Boudica aside and incorporated the kingdom of the Iceni directly into the Roman state. Emboldened by their new dominance over the Iceni, the agents of the tyrannical Roman governor abused Boudica and raped her daughters.

The queen then led her forces into open rebellion. With the aid of several neighboring tribes who also resented the Roman presence in Britain, Boudica destroyed a legion and leveled several cities, including Camulodunum, a major imperial cult center with a temple dedicated to Rome and the emperor. Resistance ended quickly after Roman forces routed Boudica's troops and the queen took her own life.

The Britons learned that resistance to Rome was futile. The Romans learned a lesson as well: Subject peoples should be treated more justly. The next Roman governor of Britain adopted more lenient administrative policies.

The Revolt of Julius Civilis in Gaul

Like Arminius, Julius Civilis was a Germanic tribal leader who had served in the Roman army. Julius Civilis was both a Roman citizen and a prince of his tribe, the Batavi. Like the Iceni in Britain, the Batavi had supplied troops but not tribute to Rome for several decades. Civilis was serving as a commander of Roman auxiliary troops in Gaul when civil war broke out in Rome in 69 C.E. following Nero's death. Quick to seize an opportunity, Julius Civilis led an army— consisting not only of Batavians but also men from several unconquered German tribes and some restless Gallic tribes—against Roman legionary bases depleted by the civil war.

Despite his career in Roman military service and his involvement in provincial politics, Civilis presented himself to his Batavian followers in religious terms, with native-style oaths of allegiance sworn in a sacred grove. He also maintained close ties with a Batavian prophet, who may

CHRONOLOGY

Political and Military Events

31 B.C.E.	Octavian defeats Mark Antony and controls Mediterranean world
27 B.C.E.	Octavian adopts the name Augustus
9 C.E.	Varus and three legions are defeated; Romans abandon Germany
30 C.E.	Jesus executed in Palestine
63 C.E.	Revolt of Boudica crushed in Britain
66–70 C.E.	Jewish Revolt; Temple and Jerusalem destroyed
69 C.E.	"Year of the Four Emperors"
101–106 C.E.	Trajan conquers Dacia
115–116 C.E.	Trajan conquers Mesopotamia; Rome reaches greatest extent
122–128 C.E.	Hadrian's Wall built in Britain
132–135 C.E.	Hadrian crushes Jewish revolt in Judaea
168 C.E.	Marcus Aurelius defeats the Marcomanni
212 C.E.	Antonine Decree grants Roman citizenship to all free inhabitants of the empire
235 C.E.	Fifty years of political turmoil begin

have predicted that Civilis would lead his people to freedom. But unlike the revolt of Arminius, the revolt of Civilis failed. The new emperor Vespasian brought stability back to the frontier through a combination of diplomacy and swift military action.

Jewish Revolts

Augustus had created the province of Judaea and annexed it to the Empire in 6 C.E. A series of mediocre governors and heavy taxation caused Judaea's economy to decline. Famines and banditry became common, and political discontent mounted among the Jews. Open rebellion almost broke out when the emperor Caligula (r. 37–41 C.E.) ordered that his statue be placed in the Temple in Jerusalem, an unthinkable sacrilege for the Jews. Only Caligula's death in 41 C.E. prevented the beginning of war between Rome and the Jews of Judaea.

Under Roman rule, a significant divide opened up within the Jewish community. Some members of the Jewish priestly caste became devoted to Greek and Roman culture, and the landed elite benefited directly from Roman rule. Ordinary Jews, however, suffered from high taxation and viewed their leaders as collaborators with an occupying and godless power. These Jews gave their loyalty and respect to the

Arch of Titus

This triumphal arch built at the end of the first century C.E. honors the recently deceased Titus for crushing the Jewish revolt of 66–70 C.E. Marble reliefs inside the arch represent the loot from the Temple of Jerusalem carried in the triumphal parade.

scribes, men of learning who devoted their lives to copying religious texts and interpreting the Bible. These learned and religious men had little stake in preserving Roman rule.

Sixty years of Roman mismanagement combined with a desire for independence sparked a massive revolt in Judaea in 66 C.E. Jews stopped offering sacrifices for the emperor's health and formed their own government. They appointed regional military commanders, chose a leader by lot, abolished debt, and issued their own coinage imprinted with messages of freedom. Internal political conflicts within the Jewish community, however, weakened the rebellion and proved as fatal to their cause as the might of Roman legions. In 70 C.E. imperial forces captured Jerusalem, destroyed the Temple, and enslaved an estimated two million people. The victorious generals were Vespasian and his son Titus, both of whom later became emperors.

Despite their overwhelming defeat in 70 C.E., Jewish communities continued to resist Rome. During Trajan's reign, minor revolts broke out in the eastern Mediterranean (115–118 C.E.). Revolts erupted again in 132–135 C.E., prompted by Hadrian's attempt to forbid the Jewish ritual circumcision of male infants. This latter revolt was led by Simon Bar Kochba, or "Son of the Star," who may have claimed to be a messiah, a leader who would end foreign oppression and inaugurate a new era for the Jewish nation.

Other rebellions occurred under the emperors Antoninus Pius (r. 138–161 C.E.) and Septimius Severus (r. 193–211 C.E.). The last major Jewish uprising occurred in Palestine in the fourth century C.E. All of these revolts failed.

Several conclusions may be drawn from these instances of resistance. In each of the western revolts, the Romans overestimated their ability to pacify subject peoples soon after conquering them. Even a tribal leader's service in the Roman auxiliary forces did not blunt tribal identity and allegiance. The rebel leaders appealed to their fellow tribespeople in traditional rather than in Roman terms. It required more than one generation after conquest for tribal elites to embrace the imperial system.

In the case of the Jewish revolt of 66–70 C.E., the Romans misunderstood the nature of leadership and loyalty in Judaea's Jewish society. The Romans allied themselves with members of the Jewish elite whom the majority of Jews distrusted and refused to follow. The continuation of Jewish opposition to Roman rule demonstrates that a population with a strong sense of religious identity rooted in a set of sacred texts could resist—and survive—the overwhelming power of Rome. Most rebels lacked this focus. Within a few generations they assimilated fully into Roman society. The Jews never did so.

Law, Citizenship, and Romanization

In the early days of the empire, Roman law set Romans apart from the bulk of the empire's peoples, who followed their own laws. For example, Jews could live according to Jewish law or Athenians by Athenian law, as long as they paid their taxes to the emperor and did not cause trouble. If a Jew or an Athenian held Roman citizenship, however, he or she could also enjoy the rights and benefits of Roman law. A Roman citizen possessed crucial legally defined rights, including the guarantee of freedom from enslavement. Male citizens had the right to compete for public magistracies, vote in public assemblies, serve in the legions, and make an appeal in a criminal trial.

As the Roman Empire expanded during the first and second centuries C.E., conditions of peace and prosperity encouraged the spread of both Roman-style cities and Roman citizenship, and thus the dominance of Roman law. In this way, Roman law tied the vast empire together. No matter where they lived in the empire, Roman citizens took pride in their centuries-old legal tradition, and in their rights of citizenship. Roman law thus helped erode the local loyalties and traditions of the diverse provincial peoples and so furthered the process of Romanization, of creating a Roman imperial culture.

Then, in 212 C.E., Emperor Aurelius Antoninus (r. 211–217 C.E.), nicknamed Caracalla, issued what became known as the Antonine Decree°. This ruling was a milestone because it granted citizenship to all free men and women within the empire, presumably to increase the tax base. By formally eliminating the distinction between Roman conquerors and subject peoples, the Antonine Decree enabled Roman law to embrace the entire population. This legal uniformity further strengthened provincial loyalty to Rome. Provincial allegiances to their own traditions and laws that had coexisted with Roman imperial law for centuries began to diminish.

Roman law not only served as an important element in Romanization, it also had a significant role in shaping the culture of the West in three specific ways. First, Roman law distinguished between civil law and criminal law. Civil law dealt with all aspects of family life, property and inheritance, slavery, and citizenship. It also dealt with legal procedure and the settling of disputes. Civil law, therefore, defined relations among different classes of Roman society and enabled courts to judge disputes among citizens. Criminal law addressed theft, homicide, sexual crimes, treason, and offenses against the government. These distinctions between civil and criminal law created by the Romans have become standard in the legal systems of nations that are part of Western civilization.

Roman law had a second significant impact on the West in its tradition of codification and interpretation. By the time of Hadrian, a board of professional jurists—directly supervised by the emperor—directed imperial legal affairs.

Combining legal scholarship, teaching, and administrative careers, these legal experts collected and analyzed earlier laws and the opinions of their predecessors. Papinian, Paul, and Ulpian, who lived in the early third century C.E., were the greatest of these specialists. They wrote hundreds of books of commentary that shaped the interpretation of Roman law for centuries, were passed on to the lawyers of medieval Europe, and continue to influence Italian, French, and Spanish legal traditions today, as well as the legal system of the state of Louisiana.

One crucial such interpretative tradition is that under the principle of what the Romans called "equity," or fairness, jurists should consider the spirit or intent rather than simply the letter of the law. On the basis of equity, Roman jurists argued that an accuser bears the burden of proof: A defendant does not have to prove he or she is innocent; rather, he or she must be proven guilty.

Finally, and perhaps most important, the Roman concept of "the law of nature" shaped Western ideas of justice. This concept stemmed from Stoicism, with its ideal of an underlying rational order to all things. From the Stoic assumption of rational order the idea developed that certain principles of justice are part of nature itself. Ideally, at least, laws of human societies should conform to the law of nature. Hence the Romans developed the idea that codes of law, although the product of particular societies and circumstances, are based on universally applicable principles. This idea would become a foundation of Western civilization. Building on this Roman idea, later thinkers would insist that all human beings had inalienable rights and that all individuals should be treated as equals under the law.

Equality under the law did not, however, exist in the Roman imperial age. Roman citizens had more rights than noncitizens, and not all Roman citizens had the same rights. In the first century C.E. the vast differences in wealth that divided citizens began to take on legal significance. By the third century C.E., the wealthy upper class, generally called *honestiores* or "better people," and the poor, called *humiliores* or "humbler people," acquired different legal rights, especially in criminal law. For example, *honestiores* convicted of crimes could not be tortured and if they were convicted of a capital crime, they received a quick death by sword. The "humbler people" received the most gruesome punishments, such as being crucified or thrown to wild animals in the arena.

The stronger legal distinction between better and humbler peoples was only one aspect of the law that shifted to reflect the new hierarchies of imperial Rome. During the Republic the Senate gave advice on legal matters to magistrates or citizen assemblies that had official authority to issue laws. During the empire control of law shifted into the emperor's hands. Whether the emperor was issuing a decree on his own initiative, making a general policy in response to an inquiry from a provincial administrator, or making a technical ruling on a point of law in consultation with legal experts on his staff, his decisions had the same status as any law issued by a citizen assembly during the Republic. The idea that the emperor was above the law and that his wishes had the force of law was widely accepted by the early third century C.E.

The Frontier and Beyond

■ How did Romans interact with peoples living beyond the imperial borders?

In Virgil's *Aeneid,* the great god Jupiter promises Rome "imperial rule without limit." But by the time of Hadrian's reign, the limits of the empire were clear. The third concentric circle of the Roman world consisted of the frontier—the outermost regions of the empire and beyond.

Like the generals of the Republic and the Hellenistic kings, Augustus set out to conquer as much land as possible in order to win glory and demonstrate his power. During his reign large portions of Germany and the Danube River basin came under Roman rule. His successors continued to add new lands to the empire. Claudius brought Britain into the Roman fold in 43 C.E., and by 117 C.E. Trajan had conquered Dacia (modern Romania), Mesopotamia, and parts of Arabia bordering the Red Sea. At this point the empire reached its greatest territorial extent.

But after Trajan, emperors turned their attention from conquest to consolidation. Trajan's successor, Hadrian, abandoned Mesopotamia because it was too expensive to control. He organized Rome's frontier with a series of carefully planned fortifications, including the renowned wall that still crosses the north of Britain and bears his name. His successors continued to fortify both the natural and manmade borders of the empire.

By the early second century C.E., regularly spaced military bases and fortresses dotted the empire's northern border while armed naval forces patrolled the Rhine and Danube, and Hadrian's wall stretched across Britain. In the East, another line of military defenses extended from the Black Sea to the Nile. In North Africa as well, a perimeter of fortifications indicated the limits of cultivable land along the empire's southernmost edge.

These were lines of not only political but also cultural demarcation. For the Romans, the boundaries between the empire and its unconquered neighbors symbolized a cultural division between civilization and barbarism. Romans used this distinction to help define their place in the world and to justify their conquest and absorption of other peoples.

Emperors systematically and heavily fortified these lines of political and cultural demarcation. Despite the resources spent on maintaining these borders, however, they remained highly permeable. These borders represented the limits of Roman authority, but they could not prevent non-Romans from entering the empire altogether.

Hadrian's Wall

This massive fortification epitomizes the second-century-C.E. military concept of the fortified frontier; stretched across northern Britain, it separated the Roman provinces to its south from the "barbarians" to the north.

Rome and the Parthian Empire

Although the Roman Empire dominated a huge expanse of territory, it did have one formidable rival: the Parthian Empire (Parthia) to the east. This realm stretched from the Euphrates River to the Indus River (covering modern Iran and Pakistan). Unlike the poorly organized and politically unstable Celtic and Germanic tribes the Romans confronted in western Europe, the Parthian Empire was highly structured and enormously powerful. It replaced the successor states of Alexander the Great in Iran in the mid-third century B.C.E. The Parthian Empire ended in 224 C.E., when another Iranian dynasty, the Sasanian, rose to power.

The structure of the highly stratified Parthian society included a king and warrior aristocracy; a middle range of doctors, artisans, and traders; and a large class of peasants. In addition Parthia contained many subject peoples with their own cultures, such as Babylonians, Jews, and Armenians. Unlike Rome, Parthia did not permit subject peoples and internal minorities to enter the ruling elite. The Parthian Empire did tolerate practice of various religions, although Zoroastrianism was the main religion of the Parthian state.

The Romans knew the Parthians as fierce warriors. Parthia's specially bred battle horses, which were famous as far away as China, made heavily armed Parthian cavalrymen and their archers worthy opponents of Rome's legions. Glory-seeking Roman generals of the late Republic found Parthia an attractive but dangerous target. Augustus, however, inaugurated a new Roman policy toward Parthia, just as he initiated changes in so many other aspects of Roman rule. Augustus—and most of the Roman emperors after him—preferred diplomacy to open conflict with Parthia because they knew they could not conquer and assimilate such a vast territory. Trajan's ambitious conquest of the Parthian provinces of Armenia and Mesopotamia in 115–116 C.E. broke with this consensus on the advantages of diplomacy, but only briefly. Trajan's successor, Hadrian, abandoned these territories because he knew that they overextended Rome's resources.

The most important result of the rivalry between Parthia and Rome was the exchange of products, technology, and ideas between their peoples. Romans highly prized Parthian steel and leather, as well as the exotic spices traded through Parthia from even farther east. The Romans also adopted some military technology and tactics from Parthia, particularly the use of heavily armed cavalry. By the fourth century C.E. these units constituted the core of Roman military might.

There was also an erratic exchange of nonmilitary technological expertise between the two empires. From the Parthians, the Romans learned new techniques of irrigating fields. In turn, Roman hydraulic engineers and masons went to Persia to help construct a great dam for the Parthian king. *Via*, the Latin word for "paved road," entered the Persian language, an indication that other Roman specialists worked in Parthia as well.

Religious ideas also flowed in both directions. Many people in the Roman Empire studied Parthian astrology and magic, while Jewish scholars in the Roman Empire maintained close ties with the Jewish academies in the Parthian province of Babylonia. It was Christianity, however, that was the most directly influenced by this religious interchange between the Parthians and the Romans. The Persian Mani (216–276 C.E.), founder of a religion called Manichaeism, preached that an eternal conflict between forces of light and darkness caused good and evil to intermingle. God's soul had become trapped in matter, and Jesus, the son of God, had come to Earth to retrieve God's soul. Mani taught that all those who followed him and turned their back on earthly possessions would be redeemed. Mani's contempt for the material world colored much of early Christian belief.

Roman Encounters with Germanic Peoples

The peoples living north of the Rhine and Danube Rivers, not the Parthians, posed the greatest threat to Rome during the first two and a half centuries C.E. Called "Germans" by the Romans, these peoples never used that term among themselves or thought of themselves as one group. Numbering in the tens of millions, most of them spoke their own dialects and did not understand the language of other tribes. Lacking political unity, different Germanic peoples constantly grouped and regrouped, taking new names and following new leaders. Led by aristocratic warriors, they often fought bitterly among themselves.

In the early years of Augustus's reign, Roman legions conquered large portions of what is now called Germany between the Rhine and the Elbe Rivers. Arminius's successful revolt in 9 C.E. drove out the Romans, however, and Roman civilization never took root in northern Europe. The Rhine and Danube Rivers became the symbolic boundary between Romans and their northern enemies. Most of Rome's legions were stationed along this boundary to defend against attacks from their northern neighbors.

Tribes along the northern border sometimes fragmented into pro- and anti-Roman factions. Romans supported kings who would favor their cause by fighting Rome's enemies beyond the borders and supplying troops to the auxiliary regiments of the Roman army. Occasionally for short periods of time, Germanic tribes formed loose confederations under the leadership of charismatic warlords in order to invade the empire themselves. For example, the Marcomanni, meaning "men of the borderlands," constituted one of these hostile confederations during the reign of Marcus Aurelius. Seeking land and booty, this confederation of many armed groups attacked the Roman

Empire with more than a hundred thousand men. Only after fourteen years of brutal war did Marcus Aurelius crush this force.

During long periods of peace, the people on either side of the border had the opportunity to interact with one another through military service and trade. Through extensive trade with Roman merchants, mostly Italians and Syrians, many Germanic aristocrats developed a taste for Mediterranean luxuries, including wine and jewelry. By the second century C.E. some chose to live in Roman-style villas in imitation of Roman aristocrats. Many Germanic men gained exposure to Roman civilization when they served in the Roman army as auxiliary troops. Discharged after the standard twenty-five years of service, many of these men returned to their homes with Roman money in their purses, a smattering of Latin, and knowledge of the riches and power of the Roman Empire.

DOCUMENT

Tacitus, *Germania*

By the end of the second century C.E. the weight of different peoples pressing on Rome's northern borders began to crack the imperial defenses. With the end of the Severan dynasty in 235 C.E., the empire entered a period of unrelieved disasters that lasted nearly fifty years. Invading groups from north of the Rhine and Danube Rivers pushed into the empire as far south as central Italy in search of plunder and land on which to settle. The Romans ultimately marshaled the military resources to repel the invaders and restore the empire's security late in the third century C.E. As we will see in the next chapter, however, the restored Roman Empire differed radically from the system Augustus inaugurated.

Economic Encounters Across Continents

The Roman empire stood on the edge of an almost global economic web. Trade routes linked the Mediterranean basin, the East African coast, the Persian Gulf, and the Red Sea with India's western Malabar coast, as well as with lands across the Bay of Bengal in Southeast Asia and China. One Roman account from the first century C.E., *Voyage Around the Red Sea*, written by an unknown author, describes a vast international commercial network.

Encounters with China

More than 3,000 forbidding miles separated the empires of Rome and China. Chinese documents from the first century C.E. mention ambassadors sent to Rome who reached as far as the Persian Gulf, and in 166 C.E. emperor Marcus Aurelius sent ambassadors to China, but the two empires never established formal ties.

Silk, not diplomatic links, bound Rome and China together. From the second millennium B.C.E. until the sixth century C.E., when Western entrepreneurs finally succeeded in smuggling the eggs of silkworms and the seeds of mulberry trees out of China, the Chinese possessed a monopoly on silk production. Far superior to wool and linen both in texture and in its ability to retain brightly colored dyes, silk was one of the most desired commodities in Roman society. In the Republican era, silk was so rare that even the wealthiest Romans could afford only small pieces, which they tended to wear as brooches.

Then, during the age of Augustus, Romans learned to use the monsoon winds to travel from southeastern Egypt across the Indian Ocean to the western coast of India, a journey that took about 40 days. Every year approximately 120 ships made this journey, lured by the promise of vast profits from the silk trade. In India, they would exchange glass, gold, wine, copper, and other items for silk. By the time this trade occurred, the price of the silk would have multiplied several times, as payments were made to each middleman along the 8,000-kilometer "Silk Road" that ran from northern China across the sweltering deserts, towering mountains, and treacherous salt flats of southern Asia and down through modern Afghanistan to the Indian coast. Yet silk was so precious that a successful journey would guarantee a Roman merchant a profit a hundred times larger than his original investment.

Roman demand for silk, spices (especially pepper), and other luxury items from the

Wineship

Found in Germany, this energetic but unsophisticated sculpture of the second century C.E. depicts wine merchants hurrying their cargo to thirsty customers somewhere on the Rhine River. Because grapes could not be cultivated in this northern region, wine was a luxury there. Common people drank beer.

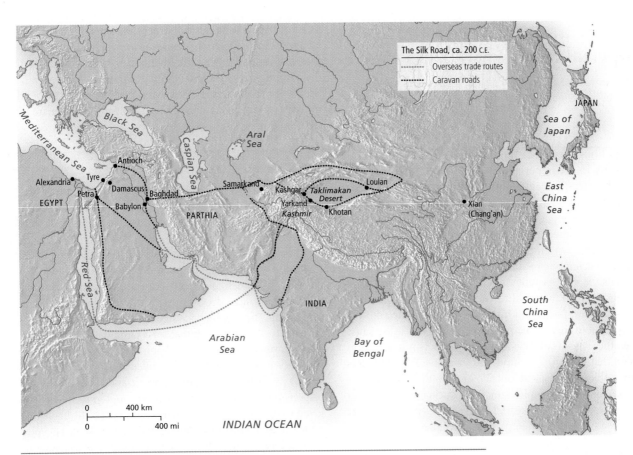

Map 5.5 The Silk Road
The first-century C.E. development of sea routes to supplement the overland parts of the journey greatly strengthened this cross-continental trading network.

Far East eventually produced a trade imbalance. As early as the first century C.E., Pliny the Elder griped, "And by the lowest reckoning India, China, and the Arabian Peninsula take from our Empire many thousands of pounds of gold every year—that is the sum which our luxuries and our women cost us." Pliny's concern was not unfounded: Many historians view the drain of hard currency to the East to pay for luxury goods as a key economic weakness of the Roman Empire, particularly from the third century onward.

Encounters with Africa

In addition to traveling to India and trading with China, Romans did some exploring in sub-Saharan Africa. Roman coins found deep in the interior of Africa suggest that they may have had commercial dealings with peoples there as well. To the Romans, however, "Africa" was one of their provinces bordering the Mediterranean Sea—the region we know as North Africa today—not the vast continent that lay to the south, beyond the Sahara Desert. Only in the European Middle Ages would the name *Africa* come to stand for the entire land mass of the continent.

The Romans knew little about sub-Saharan Africa. In 146 B.C.E., the Roman general Scipio sent the historian Polybius on an expedition down the west coast of Africa. Polybius's expedition got as far as Senegal and a place Scipio called Crocodile River. In the first century C.E., a Roman military expedition that marched south from a base in North Africa in pursuit of some raiders may have reached Chad. One hundred years later, an intrepid Roman officer named Julius Maternus traveled south for four months, reaching a place "where the rhinoceroses gather." He emerged in the Sudan, where he found the Nile and returned home.

The Romans used the word *Aethiopians* ("the People with Burned Faces") to refer to the peoples who lived south of the Sahara desert. Most of their knowledge of these peoples came from the Egyptians, who regularly traded with peoples living in the extreme south of the Nile River valley. From the Egyptians they learned of a place of fabulous wealth and exotic creatures. It would take many centuries, however, before European peoples viewed Africa as anything other than a fantasyland.

Society and Culture in the Imperial Age

■ What was the social and cultural response to the emergence and consolidation of empire?

The same central theme that characterized Roman politics after Augustus also characterized Roman society in the imperial age—the illusion of continuity with the Republic, masking fundamental change. The social pyramid described in Chapter 4 remained intact—senators at the top, followed by equestrians, plebeians and peasants, freedmen, and slaves. Important changes, however, occurred within the pyramid, as imperial rule altered social and economic relationships.

The shift from republic to empire also had a profound influence on Roman culture and religious belief. In their works, writers, poets, and historians explored the ambivalence of life under stable but autocratic rule. At the same time, the spread of religious cults promising salvation hinted that many people under Roman rule found life less than stable, and looked outside the political sphere for safety. Christianity, which emerged during the Augustan era, possessed a special appeal to the classes of society that benefited the least from imperial governance.

The Upper and Lower Classes

In the Roman Empire, aristocrats continued to stand at the top of the social pyramid, enjoying the greatest wealth, power, and prestige. Roman emperors recognized three social groups, or orders, as having aristocratic status. The first order, the senators of Rome, occupied a place of honor at the very top of the social pyramid. The Roman Senate was not a hereditary aristocracy, but Augustus encouraged the sons of senators to follow in their fathers' footsteps, and he offered financial incentives to senators to have children and perpetuate their family line. Despite these efforts, most of the oldest Roman senatorial families died out by the end of the first century C.E., due to death in war, failure to produce heirs, and falling victim to political intrigues. With the approval of the emperor, new aristocratic families emerged to take their place and serve in the Senate. These senators came from Roman families that had grown in wealth and prestige through service to the emperor. Many new senators also stemmed from the provinces and came to Rome to be in the Senate and serve as imperial officials. All senators, and their descendants for three generations, had the right to wear a broad purple stripe on their togas (formal clothing) as a badge of honor.

Below the senators stood the equestrian order, which was much larger than the senatorial order. Like senators, equestrians had to possess high birth and wealth—but to a lesser degree. The equestrian order flourished in the imperial age. Many equestrians continued to follow business careers as they had during the Republic, but the expansion of the empire provided them with new opportunities for public service. Equestrians staffed the diplomatic, fiscal, and military services, and a few were admitted to the Senate by the emperor.

The third aristocratic order consisted of the city councilors who served in the councils of every Roman city throughout the provinces. Like senators and equestrians of the city of Rome, they were expected to be wealthy, of respectable birth, and of good moral character. In many cities, the sons of freedmen (men who had once been slaves) were permitted to be city councilors.

These three aristocratic orders represented only a tiny fraction of the empire's population. Below them came the plebeians—Rome's poor but free underclass of citizens. Though not included in political life, plebeians living throughout the empire benefited in some ways from imperial rule. In the city of Rome, for example, they received a daily allotment of free grain. (Approximately half of Rome's population of one million depended on the daily gifts of grain.) With little incentive to work and deprived of the responsibilities of political participation, the plebeians enjoyed much free time. By the first century C.E., Romans had approximately 100 days designated as holidays. The plebeians demanded a steady diet of entertainment, such as the bloody gladiatorial combats in the Colosseum and the exciting chariot races in the Circus Maximus. Thus plebeian life in the city of Rome became dependent on "bread and circuses": free grain and free entertainment.

Plebeians needed bread and circuses to compensate not only for their loss of political power but also for their poor living conditions. Crowded into vile tenement slums with little light and no plumbing, the poor lived in misery. Disease kept the birth rate and life expectancy very low. Probably more than a quarter of all infants died within their first five years, and a third of those who survived were dead by age 10. The average Roman man died at age 45, and the average woman at age 34.

Poor people lived in similarly wretched conditions in every Roman city, but without the free distributions of grain. They relied on local aristocrats to provide food in times of emergency and to provide public entertainments. Plebeians in the countryside made their living primarily by farming, and they provided the bulk of troops in the Roman army.

Slaves and Freedmen

Slavery was one of the harshest facts of life in the Roman Empire. Slaves made up a huge percentage of Roman society, at the very bottom of the social order. Of the city of Rome's approximately one million inhabitants, an estimated 400,000 were slaves during the early empire. When Augustus took control of Rome, slaves constituted 35 to 40 percent of the total population of Italy.

Everyone accepted that humans could be reduced to property. Millions of slaves inhabited the empire, holding the lowest possible status in a society in which social and legal status meant everything. No Roman citizen ever objected to slavery as an institution. Some high-minded Stoic philosophers, who noted the common humanity of slaves and owners, did criticize slavery, but only because they feared its corrupting effect on the masters. They had no concern for the condition of the slaves themselves. Later Christian writers living within the empire stressed that slaves should obey their masters "with fear and trembling."

The victims of a brisk international trade in humans, most slaves entered the empire through conquest. Others were enslaved from birth, having been born of a slave mother. There was never a shortage of slaves, and sometimes after a successful military campaign, such as Trajan's defeat of the Dacians in 106 C.E., the market was glutted.

Ownership of slaves reflected a person's status. The emperor himself owned tens of thousands of slaves who labored on his estates throughout the empire. Rich men, too, possessed them in huge numbers. Even poor artisans and teachers might hold one or two. Former slaves who had gained their freedom (freedmen) also owned slaves. Slaves were permitted to earn money, with the result that even some slaves owned slaves.

Slaves used for domestic service or in commerce and crafts were the lucky ones. Many slaves worked on the great plantations, or latifundia°, as part of large slave gangs. The absentee owners cared little for the welfare of these slaves. Latifundia slaves often labored in chains and slept in underground prisons. The slaves sent to work in the mines experienced even worse conditions. For them, only a wretched death lay ahead. Female slaves were spared the horrors of working in the fields and mines, but they were valued far less than were male slaves.

Dehumanized by their enslavement and stripped of their identity when taken from family and home, slaves lived in fear of their masters, who could abuse them physically or sexually with impunity. Violence lay at the heart of this institution, for ultimate control of slaves rested on force. In 61 C.E. when Pedanius Secundus, the chief administrator of the city of Rome, was killed by one of his slaves, all the other 400 slaves in his household were executed in accordance with Roman custom, on the assumption that some of them surely must have known the killer's intention. Romans, in common with the Greeks and other ancient peoples, believed that the only way to compel a slave to tell the truth was through torture. Thus, any testimony provided by a slave in court was valid only if it was extracted by torture. In the face of such brutality, slaves had few options. Slaves could try to escape, but if caught were branded on the forehead. Slave revolts never succeeded.

Despite their utter lack of freedom, many slaves formed emotional and sexual relationships with one another. Epitaphs on graves demonstrate that they used conventional terms of affection and marriage bonds such as husband and wife, although Roman law did not recognize these informal slave marriages. Some slave owners permitted slave marriages because they understood that slaves with families would be less likely to rebel. Complete submissiveness and the goodwill of their masters were necessary to hold a slave family together.

Slavery was not, however, necessarily a permanent condition. Slaves might obtain their freedom through manumission. Through this carefully regulated legal procedure, a master granted freedom to a slave as a reward for faithful service or docile behavior, or even out of genuine affection. Of course manumission worked to the best interests of the owner: The merest hope of manumission kept most slaves docile. Moreover, Roman law established limits to manumission. No more than 100 slaves could be freed at the death of an owner, and the slave had to be at least 30 years old and the owner at least 25.

Despite these restrictions, the freedmen constituted an important class in Roman society. Freedmen made up only about 5 percent of Rome's population, but their enterprise and ambition marked them as some of the more successful members of Roman society. Many former slaves worked in business or as skilled laborers, teachers, and doctors. Unlike in other ancient societies, freedmen rid themselves of the taint of slavery in only one generation. A freed slave had only partial citizen rights, but his or her children became full Roman citizens, who could freely marry other citizens. The historian Tacitus records a remark made in a senatorial debate about this phenomenon: "Not without good reason had our ancestors, in distinguishing the position of the different orders, thrown freedom open to all." Tacitus noted that some senators and many equestrians could point to exslaves among their ancestors.

Slavery remained a part of Mediterranean economic and social life until the early Middle Ages, but in the second century C.E. the role of slaves in the economy began to diminish. As Roman emperors concentrated on consolidating rather than expanding the borders of the empire, the supply of slaves dwindled, and the cost of slaves rose. Thus, slave owning may have become less economically viable.

Women in the Roman Empire

Women in the senatorial and equestrian ranks possessed far more freedom than was usual in the ancient world. By 250 C.E., the form of marriage by which a woman passed from the control of her father to that of her husband had almost entirely died out. Women remained, at least theoretically, under the control of their father or legal guardian. In practice, this form of marriage gave a woman more freedom, in large part because her husband no longer controlled her dowry. Some women used this freedom to move more into the public view, taking part in banquets, attending the gladiatorial battles at the Colosseum and the races at the Circus Maximus, and presiding over literary salons. Wealthy women owned property, made investments, and became public benefactors. Many high-ranking women were educated in the liberal arts and lived a cultivated lifestyle. Their surviving portraits (carved in stone) reveal a restrained physical elegance. The portraits of several wives and daughters of emperors even appeared on coins.

As these coins suggest, at the highest level of society some women possessed real political power, though expressed behind the scenes. Livia, married to Augustus for fifty-two years, possessed a great deal of influence during his reign and worked actively to ensure the succession of her son Tiberius. The emperor Hadrian may have received his throne in part because of the influence of his cousin Trajan's wife, Plotina. At Plotina's funeral, Hadrian admitted, "She often made requests of me, and I never once refused her." The empress Julia Domna survived her husband Septimius Severus to become an important political power during the reign of her son Caracalla.

Lives of Luxury

A woman pours perfume in this wall painting from around 20 B.C.E. Only the wealthy could afford perfume and paintings.

The vast majority of women, of course, were not immortalized in stone or coin. We have scanty evidence about the lives of non-aristocratic women in the Roman Empire. Women do, however, appear in some records as moneylenders, shopkeepers, and investors, and there is evidence that some women became doctors while others prospered as artists. Most women probably married and gave birth to three or four children. If they survived childbirth, which many of them did not, then they would very likely see at least one or two of their children die before reaching adulthood.

Although literary evidence demonstrates that many aristocratic Roman men cherished their daughters, the practice of female infanticide remained common throughout Roman society. The expected ratio of female to male births is 105 to 100. In second-century Rome, however, the rate was 100 to 131. Unwanted babies—not only girls but also the sick and malformed, as well as some born outside marriage—were killed through exposure: The baby was left on a pile of garbage or by the roadside. Not all died; often, the babies were picked up and raised as slaves.

Literature and Empire

Writers during the reign of Augustus embodied the tensions and uncertainties of living in a society that had exchanged freedom for stability. The presence of imperial autocracy, as well as Rome's expanding might, affected literary production in different ways.

The work of the historian Livy (59 B.C.E.–12 C.E.) illustrates the fine line walked by writers in an age of autocracy. Livy wrote a massive history of Rome, called *From the Foundation of the City,* that traced Rome from its origins until his own time. Though less than a fifth of this work survives, we see that Livy presented Rome's rise to world mastery as a series of instructive moral and patriotic lessons. He showed how Rome grew to world power because of both its military and its moral strength. Although proud of Rome's greatness, Livy also believed that with power came decadence. He did not gloss over the ruthlessness with which Augustus waged the civil war that destroyed the Republic, nor did he veil his criticism of what he perceived as Rome's moral and political decline. Augustus made his displeasure with Livy's open criticism known, yet he did not punish the historian, perhaps because Livy also expressed the hope that Augustus would restore Rome's glory.

Ovid (43 B.C.E.–17 C.E.) was not so fortunate. His tragic career demonstrated the risks of offending an emperor. Ovid's brilliant love elegies had made him the darling of Rome. His lighthearted descriptions of Roman sexual life were contrary to the ideals of Augustus's legislation on marriage, while his book *Metamorphoses* developed themes of change and impermanence that indirectly challenged the idea of a stable state under Augustus's leadership. In 8 C.E., Ovid's erotic poem "The Art of Love," along with an obscure scandal involving Augustus's daughter, earned him the hostility of the emperor. Augustus exiled Ovid to a squalid village on the Black Sea, where he died in sorrow.

The poet Horace (65–8 B.C.E.), son of a wealthy freedman, walked a more careful path. He avoided political entanglements and maintained close ties to Augustus. His poetry on public themes praised Augustus for bringing peace and the hope of a moral life to the world. Throughout his work, Horace urged serene appreciation of life's transient joys. In his most famous verse (*Odes* I.11.6ff) he sings, "Be wise, taste the wine, and since our time is brief, be moderate in your aspirations. Even as we speak, greedy life slips away from us. Grasp each day (*carpe diem*) and do not pin your hopes on tomorrow."

Virgil stands as the greatest of the Roman poets. Drawing on Hellenistic poetic forms, Virgil wrote of the wisdom, safety, and serenity found in an idealized country life—with the terrible uncertainties of civil war providing a silent backdrop. At Augustus's request Virgil composed the *Aeneid*°, an epic poem that legitimized and celebrated the emperor's reign. Ostensibly the poem was about the mythic foundation of the Roman state by the hero Aeneas, a Trojan prince fleeing the destruction of his native city by the Greeks. But through a series of cinematic "flash-forwards," Virgil presented the entire history of the Roman people as culminating in the reign of Augustus. In the *Aeneid*, the emperor brings to completion the nearly unendurable efforts of his Trojan ancestor.

Although the *Aeneid* praises Augustus, Virgil was not just a propagandist for the imperial regime. Virgil praised those aspects of peace and fulfillment of duty that he genuinely valued, but he questioned the costs of warfare and empire on human beings by subtly investigating the toll imposed by the demands of public duty on individual character. In the *Aeneid* Virgil's hero Aeneas is deeply tempted by his love for the Carthaginian queen Dido to abandon his mission of founding Rome. But Aeneas overcomes his private desire in favor of the destiny of Rome: He abandons Dido to continue his divinely inspired mission. At the end of the poem, Aeneas stands victorious— but a psychological ruin. He has given everything to his duty. Virgil makes his readers wonder about the costs of such utter public service.

Seneca (ca. 4 B.C.E.–41 C.E.), who combined philosophical interests with literary skill, accepted the imperial system. He intended his writings to give sound advice to rulers. Deeply influenced by Stoicism, Seneca courageously acknowledged how hard it was to control one's human weaknesses and live a truly moral life. His integrity and rhetorical brilliance earned him the unenviable task of being Nero's tutor when the emperor was still an impressionable 12-year-old boy. For eight years Seneca guided Nero, and the empire enjoyed good government. As Nero matured, however, he found other, less decent advisers. Appalled by his student's descent into corruption, Seneca plotted to kill Nero. When he was caught, he killed himself.

Practitioners of the art of public speaking (rhetoric) had to grapple most directly with the new realities of the imperial age. Autocratic government made free political debate impossible. Nevertheless, opportunities for public speech still abounded: Law cases still had to be tried in court, and emperors had to be bathed in praise at regular intervals. Thus, rhetoric blossomed in the new imperial world. Quintilian (ca. 35–ca. 90 C.E.) exemplifies the new kind of imperial rhetorician. He rose to prominence in Rome as a teacher and speaker, becoming the tutor in the royal household of the emperor Domitian. His masterpiece, *Training in Oratory*, calls for clarity and balance in speaking. It also rather wistfully suggests that an orator might guide the Senate and the state, as Quintilian's model Cicero had done during the days of the Republic.

The historian and rhetorician Tacitus (ca. 56–ca. 118 C.E.) took a more realistic approach than Quintilian. In his *Dialogue on Orators* he argued—correctly—that political autocracy had killed true oratory, reducing it to mere public entertainment and ceremonial flourishes. Sardonic and terse, Tacitus's historical accounts covering the first century of the Augustan age displayed a deep understanding of human psychological reaction to the harsh political realities of early imperial tyranny. Although Tacitus's career flourished under the tyrannical Domitian, he hated political oppression and he never abandoned his love for the best of Roman ideals. In the *Agricola*, his biography of his father-in-law, Tacitus affirmed that good men could serve their country honorably, even under bad rulers. The *Agricola* thus inadvertently revealed an important accomplishment of Augustus's imperial system: It had tamed the competitive energies of Rome's aristocrats, transforming them into an efficient governing class.

Eager to contemplate the cultural superiority of the Roman Empire over other peoples, Rome's ruling elite took a strong interest in the habits of non-Romans. In his *Geography*, Strabo (64 B.C.E.–ca. 25 C.E.), a native Greek and a Roman citizen, wrote a detailed account of the many peoples ruled by Rome, stressing how Roman civilization could change foreign cultures for the better. He suggested that Rome's rulers and administrators should "bring together cities and peoples into a single Empire and political management." Drawing on Hellenistic and Greek traditions of writing about foreign cultures, Strabo placed the Roman Empire at the center of the inhabited world.

In addition to geography, other forms of scientific writing made great strides in the early centuries of the Roman Empire. Claudius Ptolemy of Alexandria maintained the high standards of the Hellenistic science tradition that continued to flourish under Roman rule. Writing in the second half of the second century C.E. (we do not know the dates of his birth or death), Ptolemy composed definitive works in many fields. Using the division of spheres into units of 60 first developed by the Sumerians and perfected by the Babylonians, Ptolemy's *Almagest* proved the theories and tables necessary to compute the positions of the sun, the moon, and five known planets. He accepted the Greek theory that the sun revolves around the Earth. Western astronomers used his maps of the heavens for nearly 1,500 years. His *Geography* gave readings in longitude and latitude and provided information for drawing a world map, which remained the basis of cartography until the sixteenth century. Translated from Greek into Arabic, Ptolemy's books became standard in the medieval Islamic world. Eventually they were translated into Latin and so passed back into use in western Europe during the Middle Ages.

Roman medicine also helped shape Western practices for hundreds of years. The physician Galen (131–201 C.E.) was one of the most prolific writers in the imperial period: A fire in 191 C.E. destroyed many of his manuscripts, yet enough of his work survives today to fill twenty volumes in Greek. His writings ranged from philosophy to philology, but his medical theory and practice proved the most influential. Galen sought to make medicine a science. He insisted on the importance of dissection in understanding the physical body, and stressed the need for experimentation. For most of his career Galen worked in Rome, but he served for four years as physician to the gladiators in his hometown of Pergamum, where he was able to study firsthand the impact of trauma on the human body.

Galen's influence on Western medicine was not wholly positive. He viewed disease as the result of an imbalance in the body's four "humors," or basic bodily fluids (blood, bile, urine, phlegm). Too much blood, for example, meant fever. To restore the balance, Galen taught, the physician should apply leeches or cut open a vein, and thereby drain the patient of "excess" blood. The practice of bloodletting, and the humoral theory on which it was based, remained central in Western medical practice into the early decades of the nineteenth century.

Religious Life

Religious expression in the Roman Empire took many forms. The imperial government made no effort to impose uniform belief, so subject peoples freely worshiped many gods and maintained their traditional religious rituals. Within many religious cultures, trends that first appeared in the Hellenistic Age continued, but important new changes emerged during the imperial era. Judaism was transformed during this period. At the same time, an entirely new religion, Christianity, emerged from Jewish roots. This new faith grew to become the dominant religion in the empire by 400 C.E. and eventually suppressed polytheistic religions.

DOCUMENT

Galen the Physician

Galen, the greatest physician of the imperial age, described in vivid terms how peasants in the countryside often were very close to starvation.

As soon as summer was over, those who live in the cities, in accordance with their universal practice of collecting a sufficient supply of grain to last a whole year, took from the fields all the wheat, with the barley, beans and lentils, and left to the rustics only those annual products which are called pulses and leguminous fruits; they even took away a good part of these to the city. So the people in the countryside, after consuming during the winter what had been left, were compelled to use unhealthy forms of nourishment. Through the spring they ate twigs and shoots of trees, bulbs and roots of unwholesome plants, and they made unsparing use of what are called wild vegetables, whatever they could get hold of, until they were surfeited; they ate them after boiling them whole like green grasses, of which they had not tasted before even as an experiment. I myself in person saw some of them at the end of spring and almost all at the beginning of summer afflicted with numerous ulcers covering their skin and inflamed tumours, others from spreading boils, others had an eruption resembling . . . leprosy.

Source: From Galen, translated by G. E. M. de Ste. Croix in *The Class Struggle in the Ancient Greek World.* Copyright © 1981 by G. E. M. de Ste. Croix. Reprinted by permission of Gerald Duckworth & Co. Ltd.

Polytheism in the Empire

Syncretism°, the practice of equating two gods and fusing their cults, was a common feature of imperial religious life. Like many other Mediterranean peoples, the Romans often identified a foreign god with their own deities. For example, Julius Caesar described the Gallic god of commerce as Mercury, because Mercury served the same function in Roman religion. Romans did not care that other people throughout the empire might worship Jupiter or Juno or any other Roman god in different ways, or might give the gods different attributes. Syncretism, then, helped unify the diverse peoples and regions under Roman rule. Through syncretism, shared religious experiences spread across the empire.

Imperial subjects worshiped the emperor and Rome, the protectors of the entire empire. In addition, each city in the empire had its own gods, whom people imagined as dwelling within the temples dedicated to them. Worshipers gathered in front of the temples to offer sacrifices at altars located in front of the shrines. On religious holidays, thousands of city dwellers participated in parades and feasted at the great banquets that followed the sacrifice of many specially selected animals at temple altars. Particularly elaborate celebrations attracted pilgrims and visitors from afar.

The gods worshiped in specific cities and at specific holy sites generally were of great antiquity. Gods such as Athena in Athens or Jupiter in Rome were as old as the town itself. People believed that these gods would protect and benefit their communities if the residents made the proper sacrifices. Although a deity might be associated with a similar god in another town, its worship in each city had a unique quality, deeply intertwined with the history and architecture of the town itself. For example, Hercules protected many places, but his temple in each town was connected to a different local myth about him.

Some religious cults transcended their places of origin and spread widely, particularly among slaves, freedmen, and the urban poor who felt lost in the sprawl of the empire's big cities. The anonymity of life in big cities for the poor contributed to the spread of religions that offered a measure of identity and community and a kind of salvation as well. Religions that promised victory over death or liberation from the abuses and pain of daily existence possessed a wide appeal and spread quickly across the empire.

The goddess Isis, for example, who originated in Egypt, offered freedom from the arbitrary abuses of fate to her many followers throughout the empire. The story of Isis revolved around the death and resurrection of her husband Osiris (also called Serapis); her initiates believed that they, too, would experience life after death. Moreover, Isis—often depicted holding her baby son Horus—represented the universal mother and so attracted believers with her promise of compassionate nurture.

In his work *The Golden Ass,* the Roman writer Apuleius (ca. 125–ca. 170 C.E.) describes the goddess's protective power. Full of eroticism and magic, the story tells of Lucius, a carefree young Romeo, who is turned into a miserable donkey when caught spying on a gorgeous witch. After many comic misadventures in which Lucius learns how uncertain fate can be, Isis restores him to human form. In gratitude, Lucius thanks Isis for caring "for the troubles of miserable humans with a sweet mother's love." He joins her religion and becomes her priest.

Another popular religion that promised salvation to its initiates was that of Mithras, a sun god. Artists depicted Mithras slaying a bull, an archetypal sacrifice that his followers reenacted in secret ceremonies. Limited to men, worship of Mithras took place in underground chambers in which small groups held banquets, recited sacred lessons about the celestial journey of the soul after death, and made sacrifices to the god in imitation of his killing of the bull. Because this religion stressed both physical courage and performance of duty, it particularly attracted soldiers and administrators.

The most important religion of an eastern god whose worship spread throughout the Roman Empire was that of the Unconquered Sun. Originating in Syria, this deity came to be associated with Apollo and Helios, two Greco-Roman sun gods. When Elagabalus, the high priest of the Syrian sun god (El-Gabal), became Roman emperor (r. 218–222 C.E.), he built a huge temple dedicated to his god in Rome, and designated December 25 as a special day of worship to the deity. Within fifty years, the Unconquered Sun became the chief god of imperial and official worship.

Mummy Wrapping from Egypt

This painted linen cloth was wrapped around a mummy in an Egyptian burial during the second century C.E. It shows the Egyptian god Osiris (on the left) and the jackal-headed god Anubis (on the right). Between them is the deceased man, dressed in Roman clothing. His portrait has been carefully painted and added separately. This wrapping and portrait show the continuity of ancient Egyptian religion during Roman imperial rule.

Mithras Slays the Bull

Made around 100 C.E., this sculpture shows Mithras, a god of the sun, in the sacred act of sacrificing a bull. Mithras was a savior god whose followers received salvation. Limited to men only who were organized in strict hierarchies, the worship of Mithras occurred throughout the empire. Worshipers met for fellowship, a communal meal, and worship in small, private chambers.

The greatest product of the rabbinic tradition of this era was the Mishnah, a collection of opinions, decisions, and homilies to explain the law to unlearned people. Jewish teachers had begun accumulating this material in Hellenistic times, but it was completed around the year 220 C.E. In their desire to prepare a manageable body of material for reference and teaching, rabbis undertook a task not unlike that of the Roman jurists. But unlike Roman compilations, which drew from written texts, the Mishnah drew largely from oral law that had been memorized and transmitted through many generations.

Compiled by Rabbi Judah the Prince and his school, the Mishnah consists of sixty-three books, each dealing with a particular aspect of law, ranging from matters of ritual purity to calendrical issues to civil and criminal law. Among the many moral principles stressed by the Mishnah, saving life was paramount. According to the Mishnah, no person could save his or her own life by causing another's death, and no person could be sacrificed for the welfare of the community. Moreover, to save a life, any person could break any Jewish religious law, except those forbidding idolatry, adultery, incest, or murder. In Jewish thought, saving one life symbolized saving humanity. A radical idea slowly emerged from this principle: Since all humans are made in God's image, they should all have equal rights. This idea contributed to the gradual decline of slave holding among Jews.

In addition to the rabbis who led individual Jewish communities, an official called the Patriarch represented the Jews as a whole to the emperor. The Romans appointed the Patriarch and gave him the highest political authority in Jewish affairs in the empire. The Patriarch's responsibilities included collecting taxes for Rome and choosing judges for Jewish courts. The Romans gave the Patriarch the rank of senator, as the representative of all the Jews in the empire. This arrangement, a clear example of how Roman authorities let local populations manage their own laws, continued until Christianity became the official religion of the empire in the fifth century C.E. Christian emperors then began persecuting Jews and limiting their participation in public life.

Only the rise of Christianity would displace the worship of the Unconquered Sun.

Gnosticism, which originated in the Hellenistic Age, continued its influence in the Roman Empire, affecting Judaism, Christianity, and many polytheistic religions. Gnostics believed that the material world of daily life is incompatible with the supreme god. They thought that sparks of divinity (sometimes considered the human soul) are imprisoned within the body. Only a redeemer sent from the supreme god could release these divine sparks.

The Origins of Rabbinic Judaism

Following the Roman devastation of Judaea and the destruction of the Temple in Jerusalem in 70 C.E., a new kind of community-based religious life began to develop among Jews in Judaea and other lands. Since the sixth century B.C.E., communities of Jews had lived outside Palestine, but after the Romans ransacked Judaea, the Diaspora° ("dispersion of population") came to characterize Jewish life. Jerusalem ceased to serve as the focus of Judaism's religious ceremony, although not of Jewish religious thought and aspiration. More concretely, the entire religious practice of ritual animal sacrifice centered on the Temple disappeared. So, too, did the priesthood. The rabbi ("my master" in Hebrew) gradually replaced the priest in the role of religious instructor and community guide. Scholars trained in the Jewish law, rabbis interpreted and taught the Torah, the first five books of the Hebrew Bible. By 200 C.E., synagogues emerged as communal centers in which rabbis studied Jewish law and passed judgment on disputes. Gradually synagogues developed into centers where the Jewish community would celebrate the Sabbath and pray together.

The Emergence of Christianity

The emergence of Christianity forced the Romans to deal with an entirely new community within the empire. Christianity was more than a new set of religious beliefs; Christians had a new sense of shared identity, a new sense of history, and a new perception of the Roman system. The

A Jewish Offering

According to the Greek inscription, Jacob, a local leader, left this gold medallion to the synagogue in fulfillment of a vow. Jacob made his offering somewhere in the eastern Mediterranean region some time after the third century C.E. The medallion shows a menorah, the seven-branched lampstand, and other objects of Jewish ritual.

number of Christians gradually grew until they came to dominate the religious life of the empire. Within 400 years of the death of its founder, Christianity became the official imperial religion.

The founder of Christianity was a Jew named Yeshua ben Yosef, known today as Jesus of Nazareth (ca. 4 B.C.E.– ca. 30 C.E.). Born during the reign of Augustus, Jesus grew to manhood in the Jewish community of Galilee, in northern Palestine. Around age 30 he began to travel through Palestine with a band of followers, urging men and women to repent their sins because God would soon come to rule the Kingdom of Heaven on Earth. Jesus' followers believed him to be the messiah, an important figure in Jewish prophetic writings whose coming would inaugurate a new age of freedom for God's people. Like many other contemporary Jewish teachers, Jesus insisted that having the right intent in carrying out God's law mattered more than conforming to the outward performance of the law. When asked to identify the greatest commandment, Jesus replied, "You must love the Lord your God with all your heart, with all your soul, and with all your mind. This is the greatest and the first commandment. The second resembles it: You must love your neighbor as yourself. On these two commandments hang the whole Law." Jesus urged his listeners and followers to regard themselves and others as God's children, and taught them to recognize God as their loving Father.

In 30 C.E. Jesus entered Jerusalem to preach his message. He dared to challenge some of the Jewish elites who controlled the Jewish Temple under Roman supervision, and caused a near-riot. This dangerous act led the Roman authorities to arrest, try, and convict him as a revolutionary. Sentenced to death, Jesus died by crucifixion, the usual form of capital punishment in the Roman Empire for noncitizens.

Jesus' followers, however, insisted that he still lived, that he rose from the dead three days after being executed, and that he appeared to them a number of times in the forty days between his resurrection from the dead and his ascent into Heaven. They proclaimed him as not only the Jewish messiah, but as the Son of God who died on the cross as part of the divine plan. In Christian theology, Jesus' brutal death at the hands of the Romans became a loving sacrifice: The sinless Son of God endured the punishment that sinful men and women deserved. Christians, then, regarded Jesus as their savior, as the God whose intervention in human history rescued them from their sins and whose spirit continued to guide them in their earthly lives.

Jesus recorded none of his ideas in writing, but his followers transmitted his teachings orally for several decades after his death and then in the 50s and 60s C.E. began to write them down. By about 120 C.E. they had compiled an authoritative body of texts that recorded Jesus' life and words, which Christians

DOCUMENT

The Gospel According to Luke

The Trial of Jesus in Historical Perspective

In 30 C.E. Roman authorities in the city of Jerusalem in the Roman province of Judaea tried and executed a Jewish teacher known as Jesus of Nazareth, whose teachings lie at the foundation of Christianity, the faith of hundreds of millions of people in the world today. Although an insignificant event at the time, the trial of Jesus and its interpretation made and continues to make a profound impact on Western civilization.

Information about Jesus' trial comes from the New Testament books of Matthew, Mark, Luke, and John. These narratives, called the Gospels, were written thirty to sixty years after Jesus' death. They relate that during three years of teaching and miraculous healing in the Roman provinces of Galilee and Judaea, Jesus earned the resentment of certain segments of the Jewish religious leadership by disregarding aspects of Jewish religious law. According to the Gospels, when Jesus entered the Temple precinct in Jerusalem, he angered the temple elites by denouncing their hypocrisy and by overturning the tables of money changers. The priests then conspired to kill him. They paid one of Jesus' followers to reveal his whereabouts, arrested him on either the night before or the night of the Passover feast, and tried him immediately before the Sanhedrin, the highest Jewish court, which met that same night in the house of the Jewish high priest. The Sanhedrin found Jesus guilty of the crime of blas-

phemy for claiming to be the messiah, the Son of God.

Lacking the authority to put Jesus to death, the Jewish leaders brought Jesus before Pontius Pilate, the Roman governor, and demanded that he execute Jesus. Pilate hesitated, but the priests persuaded him by insisting that Jesus threatened the emperor's authority with his claim to be king of the Jews. Pilate's soldiers crucified Jesus, but according to the Gospel accounts, the real blame for Jesus' death lay with the Jews, who had demanded his execution. In all four Gospels, Jewish crowds in Jerusalem reject Jesus and cry out, "Crucify him!" to a reluctant Pontius Pilate.

The Gospel accounts of Jesus' arrest, trial, and crucifixion offer some difficulties for historians: Portions of these narratives conflict with what scholars understand about the conduct of trials by Jewish authorities or Roman administrators. For example, the evidence that we have indicates that the Sanhedrin did not hold trials at night; it did not meet in the house of the high priest; and it did not

convene on a Jewish feast day or the night before a feast.

Far more important than these issues, however, is the question of the crime of blasphemy. According to Jewish law Jesus would not have blasphemed by claiming to be the messiah. Originating in ceremonies of anointing kings, the word *messiah* had many interpretations in Judaism as a kingly figure of power—but not as a divine being. Some scholars, though, argue that the Jewish leaders could have construed as blasphemy both Jesus' criticisms of Temple Judaism and his inferred claim to sit in God's presence (and thus to share in God's rule).

The issue of Jesus' blasphemy remains unclear but there is little debate about the importance of Jesus' confrontation with the Jewish elites in the Temple. Jesus had committed a very dangerous act by denouncing the priests in Jerusalem. These men, especially the high priest himself, owed their positions of power to the Roman overlords and were responsible for maintaining order. Many Jews in the temple elite saw Jesus as an agitator who posed a threat to their authority. Jesus was first brought before the Sanhedrin, the Jewish court permitted by the Romans to deal with affairs within the Jewish community. The Romans had appointed all seventy-one members of the court, including Caiaphas, the high priest who led it. These court members knew that if they could not control Jesus, the Romans would certainly replace them. The Sanhedrin could not punish Jesus under Jewish law, but it could send him before Roman magistrates on a

The Scales of Justice
This coin shows the goddess Aequitas, who represents the idea of fairness in Roman justice.

Early Christian Symbols
Some of the earliest Christian symbols decorate this Roman tombstone.

The anchor represents hope.

The fish stands for Jesus. The Greek word for fish, icthus, *is an anagram of the Greek words for "Jesus Christ Son of God and Savior."*

charge that the Romans would not hesitate to prosecute—stirring up rebellion.

Jesus' popularity with the common people and the disturbance in the Temple precinct would have been enough to arouse Roman suspicion. Roman officials usually responded to real or imagined threats to the political order by crucifixion. In the eyes of Pontius Pilate, a cautious magistrate, Jesus constituted a threat to public order, and so deserved execution. He would not have been reluctant to kill him.

Why, then, do the Gospels tend to shift the blame for Jesus' death from Pontius Pilate, who most certainly ordered Jesus' execution, and place it on the Jewish community? We know that the Gospel narratives began to be written down in an atmosphere of growing hostility and suspicion between Jews and Christians. Moreover, after Roman armies destroyed the Jerusalem Temple in the Jewish rebellion of 66–70 C.E.,

Christians wanted to disassociate themselves from Jews in Roman eyes, hoping to persuade Roman authorities to think of them not as rebels but rather as followers of a lawful religion. Such concerns may have shaped the Gospel writers' tendencies to emphasize the role of Jewish leaders in Jesus' death and to deemphasize Pilate's responsibility.

The Gospels also relate that before he died Jesus predicted the destruction of the Jewish Temple in Jerusalem. Many early Christians came to believe that the fall of the Temple and the savage repression of the Jewish rebellion served as divine punishment for the Jews who had caused Jesus' death. These interpretations of Jesus' trial and execution, and of the destruction of the Jewish community in Palestine, helped poison Christian-Jewish relations for two millennia. From the first century C.E. through the twentieth, important segments of the Christian community blamed "the Jews" for Jesus' crucifixion.

Questions of Justice

1. What does the trial of Jesus show about Roman methods of provincial administration—and about the limitations of these methods? Who had power in Judaea?
2. In Christian theology, Jesus died for the sins of the world. In theological terms, then, all sinners—all human beings—bear responsibility for Jesus' death. Why, then, does it matter if the Gospels place the blame for Jesus' crucifixion on Jews instead of Romans?

Taking It Further

Crossan, John Dominic. *Who Killed Jesus: Exposing the Roots of Anti-Semitism in the Gospel Story of the Death of Jesus.* 1997. A highly engaging investigation.

Johnson, Luke Timothy, John Dominic Crossan, and Werner H. Kelber. *The Jesus Controversy.* 1999. Three experts discuss the problems of finding who Jesus "really was."

Sherwin-White, A. N. *Roman Society and Roman Law in the New Testament.* 1963. A leading Roman historian puts the New Testament in its Roman context.

call the New Testament. Christians held that Jesus' teachings contained in the New Testament built on the teachings of the Hebrew Bible—the "Old" Testament. Consequently, they tended to interpret the Hebrew Bible in light of Christianity. For example, Christians read the prophetic writings of the Hebrew Bible as predictions of Jesus' birth, death, and resurrection.

For many decades after Jesus' death, his followers still thought of themselves as Jews. The word *Christian* (which comes from the Greek word *Christos,* meaning "the anointed one" or "messiah") was first used in the Syrian city of Antioch in the second half of the first century C.E. Christianity, however, eventually diverged from Judaism. Most scholars agree that the work and teaching of Paul of Tarsus (d. ca. 65 C.E.) played a crucial role in this development. An educated Jew, Paul fiercely opposed the new Christian teachings until he had a vision of Jesus calling him to Christian service. Paul became as ardent in his advocacy of Christianity as he had been in his opposition. The most effective early Christian missionary, he traveled throughout Asia Minor, inaugurating and developing Christian communities. Even more important, Paul wrote letters that circulated among these communities. These letters, written in the 50s C.E., constitute our earliest written Christian documents and articulate key doctrines of the Christian faith—doctrines that helped divide Christianity from Judaism.

In Paul's writings, the Christian view of Jesus' crucifixion as a divine sacrifice to atone for human sin was first fully developed. Paul taught that the only way a man or a woman could join God after death for an eternity of peace and happiness was by belief in Jesus as the Son of God and as the savior of humanity. Through participating in the ritual of the Eucharist (also called Holy Communion or the Lord's Supper), Christians recalled Jesus' sacrifice of himself on the cross. Paul preached this message of sacrifice and salvation to the Jews of the Diaspora and, significantly, to non-Jews. Paul encouraged Christian converts from outside Judaism to abide by certain Jewish laws, but he did not require that they be circumcised, a key Jewish initiation rite, or that they follow Jewish dietary restrictions.

Paul was executed as a troublemaker by the Romans in 65 C.E.; five years later the Roman army destroyed the Jewish Temple and devastated Judaea. After the fall of the Temple, Judaism and Christianity took their own distinctive paths. Yet, for all their fundamental differences of belief, Christianity and Judaism shared characteristics that distinguished them from other religions of antiquity. Both Christianity and Judaism combined a statement of belief with a social ethic. Their ethical systems embodied values that strengthened the religious community. Both, for example, protected the underprivileged—widows, orphans, and the poor—in their communities. Both religious communities also had an internal organization that did not depend on Rome. Their leaders (bishops for Christians and rabbis for Jews) gave judgments based on law that was separate from the Roman justice system. Finally, both Judaism and Christianity were monotheistic. Jews and Christians believed that that there is only one God, with whom contact is direct and immediate. To the Romans, who believed in many gods, this monotheism was the strangest aspect of the two faiths. Worshiping only one god made no sense to Romans, with their tradition of making sacrifices to many gods.

The Spread of Christianity

Christianity drew many of its first converts from socially marginalized groups, such as women, noncitizens, and slaves. Indeed, Jesus' message was revolutionary in the way it overturned conventional boundaries of class, gender, and ethnicity. Paul's writings in the New Testament illustrate this perspective. Paul encouraged a communal life in which all followers of Jesus were equal in the eyes of God. As he wrote to a small Christian community in Galatia in Asia Minor, "For in Christ Jesus . . . there is no longer Jew or Greek, there is no longer slave or free, there is no longer male or female; for all of you are one in Christ Jesus." Paul therefore urged the entry of gentiles (non-Jews) into the Christian community, believing that Jesus' teachings would one day unify the entire human race.

Christianity continued to attract the poor and outcast, but by the middle of the second century C.E., an important change occurred within the ranks of Christian adherents. Many new converts to the faith were men and women who had already been educated in Greek philosophy. They began to analyze and understand Christianity in the terms with which they were familiar: the abstract ideas of the Hellenistic philosophical tradition. Rather than dismiss the philosopher Plato, for example, they argued that his ideas about the supremacy of the soul and what it meant to lead a good life anticipated the teachings of Jesus.

Because it eventually led to Christianity's assimilation of much of classical culture, this encounter between Christians and the intelligentsia of the Mediterranean world transformed the Christian faith. As Christians explained their faith to educated gentiles in the language of traditional philosophical education, they won even more converts. They developed methods of analyzing biblical texts drawn from philosophy and rhetoric. The language of Christianity and Greek and Latin intellectual life fused.

Much of this development centered on the works of a group of Christian writers, whom historians call Apologists°. The Apologists publicly defended their faith to learned non-Christian audiences (just as Socrates had defended his beliefs in Plato's *Apology*—hence the name *Apologists*). In the process, they helped shape the Christian response to the challenges of Hellenist philosophy and cosmology. One of the most important of the Apologists, Justin Martyr (ca. 100–165 C.E.), sought to make Christianity comprehensible to other intellectuals like himself who had not grown up as Christians. Justin insisted that Christian beliefs accorded with rational thought and that Christianity was the culmination of intellectual developments that had begun in the classical past.

Justin Martyr's embrace of Greek philosophy was typical of Apologist thought. Another Apologist, Clement of Alexandria (ca. 150–216 C.E.), wrote that the study of Greek philosophy could prepare a Christian to understand Jesus' teachings. Origen (ca. 184–255 C.E.), the most profound thinker among the Apologists, was as much a classical scholar as a churchman. A talented editor and commentator on biblical texts, he also made significant contributions to Christian theology. He and Clement laid the groundwork for the integration of classical Greek philosophy and culture with Christianity. This complex step was of great importance in the development of Western civilization because it not only enhanced the appeal of Christianity among educated believers but also ensured the transmission of many Greek philosophical ideas to what would become Western culture.

The Apologists faced stiff opposition from within the Christian community because many churchmen viewed classical learning with deep suspicion. Tertullian (ca. 160–240 C.E.), Origen's influential contemporary, argued forcefully for the separation of Christianity from the learning and culture of the non-Christian world. He worried that the mingling of religious cults so common in his day might corrupt Christianity. Tertullian summed up his opposition to classical culture: "What has Athens to do with Jerusalem? What is there in common between the philosopher and the Christian? . . . After the Gospel we have no need for further research." Christians like Tertullian mistrusted the power of the human intellect and stressed the need to remain focused on the divine revelation of the Christian Scriptures. Yet Tertullian could not stop the integration of Christianity with classical learning. By the third century C.E. Christians could no longer ignore the Mediterranean world in which they lived.

And that world could no longer ignore them. Many of Christianity's core concepts, such as its ideas about personal salvation, the equality of individual men and women before God, and the redemption of humanity from sin, distinguished it from the empire's polytheistic faiths. Most strikingly, Christianity firmly rejected the existence of multiple gods and sought to convince followers of other religions that they stood in error. This conversionist impulse (called *proselytizing*), in addition to Christians' close community life and failure to engage in the public life of Roman culture, won them suspicion and persecution. Claudius expelled Christians from Rome, and in 64 C.E., Nero blamed Christians for a destructive fire that consumed central Rome. (Popular legend blamed him, equally wrongly.) Hundreds of Christians died in the arena before cheering crowds.

By the second half of the first century C.E., many Roman officials perceived Christians as potential enemies of the state because they refused to join in the worship of the emperor. Christians called the men and women who died rather than renounce their beliefs *martyrs*, or witnesses for their faith. Tertullian chided his Roman persecutors, "We multiply whenever we are mown down by you; the blood of Christians is [like] seed."

In their vision of all humanity united under a single God and their desire to replace other forms of religious expression with the worship of this one God, Christians were truly revolutionary. Christians eventually succeeded in displacing all polytheist religions within the Roman Empire. Although polytheism still exists in many parts of the world today, it is nearly absent from the West. A fundamental part of how many peoples understood the world changed radically as a result of the Christian revolution.

Conclusion

Rome Shapes the West

The map of the Roman Empire outlined the heart of the regions included in the West today. Rome was the means by which cultural and political ideas developed in Mediterranean societies and spread into Europe. This quilt of lands and peoples was acquired mostly by conquest. An autocratic government held the pieces together. Although Roman authorities permitted no dissent in the provinces, they allowed provincial peoples to become Roman. Being Roman meant that one had specific legal rights of citizenship, not that one belonged to a particular race or ethnic group. Thus, in addition to expanding the boundaries of the empire and patrolling its borders, the Roman army brought a version of Roman society to subject peoples. By imitating Roman styles of architecture and urban life, the cities, too, helped spread Roman civilization. Moreover, the elites of these cities helped funnel the resources of the countryside into the emperor's coffers, and so sustain the imperial system.

For two and a half centuries the *Pax Romana* inaugurated by Augustus fostered a remarkable degree of cultural uniformity within the empire's boundaries. Rome's civilization, including its legal system, its development of cities, and its literary and artistic legacy, made it the foundation of Western civilization as we know it today. The legal precedents established by Roman jurists remain valid in much of Europe. Latin and Greek literature of the early Roman Empire has entertained, instructed, and inspired readers in the West for nearly 2,000 years. Until very recently all educated people in the West could read Latin and many could read Greek, and looked to the works of the Romans for their model in prose style. Many of our public buildings and memorial sculptures continue to adhere to the artistic and architectural models first outlined in Rome. The Roman Empire was the most important and influential model of an imperial system for Europeans until modern times. Of equal importance, the monotheism and ethical teachings of Judaism and Christianity have been prominent forces in shaping Western ideals and attitudes.

A debilitating combination of economic weakness, civil war, and invasions by northern peoples would almost destroy the Roman Empire in the third century C.E. How the Roman Empire recovered and was transformed in the process is the story of the next chapter.

Suggestions for Further Reading

For a comprehensive list of suggested readings, please go to www.ablongman.com/levack2e/chapter5

Beard, Mary, John North, and Simon Price. *Religions of Rome.* 1995. The first volume contains essays on polytheist religions, and the second contains translated ancient sources.

Gardner, Jane F. *Women in Roman Law and Society.* 1987. Discusses issues pertaining to women in Rome.

Garnsey, Peter, and Richard Saller. *The Roman Empire: Economy, Society, and Culture.* 1987. Stresses the economic and social foundations of the Roman Empire.

Hornblower, Simon, and Antony Spawforth, eds. *The Oxford Classical Dictionary,* 3rd ed. 1996. This encyclopedia treats all aspects of Roman culture and history.

Isaac, Benjamin. *The Creation of Racism in Classical Antiquity.* 2004. A highly readable discussion of ancient social prejudices and discriminatory stereotypes that influenced the development of modern racism.

Markus, Robert. *Christianity in the Roman World.* 1974. An excellent study of the growth of Christianity.

Ramage, Nancy H., and Andrew Ramage. *Roman Art,* 4th ed. 2005. An excellent, beautifully illustrated introduction to Roman art and architecture.

Romm, James. *The Edges of the Earth in Ancient Thought: Geography, Exploration, and Fiction.* 1992. An exciting introduction to the Roman understanding of real and imaginary peoples.

Scott, Sarah, and Jane Webster, eds. *Roman Imperialism and Provincial Art.* 2003. A collection of essays that explores new approaches to the cultural interconnections between the Romans and the peoples they ruled.

Talbert, Richard, ed. *The Barrington Atlas of the Classical World.* 2000. This atlas contains the best maps available.

Webster, Graham. *The Roman Imperial Army,* 3rd ed. 1985. Discusses military organization and life in the empire.

Wiedemann, Thomas. *Emperors and Gladiators.* 1992. An important study of the ideology and practice of gladiatorial combat.

Wolfram, Herwig. *The Roman Empire and Its Germanic Peoples.* 1997. Examines the interrelation of Romans and Germans over several centuries.

Woolf, Greg. *Becoming Roman: The Origins of Provincial Civilization in Gaul.* 1998. The best recent study of Romanization.

Late Antiquity: The Age of New Boundaries, 250–600

6

DURING THE LAST WEEK OF AUGUST IN 410, AN EVENT OCCURRED THAT stunned the Roman world. A small army of landless warriors—no more than a few thousand men—led by their king Alaric, forced their way into the city of Rome and plundered it for three days. For more than a year Alaric had been threatening the city in an attempt to extort gold and land for his people. When his attempts at extortion failed, he resorted to attacking the city directly. Because Alaric's followers, the Visigoths, were Christian, they spared Rome's churches and took care not to violate nuns. But that left plenty of loot—gold, silver, and silks—for them to cart away.

For these warriors and their families, who had first invaded the Roman Empire from their homelands in southern Russia thirty years earlier, pillaging the most opulent city in the Mediterranean world was a pleasant interlude in a long struggle to secure a permanent home. For the Romans, however, the looting of Rome was an unfathomable disaster. They could scarcely believe that their capital city, the gleaming symbol of world rule, had fallen to an army of people they considered barbarian thugs, one of several Germanic tribes that invaded the Roman Empire. "If Rome is sacked, what can be safe?" lamented the Christian theologian Jerome when he heard the news in far-off Jerusalem. His remark captures the outrage and astonishment felt by Roman citizens everywhere, Christian and non-Christian alike, who believed that their empire was divinely protected and would last forever.

To understand how the Visigoths managed to sack Rome, we must examine late antiquity, the period between about 250 and 600, which bridged the classical world and the Middle Ages. During this critical era in the

---

The Vienna Genesis Written in silver ink on purple-dyed parchment, this sumptuous manuscript of the first book of the Bible, now in a museum in Vienna, Austria, was created in the sixth century, probably for a member of the imperial court in Constantinople. The Greek text at the top portion of the page tells the story of Susanna at the Well, which is illustrated at the bottom of the page. Though the illustration tells a biblical story, certain details reflect conditions in late antiquity, such as fortified cities and the growing importance of camels in travel and commerce. The seated, semi-nude female in the lower left is derived from polytheist religion. She personifies the stream from which the more modestly dressed Susanna gathers water.

development of Western civilization, the Roman Empire underwent radical transformation. After its recovery from a half century of near-fatal civil war, foreign invasion, and economic crisis, Rome experienced a hundred years of political reform and economic revival. Yet by the middle of the fifth century, the political unity of the Mediterranean world had come to an end. The Roman Empire collapsed in western Europe. In its place, new Germanic kingdoms developed in Italy, Gaul, Britain, Spain, and North Africa. These kingdoms would serve as the foundation of western medieval Europe.

In contrast, the Roman Empire in the East managed to hold together and prosper. The empire's eastern provinces were held together by the new capital, the city of Constantinople (modern Istanbul in Turkey). Until their empire fell to the Turks in 1453, the inhabitants of this eastern realm considered themselves Romans. In both Constantinople (where Roman political administration was maintained) and the new kingdoms of the West (where it was not) Rome's cultural legacy continued.

Late antiquity witnessed not only the collapse of the Roman Empire in the western provinces but also the emergence of Christianity as the dominant religion throughout the imperial realm. From there it spread beyond the imperial borders, bringing new notions of civilization to the people of Europe, North Africa, and the Middle East. In this era one did not have to be Roman to be Christian, but it was necessary to be Christian to be civilized. Once Christianity became dominant the cultural boundaries between Christians, Jews, and polytheists hardened. Henceforth, Western civilization was for most people a Christian civilization, and the borders that separated peoples were not just political ones, as in the ancient world, but religious ones. The encounter between the Roman Empire and Christianity raised the question, how were both the culture of the empire and the practice of Christianity transformed?

- How did the Roman Empire successfully reorganize following the instability of the third century?
- How did Christianity become the dominant religion in the Roman Empire, and what impact did it exert on Roman society?
- How did Christianity enable the transformation of communities, religious experience, and intellectual traditions inside and outside the empire?
- How and why did the Roman Empire in the West disintegrate?

Crisis and Recovery in the Third Century

- How did the Roman Empire successfully reorganize following the instability of the third century?

In the years between 235 and 284, the Roman Empire staggered under waves of political and economic turmoil. The very institutions of the army and the office of the emperor, which had made the Roman Empire the dominant power in the Mediterranean, seemed incapable of standing up to new threats. Rival generals competed for the throne, chronic civil war shook the empire's very foundation, and invaders hungry for land and plunder broke through the weakened imperial borders. As a consequence the economy collapsed and the imperial administration broke down. However, by the end of the third century, the emperor Diocletian managed to arrest the process of disintegration by shoring up the empire with drastic administrative and social reforms.

The Breakdown of the Imperial Government

In 235, the assassination of Emperor Severus Alexander, the last member of the Severan dynasty, precipitated a crisis in the imperial administration. Military coup followed military coup as ruthless generals with nicknames like "Sword-

The Walls of Rome

The emperor Aurelian built a twelve-mile circuit of walls around Rome in the 270s to protect the city from Germanic invaders. Twenty feet high and twelve feet thick, the walls had eighteen major gates. The Gate of Saint Sebastian, seen here, had additional towers added in later years. That Rome should need protective walls would have been unthinkable during the early empire.

Subjugation of Valerian
Persian kings built their tombs in a cliff six miles north of Persepolis, the old Persian capital. Here at Naqsh-i Rustam, a carving depicts the Great King Shapur I (239–272) on horseback holding the arm of his prisoner, the Roman emperor Valerian. The previous Roman emperor, Philip (known as "the Arab"), kneels in supplication. Shapur bragged about his accomplishments: "When I first came to rule, the Roman emperor Gordian gathered an army from the whole empire of the Romans, Goths, and Germans and came to Mesopotamia against my empire. . . . and we annihilated the Roman army. Then the Romans proclaimed Philip the new emperor . . . and he came to plead with me, and he paid 500,000 gold pieces as ransom and became our tributary. . . . And when I marched against Carrhae and Edessa [Roman cities in Syria], the Emperor Valerian advanced against us. . . . We fought a great battle . . . and I captured the Emperor Valerian myself with my own hands."

in-Hand" competed for the throne. In the latter half of the third century, not one of more than four dozen emperors and would-be emperors died a natural death. Gallienus clung to the throne longest: his reign lasted fifteen years (253–268). Most emperors held power for only a few months. Preoccupied with merely staying on the throne, they neglected the empire's borders, leaving them vulnerable to attack.

This situation had dire consequences for the empire. Foreign invaders attacked both eastern and western provinces throughout late antiquity. To the Romans' deep shame, Emperor Valerian was captured in battle by the Great King of Persia in 260. Warbands from across the Rhine River reached as far south as Italy, forcing the em-

peror Aurelian to build a great wall around the city of Rome in 270. Many other cities across the empire constructed similar defenses. The Roman military system and the Roman economy buckled under the pressure of invasions and civil war. Inflation spun out of control and coins lost their value. With the decline of the value of money the government was forced to pay soldiers in produce and supplies rather than cash. Not surprisingly, resentment boiled among the troops.

As a consequence of the political turmoil in the empire, the seat of power shifted from Rome to provincial cities. Unlike their predecessors, the soldier-emperors of this era, who came mostly from frontier provinces, had little time to cultivate the support of the Roman Senate. Instead, they held court in cities close to the embattled frontiers. Towns far from Rome, such as York in Britain or Trier in Gaul, had long functioned as military bases and supply distribution centers. Now they served as imperial capitals whenever the emperor resided there.

With the emperor on the move and with armies slipping from imperial control, political power fragmented. Political decentralization injured the empire further. Some cities and provinces took advantage of the weakened government to try to break away from Roman control. In the early 260s and 270s a large portion of Gaul known as the Gallic Empire briefly established independence. A few years later, Zenobia, the queen of Palmyra (r. 267–272), a city in Syria that had grown wealthy from the caravan trade, rebelled against Rome, and a bitter war ensued. The emperor Aurelian's troops finally crushed Palmyra in 272 and led Zenobia in chains through the streets of Rome in a triumphal procession. Such triumphs, however, were few and far between in these years.

The Restoration of Imperial Government

Diocletian (r. 284–305) stepped in to rescue the empire from its chaotic condition near the end of the third century. Drawing partly on innovations of his immediate predecessors and partly on his brilliant organizational talents, he launched a succession of military, administrative, and economic reforms that had far-reaching consequences. Not since the reign of Augustus had the Roman Empire been so fundamentally transformed.

Diocletian's Reforms

After ruling alone for two years, Diocletian recognized that the enormous responsibilities of imperial rule overburdened a single ruler, and so he took the dramatic step of dividing the administration of the empire into two parts. In 286 he chose a co-ruler, Maximian, to govern the western half of the empire, while he continued to rule in the east, residing for much his early rule in the city of Nicomedia (in modern Turkey), strategically located at the point where Asia meets Europe. Based in Rome, Maximian maintained a separate administrative system and his own army. Then, in 293, Diocletian and Maximian subdivided their territories by appointing two junior-level emperors. These junior rulers administered their territories in the eastern and western parts of the empire with their own bureaucracies and armies.

Through this system of shared government called the tetrarchy° or rule of four, Diocletian hoped not only to make the imperial government more efficient, but also to put an end to the bloody cycle of imperial assassinations. Although he had gained the throne by murdering his predecessor, he knew that the empire's survival depended on a

The Tetrarchs

Stolen by crusaders during the Middle Ages from its original site near Constantinople, this statue of the tetrarchs now is built into a wall of the cathedral of San Marco in Venice. To depict their solidarity and readiness for war, the tetrarchs are presented as fierce soldiers in military uniform, holding their swords with one hand and clasping their colleague's shoulder with the other. Each pair of figures shows one junior emperor and one senior emperor, who has more worry lines in his forehead as a sign of his greater responsibilities.

reliable succession strategy. To that end, Diocletian dictated that the junior emperors were to step into the senior emperors' place when they retired. Then they themselves were to select two new talented and reliable men to be junior emperors and their eventual replacements. Thus supreme power was to be handed down from capable ruler to capable ruler, and the constant cycle of assassinations and civil wars was to be broken.

Diocletian sought to enhance imperial authority by heightening the grandeur of the emperor's office. He used the title *dominus*, or lord, more freely than any emperor before him. Everything that had to do with the emperor was referred to as sacred or divine, suggesting his closeness to the gods. During public ceremonies he arrayed himself in gorgeous robes of purple silk. He required his officials to prostrate themselves before him and kiss the hem of his gown before they spoke to him. Diocletian as well as his fellow tetrarchs claimed that specific gods had singled them out for glory and victory. Jupiter was Diocletian's special protector, while Mars (the god of war) and Hercules guarded other tetrarchs. By emphasizing his special ties to the mightiest god of Rome, Diocletian set himself apart from the rest of the imperial court, thereby heightening his authority and prestige.

To restore Roman military power that had been weakened during the crises of earlier decades, Diocletian reorganized the Roman army, raising its size to about 400,000 men, an increase of 50,000 soldiers. In order to protect the empire from invaders, he stationed most of these troops along the borders of the empire and built several new mili-

tary roads in the western and eastern parts of the empire. He also supported forces of heavily armed cavalry that could race to trouble spots whenever necessary. At the same time, Diocletian sought to reduce the army's involvement in political affairs. Although he was a soldier himself, he recognized that the army had played a disruptive role in earlier decades by constantly engaging in civil wars. He created many new legions but reduced the size of each in order to limit its commander's power as well as to increase its maneuverability. He placed the legions under new, loyal commanders. With these military reforms in place, Diocletian was able to secure the empire's borders once again and suppress internal revolts (see Map 6.1).

Reorganizing the army was only one part of Diocletian's vision of reform. To restore efficient government, he also embarked on a thorough reorganization of the empire's administrative system. He redrew the map of the realm, drastically reducing the size of provinces. He set up a civil governor and a military commander within each province and

Map 6.1 The Roman Empire in Late Antiquity

Following the reforms of Diocletian, the Roman Empire enjoyed a century of stable government, with the same borders as in earlier centuries.

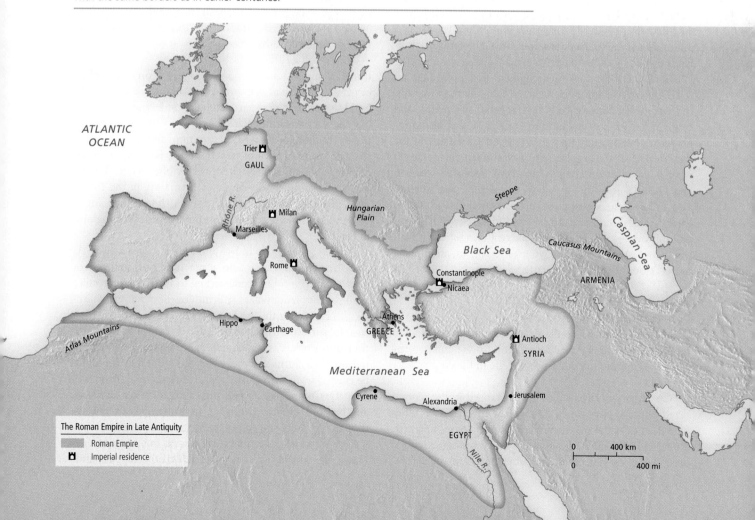

gave them separate civilian and military bureaucracies. These changes further reduced the risk of rebellion by limiting the power of any single civilian official. This administrative overhaul resulted in a significant expansion of the numbers of bureaucrats and military commanders.

Maintaining the expanded civilian and military apparatus created by the tetrarchy, especially in an era of rampant inflation, demanded full use of the empire's financial resources as well as far-reaching economic reforms. To halt the declining value of money, Diocletian attempted to freeze wages and prices by imperial decree. He also increased taxes and endeavored to make tax collection more effective through the establishment of a regular—and deeply resented—census to register all taxpayers. Despite the fact that senators, army officers and other influential citizens were undertaxed or not taxed at all, the new tax system generated enough revenues to fund the now enormous machinery of government.

The greatest tax burden fell on those least able to pay it: the peasants. These agricultural workers were required by law to remain in the places in which they were registered by the census. Sons were supposed to follow in their fathers' professions. This attempt to maintain the agricultural tax base was successful, but it lessened social mobility, and the gap between rich and poor continued to grow, a feature characteristic of late antique society. Fewer rich men controlled more of the empire's land and the wealth it generated than ever before. The emperor himself was the wealthiest of all, adding to his possessions through confiscation of lands owned by cities and private individuals.

Diocletian took steps to strengthen the empire that led to religious persecution. He believed that failure to worship the traditional Roman gods had angered the deities and brought hardship to the empire. In 303, he and his junior emperor Galerius initiated an attack on Christians in the eastern part of the empire, which was under their rule. In what is now known as the Great Persecution°, Diocletian and Galerius forbade Christians to assemble for worship and ordered the destruction of all churches and sacred books. Several thousand women and men refused to cooperate and were executed. Due to the religious sensibilities of the two co-emperors in the western provinces, attempts at persecution there were halfhearted.

Foundations of Late Antique Government and Society

Diocletian's reforms stabilized and preserved the Roman Empire, establishing a new foundation for life and government in late antiquity. All aspects of life in the empire were affected.

The quality of urban life slowly changed in the reorganized imperial government. As we saw in Chapter 5, cities played an essential role in imperial Rome's economic, religious, and cultural life: Romans saw themselves as civilized because they lived in cities. The number of Roman cities remained largely unchanged in late antiquity, but the weight of the new tax system and the costly bureaucracy of the increasingly centralized imperial government transformed many traditions of urban daily life. To finance imperial projects, emperors confiscated most city-owned lands and revenues, resulting in a reduction of funds to spend on civic life: games, chariot races, public buildings, and maintenance of urban infrastructure, such as roads and aqueducts.

Furthermore, the city councilors, who had the responsibility of raising the tax revenues required by the central government, grew increasingly frustrated. If they could not gather the amount of tax revenues that the government demanded every year, they would have to pay the difference from their own pockets. Failure to do so could lead to public flogging with lead-tipped whips—a punishment as humiliating as it was painful. Once considered a great honor, being a city councilor began to lose its appeal. Because a position in the imperial bureaucracy granted immunity from service in city government, with its crushing fiscal obligations, many ambitious men turned to the imperial bureaucracy to win the honors, status, and power that used to come with positions in the city government. Some cities benefited from the newly expanded imperial superstructure, especially administrative centers and the capitals of the many new provinces. Most cities, however, lost a great deal of their autonomy because of the growth of the imperial bureaucracy. Meanwhile, both the wealth and numbers of city aristocrats, the traditional leaders and patrons of their communities, dwindled.

One result of this shift in power away from the traditional urban aristocracy was the deterioration of the fabric of urban life. The inscriptions in marble attached to public buildings reveal a gradual decline in public spending by all but the very wealthiest citizens. As civic monuments and public buildings decayed, restoration and repair rather than the construction of new buildings became the order of the day in cities throughout the empire. When the empire's governing elite turned to Christianity in the course of the fourth century, private donors shifted their interests and built many churches and monasteries throughout the empire.

The life of peasants in late antiquity changed as well. As some men grew richer and more powerful, many poor peasants in the countryside turned to them for protection against other landowners and ruthless imperial tax collectors. In return for this protection, these peasants gave their wealthy patrons ownership of the farms on which they continued to work. These peasants, called *coloni*, lost the right to leave their farms and move elsewhere, but they could not be evicted from their farms, which gave them a measure of security. Coloni had to perform labor for their landlords and had only limited control of their own possessions, although they were still considered free Roman citizens.

The imperial government supported this form of economic dependency because it benefited the biggest landholders—including the emperor—who needed a stable workforce tied to the land to make agriculture profitable and to supply recruits for the army. The coloni system (called the colonate) also promised the emperor a reliable source of tax revenues. Over time, landowners particularly in the western provinces began to develop private armies to protect their vast country estates and the peasants who labored on them. This usurpation of the role of the central government weakened the authority of the emperor and his administration in the western provinces. In contrast, the eastern provinces of the empire remained prosperous into the sixth century. Private estates grew in size, but the imperial administrators maintained tight control of the economy.

The economic strength of the eastern provinces was matched by the development of political strength in that part of the empire. In late antiquity, the center of power within the empire shifted decisively to the east, where wealth and political might were increasingly concentrated. Cities such as Antioch in Syria and eventually the new capital of Constantinople became the wealthiest and most powerful urban centers in the empire.

Christianizing the Empire

■ How did Christianity become the dominant religion in the Roman Empire, and what impact did it exert on Roman society?

When Diocletian died, he left the eastern provinces of the empire, at least, stronger militarily, administratively, and economically than they had been for nearly a century. The steps he had taken to eradicate Christianity, however, turned out to be a failure. The new faith gathered momentum despite the hostility of Diocletian and other polytheist emperors. Within a year of Diocletian's resignation as emperor, an ambitious young man began his quest to become the sole emperor of Rome, and his subsequent conversion transformed the Christians from a persecuted minority to the dominant force in the empire.

Constantine: The First Christian Emperor

In 305, Diocletian stepped down from the imperial throne and insisted that his co-emperor in the west, Maximian, retire as well. Diocletian expected a peaceful succession to occur. It did, but just barely. As planned the two junior emperors, Galerius and Constantius, took Diocletian's and Maximian's places. But just one year later, Constantius died in Britain. Abandoning the principles of the tetrarchy, the

troops stationed in Britain in 306 proclaimed Constantius's son, Constantine (ca. 280–337), to be his replacement. The ambitious young general set out to assert sole rule over the Roman Empire. In 312 he smashed the army of Maxentius, his last rival in the west, at the battle of the Milvian Bridge over the Tiber River at Rome. Twelve years later he defeated Licinius, the tetrarch ruling in the east. Constantine then rejoined the western and eastern halves of the empire together with himself as absolute ruler. Thus both the divided rule of the empire and the system of succession through co-emperors that Diocletian implemented came to an end.

In other ways, however, Constantine continued along Diocletian's reformist path. Under Constantine the empire's eastern and western sectors retained separate administrations. To improve the administrative chain of command, Constantine installed new officials called praetorian prefects in each sector. These rulers were directly accountable to the emperor. He also retained Diocletian's emphasis on a large field army, but ensured that heavily armored cavalry troops were trained for rapid deployment to trouble spots.

The imperial bureaucracy and army remained immense, and so taxes remained high. Under Diocletian coins had been losing their value, which contributed to the rampant inflation of prices and made the burden of taxes on the poor ever harder to sustain. To remedy the situation, Constantine reformed the coinage system. He recognized that the existing coins had become so debased they were effectively worthless, so he created a new gold coin—the *solidus*, which had a fixed weight of gold content. The creation of the solidus stabilized the economy by restoring the value of currency. The new coin ended the inflationary spiral that had contributed so much to the political and social turmoil of the third century and remained the standard coin in the Mediterranean world for 800 years.

Unlike Diocletian, Constantine embraced the new religion of Christianity. Most emperors had associated themselves with a divine protector. Constantine chose the sun god Apollo as his first divine companion. But the night before the pivotal battle at the Milvian Bridge in 312, Constantine experienced a revelation, which he interpreted as a sign from the Christian God. After triumphing in battle, Constantine attributed his success to Christ's favor. Later in his reign, writers described Constantine's victory as a miracle. Though it was not unusual for an emperor to embrace a new god, Constantine's particular choice made a difference. Because monotheistic Christianity repudiated rival gods and alternative forms of worship, Constantine's conversion led to the eventual Christianization of the entire empire. Constantine did not order his subjects to accept Christianity or forbid polytheist worship. He did, however, encourage widespread and public practice of his new faith. Before Constantine Christian worship had been conducted in the privacy of homes, but he lavished funds on church buildings. He obtained the gold for his new solidus coinage

DOCUMENT

Eusebius on the Vision and Victory of Constantine

by looting the treasures that had been stored for centuries in polytheist temples. Now yoked to the imperial office, Christianity quickly gained strength across the empire and became a potent challenge to traditional modes of religious expression.

To glorify his name, Constantine founded a new capital city, Constantinople, the "City of Constantine," on the site of the Greek city Byzantium in 324. Constantine's choice of location reveals a shrewd eye for strategy. The city lay at the juncture of two military roads that linked Europe and Asia and controlled access to the Black Sea. From this convenient spot the emperor could monitor the vast resources of the empire's eastern provinces. Like Diocletian, Constantine recognized that the wealth and power of the empire lay in the East.

The growth of Constantine's new city of Constantinople paralleled the growth of Christianity. Constantine did not intend to establish an exclusively Christian city as an alternative to Rome. He built no more than three churches and left the city's many temples to older gods intact. Within a generation, however, Constantinople became a Christian center, and the traces of polytheism in the city disappeared. Constantinople continued to grow in size and splendor, as palaces, monuments, churches, bathhouses, public buildings, and colonnaded streets appeared on a scale befitting the New Rome, as Constantinople came to be known. In addition to serving as an administrative center and an imperial capital, Constantinople came to symbolize the kingdom of Heaven in the minds of Christians. As God ruled from his throne in the court of Heaven, so the emperor ruled in Constantinople. The emperor, whom God had chosen to rule, thus provided the essential link between the celestial and earthly kingdoms. Christian monotheism created a new conception of the Roman Empire. One Roman law was wedded to one faith shared by all its subjects and led by one emperor who was God's representative on Earth.

Constantine's capital also became a strongly fortified city. In response to the threat of attack by Vandal pirates, the emperor Theodosius II erected massive defensive walls around the city in 413. In future centuries these fortifications would protect the city—and indeed, the empire—from ruin on several occasions. With a new Senate formed on the model of the Senate of the city of Rome, a steady supply of grain from Egypt to feed the capital's inhabitants, and plenty of opportunities for trade, Constantinople attracted people from all over the empire. The city rapidly grew in size, reaching perhaps several hundred thousand inhabitants by the early sixth century.

The Spread of Christianity

Before the fourth century Christianity had grown through traveling missionaries who established congregations in most cities of the empire. After Constantine successive em-

perors promoted Christianity, which mushroomed rapidly throughout the empire during the fourth century. With imperial support, church leaders transformed the face of cities by building churches and leading attacks on the institutions and temples of polytheist worship.

Spread of Latin Christianity in Western Europe

The Rise of the Bishops

As Christianity spread, it grew more complex in its internal organization. Shortly after Paul of Tarsus (ca. 5–67) had established the theological grounding of the new religion, a distinction developed between the laity—the ordinary worshipers—and the priests, who led the worship, administered the sacraments, and acted as pastors for the laity. This distinction between the laity and the priesthood remained a central feature of the administration of Christianity. Much of the early growth of Christianity occurred in cities. In imitation of the hierarchic Roman urban administration, Christian priests developed their own structures to exercise authority over the laity. Just as an imperial official directed each city's political affairs with a staff of assistants, so each city's Christian community came to be led by a chief pastor, called a bishop, who in turn had a staff of subordinate priests and deacons. Just as a provincial governor controlled the political affairs of all of the cities and rural regions in his province, so the bishop of the main city of a province held authority over the other bishops and priests in the province. This main or head bishop came to be called a *metropolitan* (because he resided in the chief city, the metropolis, of the province) in the east, an *archbishop* in the west. Through this hierarchy of metropolitans, archbishops/bishops, priests, and deacons, the scattered communities of believers were linked together into what emerged as the Christian Church.

With its sophisticated administrative structure, the Church grew quickly, and bishops became important authorities in their cities. A bishop's main task was to supervise the religious life of his *see* or diocese, which comprised not only the city itself but also its surrounding villages and agricultural regions. Such supervision involved explaining Christian principles and teaching the Bible to these communities. Bishops soon became far more than religious teachers. As the Church grew wealthy from the massive donations of emperors such as Constantine and the humbler offerings of pious women and men throughout the empire, bishops used these resources to help the poor. They cared for the general welfare of orphans, widows, sick people, prisoners, and travelers. When famine struck southern Gaul in the fifth century, for example, the bishop of Lyons sent so much food from his church estates that the Rhône and Saône Rivers as well as all the roads to the south were jammed with grain transports.

Constantine incorporated the Church's bishops into the imperial government by permitting them to act as judges in civil actions. This policy soon entangled them in secular politics. Litigants could choose to be tried before a bishop rather than a civil judge. The decisions of a bishop had the same legal authority as those made by civil judges and could not be appealed. Using the rhetorical skills they had learned in Roman schools, bishops were also the advocates of their cities before provincial governors or the imperial court. In many ways they usurped the role of the traditional urban aristocracy. For example, when the people of Antioch in Syria rioted and smashed a statue of the emperor, it was the local bishop, not a local aristocrat, who intervened with the emperor to prevent imperial troops from massacring the city's people.

Bishops also administered the financial affairs of their communities. Sometimes bishops used this money for political purposes. In an attempt to win influence and political support, Cyril, bishop of Alexandria from 412 to 444, spent 2,500 pounds of gold on general expenses and bribes to court officials and other clergymen during just one visit to Constantinople. In contrast, in regions without wealthy cities, the bishops were often hard pressed to find enough money to function effectively. British bishops going to a Church conference in 359 could do so only with financial assistance from the government.

By 400 Rome had become the most important see in western Europe. The bishop of Rome came to be called the "pope"—the papa or father of the other western bishops. By the middle of the fifth century the emperor formally recognized the pope's claim to have preeminence over other bishops. A number of factors explain why the office of the bishop of Rome evolved into the papacy°. Together with Jerusalem, Rome was a site of powerful symbolic importance to Christians. Both the Apostle Peter, the first among Jesus' disciples, and Paul of Tarsus, the traveling teacher who took a leading role in spreading Christianity beyond its Jewish origins, died as martyrs in Rome. Early Christians considered Peter to have been the first bishop of Rome who passed on his authority to all subsequent popes.

The tradition that Peter was the first among the disciples received support from a conversation between Jesus and Peter recorded in the Gospel of Matthew. Punning on Peter's name, Jesus told him, "You are Peter [*petrus*] and upon this rock [*petram*] I will build my church, and the gates of Hell shall not avail against it. And I will give to you the keys of the kingdom of heaven." Early Christians interpreted these words to mean that Jesus had given Peter special authority, including the power to absolve a sinner's guilt, and that the Church was to be led by those who inherited Peter's position. What came to be called the doctrine of the Petrine Succession declared that just as Peter was specially anointed by Jesus, so subsequent bishops in Rome (the popes) were anointed with special, God-given powers.

In this way popes claimed to be the chief bishops of the Christian world. They insisted that their spiritual authority took precedence over that of rival bishops in four other imperial cities: Constantinople, Jerusalem, Alexandria in Egypt, and Antioch in Syria. The bishops of these leading religious centers, however, also claimed spiritual descent from Jesus' apostles. They did not accept papal authority and often quarreled bitterly with the pope over matters of faith and politics. The tensions among these bishops of the empire's most important Christian communities led to divisions between the eastern and western parts of the empire that have lasted until the present day.

Through the authority of the bishops, the Church began functioning almost as an administrative arm of the government, although it still had its own internal organization. Indeed, when Roman rule collapsed in western Europe in the fifth century, the Church survived the crisis and stepped in to fill the vacuum of public leadership.

Christianity and the City of Rome

Christianity transformed the appearance of Roman cities. Constantine set an example of public and private spending on churches, hospitals, and monastic communities that conformed to Christian values. The first churches in Rome were built to honor Christian martyrs of earlier centuries, including the great basilicas built over the presumed burial sites of Sts. Paul and Peter. One of the great churches that

Central Nave of Santa Maria Maggiore

The church of Santa Maria Maggiore, dedicated to Mary, the mother of Jesus, was built in Rome in the 430s. Like other churches of the late antique period, Santa Maria Maggiore followed the plan of a Roman public building, a basilica, but added an altar in the semicircular apse at one end. Stories from the Bible were presented in mosaics on the walls above the columns. They decorated the church and provided lessons for illiterate worshipers.

Constantine built in Rome was called "Saint Paul Outside the Walls." This imposing structure marked the burial spot of Paul of Tarsus. Constantine also financed the construction of another grand church on the presumed site of Peter's martyrdom and burial, in an obscure cemetery on what was called the Vatican hill, just outside Rome's wall and across the Tiber River. St. Peter's Basilica was an imposing structure, with five aisles punctuated with marble columns. Its altar rested over Peter's grave. (Today the papal cathedral of St. Peter stands on that same spot, in the heart of the Vatican, the city of the pope.) The construction of these churches signaled that Jesus' disciples Peter and Paul had replaced Rome's mythical founders Romulus and Remus as the city's sacred patrons. In other places, too, Christian saints took the place of traditional gods and heroes as protectors of city life. With the construction of Christian churches, spending and construction on traditional buildings such as temples, bathhouses, and public entertainment facilities such as the circuses gradually declined.

Although Rome became a vital center of Christianity, the city's inhabitants did not adopt the Christian faith overnight. Throughout the fourth century, the huge temples and shrines of the old gods clustered in Rome's center continued to attract many worshipers, including influential senators. Church authorities hesitated to close these time-honored places of worship because they did not have legal authority to do so. Even after imperial laws in 391 and 392 forbade polytheist worship, sacrifices, and other religious rites, the ancient temples stood empty for a long time, because Christians believed that demons inhabited them. At the prompting of Rome's bishops, other public buildings, such as the large basilicas that had been used to conduct public business of many sorts, including legal trials, were turned into churches.

With the proliferation of new Christian houses of worship in Rome and other cities came new religious festivals and rituals, which gradually replaced traditional celebrations. Christians marked the anniversaries of the martyrdom of saints on the calendar. Sometimes a Christian holiday (a holy day) competed with a non-Christian holiday. For example, Rome's churchmen designated December 25 as the birthday of Christ to challenge the popular festival of the Unconquered Sun, which fell on the same day. Other Christian holidays also aimed to draw worshipers away from the rites of older gods. By the early sixth century the Church had filled the calendar with many days devoted to Christian ceremonies. Christmas and Easter (which commemorates Jesus' death and resurrection) as well as days for worshiping specific martyrs supplanted traditional Roman holidays. These festivals thus changed the patterns of urban community life throughout the empire. Not all of the traditional Roman holidays disappeared, however. Those that Christians considered harmless continued to be observed as civic holidays. These included New Year's Day, the accession days of the emperors, and the days that celebrated the founding of Rome and Constantinople.

One additional development in the Christian shaping of time was the use of the letters A.D. as a dating convention. A.D. stands for *anno domini,* or "in the year of our Lord," referring to the year of Jesus' birth. The convention began in 531, when Dionysius Exiguus, a monk in Rome, established a simple system for determining the date of Easter every year. He began his calendar with the birth of Jesus in the year 1 (zero was unknown in Europe at this time) and started counting from there. Although he was probably a few years off in his determination of the year of Jesus' birth, his system slowly came into general use by the tenth century. In modern secular societies where Christianity is not the universal belief, the abbreviation A.D. has been replaced by C.E.—meaning "in the Common Era"—to designate years (as is done in this textbook). In both systems, however, the year 1 still refers to Jesus' birth. Regardless of what designation is used—A.D. or C.E.—the Christian system has become the standard dating convention around the world.

Old Gods Under Attack

Many people today identify themselves as members of a religious community—as Christians, Buddhists, Hindus, Jews, or Muslims. For the most part these faiths are mutually exclusive—there are no Muslim Christians, for example. In late antiquity, however, before Christianity became the dominant religion in the Roman Empire, people prayed to gods of all sorts. Different deities met different needs, and the worship of one did not preclude worship of another. Some divinities—such as Isis, who promised life after death—had elaborate cults throughout the empire. The empire's great gods—Jupiter, Juno, and Minerva—had temples in cities everywhere and were formally worshiped on state occasions. In the countryside as well a variety of deities protected laborers and ensured fertility of plants, animals, and the farmers themselves.

To Christians, this diverse range of religious expression was intolerable. They labeled all polytheistic worship with the derogatory term paganism° and made a determined effort to eradicate it.

After converting to Christianity in 312, Constantine ordered the end of the persecution of Christians. Although Christianity did not become the "official" religion of the empire for nearly a century, tolerance for non-Christian beliefs and practices began to fade. In the fourth century, imperial laws forbade sacrificing animals on the altars outside the old gods' temples. Constantine's son, Constantius II (r. 337–361), ordered the Altar of Victory removed from the Senate House in Rome. Since Augustus's reign, generals had sworn oaths of allegiance to the emperor at this altar before marching to battle. State funding for polytheistic worship gradually stopped. Instead of temples, emperors built churches with money collected from the taxpayers.

During the fourth century bishops and monks, often in collusion with local administrators, led attacks on polytheist shrines and holy places. For example, in 392 the bishop and parishioners of Alexandria destroyed the city's Temple of Serapis, known for its huge size, its magnificent architecture, and the devotion of the local community to it. Similar clashes erupted in many cities across the empire. Libanius, an aristocrat from Antioch, complained to Emperor Theodosius in 390 about the destruction caused by gangs of zealous monks: "This black-robed tribe . . . hasten to attack the temples with sticks and stones and bars of iron, and in some cases, disdaining these, with hands and feet. Then utter desolation follows, with the stripping of roofs, demolition of walls, the tearing down of statues and the overthrow of altars, and the [polytheist] priests must either keep quiet or die."[1]

One emperor tried to restore traditional religion. Julian the Apostate (r. 360–363), who had been raised as a Christian in Constantine's court, rejected Christianity and tried to reinstate the old religions when he came to the throne. But his death during a campaign against Persia eliminated any hope for a restoration of pre-Christian ways. Emboldened by this turn of events, an increasingly zealous Church establishment attacked polytheism with renewed vigor. Emperor Theodosius I (r. 379–395) and his grandson Theodosius II (r. 402–450) forbade all forms of polytheistic worship, and non-Christian practice lost the protection of the law.

Because polytheism was not a single, organized religion, it offered no systematic opposition to government-supported attacks, but there were influential opponents to the Christianization of the empire. In sharp contrast to the pious Christian court at Constantinople, the conservative aristocracy of the city of Rome clung hard to the old gods. In 384, their spokesman unsuccessfully begged the emperor for tolerance. Quintus Aurelius Symmachus, a highly respected nobleman who had pleaded unsuccessfully for the return of the Altar of Victory, argued that Rome's greatness had resulted from the observance of ancient rites. His pleas fell on deaf ears. By the middle of the fifth century the aristocracy of the city of Rome had accepted Christianity.

A Female Priest

This foot-high ivory panel shows a female priest making a sacrifice at an altar to an unnamed god or goddess. *Symmachorum* means "of the family of the Symmachi," an aristocratic Roman clan in which some members defended the old gods in the face of Christianity. This elegant plaque commemorates some now-forgotten event in the family's life.

Many less influential people also struggled to maintain ancient forms of worship. Sometimes they fought with monks to preserve the shrines of the gods their families had worshiped for generations. But with the empire's resources pitted against them, they could not resist for long. People increasingly began to join Christian communities, though often without fully understanding what the religion required of them. Surviving records of sermons reveal that church leaders preached for centuries afterward against the surprising persistence of "pagan" habits among their congregants. Priests repeatedly explained the risks to salvation that lurked in age-old festivals, bawdy public entertainments, and even regular bathing, which was considered a sinful pleasure.

Eventually, this priestly diligence paid off. The pace of conversion accelerated in the fifth and sixth centuries. Emperor Justinian (r. 527–565) sponsored programs of forced conversion in the countryside of Asia Minor, where tens of thousands of his subjects still followed ancient ways. Eradicating polytheism in the Roman Empire meant far more than the substitution of one religion for another. Polytheism lay at the heart of every community, influencing every activity, every habit of social life, in the pre-Christian world. To replace the worship of the old gods required a true revolution in social and intellectual life. Completing that revolution became the challenge of the new Christian communities.

New Christian Communities and Identities

■ How did Christianity enable the transformation of communities, religious experience, and intellectual traditions inside and outside the empire?

The spread of Christianity produced new kinds of identities based on faith and language. Christianity solidified community loyalties and allegiances by providing a shared belief system and new opportunities for participation in religious culture. Yet at the same time, Christianity opened up new divisions and gave rise to new hostilities. Certain new groups were respected and revered; others found themselves marginalized or persecuted. As Christians debated how to interpret the doctrines of their faith, sharp divisions emerged among them. Because Christians spoke Greek, Latin, Coptic, Syriac, Armenian, and other languages, different religious interpretations and rituals sometimes took hold, creating distinct communities. As a result, new religious zones identified with different spoken languages and different interpretations of Christian texts appeared within the empire.

The Creation of New Communities

Christianity fostered the growth of large-scale communities of faith by providing a well-defined set of beliefs and values. These basic beliefs and values had to be integrated with daily life and older ways of thinking. Thus Christianity required followers to study and interpret the Bible, the religion's sacred text. The religion also demanded allegiance to one God and a complex set of doctrines. Weaving these elements into daily life resulted in a strong sense of Christian identity and common purpose. This new Christian identity competed with and at times replaced older identities linked to Roman citizenship or shaped by regional or urban loyalties.

Christian Doctrine and Heresy

The foundations of Christian doctrine were in two texts, the Hebrew Bible, which Christians called the Old Testament, and Jesus' teachings, contained in the New Testament. The Old and New Testaments gave a focal point to Christian worship, and their interpretation shaped Christian communities. Both testaments contained powerfully evocative narratives, moral teachings, poems, and parables, the precise meanings of which were not always self-evident. Every week the priest read to parishioners from these sacred texts. As Christian communities developed, interpretation of that faith by its followers became all-important. The Church decided what interpretations of the Bible were correct and expected all members of the community to accept these doctrines. In this way, Christian teaching contrasted sharply with secular (nonreligious) education in the Roman Empire, which was intended only for the urban elite. Christian teaching was meant for all. It required all people to live according to a shared interpretation of the Bible and the meaning of Jesus' life, death, and resurrection.

The Church soon ran into difficulties over interpretation of the texts, as Church leaders disagreed about the meanings of many biblical passages. Councils of bishops met frequently to try to resolve doctrinal differences and produce statements of the faith that all parties could accept. Two theological questions generated the most disagreement—the nature of the Trinity and the nature of Jesus Christ.

Christians believe that one God created and governs Heaven and Earth. This monotheistic foundation, however, undergirded a complex theological system in which the one God was understood to exist in three distinct "persons," each fully and absolutely God—God the Father, God the Son, and God the Holy Spirit—or the Holy Trinity. Church leaders argued about the precise relation of the three persons to one another and within the Trinity. Were the Son and the Holy Spirit of the same essence as the Father? Were they equally divine? Did the Father exist before the Son?

These debates over the Trinity were intimately connected to the second issue of contention with the early Church—the question of the nature of Jesus. At one extreme, some Christian scholars believed that Jesus was entirely divine and had no human nature. This emphasis on Jesus' divinity made his death on the cross and his resurrection irrelevant, for God could not suffer and die. It also severed the links between Jesus and his human followers by emphasizing that Jesus was entirely "transcendent" or "other," entirely beyond human comprehension or human limitations. At the other extreme, some Christians taught that Jesus was entirely human and not at all divine, thus challenging both the belief in the Trinity and what most other Christians understood as Jesus' mission on Earth.

The questions of the nature of the Trinity and the nature of Jesus erupted in the first great Christian controversy of late antiquity: the dispute between the Arians and the Athanasians. The Arians followed Arius of Alexandria (ca. 250–336), a priest steeped in Greek philosophy. Arians asserted that God the Father created Jesus and so Jesus could not be equal to or of the same essence as God the Father. Arians argued that the Trinitarian idea that Jesus as God the Son was both fully divine and fully human was illogical. The Athanasians, followers of the Bishop Athanasius of Alexandria (293–373), were horrified by what they saw as the Arians' attempt to degrade Jesus' divinity. They argued that Christian truths were beyond human logic and that Jesus was fully God, equal to and of the same substance as God the Father, yet also fully human.

The Arian-Athanasian dispute resulted in perhaps the most influential of the many church meetings held in late antiquity: the Council of Nicaea. In 325, Emperor Constantine summoned the bishops to Nicaea, a town near Constantinople, to reach a decision about the relationship among the divine members of the Holy Trinity. The bishops produced the Nicene Creed, which is still recited in Christian worship today. The creed states that God the Son (Jesus Christ) is identical in nature and essence to God the Father, Athanasian belief. More than a century later, the Council of Chalcedon of 451 reinforced the Nicene Creed. The assembled bishops agreed that Jesus was both fully human and fully divine, and that these two natures were entirely distinct though united.

The Nicene Creed and the decisions of the Council of Chalcedon became the correct, or orthodox°, interpretation of Christian teaching because they had the support of most bishops and the imperial court. Still, some bishops and other religious leaders continued to debate conflicting interpretations of the Bible, and many ordinary Christians continued to hold beliefs that clashed with those defined as orthodox. People who held the orthodox point of view considered such alternative doctrines to be false beliefs, or heresies°, and they labeled the supporters of such alternative beliefs *heretics*.

Communities of Faith and Language

The doctrinal differences between orthodox and unorthodox or heretical Christian groups helped cement different communal and even ethnic identities in late antiquity. Several geographic zones of Christians emerged that held different interpretations of Christian doctrine. They produced Bibles, sermons, and religious ceremonies in their native languages. A central zone based in Constantinople and including North Africa, Gaul, Italy, the Balkans, and much of western Europe contained Christians called Chalcedonians°, or orthodox. (In the Latin-speaking western provinces they were also called Catholics.) These believers followed the decision of the Council of Chalcedon in 451 that defined Christ's divine and human natures as equal but entirely distinct. In late antiquity, the emperors in Constantinople and the popes in Rome—as well as the most of the population of the Roman Empire—were Chalcedonian Christians.

Although the Christians in this zone agreed on fundamental matters of doctrine, they differed culturally by producing Bibles, delivering sermons, and conducting religious ceremonies in their native languages—Latin in the western part of the central zone, mostly Greek (but also Syriac, Armenian, and Coptic) in the eastern. In western Europe, Latin was the language of Christian literature and church ritual. About 410, the monk Jerome finished a new Latin translation of the Bible, which replaced earlier Latin versions. This translation, called the Vulgate Bible, became the standard Bible in European churches for many centuries.

The western Church's use of Latin kept the door open for the transmission of all Latin texts into a world defined by Christianity. This ensured the survival of Roman legal, scientific, and literary traditions, even after Roman rule had evaporated in western Europe. Latin also forged a common bond among different political communities of the empire's western sector. Latin served as an international language among the ruling elites in western Europe, even though they spoke different languages in their daily lives. Thus, church-based Latin served as a powerful unifying and stabilizing influence. The Latin language combined with Christianity to spur the development of Latin Christendom°—the many peoples and kingdoms in western Europe united by their common religion and shared language of worship and intellectual life.

In the eastern provinces of the Roman Empire, Christianity had a different voice. There a Greek-based Church developed. Greek was the language of imperial rule and common culture in that region, and Greek became the language of the eastern Christian Church. In addition to the New Testament, which had been originally written in Greek, eastern Christians used a Greek version of the Hebrew Bible (the Old Testament) called the Septuagint, which Greek-speaking Jews had prepared in Alexandria in the second century B.C.E. for their own community. The Septuagint combined with the Greek New Testament to become the authoritative Christian Bible throughout most of Rome's eastern provinces.

In a second zone in the eastern Mediterranean and beyond were Anti-Chalcedonians, usually known by the derogatory term of Monophysites° (literally "one nature"). They did not accept the teaching of the Council of Chalcedon about the combination of the divine and the human in Christ as being "in two natures." Instead, they believed that Christ had one nature in which the divine and human coexist, though neither mixed nor divided. As a leading Anti-Chalcedonian bishop in Alexandria explained, "if there are two natures, there are necessarily two persons, but if there are two persons, there are also two Christs." Three Anti-Chalcedonian communities had developed by the end of late antiquity. The kingdom of Armenia in the Caucasus mountain region of eastern Asia Minor, which had become in about 300 the first kingdom in the world to accept Christianity, which was a dozen years before Constantine's conversion, eventually accepted the doctrines of Anti-Chalcedonian Christianity in the late fourth century. When the Bible was translated into Armenian about 400, a rich Christian literature developed among the peoples of Armenia. Christianity in its Anti-Chalcedonian form helped foster a strong sense of ethnic identity among the Armenians.

An Anti-Chalcedonian community also appeared in Egypt, among the native Egyptian speakers, called Copts. Like the Armenians, the Copts developed a vibrant Christian culture expressed in the Egyptian language. Christianity took root in Egypt during the first century, and a Coptic Bible, completed in late antiquity, solidified a Coptic community that has survived to the present day.

In the Middle East, another distinctively Anti-Chalcedonian community was forged among the inhabitants of Syria. These Christians spoke Syriac, a Semitic language spoken by many people within the region. The Syriac Bible probably appeared in the second century. As was the case with Armenian and Coptic peoples, a vast literature of biblical interpretation, sermons, commentaries, and church documents was gradually created, forming the basis of Syriac-speaking Christian culture. In the sixth century the Syriac church developed its own hierarchy of priests and bishops independent of the Chalcedonian church in Constantinople.

The Ascetic Alternative

The idea that the human body, with all its physical needs, stands in the way of spiritual progress had long existed in the ancient Mediterranean world. Over the centuries, it has become deeply rooted in Western culture. As we saw in Chapter 3, in the fifth century B.C.E. Plato had argued that human souls are only bits of the great Soul that dwells in an unchanging celestial realm far above our earthly world. These bits of soul reside only temporarily in the human body during a person's life. By pursuing the philosophical life people might overcome the constraints of the human body and the material world and free these bits of soul to return to their source. Living a philosophical life meant combining a rigorous intellectual pursuit of knowledge with a disregard for physical needs. Greek and Roman philosophers following Plato dreamed of freeing their souls to ascend to a higher realm.

Christian ascetics took a different direction. They sought to suppress their physical needs to the extent that God might enter their bodies and work through them. Making contact with God required constant preparation, as one might prepare for an athletic competition. For this reason Christian ascetics struggled to deny the physical self in all its manifestations. Many relied on deprivation, going without food and sleep. They would also punish their bodies through self-flagellation. Still others rejected human contact, living in uncomfortable places such as atop a pillar or at the bottom of a dry well. All ascetics struggled to abstain from sex and to reject social standards of cleanliness, which they viewed as mere vanity.

Christian ascetic practice could also take subtler forms than physical abuse. Some followers rejected their families and communities, spurned all knowledge except for the content of the Bible, and even denied the significance of the passage of time by insisting that each day was a new beginning. In all of these ways ascetics freed themselves from the practices that ordered and gave meaning to everyday life. In monasteries and nunneries men and women submitted to the absolute rule of abbots and abbesses in their quest to suppress individual aspirations.

Winning the endless battles against the desires of the self and the lures of the Devil made ascetics holy in the eyes of their fellow Christians. Once an ascetic achieved communion with God, that divine presence within the ascetic radiated a curative power. Uniquely situated on the border between the divine and the human, holy ascetics sometimes channeled their power to the benefit of the human community by performing healing miracles and mediating disputes.

The ascetic movement revealed a profound shift in ideas about the body, the accessibility of divinity, and the nature of sexuality. From the ascetic perspective, the human body ceased to be a beautiful gift to be glorified in statuary and song. Instead it became an obstacle to spiritual communion with God. An ascetic life was not just a suppression of sexual desires but a victory over them. For Christians, following an ascetic life was not a cowardly flight from the problems of the world. Rather, it represented a courageous encounter with personal demons and the evils of society. Through ascetic discipline, men and women challenged their own physical existence as well as the basic values of the everyday Mediterranean world.

For Discussion

How did religious beliefs affect the ways that Christians understood their bodies in late antiquity? What do these beliefs about the human body and sexuality tell us about late antique society?

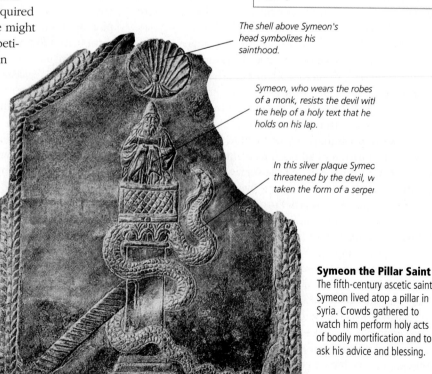

The shell above Symeon's head symbolizes his sainthood.

Symeon, who wears the robes of a monk, resists the devil with the help of a holy text that he holds on his lap.

In this silver plaque Symeon threatened by the devil, w taken the form of a serpent

Symeon the Pillar Saint
The fifth-century ascetic saint Symeon lived atop a pillar in Syria. Crowds gathered to watch him perform holy acts of bodily mortification and to ask his advice and blessing.

In addition to the Chalcedonian and Anti-Chalcedonian regions in late antiquity, a third zone of Christians consisted of the Arians. As described earlier, Arians° believed that Jesus was not equal to or of the same essence as God the Father. Most of the people who followed Arian Christianity were the Goths and other Germanic settlers who converted to Christianity in the fourth century, when they still lived north of the Danube River and in southern Russia. When they invaded the Roman Empire in the fifth century, they seized political control of Rome's western provinces. Because of religious differences with the Roman Christians who followed Chalcedonian Christianity, the two groups did not intermarry, and the Arians were able to maintain their ethnic identity in the face of the much larger Roman population whom they ruled. While the Goths were still north of the Danube, a Gothic priest named Ulfila devised a Gothic alphabet and used it to translate the Bible. A Christian Gothic culture thrived in the western zone despite its minority status.

In all of these three zones, variations of the Christian faith expressed in different languages formed the seedbed of ethnic communities, some of which survive to the present day, such as the Armenians, Copts, and Greek-speaking Orthodox Christians. Yet at the same time, the spread of Christianity weakened other local groupings. As language-based Christian communities spread inside and outside the empire, many local dialects and languages disappeared. Throughout most of western Europe the Celtic languages began to fade away during late antiquity. In the east the old languages of Asia Minor were gone by the end of the sixth century. Only the languages in which Christianity found textual expression survived.

The Monastic Movement

Near the end of the third century, a new Christian spiritual movement took root in the Roman Empire. Known today as asceticism°, this movement called for Christians to subordinate their physical needs and desires to a quest for spiritual union with God. Asceticism both challenged the emerging connection between the political and religious authorities and rejected the growing wealth of the Church.

The life of an Egyptian Christian, Antony, provided a model for future ascetics. Around 280 Antony sold all his property and walked away from his crowded village near the Nile into the desert in search of a higher spirituality. A few decades later, Athanasius, the Bishop of Alexandria who had argued against the Arians, composed a biography, the *Life of Antony*, telling how Antony overcame all the temptations the Devil could conjure up, from voluptuous naked women to opportunities for power and fame. Vividly describing the struggle between asceticism ("the discipline") and the lures of everyday life ("the household"), Athanasius's work became one of the most influential books in Western literature. It captured the spiritual yearnings of thousands of men and women, inspiring them to imitate Antony by following "the discipline" to seek God through a rejection of the ties of the household and material world. Asceticism appealed to those who desired an alternative to everyday political and social life, especially family life with its coercive parental authority, marriage, sexuality, and children that distracted from the contemplation of God.

Ascetic discipline required harsh and often violent treatment of the body. The first ascetics, called anchorites or hermits, lived alone in the most inaccessible and uncomfortable places they could find, such as a cave in a cliffside, a hole in the ground, or on top of a pillar. In addition to praying constantly in their struggle to overcome the Devil and to empty themselves of human desires so that God could enter and work through them, these men and women starved and whipped themselves, rejecting every comfort, including human companionship.

Over time, however, many Egyptian ascetics began to construct communities for themselves. The result was the monastic movement°. Because these communities, called monasteries, often grew to hold a thousand or more members, they required organization and guidance. Leaders like the Egyptian Pachomius (ca. 292–346), known as the "Searcher of Hearts," emerged to provide clear instructions for regulating monastic life and to offer spiritual guidance to the members of the monasteries. (The male inhabitants of monasteries are called monks, or solitary men; women are called nuns.)

Monastic communities soon multiplied in the eastern provinces of the Roman Empire, especially near Jerusalem in Palestine, where Jesus had lived centuries earlier. Basil of Caesarea (ca. 330–379) wrote a set of guidelines that was widely followed in eastern lands. Highly educated in Greek and Roman literature and philosophy as well as Christian theology, Basil repudiated extreme ascetic practices. He viewed the monastery as a community of individuals living and working together while pursuing their individual spiritual growth. Through his writings, Basil encouraged monks to discipline their souls through productive labor and voluntary poverty rather than through long bouts of self-inflicted physical tortures. He also insisted that monks should devote the greater part of their day to religious contemplation and prayer. In the monasteries, the monks typically shared meals and worship but engaged in ascetic discipline and prayer alone.

After spreading throughout the eastern provinces, monasticism made its way into western Europe. The desert, so accessible to monks in Egypt, became a metaphor for any desolate place where a person could live as an ascetic in the quest for God. John Cassian (ca. 365–ca. 433), for example, carried monastic ideas from Egypt to Gaul, where he found his "desert" in the rugged islands of the coast near modern Marseilles. He established two monasteries there. Cassian and other monks wrote rule books explaining how to organize and govern monastic life for the many communities that sprang up in Italy and Gaul.

Drawing from the ideas of these earlier monastic rules written in Greek, Benedict of Nursia (ca. 480–547) wrote a Latin *Rule* that became the foundation of monasticism in western Europe. Benedict built a monastery on Monte Cassino near Naples in 529. Like Basil of Caesarea, Benedict emphasized voluntary poverty and a life devoted to prayer. Benedict, however, placed a greater stress on labor. Fearing that the Devil could easily tempt an idle monk, Benedict wanted his monks to keep busy. He therefore ordered that all monks perform physical labor for parts of every day when they were not sleeping or praying.

Rule of
St. Benedict

In the western Roman Empire monasticism played a central role in preserving classical learning and thus allowing its integration into Christian culture in later centuries. Much of the responsibility for the preservation of the classical intellectual tradition lay with the monasteries founded by Benedict. This group of monks, called the Benedictine order, established many monasteries throughout western Europe, modeled on Benedict's original monastery of Monte Cassino. Benedict himself was wary of classical teaching, but he wanted the monks and nuns under his supervision to be able to read religious books. At least basic education had to become part of monastic life. Benedictine monasteries provided an education not only to their inhabitants but also to any eager scholar from the surrounding communities. The Benedictine definition of "manual labor" expanded to include the copying of ancient manuscripts and Benedictine monasteries developed significant libraries. As monasteries that followed Benedict's *Rule* spread throughout Europe, they served as centers of education and also succeeded in preserving much Latin literature.

Monasticism, Women, and Sexuality

The monastic movement opened new avenues for female spirituality and offered an alternative to marriage and childbearing. In the first monastic communities, men and women lived separately to reduce sexual temptation, but within the confines of these communities, gender was irrelevant. It was just one more difficult physical boundary to cross over on the path to finding God. By joining monastic communities and leaving the routines of daily life behind, women could gain independence from the obligations of male-dominated society. As Christian monasticism spread, ascetic women began to create communities of their own. They lived as celibate sisterhoods of nuns, dedicated to spiritual quest and service to God.

The wives or daughters of wealthy and powerful families were typically the founders of female monastic communities. Such women wielded an authority and influence that would not have been available to them otherwise. For example, Melania the Younger (383–439), the daughter of a wealthy Roman senatorial family, decided to sell her vast estates and spend the proceeds in religious pursuits. When the Roman Senate objected to the breaking up of Melania's family estates, Melania successfully appealed to the empress, who interceded with the legal authorities to enable her to dispose of her property. (Melania's slaves also objected because they did not want to be sold separately to raise cash for her religious projects, but Melania ignored them.) Melania spent her fortune on building monasteries in the Holy Land of Palestine. Most women lacked the financial resources to make such dramatic gestures, but they could imitate Melania's accomplishment on a modest scale.

Monasticism also reinforced negative ideas about women and sexuality in the Church. During the late antique era an increasingly negative view of women emerged in the writings of churchmen. Christian writers branded women as disobedient, sexually promiscuous, innately sinful, and naturally inferior to men. They interpreted Genesis, the first book of the Bible, to mean that women bore a special curse. In their reading of the Genesis account, Eve, the first woman, seduced Adam, the first man. For this reason late

DOCUMENT

An Aristocratic Woman Chooses Poverty and a Religious Life

Melania the Younger (383–439) became a saint because of her generosity and piety. The daughter of an enormously wealthy senatorial family in Rome, she married at an early age but remained loyal to ascetic principles of poverty and virginity. In their early twenties, she and her husband, who was equally rich, sold their estates and gave their money to charity. This description comes from a biography of Melania written by one of the nuns in a monastery founded by Melania in Jerusalem:

It was as if she hoped that by the virtuous practice of almsgiving alone she might obtain mercy; as the Lord said, "blessed are the merciful, for they shall obtain mercy." Her love for poverty exceeded everyone else's. As she testified to us shortly before her departure of the Lord, she owned nothing at all except for about fifty coins of gold for the offering and even this she sent to a very holy bishop, saying "I do not wish to possess even this from our patrimony." Nor only did she offer to God that which was her own, she also helped others to do the same. Thus many of those who loved Christ furnished her with their money, since she was a faithful and wise steward. She commanded these monies to be distributed honestly and judiciously according to the request of the donor.

Source: *Life of Melania the Younger*, 30.35, trans. Elizabeth A. Clark (NY/Toronto: Mellon Press, 1984), 48, 51.

antique Christians blamed Eve—and women collectively—for humanity's expulsion from the Garden of Eden and for all the woes human beings had suffered ever since. Yet at the same time Christians also believed that God would save the souls of women as well as men, and they honored Mary for her role in bringing Jesus, and therefore salvation, into the world. In many ways women occupied a position in the Christian religious imagination comparable to that held by Jews: They were considered guilty as a group of a terrible deed, yet they were accepted as a necessary part of God's plan for humanity.

Male ascetics preached and practiced sexual abstinence as an important self-denying discipline. In ascetic thought, women were linked to the corrupt world of the flesh against which the Christian must exercise unceasing vigilance. The ascetic retreat into the desert or monastery was a flight from temptation, and that meant a flight from women. As ascetic ideas gained in prominence, celibacy became a Christian ideal, with sexual relations within the confines of marriage viewed as distinctly second-best.

Jews in a Christian World

Until Christianity became the official religion of the Roman Empire, Jews had been simply one among hundreds of religious and ethnic groups who lived under Roman rule. Although polytheist Romans considered Jews eccentric because they worshiped only one god and refused to make statues of him, they still respected the Jewish people's faith. Prior to the fourth century, Jews had enjoyed full citizenship rights and appeared in all professions and at all levels of society.

Christianity slowly erased all this. According to Christian belief, Jews had been the chosen people of God until the appearance of Jesus, who displaced them from their place in God's plan. Christians criticized Jews for failing to accept that Jesus' teachings had supplanted those of the Hebrew Bible, and blamed them collectively for Jesus' crucifixion. Christians viewed the Diaspora (the dispersion of Jews around the world after the destruction of Jerusalem by the Roman army in 70) as God's way of punishing the Jews.

With the advance of Christianity within the empire, conditions for Jews declined. Beginning in the fourth century, Roman laws began to discriminate against Jews, forbidding them to marry Christians, own Christian slaves, or accept converts into their faith. With the support of Christian imperial officials, Church leaders sometimes forced entire communities of Jews to convert to Christianity on pain of death. A notable exception to this downward spiral was that Jews still retained the right to remain members of city councils. Although organized resistance among scattered Jewish communities was impossible, many Jews refused to accept the deepening oppression. Their resistance ranged from acts of violence against Jews who had converted to Christianity to armed revolt against Roman authorities.

DOCUMENT

A Christian Bishop's Attitude Toward Women

Ambrose was an extremely influential bishop of Milan from 373 to 397. He believed, as did others, that women were not made entirely in God's image and that as descendants of Eve they shared her sin:

Since she is not the image of God, a woman ought, therefore, to veil her head, to show herself subject. And since falsehood began through her, she ought to have this sign, that her head be not free, but covered with a veil out of reverence for the bishop. For the bishop has the role of Christ. Because for the beginning of crime, she ought to appear subject before a bishop, since he is the vicar of the Lord, just as she would before a judge.

Source: Ambrose, *Commentary on Paul's First Letter to the Corinthians,* 148. Trans. Karl Frederick Morrison, *Rome and the City of God* TAPA ns.54.1, Philadelphia, 1964, pp. 46–47.

Despite their marginal position in the empire, Jews did retain some security because most emperors honored traditional obligations to protect all their subjects. Roman emperors repeatedly issued laws forbidding the destruction of synagogues. They permitted Jews to worship on the sabbath and excused them from performing public or private business on that day, as Jewish law required. Zealous bishops often objected to such treatment of Jews, and some bishops goaded Christians into attacking synagogues. For example, in 388 the bishop of Callinicum, a town on the Euphrates River, destroyed the local synagogue with the assistance of his Christian congregation. When the emperor Theodosius I tried to punish the guilty citizens, Bishop Ambrose of Milan wrote a long letter stiffly rebuking the emperor: "Will you give the Jews this triumph over the Church of God, this victory over the people of Christ?" The emperor backed down, and the Christians of Callinicum went unpunished.

In 429, Roman officials abolished the office of Jewish Patriarch, the head of the Jewish community who enjoyed high official rank in the empire. The Roman emperors had long recognized the Patriarch as leader of the many Jews who were dispersed throughout the empire, and had given the Patriarch certain legal and administrative duties. With the office abolished, the Roman treasury now collected for itself the special taxes that had been paid by Jews for the Patriarch's administration. The end of the Patriarchate shows that Jews had lost their status as a legally recognized religious community in the eyes of the empire.

Individual Jewish communities continued to administer their own affairs under the leadership of rabbis—men who served as teachers and interpreters of Jewish law. With the completion of the Mishnah°, the final organization and transcription of Jewish oral law, by the end of the third century and the production of the Jerusalem and Babylonian Talmuds°, or commentaries on the law, by the end of the fourth and fifth centuries, rabbis and their courts now dominated Jewish communities. These learned men established academies of legal study in Roman Palestine and Persian Babylonia, where they produced authoritative interpretations of law that guided everyday Jewish life.

Although some Jewish women served as leaders of synagogues in late antiquity, in general rabbinic Judaism subordinated women in Jewish society. For example, Jewish women did not receive an education at the Jewish academies. Excluded from the formal process of interpreting the Bible, Jewish women did not acquire highly prized religious knowledge. Instead, men expected them to conform to submissive roles as daughters, wives, and mothers, much as women in other religious communities were expected to do.

A Greek Zodiac in a Synagogue

In late antiquity, Jews living in Palestine sometimes decorated their synagogues with mosaic floors depicting the zodiac. Although these mosaics appeared in synagogues and often contained Hebrew writing, the scenes and style of the mosaics were typical of Greek and Roman art. This blending demonstrates that members of the Jewish congregation also participated in the general non-Jewish culture of the province.

Access to Holiness: Christian Pilgrimage

Christianity not only created new communities and condemned others, it also offered new avenues of participation in religious culture. In late antiquity, Christians of all social ranks began to make religious journeys, or pilgrimages°. Their goal was to visit sacred places, especially places where holy objects, known as relics°, were housed. They believed these relics were inherently holy because they were physical objects associated with saints and martyrs, or with Jesus himself. The most highly valued relics were bones from the venerated person. Christians believed that contact with such relics could cure them of an illness, heighten their spiritual awareness, or improve their lives.

The mortal remains of Christian martyrs provided the first relics and the first objects of veneration for pilgrims, but after persecution of Christians ceased in 312, believers resorted to the bodies of great bishops and ascetic monks and nuns. From the fourth century onward, Christians regularly dug up saintly skeletons, chopped them up, and distributed the pieces to churches. The more important the holy person, the fiercer the competition for the bones and other objects associated with him or her. Churches in the largest cities of the empire, such as Rome, Constantinople, Alexandria, and Jerusalem, acquired fine collections. For example, the robe of the Virgin Mary, the mother of Jesus, was kept in a church in Constantinople. Residents of the city believed that the Virgin's robe drove away enemies when it was carried in procession along the city's battlements.

Emperors and important bishops acquired the greatest and most powerful relics of all—those that had reportedly touched Jesus himself. These included the crown of thorns he wore when crucified, the cross on which he died, and the nails that fastened him to the wood. Relics reminded Christians that Jesus' own death was symbolically repeated in the martyrdom of his followers. For this reason church altars where followers celebrated the Eucharist, the rite in which bread and wine are offered as Jesus' body and blood in memory of his death, were built over the graves or relics of martyrs.

Traveling to touch a relic was the primary motive for going on a pilgrimage. Palestine became a frequent destination of Christian pilgrims because it contained the greatest number of sacred sites and relics associated with events described in the Bible and particularly with Jesus' life and death. Between the fourth and seventh centuries, thousands of earnest Christian pilgrims flocked to Palestine to visit holy sites and pray for divine assistance and forgiveness for their sins. Helena, the mother of Emperor Constantine, made pilgrimage fashionable. In the early fourth century she visited Jerusalem, where she reportedly found remnants of the cross on which Jesus was crucified, as well as many of the sites pertaining to Jesus' life.

Inspired by his mother's journey, Constantine funded the construction of lavish shrines and monasteries at these sites, as well as guest houses for pilgrims. Practically overnight Palestine was transformed from a provincial backwater to the spiritual focus of the Christian world. Religious men and women—rich and poor, old and young, sick and healthy—streamed to Palestine and Jerusalem. There they joined processions that made their way from holy place to holy place. At each site clergymen permitted them to view and sometimes kiss or touch holy relics. On the most important holidays, such as Easter, priests held special ceremonies at the different sites of Jesus' last day on Earth—at the Mount of Olives where he was arrested by Roman soldiers, at the place of his trial, at the hill of his crucifixion, and at his tomb, called the Holy Sepulchre.

Palestine did not have a monopoly on holy places, however. Pilgrims traveled to places throughout the Roman world wherever saints had lived and died and where their relics rested. Their pilgrimages contributed to the growth of a Christian view of the world in several ways. Because pilgrimage was a holy enterprise, Christian communities gave hospitality and lodging to religious travelers. This fostered a shared sense of Christian community among people from many lands. Christians envisioned a Christian "map" dominated by spiritually significant places. Travel guides that explained this "spiritual geography" became popular among pilgrims. Most of all, pilgrims who returned home enriched in their faith and perhaps cured in mind or spirit inspired their home communities with news of a growing Christian world directly linked to the biblical lands they heard about in church.

Christian Intellectual Life

During the first three centuries after Jesus' death, when Christians were marginalized and at times persecuted in Roman society, many church leaders strongly criticized classical learning. Churchmen argued that the learning of pagan intellectuals was false wisdom, that it distracted the Christian from what was truly important—contemplation of Jesus Christ and the eternal salvation he offered—and therefore that it corrupted young Christians. However, after the persecutions ceased, many Christian thinkers began to participate actively in the empire's intellectual life. Highly educated in Christian learning as well as the traditional studies of the Roman elite, these writers examined the meaning of Christianity in the context of classical history and philosophy. In so doing they profoundly influenced every aspect of Christian thought, making Christian intellectual life compatible with classical learning at the highest level.

The Reconciliation of Christianity and the Classics

In Roman schools, the sons of wealthy families, as well as some poor boys with ambition and talent, studied the poets, dramatists, philosophers, and rhetoricians of the classi-

---

DOCUMENT

Bring Me the Head of Saint Paul!

Pope Gregory the Great (r. 590–604) tactfully responded to the request of Constantina, the empress in Constantinople, for the head of Saint Paul. He points to some differences between the cult of relics in the eastern and western Mediterranean, evidence of the growing cultural differences between the Latin West and the Greek East:

The Serenity of your Piety [the empress], conspicuous for religious zeal and love of holiness has charged me to send to you the head of Saint Paul, or some other part of his body, for the church which is being built in his honor in the palace in Constantinople. . . . [but] I neither can nor dare to do what you want. For the bodies of the apostles Saint Peter and Saint Paul glitter with so great miracles and terror in their churches that one cannot even go to pray there without great fear. . . . In the Roman and all the western parts [of the empire] it is unendurable and sacrilegious for any one by any chance to desire to touch the bodies of saints: and if one should presume to do this, it is certain that this temerity will by no means remain unpunished. For this reason we greatly wonder at the custom of the Greeks, who say that they pick up the bones of saints; and we scarcely believe it. . . . But since so religious a desire of my most serene lady ought not be wholly unsatisfied, I will make haste to transmit to you some portions of the chains which Saint Peter the Apostle himself bore on his neck and his hand, from which many miracles are displayed among the people, if at least I should succeed in removing it by filing. . . .

Source: With some changes from: Gregory the Great, *Selected Epistles*, Trans. James Barmby, in *Nicene and Post-Nicene Fathers*, vol. 12, ed. P. Schaff and H. Wace, 1895/1995, pp. 154–156.

---

cal Greek, Hellenistic, and Roman periods. By late antiquity this curriculum had become formalized into seven liberal arts: grammar, logical argument, and rhetoric (collectively called the Trivium); and geometry, arithmetic, astronomy, and music (the Quadrivium). Law and medicine were taught separately for those who aspired to those professions. This education prepared students for careers in the imperial bureaucracy and various other fields. Equally important, it provided aristocratic men with a common cultural bond—a shared version of history, a value system that legitimized their exercise of power, an appreciation of the benefits of civilized life, and a common understanding of how the universe functioned. No other institution before the rise of Christianity, not even the army, exerted such a powerful influence on the minds of the men who controlled Rome's destiny.

Classical learning and the educational system that kept it alive posed a challenge to Christian educators. Specifically, how should Christians reconcile classical teachings with the doctrines of their faith, particularly when the two conflicted? Did the classics of Greek and Roman philosophy constitute a threat to Christianity? Could Christians learn anything of value from non-Christian cultures? Should educated men turn their backs on classical learning in order to avoid being corrupted by it?

After Constantine's conversion in 312, influential voices in the Church began to answer these questions. To them classical learning no longer seemed as threatening to Christianity has it had before. Many church leaders now came from the empire's urban elite, where they had benefited from classical learning. Christian officials grudgingly approved secular education as they recognized that the traditional curriculum still had practical value because it was useful for the administration of the Church and for the law. Training in classical rhetoric, grammar, and literature became an integral part of upper-class Christian life. By the fifth century traditional schooling for Christians was accepted as a useful if risky enterprise. As Basil the Great (ca. 330–379), bishop of Caesarea in Cappadocia (in modern Turkey), explained to young men about to embark on their studies, classical learning had both benefits and dangers. Although pagan learning, he advised, had some spiritual value, the charm of words can be dangerous and poison the Christian's heart.

Writing in Greek and Latin, churchmen now drew freely from classical texts and methods of discussion, even though they considered the Christian scriptures the sole source of truth. In the process both how they understood classical learning and Christianity itself changed. For example, Christianity reshaped how Romans understood the empire's place in human history. Eusebius, the bishop of Caesarea in Palestine from 313 to 339 and an adviser to Constantine, developed a theory of history that linked the development of the Roman Empire to a divine plan for humanity's salvation. Like other Christians before him, Eusebius believed that the Bible described the main events of human history, such as the creation of the first man and woman, God's revelation of his law to the Hebrews, and the great flood. Events still to come, according to Eusebius, included the appearance of the Antichrist, who would inaugurate a brutal reign of evil on Earth, the return of Jesus, the overthrow of the Antichrist, and the End of Days, when God would judge all human beings, reward the pious, and punish the wicked.

Eusebius added the Roman Empire to this historical plan. He argued that God had sent Jesus to Earth at a divinely appointed place and time—during the reign of the emperor Augustus and thus at a time when much of the known world had been united under imperial rule. The *Pax Romana,* according to Eusebius, provided the perfect, indeed the divinely ordained, conditions for the rapid spread of Christian teaching and the rapid growth of the Christian Church. In Eusebius's view, Constantine's conversion to Christianity marked the next step in God's plan. With one world empire now united under the one true religion, it would be the emperor's job to bring this religion to all of humankind. This triumphal vision of history struck a powerful chord among the empire's Christian elite. It gave Rome a crucial role to play in human destiny. It also enabled aristocrats to justify their traditional roles as political leaders.

By the fifth century, many Romans especially in the western provinces found Eusebius's triumphalism less satisfying as troubling questions surfaced. As we saw in the chapter introduction, in 410 the Visigoths plundered the city of Rome itself. This disastrous event challenged Christians' confidence in Eusebius's vision. Did Rome really have a special role in God's divine plan for humanity? If God favored Rome, as Eusebius explained, why had he allowed Visigoths to humiliate the great city? Was God punishing Romans because they had not eradicated paganism?

Questions such as these prompted Augustine of Hippo (354–430) to reexamine conventional notions about Rome's place in the world. By examining the most troubling philosophical and historical questions in light of the scriptures, Augustine became the most influential Latin Father of the Church, a term reserved for the early Christian writers who sought to reconcile Christianity with classical learning.

Born to parents of modest means, Augustine attended traditional Roman schools as a youth, an education that made him thoroughly familiar with the classics. His talent and schooling had prepared him for a high position in public life. After his conversion to Christianity, Augustine became the influential bishop of the city of Hippo Regius in North Africa. He recounted his spiritual experiences and conversion in the *Confessions* (397), an autobiography written in his middle age. Drawing on the ideas of the Greek philosopher Plato and Christian scriptures, Augustine in the *Confessions* meditated on the meaning of life, especially on sin and redemption. To modern readers his sins may seem petty things, but for him the real message was the power of redemption that made possible eternal life. Augustine showed that intellect alone was incapable of bringing about the spiritual growth that he desired. God's intervention was necessary to achieve his spiritual goals. For a spiritual conversion to be complete he had to cleanse himself of the desires of the flesh, which led him to renounce sexuality completely. Using his episcopal office as a platform from which to defend Christianity from polytheist philosophers and to define all aspects of the Christian life, Augustine displayed a sincere respect for certain aspects of Roman cultural and intellectual accomplishments—especially rhetoric and history. But he always believed Christianity was superior. For Augustine, the most dangerous enemy of all true Christians was "antiquity, mother of all evils"—the source of false beliefs.

In his book *The City of God,* completed in 423, Augustine developed a new interpretation of history. Though Augustine admired the Romans for their many virtues, he disagreed with Eusebius, concluding that Rome played no significant role in salvation history. Even the sack of Rome in 410 had no special meaning for Christians. Augustine's historical theory disconnected Christian ideas of human destiny from the fate of the Roman Empire. In his view, the Roman Empire was just one among many that had existed and that would exist before Jesus' return. According to Augustine, the only dates humanity should view as spiritually significant were Jesus' time on Earth and the End of Days sometime in the future. The significance of all events in between remained known only to God.

Augustine's theory proved quite timely. Within a few years of his death the Vandals seized North Africa and the Roman Empire lost control of all of its provinces in western Europe. Augustine thus gave Roman Christians a new perspective with which to view this loss: Rome had contributed to world civilization and to the growth of the Christian Church, but now Christianity would grow on its own without the support of Roman emperors.

Other churchmen explained the collapse of Roman power in western Europe differently. Salvian, a clergyman from the south of France who found himself living in a new Germanic kingdom of the visigoths in the first half of the fifth century, believed that the Romans deserved to lose their empire in the West because of their sinful lives and oppressive social order. The Visigoths, while less sophisticated than Romans, were nevertheless purer at heart—better Christians despite their heretical Arian views. Salvian's views demonstrate that for many devout Christians, Roman civilization had come to the end of the road. In their eyes, it was time to build a new, Christian world.

After the collapse of the Roman Empire in the western provinces, the challenge for Christian thinkers came less from reconciling Christianity with the power of classical learning than from keeping classical learning alive at all. Like Augustine, Cassiodorus (ca. 490–ca. 585), an Italian statesman in the court of Ostrogothic rulers of Italy, regarded classical learning as an intellectual inheritance of high value. Cassiodorus was appalled by the waning of the traditional classical educational system in the chaotic final days of the Roman Empire in the West. In response, he founded a monastery at Vivarium in the south of Italy, to which he retired at the end of his political career. Eager to preserve the liberal arts, Cassiodorus instructed his monks to copy classical literature in the monastery's library. "Let the task of the ancients be our task,"[2] he told them.

Outside the monasteries traditional schooling in the classics survived only as long as cities could afford to pay for teachers. In most of the towns of the western provinces of the empire, schools gradually disappeared in the course of the fifth century as a result of the Germanic invasions. With the exception of a few major urban centers, such as Carthage in North Africa, where traditional Roman schooling continued after the establishment of the Vandal kingdom, cities no longer had the funds to pay for teachers.

In contrast in the eastern half of the empire, classical learning lasted well into the sixth century as a basic part of elite education. Traditional education declined in the eastern empire not because of invasions or poverty as in the west but because of the growing influence of Christianity on daily life. After the emperor Justinian (r. 527–565) forbade non-Christians to teach, the number of schools decreased. By the end of the seventh century, traditional schools of grammar and rhetoric had disappeared. The Psalter (the collection of Psalms in the Bible) became the primer for reading, and religious literature supplanted classical works.

Neoplatonism and Christianity

Greek and Roman philosophy continued to be enormously influential. One branch of this tradition, called Neoplatonism°, originated with Plotinus (205–270), a non-Christian philosopher. His teachings greatly influenced Christianity, an example of how classical and Christian thought intertwined in late antiquity. Plotinus, who taught in the city of Rome, traced his intellectual roots primarily to the works of Plato (ca. 429–327 B.C.E.). He also drew ideas from Aristotle (384–322 B.C.E.) and various Stoic philosophers (third century B.C.E.), as well as the writings of their followers. In a series of essays called the *Enneads,* Plotinus applied Plato's views to the issues addressed in ancient philosophy, but Plotinus's greatest influence came from interpreting Neoplatonism in religious terms. He argued that all things that exist, whether intangible ideas or tangible matter, originate in a single force called the One.

According to Neoplatonists, the One has no physical existence; it is eternal and unchanging. The One is separated from the world of matter and physical change in which humans live by three descending grades of reality: the World Mind, the World Soul, and finally Nature. The World Mind contains the Forms that Plato described (see Chapter 3). The Forms are eternal, unchanging absolutes such as Truth, Justice, and Beauty that represent true reality, as opposed to the approximations of reality that humans encounter in everyday life. The Neoplatonists argued that the World Mind holds these Forms together as pure knowledge. The World Soul produces time and space, the dimensions that humans experience as history, Earth, and the planetary bodies. Nature is the lowest of these creative principles, consisting of things that come into being, change, and go out of existence, including living things. In Neoplatonic thinking, the human soul is a microcosm of these three levels of reality. The human soul "fell" from the One through the World Mind, the World Soul, and Nature into the human body, thereby losing its connection with the One. Yet the human soul can be redeemed. Humans have the potential to reunite their souls with the One by overcoming their passions and physical desires that are governed by the body. Many Neoplatonists believed that by gaining the help of the gods through magical rites (called theurgy) and by studying divine revelations, the human soul can reconnect with the One and fulfill its fullest potential.

With its emphasis on the fall and return of the soul to the One, Neoplatonism appealed to many Christians. For them, the One was God, and the Bible provided the divine revelations that could lead to the salvation of the human soul and reunification with God. The churchmen Gregory of Nyssa in the Greek East and Augustine in the Latin West were only two of the many churchmen who incorporated Neoplatonism into their own works in the later fourth century. Yet Christian and non-Christian Neoplatonists soon argued over such issues as whether the identity of "the One" could be equated with the Christian God and whether the use of theurgy constituted a pagan practice. In 529 the emperor Justinian closed Plato's Academy in Athens and forbade non-Christians to teach philosophy.

Nevertheless, the impact of Neoplatonism on Christian theology remained profound. Neoplatonic thought helped shape the Christian doctrine of the immortality of the human soul. It also reinforced the ascetic ideal practiced by

monks and nuns. Thus contempt for the material, temporal world and the physical body took deep root in Christian culture.

The Breakup of the Roman Empire

■ How and why did the Roman Empire in the West disintegrate?

During the fifth century, the Roman Empire split into two parts: the Latin-speaking provinces in western Europe, and the largely Greek- and Syriac-speaking provinces in the east. As the Roman government lost control of its western domains, independent Germanic kingdoms emerged. The eastern provinces remained under the control of the Roman emperor, whose capital city was not Rome, but Constantinople. The definitive split of the Roman Empire marked the end of late antiquity. In future centuries the legacy of the Roman Empire survived in the West through Latin culture and Latin Christianity. In the East it survived as a political reality until its final collapse a thousand years later in 1453.

The Fall of Rome's Western Provinces

Why did Roman rule remain strong in the eastern Mediterranean while collapsing in western Europe? This is one of the most hotly debated subjects in all of history.

Most Christians of the time attributed the collapse of Roman rule to God's anger at the stubborn persistence of polytheist worship. Polytheists, for their part, blamed Christians for destroying the temples of the gods who had protected Rome so well in the past. In later centuries, the explanations varied. Edward Gibbon, an eighteenth-century writer whose *Decline and Fall of the Roman Empire* has influenced all historians of Rome and remains one of the most widely read history books of all time, criticized the Catholic Church for diverting able men away from public service and into religious life. Other historians attributed Rome's collapse in the West to enormous waves of savage barbarian invasions. The reason the Romans lost their western provinces is, however, more complicated and less dramatic than any of these one-dimensional explanations.

Loss of Imperial Power in the West

The end of Roman rule in western Europe came in a haphazard and gradual fashion as the cumulative result of unwise decisions, weak leadership, and military failure. During the first century, the Romans established the northern limits of their empire on the European continent along the Rhine and Danube Rivers. From that time forward, Roman generals and emperors withstood invasions of many different northern tribes looking for plunder and new lands. The Roman legions parried their attacks, maintaining a relatively stable northern frontier through not only military might and but also diplomacy. Since the time of Augustus, Roman emperors had made treaties with newcomers, permitting them to settle on Roman lands. The empire had always been able to absorb the settlers until the situation changed in the fourth century.

In the fourth century, the sudden appearance in southern Russia of the Huns, a fierce nomadic people from central Asia, set in motion a series of events that helped bring about the eventual collapse of Roman rule in western Europe. Unlike the settled farmers who lived in Europe, the Huns were nomads who herded their flocks over the plains (or *steppes*) that stretched from southern Russia to central Asia. Able to travel vast distances very quickly on their rugged horses, the highly mobile Huns consistently overran adversaries from settled agricultural communities who were attempting to protect their farms and families. They also earned a reputation for ferocity in battle. Always living under the specter of starvation, they lusted after the great riches and easy lifestyles they observed in the urbanized empires of Rome and Persia.

In 376, in what is now south Russia, an army of Huns drove a group of Visigoths from their farmlands. The refugees gained permission from the Roman emperor Valens to cross the Danube and settle in the Balkans in return for supplying troops to the Roman army. In the past, Roman rulers had frequently made this sort of arrangement with newcomers eager to settle in the empire. The Roman officials in charge of this resettlement, however, flagrantly exploited the refugees by charging

them exorbitant fees for food and supplies. The situation grew so intolerable that in 378 the Visigoths revolted. At the battle of Adrianople in Thrace they killed Valens and destroyed an entire Roman army and the emperor who led it.

The Visigoths' successful rebellion wounded the empire, but not fatally. Rome's response to the disaster, however, sowed the seeds for a serious loss of imperial power in the west. Necessity forced the new emperor, Theodosius the Great (r. 379–395), to permit Visigothic soldiers to serve in the Roman army under their own Visigothic commanders. But this precedent of allowing independent military forces of dubious loyalty operate freely within the empire was a terrible mistake. The consequences of Theodosius's decision to allow the Visigoths their own commanders became all too clear in the mid-390s when Alaric, the new Visigothic king, adopted a new policy toward the empire and began to attack and plunder Roman cities in the Balkans and Greece. In 401 Alaric invaded Italy, but was driven out by Roman soldiers under the leadership of Stilicho, Rome's most powerful general in the West. Stilicho served Rome loyally, defending it against Alaric and other menacing barbarians. The Roman Senate turned on him in 408, however, because he could not eliminate Alaric's forces. Rather than plunge

Stilicho and His Family

Between 395 and 408 the general Stilicho ruled the western half of the empire as the regent for Honorius, the son of Theodosius I. Though his father was a Vandal, Stilicho was completely loyal to Rome. Carved in traditional Roman style, these ivory panels show Stilicho dressed in Vandal clothing, accompanied by his wife and son.

Italy into civil war, Stilicho bravely accepted a death sentence. Two years later Alaric reappeared at the walls of Rome, demanding a huge payment of gold and pepper, a precious spice. Without Stilicho to protect them, the powerless senators yielded to Alaric's extortion.

Alaric's success at extortion only expanded his ambitions. For two years following this success, Alaric became involved in a long series of negotiations with the Senate in Rome and the emperor of the west, who now lived in Ravenna. He wanted to be appointed to the highest military rank in the western empire, but the emperor refused. Finally a new emperor granted his request. In 410, however, when the Roman senate denied him parts of northern Italy and the western coast of the Balkans, and when imperial forces attacked him, Alaric and his troops sacked Rome for three days. Disbelieving senators and citizens alike could only watch as the Visigoths rampaged through their streets. Because Alaric died soon after his triumph, he was unable to follow up on his great victory. To keep his burial place secret, his followers diverted the Busento River in Italy, buried their fallen leader and all his loot, and then executed the grave diggers. Finally, they returned the river to its original course. The exact location of Alaric's grave remains a mystery to this day, awaiting an archaeologist's spade.

The Visigoths' sack of Rome not only dealt a psychological blow to the empire's inhabitants, it also led indirectly to the loss of many of Rome's western provinces. To fight Alaric, Rome's armies withdrew from the empire's northwestern defenses, leaving the frontier in Britain and along the Rhine vulnerable.

In Britain, Rome abandoned its control entirely after an ambitious general, styling himself Constantine III, led Britain's last legions across the English Channel in an unsuccessful attempt to grab the imperial throne. This action left Britain defenseless, vulnerable to groups of Germanic tribesmen known as the Saxons already settled on British soil. Originally from the shores of the North Sea near modern Denmark, the Saxons had been fighting in Britain as allies of Roman forces. Now they turned on their former partners and attacked Roman-held Britain. The desperate inhabitants begged for help from the emperor Honorius. According to one contemporary, in 410 the beleaguered ruler merely told the Britons to fend for themselves.

Elsewhere the chaos spread. In December 406, the Rhine River froze, enabling an array of migrating Germanic tribes to enter the empire with little opposition from Roman forces. Small bands of these marauding tribes such as Alans, Burgundians, and Sueves roamed through Gaul, while the Vandals and their allies raided their way through Spain. For more than a decade, the various invaders tried to secure territory for themselves within the imperial borders by force. Vastly outnumbered by the provincial populations, they survived by plundering the farms of the Romans.

Although the invading bands were small, the imperial government in the west no longer possessed the administrative capacity to marshal its military resources and push the invaders out. Instead, it turned to diplomacy, offering the invaders a place within the Roman Empire. In Gaul, for example, the treaty of 418 granted the Visigoths a home in Aquitania (a region of southwestern Gaul). According to the treaty, the Visigoths received lands on which to settle permanently, something they had sought for nearly two generations. In return they would pay taxes and fight under Rome's banner to combat peasant rebels and other invading tribes. Within a generation, however, the Visigoths shook off their subordinate status to Rome. Refusing to pay taxes to Roman officials or send troops to fight in Roman armies, they established a kingdom of their own in Gaul by 450. A similar process of encroachment and settlement took place elsewhere in the western provinces. In 429 the Vandals moved from Spain to North Africa, where they soon established an independent kingdom. In 439 they seized Carthage and made it their capital.

Thus, encroaching bands of Germanic peoples established independent kingdoms in the regions of Britain, Gaul, Spain, and North Africa through a gradual process (see Map 6.2). The empire was not invaded by overwhelming numbers of savage invaders. In fact, their numbers were puny compared to the millions of Roman provincials against whom they pitted themselves. And although the Germans plundered and pillaged, they could not hold on to imperial lands and settle there without the active cooperation of Roman administrators who thought they could bargain with the tribesmen. Once they put down roots, however, they steadily consolidated their strength and established rule on their own. By then, Roman authorities lacked both the organization and the strength to defeat them.

DOCUMENT

Excerpt from Salvian: *The Governance of God*

Even though most of the western provinces had fallen to invaders by 450, the Romans managed to hold on to Italy for a short while longer. The city of Rome remained the home of the Senate, while the emperor of the western provinces resided in Ravenna, a town on Italy's northeast coast. Warlords, however, held the real power in Italy, although they were formally subordinate to the emperor. These soldiers were usually not Romans by birth, but they adopted Roman culture and fought for Rome's advantage. In 476 one of these warlords, a Germanic general named Odovacar, ended the charade of obedience to the emperor. He deposed the last emperor in the west, a boy named Romulus Augustulus. Odovacar then assumed full power over the Italian peninsula, naming himself king of Italy. For many historians the year 476 used to symbolize the end of the Roman Empire in the west. In actuality, however, 476 is a date of little significance. The Romans' control of their western provinces had all but slipped away decades earlier.

The Empire of Attila

The Huns, who had driven the Visigoths into the Balkans and sparked the series of events that led to Rome's loss of

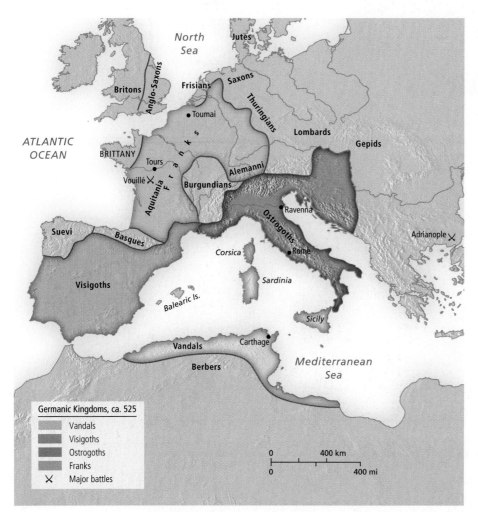

Map 6.2 Germanic Kingdoms, ca. 525

In little more than a century after their entry into the Roman Empire, different Germanic peoples had established several powerful kingdoms in western Europe.

its western provinces, continued to advance on Europe. By 400 they had carved out a powerful kingdom on the great plain of Hungary, where they could graze their horses and flocks. Throughout the first half of the fifth century the Huns remained a violent and disruptive presence on the European continent, relentlessly raiding the Balkans and western Europe.

By 445, the charismatic and ruthless king Attila (r. 434–453) emerged as the sole leader of the Hunnic tribes and their allies. Attila expanded the Huns' empire to extend from southern Russia to France. His aggression brought him face to face with the Roman Empire in the east. To their surprise, Roman diplomats from Constantinople who visited Attila's court found the Hunnic king to be a sophisticated bargainer as well as an able administrator. Attila, they discovered, included chieftains of subject peoples among his trusted assistants. The diplomats also found Roman merchants and craftsmen who had been attracted to Attila's camp, where they enjoyed freedom from oppressive Roman taxation and corrupt Roman officials.

Yet the Hunnic ruler had a shockingly brutal side as well. From his base of operations on the Hungarian plain, Attila

hammered the Balkan provinces and forced the Roman emperor in Constantinople to pay him tribute in gold every year. In 450, when a new emperor refused to submit any longer to Attila's extortion, the Hun turned westward and invaded Gaul with an immense army. The savagery of his attack and the fear he inspired earned him the title "the Scourge of God."

The next year, the tide began to turn against Attila. A force of Visigoths (who still hated the Huns for having driven them from their homelands in south Russia nearly a century earlier) joined with Romans and other allies from the Germanic kingdoms in western Europe. This allied force stopped Attila's advance in a battle at the Catalaunian Fields in central Gaul in 451. The following year the tenacious warrior launched a new attack on Italy but failed to take the city of Rome, perhaps because his army was weakened by disease.

Soon after the ill-fated invasion of Italy, Attila died while in bed with a young bride. His sons divided the Hunnic Empire among themselves, but the realm could not endure without its great leader. Soon the Huns' subject peoples rebelled against their oppressors and reclaimed

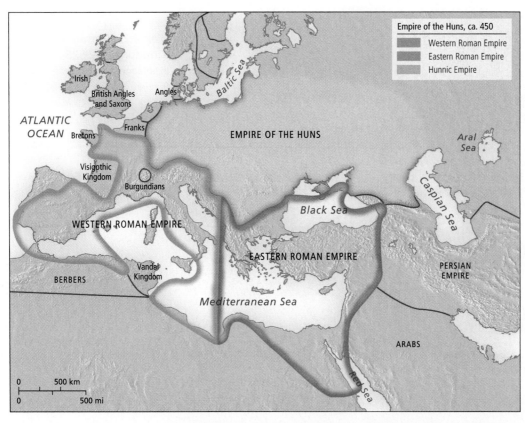

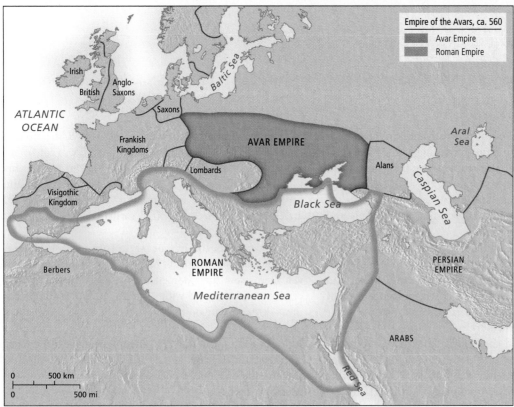

Map 6.3 Nomad Empires

During late antiquity, the Huns and later the Avars established powerful empires based on the Hungarian plain. These fierce horsemen terrified the settled peoples of the Roman world.

their independence. The mighty empire of the Huns fragmented and disappeared. Within a century another nomadic people, the Avars, replaced the Huns as the biggest menace to the Roman Empire and its successor kingdoms (see Map 6.3). The Huns seem to have made no material or intellectual contribution to Western civilization. But they did leave a chilling cultural legacy. As a common enemy of the peoples of the settled Mediterranean world, they embedded in Western culture a frightening memory of bloodthirsty steppe peoples who attacked from the east.

Cultural Encounters After the End of Roman Rule

By the mid-fifth century, when the fighting between Germanic invaders and the Romans ended, the two sides had to learn to live with one another. The rulers of Germanic tribes of Vandals, Ostrogoths, and Visigoths possessed military power but were vastly outnumbered by the Romans. For example, only 40,000 Vandals controlled North Africa, which had a population of several million Romans. Although the Romans had no military power, they dominated urban life and agricultural production. The Romans continued to enjoy urban life and education but were ruled by Germanic masters who maintained separate churches because they were Arian Christians. Their law courts were separate from the Romans' as well so that the two communities could live by their own legal traditions. Both sides faced challenges in adapting to the new situation.

In Britain the Germanic invaders were polytheists who snuffed out the Roman Christians. Yet legends hint at a fierce resistance against the invaders. The stories about King Arthur that have captivated English-speaking audiences since the Middle Ages are based on memories of valiant resistance to the Saxon invaders in the mid-fifth century. In Gaul, North Africa, Italy, and Spain, the new settlers were Christian, but followed Arian Christianity, a creed that viewed Jesus Christ as subordinate to God the Father. The Romans, on the other hand, followed Chalcedonian (Catholic) Christianity and thus saw the invaders as heretics. Although this religious difference caused considerable friction between the two peoples, it also worked to their mutual advantage. Roman law forbade marriage with Arian Christians, so the conquerors remained a distinctive minority in their new domains. This enabled them to maintain a separate Arian clergy and separate churches and hence a distinct identity in the midst of the vastly larger numbers of Roman provincials they ruled.

Confident in their position of power, the newcomers easily slipped into the role of military protectors of the Roman provincials they now ruled. For example, Vandal forces fought against Berber nomads from the foothills of the Atlas Mountains who tried to raid North Africa's fertile farmlands. To many Roman peasants, the new masters provided a welcome alternative to the callous imperial officials who had exploited them for so long.

Of all the former empire's western provinces, Italy prospered the most under Germanic rule, particularly under the long reign of Theodoric the Ostrogoth (r. 493–526). In 493 Theodoric left the Balkans for Italy at the instigation of the Roman emperor in Constantinople. The emperor told Theodoric that he could rule Italy if he was able to capture it from Odovacar, who was currently ruling there. The crafty emperor calculated that if Odovacar defeated Theodoric, the situation in Italy would remain unchanged, but the menace Theodoric presented would be gone from the Balkans. If Theodoric won, the Balkans would still be safe and there would be another barbarian ruling Italy, which was less of a threat to Constantinople. Either way he had little to lose and much to gain. Theodoric accepted the challenge and murdered Odovacar in Italy. Once on the

---

DOCUMENT

Romans Deserve Their Fate

Salvian, a priest at Marseilles, believed that the Arian Christian "barbarians," even though they were not orthodox Christians, had seized Rome's western provinces because the Romans had sinned and were being punished by God. He condemned Roman oppression of the poor as a sin:

Almost all barbarians . . . love one another; almost all Romans persecute each other. . . . The Roman poor are despoiled, the widows groan, the orphans are tread underfoot, so much so that many of them, and they are not of obscure birth and have received a liberal education, flee to the enemy lest they die from the pain of public persecution. They seek among the barbarians the dignity of the Roman because they cannot bear barbarous indignity among the Romans. Although these Romans differ in religion and language from the barbarians to whom they flee, and differ from them in respect to filthiness of body and clothing, nevertheless, they prefer to bear among the barbarians a worship unlike their own rather than rampant injustice among the Romans. Thus far and wide they migrate to the barbarians everywhere in power. . . . They prefer to live as free men under an outward form of captivity than as captives under an appearance of liberty. Therefore, the name of Roman citizens, at one time not only greatly valued but acquired with great effort, is now repudiated and fled from, and it is almost considered not only base but even deserving of abhorrence.

Source: Salvian, *On the Governance of God* 5.4-7. Trans. Jeremiah O'Sullivan. *Fathers of the Church. The Writings of Salvian the Presbyter.* NY: CIMA, 1947, 131–137, with some changes.

gave way to oaths of loyalty to local chieftains. Over time, new warrior-based aristocracies took shape in which landowning noblemen forged ties of personal loyalty to their local king.

Roman culture did not abruptly come to an end with the last vestiges of Roman rule. It remained a vital presence in most regions, but it took different forms in the various lands now ruled by Germanic leaders. In Britain, Roman culture perhaps fared the worst and little of it survived into later ages. There the Germanic language the Saxon invaders and their Angle allies spoke took hold and began developing into the English spoken today. In Gaul, Italy, and Spain, the Germanic settlers quickly learned the tongues of the Romans they ruled. Within several centuries these Latin-based "Romance" (based on the Roman speech) languages grew into the early versions of French, Italian, Spanish, and Portuguese. Latin continued as the language of literacy, and the settlers borrowed heavily from Roman literary forms. Writing in Latin, they produced histories of their tribal kingdoms in imitation of Roman historians. They also developed law codes composed in Latin influenced by Roman models.

throne of Italy, Theodoric took care to acknowledge the emperor's superior status. In politics, Theodoric sought to create an atmosphere of mutual respect between Ostrogoths and Romans by maintaining two separate administrations—one for his Ostrogoths, the other for the Romans—so that both communities could manage their own affairs under his supervision. He also included aristocratic Romans among his closest advisers and most trusted administrators. Even in his religious policies Theodoric pursued mutual tolerance. As an Arian Christian, Theodoric supported the separate Arian clergy, but he also maintained excellent ties with the pope, leader of the Roman Christians. Theodoric united Visigothic kingdoms in Spain and Gaul with his own in Italy, ultimately wielding great influence throughout western Europe. Italy prospered under his rule, and the communities of Ostrogoths and Romans lived together amicably.

Throughout the western provinces links to the Roman Empire in the east began to weaken. Most of the invaders had brought their traditional practice of pledging fidelity and obedience to a local chieftain, and this tradition began to erode loyalty to the far-off Roman emperor in Constantinople. By pledging themselves to a Germanic king, men gained a place in the "tribe" of their new chieftain. Many of these men had been soldiers who served in units of the Roman army under their own Germanic officers, but now they looked to their king—not to the emperor—to provide gifts and the opportunities to win prestige, honor, and land. Thus service to the empire gradually

The Survival of Rome's Eastern Provinces

Despite the profound alterations wrought by Christianity and Rome's loss of the western provinces, the Roman Empire endured in the eastern Mediterranean without interruption. Constantinople, the imperial city founded by Constantine in 324, became the center of a remodeled empire that over several centuries merged Christian and Roman characteristics. Inhabitants of the realm continued to think of themselves as citizens of the Roman Empire for another thousand years. The remodeled Roman Empire in the east is referred to as the Byzantine Empire.

Christianity and Law Under Justinian

The most important amalgamation of Christian and Roman traditions took place during the reign of the emperor Justinian (r. 527–565). Born in the Balkans, Justinian was the last emperor to speak Latin as his native language. He combined a powerful intellect, an unshakable Christian faith, and a driving ambition to reform the empire. He defied convention by marrying Theodora, a strong-willed former actress, and included her in imperial decision making once he became emperor in 527.

Emperor Justinian

Justinian inaugurated a number of changes that highlighted his role as a Christian emperor. First of all, he emphasized the position of the emperor at the center of society

Consular Diptych?

This ivory panel celebrates a consul at Constantinople in the early sixth century. He holds the mappa, a ceremonial cloth that symbolizes his office, in his right hand. Behind him stand personifications of Rome (on his left) and Constantinople (on his right). Such panels were given as gifts when consuls took office; this one demonstrates Roman traditions continuing in the new world of Byzantium.

in explicitly Christian terms. He was the first emperor to use the title "Beloved of Christ" and he amplified the emperor's role in Church affairs. Justinian considered it his duty as emperor to impose uniform religious belief throughout the empire by enforcing the decrees of the Council of Chalcedon as he interpreted them. In the east this meant stamping out the survivals of polytheist worship and struggling to find a common ground with the Anti-Chalcedonians. After he reconquered some of the western domains of the empire it meant dealing with the Arian Christian Vandals and Ostrogoths living there. In the east he succeeded in suppressing polytheism, but he never

reached an agreement with the Anti-Chalcedonian communities in Syria and Egypt. After these regions were conquered by the armies of Islam in the following century, the Christian churches there fell out of imperial control (see Chapter 7). In the west the bishops of North Africa and Italy deeply resented Justinian's attempts to meddle in ecclesiastical affairs by determining doctrine. As a result a bitter division arose between Christian churches in the eastern and western Mediterranean over the rights of bishops to resist imperial authority on religious matters.

Justinian attempted to create a Christian society by using Roman law coupled with military force. Unlike rulers of Rome's early empire, who permitted subject peoples to maintain their own customary laws, Justinian suppressed local laws throughout his realm. He envisioned all of his subjects obeying only Roman law—law that he defined and that God approved. (Justinian was sure that if God did not approve of his legislative changes, God would not allow him to continue as emperor.)

Thus, in his God-given mission as emperor-legislator, Justinian reformed Roman law. In an effort to simplify the vast body of civil law, he ordered his lawyers to sort through all the laws that had accumulated over the centuries and determine which of them should still be enforced. This monumental effort, which was completed in 534, is known as the *Code of Justinian.* His lawyers also prepared a handbook of basic Roman law for law students, called the *Institutes,* as well as the *Digest,* a collection and summary of several centuries' worth of commentary on Roman law by legal experts. Justinian then banned any additional commentary on the law, naming himself as the only interpreter of existing laws and the sole source of new laws. While the *Code, Digest,* and *Institutes* were composed in Latin, the traditional legal language of Rome, Justinian's new legislation, called the *Novels,* was issued in Greek, the common language of the eastern empire. Collectively, this legal work is now called the *Corpus of Civil Law°.* The body of Roman law passed down to later generations primarily through this compilation. At the end of the eleventh century, scholars in Italy discovered manuscripts of Justinian's legal works in church libraries, and interest in Roman law began to revive. The *Digest* became the most influential

Two Martyrdoms: Culture and Religion on Trial

Between the reigns of Diocletian (r. 284–305) and Justinian (r. 527–565), the status of Christians changed dramatically. Christians went from being a religious minority persecuted by the imperial government to a majority that persecuted non-Christians with the Roman government's backing. One thing did not change during this period, however. Whether polytheist or Christian, emperors used force to compel their subjects to believe and worship in prescribed ways, hoping to keep the empire in the gods' good graces. To ensure religious conformity, emperors used the Roman judicial system. A comparison of the trials of a Christian soldier named Julius in 303, and Phocas, an aristocrat in Constantinople accused of paganism in 529 and 545, illustrates the objectives and methods of the Roman government's religious prosecution.

In 303 officials arrested a veteran soldier named Julius and brought him before the prefect Maximus. The following excerpt comes from a description of the trial:

"Who is this?" asked Maximus. One of the staff replied: "This is a Christian who will not obey the laws." "What is your name?" asked the prefect. "Julius," was the reply. "Well, what say you, Julius?" asked the prefect. "Are these allegations true?" "Yes, they are," said Julius. "I am indeed a Christian. I do not deny that I am precisely what I am." "You are surely aware," said the prefect, "of the emperors' edicts which order you to sacrifice to the gods?" "I am aware of them," answered Julius. "I am indeed a Christian and cannot do what you want; for I must not lose sight of my living and true God." . . . "If you think it a sin," answered the prefect Maximus, "let me take the blame. I am the one who is forcing you, so that you may not give impression of having consented voluntarily. Afterwards you can go home in peace, you will pick up your ten-year bonus, and no one will ever trouble you again. . . . If you do not respect the imperial decrees and offer sacrifice, I am going to cut your head off." "That is a good plan," answered Julius, "Only I beg . . . that you execute your plan and pass sentence on me so that my prayers may be answered. . . . I have chosen death for now so that I might live with the saints forever." The prefect Maximus then delivered the sentence as follows: "Whereas Julius has refused to obey the imperial edicts, he is sentenced to death."[3]

After Constantine's conversion to Christianity in 312, persecution of Christians stopped, and Christian officials began to attack polytheism with the government's support. The emperor Justinian severely enforced laws against polytheists, executing anyone who sacrificed animals to non-Christian gods. During Justinian's reign, the imperial government launched three major persecutions of polytheists. In the first episode of persecution in 528–529, one year after Justinian ascended to the throne, a handful of government officials were charged with the crime of worshiping pagan gods.

One of these men was Phocas the Patrician, an aristocratic lawyer with an illustrious career in the emperor's service. After serving as the chief of protocol at court, he was sent to Antioch with funds to rebuild the city after a ruinous earthquake in 526. Cleared of charges of practicing paganism in 529, he continued to enjoy Justinian's trust and earn further promotions. In 532 he served for a year as Praetorian Prefect, the most powerful position in the realm after that of emperor. During this time, Phocas was responsible for raising revenues and administering the empire. He assisted in the construction of the new Cathedral of Holy Wisdom (see Haghia Sophia illustration in Chapter 7) in Constantinople by raising revenues. He also spent his personal funds in supporting smaller churches and ransoming hostages captured by Byzantium's enemies. Justinian next made him a judge and sent him on a mission to investigate the murder of a bishop. Then, in 545–546, during the second wave of persecution, despite his publicly recognized activities in support of the church and his faithful service to Justinian, Phocas was arrested again. He was among the doctors, teachers, and government officials suddenly charged with being pagans. A contemporary historian described a time of terror in Constantinople, when officials accused of worshiping the old gods in secret were driven from public office, had their property confiscated by the emperor, and were executed. In a panic, some of the accused men took their own lives. Phocas was one of them. Rather than undergo the humiliation of public execution, Phocas committed suicide. The furious emperor ordered that Phocas's body be buried in a ditch like an animal, without prayer or ceremony of any sort.

Phocas thus missed the third purge of 562, when polytheists were arrested throughout the empire, paraded in public, imprisoned, tried, and sentenced. Zealous crowds threw thousands of non-Christian books into bonfires in the empire's cities.

A representation of Jesus holding a cross and making a gesture of blessing.

An angel of victory hovers next to the emperor, another supports his foot. An attendant carries a statue adorned with wreath of victory.

Subject barbarians in native clothing bring offerings of gold and ivory.

Justinian
This mid-sixth-century ivory panel depicts the emperor Justinian in a standard pose of Roman emperors. The panel sends the message that Justinian rules the world with the approval and support of God.

The official reason for persecuting Christians, such as Maximus, was relatively simple: Christians broke the law by refusing to make sacrifices to the Roman gods. But why did the later Christian governments use such a heavy hand in persecuting polytheists? Men like Phocas who were attacked as pagans were highly educated in the traditional learning of the Greco-Roman world. Indeed, it was this learning that was really on trial. Phocas and other victims had a deep commitment to traditional Roman culture; their "paganism" was not the furtive worship of old gods like Zeus or Apollo. Rather, Phocas was considered a pagan because he was loyal to classical philosophy, literature, and rhetoric, without any Christian overlay or interpretation. In Justinian's eyes, this sort of classical learning had no place in a Christian empire.

Question of Justice

1. Why did both polytheist and Christian governments of Rome think it was necessary to persecute adherents of non-official religions?

Taking It Further

Helgeland, John. *Christians in the Military: The Early Experience.* 1985. An introduction to the persecutions of Christians in the Roman army and their depiction in Christian literature.

Maas, Michael. *John Lydus and the Roman Past: Antiquarianism and Politics in the Age of Justinian.* 1992. This book explains how Justinian's policies about religion also involved an encounter with the empire's classical heritage.

legal text in medieval Europe. Thus the *Corpus of Civil Law* became a pillar of Latin-speaking European civilization.

Reconquering the Provinces in the West

Once he had reorganized Byzantium's legal system, Justinian turned his attention to Rome's fallen western provinces. He wanted to reestablish imperial control over these territories, now ruled by Germanic kings. Once the empire was restored to its former glory, Justinian's plan was to impose his version of Christian orthodoxy upon the Arian Christian Vandals and Ostrogoths still living in his western domains. He would also force them to live under his version of Roman law and government.

In 533, Justinian sent a fleet of 10,000 men and 5,000 cavalry under the command of his general Belisarius to attack the Vandal kingdom in North Africa. The Vandal kingdom fell quickly, and within a year Belisarius celebrated a triumph in Constantinople. Encouraged by this easy victory, Justinian set his sights on Italy, where the Ostrogothic ruling family was embroiled in political infighting. This time Justinian had underestimated his opponents. The Ostrogoths, who had won the support of the Roman population in Italy, mounted a fierce resistance to Belisarius's invasion in 536. Justinian, for his part, did not trust his own general and failed to support him with adequate funds and soldiers. Bitter fighting between Justinian's troops and the Ostrogothic armies dragged on for two decades. Justinian's armies eventually wrestled Italy back under imperial control, but the long-term effects of the protracted reconquest had disastrous consequences for Justinian's empire. The many years of fighting devastated Italy's cities and countryside. Between pouring precious financial resources into the Italy campaign and maintaining his grip on North Africa, Justinian was draining his empire's resources dry.

One of the reasons Justinian's reconquest of Italy took decades was the visitation of a lethal plague. The plague struck the empire in 542 and spread throughout Justinian's realm, migrating swiftly to Italy, North Africa, and Gaul. The first onslaught took the lives of about a quarter of a million people, which was half the population of Constantinople. An estimated one-third of the entire population of the empire's inhabitants succumbed to the dreaded disease. With the population devastated by the plague, Justinian's army could not recruit the large number of soldiers it needed to fight on several fronts; the protracted battle for Italy was the result. The plague also weakened the economy. In many provinces farms lay deserted and city populations shriveled. Commercial ties between the eastern and western Mediterranean declined, and in the western provinces economies became more "local" and self-sufficient (see Map 6.4).

The Struggle with Persia

Although Justinian's greatest military successes were in the western Mediterranean, his most dangerous enemy was the Persian Empire on his eastern flank. This huge, multi-ethnic empire, under the rule of the Sasanian dynasty (ca. 220–633), had been Rome's main rival throughout late antiquity (see Map 6.5). The tension stemmed chiefly from competition over Armenia, which was a rich source of troops, and Syria, which possessed enormous wealth. From the time that Emperor Julian died in combat against Persia in 363, emperors at Constantinople kept up their guard against this eastern threat. Though wars were frequent, neither side could win permanent superiority over the other.

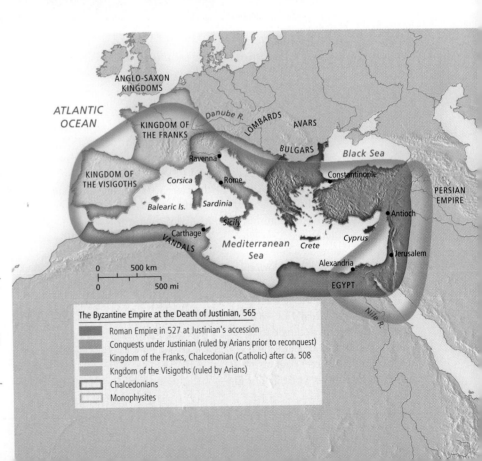

Map 6.4 The Byzantine Empire at the Death of Justinian

When Justinian died in 565, the territories of Italy, North Africa, and part of Spain that had been lost in the fifth century were restored, temporarily, to imperial rule.

The Byzantine Empire at the Death of Justinian, 565

- Roman Empire in 527 at Justinian's accession
- Conquests under Justinian (ruled by Arians prior to reconquest)
- Kingdom of the Franks, Chalcedonian (Catholic) after ca. 508
- Kngdom of the Visigoths (ruled by Arians)
- Chalcedonians
- Monophysites

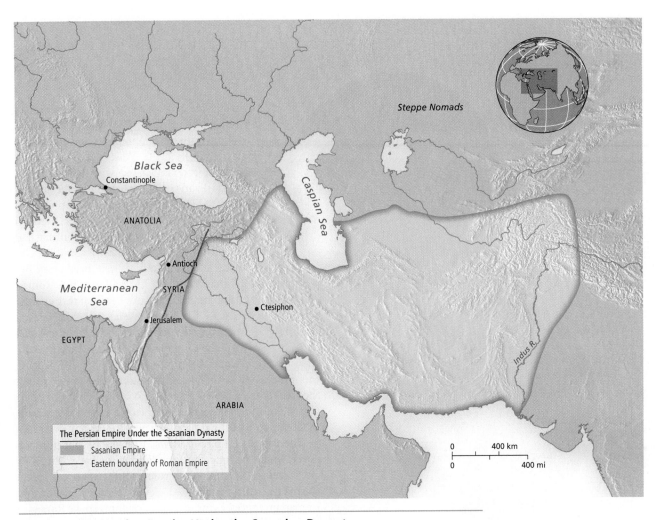

Map 6.5   The Persian Empire Under the Sasanian Dynasty

Under the dynamic Sasanian dynasty, the Persian Empire fought many wars with the Roman Empire. Neither empire had an advantage because they were roughly the same size and possessed equivalent resources of wealth and manpower.

Justinian fought several brutal wars with Persia. The emperor gave top priority to the struggle on his eastern frontier by supplying more than half of his troops, led by his best generals. He also provided more financial resources to the struggle in the east than to the wars of reconquest in the west. Chosroes I, the aggressive and ambitious Great King of Persia, proved to be a worthy adversary for Justinian. Chosroes repeatedly invaded the Roman Empire, causing great damage. In 540, for example, he sacked Antioch, the wealthiest city in Syria. Because war with Persia was extraordinarily expensive, Justinian made peace by paying thousands of pounds of gold to the Persian monarch in order to bring the fighting to a close. Even this great cost was less than continuing to fight every year.

By the time of Justinian's death, the two superpowers had established an uneasy coexistence, but the basic animosity between them remained unresolved. For the next half century, Justinian's successors engaged in intermittent bitter warfare with the Persian rulers. This protracted struggle between Constantinople and Persia demonstrates how the most important enemies lay to the east. Fighting to regain provinces in the west brought glory, but war with Persia was a matter of life and death for the eastern Roman Empire.

By fighting expensive wars on the eastern and western flanks of his empire, Justinian hastened the disintegration of imperial rule beyond the eastern provinces. The overextension of resources ensured that Constantinople could not maintain lasting control of the western Mediterranean region. When new invaders descended on Italy and the Balkans in the late sixth century, the empire would not have the strength to resist them. The drain of resources on

Persian Coins and the Religion of Zoroaster

This silver Persian coin depicts the Sasanian Great King Ohrmazd II (r. 302–309). He wears an elaborate crown. On the coin's other side two Zoroastrian priests tend a fire altar. Zoroastrianism was the state religion of the Persian Empire in late antiquity.

the Persian front also helped weaken the empire, and in the seventh century the remaining Roman provinces in North Africa, Egypt, and Syria were lost. Nevertheless, in what remained of the Roman Empire Justinian succeeded in creating a Christian-Roman society, united under one God, one emperor, and one law.

CHRONOLOGY

The Reign of Justinian

527–565	Reign of Justinian
529	Plato's Academy in Athens closed
529–532	War with Persia
527–533	Law Code of Justinian
534	Reconquest of North Africa
542	Plague strikes empire

Conclusion

The Age of New Boundaries

During late antiquity the transformation of the Roman world into new political configurations with new boundaries helped create a new conception of the West. Henceforth, the West was closely associated with the legacy of Roman civilization filtered through the lens of Christianity. The most lasting development of the period came from the encounter between Christianity, which before the fourth century had been the faith of a persecuted minority, and the civilization of the Roman Empire. As Christianity became the dominant religion throughout the Roman Empire, it was itself transformed, not the least through the attempts to reconcile Christian revelation with classical learning. Christian thinkers assimilated much of classical culture, and with the support of the Roman emperors Christianity became the official religion by 400. During this process of assimilation, Christians disagreed among themselves over how they explained the divinity of Jesus Christ, and these disagreements led to distinctive strains of Christian belief that have survived to this day.

The Roman Empire itself was irreparably split into two parts, which became the foundations for two distinctive civilizations. After Roman rule in the west collapsed, Germanic rulers established new kingdoms in the old Roman provinces. Some of these kingdoms spoke Romance languages derived from Latin, and all of them used Latin for religious worship. Latin remained the language of learning and the law, even in places such as Britain where the spoken language derived from a Germanic language. Through the spread of the Latin Christianity that developed in the western provinces of the Roman Empire during late antiquity, Latin civilization spread to parts of central, eastern, and northern Europe that had never been part of the Roman Empire. In the eastern Mediterranean, the Roman Empire survived as the Byzantine Empire (discussed in the next chapter) and became the home of Greek Orthodox Christianity. In Byzantium Greek remained the dominant tongue of daily life, learning, and Christian worship.

When Islam emerged as a powerful religious and political entity at the end of the late antique period, as we will discuss in the next chapter, its adherents were also influenced by classical learning and Roman institutions. But the Muslim and Christian Empires became enemies, a tendency that created the most lasting borders among the peoples who had once been citizens of the Roman Empire. The North African and Middle Eastern lands that Islamic conquerors seized from the Byzantine Empire lost their place in the roster of "Western" communities, while those lands not conquered by Islam became the bastion of a medieval civilization that defined itself primarily as European and Christian.

Suggestions for Further Reading

For a comprehensive listing of suggested readings, please go to www.ablongman.com/levack2e/chapter6

Bowersock, G. W. *Hellenism in Late Antiquity.* 1990. Explains the important role of traditional Greek culture in shaping late antiquity.

Bowersock, G. W., Peter Brown, and Oleg Grabar, eds. *Late Antiquity: A Guide to the Postclassical World.* 1999. An indispensable handbook containing synthetic essays and shorter encyclopedia entries.

Brown, Peter. *The Cult of the Saints: Its Rise and Function in Late Antiquity.* 1981. A brilliant and highly influential study.

Brown, Peter. *The Rise of Western Christendom: Triumph and Diversity.* 1996. An influential and highly accessible survey.

Brown, Peter. *The World of Late Antiquity.* 1971. A classic treatment of the period.

Cameron, Averil. *The Later Roman Empire.* 1993. *The Mediterranean World in Late Antiquity.* 1997. Excellent textbooks with bibliography and maps.

Clark, Gillian. *Women in Late Antiquity: Pagan and Christian Life-Styles.* 1993. The starting point of modern discussion; lucid and reliable.

Harries, Jill. *Law and Empire in Late Antiquity.* 1999. Explores the presence and practice of law in Roman society.

Lee, A. D. *Information and Frontiers: Roman Foreign Relations in Late Antiquity.* 1993. An exciting and original investigation.

Maas, Michael. *The Cambridge Companion to the Age of Justinian.* 2005. A collection of twenty chapters by different experts on all aspects of the Mediterranean world in the sixth century.

Maas, Michael. *Readings in Late Antiquity: A Sourcebook.* 2000. Hundreds of ancient sources in translation illustrating all aspects of late antiquity.

Markus, Robert. *The End of Ancient Christianity.* 1995. Excellent introduction to the transformation of Christianity in late antiquity.

Rich, John, ed. *The City in Late Antiquity.* 1992. Important studies of changes in late antique urbanism.

Thompson, E. A. *The Huns,* rev. Peter Heather. 1996. The best introduction to major issues.

Notes

1. Libanius, *On the Temples,* in A. F. Norman, *Libanius: Selected Works* (1977), 107–109.

2. Marcia L. Colish, *Medieval Foundations of the Western Intellectual Tradition* (1997), 49.

3. John Helgeland, *Christians in the Military: The Early Experience* (1985), 64–65.

Medieval Empires and Borderlands: Byzantium and Islam

7

I
N 860 FIERCE RUS TRIBESMEN ABOARD A FLEET OF SLEEK DRAGON SHIPS RAIDED the villages along the shores of the Black Sea and then stomped up to the gates of Constantinople, ready for pillage and rape. Taken by surprise, the inhabitants were gripped with panic. The Patriarch of Constantinople, Photius, called upon the people to repent of their sins to avoid God's wrath, and when the Rus unexpectedly broke camp and departed, it was interpreted as an act of divine intervention.

Strategically located where the Black Sea meets the Mediterranean, Constantinople was the shining remnant of the Roman Empire. The western provinces of the empire, including Rome itself, had been lost during the fifth century to Germanic tribes. Historians call the vestige of the Roman Empire in the east with its capital at Constantinople the Byzantine Empire because Constantinople was founded on the site of the ancient Greek city of Byzantium. Roman rule continued uninterrupted in the Byzantine Empire for a thousand years after the collapse of Roman rule in the west, and its citizens continued to call themselves the Romans.

Constantinople was the largest and richest city in the western world. Its Greek-speaking inhabitants clearly considered the Rus merchants as little more than savages, prone to the worst kinds of violence, and tried to keep them under control by signing treaties. The treaties stipulated that no more than fifty Rus could enter the city at one time, all must be unarmed, and they all had to leave by autumn. In exchange for civilized behavior, however, the Rus received during their stay free baths, food, provisions for a month, and equipment for their return. By the ninth century the Rus had established a regular pattern. Each spring after spending the winters along the river valleys of the north collecting tribute from the Slavic tribes, the Rus set off in their boats, risking dangerous rapids and waterfalls on the Dnieper River and ambush from hostile tribes, to reach the Black Sea and the splendid emporium

VIDEO

Haghia Sophia

The Cathedral of Holy Wisdom (Haghia Sophia) When Justinian entered his newly completed cathedral of Holy Wisdom (Haghia Sophia) in Constantinople, he boasted, "Solomon, I have outdone you!" He meant that his church was bigger than the Jerusalem Temple built by the biblical King Solomon. For centuries Haghia Sophia was the largest building in Europe. In 1453 the church became a mosque. Today it is a public museum.

of the world, Constantinople, which they called simply the "Great City."

Accustomed to the rough life of long winter treks, grubby little villages, and constant danger, they were dazzled by the sight of the Great City, with its half a million inhabitants, the gilded cupolas of its churches, the marble palaces of the aristocrats and emperor, the cavernous wharves and warehouses of its merchants, and the twelve miles of fortifications and walls that protected the city. The people of Constantinople were equally astonished by the sight of the Rus merchants—sun-worn, fur-clad, and armed to the teeth—whom they met with fascination and fear. To them the Rus seemed like so many other barbarian peoples: They could not speak Greek, were not Christians, and did not recognize the authority of the Byzantine Emperor, which the Greeks believed came directly from God. Despite constant threats to their borders by barbarian raiders and the armies of other civilized empires, Byzantium managed to thrive for many centuries and to survive for many more.

The usual purpose of these repeated barbarian visits was trade. The merchants of Constantinople traded Byzantine and Chinese silks, Persian glass, Arabic silver coins (highly prized by the Rus), and Indian spices for honey, wax, slaves, and musty bales of furs from Scandinavia and what is now northern Russia. Despite their sense of superiority, the Byzantines needed the barbarians. In the merchant stalls of Constantinople, traders from many cultures met, haggled, and came to know something of one another. None perhaps were more unlike each other than the rough Rus and the refined Byzantines, but their mutual desires for profit kept them in a persistent, if tentative, embrace. These repeated interactions among very different peoples who traded, competed, and fought with one another offer clues for understanding the medieval world, also known as the Middle Ages.

The term *Middle Ages* refers to the period between the ancient and modern civilizations from about the fifth to fifteenth centuries. Medieval culture rested on the foundations of three great civilizations: the Greek Christianity of Byzantium; the Arabic-speaking Islamic caliphates of the Middle East, North Africa, and Spain; and the Latin Christian kingdoms of western Europe. The dynamic interactions among these three civilizations, distinguished by religion and language, lay at the heart of medieval culture. From the seventh to eleventh centuries, the most energetic and creative of these three civilizations was Islam, which threatened militarily both Byzantium and the Latin Christian kingdoms. In the century after the death of its founder, the prophet Muhammad, in 632, Islam's followers burst from their home in Arabia to conquer an empire stretching from Spain to central Asia. Especially during the tenth and eleventh centuries, the Islamic empire supported important philosophical and scientific work, and produced a thriving economy.

These civilizations build empires. From the interaction and competition among them, the West created new borders that were both political and cultural. All the empires drew from Rome's legacy. The very concept of a universal empire derived from Roman political theory. The Byzantines thought of themselves as Romans and their empire as the Roman Empire. Although Muslims tended to create distinctively new forms of government and did not accept Roman law, in the cities that had once been part of the Roman Empire Muslim rulers adapted Roman administrative traditions for their own use. As we shall see in Chapter 8, the Latin rulers of the West attempted to revive the Roman Empire as a means of unifying their territories. The most distinctive feature of the medieval period was that all these civilizations were based on monotheistic religions that shared basic beliefs about God and the origin of their faiths. All struggled to eliminate either by persuasion or force vestiges of polytheism. However, because each of these medieval civilizations defined itself as an exclusive community of faith, cultural boundaries developed between them that are still visible today. The most important question raised by these encounters is, "how did the competition among the great medieval empires transform the idea of the West?"

■ **How did the Roman Empire's eastern provinces evolve into the Byzantine Empire?**

■ **How did Islam develop in Arabia, and how did its followers create a vast empire so quickly?**

Byzantium: The Survival of the Roman Empire

■ **How did the Roman Empire's eastern provinces evolve into the Byzantine Empire?**

The emperor Justinian (r. 527–565) tried to restore the glory of the Roman Empire by reconquering Roman provinces in North Africa, Italy, and parts of Spain from Germanic rulers who had established kingdoms in these territories in the fifth century. When Justinian died, his realm extended from southern Spain to the Persian frontier. As we saw in Chapter 6, it was an empire in which many of the institutions and traditions of the late antique Roman state, such as the imperial bureaucracy and provincial organization, still functioned. Despite these continuities with the Roman Empire of earlier centuries, Justinian brought profound changes. By insisting that his subjects follow Orthodox Christianity, eradicating the last traces of polytheist worship, and emphasizing the role of Christian faith in every aspect of government and education, he integrated classical culture and Christianity to a new degree. But he failed in his goal to unify the empire through Orthodox Christianity and completely alienated the bishops who disagreed with him.

Justinian's rule also represented a watershed in the military fortunes of the empire. After Justinian's death in 565, the Byzantine Empire still faced powerful enemies who surrounded it on all sides. To thwart its many adversaries, emperors reorganized Byzantium for military purposes. Byzantine institutions remained principally defensive, but they were effective in helping the empire survive formidable challenges.

In late antiquity Constantinople and Rome symbolized the two halves of the Roman Empire. Once joined in a common Christian culture, eastern and western Christians began to grow apart so that by the late ninth century they began to constitute separate civilizations. There were still cultural exchanges among them as merchants, pilgrims, and scholars crossed back and forth, but the two civilizations had ceased to understand one another. They held different opinions about religious matters, such as the dating of Easter, the rituals of the liturgy, the role of images in worship, and the extent of the authority of the bishop in Rome, the pope. The East and West also spoke different languages. In the East, Greek was the language of most of the population, and Latin had been largely forgotten by the end of the sixth century. In the West, Latin or local dialects of Latin prevailed; except in southern Italy and Sicily, only a tiny few knew some Greek.

As an extension of the great Eurasian steppes inhabited by polytheist farmers and nomads, eastern Europe became an unstable borderland on the flanks of Byzantium. In eastern Europe rival missionaries practicing Greek and Latin forms of Christianity competed for converts and allies to their respective sides, and the struggle between the two has left permanent scars in the cultural divisions of the region. One of the most long-lasting achievements of Byzantium was the conversion of many of the Slavic peoples to Orthodox Christianity, a faith that survived even after the collapse of Byzantium itself.

An Embattled Empire

After Justinian the Byzantine Empire was gradually reduced to a much smaller regional power struggling for survival against many enemies. Some of the threats came from nomadic tribes from the Eurasian steppes, such as the Avars, Slavs, and Bulgars, who migrated into the Balkans and permanently settled within the borders of the empire. These peoples became the ancestors of some of the current inhabitants of the region. In the west the Byzantines faced the Germanic kingdom of the Lombards who eroded the imperial rule over northern Italy that Justinian had reestablished. To the east the Byzantines confronted their old rival,

the Persian Empire. And from the south an entirely new threat arose out of the Arabian peninsula from the armies of Islam. The encounters between these diverse enemies and Byzantium were usually hostile, and their encirclement of Byzantium forced important changes in Byzantine administration and military policy.

Out of the Steppes: Borderlands in Eastern Europe

Like so many others before and after them, raiders and migrants poured out of the Eurasian steppes, a band of grasslands that spread some 5,000 miles from what is now Hungary and the Ukraine in Europe into Central Asia. Nomads could easily cross the grasslands on horseback. In much of the Balkan peninsula from the late sixth through ninth centuries, the weakness of Byzantium created a power vacuum that made the settled inhabitants who were Christians and still considered themselves subjects of the Roman Empire vulnerable to polytheist invaders from the steppes. The nomadic Avars, who first appeared on the steppes north of the Black Sea in the sixth century, had a bone-chilling reputation for cruelty and ferocity in warfare. They suddenly and violently arrived in the plains of present-day Hungary, from which they extended their territory into central Europe and the Balkans. These tenacious warriors dominated the region until the early ninth century and posed a constant menace to Byzantium and the new kingdoms taking shape in Italy and France (see Map 7.1).

The Avars created an empire by forcing conquered peoples to serve in their armies. Some of the peoples were Slavs. Between about 400 and 600, Slavic societies had formed from a blending of many cultures and ethnic groups. The Slavic communities that developed in eastern Europe between the Baltic Sea and the Balkans lay outside Byzantium's borders. Their Avar conquerors ruled by brute force, and most Slavs could not win back their independence. However, a few Slavic communities managed to overthrow Avar rule. In the middle of the seventh century, for example, in the territory of the modern Czech Republic, the Slavic king Samo led a successful revolt against the Avars and ruled a small, independent kingdom for nearly forty years.

In the second half of the sixth century, bands of Slavs began to migrate south across the Danube River into the Balkans, searching for new homes. Collaborating with groups of marauding Avars, the Slavs settled in sparsely populated frontier lands in the northern Balkans in what is now Croatia and Serbia. As the Slavs pushed south, many Byzantines fled their cities, abandoning them to the invaders.

By 600, Slavic and Avar groups had seized most Byzantine lands from the Danube to Greece. In 626, Slav and Avar forces attacked Constantinople from the northwest, while their Persian allies approached from the east.

The capital city survived their combined assault, but it took the Byzantines nearly four hundred years to reassert control over the Balkans.

By the ninth century, however, most of these tribes began to convert to one or another form of Christianity, and the patterns of those conversions have had lasting consequences to this day. The religious dividing line between those who adhered to Roman Catholicism and those who followed Orthodox rites cut directly through eastern Europe. The various tribes in eastern Europe were extremely fragmented politically, which mirrored the intricate distribution of ethnic and linguistic groups. State building was especially complicated in eastern Europe because most of the region had never been under Roman rule and lacked the legacies of Roman cities, institutions, and law that made the survival of Byzantium possible and the Germanic kingdoms of western Europe viable.

Fast on the heels of the Avars and Slavs from the steppes came the nomadic peoples called the Bulgars who established rule over the largely Slavic inhabitants of the Balkans by the eighth century. The Bulgars destroyed the surviving old Roman cities there, expelled what Christians remained, and attacked the Byzantine Empire. In 811, after annihilating the Byzantine army, the Bulgarian khan (the head of a confederation of clans) Krum (r. 808–814) had the Byzantine emperor murdered and lined his skull with silver in order to turn the rival's head into a drinking cup. With this symbolic act of debasement, the Bulgarians gained a fierce reputation as enemies of Christianity and Byzantium.

In 865, however, Khan Boris I (r. 852–889) dramatically changed course by accepting the Orthodox Christianity of his former enemies in Byzantium. His conversion illustrates the politics of the period. During the ninth century Christianity began to acquire a powerful allure among the

Map 7.1 The Byzantine Empire, ca. 600

By 600 the Byzantine Empire consisted of Anatolia, Greece, part of the Balkans, Syria, Egypt, and some territories in North Africa and Spain. Until the rise of Islam, the Persian Empire remained its greatest enemy.

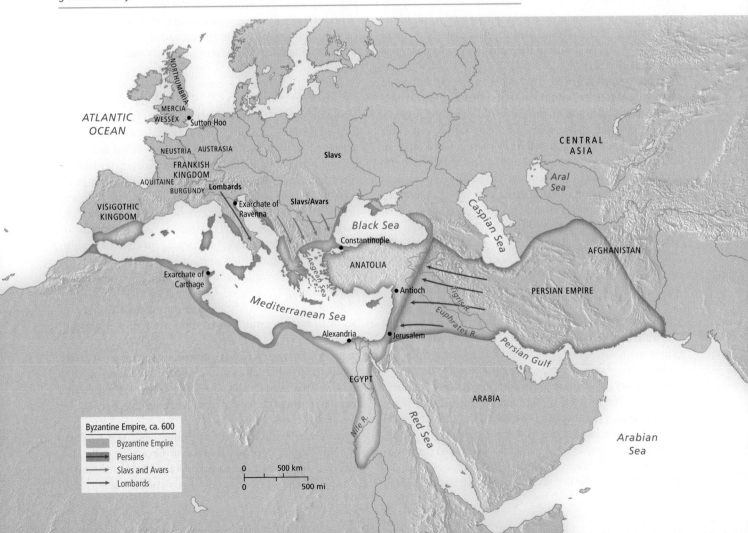

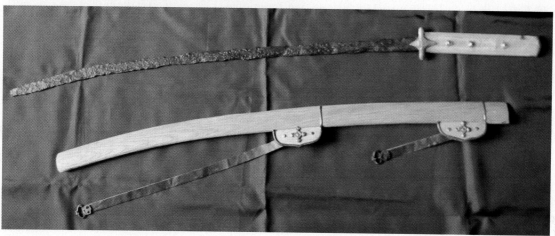

Avar Stirrups and Saber
Originally a nomadic people from central Asia, the Avars settled in Hungary and created an empire in central Europe. They depended on their heavily armed cavalry in battle. Byzantine military writers carefully studied Avar cavalry tactics and maneuvers. This pair of iron stirrups supported the weight of heavily armed cavalry and gave an Avar rider extra striking power with a slashing saber.

polytheistic tribes, not the least because Christian rulers considered so-called pagans legitimate objects of aggression, and their acceptance of Christianity opened the possibility for diplomatic ties and alliances. For Boris, therefore, conversion was a way to ward off Byzantine aggression and to make peace. For four years, Boris brilliantly negotiated with Rome, Constantinople, and German missionaries, all of whom sought to convert the Bulgars. In the end Boris got what he wanted—a Bulgarian Church that recognized the ultimate authority of the patriarch of Constantinople but was essentially autonomous.

The autonomy of the Bulgarian Church was further guaranteed later in the ninth century by the adoption of a Slavic rather than Latin or Greek liturgy. This was made possible by the missionary work in neighboring Moravia of Cyril (ca. 826–869) and his brother Methodius (815–885), who had invented an alphabet to write the Slavic language. They translated a Greek church liturgy into a version of the Slavic language now known as Old Church Slavonic. The acceptance of the Slavonic liturgy gradually led the ethnically and linguistically mixed peoples of Bulgaria to identify

with Slavic culture and language. From a string of monasteries established by the Bulgarians, the Old Church Slavonic liturgy spread among the Serbs, the Romanians, and eventually the Russians, creating cultural ties among these widespread peoples that have survived to the present.

Despite their conversion to Orthodox Christianity, the Bulgarians remained military rivals of Byzantium. A foolhardy Bulgarian attempt to capture impregnable Constantinople, safe behind its massive circuit of walls, provoked a formidable military reaction. By 1018 Bulgaria had lost its independence and was reincorporated into the Byzantine Empire.

Unlike the Bulgarians, the Rus did not represent an organized military threat to Byzantium even if their annual visits to Constantinople seemed vaguely threatening to the inhabitants of the city. From their trade with Constantinople, the Rus came to admire Byzantine culture. They established a headquarters at Kiev on the Dnieper River and gradually extended their domination over the local Slav tribes. From among the merchant-warriors of the Rus arose the forebears of the princes of Kiev, who by the end

DOCUMENT

Constantinople and the Avars: A Change in Tactics

After the death of Justinian in 565, the new emperor Justin II (565–578), confronted by an empty treasury, changed his policy toward the Avars. He refused to pay them their annual subsidies of gold to maintain peace with them, and so in 566 a delegation of Avars came to the palace to demand their gold. When the Avars were brought into the palace to meet the emperor, everything possible was done to impress them with the wealth and power of Constantinople and so subtly threaten them. A poet at court named Corippus described the Avar embassy's visit to the huge and gleaming palace:

The imperial throne ennobles the inmost sanctum, girded with four marvelous columns over which in the middle a canopy shining with liquid gold, like the vault of the curving sky, shades over the immortal head and throne of the emperor as he sits there.... Guards stood at the high entrance and kept out the unworthy.... When the officials had filled the decorated palace with their groups arranged in order, a glorious light shone from the inner chamber and filled all the meeting place. The emperor came forth surrounded by the great senate.... When the happy emperor had ascended the lofty throne and settled his limbs high up with his purple robes, the master of offices ordered the Avars to enter and announced that they were before the first doors of the imperial hall begging to see the holy feet of the merciful emperor.... The barbarian warriors marveled as they crossed the first threshold and at the great hall. They saw the tall men standing there, the golden shields, and looked up at their gold javelins as they glittered with their long iron tips and at the gilded helmet tops and red crosses. They shuddered at the sight of the lances and cruel axes and saw the other wonders of the noble procession. And they believed that the Roman palace was another heaven. But when the curtain was drawn aside and the inner part was revealed, and when the hall of the gilded building glittered and Tregazis the Avar looked up at the head of the emperor shining with the holy diadem, he lay down three times in adoration and remained fixed to the ground. The other Avars followed him in similar fear and fell on their faces, and brushed the carpets with their foreheads....

Source: Corippus, *In Laudem Justini Minoris,* ed. Averil Cameron (London: 1976), 3.190–270 (pp. 106–107).

---

of the tenth century ruled a vast steppe and forest domain through a loose collective of principalities. The term *Rus* (later *Russian*) came to be applied to all the lands ruled by the princes of Kiev.

The zenith of Kievan Rus was under Vladimir the Great (r. 980–1015) and his son Iaroslav the Wise (r. 1019–1054). A ruthless fighter, Vladimir consolidated into a single state the provinces of Kiev and Novgorod, a city in the far north that had grown rich from the fur trade. A polytheist by birth, Vladimir had seven wives and took part in human sacrifices. However, when offered a military alliance with Byzantium in 987, he abandoned his other wives, married the Byzantine emperor's sister, and accepted conversion to Orthodox Christianity. He then forced the inhabitants of Kiev and Novgorod to be baptized and had their idols cast into the rivers. The Byzantine Church established administrative control over the Rus Church by appointing an Orthodox archbishop for Kiev. The liturgy was in Old Church Slavonic, which provided a written language and the stimulus for the literature, art, and music at the foundations of Russian culture.

The religious and political connection between the Rus and Byzantium influenced the course of Russian history, and it limited the eastward spread of Latin Christianity or Roman Catholicism. Iaroslav helped establish a bulwark of Orthodox culture throughout the Kievan state by collecting books, employing scribes to translate Greek religious books into Old Slavonic, and founding new churches and monasteries (see Map 7.2).

The Loss of the Western Provinces

Justinian reconquered the western provinces of the Roman Empire in North Africa, parts of Spain, and Italy. The Byzantine emperors after Justinian tried to hold on to the western provinces by reorganizing the administration of North Africa and Italy into two new units called *exarchates*—the Exarchate of Carthage and the Exarchate of Ravenna. Because of their long distance from Constantinople and the immediate press of the local problems they confronted, the two exarchates had a certain autonomy from the rest of the Byzantine Empire. The exarchs (or governors) ruled the exarchates, holding authority over civilian as well as military affairs—a break from Roman tradition that had kept these two spheres separate. This joint command augmented the exarch's authority and independence, but the unity of civil administration and the army under one command was a sign of how grave were the problems the exarchs faced. The Exarchate of Carthage administered southern Spain and North Africa, but it failed to resist the onslaught of enemies. Southern Spain fell to the Visigoths in the 630s, and North Africa lasted until 698 when it was lost to Muslim armies.

In Italy, the exarchate was based in Ravenna, a city located in an easily defensible marshy area on the northeastern coast. The Exarchate of Ravenna administered the Byzantine possessions in Italy and Sicily, including the city of Rome, where because of his prestige the support of the pope was important for implementing Byzantine policies. But in 751 the Germanic Lombards captured Ravenna, put an end to the exarchate, and eliminated forever the tenuous vestiges of authority the Byzantines had managed to preserve in Italy since the conquests of Justinian.

The Old Enemy: Persia

On the southeastern front, Persia, ruled by the Sasanian dynasty (224–651), continued to threaten Byzantium after Justinian's death. The two powers fought intermittently for the rest of the sixth century. In 602 the struggle entered a new and final phase when the Persian ruler Chosroes II launched a series of devastating attacks against Byzantium. In 614 Chosroes seized Antioch, the richest Byzantine city in Syria. Then he captured Jerusalem, the holiest Christian city in the Byzantine Empire, and stole the holiest relic in the Christian world: a fragment of the cross on which Jesus reportedly had been crucified, known as the True Cross.

Motivated by a desire to avenge these losses and regain the holy relics, the Byzantine emperor Heraclius (r. 610–641) devoted his life to crushing the Persians once and for all. This resourceful and tenacious emperor spent most of his reign locked in a life-and-death struggle against Persia. In 622 Heraclius took a huge gamble. Leaving Constantinople in the hands of its capable patriarch Sergius, he led the Byzantine army deep into Persian territory, where he campaigned for years. Believing that Constantinople now lay vulnerable due to the emperor's absence, the Persians made an alliance with the Avars in 626 and attacked the Byzantine capital. The city's massive walls, however, thwarted their assault. After two more years of desperate fighting, Heraclius finally defeated Chosroes on Persian territory.

When Heraclius defeated the Persian emperor, he recovered the fragment of Jesus' cross that had been stolen from Jerusalem. When the Byzantine emperor returned the cherished relic to Jerusalem, he won a spiritual as well as a military and political triumph. Writers of the day described his struggle with Persia as a victory of Christianity. Heraclius announced his victory to the inhabitants of Constantinople with these words: "Let all the earth raise a cry to God . . . and let all we Christians, praising and glorifying, give thanks to the one God, rejoicing with great joy in his holy name, for fallen is the arrogant Chosroes, opponent of God." Heraclius's victory over Persia, however, had exacted a huge toll. It left the Byzantines (and the Persians) too

Map 7.2 The Expanding States of Eastern and Northern Europe
Eastern Europe during the Early Middle Ages was home to a very diverse population of tribes and fledgling states. Within this diversity the states of Bulgaria, Kievan Rus, and Poland emerged by the beginning of the eleventh century.

The Expanding States of Eastern and Northern Europe

DOCUMENT

Relics and International Diplomacy: Constantinople and the West

Emperors in Constantinople distributed relics in order to maintain relations with the rulers of the Latin kingdoms of western Europe. Queen Radegund of Poitiers (520–587), after several years of childless marriage to King Clothar (d. 561), left the royal court to found a nunnery in the city of Poitiers, where she devoted her life to charity and the ascetic life. Because of her piety she eventually was made a saint, the first female ruler ever to be honored in this way. Even while in the nunnery she played a role in domestic and international politics. The following excerpt, taken from her biography, describes how she obtained a fragment of what was believed to be the True Cross, on which Jesus had been crucified, as well as other gifts, from the reigning Byzantine emperor, Justin II, about the year 570. The passage illustrates the Mediterranean-wide scope of diplomacy and the importance of Constantinople as a source of prestige. Justin II sent the gifts to demonstrate his influence in the West.

. . . Because [Radegund] did not wish to do anything without counsel as long as she lived, she sent letters to the most excellent lord king Sigibert (her stepson), under whose power our land of Gaul is ruled, that he might permit her, for the safety of the whole land and the stability of his kingdom, to see the wood of the Lord's (Jesus's) cross from the emperor in Constantinople. Sigibert gave his consent most graciously to the petition of the holy queen. She, full of devotion, on fire with longing, sent no gifts to the emperor, since she had made herself poor for the sake of God, but with prayer prevailing, and with the presence of the saints, whom she invoked ceaselessly, she sent her messengers. And she obtained that which her vows had requested, namely that she, remaining in one place, gloried in the possession of the blessed wood of the Lord's cross, adorned with gold and gems, and many relics of the saints, which the East used to have. In response to the petition of the holy woman, the emperor sent representatives with the Gospels adorned in gold and gems.

Source: Based on the translation of the *Life of Radegund* II.16, by Martha Jenks, in *From Queen to Bishop, A Political Biography of Radegund of Poitiers* (Diss. U.C. Berkeley, 1999), p. 181.

---

exhausted to resist the sudden onslaught of a new enemy, the Muslim Arab armies.

The New Enemy: Islam

After the defeat of the Persian emperor, a ferocious new enemy challenged Byzantium: the armies of Islam. The military vigor of the Muslim Arab armies derived from the new religion of Islam that appeared in the Arabian peninsula in the seventh century. Islam is discussed in detail later in this chapter, but for the Byzantines the Muslim armies represented a new and what would prove to be a persistent threat. After the 630s, Islamic armies attacked the Byzantine Empire continually from the east, raiding deep into Anatolia (modern Turkey) and sometimes threatening Constantinople itself. In 636, the formidable Arab enemy crushed a Byzantine army at the battle of the Yarmuk River, forcing the Byzantines to abandon the wealthy province of Syria. A few years later Arab troops seized Egypt from Byzantine hands. Encouraged by their victories, an enormous Arab force of more than 100,000 men and 1,800 ships besieged Constantinople itself between 716 and 718. The attack failed because of the strength of Constantinople's walls, the courage of the defenders, and logistical problems among the Arabs. However, the Byzantines were certain their salvation was a miracle, a sign of God's favor. They claimed that the Virgin Mary had personally helped defend their capital.

Unfazed by their failure to capture Constantinople, Arab troops soon resumed their annual raids into Byzantine territory, defeating every Byzantine army that opposed them. Finally, in 740, Emperor Leo III (r. 717–741) won the Byzantine Empire's first important victory over the Muslim armies at the battle of Akroinon in western Asia Minor. Exhausted Byzantine troops could not go on the offensive, but they had slowed Arab momentum against their empire. The Byzantines were no more often at war with Muslim armies than with others, but the Muslims came to represent a singular threat in the eyes of Byzantine Christians largely because Muslim armies were so persistently successful against them. The Muslims quickly conquered all of North Africa, the Middle East, southern Spain, and Sicily, chipping away huge parts of what had once been Byzantine territory.

One of the lasting fruits of these conflicts were legends of great heroes. These legends began as stories recited in verse to entertain Byzantine aristocrats whose ancestors had fought the Arabs, and several of these oral legends were eventually refashioned into epic poems that became extremely popular and much imitated. The epic tenth-century Greek poem *Digenes Akritas* describes the heroic feats of soldiers during the late eighth century on the eastern

King David Plate

Nine silver plates made in Constantinople about 630 illustrate scenes from the career of the biblical King David. The largest plate (about 20 inches in diameter) shows David battling the giant Goliath. Though the subject matter is biblical, the style of representing clothing, human bodies, and spatial relationships comes directly from the classical tradition. The artist may have intended to show a connection between the warrior king of the Bible and the emperor Heraclius, who defeated the mighty Persian emperor Chosroes II.

which provided spiritual guidance and resolved the religious controversies. Each of these institutions contributed to stability in a world of turmoil. The Byzantine system was perhaps most successful in reorganizing its military institutions, which made it possible to respond to armed threats on the frontiers without direct authorization from Constantinople. Despite terrible losses Byzantium endured.

Imperial Administration and Economy

Based in the capital city of Constantinople, the emperor stood at the very center of Byzantine society. His authority, which his people believed had been granted by God, reached to every corner of the empire. This supreme ruler governed with the assistance of a large bureaucracy that he tightly controlled. In this hierarchical bureaucracy different clothing indicated different levels of importance. Only the emperor or members of his household, for example, could wear the color purple, a symbol of royalty. High dignitaries wore silk garments of distinctive colors encrusted with jewels; the higher the official, the more gems he was permitted to display. Bureaucrats and courtiers (members of the emperor's personal retinue) lined up in elaborate processions in order of their importance, as indicated by the color of their clothing and shoes. Through these ceremonial processions the emperor displayed the government to the people. Such processions were not just a form of political propaganda. They made the constitution of the empire evident through the hierarchic order of the procession, and they provided an indicator of the politics of the court as favored courtiers moved to a higher-ranked position in the procession and those out of favor moved to a lower-ranked place or disappeared from the procession altogether.

Men fortunate enough to obtain an office in the imperial government acquired considerable wealth and influence. For this reason leading provincial families sent their sons to Constantinople in search of positions in the imperial hierarchy. Through this method of recruitment Constantinople remained in close touch with the outlying regions of the

frontier of the empire, where Byzantine and Arab populations both fought and cooperated in a complex symbiosis. The father of the hero of the poem was an Arab soldier who abducted the daughter of a Byzantine general, married her, and converted to Christianity. The son of this mixed marriage was Digenes ("two-blooded"), a man of two peoples and two religions, who became a border fighter. This greatest Byzantine hero, who lived between two cultures, was the poetic embodiment of the engagement between Byzantium and Islam at a time when the former seemed clearly in the ascendant. The legends surrounding *Digenes Akritas* had a profound influence on Greek literature. Later writers referred to it and retold its stories again and again.

Byzantine Civilization

In addition to assaults from so many directions, the Byzantine Empire faced turmoil from within. The loss of territories caused economic suffering, and doctrinal controversies during the eighth century severely divided the Orthodox Christian Church. It seems remarkable that the Byzantine Empire survived at all, but it did. Its survival points to the strength of three institutions that held the empire together: the emperor, who set policies and safeguarded his subjects' welfare; the army that defended the realm's frontiers; and the Orthodox Christian Church, empire. This aspect of the system was a strength because it gave both provincial families a stake in the success of the imperial system and the provinces a voice in the capital. However, the governmental system was also vulnerable to corruption. Many men obtained their positions by bribing court officials who worked for the emperor. Many office-holders probably owed their jobs to family influence or bribes rather than talent, but even a corrupt system can be an effective form of government because official corruption made loyalty to the emperor more rewarding than opposition to him.

From his position at the head of this elaborate hierarchy, the emperor controlled Byzantium's economy. The Byzantine economy was monopolistic in that official monopolies controlled the production and distribution of specific commodities. These monopolies were designed to protect the interests of the emperor and those he rewarded by stifling all forms of competition. As long as the monopolies flourished the government had a source of revenue through taxation. When Justinian died, the imperial taxation system that Constantine had established in the early fourth century still generated sufficient funds to keep the imperial system working. Trade within the empire was stimulated by the ready availability of imperial coinage, which spurred a flourishing cash-based economy.

By the end of the seventh century, however, when the rich provinces of Egypt and Syria and the wealthy cities of Alexandria, Antioch, Jerusalem, and many others had fallen to the Arabs, the Byzantine economy stumbled. Thousands of refugees from lands conquered by Muslims streamed into the empire and strained its dwindling resources. In conquered provinces, Muslim rulers monopolized Middle Eastern trade revenues and prevented Byzantine merchants from participating in long-distance commerce, which badly hurt the official monopolies. Cut off from foreign markets, Byzantines stopped manufacturing goods for export. As the economy shriveled, Byzantines stopped building new homes and churches. By 750, the standard of living in most Byzantine cities steeply declined.

The Military System of the Themes

In response to the many external threats, Byzantine society was reorganized for constant preparation for war. Emperors relied on their armies to protect Constantinople, the nerve center of the shrinking Byzantine state, and to defend the borders against invaders. By about 650 in Anatolia, emperors abandoned the late antique system of relying on the provincial governors to protect the frontiers. In place of the Anatolian provinces the emperors created buffer territories against Muslim armies—the four military districts called themes. Each of the themes had its own army and administration commanded by a general chosen by the emperor. The themes' armies developed strong traditions of local identity and prided themselves on their expert military skills, a legacy the Byzantine Empire had inherited from the

Roman legions. These military forces remained effective enough to keep the empire from collapsing in spite of devastating losses to Islamic armies throughout the seventh century.

By 750 the themes developed considerable independence from Constantinople and were the basis of further reorganization of the agricultural economy and procedures for recruitment. Soldiers and sailors who were once paid in cash from the emperor's tax revenues now were granted land on which to support themselves. Fighting men had to provide their own weapons from their income as farmers, and the theme system enabled the various parts of the empire to function without direct support from the imperial treasury. The theme system created some measure of defensive flexibility for the empire. While it could no longer launch large-scale offensive conquests, as was possible in the time of Justinian, Byzantium could at least make an attempt at defending its shrinking borders.

Over time the four original themes were subdivided and new ones added in other regions until by the end of the eleventh century there were thirty-eight themes. The military strength of the empire came to depend on the theme system in which free, tax-paying soldier-farmers lived in villages under the supervision of a military commander who was also civil administrator. These soldier-farmers usually fought in their own districts, which meant they were defending their homes and families, and they provided a formidable bulwark against invaders. Because of their strong local roots the themes were more effective for defending against aggressors than conducting offensive campaigns.

Even with reorganized territorial defenses in the themes, Constantinople could not be protected without naval power. During the seventh and eighth centuries, the Byzantine fleet successfully kept Arab forces at bay through the use of "Greek Fire," a kind of napalm hurled against enemy ships to ignite them. Muslims soon learned how to use "Greek Fire," but the Byzantines used it more effectively in battle. Byzantine naval policy was also primarily defensive. Byzantium did not attempt great naval expeditions that landed troops abroad, but the navy was capable of maintaining a fleet that kept the capital safe from Muslim fleets.

The Byzantine borders were especially harassed by Muslim enemies, but from the first thrust of Muslim armies against Byzantium's frontier in the seventh century until its final collapse more than eight hundred years later, Constantinople held on. While Persia and other territories fell to Arab armies, Byzantium survived. That fact is perhaps the most important measure of the success of its military reorganization and defensive strategy.

The Church and Religious Life

Most Byzantines identified themselves as Orthodox Christians, meaning that like the emperor they accepted the doctrines established by the first seven church councils, especially the Council of Chalcedon in 451. That important council defined Christ's human and divine natures as being united in one divine "person" without any separation, division, or change. This distinguished Byzantine Christians from other Christian communities that interpreted the nature of Christ differently, as discussed in Chapter 6.

Constantinople boasted so many churches and sacred relics that by 600 Byzantines had begun to think of it as a holy city, protected by God and under the special care of the Virgin Mary, Jesus' human mother. Churchmen taught that Constantinople was a "New Jerusalem" that would be at the center of events at the end of days when God would bring history to an end and judge humanity.

One of the institutional pillars of the Orthodox Church was that the clergy were organized hierarchically like the imperial bureaucracy. The Patriarch, or chief bishop, of Constantinople led the Orthodox Church, administering several thousand clergymen in the capital and directing church affairs throughout the empire. Emperors generally controlled the appointment of new Patriarchs, and often they worked closely together, serving Byzantium's spiritual needs. The Patriarch helped impose religious unity throughout the empire by controlling the network of bishops based in cities. As the leader of urban religious life, a city's bishop supervised the veneration of the saints' relics housed in its churches. Byzantines believed that relics protected their communities, as the polytheist gods had done in the pre-Christian past. Because bishops usually came from the city's elite, they were influential local leaders, responsible for many kinds of decisions for the public good, not just religious ones.

Many cities were also home to monasteries, which played a significant role in the empire's daily life. Men and women went to separate monasteries to live a spiritual life, praying for their salvation and that of other people. People in need of assistance, such as orphans, the elderly, battered wives, and the physically and mentally ill, found refuge and assistance in monasteries. Monks and nuns regularly distributed food and clothing to the needy outside the monastery walls. Generous donors gave lavishly to monasteries to fund these activities, and many monasteries grew extremely wealthy through these gifts.

Monastery of the Holy Trinity in Meteora, Greece

During the seventh and eighth centuries, Christian instruction under the supervision of the Church replaced the traditional Roman educational system. By about 600, financially strapped city leaders had stopped paying schoolmasters to offer traditional instruction. Learning so declined that most Byzantines could neither read nor write. Pious Christians also developed a deep suspicion of classical

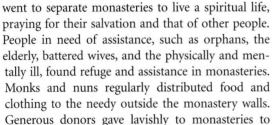

Christ on Byzantine Coins: An Emperor's Piety

Coins often indicate beliefs important to the society that minted them. The emperor Justinian II (r. 685–695) introduced a new kind of coin that for the first time depicted the head of Christ. The emperor moved his own image holding a cross to the back of the coin, a statement of his subordination to Christ.

learning, with its references to ancient gods and customs frowned on by the Church. Those few who learned how to read did so by studying the Bible, not the classics of Greek antiquity. As a result of this general decline in learning, the Church monopolized all culture and thought. Knowledge of classical literature, history, and science disappeared everywhere except in Constantinople, and even there the academic community was tiny. Many Byzantines, for example, had no memory of the polytheist religions and thought that the marble statues from earlier centuries adorning their cities were sinister demons.

Icons and the Iconoclastic Controversy

The Orthodox Church created unity of faith and culture, but that unity was broken in the eighth century by controversy within the church itself. As enemies tore at the borders of the empire, Byzantines wondered why God was punishing them so severely. Their answer was that somehow they were failing God. Convinced that only appeasing God could save them, Emperor Leo III (r. 717–741) took action. In order to make Byzantium a completely Christian empire, he forcibly converted communities of Jews. His most important move was to challenge the use of icons°, the images of Christ and saints found everywhere in Byzantine worship.

In contrast to Byzantine practice, the first Christians had refused to make images of Christ and other holy individuals. They had two reasons for banning such representations. First, the Hebrew Bible forbids creating any representations of God, and they considered this aspect of the old law of the Hebrews still in effect for Christians. Second, they thought that Christians might start to worship their images in the same way that polytheists worshiped statues in their temples. "When images are put up, the customs of the pagans do the rest," wrote one church leader in the fourth century.

Despite such warnings, many Christians responded aesthetically to the beautiful polytheist statues and images that filled the cities in which they lived. Christian sculptors and painters started to create a distinctive Christian art that combined religious images with the styles and techniques of classical art. After Constantine converted to Christianity in 312 and put an end to the persecutions of Christians, this new art flourished. Artists routinely portrayed Christ and the saints in churches. During the sixth and seventh centuries Byzantines used religious images with greater zeal than ever before. By 600, for example, the emperor placed a large image of Christ above the Bronze Gate, the main entrance to the imperial palace in Constantinople. Smaller paintings became intensely popular in churches and in people's homes.

Byzantine theologians defended icons as doorways through which the divine presence could make itself accessible to believers. Churchmen cautioned that God or saints do not actually reside within the icons, and so believers should not worship the images themselves. Rather, they should consider icons as openings to a spiritual world, enabling believers to encounter a holy presence. Thus Byzantines treated icons with great love and respect.

However, by the eighth century some Byzantine religious thinkers thought matters had gone too far and sought to revive the early Christian prohibitions against religious images. They advised Emperor Leo that icon veneration should be halted because too many uneducated people believed icons were divine themselves. These simple believers confused the image of the icon with what it represented and worshiped icons as polytheists had worshiped statues in their temples. Besides following the advice of these theologians, Leo decided to act after a volcanic eruption destroyed the island of Santorini, proving in his mind that God had

been angered by icon veneration. Leo prohibited the veneration and ordered the destruction of holy images (except for crucifixes) throughout the empire, but public resistance forced him to move very carefully. For example, when he ordered workers to remove the image of Christ from the Bronze Gate at the imperial palace in 726, the people of Constantinople rioted. Four years later, Leo renewed the general prohibition. The destruction of icons, known as iconoclasm° (image breaking), sparked a bitter controversy that divided Byzantine society until 842.

Epitome of the Iconoclastic 7th Synod (754)

Leo's iconoclasm backfired because the veneration of icons was such a vital part of popular religious life. He found it difficult to enforce iconoclasm outside Constantinople. Revolts broke out in Greece and southern Italy when imperial messengers arrived with orders to destroy images. The iconoclastic controversy affected international politics as well. Outraged by the Byzantine emperor's prohibition of icons, the Roman pope, by then the dominant religious and political figure in the West, excommunicated Leo. In retaliation Leo deprived the pope of political authority over southern Italy, Sicily, and Illyricum (the Balkan coast of the Adriatic Sea), a political authority the popes claimed they had inherited from long-gone Roman emperors of the west. The Roman popes never forgave the emperor for this slight. This conflict contributed to a growing rift between Greek Orthodox and Latin Christianity.

After years of turmoil, two Byzantine empresses who sympathized with their subjects' religious convictions restored icons to churches. In 787, the empress Irene called a general church council that reversed Leo's ruling. After a brief renewal of iconoclasm, in 843 the empress Theodora introduced a religious ceremony for commemorating images, which Orthodox Christians still celebrate annually. Icons remain an integral part of Orthodox worship today. The iconoclastic controversy may have widened the gap between Greek Orthodoxy and Latin Christianity, but its resolution created even greater religious unity within the Byzantine world. A common religious culture not only unified the Byzantines, but also provided solace and a spiritual connection to Byzantium for many Christians who found themselves in the former Byzantine territories that had been conquered by Islamic rulers.

The Macedonian Renaissance

Byzantium's losses to external enemies were reversed during the Macedonian dynasty (867–1056), the term for a line of emperors from the Makedonikon Theme that lasted six generations. Before the Macedonians there was always the potential for instability when an emperor died because powerful families struggled over who would become the new emperor. But after Basil I (r. 867–886) murdered his way to the throne, he kept his family in power by naming

Byzantine Manuscript

In this ninth-century Byzantine manuscript the figure with a pole is shown whiting out an image of Christ.

**An Icon that Survived Iconoclasm:
St. Peter in the Monastery at Mount Sinai**
This image of St. Peter, painted sometime during the sixth century, is in the Monastery of St. Catherine on Mount Sinai in Egypt. Because Egypt was in Muslim hands when the iconoclastic controversy broke out, this image survived.

retook the island of Cyprus and kept the Muslims from southern Italy, although they were unable to prevent Muslim conquests of Crete and Sicily, which became thriving centers of Muslim culture.

Whereas on the eastern borders the only option against the Muslims was a military one, in the polytheistic Balkans missionary efforts helped create new alliances. As discussed previously, the conversion of the southern Slavs and the Bulgars was well underway before the Macedonian Renaissance, which enhanced the cultural allure of Byzantium for these newly converted peoples. The Bulgars were incorporated into the Byzantine sphere of influence, but they proved inconstant allies. Perhaps the greatest achievement in the spread of Christianity under the Macedonians was the conversion of the Rus, which made them less isolated and more open to Byzantine influence.

The Byzantine success at converting the Slavs, Bulgars, and Rus magnified a growing bitterness with the Latin or Catholic Christians in western Europe. For their part, the Byzantines under the Macedonian dynasty took heart from their military successes and assumed it was only a matter of time before the West returned to obedience to the one true emperor in Constantinople. Needless to say, Latin Christians did not accept the Byzantine vision of an empire in which they played a subordinate role, and relations between East and West soured during the tenth and eleventh centuries. Especially after the Saxon king Otto I was crowned Roman emperor in 962, the Macedonian dynasty was hostile to the Latins. Visiting western ambassadors were treated with scorn and a superior attitude that precluded cooperation between Orthodox and Catholic Christians, especially against their common Muslim foes.

Under the Macedonian dynasty, the economy of Constantinople thrived. Home to more than half a million people by the tenth century, the city became a great marketplace where goods from as far away as China and the British Isles were exchanged. It was also a center for the production of luxury goods, especially silk cloth and brocades, which were traded throughout Europe, Asia, and northern Africa. During this period aristocratic families, the Church, and monasteries became immensely rich, and devoted themselves to embellishing the city with magnificent buildings, mosaics, and icons, creating the Macedonian Renaissance°.

The settlement of the iconoclastic controversy in 842 by Empress Theodora released great creative energies by defining the religious beliefs of Orthodoxy and creating unity within the Orthodox Church. Some of those energies went into missionary work, but the educated classes of courtiers, churchmen, monks, and scholars also produced a remarkable body of work. The most original work was spiritual in nature, embodied in sermons, theological scholarship, and especially hymns, but thanks to generous imperial patronage Constantinople also became a center for philosophical study. The accumulation of ancient manuscripts and the

his sons co-emperors and encouraging the principle of dynastic succession.

Byzantium and Islam had been engaged in a life-and-death struggle since the seventh century. Under the Macedonian emperors from the middle of the ninth century to the late tenth century, Byzantine armies and fleets fought Muslim armies on several fronts. In the East the Byzantines pushed into Syria and Palestine almost to Jerusalem. A large portion of the Mesopotamian river valley fell into their hands. They annexed the kingdom of Georgia and part of Armenia. In the Mediterranean the Byzantines compilations of ancient philosophy created an important cultural link between the ancient and medieval worlds.

The Patriarch Photius (ca. 810–ca. 893) became the most eminent scholar in the history of Byzantium. Photius maintained a huge library, which became a major center for the study of ancient Greek literature based on the rare manuscripts he had collected. Photius was the author of several important works, including the *Library*, an encyclopedic compendium of classical, late antique, and early Byzantine writers in both theology and secular literatures. Photius's summaries and analyses of these writers remain especially vital to this day because many of these books have been lost since his time. In addition to writing, Photius was deeply involved in church politics. Photius's election as Patriarch while still a layman was strongly opposed by the Roman pope. Photius was twice deposed from office due to the shifts of political winds in Constantinople. A bitter critic of the Latin Christians on matters of religious doctrine, Photius is often blamed for widening the gap, called the Photian Schism, between the two main branches of Christianity.

The quasi-sacred office of the emperor came to be magnified in elaborate court ceremonies under the Macedonian dynasty. The historian Emperor Constantine VII Porphyrogenetus (r. 912–959) wrote *On the Administration of the Empire*, an important source for Byzantine history. He also wrote the *Book of Ceremonies*, which became a model for royal ceremony throughout the Christian world and was adapted in kingdoms across Europe from Spain to Russia. The *Book of Ceremonies* disseminated Byzantine concepts of rulership, which suggested that the emperor, like Christ, had two natures. One of these natures was human and fallible, but the other was derived from God, which gave the properly consecrated ruler divine authority over his subjects. In fact, Byzantine emperors were anointed with holy oil in a ceremony that was very similar to the ordination of priests. The divine authority of emperors represented by their anointment became a central feature of political thought during the Middle Ages.

The Byzantine Portrait
This ivory plaque shows the emperor Constantine VII Porphyrogenetus being crowned by Christ. It was probably made in 944 to commemorate his becoming the sole ruler of the Byzantine Empire. Under the emperor's left hand the inscription reads "Emperor of the Romans."

Despite the achievements of the Macedonians, new threats loomed on the horizon. Under the Macedonian emperors, Byzantium had never been completely free from the external threat of invasions. The extent to which the empire succeeded in meeting these threats had depended on two factors—the political stability guaranteed by the Macedonian dynasty, and the organization and recruitment of the army through the military districts of the themes.

Emperor Basil II died in 1025 and left no direct heirs. But members of his family continued to rule until 1056, largely because of the general assumption that the peace and prosperity of the empire depended on the dynasty. Basil's successors, however, were not the strong leaders that had distinguished the earlier Macedonian dynasty. Administration of the empire was highly centralized, with a tangled bureaucracy that supervised everything from diplomatic ceremony to the training of lowly artisans. Without energetic leadership, the Byzantine bureaucracy quickly degenerated into routine and failed to respond to new challenges.

The early Macedonian emperors' success in checking invasions had been largely the result of Byzantium's superior military capacities, guaranteed by the systematic organization of the army in the themes, the steady support of the navy, and the strength of the economy. As discussed earlier, the success of the themes depended on a system in which free, tax-paying soldier-farmers fought in their own districts, defending their homes and families. However, by the eleventh century the independence of these soldier-farmers was threatened by deteriorating economic conditions. Every time a crop failed or a drought or famine struck, starving soldier-farmers in the themes were forced to surrender their land and their independence to one of the prosperous aristocrats who offered them food. As the great landowners acquired more land, the small farmers who were the backbone of the army began to disappear or lose their freedom. Because only free landholders could perform military service, the concentration of land in the hands of a few was disastrous for the army. Qualified soldiers with the land to support them became rare. The late Macedonian emperors lacked the will to initiate reforms that would have arrested this dangerous trend in which the land-grabbing of the aristocrats led to the decay of the army. These emperors found themselves in a difficult bind. Their income largely depended on their control of virtually all industry and trade, but that control meant that the only profitable alternative form of investment for the aristocrats was the acquisition of land. Because economic reforms that opened up the economy might have hurt their own incomes, the emperors failed to do what was necessary to protect the empire.

To make matters worse, after 1025 Byzantium faced formidable new enemies. In the west the Normans advanced on southern Italy and Sicily, crushing Byzantine power in Italy forever. The Normans, however, preserved a great deal of Byzantine culture in these regions, even as the Byzantine Empire became a distant memory. Official documents were issued in Latin, Greek, and Arabic, and the Norman princes acted as patrons of the Greek monasteries. Greek continued to be spoken in southern Italy for many centuries as remnants of Byzantine civilization survived alongside other languages and cultures.

In the east Byzantium faced an even more dangerous enemy. In 1071, the Seljuk Turks, who had converted to Sunni Islam in the previous century, captured the Byzantine emperor himself at the battle of Manzikert in Armenia. After their victory the Seljuks advanced across Asia Minor and threatened the very survival of Byzantium. The situation looked bleak indeed, and over the succeeding centuries, western European armies and the Turks ate away at Byzantium until its final collapse in 1453.

The New World of Islam

■ How did Islam develop in Arabia, and how did its followers create a vast empire so quickly?

The Muslim armies that battered Byzantium created a thriving civilization that transformed the Mediterranean world. Today more than one billion Muslims around the globe adhere to Islam, playing a significant role in world affairs. This rapidly growing faith has left an indelible stamp not only on the West but also on the rest of the world.

CHRONOLOGY

The Byzantine Empire

527–565	Reign of Justinian I
614–616	Persians take Jerusalem and Egypt
626	Avars and Persians besiege Constantinople
630	Heraclius defeats Persian king and restores True Cross to Jerusalem
636	Byzantines lose Battle of Yarmuk, Arabs take Syria and Jerusalem
642	Muslims take Egypt
698	Muslims take Carthage
716–718	Muslims besiege Constantinople
740	Byzantines defeat Arabs at Akroinon
751	Lombards conquer Ravenna and end the Exarchate of Italy
ca. 810–ca. 893	Life of Photius, Patriarch of Constantinople
867–1056	Macedonian dynasty
1071	Seljuk Turks defeat Byzantine army at the Battle of Manzikert

Islam originated in the early seventh century among the inhabitants of the Arabian peninsula. Through conquest and expansion, Muslims created a single Islamic Empire stretching from Spain to central Asia by 750 (see Map 7.3).

Arabs Before Islam

Before the emergence of Islam, Arabs were tribal people from the Arabian peninsula and the Middle East who spoke Arabic, a semitic language related to Hebrew (the ancient language of the Jews), Aramaic (the language spoken by Jews and other peoples at the time of Jesus), and Akkadian. Despite their shared language, Arab communities varied from nomadic bands to sophisticated cities. Those living in the interior of the Arabian peninsula led a nomadic life herding camels. On the edges of the desert they raised goats and sheep. In south Arabia, they farmed, lived in towns, and developed extensive commercial networks. During the late Roman Empire some Arabs had lived within the empire while others traded there, an experience that gave them considerable knowledge of both Roman civilization and Christianity. The communities of Arabia and the Middle East, however, were not unified into a single state.

Arabs have a long history in the Middle East. They were first mentioned in the Hebrew Bible about 1000 B.C.E., and

Ships of the Desert: Camels from Morocco to Central Asia

A remarkable thing happened when the Arab followers of the dynamic new religion of Islam encountered the humble beast of burden the camel. The camel helped make Arab armies lethal in battle, which meant that the message of Islam spread rapidly through conquest. In addition the caravan trade that transported goods on the backs of camels brought the Arabs into contact with a vast stretch of the world from Spain to China. In the exchanges that took place along the caravan routes, Islamic religious ideas were widely disseminated, and Arab merchants gained access to a lucrative trade that enriched Muslim cities. The success of the caravan trade changed the very appearance of large parts of the West by making obsolete the old Roman roads and the shipping lanes that had unified the Mediterranean, Europe, and North Africa in the ancient world. Narrow camel tracks replaced roads; oases and cities along the caravan routes supplanted ports in economic significance.

Before Muhammad began to recite, the camel had already transformed the life of Arabia. Camels were highly efficient beasts of burden, especially in arid regions, because of their bodies' capacity to conserve water. Able to drink as much as twenty-eight gallons at a time, camels can last four to nine days without water and travel great distances in this period. The fat in their humps allows camels to survive for even longer without food. As pack animals, camels are more efficient than carts pulled by animals because they can traverse roadless rough terrain and cross rivers without bridges. They require fewer people to manage them on a journey than do wheeled vehicles.

Arab fighters were especially menacing because they developed the "North Arabian saddle" that let them ride the one-humped Arabian camel with comfort in battle. The new saddle required only one rider who could grasp the camel's reins with one hand while slashing downward at enemy troops with a sword in his other hand. Warriors on camels could attack infantry with speed and crushing force. By 300 C.E., camel-breeding Arab tribesmen, empowered by their new military technology, inaugurated the "Caravan Age." The Arabs seized control of the lucrative spice trade routes and became an economic, military, and political force by exploiting and guarding the wealth of the caravans.

After Muhammad established his community in Mecca, Islam literally "took off" on camelback. Tribesmen on camels proved an unstoppable force as they spread Islam first throughout Arabia and the Middle East, and then with lightning speed across North Africa into Spain and Central Asia. Camels played a significant role in the expanding Islamic economy because they made long-distance trade extremely profitable. The transformations the camel brought were most evident in the former Roman provinces where the famous Roman roads had been a primary conduit of land trade. Thousands of miles of roads connected the provinces of the Roman Empire and let troops march easily from one front to another. However, camels changed all of that. Because these "ships of the desert" do not need paved roads, caravan routes did not have to stick to Roman road systems, and merchants bypassed them altogether. New trade routes across the desert and other harsh terrains well suited to camels quickly developed from Morocco to Central Asia, with the astonishing consequence that after 700 paved roads started to disappear. Because camels can easily walk on narrow paths, the broad streets and wide markets suited to carts and wagons that typified Greek and Roman cities fell out of use. Bazaars with narrow, winding lanes appropriate to camel traffic sprung up to replace them; carts and wheeled vehicles all but disappeared in these lands. It was not just roads and the shape of cities that changed. There were cultural consequences as well. In particular, caravan traffic reached as far as China, bringing Chinese goods and Chinese ideas to the West.

Question for Discussion

How might the history of the West have differed had not camel caravans replaced the system of Roman roads?

The Camel Caravan
This modern photograph shows a string of camels crossing sand dunes in the desert, carrying heavy loads, just as camel caravans would have in antiquity.

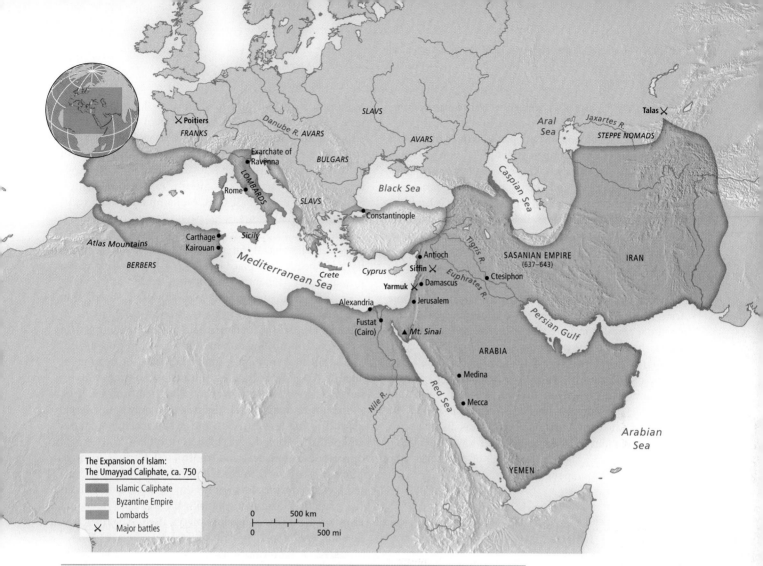

Map 7.3   The Expansion of Islam: The Umayyad Caliphate, ca. 750

By about 750 the Umayyad caliphate had reached its greatest extent. It provided political unity to territories stretching from central Asia to Spain. Islam became the dominant religion in this vast empire.

Middle Eastern, Greek, and Roman historical records continued to describe them for 1,500 years as raiders of settled communities but never as serious military threats. The Arabs became more threatening to their enemies after 300 B.C.E. because of an innovation in military technology that allowed them to fight effectively from the backs of camels. Military strength combined with trade in luxury goods made some Arab communities wealthy and powerful. By the first century B.C.E. Arabs had seized control of Petra, a merchant city in modern Jordan that controlled the incense trade. Merchants brought this precious, fragrant spice used in religious rituals across the Arabian peninsula from ports on the Red Sea and the Persian Gulf to Petra, where it was sold to other merchants from throughout the Middle East and the Mediterranean region. Petra also received merchandise such as ivory and gold from Egyptian traders. Other Arab cities such as Medina, located on the western coast of the Arabian peninsula, also flourished due to long-

distance caravan trade. Their merchants traded throughout the Middle East, sailed to India, and had extensive contacts with eastern Africa. At the same time, Arabs in north Arabia bred sturdier camels that could endure the harsh, arid terrain of central Asia. This enabled Arab merchants to travel to China along the silk route.

Most Arab communities organized themselves into tribes, each of which claimed descent from a common male ancestor. There was no formal government holding each tribe together. The chiefs who led their tribes did so by personal prestige and by the common consent of the tribesmen. Arab tribes, however, performed many of the functions of a state, which included protecting the lives and property of all their members. Arab tribesmen frequently feuded with one another, killing the men and stealing the herds and women of other tribes. Honor required retribution for every grievance, and so cycles of violence often lasted for generations. An injury to any member of a tribe obliged fellow tribesmen to seek either vengeance or compensation. Some feuding men chose to settle their grievances through mediation. If both parties agreed, mediators would set fair terms of compensation.

Before the rise of Islam in the seventh century, most Arabs worshiped many gods, including natural objects such as the sun and certain rocks or trees. Unlike their Egyptian and Greco-Roman neighbors, however, they did not erect huge temples to these deities. While most Arabs were probably polytheists, there was a strain of monotheism within Arab culture, which was reinforced through encounters with Jews, Christians, and Zoroastrians in Syria, Palestine, Mesopotamia, and Arabia. From these encounters some Arabs learned about different versions of monotheism, especially as revealed in sacred texts such as the Bible and the Avesta, the sacred text of Zoroastrians. Large Jewish communities existed in the cities of western Arabia as well as in Yemen, the southwest corner of the Arabian peninsula. Christianity had spread on Arabia's southern coast, and small groups of Zoroastrians lived in eastern Arabia. The Jewish and Christian Arabs developed ideas about heaven and hell and about the judgment of individuals after death that opened the way to the teachings of a prophet who many came to believe spoke directly for God.

The Rise of Islam

Islam is based on the Qur'an and the sayings of the prophet Muhammad (ca. 570–632). Muhammad was born in 570 to the powerful Hashimite clan of the Quraysh tribe in the cosmopolitan and wealthy west Arabian trading city of Mecca. This city was the site of the Kaaba, a sacred stone where polytheist Arabs worshiped various deities. As a young man Muhammad married a widowed businesswoman, Khadija, and worked as a caravan merchant. In this profession he earned a reputation as a skilled arbitrator of disputes among feuding tribes. At about age 40, Muhammad reported that while he was meditating in solitude an angel appeared before him, saying, "Muhammad, I am Gabriel and you are the Messenger of God. Recite!" According to Muhammad's account the angel gave him a message to convey to the people of Mecca. Muhammad's message was a call to all Arabs to worship the one true God (the god of Abraham) and to warn of the fires of hell if they failed to answer that call. Muhammad continued to report what he considered revelations for the rest of his life. They were written down as the Qur'an (meaning "recitation"), the holy book of Islam. Though Muhammad won some followers among friends and family, the people of Mecca initially did not accept his monotheist message and some were openly hostile to him.

In 622, Muhammad and his followers moved from Mecca to Medina, a city 200 miles to the north. Aware of Muhammad's skill as a mediator, several feuding tribes in

Medina had invited him to settle their long-lasting disputes. Muhammad's emigration to Medina, known as the *Hijra*, is the starting date of the Muslim calendar. The event marks a historical turning point in the development of Islam. For the first time Muhammad and his followers lived as an independent community. Accepted by his followers as the prophet of God, Muhammad strictly regulated the internal affairs of his new community and its relations with outsiders, creating a society that was political as well as religious. At the center of this Islamic community lay the mosque°, the place where his followers gathered to pray and hear Muhammad recite the Qur'an.

Initially, Muhammad and his followers enjoyed good relations with the Jews who controlled the markets in Medina. He and his followers even abided by some Jewish rituals, such as turning toward Jerusalem while praying. But as his influence among the Arab tribes grew, he became involved in a series of disputes with the Jewish tribes who refused to accept him as a prophet. Alienated from the Jews, Muhammad changed the direction of prayer to Mecca, expelled some Jewish tribes, and massacred the men and enslaved the women and children of others. With Jewish opposition eliminated and control of Medina secured, Muhammad turned to his old enemies in Mecca and attempted to convince them of his divine mission. After a series of military engagements with the Meccans, he led an army of his followers against Mecca itself, which surrendered in 630.

Using a combination of force and negotiation, Muhammad drew many Arab tribes into his new religious community. His authority rested both on his ability as a military leader who was successful at raiding caravans and defeating enemy tribes and his reputation as a prophet. By the time of his death in 632 he had unified most of Arabia under Islam. Muhammad created a tightly controlled community that was inspired by his teachings.

Muhammad's Teachings

Islam teaches that Allah (which means "God" in Arabic) revealed his message to Muhammad, the last in a line of prophets. Such prophets included Abraham, Moses, and David, all pivotal biblical figures in the Jewish tradition who transmitted divine instruction to humanity, and Jesus Christ, whom Muslims accept as a prophet but not the son of God. Muslims claimed Abraham as their ancestor because he was the father of Ishmael, whom they consider to be the father of the Arab peoples. Thus, Islam shares some of the fundamental religious beliefs of Judaism and Christianity.

Muhammad taught his followers basic principles that eventually came to be called the five Pillars of Islam°. *Islam means "submission,"* and by performing these acts of faith Muslims demonstrate submission to the will of God. First, all Muslims must acknowledge that there is only one God and that Muhammad is his prophet. Second, they must state this belief in prayer five times a day. On Fridays, the noon prayers must be recited in the company of other believers. Muslims may say their prayers anywhere. Third, Muslims must fast between sunrise and sunset during Ramadan, the ninth month of the Muslim calendar. Fourth, Muslims must give generous donations of money and food to the needy in their community. Islam expects its followers to be kind to one another, especially to orphans and widows, and to work for the good of the entire Islamic community. Fifth, Muslims must make a pilgrimage to Mecca at least once in their lives if it is possible. As the focus of prayer and pilgrimage, Mecca quickly became the center of the Muslim world. The Qur'an affirmed Mecca's special role in Islam with these words:

> Announce the Pilgrimage to the people. They will come to you on foot and riding along distant roads on lean and slender beasts, in order to reach the place of advantage (the Kaaba) for them, and to pronounce the name of God on appointed days over cattle he has given them as food; then eat the food and feed the needy and the poor. (Qur'an 22:26)

With the spread of Islam to Persia, Asia, and parts of Europe in the seventh century, Muslims from many different lands encountered one another in Mecca, developing a shared Islamic identity.

While the Qur'an contains many examples of proper behavior for the community to follow, Muslims also looked to the prophet Muhammad's example as a guide. Muhammad taught his followers to struggle for the good of the Muslim community. This struggle is called *jihad*. Islam teaches that the duty of *jihad* should be fulfilled by the heart, the tongue, the hand, and the sword. The *jihad* of the heart consists of a spiritual purification by doing battle with the Devil and avoiding temptations to do evil. *Jihad* of the tongue requires believers to propagate the faith and of the hand to correct moral wrongs. The fourth way to fulfill one's duty is to employ the sword by waging war against unbelievers and enemies of Islam. They could either convert to Islam or submit to Islamic political rule by paying special taxes. If they rejected both options, they became subject to *jihad* of the sword. Most modern Muslim scholars understand *jihad* as waging war with one's inner self, but some Muslims have revived the concept of *jihad* of the sword in support of military engagements.

The Succession Crisis After Muhammad: Sunnis and Shi'ites

Muhammad had demonstrated a remarkable talent for leadership during his lifetime, but he did not choose anyone to succeed him. His death in 632 caused a profound crisis among his followers. Would the Islamic community stay united under a single new leader or break up into smaller groups? After many deliberations, Muslim elders chose the prophet's father-in-law, Abu Bakr, to lead them. Abu Bakr (r. 632–634) became the first caliph, or successor to Muhammad. The form of Islamic government that evolved under his leadership is called the caliphate°.

Most Muslims supported Abu Bakr, but some opposed him. One group claimed that Muhammad's son-in-law and cousin, Ali, should have become the first caliph instead. Other Arab tribes rejected not only Abu Bakr's succession, but Islam itself. They rebelled, claiming that their membership in the Islamic community had been valid only when Muhammad was alive. Abu Bakr crushed these forces in a struggle called the Wars of Apostasy (a word meaning renunciation of a previous faith). By the time of his death in 634, Abu Bakr had brought most of Arabia back under his

The Kaaba in Mecca

In pre-Islamic times, Arabs worshiped a large, black stone at the Kaaba shrine in the center of Mecca. When Muhammad established Islam in Mecca in 629, he rejected the polytheist past and transformed the Kaaba into the holiest place in the Islamic world, revered as the House of God. Muslim teachers interpreted polytheist rituals that continued under Islam, such as walking around the Kaaba seven times, as symbols of the Muslim believer's entry into God's presence. Muslims from all over the world make pilgrimages to the Kaaba. These journeys foster a sense of shared religious identity among them, no matter where their homelands lie.

"Judgment Belongs to God Alone": The Battle and Arbitration at Siffin

On a spring day in 657, two Muslim armies confronted each other at Siffin, a village on the Euphrates River in Mesopotamia. The armies were commanded by men who had been longtime rivals, the caliph Ali (r. 656–661) and Muawiya, the governor of Syria. Their rivalry stemmed from Muawiya's refusal to accept Ali's authority as caliph. The Battle of Siffin became a defining moment in the development of the Islamic state. Basic Islamic ideas about divine judgment were put to the test, leading to passionate debate about how God makes his judgment known to Muslims.

Ali had taken power after the assassination of his predecessor, Caliph Uthman, in 656. The murder went unpunished, but many people considered Ali responsible because when he became caliph he appointed officials known to have taken part in the murder and because he had never disavowed the crime. Uthman belonged to the influential Umayyad clan, and his supporters and family felt an obligation to avenge their kinsman's death. Chief among Ali's opponents was Muawiya, a leading member of the Umayyad clan. Muawiya maintained a strong army and powerful support in Syria.

The immediate provocation of the confrontation between Muawiya and Ali was Uthman's murder, but the men's quarrel also stemmed from tensions about status and membership in the Muslim community. The earliest converts to Islam and their descendants believed that their association with Muhammad entitled them to greater status than the many new non-Arab converts to the religion, most of whom supported Ali. Resenting Ali's popularity among the newer members of the Islamic community, the early converts supported Muawiya. Further support for Muawiya came from many tribal leaders who opposed the caliph's growing authority.

The new converts to Islam also had complaints. In their view, the earliest Muslims, including the Umayyad clan, unfairly enjoyed a privileged position in the Islamic community even though all Muslims were supposed to be treated equally.

When Ali and Muawiya confronted each other at Siffin, they hesitated to fight because many of their soldiers felt strongly that Muslims should not shed the blood of other Muslims. As one of Ali's followers said,

It is one of the worst wrongs and most terrible trials that we should be sent against our own people and they against us. . . . Yet, if we do not assist our community and act faithfully toward our leader, we deny our faith, and if we do that, we abandon our honor and extinguish our fire.[1]

So for three months, the armies engaged in only occasional skirmishes.

Finally, in July 657, real fighting broke out. Ali encouraged his men with these words: "Be steadfast! May God's spirit descend on you, and may God make you firm with conviction so that he who is put to flight knows that he displeases his God. . . . "

The furious battle came to a sudden halt in July when Muawiya's soldiers held up pages of the Qur'an on the ends of their spears and appealed for arbitration. When Ali's men saw this symbolic gesture, they stopped fighting and demanded that their leader settle his differences with Muawiya peacefully through arbitration.

Mediation of conflicts by third-party arbitrators frequently occurred among Arab tribes. Muhammad himself had earned renown as a skilled mediator before Islam was revealed to him. However, the arbitration between Ali and Muawiya failed to resolve the conflict. The two men and their armies separated without having reached an agreement. Ali continued to rule as caliph for six more years, but his authority declined rapidly because many Arabs interpreted his willingness to go to arbitration as a sign of weakness. In 661 Ali was assassinated.

In contrast, Muawiya's power grew after the Battle of Siffin. He openly claimed the caliphate for himself and began making deals with the tribal leaders for their support in order to form his own coalition. After Ali's assassination, Muawiya became caliph.

The fact that the arbitration at Siffin occurred at all had long-lasting consequences. Most important, a small but influential Muslim faction emerged when the two leaders first confronted one another. They objected to Ali's initial agreement to arbitration, arguing that God was the only true arbitrator. They believed that Ali should pull out of the arbitration and submit to God's judgment, which they believed could be known only through battle. These Muslims wanted to fight Muawiya in order to find out what God wanted. This splinter group became known as the Kharijites or "seceders." The Kharijites expressed their view in the phrase "Judgment belongs to God alone."

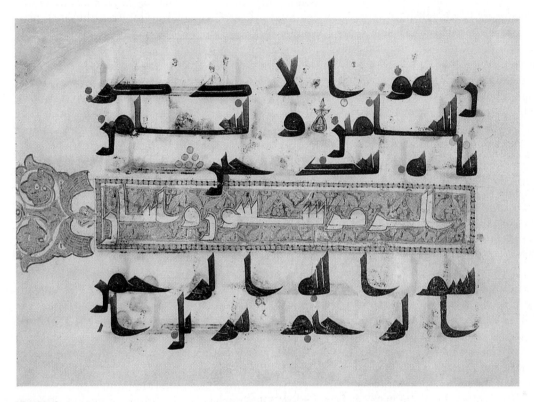

The Qur'an
Muslim artists devised elaborate Arabic scripts to enhance the beauty of the Qur'an, the holiest text of their faith. This page of the Qur'an, dating to the Umayyad caliphate, is written in the elegant and highly decorative Kufic script.

The Kharijites went one step further in their beliefs. They declared not only that Ali was wrong to accept human arbitration, but that he and his supporters should no longer be considered Muslims. In their view, Ali and his supporters had committed an unpardonable grave sin by accepting arbitration. The Kharijites claimed that they were the only true Muslims. Small in numbers, they established several independent communities in the Islamic Empire and turned their backs on Islamic society. They lived as bandits until the tenth century, when they disappeared from the historical record.

Other Muslims who disagreed with the Kharijites proclaimed that neither the Kharijites nor any other human being could know whether sinners were still Muslims in the eyes of God. In their opinion, believers would discover God's judgment on these matters only at the End of Days, when God will judge all humanity.

Question of Justice

During this early period of the Islamic Empire, how did different Arab beliefs about how God makes his judgment known influence the Arabic sense of the proper forms of human justice?

Taking It Further

W. M. Watt. *The Formative Period of Islamic Thought.* 1973. This account discusses the formation of sects and political groups in early Islamic history.

control, but disputes between the followers of Ali and those of Abu Bakr led to a permanent split within Islam between the minority Shi'ites, who followed Ali, and the majority Sunnis, who followed Abu Bakr. While the Shi'ites and Sunnis both considered the caliphate a hereditary office restricted to members of Muhammad's Hashimite clan of the Quraysh tribe, the Shi'ites believed that only direct descendants of Muhammad through his daughter Fatima and son-in-law Ali should rule the Islamic community. The Sunnis, in contrast, devised a more flexible theory of succession that allowed them later to accept the Abbasid caliphs and even foreign caliphs. The caliphate developed into an office that combined some governmental and some religious responsibilities.

In the course of the wars among Muslims after the death of Muhammad, Abu Bakr created a highly trained Muslim army eager to spread the faith and gain additional wealth and power. The rich Persian and Byzantine Empires became irresistible targets. Under the leadership of the second caliph, Umar (r. 634–644), Muslim forces moved north from the Arabian peninsula and invaded the rich territories of the Byzantine and Persian Empires. As discussed earlier, they seized Syria in 636. The next year they crushed the main Persian army and captured the Persian capital city, Ctesiphon. Within just a decade Islamic troops had conquered Egypt and all of Persia as far east as India. Meanwhile, Muslim navies, manned by subject Egyptian and Syrian sailors and Arab troops, seized Cyprus, raided in the eastern Mediterranean, and defeated a large Byzantine fleet. Muslim armies were racing across North Africa without serious opposition when civil war broke out in 655 and temporarily halted their advance.

Two groups struggled for control of the caliphate during this six-year civil war. On one side were Muhammad's son-in-law Ali, who had become caliph in 656, and his supporters, the Shi'ites. On the other side was the wealthy Umayyad family, who opposed him and whose supporters were Sunnis. The lasting cracks in the unity of Islam broke open over the proper succession to the caliphate, represented in the two parties of Shi'ites and the Sunnis. In 661 the Umayyads arranged Ali's assassination and took control of the caliphate, creating a new dynasty that would last until 750. The Umayyads established Damascus in Syria as their new capital city, which shifted Islam's power center away from Mecca.

The Umayyad Caliphate

The Umayyad dynasty produced brilliant administrators and generals. At the end of the civil war in 661, these talented leaders consolidated their control of conquered territories and established peaceful conditions in the empire. Then they resumed wars of conquest to enhance the Islamic state's power and to gain wealth.

The "House of War"

As we saw in Chapter 5, the Romans distinguished themselves from uncivilized "barbarians" who had not yet come under Roman rule. In a similar fashion, the Umayyads viewed the world as consisting of two parts: the "House of Islam," which contained the territories under their political control, and the "House of War," which included all non-Muslim lands, which they hoped to conquer. By 700, Muslim armies had rolled west across North Africa as far as the Atlantic Ocean in order to conquer non-Muslim lands.

Eleven years later, they invaded much of Spain and overthrew the Visigothic kingdom in just one battle. From Spain they attacked France, but in 732, Charles Martel "the Hammer," leading a Frankish army, stopped their advance into Europe at the Battle of Poitiers. After their defeat, the Umayyad armies retreated to their territories in Spain.

Umayyad caliphs attempted to conquer the Christian kingdom of Nubia south of Egypt to obtain its gold and spread Islam. The Nubians successfully repelled the Muslim invaders, however, and in 661 a lasting peace treaty was signed between the Umayyad caliphate and Nubian kingdoms. This treaty was unique, because the Nubians belonged to the "House of War," which meant that they were enemies still to be conquered. While struggling with the Nubians, Umayyad armies continued to strike at the Byzantine Empire. After seizing Egypt and Syria, they made regular attacks on the Byzantine territories, sometimes reaching as far as Constantinople, which remained protected by its formidable walls.

Umayyad armies moved eastward with equal speed and success. They reached the territories of modern Pakistan and India and even penetrated central Asia, where they captured the caravan city of Samarkand. During the Umayyad caliphate, this city served as a commercial hub on the trade route to China. In 751, just after the death of the last Umayyad caliph, Muslim armies defeated Chinese troops of the expansionist Chinese Tang dynasty at the Battle of Talas in central Asia. Despite their victory, the Muslims decided to halt their expansion and did not advance further into Chinese-controlled areas in central Asia. One consequence of this encounter was the introduction of paper from China into the Islamic world, from where it spread into Europe 500 years later.

Like the battle of Poitiers, which marked the limit of the Umayyads' expansion into western Europe, the battle of Talas marked the limit of Muslim military expansion into central Asia. For the next four centuries, these borders would define the Islamic world.

Governing the Islamic Empire

In less than a century the Umayyads had built an empire that reached from southern Spain to central Asia and India.

The Umayyads developed a highly centralized regime that changed the political character of the Muslim community. The first Umayyad caliph, Muawiya (r. 661–680), established a hereditary monarchy to ensure orderly succession of power. This was a major change in the caliphate. Unlike the first four caliphs, who ruled by virtue of their prestige (as did Arab tribal chiefs) and more importantly by the consent of the community, the Umayyads made the caliphate an authoritarian institution. Because of this, the soldiers protested that the Umayyads had turned "God's servants into slaves," corrupted the faith, and seized the property of God. A second civil war broke out (683–692) between these protestors and the Umayyads, but the Umayyads emerged victorious.

To control their vast empire, Umayyad rulers were obliged to create a new administrative system that both borrowed from and supplanted Byzantine and Persian institutions. The Umayyads designed new provinces that replaced old Byzantine and Persian administrative units. In addition, the Umayyads created a professional bureaucracy based in the capital of Damascus to meet their expanding financial needs and to ensure that the taxes collected in the provinces came to the central treasury. Most of the administrators were local officials who had served the Byzantine or Persian Empire. Many of them were non-Muslims, but a large number converted to Islam with Umayyad encouragement. These officials provided significant administrative continuity between the conquered empires and the caliphate.

After the Umayyads made Arabic the official language of their empire, Arabic gradually replaced the languages of the conquered peoples. Only in Iran did Persian survive as a widely spoken language, and even there Arabic served as the language of government. In the Umayyad caliphate, the Arabic language functioned as Latin had done in the ancient Roman Empire: It provided a common language for diverse subject peoples. By 800 Arabic had become the essential language of administration and international commerce in lands from Morocco to central Asia.

The rapid expansion of Islam created problems for Umayyad rulers eager to consolidate their power. Arab armies had conquered enormous territories, but Arabs were only a small minority among the huge non-Muslim populations. Umayyad policy was to establish garrison cities in conquered lands to hold down the more numerous local populations. Just as Greek colonists followed in the footsteps of Alexander the Great in the fourth century B.C.E., Arab settlers from the Arabian peninsula migrated to newly conquered lands in great numbers. They established themselves first in the garrison towns where government officials were based and then became a significant presence in major cities, such as Alexandria, Jerusalem, and Antioch. Some immigrants were nomadic tribes that adopted a settled way of life for the first time. Others were farmers from the highlands of Yemen, who brought sophisticated irrigation systems and agricultural traditions to their new homes. Arab migrations to cities ended many old Arab traditions of nomadic life.

DOCUMENT

The Rules of War According to the Muslim Conquerors

In 632, Abu Bakr composed a book called the Rules of War that makes clear how the warriors of Islam were to conduct themselves in battle:

O people! I charge you with ten rules; learn them well!

Do not betray or misappropriate any part of the booty; do not practice treachery or mutilation. Do not kill a young child, an old man, or a woman. Do not uproot or burn palms or cut down fruitful trees. Do not slaughter a sheep or a cow or a camel, except for food. You will meet people who have set themselves apart in hermitages; leave them to accomplish the purpose for which they have done this. You will come upon people who will bring you dishes with various kinds of foods. If you partake of them, pronounce God's name over what you eat. You will meet people who have shaved the crown of their heads, leaving a band of hair around it (monks). Strike them with the sword.

Go in God's name, and may God protect you from sword and pestilence.

Source: Al-Tabari, *The History of the Prophets and Kings* I.1850, in Bernard Lewis, ed., *Islam from the Prophet Muhammad to the Capture of Constantinople, vol. 1: Politics and War* (New York: Walker and Company, 1974), p. 213.

In addition to settling in existing cities, Arabs founded many new ones. In Egypt they built Fustat, which would later become Cairo. In North Africa, they established Kairouan in Tunisia. In Mesopotamia they created Basra, an important port city, as well as Kufa on the Euphrates River. Though built on a smaller scale than the major urban centers of the Roman and Persian Empires, most new Arab cities drew from Hellenistic town planning. They had a square shape, walls with gates on all four sides, towers, and a central plaza. In the heart of all of these cities, Umayyad caliphs built a mosque to emphasize the central role of Islam in community life and to celebrate their own authority. The magnificent mosques in Damascus, Jerusalem, and other cities were intended to surpass the grand Christian churches in prestige.

Interior of the Blue Mosque in Istanbul, Turkey

In formerly Byzantine cities such as Jerusalem, Antioch, and Alexandria, Muslim officials introduced or permitted significant structural changes, especially in urban street patterns. Winding, narrow alleys in which camels could easily maneuver replaced the long, straight, wide streets

The Dome of the Rock in Jerusalem

The Dome of the Rock, an eight-sided building with a gilded dome, dominates Jerusalem's skyline. Completed in 692 on the Temple Mount (the site of the Jewish Temple destroyed by the Romans in 69 C.E.), the building encloses a rock projecting from the floor. Scholars disagree about the structure's original purpose. A Muslim of the tenth century thought it had been built as a statement of Islam's triumph at the heart of the holiest Christian city. During the sixteenth century the story began to circulate that when Muhammad ascended to heaven at night, his winged horse took one leap from Mecca to the rock and then sprang skyward. The artists who completed the dome's interior mosaics probably came from Constantinople, the only place where art of such high quality was being produced. The mosaic patterns also draw from contemporary styles in the Mediterranean world and Persia.

appropriate for wagons that typified Hellenistic and Roman cities. Wheeled vehicles gradually disappeared from use in cities where alleys predominated. Especially in markets, the old, wide streets and sidewalks filled up with small shops, and pedestrians walked through narrow alleys behind the shops. In many of these cities, tightly packed bazaars connected by narrow alleys persist to this day.

Patterns of daily activity also changed under Muslim rule. With Islam now dominating public life, cities ceased to celebrate Greco-Roman culture. Theaters fell out of use because there was no Arabic tradition of publicly performed drama and comedy. The exercise fields, sports buildings, libraries, schools, and gymnasiums surviving from the Classical Age were also abandoned or adapted for other purposes. Revenues once earmarked for gymnasiums and public buildings now went to local mosques. These centers of Islamic urban culture replaced the forums and agoras of the Roman and Greek world as the chief public space for men. Mosque schools provided education for the community. Muslims gathered at mosques for public festivals and,

of course, for religious worship. In their capacity as administrative centers, mosques provided courtrooms, assembly halls, and treasuries for the community. Judges, tax collectors, bureaucrats, and emissaries from the caliph conducted their affairs in the mosque precinct.

During the Umayyad caliphate, the majority of Muslims were farmers and artisans who lived in prosperous villages. Many of these small communities stood on the vast estates of rich landowners who controlled the workers' labor. The caliphate also sponsored huge land reclamation projects on the edges of the desert in Syria and Mesopotamia. Officials of the imperial government drew revenues directly from the villages that sprang up in these new farmlands.

Becoming Muslims

Islam sharply defined the differences between Muslims and their non-Muslim subjects. The conquerors understood themselves as a community of faith. Only individuals who converted to Islam could gain full participation in the Islamic community. Their ethnicity did not matter. Therefore Muslims defined their new subjects by their religions, something Egyptians, Assyrians, Persians, Greeks, or Romans before Constantine had never done. The Qur'an states that "there is no compulsion in religion," meaning that monotheists (Jews, Christians, and Zoroastrians) cannot be forced to convert to Islam. These monotheists were required to accept Islamic political authority, pay a special tax, and accept some other restrictions. However, Muslims viewed polytheists differently. Polytheists could not be tolerated and had the choice of conversion to the Muslim faith or death.

Throughout the Umayyad period, the number of Muslims grew slowly, reaching perhaps only 10 percent of the total population. Perhaps most of the first converts had been Christians, Jews, and Zoroastrians who willingly accepted the new religion. Other converts were slaves in the households of their Muslim owners whose willingness to convert is less easy to determine. Still others were villagers who migrated to garrison cities and converted in the hope of sharing in the spoils of conquest—and avoiding the taxes demanded of non-Muslims. Their eagerness to convert so threatened the tax base that some Muslim officials refused to acknowledge their conversion and sent them back to their villages.

Conversion to Islam increased as Muslim armies fought their way across North Africa. In the huge area that stretches from Egypt to the Atlantic Ocean, the Muslims conquered many distinct polytheist ethnic groups whom the Arab conquerors collectively called Berbers. Faced with the choice of conversion or death, huge numbers of Berbers joined the victorious Muslim armies. Islam unified the Berber populations and brought them into a wider Islamic world. With the aid of these troops, Islamic power spread even more quickly across North Africa and into Spain.

Peoples of the Book

How do empires govern subject peoples? Do they have the same privileges and obligations as their rulers? Can they freely enter into the society of their masters? Previous chapters show how the Assyrians, Persians, Hellenistic Greeks, and Romans answered these questions. Though their solutions differed, none of these great empires considered the religions of their subjects when deciding their place in society.

By distinguishing their subjects on religious, not ethnic grounds, the Umayyad caliphate took a different approach to governing their subject peoples. Jews, Christians, and Zoroastrians constituted the main religions among conquered peoples. Islamic law called them "Peoples of the Book" because each of these religious communities had a sacred book. They had lower status than Muslims, but they were free to practice their religion. Islamic law forbade their persecution or forcible conversion. For this reason, large communities of Jews, Christians, and Zoroastrians lived peacefully under Muslim rule.

Several Christian communities, separated by old controversies about doctrinal issues, coexisted within the Islamic Empire because the caliphate was indifferent to which Christian doctrine they followed. Followers of the Chalcedonian Orthodox church changed the language of prayer from Greek to Syriac and then to Arabic. Though these Christians had no direct ties with Constantinople, they followed the Byzantine emperors' Chalcedonian Orthodoxy. Thus their church was called the Melkite, or Royal, church. The Melkite church continues to be the largest Christian community in Muslim lands in the Middle East today. Another Christian church, called the Jacobite church, was formed by Anti-Chalcedonian (Monophysite) Christians in the late sixth century, as discussed in Chapter 6. The Jacobite Bible and prayers are in Syriac. The Nestorian church, comprising Christians who emphasized Jesus' humanity rather than the combination of his humanity and divinity, also flourished under Muslim rule in Persia, Syria, and northern Arabia. Nestorians established communities in India, central Asia, and China. The variety of Christian communities in the caliphate was greater than in Byzantium and the Latin Christian kingdoms where conformity to the dogmas of one particular Church, Orthodox or Catholic, was enforced by law.

Jewish communities also flourished throughout Umayyad lands, notably in southern Spain and Mesopotamia. Jews found their subordinate but protected status under Islam preferable to the open persecution they suffered in many Christian kingdoms. In Persia, Zoroastrian communities fared less well under Islamic rule. As they were slowly forced into remote regions of central Iran, their numbers gradually dwindled. In the tenth century, many Zoroastrians migrated to India, where they are known today as Farsis, a word that means "Persians."

Commercial Encounters

The Umayyads managed to transform the economic system of the empire to strengthen their hand as rulers. From the time of the first conquests, revenues were derived primarily from the huge amounts of gold and silver taken in war, taxes, and contributions made by Muslims to support widows and orphans. To increase their revenues further, Umayyad rulers introduced a land tax for Muslim landowners, in imitation of Byzantine and Persian systems of taxation. Even the proud Arab tribesmen, for whom paying taxes was a humiliation because it implied subordination to a greater authority, had to pay taxes, though not as much as non-Muslims. With land tax revenues Umayyad caliphs could afford to establish a standing professional army. This further reduced the fighting role of individual Arab tribes, enabling caliphs to cement their authority more firmly.

Long-distance overland trade rapidly expanded due to the peaceful conditions achieved after years of fighting. Although merchants could travel safely from Morocco to central Asia and earn great sums, such long-distance expeditions were expensive. The Qur'an approves of mercantile trading, and Islamic law permitted letters of credit, loans, and other financial instruments that made commerce over huge distances possible long before they were known in Christian Europe.

Umayyad rulers further stimulated international commerce by creating a new currency that imitated Persian and Byzantine coinage. The Persian silver *drahm* (a word derived from the Greek *drachma*) inspired the Umayyad *dirham*, which became the standard coin throughout the caliphate by the 780s. Muslim merchants, as well as businessmen as far away as western Europe, Scandinavia, and Russia, used silver dirhams to pay for goods. For gold coinage the Umayyads minted the *dinar* (a word derived from a Roman coin, the *denarius*). Like the dirham, the dinar also became a standard coin in the caliphate as well as in distant lands. Merchants could depend on the value of this currency wherever they did business.

In addition to supporting long-distance overland trade by camel caravans, Umayyad caliphs also developed maritime trade. The Egyptian city of Alexandria became the chief Mediterranean naval base for Arab commercial shipping. The Syrian port cities of Acre and Tyre also contributed to maritime shipping in the eastern Mediterranean region. The Umayyads maintained peaceful conditions in the Persian Gulf and the Indian Ocean. Arab merchants

Designing Muslim Coins: The Encounter with Byzantine Prototypes

In the early years of the Umayyad state, caliphs experimented with the design of Islamic coins. Because Arabs had no tradition of minting coins, they borrowed freely from the images they saw on Persian and Byzantine coins. Then they made the necessary adjustments to change Christian or Persian symbols to Islamic ones. On a dinar of Abd al-Malik (r. 685–705) (top), the artist changed the Byzantine emperor Heraclius and his heirs, who carry globes with small crosses (shown on the back of a Byzantine coin at bottom left), to the caliph and his heirs, holding globes without crosses. On the Islamic coin's reverse side, Muhammad's scepter replaced the Christian cross (shown bottom right, on the back of another Byzantine coin). By the end of his reign, Abd al-Malik did away with images altogether and decorated his coins entirely with written quotations from the Qur'an.

Islamic coin

(front)

(back)

Byzantine prototypes

(back)

(back)

sailed past Zanzibar and India to Canton in southern China, following sea routes established by Persian navigators. Arab traders also sailed down the coast of East Africa to obtain slaves and natural resources brought from the interior. In later centuries Muslim navigators reached Malaysia, Indochina, and eventually Indonesia and the Philippines.

By 850, Muslims in cities throughout the caliphate could buy many exotic luxuries. These goods included panther skins, rubies, and coconuts from India; paper, silk, fine ceramics, eunuchs (castrated men), slaves, and marble workers from China; hawks from North Africa; Egyptian papyrus; and furs and sugar cane from central Asia. People could also buy less-expensive fabrics and manufactured items crafted locally.

Arab traders also brought back valuable ideas and scientific knowledge from the peoples encountered through trade in the East. Many Arabic nautical terms, which were picked up by sailors, derive from Persian. By late in the eighth century Arabic intellectual life became much more

sophisticated as scholars translated Persian and Indian astronomical works into Arabic, the beginning of an explosion of scientific knowledge in the Islamic world.

Throughout the formative period of Islam and the Umayyad caliphate, Muslims took firm hold of territories stretching from North Africa to central Asia, creating a single political realm there for the first time in history. The inhabitants of the entire Arabian peninsula, with their trade connections to Africa and Asia, joined the peoples of the Middle East and the Mediterranean in an intricate system of commerce and government.

The principal reason for the rapid spread of the religion of the prophet Muhammad was the capacity of his message to unify many diverse communities in Arabia. Especially during its early centuries, Islam disseminated Muhammad's message by both force and persuasion.

The Breakup of the Umayyad Caliphate

The Umayyad clan, who governed a vast Islamic Empire between 661 and 750, were never firmly in control of the en-

Mosque of Córdoba

The great mosque was one of the wonders of the world during the tenth century. Because Islam prohibited the depiction of the human body, mosques were embellished with geometrical forms and quotations from the Qur'an. The repetition of multiple arches creates an intricate pattern that changes as the viewer moves about in the space.

Granada. An able Hebrew poet, biblical commentator, and philosopher, Samuel ibn Nagrela was also an effective commander of Muslim armies. His brilliant career reflected the value Muslims placed on learning and skill.

During the early eleventh century after a series of succession disputes that led to the murder of several caliphs, the caliphate of Córdoba splintered into numerous small states. The disunity of Muslim Spain provided opportunities for the stubborn little Christian states to push against the frontiers of their opulent Muslim neighbors. The kingdom of Navarre under Sancho I (r. 1000–1035) was the first to achieve dramatic success against Muslims. After Sancho's death the division of his conquests created the three kingdoms of Navarre, Aragon, and Castile. During the reign of Alfonso VI (r. 1072–1109), Castile became the dominant military power on the peninsula. Forcing Muslims to pay tribute to him to finance further wars and gathering assistance from French knights eager for plunder and French monks ardent for converts, Alfonso launched a massive campaign known as the Spanish Reconquest° that led to the capture of Toledo in 1085. The center of Spanish Christianity before the Muslim conquests, Toledo provided Alfonso with a glorious prize that made him famous throughout Christian Europe (see Map 7.4).

The loss of Toledo so shocked the Muslim states that they invited into Spain a sect of warriors called the Almoravids from northern Africa. The Almoravids defeated Alfonso VI and temporarily halted the Spanish Reconquest in 1086.

CHRONOLOGY

The New World of Islam

ca. 570	Muhammad born in Mecca
622	Muhammad flees to Medina (the *Hijra*)
632	Muhammad dies in Medina
640–642	Byzantines abandon Alexandria; Muslims conquer Egypt
651	Muslims conquer Persia
661	Caliph Ali is assassinated
661–750	Umayyad caliphate
703–1060	Arab occupation of Sicily
713	Muslims conquer most of Spain
750–945	Abbasid caliphate
756–1031	Umayyad dynasty of Córdoba
After 870	Death of al-Kindi
1085	Christian capture of Toledo from Muslims

patronage. Despite some tensions among Muslims and Jews, many of the prominent intellectuals in the caliphs' court were Arabized Jews. Typical of the many non-Muslims who served Arab rulers, Hasdai ibn Shaprut (915–970), who was probably a Jew, became famous for his medical skills, in particular his antidotes for poisons. In the caliphs' court the demand for his cures was strong, because several princes had fallen victim to conspiracies hatched in the palace harem or had been poisoned by a lover. The trust that Hasdai gained from his medical skills led to political appointments to deal with sensitive customs and diplomatic disputes. Both Muslim and Christian rulers considered Jews like Hasdai politically neutral, making them prized as diplomatic envoys. The Jew Samuel ibn Nagrela (993–1055) astonishingly rose to the position of vizier (minister) of the neighboring Muslim kingdom of

Map 7.4 Christian Reconquest of Muslim Spain

The Spanish Reconquest refers to the numerous military campaigns by the Christian kingdoms of northern Spain to capture the Muslim-controlled cities and kingdoms of southern Spain. This long, intermittent struggle began with the capture of Toledo in 1085 and lasted until Granada fell to Christian armies in 1492.

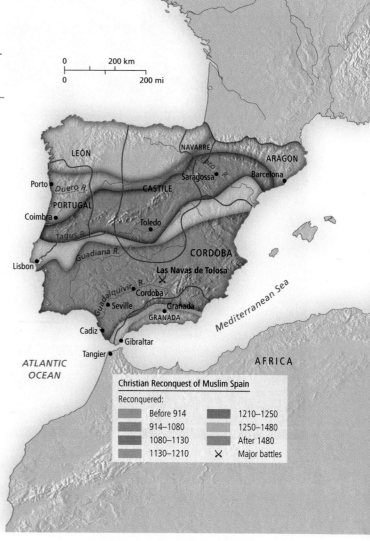

The halt of active warfare against the Muslims provided the young Christian kingdoms time to mature by establishing the basic institutions of government. After the time of Alfonso VI, the Reconquest lost steam, and a few surviving remnants of Muslim power managed to hang on in Spain for another 400 years.

Conclusion

Three Cultural Realms

The death of the Byzantine emperor Justinian I in 565 marked the last time all the territory spanning from Spain to North Africa to Asia Minor would be united under one imperial ruler. The Persian Empire still menaced Byzantium's eastern frontier, and except for Italy and some coastal areas of Spain, western Europe was now ruled by Germanic kings. During the next two centuries western Europe, the Mediterranean world, and the Middle East as far as India and central Asia were utterly reconfigured politically and culturally. Part of that reconfiguration came about as new peoples migrated into central Europe and the Balkans from the steppe frontiers. As threatening as they were these new arrivals were eventually absorbed into the civilizations of the West through conversions to Christianity. By ca. 750, three new realms had come into sharp focus: the Christian Byzantine Empire based at Constantinople; the vast Umayyad caliphate created by Muhammad's Islamic followers; and, as the next chapter examines, Latin Christendom in western Europe, which was fragmented politically but united culturally by Christianity. Each of these regions was constituted as a community of religious faith, each of which had, at best, a limited toleration of other faiths. The cultural foundations they established as well as the divisions that emerged among them are still shaping the West today.

These three cultural realms of the West each borrowed from the heritage of ancient Rome, especially its network of cities, which survived most completely in the Mediterranean and the Middle East in the Byzantine and Islamic Empires. The three realms were each influenced by the reli-

gious traditions of antiquity, especially the emphasis on monotheism in Judaism. They each adapted parts of Roman law but reshaped it to suit changing needs and new cultural influences. The heritage of Rome remained strongest in Byzantium. Indeed, the Byzantines continued to call themselves Romans. But between the sixth and eleventh centuries these three cultural realms came to be distinguished by the language that dominated intellectual and religious life and by the forms of monotheism practiced. In Byzantium the Greek language and Orthodox Christianity with its distinctively elaborate ceremonies defined the culture. By the end of the Umayyad caliphate, the Arabic language was becoming widespread and many Islamic beliefs and practices were becoming standard over a wide area. In western Europe, many languages were spoken but Latin became the universal language of the Church and government.

The year 750 saw the end of the Umayyad caliphate and the limit of Muslim expansion in western Europe and central Asia. After that the Byzantine Empire struggled for survival. In the next chapter we will see how the kingdom of the Franks arrested Muslim incursions into western Europe. However, the very survival of many western European kingdoms was put to the test during the ninth and tenth centuries by yet more invasions and migrations from the Eurasian steppes and Scandinavia. By the end of the eleventh century the Latin kingdoms of western Europe had gathered sufficient cohesion and military strength to launch a vast counterstroke against Islam in the form of the Crusades.

Suggestions for Further Reading

For a comprehensive listing of suggested readings, please go to www.ablongman.com/levack2e/chapter7

Bowersock, Glen, Peter Brown, and Oleg Grabar, eds. *Late Antiquity: A Guide to the Post-Classical World.* 1999. Interpretive essays combined with encyclopedia entries make this a starting point for discussion.

Brown, Thomas S. *Gentlemen and Officers: Imperial Administration and Aristocratic Power in Byzantine Italy, A.D. 554–800.* 1984. The basic study of Byzantine rule in Italy between Justinian and Charlemagne.

Bulliet, Richard W. *The Camel and the Wheel.* 1990. A fascinating investigation of the importance of the camel in history.

Cook, Michael. *Muhammad.* 1996. A short, incisive account of Muhammad's life that questions the traditional picture.

Cormack, Robin. *Writing in Gold: Byzantine Society and Its Icons.* 1985. An expert discussion of icons in the Byzantine world.

Donner, Fred M. *The Early Islamic Conquests.* 1981. Discusses the first phases of Islamic expansion.

Fletcher, Richard. *Moorish Spain.* 1992. Highly readable.

Franklin, Simon, and Jonathan Shepard. *The Emergence of Rus: 750–1200.* 1996. The standard text for this period.

Herrin, Judith. *The Formation of Christendom.* 2001. An exceptionally learned and lucid book; Herrin sees Byzantium as crucial both for the development of Christianity and Islam.

Hourani, George. *Arab Seafaring in the Indian Ocean in Ancient and Early Medieval Times.* 1995. The standard discussion of Arab maritime activity.

King, Charles. *The Black Sea: A History.* 2004. A comprehensive history of the Black Sea region from antiquity to the present. It is especially useful for anyone interested in this borderland among cultures.

Moorhead, John. *The Roman Empire Divided, 400–700.* 2001. A reliable and up-to-date survey of the period.

Robinson, Francis, ed. *The Cambridge Illustrated History of the Islamic World.* 1977. Many excellent and well-illustrated articles that will be useful for beginners.

Treadgold, Warren T. *A Concise History of Byzantium.* 2001. A reliable and insightful short survey.

Treadgold, Warren. *A History of the Byzantine State and Society.* 1997. A reliable narrative of Byzantine history.

Notes

1. Al-Tabari, *The History of Al-Tabari,* Vol. 17: *The First Civil War,* trans. and annotated by G. R. Hawting (1985), 50.

2. Quoted in Jane S. Gerber, *The Jews of Spain: A History of the Sephardic Experience* (1992), 28.

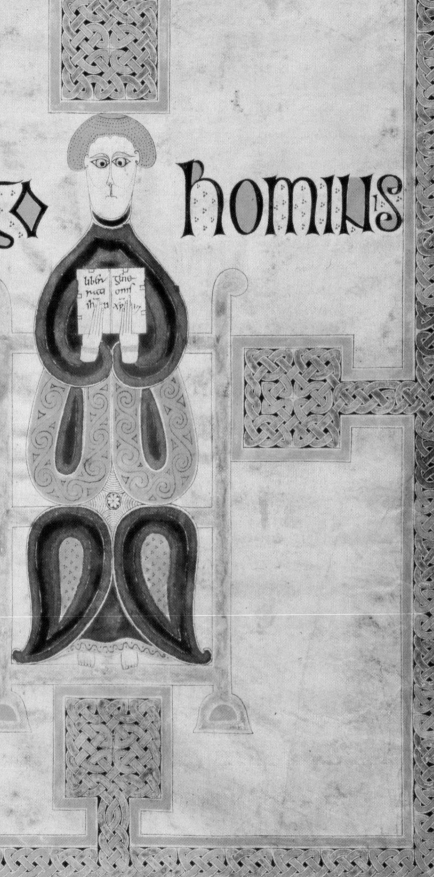

Medieval Empires and Borderlands: The Latin West

8

ONE GRAY DAY IN CENTRAL GERMANY IN 740, AN ENGLISH MONK named Boniface swung his axe at an enormous oak tree. This was the sacred Oak of Thor, where German men and women had prayed for centuries to one of their mightiest gods. Some local Christians cheered and applauded the monk. But an angry crowd of men and women gathered as well, cursing Boniface for attacking their sacred tree. Then something extraordinary occurred. Though Boniface had only taken one small chop, the entire tree came crashing down, split neatly into four parts. Boniface's biographer, a monk named Willibald, explained the strange event as God's judgment against "pagan" worshipers. In Willibald's account of the incident, the hostile crowd was so impressed by the miracle that they immediately embraced Christianity. As the news spread, more and more Germans accepted the faith, and Boniface's fame grew. According to Willibald, "The sound of Boniface's name was heard through the greater part of Europe. From the land of Britain, a great host of monks came to him—readers, and writers, and men trained in other skills."[1]

Whether or not the miracle at the Oak of Thor actually occurred, Boniface, a missionary who worked closely with the pope in Rome, played a leading role in spreading Christianity among the peoples of northern Europe. The Christian missionaries who traveled to lands far beyond the Mediterranean world brought Latin books and established monasteries. Through Christianity and the literacy that spread from these monastic centers, the monks established cultural ties among the new Germanic converts to Roman learning and the late antique world.

But Boniface was not Roman. He was English, a descendant of the Germanic settlers, called the Anglo-Saxons, who took control of much of

The Image of a Man (Imago Hominis) In Christian iconography, the image of a man symbolizes the Evangelist Matthew. The other three evangelists, Mark, Luke, and John, were symbolized by a lion, bull, and eagle. These Christian symbols were related to the fixed signs of the zodiac, created by ancient polytheist astronomers. The adaptation of Christianity to pagan symbolism conveyed the message that Christianity represented the fulfillment of ancient wisdom. This page introducing the Gospel of St. Matthew comes from an illuminated manuscript, the Echternach Gospel Book, made in Anglo-Saxon England in the first half of the eighth century.

Britain after the Roman legions abandoned it in the early fourth century. Boniface's England (as southern Britain is called after the Anglo-Saxon settlements) was just one of the former Roman provinces in western Europe that had been settled and eventually ruled by Germanic tribes. In England Roman culture had been overwhelmed and was reintroduced only indirectly through Christianity. In Spain, Italy, and France, in contrast, the Germanic settlers grafted their societies onto a still-living Roman stalk. The intermingling of these cultures produced Christian kingdoms on a Roman foundation. Historians refer to these continental kingdoms plus Britain as Latin Christendom° because they celebrated the Christian liturgy in Latin and accepted the authority of the pope in Rome.

Historians use the term *Latin Christianity* for this early period rather than *Roman Catholicism* because people at the time did not use *Catholicism* with the same meaning as today. Then they usually described themselves as "Christians" to distinguish themselves from polytheists, Jews, and Muslims, or as "Latins" to distinguish themselves from the Greek Orthodox. Now Roman Catholicism identifies itself as in the Latin Christian tradition, which for many Christians makes the terms interchangeable. Even though they no longer celebrate the liturgy in Latin as they did in the Middle Ages, Catholics today continue to accept the authority of the pope in Rome and the traditions of medieval Latin Christianity.

As discussed in Chapter 7, Latin Christianity and Orthodox Christianity gradually grew apart during the Middle Ages, primarily over theological differences and disputes about who held the ultimate authority in the Church. For most Christians, however, the crucial differences were over liturgy and language. The liturgy° consists of the forms of worship—prayers, chants, and rituals. In the Middle Ages there was a great deal of variety in the Christian liturgy, and a number of languages were used, but followers of the Roman church gradually came to identify themselves with the Latin liturgy and the Latin language. As a result, the diverse peoples of medieval western Europe began to be called the "Latin people," although they spoke many different languages. The term *Latin* came to represent more than a liturgy or language; during the Middle Ages it became a religious and even cultural identity.

The Latin Christendom that came to dominate western Europe was only one of three major civilizations that emerged on the ruins of the late antique Roman world and that constituted the West during this period. During the Middle Ages, the Latin Christian, Greek Orthodox, and Arabic Muslim kingdoms and empires began to form a distinctively Western civilization. However, recurrently pressing across the frontiers of these civilizations were barbarian peoples coming from the Eurasian steppes and Scandinavia. Like the Avars, Slavs, Rus, and Bulgars who threatened Byzantium, the raiders and invaders from the steppes and the North—the Germanic tribes, the Magyars, and the Vikings—who entered the western half of the Roman Empire eventually became Christians. Their conversions took place through missionary efforts, the profession of tribal leaders and kings who brought entire peoples with them, and military expeditions that forced the conquered to convert. By the end of the eleventh century few polytheists could still be found in Europe. With the exception of the Muslim pockets in Spain and Sicily and isolated communities of Jews, Christianity had become the dominant faith. Unlike most of the earlier invaders from the steppes who were converted to Orthodox Christianity, those who invaded western Europe eventually accepted the Latin form of Christianity.

In this crucial phase in forming Western civilization from about 350 to 1100, new political formations in western Europe made possible greater political cohesion that brought together ethnically and linguistically diverse peoples under obedience to an emperor or king. As in Byzantium and the Islamic caliphates the empires and kingdoms of the Latin West enforced or encouraged uniformity of religion, spread a common language among the ruling elite, and instituted systematic principles for governing. The Carolingian Empire, which lasted from 800 to 843 and controlled much of western Europe, reestablished the Roman Empire in the West for the first time in more than 300 years and sponsored a revival of interest in antiquity called the Carolingian Renaissance. The Carolingian Empire's collapse was followed by a period of anarchy as Europe faced wave after wave of hostile invaders. During the eleventh century, however, the Latin West recovered in dramatic fashion. By the end of the century the Latin kingdoms were strong enough to engage in a massive counterassault against Islam, in part in defense of fellow Christians in Byzantium. These wars with Islam, known as the Crusades, produced a series of wars in the Middle East and North Africa that continued throughout the Middle Ages. But the ideals of the Crusaders lasted well into modern times, long after active fighting ceased. The transformations in this period raise the question, how did Latin Christianity help strengthen the new kingdoms of the Latin West so that they were eventually able to deal effectively with both barbarian invaders and Muslim rivals?

- How did Latin Christendom—the new kingdoms of western Europe—build on Rome's legal and governmental legacies and how did Christianity spread in these new kingdoms?
- How did the Carolingian Empire contribute to establishing a distinctive western European culture?
- After the collapse of the Carolingian Empire, how did the western kingdoms consolidate in the core of the European continent and how did Latin Christianity spread to its periphery?
- What were the causes and consequences of the Crusades?

The Birth of Latin Christendom

■ How did Latin Christendom—the new kingdoms of western Europe—build on Rome's legal and governmental legacies and how did Christianity spread in these new kingdoms?

By the time the Roman Empire collapsed in the West during the fifth century, numerous Germanic tribes had settled in the lands of the former empire. These tribes became the nucleus for new kingdoms as Germanic chiefs transformed themselves into kings. By 750, several of these new kingdoms had emerged. Various Anglo-Saxon kings controlled most of England. The Franks ruled over the territories that constitute modern France, Germany,

and the Netherlands; the Visigoths Spain; and the Lombards Italy. These territories were not politically united as they had been under the Roman Empire (see Map 8.1). Though their populations were quite diverse ethnically and linguistically, they shared certain social and religious characteristics. They had enough in common that historians refer to these kingdoms collectively as Latin Christendom.

Germanic Kingdoms on Roman Foundations

These new Germanic kingdoms of Christendom borrowed from Roman law while establishing government institutions; they developed their own cultural identity and they

Map 8.1   Europe, ca. 750

By about 750 the kingdom of the Franks had become the dominant power in western Europe. The Umayyad caliphate controlled Spain, and the Lombard kingdom governed most of Italy. The Byzantine Empire held power in Greece, as well as its core lands in Asia Minor.

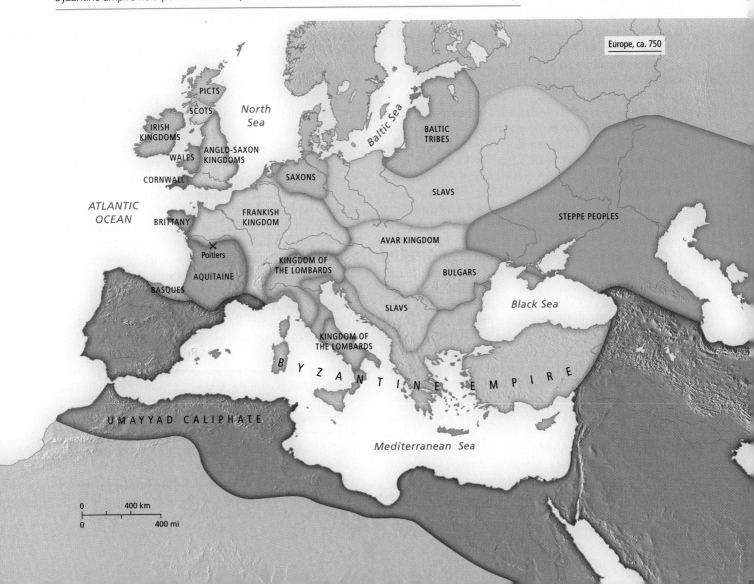

relied on their own methods of rule. Thus, they were able to unify the kingdoms in three ways. First, in the Germanic kingdoms personal loyalty rather than legal rights unified society. Kinship obligations to a particular clan of blood relatives rather than citizenship, as in the Roman Empire, defined a person's place in society and his or her relationship to rulers. Second, Christianity became the dominant religion in the kingdoms. The common faith linked rulers with their subjects. A third unifying force was Latin. Latin served as the language of worship, learning, and diplomacy in these kingdoms.

Anglo-Saxon England

Roman civilization collapsed more completely in Britain during the fifth century than it did on the European continent, largely because of Britain's long distance from Rome and the small number of Romans who had settled there. About 400, the Roman economic and administrative infrastructure of Britain fell apart, and the last Roman legions left the island to fight on the continent. Raiders from the coast of the North Sea called Angles and Saxons (historians refer to them as Anglo-Saxons) took advantage of Britain's weakened defenses and launched invasions. They began to probe the island's southeast coast, pillaging the small villages they found there and establishing permanent settlements of their own.

The economic situation in Britain continued to deteriorate. By 420 coinage had fallen out of use on the island, and barter became the sole means of exchange. By 450, cities either shrank to very small villages or lay abandoned. A century later, fortified villas in the countryside—the last vestige of Roman life—had disappeared.

Christian worship was threatened but survived in all the areas held by the Roman Britons, Wales, Cornwall, and southern Scotland. Due to the efforts of missionaries from Italy, Gaul, and Ireland, by 750 Christianity was reinvigorated and become deeply embedded in Anglo-Saxon culture.

Because the small bands of Anglo-Saxon settlers fought as often among themselves as they did against the Roman Britons, the island remained fragmented politically during the first few centuries of the invaders' rule. But by 750, three warring kingdoms managed to seize enough land to coalesce and dominate Britain: Mercia, Wessex, and Northumbria.

Because Roman culture had virtually disappeared in these areas, Roman legal traditions had to be reintroduced through the spread of Christianity. The English language derives primarily from the Germanic languages spoken by the Anglo-Saxon settlers of Britain. In contrast, the Romance (or Roman-based) languages of Spanish, Italian, and French developed from Latin spoken in Rome's former provinces on the Continent, where Roman civilization was more deeply rooted. In Wales, which the Anglo-Saxons did not conquer, the Welsh language shows a combination of Latin and the region's older Celtic tongues.

The Franks: A Dual Heritage

The encounter between Roman and Frankish cultures from the third to the seventh century produced the largest and most powerful kingdom on the continent of western Europe, that of the Franks. Yet the Franks had modest origins. In the third century a number of small tribes living in what is now the Netherlands and the northwestern part of Germany organized themselves into a loose confederation. According to Roman records, Frankish warbands launched destructive attacks on northern Gaul (now northern France) and raided Spain and North Africa during the second half of the third century. The armies of the Roman emperor Constantine finally brought the Franks under control in the early fourth century. After that the Franks who lived beyond Roman borders did not dare to attack Rome, and Franks living within the empire served faithfully as soldiers in the Roman army. These men retained dual identities, remaining both Frankish and Roman. As a third century soldier's gravestone proudly states: "I am a Frank, a Roman citizen, and an armed soldier."[2] Several Franks even became important Roman generals.

But in the course of the fifth century, as Roman imperial control of western Europe disintegrated, Frankish power grew. One group among the Franks, called Salians, gradually gained preeminence among the Frankish people. The Salians' leading family were the Merovingians. A crafty Merovingian war chief named Childeric ruled a powerful band of Salian Franks from about 460 until his death in 481.

During his long reign, Childeric set the stage for the rapid consolidation and expansion of Frankish power. Childeric gave his warriors the opportunity to participate in campaigns to seize lands in Roman Gaul, rewarding them handsomely with loot. But the complex political situation in Gaul posed a problem for the Merovingian leader. After Roman imperial government collapsed throughout most of Gaul by the 450s, some independent groups of Romans continued to fight for control of territory against Huns, Visigoths, and other peoples who had settled there. In a few places Roman churchmen and aristocrats managed to hold on to some authority. Although Childeric was not Christian, he cooperated with these Romans in an effort to win their support against their common enemies.

With the support of loyal Frankish soldiers, Childeric laid the foundation for the Merovingian kingdom. His energetic and ruthless son Clovis (r. 481–511) made the Franks one of the leading powers in the western provinces of the old Roman Empire. Clovis aggressively expanded his father's power base through conquest of northern Gaul and neighboring territories. He also murdered many of his relatives and other Frankish chieftains whom he considered rivals. In 486 he overcame the last Roman stronghold in northern Gaul.

Clovis's wife, Clotild, followed Latin Christianity, the religion of most of the inhabitants of the former Roman Empire in western Europe. Historians refer to this version of Christianity as Latin Christianity because its followers used a Latin Bible, performed church services in Latin, and at least formally accepted the authority of the pope in Rome. Latin Christianity, like the Greek-based Orthodox Christianity in the Byzantine Empire, teaches the full equality of the Father, the Son, and the Holy Spirit in the Trinity. In contrast to Latin Christianity in the western provinces was the Arian Christianity practiced by the Germanic kings, who had established new kingdoms in western Europe during the fifth century. Arians believed that Christ was divine, but inferior to God the Father in rank, authority, and glory.

The theological distinction between Latin and Arian Christians in western Europe was a crucial political issue

DOCUMENT
History of the Franks

that divided the Roman subjects from their Germanic rulers, who were usually Arians. Around 500, perhaps influenced by his wife's beliefs, the polytheist Clovis converted to Latin Christianity. About 3,000 warriors, the core of his army, joined their king in this change to the new faith. Clovis had practical reasons to convert as well. He intended to attack the Visigothic kingdom in southern Gaul. The Visigoths followed Arian Christianity, but their subjects, the Roman inhabitants of the region, followed Latin Christianity. By converting to Latin Christianity, Clovis won the support of many of the Visigoths' subjects. With their help Clovis and his Frankish army crushed the Visigothic king Alaric II, who died at the battle of Vouillé in the summer of 507. Clovis now controlled almost all of Gaul as far as Spain, but the Visigoths in Spain continued to resist and to maintain the independence of their territories.

Clovis went on to conquer other Germanic peoples. His armies overran the kingdom of the Thuringians to the east of his homeland. They also defeated the Alemanni, who lived in what are now Switzerland and southwest Germany. In order to consolidate his authority in these varied lands, Clovis needed recognition from both the emperor in Constantinople and the Roman Church in Gaul. He shrewdly achieved both. After defeating Alaric II, the Merovingian ruler won the support of Gaul's clergy by donating much of the booty from his victory to the church of the most important saint in Gaul, Martin of Tours. Clovis then earned the recognition of the Byzantine emperor by formally acknowledging his authority. At the pageant when Clovis brought the treasure to Martin's church, ambassadors of the Byzantine emperor may have made him an honorary consul. Wearing a Roman military uniform, Clovis celebrated a Roman-style victory parade in which he scattered gold coins to the crowd. For the next three centuries, Merovingian kings followed Latin Christianity and received similar honors from Byzantine emperors.

The Frankish kingdom thrived under several able monarchs in the sixth and seventh centuries. Continuing their father's expansionist policies, Clovis's sons conquered the Burgundian kingdom in 534 and acquired Provence on the southeastern coast of Gaul two years later.

Despite these successes, the Merovingian dynasty gradually grew weak as a result of conflicts among kings, their quarrelsome sons, and independent-minded aristocrats. As a result of these squabbles, Clovis's kingdom split into four separate realms: Neustria in the west; Austrasia, which included lands east of the Rhine River as well as in Gaul; Aquitaine in the southwest; and Burgundy in the southeast. These realms later reunified and separated several additional times, which is a measure of the instability of the Merovingian system. Rulers of these independent kingdoms issued their own law codes, collected taxes from their subjects—and quarreled bitterly with one another. As they went their separate ways politically, striking linguistic differences emerged. For example, in Neustria, the people spoke an early form of French, while in Austrasia they spoke a German language. While the political divisions of Merovingian Gaul were never made permanent, the cultural distinctions have had lasting effects.

Though Merovingian kings still ruled Gaul, they had become so ineffectual that real power passed to the official in charge of the royal household called the "Mayor of the Palace." One of these mayors, Charles Martel "the Hammer" (r. 719–741), established his personal power by regaining control over regions that had slipped away from Merovingian rule and by defeating an invading Muslim army at Poitiers in 732. Martel's son, Pepin the Short (r. 741–768), succeeded his father as Mayor of the Palace, but dethroned the last of the Merovingian monarchs and in 751 made himself king of the Franks.

Visigoths in Spain

In contrast to the Frankish kings who after Clovis accepted Latin Christianity, during the sixth century the Visigothic kings, who controlled southern Gaul and most of Spain, adhered to Arian Christianity. By favoring Arianism these kings generated animosity among the subject population, most of whom were Latin Christians. When the Frankish king, Clovis, invaded southern Gaul in 507, many Latin Christians welcomed him and provided the invaders with military assistance. As a consequence of defeat, the Visigoth kings retreated to Spain, where they concentrated on unifying the people through the spread of Arianism and the acceptance of Roman law, which influenced the Visigoth law codes.

By 600, Visigoth kings ruled over most of the Spanish peninsula and had even managed to drive the last Byzantine forces from its southern coast. Under the Visigoths Spain thrived. From its vast, rich estates, surpluses of grain, olive oil, and leather were exported by international merchants, including a substantial community of Jews as well as Greeks and even Syrians. By taxing this trade the Visigoth kings filled their treasuries with gold and became the envy of their neighbors.

The Visigoth kings failed to spread Arianism among the population, and when King Reccared (r. 586–601) converted to Latin Christianity most of the remaining Arians followed. The kings began to imitate the Byzantine emperors with the elaborate court ceremonies of Constantinople and used frequent church councils as assemblies that enforced their will. Thus the key to their success was the ability to employ the spiritual authority of the Church to enhance the secular authority of the king. However, the autocratic instincts of the Visigoth kings alienated many of the substantial landowners who were easily lured by the promises of invaders to treat them more favorably.

In 711 invading armies of Muslims from North Africa vanquished the last Visigothic king. As a result, Spain became part of the Umayyad caliphate. The Jews, in particular, welcomed the Muslim conquerors because Islam granted them a measure of religious toleration they had not experienced under the Christian Visigoths. Many Christians from the upper classes converted to Islam to preserve the property and offices of authority. Some survivors of the Visigoth kingdoms held on in the northwest of Spain, where they managed to keep Christianity alive.

Lombards in Italy

Between 568 and 774, a Germanic people known as the Lombards controlled most of northern and central Italy. They were called *Langobardi*, or "Long Beards," from which the name *Lombard* derives. In the first part of the sixth century under their ruler Waccho, Lombards established a kingdom in the area of modern Hungary. As we have seen, Justinian's wars and a devastating plague drained the Byzantine Empire's strength. Without imperial troops to defend Italy, the peninsula became vulnerable to invasion. The Lombard king Alboin (r. ca. 565–572) took advantage of the situation and invaded Italy in 568. Alboin's army contained soldiers of different ethnic backgrounds. In addition to Lombards, his forces included smaller bands of Goths, Avars, Saxons, and other non-Romans. Some were Arian Christians; others were Latin Christians. Still others practiced polytheism. Alboin's highly diverse army indicated his ability to attract followers but also implied a lack of common purpose among them other than taking the opportunity to pillage. That lack of unity made it impossible for Alboin to build a strong, lasting kingdom.

The Romans living in Italy put up a feeble resistance. Within three years Alboin controlled all of northern Italy, Tuscany, and parts of southern Italy in the region of Spoleto, near Naples. Yet until 700, the Lombard kings proved weak rulers. Throughout their lands real power lay in the hands of semi-independent dukes based in the most populated urban centers such as Benevento and Spoleto. These dukes gradually expanded their possessions within Italy, jockeying among themselves for land and power. After 700, the Lombard kings reasserted their authority by developing a royal bureaucracy of judges and legal officials, compensating somewhat for the weaknesses of the Lombard system evident in the initial conquest. The new infrastructure enabled them to overshadow the dukes' local authority.

Despite the Lombard kings' newfound strength, they still faced two formidable external enemies. The most dangerous of these were the Byzantine forces who remained in the Exarchate of Ravenna. These soldiers hoped to crush the Lombards and regain control of Italy in the name of the Byzantine emperors. Again and again they battled with Lombards, but their efforts proved futile. In 751 the Lombard ruler Aistulf defeated the Exarchate of Ravenna, leading to its abandonment as the Byzantine capital in the West.

The Franks posed the second threat to the Lombards. These hardy warriors marched into Italy several times during the seventh century, trying to crush the Lombards and seize their lands. Sometimes they joined with Byzantine forces from the Exarchate of Ravenna. During other attacks, the Franks had the backing of the popes in Rome, who resented the Lombards' power. Despite their diplomatic and military efforts, however, the Franks failed to achieve their goals of conquest.

The tide of battle soon turned against the Lombards. In the middle of the eighth century, internal political disputes once again tore at the kingdom. The Lombards' diplomatic relations with the papacy and their uneasy standoff with the Franks deteriorated. As will be discussed shortly, the Frankish king Charlemagne, responding to a call for assistance from Pope Leo III, invaded Italy and crushed the Lombards in 774.

Different Kingdoms, Shared Traditions

With the exception of England, where Anglo-Saxon invaders overwhelmed the Roman population, the leaders of the new Germanic kingdoms faced a common problem: how should the Germanic minority govern subject peoples who vastly outnumbered them? These rulers found a solution to this problem by blending Roman and Germanic traditions. For example, the kings served as administrators of the civil order in the style of the Roman emperor, issuing laws and managing a bureaucracy. They also served as war leaders in the Germanic tradition, leading their men into battle in search of glory and loot. As the Germanic kings defined new roles for themselves, they discovered that Christianity could bind all their subjects together into one community of believers. The merging of Roman and Germanic traditions could also be traced in the law, which eventually erased the distinctions between Romans and Germans, and in the ability of women to own property, a right far more common among the Romans than the Germans.

Civil Authority: The Roman Legacy

In imitation of Roman practice, the monarchs of Latin Christendom designated themselves the source of all law and believed that they ruled with God's approval. Kings controlled all appointments to civil, military, and religious office. Accompanied by troops and administrative assistants, they also traveled throughout their lands to dispense justice, collect taxes, and enforce royal authority.

Frankish Gaul provides an apt example of how these monarchs adopted preexisting Roman institutions. When Clovis conquered the Visigoths in Gaul, he inherited the nearly intact Roman infrastructure and administrative system that had survived the collapse of Roman imperial authority. Merovingian kings (as well as Visigoth and Lombard rulers in Spain and Italy) found it useful to maintain parts of the preexisting system and kept the officials who ran them. For instance, Frankish kings relied on the bishops and counts in each region to deal with local problems. Because Roman aristocrats were literate and had experience in Roman administration on the local level, they often served as counts. Based in cities, these officials presided in local law courts, collected revenues, and raised troops for the king's army. Most bishops also stemmed from the Roman aristocracy. In addition to performing their religious responsibilities, bishops aided their king by providing for the poor, ransoming hostages who had been captured by enemy warriors from other kingdoms, and bringing social and legal injustices to the monarch's attention. Finally, the kings used dukes, most of whom were Franks, to serve as local military commanders, which made them important patrons of the community. Thus, the civil and religious administration tended to remain the responsibility of the Roman counts and bishops, but military command fell to the Franks.

War Leaders and *Wergild*: The Germanic Legacy

The kingdoms of Latin Christendom developed from war bands led by Germanic chieftains. By rewarding brave warriors with land and loot taken in war, as well as with revenues skimmed from subject peoples, chieftains created political communities of loyal men and their families, called clans° or kin groups°. Though these followers sometimes came from diverse backgrounds, they all owed military service to the clan chiefs. Because leadership in Germanic society was hereditary, networks of loyalty and kinship expanded through the generations.

Though the principle of loyalty to a superior defined life in these Germanic communities, many men ignored this principle in the pursuit of their own interests. Rivalries among warriors unwilling to follow their chieftain and among power-hungry men who competed for the kingship within the royal families often led to bloody struggles that weakened the political fabric of the kingdoms. Frankish leaders proved particularly vicious in their quest for power, thinking nothing of betrayal and assassination of their rivals, including members of their own families. Despite the bloodshed and brutal competition for power, the various political communities gradually evolved into distinct ethnic groups led by a king, such as the Lombards and the Franks.

These ethnic groups developed a sense of shared history, kinship, and culture. The coalescence of these kingdoms resulted from the Germanic settlers' pride in their new homelands as well as from their allegiance to their monarchs who governed them fairly at home and who protected them from foreign enemies.

The new Germanic kingdoms had highly hierarchic societies geared for warfare. Kinship-based clans stood as the most basic unit of Germanic society. The clan consisted of all the households and blood relations loyal to the clan chief, and a warrior who protected them and spoke on their behalf before the king on matters of justice. Clan chieftains in turn swore oaths of loyalty to their kings and agreed to fight for him in wars against other kingdoms. The clan leaders formed an aristocracy among the Germanic peoples. Like the Roman elites before them, the royal house and the clan-based aristocracy consisted of rich men and women who controlled huge estates. The new Germanic aristocrats intermarried with the preexisting Roman elites of wealthy landholders, thus maintaining control of most of the land. These people stood at the very top of the social order, winning the loyalty of their followers by giving them gifts and parcels of land. Under the weight of this new upper class, the majority of the population, the ordinary farmers and artisans, slipped into a deepening dependence on these nobles. Eventually, ordinary farmers merged with the Roman peasantry. Most peasants could not enter into legal transactions in their own name, and they had few protections and privileges under the law. Even so, they were better off than the slaves who toiled at society's very lowest depths. Valued simply as property, these men, women, and children had virtually no rights in the eyes of the law.

Though this social hierarchy showed some similarities to societies in earlier Roman times, the new kingdoms' various social groups were defined by law in a fundamentally different way. Unlike Roman law, which defined people by citizenship rights and obligations, the laws of the new kingdoms defined people by their wergild°. A Germanic concept, *wergild* referred to what an individual was worth in case he or she suffered some grievance at the hands of another. If someone injured or murdered someone else, wergild was the amount of compensation in gold that the wrongdoer's family had to pay to the victim's family.

In the wergild system, every person had a price that depended on social status and perceived usefulness to the community. For example, among the Lombards service to the king increased a free man's worth—his wergild was higher than that of a peasant. In the Frankish kingdom, if a freeborn woman of childbearing age was murdered, the killer's family had to pay 600 pieces of gold. Two-thirds of that sum went to the victim's family. The king received the rest. Noble women and men had higher wergild than peasants, while slaves and women past childbearing age were worth very little.

If proper wergild was not paid, the injured party's kin group felt obligated to gain vengeance for their loss. The desire for revenge and compensation frequently led to vicious feuding. In order to minimize the bloodletting that could sometimes drag on for generations after a crime had been committed, representatives of the king or a local aristocrat urged families to accept wergild.

Unity Through Law and Christianity

Within the kingdoms of Latin Christendom, rulers tried to achieve unity by merging Germanic and Roman legal principles and by accepting the cultural influence of the Church. Religious diversity among the peoples in their kingdoms made this unity difficult to establish. As discussed in Chapter 6, many of the tribes that invaded the Roman Empire during the fifth century practiced Arian Christianity. They kept themselves apart from the Latin Christians by force of law. For example, they declared marriage between Arian and Latin Christians illegal.

These barriers began to collapse when some Germanic kings converted to the Latin Christianity of their Roman subjects. Some converted for reasons of personal belief, or because their wives were Latin Christians. Others decided to become Latin Christians to gain wider political support. For instance, when Clovis converted about 500, laws against intermarriage between Arians and Latin Christians in Gaul disappeared. More and more Franks and Romans began to marry one another, blending the two formerly separate communities into one and reinforcing the strength of the Latin Church. Similarly in 587, when the Visigothic king Reccared converted from Arianism to Latin Christianity, he made it the official religion of Spain. Soon Visigoths and Romans began to intermarry legally. Many of the Lombards had already converted to Latin Christianity when they entered Italy so they, too, began to marry Romans. By 750 most of the western European kingdoms had officially become Latin Christian, even if substantial pockets of polytheist practice survived and communities of Jews were allowed to practice their faith.

Germanic kings adopted Latin Christianity, but they had no intention of abandoning their own Germanic law, which differed from Roman law on many issues, especially relating to the family and property. Instead, they offered their Roman subjects the opportunity to live under the Germanic law that governed the king. Clovis's *Law Code* or *Salic Law,* published sometime between 508 and 511, illustrates this development. The *Law Code* applied to Franks and to any other non-Roman peoples in his realm who chose to live according to Frankish law. Because the Romans dwelling in the Frankish kingdom technically still followed the laws of Byzantium, Clovis did not presume to legislate for them. Romans could follow their own law if they wished, or they could follow his laws and become Franks.

Permitting his subjects to switch to Frankish law helped Clovis strengthen his kingdom. It fostered a shared sense of Frankish identity throughout his kingdom. Eventually the Frankish king's policies eroded distinctions among Romans, Franks, and other ethnic groups within his realm. By 750, most Romans had chosen to abandon their legal identity as Romans and live according to Frankish law, and the distinction between Roman and Frank lost all meaning.

A similar process occurred in other Germanic kingdoms. The Lombards slowly mixed with the Romans living in Italy. By 750 their law, which originally protected only Lombards, now applied to all the Latin Christian inhabitants of Italy. In Spain, the Roman and Visigothic populations merged once the religious barriers came down. In 654 the Visigothic king Recceswinth abolished the separate Roman law entirely and brought his entire population under Visigothic law. As in the Frankish and Lombard kingdoms, this unification of two peoples under one law happened without protest, a sign that various groups had blended politically, religiously, and culturally.

Women and Property

Roman law influenced more than just local administration in Latin Christendom. It also prompted Germanic rulers to reconsider the question of a woman's right to inherit land. In the Roman Empire, women had inherited land without difficulty. Indeed, perhaps as much as 25 percent of the land in the entire realm had been owned by women. In many Germanic societies, however, men could inherit land and property far more easily than women. Attitudes about female inheritance began to shift when the Germanic settlers established their homes in previously Roman provinces—and began to marry Roman women who owned property.

By comparing the law codes of the new kingdoms over time, historians have detected the impact of Roman customs on Germanic inheritance laws. By the late eighth century women in Frankish Gaul, Lombard Italy, and Visigothic Spain could inherit land, though often under the restriction that they must eventually pass it on to their sons. Germanic rulers adopted the custom of female inheritance because it enabled the new settlers to keep within their own families the property that their Roman wives had inherited and brought to the marriage. Despite these limitations, the new laws transformed women's lives. A woman who received an inheritance of land could live more independently, support herself if her husband died, and have a say in the community's decisions.

The Spread of Latin Christianity in the New Kingdoms of Western Europe

As Latin Christianity spread as the official religion through the new kingdoms, churchmen decided that they had a moral responsibility to convert all the people of these kingdoms and beyond to their faith. They sent out missionaries to explain the religion to nonbelievers and challenge the worship of polytheist gods.

Meanwhile, bishops based in cities directed people's spiritual lives, instilling the moral and social conventions of Christianity through sermons delivered in church. Monks such as Boniface, who introduced this chapter, traveled from their home monasteries in Ireland, England, and Gaul to spread the faith to Germanic tribes east of the Rhine. Monasteries became centers of intellectual life, and monks replaced urban aristocrats as the keepers of books and learning.

The Growth of the Papacy

In theory, the Byzantine emperors still had political authority over the city of Rome and its surrounding lands during this violent time. However, strapped for cash and troops, these distant rulers proved unequal to the task of defending the city from internal or external threats. In the resulting power vacuum, the popes stepped in to manage local affairs and became, in effect, princes who ruled over a significant part of Italy.

Gregory the Great (r. 590–604) stands out as the most powerful of these popes. The pragmatic Gregory wrote repeatedly to Constantinople, pleading for military assistance that never came. Without any succor from the Byzantines, Gregory had to look elsewhere for help. Through clever diplomacy, Gregory successfully cultivated the goodwill of the Christian communities of western Europe by offering religious sanction to the authority of friendly kings. He negotiated skillfully with his Lombard, Frankish, and Byzantine neighbors to gain their support and establish the authority of the Roman church. He also encouraged Christian missionaries to spread the faith in England and Germany. In addition, he took steps to train educated clergymen for future generations, in this way securing Christianity's future in western Europe.

Gregory had set the stage for a dramatic increase in papal power. As his successors' authority expanded over the next few centuries, relations between Rome and the Byzantine emperors slowly soured, especially during the Iconoclastic Controversy discussed in Chapter 7. By the early eighth century the popes abandoned the fiction that they were still subject to the Byzantines and sought protection from the Frankish kings. The popes established political independence during the period but remained dependent on the Franks for military assistance when necessary.

Converting the Irish

Though the Romans had conquered most of Britain during the imperial period, they never attempted to bring Ireland into their empire. Thus the island off Britain's west coast had had only minimal contact with Christianity. Little is known for certain of how Christianity came to Ireland. There were probably missionaries who traveled with traders from the Roman Empire, but the earliest firm date is 431 when Palladius was supposedly sent to administer to those in Ireland who were already Christians. Subsequent missionary history in Ireland is dominated by the figure of Patrick (died ca. 492 or 493), whose later biographers improbably gave him credit for converting all the Irish to Christianity. A ninth-century record describes his capture from a Roman villa in Britain by Irish raiders, who sold him into slavery in Ireland. Patrick learned Irish during his years in captivity. He managed to escape to Britain, where he was ordained into the priesthood and sent back to Ireland as a missionary. A great deal of confusion exists regarding Patrick's life, and some scholars argue that tradition merged the experiences of the two missionaries Palladius and Patrick. However, by the end of the fifth century Christianity had a firm foothold in Ireland.

But Ireland was still a rural place. The early missionaries wondered how to Christianize the Irish without a Roman urban foundation to build on. Elsewhere in the West Christianity spread out into the countryside from cities, with bishops administering the local church from their city cathedrals. However, the island lacked cities in which to build churches and housing for bishops. No one living in Ireland knew Latin, Greek, or any of the other languages into which the Bible had been translated. And no schools existed where churchmen might teach the Gospel to new converts.

Irish churchmen found solutions to these problems in monasteries, places where priests could receive training and men and women from the surrounding communities could learn to read Latin and absorb the basics of Christian education. By 750, the Irish scholars produced by these monasteries gained a high reputation for their learning in their own lands as well as across western Europe. Irish monasteries sent out dozens of missionaries, who in turn founded new monasteries in England, France, and Germany. Irish scholars produced magnificently illustrated manuscripts in their libraries. These books brought Irish art to all the lands where the missionaries traveled.

Irish monasteries sometimes grew rich from the gifts of money and property provided by kings and other pious folk. Such centers, especially those that became bishops' headquarters, acquired substantial economic and political influence in their local communities by settling disputes, caring for the sick, and employing local laborers. Having proved its value in Ireland, the monastery system spread from the island to England and then to the European continent.

Converting the Anglo-Saxons

By 600, numerous Irish missionaries had begun to travel to England and the European continent to establish new monasteries. Columbanus (543–615), for example, founded several monasteries on the Irish model in the kingdom of Burgundy. The most notable among these were the monastery of Luxeuil in the Rhône River valley, and Bobbio in northern Italy. These centers inspired the founding of many additional nunneries and monasteries in northern Gaul. From there Latin Christianity spread east of the Rhine River, into lands where the religion had not yet penetrated.

Irish missionaries also expanded their monastic network in their own land. Columba (521–597), for instance, founded several new monasteries in Ireland as well as one on the island of Iona, off Scotland's western coast. From this thriving community missionaries began to bring Christianity to the peoples of Scotland. The offshoot monastery of Lindisfarne in northern England also became a dynamic center of learning and missionary activity. During the seventh century, missionaries based there carried Christianity to many other parts of England. They also began converting the people of Frisia on the North Sea, in the area of the modern Netherlands.

Besides the Irish monks who went to Anglo-Saxon England, Pope Gregory the Great (r. 590–604) and his successors sent other missionary monks from Rome. Through missionary efforts Gregory hoped to save souls and in so doing forged a Christian community not just in England but throughout Europe. Gregory understood that the first step in creating the new community was to convert as many people as possible to the faith; deep learning about the religion could come later. To that end he instructed missionaries to permit local variations in worship and to accommodate harmless vestiges of pre-Christian worship practices. "Don't tear down their temples," Gregory advised; "put a cross on the roofs!"

Following Gregory's pragmatic suggestion, missionaries in England accepted certain Anglo-Saxon calendar conventions that stemmed from polytheist worship. For example, in the Anglo-Saxon calendar, the weekdays took their names from old gods: Tuesday derived from Tiw, a war god; Wednesday from Woden, king of the gods; Thursday from Thor, god of thunder; and Friday from Freya, goddess of agriculture. Anglo-Saxon deities eventually found their way into the Christian calendar as well. Eostre, for example, a goddess whose festival came in April, gave her name to the Christian holiday Easter.

Despite their common commitment to Latin Christianity, the Irish and Roman monks working throughout England disagreed strongly about proper Christian practice. For instance, they argued over how to perform baptism, the ritual of anointing someone with water to admit him or her into the Christian community. They bickered about how monks should shave the tops of their heads to show their religious dedication, and they squabbled about the correct means of calculating the date of Easter. These disputes threatened to create deep divisions among England's Christians. The overall conflict finally found resolution in 664 in the Anglo-Saxon kingdom of Northumbria, where monastic life flourished. At a council of monks and royal advisers called the Synod of Whitby, the Northumbrian monarch commanded that the Roman version of Christianity would prevail in his kingdom. His decision eventually was accepted throughout England.

Monastic Intellectual Life

The missionaries from Rome were members of the vigorous monastic movement initiated by Benedict of Nursia (ca. 480–547) from his monastery at Monte Cassino in Italy (see Chapter 6). These monks followed Benedict's *Rule*, a guidebook for the management of monastic life and spirituality. In the *Rule* Benedict had written that individual monks should live temperate lives devoted to spiritual contemplation, communal prayer, and manual labor. So that their contemplations might not depart from the path of truth, Benedict had encouraged monks to seek guidance in the Bible, in the writings of the renowned theologians, and in works of spiritual edification. For Benedict, contemplative reading constituted a fundamental part of monastic life. Thus monks had to be literate in Latin. They needed training in the Latin classics, which required books.

Medieval monasteries set aside at least two rooms—the scriptorium° and the library—to meet the growing demand for books. In the scriptorium, scribes laboriously copied Latin and Greek manuscripts as an act of religious devotion. Monastery libraries were small in comparison to the public libraries of classical Rome, but the volumes were cherished and carefully controlled. Because books were precious possessions, these libraries set forth strict rules for their use. Some librarians chained books to tables to prevent theft. Others pronounced a curse against anyone who failed to return a borrowed book. Nevertheless, librarians also generously lent books to other monasteries to copy.

Monks preferred to read Christian texts with a spiritual message, so these books were the most frequently copied. In many monasteries, however, monks preserved non-Christian texts. By doing so, they helped to keep knowledge of Latin and classical learning alive. Indeed, many of the surviving works by authors of the Classical Age were copied and passed on by monks in the sixth and seventh centuries. In addition to Christian works, monks also studied the writings of Latin poets such as Virgil and Juvenal, scientists such as Pliny the Elder, and philosophers such as Boethius and Cicero, as well as the works of grammarians, mathematicians, scientists, and physicians from the ancient world. Without the monasteries and scriptoria, knowledge today of the literature of the classical world would be greatly reduced.

Sometimes classical works survived merely by accident. Because parchment, the specially prepared sheepskin on which writers copied their manuscripts, was expensive, many monks scrubbed old manuscripts clean and reused them to copy religious texts. By studying these reused parchment sheets, called palimpsests°, modern scholars have succeeded in reclaiming vital classical texts or portions of them that otherwise would have been lost forever. Cicero's treatise *On the Republic*, which has influenced many political thinkers including the writers of the U.S. Constitution, is one example. Although other parts had survived since antiquity and the whole is still not known, sections of this work survived only because in the seventh century, at the monastery of Bobbio in northern Italy, a monk erased Cicero's text and copied an interpretation of the Psalms by Augustine onto the parchment. Modern scholars can read Cicero's words below Augustine's.

Monks did far more than merely copy ancient texts, however. Some wrote original books of their own. At the English monastery at Jarrow, for example, Bede (d. 735) became the most distinguished scholar in eighth-century Europe. He wrote many books, including the *History of the English Church and People.* This work provides an invaluable source of information about the early Anglo-Saxon kingdoms.

Monks carried books with them when they embarked on missionary journeys. They also acquired new books during their travels. For instance, Benedict Biscop, the founder of the monasteries of Wearmouth (674) and Jarrow (682) in England, made six trips to Italy. Each time he brought back crates of books on all subjects, including works written by classical authors whom monks studied with interest. Other Anglo-Saxon missionaries transported this literary heritage to the monasteries they founded in Germany during the eighth century. As monks avidly read, copied, wrote, and transported books of all sorts, knowledge and intellectual discourse flourished in the monasteries.

Monks shared their expanding knowledge with Christians outside the monastery walls. They established schools at monasteries where boys (and in some places girls) could learn to read and write. In Italy some public schools survived from antiquity, but elsewhere most of the very few literate people who lived between 550 and 750 gained their education at monastery schools. The men trained in these schools played an important role in society as officials and bureaucrats. Their skills in reading and writing were necessary for keeping records and writing business and diplomatic letters.

Jews in a Christian World

For Jews during this era, quality of life varied in the different western European kingdoms. Jews continued to work in every profession, own land, serve in the army, and engage in trade. The vast majority of monarchs protected the Jewish minorities living in their kingdoms. Thus many Jews prospered in the Frankish, Visigothic, and Lombard realms (no Jews lived in England during this period). At times, theological curiosity led to intellectual encounters between Jews and Christians. In Lombard Italy, for example, Jews and Christians sometimes engaged in public debates about their religious beliefs.

Christian churchmen still blamed Jews collectively for Jesus' death and especially feared that Christians might be tempted to convert to Judaism. Some bishops advocated persecuting Jews, but only a few rulers were willing to follow their advice. Leading churchmen in the western kingdoms also developed theological reasons for wanting Jews to convert to Christianity. Pope Gregory urged conversion

CHRONOLOGY

The Birth of Latin Christendom

481–511	Clovis reigns; Frankish kingdom divided at his death
ca. 525	Benedict founds monastery at Monte Cassino
568	Lombards invade Italy
587	Visigothic king of Spain converts to Latin Christianity; Columbanus travels to Gaul from Ireland
ca. 700	Lombards accept Latin Christianity
732	Charles Martel defeats Muslims at Poitiers
751	Pepin overthrows last Merovingian king; Exarchate of Ravenna falls to Lombards

because he believed that Christ would return to Earth only when Jews embraced Christianity. Nevertheless, Gregory advocated the use of persuasion and kindness to encourage conversion, rather than force or terror. On numerous occasions he intervened to stop Christians from committing violence against Jews. Other Christian writers, such as Isidore of Seville (in Spain), further developed the idea that Jews had a place in Christian society because of their role in bringing about Christ's return and then the Day of Judgment. Highly ambivalent about the Jews, Christians both persecuted and protected them.

The Carolingians

■ How did the Carolingian Empire contribute to establishing a distinctive western European culture?

Among the successor kingdoms to the Roman Empire in the West, discussed in the previous section, none was more powerful militarily than the Merovingian kingdom of the Salian Franks, which ruled the northern part of the ancient Roman province of Gaul and at various periods most of the rest of Gaul from the late fifth through the middle of the eighth centuries. The Merovingian dynasty was plagued by factions, royal assassinations, and do-nothing kings. When Pepin the Short deposed the last of the Merovingian kings in 751, he made himself king of the Franks and inaugurated the Carolingian dynasty.

Both the weak Merovingians and the strong Carolingians illustrated how the problem of succession from one king to another destabilized early medieval monarchies. The kingdom was considered the private property of the royal family, and according to Frankish custom, a father was obliged to divide his estates among his legitimate sons. As a result, whenever a king of the Franks died, the kingdom was divided up as happened numerous times under the Merovingians. When Pepin died in 768, the kingdom was divided between his sons, Charlemagne and Carloman. When Carloman died suddenly in 771, Charlemagne ignored the inheritance rights of Carloman's sons and may even have had them killed, making himself the sole ruler of the Franks.

The Leadership of Charlemagne

Charlemagne's (r. 768–814) ruthlessness with his own nephews epitomized the crafty leadership that made him the mightiest ruler in western Europe and gave him the

nickname of Charles the Great. One of his court poets labeled him "The King Father of Europe"; no monarch in European history has enjoyed such posthumous fame.

An unusually tall and imposing figure, Charlemagne was a superb athlete and swimmer, a lover of jokes and high living, but also a deeply pious Christian. As Pepin's eldest son, he had frequently accompanied the army during his father's campaigns, and these youthful experiences gave him an unbending will and a fighting spirit.

During his reign, Charlemagne engaged in almost constant warfare, especially against polytheistic tribes that when defeated were usually compelled to accept Christianity. He went to war eighteen times against the Germanic tribe the Saxons, whose forced conversion only encouraged subsequent rebellions. The causes for Charlemagne's persistent warfare were complex. He believed he had an obligation to spread Christianity. He also needed to protect his borders

Map 8.2 Carolingian Empire

Charlemagne's conquests were the greatest military achievement of the Early Middle Ages. The Carolingian armies successfully reunified all western European territories of the ancient Roman Empire except for southern Italy, Spain, and Britain. However, the empire was fragile due to Frankish inheritance laws that required all legitimate sons to inherit lands from their father. By the time of Charlemagne's grandsons the empire began to fragment.

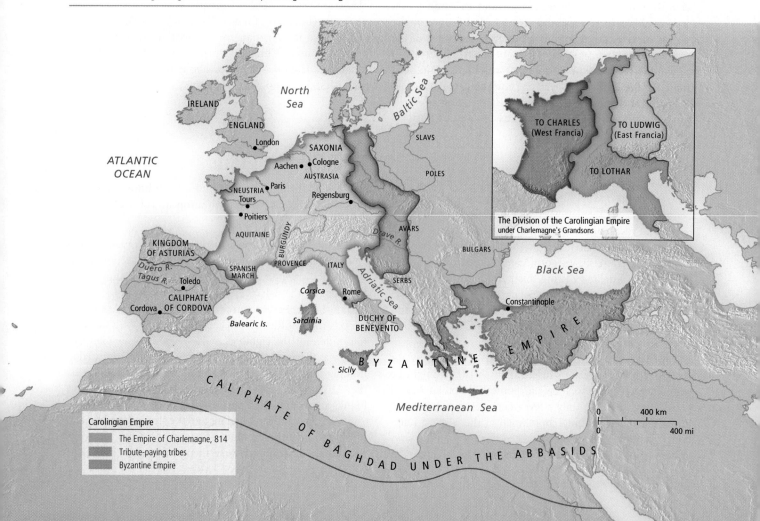

DOCUMENT

The Coronation of Charlemagne

Previous rulers of the Franks had styled themselves kings and none had challenged the Byzantine Emperor's claim to be the sole heir to the emperors of ancient Rome. However, in 800 when the pope crowned Charlemagne emperor, the Byzantines took it as an attempt to usurp the throne. Charlemagne's biographer, Einhard, described Charlemagne's support of the pope and the controversial circumstances of his imperial coronation. Einhard's Life of Charlemagne *is an example of how Carolingian Renaissance literature imitated ancient literary models, in this case to show that Charlemagne acted like an ancient emperor.*

Beyond all other sacred and venerable places he loved the church of the holy Apostle Peter at Rome, and he poured into its treasury great wealth in silver and gold and precious stones. He sent innumerable gifts to the Pope; and during the whole course of his reign he strove with all his might (and, indeed, no object was nearer to his heart than this) to restore to the city of Rome her ancient authority, and not merely to defend the church of Saint Peter but to decorate and enrich it out of his resources above all other churches. But although he valued Rome so much, still, during all the forty-seven years that he reigned, he only went there four times to pay his vows and offer up his prayers.

But such were not the only objects of his last visit; for the Romans had grievously outraged Pope Leo, had torn out his eyes and cut off his tongue, and thus forced him to throw himself upon the protection of the King. He, therefore, came to Rome to restore the condition of the church, which was terribly disturbed, and spent the whole of the winter there. It was then that he received the title of Emperor and Augustus, which he so disliked at first that he affirmed that he would not have entered the church on that day—though it was the chief festival of the church—if he could have foreseen the design of the Pope. But when he had taken the title he bore very quietly the hostility that it caused and the indignation of the Roman emperors [in Byzantium]. He conquered their ill-feeling by his magnanimity, in which doubtless, he far excelled them, and sent frequent embassies to them, and called them his brothers.

Source: Early Lives of Charlemagne by Einhard and the Monk of St. Gall, trans. A. J. Grant (1922): 43–44.

from incursions by hostile tribes. Perhaps most important, however, was his need to satisfy his followers, especially the members of the aristocracy, by providing them with opportunities for plunder and new lands. As a result of these wars, he established a network of subservient kingdoms that owed tribute to the Carolingian Empire (see Map 8.2).

The extraordinary expansion of the Carolingian Empire represented a significant departure from the small, loosely governed kingdoms that had prevailed in the wake of the collapse of the Roman Empire. Charlemagne's empire covered all of western Europe except for southern Italy, Spain, and the British Isles. His military ambitions had brought the Franks into direct confrontation with other cultures—the polytheistic German tribes, Scandinavians, and Slavs; the Orthodox Christians of Byzantium; and the Muslims in Spain. These confrontations were usually hostile and violent, characterized as they were by the imposition of Frankish rule and Latin Christian faith.

Coronation of Charlemagne as Emperor

Charlemagne's coronation as Roman emperor at the hands of Pope Leo III (r. 795–816) conferred extraordinary authority on the Frankish kingdom. In 799 Pope Leo found himself embroiled in a vicious dispute with a faction of Roman nobles who accused him of adultery and lying. Kidnapped on the streets of Rome, the pope was beaten and perhaps maimed before he was rescued by some of his attendants. Charlemagne put together a commission of prominent churchmen and nobles to conduct a judicial inquiry into the charges against the pope, and then in the autumn of 800 the king himself set out for Rome to restore order to the Church. After Leo was cleared of the accusations against him, on Christmas Day 800 in front of a large crowd at St. Peter's Basilica, the pope presided over a ceremony in which Charlemagne was crowned emperor. Historians have debated exactly what happened, but according to the most widely accepted account, the assembled throng acclaimed Charlemagne as Augustus and emperor, and the pope prostrated himself before the new emperor in a public demonstration of submission. Charlemagne's biographer Einhard later stated that the coronation came as a surprise to the king. Certainly there were dangers in accepting the imperial crown because the coronation was certain to antagonize Constantinople, where there already was a Roman emperor. Nevertheless, Charlemagne became the first Roman emperor in the West since the fifth century.

The coronation exemplified two of the most prominent characteristics of the Carolingians. The first was the conscious imitation of the ancient Roman Empire, especially the Christian empire of Constantine. Charlemagne's conquests acquired much of the former territory of the western Roman Empire, and the churches built during his reign were modeled after the fourth- and fifth-century basilicas of Rome. The second characteristic of Carolingian rule was the obligation of the Frankish kings to protect the Roman popes, an obligation that began under Charlemagne's father Pepin. In exchange for this protection, the popes offered the Carolingian monarchs the legitimacy of divine sanction.

The imperial title bestowed on Charlemagne tremendous prestige and tremendous risk. With the imperial crown came the rulership of northern Italy and theoretical superiority over all other rulers in the West. But it made dangerous enemies of the Byzantine emperors. They had been calling themselves Roman emperors since the fourth century and justly claimed to be the true heirs of the legal authority of the ancient Roman Empire. To them Charlemagne was nothing more than a barbarian usurper of the imperial crown. In their minds the pope had no right to crown anyone emperor. Instead of reuniting the eastern and western halves of the ancient Roman Empire, the coronation of Charlemagne drove them further apart.

Carolingian Rulership

Even under the discerning and strong rulership of Charlemagne, the Carolingian Empire never enjoyed the assets that had united the ancient Roman Empire for so many centuries. The Carolingians lacked a standing army and navy, professional civil servants, properly maintained roads, regular communications, and a money economy, a stark contrast with Byzantium and the Muslim caliphates, which could also boast splendid capital cities of Constantinople, Damascus, Baghdad, and Córdoba. However, Charlemagne governed very effectively without a capital, spending much of his time ruling from the saddle. From Christmas to Easter and sometimes longer, Charlemagne wintered in one of the imperial palaces, usually in the Frankish heartland. In the summer he and his court traveled about, camping out or living as guests in the castles of friendly lords, where he dispensed justice, decided disputes, and enforced obedience to his rule. During these summer travels he frequently conducted campaigns against the Saxon tribes.

Such a system of government depended more on personal than institutional forms of rule. Personal loyalty to the Carolingian monarch, expressed in an oath of allegiance, provided the strongest bonds unifying the realm, but betrayals were frequent. The Carolingian system required a monarch with outstanding personal abilities and unflagging energy, such as Charlemagne possessed, but a weak monarch threatened the collapse of the entire empire. Until the reign of Charlemagne, royal commands had been delivered orally, and there were few written records of what decisions had been made. Charlemagne's decrees (capitularies) gradually came to be written out. The written capitularies began to strengthen and institutionalize governmental procedures through written aids to memory. In addition, Charlemagne's leading adviser, Alcuin, insisted that all official communications be stated in the appropriate Latin form, which would help prevent falsification be-

cause only the educated members of Charlemagne's court were well enough educated to know the proper forms.

One of the weaknesses of the Merovingian dynasty had been the decentralization of power, as local dukes appropriated royal resources and public functions for themselves. To combat this weakness, Charlemagne followed his father's lead in reorganizing government around territorial units called counties°, each administered by a count. The counts were rewarded with lands from the king and sent to areas where they had no family ties to serve as a combined provincial governor, judge, military commander, and representative of the king. To check on the counts, traveling circuit inspectors reviewed the counts' activities on a regular basis and remedied abuses of office. On the frontiers of their sprawling kingdom, the Franks established special territories called marches°, which were ruled by margraves with extended powers necessary to defend vulnerable borders.

In many respects, however, the Church provided the most vital foundations for the Carolingian system of rulership. As discussed in Chapter 6, during the last years of the ancient Roman Empire the administration of the Church was organized around the office of the bishop. By the late seventh century this system had almost completely collapsed, as many bishoprics were left vacant or were occupied by royal favorites and relatives who lacked qualifications for church office. Because Carolingian monarchs considered themselves responsible for the welfare of Christianity, they took charge of the appointment of bishops and reorganized church administration into a strict hierarchy of archbishops who supervised bishops who, in turn, supervised parish priests. Pepin and Charlemagne also revitalized the monasteries and endowed new ones, which provided the royal court with trained personnel—scribes, advisers, and spiritual assistants. Most laymen of the time were illiterate, so monks and priests wrote the emperor's letters for him, kept government records, composed histories, and promoted education—all essential for Carolingian rule.

The Carolingian Renaissance

In addition to organizing efficient political administration, Charlemagne sought to make the royal court an intellectual center. He gathered around him prominent scholars from throughout the realm and other countries. Under Charlemagne's patronage, these scholars were responsible for the flowering of culture that is called the Carolingian Renaissance.

The Carolingian Renaissance° ("rebirth") was one of a series of revivals of interest in ancient Greek and Latin literature. Charlemagne understood that both governmental efficiency and the propagation of the Christian faith required the intensive study of Latin, which was the language of the law, learning, and the Church. The Latin of everyday speech had evolved considerably since antiquity. During Charlemagne's time, spoken Latin had already been transformed into early versions of the Romance languages of Spanish, Italian, Portuguese, and French. Distressed that the poor Latin of many clergymen meant they misunderstood the Bible, Charlemagne ordered that all prospective priests undergo a rigorous education and recommended the liberal application of physical punishment if a pupil was slow in his lessons. However, due to the lack of properly educated teachers the Carolingian reforms did not penetrate very far into the lower levels of the clergy, who taught by rote the rudiments of Christianity to the nonliterate peasants.

Charlemagne's patronage was crucial for the Carolingian Renaissance, which took place in the monasteries and the imperial court. Many of the heads of the monastic writing rooms wrote literary works of their own, including poetry and theology. The Carolingian scholars developed a beautiful new style of handwriting called the Carolingian minuscule, in which each letter was carefully and clearly formed. Texts collected by Carolingian librarians provided the foundation for the laws of the Church (called *canon law*) and codified the liturgy, which consisted of the prayers offered, texts read, and chants sung on each day of the year.

During the Carolingian period, the copying and studying of ancient Latin texts intensified. The works of some seventy ancient authors were preserved by Carolingian scribes. Some 8,000 Carolingian manuscripts still exist, a small portion of the total number known to have been produced.

The brighter young clerics and some promising laymen required instruction more advanced than the typical monastery could provide; to meet this need, Charlemagne established a school in his palace in Aachen. To staff his school and to serve as advisers, Charlemagne sought the best talent from within and outside the empire. Grammarians, historians, geographers, and astronomers from Ireland, England, Italy, Germany, and Spain flocked to Charlemagne's call.

The man most fully responsible for the Carolingian Renaissance was the English poet and cleric Alcuin of York (ca. 732–804), whom Charlemagne invited to head the palace school. Charlemagne himself joined his sons, his friends, and his friends' sons as a student, and under Alcuin's guidance the court became a lively center of discussion and exchange of knowledge. They debated issues such as the existence or nonexistence of Hell, the meaning of solar eclipses, and the nature of the Holy Trinity. After fifteen years at court, Alcuin became the abbot of the monastery of St. Martin at Tours, where he expanded the library and produced a number of works on education, theology, and philosophy.

A brilliant young monk named Einhard (ca. 770–840), who studied in the palace school, quickly became a trusted friend and adviser to Charlemagne. Based on twenty-three years of service to Charlemagne and research in royal documents, Einhard wrote the *Life of Charlemagne* (830–833), which describes Charlemagne's family, foreign policy, con-

The Palatine Chapel of Charlemagne

The Palatine Chapel, which is now a component of the cathedral of Aachen, Germany, is the most significant surviving example of Carolingian architecture. Consecrated in 805, it served as Charlemagne's imperial chapel and his resting place. The intricate design of the octagonal core was modeled after the Byzantine church of San Vitale in Ravenna, Italy.

quests, administration, and personal attributes. In Einhard's vivid Latin prose, Charlemagne comes alive as a great leader, a lover of hunting and fighting, who unlike his rough companions possessed a towering sense of responsibility for the welfare of his subjects and the salvation of their souls. In Einhard's biography, Charlemagne appears as an idealist, the first Christian prince in medieval Europe to imagine that his role was not just to acquire more possessions but to better humankind.

DOCUMENT

Einhard, *Life of Charlemagne*

Charlemagne's rule and reputation have had lasting significance for western Europe. Around 776 an Anglo-Saxon monk referred to the vast new kingdom of the Franks as the

Carolingian Renaissance Art
This exquisitely carved bookcover for the Psalter of Dagulf was made for Pope Hadrian (d. 795) in the workshops of Charlemagne's palace. In the upper left side panel, King David orders the psalms be written down. In the lower left he sings them. In the upper right the pope orders Saint Jerome to edit the psalms for inclusion in the Bible, which he does in the lower right.

Kingdom of Europe, reviving the Roman geographical term *Europa*. Thanks to the Carolingians, Europe became more than a geographical expression. It became the geographical center of a new civilization that supplanted the Roman civilization of the Mediterranean and transformed the culture of the West.

The Division of Western Europe

None of Charlemagne's successors possessed his personal skills, and without a permanent institutional basis for administration, the empire was vulnerable to fragmentation and disorder. When Charlemagne died in 814, the imperial crown passed to his only surviving son, Louis the Pious (r. 814–840). Louis's most serious problem was dividing the empire among his own three sons, as required by Frankish inheritance laws. Disputes among Louis's sons led to civil war, even before the death of their father, and while they were fighting the administration of the empire was neglected.

CHRONOLOGY

The Carolingian Dynasty

751	Pepin the Short deposes last Merovingian king
800	Charlemagne crowned emperor in Rome
843	Treaty of Verdun divides Frankish kingdom
987	Death of the last Carolingian king

After years of fighting, the three sons—Charles the Bald (d. 877), Lothair (d. 855), and Louis the German (d. 876)—negotiated the Treaty of Verdun, which divided the Frankish kingdom. Charles the Bald received the western part of the territories, the kingdom of West Francia. Louis the German received the eastern portion, the kingdom of East Francia. Lothair obtained the imperial title as well as the central portion of the kingdom, the "Middle Kingdom," which extended from Rome to the North Sea (see Map 8.2). In succeeding generations, the laws of inheritance created further fragmentation of these kingdoms, and during the ninth and tenth centuries the descendants of Charlemagne died out or lost control of their lands. By 987 none were left.

The Carolingian Empire lasted only a few generations. Carolingian military power, however, had been formidable, providing within the Frankish lands an unusual period of security from hostile enemies, measured by the fact that few settlements were fortified. After the empire's collapse virtually every surviving community in western Europe required fortifications, represented by castles and town walls. Post-Carolingian Europe became fragmented as local aristocrats stepped into the vacuum created by the demise of the Carolingians—and it became vulnerable, as a new wave of raiders from the steppes and the North plundered and carved out land for themselves.

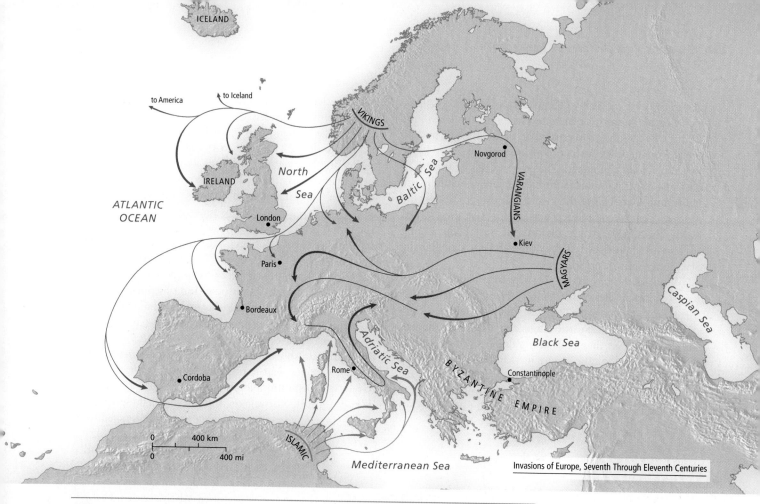

Map 8.3 Invasions of Europe, Seventh Through Eleventh Centuries

Especially after the division of the Carolingian empire, Europe came under severe pressure from invading Viking bands from Scandinavia. The effects of the Viking invasions were felt most gravely in the British Isles and northern France. From the east came the Magyars, who eventually settled in the vast Hungarian plain. From the south there were persistent raids and conquests from various Islamic states, some of which established a rich Muslim civilization in Europe.

Invasions and Recovery in the Latin West

■ **After the collapse of the Carolingian Empire, how did the western kingdoms consolidate in the core of the European continent and how did Latin Christianity spread to its periphery?**

Despite Charlemagne's campaigns of conquest and conversion, the spread of Christianity throughout western Europe remained uneven and incomplete. By 900, Latin Christianity was limited to a few regions that constituted the heartland of western Europe—the Frankish lands, Italy, parts of Germany that had been under Carolingian rule, the British Isles, and a fringe in Spain. During the ninth and tenth centuries, hostile polytheistic tribes raided deep into the tightly packed Christian core of western Europe (see Map 8.3). Despite these attacks

Christianity survived, and the polytheist tribes eventually accepted the Christian faith. These conversions were not always the consequence of Christian victories in battle, as had often been the case during late antiquity and the Carolingian period. More frequently they resulted from organized missionary efforts by monks and bishops.

The Polytheist Invaders of the Latin West

Some of the raiders during the eighth to eleventh centuries plundered what they could from the Christian settlements of the West and returned home. Others seized lands, settled down, and established new principalities. The two groups who took advantage of the weakness of the Latin West most often during this period were the Magyars and Vikings.

The original homeland of the Magyars, later known as the Hungarians, was in the central Asian steppes. Gradually driven by other nomads to the western edge of the steppes, the Magyars began to penetrate Europe in the late ninth century. By 896 they had crossed en masse into the middle of the Danube River basin, occupying sparsely settled lands that were easily conquered. The grassy plains of this basin had long attracted nomads from the steppes, including the Huns and Avars before them, and like other nomads, the Magyars were accomplished horsemen. Once they settled down, the Magyar tribes divided the vast plain among themselves and pushed at the borders of the neighboring Slavic and German principalities.

Mounted raiding parties of Magyars ranged far into western Europe. Between 898 and 920 they sacked settlements in the prosperous Po River valley of Italy and then descended on the remnant kingdoms of the Carolingian Empire. Wherever they went they plundered for booty and took slaves for domestic service or sale. The kings of western and central Europe were powerless against these fierce raiders, who were unstoppable until 955 when the Saxon king Otto I (who later became emperor) destroyed a band of marauders on their way home with booty. After 955, Magyar raiding subsided.

The definitive end of Magyar forays, however, may have had less to do with Otto's victory than with the consolidation of the Hungarian plain into its own kingdom under the Árpád dynasty, named after Árpád (d. 907), who had led seven Magyar tribes in their migration to Hungary. Both Orthodox and Latin missionaries vied to convert the Magyars, but because of an alliance with German monarchs, the Árpáds accepted Roman Christianity. On Christmas Day 1000, the Árpád king Stephen I (r. 997–1038) received the insignia of royalty directly from the pope and was crowned king. To help convert his people, King Stephen laid out a network of bishoprics and lavishly endowed monasteries.

The most devastating of the eighth- to eleventh-century invaders of western European settlements were the Vikings, also called Norsemen or Northmen. (These Viking warriors were ethnically related to the Rus who harassed Constantinople at the same time.) During this period, Danish, Norwegian, and Swedish Viking warriors sailed on long-distance raiding expeditions from their homes in Scandinavia. Every spring the long Viking dragon ships sailed forth, each carrying 50 to 100 warriors avid for loot. Propelled by a single square sail or by oarsmen when the winds failed or were blowing in the wrong direction, Viking ships were unmatched for seaworthiness and regularly sailed into the wild seas of the North Atlantic. The shallow-draft vessels could also be rowed up the lazy rivers of Europe to plunder monasteries and villages far into the interior.

The Viking Ship Museum in Oslo

The causes for the enormous Viking onslaught were complex. Higher annual temperatures in the North may have stimulated a spurt in population that encouraged raiding and eventually emigration. But the primary motive seems to have been an insatiable thirst for silver, which was deemed the essential standard of social distinction in Scandinavian society. As a result, monasteries and cathedrals with their silver liturgical vessels were especially prized sources of plunder for Viking raiding parties. In 793, for example, the great English monastery at Lindisfarne was pillaged for silver and largely destroyed in the process.

By the middle of the ninth century, the Vikings began to maintain winter quarters in the British Isles and on the shores of the weak Carolingian kingdoms—locations that enabled them to house and feed ever-larger raiding parties. These raiders soon became

Viking Ship

This reconstructed Viking ship, discovered at Oseberg, Norway, dates from ca. 800. It would have been propelled by a single square sail or rowed by oarsmen. Horses and warriors crowded into the ship. The tiller was mounted on the starboard side toward the stern. Stern-mounted rudders, which gave the helmsman much greater control of the direction of the ship, were gradually introduced during the twelfth century.

Viking Treasure Hoard
The Vikings were engaged in long-distance trading and raiding. One of the principal motives for their long treks was the accumulation of silver. This hoard from an eleventh century site is mainly made up of Byzantine and Islamic silver coins.

invading armies that took land and settled their families on it. As a result, the Vikings moved from disruptive pillaging to permanent occupation, which created a lasting mark on Europe. Amid the ruins of the Carolingian Empire, Viking settlements on the Seine River formed the beginnings of the duchy of Normandy ("Northman land"), whose soldiers would conquer during the eleventh century England, Sicily, and much of southern Italy.

The most long-lasting influence of the Vikings outside Scandinavia was in the British Isles and North Atlantic. In 865 a great Viking army conquered large parts of northeastern England, creating a loosely organized network of territories known as the Danelaw. The Danish and Norse conquests in the British Isles left deep cultural residues in local dialects, geographical names, personal names, social structure, and literature. The most enduring example in Old English, the earliest form of spoken and written English, remains the epic of *Beowulf*, which recounts the exploits of a great Scandinavian adventurer in combat with the monster Grendel, Grendel's mother, and a fiery dragon.

In the North Atlantic, Vikings undertook long voyages into the unknown across cold rough seas. Beginning about 870, settlers poured into unsettled Iceland. Using Iceland as a base, they ventured farther and established new colonies in Greenland. In Iceland the adventures of these Viking warriors, explorers, and settlers were celebrated in poetry and sagas. The sagas of Erik the Red and the Greenlanders recount hazardous voyages to the coasts of Canada. These Europeans arrived in America 500 years before Christopher Columbus. In 930 the fiercely independent Icelanders founded a national parliament, the *althing*, an institution at which disputes were adjudicated through legal procedures rather than combat.

After the mid-ninth century, the kings of Scandinavia (Norway, Denmark, and Sweden) began to assert control over the bands of raiders who had constituted the vanguard of the Viking invasions. By the end of the tenth century, the great age of Viking raiding by small parties ended. The Scandinavian kings established firm hold over the settled population and converted to Christianity, bringing their subjects with them into the new faith. Henceforth, the descendants of the Viking raiders settled down to become peaceable farmers and shepherds.

The Rulers in the Latin West

As a consequence of the disintegration of the Carolingian order and the subsequent invasions, people during the ninth and tenth centuries began to seek protection from local warlords who assumed responsibilities once invested in royal authorities.

Lords and Vassals

The society of warlords derived from Germanic military traditions in which a great chief attracted followers who fought alongside him. The relationship was voluntary and egalitarian. By the eighth century, however, the chief had become a lord° who dominated others, and his dependents were known as vassals°.

The bond of loyalty between lord and vassal was formalized by an oath. In the Carolingian period the vassal proved his loyalty to the lord by performing an act of homage, which made the vassal the "man" of the lord. The act of homage was a ritual in which the kneeling vassal placed his clasped hands between the hands of the lord and made a verbal declaration of intent, usually something such as, "Sir, I become your man." In return for the vassal's homage or fealty, as it came to be called, the lord swore to protect the vassal. The oath established a personal relationship in which the lord reciprocated the vassal's loyalty and willingness to obey the lord with protection and in some cases with a land grant called a fief°. Lords frequently called on their vassals for military assistance to resist invaders or to fight with other lords. The fief supplied the vassal with an income to cover the expenses of armor and weapons and of raising and feeding horses, all of which were necessary to be an effective mounted soldier, known by the twelfth century as a knight°. This connection between lord-vassal relations and the holding of a fief is called feudalism°.

Revealing the Truth: Oaths and Ordeals

No participant in a lawsuit or criminal trial today would dream of entering the courtroom without an accompanying pile of documents to prove the case. In modern society we trust written over oral evidence because we are aware of how easily memories can be distorted. In an early medieval court, however, the participants usually arrived with nothing more than their own sworn testimony and personal reputations to support their cause. Papers alleging to prove one thing or another meant little in a largely illiterate society. Unable to read and perhaps aware that the few who could read might deceive them, most people trusted what they had personally seen and heard. Count Berthold of Hamm expressed the opinion of many when, after being presented with documents opposing his claim to a piece of land, he "laughed at the documents, saying that since anyone's pen could write what they liked, he ought not to lose his rights over it."

To settle disputes, medieval courts put much more faith in confession or in eyewitness testimony than in documents. In 1124 Pope Calixtus II pronounced that "we put greater faith in the oral testimony of living witnesses than in the written word."

Under normal trial procedures, a man would give his oath that what he was saying was true. If he was an established and respected member of the community, he would also have a number of "oath-witnesses" testify for his reliability, although not to the truth or falsehood of his evidence. The court would also hear from witnesses in the case. This system worked well enough when two local men, known in the community, were at odds. But what happened when there was a trial involving a person who had a bad reputation, was a known liar, or was a stranger? What would happen in a case with no witnesses?

In these instances, medieval courts sometimes turned to trial by ordeal to settle the matter. The judicial ordeal was used only as a last resort, as a German law code of 1220 declared: "It is not right to use the ordeal in any case, except that the truth may be known in no other way." The wide range of situations and people handed over to the ordeal makes clear that in the eyes of the medieval courts, the ordeal was a fallback method when all else failed to reveal the truth.

What was a trial by ordeal? There were several types. The most common was trial by fire. The accused would plunge his or her arm into a cauldron of boiling water to retrieve a coin or a jewel, or alternately would pick up a red-hot iron and walk nine paces. A variation of this method was to walk over hot coals or red-hot plowshares. After the accused suffered this ordeal, his or her hand or foot would be bound for three days and then examined. If the wound was healing "cleanly," meaning without infection, the accused was declared innocent. If not, he or she was adjudged guilty. Another common form of the ordeal was immersion in cold water, or "swimming," made famous in later centuries by its use in witch trials. The accused would be thrown into a river or lake. If the water "rejected" her and she floated, then she was guilty. If the water "embraced" her and she sank, then she was innocent. The obvious complication that a sinking person, even though innocent, may have also been a drowning person did not seem to deter use of trial by water.

The ordeal was especially widespread in judging crimes such as heresy and adultery and in assigning paternity. In 1218, Inga of Varteig carried the hot iron to prove that her son, born out of wedlock, was the son of deceased King Hakon III, which if true would change the line of succession in Norway. The ordeal was also used to decide much more pedestrian matters. In 1090, Gautier of Meigné claimed a plot of land from the monks of Saint Auban at Angers, arguing that he had traded a horse in return for the property. He too carried a hot iron to prove his claim.

The belief that an ordeal could effectively reveal guilt or innocence in a judicial matter was based on the widespread conviction that God constantly and actively intervened in earthly affairs and that his judgment could be seen immediately. To focus God's attention on a specific issue, the participants performed the ordeal in a ritual manner. A priest was usually present to invoke God's power and to bless the implements employed in the ordeal. In one typical formula, the priest asked God "to bless and sanctify this fiery iron, which is used in the just examination of doubtful issues." Priests would also inform the accused, "If you are innocent of this charge . . . you may confidently receive this iron in your hand and the Lord, the just judge, will free you." The ritual element of the judicial ordeal emphasized the judgment of God over the judgment of men.

During the eleventh and twelfth centuries, the use of the ordeal waned. The recovery of Roman law, the rise of literacy and written documents in society at large, and a greater confidence in the power of courts to settle disputes all con-

Trial by Ordeal

This fifteenth-century painting by Dieric Bouts (c. 1415–1475), was commissioned by the city of Louvain in 1468 for a large project on the theme of the Last Judgment.

This panel illustrates an episode from the legend of the Holy Roman emperor Otto III (980–1002) who presided over the trial.

The woman, accused of murdering her husband, embraces his head with her right arm and holds a red-hot iron in her left hand in a trial by ordeal.

tributed to the gradual replacement of the ordeal with the jury trial or the use of torture to elicit a confession from the accused. In England the common law began to entrust the determination of the truth to a jury of peers who listened to and evaluated all the testimony. The jury system valued the opinions of members of the community over the reliability of the ordeal to reveal God's judgment. These changes mark a shift in medieval society toward a growing belief in the power of secular society to organize and police itself, leaving divine justice to the afterlife. But the most crucial shift came from within the Church itself, which felt its spiritual mission compromised by the involvement of priests in supervising ordeals. In 1215 the Fourth Lateran Council forbade priests from participating, and their absence made it impossible for the ordeal to continue as a formal legal procedure.

Questions of Justice

1. Why was someone's reputation in the community so significant for determining the truth in a medieval trial? How do reputations play a role in trials today?
2. What do oaths and the trial by ordeal reveal about the relationship between human and divine justice during the Middle Ages?

Taking It Further

Bartlett, Robert. *Trial by Fire and Water: The Medieval Judicial Ordeal.* 1986. Associates the spread of the trial by ordeal with the expansion of Christianity. The best study of the ordeal.

van Caenegen, R. C. *An Historical Introduction to Private Law.* 1992. A basic narrative from late antiquity to the nineteenth century that traces the evolution of early medieval trial procedures.

During the ninth and tenth centuries, the lords often became the only effective rulers in a particular locality. After the collapse of public authority during the invasions and the dissolution of the Carolingian Empire, lordship implied political and legal jurisdiction over the inhabitants of the land. These lords came to exercise many of the powers of the state, such as adjudicating disputes over property or inheritance and punishing thieves and murderers. The rendering of justice represented the most elementary attribute of government, and in the absence of a formal legal system and systematic record keeping, local lords rendered a rough and ready justice. The personal loyalties of those involved in a dispute were crucial for determining the outcome. Those well-connected to the lord, especially those who were his vassals, were always better off than those who were outsiders or had fallen into his disfavor. In a society in which personal ties meant everything, the truth of conflicting testimonies was often determined by the public reputations and personal connections of those who testified. When the reputations of disputants or an alleged criminal could not determine whom to believe, lords acting as judges relied on oaths and ordeals to determine the truth.

The mixture of personal lord-vassal obligations, property rights conveyed by the fief, and legal jurisdiction over communities caused endless complications. The king's vassals were also lords of their own vassals, who in turn were lords over lesser vassals down to the level of simple knight. In theory such a system created a hierarchy of authority that descended down from the king, but reality was never that simple. In France, for example, many of the great lords enjoyed as much land as the king, which made it very difficult for the king to force them to enact his will. Many vassals held different fiefs from different lords, which created a confusion of loyalties, especially when two lords of the same vassal went to war against one another.

Women could inherit fiefs and own property of their own, although they could not perform military services. They often managed royal and aristocratic property when men were absent or dead, decided how property would be divided up among heirs, and functioned as lords when receiving the homage of male vassals. The lineage and accomplishments of prominent ladies enhanced their husbands' social prestige. A number of aristocratic families traced their descent from the female line, if it was more prestigious than the male line, and named their children after the wife's illustrious ancestors.

Lord-vassal relationships infiltrated many medieval social institutions and practices. Since most vassals owed military service to their lords, medieval armies were at least partially composed of vassal-knights who were obliged to fight for their lord for a certain number of days (often forty) per year. Vassals were required to provide their lord with other kinds of support as well. When summoned, they had to appear at the lord's court to offer advice or sit in judgment of other vassals who were their peers. When the

DOCUMENT

An Oath of Voluntary Submission to a Lord

Many men who found themselves in desperate circumstances became vassals in order to feed themselves and to find protection from someone richer and stronger. This voluntary oath of obedience reflects the origins of the relationship of dominance and submission between lords and vassals. In the eighth century according to the prescribed formula a destitute man was supposed to address his "magnificent lord" as follows:

Inasmuch as it is known to all and sundry that I lack the wherewithal to feed and clothe myself, I have asked of your pity, and your goodwill has granted to me permission to deliver and commend myself into your authority and protection . . . in return you have undertaken to aid and sustain me in food and clothing, while I have undertaken to serve you and deserve well of you as far as lies in my power. And for as long as I shall live, I am bound to serve you and respect you as a free man ought, and during my lifetime I have not the right to withdraw from your authority and protection, but must, on the contrary for the remainder of my days remain under it.

And in virtue of this action, if one of us wishes to alter the terms of the agreement, he can do so after paying a fine of ten solidi to the other. But the agreement itself shall remain in force. Whence it has seemed good to us that we should both draw up and confirm two documents of the same tenor, and this they have done.

Source: This example of a voluntary oath of obedience comes from Tours, in the eighth century.

lord traveled, his vassal was obliged to provide food and shelter in the vassal's castle, sometimes for a large entourage of family and retainers who accompanied the lord. Vassals were obliged to pay their lord certain fees on special occasions, such as the marriage of the lord's daughter. If the lord was captured in battle, his vassals had to pay the ransom.

The Western European Kingdoms After the Carolingians

At a time when the bonds of loyalty and support between lords and vassals were the only form of protection from invaders and marauders, lordship was a stronger social institution than the vague obligations all subjects owed to their kings. To rule effectively, a king was obliged to be a strong lord, in effect to become the lord of all the other lords, who in turn would discipline their own vassals. Achieving this difficult goal took several steps. First, the king had to establish a firm hand over his own lands, the royal domain. With the domain supplying food, materiel, and fighting men, the king could attempt the second step—establishing control over lords who lived outside the royal domain. To hold sway over these independent-minded lords, kings sometimes employed force but frequently offered lucrative rewards by giving out royal prerogatives to loyal lords. These prerogatives included the rights to receive fines in courts of law, to collect taxes, and to perform other governmental functions. As a result, some medieval kingdoms, such as France and England, began to combine in the hands of the same people the personal authority of lordship with the legal authority of the king, creating feudal kingship.

The final step in the process of establishing royal authority was to emphasize the sacred character of kingship. With the assistance of the clergy, kings emulated the great Christian emperors of Rome, Constantine and Justinian. Medieval kings became quasi priests who received obedience from their subjects because they believed kings represented the majesty of God on Earth. The institution of sacred kingship gave kings an additional weapon for persuading the nobles to recognize the king's superiority over them.

Under the influence of ancient Roman ideas of rulership, some kings began to envision their kingdoms as something grander than private property. As the Germanic king and later emperor Conrad II (r. 1024–1039) put it, "If the king is dead the kingdom remains, just as the ship remains even if the helmsman falls overboard."[3] The idea slowly began to take hold that the kingdom had an eternal existence separate from the mortal person of the king and that it was superior to its component parts—its provinces, tribes, lords, families, bishoprics, and cities. This profound idea reached its fullest theoretical expression many centuries later. Promoting the sacred and eternal character of kingship required monarchs to patronize priests, monks, writers, and artists who could formulate and express these ideas.

The kingdoms of East and West Francia, which arose out of the remnants of the Carolingian Empire, produced kings who attempted to expand the power of the monarchy and enhance the idea of kingship. East Francia largely consisted of Germanic tribes, each governed by a Frankish official called a duke. During the tenth century, several of these dukes became powerful lords, but they had to rule from the saddle, constantly on the road—being seen, making judgments, suppressing revolts, punishing disloyal vassals, and rewarding loyal ones.

After 919 the dukes of Saxony were elected the kings of East Francia, establishing the foundations for the Saxon dynasty. With few lands of their own, the Saxon kings maintained their power by acquiring other duchies and controlling appointments to high church offices, which went to family members or loyal followers. The greatest of the Saxon kings, Otto I the Great (936–973), combined deep Christian piety with formidable military ability. More than any other tenth-century king, he supported the foundation of missionary bishoprics in polytheist Slavic and Scandinavian lands, thereby pushing the boundaries of Christianity beyond what they had been under Charlemagne. Otto launched a major expedition to Italy, where he reestablished order in anarchic Rome, deposed one pope, and nominated another. As a consequence of his intervention in Italy, the new pope crowned him emperor in 962, reviving the Roman Empire in the West, as Charlemagne had done earlier. Otto and his successors in the Saxon dynasty attempted to rule a more restricted version of the western empire than had Charlemagne. By the 1030s the German Empire consisted of most of the Germanic duchies, north-central Italy, and Burgundy. In later centuries these regions collectively came to be called the Holy Roman Empire.

As had been the case under Charlemagne, effective rulership in the new German Empire included the patronage of learned men and

Otto III

The Emperor Otto III is represented here in a form usually reserved for Christ. The emperor sits on a throne, is surrounded by a mandorla (lines surrounding his body in the shape of an almond), and reaches out to the four evangelists—Matthew, Mark, Luke, and John—who are signified by the winged figures of an eagle, lion, bull, and man. The hand of God reaches down from the heavens to crown Otto. The idea of divine sanction of kingship could not be more graphic.

women who enhanced the reputation of the monarch. Otto and his able brother Bruno, the archbishop of Cologne, initiated a cultural revival, the Ottonian Renaissance°, which centered on the imperial court. Learned Irish and English monks, Greek philosophers from Byzantium, and Italian scholars found positions there. Among the many intellectuals patronized by Otto, the most notable was Liutprand of Cremona (ca. 920–ca. 972), a vivid writer whose unabashed histories reflected the passions of the troubled times. For example, his history of contemporary Europe vilified his enemies and was aptly titled *Revenge.*

Like East Francia, West Francia included many groups with separate ethnic and linguistic identities, but the kingdom had been Christianized much longer because it had been part of the Roman Empire. Thus West Francia, although highly fragmented, possessed the potential for greater unity by using fully established Christianity to champion the authority of the king.

Strengthening the monarchy became the crucial goal of the Capetian dynasty, which succeeded the last of the Carolingian kings. Hugh Capet (r. 987–996) was elevated king of West Francia in an elaborate coronation ceremony in which the prayers of the archbishop of Reims offered divine sanction to the new dynasty. The involvement of the archbishop established an important precedent for the French monarchy: From this point on, the monarchy and the church hierarchy were closely entwined. From this mutually beneficial relationship, the king received ecclesiastical and spiritual support while the upper clergy gained royal protection and patronage. The term *France* at first applied only to Capet's feudal domain, a small but rich region around Paris, but through the persistence of the Capetians West Francia became so unified that the name France came to refer to the entire kingdom.

The Capetians were especially successful in soliciting homage and services from the great lords of the land—despite some initial resistance. Hugh and his successors distinguished themselves by emphasizing that unlike other lords, kings were appointed by God. Shortly after his own coronation, Hugh had his son crowned—a strategy that ensured the succession of the Capetian family. Hugh's son, Robert II, the Pious (r. 996–1031), was apparently the first to perform the king's touch, the reputed power of the king to cure certain skin diseases. The royal coronation cult and the king's touch established the reputation of French kings as miracle workers.

Anglo-Saxon England had never been part of the Carolingian Empire, but because it was Christian, England shared in the culture of the Latin West. England suffered extensive damage at the hands of the Vikings. After England was almost overwhelmed by a Danish invasion during the winter of 878–879, Alfred the Great (r. 871–899) finally defeated the Danes as spring approached. As king of only Wessex (not of all England), Alfred consolidated his authority and issued a new law code. Alfred's able successors

cooperated with the nobility more effectively than the monarchs in either East or West Francia and built a broad base of support in the local units of government, the hundreds and shires. The Anglo-Saxon monarchy also enjoyed the support of the Church, which provided it with skilled servants and spiritual authorization.

During the late ninth and tenth centuries, Anglo-Saxon England experienced a cultural revival under royal patronage. King Alfred proclaimed that the Viking invasions had been God's punishment for the neglect of learning, without which God's will could not be known. Alfred accordingly promoted the study of Latin. He also desired that all men of wealth learn to read the language of the English people. Under Alfred a highly sophisticated literature appeared in Old English. This literature included poems, sermons, commentaries on the Bible, and translations of important Latin works. The masterpiece of this era was a history called the *Anglo-Saxon Chronicle.* It was begun during Alfred's reign but maintained over several generations.

During the late tenth and early eleventh centuries, England was weakened by another series of Viking raids and a succession of feeble kings. In 1066 William, the duke of Normandy and a descendant of Vikings who had settled in the north of France, defeated King Harold, the last Anglo-Saxon king. William seized the English throne. William the Conqueror opened a new era in which English affairs became deeply intertwined with those of the duchy of Normandy and the kingdom of France.

DOCUMENT

Battle of Hastings (1066)

The Conversion of the Last Polytheists

As the core of the Latin West became politically stronger and economically more prosperous during the tenth and eleventh centuries, Christians made concerted attempts to convert the invaders, especially the polytheistic tribes in northern and eastern Europe. Through conversion, Latin Christianity dominated northern Europe up to the Russian border where Orthodox Christianity adopted from Byzantium held sway.

Among the polytheistic tribes in Scandinavia, the Baltic Sea region, and parts of eastern Europe, the first Christian conversions usually took place when a king or chieftain accepted Christianity. His subjects were expected to follow. Teaching Christian principles and forms of worship required much more time and effort, of course. Missionary monks usually arrived after a king's conversion, but these monks tended to take a tolerant attitude about variations in the liturgy. Because most Christians were isolated from one another, new converts tended to practice their own local forms of worship and belief. Missionaries and Christian princes discovered that the most effective way to combat this localizing tendency was to found bishoprics. The bishopric was a territorial unit (called the *diocese*), presided

Christian Church Imitates Polytheist Temple

The stave church was a type of wooden church built in northern Europe during the Middle Ages. Most of the surviving examples in Scandinavia are generally assumed to be modeled on polytheist temples. The Borgund church in Norway pictured here dates from about 1150.

over by an official (called the *bishop*), who was responsible for enforcing correct worship, combating the vestiges of polytheism and false Christian beliefs (known as *heresy*), and disciplining immorality. Especially among the nonliterate, formerly polytheist tribes in northern and eastern Europe, the foundation of bishoprics created cultural centers of considerable prestige that attracted members of the upper classes. Those educated under the supervision of these new bishops became influential servants to the ruling families, further enhancing the stature of Christian culture.

From the middle of the tenth century along the eastern frontiers of Germany, a line of newly established Catholic bishoprics became the base for the conversion of the polytheist Slavic tribes. Over a period of about sixty years, these German bishoprics pushed the Latin form of Christianity deep into east-central Europe. This effort ensured that the Poles, Bohemians (Czechs), and Magyars (Hungarians) looked to the West and the pope for their cultural models and religious leadership. These peoples remain overwhelmingly Catholic to this day.

The first bishoprics in Scandinavia were also established in the last half of the tenth century. Whereas Germans were primarily responsible for the spread of Latin Christianity among the Slavs, it was English missionaries who evangelized Scandinavia. Denmark had the first completely organized church in Scandinavia, represented by the establishment of nine bishoprics by 1060. The diffusion into Sweden, Norway, and Iceland came later after the strong kingdoms developed in those countries and a pro-Christian dynasty could assist the spread of the new religion. Christian conversion especially benefited women through the abandonment of polygamous marriages, common among the polytheist peoples. As a result, aristocratic women played an important role in helping convert their peoples to Christianity. That role gave them a lasting influence in the churches of the newly converted lands, both as founders and patrons of convents and as writers on religious subjects. By the end of the fourteenth century organized polytheistic worship had disappeared.

Unlike Bulgaria and Kievan Rus, Poland favored Latin Christianity, an association that helped create strong political and cultural ties to western Europe. The Slavic Poles inhabited a flat plain of forested land with small clearings for farming. First exposed to missionaries tied to Saint Methodius, Poland resisted Christianity until Prince Mieszko (ca. 960–992) created the most powerful of the Slav states and accepted Latin Christianity in 966 in an attempt to build political alliances with Christian princes. A new bishopric was established at Poznan with the design of coordinating missionary activities throughout the country. However, German dukes interfered with the administration of the Polish church in an attempt to expand their influence at Poland's expense. To gain outside assistance to counter the German threat, Mieszko formally subordinated his country to the Roman pope with the Donation of Poland (ca. 991). Thus began Poland's long and special relationship with the

CHRONOLOGY

The Western European Kingdoms Emerge

843–911	Carolingian dynasty in East Francia
843–987	Carolingian dynasty in West Francia
919–1024	Saxon or Ottonian dynasty
955	Otto I defeats Magyars
962	Otto crowned emperor in Rome
987–1328	Capetian dynasty in France
1066	William the Conqueror defeats last Anglo-Saxon king

papacy. At Mieszko's death, the territory of Poland approximated what it was at the end of World War II.

Mieszko's successor, Boleslaw the Brave (992–1025), expanded his territories through conquest, making Poland one of the largest European kingdoms. He guaranteed the independence of the Polish church from German ecclesiastical control by obtaining the pope's approval for a Polish archdiocese, and within a few years a string of bishoprics were set up across Poland. In 1000 the German emperor recognized the independence of Poland. In 1025 the pope gave Boleslaw a royal crown, making him the equal of any monarch in Europe. Boleslaw's immediate successors, however, allowed the central authority of the government to slip away into the hands of the local nobility and even lost the title of king.

The West in the East:
The Crusades

■ **What were the causes and consequences of the Crusades?**

On a chilly November day in 1095 in a bare field outside Clermont, France, Pope Urban II (r. 1088–1099) delivered a landmark sermon to the assembled French clergy and laypeople eager to hear the pope. In stirring words Urban recalled that Muslims in the East were persecuting Christians and that the holy places in Palestine had been ransacked. He called upon the knights "to take up the cross" to defend their fellow Christians in distress.

Urban's appeal for a Crusade was stunningly successful. When he finished speaking, the crowd chanted back, "God wills it." The news of Urban's call for a holy war in the East spread like wildfire, and all across France and the western part of the German Empire knights prepared for the journey to Jerusalem. Unexpectedly and probably contrary to the pope's intentions, the poor and dispossessed also became enthused about an armed pilgrimage to the Holy Land. The zealous Peter the Hermit (ca. 1050–1115) preached the Crusade among the poor and homeless and gathered a huge unequipped, undisciplined army, which left for Jerusalem well in advance of the knights. The army was annihilated along the way.

Urban's call for a Crusade gave powerful religious sanction to the western Christian military expeditions against Islam. From 1095 until well into the thirteenth century, there were recurrent, large-scale Crusading expeditions as Christian knights from the Latin West attempted to take, retake, and protect Christian Jerusalem (see Map 8.4). But the ideal of going on a Crusade lasted long after the thirteenth century into modern times.

IMAGE

Crusaders Besieging a Medieval Castle

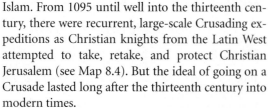

DOCUMENT

Pope Urban II Calls for the Crusades

Robert the Monk recorded what Pope Urban said to the assembly at the Council of Clermont in 1095. He addressed the crowd as the "race of Franks, race from across the mountains, race beloved and chosen by God." He went on to describe the situation in Jerusalem.

From the confines of Jerusalem and from the city of Constantinople a grievous report has gone forth and has repeatedly been brought to our ears; namely, that a race from the kingdom of the Persians, an accursed race, a race wholly alienated from God, "a generation that set not their heart aright, and whose spirit was not steadfast with God," has violently invaded the lands of those Christians and has depopulated them by pillage and fire. They have led away a part of the captives into their own country, and a part they have killed by cruel tortures. They have either destroyed the churches of God or appropriated them for the rites of their own religion. They destroy the altars, after having defiled them with their uncleanness. . . .

Let hatred therefore depart from among you, let your quarrels end, let wars cease, and let all dissensions and controversies slumber. Enter upon the road to the Holy Sepulcher; wrest that land from the wicked race, and subject it to yourselves. That land which, as the Scripture says, "floweth with milk and honey" was given by God into the power of the children of Israel. Jerusalem is the center of the earth; the land is fruitful above all others, like another paradise of delights. This spot the Redeemer of mankind has made illustrious by his advent, has beautified by his sojourn, has consecrated by his passion, has redeemed by his death, has glorified by his burial.

This royal city, however, situated at the center of the earth, is now held captive by the enemies of Christ and is subjected, by those who do not know God, to the worship of the heathen. She seeks, therefore, and desires to be liberated and ceases not to implore you to come to her aid. . . . Accordingly, undertake this journey eagerly for the remission of your sins, with the assurance of the reward of imperishable glory in the kingdom of heaven.

Source: Dennis Sherman, A. Tom Grunfeld, Gerald Markowitz, David Rosner, and Linda Heywood, eds. *World Civilizations: Sources, Images, and Interpretations*, 3rd ed. Copyright 2002, 1998, vol. 1, pp. 201–202.

The Origins of Holy War

The original impulse for the Crusades° was the threat that Muslim armies posed to Christian peoples, pilgrims, and holy places in the eastern Mediterranean. By the middle of the eleventh century the Seljuk Turks, who had converted to Islam, were putting pressure on the Byzantine empire. In 1071 the Seljuks defeated the Byzantine army at Manzikert; their victory opened all of Asia Minor to Muslim occupation. Pope Urban's appeal for a Crusade in 1095 came in response to a request for military assistance from the Byzantine emperor Alexius Comnenus, who probably thought he would get yet another band of Western mercenaries to help him reconquer Byzantine territory lost to the Seljuks. Instead, he got something utterly unprecedented, a massive volunteer army of perhaps 100,000 soldiers devoted less to cooperating with their Byzantine Christian brethren than to wresting Jerusalem from Muslim hands.

To people in the eleventh century, the very idea of Jerusalem had a mystical allure. Enhancing this allure was a widespread confusion between the actual earthly city of Jerusalem in Palestine, where Jesus had been crucified more than a millennium before, and the fantastic heavenly city of Jerusalem with walls of dazzling precious stones as promised in the Bible (Revelation 21:10ff). Many of the crusaders probably could not distinguish between the earthly and the heavenly cities and thought that when they abandoned their homes for Jerusalem, they were marching directly to Paradise. The promise of an eternal reward was reinforced by a special offer Pope Urban made in his famous sermon at Clermont to remit all penance for sin for those who went on the Crusade. Moreover, a penitential pilgrimage to a holy site such as Jerusalem provided a sinner with a pardon for capital crimes such as murder.

There was a significant difference between a pilgrim and a crusader, however. A pilgrim was always unarmed. A crusader carried weapons and was willing not just to

---

Map 8.4   The Major Crusades

During the first three Crusades, Christian armies and fleets from western Europe attacked Muslim strongholds and fortresses in the Middle East in an attempt to capture and hold Jerusalem. The Fourth Crusade never arrived in the Middle East, as it was diverted to besiege Constantinople.

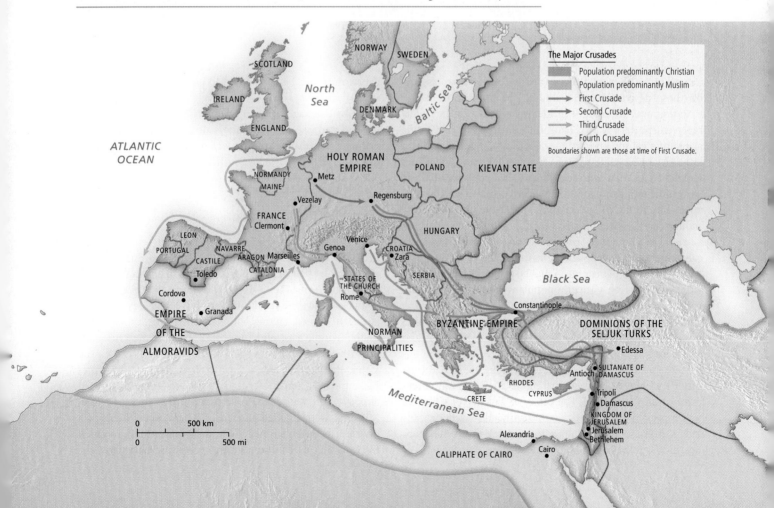

Jesus Christ Leading the Crusaders

The rider on the white horse is Jesus, who holds the Gospels in his right hand and the sword of righteousness in his teeth. The crusading knights bearing banners and shields emblazoned with the cross follow him. The figure in the upper left-hand corner represents St. John the Evangelist, whose writings were understood to prophesy the Crusades. This manuscript illumination dates from ca. 1310–1325.

defend other pilgrims from attack but to launch an assault on those he considered heathens. The innovation of the Crusades was to create the idea of armed pilgrims who received special rewards from the Church. The merger of a spiritual calling and military action was strongest in the knightly orders—Templars, Hospitallers, and Teutonic Knights. The men who joined these orders were soldiers who took monastic vows of poverty, chastity, and obedience. But rather than isolating themselves to pray in a monastery, they went forth, sword in hand, to conquer for Christ. These knightly orders exercised considerable political influence in Europe and amassed great wealth.

In the minds of crusader-knights, greed probably jostled with fervent piety. Growing population pressures and the spread of primogeniture (passing landed estates on to the eldest male heir) left younger sons with little to anticipate at home and much to hope for by seeking their fortunes in the Crusades.

Nevertheless, crusaders testified to the sense of community they enjoyed by participating in "the common enterprise of all Christians." The crusader Fulcher of Chartres was especially captivated by the unity displayed by crusaders from so many different countries: "Who has ever heard of speakers of so many languages in one army . . . If a Breton or a German wished to ask me something, I was utterly without words to reply. But although we were divided by language, we seemed to be like brothers in the love of God and like near neighbors of one mind."[4] For many crusaders the exhilarating experience of brotherhood in the love of God seemed to be a sufficient motive.

Crusading Warfare

The crusaders' enthusiasm for getting to Jerusalem impelled them to capture the holy city from the Muslims soon after they landed in the Middle East. In achieving this goal, the First Crusade (1095–1099) was strikingly successful, but it was as much the result of Muslim weakness as Christian strength. Several factors had weakened Muslim solidarity in the Middle East and the ability to resist the crusaders. First, the onslaught of the Seljuk Turks threatened the Arab states that controlled access to Jerusalem as much as Byzantium. When the crusaders arrived, these states had already been weakened from fighting the Turks. Second, Muslims were divided internally. There were theological divisions between Sunni and Shi'ite Muslims that prevented the Muslim caliphs from uniting against the Christians.

In 1099, after a little more than a month's siege, the crusaders scaled the walls of Jerusalem and took possession of the city, which was also holy to Muslims and Jews and previously largely inhabited by them. The Christian triumph led to the establishment of the Latin principalities, which were devoted to maintaining a Western foothold in the Holy Land. The Latin principalities included all of the territory in contemporary Lebanon, Israel, and Palestine.

The subsequent crusades never achieved the success of the first. In 1144 Muslims captured the northernmost Latin principality, the county of Edessa—a warning to westerners of the fragility of a defensive system that relied on a few scattered fortresses strung along a thin strip of coastline. In response to the loss of Edessa, Christians launched the Second Crusade (1147–1149). The ambitious offensive on several fronts failed disastrously. In 1187, the sultan of Egypt and Syria, Saladin (1137–1193), recaptured Jerusalem for Islam. In response to this dispiriting loss, the Third Crusade (1189–1192) assembled the most spectacular army of European chivalry ever seen, led by Europe's three most powerful kings: German emperor Frederick Barbarossa, Philip Augustus of France, and Richard the Lion-Heart of England. After Frederick drowned wading in a river en route and Philip went home, Richard the Lion-Heart negotiated a truce with Saladin.

The Fourth Crusade proved a particular disaster, at least for the integrity of the Crusading ideal. In 1199, Pope Innocent III called for yet another Crusade to recapture Jerusalem, but the Frankish knights and Venetian fleet were diverted to intervene in a disputed imperial succession in Byzantium. In 1204 they besieged and captured Constantinople. After the conquest the Westerners divided up among themselves the Byzantine Empire, set up a Latin regime that lasted until 1261, and neglected their oaths to reconquer Jerusalem. The Fourth Crusade dangerously weakened the Byzantine Empire by making it a prize for Western adventurers. None of the subsequent Crusades achieved lasting success in the Middle East, but the idea of

DOCUMENT

A Muslim Appeal for Jihad Against the Crusaders

After the Second Crusade (1147–1149) failed to conquer Damascus, Syria, an important Muslim city inland from the crusader states established in what is now Lebanon, an anonymous Muslim author called on all Muslims to resist another attack. In this appeal he calls for a defensive jihad. The passage begins with a quotation from Abu Hamid Al Ghazali (1058–1128), a prominent Muslim scholar.

All Muslims who were free, responsible for their acts and capable of bearing arms must march against [the unbelievers] until they form a force large enough to smite them. This war is to glorify the Word of God and to make His religion victorious over its enemies. . . . If the enemy attacks a town [in Syria] that is incapable of self-defense, all the towns in Syria must raise an army that could drive him back. . . . If, however, the soldiers in Syria are insufficient for the task, the inhabitants of the nearer surrounding countries have the duty to assist them, while those of the more remote lands are free from this obligation.

Apply yourself to carry out the precept of jihad! Help one another in order to protect your religion and your brothers! Seize this opportunity and march forth against the unbelievers, for it does not require too great an effort and God has prepared you for it! . . . Commit jihad to make combat in your soul before committing jihad against your enemies because your souls are worse enemies for you than your foes. Turn your soul away from disobedience to its creator so that you would achieve the much desired victory. . . . Forsake the sins that you insist on committing and then begin to do good deeds. . . . Fight for God as He deserves it!

Source: Richard Lim and David Kammerling Smith, eds. *The West in the Wider World: Sources and Perspectives*, vol. 1 (2003): 278.

Krak des Chevaliers
This crusader castle survives in northern Syria in what was once the County of Edessa, a Latin Christian principality constructed to defend the Holy Land. The word *krak* derives from an Arabic word meaning "strong fort."

Legends of the Borderlands: Roland and El Cid

From the eighth to the fifteenth centuries, Muslim and Latin Christian armies grappled with one another in the borderlands between their two civilizations in the Iberian peninsula, the territory now called Spain. The borderlands, however, were more than just places of conflict. During times of peace, Christians and Muslims traded with and even married one another, and in the confused loyalties typical of the times, soldiers and generals from both faiths frequently switched sides. These borderland clashes produced legends of great heroes, which once refashioned into epic poems created a lasting memory of Muslim and Christian animosity.

The Song of Roland, an Old French epic poem that dates from around 1100, tells a story about the Battle of Roncesvalles, which took place in 778. The actual historical battle had been a minor skirmish between Charlemagne's armies and some local inhabitants in Spain who were not Muslims at all, but *The Song of Roland* transforms this sordid episode into a great epic of Christian-Muslim conflict. In the climax of the poem, the Christian hero Roland, seeking renown for his valor, rejects his companion Oliver's advice to blow a horn to alert Charlemagne of a Muslim attack. The battle is hopeless, and when the horn is finally sounded it is too late to save Roland or Oliver. Roland's recklessness made him the model of a brave Christian knight.

In the subsequent Spanish border wars, the most renowned soldier was Rodrigo Díaz de Vivar (ca. 1043–1099), known to history as El Cid (from the Arabic word for "lord"). He is remembered in legend as a heroic knight fighting for the Christian Reconquest of the peninsula, but the real story of El Cid was much more self-serving. El Cid repeatedly switched allegiances to the Muslims. Even when a major Muslim invasion from North Africa threatened the very existence of Christian Spain, El Cid did not come to the rescue and instead undertook a private adventure to carve out a kingdom for himself in Muslim Valencia.

Soon after El Cid's death and despite his inconstant loyalty to Castile and Christianity, he was elevated to the status of the great hero of Christian Spain. The popularity of the twelfth-century epic poem *The Poem of My Cid* transformed this cruel, vindictive, and utterly self-interested man into a model of Christian virtue and self-sacrificing loyalty.

The medieval borderlands created legends of heroism and epic struggles that often stretched the truth. The borderlands were a wild frontier, not unlike the American frontier, into which desperate men fled to hide or to make opportunities for themselves. However, the lasting significance of the violent encounters that took place in these borderlands is not the nasty realities but the heroic models they produced. Poetry transformed reality into a higher truth that emphasized courage and faithfulness. Because these poems were memorized and recited in the vernacular languages of Old French and Castilian (now Spanish), they became a model of aristocratic values in medieval society and over the centuries a source for a national literary culture. Thus, becoming French or Spanish meant, in some respects, rejecting Islam, which has created a lasting anti-Muslim strain in western European culture.

Question for Discussion

How did transforming the accounts of battles between Christian and Muslims into heroic poems change how these events would be remembered among Christians?

The Death of Roland
No legend from the borderlands between Christianity and Islam had a greater influence on European Christian society than that of Roland.

He hands his glove, symbolizing a knight's honor, to God the Father. The gesture captures the concept that God accepted Roland's sacrifice for Christianity.

With his horn he slays a Muslim warrior.

In this fourteenth-century illuminated chronicle of the reign of Charlemagne, Roland is shown mortally wounded.

the Crusade continued to spark the imagination of Latin Christians for centuries.

The Significance of the Crusades

Despite the capture of Jerusalem during the First Crusade, the crusaders could not maintain control of the city and for more than two centuries wasted enormous efforts on what proved to be a futile enterprise. Neither did any of the Latin principalities in the Middle East survive for very long. The crusaders who resided in these principalities were obliged to learn how to live and trade with their Muslim neighbors, but few of them learned Arabic or took seriously Muslim learning. The strongest Islamic cultural and intellectual influences on Christian Europe came through Sicily and Spain rather than via returning crusaders.

The most important immediate consequence of the Crusades was not the tenuous Western possession of the Holy Land but the expansion of trade and economic contacts the expeditions facilitated. No one profited more from the Crusades than the Italian cities that provided transportation and supplies to the crusading armies. During the Crusades, Genoa, Pisa, and Venice were transformed from small ports of regional significance into hubs of international trade. Genoa and Venice established their own colonial outposts in the eastern Mediterranean, and both vied to monopolize the rich commerce of Byzantium. The new trade controlled by these cities included luxury goods, such as silk, Persian carpets, medicine, and spices, all expensive, exotic consumer goods found in the bazaars of the Middle East. Profits from this trade helped galvanize the economy of western Europe, leading to an era of exuberant economic growth during the twelfth and thirteenth centuries.

During the Crusades Muslims and Christians mixed mutual curiosity with militant hostility. Their tentative appreciation of each other was undermined by grotesque misunderstandings. The complexity of the relationship became especially clear in spiritual centers such as the mosques and churches of Jerusalem. While Jerusalem was occupied by Christian crusaders, an Arab nobleman named Ousama made a business trip to Jerusalem. To fulfill the obligation of his Muslim faith to pray daily, Ousama went to the Al-Aksa mosque, the oldest Muslim shrine in Jerusalem. He was struck by the contrast between the crusaders who had resided in Jerusalem for some time and had an understanding of Islam and those who had just arrived and "show themselves more inhuman." Some of the old-timers had even befriended him and made certain he had a place to pray. But the newcomers were far less friendly. Ousama reported, "One day I went into [the mosque] and glorified

DOCUMENT

An Arab-Syrian Gentleman Discusses the Franks

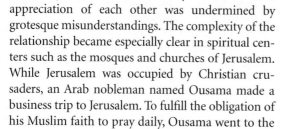

CHRONOLOGY

The Crusades

1071	Battle of Manzikert; Seljuk Turks defeat the Byzantine emperor
1095	Council of Clermont; Urban II calls First Crusade
1095–1099	First Crusade
1099	Christians capture Jerusalem
1147–1149	Second Crusade
1189–1192	Third Crusade, led by Emperor Frederick Barbarossa (who drowned), King Richard the Lion-Heart of England, and King Philip II of France
1202–1204	Fourth Crusade, culminates in capture of Constantinople by Western crusaders

Allah. I was engrossed in my praying when one of the Franks [as Muslims called all western Europeans] rushed at me, seized me and turned my face to the East, saying, 'That is how to pray!'" At that time Christians were supposed to pray facing the rising sun in the East. Muslims pray facing Mecca to the south of Jerusalem. On two occasions the Templars, members of the Christian military order who guarded the mosque, had to expel the zealous Frank from the mosque so Ousama could return to his prayers. The Templars apologized to Ousama, saying, "He is a stranger who has only recently arrived from Frankish lands. He has never seen anyone praying without turning to the East."

An uneasy familiarity developed among the Christians and Muslims in Jerusalem during this period. It was possible for an Arab such as Ousama to describe the Templars as his "friends," and they in turn protected him from the intolerance of the newly arrived Europeans. This peculiar mixture of friendliness and intolerance cut both ways. Ousama recounted another scene he witnessed at the Dome of the Rock, the place from which it was believed that Muhammad had ascended to heaven but which the crusaders had transformed into a Christian church. A Templar approached a Muslim and asked if he would like to see God as a child. When the Muslim answered "yes," the Templar displayed a painting of the Virgin Mary with the Christ child on her lap. The Muslims were shocked at the Christian's idolatry of referring to an image as God. Ousama exclaimed, "May Allah raise himself high above those who speak such impious things!"[5]

Conclusion

An Emerging Unity in the Latin West

The most lasting legacy of the Early Middle Ages was the distinction between western and eastern Europe, established by the patterns of conversion to Christianity. Slavs in eastern Europe, such as the Poles, who were converted to Latin Christianity looked to Rome as a source for inspiration and eventually considered themselves part of the West. Those who converted to Orthodox Christianity, such as the Bulgarians and Russians, remained Europeans certainly but came to see themselves as culturally distinct from their Western counterparts. The southern border of Christian Europe was defined by the presence of the Islamic caliphates, which, despite recurrent border wars with Christian kingdoms, greatly contributed to the cultural vitality of the West during this period.

During this same period, however, a tentative unity began to emerge among western European Christians, just as Byzantium fell into decline and Islam divided among competing caliphates. That ephemeral unity was born in the hero worship of Charlemagne and the resurrection of the Roman Empire in the West, symbolized by his coronation in Rome. The collapse of the Carolingian Empire created the basis for the European kingdoms that dominated the political order of Europe for most of the subsequent millennium. These new kingdoms were each quite distinctive, and yet they shared a heritage from ancient Rome and the Carolingians that emphasized the power of the law on the one hand and the intimate relationship between royal and ecclesiastical authority on the other. The most distinguishing mark of western Europe became the practice of Latin Christianity, a distinctive form of Christianity identifiable by the use of the Latin language and the celebration of the church liturgy in Latin.

In the wake of the Carolingian Empire, a system of personal loyalties associated with lordship and vassalage came to dominate the military and political life of Latin Christendom. All medieval kings were obliged to build their monarchies on the social foundations of lordship, which provided cohesion in kingdoms that lacked bureaucracies and sufficient numbers of trained officials. In addition to the lords and vassals the Latin kingdoms relied on the support of the Church to provide unity and often to provide the services of local government. By the end of the eleventh century, emerging western Europe had recovered sufficiently from the many destructive invaders and had built new political and ecclesiastical institutions that enabled it to assert itself on a broader stage. The first move was sensational: The leaders of the Latin Church declared their intention to achieve what the Byzantines had failed to do—recapture Jerusalem from Islam. With the Crusades, western Europeans began an aggressive engagement outside their own continent.

Suggestions for Further Reading

For a comprehensive listing of suggested readings, please go to www.ablongman.com/levack2e/chapter8

Bachrach, Bernard S. *Early Medieval Jewish Policy in Western Europe.* 1977. A significant revisionist view of the history of the Jews in Latin Christian Europe.

Bartlett, Robert. *The Making of Europe: Conquest, Colonization and Cultural Change: 950–1350.* 1993. The best, and often greatly stimulating, analysis of how Latin Christianity spread in post-Carolingian Europe.

Brown, Peter. *The Rise of Western Christendom: Triumph and Diversity* A.D. *200–1000.* 2001. A brilliant interpretation of the development of Christianity in its social context.

Cohen, Jeremy. *Living Letters of the Law: Ideas of the Jew in Medieval Christianity.* 1999. A masterful investigation of early medieval Judaism.

Geary, Patrick J. *The Peoples of Europe in the Early Middle Ages.* 2002. Discusses the emergence of the new kingdoms of Europe, stressing the incorporation of Roman elements.

Hollister, C. Warren. *Medieval Europe: A Short History.* 1997. This concise, crisply written text presents the development of Europe during the Middle Ages by charting its progression from a primitive rural society, sparsely settled and impoverished, to a powerful and distinctive civilization.

Jones, Gwyn. *A History of the Vikings.* 2001. A comprehensive, highly readable analysis.

Keen, Maurice, ed. *Medieval Warfare: A History.* 1999. Lucid specialist studies of aspects of medieval warfare.

Lawrence, C. H. *Medieval Monasticism.* 2001. A fine introduction to the phenomenon of Christian monasticism.

Mayr-Harting, Henry. *The Coming of Christianity to Anglo-Saxon England.* 1991. How a Germanic people were converted to Christianity.

McKitterick, Rosamond. *The Early Middle Ages.* 2001. The best up-to-date survey for the period 400–1000. It is composed of separate essays by leading specialists.

Moorhead, John. *The Roman Empire Divided, 400–700.* 2001. The best recent survey of the period.

Reuter, Timothy. *Germany in the Early Middle Ages, c. 800–1056.* 1991. A lucid explanation of the complexities of German history in this period.

Reynolds, Susan. *Fiefs and Vassals: The Medieval Evidence Reinterpreted.* 1994. The most important reexamination of the feudalism problem.

Riché, Pierre. *The Carolingians: A Family Who Forged Europe.* 1993. Translated from the 1983 French edition, this book traces the rise, fall, and revival of the Carolingian dynasty, and shows how it molded the shape of a post-Roman Europe that still prevails today. This is basically a family history, but the family dominated Europe for more than two centuries.

Riché, Pierre. *Education and Culture in the Barbarian West, Sixth Through Eighth Centuries,* translated from the 3rd French ed.

by John J. Contreni. 1975. Demonstrates the rich complexity of learning during this period, once thought to be the Dark Ages of education.

Riley-Smith, Jonathan Simon Christopher. *The Crusades: A Short History.* 1987. Exactly what the title says.

Riley-Smith, Jonathan Simon Christopher. *The Oxford Illustrated History of the Crusades.* 2001. An utterly engaging, comprehensive study.

Stenton, Frank M. *Anglo-Saxon England.* 2001. This classic history covers the period ca. 550–1087 and traces the development of English society from the oldest Anglo-Saxon laws and kings to the extension of private lordship.

Strayer, Joseph B., ed. *Dictionary of the Middle Ages.* 1986. An indispensable reference work.

Webster, Leslie, and Michelle Brown, eds. *The Transformation of the Roman World, A.D. 400–900.* 1997. A well-illustrated synthesis with maps and bibliography.

Wickham, Chris. *Early Medieval Italy: Central Government and Local Society, 400–1000.* 1981. Examines the economic and social transformation of Italy.

Notes

1. Willibald, *The Life of Boniface,* in Clinton Albertson, trans., *Anglo-Saxon Saints and Heroes* (1967), 308–310.

2. Kent Rigsby, *Zeitschrift für Papyrologie and Epigraphik,* 126 (1999), 175–176.

3. Quoted in Edward Peters, *Europe and the Middle Ages* (1989), 158.

4. Fulcher of Chartres, *Historia Hierosolymitana,* ed. Heinrich Hagenmeyer (1913), 202–203.

5. *The Autobiography of Ousama* (1995–1188), trans. G. R. Potter, in Brian Tierney, ed., *The Middle Ages,* Vol. 1: *Sources of Medieval History,* 3rd ed. (1978), 162.

Medieval Civilization: The Rise of Western Europe

FRANCIS OF ASSISI (CA. 1182–1226) WAS THE SON OF A PROSPEROUS MERchant in a modest-sized town in central Italy. As a young man of 20, Francis joined his friends and neighbors as a member of the Assisi forces in a war with the nearby town of Perugia. Taken prisoner, he spent nearly a year in captivity; on his release he became seriously ill, the first of many painful illnesses that afflicted him periodically throughout his life. During a journey to join another army, he had the first of his many visions or dreams that led him to give up fighting and to convert to a life of spirituality and service to others. Initially he searched about for what to do. He went on a pilgrimage to Rome as a beggar, and although lepers personally disgusted him he not only gave alms to a leper but kissed his hand. Then, according to his earliest biographer, while praying in the dilapidated chapel of San Damiano outside the gates of Assisi, he received a direct command from the crucifix above the altar: "Go Francis, and repair my house which, as you see, is nearly in ruins."

At first, Francis understood this command literally and began to repair churches and chapels. To raise money he took some of the best cloth from his father's shop and rode off to a nearby town where he sold the cloth and the horse. When the priest of San Damiano rejected the funds, Francis threw the money out the window. Angered by the theft of cloth, his father denounced him to the town's authorities, and when Francis refused the summons to court, his father had him brought to be interrogated by the bishop of Assisi. Before his father could say anything to the bishop, Francis "without a word stripped off his clothing even removing his pants and gave them back to his father." Stark naked, Francis announced that he was switching his obedience from his earthly to his heavenly father. The astonished bishop gave him a cloak, but Francis renounced all family ties and worldly goods to live a life of complete poverty. Henceforth, he seemed to understand the command to "repair my house" as a metaphor for the entire Church, which he intended to serve in a new way.

Interior of a Gothic Cathedral The narrow columns and pointed arches of the Gothic style drew the worshipers' eyes upward toward Heaven. The play of light from the stained-glass windows created mysterious visual effects.

Dressed in rags, he went about town begging for food, preaching repentance in the streets, and ministering to outcasts and lepers. Without training as a priest or license as a preacher, Francis at first seemed like a devout eccentric or even a dangerous heretic, but his rigorous imitation of Jesus began to attract like-minded followers. In 1210 Francis and twelve of his ragged brothers showed up in the opulent papal court of Pope Innocent III seeking approval of Francis's rule for a new religious order. A less discerning man than Innocent would have sent the strange band packing or thrown them in prison as a danger to established society, but Innocent was impressed by Francis's sincerity and his willingness to profess obedience to the pope. Innocent's provisional approval of the Franciscans was a brilliant stroke, in that it gave the papacy a way to manage the widespread enthusiasm for a life of spirituality and purity.

The life of Francis of Assisi and the religious order he founded, the Friars Minor (Lesser Brothers), known as the Franciscans, epitomized the strengths and tensions of medieval Europe. Francis was a product of the newly prosperous towns of Europe, which began to grow at an unprecedented rate after about 1050. In the streets of the towns like Assisi that thrived on profits from the international cloth trade, the extremes of wealth and poverty were always on display. Rich merchants such as Francis's father lived in splendid comfort and financed an urban building boom that had not been seen in the West for more than a thousand years. The most lasting manifestations of that building boom were the vast new cathedrals, the pride of every medieval city. At the same time wretchedly poor people, many of them immigrants from the overpopulated countryside, starving, and homeless, lined the steps into the great churches begging for alms. Francis abhorred the immorality of this contrast between wealth and poverty. His reaction was to reject all forms of wealth, to give away all his possessions, and to distain money as if it were some kind of poison. He and his followers devoted themselves to the poor and abandoned. They became traveling street preachers who relied entirely on the charity of others for food and shelter. Francis's rejection of the material world was not just a protest against the materialist values of his times. It was a total denial of the self, or to put it in modern terms, a rejection of all forms of egotism.

In a period that placed great emphasis on hierarchic authority and on the privileges of rank in both society and the Church, Francis insisted on absolute equality within his order. Unlike other orders in which the educated, aristocratic monks prayed and sang while the uneducated lay brothers performed physical labor, the Franciscans made no distinctions on the basis of learning or social rank among its members. Francis's commitment to equality was stunningly revolutionary for his times. Just as revolutionary was his brave commitment to convert the Muslims through persuasion rather than force. During Francis's lifetime, crusaders from western Europe had been fighting Muslims on and off for more than a century. After several attempts to travel to Muslim lands, Francis went to Egypt, where crusaders were besieging Damietta. He managed to enter the Muslim camp and preached to the sultan himself, who was reportedly so impressed that he gave Francis permission to travel to the Holy Land.

Based on the efforts of the knights who fought in the Crusades, European merchants, and Latin Christian preachers and thinkers, the Catholic West began to assert itself militarily, economically, and intellectually both in Byzantium and against the Muslim world. As a result, western Europeans more sharply distinguished themselves from the Orthodox and Muslim worlds. The West became more exclusively Latin and Catholic.

St. Francis of Assisi Asks Pope Innocent III for a License to Preach
The drama of the meeting between the simple brothers shown kneeling, presenting their rule to the pope, and the sumptuous prelates of the curia is captured by the greatest of all medieval painters, Giotto. This fresco was painted in the Franciscan church in Assisi shortly before 1300.

The consolidation of a distinctive Western identity and the projection of Western power outside Europe were made possible by internal developments within Europe. The agricultural revolution of the eleventh century stimulated population growth and urbanization. Fed by more productive farms, the expanding cities began to produce industrial goods, such as woolen cloth, that could be sold abroad in exchange for luxury goods from the Middle East and Asia. A number of vigorous kings created political stability in the West by consolidating their authority through financial and judicial bureaucracies. The most effective of these kings used a variety of strategies to force the most dangerous element in society, the landed aristocrats, to serve the royal interest. At the same time, the West experienced a period of creative ferment unequaled since antiquity. The Roman Catholic Church played a central role in encouraging intellectual and artistic activity, but there was also a flourishing literature in the vernacular languages such as French, German, and Italian. All these developments lead to the question, how did western European civilization mature during the eleventh through thirteenth centuries?

- How was medieval western European economy and society organized around manors and cities?
- How did the Catholic Church consolidate its hold over the Latin West?
- How did the western European monarchies strengthen themselves?
- What made western European culture distinctive?

Two Worlds: Manors and Cities

- How was medieval western European economy and society organized around manors and cities?

After the end of the destructive Magyar and Viking invasions of the ninth and tenth centuries, the population of western Europe recovered dramatically. Technological innovations created the agricultural revolution° that increased the supply of food. With more food available, people were better nourished than they had been in more than 500 years. As a result of more and better food, the population began to grow. In the seventh century all of Europe was home to only 14 million inhabitants. Much of the land cultivated in the ancient world had reverted to wild forests, simply because there were not enough people left to farm it due to the deaths from plague and the Germanic invasions. By 1300 the population had exploded to 74 million. From the seventh to the fourteenth centuries, then, the population grew many times over, perhaps as much as 500 percent. The most dramatic signs of population growth began after the year 1000.

The Medieval Agricultural Revolution

At the beginning of the eleventh century, the vast majority of people lived in small villages or isolated farmsteads. Peasants literally scratched out a living from a small area of cleared land around the village by employing a light scratch plow that barely turned over the soil. The farms produced mostly grain, which was consumed as bread, porridge, and ale or beer. Vegetables were rare, meat and fish uncommon. Over the course of the century, the productivity of the land was greatly enhanced by a number of innovations that came into widespread use.

Technological Innovations

The invention of new labor-saving devices ushered in the power revolution. This development, which occurred in the

A Scratch Plow

This illumination, dated 1028 from the Abbey of Montecassino in Italy, depicts the labor of the four seasons. The plowman on the right uses a light, unwheeled scratch plow that could not dig deeply into the soil, providing less efficient aeration than the heavy *carruca* plow, which was introduced later in the eleventh century.

tenth to twelfth centuries, harnessed the first new sources of power since the domestication of oxen and the invention of the ship in the ancient world. There would not be a technological discovery of similar magnitude until the development of steam power in the eighteenth century. Perhaps the most notable innovation was the exploitation of non-animal sources of power from water and wind. The water mill was invented in late Roman times, but it came into widespread use only in the tenth and eleventh centuries. Water mills were first used to grind grain but were gradually adapted to a wide variety of tasks, including turning saws to mill timber. By the end of the twelfth century windmills also began to appear, which were used for similar purposes.

As important as the harnessing of water and wind power was the enhanced ability to use animal power. Knights began to breed large, powerful war-horses. They equipped their horses with metal armor and stirrups, which kept knights on their horses, and metal horseshoes (until then, horses' hooves had been bound in cloth), which gave horses better footing and traction. The exploitation of power of animals also became more efficient with the introduction of a new type of horse collar, which increased the animal's pulling power. Earlier collars fit tightly around a horse's neck, which choked the animal if it pulled too great a weight. The new collar transferred the pressure points from the throat to the shoulders. Originally devised to make horses more effective at fighting, the collar was adapted to make both horses and oxen more efficient farm draft animals. With enhanced animal pulling power, farmers could plow the damp, heavy clay soils of northern Europe much more efficiently.

The centerpiece of the agricultural revolution was the heavy plow, which replaced the widely used Mediterranean scratch plow. Developed for light, sandy soils that were easily broken up, the scratch plow was barely able to dig into the poorly drained soils of the northern European plain.

The heavy plow had several distinctive advantages. It cut through and lifted the soil, aerating it and bringing to the surface minerals vital for plant growth. It created a furrow that channeled drainage, preventing the fields from being flooded by the frequent rains of northern Europe. The heavy plow was very cumbersome, however. It required six or eight horses or oxen to pull it, and no single peasant family in the tenth or eleventh century was able to afford that many draft animals. Farmers had to pool their animals to create plow teams, a practice that required mutual planning and cooperation. A two-wheeled heavy plow pulled by a team of eight oxen was difficult to turn, which meant it was best to continue plowing in a straight line for as long as possible. Thus, the heavy plow required peasants to cooperate further in redesigning their fields—from compact square fields, which had been cross-plowed with the older scratch plow, to long narrow fields that minimized the number of turns and provided a headland at the end to permit the draft team to make a wide turn. The new plow created the elongated fields that were distinctive to northern Europe.

The necessity to replenish the soil meant that half the arable land lay fallow while the other half was planted with crops. The fields would be reversed in the following year. In northern Europe farm animals were allowed to graze in the fallow field, what was called the open field, leaving their manure to recondition its soil. This practice, the two-field system, was gradually supplanted by the three-field system. In the three-field system one field was planted in the fall with grain; one was planted in the spring with beans, peas, or lentils; and one lay fallow. Both fall and spring plantings were harvested in the summer, after which all the fields shifted. The open three-field system produced extraordinary advantages: the amount of land under cultivation was increased from one-half to two-thirds; beans planted in the spring rotation returned nitrogen to the soil; and the crop

A Heavy *Carruca* Plow

At the center of the two-wheeled plow is a sturdy timber from which the coulter projects just in front of the plowshare, which is hidden by the earth.

rotation combined with animal manure reduced soil exhaustion from excessive grain planting.

The agricultural revolution had a significant effect on society. First, villagers learned to cooperate—by pooling draft animals for plow teams, redesigning and elongating their fields, coordinating the three-field rotation of crops, and timing the harvest schedule. To accomplish these cooperative ventures, they created village councils and developed habits of collective decision making that were essential for stable community life. Second, the system produced not only more food, but better food. Beans and other vegetables grown in the spring planting were rich in proteins. Slaughtering cattle for meat was still out of the question for peasants, but a plate of beans had a nutritional value similar to that of beef.

Manors and Peasants

The medieval agricultural economy bound landlords and peasants together in a unit of management called the manor. A manor referred to the holding of a single lord and the community of farmers who worked it. A single village might be divided up to serve several small manors, or a large manor might draw from several villages. Some lords possessed several manors and traveled from one to another throughout the year. The lord of the manor usually had his own large house or stone castle and served as the presiding judge of the community. However, most lords probably did not dictate what happened at the sessions of the manor court, which probably functioned as a kind of village meeting in most cases. Although the lord was clearly the social superior of the peasants on his manor, he could not rule effectively without their cooperation. The lord typically appointed the priest of the parish church and was responsible for enforcing church attendance and maintaining the church buildings. The parish priest worked land loaned to him by the lord in exchange for his religious services to the village and manor.

Unlike in the ancient world, in which slaves performed most of the heavy farm work, slaves seldom worked on farms during the Middle Ages. A much more common status for a farm worker or peasant was that of serf. Unlike slaves, serfs° were not owned, but they were tied to a specific manor, which they could not leave. They had certain legal rights denied slaves, such as the right to a certain portion of what they produced, but they were obliged to subject themselves to the lord's will. In theory, at least, the relationship between the lord and his serfs was reciprocal. The lord supplied the land, sometimes tools and seed, and protection from invaders and bandits. In return serfs supplied the labor necessary to work the land. Serfs were most common in England and northern France.

There were also peasants, known as freeholders, who worked as independent farmers and owned their land outright. Freeholders appeared in Scandinavia, northern Germany, southern France, Switzerland, and northern Italy. In many villages of Europe freeholders could be found scattered among larger communities of serfs.

At the bottom of rural peasant society were the numerous impoverished cottagers who farmed smaller plots of land than serfs or free peasants but who did not have the right to pass the land down to succeeding generations as serfs and free peasants did. Even serfdom, which was onerous, was preferable to being a cottager or completely landless; at least serfdom provided peasants with the means to feed themselves and their families.

The most important social units on a medieval manor were families who worked the land together, each member performing tasks suitable to their abilities, strength, and age. The rigors of medieval farm labor did not permit a fastidious division of labor between women and men. Women did not usually drive the heavy plow, but they toiled at other physically demanding tasks. The life of one young girl—documented because she later achieved sainthood as Saint Alpaix—was probably typical. From age 12, Alpaix

Twelfth-Century Manor Made Possible by the Heavy Plow

Aerial photograph of the manor of West Whelpington North (England), which was settled in the twelfth century but whose inhabitants died out during the Black Death of the fourteenth century (see Chapter 10). Outlines of the individual families' farm gardens can be seen in the left center. On the lower right are the ridges and furrows of the elongated fields required by the use of the heavy plow.

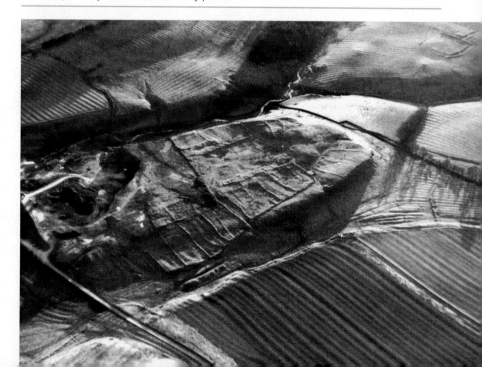

worked with her father in the fields, carrying heavy baskets of manure and sheep dung to fertilize the garden. When her arms became exhausted, she was harnessed to a sledge by a rope so that she could drag manure to the fields. During the critical harvest times, women and children worked alongside men from dawn to dusk. Young girls typically worked as gleaners, picking up the stalks and kernels that the male harvesters dropped or left behind, and girls were responsible for weeding and cleaning the fields. Before the use of water mills and windmills, women ground the grain by hand.

The Great Migrations and the Hunger for Land

During the Middle Ages most peasant families, whether serfs or freeholders, were considerably better off than had been their ancestors before the new technological innovations. After the agricultural revolution nutritional levels improved so dramatically that the condition of permanent famine that had plagued Europe for centuries was over. At first the population seems to have grown through a decrease in death rates but after 1100 a "baby boom" led to even greater increases in the population.

The effect of the baby boom meant that the amount of land available to farm was insufficient to support the expanding population of the manors. As more and more young people entered the workforce, they either sought opportunities in the cities or sought land of their own. Both options meant that many young people and whole families had to migrate. On the rutted old Roman roads and the paths that had sprung up where the roads did not go was a continuous traffic of travelers—the younger sons of nobles, demobilized soldiers, merchants, monks, pilgrims, and innumerable peasants—all moving from village to village, from village to town, and even to distant lands. For example, in an English village in 1247 there were forty-seven heads of families, three of whom were recent immigrants. Among their sons twelve boys went away to join the Church, seven sought jobs in town, twenty-four wandered off to places unknown in search of their fortunes, and only twenty-three were still there. In other words, two-thirds of the boys left home. Among the daughters twenty-seven, a little less than half, married outside the village.

Where did all these people go? At first, many invaded the "common lands." Surrounding every cultivated manor were common lands consisting of pastures, wetlands, scrub, and forests, reserved to common use. Cattle grazed in the pastures, anyone could gather reeds or berries in the wetlands or scrub, and the forests supplied wood for fuel and building materials as well as forage for pigs. The common lands, especially the scrub and forests, were the first to be cleared and put under the plow to grow more grain. Some of these lands had been plowed in ancient times but allowed to revert to the forest during the centuries of declining and stagnant population before 1000. Other clearings pushed into virgin forests and mountain slopes that had been avoided because of the difficulty of farming them. But another solution was also at hand: invading someone else's land.

Migrants seeking to clear new lands for agriculture moved in three directions: Germans into the Slavic lands to the east, Scandinavians to the far north and north Atlantic islands, and Christian Spaniards to the south into previously Muslim territories. In east-central Europe Germanic and Slavic-speaking peoples had fought for centuries for control of the productive farm lands. Up until about 1100 the struggle had been fairly balanced, especially after Poland unified and became Christian. During the twelfth and thirteenth centuries, however, the balance decisively shifted in favor of the Germans, who launched a concerted assault on Polish lands. The German invasion of Poland involved the most dramatic example of racism found in the Middle Ages as the Poles, despite their conversion to Christianity, were described in propaganda as "pagans" and "repulsive beasts." The German peasants who migrated had military support and were encouraged by ambitious princes with names such as Albert the Bear and Henry the Lion. The German movement eastward was steady and relentless, especially after the crusading knights of the Teutonic Order spread fire and sword across northern Poland into Estonia until they completely cut off the rest of Poland from access to the sea. To attract immigrants in these newly acquired lands, peasants were offered lower feudal dues than in Germany and granted very large plots. Scattered across Poland and Bohemia, German-speaking villages sprung up that were autonomous enough to ignore the laws of the host country.

In the north Vikings in the ninth, tenth, and early eleventh centuries had raided and invaded deep into northern Europe and the British Isles and had established settlements as far as Normandy in France and Sicily, where they had taken over already occupied lands. When Vikings arrived in Iceland there was not a single living soul there and in Greenland only a few Eskimos from Baffin Island. After 1100 their descendants in Scandinavia launched a new phase of expansion as they cleared lands for farming on the Scandinavian peninsula, which except for Denmark was barely settled at all. During the twelfth and thirteenth centuries, families hungry for land pushed into the inland forests of Scandinavia and up the coast of Norway. Because of the difficulties of living in the far north, these villages were almost completely independent from obligations to the king and created strong collective obligations, unknown elsewhere in the West.

Whereas the Germans killed off or drove away the Poles, and the Scandinavians cleared uninhabited lands, in Spain a very different kind of process took place. Chapters 7 and 8 discussed the Spanish Reconquest, the military efforts of the Christian kings of northern Spain to reconquer the parts of southern and central Spain under Muslim caliphates. The Reconquest was a military and ideological enterprise that lasted from the eleventh to fifteenth centuries, but in the van of the soldiers followed a much more peaceful process of settlement and assimilation. Once the caliphs were defeated, massacres and expulsions of Muslims ceased as Christian settlers moved into the newly reconquered lands. The population was regrouped into separate Muslim and Christian neighborhoods and villages, and with much less violence than the Germans in Poland, Christian Spaniards migrated into formerly Muslim lands in large numbers.

Between 1100 and 1300, while the population was growing enormously, between 15 and 40 percent more land was brought under cultivation in Europe. The new land either had been untouched for farming as in northern Scandinavia or was taken from peoples who had lived on the borders of Latin Christendom, especially in the East. As Chapter 10 discusses, by about 1300 all the new lands potentially available for cultivation were gone. At that point the ability of Europe to sustain its population growth was compromised and a massive demographic catastrophe followed in the fourteenth century. However, the vibrant civilization discussed in the rest of this chapter was the direct consequence of the European demographic success of the eleventh through thirteenth centuries.

The Growth of Cities

Before the eleventh century the vast majority of people in Europe lived on manors, in rural villages, or perhaps in small market towns of a few thousand people. The cities that survived from the ancient world remained small, except in the Mediterranean. Constantinople was by far the largest city, with a population in the hundreds of thousands. The vibrant Islamic cities of Spain were the largest in western Europe, and it was said that more people could fit into the mosque of Córdoba than lived in Rome. When the population began to grow as a consequence of the agricultural revolution, migrants from the manors and villages swelled the small market towns into cities and repopulated the few cities that had survived from antiquity.

The Challenge of Free Cities

The newly thriving cities proved to be troublesome for the lords, bishops, and kings who usually had legal authority over them. As the population grew and urban merchants, such as Francis of Assisi's father, became increasingly rich, the cities in which they lived enjoyed even greater resources in people and money than those available to the rural lords. In many places the citizens of the new enlarged towns attempted to rid themselves of their lords to establish self-rule or, at least, substantial autonomy for their city. In the cities of north-central Italy, for example, the prominent townsmen began to chafe at the violent authority the rural lords held over them. The lords taxed or even stole the wealth that the townsmen earned through manufacturing

and trade. The lords made life unsafe and unbearable, fighting among themselves and abusing the unarmed townsmen. To counter the power of the lords, townsmen formed sworn defensive associations called communes°, which quickly became the effective government of the towns. The communes evolved into city-states, which were self-governing cities that became small states by seizing control of the surrounding countryside. Perhaps as many as a hundred or more cities in north-central Italy formed communes after 1070.

The Italian communes created the institutions and culture of self-rule. They were not fully democratic, but in many of them a significant percentage of the male population, including artisans, could vote for public officials, hold office themselves, and have a voice in important decisions such as going to war or raising new taxes. They also developed a new ethic that emphasized the civic responsibilities of citizens to protect the weakest members of the community, to beautify the city with public buildings and monuments, and to defend it by serving in the militia and paying taxes. These cities created vital and lasting community institutions, some of which survive to this day.

Outside Italy the movement for urban liberty was strongest in southern France, the Christian parts of Spain, and the Netherlands. Kings fiercely resisted attempts to establish urban autonomy. Especially in northern Europe, urban liberty was often extracted at a high price. Townsmen bought their freedom by agreeing to pay higher taxes to kings, who were always desperate for cash. London, an ancient Roman city that revived by the end of the eleventh century, bartered with several kings for civic autonomy, which it never entirely achieved.

In the wake of the Crusades several north Italian cities, especially Venice, Genoa, and Pisa, became ports of international significance. Sailors from these cities had transported the Crusading knights to the Holy Land, Egypt, Syria, and Byzantium. Even after the Latin kingdoms of the Levant collapsed, these cities kept footholds in the eastern Mediterranean, some of which evolved into colonies. Through these trading cities western Europe became integrated into the international luxury trade, which they carried out with ships crisscrossing the Mediterranean. By the thirteenth century the Italian shipping merchants began to challenge the domination of the Muslim caravan trade.

The Economic Boom Years

The cities of the medieval West thrived on an economic base of unprecedented prosperity. What made possible the twelfth- and thirteenth-century economic boom? Besides the agricultural revolution of the eleventh century that enabled population growth, three other factors proved crucial.

First, there were advances in transportation networks. Trade in grain, woolen cloth, and other bulk goods depended on the use of relatively cheap water transportation for hauling goods. Where there were neither seaports nor

A Medieval Town
Painted on the wall of the city council chambers in Siena, Italy, this fresco from 1338–1339 depicts what a well-governed medieval town should look like. Workers repair buildings, merchants bring goods into the bustling city, students quietly study, and the streets are so safe that young women dance in the streets on their way to a wedding.

navigable rivers, goods had to be hauled cross-country by pack train, a very expensive enterprise. In western Europe there were no land transportation routes or pack animals that rivaled the efficiency of the camel in the deserts of North Africa and the steppes of Asia. To address the problem and to facilitate transportation and trade, new roads and bridges were built, and old Roman roads that had been neglected for a thousand years were repaired. These improvements, however, were unevenly distributed, leaving large parts of Europe without any effective form of transportation. Many roads were little more than rutted tracks, blocked in places by bogs of mud or fallen trees. Few lords or cities were willing to make the investment to repair the roads and clear the blockages. Without a cheap way to move grain to places of scarcity, one village could be suffering from famine while another nearby enjoyed a surplus.

The most lucrative trade was the international commerce in luxury goods. Because these goods were lightweight and high-priced, they could sustain the cost of long-distance transportation across land. Italian merchants virtually monopolized the European luxury trade. The Genoese distributed rare alum—the fixing agent for dyeing cloth—from the west coast of Asia Minor to the entire European cloth industry. Venetians and Genoese imported cotton from the Middle East. Raw silk, transported aboard camel caravans from China and Turkestan, was sold at trading posts on the shores of the Black Sea and in Constantinople to Italian merchants who shipped the goods across the Mediterranean and then earned enormous profits selling shimmering silk fabric to the ladies and gentlemen of the western European aristocracy. The silk trade was quite small in quantity, but it was of great value to international commerce because silk was so highly prized. One ounce of fine Chinese black silk sold on the London market for as much as a highly skilled mason would earn in a week's labor.

Rubies, pearls, coral, and diamonds were also easily transported for fantastic profits. Marco Polo of Venice, for example, specialized in trading jewels, which he sewed into the linings of his clothing for safety when he trekked across Asia from Venice to China and back. During the thirteenth century, he was one of countless European merchants who crisscrossed the caravan routes of Asia and North Africa. Italian merchant fleets sailed the Mediterranean, but transportation from the European ports in the Mediterranean to northern Europe still employed costly pack trains traversing the Alpine passes north. By the end of the thirteenth century, however, first Genoese and then other Italian fleets regularly ventured beyond the Straits of Gibraltar into the stormy Atlantic, dramatically improving transportation between northern and southern Europe.

Even the bulk commodities the Italians brought from the East were valuable enough to sustain the high transportation costs. Known by the generic term "spices," these included hundreds of exotic items: True spices such as pepper, sugar, cloves, nutmeg, ginger, saffron, mace, and cinnamon were used to enhance the otherwise boring, bland cuisine; for dyeing cloth indigo was used for blue and madder root for red; and medicinal herbs including opiates were used as pain relievers. The profits from spices generated most of the capital in European financial markets.

The second factor responsible for the economic boom of the twelfth and thirteenth centuries was the creation of new business techniques that long-distance trade necessitated. For example, the expansion of trade and new markets required a moneyed economy. Coins had almost disappeared in the West for nearly 400 years during the Early Middle Ages, when most people lived self-sufficiently on manors and bartered for what they could not produce for themselves. The few coins that circulated came from Byzantium or the Muslim caliphates. By the thirteenth century Venice and Florence were minting their own gold coins, which became the medium for exchange across much of Europe.

Merchants who engaged in long-distance trade began to develop the essential business tools of capitalism during this period. They created business partnerships, uniform accounting practices, merchants' courts to enforce contracts and resolve disputes, letters of credit (used like modern traveler's checks), bank deposits and loans, and even insurance policies. The Italian cities established primary schools to train merchants' sons to write business letters and keep accounts—a sign of the growing professional character of business. Two centuries earlier an international merchant had been an itinerant peddler who led pack trains over dusty and muddy tracks to customers in small villages and castles. But by the end of the thirteenth century an international merchant could stay at home behind a desk, writing letters to business partners and ship captains and enjoying the profits from his labors in the bustling atmosphere of a thriving city.

At the center of the European market were the Champagne fairs in France, where merchants from northern and southern Europe met every summer to bargain and haggle (see Map 9.1). The Italians exchanged their spices for English raw wool, Dutch woolen cloth, German furs and linens, and Spanish leather. From the Champagne fairs, prosperity spread into previously wild parts of Europe. Cities along the German rivers and the Baltic coast thrived through the trade of raw materials such as timber and iron, livestock, salt fish, and hides. The most prominent of the North German towns was Lübeck, which became the center of a loose trade association of cities in Germany and the Baltic coast known as the Hanseatic League. Never achieving the level of a unified government, the league nonetheless provided its members mutual security and trading monopolies—necessary because of the weakness of the German imperial government.

The third factor in the economic prosperity of the period was the cities themselves. Cities both facilitated the commercial boom and were the primary beneficiaries of it. All across Europe, especially in Flanders, the Netherlands, and north-central Italy, cities exploded in size from what they had been. Exact population figures are difficult to determine, and by contemporary standards most of these cities were modest in size—numbering in the tens of thousands rather than hundreds of thousands—but there is ample evidence of stunning growth. Between 1160 and 1300 Ghent had to expand its city walls five times to accommodate all its inhabitants. During the thirteenth century the population of Florence grew by an estimated 640 percent.

Urban civilization, one of the major achievements of the Middle Ages, was an outgrowth of commerce. From urban civilization came other achievements. All the cities built a large new cathedral to flaunt their accumulated wealth and to honor God. New educational institutions, especially universities, trained the sons of the urban, commercial elite in

Map 9.1   European Fairs and Trade Routes

Trade routes crisscrossed the Mediterranean Sea and hugged the Atlantic Ocean, North Sea, and Baltic Sea coastlines. Land routes converged in central France at the Champagne fairs. Other trade routes led to the large market cities in Germany and Flanders.

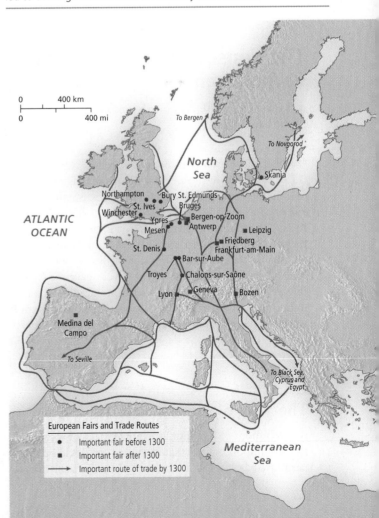

the professions. However, these merchants who commanded the booming urban economy were not necessarily society's heroes. The populace at large viewed them with deep ambivalence, despite the immeasurable ways in which they enriched society. The landed aristocrats treated merchants with withering disdain even when forced to borrow money from them and to tax them to finance grandiose expenditures. Many merchants themselves were ambivalent about trade and aspired to retire as soon as they could afford to buy land and take up life as a country gentleman.

Churchmen worried about the morality of making profits. Church councils condemned usury—the lending of money for interest—even though papal finances depended on it. Theologians promulgated the idea of a "just price," the idea that there should be a fixed price for any particular commodity. The just price was anathema to hardheaded merchants who were committed to the laws of supply and demand. Part of the ambivalence toward trade and merchants came from the inequities created in all market-based economies—the rewards of the market were unevenly distributed, both socially and geographically. The prosperous merchants were the most visible signs of puzzling social changes, but they were also the dynamic force that made possible the intellectual and artistic flowering of the High Middle Ages.

The Consolidation of Roman Catholicism

■ How did the Catholic Church consolidate its hold over the Latin West?

The late eleventh through thirteenth centuries witnessed one of the greatest periods of religious vitality in the history of Roman Catholicism. Manifest by the rise of new religious orders, remarkable intellectual creativity, and the final triumphant battle with the surviving polytheistic tribes of northern and eastern Europe, the religious vitality of the era was due in no small part to the effective leadership of a series of able popes. They gave the Church the benefits of the most advanced, centralized government in Europe. However, the papacy's successful intervention in worldly affairs helped undermine its spiritual authority, opening the way to the degradation of the papacy in the fourteenth century.

The Task of Church Reform

As the bishops of the Church accepted many of the administrative responsibilities that in the ancient world had been performed by secular authorities, their spiritual mission sometimes suffered. They become overly involved in the business of the world. In addition, over the centuries many wealthy and pious people had made large donations of land to the Church, making many monasteries, in particular, immensely wealthy. Such wealth tempted the less pious to corruption, and some of the Roman popes who had benefited from the wealth of the Church were reluctant to promote reforms that would have reduced corruption. Even those who wanted to eliminate the temptations of wealth were slow to assemble the administrative machinery necessary to enforce their will across the unruly lands of Latin Christianity.

As discussed in Chapter 8, Pope Gregory the Great (r. 590–604) became the moral guidepost of the western Church and the model for a strong papacy. But after Gregory the papacy gradually fell into a degraded moral state. Popes were caught in a web of scandal spun by the ambitious aristocratic families of Rome that involved the theft of church property, sexual intrigue, and even murder. During the tenth century the Crescentii family became the virtual dictators of papal administration, were rumored to have murdered popes who got in their way, and set members of their own clan on the papal throne. The slow but determined progress of the popes from the eleventh to thirteenth centuries to regain prominence as moral reformers is one of the most remarkable achievements of the medieval papacy.

The movement for reform, however, did not begin with the popes. The idea and energy for the reform of the Church came out of the monasteries. Monks thought the best way to clean up corruption in the Church would be to improve the morals of individuals. If men and women conducted themselves with a sense of moral responsibility, the whole institution of the Church could be purified. The model for self-improvement was that provided by monks and nuns themselves, who set an example for the rest of the Church and for society at large. The most influential of the reform-minded monasteries was that of Cluny° in Burgundy, which was established in 910. Cluny itself became the center of a far-reaching reform movement that was sustained in more than 1,500 Cluniac monasteries.

From the very beginning Cluny was exceptional, for several reasons. First, its aristocratic founder offered the monastery as a gift to the pope. As a result, it was directly connected to Rome and completely independent from local political pressures, which so often caused corruption. The Rome connection positioned Cluniacs to assist in reforming the papacy itself. Second, the various abbots who headed Cluny over the years closely coordinated reform activities of the various monasteries in the Cluniac system. Some of these abbots were men of exceptional ability and learning who had a European-wide reputation for their moral stature. Third, Cluny regulated the life of monks much more closely than did other monasteries, so the monks there were models of devotion. To the Cluniacs moral purity required as complete a renunciation of the benefits of the material world as possible and a commitment to stimulating spiritual experiences. Cluniac purity was symbolized by the elegantly simple liturgy in which the monks themselves sung the text of the mass and other prayers. The beauty of the music enhanced the spiritual experience, and its simplicity clarified rather than obscured the meaning of the words. The Cluniac liturgy spread to the far corners of Europe.

The success of Cluny and other reformed monasteries provided the base from which reform ideas spread beyond the isolated world of monks to the rest of the Church. The first candidates for reform were parish priests and bishops. Called the *secular clergy* (in Latin *saeculum,* meaning "secular") because they lived in the secular world, they differed from the regular clergy (in Latin *regula,* those who followed a "rule") who lived in monasteries apart from the world. The lives of many secular clergy differed little from their lay neighbors. (*Laypeople* or *the laity* referred to all Christians who had not taken religious vows to become a priest, monk, or nun.) In contrast to celibate monks, who were sexually chaste, many priests kept concubines or were married and tried to bequeath church property to their children. In contrast to the Orthodox Church, in which priests were allowed to marry, the Roman Church had repeatedly forbidden married priests, but the prohibitions had been ineffective until Cluniac reform stressed the ideal of the sexually pure priest. During the eleventh century Roman bishops, church councils, and reformist popes began to insist on a celibate clergy.

The other objective of the clerical reform movement was the elimination of the corrupt practices of simony and lay investiture. Simony° was the practice of buying and selling church offices. Lay investiture° took place when nobles, kings, or emperors actually installed churchmen and gave them their symbols of office ("invested" them). Through this practice, the powerful laity dominated the clergy and usurped the property of the Church for their own use. Many nobles conceived of church offices as a form of vassalage and expected to be able to name their own candidates as priests and bishops in exchange for protecting the Church. The reformers saw as sinful any form of lay authority over the Church—whether that of the local lord or the emperor himself. The reformers wanted the emperor and all other lords to keep their hands off. As a result of this controversy, the most troublesome issue of the eleventh century became establishing the boundaries between temporal and spiritual authorities.

The Pope Becomes a Monarch

Religious reform and vitality required unity within the Church. The most important step in building unity was to define what it meant to be a Catholic. Catholics began to define themselves in two ways. First, the Church insisted on conformity in rites. Rites consisted of the forms of public worship called the liturgy, which included certain prescribed prayers and chants, usually in Latin. Uniform rites meant that Catholics could hear the Mass celebrated in essentially the same way everywhere from Poland to Portugal, Iceland to Croatia. Conformity of worship created a cultural unity that transcended differences in language and ethnicity. When Catholics from far-flung locales encountered one another, they shared something meaningful to them all because of the uniformity of the rites. The second thing that defined a Catholic was obedience to the pope. Ritual uniformity and obedience to the pope were closely interrelated because both the ritual and the pope were Roman. There were many bishops in Christianity, but as one monk put it, "Rome is . . . the head of the world."

The task of the medieval popes was to make this theoretical claim to authority real—in short, to make the papacy a religious monarchy. In the last half of the eleventh century under a series of dynamic reformers, the papacy firmly reasserted itself as the head of the Roman Catholic world. Among the reformers who gathered in Rome was Hildebrand (ca. 1020–1085), one of the most remarkable figures in the history of the Church, a man beloved as saintly by his admirers and considered an ambitious, self-serving megalomaniac by many others. From 1055 to 1073 during the pontificates of some four popes, Hildebrand became the power behind the throne, helping enact wide-ranging reforms that enforced uniformity of worship and establishing the rules for electing new popes by the college of cardinals. In 1073 Hildebrand was himself elected pope and took the name Gregory VII (r. 1073–1085).

Gregory's greatness lay in his leadership over the internal reform of the Church. Every year he held a Church council in Rome where he decreed against simony (the buying and selling of church offices) and priests who married and attempted to bequeath church property to their children. Gregory centralized authority over the Church itself by sending out papal legates, representatives who delivered orders to local bishops, and attempted to free it from external influence by asserting the superiority of the pope over all other authorities. Gregory's theory of papal supremacy led him into direct conflict with the German emperor Henry IV (r. 1056–1106). The issue was lay investiture, the power of kings and emperors to pick their own candidates for ecclesiastical offices, especially bishoprics. During the eighth and ninth centuries weak popes relied on the Carolingian kings and emperors to name suitable candidates for these offices in order to keep them out of the hands of local aristocrats. At stake was not only power and authority, but also the income from the enormous amount of property controlled by the Church, which the emperor was in the best position to protect. During the eleventh century, Gregory VII and other reform-minded popes sought to regain control of this property. Without the ability to name his own candidates as bishops, Gregory recognized that his whole campaign for church reform would falter.

When Pope Gregory tried to negotiate with the emperor over the appointment of the bishop of Milan, Henry was defiant, ordering Gregory to resign the papacy in a letter with the notorious salutation, "Henry, King not by usurpation, but by the pious ordination of God to Hildebrand now not Pope but false monk."

Gregory struck back in an escalating confrontation now known as the Investiture Controversy°. He deposed Henry from the imperial throne and excommunicated him. Excommunication° prohibited the sinner from participating in the sacraments and forbade any social contact whatsoever with the surrounding community. People caught talking to an excommunicated person or writing a letter or even offering a drink of water could themselves be excommunicated. Excommunication was a form of social death, a dire punishment indeed, especially if the excommunicated person was a king. Both sides marshaled arguments from

The Investiture Controversy
When Pope Gregory VII sought refuge at Canossa in 1177, his host was his strong supporter, Countess Matilda of Tuscany. In this illumination in a chronicle of the life of Matilda, Emperor Henry IV kneels at her feet asking her to intercede for him with Pope Gregory. Another of the pope's supporters, Abbot Hugo of Cluny, sits behind the emperor holding a staff. The image of an emperor humbling himself before a mere countess conveyed the idea to medieval viewers of the complete subordination of the imperial authority to that of the pope and his allies.

Scripture and history, but the excommunication was effective. Henry's friends started to abandon him, rebellion broke out in Germany, and the most powerful German lords called for a meeting to elect a new emperor. Backed into a corner, Henry plotted a clever counterstroke.

Early in the winter of 1077 Pope Gregory set out to cross the Alps to meet with the German lords. When Gregory reached the Alpine passes, however, he learned that Emperor Henry was on his way to Italy. In fear of what the emperor would do, Gregory retreated to the castle of Canossa, where he expected to be attacked. Henry surprised Gregory, however, by arriving not with an army but as a supplicant asking the pope to hear his confession. As a priest Gregory could hardly refuse to hear the confession of a penitent sinner, but he nevertheless attempted to humiliate Henry by making him wait for three days, kneeling in the snow outside the castle. Henry's presentation of himself as a penitent sinner posed a dilemma for Gregory. The German lords were waiting for Gregory to appear in his capacity as the chief justice of Christendom to judge Henry, but Henry himself was asking the pope to act in his capacity as priest to grant absolution for sin. The priest in Gregory won out over the judge, and he absolved Henry.

Even after the deaths of Gregory and Henry, the Investiture Controversy continued to poison relations between the popes and emperors until the Concordat of Worms in 1122 resolved the issue in a formal treaty. The emperor retained the right to nominate high churchmen, but in a concession to the papacy, the emperor lost the ceremonial privileges of investiture that conveyed spiritual authority. Without the ceremony of investiture, no bishop could exercise his office. By refusing to invest unsuitable nominees, the popes had the last word. Gregory VII's vision of papal supremacy over all kings and emperors persevered.

How the Popes Ruled

The most lasting accomplishment of the popes during the twelfth and thirteenth centuries derived less from dramatic confrontations with emperors than from the humdrum routine of the law. Beginning with Gregory VII, the papacy became the supreme court of the Catholic world by claiming authority over a vast range of issues. To justify these claims, Gregory and his assistants conducted massive research among old laws and treatises. These were organized into a body of legal texts called canon law°.

Canon law came to encompass many kinds of cases, including all those involving the clergy, disputes about church property, and donations to the Church. The law of the Church also touched on many of the most vital concerns of the laity—all those who were not priests, monks, or nuns—including annulling marriages, legitimating bastards, prosecuting bigamy, protecting widows and orphans, and resolving inheritance disputes. Most of the cases originated in the courts of the bishops, but the bishops' decisions could be appealed to the pope and cardinals sitting together in the papal consistory. The consistory could make exceptions from the letter of the law, called dispensations, giving it considerable power over kings and aristocrats who wanted to marry a cousin, divorce a wife, legitimate a bastard, or annul a will. By the middle of the twelfth century, Rome was awash with legal business. The functions of the canon law courts became so important that those who were elected popes were no longer monks but trained canon lawyers, men very capable in the ways of the world.

The pope also presided over the curia°, the administrative bureaucracy of the Church. The cardinals served as ministers in the papal administration and were sent off to foreign princes and cities as ambassadors, or legates. Because large amounts of revenue were flowing into the coffers of the Church, Rome became the financial capital of the West.

In addition to its legal, administrative, and financial authority, the papacy also made use of two powerful spiritual weapons against the disobedient. Any Christian who refused to repent of a sin could be excommunicated, as the Emperor Henry IV had been. The second spiritual weapon was the interdict°, which usually applied to a whole city or kingdom whose ruler had displeased the pope. During an interdict, the sacraments were not celebrated and the churches closed their doors, creating panic among the faithful who could not baptize their children or bury their dead. The interdict, which encouraged a public outcry, could be a very effective weapon for undermining the political support of any monarch who ran afoul of the pope.

The Pinnacle of the Medieval Papacy: Pope Innocent III

The most capable of the medieval popes was Innocent III (r. 1198–1216). Only 37 when elected, Innocent was tough-minded and the ideal candidate to bolster the papal monarchy, because of both his extensive family connections in Italy and Germany and his training in theology and canon law. Innocent possessed a clear-sighted concept of the papal monarchy. To him the pope was the overlord and moral guide of the Christian community, with authority over the entire world. He recognized the right of kings to rule over the secular sphere, but he considered it his duty to prevent and punish sin, a duty that gave him wide latitude to meddle in the affairs of kings and princes. The indefatigable pope pummeled the world with commands and advice, which were not to be taken lightly. Under Innocent, the

Map 9.2   Universal Monarchy of Pope Innocent III
Besides his direct control of the Papal States in central Italy, Pope Innocent III made vassals of many of the kings of Catholic Europe. These feudal ties provided a legal foundation for his claim to be the highest authority in Christian Europe.

sheer volume of correspondence to Spain, for example, increased by some twenty-five times over what it had been under the hyperactive Pope Gregory VII.

Innocent's first task was to provide the papacy with a strong territorial base of support so that the popes could act with the same freedom as kings and princes. Innocent is generally considered to be the founder of the Papal State in central Italy, an independent state that lasted until 1870 and survives today in a tiny fragment as Vatican City.

Innocent's second task was keeping alive the Crusading ideal. He called the Fourth Crusade, which went awry when the crusaders attacked Constantinople. He also expanded the definition of Crusading by calling for a Crusade to eliminate heresy within Christian Europe. Innocent was deeply concerned about the spread of new heresies, which attracted enormous numbers of converts, especially in the growing cities of southern Europe. By Crusading against Christian heretics, the Cathars and Waldensians, Innocent authorized the use of military methods to enforce uniformity of belief.

The third objective of this ambitious and energetic pope was to assert the power of the papacy over political affairs. Innocent managed the election of Emperor Frederick II; he also assumed the right to veto imperial elections. He excommunicated King Philip II of France to force him to take back an unwanted wife. And he placed England under the interdict to compel King John to cede his kingdom to the papacy and receive it back as a fief, a transaction that made the king of England the vassal of the pope. Using whatever means necessary, he made papal vassals of the rulers of Aragon, Bulgaria, Denmark, Hungary, Poland, Portugal, and Serbia. Through the use of the feudal law of vassalage, Innocent brought the papacy to its closest approximation of a universal Christian monarchy (see Map 9.2).

Innocent's fourth and greatest accomplishment was to codify the rites of the liturgy and to define the dogmas of the faith. This monumental task was the achievement of the Fourth Lateran Council, held in Rome in 1215. This council, attended by more than 400 bishops, 800 abbots, and the ambassadors of the monarchs of Catholic Europe, issued decrees that reinforced the celebration of the sacraments as the centerpiece of Christian life. They included rules to educate the clergy, define their qualifications, and govern elections of bishops. The council condemned heretical beliefs, and it called yet another Crusade. It became the guidepost that has governed many aspects of Catholic practice, especially with regard to the sacraments. It did more than any other council to fulfill the goal of uniformity of rites in Catholicism, and its influence survives to this day.

The Troubled Legacy of the Papal Monarchy

Innocent was a crafty, intelligent man who in single-minded fashion pursued the greater good of the Church as he saw it. His policies, however, had ruinous results in the hands of his less able successors. Their blunders undermined the pope's spiritual mission, especially when they attempted to influence the fate of the kingdom of Sicily, which lay on the southern border of the Papal State. Innocent's successors went beyond defending the Papal

State and embroiled all Italy in a series of bloody civil wars between the Guelfs, who supported the popes, and the Ghibellines, who opposed them. The pope's position as a monarch superior to all others collapsed under the weight of immense folly and hypocrisy during the pontificate of Boniface VIII (r. 1294–1303). His personal faults, which included breathtaking vanity and rudeness, did little to help the papacy's blemished reputation. Widely believed to be a religious skeptic addicted to amulets and magic, Boniface enjoyed the company of riotous companions and loved to dress up in the regalia of an emperor.

In 1302 Boniface promulgated the most extreme theoretical assertion of papal superiority over lay rulers. Behind the statement was a specific dispute with King Philip IV of France (r. 1285–1314), who was attempting to try a French bishop for treason. The larger issue behind the dispute was similar to the Investiture Controversy of the eleventh century, but this time no one paid much attention to the pope. The loss of papal moral authority had taken its toll. In the heat of the confrontation, King Philip accused Pope Boniface of heresy, one of the few sins of which he was not guilty, and sent his agents to arrest the pope. They forced their way into his rooms at the papal palace of Anagni in 1303, where they found the 70-year-old Boniface in bed. Traumatized by the arrest and the threats of violence against him, the old man died shortly after he was released. With Boniface the papal monarchy died as well. It took more than a century for the popes to recover their complete independence from French influence and longer still to recapture their dignity.

DOCUMENT

Pope Boniface VIII, Unam Sanctum (1302)

Discovering God in the World

Even before the First Crusade, Catholic Europe began to experience an unprecedented spiritual awakening. The eleventh-century papal campaign to reform the morals of the clergy helped make priests both more respectable and better educated. At the same time, many laypeople who had previously been Christians in name only began to show genuine enthusiasm for the Church. A better-educated clergy educated the laity more effectively, and the teachings of Christianity became less a matter of public conformity, manifest by attendance at Mass, than of personal devotion. In large numbers Latin Christians began to internalize the teachings of the Church. The most devout were drawn to dedicating their lives to religion. In England, for example, the number of monks increased tenfold from the late eleventh century to 1200. The newly expanding cities built loyalty and encouraged peaceable behavior through the veneration of civic patron saints. The most vital indication of spiritual renewal was the success of new religious orders, which satisfied a widespread yearning to discover the hand of God in the world.

CHRONOLOGY

The Papal Monarchy

1073–1085	Reign of Pope Gregory VII
1075–1122	The Investiture Controversy
1198–1216	Reign of Pope Innocent III
1215	Fourth Lateran Council
1294–1303	Reign of Pope Boniface VIII

The Patron Saints

Saints are holy people whose moral perfection gives them a special relationship with the sacred. Ordinary Christians venerated saints to gain access to supernatural powers, protection, and intercession with God. A saintly intercessor was someone who could be trusted to obtain God's favor. In many places the newly converted simply transformed polytheistic deities into saints, a process that greatly facilitated the adoption of Christianity.

The relationship between Christian believers and the saints was profoundly intimate and intertwined with many aspects of life: Christian children were named after saints who became their special protectors; every church was dedicated to a saint; every town and city adopted a patron saint. And even entire peoples cherished a patron saint; for example, the Irish adopted Saint Patrick, who supposedly brought Christianity to the island.

A city gained protection from a patron saint by obtaining the saint's corpse or skeleton or part of the skeleton or some object associated with the saint. These body parts and material objects, called relics, served as contacts between Earth and Heaven and were said to have been verified by miracles. The belief in the miraculous powers of relics created an enormous demand for them in the thriving medieval cities. But because the remains of the martyrs and early saints of the church were spread across the Middle East and Mediterranean from Jerusalem to Rome, relics first had to be discovered and transferred from where they were buried to new homes in the churches of the growing western European cities. The demand created a thriving market in saints' bones and body parts. They were bought or stolen, and there was ample room for fraud in passing off unauthentic bones to gullible buyers. During the Crusades the supply of relics greatly increased, both because the Crusading knights had access to the tombs of early Christian saints and martyrs and because the thriving cities of the West produced a great demand for them.

Possessing relics was also important for establishing the legitimacy of political authority. For example, the ruler of the city of Venice, the doge, claimed to possess the relics of St. Mark, one of the four evangelists who wrote the gospels of the New Testament. Based on their possession of these prestigious relics, the Venetians argued that God had authorized the city's liberty from outside interference. They used this argument against their one-time imperial masters in Constantinople, against the Carolingians who attempted to conquer the thriving city, against bishops from the mainland who claimed authority over Venice's churches, and eventually even against the pope when he attempted to control the Venetian church. The great basilica of St. Mark in Venice became a pilgrimage shrine visited by Christians from all over Europe on their way to the Holy Land. Each pilgrim learned of Venice's intimate association with St. Mark from the magnificent mosaics that adorned the basilica's ceilings and walls.

During the twelfth and thirteenth centuries, public veneration of saints also began to undergo a subtle shift of emphasis, away from the cults of the local patron saints toward more universal figures such as Jesus and the Virgin Mary. The patron saints had functioned almost like the family deities of antiquity who served the particular interests of individuals and communities, but the papal monarchy

Mosaics in the Basilica of St. Mark in Venice

Pilgrims learned of Venice's intimate association with St. Mark from the magnificent mosaics that adorned the basilica's ceilings and walls. This scene shows a miracle that occurred after St. Mark's body was lost during a fire in the basilica. After the leaders of Venice spent days in prayer, shown on the left, St. Mark opened a door in a column shown at the far right to reveal the place where his body was hidden. In between these two scenes, those who witnessed the miracle turn to one another in amazement.

A Tale of Two Marys

Medieval thinking about women began with the fundamental dichotomy between Eve, the symbol of women as they are, and Mary, the ideal to which all women strived. Eve brought sin and sex into the world through her disobedience to God. Mary, the Virgin Mother, kept her body inviolate.

Into the gap between the two natures of women emerged Mary Magdalen, a repentant prostitute whose veneration reached a pinnacle in the twelfth century. In contrast to the perpetually virginal ideal of Mary, the mother of Christ, Magdalen offered the possibility of redemption to all women. The clerical discussion of the natures of these two Marys—the Virgin Mary and Mary Magdalen—reveals a complex and changing medieval discussion about the nature of women. This discussion was pursued through a theoretical examination of women's bodies and their sexuality.

The precise significance of Mary's virginity long preoccupied Christian thinkers. Two of the Gospels simply assert that Mary had not known a man before she became pregnant with the Christ child. Later Christian thinkers extended this idea to assert that she remained a virgin after the birth of Jesus and even that she miraculously managed to preserve her virginity "before, during, and after delivery" of the infant. By discussing her as a virgin who gave birth and still remained a virgin, these Christian thinkers relegated Mary to a heavenly realm where the physical facts of real women's lives did not apply.

Geoffroy of Vendôme (d. 1132), a cleric educated in a cathedral school, drew an astonishing conclusion from these speculations about Mary's reproductive anatomy:

Virtuous Mary gave birth to Christ, and in Christ she gave birth to Christians. Hence the mother of Christ is the mother of all Christians. If the mother of Christ is the mother of all Christians, then clearly Christ and Christians are brothers. Not only is Christ the brother of all Christians, he is also the father of all men and primarily of Christians. From which it follows that Christ is the Virgin's father and husband as well as her son.[1]

Geoffroy collapsed all male family relationships into one: the lineage of father, husband, and son merges with the equality of brotherhood among all Christians. What is most remarkable about Geoffroy's way of thinking is that this great Christian drama takes place within the confines of a mother's womb, invisible to sight yet so mysteriously open to speculative examination. The problem with this way of thinking was that its implications were not merely theoretical. Geoffroy and other priests were pastors who offered practical advice to real women. The model of the Virgin Mary left them with only one avenue for giving advice: They recommended that women remain lifelong virgins, which was rather impractical advice for the vast majority of women who were married.

Mary Magdalen's life provided an alternative, more practical model to follow. Known in the early Church, her veneration spread after the abbey at Vézelay, Burgundy, changed its dedication from the Virgin Mary to Mary Magdalen in 1095 and began to flourish as a pilgrimage site. Throughout France, "Madeleine" became a popular name for girls. In 1105 Geoffroy of Vendôme assembled most of the known and presumed information about her in a sermon, "In Honor of the Blessed Mary Magdalen." All writers agreed she had been a prostitute. But she had redeemed herself. By confessing her sins, she saved herself, and Christ forgave her. Thus, a woman whose body had once been corrupted saved not only herself but through her example brought others to repentance. If Magdalen could achieve redemption from her degraded state, did she not offer hope to all women?

For Discussion

What did the medieval depiction of the two Marys reveal about the way people thought about women, sexuality, and moral worth?

Mary Magdalen represented the possibility of redemption for all sinners.

The Virgin Mary suckles the baby Jesus, an image of the Christian ideal of selfless Charity.

Saint Anthony of Padua holds a lily, symbolizing purity and innocence.

The Two Marys: The Mother of God and the Repentant Prostitute

encouraged uniform rites that were universal throughout Catholicism.

Christians had always honored the Virgin Mary, but beginning in the twelfth century her immense popularity provided Catholics with a positive female image that contradicted the traditional misogyny and mistrust associated with Eve. Clerics and monks had long depicted women as deceitful and lustful in luring men to their moral ruin. In contrast, the veneration of the Virgin Mary promoted the image of a loving mother who would intervene with her son on behalf of sinners at the Last Judgment. Theologians still taught that the woman Eve had brought sin into the world, but the woman Mary offered help in escaping the consequences of sin.

The popularity of Mary was evident everywhere. Most of the new cathedrals in the burgeoning cities of Europe were dedicated to her. She became the favorite example of preachers as a model for women, and numerous miracles were attributed to her. Part of her appeal derived from her image as the ideal mother with the bouncing Christ child on her knee. Countless paintings and sculptures of the Madonna and child adorned the churches of Europe, and Mary's tender humanity stimulated artists to find new ways to evoke human emotions. Mary became the center of a renewed interest in the family and the Christian value of love within the family.

Mary became a model with whom women could identify, presenting a positive image of femininity. In images of her suckling the Christ child, she became the perfect embodiment of the virtue of charity, the willingness to give without any expectation of reward. Through the image of the nursing Virgin Mary, the ability to nurture became associated not just with Mary but with Christ himself. In contrast to the early Christian saints who were predominantly martyrs and missionaries, during the twelfth and thirteenth centuries saints exhibited sanctity more through nurturing others, especially by feeding the poor and healing the sick. Nurturing was associated with women, and many more women became saints during this period than during the entire first millennium of Christianity. In 1100 fewer than 10 percent of all the saints were female. By 1300 the percentage had increased to 24 percent. During the fifteenth century about 30 percent were women. Far from a feminist religion, Catholicism nevertheless developed a sacred female principle and offered an ideal woman for veneration much more prominently than did Judaism or Islam.

The New Religious Orders

By the eleventh century many men attracted to the religious life found the Benedictines too lax in their discipline and the Cluniacs too worldly with their elaborate liturgy and decorated churches. In 1098 a small group of Benedictine monks removed themselves to an isolated wasteland to establish the Cistercian Order. The Cistercians practiced a very strict discipline. They ate only enough to stay alive.

DOCUMENT

The Position of Women in the Eyes of the Medieval Church

In the view of the medieval Church, women were spiritually equal to men but legally and socially inferior. Women were to be subject to male control. The Decretum, *written by the jurist Gratian in about 1140, codified the canon law. In this passage Gratian defines the legal status of women in Christian society.*

Women should be subject to their men. The natural order for mankind is that women should serve men and children their parents, for it is just that the lesser serve the greater.

The image of God is in man and it is one. Women were drawn from man, who has God's jurisdiction as if he were God's vicar, because he has the image of the one God. Therefore woman is not made in God's image.

Woman's authority is nil; let her in all things be subject to the rule of man. . . . And neither can she teach, nor be a witness, nor give a guarantee, nor sit in judgment.

Adam was beguiled by Eve, not she by him. It is right then that he whom woman led into wrongdoing should have her under his direction, so that he may not fail a second time through female levity.

Source: From Julia O'Faolain and Lauro Martines, *Not in God's Image* (1973).

Each monk possessed only one robe. Unlike other orders that required monks to attend frequent and lengthy services, the Cistercians spent more time in private prayer and manual labor. Their churches were bare of all decoration. Under the brilliant leadership of Bernard of Clairvaux (1090–1153), the Cistercians grew rapidly, as many men disillusioned with the sinful and materialistic society around them joined the new order. Bernard's asceticism led him to seek refuge from the affairs of the world, but he was also a religious reformer and activist, engaged with the important issues of his time. He even helped settle a disputed papal election and preached a crusade.

The Cistercians established their new monasteries in isolated, uninhabited places where they cleared forests and worked the land so that they could live in complete isolation from the troubled affairs of the world. Their hard work had an ironic result. By bringing new lands under the plow and by employing the latest technological innovations, such as water mills, many of the Cistercian monasteries produced more than was needed for the monks, and the sale of excess produce made the Cistercians very rich. The economic success of the Cistercians helped them expand even more rapidly. In their first century, the Cistercians built more than 500 new monasteries, many in places previously untouched by Western monasticism. Numerous colonies of Cistercian monks moved into northeastern Europe in areas recently converted to Latin Christianity. English Cistercians moved into the newly settled parts of Norway, Germans into the confiscated lands of Poland. There were also foundations in Greece and Syria, both bastions of Eastern Orthodoxy. The rapid Cistercian push beyond the frontiers of Latin Europe helped disseminate the culture of Catholic Christianity through educating the local elites and attracting members of the aristocracy to join the Cistercians. By recruiting lay brothers, known as *converse*, the Cistercians made important connections with the peasants.

More than a century after the foundation of the Cistercians in France, the Spaniard Dominic and the Italian Francis formulated a new kind of religious order composed of mendicant friars°. From the very beginning the friars wanted to distinguish themselves from monks. As the opening of this chapter indicated, instead of working in a monastery to feed themselves as did the Cistercians, friars ("brothers") wandered from city to city and throughout the countryside begging for alms (*mendicare* means "to beg," hence *mendicant*). Unlike monks who remained in a cloister, friars tried to help ordinary laypeople with their problems by preaching and administering to the sick and poor.

The Spaniard Dominic (1170–1221) founded the Dominican Order to convert Muslims and Jews and to combat heresy among Christians against whom he began his preaching mission while traveling through southern France. The ever-perceptive Pope Innocent III recognized Dominic's talents while he was visiting Rome and gave his new order provisional approval. Dominic believed the task of conversion could be achieved through persuasion and argument. To hone the Dominicans' persuasive skills, they created the first multigrade, comprehensive educational system. It connected schools located in individual friaries with more advanced regional schools that offered specialized training in languages, philosophy, and especially theology. Most Dominican friars never studied at a university but enjoyed, nevertheless, a highly sophisticated education that made them exceptionally influential in European intellectual life. Famed for their preaching skills, Dominicans were equally successful in moving the illiterate masses and debating sophisticated opponents.

From the beginning, the Dominican Order synthesized the contemplative life of the monastery and the active ministry of preaching to laypeople. In contrast to traditional monastic orders, the Dominican Order was organized like an army. Each province was under the supervision of a master general, and each Dominican was ready to travel wherever needed to preach and convert.

The Franciscan Order enjoyed a similar success. Francis of Assisi (1182–1226), whose story opened this chapter, deeply influenced Clare of Assisi (1194–1253), who founded a parallel order for women, the Poor Clares. Like the Franciscans, she and her followers enjoyed the "privilege of perfect poverty," which forbade the ownership of any property even by the community itself. Clare devoted herself to penitential prayer, which was said to have twice saved the town of Assisi from besieging armies.

Both the Dominican and Franciscan Orders spread rapidly. Whereas the successful Cistercians had founded 500 new houses in their first century, the Franciscans established more than 1,400 in their first hundred years. Liberated from the obligation to live in a monastery, the mendicant friars traveled wherever the pope ordered them, making them effective agents of the papal monarchy. They preached Crusades. They pacified the poor. They converted heretics and non-Christians through their inspiring preaching revivals. Even more effectively than the Cistercians before them, they established Catholic colonies along the frontiers of the West and beyond. They became missionary scouts looking for opportunities to disseminate Christian culture. In 1254 the Great Khan in Mongolia sponsored a debate on the principal religions of the world. There, many

DOCUMENT

The Song of Brother Sun

Francis of Assisi is known as a nature mystic, which means he celebrated God's Creation through a love of nature. In one of the most renowned celebrations of nature ever written, "The Song of Brother Sun," Francis transforms the inanimate forces of nature into his spiritual brothers and sisters.

Be praised, my Lord, with all Your creatures,
Especially Sir Brother Sun,
By whom You give us the light of day!
And he is beautiful and radiant with great splendor.
Of You, Most High, he is a symbol!
Be praised, my Lord, for Sister Moon and the Stars!
In the sky You formed them bright and lovely and fair.
Be praised, my Lord, for Brother Wind
And for the Air and cloudy and clear and all Weather,
By which You give sustenance to Your creatures!
Be praised, my Lord, for Sister Water,
Who is very useful and humble and lovely and chaste!
Be praised, my Lord, for Brother Fire,
By whom You give us light at night,
And he is beautiful and merry and mighty and strong!
Be praised, my Lord, for our Sister Mother Earth,
Who sustains and governs us,
And produces fruits with colorful flowers and leaves!

Source: From *The Little Flowers of St. Francis* by St. Francis of Assisi, translated by Raphael Brown, copyright © 1958 by Beverly Brown. Used by permission of Doubleday, a division of Random House, Inc.

thousands of miles from Catholic Europe, was a Franciscan friar ready to debate the learned men representing Islam, Buddhism, and Confucianism.

The Flowering of Religious Sensibilities

During the twelfth and thirteenth centuries the widespread enthusiasm for religion exalted spiritual creativity. Experimentation pushed Christian piety in new directions, not just for aristocratic men, who dominated the Church hierarchy and the monasteries, but for women and laypeople from all social levels.

Catholic worship concentrated on the celebration of the Eucharist°. The Eucharist, which was the crucial ritual moment during the Mass, celebrated Jesus' last meal with his apostles. The Eucharistic rite consecrated wafers of bread and wine as the body and blood of Christ. After the consecration, the celebrating priest distributed to the congregation the bread, called the host. Drinking from the chalice of wine, however, was a special privilege of the priesthood. More than anything else, belief in the miraculous change from bread to flesh and wine to blood, along with the sacrament of baptism, distinguished Christian believers from others. The Fourth Lateran Council in 1215 obligated all Christians to partake of the Eucharist:

All the faithful of both sexes shall after they have reached the age of discretion faithfully confess all their sins at least once a year to their own priest, and perform to the best of their ability the penance imposed, receiving reverently, at least at Easter, the sacrament of the Eucharist, unless perchance at the advice of their own priest they may for a good reason abstain for a time from its reception; otherwise they shall be cut off from the Church during life, and deprived of Christian burial in death.[2]

This statement in its stark simplicity defined the core obligation of all medieval Catholics. As simple as it was as a ritual observance, belief in the Eucharistic miracle presented a vexing and complex theological problem—why the host still looked, tasted, and smelled like bread rather than flesh, and why the blood in the chalice still seemed to be wine rather than blood. After the Fourth Lateran Council, Catholics solved this problem with the doctrine of transubstantiation°. The doctrine rested on a distinction between the outward appearances of the object, which the five senses can perceive, and the substance of an object, which they cannot perceive. When the priest spoke the words of consecration during the Mass, the bread and wine were changed into the flesh and blood of Christ in substance ("transubstantiated") but not in outward appearances. Thus, the substance of the Eucharist literally became God's body, but the senses of taste, smell, and sight perceived it as bread.

Veneration of the Eucharist enabled the faithful to identify with Christ because believers considered the consecrated Eucharistic wafer to be Christ himself. By eating the host, they had literally ingested Christ, making his body

part of their bodies. Eucharistic veneration became enormously popular in the thirteenth century and the climax of dazzling ritual performance. Priests enhanced the effect of the miracle by dramatically elevating the host at the moment of consecration, holding it in upraised hands. Altar screens had special peepholes so that many people could adore the host at the elevation, and the faithful would rush from altar to altar or church to church to witness a succession of host elevations.

Many Christians became attracted to mysticism, the attempt to achieve union of the self with God. To the mystic, complete understanding of the divine was spiritual, not intellectual, an understanding best achieved through asceticism, the repudiation of material and bodily comforts. Both men and women were mystics, but women concentrated on the more extreme forms of asceticism. For example, some women allowed themselves to be walled up in dark chambers to achieve perfect seclusion from the world and avoid distractions from their mystical pursuits. Others had themselves whipped, wore painful scratching clothing, starved themselves in a form of holy anorexia, or claimed to survive with the Eucharist as their only food. Female mystics, such as Juliana of Norwich (1342–ca. 1416), envisioned a holy family in which God the Father was almighty but the Mother was all wisdom. Some female mystics believed that Christ had a female body because he was the perfect nurturer, and they ecstatically contemplated spiritual union with him.

Mystics, however, were exceptional people. Most Christians contented themselves with the sacraments, especially baptism, penance, and the Eucharist; perhaps a pilgrimage to a saint's shrine; and a final attempt at salvation by making a pious gift to the Church on their deathbed. The benevolent process of discovering God also stimulated a related malevolent process of attempting to detect the influence of the Devil in the world. To eradicate the Devil's influence, Christians made some people the outcasts of Western society.

Creating the Outcasts of Europe

As churchmen and kings sought to enforce religious unity and moral reform during the twelfth and thirteenth centuries, they were disturbed by peoples who did not seem to fit into official notions of Christian society. Some of these people, such as lepers and male homosexuals, were physically or socially different; others, such as heretics and Jews, actively rejected church authority. The papacy began a dramatic wave of military expeditions against heretical lords in order to deprive them of their lands and to inquire into the beliefs that they had allowed to flourish in their territories. Follow-up campaigns attempted to convert, control, or suppress these religious minorities, who were made social outcasts.

The Heretics: Cathars and Waldensians

In its efforts to defend the faith, the Church during the first half of the thirteenth century began to authorize bishops and other clerics to conduct inquisitions (formal inquiries) into specific instances of heresy or perceived heresy. The so-called heretics tended to be faithful people who sought a form of religion purer than what the Church provided. During the thirteenth and early fourteenth centuries, inquisitions and systematic persecutions targeted the Cathars and Waldensians, who at first had lived peacefully with their Catholic neighbors and shared many of the same beliefs with them.

The Cathars were especially strong in northern Italy and southern France. The name *Cathar* derives from the Greek word for purity. Heavily concentrated around the French town of Albi, the Cathars were also known as Albigensians. They departed from Catholic doctrine, which held that God created the Earth, because they believed that an evil force had created all matter. To purify themselves, an elite few—known as "perfects"—rejected their own bodies as corrupt matter, refused to marry and procreate, and in extreme cases gradually starved themselves. These purified perfects provided a dramatic contrast to the more worldly Catholic clergy. For many, Catharism became a form of protest against the wealth and power of the Church. By the 1150s the Cathars had organized their own churches, performed their own rituals, and even elected their own bishops. Where they became deeply rooted, as in the south of France, they practiced their faith openly until Pope Innocent III authorized a Crusade against them.

The Waldensians were the followers of Peter Waldo (d. ca. 1184), a merchant of Lyons, France, who like Francis of Assisi had abandoned all his possessions and taken a vow of poverty. Desiring to imitate the life of Jesus and live in simple purity, the Waldensians preached and translated the Gospels into their own language so that laypeople who did not know Latin could understand them. At first the Waldensians' seemed similar to the Franciscans, but because of the Waldensians' failure to obtain licenses to preach as the Franciscans had done, they came to be depicted by Church authorities as heretics. In response the Waldensians created an alternative church that became widespread in southern France, Rhineland Germany, and northern Italy.

Catholic authorities, who were often the objects of strong criticisms from the Cathars and Waldensians, grew ever more hostile to them. Bishops declared heretics liable to the same legal penalties as those guilty of treason, which authorized the political authorities to proceed against them. In 1208 Pope Innocent III called the Albigensian Crusade, the first of several holy wars launched against heretics in the south of France. The king of France was only too happy to fight the Albigensian Crusade because he saw it as a means of expanding royal power in a region of France where his authority was weak. To eradicate the remaining Cathars and Waldensians, several kings and popes initiated inquisitions. By the middle of the thirteenth century the Cathars had been converted or exterminated except for a few isolated pockets in the mountains, which were stamped out by later inquisitors. The Waldensians were nearly wiped out by inquisitorial campaigns, but a few scattered groups have managed to survive to this day, mostly by retreating to the relative safety of the high Alps and later to the Americas.

Systematic Persecution of the Jews

Before the Crusades, Christians and Jews had lived in relative harmony in Europe. In fact, during the Carolingian period the Frankish kings and emperors had protected Jewish communities from the occasional hostility of bishops who sought to expel them. The Crusades, however, fomented increased violence against Jews. Discrimination and assaults against Jews soon became far more common than ever before. In 1182 Jews were expelled from France and allowed to return only under dire financial penalties. In England the monarchy discriminated against the Jews, opening the way for the massacre and mass suicide of the entire Jewish community of York in 1190. The 1215 decrees of the Fourth Lateran Council, which were the centerpiece of Innocent III's pontificate, attempted to regulate the activities of the Jews of Europe. These decrees prohibited Jews from holding public offices and required them to wear distinctive dress.

Christians justified their persecution of Jews during the twelfth and thirteenth centuries in two ways. First, they depicted Jews as the enemies of Christ. This bias was based on the belief that Jews were members of a conspiratorial organization devoted to the destruction of Christianity. Second, jurists began to consider Jews as royal serfs because they lived in a Christian kingdom at the king's sufferance. By classifying Jews as serfs, the law deprived them of the rights of private property. As the jurist Bracton put it, "The Jew can have nothing of his own, for whatever he acquires he acquires not for himself but for the king; for the Jews live not for themselves but for others and so they acquire not for themselves but for others."[3] This precept, which was promulgated in Spain, England, and the German Empire, justified the repeated royal confiscations of Jewish property. Especially when faced with a fiscal shortfall, kings were inclined to solve their financial problems by expropriating the property of the Jewish community. As a result of these policies most Jews were desperately poor. Because they were prohibited from owning land or joining craft guilds, Jews were forced to seek other means of support. Because Christians were barred from loaning money at interest, running pawn shops and banking were some of the few economic activities open to European Jews.

DOCUMENT

The Church's Policy Toward the Jews

At the Fourth Lateran Council of 1215, Pope Innocent III presided over a number of decrees that regulated the lives of Jews. Many of the decrees of the council were based on earlier laws, but by bringing all these laws together the council attempted to separate the Jews entirely from Christians. The first passage treats the issue of usury, the taking of interest payments on loans. The second orders Jews and Muslims to wear distinctive clothing in order to prevent sexual relations among adherents to different faiths.

The more the Christian religion is restrained in the exaction of interest so much more does the knavery of the Jews in this matter increase, so that in a short time they exhaust the wealth of Christians. Wishing therefore to provide for Christians in this matter lest they be burdened excessively by the Jews, we ordain through synodal decree that if they hereafter extort heavy and unrestrained interest, no matter what the pretext be, Christians shall be withdrawn from association with them until the Jews give adequate satisfaction for their unmitigated oppression. Also the Christians shall be compelled, if necessary, through Church punishment from which an appeal will be disregarded, to abstain from business relations with the Jews. . . .

In some provinces a difference in dress distinguishes the Jews or Saracens [Muslims] from the Christians, but in certain others such a confusion has grown up that they cannot be distinguished by any difference. Thus it happens at times that through error Christians have relations with the women of Jews or Saracens, and Jews or Saracens with Christian women. Therefore, that they may not, under pretext of error of this sort excuse themselves in the future for the excesses of such prohibited intercourse, we decree that such Jews and Saracens of both sexes in every Christian province and at all time shall be marked off in the eyes of the public from other peoples through the character of their dress.

Source: From Richard Lim and David Kammerling Smith, eds. *The West in the Wider World: Sources and Perspectives*, vol. 1 (2003): 298.

"The Living Dead": Lepers

The widespread presence of lepers produced dramatically conflicting emotions in medieval Europe. Leprosy (Hansen's disease), which destroys the blood vessels, skin tissues, and ligaments of those who have it, creating grotesque disfigurements and bone deformations, was greatly feared. The exact means of transmission of leprosy is still unclear, and it can probably be contracted from another person only after long physical contact. Even though it was not particularly contagious, lepers were shunned. Leviticus 13:45–46 says of the leper, "he is unclean: he shall dwell alone." Following these biblical precepts, many communities during the twelfth century established leper houses to segregate people with leprosy and other disfiguring or repellent diseases. Lepers' separation from the world made them objects of admiration for some pious Christians. To wash the sores and kiss the lesions of lepers constituted a charitable act of special merit, especially for pious women.

Some medieval thinkers equated lepers with heretics and Jews. A monk was reported to have shouted to a heretical preacher, "you too are a leper, scarred by heresy, excluded from communion by the judgment of the priest, according to the law, bare-headed, with ragged clothing, your body covered by an infected and filthy garment." In 1321 rumors alleged that a conspiracy between lepers and Jews had poisoned the wells in France. Heretics, lepers, and Jews became interchangeable co-conspirators in league with the Devil to destroy Christianity. As the assumed common enemy, they all became subject to persecution.

The Creation of Sexual Crimes

The Christian disapproval of men who engaged in sexual relations with other men derived from a medieval interpretation of the biblical condemnation of the Sodomites, the people of the city of Sodom and its sister cities. Ezekiel 16:49 states, "This was the guilt of your sister Sodom: she and her daughters had pride, excess of food, and prosperous ease, but did not aid the poor and needy." According to this passage, the sin of the people of Sodom was the failure to be charitable; sexual behavior was not mentioned. In fact, during the first thousand years of Christianity, there was no particular concern about homosexuality. Christian theologians advocated chastity for everyone and did not consider homosexual relations between men to be any more sinful than any other form of sexual behavior.

During the eleventh century, however, the sin of Sodom came to be associated with homosexual relations, prompted perhaps by reports of forced child prostitution in Muslim lands. The first church legislation against the practice came in 1179. The reasons for this dramatic shift of opinion—from treating such behavior as sinful but tolerable to treating it as criminal—are obscure, but the language of the time paired sodomy with leprosy. Male sodomites began to be persecuted, and by 1300 most governments had made male sodomy punishable by death, in many statutes death

Inquiring into Heresy: The Inquisition in Montaillou

In 1208 Pope Innocent III issued a call for a Crusade against the Cathars or Albigensians. Fighting on behalf of French King Philip II, Simon de Montfort decisively defeated the pro-Cathar barons of southern France at Muret in 1213. Catharism retreated to the mountains, where it was kept alive by a clandestine network of adherents. The obliteration of these stubborn remnants required methods more subtle than the blunt instrument of a Crusade. It required the techniques of inquisitors adept at interrogation and investigation.

Against the Cathar underground, the inquisition conducted its business through a combination of denunciations, exhaustive interrogations of witnesses and suspects, and confessions. Because its avowed purpose was to root out doctrinal error and to reconcile heretics to the Church, eliciting confessions was the preferred technique. But confessed heretics could not receive absolution until they informed on their friends and associates.

One of the last and most extensively documented inquisition cases against Catharism took place in Montaillou, a village in the Pyrenees Mountains, near the border of modern France and Spain. The Montaillou inquisition began in 1308, a century after the launch of the Albigensian Crusade and long after the heyday of Catharism.

However, the detailed records of the inquisitors provide a revealing glimpse into Catharism and its suppression as well as the procedures of the inquisition. The first to investigate Montaillou was Geoffrey d'Ablis, the inquisitor of Carcassone. In 1308 he had every resident over age 12 seized and imprisoned. After the investigation, the villagers suffered the full range of inquisitorial penalties for their Cathar faith. Some were burned at the stake or sentenced to life in prison. Many who were allowed to return to Montaillou were forced to wear a yellow cross, the symbol of a heretic, sewn to the outside of their garments.

Unfortunately for these survivors, Montaillou was investigated again from 1318 to 1325 by the most fearsome inquisitor of the age, Jacques Fournier, who was later elected Pope Benedict XII. Known as an efficient, rigorous opponent of heresy, Fournier forced virtually all the surviving adults in Montaillou to appear before his tribunal. When the scrupulous Fournier took up a case, his inquiries were notoriously lengthy and rigorous. Both witnesses and defendants spoke of his tenacity, skill, and close attention to detail in conducting interrogations. If Fournier and his assistants could not uncover evidence through interrogation and confession, they did not hesitate to employ informers and spies to obtain the necessary information. When Pierre Maury, a shepherd who had been sought by the inquisitors for many years, returned to the village for a visit, an old friend received him with caution: "When we saw you again we felt both joy and fear. Joy, because it was a long time since we had seen you. Fear, because I was afraid lest the Inquisition had captured you up there: if they had they would have made you confess everything and come back among us as a spy in order to bring about my capture."[4]

Fournier's success in Montaillou depended on his ability to play local factions against each other by encouraging members of one clan to denounce the members of another. Fournier's persistence even turned family members against one another. The clearest example of this convoluted play of local alliances and animosities, family ties, religious belief, and self-interest is the case of Montaillou's wealthiest family, the Clergues.

Bernard Clergue was the count's local representative, which made him a kind of sheriff, and his brother Pierre was the parish priest. Together they represented both the secular and religious arms of the inquisition in Montaillou. In his youth, Pierre had Cathar sympathies, and he reportedly had kept a heretical book or calendar in his home. Nevertheless, at some time before 1308, he and Bernard betrayed the local Cathars to the inquisition. In the proceedings that followed, they had the power to either protect or expose their neighbors and family members. When one of his relatives was summoned to appear before the inquisition, Bernard warned her to "say you fell off the ladder in your house; pretend you have broken bones everywhere. Otherwise it's prison for you."[5] Pierre relentlessly used his influence for his own and his family's benefit. A notorious womanizer, Pierre frightened women into sleeping with him by threatening to denounce them to the inquisition. Those he personally testified against were primarily from other prominent Montaillou families who represented a challenge to the Clergues' power. As one resident bitterly testified, "the priest himself cause[s] many inhabitants of Montaillou to be summoned by the Lord Inquisitor of Carcassone.

Burning of the Heretical Books of the Cathars
In this fifteenth-century painting, St. Dominic presides over the burning of the heretical books of the Cathars.

A Catholic book, which contains the truth, miraculously floats above the flames.

St. Dominic is depicted with a halo.

It is high time the people of the priest's house were thrust as deep in prison as the other inhabitants of Montaillou."[6]

Despite the Clergues' attempted misuse of the inquisitorial investigation for their own purposes, the inquisitor Fournier persevered according to his own standards of evidence. In 1320 he finally had Pierre Clergue arrested as a heretic. The sly priest died in prison.

Questions of Justice

1. How did the methods of the inquisition help create outcasts from Catholic society? How did these methods help consolidate Catholic identity?
2. The primary function of the inquisition was to investigate what people believed. What do you think the inquisitors thought justice to be?

Taking It Further

Lambert, Malcolm. *The Cathars.* 1998. The best place to investigate the Cathar movement in the full sweep of its troubled history.

Le Roy Ladurie, Emmanuel. *Montaillou: The Promised Land of Error,* trans. Barbara Bray. 1978. The best-selling and fascinating account of life in a Cathar village based on the records of Fournier's inquisition.

Moore, R. I. *The Formation of a Persecuting Society: Power and Deviance in Western Europe, 950–1250.* 1987. Places the harassment of heretics in the broader context of medieval persecutions.

Medieval Religious Developments

1098	Founding of Cistercian Order
1221	Death of Dominic
1226	Death of Francis of Assisi
1208–1213	Albigensian Crusade
1215	Fourth Lateran Council promulgates dogma of transubstantiation

by burning. In the process of creating new outcasts, however, female homosexuals were never mentioned. It appears that the male authors of penal legislation could not imagine that erotic relationships between women were even possible.

By the thirteenth century, heretics, Jews, lepers, and male sodomites were identified as outcasts and subjected to legal discrimination, persecution, and violence. The so-called cleansing of Christian Europe of its outcasts was a particularly violent example of the use of power by the dominant society over certain minority groups within it. One of the ways medieval Christian society became more uniform was by ostracizing certain groups of people from within its midst.

Strengthening the Center of the West

■ How did the western European monarchies strengthen themselves?

During the twelfth and thirteenth centuries, Catholic western Europe became the supreme political and economic power in the Christian world, eclipsing Byzantium—an achievement that made it a potent rival to the Islamic states. One reason was stronger political unity.

The three forms of government during the Middle Ages were empires, city-states, and monarchies. The best example of an empire was Byzantium, a potentially formidable military power, but too diverse and far-flung to maintain the loyalty of its subjects. It remained on the defensive, especially against the powerful Islamic caliphates, which also were empires. The other Christian empire was the German Empire, which boasted some impressive monarchs but lacked unity and thus never achieved its potential as the dominant power in Europe. Italian city-states, such as Venice, Milan, Florence, Pisa, and Genoa, thrived as the engines of economic innovation and vitality, but they were vulnerable to foreign conquest and frequently enfeebled by

internal rivalries and feuds. In contrast to overextended empires and underdefended city-states, the western European monarchies gathered the military resources and created the bureaucratic structures necessary to surpass all other forms of government. These kingdoms created the foundations of the modern nation-states, which remain to this day the dominant forms of government around the globe. What happened in France and England during the twelfth and thirteenth centuries, therefore, represents one of the most important and lasting contributions of the West to world history.

The Monarchies of Western Europe

During the High Middle Ages, France and England began to exhibit the fundamental characteristics of unified kingdoms. Several developments explain how these kingdoms strengthened themselves. First, they formed political units that persisted. These units had borders that survived despite changes in rulers and dynasties. Second, these kingdoms developed lasting, impersonal institutions that managed finances and administration. We can blame this period for the rise of bureaucracies. Third, they established a system for resolving disputes and rendering justice in which the final authority was the king—the principle of sovereignty. Fourth, the medieval monarchies resolved that the fundamental loyalty of subjects should be to the laws of the state, a loyalty greater than the obligations of a vassal to a lord or even a son to a father. Stable borders, permanent bureaucracies, sovereignty, and the rule of law were the foundations on which France and England became the most powerful kingdoms in Europe during the twelfth and thirteenth centuries (see Map 9.3).

Expansion of Power: France

For the French kings, the pressing task was to unify their hodge-podge kingdom. Through most of the twelfth century the only part of France the kings ruled directly was the royal domain, the Ile-de-France, an area roughly the size of Vermont but with the fertile soil of Illinois. Over the rest of the kingdom, the king of France was merely the overlord with vague obligations from his vassals, one of whom, the king of England, directly controlled more French territory than he did. On these unpromising foundations, the twelfth- and thirteenth-century French monarchs built the most powerful kingdom in Europe and one of the most unified. The kings of France achieved unity through military conquests and shrewd administrative reforms.

France enjoyed a continuous succession of kings who ruled for long periods of time, produced male heirs, and avoided succession disputes. In the turbulent Middle Ages, dynastic continuity was a key ingredient in building loyalty and avoiding chaos. The vigorous Philip I (r. 1060–1108) initiated a succession of extremely effective kings.

Unpopular with the clergy because of his alleged adultery, Philip took charge of his own domain, where he countermanded the arbitrary justice of local lords by extending royal justice. By focusing his attention on establishing himself as the undisputed lord of his own domain, Philip provided his descendants with a powerful lordship on which they built the French monarchy.

Louis VI, the Fat (r. 1108–1137), secured complete control of the Ile-de-France, thus providing the dynasty with a dependable income from the region's abundant farms and the thriving trade of Paris. He shoved aside the great barons who had dominated the royal administration and replaced them with career bureaucrats who were loyal only to the king. The most prominent of these was the highly talented Suger, a lower-class priest who had been Louis's tutor and served the king as a statesman of vision.

Louis's grandson, Philip II Augustus (r. 1180–1223), proved himself a shrewd realist who outmaneuvered his vassal, the English king John, to recover much of western France for himself. To administer his domain and newly ac-

quired lands, Philip introduced new royal officials, the *baillis,* who were paid professionals; some were trained in Roman law. Directly responsible to the king, they had full administrative, judicial, and military powers in their districts. Philip tolerated considerable regional diversity, but the *baillis* laid the foundation for a bureaucracy that centralized French government. Many historians consider Philip Augustus the most important figure in establishing the unity of the French state.

The medieval French king who came closest to exemplifying the moral ideals of kingship was Louis IX (r. 1226–1270), who was canonized St. Louis in 1297 for his exemplary piety and reputation for justice. A tall imposing figure, Louis was blessed with impeccable manners and a chivalrous nature. Prompted by an ardent desire to lead a Crusade to the Holy Land, he sought to strengthen the kingdom so that it could operate and survive in his absence. He introduced a system of judicial appeals that expanded royal justice and investigated the honesty of the *baillis.*

Map 9.3 Western European Kingdoms in the Late Twelfth Century

The kings of England occupied Ireland as well as much of western France. France itself was consolidated around the Ile-de-France, the area around Paris. The kingdoms of Germany, Bohemia, Burgundy, and Italy were ruled by the German emperors.

The reputation of the monarchy so carefully burnished by Louis IX suffered during the reign of his grandson, Philip IV, the Fair (r. 1285–1314)—known for his ruthless use of power. Philip greatly expanded the king's authority and also managed to bring the Church under his personal control, making the French clergy largely exempt from papal supervision. To pay for his frequent wars, Philip expelled the Jews after stripping them of their lands and goods, and then turned against the rich Order of the Knights Templar, a crusader order that had amassed a fortune as the papal banker and creditor of Philip. He confiscated the Templars' lands and tortured the knights to extort confessions to various crimes in a perverse campaign to discredit them. Philip was perhaps most effective in finding new ways to increase taxation. Under Philip, royal revenues grew tenfold from what they had been in the saintly reign of Louis IX.

Lord of All Lords: The King of England

When William I, the Conqueror (r. 1066–1087), seized England in 1066, he claimed all the land for himself. The new king kept about one-fifth of the land under his personal rule and parceled out the rest to the loyal nobles, monasteries, and the churches. This policy ensured that every bit of England was held as a fief, directly or indirectly, from the king, a principle of lordship enforced by an oath of loyalty to the crown required of all vassals. About 180 great lords from among the Norman aristocracy held land directly from the king, and hundreds of lesser nobles were vassals of these great lords. William accomplished what other kings only dreamed about: He had truly made himself the lord of all lords. William's hierarchy of nobles transformed the nature of the English monarchy, giving the Norman kings far greater authority over England than any of the earlier Anglo-Saxon kings had enjoyed and creating a more unified realm than any kingdom on the continent.

The legacy of the conquest provided William's successors with a decided advantage in centralizing the monarchy. Nevertheless, the system required the king's close personal attention. King Henry II (r. 1154–1189) proved himself an indefatigable administrator and calculating realist who made England the best-governed kingdom in Europe at the time. Reacting to the anarchy that prevailed when he ascended to the throne, he strengthened the government of England and extended English authority—with varying degrees of success—over Ireland, Wales, and Scotland.

The greatest innovations of Henry's rule were judicial. His use of sheriffs to enforce the royal will produced the legends of Robin Hood, the bandit who resisted the nasty sheriff of Nottingham on behalf of the poor. But in reality the sheriffs probably did more good than harm in protecting the weak against the powerful. In attempting to reduce the jurisdiction of the nobles, Henry made it possible for almost anyone to obtain a writ that moved a case to a royal court. To make justice more available to those who could not travel to Westminster, just outside London where the royal court usually sat, Henry introduced a system of itinerant circuit court° judges who visited every shire in the land four times a year. When this judge arrived, the sheriff was required to assemble a group of men familiar with local affairs to report the major crimes that had been committed since the judge's last visit. These assemblies were the origins of the grand jury° system, which persists to this day as the means for indicting someone for a crime.

For disputes over the possession of land, sheriffs assembled a group of twelve local men who testified under oath about the claims of the disputants, and the judge made his decision on the basis of their testimony. These assemblies were the beginning of trial by jury°. The system was later extended to criminal cases and remains the basis for rendering legal verdicts in common-law countries, including Britain, the United States, and Canada.

With his usual directness, Henry tackled the special legal privileges of the clergy, the thorn in the side of medieval kings everywhere. According to canon law, priests could be tried only in church courts, which were notoriously easygoing in punishing even murderers with a simple penance. Moreover, these verdicts—however trivial—could be appealed to Rome, a process that could delay justice for years. Henry wanted to subject priests who had committed crimes to the jurisdiction of the royal courts in order to establish a universal justice that applied to everyone in the realm, a principle fiercely opposed by Thomas Becket, the archbishop of Canterbury. When four knights—believing they were acting on the king's wishes—murdered Becket before the altar of Canterbury cathedral, the public was outraged, and Henry's attempts to subject the Church to royal justice were ruined. Becket was soon canonized and revered as England's most famous saint.

The royal powers assembled by Henry met strong reaction under King John (r. 1199–1216). In 1204 John lost to King Philip II of France the duchy of Normandy, which had been one of the foundations of English royal power since William the Conqueror. After the French defeated King John at the Battle of Bouvines in 1214, the barons of England grew tired of being asked to pay for wars the king lost. In 1215 some English barons forced John to sign Magna Carta° ("great charter," in reference to its size), in which the king pledged to respect the traditional feudal privileges of the nobility, towns, and clergy. Contrary to widespread belief, Magna Carta had nothing to do with asserting the liberty of the common people or guaranteeing universal rights. It addressed only the privileges of a select few rather than the rights of the many. Subsequent kings, however, swore to uphold it, thereby accepting the fundamental principle that even the king was obliged to respect the law. After Magna Carta the lord of all lords became less so.

English government boasted two important innovations under King Edward I (r. 1272–1307). The first was the foundation of the English Parliament (from the French "talking together"). Edward called together the clergy, barons, knights, and townsmen in Parliament in order to raise large sums of money for his foreign wars. The members of Parliament had little choice but to comply with the king's demands, and all they received in return was Edward's explanation of what he was going to do with their money. The English Parliament differed from similar assemblies on the Continent in that it more often included representatives of the "commons." The commons consisted of townsmen and prosperous farmers who lacked titles of nobility but whom the king summoned because he needed their money. The second governmental innovation during Edward's reign consisted of an extensive body of legal reforms. Edward curtailed the power of the local courts, which were dominated by rural landlords and aristocrats. He began to issue statutes that applied to the entire kingdom. Under Edward, lawyers began to practice at the Inns of Court in London, where they transformed customary legal practices into the common law that still survives as the foundation of Anglo-American law.

A Divided Regime: The German Empire

Heir to the old Carolingian kingdom of East Francia, the German Empire suffered from the division between its principal component parts in Germany and northern Italy. Germany itself was an ill-defined region, subdivided by deep ethnic diversity and powerful dukes who ruled their lands with a spirit of fierce independence. As a result, emperors could not rule Germany directly but only by demanding homage from the dukes who became imperial vassals. These feudal bonds were fragile substitutes for the kinds of monarchic institutions that evolved in France and England. An effective emperor could call on the dukes to help him crush rivals, but he could neither dictate to his vassals nor claim vacant fiefs for the crown, as in France and England. The emperor's best asset was the force of his personality and his willingness to engage in a perpetual show of force to prevent rebellion. In northern Italy, the other part of the emperor's dominion, he did not even enjoy these extensive ties of vassalage and could rely only on vague legal rights granted by the imperial title and his ability to keep an army on the scene.

The century between the election of Frederick I (r. 1152–1190), known as Barbarossa or "red-beard," and the death of his grandson Frederick II (r. 1212–1250) represented the great age of the medieval German Empire, a period of relative stability preceded and followed by disastrous phases of anarchy and civil war. Both of these Hohenstaufen emperors, however, faced hostility from the popes whose own monarchic pretensions clashed with imperial rule in Italy.

Barbarossa projected enormous personal charisma that helped him awe recalcitrant vassals. He became a careful student of the imperial dignities encoded in Roman law, surrounded himself with experts in that law, and considered himself the heir of the great emperors Constantine, Justinian, and Charlemagne. He even managed to have Charlemagne canonized a saint.

Barbarossa's lofty ambitions contrasted with the flimsy base of his support. His own ancestral lands were in Swabia, an impoverished region barely capable of subsistence let alone supporting Frederick's imperial adventures. To set himself on a firmer financial footing, Frederick launched a series of expeditions across the Alps to subdue the enormously wealthy Italian cities that were technically part of his realm, even though they acted as if they were independent. The campaign proved a disaster. It galvanized papal opposition to him and forced the Italian city-states to put aside their rivalries to form an anti-imperial coalition, the Lombard League. At the Battle of Legnano in 1176 the League decisively defeated the German imperial army, forcing Barbarossa to recognize the autonomy of the city-states.

Barbarossa's young grandson, Frederick II, turned the traditional policy of the German emperors upside down. Instead of residing in Germany and attempting to influence Italian affairs from afar, Frederick, who loved the warm climate and engaging society of the South, lived in Sicily and left Germany alone.

Frederick has long enjoyed a remarkable historical reputation as the "wonder of the world," the most cosmopolitan monarch of the Middle Ages, who laid out grand plans for a united Italy embodied in the Constitutions of Melfi, which he put forth in 1231 (see Map 9.4). Through them, he proposed to rule through a professional imperial bureaucracy, to employ itinerant inspectors to check corruption, and to introduce uniform statutes based on Roman law. In effect, he sought a level of uniformity similar to what France and England had achieved during this period, and he was probably subject to similar influences derived from ancient Roman political theory and law. However, the popes' enduring antagonism to these plans and Frederick's own despotic tendencies undermined these ambitious and potentially fruitful reforms. He cut himself off from honest advice by declaring it an act of sacrilege even to discuss, let

CHRONOLOGY

Strengthening the Center of the West

1170	Murder of Thomas Becket
1176	Battle of Legnano; Lombard League defeats Emperor Frederick I (Barbarossa)
1214	Battle of Bouvines; Philip II of France, allied to Emperor Frederick II, defeats John of England and his allies
1215	Magna Carta
1231	Constitutions of Melfi

alone question, any of his decisions. He so overtaxed southern Italy and Sicily that these lands, which were once the richest in Italy, became an economic backwater. His abandonment of Germany to its feuding princes prevented the centralization and implementation of legal reforms that took place in France and England.

After Frederick II's death, his successors lost their hold on both Italy and Germany. During the nearly constant warfare and turmoil of the late thirteenth century, the exceedingly inappropriate name of "Holy Roman Empire" came into general use for the German Empire. The term suggested a universal empire ordained by God and descended from ancient Rome, but the lofty claims embedded in the name found no basis in the crude reality of the rebellious, disunited lands of Germany and Italy.

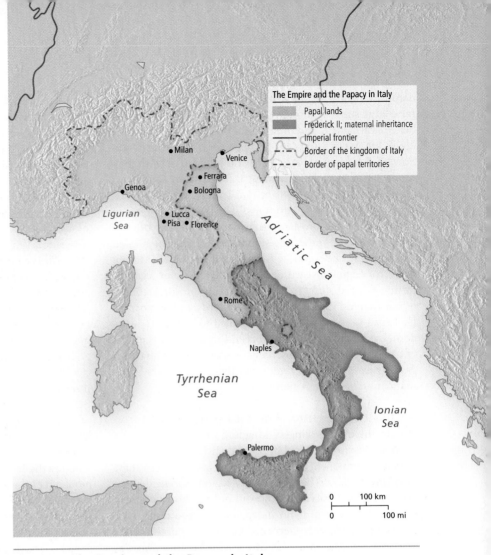

Map 9.4   The Empire and the Papacy in Italy
During the reign of Emperor Frederick II, the kingdom of Sicily became the most potent power in Italy and presented a challenge to the papacy. After Frederick's death, the peninsula suffered from a long series of wars as rival claimants attempted to replace him in Sicily and the popes attempted to control events.

Medieval Culture: The Search for Understanding

■ What made western European culture distinctive?

Cultural encounters during the High Middle Ages took many forms. Some were direct exchanges, as when Christians and Muslims in crusader Jerusalem discovered their different ways of praying. Other encounters were more indirect, as when medieval thinkers read the books of ancient philosophers and so were confronted with challenging ideas that did not fit easily into their view of the world. During the twelfth and thirteenth centuries, this second kind of encounter, based on the renewed availability of works of classical Greek philosophy, opened creative possibilities, especially in theology. The Greek philosophers had been dead for nearly 1,500 years, but the medieval thinkers who rediscovered ancient philosophy experienced a profound cultural shock. First Muslim and then Jewish and Christian writers struggled to reconcile the rational approach of Aristotle and other Greek philosophers with the faith demanded by Islam, Judaism, and Christianity. Some suffered from a crisis of faith. Others confronted the challenge presented by ancient philosophy and attempted to reconcile reason and faith by creating new philosophical systems.

The medieval intellectual engagement with new ideas spread in many directions. Lawyers began to look back to ancient Roman law for guidance about how to settle disputes, adjudicate crimes, and create governmental institutions. Muslim influences reinvigorated the Christian understanding of the sciences. Themes found in Persian love poetry, which were echoed in Arabic poems, found their way into the Christian notion of courtly love. Catholic western Europe experienced a cultural flowering through the spread of education, the growing power of Latin learning, and the invention of the university. Distinctively Western forms developed in literature, music, drama, and above all the Romanesque and Gothic architecture of Europe's great cathedrals.

The city of Paris was the breeding ground for much creative activity. The dynamism of Paris attracted thinkers and artists from all over Europe. Thirteenth-century Paris represented the cultural pinnacle of the High Middle Ages, comparable to Athens in the fifth century B.C.E. or Florence in the fifteenth century.

Revival of Learning

The magnitude of the educational revolution in medieval western Europe is clear from simple statistics. In 1050 less than 1 percent of the population of Latin Christian Europe could read, and most of these literate people were priests who knew just enough Latin to recite the offices of the liturgy. Four hundred years later, as much as 40 percent of men and a smaller percentage of women were literate in the cities of western Europe. Europeans had embraced learning on a massive scale even before inexpensive printed books became available in the late fifteenth century. In fact, the printing revolution of the fifteenth century was not so much the stimulus for new learning as a response to the escalating demand for more books. How did this demand come about?

In 1050 education was available only in monasteries and cathedral schools, and the curriculum was very basic, usually only reading and writing. These two kinds of schools had different educational missions. Monastic education trained monks to read the books available in their libraries as an aid to contemplating the mysteries of the next world. In contrast, the cathedral schools, which trained members of the ecclesiastical hierarchy, emphasized the practical skills of rational analysis that would help future priests, bishops, and royal advisers solve the problems of this world.

By 1100 the number of cathedral schools had grown significantly and the curriculum expanded to include the study of the ancient Roman masters, Cicero and Virgil, who became models for clear Latin composition. These schools met the demand for trained officials from various sources—the thriving cities, the growing church bureaucracy, and the infant bureaucracies of the Western kingdoms. As the number of schools expanded, they became less exclusively devoted to religious training and began to provide a practical education for laypeople. But the Church was still the dominant force.

Scholasticism: A Christian Philosophy

In addition to teaching Latin grammar, cathedral schools recognized a growing need for training in logic as well. Refuting heresies required precise logical arguments. Anselm of Canterbury (ca. 1033–1109), for example, employed strict logic in an attempt to prove the existence of God. He began with the question of how the mind conceived ideas. He could not imagine ideas coming from

nothing, arguing that they must have some basis in reality. Did not the very presence of the idea of God in the mind, Anselm concluded, demonstrate that God must exist? Intrigued by such arguments, students began to seek more advanced instruction than that provided by the standard curriculum. They tended to gather around popular lecturers in the cathedral schools, where they were trained in scholasticism, which emphasized the critical methods of reasoning, pioneered by Anselm.

Scholasticism° literally means "of the schools," but the term also refers to a broad philosophical and theological movement that dominated medieval thought. In this broader sense, scholasticism refers to the use of logic learned from Aristotle to interpret the meaning of the Bible and the writings of the Church Fathers, who created Christian theology in its first centuries. Books were scarce in the cathedral schools because the only means of duplication before the invention of the printing press was hand copying onto expensive sheepskin parchment. So the principal method of teaching and learning was the lecture. Teachers read Latin texts out loud, and students were obliged to memorize what they heard. In the classroom the lecturer would recite a short passage, present the comments of other authorities on it, and draw his own conclusions. He would then move on to another brief passage and repeat the process. Students heard the same lectures over and over again until they had thoroughly memorized the text under discussion. In addition to lectures, scholastics engaged in disputations. Participants in a disputation presented oral arguments for or against a particular thesis, a process called dialectical reasoning. Disputants were evaluated on their ability to investigate through logic the truth of a thesis. Disputations required several skills—verbal facility, a prodigious memory so that apt citations could be made, and the ability to think quickly. The process we know today as debate originated with these medieval disputations. Lectures and disputations became the core activities of the scholastics, who considered all subjects, however sacred, as appropriate for reasoned examination.

None of the scholastic teachers was more popular than the acerbic, witty, and daring Peter Abelard (1079–1142). Students from all over Europe flocked to hear Abelard's lectures at the cathedral school of Paris. Abelard's clever criticisms of the ideas of other thinkers delighted students. In *Sic et Non* ("Yes and No"), Abelard boldly examined some of the foundations of Christian truth. Employing the dialectical reasoning of a disputation, he presented both sides of 150 theological problems discussed by the Church Fathers. He left the conclusions open in order to challenge his students and readers to think further, but his intention seems to have been less to undermine accepted biblical truths than to point out how apparent disagreements among the experts masked a deeper level of agreement about Christian truth.

Universities: Organizing Learning

From the cathedral schools arose the first universities. The University of Paris evolved from the cathedral school where Abelard once taught. Initially the universities were little more than guilds (trade associations), organized by either students or teachers to protect their interests. As members of a guild, students bargained with their professors and townspeople, as would other tradesmen, over costs and established minimum standards of instruction. The guild of the law students at Bologna received a charter in 1158, which probably made it the first university. Some of the early universities were professional schools, such as the medical faculty at Salerno, but true to their origins as cathedral schools, most emphasized theology over other subjects.

The medieval universities formulated the basic educational practices that are still in place today. They established a curriculum, examined students, conferred degrees, and conducted graduation ceremonies. Students and teachers wore distinctive robes, which are still worn at graduation ceremonies. Teachers were clergymen—that is, they "professed" religion; hence the title of *professor* for a university instructor. In their first years students pursued the liberal arts curriculum, which consisted of the *trivium* (grammar, rhetoric, and logic) and the *quadrivium* (arithmetic, geometry, astronomy, and music). This curriculum is forerunner of the arts and sciences faculties and distribution requirements in modern universities. Medieval university students devoted many years to rigorous study and rote memoriza-

tion. Completion of a professional doctorate in law, medicine, or theology typically required more than ten years.

Medieval universities did not admit women, in part because women were barred from the priesthood and most university students were training to become priests. (Women did not attend universities in significant numbers until the nineteenth century.) There was also a widespread fear of learned women who might think on their own. The few women who did receive advanced educations had to rely on a private tutor.

The Ancients: Renaissance of the Twelfth Century

The scholastics' integration of Greek philosophy with Christian theology represents a key facet of the Twelfth-Century Renaissance°, a revival of interest in the ancients comparable in importance to the Carolingian Renaissance of the ninth century and the Italian Renaissance of the fifteenth. During Peter Abelard's lifetime, very few western Europeans knew Greek, the language of ancient philosophy, and only a few works of the Greeks were available in Latin translations. Between about 1140 and 1260 this cultural isolation dramatically changed.

A flood of new Latin translations of the Greek classics came from Sicily and Spain, where Christians had close contacts with Muslims and Jews. Muslim philosophers had translated into Arabic the Greek philosophical and scientific classics, which were readily available in the Middle East and North Africa. These Arabic translations were then translated into Latin, often by Jewish scholars who knew both languages. Later a few Catholic scholars traveled to Byzantium, where they learned enough Greek to make even better translations from the originals.

As they encountered the philosophy of the ancients, Muslim, Jewish, and Christian thinkers faced profoundly disturbing problems. The principles of faith revealed in the Qur'an of Islam and the Hebrew and Christian Bibles were not easily reconciled with the philosophical method of reasoning found in Greek works, especially those by Aristotle. These religious thinkers recognized the superiority of Greek thought over their own. They worried that the power of philosophical reasoning undermined religious truth. As men of faith they challenged themselves to demonstrate that philosophy did not contradict religious teaching, and some of them went even further to employ philosophical reasoning to demonstrate the truth of religion. They always faced opposition within their own religious faiths, how-

A Lecture in a Medieval University
Some of the students are sleeping and others are chatting with their neighbors. The most earnest students are sitting in the front row. Some things never change.

ever, especially from people who thought philosophical reason was an impediment to religious faith.

Avicenna (980–1037) was the first Muslim thinker to confront the questions raised by Greek philosophy, such as how to prove the existence of God or account for the creation of the world. An Iranian physician, Avicenna's commentaries on Aristotle deeply influenced the Catholic scholastics, who quoted him extensively. Avicenna attempted a rational proof of the existence of God based on the "necessary existent." Without God nothing exists; therefore, if we exist, so must God.

Following Avicenna's lead, Al-Ghazali (1058–1111) taught the ancient Greek philosophers to Muslim students. But from the daunting task of reconciling philosophy and religion he suffered a nervous breakdown, which forced him to abandon lecturing temporarily and turn to religious mysticism. After this experience, he wrote *The Incoherence of the Philosophers,* in which he argued that religious truth was more accessible through mystical experience than through rational and systematic analysis.

The most powerful answer to Al-Ghazali's critique of philosophy came from Averroës (1126–1198), who rose to become the chief judge of Córdoba, Spain, and an adviser to the caliph. In *The Incoherence of the Incoherence* (1179–1180), Averroës argued that the aim of philosophy is to explain the true, inner meaning of religious revelations. This inner meaning, however, should not be disclosed to the unlettered masses, which must be told only the simple, literal stories and metaphors of Scripture. Although lively and persuasive, Averroës's defense of philosophy failed to revive philosophical speculation within Islam. Once far superior to that of the Latin Christian world, Islamic philosophy and science declined as Muslim thinkers turned to mysticism and rote learning over rational debate. Averroës received a more sympathetic hearing among Jews and Catholics than among Muslims.

DOCUMENT

Ibn Rushd (Averroës) (12th c.)

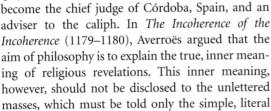

Within Judaism, many had attempted unsuccessfully to reconcile Greek philosophy with Hebrew law and scripture. Success was achieved by a contemporary of Averroës, also from Córdoba—the Jewish philosopher, jurist, and physician Moses Maimonides (1135–1204). His most important work in religious philosophy was *The Guide for the Perplexed* (ca. 1191), which synthesized Greek philosophy, science, and Judaism. Widely read in Arabic, Hebrew, and Latin versions, the book stimulated both Jewish and Christian philosophy. Maimonides's efforts, like those of Averroës, distressed many of his fellow Jews, some of whom desecrated his tomb, but as controversy abated he came to be recognized as a pillar of Jewish thought.

For medieval Catholic philosophers, one of the most difficult tasks was reconciling the biblical account of the divine creation with Aristotle's teaching that the universe was eternal. Even in this early clash between science and religion, creationism was the sticking point. Following the lead

established by Avicenna, Averroës, and Maimonides, the great project of the scholastics became to demonstrate the fundamental harmony between Christian faith and the philosophical knowledge of the ancients.

The most effective resolution of the apparent conflict between faith and philosophy was found in the work of Thomas Aquinas (1225–1274), whose philosophy is called Thomism°. A Dominican friar, Aquinas spent most of his career developing a school system for the Dominicans in Italy, but he also spent two short periods teaching at the University of Paris. Aquinas avoided distracting controversies and academic disputes to concentrate on his two great summaries of human knowledge—the *Summary of the Catholic Faith Against the Gentiles* (1261) and the *Summary of Theology* (1265–1274). In both of these massive scholastic works, reason fully confirmed Christian faith. Encyclopedias of knowledge, they rigorously examined whole fields through dialectical reasoning. Aquinas's method was to pose a question derived from the Bible—such as "Whether woman was made from man?"—and then draw on the accumulated thought of the past to suggest answers, raise critical objections to the answers, refute the objections, and reach a conclusion. Then he proceeded to the next question, "Whether [woman was made] of man's rib?"

Building on the works of Averroës, Aquinas solved the problem of reconciling philosophy and religion by drawing a distinction between *natural truth* and *revealed truth*. For Aquinas, natural truth meant the kinds of things anyone can know through the operation of human reason; revealed truth referred to the things that can be known only through revelation, such as the Trinity and the incarnation of Christ. Aquinas argued that these two kinds of truths could not possibly contradict one another because both came from God. Apparent contradictions could be accommodated by an understanding of a higher truth. On the issue of Creation, for example, Aquinas argued that Aristotle's understanding of the eternal universe was inferior to the higher revealed truth of the Bible that God created the universe in seven days.

The most influential of the scholastic thinkers, Aquinas asserted that to achieve religious truth one should start with faith and then use reason to reach conclusions. He was the first to understand theology systematically in this way, and in doing so he raised a storm of opposition among Christians who were threatened by philosophical reason. Like the work of Avicenna and Maimonides before him, Aquinas's writings were at first prohibited by the theological faculties in universities. Nevertheless, his method remains crucial for Catholic theology to this day.

Just as scholastic theologians looked to ancient Greek philosophy as a guide to reason, jurists revived ancient Roman law, especially at the universities of Bologna and Pavia in Italy. In the law faculties, students were required to learn the legal work of the Emperor Justinian—the text of the *Body of the Civil Law,* together with the commentaries on it. The systematic approach of Roman law provided a way to make the legal system less arbitrary for judges, lawyers, bureaucrats, and advisers to kings and popes. Laws had long consisted of a contradictory mess of municipal regulations, Germanic customs, and feudal precepts. Under Roman law, judges were obliged to justify their verdicts according to prescribed standards of evidence and procedure. The revival of Roman law in the twelfth century made possible the legal system that still guides most of continental Europe.

Epic Violence and Courtly Love

In addition to the developments in philosophy, theology, and the law, the Twelfth-Century Renaissance included a remarkable literary output in the vernacular languages, the tongues spoken in everyday life. The great heroic epics, most of which were adapted from oral tradition or composed between 1050 and 1150, were in English, German, Celtic, Slavonic, Nordic, Icelandic, French, and Spanish. These epics, often repeated from memory as popular entertainment, recounted adventure stories about medieval warriors. They were manly stories that celebrated the beauty and terror of battle and glorified cracked skulls and brutal death: "Now Roland feels that he is at death's door; Out of his ears the brain is running forth." Women hardly appear at all in these epics, except as backdrops to the battles among men or as battered wives.

By the end of the twelfth century, however, a new vernacular literature appeared, created by poets called troubadours°. Unlike the creators of vernacular epics, the troubadour poets included women as well as men, and their literature reflected an entirely new sensibility about the relationships between men and women. The troubadours wrote poems of love, meant to be sung to music; their literary movement is called courtly love°. They composed in Provençal, one of the languages of southern France, and the first audience for their poems was in the courts of southern France. These graciously elegant poems clearly show influences from Arabic love poetry and especially from Muslim mystical literature in which the soul, depicted as feminine, seeks her masculine God/lover. The troubadours secularized this theme of religious union by portraying the ennobling possibilities of the love between a woman and a man. In so doing, they popularized the idea of romantic love, one of the most powerful concepts in all of Western history, an ideal that still dominates popular culture to this day.

An innovative aspect of the courtly love poems of the troubadours was their idealization of women. The male troubadours, such as Chrétien de Troyes (1135–1183), placed women on a pedestal and treated men as the "love vassals" of beloved women to whom they owed loyalty and service. Female troubadours, such as Marie de France (dates unknown), did not place women on a pedestal but idealized emotionally honest and open relationships between lovers. Unlike the epics in which women were brutalized, the troubadours typically saw women as holding power over men or acting as their equals. From southern France, courtly love spread to Germany and elsewhere throughout Europe. Based on a now lost version in Old French, Gottfried von Strassburg recomposed in German the romance of Tristan and Iseult. At first the two lovers struggle to resist temptation and to doubt the other's love, but they find themselves unable to keep away from one another. His resistance is motivated by a sense of honor and hers by "maiden shame," but the power of love triumphs over prudence and the two consummate the relationship. Many of the German poems were romances that reinterpreted the stories of the epics to conform to the values of courtly love. The courtly love ideal has persisted across the centuries in innumerable popular revivals.

The Center of Medieval Culture: The Great Cathedrals

When tourists visit a European city today, they usually want to see its cathedral. Most of these imposing structures were built between 1050 and 1300 and symbolize the soaring ambitions and imaginations of their largely unknown builders. During the great medieval building boom, old churches, which were often perfectly adequate but out of style, were ripped down. In their place hundreds of new cathedrals and thousands of other churches were erected, sparing no expense and reflecting the latest experimental techniques in architectural engineering and artistic fashion. These buildings became multimedia centers for the arts—incorporating architecture, sculpture, stained glass, and painting in their structure and providing a setting for the performance of music and drama. The medieval cathedrals took decades, sometimes centuries, to build at great cost and sacrifice. They are magnificent examples of the pious devotion to God of the people who built them.

Architecture: The Romanesque and Gothic Styles

The Romanesque° style spread throughout western Europe during the eleventh century and the first half of the twelfth century because the master masons who understood sophisticated stone construction techniques traveled from one building site to another, bringing with them a uniform style. The principal innovation of the Romanesque was the arched stone roofs, which were more aesthetically pleasing and less vulnerable to fire than the flat roofs they replaced. The rounded arches of these stone roofs were called barrel vaults because they looked like the inside of a barrel.

Romanesque Cathedral Architecture

The rounded arches, the massive columns, the barrel vaults in the ceilings, and the small windows were characteristic of the Romanesque style. Compare the massiveness of this interior with the Gothic style of the Abbey Church of St. Denis in the next illustration. This Romanesque church in Vezelay, France, was dedicated to Mary Magdalen and became a center for her veneration during the Middle Ages.

Romanesque churches employed transepts, which fashioned the church into the shape of a cross if viewed from above, the vantage point of God. The intersection of the transept with the nave of the church required a cross vault, a construction that demanded considerable expertise. The high stone vaults of Romanesque churches and cathedrals required the support of massive stone pillars and thick walls. As a result, windows were small slits that imitated the slit windows of castles. Romanesque churches had a dark, yet cozy appearance, which was sometimes enlivened by painted walls or sculpture.

The religious experience of worshiping in a Romanesque cathedral had an intimate, almost familiar quality to it. The worshiper was enveloped by a comforting space, surrounded by family and neighbors, and close to deceased rel-

atives buried beneath the pavement or in tombs that lined the walls. Romanesque churches and cathedrals were the first architectural expression of the new and growing medieval cities, proud and wealthy places. In such a building, God became a fellow townsman, an associate in the grand new project of making cities habitable and comfortable.

More than a century after the urban revival began, the Gothic° style replaced the Romanesque during the late twelfth and thirteenth centuries. The innovation of this style was the ribbed vault and pointed arches, which superseded the barrel vault of the Romanesque. These narrow pointed arches drew the viewer's eye upward toward God and gave the building the appearance of weightlessness that symbolized the Christian's uplifting reach for heaven. The neighborly solidity of the Romanesque style was abandoned for an effect that stimulated a mystical appreciation of God's utter otherness, the supreme divinity far above mortal men and women. The Gothic style also introduced the innovation of the flying buttress, an arched construction on the outside of the walls that redistributed the weight of the roof. This innovation allowed for thin walls, which were pierced by windows much bigger than was possible with Romanesque construction techniques.

IMAGE

Notre-Dame, Paris

The result was stunning. The stonework of a Gothic cathedral became a skeleton to support massive expanses of stained glass, transforming the interior spaces into a mystical haven from the outside world. At different times of the day, the multicolored windows converted sunlight into an ever-changing light show that offered sparkling hints of the secret truths of God's Creation. See, for example, the image on page 304. The light that passed through these windows symbolized the light of God. The windows themselves contained scenes that were an encyclopedia of medieval knowledge and lore. In addition to Bible stories and the lives of saints, these windows depicted common people at their trades, animals, plants, and natural wonders. These windows celebrated not only the promise of salvation but all the wonders of God's creation. They drew worshipers out of the busy city in which they lived and worked toward the perfect realm of the divine.

The first Gothic church was built at the abbey of St. Denis, outside Paris, under the direction of the abbot Suger. From northern France the style spread all across Europe. In France, Germany, Italy, Spain, and England, cities made enormous financial sacrifices to construct new Gothic cathedrals during the economic boom years of the thirteenth century. Gothic cathedrals expressed civic pride as well as Christian piety, and cities vied to build taller and taller cathedrals with ever more daringly thin walls. The French city of Beauvais pushed beyond reasonable limits by building its cathedral so high that it collapsed. Because costs were so high, many cathedrals, such as the one in Siena, Italy, remained unfinished, but even the incomplete ones became vital symbols of local identity.

Flying Buttresses of Chartres Cathedral
The flying buttress did more than hold up the thin walls of Gothic cathedrals. The buttress created an almost lacelike appearance on the outside of the building, magnifying the sense of mystery evoked by the style.

Gothic Vaults
The delicately ribbed ceiling vaults and vast expanses of stained glass in the Abbey Church of St. Denis, France, contrast with the heavy barrel vaults of the Romanesque Cathedral in Vezelay.

Music and Drama: Reaching God's Ear and the Christian's Soul

The churches and cathedrals were devoted to the celebration of the Latin liturgy, which at the time was a chanted form of prayer. Because the function of chant was worship, music was one of the most exquisite expressions of medieval religious life. The liturgical chant that survives from the Middle Ages can still be sung today because the Benedictine monk Guido of Arezzo (ca. 990–1050) devised a system of musical notation, which forms the basis for modern Western musical notation. In Guido's time, chant was primarily plainchant°, a straightforward melody sung with simple harmony by a choir to accompany the recitation of the text of the liturgy. The simple clarity of plainchant matched the solid familiarity of the Romanesque style in church architecture.

In the Paris cathedral around 1170, however, musical experiments led to an important new breakthrough. Instead of using a simple plainchant melody to sing the liturgy, the simultaneous singing of two melodies was employed. This new form was called polyphony°, the singing of two or more independent melodies at the same time. Polyphony represented a major innovation in music by creating an enchanting sound to echo throughout the vast stone chambers of Gothic cathedrals, a musical form of praise that enhanced the mystical experience of worship.

In addition to its advances in architecture and music, Paris became the center for innovation in liturgical drama. Some time during the twelfth century, portions of the liturgy began to be acted out in short Latin plays, usually inside the church. These rudimentary plays were soon translated into the vernacular language so that everyone in the congregation could understand them. As they became more popular, the performances moved outside in front of the church. The function of these liturgical dramas was to educate as well as to worship. The priests who put on the plays wanted to teach Christian stories and provide moral examples to the young and to the uneducated laity. From these early liturgical plays arose the Western dramatic tradition that evolved into the secular theater of Shakespeare and the ubiquitous dramas of modern television and film.

Conclusion

Asserting Western Culture

During the twelfth and thirteenth centuries, western Europe matured into its own self-confident identity. Through penal laws and discrimination heretical groups within Europe were systematically transformed into outcasts or eliminated altogether. The processes of creating outcasts within Europe and defining what it meant to be a Catholic accompanied the external assertion of Latin power. The West looked both inward and outward as it measured itself, defined itself, and promoted itself, especially through the Crusades.

Less a semibarbarian backwater than it had been even in the time of Charlemagne, western Europe cultivated modes of thought that revealed an almost limitless capacity for creative renewal and critical self-examination. That capacity, first evident during the Twelfth-Century Renaissance, is what has most distinguished the West ever since. Part of the reason for this creative capacity rested in the cultivation of critical methods of thinking based on applying the logic of ancient Greek philosophy to the Bible and on defending the conclusions drawn through disputations. These methods were codified in scholasticism. No medieval thinker followed these critical methods consistently, and they repeatedly caused alarm among some believers. However, this tendency to question basic assumptions is among the greatest achievements of Western civilization. The western European university system, which was based on teaching methods of critical inquiry, differed from the educational institutions in other cultures, such as Byzantium or Islam, that were devoted to passing on received knowledge. This distinctive critical spirit connects the cultures of the ancient, medieval, and modern West.

Suggestions for Further Reading

For a comprehensive listing of suggested readings, please go to www.ablongman.com/levack2e/chapter9

Bony, Jean. *French Gothic Architecture of the Twelfth and Thirteenth Centuries.* 1983. With many beautiful illustrations, this is a good way to begin an investigation of these magnificent buildings.

Colish, Marcia L. *Medieval Foundations of the Western Intellectual Tradition, 400–1400.* 1997. The best general study.

Gimpel, Jean. *The Medieval Machine: The Industrial Revolution of the Middle Ages.* 1976. A short, lucid account of the power and agricultural revolutions.

Keen, Maurice. *Chivalry.* 1984. Readable and balanced in its coverage of this sometimes misunderstood phenomenon.

Lambert, Malcolm. *Medieval Heresy: Popular Movements from the Gregorian Reform to the Reformation.* 2nd ed. 1992. The best general study of heresy.

Lawrence, C. H. *The Friars: The Impact of the Early Mendicant Movement on Western Society.* 1994. The best general study of the influence of Dominicans and Franciscans.

Moore, R. I. *The Formation of a Persecuting Society: Power and Deviance in Western Europe, 950–1250.* 1987. A brilliant analysis of how Europe became a persecuting society.

Morris, Colin. *The Papal Monarchy: The Western Church from 1050 to 1250.* 1989. A thorough study that should be the beginning point for further investigation of the many fascinating figures in the medieval Church.

Mundy, John H. *Europe in the High Middle Ages, 1150–1309.* 3rd ed. 1999. A comprehensive introduction to the period.

Peters, Edward. *Europe and the Middle Ages.* 1989. An excellent general survey.

Strayer, Joseph R. *On the Medieval Origins of the Modern State.* 1970. Still the best short analysis.

Notes

1. Cited in Jacques Dalarun, "The Clerical Gaze," in Christiane Klapisch-Zuber, ed., *A History of Women in the West,* Vol. 2: *Silences of the Middle Ages* (1992), 27.

2. Edward Peters, *Heresy and Authority in the Middle Ages* (1980), 177.

3. A. F. Pollock and F. W. Maitland, *The History of English Law,* Vol. 1 (1895), 468.

4. Cited in Emmanuel Le Roy Ladurie, *Montaillou: Promised Land of Error,* trans. Barbara Bray (1978), 130.

5. Ibid., 56.

6. Ibid., 63.

The Medieval West in Crisis

10

THE FOURTEENTH CENTURY DAWNED WITH A CHILL. IN 1303 AND THEN again during 1306–1307, the Baltic Sea froze over. No one had ever heard of that happening before, and the freezings foretold worse disasters. The cold spread beyond its normal winter season, arriving earlier in the autumn and staying later into the summer. Then it started to rain and did not let up. The Caspian Sea began to rise, flooding villages along its shores. In the summer of 1314 all across Europe, crops rotted in sodden fields. The meager harvest came late, precipitating a surge in prices for farm produce and forcing King Edward II of England to impose price controls. But capping prices did not grow more food.

In 1315 the situation got worse. In England during that year, the price of wheat rose 800 percent. Preachers compared the ceaseless rains to the great flood in the Bible, and floods did come, overwhelming dikes in the Netherlands and England, washing away entire towns in Germany, turning fields into lakes in France. Everywhere crops failed.

Things got much worse. Torrential rains fell again in 1316, and for the third straight year the crops failed, creating the most severe famine in recorded European history. The effects were most dramatic in the far north. In Scandinavia agriculture almost disappeared, in Iceland peasants abandoned farming and turned to fishing and herding sheep, and in Greenland the European settlers began to die out. Already malnourished, the people of Europe became susceptible to disease and starvation. Desperate people resorted to desperate options. They ate cats, rats, insects, reptiles, animal dung, and tree leaves. Stories spread that some ate their own children. In Poland the starving were said to cut down criminals from the gallows for food.

By the 1340s, nearly all of Europe was gripped by a seemingly endless cycle of disease and famine. Then came the deadliest epidemic in European history, the Black Death, which killed at least one-third of the total population.

The Mongol Threat This detail from the "Martyrdom of the Franciscans at Ceuta" shows a stereotypical Mongol, the man in the middle with a tall peaked hat. Ceuta is in North Africa, far from Mongol lands, but the depiction of a Mongol among the Muslims who executed Franciscan missionaries illustrates how Christians felt as threatened by the distant Mongols as by the nearby Muslims. The fresco is in the Franciscan church in Siena, Italy.

The economy collapsed. Trade disappeared. Industry shriveled. Hopeless peasants and urban workers revolted against their masters, demanding relief for their families. Neither state nor church could provide it. The two great medieval kingdoms of France and England became locked in a struggle that depleted royal treasuries and wasted the aristocracy in a series of clashes that historians call the Hundred Years' War. The popes left the dangerous streets of Rome for Avignon, France, where they were obliged to extort money to survive. After the pope returned to Rome, a group of French cardinals refused to go and elected a second pope, leading to the Great Schism when Europe was divided by allegiances to two different popes.

Of all the frightening elements of these disasters, perhaps most frightening was that their causes were hidden or completely unknowable given the technology and medical understanding that became available only a century ago. In many respects, the West was held captive by the climate, economic forces that no one completely understood, and microbes that would not be identified for another 550 years. During the twelfth and thirteenth centuries the West had asserted itself against Islam through the Crusades and spread Catholic Christianity to the far corners of Europe. During the fourteenth and early fifteenth centuries, however, the West drew into itself due to war, epidemics, and conflicts with the Mongol and Ottoman Empires. Western European contact with Russia became more intermittent, and the Byzantine Empire, once the bastion of Orthodox Christianity, fell to the Muslim armies of the Ottomans. The contact during the fourteenth and fifteenth centuries between Europe and the powerful Asian empires and between Europe and epidemic diseases raises the question of how such encounters could so profoundly transform the identity of the West.

- ■ **What caused the deaths of so many Europeans?**
- ■ **How did forces outside Europe, in particular the Mongol and Ottoman Empires, influence conditions in the West?**
- ■ **How did disturbances in the rudimentary global economy of the Middle Ages precipitate almost complete financial collapse and widespread social discontent in Europe?**
- ■ **How did incessant warfare transform the most powerful medieval states?**
- ■ **Why did the church fail to provide leadership and spiritual guidance during these difficult times?**
- ■ **How did European culture offer explanations and solace for the otherwise inexplicable calamities of the times?**

A Time of Death

■ **What caused the deaths of so many Europeans?**

Because of demographic research, we know a great deal about life and death during the fourteenth century. The magnitude of Europe's demographic crisis is evident from the raw numbers. In 1300 the population of Europe was about 74 million—roughly 15 percent of its current population. Population size can be an elementary measure of the success of a subsistence economy to keep people alive, and by this measure Europe had been very successful up to about 1300. It had approximately doubled its population over the previous 300 years. After the 1340s, however, Europe's ability to sustain its population evaporated. Population fell to just 52 million.

The raw numbers, however, hardly touch the magnitude of human suffering, which fell disproportionately on the poor, the very young, and the old. Death by starvation and disease became the fate of uncomprehending millions. The demographic crisis of the fourteenth century was the greatest natural disaster in Western civilization since the epidemics of antiquity. How did it happen?

Mass Starvation

Widespread famine began during the decade of 1310–1320. During the famines in 1315 and 1316 alone, more than 10 percent of Europe's population probably died. One eyewitness described bands of people as thin as skeletons in 1315:

> We saw a large number of both sexes, not only from nearby places but from places as much as five leagues away, barefooted, and many even, except the women, in a completely nude condition, with their priests coming together in procession at the church of the holy martyrs, and they devoutly carried bodies of the saints and other relics to be adored.[1]

A crisis in agriculture produced the Great Famine.

The agricultural revolution of the eleventh century had made available more food and more nutritious food, triggering the growth of the population during the Middle Ages. During the twelfth and thirteenth centuries, vast tracks of virgin forests were cleared for farming, especially in eastern Europe. By the thirteenth century this region resembled the American frontier during the nineteenth century, as settlers flocked in, staked out farms, and established new towns. The additional land under the plow created an escape valve for population growth by preventing large numbers of people from going hungry. But by the fourteenth century no more virgin land was available for clearing, which meant that an ever-growing population tried to survive on a fixed amount of farming land. Because of the limitations of medieval agriculture, the ability of farmers to produce food could not keep up with unchecked population growth.

At the same time there was probably a change in climate, known as the "Little Ice Age." The mean annual temperatures dropped just enough to make it impossible to grow crops in the more northerly parts of Europe and at high elevations such as the Alps. Before the fourteenth century, for example, grapes were grown in England to produce wine, but with the decline in temperatures, the grape vineyards ceased to produce. Growing grapes in England became possible again only with global warming in the late twentieth century. The result of the Little Ice Age was twofold. First, there was less land available for cultivation as it became impossible to grow crops in marginal areas. Second, a harsher climate shortened the growing season, which meant that even where crops could still grow they were less abundant.

The imbalance between food production and population set off a dreadful cycle of famine and disease. Insufficient food resulted in either malnutrition or starvation. Those who suffered from prolonged malnutrition were particularly susceptible to epidemic diseases, such as typhus, cholera, and dysentery. By 1300, children of the poor faced the probability of extreme hunger once or twice during the course of their childhood. In Pistoia, Italy, priests kept the *Book of the Dead,* which recorded the pattern: famine in 1313, famine in 1328–1329, famine and epidemic in 1339–1340 that killed one-quarter of the population, famine in 1346, famine and epidemic in 1347, and then the killing hammer blow—the Black Death in 1348 (see Map 10.1).

The Black Death

Following on the heels of the Great Famine, the Black Death arrived in Europe in the spring of 1348 with brutal force. In the lovely hilltop city of Siena, Italy, all industry stopped, carters refused to bring produce and cooking oil in from the countryside, and on June 2 the daily records of the

---

Map 10.1 Spread of the Black Death

After the Black Death first appeared in the ports of Italy in 1348, it spread relentlessly throughout most of Europe, killing at least 20 million people in Europe alone.

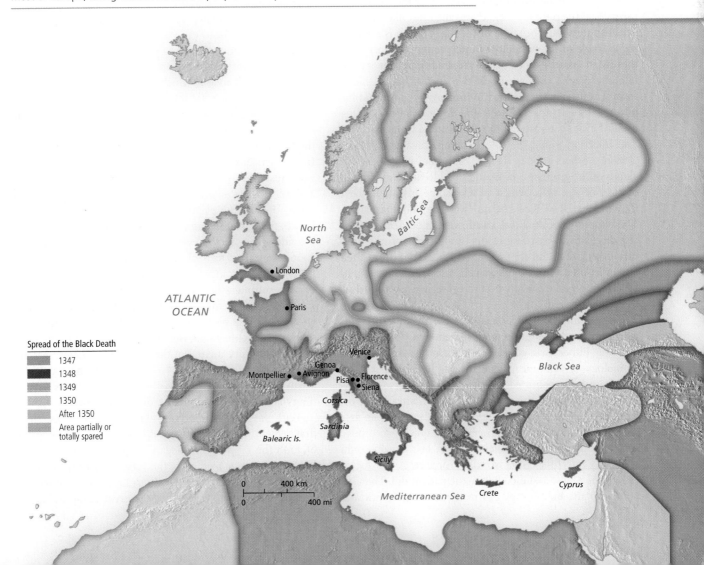

city council and civil courts abruptly ended, as if the city fathers and judges had all died or rushed home in panic. A local chronicler, Agnolo di Tura, wrote down his memories of those terrible days:

> *Father abandoned child, wife husband, one brother another; for this illness seemed to strike through the breath and sight. And so they died. And none could be found to bury the dead for money or friendship. Members of a household brought their dead to a ditch as best they could, without priest, without divine offices. Nor did the [death] bell sound. And in many places in Siena great pits were dug and piled deep with the multitude of dead. . . . And I, Agnolo di Tura, called the Fat, buried my five children with my own hands. And there were also those who were so sparsely covered with earth that the dogs dragged them forth and devoured many bodies throughout the city.*[2]

During the summer of 1348 more than half of the Sienese died. The construction of Siena's great cathedral, planned to be the largest in the world, stopped and was never resumed due to a lack of workers. In fact, Siena, once among the most prosperous cities in Europe, never fully recovered and lost its economic preeminence to other cities.

Experts still dispute the cause of the Black Death, but there is growing doubt about the validity of the traditional theory that the bubonic plague° was the most likely culprit. The dispute about the cause of the Black Death is a revealing example of the difficulty of interpreting evidence from the distant past. According to the traditional theory the bubonic plague can appear in two forms. In the classic form it is usually transmitted to humans by a flea that has bitten a rodent infected with the *Yersinia pestis* bacillus, usually a rat. The infected flea then bites a human victim. The infection enters the bloodstream, causing inflamed swellings called buboes (hence, "bubonic" plague) in the glands of the groin or armpit, internal bleeding, and discoloration of the skin, which is why some historians have thought that the "Black Death" was the bubonic plague. The symptoms of the Black Death were, indeed, exceptionally disgusting, according to one quite typical contemporary description: "all the matter which exuded from their bodies let off an unbearable stench; sweat, excrement, spittle, breath, so fetid as to be overpowering; urine turbid, thick, black or red. . . . "[3]

The second form of plague was the pneumonic type, which infected the lungs and spread by coughing and sneezing. Either form could be lethal, but the complex epidemiology of bubonic plague meant that the first form could not be transmitted directly from one person to another. According to the traditional theory, after being infected, many victims probably developed pneumonia as a secondary symptom, which then spread quickly to others. As one contemporary physician put it, one person could seemingly infect the entire world. In some cases, the doctor caught the illness and died before the patient did. The visitations of the bubonic plague in the late nineteenth and

twentieth centuries, which have been observed by physicians trained in modern medicine, formed that basis for this theory. Alexandre Yersin discovered the bubonic plague bacillus in Hong Kong in 1894 and traced its spread through rats and fleas. For more than a century most historians and epidemiologists have thought that something similar to this must have happened in 1348.

However, there are problems with the traditional theory that the Black Death was caused by bubonic plague. The Black Death spread much more rapidly from person to person and place to place than the bubonic plague does in modern epidemics. For example, rats do not travel very fast, and in modern examples the bubonic plague has rarely spread more than twelve miles per year. In 1348, however, the Black Death traveled as far in a day as rat-borne bubonic plague does in a year. Many of the reported symptoms from the fourteenth century do not match the symptoms observed in modern plague victims. Moreover, the Black Death, unlike the bubonic plague, seems to have had a long incubation period before the first symptoms appeared. Because of the long incubation, those who had the disease transmitted it to others before they knew they were sick, which helps explain why the disease was so lethal despite attempts to quarantine those afflicted with it. The most recent revisionist research suggests that the Black Death may have been caused by an unidentified virus that produced bleeding similar to the Ebola virus that has appeared in Africa in recent years.

Why does it matter which theory for the cause of the Black Death is correct—the traditional one about bubonic plague or the revisionist one about a bleeding virus? In one sense it does not matter because it is clear that the effects of the Black Death were devastating no matter what the cause. In another sense, it does matter because if the Black Death was caused by a virus, it could reappear again at any time and kill many millions again. There is now medical treatment for bubonic plague, but if a virus caused the Black Death, then extensive research would need to take place to provide a cure in the event it reappeared. Thus, a debate about events that took place more than 650 years ago could have vital importance for the future.

Two summers before the Black Death's appearance in Europe, sailors returning from the East had told stories about a terrible pestilence in China and India. Entire regions of India, they said, were littered with corpses with no survivors to bury them. But the vague information that arrived in European seaports in 1346 caused no particular alarm. Asia was far away and the source of stories so baffling that most people could hardly credit them.

With the galley slaves dying at their oars, Genoese ships first brought the disease to ports in Italy, and by the spring of 1348 the Black Death began to spread throughout the Italian peninsula. Ironically, the very network of shipping that had connected the Mediterranean with northern European waters and propelled the great economic boom of the Middle Ages spread the deadly disease. By summer the pestilence had traveled as far north as Paris; by the end of the year it had crossed the English Channel, following William the Conqueror's old route from Normandy to England. From Italy the Black Death passed through the rugged Alpine passes into Switzerland and Hungary. In 1349 the relentless surge continued, passing from France into the Netherlands and from England to Scotland, Ireland, and Norway, where a ghost ship of dead men ran aground near Bergen. From Norway the deadly disease migrated to Sweden, Denmark, Prussia, Iceland, and Greenland. By 1351 it had arrived in Russia.

Modern estimates indicate that during the late 1340s and early 1350s from India to Iceland, about one-third of the population perished. In Europe this would have meant that about 20 million people died, with the deaths usually clustered in a matter of a few weeks or months after the disease first appeared in a particular locale. The death toll, however, varied erratically from place to place, ranging from about 20 to 90 percent. So great was the toll that entire villages were depopulated or abandoned. In Avignon 400 died daily, in Pisa 500, in Paris 800. Paris lost half its population, Florence as much as four-fifths, and Venice two-thirds. In the seaport of Trapani, Italy, everyone apparently died or left. Living in enclosed spaces, monks and nuns were especially hard hit. All the Franciscans of Carcassonne and Marseille in France died. In Montpellier, France, only 7 of the 140 Dominicans survived. In isolated Kilkenny, Ireland, Brother John Clyn found himself left alone among his dead brothers, and he began to write a diary of what he had witnessed because he was afraid he might be the last person left alive in the world.

Civic and religious leaders had neither the knowledge nor the power to prevent or contain the disease. Following the biblical passages that prescribed ostracizing lepers, governments began to treat Black Death victims as temporary lepers and quarantined them for forty days. Because such measures were ineffective, the Black Death kept coming back. In the Mediterranean basin where the many port cities formed a network of contagion, the plague reappeared between 1348 and 1721 in one port or another about every fifteen to twenty years. Some of the later outbreaks were just as lethal as the initial 1348 catastrophe. Florence lost half its population in 1400; Venice lost a third in 1575–1577 and a third again in 1630–1631. Half a million people died in northern Spain from an epidemic in 1596–1602. Less exposed than the Mediterranean, northern Europe suffered less and saw the last of the dread disease in the Great Plague of London of 1665–1666.

No matter which theory of the cause of the Black Death is correct, both demonstrate how the fate of the West was largely in the hands of unknown forces that ensnared Eurasia and Africa in a unified biological web. If the revisionist theory is correct, then the disease came out of Africa, afflicting Europe via Italy, which had regular contacts with North Africa and where the disease first appeared. If the

Flagellants

During the Black Death many people believed God was punishing them for their sins. In order to expiate those sins some young men practiced flagellation, a practice once reserved for monks who whipped themselves as a form of penance. In order to control the practice among laymen, confraternities were formed in which collective flagellation was organized and carried out under the supervision of a priest. These confraternities took on a variety of charitable obligations, including succoring the sick, building hospitals and orphanages, and burying the dead.

The Black Death: The Signs of Disease

Infectious diseases are invisible. They are carried by viruses or bacteria that infect the body, but until the invention of the microscope in the seventeenth century and the development of epidemiology in the nineteenth the disease itself could not be directly observed. Diseases manifest themselves indirectly through symptoms: fevers, cold sweats, pain, coughing, vomiting, diarrhea, paleness, glandular swellings, skin lesions, and rashes. Through these symptoms, the disease leaves a distinctive sign on the body.

No disease left more distinctive and disturbing signs on the body than the Black Death. In the introduction to *The Decameron*, Giovanni Boccaccio described what he had witnessed of the symptoms:

> In the year 1348 after the fruitful incarnation of the Son of God, that most beautiful of Italian cities, noble Florence, was attacked by deadly plague. . . . The symptoms . . . began both in men and women with certain swellings in the groin or under the armpit. They grew to the size of a small apple or an egg, more or less, and were vulgarly called tumors. In a short space of time these tumors spread from the two parts named [to] all over the body. Soon after this the symptoms changed and black or purple spots appeared on the arms or thighs or any other part of the body, sometimes a few large ones, sometimes many little ones. These spots were a certain sign of death, just as the original tumor had been and still remained.[4]

The fear of the Black Death and the inability to discern its causes

focused the attention of contemporaries on the bodies of the sick, and when someone fell ill there was intense concern to determine whether the signs of the Black Death were present. As a result, almost any discoloration of the skin or glandular swellings could be interpreted as a sign of its presence, and other diseases, such as smallpox, could be diagnosed as the Black Death. Physicians and surgeons, of course, were the experts in reading the signs of the body for disease. As victims and their distraught families soon discovered, however, physicians did not really know what the glandular swellings and discolorations of the skin meant. Boccaccio reported that "No doctor's advice, no medicine could overcome or alleviate this disease. . . . Either the disease was such that no treatment was possible or the doctors were so ignorant that they did not know what caused it, and consequently could not administer the proper remedy."[5]

On the advice of physicians, governmental authorities tried to stop the contagion by placing the houses of the sick and sometimes entire neighborhoods under quarantine when plague was suspected. Within the councils of city governments, greater attention began to be paid to the poor, largely

because their bodies were more likely to manifest deformities and skin problems because of malnutrition and poor living conditions. The bodies of the poor became subject to systematic regulation. In general, the poor were much more likely to be quarantined than the rich. The deformed might even be driven out of town. Cities established hospitals to segregate the most wretched of the poor, and health officials set up border guards to prevent poor vagabonds from entering towns. To maintain quarantines and bury the dead, a public health bureaucracy was created, complete with its own staff physicians, grave diggers, and police force. The extraordinary powers granted to the public health authorities helped expand the authority of the state over its citizens in the name of pursuing the common good. The expansion of governmental bureaucracy that distinguished modern from medieval states was partly the result of the need to keep human bodies under surveillance and control—a need that began with the Black Death.

For Discussion

How did the government's need to control the Black Death contribute to the expansion of the state? How did it reveal the limits of the power of the state?

The Triumph of Death
A detail from Francesco Traini's fresco *The Triumph of Death*, in the Camposanto, Pisa, ca. 1350. Frescoes such as this reflect the horror of the Black Death.

traditional theory is correct then Europe was victimized by a disease from Asia. Modern research has suggested that the homeland of the *Yersinia pestis* bacillus is an extremely isolated area in Central Asia, from which the plague could have spread during the fourteenth century. The strongest strands in that web were those of merchant traders and armies who were responsible for accidentally disseminating microbes. Whether or not they were the means for transmitting the Black Death, no armies were as important for the fate of Europe as the mounted warriors of the distant Mongol tribes, whose relentless conquests drove them from Outer Mongolia across central Asia toward Europe.

A Cold Wind from the East

■ How did forces outside Europe, in particular the Mongol and Ottoman Empires, influence conditions in the West?

The Mongols and Turks were nomadic peoples from central Asia. Closely related culturally but speaking different languages, these peoples exerted an extraordinary influence on world history despite a rather small population. Map 10.2 shows the place of origin of the

Map 10.2 The Mongol Empire, 1206–1405

The Mongols and Turks were nomadic peoples who spread out across Asia and Europe from their homeland in the region of Mongolia. The Mongol armies eventually conquered vast territories from Korea to the borders of Hungary and from the Arctic Ocean to the Arabian Sea.

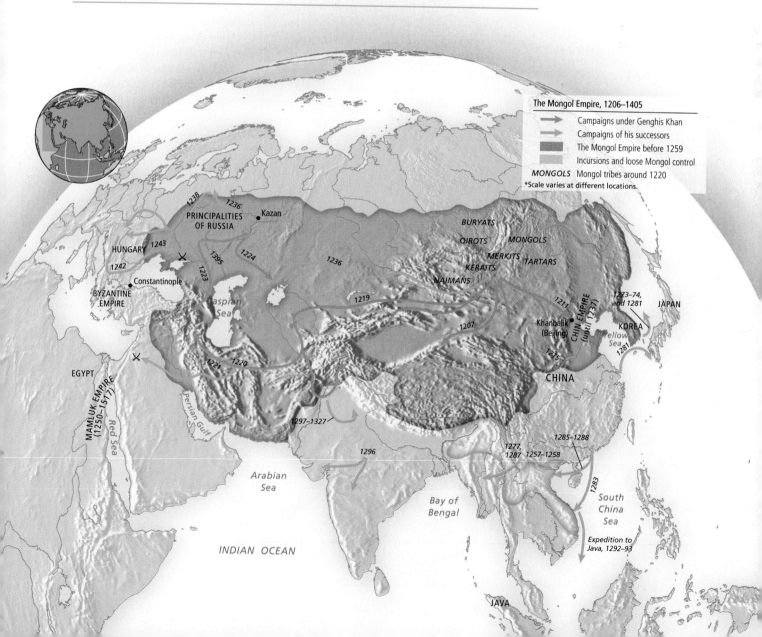

Mongols and Turks and where they spread across a wide belt of open, relatively flat steppe land stretching from the Yellow Sea between China and the Korean peninsula to the Baltic Sea and the Danube River basin in Europe. Virtually unwooded and interrupted only by a few easily traversed mountain ranges, the broad Eurasian steppes have been the great migration highway of world history from prehistoric times to the medieval caravans and the modern trans-Siberian railway.

As the Mongols and Turks charged westward out of central Asia on their fast ponies, they put pressure on the kingdoms of the West. Mongol armies hobbled Russia, and Turks conquered Constantinople. As a consequence the potential Orthodox allies in the East of the Catholic Christian West were weakened or eliminated. Under the Ottomans, adherents to Islam were reinserted into the West, this time in the Balkans. In contrast to the era of the twelfth-century Crusades, Catholic Europe found itself on the defensive against a powerful Muslim foe.

The Mongol Invasions

Whereas the Europeans became successful sailors because of their extensive coastlines and close proximity to the sea, the Mongols became roving horsemen because they needed to migrate several times a year in search of grass and water

for their ponies and livestock. They also became highly skilled warriors because they competed persistently with other tribes for access to the grasslands.

Between 1206 and 1258, the Mongols transformed themselves from a collection of disunited tribes with a vague ethnic affinity to create the most extensive empire in the history of the world. The epic rise of the previously obscure Mongols was the work of a Mongol chief who succeeded in uniting the various quarreling tribes and transforming them into a world power. In 1206 he was proclaimed Genghis Khan (ca. 1162–1227) ("Very Mighty King"), the supreme ruler over all the Mongols. Genghis broke through the Great Wall of China, destroyed the Jin (Chin) empire in northern China, and occupied Beijing. His cavalry swept across Asia as far as Azerbaijan, Georgia, northern Persia, and Russia. Eventually, Mongol armies conquered territories that stretched from Korea to Hungary and from the Arctic Ocean to the Arabian Sea. They even attempted seaborne expeditions to overpower Japan, which ended in disaster, and Java, which they were able to hold only temporarily. These failures indicated that Mongol strength was in their army rather than their navy.

The Mongol success was accomplished through a highly disciplined military organization, tactics that relied on extremely mobile cavalry forces, and a sophisticated intelligence network. During the Russian campaign in the winter of 1223, the Mongol cavalry moved with lightning speed

Mongol Horseman
Unlike the fourteenth-century European representations of the Mongols, this contemporary Chinese illustration of a Mongol archer on horseback accurately depicts their appearance, dress, and equipment.

across frozen rivers to accomplish the only successful winter invasion of Russia in history. Although the Russian forces outnumbered the Mongol armies and had superior armor, they were crushed in every encounter with the Mongols.

The Mongol armies employed clever tactics. First they unnerved enemy soldiers with a hail of arrows. Then the Mongols would appear to retreat, only to draw the enemy into false confidence before the Mongol horsemen delivered a deadly final blow. European chroniclers at the time tried to explain their many defeats at the hands of the Mongols by reporting that the Mongol "hordes" had overwhelming numbers, but evidence clearly shows that their victories were the result not of superior numbers but of superior discipline and the sophistication of the Mongol intelligence network.

The Mongol invasions completely altered the composition of Asia and much of eastern Europe—economically, politically, and ethnically. Once they had conquered new territories, they established the Mongol Peace by reopening the caravan routes across the Asian steppes, making trans-Eurasian trade possible and merchants safe from robbers. The most famous of the many merchants who traversed this route were the Venetians from the Polo family, including Marco Polo, who arrived at the court of the Great Khan in China in 1275. Marco Polo's book about his travels offers a vivid and often remarkably perceptive account of the Mongol Empire during the Mongol Peace. It also illustrates better than any other source the cultural engagement of the Christian West with the Mongol East during the late thirteenth century, an encounter in which both sides demonstrated an abiding fascination with the other's religion and social mores.

Mongol power climaxed in 1260. In that year the Mongols suffered a crushing defeat in Syria at the hands of the Mamluk rulers of Egypt, an event that ended the Mongol reputation for invincibility. Conflicts and succession disputes among the various Mongol tribes made them vulnerable to rivals and to rebellion from their unhappy subjects. The Mongol Empire did not disappear overnight, but its various successor kingdoms never recaptured the dynamic unity forged by Genghis Khan. During the fourteenth century the Mongol Peace fitfully sputtered to an end.

In the wake of these upheavals, a warrior of Mongol descent known as Tamerlane (r. 1369–1405) created an army composed of Mongols, Turks, and Persians, which challenged the established Mongol khanates. Tamerlane's conquests rivaled those of Genghis Khan, but with very different results. His armies pillaged the rich cities that supplied the caravan routes. Thus, in his attempt to monopolize the lucrative trans-Eurasian trade, Tamerlane largely destroyed it. The collapse of the Mongol Peace broke the thread of commerce across Eurasia and stimulated the European search for alternative routes to China that ultimately resulted in the voyages of Christopher Columbus in 1492.

CHRONOLOGY

The Mongols

1206–1227	Reign of Genghis Khan
1206–1258	Mongol armies advance undefeated across Eurasia
1260	Defeat in Syria of Mongols by Mamluks of Egypt
1369–1405	Reign of Tamerlane

The Rise of the Ottoman Turks

The Mongol armies were never very large, so the Mongols had always augmented their numbers with Turkish tribes. The result was that outside Mongolia, Turks gradually absorbed the Mongols. Turkish replaced Mongolian as the dominant language, and the Turks took over the government of the central Asian empires that had been scraped together by the Mongol conquests. In contrast to the Mongols, many of whom remained Buddhists, the Turks became Muslims and created an exceptionally dynamic, expansionist society of their own (see Map 10.3).

Among the Turkish peoples, the most successful state builders were the Ottomans. Named for Osman I (r. 1281–1326), who brought it to prominence, the Ottoman dynasty endured for more than 600 years, until 1924. The nucleus of the Ottoman state was a small principality in Anatolia (a portion of present-day Turkey), which in the early fourteenth century began to expand at the expense of its weaker neighbors, including the Byzantine Empire. The Ottoman state was built not on national, linguistic, or ethnic unity, but on a purely dynastic network of personal and military loyalties to the Ottoman prince, called the sultan. Thus the vitality of the empire depended on the energy of the individual sultans. The Ottomans thought of themselves as *ghazis*, warriors for Islam devoted to destroying polytheists, including Christians. (To some Muslims in this period the Christian belief in the Trinity and veneration of numerous saints demonstrated that Christians were not true monotheists.) During the fourteenth century, incessant Ottoman guerilla actions gradually chipped away at the Byzantine frontier.

The Byzantine Empire in the middle of the thirteenth century was emerging from a period of domination by Frankish knights and Venetian merchants who had conquered Constantinople during the Fourth Crusade in 1204. In 1261, the Byzantine emperor Michael VIII Palaeologus (r. 1260–1282) recaptured the great city. The revived Byzantine Empire, however, was a pale vestige of what it once had been, and the Palaeologi emperors desperately sought military assistance from western Europe to defend themselves from the Ottomans. Dependent on mercenary armies and divided by civil wars, the Byzantines offered only pathetic resistance to the all-conquering Ottomans.

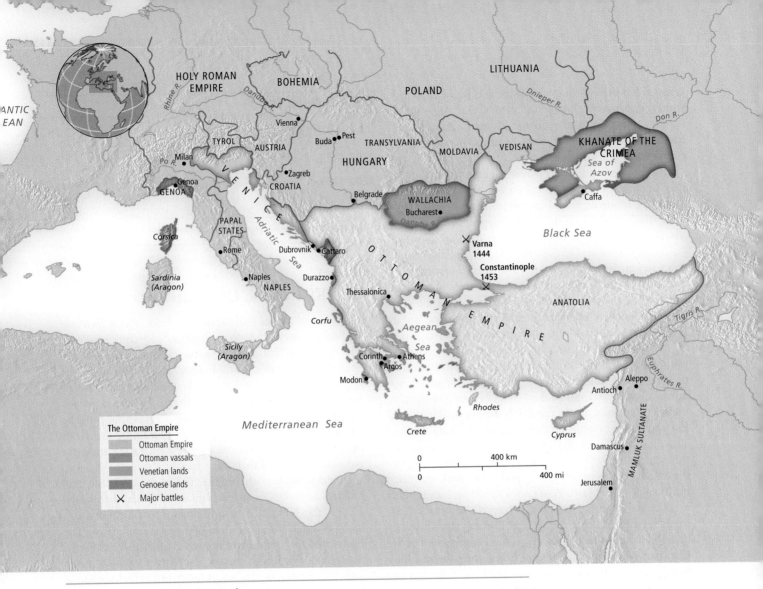

Map 10.3   The Ottoman Empire

The Ottoman state expanded from a small principality in Anatolia, which is south of the Black Sea. From there the Ottomans spread eastward into Kurdistan and Armenia. In the West they captured all of Greece and much of the Balkan peninsula.

From their base in Anatolia, the Ottomans raided far and wide, launching pirate fleets into the Aegean and gradually encircling Constantinople after they crossed over into Europe in 1308. By 1402 Ottoman territory had grown to forty times its size a century earlier. During that century of conquests, the frontier between Christianity and Islam shifted. The former subjects of the Byzantines in the Balkans fell to the Ottoman Turks. Fragile Serbia, a bastion of Orthodox Christianity in the Balkans, broke under Ottoman pressure. First unified in the late twelfth century, Serbia established political independence from Byzantium and autonomy for the Serbian church. Although the Serbs had taken control over a number of former Byzantine provinces, they fell to the invincible Ottomans at the Battle of Kosovo in 1389. Lamenting the Battle of Kosovo has remained the bedrock of Serbian national identity to this day.

Serbia's western neighbors, the kingdoms of Bosnia and Herzegovina, deflated under Ottoman pressure during the late fifteenth century. Unlike Serbia, where most of the population remained loyal to the Serbian Orthodox Church, Bosnia and Herzegovina had long been divided by religious schisms. The dominant, educated classes were Serbian-speaking Muslims; the subjugated peasants, also Serbian-speaking, were Orthodox Christians who turned over one-third of everything they raised to their Muslim lords. The parallel divisions along religious and class lines long enfeebled Bosnian unity.

When Mehmed II, "The Conqueror" (r. 1451–1481), became the Ottoman sultan, he began to obliterate the last remnants of the Byzantine Empire. During the winter of 1451–1452, the sultan ordered the encirclement of Constantinople, a city that had

Mehmed II

once been the largest in the world but now was reduced from perhaps a million people to fewer than 50,000. The Ottoman siege strategy was to bombard Constantinople into submission with daily rounds from enormous cannons. The largest was a monster cannon, twenty-nine feet long, that could shoot 1,200-pound stones. It required a crew of 200 soldiers and sixty oxen to handle it, and each firing generated so much heat that it took hours to cool off before it could be fired again. The siege was a gargantuan task because the walls of Constantinople, which had been built, repaired, and improved over a period of a thousand years, were formidable. However, the new weapon of gunpowder artillery had rendered city walls a military anachronism. Brought from China by the Mongols, gunpowder had gradually revolutionized warfare, and breaching city walls in sieges was merely a matter of time as long as the heavy metal cannons could be dragged into position. Quarrels among the Christians also hampered the defense of the walls. Toward the end, the Byzantine emperor was forced to melt down church treasures so "that from them coins should be struck and given to the soldiers, the sappers and the builders, who selfishly cared so little for the public welfare that they were refusing to go to their work unless they were first paid."[6]

The final assault came in May 1453 and lasted less than a day. When the city fell, the Ottoman army spent the day plundering, raping, and enslaving the populace. The last Byzantine emperor, Constantine XI, was never found amid the multitude of the dead. The fall of Constantinople ended the Christian Byzantine Empire, the continuous remnant of the ancient Roman Empire. But the idea of Rome was not so easily snuffed out. The first Ottoman sultans residing in Constantinople continued to be called "Roman emperors."

DOCUMENT

Nestor-Iskander on the Fall of Constantinople

Although the western European princes had done little to save Byzantium, its demise was a profound shock, rendering them vulnerable to the Ottoman onslaught. For the next 200 years the Ottomans used Constantinople as a base to threaten Christian Europe. Hungary and the eastern Mediterranean empire of Venice remained the last lines of defense for the West, and at various times in succeeding

---

DOCUMENT

The Ottoman Conquest of Constantinople

The Turkish sultan Mehmed II led the Ottoman army and navy in the final siege of Constantinople. A brilliant leader and strategist, he succeeded in taking the capital of Byzantium, which had been unsuccessfully attacked so many times before. This account of what he said to inspire his troops before the final assault on the walls on Constantinople is by a Greek named Kritovoulos who began to work for Mehmed shortly after the conquest. He gathered this account from many eyewitnesses. Notice how Mehmed emphasizes the various rewards promised by the conquest of the city.

My friends and my comrades in the present struggle! I have called you together here . . . to show you how many and how great [are the rewards] and what great glory and honor accompany the winning. And I also wish that you may know well how to carry on the struggle for the very highest rewards.

First, then, there is a great wealth of all sorts in this city, some in the royal palaces and some in the houses of the mighty, some in the homes of the common people and still other, finer and more abundant, laid up in the churches as votive offerings and treasures of all sorts, constructed of gold and silver and precious stones and costly pearls.

Then too, there are very many noble and distinguished men, some of whom will be your slaves, and the rest will be put up for sale; also very many and very beautiful women, young and good-looking, and virgins lovely for marriage, noble, and of noble families, and even till now unseen by masculine eyes, some of them, evidently intended for the weddings of great men. . . .

And you will have boys, too, very many and very beautiful and of noble families.

Further, you will enjoy the beauty of the churches and public buildings and splendid houses and gardens, and many such things, suited to look at and enjoy and take pleasure in and profit by.

And the greatest of all is this, that you will capture a city whose renown has gone out to all parts of the world. It is evident that to whatever extent the leadership and glory of this city has spread, to a like extent the renown of your valor and bravery will spread for having captured by assault a city such as this. . . .

And, best of all, we shall demolish a city that has been hostile to use from the beginning and is constantly growing at our expense and in every way plotting against our rule. . . .

I myself will be in the van of the attack [applause by all the gathering]. Yes, I myself will lead the attack, and will be fighting by your side and will watch to see what each one of you does."

Source: From Kritovoulos, *History of Mehmed the Conqueror,* translated by Charles T. Riggs (Westport, Conn.: Greenwood Press, 1970), 61–64.

CHRONOLOGY

The Conquests of the Ottoman Turks

1281–1326	Reign of Osman I
1308	Ottoman Empire advances into Europe
1389	Battle of Kosovo; Serbia becomes vassal state of the Ottomans
1451–1481	Reign of Mehmed II, "The Conqueror"
1453	Fall of Constantinople and death of last Byzantine emperor

centuries the Ottomans launched expeditions against Europe, including two sieges of Vienna (1529 and 1683) and several invasions of Italy.

Hundreds of years of attacks by the Mongol and Ottoman Empires redrew the map of the West. Events in western Europe did not and could not take place in isolation from the eastern pressures and influences. For more than 200 years Christian Russia was isolated from cultural influences in the rest of the Christian world. The experience made the Russians much more aware of their eastern neighbors, and when they did recover from the Mongol conquests in the fifteenth century, much of their energy and military might was directed toward expanding eastward into the void left by the collapse of the Mongol Empire. The Ottoman conquests also created a lasting Muslim presence within the borders of Europe, especially in Bosnia and Albania. In succeeding centuries Christian Europe and the Muslim Ottoman Empire would be locked in a deadly competitive embrace, but they also benefited from innumerable cultural exchanges and regular trade. Hostility between the two sides was recurrent but never inevitable and was broken by long periods of peaceful engagement. In fact, the Christian kingdoms of western Europe went to war far more often with one another than with the Turks.

Economic Depression and Social Turmoil

■ How did disturbances in the rudimentary global economy of the Middle Ages precipitate almost complete financial collapse and widespread social discontent in Europe?

Adding insult to injury in this time of famine, plague, and conquest, the West began to suffer a major economic depression during the fourteenth century. The economic boom fueled by the agricultural revolution and the revitalization of European cities during the eleventh century and the commercial prosperity of the twelfth and thirteenth centuries petered out in the fourteenth. The causes of this economic catastrophe were complex, but the consequences were obvious. Businesses went bust, banks collapsed, guilds were in turmoil, and workers rebelled.

At the same time, the effects of the depression were unevenly felt. The economic conditions for many peasants actually improved because there was a labor shortage in the countryside due to the loss of population. Forced to pay their peasants more for their labor and crops, landlords saw their own fortunes decline. Finding it harder to pay the higher prices for food, urban workers probably suffered the most because their wages did not keep up with the cost of living.

The Collapse of International Trade and Banking

The Mongol Peace during the thirteenth century had stimulated vast, lucrative trade in exotic luxury items between Europe and Asia. When the Mongol Empire began to break up in the fourteenth century, the trade routes were cut off or displaced. Later in the century, Tamerlane's forcible channeling of the caravan trade through his own territory created a narrow trade corridor with outlets on the coast of the Middle East. Rulers along this path, such as the Mamluks in Egypt, took advantage of the situation to levy heavy tolls on trade, raising the price of goods beyond what the market could bear. As a result, trade dwindled. Alternative routes would have taken merchants through Constantinople, but Ottoman pressure on Byzantium endangered these routes.

The financial infrastructure of medieval Europe was tied to international trade in luxury goods. The successful, entrepreneurial Italian merchants who dominated the luxury trade deposited their enormous profits in Italian banks. The Italian bankers lent money to the aristocracy and royalty of northern Europe to finance the purchases of exotic luxuries and to fight wars. The whole system was mutually reinforcing, but it was very fragile. With the disruption of supply sources for luxury goods, the financial networks of Europe collapsed, precipitating a major depression.

For most of the thirteenth century the Italian city of Siena had been one of the principal banking centers of the world, the equivalent of New York or Tokyo today. In 1298, however, panic caused a run on its largest bank, which failed. Soon the lesser Sienese banks were forced to close, and the entire city fell into a deep economic depression. Siena never recovered its economic stature and is a major tourist attraction today simply because it is largely unchanged from the time when the banks went broke.

In nearby Florence, several local banks took advantage of Siena's collapse and became even bigger than the Sienese banks had been. Through these banks, the coinage of Florence, the florin, became the common currency of Europe. By 1346, however, all of these banks crashed due to a series of bad loans to several kings of Europe. With the bank crash, virtually all sources of credit dried up all across Europe. At the same time, wars between France and England deprived their aristocracies of the money to buy luxuries from the Italian merchants whose deposits had been the principal source of capital for the banks. With disruptions in the supply of Asian luxury goods, a catastrophic loss of capital by Italian bankers, and a decline in demand for luxuries in France and England, Europe entered a major depression.

Rebellions from Below

The luxury trade that brought exotic items from Asia to Europe represented only half of the economic equation. The other half was the raw materials and manufactured goods that Europeans sold in exchange, principally woolen cloth. The production of woolen cloth depended on a highly sophisticated economic system that connected shepherds in England, the Netherlands, and Spain with woolen cloth manufacturers in cities. The manufacture of cloth and other commodities was organized by guilds. The collapse of the luxury trade reduced the demand for the goods produced by the guilds, depriving guildsmen and urban workers of employment at a time when the cost of food to feed their children was rising. The situation must have seemed ironic. Workers knew that the population decline from famine and pestilence had created a labor shortage, which according to the elementary laws of supply and demand should have produced higher wages for the workers who survived. However, wages stagnated because of the decline in business. Royal and local governments made matters worse by trying to control wages and raise taxes in a period of declining revenues. Frustrated and enraged, workers rebelled.

An Economy of Monopolies: Guilds

Central to the political and economic control of medieval cities were the guilds°. Guilds were professional associations devoted to protecting the special interests of a particular trade or craft and to monopolizing production and trade in the goods the guild produced. There were two dominant types of guilds. The first type, merchant guilds, attempted to monopolize the local market for a particular commodity. There were spice guilds, fruit and vegetable guilds, and apothecary guilds. The second type, craft guilds, regulated the manufacturing processes of artisans, such as carpenters, bricklayers, woolen-cloth manufacturers, glass blowers, and painters. These guilds were dominated by master craftsmen, who ran their own shops. Working for wages in these shops

were the journeymen, who knew the craft but could not yet afford to open their own shops. Under the masters and journeymen were apprentices, who worked usually without pay for a specific number of years to learn the trade.

Guild regulations governed virtually all aspects of guildsmen's lives. In fact, until a youth passed from apprenticeship to become a journeyman, he could not marry or own property. Craft guilds functioned like a modern professional association by guaranteeing that producers met certain standards of training and competence before they could practice a trade. Like merchant guilds, they also regulated competition and prices in an attempt to protect the masters' local monopoly in the craft.

In many cities the guilds expanded far beyond the economic regulation of trade and manufacturing to become the backbone of urban society and politics. The masters of the guilds constituted part of the urban elite, and guild membership was often a prerequisite for holding public office. One of the obligations of city government was to protect the interests of the guildsmen, who in turn helped stabilize the economy through their influence in city hall. The guilds were often at the center of a city's social life as well, countering the anonymity of city life by offering fellowship and a sense of belonging. Medieval festivals were often organized by the guilds, whose members engaged in sports competitions with other guilds. In Nuremberg, for example, the butchers' guild organized and financed the elaborate carnival festivities that absorbed the energies of the entire city for days on end. In many places guilds supplied the actors for the Corpus Christi plays that acted out stories from the Bible or the lives of the saints for the entertainment and edification of their fellow citizens. In Florence the church of the guildsmen became a display case for works of sculpture by the city's most prominent artists, each work sponsored by a specific guild. The guilds endowed magnificent chapels and provided funeral insurance for their members and welfare for the injured and widows of masters.

When the economy declined during the fourteenth century, the urban guilds became lightning rods for mounting social tension. Guild monopolies produced considerable conflict, provoking anger among those who were blocked from joining guilds, young journeymen who earned low wages, and those who found themselves unemployed due to the depression. These tensions exploded into dangerous revolts.

"Long Live the People, Long Live Liberty"

Economic pressures erupted into rebellion most dramatically among woolen-cloth workers in the urban centers in Italy, the Netherlands, and France. The most famous revolt involved the Ciompi, the laborers in the woolen-cloth industry of Florence, Italy, where guilds were the most powerful force in city government. The Ciompi, who performed the heaviest jobs such as carting and the most noxious tasks such as dyeing, had not been allowed to have their own guild and were therefore deprived of the political and economic rights of guild membership.

Fueling the Ciompi's frustration was the fact that by the middle of the fourteenth century woolen-cloth production in Florence dropped by two-thirds, leaving many workers unemployed. In 1378 the desperate Ciompi rebelled. A crowd chanting, "Long live the people, long live liberty," broke into the houses of prominent citizens, released political prisoners from the city jails, and sacked the rich convents that housed the pampered daughters of the wealthy. Over the course of a few months, the rebels managed to force their way onto the city council, where they demanded tax and economic reforms and the right to form their own guild. The Ciompi revolt is one of the earliest cases of workers demanding political rights. The disenfranchised workers did not want to eliminate the guilds' monopoly on political power; they merely wanted a guild of their own so that they could join the regime. That was not to be, however. After a few weeks of success, the Ciompi were divided and defeated.

Shortly after the Ciompi revolt faded, troubles broke out in the woolen-cloth centers of Ghent and Bruges in Flanders and in Paris and Rouen in France. In these cases, however, the revolt spread beyond woolen-cloth workers to voice the more generalized grievances of urban workers. In Ghent and Bruges the weavers attempted to wrest control of their cities from the local leaders who dominated politics and the economy. In Paris and Rouen in 1380, social unrest erupted in resistance to high taxes and attacks by the poor on the rich. The pinnacle of the violence involved the *Maillotins* ("people who fight with mallets") in Paris during March 1382, when the houses of tax collectors were sacked and the inhabitants murdered. Although the violence in Flanders and France was precipitated by local issues, such as control of the town council and taxes, both cases were symptomatic of the widespread social conflicts that followed in the wake of the great depression of the fourteenth century that profoundly affected the crucial woolen-cloth industry.

Like urban workers, many rural peasants also rebelled during the troubled fourteenth century. In France in 1358 a peasant revolt broke out that came to be called the *Jacquerie*, a term derived from "Jacques Bonhomme" ("James Goodfellow"), the traditional name for the typical peasant. Jacquerie became synonymous with extreme, seemingly mindless violence. Filled with hatred for the aristocracy, the peasants indulged in pillaging, murder, and rape, but they offered no plan for an alternative social system or even for their own participation in the political order, so their movement had no lasting effects. They were quickly defeated by a force of nobles.

Unlike the French Jacquerie, the peasants who revolted in England in 1381 had a clear political vision for an alternative society, a fact that makes their revolt far more significant. In England the rebels' motives stemmed from the frustration of rising expectations that were never realized.

DOCUMENT

Worker Rebellions in Flanders and France

A Florentine businessman, Buonaccorso Pitti, who had witnessed the Ciompi revolt in Florence in 1378, found himself in Paris when the Maillotins *revolt broke out. Like his contemporaries, he concluded that the violence in Bruges and Ghent was somehow connected to the outbreak of violence in Rouen and Paris. This was a reasonable assumption, because the count of Flanders and the French royal court had many intimate ties. Thus, rebellion in one place had political implications elsewhere. Here is what Pitti reported.*

In 1381 the people of Ghent rebelled against their overlord, the count of Flanders, who was the father of the duchess of Burgundy. They marched in great numbers to Bruges, took the city, deposed the Count, robbed and killed all his officers, and dealt in the same way with all the other Flemish towns which fell into their hands. Their leader was Philip van Artevelde. As the number of Flemings rebelling against their overlords increased, they sent secret embassies to the populace of Paris and Rouen, urging them to do the like with their own lords, and promising them aid and succor in this undertaking. Accordingly, these two cities rebelled against the King of France. The first insurrection was that of the Paris mob, and was sparked off by a costermonger [someone who sells produce from a cart] who, when an official tried to levy a tax on the fruit and vegetables he was selling, began to roar "Down with the *gabelle* [a food tax]." At this cry the whole populace rose, ran to the tax-collectors' houses and robbed and murdered them. Then, since the mob was unarmed, one of their number led them to the Chatelet where Bertrand du Guesclin, a former High Constable, had stored 3000 lead-tipped cudgels in preparation for a battle which was to have been fought against the English. The rabble used axes to break their way into the tower where these cudgels or mallets (in French, *maillets*) were kept and, arming themselves, set forth in all directions to rob the houses of the King's representatives and in many cases to murder them. The . . . men of substance who in French are called *bourgeois,* fearing lest the mob (who were later called *Maillotins* and were of much the same kidney [nature] as the *Ciompi* in Florence) might rob them too, took arms and managed to subdue them. They then proceeded to take government into their own hands, and together with the *Maillotins*, continued the war against their royal lords.

Source: Reprinted by permission of Waveland Press, Inc. from Gene Brucker, ed., *Two Memoirs of Renaissance Florence: The Diaries of Buonaccorso Pitti and Gregorio Dati,* translated by Julia Martines (Prospect Heights, IL: Waveland Press, Inc., 1967, reissued 1991). All rights reserved.

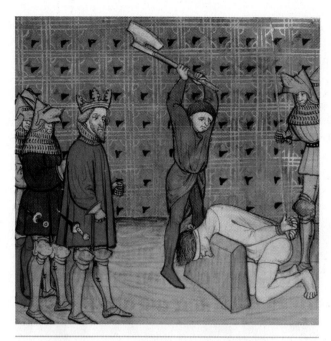

Jacquerie
A leader of the Jacquerie is beheaded while the king looks on.

The peasants believed that the labor shortage caused by the Black Death should have improved their condition, but the exact opposite was happening. Landlords clung to the old system that defined peasants as serfs who were tied to the land and unable to bargain for the price of their labor. Although the English peasants were probably better off than their fathers and grandfathers had been, their expectations of an even better life were blocked by the land-holding aristocracy. The clashing interests of the peasants and the aristocrats needed only a spark to ignite a conflagration. That spark came from the Poll Tax controversy.

The traditional means of raising revenue in England had been a levy on the more well-to-do landowners, who were taxed according to the size and value of their holdings. In 1381, however, the crown attempted to levy a Poll Tax, which taxed with little concern for the ability of each person to pay. The Poll Tax, in effect, shifted the burden of taxation to a lower social level, and the peasants bitterly resented it. As agents came to collect the Poll Tax in June 1381, riots broke out throughout eastern England, and rioters burned local tax records. The rebels briefly occupied London, where they lynched the lord chancellor and treasurer of the kingdom. The rebels demanded lower rents, higher wages, and the abolition of serfdom—all typical peasant demands—but to these they added a class-based argument against the aristocracy. They had been influenced by popular preachers who told them that in the Garden of Eden there had been no aristocracy. Following these preachers, the English rebels imagined a classless society, a utopian vision of an alternative to medieval society that was entirely structured around distinctive classes.

The 15-year-old English king, Richard II (r. 1377–1399), promised the rebels that their demands would be met. Satisfied that they had gotten what they wanted, including the abolition of serfdom, the peasants disbanded. The king then rescinded his promises and ordered that the peasant leaders be hunted down and executed. Thus, the greatest peasant rebellion in medieval English history ended with broken promises and no tangible achievements.

None of the worker or peasant revolts of the fourteenth century met with lasting success. The universal failure of lower-class rebellion was due, in part, to the lack of any clear alternative to the existing economic and political system. The Ciompi wanted to join the existing guild system. The weavers of Ghent and Bruges were as much competing with one another as rebelling against the Flanders establishment. The extreme violence of the Jacquerie frightened away potential allies. Only the English rebels had precise revolutionary demands, but they were betrayed by King Richard. However, the rebellions revealed for the first time in the West a widespread impulse among the lower classes to question and protest the existing social and economic order. The tradition of worker protest became common and recurrent during subsequent centuries.

An Age of Warfare

■ How did incessant warfare transform the most powerful medieval states?

Western Europe was further weakened during the fourteenth century by prolonged war between its two largest and previously most stable kingdoms, England and France. The Hundred Years' War° (1337–1453) was a struggle over England's attempts to assert its claims to territories in France. The prolonged conflict drained resources from the aristocracies of both kingdoms, deepening and lengthening the economic depression. The Hundred Years' War sowed the seeds of a military revolution that by the sixteenth century transformed the kingdoms of western Europe. In that transformation monarchies, ruled by relatively weak kings and strong aristocracies, evolved into modern states, ruled by strong monarchs who usurped many of the traditional privileges of the aristocracy in order to centralize authority and strengthen military prowess.

The Fragility of Monarchies

The most dangerous threat to the kings of France and England during the fourteenth and fifteenth centuries came less from worker and peasant rebellions than from members of the aristocracy, who were fiercely protective of their jurisdictional privileges over their lands. The privilege of jurisdiction allowed aristocrats to act as judges for crimes committed in their territories, a privilege that was a crucial source of their power. In both kingdoms, royal officials asserted the legal principle that aristocratic jurisdictions originated with the crown and were subordinate to it. The problem in enforcing this principle, however, was that there were overlapping, conflicting, and sometimes contradictory jurisdictions and loyalties, which were produced by many generations of inheritance. The system bred strife and limited the power of the monarch. Thus the Hundred Years' War was both a conflict between two kingdoms and a series of civil wars between aristocratic factions and imperiled monarchs.

Medieval monarchies depended on the king to maintain stability. Despite the remarkable legal reforms and bureaucratic centralization of monarchies in England and France during the twelfth and thirteenth centuries (see Chapter 9), weak or incompetent kings were all too common during the fourteenth. Weak kings created a perilous situation made worse by disputed successions. The career of Edward II (r. 1307–1327) of England illustrates the peril. Edward was unable to control the vital judicial and financial sinews of royal power. He continued the policy of his father, Edward I, by introducing resident justices of the peace who had replaced the inadequate system of itinerant judges who traveled from village to village to hear cases. In theory, these justices of the peace should have prevented the abuses of justice typical of aristocratic jurisdictions, but even though they were royal officials who answered to the king, most of those appointed were also local landowners who were deeply implicated in many of the disputes that came before them. As a result, justice in England became notoriously corrupt and the cause of discontent. Edward II was so incompetent to deal with the consequences of corrupted justice that he provoked a civil war in which his own queen joined his aristocratic enemies to depose him.

The French monarchy was no better. In fact, the French king was in an even weaker constitutional position than the

Royal Justice
English kings were preoccupied with extending their prerogatives over the judiciary as a way to express royal power. Despite the corruption of the many lower courts, the Court of the King's Bench attempted to assert a level of uniform procedures and royal control of justice.

English monarch. In France the king had effective jurisdiction over only a small part of his realm. Many of the duchies and counties of France were quasi-independent principalities, paying only nominal allegiance to the king, whose will was ignored with impunity. In these regions the administration of justice, the collection of taxes, and the recruitment of soldiers all remained in the hands of local lords. To explain why he needed to raise taxes, Philip IV, "The Fair" (r. 1285–1314), created a representative assembly, the Estates General, which met for the first time in 1302, but he still had to negotiate with each region and town individually to collect the taxes. Given the difficulty of raising taxes, the French kings resorted to makeshift solutions that hurt the economy, such as confiscating the property of vulnerable Jewish and Italian merchants and debasing the coinage to increase the value of scarce silver. Such a system made the finances of the kingdom of France especially shaky because the king lacked a dependable flow of revenue.

The Hundred Years' War

The Hundred Years' War revealed the fragility of the medieval monarchies. The initial cause of the war involved disputes over the duchy of Aquitaine. The king of England also held the title of duke of Aquitaine, who was a vassal of the French crown, which meant that the English kings technically owed military assistance to the French kings whenever they asked for it. A long succession of English kings had reluctantly paid homage as dukes of Aquitaine to the king of France, but the unusual status of the duchy was a continuing source of contention.

The second cause of the war derived from a dispute over the succession to the French crown. When King Charles IV died in 1328, his closest surviving relative was none other than the archenemy of France, Edward III (r. 1327–1377), king of England. To the barons of France, the possibility of Edward's succession to the throne was unthinkable, and they excluded him because his relation to the French royal family was through his mother. Instead the barons elected to the throne a member of the Valois family, King Philip VI (r. 1328–1350), and at first Edward reluctantly accepted the decision. However, when Philip started to hear judicial appeals from the duchy of Aquitaine, Edward changed his mind. He claimed the title of king of France for himself, sparking the beginning of more than a century of warfare (see Map 10.4).

The Hundred Years' War (1337–1453) was not a continuous formal war but a series of occasional pitched battles, punctuated by long truces and periods of general exhaustion. The term *Hundred Years' War* was invented by nineteenth-century historians to describe the prolonged time of troubles between the two countries. In terms of its potential for warfare, France, far richer and with three times the population, held the advantage over sparsely populated England. In nearly every battle the French outnumbered the English, but the English were usually victorious because of superior discipline and the ability of their longbows to break up cavalry charges. As a rule, the English avoided open battle, preferring raids, sieges of isolated castles, and capturing French knights for ransom. For many Englishmen the objective of fighting in France was to get rich by looting. Because all the fighting took place on French soil, France suffered extensive destruction and significant civilian casualties from repeated English raids.

From English Victories to French Salvation

In the early phases of the war, the English enjoyed a stunning series of victories. At the Battle of Sluys in 1340, a

Siege Warfare
English soldiers pillaging and burning a French town.

small English fleet of 150 ships carrying the English invasion forces ran into a French blockade of more than 200 ships. In the heavy hand-to-hand combat, the English captured 166 French ships and killed some 20,000 men, so many that it was later said, "If fish could talk, they would speak French." At Crécy in 1346, the English longbowmen shot thousands of arrows "like thunderbolts" into the flanks of the charging French knights, killing men and horses in shocking numbers. The French knights mounted one disorderly, hopeless charge after another, until the piles of dead blocked further charges. Though wounded, King Philip escaped, leaving 3,000 of his men dead on the field, including 1,500 knights. The aristocracy of France was decimated. At Poitiers in 1356, King John of France (r. 1350–1364) encircled 6,000 English with a vastly superior royal army of 15,000, but—as at Crécy—the English archers broke up the overly hasty French cavalry charge, and the English counterassault crushed the French. Two thousand French knights died and another 2,000 were captured, including King John himself. With its king imprisoned in England, France was forced to pay a huge ransom and grant formal sovereignty over a third of France to the king of England.

At Agincourt in 1415, King Henry V (r. 1413–1422) and England's disease-racked army of 6,000 were cut off by a French force of about 20,000. In the ensuing battle the English archers repelled a hasty French cavalry charge and

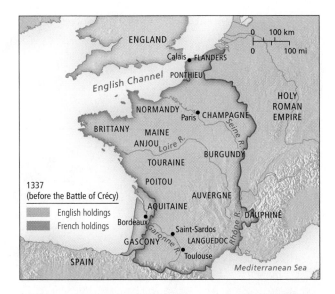

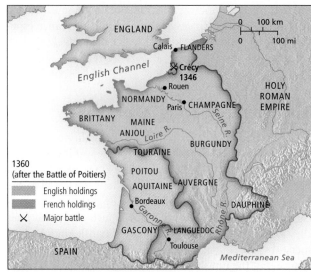

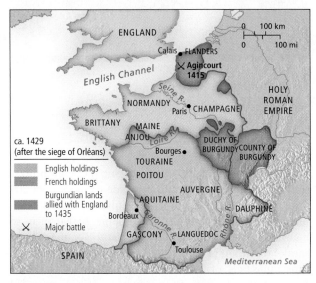

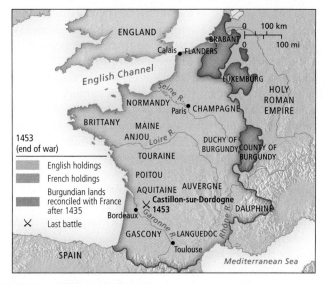

Map 10.4 The Hundred Years' War

This map illustrates four phases of the Hundred Years' War. In the first phase (1337), England maintained a small foothold in the southwest of France. In the second phase (1360), England considerably expanded the territory around Aquitaine and gained a vital base in the north of France. In the third phase (ca. 1429), England occupied much of the north of France, and England's ally Burgundy established effective independence from French authority. In the fourth phase at the end of the war (1453), England had been driven from French soil except at Calais, and Burgundy maintained control over its scattered territories.

the fleeing, terrified horses trampled the French men-at-arms as they advanced. The English lost only a few hundred, but the French suffered nearly 10,000 casualties. After Agincourt, the French never again dared challenge King Henry in open battle, and were forced to recognize him as the heir to the French throne. By 1420 the English victory appeared complete. Now with the responsibility of ruling rather than conquering France, the English could no longer

rely on their old strategy of mounted raiding and had to hold the French cities, which proved exceedingly difficult. By 1422, however, Henry V was dead, leaving two claimants to the French throne. The English asserted the rights of the infant King Henry VI of England, son of King Henry V, the victor at Agincourt. Most of the French defended the claim of the Dauphin (the title of the heir to the throne) Charles, the only surviving son of the late King Charles VI of France.

English Archers

English archers practicing the longbow. Note that the unpulled bows are the height of a man.

The Hundred Years' War entered a new phase with factions of the French aristocracy supporting the two rivals in a bloody series of engagements.

By 1429 the English were on the verge of final victory. They occupied Paris and Rheims, and their army was besieging Orleans. The Dauphin Charles was penniless and indecisive. Even his own mother denied his legitimacy as the future king. At this point a 17-year-old illiterate peasant from Burgundy, Joan of Arc (Jeanne d'Arc, ca. 1412–1431), following "divine voices," went to Orleans to lead the French armies. Under her inspiration Orleans was relieved, French forces began to defeat the English, much of the occupied territory was regained, and the Dauphin was crowned King Charles VII (r. 1429–1461) in the cathedral of Rheims. After Joan failed to recapture Paris, however, her successes ceased. The final success of the French came from the leadership of King Charles and the general exhaustion of the English forces.

Charles VII reorganized the French army and gradually chipped away at the English holdings in France, eventually taking away Aquitaine in 1453. The English lost all their possessions in France except Calais, which was finally surrendered in 1558. There was no peace treaty, just a fading away of war in France, especially after England stumbled into civil war—the War of the Roses (1455–1485).

The Hundred Years' War in Perspective

The Hundred Years' War had broad consequences. First, nearly continuous warfare between the two most powerful kingdoms in the West exacerbated other conflicts as well. Scotland, the German princes, Aragon, Castile, and most importantly Burgundy were drawn into the conflict, making the English-French brawl a European-wide war at certain stages. The squabble between France and England made it much more difficult to settle the Great Schism that split the Church during the same period. Second, the war devastated France, which eventually regained control of most of its territory but still suffered the most from the fighting. During the century of the war, the population dropped by half, due to the ravages of combat, pillage, and plague. Agriculture languished after the English repeatedly mounted raids that destroyed crops and sacked peasant villages. Third, the deaths of so many nobles and destruction of their fortunes diminished the international luxury trade; merchants and banks as far away as Italy went broke; and the Flemish woolen industry was disrupted, causing further economic damage. Finally, the war helped make England more English. Before the war the Plantagenet dynasty in England was more French than English. The monarchs possessed extensive territories in France and were embroiled in French affairs. English aristocrats also had business in France, spoke French, and married their French cousins. After 1450 the English abandoned the many French connections that had stretched across the English Channel since William the Conqueror sailed from Normandy to England in 1066. Henceforth, the English upper classes cultivated English rather than French language and culture.

CHRONOLOGY

An Age of Warfare

1285–1314	Reign of Philip IV, "The Fair," of France
1307–1327	Reign of Edward II of England
1327–1377	Reign of Edward III of England
1328–1350	Reign of Philip VI of France
1337–1453	Hundred Years' War
1340	Battle of Sluys
1346	Battle of Crécy
1356	Battle of Poitiers
1377–1399	Reign of Richard II of England
ca. 1412–1431	Life of Joan of Arc
1413–1422	Reign of Henry V of England
1415	Battle of Agincourt
1429–1461	Reign of Charles VII of France
1455–1485	War of the Roses in England

The Trial of Joan of Arc

After only fifteen months as the inspiration of the French army, Joan of Arc fell into the hands of the English, who brought her to trial for witchcraft. The English needed to stage a kind of show trial to demonstrate to their own demoralized forces that Joan's remarkable victories had been the result not of military superiority but rather of witchcraft. In the English trial, conducted at Rouen in 1431, Joan testified that her mission to save France was in response to voices she heard that commanded her to wear men's clothing. On the basis of this evidence of a confused or double gender identity, the ecclesiastical tribunal declared her a witch and a relapsed heretic. The court sentenced her to be burned at the stake.

Political motivations governed the 1431 English trial for witchcraft, but Joan's testimony provides some clues to her own identity conflicts. The two pieces of evidence against Joan ultimately resulted in her condemnation: the spiritual "voices" she claimed to hear and her cross-dressing in men's clothing.

From the beginning of her emergence onto the political scene, Joan's voices intrigued all who came into contact with her. Joan claimed that she was guided by the voices of St. Catherine, St. Margaret, and the Archangel Michael. To Joan, these voices had the authority of divine commands. The problem the English judges faced was to demonstrate that the voices came not from God but from the Devil. If they could prove that, then they had evidence of witchcraft and sorcery. Following standard inquisitorial guidelines, the judges knew that authentic messages from God would always conform to church dogma. Any deviation from official doctrines would constitute evidence of demonic influence. Thus, during Joan's trial the judges demanded that she make theological

distinctions that were alien to her. When they wanted to know if the voices were those of angels or saints, Joan seemed perplexed and responded, "This voice comes from God . . . I am more afraid of failing the voices by saying what is displeasing to them than answering you."[7] The judges kept pushing, asking if the saints or angels had heads, eyes, and hair. Exasperated, Joan simply replied, "I have told you often enough, believe me if you will."

The judges reformulated Joan's words to reflect their own rigid scholastic categories and concluded that her "veneration of the saints seems to partake of idolatry and to proceed from a pact made with devils. These are less divine revelations than lies invented by Joan, suggested or shown to her by the demon in illusive apparitions, in order to mock at her imagination while she meddled with things that are beyond her and superior to the faculty of her condition."[8] In other words, Joan was just too naive and uneducated to have authentic visions. But the English judges were on dangerous ground because during the previous fifty years there had been a number of notable female mystics, including St. Catherine of Siena and St. Bridget of Sweden, whose visions had been accepted as authentic by the pope. The English could not take the chance that they were executing a real saint. They had to prove Joan was a witch by showing that her visions were theologically unsound. But that they could not do.

If they could not convict her for bad theology, the English needed evidence for superstitious practices. In an attempt to do that, they drew up seventy charges against her. Many of these consisted of allegations of performing magic, such as chanting spells, visiting a magical tree at night, and invoking demons. They attempted

to prove bad behavior by insinuating that a young man had refused to marry her on account of her immoral life. They asserted that her godmother was a notorious witch who had taught her sorcery. None of these ploys worked, however, because Joan consistently denied these charges. She did, however, admit to one allegation: she cross-dressed as a man.

Some of the charges against her and many of the questions she was asked concerned how she dressed:

> The said Joan put off and entirely abandoned women's clothes, with her hair cropped short and round in the fashion of young men, she wore shirt, breeches, doublet, with hose joined together, long and fastened to the said doublet by twenty points, long leggings laced on the outside, a short mantle reaching to the knee, or thereabouts, a close-cut cap, tight-fitting boots or buskins, long spurs, sword, dagger, breastplate, lance and other arms in the style of a man-at-arms.[9]

The judges explained to her that "according to canon law and the Holy Scriptures" a woman dressing as a man or a man as a woman is "an abomination before God."[10] She replied simply and consistently that "everything that I have done, I did by command of the voices" and that wearing male dress "would be for the great good of France."[11] When they asked her to put on a woman's dress in order to take the Eucharist on Easter Sunday, she refused, saying the miracle of the Eucharist did not depend on whether she wore a man's or a woman's clothing. On many occasions she had been asked to put on a woman's dress and refused. "And as for womanly duties, she said there were enough other women to do them."[12]

After a long imprisonment and psychological pressure from her in-

The Execution of Joan of Arc
There are no contemporary portraits of Joan, and this image is clearly a generalized one of a young woman rather than a portrait taken from the real Joan.

The bundle of stakes will be used for the fire that will consume her.

Joan of Arc is tied to the stake before her execution.

These onlookers are holding sticks for the fire.

quisitors, Joan confessed to charges of witchcraft, signed a recantation of her heresy, and agreed to put on a dress. She was sentenced to life imprisonment on bread and water. Why did she confess? Some historians have argued that she was tricked into confessing because the inquisitors really wanted to execute her but could not do so unless she was a *relapsed* heretic. To be relapsed she had to confess and then somehow return to her heretical ways. If that was the inquisitors' intention, Joan soon obliged them. After a few days in prison, Joan threw off the women's clothes she had been given and resumed dressing as a man. As a witness put it, "The said Catherine and Margaret [instructed] this woman in the name of God to take and wear a man's clothes, and she had worn them and still wears them, stubbornly obeying the said command, to such an extent that this woman had declared she would rather die than relinquish these clothes."[13]

Joan was willing to be burned at the stake rather than disobey her voices. Why? Historians will never know for sure, but dressing as a man may have been necessary for her to fulfill her role as a military leader. The men who followed her into battle and trusted her voices accepted the necessity of this mutation of gender. In her military career, Joan had adopted the masculine qualities of chivalry: bravery, steadfastness, loyalty, and a willingness to accept pain and death. She made herself believable by dressing as a knight. A number

of soldiers who had served with her testified that although they knew Joan was a woman, they had never felt any sexual desire for her, which suggests that she seemed androgynous to them. It was precisely Joan's gender ambiguity that the inquisitors found a dangerous sign of Satan's hand. And it was Joan's refusal to abandon her ambiguous gender identity that provided the inquisitors with the evidence they needed.

Joan's condemnation was much more than another example of men's attempt to control women. The inquisitors needed evidence of demonic influence, which to their minds Joan's transgressive gender behavior supplied. Joan's confused gender identity threatened the whole system of neat hierarchical distinctions upon which scholastic theology rested. To the theologians, everything in God's Creation had its own proper place and anyone who changed his or her divinely ordained position in society presented a direct affront to God.

The English verdict and Joan's tragic fate greatly wounded French pride. In 1456 at her mother's instigation the French clergy reopened her case in a posthumous trial that sought to rehabilitate her

in the eyes of the church. To these churchmen, she was an authentic visionary and a saint who listened to a direct command from God. To the French people ever since, she has become a national symbol of pride and of French unity against a foreign invader. In our own time, Joan has been characterized as many things—a saint, a madwoman, a female warrior, a woman exercising power in a male world, and a woman openly transgressing gender categories by dressing in men's clothes.

Questions of Justice

1. In medieval ecclesiastical trials such as this one, what kinds of evidence were presented and what kind of justice was sought?
2. What did Joan's claim that she heard voices reveal about her understanding of what constituted the proper authority over her life?

Taking It Further

Joan of Arc. *In Her Own Words,* trans. Willard Trask. 1996. The record of what Joan reputedly said at her trials.

Warner, Marina. *Joan of Arc: The Image of Female Heroism.* 1981. A highly readable feminist reading of the Joan of Arc story.

The Military Revolution

The "military revolution," whose effects first became evident during the Hundred Years' War, refers to changes in warfare that marked the transition from the late medieval to the early modern state. The heavily armored mounted knights, who had dominated European warfare and society since the Carolingian period, were gradually supplanted by foot soldiers as the most effective fighting unit in battle. Infantry units were composed of men who fought on foot in disciplined ranks, which allowed them to break up cavalry charges by concentrating firepower in deadly volleys. Infantry soldiers could fight on a greater variety of terrains than mounted knights, who needed even ground and plenty of space for their horses to maneuver. The effectiveness of infantry units made battles more ferocious but also more decisive, which was why governments favored them. Infantry, however, put new requirements on the governments that recruited them. Armies now demanded large numbers of well-drilled foot soldiers who could move in disciplined ranks around a battlefield. Recruiting, training, and drilling soldiers made armies much more complex organizations than they had been, and officers needed to possess a wide range of management skills. Governments faced added expenses as they needed to arrange and pay for the logistical support necessary to feed and transport those large numbers. The creation of the highly centralized modern state resulted in part from the necessity to maintain a large army in which infantry played the crucial role.

Infantry used a variety of weapons. The English demonstrated the effectiveness of longbowmen during the Hundred Years' War. Capable of shooting at a much more rapid rate than the French crossbowmen, the English longbowmen at Agincourt protected themselves behind a hurriedly erected stockade of stakes and rained a shower of deadly arrows on the French cavalry to break up charges. In the narrow battlefield, which was wedged between two forests, the French cavalry had insufficient room to maneuver, and when some of them dismounted to create more room, their heavy armor made them easy to topple over and spear through the underarm seam in their armor. Some English infantry units deployed ranks of pikemen who created an impenetrable wall of sharp spikes.

The military revolution of the fourteenth and fifteenth centuries also introduced gunpowder to European warfare. Arriving from China with the Mongol invasions, gunpowder was first used in the West in artillery. Beginning in the 1320s huge wrought-iron cannons were used to shoot stone or iron against fortifications during sieges. By the early sixteenth century bronze muzzle-loading cannons were used in field battles. With the introduction during the late fifteenth century of the first handgun and the harquebus (a matchlock shoulder gun), properly drilled and disciplined infantrymen could deliver very destructive firepower.

Gunshot pierced plate armor, whereas arrows bounced off. The slow rate of fire of these guns, however, necessitated carefully planned battle tactics. Around 1500 the Spanish introduced mixed infantry formations that pursued "shock" and "shot" tactics. Spanish pikemen provided the shock, which was quickly followed up by gunshot or missile fire. Spanish infantry formations were capable of defeating cavalry even in the open field without defensive fortifications, an unprecedented feat. By the end of the fifteenth century, trained infantry were necessary in every army.

The chivalric aristocrats, who made up the heavily armored cavalry forces and whose fighting ability justified their social privileges, tried to adapt to the changes by improving plate armor, employing longer lances, and drilling their horses for greater maneuverability. They were successful enough and retained enough political influence that heavy cavalry remained necessary in the professional armies that began to appear in the fifteenth century. However, the military revolution precipitated a major shift in European society as well as in battlefield tactics. The successful states were those that created the financial base and bureaucratic structures necessary to put into the field a well-trained professional army composed of infantry units and artillery. Armies now required officers who were capable of drilling infantry or understanding the science of warfare in order to serve as an artillery officer. The traditional landed aristocrats, accustomed to commanding armored knights, found that noble lineage was not as important as technical skills and talents.

A Troubled Church and the Demand for Religious Comfort

■ Why did the church fail to provide leadership and spiritual guidance during these difficult times?

In reaction to the suffering and widespread death during the fourteenth century, many people naturally turned to religion for spiritual consolation and for explanations of what had gone wrong. But the spiritual authority of the Church was so dangerously weakened during this period that it failed to satisfy the popular craving for solace. The moral leadership that had made the papacy such a powerful force for reform during the eleventh through thirteenth centuries was completely lacking in the fourteenth. Many laypeople gave up looking to the pope for guidance and found their own means of religious expression, making the Later Middle Ages one of the most religiously creative epochs in Christian history. Some of the new religious movements, especially in England and Bohemia, veered onto the dangerous shoals of heresy, breaking the fragile unity of the Church.

The Babylonian Captivity of the Church and the Great Schism

Faced with anarchy in the streets of Rome as local aristocrats engaged in incessant feuding, a succession of seven consecutive popes chose to reside in the relative calm of Avignon, France. This period of voluntary papal exile is known as the Babylonian Captivity of the Church° (1305–1378), a biblical reference recalling the captivity of the Jews in Babylonia (587–539 B.C.E.). The popes' presumed subservience to the kings of France during this period dangerously politicized the papacy, destroying its ability to rise above the petty squabbles of the European princes. Even though these popes were never the French kings' lackeys, the enemies of the kings of France did not trust popes who were residing in France and who were themselves French. The loss of revenues from papal lands in Italy lured several popes into questionable financial schemes, which included accepting kickbacks from appointees to church offices, taking bribes for judicial decisions, and selling indulgences°. Indulgences were certificates that allowed penitents to atone for their sins and reduce their time in Purgatory.

When Pope Urban VI (r. 1378–1389) was elevated to the papacy in 1378 and announced his intention to reside in Rome, a group of disgruntled French cardinals returned to Avignon and elected a rival French pope. The Church was then divided over allegiance to Italian and French claimants to the papal throne, a period called the Great Schism° (1378–1417). Toward the end of the schism there were actually four rival popes. Some of these antipopes completely lacked spiritual qualities. The most infamous was Baldassare Cossa, whom a faction of cardinals elected Pope John XXIII (r. 1410–1415) because he had been an effective commander of the papal troops. The cardinals who supported rival popes charged Pope John with the crimes of piracy, murder, rape, sodomy, and incest—charges without much substance—but the publication of the allegations further undermined the moral reputation of the papacy. During the Great Schism the kings, princes, and cities of Europe divided their allegiances between the rival candidates. The Church was split not because of doctrinal differences but because competing systems of political alliances sustained the schism. The French king and the allies of France supported the French pope. The enemies of France gave aid and comfort to the Italian pope.

Urban VI's decision to return the papacy to Rome and attempt to end the Babylonian Captivity of the Church resulted from an intense demand for his presence in Italy. Part of the reason was the growing influence of a young woman mystic. Catherine Benincasa (1347–1380), now known as St. Catherine of Siena, demonstrated her mystic tendencies at an early age by locking herself in a room of her parents' house for a year to devote herself to prayer and fasting. She soon became famous for her holiness and severe asceticism, which during the troubled times of the Babylonian Captivity gave her a powerful moral authority. She went to Avignon, and although the pope ignored her, she attracted the attention of others in the papal court. Catherine became the most important advocate for encouraging the return of the pope from Avignon to Rome and launching a new crusade against the Muslims. She helped Pope Urban VI reorganize the Church after he returned to Rome, and she sent out letters and pleas to the kings and queens of Europe to gain support for him during the schism. Catherine dictated an influential body of letters,

The Babylonian Captivity of the Church
From 1303 to 1378 the popes lived in exile from Rome in this fortress-like Palace of the Popes in Avignon, France. The French claimants to the papal throne continued to live here during the Great Schism until 1417.

prayers, and treatises that attempted to remind the popes and kings of Europe of their religious responsibilities.

The Great Schism created the need for a mechanism to sort out the competing claims of rival popes. That need led to the Conciliar Movement°. The conciliarists argued that a general meeting or council of the bishops of the Church had authority over the pope, it could be called to order by a king, and it could pass judgment on a standing pope or order a conclave to elect a new one. Several general councils were held during the early fifteenth century to resolve the schism and initiate reforms, but solutions were difficult to achieve because politics and the affairs of the Church were so closely intertwined. The Council of Constance (1414–1417) finally succeeded in restoring unity to the Church and also in formally asserting the principle that a general council is superior to the pope and should be called frequently. The Council of Basel (1431–1449) approved a series of necessary reforms, although these were never implemented due to the hostility to conciliarism by Pope Eugene IV (r. 1431–1447). The failure of even the timid reforms of the Council of Basel opened the way for the more radical rejection of papal authority during the Protestant Reformation of the sixteenth century. The Conciliar Movement, however, was not a complete failure because it provided a model for how reform could take place. This model would later become central to the Catholic Reformation and the foundation of modern Catholicism (see Chapter 13).

The Search for Religious Alternatives

The popes' loss of moral authority during the Babylonian Captivity and the Great Schism opened the way for a remarkable variety of reformers, mystics, and preachers, who appealed to lay believers crying out for a direct experience of God and a return to the message of the original apostles of Christ. Most of these movements were quite traditional in their doctrines, but some were heretical, and the weakened papacy was unable to control them, as it had successfully done during the thirteenth-century crusade against the Albigensians.

Protests Against the Papacy: New Heresies

For most Catholic Christians during the fourteenth century, religious life consisted of witnessing or participating in the seven sacraments, which were formal rituals celebrated by duly consecrated priests usually within the confines of churches. After baptism, which was universally performed on infants, the most common sacraments for lay adults were penance and communion. Both of these sacraments emphasized the authority of the clergy over the laity and therefore were potential sources for resentment. The sacrament of penance required the layperson to confess his or her sins to a priest, who then prescribed certain penalties to satisfy

the sin. At communion, it was believed, the priest changed the substance of an unleavened wafer of bread, called the Eucharist, into the body of Christ and a chalice of wine into his blood, a miraculous process called transubstantiation. Priests and lay recipients of communion both ate the wafer, but the chalice was reserved for the priest alone. More than anything else, the reservation of the chalice for priests profoundly symbolized the privileges of the clergy. Because medieval Catholicism was primarily a sacramental religion, reformers and heretics tended to concentrate their criticism on sacramental rituals, especially of their spiritual value compared to other kinds of worship such as prayer.

The most serious discontent about the authority of the popes, the privileges of the clergy, and the efficacy of the sacraments appeared in England and Bohemia (a region in the modern Czech Republic). An Oxford professor, John Wycliffe (1320–1384), criticized the power and wealth of the clergy, played down the value of the sacraments for encouraging ethical behavior, and exalted the benefits of preaching, which promoted a sense of personal responsibility. During the Great Schism, Wycliffe rejected the authority of the rival popes and asserted instead the absolute authority of the Bible, which he wanted to make available to the laity in English rather than in Latin, which most laypeople could not understand.

The Execution of Jan Hus
Despite a safe-conduct from the emperor, Jan Hus was arrested and convicted as a heretic at the Council of Constance in 1415. This miniature from later in the fifteenth century depicts his burning.

Outside England Wycliffe's ideas found their most sympathetic audience among a group of reformist professors at the University of Prague in Bohemia, where Jan Hus (1369–1415) regularly preached to a large popular following. Hus's most revolutionary act was to offer the chalice of consecrated communion wine to the laity, thus symbolically diminishing the special status of the clergy. When Hus also preached against indulgences, which he said converted the sacrament of penance into a cash transaction, Pope John XXIII excommunicated him. Hus attended the Council of Constance to defend his ideas. Despite the promise of a safe-conduct from the Holy Roman emperor (whose jurisdiction included Bohemia and Constance) that would have made him immune from arrest, Hus was imprisoned, his writings were condemned, and he was burned alive as a heretic.

Imitating Christ: The Modern Devotion

In the climate of religious turmoil of the fourteenth and fifteenth centuries, many Christians sought deeper spiritual solace than the institutionalized Church could provide. Most of these people pursued deeply traditional forms of piety, exhibiting how medieval spirituality was capable of seemingly infinite renewal and vitality. By stressing individual piety, ethical behavior, and intense religious education, a movement called the Modern Devotion° built on the existing traditions of spirituality and became highly influential. Promoted by the Brothers of the Common Life, a religious order established in the Netherlands, the Modern Devotion was especially popular throughout northern Europe. In the houses for the Brothers, clerics and laity lived together without monastic vows, shared household tasks, joined in regular prayers, and engaged in religious studies. (A similar structure was devised for women.) The lay brothers continued their occupations in the outside world, thus influencing their neighbors through their pious example. The houses established schools that prepared boys for church careers through constant prayer and rigorous training in Latin. Many of the leading figures behind the Protestant Reformation in the sixteenth century had attended schools run by the Brothers of the Common Life.

The Modern Devotion was also spread by the best-seller of the late fifteenth century, the *Imitation of Christ,* written about 1441 by a Common Life brother, probably Thomas à Kempis. By emphasizing frequent private prayer and moral introspection, the *Imitation* provided a manual to guide laypeople in the path toward spiritual renewal that had traditionally been reserved for monks and nuns. There was nothing especially reformist or antisacramental about the *Imitation of Christ,* which emphasized the need for regular confession and communion. However, its popularity helped prepare the way for a broad-based reform of the Church by turning the walls of the monastery inside out, spilling out a large number of lay believers who were dedicated to becoming living examples of moral purity for their neighbors.

CHRONOLOGY

Troubles in the Church

1305–1378	Babylonian Captivity of the Church; popes reside in Avignon
1320–1384	John Wycliffe
1347–1380	Catherine of Siena
1369–1415	Jan Hus
1378–1417	Great Schism; more than one pope
1414–1417	Council of Constance
1431–1449	Council of Basel
ca. 1441	*Imitation of Christ*

The moral and financial degradation of the papacy during the fourteenth and early fifteenth centuries was countered by the persistent spirituality of the laity, manifest in the Modern Devotion. As a result, throughout Europe laypeople took responsibility not only for their own behavior but for the spiritual and material welfare of their entire community and of the Church itself. Lay spirituality remained deeply traditional rather than innovative. These pious people founded hospitals for the sick and dying, orphanages for abandoned children, and confraternities that engaged in a wide range of charitable good works—from providing dowries for poor women to accompanying condemned criminals to the gallows.

The Culture of Loss

■ How did European culture offer explanations and solace for the otherwise inexplicable calamities of the times?

During the fourteenth and early fifteenth centuries, the omnipresence of violence and death made suffering a common theme in the arts and strangely the subject matter for jokes, fancy-dress masquerades, and wild dances. The preoccupation with death revealed an anxious attachment to fleeting life.

This widespread anxiety had many manifestations. Some aristocrats sought escape from the terror by indulging in a beautiful fantasy life of gallant knights and beautiful ladies. Others went on long penitential pilgrimages to the shrines of saints or to the Holy Land. During the fourteenth century the tribulations of the pilgrim's travels became a metaphor for the journey of life itself, stimulating creative literature. Still others tried to find someone to blame for calamities. When no other explanation could be found, alleged witches became handy scapegoats. The search for scapegoats also focused on minority groups, especially Jews and Muslims.

Reminders of Death

In no other period of Western civilization has the idea of death constituted such a pervasive cultural force as during the fourteenth and fifteenth centuries. The religious justification for this preoccupation was the Reminder of Death, a theme found in religious books, literary works, and the visual arts. A contemporary book of moral guidance advised the reader that "when he goes to bed, he should imagine not that he is putting himself to bed, but that others are laying him in his grave."[14] Reminders of Death became the everyday theme of preachers, and popular woodcuts represented death in simple but disturbing images. These representations emphasized the transitory nature of life, admonishing that every created thing perishes. The Reminder of Death tried to encourage ethical behavior in this life by showing that in everyone's future was neither riches, nor fame, nor love, nor pleasure, but only the decay of death.

The most famous Reminder of Death was the Dance of Death. First appearing in a poem of 1376, the Dance of Death evolved into a street play, performed to illustrate sermons that called for repentance. It also appeared in church murals, depicting a procession led by a skeleton that included representatives of the social orders, from children and peasants to pope and emperor. All were being led to their inevitable deaths. At the Church of the Innocents in Paris, the mural depicting the Dance of Death is accompanied by an inscription that reads:

Tomb Effigy of a Knight
This effigy above the tomb of Jean d'Alluy shows the deceased as if he were serenely sleeping, still dressed in the armor of his worldly profession.

Advance, see yourselves in us, dead, naked, rotten and stinking. So will you be. . . . To live without thinking of this risks damnation. . . . Power, honor, riches are nothing; at the hour of death only good works count. . . . Everyone should think at least once a day of his loathsome end [in order to escape] the dreadful pain of hell without end which is unspeakable.[15]

In earlier centuries, tombs had depicted death as serene: On top of the tomb was an effigy of the deceased, dressed in the finest clothes with hands piously folded and eyes open to the promise of eternal life. In contrast, during the fourteenth century tomb effigies began to depict putrefying bodies or naked skeletons, symbols of the futility of human status and achievements. These tombs were disturbingly graphic Reminders of Death. Likewise, poems spoke of the disgusting smell of rotting flesh, the livid color of plague victims, the cold touch of the dead. Preachers loved to personalize death. They would point to the most beautiful young woman in the congregation and describe how she would look while rotting in the grave, how worms would crawl through the empty sockets that once held her alluring eyes.

In reminding people of the need to repent their sins in the face of their inevitable deaths, no sin was more condemned than pride, the high opinion

Decomposing Cadaver
The tomb effigy of Jean de Lagrange.

The Art of Dying

In this death scene, the dying man receives extreme unction (last rites) from a priest. A friar holds a crucifixion for him to contemplate. Above his head an devil and angel compete for his soul while behind him Death lurks waiting for his moment.

of one's own qualities and conduct. In contrast to modern times, when pride is often understood as a virtue, late medieval moralists saw pride as an affront to God, a rejection of God's will that humanity should concentrate on spiritual rather than worldly things. Pride, in fact, was often discussed as the ultimate source of all the other deadly sins: lust, gluttony, avarice, sloth, wrath, and covetousness. The theme was encapsulated by the inscription on the tomb of a cardinal who died in 1402: "So, miserable one, what cause for pride?"[16]

Late medieval society was completely frank about the unpleasant process of dying, unlike modern societies that hide the dying in hospitals and segregate mourning to funeral homes. Dying was a public event, almost a theatrical performance. The last rites of the Catholic Church and the Art of Dying served to assist souls in their final test before God and to separate the departed from their kin. According to the Art of Dying, which was prescribed in numerous advice books and illustrations, the sick or injured person should die in bed, surrounded by a room full of people, including children. It was believed that a dying person watched a supernatural spectacle visible to him or her alone as the heavenly host fought with Satan and his demon minions for the soul. The Art of Dying compared the deathbed contest to a horrific game of chess in which the Devil did all he could to trap the dying person into a checkmate just at the moment of death. In the best of circumstances, a priest arrived in time to hear a confession, offer words of consolation, encourage the dying individual to forgive his or her enemies and redress any wrongs, and perform the last rites.

Illusions of a Noble Life

Eventually death arrived for everyone, peasant and noble alike, a fact that the Reminders of Death were designed to keep foremost in the minds of all Christians. Some people, especially among the nobility, sought to ignore this fundamental truth through escapist fantasies. These fantasies shielded nobles not only from the inevitability of death but also from all the other perils of the age—the worker and peasant rebellions, the economic depression that depleted their wealth, and the military revolution that challenged their monopoly on soldierly valor. During the Later Middle Ages, many nobles indulged in chivalric escapism and idealized their class as the remedy for evil times. They thought God had placed them on Earth to purify the world.

Much of the attraction of chivalry derived from its fanciful vision of the virtues of the ascetic life, the life that practices severe self-discipline and abstains from physical pleasures. The ideal medieval knight was as much a self-denying ascetic as the ideal medieval monk. The highest expression of the chivalric ideal was the knight-errant, a warrior who roamed in search of adventure. He was poor and free of ties to home and family, a man who lived a life of perfect freedom but whose virtue led him to do the right thing. In reality most knights were hardly ascetics but rich, propertied men who were completely involved in the world and who indulged in all of its pleasures.

The ideal of the ascetic knight-errant was pursued in an elaborately developed fantasy culture that occupied much of the time and cultural energy of the aristocracy. The French nobleman Philippe de Mézières (ca. 1327–1405), whose chivalric imagination knew no bounds, dreamed of establishing a new order of knights, the Order of the Passion, whose members would be spiritually removed from worldly affairs and devoted to reconquering the Holy Land. He drew up a plan for the order, but it never became a reality. He imagined that the knights in the Order of the Passion would peacefully end all wars among Christians and bind themselves together in a great Crusade against the Mongols, Jews, Turks, and other Muslims. Several kings actually did establish new crusading orders, which aristocrats joined with unbridled enthusiasm—the Order of the Garter in England, the Order of the Stars and Order of St. Michael in France, and the most fantastic of all, the Order of the Golden Fleece in Burgundy. Members of these orders indulged in extravagant acts of self-deprivation—for example, wearing fur coats in summer but refusing to wear a

A Sumptuous Aristocratic Banquet
An aristocratic banquet with scenes of fighting in the background. Dining was the principal occasion at which nobles displayed refined manners showing their commitment to the beautiful life.

coat, hat, or gloves in freezing temperatures. They loved to take vows: One knight swore he would not sleep in a bed on Sundays until he had fought the Muslims; another took an oath that he would keep his right arm bare of any armor during battle with the Turks. None of these would-be crusaders came close to fighting Turks.

Many vows were taken in the name of ladies, revealing that the chivalric ideal also included a heavy dose of erotic desire. Besides ascetic self-denial, the most persistent chivalric fantasy was the motif of the young hero who liberates a virgin, either from a dragon or from a rioting mob of peasants. The myth of the noble knight suffering to save his beloved was the product of the male imagination, revealing how men wished to be admired in the eyes of women, but the myth has had a profound and lasting influence on Western culture.

The fantasy world of the noble life especially animated the duchy of Burgundy, a quasi-independent principality that paid nominal allegiance to the French king. Burgundy set the chivalric standards for all of Europe during the fifteenth century. Famous for his lavish lifestyle, Duke Philip the Good (r. 1419–1467) was a notorious rake who seduced numerous noble ladies and produced many illegitimate children, but he also epitomized the ideals of chivalry in his love of horses, hunting, and court ceremonies. He was an extravagant patron of the arts, which made him famous throughout Europe. Musicians, manuscript illuminators, painters, tapestry makers, and historians thrived with his support and made Burgundy the center of European aristocratic fashion.

The dukes of Burgundy sustained their power through their personal ties to the nobility and elites of the cities of their dominions. They were constantly on the move, visiting palaces, castles, and towns. They created a kind of theater state, staging elaborate entry ceremonies to the towns they visited; celebrating with fantastic splendor every event in the ducal family, such as marriages and births; entertaining the nobles with tournaments and the people with elaborate processions; and guaranteeing the loyalty of the nobles by inviting them to join the Order of the Golden Fleece, which occupied its members by training for a crusade.

Pilgrims of the Imagination

During the Middle Ages, a pilgrimage offered a religiously sanctioned form of escape from the omnipresent suffering and peril. Pious Christians could go on a pilgrimage to the Holy Land, Rome, or the shrine of a saint, such as Santiago de Compostela in Spain or Canterbury in England. The usual motive for a pilgrimage was to fulfill a vow or promise made to God, or to obtain an indulgence, which exempted the pilgrim from some of the time spent in punishment in Purgatory after death. The pilgrimage became the instrument for spiritual liberation and escape from difficulties. As a result, going on a pilgrimage became a compelling model for creative literature, especially during the fourteenth century. Not all of these great works of literature were fictional pilgrimages, but many evoked the pilgrim's impulse to find a refuge from the difficulties of daily life or to find solace in the promise of a better life to come.

Dante Alighieri and *The Divine Comedy*
In *The Divine Comedy* an Italian poet from Florence, Dante Alighieri (1265–1321), imagined the most fantastic pilgrimage ever attempted, a journey through Hell, Purgatory, and Paradise. A work of astounding originality, *The Divine Comedy* remains the greatest masterpiece of medieval literature. Little is known about Dante's early life except that somehow he acquired an encyclopedic education that gave him

DOCUMENT

Dante, *Divine Comedy* (1321)

Dante and the Plague Victims

The ancient poet Virgil and Dante come across victims of the plague in their journey through Hell. This depiction, which comes from a sixteenth-century manuscript, is anachronistic because the Black Death arrived after Dante wrote *The Divine Comedy*, but he does describe victims of epidemic diseases in his poem.

expertise in Greek philosophy, scholastic theology (the application of logic to the understanding of Christianity), Latin literature, and the newly fashionable poetic forms in Provençal, the language of southern France. Dante was involved in the dangerous politics of Florence, which led to his exile under pain of death if he ever returned. During his exile Dante wandered for years, suffering grievously the loss of his home: "bitter is the taste of another man's bread and . . . heavy the way up and down another man's stair" (*Paradiso*, canto 17). While in exile, Dante sustained himself by writing his great poetic vision of human destiny and God's plan for redemption.

In the poem Dante himself travels into the Christian version of the afterlife, but the poetic journey displays numerous non-Christian influences. The passage through Hell, for example, derived from a long Muslim poem reconstructing Muhammad's *miraj*, a night journey to Jerusalem and ascent to heaven. Dante's poem can be read on many levels—personal, historical, spiritual, moral, theological— as it recounts an allegorical pilgrimage to visit the souls of the departed. Dante connects his personal suffering with the historical problems of Italy, the warnings of the dead who had sinned in life, and the promise of rewards to those who had been virtuous. Dante's trip, initially guided by the Latin poet Virgil, the epitome of ancient wisdom, starts in Hell. While traveling deeper into its harsh depths, Dante is

DOCUMENT

Dante Describes Hell

In The Divine Comedy, *Dante imagined a series of circles in Hell into which were cast those guilty of a certain class of sin. In the eighth circle Dante and his guide Virgil came upon those guilty of fraud. They suffered for all eternity in the depths of stinking, filthy caverns in the ground. Dante and Virgil followed a path through Hell, and at this point the path led to a series of arches that spanned over the caverns.*

Here we heard people whine in the next chasm,
and knock and thump themselves with open palms, and
blubber through their snouts as if in a spasm.

Steaming from that pit, a vapor rose
over the banks, crusting them with a slime
that sickened my eyes and hammered at my nose.

That chasm sinks so deep we could not sight
its bottom anywhere until we climbed
along the rock arch to its greatest height.

Once there, I peered down; and I saw long lines
of people in a river of excrement
that seemed the overflow of the world's latrines.

I saw among the felons of that pit
one wraith who might or might not have been tonsured—
one could not tell, he was so smeared with shit.

He bellowed: "You there, why do you stare at me
more than at all the others in this stew?"
And I to him: "Because if memory

serves me, I knew you when your hair was dry.
You are Alessio Interminelli da Lucca.
That's why I pick you from this filthy fry."

And he then, beating himself on his clown's head:
"Down to this have the flatteries I sold
the living sunk me here among the dead."

And my Guide prompted then: "Lean forward a bit
and look beyond them, there—do you see that one
scratching herself with dungy nails, the strumpet

who fidgets to her feet, then to a crouch?
It is the whore Thais . . ."

Source: From *The Divine Comedy* by Dante Alighieri, translated by John Ciardi. Copyright 1954, 1957, 1960, 1961, 1965, 1967, 1970 by the Ciardi Family Publishing Trust. Used by permission of W. W. Norton & Company, Inc.

warned of the harmful values of this world by meeting a cast of sinful characters who inhabit the world of the damned. In Purgatory his guide becomes Beatrice, Dante's deceased beloved, who stands for the Christian virtues. In this section of the poem, he begins the painful process of spiritual rehabilitation in which he comes to accept the Christian image of life as a pilgrimage. In Paradise he achieves spiritual fulfillment by speaking with figures from the past who have defied death.

The lasting appeal of this long, complex, and difficult poem is a wonder. Underlying the appeal of *The Divine Comedy* is perhaps its optimism, which expresses Dante's own cure to his depressing condition as an exile. The power of Dante's poetry established the form of the modern Italian language. Even in translation the images and stories can intrigue and fascinate.

Giovanni Boccaccio and *The Decameron*

Like Dante, Giovanni Boccaccio (1313–1375) was a Florentine. He grew up in a prosperous merchant banking family that was bankrupted during the Florentine financial crisis of the 1340s. Losing the shelter of economic and social privilege, Boccaccio's life became one of poverty and endless adversity. In the freedom from business responsibilities created by enforced poverty, Boccaccio turned to writing tales of chivalry and love, which were immediately very popular and had lasting influence on other writers.

After witnessing the ravages of the Black Death in Florence in 1348 and 1349, Boccaccio turned to polishing his masterpiece, *The Decameron*, a collection of 100 humorous, satirical, majestic, and sometimes pornographic stories. The book begins with a somber description of the social chaos created by the plague and tells how ten young people (seven women and three men) escaped the plague in Florence for a refuge in the country. *The Decameron* is less a story of a pilgrimage than the depiction of a refuge, but it is no less an escape from the cruel realities of the world. In their luxurious fantasy world of the country, each of the ten tells a story every night for ten nights. Displaying an open-minded attitude toward human weaknesses, *The Decameron* represents Boccaccio's initial response to the Black Death. Believing there was no future other than death, Boccaccio responded with a celebration of life in stories full of heroism, romance, unhappy love, wit, trickery, sexual license, and laughter. Although *The Decameron* was often read as escapist fantasy literature designed to lift the gloom of events, it was also a literary masterpiece that created a vivid, swift moving narrative.

Geoffrey Chaucer and *The Canterbury Tales*

Boccaccio profoundly influenced Geoffrey Chaucer (ca. 1342–1400), the most outstanding English poet prior to William Shakespeare. As a courtier and diplomat,

Chaucer was a trusted adviser to three successive English kings. But he is best known for his literary output, including *The Canterbury Tales,* which exhibit some of the same earthy humor and tolerance for human folly as *The Decameron.*

In *The Canterbury Tales* a group of thirty pilgrims tell stories as they travel on horseback to the shrine at Canterbury. By employing the pilgrimage as a framing device for telling the stories, Chaucer was able to bring together a collection of people from across the social spectrum, including a wife, indulgence hawker, miller, town magistrate, clerk, landowner, lawyer, merchant, knight, abbess, and monk. The variety of characters who told the tales allowed Chaucer to experiment with many kinds of literary forms, from a chivalric romance to a sermon. The pilgrimage combined the considerations of religious morality with the fun of a spring vacation more concerned with the pleasures of this world than preparing for the next, which was the avowed purpose of going on a pilgrimage. In this intertwining of the worldly and the spiritual, Chaucer brought the abstract principles of Christian morality down to a level of common understanding.

Margery Kempe and the Autobiographical Pilgrimage

As the daughter of a town mayor, Margery Kempe (1373–1440) was destined for a comfortable life as a middle-class wife in provincial England. After her first child was born, however, she experienced a bout of depression during which she had a vision of Christ. She began to experience more visions and felt a calling to lead a more spiritual life. As a married woman she could not become a nun, which would have been the normal course for a woman with her spiritual inclinations. Instead, she accepted her marital duties and bore fourteen children.

At the age of about 40 she persuaded her husband to join her in a mutual vow of chastity and embarked on her own religious vocation. Always a bit of an eccentric, Kempe became a fervent vegetarian at a time when meat was scarce but highly desired. She also developed an insatiable wanderlust, undertaking a series of pilgrimages to Jerusalem, Rome, Germany, Norway, Spain, and numerous places in England. On these pilgrimages she sought out mystics and recluses for their spiritual advice. Her own devotions took the form of loud weeping and crying, which alienated many people who feared she might be a heretic or a madwoman. Toward the end of her life she dictated an account of her difficult dealings with her husband, her spells of madness, her ecstatic visions, and her widespread travels as a pilgrim. For Kempe the actual experience of undertaking pilgrimages made it possible for her to examine the course of her own life, which she understood as a spiritual pilgrimage. Her *Book* (1436) was the earliest autobiography in English.

Christine de Pisan and the Defense of Female Virtue

The work of the poet Christine de Pisan (1364–1430) was neither escapist like Giovanni Boccaccio's nor a spiritual pilgrimage like Dante's, Chaucer's, or Kempe's but was a thoughtful and passionate commentary on the tumultuous issues of her day. At age 15 Pisan married a notary of King Charles V of France, but by age 25 she was a widow with three young children. In order to support her family, she turned to writing and relied on the patronage of the royalty and wealthy aristocrats of France, Burgundy, Germany, and England.

Christine de Pisan championed the cause of women in a male-dominated society that was often overtly hostile to them. Following the fashion of the times, she invented a new chivalric order, the Order of the Rose, whose members took a vow to defend the honor of women. She wrote a defense of women for a male readership and an allegorical autobiography. But she is most famous for the two books she wrote for women readers, *The Book of the City of Ladies* and *The Book of Three Virtues* (both about 1407). In these she recounted tales of the heroism and virtue of women and offered moral instruction for women in different social roles. In 1415 she retired to a convent where in the last year of her life she wrote a masterpiece of ecstatic lyricism that celebrated the early victories of Joan of Arc. Pisan's book turned the martyred Joan into the heroine of France.

Defining Cultural Boundaries

During the Later Middle Ages, systematic discrimination against certain ethnic and religious groups increased markedly in Europe. As European society enforced ever-higher levels of religious uniformity, intolerance spread in the ethnically mixed societies of the European periphery. Intolerance was marked in three especially troubled areas: Spain with its mixture of Muslim, Jewish, and Christian cultures; the German borderlands in east-central Europe, where Germans mingled with Slavs; and Ireland and Wales, where Celts came under the domination of the English. Within the heartland of Europe were other areas of clashing cultures—for example, Switzerland where the folk culture of peasants and shepherds living in the isolated mountains collided with the intense Christian religiosity of the cities.

During the eleventh and twelfth centuries, ethnic diversity had been more widely accepted. A Hungarian cleric wrote in an undated work from this period, "As immigrants come from various lands, so they bring with them various languages and customs, various skills and forms of armament, which adorn and glorify the royal household and quell the pride of external powers. A kingdom of one race and custom is weak and fragile."[17] By the fourteenth and fifteenth centuries, however, this optimistic celebration of

DOCUMENT

Why Women Deserve an Education as Much as Men

In the Book of the City of the Ladies *Christine de Pisan addresses the reasons offered by some men who opposed the education of women. These men did not want their daughters, wives, or sisters to receive an education because it would compromise their morals. Christine forcefully answers that objection.*

Here you can clearly see that not all opinions of men are based on reason and that these men are wrong. For it must not be presumed that mores necessarily grow worse from knowing the moral sciences, which teach the virtues, indeed, there is not the slightest doubt that moral education amends and ennobles them. How could anyone think or believe that whoever follows good teaching or doctrine is the worse for it? Such an opinion cannot be expressed or maintained. . . .

Thus, not all men (and especially the wisest) share the opinion that is it bad for women to be educated. But it is very true that many foolish men have claimed this because it displeased them that women knew more than they did. . . .

If it were customary to send little girls to school and to teach them the same subjects as are taught to boys, they would learn just as fully and would understand the subtleties of all arts and sciences. Indeed maybe they would understand them better . . . for just as women's bodies are more soft than men's, so too their understanding is more sharp. . . . If they understand less it is because they do not go out and see so many different places and things but stay home and mind their own work. For there is nothing which teaches a reasonable creature so much as the experience of many different things.

Source: Christine de Pisan, *The Book of the City of Ladies,* translated by Earl Jeffrey Richards. Copyright © 1982 by Persea Books, Inc.

diversity had faded. Ethnic discrimination and residential segregation created the first ghettos for ethnic and religious minorities.

Spain: Religious Communities in Tension

The Iberian peninsula was home to thriving communities of Muslims, Jews, and Christians. Since the eleventh century the aggressive northern Christian kingdoms of Castile and Aragon had engaged in a protracted program of Reconquest (*Reconquista*) against the Muslim states of the peninsula. By 1248 the Reconquest was largely completed, with only a small Muslim enclave in Granada holding out until 1492. The Spanish Reconquest placed former enemies in close proximity to one another. Hostilities between Christians and Muslims ranged from active warfare to tense stalemate, with Jews working as cultural intermediaries between the two larger communities.

During the twelfth and thirteenth centuries Muslims, called the Mudejars, who capitulated to the conquering Christians, received guarantees that they could continue to practice their own religion and laws. During the fourteenth century, however, Christian kings gradually reneged on these promises. In 1301 the king of Castile decreed that the testimony of any two Christian witnesses could convict a Jew or Muslim, notwithstanding any previously granted privileges that allowed them to be tried in their own courts. The Arabic language began to disappear in Spain as the Mudejars suffered discrimination on many levels. By the sixteenth century, the practice of Islam became illegal, and the Spanish state adopted a systematic policy to destroy Mudejar culture by prohibiting Muslim dress, customs, and marriage practices.

The Jews also began to feel the pain of organized, official discrimination. Christian preachers accused Jews of poisonings, stealing Christian babies, and cannibalism. When the Black Death arrived in 1348, the Jews of Aragon were accused of having poisoned the wells, even though Jews were dying just like Christians. Beginning in 1378, a Catholic prelate in Seville, Ferrant Martínez, commenced an anti-Jewish preaching campaign by calling for the destruction of all twenty-three of the city's synagogues, the confinement of Jews to a ghetto, the dislodging of all Jews from public positions, and the prohibition of any social contact between Christians and Jews. His campaign led to an attack on the Jews of Seville in 1391. Violence spread to other cities throughout the peninsula and the nearby Balearic Islands. Jews were given a stark choice: conversion or death. After a year of mob violence, about 100,000 Jews had been murdered and an equal number had gone into hiding or fled to more tolerant Muslim countries. The 1391 pogroms led to the first significant forced conversions of Jews in Spain. A century later in 1492, on the heels of the final Christian victory of the Reconquest, all remaining Jews in Spain were compelled to either leave or convert.

German and Celtic Borderlands: Ethnic Communities in Tension

Other regions with diverse populations also witnessed discrimination and its brutal consequences. During the population boom of the twelfth and thirteenth centuries, German-speaking immigrants had established colonial towns in the Baltic and penetrated eastward, creating isolated pockets of German culture in Bohemia, Poland, and Hungary. During the fourteenth and fifteenth centuries, the bias of native populations against the colonizing Germans was manifest in various ways. One Czech prince offered 100 silver marks to anyone who brought him 100 German noses. The German settlers exhibited a similar intolerance

of the natives. The Teutonic Knights, who had been the vanguard of the German migrations in the Baltic, began to require German ancestry for membership. In German-speaking towns along the colonized borderlands of east-central Europe, city councils and guilds began to restrict by ethnicity the qualification for holding certain offices or joining a guild. The most famous example was the "German Paragraph" in guild statutes, which required candidates for admission to a guild to prove German descent. As the statutes of a bakers' guild put it, "Whoever wishes to be a member must bring proof to the councilors and the guildsmen that he is born of legitimate, upright German folk." Others required members to be "of German blood and tongue," as if language were a matter of biological inheritance.[18] German guildsmen were also forbidden to marry non-Germans.

A similar process of exclusion occurred in the Celtic fringe of the British Isles. In Ireland the ruling English promulgated laws that attempted to protect the cultural identity of the English colonists. The English prohibited native Irish from citizenship in town or guild membership. The Statutes of Kilkenny of 1366 attempted to legislate ethnic purity: They prohibited intermarriage between English and Irish; they required English colonists to speak English, use English names, wear English clothes, and ride horses in the English way; and they forbade the English to play Irish games or listen to Irish music. The aggressive legislation of the English in Ireland was essentially defensive. The tiny English community was attempting to prevent its absorption into the majority culture. A similar pattern appeared in Wales, where the lines dividing the Welsh and English communities hardened during the fourteenth century.

Enemies Within

The Black Death and its aftermath transformed many segments of Europe into a persecuting society. The year 1348 represented a watershed; in the period that followed, vague biases and dislikes sharpened into systematic violence against minorities. The plague sparked assaults against lepers, people with handicaps and physical deformities, beggars, vagabonds, foreigners, priests, pilgrims, Muslims, and Jews. Anyone who looked strange, dressed differently, spoke with an accent, practiced a minority religion, or did not fit in was vulnerable to becoming a scapegoat for the miseries of others. Minorities took the blame for calamities that could not be otherwise explained.

Violence against minorities occurred in many places, but it was most systematic in German-speaking lands. Between November 1348 and August 1350, violence against Jews occurred in more than eighty German towns. Like the allegations in Aragon, the fear that Jews poisoned the wells led to massacres in German lands even *before* plague had arrived in these communities. The frequent occurrence of violence on Sundays or feast days suggests that preachers consciously or unconsciously encouraged the rioting mobs.

The troubles caused by the Great Schism (1378–1417, when there was more than one pope) also contributed to a heightened sensitivity to cultural differences. During the Council of Basel (1431–1449), German bishops and theologians in attendance began to exchange information about cases of alleged witchcraft they had heard about in the nearby Swiss Alps. What these learned priests and friars thought of as witchcraft was probably nothing more than harmless folk magic, but to them the strange details of peasant behavior seemed evidence of a vast Satanic conspiracy to destroy Christianity. For most of its history, the Catholic Church had denied that witchcraft existed, but the terrible events of the fourteenth century cried out for explanation. In 1484 Pope Innocent VIII changed official Catholic policy by calling on two Dominican professors of theology to examine the alleged spread of witchcraft in Germany. As a guide to witch hunters, they wrote a detailed handbook on witchcraft, *The Hammer of Witches,* which went through twenty-eight editions between 1486 and 1600, evidence of its enormous success and influence.

The Hammer of Witches codified the folklore of the Alpine peasants as the basis for witchcraft practices. The book condemned as heretics those who disbelieved in the power of witches and established legal procedures for the prosecution of witches. It sanctioned torture as the most effective means for obtaining confessions, and it established much lower standards of evidence than in other kinds of cases. As an anthology of mythical stories about the activities of supposed witches, *The Hammer* summed up the worst of prevailing attitudes about women: "all witchcraft comes from carnal lust, which in women is insatiable." Most witchcraft persecutions came later in the sixteenth and seventeenth centuries, but the publication of *The Hammer of Witches* represented the culmination of the frenzied search to find enemies within European society, which was quickened by the events of the fourteenth and fifteenth centuries. With the dissemination of the idea of the reality of witchcraft, virtually anyone could be hauled before a court on charges of maintaining a secret liaison with Satan.

Conclusion

Looking Inward

Unlike the more dynamic, outward-looking thirteenth century, Europeans during the fourteenth and early fifteenth centuries turned their attention inward to their own communities and their own problems. Europe faced one calamity after another, each crisis compounding the misery. In the process the identity of the West became more defensive and the fragility of Christianity itself was laid bare. The process of changing Western identities can be seen in two ways. First, as a result of the Western encounters with the Mongol and Ottoman Empires, the political and religious frontiers of the West shifted. These two empires redrew the map of the West by ending the Christian Byzantine Empire and by leaving Christian Russia on the margins of the West. With the Mongol invasions, the eastward spread of Christianity into Asia ended. The Ottoman conquests left a lasting Muslim influence inside eastern Europe, particularly in Bosnia and Albania. Peoples who were predominantly Christian and whose political institutions were a heritage of the ancient Roman Empire now survived under the domination of Asian or Muslim empires and in a tenuous relationship with the rest of the Christian West. Most of the new subjects of these empires remained Christian, but their Mongol and Ottoman masters destroyed their political autonomy. The Ottoman Empire remained hostile to and frequently at war with the Christian West for more than 200 years.

Second, most Europeans reinforced their identity as Christians and became more self-conscious of the country in which they lived. At the same time Christian civilization was becoming eclipsed in parts of eastern Europe, it revived in the Iberian peninsula, where the Muslim population, once the most extensive in the West, suffered discrimination and defeat. The northern Spanish kingdoms, for example, began to unify their subjects around a militant form of Christianity that was overtly hostile to Muslims and Jews. In many places in the West, religious and ethnic discrimination against minorities increased. A stronger sense of self-identification by country can be most dramatically seen in France and England as a consequence of the Hundred Years' War. The French rallied around a saintly national heroine, Joan of Arc. After dropping claims to France after the Hundred Years' War, the English aristocracy stopped speaking French and adopting the customs of the French court. They became less international and more English. The Western countries became more self-consciously characterized by an attitude of "us versus them."

Except for the very visible military conquests of the Mongols and the Ottomans, the causes of most of the calamities of the fourteenth century were invisible or unknown. No one recognized a climate change or understood the dynamics of the population crisis. No one understood the cause of the epidemics. No one grasped the role of the Mongol Empire in the world economy or the causes for the collapse of banking and trade. Unable to distinguish how these forces were changing their lives, western Europeans only witnessed their consequences. In the face of these calamities, European culture became obsessed with death and with finding scapegoats to blame for events that could not be otherwise explained. However, calamity also bred creativity. The search for answers to the question, "Why did this happen to us?" produced a new spiritual sensibility and a rich literature. Following the travails of the fourteenth century, moreover, there arose in the fifteenth a new, more optimistic cultural movement—the Renaissance. Gloom and doom was not the only response to troubles. During the Renaissance some people began to search for new answers to human problems in a fashion that would transform the West anew.

Suggestions for Further Reading

For a comprehensive listing of suggested readings, please go to www.ablongman.com/levack2e/chapter10

Carmichael, Ann G. *Plague and the Poor in Renaissance Florence.* 1986. An innovative study that both questions the traditional theory of the bubonic plague as the cause of the Black Death and examines how fear of the disease led to regulation of the poor.

Cohn, Samuel. *The Black Death Transformed: Disease and Culture in Early Renaissance Europe.* 2003. A well-argued case that the Black Death was not caused by the bubonic plague.

Duby, Georges. *France in the Middle Ages, 987–1460: From Hugh Capet to Joan of Arc.* 1991. Traces the emergence of the French state.

Gordon, Bruce, and Peter Marshall, eds. *The Place of the Dead: Death and Remembrance in Late Medieval and Early Modern Europe.* 2000. A collection of essays that shows how the placing of the dead in society was an important activity that engendered considerable conflict and negotiation.

Herlihy, David. *The Black Death and the Transformation of the West.* 1997. A pithy, readable analysis of the epidemiological and historical issues surrounding the Black Death.

Holmes, George. *Europe: Hierarchy and Revolt, 1320–1450.* 1975. Excellent examination of rebellions.

Huizinga, Johan. *The Autumn of the Middle Ages,* trans. Rodney J. Payton and Urlich Mammitzsch. 1996. A new translation of the classic study of France and the Low Countries during the fourteenth and fifteenth centuries. Dated and perhaps too pessimistic, Huizinga's lucid prose and broad vision still make this an engaging reading experience.

Imber, Colin. *The Ottoman Empire, 1300–1481.* 1990. The basic work that establishes a chronology for the early Ottomans.

Jordan, William C. *The Great Famine: Northern Europe in the Early Fourteenth Century.* 1996. The most comprehensive book on the famine.

Lambert, Malcolm. *Medieval Heresy: Popular Movements from the Gregorian Reform to the Reformation.* 1992. Excellent general study of the Hussite and Lollard movements.

Le Roy Ladurie, Emmanuel. *Times of Feast, Times of Famine: A History of Climate Since the Year 1000,* trans. Barbara Bray. 1971. The book that introduced the idea of the Little Ice Age and promoted the study of the influence of climate on history.

Lynch, Joseph H. *The Medieval Church: A Brief History.* 1992. A pithy, elegant survey of ecclesiastical institutions and developments.

Morgan, David O. *The Mongols.* 1986. Best introduction to Mongol history.

Nirenberg, David. *Communities of Violence: Persecution of Minorities in the Middle Ages.* 1996. An important analysis of the persecution of minorities that is deeply rooted in Spanish evidence.

Scott, Susan, and Christopher Duncan. *Biology of Plagues: Evidence from Historical Populations.* 2001. An analysis by two epidemiologists who argue that the Black Death was not the bubonic plague but probably a virus similar to Ebola.

Sumption, Jonathan. *The Hundred Years' War: Trial by Battle.* 1991. First volume goes only to 1347. When it is completed, it will be the best comprehensive study.

Swanson, R. N. *Religion and Devotion in Europe, c. 1215–c. 1515.* 1995. The best up-to-date textbook account of late medieval religious practice.

Notes

1. Quoted in Emmanuel Le Roy Ladurie, *Times of Feast, Times of Famine: A History of Climate Since the Year 1000,* trans. Barbara Bray (1971), 47.

2. Quoted in William Bowsky, "The Impact of the Black Death," in Anthony Molho, ed., *Social and Economic Foundations of the Italian Renaissance* (1969), 92.

3. Cited in Philip Ziegler, *The Black Death* (1969), 20.

4. Giovanni Boccaccio, *The Decameron,* trans. Richard Aldington (1962), 30.

5. Ibid.

6. Quoted in Mark C. Bartusis, *The Late Byzantine Army: Arms and Society, 1204–1453* (1992), 133.

7. Trial record as quoted in Marina Warner, *Joan of Arc* (1981), 122.

8. Ibid., 127.

9. Ibid., 143.

10. *The Trial of Joan of Arc,* trans. W. S. Scott (1956), 134.

11. Ibid., 106.

12. Ibid., 135.

13. Warner, *Joan of Arc,* 145.

14. Johan Huizinga, *The Autumn of the Middle Ages,* trans. Rodney J. Payton and Ulrich Mammitzsch (1996), 156.

15. Quoted in Barbara W. Tuchman, *A Distant Mirror: The Calamitous 14th Century* (1978), 505–506. Translation has been slightly modified by the authors.

16. Ibid., 506.

17. *Libellus de institutione morum,* ed. J. Balogh, *Scriptores rerum Hungaricarum 2* (1938), 625. Quoted in Robert Bartlett, *The Making of Europe: Conquest, Colonization and Cultural Change 950–1350* (1993), 239.

18. *Codex diplomaticus Brandenburgensis,* ed. Adolph Friedrich Riedel (41 vols., 1838–1869), 365–367. Cited in Bartlett, *The Making of Europe,* 238.

The Italian Renaissance and Beyond: The Politics of Culture

FOR FIFTEEN YEARS NICCOLÒ MACHIAVELLI WORKED AS A DIPLOMAT AND political adviser, a man always at the center of the action in his hometown of Florence. But in 1512 there was a change of regimes in the city-state of Florence. Distrusted by the new rulers and suspected of involvement in an assassination plot, he was abruptly fired from his job, imprisoned, tortured, and finally ordered to stay out of town. Exiled to his suburban farm, impoverished, and utterly miserable, Machiavelli survived by selling lumber from his woodlot to his former colleagues, who regularly cheated him. To help feed his family he snared birds; to entertain himself he played cards in a local inn with the innkeeper, a butcher, a miller, and two bakers. As he put it, "caught this way among these lice I wipe the mold from my brain [by playing cards] and release my feeling of being ill-treated by Fate."

In the evenings, however, Machiavelli transformed himself into an entirely different person. He entered his study, removed his mud-splattered clothes, and put on the elegant robes he had once worn as a government official. And then, "dressed in a more appropriate manner I enter into the ancient courts of ancient men and am welcomed by them kindly." Machiavelli was actually reading the works of the ancient Greek and Latin historians, but he described his evening reading as a conversation: He asked the ancients about the reasons for their actions, and in reading their books he found answers. For four hours, "I feel no boredom, I dismiss every affliction, I no longer fear poverty nor do I tremble at the thought of death: I become completely part of them."[1]

Machiavelli's evening conversations with the long-dead ancients perfectly expressed the sensibility of the Italian Renaissance. This wretched man, disillusioned with his own times and bored by his empty-headed neighbors, found in the ancients the stimulating companions he could not find in life. For him the ancient past was more alive than the present. In this sense Machiavelli was very much a Renaissance man, because feeling part of antiquity is what the Renaissance is all about. For those who were captivated

---

The Mona Lisa Leonardo da Vinci's portrait of a Florentine woman with her enigmatic smile testifies to the Renaissance fascination with portraits of individuals who appear completely natural.

by it, the ancient past and the examples of leadership and beauty it offered seemed to be a cure for the ills of a decidedly troubled time.

As discussed in Chapter 10, during the fourteenth and fifteenth centuries Europeans experienced a prevailing sense of loss, a morbid preoccupation with death, and a widespread pessimism about the human capacity for good. Yet in Florence during this same period a cultural movement began to express a different view of life that emphasized the responsibilities of humans to better their communities through social welfare, to beautify their cities, and to devote themselves to the duties of citizenship. We now call that movement the Renaissance. The movement emerged from the desire to improve the human condition during times of trouble, and that desire was first manifest in the intellectually free environment of the independent city-states of Italy. Machiavelli—despite the bleak circumstances of his later life—was one of the Renaissance thinkers who thought the world could be set right through concerted political action. Like the medieval thinkers he was pessimistic about the frailties of human nature, but he firmly believed that the weakness of most humans could be counteracted by strong leadership and strong laws. In this respect he differed from the medieval writers who thought the contemplative life of the monk was the highest calling to which a man could aspire. The Renaissance was born and developed because the political structures of the Italian city-states encouraged cultural experimentation and fostered the idea that society could be reengineered according to the principles that made ancient Greece and Rome great.

The word Renaissance°, which means "rebirth," is a term historians invented to describe a movement that sought to imitate and understand the culture of antiquity. The fundamental Renaissance principle was the need to keep everything in balance and proportion, an aesthetic ideal derived from ancient literature. In political theory, this meant building a stable society upon the foundations of well-balanced individuals who conformed to a rigorous code of conduct. In the arts it meant searching for the underlying harmonies in nature, which typically meant employing geometry and the mathematics of proportion in drawing, painting, sculpting, and designing buildings. Renaissance artists thought geometry unlocked the secrets of nature and revealed the hidden hand of God in creation.

The Italian Renaissance was not the first time the West experienced a revival of ancient learning and thought. In the Carolingian Renaissance of the ninth century, members of the emperor Charlemagne's court reinvigorated education in Latin. And the European-wide Renaissance of the twelfth century led to the foundation of the universities, the reintroduction of Roman law, and the spread of scholastic philosophy and theology. The Renaissance considered in this chapter refers to a diffuse cultural movement that occurred at different times in different regions, and as a result its dates are very approximate. Most historians date the Italian Renaissance from about 1350 to 1550. By 1500 the

cultural movement that began in Italy had spread to much of western Europe.

The Renaissance helped refashion the concept of Western civilization. From the fifth to the fourteenth centuries, the West identified itself primarily through conformity to Latin Christianity or Roman Catholicism, which meant the celebration of uniform religious rituals in Latin and obedience to the pope. The Renaissance added a new element to this identity. Although by no means anti-Christian, Renaissance thinkers began to think of themselves as the heirs of pre-Christian cultures—Hebrew, Greek, and Roman. In this sense, they began to imagine a Western civilization that was more than just Christianity but as the history of a common culture dating back to Antiquity. Through reading the texts and viewing the works of art of the long-dead ancients, people during the Italian Renaissance gained historical and visual perspective on their own world and cultivated a critical attitude about both the past and their own culture. How then did the cultural encounter during the Renaissance with the philosophy, literature, and art of the Ancient world transform the way Europeans thought?

■ In what ways did the political and social climate peculiar to the Italian city-states help create Renaissance culture?

■ How did Renaissance thinkers create historical perspective and devise methods of criticism for interpreting texts?

■ How did various attempts to imitate antiquity in the arts alter perceptions of nature?

■ How did the monarchies of western Europe gather the strength to become more assertive and more effective during the last half of the fifteenth and early sixteenth centuries?

The Cradle of the Renaissance: The Italian City-States

■ In what ways did the political and social climate peculiar to the Italian city-states help create Renaissance culture?

In comparison with the rest of Europe and other world civilizations, Renaissance Italy was distinguished by the large number and political autonomy of its thriving city-states. The Netherlands and parts of the Rhine Valley were as thoroughly urbanized, but only in Italy did cities have so much political power. The evolution of the Italian city-states can be encapsulated into two distinct phases.

The first phase in the evolution of the Italian city-states occurred during the eleventh and twelfth centuries.

During this period about one hundred Italian towns became independent republics, also known as communes, and developed the laws and institutions of self-government. The male citizens of these tiny republics gathered on a regular basis in the town square to debate important issues such as assessing new taxes, improving the city walls, or going to war. To conduct the day-to-day business of government, they elected city officials from among themselves.

The governmental practices of these city-states produced the political theory of republicanism°, which described a state in which government officials were elected by the people or a portion of the people. The theory of republicanism was first articulated by Marsilius of Padua (1270–1342) in *The Defender of the Peace,* a book that relied on the precedents established by the ancient Roman republic. Marsilius recognized two kinds of government—principalities and republics. Principalities relied upon the descending principle that political authority came directly from God and trickled down through kings and princes to the rest of humanity. According to this principle, the responsibility of government was to enforce God's laws. Marsilius, however, rejected the idea that the task of the political world was to express the will of God. His ascending principle of republicanism suggested that laws derive not from God but from the will of the people, who freely choose their own form of government and who are equally free to change it. In Marsilius's theory, citizens regularly expressed their will through voting. The first phase in the evolution of the Italian city-states established the institutions of self-government, the procedures for electing officials, and the theory of republicanism.

In the second phase of evolution, which occurred during the fourteenth century, most city-states abandoned or lost their republican institutions and came to be ruled by princes. The reasons for the transformation of these republics into principalities were related to the economic and demographic turmoil created by the international economic collapse and the Black Death. Two of the largest republics, however, did not go through this second phase and survived without losing their liberty to a prince. The Renaissance began in these two city-states, Florence and Venice (see Map 11.1). Their survival as republics, which made them exceptions to the rule by the fifteenth century, helps explain the origins of the Renaissance.

The Renaissance Republics: Florence and Venice

In an age of despotic princes, Florence and Venice were keenly aware of how different they were from other cities, and they feared they might suffer the same fate as their neighbors if they did not defend their republican institutions and liberty. In keeping alive the traditions of republican self-government, these two cities created an environment of competition and freedom that stimulated creative ingenuity. Although neither of these cities were democracies, nor were they particularly egalitarian, they were certainly more open to new ideas than cities ruled by princes. In both Florence and Venice, citizens prized discussion and debate, the skills necessary for success in business and politics. By contrast, in the principalities all cultural activity tended to revolve around and express the tastes of the prince, who monopolized much of the wealth. In Florence and Venice a few great families called the *patriciate* controlled most of the property, but these patricians competed among themselves to gain recognition

Map 11.1 Northern Italy in the Mid-Fifteenth Century

During the Renaissance the largest city-states, such as Milan, Venice, and Florence, gained control of the surrounding countryside and smaller cities in the vicinity, establishing regional territorial states. Only Venice and Florence remained republics. Milan and Savoy were ruled by dukes. The Gonzaga family ruled Mantua and the Este family Modena and Ferrara. The states of the Church were ruled by the pope in Rome.

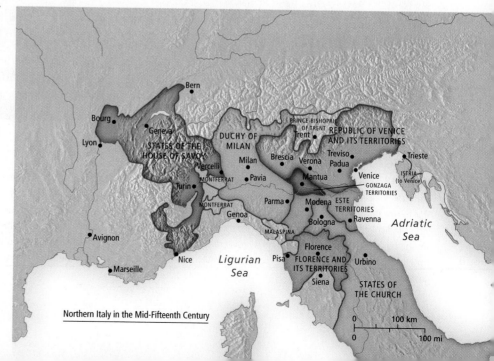

Northern Italy in the Mid-Fifteenth Century

and fame by patronizing great artists and scholars. This patronage by wealthy men and women made the Renaissance possible. Because the tastes of these patricians dictated what writers and artists could do, understanding who they were helps explain Renaissance culture.

Florence Under the Medici

The greatest patron during the early Renaissance was the fabulously rich Florentine banker Cosimo de' Medici (1389–1464). Based on his financial power, Cosimo effectively took control of the Florentine republic in 1434, ushering in a period of unprecedented domestic peace and artistic splendor called the Medicean Age (1434–1494). Cosimo's style of rule was exceedingly clever. Instead of making himself a prince, which the citizens of Florence would have opposed, he managed the policies of the republic from behind the scenes. He seldom held public office, but he made himself the center of Florentine affairs through shrewd negotiating, quiet fixing of elections, and generous distribution

of bribes, gifts, and jobs. Cosimo's behind-the-scenes rule illustrated a fundamental value of Renaissance culture—the desire to maintain appearances. In this case, the appearance of the Florentine republic was saved, even as the reality of Florentine liberty was subverted.

Cosimo's brilliant patronage of intellectuals and artists mirrored a similar ambition to maintain appearances. It helped make Cosimo appear a pious, generous man who modeled himself after the great statesmen of the ancient Roman republic. Cosimo appreciated intelligence and merit wherever he found it. He frequented the discussions of prominent scholars, some of whom became his lasting friends. Intrigued by what he learned from them, he personally financed the search for and acquisition of manuscripts of ancient Latin and Greek literature and philosophy for new libraries he helped establish. In return for his financial support, many Florentine scholars dedicated their works to Cosimo. He took particular interest in the revival of the ancient Greek philosopher Plato, and he set up the

The Medici as Magi

During the fifteenth century the Medici had the power but lacked the legitimacy to rule Florence because they neither had been elected nor were the princes of the city. To compensate for their lack of legal authority, they created the image of themselves as "wise men" similar to the three wise men or magi who first recognized the divinity of Christ. In this fresco in the Medici Palace, the artist Benozzo Gozzoli depicted Lorenzo the Magnificent as one of the magi. He is the young man wearing a crown and gold robe riding on a white horse. His father, grandfather, and other senior members of the Medici family follow, wearing the red hats of common Florentine citizens.

neo-Platonic philosopher Marsilio Ficino (1433–1499) with a house and steady income.

Cosimo's most significant patronage of the arts clustered in the neighborhood where he lived. He rebuilt the nearby monastery of San Marco. He personally selected Fra Angelico, a monk, to paint the austere yet deeply emotive frescoes throughout the monastery. As the centerpiece of his neighborhood beautification plans, Cosimo built for his own family a magnificent new palace, which he filled with innumerable objects of beauty and exquisite paintings.

Cosimo's artistic patronage helped create the image of a man who was an open-handed and benevolent godfather for his community. Because Cosimo had not been elected to rule Florence, his political influence was illegitimate and he needed to find a way to create a proper image that would justify his power. To do that he decorated the private chapel in his palace with frescoes that depicted him accompanying the magi, the wise men or kings who brought gifts to the baby Jesus. Thus Cosimo made himself appear similar to those ancient kings who first recognized the divinity of Christ. By having himself depicted with the magi, Cosimo created an image that helped justify the fact that he controlled elections and dictated policies.

Cosimo's grandson Lorenzo the Magnificent (r. 1469–1492) expanded the family's dominance in Florentine politics through what has been called "veiled lordship." Lorenzo never took the title of prince but behaved very much like one by intervening publicly in the affairs of the state. In contrast to his grandfather's commitment to public patronage, Lorenzo's interest in the arts concentrated on building private villas, collecting precious gems, and commissioning small bronze statues, the kinds of things that gave him private pleasure rather than a public reputation. A fine poet and an intellectual companion of the most renowned scholars of his age, Lorenzo created a lasting reputation as a well-rounded, accomplished Renaissance man, but his princely style of rule, which ignored the republican sensibilities of the Florentines, created discontent and undermined public support for the Medicis. There were several conspiracies against him; during an attempted assassination of Lorenzo, his brother Giuliano was killed.

During the fifteenth century Florence became the first society that dedicated itself to the production and appreciation of what we now call Renaissance culture. As a republic on the perilous edge of financial survival, Florence had surrendered to the behind-the-scenes rule of the Medici family, who supported a movement in philosophy and the arts that, as we shall see, imitated and celebrated the heritage of pre-Christian antiquity, especially the culture of Greece and Rome.

Venice, the Cosmopolitan Republic

Venice resembled Florence in that it survived into the Renaissance period with its republican institutions intact,

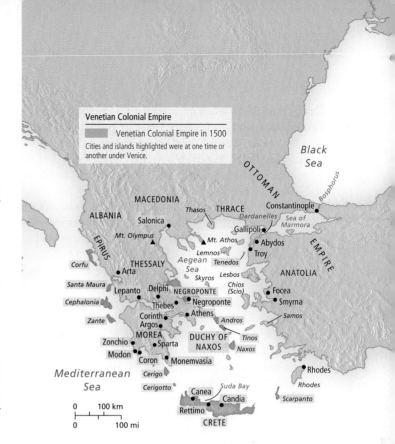

Map 11.2 Venetian Colonial Empire

The Venetian colonies included the Greek-speaking islands in the Adriatic and a number of important islands in the Aegean. Between the fifteenth and seventeenth centuries these colonies were repeatedly threatened by the Ottoman Empire, with its capital in Constantinople.

but it was far more politically stable. Situated in the midst of a vast lagoon, Venice's streets consisted of broad channels in which great seagoing merchant ships were moored and small canals choked with private gondolas for local transportation. To protect their fragile city from flooding, the Venetians recognized that they had to cooperate among themselves, and thus the imperative for survival helped create a republic that became a model of stability and ecological awareness. The Venetians, for example, created the world's first environmental regulatory agencies, which were responsible for hydrological projects, such as building dikes and dredging canals, and for forestry management to prevent soil erosion and the consequent silting up of the lagoon.

Venice was among the first European powers to have colonies abroad. To guarantee its merchant ships access to the eastern Mediterranean and Constantinople, Venice conquered a series of ports, including a significant number in Greece (see Map 11.2). Its involvement in international trade and governing distant colonies made Venice unusually cosmopolitan. Many Venetian merchants spent years living abroad and some settled in the colonies. Moreover, people from all over Europe flocked to the city of Venice— Germans, Turks, Armenians, Albanians, Greeks, Slovenes,

Croats, and Jews—each creating their own neighborhood communities and institutions. Venetian households owned Russian, Asian, Turkish, and African slaves, all of whom contributed to the remarkable diversity of the city.

Of the many foreign groups in Venice, the most influential were the Greeks. Venice had long maintained close commercial and cultural ties with the Greek world. Its churches were modeled after the huge basilicas of Constantinople, and many Venetian merchants spoke Greek. After the fall of the Byzantine Empire to the Ottoman Turks in 1453, many Greek Christian refugees found a new home in Venice and other Italian cities, including influential scholars who helped reintroduce Greek philosophy and literature to an eager Italian readership. One of these scholars was John Bessarion (1403–1472), a Byzantine archbishop who compiled a magnificent library of Greek manuscripts that he bequeathed to the republic of Venice. Venice also became the leading center in western Europe for the publication of Greek books, printing the important texts in Greek philosophy and science, and making them widely available for the first time in western Europe.

The defining characteristic of Venetian government was its social stability, a trait that made it the envy of other more troubled cities and the source of imitation by republican-minded reformers throughout Europe. Whereas the Florentine republic was notoriously unstable and subject to quiet subversion by the Medicis, Venice boasted a largely unchanging republican constitution that lasted from 1297 to 1797. Thus Venice is the longest-surviving republic in history. It was, however, a very exclusive republic. Out of a total population of nearly 150,000, only a small political elite consisting of 2,500 nobles enjoyed voting privileges. From this elite and from Venice's many wealthy religious institutions came the resources to patronize Renaissance artists.

At the top of Venetian society was the *doge*, a member of the nobility who was elected to the job for life. The most notable Renaissance doge was Andrea Gritti (r. 1523–1538), whose reputation derived from his brilliant early career as a military administrator and diplomat. Gritti sometimes bent the laws in his favor, but he never manipulated elections or managed Venice's affairs as completely as Cosimo de' Medici did in Florence a century before. Like the Medicis, however, he used his own financial resources and his personal influence to transform his city into a major center of Renaissance culture.

Gritti hired some of the most prominent European artists, musicians, and poets to come to Venice. These included Pietro Aretino (1492–1556), the greatest master of satire of the sixteenth century, and the architect and sculptor Jacopo Sansovino (1486–1570). As official architect of the city, Sansovino transformed its appearance with his sculptures, palaces, and churches that imitated the styles of classical Greece and Rome. One of his most notable buildings is the Marciana Library, which was begun in 1537 to house Bessarion's collection of Greek manuscripts.

Artistic and scholarly creativity in Florence and Venice thrived on the competition among many different patrons. Neither the Medicis in Florence nor Gritti in Venice entirely dominated the cultural scene. Artistic patronage in these republics mirrored the dynamic political life that engaged many people. The diversity of patronage gave extensive employment to painters, sculptors, and architects, thereby attracting the best artists to these two cities. Later sections of the chapter will examine the works they produced.

Princes and Courtiers

Although the Renaissance began in the relative freedom of republics, such as Florence, it soon spread to principalities, those states ruled by one man, the prince. In contrast to the multiple sources of support for the arts and learning in the republics, patronage in the principalities was more constricted, confined to the prince and members of his court. The terms *lord* and *prince* refer to rulers who possessed formal aristocratic titles, such as the Marquis of Mantua, the Duke of Milan, or the King of Naples. Most Renaissance princes came from local aristocratic families who seized control of the government by force. Some, however, had been soldiers of fortune who had held on to a city as a spoil of war or had even overthrown a government that had once employed them to defend the city. Regardless of how a prince originally obtained power, his goal was to establish a dynasty, that is, to guarantee the rights of his descendants to continue to rule the city. Some dynasties—such as that of the D'Este family, which ruled Ferrara from 1240 to 1597—were well established and quite popular.

The Ideal Prince, the Ideal Princess

Federico II da Montefeltro (1422–1482), Duke of Urbino, succeeded in achieving the lasting fame and glorious reputation that so many princes craved. Although he was illegitimate, his father gave him the best possible education by sending him to study at the most fashionable school in Italy and to apprentice as a soldier under a renowned mercenary captain. In Renaissance Italy, an illegitimate boy could not inherit his father's property. Thus he usually had two career options: He could become a priest to obtain a living from the church, or he could become a mercenary and take his chances at war. Federico became a mercenary. From among the peasants of the duchy he recruited an army, which he hired out to the highest bidder. He soon earned a European-wide reputation for his many victories and enriched the duchy with the income from mercenary contracts and plunder. When his half-brother was assassinated in 1444, Federico became the ruler of Urbino, and by 1474 he obtained from the pope the title of duke. Federico epitomized the ideal Renaissance prince—a father figure to his subjects, astute diplomat, brilliant soldier, generous patron, avid collector, and man of learning. He was a prince who combined the insights of contempla-

Federico da Montefeltro as the Ideal Prince
The papal tiara in the upper left alludes to the pope's authorization of his title as duke. Federico is shown studying a book while dressed in armor, reflecting his two sides as scholar and soldier. His dynastic ambitions are represented by the presence of his son and potential successor standing at his feet.

tive study with active involvement in the affairs of the world.

Federico's rule was paternalistic. He was concerned for the welfare of his subjects and personally listened to their complaints and adjudicated their disputes. His military adventures tripled the size of his duchy. Conquests brought the prosperity that financed his expensive building projects and his collection of Latin manuscripts. Federico's personal library surpassed that of any contemporary university library in Europe, and his wide-ranging reading interests

showed his openness to the latest developments in learning. Federico's greatest achievement, however, was the building of a vast palace. At one stage the project was supervised by the architect Luciano Laurana (ca. 1420–1479), but it was Federico who clearly deserves most of the credit for what remains the single best example of Renaissance architectural ideals in a palace. Because of Federico, the small mountainous duchy of Urbino acquired a cultural importance far greater than its size warranted.

The best candidate for the ideal princess was Isabella d'Este (1474–1539), the Marchioness of Mantua. Such was her fame as a patron that she was known during her lifetime as "the first lady of the world." Enjoying an education that was exceptional for a girl in the fifteenth century, she grew up in the court at Ferrara, where she was surrounded by famous painters and poets and where she cultivated foreign ambassadors and leading intellectuals of the time. But her influence went far beyond that. When her husband was absent and after his death, she ruled Mantua by herself, earning a reputation for her just decisions and witty charm. She gained renown for her ability as a tenacious negotiator and behind-the-scenes diplomat. An avid reader and collector, she personally knew virtually all the great artists and writers of her age. Her influence spread far beyond Mantua, in part through her voluminous correspondence, which is estimated to include 12,000 letters.

The Ideal Courtier

The Renaissance republics developed a code of conduct for the ideal citizen. The code encouraged citizens to devote their time and energies to public service. The code insisted that the most valuable services of the citizen were to hold public office, to pay taxes honestly, and to help beautify the city through patronage of the arts. In similar fashion the Renaissance principalities created a code for the ideal courtier. A courtier was a man or woman who lived in or regularly visited the palace of a prince. Courtiers helped the prince's household function by performing all kinds of services, such as taking care of the family's wardrobe, managing servants, educating children, providing entertainment, keeping accounts, administering estates, going on diplomatic missions, and fighting battles. To best serve the princely family in whatever was needed, a courtier needed to cultivate a wide range of skills. Men trained in horsemanship, swordplay, and all kinds of sports, which were useful for keeping in shape for war. Women learned to draw, dance, play musical instruments, and engage in witty conversation. Both men and women needed to be adept at foreign languages so that they could converse with visitors and diplomats. According to the ideal, men should also know Latin and Greek, which were the foundations of a formal education. Some of the women in the courts also learned these ancient languages.

The stability and efficiency of the princely states depended on the abilities of the courtiers, who performed many of the functions that elected officials did in the republics. It was also extremely important to prevent conflicts among the courtiers; otherwise the peace of the state would be compromised. The most influential guide to how a courtier should behave was *The Book of the Courtier* (composed between 1508 and 1528) by the cultivated diplomat Baldassare Castiglione (1478–1529). Underlying the behavior and conversation of the ideal courtier described in this book were two general principles that governed all courtly manners—nonchalance and ease:

> *I have found quite a universal rule which . . . seems to me valid above all others, and in all human affairs whether in word or deed: and that is to avoid affectation in every way possible as though it were some very rough and dangerous reef; and (to pronounce a new word perhaps) to practice in all things a certain nonchalance, so as to conceal all art and make whatever is done or said appear to be without effort and almost without any thought about it. . . .*
>
> *Therefore we may call that art true art which does not seem to be art; nor must one be more careful of anything than of concealing it, because if it is discovered, this robs a man of all credit and causes him to be held in slight esteem.*[2]

In other words, nonchalance is the ability to do something that requires considerable training and effort while making it appear to be natural and without effort. The need to maintain appearances, which we first saw in the disguised rulership of Cosimo de' Medici in Florence, became one of the distinguishing traits of Italian Renaissance culture. According to Castiglione, all human action and communication should be moderate and balanced, creating the effect of ease. In effect, *The Book of the Courtier* translated the ideals of harmony and proportion so admired in Renaissance culture into a plan for human comportment. By using courtly manners, human beings governed the movements of the body according to an almost mathematical ideal of proportion.

Through *The Book of the Courtier* and its many imitators, the Renaissance ideal of courtly manners began to be widely disseminated during the sixteenth century due to the capacity of the newly invented printing press to produce inexpensive copies of the same text. Written in a lucid Italian that made for lively reading, the book was translated into Latin, English, French, and Spanish and absorbed into the literature of Europe. By studying these books, any young man or woman of talent and ambition could aspire to act and speak like a great aristocrat. The courtly ideal was completely accessible to anyone who could read, and many of its precepts were incorporated into the educational curriculum of schools, where it has survived to the present in the institution of the prom.

The Papal Prince

The Renaissance popes were the heads of the Church; they also had jurisdiction over the Papal State in central Italy. Thus they combined the roles of priest and prince. The Papal State was supposed to supply the pope with the in-

Courtiers Waiting on a Princely Family
Male courtiers pose while waiting around in the court of the Gonzaga in Mantua. These elegant gentlemen epitomized the nonchalance and ease idealized in Baldassare Castiglione's *The Book of the Courtier.*

come to run the affairs of the Church, but during the period when the popes left Rome and resided in Avignon (France) and during the Great Schism of 1305–1417, the popes lost control of the Papal State. After 1418 the popes saw that they had two main tasks—regain the revenues of the Papal State and rebuild the city of Rome, which had become a neglected ruin. To collect the taxes and revenues due them, many popes were obliged to use military force to bring the rebellious lords and cities into obedience. The popes also squabbled with the neighboring states that had taken advantage of the weakness of the papacy during the schism.

These military and diplomatic adventures thrust the popes into some very nasty quarrels—a situation that undermined the popes' ability to provide moral leadership. Pope Alexander VI (r. 1492–1503) financed his son Cesare Borgia's attempts to carve out a principality for himself along the northern fringe of the Papal State. He also married off his daughter, Lucrezia Borgia, in succession to several different Italian princes who were useful allies in the pope's military ambitions. The members of the Borgia family made many enemies who accused them of all kinds of evil deeds, including the poisoning of one of Lucrezia's husbands, brother-sister and father-daughter incest, and conducting orgies in the Vatican. Even though many of these allegations were false or exaggerated, the reputation of the papacy suffered. Alexander's successor, Pope Julius II (r. 1503–1513), continued to pursue a military strategy for regaining control of the Papal State. He took his princely role so seriously that he donned armor, personally led troops during the siege of Bologna, and rather presumptuously rewarded himself with a triumphal procession, an honor that had been granted in ancient Rome to victorious generals such as Julius Caesar.

Many of the Renaissance popes were embarrassed by the squalor of the city of Rome, an unfit place to serve as the capital of the Church. A number of popes sought to create a capital they felt worthy for Christendom. The most clear-sighted of the builders of Rome was Pope Leo X (r. 1513–1521), the second son of Lorenzo the Magnificent. Educated by the circle of scholars who surrounded the Medicis, Leo was destined for a clerical career at a young age. He received a doctorate in canon law and was made a cardinal at age 17. During Leo's pontificate, Rome was transformed into one of the centers of Renaissance culture. Leo made the University of Rome a distinguished institution through the appointment of famous professors. For his own private secretaries he chose intellectuals who had already gained an international reputation for their scholarship and learning. Leo's ambition can best be measured in his project to rebuild St. Peter's Basilica as the largest church in the world. He tore down the old basilica, which had been a major pilgrimage destination for more than a thousand years, and planned the great church that still dominates Rome today.

The Contradictions of the Patriarchal Family

The contradiction between the theory of the patriarchal family and realities of family life produced much of the creative energy of the Italian Renaissance. When theory dramatically departed from actual experience, many people began to distrust the theory and seek alternative ways of looking at society and the world. That is what happened in Renaissance Italy.

Advice books on family management, such as Leon Battista Alberti's *Four Books on the Family* (written in the 1430s), provide evidence for the widespread concern for better understanding the family. Such books propounded the theory that husbands and fathers ruled. These patriarchs were the sources of social order and discipline, and not just within the family but of all of society. Groups of male relatives

DOCUMENT

Juan Luis Vives, *The Office and Dutie of an Husband* (1529)

were responsible for rectifying injuries and especially for avenging any assault on a family member. Nearly all marriages were arranged by fathers or male guardians who sought beneficial financial and political alliances with other families, a situation that gave older men an advantage in the marriage market, as they were usually better off financially than younger ones. As a result, husbands tended to be much older than wives. In Florence in 1427, for example, the typical first marriage was between a 30-year-old man and an 18-year-old woman. Husbands were encouraged to treat their spouses with a kindly but distant paternalism. All women were supposed to be kept under strict male supervision, and the only honorable role for an unmarried woman was as a nun.

However, the reality of family life often departed from theory. A number of factors explain the disparity. First, a variety of circumstances made family life insecure and the very survival of families tenuous—death from epidemic diseases, especially the Black Death, and separations due to marital strife, which were common enough even though divorce was not possible. Second, the wide age gap between husbands and wives meant that husbands were likely to die long before their wives, and thus many women became widows at a relatively young age with children still to raise. Third, many men, especially international merchants and migrant workers, were away from their families for long periods of time. Regardless of the patriarchal assertion that

Vendetta as Private Justice

During the fourteenth and fifteenth centuries, the official justice provided by the law courts competed with the private justice of revenge. Private justice was based on the principle of retaliation. When someone was murdered or assaulted, it became the obligation of the victim's closest male relatives to avenge the injury by harming the perpetrator or one of his relatives to a similar degree. A son was obliged to avenge the death of his father, a brother the injury of his brother. Given the weakness of most governments, the only effective justice was often private justice or, as the Italians called it, *vendetta*. As the most significant source of disorder during the Renaissance, vendetta was a practice that all governments struggled to eradicate.

One of the attributes that distinguished an act of private justice from a simple violent crime was that avengers committed their acts openly and even bragged about what they had done. A criminal covered his tracks. An avenger did not. Therefore, the violence of an act of revenge was carried out in public so there would be witnesses, and often it was performed in a highly symbolic way in order to humiliate the victim as much as possible.

In Renaissance Italy private justice took many forms, but always such acts sought to do more than create another victim. They sought to deliver a message. After a period of disorder in 1342, the Florentines granted extraordinary judicial powers to a soldier of fortune, Walter of Brienne, known as the Duke of Athens. But Walter offended many Florentines by arresting and executing members of prominent families. In September of that year a crowd led by these families besieged the government palace and captured the duke's most hated henchmen, the "conservator" and his son.

Even though the conservator had been the highest judge of Florence, the Florentines repudiated his authority by obtaining revenge. An eyewitness reported what happened next:

> The son was pushed out in front, and they cut him up and dismembered him. This done, they shoved out the conservator himself and did the same to him. Some carried a piece of him on a lance or sword throughout the city, and there were those so cruel, so bestial in their anger, and full of such hatred that they ate the raw flesh.[3]

This story of revenge in the most sophisticated city in Europe on the eve of the Renaissance illustrates the brutality of private justice, especially the need to make a public example of the victim.

Another account from nearly 200 years later tells of the murder of Antonio Savorgnan, a nobleman from Friuli who had killed a number of his enemies the previous year. Rather than attempting to have Antonio arrested as they could have, the murderers avenged their dead relatives through private justice. One eyewitness recounted that Antonio was attacked while leaving church, and then, "It was by divine miracle that Antonio Savorgnan was wounded: his head opened, he fell down, and he never spoke another word. But before he died, a giant dog came there and ate all his brains, and one cannot possibly deny that his brains were eaten."[4] This time a dog did the avengers' work for them. Perhaps the strangest detail in both of these accounts is that the writers wanted readers to believe that the victim had been eaten, either by humans or by a dog. Why was this an important message to get across?

The eating of a victim was one way avengers signaled that they were killing as an act of private justice. In both of the killings just described, the killers were retaliating for the murder of one of their close relatives and symbolically announcing to others that the attack was not an unjustifiable crime but a legitimate act of revenge. To convey that message, avengers could not ambush their opponent in the dark of night but were obliged to confront him openly in broad daylight before witnesses. There had to be the appearance, at least, of a fair fight. Murderers symbolized their revenge in several ways: They butchered the corpse as if it were the prey of a hunt or fed the remains to hunting dogs or even ate it themselves in what appeared to be a frenzy of revenge.

One of the major objectives of any government, whether a tiny city-state or a great monarchy, was to substitute public justice for private justice; but the persistence of tradition was strong. During the sixteenth century as governments sought to control violence and as the Renaissance values of moderation spread, a different kind of private justice appeared—the duel. Traditionally, the duel had been a means of solving disputes among medieval knights, but during the sixteenth century duels became much more common, even among men who had never been soldiers. Dueling required potential combatants to conform to an elaborate set of rules: The legitimate causes for a challenge to a duel were few, the combatants had to recognize each other as honorable men, the actual fight took place only after extensive preparations, judges who were experts on honor had to serve as witnesses, and the combatants had to swear to accept the outcome and abstain from fighting one another in the future.

The very complexity of the rules of dueling limited the vio-

Private Justice
In Titian's painting *The Bravo* (ca. 1515/1520), a man wearing a breastplate and hiding a drawn sword behind his back grabs the collar of his enemy before assaulting him. To enact honorable revenge the attacker could not stab his enemy in the back but had to give him a chance in a fair fight.

lence of private justice, and that meant that fewer fights actually took place. Dueling, in effect, civilized private justice. Although dueling was always against the law, princes tended to wink at duels because they kept conflicts among their own courtiers under control. At the same time, governments became far less tolerant of other forms of private justice, especially among the lower classes. They at-

tempted to abolish feuds and vendettas and insisted that all disputes be submitted to the courts.

Questions of Justice

1. How did the persistence of private justice present a challenge to the emerging states of the Renaissance?
2. In what ways did private justice reflect Renaissance values, such as the value of keeping appearances?

Taking It Further

Muir, Edward. *Mad Blood Stirring: Vendetta in Renaissance Italy.* 1998. A study of the most extensive and long-lasting vendetta in Renaissance Italy. It traces the evolution of vendetta violence into dueling.

Weinstein, Donald. *The Captain's Concubine: Love, Honor, and Violence in Renaissance Tuscany.* 2000. A delightfully engaging account of an ambush and fight among two nobles over a woman who was the concubine of the father of one of the fighters and the lover of the other. It reveals the disturbing relationship between love and violence in Renaissance society.

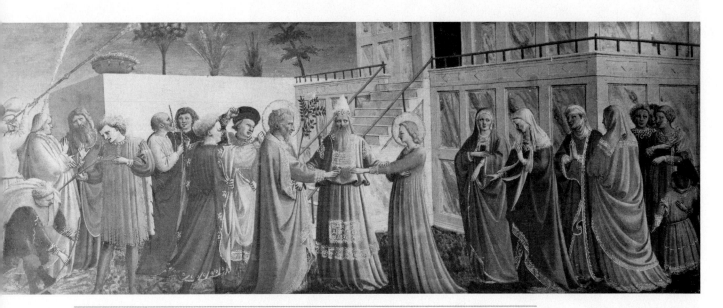

The Age Gap Between Husbands and Wives

In Renaissance Italy older men typically married much younger women. In the middle of this fresco, *Marriage of the Virgin* by Fra Angelico, the young Mary holds out her hands to a rabbi who joins her in marriage to the gray-bearded Joseph. Behind Joseph young men hold up their fists as if to strike him. Fra Angelico dramatically conveys the anger of the young men about a marriage system that made it impossible for them to compete for brides with the older men.

fathers should be in control, in reality they were often absent or dead.

The contradiction between the theory of patriarchy and the fragile reality of family life had far-reaching consequences. Instead of wielding a strong hand over their families, most fathers were remote figures who had little direct influence. Mothers who were supposed to be modest, obedient to their husbands, and invisible to the outside world not only had to raise children alone but often had to manage their dead or absent husband's business and political affairs. By necessity, many resilient, strong, and active women were deeply involved in the management of worldly affairs, and mothers had much more direct influence on children than fathers. Despite the theory of patriarchy, the families of Renaissance Italy were in fact matriarchies in which mothers ruled.

The contradictions of family life became one of the most discussed problems in the Renaissance. Making fun of impotent old husbands married to beautiful but unfulfilled young wives became a major theme in comic drama. Given the demographic ravages of the Black Death, concern for the care of babies preoccupied preachers, while the many Renaissance paintings in which little cherubs seem to fall from the sky manifested a widespread craving for healthy children. A deep anxiety produced by the contradictions of family life and by the tenuous hold many families had on survival stimulated the distinctive family theme in the culture of Renaissance Italy.

The Influence of Ancient Culture

■ How did Renaissance thinkers create historical perspective and devise methods of criticism for interpreting texts?

The need in Renaissance Italy to provide effective models for how citizens, courtiers, and families should behave stimulated a reexamination of ancient culture. The civilizations of ancient Greece and Rome had long fascinated the educated classes in the West. In Italy, where most cities were built around or on top of the ruins of the ancient past, the seduction of antiquity was particularly pronounced. During the fourteenth and fifteenth centuries many Italian thinkers and artists attempted to foster a rebirth of ancient cultures. At first they merely attempted to imitate the Latin style of the best Roman writers. Then scholars tried to do the same thing with Greek, stimulated in part by direct contact with Greek-speaking refugees from Byzantium. Artists trekked to Rome to fill their notebooks with sketches of ancient ruins, sculptures, and medallions. Wealthy collectors hoarded manuscripts of ancient philosophy, built libraries to house them, bought up every piece of ancient sculpture they could find, and dug up ruins to find more antiquities to adorn their palaces. Patrons demanded that artists produce new works that imitated the styles of the ancients and that displayed a similar concern for rendering natural forms. Especially prized were lifelike representations of the human body.

Patrons, artists, and scholars during the Renaissance not only appreciated the achievements of the past but began to understand the enormous cultural distance between themselves and the ancients. That insight made their perspective historical. They also developed techniques of literary analysis to determine when a particular text had been written and to differentiate authentic texts from ones that had been corrupted by the mistakes of copyists. That ability made their perspective critical.

Petrarch and the Illustrious Ancients

The founder of the historical critical perspective that characterized the Renaissance was Francesco Petrarca (1304–1374), known in English as Petrarch. In contrast to the medieval thinkers who admired the ancients and treated their words as repositories of eternal wisdom, Petrarch discovered that the ancients were mere men much like himself. More than anything else, that insight might distinguish what was new about the Italian Renaissance, and Petrarch was the first to explore its implications.

Petrarch's early fame came from his poetry, in both his native Italian and Latin. In an attempt to improve his Latin style, Petrarch engaged in a detailed study of the best ancient Roman writers and searched to find old manuscripts that were the least corrupted by copyists. In that search he was always watching for anything by the Roman orator Cicero (106–43 B.C.E.), who was the Latinist most revered for literary style. In 1345 Petrarch briefly visited Verona to see what he could find in the library of a local monastery. While thumbing through the dusty volumes, he excitedly happened upon a previously unknown collection of letters Cicero had written to his friend Atticus.

As Petrarch began to read the letters, however, he suffered a profound shock. Cicero had a reputation as the greatest sage of the Romans, a model of good Latin style, of philosophical sophistication, and most of all of high ethical standards. But in the letters Petrarch found not sage moral advice but gossip, rumors, and crude political calculations. Cicero looked like a scheming politician, a man of crass ambition rather than grand philosophical wisdom. Although Petrarch could never forgive Cicero for being less than what he had avowed in his philosophical writings, he had discovered the human Cicero rather than just the idealized Cicero, a man so human you could imagine having a conversation with him.

And having a conversation was precisely what Petrarch set out to do. Cicero, however, had been dead for 1,388 years. So Petrarch wrote a letter to Cicero's ghost. Adopting Cicero's own elegant Latin style, Petrarch lambasted the Roman for going against the moral advice he had given others. Petrarch quoted Cicero back to Cicero, asking him how he could be such a hypocrite:

Your letters I sought for long and diligently; and finally, where I least expected it, I found them. At once I read them, over and over, with the utmost eagerness. And as I read I seemed to hear your bodily voice, O Marcus Tullius [Cicero's given names], saying many things, uttering many lamentations, ranging through many phases of thought and feeling. I long had known how excellent a guide you have proved for others; at last I was to learn what sort of guidance you gave yourself. . . . Now it is your turn to be the listener.[5]

DOCUMENT

Petrarch, Letters to Cicero (14th c.)

Petrarch went on to lecture Cicero for his false dealings, his corruption, and his moral failures. The point of the exercise of writing a letter to a dead man was to compare the ideals Cicero had avowed in his philosophical work and the reality he seemed to have lived. Making comparisons is one of the elementary techniques of a critical method, and it became the hallmark of Petrarch's mode of analysis. Petrarch's letter reduced the stature of the ancients a bit, making them less like gods and more like other men who made mistakes and told lies. Petrarch ended this remarkable, unprecedented letter with a specific date, given in both the Roman and Christian ways, and a description of Verona's location in a way an ancient Roman would understand—as if he were making it possible for Cicero to find and answer him. This concern for historical precision typified the aspect that was most revolutionary about Petrarch's approach. No longer a repository of timeless truths, the ancient world became a specific time and place that Petrarch perceived to be at a great distance from himself. The ancients had ceased to be godlike; they had become historical figures. After his letter to Cicero, Petrarch wrote a series of letters to other illustrious ancients in which he revealed the human qualities and shortcomings of each.

Petrarch and his follower Lorenzo Valla (1407–1457) developed critical methods by editing classical texts, including parts of Livy's history of Rome, which was written about the time of Jesus. Petrarch compared different manuscript versions of Livy's work in an attempt to establish exactly the original words, a method very different from the medieval scribe's temptation to alter or improve a text as he saw fit. Petrarch strived to get the words right because he wanted to understand exactly what Livy had meant, a method now called the philological approach. Philology° is the comparative study of language, devoted to understanding the meaning of a word in a particular historical context. Valla elaborated on Petrarch's insights into philology to demonstrate that words do not have fixed meanings but take on different meanings depending on who is using them and when they were written. It was obvious, for example, that the word *virtue* had meant something quite different to the polytheist Livy than it did to readers in the fourteenth and fifteenth centuries, who understood virtue in Christian terms. A concern for philology gave Petrarch and his followers access to the individuality of a writer. In the particularity of words, Petrarch discovered the particularity of actual individuals who lived and wrote many centuries before.

An interest in the meaning of words led Petrarch to study the rhetoric° of language. Rhetoric refers to the art of persuasive or emotive speaking and writing. From his studies of rhetoric, Petrarch became less confident about the ability of language to represent truth than he was about its capacity to motivate readers and listeners to action. He came to think that rhetoric was superior to philosophy because he preferred a good man over a wise one, and rhetoric offered examples worthy of emulation rather than abstract principles subject to debate. Petrarch wanted people to behave morally, not just talk or write about morality. And he believed that the most efficient way to inspire his readers to do the right thing was to write moving rhetoric.

The Humanists: The Latin Point of View

Those who followed Petrarch's approach to the classical authors were the Renaissance humanists°. The Renaissance humanists studied Latin and sometimes Greek texts on grammar, rhetoric, poetry, history, and ethics. (The term *humanist* in the Renaissance meant something very different from what it means today—someone concerned with human welfare and dignity.) The humanists sought to resurrect a form of Latin that had been dead for more than a thousand years and was distinct from the living Latin used by the Church, law courts, and universities—which they thought was mediocre compared to ancient Latin. In this effort, humanists acquired a difficult but functional skill that opened a wide variety of employment opportunities to them and gave them great public influence. They worked as schoolmasters, secretaries, bureaucrats, official court or civic historians, and ambassadors. Many other humanists were wealthy men who did not need a job but were fascinated with the rhetorical capabilities of the new learning to persuade other people to do what they wanted them to do.

Because humanists could be found on different sides of almost all important questions of the day, the significance of their work lies less in what they said than in how they said it. They wrote about practically everything: painting pictures, designing buildings, planting crops, draining swamps, raising children, managing a household, and educating women. They debated the nature of human liberty, the virtues of famous men, the vices of infamous ones, the meaning of Egyptian hieroglyphics, and the cosmology of the universe.

How did the humanists' use of Latin words and grammar influence the understanding of this vast range of subjects? Their approach was entirely literary. When they wanted to design a building, they read ancient books on architecture instead of consulting masons and builders. By studying the ancients, humanists organized experience into new categories that changed people's perceptions of them-

selves, the society they lived in, and the universe they inhabited. Humanist writing revealed what might be called the *Latin point of view*. Each language organizes experience according to the needs of the people who speak it, and all languages make arbitrary distinctions, dividing up the world into different categories. People who study a foreign language run across these arbitrary distinctions when they learn that some expressions can never be translated exactly.

The humanists' recovery of the Latin point of view contributed new words, new sentence patterns, and new rhetorical models that often altered their own perceptions in very subtle ways. For example, when a fifteenth-century humanist examined what the ancient Romans had written about painting, he found the phrase *ars et ingenium. Ars* referred to skills that can be learned by following established rules and adhering to models provided by the best painters. Thus, the ability of a painter to draw a straight line, to mix colors properly, and to identify a saint with the correct symbol are examples of *ars* or what we would call craftsmanship. The meaning of *ingenium* was more difficult to pin down, however. It referred to the inventive capacity of the painter, to his or her ingenuity. The humanists discovered that the ancients had made a distinction between the craftsmanship and the ingenuity of a painter. As a result, when humanists and their pupils looked at paintings, they began to make the same distinction and began to admire the genius of artists whose work showed ingenuity as well as craftsmanship. Ingenuity came to refer to the ability of the painter to arrange figures in a novel way, to employ unusual colors, or to create emotionally exciting effects that conveyed piety, sorrow, or joy as the subject demanded. So widespread was the influence of the humanists that the most ingenious artists demanded higher prices and became the most sought after. In this way, creative innovation was encouraged in the arts, but it all started very simply with the introduction of new words into the Latin vocabulary of the people who paid for paintings. A similar process of establishing new categories altered every subject the humanists touched.

The humanist movement spread rapidly during the fifteenth century. Leonardo Bruni (ca. 1370–1444), who became the chancellor of Florence (the head of the government's bureaucracy), employed humanist techniques to defend the republican institutions and values of the city. Bruni's defense of republican government is called civic humanism°. He argued that the truly ethical man should devote himself to active service to his city rather than to passive contemplation in scholarly retreat or monastic seclusion. Thus Bruni formulated the ethic of responsible citizenship that remains today as necessary to sustain a free society. Given the supreme value Christianity had long placed on the passive contemplation of divine truth, Bruni's assertion that active public service constituted an even higher vocation was radical indeed.

Lorenzo Valla employed philological criticism to undermine papal claims to authority over secular rulers, such as

A Humanist Laments the Ruins of Rome

In 1430 the distinguished humanist Poggio Bracciolini (1380–1459) was working in Rome as a papal secretary. In this account he describes his and a friend's response to seeing the ruins of the once-great city of Rome. Poggio's lament and those of other humanists stimulated popes to commit themselves to the rebuilding of the city, but the enthusiasm to return Rome to its ancient splendor had some unfortunate side effects. Many of the building materials for the new Rome were pillaged from the ruins of the old Rome. As a result, much of the destruction of the ancient city of Rome occurred during the Renaissance.

Not long ago, after Pope Martin left Rome shortly before his death for a farewell visit to the Tuscan countryside, and when Antonio Lusco, a very distinguished man, and I were free of business and public duties, we used to contemplate the desert places of the city with wonder in our hearts as we reflected on the former greatness of the broken buildings and the vast ruins of the ancient city, and again on the truly prodigious and astounding fall of its great empire and the deplorable inconstancy of fortune. And once when we had climbed the Capitoline hill, and Antonio, who was a little weary from riding, wanted to rest, we dismounted from our horses and sat down together within the very enclosures of the Tarpeian ruins, behind the great marble threshold of its very doors, as I believe, and the numerous broken columns lying here and there, whence a view of a large part of the city opens out.

Here, after he had looked about for some time, sighing and as if struck dumb, Antonio declared, "Oh, Poggio, how remote are these ruins from the Capitol that our Vergil celebrated: 'Golden now, once bristling with thorn bushes.' How justly one can transpose this verse and say: 'Golden once, now rough with thorns and overgrown with briars.'"

Source: "The Ruins of Rome" by Poggio Bracciolini, translated by Mary Martin McLaughlin, from *The Portable Renaissance Reader* by James B. Ross and Mary Martin McLaughlin, editors, copyright 1953, renewed © 1981 by Viking Penguin Inc. Used by permission of Viking Penguin, a division of Penguin Group (USA) Inc.

the princes and republics of Italy. He did so by proving that a famous document, the Donation of Constantine, was a forgery. The Donation recorded that during the fourth century the emperor Constantine had transferred his imperial authority in Italy to the pope, and although Renaissance popes could not get what they wanted just by citing this document, it was part of the legal arsenal popes used against secular rulers. Valla demonstrated that the Donation had actually been forged in the ninth century, a work of detection that showed how the historical analysis of documents could be immensely useful for resolving contemporary political disputes. The controversy between defenders and enemies of the papacy that followed Valla's discovery stimulated the demand for humanist learning because it became clear that humanist methods were necessary for political debate and propaganda.

The intellectual curiosity of the humanists led them to master many fields of endeavor. This breadth of accomplishment contributed to the ideal of the "Renaissance Man," a person who sought excellence in everything he did. No one came closer to this ideal than Leon Battista Alberti (1404–1472). As a young man, Alberti wrote Latin comedies and satirical works that drew on Greek and Roman models, but as he matured he tackled more serious subjects. Although he was a bachelor and thus knew nothing firsthand about marriage, he drew upon the ancient writers to create the most influential Renaissance book on the family, which included sections on relations between husbands and wives, raising children, and estate management. He composed the first grammar of the Italian language. He dabbled in mathematics and wrote on painting, law, the duties of bishops, love, horsemanship, dogs, agriculture, and flies. He mapped the city of Rome and wrote the most important fifteenth-century work on the theory and practice of architecture. His interest in architecture, moreover, was not just theoretical. In the last decades of his life, he dedicated much of his spare time to architectural projects that included restoring an ancient church in Rome, designing Renaissance façades for medieval churches, and building a palace for his most important patron. One of his last projects was the first significant work for making and deciphering secret codes in the West.

The humanists guaranteed their lasting influence through their innovations in the educational curriculum. The objective of humanist education was to create well-rounded male pupils (girls were not usually accepted in humanist schools) who were not specialists or professionals, such as the theologians, lawyers, and physicians trained in universities, but critical thinkers who could tackle any problems that life presented. It was a curriculum well suited for the active life of civic leaders, courtiers, princes, and churchmen. The influence of the humanist curriculum persists in the general-education requirements of modern universities, which require students, now of both sexes, to obtain intellectual breadth before they specialize in narrow professional training.

Historians have identified a few female humanists from the Renaissance. Because they were so unusual, learned humanist women were often ridiculed. Jealous men accused the humanist Isotta Nogarola (1418–1466) of promiscuity and incest, and other women insulted her in public. A famous male schoolmaster said that Isotta was too feminine in her writings and should learn how to find "a man within the woman."[6] Laura Cereta (1475–1506), who knew Greek as well as Latin and was adept at mathematics, answered the scorn of a male critic with rhetorical insult worthy of Petrarch himself:

> I would have been silent, believe me, if that savage old enmity of yours had attacked me alone. . . . But I cannot tolerate your having attacked my entire sex. For this reason my thirsty soul seeks revenge, my sleeping pen is aroused to literary struggle, raging anger stirs mental passions long chained by silence. With just cause I am moved to demonstrate how great a reputation for learning and virtue women have won by their inborn excellence, manifested in every age as knowledge, the [purveyor] of honor. Certain, indeed, and legitimate is our possession of this inheritance, come to us from a long eternity of ages past.[7]

These few humanist women can be seen as among the first feminists. They advocated female equality and female education but also urged women to take control of their own lives. Nogarola answered her critics in a typical humanist fashion by reinterpreting the past. Thinking at this time suggested that all women were the daughters of Eve, who in her weakness had submitted to the temptation of the serpent, which led to the exile of humanity from the Garden of Eden. Nogarola pointed out that Eve had been no weaker than Adam, who also ate of the forbidden fruit, and therefore women should not be blamed for the Fall from God's grace. Cereta was the most optimistic of the female humanists. She maintained that if women paid as much attention to learning as they did to their appearances, they would achieve equality. Despite the efforts of Cereta and other female humanists, progress in women's education was extremely slow. The universities remained closed to talented women. The first woman to earn a degree from a university did so in 1678, and it took another 200 years before very many others could follow her example.

Through the influence of the humanists, the Latin point of view permeated Renaissance culture. They educated generations of wealthy young gentlemen whose appreciation of antiquity led them to pay to collect manuscripts of ancient literature, philosophy, and science. These patrons were also responsible for encouraging artists to imitate the ancients. What began as a narrow literary movement became the stimulus to see human society and nature through entirely new eyes. Some humanists, especially in northern Europe, applied these techniques with revolutionary results to the study of the Bible and the sources of Christianity.

Understanding Nature: Moving Beyond the Science of the Ancients

The humanists' initial concern was to emulate the language of the ancients. Most of them preferred to spend time reading a book rather than observing the world around them. In fact, their methods were ill-suited to understanding nature, and when they wanted to explain some natural phenomenon such as the movement of blood through the body or the apparent movements of the planets and stars, they looked to ancient authorities for answers rather than to nature itself. The Renaissance humanists' most prominent contributions to science consisted of recovering classical texts and translating the work of ancient Greek scientists into the more widely understood Latin. This is in contrast to the scientific method of today, in which scientists form a hypothesis and then determine whether it is correct by observing the natural world as directly as possible. In contrast, Renaissance scientists searched for ancient texts about nature, and then debated about which ancient author had been correct.

These translated texts broadened the discussion of two subjects crucial to the scientific revolution of the late sixteenth and seventeenth centuries—astronomy and anatomy. In 1543 the Polish humanist Nicolaus Copernicus (1473–1543) resolved the complications in the cosmological system of the second-century astronomer Ptolemy. Whereas Ptolemy's writings had placed Earth at the center of the universe, Copernicus cited other ancient writers who put the sun in the center. Thus the first breakthrough in theoretical astronomy was achieved not by making new observations but by comparing ancient texts. Nothing was proven, however, until Galileo Galilei (1564–1642) turned his telescope to the heavens in 1610 to observe the stars through his own eyes rather than through an ancient text.

Andreas Vesalius (1514–1564) built upon recently published studies in anatomy from ancient Greece to write a survey of human anatomy, *On the Fabric of the Human Body* (1543), a book that encouraged dissection and anatomical observations. With Vesalius, anatomy moved away from relying exclusively on the authority of ancient books to encouraging medical students and physicians to examine the human body with their own eyes. Building upon Vesalius's work, Gabriele Falloppio (ca. 1523–1562) made many original observations of muscles, nerves, kidneys, bones, and most famously the "Fallopian tubes," which he described for the first time. By the late sixteenth century, astronomy and anatomy had surpassed what the ancients had known.

Besides recovering ancient scientific texts, the most important Renaissance contributions to science came secondhand from developments in the visual arts and technology. A number of Florentine artists experimented during the early fifteenth century with the application of mathematics to the preliminary design of paintings. The goal was to make paintings more accurately represent reality by creating the visual illusion of the third dimension of depth on a two-dimensional rectangular surface, a technique known as linear perspective (see next section). These artists contributed to a more refined understanding of how the eye perceives objects, and their understanding of how the eye worked led to experiments with glass lenses. A more thorough knowledge of optics made possible the invention of the telescope and microscope.

Of all the developments in the fifteenth century, however, none matched the long-term significance of a pair of rather simple inventions—cheap manufactured paper and the printing press. Paper made from rags created an inexpensive alternative to sheepskins, which had been the preferred medium for medieval scribes. And just as paper replaced sheepskin, the printing press replaced the scribe. Several Dutch and German craftsmen had experimented with printing during the 1440s, but credit for the essential innovation of movable metal type has traditionally been accredited to Johannes Gutenberg (ca. 1398–1468) of Mainz in the 1450s. German immigrants brought printing to Italy, which rapidly became the publishing center of Europe, largely because it boasted a large, literate urban population who bought books.

Scientific books accounted for only about 10 percent of the titles of the first printed books, but the significance of printing for science was greater than the sales figures would indicate. In addition to making ancient scientific texts more readily available, print meant that new discoveries and new ideas reached a wider audience, duplication of scientific investigation could be avoided, illustrations were standardized, and scientists built upon each other's work. With the invention of the printing press, scientific work became closely intertwined with publishing, so that published scientific work advanced science, and scientific work that was not published went largely unnoticed. It is revealing that Leonardo da Vinci (1452–1519), the greatest Renaissance observer of nature, contributed nothing to science because he failed to publish his findings. The fundamental principle of modern science and, in fact, of all modern scholarship is that research must be made available to everyone through publication.

Antiquity and Nature in the Arts

■ How did various attempts to imitate antiquity in the arts alter perceptions of nature?

More than any other age in Western history, the Italian Renaissance is identified with the visual arts. The unprecedented clusters of brilliant artists active in a handful of Italian cities during the fifteenth and sixteenth centuries overshadow any other contribution of Renaissance culture. Under the influence of the humanists, Renaissance artists began to imitate the sculpture, architecture, and painting of the ancients. At first they concerned themselves with merely copying ancient styles and poses. But soon they attempted a more sophisticated form of imitation. They wanted to understand the principles that made

CHRONOLOGY	
The Influence of Ancient Culture	
106–43 B.C.E.	Marcus Tullius Cicero, Latin rhetorician
1304–1374	Francesco Petrarca (Petrarch), first humanist
ca. 1370–1444	Leonardo Bruni, chancellor of Florence
1404–1472	Leon Battista Alberti, humanist and architect
1407–1457	Lorenzo Valla, humanist
1418–1466	Isotta Nogarola, first female humanist
ca. 1454	Johannes Gutenberg begins printing books
1473–1543	Nicolaus Copernicus, humanist and cosmological theorist
1475–1506	Laura Cereta, humanist
1514–1564	Andreas Vesalius, writer on anatomy
ca. 1523–1562	Gabriele Falloppio, conducted anatomical dissections
1564–1642	Galileo Galilei, astronomer

it possible for the artists from classical Greece and Rome to make their figures so lifelike. That led them to observe more directly nature itself, especially the anatomy of the human body. Renaissance art was driven by the passionate desire of artists and their patrons both to imitate ancient models and to imitate nature. These twin desires produced a certain creative tension in their work because the ancients, whose works of art often depicted gods and goddesses, had idealized and improved on what they observed in nature. Renaissance artists sought to depict simultaneously the ideal and the real—an impossible goal, but one that sparked remarkable creativity.

All of the Renaissance arts displayed the mark of patrons, the discriminating and wealthy people who controlled the city-states and who had been educated in humanist schools. Until the end of the sixteenth century, all painters, sculptors, and even poets worked for a patron. An individual patron would commission a particular work of art, such as an altar painting, portrait bust, or palace. The patron and artist would agree to the terms of the work through a contract, which might spell out in considerable detail exactly what the artist was to do, what kinds of materials he was to use, how much they could cost, how much he was allowed to rely on assistants, how much he had to do himself, and even how he was to arrange figures. The same sort of contract was used when work was commissioned by a group—for example, a guild, lay religious society (called a confraternity), convent, or government. Michelangelo Buonarroti (1475–1564) sculpted *David*, which has become the most famous work of Renaissance art, to fulfill a contract that had been debated in a committee meeting. Regardless of their talent or ingenuity, artists were never free agents who could do whatever they wanted.

Another kind of patron supported the career of an artist for an extended period of time. Princes, in particular, liked to take on an artist—give him a regular salary and perhaps even some official title—in exchange for having him perform whatever duties the prince deemed necessary. In this kind of an arrangement, Duke Lodovico Sforza (1451–1508) brought Leonardo da Vinci to Milan, where Leonardo painted a portrait of the duke's mistress, devised plans for a giant equestrian statue of the duke's father, designed stage sets and carnival pageants, painted the interior decorations of the castle, and did engineering work. The artist Cosmè Tura (active ca. 1450–1495) probably spent more time painting furniture than canvases for the Duke of Ferrara.

Most patrons supported the arts in order to enhance their own prestige and power. Some, such as Pope Julius II, had exceptional influence on the work of artists. He persuaded the very reluctant Michelangelo, who saw himself as a sculptor, to become a painter in order to decorate the ceiling of the Sistine Chapel.

Sculpture, Architecture, and Painting: The Natural and the Ideal

Just as humanists recaptured antiquity by collecting, translating, and analyzing the writings of classical authors, so Renaissance artists made drawings of surviving classical medals, sculpture, and architecture. Collected in sketch books, these drawings often served as pattern books from which the apprentices in artists' workshops learned how to draw. Because artists believed that the classical world enjoyed an artistic tradition vastly superior to their own, these sketches became valuable models from which other artists could learn. Two of the most influential Florentine artists, the architect Filippo Brunelleschi (1377–1446) and the sculptor Donatello (1386–1466), may have gone to Rome together as young men to sketch the ancient monuments. No Roman paintings survived into the fifteenth century (Pompeii, which proved to have a treasure trove of Roman art buried under layers of volcanic ash, had not yet been excavated), and no Renaissance artist ever saw a Greek building, so the only examples of ancient art to copy were the ruins of Roman buildings and a few surviving Roman

The Competition Panels of the Sacrifice of Isaac

These two panels were the finalists in a competition to design the cast bronze doors on the north side of the Baptistery in Florence. Each demonstrates a bold new design that attempted to capture the emotional trauma of the exact moment when an angel arrests Abraham's arm from sacrificing his son Isaac (Genesis 22:1–12). Both artists went on to be closely associated with the new style of the Renaissance. The panel on the left, by Filippo Brunelleschi, lost to the one on the right, by Lorenzo Ghiberti. Notice how the Ghiberti relief better conveys the drama of the scene by projecting the elbow of Abraham's upraised arm outward toward the viewer. As a result the viewer's line of sight follows the line of the arm and knife directly toward Isaac's throat.

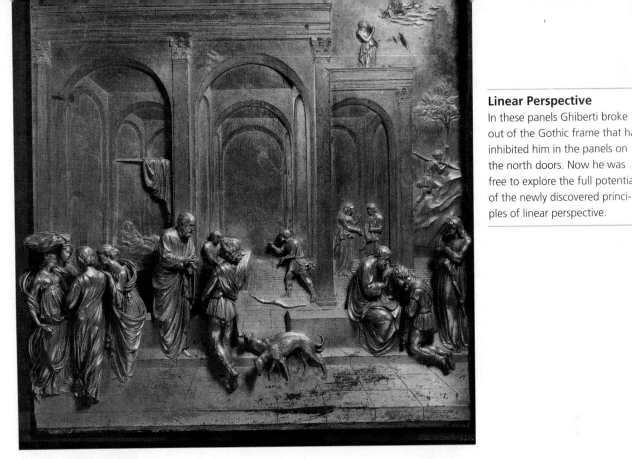

Linear Perspective

In these panels Ghiberti broke out of the Gothic frame that had inhibited him in the panels on the north doors. Now he was free to explore the full potential of the newly discovered principles of linear perspective.

states. As a result, architecture and sculpture led the way in the imitation of ancient art, but Renaissance artists imposed their own sensibilities on the ancients as much as they imitated them.

The Renaissance style evolved in Florence during the first few decades of the fifteenth century. In 1401 the 24-year-old Brunelleschi entered a competition to design bronze relief panels for the north doors of the Baptistery. He narrowly lost to the even younger Lorenzo Ghiberti (1378–1455). Look at the illustrations on page 360. The rules of the competition required both artists to fit their relief panels within a fancy decorative frame in the Gothic style, which had been in fashion for nearly 300 years. However, both competition relief panels seem constrained by the curves and angles of the frame. For example, some of the figures in the Brunelleschi panel project outside it as if trying to escape the restraints of the style. Ghiberti's relief shows the two characteristic elements of the early Renaissance style: The head of Isaac is modeled after a classical Roman sculpture, and the figures and horse on the left are depicted as realistically as possible. In these elements, Ghiberti was imitating both antiquity and nature.

Ghiberti worked on the north doors for twenty-one years and won such renown as a result that when he finished he was immediately offered a new commission to complete panels for the east portal. These doors, begun in 1425, took twenty-seven years to finish. In the east doors, Ghiberti substituted a simple square frame for the Gothic frame of the north doors, thereby liberating his composi-

tion. In the illustration above, which depicts the biblical story of Jacob and Esau, the squares in the pavement set up an underlying geometry to the scene. The background architecture of rounded arches and crisp-angled columns in the classical style creates the illusion of depth in the relief. This illusion is achieved through linear perspective°, that is, the use of geometrical principles to depict a three-dimensional space on a flat, two-dimensional surface. The rigorous geometry of the composition provided the additional benefit of allowing Ghiberti to divide up the space to depict several different scenes within one panel. In the panels of the east doors, he created the definitive Renaissance interpretation of the ancient principles of the harmony produced by geometry. Michelangelo later remarked that the doors were fit to serve as the "gates of paradise."

After failing to win the competition for the Baptistery doors, Brunelleschi turned to architecture. In his own time, Brunelleschi was considered to have revived ancient Roman principles, but it is evident now that he was less a student of antiquity than an astutely original thinker. In his buildings he employed a proportional system of design that is best seen in his masterpiece, the Pazzi Chapel. He began with a basic geometric unit represented by each of the small rectangles clustered in groups of four on the upper third of the façade of the chapel. The height of each of these was approximately the height of an average man. All the other dimensions of the building were multiples of these basic rectangles. Thus the building was formed from the proportions of a human being. Brunelleschi employed

The Natural and the Ideal Body in Renaissance Art

During the Italian Renaissance artists depicted the human body, especially the nude body, with a greater sensitivity to anatomy than at any time since antiquity. In attempting to portray the human body, Renaissance sculptors and painters explored two possible approaches. Should they attempt to imitate nature by depicting human bodies as they really appear, or should they improve upon nature by representing human bodies in an idealized way?

The Florentine sculptor Donatello (1386–1466) was the master of the first approach, the naturalistic representation of the human body. His major achievement was solving the difficult technical problem of creating a freestanding life-size statue of a human being that looked as if the person depicted were standing in a natural way. In his solution, called *contraposto,* one leg of the human form is kept straight and the other is slightly bent, with the hips slanting in the opposite direction from the slant of the shoulders. One contemporary described Donatello's statues as so lively that they appeared to move. Following Donatello's lead, Florentine sculptors dedicated themselves to "the return to nature," the attempt to make inanimate works of art imitate not just ancient sculpture, but nature itself.

During the later Renaissance, Michelangelo Buonarroti (1475–1564) perfected the second approach by idealizing the human body. He did not want just to imitate nature, he wanted to surpass nature. His figures, such as his famous *David,* often seemed superhuman. In creating figures such as this, he brought the Renaissance preoccupation with antiquity full circle because many classical sculptors had intended to achieve the same effect. After all, most of their work was for polytheist temples, and by improving on nature they wanted to create images of the perfect bodies of the gods.

With Michelangelo, Western art entered an entirely new phase. He advanced art from the simple goal of imitating classical motifs and observing nature to a more grandiose goal of improving on the ancients and on nature. According to Michelangelo, because nature alone never achieved perfection, great art can be even more powerful than nature itself.

The Naturalistic Body

In the *contraposto* pose of Donatello's David, the weight of the figure is carried on one leg of the human form, which appears straight and taut while the other seems relaxed and slightly bent.

The Idealized Body

This larger-than-life figure of the biblical warrior King David transformed the young boy who slew the giant Goliath into a kind of superman whose physical bearing was greater than any normal man. Michelangelo altered the proportions of a natural man, making the head and hands significantly larger than normal. In its original placement on a staircase in a large open square, the statue towered above viewers.

For Discussion

How might the Renaissance humanist concerns for imitation produce both the artistic conceptions of naturalism and idealized beauty?

worked in fresco. A common form of decoration in churches, fresco was the technique of applying paint to wet plaster on a wall. In his great fresco cycle for the Brancacci chapel painted in the 1420s, Masaccio depicted street scenes from Florence complete with portraits of actual people, including himself. These were examples of naturalism. On other figures—Jesus, St. Peter, and St. John—he placed heads copied from ancient sculptures of gods. These were examples of idealized beauty, which were especially suitable for saints. In Masaccio's frescoes, both realistic and idealized figures appeared in the same work. The realistic figures helped viewers identify with the subject of the picture by allowing them to recognize people they actually knew. The idealized figures represented the saintly, whose superior moral qualities made them appear different from average people.

Masaccio developed the technical means for employing linear perspective in painting. To achieve the effect of perspective, he organized the entire composition around the position he assumed a viewer would take while looking at the picture. Once he established the point of view, he composed the picture to direct the viewer's gaze through the

The Engineering of Renaissance Architecture

Filippo Brunelleschi designed the dome for the cathedral in Florence, which became the most famous engineering achievement of the Renaissance. The dome spanned the largest space without columns to support it of any structure built since antiquity.

Portraits in Renaissance Paintings

During the fifteenth century artists idealized some figures and made others appear as natural as possible. Natural effects were created by incorporating portraits of actual people into scenes. In this example from a fresco by Masaccio depicting one of the miracles of St. Peter, the crowd witnessing the event includes portraits of notable artists. Starting from the far right are portraits of Brunelleschi, Leon Battista Alberti, Masaccio, and Masolino, who helped Masaccio paint the frescoes in the Brancacci Chapel from which this detail comes.

what he saw as the natural dimensions of humanity and transformed them into principles of architectural geometry. The result was a stunning impression of harmony in all the spaces of the building. For the dome of the Cathedral of Florence he employed innovative engineering technologies to span a huge space that had been left open for more than a century because no one knew how to build a dome over such a large expanse.

Later sculptors and architects built upon the innovations of Ghiberti and Brunelleschi. Florence became renowned for its tradition of sculpture, producing the two greatest Renaissance masters of the art, Donatello and Michelangelo. In their representations of the human form, both of these sculptors demonstrated the Renaissance preoccupation with the relationship between the ideal and the natural.

Conceptions of both the ideal and the natural are evident in the work of the most important painter of the early Florentine Renaissance, Masaccio (1401–ca. 1428), who

The Tribute Money: Combining Natural and Idealized Representations

In this detail of a fresco of Christ and his apostles, Masaccio mixed naturalism and idealized beauty. The figure on the right with his back turned to the viewer is a tax collector, who is depicted as a normal human being. The head of the fourth figure to the left of him, who represents one of the apostles, was copied from an ancient statue that represents ancient ideals of beauty.

pictorial space. In *The Tribute Money*, he drew the spectator's eye to the head of Jesus, who is the figure in the middle pointing with his right hand. In addition, Masaccio recognized that the human eye perceives an object when light shines on it to form lighted surfaces and shadows. He used this understanding in creating a painting technique called *chiaroscuro* ("light and shade"). There is a single source of light in the painting coming from the same direction as the light in the room. That light defines figures and objects in the painting through the play of light and shadow. The strokes of Masaccio's paintbrush tried to duplicate the way natural light plays upon surfaces.

The techniques developed by Masaccio came to complete fulfillment in the career of Leonardo da Vinci (1452–1519). So compelling was Leonardo's curiosity and desire to tackle new problems that many of his paintings remained unfinished. He was a restless experimenter, never settling on simple solutions. Because of experiments Leonardo made with paint, his *Last Supper* fresco in Milan has seriously deteriorated. His mature works, such as *Mona Lisa*, completely reconciled the technical problems of representing human figures with realistic accuracy and the spiritual goal of evoking deep emotions. Unlike some of his predecessors, who grouped figures in a painting as if they were statues, Leonardo managed to make his figures appear to interact and communicate with one another.

DOCUMENT

Vasari on Leonardo da Vinci

IMAGE

Leonardo da Vinci, *Madonna with the Carnation*, c. 1435

The technique of painting with oils achieved new levels among painters in the Netherlands and in Flanders (in present-day Belgium, but at the time a province in the Duchy of Burgundy). By carefully layering numerous coats of tinted oil glazes over the surface of the painting, these painters created

Leonardo Invents an Airplane

Leonardo da Vinci's notebooks are filled with numerous examples of his unprecedented inventions. In this drawing he designed the fuselage of a flying machine. However, Leonardo had no influence at all on science or technology because he kept his inventions in his secret notebooks, and no one knew about them until they were discovered centuries later.

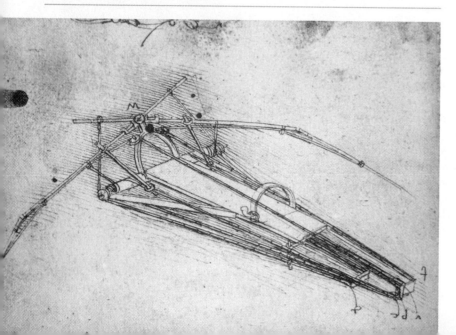

Northern Renaissance Art

In this fifteenth-century Flemish painting by Jan van Eyck, the use of oil paint and glazes made it possible to convey the shimmering surfaces of the brass chandelier and mirror hanging in the background. Shown in the mirror are the backs of the posing couple and the artist at his easel. Northern European artists delighted in using oils and glazes to create visual tricks, such as mirrored images. This is a portrait of Giovanni Arnolfini and Giovanna Cenami, who were married in 1434. Arnolfini was an Italian banker residing in the Flemish city of Bruges.

a luminous surface that gave the illusion of depth. The use of glazes enabled painters to blend brushstrokes in a way that made them virtually imperceptible. As a result Flemish and Dutch painters excelled in painting meticulous details, such as the textures of textiles, the reflections of gems, and the features of distant landscapes. Jan van Eyck (ca. 1395–1441) was the most famous Flemish painter. He worked as a court painter for the Duke of Burgundy, for whom he undertook many kinds of projects including decorating his palaces and designing stage sets and ornaments for festivals. His oil paintings were so famous that he was much praised by the Italian humanists, and numerous Italian patrons, including the Medicis, bought his works.

Most humanist theorists of painting linked artistic creativity with masculinity. By the sixteenth century, however, these theorists were proved wrong, as a number of female painters rose to prominence. The most notable was Sofonisba Anguissola (ca. 1532–1625). Born into an aristocratic family in Cremona, Italy, she received a humanist education along with her five sisters and brother. Because she was a woman, she was prohibited from studying anatomy or drawing male models. As a result she specialized in portraits, often of members of her family, and self-portraits. She developed a distinctive style of depicting animated faces. Her example inspired other aristocratic women to take up painting.

Music of the Emotions

Renaissance humanists' fascination with the visual arts of the ancients led them to assume that composers should imitate ancient music. But in attempting to turn humanist theories about music into real music, fifteenth-century composers faced a formidable problem—no one had the slightest clue what ancient Greek music actually sounded like. As a result, musical innovations lagged behind the other arts until the late sixteenth century, when a musical Renaissance finally took hold.

During the fourteenth and fifteenth centuries the principal composers came from France and the Netherlands. The greatest of them, Josquin de Prez (ca. 1440–1521), was born

and trained in the Netherlands and later found patrons in Milan, Rome, and Ferrara. His finest talent as a composer consisted of his ability to enhance musically the meaning of lyrics. In contrast to Josquin's sensitivity to matching music and lyric, most other composers relied on stereotypical rhythmic patterns and a simple melodic line that had no connection to the text. In fact, almost any lyric could be sung to the same music.

Recognizing that the music of their time did not measure up to what ancient writers had reported about the emotional intensity of their music, several prominent musician-humanists conducted extensive discussions about how to combine music and words in a way that would create a fuller aesthetic and emotional experience. The initial consequence of these discussions was the Renaissance madrigal, a type of song in which the music closely followed a poetic lyric to accentuate the shades of textual meaning. For example, when the text described a happy mood, the music would rise up the scale. A somber text would be lower-pitched. When the lyric described agitation or fear, the rhythm would quicken in imitation of the heart beating faster.

The most important consequence of the discussions about the need for a richer musical experience was the invention of opera° during the final decades of the sixteenth century. A group of humanist thinkers called the *Camerata* thought the power of ancient Greek music could be recovered by writing continuous music to accompany a full drama. The drama was performed as a kind of speech-song with the range of pitch and rhythms closely following those of natural speech. Singers were accompanied by a small ensemble of musicians. The first operas composed in this vein were by Jacopo Peri (1561–1633) and Giulio Caccini (ca. 1550–1618) and were performed in Florence

at the Grand Duke's court around 1600. These lengthy, bloated works attracted little attention among audiences, and opera likely would have sunk under its own weight had it not been for Claudio Monteverdi (1567–1643), who discovered its dramatic and lyrical potential. His sumptuous productions employed large ensembles of singers and instrumentalists, punctuated speech-song with arias (long sung solos) and dances, and included magnificent stage machines that simulated earthquakes, fires, and battles. Under Monteverdi's masterful hand, opera became the first complete multimedia art form. Arias from his productions became popular hits sung on every street corner, and opera moved from being a private amusement for princely courtiers to mass entertainment. The first public opera house opened in Venice in 1637. By the end of the seventeenth century, Venice boasted seventeen opera houses for a population of only 140,000. With the rise of opera houses and theaters for plays, the close bond between patrons and artists began to break down. Until then, artists were bound by the wishes of patrons. Now they began to serve the much larger marketplace for popular entertainment.

The Early Modern European State System

■ **How did the monarchies of western Europe gather the strength to become more assertive and more effective during the last half of the fifteenth and early sixteenth centuries?**

The civic independence that had made the Italian Renaissance possible was profoundly challenged during the Italian Wars (1494–1530). During these wars France, Spain, and the Holy Roman Empire attempted to carve up the peninsula for themselves, and the Italian city-states were thrown into turmoil. By 1530 the Italian city-states, with the exception of Venice, had lost their independence to the triumphant king of Spain. The surrender of the rich city-states of Italy was the first and most prominent sign of a major transformation in the European system of states. The age of city-states was over because they could never muster the level of materiel and manpower necessary to put and keep a large army in the field. Only the large monarchies of the West could do that. The Italian Wars revealed the outlines of the early modern European state system, which was built on the power of large countries that had been brought under control by their own kings. These kings amassed an unprecedented level of resources that not only crushed Italy but made possible the European domination of much of the globe through establishment of colonies in the Americas, Asia, and eventually Africa.

Monarchies: The Foundation of the State System

During the last half of the fifteenth century, the monarchies of western Europe began to show signs of recovery from the turmoil of the fourteenth and early fifteenth centuries, which had been marked by famine, plague, revolts, and the Hundred Years' War. France and England ended the Hundred Years' War, which had bled both kingdoms of men and resources during the century before 1453. England escaped from its civil war, the War of the Roses, in 1485. The kingdoms of Castile and Aragon joined in 1479 to create the new kingdom of Spain, which in 1492 completed the reconquest of territories from the Muslims that had been underway since the eleventh century. The Holy Roman Empire, which became allied to Spain through marriage, pursued a grand new vision for unifying the diverse principalities of Germany.

The early modern European state system was the consequence of five developments. First, governments established standing armies. As a result of the military revolution that brought large numbers of infantrymen to the field of battle and gunpowder cannons to besiege cities and castles, governments were obliged to modernize their armies or face defeat. Since the ninth century, kings had relied on feudal levies, in which soldiers were recruited to fulfill their personal obligation to a lord, but by the late fifteenth century governments began to organize standing armies. These armies enjoyed high levels of professionalism and skill, but they were very expensive to maintain because the soldiers had to be regularly paid. Moreover, the new artillery was costly, and improvements in the effectiveness of artillery bombardments necessitated extensive improvements in the walls of castles, fortresses, and cities. As a result, kings were desperate for new revenues.

The need for revenues led to the second development, the systematic expansion of taxation. Every European state struggled with the problem of taxation. The need to tax efficiently produced the beginnings of a bureaucracy of tax assessors and collectors in many states.

People naturally resisted the burden of new taxes, and monarchs naturally responded to the resistance. This tension led to the third development. Monarchs attempted to weaken the institutional seats of resistance by abolishing the tax-exempt privileges of local communities and ignoring regional assemblies and parliaments that were supposed to approve new taxes. During the twelfth and thirteenth centuries, effective government was local government, and kings seldom had the power to interfere in the affairs of towns and regions. During the fifteenth century, however, kings everywhere attempted to eliminate or erode the independence of towns and regional parliaments in order to raise taxes more effectively and to express the royal will throughout the realm.

The fourth development, closely linked to the third, can be seen in monarchs' attempts to constrain the independence of the aristocracy and the Church. In virtually every kingdom, the most significant threats to the power of the king were the powerful aristocrats. In England a civil war among aristocrats almost tore the kingdom apart. Kings everywhere struggled to co-opt or force submission from these aristocrats. Likewise, the autonomy of the Church threatened monarchical authority, and most monarchs took measures to oblige churchmen to act as agents of government policy.

The fifth development in the evolution of the European state system was the institution of resident ambassadors. During the Italian Wars, the kings of Europe began to exchange permanent, resident ambassadors who were responsible for informing their sovereign about conditions in the host country and representing the interests of their country abroad. Resident ambassadors became the linchpins in a sophisticated information network that provided intelligence about the intentions and capabilities of other kings, princes, and cities. These ambassadors typically enjoyed a humanist education, which helped them adapt to many strange and unpredictable situations, understand foreign languages, negotiate effectively, and speak persuasively. Ambassadors cultivated courtly manners, which smoothed over personal conflicts. For the development of the new state system, gathering reliable information became just as important as maintaining armies and collecting taxes.

France: Consolidating Power and Cultivating Renaissance Values

With the largest territory in western Europe and a population of more than 16 million, France had the potential to become the most powerful state in Europe if the king could figure out how to take advantage of the kingdom's size and resources. By 1453 the Hundred Years' War between France and England had come to an end. With the inspiration of Joan of Arc and with the reform of royal finances by the merchant-banker Jacques Coeur, King Charles VII (r. 1422–1461) expelled the English and regained control of his kingdom. Under Charles, France created its first professional army. Equally important, during the Hundred Years' War the Pragmatic Sanction of Bourges° (1438) guaranteed the virtual autonomy of the French Church from papal control, giving the French king unparalleled opportunities to interfere in religious affairs and to exploit Church revenues for government purposes.

Louis XI (r. 1461–1483), called the "Spider King" because of his fondness for secret intrigue, took up the challenge of consolidating power over the great nobles of his kingdom, who thwarted his state building and threatened his throne. When Louis came to power, the Duchy of

Brittany was virtually independent; one great aristocrat, René of Anjou, controlled more territory and was richer than the king himself; and, most dangerous of all, the dukes of Burgundy had carved out their own splendid principality, which celebrated extravagant forms of courtly ritual and threatened to eclipse the prestige of France itself.

Against these powerful rivals, Louis turned to an equally powerful new weapon—the *taille*. During the final years of the Hundred Years' War, in order to support the army, the Estates General (France's parliament) granted the king the *taille*, the right to collect an annual direct tax. After the war, the tax continued and Louis turned it into a permanent source of revenue for himself and his successors. Armed with the financial resources of the *taille*, Louis took on his most rebellious vassal, Charles the Bold, the Duke of Burgundy, and in 1477 professional Swiss infantrymen in the pay of Louis defeated the plumed knights of Burgundy. Charles was killed in battle, and only his daughter Mary's hurried marriage to the Habsburg Archduke Maximilian bought the protection Burgundy needed to prevent France from seizing all of the duchy.

The monarch most responsible for the spread of Renaissance culture in France was Francis I (r. 1515–1547), a sportsman and warrior who thrilled to the frenzy of battle. Much of his early career was devoted to pursuing French interests in the Italian Wars, until he was captured in battle in 1525 in Italy. Thereafter he focused more on patronizing Italian artists and humanists at his court and importing Italian Renaissance styles. He had the first Renaissance-style chateau built in the Loire Valley and hired artists, including Leonardo da Vinci. As a result of Francis's patronage, Italy was no longer the exclusive center of Renaissance culture.

Spain: Unification by Marriage

In the early fifteenth century the Iberian peninsula was a diverse place, lacking political unity. It was home to several different kingdoms—Portugal, Castile, Navarre, and Aragon, which were all Christian, and Granada, which was Muslim. Each kingdom had its own laws, political institutions, customs, and languages. Unlike France, the Christian kingdoms of medieval Iberia were poor, underpopulated, and preoccupied with the reconquest, the attempt to drive

---

DOCUMENT

The Expulsion of the Jews from Spain

In 1492 after the conquest of Granada, the last Muslim kingdom on the Iberian peninsula, Ferdinand and Isabella ordered the expulsion of all Jews, who were given three months to leave Spain. Some sought an agreement to remain in the country in return for the payment of a large sum of money. However, the Jews soon discovered that was impossible. This account was written by a Jew living in Italy in 1495 who assembled his information from the reports of Jewish refugees.

Then they saw that there was evil determined against them by the King, and they gave up the hope of remaining. But the time had become short, and they had to hasten their exodus from Spain. They sold their houses, their landed estates, and their cattle for very small prices to save themselves. The King did not allow them to carry silver and gold out of his country, so that they were compelled to exchange their silver and gold for merchandise of cloths and skins and other things. . . .

One hundred and twenty thousand of them went to Portugal, according to a compact which a prominent man, Don Vidal bar Benveniste del Cavalleria, had made with the King of Portugal, and they paid one ducat for every soul, and the fourth part of all the merchandise they had carried thither; and he allowed them to stay in his country six months. This King acted much worse toward them than the King of Spain, and after the six months had elapsed he made

slaves of all those that remained in his country, and banished seven hundred children to a remote island to settle it, and all of them died. Some say that there were double as many. . . .

Many of the exiled Spaniards went to Mohammedan countries. . . . On account of their large numbers the Moors did not allow them into their cities, and many of them died in the fields from hunger, thirst, and lack of everything. The lions and bears, which are numerous in this country, killed some of them while they lay starving outside of the cities.

When the edict of expulsion became known in the other countries, vessels came from Genoa to the Spanish harbors to carry away the Jews. The crews of these vessels, too, acted maliciously and meanly toward the Jews, robbed them, and delivered some of them to the famous pirate of that time who was called the Corsair of Genoa. To those who escaped and arrived at Genoa the people of the city showed themselves merciless, and oppressed and robbed them, and the cruelty of their wicked hearts went so far that they took the infants from their mothers' breasts.

Many ships with Jews, especially from Sicily, went to the city of Naples on the coast. The King of this country was friendly to the Jews, received them all, and was merciful towards them, and he helped them with money. The Jews that were at Naples supplied them with food as much as they could, and sent around to the other parts of Italy to collect money to sustain them. . . . Even the Dominican Brotherhood acted mercifully toward them. . . .

Source: Jacob R. Marcus, ed., *The Jew in the Medieval World: A Source Book, 315–1791* (Cincinnati: Sinai Press, 1938), 51–55.

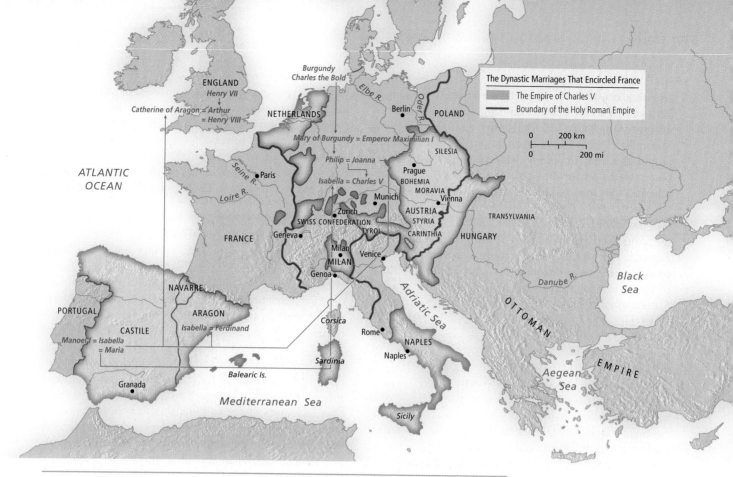

Map 11.3 The Dynastic Marriages That Encircled France

Through skillfully arranging the marriages of their sons and daughters, Ferdinand of Aragon and Isabella of Castile managed to completely surround the rival kingdom of France with a network of alliances.

the Muslims from the peninsula. There was little reason to assume that this region would become one of the greatest powers in Europe, the rival of France.

That rise to power began with a wedding. In 1469 Isabella, who later would become queen of Castile (r. 1474–1504), married Ferdinand, who later would be king of Aragon (r. 1479–1516). The objective of this arranged marriage was to solidify an alliance between the two kingdoms, not to unify them, but in 1479 Castile and Aragon were combined into the kingdom of Spain. Of the two, Castile was the larger, with a population of perhaps six million, and the richer because of the government-supported sheep-raising industry called the *Mesta*. Aragon had less than a million people and was a hybrid of three very distinct regions that had nothing in common except that they shared the same king. Together Isabella and Ferdinand, each still ruling their own kingdoms, at least partially subdued the rebellious aristocracy and built up a bureaucracy of well-educated middle-class lawyers and priests to manage the administration of the government.

The Christian kings of Iberia had long aspired to making the entire peninsula Christian. In 1492 the armies of Isabella and Ferdinand defeated the last remaining Iberian

Muslim kingdom of Granada. While celebrating the victory over Islam, the monarchs made two momentous decisions. The first was to rid Spain of Jews as well as Muslims. Isabella and Ferdinand decreed that within six months all Jews must either convert to Christianity or leave. To enforce conformity to Christianity among the converted Jews who did not leave, the king and queen authorized an ecclesiastical tribunal, the Spanish Inquisition, to investigate the sincerity of conversions. The second decision was Isabella's alone. She financed a voyage by a Genoese sea captain, Christopher Columbus, to sail west into the Atlantic in an attempt to reach India and China. Isabella's intention seems to have been to outflank the Muslim kingdoms of the Middle East and find allies in Asia. As we shall see in the next chapter, Columbus's voyage had consequences more far-reaching than Isabella's intentions, adding to the crown of Castile immense lands in the Americas.

Despite the diversity of their kingdoms, Isabella and Ferdinand made Spain a great power. The clever dynastic marriages they arranged for their children allowed Spain to encircle rival France and established the framework for the diplomatic relations among European states for the next century and a half (see Map 11.3). Their eldest daughter and, after her death, her sister were married to the king of Portugal. Their son and another daughter, Joanna, married offspring of Mary of Burgundy and the Emperor Maximilian I of the Holy Roman Empire. Joanna's marriage produced a son, Charles V, who amassed extraordinary power. He succeeded to the Habsburg lands of Burgundy, inherited the crowns of Castile and Aragon (r. 1516–1556), was elected Holy Roman Emperor (r. 1519–1558), ruled over the Spanish conquests in Italy, and was the emperor of the Indies, which included all of Spanish Central and South America. This was the greatest accumulation of territories by a European ruler since Charlemagne. The encirclement of France was completed with the wedding of Isabella and Ferdinand's daughter Catherine of Aragon to the Prince of Wales and, after his death, to his brother, King Henry VIII (r. 1509–1547) of England.

The Holy Roman Empire: The Costs of Decentralization

Like Spain, the Holy Roman Empire saw powerful France as its most dangerous enemy. And when the French king's invasion of Italy initiated the Italian Wars, it launched a struggle that pitted the empire and Spain against France for the next 200 years. Members of the Habsburg family had been elected to the throne of the Holy Roman Empire since 1438. Emperor Maximilian I (r. 1493–1519) wed Mary, the daughter of Charles the Bold of Burgundy, and although they were not able to preserve all of Burgundy from the French, they did keep substantial parts, including the extremely rich Netherlands.

In an era of coolly calculating monarchs, Maximilian cut an odd figure. Like his father-in-law, Charles the Bold, he loved chivalry and enjoyed nothing more than to play the role of a knight leading his men into battle. The problem was that he was not very good in that role. His military adventures led to a series of disasters, often at the hands of the rough Swiss mercenaries who were experts in using the pike (a long pole with a metal spearhead) to cut up aristocratic cavalrymen and who passionately hated everything about the autocratic Habsburgs who had once ruled their lands. Maximilian also came under the influence of Italian Renaissance culture and imagined himself another Caesar with a special mission to reconquer Italy for the Holy Roman Empire. The French invasion of Italy in 1494 drew him into the quagmire of Italian affairs as he attempted to counter French influence there. His erratic military policies, however, could not quite keep pace with these imperial ambitions.

Maximilian's inability to execute a consistent military policy in Italy was a consequence of the highly decentralized nature of the empire. Unlike the other European monarchs who inherited their thrones at the death of their predecessors, the emperor was selected by seven electors, who even after an election exercised considerable independent power. The German part of the Holy Roman Empire, home to 15 to 20 million people, was composed of some 300 sovereign and quasi-sovereign principalities and free cities (legally exempt from direct imperial rule). Besides the emperor, only a few institutions served to unify the empire. Most important was the imperial diet, an assembly that included the seven electors, other princes, and representatives of the imperial free cities. The imperial diet was established during the fifteenth century to control the relentless feuding among the German princes, but it often became instead a forum for resisting the emperor.

Maximilian's reign produced some limited reforms. These included a moratorium on feuds, a Supreme Court to impose ancient Roman law throughout the German-speaking portions of the empire, a graduated property and income tax, and eventually an imperial council to exercise executive functions in the absence of the emperor. In practice, however, these institutions worked only to the degree that the emperor and German princes cooperated. The empire remained a fractured, dissent-ridden jumble with no real unity. Compared to the centralizing monarchies in France, Spain, and England, or even to the better managed among the Italian city-states such as tiny Venice, which recurrently defeated Maximilian in battle, the empire under Maximilian was little more than a glorious-sounding name.

England: From Civil War to Stability Under the Tudors

At the end of the Hundred Years' War in 1453, the English crown was defeated. Thousands of disbanded mercenaries were let loose in England and enlisted with one quarreling side or the other in feuds among aristocratic families. The mercenaries brought to England the evil habits of pillage, murder, and violence they had previously practiced in the wars with France. King Henry VI (r. 1422–1461) suffered from bouts of madness that made him unfit to rule and unable to control the disorder. Under the tensions caused by defeat and revolt, the royal family fractured into the two houses of Lancaster and York, which fought a vicious civil war, now known as the Wars of the Roses (1455–1485) from the red and white roses used to identify members of the two opposing sides.

After decades of bloody conflict, the cynical but able Richard III (r. 1483–1485) usurped the throne from his 12-year-old nephew Edward V and had Edward and his brother imprisoned in the Tower of London, where they were murdered, perhaps on Richard's orders. Richard's apparent cruelty and his scandalous intent to marry Edward's young sister, now heir to the throne, precipitated open defections against him. When Henry Tudor challenged Richard, many nobles flocked to Henry's banner. At the Battle of Bosworth Field (1485), Richard was slain and his crown discovered on the field of battle. His naked corpse was dragged off and buried in an unmarked grave.

The Tower of London

When Henry Tudor became King Henry VII (r. 1485–1509), there was little reason to believe that exhausted England could again become a major force in European events. It took years of patient effort for Henry to become safe on his own throne. He revived the Court of Star Chamber as an instrument of royal will to punish unruly nobles who had long bribed and intimidated their way out of trouble with the courts. Because the king's own hand-picked councilors served as judges, Henry could guarantee that the court system became more equitable and obedient to his wishes. Henry confiscated the lands of the rebellious lords, thereby increasing his own income, and he prohibited all private armies except those that served his interests. By managing his administration efficiently, eliminating unnecessary expenses, and staying out of war, Henry governed without the need to call on Parliament for increased revenues.

England was still a backward country and, with fewer than three million people, a fraction of the size of France. By nourishing an alliance with newly unified Spain, Henry was able to bring England back into European affairs. When his son Henry VIII succeeded to the throne, the Tudor dynasty was more secure than any of its predecessors and England more stable than it had ever been before. By the reign of Henry VII's granddaughter, Elizabeth I (r. 1558–1603), England could boast of a splendid Renaissance court and a fleet that would make it a world power.

The Origins of Modern Historical and Political Thought

The revival of the monarchies of western Europe and the loss of the independence of the Italian city-states forced a rethinking of politics. As in so many other fields, the Florentines led the way. In an attempt to understand their own troubled city-state, they analyzed politics by making historical comparisons between one kind of government and another and by carefully observing current events. Two crucial figures in these developments, Francesco Guicciardini and Niccolò Machiavelli, had both served Florence as diplomats, an experience that was crucial in forming their views.

History: The Search for Causes
During the fifteenth century there were two kinds of historians. The first kind consisted of chroniclers who kept records of the important events in their city or principality. The chroniclers recorded a great deal of factual information in the simple form of one-occurrence-after-another. In so doing they established chronologies, which meant they arranged history according to a sequence of dates. But they lacked any sense of how one event caused another, and they

CHRONOLOGY

The Early Modern European State System

1422–1461	Reign of Charles VII of France
1455–1485	Wars of the Roses in England
1461–1483	Reign of Louis XI of France
1474–1504	Reign of Isabella of Castile
1479–1516	Reign of Ferdinand of Aragon
1479	Unification of Spain
1483–1485	Reign of Richard III of England
1485–1509	Reign of Henry VII of England
1492	Conquest of Granada; expulsion of the Jews from Spain; voyage of Christopher Columbus
1493–1519	Reign of Maximilian I, Holy Roman Emperor
1494–1530	The Italian Wars
1515–1547	Reign of Francis I of France
1516–1556	Reign of Charles I, king of Spain, who also became Charles V, Holy Roman Emperor (1519–1558)

failed to interpret the meaning and consequences of the decisions leaders and other people had made.

The second kind of historians consisted of the humanists. Petrarch established that the fundamental principle for writing humanist history was to maintain historical distance—the sense that the past was past and had to be reconstructed in its own terms. The most dangerous historical error in writing history became anachronism, that is, imposing present sensibilities and understandings on the past. Before the Renaissance the most common version of anachronism was for historians to interpret pre-Christian history in the light of Christian understandings of God's plan for humanity. In contrast to that approach, humanist historians attempted to offer explanations for why things had happened in human terms. When they interpreted past events, they tried to respect the limitations people had faced. For example, they understood that the moral code of the Roman orator and senator Cicero, who died two generations before Jesus was born, derived from Greek philosophy and Roman ethics rather than a premonition of Christianity. The humanists' interest in rhetoric, however, led them to make moral judgments about the past in an attempt to encourage morality among their readers. Thus, they were prone to pull especially compelling instances of good or bad conduct out of the historical context in which it had taken place and to compare it with other cases. For example, they might compare the behavior of the citizens in fifth-century-B.C.E. Athens with the actions of citizens in fifteenth-century Florence.

The shock of the Italian Wars that began in 1494 stimulated a quest for understanding the causes of Italy's fall and prompted a new kind of history writing. The first person to write a successful history in the new vein was Francesco Guicciardini (1483–1540). Born to a well-placed Florentine family, educated in a humanist school, and experienced as a diplomat, governor, and adviser to the Medicis, Guicciardini combined literary skill and practical political experience. Besides collecting information about contemporary events, Guicciardini kept a record of how his own thoughts and values evolved in response to what he observed. One of the hallmarks of his work was that as he analyzed the motives of others, he engaged in self-scrutiny and self-criticism.

From this habit of criticizing himself and others, Guicciardini developed a strong interpretive framework for his histories. His masterpiece, *The History of Italy* (1536–1540), was the first account of events that occurred across the entire Italian peninsula. In many respects, this book originated the idea that Italy is more than just a geographical term and has had a common historical experience. Like the humanist historians, Guicciardini saw human causes for historical events rather than the hidden hand of God, but he refined the understanding of causation through his psychological insights. He suggested, for example, that emotions mattered more than rational calculation and noted that nothing ever turns out quite as anticipated.

Political Thought: Considering the End Result

Guicciardini's contemporary and Florentine compatriot Niccolò Machiavelli (1469–1527) also wrote histories, but he is best known as a political theorist. Trained as a humanist, he lacked the personal wealth and family connections that allowed Guicciardini to move as a matter of birthright in high social and political circles. As seen in the story that opened this chapter, Machiavelli had worked as a diplomat and military official but was exiled for complicity in a plot against the Medici family, who had retaken Florence in 1512. While in exile he wrote a book of advice for the Medicis in the vain hope that they would give him back his job. They probably never read his little book, *The Prince* (1513), but it became a classic in political thought. In it he encouraged rulers to understand the underlying principles of political power, which differed from the personal morality expected of those who were not rulers. He thought it was important for a prince to appear to be a moral person, but Machiavelli pointed out that the successful prince might sometimes be obliged to be immoral in order to protect the interests of the state. How would the prince know when this might be the case?

DOCUMENT

Machiavelli's *The Prince*

DOCUMENT

Machiavelli on the Source of Liberty

Niccolò Machiavelli is best known for his book, The Prince, *which offers advice to princes on how to rule. His more important study, however, was* The Discourses of the First Decade of Livy *(1516–1519), which discussed how a republic should be governed. In this book he asked how the ancient Roman Republic managed to be both free and powerful. His startling answer was that all liberty and greatness in republics comes from class conflict.*

It seems to me that those who criticize the conflicts between the nobles and the plebeians [the lower classes of ancient Rome] condemn those very things which were the primary cause of Roman liberty, and that they pay more attention to the noises and cries raised by such quarrels than to the good effects that they brought forth; nor do they consider that in every republic there are two different inclinations: that of the people and that of the upper class, and that all the laws which are made in favor of liberty are born of the conflict between the two, as one can easily see from what happened in Rome. . . .

And the desires of free peoples are very rarely pernicious to liberty, for they arise from being oppressed or from the suspicion of future oppression. And should these opinions prove to be mistaken, there is the remedy of public meetings, in which some good man of influence may rise up and make a speech showing them that they are mistaken.

Source: *The Portable Machiavelli*, translated by Peter Bondanella and Mark Musa (Penguin Books, 1970), 183–84.

Machiavelli's answer was that "necessity" forced political decisions to go against normal morality. The prince "must consider the end result," which meant that his highest obligation was preserving the very existence of the state, which had been entrusted to him and which provided security for all citizens of the state. This obligation was higher even than his obligation to religion.

Machiavelli's *The Prince* has sometimes been considered a blueprint for tyrants. However, as his more learned and serious work, *The Discourses of the First Decade of Livy* (1516–1519), makes clear, Machiavelli himself preferred a free republic over a despotic princely government. In some ways, *The Discourses* is an even more radical work than *The Prince* because it suggests that class conflict is the source of political liberty: "In every republic there are two different inclinations: that of the people and that of the upper class, and . . . all the laws which are made in favor of liberty are born of the conflict between the two."[8] In this passage,

Machiavelli suggested that political turmoil was not necessarily a bad thing, because it was by provoking conflict that the lower classes prevented the upper classes from acting like tyrants.

In all his works, Machiavelli sought to understand the dynamics behind political events. To do this, he theorized that human events were the product of the interaction between two forces. One force was fortune, a term derived from the name of the ancient Roman goddess Fortuna. Fortune stood for all things beyond human control and could be equated with luck or chance. Machiavelli depicted fortune as extremely powerful, like an irresistible flood that swept all before it or like the headstrong goddess who determined the fate of men. Fortune controlled perhaps half of all human events. The problem with fortune was its changeability and unpredictability: "since Fortune changes and men remain set in their ways, men will succeed when the two are in harmony and fail when they are not in accord." How could rulers or even simple citizens put themselves in harmony with fortune and predict its shifts? The answer could be found in the characteristics of the second force, virtue, which he understood as deriving from the Roman concept of *virtus*, literally "manliness." The best description of virtue could be found in the code expected of an ancient Roman warrior: strength, loyalty, and courage. If a man possessed these traits he was most likely to be able to confront the unpredictable. As Machiavelli put it, "I am certainly convinced of this: that it is better to be impetuous than cautious."[9] The man possessing virtue, therefore, looked for opportunities to take control of events before they took control of him. In that way he put himself in harmony with fortune.

Through Guicciardini's analysis of human motivations and Machiavelli's attempt to discover the hidden forces behind events, history and political thought moved in a new direction. The key to understanding history and politics was in the details of human events. To Guicciardini these details provided clues to the psychology of leaders. To Machiavelli they revealed the hidden mechanisms of chance and planning that governed not just political decisions but all human events.

Conclusion

The Politics of Culture

The Renaissance began simply enough as an attempt to imitate the Latin style of the best ancient Latin authors and orators. Within a generation, however, humanists and artists pushed this narrowly technical literary project into a full-scale attempt to refashion human society on the model of ancient cultures. Reading about the ancients and looking at their works of art provoked comparisons with contemporary Renaissance society. The result was the development of a critical approach to the past and present. The critical approach was accompanied by an enhanced historical sensibility, which transformed the idea of the West from one defined primarily by religious identification with Christianity to one forged by a common historical experience.

During the sixteenth century, western Europeans absorbed the critical-historical methods of the Renaissance and turned them in new directions. As shown in the next chapter, Spanish and Portuguese sailors encountered previously unknown cultures in the Americas and only vaguely known ones in Africa and Asia. Because of the Renaissance, those who thought and wrote about these strange new cultures did so with the perspective of antiquity in mind. As shown in Chapter 13, in northern Europe the critical historical methods of the humanists were used to better understand the historical sources of Christianity, especially the Bible. With that development, Christianity began to take on new shades of meaning, and many thoughtful Christians attempted to make the practices of the Church conform more closely to the Bible. The humanist approach to religion led down a path that permanently divided Christians into contending camps over the interpretation of Scripture, breaking apart the hard-won unity of the Roman Catholic West.

Suggestions for Further Reading

For a comprehensive listing of suggested readings, please go to www.ablongman.com/levack2e/chapter11

Baxandall, Michael. *Painting and Experience in Fifteenth Century Italy: A Primer in the Social History of Pictorial Style*. 1988. A fascinating study of how the daily social experiences of Florentine bankers and churchgoers influenced how these individuals saw Renaissance paintings and how painters responded to the viewers' experience. One of the best books on Italian painting.

Brown, Howard M. *Music in the Renaissance*. 1976. Dated but still the best general study of Renaissance music.

Brown, Patricia Fortini. *Art and Life in Renaissance Venice*. 1997. A delightful study about how art fit into the daily lives and homes of the Venetian upper classes.

Brucker, Gene. *Florence: The Golden Age, 1138–1737*. 1998. A brilliant, beautifully illustrated history by the most prominent American historian of Florence.

Burke, Peter. *The Italian Renaissance*. 1999. A concise and readable synthesis of the most recent research.

Hale, J. R. *Renaissance Europe, 1480–1520*. 2000. A witty, engaging, and enlightening study of Europe during the formation of the early modern state system. Strong on establishing the material and social limitations of Renaissance society.

King, Margaret L. *Women of the Renaissance*. 1991. The best general study of women in Renaissance Europe. It is especially strong on female intellectuals and women's education.

Kohl, Benjamin G., and Alison Andrews Smith, eds. *Major Problems in the History of the Italian Renaissance.* 1995. A useful collection of articles and short studies of major historical problems in the study of the Renaissance.

Martines, Lauro. *Power and Imagination: City-States in Renaissance Italy.* 1988. An excellent general survey that is strong on class conflicts and patronage.

Nauert, Charles G., Jr. *Humanism and the Culture of Renaissance Europe.* 1995. The best survey of humanism for students new to the subject. It is clear and comprehensive.

Skinner, Quentin. *Machiavelli: A Very Short Introduction.* 2000. This is the place to begin in the study of Machiavelli. Always clear and precise, this is a beautiful little book.

Stephens, John. *The Italian Renaissance: The Origins of Intellectual and Artistic Change Before the Reformation.* 1990. A stimulating analysis of how cultural change took place.

Vasari, Giorgio. *The Lives of the Artists.* 1998. Written by a sixteenth-century Florentine who was himself a prominent artist, this series of artistic biographies captures the spirit of Renaissance society.

Notes

1. *The Portable Machiavelli,* trans. and ed. Peter Bondanella and Mark Musa (1979), 67–69.

2. Baldesar Castiglione, *The Book of the Courtier,* trans. Charles S. Singleton (1959), 43.

3. Giovanni Villani, *Cronica,* vol. 7 (1823), p. 52. Translation by the authors.

4. Agostino di Colloredo, "Chroniche friulane, 1508–18," *Pagine friulane* 2 (1889), 6. Translation by the authors.

5. Francesco Petrarca, "Letter to the Shade of Cicero," in Kenneth R. Bartlett, ed., *The Civilization of the Italian Renaissance: A Sourcebook* (1992), 31.

6. Quoted in Margaret L. King, *Women of the Renaissance* (1991), 197.

7. "Laura Cereta to Bibulus Sempronius: Defense of the Liberal Instruction of Women," in Margaret King and Alfred Rabil, eds., *Her Immaculate Hand: Selected Words by and About the Women Humanists of Quattrocento Italy* (1983), 82.

8. *The Portable Machiavelli,* 183.

9. Ibid., 161–162.

The West and the World: The Significance of Global Encounters, 1450–1650

12

O N A HOT OCTOBER DAY IN 1492, CHRISTOPHER COLUMBUS AND HIS men, dressed in heavy armor, clanked onto the beach of an island in the Bahamas. The captain and his crew had been at sea sailing west from the Canary Islands for five weeks, propelled by winds they thought would take them straight to Asia. As the ships under Columbus's command vainly searched among the islands of the Caribbean for the rich ports of Asia, Columbus thought he must be in India and thus called the natives he met "Indians." At another point he thought he might be among the Mongols of central Asia, which he described in his journal as the "people of the Great Khan." Both of Columbus's guesses about his location were incorrect, but they have left a revealing linguistic legacy in terms still in use: "Indians" for the native Americans, and both "cannibals" and "Caribbean" from Columbus's inconsistent spellings of Khan. Columbus believed that the people he called the Cannibals or Caribs ate human flesh. But he got that information—also incorrect—from their enemies. Thus began one of the most lasting misunderstandings from Columbus's first voyage.

Historians know very little about the natives' first thoughts of the arrival of their foreign visitors, but they know that the effects of the arrival were catastrophic. Within a few generations the Caribs almost completely died out, replaced by African slaves who worked the plantations of European masters.

Western civilization at the end of the fifteenth century hardly seemed on the verge of encircling the globe with outposts and colonies. Its kingdoms had barely been able to reorganize themselves sufficiently for self-defense, let alone world exploration and foreign conquest. The Venetian and Genoese colonies in the Mediterranean were retreating from the advancing Ottoman Turks, who would continue to occupy the Balkans for at least four more centuries. The Ottoman threat was so great that all of southern Europe was

The Encounter of Three Cultures On this wooden bottle painted in the Incan style about 1650, an African drummer leads a procession, followed by a Spanish trumpeter and an Incan official. The mixing of cultures that occurred after the arrival of the Spanish and Portuguese distinguished the Americas from other civilizations.

on the defensive. And the hostilities had blocked the traditional trade routes to Asia, which had stimulated the great medieval economic expansion of Europe. Scandinavian voyages to North America had ceased in the fourteenth century, and the isolated Western outpost of Christianity in Greenland vanished under the onslaught of advancing ice by the middle of the fifteenth. In comparison with the Ottoman Empire or Ming China, Europe's puny, impoverished states seemed more prone to quarreling among themselves than to seeking expanded horizons.

Nevertheless, by 1500 Europeans could be found fighting and trading in Africa, the Americas, and Asia. A mere fifty years later, Europeans had destroyed the two greatest civilizations in the Americas, had begun the forced migration of Africans to the Americas through the slave trade, and had opened trading posts throughout South and East Asia.

Before 1500 the West, identified by its languages, religions, agricultural technology, literature, folklore, music, art, and common intellectual tradition that stretched back to pre-Christian antiquity, was largely confined to Europe and the Middle East. After 1500, European travelers and missionaries began to export Western culture and technology to the rest of the world and to be greatly influenced themselves by the cultures they encountered abroad, especially after large numbers of European settlers moved to the Americas.

After the sixteenth century, European culture could be found in many distant lands, and western European languages and forms of Christianity were adopted by or forced upon other peoples. The West was now more of an idea than a place, a certain kind of culture that thrived in many different environments. As western Europeans came under the influence of the far-flung cultures they visited, Europe itself was transformed into a much more cosmopolitan region than it had ever been before. The European voyages integrated the globe biologically and economically. Microbes, animals, and plants that had once been isolated were now transported throughout the world. Because the Europeans possessed the ships for transport and the guns for coercion, they became the dominant players in international trade, even in places thousands of miles from the European homeland. The question raised by this first phase of the European global encounters is, how were both the West and the rest of the world transformed?

- **Why did the European incursions into sub-Saharan Africa lead to the vast migration of Africans to the Americas as slaves?**
- **How did the arrival of Europeans in the Americas transform native cultures and life?**
- **Why was the European encounter with Asian civilizations far less disruptive than those in Africa and the Americas?**
- **How was the world tied together in a global biological and economic system?**

Europeans in Africa

- **Why did the European incursions into sub-Saharan Africa lead to the vast migration of Africans to the Americas as slaves?**

Geographers of the ancient world, writing in Greek and Latin, had accumulated a substantial knowledge about all of North Africa, but they were almost completely ignorant of the region south of the Sahara desert. Medieval writers remained equally ill-informed, reporting that sub-Saharan Africa was populated by man-eaters, "great giants of twenty-eight foot long . . . and they eat more gladly man's flesh than any other flesh," and Amazons, warrior women who cut off one breast to facilitate archery.

In fact, the interior of sub-Saharan Africa had been governed for centuries by highly developed kingdoms and boasted numerous wealthy cities. By the fifteenth century, Muslim contacts with sub-Saharan Africa made it clear that the region was a rich source of gold and slaves. In search of these, Europeans, especially the Portuguese, began to journey down the west coast of Africa. Enabled by new developments in ship technology, the Europeans were capable of making long sea voyages. European settlers founded colonies in the Atlantic islands off the west coast of Africa, establishing precedents for colonies that would later be installed in the Americas.

Sub-Saharan Africa Before the Europeans Arrived

During the Middle Ages a number of kingdoms that emulated ancient Egyptian forms of rulership arose south of the Sahara desert. Some kingdoms boasted large cities and consisted of as many as a million inhabitants who were subjects of strongly centralized regimes. The kingdoms were administered by public officials who could be transferred, demoted, or promoted according to the king's will in a bureaucratic system that paralleled what the European states had achieved.

For Europeans, the principal attraction to Africa were reports of its rich deposits of gold. These reports came from the Muslim kingdom of Mali, a landlocked empire between the Upper Senegal and Niger Rivers, to the north of the Guinea coast. The source of Mali's wealth was its monopoly of the gold caravans that carried the coveted metal from the fabled city of Timbuktu across the Sahara to the gold-greedy Mediterranean. The king of Mali, known as the Mansa, never owned the gold mines, the location of which was a closely kept secret, but he controlled the gold market. The

The Catalan Map

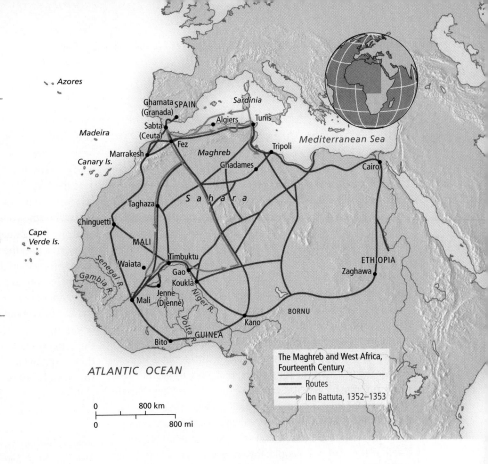

Map 12.1   The Maghreb and West Africa, Fourteenth Century

Long before the arrival of the Portuguese via sea routes, caravans of camels crisscrossed the Sahara desert during the fourteenth century, linking the sources of gold in Mali with the Maghreb (the coast of northwest Africa) and the seaports of the Mediterranean. The greatest medieval Arabic traveler, Ibn Battuta (1304–1368/69), crossed the Sahara and spent more than a year in Mali. He left the most extensive account of medieval West Africa.

gold from the mines went to the Mansa, whose agents traded it in distant lands for luxury goods. The Mansa's power rested on his cavalry, which by the middle of the fourteenth century had spread the rule of Mali from the Gambia and lower Senegal Rivers to the West through the Niger valley to the south.

The wealth of the Mansa became legendary after Mansa Musa (r. 1312–1337) conducted a spectacular pilgrimage to the Muslim holy city of Mecca in 1324. Mansa Musa made a magnificently opulent impression. A gold bird sat above the parasol that shaded him from the sun, and he carried a gilded staff, wore a goldskull cap, strung a gold quiver over his shoulder, and affixed a gold scabbard to his waist. The pilgrimage took more than a year, and Mansa Musa was so generous that his trip was remembered for centuries in Egypt, where he stayed for three months. He gave out so much gold that Egypt suffered a disastrous inflation of prices. Traveling with as many as a hundred camels, each loaded with 300 pounds of gold, the Mansa gave whole ingots of gold to officials along the way and to religious shrines he visited.

By 1400, however, the kingdom of Mali was in decline. Internal power struggles had split apart the once-vast empire. In 1482, when the Portuguese founded a gold-trading post at Elmina, some sixty miles west of the mouth of the Volta, they had to negotiate with a ruler called the Karamansa, whose title echoed the past glories of the Mansa of Mali but whose power was a mere shadow of what the rulers of Mali exercised during the fourteenth century (see Map 12.1).

Influenced by Mali, the forest kingdoms of Guinea were built on a prosperous urban society and extensive trading networks. Benin was a particularly great city, which European travelers compared favorably with the principal European cities of the time. The towns of Guinea held regu-

lar markets, similar to the periodic fairs of Europe, and carefully scheduled them so they would not compete with each other. The staples of the long-distance trade routes in this region were high-value luxury goods, especially imported cloth, kola nuts (a mild stimulant popular in Muslim countries), metalwork such as cutlasses, ivory, and of course gold. For money, African traders used cowrie shells, brought all the way from the Indian Ocean.

Unlike the kingdoms of the western sub-Sahara, which tended to be Muslim, mountainous Ethiopia was predominantly Christian. In fact, Europeans saw Ethiopians as potential allies against Islam. The Roman Catholic pope sent a delegation to Ethiopia in 1316, and Ethiopian embassies occasionally appeared in Italy and Portugal during the fifteenth century. Diplomatic contacts between Rome and Ethiopia intensified at the time of the Council of Florence in 1439, which attempted to unify Christianity in defense against the onslaught of the Muslim Ottoman Turks. Learned Ethiopian churchmen became known in western Europe and created the impression that Ethiopia was an abundant land peopled by pious Christians.

Conditions during the later Middle Ages tended to confirm this image of Ethiopia. Threatened by Muslim invaders in 1270, the Ethiopian kingdom created a powerful army, rumors of which tantalized European Christians who sought allies against Islam. As the armies expanded Ethiopian power to the south and east, missionaries proselytized among the conquered peoples and helped unify the kingdom. Ethiopian expansion greatly enriched the kingdom through the control of trade in ivory, gold, slaves, and

The Kings of West Africa

During the late sixteenth century a Dutch merchant, Pieter de Mareers, traveled to the kingdom of Guinea. During the sixteenth century what was known as the Gold Coast, now modern Ghana, was divided into more than a dozen states, some monarchies, some governed by collective councils. In this account Mareers described one of the more powerful kings.

The Kings are elected by the common people and by the highest vote; for the Kingdom does not devolve on friends or descendants, and even someone's children do not inherit. So, when the King is dead, they elect another to govern them and possess the Kingdom, and he takes possession of the Court, together with all that is in it. For his inauguration he must in the first place buy many Cows and much Palm wine and give these to his Subjects as a present; for they very much love a King who often fetes them, but hate a King who is frugal and keen on accumulating Gold. They will not respect such a King and he is not loved by the common people: they bear him great hatred and jealousy, seeking every means of taking action against him, in order to drive him out and choose a better person who is to their liking. . . .

His wives live with him in his Palace, and some also outside the Court; but these are the oldest wives, whom he does not love all that much and who can no longer please him. To each of the young and beautiful wives he normally gives separate living quarters, within his Palace, in order that they may serve him the better and [he] may have his comfort. These women do their husband the King great service and each fetes him as best she can in order to be loved by him; so he does not lack any services or comfort. Each woman has her own goods and wealth, and each also maintains and brings up her own children. Those who are the favourites of the King [do not] stand in want of anything. Whenever these women go out they lean on the shoulders of other women who serve them and are their Slaves; likewise the children are carried on the shoulders of other blacks or Slaves of the King.

Source: *Pieter de Mareers: Description and Historical Account of the Gold Kingdom of Guines* (1602), edited by A. Van Dantzig and A. Jones (1987), pp. 94–97. British Academy.

civet, a highly prized musky perfume. Portuguese visitors were duly impressed by the splendor of the emperor of Ethiopia, the Negus, who traveled with 2,000 attendants and 50,000 mules to carry provisions and tents.

By the early sixteenth century, the Ethiopian kingdom had become overextended. In the 1520s and 1530s Muslims attacked deep into the Ethiopian heartland, raiding and burning the wealthy Ethiopian monasteries. The raids severely weakened the power of the Negus. By destroying relics and religious images, the Muslims eradicated much of the great artistic heritage of Ethiopia. Ethiopia survived with the help of a Portuguese expeditionary force, but it was hobbled by competing Christian warlords and a weak central power, and it never regained its previous strength.

During the fifteenth and sixteenth centuries when European contacts with the sub-Sahara dramatically expanded, the once-strong kingdoms were either in decline or engaged in protracted struggles with regional rivals. The Europeans arrived at precisely the moment when they could take advantage of the weaknesses produced by internal African conflicts.

European Voyages Along the African Coast

Although sub-Saharan Africa represented something of a mystery to Europeans, merchants from Italy, Catalonia, Castile, and Portugal had long shown interest in the ports of the Maghreb, the collective name for the present-day regions of Morocco, Algeria, and Tunisia on the Mediterranean coast of North Africa. There they brought wool and woolen textiles, wine, dye stuffs, and clandestine items such as weapons, which they traded for various commodities, most significantly gold. Since at least the mid-thirteenth century, the Maghreb had been famous as the northern terminus of the gold caravans from Mali. In the thirteenth and fourteenth centuries, European traders obtained gold in the Maghreb in exchange for silver mined in Europe. They then resold the gold in the ports along the northern shore of the Mediterranean for more silver than they had originally paid to buy the gold. With the handsome silver profits made in the gold trade, merchants provided a steady supply that encouraged the general adoption of gold coinage throughout much of southern Europe. Gold was highly prized in Europe largely because it was rare in comparison to silver, and by the laws of supply and demand the commodity that is scarce is more valuable.

To gain more direct access to the sources of gold, European traders occasionally crossed the Sahara with camel caravans—the "ships of the desert." For example, the Florentine merchant Benedetto Dei told of traveling in 1470 as far as Timbuktu, where he saw many examples of European textiles on the local market. The efficient camel caravans created a vast trading network that stretched from Mali and Morocco in the west of Africa into central Asia,

The Lure of Gold
From the first Portuguese expeditions along the coast of West Africa to the extensive European explorations of the Americas, a persistent lure was finding gold. Columbus and the conquistadores seemed obsessed with finding gold. This illustration from the sixteenth century depicts North American native techniques for collecting gold, which involved digging in the mud of river bottoms and then sifting the soil to look for gold nuggets. Similar techniques were employed in Africa.

completely bypassing the Mediterranean. But Europeans had little hope of regularly using the "sea of sand" routes across North Africa because of the hostility of Muslim inhabitants who were wary about foreign interlopers, especially Christian ones.

The alternative for Europeans was to outflank the Muslims by crossing the sea of water. As early as the thirteenth century, European voyagers ventured down the west coast of Africa into uncharted waters. In 1291 the Vivaldi brothers left Genoa with the goal of circumnavigating Africa to reach the Indies. But their galleys were adapted to the relatively calm waters of the Mediterranean and were ill-suited for the voyage on the heavy seas of the Atlantic. Such ships, which required large crews of oarsmen, were easily swamped in the Atlantic, and the long coastline of West Africa lacked protective harbors for refuge from storms. The Vivaldi expedition disappeared without a trace.

New Maritime Technology

The disadvantages of Mediterranean galleys were surmounted during the fifteenth century through changes in the technology of ocean sailing. The Iberian peninsula (the land of present-day Portugal and Spain), situated between the Mediterranean and the Atlantic, was uniquely located to develop a hybrid ship that combined features of Mediterranean and Atlantic designs. The initial impulse for developing the shipping technology was to facilitate trade between the Mediterranean and northern Europe via the Atlantic. The resulting changes, however, also made possible much more ambitious voyages into the unknown southern regions.

The Iberians modified the cog design, the dominant ship in the Atlantic, by adding extra masts and creating a new kind of rigging that combined the square sails of Atlantic ships, suitable for sailing in the same direction as the wind was blowing, with the triangular "lateen" sails of Mediterranean galleys, which permitted sailing into the wind. The result was a ship that could sail in a variety of winds, carry large cargoes, be managed by a small crew, and be defended by guns mounted in the castle superstructure. These hybrid three-mast ships, called caravels°, appeared about 1450, and for the next 200 years Europeans sailed ships of this same basic design on long ocean voyages to the very ends of the Earth.

Also assisting European navigators were other technological innovations, the fruit of late medieval Mediterranean seafaring. The compass provided an approximate indicator of direction, and the astrolabe and naked-eye celestial navigation made it possible to estimate latitudes. Books of sailing directions, called portolanos°, included charts and descriptions of ports and recorded the location of dangerous shoals and safe harbors for future voyages. The advances in maritime technology made it possible for Europeans motivated by economic need and religious fervor to sail wherever they wanted.

Technology alone, however, does not explain the extent of the European voyages because there had been great ocean navigating efforts before. For centuries Polynesians had successfully navigated their way across the Pacific Ocean. The Vikings had regularly crossed the North Atlantic from the tenth to fourteenth centuries, and the Chinese had engaged in extensive exploratory voyages throughout the Indian Ocean earlier in the fifteenth century. The explanation for

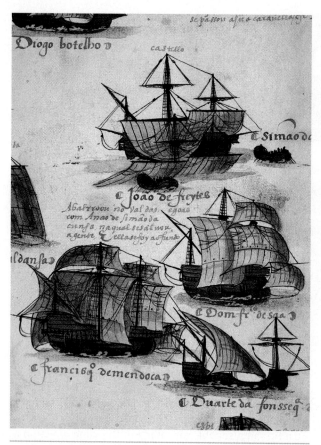

Early Caravels
The caravel was typical of the hybrid ship developed during the fifteenth century on the Iberian peninsula. The ship on the lower right is rigged with a lateen sail on its main mast.

the voyages must be sought in the European Christian imperative to profit from an expanded trade network and to outflank the Muslims who blocked the eastern trade routes.

New Colonialism

During the fifteenth century, European colonialism departed from the patterns of the past. Mediterranean colonies established during the Crusades of the twelfth and thirteenth centuries had relied on native inhabitants to produce commodities that could be expropriated by the colonizers. These were either aristocratic colonies in which a few warriors occupied castles to dominate the native population or mercantile colonies built around a trading post for foreign merchants.

As Europeans ventured into the Atlantic more frequently and expanded their contacts with sub-Saharan Africa, they established new patterns of colonization. In search of fertile lands for agriculture, Castile and Portugal founded colonies in the Canary Islands, the Madeira archipelago, the Azores, and the Cape Verde Islands. The climate of these islands was similar to that of the Mediterranean and invited the cultivation of typical Mediterranean crops, such as grains and

sugar cane, but the islands lacked a native labor force. When Europeans arrived, the Canaries had few inhabitants and the other islands were uninhabited. In response to the labor shortage, two new types of colonies emerged, both of which were later introduced into the Americas.

The first new type of colony during this period was the settler colony°. The settler colony derived from the medieval, feudal model of government, in which a private person obtained a license from a king to seize an island or some part of an island. The king supplied financial support and legal authority for the expedition. In return the settler promised to recognize the king as his lord and occasionally to pay a fee after the settlement was successful. The kings of Castile and Portugal issued such licenses for the exploitation of Atlantic islands. The actual expeditions to colonize these islands were private enterprises, and adventurers from various parts of Europe vied for a license from any king who would grant them one. For example, the first European settlement in the Canary Islands was led by a Norman knight, Jean de Béthencourt, who could not obtain sufficient support from the king of France and thus switched loyalties to the king of Castile.

After the arrival of the Europeans, all the natives of the Canaries, called the Guanches, were killed or died off from European diseases, creating the need for settler families from Europe to till the land and maintain the Castilian claim on the islands. These peasants and artisans, rather than living like islanders and adapting to the native culture, imported their own culture. They brought with them their traditional family structures, customs, language, religion, seeds, livestock, and patterns of cultivation. Wherever settler colonies were found, whether in the Atlantic islands or the Americas, which the Europeans called the New World, they Europeanized the landscape and remade the lands they cultivated in the image of the Old World.

The second new type of colony was the plantation colony°. Until the occupation of the Cape Verde Islands in the 1460s, the Atlantic island colonies had relied on European settlers for labor. However, the Cape Verdes attracted few immigrants because of the rigors of the tropical climate, and yet the islands seemed especially well-suited for growing the lucrative sugar cane crop. The few permanent European colonists there tended to be exiled criminals, and the Cape Verdes became a haven for lawless ruffians who were disinclined to work. Because there was no indigenous population to exploit on the Cape Verdes, the few European colonizers began to look elsewhere for laborers and voyaged to the African coast, where they bought slaves who had been captured from inland villages. These slaves worked as agricultural laborers in the Cape Verdes sugar cane fields. Thus in the Cape Verdes began the tragic conjunction between African slavery and the European demand for sugar. When sugar began to replace honey as the sweetener of choice for Europeans, the almost insatiable demand was supplied by sugar cultivated by slaves in plantation colonies, first in the Atlantic islands and later in the

West Indies and American mainland. Over the next 300 years, this pattern for plantation colonies was repeated for other valuable agricultural commodities, such as indigo for dyes, coffee, and cotton, which were grown to sell in European markets. The first loop of what would eventually become a global trading circuit was now completed.

The Portuguese in Africa

The first European voyages along the African coast during the fifteenth century were launched by the Portuguese. The sponsor of these voyages was Prince Henry the Navigator (1394–1460). As governor of Algarve, the southernmost province of Portugal, Henry established a headquarters at Sagres and financed numerous exploratory voyages. Driven by the quest for fame and a profound faith in astrology, Henry had two objectives above all else: In order to enhance his reputation, he wanted to steal the Canary Islands from his archrival, the king of Castile, and to reward the men who sailed his ships, he desperately needed to get his hands on more gold.

The first Portuguese expeditions along the African coast were prompted by Henry's desire to capture the Canaries. He tried armed force, negotiations with the inhabitants, and entreaties to the pope, all with no success. He even purchased phony titles to the Canaries in a transparent attempt to fool the Castilians into believing that he was really the lord of the islands. In the mid-1450s, however, Henry's disappointment over the Canaries subsided as it became evident that gold from Mali could be obtained farther south from bases near the Senegal and Gambia Rivers. Although the many voyages of Henry's sailors did not fulfill his dreams of conquest and enormous riches, he and other members of his family did help colonize Madeira and the Azores. As a source of sugar, Madeira became a valuable colony (see Maps 12.1 and 12.2).

After Henry's death, Portuguese exploration of the African coast accelerated. In only six years, a private merchant of Lisbon commissioned voyages that added 2,000 miles of coastline to what was known to the Portuguese. In 1482 the exploration policy that had been a loose and

Map 12.2 Europeans in the World, Fifteenth and Sixteenth Centuries

During the fifteenth and sixteenth centuries European sailors opened sea lanes for commerce across the Atlantic, Pacific, and Indian Oceans. Dates indicate first arrival of Europeans.

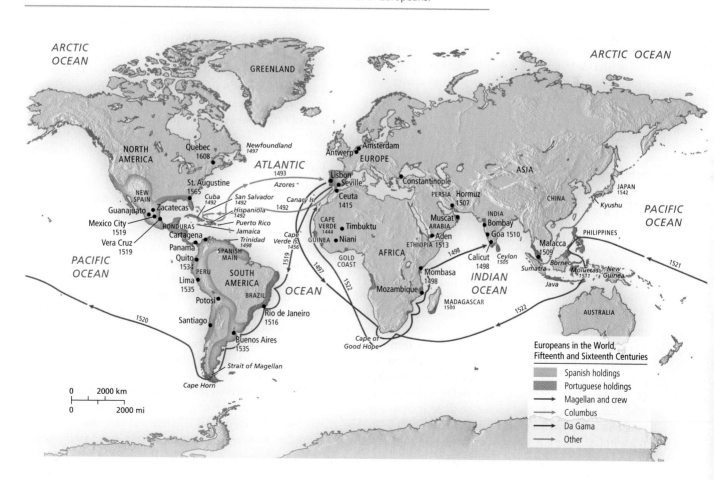

haphazard enterprise under private contractors was transformed. That year the Portuguese royal family took control of trade with Africa; they required that all sailings be authorized and all cargoes inventoried, and they built a permanent fortress at Elmina near the mouth of the Volta River in modern Ghana in West Africa. At Elmina, Portuguese traders found local sources of gold and opportunities to obtain more upriver. Rather than establishing new settler or plantation colonies, the Portuguese on the African coast relied on trading posts that supplied gold, ivory, pepper, and slaves.

Europeans in the Americas

■ How did the arrival of Europeans in the Americas transform native cultures and life?

Like the Europeans who sailed along the African coast, the first European voyagers to the Americas coveted gold and an alternative route to India and China. The European impulse to reach Asia by sailing west came from the fact that the Ottoman Empire, which was pushing into the Mediterranean after the conquest of Constantinople in 1453, blocked the traditional trade routes through the Middle East and across the Black and Red Seas. Europeans relied on Asian sources for medicines, spices, and all kinds of luxury goods that were unavailable elsewhere. Those who gained access to the source of these lucrative goods could make enormous profits. The desire to profit from this trade impelled men to take great risks to find an alternative route to East Asia. In the short run, the Americas proved to be an impediment to achieving these goals because the two continents stood in the way of getting to Asia. But in the long run, the European voyages to the Americas brought consequences unimaginable to those who first began to sail west from Europe.

The Americas Before the Conquistadores

Prior to their contact with Europeans, the peoples of the Americas displayed remarkable cultural variety. Nomadic hunters spread across the sub-Arctic regions, western North America, and the Amazon jungles, while farming settlements prevailed in much of South America and eastern North America. Some of these North American cultures, such as the Anasazi and Iroquois, developed highly sophisticated forms of political organization, but none matched the advanced civilizations of Mesoamerica and the central Andes to the south. On the eve of the arrival of Europeans, two great civilizations, the Aztecs of central Mexico and the Incas of highland Peru, had built extensive empires that dominated their neighbors.

The Aztec Empire of Mexico

Mesoamerica (the region known today as Mexico and Central America) had been the home of a series of highly urbanized, politically centralized cultures: the Mayas (300–900), the Toltecs (900–1325), and finally the Aztecs (1325 to the Spanish conquest in 1522). The Aztecs found safety from incessant warfare with neighboring tribes on an island in Lake Texcoco, where they established the city of Tenochtitlán, now Mexico City. From their base at Tenochtitlán the Aztecs followed a brilliantly successful policy of divide and conquer, first allying with powerful neighbors to attack weaker groups, then turning against former allies.

The Aztec king Montezuma I (r. 1440–1469) consolidated an empire that stretched across most of central Mexico. In order to provide food for his people during a severe famine between 1450 and 1454, Montezuma first conquered the breadbasket of Mexico, the rich coastal region of the Totonacs. In repeated attacks, swarms of Aztec warriors took city after city, captured the local chief whenever possible, burned the temple, and extorted tribute payments from the population. With the riches gained from conquest, Montezuma transformed Tenochtitlán from a dusty town of mud houses to a great imperial capital built of stone with a grand botanical garden that displayed plants taken from various climates.

The Aztecs excelled in the perpetual state of war that had long been the dominant fact of life in Mexico, and as a result they attributed great religious value to war. They practiced the "flowery war," a staged occurrence during which states agreed to a predetermined time and place for a battle, the only objective of which was to take prisoners for temple sacrifice. Sustaining the gods' hunger for human sacrifices became the most notorious feature of Aztec religion. The Aztecs attributed their military successes to their tribal god, Huitzilpochti, the giver of light and all things necessary for life, but Huitzilpochti could be nourished only with human blood, creating the need among the Aztec faithful to acquire human captives.

The rituals of sacrifice permeated Aztec society. It has been estimated that 10,000 victims were sacrificed each year, with the number rising to 50,000 on the eve of the Spanish conquest. From the very first encounters, Europeans have been baffled by the paradox of Aztec culture. Despite their apparent practice of human sacrifice, the Aztecs displayed refined manners, a sensitivity to beauty, and a highly developed religion.

The Incan Empire of the Andes

At about the same time the Aztecs were thriving in Mexico, the Incas expanded their empire in Peru and developed a comprehensive imperial ideal. Whereas the Aztecs created a loosely linked empire based on tribute payments, the Incas employed a more direct form of rulership. As they pushed out from their base in the south Andes during the fifteenth century, they imposed their authority on conquered peoples.

The first Incan emperor, Pachacuti Inca Yupanqui (r. 1438–1471), founded the empire around 1438 when he spread Incan rule beyond the valley of Cuzco. By the end of the fifteenth century, the Incas had begun to integrate by

Incan Expansion

force the distinctive cultures of the various conquered regions. In this way, they created a mountain empire 200 miles wide and 2,000 miles long, stretching from modern Chile to Ecuador and comprising a population of about ten million. From his capital at Cuzco, the Incan emperor lived in luxury and established an elaborately hierarchic political structure. His authority was carried through layers of aristocrats down to officials who were responsible for every ten families in every village. These families supplied food and tribute for the empire, worked on roads and bridges, and served in the army. State-owned warehouses of food guaranteed the peasants freedom from starvation and provided for the sick and elderly.

Emperor Huayna Capac (r. 1493–1525) founded a second capital further south at Quito, established to decentralize the overextended empire, but at his death a bitter civil war broke out between the northern and southern halves of the empire, led respectively by his rival sons. This war weakened Incan unity on the eve of the Spanish conquest.

The Incas were impressive in creating a strong imperial administration, and as rulers they were as severe as the Aztecs. Huayna Capac slaughtered 20,000 recalcitrant Caranqui and poisoned Lake Yahuar-Cocha with their corpses. After conquering a region, the Incas killed the native population or removed them to a secure area and replaced the inhabitants with loyal colonists. During the early sixteenth century, for example, Huayna Capac brought in 14,000 colonists from all over the empire to settle the Cochabamba valley. A superb network of roads and bridges covered more than 18,000 miles and made it possible to

The Aztec Rite of Human Sacrifice

Human victims had their hearts cut out by a priest at the top of the stairs to a temple.

communicate with relays of runners who could cover as much as 140 miles a day. Troops could also be quickly dispatched to trouble spots via these roads. Despite this well-organized imperial system, the Incan Empire became overly centralized because decisions could only be made by the emperor himself, a fatal flaw that allowed the Spanish invaders to crush it very quickly.

The Mission of the European Voyagers

The European arrival in the Americas was the result of a mistake suggested by Christopher Columbus's (1451–1506) ardent sense of Christian mission. Born in Genoa to an artisan family, Columbus followed the destiny of so many of his compatriots by becoming a sailor. "From my earliest youth," he reported late in life, "I went to sea and I have remained at sea until this day. It has occupied me for more than forty years. Wherever men have sailed, I too have sailed." Columbus certainly had extensive experience as a seaman, but more crucial to understanding his stubborn sense of mission was his personality, which remains an enigma that has allowed a wide variety of interpretations. Historians once depicted Columbus as a practical-minded experimenter, who was opposed by ignorant fools, but now he is understood as a more complex figure whose defining characteristic was his religious devotion. Columbus believed that he had been predestined to fulfill biblical prophecies. If he could reach China, he could outflank the Ottoman Turks and recapture Jerusalem from the Muslims who had held it since 1187, an achievement that he believed would usher in the Second Coming of Christ. In trying to persuade Queen Isabella of Castile to finance his voyage to China by sailing west, he later admitted that to make his case he ignored navigational data and, instead, relied "entirely on holy, sacred Scripture and certain prophetic texts by certain saintly persons, who by divine revelation have had something to say on this matter."[1]

It had long been recognized that it was theoretically possible to reach China by sailing west. Most educated people, and certainly all those influenced by the Renaissance humanists, agreed the world was round. The problem was not a theoretical one about the shape of the Earth but a practical one about getting around it. During Columbus's life the most widely accepted authority on the circumference of the Earth was the ancient Greek geographer Ptolemy, who had estimated that the distance across the Atlantic Ocean from Europe to Asia was more than 10,000 miles. The practical problem was that no ship in Columbus's day could hope to sail that far without landfalls along the way for finding provisions and making repairs. In fact, Ptolemy had underestimated the size of the Earth by 25 percent, but Columbus decided that Ptolemy had overestimated the distance. Columbus also imagined that the wealthy island of Japan lay farther east of the Asian continent than it actually does,

DOCUMENT

Columbus's Christian Mission

One of the most common features of Christopher Columbus's writings is the prevalence of Christian images and themes. Expectations of Christian salvation and the second coming of Christ motivated Columbus in his attempts to reach Asia by sailing west. The Introduction to the journal of his first voyage offers a glimpse of Columbus's militant Christianity. It depicts the stirring moment of Christian triumph when the Muslim king of Granada surrendered to Ferdinand and Isabella in 1492.

I saw your Highnesses' banners victoriously raised on the towers of the Alhambra, the citadel of that city [of Granada], and the Moorish king come out of the city gates and kiss the hands of your Highnesses [Ferdinand and Isabella] . . . And later in that same month, on the grounds of information I had given your royal Highnesses concerning the lands of India and a prince who is called the Great Khan—which means in Spanish "King of Kings"—and of his and his ancestors' frequent and vain applications to Rome for men learned in the holy faith who should instruct them in it, your Highnesses decided to send me, Christopher Columbus, to see these parts of India and the princes and peoples of those lands and consider the best means for their conversion. For, by the neglect of the Popes to send instructors, many nations had fallen to idolatory and adopted doctrines of perdition, and your Highnesses as Catholic princes and devoted propagators of the holy Christian faith have always been enemies of the sect of Mahomet and of all idolatries and heresies.

Your Highnesses ordained that I should not go eastward by land in the usual manner but by the western way which no one about whom we have positive information has ever followed. Therefore having expelled all the Jews from your dominions in that same month of January, your Highnesses commanded me to go with an adequate fleet to those parts of India.

Source: From *The Four Voyages of Christopher Columbus*, translated by J. M. Cohen (London: Penguin Classics, 1969). Copyright © 1969 by J. M. Cohen. Reproduced by permission of Penguin Books Ltd.

thus further minimizing the distance of the voyage. When he first proposed sailing west to Asia, King John II of Portugal consulted a committee of experts who quite correctly pointed out how seriously Columbus had miscalculated the distance. His extremely inaccurate estimate of how close China was seems to have been more the result of wishful thinking and religious fervor than geographical expertise. King John's rejection led Columbus to seek patronage elsewhere. Columbus applied to Queen Isabella of newly unified Spain, whose own advisers at first recommended against the voyage for the same reasons the Portuguese experts had rejected his plan. When the Spanish defeated the Muslim kingdom of Granada in 1492, which completed the Christian reconquest of the Iberian peninsula, Isabella succumbed to the religious enthusiasm of the moment and relented. She offered Columbus a commission for the voyage in the hope that it would ensure a final Christian victory over Islam.

On August 3, 1492, Columbus set sail with three small ships—the Niña, Pinta, and Santa Maria—and a crew of ninety men and boys. After refitting in the Canary Islands, the modest convoy entered unknown waters guided only by Columbus's faith in finding China, which was, in fact, thousands of miles farther west than he thought it would be. At two in the morning on the moonlit night of October 12, a lookout spied land, probably Watling Island in the Bahamas.

In all, Columbus made four voyages across the Atlantic (1492, 1493, 1498, 1502), exploring the Caribbean Islands, the coast of Central America, and part of the coast of South America. He never abandoned the belief that he had arrived in Asia. His four voyages were filled with adventures. On the third voyage, he was arrested by the newly appointed Spanish governor of Hispaniola on false charges and sent home in chains for trial; on the fourth he was marooned for nearly a year on Jamaica after worms weakened the timbers of his ships. He garnered considerable wealth in gold found on his voyages, but he never received the ti-tles and offices that Queen Isabella had promised him before his first voyage.

Soon after Columbus returned to Spain from his first voyage, the Spanish monarchs who had sponsored him tried to obtain a monopoly to explore the western Atlantic. They appealed to Pope Alexander VI, who was himself a Spaniard and sympathetic to their request. In an effort to give the Spanish a firm legal monopoly to the lands across the Atlantic, the pope confirmed in 1493 the right of Spanish sailors to explore all lands to the west as long as they did not infringe upon the rights of another Christian ruler. Since all involved still thought Columbus had arrived in China, the obvious other Christian ruler was the king of Portugal, whose sailors had already pushed far enough south down the African coast to realize that they could eventually reach China by sailing east. The pope ordered a line of demarcation drawn along a north-south line 100 leagues (about 300 miles) west of the Azores and Cape Verde Islands. Spain received all lands to the west of the line; Portugal obtained the lands to the east. This line of demarcation seemed to limit the Portuguese to Africa, which alarmed them and led to direct negotiations between the Portuguese and the Spaniards. The result of the negotiations was the Treaty of Tordesillas in 1494, which moved the line of demarcation to 370 leagues (about 1,110 miles) west of the Cape Verde Islands, a decision that granted to Portugal all of Africa, India, and Brazil.

Spanish Conquistadores Land on an Island in the New World

The armored Spaniards are met by the naked inhabitants who offer them jewels and gold. As one of their first acts, the Spaniards erect a cross, symbolizing the Christian conquest of the New World.

Despite Columbus's persistent faith that he had found a route to the East Indies, other voyagers began to suspect, even before Columbus's death, that he had not found Asia at all and that other routes had to be explored. Another Italian, the Florentine Amerigo Vespucci (1454–1512), met Columbus, helped him prepare for the third voyage, and later made at least two voyages of his own across the Atlantic. From his voyages, Vespucci recognized something of the immensity of the South American continent and was the first to use the term "New World." Because he coined the term and because the account of his voyages got into print before Columbus's, Vespucci's given name, Amerigo (America), came to be attached to the New World rather than Columbus's. By the 1520s, Europeans had explored the Americas extensively enough to recognize that the New World was nowhere near India or China.

After the Treaty of Tordesillas, explorers followed two distinct strategies for finding a sea route to East Asia. The first strategy was the Portuguese continued pursuit of routes to the south and east around Africa. Between 1487 and 1488, Bartholomew Dias (ca. 1450–1500) reached the Cape of Good Hope at the southern tip of the African continent. This discovery made it evident that passage to India could be achieved by sailing south, rounding the tip of Africa, and crossing the Indian Ocean. Political and financial problems in Portugal, however, prevented a followup to Dias's voyage for ten years. Between 1497 and 1499, Vasco da Gama (ca. 1460–1524) finally succeeded in sailing from Lisbon to India around the Cape of Good Hope. This celebrated voyage included a great looping westward course far out into the Atlantic to escape the doldrums, an area in the ocean where the winds died. As a consequence of the route opened by da Gama, the Portuguese were the first Europeans to establish trading posts in Asia. They reached the Malabar coast of India in 1498 and soon found their way to the Spice Islands and China. By the middle of the sixteenth century, the Portuguese had assembled a string of more than fifty trading posts° and forts from Sofala on the east coast of Africa to Nagasaki in Japan.

The second strategy for reaching Asia consisted of Spanish attempts to pursue Columbus's proposed route west. The problem faced by those sailing under the Spanish flag was to find a way around the barrier presented by the American continents. A Portuguese sailor named Ferdinand Magellan (ca. 1480–1521), who had previously sailed to Asia aboard Portuguese ships, persuaded the king of Spain to sponsor a voyage to Asia sailing west around South America. That venture (1519–1522), which began under Magellan's command, passed through the strait named after him at the tip of South America and crossed the Pacific in a voyage of extreme hardship as his men suffered from thirst and hunger and died of scurvy. Magellan himself was killed by natives in the Philippines. After three years at sea, 18 survivors from the original 240 in Magellan's fleet

reached Seville, Spain, having sailed around the world for the first time. Contemporaries immediately recognized the epic significance of the voyage, but the route opened by Magellan was too long and arduous for the Spanish to employ as a reliable alternative to the Portuguese route around Africa.

In the course of three centuries (about 1480–1780), European navigators linked the previously isolated routes of seaborne commerce, opened all the seas of the world to trade, and encountered many of the cultures and peoples of the world. Within the Indian Ocean and the western Pacific, the Europeans faced stiff competition from Arab and Chinese merchant sailors. But for the first hundred years or so, the Portuguese and Spanish effectively maintained a monopoly over the global trade routes back to Europe. Gradually English, Dutch, and French sailors also made their way around the globe. In the Americas, inadvertently made known to Europeans by Christopher Columbus, the Spanish immediately began settlements and attempted to subdue the indigenous populations.

MAP

European Empires in Latin American 1660

The Fall of the Aztec and Incan Empires

Following the seafaring captains, such as Columbus and Magellan, came the conquistadores°. They were Spanish adventurers, usually from impoverished minor noble families, who sought fortune and royal recognition through explorations and conquests of indigenous peoples. Spain was a poor land with few opportunities for advancement, a bleak situation that made the lands of the New World a powerful lure to many men seeking a fortune. Embroiled in almost continuous warfare in Europe, the Spanish crown was also perennially strapped for cash, which meant the king of Spain was highly motivated to encourage profitable foreign conquests. Many of the conquistadores launched their own expeditions with little or no legal authority, hoping to acquire sufficient riches to impress the king to give them official sanction for additional conquests. Those who did acquire legal authority from the crown received the privilege to conquer new lands in the name of the king of Spain and to keep a portion of those territories for themselves. In return they were obliged to turn over to the king one fifth—the "royal fifth"—of everything of value they acquired, an obligation enforced by a notary sent along with the conquistadores to keep a record of valuables that were found. The conquistadores also extended Spanish sovereignty over new lands and opened the way for missionaries to bring millions, at least nominally, into the Christian fold.

All conquistadores were required to read a document, called the *requerimiento*°, to the natives before making war on them. Derived from the Muslim declaration of *jihad* or holy war, this Spanish Christian document briefly explained the principles of Christianity and commanded the natives to accept them immediately along with the authority of the pope and the sovereignty of the king of Spain. If the natives refused, they were warned that they would be forced through war to subject themselves "to the yoke and obedience of the Church and of Their Highnesses. We shall take you and your wives and your children, and shall make slaves of them, and as such shall sell and dispose of them as Their Highnesses may command. And we shall take your goods, and shall do you all the mischief and damage that we can."[2] The *requerimiento* revealed the conflicting motives behind the Spanish conquest. On the one hand, the Spanish were sincerely interested in converting the natives to Christianity. On the other, the conquistadores were trying to justify the immorality of their actions by suggesting that the natives had brought the attack on themselves by refusing to obey the Spanish king.

Hernán Cortés and the Conquest of Mexico

Among the first and most successful of the conquistadores was Hernán Cortés (1485–1547). Cortés arrived on the Yucatán peninsula of present-day Mexico in February 1519, beginning a conquest that culminated in the collapse of the Aztec Empire and the Spanish colonization of Mexico. He followed a policy of divide and conquer with the natives, making alliances with peoples who hated the Aztecs and then using their warriors on the front lines of his battles where they absorbed most of the losses. If after a

reading of the *requerimiento* the native chieftains did not immediately surrender, Cortés's men attacked them, breaking through their lines on horses, which the natives had never seen before.

After a number of bloody battles, Cortés set off with 450 Spanish troops, 15 horses, and 4,000 native allies to conquer the great capital of the Aztec Empire, Tenochtitlán, a city of at least 300,000 and defended by thousands of warriors. As Cortés approached, Montezuma II was slow to set up a strong defense, because he suspected Cortés might be the white god, Quetzalcóatl, who according to prophecies would arrive one day from the east. The result was disastrous for the Aztecs. Montezuma knew his reign was doomed unless he could gain the assistance of other gods to drive Quetzalcóatl away. Thus, rather than an ardent military campaign, the king's defense primarily took the form of human sacrifices made to please the gods. Cortés captured Montezuma, who continued to rule for several months as a puppet of the conquistadores. The city revolted, however, killing Montezuma and driving out the Spanish. Cortés then gathered new troops and additional allies, built ships for use on the lake that surrounded Tenochtitlán, and besieged the city. By the time Tenochtitlán finally surrendered, the shiny jewel that had so impressed the Spanish when they first glimpsed it from the surrounding mountains lay in smoldering ruins.

By 1522 Cortés controlled a territory in New Spain—as Mexico was renamed—larger than Old Spain itself. Aztec culture and its religion of human sacrifice disappeared as Franciscan friars arrived to evangelize the surviving population.

Cortés Arrives in Mexico

The figure on the right is the native woman La Malinche, who served as Cortés's mistress and translator, a position often occupied by native women who served as mediators between the indigenous and Spanish cultures. Cortés is the bearded man in breeches. Following him is an African servant, Spanish soldiers dressed in full armor, and finally three native porters, bent over from their heavy burdens.

DOCUMENT

Why the Aztecs Lost to the Spanish Conquerors

A Spaniard named Diego Munoz Camargo married into the nobility of one of the native groups that allied with Cortés against the Aztecs. He had access to local knowledge that suggests the Aztecs feared the Spanish, not because of their technology of horses and guns, but because of portents that their world was coming to an end.

Ten years before the Spaniards came to this land, the people saw a strange wonder and took it to be an evil sign and portent. This wonder was a great column of flame which burned in the night, shooting out such brilliant sparks and flashes that it seemed to rain fire on the earth and to blaze like daybreak. It seemed to be fastened against the sky in the shape of a pyramid, its base set against the ground, where it was of vast width, and its bulk narrowing to a peak that reached up and touched the heavens. It appeared at midnight and could still be seen at dawn, but in the daytime it was quelled by the force and brilliance of the sun. This portent burned for a year, beginning in the year which the natives called 12-House—that is, 1517 in our Spanish reckoning. . . .

To the natives, these marvels augured their death and ruin, signifying that the end of the world was coming and that other peoples would be created to inhabit the earth. They were so frightened and grief-stricken that they could form no judgment about these things, so new and strange and never before seen or reported.

Source: Miguel Leon-Portilla, *The Broken Spears: The Aztec Account of the Conquest of Mexico* (Boston, Beacon Press, 1962), pp. 7, 11.

Quetzalcóatl, Aztec God of Life and Death

Quetzalcóatl took the form of a feathered snake, which in this Aztec image can be seen coiled beneath its head. According to myth, another god had expelled Quetzalcóatl, who embarked on a raft of snakes into the Atlantic and disappeared to the east. The prophecy that he would return from the east led Montezuma II to assume that Cortés was the god returned.

Francisco Pizarro and the Conquest of Peru

Like other conquistadores, Francisco Pizarro (ca. 1478–1541) was poor, but he bore the additional social liabilities of illegitimacy and illiteracy. With no prospects at home, Pizarro found his way to Panama, where he accompanied Vasco Núñez de Balboa (1475–1519) on an expedition in 1513 across the Isthmus of Panama during which Europeans got their first look at the Pacific Ocean.

In 1531 Pizarro left Panama with a small expedition of 180 men and 30 horses. Pizarro's goal was to conquer Peru, known to be a land rich with gold. Gathering additional recruits along the way, he sailed to northern Peru and sent out spies who discovered that the Incan emperor, Atahuallpa, could be found in the highland city of Cajamarca. When Pizarro and his forces arrived there, the central square was empty, but Atahuallpa was encamped nearby with a large army. Pizarro treacherously invited Atahuallpa to come for a parlay, but instead took him captive. The news of the capture plunged the overly centralized Incan Empire into a crisis because no one dared take action without the emperor's orders. In an attempt to satisfy the Spaniards' hunger for gold and to win his freedom, Atahuallpa had a room filled with gold and silver for the conquistadores, but the treasure merely stimulated their appetite for more. In July 1533 Pizarro executed the emperor, and by the following November he had captured the demoralized Incan capital of Cuzco.

The conquest of Peru vastly increased the size of the Spanish Empire and began to satisfy the craving for gold that had impelled Columbus and the conquistadores in the first place. Through the collection of the royal fifth, gold and silver flowed into the royal coffers in Spain. The discovery in 1545 of the fabulous Peruvian silver mine of Potosí (in what is now southern Bolivia) coincided with the introduction of the mercury amalgamation process that separated silver from ore. Mercury amalgamation enabled the Spaniards to replace surface gathering of silver ore with tunneling for ore, a procedure that led to greatly elevated yields of precious metals. For a century the silver of Peru helped provide otherwise impoverished Spain with the resources to become the most powerful kingdom in Europe.

Spanish America: The Transplanting of a European Culture

With the defeat of the Aztec and Incan Empires, the process of transplanting Spanish society to the Americas began in earnest. The arrival of Europeans was a catastrophe for most native peoples, some of whom—in the Caribbean, northern Argentina, and central Chile—completely disappeared through the ravages of conquest and diseases. Whereas Spanish became the language of government and education, some native traditions survived and a mixed-blood immigrant and native population called *mestizos* gradually appeared. Through this process, Spanish America became the first lasting outpost of Western civilization outside of Europe.

The basic form of economic and social organization in Spanish America was the encomienda° system, which was created as an instrument to exploit native labor. An encomienda was a royal grant awarded for military or other services that gave the conquistadores and their successors the right to gather tribute from the Indians in a defined area. In return, the encomendero (the receiver of the royal grant and native tribute) was theoretically obliged to protect the natives and teach them the rudiments of the Christian faith. Because the encomiendas were very large, only a small number of Spanish settlers were actually encomenderos. In greater Peru, which included modern Peru, Ecuador, and Bolivia, there were never more than 500 encomenderos. By the seventeenth century these encomiendas had evolved to become great landed estates called haciendas°.

There were only a few prosperous encomenderos, but the stories about those who rose from rags to riches in the New World were so compelling that during the sixteenth century alone more than 200,000 Spaniards migrated there. They came from every part of the Iberian peninsula, from

Layers of Cultures

Cuzco, Peru, was the capital of the Incan Empire before the Spanish Conquest in 1533. In this photo the heavy stone wall at the lower level was built by the Incas. Above it is a whitewashed wall built during the colonial period, and affixed to it is a sign of the contemporary global economy, Coca-Cola.

every class except the peasantry, and they practiced a wide variety of trades. There were nobles, notaries, lawyers, priests, physicians, merchants, artisans, and sailors; there were also vagabonds prone to crime and rebellion. In effect, these immigrants duplicated Spanish Catholic society in the New World, complete with its class divisions and tensions, except that the native population or African slaves substituted for the peasants as agricultural workers. Included among the immigrants were an unknown number of Jews who hid their faith and who escaped the rigors of the Spanish Inquisition by removing themselves to the Americas, where they were less likely to suffer persecution.

Only one in ten of Spanish immigrants were women, and for a long time the colonies suffered from a shortage of Spanish women. Although native Americans were usually excluded from Spanish society, many native women who were the mistresses or wives of Spaniards became partially assimilated to European culture and helped pass it on to their offspring. These native women learned Spanish and were converted to Christianity, and because of their origins they could mediate between the dominant Spanish and the subordinate native population. These women knew both languages, which made them valuable interpreters, and were familiar with both cultures, which enabled them to explain native customs to the Spanish. The progeny of

Between Indian and Christian: Creating Hybrid Religion in Mexico

As conquest passed into colonialism during the sixteenth century, Christian missionaries began to exert a profound influence on Indian moral and religious practices. However, as the Indians accepted Christianity they subtly adapted it to meet their needs and to fit into their culture. As a result native Americans created a new hybrid religion that combined both Christian and Indian elements.

No example of the hybrid nature of native Christianity is more revealing than the Indian uses of the cross. As his army marched across Mexico, Cortés had ordered the smashing of idols and their substitution with Christian crosses. Missionaries later placed crosses in churches, encouraged making the sign of the cross a ritual practice, and introduced the wearing of miniature crosses as a kind of personal talisman that offered protection from illness and evil influences.

Mayas adapted to the Christian cross so readily because Maya culture already had a symbol similar to the Christian cross. However, the Maya at first misunderstood what the missionaries meant when they preached about the cross and took the example of Christ's sacrifice on the cross too literally. Some Maya actually performed crucifixions, usually of children, whose hands were nailed or tied to the cross and whose hearts were torn out in a vestige of pre-Christian practices. There are also reports of pigs and dogs sacrificed on crosses. Needless to say, the Christian missionaries were horrified at these crucifixions. Even though the Maya had missed the point of Christ's singular sacrifice, they had understood the power behind the Christian symbol, which the Spaniards had used in their conquest of the Maya, and they wanted some of that power for themselves.

When the Franciscan friars arrived in Mexico City in 1524, they introduced the practice of flagellation, in which the missionaries whipped themselves to aid in the conversion of the recently conquered Aztec population. In Europe the ritual of self-flagellation was usually practiced by monks, friars, and small numbers of laymen who joined "confraternities of the discipline," which carefully supervised the whippings. The practice imitated the flagellation of Christ under the whips of Roman soldiers and served as a means of mortification for the penance of sins.

The friars first employed self-flagellation as a tool for impressing the natives. Fray Antonio de Roa encouraged conversions through dramatic flagellations, called "a general discipline," which was attended by everyone in the village. After a collective flagellation in which the Indians who had converted to Christianity imitated Fray Roa, he proceeded out of the church, naked from the waist up with a cord around his neck and shoeless. He walked over hot coals, and then delivered a sermon about how much greater the pains of Hell would be than those from the burning coals. After the sermon he doused his whole body with boiling water. During the sixteenth century the Indians themselves began to practice flagellation, especially during processions conducted during Holy Week. The natives flogged themselves with such evident enthusiasm that the friars had to intervene to prevent the Indians from seriously harming themselves. On many occasions during the colonial period, the Indians used self-flagellation as a means of rousing their fellows in protest against Spanish domination. Even now flagellation remains the most distinctive feature of the Mexican passion plays. By adapting European Christian rituals for their own purposes, the natives created a new hybrid religious culture that was distinctively Mexican.

Hybrid Religion
Here a priest flagellates a naked Incan in Peru. Introduced by Christian missionaries, flagellation became one of the more extreme forms of religious practice among the newly converted Indians.

Question for Discussion

Why do you think the natives of Mexico changed the practices of Christianity?

European men and Indian women constituted the mestizo, or genetically mixed, population.

Wherever they went in the Americas, the Spaniards brought African slaves with them. Most of the slaves remembered little about their original African cultures, however, because many had been born in Spain, the Caribbean, or the Cape Verde Islands, and Spanish had become their native language. At every stage from initial explorations to the building of new cities, Africans participated in helping make the Americas Spanish. In 1533, while Pizarro held the Incan emperor captive at Cajamarca, he sent to Cuzco an advance party of five men, including a black man who was entrusted to bring back a huge fortune in gold and silver. Unlike in the West Indies and the coastal regions where they became plantation workers, blacks in the interior of South America often fought and worked as partners with the Spanish, not as full equals but as necessary auxiliaries for and beneficiaries of the conquest.

The king of Spain was represented in the Americas by the two viceroys, who were the highest colonial officials. One in Mexico City governed the West Indies, the mainland north of Panama, Venezuela, and the Philippines; the other in Lima, Peru, had authority over all of Spanish South America, excluding Venezuela. However, the vast territory of Spanish America and the enormous cultural diversity within it precluded any rigorous centralized control either from Spain or from the viceregal capitals.

In Spanish America the church was a more effective presence than the state. Driven by the same religious fervor as Columbus, Catholic missionaries trekked into the farthest reaches of Spanish America, converting the native populations to Christianity with much more success than in Africa or Asia. Greed had enticed the conquistadores, but an ardent desire to spread the gospel of Christianity spurred the missionaries. As heirs to the long Christian struggle against Islam and, in particular, the reconquest of the Iberian peninsula from the Muslims, the missionaries found in the Americas an exceptional opportunity to expand Christianity. The most zealous missionaries were members of religious orders—Franciscans, Dominicans, and Jesuits—who were distinguished from the parish priests by their autonomy and special training for missionary work. Instead of answering to a bishop who had authority over a defined region, members of religious orders were organized like an army, followed the commands of the head of their order in Rome, and were willing to travel anywhere in the world.

The Spanish colonization of South America meant that missionaries did not have to contend with the opposition of local governments, as they did in Africa and Asia. Church officials generally assumed that it took ten years for the transition to a settled Christian society, a policy that meant that Christianity arrived in two stages. First, members of a religious order evangelized the population by learning the native language, then preaching and teaching in it. They also introduced the celebration of the Catholic sacraments. Once churches were built and Christianity was accepted by the local elite, the missionaries moved on to be replaced, in the second stage, by parish priests who expected to stay in one place for their entire lives. In the border regions, evangelizing never ceased and members of the missionary orders stayed on until the end of colonial times. In California, New Mexico, and Texas, missions formed outposts of Spanish society in regions that were otherwise often lawless borderlands. In Paraguay, the members of the Jesuit Order gathered the Guaraní peoples into *reductions,* highly disciplined and closed communities where the natives were subjected to a rigorous regime of labor and prayer, and even the smallest details of their daily lives were regulated.

Portuguese Brazil: The Tenuous Colony

In 1500 Pedro Cabral sighted the Brazilian coast, claiming it for Portugal under the Treaty of Tordesillas. While the Spaniards busied themselves with the conquest of Mexico and Peru, the Portuguese largely ignored Brazil, which lacked any obvious source of gold or temptingly rich civilizations to conquer. Instead, the Portuguese concentrated on developing their lucrative empire in Asia.

Brazil became a haven for pirates and castaways, especially French. In 1532 the Portuguese crown finally answered the French threat by devising a plan for Portuguese settlement and government of Brazil. Brazil was divided into fifteen captaincies, which were passed out to court favorites as compensation for services rendered or just to get them out of the way. The captains turned out to be tyrannical, incompetent, or absent, and they so completely failed to govern effectively that in 1549 the crown was forced to appoint a governor-general and to establish a capital city at Salvador in eastern Brazil.

The impetus for the further colonization of Brazil was the growing European demand for sugar. The Brazilian climate was perfectly suited for cultivating sugar cane. Between 1575 and 1600, Brazil became the Western world's leading producer of sugar, luring thousands of poor young men from Portugal and the Azores who took native women as wives, thereby producing a distinctive mestizo population. In the coastal regions, the land was cleared for vast sugar cane plantations. Sugar cane production required back-breaking, dangerous labor to weed and especially to cut the cane. To help work the plantations the Portuguese attempted to enslave the Tupí-Guaraní natives, but European diseases soon killed them off.

The Portuguese increasingly looked to Africans to perform the hard labor they were unwilling to do themselves. As a result, the Brazilian demand for slaves intensified the Portuguese presence in West Africa and the African presence in Brazil. In the search for ever more slaves, Portuguese

The Difficulties of a Transatlantic Marriage

In 1557 Francisco Noguerol de Ulloa, a Spanish conquistador who had fought in Peru, returned home to Spain. During his nearly two decades in the New World, he had amassed a sizable fortune and earned a great reputation for himself. He expected to enjoy his wealth and fame in a peaceful retirement, but instead almost immediately upon his return he was arrested on the charge of bigamy. During his long stay in Peru, he had neither seen nor heard from the Spanish woman he had married before he left, and when his sisters wrote to him that she had died he thought he was free to marry again. So he did. But when he returned to Spain, his first wife, Dona Beatriz, who was alive and well, heard about his second marriage and filed suit against him for bigamy.

The chance to escape Beatriz had impelled Francisco across the Atlantic in the first place. Many Spanish conquistadores were trying to flee troubles at home, such as a bad marriage. Francisco had married Beatriz under pressure from his widowed mother for the usual reasons parents forced their children into arranged marriages. Beatriz came with a large dowry and provided useful alliances for Francisco's mother and sisters, who felt vulnerable because of Francisco's father's untimely death.

But the marriage was a failure from the beginning. According to Francisco, they had never slept together, and in the eyes of the Church, at least, an unconsummated marriage was not a real marriage. Certainly Francisco and Beatriz never lived together, and she bore him no children. However, his lack of affection for his wife did not prevent him from accepting large payments for her dowry or from writing to his in-laws to ask for money when in his early years abroad he ran into difficulties in Peru. Even a letter of consolation on the death of his wife's sister included a request for more money. Francisco may never have had an affectionate or sexual relationship with Beatriz, but he certainly had a financial one.

Peru eventually rewarded Francisco with a great fortune. For his military prowess and devotion to the Spanish crown, he was granted one of the largest and most productive encomiendas in Peru, a vast tract of land that included the labor of thousands of Incas and a retinue of personal slaves, including a harem of female domestics. Once the false news of Beatriz's death spread throughout Peru, Francisco came to be regarded as the most eligible bachelor in the entire colony. Although many women were eager to become his wife, Francisco did not remarry for years after the news of his first wife's death.

Francisco's second wife, Dona Catalina, shared at least two attributes with his first wife: wealth and social prominence. Born into a respectable Castilian family, she was herself the widow of one of the most powerful Spaniards in Peru. She controlled her own vast fortune in property and other assets, which meant that she could bring a substantial dowry to her new husband. Her reputation as a woman of modesty and virtue was impeccable; she also possessed one vital asset that Beatriz apparently lacked—great beauty. Catalina was known as the "crown jewel of all the women of those parts." It is no wonder that Francisco chose her as his new wife. This time he consummated the marriage.

This case reveals much about the nature of marriage in imperial Spain and the relative power of men and women in Spanish and colonial society. Marriage was the union of two families, not just two people. Social standing counted for more than affection in the choice of a spouse. Francisco, in fact, had to defend himself against the charge that he had fallen in love with Catalina and had, therefore, abandoned Beatriz so that he could marry Catalina. Love was not an acceptable reason for marriage, let alone an acceptable reason for leaving one marriage for another. In his trial and subsequent litigation, he never claimed to love his new wife and in fact denied that he knew her well at all before the wedding. As an honorable and respectable widow, she had lived a secluded life that would have made it impossible for Francisco to have had much contact with her at all, or so he said.

To escape Beatriz, Francisco had to prove that the marriage had never been a real marriage. To this end, he and his lawyers highlighted the fact that he had never consummated his first marriage, a fact that would have automatically invalidated it as a legal marriage according to the canon law of the Church. To keep Francisco as her husband, Beatriz had to prove that they had had sex together at least once. Francisco's belief that Beatriz was dead had no legal bearing on the case because she was not.

Despite Francisco's arguments that the marriage had never been valid, the judges initially decided in favor of Beatriz. Francisco was sentenced to pay a heavy fine to Beatriz, to serve time in jail, and to separate from his second wife, whom he was forbidden to ever see again. Perhaps most galling of all, he was obliged to resume marital relations with Beatriz, with whom he had certainly never lived before. Beatriz won the case

A Spanish Couple

Francisco Noguerol de Ulloa and Catalina would have dressed much like this aristocratic couple out for a stroll.

largely because of the legal protection women enjoyed in sixteenth-century Spain. Husbands had obligations toward their wives that the courts consistently enforced.

One of the most important protections women had was the dowry itself. A man could enjoy the income from his wife's dowry, but legally she still had certain claims to it. If he died before she did—which was quite likely given the difference in age between men and women at first marriage—she had a claim on his estate to have the entire sum of her dowry restored to her, not to his family or his heirs but only to her. Beatriz supplied the court with extensive evidence of receipts for dowry payments, signed by Francisco himself. The judges respected the legal protections for women and would not allow Francisco to squander the dowry or relegate it entirely for himself. Francisco's repeated requests to his in-laws for more money made him look like an opportunistic fortune hunter rather than a valuable family ally. The court's judgment in favor of Beatriz had less to do with the emotions of love than the defense of the dowry system and its role in maintaining social stability.

Catalina did not accept lightly the loss of the man she considered her husband. She needed to protect her own dowry from Beatriz's claims. Catalina filed a countersuit to assert that much of Francisco's assets were profits earned from her own dowry, which could not, therefore, be transferred to Beatriz. Catalina was fighting not just for her dowry but for her good name and her marriage, and the courts eventually found a way to recognize the rights of both women—Beatriz to her dowry portion and Catalina to her honorable marriage to Francisco.

In the end, it was the women who resolved the legal struggle that surrounded Francisco. For both women, the courts and the dowry system served as a powerful form of protection for their financial well-being and their honor. Despite the overwhelming authority of men in Spanish society, women were not passive pawns. They found ways to assert control over their own lives. It is revealing that the distance between the Old and New Worlds had little bearing on the status of or legal protections for these women. Far from becoming a lawless frontier, early colonial Peru was for Spaniards at least, an extension of Spanish society.

Questions of Justice

1. In what ways did the sixteenth-century Spanish legal system protect the rights of women?
2. What does this case reveal about how Spanish society was transported to the New World?

Taking It Further

Cook, Alexandra Parma, and Noble David Cook. *Good Faith and Truthful Ignorance: A Case of Transatlantic Bigamy.* 1991. A detailed study of the Noguerol de Ulloa case.

slave buyers enlarged their area of operations in Africa south to Angola, where in 1575 they founded a trading post. This post became the embarkation point for slave traders who sailed directly to Brazil and sold slaves in exchange for low-grade Brazilian tobacco, which they exchanged for more slaves when they returned to Angola.

As in Spanish America, Portuguese authorities felt responsible for converting the natives to Christianity. In Brazil, the Jesuits took the lead during the last half of the sixteenth century by establishing a school for the training of missionaries on the site of the present city of São Paulo. São Paulo became the headquarters for the "Apostle of Brazil," José de Anchieta, who worked among the indigenous peoples. In the seventeenth century, Father Antonio Vieira established a string of missions in the Amazon valley. Once converted, natives were resettled into villages called aldeias°, which were similar to Spanish missions. The Jesuits attempted to protect the natives against the white colonists who wanted to enslave them, creating a lasting conflict between the Jesuit fathers and local landowners. Both Jesuits and colonists appealed to the king to settle their dispute; finally the king gave the Jesuits complete responsibility for all Indians in aldeias but allowed colonists to enslave Indians who had not been converted or who were captured in war. The Portuguese connected Christian conversion with settlement in aldeias, which meant that any unsettled native was, by definition, a heathen. Nevertheless, these restrictions on enslaving Indians created a perceived labor shortage and further stimulated the demand for African slaves.

More rural, more African, and less centrally governed than Spanish America, Brazil during its colonial history remained a plantation economy in which the few dominant white European landowners were vastly outnumbered by their African slaves. In certain areas a racially mixed population created its own vibrantly hybrid culture that combined native, African, and European elements, especially in the eclectic religious life that combined Catholic with polytheistic forms of worship. Although Brazil occupied nearly half of the South American continent, until the twentieth century most of the vast interior was unexplored by Europeans and unsettled except by the small native population.

North America: The Land of Lesser Interest

Compared with Central and South America, North America outside Mexico held little attraction for Europeans during the sixteenth century. European experience in North America consisted of a number of exploratory missions and several failed attempts at colonization. By 1600, when hundreds of thousands of Europeans and Africans had settled in the Caribbean, Central and South America, the only European settlements in North America (except for New Spain) consisted of a tiny Spanish garrison at St. Augustine,

Florida, a doomed Spanish colony on the upper Rio Grande in New Mexico, and a few marooned Frenchmen on Sable Island far off the coast of Nova Scotia. Even by 1700, when English, French, and Spanish colonies were finally thriving in North America, they still played a very minor role in the global picture of European economic interests.

At first the principal attraction of North America was the cod fisheries in the waters off Newfoundland, which every spring lured ships from England, France, Spain, and Portugal and which may have been frequented by Europeans even before Columbus. An Italian captain in the employ of England, John Cabot (ca. 1450–ca. 1498), landed in North America in 1497 and established the basis for an English claim in the New World, but after he disappeared on a return trip the following year no one else bothered to follow up on the claim. Occasionally fishermen dropped anchor at the harbors at St. John's, Newfoundland, and came to know the coasts of Maine and the Gulf of St. Lawrence. In 1521 some Portuguese families founded a settlement on Nova Scotia, but they soon disappeared.

The second attraction of North America lay in the vain hope of a Northwest Passage to China and India through or around the continent to the north. After Magellan's voyage (1519–1522), the Spanish knew how to sail around South America, but they preferred overland transportation from Vera Cruz, Mexico, to reach the Pacific coast at Acapulco, which became an embarkation port for Spanish trade with Asia. In 1524 the French king sent the Italian Giovanni da Verrazano (ca. 1485–1528) to find a passage around North America, which resulted in the first geographical description of the coast from North Carolina to Newfoundland. Following up on Verrazano's voyage, Jacques Cartier (1491–1557) discovered the St. Lawrence River in 1534. Hard winters defeated two French attempts to found a colony in the St. Lawrence Valley between 1541 and 1543. The English explored further north in a series of voyages that led to the discovery of Hudson Bay, which was thought for some time to be part of the Pacific Ocean. Only in 1616 did William Baffin (ca. 1584–1622) determine that there was no ice-free passage around North America.

In the competition over North America, the English arrived late, devoting themselves at first to preying on Spanish shipping rather than building their own colonies. During most of the sixteenth century England was considerably less well prepared than Spain or Portugal to sustain a campaign of conquest and colonization in the Americas. At this time the English monarchy had a fragile hold on power, its naval fleet was tiny, and it lacked the financial backing for risky expeditions. In contrast to the great convoys of Spanish and Portuguese ships that plied the Atlantic, the English were represented by a few "privateers," which was a polite word for pirates. These men sought quick, easy profits rather than the rigors of settling and pacifying the country. John Hawkins, the most famous of the early English privateers, and his nephew, Francis Drake (ca. 1543–1596), specialized in harassing the Spanish fleet, both to steal the gold and silver that was being transported back to Spain and to sustain an intermittent war against England's most powerful enemy.

During the reign of Queen Elizabeth I (r. 1558–1603), English efforts finally turned to establishing colonies in the Americas. Two prominent courtiers, Humphrey Gilbert and his stepbrother, Walter Raleigh, sponsored a series of voyages intended to establish an English colony called Virginia in honor of Elizabeth, "The Virgin Queen." The shift of English interest from piracy to colonization was made possible by Elizabeth's success in strengthening the monarchy, building up the fleet, and encouraging investments in New World colonies. In 1585 the first English colonists in the Americas landed on Roanoke Island off the coast of North Carolina, but they were so poorly prepared that their attempt and a second one in 1587 failed. The inexperienced and naive English settlers did not even make provisions for planting crops.

The successful English colonies came a generation later. Learning from past mistakes, the colonists of Jamestown in Virginia, who landed in 1607, brought seeds for planting, built fortifications for protection, and established a successful form of self-government. From these modest beginnings, the English gradually established vast plantations along the rivers of Virginia. There they raised tobacco to supply the new European habit of smoking, which had been picked up from native Americans. In 1620 religious refugees from England settled in Massachusetts Bay, but in contrast to Central and South America, most of North America by 1650 remained only marginally touched by Europeans.

Europeans in Asia

■ Why was the European encounter with Asian civilizations far less disruptive than those in Africa and the Americas?

India, the Malay peninsula, Indonesia, the Spice Islands, and China were the ultimate goal of the European explorers during the fifteenth and sixteenth centuries. They were eventually reached by many routes—by the Portuguese sailing around Africa, by the Spanish sailing around South America, and by the Russians trekking across the vastness of Siberia. Trade between Europe and Asia was very lucra-

CHRONOLOGY

Europeans in the Americas

ca. 1438	Founding of Incan Empire in Peru by Pachacuti Inca Yupanqui
1440–1469	Reign of Montezuma I of the Aztec Empire
1492–1493	First two voyages of Christopher Columbus
1497	John Cabot lands in North America
1498	Third voyage of Columbus
1500	Cabral sights Brazil
1502	Fourth voyage of Columbus
1519–1522	Spanish conquer Mexico
1524	Giovanni da Verrazano explores North American coast for France
1534	Jacques Cartier discovers St. Lawrence River
1549	Portuguese establish a governor-general at Salvador, Brazil
1585	English establish colony on Roanoke Island, North Carolina
1607	English establish colony at Jamestown, Virginia
1616	William Baffin fails to discover Northwest Passage around North America
1620	English establish colony at Massachusetts Bay

tive. Europeans were especially dependent on Asian sources for luxury goods such as silk, spices for cooking and preserving food, and medicines for pain relief and healing.

Asia Before the European Empires

After the collapse of the Mongol Empire in the fourteenth century, direct access for European merchants to China and the Indian Ocean was blocked. Plague, political unrest, and Muslim hostility to Christians reduced trade to a mere trickle of what it had been. The elaborate trade networks that had helped drive the expansion of the economy of the West during the thirteenth century were in disarray.

The greatest potential rival to the Europeans who sought access to Asian trade was Ming China (1368–1644), a highly advanced civilization with maritime technology and organizational capability to launch exploratory voyages far superior to Europe's. Even before the Portuguese began their slow progress down the west coast of Africa, the Chinese organized a series of huge maritime expeditions into the Indian Ocean that reached far down the east coast of Africa. Between 1405 and 1433 the Chinese established diplomatic contacts and demanded tribute in dozens of kingdoms in

DOCUMENT

A Ming Naval Expedition (15th c.)

India and Africa. The size and ambition of these fleets far surpassed anything that sailed from Europe at this time, and the massive crews of as many as 27,500 men (compared to Columbus's crew of 90) included a complement of scholars to communicate with foreign kings and highly skilled technicians to make repairs to the fleet. The Chinese fleets took trade goods, such as silk, tea, and porcelains, and brought back to China strange animals, hostage kings, and possible trade items. After nearly thirty years of searching the Indian Ocean ports, the Ming emperors concluded that China already possessed all the goods that were available abroad, that China was indeed the center of civilization, and that further investments in oceangoing expeditions were unwarranted.

The European and Chinese voyages of the fifteenth century differed in their objectives and in the motives of the governments that sponsored them. The Europeans were mostly privateers seeking personal profit or captains who enjoyed official government backing in return for a portion of the profits. The economic motive behind the European voyages made them self-sustaining because the Europeans sailed only to places where they could make money. In contrast, the imperial Chinese expeditions were only partially motivated by the desire for economic gain. The official purpose of the Chinese voyages was to learn about the world, and once the Chinese found out what they wanted, they ceased the official voyages. Chinese merchant traders continued to ply the seas on their own, however, and when the Europeans arrived in East Asia, they simply inserted themselves into this already developed Chinese-dominated trade network.

In contrast to the trade in Africa and America, Europeans failed to monopolize trade in Asia. The Europeans were just one among many trading groups, some working under government sponsorship, such as the Portuguese, and others working alone, such as the Chinese.

The Trading Post Empires

In 1497–1499 Vasco da Gama opened the most promising route for the Portuguese around Africa to South and East Asia. But the sailing distances were long, limiting the number of people who could be transported to Asia, and the Asian empires were well equipped to defend themselves against European conquest. As a result, European engagement with Asia was slight for 300 years. Because Europeans lacked the support system provided by colonial conquest, few Europeans settled in Asia, and even missionary work proved much more difficult than in the Americas.

Unlike Brazil, where the Portuguese established colonial plantations, in Asia they established trading posts along the coasts of India, China, and the Spice Islands. When the Portuguese first arrived at a location with a safe harbor and easy access to the hinterland, they built a fort and forced,

bribed, or tricked the local political authority, usually a chieftain, to cede the land around the post to Portugal. The agents sent to trade in Asia were called factors and their trading posts were called factories. But they were not factories in the modern sense of sites for manufacturing; they were safe places where merchants could trade and store their merchandise. The factors lived in the factories with a few other Portuguese traders, a small detachment of troops, and servants recruited from the local population. Nowhere did Portuguese authority extend very far into the hinterland. The traditional political structures of local chieftains remained, and the local elites usually went along with the arrangement because they profited by reselling European wares, such as cloth, guns, knives, and many kinds of cheap gadgets. The factors acquired silks, gold, silver, raw cotton, pepper, spices, and medicines. Some of these outposts of the Portuguese Empire survived until late in the twentieth century, but their roots remained exceedingly shallow. Even in places such as East Timor, an island in Indonesia, and Macao on the south China coast, which were Portuguese outposts for more than four centuries, only a small native elite ever learned the Portuguese language or adapted to European culture.

The Portuguese and later other Europeans were motivated to establish colonies in Asia primarily by commercial considerations. Consider the search for the spice nutmeg, which illustrates something of the enticement of the Asia trade. In an account published in 1510, an Italian traveler, Ludovico di Varthema, described for the first time in a European language nutmeg trees, which he found growing in the Banda Islands, a small archipelago some thousand miles east of Java. These were the only places in the world where nutmeg grew. Besides adding flavor to foods, nutmeg was believed to possess powers to cure all kinds of diseases and to induce a hallucinatory euphoria. The demand for nutmeg was so great and the supply so limited that exporting it yielded enormous profits. At one time, nutmeg was the most valuable commodity in the world after gold and silver. In the early seventeenth century the markup on a pound of nutmeg transported from the Banda Islands to Europe was 60,000 percent. It is no wonder European traders were willing to risk their lives on long, dangerous sea voyages to obtain nutmeg and other spices.

In return for raw materials such as nutmeg, European merchants typically traded manufactured goods, and they made every effort to ensure that other European powers were excluded from competing in this trade in Asia. Given the high profit potential, there was a great temptation to break a European rival's trading monopoly on a rare commodity such as nutmeg. Crucial to enforcing the system was a network of factories and a strong navy, which was primarily used against other European and occasionally Muslim interlopers. Through the trading post empires, commercial rivalries among European states extended abroad to Asia. Competition over these trading posts foreshadowed the beginnings of a global economy dominated by Europeans. It also demonstrated the Europeans' propensity to transform European wars into world wars.

In addition to trade, the Portuguese and other European powers sought to spread Christianity among the local Asian populations. Franciscan, Dominican, and later Jesuit missionaries preached to the indigenous peoples. To accomplish conversions, they tried persuasion, because without the backing of a full-scale conquest as in the Americas, resorting to force was usually not an option. The missionaries frequently drew the ire of local rulers, who viewed the converts as traitors—a situation that led to the persecution of some of the new Christians. To accomplish their task of conversion, Christian missionaries had to learn the native languages and something of the native culture and religion. In this effort, the Jesuits were particularly dedicated; they sent members of their order to the Chinese imperial court, where they lived incognito for decades, although they made few converts. Jesuits also traveled to Japan, where they established an outpost of Christianity at Nagasaki. With the exception of the Spanish Philippines, which was nominally converted to Catholicism by 1600, Christian missionaries in Asia were far less successful than in the Americas. Perhaps one million Asians outside the Philippines had been converted during this period, but many of these conversions did not last. Christians were most successful in converting Buddhists and least effective among Muslims, who almost never abandoned their faith.

St. Francis Xavier, Jesuit in India (1530s–1550s)

By the end of the sixteenth century, Portuguese and Spanish shipping in Asian waters faced recurrent harassment from the English, French, and Dutch. The Dutch drove the Portuguese from their possessions in Ceylon, India, and the Spice Islands, except for East Timor. But none of these sixteenth-century European empires was particularly effective at imposing European culture on Asia in a way comparable with the Americas. In the Spanish Philippines, for example, few natives spoke Spanish, and there were fewer than 5,000 Spanish inhabitants as late as 1850. European states competed among themselves for trade and tried to enforce monopolies, but the Europeans remained peripheral to Asian culture until the late eighteenth and early nineteenth centuries, when the British expanded their power in India and colonized Australia and New Zealand.

The expansion of the Russian Empire into Asia depended not on naval power but on cross-country expeditions. The heartland of the Russian Empire was Muscovy, the area around Moscow, but the empire would eventually spread from the Baltic Sea to the Pacific Ocean. After 1552 Russians began to push across the Ural mountains into Siberia, lured by the trade in exotic furs, which were in great demand among the upper classes of northern Europe, both to keep warm and as fashion statements. The Russians' search for furs was equivalent to the Spanish search for

gold; like gold, fur attracted adventurous and desperate men. Following the navigable rivers and building strategic forts along the way, expeditions collected furs locally and then advanced deeper into the frozen wilds of Siberia. Several of the great aristocratic families of Russia acquired enormous wealth from the Siberian fur trade, which was so lucrative that Russian trappers kept pushing farther and farther east. In this quest for furs, expeditions reached the Pacific coast in 1649, by which time Russia had established a network of trading posts over all of northern Asia.

The significance of the European trading post empires lies less in the influence of Europe on Asia than in the influence of Asia on Europe. Asian products from spices and opium to silk cloth and oriental rugs became commonplace items in middle- and upper-class European households. European collectors became fascinated with Chinese porcelains, lacquered boxes, and screen paintings. At the same time, Asians began to visit Europe, a tradition begun when four Japanese converts to Christianity arrived in Lisbon in 1586 and made a celebrated tour of Europe.

CHRONOLOGY

Europeans in Asia

1487–1488	Bartholomew Dias reaches Cape of Good Hope
1497–1499	Vasco da Gama reaches India via Cape of Good Hope
1498	Portuguese reach Malabar coast of India
1514	Portuguese reach China
1519–1522	Ferdinand Magellan's crew circumnavigate the globe

The Beginnings of the Global System

■ How was the world tied together in a global biological and economic system?

As a result of the European voyages of the fifteenth and sixteenth centuries, a network of cultural, biological, and economic connections formed along intercontinental trading routes. These connections created a global system that has been sustained ever since. Today's global economy, based on cellular telephones, the World Wide Web, air transportation, and free trade, operates much more efficiently and quickly than its predecessors, but it is merely an extension and elaboration of a system that first appeared on a global scale during the sixteenth century. For many thousands of years, Europe, northern Africa, and Asia had been in contact with each other, but the system that took form during the sixteenth century began to encompass most of the globe, including sub-Saharan Africa and the Americas. Unlike earlier international trading systems that linked Europe and Asia, the new global system was dominated by Europeans. They turned large parts of the Americas into plantations that used African slave labor to grow crops for European consumers. This system transformed human society by bringing into contact elements that had previously been separate and isolated—regional cultures, biological systems, and local economies.

The Columbian Exchange

The most dramatic changes were at first produced by the trade of peoples, plants, animals, microbes, and ideas between the Old and New Worlds—a process known as the Columbian Exchange°. For the native Americans, the importation of Europeans, Africans, and microbes had devastating consequences—threatening indigenous religions, making native technology irrelevant, disrupting social life, and destroying millions of lives. For Europeans, the discovery of previously unknown civilizations profoundly shook their own understanding of human geography and history. Neither the ancient philosophers nor the Bible, which was understood to be an accurate history of humankind since the creation of the world, had provided a hint about the peoples of the Americas.

The Slave Trade

All of the ancient civilizations had been slave societies with as many as one-third of the population in bondage. During the Middle Ages a small number of slaves were employed as domestic servants and concubines in the Christian cities of the Mediterranean, and in Muslim countries large numbers of slaves were found in harems, used as laborers, and even trained as soldiers. Many of the slaves in Christian cities were Muslims, and many slaves in Muslim countries were Christians, because both religions considered it legitimate to enslave members of the opposing faith. In the wars between Christians and Muslims, captives were habitually enslaved or held for ransom. Large-scale transportation of black Africans began during the ninth and tenth centuries, when Muslim traders took tens of thousands from the island of Zanzibar off the east coast of Africa to lower Iraq, where they performed the heavy labor of draining swamps and cutting sugar cane. Slavery was also widespread in Islamic West Africa. Mali depended heavily on slave labor, and in Muslim Ghana slaves constituted about one-third of the population. Thus the institution of slavery was well established in Africa long before the beginning of the trans-atlantic slave trade dominated by Europeans.

Slave Trading Factory
Built by the Portuguese in 1482, the Elmina castle became a base for the slave trade on the Guinea coast of Africa. It was later used by the Dutch and English.

The slave trade flourished only when and where it was profitable. The necessary conditions for profitability were a strong demand for labor-intensive agricultural commodities, a perceived shortage of local labor, a supply of people who could be captured elsewhere, and a moral and legal climate that permitted slavery. These conditions, which came together for Europeans during the colonization of the Cape Verde Islands, were all present in the late fifteenth and sixteenth centuries. The growing population of Europe developed a taste for exotic products such as sugar, tobacco, coffee, and indigo dye. The European colonizers who sought to supply the demand for these goods needed agricultural workers, first for the colonies in the Atlantic islands and then for plantations in the Americas. In the Americas, European diseases decimated the indigenous population, creating a labor shortage. Europeans also found it difficult to enslave the native peoples, who knew the territory and could easily escape.

The flourishing demand for labor was supplied by the population of Africa. Once Europeans started to buy up slaves in the coastal trading posts, enterprising African chieftains sent slave-hunting expeditions into the interior. As a consequence, the slave-trading states of the Guinea coast gained power at the expense of their neighbors and spread the unwelcome web of the slave trade deep into the African interior. The slave hunters sold captives to the Europeans for transportation across the Atlantic. Following the Portuguese in the trade came the Dutch, English, French, and Danes, who eventually established their own trading posts to obtain slaves.

In addition to the economic incentive for slavery, both Christianity and Islam provided a moral justification and legal protection for it. Enslaving others was considered legitimate punishment for unbelievers. Of all the Western religions, only Judaism demonstrated a consistent moral resistance to the slave trade because Jewish identity depended heavily on remembering the biblical account of the enslavement of the ancient Hebrews in Egypt. Notable exceptions were the few Jewish plantation owners in Surinam, who did use slave labor. The problem for Christian and Muslim slavers was that when a slave converted to Christianity or Islam, the pretext for enslavement disappeared. To solve this problem, Christians created a new rationalization by connecting slavery to race. As the African slave trade expanded during the seventeenth and eighteenth centuries, Europeans began to associate slavery with "blackness," which was considered inferior to "whiteness." Among Muslims, the justification for enslavement remained a religious one, and when a slave converted to Islam he or she was, at least theoretically, supposed to be freed.

During the nearly 400 years of the European slave trade (ca. 1500–1870), more than ten million Africans were transported to the Americas, the result of which was that large slices of the Americas were transformed into outposts of sub-Saharan African cultures. Blacks came to outnumber native Americans and constituted the majority of the colonial population in most of the Caribbean, and broad parts of coastal Central America, Venezuela, Guyana, and Brazil. Much of the male population of Angola was transported directly to Brazil, a forced migration that resulted in a dramatic excess of females over males in the most heavily depopulated areas of Angola. In the process, Portuguese Brazil became the single largest recipient of African slaves. It was the destination of 3.6 million Africans—nearly ten times the number brought to all of English-speaking North America.

The slave ships that sailed the infamous Middle Passage across the Atlantic were so unhealthy, with Africans "stacked like books on a shelf," that a significant portion of the human cargo died en route. The physical and psychological burdens that slavery placed on its victims can scarcely be imagined, in large part because few slaves were ever allowed to learn to read and write, and thus direct records of their experiences are rare. Documents from ship surgeons, overseers, and slave masters, however, indicate that slaves were subjected to unhealthy living conditions, back-breaking work, and demoralization.

The plantations of the New World mixed together Africans from different cultures and language groups, making it difficult for slaves to build the solidarity necessary to rebel successfully. In a few places, runaways established their own self-governing communities, such as the Saramakas of Surinam or the Cimarrón republic in Peru, but most found escape impossible because they had no place to go and certainly no way to return to their homeland. Despite these crushing hardships, and even within the harsh confines of white-owned plantations, black slaves created their own institutions, family structures, and cultures.

Biological Exchanges

Europeans certainly perpetuated atrocities in the New World, but the intentional genocide of whole peoples was rare. Except for the first colonizers of the Canary Islands, even the most vicious colonizers wanted to enslave or exploit the natives, not destroy them. Nevertheless, the introduction of new diseases to the Americas and the disruption of traditional economies led to a form of unintentional genocide that resulted in the deaths of millions. The European, Asian, and African continents, on the one hand, and the Americas, on the other, had been isolated from each other for so long that they had become two biologically distinct worlds. After the voyages of Christopher Columbus they were rejoined in ways that—for good or for ill—made them more alike culturally and, especially, biologically. As one historian has put it, the "trend toward biological homogeneity is one of the most important aspects of the history of life on this planet since the retreat of the continental glaciers."[3]

How did a few thousand Europeans so easily conquer the civilizations of the Americas, which were populated by millions of people? After all, the Aztecs, Incas, and others put up a stubborn resistance to the conquistadores, and yet the Europeans triumphed time after time. The answer: epidemics. Along with their gunpowder weapons, the conquistadores' most effective allies were the invisible microbes of Old World diseases, such as smallpox. A native of the Yucatán peninsula recalled the better days before the conquest:

> There was then no sickness; they had no aching bones; they had then no high fever; they had then no smallpox; they had then no burning chest; they had then no abdominal pain; they had then no consumption; they had then no headache. At that time the course of humanity was orderly. The foreigners made it otherwise when they arrived here.[4]

Nearly every chronicler of the New World conquests was stunned by the toll that epidemic disease had on the natives soon after their initial contact with Europeans. Between 1520 and 1600, Mexico suffered fourteen major epidemics, and Peru seventeen. By the 1580s the populations of the Caribbean islands, the Antilles, and the lowlands of Mexico and Peru had almost completely died off.

Historians estimate the deaths in the tens of millions. The preconquest population of Mexico, which has been estimated at about 19 million, dropped in eighty years to 2.5 million. Even the infrequent contacts between European fishermen and fur traders with natives on the coast of what is now Canada led to rapid depopulation.

The most deadly culprit was smallpox, but measles, typhus, scarlet fever, and chicken pox also contributed to the devastation. All of these were dangerous and even life-threatening to Europeans and Africans alike, but from exposure, people of the Old World had either died young or survived the illness with a resistance to infection from the disease. However, native Americans had never been exposed to these diseases, and as a population completely lacked immunities to them. As a result, all it took was for one infected person to arrive from the Old World to kill off many millions in the New World. After Cortés's men were first driven from Tenochtitlán, a Dominican friar reported that a new ally appeared: "When the Christians were exhausted from war, God saw fit to send the Indians smallpox, and there was a great pestilence in the city. . . . "[5] The epidemic undoubtedly impaired the fighting ability of the Aztecs. The Spaniards' immunity to the very diseases that killed off so many Indians reinforced the impression that the Europeans were favored agents of the gods or gods themselves. As a Maya put it, "we were born to die."[6]

In exchange, the New World gave the Old World syphilis, or at least contemporary Europeans thought so. Historians and epidemiologists have long debated what they call the Columbian question° about the origins of syphilis. Some argue that syphilis or a venereal disease that might be classified as its ancestor came back from the New World with Columbus's sailors; others assert that syphilis was widespread in the Old World long before 1492. Scholars still do not know the answer to the Columbian question, but it is true that after about 1492 there were epidemic outbreaks of sexually transmitted diseases, leading many to assume an American origin.

The exchange of other forms of life was less obviously disastrous. Following the European settlers came a flood of European animals and plants. With the conquistadores came pigs, cattle, goats, sheep, donkeys, and horses—all previously unknown in the New World. Pigs that escaped from the first Spanish ships to land in Florida were the ancestors of the ubiquitous wild razorback pigs of the southern United States. Vast areas of Mexico and Peru depopulated of humans were repopulated with enormous herds of sheep. The cattle herded by the present-day gauchos of Argentina derive from Iberian stock. The characteristic Latin American burro came from Europe as did the horse, which came to be so prized by the plains Indians of North America. Sheep, cattle, and horses, in particular, completely changed the way of life of the native American peoples.

From Europe came the lucrative plantation crops of sugar, cotton, rice, and indigo, crops that required a large supply of field hands. European varieties of wheat, grapes, and olives soon appeared as major crops in Mexico and elsewhere. In exchange, the Americas offered new crops to the Old World such as tobacco, cocoa, paprika, American cotton, pumpkins, beans, maize (corn), and potatoes.

The Demand for Sugar

This engraving from 1540 shows enslaved Indians performing back-breaking work in a sugar mill. African slaves very quickly replaced Indians in the sugar industry. The European demand for sugar stimulated the transportation of Africans to work in the sugar plantations of the Caribbean and Central and South America.

European peasant farmers discovered that maize and the potato provided an attractive substitute for wheat. In many places, the potato replaced wheat as the staple in the diet of the poor. By yielding more calories per acre than wheat or virtually any other traditional grain, the potato made it possible to support more people on a given amount of land. With the spread of the potato as a food source, European populations began to increase rapidly, a trend that created population pressures, which in turn stimulated additional European migrations to the Americas.

The Problem of Cultural Diversity

Before Columbus sailed west, Europeans possessed two systems of thought that seemed to explain everything to them—the Aristotelian and the Christian. The ancient Greek philosopher Aristotle and his followers provided a systematic explanation of geography and cosmology based on what they knew of the world. They had named the continents, described their peoples, and estimated the size of the globe. Particularly in the European universities, Aristotle was still considered practically infallible, the primary source of all human knowledge. But Aristotle had not even imagined the Americas, and that fact raised the possibility that he was wrong on other matters as well. He knew nothing of the llama, the potato, or syphilis—common knowledge to even the most ignorant conquistador. Aristotle had assumed that the heat of the equatorial zone was so great that no one could live there, but the Spanish had found great civilizations thriving astride the equator. In 1570, when Joseph de Acosta felt a chill in the tropics on his way to America, he observed, "what could I else do then but laugh at Aristotle's Meteors and his Philosophy."[7] Travelers to the New World began to realize that the ancients had not known half the truth about the world.

For Christians and Jews, the Bible remained the unchallenged authority on the origins of the whole world, but the New World created numerous problems for biblical interpretation. The book of Genesis told of the Creation and the great flood, which had destroyed all people and all animals except those saved in Noah's ark. The New World brought into question that vision of a single creation and cleansing flood simply because it could not explain why the plants and animals of the Americas were so different. If the only animals on Earth were those Noah preserved, then why were they different on the two sides of the Earth? About the New World a French writer asked, "How falls it out that the nations of the world, coming all of one father, Noah, do vary so much from one another, both in body and mind?"[8] Thinkers argued either that there must have been more than one creation or that the great flood must have covered only Palestine rather than the entire Earth. However, these solutions tacitly recognized that a literal reading of the words of Scripture could not produce a satisfactory account of the history of the world.

The greatest conceptual challenges to Christian Europe were the New World peoples themselves. If these people were not the children of God's Creation, then how did they get there? If they were God's children, then why were they so different from Europeans? In the terms available to sixteenth-century thinkers, there were three possible ways to answer these questions. One was to assume that the native Americans were subhumans, demons, or some strange form of animal life. This answer was the most convenient one to those who sought to exploit the natives. Often with little or no foundation, these Europeans believed that the natives practiced devil worship, incest, sexual promiscuity, polygamy, sodomy, and cannibalism—all signs of their demonic nature. If not demons, the natives must be unnatural beasts: wild men, dog men, or satyrs. In this extreme form of European belief, the natives did not even possess a human soul and were neither capable of converting to Christianity nor worthy of human rights. Most European thinkers insisted that the natives must be descendants of Adam and Eve, and thus they possessed souls, could be redeemed, and were subject to divine law. But even among otherwise intelligent thinkers, some of the subhuman prejudice survived. The English philosopher Francis Bacon (1561–1626), who did not wallow in the common intolerance of his day, shared the view that as naked cannibals, Indians had defaced humanity.

A second answer to why the peoples of the New World were so different sprung from a belief that the natives were complete innocents. The native peoples lived in a kind of earthly Paradise, unspoiled by the corruption of European society. Some of the early English explorers of Virginia found the natives "most gentle, loving and faithful, void of any guile or treason," and one missionary found them "all the more children of God owing to their very lack of capacity and skill."[9] A tiny number of unconventional theological thinkers hypothesized that the native Americans had been created before the Hebrews as reported in the Bible, and, therefore, had not been subject to the Fall of Man and still lived in the earthly Paradise. The English humanist Thomas More (1478–1535) located his Utopia, an imagined ideal community, in the New World to demonstrate how corrupt the social institutions of the Old World had become.

The most influential spokesman during the sixteenth century for this idea of native innocence was the powerful advocate of human rights Bartholomew de Las Casas (1474–1566), the bishop of arid, impoverished Chiapas in Mexico. Throughout his career, Las Casas forcefully argued against the enslavement and ill treatment of the native Americans, which he chronicled in his most important published work, *The Brief Relation of the Destruction of the West Indies* (1542). Through Las Casas's influence, Spanish royal policy toward the Indians became more peaceful and sympathetic. As beneficent as he was toward the natives, however, Las Casas did not accept native culture as in any way equal or superior to European. He merely saw the natives as innocents who needed to be guided rather than forced to accept Christianity and who did not deserve to be slaves. He

DOCUMENT

Excerpt from Bartholomew de las Casas's *In Defense of the Indians*

Mutilation of Native Americans

In this illustration for one of Bartholomew de Las Casas's books condemning Spanish policy in America, a conquistador is shown terrorizing the natives with vicious dogs, a frequently employed technique. The conquistador dangles two infants while the dogs bite them. To the left a priest baptizes a young child whose mother has been hanged.

did not, however, bother to make the same argument on behalf of black Africans.

The third response to the question of how to explain the "differentness" of New World peoples neither dehumanized them nor assumed them innocent but simply recognized their differences as the natural consequence of human diversity. Advocates of this position proposed some form of cultural toleration. The inconvenient facts of the New World brought to the forefront the inadequacy of traditional moral standards for judging the behavior of other people. Deciding whether a particular people were bad or good raised questions about the criteria for making such judgments, and these questions introduced the principle of cultural relativism. Cultural relativism° recognized that many (but not necessarily all) standards of judgment are specific to particular cultures rather than the fixed truths established by natural or divine law. Cultural relativists attempt to understand why other people think and act the way they do before they judge them. Such an approach can be traced to a small group of sixteenth-century European thinkers who tried to make sense of the new discoveries. Perplexed by the cultural diversity he had observed in the New World, Peter Martyr D'Anghiera (1457–1526), a pious priest and astute historian of Spanish explorations, noted that different peoples made judgments on the basis of different criteria: "the Ethiopian thinks the black color to be fairer than the white, and the white man thinks otherwise.... The bearded man supposes he is more comely than he that wants a beard. As appetite therefore moves, not as reason persuades, men run into these vanities, and every province is ruled by its own sense...."[10] What others

thought fundamental moral truths, Martyr considered manifestations of superficial cultural differences.

The most eloquent voice for cultural toleration during the sixteenth century was Michel de Montaigne (1533–1592), the brilliant French essayist. After a career as a hardworking public official, he retired at age 38 to his estate to a life of study and contemplation. Among his many interests, he especially loved to read about travels to the New World. His essay "On Cannibals" pointed to the hypocrisy of Christians who condemned the alleged cannibalism of the native Americans but justified the torture and murder of other Christians over some minor theological dispute. Montaigne argued that a truly ethical, truly Christian person was not a rigid follower of biblical laws but was capable of understanding and tolerating cultural differences. The discovery in the New World that non-Christians could lead moral lives, love their families, practice humility and charity, and benefit from highly developed religious institutions shook the complacent sense of European superiority.

The Capitalist Global Economy

During the sixteenth century a truly global economy began to take shape as a consequence of the European encounters with the rest of the world. As the Europeans sailed the oceans of the world in search of profits, they pioneered a new form of economic organization—agrarian capitalism°. In agrarian capitalism Europeans organized the production of certain kinds of commercial crops, such as sugar, tobacco, and indigo, which were raised for sale to an expanding population in Europe. With land expropriated from native peoples in the Atlantic islands, the Americas, and parts of Asia, European capitalists began to raise commercial crops on an unprecedented scale. Unlike other forms of capitalism, which relied on workers who were paid a wage, agrarian capitalism relied on slave labor, mostly provided by transplanted Africans.

Agrarian capitalism depended on the creation of European empires—the settler colonies, plantation colonies, and trading post empires of the Portuguese, Spanish, Dutch, French, English, and Russians. These empires, however, were very different from those of the ancient world, medieval Europe, preconquest Americas, and Asia. In ancient Rome, medieval Byzantium, and early modern China, for example, imperial governments promoted monopolies and inhibited free access to the market and thus stymied the development of capitalism. These empires produced economic stagnation instead of growth. But in the European global empires of the sixteenth century, the organization of trade and the division of labor took place outside the authority of any one state, a fact that made it impossible for a single imperial government to monopolize completely economic resources. It was the competition among imperialist states, rather than control by a single powerful empire, that was new.

The creation of the European empires during the sixteenth century made it possible for capitalists to maximize their profits through regional specialization. Western Europe became the *core* of the global economy, the center of a complex variety of economic activities and institutions—banking, insurance, trade companies, gun manufacture, shipbuilding, and the production of cloth. In Europe agriculture was more and more devoted exclusively to producing food, and the labor supply was free—neither serfs, as had been the case in the Middle Ages, nor slaves, as was the case in parts of the Americas. The distant colonies, especially in Spanish and Portuguese America, became the *periphery* devoted to raising single cash crops, such as sugar, tobacco, cotton, coffee, or indigo for dyes. Agriculture in the periphery was produced on large estates by slaves. Even after the end of slavery in the nineteenth century and the European empires in the nineteenth and twentieth centuries, the heritage of agrarian capitalism has left radical imbalances between the core and the periphery in the global economy.

The capitalist global economy has steadily and relentlessly expanded throughout the world since the sixteenth century. Much of the subsequent history of Western civilization can be understood only in terms of the triumph of capitalism and the economic integration of a world dominated by Westerners. The capitalist global economy has yielded many benefits in enhancing the material well-being of the middle classes of the West, increasing the available food supply of the world, and stimulating technological innovation. But there have been costs. Since the sixteenth

century, the gap between rich and poor individuals and rich and poor countries has widened, and societies on the agrarian periphery have found it enormously difficult to break out of their disadvantaged position in the world economy.

Conclusion

The Significance of the Global Encounters

The world was forever changed by the European voyages from about 1450 to 1650. The significance of these encounters lay not so much in the Europeans' geographical discoveries as in the scale of permanent contact these voyages made possible among previously isolated peoples of the world. Vikings had been to the Americas before Columbus, and the Chinese had earlier engaged in long-distance voyages of reconnaissance as far as the east coast of Africa. But none of these early voyages had created a lasting economic system or lasting cultural contacts. The European voyages of the fifteenth and sixteenth centuries did.

As a result of the Portuguese slaving enterprises on the coast of West and Central Africa, millions of Africans were uprooted, transported in chains to a strange land, and forced to toil in subhuman conditions on plantations. There they grew crops for the increasingly affluent European consumers and generated profits often used to buy more slaves in Africa, parts of which became depopulated in the process. In Europe until well into the nineteenth century, every cup of coffee, every puff of tobacco, every sugar candy, and every cotton dress of indigo blue came from the sweat of a black slave.

Many of the native Americans lost their lives, their land, and their way of life as a result of European encounters. The most isolated of them retained their languages and religion, but other groups were assimilated to the point of nearly complete cultural loss. Everywhere in the Americas, native peoples suffered from the invasion of Old World microbes even more than from the invasion of Old World conquerors. The destruction of the Aztec and Incan Empires were certainly the most dramatic, but everywhere native peoples struggled to adapt to an invasion of foreign beings from a foreign world.

Asia was far less altered by contact with Europeans. The most thorough European conquest in Asia—the Russians in Siberia—was of the least populated region of the entire continent. European civilization remained on the cultural periphery of Asia. But European access to Asian luxury goods remained a crucial component in the expanding global economy that became one of the first fruits of European capitalism.

Coming to terms with the variety of world cultures became a persistent and absorbing problem in Western civilization. Most Europeans retained confidence in the inherent superiority of their civilization, but the realities of the world began to chip away at that confidence, and economic globalization profoundly altered Western civilization itself. Westerners began to confront the problem of understanding "other" cultures and in so doing changed themselves. The West came to mean less a place in Europe than a certain kind of culture that was exported throughout the world through conversion to Christianity, the acquisition of Western languages, and the spread of Western technology.

Suggestions for Further Reading

For a comprehensive listing of suggested readings, please go to www.ablongman.com/levack2e/chapter12

Chaudhuri, K. N. *Trade and Civilization in the Indian Ocean: An Economic History from the Rise of Islam to 1750.* 1985. Arguing for the long-term unity of trade routes, the book lays out the importance of Asian merchants to maritime trade networks from the South China Sea to the Mediterranean.

Clendinnen, Inga. *Aztecs: An Interpretation.* 1991. A provocative, sometimes disturbing book that directly confronts the implications of human sacrifice and cannibalism among the Aztecs and offers an explanation for it by analyzing Aztec religion.

Crosby, Alfred W., Jr. *The Columbian Exchange: Biological and Cultural Consequences of 1492.* 1973. The most significant study on the implications of the biological exchanges for the cultural history of both the Old and New Worlds. It has the benefit of being an exciting book to read.

Curtin, Philip D. *African History: From Earliest Times to Independence.* 1995. An excellent survey by one of the most distinguished comparative historians.

Elvin, Mark. *The Pattern of the Chinese Past: A Social and Economic Interpretation.* 1973. An excellent overview of Chinese history that covers Chinese responses to Western encounters.

Fernández-Armesto, Felipe. *Before Columbus: Exploration and Colonization from the Mediterranean to the Atlantic, 1229–1492.* 1987. Engagingly written and original in scope, this is the best single account of early European colonization efforts.

Fernández-Armesto, Felipe. *Columbus.* 1991. The 500th anniversary of Columbus's voyage in 1492 provoked a wide-ranging reappraisal of his motives and career. This pithy, engaging book is by far the most convincing in revising Columbus's image, but it deflated much of the Columbus myth and caused considerable controversy.

Oliver, Roland. *The African Experience from Olduvai Gorge to the 21st Century.* 2000. A highly readable general survey.

Pagden, Anthony. *European Encounters with the New World: From Renaissance to Romanticism.* 1993. A fascinating examination of how Europeans interpreted their encounters with America.

Parry, J. H. *The Age of Reconnaissance.* 1982. An analysis of European shipping technology and the causes behind European explorations. It covers all the major voyages.

Parry, J. H. *The Spanish Seaborne Empire.* 1990. The standard study on the subject. It brings together an enormous range of material and presents it clearly and cogently.

Phillips, William D., Jr., and Carla Rahn Phillips. *The Worlds of Christopher Columbus.* 1992. A balanced analysis of Columbus's attempts to find financing for his voyage that pays equal attention to his personal ambition, Christian zeal, and navigational skills.

Notes

1. Christopher Columbus, quoted in Felipe Fernández-Armesto, *Columbus* (1991), 154.

2. Sir Arthur Helps, *The Spanish Conquest in America,* Vol. 1 (1900), 1, 264–267.

3. Alfred W. Crosby, Jr., *The Columbian Exchange: Biological and Cultural Consequences of 1492* (1973), 3.

4. *The Book of Chilam Balam of Chumayel,* ed. and trans. Ralph L. Roy (1933), 83.

5. *The Conquistadores: First-Person Accounts of the Conquest of Mexico,* ed. and trans. Patricia de Fuentes (1963), 159.

6. *The Annals of the Cakchiquels and Title of the Lords of Totnicapán,* trans. Adrian Recinos, Dioniscio José Chonay, and Delia Goetz (1953), 116.

7. Quoted in Margaret T. Hodgen, *Early Anthropology in the Sixteenth and Seventeenth Centuries* (1964), 9.

8. Quoted in ibid., 207. Spelling has been modernized.

9. Quoted in ibid., 369.

10. Quoted in ibid., 373–374. Spelling and syntax have been modernized.

1500

AD

ALBERTVS DVRERVS NORICVS
ipfum me proprijs fic effin
gebam coloribus ætatis
anno XXVIII.

The Reformations of Religion

13

N OCTOBER 31, 1517, AN OBSCURE MONK-TURNED-UNIVERSITY-professor was reported to have nailed on the door of the cathedral in Wittenberg, Germany, an announcement containing ninety-five theses or debating propositions. Martin Luther had no hint of the ramifications of this simple act—as common then as posting an announcement for a lecture or concert on a university bulletin board now. But Luther's seemingly harmless deed would spark a revolution. Within weeks all Germany was ablaze over what was widely seen as Luther's daring attack on the pope. Within a few short years Wittenberg became the European center for a movement to reform the Church. As the pope and high churchmen resisted Martin Luther's call for reform, much of Germany and eventually most of northern Europe and Britain broke away from the Catholic Church in a movement called the Protestant Reformation, which dominated European affairs from 1517 until 1560.

Martin Luther was successful because he expressed in print what many felt in their hearts—that the Church was failing in its most fundamental obligation to help Christians achieve salvation. In contrast, many Catholics considered the Protestants dangerous heretics who offended God with their errors and whose heresies made salvation impossible. Moreover, many Catholics had long recognized the need for reforms in the Church and had been diligently working on achieving them. To them the intemperate Martin Luther only made matters worse.

The division between Protestants and Catholics split the West into two distinctive religious cultures. The result was that the hard-won unity of the West, which had been achieved during the Middle Ages through the expansion of Christianity to the most distant corners of the European continent and through the leadership of the papacy, was lost. Catholics and Protestants continued to share a great deal of the Christian tradition, but fateful issues

The Imitation of Christ In Albrecht Dürer's self-portrait at age 28, he literally shows himself imitating Christ's appearance. The initials AD are prominently displayed in the upper left-hand corner. They stand for Albrecht Dürer but also for *anno domini*, "the year of our Lord."

divided them: their understanding of salvation, the function of the sacraments in promoting pious behavior, the celebration of the liturgy in Latin, and obedience to the pope. After the Reformation of the sixteenth century, the common Christian culture was permanently severed by the Protestants' refusal to accept the authority of the pope on these issues.

Throughout western Europe, countries officially became either Catholic or Protestant—a situation that enforced obedience to the official faith through the police powers of the state and caused considerable suffering among adherents to unofficial religions. The fundamental conflict during the Reformation was about religion, but religion can never be entirely separated from politics or society. The competition among the kingdoms and the social tensions within the cities of central and northern Europe magnified the religious controversies, making the Reformation a broad cultural movement that seeped into all aspects of life. The Reformation raises the question, how did encounters between Catholics and Protestants permanently transform religious unity into religious division in the West?

- What caused the religious rebellion that began in German-speaking lands and spread to much of northern Europe?
- How did the Lutheran Reformation create a new kind of religious culture?
- How and why did Protestant denominations multiply to such an extent in northern Europe and Britain?
- How did the Catholic Church respond to the unprecedented threat to its dominance of religious authority in the West?
- How did the religious turmoil of the sixteenth century transform the role of the visual arts and music in public life?

Causes of the Reformation

- What caused the religious rebellion that began in German-speaking lands and spread to much of northern Europe?

The Protestant Reformation was the culmination of nearly 200 years of turmoil within the Church. During the fourteenth and fifteenth centuries the Church was especially hampered by the contradiction between its divine mission and its obligations in this world. On the one hand, the Church taught that its mission was otherworldly, as the source of spiritual solace and the guide to eternal salvation. On the other hand, the Church was thoroughly of this world. It owned vast amounts of property, maintained a far-reaching judicial bureaucracy to enforce canon

(Church) law, and was headed by the pope, who was also the territorial prince of the Papal State in central Italy. Whereas from the eleventh to the thirteenth centuries the popes had been the source of moral reform and spiritual renewal in the Church, by the fifteenth century they had become part of the problem. The problem was not so much that they had become corrupt but that they were unable to respond effectively to the demands of ordinary people who were increasingly concerned with their own salvation and the effective government of their communities.

Three developments, in particular, contributed to the demand for religious reform: the search for the freedom of private religious expression; the print revolution; and the northern Renaissance interest in the Bible and sources of Christianity.

The Search for Spiritual and Fiscal Freedom

A series of events during the fourteenth century had weakened the authority of the popes and driven the Church to the point of splitting apart, more for political than theological reasons (see Chapter 10). Between 1305 and 1378 seven popes in a row abandoned Rome, which was plagued by dangerous feuds among its aristocratic families, and chose to reside in the relative calm of Avignon, France. The period came to be called the Babylonian Captivity of the Church, a pejorative term that reflected the widespread opinion outside France that the popes had become subservient to the kings of France. The loss of revenues from the Papal State in Italy forced the financial advisers of the popes into various shady financial schemes, which undermined the moral reputation of the papacy. The Babylonian Captivity was followed by an equally contentious period between 1378 and 1417, the Great Schism, when the Church was divided over allegiance to rival Italian and French popes, and eventually to three and four competing popes.

The degradation of the papacy during the Babylonian Captivity and the Great Schism led to the Conciliar Movement, an attempt by a group of bishops to solve the schism and to liberate the Church from the abuses of papal authority. The conciliarists argued that at a general meeting or council (hence, "conciliar") the bishops would have authority over the pope and could depose him and arrange for the election of a new pope. Accordingly, the Council of Constance (1414–1417) ended the Great Schism, and the Council of Basel (1431–1449) voted for reforms. But the reforms were never implemented because of the uncompromising attitude of Pope Eugeneus IV (1431–1447). The failure of the moderate reforms of the Council of Basel opened the way for the more radical rejection of papal authority during the Protestant Reformation of the sixteenth century.

While the papacy's moral authority precipitously declined, lay Christians were drawn to new forms of worship.

tion the moral authority of the papacy. They began to see the pope as a thieving foreigner who extorted money that could be better spent locally. German communities, in particular, protested against the financial demands and the questionable practices of the pope and higher clergy. Some bishops neglected their duties regarding the spiritual guidance of their flock. Some never resided in their dioceses (the district under the bishop's care), knew nothing of the problems of their people, and were concerned only with retaining their incomes and lavish living standards. Living amid the pleasures of Rome, these high clergymen were in no position to discipline parish priests, some of whom also ignored their moral responsibilities by living openly with concubines and even selling the sacraments. Although immorality of this sort was probably not widespread, a few notorious examples bred enormous resentment among the laity.

In an effort to assert control over the church in their own communities, city officials known as magistrates attempted to stem the financial drain and end clerical abuses. They restricted the amount of property ecclesiastical institutions could own, tried to tax the clergy, made priests subject to the town's courts of law, and eliminated the churchmen's exemption from burdensome duties, such as serving in the town militia or providing labor for public works. On the eve of the Reformation—especially in the cities of Germany and the Netherlands—magistrates had already begun to assert local control over the church, a tendency that prepared the way for the Protestants' efforts. For many laypeople, the overriding desire was to obtain greater spiritual and fiscal freedom from the Church.

Vision of the Other World

Hieronymus Bosch (ca. 1450–1516) attempted to visualize in this painting the concern of all Christians for transcendence. In the panel on the left, angels offer those who have been saved a vision of Heaven. In the panel on the right, the angels assist the saved on their ascension through a tunnel that divides this world from the pure light of God.

Particularly influential were the Modern Devotion, which was promoted by the Brothers of the Common Life, and the *Imitation of Christ*, written by a Common Life brother about 1441. By emphasizing frequent private prayer and moral introspection, the *Imitation* provided a kind of spiritual manual that helped laypeople follow the same path toward spiritual renewal that traditionally had been reserved for monks and nuns. The goal was to imitate Christ so thoroughly that Christ entered the believer's soul. For example, the 1500 self-portrait of Albrecht Dürer (1471–1528), a work influenced by the Modern Devotion, portrayed the artist as if he were Christ himself. This portrait is the opening image in this chapter.

The religious fervor that drew many Christians to such profound forms of religious expression led them to ques-

The Print Revolution

Until the mid-fifteenth century, the only way in the West to reproduce any kind of text—a short business record or a long philosophical book—was to copy it laboriously by hand. As medieval scribes made copies on parchment, however, they often introduced errors or "improved" the original text as they saw fit. Thus, two different copies of the same text could read differently. Parchment books were also very expensive; a book as long as the Bible might require the skins of 300 sheep to make the parchment sheets and hundreds of hours of labor to copy the text. The high cost meant that books were limited to churchmen and to the very rich. Few Christians ever actually read the Bible simply because Bibles—like all books—were so rare.

Two fifteenth-century inventions revolutionized the availability of books. First, movable metal type was introduced around 1450, and after that time printed books first began to appear. Perhaps the very first was a Bible printed by Johannes Gutenberg in Mainz, Germany. Equally important, cheap manufactured paper replaced expensive sheepskins. These two developments reduced the cost of books to a level that made them available even to artisans of modest incomes.

Gutenberg Bible

The demand for inexpensive printed books was astounding. During the first forty years of print, more books were produced than had been copied by scribes during the previous thousand years. By 1500, presses in more than 200 cities and towns had printed six million books. Half of the titles were on religious subjects, and because the publishing industry (then as now) produced only what people wanted to buy, the predominance of religion is a telling indication of what was on the minds of the reading public.

The buyers of printed books included, of course, the traditionally literate classes of university students, churchmen, professionals, and aristocratic intellectuals. Remarkably, however, there was also an enormous demand among people for whom books had previously been an unimaginable luxury. During the fourteenth and fifteenth centuries literacy rates had steadily risen and the power of literate culture was strongly felt even by those who could not write. For example, an illiterate farmer near Siena, Italy, had someone else keep a farming diary for him because he recognized that a written record would give him greater power over his own affairs. Literacy rates varied enormously across Europe. They were highest in the cities, especially in northern Italy, Germany, and the Netherlands. In the rural areas, literacy was still rare, probably limited to the village priest, the notary, and perhaps the local nobility. Everywhere men were more often literate than women. However, the knowledge of what was in books spread widely beyond the literate few. The reason was that reading for most people in the fifteenth and sixteenth centuries was an oral, public activity rather than a silent, private one. In parish churches, taverns, and private houses the literate read books out loud to others for their entertainment and edification.

The expansion of the university system during this period also created more demand for books. Between 1300 and 1500 the number of European universities grew from twenty to seventy. The universities also developed a new way of reading. During the fifteenth century the Sorbonne in Paris and Oxford University decreed that libraries were to be quiet places, an indication of the spread of silent reading among the most highly educated classes. Compared to the tradition of reading aloud, silent reading was faster and more private. The silent reader learned more quickly and also decided independently the meaning of what had been read. Once many cheap books were available to the silent readers among the best educated, the interpretation of texts, especially the notoriously difficult text of the Bible, could no longer be easily regulated.

Would the Reformation have succeeded without the print revolution? It is impossible to imagine that it could have. Print culture radically changed how information was disseminated and gave people new ways to interpret their experiences. Between 1517 and 1520, Martin Luther wrote some thirty tracts, mostly in a riveting colloquial German; 300,000 copies were printed and distributed throughout Europe. No other author's ideas had ever spread so fast to so many.

The First Printing Press

The first printing press, invented by Johannes Gutenberg in Mainz, Germany, probably looked very much like this reconstructed model. The metal blocks with interchangeable letters were inked and then pressed onto each sheet of paper. Then the sheets were hung up while the ink dried.

The Northern Renaissance and the Christian Humanists

As discussed in Chapter 11, the humanists were writers devoted to rediscovering the lost works of antiquity and imitating the style of the best Greek and Latin authors of the ancient world. As the humanists examined these ancient texts, they developed the study of philology, of how the meanings of words change over time. These endeavors stimulated a new kind of approach to the sources of Christianity. The humanist Lorenzo Valla (ca. 1407–1457), for example, evaluated the historical sources of papal authority, including the Donation of Constantine—a document that provided the legal justification for the Papal State and papal assertions of supreme authority in Italy. Because the Donation of Constantine used words that were not current during the time when it was supposedly written, Valla argued that it was a forgery. He went on to question the accuracy of the Vulgate, the Latin translation of the Bible accepted by the Church.

The humanists who specialized in subjecting the Bible to philological study are called the Christian humanists°. In examining the sources of Christianity, their goal was not to criticize Christianity or the Church but to understand the precise meaning of its founding texts, especially the Bible and the writings of the Church fathers, who wrote in Greek and Latin and commented on the Bible during the early centuries of Christianity. The Christian humanists sought to correct what they saw as mistakes in interpreting Christian doctrine and by making the proper interpretations they tried to improve the morals of all. They believed that the path to personal morality and to Church reform lay in imitating "the primitive church," which meant the practices of Christianity at the time of Jesus and the apostles. Most of the Christian humanists came from northern Europe. They constituted the most influential wing of the northern Renaissance, a movement that built on the foundations of the Italian Renaissance. Through their efforts, the foundations of Christianity came under intense scrutiny during the early sixteenth century.

By far the most influential of the Christian humanists was a Dutchman, Desiderius Erasmus (ca. 1469–1536). To remedy the evils of the world, Erasmus became an ardent advocate of education, especially for future priests, whom he wanted to learn "the philosophy of Christ." As a guide to that philosophy, he published an annotated text of the Greek New Testament, which he opened with the optimistic preface: "If the Gospel were truly preached, the Christian people would be spared many wars." He later translated the

Albrecht Dürer, *The Knight, Death, and the Devil*
This engraving of 1513 illustrates Erasmus's *Handbook for the Militant Christian* by depicting a knight steadfastly advancing through a frightening landscape. A figure of death holds an hourglass, indicating that the knight's time on Earth is limited. A devil follows behind him threateningly. His valiant horse and loyal dog represent the virtues that a pious Christian must acquire.

Greek New Testament into a new Latin version. His critical studies were the basis of many translations of the Hebrew and Greek Bible into vernacular languages, including the popular English translation, the King James Bible. His lasting fame rests on his perceptive philological analysis of the Bible and other early Christian texts.

Exploiting the potential of the relatively new printing industry, Erasmus became the most inspiring moral critic of his times. During times of war he eloquently called for peace; he published a practical manual for helping children develop a sense of morality; and he laid out easy-to-follow guidelines for spiritual renewal in the *Handbook for the Militant Christian*. He was most popular for his biting criticisms of the Church that revealed a genuine spiritual sorrow shared by many of his readers:

I could see that the common body of Christians was corrupt not only in its affections but in its ideas. I pondered on the fact that those who profess themselves pastors and doctors for the most part misuse these titles, which belong to Christ, for their own advantage. . . . Is there any religious man who does not see with sorrow that this generation is far the most corrupt there has ever been?[1]

Erasmus's penchant for moral criticism reached the level of high satire in his masterpiece, *The Praise of Folly* (1514). In it he attacked theologians preoccupied by silly questions, such as whether the Resurrection could take place at night; he lampooned corrupt priests who took money from dying men to read the last rites; he ridiculed gullible pilgrims who bought phony relics as tourist souvenirs; and he parodied the vanity of monks who thought the color of their robes more important than helping the poor. He saved some of his most biting sarcasm for the monks by pointing out "their filthiness, their ignorance, their bawdiness, and their insolence."[2]

Despite these criticisms Erasmus refused to abandon Catholicism and engaged in a very public conflict with Luther and the Protestants. He thought the militants on both sides were driven more by egotism than by Christian humility. In the combative age of the Reformation, Erasmus stood virtually alone as a voice of peace and moderation, and like many nonviolent people since that time, he was deeply hated. Erasmus was an eloquent popularizer, some-

one who demonstrated to a large public how individuals could apply to their daily lives previously obscure trends in humanist learning and how a better understanding of the Bible could purify faith and combat corruption within the Church.

Erasmus's friend, the Englishman Thomas More (1478–1535), is best known for his book *Utopia* (1516). More's little book established the genre of utopian fiction, which describes imaginary, idealized worlds. It depicted a fantasy island in the New World, "Utopia," which in Greek means "nowhere." Utopia was inhabited by monotheists who, although not Christians, intuitively understood pure religion, lived a highly regulated life, and shared their property in common. Utopia represented More's understanding of what a society based on the primitive church might look like. In particular he took the idea of abolishing all private property from Scripture, which states that the believers in Christ "were of one heart and soul, and no one claimed private ownership of any possessions, but everything they owned was held in common" (Acts 4:32). More shared some of Erasmus's ideas about the critical study of Scripture and a purer Church, but unlike Erasmus he was no pacifist. In his capacity as chancellor of England, he ruthlessly persecuted Protestants.

Erasmus and More remained loyal Catholics, and More even sacrificed his own life to the faith. Nevertheless, their

---

DOCUMENT

Thomas More's Argument Against Capital Punishment

In sixteenth-century England, there were hundreds of offenses, including simple theft, that could lead to capital punishment. Among the many aspects of contemporary society that Thomas More criticized in Utopia (1516), capital punishment especially offended him because it was so clearly prohibited in the Bible. More combined moral precepts derived from Scripture and reasoned argument, a combination that is especially characteristic of the Christian humanists. Thomas More was himself a victim of capital punishment, executed by the courts of King Henry VIII.

God said, "Thou shalt not kill"—does the theft of a little money make it quite all right for us to do so? If it's said that this commandment applies only to illegal killing, what's to prevent human beings from similarly agreeing among themselves to legalize certain types of rape, adultery, or perjury? Considering that God has forbidden us even to kill ourselves, can we really believe that purely human arrangements for the regulation of mutual slaughter are enough, without any divine authority, to exempt execu-

tioners from the sixth commandment? Isn't that rather like saying that this particular commandment has no more validity than human laws allow it?—in which case the principle can be extended indefinitely, until in all spheres of life human beings decide just how far God's commandments may conveniently be observed.

. . .

Well, those are my objections on moral grounds. From a practical point of view, surely it's obvious that to punish thieves and murderers in precisely the same way is not only absurd but also highly dangerous for the public. If a thief knows that a conviction for murder will get him into no more trouble than a conviction for theft, he's naturally impelled to kill the person that he'd otherwise merely have robbed. It's no worse to him if he's caught, and it gives him a better chance of not being caught, and of concealing the crime altogether by eliminating the only witness. So in our efforts to terrorize thieves we're actually encouraging them to murder innocent people.

Source: From *Utopia*, by Thomas More, translated by Paul Turner (Penguin Classics, 1961). Copyright © 1961 by Paul Turner. Reproduced by permission of Penguin Books Ltd.

work helped popularize some of the principles that came to be associated with the Protestant reformers. To them, the test for the legitimacy of any religious practice was twofold: First, could it be found in the Bible; second, did it promote moral behavior? The Christian humanists' preoccupation with textual criticism focused attention on the sources of Christianity, and some readers were profoundly shaken by the deep disparity they perceived between the Christianity of the New Testament and the state of the Church in their own time.

The Lutheran Reformation

■ How did the Lutheran Reformation create a new kind of religious culture?

The Protestant Reformation began with the protests of Martin Luther against the pope and certain Church practices. Like Erasmus and More, Luther used the Bible as the litmus test of what the Church should do. If a practice could not be found in the Bible, Luther thought, then it should not be considered Christian. But unlike Erasmus and More, he also introduced theological innovations that made compromise with the papacy impossible.

Luther and his followers would not have succeeded without the support of local political authorities, who had their own grievances against the pope and the Holy Roman Emperor, a devout defender of the Catholic faith. The Lutheran Reformation first spread in Germany with the assistance and encouragement of those local authorities: the town magistrates and the territorial princes. Luther's ideas had a magnetic appeal to a wide spectrum of the population, especially women and peasants. When the peasants thought that Luther's ideas about the freedom of the Christian also meant economic freedom, they revolted against their feudal lords. The violence of that revolt forced Luther to retreat and to back the forces of order, the lords and princes. In so doing he made it clear that the Reformation was not to be a social revolution but a religious reform. Lutheranism would not threaten the established political order. Under the sponsorship of princes and kings, Lutheranism spread from Germany into Scandinavia.

Martin Luther and the Break with Rome

Martin Luther (1483–1546) suffered a grim childhood and uneasy relationship with his father, a miner who wanted his son to become a lawyer. During a break from the University of Erfurt, where he was studying law, Luther was thrown from his horse in a storm and nearly died. That frightening experience impelled him to become a monk, a decision that infuriated his father because it meant young Luther abandoned a promising professional career. By becoming a monk, Luther replaced the control of his father with obedience to his superiors in the Augustinian Order. They sent him back to the University of Erfurt for advanced study in theology and then transferred him from the lovely garden city of Erfurt to Wittenberg in Saxony, a scruffy town "on the edge of beyond," as Luther described it. At Wittenberg Luther began to teach at an undistinguished university, far from the intellectual action. Instead of lamenting his isolation, Luther brought the world to his university by making it the center of the religious reform movement.

As a monk, Luther had been haunted by a deep lack of self-worth: "In the monastery, I did not think about women, or gold, or goods, but my heart trembled, and doubted how God could be gracious to me. Then I fell away from faith, and let myself think nothing less than that I had come under the Wrath of God, whom I must reconcile with my good works."[3] Obsessed by the fear that no amount of charitable good works, prayers, or religious ceremonies would compensate for God's contempt of him, Luther suffered from anxiety attacks and prolonged periods of depression. He understood his psychic turmoil and shaky faith as any monk would—the temptations of the Devil, who was a very powerful figure in Luther's imagination.

Over several years, while preparing and revising his university lectures on St. Paul, Luther gradually worked out a solution to his own spiritual crisis by reexamining the theology of penance. The sacrament of penance provided a way to confess sins and receive absolution for them. If a penitent had lied, for example, he could seek forgiveness for the sin by feeling sorry about it, confessing it to a priest, and receiving a penalty, usually a specified number of prayers. Penance took care of only those penalties the Church could inflict on sinners; God's punishment for sins would take place in Purgatory (a place of temporary suffering for dead souls) and at the Last Judgment. But Catholic theology held that penance in this world would reduce punishment in the next. In wrestling with the concept of penance, Luther long meditated on the meaning of a difficult passage in St. Paul's epistle to the Romans (1:17): "The just shall live by faith." Luther came to understand this passage to mean that eternal salvation came not from performing the religious good works of penance but as a gift from God. That gift was called "grace" and was completely unmerited. Luther called this process of receiving God's grace "justification by faith alone°," because the ability to have faith in Christ was a sign that one had received grace.

Luther's emphasis on justification by faith alone left no room for human free will in obtaining salvation, because Luther believed that faith could come only from God's grace. This did not mean that God controlled every human action, but it did mean that humans could not will to do good. They needed God's help. Those blessed with God's grace would naturally perform good works. This way of thinking about God's grace had a long tradition going back to St. Augustine, the Church father whose work profoundly influenced Luther's own thought. In fact, many Catholic thinkers had embraced a similar position, but they did not draw the same conclusions about free will that Luther did. In the turmoil of the Reformation Luther's interpretation of St. Augustine separated Lutheran from Catholic theology. The issue of free will became one of the most crucial differences between Protestants and Catholics. Based on his rejection of free will, Luther eventually concluded that the sacraments of the Church could work only if the person receiving them had received God's grace. One could not will for them to work. He abandoned all but two of the sacraments because sacraments were examples of vain works that deluded people into thinking they could earn salvation by performing them. He was obliged to retain communion and baptism because they were clearly authorized by the Bible, but disputes over the meaning of these two sacraments created divisions within the Protestant Reformation movement itself.

Communion in Both Kinds

In this woodcut by Lucas Cranach the Elder, Lutheran ministers offer both the communion wine and bread to the laity. Catholics reserved the wine for the priests, which set them apart from the laity. Changes in the rituals of the Eucharist or communion were among the most divisive issues separating Catholic from Protestant.

For Luther this seemingly bleak doctrine of denying the human will to do good liberated him from his persistent fears of damnation. He no longer had to worry whether he was doing enough to please God or could muster enough energy to fight the Devil. All he had to do was trust in God's grace. After this breakthrough, Luther reported that "I felt myself to be born anew, and to enter through open gates into paradise itself. From here, the whole face of the Scriptures was altered."[4]

The Ninety-Five Theses

In 1517 Luther became embroiled in a controversy that led to his and his followers' separation from the Roman Catholic Church. In order to finance the building of a new St. Peter's Basilica in Rome, Pope Leo X had issued a special new indulgence. An indulgence was a particular form of penance whereby a sinner could remove years of punishment in Purgatory after death by performing a good work here on Earth. For example, pilgrims to Rome or Jerusalem were often in search of indulgences, which were concrete measures of the value of their penances. Indulgences formed one of the most intimate bonds between the Church and the laity because they offered a means for the forgiveness of specific sins.

During the fourteenth century popes in need of ready cash had begun to sell indulgences. But Pope Leo's new indulgence went far beyond the promise of earlier indulgences by offering a one-time-only opportunity to escape penalties in Purgatory for all sins. Moreover, the special indulgence could apply not only to the purchaser but to the dead already in Purgatory. The new indulgence immediately made all other indulgences worthless because it removed all penalties for sin whereas others removed only some.

Frederick the Wise, the Elector of Saxony (a princely title indicating that he was one of those who elected the emperors of the Holy Roman Empire) and the patron of Martin Luther's university, prohibited the sale of Pope Leo's special indulgence in Electoral Saxony, but it was sold just a few miles away from Wittenberg, across the border in the domain of Archbishop Albrecht of Mainz. Albrecht needed the revenues that the sale of indulgences would bring because he was in debt. He had borrowed enormous sums to bribe Pope Leo to allow him to hold simultaneously three ecclesiastical offices—a practice that was against Church law. To help Albrecht repay his debts, the pope allowed Albrecht to keep half of the revenue from the indulgence sale in his territories. Wittenbergers began to trek over the border to Albrecht's lands to listen to the sales pitch of a shameless indulgence hawker, the Dominican John Tetzel (1470–1519). Tetzel staged an ecclesiastical version of a carnival barker's act in which he harangued the crowd about their dead parents who could be immediately released from the flames of Purgatory for the sacrifice of a few coins. He allegedly ended his sermons with the notorious jingle,

As soon as gold in the basin rings,
Right then the soul to heaven springs.[5]

A group of the Wittenbergers who heard Tetzel asked Martin Luther for his advice about buying the indulgence. Luther responded less as a pastor offering comforting advice to his flock than as a university professor keen for debate. He prepared in Latin ninety-five theses—arguments or talking points—about indulgences that he announced he was willing to defend in an academic disputation. Luther had a few copies printed and, according to Lutheran tradition, dramatically posted one on the door of Wittenberg Cathedral. In fact, his posting of the theses makes a good story, but there is no evidence that he actually did so. It was just standard practice for debates. The Ninety-Five Theses were hardly revolutionary in themselves. They argued a simple point that salvation could not be bought and sold, a proposition that was sound, conservative theology, and they explicitly accepted the authority of the pope even as they set limits on that authority. On that point, Luther was merely following what the Church councils of the fifteenth century had decreed. Luther's tone was moderate. He simply suggested that Pope Leo may have been misled in issuing the new indulgence. No one showed up to debate Luther, but someone translated the Ninety-Five Theses into German and printed them, and within a few weeks, a previously unknown professor from an obscure university was the talk of the German-speaking lands.

The Dominicans counterattacked. Tetzel himself drew up opposing theses, which provoked a public clamor that Luther had tried to avoid. In 1519 at Leipzig before a raucous crowd of university students, Luther finally debated the theses and other issues with Johann Eck, a professor from the University of Ingolstadt. When Eck cleverly backed him into a logical corner, Luther refused to retreat; he insisted that the Bible was the sole guide to human conscience, and he questioned the authority of both popes and councils. This was the very teaching for which earlier heretics had been burned at the stake. At this point Luther had no choice but to abandon his allegiance to the Church to which he had dedicated his life. By this time, Luther also had a large following in Wittenberg and beyond. The core of this group, who called themselves "evangelicals," were university students, younger humanists, and the well-educated, reform-minded priests and monks.

The Path to the Diet of Worms

In the wake of the Leipzig debate and Pope Leo's rejection of Luther's objections to indulgences, Luther abandoned his moderate tone and launched an inflammatory pamphlet campaign. Some pamphlets were first written in Latin, for learned readers, but all soon became available in Luther's acerbic German prose, which delighted readers. *Freedom of a Christian* (1520) argued that the Church's emphasis on good works had distracted Christians from the only source of salvation—God's grace, which was manifest in the faith of the Christian. It proclaimed the revolutionary doctrine of the "priesthood of all believers°," which reasoned that all those of pure faith were themselves priests, a doctrine that undermined the authority of the Catholic clergy over the laity. The most inspirational pamphlet, *To the Christian Nobility of the German Nation* (1520), called upon the German princes to reform the Church and to defend Germany from exploitation by the corrupt Italians who ran the Church in Rome. When Pope Leo ordered Luther to retract his writings, Luther responded with a defiant demonstration in which he and his students burned the pope's decree and all of the university library's books of Church law. The die was cast.

The pope demanded that Luther be arrested, but Luther's patron, the Elector Frederick, answered by defending the professor. Frederick refused to make the arrest without first giving Luther a hearing at the Imperial Diet (parliament), which was set to meet at the town of Worms in 1521. Assembled at the Diet of Worms were haughty princes, grave bishops, and the resplendent young emperor Charles V (r. 1519–1558), who was presiding over his first Imperial Diet. The emperor ordered Luther to disavow his writings, but Luther refused to do so. For several days the diet was in an uproar, divided by friends and foes of Luther's doctrines. Just before he was to be condemned by the emperor, Luther disappeared, and rumors flew that he had been assassinated. For days no one knew the truth. Frederick the Wise had kidnapped Luther for his own safety and hidden him in the castle at Wartburg, where for nearly a year he labored in quiet seclusion translating the New Testament into German.

The Lutheran Reformation in the Cities and Principalities

Luther had escaped arrest and execution at the hands of the emperor, but he could not control his own followers and allies. The Reformation quickly became a vast, sprawling movement far beyond the control of any individual, even in Luther's own Wittenberg. One of the characteristics of the Protestant Reformation was that once reformers rejected the supreme authority of the papacy, differences about forms of worship or biblical interpretation led to division within the movement and eventually to the formation of separate churches.

DOCUMENT

Martin Luther, *The German Mass* (1526)

In its early phases the Reformation spread most rapidly among the educated urban classes. During the sixteenth century, fifty of the sixty-five German imperial cities, at one time or another, officially accepted the Protestant Reformation. Besides these large imperial cities, most of the 200 smaller German towns with a population of more than

DOCUMENT

Martin Luther's Powers of Persuasion

Part of Martin Luther's appeal derived from his polemical style. The Freedom of a Christian (1520) was probably Luther's last serious attempt to reconcile himself with Pope Leo X. In the open letter to Pope Leo that introduces the tract, Luther asserts that he is criticizing corrupt advisers in the papal curia rather than the pope himself, but Luther's language seems more designed to embolden his own followers than to persuade the pope.

Living among the monsters of this age with whom I am now for the third year waging war, I am compelled occasionally to look up to you, Leo, most blessed father, and to think of you. Indeed, since you are occasionally regarded as the sole cause of my warfare, I cannot help thinking of you. To be sure, the undeserved raging of your godless flatterers against me has compelled me to appeal from your see [officials] to a future council [of all the bishops of the Church], despite the decrees of your predecessors Pius and Julius, who with a foolish tyranny forbade such an appeal.

. . .

I have truly despised your see, the Roman Curia, which, however, neither you nor anyone else can deny is more corrupt than any Babylon or Sodom [places condemned for sinfulness in the Bible] ever was, and which, as far as I can see, is characterized by a completely depraved, hopeless, and notorious godlessness. I have been thoroughly incensed over the fact that good Christians are mocked in your name and under the cloak of the Roman church. I have resisted and will continue to resist your see as long as the spirit of faith lives in me.

. . .

I never intended to attack the Roman Curia or to raise any controversy concerning it. But when I saw all efforts to save it were hopeless, I despised it, gave it a bill of divorce, and said, "let the evildoer still do evil, and the filthy still be filthy" [Revelations 22:11]. Then I turned to the quiet and peaceful study of the Holy Scriptures so that I might be helpful to my brothers around me. When I had made some progress in these studies, Satan opened his eyes and then filled his servant Johann Eck, a notable enemy of Christ, with an insatiable lust for glory and thus aroused him to drag me unawares to a debate, seizing me by means of one little word which I had let slip concerning the primacy of the Roman church. Then that boastful braggart, frothing and gnashing his teeth, declared that he would risk everything for the glory of God and the honor of the Apostolic See. Puffed up with the prospect of abusing your authority, he looked forward with great confidence to a victory over me. . . . When the debate ended badly for the sophist, an unbelievable madness overcame the man, for he believed that it was his fault alone which was responsible for my disclosing all the infamy of Rome.

Source: Excerpt from *Luther's Works, vol. 31, Career of the Reformer: I*, edited by Harold J. Grimm (Philadelphia: Muhlenberg Press, 1957). Translated by W. A. Lambert and revised by Harold J. Grimm.

1,000 experienced some form of the Protestant movement. During the 1520s and 1530s, the magistrates (mayors and other office holders) of these towns took command of the Reformation movement by seizing control of the local churches. The magistrates implemented Luther's reform of worship, disciplined the clergy, and stopped the drain of revenues to irresponsible bishops and the distant pope.

The German princes of the Holy Roman Empire had their own reasons to resent the Church. They wanted to appoint their own nominees to ecclesiastical offices and to diminish the legal privileges of the clergy. During the 1520s Luther's enormous popularity gave many German princes the opportunity they had been waiting for. Despite his steadfast Catholicism, Emperor Charles V was in no position to resist their demands. During most of his reign, Charles faced a two-front war—against France and against the Ottoman Turks. Charles could ill afford additional trouble with the German princes because he desperately needed their military assistance. At the first Imperial Diet of Speyer in 1526, Charles granted the princes territorial sovereignty in religion by allowing them to decide whether they would enforce the imperial edict of the Diet of Worms against Luther and his followers. To preserve the empire from external enemies, Charles was forced to allow its internal division along religious lines.

The Appeal of the Reformation to Women

As divisive as Reformist theology was to imperial politics, it had a particular appeal to people who were habitually excluded from the political world and governance of the Church, especially women and peasants. In the early days of the movement, women felt that Luther's description of "the priesthood of all believers" meant that women as well as men could participate fully in the religious life of the Church. Women understood Luther's phrase "the freedom of a Christian" as freeing them from the restrictive roles that had traditionally kept them silent and at home. Moreover, Luther and the other major reformers saw positive religious value in the role of wife and mother. Abandoning the Catholic Church's view that celibate monks and nuns were morally superior to married people, Luther declared marriage holy and set an example by taking a wife, the ex-nun Katherine von Bora. The wives of the reformers often became partners in the Reformation, taking particular responsibility for organizing charities and administering to the poor.

In the early phases of the Reformation, women preached and published on religious matters. These women demanded to be heard in churches and delivered inspiring sermons. They asked that their writings be accepted as authentic products of the Holy Spirit. In some cases, female rulers brought their entire land over to the Reformation. Elisabeth of Brunswick-Calenburg reformed the local church and invited Protestant preachers into her lands. The noblewoman Argula von Grumbach argued that even though St. Paul had warned that women should be silent in church, she felt driven by the word of God to profess her faith publicly. Marie Dentière, a former abbess of a French convent who joined the Reformation cause, asked, "Do we have two Gospels, one for men and the other for women? . . . For we [women] ought not, any more than men, hide and bury within the earth that which God has . . . revealed to us women?"[6]

Most women were soon disappointed. Women's preaching and writing threatened the male religious and political authorities. They ordered Argula von Grumbach's husband to make her stop writing. Other women who defended the Reformation were silenced by the reformers themselves, and women who spoke up in church were widely condemned. In some places laws were passed that prohibited groups of women from discussing religious questions. In England, noblewomen were even prevented from reading the Bible aloud to others. One kind of writing could not be controlled, however—the private diary. The Protestant imperative to discover the workings of faith within oneself helped promote writing private diaries. The practice spread rapidly with Protestantism, and many women used diaries as an outlet for personal expression and a way to develop a sense of their own personal identities.

The few women who were able to speak and act openly in public were either from the upper classes or the wives of prominent reformers. No man could silence Marguerite of Navarre and her daughter Jeanne d'Albret, who used their authority as queens to promote the Reformation. A body of religious literature developed that held up as models more

Martin Luther and Katherine von Bora
For many pious Lutherans the images of Luther and his wife, herself a former nun, replaced the images of the Virgin Mary and the saints favored by the Catholics.

humble women such as Katherine Zell, the wife of one of Strasbourg's reformers.

For most women participation in the Reformation was confined to the domestic sphere, where they instructed children, quietly read the Bible, and led prayer circles. Protestant authorities also allowed divorce, which was prohibited by Catholic Church law. However, the reform leaders were quite reluctant to grant women the same rights as their husbands in obtaining a divorce. During the early years of the Reformation, there were many marriages in which one spouse followed the old faith and the other the new. But if the woman converted and her husband did not, the Protestant reformers counseled that she obey her husband even if he forced her to act contrary to God's will. She could pray for his conversion but could not leave or divorce him. Most women were forced to remain married regardless of their feelings. A few exceptional women left their husbands anyway and continued to proclaim their religious convictions to the world. One such woman, Anne Askew from England, was tortured and executed for her beliefs.

The German Peasants' Revolt

The Reformation also appealed to many peasants simply because it offered them a simplified, purified religion and, most important, local control of their churches. The peasants of Wendelstein, a typical South German village, had been complaining about the conduct of its priests for some time. In 1523, they hired a "Christian teacher" and told him in no uncertain terms: "We will not recognize you as a lord, but only as a servant of the community. We will command you, not you us, and we order you to preach the gospel and the word of God purely, clearly, and truthfully—without any human teachings—faithfully and conscientiously."[7] These villagers understood the Reformation to mean that they could take control of their local church and demand responsible conduct from the minister they hired. However, other peasants understood the Reformation in more radical terms as licensing social reforms that Luther himself never supported.

In June 1524 a seemingly minor event sparked a revolt of peasants in many parts of Germany. When an aristocratic lady demanded that the peasants in her village abandon their grain harvest to gather snails for her, they rebelled and set her castle on fire. Over the next two years, the rebellion spread as peasants rose up against their feudal lords to demand the adoption of Lutheran reforms in the Church, a reduction of feudal privileges, the abolition of serfdom, and the self-government of their communities. Their rebellion was unprecedented: the largest and best-organized peasant movement up to that time in European history, a measure of the powerful effect of the Protestant reform message. Like the Reformation, the revolt was the culmination of a long period of discontent, but unlike the Reformation, it was a tragic failure.

These peasants were doing exactly what they thought Luther had advocated when he wrote about the "freedom of the Christian." They interpreted his words to mean complete social as well as religious freedom. However, Luther had not meant anything of the sort. To him the freedom of the Christian referred to inner, spiritual freedom, not liberation from economic or political bondage. Instead of supporting the rebellion begun in his name, Luther and nearly all the other reformers backed the feudal lords and condemned in uncompromising terms the violence of the peasant armies. In *Against the Thieving, Murderous Hordes of Peasants* (1525), Luther expressed his own fear of the lower classes and revealed that despite his acid-tongued attacks on the pope, he was fundamentally a conservative thinker who was committed to law and order. He urged that the peasants be hunted down and killed like rabid dogs. And so they were. Between 70,000 and 100,000 peasants died, a slaughter far greater than the Roman persecutions of the early Christians. To the peasants, Luther's conservative position on social and economic issues felt like betrayal, but it enabled the Lutheran Reformation to retain the support of the princes, which was essential for its survival.

Lutheran Success

Soon after the crushing of the Peasants' Revolt, the Lutheran Reformation faced a renewed threat from its Catholic opponents. In 1530 Emperor Charles V bluntly commanded all Lutherans to return to the Catholic fold or face arrest. Enraged, the Lutherans refused to comply. The following year the Protestant princes formed a military alliance, the Schmalkaldic League, against the emperor. Renewed trouble with France and the Turks prevented a military confrontation between the league and the emperor for fifteen years, giving the Lutherans enough breathing space to put the Reformation on a firmer basis in Germany by training ministers and educating the laity in the new religion. In place of the Catholic bishops, Lutherans established regional consistories (boards of clerics) to supervise the new Protestant churches. Educational reforms introduced a humanist curriculum, established schools for girls, and organized religious instruction for the laity. In the meantime Lutheranism spread beyond Germany into Scandinavia, where it received support from the kings of Denmark and Sweden as it had among the princes of northern Germany.

After freeing himself yet again from foreign wars and failing to effect a compromise solution in Germany, Charles V turned his armies against the Protestants. However, in 1552 the Protestant armies defeated in battle the Catholic forces of the emperor, and Charles was forced to relent. In 1555 the Religious Peace of Augsburg° established the principle of *cuius regio, eius religio*, which means "he who rules determines the religion of the land." Protestant princes were permitted to retain all church lands seized before 1552 and to enforce Protestant worship, but Catholic princes were also allowed to enforce Catholic worship in their territories. Those who disagreed with the religion of their ruler would not be tolerated; their options were to change religious affiliations or to emigrate elsewhere. With the Peace of Augsburg the religious division of the Holy Roman Empire became permanent, and the legal foundations were in place for the development of the two distinctive religious cultures—Protestant and Catholic.

The following year, Emperor Charles, worn out from ceaseless warfare, the anxieties of holding his vast territories together, and nearly forty years of trying to stamp out Protestantism, abdicated and retired to a monastery, where he died in 1558.

CHRONOLOGY

The Lutheran Reformation

1517	Luther posts the Ninety-Five Theses
1519	Luther debates Johann Eck at Leipzig; election of Charles V as Holy Roman Emperor
1521	Diet of Worms
1524–1525	German peasants revolt
1531	Formation of the Schmalkaldic League
1555	The Religious Peace of Augsburg

The Diversity of Protestantism

■ How and why did Protestant denominations multiply to such an extent in northern Europe and Britain?

The term *Protestant* originally applied only to the followers of Luther who *protested* the decisions of the second Imperial Diet of Speyer in 1529, which attempted to force them back into the Catholic fold, but the term came to describe much more than that small group. It designated all western European Christians who refused to accept the authority of the pope. Protestantism encompassed innumerable churches and sects. Many of these have survived since the Reformation; some disappeared in the violence of the sixteenth century; others have sprung up since, especially in North America, where Protestantism has thrived.

The varieties of Protestantism can be divided into two types. The first type was the product of the Magisterial Reformation°, which refers to the churches that received official government sanction. These included the Lutheran churches (Germany and Scandinavia); the Reformed and Calvinist churches (Switzerland, Scotland, the Netherlands, and a few places in Germany); and the Anglican church (England, Wales, parts of Ireland, and later in England's colonies). The second type was the product of the Radical Reformation° and includes the movements that failed to gain official recognition and were at best tolerated, at worst persecuted. This strict division into Magisterial and Radical Protestantism broke down in eastern Europe, where the states were too weak to enforce religious conformity. In eastern Europe religious variety prevailed over rigid conformity, at least for the sixteenth century (see Map 13.1).

The Reformation in Switzerland

The governmental independence of Switzerland from the Holy Roman Empire meant that from the beginning of the Reformation local authorities could cooperate with the reformers without opposition from the emperor. The Swiss Confederation bound together thirteen fiercely proud regions, called cantons, which had established their independence from the Habsburg dynasty of the Holy Roman Empire. Except for the leading cities of Zürich, Basel, and Geneva, Switzerland remained an impoverished land of peasants who could not fully support themselves from the barren mountainous land. To supplement their meager incomes, young Swiss men fought as mercenaries in foreign armies, often those of the pope. Each spring, mercenary captains recruited able-bodied Swiss men from the mountain villages. The Swiss men left the women behind to tend the animals and farms. By summer, the villages were emptied of all men except the old and invalid. Each fall at the end of the fighting season, the survivors of that season's campaign trudged home, always bringing bad news to a fresh group of widows. The strain created by the mercenary's life stimulated the desire for sweeping reforms in Switzerland.

Zwingli's Zürich

Ulrich Zwingli (1484–1531) had served as a chaplain with the Swiss mercenaries serving the pope in Italy. In 1520, after being named the People's Priest of Zürich, Zwingli criticized his superior bishop for recruiting local young men to die in the papal armies. That same year he began to call for reform of the Church, advocating the abolition of the Roman Catholic mass, the marriage of priests, and the closing of monasteries. One of the novel features of Zwingli's reform was the strict emphasis on preaching the Word of Scripture during Church services, in contrast to the emphasis on ritual in the traditional Catholic liturgy. He ordered the removal of all paintings and statues from churches because they were too powerful a distraction from concentrating on the preaching. Zwingli was certainly influenced by the writings of Erasmus, but he denied that Luther had any effect on him at all. The Zwinglian Reformation began independently of the Lutheran Reformation and created a separate reform center from

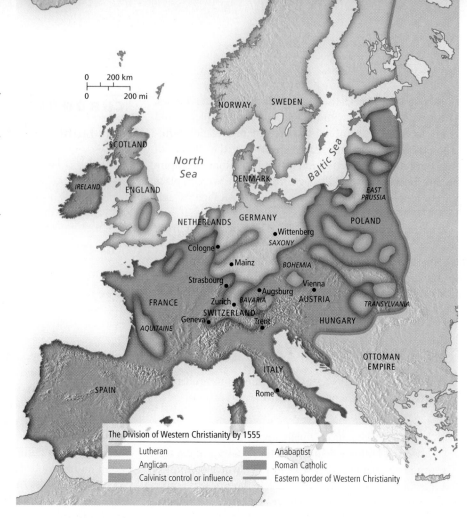

Map 13.1 The Division of Western Christianity by 1555

The West, which had been culturally unified by Christianity for more than a thousand years, split apart during the sixteenth century. These religious divisions persist to this day.

The Division of Western Christianity by 1555

- Lutheran
- Anglican
- Calvinist control or influence
- Anabaptist
- Roman Catholic
- Eastern border of Western Christianity

which initiatives spread throughout Switzerland, southern Germany, and England.

Two features distinguished the Zwinglian from the Lutheran Reformation. One was Zwingli's desire to have reformed ministers participate in governmental decisions. In Lutheran Germany, church and state supported each other, but they remained legally separate, and the prince alone had the authority to determine the religion of the land. In Zürich, the moral Christian and the good citizen were one and the same, and Zwingli worked with the magistrates of the city council, who step-by-step legalized the Reformation and enforced conformity through its police powers.

Luther and Zwingli also differed in their understanding of the nature of the Eucharist, the communion sacrament that reenacted Christ's Last Supper with his apostles. Luther believed that Christ's body was spiritually present in the communion bread. "You will receive," as he put it, "as much as you believe you receive."[8] This emphasis on the inner, spiritual state of the believer was very characteristic of Luther's introspective piety. In contrast to Luther, Zwingli could not accept the idea of Almighty God making himself present in a humble piece of bread. To Zwingli the Eucharistic bread was just a symbol that stood for the body of Christ. The problem with the symbolic interpretation of the Eucharist was that the various reformers could not agree with Zwingli on exactly what the Eucharist symbol-

ized. As early as 1524, it became evident that each reformer was committed to a different interpretation, and these different interpretations became the basis for different Protestant churches.

In 1529 Count Philip of Hesse (1504–1567) tried to forge a military alliance between the Protestants of Germany and Switzerland against the Catholics. The theological disputes over the Eucharist blocked full cooperation, however. Philip brought together Luther, Zwingli, and the other principal reformers for a formal discussion at the new Protestant University of Marburg. But Luther adamantly refused to compromise and shrugged off Zwingli's tearful pleas for cooperation. The failure of the Marburg Colloquy marked the permanent rupture of the Reformation movement.

Calvin's Geneva

In the next generation the momentum of the Reformation shifted to Geneva, Switzerland, under the leadership of John Calvin (1509–1564). Calvin arrived in French-speaking Geneva as a religious refugee in 1536 and came to support the city's long struggle for independence from the Duke of Savoy, who had been rejected as the city's lord a few years before. Calvin worked with the Genevan magistrates who attempted to build a holy community that was independent of the dictates of the city's Catholic bishop. But Calvinism spread far beyond its Swiss home, becoming the dominant form of Protestantism in France, the Netherlands, Scotland, and New England.

Trained as a lawyer and exiled from his home in France in 1533 for his reformist views, Calvin spent several years wandering, searching for a quiet retreat and collaborating with other reformers. After he settled in Geneva, Calvin spent the rest of his life transforming the town into the City of God. The linchpin of the Genevan reform was the close cooperation between the magistrates of the city council and the clergy in enforcing the moral discipline of the citizens. To achieve this goal, Calvin persuaded the magistrates in 1555 to grant the clergy the right to excommunicate sinners as well as those who disagreed with Calvinist theology. And in the Calvinist construction, excommunication meant more than banishment from church. Excommunicated people were completely shunned; no one could talk to them, including members of their own family; they effectively lost their property and ability to conduct business. Excommunication became a form of exile. The financial and psychological consequences of excommunication were deeply feared because the excommunicated were, in effect, socially dead.

Calvin's theology extended the insights of Luther and Zwingli to their logical conclusion. This pattern was most obvious in Calvin's understanding of justification by faith. Luther had argued that the Christian could not earn salvation through good works and that faith came only from God. Calvin reasoned that if an all-knowing, all-powerful God knew everything in advance and caused everything to happen, then the salvation of any individual was predetermined or, as Calvin put it, "predestined." Calvin's doctrine of predestination° was not new. In fact, it had long been discussed among Christian theologians. But for Calvin two considerations made it crucial. First was Calvin's certainty that God was above any influence from humanity. The "majesty of God," as Calvin put it, was the principle from which everything else followed. Second, Calvin and other preachers had noticed that in a congregation attending a sermon, only a few paid attention to what was preached, while the vast majority seemed unable or unwilling to understand. The reason for this disparity seemed to be that only the Elect could truly follow God's Word. The Elect were those who had received God's grace and would be saved. The Elect were known only to God, but Calvin's theology encouraged the converted to feel the assurance of salvation and to accept a "calling" from God to perform his will on Earth. God's calling° gave Calvinists a powerful sense of personal direction, which committed them to a life of moral activity, whether as preacher, wife, or shoemaker.

Calvin composed an elegant theological treatise, the *Institutes of the Christian Religion,* first published in six chapters in 1535 but constantly revised and expanded until it reached eighty chapters in the definitive 1559 edition.

DOCUMENT

Calvin on Predestination (16th c.)

Calvin the lawyer wrote a tightly argued and reasoned work, like a trial attorney preparing a case. In Calvin's theology the parts fit neatly together like a vast, intricate puzzle. Calvin's work aspired to be a comprehensive reformed theology that would convince through reasoned deliberation, and it became the first systematic presentation of Protestant doctrine. Whereas Luther spun out his sometimes contradictory ideas in a series of often polemical pamphlets, Calvin devoted himself to perfecting his comprehensive theology of Protestantism.

Given its emphasis on building a holy community, Calvinism helped transform the nuclear family into a social unit for training and disciplining children, a family in which women had a vital educational function that in turn encouraged women's literacy. Calvinist communities also began to allow divorce for women who had been abused by their husbands. Calvinist women and men were both disciplined and liberated—disciplined to avoid physical and material pleasures, liberated from the necessity to do good works but guided by God's grace to do them anyway.

The Reformation in Britain

Great Britain, as the island kingdom is known today, did not exist in the sixteenth century. The Tudor dynasty, which began in 1485 with Henry VII (see Chapter 11), ruled over England, Wales, and Ireland, but Scotland was still a separate kingdom with its own monarch and church institutions. These countries had distinctive political traditions, culture, and language, and as a result their Reformation experiences differed considerably. The Tudors imposed the Reformation as a matter of royal policy, and they were mostly successful in England and Wales. But they hardly made a dent in the religious culture of Ireland, which was a remarkable exception to the European pattern of conformity to the religion of the ruler. There the vast majority of the population were Catholics, a faith different from that of their Protestant monarch. Scotland, also an exception to the rule, wholeheartedly accepted the Protestant Reformation against the will of its Catholic queen and most of the clergy.

The Tudors and the English Reformation

In 1527 the rotund, self-absorbed, but crafty King Henry VIII (r. 1509–1547) announced that he had come to the pious conclusion that he had gravely sinned by marrying his brother's widow, Catherine of Aragon. By this time the couple had been married for eighteen years, their only living child was the princess Mary, and at age 42 Catherine was unlikely to give birth to more children. Henry let it be known that he wanted a son to secure the English throne for the Tudor dynasty. He also had his eye on the most engaging woman of the court, Anne Boleyn, who was less than half Catherine's age. In the past popes had usually been cooperative when a powerful king needed an annulment, but Pope Clement VII (r. 1523–1534) was in no position to oblige Henry. At the time of the marriage, the papal curia had issued a dispensation for Henry to marry his brother's widow, a practice that is prohibited in the Bible. In effect, Henry was asking the papacy to admit it had made a mistake. In addition, at the moment when Henry's petition for divorce arrived, Clement was under the control of Catherine's nephew, the Emperor Charles V, whose armies had recently captured and sacked the city of Rome. In 1531 Henry gave up trying to obtain papal approval and definitively separated from Catherine. Eighteen months later he secretly married Anne Boleyn. England's compliant Archbishop Thomas Cranmer (1489–1556) pronounced the marriage to Catherine void and the one to Anne valid. But the marriage to Anne did not last. When she began to displease him, Henry had her arrested, charged with incest with her brother and adultery with other men. She was convicted and beheaded.

The English separation from the Roman Catholic Church, which took place in 1534 through the Acts of Supremacy and Succession, passed at Henry's request by the English Parliament, has often been understood as a by-product of Henry's capricious lust and the plots of his brilliant minister, Thomas Cromwell (ca. 1485–1540). It is certainly true that Henry's desire to rid himself of Catherine led him to reject papal authority and to establish himself as the head of the Church of England. It is also certainly true that Henry was an inconstant husband: Of his six wives, two were divorced and two beheaded. However, the English Reformation cannot be explained simply as the consequence of royal whim or the machinations of a single minister.

The English Reformation began as a declaration of royal independence from papal supervision rather than an attempt to reform the practices of the Church. Under Henry VIII the English Reformation could be described as Catholicism without the pope. Protestant doctrine, at first, had little role in the English Reformation, and Henry had himself been one of the most vociferous critics of Martin Luther. Royal supremacy established control over the Church by granting to the king supervising authority over liturgical rituals and religious doctrines. Thomas Cromwell, who worked out the practical details for parliamentary legislation, was himself a Protestant, and no doubt his religious views emboldened him to reject papal authority. But the principal theorist of royal supremacy was a Catholic, Thomas Starkey (ca. 1499–1538). A sojourn in Italy had acquainted Starkey with Italian Renaissance political theory, which emphasized concepts of civic liberty. In fact, even many English Catholics found the change acceptable as long as it meant only abandoning submission to the pope in distant Rome. Those who opposed cutting the connection to Rome suffered for their opposition, however. Bishop John Fisher (ca. 1469–1535) and Sir Thomas More, the humanist author of *Utopia* and former chancellor of England,

were both executed for their refusal to go along with the king's decision.

With this display of despotic power, Henry seized personal control of the English church and then closed and confiscated the lands of the monasteries. He redistributed the monastic lands to the nobility in an effort to purchase their support and to make money for the crown. Henry's officials briefly flirted with some Protestant reforms, but theological innovations were largely avoided. The Reformation of Henry VIII was more significant for consolidating the dynastic power of the Tudors than for initiating wide-ranging religious reform. On the local level many people embraced the Reformation for their own reasons, often because it gave them a sense of control over the affairs of their community. Others went along simply because the power of the king was too strong to resist.

Henry's six wives bore three surviving children. As each succeeded to the throne, the official religion of England gyrated wildly. Because his youngest child, Edward, was male, Henry designed him successor to the throne. His two daughters, Mary and Elizabeth, were to succeed only if Edward died without an heir, which he did. Only 10 years old when he followed his father to the throne, King Edward VI (r. 1547–1553) was the pawn of his Protestant guardians, some of whom pushed for a more thorough Protestant Reformation in England than Henry had espoused. After Edward's premature death, his half-sister, Queen Mary I (r. 1553–1558), daughter of Henry and Catherine of Aragon, attempted to bring England back to obedience to the pope. Her unpopular marriage to the king of Spain and her failure to retain the support of the nobles, who were the foundation of Tudor government, damaged the Catholic cause in England.

Mary's successor and half-sister, Elizabeth Tudor, the daughter of Henry and Anne Boleyn, was an entirely different sort. Queen Elizabeth I (r. 1558–1603), raised as a Protestant, kept her enemies off balance and her quarrelsome subjects firmly in hand with her tremendous charisma and shrewd political judgments. Elizabeth became one of the most successful monarchs to ever reign anywhere. Without the considerable talents of Elizabeth, England could easily have fallen into civil war over religion—as the Holy Roman Empire and France did and as England itself did some forty years after her death.

Between 1559 and 1563, Elizabeth repealed the Catholic legislation of Mary and promulgated her own Protestant laws, collectively known as the Elizabethan Settlement, which established the Church of England, known as the Anglican Church (Episcopalian in the United States). Her principal adviser, William Cecil (1520–1598), implemented the details of the reform through reasonable debate and compromise rather than by insisting on doctrinal purity and rigid conformity. The touchstone of the Elizabethan Settlement was the Thirty-Nine Articles (finally approved by Parliament in 1571), which articulated a moderate version of Protestantism. It retained the ecclesiastical hierarchy of bishops as well as an essentially Catholic liturgy translated into English. This "middle way" between Roman Catholicism and militant Calvinism was ably defended by the Calvinist Richard Hooker (1553–1600), whose *Laws of Ecclesiastical Polity* emphasized how the law as promulgated by the royal government manifested the divine order.

The Church of England under Elizabeth permitted a wide latitude of beliefs, but it did not tolerate "recusants," those who as a matter of principle refused to attend Church of England services. These were mostly Catholics who set up a secret network of priests to serve their sacramental needs and whom the government considered dangerous agents of foreign powers. Many others were militant Protestants who thought the Elizabethan Settlement did not go far enough in reforming religion. The most vocal and influential of the Protestant dissenters were the Puritans, who were influenced by Calvinism and demanded a church purified of what they thought were remnants of Roman Catholicism.

Scotland: The Citadel of Calvinism

While England groped its way toward moderate Protestantism, neighboring Scotland became one of the most thoroughly Calvinist countries in Europe. In 1560 the parliament of Scotland, with encouragement from Queen Elizabeth of England, overthrew Roman Catholicism against the will of Mary Stuart, Queen of Scots (1542–1587). The wife of the French king, Francis II, Mary was absent in France during the crucial early phases of the Reformation and returned to Scotland only after her husband's death in 1561. Despite her Catholicism, Mary proved remarkably conciliatory toward the Protestants by putting royal funds at the disposal of the new Reformed Kirk (Church) of Scotland. But the Scottish Calvinists never trusted her, and their mistrust would bring about her doom when they rebelled against her and drove her into exile in England, where Queen Elizabeth had her imprisoned and eventually executed for treason against the English crown.

The Scots Confession of 1560, written by a panel of six reformers, established the new church. John Knox (ca. 1514–1572) breathed a strongly Calvinist air into the church through his many polemical writings and the official liturgy he composed in 1564, the *Book of Common Order*. Knox emphasized faith and individual Christian conscience over ecclesiastical authority, a priority that discouraged compromise among the Scots. Instead of the episcopal structure in England, which granted bishops the authority over doctrine and discipline, the Scots Kirk established a Presbyterian form of organization, which gave organizational authority to the pastors and elders of the congregations, all of whom had equal rank. As a result the Presbyterian congregations were more independent and subject to local variations than the episcopal structure allowed in the Anglican Church.

The Radical Reformation

The magisterial reformers in Germany, Switzerland, England, and Scotland managed to obtain official sanction for their religious reforms, often at the cost of some compromise with governmental authorities. As a result of those compromises, the magisterial reformers were challenged by radicals from among their own followers who demanded faster, more thorough reform. In most places the radicals represented a small minority, perhaps never more than 2 percent of all Protestants. But their significance outstripped their small numbers, in part because they forced the magisterial reformers to respond to their arguments and because their enemies attempted to eradicate them through extreme violence.

The radicals can be divided into three categories: Anabaptists, who attempted to construct a holy community on the basis of literal readings of the Bible; Spiritualists, who abandoned all forms of organized religion to allow individuals to follow the inner voice of the Holy Spirit; and Unitarians, who advocated a rational religion that emphasized ethical behavior over ceremonies.

Anabaptists: The Holy Community

For Anabaptists, the Bible was a blueprint for reforming not just the church but all of society. Because the Bible reported that Jesus was an adult when he was baptized, the Anabaptists rejected infant baptism and adopted adult baptism (Anabaptism° means to rebaptize). An adult, they believed, could accept baptism as an act of faith, unlike an oblivious infant. Anabaptists saw the sacraments of baptism and communion as symbols of faith, which had no purpose or meaning unless the recipient was already a person of faith. Adult baptism reserved for the faithful allowed the creation of a pure church, isolated from the sinfulness of the world.

Because they did not want the faithful to be tainted by contact with the sinful, Anabaptists advocated the complete separation of Church and state. Anabaptists sought to obey only God and completely rejected all established religious and political authorities; they required adherents to refuse to serve in government offices, swear oaths, pay taxes, or serve as soldiers. Anabaptists sought to live in highly disciplined "holy communities," which excommunicated errant members and practiced simple services based on scriptural readings. Because the Anabaptist communities consisted largely of uneducated peasants, artisans, and miners, a dimension of economic radicalism colored the early Anabaptist movement. For example, some Anabaptist radicals advocated the elimination of all private property and the sharing of wealth. On the position of women, however, Anabaptists were staunchly conservative, denying women any public role in religious affairs and insisting that they remain under the strict control of their fathers and husbands.

The Trial of Anne Boleyn: The Dynastic Crime

Anne Boleyn, the first of Henry VIII's wives to be executed, was beheaded in the Tower of London's courtyard in May 1536, just a few hundred feet from the hall in which she had celebrated her coronation three years earlier. She had been tried by a court of peers and unanimously convicted of high treason. The evidence against her was for adultery, but the alleged adultery of a queen was considered treason because it put in question the paternity of potential heirs to the throne. Queen Anne insisted on her innocence until the end, but her final address to the crowd did not protest her execution. Instead, she said, "According to the law and by the law I am judged to die, and therefore I will speak nothing against it."[9] To twenty-first-century observers, Anne seems to accept her unjust fate passively. To sixteenth-century observers, however, she died "boldly," and her refusal to admit guilt and to accept the law was one of the best indicators of her innocence.

To understand Anne Boleyn's scaffold statement, it is necessary to look at the idea of a "fair trial" in sixteenth-century England. She was condemned for high treason because of her supposed adultery with five men, including her own brother. But her supposed lovers were in other places when the adulteries were alleged to take place—evidence that casts doubt on their truth. She was unable to present this evidence, which today would serve as an alibi for the defendant, because she heard the charges against her for the first time at the actual trial. The queen enjoyed no counsel for the defense, had no opportunity to call witnesses on her own behalf, and had no protection against self-incrimination. Because she was

the queen of England, her trial was unusual, but these procedures were standard in the sixteenth century.

It was widely known that the king wished her death, but because her trial followed the accepted legal procedures, it was considered a fair trial by the standards of the sixteenth century. When Anne married Henry, who had recently divorced Catherine of Aragon, Anne's most important role was to provide the king with a male heir. Anne soon gave birth to a daughter, Elizabeth, but she then suffered two miscarriages. Some historians argue that Henry wanted to get rid of Anne in favor of her younger rival, Jane Seymour, but others have suggested that because the fetus of Anne's second miscarriage was deformed, she was suspected of witchcraft. Henry himself stated that he had been seduced by witchcraft, which was why God had not permitted him to have a son. He considered the marriage null and void because Anne's witchery had coerced him into the liaison. As far as Henry was concerned, Anne's failure to bear him a son was evidence of some sort of wrongdoing on her part. It remained only to construct a case against her.

The king and his prosecutors assembled a large number of statements about Anne's infidelity, which shocked observers of the trial. John Husee wrote, "I think

Portrait of King Henry VIII
This portrait by Hans Holbein the Younger depicts Henry as he looked shortly after Queen Anne's execution.

Portrait Sketch of Anne Boleyn
This portrait of Anne Boleyn may be by Hans Holbein the Younger. It was probably painted while Anne was queen of England.

same."[11] Most telling was the opinion of Chapuys, the ambassador of Emperor Charles V to Henry's court. Chapuys had previously been hostile to Anne, but he considered the whole trial a sham. After the jury returned a guilty verdict, Anne herself shrewdly observed, "I believe you have reasons . . . upon which you have condemned me: but they must be other than those that have been produced in court."[12]

The trial of Anne Boleyn was a classic example of the triumph of judicial form over the substance of evidence. Because Henry and the prosecutors had followed the proper trial procedures, they believed they were above reproach on legal grounds. Anne had been justly condemned even if the evidence against her had been faked.

Questions of Justice

1. Assuming that the evidence against Anne was false, why was her alleged treason defined as adultery rather than something else, such as witchcraft or heresy?
2. What do these charges tell us about the nature of early modern conceptions of kingship?

Taking It Further

Guy, John. *Tudor England.* 1990. Taking account of recent scholarship, this is the best general history of the period. It includes illuminating portraits of the principal figures.

Warnicke, Retha M. *The Rise and Fall of Anne Boleyn: Family Politics at the Court of Henry VIII.* 1991. Based on a careful examination of all the available evidence, Warnicke shows how the trial was a consequence of Henry VIII's desire to preserve his dynasty.

verily, if all the books and chronicles . . . which against woman hath been penned, contrived, and written since Adam and Eve, those same were, I think, verily nothing in comparison of that which hath been done and committed by Anne the Queen." James Spelman commented, "All the evidence was of bawdery and lechery, so that there was no such whore in all the realm."[10]

The quantity and offensive nature of the evidence was part of a propaganda campaign Henry orchestrated to convince the members of the nobility and the English people that Anne's execution was justified.

Despite the careful orchestration of the trial, the preponderance of the evidence, and the procedures that denied her systematic defense, Anne Boleyn managed to convince a number of observers that she was innocent. Charles Wriothesley recounted, "She made so wise and discreet answers to all things laid against her, excusing herself through her words so clearly as though she had never been faulty to the

Because the Anabaptists promoted such a radical reorganization of society along biblical lines, they provoked a violent reaction. In Zürich the city council decreed that the appropriate punishment for all Anabaptists was to be drowned in the local river where they had been rebaptizing themselves. By 1529 it became a capital offense in the Holy Roman Empire to be rebaptized, and during the sixteenth century perhaps as many as 5,000 Anabaptists were executed for the offense, a persecution that tended to fragment the Anabaptists into isolated, secretive rural communities.

During a brief period in 1534 and 1535, Anabaptists managed to seize control of the city of Münster in northern Germany. An immigrant Dutch tailor, John of Leiden, set up a despotic regime in Münster that punished with death any sin, even gossiping or complaining. John of Leiden introduced polygamy and collective ownership of property. John set an example by taking sixteen wives, one of whom he beheaded for talking back, stomping on her body in front of the other frightened wives. As the besieging armies closed in, John forced his followers to crown him king and worship him. After his capture, John was subjected to an excruciating torture, and as a warning to others his corpse was displayed for many years hanging in an iron cage.

"God opened the eyes of the governments by the revolt at Münster," as the Protestant reformer Heinrich Bullinger put it, "and thereafter no one would trust even those Anabaptists who claimed to be innocent."[13] The surviving Anabaptists abandoned the radicalism of the Münster community, embracing pacifism and nonviolent resistance. A Dutchman, Menno Simons (1496–1561), tirelessly traveled about the Netherlands and Germany, providing solace and guidance to the isolated survivors of the Münster disaster. His followers, the Mennonites, preserved the noblest features of the Anabaptist tradition of quiet resistance to persecution. Both the Mennonites and the Amish in North America are direct descendants of sixteenth- and seventeenth-century Anabaptist groups. Under Mennonite influence, Thomas Helwys founded the first Baptist church in England in 1612. As the leader of the English Baptists, Helwys wrote an unprecedented appeal for the absolute freedom of religion. In it he defended the religious rights of Jews, Muslims, and even atheists as well as all varieties of Christians. He was almost immediately put in prison, where he died.

The most significant measure of the influence of the Anabaptists is the fact that the largest number of Protestants in the United States are Baptists. The modern Baptist movement has lost the social radicalism of its Anabaptist forebearers and no longer advocates the communal ownership of property as the Anabaptists did in the sixteenth century. Baptists no longer refuse to pay taxes or accept the authority of the government. Most Baptists have also forsaken pacifism and will serve in the military, but during the civil rights movement of the 1950s and 1960s, it was a Baptist

Cages for the Anabapist Leaders of Münster
The bodies of John of Leiden and two other Anabaptist leaders were displayed after their execution in these three cages, hanging on the tower of St. Lambert Church in Münster, Germany. The slaughter of the Anabaptists after the fall of Münster was one of the most violent episodes in the Reformation.

preacher, Dr. Martin Luther King, Jr., who reintroduced the principle of nonviolent resistance to persecution.

Spiritualists: The Holy Individual

Whereas the Anabaptists radicalized the Swiss Reformation's emphasis on building a godly community, the Spiritualists° radicalized Luther's commitment to personal introspection. Perhaps the greatest Spiritualist was the aristocratic Caspar Schwenckfeld (1490–1561), who was a friend of Luther's until he broke with the reformer over what he considered the weak spirituality of established Lutheranism. Schwenckfeld believed that depraved humanity was incapable of casting off the bonds of sin, which only a supernatural act of God could achieve. This separation from sinfulness was revealed through an intense conversion experience, after which the believer gained spiritual illumination. Schwenckfeld called this illumination the "inner Word," which he understood as a living form of the Scriptures written directly on the believer's soul by the hand of God. Schwenckfeld also prized the "outer Word," that is, the Scriptures, but he found the emotional experience of the inner Word more powerful than the intellectual experience that came from reading the Bible. Spiritualists reflected an inner peace evident in their calm physical appearance, lack of anxiety, and mastery of bodily appetites—a state Schwenckfeld called the "castle of peace."

The most prominent example of the Spiritualist tendency in the English-speaking world is the Quakers, who first appeared in England a century after the Lutheran Reformation. The Quakers, or Society of Friends, interpreted the priesthood of all believers to mean that God's spirit, which they called the Light of Christ, was given equally to all men and women. This belief led them to abandon entirely a separately ordained ministry and to replace organized worship with meetings in which any man, woman, or child could speak, read Scripture, pray, or sing, as the spirit moved them. The Quakers' belief in the sacredness of all human beings also inclined them toward pacifism and egalitarianism.

In no other religious tradition have women played such a prominent role for so long. From the very beginning of the movement, female Friends were prominent in preaching the Quaker gospel. In Quaker marriages, wives were completely equal to their husbands—at least in religious matters. Quakers long played a prominent role in various social reform movements as well. In the eighteenth century, they were the first to campaign for the abolition of slavery; in the nineteenth century, Quaker women were prominent in the movement to establish women's rights; and in the twentieth century they led antiwar movements and the campaign for nuclear disarmament.

Unitarians: A Rationalist Approach

The universal acceptance of the Trinity among Christians changed in the middle of the sixteenth century with the emergence of numerous radical sects that rejected the divinity of Christ. They were called Arians, Socinians, Anti-Trinitarians, or Unitarians°. Distinctive to Christian theology—in comparison to other monotheistic religions, such as Judaism and Islam—is the doctrine of the Trinity, which posits that the one God has three identities: God the Father, God the Son, and God the Holy Spirit. The doctrine of the Trinity made it possible for Christians to believe that God the Son "took on flesh" in what is called the *incarnation*. At a particular moment in history, God became the human being Jesus Christ. The doctrine of the Trinity was officially established as Christian dogma at the Council of Nicaea in

325, in response to the Arians who accepted Jesus as a religious leader but denied that he was "co-eternal" with God the Father. The Trinitarian Christians denounced the Arian doctrine because they thought it rejected Christ's full divinity.

During the sixteenth-century Reformation various forms of the Arian doctrine were revived. The Italian Faustus Socinus (1539–1604) taught a rationalist interpretation of the Scriptures and argued that Jesus was a divinely inspired man, not God-become-man. Socinus's followers thus rejected the doctrine of the Trinity, which they found contrary to simple common sense and without support in Scripture. Socinus's ideas remain central to Unitarianism—the specific rejection of Trinitarian doctrine and the general emphasis on rationality.

Catholics and magisterial Protestants alike were extremely hostile to Unitarians, who tended to be well-educated humanists and men of letters. Unitarian views thrived in advanced intellectual circles in northern Italy and eastern Europe, but the most famous critic of the Trinity was the brilliant, if eccentric, Spaniard Michael Servetus (1511–1553). Trained as a physician and widely read in the literature of the occult, Servetus published influential Anti-Trinitarian works and daringly sent his provocative works to the major Protestant reformers. Based on a tip from the Protestants in Geneva, the Catholic inquisitor-general in Lyons, France, arrested Servetus, but he escaped from prison during his trial. While passing through Protestant Geneva on his way to refuge in Italy, he was recognized while attending a church service and again imprisoned. Although no law in Geneva allowed capital punishment, Servetus was convicted of heresy and burned alive.

The Anabaptists and Unitarians shared some early connections and similarities, but the two groups soon parted ways. Both Anabaptists and Unitarians followed the logic of their own beliefs and were unwilling to compromise with other Protestants. Anabaptists isolated themselves in their own communities and avoided contact with outsiders to avoid pollution from sinners and persecution from the authorities. Unitarians were more open to public debate, and in eastern Europe they attracted support from the powerful.

The Free World of Eastern Europe

During the sixteenth century eastern Europe offered a measure of religious freedom and toleration unknown elsewhere in Europe. As a result, eastern Europe was open to considerable religious experimentation and attracted refugees from the oppressive princes of western Europe, none of whom tolerated more than one religion in their territories if they could help it. Such religious toleration was made possible by the relative weakness of the monarchs in Bohemia, Hungary, Transylvania, and especially Poland-Lithuania, where the great land-owning aristocrats exercised nearly complete freedom on their estates. All of these kingdoms had Catholic monarchs, but the Reformation radicalized the aristocrats who dominated the parliaments, enabling Protestantism to take hold even against the wishes of the monarch.

In Bohemia (now in the Czech Republic), the Hussite movement in the fourteenth century had rejected papal authority and some of the sacramental authority of the priesthood long before the Protestant Reformation. After the Lutherans and Calvinists attracted adherents in Bohemia, the few surviving old Hussites and the new Protestants formed an alliance in 1575, which made common cause against the Catholics. In addition to this formal alliance, substantial numbers of Anabaptists found refuge from persecution in Bohemia and lived in complete freedom on the estates of tolerant landlords who were desperate for settlers to farm their lands.

The religious diversity of Hungary was also remarkable by the standards of the time. By the end of the sixteenth century, much of Hungary's diverse population had accepted some form of Protestantism. Among the German-speaking city dwellers and the Hungarian peasants in western Hungary, Lutheranism prevailed, whereas in eastern Hungary Calvinism was dominant.

No other country was as tolerant of religious diversity as Transylvania (now in Romania), largely because of the weak monarchy, which could not have enforced religious uniformity even if the king had wanted to do so. In Transylvania, Unitarianism took hold more firmly than anywhere else. In 1572 the tolerant ruler Prince István Báthory (r. 1571–1586) granted the Unitarians complete legal equality to establish their own churches along with Catholics, Lutherans, and Calvinists—the only place in Europe where equality of religions was achieved. Transylvania was also

home to significant communities of Jews, Armenian Christians, and Orthodox Christians.

The sixteenth century was the golden age of the Polish-Lithuanian Commonwealth, which was the largest state in the size of its territory in Europe. It escaped both the Ottoman invasions and the religious wars that plagued the Holy Roman Empire. From the Lutheran cities in the German-speaking north to the vast open plains of Great Poland, where Calvinism took hold among the independent-minded nobility, religious lines often had been drawn along ethnic or class divisions. When Sigismund August (r. 1548–1572) became king, he declared, "I am not king of men's conscience," and inaugurated extensive toleration of Protestant churches, even while the vast majority of peasants remained loyal to Orthodoxy or Catholicism. Fleeing persecution in other countries, various Anabaptist groups and Unitarians found refuge in Poland. This extensive religious diversity in Poland was later snuffed out during the Catholic Reformation.

The Catholic Reformation

■ How did the Catholic Church respond to the unprecedented threat to its dominance of religious authority in the West?

The Catholic Reformation, also known as the Counter Reformation, profoundly revitalized the Catholic Church and established an institutional and doctrinal framework that persisted into the late twentieth century. The Catholic Reformation° was a series of efforts to purify the Church; these efforts were not necessarily just a reaction to the Protestant Reformation but evolved out of late medieval spirituality, driven by many of the same impulses that stimulated the Protestants. The most important of these efforts was the creation of new religious orders, especially the Society of Jesus, whose members are known as the Jesuits. They promoted a vast educational program that improved understanding of the faith and a missionary effort that spread Christianity throughout the world. However, the Church also responded to the challenge of the Protestant Reformation by establishing the Holy Office of the Inquisition, promulgating the *Index of Forbidden Books*, and implementing the decrees of the Council of Trent (1545–1563).

The Catholic Reformation came both from the religious enthusiasm that welled up from the laity and lower clergy and the leadership of a series of influential popes who gave the movement a strongly international character. Catholicism retained Latin, in contrast to Protestantism, which conducted services in vernacular languages such as German or English. The success of the Catholic

---

CHRONOLOGY

The Diversity of Protestantism

1520	Zwingli declared the People's Priest in Zürich
1529	Marburg Colloquy
1534	Parliament in England passes the Acts of Supremacy and Succession
1534–1535	Anabaptist control of Münster, Germany
1535	Execution of John Fisher and Thomas More; first edition of John Calvin's *Institutes of the Christian Religion*
1559–1563	The Elizabethan Settlement of the Anglican Church
1560	Scots Confession

Reformation tended to obliterate differences in religious culture from one Catholic country to another, creating greater uniformity in Catholic practice and doctrine than had been the case in the medieval period. The international spread of the Catholic Reformation was a source of tremendous strength in revitalizing the Church and in creating a distinctively Catholic culture. For 400 years after the Catholic Reformation, Catholics who found themselves in a foreign land could experience something very familiar merely by attending a mass, spoken or chanted in the ancient Latin of the Church.

The Religious Orders in the Catholic Reformation

The most dramatic and effective manifestation of the Catholic Reformation was the founding of new religious orders. These orders exhibited a religious vitality that had little to do with the Protestant threat. In fact, none of the new orders began near the centers of Protestantism, such as Germany. Italy, which remained strongly Catholic, produced the largest number of new orders, followed by Spain and France. All of the new orders remained committed to a very traditional Catholic theology, but they differed from the prayerful isolation of the traditional monastic orders by their commitment to an active ministry in the world.

Jesuits: The Soldiers of God

By far the most influential new order was the Society of Jesus, also known as the Jesuits. In 1534 a group of seven students at the University of Paris took a vow to go on a pilgrimage to Jerusalem after graduation. They were an international lot—a Portuguese, a Savoyard, an Aragonese, two Basques, and two Castilians. When the original seven plus some French companions gathered in Venice to take a ship to Palestine, they found their way blocked by a war, a turn of events that led them to place themselves at the disposal of the pope. This loosely organized group of kindred spirits became the core of a new order. In 1540 they officially organized the Society of Jesus and elected Ignatius Loyola (1491–1556) the first General of the Society.

Loyola's dynamic personality and intense spirituality gave the new order its distinctive commitment to moral action in the world. Loyola began his career as a courtier to King Ferdinand of Aragon and a soldier. In 1521 during a French attack on the Spanish garrison at Pamplona, Loyola's leg was shattered by a cannonball. Driven by vanity to keep his leg from looking deformed, he insisted on having his leg rebroken and reset several times despite the excruciating pain of the procedure. During the boredom of his convalescence, he turned to reading a life of Christ and the lives of the saints. From these he discovered tales of heroism superior to anything he had read of medieval knights. These revelations converted Loyola to Christ.

Loyola's background as a courtier and soldier deeply influenced his religiosity. The Society of Jesus that he helped found preserved some of the values Loyola had acquired as a courtier-soldier—social refinement, loyalty to authority, sense of duty, and high-minded chivalry.

Loyola's most impressive personal contribution to religious literature was the *Spiritual Exercises* (1548), which became the foundation of Jesuit practice. Republished in more than 5,000 editions in hundreds of languages, the *Exercises* prescribe a month-long retreat devoted to a series of meditations in which the participant mentally reexperiences the spiritual life, physical death, and miraculous resurrection of Christ. Much of the power of the *Exercises* derives from the systematic employment of each of the five senses to produce a defined emotional, spiritual, and even physical response. Participants in the *Exercises* seem to hear the blasphemous cries of the soldiers at Christ's crucifixion, feel the terrible agony of his suffering on the cross, and experience the blinding illumination of his resurrection from the dead. Those who participated in the *Exercises* considered the experience life-transforming and usually made a steadfast commitment to serve the Church.

The Jesuits distinguished themselves from other religious orders by extending their personal spirituality to minister to others. They did not wear clerical clothing, and on foreign missions they devoted themselves to learning the language and culture of the peoples they hoped to convert. Jesuits became famous for their loyalty to the pope, and some took a special fourth vow (in addition to the three traditional vows of poverty, chastity, and obedience) to go on a mission if the pope requested it. Many traveled as missionaries to distant parts of the globe, such as China and Japan. In Europe and the Americas the Jesuits established a vast network of colleges, most similar to modern high schools but some became universities. These colleges offered free tuition, which made them open to the poor who had few other opportunities for education. The Jesuit colleges combined a thorough training in languages, humanities, and sciences with religious instruction and moral guidance. They became especially popular because the Jesuit fathers were much more likely to pay personal attention to their students than professors in the established universities. In Europe the Jesuit college system transformed the culture of the Catholic elite. These colleges attracted the sons of the aristocrats and the wealthy who absorbed from the Jesuit instructors the values of Renaissance humanism and the Catholic Reformation. By 1615 there were 372 Jesuit colleges in Europe, and the demand for new colleges was so great that the Jesuits could not recruit and train enough qualified instructors. With the success of these colleges, education gradually replaced missionary work as the most important Jesuit activity.

The Jesuit order grew rapidly. At Loyola's death in 1556 there were about a thousand Jesuits, but by 1700 there were nearly 20,000, and many young men who wished to join

The Ecstasy of Teresa of Avila: The Body and the Soul

Teresa of Avila (1515–1582, canonized St. Teresa in 1622) eloquently expressed the intimate connection between physical and spiritual experiences that was a common feature of Catholic mysticism. She was a Spanish Carmelite nun whose accounts of her own mystical experiences made her a model for other nuns throughout the world. Filled with religious ardor, she devoted herself to an ascetic regime of self-deprivations so intense that she fell ill and suffered paralysis.

Often afflicted by an intense pain in her side, Teresa reported that an angel had stuck a lance tipped with fire into her heart. This "seraphic vision," which became the subject of Gianlorenzo Bernini's famous sculpture in Santa Maria della Vittoria in Rome (1645–1652), epitomized the Catholic Reformation sensibility of understanding spiritual states through physical feelings. In Teresa's case, her extreme bodily deprivations, paralysis, and intense pain conditioned how she experienced the spiritual side of her nature. Many have seen an erotic character to the vision, which may be true, but the vision best demonstrates a profound psychological awareness that bodily and spiritual sensations cannot be precisely distinguished. As Teresa put it, "it is not bodily pain, but spiritual, though the body has a share in it—indeed, a great share." She described the paralysis of her soul and her body as interconnected: "The soul is unable to do either this or anything else. The entire body contracts and neither arm nor foot can be moved." She then described, in remarkably graphic terms, her repeated vision:

It pleased the Lord that I should sometimes see the following vi-sion. I would see beside me, on my left hand, an angel in bodily form—a type of vision which I am not in the habit of seeing, except very rarely. . . . I pleased the Lord that I should see this angel in the following way. He was not tall, but short, and very beautiful, his face so aflame that he appeared to be one of the highest types of angel who seem to be all afire. . . . In his hands I saw a long golden spear and at the end of the iron tip I seemed to see a point of fire. With this he seemed to pierce my heart several times so that it penetrated to my entrails. When he drew it out, I thought he was drawing them out with it and he left me completely afire with a great love for God. The pain was so sharp that it made me utter several moans; and so excessive was the sweetness caused me by this intense pain that one can never wish to lose it, nor will one's soul be content with anything less than God. . . . So sweet are the colloquies of love which pass between the soul and God that if anyone thinks I am lying I be-seech God, in His goodness, to give him the same experience.[14]

Visions such as this one were difficult to interpret. Exactly what was going on in those sweet colloquies between Teresa's soul and God? Teresa associated these visions with intense physical pain, as if she had to suffer in order to receive divine illumination, which she described as a sweet conversation between her soul and God. Her sensibility about the necessary relationship between physical pain and spiritual experiences was especially pronounced among sixteenth-century Catholics. Pain and suffering were understood as a form of penance, and thus the body could play a positive and redemptive role in enabling spirituality. The best way to transcend this world was in bodily pain, because through pain the Christian escaped the temptations of the flesh and renounced the attractions of the world.

For Discussion

How was pain understood to have religious value? What was happening around Teresa that might explain her preoccupation with pain?

An angel is about to pierce her side with an arrow.

St. Teresa lies suspended in the air in a swoon induced by a vision.

The Ecstasy of St. Teresa

DOCUMENT

The Constitution of the Society of Jesus

In 1540, Pope Paul III approved the Constitution of the Society of Jesus. This excerpt includes some of the characteristics of the society that help explain its success, including to go on a mission to distant lands if the pope so orders.

He who desires to fight for God under the banner of the cross in our society—which we wish to distinguish by the name of Jesus—and to serve God alone and the Roman pontiff, his vicar on earth, after a solemn vow of perpetual chastity, shall set this thought before his mind, that he is a part of a society founded for the especial purpose of providing for the advancement of souls in Christian life and doctrine and for the propagation of faith through public preaching and the ministry of the word of God, spiritual exercises and deeds of charity, and in particular through the training of the young and ignorant in Christianity and through the spiritual consolation of the faithful of Christ in hearing confessions; and he shall take care to keep first God and next the purpose of this organization always before his eyes . . .

All members shall realize, and shall recall daily, as long as they live, that this society as a whole and in every part is fighting for God under faithful obedience to one most holy lord, the pope, and to the other Roman pontiffs who succeed him. And although we are taught in the gospel and through the orthodox faith to recognize and steadfastly profess that all the faithful of Christ are subject to the Roman pontiff as their head and as the vicar of Jesus Christ, yet we have adjudged that, for the special promotion of greater humility in our society and the perfect mortification of every individual and the sacrifice of our own wills, we should each be bound by a peculiar vow, in addition to the general obligation, that whatever the present Roman pontiff, or any future one, may from time to time decree regarding the welfare of souls and the propagation of the faith, we are pledged to obey without evasion or excuse, instantly, so far as in us lies, whether he send us to the Turks or any other infidels, even to those who inhabit the regions men call the Indies; whether to heretics or schismatics, or, on the other hand, to certain of the faithful.

Source: From James Harvey Robinson, ed. Readings in European History, vol. 2 (Boston: Ginn, 1904), pp. 162–63.

had to be turned away because there were insufficient funds to train them. The influence of the Jesuits was even greater than their numbers would indicate, however. Besides their success in education, which shaped the values of the upper classes and guided intellectual life throughout Catholic Europe, Jesuits often served as the personal confessors to powerful figures, including several kings of France and Holy Roman Emperors. By giving private advice on spiritual matters, confessors had many opportunities to influence royal policy, an influence the Jesuits were not shy to exercise.

Women's Orders: In But Not of the World

Creating a ministry that was active in the world was much more difficult for the female orders than for the Jesuits and the other male orders. Women who sought to reinvigorate old orders or found new ones faced hostility from ecclesiastical and civic authorities, who thought women had to be protected by either a husband or the cloister wall. Women in convents were supposed to be entirely separated from the world, "as if they were dead," but this principle was at odds with the desires of many devout women who wanted to help make the world a better place.

The cloistering of women was a highly controversial issue during the sixteenth century. Because it was cheaper to place a daughter in a convent than to provide her with a dowry for marriage, about one-third of the women of aristocratic families in Catholic countries found themselves in convents rather than on the marriage market. In some places, such as Venice during the late sixteenth century, more than three-quarters of the noblewomen were cloistered. In many convents, aristocratic women tried to live much as they would have in secular society, enjoying private apartments, servants, regular visits with relatives, musical entertainments, and even vacations. Many of these women felt like involuntary inmates living in a "Convent Hell," to quote the title of Arcangela Tarabotti's famous exposé of the nun's life (1654). The dreary experience of these reluctant nuns, however, contrasted with the genuine enthusiasm for convent life of many other women who were caught up in the religious enthusiasm of the Catholic Reformation.

The first task of those who were ardently religious was to reform convent life. The most famous model was provided by Teresa of Avila (1515–1582), who wrote a strict new rule for the Carmelites, who had been established in 1452. The new rule required mortifications of the flesh and complete withdrawal from the world. Teresa described her own mystical experiences in her *Autobiography* (1611) and in the *Interior Castle* (1588), a compelling masterpiece in the literature of mysticism. Teresa advocated a very cautious brand of mysticism, which was checked by regular confession and skepticism about extreme acts of self-deprivation. For example, she recognized that a nun who fell into an apparent rapture after extensive fasting was probably just having hallucinations from the hunger.

The many orders of nuns during the sixteenth century presented many contradictions. On the one hand, they housed some women who had no special religious vocation, who did not want to be locked away from family and friends, and who suffered from the stifling boredom of living without apparent purpose. On the other hand, many women who willingly chose the religious life thrived in a community of women, were liberated from the rigors of childbearing, and were freed from direct male supervision. These women could devote themselves to cultivating musical or literary talents to a degree that would have been impossible in the outside world. Nuns created their own distinctly female culture, producing a number of learned women and social reformers who had considerable influence in the arts, education, and charitable work such as nursing.

Paul III, The First Catholic Reformation Pope

Despite the many earlier attempts at reform and the Protestant threat, the Church was slow to initiate its own reforms because of resistance among bishops and cardinals of the Church hierarchy who worried that reform would threaten their income. More than twenty years after Luther's defiant stand at the Diet of Worms in 1521, Pope Paul III (r. 1534–1549) finally launched a systematic counterattack. As a member of the powerful Farnese family, who had long treated church offices as their private property, Paul seemed an unlikely reformer. But more than any other pope, Paul understood the necessity to respond to the political winds of change. It was Pope Paul, for example, who formally approved the Jesuits and began to employ them as missionary soldiers for the Church.

In 1541, in an attempt to resolve the dangerous religious disputes provoked by the Lutherans, Paul sent a representative to a discussion between Catholic and Protestant theologians held in conjunction with the Imperial Diet of Regensburg. Despite the best efforts of the pope's reform-minded representative, the meeting failed, making it stunningly clear how wide the gap had become between Protestant and Catholic theology. The failure of Regensburg shifted Pope Paul's efforts from a plan of hesitant accommodation to a defensive strategy devoted to building a Catholic bulwark against Protestant ideas.

The following year, on the advice of an archconservative faction of cardinals, Paul III reorganized the Roman Inquisition, called the Holy Office. The function of the Inquisition was to inquire into the beliefs of all Catholics primarily to discover indications of heresies such as those of the Protestants. Jews, for example, were exempt from its authority, although Jews who had converted or been forced to convert to Christianity did fall under the jurisdiction of the Inquisition. There had been other inquisitions, but most had been local or national. The Spanish Inquisition was controlled by the Spanish monarchs, for example. In contrast, the Holy Office came under the direct control of the pope and cardinals and termed itself the Universal Roman Inquisition. Its effective authority did not reach beyond northern and central Italy, but it set the tone for the entire Catholic Reformation Church.

The Inquisition immediately began to crack down on suspected heretics. One of the first to be investigated was Bernardino Ochino (1487–1563), the most popular preacher in Rome and the Minister General of the Capuchin order. When summoned to answer questions before the Holy Office, he fled to Geneva. His defection to Calvin's Geneva caused an enormous sensation and fueled the clamor for more extensive investigations. Any form of criticism of the Church within earshot of an informant of the Inquisition became very dangerous. The Inquisition could subject defendants to lengthy interrogations and stiff penalties, including prison sentences and even execution in exceptional cases.

A second effort to stop the spread of Protestant and other ideas deemed heretical led to the first *Index of Forbidden Books,* drawn up in 1549 in Venice, the capital of the publishing industry in Italy. The *Index* censored or banned many books that the Church considered detrimental to the faith and the authority of the Church. Most affected by the strictures were books about theology and philosophy, but books of moral guidance were also prohibited or butchered by the censors, such as the works of Erasmus, and classics of literature, such as Giovanni Boccaccio's *The Decameron.* The official papal *Index* of 1559 prohibited translations of the Bible into vernacular languages such as Italian. The prohibition of vernacular Bibles was especially important because the Church insisted that laypeople required a trained intermediary in the person of a priest to interpret and explain the Bible. The Church's protective attitude about biblical interpretation clearly distinguished the Catholic from the Protestant attitude of encouraging widespread Bible reading. It remained possible to buy certain heretical theological books "under the counter," much as people today find ways to obtain illegal drugs, but possessing such books could be dangerous if agents of the Inquisition conducted a raid.

The Council of Trent

By far the most significant of Pope Paul III's contributions to the Catholic Reformation was his call for a general council of the Church, which began to meet in 1545 in Trent on the border between Italy and Germany. The Council of Trent established principles that guided the Catholic Church for the next 400 years.

DOCUMENT

Council of Trent (1545–1563)

Between 1545 and 1563 the council met under the auspices of three different popes in three separate sessions, with long intervals of as much as ten years between sessions. The objective of these sessions was to find a way to respond to the Protestant criticisms of the Church, to reassert the authority of the pope, and to launch reforms that would guarantee a well-educated and honest clergy. The decrees of the Council of Trent, which had the force of legislation for the entire Church, defied the Protestants by refusing to yield any ground on the traditional doctrines of the Church. The decrees confirmed the efficacy of all seven of the traditional sacraments, the reality of Purgatory, and the spiritual value of indulgences. In order to provide better supervision of the Church, bishops were ordered to reside in their dioceses or regions. Trent decreed that every diocese should have a seminary to train priests, providing a practical solution to the problem of clerical ignorance.

The Council of Trent represented a dramatic reassertion of the authority of the papacy, the bishops, and the priesthood. The actual implementation of the decrees varied considerably from country to country and from diocese to diocese, however. The model for enforcing the decrees was Archbishop Carlo Borromeo (r. 1565–1584) of Milan. His energetic visitations of his diocese and attention to administrative detail became an example for others. Despite the hopes of some of the participants in the council, it had no effect whatsoever in luring Protestants back into the Catholic fold.

The Reformation in the Arts

■ How did the religious turmoil of the sixteenth century transform the role of the visual arts and music in public life?

Most of the paintings, sculptures, and musical compositions created before and during the sixteenth century were destined for churches or had some kind of religious function. But with the tensions brought about during the Reformation, one of the major issues dividing Protestants and Catholics was defining the proper role of the arts in Christian worship. Except among the most radical Protestants, who entirely rejected any role for the arts in religious worship, the difference between the two was more one of degree than of kind. Catholics considered religious images, properly regulated, vital for devotion. Protestants, however, were uneasy about religious art because they worried about confining divine truths within any kind of visual representation.

Protestant Iconoclasm

Protestants sometimes initiated reform by vandalizing churches through acts of iconoclasm—the removing,

CHRONOLOGY

The Catholic Reformation

1534–1549	Pontificate of Pope Paul III
1540	Founding of the Society of Jesus
1541	Imperial Diet of Regensburg
1542	Reorganization of the Roman Inquisition or Holy Office
1545–1563	Meetings of the Council of Trent
1548	*Spiritual Exercises* of Ignatius Loyola
1549	*Index of Forbidden Books*

breaking, or defacing of religious statues, paintings, and symbols such as crucifixes. The destruction of religious works of art more often than not took place even when the reformers themselves discouraged or denounced it. Nevertheless, in town after town in the thrall of reform enthusiasm, laypeople destroyed religious art, including some of the greatest masterpieces of the Middle Ages and Renaissance. Their violence against property was seldom matched by violence against people. Protestant mobs were much more likely to rip down an altar painting than to attack a priest.

Three factors likely explain iconoclasm. One was that people feared the power of such images. Guillaume Farel, the reformer of Geneva before Calvin, told how his parents had taken him as a child to the shrine of the Holy Cross at Tallard in southern France. A priest stationed at the shrine told the pilgrims that the cross shook violently during storms. What Farel remembered most about the cross was his fear, reinforced by the apprehension of his parents. The implication was that images possessed great powers that could be used both to protect and to destroy. The problem with religious images, therefore, was not that they were idols, which were by definition without power. They were dangerous because they were perceived to be *too* powerful.

A second reason for iconoclasm was that religious images devoured financial resources that could be better spent on the poor. Ulrich Zwingli was especially articulate on this point. He hoped that the assets devoted to paying for paintings and statues could be transformed into "food of the poor." In this sense iconoclasm was part of a pious project to redirect the energy of Christians toward solving the social problems of the community. Great paintings were given to hospitals to serve as fuel, and crucifixes were sold as lumber with the proceeds going to the indigent.

Many reformers spoke of a third concern about images. They worried that a church filled with works of art distracted worshipers from paying attention to the Word of

Iconoclasm in the Netherlands

This engraving shows statues being hauled down by the men on the left of the church pulling ropes. Note that one statue is already lying on the ground. On the right side of the church, men are breaking the stained glass windows with clubs.

Scripture. They found the meaning of images too ambiguous, too subject to misinterpretation. Instead they wanted to ensure that their preaching provided the interpretation of Scripture. In effect, they wanted to substitute the Word of God for the image of God. In many reformed Dutch churches, for example, the walls were stripped bare of images and whitewashed. Passages of Scripture were then painted on the walls in place of the images.

Although skeptical of the role of images in churches, propagandists for the Reformation had no such reservation about woodcuts and engravings, which could be reproduced in multiple copies and cheaply sold to thousands of people. These images, the visual by-product of the printing revolution, promoted the Reformation to the masses in a simple graphic way by lampooning the pope and ridiculing the wealth of the clergy. These images were the prototype for modern political cartoons. Also popular were portraits of the reformers. Many a pious Lutheran household replaced an image of the Madonna with an engraving of Martin Luther and his wife, Katherine von Bora.

Ego sum Papa
(Ich bin der Papst).

Französischer Holzschnitt gegen den lasterhaften Papst Alexander VI.

Anti-Catholic Propaganda

This woodcut, titled *I Am the Pope*, satirizes the papacy by depicting Pope Alexander VI as a monster. Alexander was infamous for allegedly conducting orgies in the Vatican. This kind of visual propaganda was an effective way to undermine support for the papacy.

Catholic Reformation Art

The Catholic Church retained a strong commitment to the religious value of the arts. However, the Catholic Reformation recognized that abuses had taken place in works of art that depicted events that did not appear in Scripture. The Church placed artists under much closer surveillance than before. The Council of Trent enjoined artists to avoid representing impieties of any sort and to use their art to teach correct doctrine and to move believers to true piety. Religious art had to convey a message simply, directly, and in terms that unlettered viewers could understand. The best Catholic art employed dramatic theatrical effects in lighting and the arrangement of figures to represent deep emotional and spiritual experiences. Through contemplating these pictures, viewers were supposed to create similar experiences within themselves. In this sense an aesthetic and a spiritual appreciation of art were inseparable.

The Council of Trent forced a reevaluation of previous trends in the arts and a number of existing works of art. The Italian Renaissance, in particular, had glorified the human body, often represented in the nude. In earlier generations churchmen and popes had not objected to the display of naked figures in churches and chapels because after all, the human body was God's finest creation. However, after the Council of Trent many influential ecclesiastics disapproved this practice in the strongest terms. Michelangelo's *The Last Judgment*, a fresco painted in the Sistine Chapel in the Vatican in Rome between 1534 and 1541, came under severe attack the year after the last session of Trent. The

The Last Judgment
In this fresco by Michelangelo, the figure with the raised hand in the upper center is Christ. On his right sits the Virgin Mary. Both figures were painted over with clothing to hide their nudity.

The Inquisition Criticizes a Work of Art

This painting was originally intended to represent the Last Supper when Christ introduced the mass to his apostles. Because there are many figures in it who are not mentioned in the biblical account and the supper appears as if it were a Renaissance banquet, the artist, Paolo Veronese, was obliged to answer questions from the Inquisition. Ordered to remove the offending figures, Veronese instead changed the name of the painting to depict the less theologically controversial supper in the house of Levi.

polemical *Dialogue on the Errors of Painters* criticized Michelangelo for subordinating the representation of Christian truths to his own stylistic interests in the human nude. Genitals and bare breasts in *The Last Judgment* were painted over, disfiguring one of the greatest masterpieces of the Renaissance. The crude overpainting was not removed until the fresco was cleaned during the 1990s.

Everywhere in Catholic Europe, offending body parts were painted over and paintings of indecorous subject matter removed from churches. In the Catholic parts of the Netherlands, paintings and statues deemed indecent were even destroyed, in an odd echo of Protestant iconoclasm. In Venice the Inquisition got involved. In a celebrated inquiry in 1573, the inquisitor called in the painter, Paolo Veronese, to answer why he put into a painting of the Last Supper various figures that did not appear in the Bible. The inquisitor noticed a figure dressed like a German and badgered Veronese with the allegation that this might indicate Lutheran sympathies. Ordered to change the painting, Veronese quietly changed its title instead.

Because artists' livelihoods depended on the patronage of aristocrats and high ecclesiastical officials, most quickly fell into line with the new requirements. Artistic rebels were unknown in the late sixteenth-century Catholic world. In

1577 the pope founded a new academy in Rome to create guidelines for artists in promoting Christianity, and the Jesuits proved very influential in defining a new path for artists. Many prominent artists across Europe enthusiastically embraced the Catholic Reformation. Some became friends of Jesuits, undertook commissions for Jesuits, and practiced the *Spiritual Exercises*, thereby suffusing a Jesuit sensibility throughout Catholic culture.

Ignatius of Loyola

Sacred Music: Praising God

The Protestants' concern that the Word of God be intelligible to ordinary believers also influenced their attitude toward music. Luther, in particular, recognized the power of music to move the souls of the congregation. In the Lutheran mass he retained much of the traditional chant, but he translated the words into German and encouraged congregational singing so that believers sang the text themselves rather than passively listened to a choir. A number of new hymns were composed for the Lutheran service, some by Luther himself. One of the lasting masterpieces of the Reformation is Luther's great hymn "A Mighty Fortress Is

Our God." The Lutheran hymnbook laid the foundations for the magnificent tradition of Protestant church music that culminated in the compositions of Johann Sebastian Bach (1685–1750).

Zwingli, less certain about the value of music, banished organs from churches because he thought they obscured the clarity of the biblical text. Some radicals eliminated all music from churches, creating an austere form of worship practiced in houses or bare chapels, in which nothing was allowed to distract from the preaching of God's Word and the direct influence of the Holy Spirit. In these radical sects, the intimate connection between Western Christianity and the arts, which had been so pronounced for centuries, came to an abrupt end. Radical Protestants such as Anabaptists left a lasting legacy of hostility toward creative artists.

The Council of Trent spent more than a year debating the reform of sacred music. The Council decreed that the purpose of liturgical music was to encourage a sense of worship in the congregation. This meant that unlike Protestant music, which appealed to the laity by employing folk tunes, Catholic compositions should not borrow from secular music, but like Protestant music, the style of composition must allow for the words to be clearly heard. The Catholics did not follow the Protestant emphasis on congregational singing and rejected virtuoso vocal or instrumental displays. Catholic liturgical performances consisted only of the organ either accompanying voices or playing solos.

The new music of the Catholic Reformation remained firmly rooted in the innovations of Renaissance music and consisted of compositions for various forms of the Latin mass. The most important Catholic composer of church music in the later sixteenth century was Giovanni Pierluigi da Palestrina (ca. 1525–1594). Palestrina spent most of his career in Rome, where he worked as an organist and choir master. His more than 100 masses demonstrated to the often skeptical prelates, who wanted to abolish all elaborate compositions, that music could reflect the meaning of the words while not obscuring their audibility. Palestrina amplified the sumptuous effects of the unaccompanied choir, employing an exotic mixture of harmonic and melodic purity, carefully controlled dissonance, and a sensuous sound. For many generations his music served as the model for Catholic composers.

Conclusion

Competing Understanding

During the Reformation the West was permanently divided into two discordant religious cultures of Protestant and Catholic. The religious unity of the West achieved during the Middle Ages had been fruit of many centuries of diligent effort by missionaries, monks,

popes, and crusading knights. That unity was lost through the conflicts between, on the one hand, reformers, city magistrates, princes, and kings who wanted to control their own affairs and, on the other, popes who continued to cling to the medieval concept of the papal monarchy. In the West, Christians no longer saw themselves as dedicated to serving the same God as all other Christians. Instead, Catholics and Protestants emphasized their differences.

The differences between these two cultures had lasting implications for how people understood and accepted the authority of the Church and the state, how they conducted their family life, and how they formed their own identities as individuals and as members of a larger community. The next chapter will explore all of these themes.

As the result of intransigence on the part of both confessional cultures, the division had tragic consequences. From the late sixteenth century to the late seventeenth century, European states tended to create diplomatic alliances along this ideological and religious divide, allowed disputes about doctrine to prevent peaceful reconciliation, and conducted wars as if they were a fulfillment of God's plan. Even after the era of religious warfare ended, Protestant and Catholic confessional cultures remained ingrained in all aspects of life, influencing not just government policy but painting, music, literature, and education. This division completely reshaped the West into a place of intense religious and ideological conflict, which by the eighteenth century drove many thoughtful people to reject the traditional forms of Christianity altogether and to advocate religious toleration and the separation of Church and state, ideas that were barely conceivable in the sixteenth century.

Suggestions for Further Reading

For a comprehensive listing of suggested readings, please go to www.ablongman.com/levack2e/chapter13

Bireley, Robert. *The Refashioning of Catholicism, 1450–1700: A Reassessment of the Counter Reformation.* 1999. A fair reappraisal of the major events by one of the most prominent historians of Catholicism in this period.

Bossy, John. *Christianity in the West, 1400–1700.* 1985. A short study not of the institutions of the Church but of Christianity itself, this book explores the Christian people, their beliefs, and their way of life. The book demonstrates considerable continuities before and after the Reformation and is especially useful in understanding the attitudes of common lay believers as opposed to the major reformers and Church officials.

Cameron, Euan. *The European Reformation.* 1995. The most comprehensive general survey, this bulky book covers all the major topics in considerable detail. It is excellent in explaining theological issues.

Hsia, R. Po-chia. *The World of Catholic Renewal, 1540–1770.* 1998. An excellent survey of the most recent research.

Koenigsberger, H. G., George L. Mosse, and G. Q. Bowler. *Europe in the Sixteenth Century,* 2nd ed. 1989. A good beginner's survey. Strong on political events.

McGrath, Alister E. *Reformation Thought: An Introduction,* 3rd rev. ed. 1999. Indispensable introduction for anyone seeking to understand the ideas of the European Reformation. Drawing on the most up-to-date scholarship, McGrath offers a clear explanation of these ideas, set firmly in their historical contexts.

Muir, Edward. *Ritual in Early Modern Europe.* 2nd ed. 2005. A broad survey of the debates about ritual during the Reformation and the implementation of ritual reforms.

Oberman, Heiko A. *Luther: Man Between God and the Devil,* trans. Eileen Walliser-Schwarzbart. 1992. First published to great acclaim in Germany, this book argues that Luther was more the medieval monk than history has usually regarded him. Oberman claims that Luther was haunted by the Devil and saw the world as a cosmic battleground between God and Satan. A brilliant, intellectual biography that is sometimes challenging but always clear and precise.

O'Malley, John. *Trent and All That: Renaming Catholicism in the Early Modern Era.* 2000. O'Malley works out a remarkable guide to the intellectual and historical developments behind the concepts of Catholic reform and, in his useful term, Early Modern Catholicism. The result is the single best overview of scholarship on Catholicism in early modern Europe, delivered in a pithy, lucid, and entertaining style.

Ozment, Steven. *The Age of Reform, 1250–1550: An Intellectual and Religious History of Late Medieval and Reformation Europe.* 1986. Firmly places the Protestant Reformation in the context of late medieval spirituality and theology; particularly strong on pre-Reformation developments.

Reardon, Bernard M. G. *Religious Thought in the Reformation.* 2nd ed. 1995. A good beginner's survey of the intellectual dimensions of the Reformation.

Scribner, R. W. *For the Sake of the Simple Folk: Popular Propaganda for the German Reformation.* 1994. An innovative and fascinating study of the Lutheran use of visual images.

Scribner, R. W. *The German Reformation.* 1996. A short and very clear analysis of the appeal of the Reformation by the leading social historian of the period. Pays attention to what people actually did rather than just what reformers said they should do.

Notes

1. *Correspondence of Erasmus,* trans. R. A. B. Mynors and D. F. S. Thomson, annotated by Wallace K. Ferguson (1974–1994), no. 858, 167–177.

2. *Desiderius Erasmus, The Essential Erasmus,* ed. John P. Dolan (1964), 148.

3. Quoted in Gordon Rupp, *Luther's Progress to the Diet of Worms* (1964), 29.

4. Ibid., 33.

5. Quote from an anonymous caricature reproduced in A. G. Dickens, *Reformation and Society in Sixteenth-Century Europe* (1966), Figure 46, 61.

6. Translated and quoted in Thomas Head, "Marie Dentière: A Propagandist for the Reform," in Katharina M. Wilson, ed., *Women Writers of the Renaissance and Reformation* (1987), 260.

7. Quoted in Peter Blickle, "The Popular Reformation," in *Handbook of European History 1400–1600: Late Middle Ages, Renaissance and Reformation*, Vol. 2: *Visions, Programs and Outcomes*, eds. Thomas A. Brady, Jr., Heiko A. Oberman, and James D. Tracy (1995), 171.

8. Quoted in Heiko A. Oberman, *Luther: Man Between God and the Devil*, trans. Eileen Walliser-Schwarzbart (1989), 240.

9. E. W. Ives, *Anne Boleyn* (1986), 398.

10. Quoted in Margery Stone Schauer and Frederick Schauer, "Law as the Engine of State: The Trial of Anne Boleyn," *William and Mary Law Review* 22 (1992): 68.

11. Quoted in Ives, "Anne Boleyn," 387.

12. Quoted in Schauer and Schauer, "Law as the Engine of State," 70.

13. Quoted in Dickens, *Reformation and Society*, 134.

14. Quoted in Irving Lavin, *Bernini and the Unity of the Visual Arts* (1980), 107.

The Age of Confessional Division

14

O
N JULY 10, 1584, CATHOLIC EXTREMIST FRANÇOIS GUION, WITH A brace of pistols hidden under his cloak, surprised William the Silent, the Prince of Orange, as he was leaving the dining hall of his palace and shot him at point-blank range. William had been the leader of the Protestant nobility in the Netherlands, which was in revolt against the Catholic king of Spain. Guion masqueraded as a Protestant for seven years in order to ingratiate himself with William's party, and before the assassination he had consulted three Catholic priests who had confirmed the religious merit of his plan. Spain's representative in the Netherlands, the Duke of Parma, had offered a reward of 25,000 crowns to anyone who killed William, and at the moment of the assassination four other fanatics were in Delft trying to gain access to the Prince of Orange.

The murder of William the Silent exemplified an ominous figure in Western civilization—the religiously motivated assassin. There had been many assassinations before the late sixteenth century, but the assassins tended to be motivated by the desire to gain political power or to avenge a personal or family injury and less often by religious differences. In the wake of the Reformation the idea that killing a political leader of the opposing faith would serve God's plan became all too common. The assassination of William illustrated patterns of violence that have become the modus operandi of the political assassin—the use of deception to gain access to the victim, the vulnerability of leaders who wish to mingle with the public, the lethal potential of easily concealed pistols (a new weapon at that time), the corruption of politics through vast sums of money, and the obsessive hostility of zealots against their perceived enemies. The widespread acrimony among the varieties of Christian faith created a climate of religious extremism during the late sixteenth and early seventeenth centuries. After the Protestant and Catholic Reformations, the various forms of Christianity

Procession of the Catholic League During the last half of the sixteenth century, Catholics and Protestants in France formed armed militias or leagues. Bloody confrontations between these militias led to prolonged civil wars. In this 1590 procession of the French Catholic League, armed monks joined soldiers and common citizens in a demonstration of force.

came to be called confessions° because their adherents believed in a particular confession of faith, or statement of religious doctrine.

Religious extremism was just one manifestation of an anxiety that pervaded European society at the time—a fear of hidden forces controlling human events. In an attempt to curb that anxiety, the European monarchs created confessional states. The combined effort of state and church sought to discipline common people, persecute deviants of all sorts, and combat enemies through a religiously driven foreign policy. During this age of confessional division, European countries polarized along confessional lines, and governments persecuted followers of minority religions, whom they saw as threats to public security. Anxious believers everywhere were consumed with pleasing an angry God, but when they tried to find God within themselves many Christians seemed only to find the Devil in others. The bloody history of confessional conflicts during the sixteenth and seventeenth centuries, in fact, eventually stimulated the formation of the modern ethical principles of religious toleration, separation of church and state, and human rights during the eighteenth.

By attempting to discipline the people of Europe and make them better Christians, educated and elite society directly confronted a thriving popular culture. In many respects, the culture they encountered was nearly as alien as the native cultures in the newly discovered America. Certainly, the peoples of early modern Europe considered themselves Christian, but what they meant by Christianity was quite at odds with that of the Protestant and Catholic reformers. In a confused, haphazard, and sometimes violent fashion, members of the elite attempted to blot out many elements of popular culture that they suspected might be remnants of pre-Christian beliefs and practices. One of the most curious consequences of the Reformations during the sixteenth and seventeenth centuries was a dramatic conflict between two cultures, that of the educated elite and that of the ordinary people. However, the disciplining of the people was primarily confined to western Europe. In eastern Europe religious diversity and popular culture thrived largely due to the relative weakness of the monarchs.

The religious controversies of the age of confessional division redefined the West. During the Middle Ages, the West came to be identified with the practice of Roman Catholic Christianity. The Reformation of the early sixteenth century broke up the unity of medieval Christian Europe by dividing westerners into Catholic and Protestant camps. During the late sixteenth and seventeenth centuries, governments reinforced religious divisions and attempted to unify their peoples around a common set of beliefs. By the end of the eighteenth century, these confessional religious identities changed in some places into more secular political ideologies, such as the belief in the superiority of a republic over a monarchy, but the assumption that all citizens of a state should believe in some common ideology remained. The period from about 1500 to 1750—the Early Modern period in European history—produced the lasting division of the West into national camps that were based on either religious confessions or ideological commitments. How did the encounter between the confessions and the state transform Europe into religiously driven camps?

■ **How did the expanding population and price revolution exacerbate religious and political tensions?**
■ **How did religious and political authorities attempt to discipline the people?**
■ **How did religious differences provoke violence and start wars?**
■ **How did the countries of eastern Europe during the late sixteenth century become enmeshed in the religious controversies that began in western Europe during the early part of the century?**

The Peoples of Early Modern Europe

■ **How did the expanding population and price revolution exacerbate religious and political tensions?**

During the tenth century if a Russian had wanted to see the sights of Paris—assuming he had even heard of Paris—he could have left Kiev and walked under the shade of trees all the way to France, so extensive were the forests and so sparse the human settlements of northern Europe. By the end of the thirteenth century, the nomadic Russian would have needed a hat to protect him on the shadeless journey. Instead of human settlements forming little islands in a sea of forests, the forests were by then islands in a sea of villages and farms, and from any church tower the sharp-eyed traveler could have seen other church towers, each marking a nearby village or town. At the end of the thirteenth century, the European continent had become completely settled by a dynamic, growing population, which had cleared the forests for farms.

During the fourteenth century all of that changed. A series of crises—periodic famines, the catastrophic Black Death, and a general economic collapse—left the villages and towns of Europe intact, but a third or more of the population was gone. In that period of desolation, many villages looked like abandoned movie sets, and the cities did not have enough people to fill in the empty spaces between the central market square and the city walls. Fields that had once been put to the plow to feed the hungry children of the thirteenth century were neglected and overrun with bristles and brambles. During the fifteenth century a general European depression and recurrent epidemics kept the population stagnant.

In the sixteenth century the population began to rebound, but the sudden swell brought dramatic and destabilizing consequences that contributed to pervasive anxiety. An important factor in the population growth was the transformation of European agriculture from subsistence to commercial farming, an uneven transformation that impoverished some villages while it enriched others. Moreover, the expanded population transformed the balance of power, as northern Europe recovered its population more successfully than southern Europe. As the population grew, young men and women flocked to the cities, creating enormous social strains and demands on local governments. Perhaps most disruptive was the price revolution, which brought inflation that ate away at the buying power of everyone from working families to kings and queens. The anxiety produced by these circumstances lasted into the seventeenth century.

The Population Recovery

During a period that historical demographers call the "long sixteenth century" (ca. 1480–1640), the population of Europe began to grow consistently again for the first time since the late thirteenth century. In 1340, on the brink of the Black Death, Europe had about 74 million inhabitants, or 17 percent of the world's total. By 1400 the population of all of Europe had dropped to 52 million (less than one-fifth of the population of the United States today), or 14 percent of the world's total. Over the course of the long sixteenth century, Europe's population grew from 60.9 million to 77.9 million, just barely surpassing the pre–Black Death level.

The table to the right shows some representative population figures for the larger European countries during the sixteenth century. Two stunning facts emerge from these data. The first is the much greater rate of growth in northern Europe compared to southern Europe. England grew by 83 percent, Poland grew by 76 percent, and even the tiny, war-torn Netherlands gained 58 percent. During the same period Italy grew by only 25 percent and Spain by 19. These trends signal a massive, permanent shift of demographic and economic power from the Mediterranean countries of Italy and Spain to northern, especially northwestern, Europe. The second fact to note from these data is the overwhelming size of France, which was home to about a quarter of Europe's population. Once France recovered from its long wars of religion, its demographic superiority overwhelmed competing countries and made it the dominant power in Europe, permanently eclipsing its chief rival, Spain. Because the Holy Roman Empire and especially its core regions in the German-speaking lands lacked political unity, it was unable to take advantage of its position as the second-largest state.

What explains the growth in the population and the economy? To a large extent, it was made possible by the

European Population, 1500–1600 (in millions)			
	1500	**1550**	**1600**
England	2.30	3.10	4.20
Germany	12.00	14.00	16.00
France	16.40	19.00	20.00
Netherlands	0.95	1.25	1.50
Belgium	1.25	1.65	1.30
Italy	10.50	11.40	13.10
Spain	6.80	7.50	8.10
Austria-Bohemia	3.50	3.60	4.30
Poland	2.50	3.00	3.40

Source: Jan de Vries, "Population," in *Handbook of European History 1400–1600: Late Middle Ages, Renaissance and Reformation,* Vol. 1: *Structures and Assertions,* eds. Thomas A. Brady, Jr., Heiko A. Oberman, and James D. Tracy (1994), Table 1, 13.

transformation from subsistence to commercial agriculture in certain regions of Europe. Subsistence farmers, called peasants, had worked the land year in and year out, raising grains for the coarse black bread that fed their families, supplemented only by beer, grain porridge, and occasionally vegetables. Meat was rare and expensive. Peasants consumed about 80 percent of everything they raised, and what little was left over went almost entirely to the landlord as feudal dues and to the church as tithing—the obligation to give to God one-tenth of everything earned or produced. Peasant families lived on the edge of existence. In a bad year some starved to death, usually the vulnerable children and old people. But during the sixteenth century, in areas with access to big cities, subsistence agriculture gave way to commercial crops, especially wheat, which was hauled to be sold in town markets. Profits from this market agriculture stimulated farmers to raise even greater surpluses in the agricultural regions around the great cities—London, Antwerp, Amsterdam, Paris, Milan, Venice, Barcelona, and scattered places in Germany. Commercial crops and the cash income they produced meant fewer starving children and a higher standard of living for those who were able to take advantage of the new opportunities. As commercial agriculture spread, the population grew because the rural population was better fed and more prosperous.

The Prosperous Villages

Success in commercializing agriculture could make an enormous difference in the lives of peasants. The village of Buia tells the story of many similarly prosperous hamlets.

Situated in Friuli, a region in the northeast corner of Italy, it served as part of the agricultural hinterland of the great metropolis of Venice. For centuries the peasants of hilly and pleasant Buia had lived in thatched hovels surviving at the subsistence level. But during the fourteenth and fifteenth centuries serfdom disappeared in the region and the peasants' legal status changed. Now free to sell their labor to the highest bidder, peasant families contracted with a landlord to lease a plot of land for a certain number of years in exchange for annual rent payments in kind. A typical yearly rent might include two bushels of wheat, two of oats, one of beans, one of millet, three barrels of wine, two chickens, one ham, three guinea hens, thirty eggs, two cartloads of firewood, and two days' work mowing hay. In contrast to the servitude of serfdom, which tied peasants to the land, agricultural leases created a measure of economic freedom. They allowed landlords to find labor at a time when laborers were scarce, and they enabled peasants to negotiate for a better reward for their labor.

Unlike some neighboring villages that were still under the heel of their lords, Buia had incorporated as a town, a status that provided it with more autonomy from its lords, the Savorgnan family. Moreover, Buia had diversified its economy, branching out into cattle raising and marketing its fierce pear brandy and smooth white wine. But Buia's crucial economic advantage derived from its access to capital. The Savorgnan lords liberally lent money to their tenants in Buia, which enabled them to survive hard times and to invest in commercial profit-making enterprises. Unlike other families, the Savorgnans were willing to invest in their tenants, because they had established political and economic ties with the nearby commercial metropolis of Venice, whose bankers were more than happy to bankroll the Savorgnan family. From the commercial banks of Venice, money flowed through the hands of the Savorgnan to the peasants of the little village of Buia, who in turn produced crops that could be sold in the markets of Venice, a flow of money and goods that enriched, although unequally, everyone involved—the peasants, their Savorgnan landlords, and the Venetian bankers. With the increased income from commercial agriculture, Buia even began to look more affluent during the sixteenth century, boasting a substantial church, a tavern, and a simple one-room town hall where citizens could gather to debate their affairs.

The success of commercial agriculture during the sixteenth century depended on a free and mobile labor supply, access to capital for investment, and proximity to the markets of the big cities. What happened in Buia happened in many places throughout Europe, but overall the amount of

The Rise of Commercial Agriculture
During the sixteenth century commercial agriculture began to produce significant surpluses for the expanding population of the cities. This scene depicts a windmill for grinding grain and a train of wagons hauling produce from the country to be marketed in a city.

land available could not provide enough work for the growing farm population. As a result, the growth of the rural population created a new class of landless, impoverished men and women, who were forced to take to the road to find their fortunes. These vagabonds, as they were called, exemplified the social problems that emerged from the uneven distribution of wealth created by the new commerce.

The Regulated Cities

By the 1480s cities began to grow, largely through migration from the more prosperous countryside, but the growth was uneven with the most dramatic growth occurring in the cities of the North, especially London, Antwerp, and Amsterdam (see Map 14.1). The surpluses of the countryside, both human and agricultural, flowed into the cities during the sixteenth century. Compared to even the prosperous rural villages, such as Buia, the cities must have seemed incomparably rich. Half-starved vagabonds from the countryside would have marveled at shops piled high with food (white bread, fancy pies, fruit, casks of wine, roasting meats); they would have wistfully passed taverns full of drunken, laughing citizens; and they would have begged for alms in front of magnificent, marble-faced churches.

Every aspect of the cities exhibited dramatic contrasts between the rich and poor, who lived on the same streets and often in different parts of the same houses. Around 1580 Christian missionaries brought a Native American chief to the French city of Rouen. Through an interpreter he was asked what impressed him the most about European cities, so unlike the villages of North America. He replied that he was astonished that the rag-clad, emaciated men and women who crowded the streets did not grab the plump, well-dressed rich people by the throat.

The wretched human surplus from the farms continuously replenished and swelled the populations of the cities, which were frequently depleted by high urban death rates. As wealthy as the cities were, they were unhealthy places: human waste overflowed from open latrines because there were no sewage systems; garbage, manure, dead animals, and roaming pigs and dogs made the streets putrid and dangerous; and water came from polluted rivers or sat stale in cisterns for months. Under such conditions, entire neighborhoods could be wiped out in epidemics. Both ends of the life span were vulnerable: one in three babies died in the first year of life; old people did not last long in cold, drafty houses. When the epidemics appeared, which they continued to do about every twenty years until 1721, the rich escaped to their country retreats while the poor died in the streets or in houses locked up and under quarantine.

Despite the danger from disease in the cities, rural immigrants were less likely to starve than those who remained in small villages where they lacked land. Every city maintained storehouses of grain and regulated the price of bread and the size of a loaf so that the poor could be fed. The impulse to feed the poor was less the result of humanitarian motives than a recognition that nothing was more dangerous than a hungry mob. Given the contrasts in wealth among its inhabitants, cities guarded carefully against revolts and crime. Even for petty crime, punishment was

Map 14.1 Population Distribution in the Sixteenth Century
The population of Europe concentrated around the cities of northern Italy, the Danube and Rhine River valleys, Flanders and northern France, and southeastern England. During the late sixteenth century, northwestern Europe began to grow significantly more rapidly than southern Europe.

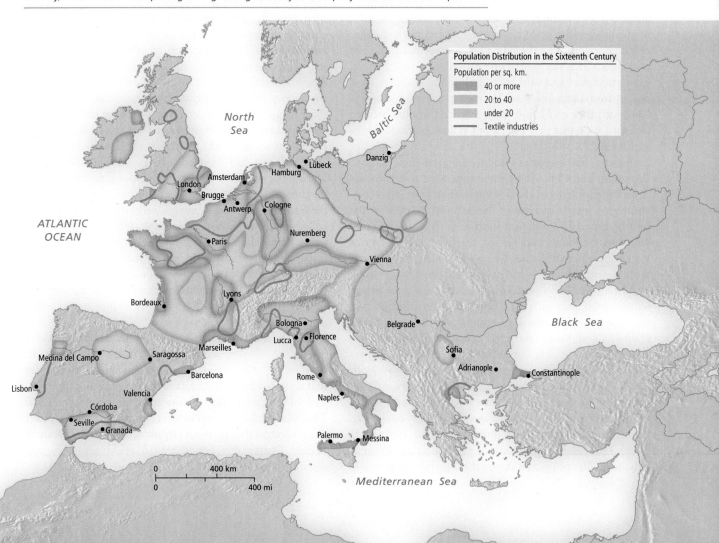

swift, sure, and gruesome. The beggar who stole a loaf of bread from a baker's cart would have his hand amputated on a chopping block in the market square. A shabbily dressed girl who grabbed a lady's glittering trinket would have her nose cut off so that she could never attract a man. A burglar would be tortured, drawn, and quartered, and have his severed head impaled on an iron spike at the town gate as a warning to others.

To deal with the consequences of commerce and massive immigration, European cities attempted to regulate the lives of their inhabitants. Ringing bells measured each working day, and during the sixteenth century many cities erected a large mechanical clock in a prominent place so that busy citizens could keep to their schedules. Municipal officers inspected the weights and measures in the city market, regulated the distribution of produce to guarantee an abundant food supply, and repaired the streets and city walls. However talented or enterprising, new arrivals to the city had very limited opportunities. They could hardly start up their own business because all production was strictly controlled by the guilds, which were associations of merchants or artisans organized to protect their interests. Guilds rigidly regulated their membership; they required an apprenticeship of many years, prohibited technological innovations, guaranteed certain standards of workmanship, and did not allow branching out into new lines. A member of the goldsmiths' guild could not make mirrors; a baker could not sell fruit on the side; a house carpenter could not lay bricks. Given the limited opportunities for new arrivals, immigrant men and women begged on the streets or took charity from the public dole. The men picked up any heavy-labor jobs they could find. Both men and women became servants, a job that paid poorly but at least guaranteed regular meals.

Among the important social achievements of both Protestant and Catholic Reformations were efforts to address the problems of the destitute urban poor, who constituted at least a quarter of the population, even in the best of times. In Catholic countries such as Italy, Spain, southern Germany, and France, there was an enormous expansion of credit banks, which were financed by charitable contributions in order to provide small loans to the poor. Catholic cities established convents for poor young women who were at risk of falling into prostitution and for other women who had retired from the sex trade. Catholic and Protestant cities established orphanages, hospitals for the sick, hospices for the dying, and apartments lent out for a modest rent to poor widows. Both Catholic and Protestant cities attempted to distinguish between the "honest" poor—those who were disabled and truly deserving—and the "dishonest" poor who were thought to be malingerers. Protestant cities established poorhouses, which segregated the poor, subjected them to prisonlike discipline, and forced the able-bodied to work.

The more comfortable classes of the cities enjoyed large palaces and luxurious lifestyles. They hired extensive staffs of servants, feasted on meat and fine wines, and purchased exotic imports such as silk cloth, spices from the East, and, in the Mediterranean cities, slaves from eastern Europe, the Middle East, or Africa. The merchants whose fortunes came from cloth manufacturing, banking, and regional or international trade maintained their status by marrying within their own class, providing municipal offices to those whose fortunes had fallen, and educating their children in the newly fashionable humanist schools. The wealthy of the cities were the bastions of social stability. They possessed the financial resources and economic skills to protect themselves from the worst consequences of economic instability, especially the corrosive wave of price inflation that struck the West after about 1540.

The Price Revolution

Price inflation became so pervasive during the last half of the sixteenth century that it contributed to the widespread fear that events were being controlled by hidden forces. The effects of inflation are illustrated by the experience of the students at Winchester College in England. These young men were the privileged sons of English aristocrats and country gentlemen, destined for leisured wealth and public responsibility. The curriculum of Winchester emphasized the unchanging values of aristocratic privilege and Christian rectitude, but the dusty account books, kept in meticulous detail by generations of college stewards, reveal that change was very much a fact of college life during the sixteenth century. For example, in 1500 a piece of cloth large enough to make a student's uniform cost forty shillings. By 1580 the cost had doubled, and by 1630 it had tripled. During the sixteenth century the cost of a dozen sheets of parchment doubled, the cost of a dozen candles quadrupled, and the cost of a twelve-gallon barrel of wine (yes, the college served wine to its teenaged students) rose from eight to sixty-four shillings. English masons' experience of price inflation during this period was far more painful. Over the course of the century their wages doubled, but the price of bread increased four- or fivefold, and because the survival of their families depended on the cost of bread, price inflation seriously threatened their lives.

The finances of English college students and masons reveal the phenomenon that historians call the Price Revolution°. After a long period of falling or stable prices that stretched back to the fourteenth century, Europe experienced sustained price increases, beginning around 1540. The inflation lasted a century, forcing major economic and social changes that permanently altered the face of Western society. During this period overall prices across Europe multiplied five- or sixfold.

What caused the inflation? The basic principle is simple. The price paid for goods and services is fundamentally the result of the relationship between *supply* and *demand*. If the number of children who need to be fed grows faster than the supply of grain, the price of bread goes up. This happens simply because mothers who can afford it will be willing to pay a higher price to save their children from hunger. If good harvests allow the supply of grain to increase at a greater rate than the demand for bread, then prices go down. The equation gets somewhat more complicated when taking into account two other factors that can influence price. One factor is the *amount of money in circulation*. If the amount of gold or silver available to make coins increases, there is more money in circulation. When more money is circulating, people have more money to buy more things, which creates the same effect as an increase in demand—prices go up. The other factor is called the *velocity of money in circulation,* which refers to the number of times money changes hands to buy things. When people buy commodities with greater frequency, it has the same effect as increasing the amount of money in circulation or of increasing demand—again, prices go up.

The precise combination of these factors in causing the great Price Revolution of the sixteenth century has long been a matter of considerable debate. Most historians would now agree that the primary cause of inflation was population growth, which increased demand for all kinds of basic commodities, such as bread and woolen cloth for clothing. As Europe's population finally began to recover, it meant that more people needed and desired to buy more things. This explanation is most obvious for commodities that people need to survive, such as grain to make bread. These commodities have what economists call *inelastic demand,* that is, consumers do not have a great deal of discretion in purchasing them. Everybody has to eat. The commodities that people could survive without if the price is too high are said to have *elastic demand,* such as dancing shoes and lace collars. In England between 1540 and 1640 overall prices rose by 490 percent. More telling, however, is that the price of grain (inelastic demand) rose by a stunning 670 percent, whereas the price of luxury goods (elastic demand) rose much less, by 204 percent. Thus, inflation hurt the poor, who needed to feed their children, more than the rich, whose desires were more elastic.

Monetary factors also contributed to inflation. The Portuguese brought in significant amounts of gold from Africa, and newly opened mines in central Europe increased the amount of silver by fivefold as early as the 1520s. The discovery in 1545 of the fabulous silver mine of Potosí (in present-day Bolivia) brought to Europe a flood of silver, which Spain used to finance its costly wars. As inflation began to eat away at royal incomes, financially strapped monarchs all across western Europe debased their money because they believed, mistakenly, that producing more coins

containing less silver would buy more. In fact, the minting of more coins meant each coin was worth less and would buy less. In England, for example, debasement was the major source of inflation during the 1540s and 1550s.

During the sixteenth century, no one understood these causes, however. People only experienced the effects of inflation, and then only gradually. The real wages of workers declined, causing widespread suffering and discontent. Incomes eroded for those dependent on fixed incomes— clergymen, pensioners, government clerks, and landlords who rented out land on long leases. Landlords who were willing to be ruthless and enterprising survived and even prospered. Those who were more paternalistic or conservative in managing their estates often lost their land to creditors.

The Price Revolution severely weakened governments. Most monarchs derived their incomes from their own private lands and from taxes on property. As inflation took hold, property taxes proved dangerously inadequate to cover royal expenses. Even frugal monarchs such as England's Elizabeth I were forced to take extraordinary measures, in her case to sell off royal lands. Spendthrift monarchs faced disaster. Spain was involved in the costly enterprise of nearly continuous war during the sixteenth century. To pay for the wars, Charles V resorted to a form of deficit financing in which he borrowed money by issuing *juros,* which provided lenders an annuity yielding between 3 and 7 percent on the amount of the principal. By the 1550s, however, the annuity payments of the *juros* consumed half of the royal revenues. Charles's son, Philip II, inherited such an alarming situation that in 1557, the year after he assumed the throne, he was forced to declare bankruptcy. Philip continued to fight expensive wars and borrow wildly, and thus failed to get his financial house in order. He declared bankruptcy again in 1575 and 1596. Philip squandered Spain's wealth, impoverishing his own subjects through burdensome taxes and contributing to inflation by borrowing at high rates of interest and debasing the coinage. Although the greatest power of the sixteenth century, Spain sowed the seeds of its own decline by fighting on borrowed money.

Probably the most serious consequence of the Price Revolution was that the hidden force of inflation caused widespread human suffering. During the late sixteenth and early seventeenth centuries, people felt their lives threatened, but they did not know the source and so they imagined all kinds of secret powers at work, especially supernatural ones. The suspicion of religious differences created by the Reformation provided handy, if utterly false, explanations for what had gone wrong. Catholics suspected Protestants, Protestants suspected Catholics, both suspected Jews, and they all worried about witches. Authorities sought to relieve this widespread anxiety by looking in all the wrong

DOCUMENT

Michel de Montaigne, *Essays* (1575)

places, disciplining the populace, hunting for witches, and battling against enemies from the opposite side of the confessional divide.

Disciplining the People

■ How did religious and political authorities attempt to discipline the people?

The first generation of the Protestant and Catholic Reformations had been devoted to doctrinal disputes and to either rejecting or defending papal authority. Subsequent generations of reformers in the last half of the sixteenth and the early seventeenth centuries faced the formidable task of building the institutions that would firmly establish a Protestant or Catholic religious culture. Leaders of all religious confessions attempted to revitalize the Christian community by disciplining nonconformists and enforcing moral rigor. Members of the community came to identify responsible citizenship with conformity to a specific Christian confession.

Whether Lutheran, Calvinist, Catholic, or Anglican, godly reformers sought to bring order to society, which meant they often felt obliged to attack popular culture. They reformed or abolished wild festivals, imprisoned town drunks, decreased the number of holidays, and tried to regulate sexual behavior. Many activities that had once been accepted as normal came to be considered deviant or criminal. The process of better ordering society required that the common people accept a certain measure of discipline. Discipline required cooperation between church and secular authorities, but it was not entirely imposed from above. Many people wholeheartedly cooperated with moral correction and even encouraged reformers to go further. Others passively, actively, or resentfully resisted it.

Establishing Confessional Identities

Between 1560 and 1650 religious confessions reshaped European culture, and loyalty to a single confession governed the relationships between states. A confession consisted of the adherents to a particular statement of religious doctrine—the Confession of Augsburg for Lutherans, the Helvetic Confessions for Calvinists, the Thirty-Nine Articles for Anglicans, and the decrees of the Council of Trent for Catholics. Based on these confessions of faith, the clergy disciplined the laity, exiled nonconformists, and promoted distinct religious institutions, beliefs, and culture.

The process of establishing confessional identities did not happen overnight; it lasted for centuries and had far-reaching consequences. During the second half of the sixteenth century, Lutherans turned from the struggle to survive within the hostile Holy Roman Empire to establishing a confessional identity in the parts of the empire where Lutheranism was the chosen religion of the local prince. They had to recruit Lutheran clergy and provide each clergyman with a university education, which was made possible by scholarship endowments from the Lutheran princes of the empire. Once established, the Lutheran clergy became a branch of the civil bureaucracy, received a government stipend, and enforced the will of the prince. Calvinist states followed a similar process, but where they were in a minority, as in France, Calvinists had to go it alone, and the state often discriminated against them. In those places confessional identities were established in opposition to the state and the dominant confession.

Catholics responded with their own aggressive plan of training new clergymen, educating the laity, and reinforcing the bond between church and state. Just as with the Lutheran princes, Catholic princes in the Holy Roman Empire associated conformity to Catholicism with loyalty to themselves, making religion a pillar of the state. Everywhere in western Europe (except for Ireland, a few places in the Holy Roman Empire, and for a time France) the only openly practiced religion was the religion of the state.

The authorities primarily formed confessional identities among the laity by promoting distinctive ritual systems. These ritual systems embodied ways of acting and even of gesturing that transformed the way people moved their bodies so that a Catholic and a Protestant might be instantly recognized by certain telltale signs of posture, speech, and comportment.

The Catholic and Protestant ritual systems differed primarily in their attitude toward the sacred. Whereas Catholic ritual behavior depended on a repertoire of gestures that indicated reverence in the presence of the sacred, Protestant ritual depended on a demonstration of sociability that identified people as members of a certain congregation or church. For example, until the late sixteenth century Europeans greeted one another either by raising a hand, palm outward, which meant "welcome," or with a bow by which someone of lower status recognized the superiority of another. Some radical Protestants, however, insisted that all gestures of deference, such as bows and curtsies, were an affront to God and introduced a new form of greeting, the handshake. Shaking hands was completely egalitarian, and one could identify English Quakers or Scottish Calvinists, for example, simply by the fact that they shook hands with one another.

A particularly revealing ritual difference can be seen in the contrasting ways that Scottish Calvinists and Spanish Catholics reintegrated repentant sinners into the Church. In Calvinism disciplinary authority rested with the presbytery, a board of pastors and elders elected by the community. If a Scottish Calvinist blasphemed God, the presbytery could discipline him, shun him, or banish him from the community. If he wished to be reinstated and the presbytery agreed, he would be obliged to come before the entire congregation to confess sincerely his wrongs and beg forgiveness. The congregation would make a collective judgment about his acceptability for renewed membership. The pain inflicted on the Calvinist sinner was the social pain of having his transgression openly discussed and evaluated by his friends and neighbors.

If a Spanish Catholic blasphemed, he would be subjected to an extended ritual of penance, the auto-da-fé°, which meant a theater of faith. The auto-da-fé was designed to promote fear and to cause physical pain because, according to Catholic doctrine, bodily suffering in this world was necessary in order to free the soul from worse suffering in the next. An *auto* was a public performance in which dozens or sometimes hundreds of sinners and criminals were paraded through the streets in a theatrical demonstration of the authority of the Church and the power of penance. The *auto* culminated in a mass confirmation of faith in which the repentant sinners utterly subjected themselves to the authority of the clergy, while those who refused to repent or were relapsed heretics were strangled and their corpses burned.

Whereas the punishment of the Calvinist community was primarily a rite of social humiliation, the auto-da-fé involved physical torture as well as social degradation. The nub of the difference was that Calvinists had to demonstrate the sincerity of their social conformity; Catholics had to go through a performance that emphasized the authority of the clergy and that purified sin with physical pain.

Regulating the Family

One matter on which Calvinists, Lutherans, and Catholics agreed was that the foundation of society should be the authority fathers had over their families. This principle, known as patriarchy, was very traditional. The confessions that emerged from the Reformation further strengthened patriarchy because it so usefully served the needs of church and state to establish social order and encourage morality. According to an anonymous treatise published in 1586 in Calvinist Nassau, the three pillars of Christian society were the church, the state, and the household. This proposition made the father's authority parallel to the authority of clergy and king—a position that all the confessions would have accepted. Enforcing patriarchy led to regulating sexuality and the behavior of children.

Marriage and Sexuality: The Self-Restrained Couple

However, regional differences in the structure of the family itself meant that despite the near universal acceptance of the theory of patriarchy, the reality of the father's authority varied a great deal. Since the early Middle Ages in northwestern Europe—in Britain, Scandinavia, the Netherlands, northern France, and western Germany—couples tended to

wait to marry until their mid- or late twenties, well beyond the age of sexual maturity. When these couples married, they established their own household separate from either of their parents. Husbands were usually only two or three years older than their wives, and that proximity of age tended to make those relationships more cooperative and less authoritarian than the theory of patriarchy might suggest. In northwestern European the couple had to be economically independent before they married, which meant both had to accumulate savings or the husband needed to inherit from his deceased father before he could marry. By contrast, in southern Europe, men in their late twenties or thirties married teenaged women over whom they exercised authority by virtue of their age. In the South patriarchy meant husbands ruled over wives. In eastern Europe, both spouses married in their teens and resided in one of the parental households for many years, which placed both spouses for extended periods under the authority of the husband's parents.

The marriage pattern in northwestern Europe required prolonged sexual restraint by young men and women until they were economically self-sufficient. In addition to individual self-control, sexual restraint required social control by church and secular authorities, who seem to have been more vigilant about regulating sexual behavior than in southern and eastern Europe. Their efforts seem to have been generally successful. For example, in sixteenth-century Geneva, where the elders were especially wary about sexual sins, the rates of illegitimate births were extremely low. The elders were particularly vigilant about disciplining women and keeping them subservient, often making and enforcing highly minute regulations. In 1584 Calvinist elders in another Swiss town excommunicated Charlotte Arbaleste and her entire household because she wore her hair in curls, which the elders thought were too alluring.

Northwestern European families also tended to be smaller. Married couples in northwestern Europe began to space their children through birth control and family planning. These self-restrained couples practiced withdrawal, the rhythm method, or abstinence. When mothers no longer relied on wet nurses and nursed their own infants, often for long periods, they also reduced their chances of becoming pregnant. Thus, limiting family size became the social norm in northwestern Europe, especially among the educated and urban middle classes. Protestant families tended to have fewer children than Catholic families, but Catholics in this region also practiced some form of birth control, even though Church law prohibited all forms except abstinence.

For prospective couples, parental approval remained more important than romantic love. In fact, a romantic attachment between a husband and wife was frowned upon as unseemly and even dangerous. More highly prized in a marriage partner were trust, dependability, and the willingness to work. Many married couples certainly exhibited

The *Auto-da-Fé:* The Power of Penance

Performed in Spain and Portugal from the sixteenth to eighteenth centuries, the auto-da-fé merged the judicial processes of the state with the sacramental rituals of the Catholic Church. An *auto* took place at the end of a judicial investigation conducted by the inquisitors of the Church after the defendants had been found guilty of a sin or crime. The term *auto-da-fé* means "theater of faith," and the goal was to persuade or force a person who had been judged guilty to repent and confess. Organized through the cooperation of ecclesiastical and secular authorities, autos-da-fé brought together an assortment of sinners, criminals, and heretics for a vast public rite that dramatized the essential elements of the sacrament of penance: contrition, by which the sinner recognized and felt sorry for the sin; confession, which required the sinner to admit the sin to a priest; and satisfaction or punishment, by which the priest absolved the sinner and enacted some kind of penalty. The auto-da-fé transformed penance, especially confession and satisfaction, into a spectacular affirmation of the faith and a manifestation of divine justice.

The *auto* symbolically anticipated the Last Judgment, and it provoked deep anxiety among those who witnessed it about how God would judge them. By suffering bodily pain in this life the soul might be relieved from worse punishments in the next. The sinners, convicts, and heretics, now considered penitents, were forced to march in a procession that went through the streets of the city from the cathedral to the town hall or place of punishment. These processions would typically include some thirty or forty penitents, but in moments of crisis they could be

far larger. In Toledo in 1486 there were three *autos*—one parading 750 penitents and two displaying some 900 each.

A 1655 *auto* in Córdoba illustrates the symbolic character of the rites. Soldiers bearing torches that would light the pyre for those to be burnt led the procession. Following them came three bigamists who wore on their heads conical miters or hats painted with representations of their sin, four witches whose miters depicted devils, and three criminals with harnesses around their necks to demonstrate their status as captives. The sinners carried unlit candles to represent their lack of faith. Criminals who had escaped arrest were represented in the procession by effigies made in their likeness, and those who had died before punishment were carried in their coffins. The marching sinners appeared before their neighbors and fellow citizens stripped of the normal indicators of status, dressed only in the emblems of their sins. Among them walked a few who wore the infamous *sanbenitos,* a kind of tunic or vest with a yellow strip down the back, and a conical hat painted with flames. These were the *relajados,* the unrepentant or relapsed sinners who were going to be "relaxed" (released into the hands of the secular authorities) at the culminating moment of the *auto* when they were strangled and burned.

The procession ended in the town square at a platform from which penances were performed as on the stage of a theater. Forced to their knees, the penitents were asked to confess and to plead for readmission into the bosom of the church. For those who did confess, a sentence was an-

nounced that would rescue them from the pains of Purgatory and the flames of the *auto*. The sentence required them to join a penitential procession for a certain number of Fridays, perform self-flagellation in public, or wear a badge of shame for a prescribed period of time. Those who failed to confess faced a more immediate sentence.

The most horrendous scenes of suffering awaited those who refused to confess or who had relapsed into sin or heresy, which meant their confession was not considered sincere. If holdouts confessed prior to the reading of the sentence, then the *auto* was a success, a triumph of the Christian faith over its enemies, and everything that could possibly elicit confessions was attempted, including haranguing, humiliating, and torturing the accused until their stubborn will broke. If the accused finally confessed after the sentence was read, then they would be strangled before burning, but if they held out to the very end, they would be burned alive. From the ecclesiastics' point of view, the refusal to confess was a disaster for the entire Church because the flames of the pyre opened a window into Hell. They would certainly prefer to see the Church's authority acknowledged through confession than to see the power of Satan manifest in such a public fashion.

It is reported that crowds witnessed the violence of the autos-da-fé with silent attention in a mood of deep dread, not so much of the inquisitors, it seems, as for the inevitability of the final day of divine judgment that would arrive for them all. The core assumption of the auto-da-fé was that bodily pain could save a soul from damnation. As one contemporary

Relapsed heretics were burned on a pyre.

The conical hats were painted with the representation of the sinner's sin.

Sinners wearing the sanbenitos.

A procession conducted the sinners to the town square.

Auto-da-fé in Lisbon

witness put it, the inquisitors removed "through external ritual [the sinners'] internal crimes." It was assumed that the public ritual framework for the sacrament of penance would have a salutary effect on those who witnessed the *auto* by encouraging them to repent before they too faced divine judgment.

Questions of Justice

1. How did the auto-da-fé contribute to the formation of an individual and collective sense of being a Catholic?
2. In the auto-da-fé, inflicting physical pain was more than punishment. How was pain understood to have been socially and religiously useful?

Taking It Further

Flynn, Maureen. "Mimesis of the Last Judgment: The Spanish *Auto da fe*," *Sixteenth Century Journal* 22 (1991): 281–97. The best analysis of the religious significance of the auto-da-fé.

Flynn, Maureen. "The Spectacle of Suffering in Spanish Streets," in Barbara A. Hanawalt and Kathryn L. Reyerson, eds., *City and Spectacle in Medieval Europe.* 1994. In this fascinating article Flynn analyzes the spiritual value of physical pain.

signs of affection—addressing one another lovingly in letters, nursing a sick mate, mourning a dead one—but overly sentimental attachments were discouraged as contrary to the patriarchal authority that ideally characterized family life. Most husbands and wives seem to have treated one another with a certain coolness and emotional detachment.

The moral status of marriage also demonstrated regional variations during the early modern period. Protestants no longer considered husbands and wives morally inferior to celibate monks and nuns, and the wives of preachers in Protestant communities certainly had a respected social role never granted to the concubines of priests. But the favorable Protestant attitude toward marriage did not necessarily translate into a positive attitude toward women. In Germany the numerous books of advice, called the Father of the House literature, encouraged families to subordinate the individual interests of servants, children, and the mother to the dictates of the father, who was encouraged to be just but who must be obeyed. Even if a wife was brutally treated by her husband, she could neither find help from authorities nor expect a divorce.

Children: Naturally Evil?

Although families had always cherished their children, during the Reformation both Protestant and Catholic preachers placed even greater emphasis on the welfare, education, and moral upbringing of children. Protestants contributed to this process by emphasizing the family's responsibility for their children's moral guidance and religious education. One of the obligations of Protestant fathers was to read and teach the Bible in the home. This directive may have been more a theoretical ideal than a practical reality, but the rise in literacy among both boys and girls in Protestant countries attests to the increased importance of education.

Discipline also played a large role in the sixteenth-century family. Parents had always demonstrated love toward their children by indulging them with sweets and toys and protecting them from danger. But during the sixteenth century some authors of advice books and many preachers began to emphasize that parental love must be tempered by strict discipline. In effect, the clergy attempted to impose their own authoritarian impulses on the emotional lives of the family. The Protestant emphasis on the majesty of God and a belief in original sin translated into a negative view of human nature. Calvinist theologians who held such a view placed a special emphasis on family discipline. The *Disquisition on the Spiritual Condition of Infants* (1618) pointed out that from a theological point of view, babies were naturally evil. The godly responsibility of the father was to break the will of his evil offspring, taming them so that they could be turned away

The Domestic Ideal
During the late sixteenth and seventeenth centuries, idealized depictions of harmonious family life became very popular, especially in the Netherlands. In this painting by Pieter De Hooch a young child is learning to walk.

from sin toward virtue. The very title of a 1591 Calvinist treatise revealed the strength of the evil-child argument: *On Disciplining Children: How the Disobedient, Evil, and Corrupted Youth of These Anxious Last Days Can Be Bettered*. The treatise also advised that the mother's role should be limited to her biological function of giving birth. It directed fathers to be vigilant so that their wives did not corrupt the children, because women "love to accept strange, false beliefs, and go about with benedictions and witches' handiwork. When they are not firm in faith and the Devil comes to tempt them . . . they follow him and go about with supernatural fantasies."[1]

In order to break the will of their infants, mothers were encouraged to wean them early and turn them over for a strict upbringing by their fathers. The ideal father was to cultivate both love and fear in his children by remaining unemotional and firm. He was to be vigilant to prevent masturbation, to discourage frivolity, and to toughen little children by not allowing them to eat too much, sleep too long, or stay too comfortably warm. Although discouraged from being unnecessarily brutal, the godly father was never to spare the rod on either his children or his wife.

It is clear that disciplining children was an important theoretical guideline in sixteenth- and seventeenth-century Europe. It is less clear whether this was as true in practice as in theory. Historians disagree on the issue. It is likely that then, as now, there were many different ways of raising children, and each family exhibited its own emotional chemistry. And it is also likely that sixteenth-century parents did considered firm discipline loving.

Suppressing Popular Culture

The family was not the only institution that sixteenth-century educated reformers sought to discipline. Their efforts also targeted many manifestations of traditional popular culture. The reformers or puritans, as they came to be called in England, wanted to purify both the church and society, to transform them into a "godly community" by encouraging and even enforcing moral behavior, particularly in rowdy youths and members of the lower classes. The suppression of popular culture had two aspects. One was a policing effort, aimed at ridding society of presumably unChristian practices. The other was a missionary enterprise, an attempt to bring the Protestant and Catholic Reformations to the people through instruction and popular preaching.

Overall the reformers sought to encourage an ethic of moderation, which valued thrift, modesty, chastity, and above all self-control. This ethic was neither Protestant nor Catholic but was promoted by clerics of all religious confessions. The traditional popular culture they so distrusted stressed other values such as spontaneity and emotional freedom, values that were hardly subject to control and could have dangerous, often violent consequences.

Once the reformers had cleaned up the churches by eliminating idolatry, unnecessary holidays, and superfluous rituals, they turned to the secular world, and they found much to criticize. The reformers saw impiety in comedians, dancing, loud music, rough sports, dice and card games, public drinking, dressing up in costumes, puppets, and above all actors. The Catholic Bishop of Verona condemned preachers who told stories that made the congregations laugh. To the reformers, these things were despicable because they seemed to be vestiges of pre-Christian practices and because they led people into sin.

The festival of Carnival° came under particularly virulent attack. The most popular annual festival, Carnival took place for several days or even weeks before the beginning of Lent and included all kinds of fun and games—silly pantomimes, bear baiting, bullfights, masquerades, dances, lots of eating and drinking, and illicit sex. The *Discourse Against Carnival* (1607) complained about the temptations to sin and the money wasted in Carnival play. Catholics attempted to reform Carnival by eliminating the most offensive forms of behavior, especially those that led to violence or vice. Other popular festivals and entertainments suffered a similar fate of scornful criticism, regulation, or even abolition.

Pieter Brueghel the Elder's painting *The Battle Between Carnival and Lent* (1559) illustrates the role of festivals in the popular culture. In the painting, a fat man riding on a wine barrel engages in a mock joust with an emaciated, stooped figure of uncertain gender who rides a wheeled cart pulled by a monk and nun. The two figures in the painting symbolize the two festival seasons. The fat man represents Carnival, a time of joyous, gluttonous, drunken feasting; the lean one represents Lent, a period of sexual abstinence and fasting that precedes Easter. During the

The Battle Between Carnival and Lent

In this allegory, called *The Battle Between Carnival and Lent* (1559) by Pieter Brueghel the Elder, the festive season of Carnival is represented on the left by a fat man riding a wine barrel wielding as a lance a roasted pig on a spit. He is engaged in a mock joust with an emaciated figure holding a paddle of fish representing Lent, the season for fasting and giving up meat. On the Carnival side are cards, dice, and people dressed in the funny costumes of Carnival. On the Lent side are pretzels and flatbread, the unleavened breads of the fasting season.

The Introduction of the Table Fork: The New Sign of Western Civilization

Sometime in the sixteenth century, western Europeans encountered a new tool that would initiate a profound and lasting transformation in Western society: the table fork. Before people used the table fork and practiced the refined dining manners that accompanied its use, they dined in a way that, to our modern sensibilities, would seem disgusting. Meat was a luxury available only to people in the upper classes, who indulged themselves by devouring it in enormous quantities. Whole rabbits, lambs, and pigs roasted on a spit would be placed before diners. A quarter of veal or venison or even an entire roast beef, complete with its head, might be heaved onto the table. Diners would use knives to cut off a piece of meat that they would then eat with their hands, allowing the juices to drip down their arms. The long sleeves of their shirts were used to wipe meat juices, sweat, and spittle from their mouths and faces. These banquets celebrated the direct physical contact between the body of the dead animal and the bodies of the diners themselves who touched, handled, chewed, and swallowed it.

During the sixteenth century, reformers who were trying to abolish the cruder aspects of popular culture also promoted new table manners that treated the eating of meat as discomforting, if not shameful. Well-mannered people increasingly felt the need to distance themselves from the fact that they were consuming a dead animal. To accomplish this, new implements made certain that diners did not come into direct physical contact with their food

before they placed it in their mouths. In addition to napkins—which came into widespread use to replace shirt sleeves for wiping the mouth—table forks appeared on upper-class tables. It became impolite to transfer food directly from the table or common serving plate to the mouth. Food first had to go onto each individual's plate and then be cut into small portions and raised to the mouth. A French treatise of 1672 warns that "meat must never be touched . . . by hand, not even while eating."[2] This prohibition had nothing to do with cleanliness, because bacteria were not discovered until the end of the nineteenth century. The fear was not of disease, but of direct contact with the bodies of dead animals. The fear, it seems, derived from a growing sense of revulsion with the more physical aspects of human nature, including sexuality, which was regulated by church authorities, and the killing of animals in order to survive, which was regulated by table manners. The table fork made it possible to eat meat without ever touching it. Forks enabled diners to avoid their growing sense of discomfort with the textures and juices of meats that perhaps reminded them of the flesh and blood of the dead animal.

The use of the table fork, therefore, has more to do with civility than hygiene, which can be demonstrated by the fact that certain foods, such as bread, cherries, or chocolates, are always eaten with the hands, even by the Queen of England. In determining when to use a fork it is not cleanliness that matters but the kind of food consumed. Moreover, the civility that resulted from use of the table fork promoted individualism, because everyone—regardless of their social origins—could learn how to use it. A clerk or governess could disguise a humble background simply by learning how to eat properly. In the end, the transformations that occurred in Western society because of its encounter with the table fork—the blurring of class distinctions and creation of a universal code of manners—were so gradual and subtle that few of us who use a table fork daily are even aware of its profound significance.

For Discussion

How do manners, both good and bad, communicate messages to other people? Does it matter to have good manners?

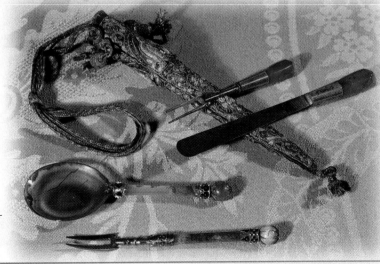

The Introduction of the Table Fork
During the late sixteenth century the refinement of manners among the upper classes focused on dining. No innovation was more revolutionary than the spread of the use of the table fork. Pictured here are the travel cutlery, including two table forks, of Queen Elizabeth I.

sixteenth century contemporaries understood the contrast between Carnival, which was devoted to bodily pleasure, and Lent, during which the bodily desires were ignored to enable repentance, as the battle between two divergent ideas of society. The battle was not just a symbol but a reality that took place through the attempts to suppress popular culture.

What Catholics reformed, Protestants abolished. Martin Luther had been relatively tolerant of popular culture, but later reformers were not. The most famous German Carnival, the *Schembartlauf* of Nuremberg, was abolished; in England the great medieval pageants of York, Coventry, Chester, Norwich, and Worcester disappeared; in Calvinist Holland, the Christmas tradition of giving children gifts was strongly denounced.

The Carnival festival was highly resilient, however. Along with many other forms of popular culture, it persisted, even if less openly public. The moralist attack on popular culture meant that some activities retreated from outside to inside—into sports arenas, taverns, theaters, and opera houses. And some were professionalized by athletes, entertainers, actors, and singers. The attempts of mayors and clerics to abolish fun also provoked open resistance. In 1539 in Nuremberg the Lutheran pastor Andreas Osiander, who had preached against Carnival, found himself lampooned by a float in the shape of a ship of fools, in which he was depicted as the captain.

The attempts to suppress popular culture produced a confrontation between the educated elites of Europe and the workers, peasants, servants, and artisans who surrounded them and served them. Although not entirely successful, by the late sixteenth century the suppression had the effect of broadening the cultural gap between the educated few and the masses. Practices that previously had been broadly accepted forms of public entertainment, in which even members of the clergy participated, came to be seen as unworthy of educated people.

Hunting Witches

The most catastrophic manifestation of the widespread anxiety of the late sixteenth and seventeenth centuries was the great witch-hunt°. The judicial prosecution of alleged witches in either church or secular courts dramatically increased about the middle of the sixteenth century and lasted until the late seventeenth, when the number of witchcraft trials rapidly diminished and stopped entirely in western Europe.

Throughout this period, people accepted the reality of two kinds of magic°. The first kind was natural magic, such as the practice of alchemy or astrology, which involved the manipulation of occult forces believed to exist in nature. The fundamental assumption of natural magic was that everything in nature is alive. The trained magician could coerce the occult forces in nature to do his bidding. During the Renaissance many humanists and scientific thinkers were drawn to natural magic because of its promise of power over nature. Natural magic, in fact, had some practical uses. Alchemists, for example, devoted themselves to discovering what they called the "philosopher's stone," the secret of transmuting base metals into gold. In practice this meant that they learned how to imitate the appearance of gold, a very useful skill for counterfeiting coins or reducing the content of precious metals in legal coins. Natural magic was practiced by educated men and involved the human manipulation of the occult, but it did not imply any kind of contact with devils. Most practitioners of natural magic desired to achieve good, and many considered it the highest form of curative medicine.

Many people of the sixteenth and seventeenth centuries also believed in a second kind of magic—demonic magic. The practitioner of this kind of magic—usually but not always a female witch—called upon evil spirits to gain access to power. Demonic magic was generally understood as a way to work harm by ritual means. Belief in the reality of harmful magic and of witches had been widespread for centuries, and there had been occasional witch trials throughout the Middle Ages. Systematic witch-hunts, however, began only when ecclesiastical and secular authorities showed a willingness to employ the law to discover and punish accused witches. The Reformation controversies of the late sixteenth century and the authorities' willingness to discipline deviants of all sorts certainly intensified the hunt for witches. Thousands of people were accused of and tried for practicing witchcraft. About half of these alleged witches were executed, most often by burning. Cases of alleged witchcraft rarely occurred in a steady flow, as one would find for other crimes. Typically, witchcraft trials took place during localized hunts when a flare-up of paranoia and torture multiplied allegations against vulnerable members of the community. Most allegations were against women, in particular young unmarried women and older widows, but men and even young children could be accused of witchcraft as well.

People in many different places—from shepherds in the mountains of Switzerland to Calvinist ministers in the lowlands of Scotland—thought they perceived the work of witches in human and natural events. The alleged demonic magic of witchcraft appeared in two forms: *maleficia* (doing harm) and *diabolism* (worshiping the devil). The rituals of *maleficia* consisted of a simple sign or a complex incantation, but what made them *maleficia* was the belief that the person who performed them intended to cause harm to someone or something. There were many kinds of *maleficia*, including coercing an unwilling lover by sprinkling dried menstrual blood in his food, sickening a pig by cursing it, burning a barn by marking it with a hex sign, bringing wasting diarrhea to a child by reciting a spell, and killing an enemy by stabbing a wax statue of him. Midwives and women who specialized in healing were especially vulnerable to accusations of witchcraft. The intention behind a particular action they might have performed was often obscure, making it difficult to distinguish between magic designed to bring beneficial results, such as the cure of a child, and *maleficia* designed to bring harmful ones. With the high infant mortality rates of the sixteenth and seventeenth centuries, performing magical rituals for a sick baby could be very risky. The logic of witchcraft beliefs implied that a bad ending must have been caused by bad intentions.

While some people certainly attempted to practice *maleficia*, the second and far more serious kind of ritual practice associated with demonic magic, diabolism, almost certainly never took place. Diabolism was a fantasy that helped explain events that could not otherwise be explained. The theory behind diabolism asserted that the witch had sold her soul to the Devil, whom she worshiped as her god. These witches had made a pact with the Devil, worshiped the Devil in the ritual of the witches' sabbath, flew around at night, and sometimes changed themselves into animals. The two core beliefs of the pact with the Devil and the witches' sabbath created the intellectual and legal conditions for the great witch-hunts of the sixteenth and seventeenth centuries.

A pact with the Devil was believed to give the witch the ability to accomplish *maleficia,* in exchange for which she was obliged to serve and worship Satan. The most influential witchcraft treatise, *The Hammer of Witches* (1486), had an extensive discussion of the ceremony of the pact. After the prospective witch had declared her intention to enter his service, Satan appeared to her, often in the alluring form of a handsome young man who offered her rewards, including a demonic lover, called an *incubus*. To obtain these inducements, the witch was obliged to renounce her allegiance to Christ, usually signified by stomping on the cross. The Devil rebaptized her in a disgusting substance, guaranteeing that her soul belonged to him. To signify that she was one of his own, the Devil marked her body in a hidden place, creating a sign, which could easily be confused with a birthmark or blemish. To an inquisitor or judge almost any mark on the skin might confirm guilt.

One of the fullest accounts of beliefs in the witches' sabbath comes from the tragic trial of the Pappenheimer family in Bavaria in 1600. The Pappenheimers, consisting of a mother, a father, and their sons, were vagrants arrested for killing babies and cutting off their hands for the purposes of witchcraft. In her confession under torture, Anna Pappenheimer gave a full account of her participation in a fantastic witches' sabbath that supposedly took place at night on a hill outside of the village of Tettenwang. She claimed that witches arrived from near and far flying in on broomsticks and pitchforks. The assembled company largely consisted of women, young and old and most of them naked, but there were a few male witches (known as warlocks) and even some children. With a clap of thunder

DOCUMENT

How Women Came to Be Accused of Witchcraft: A Witch's Confession

Walpurga Hausmännin, an elderly widow and midwife from a small town near Augsburg in the Holy Roman Empire, was accused in 1587 of killing more than forty children. Her confession, extracted out of her through fear and torture, is tragic but typical, complete with lurid details of sexual intercourse with the Devil, the Devil's mark, a pact with the Devil, and riding on a broomstick to a witches' sabbath. This excerpt from her confession, which lists some of her alleged victims, illustrates how the collective fears of the community were channeled into imagined crimes against children.

[T]he Devil] also compelled her to do away with and to kill young infants at birth, even before they had been taken to Holy Baptism. This she did, whenever possible. These as follows:

1 and 2. About ten years ago, she had rubbed Anna Hämännin, who dwelt far from Dursteigel, with her salve on the occasion of her first childbirth and also otherwise damaged her so that mother and child remained together and died.

3. Dorothea, the stepdaughter of Christian Wachter, bore her first child ten years before; at its birth she made press on its little brain so that it died. The Devil had specially bidden her destroy the first-born.

5. When, four years ago, the organist's wife was awaiting her confinement, she touched her naked body with her salve whereby the child promptly died and came stillborn.

8. Three years ago when she was called to a mill to the miller's wife there she had let the child fall into the water and drown.

11. When six years ago, she partook of food with Magdalena Seilerin, called *Kammerschreiberin* (wife of the chamber scribe), she had put a salve in her drink, so that she was delivered prematurely. This child she, Walpurga, secretly buried under the doorway of the said wife of the scribe on the pretext that then she would have no other miscarriage. The same she also did with many others. When she was questioned under torture for the reasons of this burial, she admitted that it was done in order to cause disunion between two spouses. This her Devil-Paramour had taught her.

15. She had also rubbed a salve on a beautiful son of the late Chancellor, Jacob by name: this child had lovely fair hair and she had given him a hobby-horse so that he might ride on it till he lost his senses. He died likewise.

Source: From George T. Matthews, ed., *News and Rumor in Renaissance Europe: The Fugger Newsletters*, pp. 137–143. Copyright © 1959 by G. P. Putnam's Sons.

The Witches' Kitchen

During the sixteenth and seventeenth centuries it was widely believed that witches were women who practiced *maleficia* and worshiped Satan. Both attractive young and wrinkled old women appear here as witches. From the right an old witch embraces her naked demon lover, a young woman opens her blouse for her approaching lover, another young woman points to the witch's mark on her leg, a hag reads spells from a book in front of a human skull, a witch brews noxious substances in a large kettle, and a kneeling woman worships a satanic idol. In the background is a house fire, the product of the witches' evil work.

and a profusion of smoke, Satan himself suddenly appeared with his eyes glowing, dressed in black and smelling horribly. The assembled witches and warlocks bowed low before him, praying in a travesty of the Lord's Prayer, "Our Satan which art in Hell. . . ." There followed an infernal banquet of disgusting foods, including horse meat, ravens, crows, toads, frogs, and boiled and roasted infants. After the feast, an orchestra of demons played tuneless, screeching dance music that aroused a mad lust in the witches and their demon lovers, who began a wild spinning dance that finally broke

down into a indiscriminate orgy. The family and some other drifters were grotesquely tortured and burned alive.

Between about 1550 and 1650, approximately 100,000 people in Europe were tried for witchcraft. About 50,000 of these were executed. Approximately half of the trials were in the German-speaking lands of the Holy Roman Empire. Prosecutions were also extensive in Switzerland, France, Scotland, Poland, Hungary, Transylvania, and Russia. 10,000 people were tried in Spain and Italy, but these were mostly for minor offenses of *maleficia*, and very few people

Burning of Witches at Dernberg in 1555

One of the witches is being taken away by a flying demon to whom she had sold her soul.

were executed, probably none in Italy. As the product of collective beliefs and collective paranoia, witchcraft beliefs could be applied to all kinds of people, but allegations were most commonly lodged against poor, older women in small rural villages. Perhaps most tragic is the fact that these women were the members of the community most dependent on their neighbors for kindness and charity.

The Confessional States

■ How did religious differences provoke violence and start wars?

The Religious Peace of Augsburg of 1555 provided the model for a solution to the religious divisions produced by the Reformation. According to the principle of *cuius regio, eius religio* (he who rules determines the religion of the land), each prince in the Holy Roman Empire determined the religion to be followed by his subjects, and those who disagreed were obliged to convert or emigrate elsewhere. Certainly, forced exile was economically and personally traumatic for those who emigrated, but it preserved what was almost universally believed to be the fundamental principle of successful rulership—one king, one faith, one law. In other words, each state should have only one church. Except in the notoriously weak states of eastern Europe and a few small troubled principalities in the Holy Roman Empire, few thought it desirable to allow more than one confession in the same state.

The problem with this political theory of religious unity, of course, was the reality of religious divisions created by the Reformation. In some places there were as many as three active confessions—Catholic, Lutheran, and Calvinist—in addition to the minority sects, such as the Anabaptists and the Jewish communities. The alternative to religious unity would have been religious toleration, but hardly anyone in a position of authority was willing to advocate that. Calvin had expelled advocates of religious toleration, and Luther had been aggressively hostile to those who disagreed with him on seemingly minor theological points. After 1542 with the establishment of the Universal Inquisition, the Catholic Church was committed to exposing and punishing anyone who professed a different faith, with the exception of Jews in Italy, who were under papal protection. Geneva and Rome became competing missionary centers, each flooding the world with polemical tracts and specially trained missionaries willing to risk their lives by going behind the enemy lines to console their co-religionists and evangelize for converts.

Wherever there were significant religious minorities within a state, the best that could be hoped for was a condition of anxious tension, omnipresent suspicion, and peri-odic hysteria (see Map 14.2). The worst possibility was civil war in which religious affiliations and political rivalries were intertwined in such complicated ways that finding peaceful solutions was especially difficult. Between 1560 and 1648 several religious civil wars broke out, including the French Wars of Religion, the Dutch revolt against Spain, the Thirty Years' War in Germany, and the English Civil War. (The latter two will be discussed in Chapter 15.)

During the late sixteenth century a new word appeared to describe a personality type that may not have been entirely new but was certainly much more common—the fanatic°. Originally referring to someone possessed by a demon, *fanatic* came to mean a person who expressed immoderate enthusiasm in religious matters, a person who pursued a supposedly divine mission, often to violent ends. Fanatics from all sides of the religious divide initiated waves of political assassinations and engaged in grotesque massacres of their opponents. François Guion, the assassin of William the Silent, whose story began this chapter, was in many ways typical of fanatics in his steadfast pursuit of his victim and his willingness to masquerade for years under a false identity. During the sixteenth and seventeenth centuries, no religious community had a monopoly on fanatics. They presented themselves as serving the pope as well as the Protestant churches.

The sharp confessional divisions that produced fanatics and assassins also stimulated writers, poets, and dramatists to examine the human condition. Perhaps no period in the history of the West produced so many great works of literature as the late sixteenth and early seventeenth centuries.

The French Wars of Religion

When King Henry II (r. 1547–1559) of France died unexpectedly from a jousting accident, he left behind his widow, the formidable Catherine de Médicis (1519–1589), and a brood of young children—including his heir, Francis II (r. 1559–1560), who was only 15. Henry II had been a peacemaker. He succeeded in keeping France from civil war by carefully pacifying the quarrelsome nobles of the realm, and at the Peace of Cateau-Cambrésis (1559) he finally ended more than sixty years of war with Spain. In contrast, Catherine and her children, including three sons who successively ascended to the throne, utterly failed to keep the peace, and for some forty years France was torn apart by a series of desperate civil wars.

The Huguenots: The French Calvinist Community

By 1560 Calvinism had made significant inroads into predominantly Catholic France. Pastors sent from Geneva had been especially successful in the larger provincial towns, where their evangelical message appealed to enterprising

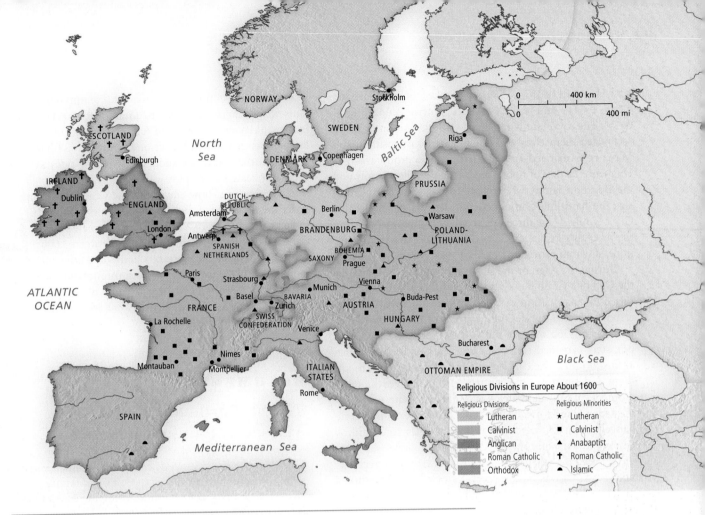

Map 14.2 Religious Divisions in Europe About 1600

After 1555 the religious borders of Europe became relatively fixed, with only minor changes in con-fessional affiliations to this day.

Religious Divisions in Europe About 1600

Religious Divisions	Religious Minorities
Lutheran	★ Lutheran
Calvinist	■ Calvinist
Anglican	▲ Anabaptist
Roman Catholic	✝ Roman Catholic
Orthodox	▲ Islamic

merchants, professionals, and skilled artisans. One in ten of the French had become Calvinists, or Huguenots° as French Protestants were called. The political strength of the Huguenots was greater than their numbers might indicate, because between one-third and one-half of the lower nobility professed Calvinism. Calvinism was popular among the French nobility for two reasons. One involved the imitation of social superiors. The financial well-being of any noble depended on his patron, an aristocrat of higher rank who had access to the king and who could distribute jobs and lands to his clients. When a high aristocrat converted to Protestantism, he tended to bring into the new faith as well his noble clientele, who converted through loyalty to their patron or through the patron's ability to persuade those who were financially dependent on him. As a result of a few aristocratic conversions in southwest France, Calvinism spread through "a veritable religious spider's web,"³ as one contemporary put it.

Even more important than networks of male patrons was the influence of aristocratic women. The sister of King Francis I of France (r. 1515–1547), Marguerite of Angoulême (1492–1549), married the King of Navarre (an independent kingdom situated between France and Spain) and created a haven in Navarre for Huguenot preachers and theologians. Her example drew other aristocratic ladies to the Huguenot cause, and many of the Huguenot leaders during the French Wars of Religion were the sons and grandsons of these early female converts. Marguerite's daughter, Jeanne d'Albret, sponsored Calvinist preachers for several years before she publicly announced her own conversion in 1560, and her son, Henry Bourbon, became the principal leader of the Huguenot cause during the French Wars of Religion° and the person responsible for eventually bringing the wars to an end.

The Origins of the Religious Wars

Like all civil wars, the French Wars of Religion exhibited a bewildering pattern of intrigue, betrayal, and treachery. Three distinct groups constituted the principal players. The first group was the royal family, consisting of Queen Catherine de Médicis and her four sons by Henry II—King Francis II (r. 1559–1560), King Charles IX (r. 1560–1574),

King Henry III (r. 1574–1589), and Duke Francis of Alençon (1554–1584)—and her daughter, Marguerite Valois (1553–1615). The royal family remained Catholic but on occasion reconciled themselves with the Huguenot opposition, and Marguerite married into it. The second group was the Huguenot faction of nobles led by the Châtillon family and the Bourbon family who ruled Navarre. The third group was the hard-line Catholic faction led by the implacable Guise family. These three groups vied for supremacy during the successive reigns of Catherine de Médicis's three sons, none of whom proved to be effective monarchs.

During the reign of the sickly and immature Francis II, the Catholic Guise family dominated the government and raised the persecution of the Huguenots to a new level. In response to that persecution, a group of Protestant nobles plotted in 1560 against the Guises, and some Calvinist ministers provided scriptural justifications for vengeance against tyrants. The Guises got wind of a conspiracy to kill them and surprised the plotters as they arrived in small groups at the royal chateau of Amboise. Some were ambushed, some drowned in the Loire River, and some hanged from the balconies of the chateau's courtyard. A tense two years later in 1562, the Duke of Guise was passing through the village of Vassy just as a large congregation of Protestants was holding services in a barn. The duke's men attacked the worshipers, killing some 740 of them and wounding hundreds of others.

Following the massacre at Vassy, civil war broke out in earnest. For nearly forty years a series of religious wars sapped the strength of France. Most of the battles were indecisive, which meant neither side sustained military superiority for long. Both sides relied for support on their regional bases: The Protestant strength was in the southwest, the Catholic in Paris and the north. Besides military engagements, the French Wars of Religion were characterized by political assassinations and massacres.

Massacre of St. Bartholomew's Day

After a decade of bloody yet inconclusive combat, the royal family tried to resolve the conflict by making peace with the Protestants, a shift of policy signified by the announcement of the engagement of Marguerite Valois, daughter of Henry II and Catherine de Médicis, to Henry Bourbon, the son of the Huguenot King of Navarre. At age 19, Marguerite—or Queen Margot, as she was known—was already renowned for her brilliant intelligence. But she was renowned also for her wanton morals, and to complicate the situation further, on the eve of the wedding she was having an affair with another Henry, the young new Duke of Guise who was the leader of the intransigent Catholic faction. The marriage between Marguerite and Henry of Navarre was to take place in Paris in August 1572, an event that brought all the Huguenot leaders to the heavily armed Catholic capital for the first time in many years. The gathering of all their ene-

mies in one place presented too great a temptation for the Guises, who hatched a plot to assassinate the Huguenot leaders. Perhaps because she had become jealous of the Huguenots' growing influence on her son, King Charles IX, the mercurial Catherine suddenly switched sides and became implicated in the plot.

Catherine somehow convinced the weak-willed king to order the massacre of the Huguenot nobles gathered in Paris. On August 14, 1572, St. Bartholomew's Day, the people of Paris began a slaughter. Between 3,000 and 4,000 Huguenots were butchered in Paris and more than 20,000 were put to death throughout the rest of France. Henry of Navarre saved his life by pretending to convert to Catholicism, while most of his companions were murdered.

St. Bartholomew's Day Massacre (1572)

St. Bartholomew's Day Massacre

This Protestant painter, François Dubois, depicted the merciless slaughter of Protestant men, women, and children in the streets of Paris in 1572. The massacre was the most bloody and infamous in the French Wars of Religion and created a lasting memory of atrocity.

litical revolution: François Hotman in *Francogallia* (1573) and Théodore de Bèze in *Right of Magistrates* (1579). They argued that because the authority of all magistrates, including even low-ranking nobles, came directly from God, the Huguenot nobles had the right and obligation to resist a tyrannical Catholic king. During the same period, Catholic moderates known as the *politiques* rejected the excesses of the Guises and argued for an accommodation with the Huguenots.

The wars of religion continued until the assassination of King Henry III, brother of the late Charles IX. Both Charles and Henry had been childless, a situation that made Henry Bourbon of Navarre the rightful heir to the throne, even though he was a Huguenot. Henry Bourbon became King Henry IV (r. 1589–1610) and recognized that predominantly Catholic France would never accept a Huguenot king, and so in 1593 with his famous quip, "Paris is worth a mass," Henry reconverted to the ancient faith, and most opposition to him among Catholics collapsed. Once he returned to Catholicism he managed to have the pope annul his childless marriage to Marguerite so that he could marry Marie de' Medici and obtain her huge dowry. Affable, witty, generous, and exceedingly tolerant, "Henry the Great" became the most popular king in French history, reuniting the war-torn country by ruling with a very firm hand. With the Edict of Nantes° of 1598, he allowed the Huguenots to build a quasi state within the state, giving them the right to have their own troops, church organization, and political autonomy within their walled towns, but they were banned from the royal court and the city of Paris.

Henry encouraged economic development under his minister the Duke of Sully, who retired the crushing state debt and built up a fiscal surplus by reforming finances and eliminating corruption. Henry declared that his ambition was for even the poorest peasant to be able to afford a chicken in his pot every Sunday, and even though he did not achieve this laudatory goal, his public works included the beautification of Paris and an impressive canal system to facilitate transportation.

Despite his enormous popularity, Henry too fell victim to fanaticism. After surviving eighteen attempts on his life, in 1610 the king was fatally stabbed by a Catholic fanatic, who took advantage of the opportunity presented when the royal coach unexpectedly stopped behind a cart loading hay. Unlike the aftermath of the St. Bartholomew's Day massacre, Catholics all over France mourned Henry's death and considered the assassin mad. Henry's brilliant conciliatory nature and the horrors of the religious wars had tempered public opinion.

After the massacre of St. Bartholomew's Day, both sides tried to interpret the events to their own advantage. Catholics celebrated. The pope marked the occasion by having a medal struck and frescoes painted in the Vatican. King Philip II of Spain wrote that the massacre "was indeed of such value and prudence and of such service, glory, and honor to God and universal benefit to all Christendom that to hear of it was for me the best and most cheerful news which at present could come to me."[4] For Catholics the massacre was a great service to God. Protestants had a very different reaction, and presented it as a great affront to God.

Catherine's attempted solution for the Huguenot problem failed to solve anything, however. Henry of Navarre escaped his virtual imprisonment in the royal household, set Marguerite up in an isolated castle, returned to Navarre and his faith, and reinvigorated Huguenot resistance. Two Huguenot political thinkers laid out a theory justifying po-

Philip II, His Most Catholic Majesty

France's greatest rivals were the Habsburgs, who possessed vast territories in the Holy Roman Empire, controlled the elections for emperor, and had dynastic rights to the throne of Spain. As archenemies of the Protestant Reformation, they had regularly helped finance the Catholic cause during the French Wars of Religion. During the late sixteenth century, Habsburg Spain took advantage of French weakness to establish itself as the dominant power in Europe. When Emperor Charles V (who had been both Holy Roman Emperor and king of Spain) abdicated his thrones in 1556, the Habsburg possessions in the Holy Roman Empire and the emperorship went to his brother, Ferdinand I, and the balance of his vast domain to his son, Philip II (r. 1556–1598). Philip's inheritance included Milan, Naples, Sicily, the Netherlands, scattered outposts on the north coast of Africa, colonies in the Caribbean, Central America, Mexico, Peru, the Philippines, and most important of all, Spain. In 1580 he also inherited Portugal and its far-flung overseas empire, which included a line of trading posts from West Africa to the Spice Islands and the vast colony of unexplored Brazil.

Ruling over these enormous territories was a gargantuan task that Philip undertook with obsessive seriousness. From the rambling palace of El Escorial, which was also a mausoleum for his father and a monastery, Philip lived in semimonastic seclusion and ruled as the "King of Paper," an office-bound bureaucrat rather than the rule-from-the-saddle warrior his father had been and many of his contemporary monarchs remained. Philip kept himself to a rigid daily work discipline that included endless committee meetings and long hours devoted to poring over as many as 400 documents a day, which he annotated extensively in his crabbed hand. Because of his inability to delegate authority and his immersion in minutiae, Philip tended to lose his grasp of the larger picture, especially the shaky finances of Spain.

This grave, distrustful, rigid man saw himself as the great protector of the Catholic cause and committed Spain to perpetual hostility toward Muslims and Protestants. On the Muslim front he first bullied the Moriscos, the descendants of the Spanish Muslims. The Moriscos had received Christian baptism, but they were suspected of secretly practicing Islam, and in 1568 Philip issued an edict that banned all manifestations of Muslim culture and ordered the Moriscos to turn over their children to Christian priests to educate. The outraged Moriscos of Granada rebelled but were soundly defeated. At first dispersed throughout Spain, the surviving Moriscos were eventually expelled from the country in 1609. Philip hardened his policy toward the Moriscos because he feared, not unreasonably, that they would become secret agents on Spanish soil for his great Mediterranean rivals, the Ottoman Turks. To counter the Turkish threat, Philip maintained expensive fortresses on the North African coast. In 1571 he joined the Venetians and the pope to check Turkish advances after the Ottomans captured Cyprus, Venice's richest colony. The Christian victory at Lepanto in the Gulf of Corinth, which destroyed more than one-third of the enemy's fleet, was heralded as one of the greatest events of the sixteenth century, proving that the Turks could be beaten. Lepanto renewed the crusading spirit in the Catholic world. Although the victory at Lepanto was a valuable propaganda tool, it had slight military significance because the Turks quickly rebuilt their fleet and forced Venice to cede Cyprus to them. The island remains divided between Christian and Muslim populations to this day.

Philip once said he would rather lose all his possessions and die a hundred times than be the king of heretics. His attitude toward Protestants showed that he meant what he said. Through his marriage to Queen Mary I of England (r. 1553–1558), Philip encouraged her persecutions of Protestants, but they got their revenge. After Mary's death her half-sister, Queen Elizabeth I, refused his marriage proposal and in 1577 signed a treaty to assist the Protestant Netherlands, which was in rebellion against Spain. To add insult to injury, the English privateer Sir Francis Drake (ca. 1540–1596) conducted a personal war against Catholic Spain by raiding the Spanish convoys bringing silver from the New World. In 1587 Drake's embarrassing successes culminated with a daring raid on the great Spanish port city of Cadiz, where, "singeing the king of Spain's beard," he destroyed the anchored Spanish fleet and many thousands of tons of vital supplies. Philip retaliated by building a huge fleet of 132 ships armed with 3,165 cannons, which sailed from Portugal to rendezvous with the Spanish army stationed in the Netherlands and launch an invasion of England in 1588. As the Invincible Armada, as it was called, passed through the English Channel, it was met by a much smaller English fleet, assembled out of merchant ships refit for battle. Unable to maneuver as effectively as the English in the fluky winds of the channel and mauled by the rapid-firing

DOCUMENT

John Hawkins Reports on the Spanish Armada (1588)

Defeat of the Spanish Armada

The smaller English ships on the left outmaneuvered the Spanish Armada arrayed in the formal curved line of galleons in the middle.

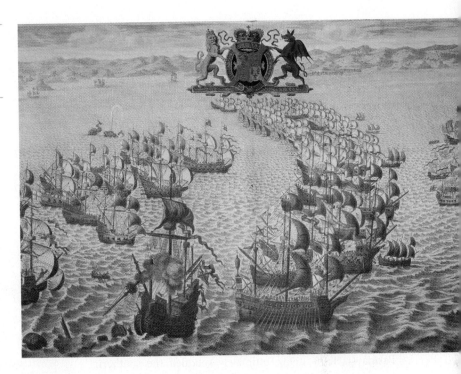

English guns, the Spanish Armada° suffered heavy losses and was forced to retreat to the north, where it sustained further losses in storms off the coast of Scotland and Ireland. Barely more than half of the fleet finally straggled home. The defeat severely shook Philip's sense of invincibility.

The reign of Philip II illustrated better than any other the contradictions and tensions of the era. No monarch had at his grasp as many resources and territories as Philip, and yet defending them proved extremely costly. The creaky governmental machinery of Spain put a tremendous burden on a conscientious king such as Philip, but even his unflagging energy and dedication to his duties could not prevent military defeat and financial disaster. Economic historians remember Philip's reign for its series of state bankruptcies and for the loss of the Dutch provinces in the Netherlands, the most precious jewel in the crown of Spain.

The Dutch Revolt

The Netherlands boasted some of Europe's richest cities, situated amid a vast network of lakes, rivers, channels, estuaries, and tidal basins that periodically replenished the exceptionally productive soil through flooding. The Netherlands consisted of seventeen provinces, each with its own distinctive identity, traditions, and even language. The southern provinces were primarily French-speaking; those in the north spoke a bewildering variety of Flemish dialects. In 1548 Emperor Charles V annexed the northern provinces that had been part of the Holy Roman Empire to the southern provinces he had inherited from his father. His decision meant that when his son, Philip II, became king of Spain, all of the Netherlands was included with the Spanish crown. With his characteristic bureaucratic mentality, Philip treated Dutch affairs as a management problem rather than a political sore spot, an attitude that subordinated the Netherlands to Spanish interests. Foreign rule irritated the Dutch, who had long enjoyed ancient privileges including the right to raise their own taxes and muster their own troops.

Consolidating the Netherlands under the Spanish crown deprived the Dutch princes of the right to chose the official religion of their lands, a right they would have enjoyed had the provinces remained in the Holy Roman Empire, where the Religious Peace of Augsburg granted princes religious freedom. Philip's harsh attitude toward Protestants upset the Netherlands' delicate balance among Catholic, Lutheran, Calvinist, and Anabaptist communities. Huguenot refugees from the French Wars of Religion heightened the anti-Catholic fanaticism of the local Calvinists, who in 1566 occupied many Catholic churches and destroyed paintings and statues.

In response to the rapidly deteriorating situation in the Netherlands, Philip issued edicts against the heretics and strengthened the Spanish Inquisition. The Inquisition in Spain was an arm of the monarchy charged with ensuring religious conformity among the extremely diverse cultures of the Iberian peninsula. The Spanish Inquisition had been preoccupied with investigating the Christian sincerity of former Jews, who after the expulsions of 1492 had converted to Christianity in order to stay in Spain. When introduced in the Netherlands, the Inquisition became an investigating agency devoted to finding, interrogating, and, if necessary, punishing Protestants. Philip also dispatched 20,000 Spanish troops under the command of the Duke of Alba (1508–1582), a veteran of the Turkish campaigns in North Africa and victories over the Lutheran princes in the Holy Roman Empire. Alba directly attacked the Protestants. He personally presided over the military court, the Council of Troubles, which became so notoriously tyrannical that the people called it the Council of Blood. As an example to others, he systematically razed several small villages where there had been incidents of desecrating Catholic images, slaughtering every inhabitant. Alba himself boasted that during the campaign against the rebels, he had 18,000 people executed, in addition to those who died in battle or were massacred by soldiers. The Prince of Orange, William the

Silent (1533–1584), accompanied into exile some 60,000 refugees, who constituted about 2 percent of the population. While abroad William began to organize resistance to Alba.

Alba's cruelty backfired by steeling Protestant opposition to the Spanish. Alba also lost support among otherwise loyal Catholics when he attempted to introduce a 10 percent tax on trade. His policies a failure, Alba was recalled to Spain in 1573. Meanwhile the sea-beggars, as the Dutch Calvinist privateers were called, had begun to achieve some success against the Spanish. Within a few short years, William the Silent seized permanent control of the provinces of Holland and Zealand, which were then flooded by Calvinist refugees from the southern provinces. After Alba's departure, no one kept control of the unpaid Spanish soldiers, who in mutinous rage turned against cities loyal to Spain, including Brussels, Ghent, and most savagely Antwerp, the rich center of trade. Antwerp lost 7,000 citizens and one-third of its houses to the "Spanish fury," which permanently destroyed its prosperity. Alba's replacement, the shrewd statesman and general the Duke of Parma (r. 1578–1592), ultimately subdued the southern provinces, which remained a Spanish colony. The seven northern provinces, however, united in 1579 and declared independence from Spain in 1581 (see Map 14.3). William the Silent became the *stadholder* (governor) of the new United Provinces, and after his assassination his 17-year-old son, Maurice of Nassau, inherited the same title.

The Netherlands' struggle for independence transformed the population of the northern provinces from mixed religions to staunch Calvinism. The Dutch Revolt°

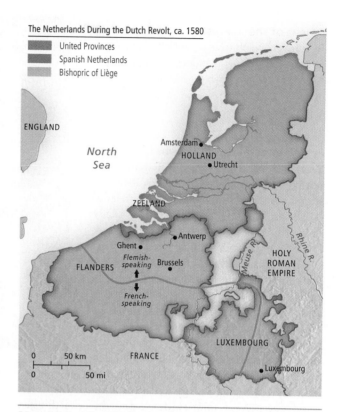

Map 14.3   The Netherlands During the Dutch Revolt, ca. 1580
During the late sixteenth century the northern United Provinces separated from the Spanish Netherlands. The independence of the United Provinces was not recognized by the other European powers until 1648.

CHRONOLOGY

Spain and the Netherlands

1548	Annexation of the northern provinces of the Netherlands to the Spanish crown
1568	Edict against Morisco culture
1571	Christian victory over Ottoman Turks at Lepanto
1580	King Philip II inherits Portugal and the Portuguese Empire
1581	Seven northern provinces of the Netherlands declare independence from Spain
1584	Assassination of William the Silent
1588	Defeat of the Spanish Armada
1609	Expulsion of the Moriscos from Spain
1648	Treaty of Westphalia recognizes independence of the Netherlands

became ensnared in the French Wars of Religion through Huguenot refugees, and the alliance with England, which provided much-needed financial and moral support, reinforced the Protestant identity of the Dutch. The international Protestant alliance created by the Dutch Revolt and centered in the Netherlands withstood both Philip's fury and Parma's calm generalship. The failure of the Spanish Armada to land Parma's men in England guaranteed the survival of an independent Netherlands. The Dutch carried on a sporadic and inconclusive war against Spain until the end of the Thirty Years' War in 1648, when the international community recognized the independent Republic of the United Provinces.

Literature in the Age of Confessional Division

Churches and monarchs everywhere demanded religious conformity in word and deed, a situation that would seem to stifle creativity, and yet the late sixteenth and early seventeenth centuries were one of the most remarkable periods in the history of creative literature. During this period the native or vernacular languages of western Europe became literary languages, replacing Latin as the dominant form of expression, even for the educated elite. Italian was the first vernacular to be prized for its literary qualities and considered a worthy alternative to Latin. The availability of cheap printed books and the Bible reading encouraged by the Protestant Reformation stimulated literature in other vernacular languages so that by the late sixteenth century great literary figures were writing in French, Portuguese, Spanish, and English.

French Literature During the Religious Turmoil

In France royal decrees in 1520 and 1539 substituted French for Latin in official legal and government documents. A century later with the founding of the Académie Française, it became government policy to promote, protect, and refine the French language. The greatest masters of French prose during this crucial period were François Rabelais (ca. 1483–1553) and Michel de Montaigne (1533–1592). Trained as a lawyer, Rabelais became a friar and priest but left the Church under a cloud of heresy to become a physician. Rabelais's satirical masterpiece, a series of novels recounting the fantastic and grotesque adventures of the giants Gargantua and Pantagruel, combined an encyclopedic command of humanist thought with stunning verbal invention that has had a lasting influence on humorous writers to this day. One of Rabelais's most remarkable creations was the imaginary Abbey of Thélème, inhabited by a kind of antimonastic community of monks and nuns for whom "all their life was regulated not by laws, statutes, or rules, but according to their free will and pleasure." This was an abbey for hedonists who lived by the motto, "DO WHAT YOU WILL, because people who are free, well-born, well-bred, and easy in honest company have a natural spur and instinct which drives them to virtuous deeds and deflects them from vice."[5] Rabelais's optimistic vision of human nature represented a startling contrast to the growing anxiety provoked by the religious controversies of his time. Rabelais's controversial work was banned, and he was briefly forced into exile.

It is ironic that Montaigne became a master of French prose. His mother was a Catholic of Spanish-Jewish origins, and the young Michel spoke only Latin for the first six years of his life because his German tutor knew no French. After a modestly successful legal career, Montaigne retired to the family chateau to discover himself by writing essays, a literary form well suited to reflective introspection. In his essays, Montaigne struggled with his lasting grief over the premature death from dysentery of a close friend, reflected on his own experience of the intense physical pain of illness, and diagnosed the absurd causes of the French Wars of Religion. Montaigne's essays are a profound series of

DOCUMENT

Men Are the Source of the Epidemic of Violence

Lucrezia Marinella (1571–1653) was a brilliant, well-educated intellectual who wrote passionately on moral issues of the day. Her masterpiece was The Nobility and Excellence of Women, and the Defects and Vices of Men, *first published in 1600. The book was an answer to the alleged defects of women in which she argued that morally and in many other ways women are superior to men. Marinella depicts violence as the product of male swagger and feelings of insecurity. She contrasts male bluster with women's use of cosmetics. If women were in charge, she implies, the civil wars and violence of the age would be quickly resolved.*

Since beauty is women's special gift from the Supreme Hand, should she not seek to guard it with all diligence? And when she is endowed with but a small amount of that excellent quality, should she not seek to embellish it by every means possible, provided it is not ignoble? I certainly believe that it is so. When man has some special gift such as physical strength, which enables him to perform as a gladiator or swagger around, as is the common usage, does he not seek to conserve it? If he were born courageous, would he not seek to augment his natural courage with the art of defense? But if he were born with little courage would he not practice the martial arts and cover himself with plate and mail and constantly seek out duels and fights in order to demonstrate his courage rather than reveal his true timidity and cowardice?

I have used this example because of the impossibility of finding a man who does not swagger and play the daredevil. If there is such a one people call him effeminate, which is why we always see men dressed up like soldiers with weapons at their belts, bearded and menacing, and walking in a way that they think will frighten everyone. Often they wear gloves of mail and contrive for their weapons to clink under their clothing so people realize they are armed and ready for combat and feel intimidated by them.

What are all these things but artifice and tinsel? Under these trappings of courage and valor hide the cowardly souls of rabbits or hunted hares, and it is the same with all their other artifices. Since men behave in this way, why should not those women who are born less beautiful than the rest hide their less fortunate attributes and seek to augment the little beauty they possess through artifice, provided it is not offensive?

Source: From Lucrezia Marinella, *The Nobility and Excellence of Women, and the Defects and Vices of Men,* edited and translated by Anne Dunhill, Chicago: University of Chicago Press, 1999, pp. 166–67.

meditations on the meaning of life and death, presented in a calm voice of reason to an age of violent fanaticism. In one essay, for example, he exposed the presumption of human beings: "The most vulnerable and frail of all creatures is man, and at the same time the most arrogant." Montaigne thought it presumptuous that human beings picked themselves out as God's favorite creatures. How did they know they were superior to other animals? "When I play with my cat, who knows if I am not a pastime to her more than she is to me?"[6] His own skepticism about religion insulated him from the sometimes violent passions of his era.

Stirrings of the Golden Age in Iberia

The literary tradition in the Iberian peninsula differed from that of other regions in Europe in that Iberia is a polyglot region in which several languages are spoken—Basque, Galician, Portuguese, Castilian, and Catalan. The greatest lyric poet of the peninsula, Luís Vaz de Camões (1524–1580), lost an eye in battle and was sent to the Portuguese East Indies after he killed a royal official in a street brawl. When he returned years later, he completed his epic poem *The Lusiads* (1572), which became the national poem of Portugal by celebrating Vasco da Gama's discovery of the sea route to India. This great work was modeled on the ancient epics, especially the *Aeneid*, the greatest Latin epic of ancient Rome, and even included the gods of Olympus as commentators on the human events of Camões's time. In the opening lines, Jupiter spoke of contemporary Portugal:

> *Eternal dwellers in the starry heavens, you will not have forgotten the great valor of that brave people the Portuguese. You cannot therefore be unaware that it is the fixed resolve of destiny that before their achievements those of Assyrians, Persians, Greeks and Romans shall fade into oblivion. Already with negligible forces—you were witnesses—they have expelled the Moslem, for all his strength and numbers . . . while against the redoubtable Castilians they have invariably had heaven on their side. Always, in a word, they have known victory in battle and have reaped, with its trophies, fame and glory too.*[7]

By connecting Portugal directly to the glories of the ancient empires, Camões managed to elevate the adventures of his fellow Portuguese in Asia to an important moment in the history of the world.

Because Spain was unified around the crown of Castile, the Castilian language became the language we now call Spanish. The period when Spain was the dominant power in Europe coincided with the Golden Age of Spanish literature. The greatest literary figure was Miguel de Cervantes Saavedra (1547–1616), an impoverished son of an unsuccessful doctor with little formal education. Like Camões, Cervantes survived many adventures, losing the use of his left hand at the naval battle of Lepanto and spending five years languishing in a Turkish prison after he was captured by Algerian pirates. In order to survive, the disabled veteran was forced to write plays for the Madrid theater and to work as a tax collector, but he was still imprisoned several times for debts. Desperate to make money, Cervantes published a serial novel in installments between 1605 and 1615. It became the greatest masterpiece in Spanish literature, *Don Quixote*.

The prototype of the modern novel form, *Don Quixote* was a satire of chivalric romances. Cervantes presented reality on two levels, the "poetic truth" of the master and dreamer Don Quixote and the "historic truth" of his squire and realist Sancho Panza. Don Quixote's imagination persistently ran away with him as he tilted at windmills, believing they were fierce dragons. It remained to Sancho Panza to point out the unheroic truth. Cervantes pursued the interaction between these two incongruous views of truth as a philosophical commentary on existence. For Cervantes there was no single, objective truth, only psychological truths revealed through the interaction of the characters, an idea that contrasted with the notion of dogmatic religious truth that dominated the time. Despite the extensive popularity of *Don Quixote*, Cervantes died a pauper, buried in an unmarked grave in Madrid.

The Elizabethan Renaissance

During the reign of Elizabeth I (r. 1558–1603), the Renaissance truly arrived in England. The daughter of Henry VIII and Anne Boleyn, Elizabeth faced terrible insecurity as a girl. Her father had her mother beheaded, she was declared illegitimate, and her sister Mary imprisoned her for treason in the Tower of London. After she ascended to the throne in 1558, however, she proved to be a brilliant leader. She prevented the kind of religious civil wars that broke out in France by establishing a moderate form of Protestantism as the official religion. She presided over the beginnings of England's rise as a major European power. Perhaps most remarkably, she became the patron and inspiration for England's greatest age of literature. Never married, Elizabeth used her eligibility for marriage as a lure in diplomacy, and even though she may have had real lovers, she addressed her subjects as if they were her only love. Her "golden speech" delivered before a troublesome House of Commons in 1601 exemplifies her ability to inspire exuberant loyalty:

> *Though God hath raised me high, yet this I account the glory of my crown, that I have reigned with your loves. . . . It is not my desire to live or reign longer than my life and reign shall be for your good. And though you have had, and may have, many mightier and wiser princes sitting in this seat, yet you never had, nor shall have any that will love you better.*[8]

Among Elizabeth's courtiers were major literary figures, including the adventurer-poet Sir Walter Raleigh (ca. 1552–1618), the soldier-poet Sir Philip Sidney (1554–1586), and Edmund Spenser (ca. 1552–1599), whose great poem *The Faerie Queen* was a personal tribute to Elizabeth.

Queen Elizabeth I of England
Elizabeth presided over the greatest
age of English literature.

The principal figure of the Elizabethan Renaissance, however, was not a courtier but a professional dramatist, William Shakespeare (1564–1616). In a series of theaters, including the famous Globe on the south side of the Thames in London, Shakespeare wrote, produced, and acted in comedies, tragedies, and history plays. Shakespeare's enormous output of plays, some of which made veiled allusions to the politics of Elizabeth's court, established him not only as the most popular dramatist of his time but the greatest literary figure in the English language. The power of his plays derives from the subtle understanding of human psychology found in his characters and the stunning force of his language. For Shakespeare, as for Montaigne, the source of true knowledge was self-knowledge. One character advises,

> *Neither a borrower nor a lender be,*
> *For loan oft loses both itself and friend*
> *And borrowing dulls the edge of husbandry.*
> *This above all: To thine own self be true,*
> *And it must follow, as the night the day,*
> *Thou canst not then be false to any man.*
> (Hamlet I, iii, 75–80)

Unlike most contemporary authors, Shakespeare wrote for a broad audience of paying theatergoers that included common workers as well as highly educated members of Elizabeth's court. This need to appeal to a large audience who gave instant feedback helped him hone his skills as a dramatist.

Some of these literary figures found their works banned, as did Rabelais. Some had political or personal troubles with their monarch, as did Montaigne, Camões, Raleigh, and Sidney. But the controversies of the day seemed to have stimulated rather than inhibited these writers. Political and religious turmoil led them to ask penetrating questions about the meaning of life and to rise above the petty squabbles that preoccupied so many of their contemporaries.

States and Confessions in Eastern Europe

■ How did the countries of eastern Europe during the late sixteenth century become enmeshed in the religious controversies that began in western Europe during the early part of the century?

In contrast to the confessional states of western Europe where rulers demanded religious conformity, the weak states of eastern Europe during the early sixteenth century were less successful in linking religious conformity to political loyalty. Whereas in the West the religious controversies stimulated writers to investigate deeply the human condition but made them cautious about expressing nonconforming religious opinions, writers and creative people in the East during this period were able to explore a wide range of ideas in a relatively tolerant atmosphere. Bohemia and Poland, in particular, allowed levels of religious diversity unheard of in the West. During the last decades of the sixteenth century and early decades of the seventeenth, however, dynastic troubles compromised the relative openness of the eastern states, enmeshing them in conflicts among themselves that had an increasingly strong religious dimension. In the Holy Roman Empire, the weakness of the mad Emperor Rudolf permitted religious conflicts to fester, setting the stage for the disastrous Thirty Years' War (1618–1648) that pitted Catholic and Protestant princes against one another.

Around the Baltic Sea, rivalries among Lutheran Sweden, Catholic Poland-Lithuania, and Orthodox Russia created a state of almost permanent war in a tense standoff among three very different political and religious states. The enormous confederation of Poland-Lithuania struggled to sustain the most decentralized, religiously diverse state anywhere in Europe. By the end of the century, it remained politically decentralized but had become an active theater of the Catholic Reformation where dynastic policy firmly supported the Roman Church. Russia began to strengthen itself from obscurity under the authoritarian rule of the tsars, who began to transform it into a major European power.

The Dream World of Emperor Rudolf

In Goethe's *Faust,* set in sixteenth-century Germany, drinkers in a tavern sing:

> *The dear old Holy Roman Empire,*
> *How does it hang together?*[9]

Good question. How did this peculiarly decentralized state—neither holy, nor Roman, nor an empire—hang together? In the late sixteenth century the empire consisted of the following components: 1 emperor; 7 electors, comprising 4 secular princes and 3 archbishops; 50 other bishops and archbishops; 21 dukes, margraves, and landgraves; 88 independent abbots and assorted prelates of the Church; 178 counts and other sovereign lords; about 80 free imperial cities; and hundreds of free imperial knights. The emperor presided over all, and the Imperial Diet served as a parliament, but the Holy Roman Empire was, in fact, a very loose confederation of semi-independent, mostly German-speaking states, many of which ignored imperial decrees that did not suit them. During the first half of the sixteenth century the empire faced a number of challenges—the turmoil within the empire created by Lutheranism, endless French enmity on the western borders, and the tenacious Ottoman threat on the eastern frontier. Only the universal vision and firm hand of Emperor Charles V kept the empire together. The universal vision and firm hand disappeared in the succeeding generations of emperors, to be replaced by petty dynastic squabbles and infirm minds.

The crippling weakness of the imperial system became most evident during the reign of Rudolf II (r. 1576–1612).

The Habsburg line had a strain of insanity going back to Joanna "The Mad," the mother of Emperors Charles V (r. 1519–1558) and Ferdinand I (r. 1558–1564), who happened to be Rudolf's two grandfathers, giving him a double dose of Habsburg genes. Soon after his election to the imperial throne, Rudolf moved his court from bustling Vienna to the lovely quiet of Prague in Bohemia. Fearful of noisy crowds and impatient courtiers, standoffish toward foreign ambassadors who presented him with difficult decisions, paranoid about scheming relatives, and prone to wild emotional gyrations from deep depression to manic grandiosity, Rudolf was hardly suited for the imperial throne. In fact, many contemporaries, who had their own reasons to underrate him, described him as hopelessly insane. Rudolf certainly suffered from moments of profound melancholy and irrational fears that may have had genetic or organic causes, but he was probably unhinged by the conundrum of being the emperor, a position that trapped him between the glorious universal imperial ideal and the ignoble reality of unscrupulous relatives and petty rivalries.

Rudolf was not the only sixteenth-century prince in the Holy Roman Empire driven to distraction by the pressures of court life. At least twenty German princes and princesses were confined or deposed due to symptoms of serious mental disorder. Certainly inbreeding within a small pool of princely families contributed to the patterns of madness, but the most unhealthy emotional pressure was produced by the code of manners required of all courtiers, most particularly princes and princesses. This strictly maintained code demanded the repression of all spontaneous feelings, a repression that resulted in a prevailing sense of shame. When religious rigidity and extreme political conflict were mixed into this volatile psychological concoction, it is not surprising that some personalities shattered. Because the entire political system depended on the prince's guidance, a mad prince could seriously disrupt an entire society.

Incapable of governing, Rudolf transmuted the imperial ideal of universality into a strange dream world. In Prague he gathered around him a brilliant court of humanists, musicians, painters, physicians, astronomers, astrologers, alchemists, and magicians. These included an eclectic assortment of significant thinkers—the great astronomers Tycho Brahe and Johannes Kepler, the notorious occult philosopher Giordano Bruno, the theoretical mathematician and astrologer John Dee, and the remarkable inventor of surrealist painting Giuseppe Arcimboldo. Many of these figures are considered the immediate forerunners of the Scientific Revolution, but Rudolf also fell prey to fast-talking charlatans. These included the illusionist and opera-set designer Cornelius Drebber, who claimed to have invented a perpetual-motion machine. This weird court, however, was less the strange fruit of the emperor's hopeless dementia than the manifestation of a striving for universal empire. Rudolf sought to preserve the cultural and political unity of the

The Strange Court of Emperor Rudolf II
Among the many creative people in the Emperor Rudolf's court was the Italian surrealist painter Giuseppe Arcimboldo, who specialized in creating images out of fruits, vegetables, flowers, and animals. This is a portrait of the Emperor Rudolf.

empire, to eradicate religious divisions, and to achieve peace at home. Rudolf's court in Prague was perhaps the only place left during the late sixteenth century where Protestants, Catholics, Jews, and even radical heretics such as Bruno could gather together in a common intellectual enterprise. The goal of such gatherings was to discover the universal principles that governed nature, principles that would provide the foundations for a single unifying religion and a cure for all human maladies. It was a noble, if utterly improbable, dream.

While Rudolf and his favorite courtiers isolated themselves in their dream world, the religious conflicts within the empire reached a boiling point. Without a strong emperor, the Imperial Diets were paralyzed by confessional squabbles. In 1607 in the imperial free city of Donauworth in south Germany, a conflict between the Lutheran town council and the substantial Catholic minority gave the Catholic Duke of Bavaria the excuse to annex the city to his own territories. Despite the illegality of the duke's action,

Rudolf passively acquiesced, causing fear among German Protestants that the principles of the Religious Peace of Augsburg of 1555 might be ignored. In the following decade, more than 200 religious revolts or riots took place. In 1609 the insane Duke John William of Jülich-Cleves died without a direct heir, and the most suitable claimants to the Catholic duchy were two Lutheran princes. Were one of them to succeed to the dukedom, the balance between Catholics and Protestants in Germany would have been seriously disrupted. Religious tensions boiled over. As Chapter 15 will describe, in less than a decade the empire began to dissolve in what became the Thirty Years' War.

The Renaissance of Poland-Lithuania

During the late sixteenth and early seventeenth centuries, Poland-Lithuania experienced a remarkable cultural and political renaissance. It was inspired by influences from Renaissance Italy linked to strong commercial and diplomatic ties to the Republic of Venice and intellectual connections with the University of Padua. As the major power in eastern Europe, Poland-Lithuania engaged in a tug-of-war with Sweden over control of the eastern Baltic and virtually constant warfare against the expansionist ambitions of Russia (see Map 14.4). The most remarkable achievement of Poland-Lithuania during this contentious time was its unparalleled and still controversial experiments in government. Poland-Lithuania had an elected king but called itself a republic. The king was a figurehead, and Poland-Lithuania was a republic in the sense that it was effectively governed by assemblies of nobles.

Very loosely joined since 1336, Poland and Lithuania created a constitutional union in 1569, creating a confederation in which Poland supplied the king, but the Grand Duchy of Lithuania was considered an equal partner and allowed to retain its own laws, administration, and army. The novel feature of the confederation was how the nobles reserved power for themselves through their control of regional assemblies, which in turn dominated the central parliament called the Sejm. These nobles elected the king and treated him, at best, as a hired manager. They resisted all attempts to exert royal power by asserting the legal right to form local armed assemblies against the king and by exercising the principle of unanimity in the Sejm, which prevented the king or a strong faction from dominating affairs. In the last half of the seventeenth century Poland-Lithuania fell into chaos under this system, but for nearly three-quarters of a century it worked well enough—at least for the nobles.

The rule of the nobles in Poland-Lithuania came at a great cost to the Polish peasants, however, who were ruthlessly forced into serfdom and deprived of their legal rights.

Peasants were prohibited from leaving the land without permission from their landlords, and they were denied the ability to appeal the legal judgments of their local lords. In this regard, Poland-Lithuania moved in the opposite direction from western European states, which at this time were extending the right of judicial appeal and allowing serfdom to fade away. Moreover, the Polish kings could not stop the gradual erosion of their authority so that Poland-Lithuania, the greatest power in the East, enfeebled itself through the grasping hands of a notoriously self-interested and proud nobility.

Poland-Lithuania contained an incomparable religious mixture of Roman Catholics, Lutherans, Calvinists, Russian Orthodox, Anabaptists, Unitarians, and Jews, but these communities were strongly divided along geographic and class lines. Lutheranism was a phenomenon of the German-speaking towns, the peasants of Poland remained Catholic, those in Lithuania were Orthodox, and many of the nobles were attracted to Calvinism. During the late sixteenth century, however, Christians in Poland almost completely returned or converted to the Roman Catholic faith. The key to the transformation was the changing attitude of the Polish nobles, who had tolerated religious diversity because they believed that religious liberty was the cornerstone of political liberty. The return to Catholicism owed a great deal to Stanislas Hosius (1504–1579), who had studied in Italy before he returned to Poland to become successively a diplomat, bishop, and cardinal. Imbued with the zeal of the Italian Catholic Reformation, Hosius invited the Society of Jesus into Poland and worked closely with the papal *nuncios* (the diplomatic representatives of the pope), who organized a campaign to combat all forms of Protestantism.

Map 14.4 Poland-Lithuania and Russia

These countries were the largest in Europe in the size of their territories but were relatively underpopulated compared to the western European states.

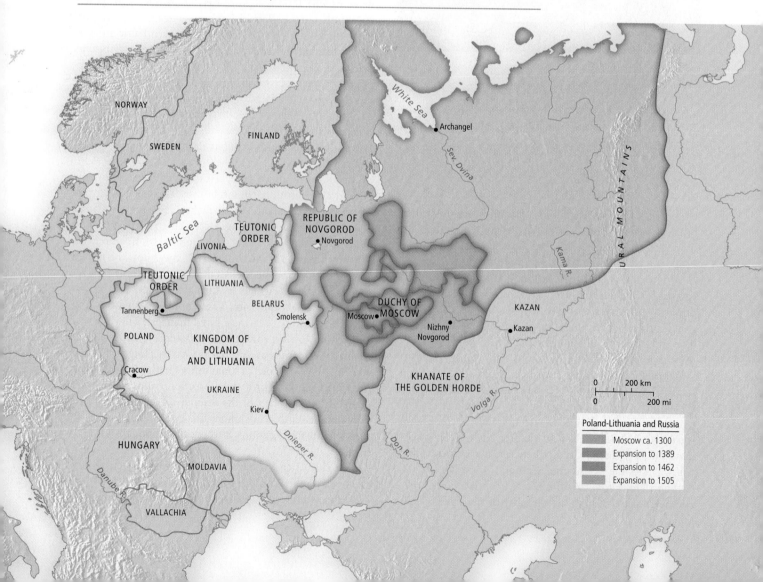

Poland-Lithuania and Russia
Moscow ca. 1300
Expansion to 1389
Expansion to 1462
Expansion to 1505

Between 1565 and 1586, forty-four young Polish nobles studied at the Jesuit college in Rome and when they returned took up the most influential church and government offices in Poland. Jesuit colleges sprouted up in many Polish towns, attracting the brightest sons of the nobility and urban bourgeoisie. A close alliance between the kings of Poland and the Jesuits enhanced the social prestige of Catholicism.

The cultural appeal of all things Italian helped lure the Polish nobility back to Catholicism. Through the spread of elite education, Catholicism returned to Poland largely through persuasion rather than coercion. But the transformation did not occur without violent repercussions. Lutheran, Calvinist, and Bohemian Brethren churches were burned. In Cracow armed confrontations between Protestant and Catholic militants led to casualties. However, Poland did not degenerate into civil war, as did France or the Netherlands over much the same issues. As the monarchy progressively weakened, the Catholic Church became the only solid institutional pillar of Polish national identity and Polish culture.

The Troubled Legacy of Ivan the Terrible

While Poland experimented with a decentralized confederation dominated by nobles that severely restricted the king's initiative, Russia evolved in the opposite direction. During the late fifteenth and sixteenth centuries, the grand dukes of Moscow who became the tsars of Russia eclipsed the authority of the great landed nobles and snuffed out the independence of the towns. The authoritarian tendencies of the tsars harmed the Russian peasants, however, just as royal weakness harmed the Polish peasants. After 1454 Moscow's creation of military fiefs (*pomestye*) to supply soldiers against the Tartars (Mongol tribes) allowed the nobles to push the peasants back into serfdom. Refusing to accept enserfment, the peasants fled the fields in massive numbers, depopulating central Russia as they found refuge among the Cossack colonies along the borders to the southeast.

Russia was already well integrated into the European diplomatic community and engaged in trade with its western neighbors. But for more than 300 years Russia had been under the "Tartar Yoke," a term describing the Mongolian tribes that overran the country, pillaging and depopulating it. Ivan III, "The Great" (1462–1505), succeeded in gradually throwing off the Tartar Yoke by refusing to continue to pay tribute to the Mongols. Ivan married Zoë, the niece of the last Greek emperor of Constantinople. The marriage gave him the basis for claiming that the Russian rulers were the heirs of Byzantium and the exclusive protectors of Orthodox Christianity, the state religion of Russia. Following the Byzantine tradition of imperial pomp, Ivan practiced Byzantine court ceremonies, and his advisers developed the theory of the Three Romes. According to this theory, the authority of the ancient Roman Empire had passed first to the Byzantine Empire, which God had punished with the Turkish conquest, and then to Moscow as the third and last "Rome." Ivan celebrated this theory by assuming the title of tsar (or "Caesar"). With his wife's assistance, he hired Italian architects to rebuild the grand ducal palace, the Kremlin. Ivan captured the vast northern territories of the city-state of Novgorod, expanding the Russian state north to the White Sea and east to the Urals. Ivan's invasion of parts of Lithuania embroiled Russia in a protracted conflict with Poland that lasted more than a century. Like his fellow monarchs in western Europe, Ivan began to bring the aristocrats under control by incorporating them into the bureaucracy of the state.

Ivan III's grandson, Ivan IV, "The Terrible" (1533–1584), succeeded his father at age 3 and became the object of innumerable plots, attempted coups, and power struggles among his mother, uncles, and the boyars (the upper-level nobles who dominated Russian society). The trauma of his childhood years and a painful disease of the spine made him inordinately suspicious and prone to acts of impulsive violence. When at age 17 Ivan was crowned, he reduced the power of the dukes and the boyars by forcing them to exchange their hereditary estates for lands that obligated them to serve the tsar in war. In weakening the boyars, Ivan gained considerable support among the common people and was even remembered in popular songs as the people's tsar. Nevertheless, Ivan distrusted everyone. He often arrested people on charges of treason, just for taking a trip abroad. In a cruel revenge on his enemies among the boyars, he began a reign of terror in which he personally committed horrendous atrocities. His massacre in 1570 of the inhabitants of Novgorod, whom he suspected of harboring Polish sympathies, contributed to his reputation as a bloody tyrant. By setting aside half of the realm as his personal domain, he created a strong financial base for the army, which led to military successes in the prolonged wars against Poland-Lithuania and Sweden. During his reign, however, the Polish threat and boyar

CHRONOLOGY	
States and Confessions in Eastern Europe	
1480	Grand Duke and later Tsar Ivan III, "The Great," of Russia refuses to pay tribute to Tartars
1569	Constitutional Union of Poland and Lithuania
1604–1613	Time of Troubles in Russia
1613	Michael Romanov elected Tsar of Russia

The Kremlin

The Kremlin was the seat of government for the Russian tsars until 1712. Originally built in 1156, the present enclosure of the Kremlin dates from the sixteenth century and reflects the influence of Italian architects brought to Moscow as well as traditional Byzantine styles.

opposition to his rule revealed signs of the fragility of Russian unity.

During the "Time of Troubles°" (1604–1613), Russia fell into chaos. Boyar families struggled among themselves for supremacy, the Cossacks from the south led a popular revolt, and Poles and Swedes openly interfered in Russian affairs. Finally, the Time of Troubles ended when in 1613 the national assembly elected Tsar Michael Romanov, whose descendants ruled Russia until they were deposed in 1917. During the seventeenth century the Romanovs gradually restored order to Russia, eroded the independence of local governments, and strengthened the institution of serfdom. By the end of the seventeenth century Russia was strong enough to reenter European affairs as a major power.

Conclusion

The Divisions of the West

During the late sixteenth and early seventeenth centuries, hidden demographic and economic pressures eroded the confidence and security of many Europeans, creating a widespread sense of unease. Most people retreated like confused soldiers behind the barricades of a rigid confessional faith, which provided reassurance that was unavailable elsewhere. To compensate for the absence of predictability in daily life, societies everywhere imposed strict discipline—discipline of women, children, the poor, criminals, and alleged witches. The frenzy for social discipline displaced the fear of those things that could

not be controlled onto the most easily controllable people, especially the weak, the subordinate, and those perceived to be different in some way.

The union between religion and political authority in the confessional states bolstered official religious faith with the threat of legal or military coercion. Where different religious confessions persisted within one state—most notably France and the Netherlands—the result was riots, assassinations, and civil war. The West had become divided along religious lines in two ways. The first kind of division was within countries with religiously mixed populations, where distinctive religious communities competed for political power and influence. In these countries religion became the cornerstone to justify patriotism or rebellion, loyalty or disloyalty to the monarch. The second kind of division was international. The confessional states formed alliances, crafted foreign policies, and went to war, with religion determining friend and foe. The West split into religiously driven camps. Over the subsequent centuries, religious differences mutated into ideological differences, but the sense that alliances among states should be linked together by a common set of beliefs has persisted to this day as a legacy from the sixteenth century.

During the period of the middle seventeenth to eighteenth centuries, confessional identity and the fear of religious turmoil led monarchs throughout Europe to build absolutist regimes, which attempted to enforce stability through a strengthened, centralized state. The principles of religious toleration and the separation of church and state were still far in the future. They were made possible only as a consequence of the hard lessons learned from the historical turmoil of the late sixteenth and seventeenth centuries.

Suggestions for Further Reading

For a comprehensive listing of suggested readings, please go to www.ablongman.com/levack2e/chapter14

Anderson, M. S. *The Origins of the Modern European State System, 1494–1618.* 1998. The best short study for students new to the subject of the evolution of the confessional states in Europe. This book is very good at establishing common patterns among the various states.

Burke, Peter. *Popular Culture in Early Modern Europe.* 1994. This wide-ranging book includes considerable material from eastern Europe and Scandinavia, as well as the more extensively studied western European countries. Extraordinarily influential, it practically invented the subject of popular culture by showing how much could be learned from studying festivals and games.

Davies, Norman. *God's Playground: A History of Poland.* Rev. ed., 2 vols. 1982. By far the most comprehensive study of Polish history, this is particularly strong for the sixteenth and seventeenth centuries. Davies offers a Polish-centered view of European history that is marvelously stimulating even if he sometimes overstates his case for the importance of Poland.

Dukes, Paul. *A History of Russia: Medieval, Modern, Contemporary, ca. 882–1996.* 3rd ed. 1998. A comprehensive survey that synthesizes the most recent research.

Dunn, Richard S. *The Age of Religious Wars, 1559–1715.* 2nd ed. 1980. An excellent survey for students new to the subject.

Evans, R. J. W. *Rudolf II and His World: A Study in Intellectual History, 1576–1612.* 1973. A sympathetic examination of the intellectual world Rudolf created. Evans recognizes Rudolf's mental problems but lessens their significance for understanding the period.

Holt, Mack P. *The French Wars of Religion, 1562–1629.* 1996. A lucid short synthesis of the events and complex issues raised by these wars.

Hsia, R. Po-chia. *Social Discipline in the Reformation: Central Europe, 1550–1750.* 1989. An excellent, lucid, and short overview of the attempts to discipline the people in Germany.

Huppert, George. *After the Black Death: A Social History of Early Modern Europe.* 1986. Engaging, entertaining, and elegantly written, this is the best single study of European social life during the Early Modern period.

Levack, Brian P. *The Witch-Hunt in Early Modern Europe.* 2nd ed. 1995. The best and most up-to-date short examination of the complex problem of the witch-hunt. This is the place to begin for students new to the subject.

Ozment, Steven E. *Ancestors: The Loving Family in Old Europe.* 2001. This comprehensive study of family life demonstrates that families were actually far more loving than the theory of patriarchy would suggest.

Parker, Geoffrey. *The Dutch Revolt.* Rev. ed. 1990. The classic study of the revolt by one of the most masterful historians of the period. This study is especially adept at pointing to the larger European context of the revolt.

Parker, Geoffrey. *The Grand Strategy of Philip II.* 1998. Rehabilitates Philip as a significant strategic thinker.

Wiesner, Merry E. *Women and Gender in Early Modern Europe.* 1993. The best short study of the subject. This is the best book for students new to the subject.

Notes

1. Quoted in R. Po-Chia Hsia, *Social Discipline in the Reformation: Central Europe, 1550–1750* (1989), 147–148.

2. Quoted in Norbert Elias, *The Civilizing Process,* Vol. 1: *The History of Manners,* trans. Edmund Jephcott (1978), 119.

3. Quoted in R. J. Knecht, *The French Wars of Religion, 1559–1598,* 2nd ed. (1996), 13.

4. Quoted in John Neale, "The Massacre of St. Bartholomew," reprinted in Orest Ranum, ed., *Searching for Modern Times,* Vol. 1, *1500–1650* (1969), 176.

5. François Rabelais, *The Histories of Gargantua and Pantagruel,* trans. J. M. Cohen (1955), 159.

6. Michel de Montaigne, *Essays and Selected Writings,* trans. and ed. Donald M. Frame (1963), 219–221.

7. Luís Vaz de Camões, *The Lusiads,* trans. William C. Atkinson (1952), 42.

8. Quoted in "Elizabeth I," *Encyclopedia Britannica* 8 (1959), 364b.

9. Quoted in Norman Davies, *Europe: A History* (1996), 529.

Absolutism and State Building, 1618–1715

IN 1651 THOMAS HOBBES, AN ENGLISH PHILOSOPHER LIVING IN EXILE IN France, was convinced that the West had descended into chaos. As he looked around him, Hobbes saw nothing but political instability, rebellion, and civil war. The turmoil had begun in the late sixteenth century, when the Reformation sparked the religious warfare described in the last chapter. In 1618 the situation deteriorated when another cycle of internal political strife and warfare erupted. The Thirty Years' War (1618–1648) began as a religious and political dispute in Germany but soon became an international conflict involving the armies of Spain, France, Sweden, and England as well as those of many German states. The war wreaked economic and social havoc in Germany, decimated its population, and forced governments throughout Europe to raise large armies and tax their subjects to pay for them. The entire European economy suffered as a result.

During the 1640s, partly as a result of that devastating conflict, the political order of Europe virtually collapsed. In England a series of bloody civil wars led to the destruction of the monarchy and the establishment of a republic. In France a civil war over constitutional issues drove the royal family from Paris. In Spain the king faced rebellions in no fewer than four of his territories, while in many European kingdoms peasants had risen in protest against the taxes their governments were collecting. Europe was in the midst of a profound and multifaceted crisis.

Hobbes, a man plagued by anxiety even since he was a child, proposed a solution to this crisis. In 1651 he published a book, *Leviathan,* about the origin and exercise of political power. He began by observing that people had a natural tendency to quarrel among themselves and seek power over each other. If left to their own devices in a hypothetical state of nature, in which government did not exist, they would find themselves in constant conflict. In these circumstances, which Hobbes referred to as a state of war, people would be unable to engage in trade or agriculture or pursue cultural

Louis XIV Portrait of Louis XIV in military armor, with his plumed helmet and his crown on the table to the right. The portrait was painted during the period of French warfare. In the background is a French ship.

interests. Life would soon become, in Hobbes's famous words, "solitary, poor nasty, brutish, and short."[1] The only way for people to find peace in this dangerous and unproductive world would be to agree with their neighbors to form a political society, or a state, by surrendering their independent power to a ruler who would make laws, administer justice, and maintain order. In this state the ruler would wield great power, and he would not share it with others. His subjects, having agreed to endow him with such extensive power, and having agreed to submit to his rule, could not resist or depose him.

Hobbes wrote *Leviathan* not simply as an abstract study of political philosophy but as a solution to the problems that plagued the West in the middle of the seventeenth century. He was suggesting that the best way to achieve peace and security was for people to submit themselves to the authority of a single ruler. The term used to designate this type of government is absolutism°. In the most general terms, absolutism means a political arrangement in which one ruler possesses complete and unrivaled power.

The political history of the West during the seventeenth and early eighteenth centuries can be written largely in terms of the efforts made by European monarchs to introduce absolutism. Those efforts were accompanied by policies intended to make the states they ruled wealthier and more powerful. Attempts to introduce absolutism and to strengthen the state took place in almost every country in Europe. In all these countries a succession of encounters took place between rulers who were trying to enlarge the power of the state and those who resisted their efforts. The outcome of these encounters varied from country to country, but for the most part the advocates of state building and absolutism prevailed. By the end of the seventeenth century the West comprised a number of large states, governed by rulers who had achieved unrivaled power and who commanded large, well-equipped armies. The West had entered the age of absolutism, which lasted until the outbreak of the French Revolution in 1789.

Not only did the West acquire a clear political identity during the seventeenth century, but its geographical boundaries also began to shift. Russia, which Europeans thought of as part of the East, began a program of imitating Western governments and became a major player in European diplomacy and warfare. At the same time Russia's southern neighbor, the Ottoman Empire, which had long straddled the boundary between East and West, was increasingly viewed by Europeans as part of a remote, Asian world.

The overarching question that this chapter addresses is: How did Western rulers strengthen the administrative and military capacities of the states they governed during this

The Frontispiece of Thomas Hobbes's Treatise *Leviathan,* **Published in London in 1651**
The ruler is depicted as incorporating the bodies of all his subjects, as they collectively authorized him to govern.

period? The individual sections of the chapter will answer the following questions:

- **What did absolutism mean, both as a political theory and as a practical program, and how was absolutism related to the growth of the power of the state?**
- **How did the encounters that took place in France and Spain during the seventeenth century result in the establishment of absolutism, and how powerful did those two states become in the seventeenth century?**
- **What was the nature of royal absolutism in central and eastern Europe, and how did the policies of the Ottoman Empire and Russia help establish the boundaries of the West during this period?**
- **Why did absolutism fail to take root in England and the Dutch Republic during the seventeenth century?**

The Nature of Absolutism

■ What did absolutism mean, both as a political theory and as a practical program, and how was absolutism related to the growth of the power of the state?

Seventeenth-century absolutism had both a theoretical and a practical dimension. Theoretical absolutists included writers like Hobbes who described the nature of power in the state and explained the conditions for its acquisition and continuation. Practical absolutists were the rulers who took concrete political steps to subordinate all other political authorities within the state to themselves. Efforts to introduce royal absolutism in Europe began in the late sixteenth and early seventeenth centuries, but only in the late seventeenth century, after the Thirty Years' War and the political turmoil of the 1640s, did many European rulers consolidate their political positions and actually achieve absolute power.

The word *absolutism* usually conjures up images of despotic kings terrorizing every segment of the population, ruling by whim and caprice, and executing their subjects at will. Nothing could be further from the truth. Absolute monarchs succeeded in establishing themselves as the highest political authorities within their kingdoms, but they never attained unlimited power. Nor could they exercise power in a completely arbitrary manner. Theoretical absolutists never sanctioned this type of arbitrary rule, and the laws of European states never permitted it. Even if European monarchs had wished to act in this way, they usually could not because they did not have the political or judicial resources to impose their will on the people. The exercise of royal power in the seventeenth century, even when it was considered absolute, depended on the tacit consent of noblemen, office holders, and the members of local political assemblies. Kings usually could not afford to risk losing the support of these prominent men by acting illegally or arbitrarily, and when they did, they found themselves faced with rebellion.

The Theory of Absolutism

When seventeenth-century political writers referred to the monarch as having absolute power, they usually meant that he possessed the highest legislative power in his kingdom. In particular, they meant that he did not share the power to make law with representative assemblies such as the English Parliament. The French magistrate Jean Bodin (1530?–1596), who was one of the earliest proponents of absolutist theory, argued in *Six Books of a Commonweal* (1576) that absolute power consisted of several attributes, the most important of which was the power to make law. In similar fashion Hobbes referred to the absolute ruler as "sole legislator." Absolute monarchs, therefore, were rulers who could make law by themselves.

In order to bolster their authority, absolute monarchs frequently asserted that they received their power directly from God and therefore ruled by divine right. This idea was hardly new in the seventeenth century. The Bible proclaimed that all political authorities were "of God" and that people must therefore be obedient to them. In the fourteenth century European monarchs asserted that because God had given them the right to rule, the pope could not depose them. In the sixteenth century the idea of divine right was used to discourage rebellion, for to resist the king was to attack God's representative on Earth. In the seventeenth century many theorists of absolutism—although not Hobbes—used the idea of divine right to insist that kings were accountable only to God, rather than to their subjects.

Absolute rulers often claimed that they were above the law. This meant that when monarchs acted for reason of state, that is, for the benefit of the entire kingdom, they were not strictly bound by the law of their kingdoms. Being above the law also meant that they could not be held legally accountable for their actions, as they were the highest judges in the land. Being above the law did not mean kings or queens could act arbitrarily, illegally, or despotically, even though some of them did so from time to time. Absolute rulers, no less than those who shared power with representative assemblies, were always expected to observe the individual rights and liberties of their subjects as well as the moral law established by God. They were expected, for example, to try people in a court of law rather than execute them at will. The French preacher Jacques Bossuet (1627–1704), who wrote an absolutist treatise on the authority of kings in 1670, insisted that even though kings were not subject to the penalties of the law, they still were not freed from the obligation to observe that law. No less than their subjects, kings were subject to the "equity of the laws." This meant that they should not rule despotically or arbitrarily.

Theorists of absolutism distinguished between European monarchs and rulers in other parts of the world, such as Turkish sultans, Russian tsars, and the kings of Asian and African lands. In those so-called Eastern countries, according to Bodin, "the prince has become the lord of the goods and the persons of his subjects," by which Bodin meant that the rulers of those lands could seize the possessions of their subjects or execute them without due process of law.[2] Only in the West, wrote Bodin, did royal subjects live under a regime that abided by the rule of law. Bodin exaggerated the powers of both Turkish sultans and Russian tsars, who had much in common with the absolute rulers of western and central Europe. But by emphasizing the rule of law and the king's obligation to abide by it, Bodin identified one of the distinctive features of Western politics during the age of absolutism.

The Practice of Absolutism

What steps did the European monarchs who claimed absolute power take to establish and maintain themselves as the supreme authorities within the state? The first strategy they employed was the elimination or the weakening of national representative assemblies, such as Parliament in England, Diets in German states, and the Cortes in Spain and Portugal. In France, which is considered to have been the most absolutist state in seventeenth-century Europe, the monarchy stopped summoning its national assembly, the Estates General, in 1614. This assembly did not meet again until the late eighteenth century.

The second strategy of absolutist rulers was to subordinate the nobility to the king and make them dependent on his favor. The political and social power of the nobility often led them to participate in rebellions and conspiracies against the king. Monarchs who aspired to a position of unrivaled power in their kingdoms therefore took steps to keep the nobility in line, not only by suppressing challenges to their authority but also by appointing men from different social groups as their chief ministers, At the same time, however, the king could not afford to alienate these wealthy and high-ranking men, upon whom he still relied for running his government and maintaining order in the localities. Absolute monarchs, therefore, offered nobles special privileges, such as exemption from taxation, positions in the king's household, and freedom to exploit their peasants in exchange for their recognition of the king's superiority and their assistance in maintaining order in the localities. In this way nobles became junior partners in the management of the absolutist state.

The final strategy of absolute monarchs was to gain effective control of the administrative machinery of the state and to use it to enforce royal policy throughout their kingdoms. Absolute monarchs were by nature state builders. They established centralized bureaucracies that extended the reach of their governments down into the smallest towns and villages and out into the most remote regions of their kingdoms. The business conducted by these centrally controlled bureaucracies included collection of taxes, recruitment of soldiers, and operation of the judicial system. Some absolute monarchs used the central machinery of the state to impose and maintain religious conformity. As the seventeenth century advanced, they also used the same machinery to regulate the price of grain, stimulate the growth of industry, and relieve the plight of the poor. In these ways the policies pursued by absolute monarchs had an impact on the lives of all royal subjects, not just noblemen and royal councilors.

Warfare and the Absolutist State

Much of the growth of European states in the seventeenth century can be related in one way or another to the conduct of war. During the period from 1600 to 1721, European powers were almost constantly at war. The entire continent was at peace for only four of those years. To meet the demands of war, rulers kept men under arms at all times. By the middle of the seventeenth century, after the Thirty Years' War had come to an end, most European rulers had acquired such standing armies. These armies not only served their rulers in foreign wars but also helped them maintain order and enforce royal policy at home. Standing armies thus became one of the main props of royal absolutism.

During the seventeenth and early eighteenth centuries European armies became larger, in many cases tripling in size. In the 1590s Philip II of Spain had mastered Europe with an army of 40,000 men. By contrast, in the late seventeenth century Louis XIV of France needed an army of 400,000 men to become the dominant power on the continent. The increase in the size of these forces can be traced to the invention of gunpowder and its more frequent use in the fifteenth and sixteenth centuries. Gunpowder led to the widespread use of the musket, a heavy shoulder firearm carried by a foot soldier. The use of the musket placed a premium on the recruitment and equipment of large armies of infantry, who marched in square columns with men holding long pikes (long wooden shafts with pointed metal heads) to protect the musketeers from enemy attacks. As the size of these armies of foot soldiers grew, the role of mounted soldiers, who had dominated medieval warfare, was greatly reduced.

Changes in military technology and tactics also necessitated more intensive military training. In the Middle Ages mounted knights had acquired great individual skill, but they did not need to work in precise unison with other men under arms. Seventeenth-century foot soldiers, however, had to learn to march in formation, to coordinate their maneuvers, and to fire without harming their comrades in arms. Therefore they needed to be drilled. The introduction of volley fire, by which each successive line of soldiers stepped forward to fire while the others were reloading, placed an even greater premium on precise drilling. Drilling took place in peacetime as well as during war. The wearing of uniforms, which began when the state assumed the function of clothing its thousands of soldiers, gave further unity and cohesion to the trained fighting force.

The cost of recruiting, training, and equipping these mammoth armies was staggering. In the Middle Ages individual lords often had sufficient financial resources to assemble their own private armies. By the beginning of the seventeenth century the only institution capable of putting the new armies in the field was the state itself. The same was true for navies, which now consisted of heavily armed sailing ships, each of which carried as many as 400 sailors. To build these large armies and navies, as well as to pay the increasing cost of waging war itself (which rose 500 percent between 1530 and 1630), the state had to identify new methods of raising and collecting taxes. In times of war as much as 80 percent of the revenue taken in by the state went for military purposes.

The equipment and training of military forces and the collection and allocation of the revenue necessary to subsidize these efforts stimulated the expansion and refinement of the state bureaucracy. Governments found it necessary to employ thousands of new officials to supervise the collection of new taxes, and in order to make the system of tax collection more efficient, governments often introduced entirely new administrative systems. Some states completely reorganized their bureaucracies to meet the demands of war. New departments of state were created to supervise the recruitment of soldiers, the manufacture of equipment and uniforms, the building of fleets, and the provisioning of troops in time of war. Rulers of European states recognized that the exercise of absolute power greatly facilitated the utilization of state power for these purposes.

The Absolutist State in France and Spain

- How did the encounters that took place in France and Spain during the seventeenth century result in the establishment of absolutism, and how powerful did those two states become in the seventeenth century?

The two European countries in which royal absolutism first became a political reality were France and Spain. The histories of these two monarchies in the seventeenth century followed very different courses. The kingdom of France, especially during the reign of Louis XIV (r. 1643–1715), became a model of state building and gradually emerged as the most powerful country in Europe. The Spanish monarchy, on the other hand, struggled to introduce absolutism at a time when the overall economic condition of the country was deteriorating and its military forces were suffering a series of defeats. Spain established the forms of absolutist rule, but the monarchy was not able to match the political or military achievements of France in the late seventeenth century.

The Foundations of French Absolutism

Efforts to make the French monarchy absolute began in response to the disorder that occurred during the wars of religion in the late sixteenth century. Bodin wrote his treatises during those wars, and the threat of renewed civil war between Protestants and Catholics affected French politics throughout the seventeenth century. The first steps toward the achievement of absolutism were taken during the reign of Henry IV (r. 1589–1610), the Huguenot who converted to Catholicism in 1594 and who ended the wars of religion by granting freedom of worship and full civil rights to

French Protestants by the Edict of Nantes (1598). This decree brought internal religious peace to the kingdom, while the progressive financial and economic policies of Henry's brilliant minister, the Duke of Sully, helped restore the financial strength of the crown and involve the government in a process of commercial recovery and expansion. Despite this success, Henry could not prevent the great nobles from conspiring against him, and his policy of religious toleration encountered resistance from Catholics committed to the suppression of Protestantism. In 1610 a fanatical Catholic, François Ravaillac, stabbed the king to death in his carriage on a Parisian street.

On Henry's death the crown passed to his young son, Louis XIII (r. 1610–1643), while the queen mother, Marie de' Medici, assumed the leadership of a government acting in the king's name during his youth. This period of regency, in which aristocratic factions vied for supremacy at court, exposed the main weakness of the monarchy, which was the rival power of the great noble families of the realm. The statesman who addressed this problem most directly was Louis's main councilor, Cardinal Armand Jean du Plessis de Richelieu (1585–1642). A member of an old and wealthy family, Richelieu rose to power through the patronage of the queen mother and then, after losing her support, maintained his preeminent position with the support of the king himself. He became the king's chief minister in 1628. Richelieu was arguably the greatest state builder of the seventeenth century. He directed all his energies toward centralizing the power of the French state in the person of the king.

Richelieu's most immediate concern was bringing the independent nobility to heel and subordinating their local power to that of the state. This he accomplished by suppressing several conspiracies and rebellions led by noblemen and by restricting the independent power of the provincial assemblies and the eight regional parlements°, which were the highest courts in the country. His great administrative achievement was the strengthening of the system of the intendants°. These paid crown officials, who were recruited from the professional classes and the lower ranks of the nobility, became the main agents of French local administration. Responsible only to the royal council, they collected taxes, supervised local administration, and recruited soldiers for the army. Because they could not come from the districts to which they were assigned, they had no vested interest in maintaining local customs or privileges.

Richelieu also modified the religious policy embodied in the Edict of Nantes. According to that document, Huguenots not only had freedom of worship but could also fortify the towns in which they lived. Richelieu resented the maintenance of these citadels of local power, which represented a challenge to the type of absolutist state he envisioned. He also suspected that rivals of the king from the nobility were using the Huguenot towns as a means of maintaining their independent power. A series of military confrontations between the government and the

Cardinal Richelieu

Triple portrait of Cardinal Richelieu, who laid the foundations of French absolutism.

Protestants in the late 1610s and 1620s brought the country to the brink of civil war. Following the successful siege of the town of La Rochelle in 1627–1628, the government razed the fortifications of the Huguenot cities, melted down their cannons, and disarmed their Protestant citizens. A peace treaty signed in 1629 ratified the government's victory, but it did not deny the Huguenots their right to worship freely.

CHRONOLOGY

France in the Age of Absolutism

1598	The Edict of Nantes grants toleration to French Calvinists, known as Huguenots
1610	Assassination of Henry IV of France, who was succeeded by Louis XIII (r. 1610–1643)
1628	Cardinal Richelieu becomes chief minister of Louis XIII of France
1643	Death of Louis XIII of France and accession of Louis XIV; Louis's mother, Anne of Austria, becomes queen regent with Cardinal Mazarin as his minister
1648–1653	The Fronde
1661	Death of Cardinal Mazarin; Louis XIV assumes personal rule
1685	Revocation of the Edict of Nantes
1715	Death of Louis XIV of France; succeeded by his grandson, Louis XV

The most challenging task for Richelieu, as for all French ministers in the early modern period, was increasing the government's yield from taxation, a task that became more demanding during times of war. Levying taxes on the French population was always a delicate process, as the needs of the state conflicted with the privileges of various social groups, such as the nobles, who were exempt from taxation, and the estates of individual provinces such as Brittany that claimed the right to tax the people themselves. Using a variety of tactics, including negotiation and compromise, and relying heavily on the support of the provincial intendants, Richelieu managed to increase the yield from the *taille*, the direct tax on land, as much as threefold during the period 1635–1648. He supplemented the taille with taxes on office holding. Even then, the revenue was insufficient to meet the extraordinary demands of war.

Opposition to Richelieu's financial policies lay at the root of the main problem the government faced after the cardinal's death in 1642. The minister who succeeded him was his protégé Jules Mazarin (1602–1661), a diplomat of Italian birth who had entered French government service during Richelieu's administration. Mazarin dominated the government of Louis XIV when the king, who inherited the throne at age 5, was still a boy and while his mother was serving as regent. Mazarin continued the policies of his predecessor, but he was unable to prevent civil war from breaking out in 1648. This challenge to the French state, known as the *Fronde* (a pejorative reference to a Parisian game in which children flung mud at passing carriages), had two phases. The first, the Fronde of the Parlement (1648–1649), began when the members of the Parlement of Paris, the most important of all the provincial parlements, refused to register an edict of the king that had required them to surrender four years' salary. This act of resistance led to demands that the king sign a document limiting royal authority. Barricades went up in the streets of Paris, and the royal family was forced to flee the city. A blockade of the city by royal troops led to an uneasy compromise in 1649. Revolts in three other parlements, each of which had its own dynamic and which were not coordinated with that of Paris, came to a similar resolution. The second and more violent phase was the Fronde of the Princes (1650–1653), during which the Prince de Condé and his noble allies waged war on the government and even formed an alliance with

France's enemy, Spain. Only after Condé's military defeat did the entire rebellion collapse.

The Fronde stands as the great crisis of the seventeenth-century French state. It revealed the strength of the local, aristocratic, and legal forces with which the king and his ministers had to contend. These forces managed to disrupt the growth of the French state, drive the king from his capital, and challenge his authority throughout the kingdom. But in the long run they could not destroy the achievement of Richelieu and Mazarin. By the late 1650s the damage had been repaired and the state had resumed its growth.

Absolutism in the Reign of Louis XIV

The man who presided over the development of the French state for the next fifty years was the king himself, Louis XIV, who assumed direct control of his government after the death of Mazarin in 1661. In an age of absolute monarchs, Louis towered among his contemporaries. He is widely regarded as the most powerful king of the seventeenth century. This reputation comes as much from the image he conveyed as from the policies he pursued. Artists, architects, dramatists, and members of his immediate entourage helped the king project an image of incomparable majesty and authority. Paintings and sculptures of the king depicted him in sartorial splendor, holding the symbols of power and displaying expressions of regal superiority that bordered on arrogance. At Versailles, about ten miles from Paris, Louis constructed a lavishly furnished palace that be-

came his main residence and the center of the glittering court that surrounded him. The palace was built in the baroque° style, which emphasized the size and grandeur of the structure while also conveying a sense of unity and balance among its diverse parts. The sweeping façades of baroque buildings gave them a dynamic quality that evoked an emotional response from the viewer. The baroque style, criticized by contemporaries for its exuberance and pomposity, appealed to absolute monarchs who wished to emphasize their unrivaled position within society and their determination to impose order and stability on their kingdoms.

Court life at Versailles revolved entirely around the king. Court dramas depicted Louis, who styled himself "the sun king," as Apollo, the god of light. The paintings in the grand Hall of Mirrors at Versailles, which recorded the king's military victories, served as reminders of his unrivaled accomplishments. Louis's formal routine in receiving visitors created appropriate distance between him and his courtiers while keeping his subjects in a state of subservient anticipation of royal favor. His frequent bursts of anger achieved the same effect. When an untitled lady took the seat of a noblewoman at a dinner in his presence, he described the act as one of "incredible insolence" that "had thrown him into such a rage that he had been unable to eat." After rebuking the offending lady for her "impertinence," he became so angry that he left the room.[3]

The image of magnificence and power that Louis conveyed in art and ceremony mirrored and reinforced his more tangible political accomplishments. His greatest

Versailles Palace, Center of the Court of Louis XIV After 1682
The palace was constructed between 1669 and 1686. Its massiveness and grandeur and the order it imposed on the landscape made it a symbol of royal absolutism.

achievement was to solve the persistent problem of aristocratic independence and rebellion by securing the complete loyalty and dependence of the old nobility. This he achieved first by requiring the members of these ancient families to come to Versailles for a portion of every year, where they stayed in apartments within the royal palace itself. At Versailles Louis involved them in the elaborate cultural activities of court life and in ceremonial rituals that emphasized their subservience to the king. At the same time, he excluded the nobles from holding important offices in the government of the realm, a strategy designed to prevent them from building an independent power base within the bureaucracy. Instead he recruited men from the mercantile and professional classes to run his government. This policy of taming the nobility and depriving them of central administrative power could work only if they received something in return. Like all the absolute monarchs of western Europe, Louis used the patronage at his disposal to grant members of the nobility wealth and privileges in exchange for their loyalty to the crown. In this way the monarchy and the nobility served each other's interests.

In running the actual machinery of government Louis built upon and perfected the centralizing policies of Richelieu and Mazarin. After the death of Mazarin in 1661

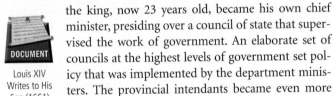

DOCUMENT

Louis XIV Writes to His Son (1661)

the king, now 23 years old, became his own chief minister, presiding over a council of state that supervised the work of government. An elaborate set of councils at the highest levels of government set policy that was implemented by the department ministers. The provincial intendants became even more important than they had been under Richelieu and Mazarin, especially in providing food, arms, and equipment for royal troops. It was the intendants' job to secure the cooperation of the local judges, city councils, and parish priests as well as the compliance of the local population. If necessary they could call upon royal troops in order to enforce their will, but for the most part they preferred to rely on the more effective tactics of negotiation and compromise with local officials. The system, when it worked properly, allowed the king to make decisions that directly affected the lives and beliefs of his 20 million subjects.

A further manifestation of the newfound power of the French state in the late seventeenth century was the government's active involvement in the economic and financial life of the country. The minister who was most responsible for this series of undertakings was Jean Baptiste Colbert (1619–1683), a protégé of Mazarin who in 1661 became controller general of the realm. Born into a family of merchants, and despised by the old nobility, Colbert epitomized the type of government official Louis recruited into his service. Entrusted with the supervision of the entire system of royal taxation, Colbert managed to increase royal revenues dramatically simply by reducing the cut taken by the agents whom the government hired to collect taxes.

Even more beneficial to the French state was the determination of Colbert to use the country's economic resources for its benefit. The theory underlying this set of policies was mercantilism°, which held that the wealth of the state depended on its ability to import fewer commodities than it exported. Its goal was to secure the largest possible share of the world's monetary supply. In keeping with those objectives, Colbert increased the size of France's merchant fleet, founded overseas trading companies, and levied high tariffs on France's commercial rivals. To make France economically self-sufficient he encouraged the growth of the French textile industry, improved the condition of the roads, built canals throughout the kingdom, and reduced some of the burdensome tolls that impeded internal trade.

The most intrusive exercise of the power of the state during Louis XIV's reign was the decision to enforce religious uniformity. The king always considered the existence of a large Huguenot minority within his kingdom an affront to his sense of order. Toleration was divisive and dangerous, especially to someone who styled himself as "Most Christian King." Even after Richelieu had leveled the walls of the fortified Huguenot towns, the problem of religious pluralism remained. In 1685 Louis addressed this problem by revoking the entire Edict of Nantes, thereby denying freedom of religious worship to about one million of his subjects. The enforcement of this policy was violent and disruptive, with the army being called upon to enforce public conversions to Catholicism. Protestant churches were closed and often destroyed, while large numbers of Huguenots were forced to emigrate to the Netherlands, England, and Protestant German lands. Few exercises of absolute power in the seventeenth century caused more disruption in the lives of ordinary people than this attempt to realize the king's ideal of "one king, one law, one faith."

Louis XIV and the Culture of Absolutism

A further manifestation of the power of the French absolutist state was Louis's success in influencing and transforming French culture. Kings had often served as patrons of the arts by providing income for artists, writers, and musicians while endowing cultural and educational institutions. Louis took this type of royal patronage to a new level, making it possible for him to control the dissemination of ideas and the very production of culture itself. During Louis's reign royal patronage, emanating from the court, extended the king's influence over the entire cultural landscape. The architects of the palace at Versailles, the painters of historical scenes that hung in its hallways and galleries, the composers of the plays and operas that were performed in its theaters, the sculptors who created busts of the king to decorate its chambers, and the historians and pamphlet

DOCUMENT

Revocation of the Edict of Nantes, October 25, 1685

In 1685 King Louis XIV of France revoked the Edict of Nantes, the decree of King Henry IV that had granted freedom of worship to French Protestants in 1598. Before the revocation was published, the government sent dragoons (cavalry who arrived on horseback but fought on foot) to terrorize Protestant households and make them convert to Catholicism. The terms of the revocation were particularly harsh, and despite the prohibition against leaving the country, hundreds of thousands of Huguenots emigrated to England, the Dutch Republic, and North America.

. . . Therefore we decided that there was nothing better we could do to erase from memory the troubles, the confusion, and the evils that the growth of this false religion had caused in our kingdom and that gave rise to the said Edict and to so many other edicts and declarations that preceded it . . . than to revoke entirely the said Edict of Nantes and the detailed articles attached to it and everything that has been done since on behalf of the said Supposedly Reformed Religion [Calvinism].

1. We therefore for these reasons and in full knowledge, power, and Royal authority, by means of the present perpetual and irrevocable edict, do suppress and revoke the Edict of the king, our grandfather, issued at Nantes in April 1598. . . . As a result we desire and it is our pleasure that all the temples of the Supposedly Reformed Religion situated in our kingdom, county, lands and seigneuries within our obedience be immediately demolished. . . .

2. Our subjects of the Supposedly Reformed Religion are not to assemble for worship in any place or house for any reason.

3. Noble lords are not to hold worship services in their houses or fiefs of any sort on pain of confiscation of goods and property.

4. Ministers of the Supposedly Reformed Religion who have not converted are to leave the kingdom within fifteen days and are not to preach or perform any functions in the meantime, or they will be sent to the galleys.

5. Ministers who convert, and their widows after their death, are to enjoy the same exemptions from taxes and troop lodgings that they had as ministers. . . .

6. Converted ministers can become lawyers or doctors of law without the usual three years of study and for half the fees usually charged by the universities.

7. Special schools for the children of the Supposedly Reformed Religion are prohibited.

8. Children of [Huguenot] parents are to be baptized by the chief priests of their parishes and raised as Catholics, and local judges are to oversee this.

9. If Protestants who left the kingdom before this edict was issued return within four months, they can regain their property and resume their lives. If, however, they do not return within four months, their goods will be confiscated.

10. All subjects belonging to the Supposedly Reformed Religion and their wives and children are forbidden to leave the country or to send out their property and effects. The penalty for men is the galleys and women confiscation of their persons and property.

11. The declarations already issued concerning those who relapse are to be executed in full.

And, in addition, those who adhere to the Supposedly Reformed Religion, while waiting until it pleases God to enlighten them like the others, may continue to live in the cities and communities of our realm, continue their commerce, and enjoy their property without being bothered or hindered because of the Supposedly Reformed Religion, on condition, however, of not practicing their religion or assembling for prayers or worship or for any other pretext, with the penalties stated above.

Source: Copyright © 2000 by Bedford/St. Martin's. From *Louis XIV & Absolutism: A Brief Study with Documents* by William Beik. Reprinted with permission of Bedford/St. Martin's.

writers who celebrated the king's achievements in print all benefited from Louis's direct financial support.

Much of Louis's patronage went to cultural institutions, thereby enabling the king to influence a wider circle of artists and have a greater effect on the cultural life of the nation. He took over the Academy of Fine Arts in 1661, founded the Academy of Music in 1669, and chartered a theater company, the *Comédie Française,* in 1680. Two great French dramatists of the late seventeenth century, Jean Baptiste Molière (1622–1673), the creator of French high comedy, and Jean Racine (1639–1699), who wrote tragedies in the classical style, benefited from the king's patronage. Louis even subsidized the publication of a new journal, the *Journal des savants,* in which men of letters advanced their ideas. In 1666 Louis extended his patronage to the sciences with the founding of the *Académie des Sciences,* which had the twofold objective of advancing scientific knowledge and glorifying the king. It also benefited the state by devising improvements in ship design and navigation.

Of all the cultural institutions that benefited from Louis XIV's patronage, the *Académie Française* had the most enduring impact on French culture. This academy, a society of literary scholars, had been founded in 1635 with the support of Cardinal Richelieu. Its purpose was to standardize the French language and serve as the guardian of its integrity. In 1694, twenty-two years after Louis became the academy's patron, the first official French dictionary appeared in print. This achievement of linguistic uniformity, in which words received authorized spellings and definitions, reflected the pervasiveness of Louis's cultural influence as well as the search for order that became the defining characteristic of his reign.

Louis introduced order and uniformity into every aspect of his own life and that of his country. He followed a precise routine in ordering his daily life, created ceremonies that ordered the life of his court, and insisted on the court's adoption of table manners that followed strict rules of politeness. He created a bureaucracy that was organized along rational, orderly principles, and he sought to ensure that all his subjects would practice the same religion. The establishment of a clearly defined chain of command in the army, which Louis's minister the Marquis de Louvois introduced, gave organizational cohesion and hierarchical order to the large military force the king and his ministers assembled. Nearly all areas of French public life were transformed by the king's desire to establish order and uniformity and his use of the power of the state to enforce it.

One indication of the extent of Louis's achievement was the conspicuous attempt of other monarchs to imitate France, even in the eighteenth century. The absolute monarchs in Prussia, Austria, and Russia, as well as aspiring ones in England and Sweden, not only experimented selectively with French political methods but imported many of the features of French culture that Louis had supported. They built palaces in the same architectural style as that of Versailles, designed French gardens to surround them, imported the fashions and decorative styles of the French court, staged French ballets and operas in their capitals, and even spoke French, which had replaced Latin as the language of international diplomacy, when conducting official business. The power of the French monarchy had made French culture the dominant influence in the courts and capitals of Europe.

The Wars of Louis XIV, 1667–1714

The seventeenth-century French state was designed not only to maintain internal peace and order but also to wage war against other states. Colbert's financial and economic policies, coupled with the military reforms of the Marquis de Louvois, had laid the foundations for the creation of a

formidable military machine. In 1667 Louis XIV began unleashing its full potential. Having assembled an army that was twenty times larger than the French force that had invaded Italy in 1494, Louis deployed this armed force against an array of European powers in four separate wars between 1667 and 1714. His goal in all these wars, as it had been in all French international conflicts since 1635, was territorial acquisition (see Map 15.1). In this case Louis set his sights mainly on the German and Spanish territories in the Rhineland along the eastern borders of his kingdom. Contemporaries suggested, however, that he was thinking in grander terms than traditional French dynastic ambition. Propagandists for the king in the late 1660s claimed that Louis harbored visions of establishing a "universal monarchy" or an "absolute empire," reminiscent of the empires of ancient Rome, Charlemagne in the ninth century, and Charles V in the sixteenth century.

Louis never attained the empire of his dreams, but concerted action by almost all the other European powers was required to stop him. France's acquisition of new territories

---

Map 15.1 French Territorial Acquisitions, 1679–1714
The main acquisitions were lands in the Spanish Netherlands to the north and Franche Comté, Alsace, and Lorraine to the east. Louis thought of the Rhine River as France's natural eastern boundary, and territories acquired in 1659 and 1697 allowed it to reach that limit.

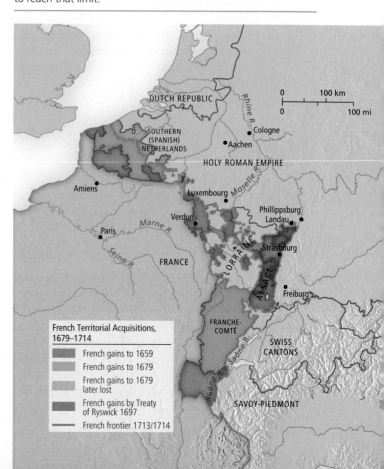

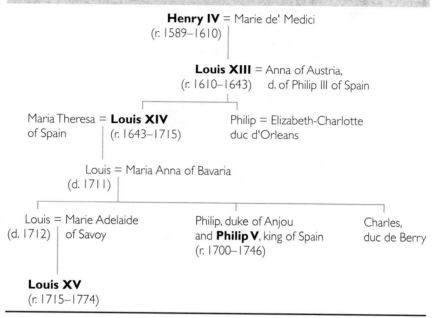

The French Bourbons and the Spanish Succession 1589–1700

Henry IV = Marie de' Medici
(r. 1589–1610)

Louis XIII = Anna of Austria,
(r. 1610–1643)   d. of Philip III of Spain

Maria Theresa = **Louis XIV**   Philip = Elizabeth-Charlotte
of Spain   (r. 1643–1715)   duc d'Orleans

Louis = Maria Anna of Bavaria
(d. 1711)

Louis = Marie Adelaide   Philip, duke of Anjou   Charles,
(d. 1712)   of Savoy   and **Philip V**, king of Spain   duc de Berry
(r. 1700–1746)

Louis XV
(r. 1715–1774)

---

along its eastern boundaries between 1668 and 1684 confirmed the fears of other European states that the king had imperial ambitions. After Louis had launched an offensive against German towns along the Rhine River in 1688, signaling the beginning of yet another round of European warfare, Great Britain, the Dutch Republic, Spain, and Austria formed a coalition against him. Finally matched by the combined military forces of these allies, forced to wage war on many different fronts (including North America), and unable to provide adequate funding of the war on the basis of its system of taxation, France felt compelled to conclude peace in 1697. The Treaty of Ryswick marked the turning point in the expansion of the French state and laid the groundwork for the establishment of a balance of power° in the next century, an arrangement whereby various countries form alliances to prevent any one state from dominating the others.

The Treaty of Ryswick, however, did not mark the end of French territorial ambition. In 1701 Louis went to war once again, this time as part of an effort to place a French Bourbon candidate, his grandson Duke Philip of Anjou, on the Spanish throne. The impending death of the mentally weak, sexually impotent, and chronically ill King Charles II of Spain (r. 1665–1700) without heirs had created a succession crisis. In 1698 the major European powers had agreed to a treaty in which Spanish lands would be divided between Louis himself and the Holy Roman Emperor, both of whom happened to be Charles's brothers-in-law. By his will, however, Charles left the Spanish crown and all its overseas possessions to Philip. This bequest offered France

more than it would have received on the basis of the treaty. If the will had been upheld, the Pyrenees mountains would have disappeared as a political barrier between France and Spain, and France, as the stronger of the two kingdoms, would have controlled unprecedented expanses of European and American territory.

Dreaming once again of universal monarchy, Louis rejected the treaty in favor of King Charles's will. The British, Dutch, and Austrians responded by forming a Grand Alliance against France and Spain. After a long and costly conflict, known as the War of the Spanish Succession (1701–1713), the members of this coalition were able to dictate the terms of the Treaty of Utrecht (1713). Philip, who suffered from fits of manic depression and went days without dressing or leaving his room, remained on the Spanish throne as Philip V (r. 1700–1746), but only on the condition that the French and Spanish crowns would never be united. Spain ceded its territories in the Netherlands and in Italy to the Austrian Habsburg Monarchy and its strategic port of Gibraltar at the entrance to the Mediterranean to the British. The treaty not only confirmed the new balance of power in Europe but also resulted in the transfer of large parts of French Canada, including Newfoundland and Nova Scotia, to Great Britain.

The loss of French territory in North America, the strains placed on the taxation system by the financial demands of war, and the weakening of France's commercial power as a result of this conflict made France a less potent state at the time of Louis's death in 1715 than it had been in the 1680s. Nevertheless the main effects of a century of

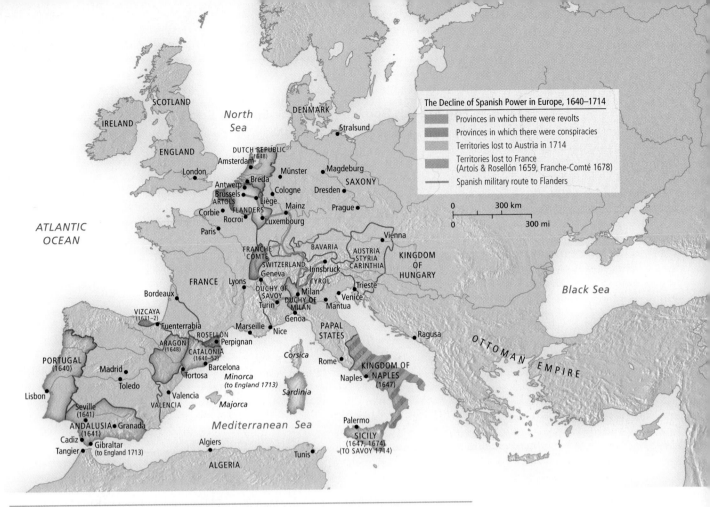

Map 15.2 The Decline of Spanish Power in Europe, 1640–1714
Revolts in the United Provinces of the Netherlands and Portugal account for two of the most significant losses of Spanish territory. Military defeat at the hands of the French in 1659 and Austria in 1714 account for the loss of most of the other territories.

French state building remained, including a large, well-integrated bureaucratic edifice that allowed the government to exercise unprecedented control over the population and a military establishment that remained the largest and best equipped in Europe.

Absolutism and State Building in Spain

The history of Spain in the seventeenth century is almost always written in terms of failure, as the country endured a long period of economic decline that began in the late sixteenth century with a precipitate drop in the size of its population and stretched well into the eighteenth century. The monarchy became progressively weaker during the seventeenth century, as it was occupied by a succession of ineffective kings who exercised far less power than their French counterparts. To make matters worse, Spain in the seventeenth century suffered a long series of military defeats, most of them at the hands of the French, and it lost the position it had held in the sixteenth century as the major

European power (see Map 15.2). By the early eighteenth century Spain was a shadow of its former self, and its culture reflected uncertainty, pessimism, and nostalgia for former imperial greatness. None of this failure, however, should obscure the fact that Spain, like France, underwent a period of state building during the seventeenth century, and that its government, like that of France, gravitated toward absolutism.

The Spanish monarchy in 1600 ruled more territory than did France, and the various kingdoms and principalities that it comprised possessed far more independence than even the most remote and peripheral French provinces. The center of the monarchy was the kingdom of Castile, with its capital at Madrid. This kingdom, the largest and wealthiest territory within the Iberian peninsula, had been united with the kingdom of Aragon in 1479 when King Ferdinand II of Aragon (r. 1479–1516), the husband of Queen Isabella of Castile (r. 1474–1504), ascended the throne. These two kingdoms, however, continued to exist as separate states after the union, each having its own representative institutions and administrative systems. Each of them, moreover, contained smaller, semiautonomous kingdoms and provinces that retained their own distinctive political institutions. The kingdom of Valencia and the principality of Catalonia formed part of the Crown of Aragon, while in the sixteenth century the kingdoms of Navarre and Portugal had been annexed to the Crown of Castile. Outside the Iberian peninsula the Spanish monarchy ruled territories in the Netherlands, Italy, and the New World.

The only institution besides the monarchy itself that provided any kind of administrative unity to all these Spanish territories in the seventeenth century was the Spanish Inquisition, a centralized ecclesiastical court with a supreme council in Madrid and twenty-one regional tribunals in different parts of Spain, Italy, and America. Its function was to enforce religious uniformity and maintain the purity of the Catholic faith.

The great challenge for the Spanish monarchy in the seventeenth century was to integrate the various kingdoms and principalities of Spain into a more highly centralized state while at the same time making the machinery of that state more efficient and profitable. The statesman who made the most sustained efforts at realizing these goals was the energetic and authoritarian Count-Duke of Olivares (1587–1645), the contemporary and counterpart of Richelieu during the reign of the Spanish king Philip IV (1621–1665). The task Olivares faced was more daunting than anything the French cardinal had ever confronted. As a result of decades of warfare, the Spanish monarchy in the 1620s was penniless, the kingdom of Castile had gone bankrupt, and the entire country had already entered a period of protracted economic decline.

To deal with these deep structural problems Olivares proposed a reform of the entire financial system, the establishment of national banks, and the replacement of the main tax, the *millones,* which was levied on the consumption of basic commodities such as meat and wine, with proportional contributions from all the towns and villages in the kingdom. At the same time he tried to address the problem of ruling a disparate and far-flung empire, making all the kingdoms and principalities within the monarchy contribute to national defense on a proportionate basis. His ultimate goal was to unify the entire peninsula in a cohesive Spanish national state, similar to that of France. This policy involved suppression of the individual liberties of the various kingdoms and principalities and direct subordination of each area to the king himself. It was, in other words, a solution based on the principles of absolutism.

Olivares was unable to match the state-building achievement of Richelieu in France. His failure, which was complete by the time he fell from office in 1643, can be attributed to three factors. The first was the opposition he confronted within Castile itself, especially from the cities represented in the Cortes, over the question of taxation. The second, a problem facing Spain throughout the seventeenth century, was military failure, in this case the losses to France during the final phase of the Thirty Years' War. That failure aggravated the financial crisis and prevented the monarchy from capitalizing on the prestige that usually attends military victory. The third and most serious impediment was opposition to the policy of subordinating the outlying Spanish regions to the kingdom of Castile. The kingdoms and provinces on the periphery of the country were determined to maintain their individual laws and liberties, especially the powers of their own Cortes, in the face of the pressures to centralize power in Madrid. The problem became more serious as Olivares, in the wake of military defeat by the French and Dutch, put more pressure on these outlying kingdoms and provinces to contribute to the war effort.

Provincial resistance to a policy of Castilian centralization lay at the root of the Spanish crisis of the seventeenth

CHRONOLOGY

International Conflict in the Seventeenth Century

1609	Truce between the seven Dutch provinces and Spain
1618	Bohemian revolt against Habsburg rule; beginning of the Thirty Years' War
1620	Imperial forces defeat Bohemians at Battle of White Mountain
1648	Treaty of Westphalia, ending the Thirty Years' War; Treaty of Münster, ending the Dutch War of Independence
1667	Beginning of the wars of Louis XIV
1672	William III of Orange-Nassau becomes captain-general of Dutch; beginning of the war against France (1672–1678)
1688–1697	War of the League of Augsburg (Nine Years' War); England and Scotland join forces with Prussia, Austria, the Dutch Republic, and many German states against France
1697	Treaty of Ryswick
1700–1721	Great Northern War in which Russia eventually defeated Sweden; emergence of Russia as a major power
1701–1713	War of the Spanish Succession
1713	Treaty of Utrecht

century. This crisis did not throw Castile itself into a state of civil war. Unlike Paris during the Fronde, Madrid itself remained peaceful. Throughout the 1640s the crown managed to maintain order within its main kingdom, probably because it had learned the art of negotiating directly with the thousands of towns and villages that ran local government. Instead, the Spanish crisis took the form of separatist revolts in Portugal, Catalonia, Sicily, and Naples. With the exception of Portugal, which recovered its sovereignty in 1640, the monarchy met this test and managed to maintain control of its provincial and Italian territories. In the aftermath of the revolts, however, the monarchy failed to bring the areas within the sphere of effective central government control.

The relative weakness of the Spanish monarchy, especially in comparison with that of France, became most apparent in the late seventeenth century, the age of Louis XIV. In two important respects the Spanish government failed to match the achievement of the French. First, it could never escape the grip that the old noble families had on the central administration. The unwillingness of the nobility to recruit ministers and officials from the mercantile and professional groups within society (which were small to begin with in Spain) worked against the achievement of bureaucratic efficiency and made innovation virtually impossible. Second, unlike the French government during Colbert's ministry, the Spanish government failed to encourage economic growth. The hostility of the aristocratic ruling class to mercantile affairs, coupled with a traditional Spanish unwillingness to follow the example of foreigners (especially when they were Protestants) prevented the country from stemming its own economic decline and the government from solving the formidable financial problems facing it. To make matters worse, the Spanish government failed to make its system of tax collection more efficient.

The mood that prevailed within the upper levels of Castilian society in the seventeenth century reflected the failure of the government and the entire nation. The contrast between the glorious achievements of the monarchy during the reign of Philip II (r. 1555–1598) and the somber realities of the late seventeenth century led most members of the ruling class to retreat into that past, a nostalgia that only encouraged further economic and political stagnation. The work of Miguel de Cervantes (1547–1616), the greatest Spanish writer of the seventeenth century, reflected this change in the Spanish national mood. In 1605 and 1615 Cervantes published (in two parts) *Don Quixote*, the story of an idealistic wandering nobleman who pursued dreams of an

elusive military glory. This work, which as we have seen in Chapter 14 explored the relationship between illusion and reality, served as a commentary on a nobility that had lost confidence in itself.

Spanish painting, which paradoxically entered its Golden Age at the time the country began to lose its economic, political, and military vitality, was less willing to accept the decline of Spain. There was very little in the paintings of the great Spanish artist Diego de Velázquez (1599–1660) that would suggest the malaise that was affecting Spain and its nobility at the time. Velázquez painted in the baroque style that was in favor at court throughout Europe, depicting his subjects in heroic poses and imbuing them with a sense of royal or aristocratic dignity. One of his historical paintings, *The Surrender of Breda* (1634), commemorated a rare Spanish military victory over the Dutch in 1625 and the magnanimity of the Spanish victors toward their captives. All this was intended to reinforce the prestige

Diego de Velázquez, Portrait of the Prince Baltasar Carlos, Heir to the Spanish Throne
The depiction of the six-year-old prince on a rearing horse was intended to suggest military and political power at a time when the monarchy was losing both. The prince died in 1646, before he could succeed to the throne.

of the monarchy, the royal family, and the nation itself at a time when the imperial grandeur of the past had faded. Velázquez's painting reflected the ideals of absolutism but ignored the realities of Spanish political and military life.

Absolutism and State Building in Central and Eastern Europe

■ What was the nature of royal absolutism in central and eastern Europe, and how did the policies of the Ottoman Empire and Russia help establish the boundaries of the West during this period?

The forces that led to the establishment of absolutism and state building in France and Spain also made an impact on central and eastern Europe. In Germany the Thirty Years' War led to the establishment of two absolutist states, Prussia and the Austrian Habsburg Monarchy. Further to the East, the Ottoman and Russian Empires, both of them on the margins of the West, also developed absolutist political systems that shared many of the same characteristics as those in western and central Europe. Russia, previously thought of as belonging to an Eastern, Asian world, entered upon a program of westernization and staked a claim to be considered a Western power. At the same time the Ottoman Empire, whose political develop-

ment followed a Western pattern in many respects, was increasingly dismissed by Europeans as part of a distant, non-Western world.

Germany and the Thirty Years' War, 1618–1648

Before 1648 the main political power within the geographical area known as Germany was the Holy Roman Empire. This large political formation was a loose confederation of kingdoms, principalities, duchies, ecclesiastical territories, and cities, each of which had its own laws and political institutions. The emperor, who was elected by a body of German princes, exercised immediate jurisdiction only in his own dynastic possessions and in the imperial cities. He also convened a legislative assembly known as the *Reichstag*, over which he exercised limited influence. But the emperor did not have a large administrative or judicial bureaucracy through which he could enforce imperial law in the localities. The empire was not in any sense a sovereign state, even though it had long been a major force in European diplomacy. It had acquired and maintained that international position by relying on the military and financial contributions of its imperial cities and the lands controlled directly by the Habsburg emperors.

The Thirty Years' War permanently altered the nature of this vast and intricate political structure. That war began as a conflict between Protestant German princes and the Catholic emperor over religious and constitutional issues. The incident that triggered it in 1618 was the so-called Defenestration of Prague, when members of the predominantly Protestant Bohemian legislature, known as the Diet, threw two imperial officials out a castle window as a protest against the religious policies of their recently elected king, the future emperor Ferdinand II. The Diet proceeded to depose Ferdinand, a Catholic, and elect a Protestant prince, Frederick V of the Palatinate, to replace him. The war soon broadened into a European-wide struggle over the possession of German and Spanish territory, as the Danes, Swedes, and French successively entered the conflict against the emperor and his Spanish Habsburg relatives. For a brief period in the late 1620s England also entered the conflict against Spain. The war, which was fought mainly on German soil, had a devastating effect on the country. More than one million soldiers marched across German lands, sacking towns and exploiting the resources of local communities. Germany lost up to one-third of its population, while the destruction of property retarded the economic development of the country for more than fifty years.

The political effects of the war were no less traumatic. By virtue of the Treaty of Westphalia, which ended the war in 1648, the empire was permanently weakened, although it continued to function until 1806 (see Map 15.3). The individual German territories within the empire developed more institutional autonomy than they had before the war. They became sovereign states themselves, with their own armies, foreign policies, and central bureaucracies. Two of these German states soon surpassed all the others in size and military strength and became major European powers. The first was Brandenburg-Prussia, a collection of various territories in northern Germany that was transformed into the kingdom of Prussia at the beginning of the eighteenth century. In the nineteenth century Prussia would unify Germany under its leadership. The second state was the Austrian Habsburg Monarchy, which in the eighteenth century was usually identified simply as Austria. The Habsburgs had long dominated the Holy Roman Empire and continued to secure election as emperors after the Treaty of Westphalia. In the late seventeenth century, however, the Habsburg Monarchy acquired its own institutional identity, distinct from that of the empire. It consisted of the lands that the Habsburgs controlled directly in the southeastern part of the empire and other territories, including the kingdom of Hungary, which lay outside the territorial boundary of the empire. Both Prussia and Austria developed their own forms of absolutism during the second half of the seventeenth century.

The Growth of the Prussian State

In 1648, at the end of the Thirty Years' War, Prussia could barely have claimed the status of an independent state, much less that of an absolute monarchy. The core of the

Defenestration of Prague, May 23, 1618
The Thirty Years' War was touched off when Protestant nobles in the Bohemian legislature threw two Catholic imperial governors out the window of a castle in Prague.

Spanish dominions
Austrian dominions
Brandenburg-Prussia
Swedish dominions
—— Boundary of Holy Roman Empire

Map 15.3   Europe After the Treaty of Westphalia, 1648
The Holy Roman Empire no longer included the Dutch Republic, which was now independent of Spain. Some of the lands of the Austrian Habsburg Monarchy and Brandenburg-Prussia lay outside the boundaries of the Holy Roman Empire. Italy was divided into a number of small states in the north, while Naples, Sicily, and Sardinia were ruled by Spain.

Prussian state was Brandenburg, which claimed the status of an electorate because its ruler cast one of the ballots to elect the Holy Roman Emperor. The lands that belonged to the elector of Brandenburg lay scattered throughout northern Germany and stretched into eastern Europe. As a result of the Thirty Years' War, the archbishoprics of Magdeburg and East Pomerania were annexed to Brandenburg. The Hohenzollern family, in whose line the electorate of Brandenburg passed, also owned or controlled various parcels of German territory in the Rhineland, near the borders of the Spanish Netherlands. In 1618 the Hohenzollerns had acquired the much larger but equally remote duchy of Prussia, a Baltic territory lying outside the boundaries of the Holy Roman Empire. As ruler of these disparate and noncontiguous lands, the elector of Brandenburg had virtually no state bureaucracy, collected few taxes, and commanded only a small army. Most of his territories, moreover, lay in ruins in 1648, having been devastated by Swedish and imperial troops at various times during the war.

The Great Elector Frederick William (r. 1640–1688) began the long process of turning this ramshackle structure into a powerful and cohesive German state (see Map 15.4). His son King Frederick I (r. 1688–1713) and grandson Frederick William I (r. 1713–1740) completed the transformation. The key to their success, as it was for all aspiring absolute monarchs in eastern Europe, was to secure the compliance of the traditional nobility, who in Prussia were known as Junkers°. The Great Elector Frederick William achieved this end by granting the Junkers a variety of privileges, including exemption from import duties and the excise tax. The most valuable concession was the legal confirmation of their rights over the serfs. During the previous 150 years Prussian peasants had lost their freedom, becoming permanently bound to the estates of their lords and completely subject to the Junkers' arbitrary brand of local justice. The Junkers had a deeply vested interest in perpetuating this oppressive system of serfdom, and the lawgiver Frederick was able to provide them with the legal guarantees they required.

DOCUMENT

A German Writer Describes the Horrors of the Thirty Years' War

In 1669 the German writer H. J. C. Grimmelshausen (1625–1676) published an imaginary account of the adventures of a German vagabond, to whom he gave the name Simplicissimus. The setting of the book was the Thirty Years' War in Germany, which Grimmelshausen had experienced firsthand. At age 10 Grimmelshausen, like the character Simplicissimus in the book, was captured by Hessian troops and later became a camp-follower. In this chapter Simplicissimus describes how the palace of his father was stormed, plundered, and ruined.

The first thing that these troops did was, that they stabbed their horses; thereafter each fell to his appointed task, which task was either more or less than ruin and destruction. For though some began to slaughter and to boil and to roast, so that it looked as if there should be a merry banquet forward, yet others there were who did but storm through the house above and below the stairs. . . . All that they had no mind to take with them they cut in pieces. Some thrust their swords through the hay and straw as if they had not enough sheep and swine to slaughter; and some shook the feathers out of the beds and in their stead stuffed in bacon and other dried meat and provisions as if such were better and softer to sleep upon. Others broke the stove and the windows as if they had a never-ending summer to promise. Housewares of copper and tin they beat flat, and packed such vessels, all bent and spoiled, in with the rest. Bedsteads, tables, chairs and benches they burned, though there lay many cords of dry wood in the yard. . . .

Our maid was so handled in the stable that she could not come out; which is a shame to tell of. Our man they laid bound upon the ground, thrust a gag into his mouth, and poured a pailful of filthy water into his body; and by this, which they called a Swedish draught, they forced him to lead a party of them to another place where they captured men and beasts, and brought them back to our farm, in which company were my dad, my mother, and our Ursula.

And now they began first to take the flints out of their pistols and in place of them to jam the peasants' thumbs in and so to torture the poor rogues as if they had been about the burning of witches. For one of them they had taken they thrust into the baking oven and there lit a fire under him, although he had as yet confessed no crime; as for another, they put a cord round his head and so twisted it tight with a piece of wood that the blood gushed from his mouth and nose and ears. In a word each had his own device to torture the peasants, and each peasant his several torture.

Source: Reprinted from The Adventurous Simplicissimus: Being the Description of the Life of a Strange Vagabond Named Melchior Sternfels Von Fuchshaim *by H. J. C. Grimmelshausen. Published by the University of Nebraska Press.*

With the loyalty of the Junkers secure, Frederick William went about the process of building a powerful Prussian state. A large administrative bureaucracy, centralized under a General Directory in Berlin, governed both financial and military affairs throughout the elector's lands. At first it was staffed by members of the nobility, but eventually educated commoners were recruited into the system. The taxes that the government collected, especially from the towns, went in large part to fund a standing army, which had come into being in the late 1650s.

The Prussian army grew rapidly, rising to 30,000 men in 1690 and 80,000 by 1740. It consisted of a combination of carefully recruited volunteers, foreign mercenaries, and, after 1713, conscripts from the general population. Its most famous regiment, known as the Blue Prussians or the Giants of Potsdam, consisted of 1,200 men, each of whom was at least six feet tall. Commanded by officers drawn from the nobility and reinforced by Europe's first system of military reserves, this army quickly became the best trained fighting force in Europe. Prussia became a model military state, symbolized by the transformation of the royal gardens into an army training ground during the reign of Frederick William I.

As this military state grew in size and complexity, its rulers acquired many of the attributes of absolute rule. Most significantly they became the sole legislators within the state. The main representative assembly in the electorate, the Diet of Brandenburg, met for the last time in 1652. Frederick William and his successors, however, continued to consult with smaller local assemblies, especially in the matter of taxation. The elevation of Frederick I's status to that of king of Prussia in 1701 marked a further consolidation of power in the person of the ruler. His son's style of rule, which included physical punishment of judges whose decisions displeased him, suggested that the Prussian monarchy not only had attained absolute power but could occasionally abuse it.

The Austrian Habsburg Monarchy

The Austrian Habsburgs were much less successful than the Hohenzollerns in building a centralized, consolidated state along absolutist lines. The various territories that made up the Austrian Habsburg Monarchy in the late seventeenth century were larger and more diverse than those that belonged to the king of Prussia. In addition to the collection of duchies that form present-day Austria and that then served as the core of the monarchy, it embraced two subordinate kingdoms, which were themselves composed of various semiautonomous principalities and duchies. The first of these, lying to the north, was the kingdom of Bohemia, which had struggled against Habsburg control for nearly a century and included Moravia and Silesia. The second, lying to the southeast, was the kingdom of Hungary, including the large semiautonomous principality of Transylvania. The Habsburgs regained Hungary from the Ottoman Empire in stages between 1664 and 1718. In 1713 the monarchy also acquired the former Spanish Netherlands and the Italian territories of Milan and Naples.

The Austrian Habsburg monarchs of the seventeenth and early eighteenth centuries never succeeded in integrating these ethnically, religiously, and politically diverse lands into a unified, cohesive state similar to that of France. The problem was a lack of a unified bureaucracy. The only centralized administrative institutions in this amalgam of kingdoms were the Court Chamber, which superintended the collection of taxes throughout the monarchy, and the Austrian army, which included troops from all Habsburg lands. Like many European military forces it had become a standing army in 1648, and by 1716 it had a troop strength of 165,000 men. Even these centralized institutions had difficulty operating smoothly. The council of the army had trouble integrating units drawn from separate kingdoms, while the Court Chamber never developed a uniform system of tax collection. For all practical purposes the Habsburgs had to rule their various kingdoms separately.

In governing its Austrian and Bohemian lands, this decentralized Habsburg Monarchy nonetheless acquired some of the characteristics of absolutist rule. This development toward absolutism began long before the Treaty of

Map 15.4   The Growth of Brandenburg-Prussia, 1618–1786

By acquiring lands throughout northern Germany, Prussia became a major European power. The process began during the early seventeenth century, but it continued well into the eighteenth century. The Prussian army, which was the best trained fighting force in Europe in the eighteenth century, greatly facilitated Prussia's growth.

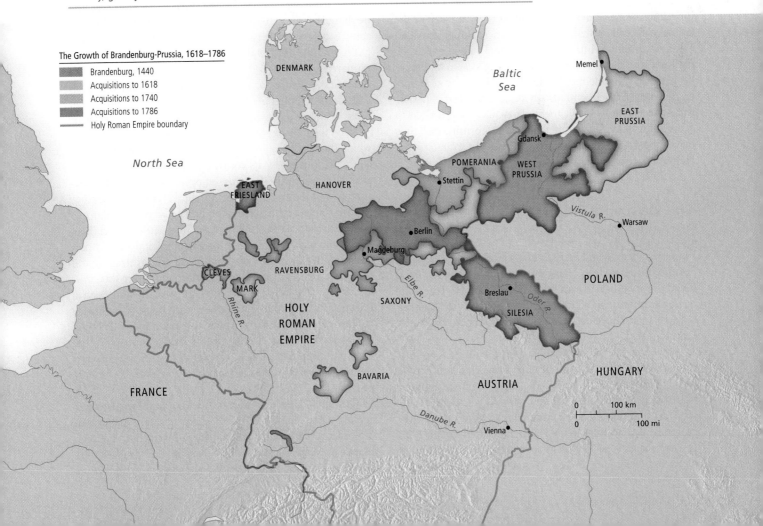

The Growth of Brandenburg-Prussia, 1618–1786

- Brandenburg, 1440
- Acquisitions to 1618
- Acquisitions to 1740
- Acquisitions to 1786
- Holy Roman Empire boundary

Westphalia in 1648. After defeating the Bohemians at the Battle of White Mountain in 1620 during the Thirty Years' War, Emperor Ferdinand II (r. 1618–1637) had decided to strengthen his authority in the areas under his direct control. Bohemia, which had led the revolt against him, was the main target of this policy, but the emperor used this opportunity to increase his power throughout his territories. After punishing the rebels and exiling many of the Protestant nobility, he undertook a deliberate expansion of his legislative and judicial powers, and he secured direct control over all his administrative officials.

A policy of severe religious repression accompanied this increase in the emperor's authority. Like Cardinal Richelieu of France, Ferdinand assumed that Protestantism served as a justification for rebellion, and he therefore decided that its practice could not be tolerated. Protestants in all the emperor's territories were forced to take a Catholic loyalty oath, and Protestant education was banned. Protestant towns were destroyed at exactly the same time that Richelieu was razing the fortifications of the Huguenot town of La Rochelle. These efforts at reconversion continued right through the seventeenth century. They amounted to a policy of religious or "confessional" absolutism.

While the Habsburgs succeeded in imposing some elements of absolutist rule on the Austrians and the Bohemians in the early seventeenth century, they encountered much more resistance when they attempted to follow the same course of action with respect to Hungary in the late seventeenth and eighteenth centuries. Hungarians had a long tradition of limited, constitutional rule in which the national Diet had exercised powers of legislation and taxation, just as Parliament did in England. Habsburg emperors made some limited inroads on these traditions but they were never able to break them. They also were unable to achieve the same degree of religious uniformity that they had imposed on their other territories. In Hungary the Habsburgs encountered the limits of royal absolutism.

The Ottoman Empire: Between East and West

In the seventeenth and early eighteenth centuries the southeastern border of the Habsburg monarchy separated the kingdom of Hungary from the Ottoman Empire. This militarized frontier marked not only the political boundary between two empires but a deeper cultural boundary between East and West.

As we have seen in previous chapters, the West is not just a geographical but also a cultural realm, and the people who inhabit this realm, although distinct from one another, share many of the same religious, political, legal, and philosophical traditions. The Ottoman Turks, who posed a recurrent military threat to the Habsburg monarchy and who reached the gates of Vienna in 1683, were generally thought of as not belonging to this Western world. Because the Ottoman Turks were Muslims, Europeans considered them enemies of Christianity, infidels who were bent on the destruction of Christendom. In the sixteenth century Catholics and Protestants alike claimed that the military victories of the Turks over European forces were signs of divine punishment for the sins European Christians had committed. Ottoman emperors, known as sultans, were considered despots who ruled over their subjects as slaves. The sultans were also depicted in Western literature as cruel and brutal tyrants, the opposite of the ideal Christian prince of Europe. One French play of 1612 depicted the mother of the sultan Mehmed the Conquerer (r. 1451–1481) as drinking the blood of a victim.

These stereotypes of the Turks served the function of giving Europeans a sense of their own Western identity. Turks became a negative reference group with whom Europeans could favorably compare themselves. The realities of Ottoman politics and culture, however, were quite different from the ways in which they were represented in European literature. Turkish despotism, the name Europeans gave to the Ottoman system of government, existed only in theory. Ever since the fourteenth century Ottoman writers had claimed for the sultan extraordinary powers, including the right to seize the landed property of his subjects at will. In practice he never exercised unlimited power. His prerogatives were limited by the spirit of Muslim law, and he shared power with the grand vizier, who was his chief executive officer. In practice there was little difference between the rule of the sultans and that of European absolute monarchs. As far as religious policy is concerned, the Ottoman practice of tolerating non-Muslim religions within the empire made the sultans less absolutist than most of their seventeenth-century European counterparts.

DOCUMENT

Venetian Observations on the Ottoman Empire (late 16th c.)

Even the high degree of administrative centralization for which the Ottoman Empire was famous did not encompass all the regions under its control. Many of its provinces, especially those in the Balkans, enjoyed a considerable measure of autonomy, especially in the seventeenth century. The Balkans, which were geographically part of Europe, never experienced the full force of direct Turkish rule. In all the Ottoman provinces there was a complex pattern of negotiation between the central imperial administration and local officials. In this respect the Ottoman Empire was similar to the absolutist monarchies of western and central Europe. The Ottoman Empire bore the closest resemblance to the Spanish monarchy, which also ruled many far-flung territories in Europe. Like the Spanish monarchy, the Ottoman Empire declined in power during the seventeenth century and lost effective control of some of its outlying provinces.

Ottoman Turks and Europeans frequently went to war against each other, but there was a constant pattern of diplomatic, economic, and cultural interaction between them. The Turks had been involved in European warfare since the fifteenth century, and they had formed diplomatic alliances with the French against the Austrian Habsburgs on a number of occasions. Europeans and Ottomans often borrowed military technology from each other, and they also shared knowledge of administrative techniques. Trade between European countries and the Ottoman Empire remained brisk throughout this period. Europe supplied hardware and textiles to the Turks while they in turn shipped coffee, tobacco, and tulips to European ports. Communities of Turks and other Muslims lived in European cities, while numerous European merchants resided in territories under Ottoman control.

These encounters between Turks and Europeans suggest that the militarized boundary between the Habsburgs and the Ottoman Empire was much more porous than its fortifications would suggest. Military conflict and Western contempt for Muslim Turks disguised a much more complex process of political and cultural interaction between the two civilizations. Europeans tended to think of the Ottoman Empire as "oriental," but it is more accurate to view it as a region lying between the East and the West.

Russia and the West

The other seventeenth-century power that marked the boundary between East and West was the vast Russian Empire, which stretched from its boundary with Poland in the west all the way to the Pacific Ocean in the east. Until the end of the seventeenth century, the kingdom of Muscovy and the lands attached to it seemed, at least to Europeans, part of the Asiatic world. Dominated by an Eastern Orthodox branch of Christianity, Russia drew very little upon the cultural traditions associated with western Europe. Unlike its neighboring Slavic kingdom of Poland, it had not absorbed large doses of German culture. It also appeared to Europeans to be another example of "oriental despotism," a state in which the ruler, known as the tsar, could rule his subjects at will, "not bound up by any law or custom."

DOCUMENT

Adan Olearius: A Foreign Traveler in Russia (early 17th c.)

During the reign of Tsar Peter I, known as Peter the Great (r. 1682–1725), Russia underwent a process of westernization, bringing it more into line with the culture of European countries and becoming a major European power. This policy began after Peter visited England, Holland, northern Germany, and Austria in 1697 and 1698. Upon his return he directed his officials and members of the upper levels of Russian society to adopt Western styles of dress and appearance, including the removal of men's beards. (Scissors were kept in the customs house for this purpose alone.) Beards symbolized the backward, Eastern, Orthodox culture from whose grip Peter hoped to extricate his country. Young Russian boys were sent abroad for their education. Women began to participate openly in the social

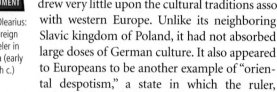

IMAGE

Peter the Great

and cultural life of the cities, in violation of Orthodox custom. Smoking was permitted despite the Church's insistence that Scripture condemned it. The calendar was reformed and books were printed in modern Russian type. Peter's importation of Western art and the imitation of Western architecture complemented this policy of enforced cultural change. Westernization, however, involved more than a change of manners and appearance. It also involved military and political reforms that changed the character of the Russian state.

During the first twenty-five years of his reign Peter had found himself unable to achieve sustained military success against his two great enemies, the Ottoman Turks to the south and the Swedes to the west. During the Great Northern War with Sweden (1700–1721) Peter introduced a number of military reforms that eventually turned the tide against his enemy. These reforms were based on the knowledge he had acquired of military technology, organization, and tactics of western European states, especially Prussia and, ironically, Sweden itself. Having introduced a program of conscription, Peter assembled a large standing army of more than 200,000 men, which he trained and disciplined in the Prussian manner. All of this was supported by the imposition of new taxes on a variety of commodities, including beards, and the encouragement of Russian industry in much the same way that Colbert had encouraged French industry. A central council, established in 1711, not only directed financial administration but also levied and supplied troops, not unlike the General Directory of the electorate of Brandenburg.

This new military state also acquired many of the centralizing and absolutist features of western European

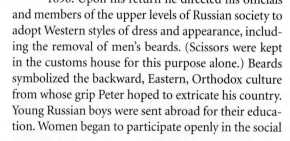

CHRONOLOGY

The Age of Absolutism in Central and Eastern Europe

1618	Ferdinand II becomes Holy Roman Emperor (r. 1618–1637)
1640	Beginning of the reign of Frederick William, the Great Elector of Brandenburg Prussia (r. 1640–1688)
1657	Leopold I becomes Holy Roman Emperor (r. 1657–1705)
1682	Accession of Tsar Peter the Great of Russia (r. 1682–1725)
1688	Accession of Frederick as elector of Prussia; becomes king of Prussia in 1701
1703	Foundation of St. Petersburg, Russia's new capital and "window on the West"
1705	Joseph I becomes Holy Roman Emperor (r. 1705–1711)
1711	Charles VI, brother of Joseph I, becomes Holy Roman Emperor (r. 1711–1740)

St. Petersburg and the West

The major encounter between Russia and the West during the reign of Peter the Great was the building of a new capital city, St. Petersburg, on the marshy delta of the Neva River, which empties into the Gulf of Finland. The land on which the city was located was seized from Sweden during the Northern War. The construction of the city, which first served as a fortress and then a naval base in that conflict, occurred at a tremendous cost in treasure and human life. Using the royal powers that he had significantly augmented earlier in his reign, Peter ordered more than 10,000 workers (and possibly twice that number) from throughout his kingdom to realize this ambitious and risky project. The harsh weather conditions, the ravages of malaria and other diseases, and the chronic shortages of provisions in a distant location resulted in the death of a few thousand workers—numbers that were often greatly exaggerated by foreigners. Beginning in 1710 Peter ordered the transfer of central governmental, commercial, and military functions to the new city. The city became the site for Peter's Winter Palace, the residences of Russia's foreign ambassadors, and the headquarters of the Russian Orthodox Church. The Academy of Fine Arts and the Academy of Sciences were built shortly thereafter. During the 1730s Russia's first bourse, or exchange, fulfilled the prophecy of a British observer in 1710 that the city, with its network of canals, "might one day prove a second Amsterdam or Venice." Thus St. Petersburg came to embody all the modernizing and westernizing achievements of Peter the Great.

Russia's encounter with the West at St. Petersburg was reflected both in the location of the new city and the styles in which the buildings were constructed. As a port with access to the Baltic Sea, the new city, often described as "a window on the West," looked toward the European ports with which Russia increased its commerce and the European powers that Russia engaged in battle and diplomacy. The architects, stonemasons, and interior decorators that Peter commissioned came from France, Italy, Germany and the Dutch Republic, and they constructed the buildings in contemporary European styles. The general plan of the city, drawn up by the French architect Le Blond, featured straight, paved streets with stone paths that are now called sidewalks. St. Petersburg thus became a port through which Western influences entered Russia. The contrast with the old capital, Moscow, which was situated in the center of the country and embodied the spirit of the old Russia that Peter strove to modernize, could not have been clearer.

The construction of St. Petersburg played a central role in transforming Russia from a medieval kingdom on the fringes of Europe into a modern, Western power. It did not, however, eliminate the conflict in Russia between those who held the West up as the cultural standard that Russia should strive to emulate and those who celebrated Russia's cultural superiority over the West. This conflict between westernizers and Slavophiles, which began in the eighteenth century, has continued to the present day. During the period of communism in the twentieth century, when St. Petersburg was renamed Leningrad and Moscow once again became the political capital of the country, the Slavophile tradition tended to prevail. It is no coincidence that the collapse of communism and the disintegration of the Union of Soviet Socialist Republics in 1989 has led to a renewed emphasis on Russia's ties with the West. The celebration of the 300th anniversary of St. Petersburg in 2003 and the restoration of its original name in 1991 constitute one more episode in the effort to integrate Russia more fully into the West.

For Discussion

How did the founding of St. Petersburg contribute to the growth of the Russian state?

How did Peter the Great's absolute power facilitate the growth of the city?

A Picture of St. Petersburg (1815)
This view of St. Petersburg from the quay in front of the Winter Palace reveals the city's Western character. The buildings lying across the Neva River, including the bourse, were designed by European architects. The gondolas, seen in the foreground docking at the quay, enhanced St. Petersburg's reputation as "Venice of the North."

monarchies. Efforts to introduce absolutism in Russia had begun during the reigns of Alexis (r. 1645–1676) and Fedor (r. 1676–1682), who had achieved limited success in strengthening the central administration, controlling the nobility, and brutally suppressing peasant rebellions. Peter built upon his predecessors' achievement. He created an entirely new structure for managing the empire, appointing twelve governors to superintend Russia's forty-three separate provinces. He brought the Church under state control. By establishing a finely graded hierarchy of official ranks in the armed forces, the civil administration, and the court, Peter not only improved administrative efficiency but also made it possible for men of nonaristocratic birth to attain the same privileged status as the old landowning nobility. At the same time he won the support of all landowners by introducing primogeniture (inheritance of the entire estate by the eldest son), which prevented their estates from being subdivided, and supporting the enserfment of the peasants. In dealing with his subjects Peter claimed more power than any other absolute monarch in Europe. During the trial of his own son, Alexis, for treason in 1718, he told the clergy that "we have a sufficient and absolute power to judge our son for his crimes according to our own pleasure."[4]

The most visible sign of Peter's policy of westernization was the construction of the port city of St. Petersburg on the Gulf of Finland, which became the new capital of the Russian Empire. One of the main objectives of Russian foreign policy during Peter's reign had been to secure access to the Baltic Sea, allowing Russia to open maritime trade with Europe and to become a Western naval power. By draining a swamp on the estuary of the Neva River, Peter laid the foundations of a city that became the new capital of his empire. Construction began in 1703, and within twenty years St. Petersburg had a population of 40,000 people. With his new capital city now looking westward, and an army and central administration reformed on the basis of Prussian and French example, Peter could enter the world of European diplomacy and warfare as both a Western and an absolute monarch.

Resistance to Absolutism in England and the Dutch Republic

■ Why did absolutism fail to take root in England and the Dutch Republic during the seventeenth century?

The kingdom of England and the northern provinces of the Netherlands stand out as the two great exceptions to the dominant pattern of political development in seventeenth-century Europe. Both of these countries successfully resisted the establishment of royal absolutism, and

neither underwent the rigorous centralization of power and the dynamic growth of the state that usually accompanied the establishment of absolutist rule. In England the encounter between the proponents and opponents of absolute monarchy was more pronounced than in any other European country. It resulted in the temporary destruction of the monarchy in 1649 and the establishment of parliamentary supremacy after the Glorious Revolution of 1688. In the northern provinces of the Netherlands, known as the Dutch Republic, an even more emphatic rejection of absolutism occurred. During their long struggle to win their independence from Spain, the Dutch established a republican, decentralized form of government, but that did not prevent them from acquiring considerable military strength and dominating the world's economy during the seventeenth century.

The English Monarchy

At various times in the seventeenth century English monarchs tried to introduce royal absolutism, but the political institutions and the political culture of the country stood as major obstacles to their designs. As early as the fifteenth century, the English writer and diplomat Sir John Fortescue (ca. 1395–1477) had celebrated England's parliamentary system of government by contrasting it with that of France, where he claimed the king could make laws by himself and impose his will on his subjects. Fortescue's treatise contributed to the pride Englishmen had in what they considered their distinctive set of political and legal traditions. The most important of these traditions was the making of law and the levying of taxes by the two Houses of Parliament, the House of Lords and the House of Commons, with the king holding the power to sign or veto the bills they passed.

In the early seventeenth century the perception began to arise, especially among certain members of the House of Commons, that this tradition of parliamentary government was under attack. The first Stuart king, James I (r. 1603–1625), who succeeded the last Tudor monarch, Elizabeth I, aroused some of these fears as early as 1604, when he called his first parliament. James thought of himself as an absolute monarch, and in a number of speeches and published works he emphasized the height of his independent royal power, which was known in England as the prerogative°. James also spoke often about his divine right to rule, and he claimed that the main function of Parliament was simply to give the king advice, rather than to make law. These statements had the effect of antagonizing members of Parliament, leading them to defend their privileges, including the right they claimed to discuss foreign policy and other affairs of state.

James believed that he was an absolute monarch, but he did not actually try to put his ideas into practice. For example, he did not try to make laws or levy taxes without the consent of Parliament or deny men their legal rights, such as freedom from arbitrary imprisonment. The real political fireworks did not begin until James's son, Charles I (r. 1625–1649), succeeded him. Charles believed in absolutism every bit as much as his father, but unlike James, Charles actually put his theories into practice. His efforts to force his subjects to lend money to the government during a war with Spain (1625–1629) and his imprisonment of men who refused to make these loans led Parliament to pass the Petition of Right in 1628. This document declared boldly that subjects possessed fundamental rights that kings could not violate under any circumstances, even when the country was at war.

Charles consented to the Petition of Right, but when Parliament met again in 1629, further conflict between the king and certain members of the House of Commons developed over taxation and the king's religious policies. Charles had been collecting duties on exports without parliamentary approval since 1625. He had also begun to favor conservative clergymen known as Arminians, leading the more zealous English Protestants, the Puritans, to fear that the English Church was leaning in the direction of Catholicism or "popery." Faced with this opposition over constitutional and religious issues, Charles decided to dismiss this parliament and to rule indefinitely without calling another one.

This period of nonparliamentary government, known as the personal rule,° lasted until 1640. During these years Charles, unable to collect taxes by the authority of Parliament, used his prerogative to bring in new revenues, especially by asking all subjects to pay "ship-money" to support the outfitting of ships to defend the country against attack. During the personal rule the king's religious policy fell under the control of William Laud, who was named archbishop of Canterbury in 1633 and who became one of the king's main privy councilors. Laud's determination to restore many of the rituals associated with Roman Catholicism alienated large numbers of Puritans and led to a growing perception that members of the king's government were engaged in a conspiracy to destroy both England's ancient constitution and the Protestant religion.

This period of absolutism might have continued indefinitely if Charles had not once again been faced with the financial demands of war. In 1636 the king tried to introduce a new religious liturgy in his northern kingdom of Scotland. The liturgy included a number of rituals that the firmly Calvinist Scottish population considered popish. The new liturgy so angered a group of women in Edinburgh that they threw their chairs at the bishop when he introduced it. In response to this affront to their religion, the Scots signed a National Covenant (1638) pledging themselves to defend the integrity of their Church, abolished episcopacy (government of the church by bishops) in favor of a Presbyterian system of church government, and mobi-

The English House of Commons in 1604
The men elected to sit in the House of Commons were known as Members of Parliament or MPs. In the early seventeenth century many of these men claimed that King James I was denying them their ancient privileges and liberties, including freedom of speech. They also objected to the claims of James that he was an absolute monarch.

lized a large army. To secure the funds to fight the Scots, Charles was forced to summon his English Parliament, thereby ending the period of personal rule.

The English Civil Wars and Revolution

Tensions between the reconvened English Parliament and Charles led to the first revolution of modern times. The Short Parliament, called in April 1640, lasted only two months, but a Scottish military victory against the English in that year forced the king to call a second parliament. The Long Parliament, which met in November 1640, impeached many of the king's ministers and judges and dismantled the judicial apparatus of the eleven years of personal rule, including the courts that had been active in the prosecution of Puritans. Parliament declared the king's nonparliamentary taxes illegal and enacted a law limiting the time between the meetings of Parliament to three years.

This legislation did not satisfy the king's critics in Parliament. Their suspicion that the king was conspiring against them and their demand to approve all royal appointments created a poisoned political atmosphere in which neither side trusted the other. After the king and his armed guards forced their way into the House of Commons to arrest five members for treason, there was little hope of reconciliation. In August 1642 civil war began between the Parliamentarians, known as Roundheads because many of the artisans who supported them had close-cropped hair styles, and the Royalists or Cavaliers, who often wore their hair in long flowing locks. Parliament, which was supported by the Scots and which benefited from the creation in 1645 of a well-trained, efficient fighting force, the New Model Army, ultimately won this war in 1646 and took Charles prisoner. The king's subsequent negotiations with the Scots and the English Presbyterians, both of whom had originally fought against him, led to a second civil war in 1648. In this war, which lasted only a few months, the New Model Army once again defeated Royalist forces.

This military victory led to a series of revolutionary changes in the English system of government. Believing with some justification that Charles could never be trusted, and eager to bring about an end to years of political uncertainty, members of the army purged Parliament of its Presbyterian members, leaving only a small group of Independents. These men, who favored a form of church government in which the congregations had a high degree of autonomy, had broken off negotiations with Charles I. The remaining members of Parliament were known as the Rump, because they were all that was left of the Long Parliament elected in 1640. This small group of Independents in Parliament, following the wishes of the army, set up a court to try Charles in January 1649. The trial resulted in Charles's conviction and execution, and shortly thereafter the Rump destroyed the House of Lords and the monarchy itself. As Parliament had already abolished the episcopal structure of the English Church in 1646, these actions completed a genuine revolution, a political transformation that destroyed the very system of government and replaced it with new institutions.

The revolution resulted in the establishment of a republic, in which the House of Commons possessed supreme legislative power in the name of the people of England. This change in the system of government, however, did not lead to the introduction of a more democratic form of government. A government of this sort, in which a very large percentage of the adult male population would be allowed to vote, was the goal of a political party, the Levellers, which originated in the New Model Army and attracted consider-

CHRONOLOGY

A Century of Revolution in England and Scotland

1603	James VI of Scotland (r. 1567–1625) becomes James I of England (r. 1603–1625)
1625	Death of James I and accession of Charles I (r. 1625–1649)
1628	Parliament passes the Petition of Right
1629–1640	Personal rule of Charles I
1638	Scots sign the National Covenant
1640	Opening of the Long Parliament
1642–1646	Civil War in England, ending with the capture of King Charles I
1648	Second Civil War; New Model Army defeats English Presbyterians and Scots
1649	Execution of Charles I of England and the beginning of the Republic
1653	End of the Long Parliament; beginning and dissolution of Barebones Parliament; Oliver Cromwell becomes Protector of England, Scotland, and Ireland
1660	Restoration of the monarchy in the person of Charles II; House of Lords and the Church of England also restored
1685	Death of Charles II and accession of his brother, James II (r. 1685–1688)
1688–1689	Glorious Revolution in England and Scotland
1707	England and Scotland politically joined to form the United Kingdom of Great Britain

able support in London and the towns. In 1647 at Putney Bridge, near London, the Levellers participated in a debate with more conservative army officers concerning the future constitution of the country. The spokesmen for the Levellers called for annual parliaments, the separation of powers between the executive and legislative branches of government, and the introduction of universal suffrage for men. The army officers argued against this proposed constitution, arguing that the vote should be entrusted only to men who owned property. The officers made sure that the Leveller program would not be accepted. The Levellers eventually mutinied in the army, their leaders were imprisoned, and the party collapsed.

The fate of the Levellers and their program underlines the fact that the English revolution was brought about by men of property, especially by the gentry or lesser aristocracy who sat in the House of Commons and who served as officers in the New Model Army. Although these men defeated and executed the king and secured the right to participate regularly in the governance of the kingdom, they

The Trial of Charles I

In January 1649, after the New Model Army had defeated Royalist forces in England's second civil war and purged Parliament of its Presbyterian members, the few remaining members of the House of Commons voted by a narrow margin to erect a High Court of Justice to try King Charles I. This trial, which resulted in Charles's execution, marked the only time in European history that a monarch was tried and executed while still holding the office of king.

The decision to try the king formed part of a deliberate political strategy. The men who arranged the proceeding knew that they were embarking upon a revolutionary course by declaring that the House of Commons, as the elected representative of the people, was the highest power in the realm. They also knew that the republican regime they were establishing did not command a large body of popular support. By trying the king publicly in a court of law and by ensuring that the trial was reported in daily newspapers (the first such trial in history), they hoped to prove the legitimacy of their cause and win support for the new regime.

The decision to bring the king to justice created two legal problems. The first was to identify a crime upon which the trial would be based. For many years members of Parliament had insisted that the king had violated the ancient laws of the kingdom. The charge read that he had "wickedly designed to erect an unlimited and tyrannical power" and had waged war against his people in two civil wars. His prosecutors claimed that those activities amounted to the crime of treason. The problem was that treason in England was a crime committed by a subject against the king, not by the king against his subjects. In order to try the king for this crime, his accusers had to construct a new theory of treason, according to which the king had attacked his own political body, which they identified with the kingdom or the state.

The second problem was to make the court itself a legitimate tribunal. According to English constitutional law, the king possessed the highest legal authority in the land. He appointed his judges, and the courts represented his authority. Parliament could vote to erect a special court, but the bill authorizing it would become law only if the king agreed to it. In this case the House of Commons had set up the court by its own authority, and it had named 135 men, most of whom were army officers, to serve as its judges. The revolutionary nature of this tribunal was difficult to disguise, and Charles made its illegality the basis of his defense. When asked how he would plead, he challenged the legitimacy of the court.

"By what power am I called hither?" he asked. "I would know by what authority—I mean lawful authority. There are many unlawful authorities in the world—thieves and robbers by the highways. And when I know what lawful authority, I shall answer. Remember I am your king, your lawful king. . . . I have a trust committed to me by God by old and lawful descent; I will not betray it to answer to a new unlawful authority."

By taking this position Charles put himself on the side of the law, and by refusing to enter a plea he also prevented his prosecutors from presenting the evidence against him.

The arguments that King Charles and John Bradshawe, the president of the court, presented regarding the legitimacy of the court reflected the main constitutional conflict in seventeenth-century England. On the one hand was the doctrine of divine-right absolutism, according to which the king received his authority from God. He was therefore responsible to God alone, not to the people. His subjects could neither try him in a court of law nor fight him on the battlefield. "A king," said Charles, "cannot be tried by any superior jurisdiction on earth." On the other hand was the doctrine of popular sovereignty, which held that political power came from the people. As Bradshawe said in response to Charles's objection, "Sir, as the law is your superior, so truly Sir, there is something that is superior to the law, and that is indeed the parent or author of law, and that is the people of England." This trial, therefore, involved not only a confrontation between Charles and his revolutionary judges but an encounter between two incompatible political ideologies.

In 1649 the advocates of popular sovereignty triumphed over those of divine right. Charles was convicted as a "tyrant, traitor, murderer, and public enemy of the good people of this nation." The verdict was never in doubt, although only 67 of the 135 men originally appointed as judges voted to convict the king, and a mere 59 signed the death warrant. The trial succeeded only to the extent that it facilitated the establishment of the new regime. With Charles gone, the Rump could move ahead with the abolition of the monarchy and the establishment of a republic. But in dramatic terms the trial was a complete failure. Charles, a small shy man with a nervous stammer, was expected to make a poor impression, but he spoke eloquently when he refused to plead, and he won support from spectators in the gallery. In the greatest show trial of the seven-

Trial of Charles I at Westminster Hall, January 1649
The king is sitting in the prisoner's box in the foreground, facing the commissioners of the High Court of Justice. His refusal to plead meant that a full trial could not take place.

teenth century, the royal defendant stole the show.

When Charles's son, Charles II, was restored to the throne in 1660, Royalists finally had their revenge against the judges of this court. Those who could be found alive were hanged, disemboweled, and quartered. For those who were already dead, there was to be another type of justice. In 1661 Royalists exhumed the badly decomposed corpses of Bradshawe, Henry Ireton, and Oliver Cromwell, the three men who bore the largest responsibility for the execution of the king. The three cadavers were hanged and

their skulls were placed on pikes on top of Westminster Hall. This macabre ritual served as the Royalists' way of vilifying the memory of the judges of this illegal and revolutionary trial, and their unpardonable sin of executing an anointed king.

Questions of Justice

1. The men who brought King Charles to trial often spoke about bringing him to "justice." How is justice best understood in this context?
2. How does this trial reveal the limitations of divine-right absolutism in England?

Taking It Further

Peacey, Jason, ed. *The Regicides and the Execution of Charles I.* 2001. A collection of essays on various aspects of this episode and the men who signed the death warrant.

Wedgewood, C. V. *The Trial of Charles I.* 1964. Presents a full account and analysis of the trial by one of the great historical stylists of the twentieth century.

were also determined to keep political power in the hands of their own class.

The republican government established in 1649 did not last. Tension between the army and the Rump, fueled by the belief that the Rump was not creating a godly society, resulted in the army's dissolution of the Long Parliament in 1653 and the selection of a small parliament of zealous Puritans, nominated by the army. Known as the Barebones Parliament for one of its members, Praise-God Barebones, this assembly soon became hopelessly divided between radicals who wished to eliminate state support of the Church, the Court of Chancery, and the universities, and the moderates who opposed these measures. Unable to overcome its divisions, it too was dissolved after sitting for only five months.

At that point Oliver Cromwell (1599–1658), the commander in chief of the army and the most prominent member of the Council of State after 1649, had himself proclaimed Protector of England, Scotland, and Ireland.

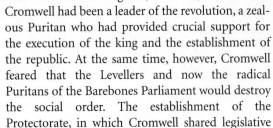

Allegorical View of Cromwell as Savior of England

Cromwell had been a leader of the revolution, a zealous Puritan who had provided crucial support for the execution of the king and the establishment of the republic. At the same time, however, Cromwell feared that the Levellers and now the radical Puritans of the Barebones Parliament would destroy the social order. The establishment of the Protectorate, in which Cromwell shared legislative power with Parliament, represented an effort to return to a more traditional system of government. Cromwell would not, however, go so far as to accept a petition of 1657 to make him king. After Cromwell's death in 1658 and the brief rule of his son Richard, the Protectorate collapsed. A period of political instability, in which there was renewed hostility between the army and the members of Parliament, led the army to restore the monarchy in 1660.

Later Stuart Absolutism and the Glorious Revolution

Charles II (r. 1660–1685) and his brother James II (r. 1685–1688) were both absolutists who admired the political achievement of their cousin, Louis XIV of France. At the same time, however, they realized that they could never return to the policies of their father, much less adopt those of Louis. Neither of them attempted to rule indefinitely without Parliament, as Charles I had. Their main objective was to destroy the independence of Parliament by packing it with their own supporters and use the prerogative to weaken the force of the parliamentary statutes to which they objected.

The main political crisis of Charles II's reign was the attempt by a group of members of Parliament, headed by the Earl of Shaftesbury (1621–1683) and known by their

DOCUMENT

John Locke Justifies the Glorious Revolution

John Locke wrote Two Treatises of Government *between 1679 and 1682, during the reign of Charles II. The main purpose of the book was to justify armed resistance against Charles, who was pursuing absolutist policies, including attacks on the freedom of the English Parliament. Locke did not publish the* Two Treatises, *however, until after the Glorious Revolution of 1688. In order to justify that revolution, Locke wrote two new paragraphs, claiming that when a king abandons his responsibility to enforce the law, as James II had when he fled to France in December 1688, the government was dissolved and the people had the right to form a new one, as they had when they offered the crown to William and Mary in February 1689.*

There is one more way whereby such a government may be dissolved, and that is when he who has the supreme executive power neglects and abandons that charge, so that the laws already made can no longer be put in execution. This is demonstrably to reduce all to anarchy, and so effectually to dissolve the government. For laws not being made for themselves, but to be by their execution the bonds of the society, to keep every part of the body politic in its due place and function, when that totally ceases, the government visibly ceases, and the people become a confused multitude, without order or connection. Where there is no longer the administration of justice, for the securing of men's rights, nor any remaining power within the community to direct the force, or provide for the necessities of the public, there is certainly no government left. Where the laws cannot be executed, it is all one as if there were no laws, and a government without laws is, I suppose, a mystery in politics, unconceivable to human capacity, and inconsistent with human society.

In these and in the like cases, when the government is dissolved, the people are at liberty to provide for themselves, by erecting a new legislative, differing from the other by the change of persons or form, or both, as they shall find it most for their safety and good. For the society can never, by the fault of another, lose the native and original right it has to preserve itself, which can only be done by a settled legislative and a fair and impartial execution of the laws made by it.

Source: From *Two Treatises of Government* by John Locke, 1698.

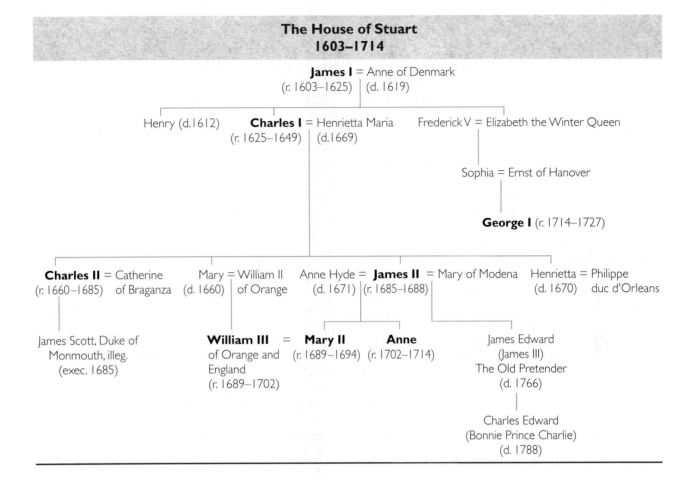

The House of Stuart
1603–1714

James I = Anne of Denmark
(r. 1603–1625) (d. 1619)

Henry (d.1612)   **Charles I** = Henrietta Maria   Frederick V = Elizabeth the Winter Queen
(r. 1625–1649) (d.1669)

Sophia = Ernst of Hanover

George I (r. 1714–1727)

Charles II = Catherine   Mary = William II   Anne Hyde = **James II** = Mary of Modena   Henrietta = Philippe
(r. 1660–1685) of Braganza   (d. 1660) of Orange   (d. 1671) (r. 1685–1688)   (d. 1670) duc d'Orleans

James Scott, Duke of   **William III** = **Mary II**   **Anne**   James Edward
Monmouth, illeg.   of Orange and   (r. 1689–1694) (r. 1702–1714)   (James III)
(exec. 1685)   England   The Old Pretender
   (r. 1689–1702)   (d. 1766)

Charles Edward
(Bonnie Prince Charlie)
(d. 1788)

opponents as Whigs, to exclude the king's brother, James, from the throne on the grounds that he was a Catholic. Charles opposed this strategy because it violated the theory of hereditary divine right, according to which God sanctioned the right of the king's closest heir to succeed him. Those members of Parliament who supported Charles on this issue, whom the Whigs called Tories, thwarted the designs of the Whigs in three successive parliaments between 1679 and 1681.

An even more serious political crisis occurred after James II succeeded to the throne in 1685. James began to exempt his fellow Catholics from the penal laws, which prevented them from worshiping freely, and from the Test Act of 1673, which had denied them the right to hold office under the crown. Catholics began to secure appointments in the army, the court, and local government. These efforts by the monarchy to grant toleration and political power to Catholics revived the traditional English fears of absolutism and popery. Not only the Whigs but also the predominantly Anglican Tories became alarmed at the king's policies. The birth of a Catholic son to James by his second wife, the Italian princess Mary of Modena, in June 1688 created the fear that the king's religious policy might be continued indefinitely. A group of seven Whigs and Tories, including the Bishop of London, drafted an invitation to William III of Orange, the captain-general of the military forces of the

Dutch Republic and James's nephew, to come to England to defend their Protestant religion and their constitution. William was married to James's eldest daughter, the Protestant Princess Mary, and as the king's nephew he also had a claim to the throne himself.

Invading with an international force of 12,000 men, William gathered substantial support from the English population, and when James's army defected, he was forced to flee to France without ever engaging William's forces in battle. The Convention, a special parliament convened by William in 1689, offered the crown to William and Mary while at the same time securing their assent to the Declaration of Rights, a document that later became the parliamentary statute known as the Bill of Rights. This bill, which is considered a cornerstone of the English constitution, corrected many of the abuses of royal power at the hands of James and Charles, especially the practice of exempting individuals from the penalties of the laws made by Parliament. By proclaiming William king and by excluding Catholics from the throne, the Bill of Rights also destroyed the theory of hereditary divine right.

It would be difficult to argue that this sequence of events, which is known as the Glorious Revolution, amounted to a revolution in the full sense of the word, because it did not change the basic institutions of English government. The revolution simply replaced one monarch with a king and queen who were more acceptable to the nation's political elite. But the events of 1688–1689 were decisive in defeating once and for all the absolutist designs of the Stuart kings and in guaranteeing that Parliament would form a permanent and regular place in English government. That Parliament has in fact met every year since 1689, and its legislative power grew considerably when the crown vetoed a bill for the last time in 1707.

For the English aristocracy, the peers and gentry who sat in Parliament, the revolution guaranteed that they would occupy a paramount position within English politics and society for more than a hundred years. The revolution also had profound effects on British and European diplomacy, as it quickly brought England and Scotland into a war against Louis XIV of France, the great antagonist of William III. The main reason William had come to England and secured the crown in the first place was to secure British entry into the European alliance he was building against France.

Even if the Glorious Revolution has been misnamed, it prompted the publication of a genuinely revolutionary political manifesto, John Locke's *Two Treatises of Government* (1690). Locke was a radical Whig; he had written the *Treatises* in the early 1680s as a protest against the absolutist policies of Charles II, but only after the abdication and flight of James II could he safely publish his manuscript. Like Hobbes, Locke argued that men left the state of nature and agreed to form a political society in order to protect their property and prevent the chaos that characterized a state of war. But unlike Hobbes, Locke asserted that the government they formed was based on trust and that governments that acted against the interests of the people could be dissolved. In these circumstances the people, in whom sovereignty was always vested, could establish a new regime. Locke's treatises constituted an uncompromising attack on the system of royal absolutism, which he equated with slavery. His work gave the people permission to take up arms against an oppressive regime even before that regime had consolidated its power. Since its publication, the *Two Treatises of Government* has been pressed into the service of various revolutionary and radical causes, most notably in the Declaration of Independence by the United States of America in 1776.

The Glorious Revolution had a direct bearing on the growth of the English state. As long as Parliament had remained suspicious of the Stuart kings, it had been reluctant to facilitate the growth of the state, which until 1688 was under direct royal control. Once the king's power had been permanently restricted, however, and Parliament had begun to emerge as the highest power within the country, Members of Parliament had less to fear from the executive branch of government. The inauguration of a long period of warfare against France in 1689 required the development of a large army and navy, the expansion of the bureaucracy, government borrowing on an unprecedented scale, and an increase in taxes. Members of Parliament, especially those in the Whig party, which had formed the main opposition to the monarchy before the revolution and had long opposed standing armies as a threat to English liberty, supported this expansion of the state as well as the war effort itself. By 1720 the kingdom of Great Britain, which had been created by the parliamentary union of England and Scotland in 1707, could rival the French state in military power, wealth, and diplomatic prestige. In fact, with its system of parliamentary government, Great Britain proved to be more successful than absolutist France in tapping the wealth of the people in the form of taxation to support its military establishment.

The Dutch Republic

In many respects the United Provinces of the Netherlands, known as the Dutch Republic, forms the most striking exception to the pattern of state building in seventeenth-century Europe. Formally established in 1588 during its revolt against Spanish rule, the Dutch Republic was the only major European power to maintain a republican form of government throughout the entire seventeenth century. As a state it also failed to conform to the pattern of centralization and consolidation that became evident in virtually all European monarchies. Having successfully resisted the centralizing policies of a large multinational Spanish monarchy, the Dutch Republic never acquired much of a centralized bureaucracy of its own. The provinces formed little more than a loose confederation of sovereign republican states. Each of the provinces sent deputies to the States General, where unanimity was required on all important issues, such as the levying of taxes, the declaration of war, and the ratification of treaties. Executive power was vested in a Council of State, which likewise consisted of deputies from the provinces. Even the individual provinces, the most important of which was Holland, were themselves decentralized, with the cities and rural areas sending delegates to a provincial assembly known as the States. Only the province of Holland invested one official, known as the grand pensionary, with extraordinary executive power.

This system of decentralized republican rule was much better suited for domestic affairs than the conduct of foreign policy. During most of the seventeenth century the Dutch were at war. After finally securing Spanish recognition of their independence by the Treaty of Münster in 1648, the Republic engaged in three commercial naval wars against England (1652–1654, 1665–1667, 1672–1674) and a much longer struggle against the territorial ambitions and economic policies of Louis XIV of France (1672–1678, 1689–1697, 1701–1713). The conduct of Dutch foreign policy and the coordination of the military forces of the seven provinces required some kind of central direction. During the 1650s John de Witt, the grand pensionary of Holland, assumed an informal presidency of the republic and directed the state's foreign policy in the first two wars against England. After 1672 William III, a prince of the hereditary house of Orange-Nassau, gave further unity and coordination to Dutch state policy. William, who served as the stadholder or governor of each of the seven provinces, became the captain-general of the republic's military forces when war with France began in 1672.

The House of Orange, which had a permanent vote in the States General, represented the royal, centralizing force within the Dutch Republic, and it led a party within the republic that favored a modification of republican rule. These princes never acquired the same type of constitutional authority that monarchs exercised in other European states. William III of Orange, who became William III of England and Scotland in 1689, exercised far more power in his new British kingdoms than he did in the Dutch Republic. Nevertheless the House of Orange played a crucial role in the rise of this tiny republic to the status of a world power. During the period of its influence the size of the Dutch military forces increased dramatically, from 50,000 men in 1670 to 73,000 in 1690 and 130,000 in 1710. During the same period of time the size of the Dutch navy doubled. In this one respect the republican, decentralized United Provinces participated in the same process of state building as the other great powers of Europe. The main reason the government was able to support this large standing army was the enormous wealth it had accumulated by virtue of the country's thriving international trade.

Political power in the Dutch Republic lay mainly with the wealthy merchants and bankers who served as regents in the councils of the towns. These same men represented the towns in the States of each province. The rural areas, which predominated only in the eastern provinces, were represented by the aristocracy. The country was therefore ruled by an oligarchy, but the men who belonged to it represented a predominantly urban, mercantile elite rather than a rural nobility. The members of this bourgeois elite did not tend to seek admission to landed society in the way that successful English merchants often did. Nor were they lured into becoming part of an ostentatious court in the manner of the French nobility. As men completely immersed in the world of commerce, they remained part of mercantile society and used their political power to guarantee that the Dutch state would serve the interests of trade.

The political prominence of Dutch merchants reflected the highly commercial character of the Dutch economy. Shortly after its truce with Spain in 1609, the Dutch cities, especially the rapidly expanding port city of Amsterdam in Holland, began to dominate European and world trade. The Dutch served as middlemen and shippers for all the other powers of Europe, transporting grain from the Baltic, textiles from England, timber from Scandinavia, wine from Germany, sugar from Brazil and Ceylon, silk from Persia and China, and porcelain from Japan to markets throughout the world. The Dutch even served as middlemen for their archenemy Spain, providing food and manufactured goods to the Spanish colonies in the New World in exchange for silver from the mines of Peru and Mexico. As part of this process Dutch trading companies, such as the Dutch East India Company, began to establish permanent outposts in India, Indonesia, North America, the Caribbean, South America, and South Africa. Thus a relatively small country, with one-tenth the population of France and one-third that of Great Britain, became a colonial power.

The Amsterdam Stock Exchange in 1668

Known as the Bourse, this multipurpose building served as a gathering point for merchants trading in different parts of the world. The main activity was the buying and selling of shares of stock in trading companies during trading sessions that lasted for two hours each day.

To support their dynamic mercantile economy, Dutch cities developed financial institutions favorable to trade. An Exchange Bank in Amsterdam, which had a monopoly on the exchange of foreign currencies, allowed merchants to make international transactions by adding sums to or deducting sums from their accounts whenever they imported or exported goods. The Dutch also developed rational and efficient methods of bookkeeping. A stock market, also situated in Amsterdam, facilitated the buying and selling of shares in commercial ventures. Even lawyers contributed to these commercial enterprises. In *The Freedom of the Sea* (1609), the great legal and political philosopher Hugo Grotius (1583–1645) defended the freedom of merchants to use the open seas for trade and fishing, thereby challenging the claims of European monarchs who wished to exclude foreigners from the waters surrounding their countries. Grotius, who also wrote *The Law of War and Peace* (1625), gained a reputation as the father of modern international law.

One of the most striking contrasts between the Dutch Republic and the kingdom of France in the seventeenth century lay in the area of religious policy. Whereas in France the revocation of the Edict of Nantes represented the culmination of a policy enforcing religious uniformity and the suppression of Protestant dissent, the predominantly Calvinist Dutch Republic gained a reputation for religious toleration. The Dutch Reformed Church did not always deserve this reputation, but secular authorities, especially in the cities, proved remarkably tolerant of different religious groups. Amsterdam, which attracted a diverse immigrant population during its period of rapid growth, contained a large community of Jews, including the

philosopher Baruch Spinoza (1632–1677). The country became the center for religious exiles and political dissidents, accommodating French Huguenots who fled their country after the repeal of the Edict of Nantes in 1685 as well as English Whigs (including the Earl of Shaftesbury and John Locke) who were being pursued by the Tory government in the 1680s. In keeping with this Dutch tradition of toleration, Dutch courts became the first to stop the prosecution of witches, executing the last person for this crime in 1608.

This tolerant bourgeois republic also made a distinct contribution to European culture during the seventeenth century, known as its Golden Age. The Dutch cultural achievement was greatest in the area of the visual arts, where Rembrandt van Rijn (1606–1669), Franz Hals (ca. 1580–1666) and Jan Steen (1626–1679) formed only part of an astonishing concentration of artistic genius in the cities of Amsterdam, Haarlem, and Leiden. Dutch painting of this era reflected the religious, social, and political climate in which painters worked. The Protestant Reformation had brought an end to the tradition of didactic and devotional religious painting that had flourished during the Middle Ages, leading many Dutch artists to adopt more secular themes for their work. At the same time the absence of a baroque court culture, such as that which still flourished in Spain and France as well as in the Spanish Netherlands, reduced the demand for royal and aristocratic portraiture as well as for paintings of heroic classical, mythological, and historical scenes. Instead the Dutch artists of the Golden Age produced intensely realistic portraits of merchants and financiers, such as Rembrandt's famous *Syndics of the Clothmakers of Amsterdam* (1662).

Rembrandt, *Syndics of the Clothmakers of Amsterdam* (1662)
Rembrandt's realistic portrait depicted wealthy Dutch bourgeoisie, who had great political as well as economic power in the Dutch Republic.

Realism became one of the defining features of Dutch painting, evident in the numerous street scenes, still lifes, and landscapes that Dutch artists painted and sold to a largely bourgeois clientele. At the same time Dutch engravers perfected the art of political printmaking, much of it highly satirical, an achievement that was encouraged by the political tolerance of the country.

In the early eighteenth century the Dutch Republic lost its position of economic superiority to Great Britain and France, which developed even larger mercantile empires of their own and began to dominate world commerce. The long period of war against France, which ended in 1713, took its toll on Dutch manpower and wealth, and the relatively small size of the country and its decentralized institutions made it more difficult for it to recover its position in European diplomacy and warfare. As a state it could no longer fight above its weight, and it became vulnerable to attacks by the French in the nineteenth century and the Germans in the twentieth. But in the seventeenth century this highly urbanized and commercial country showed that a small, decentralized republic could hold its own with the absolutist states of France and Spain as well as with the parliamentary monarchy of England.

Conclusion

The Western State in the Age of Absolutism

Between 1600 and 1715 three fundamental political changes, all related to each other, helped redefine the West. The first was the dramatic and unprecedented growth of the state. During these years all Western states grew in size and strength. They became more cohesive as the outlying provinces of kingdoms were brought more firmly under central governmental control. The administrative machinery of the state became more complex and efficient. The armies of the state could be called upon at any time to take action against internal rebels and foreign enemies. The income of the state increased as royal officials collected higher taxes, and governments became involved in the promotion of trade and industry and in the regulation of the economy. By the beginning of the eighteenth century one of the most distinctive features of Western civilization was the prevalence of these large, powerful, bureaucratic states. There was nothing like them in the non-Western world.

The second change was the introduction of royal absolutism into these Western states. From one end of the European continent to the other, efforts were made to establish the monarch as a ruler with complete and unrivaled power. These efforts achieved varying degrees of success, and in two states, England and the Dutch Republic, they ended in failure. Nevertheless, during the seventeenth and eighteenth centuries the absolutist state became the main form of government in the West. For this reason historians refer to the period of Western history beginning in the seventeenth century as the age of absolutism.

The third change was the conduct of a new style of warfare by Western absolutist states. The West became the arena where large armies, funded, equipped, and trained by the state, engaged in long, costly, and bloody military campaigns. The conduct of war on this scale threatened to drain the state of its financial resources, destroy its economy, and decimate its civilian and military population. Western powers were not unaware of the dangers of this type of warfare. The development of international law and the attempt to achieve a balance of power among European powers represented efforts to place restrictions on the conduct of seventeenth-century warfare. These efforts, however, were not completely successful, and in the eighteenth and nineteenth centuries warfare in the West entered a new and even more dangerous phase, aided by the technological innovations that the Scientific and Industrial Revolutions made possible. To the first of those great transformations, the revolution in science, we now turn.

Suggestions for Further Reading

For a comprehensive listing of suggested readings, please go to www.ablongman.com/levack2e/chapter15

Aylmer, G. E. *Rebellion or Revolution.* 1986. A study of the nature of the political disturbances of the 1640s and 1650s.

Beik, William. *Louis XIV and Absolutism: A Brief Study with Documents.* 2000. An excellent collection of documents.

Collins, James B. *The State in Early Modern France.* 1995. The best general study of the French state.

Elliott, J. H. *Richelieu and Olivares.* 1984. A comparison of the two contemporary absolutist ministers and state builders in France and Spain.

Harris, Tim. *Politics Under the Later Stuarts.* 1993. The best study of Restoration politics, including the Glorious Revolution.

Hughes, Lindsey. *Russia in the Age of Peter the Great.* 1998. A comprehensive study of politics, diplomacy, society, and culture during the reign of the "Tsar Reformer."

Israel, Jonathan. *The Dutch Republic: Its Rise, Greatness and Fall, 1477–1806.* 1996. A massive and authoritative study of the Dutch Republic during the period of its greatest global influence.

Lincoln, W. Bruce. *Sunlight at Midnight: St. Petersburg and the Rise of Modern Russia.* 2000. The best study of the building of Peter the Great's new capital city.

Parker, David. *The Making of French Absolutism.* 1983. A particularly good treatment of the early seventeenth century.

Parker, Geoffrey. *The Military Revolution.* 1988. Deals with the impact of the military revolution on the world as well as European history.

Rabb, Theodore K. *The Struggle for Stability in Early Modern Europe.* 1975. Employs visual as well as political sources to illustrate the way in which Europeans responded to the general crisis of the seventeenth century.

Schama, Simon. *The Embarrassment of Riches: An Interpretation of Dutch Culture in the Golden Age.* 1987. Contains a wealth of commentary on Dutch art and culture during its most influential period.

Wilson, Peter H. *Absolutism in Central Europe.* 2000. Analyzes both the theory and the practice of absolutism in Prussia and Austria.

Notes

1. Thomas Hobbes, *Leviathan,* ed. C. B. Macpherson (1968), 186.

2. Jean Bodin, *The Six Books of the Commonweale* (1606), Book II, Chapter 2.

3. Louis de Rouvroy, duc de Saint-Simon, *Memoirs of Louis XIV and the Regency* trans. Bayle St. John (1901) vol. 2, p. 11.

4. Quoted in Lindsey Hughes, *Russia in the Age of Peter the Great* (1998), 92.

The Scientific Revolution

16

I N 1609 Galileo Galilei, an Italian mathematician at the University of Padua, introduced a new scientific instrument, the telescope, which revealed a wealth of knowledge about the stars and planets that filled the night skies. Having heard that a Dutch artisan had put together two lenses in such a way that magnified distant objects, Galileo built his own such device and directed it toward the heavens. Anyone who has looked through a telescope or seen photographs taken from a satellite can appreciate Galileo's excitement at what he saw. Objects that appeared one way to the naked eye looked entirely different when magnified by his new "spyglass," as he called it. The Milky Way, the pale glow that was previously thought to be a reflection of diffused light, turned out to be composed of a multitude of previously unknown stars. The surface of the moon, long believed to be smooth, uniform, and perfectly spherical, now appeared to be full of mountains, craters, and other irregularities. The sun, which was also supposed to be perfect in shape and composed of matter that could not be altered, was marred by spots that appeared to move across its surface. When turned toward Jupiter, the telescope revealed four moons never seen before. Venus, viewed over the course of many months, appeared to change its shape, much in the way that the moon did in its various phases. This latter discovery provided evidence for the relatively new theory that the planets, including Earth, revolved around the sun rather than the sun and the planets around the Earth.

Galileo shared the discoveries he made not only with fellow scientists but with other Europeans. In 1610 he published *The Starry Messenger,* a treatise in which he described his discovery of the new moons of Jupiter. Twenty-two years later he included the evidence he had gained from his telescope in another book, *Dialogue Concerning the Two Chief World Systems,* to support the claim that the Earth orbited the sun. He also staged a number of public demonstrations of his new astronomical instrument, the first of which took place on top of one of the city gates of Rome in 1611. To convince those who doubted the reality of the images they saw, Galileo turned

The Telescope The telescope was the most important of the new scientific instruments that facilitated discovery. This engraving depicts an astronomer using the telescope in 1647.

the telescope toward familiar landmarks in the city. Interest in the new scientific instrument ran so high that a number of amateur astronomers acquired telescopes of their own.

Galileo's observations and discoveries formed one facet of the development that historians call the Scientific Revolution. A series of remarkable achievements in astronomy, physics, chemistry, and biology formed the centerpieces of this revolution, but its effects reached far beyond the observatories and laboratories of seventeenth-century scientists. The Scientific Revolution brought about fundamental changes in Western thought, altering the way in which Europeans viewed the natural world, the supernatural realm, and themselves. It stimulated controversies in religion, philosophy, and politics and brought about changes in military technology, navigation, and economic enterprise. The revolution added a new dimension to Western culture and provided a basis for claims of Western superiority over people in other lands. For all these reasons the Scientific Revolution marked a decisive turning point in the history of Western civilization, and it set the West apart from contemporary civilizations in the Middle East, Africa, and Asia.

The scientific culture that emerged in the West by the end of the seventeenth century was the product of a series of cultural encounters. It resulted from a complex interaction among scholars proposing different accounts of how nature operated. In some cases the scientists who advanced the revolutionary ideas were themselves influenced by ideas drawn from different cultural traditions. Some of these ideas had originated in Greek philosophy, while others came from orthodox Christian sources. Still other ideas came from a tradition of late medieval science, which had in turn been heavily influenced by the scholarship of the Islamic Middle East. A skeptical refusal to rely on any inherited authority whatsoever had its own religious and philosophical sources.

The main question this chapter seeks to answer is how European scientists in the sixteenth and seventeenth centuries changed the way in which people in the West viewed the natural world. Five specific questions, each of which will be addressed in a separate section of the chapter, will structure our exploration of this subject:

- **What were the scientific achievements and discoveries of the late sixteenth and seventeenth centuries that historians refer to as the Scientific Revolution?**
- **What methods did scientists use during this period to investigate nature, and how did they think nature operated?**
- **Why did the Scientific Revolution take place in western Europe at this particular time?**
- **How did the Scientific Revolution influence the development of philosophical and religious thought in the seventeenth and early eighteenth centuries?**
- **How did the Scientific Revolution change the way in which seventeenth- and eighteenth-century Europeans thought of their relationship to the natural world?**

The Discoveries and Achievements of the Scientific Revolution

- **What were the scientific achievements and discoveries of the late sixteenth and seventeenth centuries that historians refer to as the Scientific Revolution?**

Unlike political revolutions, such as the English Revolution of the 1640s discussed in the last chapter, the Scientific Revolution developed gradually and over a long period of time. It began in the middle and later decades of the sixteenth century and continued into the early years of the eighteenth century. Even though it took a relatively long time to unfold, it was revolutionary in the sense that it brought about a radical transformation of human thought, just as political revolutions have produced fundamental changes in systems of government. The most important changes in seventeenth-century science took place in the fields of astronomy, physics, chemistry, and biology.

Astronomy: A New Model of the Universe

The most significant change in astronomy was the acceptance of the view that the sun, not the Earth, was the center of the universe. Until the middle of the sixteenth century, most natural philosophers—as scientists were known at the time—subscribed to the writings of the Greek astronomer Claudius Ptolemy (100–170 C.E.). Ptolemy's observations and calculations had given considerable support to the cosmology° (a theory regarding the structure and nature of the universe) proposed by the Greek philosopher Aristotle (384–322 B.C.E.). According to Ptolemy and Aristotle, the center of the universe was a stationary Earth, around which the moon, the sun, and the other planets revolved in circular orbits. Beyond the planets a large sphere carried the stars, which stood in a fixed relationship to each other, around the Earth from east to west once every twenty-four hours, thus accounting for the rising and setting of the stars. Each of the four known elements—earth, water, air, and fire—had a natural place within this universe, with the heavy elements, earth and water, being pulled down toward the center of the Earth and the light ones, air and fire, hovering above it. All heavenly bodies, including the sun and the planets, were composed of a fifth element, called ether, which unlike matter on Earth was thought to be eternal and could not be altered, corrupted, or destroyed.

This traditional view of the cosmos had much to recommend it, and some educated people continued to subscribe to it well into the eighteenth century. The authority

(a)   (b)

Two Views of the Ptolemaic or Pre-Copernican Universe

(a) In this sixteenth-century engraving the Earth lies at the center of the universe and the elements of water, air, and fire are arranged in ascending order above the Earth. The orbit that is shaded in black is the firmament or stellar sphere. The presence of Christ and the saints at the top reflects the view that Heaven lay beyond the stellar sphere. (b) A medieval king representing Atlas holds a Ptolemaic cosmos. The Ptolemaic universe is often referred to as a two-sphere universe: The inner sphere of the Earth lies at the center and the outer sphere encompassing the entire universe rotates around the Earth.

of Aristotle, predominant in late medieval universities, was reinforced by the Bible, which in a few passages referred to the motion of the sun. The motion of the sun could be confirmed by simple human observation. We do, after all, see the sun "rise" and "set" every day, while the idea that the Earth rotates at a high speed and revolves around the sun contradicts the experience of our senses. Nevertheless, the Earth-centered model of the universe failed to provide an explanation for many patterns that astronomers observed in the sky, most notably the paths followed by planets. In the sixteenth century natural

philosophers began to consider alternative models of the universe.

The first major challenge to the Ptolemaic system came from a Polish cleric, Nicolaus Copernicus (1473–1543), who in 1543 published *The Revolutions of the Heavenly Spheres*, in which he proposed that the center of the universe was not the Earth but the sun. The book was widely circulated, but it did not win much support for the sun-centered theory of the universe. The mathematical arguments Copernicus presented in the book were so abstruse

DOCUMENT

Nicolaus Copernicus, *On the Revolution of Heavenly Spheres* (1500s)

that only the most erudite astronomers could understand them. Even those who could appreciate his detailed plotting of planetary motion were not prepared to adopt the central thesis of his book. In the late sixteenth century the great Danish astronomer Tycho Brahe (1546–1601) accepted the argument of Copernicus that the planets revolved around the sun but still insisted that the sun continued to revolve around the Earth.

Significant support for the Copernican model of the universe among scientists began to materialize only in the seventeenth century. In 1609 a German astronomer, Johannes Kepler (1571–1630), using data that Brahe had collected, confirmed the central position of the sun in the universe. In his treatise *New Astronomy*, Kepler also demonstrated that the planets, including the Earth, followed elliptical rather than circular orbits and that the planets moved in accordance with a series of physical laws. Kepler's book, however, did not reach a large audience, and his achievement was not fully appreciated until many decades later.

Galileo Galilei (1564–1642) was far more successful than Kepler in gaining support for the sun-centered model of the universe. In some respects Galileo was more conservative than Kepler. For example, Galileo never took issue with the traditional idea that the planets followed circular orbits. But Galileo had the literary skill, lacking in Kepler, of being able to write for a broad audience. Using the evidence gained from his observations with the telescope, and presenting his views in the form of a dialogue between the advocates of the two competing worldviews,

(a)

Two Early Modern Views of the Sun-Centered Universe

(a) The depiction by Copernicus. Note that all the orbits are circular, rather than elliptical, as Kepler was to show they were. The outermost sphere is that of the fixed stars. (b) A late-seventeenth-century depiction of the cosmos by Andreas Cellarius in which the planets follow elliptical orbits. It illustrates four different positions of the Earth as it orbits the sun.

(b)

he demonstrated the plausibility and superiority of Copernicus's theory.

The publication of Galileo's *Dialogue Concerning the Two Chief World Systems—Ptolemaic and Copernican* in 1632 won many converts to the sun-centered theory of the universe, but it lost him the support of Pope Urban VIII, who had been one of his patrons. Urban believed that by naming the character in *Dialogue* who defended the Ptolemaic system Simplicio (that is, a simple person), he was mocking the pope himself. In the following year Galileo was tried before the Roman Inquisition, an ecclesiastical court whose purpose was to maintain theological orthodoxy. The charge against him was that he had challenged the authority of Scripture and was therefore guilty of heresy, the denial of the theological truths of the Roman Catholic Church. (See "Justice in History: The Trial of Galileo" later in this chapter.)

As a result of this trial Galileo was forced to abandon his support for the Copernican model of the universe, and *Dialogue* was placed on the Index of Prohibited Books, a list compiled by the papacy of all printed works containing heretical ideas. Despite this setback, support for Copernicanism grew during the seventeenth century, and by 1700 it commanded widespread support among scientists and the educated public. *Dialogue*, however, was not removed from the Index until 1822.

Physics: The Laws of Motion and Gravitation

Galileo made his most significant contributions to the Scientific Revolution in the field of physics, which deals with matter and energy and the relationship between them. In the seventeenth century the main branches of physics were mechanics (the study of motion and its causes) and optics (the study of light). Galileo's most significant achievement in physics was to formulate a set of laws governing the motion of material objects. His work, which laid the foundation of modern physics, effectively challenged the theories of Aristotle regarding motion.

According to Aristotle, whose views dominated science in the late Middle Ages, the motion of every object except the natural motion of falling toward the center of the Earth required another object to move it. If the mover stopped, the object fell to the ground or simply stopped moving. One of the problems with this theory was that it could not account for the continued motion of a projectile, such as a discus or a javelin, after it left the hand of the person who threw it. Galileo's answer to that

question was a theory of inertia, which became the basis of a radical new theory of motion. According to Galileo, an object continues to move or to lie at rest until something external to it intervenes to change its motion. Thus motion is neither a quality inherent in an object nor a force that it acquires from another object; it is simply a state in which the object finds itself.

Galileo also discovered that the motion of an object occurs only in relation to things that do not move. A ship moves through the water, for example, but the goods carried by that ship do not move in relationship to the moving ship. This insight served the immediate purpose of explaining to the critics of Copernicus how the Earth can move even though we do not experience its motion. Galileo's most significant contribution to the study of mechanics was his formulation of a mathematical law of motion that explained how the speed and acceleration of a falling object are determined by the distance it travels during equal intervals of time.

The greatest achievements of the Scientific Revolution in physics belong to English scientist Sir Isaac Newton (1642–1727). Newton was one of those rare geniuses whose research changed the way future generations viewed the world. As a boy Newton found himself out of place while working on his mother's farm in a small hamlet in

CHRONOLOGY

Discoveries of the Scientific Revolution

1543	Andreas Vesalius publishes *On the Fabric of the Human Body*, the first realistic depiction of human anatomy; Copernicus publishes *The Revolutions of the Heavenly Spheres*, challenging the traditional Earth-centered cosmos
1609	Johannes Kepler publishes *New Astronomy*, identifying elliptical orbits of the planets
1628	William Harvey publishes *On the Motion of the Heart and Blood in Animals*, demonstrating the circulation of the blood
1632	Galileo publishes *Dialogue Concerning the Two Chief World Systems*, leading to his trial
1638	Galileo publishes *Discourses on the Two New Sciences of Motion and Mechanics*, proposing new laws of motion
1655	Evangelista Torricelli conducts experiments on atmospheric pressure
1659	Robert Boyle invents the air pump and conducts experiments on the elasticity and compressibility of air
1673	Christian Huygens publishes *On the Motion of Pendulums*, developing his theories of gravitation and centrifugal force
1687	Newton publishes his *Mathematical Principles of Natural Philosophy*, presenting a theory of universal gravitation

Lincolnshire and while attending school in the same county. Fascinated by mechanical devices, he spent much of his time building wooden models of windmills and other machines. When playing with his friends he always found ways to exercise his mind, calculating, for example, how he could use the wind to win jumping contests with his classmates. While he was still an adolescent, it had become obvious to all his acquaintances that the only place where he would be comfortable would be at a university. In 1661 he entered Trinity College, Cambridge, a step that introduced him to the broader world of ideas. In 1667 he became a fellow of the college and two years later, at age 27, he became the Lucasian Professor of Mathematics.

At Cambridge Newton pursued a wide range of intellectual interests, including the study of biblical prophecy. His great discoveries, however, were in the disciplines of mathematics and natural philosophy. During the 1680s Newton formulated a set of mathematical laws that governed the operation of the entire physical world. In 1687 he published his theories in *Mathematical Principles of Natural Philosophy*. The centerpiece of this monumental work was the universal law of gravitation°, which demonstrated that the same force holding an object to the Earth also holds the planets in their orbits. Newton established that any two bodies attract each other with a force that is directly proportional to the product of their masses and inversely proportional to the square of the distance between them. This law represented a synthesis of the work by Kepler on planetary motion, Galileo on inertia, the English physicist Robert Hooke (1635–1703) on gravity, and the Dutch scientist Christian Huygens (1629–1695) on centrifugal force. Newton's *Mathematical Principles* superseded the works of all these scientists by establishing the existence of a single gravitational force and by giving it precise mathematical expression. At the same time it revealed the unity and order of the entire physical world. It provided, in Newton's words, "a system of the world."

Newton extended his study of motion to the science of optics by demonstrating that light consists of small particles that also follow the laws of motion. Newton's theory prevailed until the early nineteenth century, when a series of experiments provided support for a new theory of light, according to which light should be thought of as waves, similar to those that cross a pond after a stone is dropped. Later in the nineteenth century the wave theory itself gave way to the view that light is a form of electromagnetic radiation. The most revolutionary change in our understanding of light, however, came with Newton in the seventeenth century.

Chemistry: Discovering the Elements of Nature

At the beginning of the seventeenth century, the branch of science today called chemistry had little intellectual respectability. It was not even an independent discipline, because it was considered a part of either medicine or

alchemy°, the magical art of attempting to turn base metals into precious ones. The most famous chemist of the sixteenth century was the Swiss physician and natural magician Paracelsus (1493–1541), who rejected the theory advanced by the Greek physician Galen (129–200 C.E.) that diseases were caused by the imbalance of the four "humors" or fluids in the body—blood, phlegm, black bile, and yellow bile. The widespread medical practice of drawing blood from sick patients to cure them was based on Galen's theory. Paracelsus began instead to treat his patients with chemicals, such as mercury and sulfur, to cure certain diseases. Paracelsus and his followers also believed that chemistry would provide a new basis for the understanding of nature, and he interpreted the biblical account of Creation as the chemical unfolding of nature. Paracelsus is often dismissed for his belief in alchemy, but his prescription of chemicals to treat specific diseases helped give chemistry a respectable place within medical science.

During the seventeenth century chemistry became a legitimate field of scientific research, largely as the result of the

Sir Isaac Newton
This portrait was painted by Sir Godfrey Kneller in 1689, two years after the publication of *Mathematical Principles of Natural Philosophy*.

Portrait of Robert Boyle with His Air Pump in the Background (1664)
Boyle's pump became the center of a series of experiments carried on at the Royal Society in London.

work of the English natural philosopher Robert Boyle (1627–1691). Boyle destroyed the prevailing idea that all basic constituents of matter share the same structure. He contended that the arrangement of their components, which Boyle identified as corpuscles or atoms, determines their characteristics. Boyle also conducted experiments on the volume, pressure, and density of gas and the elasticity of air. His most famous experiments, undertaken with the help of an air pump, proved the existence of a vacuum. Largely as a result of Boyle's discoveries, chemists won acceptance as legitimate members of the company of scientists.

Biology: The Circulation of the Blood

The English physician William Harvey (1578–1657) made one of the great medical discoveries of the seventeenth century by demonstrating in 1628 that blood circulates throughout the human body. Harvey, who had studied medicine at the University of Padua and who became the royal physician to both James I and Charles I in England,

challenged the traditional theory regarding the motion of the blood advanced by Galen and perpetuated by medieval philosophers. According to this traditional theory, blood originated in the liver, where it was converted from food and then flowed outward through the veins, providing nourishment to the organs and the other parts of the body. A certain amount of blood was also drawn from the liver into the heart, where it passed from one ventricle to the other and then traveled through the arteries to different parts of the body. During its journey this arterial blood was enriched by a special *pneuma* or "vital spirit" that originated in the atmosphere and was necessary to sustain life. When this enriched blood reached the brain, it became the body's "psychic spirits," which eventually traveled to the nerves and influenced human behavior.

During the late sixteenth century a succession of Italian scientists called specific aspects of Galen's theory into question. It was Harvey, however, who proposed an entirely new framework for understanding the motion of the blood. Through a series of experiments on human cadavers and live animals in which he weighed the blood that the heart pumped every hour, Harvey demonstrated that the blood circulates throughout the body, traveling outward from the heart through the arteries and returning to the heart through the veins. The heart, rather than sucking in blood, performed the essential function of pumping it by means of its contraction and constriction. The only gap in Harvey's theory was the question of how blood goes from the ends of the arteries to the ends of the veins. The answer to this question came in 1661, when scientists, using another new magnifying instrument known as a microscope, could see the capillaries connecting the veins and arteries. Harvey, however, had provided the basis for understanding how blood circulates through the body, and he had set a standard for the conduct of future biological research.

The Search for Scientific Knowledge

■ **What methods did scientists use during this period to investigate nature, and how did they think nature operated?**

The natural philosophers who made these various scientific discoveries worked in different academic disciplines, and each followed his own procedures for discovering scientific truth. In the sixteenth and seventeenth centuries there was no such thing as a single "scientific method." Many natural philosophers, however, shared similar views regarding the way in which nature operated and the means by which humans could acquire knowledge of it. In searching for scientific knowledge, these scientists engaged in extensive observation and experimentation, used a process of deductive reasoning to solve scientific problems,

Dissecting the Human Corpse

As medical science developed in the sixteenth and seventeenth centuries, the dissection of human corpses became a standard practice in European universities and medical schools. Knowledge of the structure and composition of the human body, which was central to the advancement of physiology, could best be acquired by cutting open a corpse to reveal the organs, muscles, and bones of human beings. The practice reflected the emphasis scientists placed on observation and experimentation in conducting scientific research. In the sixteenth century the great Flemish physiologist Andreas Vesalius (1514–1564), who published the first realistic drawings of human anatomy in 1543, cut limbs and extracted organs in his lectures on anatomy at the University of Padua. A century later, the English physician William Harvey dissected human cadavers in his path-breaking study of the circulation of the blood.

The physicians who performed dissections had difficulty securing an adequate supply of corpses. A preference developed for the bodies of recently hanged criminals, mainly because rulers claimed jurisdiction over the bodies of the condemned and could dispose of them at will. Criminals, moreover, were generally young or middle-aged and in fairly good health, thus making them desirable specimens for dissection. Demand for corpses became so great in the late seventeenth and eighteenth centuries that surgeons were willing to pay a price for them, thus turning the dead human body into a commodity. In eighteenth-century England the demand for bodies of the hanged often resulted in brawls between the agents whom the surgeons paid to snatch the bodies from the scaffold and the relatives and friends of the deceased, who wanted to claim the corpses in order to guarantee a decent burial.

During the sixteenth and seventeenth centuries, dissection underwent two transformations. The first was the expansion of the audience from a small group of medical students to a large cross-section of scholars who attended in order to learn more about the relationship between human beings and the natural world. The audiences also began to include artists, who learned from these exercises how to depict the human body more accurately. The second change was the transformation of dissection into a public spectacle, controlled by municipal authorities. During the seventeenth century, the city of Bologna staged dissections every year before crowds of as many as 200 people.

To these public dissections, which took place in many other European cities, people from the lower classes were often admitted together with scholars, students, and artists. The uneducated men and women who attended were attracted by the entertaining aspects of the event and the eagerness to witness the violence done to the corpse, just as they were at public executions. They were particularly eager to see the dissection of the genital organs, so much so that some authorities restricted access to that part of the dissection in the interest of public decency.

The holding of public anatomy lessons had much less to do with the popularization of science than with the satisfaction of the popular taste for blood and sex. Only in the late eighteenth century, during the age of the Enlightenment, did a new sensitivity to blood and human torment and an unprecedented repugnance toward death bring about an end to public dissections, together with the public executions with which they were closely associated.

For Discussion

What interests were served by holding public dissections of human corpses in the seventeenth and eighteenth centuries?

Dissection
The English surgeon William Cheselden giving an anatomical demonstration to spectators in London ca. 1735.

expressed their theories in mathematical terms, and argued that nature operated like a machine. Taken together, these common features of scientific research ultimately defined a distinctly Western approach to solving scientific problems.

Observation and Experimentation

The most prominent feature of scientific research in sixteenth- and seventeenth-century Europe was the extensive observation of nature, combined with the testing of hypotheses by means of rigorous experimentation. This was primarily a process of induction°, in which theories emerged only after the systematic accumulation and analysis of large amounts of data. It assumed a willingness to abandon all preconceived notions, whether they were those of Aristotle, Galen, or medieval philosophers, and to base scientific conclusions on experience and observation.

The English philosopher Francis Bacon (1561–1626) promoted this empirical, experimental approach in his book *New Organon* (1620), in which he complained that all previous scientific endeavors, especially those of ancient Greek philosophers, relied too little on experimentation. By contrast, Bacon's approach involved the thorough and systematic investigation of nature, a process that Bacon, who was a lawyer and judge, compared to the interrogation of a person suspected of committing a crime. Bacon claimed that scientific experimentation was "putting nature to the question" in order to obtain the truth, a phrase that referred to questioning a prisoner under torture to determine the facts of a case.

Francis Bacon, *Novum Organum* (1620)

All the great scientists of the sixteenth and seventeenth centuries abandoned preconceived notions and based their theories on the facts of nature, but the most enthusiastic practitioners of carefully planned and controlled experimentation came from England. Two of its most tireless advocates were Boyle, who performed a succession of experiments with an air pump to prove the existence of a vacuum, and Robert Hooke, whose experiments with a pendulum provided one of the foundations for Newton's theory of universal gravitation. Harvey belongs to the same English experimental tradition, although his commitment to this methodology originated at the University of Padua. Galileo and some other Italian scientists matched the English in their insistence on experimentation, but Galileo's experiments were designed more to demonstrate the validity of his theories than to help him establish them in the first place.

Deductive Reasoning

The second feature of sixteenth- and seventeenth-century scientific research was the application of deductive reasoning to scientific problems. Unlike the inductive experimental approach, which found its most enthusiastic practitioners in England, the deductive approach had its most zealous advocates on the European continent. The men who took this approach were just as determined as Bacon and Boyle to replace the testimony of human authorities with what they discovered from nature itself. Their main method, however, was to establish basic scientific truths or propositions from which other ideas or laws could be deduced logically. The French philosopher and mathematician René Descartes (1596–1650) became the champion of this methodology. In his *Discourse on the Method* (1637) he recommended that in solving any intellectual problem a person should first establish fundamental principles or truths and then proceed deductively from those ideas to more specific conclusions.

The model for deductive reasoning was mathematics, in which one also moves logically from certain premises to conclusions by means of equations. Rational deduction° proved to be an essential feature of scientific methodology, although some scientists relied too heavily on it at the expense of a more experimental approach. The limitations of an exclusively deductive approach became apparent when Descartes and his followers deduced a theory of gravitation from the principle that objects could influence each other only if they actually touched. The theory, as well as the principle upon which it was based, lacked an empirical foundation, which is one based on observation and experience, and eventually had to be abandoned.

Mathematics and Nature

The third feature of scientific research in the sixteenth and seventeenth centuries was the application of mathematics to the study of the physical world. The mathematical treatment of nature was undertaken by scientists working in both the experimental and the deductive traditions. Descartes shared with Galileo, Kepler, and Huygens the conviction that nature had a geometrical structure and that it could therefore be understood in mathematical terms. The physical dimensions of matter, which Descartes claimed were its only properties, could of course be expressed mathematically. Galileo claimed that mathematics was the language in which philosophy was written in "the book of the universe."

This mathematical way of looking at the physical world had a long history. The Greek philosophers Pythagoras (582–507 B.C.E.) and Plato (ca. 428–348 B.C.E.) had both emphasized the geometric structure of the cosmos and therefore considered numbers to hold the key to its secrets. In the fifteenth century Renaissance philosophers revived this ancient Greek emphasis on mathematics. Copernicus, who was influenced by Platonic thought, criticized the Islamic and western European medieval philosophers who had accepted an Earth-centered universe for their mathematical miscalculations. Copernicus advocated a rigorous application of mathematics to astronomical writing. One of the reasons his book *The Revolutions of the Heavenly Spheres* was so demanding was that he described planetary motion in technical, mathematical terms.

In the seventeenth century Isaac Newton's work provides the best illustration of the application of mathematics to scientific problems. Newton used observation and experimentation to confirm his theory of universal gravitation, but the work in which he presented his theory, *Mathematical Principles of Natural Philosophy,* was written in the language of mathematics. Just as Newton had synthesized previous work in physics to arrive at the law of universal gravitation, he also combined the experimental and deductive approaches to acquire scientific truth. His approach to solving scientific problems, which became a model for future scientific research, involved generalization on the basis of particular examples derived from experiments and the use of deductive, mathematical reasoning to discover the laws of nature.

The Mechanical Philosophy

Much of the scientific experimentation and deduction undertaken in the seventeenth century proceeded on the assumption that the natural world operated as if it were a machine made by a human being. This philosophy of nature, which is often referred to as the mechanical philosophy°, cannot be attributed to a single person, but its most comprehensive statement can be found in the work of Descartes. The scholastic philosophers of the fourteenth and fifteenth centuries insisted that nature was fundamentally different from a machine or any other object built by humans. According to the scholastics, natural bodies had an innate tendency to change, whereas artificial objects, that is, those constructed by humans, did not. Descartes, Kepler, Galileo, and Bacon all denied that assumption, arguing that nature operated in a mechanical way, just like a clock or some other piece of machinery. The only difference was that we cannot readily observe the structures of natural mechanisms, in the way that we can see the structure of a pump or a wagon.

According to mechanists—scientists who subscribed to the mechanical philosophy—nature consisted of many machines, some of them extremely small. The human body was itself a machine, and the center of that human machine, the heart, was in Harvey's words "a piece of machinery in which, though one wheel gives motion to another, yet all the wheels seem to move simultaneously." Because the human body was made by God, it was superior to any human-made machine, but it was still nothing more than a machine.

According to Descartes, the only part of a human being that was not a machine was the mind, which was completely different from the body and the rest of the material world. Unlike the body, the mind was an immaterial substance that could be neither extended in space nor divided. Nor could it

be measured mathematically, in the way one could record the dimensions of the human body. Because Descartes made this sharp distinction between the mind and the human body, we speak of his philosophy as being dualistic°.

The mechanical philosophy presented just as bold a challenge to the philosophers known as Neoplatonists° as it did to the scholastics. Neoplatonists were inspired by the work of Plotinus (205–270 C.E.), the last great philosopher of antiquity who had synthesized the work of Plato with that of other Greek philosophers. Plotinus also drew on many traditions of ancient Persian religion. Neoplatonic thought experienced a revival in the fifteenth and sixteenth centuries at the time of the Renaissance (see Chapter 11). Neoplatonists believed that the natural world was animistic—that is, it possessed a soul (known to them as a world soul) and was charged with various occult forces and spirits. The English natural philosopher William Gilbert (1544–1603), who wrote extensively on the phenomenon of magnetism, adopted a Neoplatonic worldview when he declared that the Earth and other planets were actually alive. Kepler clearly recognized the incompatibility of this outlook with that of the mechanical philosophy when he insisted that "the machine of the universe is not similar to a divine animated being but similar to a clock."[1]

René Descartes
Although Descartes was a scientist who made contributions to the study of biology and optics, he is best known for the method he proposed to attain certain knowledge and his articulation of the mechanical philosophy.

Descartes and other mechanists argued that matter was completely inert or dead. It had neither a soul nor any innate purpose. Its only property was extension, or the physical dimensions of length, width, and depth. Without a spirit or any other internal force directing its action, matter simply responded to the power of the other bodies with which it came in contact. According to Descartes, all physical phenomena could be explained by reference to the dimensions and the movement of particles of matter. He once claimed, "Give me extension and motion and I will construct the universe."[2] Even the human body contained no "vital spirits." It consisted only of flesh and the blood pumped by the mechanism of the heart. The only difference between the human body and other machines was that the mind (or soul) could move it, although how it did so was a matter of great controversy, as we shall see in a later section.

The view of nature as a machine implied that it operated in a regular, predictable way in accordance with unchanging laws of nature. Scientists could use reason to discover what those laws were and thus learn how nature performed under any circumstances. The scientific investigations of Galileo and Kepler were based on those assumptions, and Descartes made them explicit. The immutability of the laws of nature implied that the entire universe was uniform in structure, an assumption that underlay Newton's formulation of the laws of motion and of universal gravitation. Newton's theory of gravity denied Descartes's view of matter as inert, but he nonetheless accepted his view that the universe operated like a machine.

The Causes of the Scientific Revolution

■ Why did the Scientific Revolution take place in western Europe at this particular time?

Why did the Scientific Revolution take place at this particular time, and why did it originate in western European countries? What prompted natural philosophers in Italy, France, England, and the Dutch Republic to develop new ways of looking at the world? There are no simple answers to these questions. We can, however, identify a number of developments that inspired this remarkable set of scientific discoveries. Some of these developments were internal to science, in the sense that they arose out of earlier investigations conducted by natural philosophers in the late Middle Ages, the Renaissance, and the sixteenth century. Others were external to the development of science, arising out of the religious, political, social, and economic life of Europe during the early modern period.

Developments Within Science

The three internal causes of the Scientific Revolution were the research into motion conducted by scholastic natural philosophers in the fourteenth century, the scientific investigations conducted by humanists at the time of the Renaissance, and the collapse of the dominant conceptual frameworks that had governed scientific inquiry and research for centuries.

Late Medieval Science

Modern science can trace some of its origins to the fourteenth century, when the first significant modifications of Aristotle's scientific theories began to emerge. These challenges came not only from theologians, who objected that Aristotle was a pagan philosopher, but from natural philosophers, who refined some of the basic ideas of Aristotle's physics.

The most significant of these refinements was the theory of impetus. Aristotle, as we have seen, had argued that an object would stop as soon as it lost contact with the object that moved it. The scholastic philosophers who modified this principle claimed that objects in motion acquire a force that stays with them after they lose contact with the mover. The theory of impetus did not bring about a full-scale demolition of Aristotle's mechanics, but it did begin to call Aristotle's authority into question. The theory of impetus was known in Galileo's day, and it influenced some of his early thought on motion.

Scholastic philosophers of the fourteenth century also began to recommend direct, empirical observation in place of the traditional scholastic tendency to accept preconceived theories regarding the operation of nature. This approach to answering scientific questions did not result in the type of rigorous experimentation that Bacon demanded three centuries later, but it did encourage scientists to base their theories on the facts that emerged from an empirical study of nature.

The contribution of late medieval science to the Scientific Revolution should not be exaggerated. Scholastic natural philosophers continued to accept the cosmology of Ptolemy. They still perpetuated the anatomical theories of Galen. The restraints that theology exercised over scientific thought in the Middle Ages also prevented the emergence of new scientific ideas.

Renaissance Science

Natural philosophers during the Renaissance made more tangible contributions to the rise of modern science than the scholastics of the late Middle Ages. Renaissance natural philosophers made those contributions despite the fact that the Renaissance, the revival of classical antiquity in the fifteenth and sixteenth centuries, was not conducive to the type of scientific research that Galileo, Descartes, Boyle, and Newton conducted. Renaissance humanism was mainly a literary and artistic movement, and humanists were not particularly interested in scientific knowledge. Humanism also cultivated a tradition of deferring to the superior wisdom of classical authors, whereas the new science defined itself largely in opposition to the theories of the ancients, especially Aristotle, Ptolemy, and Galen. The main philosophical movement of the Renaissance, moreover, was Neoplatonism, which, as we have seen, promoted an animistic view of nature that mechanists such as Descartes and Kepler rejected.

The natural philosophers of the Renaissance did nonetheless make a number of important contributions to the birth of modern science. Many of the discoveries of the late sixteenth and seventeenth centuries drew their inspiration from Greek scientific works that had been recovered in their original form during the Renaissance. Copernicus found the original idea of his sun-centered universe in the writings of Aristarchus of Samos, a Greek astronomer of the third century B.C.E. whose work had been unknown during the Middle Ages. The theory that matter was divisible into small measurable particles known as atoms was inspired at least in part by the recovery of the texts of the ancient philosophers, most notably Democritus, who flourished around 480 B.C.E. Sixteenth-century editions of the works of Archimedes (287–212 B.C.E.), which had been virtually unknown in the Middle Ages, stimulated interest in the science of mechanics. The recovery and translation of previously unknown texts also made scientists aware that Greek scientists did not always agree with each other and thus provided a stimulus to independent observation and experimentation as a means of resolving their differences.

The Renaissance philosophy of Neoplatonism, despised by mechanists, also played an important role in the Scientific Revolution. In addition to the belief that the natural world had a soul, Neoplatonists adopted a geometric view of the universe and therefore encouraged the application of mathematics to the study of the natural world. Kepler developed his third law of planetary motion by applying to the cosmos the Neoplatonic idea of a harmony between numbers. The Neoplatonic tendency to think in terms of large, general categories also encouraged scientists such as Kepler, Galileo, and Newton to discover universal laws of nature. Even alchemy, which many Neoplatonists practiced during the Renaissance, involved natural philosophers in experiments that gave them a limited sense of control over the operations of nature. The followers of Paracelsus, whose alchemy was tinged with Neoplatonic mysticism, were firm advocates of the observation of nature and experimentation.

Some of the most prominent natural philosophers of the seventeenth century were influenced to some extent by the cultural traditions that we associate with the Renaissance. Kepler became involved in the study of magic at the court of the Holy Roman Emperor Rudolf II. From his reading in Neoplatonic sources, Kepler acquired his belief that the universe was constructed according to geometric principles.

DOCUMENT

Copernicus Proposes His Sun-Centered Theory of the Universe

In the dedication of his book On the Revolution of the Heavenly Spheres *(1543) to Pope Paul III, Copernicus explains that in his search for an orderly model of the universe he drew inspiration from a few ancient philosophers who had imagined that the Earth moved. He then explained how he had bolstered his theory through long and frequent observations. Anticipating condemnation from those who based their astronomical theories on the Bible, he appeals to the pope for protection while showing contempt for the theories of his opponents.*

. . . I began to chafe that philosophers could by no means agree on any one certain theory of the mechanism of the Universe, wrought for us by a supremely good and orderly Creator . . . I therefore took pains to read again the works of all the philosophers on whom I could lay my hand to seek out whether any of them had ever supposed that the motions of the spheres were other than those demanded by the mathematical schools. I found first in Cicero that Hicetas had realized that the Earth moved. Afterwards I found in Plutarch that certain others had held the like opinion. . . .

Taking advantage of this I too began to think of the mobility of the Earth; and though the opinion seemed absurd, yet knowing now that others before me had been granted freedom to imagine such circles as they chose to explain the phenomena of the stars, I considered that I also might easily be allowed to try whether, by assuming some motion of the Earth, sounder explanations than theirs for the revolution of the celestial spheres might so be discovered.

Thus assuming motions, which in my work I ascribe to the Earth, by long and frequent observations I have at last discovered that, if the motions of the rest of the planets be brought into relation with the circulation of the Earth and be reckoned in proportion to the circles of each planet . . . the orders and magnitudes of all stars and spheres, nay the heavens themselves, become so bound together that nothing in any part thereof could be moved from its place without producing confusion of all the other parts and of the Universe as a whole. . . .

It may fall out, too, that idle babblers, ignorant of mathematics, may claim a right to pronounce a judgment on my work, by reason of a certain passage of Scripture basely twisted to serve their purpose. Should any such venture to criticize and carp at my project, I make no account of them; I consider their judgment rash, and utterly despise it.

Source: From Nicolaus Copernicus, *De Revolutionibus Orbium Caelestium* (1543), translated by John F. Dobson and Selig Brodetsky in *Occasional Notes of the Royal Astronomical Society*, Vol. 2, No. 10, 1947. Reprinted by permission of Blackwell Publishing.

Bacon gained some of his enthusiasm for experimentation from his interest in natural magic°, which was the use of magical words and drawings to manipulate forces in the physical world without calling on supernatural beings for assistance. Newton was fascinated by the subject of magic and studied alchemy intensively. The original inspiration of Newton's theory of gravitation probably came from his professor at Cambridge, the Neoplatonist Henry More, who insisted on the presence of spiritual and immaterial forces in the physical world.

These contributions of the Renaissance to the new science were so important that some historians have identified the sixteenth century, when learned magic was in vogue and when the mechanical philosophy had not yet taken hold, as the first stage of the Scientific Revolution, to be followed by the mechanical phase when the discoveries of Galileo, Boyle, and Newton took center stage. Modern science resulted not so much from the victory of the mechanical philosophy over its Neoplatonic predecessor but from this encounter between these two worldviews.

The Collapse of Paradigms

The third internal cause of the Scientific Revolution was the collapse of the intellectual frameworks that had governed the conduct of scientific research since antiquity. The key to understanding this development is the recognition that scientists in all historical periods do not strive to introduce new theories but prefer to work within an established conceptual framework, or what the scholar Thomas Kuhn has referred to as a paradigm°. Scientists strive to solve puzzles that are presented by the paradigm. Every so often, however, the paradigm that has governed scientific research for an extended period of time collapses because it can no longer account for many different observable phenomena. A scientific revolution occurs when the old paradigm collapses and a new paradigm takes its place.[3]

The revolutionary developments we have studied in astronomy and biology can be explained at least in part by the collapse of old paradigms. In astronomy the paradigm that had governed scientific inquiry in antiquity and the Middle Ages was the Ptolemaic system, in which the sun and the planets revolved around the Earth. Whenever ancient or medieval astronomers confronted a new problem as a result of their observations, they tried to accommodate the results to the Ptolemaic model. In the process they had to refine the basic concept that Ptolemy had presented. By the sixteenth century the paradigm had been modified or adjusted so many times that it no longer made sense. As scientists gradually added numerous "epicycles" of planetary motion outside the prescribed spheres, and as they identified numerous "eccentric" or noncircular orbits around the Earth, Ptolemy's paradigm of a harmoniously functioning universe gradually became a confused collection of planets and stars following different motions. Faced with this situation, Copernicus began to look for a simpler and more plausible model of the universe. The sun-centered theory that he proposed became the new paradigm within which Kepler, Galileo, and Newton all worked.

In the field of biology a parallel development occurred when the old paradigm constructed by Galen, in which the blood originated in the liver and was drawn into the heart and from there traveled through the arteries to the brain and nerves, also collapsed. By the seventeenth century the paradigm of Galen could no longer satisfactorily explain the findings of medical scholars, such as the recognition that blood could not easily pass from one ventricle of the heart to the other. It was left to Harvey to introduce an entirely new paradigm, in which the blood circulated through the body. As in astronomy, the collapse of the old paradigm led to the Scientific Revolution, and Harvey's new paradigm served as a framework for subsequent biological research.

Developments Outside Science

A number of nonscientific developments also encouraged the development and acceptance of new scientific ideas. These developments outside science include the spread of Protestantism, the patronage of scientific research, the invention of the printing press, military and economic change, and voyages of exploration.

Protestantism

The growth of Protestantism in the sixteenth and seventeenth centuries encouraged the rise of modern science. Catholics as well as Protestants engaged in scientific research, and some of the most prominent European natural philosophers, including Galileo and Descartes, were devout Catholics. Protestantism, however, encouraged the emergence of modern science in three indirect ways.

First, Protestant countries proved to be more receptive than Catholic ones to new scientific ideas. Protestant churches, for example, did not prohibit the publication of books that promoted novel scientific ideas on the grounds that they were heretical, as the Papal Index did. The greater willingness of Protestant governments, especially those of England and the Dutch Republic, to tolerate the expression of unorthodox ideas helps to explain why the main geographical arena of scientific investigation shifted from the Catholic Mediterranean to the Protestant North Atlantic in the second half of the seventeenth century.

The second connection between Protestantism and the development of science was the emphasis Protestant writers placed on the idea that God revealed his intentions not only in the Bible but also in nature itself. Protestants claimed that individuals had a duty to discover what God had revealed to them in this way, just as it was their duty to read Scripture to gain knowledge of God's will. Kepler's claim that the astronomer was "as a priest of God to the book of nature," a reference to the Protestant idea of the priesthood of all believers, serves as an explicit statement of this Protestant outlook.

The third contribution of Protestantism to the new science was the strong Protestant belief in the millennium, the second coming of Christ predicted in the book of Revelation in the New Testament. Many Protestants believed that the event was about to occur and after Christ's arrival he would rule the world with the saints for a thousand years. In preparation for this climactic event, many English scientists, including Boyle and Newton, called for the use of scientific knowledge to achieve the general improvement of society. They also took seriously the biblical prediction that as the millennium approached, knowledge and understanding would increase.

Patronage

Although the intellectual problems that scientists grappled with may have inspired them to pursue their research and conduct experiments, they could not have succeeded without some kind of financial and institutional support. Only with the acquisition of an organizational structure could science acquire a permanent status, develop as a discipline, and give its members a professional identity. The universities, which today are known for their support of scientific research, did not serve as the main source of that support in the seventeenth century. One reason was that most universities, which were predominantly clerical institutions, had a vested interest in the defense of scholastic theology and Aristotelian science. They were therefore unlikely to provide the type of free academic atmosphere in which new scientific ideas might flourish. Moreover, within the university the only subject that allowed for the exploration of nature was that of philosophy. As long as science was considered a branch of philosophy, it could not establish its autonomy as a discipline and gain recognition as a legitimate pursuit in its own right.

Given limited support from the universities, scientists became dependent upon the patronage of wealthy and politically influential individuals. For the most part this patronage came from the kings, princes, and great noblemen who ruled European territorial states. During the seven-

teenth century, scientists found this type of patronage in two different types of institutions. The first were the courts of Italian and German princes. Galileo, for example, was the beneficiary of the patronage of Vincenzio Pinelli of Padua, the Venetian patrician Giovanfrancesco Sagredo, the Grand Duke of Tuscany Cosimo II de' Medici, the Roman aristocrat Prince Federico Cesi, and even Pope Urban VIII. These patrons, who were eager to display their interest in and support of learning, were actually responsible for securing Galileo's university appointments.

The terms of these appointments could be very generous. Galileo's appointment as Chief Mathematician at the University of Pisa, which Cosimo II secured for him in 1610, did not even require him to reside or teach there. Galileo's patrons gave him the opportunity to engage in his scientific work, and they circulated his publications at foreign courts. They did not, however, provide him with a permanent institutional base in which he could work.

Patronage from one politically powerful ruler rarely outlived the death of the patron, and the client could also lose the support of his patron, as Galileo did when he fell out of favor with Pope Urban VIII in 1632. Scientists who secured their livelihood at court also had to conduct themselves and their research in such a way as to maintain the favor of their patrons. Galileo referred to the new moons of Jupiter that he observed through his telescope as the Medicean stars in order to add luster to the image of the Medici family. His publications were inspired as much by his obligation to glorify Cosimo as by his belief in the validity of the sun-centered theory.

The second type of scientific institutions that provided patronage to scientists were academies in which groups of scientists could share ideas and work collectively. One of the earliest of these institutions was the Academy of the Lynxes in Rome, founded in 1603 by Prince Cesi. In keeping with the aristocratic values of its founder, it was modeled on an order of knights. Galileo became a member of this academy in 1611, and it published many of his works. In 1657 Cosimo II founded a similar institution, the Academy of Experiment, in Florence. These academies offered a more regular source of patronage than scientists could acquire from individual positions at court, but they still served the function of glorifying their founders, and they depended on patrons for their continued existence. The royal academies established in the 1660s, however, especially the Royal Academy of Sciences in France and the Royal Society in England, reduced that dependence on their patrons. These academies became in effect public institutions; even though they were established by the crown, they operated with a minimum of royal intervention. The royal academies also acquired a permanent location that made possible a continuous program of work.

The mission of the Royal Society in England was the promotion of scientific knowledge through a program of experimentation. It also served the political purpose of placing the results of scientific research at the service of the

CHRONOLOGY

The Formation of Scientific Societies

1603	Prince Cesi founds the Academy of the Lynxes in Rome
1657	Cosimo II de' Medici founds the Academy of Experiment in Florence
1662	Founding of the Royal Society of London under the auspices of Charles II
1666	Founding of the Academy of Sciences in Paris

state, as we shall see shortly. This had been Francis Bacon's objective in his *New Organon,* and many of the members of the society, including Robert Boyle and Robert Hooke, were committed to the implementation of Bacon's plans. The research that members of the Royal Society did on both ship construction and military technology gave some indication of this commitment. These attempts to use scientific technology to strengthen the power of the state show that two of the most important developments of the seventeenth century, the growth of the modern state and the emergence of modern science, were related.

The Printing Press

The scientific academies and societies of the seventeenth century gave natural philosophers an opportunity to discuss their findings among themselves, but these scientists also needed to communicate the results of their research to scientists in more distant localities. The introduction and spread of printing throughout Europe made it much easier for scientists to share their discoveries with others who were working on similar problems. During the Middle Ages, when books were handwritten, the dissemination of scientific knowledge was limited by the number of copies that could be made of a manuscript. Moreover, errors could easily creep into the text as it was being copied. The advent and spread of printing helped to correct this problem: Scientific achievements could be preserved in a much more accurate form and presented to a broader audience. The availability of printed copies also made it much easier for other scientists to correct or supplement the data that the authors supplied. In this way the entire body of scientific knowledge became cumulative, as it is today. Printing also made possible the reproduction of illustrations, diagrams, tables, and other schematic drawings that helped to convey the author's findings.

It remains uncertain how large a role printed materials played in the development of science. Scientists certainly read the work of others, but they also devoted large amounts of time to their own experiments, and those experiments in the long run were more important than books in the development of scientific knowledge. Printing may have accomplished more by making members of the nonscientific community aware of the latest advances in physics and astronomy than by leading scientists themselves to make new discoveries. In this way printing helped to make science an integral part of the culture of educated Europeans. The printing press also facilitated the growth of opposition to the new science, since it made possible the publication of treatises attacking the theories of Copernicus, Galileo, and Descartes.

Military and Economic Change

The Scientific Revolution occurred at roughly the same time that both the conduct of warfare and the European economy were undergoing dramatic changes. As territorial states increased the size of their armies and their military arsenals, they naturally demanded more accurate weapons with longer range. Some of the work undertaken by physicists during the seventeenth century, especially concerning the trajectory and velocity of missiles, gravitation, and air resistance, had the specific intention of improving military weaponry. Members of the Royal Society in England conducted extensive scientific research on these topics, and in so doing followed Francis Bacon's recommendation that scientists place their research at the service of the state.

The practical needs of capitalist enterprise also had a bearing on the direction of scientific research. The seventeenth century was a formative period in the emergence of a new capitalist economy, one in which private individuals engaged in trade, agriculture, and industry in order to realize ever-increasing profits. Some of the questions discussed at the meetings of the Royal Society suggest that its members undertook research with the specific objective of making such capitalist ventures more productive and profitable. The research did not always produce immediate results, but ultimately it increased economic profitability and contributed to the growth of the English economy in the eighteenth century. Knowledge of the displacement of water by ships led to improvements in methods of ship construction, which benefited merchants engaged in overseas trade. The determination of longitude by means of an accurate measurement of time at sea, a problem with which many seventeenth-century scientists grappled and which was finally solved in the eighteenth century with the invention of the chronometer, improved navigation. The study of mechanics led to new techniques to ventilate mines and raise coal or ore from them, thus making mining more profitable.

Voyages of Exploration

Closely related to the economic causes of the Scientific Revolution were the oceanic voyages of exploration that European mariners began to make in the late fifteenth century. As these voyages began long before the seventeenth century, they did not exercise an immediate or direct influence on the development of science. Most of the voyages, moreover, were undertaken by Portuguese and Spaniards, who did not play a major role in the Scientific Revolution. Nevertheless, these voyages revealed to mariners a number of natural phenomena that conflicted with the inherited traditions of Greek and late medieval science. They disproved, for example, much of what Ptolemy had written about the moistness of land in the Southern Hemisphere and what Aristotle had written about the difficulty of living in tropical areas. These inconsistencies led European natural philosophers to call into question the inherited authority of the Greeks on a variety of scientific matters and to base their views on the empirical observation of nature. In writing about the experimental method, Bacon frequently cited the body of evidence that had come from these voyages.

The Intellectual Effects of the Scientific Revolution

■ How did the Scientific Revolution influence the development of philosophical and religious thought in the seventeenth and early eighteenth centuries?

The Scientific Revolution had a profound impact on the intellectual life of educated Europeans. The discoveries of Copernicus, Kepler, Galileo, and Newton, as well as the assumptions upon which their work was based, influenced the subjects that people in the West studied, the way in which they approached intellectual problems, and their views regarding the supernatural realm.

Education

The philosophy of Aristotle, especially in its Christianized, scholastic form, had proved remarkably durable at European universities during the sixteenth century. It had successfully withstood the challenge of Neoplatonism, but the new science and the mechanical philosophy represented a more potent challenge to its supremacy. Over the course

CHRONOLOGY

The Impact of the Scientific Revolution

1620	Sir Francis Bacon publishes *The New Organon,* arguing for the necessity of rigorous experimentation
1633	Galileo tried by the Roman Inquisition
1637	René Descartes publishes *Discourse on the Method,* recommending the solution of intellectual problems through a process of deduction
1670	Baruch Spinoza publishes *Treatise on Religion and Political Philosophy,* challenging the distinction between spirit and matter
1682	Edict of Louis XIV ending most witchcraft trials in France
1685	Last execution for witchcraft in England
1686	Bernard de Fontenelle publishes *Treatises on the Plurality of Worlds,* a fictional work exploring the possibility of extraterrestial life
1691–1693	Balthasar Bekker publishes *The Enchanted World* in four volumes, denying the intervention of the Devil in the operation of the natural world
1709	Thomas Newcomen invents the first steam engine

of the seventeenth and early eighteenth centuries, especially between 1680 and 1720, science and the new philosophy that was associated with it acquired academic respectability and became an important component of university education. Outside academia, knowledge of science increased as the result of its promotion by learned societies, attendance at public lectures, the discussion of science in coffeehouses, and the publication of scientific textbooks. As this knowledge was diffused among the educated classes, science secured a permanent foothold in Western culture.

The spread of science did not go unchallenged. It encountered academic rivals committed not only to traditional Aristotelianism but also to Renaissance humanism, which had gradually penetrated the curriculum of the universities during the sixteenth and seventeenth centuries. Beginning in the late seventeenth century a conflict arose between "the ancients," who revered the wisdom of classical authors, and "the moderns," who emphasized the superiority of the new scientific culture. The most concrete expression of this conflict was the Battle of the Books, an intellectual debate that raged in England and on the Continent in the late seventeenth and early eighteenth centuries over the question of which group of thinkers had contributed more to human knowledge. The battle accentuated the differences between two distinct components of western European culture. The Battle of the Books ended with no clear winner, and the conflict between the ancients and the moderns has never been completely resolved. The humanities and the sciences, while included within the same curriculum at many universities, are still often regarded as representing two separate cultural traditions.

Skepticism and Independent Reasoning

One of the most significant intellectual effects of the Scientific Revolution was the encouragement it gave to the habit of skepticism, the tendency to doubt what we have been taught and are expected to believe. This skepticism formed part of the method that seventeenth-century scientists adopted in their efforts to solve philosophical problems. As we have seen, Descartes, Bacon, Galileo, and Kepler all refused to acknowledge the authority of classical or medieval texts, preferring instead to rely upon the knowledge they acquired from the observation of nature and the use of their own rational faculties.

In *Discourse on the Method,* Descartes showed the extremes to which this skepticism could be taken by doubting the reality of his own sense perceptions and even his own existence. He eventually found a way out of this dilemma when he real-

Baruch Spinoza

Spinoza was one of the most radical thinkers of the seventeenth century. His followers in the Dutch Republic, who were known as freethinkers, laid the foundations for the Enlightenment in the eighteenth century.

ized that the very act of doubting proved his existence as a thinking being. As he wrote in words that have become famous, "I think, therefore I am."[4] Upon this foundation Descartes went on to prove the existence of God and the material world, thereby conquering the skepticism with which he began his inquiry. In the process, however, Descartes had promoted an approach to solving intellectual problems that asked people to question the authority of others and to think clearly and systematically for themselves. The effects of this method began to become apparent in the late seventeenth century, when Descartes's methodology was invoked in challenging a variety of orthodox opinions regarding the supernatural world.

Some of the most radical of those opinions came from the mind of Baruch Spinoza (1632–1677), who grew up in Amsterdam in a community of Spanish and Portuguese Jews who had fled the Inquisition. Although educated in the Orthodox Jewish manner, Spinoza also studied Latin and read the works of Descartes and other Christian writers of the period. From Descartes, Spinoza had learned "that nothing ought to be admitted as true but what has been proved by good and solid reason." This skepticism and independence of thought led to his excommunication from the Jewish community at age 24, at which time he changed his first name from its Jewish form, Baruch, to Benedict. A skilled lens grinder by trade, Spinoza spent much of his life developing his philosophical ideas.

Spinoza challenged Descartes's separation of the mind and the body and the radical distinction between the spiritual and the material. For Spinoza there was only one substance in the universe, which he equated with nature or God. This pantheism, in which all matter became spirit and was comprehended within God, challenged not only the ideas of Descartes but also a fundamental tenet of Christianity—the distinction between God as pure spirit and the material world that he had created. In his most famous book, *A Treatise on Religion and Political Philosophy* (1670), Spinoza developed these ideas and also called for complete freedom from intellectual restraints.

The type of freethinking that Spinoza advocated aroused considerable suspicion. His followers, most of whom lived in the Dutch Republic, were constantly exposed to the danger of prosecution for atheism and blasphemy. Spinoza's skeptical approach to solving philosophical and scientific problems revealed the radical intellectual potential of the new science. The freedom of thought that Spinoza advocated, as well as the belief that nature followed immutable laws and could be understood in mathematical terms, served as important links between the Scientific Revolution and the Enlightenment of the eighteenth century. Those connections will be studied more fully in Chapter 18.

Science and Religion

The most profound intellectual effects of the Scientific Revolution occurred in the area of religious thought. The claims of the new science presented two challenges to traditional Christian belief. The first involved the apparent contradiction between the sun-centered theory of the universe and biblical references to the sun's mobility. Because the Bible was considered the inspired word of God, the Church took everything it said, including any passages regarding the operation of the physical world, as literally true. The Bible's reference to the sun moving across the sky served as the basis of the official papal condemnation of sun-centered theories in 1616 and the prosecution of Galileo in 1633.

The second challenge to traditional Christian belief was the implication that if the universe functioned as a machine, on the basis of immutable natural laws, then God apparently played a very small role in its operation. This position, which was adopted by the late-seventeenth- and eighteenth-century thinkers known as Deists°, was considered a denial of the Christian belief that God superintended the operation of the world and was continually active in its governance. None of the great scientists of the seventeenth century actually adopted this position, but the acceptance of the mechanical philosophy made them vulnerable to the charge that they denied Christian doctrine. Because of his support for the mechanical philosophy, Descartes was suspected of atheism.

Although the new science and seventeenth-century Christianity appeared to be on a collision course, a number of scientists and theologians insisted that there was no conflict between them. One argument they made was that religion and science were separate disciplines that had very different concerns. Religion dealt with the relationship between humans and God, while science explained how nature operated. As Galileo wrote in a letter to the Grand Duchess Christina of Tuscany in 1615, "The intention of the Holy Ghost is to teach us how one goes to heaven, not how the heaven goes."[5] Scripture was not intended to explain natural phenomena, but to convey religious truths that could not be grasped by human reason. In making these points Galileo was pleading for the separation of religion and science by freeing scientific inquiry from the control of the

DOCUMENT

Galileo Galilei,
*Letter to the
Grand Duchess
Christina*

Church. To some extent, that separation has taken place over the course of the last three centuries. Theology and science have gradually become separate academic disciplines, each with its own objectives and methodology. Even the papacy eventually accepted the position of Galileo on this question in 1992. Nevertheless, conflicts between the claims of science and those who believe in the literal truth of the Bible have not disappeared, especially regarding the theory of evolution.

Another argument for the compatibility of science and religion was the claim that the mechanical philosophy, rather than relegating God to the role of a retired engineer, actually manifested his unlimited power. In a mechanistic universe God was still the creator of the entire physical world and the formulator of the laws of nature that guaranteed its regular operation. He was still all-powerful and present everywhere. According to Boyle and Newton, moreover, God played a supremely active role in governing the universe. Not only had he created the universe, but, in a theory developed by Boyle, he also continued to keep all matter constantly in motion. This theory served the purpose of redefining God's power without diminishing it in

---

DOCUMENT

Science and the Preternatural

Thomas Sprat (1635–1713), an English clergyman who rose to be bishop of Rochester, was elected a member of the Royal Society of London in 1663, and in 1667 he published a history of that society. Sprat praised the tradition of experimentation that became the hallmark of the society, and in this passage he claimed that the empiricism of modern science eliminated the imaginary creatures, such as fairies and ghosts, that classical writers had invented and medieval theologians had continued to claim were the causes of unusual phenomena. According to Sprat, all such phenomena can be explained by natural causes and effects, through which God governed the universe. Sprat claims that by showing these creatures to be mere phantasms, science has eliminated the fear that people have had of them from early childhood.

And as for the terrors and misapprehensions which commonly confound weaker minds and make men's minds to fail and boggle at trifles, there is so little hope of having them removed by speculation alone that it is evident they were first produced by the most contemplative men among the ancients and chiefly prevailed of late years, when that way of learning flourished. The poets began of old to impose the deceit. They to make all things look more venerable than they were devised a thousand false chimeras; on every field, river, grove and cove, they bestowed a phantasm of their own making. With these they amazed the world; these they clothed with what shapes they pleased. By these they pretended that all wars and counsels and actions of men were administered. And in the modern ages these fantastical forms were revived and possessed Christendom in the very height of the schoolmen's time. An infinite number of fairies haunted every house; all churches were filled with apparitions; men began to be frightened from their cradles, which fright continued to their graves, and their names also were made the causes of scaring others. All which abuses if those acute philosophers did not promote, yet they were never able to overcome; nay, even not so much as King Oberon and his invisible army.

But from the time in which the real philosophy [science] appeared, there is scarce any whisper remaining of such horrors. Every man is unshaken at those tales at which his ancestors trembled. The course of things goes quietly along, in its own true channel of causes and effects. For this we are beholden to experiments, which though they have not yet completed the discovery of the true world, yet they have already vanquished those wild inhabitants of the false worlds that used to astonish the minds of men. A blessing for which we ought to be thankful, if we remember, that it is one of the greatest curses that God pronounces on the wicked, that they shall fear where no fear is.

Source: From *History of the Royal Society of London* by Thomas Sprat, 1702, pp. 339–341.

any way. Newton arrived at a similar position in his search for an immaterial agent who would cause gravity to operate. He proposed that God himself, who he believed "endures always and is present everywhere," made bodies move according to gravitational laws. Throughout the early eighteenth century this feature of Newtonian natural philosophy served as a powerful argument for the existence and immanence of God.

As the new science became more widely accepted, and as the regularity and immutability of the laws of nature became more apparent, religion itself began to undergo a transformation. Instead of denying the validity of the new science, many theologians, especially Protestants, accommodated scientific knowledge to their religious beliefs. Some Protestants welcomed the discoveries of science as an opportunity to purify the Christian religion by combating the superstition, magic, and ignorance that they claimed the Catholic Church had been promoting. Clerics who accepted the new science, including those who became members of the Royal Society, argued that because God worked through the processes of nature, human beings could acquire theological knowledge of him by engaging in scientific inquiry. For them religion and science were not so much separate but complementary forms of knowledge, each capable of illuminating the other.

The most widespread effect of the new science on religion was a new emphasis on the compatibility of reason and religion. In the Middle Ages scholastic theologians such as Thomas Aquinas had tried to reconcile the two, arguing that there was a body of knowledge about God, called natural theology, that could be obtained without the assistance of revelation. Now, however, with the benefit of the new science, theologians and philosophers began to expand the role that reason played in religion. In the religious writings of the English philosopher John Locke, the role of reason became dominant. In *The Reasonableness of Christianity* (1695), Locke argued that reason should be the final arbiter of the existence of the supernatural and it should also determine the true meaning of the Bible. This new emphasis on the role of reason in religion coincided with a rejection of the religious zeal that had characterized the era of the Reformation and the wars of religion. Political and ecclesiastical authorities looked down on religious enthusiasm not only as politically dangerous, as it had inspired revolution and rebellion throughout Europe, but as a form of behavior that had no rational basis.

The new emphasis on the reasonableness of religion and the decline of religious enthusiasm are often viewed as evidence of a broader trend toward the secularization of European life, a process in which religion gave way to more worldly concerns. In one sense this secular trend was undeniable. By the dawn of the eighteenth century, theology had lost its dominant position at the universities, the sciences had become autonomous academic disciplines, and religion had lost much of its intellectual authority. Religion also began to exercise less influence on the conduct of politics and diplomacy and on the regulation of economic activity.

Religion had not, however, lost its relevance. Throughout the eighteenth century it remained a vital force in the lives of most European people. Religious books continued to be published in great numbers. Many of those who accepted the new science continued to believe in a providential God and the divinity of Christ. Moreover, a small but influential group of educated people, following the lead of the French mathematician, physicist, and religious philosopher Blaise Pascal (1623–1662), insisted that although reason and science have their place, they represent only one sphere of truth. In his widely circulated book *Reflections,* which lay unfinished at his death but was published in 1670, Pascal argued that religious faith occupied a higher sphere of knowledge that reason and science could not penetrate. Pascal, the inventor of a calculating machine and the promoter of a system of public coach service in Paris, had been an advocate of the new science. He endorsed the Copernican model of the universe and opposed the condemnation of Galileo. But on the question of the relationship between science and religion, Pascal presented arguments that could be used against Spinoza, Locke, and all those who considered reason the ultimate arbiter of truth.

Magic, Demons, and Witchcraft

The new science not only changed many patterns of religious thought but also led to a denial of the reality and effectiveness of magic. Magic is the use of a supernatural, occult, or mysterious power to achieve extraordinary effects in the physical world or to influence the course of human events. The effects can be beneficial or harmful. Magicians claimed to be able to use their special powers to cure a person or inflict disease, acquire political power, stimulate love or hatred in another individual, predict the future, or produce any number of natural "marvels," including changes in the weather. In the sixteenth and seventeenth centuries men and women believed in and practiced two forms of magic. Natural magic, such as the practice of alchemy, involved the manipulation of occult forces that were believed to exist in nature. As we have seen, many Neoplatonists believed in the possibility of this type of magic, and many of them actually practiced it. Demonic magic°, on the other hand, involved the invocation of evil spirits so that one might gain access to their supernatural power. The men who were most committed to the mechanical philosophy denied the effectiveness of both types of magic. By claiming that matter was inert, they challenged the central notion of natural magic, which is the belief that material objects are animated by occult forces, such as an innate attraction to another object. If matter was not alive, it contained no forces for a magician to manipulate.

The Trial of Galileo

The events leading to the trial of Galileo for heresy in 1633 began in 1616, when a committee of eleven theologians reported to the Roman Inquisition that the sun-centered theory of Copernicus was heretical. Those who accepted this theory were declared to be heretics not only because they called the authority of the Bible into question but because they denied the exclusive authority of the Catholic Church to determine how the Bible should be interpreted. The day after this report was submitted, Pope Paul V instructed Cardinal Robert Bellarmine, a theologian who was on good terms with Galileo, to warn him to abandon his Copernican views. Galileo had written extensively in support of the sun-centered thesis, especially in his *Letters on Sunspots* (1613) and his *Letter to the Grand Duchess Christina* (1615), although he had never admitted that the theory was proved conclusively. Now he was being told that he should not hold, teach, or defend in any way the opinion of the sun's stability or the Earth's mobility. If he were to ignore that warning, he would be prosecuted as a heretic.

During the next sixteen years Galileo published two books. The first, *The Assayer* (1623), was an attack upon the views of an Italian philosopher regarding comets. The book actually won Galileo considerable support, especially from the new pope, Urban VIII, who was eager to be associated with the most fashionable intellectual trends. Urban took Galileo under his wing and made him the intellectual star of his court. Urban even went so far as to declare that support for Copernicanism was not heretical but only rash.

The patronage of the pope may have emboldened Galileo to exercise less caution in writing his second book of this period, *Dialogue Concerning the Two Chief World Systems* (1632). This treatise was ostensibly an impartial presentation of the rival Ptolemaic and Copernican cosmologies, but in its own quiet way it served the purpose of promoting Copernicanism. Galileo sought proper authorization from ecclesiastical authorities to put the book in print, but he eventually allowed it to be published in Florence before it received official approval from Rome.

The publication of *Dialogue* precipitated Galileo's fall from the pope's favor. Urban, who at this time was coming under criticism for leniency with heretics, ordered the book taken out of circulation in the summer of 1632 and appointed a commission to investigate Galileo's activities. After receiving the report from the committee a few months later, he turned the matter over to the Roman Inquisition, which charged Galileo with heresy.

The Roman Inquisition had been established in 1542 to preserve the Catholic faith. Its main concern was the prosecution of heresy. Like the Spanish Inquisition, this Roman ecclesiastical court has acquired a reputation for being harsh and arbitrary, for administering torture, for proceeding in secrecy, and for denying the accused the right to know the charges in advance of the trial. There is some validity to these criticisms, although the Roman Inquisition did not torture Galileo or deny him the opportunity to present a defense. The most unfair aspect of the proceeding, and of inquisitorial justice in general, was the determination of the outcome of the trial by the same judges who had brought the charges against the accused and conducted the interrogation. This meant that in a politically motivated trial such as

Galileo's, the verdict was a foregone conclusion. To accept Galileo's defense would have been a sign of weakness and a repudiation of the pope.

Although the underlying substantive issue in the trial was whether Galileo was guilty of heresy for denying the sun's motion and the Earth's immobility, the more technical question was whether by publishing *Dialogue* he had violated the prohibition of 1616. In his defense Galileo claimed that the only reason he had written *Dialogue* was to present "the physical and astronomical reasons that can be advanced for one side or the other." He denied holding Copernicus's opinion to be true.

In the end the court determined that by publishing *Dialogue*, Galileo had violated the injunction of 1616. He had disseminated "the false opinion of the Earth's motion and the sun's stability" and he had "defended the said opinion already condemned." Even Galileo's efforts "to give the impression of leaving it undecided and labeled as probable" was still a very serious error, because there was no way that "an opinion declared and defined contrary to divine Scripture may be probable." The court also declared that Galileo had obtained permission to publish the book in Florence without divulging to the authorities there that he was under the injunction of 1616.

Throughout the trial every effort was made to distance the pope from his former protégé. There was real fear among the members of the papal court that because the pope had been Galileo's patron and had given him considerable latitude in developing his ideas, he himself would be implicated in Galileo's heresy. Every step was taken to guarantee

The Trial of Galileo, 1633
Galileo is shown here presenting one of his four defenses to the Inquisition. He claimed that his book *Dialogue Concerning the Two Chief World Systems* did not endorse the Copernican model of the universe.

that information regarding the pope's support for Galileo did not surface. The court made sure, for example, that no one from the Medici court, which had provided support for Galileo, would testify on Galileo's behalf. The trial tells us as much about the efforts of Urban VIII to save face as about the Catholic Church's hostility to the new science.

Galileo was required to formally renounce his views and to avoid any further defense of Copernicanism. After making this humiliating submission to the court, he was sent to Siena and later that year was allowed to return to his villa in Arcetri near Florence, where he remained under house arrest until his death in 1642.

Questions of Justice

1. Galileo was silenced because of what he had put into print. Why had he published these works, and why did the Church consider his publications a serious threat?
2. Is a court of law an appropriate place to resolve disputes between science and religion? Why or why not?

Taking It Further

Finocchiaro, Maurice, ed. *The Galileo Affair: A Documentary History*. 1989. A collection of original documents regarding the controversy between Galileo and the Roman Catholic Church.

Sharratt, Michael. *Galileo: Decisive Innovator*. 1994. A study of Galileo's place in the history of science that provides full coverage of his trial and papal reconsiderations of it in the late twentieth century.

The denial of the reality of demonic magic was based on a rejection of the powers of demons. Seventeenth-century scientists did not necessarily deny the existence of angelic or demonic spirits, but the mechanical philosophy posed a serious challenge to the belief that those spirits could influence the operation of the physical world. The belief in demons experienced a slow death. Many scientists struggled to preserve a place for them in the physical world, arguing that the Devil, like God, could work through the processes of nature. Ultimately, however, the logic of the mechanical philosophy expelled demons from the worldview of the educated classes. By the beginning of the eighteenth century, scientists and even some theologians had labeled the belief in demons as superstition, which originally had meant false or erroneous religion but which was now redefined to mean ignorance of natural causes.

The denial of the power of magic, together with the rejection of the belief in the power of demonic spirits, also explains why many educated Europeans began to deny the reality of witchcraft in the second half of the seventeenth century. As we have seen in Chapter 14, witches were individuals, mostly women, who stood accused of using magic to harm their neighbors, their animals, or their crops. They were also accused of having made a pact with the Devil, the means by which they received their magical powers. In many cases it was claimed that witches worshiped the Devil collectively at nocturnal orgies known as sabbaths. To someone who subscribed to the mechanical philosophy, this entire set of beliefs about witches was highly questionable. Demons could not intervene in the operation of the physical world, nor could human beings perform magic with or without their assistance.

Science also played a major role in challenging the belief that demons could invade a human body and control the person's movements and behavior. During the seventeenth century Europe experienced a wave of such demonic possessions, in which individuals—often young girls—experienced fits and convulsions, spoke in deep, gruff voices, displayed preternatural strength, vomited foreign objects such as pins, and experienced temporary blindness and deafness. Believing that demons were the cause of these symptoms, clerics attempted to dispossess or exorcise them through either an elaborate ritual in Roman Catholic countries or a program of prayer and fasting in Protestant communities. By the end of the seventeenth century the belief that demons were responsible for such possessions had given way to the assumption that the behavior of the possessed person or demoniac had natural, medical causes. The range of possible maladies afflicting demoniacs included the disease known then as hysteria, in which the body of a person displayed such symptoms as a reaction to unbearable stress.

The most emphatic, comprehensive, and unequivocal attack on the entire body of beliefs regarding the Devil during the seventeenth century came from the pen of a Dutch minister and follower of Descartes, Balthasar Bekker. In his four-volume study, *The Enchanted World* (1691–1693), Bekker denied that the Devil could exercise any jurisdiction over the natural world. The mechanical philosophy was not the only basis for Bekker's skepticism. A biblical scholar, Bekker produced many passages from Scripture indicating that God exercised complete sovereignty over the Devil and had in fact chained him up in Hell. In this way the Devil had been rendered incapable of causing physical destruction in the world, either with or without the assistance of witches.

The skeptical views that many educated people acquired regarding demons and magic were usually not shared by people who remained illiterate. For them magic and witchcraft remained very real, and they continued to suspect and accuse their neighbors of engaging in diabolical practices until the early nineteenth century. In a number of instances they took the law into their own hands, stoning accused witches, drowning them, or burning them alive. All of this served to highlight a widening gap between the views of the educated and those of the common people. There had always been differences between learned and popular culture, but many aspects of culture were shared by educated and uneducated people. Both groups, for example, took part in the same religious services and rituals, and both groups also held some of the same beliefs about magic and witchcraft. In the late seventeenth century, however, this common cultural ground began to disappear, and members of the educated classes began to develop unprecedented contempt for the ignorance and superstition of the common people. The education of the upper classes in the new science and in Descartes's philosophy only aggravated what was already a noticeable trend.

The development of two separate realms of culture became one of the main themes of eighteenth-century history, and it contributed directly to the formation of class divisions. On the one side were the educated upper classes who prided themselves on their rational and enlightened views; on the other were the illiterate peasants who continued to believe in magic, witchcraft, and what the educated referred to as "vulgar superstition."

Humans and the Natural World

■ **How did the Scientific Revolution change the way in which seventeenth- and eighteenth-century Europeans thought of their relationship to the natural world?**

The spread of scientific knowledge not only redefined the views of educated people regarding the supernatural realm, but it also led them to reconsider their relationship to nature. This process involved three separate but related inquiries. The first was to determine the place of human beings in a sun-centered universe; the second to investigate how science and technology had given human beings greater control over nature; and the third to reconsider the relationship between men and women in light of new scientific knowledge regarding the human mind and body.

The Place of Human Beings in the Universe

The astronomical discoveries of Copernicus and Galileo offered a new outlook regarding the position of human beings in the universe. The Earth-centered Ptolemaic cosmos that dominated scientific thought during the Middle Ages was also human-centered. Not only was the planet that human beings inhabited situated at the center of the universe, but on Earth humans occupied a privileged position. This is not to say that the human condition was always viewed in positive terms. Trapped on a stationary Earth, which itself was corruptible, individuals were always vulnerable to the temptations of the demonic spirits that medieval clerics told them were constantly hovering in the atmosphere. But human beings nonetheless remained the absolute physical and moral center of this universe. They were, after all, created in the image of God, according to Christian belief. Renaissance Neoplatonism reinforced this medieval view. By describing human beings as having the characteristics of both angels and beasts, with the capacity to ascend toward God or descend to the level of animals, Neoplatonists accentuated the centrality and importance of humankind in the world.

The acceptance of a sun-centered model of the universe began to bring about a fundamental change in these views of humankind. Once it became apparent that the Earth was not the center of the universe, human beings began to lose their privileged position in nature. The Copernican universe was neither Earth-centered nor human-centered. Scientists such as Descartes continued to claim that human beings were the greatest of nature's creatures, but their habitation of a tiny planet circling the sun inevitably reduced the sense of their own importance. Moreover, as astronomers began to recognize the incomprehensible size of the cosmos, the possibility emerged that there were other habitable worlds in the universe, calling into further question the unique status of humankind.

In the late sixteenth and seventeenth centuries a number of literary works explored the possibility of other inhabited worlds and forms of life. In *The Infinite Universe and World* (1584), the Neoplatonist monk Giordano Bruno (1548–1600), who was eventually burned as a heretic, postulated the existence of other rational beings and suggested that they might be more intelligent than humans. Kepler's *Somnium,* or *Lunar Astronomy* (1634), a book that combined science and fiction, described various species of moon dwellers, some of whom were rational and superior to humans. This was followed by a number of works of fiction on travel to the moon, including Francis Godwin's *The Man in the Moon* (1638) and Cyrano de Bergerac's *The Other World* (1657). The most ambitious and fascinating of all these books was a fictional work by the French dramatist and poet Bernard de Fontenelle, *Conversations on the Plurality of Worlds* (1686). This work, which became immensely popular throughout Europe, was more responsible than any purely scientific discovery of the seventeenth century for leading the general reading public to call into question the centrality of humankind in Creation.

The Control of Nature

The Scientific Revolution bolstered the confidence human beings had in their ability to control nature. By disclosing the laws governing the operation of the universe, the new science gave humans the tools they needed to make nature serve their own purposes more effectively than it had in the past. This confidence in human mastery over nature found its most articulate expression in the writings of Francis Bacon. Instead of accepting the traditional view that humans were either passively reconciled with nature or victimized by it, Bacon believed that knowledge of the laws of nature could restore the dominion over nature that humans had lost in the biblical Garden of Eden. Bacon believed that nature existed for human beings to control and exploit for their own benefit. His famous maxim, "knowledge is power," conveyed his confidence that science would give human beings this type of control over nature.

In the same spirit Descartes announced that as human beings we had the capacity "to turn ourselves into the masters and possessors of nature."[6] For him nature included animals or beasts, which, unlike human beings, did not have souls and were therefore merely corporal machines. (For this reason, he was not at all reluctant to dissect live animals.) Later in the seventeenth century the members of the Royal Society proclaimed their intention to make scientific knowledge "an instrument whereby mankind may obtain a dominion over things." This optimism regarding human control of nature found support in the belief that God permitted such mastery, first by creating a regular and uniform universe and then by giving people the rational faculties by which they could understand nature's laws.

Many scientists of the seventeenth century emphasized the practical applications of their research, just as scientists often do today. Descartes, who used his knowledge of optics to improve the grinding of lenses, contemplated ways in which scientific knowledge might improve the drainage of marshes, increase the velocity of bullets, and use bells to make clouds burst. In his celebration of the French Academy of Sciences in 1699, Fontenelle wrote that "the application of science to nature will constantly grow in scope and intensity and we shall go on from one marvel to the next; the day will come when man will be able to fly by

The Founding of the French Acadèmie des Sciences
Like the Royal Society in England, the French Académie of Sciences was dependent upon royal patronage. Louis XIV, seen sitting in the middle of the painting, used the occasion to glorify himself as a patron of the sciences as well as the arts. The painting also commemorates the building of the Royal Observatory in Paris, which is shown in the background.

fitting on wings to keep him in the air . . . till one day we shall be able to fly to the moon."[7] As we mentioned earlier, members of the Royal Society discussed how their experiments would help miners, farmers, and merchants. They even discussed the possibility of making labor-saving machines. These efforts to apply scientific knowledge to practical problems encouraged the belief, which has persisted to the present day, that science could improve human life.

The hopes of seventeenth-century scientists for the improvement of human life by means of technology remained in large part unfulfilled until the eighteenth century. Only then did the technological promise of the Scientific Revolution begin to be realized, most notably with the innovations that preceded or accompanied the Industrial Revolution. The first steam engine, for example, which utilized the scientific study of atmospheric pressure conducted by a student of Galileo in the 1650s, was not invented until 1709. The great improvements in the construction of canals and the use of water power to drive machinery, which were based upon the study of Newtonian mechanics, likewise did not take place until the eighteenth century. In similar fashion, research on the internal structure of grains and the breeding of sheep did not significantly increase food production until the eighteenth century, at the time of the agricultural revolution.

By the middle of the eighteenth century, the belief that science would lead to an improvement of human life became an integral part of Western culture. Much less apparent at that time, however, was a recognition of the destructive potential of applied science. Governments supported scientific research on ballistics to gain military advantage,

but it was not until the twentieth century, especially with the construction of engines of mass destruction, that people began to recognize technology's potential to cause permanent harm to the human race. In the seventeenth and eighteenth centuries, those who possessed scientific knowledge thought mainly in terms of the benefits that science and technology could confer. Their faith in human progress became one of the main themes of the Enlightenment, which will be discussed in Chapter 18.

Women, Men, and Nature

The new scientific and philosophical ideas of the seventeenth century challenged ancient and medieval notions regarding women's physical and mental inferiority to men. At the same time the new science left other traditional ideas about the roles of men and women unchallenged.

Until the seventeenth century, a woman's sexual organs were thought to be imperfect versions of a man's, an idea that made woman an inferior version of man and in some respects a freak of nature. During the sixteenth and seventeenth centuries, a body of scientific literature advanced the new idea that women had sexual organs that were perfect in their own right and served distinct functions in reproduction. Another traditional biological idea that came under attack during this period was Aristotle's view that men made a more important contribution to reproduction than did women. The man's semen was long believed to contain the form of the body as well as the soul, while the only contribution the woman was believed to make to the process

DOCUMENT

Elisabeth of Bohemia Challenges Descartes

Elisabeth of Bohemia, the daughter of King Frederick of Bohemia and granddaughter of King James I of England, engaged in a long correspondence with Descartes regarding his philosophy. Privately educated in Greek, Latin, and mathematics, Elisabeth was one of a small group of noblewomen who participated in the scientific and philosophical debates of the day. The letter concerns the relationship between the soul (or mind), which Descartes claimed was immaterial, and the body, which is entirely composed of matter. One of the problems for Descartes was to explain how the mind could move that body to perform certain functions. In the letter Elisabeth plays a deferential, self-effacing role but in the process exposes one of the weaknesses of Descartes's dualistic philosophy.

The Hague, 20 June 1643

Monsieur Descartes,

. . . The life I am forced to lead does not leave me the disposition of enough time to acquire a habit of meditation according to your rules. So many interests of my family that I must not neglect, so many interviews and civilities that I cannot avoid, batter my weak spirit with such anger and boredom that it is rendered for a long time afterward useless for anything else. All of which will excuse my stupidity, I hope, not to have been able to understand the idea by which we must judge how the soul (not extended and immaterial) can move the body by an idea we have in another regard of heaviness, nor why a power—which we have falsely attributed to things under the name of a quality—of carrying a body toward the center of the Earth when the demonstration of a contrary truth (which you promised in your Physics) confirms us in thinking it impossible. The idea of a separate independent quality of heaviness—given that we are not able to pretend to the perfection and objective reality of God—could be made up out of ignorance of that which truly propels bodies towards the center of the Earth. Because no material cause represents itself to the senses, one attributes heaviness to matter's contrary, the immaterial, which nevertheless I would never be able to conceive but as a negation of matter and which could have no communication with matter.

I confess that it is easier for me to concede the matter and the extension of the soul than to concede that a being that is immaterial has the capacity to move a body and to be moved by it. For if the former is done by giving information, it is necessary that the spirits which make the movement be intelligent, which you do not accord to anything corporal. And although, in your meditations, you show the possibility of the soul being moved by the body, it is nevertheless very difficult to comprehend how a soul, as you have described it, after having had the faculty and habit of good reasoning, would lose all that by some sort of vapors, or that being able to subsist without the body and having nothing in common with it, would allow itself to be so ruled by the body.

Source: From The Princess and the Philosopher: Letters of Elisabeth of the Palatine to René Descartes *by Andrea Nye. Copyright © 1999 by Rowman & Littlefield Publishers, Inc. Reprinted by permission.*

---

was the formless matter upon which the semen acted. By the beginning of the eighteenth century, a scholarly consensus had emerged that recognized equal contributions from both sexes to the process of reproduction.

Some seventeenth-century natural philosophers also called into question ancient and medieval ideas regarding women's mental inferiority to men. In this regard Descartes supplied a theory that presupposed intellectual equality between the sexes. In making a radical separation between the mind and the human body, Descartes found no difference between the minds of men and women. As one of his followers wrote in 1673, "The mind has no sex."[8] A few upper-class women provided solid evidence to support this revolutionary claim of female intellectual equality. Princess Elisabeth of Bohemia, for example, carried on a long correspondence with Descartes during the 1640s and challenged many of his ideas on the relationship between the body and the soul. The privately educated English noblewoman Margaret Cavendish (1623–1673) wrote scientific and philosophical treatises and conversed with the leading philosophers of the day. In early eighteenth-century France, small groups of women and men gathered in the salons or private sitting rooms of the nobility to discuss philosophical and scientific ideas. In Germany it was not uncommon for women to help their husbands run astronomical observatories.

Although seventeenth-century science laid the theoretical foundations for a theory of sexual equality, it did not challenge other traditional ideas that compared women unfavorably to men. Most educated people continued to ground female behavior in the humors, claiming that because women were cold and wet, as opposed to hot and dry, they were naturally more deceptive, unstable, and melancholic than men. They also continued to identify women with nature itself, which had always been depicted as female. Bacon's use of masculine metaphors to describe science and his references to "man's mastery over nature" therefore seemed to reinforce traditional ideas of male dominance

Eighteenth-Century Midwifery

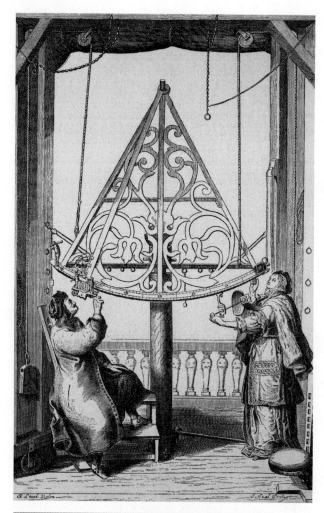

Astronomers in Seventeenth-Century Germany
Elisabetha and Johannes Hevelius working together with a sextant in a German astronomical observatory. More than 14 percent of all German astronomers were female. Most of them cooperated with their husbands in their work.

over women. His language also reinforced traditional notions of men's superior rationality.[9] In 1664 the secretary of the Royal Society, which excluded women from membership, proclaimed that the mission of that institution was to develop a "masculine philosophy."[10] At the same time the tradition of depicting science as a female goddess, such as Minerva, began to disappear.

The new science provided the theoretical foundations for the male control of women at a time when many men expressed concern over the "disorderly" and "irrational" conduct of women. In a world populated with witches, rebels, and other women who refused to adhere to conventional standards of proper feminine behavior, the adoption of a masculine philosophy was associated with the reassertion of patriarchy.

Conclusion

Science and Western Culture

The Scientific Revolution was a uniquely Western phenomenon. It had no parallel in the Eastern world. During the Middle Ages the Islamic civilizations of the Middle East produced a rich body of scientific knowledge that had influenced the development of science in western Europe, but by the time of the Scientific Revolution Islamic science had entered a period of decline. Other civilizations, most notably in China and India, also possessed impressive scientific traditions, but they too failed to undergo a transformation similar to that which occurred in western Europe in the seventeenth century.

In all these non-Western civilizations, religious traditions had prevented philosophers from undertaking an objective study of the natural world. Either nature was viewed as an entirely secular (that is, not religious) entity and hence not worthy of study on its own terms, or it was viewed as something so heavily infused with spiritual value that it could not be subjected to rational analysis. Only in Europe did religious and cultural traditions allow the scientist to view nature as both a product of supernatural forces and something that was separate from the supernatural realm. Nature could therefore be studied objectively without losing its religious significance. Only when nature was viewed in this dual way, as both the creation of God and as something independent of the deity, could it be subjected to mathematical analysis and brought under human domination.

The Scientific Revolution gave the West a new source of identity. The West could be distinguished not only by its Christianity, its capitalist economic system, its large bureaucratic states, and its massive standing armies, but also by the scientific content of its education, its approach to the natural world, and its science-based technology. By the beginning of the eighteenth century, modern science became an essential component of Western culture. It also laid the foundations of the Enlightenment, another distinctively Western phenomenon, which will be discussed in Chapter 18.

The rise of Western science and technology had profound implications for the encounters that took place between Western and non-Western peoples in Africa, Asia, and the Americas. By the eighteenth century, European science provided explicit support for European empires, which will be discussed in Chapters 17 and 23. Science gave Western states the military and navigational technology that allowed them to establish their control over non-Europeans. Knowledge of botany and agriculture allowed Western powers to develop the resources of the areas they colonized and to use these resources for the improvement of their own societies. Most important, the possession of scientific knowledge and technology encouraged people in the West to think of themselves as superior to the people they subjugated or controlled. Scientific theories regarding biological and physiological differences between the people who inhabited the West and natives of other countries also contributed to those attitudes. Western imperialism had its roots in the Scientific Revolution of the seventeenth century.

Suggestions for Further Reading

For a comprehensive listing of suggested readings, please go to www.ablongman.com/levack2e/chapter16

Biagioli, Mario. *Galileo, Courtier: The Practice of Science in the Culture of Absolutism.* 1993. Argues that Galileo's desire for patronage determined the type of research he engaged in and the scientific questions he asked.

Cohen, H. Floris. *The Scientific Revolution: A Historiographical Inquiry.* 1995. A thorough account of all the different interpretations of the causes and significance of the Scientific Revolution.

Dear, Peter. *Discipline and Experience: The Mathematical Way in the Scientific Revolution.* 1995. Explains the importance of mathematics in the development of seventeenth-century science.

Debus, Allen G. *Man and Nature in the Renaissance.* 1978. Deals with the early history of the Scientific Revolution and develops many of its connections with the Renaissance.

Drake, Stillman, ed. *Discoveries and Opinions of Galileo.* 1957. Includes four of Galileo's most important writings, together with a detailed commentary.

Easlea, Brian. *Magic, Witch-Hunting and the New Philosophy.* 1980. Relates the end of witch hunting to the spread of the mechanical philosophy.

Feingold, Mordechai. *The Newtonian Moment: Isaac Newton and the Making of Modern Culture.* 2004. A richly illustrated volume that contains valuable material on the reception of Newtonian ideas in the eighteenth century as well as a chapter on Newtonian women.

Kuhn, Thomas S. *The Copernican Revolution.* 1957. The most comprehensive and authoritative study of the shift from an Earth-centered to a sun-centered model of the universe.

Popkin, Richard. *The History of Scepticism from Erasmus to Spinoza.* 1979. Discusses skepticism as a cause as well as an effect of the Scientific Revolution.

Schiebinger, Londa. *The Mind Has No Sex? Women in the Origins of Modern Science.* 1989. Explores the role of women in all aspects of scientific endeavor.

Shapin, Steven. *The Scientific Revolution.* 1996. A study of the origins of the modern scientific worldview that emphasizes the social influences on the production of knowledge and the social purposes for which scientific knowledge was intended.

Shapin, Steven, and Simon Schaffer. *Leviathan and the Air Pump.* 1989. Discusses the difference between Robert Boyle and Thomas Hobbes regarding the value of experimentation.

Thomas, Keith. *Man and the Natural World: A History of the Modern Sensibility.* 1983. A study of the shifting attitudes of human beings toward nature during the period from 1500 to 1800.

Webster, Charles. *The Great Instauration: Science, Medicine and Reform, 1626–1660.* 1975. Explores the relationship between Puritanism and the Scientific Revolution in England.

Westfall, Richard S. *Never at Rest: A Biography of Isaac Newton.* 1980. A superb biography of the most influential scientist in the history of the West.

Notes

1. Quoted in Steven Shapin, *The Scientific Revolution* (1996), 33.

2. René Descartes, *Le Monde,* Book VI.

3. Thomas S. Kuhn, *The Structure of Scientific Revolutions* (1970).

4. René Descartes, *Discourse on the Method and Meditations on First Philosophy,* ed. David Weissmann (1996), 21.

5. Galileo, "Letter to the Grand Duchess Christina," in *Discoveries and Opinions of Galileo,* ed. Stilman Drake (1957), 186.

6. Descartes, *Discourse on the Method,* 38.

7. Quoted in W. Hazard, *The European Mind, 1680–1715* (1964), 362.

8. François Poullain, *De l'égalite des deux sexes* (1673), 85.

9. Francis Bacon, *The Works of Francis Bacon,* ed. J. Spedding (1857–1874), vol. 3, 524–539.

10. Henry Oldenburg, "To the Reader," in Robert Boyle, *Experiments and Considerations in Touching Colours* (1664).

The West and the World: Empire, Trade, and War, 1650–1815

17

N 1789 OLAUDAH EQUIANO, A FREED SLAVE LIVING IN GREAT BRITAIN, published an autobiographical account of his experiences in captivity. In this narrative Equiano recounted his seizure in the Gambia region of Africa and his transportation on a slave ship to the British Caribbean colony of Barbados. He described the unmerciful floggings to which the Africans on his ship were subjected, the unrelieved hunger they experienced, and the insufferable heat and smells they endured in the hold of the ship. He witnessed the suicide of those who threw themselves into the sea in order to avoid further misery. He was terrified that his white captors would eat him, and he wished for a merciful death.

Once the ship had reached its destination Equiano related how the Africans were herded into pens where white plantation owners examined, purchased, and branded them. The most moving part of Equiano's narrative is his account of the cries he heard as family members were sold to different masters. "O you nominal Christians," wrote Equiano, "might not an African ask you, learned you this from your God? Is it not enough that we are torn from our country and friends to toil for your luxury and lust of gain? Must every tender feeling be sacrificed to your avarice? Surely this is a new refinement in cruelty, which, while it has no advantage to atone for it, thus aggravates distress and adds fresh horrors to the wretchedness of slavery."[1]

The journey that Equiano was forced to take across the Atlantic Ocean and the emotions he described were experienced by millions of African men and women during the period from 1650 to 1815. The forced emigration of Africans from their homelands, their sale to white landlords, and their subjection to inhumane treatment number among the abiding horrors of Western civilization. To understand how these horrors could have occurred, especially at the hands of men who proclaimed a commitment to human freedom, we must study the growth of European empires during these centuries.

As European states grew in size, wealth, and military power in the sixteenth and seventeenth centuries, the most powerful of them acquired large

---

Samuel Scott, *A Thames Wharf* (1750s) British merchants conducted a brisk trade with Asia and the Americas in the eighteenth century.

overseas empires. By the end of the seventeenth century the British, French, and Dutch had joined the Portuguese and the Spanish as overseas imperial powers. As we discussed in Chapter 12, the first stage of empire building, which lasted from 1500 until about 1650, had many different motives. The search for gold and silver, the mission to Christianize the indigenous populations, the desire of some colonists to escape religious persecution, the urge to plunder, the efforts of monarchs to expand the size of their dominions, and the desire to profit from international trade all figured in the process. In 1625 the English government recognized many of these motives when it declared the purpose of the colony of Virginia to be "the propagation of the Christian religion, the increase of trade, and the enlarging of the royal empire."[2]

During the second stage of empire building, which lasted from roughly 1650 to 1815, the economic motive for acquiring overseas possessions became dominant. More than anything else, imperial policy was shaped by the desire for profit within a world economy. As far as the governments of western Europe were concerned, all colonies were economic enterprises. Whether these colonies were primarily involved in commerce or agriculture or mining was only a minor distinction. The main consideration was that they provided economic benefits to the European countries. They supplied the parent country, often referred to as the metropolis°, with agricultural products, raw materials, and minerals. Overseas colonies also provided the metropolis with markets for its manufactured goods.

The growth of these empires resulted in the expansion of the geographical boundaries of the West. It also resulted in the spread of Western ideas, political institutions, and economic systems to Asia and the Americas. At the same time, encounters between Europeans and non-Western peoples, especially those of Asia, brought about significant changes in the cultures of the West.

The main question that this chapter will address is how the growth of European empires in Asia and the Americas, the expansion of international trade, and the wars fought over empire and trade during the period 1650–1815 changed Western culture and politics. More specifically, the individual sections of the chapter will ask the following questions:

- How did the composition and organization of European empires change during the seventeenth and eighteenth centuries?
- In what ways did the wars waged by European powers during this period involve competition for overseas possessions and trading routes?
- How did European empires create an Atlantic economy in which the traffic in slaves was a major feature?
- What cultural encounters took place between European and Asian peoples during this period of empire building, and how did these encounters change Western attitudes toward outsiders?

- Why did European powers begin to lose control of some of their colonies, especially those in the Americas, between 1775 and 1825?

European Empires in the Americas and Asia

- How did the composition and organization of European empires change during the seventeenth and eighteenth centuries?

The main political units in Europe during this long period of history are usually referred to as states°. A state is a consolidated territorial area that has its own political institutions and recognizes no higher authority. Thus we refer to France, England (which became Great Britain after its union with Scotland in 1707), Prussia, the Dutch Republic, and Portugal as states. As we have discussed in Chapter 15, most of these states acquired larger armies and administrative bureaucracies during the sixteenth and seventeenth centuries, mainly to meet the demands of war. Consequently they became more highly integrated and cohesive political structures.

Many European states formed the center or core of much larger political formations known as empires°. The main characteristic of an empire in the seventeenth and eighteenth centuries was that it comprised many different kingdoms or territorial possessions outside the geographical boundaries of the state itself. These imperial territories were controlled by the metropolis, but they were not fully integrated into its administrative structure. Some of the territories that formed a part of these empires were located in Europe. The Austrian Habsburg monarchy, for example, had jurisdiction over a host of separate kingdoms and principalities in central and eastern Europe, including Hungary and Bohemia. This arrangement made Austria an empire, a designation it formally acquired in 1806. In like manner the Spanish monarchy, which also was an empire, controlled many different kingdoms and provinces in the Iberian peninsula as well as territories in southern Italy and the Netherlands. On the eastern and southeastern periphery of Europe lay two other empires: the Russian and the Ottoman, which controlled vast expanses of land not only in eastern Europe but also in the adjacent areas of Asia. As in previous centuries, the Russian and Ottoman empires marked the ever-shifting and often blurred boundaries between East and West.

Beginning in the fifteenth century, as the result of transoceanic voyages of exploration and the establishment of overseas colonies, western European states acquired, settled, or controlled territories in the Americas, Africa, and Asia. Mastery of these lands came much more quickly in the

New World than in Asia. The peoples of North and South America whom the Europeans encountered when they arrived were able fighters, but they were not organized politically, and diseases introduced by the Europeans drastically reduced their numbers. European settlers, who had the added advantage of superior military technology, were able to gain the upper hand in battle, seize or purchase their lands, and force those who survived to retreat into less inhabited areas.

When Europeans started to develop extensive trading routes in Asia, however, that continent was already highly developed politically and militarily. Three Muslim empires—the Ottoman, the Safavid (Persia), and the Mughal (India)—as well as the neighboring Chinese Empire in East Asia occupied the mass of land from the Balkans to the Pacific Ocean. Only when these Asian empires began to fall apart, giving greater autonomy to the smaller, subordinate states within their boundaries, were Europeans able to exploit the situation and secure favorable trading arrangements and ultimately control of Asian territory itself.

Until the late eighteenth century European governments usually allowed their colonies a considerable degree of political autonomy. Although monarchs claimed sovereignty over all their imperial possessions, the distance of these lands from the metropolis made direct rule difficult. The solution to this problem was to delegate the functions of government either to officials who represented royal authority in the colony or to some corporate body. In the British, Dutch, and French empires, trading companies that engaged in commerce with the East Indies assumed many of these functions. These companies could negotiate treaties, raise military forces, and govern the population of the colonies. In many ways the companies became small states themselves, operating under the authority of the Crown. In North America and the Caribbean, imperial governments usually granted charters to their colonies, authorizing them to establish their own legislative assemblies.

Colonists were granted considerable autonomy as long as they conducted trade exclusively with the metropolis. Metropolitan governments were determined to use the colonies to realize the objectives of gaining the largest possible share of world trade, acquiring a supply of gold and other precious metals, and collecting import and export duties on the colonial trade. To accomplish these ends they passed legislation forcing the colonists to trade exclusively with the metropolis. When colonists tried to break this monopoly by trading with other nations or colonies, they came into direct conflict with their own governments in Europe.

The earliest of the European overseas empires were established by the Spanish and the Portuguese. During the period under consideration, three rising European powers—Great Britain, France, and the Dutch Republic—began to rival the older empires. By the end of the period the British had emerged as the dominant imperial power. During the third period of imperial expansion in the late nineteenth and early twentieth centuries, the imperial rivalries that had developed in earlier years continued in different forms, and new European powers, most notably Germany and Italy, joined in the competition.

The Rise of the British Empire

The fastest-growing of these new European overseas empires during this period was that of Great Britain. England had begun its overseas empire in the late twelfth century, when it conquered the neighboring island of Ireland, but only in the seventeenth century did it begin to acquire lands in the New World and Asia. Attempts to establish colonies on the Atlantic coast of North America in the late sixteenth century had failed, most notably at Roanoke (in present-day North Carolina) in 1584. After Spain agreed not to contest English claims of territory north of Florida, the English succeed in settling a series of colonies along the Atlantic seaboard, the first of which was at Jamestown, Virginia, in 1607.

By 1700 this English empire in the New World included a number of colonies on the North American mainland, a vast territory in the northern part of Canada, and a cluster of islands in the Caribbean, most notably Barbados, Jamaica, and the Bahamas. These West Indian colonies developed an economy that used slave labor, and therefore blacks brought there from Africa soon outnumbered Europeans by a significant margin. In the colonies on the mainland of North America, however, most of the colonists were white. This was true even in the southern colonies, where slave labor was also introduced. Only in South Carolina, which was settled by Caribbean planters, did the black population exceed 50 percent.

A number of English colonists, especially in the northern colonies, had emigrated so that they might practice their religion without legal restraint. During the 1630s communities of English Protestants known as Puritans settled in New England. They objected to the control of the English Church by bishops, especially during the period from 1633 to 1641, when William Laud served as archbishop of Canterbury. Their main complaint was that the church services authorized by Laud too closely resembled those of Roman Catholicism. At the same time small groups of English Catholics, who often faced prosecution in English courts for practicing their religion, had taken refuge in Maryland. In the late seventeenth century a dissenting Protestant sect known as Quakers (so called because their founder, George Fox, told them to quake at the word of the Lord), smarting under legislation that denied them religious freedom and political power, emigrated to Pennsylvania.

Many other British colonists had come to America as indentured servants, usually serving for seven years in order to gain their freedom. By this time the size of the indigenous American population in the colonies had become negligible. The Indians of North America either had been pushed westward beyond the frontiers of these colonies, had died of diseases to which they were highly vulnerable, or had been killed in skirmishes with the English.

During the seventeenth century the English also established a number of trading posts, known as factories°, along the coast of India. The first of these factories was Surat, which was settled in 1612, and it was soon followed by Madras (1640), Bombay (1661), and Calcutta (1690). There were significant differences between these mercantile outposts and the colonies in the Caribbean and the North American mainland. The number of British settlers in India, most of whom were members of the East India Company, remained extremely small, and they did not establish large plantations like those in the Caribbean colonies and the southern mainland colonies. Consequently they did not introduce slave labor into these countries.

In contrast to the situation in North America and the Caribbean, the British in India had to deal with a large native population. At first they had contact with that population only when they were engaged in trade. In the second half of the eighteenth century, however, the British began to gain direct political control of Indian provinces, and by 1850 they controlled a large portion of the South Asian subcontinent. Not only did the British eventually subject the Indians to their rule, but they also drove out their French and Dutch

DOCUMENT

Arrival of
the British in
the Punjab
(mid-19th c.)

commercial rivals, who had established their own factories along the coast.

In addition to their settlements in America and India, the British acquired influence and ultimately political control of the area from Southeast Asia stretching down into the South Pacific. In the late seventeenth century the British began to challenge the Dutch and the Portuguese for control of the trade with Indonesia, and in the second half of the eighteenth century British merchants established a thriving trade with the countries on the Malay peninsula. In the late eighteenth century the British also began to explore the South Pacific, which remained the last part of the inhabited world that Europeans had not yet visited and settled. In 1770 the British naval officer and explorer Captain James Cook (1728–1779) claimed the entire eastern coast of Australia for Great Britain, and in 1788 the British established a penal colony in the southeastern corner of the continent at Botany Bay. Cook also visited New Zealand and many of the islands in the South Pacific, including Fiji, but colonies were not established at those locations until the middle of the nineteenth century.

The British Empire of the late seventeenth and eighteenth centuries possessed little administrative coherence; it was a hodgepodge of colonies, factories, and territories that had different relationships to the royal government in Britain (see Map 17.1). In India the provinces brought un-

Map 17.1 European Empires in 1763

This map shows the overseas possessions of Britain, France, the Dutch Republic, Spain, and Portugal. Russian overseas expansion into North America had not yet begun.

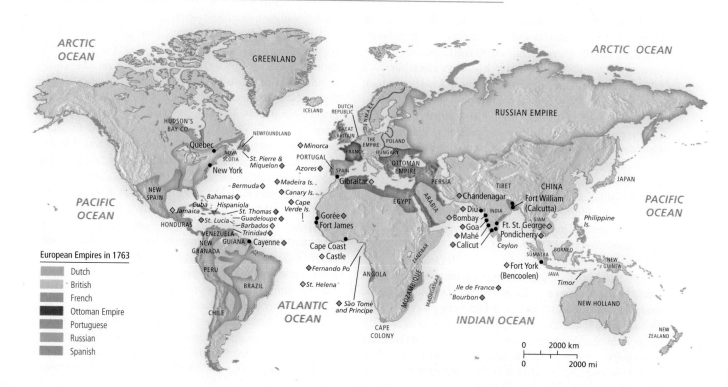

European Empires in 1763
- Dutch
- British
- French
- Ottoman Empire
- Portuguese
- Russian
- Spanish

der British control were run by a trading corporation that exercised many functions of government. Some colonies in America, such as Maryland and Pennsylvania, operated under charters granted to members of the aristocracy. Most of the colonies on the North American mainland and in the Caribbean had their own legislatures. None of these colonies, however, sent representatives to the British Parliament. The only bond of unity among all the colonists is that they, like British subjects living in England or Scotland, owed their allegiance to the monarch and were under the monarch's protection. All of these colonists were therefore British subjects.

The Scattered French Empire

French colonization of North America and India paralleled that of Great Britain, but it never achieved the same degree of success. As the British were establishing footholds in the West Indies and the mainland of North America, the French acquired their own islands in the Caribbean and laid claim to large sections of Canada and the Ohio and Mississippi River valleys in the present-day United States. In the West Indies the French began the process of colonization by introducing indentured servants for periods of three years, but in the eighteenth century they began to follow the British and Spanish pattern of importing slaves to provide the labor for the sugar plantations. In North America French settlers did not require a large labor supply, as their main economic undertakings were the fur trade and fishing. Consequently slaves were not introduced to those areas. The European population of French possessions in North America also stayed well below that of the British colonies.

The parallel between French and British overseas expansion extended to India, where in the early eighteenth century the French East India Company established factories at Pondicherry, Chandenagar, and other locations. Rivalry with the British also led the French to make alliances with native governors of Indian provinces, and with this support the French fought the British both on land and at sea at different critical times between 1744 and 1815. The British ultimately prevailed in this struggle, and by the turn of the nineteenth century the French presence in India had been reduced to a few isolated factories.

The waning of French influence in India coincided with a series of territorial losses in the New World. Defeats suffered at the hands of the British during the Seven Years' War (1756–1763) resulted in the transfer of French Canada and the territory east of the Mississippi River to Great Britain. During that conflict France also ceded the vast region of Louisiana between the Mississippi River and the Rocky Mountains to Spain. France regained Louisiana in 1801 but then promptly sold the entire territory to the United States in 1803. The following year the French Caribbean colony of Saint Domingue became independent, although France retained possession of its other West Indian colonies.

The only overseas area where France continued to expand after 1800 was much closer to home, on the Mediterranean shores of North Africa. French influence in this area had begun in the seventeenth century, and it persisted until the twentieth century. France occupied Egypt briefly from 1798 until 1801, and it acquired Algeria in 1830. It was not until the third stage of imperialism in the late nineteenth century that France took possession of large territories in the interior of Africa and in Asia (see Chapter 23).

The Commercial Dutch Empire

The tiny Dutch Republic acquired almost all of its overseas possessions in the first half of the seventeenth century, at about the same time that the British and French were establishing their first colonies in Asia and the New World. The formation of the Dutch empire went hand in hand with the explosive growth of the Dutch economy in the seventeenth century. At that time the Dutch Republic became the center of a global economy, and its overseas colonies in the New World, Asia, and Africa helped the republic maintain its commercial supremacy. Dutch overseas settlements, just like the port cities of the metropolis, were dedicated almost exclusively to serving the interests of trade.

The Dutch were more eager than other European powers to use military and naval power to acquire and fortify trading depots. They also used military force to seize factories that had been established earlier by other countries, especially Portugal. With more than 1,400 vessels that could be used as warships and 250,000 sailors, they had a distinct military advantage over the Portuguese, who could not muster half those numbers. They seized two trading posts from the Portuguese on the West African coast in 1637, and in 1641 they also acquired from Portugal the African islands of São Tomé and Principe. In 1624 the Dutch, operating through their West Indian Company, seized the northern coast of Brazil, and after its return to Portugal in 1654 they acquired two small West Indian islands and a number of small plantation colonies on the Guiana coast of South America, mainly in present-day Surinam. From these small settlements in Africa and the Caribbean the Dutch carried on trade with the Spanish, Portuguese, French, and British colonies. Through these ports the Dutch brought more than 500,000 slaves to Brazil, the Spanish colonies, and the French and British West Indies.

In addition to their African and Caribbean possessions, the Dutch established a presence in three other parts of the world. In the early seventeenth century they settled a colony in the Hudson River valley on the North American mainland. They named the colony New Netherland and its main port, at the mouth of the river, New Amsterdam. In 1664 the Dutch lost the colony to the English, who renamed the colony and the port New York. The second area was in Asia, where the Dutch East India Company established a fort at Batavia (now Jakarta in Indonesia) and factories in India,

The Trial of the Mutineers on the *Bounty*

Justice in History

In December 1787 a British ship named the *Bounty,* under the captainship of William Bligh, left Portsmouth, England, on a momentous journey to Tahiti, an island in the South Pacific that Captain James Cook had first visited in 1769. The goal of the voyage of the *Bounty* was neither exploration nor colonial expansion but to bring home breadfruit trees that Cook had discovered on his second trip to the island in 1773. The trees, so it was hoped, would be introduced to the West Indies as a source of food for the slaves and hence the survival of the plantation economy. The voyage of the *Bounty* was therefore part of the operation of the new global economy that European expansion had made possible. The total size of the crew, all of whom had volunteered for service, was forty-six. The master's first mate, who became the main leader of a mutiny against Bligh, was Fletcher Christian.

The mutiny did not take place until after the ship had remained at Tahiti for a number of months, loaded its cargo of more than a thousand breadfruit plants, and begun its return voyage. The main reason for the mutiny was Captain Bligh's abusive and humiliating language. Unlike many other officers who faced the task of maintaining order on their ships and commanding the obedience of their crews, Bligh did not flog his men. In that regard Bligh's behavior was mild. Instead he went into tantrums and verbally abused them, belittling them and calling them scoundrels. Just before the mutiny Bligh called Fletcher Christian a cowardly rascal and falsely accused him of stealing from him. On the morning of April 28, 1788, Christian arrested Bligh at bayonet point, tied his hands

behind his back, and threatened him with instant death if he should speak a word. Claiming that "Captain Bligh had brought all this on himself," Christian and his associates put Bligh and eighteen other members of the crew into one of the ship's small launch boats and set them adrift, leaving them to reach a nearby island by their own power.

The mutineers sailed on to the island of Tubuai, where after a brief stay they split into two groups. Nine of them, headed by Christian and accompanied by six Tahitian men and twelve women, established a settlement on Pitcairn Island. The remaining sixteen mutineers returned to Tahiti. All but two of these men were apprehended in 1791 by Captain Edwards of the H.M.S. *Pandora,* which had been sent to Tahiti with the objective of arresting them and returning them to England for trial. At the beginning of its return voyage the *Pandora* was shipwrecked, and four of the prisoners drowned. The rest reached England aboard another ship in 1792. They were

promptly charged before a navy court-martial with taking the *Bounty* away from its captain and with desertion, both of which were offenses under the Naval Discipline Act of 1766.

The trial took place aboard a British ship, H.M.S. *Duke,* in Portsmouth harbor in September 1792. The proceeding had all the markings of a state trial, one initiated by the government for offenses against the Crown. Mutiny and desertion represented challenges to the state itself. During the second period of imperial expansion navies became major instruments of state power. Even when ships were used for purposes of exploration rather than naval combat, they served the interests of the state. The captain of the ship represented the power of the sovereign at sea. Because of the difficulty of maintaining order in such circumstances, he was given absolute authority. He could use whatever means necessary, including the infliction of corporal punishment, to preserve order. To disobey or challenge

Sextant
Eighteenth-century ships like the *Bounty* used this instrument to determine nautical position by means of the stars.

The Mutineers Casting Bligh Adrift in the Launch, **Engraving by Robert Dodd (1790)**
This was the central act in the mutiny led by Fletcher Christian. Captain Bligh is standing in the launch in his night-clothes. Some of the breadfruit trees loaded on the ship at Tahiti can be seen on the top deck.

him was interpreted as an act of rebellion.

The trial was based on the assumption that the mutiny was illegal and seditious. The only question was the extent of individual involvement in the act itself. The degree of involvement was measured by evidence of one's co-operation with Christian or his loyalty to Bligh. The mere fact that some men had remained with Christian on the *Bounty* did not prove that they had supported the mutiny. Four of those men gave little evidence of having voluntarily cooperated with Christian, and those four men were eventually acquitted. The testimony of Captain Bligh, who declared that those four crew members had been reluctant to put him in the launch boat, was decisive in securing their nonguilty verdicts.

The remaining six men were convicted and sentenced to die by hanging. Three of those men were eventually spared their lives. Peter Heywood and James Morrison were well connected to influential people in the navy and the government and received royal pardons. William Muspratt, one of only three mutineers to hire a lawyer, entered a protest against the procedures of the court. In a court-martial, unlike a criminal trial at the common law, a prisoner could not call witnesses in his own defense. At the time of his conviction Muspratt protested that he had been "debarred calling witnesses whose evidence I have reason to believe would have tended to prove my innocence." The difference between the two systems of criminal justice, he claimed, "is dreadful to the subject and fatal to me." On this ground Muspratt was reprieved.

The three men who were executed died as model prisoners, proclaiming the illegality of their rebellion. Although the govern-ment had executed only a small minority of the mutineers, by securing their conviction and drama-tizing it with a widely publicized hanging, it had upheld its author-ity and thus reinforced the power of the Crown.

Questions of Justice

1. How would you characterize the different ideals of justice adhered to by the mutineers on the *Bounty* and the British admiralty court that tried them?
2. What does the journey of the *Bounty* tell us about the role of the British navy in the process of imperial expansion? What problems were inherent in using British ships for these purposes?

Taking It Further

Rutter, Owen, ed. *The Court-Martial of the "Bounty" Mutineers.* 1931. Contains a full transcript of the trial.

The Dutch Factory of Batavia in Indonesia, ca. 1665
The Dutch Republic dominated the Asian trade in the seventeenth century. Batavia (now Jakarta) was the most important of their settlements in Southeast Asia. The efforts of the Dutch to transplant their culture is evident in this building's Dutch style of architecture.

China, and Japan. These possessions allowed the Dutch to engage in trade throughout Asia. In the eighteenth century, however, the British began to take control of Dutch trading routes.

The third area was the southern tip of Africa, where in 1652 the Dutch settled a colony at the Cape of Good Hope, mainly to provide support for ships engaged in commerce with the East Indies. In this colony some 1,700 Dutch settlers, most of them farmers known as boers°, developed an agricultural economy on plantations that employed slave labor. The loss of this colony to the British at the end of the eighteenth century reflected a more general decline of Dutch military and imperial strength.

The Vast Spanish Empire

Of all the European overseas empires, the lands under the control of the Spanish monarchy were the most extensive. At the height of its power in 1650, the Spanish Empire covered the western part of North America from California to Mexico and from Mexico down through Central America.

It also included Florida and the Caribbean islands of Cuba, San Domingo, and Puerto Rico. It embraced almost all of South America except Brazil, which was under Portuguese control. In Asia the main Spanish possessions were the Philippine Islands, named for the future King Philip II in 1542 and conquered with little bloodshed after 1564. The Philippines served as the main base from which the Spanish engaged in trade with other Asian countries.

Spanish overseas possessions were never ruled as closely as the royal government in Madrid ruled the smaller kingdoms and principalities on the Iberian peninsula. Spanish overseas possessions were, however, integrated into a much more authoritative imperial system than were those of the British. Until the eighteenth century a hierarchy of councils, staffed by men appointed by the Crown, exercised political control of the various large territories or viceroyalties into which the empire was divided. Like all mercantilist enterprises, the Spanish colonial empire was designed to serve the purposes of trade. Until the eighteenth century a council known as the House of Trade, situated in Seville, exercised a monopoly over all colonial commerce. It funneled trade with the colonies from the southwestern Spanish port of Cadiz and to selected ports on the eastern coasts of Spanish America, from which it was then redirected to other ports. The ships returned to Spain carrying the gold and silver that had been extracted from the mines of Mexico and Peru. The entire journey was made under the protection of Spanish warships.

The Bourbon kings of Spain, who were installed on the throne in 1700, introduced a number of political reforms that were intended to increase the volume of the colonial trade and prevent the smuggling that had always threatened to undermine it. On the one hand, they opened up the colonial trade to more Spanish and American ports and also permitted more trade within the colonies. On the other hand, the Bourbons, especially Charles III (r. 1759–1788), brought the viceroyalties under more direct control of Spanish royal officials and increased the efficiency of the tax collection system. These Bourbon reforms made the empire more manageable and profitable, but they also created tension between the Spanish-born bureaucrats and the creoles°, the people of Spanish descent who had been born in the colonies. These tensions eventually led in the early nineteenth century to a series of wars of independence from Spain that we shall discuss in a later section.

The Declining Portuguese Empire

The Portuguese had been the first European nation to engage in overseas exploration and colonization. During the late fifteenth and sixteenth centuries they had established colonies in Asia, South America, and Africa (see Chapter 12). By the beginning of the eighteenth century, however, the Portuguese Empire had declined in size and wealth in relation to its rivals. The Portuguese continued to hold a few ports in India, most notably the small island of Goa. They also retained a factory at Macao off the southeastern coast of China. In the New World the major Portuguese plantation colony was Brazil, which occupied almost half the land mass of South America and which supplied Europe with sugar, cacao (from which chocolate is made), and other agricultural commodities. Closely linked to Brazil were the Portuguese colonies along and off the West African coast. These possessions were all deeply involved in the transatlantic trade, especially in slaves. The Portuguese also had a series of trading stations and small settlements on the southeastern coast of Africa, including Mozambique.

The contraction of the Portuguese Empire in the seventeenth and eighteenth centuries resulted in the transfer of land to other European countries. A relatively weak European power, Portugal did not fare well in the fierce military conflicts that ensued in South America and Asia over control of the colonial trade. Portugal's main military and economic competition came from the Dutch, who seized many of its Asian, African, and South American colonies, and who acquired many Portuguese trading routes. Most of those losses took place in Asia between 1600 and 1670. The Portuguese Empire suffered further losses when the crown relinquished Bombay and the northern African port of Tangier to the English as part of the dowry for the Portuguese princess Catherine of Braganza when she married King Charles II in 1661.

Brazil remained by far the most important of the Portuguese possessions during the late seventeenth and eighteenth centuries. The colony suffered from an unfavorable balance of trade with Portugal, but it expanded in population and wealth during this period, especially after the discovery of gold and diamonds led to large-scale mining in the interior. The slave trade increased in volume in order to provide additional labor in the mines and on the sugar plantations. In the first quarter of the nineteenth century, as the British slave trade declined and came to an end, Portuguese ships carried 871,600 slaves to Brazil. Between 1826 and 1850 the number increased to an astonishing 1,247,700. As a result of this massive influx of Africans, slaves accounted for approximately 40 percent of the entire Brazilian population by the beginning of the nineteenth century.

Like most other European countries, Portugal tightened the control of its imperial possessions during the second half of the eighteenth century. During the ministry of the dictatorial Marquis of Pombal from 1755 to 1777, efforts were made to increase the control exercised by the Crown over all aspects of colonial life. Pombal also took steps to encourage the growth of the colonial trade, and he legalized intermarriage between whites and indigenous peoples. Like the Bourbon reforms in Spanish America, this legislation created considerable resentment among the creoles against the Portuguese bureaucrats who controlled the govern-

ment. As in Spanish America, these tensions led to demands for Brazil's autonomy in the nineteenth century.

The Russian Empire in the Pacific

The only eastern European state that established an overseas empire during the eighteenth century was Russia. Between the fifteenth and the early eighteenth centuries Russia had gradually acquired a massive overland empire stretching from St. Petersburg in the west across the frigid expanse of Siberia to the Pacific Ocean. The main impulse of Russian expansion had been the search for exotic furs that were in high demand in the colder climes of Russia and northern Europe. During the reign of the empress Catherine the Great (r. 1762–1796), Russia entered a period of further territorial expansion. On its western frontier it took part in the successive partitions of Poland between 1772 and 1795, while to the south it held the Crimean region within the Ottoman Empire between 1783 and 1792.

During the late eighteenth and early nineteenth centuries Russia also extended its empire overseas. Russian traders and explorers undertook numerous expeditions to Hawaii and other islands in the Pacific Ocean, sailing as far south as Mexico. They did not, however, establish colonies in these locations. Further expeditions brought Russia across the northern Pacific, where they encroached upon the hunting grounds of the native Aleuts in Alaska. The Russian-American Company, established in 1789, built a number of trading posts along the Pacific seaboard from Alaska down to Fort Ross in northern California. These claims led to a protracted territorial dispute with Spain, which had established a string of missions and settlements on the California coast as far north as San Francisco. In this way the two great European empires of Russia and Spain, advancing from opposite directions, confronted each other on the western coast of North America. Russian expansion into Alaska and California also led to territorial disputes with the United States, which was engaged in its own process of territorial expansion westward toward the Pacific during the nineteenth century.

Warfare in Europe, North America, and Asia

■ In what ways did the wars waged by European powers during this period involve competition for overseas possessions and trading routes?

Until the middle of the seventeenth century, European states engaged each other in battle almost exclusively within their own continent. The farthest their armies ever traveled was to the Middle East to fight the Turks or to Ireland to conquer the native Celts. The acquisition of overseas empires and the conflicts that erupted between European powers over the control of global trade brought those European conflicts to new and distant military theaters. Wars that began over territory in Europe were readily extended to America in one direction and to Asia in the other. The military forces that fought in these imperial battles consisted not only of metropolitan government troops but also those of the colonists. These colonial forces were often supplemented by the troops drawn from the local population, such as when the French recruited Native Americans to fight with them against the British in North America. This pattern of recruiting soldiers from the indigenous population, which began in the eighteenth century, became the norm during the third and final phase of empire building in the nineteenth and early twentieth centuries.

Wars fought overseas placed a premium on naval strength. Ground troops remained important, both in Europe and overseas, but naval power increasingly proved to be the crucial factor. All of the Western imperial powers either possessed or acquired large navies. Great Britain and the Dutch Republic rose to the status of world powers on the basis of sea power, while the French strengthened their navy considerably during the reign of Louis XIV. The Dutch used their naval power mainly against the Portuguese and the British, while the British directed theirs against the French and the Spanish as well as the Dutch. The overwhelming success that the British realized in these conflicts resulted in the establishment of British maritime supremacy.

Mercantile Warfare

An increasingly important motive for engaging in warfare in the late seventeenth and eighteenth centuries was the protection and expansion of trade. The theory that underlay and inspired these imperial wars was mercantilism. As we discussed in Chapter 15, those who subscribed to this theory, such as Louis XIV's minister Jean-Baptiste Colbert, believed that the wealth of the state depended on its ability to import fewer commodities than it exported and thus to acquire the largest possible share of the world's monetary supply. In order to achieve this goal, mercantilists encouraged domestic industry and placed heavy customs duties or tariffs on imported goods. Mercantilism was therefore a policy of protectionism°, the shielding of domestic industries from foreign competition. Mercantilists also sought to increase the size of the country's commercial fleet, establish colonies in order to promote trade, and import raw materials from the colonies to benefit domestic industry. The imperial wars of the seventeenth and eighteenth centuries, which were fought over the control of colonies and trading routes, thus formed part of a mercantilist policy.

Of course the older, more traditional motives for waging war, especially the desire of rulers for territorial expansion, did not disappear. The acquisitive impulses of France, Prussia, Austria, and Russia remained a recurrent source of international conflict throughout this period. But the mercantile motive, which began to emerge only in the 1650s, soon became a major feature of European warfare, and it explains why military conflict was extended from Europe to the colonies. As this motive for going to war became more important, wars fought primarily for religious or ideological reasons, which had been the norm during the period of the Reformation, virtually disappeared.

The first of the great mercantile wars that involved conflict overseas arose between England and the Dutch Republic in the middle and late seventeenth century (1652–1654, 1664–1667, 1672–1675). As these wars were fought between two Protestant powers, little about these conflicts could be attributed to religious zeal. Instead they were fought mainly for mercantile advantage between the two emerging commercial giants of Europe. The two countries were engaged in heated competition for control of the transatlantic trade, and the Dutch resented the passage of English laws, known as the Navigation Acts, that excluded them from trade with the English colonies. The Dutch claimed the right to trade with all ports in the world as well as to fish in the waters off British shores. Not surprisingly, many of the engagements in these wars took place at sea and in the colonies. The most significant outcome of these Anglo-Dutch wars was the loss of the port city of New Amsterdam to the English. That city, renamed New York, later became the leading port and financial center in the Western Hemisphere.

Shortly after the first Anglo-Dutch War, England also went to war against Spain (1655–1657). Although this conflict pitted a Protestant against a Catholic power, it too reflected the new emphasis on mercantile objectives. The main battles of this war were not fought in the English Channel, as they had been when the Spanish Armada had descended on England in 1588, but in the Caribbean. The war resulted in the British acquisition of one of its most important Caribbean colonies, Jamaica, in 1655. The Anglo-Spanish tensions that surfaced in this conflict continued into the eighteenth century, when Britain tried to smuggle more goods than it was allowed by the Treaty of Utrecht (1713) into the Spanish trading post of Portobelo on the isthmus of Panama. The Spanish retaliated by cutting off the ear of Robert Jenkins, an English captain, and this incident led to the War of Jenkins' Ear in 1739. In 1762, during another war against Spain (as well as France), armed forces from Britain and the North American colonies seized the Cuban port of Havana as part of an effort to monopolize the Caribbean trade. The following year, however, Britain returned the city to Spain in exchange for Florida. This acquisition gave the British control of the entire North American eastern seaboard.

Anglo-French Military Rivalry

Anglo-Spanish conflict paled in comparison with the bitter commercial rivalry between Great Britain and France during the eighteenth century. Anglo-French conflict was one of the few consistent patterns of eighteenth-century European warfare. It lasted so long and had so many different phases that it is known as the second Hundred Years' War, a recurrence of the bitter period of warfare between England and France from the middle of the fourteenth to the middle of the fifteenth century. The great difference between the two periods of warfare was that the first Hundred Years' War involved military conflicts in France, while the second was marked by periodic naval and military engagements not only in Europe but in Asia and North America as well.

The Wars of the Spanish and Austrian Successions, 1701–1748

This eighteenth-century Anglo-French rivalry had its roots in the war of the Spanish Succession (1701–1713). The war began as an effort to prevent France from putting Louis XIV's grandson, Philip, on the Spanish throne (see Chapter 15). The implications of this dynastic conflict for the British and French colonial empires were monumental. By uniting French and Spanish territory the proposed succession would have created a massive French-Spanish empire not only in Europe but in the Western Hemisphere as well. This combination of French and Spanish territory and military power threatened to eclipse the British colonies along the North American coast and deprive British merchants of much of their valuable trade.

The ensuing struggle in North America, known by British colonists as Queen Anne's War, was settled in Britain's favor by the Treaty of Utrecht in 1713. Philip V, the first Spanish king from the Bourbon dynasty (r. 1700–1746), was allowed to remain on the throne, but French and Spanish territories in Europe and America were kept separate. Even more important, the French ceded their Canadian territories of Newfoundland and Nova Scotia to the British. The treaty, which also gave Britain the contract to ship slaves to the Spanish colonies for thirty years, marked the emergence of Britain as Europe's dominant colonial and maritime power.

The next phase of Anglo-French warfare, the War of the Austrian Succession (1740–1748), formed part of a European conflict that engaged the forces of Austria, Prussia, and Spain as well as those of Britain and France. In this conflict European dynastic struggles once again intersected with competition for colonial advantage overseas. The ostensible cause of this war was the impetuous decision by the new king of Prussia, the absolutist

CHRONOLOGY

A Century of Anglo-French Warfare

1701–1713	War of the Spanish Succession (Queen Anne's War in North America): Spain is allied with France
1740–1748	War of the Austrian Succession (Europe): France is allied with Spain and Prussia; Britain is allied with Austria and the Dutch Republic
1744–1748	King George's War (North America)
1754–1763	French and Indian War (North America): French and British are allied with different Indian tribes
1756–1763	Seven Years' War (Europe): France is allied with Austria; Britain is allied with Prussia
1775–1783	American War of Independence: France is allied with United States against Britain in 1778
1781–1783	Warfare in India
1792–1815	French Revolutionary and Napoleonic Wars: Britain is allied at various times with Austria, Prussia, Spain, and the Dutch Republic; warfare at times in the West Indies as well as in India

Frederick II (r. 1740–1786), to seize the large German-speaking province of Silesia from Austria upon the succession of Maria Theresa (r. 1740–1780) as the ruler of the hereditary Habsburg lands (see Map 17.2). Using the large army that his militaristic father Frederick William I had assembled, Frederick struck with devastating effectiveness, and by terms of the treaty that ended the war he acquired most of the province.

Frederick's aggression enticed other European powers to join the conflict. Eager to acquire some of the Habsburg territories in different parts of Europe, France and Spain both declared war on Austria. Britain then entered the war against France, mainly to keep France from acquiring Austria's possessions in the Netherlands. Britain's main concern in the European phase of this war, as it had been in the War of the Spanish Succession, was to maintain the balance of power among European states.

The colonial phase of this war, known in British North America as King George's War, opened in 1744, when the French supported the Spanish in a separate war that Spain had been waging against Britain since 1739 over the Caribbean trade. Clashes between French and British trading companies in India also began in the same year. The main military engagement of this war was the seizure of the French port and fortress of Louisbourg on Cape Breton Island in Canada by 4,000 New England colonial troops and a large British fleet. At the end of the war, however, the British returned Louisbourg to the French in exchange for

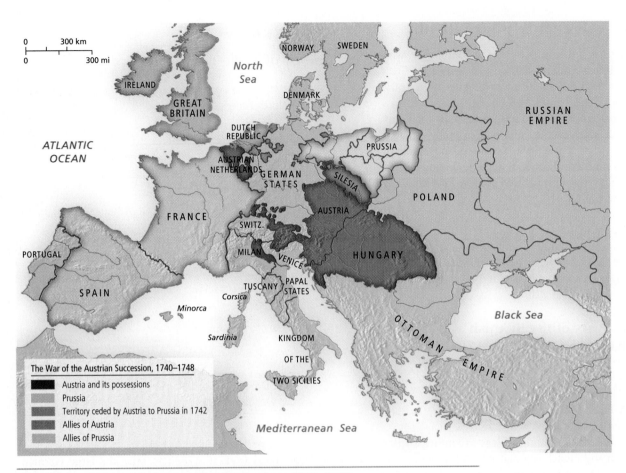

Map 17.2 The War of the Austrian Succession, 1740–1748
Austria lost Silesia to Prussia during the War of the Austrian Succession in 1742. Maria Theresa's efforts to regain the province in the Seven Years' War were unsuccessful.

the factory of Madras in India, which the French had taken during the war.

The Seven Years' War, 1756–1763

European and colonial rivalries became even more entangled in the next round of Anglo-French warfare, known as the Seven Years' War (1756–1763) in Europe and the French and Indian War (1754–1763) in North America. In Europe the conflict arose as a result of Maria Theresa's eventually unsuccessful attempt to regain Silesia. In this encounter, however, she joined forces with her former enemies, France and Russia, after Great Britain signed a defensive alliance with Prussia. This "diplomatic revolution" of 1756 shifted all the traditional alliances among European powers, but it did not affect Anglo-French rivalry in the colonies, which continued unabated.

The fighting in this North American theater of the war was particularly brutal and inflicted extensive casualties. In their struggle to gain control of eastern port cities and interior lands, the British and the French secured alliances with different Indian tribes. Among the many victims were some

of France's Indian allies who contracted smallpox when British-American colonists sold them blankets deliberately contaminated with the disease—the first known use of germ warfare in the West. This colonial war also had an Asian theater, in which French and British forces, most of them drawn from the trading companies of their respective countries, vied for mercantile influence and the possession of factories along the coast of the Indian Ocean. This conflict led directly to the British acquisition of the Indian province of Bengal in 1765.

The Treaty of Paris, which ended this round of European and colonial warfare in 1763, had more profound implications in the colonies than in Europe. In Europe, Prussia managed to hold on to Silesia, although its army incurred heavy casualties and its economy suffered from the war. In North America, however, monumental changes occurred. As a result of British naval victories, all of French Canada east of the Mississippi, including the entire province of Quebec, with its predominantly French population and French system of civil law, passed into British control (see Map 17.3). Even more important, the treaty secured British naval and mercantile superiority in the Atlantic, Caribbean, and Indian oceans. By virtue of its victories over France, Britain gained control of the lion's share of world commerce. This commercial superiority had profound implications for the economic development of Britain. Partially because of its ability to acquire raw materials from its colonies and to market its products throughout the world, Britain became the first country to experience the Industrial Revolution, as shall be discussed fully in Chapter 20.

The American and French Revolutionary Wars, 1775–1815

Despite the British victory over the French in 1763, the long conflict between the two countries continued into the early nineteenth century. During the American War of Independence (1775–1783), which we shall consider later, the North American colonists secured French military aid. During that war a British fleet attacked the French colony of Martinique, while the French dispatched an expedition against the British at Savannah that included hundreds of Africans and mulattos, or people of mixed race, drawn from the population of the West Indies. In India further conflicts between the French and British occurred, mainly between 1781 and 1783. These simultaneous military engagements in various parts of the world turned this phase of Anglo-French conflict into the first truly global war.

Anglo-French rivalry entered yet another phase between 1792 and 1815, during the era of the French Revolution (see Chapter 19). The British were able to

---

Map 17.3   British Possessions in North America and the Caribbean After the Treaty of Paris, 1763

The British acquisition of French territory marked a decisive moment in the expansion of the British Empire.

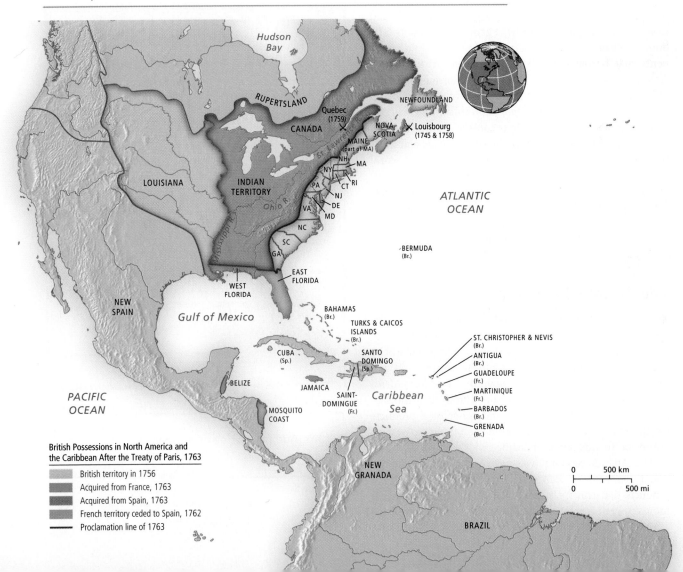

maintain their military and naval superiority, although once again it required an alliance with many European powers and the creation of a new balance of power against France. Even during this later phase of this French-British rivalry the British pursued imperial objectives. They expanded their empire in India and consolidated their territory there under the governorship of Richard Wellesley (1760–1842). In 1795, in the midst of the war against France, the British also acquired the Dutch colony at the Cape of Good Hope, giving them a base for their claims to much larger African territories in the nineteenth century.

The Atlantic World

■ How did European empires create an Atlantic economy in which the traffic in slaves was a major feature?

By the beginning of the eighteenth century, the territorial acquisitions of the five European maritime powers had moved the geographical center of the West from the European continent to the Atlantic Ocean itself. The Atlantic, rather than separating large geographical land masses, became a central, unifying geographical entity. The boundaries of this new Western world were the four continents that bordered the Atlantic: Europe, Africa, North America, and South America. The main thoroughfares that linked them were maritime routes across the Atlantic and up and down its coasts. The main points of commercial and cultural contact between the four continents, until the end of the eighteenth century, were the coastal areas and ports that bordered on the ocean. Within this Atlantic world arose new patterns of trade and economic activity, new interactions between ethnic and racial groups, and new political institutions. The Atlantic world also became the arena in which political and religious ideas were transmitted across the ocean and developed within a new environment.

The Atlantic Economy

The exchange of commercial goods and slaves between the western coasts of Europe, the African coasts, and the ports of North and South America created an economic enterprise that became one of the most active in the entire world (see Map 17.4). The ships that had brought the slaves from Africa to the Americas used the profits gained from their transactions to acquire precious metals and agricultural products for the European market. They then returned to western European Atlantic ports, where the goods were sold.

This Atlantic economy was fueled ultimately by the demand of a growing European population for agricultural products that could not be obtained in Europe and were more costly to transport from Asia. Sugar was the most important of these commodities, but tobacco, cotton, rice,

cacao, and coffee also became staples of the transatlantic trade. At the same time the North and South American colonists created a steady demand for manufactured goods, especially cutlery and metal tools, that were produced in Europe.

Two of the commodities that were imported from the colonies, tobacco and coffee, were criticized for the harmful effects they had on the human body. Tobacco, which came from the Americas, was the target of a number of criticisms in the seventeenth century. Even at that early date critics recognized the adverse physical effects of this product, which had been used widely among Native Americans. "Tobacco, that outlandish weed," read one popular rhyme, "It spends the brain and spoils the seed." Critics also believed that it had a hallucinatory effect on those who inhaled its smoke.

Coffee was a stimulant that originally came exclusively from the Middle East but later began to be shipped from Haiti and after 1809 from Brazil. Like tobacco, coffee was controversial because of the effects it had on the human

A Satire Against Coffee and Tobacco
A seventeenth-century satirical depiction of two European women smoking tobacco and drinking coffee. Turkey, represented by the figure to the right, was the main source of coffee in the seventeenth century. An African servant, to the left, pours the coffee. Tobacco came from the Americas.

Hudson
Bay

NEW FRANCE

LOUISIANA

QUEBEC

NEWFOUNDLAND
(to Great Britain, 1713)

ACADIA
(NOVA SCOTIA)
(to Great Britain, 1713)

Furs

GREAT
BRITAIN   NETH.

FRANCE

PORTUGAL   SPAIN

Manufactured goods

MEXICO

Mississippi R.

FLORIDA

Silver

Tobacco, Rice, Timber

Sugar, Cacao, Coffee

CUBA

JAMAICA

HISPANIOLA

PUERTO RICO

ASIENTO
(Spain to
Great Britain, 1713)

Portobelo

LESSER
ANTILLES
(English and French
since about 1630)

ATLANTIC
OCEAN

Canary Is.
(Spain)

AFRICA

Cape Verde Is.
(Port.)

Cape Verde

European forts and trading stations

NEW
GRANADA

DUTCH
GUIANA

FRENCH
GUIANA

Sugar

Slaves

Amazon R.

PERU

BRAZIL

ANGOLA

PACIFIC
OCEAN

The Atlantic Economy in the Mid-Eighteenth Century

British
Dutch
French
Portuguese
Spanish

* Scale varies with perspective.

Map 17.4   The Atlantic Economy in the Mid-Eighteenth Century
Commodities and African slaves were exchanged between the four continents of North America,
South America, Europe, and Africa.

body. In the late seventeenth and eighteenth centuries it was believed to be a source of political radicalism, probably because the coffeehouses where it was consumed served as gathering places for political dissidents. Contemporaries also identified coffee's capacity to produce irritability and depression.

The Atlantic economy had its own rhythms, but it was also part of a global economy that had taken shape during the seventeenth century. As Europeans had expanded the volume of their imports from Asia, those markets were fully integrated into this world system. The system was capitalist in the sense that the production and distribution of

Chocolate in the New World and the Old

One product of the encounters that took place between Spaniards and the indigenous people of the New World was the widespread consumption of chocolate among western Europeans in the seventeenth century. Chocolate was produced from the seeds of the cacao tree, which was indigenous to South America. Consumed mainly as a beverage, chocolate had been in widespread use among Aztecs and Mayans for centuries before the Spanish Conquest in the sixteenth century; like another native American plant, tobacco, it was used in religious and political ceremonies as well as for medicinal purposes. Spanish colonists received gifts of chocolate from Indians and soon began to enjoy the pleasurable physiological effects of this commodity, which contains chemical agents that act like amphetamines. Because it had such pleasurable effects, it was used in rituals of worship, friendship and courtship.

By the beginning of the seventeenth century, chocolate made its way from colonial America across the Atlantic to Spain. Shortly thereafter it became available in other western European countries. Its widespread use prepared the way for the introduction of two stimulants that came originally from the Middle East and Asia in the latter half of the seventeenth century: coffee and tea.

Because chocolate was grown in non-Christian lands where Spaniards believed that demons inhabited the landscape, and because it was associated with sexual pleasure, it met with harsh disapproval. Clerics denounced it— together with tobacco—as an inducement to vice and the work of Satan. Gradually, however, chocolate came to be viewed in purely secular terms as a commodity, without any religious significance.

The European demand for chocolate contributed to three major transformations of Western life. The first was the growth of the Atlantic trade and a global economy. Among the products that were shipped from the Americas to Europe in exchange for slaves and manufactured goods, cacao was second only to sugar in volume. In preconquest America cacao had often served as an exchange currency; now it was assigned a specific value in the world marketplace. As the price of chocolate escalated Spain established a monopoly over the trade, thus integrating it into the mercantilist system.

Second, the introduction of chocolate into Europe transformed the drinking patterns of Europeans. There had been nothing like chocolate in the diets of Europeans before its arrival, and when it was introduced, new rituals of consumption developed around its use. Cups with handles were designed specifically for drinking the hot beverage, the same cups later used for coffee and tea. The Aztec custom of scooping the foam from the top of a chocolate drink was adopted in Europe. The European desire to sweeten chocolate, as well as coffee and tea, increased the demand for sugar, which in turn encouraged the growth of slavery on the sugar plantations in the West Indies. Sweetened chocolate eventually began to be served as a candy, and by the nineteenth century chocolate candy became the main form in which the commodity was consumed.

Finally, chocolate became a part of the emerging bourgeois sexual culture of eighteenth-century France and England. Just as in preconquest Spanish America, it began to play a role in rituals of sexual seduction. It is no accident that boxes of chocolate are popular gifts on Valentine's Day and that the most well-known chocolate candy in the United States, Godiva, features the English noblewoman who rode naked through the streets of Coventry in 1140. The sustained exchange of a delectable commodity between the New World and the Old World thus contributed to a transformation of Western culture.

For Discussion

To what extent did the tastes of European consumers determine the nature of the Atlantic economy in the seventeenth and eighteenth centuries?

The Chocolate House (1787)
Men and women drinking chocolate, tea, and coffee at the White Conduit House, Islington, London.

commodities were undertaken by private individuals, in a systematic way, for the purposes of profit. European governments had an interest in this capitalist economy because as mercantilists they wanted their countries to acquire the largest possible share of world trade, but they did not control the actual operations of the marketplace. Their role was mainly to authorize individuals or trading companies to conduct trade in a particular geographical area.

The Atlantic Slave Trade

The slave trade became the very linchpin of the Atlantic economy, and all five Western European imperial powers—Britain, France, the Dutch Republic, Spain, and Portugal—engaged in it. The trade arose to meet the demand of plantation owners in the New World for agricultural labor. In the seventeenth century, after the indigenous Indian population had been ravaged by disease and the indentured whites who had emigrated from Europe in search of a more secure future had gained their freedom, this demand became urgent. Slave labor possessed a number of advantages over free labor. Slaves could be disciplined more easily, they could be forced to work longer hours, and they could be used to build a plantation economy in which the growing, harvesting, and processing of sugar and other agricultural commodities could be directed by one authority. The use of slave labor also allowed the economies of

European countries, especially Great Britain, to develop. Those who had invested in the colonial trade received attractive returns on their investment, while agricultural profits acquired from crops produced by slaves encouraged the growth of domestic manufacturing.

The slave trade formed the crucial link in the triangular pattern of commercial routes that began when European vessels traveled to ports along the western coast of Africa. There they exchanged European goods, including guns, for slaves that African merchants had captured in the interior and had marched to the sea. At these ports the slaves were branded with initials indicating to which nation they belonged. They were then crowded into ships that transported them across the Atlantic to the coast of South America, to the Caribbean, or as far north as Maryland. This was the famous and often deadly Middle Passage, the second leg of the triangular journey, which was completed when the ships returned to their point of origin. Once they had arrived in the Americas, the slaves were sold to the owners of plantations in the tropical areas of the Caribbean and the south Atlantic and in the more moderate climates of the North American mainland.

DOCUMENT

Mungo Park on Slavery in the Atlantic (late 1700s)

Slavery has been present throughout world history. It was a major feature of classical civilization and it was also present in medieval Europe before 1200. In Greece and Rome it had often been the result of captivity in war, whereas in the Middle Ages it was reserved for individuals

---

DOCUMENT

A Former Slave Protests African Slavery

In 1787 Quobna Ottobah Cugoano (1757–1791), a former slave, published an abolitionist treatise, Thoughts and Sentiments on the Evil and Wicked Traffic of the Slavery and Commerce of the Human Species. *Like the narrative written by Olaudah Equiano quoted at the beginning of this chapter, Cugoano's account describes the horrors of the African slave trade that he himself had experienced. In this passage Cugoano deplores the effect that the slave trade had on his native Africa.*

That base traffic of kid-napping and stealing men was begun by the Portuguese on the coast of Africa, and as they found the benefit of it for their own wicked purposes, they soon went on to commit further depredations. The Spaniards followed their infamous example, and the African slave trade was thought most advantageous for them, to enable themselves to live in ease and affluence by the cruel subjection and slavery of others. The French and English, and some other nations in Europe, as they founded

settlements or colonies in the West Indies or in America, went on in the same manner, and joined hand in hand with the Portuguese and Spaniards to rob and pillage Africa as well as to waste and desolate the inhabitants of the western continent. But the European depredators and pirates have not only robbed and pillaged the people of Africa themselves; but, by their instigation, they have infested the inhabitants with some of the vilest combinations of fraudulent and treacherous villains, even among their own people, and have set up their forts and factories as a reservoir of public and abandoned thieves and as a den of desperadoes, where they may ensnare, entrap and catch men. So that Africa has been robbed of its inhabitants, its freeborn sons and daughters have been stole, and kid-napped and violently taken away and carried into captivity and cruel bondage. And it may be said in respect to that diabolical traffic which is still carried on by the European depredators, that Africa has suffered as much and more than any other quarters of the globe.

Source: Quobna Ottobah Cugoano, Thoughts and Sentiments on the Evil and Wicked Traffic of the Slavery and Commerce of the Human Species *(London, 1787).*

who had been denied certain liberties. As Islam expanded in the ninth century, Arabs began the enslavement of foreign peoples, including black slaves from eastern Africa, and they continued that traffic into the early modern period. In the sixteenth and seventeenth centuries Barbary pirates in the Mediterranean captured approximately 850,000 white Europeans during sea raids and forced them into slavery in Muslim North Africa.

Within this long history of world slavery, the African slave trade conducted by Europeans is unique in three respects. The first distinction is its size. As a demographic phenomenon this involuntary transportation of Africans to the New World is without parallel in world history. It is the largest transoceanic migration recorded in written documents. Between 1519 and 1867 more than 11 million slaves were shipped from Africa to the New World. Deaths at sea reduced the number of slaves who actually arrived in the Americas to about 9.5 million. The peak years of the trade were from 1751 to 1800, when nearly four million slaves left African shores. As the volume of the slave trade increased during the eighteenth century, the percentage of African slaves among all immigrants arriving in the New World rose to more than 75 percent. Nine out of every ten slaves were sent to Brazil or the Caribbean region, including the northern coast of South America. The great majority of these slaves were sold to the owners of sugar and coffee plantations. Only about 4 percent of all slaves were destined for the British colonies on the North American mainland (after 1776 the United States), and almost all of those slaves were sent to the southern colonies.

The second distinctive feature of African slavery in the Americas was its racial character. It differed from the forms of slavery that had existed in ancient Greece and Rome as well as in medieval Europe, in which people of different races and ethnicities had been enslaved. It even differed from Muslim slavery, which involved the enslavement of European Christians as well as black Africans. As the slave trade brought millions of Africans into the Americas, and as indigenous Indian slavery diminished in size, slavery came to be equated with being black, while race was used to justify the inferiority of all African slaves.

The third distinctive feature of the Atlantic slave trade was its commercial character. Its sole function was to provide slave traders with a profit and slave owners with a supply of unfree labor. From the very beginning of their captivity African slaves were considered objects to be sold and their labor exploited. Acting in concert with African chieftains, European slave traders seized people who had performed no acts of aggression in their homelands, transported them overseas, and sold them to the highest bidders. Theories of private property developed in Europe in the seventeenth and eighteenth centuries established the right of slave masters to own their slaves as they would other pieces of property. In this way African slaves were turned into commercial commodities and treated in a manner that

Volume of the Transatlantic Slave Trade from Africa, 1519–1867	
1519–1600	266,100
1601–1650	503,500
1651–1675	239,800
1676–1700	510,000
1701–1725	958,600
1725–1750	1,311,300
1751–1775	1,905,200
1776–1800	1,921,100
1801–1825	1,645,100
1826–1850	1,621,000
1851–1867	180,800
Total	11,062,000

Source: David Eltis, "The Volume and Structure of the Transatlantic Slave Trade: A Reassessment," *William and Mary Quarterly,* 3rd series, 58 (2001), Table II.6.

deprived them of all human dignity. To justify such treatment their owners insisted that they "were beasts and had no more souls than beasts."[3] Slaves have never been treated well in any society, but slavery in the Americas acquired a reputation for being particularly exploitative and barbaric, and this has much to do with its commercial character.

One harrowing incident on the British slave ship *Zong* reveals the way in which financial calculations determined the fate of slaves. The *Zong* set sail in 1781 from the African island of São Tomé with 442 African slaves on board. When the slaves began to fall ill and die from malnutrition and disease, the captain of the ship, Luke Collingwood, feared that the owners of the ship would suffer a financial loss. If, however, the slaves were to be thrown overboard on the pretext that the safety of the crew was in jeopardy, the loss would be absorbed by those who had insured the voyage. Accordingly Collingwood decided to tie 132 slaves together, two by two, and fling them into the sea. When the ship owners went to court to collect the insurance, they argued that slaves were no different from horses and that they had a perfect right to throw the slaves overboard in order to preserve the safety of the ship.

Differences in the treatment and survival of slaves in the various parts of the New World had more to do with economic conditions, climate, and population trends than with the nationality or the religion of the slave masters. The crucial factor was the nature of the labor to which the slaves were subjected. Slaves who worked on plantations, especially those growing sugar, usually died within a few years. They were—simply said—worked to death. In the French colony of Saint Domingue, more than 500,000 of the 800,000 slaves brought to the colony between 1680 and 1780 perished. As long as the slave trade was still open, it was more profitable simply to replace those who died with new slaves than to try to extend the life of those the plantation owners already had. It was for this reason that the slave population did not start to grow internally in most areas until the slave trade ended in the nineteenth century.

Another factor influencing the treatment and survival of slaves was the ratio of the black to the white populations. When that ratio was high, as in all the Caribbean colonies, the codes regulating slave life were particularly harsh and created a reign of terror within the slave community. Yet another factor was climate. The absence of tropical diseases in the more temperate zone of the North American colonies provides the best explanation why in these colonies the numbers of births equaled and eventually exceeded the number of deaths long before they did in the Caribbean and South American colonies.

The slave trade itself became the object of intense competition, as each country tried to establish a monopoly over certain routes. During the seventeenth century the British managed to make inroads into the French slave trade, and eventually they surpassed the Portuguese and the Dutch as well. By 1700 British ships were transporting more than 50 percent of all slaves to the Americas. The dominance that Britain established in the slave trade was closely related to its growing maritime and commercial strength. With an enormous merchant marine and a navy that could support it, the British came to dominate the slave trade in the same way they came to dominate the entire world economy. Both revealed how far mercantile capitalism had triumphed in Britain and its overseas possessions.

For the British merchants who engaged in this trade there was no conflict between their traditional beliefs in individual liberty and their subjugation of African slaves. Theories of racial and national superiority removed Africans as well as other non-Europeans from the category of human beings who lived in a free society and who enjoyed individual rights. As long as those rights were tied to a particular national or racial group, such as freeborn Englishmen, slavery presented no challenge to British political ideas.

Not until the late eighteenth century did the enslavement of black Africans become a source of widespread moral concern. The movement to end the slave trade and slavery itself arose almost simultaneously in all European countries. It was inspired mainly by religious zeal, especially from evangelical Protestants in Great Britain and

The Slave Ship by J. M. W. Turner (1840)
The English painter J. M. W. Turner captured the horror of the incident that took place aboard the slave ship *Zong*, when the crew threw 132 slaves overboard in 1781.

the Jesuits in Spain and Portugal. Societies were formed to campaign for the legislative prohibition of the transportation and sale of slaves. These appeals found support in the calculations by European capitalists, especially in Britain, that slavery was no longer economically advantageous. Goods produced by free labor, especially by machine, made slavery appear less cost-effective than in the past, and the entire system of slavery began to be viewed as a costly encumbrance.

By the first decade of the nineteenth century opposition to slavery began to achieve limited success, and by 1851 it had brought about an end to the entire slave trade. The United States refused to allow any of its ports to accept slave ships after 1808, the same year in which the British parliament legislated an end to the trade within its empire. The Dutch ended their slave trade in 1814, the French in 1815, and the Spanish in 1838. The Portuguese continued to import slaves to Brazil until 1851 and ended the practice only because the British were subjecting Portuguese slave traders to constant harassment. Liberation of the slaves generally came later, except in Haiti (formerly Saint Domingue), where slavery was abolished in 1794. The British dismantled the system within their empire between 1834 and 1838. Slavery persisted until 1848 in the French Caribbean, 1863 in the southern United States, 1886 in Cuba, and 1888 in Brazil.

Carlos Julião, *Extraction of Diamonds*
In addition to their labor on plantations, slaves in Latin America were put to work mining precious metals and jewels. This watercolor depicts African slaves mining diamonds in eighteenth-century Brazil.

The ethnicity of colonial populations was more varied in Latin American colonies than in North America. The higher proportion of Africans in those colonies, more extensive patterns of intermarriage, and the free status achieved by large numbers of blacks and mulattos created highly stratified societies by the end of the eighteenth century. In these colonies divisions arose not only between the recently arrived Europeans and the creoles, but between the various groups considered by Europeans to be below them. The social structure of Brazil was more complex than that of any other country in the New World. At the top of the social hierarchy were Portuguese bureaucrats and below them was a large and wealthy group of planter creoles. These two elite groups dominated a lower-class social hierarchy of mestizos (people of mixed white and Indian ancestry), indigenous people, mulattos, freed blacks, and slaves.

Encounters between Europeans and Africans in the New World fostered the growth of ideas of white racial superiority that were grounded in the unbalanced power relationship between the dominant white and subordinate black populations. The circumstances under which physical contact between the races took place made the imbalance of this relationship readily apparent. Blacks appeared at the slave-trading stations having already been beaten into submission by their captives and forced to march hundreds of miles. The demeaning medical exams to which the slaves were subjected and their reduction to the status of a commodity for sale could readily deprive them of any sense of pride or self-respect. Their lack of formal education and literacy put them in a position of cultural inferiority, further reducing them to the status of beasts in the eyes of their white masters. In such circumstances references to the reputed blackness of the biblical Cain (Adam and Eve's first son, who murdered his brother Abel) only confirmed or reinforced the sense of superiority that white people took for granted.

Cultural Encounters in the Atlantic World

European countries had always possessed some ethnic diversity, but the emigration of people from many different parts of Europe and Africa to America, followed by their intermarriage, created societies of much greater complexity. Even the composition of the white European communities in the colonies was more varied than in the metropolis. In the British colonies, for example, English, Scots, and Irish were joined by large numbers of Germans, French, and Swiss. In 1776 Thomas Paine argued that all of Europe, rather than just England, was the true parent country of North American colonists. Ethnic divisions were further complicated by those of religion, especially in North America, where Protestants of many different denominations, as well as Roman Catholics, lived in close proximity to each other.

The Transmission of Ideas

The Atlantic Ocean became a corridor for the transmission of political and religious ideas. Political ideologies that developed in Europe were spread from the Old World to the New World mainly by the large volume of printed works that were exported during the eighteenth century. The ancient idea that a republic was the best form of government, which had found widespread support in Renaissance Italy and in seventeenth-century England, appealed to many political leaders in colonial North America. Eighteenth-century French and Scottish ideas regarding the rights of man and the responsibility of the government to bring about the improvement of society found fertile ground in many parts of North and South America. At the time of the French Revolution, ideals of liberty and equality spread not only throughout Europe but in the Americas as well. Legal ideas embodied in English common law, French civil law, and Spanish customary law were also transported to the New World and became the legal foundation of the new societies that were formed there.

The traffic in political ideas did not flow in only one direction. Political ideologies that were formed out of British and European ideas of liberty at the time of the American Revolution were sent back to European countries in a new form, where they inspired reform and revolution in Britain, France, and Ireland. These same ideas of liberty exerted a powerful influence in the Caribbean colonies and in South America. In Haiti, where French and American ideas of liberty inspired a revolution in the 1790s, radical ideas of racial equality developed within the new republic and then spread outward to other colonies and the United States.

Religious ideas experienced a similar transmission and transportation. The Calvinist belief in predestination, which had been formulated in Switzerland and modified by Puritans in England during the sixteenth century, was adopted and further modified by colonists in New England during the seventeenth century. Catholic theological ideas that were introduced into Spanish and Portuguese America, including those regarding the role of the Devil in human society, interacted with those of indigenous peoples and African slaves and produced new religious syntheses. In religion as well as politics, these exchanges of ideas enriched the intellectual worlds of Europeans and colonists alike.

Encounters Between Europeans and Asians

■ **What cultural encounters took place between European and Asian peoples during this period of empire building, and how did these encounters change Western attitudes toward outsiders?**

The period from 1650 to 1815 was decisive in the development of European empires in Asia. These overseas possessions, like the American colonies, formed important components of the empires of European states and were also essential to the operation of the global economy. European dominance of world trade was exercised not only in the Atlantic world but also in the Middle East and Asia. The history of the European presence in these areas, however, is very different from that which occurred in the New World. A first difference was that of simple numbers. Prior to the eighteenth century the European presence in Asia had been limited to the activities of missionaries and merchants in places such as Jakarta, Macao, and Manila. During the eighteenth century the number of European colonists in Asia, even in India, remained relatively small in comparison with the numbers who settled in America, especially in British North America.

A second major difference between European empires in the East and in the West during the period from 1650 to 1850 is that in Asia European powers initially did not try to acquire and govern large land masses and subjugate their populations. Europeans first came to Asia to trade, not to conquer. They did not engage in fixed battles with Asians, take steps to reduce the size of their populations, or force them to migrate, as they did in the New World. Only in a handful of Southeast Asian islands did a pattern of conquest, similar to that which had occurred in the New World, take place. When Europeans used military force in Asia, it was almost always against rival European powers, not the indigenous population. When European countries did eventually use force against Asians, they discovered that victory was much more difficult than it had been in the New World. Indeed, Asian peoples already possessed or were acquiring sufficient military strength to respond to European military might. In China and Japan the possession of this military power prevented Europeans from even contemplating conquest or exploitation until the nineteenth century. Establishment of European hegemony in Asia, therefore, took longer and was achieved more gradually than in the Americas.

Political Control of India

Despite their original intentions, Europeans eventually began to acquire political control over large land masses in Asia and subject Asians to European rule. The first decisive steps in this process took place in India during the second half of the eighteenth century. Until that time the British in India, most of whom were members of the British East India Company, remained confined to the factories that were established along the Indian coast. The main purpose of these factories was to engage in trade not only with Europe but also with other parts of Asia. In conducting this trade the British had to deal with local Indian merchants and to compete with the French, the Portuguese and the Dutch, who had established factories of their own. They also found it advantageous to make alliances with the provincial governors, known as nawabs°, who controlled the interior of the country. It became customary for each European power to have its own candidate for nawab, with the expectation that he would provide favors for his European patrons once he took office.

Military Conflict and Territorial Acquisitions, 1756–1856

In 1756 this pattern of trading and negotiating resulted in armed military conflict in the city of Calcutta in the northeastern province of Bengal. The British had established a factory at Calcutta in 1690, and they continued to carry on an extensive trade there with Indian merchants, many of whom were Hindus. The nawab of Bengal, the Muslim

Warren Hastings

Warren Hastings (1732–1818), who was appointed the first governor-general of India in 1773, represented the ambiguities of early British rule in that country. An officer in the British East India Company, he was sympathetic to Indian culture. He was, however, accused of gross misconduct in the management of Indian affairs. His impeachment by the British Parliament in 1786 for corruption in his administration and cruelty toward some of the native people in Bengal lasted 145 days but resulted in an acquittal in 1787.

Siraj-ud-Daulah, had contempt for all Europeans, especially the British, and he was determined that he would not be beholden to any of them. He was also deeply hostile to the Hindu merchants who were trading with the British. In June 1756 he sent an army of 50,000 Muslims against Calcutta, burning and plundering the city and beginning a siege of the East India Company's Fort William, which was manned by 515 troops in the service of the company. The entire British population of the city, together with more than 2,000 Hindus, had taken refuge in the fort. After a long struggle, which resulted in the death of hundreds of Indians, the fort fell to the nawab's forces, and some of the British officers and magistrates, including the governor of Calcutta, fled by sea.

During this siege the shooting death of a Bengali guard led to an incident that became permanently emblazoned on the emerging imperial consciousness of the British people. Officers in the nawab's army crammed the entire remaining British contingent, a total of 146 men and women, into the fort's lockup or prison, known as the Black Hole of Calcutta. Measuring 18' × 14' 10", it was meant to hold only three or four prisoners overnight. The British prisoners were stifled by the insufferable heat and a lack of water and air. The stench was so bad that many prisoners vomited on the people squeezed next to them. Only twenty-two men and one woman survived until the next morning, when the nawab released them. The remainder either had been trampled to death or had asphyxiated.

The deaths of these British men and women in the Black Hole of Calcutta led the British to seek swift and brutal retribution against the nawab. In 1757, under the direction of the British military officer Robert Clive, a force of 800 British troops and 2,000 native Indian soldiers known as sepoys° retook Calcutta and routed Siraj-ud-Daulah's army of 50,000 men at the battle of Plassey. Siraj-ud-Daulah was executed and replaced by a nawab more amenable to the British. A few years later the British East India Company secured the right to collect taxes and thus exercised political control over the entire province of Bengal. The enormous revenue from these taxes enabled the company to acquire a large army, composed mainly of sepoys. This force grew to 115,000 men by 1782. The British then used these military forces, which were equipped with Western military technology, to gain control of other provinces in India as well as to defeat their French rivals in subsequent engagements during the early nineteenth century.

These further acquisitions of Indian territory led to the eventual establishment of British rule throughout the South Asian subcontinent (see Map 17.5). New territories were brought under British control in the early years of the nineteenth century, and during the tenure of Lord Dalhousie as governor-general of India from 1848 to 1856 the British annexed eight Indian states, including the great Muslim state of Oudh in 1856. This policy of annexation went hand in hand with the introduction of Western technology and literature, the English language, and British criminal procedure.

The Sepoy Mutiny

The British policy of annexation in India, coupled with the attitude of cultural superiority it encouraged, lay at the root of the greatest act of rebellion by Indians against British rule in the nineteenth century. This rebellion, which began in 1857, is often known as the Sepoy Mutiny, because it originated in the ranks of the Indian troops serving in the armed forces of the British East India Company. The main source of resentment was the British annexation

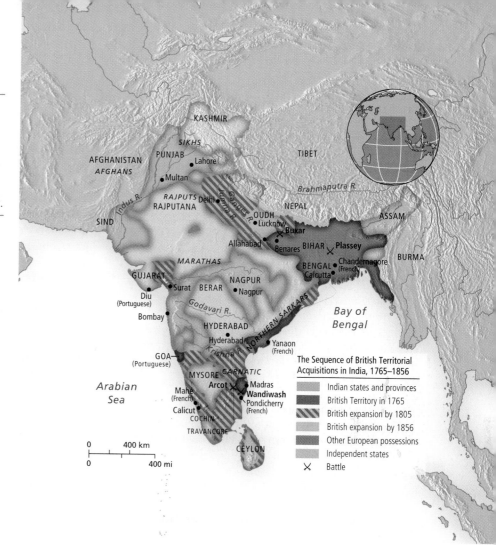

Map 17.5 The Sequence of British Territorial Acquisitions in India, 1765–1856

British political control of large territories on the South Asian subcontinent began more than a century after the establishment of the first factories along the coast.

The Sequence of British Territorial Acquisitions in India, 1765–1856

- Indian states and provinces
- British Territory in 1765
- British expansion by 1805
- British expansion by 1856
- Other European possessions
- Independent states
- ✕ Battle

of Oudh, which many sepoys considered their homeland. The incident that actually provoked the rebellion was the issue of rifle cartridges coated with beef fat, which violated Hindu law, and pork fat, which violated Muslim law. Although this insensitivity to native Indian culture was not unprecedented, in this case it struck a particularly raw nerve and led to a mutiny by the Bengali army. The cities of Delhi and Lucknow came under siege, and dreadful atrocities, including the hacking to death of British women and children, occurred. British reprisals were equally savage and eventually succeeded in suppressing the rebellion.

In the wake of the mutiny the British government abolished the British East India Company and assumed direct rule of India. Queen Victoria (r. 1837–1901), the constitutional monarch of the United Kingdom, acquired much greater power over her Indian empire. Although the British government did take steps to confirm the lands and titles of Indian princes and to give them local power, their relationship with their British overlords remained one of strict subordination.

Changing European Attitudes Toward Asian Cultures

This second phase of European imperialism in Asia played a crucial role in the formation of Western identity. The steadily increasing numbers of Europeans who had contact with these lands—merchants, missionaries, writers, and colonial administrators—and to a lesser extent the public who read about these foreign places gained a clearer sense of who they were once they compared themselves to Indians, Chinese, and Polynesians. Until the seventeenth century Europeans thought of "the East" mainly as the Middle East, an area that was largely subsumed within the Ottoman Empire. Europeans expressed a generally negative

view of the culture of this region (see Chapter 15), and over the years that perception had not changed. The political system of the Ottoman Empire was considered despotic and its religion, Islam, the antithesis of Christianity. The Far East, comprising South Asia (India), East Asia (China, Japan), and Southeast Asia (Burma, Siam, Indonesia), generally did not enter into these perceptions of "the Orient." There was little contact with this part of the world, and much of what was known about it was shrouded in mystery. During this period Europeans viewed the Far East mainly as an exotic land, rich in spices, silk, and other luxury commodities.

As Western missionaries and merchants made more frequent contacts with Asian society, Europeans developed more informed impressions of these distant lands and peoples. Some of those impressions were negative, especially when the power of Asian rulers was discussed, but many other characterizations of the East were positive. Interest in and admiration for both Indian and Chinese culture were most widespread during the middle years of the eighteenth century. The systematic study of Asian languages, especially Chinese and Sanskrit, began during this period. A preference for things Asian became characteristic of Enlightenment thinkers such as Voltaire (1694–1778), who regarded Asian cultures as superior to

DOCUMENT

The East India Company and the British Government

In the eighteenth century the control of British factories in India was entrusted to the East India Company, which had its own administrative bureaucracy and armed forces. Responding to reports of widespread corruption and other abuses by the company, the British Parliament passed an act regulating the company's affairs in 1773. This arrangement did not satisfy many critics of the company, who demanded that the British government assume direct rule of its Indian territories, at a time when the company was acquiring new provinces. The government, however, was reluctant to assume these responsibilities, and in this paper, written in 1778, John Robinson, the secretary to the treasury, set down his reasons for leaving the government of British India in the hands of the East India Company.

As far as I am hitherto informed, my opinion is that the government should not take the management of these acquisitions in their own hands but should leave them in the hands of the company, reforming and altering the government of the company, so as to make it more fit than it is at present for the management of such a concern.

My reasons . . . are as follows:

First, I have never yet seen any plan to my satisfaction by which these acquisitions can be properly transferred from the Company to the government in a better manner than they may be by the Company, provided the government of it be amended and made subject to the superintendence and frequent control of the legislature.

Secondly, the change itself would be very difficult and even dangerous in the present moment when we have a rebellion in our colonies, a foreign war and many other difficulties to contend with. . . .

Fourthly, I am violently against pledging the revenues and substance of this country for the security of these acquisitions, in return for any advantage by way of revenue that may be derived from them; and yet this must be the case, if the government take the management of them into their own hands.

Fifthly, I think that the errors which must be committed in the management of such acquisitions, at so great a distance from the seat of government, had better fall upon the directors of the Company than fall directly upon the ministers of the king, who in the midst of the difficulties that at present surround them, and of the calumnies to which they are necessarily subject, can hardly now retain a sufficient degree of authority and respect for the government of this country.

Source: British Library, Additional Manuscript 38398, folios 108–17.

---

those of a corrupt Europe in many respects. Voltaire also found the East unaffected by the superstition and the fanaticism that characterized Western Christianity, which he loathed. To him, the main philosophical tradition of China, Confucianism, which embodied a strict moral code, was a more attractive alternative. Eastern religion, especially Hinduism, was also admired for its ethical content and its underlying belief in a single deity.

This mid-eighteenth-century admiration of Asian culture even extended to Chinese and Indian political institutions. The despotic Chinese Empire was transformed through Voltaire's perceptions into an enlightened monarchy. There was less to admire in the Mughal Empire in India, but in his history of European colonialism the French Jesuit priest Guillaume Thomas Raynal (1713–1796) idealized the "purity and equity" of the ancient Indian political system. Comparison of contemporary Indian politics with the corruption of governments in Europe made native Asian political systems look good by comparison. In Britain there was more disrespect for the members of the East India Company known as nabobs°, who returned to England to flaunt the wealth they had recently acquired in India, than there was for native Indian officials. There was also more interest in reforming the British East India Company than in reforming Indian politics.

This intellectual respect for Asian philosophy and politics coincided with a period of widespread Asian influences on Western art, architecture, and design. Eastern themes began to influence British buildings, such as in the Brighton Pavilion, designed by John Nash. Small cottages, known as bungalows, owed their inspiration to Indian models. French architects built pagodas (towers with the roof of each story turning upward) for their clients. Chinese gardens, which unlike classical European gardens were not arranged geometrically, became popular in England and France.

A new form of decorative art that combined Chinese and European motifs, known in French as chinoiserie°, became highly fashionable. Wealthy French people furnished their homes with Chinese wallpaper and hand-painted folding screens. The demand for Chinese porcelain, known in English simply as china, was insatiable. Vast quantities of this porcelain, which was technically and aesthetically superior to the stoneware produced in Germany and England, left China for the ports of western Europe. Even the dress of Europeans was influenced by Asian styles. Indian and Chinese silks were in high demand, and Europeans ex-

Brighton Pavilion

This building, designed by John Nash, reflected the incorporation of Eastern styles into English architecture, and was inspired by the description of Kubla Khan's palace in Samuel Taylor Coleridge's poem "Kubla Khan" (1816).

pressed a preference for Indian cotton over that produced in the New World. A style of Indian nightwear known as pajamas became popular in England. Even a new sport, polo, which had originated to India, made its entry into upper-class European society at this time.

During the late eighteenth and early nineteenth centuries the high regard in which many Europeans held Asian culture began to wane. As the European presence in Asia became larger and more powerful, as the British began to exercise more control in India, and as merchants began to monopolize the Asian trade, Western images of the East became more unfavorable. Chinese philosophy, instead of being viewed as a repository of ancient ethical wisdom, was labeled as irrational when compared with that of the West. Confucianism fell out of favor, and Eastern religion in general was despised as being inferior to Christianity. Enlightenment thinkers ranked Asian political systems below those of the more "advanced" countries of Europe. The English scholar George Anson claimed that the Chinese reputation for industry and ingenuity was undeserved and that their scientific thought was inferior to that of Europeans. The English writer Samuel Johnson (1709–1784) expressed this

DOCUMENT

Thomas Babington Macaulay's "Minute on Education" (1834)

sense of Western intellectual superiority when he had an Arab poet in his novel *Rasselas* (1759) state that Europeans "are more powerful . . . than we, because they are wiser; knowledge will always predominate over ignorance."[4]

Expressions of Western superiority over Asians were reinforced by emerging ideas of racial difference. Sixteenth- and seventeenth-century ideas of Europeans' superiority over black Africans and the indigenous peoples of the Americas on the basis of differences in skin color and facial features were now extended to the Chinese, dark-skinned South Asians, and Polynesians. Intellectual theories of race, which are a distinctly Western creation and were developed mainly during the late eighteenth century, provided an apparently empirical and scientific foundation for these assumptions. The color of one's skin in India, which had determined the position of a person in the Hindu caste system, was now used by Westerners to identify South Asians as "coloreds."

By the same token Chinese people, previously described as white by Westerners who admired China, were now referred to as being nonwhite or yellow. By the beginning of the nineteenth century, Westerners had acquired an ideology of superiority over Asians as well as Africans and indigenous

American people that included racial difference as one of its main components. This ideology prepared Europeans intellectually and emotionally for the conquest of numerous countries in Asia and Africa in the second half of the nineteenth century. This third and final period of European imperial expansion, which began around 1870 and reached its peak around 1900, brought 84 percent of the Earth's surface under Western control.

The Crisis of Empire and the Atlantic Revolutions

■ Why did European powers begin to lose control of some of their colonies, especially those in the Americas, between 1775 and 1825?

During the period from 1780 to 1825, European empires experienced a crisis that marked the end of the second stage of European overseas expansion. As a result of this crisis British, French, and Spanish governments lost large segments of their empires, all in the Americas. New states and nations were carved out of the older sprawling empires. The crisis was to some extent administrative. Having acquired large expanses of territory overseas, European states were faced with the challenging problem of governing them from a distance. They not only had to rule large areas inhabited by non-European peoples (Indians and African slaves), but they also faced the difficulty of maintaining the loyalty of people of European descent who were born in the colonies.

These European colonials or creoles became the main protagonists in the struggles that led to the independence of the North American colonies from Britain in 1776 and the South American colonies from Spain a generation later. In the French colony of Saint Domingue, the location of the only successful revolution in the Caribbean region during this period, a very different set of pressures led to independence. In this colony, which became the republic of Haiti in 1804, the revolution was led not by white creoles but by people of color, including the slaves who worked on the plantations. In Britain's European colony of Ireland, where an unsuccessful revolution against British rule took place in 1798, the urge for independence came both from settlers of British descent and the native Irish population.

The American Revolution, 1775–1783

The first Atlantic revolution was the revolt of the thirteen North American colonies and the establishment of their independence from British rule. During the second half of the eighteenth century, a number of tensions arose between the British government and its transatlantic colonies. All of these overseas colonies had developed traditions of self-government, and all of them had their own representative assemblies. At the same time the colonies were controlled by various governmental bodies responsible to the British Parliament, such as the Board of Trade. The colonies had their own militias, but they also received protection from British troops when conflicts developed with the French or other hostile powers.

The crisis that led to the American Revolution had its roots in the situation that emerged at the end of the French and Indian War. In order to maintain the peace agreed to in 1763, the government stationed British troops on the frontiers of the colonies. It argued that because the troops were protecting the colonists, they should contribute financially to their own defense. To this end the government began imposing a number of new taxes on the colonists. In 1765 the British Parliament passed the Stamp Act, which forced

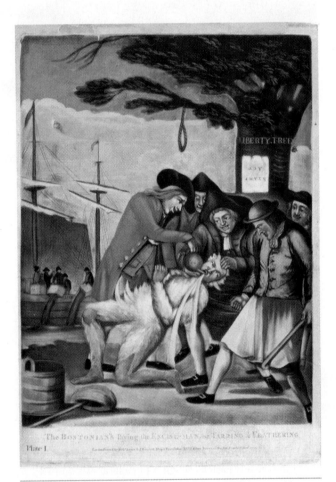

***The Bostonian's Paying the Excise Man or Tarring and Feathering* (1774)**
This satirical engraving reflects the hatred of colonial Americans at the collection of taxes levied on them without their consent. The Boston Tea Party is depicted in the background. The colonists are forcing the tax collector to drink the tea on which he is trying to collect taxes.

The British Surrender at Yorktown in 1781
This battle ended the American War of Independence, although the peace treaty was not signed
for another two years.

colonists to purchase stamps for almost anything that was printed. This piece of legislation raised the central constitutional issue of whether Parliament had the power to legislate for British subjects in lands that did not elect members of that Parliament. "Taxation without representation is tyranny" became the main rallying cry of the colonists. Opposition to the Stamp Act was so strong that Parliament repealed the act the following year, but at the same time it passed a statute declaring that it had the authority to tax the colonists as it pleased. When the government imposed new taxes on the tea imported from Britain in 1773, a number of colonists, dressed as Indians, threw the tea into the Boston Harbor.

The government responded to this "Boston Tea Party" by passing a series of statutes, known in the colonies as the Intolerable Acts, in 1774. One of these acts specified that the port of Boston be closed until the colonists had repaid the cost of the tea. The Intolerable Acts led to organized resistance to British rule, and in the following year military conflict broke out at Lexington and Concord in Massachusetts. On July 4, 1776, thirteen of the colonies on the North American mainland, stretching from New Hampshire to Georgia, approved a Declaration of Independence from Great Britain. A long revolutionary war, in which the colonists received assistance from France in 1778, ended with the defeat of British troops at Yorktown in 1781 and the recognition of the republic of the United States of America in the Treaty of Paris in 1783.

The case that the American colonists made for independence from Britain drew upon the political theories of John Locke, who justified resistance against the Stuart monarchy at the time of the Glorious Revolution. Locke, who placed limits on legislative as well as executive power, became the main inspiration of the Declaration of Independence, which was drafted by Thomas Jefferson. The Revolution also found support in the customs and traditions embodied in the English common law, especially the principle that men could not be deprived of their rights without their own consent. Republican ideas, drawn both from ancient Greece and Rome and revived at the time of the Renaissance, gave colonists a model of a community of virtuous men joined in a commitment to the body politic, which they defined in colonial terms. Finally there was the influence of the ideas of the Enlightenment, which empha-

DOCUMENT

Thomas Paine Supports the American Cause

Thomas Paine (1737–1809) was a radical Whig reformer who supported the cause for American independence. In Common Sense *(1776), a pamphlet written to support the American cause in the year of the Declaration of Independence, Paine refutes the arguments of the British that they served the interests of the American colonists. Paine protests not only the commercial exploitation of the colonies but also the way in which Great Britain has involved them in warfare with continental rivals.*

I have heard it asserted by some, that as America has flourished under her former connection with Great Britain, the same connection is necessary towards her future happiness, and will always have the same effect. Nothing can be more fallacious than this kind of argument. We may as well assert that because a child has thrived upon milk, that it is never to have meat, or that the first twenty years of our lives is to become a precedent for the next twenty. But even this is admitting more than is true; for I answer roundly that America would have flourished as much, probably much more, had no European power taken any notice of her. The commerce by which she hath enriched herself are the necessaries of life and will always have a market while eating is the custom of Europe.

But she has protected us, say some. That she hath engrossed us is true, and defended the Continent at our expense as well as her own, is admitted; and she would have defended Turkey from the same motive, *viz.* for the sake of trade and dominion.

Alas! We have been long led away by ancient prejudices and made large sacrifices to superstition. We have boasted the protection of Britain without considering that her motive was *interest,* not *attachment;* and that she did not protect us from *our* enemies on *our account* but from *her enemies* on *her own account,* from those who had no quarrel with us on any *other account,* and who will always be our enemies on the *same account.* Let Britain waive her pretensions to the Continent, or the Continent throw off the dependence, and we should be at peace with France and Spain, were they at war with Britain. The miseries of Hanover last war ought to warn us against connections.

Source: From Thomas Paine, *Common Sense* (Philadelphia: W. T. Bradford, 1776).

---

sized the natural right of all men to life, liberty, and the pursuit of happiness (see Chapter 18).

Although the American Revolution was inspired by many of the ideas that had originated in the two English revolutions of the seventeenth century, it differed from those earlier revolutions in that it was directed more against the British Parliament than the king. The Declaration of Independence severed the bonds between the colonists and King George III, to whom they formally owed allegiance, but the constitutional powers against which they protested, especially that of taxation, were those of Parliament. It was taxation by the British Parliament, rather than nonparliamentary taxes like those levied in the 1640s, that led to the American Revolution.

The Haitian Revolution, 1789–1804

The second successful revolution in the Atlantic world took place in the French Caribbean colony of Saint Domingue, known later as Haiti, which occupied the western portion of the island of Hispaniola. This revolution resulted in the establishment of the colony's independence, but the revolt was directed not so much against French rule as against the island's white planters. Just like their counterparts in Spanish and British Caribbean colonies, these planters, known in Haiti as colons°, had little desire for national independence. They wished to remain within the protective custody of the French state. Because they formed a distinct minority of the total population, they did not think of themselves as constituting a separate national community. Any resistance to imperial rule, moreover, would have required that they arm their slaves in order to make the movement succeed, and that would have threatened their control of the black population.

The real threat of revolution in all the Caribbean colonies came not from the elite or ruling class but from the subordinate members of the population. In Saint Domingue the revolution began in 1789 with a rebellion of people defined legally as free coloreds, most of whom were mulattos. The development that triggered this revolt, organized under the leadership of Vincent Ogé, was the refusal of the white planters, who were creoles, to give the free coloreds representation in the revolutionary French National Assembly as well as in local assemblies in Saint Domingue.

The free colored rebellion of 1789 led directly to a massive slave revolt in 1791. At that time slaves constituted about 90 percent of the population. Their uprising took place after the French National Assembly voted to abolish slavery in France but not in the French colonies. In this revolt 12,000 African slaves, armed with machetes and reacting to their brutal treatment by their masters, destroyed a thousand plantations and killed hundreds of whites. Their tactics, which included cutting white planters in half, raping their wives and daughters, and decapitating their children, were matched by those of the planters, who retaliated by torturing blacks and hanging them in the streets.

Spanish and British armies, frightened that this slave rebellion would spread to their colonies, occupied Saint Domingue and massacred thousands of slaves, many of them after they surrendered. In 1795, however, the Spanish withdrew from Saint Domingue and ceded their portion of the island of Hispaniola to France. The British were likewise forced to leave the colony in 1798, having lost as many as 40,000 soldiers, most of them from disease. The man who had assumed the leadership of the slave revolt, the freed slave Toussaint L'Ouverture, then proceeded to conquer the entire island in 1801, abolish slavery, and proclaim himself the governor-general of an autonomous province.

In 1801, after Napoleon had assumed control of the French government and the idealism of the French Revolution had evaporated, a French army of 20,000 men occupied Saint Domingue. The purpose was to make the colony the centerpiece of a restored French Empire, including Florida, Louisiana, French Guiana, and the French West Indies. This assertion of French imperial control secured the surrender of L'Ouverture. When it was learned that the French were planning to reintroduce slavery, however, two black generals, Jean-Jacques Dessalines and Henri Christophe, whom the French had enlisted to suppress the revolt, united freed blacks and slaves against the French forces. In 1803 these united forces drove the French out of the colony, and in 1804 they established an independent state of Haiti.

This new state of Haiti was far different from the United States, in that it was governed entirely by people of color and it banned slavery. It proclaimed racial equality by defining all Haitians as black. The plantation system was destroyed and the land was redistributed among free blacks; foreigners were forbidden to hold property. Deciding upon the form of government took time, however, as the new rulers of the country were divided between those who wished to establish a monarchy and those who favored a republic. Those divisions led to a prolonged civil war from 1807 until 1822, when the warring northern and southern provinces were integrated into a single republic.

The Haitian revolution was the most radical and egalitarian of the Atlantic revolutions of the late eighteenth and early nineteenth centuries. Whereas the American Revolution was mainly a political movement that established a new republic, the Haitian revolution was a genuine social and economic revolution as well. Its unqualified declaration of human equality and its abolition of slavery served as an inspiration to abolitionist movements in other countries, including the United States, throughout the nineteenth century. The destruction of the plantation system, however, brought about a revolutionary transformation of the country's economy. As a French possession Saint Domingue was quite possibly the richest colony in the world, producing about two-fifths of the world's sugar and half of its coffee. After the revolution, with its economy severed from that of France, the country could no longer compete successfully in the Atlantic economy.

The Irish Rebellion, 1798–1799

Within the British Empire the country that was most directly inspired by the success of the American Revolution was the kingdom of Ireland. Unlike the residents of the thirteen colonies in North America, the Gaelic people of Ireland had long thought of themselves as a distinct nation. The English, however, had begun a conquest of this Irish nation in the twelfth century, and during the next 500 years they had struggled to rule it effectively. One of their methods was to settle English landlords on Irish lands. They had done this in the Middle Ages by giving large estates to English feudal lords, but those old Anglo-Irish families had gradually begun to think of themselves as Irish, and after the Reformation they had remained Catholic, while most English people had become Protestant.

In the sixteenth century the English government had begun to settle colonies of English Protestants on plantations in various parts of Ireland. The purpose of this policy was to gain tighter control over the country and to promote the loyalty of Irish landowners to the English government. In the early seventeenth century James VI of Scotland (who had also become James I of England in 1603) had settled both Scottish Presbyterians, later known as the Scots Irish, as well as English Anglicans, in the northern Irish province of Ulster. These Protestants of Scottish and English descent had become the core of the ruling establishment throughout Ireland, especially after Catholic rebellions in 1641–1649 and again in 1689–1690 had failed.

In the eighteenth century Irish Protestants began to resent their subservient relationship to the British government. Just like the American colonists, they recognized the way in which the Irish economy was serving British rather than Irish interests, and they resented the control that Britain had over the Irish parliament. A reform association known as the Society of United Irishmen, led by the Protestant Ulsterman Wolfe Tone, succeeded in building common ground between Protestants and Catholics. The United Irishmen demanded the repeal of the laws that denied Catholics the right to hold office and sit in the Irish parliament.

The ideals of the United Irishmen drew on many different sources. A long tradition of Presbyterian republican radicalism found reinforcement in the ideals of the American Revolution. The Irish objected to paying tithes to the established Anglican church, and like the American colonists in the 1760s they resented the taxes they were asked to pay to aid in the British war against the French during the 1790s.

French revolutionary ideas of liberty, equality, and fraternity had a pervasive influence in Ireland as well.

In 1798 the United Irishmen aligned themselves with lower-class Catholic peasants known as Defenders, and these Irish groups staged a rebellion against British rule with the intention of establishing an Irish republic. Like the American colonists, the Irish revolutionaries sought French aid, but it came too little and too late, and the rebellion failed. The revolt, which was marred by atrocities on both sides, resulted in the deaths of 30,000 people.

The British government recognized that its arrangement for ruling Ireland, in which the nationalist republican movement had originated, could no longer work. The British government decided therefore to bring about a complete union between Great Britain and Ireland. By the terms of this arrangement, which took effect in 1801, Ireland's parliament ceased to meet; instead the Irish were to elect a limited number of representatives to sit in the British parliament. Ireland thus became a part of the United Kingdom, just as Scotland had done in 1707. The proximity of Ireland to Britain, which made the prospect of Irish independence much more dangerous, was a major factor in making the British determined to hold on to this "internal colony." The forces of Irish nationalism could not be contained, however, and during the nineteenth century new movements for Irish independence arose.

National Revolutions in Spanish America, 1810–1824

The final set of revolutions against European imperial powers occurred between 1810 and 1824 in a number of Spanish American colonies. These struggles, like the American Revolution, turned colonies into new states and led to the building of new nations. The first of these revolutions began in Mexico in 1810; others soon arose in Argentina, Colombia, Chile, and Peru. In these revolutions creoles played a leading role, just as they had in the American War of Independence. The main sources of creole discontent were the Bourbon reforms, which ironically had been intended to make the Spanish Empire more efficient and thus to preserve it. The reforms had achieved this goal, however, by favoring commercial interests at the expense of the traditional aristocracy, thereby reversing or threatening the position of many creole elites. The creoles also faced increasingly heavy taxation, as the Spanish government sought to make them support the expenses of colonial administration.

During the late eighteenth century Spanish creole discontent had crystallized into demands for greater political autonomy, similar to the objectives of British American colonists. South American creoles began to think of themselves as Spanish Americans and sometimes simply as Americans. Like British American colonists, they also read and were inspired by the works of Enlightenment political philosophers. They protested against the Bourbon reforms. Nevertheless, the Spanish creole struggle against imperial rule did not commence until some thirty years after the North American colonies had won their independence. One reason for this slow development of revolutionary action was that Spanish American creoles still looked to the Spanish government to provide them with military support against the threat of lower-class rebellion. When, for example, a rebellion of this sort against Spanish rule occurred in Peru in 1780, creole planters not only refused an invitation to join the revolt but also supported the Spanish forces that crushed it. Faced with this lower-class threat, which continued to plague them even after independence, creoles were cautious about abandoning the military and police support provided by the metropolis.

The event that eventually precipitated these wars for national independence was the collapse of the Spanish monarchy after Napoleon's French army invaded Spain in 1808 (see Chapter 19). This development left the Spanish Empire, which had always been more centralized than the British Empire, in a weakened position. In an effort to reconstitute the political order in their colonies, creoles sought to establish greater autonomy. Once the monarchy was restored, this demand for autonomy led quickly to armed resistance. This resistance began in Mexico, but it soon spread throughout Spanish America and quickly acquired popular support.

DOCUMENT

The Plan of Iguala (1821)

The man who took the lead in these early revolts against Spanish rule was the fiery Venezuelan aristocrat Símon Bolívar (1783–1830). Educated in the ideas of the Enlightenment, Bolívar led uprisings in his homeland in 1812 and 1814 and eventually defeated the Spanish there in 1819. Unlike most creoles, Bolívar was not afraid to recruit free coloreds and blacks into his armies. His hatred of European

CHRONOLOGY

The Atlantic Revolutions, 1775–1824

1775–1783	United States of America
1789–1804	Haiti
1798–1799	Ireland
1810–1821	Mexico
1810–1819	Colombia
1810–1821	Venezuela
1810–1816	Argentina
1810–1818	Chile
1821–1824	Peru

Símon Bolívar Presenting the Flag of Liberation to Soldiers After the Battle of Carabobo, 1821

Bolívar was the man most directly responsible for liberating South American countries from Spanish rule. He liberated his native Venezuela in 1821 and defeated Spanish forces in Peru in 1824.

colonial governors knew few boundaries. At one point he reportedly commanded his soldiers to shoot and kill any European on sight. He vowed never to rest until all of Spanish America was free. Bolívar carried the struggle for liberation to Peru, which became independent in 1824, and created the state of Bolivia in 1825. Often compared to George Washington, he was more responsible than any one individual for the liberation of Spanish America from Spanish rule. Independent states were established in Argentina in 1816, Chile in 1818, Colombia in 1819, and Mexico in 1821. By then the Spanish, who in the sixteenth century had the largest empire in the world, retained control of only two colonies in the Western Hemisphere: Puerto Rico and Cuba.

Conclusion

The Rise and Reshaping of the West

During the second period of European empire building, the West not only expanded geographically but also acquired a large share of the world's resources. By dominating the world's carrying trade, and by exploiting the agricultural and mineral resources of the Americas, Western states gained control of the world economy. The slave trade, with all its horrors, formed an important part of this economy and served as one of the main sources of Western wealth.

Western economic power laid the foundations for Western political control. In Asia European states assumed political control over territories slowly and reluctantly, as Britain's gradual and piecemeal acquisition of territory in India revealed. In the Americas, European powers acquired territory with relative ease, and European possessions in the New World soon became part of the West. By 1700, as we have seen, the geographical center of the West had become the Atlantic Ocean.

The American territories that were brought under European political control also became, at least to some extent, culturally part of the West. The European colonists who settled in the Americas preserved the languages, the religions, and many of the cultural traditions of the European countries from which they came. When some of the British and Spanish colonies in the Americas rebelled against European regimes in the late eighteenth and early nineteenth centuries, the identity of the colonists who led the resistance remained essentially Western. Even the political ideas that inspired national resistance to European regimes had their origins in Europe.

The assertion of Western political and economic power in the world cultivated a sense of Western superiority. The belief that Europeans, regardless of their nationality, were superior to those from other parts of the world originated in the encounters that took place between Europeans and both African slaves and the indigenous peoples in the

Americas. In the late eighteenth century a conviction also developed, although much more slowly, that the West was culturally superior to the civilizations of Asia. This belief in Western superiority became even more pronounced when the economies of Western nations began to experience more rapid growth than those of Asia. The main source of this new Western economic strength was the Industrial Revolution, which will be the subject of Chapter 20.

Suggestions for Further Reading

For a comprehensive listing of suggested readings, please go to www.ablongman.com/levack2e/chapter17

Bailyn, Bernard. *Ideological Origins of the American Revolution.* 1967. A probing analysis of the different intellectual traditions upon which the American colonists based their arguments for independence.

Blackburn, Robin. *The Making of New World Slavery: From the Baroque to the Modern, 1492–1800.* 1997. Places European slavery in a broad world perspective.

Boxer, C. R. *The Dutch Seaborne Empire, 1600–1800.* 1965. A thorough account covering the entire period of Dutch expansion.

Davis, Ralph. *The Rise of the Atlantic Economies.* 1973. A readable study of economic development on both sides of the Atlantic.

Eltis, David, *The Rise of African Slavery in the Americas.* 2000. An analysis of the different dimensions of the slave trade based on a database of slave ships and passengers.

Goody, Jack. *The East in the West.* 1996. Challenges the idea that Western cultures are more rational than those of Asia.

Greene, Jack P. *Peripheries and Center: Constitutional Development in the Extended Polities of the British Empire and the United States, 1607–1788.* 1986. A study of the composition of the British Empire and its disintegration in North America.

Kamen, Henry. *Empire: How Spain Became a World Power.* 2003. Explains how Spain established the most extensive empire the world had ever known.

Langley, Lester D. *The Americas in the Age of Revolution, 1750–1850.* 1996. A broad comparative study of revolutions in the United States, Haiti, and Latin America.

Liss, Peggy K. *The Atlantic Empires: The Network of Trade and Revolutions, 1713–1826.* 1983. Places the American Revolution in a broader comparative setting and includes material on early Latin American independence movements.

Mungello, D. E. *The Great Encounter of China and the West, 1500–1800.* 1999. Studies China's acceptance and rejection of Western culture as well as the parallel Western reception of China.

Pagden, Anthony. *Lords of All the World: Ideologies of Empire in Spain, Britain and France, ca. 1500–ca. 1800.* 1996. Discusses the theoretical foundations of the Atlantic Empires.

Said, Edward. *Orientalism.* 1979. A study of the way in which Western views of the East have assumed its inferiority.

Notes

1. Olaudah Equiano, *The Interesting Narrative of the Life of Olaudah Equiano, or Gustavus Vassa the African* (1789).

2. Thomas Rymer (ed.), *Foedera* (1704–1735), vol. 18, 72.

3. Quoted in Robin Blackburn, *The Making of New World Slavery* (1997), 325.

4. Samuel Johnson, *Rasselas* (1759), 47.

Eighteenth-Century Society and Culture

18

I N 1745 THOMAS BROWN AND ELEVEN OTHER MEN LIVING ON THE ESTATE OF the Earl of Uxbridge, an English nobleman, were jailed for up to one year for shooting deer and rabbits on the earl's land. All twelve defendants were poor. Brown eked out a living as a coal miner in the earl's mines and rented a cottage and five acres of land from him. Like many of his fellow villagers, Brown supplemented his family's diet by shooting game from time to time, usually as he was walking to work through the earl's vast estate. This poaching violated a set of English parliamentary statutes known as the game laws, which restricted the shooting or trapping of wild animals to the members of the landed class.

The earl and other noblemen defended the game laws on the grounds that they were necessary to protect their property. The laws, however, served the even more important purpose of maintaining social distinctions between landowners and the common people. Members of the landed class believed that only they should have the right to hunt game and to serve deer, pheasants, and hares at lavish dinners attended by their social equals. For a poor person like Thomas Brown, who was described in a court document as "a rude disorderly man and a most notorious poacher," to enjoy such delicacies was a challenge to the social order.

This mid-eighteenth-century encounter between the Earl of Uxbridge and his tenants, which took the form of a criminal prosecution, reflected the tensions that simmered beneath the calm surface of eighteenth-century European society. These tensions arose between the members of the aristocracy, a small but wealthy governing elite, and the masses of tenants and laborers who formed the overwhelming majority of the European population. The aristocracy occupied a dominant position in eighteenth-century society. They controlled an enormous portion of the wealth in their countries, much of it in land. They staffed the state bureaucracies, the legislative assemblies, the military officer corps, and the judiciaries of almost all European states. They dominated and set the tone of high cultural life in Europe. Together

First Lecture in the Salon of Madame Geoffrin, 1755 The speaker is lecturing on Voltaire's *The Orphan of China* before a predominantly aristocratic audience of men and women.

with the monarchy and the church, with which they were socially and politically linked, the aristocracy formed what today is often referred to as "the Establishment."

By 1800 the social and political dominance of the aristocracy had begun to wane. Their legitimacy as a privileged elite was increasingly called into question. In a few countries political power began to pass from them to different social groups. The aristocracy did not surrender all their power, but they lost their stranglehold over society. This change began during a period of political stability between 1750 and the outbreak of the French Revolution in 1789.

The decline of the aristocracy was the result of a series of cultural encounters. The first were the tense and occasionally violent interactions between landowners and peasants who resented the repressive features of upper-class rule. The second were criticisms of the aristocracy and the demands for reform that came from the increasingly literate, politically active people from the middle ranks of society, such as merchants, financiers, industrialists, and skilled artisans. The third was the cultural and intellectual movement known as the Enlightenment. Even though many of the Enlightenment's most prominent thinkers came from the ranks of the aristocracy, they advanced a set of political, social, economic, and legal ideas that ultimately inspired the creation of a more egalitarian society.

The aristocracy did not relinquish power willingly or quickly. Although they faced severe criticism and challenges to their dominance, they managed to preserve much of their wealth and maintain at least some of their political influence. To insulate themselves from criticisms from less powerful social groups, they adopted many of the values of the people who occupied the middle ranks of society and subscribed to many of the ideas of the Enlightenment, including those that criticized their own class. Internal encounters between different social groups, just like external encounters between Western and non-Western peoples, rarely result in total domination of one group over the other. Instead both parties change their thinking and behavior as a result of their interaction.

These encounters, especially those that took place at the time of the Enlightenment, resulted in a redefinition of the West. In Chapter 16 we saw how the Scientific Revolution completely changed the face of Western culture. In the eighteenth century the Enlightenment, which was inspired to a great extent by the ideas of the Scientific Revolution, produced a set of political and social ideals that served as the basis for a new Western identity.

This chapter will explore the ways in which these social and cultural encounters changed the political and intellectual culture of the West. In doing this the individual sections of the chapter will address the following questions:

■ **What social groups belonged to the aristocracy and how did they exercise their power and influence during the eighteenth century?**

■ **How did subordinate social groups, most notably the rural peasantry and those who lived in the towns, challenge the aristocracy during the late eighteenth century?**

■ **What were the main features of Enlightenment thought and how did it present a threat to the old order?**

■ **What impact did the Enlightenment have on Western culture and politics?**

The Aristocracy

■ **What social groups belonged to the aristocracy and how did they exercise their power and influence during the eighteenth century?**

During the eighteenth century a relatively small, wealthy group of men dominated European society and politics. This social and ruling elite is often referred to as the aristocracy°, a term derived from a Greek word meaning the people who were the most fit to rule. In the eighteenth and nineteenth centuries the term *aristocracy* began to be applied not just to those few men who exercised political power but to the wealthiest members of society, especially those who owned land.

Within the aristocracy those who received official recognition of their hereditary status, including their titles of honor and special legal privileges, were known as the nobility°. In the Middle Ages the nobility consisted mainly of warriors who prided themselves on their courage and military skill. Over the course of many centuries these military functions became less important, although many noblemen, especially in central and eastern Europe, continued to serve as military officers in the armies of the state during the eighteenth century.

The aristocracy for the most part lived on their estates in the countryside, but they also spent time in the cities and towns, where many of them maintained townhouses or even large palaces. In cities that were centers of national government, such as Madrid and Berlin, aristocrats were prominent members of the royal court. As royal judges, some members of the aristocracy also took an active part in the administration of the law in the cities, just as they did in the provinces. The aristocracy, therefore, maintained a visible and powerful presence in urban society.

By the eighteenth century most European aristocracies included a relatively small group of titled noblemen (such as dukes and counts) who possessed great wealth and political influence and a much larger group of lesser aristocrats, occasionally referred to as gentry, who sometimes did not even bear hereditary titles. In Spain a vast gulf separated a few hundred titled noblemen, the *titulos,* and thousands of sometimes poverty-stricken *hidalgos.* In Britain a few hun-

DOCUMENT

Merchants Become Members of the Aristocracy in England

Daniel Defoe is most famous for his novels, such as Robinson Crusoe *(1719) and* Moll Flanders *(1722), but he also wrote commentaries on contemporary English politics and society. In* The English Tradesman *(1726), which is excerpted here, Defoe argued that the wealth of England "lies mainly among the trading part of the people." To support his argument he presented evidence that many members of the English aristocracy came from trading backgrounds. England was unusual in the opportunities it offered for this type of upward social mobility, but Defoe nonetheless overstated his case. Even the English aristocracy of the eighteenth century was not open to such frequent entry from below.*

This being the case in England, and our trade being so vastly great, it is no wonder that the tradesmen in England fill the lists of our nobility and gentry; no wonder that the gentlemen of the best families marry tradesmen's daughters, and put their younger sons' apprentices to tradesmen; and how often do these younger sons come to buy the elder sons' estates, and restore the family, when the elder and head of the house, proving rakish and extravagant, has wasted his patrimony, and is obliged to make out the blessing of Israel's family, where the younger son brought the birthright, and the elder was doomed to serve him?

Trade is so far here from being inconsistent with a gentleman, that in short trade in England makes gentlemen, and has peopled this nation with gentlemen; for after a generation or two the tradesmen's children, or at least their grand-children, come to be as good gentlemen, statesmen, parliament-men, privy counselors, judges, bishops and noblemen, as those of the highest birth and the most ancient families; and nothing too high for them. Thus the earl of Haversham was originally a merchant; the late Secretary Craggs was the son of a barber; the present Lord Castlemaine's father was a tradesman, the great grandfather of the present Duke of Bedford the same, and so of several others. . . .

We see the tradesmen of England, as they grow wealthy, coming every day to the herald's office, to search for the coats of arms of their ancestors, in order to paint them upon their coaches, and engrave them upon their furniture, or carve them upon the pediments of their new houses; and how often do we see them trace the registers of their families up to the prime nobility, or the most ancient gentry of the kingdom?

Source: From Daniel Defoe, The Complete English Tradesman, *Volume I, 1726.*

dred titled noblemen, known as peers, took precedence over some 50,000 families that belonged to the gentry. In Poland the nobility, known as the *szlachta*, was divided between a tiny, powerful group of magnates and some 700,000 noblemen of much more modest means who constituted more than 10 percent of the entire population.

The aristocracy was not completely closed to outsiders. Commoners could gain entrance to it, especially its lower ranks, on the basis of acquired wealth or government service. It was not unusual for lawyers, wealthy merchants, or accomplished state servants to accumulate wealth during their careers, use that wealth to purchase land, and then receive a recognition of their new status in the form of a title of nobility. Many of the men to whom Peter the Great of Russia gave titles of nobility in the early eighteenth century were commoners. In France, where the old "nobility of the sword" could be distinguished from the "nobility of the robe" that ascended through state service, more than 20 percent of mid-eighteenth-century noblemen could not trace their noble status back further than two generations.

It was also possible for prosperous farmers to enter the aristocracy by purchasing land, hiring manual laborers to perform agricultural work, and then adopting the leisured lifestyle, dress, and manners of aristocrats. These men did not bear titles, but they expected to be regarded as having the same status as other members of the lesser aristocracy. Occasionally women of nonnoble birth gained entry into aristocratic society by marriage. This usually occurred when a nobleman who was greatly in debt arranged to marry his son to the daughter of a wealthy merchant in order to secure the dowry from the father of the bride. The dowry became the price of the daughter's admission to the nobility.

In the sixteenth and seventeenth centuries the size of the aristocracy had grown faster than the general population, as a result of both economic prosperity and the expansion of the state bureaucracy. In eastern Europe monarchs had increased the number of hereditary noblemen in order to gain their services for the state. In the eighteenth century the size of the aristocracy stabilized and in many countries declined, as nobles took steps to restrict the number of newcomers from the lower orders. It was never a very large social group. The number of titled nobles was almost always less than 1 percent of the total population, and even when lesser nobles or gentry are taken into account, their total numbers usually amounted to no more than 4 percent. Only in Poland and Hungary did the percentages climb to more than 10 percent. Because of the small size of this social group, many nobles knew each other, especially those who were members of the same political assembly or who served together at court. The aristocracy was in fact the only real class° in European society before the early nineteenth century, in the sense that they formed a cohesive social group with similar economic and political interests, which they were determined to protect.

The Wealth of the Aristocracy

The aristocracy was without question the wealthiest social group in all European countries, and during the eighteenth century many members of this group became even wealthier. The most prosperous aristocratic families lived in stupendous luxury. They built magnificent homes on their country estates and surrounded them with finely manicured gardens. In the cities, where service at court demanded more of their time, they built spacious palaces, entertained guests on a lavish scale, and purchased everything from expensive clothes to artistic treasures. They consumed the best food and wines they could find at home or abroad. This ostentatious display of wealth was intended to confirm their social importance and status.

Most of the income that supported the lifestyle of the aristocracy came directly or indirectly from land. In all European countries the aristocracy owned at least one-third of all the land, and in some countries, such as England and Denmark, they owned more than four-fifths of it. Even in the Italian states, where many of the nobility had come from families of merchants, they controlled large estates. Land provided the aristocracy with either feudal dues or rents from the peasants who lived and worked on their estates. Because noblemen did not engage in manual labor themselves, it is not surprising that they later came to be seen as unproductive parasites living off the labor of others.

During the first half of the eighteenth century the collective wealth of the European aristocracy reached new heights. In eastern Europe that increase in wealth derived mainly from the dramatic increase in the size of the population. With more serfs under their control, the landed nobility could increase the wealth they gained from their labor and dues. In western European countries, most notably Britain and France, the members of the aristocracy increasingly participated in other forms of economic activity. They operated rural industries such as mining and forestry. They entered the financial world by lending money to the government, thus serving the state in the process. They became involved in urban building projects and in the economic development of overseas colonies. Those who came from old families considered these pursuits to be beneath the status of a nobleman, but by investing at a distance nobles could give the impression that they were not actually engaged in the sordid transactions of the marketplace.

Size of the Aristocracy in European States in the Eighteenth Century

Country	Date	Number of Nobles and Lesser Aristocrats	Percent of the Population
Austria	1800	90,000	1.15%
France	1775	400,000	1.60
Great Britain & Ireland	1783	50,000	3.25
Hungary	1800	400,000	11.25
Poland	1800	700,000	11.66
Russia	1800	600,000	1.66
Spain	1797	402,000	3.80
Sweden	1757	10,000	0.50
Venice	1797	1,090	0.80

Sources: A. Corvisier, *Armies and Society in Europe, 1494–1789* (1976), pp. 113, 115; J. Meyer, *Noblesses et pouvoirs dans l'Europe d'Ancien Régime* (1973); M. Reinard and A. Armenguard, *Histoire Générale de la Population Modiale* (1961); J. Dewald, *The European Nobility* (1996), pp. 22–27.

The members of the eighteenth-century aristocracy are often described as social and economic conservatives who were unable or unwilling to act in an entrepreneurial manner. The financial and commercial projects that many noblemen engaged in suggest that this reputation of the aristocracy is not fully deserved. Even on their landed estates, the aristocracy often behaved in a capitalistic manner during the seventeenth and eighteenth centuries. Many members of the aristocracy, both titled and untitled, adopted capitalist techniques of estate management to make their lands more productive. In England a nobleman, Charles Townshend, became widely known as "Turnip Townshend" when he introduced a crop rotation that included the lowly turnip. This type of agrarian entrepreneurship accounts for the accumulation of many great eighteenth-century aristocratic fortunes.

The Political Power of the Aristocracy

The mid-eighteenth century also marked the apex of political power for the aristocracy in Europe. Having recovered from the economic and political turmoil of the mid-seventeenth century, when they suffered economic losses and experienced a temporary eclipse of their power, noblemen pursued various strategies to increase or preserve their share of local and national political power. In

Marriage into the Nobility

This painting by William Hogarth, in a series titled *Marriage à la Mode,* depicts the negotiation of a marriage contract between an English earl and a wealthy London merchant. The earl, seated to the left and pointing to his family tree, is negotiating with the merchant sitting across the table. The marriage will take place between the earl's vain son, sitting to the far right, and the distracted daughter of the merchant, sitting next to him. The two individuals who are about to be married have no interest in each other. The earl has incurred large debts from building the large mansion depicted in the rear, and he intends to use the dowry to recover financially. By virtue of this transaction the daughter will enter aristocratic society.

England, where royal power was greatly restricted as a result of the Glorious Revolution, the aristocracy gained political dominance. A small group of noblemen sat in the House of Lords, while the gentry formed the large majority of members of the House of Commons. After 1689 the English king could not rule without the cooperation of these two Houses of Parliament. The monarchy tried to control the proceedings of that assembly by creating parties of royal supporters within both houses. Because those parties were controlled by the king's ministers, who were themselves members of the nobility, the system allowed the aristocracy to dominate.

A similar situation prevailed in Poland and Hungary, where only the nobility were represented in the legislative assemblies of those countries. In Sweden and most German states the nobility formed a separate group that voted by themselves within the representative assemblies of those kingdoms. The country in Europe where members of the aristocracy exercised the least power and influence was the Dutch Republic. The traditional Dutch landed nobility remained a force to be reckoned with in eighteenth-century politics, but wealthy merchants and bankers held the balance of power in the seven Dutch provinces.

In absolute monarchies, where rulers had succeeded in restricting independent aristocratic power, members of the aristocracy exercised political power by controlling the institutions through which royal power was exercised. As we have seen in Chapter 15, absolute monarchs appeased the aristocracy by giving them control over provincial government and by recruiting them to occupy offices in the central bureaucracy of the state. The large bureaucracy of the eighteenth-century French state, for example, was run mainly by noblemen of the robe, a privileged group of approximately 2,000 officials who owed their noble status to their appointment to office rather than to heredity. In Russia during the early eighteenth century, tsars granted the nobility privileges and strengthened their powers over their serfs in order to secure the assistance the tsars needed to administer the Russian state at the local level.

The aristocracy also exercised political power through the judiciary. Members of the aristocracy often served as judges of the law courts of their kingdoms. In England noblemen and gentry served as the judges of almost all the common law courts, hearing cases both at the center of government at Westminster and in the provinces. In France noblemen staffed the nine regional *parlements* that registered royal edicts and acted as a court of appeal in criminal cases. The nobility controlled the central tribunals of the German kingdoms and principalities. At the local level the nobility exercised either a personal jurisdiction over the peasants who lived on their lands or an official jurisdiction as magistrates, such as the justices of the peace in each English county.

Britain provides a vivid example of the way in which the members of the landed class could use their judicial power to keep the lower classes in line: punishing petty crimes with harsh penalties. During the eighteenth century the incidence of crimes against property increased, especially when war created shortages of basic commodities. Those who occupied the middle ranks of society were the most frequent victims of these crimes, but as men of great wealth the aristocracy believed that all crimes against property threatened them as well. The aristocracy responded to this threat by passing legislation making even minor crimes against property, such as petty theft, capital offenses punishable by death. One victim of this harsh policy was John Burton, a lowly paid wagon driver who was hanged in 1744 for stealing two woolen caps.

Not all those convicted of such petty crimes suffered the same punishment as Burton. A few public executions every year were deemed sufficient to deter crime in a country that did not have a police force. Most convicted criminals were pardoned or had their sentences reduced. These displays of judicial mercy also served the purposes of the aristocracy by making people from the lower ranks of society dependent upon them for their lives. Exercising the power of pardon also strengthened their authority and made them appear sympathetic to the poor. In this way the British aristocracy helped to maintain the traditional deference paid to them from the lower ranks of society.

The Cultural World of the Aristocracy

During the eighteenth century the aristocracies in western European countries followed a lifestyle that emphasized their learning, refinement, and appreciation of the fine arts. It had not always been that way. As late as the fifteenth century the aristocracy, which in the Middle Ages had been a warrior class, had a reputation for their indifference or even hostility to learning, and their conduct was often uncouth if not boorish. In eastern Europe a tradition of aristocratic illiteracy persisted into the eighteenth century. In western and central Europe, however, the pattern began to change in the sixteenth century, when members of the aristocracy started providing for the education of their children either at universities or in private academies. Even more important, aristocratic families began to acquire the manners and social graces that would be acceptable at court. By the eighteenth century the aristocracy, especially its upper ranks, became the backbone of what was then called "polite society."

The aristocracy also developed a sophisticated appreciation of high culture. Their homes housed large private collections of artwork that occasionally rivaled or even surpassed those of contemporary European monarchs. They were the main participants in the cultural life of European cities, especially Paris, London, Rome, Vienna, and Berlin. They formed the audiences of musical recitals, attended plays and operas in large numbers, and frequented the art galleries that were established in all the capitals of Europe. They also became the patrons of musicians, writers, and artists.

The homes of the eighteenth-century aristocracy reflected their preference for classicism°, a style in art, architecture, music, and literature that emphasizes proportion, adherence to traditional forms, and a rejection of emotion and enthusiasm. The classicism of the eighteenth century marked a step away from the more dynamic, imposing baroque style, which had flourished in the seventeenth century. Classicism celebrated the culture of ancient Greece and Rome. The revival of that culture in the eighteenth century in art and architecture is often referred to as neoclassicism°. The residences of the eighteenth-century aristocracy built in the classical style were perfectly proportioned and elegant without being overly decorated. Their Greek columns and formal gardens, lined with statues of classical figures, served as symbols of their cultural heritage. The classical architecture of the eighteenth century reflected the quiet confidence of the aristocracy that they, like their Greek and Roman forebears, occupied a dominant position in society.

Eighteenth-century music, which is likewise referred to as classical, reflected a concern for formal design, proportion, and concise melodic expression. The two greatest composers of the eighteenth century, Franz Joseph Haydn (1732–1809) and Wolfgang Amadeus Mozart (1756–1791), whose music was played before predominantly aristocratic audiences, became the most famous composers in this tradition. Classical music appealed less to the emotions than either the baroque music of the seventeenth century or the romantic music of the nineteenth century. The dominance of classicism in music as well as architecture during the eighteenth century reflected broader cultural currents in

Chiswick House

This house was built by Lord Burlington as a library and reception hall on his estate near London about 1725. Symmetrical, balanced, and restrained, the building embodies many of the features of classicism. Chiswick House was modeled on the architecture of the Italian Andrea Palladio (1518–1580), who in turn drew his inspiration from the buildings of ancient Rome.

European intellectual life, when science and philosophy placed the highest value on the rationality and order of all material and human life.

Challenges to Aristocratic Dominance

■ How did subordinate social groups, most notably the rural peasantry and those who lived in the towns, challenge the aristocracy during the late eighteenth century?

Starting around the middle of the eighteenth century, the aristocracy endured increasingly acrimonious challenges to their power and criticisms of their values and lifestyles. They gradually lost the respect that they commanded from the lower ranks of society. By the end of the century European aristocracies had been significantly weakened. Their values had been called into question, while their political power and privileges had been eroded. A claim of nobility began to be viewed more as a sign of vanity than as a natural right to rule. The revolution that took place in France in the last decade of the eighteenth century, followed by the reform movements that developed in its wake throughout Europe in the early nineteenth century, brought the age of aristocracy to an end. Members of the aristocracy managed to regain some of what they had lost in the French Revolution, and they also showed their resourcefulness by accommodating themselves to the new order, but they never recovered the dominant position they had held in the eighteenth century.

Encounters with the Rural Peasantry

One set of challenges to the aristocracy came from the peasants and serfs who lived and worked on landed estates. This was the social group over whom the aristocracy exercised the most direct control. The control was most oppressive in central and eastern Europe, where the rural masses were serfs and therefore had no personal freedom. Landlords not only determined where serfs lived and when they married, but they also collected burdensome financial duties from them. Their plight was relieved only partially by the elimination of some of the burdens of serfdom. In Prussia and Austria these obligations were abolished by royal edict. The monarchs who instituted these reforms may have been responding to the demands of philosophes°, the intellectuals and writers of the age, who condemned the institution of serfdom for its cruelty and inefficiency. (See the section on the Enlightenment later in this chapter.) A more powerful motive, however, was the desire of monarchs to collect taxes from a peasantry that was spending the greater part of its income on financial duties owed to aristocratic landowners. Because the peasants still remained overburdened by financial obligations, emancipation did little to improve their lot.

In western Europe, where serfdom had for the most part given way to tenant ownership and leasehold tenure, the condition of the rural masses was only marginally better. After 1720, famines became less common than they had been in the late seventeenth century, making it possible for peasants to eke out an existence, but other economic pressures, including the elimination of common pasture rights and an increase in taxation, continued to weigh down on them. Over the course of the eighteenth century the number of peasants owning small plots of land declined. Many of those who leased land were forced to sell it as landowners consolidated their holdings. Consequently the number of landless laborers who worked for wages increased. By 1789 almost half the peasants in France had no land at all.

Under these circumstances the relationship between peasants and landowners continued to deteriorate. The realities of the marketplace gradually eroded the paternalistic concern that the nobility had traditionally shown for the welfare of their serfs or tenants. As the relationship between landlord and peasant became predominantly economic, the two parties became more distant. At the same time the gap between the culture of the elite and that of the common people, which as we have seen in Chapter 16 began in the seventeenth century, became more pronounced. The distance between landlord and peasant assumed real geographical form as landlords built their mansions away from the local village. By surrounding their homes with acres of parkland and gardens, they shielded themselves from the sight of the peasants working in the fields. Visual and personal contact between lord and peasant therefore became less frequent. The most direct contact a landlord made with the members of the lower classes was with the servants who worked in their homes.

As economic pressures on the peasants mounted, conflict between them and the aristocracy increased. Peasant resistance to their landlords could take a number of different forms. In some countries, most notably France, peasants could bring their grievances before village assemblies. These democratic institutions often succeeded in upholding peasants' demands, especially when royal officials in the provinces, who wished to collect their own taxes from the peasants, sided with them against the nobility.

Another option was to file a lawsuit against the lord, often with the assistance of the royal government. In Burgundy numerous peasant communities hired lawyers to take their seigneurs° or lords to court in order to prevent the imposition of new financial dues or the confiscation of communal village land. They were often aided in these efforts by the agents of the royal government, who wanted the peasants to be able to pay higher taxes imposed by the king. In these lawsuits, which became very common in the second half of the eighteenth century, peasants challenged not only the imposition of seigneurial dues but the very institution of aristocratic lordship. In 1765 one lawyer representing a peasant community in Champagne argued that the

rights claimed by landowners "derive from the violence of seigneurs" and had always been "odious." The language used in these cases inspired much of the rhetoric employed in the abolition of feudal privilege at the time of the French Revolution (see Chapter 19).

Peasants occasionally took more direct action against their landlords. In eastern France the number of incidents of rural violence against the property of seigneurs who tried to collect new duties increased toward the end of the eighteenth century. In Ireland a group known as the Whiteboys maimed cattle and tore down fences when landowners denied tenants their common grazing rights. Other forms of peasant action included poaching on the lands of landowners who claimed the exclusive right to hunt or trap game on their estates. The hunting activities of the tenants of the Earl of Uxbridge discussed at the beginning of this chapter are just one example of this type of lower-class resistance to aristocratic privilege.

In western Europe these acts of resistance did not develop into widespread peasant rebellion until the outbreak of the French Revolution in 1789. During the late eighteenth century incidents of rural violence were largely confined to individual villages. The reduction in the incidence of famine in the eighteenth century provides one possible explanation for this pattern of isolated, localized resistance. Without recurrent subsistence crises, the plight of the rural masses was not sufficiently desperate to provoke large-scale rebellion. The only expressions of collective unrest over the supply of food in western Europe during the eighteenth century were urban riots. These food riots usually took place in market towns or ports where grain was being exported. The violence was not directed against landlords but merchants or officials who were suspected of hoarding grain or fixing the price of bread.

The economic and social situation in eastern Europe differed from that of France, Britain, and other western European countries. In the east the deteriorating economic condition of the peasantry led to large-scale rebellion. Bohemia, Hungary, and Croatia, all of which lay within the boundaries of the Austrian Habsburg monarchy, witnessed large peasant revolts in the 1780s. The bloodiest of these revolts occurred in the province of Transylvania in 1784, when 30,000 peasant rebels butchered hundreds of noblemen and their families after those landowners had raised the dues owed to them as much as 1,000 percent.

The largest eastern European rural rebellion took place in Russia between 1773 and 1774. Pretending to be the murdered Tsar Peter III (d. 1762), the Cossack Emelian Pugachev (1726–1775) set out to destroy the Russian government of Catherine the Great and the nobility that served it. Pugachev assembled an army of 8,000 men, which staged lightning raids against government centers in the southern Urals. The most serious phase of this uprising took place when these troops marched into the agricultural regions of the country and inspired as many as three million serfs to revolt. Pugachev promised to abolish serfdom, end taxation, and eliminate the lesser aristocracy. The rebellion took a heavy toll, as the serfs and soldiers murdered some 3,000 nobles and officials. The Russian upper class feared that the rebellion would spread and destroy the entire social order, but government troops prevented that from happening by brutally suppressing the rising. Pugachev was transported to Moscow in an iron cage, where he was hanged, quartered, and burned.

Neither Pugachev nor the serfs who joined his rebellion envisioned the creation of a new social order. They still spoke in conservative terms of regaining ancient freedoms that had been lost. But this massive revolt, like others that resembled it, reflected the depth of the tension that prevailed between landlord and peasant, between nobleman and serf, in the apparently stable world of the eighteenth century. That tension serves as one of the most striking and ominous themes of eighteenth-century social history.

The Social Position of the Bourgeoisie

In the cities and towns the most serious challenges to the aristocracy came not from the urban masses, who posed an occasional threat to all urban authorities, but from the bourgeoisie°. This social group was more heterogeneous than the aristocracy. It consisted of untitled people of property who lived in the cities and towns. The word *bourgeoisie* refers to those who were burghers—or those who had voting rights in the towns. Prosperous merchants and financiers formed the upper ranks of the bourgeoisie, while members of the legal and medical professions, second-tier government officials, and emerging industrialists occupied a social niche just below them. The bourgeoisie also included some skilled artisans and shopkeepers, sometimes referred to as the "petty bourgeoisie," who were far more prosperous than the large mass of urban laborers. The size of the bourgeoisie grew as the urban population of Europe expanded during the eighteenth century, even before the advent of industrialization. This social group was far more numerous in the North Atlantic countries of France, the Dutch Republic, and Britain than in the states of central and eastern Europe. In England the bourgeoisie accounted for about 15 percent of the total population in 1800, whereas in Russia they constituted no more than 3 percent.

Because it was possible for some members of the bourgeoisie to achieve upward social mobility and join the ranks of the aristocracy, the social and economic boundaries separating these wealthy townsmen from the lower ranks of the nobility could become blurred. In French towns it was often difficult to distinguish between wealthy financiers and noble bureaucrats. Although the two groups received their income from different sources, they both belonged to a wealthy, propertied elite. The middle and lower ranks of the

Joshua Reynolds, *Mary, Duchess of Richmond* (ca. 1765)
At a time when most European noblewomen were attracting criticism for their luxury and vanity, this prominent English duchess was depicted as being engaged in the simple domestic task of needlepoint. Some members of the aristocracy were able to deflect criticism of their lifestyle by adopting the habits of the bourgeoisie.

bourgeoisie, however, gradually emerged as a social group that acquired its own social, political, and cultural identity distinct from that of the aristocracy.

Bourgeois identity was rooted in the towns, which had their own political institutions and their own social hierarchies. The bourgeoisie also possessed the means of effectively communicating with each other and thus were capable of forming common political goals. Their high rates of literacy made them the core of the new political force of public opinion that emerged in the cities and towns in the eighteenth century. The bourgeoisie made up the main audience of the thousands of newspapers, pamphlets, and books that rolled off the presses during the eighteenth century. A "public sphere" of activity, in which politically conscious townsmen participated, became a peculiar feature of bourgeois society. During the eighteenth and early nineteenth centuries the bourgeoisie became the leaders of movements seeking political change. They organized and became the main participants in the protest movements,

Bathing in the West

One of the personal habits that members of the European aristocracy and bourgeoisie began to adopt in the eighteenth century was frequent bathing. Until that time people in the West had been reluctant to immerse their bodies in water. In this respect there was a clear difference between Western and Eastern practice. Among Asians who practiced the Hindu religion, bathing had deep religious significance and was a daily ritual. The same was true for Muslims, for whom water possessed a sacred purifying role and prepared the bather for prayer or sacrifice. In the West bathing was not invested with similar religious significance. Christianity had emphasized purity of heart, not of the body. Without a religious inspiration, bathing the body rarely occurred in Western nations during the early modern period. Europeans might wash various parts of their body, especially the hands and face, but total immersion was almost unheard of. The few who did bathe usually did so no more than once a year, and tubs and basins were not widely available. Swimming in rivers and lakes was dangerous and often resulted in drowning. Even medical opinion conspired against bathing. According to one seventeenth-century French doctor, "bathing outside the practice of medicine was not only superfluous but very damaging to health."

By the beginning of the nineteenth century, many Europeans had begun to take regular baths. The sale of washbasins and commercially produced soap soared. This change occurred as a result of three distinct factors. The first was the insistence by many eighteenth-century Protestants that Christianity did indeed demand a clean body as well as a clean soul. The eighteenth-century founder of Methodism, the English preacher

John Wesley, coined a new proverb when he declared that "cleanliness is indeed next to godliness."

A second reason was that cleanliness became associated with gentility and good manners. Bodily cleanliness became one of the ways in which members of society who considered themselves civilized made themselves attractive to the people with whom they associated. This explains why bathing the body all over was first adopted by the upper classes, who contrasted themselves with the dirty lower classes. It also became more common among women than men. The third reason was a change in medical opinion, which began to view bathing as a means to keep the pores of the skin open and thus promote perspiration. Bathing came to be viewed as a means of curing numerous diseases and as a key to long life.

The acceptance of bathing in the West owed something to Eastern influence. Eighteenth-century Western writers often commented on the daily bathing of Turks and Hindus, and Europeans who lived in the East had the opportunity to witness firsthand a custom that contrasted strikingly with their own. The period of most pro-

nounced influence was the mid-eighteenth century, when many other features of Eastern culture penetrated the West. In the early nineteenth century a Hindu noted that bathing in the West was still very different from that practiced in his own country. Nevertheless, the reluctant European adoption of immersing the body in water had brought about a minor accommodation between Eastern and Western practice.

For Discussion

What does the widespread practice of bathing in Asia and the reluctance of Europeans to adopt this practice tell us about the differences between Eastern and Western cultures in the eighteenth century?

Jean-Jacques Henner, *Chaste Susanna at Her Bath* (1865)
By the nineteenth century, Europeans had adopted the practice of bathing the entire body.

petitioning drives, and ultimately the revolutionary steps taken to challenge and replace established regimes.

The Bourgeois Critique of the Aristocracy

At the core of bourgeois identity lay a set of values that contrasted with those attributed to the aristocracy, especially the noblemen and noblewomen who gathered at court. Not all members of the bourgeoisie shared these values, nor did all members of the nobility embody those attributed to them. Nonetheless, the bourgeois critique of aristocratic society, which flourished mainly among the lower or petty bourgeoisie rather than the great merchants and financiers, contributed to the formation of bourgeois identity and helped to erode respect for the traditional aristocracy.

The bourgeois critique of the aristocracy consisted of three related themes. First was the allegation that the aristocracy lived a life of luxury, hedonism, and idleness that contrasted with the thrifty, sober, hardworking petty bourgeoisie. Unlike the aristocracy, the bourgeoisie did not display their wealth. Second, court nobles were accused of being sexually promiscuous and immoral, while their wives were depicted as vain flirts. There was some foundation to this charge, especially because the predominance of arranged marriages within the nobility had induced many noble husbands and wives to seek sexual partners outside marriage, a practice that was widely tolerated within aristocratic circles. By contrast, the bourgeoisie tended to enter into marriages in which both partners remained faithful to each other. Third, the members of the aristocracy were considered participants in a decadent international culture that often ignored or degraded the more wholesome, patriotic values of the bourgeoisie.

This critique of the aristocracy had profound political implications. It laid the foundation for the demands for equal political rights and the advancement of careers on the basis of talent rather than inherited wealth. These demands came not from the wealthy financiers, merchants, and capitalists who had the opportunity to ascend into the ranks of the nobility but from men of more modest wealth: holders of minor political offices, shopkeepers, and even skilled artisans. These people from the middle ranks of society, especially those who lived in the cities and towns, were most responsible for eventually reducing the influence of the aristocracy in European political and social life.

Criticism of aristocratic values and demands for liberty and equality received support from intellectuals who are usually identified with the movement known as the Enlightenment°. Not all of these thinkers and writers came from the middle ranks of society. Many of them were in fact members of the aristocracy or the beneficiaries of aristocratic patronage. Nevertheless their goal was to bring about the reform of society, and that inevitably led to a critique of aristocratic values and practices.

The Enlightenment

■ **What were the main features of Enlightenment thought and how did it present a threat to the old order?**

The Enlightenment was the defining intellectual and cultural movement of the eighteenth century. This complex movement had roots in the seventeenth century; the Scientific Revolution and the growth of philosophical skepticism were particularly important influences (see Chapter 16). Contemporaries used the word *Enlightenment* to describe their own intellectual outlook and achievements. For Immanuel Kant (1724–1804), the renowned German philosopher and author of *Critique of Pure Reason* (1781), enlightenment was the expression of intellectual maturity, the attainment of understanding solely by using one's reason without being influenced by dogma, superstition, or another person's opinion. For Kant enlightenment was both the process of thinking for oneself and the knowledge of human society and human nature that one achieved as a result. His famous exhortation, "Have the courage to know!" could serve as a slogan for the entire Enlightenment.

The Enlightenment is often referred to as a French movement, and it is true that the most famous of the European writers and thinkers of the Enlightenment, known as philosophes, were French. It was also in France that the Enlightenment first became a campaign to change people's minds and reform institutions. But French philosophes were inspired by seventeenth-century English sources, especially the writings of Isaac Newton (1647–1727) and John Locke (1632–1704), while German, Scottish, Dutch, Swiss, and Italian writers made their own distinctive contributions to Enlightenment thought. The ideas of the Enlightenment also spread to the Americas, where they inspired movements for political reform and national independence. The men and women of the Enlightenment thought of themselves not so much as French, British, or Dutch but as members of an international Republic of Letters, not unlike the international community of scholars that had arisen within the ancient Roman Empire and again at the time of the Renaissance. This cosmopolitan literary republic knew no geographical boundaries, and it was open to ideas from all lands (see Map 18.1). Its literary achievements, however, bore a distinctly Western stamp, and the ideas its members promoted became essential components of Western civilization.

Themes of Enlightenment Thought

Because the Enlightenment spanned the entire continent and lasted for more than a century, it is difficult to establish characteristics that all its participants shared. The Enlightenment was more a frame of mind, an approach to

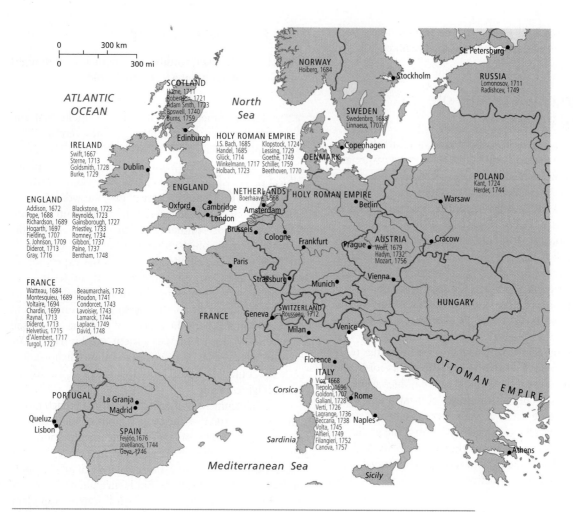

Map 18.1 The European Enlightenment

The map shows the birthplaces of thinkers and writers of the Enlightenment. The greatest number of them came from France and Britain, but all European countries were represented, and the men and women of the Enlightenment thought of themselves as belonging to an international "Republic of Letters" that knew no political boundaries.

obtaining knowledge, as Kant claimed, than a set of clearly defined beliefs. Enlightenment writers, however, emphasized several intellectual themes that gave the entire movement a certain degree of unity and coherence.

Reason and the Laws of Nature

The first theme emphasized by Enlightenment thinkers was the elevation of human reason to a position of paramount philosophical importance. Enlightenment thinkers placed almost unlimited confidence in the ability of human beings to understand how the world operates. In previous ages philosophers had always found a place for human reason, but they also placed limits on it, especially when it came into conflict with religious faith. Medieval scholastic philosophers had tried to reconcile faith and reason, and that effort continued through the seventeenth century, par-

ticularly in scientific circles. In the eighteenth century, however, greater emphasis was placed on reason alone, which was believed to be superior to religious faith and the final arbiter of all disputes.

Confidence in human reason was closely associated with the belief that the operation of the entire universe was governed by natural laws that human reason could discover. This belief in natural law can be traced back to the ancient Greeks and to its revival and assimilation to Christian theology by the scholastics in the Middle Ages. Natural law acquired a distinctive character at the time of the Scientific Revolution. The search for and discovery of the laws governing such phenomena as gravitation, the circulation of the blood, and dynamics gradually led to the belief that all activity, including the behavior of human beings, was governed by similar laws.

The application of natural law to human society was the most novel and distinctive feature of Enlightenment thought. According to Enlightenment thinkers, scientific laws governed the functioning of society. There were even laws governing the passions and the operation of the human psyche. In his *Treatise of Human Nature* (1739–1740), the Scottish philosopher David Hume (1711–1776) offered a science of the human mind, which could be applied to politics and other human endeavors. Economics, too, received the same treatment. The Scottish economist Adam Smith (1723–1790), who described the operation of economic life in *The Wealth of Nations* (1776), believed that the economy was subject to inviolable laws, just like those that governed the movement of the heavens. The Enlightenment therefore gave birth to modern social science. Economics, political science, sociology, anthropology, and psychology all trace their origins as intellectual disciplines to this time. They were all based on the premise that reason could discover the laws or principles of human nature.

The search for natural laws governing all human life provides one explanation for the unprecedented interest of eighteenth-century writers in non-European cultures. During the Enlightenment a vast literature subjected the

DOCUMENT

Adam Smith, Introduction to *The Wealth of Nations* (1776)

peoples of the world to detailed description, classification, and analysis. The first thorough, scholarly studies of Indian, Chinese, and Arab cultures were published during the middle and late eighteenth century. Egypt, a country that had been a part of the Ottoman Empire and isolated from the West since the sixteenth century, became the subject of a sizable literature, especially after the French occupied the country in 1798. There also was an increase in travel literature describing the societies that Europeans were encountering, some of them for the first time. Descriptions of the indigenous peoples of northwestern Canada, Australia, and Tahiti became readily available in the bookshops of Paris and London.

This cross-cultural scholarship, which was facilitated by the rapid growth of overseas empires after 1660, served the purpose of providing intellectuals with information enabling them to discover laws governing the behavior of all people. Some of the non-European countries that these scholars studied, such as China, had highly developed civilizations, whereas those of Native Americans and the indigenous people of the South Sea islands were far less developed. In both cases, however, educated people in the West began to consider these non-Western societies valid subjects of intellectual inquiry.

Religion and Morality

The spread of scientific knowledge in the eighteenth century gave the thinkers of the Enlightenment a new understanding of God and his relationship to humankind. The Christian God of the Middle Ages and the Reformation period was an all-knowing, personal God who often intervened in the life of human beings. He could be stern and severe or gentle and merciful, but he was always involved in the affairs of humankind, which he governed through Providence. The gradual recognition that the universe was of unfathomable size and that it operated in accordance with natural laws made God appear more remote. Most philosophes believed that God was still the creator of the universe and the author of the natural laws that governed it, but they did not believe that he was still actively involved in its operation. God was the playwright of the universe, but not its director. This belief that God had created the universe, given it laws, and then allowed it to operate in a mechanistic fashion is known as deism°. In deism there was no place for the traditional Christian belief that God became human in order to redeem humankind from original sin.

Enlightenment thinkers, especially those who were deists, believed that human beings could use reason to discover the natural laws God had laid down at the time of creation. This inquiry included the discovery of the principles of morality, which no longer were to be grounded in Scripture. To observe the laws of God now meant not so much keeping his commandments but discovering what was natural and acting accordingly. In a certain sense God

David Hume, Scottish Philosopher

Like John Locke, Hume explored the process by which the human mind reaches an understanding of the material world. Hume was committed to the application of science to the human psyche.

was being remade in a human image and was being identified with the natural instincts of human beings. In this way religion could become equated with the pursuit of human happiness.

If one believed that God established natural laws for all humanity, then doctrinal differences between religions became less important. All religions were valid to the extent that they led to an understanding of natural law. There was no one true religion, a point that the German dramatist and philosopher Gotthold Lessing (1729–1781) made in his play *Nathan the Wise* (1779) in response to the persistent questioning of a fictional Turkish sultan. This denial of the existence of one true religion led naturally to a demand for toleration of all religions, including those of non-Western peoples.

Enlightenment thinkers were highly critical of the superstitious and dogmatic character of contemporary Christianity, especially Roman Catholicism. French philosophes in particular had little use for priests, whom they castigated relentlessly in their letters and pamphlets. They minimized the importance of religious belief in the con-

duct of human life and substituted rational for religious values. They had little respect for the academic discipline of theology. The German-born Parisian writer Baron d'Holbach (1723–1789), one of the few philosophes who could be considered an atheist—denying the existence of God at all—dismissed theology as a "pretended science." He claimed that its principles were "only hazardous suppositions, imagined by ignorance, propagated by enthusiasm or knavery, adopted by timid credulity, preserved by custom which never reasons, and revered solely because not understood."[1]

Epitomizing the new religious outlook of the Enlightenment was the Scottish moral philosopher David Hume, who is most famous for his treatise *An Enquiry Concerning Human Understanding* (1748). In that work he challenged the argument of the great rationalist philosopher René Descartes that God implants a number of clear and distinct ideas in our minds, from which we are able to deduce other truths. Hume's position was that our understanding derives from sense perceptions, not innate ideas. Even more important, he denied that there was any certain knowledge,

CREDULITY, SUPERSTITION, & FANATICISM.

Hogarth pinxt. *T. Cook sculpt.*

Published by Longman, Hurst, Rees, & Orme, Jan.y 1.st 1809.

William Hogarth, *Credulity, Superstition, and Fanaticism* (1762)

Hogarth was a moralist who embodied the rationalism and humanitarianism of the Enlightenment. In this engraving he exposes the effects of fanatical religion, witchcraft, and superstition. The sermon has whipped the entire congregation into a highly emotional state. The woman in the foreground is Mary Tofts, who was believed to have given birth to rabbits. The boy next to her, allegedly possessed by the Devil, vomits pins. The Protestant preacher's wig falls off, exposing the shaven head of a Roman Catholic monk. An unemotional Turk observes this scene from outside the window.

thereby calling into question the authority of revealed truth and religious doctrine.

Hume's writing on religion reflected his skepticism. Raised a Presbyterian, he nevertheless rejected the revealed truths of Christianity on the ground that they had no rational foundation. The concept of Providence was completely alien to his philosophical position. An avowed deist, he expressed contempt for organized religion, especially Catholicism in France and Anglicanism in England. Organized religion, according to Hume, "renders men tame and submissive, is acceptable to the magistrate, and seems inoffensive to the people; till at last the priest, having firmly established his authority, becomes the tyrant and disturber of human society."[2]

Progress and Reform

Theories regarding the stages of human development, coupled with the commitment of philosophes to the improvement and ultimate transformation of society, contributed to a belief in the progress of civilization. Until the eighteenth century the very notion of progress was alien to even the most highly educated Europeans. Those who held political power had dedicated themselves to maintaining the social and political order, not its transformation. Programs of reform were almost always associated with the restoration of a superior golden age rather than the realization of something new and different. If movement took place, it was cyclical rather than progressive. Even the original meaning of the word *revolution* was the path of a planet that came full circle in its orbit, not the creation of a new order. Now, however, the possibility of improvement began to dominate philosophical and political discussion. The Enlightenment was largely responsible for making this belief in progress, especially toward the attainment of social justice, a prominent feature of modern Western culture.

Some Enlightenment thinkers, using evidence gained from encounters with non-Western people, argued that all civilizations progressed gradually from relatively simple to more complex economies and societies. David Hume, Adam Smith, and their fellow Scotsman Adam Ferguson (1723–1816) identified four stages of human development. The first was characterized by hunting and gathering, the second by pastoral farming, the third by agriculture, and the last by commerce. The French philosophe the Marquis de Condorcet (1743–1794) focused more on intellectual progress. In *A Sketch for a Historical Picture of the Progress of the Human Mind* (1795), Condorcet identified nine distinct epochs in human history. He predicted that in the tenth and final epoch humankind would achieve a state of perfection in which rational moral judgments would inform efficient government policy.

Another source of the Enlightenment's belief in progress was the conviction that corrupt institutions could be reformed, thereby allowing societies to advance to a higher level and realize their full potential. The system of taxation, bureaucratic institutions, established churches, and the institution of monarchy itself all became the targets of Enlightenment reformers. The judicial institutions of government were particularly susceptible to this type of reforming zeal. Campaigns arose to eliminate the administration of judicial torture as well as capital punishment. All of this was intended to establish a more humane, civilized society.

The intellectual inspiration to this movement for legal reform was the work of the Italian jurist Cesare Beccaria (1738–1794). In his *Essay on Crimes and Punishments* (1764), Beccaria argued that punishment should be used not to exact retribution for crimes but to rehabilitate the criminal and to serve the interests of society. "In order that every punishment may not be an act of violence committed by one or by many against a private member of society," wrote Beccaria, "it should be above all things public, immediate, and necessary, the least possible in the case given, proportioned to the crime, and determined by the laws."[3] He called for the abolition of capital punishment and the imprisonment of convicted felons. The prison, which prior to the eighteenth century had been little more than a jail or holding facility, was now to become a symbol of the improvement of society.

Voltaire and the Spirit of the Enlightenment

The philosophe who captured all the main themes as well as the spirit of the Enlightenment was the writer and philosopher François Marie Arouet (1694–1778), known universally by his pen name, Voltaire. Born into a French bourgeois family, Voltaire became one of the most prominent and prolific writers of the eighteenth century. Although he wrote for a fairly broad, predominantly bourgeois audience, and although he waged war against the injustices of aristocratic society, he was comfortable in the homes of the nobility and at the courts of European monarchs, especially that of Frederick the Great of Prussia. Voltaire's main career was as an author. He wrote plays and novels as well as poems, letters, essays, and history. These writings revealed his commitment to scientific rationality, his contempt for established religion, and his unflagging pursuit of liberty and justice.

DOCUMENT

Voltaire on the Relations Between Church and State (mid-18th c.)

Like many men of the Enlightenment, Voltaire developed a deep interest in science. He acquired much of his scientific knowledge from a learned noblewoman, Madame du Châtelet (1706–1749), a scientist and mathematician who translated the works of Newton into French. Madame du Châtelet became Voltaire's mistress, and the two lived together with her tolerant husband in their country estate in eastern France. The sexual freedom they experienced was characteristic of many Enlightenment figures, who rejected the Christian condemnation of

A Case of Infanticide in the Age of the Enlightenment

A mid-eighteenth-century trial of a young French woman charged with killing her newborn child provides a window into the life of women who occupied the lower rungs of French society, in contrast to those who frequented the court and met in salons. The trial also raises the larger questions, debated in French and European judicial circles during the time of the Enlightenment, of how society should deal with the mothers of illegitimate children and whether the punishments prescribed for infanticide, or the killing of a young child, were proportionate to the crime.

In August 1742 Marie-Jeanne Bartonnet, a 21-year-old unmarried woman from a small French village in Brie, moved to Paris, where she took up residence with Claude le Queux, whom she had known in her youth, and Claude's sister. At that time Bartonnet was seven months pregnant. On October 22 Bartonnet caused a ruckus in the middle of the night when she went to the toilet and began groaning loudly and bleeding profusely. When her neighbors found her, and when she asked for towels for the blood, they suspected that she had had a miscarriage and called for a midwife. By the time the midwife arrived, it was clear that the delivery had already taken place and that the infant had fallen down the toilet to the cesspool five stories below. Suspecting that Bartonnet had killed the baby, the proprietress of the building reported her to the nearest judicial officer. The next day judicial authorities returned to the building and found the dead infant in the cesspool. An autopsy revealed that the child's skull had been dented by either a blunt instrument or a fall. After a med-

ical examination of Bartonnet revealed the signs of having just delivered a baby, she was arrested and imprisoned for the crime of infanticide.

Bartonnet came very close to being executed, but the strict procedures of French justice saved her from paying the ultimate price for her apparent crime. In the seventeenth and eighteenth centuries French criminal justice had established clear criteria for determining the guilt or innocence of a person accused of a crime. These procedures involved a systematic interrogation of the accused (only rarely under torture), the deposition of witnesses, the evaluation of physical evidence, and the confrontation of the accused with the witnesses who testified against her. There also was a mandatory review of the case, which involved a further interrogation of the defendant, before the Parlement of Paris, the highest court in northern France.

The interrogations of Bartonnet did not give her judges much evidence on which they could convict her. When asked the name of the village where she had lived in Brie, she told her interrogators, "It's none of your business." She denied that she had even known she was pregnant, refused to name the man with whom she had had intercourse, and claimed that she had mistaken her labor pains for colic or diarrhea. She denied picking her baby off the floor of the toilet after the delivery and throwing it into the cesspool. When presented with the baby's corpse, she claimed she did not recognize it.

After this interrogation, Bartonnet was given the opportunity to challenge the testimony of the witnesses who had seen her

the night of the delivery. The most damning testimony came from Madame Pâris, the wife of the proprietor, who had found Bartonnet on the toilet and thus could verify the circumstances of the clandestine delivery. Bartonnet's inability to challenge the testimony of Madame Pâris led directly to her initial conviction. After reviewing the entire dossier of evidence, the king's attorney recommended conviction for concealing her pregnancy, hiding her delivery, and destroying her child. French criminal procedure entrusted the decision of guilt or innocence to the judges themselves, and on November 27 they voted that Bartonnet should be executed by hanging.

Marie-Jeanne Bartonnet's fate, however, was not yet sealed. When her case went on appeal to the Parlement of Paris, Bartonnet repeated her statement that she had gone to the toilet but did not know whether she had given birth. Even though her execution was warranted by terms of an edict of 1557 that defined the crime of infanticide, the judges of this court voted to commute her sentence to a public whipping, banishment from the jurisdiction of the Parlement of Paris, and confiscation of her property. The basis of this decision appears to have been the absence of any proof that she had deliberately killed her baby. Indeed, its injuries could have been caused by its fall down the drain pipe into the cesspool. There was also the persistent refusal of the defendant to make a confession. She may have been lying, but it is equally possible that once she had delivered the baby, which happened very quickly, she convinced herself that it had not happened.

Bartonnet's trial for infanticide stands at the end of a long period of intense prosecution of this crime. Trials of this sort declined as cities and towns built foundling hospitals for abandoned infants and as the moral outrage for illegitimacy was redirected from the pregnant mother to the illegitimate father. The new legal values promoted at the time of the Enlightenment, moreover, made it less likely that any woman or man would be executed for this or any other crime.

Questions of Justice

1. As in many trials, the facts of this case can be used to support different claims of justice. If you had been the prosecutor in this trial, what position would you have taken to prove the crime of infanticide? If you had been defending Marie-Jeanne Bartonnet, what arguments would you have used in her defense?

2. In his *Essay on Crimes and Punishments* (1764), Beccaria recommended that punishments be determined strictly in accordance with the social damage committed by the crime. What would Beccaria have said about the original sentence of death in this case? What would he have said about the modified sentence handed down by the Parlement of Paris?

Taking It Further

Michael Wolfe, ed. *Changing Identities in Early Modern France.* 1997. Gives a full account of Marie-Jeanne Bartonnet's trial for infanticide.

A Woman Accused of Murder in the Eighteenth Century
With the exception of infanticide—the crime for which Marie-Jeanne Bartonnet was tried and convicted—few women were tried for capital crimes in the eighteenth century. One exception was Sarah Malcolm, a 22-year-old Englishwoman, shown here in a portrait by William Hogarth (1733). Malcolm was executed for slitting the throat of a wealthy lady in London.

sexual activity outside marriage and who justified their behavior on the basis of natural law and the pursuit of happiness. From Madame du Châtelet, Voltaire acquired not only an understanding of Newton's scientific laws but also a commitment to women's education and equality. Voltaire lived with her until she died in 1749 while giving birth to a child that was fathered neither by Voltaire nor her husband.

Voltaire's belief in a Newtonian universe—one governed by the universal law of gravitation—laid the foundation for his deism and his attacks on contemporary Christianity. In his *Philosophical Dictionary* (1764), he lashed out at established religion and the clergy, Protestant as well as Catholic. In a letter to another philosophe attacking religious superstition he pleaded, "Whatever you do, crush the infamous thing." In Voltaire's eyes Christianity was not only unreasonable; it was vulgar and barbaric. He condemned the Catholic Church for the slaughter of millions of indigenous people in the Americas on the grounds that they had not been baptized, as well as the executions of hundreds of thousands of Jews and heretics in Europe. All of these people were the victims of "barbarism and fanaticism."[4]

Voltaire's indictment of the Church for these barbarities was matched by his scathing criticism of the French government for a series of injustices, including his own imprisonment for insulting the regent of France. While living in England for three years, Voltaire became an admirer of English legal institutions, which he considered more humane and just than those of his native country. Using England as a model, he appealed for the implementation of various political reforms in France. He deplored those "who reduce men to a state of slavery by force and downright violence." A tireless advocate of individual liberty, he became a regular defender of victims of injustice, including Jean Calas, a Protestant shopkeeper from Toulouse who had been tortured and executed for allegedly murdering his son because he had expressed a desire to convert to Catholicism. The boy had in fact committed suicide.

Voltaire showed a commitment to placing his knowledge in the service of humanitarian causes. In his most famous novel, *Candide* (1759), the character by that name challenges the smug confidence of Dr. Pangloss, the tutor who repeatedly claims that they lived in "the best of all possible worlds." At the end of the novel Candide responds to this refrain by saying that "we must cultivate our garden." Voltaire, instead of being content with the current condition of humankind, was demanding that we work actively to improve society.

Madame du Châtelet

In her *Institutions de physique* (1740) this French noblewoman, the mistress of Voltaire, made an original and impressive attempt to give Newtonian physics a philosophical foundation.

Enlightenment Political Theory

Enlightenment thinkers are known most widely for their political theories, especially those that supported the causes of liberty and reform. The men and women of the Enlightenment did not, however, share a common political ideology, nor did they agree on the most desirable type of political society. They did share a belief that politics was a science that, like the cosmos, had its own natural laws. The title of one of David Hume's treatises, *That Politics May Be Reduced to a Science* (1741), reflects a belief that most Enlightenment political writers endorsed. They also thought of the state in secular rather than religious terms. There was little place in Enlightenment thought for the divine right of kings. Nor was there a place for the Church in the government of the state. On other issues, however, there was little consensus. Three thinkers in particular illustrate the range of Enlightenment political thought: Montesquieu, Rousseau, and Paine.

Baron de Montesquieu: The Separation of Powers

The most influential political writer of the Enlightenment was the French philosophe Charles-Louis de Secondat, Baron de Montesquieu (1689–1755). The son of a nobleman of the robe from Bordeaux, Montesquieu had a legal education and also developed an early interest in science. His political thought owed as much to his study of history and anthropology as to the study of law and science. His first book, *The Persian Letters*, published anonymously in Holland in 1721, was a brilliant satire of Western government and society through the eyes of two Persian aristocrats traveling in Europe. It laid the groundwork for a much more scholarly and substantial contribution to political theory, *Spirit of the Laws* (1748). Often compared to Aristotle because of the range of his thought, Montesquieu interwove commentaries on natural law, religion, morals, virtue, climate, and liberty. Unlike Hobbes, Locke, and the other natural-law philosophers who preceded him, Montesquieu was not concerned with the origin of government or with the establishment of a universal model of politics. Rather, he treated the laws of a country in historical perspective and within the context of that country's religion, morality, climate, geography, and culture. His political writing was scientific mainly in its empirical approach to its subject, and in the comparisons it made between politics on the one hand and Newtonian physics on the other.

Montesquieu argued that there were three forms of government: republics, monarchies, and despotisms, each of which had an activating or inspirational force. In republics that force was civic virtue, in monarchies it was honor, and in despotisms it was fear. In each form of government there was a danger that the polity could degenerate: The virtue of republics could be lost, monarchies could become corrupt, and despotisms could lead to repression. The key to maintaining moderation and preventing this degeneration of civil society was the law of each country. Ideally the law of a country should provide for the separation and balance of political powers. Only in that way could degeneration be avoided and moderation ensured.

Montesquieu used his knowledge of the British political system, which he had studied firsthand while living in England for two years, to propose that the key to good government was the separation of executive, legislative, and judicial power. He was particularly concerned about the independence of the judiciary. Montesquieu was unaware of

CHRONOLOGY

Literary Works of the Enlightenment

1687	Isaac Newton, *Mathematical Principles of Natural Philosophy*
1690	John Locke, *An Essay Concerning Human Understanding*
1721	Baron de Montesquieu, *The Persian Letters*
1738	Voltaire, *Elements of the Philosophy of Newton*
1739	David Hume, *Treatise of Human Nature*
1748	Baron de Montesquieu, *Spirit of the Laws*
1748	David Hume, *An Enquiry Concerning Human Understanding*
1751	First volume of Diderot and d'Alembert's *Encyclopedia*
1755	Jean-Jacques Rousseau, *Discourse on the Origin of Inequality Among Men*
1759	Voltaire, *Candide*
1762	Jean-Jacques Rousseau, *The Social Contract* and *Emile, or on Education*
1763	Voltaire, *Treatise on Toleration*
1764	Cesare Beccaria, *Essay on Crimes and Punishments*
1764	Voltaire, *Philosophical Dictionary*
1776	Adam Smith, *The Wealth of Nations*
1781	Immanuel Kant, *Critique of Pure Reason*
1791	Thomas Paine, *The Rights of Man*
1792	Mary Wollstonecraft, *A Vindication of the Rights of Woman*
1795	Marquis de Condorcet, *Progress of the Human Mind*

how legislative and executive powers actually overlapped in eighteenth-century Britain, but his emphasis on the importance of a separation of powers became the most durable of his ideas. It had profound influence on the drafting of the Constitution of the United States of America in 1787.

Jean-Jacques Rousseau: The General Will

Also influential as a political theorist was the Swiss philosophe Jean-Jacques Rousseau (1712–1778), who as a young man moved from Geneva to Paris and became a member of a prominent intellectual circle. Rousseau does not conform to the model of the typical Enlightenment thinker. His distrust of human reason and his emotionalism separated him from Hume, Voltaire, and another

Differences Among the Philosophes

This satirical print shows Rousseau, to the left, and Voltaire engaged in heated debate. The two men were both major figures in the Enlightenment, but they differed widely in temperament and in their philosophical and political views. Rousseau was very much the rebel; unlike Voltaire, he distrusted reason and articulated highly egalitarian political principles.

of recreating an idealized golden age when they were not yet alienated from themselves and their environment.

Rousseau's political theories were hardly conventional, but they appealed to some segments of the reading public. In his *Discourse on the Origin of Inequality Among Men* (1755) and *The Social Contract* (1762) he challenged the existing political and social order with an uncompromising attack on aristocracy and monarchy. He linked absolute monarchy, which he referred to as despotism, with the court and especially with the vain, pampered, conceited, and overdecorated aristocratic women who wielded political influence with the king and in the salons. As an alternative to this aristocratic, monarchical, and feminized society Rousseau proclaimed the sovereignty of the people. Laws were to be determined by the General Will, by which he meant the consensus of a community of citizens (but not necessarily the vote of the majority).

As a result of his writings Rousseau became associated with radical republican and democratic ideas that flourished at the time of the French Revolution. One indication of that radicalism was the fact that *The Social Contract* was banned not only in absolutist France but in the republics of the Netherlands and Switzerland as well. Rousseau was also criticized for justifying authoritarian rule. His argument that the General Will placed limits on individual civil liberty encouraged autocratic leaders, such as the radical Maximilien Robespierre

great French philosophe, Denis Diderot (1713–1784). That distrust laid the foundations for the romantic reaction against the Enlightenment in the early nineteenth century (see Chapter 21). Instead of celebrating the improvement of society as it evolved into higher forms, Rousseau had a negative view of the achievements of civilization. In his novel *Emile, or on Education* (1762) he wrote, "All our wisdom consists of servile prejudices, all our customs are but enslavement, constraint, or bondage. Social man is born, lives and dies enslaved. At birth he is bound up with swaddling clothes; at his death he is nailed down in a coffin. For the whole of his existence as a human being he is chained up by our institutions."[5] Rousseau idealized the uncorrupted condition of human beings in the state of nature, supporting the theory of the "noble savage." Human beings could not ever return to that original natural state, but Rousseau held out the hope

at the time of the French Revolution, to claim that their dictatorial rule embodied that General Will.

Thomas Paine: The Rights of Man

Of all the Enlightenment political theorists, the English publicist and propagandist Thomas Paine (1737–1809) was arguably the most radical. Paine was influenced by Rousseau, Diderot, and Voltaire, but his radicalism was cultivated mainly by his intense involvement in the political world of revolutionary America, where he became politically active in the 1770s. In *Common Sense* (1776) Paine presented the case for American independence from Britain. This included a passionate statement of human freedom, equality, and rationality. It also involved a vicious attack on hereditary monarchy and an eloquent statement for the sovereignty of the law. At the time of the French Revolution, Paine continued to call for the establishment

Rousseau Places Limits on Civil Liberty

In his Social Contract *(1762) Rousseau discussed the effect that the formation of the civil state had on individual liberty. Rousseau is careful to distinguish between the liberty one enjoys in the state of nature and the liberty one acquires by entering civil society. As he explains in this passage, the establishment of the civil state limits one's natural liberty, but contrary to what some scholars have maintained, he does not justify totalitarian rule. Passionately committed to human liberty, Rousseau claims that the democratic and egalitarian society he envisions would serve as an alternative to the despotic systems of government that existed in late-eighteenth-century Europe.*

The passage from the state of nature to the civil state produces a very remarkable change in man, by substituting justice for instinct in his conduct and giving his actions the morality they had formerly lacked. Then only, when the voice of duty takes the place of physical impulses and right of appetite, does man who so far had considered only himself, find that he is forced to act on different principles, and to consult his reason before listening to his inclinations. Although in this state he deprives himself of some advantages which he got from nature, he gains in return others so great, his facilities are so stimulated and developed, his ideas so extended, his feelings so ennobled, and his whole soul so uplifted that, did not the abuses of this new condition often degrade him below that which he left, he would be bound to bless continually the happy moment which took him from it forever and, instead of a stupid and unimaginative animal, made him an intelligent being and a man.

Let us draw up the whole account in terms easily commensurable. What man loses by the social contract is his natural liberty and an unlimited right to everything he tries to get and succeeds in getting; what he gains is civil liberty and the proprietorship of all he possesses. If we are to avoid mistake in weighing one against the other, we must clearly distinguish natural liberty, which is bounded only by the strength of the individual, from civil liberty, which is limited by the general will; and possession, which is merely the effect of force or the right of the first occupier, from property, which can be founded only on a positive title.

Source: Jean-Jacques Rousseau, *The Social Contract* (1762).

of a republic in France and in his native country. In his most widely circulated work, *The Rights of Man* (1791), he linked the institution of monarchy with the aristocracy, which he referred to as "a seraglio of males, who neither collect the honey nor form the hive but exist only for lazy enjoyment."

The title of *The Rights of Man* identified a theme that appeared in much Enlightenment writing. Like Diderot and Rousseau, Paine spoke the language of natural rights. Until the Enlightenment, rights were considered legal privileges acquired by royal charter or by inheritance. One had a right, for example, to a particular piece of land or to elect representatives from one's county or town. Those rights could be surrendered under certain circumstances, such as when a person sold land. The new emphasis on natural law, however, led to the belief that simply by being a human being one acquired natural rights that could never be taken away. The American Declaration of Independence (1776), drafted by Thomas Jefferson, presented an eloquent statement of these God-given inalienable rights, which included "life, liberty and the pursuit of happiness." In defending that independence, Paine claimed that "a government of our own is our natural right." Since the eighteenth century those rights have been extended to include newly defined activities, such as the right to privacy, but the language in which such rights are asserted is a legacy of the Enlightenment.

Women and the Enlightenment

The claim advanced by Enlightenment thinkers that all human beings are equal in a state of nature did not lead to a widespread belief that on the basis of natural law men and women are equal. Quite to the contrary, many philosophes, including Diderot and Rousseau, argued that women are different in nature from men and that they should be confined to an exclusively domestic role as chaste wives and mothers. Rousseau also insisted on the separate education of girls.

This patriarchal argument supported the emerging theory of separate spheres°, which held that men and women should conduct their lives in different social and political environments. The identification of women with the private, domestic sphere laid the foundation for the ideology of female domesticity, which became popular in bourgeois society in the nineteenth century. But it denied them the freedom that aristocratic women in France had acquired during the eighteenth century, especially those who participated in polite society. It also continued to deny them civil rights. Like women in ancient Sparta, whose situation served as the model for a number of Enlightenment thinkers, eighteenth-century women could not vote and could not initiate lawsuits on their own authority. They were not full members of civil society.

DOCUMENT

Montesquieu Satirizes European Women

Montesquieu's first publication, The Persian Letters *(1721), is a clever satire on French society. The book consists of a series of letters written to and from two fictional Persian travelers, Usbek and Rica. Because the characters come from a radically different culture, Montesquieu was able to avoid official censure for presenting his irreverent views. The Persians refer to the king as a great magician who has the power to persuade men to kill one another though they have no quarrel, and to the pope as "an old idol worshipped out of habit." Montesquieu's satire was all the more biting because Europeans harbored deep contempt for the world of the Middle East, which they thought of as a region ruled by oriental despots and inhabited by people with lax standards of sexual morality. In this passage from one of Usbek's early letters to one of his wives in the harem, Montesquieu presents a favorable image of the oriental harem to contrast with the aristocratic women of eighteenth-century France.*

Usbek to Roxana, at the seraglio in Ispahan

How fortunate you are, Roxana, to live in the gentle land of Persia and not in these poisoned regions where neither shame nor virtue are known! You live in my seraglio as in the bower of innocence, inaccessible to the assaults of mankind; you rejoice in the good fortune that makes it impossible for you to fall. No man has sullied you with lascivious glances;

even your father-in-law, during the freedom of the festivals, has never seen your lovely mouth, because you have never failed to cover it with a sacred veil . . . .

If you had been raised in this country, you would not have been so troubled. Women here have lost all restraint. They present themselves barefaced to men, as if inviting conquest; they seek attention, and they accompany men to the mosques. On walks, even to their rooms; the service of eunuchs is unknown. In place of the noble simplicity and charming modesty which is the rule among you, one finds here a barbaric impudence, to which one cannot grow accustomed. . . .

When you enhance the brilliance of your complexion with lovely coloring, when you perfume all your body with the most precious essences, when you dress in your most beautiful garments, when you seek to distinguish yourself from your companions by the charm of your dancing or the delight of your song, when you graciously compete with them in beauty, sweetness and vivacity, then I cannot imagine that you have any other object than that of pleasing me. . . .

But what am I to think of European women? Their art in making up their complexions, the ornaments they display, the care they give to their bodies, their preoccupation with pleasing are so many stains on their virtue and outrages to their husbands.

Source: From Baron de Montesquieu, *The Persian Letters,* translated by George R. Healy (Hackett, 1999), Letter 26. Reprinted by permission of Hackett Publishing Company, Inc. All rights reserved.

Only in the 1790s did writers begin to use the language and ideas of the Enlightenment to advance the argument for the full equality of men and women. The first of these appeals came from Condorcet, who published *On the Admission of Women to the Rights of Citizenship* in 1789. In that pamphlet he proposed that all women who own property be given the right to vote. He later called for universal suffrage for all men and women on the grounds that they all shared a common human nature. A similar appeal came from the French dramatist and revolutionary activist Marie Olympe Aubrey de Gouges (1748–1793). At the very beginning of the French Revolution, de Gouges, the daughter of a butcher, proposed that the revolutionary manifesto adopted by the French National Assembly, *Declaration of the Rights of Man and Citizen* (1789), be extended to include women as well as men.

De Gouges drafted her most famous publication, *The Rights of Woman* (1791), as a proposed appendix to that constitutional document. She took the authors of the *Declaration* to task for their failure to address the problem of women's civil rights and responsibilities with the same

determination and enthusiasm they had manifested in proclaiming the rights of men. Revealing her debt to Rousseau, she proposed in Article VI of her document that "the law must be the expression of the general will. All citizens, men and women, must concur, personally or through their representatives, in its creation. It must be the same for everyone: every citizen, man and woman, being equal in its eyes, must be equally eligible for all high honors, public offices, and positions according to their merits. . . . " Using more of Rousseau's language, she went on to propose a "social contract" between man and woman that recognized, among other things, common ownership of property. None of de Gouges's proposals were implemented by the French government, but she did succeed in drawing attention to the contradictions between the rhetoric and the reality of natural rights.

De Gouges's English contemporary, Mary Wollstonecraft (1759–1797), was the most famous of the Enlightenment's advocates of women's rights. Inspired by the events of the French Revolution and angered by the conservative English response to the events taking place in France,

Wollstonecraft wrote *A Vindication of the Rights of Woman* (1792). This treatise, which embodies a stinging critique of eighteenth-century polite society, has become a founding document of modern feminism. In it Wollstonecraft made an eloquent appeal for extending civil and political rights to women and even proposed that women elect their own representatives to legislatures. Her most original and innovative proposals, however, dealt with education. She claimed that in order for women to take control of their lives and to become the full equals of men within marriage and in the political realm, girls had to acquire greater knowledge and skill and learn how to support themselves. Wollstonecraft insisted that the education of women must be made equal and identical to that of men. In this way she challenged the arguments presented by Rousseau and many other male Enlightenment thinkers that cultural and social differences between men and women should be maintained because they were "natural."

The Enlightenment and Sexuality

One facet of Enlightenment thought that had a profound effect on the position of women in society was the appeal for greater sexual permissiveness. Many philosophes, including Voltaire, Diderot, and Holbach, remained openly critical of the strict standard of sexual morality enforced by Christian churches. The basic argument of the philosophes was that sexual activity should not be restricted, because it was pleasurable and a source of happiness. The arbitrary prohibitions imposed by the Church contradicted human nature. European encounters with pagan natives of the South Pacific, who were reported to have enjoyed great sexual permissiveness, were used to reinforce this argument based on human nature. Diderot appealed to the sexual code of the Tahitians in his attack on Christian sexual morality.

Many philosophes, including Voltaire, practiced what they preached and lived openly with women out of wedlock. Other members of wealthy society adopted an even more libertine lifestyle. The Venetian adventurer and author Giacomo Casanova (1725–1798), who was expelled from a seminary for his immorality, gained fame for his life of gambling, spying, and seducing thousands of women. To one young Spanish woman, who resisted his advances in order to protect her virginity, he said: "You must abandon yourself to my passion without any resistance, and you may rest assured I will respect your innocence." Casanova's name soon became identified with sexual seduction.

The violent excesses to which this type of eighteenth-century sexual permissiveness could lead can be seen in the career of Alphonse Donatien François, the Marquis de Sade (1740–1814). The author of licentious libertine narratives, including his own memoirs and an erotic novel, *Justine* (1793), de Sade described the use of violence in sexual en-

counters and thus gave rise to the word *sadism* to describe the pleasurable administration of pain. He spent twenty-seven years in prison for his various sexual offenses.

It makes sense that noblemen like Casanova and de Sade would have adopted the libertine values of the Enlightenment thinkers. Somewhat more remarkable was the growth of public sexual permissiveness among all social groups, including the rather prim and proper bourgeoisie and the working poor. Erotic literature, such as John Cleland's *Memoirs of a Woman of Pleasure* (1749), and pornographic prints achieved considerable popularity in an increasingly commercialized society, while prostitution became more open and widespread. Voltaire and Diderot might not have approved of this literature or these practices, but their libertine, anti-Christian, materialist outlook helped to prepare the ground for their acceptance.

The Impact of the Enlightenment

■ **What impact did the Enlightenment have on Western culture and politics?**

The ideas of the Enlightenment spread to every country in Europe as well as to the Americas. They inspired programs of reform and radical political movements. Enlightenment thought, however, did not become the property of the entire population. It appealed mainly to the educated and the relatively prosperous and failed to penetrate the lower levels of society.

The Spread of Enlightened Ideas

The ideas of the Enlightenment spread rapidly among the literate members of society, mainly by means of print. During the eighteenth century, print became the main medium of formal communication. The technology of printing allowed for the publication of materials on a scale unknown a century before. Pamphlets, newspapers, and books poured off presses, not only in the major cities but in provincial towns as well. Literacy rates increased dramatically throughout western Europe. The highly educated still constituted a minority of the population, but the better part of the aristocracy and many of those who occupied the middle ranks of society could read and write. By 1750 more than half the male population of France and England could read basic texts. The foundation of public libraries in all the major cities of western Europe made printed materials more widely available. In many bookshops, rooms were set aside for browsing in the hope that readers would eventually purchase the books they consulted.

One of the most widely circulated publications of the Enlightenment was the *Encyclopedia* compiled by the philosophe Denis Diderot and the mathematician Jean le Rond d'Alembert. This massive seventeen-volume work, which was published between 1751 and 1765, contained thousands of articles on science, religion, politics, and the economy. The entries in the *Encyclopedia* were intended not only to promote knowledge but also to advance the ideas of the Enlightenment. Included, for example, were two entries on natural law, which was described as being "perpetual and unchangeable." The entry on intolerance makes a passionate plea against religious persecution, asserting that "If we may tear out one hair of anyone whose opinions differ from ours, we could also claim the whole head, for there is no limit to injustice." Other articles praised the achievements of science and technology and gave special attention to industrial crafts and trades. Underlying the entire enterprise was the belief that knowledge was useful, that it could contribute to the improvement of human life. In these respects the *Encyclopedia* became the quintessential statement of the worldview of the Enlightenment, and its publication stands as a crowning achievement of the entire movement.

Diderot's *Encyclopedia*, Plate Illustrating Agricultural Techniques

Encyclopedias, pamphlets, newspapers, and novels were not the only means by which the ideas of the Enlightenment spread. A number of informal institutions promoted the exchange of ideas. Literary societies and book clubs, which proliferated in the major cities of western Europe, encouraged the public reading and discussion of the latest publications. Scientific societies sponsored lectures on the latest developments in physics, chemistry, and natural history. One of the most famous of these lectures demonstrated the power of electricity by charging a young boy, suspended from the ground, with static electricity. This "electrified boy," who was not harmed in the process, attracted objects from a stool placed below him. Lectures like this one attracted large crowds.

Equally important in the spread of the scientific and cultural ideas of the Enlightenment were museums, where scientific and cultural artifacts, many of them gathered from around the world, could be viewed by an increasingly curious and educated public. The museums often sponsored exhibits and lectures. Paris became home to a number of these museums in the 1780s, and they could be found in all the major cities of Europe by the end of the eighteenth century. A more informal set of cultural institutions were the coffeehouses that sprang up in cities across Europe. These commercial establishments were open to everyone who could pay the fare, and therefore they proved immensely successful in facilitating the spread of ideas within the bourgeoisie. Newspapers were often read aloud at coffeehouses, and they became the setting for many political debates.

Another set of institutions that promoted the ideas of the Enlightenment were the secret societies of men and women known as freemasons°. Freemasons strove to create a society based on reason and virtue, and they were committed to the principles of liberty and equality. Freemasonry first appeared in England and Scotland in the seventeenth century and then spread to France, the Dutch Republic, Germany, and as far east as Poland and Russia during the eighteenth century. Some of the most famous figures of the Enlightenment, including Voltaire, belonged to masonic lodges. In the 1770s there were more than 10,000 freemasons in Paris alone. The lodges were places where philosophes interacted with merchants, lawyers, and government leaders. The pope condemned the freemasons in 1738, and many civil authorities expressed deep suspicion of the political and religious ideas they fostered.

The most famous informal cultural institutions of the Enlightenment were the salons, the private sitting rooms or parlors of wealthy women where discussions of philosophy, science, literature, and politics took place. Salons became particularly prominent in Paris, where the salons of Madame Geoffrin and Madame du Deffand won international fame. The women who hosted these meetings invited the participants, entertained those who attended, and used their conversational skills to direct and facilitate the discussions that took place in the salons. They also used their influence to secure aristocratic patronage of the young male writers and scientists whom they cultivated. The success of a new book was often determined by its initial reception in the salon. Most of the prominent male figures of the French Enlightenment participated in these meetings, at least during the early years of their careers. (See the illustration at the beginning of this chapter.)

Madame Geoffrin
Her salon was called "one of the wonders of the social world."

The salons became the target of contemporary criticism not only because they allowed women to participate in public life but also because they were bastions of aristocratic society. While most of the salon women came from the aristocracy, many of their fathers had recently risen into the nobility or had merely purchased their noble status. The men who attended the meetings had even fewer ties to the traditional aristocracy. The salons were places where old and new noble blood intermingled, where social refinement was even more important than inherited nobility. What mattered most in the salons was the quickness of one's wit, the quality of one's conversational skills, and the appeal of one's views. Thus the salon succeeded in opening elite society to the talented. In this way the salons helped to dissolve the bonds that held together the Old Regime and contributed to the creation of a society based on merit rather than birth alone.

The Limits of the Enlightenment

The ideas of the Enlightenment spread rapidly across Europe, but their influence was limited. The market for books by philosophes such as Voltaire and Rousseau was quite small. Diderot and d'Alembert's *Encyclopedia* sold a remarkable 25,000 copies by 1789, but that was exceptional, and many sales were to libraries. Paine's *The Rights of Man* also reached a fairly broad audience, mainly because it was written in a simple direct style and its price was deliberately kept low. Most books on social and political theory, however, like scholarly works on science, did not sell very well. Rousseau's *The Social Contract* was a commercial failure.

Books on other topics had much better sales. Inspirational religious literature continued to be published in large quantities, indicating the limits of Enlightenment secularism. Novels, a relatively new genre of fiction that appealed to the bourgeoisie, were almost as successful. We can readily see why Rousseau and Voltaire both used novels to advance their radical social views. In France, books that were banned because of their pornographic content or their satirical attacks on the monarchy, the clergy, or ministers in the government also proved to be best-sellers in the huge underground French book market.

One segment of the popular press that revealed a limited influence of the Enlightenment was the literature on popular science. The reading public did not show much interest in technical scientific books, but they did purchase publications on such technological developments as hot-air balloons, which became a new fad in the 1780s. Descriptions of monsters found in distant lands and other extraordinary natural occurrences also sold thousands of copies. Some of this interest in the preternatural originated in the work of highly educated scholars, but the reports of new discoveries increasingly lent themselves to sensational treatment in the popular press.

Another subject of popular literary interest was mesmerism°. The Viennese physicist and physician Franz Anton Mesmer (1734–1815), who moved to Paris in 1778, claimed that he had discovered a fluid that permeated and surrounded all bodies and was the source of heat, light, electricity, and magnetism. Sickness was caused by the obstruction to the flow of this fluid in the human body. To restore this flow patients were massaged, hypnotized, or "mesmerized" with the intention of producing a convulsion or crisis that restored health. Mesmerism developed into a form of spiritualism in which its patients engaged in séances with spirits, and its practitioners dabbled in the occult. This pseudoscience, which was rejected by the French Academy of Science as a hoax, became the subject of numerous pamphlets and newspaper articles that fascinated the reading public.

Those who read books about mesmerism had only a tenuous connection with the learned world of the Enlightenment. Among those who were illiterate or barely literate, Enlightened ideas made even fewer inroads. The only exposure these people may have had to the ideas we associate with the Enlightenment would be through the actions and attitudes of their social superiors. From the elitist perspective of the philosophes, the intellectual world of the illiterate was characterized by the superstition and ignorance that the philosophes were determined to eliminate.

The growing gap between a learned culture shared by philosophes and members of salons on the one hand and the popular culture of the lower classes on the other can be seen in the perpetuation of beliefs regarding magic and witchcraft among the uneducated. During the late seventeenth and eighteenth centuries, educated people in Europe gradually abandoned their belief in magic and witchcraft. As we have seen in Chapter 16, belief in the operation of a mechanical universe, religious skepticism, and rationalism had gradually eroded many beliefs regarding the operation of a supernatural realm, especially the possibility of demonic intervention in the natural world. Among the lower classes, however, this skeptical outlook found very little fertile ground. Popular belief in a world charged with supernatural and magical forces continued to lead villagers to accuse their neighbors of having harmed them by means of witchcraft. After European courts stopped prosecuting witches in the late seventeenth and early eighteenth centuries, local communities often took justice into their own hands and lynched the suspects themselves. It was left to the government to prosecute those who engaged in this illegal form of local justice.

The gap between the high culture of the Enlightenment and that of the lower classes can also be seen in the condemnations of certain sports and amusements. Popular culture was known for its blood sports, especially cockfighting, and the baiting of bulls, bears, and badgers by tying the animals down and allowing dogs to attack them. These blood sports, which could attract thousands of spectators at a single event, resulted in the serious injury or death of animals. Enlightenment thinkers, especially those from the bourgeoisie, condemned this activity for its cruelty and its barbarism. Just like the torture and execution of criminals, these "barbarous" pastimes had no place in polite society. Popular sports, however, could not be easily eradicated. It was not until the nineteenth century that they began to disappear, often as the result of campaigns conducted by clergymen rather than philosophes. The persistence of blood sports reveals the strength of popular culture and the inability of the Enlightenment to transform it.

Enlightened Absolutism

When we turn to Enlightened political ideas, we confront an even more difficult task of determining the extent of their impact. The main figures of the Enlightenment were intellectuals—men of letters who did not occupy positions of great political importance and who did not devote much thought to the challenging task of putting their theories into practice. The audience for their books did not always include people with the power to implement their proposals. Rulers often treated Enlightenment thinkers with suspicion, if only because they criticized established authority. Nevertheless, Enlightenment thought did make its mark on eighteenth-century politics in two strikingly different ways.

The first was through the reforms enacted by rulers who are often referred to as enlightened despots°. These rulers exercised absolute power and used that power to implement changes that Enlightenment thinkers had proposed. The term *despot* is misleading, as these enlightened rulers were rarely despotic in the sense of exercising power cruelly and arbitrarily. The connection between Enlightenment and royal absolutism is not as unnatural as it might appear. It is true that philosophes tended to be critical of the Old Regime°, the eighteenth-century political order that was dominated by an absolute monarch and a privileged nobility and clergy. But many of them, including Voltaire, had little sympathy with democracy and social equality, and preferred to entrust absolute monarchs with the implementation of the reforms they advocated. Among the philosophes the prospect of a philosopher-king had widespread appeal.

Rulers of central and eastern European countries were particularly open to Enlightenment thought. These monarchs had read widely in the literature of the Enlightenment and introduced Western intellectuals to their courts. The most famous of the enlightened absolutists was King Frederick II of Prussia, known as Frederick the Great (r. 1740–1786). Frederick, a deist who wrote poetry and played the flute, was enamored of all things French. When the French philosophe d'Alembert visited his court, the king hosted a dinner at which he spoke only French, leaving many of the Prussian guests to sip their soup in stunned silence. Frederick corresponded extensively with Voltaire and invited him to take up residence at his French-style royal palace, "Sans Souci," at Potsdam. The relationship between king and philosopher, however, was often stormy, and when Frederick publicly burned a publication in which Voltaire had lampooned a royal favorite, Voltaire left Potsdam in 1752.

The departure of Voltaire did not weaken Frederick's determination to implement a number of policies that reflected the ideals of the Enlightenment. The most noteworthy of these was the introduction of religious toleration throughout his predominantly Lutheran kingdom. Protestants of all denominations and Catholics (but not Jews) received the protection of the law and even benefited from royal patronage. Frederick also introduced a number of legal reforms with the intention of realizing the Enlightenment ideal of making the law both rational and humane. He authorized the codification of Prussian law (which was completed after his death in 1794), abolished judicial torture, and eliminated capital punishment. In order to provide for the training of future servants of the state, he began a system of compulsory education throughout the country. Like most enlightened rulers, Frederick never abandoned his commitment to absolute rule, which he strengthened by winning the support of the nobility. He also remained committed to the militaristic and expansionist policies of his father, Frederick William I. For him there was no contradiction between his style of rule and his commitment to Enlightenment ideals.

In neighboring Austria two Habsburg rulers, Maria Theresa (r. 1740–1780) and her son Joseph II (r. 1780–1790), pursued reformist policies that gave them the reputation of being enlightened monarchs. Most of Maria Theresa's reforms were of an administrative nature. Stunned by the Prussian invasion and occupation of the Habsburg province of Silesia in 1740, Maria Theresa set out to strengthen the Habsburg monarchy by gaining complete control over taxation and by reorganizing the military and civil bureaucracy. She also took steps to make the serfs more productive, mainly by restricting the work they performed on their lords' lands and by abolishing the feudal dues they paid.

These efforts won the applause of philosophes, but the policies of Maria Theresa's that most clearly bore the stamp of the Enlightenment were her legal reforms. Inspired by Beccaria and Montesquieu, she established a commission to reform the entire corpus of Austrian law. A new code of criminal law was promulgated in 1769, and seven years later Maria Theresa issued an edict abolishing judicial torture. Joseph continued this program of legal reform by reorganizing the entire central court system and by eliminating capital punishment. He also revealed the influence of the Enlightenment by granting religious toleration, first to Protestants and eastern Orthodox

Torture

The torture of a defendant as depicted in the published version of the criminal code promulgated by Empress Maria Theresa in 1769. This form of torture, the *strappado,* used a pulley to hang the accused from the ceiling. Weights could be attached to the feet to make the pain more excruciating. The purpose of judicial torture was to extract a confession. Torture was eliminated from the law codes of most continental European countries during the Enlightenment.

Christians in 1781, and then to Jews in 1782. With respect to social issues, he completed his mother's work of abolishing serfdom altogether.

The efforts of Catherine II of Russia (r. 1762–1796) to implement the ideas of the Enlightenment followed a different course from those of Maria Theresa and Joseph. The daughter of a German prince, Catherine received an education grounded in a traditional curriculum of history, geography, and Lutheran theology. In 1745 she was married to a distant cousin, Peter, who was in line to inherit the Russian throne from his aunt, the childless Empress Elizabeth (r. 1741–1762). After arriving in St. Petersburg Catherine

not only acquired a knowledge of Russian language, literature, and religion but also read widely in western European sources, including the works of Enlightenment thinkers. She later corresponded with Voltaire and d'Alembert and employed the famous salon hostess Madame Geoffrin at her court. At Catherine's invitation Diderot visited St. Petersburg for six months.

Early in her reign, Catherine embarked on a program of reform similar to those of other enlightened absolutists. In 1767 she appointed a commission to codify Russian law on the basis of western European principles. Her recommendations to the commission included the abolition of torture and inhumane punishment and the establishment of religious toleration. She was eventually forced to disband the commission, which could not agree on a new code, but she later abolished torture and capital punishment on her own authority. Like Maria Theresa, she instituted a number of administrative and educational reforms, including the introduction of primary schooling in the provinces. Catherine, who became known as Catherine the Great, also tried unsuccessfully to provide for the education of girls as well as boys.

DOCUMENT

Catherine the Great's Constitution (1767)

Catherine gained a reputation for being an enlightened European monarch, but her acceptance of traditional Russian culture and the need to maintain her rule prevented her from fully embracing the ideals of the Enlightenment. She even admitted that it was much easier to subscribe to the ideals of the Enlightenment than actually to implement them. The strength of vested interests within Russian society accounted for the failure of the law commission of 1767. After putting down the Pugachev rebellion in 1774, she began to question the desirability of social reform, and the experience of the French Revolution in the 1790s (see Chapter 19) led her to disavow the ideals of the Enlightenment.

On the issue of serfdom, which most Enlightenment thinkers wished to see abolished, she would not yield. She preserved that social system in order to secure the loyalty of the Russian nobility, and she extended it to Ukraine and parts of Poland after Russia incorporated those regions into the empire. Catherine also catered to the imperialistic ambitions of the Russians, gaining vast territories in eastern Europe, East Asia, and Alaska. Thus she expanded the Russian Empire at the very time when the ideals of the Enlightenment were leading some philosophes to call for the dissolution of large imperial structures.

The Enlightenment and Revolution

The second mark that Enlightenment thought made on eighteenth-century politics was the inspiration it gave to movements for reform and revolution in western Europe and the Americas. The emphasis placed by Enlightenment

Catherine the Great

Catherine II of Russia on the day she succeeded in taking the throne from her husband, Peter III, at Peterhof in 1762. Catherine, who despised her husband, joined a conspiracy against him right after his accession to the throne. Catherine, like Peter, had a number of lovers, and her two children, including the future emperor Paul, were reputedly conceived by members of the nobility.

thinkers on individual liberty, natural rights, and political reform put pressure on both monarchs and the traditional nobility either to make concessions or to relinquish power altogether.

In Britain, for example, the movement for parliamentary reform and the expansion of the franchise°, as well as the first appeals for women's rights, were partially inspired by the Enlightenment. The radical democrat Thomas Paine, the feminist Mary Wollstonecraft, and the parliamentary reformer Joseph Priestley all based their demands for political reform on Enlightenment ideas of natural rights and civil liberty. It took considerable time, however, for these reforms to be realized. Only in 1832 did the British Parliament agree to a modest extension of the franchise, and women did not receive the vote until the early twentieth century. Nevertheless the movements to achieve these reforms were inspired by ideals born of the Enlightenment.

In France the influence of the Enlightenment on the momentous changes that took place during the French Revolution (1789–1799) has been a matter of debate among historians. The complexity of the revolution, which will be discussed in Chapter 19, and the diversity of Enlightenment thought make this a particularly difficult debate to resolve. Many of the revolutionaries of the 1790s were steeped in the ideas of the Enlightenment, but those ideas did not necessarily inspire the revolution itself. The French philosophes of the eighteenth century denounced the evils of the Old Regime and proposed many ideas about how governments should function, but they did not make serious efforts to introduce actual reforms, much less topple the government. Many philosophes, including Voltaire, had personal connections with aristocratic society, and very few shared the democratic and egalitarian ideas that came to the fore at the time of the Revolution. Some lesser journalists and literary hacks were more successful than the most renowned philosophes in fostering contempt for the Old Regime before the Revolution. Their merciless satires of the court and the clergy were more responsible than the grand treatises of the philosophes for stimulating a crisis of confidence in the French government and eroding the traditional respect for authority that made possible the violent overthrow of the Old Regime.

We can nevertheless establish some connections between the ideas and programs of the philosophes and the events that transpired in France during the 1790s. Some of the figures of the Enlightenment contributed to the new critical spirit evident after 1750 or provided some inspiration for the creation of a new political culture once the revolution began. The towering reputation of Voltaire during the French Revolution—and the anger of conservatives who exhumed and burned his bones after it had ended—suggest that his passionate criticisms of the Old Regime and his pleas for human freedom at the very least helped to set the stage for the revolutionary events of the 1790s. The same is true of the radical Rousseau, whose concept of the General Will served as the basis of a revolutionary ideology. Rousseau's democratic and republican ideas were used to justify some of the most important changes that took place during the revolution. Contemporaries glorified or attacked him, depending on their political philosophy, for having actually caused the revolution. One book published in 1791 was titled *On Jean-Jacques Rousseau Considered as One of the First Authors of the Revolution.*

Yet another application of enlightened ideas to politics took place in the Americas. The advocates of colonial independence from their mother countries, such as Thomas Jefferson in Virginia and Símon Bolívar in Venezuela and Colombia, were all deeply influenced by the Enlightenment concepts of natural law, natural rights, liberty, and popular sovereignty. The Declaration of Independence, which was written by Jefferson, betrayed its debt to the Enlightenment in its reference to the inalienable rights of all men and to the foundation of those rights in "the law of nature and Nature's God." Of course the American Revolution cannot be explained solely in terms of these Enlightenment ideas. The colonists found inspiration in many different sources, including English common law. But the American colonists did wish to create an entirely new world order, just as did many Enlightenment thinkers. They also adopted some of the most radical political ideas of the Enlightenment, which identified the people as the source of political power.

More generally, the Enlightenment fostered a critique of all efforts to establish overseas empires. The French priest Guillaume Thomas Raynal, mentioned in Chapter 17, wrote a condemnation of colonialism titled *The Philosophical and Political History of the Settlement and Commerce of Europeans in the Two Indies* (1770). Diderot and a number of lesser-known philosophes contributed to the final version of this massive work, which was published at Geneva in 1780. The book, which was the first to treat European imperialism in both hemispheres in the same context, praised the civilizing effects of commerce but condemned colonialism for the effects it had on those who emigrated. Cut off from their homeland, colonists brought with them only the prejudices of the civilizations they left behind and became hopelessly corrupt and degenerate. The English political theorist Richard Price developed a similar critique of all overseas empires, claiming that simply by their size and their diversity they could not promote the happiness of a community and the "fellow-feeling that takes place between persons in private life." According to Price, sprawling overseas empires by their very nature violated the standards of humanity.

Conclusion

The Enlightenment and Western Identity

The Enlightenment was a distinctly Western phenomenon. It arose in the countries of western Europe and then spread to central and eastern Europe (Germany, Austria, Poland, and Russia) and to the Americas. Most traditions that are identified today as "Western values" either had their origin or received their most cogent expression in the Enlightenment. In particular, the commitment to individual liberty, civil rights, toleration, and rational decision making all took shape during this period.

It would be misleading to make a simple equation between the ideas of the Enlightenment and the Western intellectual tradition. First, the ideals of the Enlightenment have never been fully accepted within Western societies. Ever since their original formulation, the ideas of the philosophes and publicists of the Enlightenment have been challenged by conservatives who argued that those ideas would lead to the destruction of religion and the social order. Those conservative criticisms, which are voiced even today, became intense at the time of the French Revolution and during the early years of the nineteenth century, and we shall discuss them in Chapters 19 and 21. Second, claims that the ideas promoted by the Enlightenment are exclusively Western can also be disputed. A celebration of reason and an insistence on religious tolerance, for example, can be found in the cultures of ancient India and China. The claim that the West is more rational than the East is itself a product of long-standing Western prejudice, an assertion that studies of other cultures undertaken by Enlightenment writers only served to strengthen.

Nevertheless, the ideas and traditions of the Enlightenment, despite the challenges they have endured, have become deeply ingrained in Western law and politics. They are less often found embedded in the political and legal traditions of non-Western lands, and when they are, such as in the twentieth-century socialist legal system of China, their presence is more often the result of Western influence than the legacy of native Eastern thought.

The acquisition of the values of the Enlightenment, even though they were never universally adopted, gave Europeans a clear sense of their own identity with respect to the rest of the world. Educated people who prided themselves on being enlightened knew that their scientific, rational worldview was not shared by Asians, Africans, indigenous Americans, or South Pacific islanders. It did not matter whether Enlightenment thinkers had a positive view of those other cultures, like Voltaire or Rousseau, or a negative one, like Montesquieu. What mattered was that they shared a similar mental outlook and a commitment to individual liberty, justice, and the improvement of civilization. For all of them religious faith was less important, both as an arbiter of morality and as a source of authority, than it was in these other cultures. The men and women of the Enlightenment all looked to the law as a reflection of natural law and as the guardian of civil liberty. Their writings helped their European and colonial public audiences think of themselves as even more distinct from non-Western people than they had in the past.

As these enlightened Western cultural values were spreading, the boundaries between East and West remained fluid and contested. The geographical region where this contest took place was what we now call eastern Europe. As we have seen in Chapter 15, the countries that occupied this buffer zone between East and West had long-standing cultural ties with Asia, especially the Middle East, but they also developed an attraction to Western culture beginning in the late seventeenth century. In Russia, this process of westernization began with Peter the Great, who integrated his country into European social, political, and diplomatic life. But it was carried further by Catherine the Great, who invited *philosophes* to her court and introduced Western reforms. This adoption of Western ideas made her appear to be a model Enlightened ruler and her country part of the Western world, but Russia's inclusion became and has remained a matter of debate. The very term "eastern Europe," which was coined during the Enlightenment, reflected the ambiguous relationship between this part of the world and the West. It provides a further illustration of the fact that the West was a cultural realm whose geographical boundaries have frequently changed.

Suggestions for Further Reading

For a comprehensive listing of suggested readings, please go to www.ablongman.com/levack2e/chapter 18

Alexander, John T. *Catherine the Great: Life and Legend.* 1989. A lively biography of the remarkable "enlightened despot."

Beckett, J. V. *The Aristocracy in England, 1660–1914.* 1986. A comprehensive study of this landholding and governing elite. Makes the important distinction between the aristocracy and the nobility.

Darnton, Robert. *The Forbidden Best-Sellers of Pre-Revolutionary France.* 1995. A study of the salacious, blasphemous, and subversive books that sold more copies than those of the philosophes in eighteenth-century France.

Dewald, Jonathan. *The European Nobility, 1500–1800.* 1996. A comprehensive study of this social class that emphasizes its adaptability.

Doyle, William. *The Old European Order, 1660–1800.* 2nd ed. 1999. The best general study of the period.

Houston, R. A. *Literacy in Early Modern Europe: Culture and Education.* 1991. The best survey of the subject for the entire period.

Lugee, Carolyn. *Le Paradis des Femmes: Women, Salons and Social Stratification in 17th-Century France.* 1976. A social study of the women of the salons.

Outram, Dorinda. *The Enlightenment.* 1995. A balanced assessment of the major historiographical debates regarding the Enlightenment.

Root, Hilton. *Peasants and King in Burgundy: Agrarian Foundations of French Absolutism.* 1979. A study of peasant communal institutions and their relationship with the crown as well as the nobility.

Williams, David, ed. *The Enlightenment.* 1999. An excellent collection of political writings with a long introduction.

Notes

1. Baron d'Holbach, *Good Sense* (1753).

2. David Hume, *Essays Moral, Political, and Literary* (1742), Essay X: "Of Superstition and Enthusiasm."

3. Cesare Beccaria, *An Essay on Crimes and Punishments* (1788), Chapter 47.

4. Voltaire, "Religion," in *The Philosophical Dictionary* (1802).

5. Jean-Jacques Rousseau, *Emile, or on Education* (1762).

The Age of the French Revolution, 1789–1815

19

On July 12, 1789, the French journalist Camille Desmoulins addressed an anxious crowd of Parisian citizens gathered outside the Palais-Royal, where public debate often took place. Playing upon fears that had been mounting during the past two months, Desmoulins claimed that the royal government of Louis XVI was preparing a massacre of Parisians. "To arms, to arms," Desmoulins cried out, as he roused the citizens to their own defense. That night Parisians responded to his call by invading arsenals in the city in anticipation of the violence they thought was about to descend upon them. The next day they continued to seize weapons and declared themselves members of the National Guard, a volunteer militia of propertied citizens.

On the morning of July 14, crowds of Parisians moved into a district of the city where royal troops were stationed in an ancient fortress known as the Bastille. The Parisians feared that the troops in the Bastille would take violent action against them, and they also wanted to capture the ammunition stored inside the building, which served as both an arsenal and a prison. Negotiations with the governor of the Bastille were interrupted when some of the militia, moving into the courtyard of the fortress, demanded the surrender of the troops. Shots were fired from both sides, and the exchange led to a full-scale assault upon the Bastille by the National Guard.

After three hours of fighting and the death of eighty-three people, the governor surrendered. He was then led by his captors, bearing the arms they had seized, to face charges before the officers of the city government. The crowd, however, crying for vengeance against their oppressors, attacked the soldiers and crushed some of them underfoot. The governor was stabbed hundreds of times, hacked to pieces, and decapitated. The chief magistrate of the city suffered the same fate for his reluctance to issue arms to its citizens. The crowd then placed the heads of the two men on pikes and paraded through the city.

Jacques-Louis David, *The Oath of the Tennis Court* The oath taken by the members of the Third Estate not to disband until France had a constitution led to the creation of the National Assembly and the legislation that destroyed royal absolutism and feudalism.

The storming of the Bastille was the first of many violent episodes that occurred during the sequence of events called the French Revolution. That revolution brought about some of the most fundamental changes in European political life since the end of Roman rule. It heralded the destruction of the Old Regime, the eighteenth-century political order that had been dominated by an absolute monarch and a privileged nobility and clergy. It led to the submission of the Catholic Church to state control. A more radical phase of the revolution, beginning in 1792, resulted in the destruction of the French monarchy and the declaration of a republic. It also led to a period of state-sponsored terrorism in 1793 and 1794, during which one group of revolutionaries engaged in a brutal campaign to eliminate their real and imagined enemies.

The excesses of the revolution led to a conservative reaction. Between 1795 and 1799 a moderate republican government, known as the Directory, modified the egalitarianism of the revolution by limiting the right to vote to men of property. Between 1799 and 1814 the reaction continued under the direction of Napoleon Bonaparte, a military officer who dominated the Consulate, a new political structure established in 1799, and then proclaimed himself emperor in 1804. Although Napoleon declared his loyalty to many of the principles of the revolution, his authoritarian rule undermined or reversed many of its achievements. In 1815 Napoleon fell from power and the monarchy was restored, marking the end of the revolutionary period. The ideas of the revolution, however, especially its commitment to democratic republicanism and its concept of the nation, continued to dominate politics in the West for the next hundred years. The French Revolution permanently changed the political culture of the West.

This chapter will address the question of how the encounters between different political and social groups in France at the end of the eighteenth century brought about some of the most important and far-reaching changes in the history of the West. In pursuing this broad objective, the individual chapter sections will address the following questions:

The Storming of the Bastille, July 14, 1789
The Bastille was attacked not because it was a symbol of the Old Regime, but because it contained weapons that the Parisian citizens needed to protect themselves from royalist troops.

- Why did the Old Regime in France collapse in 1789, and what revolutionary changes took place in French government and society during the next two years?
- How did a second, more radical revolution, which began with the establishment of the Republic in 1792, lead to the creation of a regime that used the power of the state to institute the Reign of Terror?
- In what ways did the political events of the revolution change French cultural institutions and create a new political culture?
- How did the authoritarian rule of Napoleon Bonaparte from 1799 to 1814 confirm or betray the achievements of the French Revolution, and what impact did his military conquests have on Europe and the world?

■ What did the French Revolution ultimately achieve and in what ways did it change the course of European and Western history?

The First French Revolution, 1789–1791

■ Why did the Old Regime in France collapse in 1789, and what revolutionary changes took place in French government and society during the next two years?

One of the main characteristics of political revolutions is that they involve a fundamental change in the political *system,* not simply in the personnel of government. On the basis of this criterion the French Revolution consisted of two distinct revolutions. The first revolution, which began in 1789, resulted in a destruction of royal absolutism and the drafting of a constitution. The second and more radical revolution began in 1792 with the abolition of the monarchy and the formation of the French Republic.

Like all revolutions, the first French revolution had deep-seated causes. As we discussed in Chapter 18, a constant barrage of satirical literature directed at the royal family and the court lowered the prestige of the government and thus weakened its authority. The publication of thousands of pamphlets advocating reform, including many written by philosophes of the Enlightenment, fostered a critical attitude toward the French government and led to demands for political and economic change. Conflicts between the nobility and the crown over constitutional issues, a source of tension throughout the age of absolutism, led to charges that the government was acting despotically. Encounters between the landowning nobility and the peasantry, which increased in the last half of the eighteenth century, also contributed to the disaffection with the Old Regime and played a major role in stimulating demands for a restriction of the privileges enjoyed by the nobility. Ongoing food shortages in the cities created a militant citizenry ready to take action against authorities they considered responsible for the high price of bread.

DOCUMENT

De Stael on the Ancien Regime (1789)

The immediate cause of the revolution was a major economic crisis that bankrupted the monarchy and deprived it of its authority. This crisis led to a revolt of the nobles against the crown and brought down the entire system of royal absolutism. Only after this collapse of royal government did various groups that had had long-standing grievances against the regime take the initiative and establish a new political system. These groups never actually planned the revolution; they simply filled a void created by the absence of effective governmental power.

The Beginning of the Revolution

The financial crisis that brought about the collapse of the French government peaked in the late 1780s. The government of Louis XVI (r. 1774–1792) had inherited considerable debts from that of his grandfather, Louis XV (r. 1715–1774) as a result of protracted periods of warfare with Great Britain. The opening of a new phase of this warfare in 1778, when France intervened in the American War of Independence on the side of the United States, pushed the government further into debt and put a strain on the entire French economy. Attempts to solve the crisis by implementing financial reforms made the situation only worse. In 1787 the government had a revenue of 475 million livres and expenses of just under 600 million livres. More than half of the revenue went to pay interest on the accumulated debt. As the crisis deepened, protests from the ranks of the nobility against royal policy became more vocal.

In 1787 the king made efforts to win the support of the nobility by convening an Assembly of Notables, a hand-picked group of 144 nominees, the great majority of whom were noblemen. The purpose of the meeting was to gain approval for a new system of taxation that would include a direct tax on all landowners. These proposals encountered formidable opposition from the members of the assembly, and the meeting was adjourned. Some of the nobles in the assembly had been willing to pay the taxes, but only if the king would convoke the Estates General, a national legislative body that had not met since 1614. Convening the Estates General, they argued, would provide them with guarantees against royal despotism. Louis resisted these pressures because he did not want to give up the right to make law by his own authority.

The king then tried to gain approval of new taxes from the regional parlements, the provincial law courts whose powers included the registration of royal edicts. There too the crown met resistance. The Parlement of Paris, which was the most important of all the parlements, refused to comply with the king's request. The other parlements followed suit, claiming that only the Estates General had the power to approve new taxes. Constitutional tension was heightened when the king demanded the registration of edicts for new loans without the approval of the parlements, a step that even he acknowledged was illegal. He then suspended the parlements, thereby deepening the constitutional crisis.

The deterioration of the government's financial condition finally forced the king to yield to the demands of the nobles and the increasingly hostile popular press. When tax returns dried up as the result of an agricultural crisis in the summer months of 1788, the government could no longer pay its creditors. In a desperate effort to save his regime, Louis announced that he would convene the Estates General. By this time there was little hope for Louis. His absolutist government had completely collapsed.

CHRONOLOGY

The First French Revolution, 1789–1791

1787

February 22	Convening of the Assembly of Notables

1788

August 8	Announcement of the meeting of the Estates General

1789

May 5	The Estates General opens at Versailles
June 17	The Third Estate adopts the title of the National Assembly
June 20	Oath of the Tennis Court
July 11	The king dismisses his finance minister, Jacques Necker
July 14	The storming of the Bastille
Late July	The Great Fear in rural areas
August 4	Abolition of feudalism and privileges
August 26	*Declaration of the Rights of Man and Citizen*
October 5	March to Versailles; Louis XVI and National Assembly move to Paris
November 2	Church property is nationalized

1790

July 12	Civil Constitution of the Clergy
July 14	Feast of the Federation
November 27	Decree requiring oath of loyalty from the clergy

1791

June 20	Royal family flees to Varennes, is apprehended by the National Guard
October 1	Newly elected Legislative Assembly opens

The meeting of the Estates General was set for May 1789, and during the months leading up to its opening, public debates arose over how the delegates should vote. The Estates General consisted of representatives of the three orders or social groups, known as estates, that made up French society: the clergy, the nobility, and the Third Estate. The Third Estate technically contained all the commoners in the kingdom (about 96 percent of the population), ranging from the wealthiest merchant to the poorest peasant. The elected representatives of the Third Estate, whose num-

bers had doubled by a recent order of the king, were propertied nonnoble elements of lay society, including many lawyers and military officers.

Before the meeting a dispute arose among the representatives whether the three groups would vote by estate, in which case the first two estates would dominate the assembly, or by head, in which case the Third Estate would have numerical parity. Each side claimed that it was the best representative of the "nation," a term meaning the entire body of French people. The nobles maintained that the nation was represented by the nobility and clergy from all the provinces, especially the members of the provincial parlements, who had been critical of royal power during the past few decades. The members of the Third Estate advanced the claim that *they* represented the nation. The cleric Emmanuel-Joseph Sieyès (1748–1836), who joined the Third Estate during this dispute, claimed that it "has within itself all that is necessary to constitute a nation. . . . Nothing can go on without it, and everything would go on far better without the others. . . . This privileged class (nobility and clergy) is assuredly foreign to the nation by its do-nothing uselessness."[1]

The question of voting within the Estates General was not resolved when that body met at Versailles on May 5, 1789. After the king indicated that he would side with the clergy and nobility, the Third Estate took the dramatic step of declaring itself a National Assembly and asking members of the other estates to vote with them on the basis of "one man, one vote." Many members of the lower clergy and a few noblemen accepted this invitation. In a conciliatory response to this challenge, the king planned to summon all three estates to a special "royal session" to announce some concessions. In preparation for this meeting, however, he locked the Third Estate out of its meeting hall without explanation. The outraged members of the Third Estate went to a nearby indoor tennis court and took a solemn oath that they would not disband until the country had been given a constitution. One week later, after more clerics and noblemen had joined the ranks of the Third Estate, the king ordered the nobility and the clergy to join the National Assembly.

As this political crisis was reaching a climax, a major social crisis fueled by the high price of bread was causing a breakdown of public order. For many years French agriculture had had difficulty meeting the demands of an expanding population. These problems, aggravated in the 1780s by a succession of poor harvests, climaxed in a widespread harvest failure in 1788. As the price of bread soared, demand for manufactured goods shrank, thus causing widespread unemployment among artisans. An increasing number of bread riots, peasant revolts, and urban strikes contributed to a sense of panic at the very time that the government's financial crisis deepened. In Paris the situation reached a critical point in June 1789.

At this point the king, a man with little political sense, made two ill-advised decisions. The first was to send 17,000 royal troops to Paris to restore order. The arrival of the troops gave the impression that the government was planning an attack on the people of the city. The second decision was the dismissal of the king's popular finance minister, Jacques Necker, who had favored the meeting of the Estates General and demonstrated real concern for the welfare of the populace. His dismissal sent a signal that the king was contemplating a move against the National Assembly. It was in this atmosphere of public paranoia that Parisians formed the National Guard and stormed the Bastille.

The fall of the Bastille unnerved the king. When he asked one of his aides, "Is it a revolt?" the aide replied, "No, sire, it is a revolution." The revolution had just begun. It moved into high gear two weeks later when the National Assembly responded to the outbreak of social unrest in the provinces. The scarcity of grain in the countryside gave rise to false rumors that the nobles were engaged in a plot to destroy crops and starve the people into submission. Peasants armed themselves and prepared to fight off the hired agents of the nobility. Some of these peasants burned the mansions of noblemen, together with the deeds that gave the nobles title to their lands and the right to collect dues from their tenants. A widespread panic, known as the "Great Fear," gripped many parts of the country. Townspeople and peasants amassed in large numbers to defend themselves and save the harvest. In response to this panic, which reached its peak in the last two weeks of July, the National Assembly began to pass legislation that destroyed the Old Regime and created a new political order.

The Creation of a New Political Society

Between August 1789 and September 1790 the National Assembly took three revolutionary steps. The first was the elimination of noble and clerical privilege. In August the assembly abolished the feudal dues that peasants paid their lords, the private legal jurisdictions of noblemen, the collection of tithes by the clergy, and the exclusive rights of noblemen to hunt game on their lands. The privileges of provinces and local towns met the same fate, and ten months later the nobility lost their titles. Instead of a society divided into various corporate groups, each with its own privileges, France would now have only citizens, all of them equal at law. Social distinctions would be based on merit rather than birth. There were no longer any intermediary powers between the king and the individual subject.

The second step, taken on August 26, was the promulgation of the *Declaration of the Rights of Man and Citizen.* This document reveals the main influence of the Enlightenment on the revolution. It declared that all men, not just Frenchmen, had a natural right to liberty, property, equality before the law, freedom from oppression, and religious toleration. The statement that the "law is the expression of the general will" reflects the influence of Rousseau's *The Social Contract* (1762), while the statement that every citizen has the right to participate in the formation of that law either personally or through a representative embodies the basic principle of democracy. The *Declaration* differed from the English Bill of Rights of 1689 by grounding the rights it proclaimed in natural law rather than in the law of one country. The provisions of the French document therefore serve as statements of broad principle rather than as confirmations of specific rights that the government had allegedly been violating.

The third step in this revolutionary program was a complete reorganization of the Church. In order to solve the problem of the national debt, the National Assembly placed land owned by the Church (about 10 percent of all French territory) at the service of the nation. The Civil Constitution of the Clergy of July 1790 in effect made the Church a department of the state, with the government paying the clergy directly. In order to retain their positions, the clergy were required to take an oath of loyalty to the nation. At the same time the Church was reorganized into eighty-three dioceses, one for each of the departments or administrative units into which the country was also now divided. The bishops of these dioceses were to be elected by laymen. The parishes, which were the basic units of ecclesiastical administration, would become uniform in size, each administering to some 6,000 parishioners.

In 1791 a newly elected Legislative Assembly—replacing the National Assembly—confirmed and extended many of these changes. A constitution, put into effect in October, formalized the end of royal absolutism. The king became a constitutional monarch, retaining only the power to suspend legislation, direct foreign policy, and command the armed forces. The constitution did not, however, give all men the right to vote. Only "active citizens," who paid the equivalent of three days' wages in direct taxes, had the right to vote for electors, who in turn chose representatives to the legislature.

The new constitution formally abolished hereditary legal privileges, thus providing equality of all citizens before the law. Subsequent legislation granted Jews and Protestants full civil rights and toleration. A law eliminating primogeniture (inheritance of the entire estate by the eldest son) gave all heirs equal rights to inherited property.

DOCUMENT

Declaration of the Rights of Man and Citizen (1789)

The passage of the Declaration of the Rights of Man and Citizen *by the National Assembly on August 26, 1789, is one of the earliest and most enduring acts of the French Revolution. A document of great simplicity and power, it was hammered out during many weeks of debate. Its concern with the natural rights of all people and equality before the law reflected the ideas of the Enlightenment.*

1. Men are born free and remain free and equal in rights. Social distinctions may be founded only on the common good.

2. The aim of all political association is the preservation of the natural and imprescriptible rights of man. These rights are liberty, property, security and resistance to oppression.

3. The principle of all authority rests essentially in the nation. No body nor individual may exercise any authority which does not emanate expressly from the nation.

4. Liberty consists in the freedom to do whatever does not harm another; hence the exercise of the natural rights of each man has no limits except those which assure to the other members of society the enjoyment of the same rights. These limits can only be determined by law. . . .

6. Law is the expression of the general will. Every citizen has the right to participate personally or through his representative in its formation. It must be the same for all, whether it protects or punishes. All citizens, being equal in the eyes of the law, are equally eligible to all dignities and to all public positions and occupations, according to their abilities, and without distinction except that of their virtues and talents.

7. No man may be indicted, arrested, or imprisoned except in cases determined by the law and according to the forms prescribed by law. . . .

10. No one should be disturbed for his opinions, even in religion, provided that their manifestation does not trouble public order as established by law.

11. The free communication of thoughts and opinions is one of the most precious of the rights of man. Every citizen may therefore speak, write, and print freely, but shall be responsible for any abuse of this freedom in the cases set by the law. . . .

17. Property being an inviolable and sacred right, no one may be deprived of it except when public necessity, determined by law, obviously requires it, and then on the condition that the owner shall have been previously and equitably compensated.

Source: From P.-J.-B. Buchez and P.-C. Roux, *Histoire parlementaire de la Révolution française.* (Paris: Paulin, 1834).

The establishment of marriage as a civil contract and the right to end a marriage in divorce supported the idea of the husband and wife as freely contracting individuals. The largely symbolic abolition of slavery in France was consistent with the proclamation of equality of all men, but the failure to extend that emancipation to French colonies suggests that there were limits to the concept of liberty proclaimed by the assembly.

This body of legislation amounted to nothing less than a revolution. The Old Regime had been destroyed and a new one had taken its place. Although the form of government remained a monarchy, the powers of that monarchy were drastically curtailed. Unlike the English revolutions of the 1640s and 1688, this revolution did not disguise the extent of the changes that had transpired by using the language of conservatism, claiming that the revolution had recovered lost freedoms. It did not appeal to the French past at all. It promoted a new view of French society as a nation composed of equal citizens possessing natural rights, in place of the older concept of a society consisting of different corporate groups, each with its own privileges. Contemporaries recognized the significance of these changes. The Portuguese ambassador to France, who witnessed the events of 1789 firsthand, reported back to his government, "In all the world's annals there is no mention of a revolution like this."

Responses to the First French Revolution

During the early years of the revolution, events in Paris and Versailles dominated the political scene. The revolution was not confined, however, to the metropolis. In the provinces groups of ordinary townspeople and peasants, frightened that the members of the nobility might be taking counteraction against them, took the law into their own hands and brought about a new revolutionary political and social order. In many places the local rulers who had exercised political power in towns and villages were overthrown and replaced by supporters of the new regime. At the same time there was considerable opposition to the revolutionary government. In many parts of the country the clergy's refusal to take the oath of loyalty to the nation led to violent clashes with the provincial authorities. In the south nobles began to organize resistance to the new regime, while militant Catholics attacked Protestants, who had been granted toleration and who generally supported the revolution.

The revolutionary events of 1789–1791 quickly gained the attention of countries outside France. In England the nonconformist Protestant minister Richard Price urged members of the British Parliament to follow the example of their French neighbors and abolish the laws that restricted

DOCUMENT

Edmund Burke Deplores the Events of the French Revolution

The first French Revolution met with both praise and criticism abroad. The strongest attack came from Edmund Burke, an Irish-born lawyer who sat in the British Parliament. Burke, who is recognized as the father of modern conservatism, attacked the leaders of the revolution for destroying religion and the social order in the interests of an abstract philosophy, subverting the law, and introducing a new tyranny.

. . . France has bought undisguised calamities at a higher price than any nation has purchased the most unequivocal blessings. France has bought poverty by crime. France has not sacrificed her virtue to her interest; but she has abandoned her interest that she might prostitute her virtue. All other nations have begun the fabric of a new government, or the reformation of an old, by establishing originally, or by enforcing with greater exactness, some rites or other of religion. All other people have laid the foundation of civil freedom in severer manners and a system of a more austere and masculine morality. France, when she let loose the reins of regal authority, doubled the license of a ferocious dissoluteness in manners, and of an insolent religion in opinions and practices; and has extended through all ranks of life, as if she were communicating some privilege or laying open some secluded benefit, all the unhappy corruptions that usually were the disease of wealth and power. This is one of the new principles of equality in France.

France, by the perfidy of her leaders, has utterly disgraced the tone of lenient council in the cabinets of princes, and disarmed it of its most potent topics. She has sanctified the dark, suspicious maxims of tyrannous distrust, and taught kings to tremble at . . . the delusive plausibilities of moral politicians. Sovereigns will consider those who advise them to place an unlimited confidence in their people as subverterrs of their thrones—as traitors who aim at their destruction, by leading their easy good—nature, under specious pretenses, to admit combinations of bold and faithless men into a participation of their power. . . . They have seen the French rebel against a mild and lawful monarch, with more fury, outrage, and insult than ever any people has been known to rise against the most illegal usurper or the most sanguinary tyrant. . . .

They have found their punishment in their success. Laws overturned; tribunals subverted; industry without vigour; commerce expiring; the revenue unpaid, yet the people impoverished; a church pillaged, and a state not relieved; civil and military anarchy made the constitution of the kingdom; everything human and divine sacrificed to the idol of public credit, and national bankruptcy the consequence. . . .

Were all these dreadful things necessary? Were they the inevitable results of the desperate struggle of determined patriots, compelled to wade through blood and tumult to the quiet shore of a tranquil and prosperous liberty? No! Nothing like it. The fresh ruins of France, which shock our feelings wherever we can turn our eyes, are not the devastation of civil war: they are the sad, but instructive monuments of rash and ignorant counsel in a time of profound peace. . . .

Source: Edmund Burke, Reflections on the Revolution in France *(1790).*

hunting on aristocratic lands. Prussian reformers took heart that the events of the revolution would portend the destruction of absolutism in their country and in other European lands. A Prussian official who had studied with the philosopher Immanuel Kant called the revolution "the first practical triumph of philosophy . . . the hope and consolation for so many of those ancient ills under which mankind has suffered."

Not all foreign assessments of the revolution were positive. In November 1790 the British politician Edmund Burke published *Reflections on the Revolution in France,* in which he expressed horror at the way in which abstract philosophy had destroyed the traditional social order in France. Pope Pius VI condemned the *Declaration of the Rights of Man and Citizen* and then, outraged at the attack upon the Roman Catholic Church, issued a sweeping condemnation of the Civil Constitution of the Clergy. The absolute monarchs of western Europe, sensing rightly that their regimes were in danger of a contagious revolutionary ideology, not only planned an invasion of France to restore the old order but took action against dissent in their own territories. When Polish legislators wrote a new constitution in 1791, modeled on that of France, Catherine the Great of Russia, who controlled a portion of Poland at the time, claimed that it was the product of French radicalism. She shut down the presses, revived censorship, turned against the philosophes whom she had admired, and banned the works of Voltaire.

The French Republic, 1792–1799

■ How did a second, more radical revolution, which began with the establishment of the Republic in 1792, lead to the creation of a regime that used the power of the state to institute the Reign of Terror?

Beginning in 1792 France experienced a second revolution that was much more radical than the first. During this revolution France was transformed from a constitutional monarchy into a republic. The state claimed far greater power than it possessed under the constitutional monarchy established in 1791, and it used that power to bring about a radical reform of French society.

The Establishment of the Republic, 1792

During the first two years of the revolution it appeared that the building of a new French nation would take place within the framework of a constitutional monarchy. Absolutism had suffered an irreversible defeat, but there was little sentiment among the members of the Legislative Assembly, much less among the general population, in favor of abolishing the institution of monarchy. The only committed republicans—those supporting the establishment of a republic—in the Legislative Assembly belonged to a party known as the Jacobins°, who found support in political clubs in Paris and in other parts of the country. By the late summer of 1792 this group of radicals, drawing upon the support of militant Parisian citizens known as *sans-culottes* (literally, those without breeches, the pants worn by noblemen), succeeded in bringing about the second, more radical revolution.

King Louis himself was in part responsible for this destruction of the monarchy. The success of constitutional monarchy depended on the king's willingness to play the new role assigned to him as a constitutional figurehead. In October 1789 Louis had agreed, under considerable pressure, to move his residence from Versailles to Paris, where the National Assembly had also relocated. The pressure came mainly from women, who formed the large majority of 10,000 demonstrators who marched from Paris to Versailles demanding a reduction in the price of bread. The king yielded to their demands and came to Paris. As he entered the city, accompanied by soldiers, monks, and women carrying guns and pikes, he reluctantly agreed to wear the tricolor cockade (a badge) to symbolize his acceptance of the revolution. Louis, however, could not disguise his opposition to the revolution, especially to the ecclesiastical settlement. This opposition led many people to suspect that he was encouraging the powers of Europe to invade France to restore the Old Regime.

Louis XVI had few personal resources upon which he might draw to win the confidence of his subjects. He was not as intelligent as his grandfather, Louis XV, nor did he have the skills necessary to dispel his subjects' growing distrust of him. Neither Louis nor his Austrian wife, Marie Antoinette, commanded much respect among the people. For many years the royal couple had been the object of relentless, sometimes pornographic satire. He had been lampooned for his rumored sexual inadequacies and she for a series of alleged infidelities with the king's brother and a succession of female partners. Whatever confidence Parisian citizens might have retained in the royal couple evaporated in June 1791, when the king and queen attempted to flee the country. The National Guard apprehended them at Varennes, close to the eastern French border, and forced them to return to Paris, where they were kept under guard at the palace of the Tuileries. Even that development, however, failed to destroy the monarchy,

Sans-Culottes

Male and female dress of the *sans-culottes,* the armed Parisian radicals who supported the Republic. The men did not wear the breeches (*culottes*) that were in style among the members of the French nobility.

which had been preserved in the constitution implemented in October.

The development that actually precipitated the downfall of the monarchy and led to the establishment of a republic was the decision to go to war. Until the summer of 1791 European powers had been involved in various conflicts and had resisted pleas from French émigrés to support a counterrevolutionary offensive against the new French regime. After the flight to Varennes and the capture of the royal family, however, Frederick William II of Prussia (r. 1786–1797) and Emperor Leopold II of Austria (r. 1790–1792), the brother of Marie Antoinette, signed an alliance and called upon the other monarchs of Europe "to restore to the King of France complete liberty and to consolidate the bases of monarchical government." No action would be taken, however, unless all European sovereigns agreed to cooperate.

The actual declaration of war came not from the monarchs of Europe but from the French Legislative Assembly. A small group of republicans, headed by the eloquent orator Jacques-Pierre Brissot (1754–1793), convinced the assembly that an international conspiracy against the revolution would end in an invasion of their country. Brissot and his supporters also believed that if France could be lured into a foreign war, the king and queen would be revealed as traitors and the monarchy would be destroyed. Exploiting xenophobic as well as revolutionary sentiment, and claiming that the strength of a citizen army would win a quick and decisive victory, Brissot and his allies won the support of the entire assembly. They also appealed to the international goals of the revolution, claiming that the French army would inspire revolution against "the tyrants of Europe" everywhere they went.

The Legislative Assembly declared war on Austria in April 1792. Instead of a glorious victory, however, the war resulted in a series of disastrous defeats at the hands of Austrians and their Prussian allies in the Netherlands. This military failure contributed to a mood of paranoia in France, especially in Paris. Fears arose that invading armies, in alliance with nobles, would undermine the revolution. In May members of the assembly learned that the Austrian minister, in cooperation with a group of the king's advisers, was plotting the destruction of the assembly itself. In July the assembly officially proclaimed the nation to be in danger, calling for all citizens to rally against the enemies of liberty at home and abroad. Women petitioned for the right to bear arms. When the Austrians and Prussians threatened to

Tricolor Cockade
Louis XVI wearing the red liberty bonnet with the tricolor cockade on October 20, 1792. Refusing to be intimidated by a crowd of 20,000 people outside the royal palace, he donned the cap and proclaimed his loyalty to the constitution.

torch the entire city of Paris and slaughter its population if anyone laid a hand on the royal family, citizens in Paris immediately demanded that the king be deposed.

On August 10 a radical republican committee overthrew the Paris commune, the city government that had been installed in 1789, and set up a new, revolutionary commune. A force of about 20,000 men, including volunteer troops from various parts of the kingdom, invaded the Tuileries, which was defended by about 900 Swiss guards. When the members of the royal bodyguard fled, they were pursued by members of the Paris crowds, who stripped them of their red uniforms and hacked 600 of them to death with knives, pikes, and hatchets. The attack on the Tuileries forced the king to take refuge in the nearby Legislative Assembly. The assembly promptly suspended the monarchy and turned the royal family over to the commune, which imprisoned them in the Temple, a medieval fortress in the northeastern part of the city. The assembly then ordered its own dissolution and called for the election of a new legislative body that would draft a new constitution.

The fall of the monarchy did nothing to allay the siege mentality of the city, especially after further Prussian victories in early September escalated fears of a Prussian invasion. Individuals suspected of plotting against the regime were imprisoned, and when it was rumored that they would escape and support the Prussian enemy, angry crowds pulled 1,200 prisoners (most of whom were being held for nonpolitical crimes) from their cells and killed them. The feared foreign invasion that had inspired this "September Massacre" never did materialize. On September 20, 1792, a surprisingly well-disciplined and well-trained army of French citizens, inspired by dedication to France and the revolution, repulsed the armies of Austria and Prussia at Valmy. This victory saved the revolution. The German poet Johann Wolfgang von Goethe (1749–1832) claimed that the battle marked the beginning of "a new epoch in the history of the world." Delegates to a new National Convention, elected by universal male suffrage°, had already arrived in

The Attack on the Palace of the Tuileries

On the night of August 10, 1792, Parisian crowds and volunteer soldiers attacked the royal palace in Paris. The puffs of smoke in the building are coming from the Swiss guards, who were entrusted with the defense of the royal family and the palace. The royal family escaped and took refuge in the Legislative Assembly, but 600 of the Swiss guards were killed. Those that retreated were hunted down in the streets of Paris and stripped of their uniforms, and their heads were placed on the ends of pikes.

Paris to write a new constitution. On September 22 the convention declared that the monarchy was formally abolished and that France was a republic. France had now experienced a second revolution, more radical than the first, but dedicated to the same principles of liberty, equality, and fraternity.

The Jacobins and the Revolution

Before the Republic was established, different political factions had begun to vie for power, both in the Legislative Assembly and in the country at large. The first major division to emerge was between the Feuillants, who supported a constitutional monarchy, and the Jacobins, many of whom favored the creation of a democratic republic. By the time the Republic had been declared, the Jacobins had become the major political party. Soon, however, factional divisions began to develop within Jacobin ranks. The main split occurred between the followers of Brissot, known as Girondins°, and the radicals known as Montagnards°, or "the Mountain." The latter acquired their name because they occupied the benches on the side of the convention hall, where the floor sloped upward. The Girondins occupied the lower side of the hall, while the uncommitted deputies, known as "the Plain," occupied the middle. Both the Mountain and the Girondins claimed to be advancing the goals of the revolution, but they differed widely on which tactics to pursue. The Mountain took the position that as long as the state was endangered by internal and external enemies, the government needed to centralize authority in the capital. The Mountain thought of themselves as the representatives of the common people, especially the *sans-culottes* in Paris. Many of their leaders, including

Georges-Jacques Danton (1759–1794), Jean-Paul Marat (1743–1793), and Maximilien Robespierre (1758–1794), were in fact Parisians. Their mission was to make the revolution even more egalitarian and to establish a republic characterized by civic pride and patriotism, which they referred to as the Republic of Virtue.

The Girondins, known as such because many of their leaders came from the southwestern department of Gironde, took a more conservative position than the Mountain on these issues. Favoring the economic freedom and local control desired by merchants and manufacturers, they were reluctant to support further centralization of state power. They believed that the revolution had advanced far enough and should not become more radical. They were also afraid that the egalitarianism of the revolution, if unchecked, would lead to a leveling of French society and result in social anarchy.

The conflict between the Girondins and the Mountain became apparent in the debate over what to do with the deposed king. Louis had been suspected of conspiring with the enemies of the revolution, and the discovery of his correspondence with the Austrian government led to his trial for treason against the nation. The Girondins had originally expressed reluctance to bring him to trial, preferring to keep him in prison. Once the trial began, they joined the entire National Convention in voting to convict him, but they opposed his execution. This stance led the Mountain to accuse the Girondins of being secret collaborators with the monarchy. By a narrow vote the convention decided to put the king to death, and on January 21, 1793, Louis was executed at the Place de la Révolution.

The instrument of death was the guillotine, an efficient and merciful but nonetheless terrifying decapitation machine first pressed into service in April 1792. It took its name from Dr. Joseph-Ignace Guillotin, who had the original idea for such a device, although he did not invent it. The guillotine was inspired by the conviction that all criminals, not just those of noble blood, should be executed in a swift, painless manner. The new device was to be put to extensive use during the next eighteen months, and many Girondins fell victim to it.

The split between the Mountain and the Girondins became more pronounced as the republican regime encountered increasing opposition from foreign and domestic enemies. Early in 1793 Great Britain and the Dutch Republic allied with Prussia and Austria to form the First Coalition against France, and within a month Spain and the kingdoms of Sardinia and Naples joined them. The armies of these allied powers defeated French forces in the Austrian Netherlands in March of that year, and once again an invasion seemed imminent. At the same time internal rebellions against the revolutionary regime took place in various outlying provinces, especially in the district of the Vendée in western France. These uprisings were led by noblemen and clerics, but they also had popular support, especially from tenant farmers who resented the increased taxation imposed by the new revolutionary government.

In the minds of Robespierre and his colleagues, the Girondins were linked to these provincial rebels, whom they labeled as federalists° because they opposed the centralization of the French state and thus threatened the unity of the nation. In June twenty-nine Girondins were expelled from the convention for supporting local officials accused of hoarding grain. This purge made it apparent that any political opponent of the Mountain, even those with solid republican credentials, could now be identified as an enemy of the revolution.

CHRONOLOGY

The French Republic and the Terror, 1792–1794

1792

April 20	Declaration of war against Austria
August 10	Attack on the Tuileries; monarchy is suspended
September 2–6	September Massacre of prisoners in Paris
September 20	French victory at the Battle of Valmy
September 21	National Convention meets
September 22	Abolition of the monarchy and establishment of the Republic

1793

January 21	Execution of Louis XVI
February 1	Declaration of war against Great Britain and the Dutch Republic
March 11	Beginning of rebellion in the Vendée
June 2	Purge of Girondins from the Convention
June 24	Ratification of a republican constitution
July 27	Robespierre elected to the Committee of Public Safety
August 23	The Convention decrees the *levée en masse*
October 5	Adoption of the revolutionary calendar
October 16	Execution of Marie Antoinette

1794

July 28	Tenth of *Thermidor;* execution of Robespierre
November 12	Jacobin clubs are closed

The Trial of Louis XVI

After the abolition of the monarchy and the proclamation of the French Republic in September 1792, the National Convention considered the fate of the deposed king. There was a broad consensus that Louis was guilty of treason against the nation and that he should answer for his crimes, but how he should do so was a matter of heated debate. The convention was divided between the Girondins and the Mountain. Of the two, the Girondins were more inclined to follow legal forms, whereas those of the Mountain considered themselves to be acting as a revolutionary tribunal that should adhere to standards of justice not specifically included in the law of the land. The convention thus became a forum where Louis's accusers expressed competing notions of revolutionary justice.

The most divisive and revealing issue was whether there should be a trial at all. The Mountain originally took the position that because the people had already judged the king on August 10, when the monarchy had fallen and the king taken prisoner, there was no need for a second judgment. They should proceed immediately to carrying out the death sentence. Robespierre argued that to have a trial would be counterrevolutionary, for it would allow the revolution itself to be brought before the court to be judged. A centrist majority, however, decided that the king had to be charged with specific offenses in a court of law and found guilty by due process before being sentenced.

A second issue, closely related to the first, was the technical legal question of whether the king could be subject to legal action. Even if the legislative branch of the government was considered the equal of the king in a constitutional monarchy, it did not possess authority over him. A further argu-

ment was that the king could not be tried for actions for which he had already suffered abdication. This claim was challenged on the most basic principle of the revolution—that the nation was higher than the king and his crimes were committed against that nation, which is the people. The king, moreover, was no longer king but was now a citizen and therefore subject to the law in the same way as anyone else.

The third issue was Louis's culpability for the specific charges in the indictment. These crimes included refusing to call the Estates General, sending an army to march against the citizens of Paris, and conducting secret negotiations with France's enemies. The journalist and deputy Jean-Paul Marat added that "he robbed the citizens of their gold as a subsidy for their foes" and "caused his hirelings to hoard, to create famine, to dry up the sources of abundance that the people might die from misery and hunger."

Nonetheless the king, who appeared personally to hear the indictment and then to respond to the charges on December 26, presented a plausible defense. He based it on the laws in force at the various times he was supposed to have committed his crimes. Thus he defended his sending of troops to Paris on the grounds that in June and July 1789 he could order troops wherever he wanted. In the same vein he argued that he had used force solely in response to illegal intimidation. These legalisms, however, only made the members of the convention more contemptuous of the king. His defense failed to persuade a single convention deputy. He was convicted of treason by a vote of 693–0.

This unanimous conviction of the king did not end the factional debates over the king's fate. Knowing that there was extensive

support for the king in various parts of the country, the Girondins asked that the verdict be appealed to the people. Their argument was that the convention, dominated by the Mountain and supported by militants in Paris, had usurped the sovereignty of the people. Pierre-Victurnien Vergniaud, a lawyer from Bordeaux, pleaded that "To take this right from the people would be to take sovereignty from them, to transfer it . . . to the hands of the representatives chosen by the people, to transform their representatives into kings or tyrants." Vergniaud's motion to submit the verdict to the people for ratification lost by a vote of 424–283.

The last vote, the closest of all, determined the king's sentence. Originally it appeared that a majority might vote for noncapital punishment. The Marquis de Condorcet, for example, argued that although the king deserved death on the basis of the law of treason, he could not bring himself to vote for capital punishment on principle. The radical response to this argument came from Robespierre, who appealed to the "principles of nature" in stating that the death penalty could be justified "only in those cases where it is vital to the safety of private citizens or of the public." Robespierre's impassioned oratory carried the day. By a vote of 361–334 the king was sentenced to "death within 24 hours" rather than the alternatives of imprisonment followed by banishment after the war or imprisonment in chains for life. The following day Louis was led to the guillotine.

All public trials, especially those for political crimes, are theatrical events, in that the various parties play specific roles and seek to convey certain messages to their audiences. The men who voted to put Louis XVI on trial

Execution of Louis XVI, January 21, 1793
Although the king was convicted of treason by a unanimous vote, the vote to execute him carried by a slender majority of only twenty-seven votes.

wanted to create an educational spectacle in which the already deposed monarch would be stripped of any respect he might still have commanded among the people. Louis was to be tried like any other traitor, and he was to suffer the same fate, execution by the guillotine. The attempt to strip him of all privilege and status continued after his death. His corpse, with his head placed between his knees, was taken to a cemetery, placed in a wooden box, and buried in the common pit. The revolutionaries were determined to guarantee that even in death the king would have the same position as the humblest of his former subjects.

Questions of Justice

1. How would you describe the standard of justice that the members of the National Convention upheld in voting to execute the king? How did this standard of justice differ from the standard to which King Louis XVI appealed?
2. Evaluate the argument of Robespierre that the death penalty can be justified only in cases of public safety. Compare his argument to that of Enlightenment thinkers such as Cesare Beccaria that capital punishment was an unjust, unnecessary, and uncivilized punishment.

Taking It Further

Jordan, David P. *The King's Trial: The French Revolution vs. Louis XVI.* 1979. The most thorough account of the trial.

Walzer, Michael, ed. *Regicide and Revolution: Speeches at the Trial of Louis XVI.* 1974. A valuable collection of speeches with an extended commentary.

In order to repel the coalition of foreign powers, the convention ordered a *levée en masse,* a conscription of troops from the entire population. This step, taken in August 1793, created an unprecedented military force, a massive citizen army drawn from all segments of the population and committed to the prosecution of the war. In the past the rank and file of European armies, whether mercenaries or regular troops, had been filled with men on the margins of society: the poor, the unemployed, and even criminal outcasts. The conscription of males from all ranks of society might have promoted a sense of national unity among the troops, but it also caused resentment and resistance against this use of state power. It led to increased federalist resistance to the radical Jacobin government.

The Reign of Terror, 1793–1794

In order to deal with its domestic enemies, the republican government claimed powers that far exceeded those exercised by the monarchy in the age of absolutism. The convention passed laws that set up special courts to prosecute enemies of the regime and authorized special procedures that deprived those accused of their legal rights. These laws laid the legal foundation for the Reign of Terror°, a campaign to rid the state of its internal enemies. A Committee of Public Safety, consisting of twelve members entrusted with the executive power of the state, superintended this process. Although technically subordinate to the convention, the Committee of Public Safety became in effect a revolutionary dictatorship.

The man who emerged as the main figure on the Committee of Public Safety was Maximilien Robespierre. A brilliant student as a youth, Robespierre was affronted when the king's carriage splashed him with mud as he was waiting to read an address to the king. A man with little sense of humor, he was passionate in his quest for justice. As a lawyer who defended indigent clients, Robespierre was elected to the Third Estate in 1789 and became a favorite of the *sans-culottes,* who called him "The Incorruptible." That

DOCUMENT

Saint-Just on Democracy, Justice and the Terror (1790s)

he may have been, but he was also susceptible to the temptation to abuse power for partisan political purposes. Like Rousseau, whose work he admired, he was also willing to sacrifice individual liberty in the name of the collective General Will. His logic was that since the General Will was indivisible, it could not accommodate dissent. Robespierre was primarily responsible for pushing the revolution to new extremes and for establishing the program of state repression that began in the autumn of 1793.

The most intense prosecutions of the Terror took place between October 1793 and June 1794, but they continued until August 1794. By that time the revolutionary courts had executed 17,000 people, while 500,000 had suffered imprisonment. Another 20,000 either died in prison or were killed without any form of trial. Among the victims of the Terror were substantial numbers of clergy and nobility, as we might expect, but the overwhelming majority were artisans and peasants. One Parisian stableboy was guillotined for having said "f . . . the Republic," while a baker from Alsace lost his head for predicting that "the Republic will go to hell with all its partisans."[2] Many of the victims came from the outlying regions of the country, especially the northeast, where foreign armies were threatening the Republic, and the west, where a brutal civil war between the French army and Catholics and Royalists was raging. These provincial enemies of the regime were identified by special surveillance committees and then were tried by revolutionary tribunals. The guillotine was by no means the only method of execution. In November and December 1793, about 1,800 rebels captured during the uprising in the Vendée were tied to other prisoners, placed in sinking boats, and drowned in the chilly waters of the Loire River.

The most visible and alarming of the executions took place in the capital. The execution of Marie Antoinette and other royalists might have been justified on the basis of their active subversion of the regime, but trumped-up charges against Girondins exposed a process that would destroy republicans as well. As one Girondin said in a speech to the Convention, the revolution, like the mythical Roman god Saturn, devoured its own children. Some of the most prominent figures of the Enlightenment fell victim to this paranoia. Among them was the Marquis de Condorcet, who believed passionately that all citizens, including women, had equal rights. Having campaigned against capital punishment, he committed suicide in a Parisian prison, just before he was to be executed. Another figure of the Enlightenment, the famous chemist Antoine Lavoisier (1743–1794), who had devoted himself to improving social and economic conditions in France, was executed at the same time. So too was the feminist Olympe de Gouges, who as we discussed in Chapter 18 had petitioned for the equal political rights of women. Many French revolutionaries, including Robespierre, used the political ideas of the Enlightenment to justify their actions, but the Terror struck down some of the most distinguished figures of that movement. In that sense the Terror marked the end of the Enlightenment in France.

The Committee of Public Safety then went after Danton and other so-called "Indulgents," who had decided that the Terror had gone too far. Danton's execution made everyone, especially moderate Jacobins, wonder who would be the next victim of a process that had spun completely out of control. In June 1794 the Terror reached a climax, as 1,300 people were sent to their deaths. In order to stop the process, a group of Jacobins in the convention, headed by Joseph Fouché (1759–1820) and Paul Barras (1755–1829), organized a plot against Robespierre. Calling him a tyrant, they arrested him and more than 100 of his followers and guillotined them in late July 1794. An equally swift retaliation was exacted against the Jacobins in the provinces, when members of the White Terror, so named for the white Bourbon flag they displayed, executed leaders of the local revolutionary tribunals. With these reprisals, which used the very same methods that had been perfected by Robespierre and his followers, the most violent and radical phase of the French revolution came to an end.

The Reign of Terror had ended, but its memory would never be extinguished. Its horrors served as a constant warning against the dangers inherent in revolutionary movements. The guillotine, the agent of a dysfunctional and indiscriminate state terrorism, became just as closely identified with the French Revolution as its famous slogan of "Liberty, Equality, Fraternity." The contrast between those two symbols, each of them emblematic of a different stage of the revolution, helps to explain how both conservatives and liberals in the nineteenth century would be able to appeal to the experience of the revolution to support their contradictory ideologies.

The Directory, 1795–1799

A desire to end the violence of the Terror allowed moderates in the National Convention to regain control of the state apparatus that Robespierre and his allies had used to such devastating effect. The Paris Commune was dismantled and the Committee of Public Safety stripped of most of its powers. In November 1794 the Jacobin clubs throughout the country, which had provided support for the Terror, were closed. The moderates who now controlled the government still hoped to preserve the gains of the revolution, while returning the country to more familiar forms of authority. A new constitution of 1795 bestowed executive power on a five-man Directorate, while an assembly consisting of two houses, the Council of Elders and the Council of Five Hundred, proposed and voted on all legislation. The franchise was limited to property holders, allowing only 2,000,000 men out of an adult male population of 7,000,000 to vote. A system of indirect election, in which a person voted for electors who then selected representatives, guaranteed that only the wealthiest members of the country would sit in the legislative assembly.

The establishment of the Directory formed part of a more general reaction against the culture of the republic. The austere, egalitarian dress of the *sans-culottes* gave way once again to fancy and opulent clothes, at least among the bourgeoisie. Low

necklines, officially out of favor during the Reign of Terror, once again came back into fashion among wealthier members of society. The high social life of the capital experienced a revival. Some dances took place on the sites of churches that Jacobins had desecrated. Jacobin theaters were shut down and Jacobin works of art destroyed. France was still a republic, but it was no longer Robespierre's Republic of Virtue.

Some of the more entrepreneurial citizens of Paris welcomed the new regime, but opposition soon arose, mainly from Jacobins and *sans-culottes*. When the government relaxed the strict price controls that had been in effect under the Jacobins, the soaring price of bread and other commodities caused widespread social discontent among the population. This situation was aggravated by the continuation of the interminable war against the foreign powers in the First Coalition. Wherever French troops went, their constant need of food and other goods resulted in serious shortages of these commodities.

By the end of 1798 conditions had grown even worse. Inflation was running out of control. The collection of taxes was intermittent at best. The paper money known as *assignats*, first issued by the government in 1791 and backed by the value of confiscated church lands, had become almost worthless. Late in 1797 the Directory had been forced to cancel more than half the national debt, a

---

CHRONOLOGY

The Directory, 1795–1799

1795	
August 22	The National Convention approves a new constitution
October 5	Napoleon suppresses a royalist insurrection in Paris
October 26	End of the Convention; beginning of the Directory
1796	
February 19	The issuing of *assignats* is halted
April 12	Beginning of a series of victories by Napoleon in Italy
1798	
May 13	Napoleon's expedition departs for Egypt
May	Second Coalition (Britain, Austria, Russia, Naples, and Turkey) is formed against Napoleon
July 21	Napoleon wins the Battle of the Pyramids
August 1	Nelson destroys the French fleet at the Battle of the Nile
1799	
November 9–10	Napoleon's coup on the eighteenth of *Brumaire;* Consulate is established

The 25th December 1799. The Three Consuls: Bonaparte, Cambecérès and Lebrun (1856)

This painting by Louis-Charles-Auguste Couder shows the three consuls taking the oath of office before the presidents of the Assembly on December 25, 1799. Napoleon, the First Consul, stands at the center of the three to the left.

step that further alienated wealthy citizens who had lent money to the government. Military setbacks in 1798 and 1799 brought the situation to a critical point. An expedition to Egypt, which was intended to gain for France a foothold in the Middle East, had resulted in a number of victories against the Turks, but the British destroyed the French fleet at the Battle of the Nile in 1798. The next year a series of revolts against French rule in Italy and in the Austrian Netherlands pushed the French armies back to France's earlier boundaries. The formation of a Second Coalition of European powers in 1799, which included Russia, Naples, and Turkey as well as Britain and Austria, represented a formidable challenge to French power and ensured that the war would not end soon. These military events produced a swing to the political left and raised the specter of another Jacobin coup.

In the face of this instability, Emmanuel-Joseph Sieyès, who had been elected as one of the directors two years earlier, decided to overthrow the government. Sieyès provided a link between the early years of the revolution, when he had defended the Third Estate, and the current government of the Directory. Unlike many other prominent political figures, he had managed to avoid prosecution as the revolution had become more radical. When asked what he had done during the Reign of Terror, Sieyès replied, "I survived." The goal of the planned coup was to provide the country with strong government, its greatest need in a period of political, economic, and social instability. The person Sieyès selected as his partner in this enterprise, and the man who immediately assumed leadership of the coup, was Napoleon Bonaparte (1769–1821), a 30-year-old general who in 1795

had put down a royalist rebellion in Paris with a "whiff of grapeshot."

Napoleon had already established impressive credentials as a military leader. In 1796 and 1797 he had won major victories in Italy, leading to the Treaty of Campo Formio with Austria in 1797. Those victories and his short-lived success at the Battle of the Pyramids in Egypt had made him enormously popular in Paris, where he was received as a hero when he assumed command of the armed forces in the city in 1799. His popularity, his demonstrated military leadership, and his control of a large armed force made this "man on horseback" appear to have the best chance to replace the enfeebled civilian regime of the Directory.

On November 9, 1799, Napoleon addressed the two legislative councils. He reported that another Jacobin conspiracy had been uncovered and that in order to deal with such insurrections a new constitution must be written to give the executive branch of the government more authority. Napoleon encountered resistance from some members of the Council of Five Hundred, who demanded that he be declared an outlaw. At this stage the president of the council, Napoleon's brother Lucien, intervened and called in troops to evict the members who opposed him. The following day France had a new government, known as the Consulate.

Executive power in the new government was to be vested in three consuls. It soon became clear, however, that Napoleon would be the dominant member of this triumvirate, and in the new constitution of December 1799, which the electorate ratified by means of a plebiscite, Napoleon was named First Consul. This appointment made him the most powerful man in France and for all practical purposes a military dictator. Republican forms of government were preserved in the new constitution, but they were easily manipulated to produce what the consuls desired. A Senate appointed by the consuls chose men from a list of 6,000 "notables" to form a body known as the Tribunate, which would discuss legislation proposed by the consuls. Another assembly, the Legislative Body, would vote on those measures without debate.

With the establishment of the Consulate the French Republic was a thing of the past. It had been replaced by a military dictatorship in all but name. This transformation of the republic into a military dictatorship had been predicted by both the radical democrat Robespierre and the British conservative Edmund Burke many years before. The dictatorship became more apparent in 1802, when Napoleon was named Consul for Life, and in 1804, when he crowned himself emperor of the French.

Cultural Change in France During the Revolution

■ In what ways did the political events of the revolution change French cultural institutions and create a new political culture?

The French Revolution was primarily a political revolution. It brought about fundamental change in the system of government. It resulted in the destruction of the monarchy and the establishment of a republic. It inspired the drafting of new constitutions, led to the creation of new legislative assemblies, and endowed the state with unprecedented power. The French revolution also brought about profound changes in French culture. It transformed the cultural institutions of the Old Regime and created a new revolutionary culture.

The Transformation of Cultural Institutions

Between 1791 and 1794 most of the cultural institutions of the Old Regime were either destroyed or radically transformed, and new institutions under the control of the state took their place.

Schools

The confiscation of church property in 1790, followed by the abolition of the monastic religious orders, had a devastating effect on the traditional parish schools, colleges, and universities, most of which were run by the clergy. Without sufficient endowments, many of these schools were forced to close. During the Terror, schools suspected of having

aristocratic associations and teaching counterrevolutionary doctrines came under further assault. Thousands of teachers lost their salaries and sought employment elsewhere. In September 1793 the universities were suppressed.

The government gradually realized that the entire educational process was collapsing. Recognizing the necessity of using education to encourage loyalty to the republican regime, the National Convention established a system of universal primary education. Instruction would be free, and the teachers would receive their salaries from the state. Unfortunately, the state did not have enough money to pay for the system, so the schools continued to languish.

The state was only slightly more successful in providing secondary education by converting abandoned colleges, monasteries, and libraries into "central schools," which were intended to provide a standardized form of state education. By 1799, the central schools had 10,000 students, 40,000 fewer than were in the colleges in 1789. The system was improved significantly during the Napoleonic period when the government established thirty-six secondary schools known as *lycées* while also allowing private and religious schools to continue to function.

Academies

The Parisian scientific and artistic academies established by Louis XIV (see Chapter 15) had a monopoly over the promotion and transmission of knowledge in the sciences and the visual arts. The academies were the epitome of privilege. They controlled their own membership, determined the recipients of their prizes, and had a monopoly of their particular branch of knowledge. They were also heavily aristocratic institutions; as many as three-quarters of their members were nobles or clergy.

During the revolution the academies were abolished as part of a general attack on corporate bodies. The work they did was taken over by various government committees. For example, the Commission on Weights and Measures, which had been part of the Academy of Science, became an independent commission. Its task had been to provide uniform weights and measures for the entire kingdom. In 1795 it established the meter, calculated as one ten-millionth of the distance from the North Pole to the equator, as the standard measure of distance. The metric system and the decimal system, which were introduced at the same time, have subsequently been adopted as universal standards in all European countries except Great Britain.

The Royal Academy of Arts, dissolved by a vote of the National Convention in 1793, was replaced by the Popular and Republican Society of the Arts. The inspiration for this new republican society, which was open to artists of all social ranks, was Jacques-Louis David (1748–1825), the greatest painter of his generation. Employed at the court of Louis XVI, David became a vocal main critic of the academy at the time of the revolution. He painted some of the most memorable scenes of the revolution, including the oath taken at the tennis court by the members of the National Assembly in 1789. During the Republic David depicted heroes of the revolution such as Jean-Paul Marat, and after the empire was established he was appointed First Painter to Napoleon. David presided over a revival of classicism in French painting, employing Greek and Roman motifs and exhibiting a rationalism and lack of sentiment in his work.

Libraries

Shortly after the revolution had begun, thousands of books and manuscripts from the libraries of monasteries, royal castles, residences of the nobility, and academies came into the possession of the state. Many of these were funneled into the Royal Library, which grew five times in size between 1789 and 1794 and was appropriately renamed the National Library. The government also intended to inventory and catalog all the books held in libraries throughout the country. This effort to create the General Bibliography of France was never completed, and while the books were being cataloged, the government decided to get rid of those that dealt with "theology, mysticism, feudalism, and royalism" by sending them to foreign countries. This decision did not lead to the export of books to other parts of Europe, but it initiated a frenzy of book sales, mainly to private individuals. Altogether about five million books were lost or sold during these years.

Museums and Monuments

The day after the abolition of the monarchy the National Assembly created a Commission of the Museum, whose function was "to collect paintings, statues and other precious objects from the crown possessions" as well as from the churches and houses of the émigrés. The museum was to be located in the Louvre, a royal palace that also served as an art gallery. When it opened in August 1793 the Louvre included a majority of paintings with religious themes, most of them confiscated from royal and émigré residences. The incompatibility of these religious works of art with the republican rejection of Christianity can be explained only by the assumption that this museum was intended to be entirely historical and to have no relevance to contemporary politics. The Louvre and the Museum of French Monuments represented an attempt to quarantine the religious French past from its secular present, lest it contaminate the revolution itself.

The revolutionaries did not have the same respect for the bodies of their former kings. On August 10, 1793, the first anniversary of the deposition of Louis XVI, the National Convention ordered the destruction of all the tombs of past French kings. One by one the tombs were opened and the corpses, embalmed in lead, were removed. Metals and valuables were melted down for use in the war effort. The corpses were either left to disintegrate in the atmosphere or dragged unceremoniously to the cemetery, where they were

Le XI Aout 1792, les parisiens reprennent une mesure qu'ils avoient eu tort de ne pas mettre a exécution le 20 Juin 1791. Ils abbatirent les Statues de Louis XIV, Place des Victoires, et place vendome.

Destruction of the Statue of Louis XIV in the Place de Victoires, August 11, 1792

The leaders of the Republic attempted to eliminate the memory of the institution of monarchy by destroying statues as well as the tombs of France's kings.

thrown into the common pit. The corpse of Louis XIV landed on top of that of Henry IV. This disrespectful treatment of the remains of France's former kings was intended to erase the memory of monarchy.

The Creation of a New Political Culture

As the state was taking over and adapting the cultural institutions of the Old Regime, revolutionaries engaged in a much bolder and original undertaking: the production of a new, revolutionary political culture. Its sole purpose was to legitimate and glorify the new regime. It symbolized the political values of that regime: liberty, equality, and fraternity in 1789 and republicanism after 1792. This culture was almost entirely political; all forms of cultural expression were subordinated to the realization of a pressing political agenda.

One of the main characteristics of this culture was that it was popular—it was shared by the entire populace, not simply by a small upper-class or literate elite. The fundamental political doctrine of the revolution was popular sovereignty°: the claim that the people were the highest political power in the state. The revolutionaries claimed that this power could never be alienated. The move of the National Assembly from Versailles to Paris actually enabled the people to be present in the gallery during political debate, and deputies were always conscious of their presence. "Learn," claimed one of them in 1789, "that we are deliberating here in front of our masters and we are answerable to them for our opinions." The political culture that emerged—the textual and literary symbols spoken, written, and drawn to reflect this sovereignty of the people—would become the property of the entire population, especially in Paris, where the revolutionary cause found its most passionate popular support. The very words used to identify revolutionary institutions, such as the National Assembly and the National Guard, formed the texture of this new political culture.

The common people who embraced this new culture most enthusiastically were the *sans-culottes*—the radical shopkeepers, artisans, and laborers of Paris. The dress of these people influenced a change in fashion among the wealthier segments of society. A simple jacket replaced the ruffled coat worn by members of the upper classes, their powdered wigs gave way to natural hair, and they too now wore long trousers. They also donned the red liberty cap, to which a tricolor cockade was affixed. The tricolor, which combined the red and blue colors of Paris with the white symbol of the Bourbon monarchy, identified the adherents of the revolution.

Symbols of revolution could be found everywhere. The commercialization of the revolution guaranteed that the tricolor flag, portraits of revolutionary figures, and images of the Bastille would appear on household objects as constant reminders of the public's support for the revolution. By an order of the government in 1792 all men were required to wear the tricolor cockade. Liberty trees, first planted by peasants as protests against local landlords, became a symbol of the revolution. By May 1792 more than 60,000 had been planted throughout the country.

The press, no longer tightly controlled by the government and the printers' guild, became a crucial agent of revolutionary propaganda and a producer of the new culture. Pamphlets, newspapers, brochures, and posters all promoted a distinctive revolutionary language, which became one of the permanent legacies of the revolution. Political leaders used the same rhetoric in their political speeches. *Sans-culottes* sang satirical songs and ballads, many of them to the same tunes well known in the Old Regime. The most popular of the songs of the revolutionary period was the *Marseillaise,* first sung by soldiers preparing for battle against the Austrians but soon adopted by the civilian population and sung at political gatherings. The theaters, which had been privileged corporations in the Old Regime but also carefully regulated, were now free to engage in political satire that strengthened the ties of the people to the revolution.

Much of this new political culture stemmed from the conviction that the doctrine of popular sovereignty should be practiced in everyday life. *Sans-culottes* did this by joining the political clubs organized by different factions within the National Assembly, by addressing others as citizens, and by using the more familiar form of the pronoun you (*tu* rather than *vous*) in all conversations. They also participated in the revolution by taking public oaths. On the first anniversary of the fall of the Bastille, as many as 350,000 people, many of them members of the "federations" of National Guards throughout the country, gathered on the royal parade ground outside Paris to take an oath "to the Nation, to the Law, to the King." Direct democracy was not possible in a society of 27 million people, but these cultural practices allowed people to believe that they were participating actively in the political process.

The new revolutionary culture was emphatically secular. In its most extreme form, it was blatantly anti-Christian. In September 1793 the radical Jacobin and former priest Joseph Fouché inaugurated a program of de-Christianization°. Under his leadership, radical Jacobins closed churches and removed religious symbols such as crosses from cemeteries and public venues. In an effort to establish a purely civic religion, they forbade the public practice of religion and renamed churches "temples of reason." In their public pronouncements the architects of de-Christianization avoided reference to the Christian period of French history, which covered the entire national past.

This de-Christianization campaign became the official policy of the Paris Commune, and the National Convention issued a few edicts to enforce it. The program, however, did not win widespread support, and even some Jacobins

Oath Taking

On July 14, 1790, the first anniversary of the fall of the Bastille, as many as 350,000 people gathered on a field outside Paris to take an oath of loyalty to the new French nation. The event was referred to as the Feast of the Federation, because most of the oath takers were members of the regional federations of National Guards. The oath taking, which had many characteristics of a religious gathering, was led by the king himself, and it marked the most optimistic period of the revolution.

claimed that in rejecting Christianity it had undermined a belief in God and the afterlife. In 1794 Robespierre attempted to modify the excesses of de-Christianization by launching the Cult of the Supreme Being. He promoted a series of festivals acknowledging the existence of a deity and the immortality of the soul. This new cult paid lip service to traditional religious beliefs, but it still served secular purposes. In fact, the cult was designed to direct the spiritual yearnings of the French people into patriotic undertakings and promote republican virtue.

The new secular revolutionary culture incorporated many elements of the Christian culture that had prevailed before the revolution began. The new pageants and festi-vals designed to promote a civic religion were modeled on traditional Catholic processions. Revolutionaries co-opted some of the religious holy days for their own purposes. Churches were converted to temples honoring revolutionary heroes. An effigy of Jean-Paul Marat, who was murdered in 1793, appeared on the altar of a Parisian church, next to a female statue of liberty. Jacques-Louis David's portrait of the murdered Marat depicted the slain victim in the manner of the dead Christ in Michelangelo's *Pietà*. Meetings of revolutionaries often took on the atmosphere of religious revivals, as men and women wept in response to orations. Secular catechisms taught young children the virtues of republicanism in the same way that they had in-

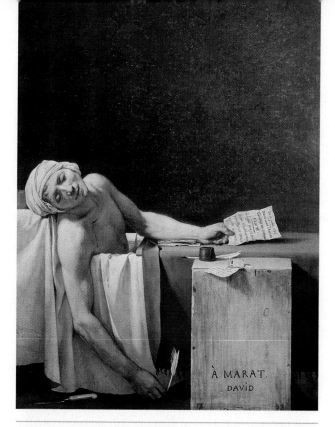

Jacques-Louis David, *The Death of Marat* (1793)
The Jacobin journalist Jean-Paul Marat was stabbed to death in his bathtub by a noblewoman, Charlotte Corday, in July 1793. The painting depicts Marat as having suffered a martyr's death. Marat holds the letter from his murderer that gave her entrance to his residence.

structed them in Christian doctrine during the Old Regime.

In order to destroy all vestiges of the Old Regime, the government also instituted a new calendar in October 1793. The dates on the calendar began with September 22, 1792, the day the Republic was established. That became the first day of the year I, while the weeks now had ten days instead of seven. The new months were given names to evoke the different seasons, such as *Brumaire* for the first month of wintry weather, *Germinal* for the season of planting, and *Thermidor* for the warmest month of the summer. Hostile British contemporaries gave their own humorous renditions of these names, translating them as Freezy, Flowery, Heaty, and so on. The new calendar was intended to make the revolution a part of people's everyday consciousness. It remained in effect until the last day of 1805.

The new revolutionary culture was disseminated widely, but it was always contested. Royalists trampled on the tricolor cockade, refused to adopt the new style of dress, and pulled up the liberty trees. This resistance from counterrevolutionary forces guaranteed that when the revolution was reversed, much of the new political culture would disappear. Napoleon did little to perpetuate it, and the restored monarchy was openly hostile to it. Like the political revolution, however, some elements of revolutionary culture, such

as the tricolor and the rhetoric of the revolutionary press, could never be suppressed. Not only did these cultural innovations inspire revolutionaries for the next hundred years, but they also became part of the mainstream of Western civilization.

Cultural Uniformity

One of the most striking features of the new revolutionary culture was its concern for standardization and simplicity. The division of France into *départements,* all roughly equal in size, population, and wealth, and the further subdivision of each *département* into uniform districts and communes, serves as one manifestation of this compulsion. The establishment of a national school system, at least on paper, serves as another. When the *lycées* were founded by Napoleon, each of the schools was given the exact same curriculum, and the same 3,000 books, chosen by a central committee, were deposited in all *lycée* libraries. The adoption of the metric system and the decimal system and the plan to establish one body of French law for the entire country, eventually brought to fruition by Napoleon, reflected the same impulse. So too did the efforts begun during the Terror to make French the official language in regions of the country that spoke Breton, Occitan, Basque, or other regional dialects.

The main source of this drive toward cultural uniformity was the desire to build a new French nation composed of equal citizens. Linguistic, legal, educational, or administrative diversity only made the realization of that program more difficult. The quest for cultural and political standardization did not, however, originate during the revolution. Many of the projects of the 1790s, especially the desire to establish standard weights and measures, began during the Old Regime. They were often the product of the rationalism of the Enlightenment, which, as we have seen in Chapter 18, sought to make society conform to the operation of universal laws.

The Napoleonic Era, 1799–1815

■ How did the authoritarian rule of Napoleon Bonaparte from 1799 to 1814 confirm or betray the achievements of the French Revolution, and what impact did his military conquests have on Europe and the world?

The coup d'état on November 9, 1799, or the eighteenth of *Brumaire* on the revolutionary calendar, marked a turning point in the political history of France. The Consulate ushered in a period of authoritarian rule. Liberty was restricted in the interest of order; republicanism gave way to dictatorship. The French Revolution had apparently run its course. But the period between 1799 and 1815 was also a time of considerable innovation, especially in the realm of politics and diplomacy. Those innovations were primarily the work of one man, Napoleon Bonaparte, who controlled the French government for the next fifteen years.

Napoleon's Rise to Power

Napoleon Bonaparte was born on the Mediterranean island of Corsica. His father, Charles-Marie de Buonaparte, was an attorney who had supported the Corsican patriot Pascale de Paoli in winning the independence of the island from the Italian state of Genoa. His mother, Letizia, had come from an old noble family from Lombardy in Italy. In 1770 the new French government, which had gained control of the island the previous year, accepted the Buonaparte family as nobility. In 1779 the young Napoleon, whose native language was Corsican, received an appointment to a French military school. He survived both the rigors of the course of study and the taunting of his classmates, who mocked him for his accent and his poverty. Displaying a natural gift for military science, he won a position in the artillery section of the national military academy in Paris.

Until the beginning of the French Revolution, Napoleon seemed destined to pursue a successful but unspectacular career as an officer in the royal army. The events of the revolution made possible his rapid ascent to military prominence and political power. When the revolution broke out, Napoleon returned to Corsica, where he organized the National Guard and petitioned the government to grant full rights of citizenship to his people. As the revolution became more radical he became a Jacobin, and he was commissioned to attack federalist and royalist positions in the south of France. Unlike many of his fellow Jacobins, he managed to survive the Terror and then found favor with the Directory. In 1796 Napoleon was given command of the Army of Italy, at which time he abandoned the Italian spelling of his name for Bonaparte. His decisive victories against the Austrians and his popularity in Paris attracted the attention of Sieyès and others who wished to give the country strong, charismatic leadership.

Napoleon's personality was ideally suited to the acquisition and maintenance of political power. A man of unparalleled ambition, he was driven by an extraordinarily high assessment of his abilities. After one of his military victories he wrote, "I realized I was a superior being and conceived the ambition of performing great things." To the pursuit of his destiny he harnessed a determined and a stubborn will. Temporary setbacks never seemed to thwart his single-minded pursuit of glory. He brought enormous energy to his military and political pursuits. He wrote more than 80,000 letters during his life, many of them transmitting orders to his officers and ministers. Authoritarian by nature, he used intimidation as well as paternal concern to cultivate the loyalty of his subordinates. Like many authoritarian leaders, he had difficulty delegating authority, a trait that was to weaken his regime. Finally, in an age dominated by high-minded causes, he exhibited an instinctive distrust of ideology and the doctrinaire pronouncements of philosophes such as Rousseau. Napoleon's military training led him to take a pragmatic, disciplined approach to politics, in which he always sought the most effective means to the desired end.

Napoleon's acquisition of power was systematic and shrewd. Playing on the need for a strong leader, and using the army he controlled as his main political tool, he maneuvered himself into the position of first consul in 1799. In 1802 he became consul for life, and two years later he crowned himself emperor of the French and his wife Josephine empress. The title of emperor traditionally denoted the height of monarchical power. It identified a ruler who not only ruled more than one kingdom or state but also did not share power with any other political authority. That was certainly the case with Napoleon. During his rule the Legislative Body, the Senate, and the Tribunate, all of which had been instituted during the Consulate, were reduced to performing only ceremonial functions.

It is certainly ironic that Napoleon, while continuing to hunt down and execute royalists, accepted a title of royalty himself and made his position, just like the French kingship, hereditary. In 1804 a group of royalists, including the members of the Bourbon family, were convicted of and executed for trying to assassinate Napoleon. One of them declared ironically, "We have done more than we hoped. We meant to give France a king, and we have given her an emperor." That emperor, moreover, appeared to the royalists and to many others to be a tyrant who would trample on the rights of the French people. Napoleon's coronation also made a negative impression outside France. The great German composer Ludwig van Beethoven, having dedicated his *Third Symphony* (1803) to Napoleon for overthrowing tyranny in France, scratched Napoleon's name from the dedication after Napoleon assumed his new position as emperor.

Napoleon and the Revolution

What was the relationship between Napoleon's rule and the French Revolution? Did Napoleon consolidate the gains of the revolution or destroy them? Did he simply redirect the revolutionary commitment to liberty, equality, and fraternity into new and more disciplined channels of expression after 1799? Or did he reverse the political trends that had prevailed from 1789 to 1799, crushing liberty in all its forms and establishing a ruthless, authoritarian dictatorship? Napoleon always thought of himself as the heir of the

Emperor Napoleon Crowning His Wife, Josephine, Empress of the French in the Cathedral of Notre Dame, 1804

This painting by Jacques-Louis David depicts secular and religious figures gathered around Napoleon not as members of privileged orders but as representatives of the nation. Pope Pius VII remains seated as Napoleon places the crown on Josephine's head. Napoleon had already crowned himself emperor of the French.

revolution rather than its undertaker. Certainly he was able to use the radical vocabulary of the revolution to characterize his domestic programs and his military campaigns. He presented himself as the ally of the common man against entrenched aristocratic privilege. He proclaimed a love for the French people and gave his support to the doctrine of popular sovereignty. He often referred to the rulers of other European countries as tyrants and presented himself as the liberator of their subjects.

This view of Napoleon as a true revolutionary, however, ignores the fact that his commitment to liberty was almost entirely rhetorical. Behind the appeals to the slogans of the revolution lurked an authoritarian will that was far stronger than that of any eighteenth-century absolute monarch. He used the language of liberty and democracy to disguise a thoroughgoing authoritarianism, just as he used the rhetoric of republicanism to legitimize his own dictatorial regime. The practice of holding carefully orchestrated and controlled elections to ratify the changes he made in French government guaranteed that his rule would appear to have

emanated from the will of the people. At the establishment of the Consulate, Napoleon paid lip service to representative forms of government, which he maintained but then proceeded to render totally ineffective. When the empire was established he told his troops that they had the freedom to vote for or against the new form of government but then told them that if they voted against it, they would be shot.

We can make a stronger case for Napoleon's egalitarianism. He spoke of equality of opportunity. He synthesized the egalitarianism of the revolution with the authoritarianism of the Old Regime. He supported the equality of all Frenchmen (but not Frenchwomen) before the law. This egalitarianism laid the foundation for the support he received from the peasants, soldiers, and workers. It might be said that he brought both equality and political stability to France in exchange for political liberty.

There are two other ways in which we might legitimately consider Napoleon the heir of the revolution. The first is that he continued the centralization and growth of state power and the rational organization of the administration

DOCUMENT

The French People Accept Napoleon as Emperor, 1804

The Countess de Rémusat was the wife of one of Napoleon's chamberlains. In this letter she explains why the French people accepted Napoleon as their emperor. Her comments reflect the fear of disorder that permeated French society at the end of the eighteenth century.

I can understand how it was that men worn out by the turmoil of the Revolution, and afraid of that liberty which had long been associated with death, looked for repose under the dominion of an able ruler on whom fortune was seemingly resolved to smile. I can conceive that they regarded his elevation as a decree of destiny and fondly believed that in the irrevocable they should find peace. I may confidently assert that those persons believed quite sincerely that Bonaparte, whether as Consul or Emperor, would exert his authority to oppose the intrigues of faction and would save us from the perils of anarchy.

None dared to utter the word Republic, so deeply had the Terror stained that name, and Directorial Government had perished in the contempt with which its chiefs were regarded. The return of the Bourbons could only be brought about by the aid of a revolution; and the slightest disturbance terrified the French people, in whom enthusiasm of every kind seemed dead. Besides, the men in whom they had trusted had one after the other deceived them; and as, this time, they were yielding to force, they were at least certain that they were not deceiving themselves.

The belief, or rather the error, that only despotism could at that epoch maintain order in France, was very widespread. It became the mainstay of Bonaparte; and it is due to him to say that he also believed it. The factions played into his hands by imprudent attempts which he turned to his own advantage; he had some grounds for his belief that he was necessary; France believed it too; and he even succeeded in persuading foreign sovereigns that he constituted a barrier against Republican influences which, but for him, might spread widely. At the moment when Bonaparte placed the imperial crown upon his head, there was not a king in Europe who did not believe that he wore his own crown more securely because of that event. Had the new emperor granted a liberal constitution, the peace of nations and of kings might, in sober seriousness, have been for ever secured.

Source: *Memoirs of Madame de Rémusat,* translated by C. Hoey and John Lillie (D. Appleton and Co., 1880).

---

that had begun in 1789. Each of the successive regimes between 1789 and 1815, even the Directory, had contributed to this pattern of state building, and Napoleon's contribution was monumental. The second was his continuation and extension of France's military mission to export the revolution to its European neighbors. The two achievements are related to each other, because the war effort necessitated the further growth and centralization of state power.

Napoleon and the French State

Once Napoleon had gained effective control of the French state, he set about the task of strengthening it, making it more efficient, highly organized, and powerful. In addition to turning the government into a de facto dictatorship, he settled the long struggle between Church and state, laid down an entirely new law code that imposed legal uniformity on the entire country, and made the civil bureaucracy more centralized, uniform, and efficient. All of this was done with the intention of making the state an effective instrument of social and political control.

Concordat with the Papacy

Napoleon's first contribution to the development of the French state, achieved during the Consulate, was to bring about a resolution of the bitter struggle between Church and state. A committed secularist, Napoleon was determined to bring the Church under the direct control of the state. This had been the main purpose of the Civil Constitution of the Clergy of 1790. Napoleon also realized, however, that this policy had divided the clergy between those who had taken an oath to the nation and those who had refused. Clerical independence had also become a major rallying cry of royalists against the new regime, thereby threatening the stability of the country.

Napoleon's solution to this problem was to reach an agreement with the Church that would satisfy clerics and royalists yet not deprive the state of its authority over the Church. With the Church safely under state control, Napoleon could also use religion to maintain respect for authority and to encourage loyalty and service to the state. "In religion," he wrote, "I do not see the mystery of the Incarnation but the mystery of the social order." In a new catechism published after Napoleon became emperor, children were taught: "Christians owe to the princes who govern them, and we owe in particular to Napoleon I, our Emperor, love, respect, obedience, fidelity, military service, and the tributes laid for the preservation and defense of the Empire."

The death of Pope Pius VI (r. 1775–1799), the implacable foe of the revolution, gave Napoleon the opportunity to address this problem. The new pope, Pius VII (r. 1800–1823), who was more sympathetic to liberal causes, was eager to come to terms with a French government that had become more moderate under the Consulate. The Concordat, which Napoleon and Pope Pius agreed to in 1801 and which was published the following year, gave something to both sides, although Napoleon gained more than he conceded. The pope agreed that all the clergy who refused to swear their loyalty to the nation would resign their posts, thus ending the bitter divisions of the past twelve years. The pope would appoint new bishops, but only with the prior approval of Napoleon. The state would pay all clerical salaries, and the Church would abandon any claims it still had to the ecclesiastical lands seized by the state at the beginning of the revolution.

These provisions represented formidable concessions to state power, and many French bishops found the terms of the Concordat too unfavorable to the Church. But the pope did manage to secure a statement that Roman Catholicism was the religion of the majority of citizens, and Napoleon agreed to scrap the secular calendar introduced in 1793, thereby restoring Sundays and holy days. Church attendance began to increase, having reached historic lows during the period of the Republic. The Church regained its respect as well as its legitimacy and its freedom to function in French society. More young recruits joined the clergy. Napoleon did not make many concessions to the Church, but they were significant enough to alienate a group of liberal philosophers and writers known as the Ideologues°, who objected to what they saw as the return of "monkish superstition."

With the pope at least somewhat appeased, Napoleon took unilateral steps to regulate the administration of the French Church. In a set of regulations known as the Organic Articles, which were added to the Concordat in 1802, the French church became a department of state, controlled by a minister of religion, just like the treasury or any other bureaucratic ministry. Pronouncements from the pope required prior government approval, and the clergy were obliged to read government decrees from the pulpit. Protestant congregations, which were also given freedom of worship and state protection by the terms of the Concordat, were likewise brought under state control, and their ministers were paid by the state. Jews received the protection of the state, but the government did not pay the salaries of rabbis.

The Civil Code

Napoleon's most enduring achievement in the realm of state building was the promulgation of a new legal code, the Civil Code of 1804, later known as the Napoleonic Code°. A legal code is an authoritative and comprehensive statement of the law of a particular country. The model for modern legal codes in Europe was the *Corpus Juris Civilis* of the Roman Empire, which Justinian decreed at Constantinople

between 529 and 534 C.E. That code had replaced the thousands of constitutions, customs, and judicial decisions that had been in effect during the Roman Republic and Empire. In compiling the new French code Napoleon, who had just proclaimed himself emperor of the French, was imitating Justinian's legal achievement.

The Napoleonic Code also met a long-standing set of demands to reform the confusing and irregular body of French law. Ever since the Middle Ages, France had been governed by a multiplicity of laws. In the southern provinces of the country, those closest to Italy, the law had been influenced by Roman law. The *Corpus Juris Civilis* had been revived in the Middle Ages and had been incorporated into the written law of these southern French provinces and municipalities. In the north the law was based on local or provincial customs that had not originally existed in written form. France needed a common law for all its people. Efforts to produce an authoritative written code began during the revolution, but Napoleon completed the project and published the code.

The Civil Code, which consisted of more than 2,000 articles, reflected the values that were ascendant in Napoleonic French society. The ideals of the revolution were enshrined in the articles guaranteeing the rights of private property, the equality of all people before the law, and freedom of religion. The values it promoted, however, did not include the equality of the sexes. It granted men control of all family property. Women could not buy or sell property without the consent of their husbands. Only adult men could witness legal documents. All male heirs were entitled to inherit equal shares of a family estate, but daughters were excluded from the settlement.

The Civil Code, which dealt only with the rights and relationships of private individuals, was the first and most important of six law codes promulgated by Napoleon. Others dealt with civil procedure (1806), commerce (1807), and criminal law (1811). Renamed the Napoleonic Code in 1806, the Civil Code had an impact on the law of several countries outside France. It became the basis for the codification of the laws of Switzerland, northern Italy, and the Netherlands, and it served as a model for the numerous codes that were compiled in the German territories controlled by France during the Napoleonic period. The Napoleonic Code also influenced the law of French-speaking North America, including the civil law of the state of Louisiana, which bears signs of its influence even today.

Administrative Centralization

Napoleon laid the foundation of modern French civil administration, which acquired the characteristics of rational organization, uniformity, and centralization. All power emanated from Paris, where Napoleon presided over a Council of State. This body consisted of his main ministers, who handled all matters of finance, domestic affairs, and war and oversaw a vast bureaucracy of salaried,

CHRONOLOGY

The Consulate and the Early Years of the Empire, 1799–1806

1799

December 15	Proclamation of the Constitution of the Consulate

1801

July 15	Signing of the Concordat with the Papacy

1802

March 27	Peace of Amiens
April 8	Organic Articles added to the Concordat

1803

May	Renewal of the war with Britain

1804

March 21	The Civil Code is promulgated
December 2	Napoleon is crowned emperor of the French

1805

August	Third Coalition (Britain, Austria, and Russia) is formed against France
October 21	Defeat of the French navy in the Battle of Trafalgar
October 29	The French defeat the Austrian army at Ulm
December 2	The French defeat Russian and Austrian armies at Austerlitz
December 31	End of the revolutionary calendar

1806

October 14	French victories at the battles of Jena and Auerstädt
November 21	Proclamation of the Continental Blockade of British goods
August 6	Formal dissolution of the Holy Roman Empire

trained officials. The central government also exercised direct control over the provinces, which lost the local privileges they had possessed under the Old Regime. In each of the departments an official known as a *prefect,* appointed by the central government, implemented orders emanating from Paris. Paid the handsome annual salary of 20,000 francs, the prefects were responsible for the maintenance of public order. The power of the prefects was far greater than that of the *intendants* of the Old Regime. The prefects enforced conscription, collected taxes, and supervised local public works, such as the construction and improvement of roads.

The men who served in the government of the French Empire belonged to one of two elaborate, hierarchical institutions: the civil bureaucracy and the army officer corps. The two were closely related, because the main purpose of the administrative bureaucracy was to prepare for and sustain the war effort. Both institutions were organized hierarchically, and those who held positions in them were trained and salaried. Appointment and promotion were based primarily on talent rather than birth.

The idea of "a career open to all talents," as Napoleon described it, ran counter to the tradition of noble privilege. This was one of the achievements of the revolution that Napoleon perpetuated during the empire. All of the twenty-six marshals who served under him in the army were of nonnoble blood. Three of them had been sergeants in the army before 1789 and another three had been privates. The new system did not amount to a pure meritocracy, in which advancement is determined solely by ability and performance, because many appointments were made or influenced by Napoleon himself on the basis of friendship or kinship. Napoleon's brother, Lucien, for example, became minister of the interior. The system did, however, allow people from the ranks of the bourgeoisie to achieve rapid upward social mobility. In order to recognize their new status, Napoleon created a new order of nonhereditary noblemen, known as *notables.* As men ascended through the ranks of the bureaucracy and army they were given the titles of duke, count, baron, and chevalier. Instead of earning status based on their ancestry, these men acquired their titles by virtue of their service to the state. Napoleon created more than 3,500 notables during his rule. In this way he encouraged service to the state while also strengthening loyalty to it.

Napoleon, the Empire, and Europe

Closely related to Napoleon's efforts to build the French state was his creation of a massive European empire. The French Empire was the product of a series of military victories against the armies of Austria, Prussia, Russia, and Spain between 1797 and 1809. By the latter date France controlled, either directly or indirectly, the Dutch Republic, the

Austrian Netherlands, Italy, Spain, and large parts of Germany and Poland. The instrument of these victories was the massive citizen army that Napoleon assembled. Building on the *levée en masse* of 1793, which he supplemented with soldiers from the countries he conquered, Napoleon had more than one million men under arms by 1812. More than three times the size of Louis XIV's army in 1700, it was the largest military force raised under the control of one man up to this time in European history.

These troops engaged in a military offensive that was more massive, wide-ranging, and sustained than Alexander the Great's invasion of Egypt, Persia, and northern India between 334 and 326 B.C.E. Napoleon's invasion began with the great victories against Austria and Prussia in 1797. Two years later, shortly after Napoleon had become first consul, he directed his army to further military successes that paved the way to French dominance of Europe. The defeat of Austria in 1800 confirmed earlier territorial gains in Italy as well as French control over the southern Netherlands, now called Belgium. With Austria defeated and Russia involved with the Ottoman Turks, France and Britain concluded peace at Amiens in 1802. This peace gave Napoleon free rein to reorganize the countries that bordered on France's eastern and southeastern boundaries. In Italy he named himself the president of the newly established Cisalpine Republic, and he transformed the cantons of Switzerland into the Helvetic Republic. These acquisitions gave substance to the title of emperor that he assumed in 1804, because now he controlled many different kingdoms. France had not had an emperor since the ninth century, when Charlemagne and his heirs had ruled as Roman emperors, and Napoleon's territories were more extensive than those under Charlemagne's jurisdiction.

These stunning military successes as well as those that were to follow have secured Napoleon's reputation as one of the most brilliant and successful military leaders in modern history. The reasons for that reputation are a matter of some controversy. Napoleon made terrible strategic blunders in many of his campaigns and tactical mistakes in many of his battles. Somehow he seemed to make up for these mistakes by his careful planning, unbounded energy, and decisive moves. He spent hours studying his opponents' position beforehand but made quick decisions once the battle had begun. "Everything," he once said, "is in the execution." The combination of infantry, artillery, and cavalry in the same units or *corps* allowed him to move these forces easily on the battlefield. He struck quickly, usually at the center of enemy lines, using superior numbers to overwhelm his opponent. Attacks on enemy lines of communication often prevented his opponents from calling up reinforcements. Once they began their retreat, he would pursue them rather than stop to celebrate. In his campaigns he benefited from the loyalty of his troops and the ideological zeal that continued to inspire them, even as his wars lost their ideological purpose of exporting the ideals of the revolution.

Napoleon was far less successful at sea than on land. With no real experience in naval warfare, he could not match the dominance of the British navy, which retained its mastery of the seas throughout the entire revolutionary period. Only in the West Indies, where Britain was never able to send sufficient naval forces, did the French navy manage to hold its own. This naval weakness also explains Napoleon's failure to build or regain an overseas empire. His expedition to Egypt in 1798, which was dominated by dreams of colonial conquest in the Middle East and South Asia, was checked by the British destruction of the French fleet at the Battle of the Nile. In the Western Hemisphere financial problems and a false hope of limiting British power induced Napoleon to sell the vast North American territory of Louisiana, which he had regained from Spain in 1800, to the United States in 1803. The following year the French Caribbean colony of St. Domingue became independent as the result of the violent revolution staged by free blacks and slaves, as discussed in Chapter 17. Informed of that loss, Napoleon shouted "Damn sugar, damn coffee, damn colonies!"

The most significant French naval defeat came in 1805, shortly after Britain, Austria, and Russia had formed the Third Coalition against France. As Napoleon was preparing for an invasion of Britain from northern French ports, the British navy, under the command of the diminutive, one-eyed Admiral Horatio Nelson, won one of the most decisive battles in the history of naval warfare. Nelson broke the line of a Franco-Spanish fleet that was preparing to strike off the Cape of Trafalgar near Gibraltar. The British destroyed or captured half the enemy ships, thus breaking the back of French sea power. The battle is commemorated at Trafalgar Square in London, which is overlooked by a towering statue of Nelson, who died of wounds inflicted during the battle. Nelson might have survived if he had not insisted on wearing glimmering medals on his uniform, thereby attracting the notice of French marksmen.

The monumental naval defeat at Trafalgar did not prevent Napoleon from continuing his wars of conquest in central Europe. In October 1805 he defeated an Austrian army at Ulm, and in December of that year he overwhelmed the combined forces of Austria and Russia at Austerlitz. These victories brought him new German and Italian territory, which he ceded to some of the larger German states; the smaller German states became satellites of France and fought with him until the collapse of his empire. A defeat of Prussian forces at Jena and Auerstädt in 1806 and the subsequent occupation of Berlin gave him the opportunity to carve the new German kingdom of Westphalia out of Prussian territory in the Rhineland and to install his brother Jerome as its ruler. In the East he created the duchy of Warsaw out of Polish lands controlled by Prussia. In 1806

The French Encounter the Egyptians, 1798–1801

Napoleon's expedition to Egypt in 1798 marked one of the few times during the revolutionary period that the French came in direct contact with non-Western peoples. The expedition resulted in the military occupation of the country for three years and set the stage for the first extensive encounters between Egyptians and Europeans since the Ottoman conquest of Egypt in the sixteenth century. At that time Egypt had become a semiautonomous province of the Ottoman Empire and had very little contact with the West. Egypt's isolation from the West meant that it had little exposure to the scientific and technological discoveries that had taken place in western Europe during the previous 300 years.

In addition to 38,000 soldiers, Napoleon brought with him 165 scholars who were organized in a Commission of Science and Arts. These men came from virtually every branch of learning: surveyors, cartographers, civil engineers, architects, botanists, physicians, chemists, and mineralogists. The commission also included artists, archaeologists, writers, and musicians. Their purpose was to give Napoleon information on the people and the resources of the country so that he could more easily subject it to French domination. A small group of these scholars set up an Institute of Egypt, whose mission was to propagate the Enlightenment and to undertake research on the history, people, and the economy of the country. This involved the scholarly study of Egyptian antiquities, including the pyramids.

This work of the institute ushered in a long period in which many artifacts of Egyptian antiquity were taken from the country and transported to European museums and palaces. Members of the institute encouraged this cultural plundering, arguing that their addition to the collections of the Louvre would embellish the glory of France. This plundering of native Egyptian antiquities represented a form of cultural imperialism that continued unabated during the nineteenth century.

Cultural imperialism of a different sort can be found in a widely disseminated description of Egypt, *Travels in Upper and Lower Egypt* (1802), by a member of the institute, Dominique Vivant-Denon. This two-volume work contained extensive descriptions of the different "races" of people in Egypt whom the expedition encountered in the thriving port town of Rosetta. Vivant-Denon described the Copts, the most ancient Egyptians, as "swarthy Nubians" with flat foreheads, high cheekbones, and short broad noses. They displayed the moral qualities of "ignorance, drunkenness, cunning, and finesse." The Arabs, who were the most numerous group, and the Turks had more appealing physical and personal characteristics, although they were often reduced to the "degraded state of animals."

Expressions of French cultural superiority permeate other contemporary accounts of Napoleon's expedition. A multivolume work, *The Description of Egypt*, claimed that Napoleon wanted to procure for Egyptians "all the advantages of a perfected civilization." It praised him for bringing modern knowledge to a country that had been "plunged into darkness." These attitudes provided a justification for the subsequent economic exploitation of Egypt, first by the French and later by the British, during the nineteenth century.

For Discussion

In what ways did Vivant-Denon's work reflect the values that were cultivated during the Enlightenment?

Jean Charles Tardieu, *The French Army Halts at Syene, Upper Egypt, on February 2, 1799*
This painting depicts a cultural encounter between French soldiers and Egyptians in the city of Syene (now Aswan) during the Egyptian campaign of 1798–1799. The soldiers are scribbling on the ruins of ancient Egypt, indicating a lack of respect for Egyptian culture.

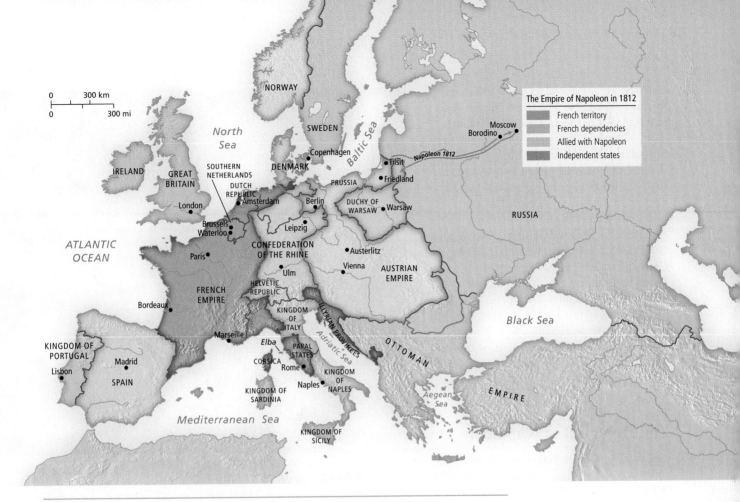

Map 19.1 The Empire of Napoleon in 1812

By establishing dependent states in Spain, Italy, Germany, and Poland, France controlled far more territory than the areas technically within the French Empire.

he formally dissolved the ancient Holy Roman Empire and replaced it with a loose association of sixteen German states known as the Confederation of the Rhine. By 1807, in the words of one historian, Napoleon had "only allies and victims" on the Continent (see Map 19.1).

Napoleon inserted the last piece in this imperial puzzle by invading and occupying the kingdom of Spain in 1808. This campaign began as an effort to crush Portugal, the ally of Britain, which he was never able to defeat. In May 1808, as French armies marched through Spain en route to Lisbon, the Portuguese capital, a popular insurrection against Spanish rule occurred in Madrid. This spontaneous revolt, which led to the abdication of King Charles IV and the succession of his son Ferdinand VII, was the first of many developments that caused the collapse of the Spanish Empire in America. In Europe it led to the absorption of Spain into the French Empire. Sensing that he could easily add one more territory to his list of conquests, Napoleon forced Ferdinand to abdicate and summoned his own brother, Joseph Bonaparte, who was then ruling the dependent kingdom of Naples, to become king of Spain.

Joseph instituted some reforms in Spain, but the abolition of the Spanish Inquisition and the closing of two-thirds of the Spanish convents triggered a visceral reaction from the Spanish clergy and the general populace. Fighting for Church and king, small bands of local guerillas subjected French forces to intermittent and effective sabotage. An invasion by British forces under the command of Arthur Wellesley, later the Duke of Wellington (1769–1852), in what has become known as the Peninsula War (1808–1813), strengthened Spanish and Portuguese resistance.

The reception of the French in Spain revealed that the export of revolution, which had begun with the French armies of 1792, was a double-edged sword. The overthrow of authoritarian regimes in other European states won the support of progressive, capitalist, and anticlerical forces in those countries, but it also triggered deep resentment against French rule. The ideology of nationalism in Germany and Italy arose more because of a reaction against French rule than because the armies of France had tried to stimulate it. In Italy during the 1790s young educated *patrioti*, imbued with enthusiasm for liberty, equality, and progress, supported the newly proclaimed republics and envisioned the establishment of a single Italian state, at least in the north of Italy. By the middle of the Napoleonic years that vision had changed. Many of the *patrioti* had become disillusioned and joined secret societies to press for further political and social change and to plot insurrections against the new republics.

In Germany many of those who supported the French cause during the early years of the Republic turned away from it during Napoleon's wars of expansion. In 1809 a German student who attempted to assassinate Napoleon shouted "Long live Germany!" at his execution. In 1813 the German writer Johann Gottlieb Fichte (1762–1814) appealed to the German nation to resist Napoleon in order to regain their liberty. For all his political astuteness, Napoleon could not comprehend that his own policies were responsible for the growth of this reactive sentiment, which formed one of the foundations of nineteenth-century nationalism. We shall discuss this topic more fully in Chapter 21.

The Downfall of Napoleon

The turning point in Napoleon's personal fortunes and those of his empire came in 1810. After securing an annulment of his marriage to Josephine in late 1809, he married Marie-Louise, the daughter of the Habsburg emperor. This marriage, which the following year produced a son and heir to the throne, should have made the French Empire more secure, but it had the opposite effect. For the first time during his rule, dissent from both the right and the left became widespread. Despite the most stringent efforts at censorship, royalist and Jacobin literature poured off the presses. The number of military deserters and those evading conscription increased. Relations with the papacy reached a breaking point when Napoleon annexed the Papal States, at which point Pope Pius VII, who had negotiated the Concordat of 1801, excommunicated him.

Dissent at home had the effect of driving the megalomaniacal emperor to seek more glory and further conquests. In this frame of mind Napoleon made the ill-advised decision to invade Russia. The motives for engaging in this overly ambitious military campaign were not completely irrational. Victory over Russia promised to give France control of the Black Sea, and that in turn would ultimately lead to the control of Constantinople and the entire Middle East. More immediately, defeating Russia would be necessary to enforce the French blockade of British goods, which Russia had refused to support.

The problem with a Russian invasion was that it stretched Napoleon's lines of communication too far and his resources too thin, despite the support of the Austrians and Prussians whom he had defeated. Even before the inva-

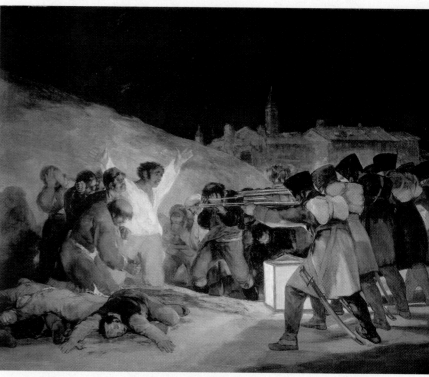

Francisco Goya, *The Third of May 1808*
This painting of the suppression of the popular revolt in Madrid in 1808 captures the brutality of the French occupation of Spain. A French unit executes Spanish citizens, including a monk in the foreground. Goya was a figure of the Enlightenment and a Spanish patriot.

VIDEO
The Art of Francisco Goya

sion it was becoming increasingly difficult to feed, equip, and train the huge army he had assembled. The Grand Army that crossed from Poland into Russia in 1812 was not the efficient military force that Napoleon had commanded in the early years of the empire. Many of his best soldiers were fighting in the guerilla war in Spain. Casualties and desertions had forced Napoleon to call up new recruits who were not properly trained. Half the army, moreover, had been recruited from the population of conquered countries, making their loyalty to Napoleon uncertain.

The tactics of the Russians contributed to the failure of the invasion. Instead of engaging the Grand Army in combat, the Russian army kept retreating, pulling Napoleon further east toward Moscow. On September 7 the two armies clashed at Borodino, suffering a staggering 77,000 casualties in all. The Russian army then continued its retreat eastward. When Napoleon reached Moscow he found it deserted, and fires deliberately set by Muscovites had destroyed more than two-thirds of the city. Napoleon, facing the onset of a dreaded Russian winter and rapidly diminishing supplies, began the long retreat back to France. Skirmishes with the Russians along the way, which cost him 25,000 lives just crossing the Beresina River, conspired with the cold and hunger to destroy his army. During the entire Russian campaign his army lost a total of 380,000 men to death, imprisonment, or desertion. In the midst of this horror Napoleon, oblivious to the suffering of his troops, reported back to Paris, "The health of the emperor has never been better."

Not to be discouraged, Napoleon soon began preparing for further conquests. Once again his enemies formed a coalition against him, pledging to restore the independence of the countries that had become his satellites or dependents. Napoleon scored a few victories in the late summer of 1813, but in October allied forces inflicted a crushing defeat on him in the Battle of the Nations at Leipzig. Austrian troops administered another blow to the French in northern Italy, and the British finally drove them out of Spain. As a result of these defeats, Napoleon's army was pushed back into France. A massive allied force advanced into Paris and occupied the city. After extensive political maneuvering, including a vote by the Senate to depose Napoleon, the emperor abdicated on April 6, 1814. The allies promptly exiled him to the Mediterranean island of Elba. As he made the journey to the coast, crowds surrounding his coach shouted "Down with the tyrant!" while some villagers hanged him in effigy.

This course of events led to the restoration of the Bourbon monarchy. By the terms of the first Treaty of Paris of May 1814, the allies restored the brother of Louis XVI, the Count of Provence, to the French throne as Louis XVIII (r. 1814–1824). Louis was an implacable foe of the revolution, and much of what he did was intended to undermine its achievements. The white Bourbon flag replaced the revolutionary tricolor. Catholicism was once again recognized as the state religion. Exiled royalists returned to their high-ranking positions in the army. Nonetheless, Louis accepted a Constitutional Charter that incorporated many of the changes made between 1789 and 1791. Representative government, with a relatively limited franchise, replaced the absolutism of the Old Regime. Equality before the law, freedom of religion, and freedom of expression were all reaffirmed. Even more important, the powers of the state that the National Assembly and the Directory had extended and Napoleon had enhanced were maintained. The administrative division of France into departments continued, and the Napoleonic Code remained in force. France had experienced a counterrevolution in 1814, but it did not simply turn the political clock back to 1788. Some of the political achievements of the previous twenty-five years were indeed preserved.

Despite his disgrace and exile, Napoleon still commanded loyalty from his troops and from large segments of the population. While in power he had constructed a legend that drew on strong patriotic sentiment. Supporters throughout France continued to promote his cause in the same way that royalists had maintained that of the Bourbon monarchy since 1792. The Napoleonic legend held great appeal among the lower classes, who were per-

CHRONOLOGY

The Downfall of Napoleon, 1807–1815

1807

November–December	French military intervention in Spain and Portugal begins

1808

| May | Beginning of the Spanish rebellion |
| July 20 | Joseph Bonaparte appointed king of Spain |

1809

| December 15 | Annulment of marriage of Napoleon and Empress Josephine |

1810

| April 2 | Marriage of Napoleon to Marie-Louise |

1812

September 7	Battle of Borodino
September 14	Napoleon enters Moscow
October	Retreat from Moscow begins

1813

| October 16–19 | Battle of the Nations at Leipzig |

1814

April 6	Abdication of Napoleon
May 30	First Treaty of Paris
September	Congress of Vienna assembles

1815

March	Napoleon escapes from Elba
June 18	Battle of Waterloo
November 20	Second Treaty of Paris

suaded that Napoleon, the patriot and the savior of the revolution, had made it possible for every Frenchman to achieve wealth and fame. The strength of the Napoleonic legend became apparent in March 1815, when Napoleon escaped from Elba and landed in southern France. Promising to rid the country of the exiled royalists who had returned and to save the revolutionary cause that he claimed had been abandoned, he won over peasants, workers, and soldiers. Regiment after regiment joined him as he marched toward Paris. By the time he arrived, Louis XVIII had gone into exile once again, and Napoleon found himself back in power.

But not for long. The allied European powers quickly began to assemble yet another coalition. Fearing that the allies would launch a massive invasion of France, Napoleon decided to strike first. He marched an army of 200,000 men into the Austrian Netherlands, where the allies responded by amassing 700,000 troops. Near the small village of Waterloo, south of Brussels, he met the British forces of the Duke of Wellington, who had turned the tide against him during the Peninsula War. Reinforced by Prussian troops, Wellington inflicted a devastating defeat on the French army, which lost 28,000 men and went into a full-scale retreat. Napoleon, captured in the battle, abdicated once again. He was

DOCUMENT

Napoleon's Exile to St. Helena (1815)

exiled to the remote South Atlantic island of St. Helena, from which escape was impossible. He died there in 1821.

Even before the battle of Waterloo, the major powers of Europe had gathered in Vienna to redraw the boundaries of the European states that had been created, dismembered, or transformed during the preceding twenty-five years (see Map 19.2). Under the leadership of the Austrian foreign minister, Prince Clemens von Metternich (1773–1859), this conference, known as the Congress of Vienna°, worked out a settlement that was intended to preserve the balance of power in Europe and at the same time uphold the principle of dynastic legitimacy. By the terms of a separate Treaty of Paris (the second in two years) the boundaries of France

Map 19.2 Europe After the Congress of Vienna, 1815

The four most important territorial changes that took place in 1815 were the scaling back of the boundaries of France to their status in 1790, the Austrian acquisition of territory in western and northeastern Italy, the establishment of the new kingdom of the Netherlands, and the formation of the new German Confederation.

Europe After the Congress of Vienna, 1815

- France
- Habsburg Empire
- Russian Empire
- German States
- Prussia
- Sardinia
- Boundary of German Confederation

were scaled back to what they had been in 1790, before it had begun its wars of expansion. To create a buffer state on the northern boundary of France, the Congress annexed the Austrian Netherlands to the Dutch Republic, which now became the kingdom of the Netherlands with William I, a prince of the House of Orange, as its king. Territory along the Rhineland in the state of Westphalia was ceded to Prussia, while Austria gained territory in Italy, both along the French border in the west and in northern Italy to the east. In place of the defunct Holy Roman Empire, the Congress established a new German Confederation, a loose coalition of thirty-nine separate territories with a weak legislative assembly, whose members were appointed and instructed by their governments. The five major powers that had drawn this new map of Europe—Britain, Austria, Prussia, Russia, and France—agreed to meet annually to prevent any one country, especially France but also Russia, from achieving military dominance of the European Continent.

The Legacy of the French Revolution

■ What did the French Revolution ultimately achieve and in what ways did it change the course of European and Western history?

With the conclusion of the Congress of Vienna a tumultuous period of European and Western history finally came to an end. Not only had France experienced a revolution, but every country in Europe and America had felt its effects. Governments were toppled in countries as far apart as Poland and Peru. Added to this turbulence was the experience of incessant warfare. France was at war for more than twenty years during the period of the Republic and the empire, and it had brought almost all European powers into the struggle. With armies constantly in need of provisions and supplies, high taxation, galloping inflation, and food shortages inflicted economic hardship on a large portion of the European population.

The cost of all this instability and warfare in terms of human life was staggering. Within the space of one generation almost two million European soldiers were killed in action, wasted by disease, or starved or frozen to death. In France alone just under 500,000 soldiers died during the revolutionary wars of 1792–1802 and another 916,000 during the wars of the empire. Internal political disturbances took the lives of hundreds of thousands of civilians from all ranks of society, not only in France but throughout Europe. The violence was fed at all levels by unprecedented fears of internal and external subversion. Government officials, col-

laborators, counterrevolutionaries, and imagined enemies of the state were all executed. This spate of violence and death—much of it in the name of liberty—was inflicted almost entirely by the state or its enemies.

What was achieved at this extraordinary price? How did the France of 1815 differ from the France of 1788? What on balance had changed? For many years historians, especially those who believed that economic forces determined the course of history, claimed that as a result of the revolution the bourgeoisie, composed of merchants, manufacturers, and other commoners of substantial wealth, had replaced the nobility as the dominant social and political class in the country. The bourgeoisie, so they argued, had started the revolution in order to acquire political power that was commensurate with their economic power, and they had ultimately prevailed.

This assessment can no longer be sustained. The nobility certainly lost many of their privileges in 1789, and many of them went into exile during the revolutionary period, but the position they had in French society in 1815 did not differ greatly from what it had been under the Old Regime. In both periods there was considerable blurring of the distinctions between nobility and bourgeoisie. Nor did the revolutionary period witness the emergence of a new class of industrial entrepreneurs. The only group who definitely profited from the revolution in the long run were men of property, regardless of their membership in any social category or "class." Men of property emerged triumphant in the Directory, found favor during the Napoleonic period, and became the most important members of political society after the monarchy was restored.

It would be difficult to argue that *women* of any social rank benefited from the revolution. During the early years of the revolution, women participated actively in public life. They were involved in many demonstrations in Paris, including the storming of the Bastille and the march to Versailles to pressure the king to move to Paris. Women as well as men filled the ranks of the *sans-culottes,* and women donned their own female version of nonaristocratic dress. During the early years of the revolution, many women joined patriotic clubs, such as the Club of Knitters or the unisex Fraternal Society of Patriots of Both Sexes. In 1790 the Marquis de Condorcet published *On the Admission of Women to the Rights of Citizenship,* and the following year Olympe de Gouges published *The Rights of Women,* in which she called for the granting of women's equal rights. Both of these advocates of women's rights had been influenced by Enlightenment thought, as we have discussed in Chapter 18.

The goal advanced by Condorcet and de Gouges was not to be realized. The radical Jacobins dealt it a terrible setback when they banned all women's clubs and societies on the grounds that their participation in public life would harm the institution of the family. This action, coupled with the imprisonment and death of both de Gouges and Condorcet during the Terror, signaled an end to the extensive participation of women in political life, which had begun during the eighteenth century, especially in the salons. During the nineteenth century women were generally considered to occupy a separate sphere of activity from that of men. They were expected to exercise influence in the private sphere of the home, but not in the public sphere of politics. As we shall discuss in Chapter 20, the changes wrought by the Industrial Revolution reinforced this segregation of men and women by excluding many married women from the workforce.

It is even more difficult to identify permanent economic changes as a result of the revolution. The elimination of the remnants of feudalism may have made France marginally more capitalist than it had been before the revolution, but agricultural and mercantile capitalism had long been entrenched in French society. Nor did the Continental System, the blockade of British goods from all European ports initiated in 1806, allow French industry to catch up with that of Great Britain. Whatever economic gains were made under the protective shield of the state were offset by the adverse economic effects of twenty-two years of nearly continuous warfare. In the long run the revolutionary period delayed the process of industrialization that had entered its preliminary stages in France during the 1780s and retarded the growth of the French economy for the remainder of the nineteenth century.

The permanent legacy of the French Revolution lies in the realm of politics. First, the period from 1789 to 1815 triggered an enormous growth in the competence and power of the state. This trend had begun before the revolution, but the desire of the revolutionaries to transform every aspect of human life in the service of the revolution, coupled with the necessity of utilizing all the country's resources in the war effort, gave the state more control over the everyday life of its citizens than ever before. Fifteen years of Napoleonic rule only accentuated this trend, and after 1815 many of those powers remained with the government.

An even more significant and permanent achievement of the French Revolution was the promotion of the doctrine of popular sovereignty. The belief that the people constituted the highest political authority in the state became so entrenched during the revolution that it could never be completely suppressed, either in France or in the other countries of Europe. Napoleon recognized its power when he asked the people to approve political changes he had already made by his own authority. He also arranged for such plebiscites to secure approval of the new states he had set up in Europe. After the restoration of the monarchy the doctrine of popular sovereignty was promoted mainly by the press, which continued to employ the new revolutionary rhetoric to keep alive the high ideals and aspirations of the revolution. The doctrine also contributed to the formation of two nineteenth-century ideologies, liberalism and nationalism, which will be discussed in Chapter 21.

The third permanent political change was the active participation of the citizens in the political life of the nation. This participation had been cultivated during the early years of the revolution, and it had been accompanied by the creation of a new political culture. Much of that culture was suppressed during the Napoleonic period, but the actual habit of participating in politics was not. The franchise was gradually expanded in Europe during the nineteenth century. The press spread political ideas to a large segment of the population. People from all walks of life participated in marches, processions, and demonstrations. All of this followed from the acceptance of the French revolutionary doctrine that the people are sovereign and have a right therefore to participate in the political life of the state.

Conclusion

The French Revolution and Western Civilization

The French Revolution was a central event in the history of the West. It began as an internal French affair, reflecting the social and political tensions of the Old Regime, but it soon became a turning point in European and Western history. Proclamations of the natural rights of humanity gave the ideals of the revolution widespread appeal, and a period of protracted warfare succeeded in disseminating those ideals outside the boundaries of France.

Underlying the export of French revolutionary ideology was the belief that France had become the standard-bearer of Western civilization. French people believed they were *la grande nation,* the country that had reached the highest level of political and social organization. They did not believe they had acquired this exalted status by inheritance. Unlike the English revolutionaries of the seventeenth century, they did not claim that they were the heirs of a medieval constitution. French republicans of the 1790s attributed none of their national preeminence to the monarchy, whose memory they took drastic steps to erase. They considered the secular political culture that emerged during the French Revolution to be an entirely novel development.

The export of French revolutionary political culture during the Republic and the empire brought about widespread changes in the established order. Regimes were toppled, French puppets acquired political power, boundaries of states were completely redrawn, and traditional authorities were challenged. Liberal reforms were enacted, new constitutions were written, and new law codes were promulgated. The Europe of 1815 could not be mistaken for the Europe of 1789.

The ideas of the French Revolution, like those of the Enlightenment that had helped to inspire them, did not go unchallenged. From the very early years of the revolution they encountered determined opposition, both in France and abroad. As the revolution lost its appeal in France, the forces of conservatism and reaction gathered strength. At the end of the Napoleonic period, the Congress of Vienna took steps to restore the legitimate rulers of European states and to prevent revolution from recurring. It appeared that the revolution would be completely reversed, but that was not the case. The ideas born of the revolution would continue to inspire demands for political reform in Europe during the nineteenth century, and those demands, just like those in the 1790s, would meet with fierce resistance.

Suggestions for Further Reading

For a comprehensive listing of suggested readings, please go to www.ablongman.com/levack2e/chapter19

Andress, David. *The French Revolution and the People.* 2004. Focuses on the role played by the common people of France— the peasants, craftsmen and those living on the margins of society—in the revolution.

Blanning, T. C. W. *The French Revolutionary Wars, 1787–1802.* 1996. An authoritative political and military narrative that assesses the impact of the wars on French politics.

Chartier, Roger. *The Cultural Origins of the French Revolution.* 1991. Explores the connections between the culture of the Enlightenment and the cultural transformations of the revolutionary period.

Cobban, Alfred. *The Social Interpretation of the French Revolution.* 1964. Challenges the Marxist interpretation of the causes and effects of the revolution.

Doyle, William. *The Oxford History of the French Revolution.* 1989. An excellent synthesis.

Ellis, Geoffrey. *Napoleon.* 1997. A study of the nature and mechanics of Napoleon's power and an analysis of his imperial policy.

Furet, François. *The French Revolution, 1770–1814.* 1992. A provocative narrative that sees Napoleon as the architect of a second, authoritarian revolution that reversed the gains of the first.

Hardman, John. *Louis XVI: The Silent King.* 2000. A reassessment of the king that mixes sympathy with criticism.

Higonnet, Patrice. *Goodness Beyond Virtue: Jacobins During the French Revolution.* 1998. Explores the contradictions of Jacobin ideology and its descent into the Terror.

Hunt, Lynn. *Politics, Culture and Class in the French Revolution.* 1984. Analyzes the formation of a revolutionary political culture.

Kennedy, Emmet. *The Culture of the French Revolution.* 1989. A comprehensive study of all cultural developments before and during the revolution.

Landes, Joan B. *Women and the Public Sphere in the Age of the French Revolution.* 1988. Explores how the new political culture of the revolution changed the position of women in society.

Lefebvre, Georges. *The Great Fear of 1789: Rural Panic in Revolutionary France.* 1973. Shows the importance of the rural unrest of July 1789 that provided the backdrop of the legislation of August 1789.

Schama, Simon. *Citizens: A Chronicle of the French Revolution.* 1989. Depicts the tragic unraveling of a vision of liberty and happiness into a scenario of hunger, anger, violence, and death.

Notes

1. Emmanuel-Joseph Sieyès, *What Is the Third Estate?* (1789).

2. H. Wallon, *Histoire du tribunal révolutionnaire de Paris* (1880–1882), Vol. 4, 511.

The Industrial Revolution

20

I N 1842 A 17-YEAR-OLD GIRL, PATIENCE KERSHAW, TESTIFIED BEFORE A BRITISH parliamentary committee regarding the practice of employing children and women in the nation's mines. When the girl made her appearance, the members of the committee observed that she was "an ignorant, filthy, ragged, and deplorable-looking object, such as one of uncivilized natives of the prairies would be shocked to look upon." Patience, who had never been to school and could not read or write, told the committee that she was one of ten children, all of whom had at one time worked in the coal mines, although three of her sisters now worked in a textile mill. She went to the pit at five in the morning and came out at five at night. Her job in the mines was to hurry coal, that is, to pull carts of coal through the narrow tunnels of the mine. Each cart weighed 300 pounds, and every day she hauled eleven of them one mile. The carts were attached to her head and shoulders by a chain and belt, and the pressure of the cart had worn a bald spot on her head. Patience hurried coal for twelve hours straight, not taking any time for her midday meal, which she ate as she worked. While she was working, the men and boys who dug the coal and put it in the carts would often beat her and take sexual liberties with her. Patience told the committee, "I am the only girl in the pit; there are about 20 boys and 15 men. All the men are naked. I would rather work in a mill than a coal pit."[1]

Patience Kershaw was one of the human casualties of an extraordinary development that historians usually refer to as the Industrial Revolution. This process, which brought about a fundamental transformation of human life, involved the extensive use of machinery in the production of goods. Much of that machinery was driven by steam engines, which required coal to produce the steam. Coal mining itself became a major industry, and the men who owned and operated the mines tried to hire workers, many of them children, at the lowest possible wage. It was this desire to maximize profits that led to the employment, physical hardship, and abuse of girls like Patience Kershaw.

Exhibit of Machinery at the Crystal Palace Exhibition in London in 1851
During the Industrial Revolution the manufacture of heavy machinery itself became an industry.

Child Labor in the Mines
A child hurrying coal through a tunnel in a mine.

The story of the Industrial Revolution cannot be told solely in terms of the exploitation of child or even adult workers. Many of its effects can be described in positive or at least morally neutral terms. The Industrial Revolution resulted in a staggering increase in the volume and range of products made available to consumers, from machine-produced clothing to household utensils. It made possible unprecedented and sustained economic growth. The Industrial Revolution facilitated the rapid transportation of passengers as well as goods across large expanses of territory, mainly on the railroads that were constructed in all industrialized countries. It brought about a new awareness of the position of workers in the economic system, and it unleashed powerful political forces intended to improve the lot of these workers.

The Industrial Revolution played a crucial role in redefining and reshaping the West. Until the late nineteenth century industrialization took place only in Western nations. During that century "the West" gradually became identified with countries that had industrial economies. When some non-Western countries introduced mechanized industry in the twentieth century, largely in imitation of Western example, the geographical boundaries of the West underwent a significant alteration.

The main question this chapter sets out to answer is why this fundamental transformation of Western civilization began in Europe in the late eighteenth and nineteenth centuries. The individual sections of the chapter will address the following questions:

■ **What do historians mean when they refer to the Industrial Revolution of the late eighteenth and nineteenth centuries?**
■ **What social and economic changes made industrial development possible?**

■ **How did industrialization spread from Great Britain to the European continent and America?**
■ **What were the economic, social, and cultural effects of the Industrial Revolution?**
■ **What was the relationship between the growth of industry and Britain's dominance in trade and imperial strength during the middle years of the nineteenth century?**

The Nature of the Industrial Revolution

■ **What do historians mean when they refer to the Industrial Revolution of the late eighteenth and nineteenth centuries?**

The Industrial Revolution was a series of economic and social changes that took place in Great Britain during the late eighteenth and early nineteenth centuries and on the European continent and in the United States after 1815. Some economic historians claim that the use of the term *revolution*, which suggests radical and abrupt change, is misleading in this context, because the economic and social changes to which the term refers occurred gradually over a long period of time. Even so, the term is still appropriate because it conveys the radical nature and profound significance of the changes it identifies. Like the Scientific Revolution of the seventeenth century, which also took place gradually, the Industrial Revolution reshaped Western civilization.

The Industrial Revolution consisted of four closely related developments: the introduction of new industrial technology, the utilization of mineral sources of energy, the concentration of labor in factories, and the development of new methods of transportation.

New Industrial Technology

The Industrial Revolution ushered in the machine age, and to this day machines are the most striking feature of modern industrial economies. In countries that have become industrialized, virtually every human-made commodity can be mass-produced by some kind of machine. In the late eighteenth century such machines were novelties, but their numbers increased dramatically in the early nineteenth century. For example, the power loom, a machine used for weaving cloth, was invented in Britain in 1787 but not put into widespread use until the 1820s. By 1836 there were more than 60,000 power looms in just one English county.

Machines became so common in Britain that machine making itself became a major industry, supplying its products to other manufacturers rather than to individual consumers. Machines were introduced in the textile, iron, printing, papermaking, and engineering industries and were used in every stage of manufacture. Machines extracted minerals that were used as either raw materials or sources of energy, transported those materials to the factories, saved time and labor in the actual manufacturing of commodities, and carried the finished products to market. Eventually machines were used in agriculture itself, facilitating both the plowing of fields and the harvesting of crops.

The most significant of the new machines, which changed the entire industrial process, were those used for spinning and weaving in the textile industry and the steam engine, first used in mining and the iron industry. These pieces of machinery became almost synonymous with the Industrial Revolution, and their invention in the 1760s appropriately marks its beginning.

Textile Machinery

Until the late eighteenth century, the production of textiles throughout Europe, which involved both the spinning of yarn and the weaving of cloth, was done entirely by hand, on spinning wheels and hand looms respectively. This was the practice for wool, which was the main textile produced in Europe during the early modern period, as well as for a new material, cotton, which became immensely popular in the early eighteenth century, mainly because of its greater comfort. The demand for cotton yarn was greater than the quantities spinners could supply. To meet this demand a British inventor, James Hargreaves, in 1767 constructed a new machine, the spinning jenny, which greatly increased the amount of cotton yarn that could be spun and thus made available for weaving. The original jenny, a hand machine used in the homes of spinners, consisted of only eight spindles, but it later accommodated as many as 120.

The spinning of yarn on the jenny required a stronger warp, the yarn that ran lengthwise on a loom. A power-driven machine, the water frame, introduced by the barber and wigmaker Richard Arkwright in 1769, made the production of this stronger warp possible. In 1779 Samuel Crompton, using tools he had purchased with his earnings as a fiddle player at a local theater, combined the jenny and the frame in one machine, called the mule. Crompton worked on his machine only at night, in order to keep it secret, and the strange noises that came out of his workshop made his neighbors think his house was haunted. The mule, which could spin as much as 300 times the amount of yarn produced by one spinning wheel, became the main spinning machine of the early Industrial Revolution. Both the water frame and the mule required power, and that requirement led to the centralization of the textile industry in large rural mills located near rivers so that their water wheels could drive the machinery.

The tremendous success of the mule eventually produced more yarn than the weavers could handle on their hand

Broadlie Mill in the 1790s
The earliest textile mills were built in the rural areas, near rivers that supplied water power. This mill was built on the Broadlie farm, near the village of Neilston in southwestern Scotland, about twelve miles from Glasgow. The power to run the mill came from the Levern River. By 1815 there were six cotton mills in the area, supporting a community of about 1,500 workers. Housing for the workers, including some houses for single women, was constructed near the mills.

looms. Edmund Cartwright, an Oxford-educated clergyman, supported by monies from his heiress wife, addressed that need with the invention of the power loom in 1787. In that same year he put his new invention to use in a weaving mill he built near the town of Doncaster. The power loom, like the spinning jenny, the water frame, and the mule, met a specific need within the industry. It also gave the producer a competitive advantage by saving time, reducing the cost of labor, and increasing production. Two power looms run by a 15-year-old boy, for example, could produce more than three times what a skilled hand loom weaver could turn out in the same time using only the old hand device, the flying shuttle. The net effect of all these machines was the production of more than 200 times as much cotton cloth in 1850 as in 1780. By 1800 cotton became Britain's largest industry, producing more than 20 percent of the world's cloth, and by 1850 that percentage had risen to more than 50 percent. Indeed, by midcentury, cotton accounted for 70 percent of the value of all British exports.

The Steam Engine

The steam engine was even more important than the new textile machinery because it was used in almost every stage of the productive process, including the operation of textile machinery itself. The steam engine was invented by a Scottish engineer, James Watt, in 1763. It represented an improvement over the engine invented by Thomas Newcomen in 1709, which had been intended mainly to drain water from deep mines. The problem with Newcomen's engine was that the steam, which was produced in a cylinder heated by coal, had to be cooled in order to make the piston return, and the process of heating and cooling had to be repeated for each stroke of the piston. The engine was therefore inefficient and expensive to operate. Watt created a separate chamber where the steam could be condensed without affecting the heat of the cylinder. The result was a more efficient and cost-effective machine that could pro-

vide more power than any other source. Watt's pride in his invention was matched only by his pride in his Scottish nationality. Upon receiving a patent for the new device, he boasted, "This was made by a Scot."

After designing the steam engine, Watt teamed up with a Birmingham metal manufacturer, Matthew Boulton, to produce it on a large scale. Boulton provided the capital necessary to begin this process and to hire the skilled laborers to assemble the machines. He also had ambitious plans for marketing the new invention throughout the world. "It would not be worth my while to make for three countries only," Boulton said, "but I find it well worth my while to make for the whole world."

The steam engine soon became the workhorse of the Industrial Revolution. Not only did it pump water from mines, but it helped raise minerals such as iron ore that were extracted from those mines. It provided the intense blast of heat that was necessary to resmelt pig iron into cast iron, which in turn was used to make industrial machinery, buildings, bridges, locomotives, and ships. Once the engine was equipped with a rotating device, it was used to drive the factory machinery in the textile mills, and it eventually powered the railroad locomotives that carried industrial goods to market.

The widespread adoption of steam power came fairly late in the Industrial Revolution. Only in the 1840s and 1850s, after its efficiency had been greatly improved, did it become the main source of energy in the textile industry. Until then rural water power was the preferred method of running the cotton mills. Only after the introduction of coal-driven steam power did the factories locate in the cities, especially those of northern England, such as Manchester. The 1840s and 1850s were also the decades when the railroads, using the steam locomotive invented by the English engineer George Stephenson in 1815, began to crisscross the European continent. By midcentury the steam engine had become the predominant symbol of the Industrial Revolution.

CHRONOLOGY

Technological Innovations of the Industrial Revolution

1763	James Watts's rotative steam engine
1767	James Hargreaves's spinning jenny
1769	Richard Arkwright's water frame
1779	Samuel Crompton's mule
1787	Edmund Cartwright's power loom
1815	George Stephenson's steam locomotive
1846	Elias Howe's sewing machine

Mineral Sources of Energy

Until the late eighteenth century, most economic activity, including the transportation of goods, was powered by either humans or beasts. Either people tilled the soil themselves, using a spade, or they yoked oxen to pull a plow. Either they carried materials and goods on their backs or they used horses to transport them. In either case the energy for these tasks came ultimately from organic sources, the food that was needed to feed farmers or their animals. If workers needed heat, they had to burn an organic material, wood or charcoal, to produce it. The amount of energy that could be generated in a particular region was therefore limited by its capacity to produce sufficient wood, charcoal, or food. By the middle of the eighteenth

Philippe Jacques de Loutherbourg, *Coalbrookdale by Night* (1801)
This painting depicts the intense heat produced by the coal bellows used to smelt iron in
Coalbrookdale, an English town in the Severn Valley that was one of the key centers of industrial
activity at the beginning of the nineteenth century.

century, for example, the forests in Britain were no longer capable of producing sufficient quantities of charcoal for use in the iron industry.

Organic sources of energy were of course renewable, in that new crops could be grown and forests replanted, but the long periods of time that these processes took, coupled with the limited volume of organic material that could be extracted from an acre of land, made it difficult to sustain economic growth. The only viable alternatives to these organic sources of energy before the eighteenth century were those that tapped the forces of nature: windmills, which were used mainly in the Netherlands for purposes of field drainage, and water wheels, which were driven by water pressure from river currents, waterfalls, or human-made channels that regulated the flow of water. The potential of those natural sources of energy was both limited and difficult to harness, and it could be tapped only in certain locations or at certain times. Moreover, those sources could not produce heat.

The decisive change in the harnessing of energy for industrial purposes was the successful use of minerals, originally coal but in the twentieth century oil and uranium as well, as the main sources of energy used in the production and transportation of goods. These minerals were not inexhaustible, as the decline of coal deposits in Europe during the twentieth century has shown, but the supplies could last for centuries, and they were much more efficient than any form of energy produced from organic materials, including charcoal and peat. Coal produced the high combustion temperatures necessary to smelt iron, and unlike charcoal it was not limited by the size of a region's forests. Coal therefore became the key to the expansion of the British iron industry in the nineteenth century. That industry's dependence on coal was reflected by the relocation of iron works from the mines that supplied the ore itself to the coal fields that supplied the energy. Coal also became the sole source of heat for the new steam engine.

As the Industrial Revolution progressed, it relied increasingly on coal as its main fuel. The change, however, occurred gradually. In 1830 a majority of factories still used water power, and steam power did not realize its most spectacular increases until after 1870. Nevertheless, largely because of the demands of the mining, textile, and metal industries, coal mining became a major industry itself with an enormous labor force. By 1850 British mines employed about 5 percent of the entire national workforce. These miners were just as instrumental as textile workers in making Britain an industrial nation.

The Growth of Factories

One of the most enduring images of the Industrial Revolution is that of the large factory, filled with workers laboring amid massive machinery driven by either water or steam power. Mechanized factory production evolved out of forms of industry that had emerged only during the early modern period (1500–1750). In the Middle Ages virtually all industry in Europe was undertaken by skilled craftsmen who belonged to urban guilds. These artisans, working either by themselves or with the assistance of apprentices or journeymen, produced everything from candlesticks and hats to oxcarts and beds. During the early modern period the urban craftsman's shop gave way to two different types of industrial workplaces, the rural cottage and the large handicraft workshop. Both of these served as halfway houses to the large factory.

Beginning in the sixteenth century, entrepreneurs began employing families in the countryside to spin and weave cloth and make nails and cutlery. By locating industry in the countryside the entrepreneurs were able to escape the regulations imposed by the guilds regarding employment and the price of finished products. They also paid lower wages, because the rural workers, who also received an income from farming, were willing to work for less than the residents of towns. Another attraction of rural industry was that all the members of the family, including children, participated in the process. In this "domestic system" a capitalist entrepreneur provided the workers with the raw materials and sometimes the tools they needed. He later paid them a fixed rate for each finished product. The entrepreneur was also responsible for having the finished cloth dyed and for marketing the commodities in regional towns.

Rural household industry was widespread not only in certain regions of Britain but also in most European countries. In the late eighteenth century it gradually gave way to the factory system. The great attraction of factory production was mechanization, which became cost-efficient only when it was introduced in a central industrial workplace. In factories, moreover, the entrepreneur could reduce the cost of labor and transportation, exercise tighter control over the quality of goods, and increase productivity by concentrating workers in one location. Temporary labor shortages sometimes made the transition from rural industry to factory production imperative.

DOCUMENT

Adam Smith Describes the Division of Labor

Adam Smith, a Scottish economist who is considered the founder of the classical school of economics, was the great theorist of modern laissez-faire *capitalism. In* An Inquiry into the Nature and Causes of the Wealth of Nations *(1776), he challenged the mercantilist assumption that there was only a fixed supply of wealth for which nations had to compete. He also argued that in an unregulated economy, the pursuit of self-interest would work in the interest of the public welfare. In this selection Smith discusses the division of labor. Smith wrote* The Wealth of Nations *during the very early stages of industrialization. The place of production that he uses in this example is not a large mechanized factory but a small urban workshop, often referred to as a manufactory.*

To take an example, therefore, from a very trifling manufacture; but one in which the division of labour has been very often taken notice of, the trade of the pin-maker; a workman not educated to this business (which the division of labour has rendered a distinct trade), nor acquainted with the use of the machinery employed in it (to the invention of which the same division of labour has probably given occasion), could scarce, perhaps, with his utmost industry, make one pin in a day, and certainly could not make twenty. But in the way in which this business is now carried on, not only the whole work is a peculiar trade, but it is divided into a number of branches, of which the greater part are likewise peculiar trades. One man draws out the wire, another straits it, a third cuts it, a fourth points it, a fifth grinds it at the top for receiving the head; to make the head requires two or three distinct operations; to put it on is a peculiar business, to whiten the pins is another; it is even a trade by itself to put them into the paper; and the important business of making a pin is in this manner, divided into about eighteen distinct operations, which in some manufactories, are all performed by distinct hands, though in others the same man will sometimes perform two or three of them. I have seen a small manufactory of this kind where ten men only were employed, and where some of them consequently performed two or three distinct operations. But though they were very poor and indifferently accommodated with the necessary machinery, they could, when they exerted themselves, make about twelve pounds of pins a day. There are in a pound upwards of four thousand pins of a middling size. Those ten persons, therefore, could make among them upwards of forty-eight thousand pins in a day. Each person, therefore making a tenth part of forty-eight thousand pins, might be considered as making four thousand eight hundred pins in a day.

Source: From Adam Smith, *An Inquiry into the Nature and Causes of the Wealth of Nations,* 5th Edition, 1789, Book I, Chapter 1.

Mule Spinning
A large mechanized spinning mill in northern England, about 1835. The workers did not require
any great skill to run the machinery.

The second type of industrial workplace that emerged during the early modern period was the large handicraft workshop. Usually located in the towns and cities, rather than in the countryside, these workshops employed relatively small numbers of people with different skills who worked collectively on the manufacture of a variety of items, such as pottery and munitions. The owner of the workshop supplied the raw materials, paid the workers' wages, and gained a profit from selling the finished products.

The large handicraft workshop made possible a division of labor°—the assignment of one stage of production to each worker or group of workers. The effect of the division of labor on productivity was evident even in the manufacture of simple items such as buttons and pins. In *The Wealth of Nations* (1776), the economist Adam Smith (1723–1790) used a pin factory in London to illustrate how the division of labor could increase per capita productivity from no more than twenty pins a day to the astonishing total of 4,800.

Like the cottages engaged in rural industry, the large handicraft workshop eventually gave way to the mechanized factory. The main difference between the workshop and the factory was that the factory did not require a body of skilled workers. When production become mechanized, the worker's job was simply to tend to the machinery. The only skill factory workers needed was manual dexterity to operate the machinery. Only those workers who made industrial machinery remained craftsmen or skilled workers in the traditional sense of the word.

With the advent of mechanization, factory owners gained much tighter control over the entire production process. Indeed, they began to enforce an unprecedented discipline among their workers, who had to accommodate themselves to the boredom of repetitive work and a timetable set by the machines. Craftsmen who had been accustomed to working at their own pace now had to adjust to an entirely new and more demanding schedule. "While the engine runs," wrote one critical contemporary, "the people must work—men, women, and children yoked together with iron and steam. The animal machine—breakable in the best case, subject to a thousand sources of suffering—is chained fast to the iron machine which knows no suffering and no weariness."[2]

Despite the growth and development of the factory system, the factory did not become the most common type of industrial workplace until the early twentieth century. In Britain, Germany, France, and the United States most manufacturing continued to take place in handicraft workshops in the cities or in rural households. Indeed, many of the industries that became mechanized spawned a variety of secondary crafts and trades, such as the dyeing and finishing of cloth and the sewing of clothes, which were conducted mainly in rural households.

New Methods of Transportation

As industry became more extensive and increased its output, transport facilities, such as roads, bridges, canals, and eventually railroads, grew in number and quality. Increased industrial productivity has always depended on efficient movement of raw materials to places of production and transportation of finished products to the market. During the early phase of the Industrial Revolution in Britain, water transportation supplied most of these needs. A vast network of navigable rivers and human-made canals, eventually more than 4,000 miles in length, was used to transport goods in areas that did not have access to the coast. The canals that were built after 1760, with their systems of locks and their aqueducts spanning roads and rivers, were a product of the technology that the Scientific Revolution had made possible. For routes that could not be reached by water, the most common method of transportation was by horse-drawn carriages on newly built turnpikes or toll roads, many of them made of stone so that they were passable even in wet weather.

The most significant innovation in transport during the nineteenth century was the railroad. Introduced as the Industrial Revolution was gaining momentum, the railroad provided quick, cheap transportation of heavy materials such as coal and iron over long distances. Its introduction in Britain during the 1820s and throughout Europe and America during the following decades serves as one of the best illustrations of the transition from an economy based on organic sources of energy to one based on mineral sources of energy. Driven by coal-burning, steam-powered locomotives, the railroads freed transport from a dependence on animal power, especially the horses that were used to pull coaches along turnpikes, barges along canals, and even carts along parallel tracks in mines. Railroads rapidly became the main economic thoroughfares of the industrial economy. They linked towns and regions that earlier had not been easily accessible to each other. They also changed the travel habits of Europeans by making it possible to cover distances in one-fifth the time it took by coach.

The construction and operation of railroads became a major new industry, employing thousands of skilled and unskilled workers and providing opportunities for investment and profit. The industry created an unprecedented demand for iron and other materials used to build and equip locomotives, tracks, freight cars, passenger cars, and signals, thus giving a tremendous boost to the iron industry and the metalworking and engineering trades. By the 1840s the railroads had become the main stimulus to economic growth throughout western Europe and the United States. Transport in industrialized economies continues to experience frequent innovation. During the twentieth century, for example, new methods of transportation, including automobiles, airplanes, and high-speed rails, have sustained economic growth in all industrialized countries, and like the railroads they have become major industries themselves.

Transport facilities, unlike factories, can seldom be built entirely by their individual owners. The cost of building locomotives and laying railroad tracks is almost always too great to come from the profits accumulated in the normal conduct of one's business. The funds for these facilities must come from either private investment, governments, or international financial institutions. In Britain the capital for

The Stockton and Darlington Railway

A locomotive and two cars used on the first major railroad in Britain, which opened in 1825. The railroad carried materials and goods to and from towns producing iron in the northern counties of England.

the railroads came entirely from individual investors. In the United States, which built the world's largest railroad system in the nineteenth century, most of the capital also came from private investment, but many state and city governments helped finance early railroads. In other industrialized countries, governments played a more important role. In Belgium, which was the second European country to experience an Industrial Revolution, and in Russia, which was one of the last, the governments of those countries assumed the responsibility for building a national railroad system.

Conditions Favoring Industrial Growth

■ What social and economic changes made industrial development possible?

The immediate causes of the Industrial Revolution were the competitive pressures that encouraged technological innovation, the transition to coal power, the growth of factories, and the building of the railroads. These developments, however, do not provide a full explanation for this unprecedented economic transformation. Certain social and economic conditions were present in Britain that allowed industrialization to progress—a large population, improved agricultural productivity, the accumulation of capital, a group of people with scientific knowledge and entrepreneurial skill, and sufficient demand for manufactured goods. In this section we will look at the historical experience of Great Britain, which was the first country to industrialize, to see how these conditions made industrial economic development possible.

Population Growth

Industrialization requires a sufficiently large pool of labor to staff the factories and workshops of the new industries. One of the main reasons why the Industrial Revolution occurred first in Britain is that its population during the eighteenth century increased more rapidly than that of any country in continental Europe. Between 1680 and 1820 the population of England more than doubled, while that of France grew at less than one-third that rate, and that of the Dutch Republic hardly grew at all. One of the reasons this growth took place was that famines, which had occurred periodically throughout the early modern period, became less frequent during the eighteenth century. The last great famine in Britain took place in 1740, only a generation before industrialization began. There was also a decrease in mortality from epidemic diseases, especially typhus, influenza, and smallpox. Bubonic plague, which had deci-

Increase in European Population, 1680–1820

Population Totals (millions)

	1680	1820
France	21.9	30.5
Italy	12.0	18.4
Germany	12.0	18.1
Spain	8.5	14.0
England	4.9	11.5
Netherlands	1.9	2.0
Western Europe	71.9	116.5

Percentage Growth Rates, 1680–1820

England	133%
Spain	64
Italy	53
Germany	51
France	39
Netherlands	8
Western Europe	73

Source: E. A. Wrigley, "The Growth of Population in Eighteenth-Century England: A Conundrum Resolved," *Past and Present* 98 (1983): 122.

mated the European population periodically since the fourteenth century, struck England for the last time in the Great Plague of London of 1665. It made its last European appearance at Marseilles in 1720 but did not spread beyond the southern parts of France.

Even more important than this reduction in mortality was an increase in fertility. More people were marrying, and at a younger age, which increased the birth rate. The spread of rural industry seems to have encouraged this early-marriage pattern. Wage-earning textile workers tended to marry a little earlier than agricultural workers, probably because wage earners did not have to postpone marriage to inherit land or to become self-employed, as was the case with farm workers.

This increase in population facilitated industrialization in two ways. First, it increased demand for the goods that were being manufactured in large quantities in the factories. The desire for these products, especially the new cottons, played an important role in enlarging the domestic market for manufactured goods, as we shall see shortly. Second, it increased the supply of labor, freeing a substantial portion of the population for industry, especially for factory labor. At the same time, however, this increase was not so large as to have had a negative effect on industrialization, as it did in a number of underdeveloped countries in the twentieth century. If population growth is too rapid, it can lead to declining incomes, put pressure on agriculture to feed more people than is possible, and prevent the accumulation of wealth. Most important, it can discourage factory owners from introducing costly machinery, because if labor is plentiful and cheap, it might very well cost less for workers to produce the same volume of goods by hand. Industrialization therefore requires a significant but not too rapid increase in population—the exact scenario that occurred in Britain during the eighteenth century.

Agricultural Productivity

Between 1700 and 1800 British agriculture experienced a revolution, resulting in a substantial increase in productivity. A major reason for this increase was the consolidation of all the land farmed by one tenant into compact fields. During the Middle Ages and most of the early modern period, each tenant on a manorial estate leased and farmed strips of land that were scattered throughout the estate. The decisions regarding the planting and harvesting of crops in these open fields were made collectively in the manorial court. Beginning in the sixteenth century, some of the wealthier tenants on these estates agreed to exchange their strips of land with their neighbors in order to consolidate their holdings into large compact fields, whose boundaries were defined by hedges, bushes, or walls. The main benefit of this process of enclosure° was that it allowed individual farmers to exercise complete control over the use of their land. In the eighteenth and nineteenth centuries the number of these enclosures increased dramatically, as the British Parliament passed legislation that divided entire estates into a number of enclosed fields. This legislation benefited all landowners, including the members of the aristocracy who passed the legislation.

With control of their lands, farmers could make them more productive. The most profitable change was to introduce new crop rotations, often involving the alternation of grains such as rye or barley with root crops such as turnips or grasses such as clover. These new crops and grasses restored nutrients to the soil and therefore made it unnecessary to let fields lie fallow once every three years. Farmers also introduced a variety of new fertilizers and soil additives that made harvests more bountiful. Farmers who raised sheep took advantage of discoveries regarding scientific breeding that improved the quality of their flocks.

More productive farming meant that fewer agricultural workers were required to feed the population. This made it possible for more people to leave the farms to work in the factories and mines. The expanded labor pool of industrial workers, moreover, was large enough that factory owners did not have to pay workers high wages; otherwise the prospect of industrializing would have lost much of its appeal. The hiring of children and women to work in the factories and mines also kept the labor pool large and the costs of labor low.

Capital Formation and Accumulation

The term capital° refers to all the assets used in production. These include the factories and machines that are used to produce other goods (fixed capital) as well as the raw materials and finished products that are sent to market (circulating capital). Other forms of capital are the railroads and barges used for transporting raw materials to the place of production and finished products to market. Mechanized industry involves the extensive and intensive use of capital to do the work formerly assigned to human beings. An industrial economy therefore requires large amounts of capital, especially fixed capital.

Capital more generally refers to the money that is necessary to purchase these physical assets. This capital can come from a number of different sources: It can come from individuals, such as wealthy landlords, merchants, or industrialists who invest the profits they have accumulated in industrial machinery or equipment. In many cases the profits derived from industrial production are reinvested in the firm itself. Alternatively, capital can come from financial institutions in the form of loans. Very often a number of individuals make their wealth available to an industrial firm by buying shares of stock in that company's operations. This of course is the main way in which most capital is accumulated today. In countries that have only recently begun to industrialize in Latin America and Southeast Asia, capital often comes from public sources, such as governments, or from international institutions, such as the International Monetary Fund.

In Great Britain the capital that was needed to achieve industrial transformation came almost entirely from private sources. Some of it was raised by selling shares of stock to people from the middle and upper levels of society, but an even larger amount came from merchants who engaged in domestic and international trade, landowners who profited from the production of agricultural goods (including those who owned plantations in America), and the industrial entrepreneurs who owned mines, ironworks, and factories. In Britain, where all three groups were more successful than in other parts of Europe, the volume of capital made available from these sources was substantial. These people could invest directly in industrial machinery and mines or, more commonly, make their wealth available to others indirectly in the form of loans from banks where they kept their financial assets.

Banks supplied a considerable amount of the funds necessary for industrialization. In Britain the possibilities for such capital were maximized in the late eighteenth century when financial institutions offered loans at low interest rates and when the development of a national banking system made these funds readily available throughout the country, especially in the new industrial cities such as Leeds, Sheffield, and Manchester. The number of English banks went from a mere dozen in 1750 to more than 300 in 1800. Many bankers had close ties with industrialists, thereby facilitating the flow of capital from the financial to the industrial sector of the economy. Banks played an even more central role in the industrialization of Germany, which was economically not as advanced as Britain and less capable, therefore, of generating capital through the accumulation of profits.

Technological Knowledge and Entrepreneurship

The process of industrialization involves the application of technological knowledge to the manufacturing process. It also involves entrepreneurship, the ability to make business ventures profitable. The mechanization of industry demanded scientifically trained people not only to introduce new forms of machinery but also to mass-produce that machinery for other manufacturers. The development of new modes of transportation required the skill of an entire class of civil engineers who could design and construct locomotives, ships, canals, railroads, and bridges. At the same time, industrialization required a group of business experts who knew how to run the factories and market their products. These requirements help explain why countries that are industrializing today often import technological and financial personnel from other countries to assist them in the process of industrialization and take steps to train and educate people from their own countries to carry on this work.

As we have discussed in Chapter 16, the geographical center of the Scientific Revolution shifted from the Mediterranean to the North Atlantic, especially to England, in the late seventeenth century. At the same time, England took the lead in making science an integral part of the nation's culture. In no other European country was so much attention given to the dissemination of scientific knowledge in public lectures, the meetings of local scientific societies, and the publication of scientific textbooks. Much of this popular scientific education focused on Newtonian mechanics and dynamics. These were precisely the areas of science that lent themselves most readily to technological application. The only area that was developed more fully in France than in Britain was thermodynamics, the branch of physics dealing with heat and its conversion into other forms of energy, such as steam power. To some extent the technological innovations and engineering achievements that took place in Britain during the Industrial Revolution can be considered the product of this unparalleled diffusion of scientific knowledge. Those who made these innovations also required extensive mathematical skill. The education

given to British schoolchildren in the eighteenth century included more instruction in mathematics than was given in any other European country.

Industrial entrepreneurs, the people who actually ran the factories and superintended the industrial process, also needed a certain level of technological and mathematical skill, but their talents lay much more in their ability to run a variety of capitalist enterprises for a profit. Britain had no shortage of this type of talent in the eighteenth century. Even before the advent of mechanization there had developed an entire class of merchant capitalists who had organized the domestic system of rural industry or run the large handicraft workshops in London and other towns.

The invention and production of the steam engine readily illustrate the way in which technological and entrepreneurial skills reinforced and complemented each other. The partnership between the Scotsman James Watt, who invented the steam engine, and the Englishman Matthew Boulton represented a dynamic British alliance of science and capitalism. Of the two men, Watt had more scientific and mathematical knowledge, having taught himself geometry and trigonometry as well as having read textbooks on mechanics. He was familiar with the work of Joseph Black, the chemist at the University of Glasgow who studied steam, and he had acquired a knowledge of scientific instruments from his father's business as an outfitter of ships. Even though he was not an academic, he thought he was as smart as the famous French chemist Antoine Lavoisier. He was also a shrewd businessman who figured out various ways to use his knowledge of engineering to turn a profit and acquire a competitive advantage over others. Boulton was the classic eighteenth-century English entrepreneur who manufactured a variety of small metal objects from toys and buttons to teakettles and watch chains. His contribution to the partnership was assembling workers with the requisite skills to mass-produce the engine. Boulton was also scientifically knowledgeable, and both he and Watt were members of the Lunar Society of Birmingham, a voluntary scientific society in which they shared similar interests. Both men thought of themselves as scientists, just as both of them acted as entrepreneurs.

Demand from Consumers and Producers

The conditions for industrialization that we have discussed so far all deal with supply°, that is, the amounts of capital, labor, food, and skill that are necessary to support the industrial process. The other side of the economic equation is demand°, that is, the desire of consumers to purchase industrial goods and of producers to acquire raw materials and machinery. Much of the extraordinary productivity of the Industrial Revolution arose from the demand for industrial products. Many of the technological innovations that occurred at the beginning of the revolution also originated as responses to the demand for more goods. For example, the demand for more cotton goods spurred the introduction of the spinning jenny, the water frame, and the mule. Likewise the demand for coal for industrial and domestic use led to the development of an efficient steam engine in order to drain mines so that those supplies of coal could be extracted.

During the early years of industrialization, only about 35 percent of all British manufactured goods were exported. This statistic indicates that as the Industrial Revolution was taking hold, the domestic market was still the main source of demand for industrial products. The demand was especially strong among the bourgeoisie. Within that group a "consumer revolution" had taken place during the eighteenth century. This revolution was based on an unprecedented desire to acquire goods of all sorts, especially clothing and housewares, such as pottery, cutlery, furniture, and curtains. The consumer revolution was fueled in large part by a desire to imitate the spending habits of the aristocracy. It was assisted by commercial manipulation of all sorts, including newspaper advertising, warehouse displays, product demonstrations, and the distribution of samples. An entirely new consumer culture arose, one in which women played a leading role. Advertisements promoting the latest female fashions, housewares, and children's toys became more common than those directed at adult male consumers. One ad in a local British paper in 1777, capitalizing on reports that mice were getting into ladies' hair at night, promoted "night caps made of silver wire so strong that no mouse or even a rat can gnaw through them." Advertisements therefore created a demand for new products as well as increasing the demand for those already on the market.

If this consumer revolution had been restricted to the middle class, it would have had only a limited effect on the Industrial Revolution. The bourgeoisie in the eighteenth century constituted at most only 20 percent of the entire population of Britain, and most of the goods they craved, with the exception of the pottery produced in Josiah Wedgwood's factories (which is still made today), were luxury items rather than the types of products that could be easily mass-produced. A strong demand for manufactured goods could develop only if workers were to buy consumer goods such as knitted stockings and caps, cotton shirts, earthenware, coffeepots, nails, candlesticks, watches, lace, and ribbon. The demand for these products came from small cottagers and laborers as well as the middle class. The demand for stockings for both men and women was particularly strong. In 1831 the author of a study of the impact of machinery on British society declared, "Two centuries ago not one person in a thousand wore stockings; one century ago not one person in five hundred wore them; now not one person in a thousand is without them."

Demand for manufactured products from the lower classes was obviously limited by the amount of money that wage earners had available for nonessential goods, and real wages did not increase very much, if at all, during the eighteenth century. Nevertheless the income of families in which the wife and children as well as the father worked for wages did increase significantly both during the heyday of rural industry and during the early years of industrialization. With these funds available, a substantial number of workers could actually afford to buy the products they desired. As the population increased, so too did this lower-class demand, which helped sustain an economy built around industrial production.

The Spread of Industrialization

■ How did industrialization spread from Great Britain to the European continent and America?

The Industrial Revolution, like the Scientific Revolution of the sixteenth and seventeenth centuries, did not occur in all European countries at the same time. As we have seen, it began in Britain in the 1760s and for more than four decades was confined exclusively to that country (see Map 20.1). It eventually spread to other European and North American countries, where many industrial innovations were modeled on those that had taken place in Britain. Belgium, France, Germany, Switzerland, Austria, Sweden, and the United States all experienced their own Industrial Revolutions by the middle of the nineteenth century. Only in the late nineteenth century did countries outside the traditional boundaries of the West, mainly Russia and Japan, begin to industrialize. By the middle of the twentieth century, industrialization had become a truly global process, transforming the economies of a number of Asian and Latin American countries.

Great Britain and the Continent

Industrialization occurred on the European continent much later than it did in Great Britain. Only after 1815 did Belgium and France begin to industrialize on a large scale, and it was not until 1840 that Germany, Switzerland, and Austria showed significant signs of industrial growth. Other European countries, such as Italy and Spain, did not begin serious efforts in this direction until the late nineteenth century. It took continental European nations even longer to rival the economic strength of Britain. Germany, which emerged as Britain's main competitor in the late nineteenth century, did not match British industrial output until the twentieth century.

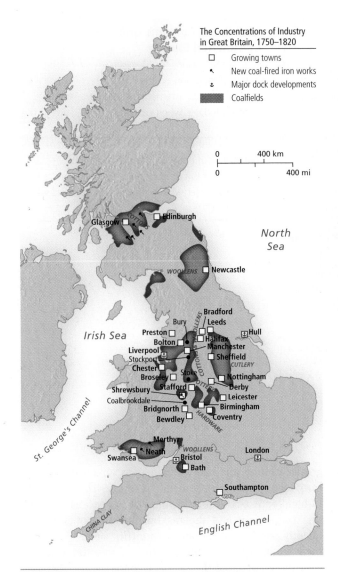

The Concentrations of Industry in Great Britain, 1750–1820

☐ Growing towns
↖ New coal-fired iron works
⚓ Major dock developments
⬛ Coalfields

Map 20.1 The Concentrations of Industry in Great Britain, 1750–1820

The most heavily industrialized regions were in northern England, where the population of cities such as Manchester, Liverpool, and Sheffield grew rapidly.

Why did it take so long for other countries to industrialize? Virtually all of them had developed extensive rural industry in the late eighteenth century. The governments of European countries, in keeping with mercantilist philosophy, had a long tradition of encouraging the development of domestic industry. Population growth on the Continent during the late eighteenth century, while less dramatic than in Great Britain, should have been sufficient to stimulate consumer demand and increase the supply of labor. Overall economic growth in France during that time almost matched that of Great Britain. Scientific education, while not as widespread as in Britain, was hardly lacking, espe-

cially in France. Nonetheless, industrialization on the Continent, especially in heavy industry, lagged far behind that of Great Britain, and the process was for the most part painfully slow.

One explanation for the slower development of industrialization on the Continent relates to the political situations in those countries. Well into the nineteenth century, most continental European countries had numerous internal political barriers that could impede the transportation of raw materials and goods from one part of the country to another. In Germany, for example, which was not politically united until 1871, scores of small sovereign territorial units charged tariffs whenever goods crossed their territorial boundaries. Only in 1834 was a customs union, the *Zollverein,* created to eliminate some of these barriers. In France, which had achieved a formal territorial unity during the reign of Louis XIV, local rights and privileges impeded internal trade until the early nineteenth century. This political situation was aggravated by the relatively poor state of continental roads and the inaccessibility of many seaports from production sites.

The contrast between the situation on the Continent and that which prevailed in Great Britain is striking. After 1707, when Scotland was united to England and freedom of internal trade was established between the two countries, the United Kingdom of Great Britain constituted the largest free-trade zone in Europe. Thus raw materials and finished products could pass from one place within Great Britain to another, up to a distance of more than 800 miles, without payment of any internal customs or duties. The system of inland waterways was complete by 1780, and seaports were accessible from all parts of the country.

The industrial potential of many continental European countries was also weakened by the imposition of protective tariffs on goods imported from other countries. The purpose of this mercantilist policy was to develop national self-sufficiency and to maintain a favorable balance of trade, but it also had the negative effect of limiting economic growth. For example, in the Dutch Republic (the kingdom of the Netherlands after 1815) a long tradition of protecting established industries prevented that country from importing the raw materials and machines needed to develop new industries. Because protectionism invited retaliation from trading partners, it also tended to shrink the size of potential overseas markets. Britain adopted a policy of free trade during the 1840s, and it pressured other European countries to adopt the same policy.

A further obstacle to European industrialization was aristocratic hostility, or at least indifference, to industrial development. In Britain the aristocracy, which consisted of noblemen and gentry, were themselves often involved in capitalist enterprise and did not have the same suspicion of industry and trade that their counterparts in France and Spain often harbored. Many members of the British aristocracy, such as

customs union
1853
DENMARK

NORWAY
& SWEDEN
customs union
1874–1890

joined German
customs union
1888

SCHLESWIG
HOLSTEIN

Hamburg
Bremen
Tax union

LUXEMBOURG

ZOLLVEREIN 1834
*united with the
Tax Union
1854*

FRANCE
*internal
duties
abolished
1790*

SWITZERLAND

*internal duties
abolished 1848–1874*

ITALY

*political and economic
unification 1860–1870*

Mediterranean Sea

RUSSIA
*Russo-Polish
customs frontier
abolished 1851*

CONGRESS
POLAND

HABSBURG
EMPIRE
*Austro-Hungarian
customs frontier
abolished 1850*

MOLDAVIA-
WALLACHIA
*customs union
1847*

Black
Sea

0   300 km
0   300 mi

Map 20.2 Customs Unions in Continental Europe

One of the reasons for the relatively slow progress of industrialization on the European continent was the existence of internal tariff barriers. This map shows the dates when customs unions, such as the *Zollverein* of 1834 in the German Confederation, were established or the customs barriers were eliminated. By contrast, all internal customs duties within Great Britain had been eliminated more than a century earlier when England and Scotland were united in 1707.

the entrepreneur "Turnip Townshend" (see Chapter 18), were agricultural capitalists who improved the productivity of their estates. Others were involved in mining. The Duke of Devonshire encouraged the exploitation of the copper mines on his estate, while the Duke of Bridgewater employed the engineer James Brindley to build a canal from the duke's coal mines in Worsley to Manchester in 1759. He later had Brindley extend the canal from Manchester to the mouth of the Mersey River, connecting the textile region of Manchester with the large northern industrial city of Liverpool.

One reason for the British aristocracy's support for economic growth was that many of its members, especially the gentry, rose into its ranks from other social and economic groups. These individuals tended to be sympathetic to the values of a commercial and an industrial society. The same attitude toward commerce and industry simply did not exist among the nobility in France before the revolution, much less among German *Junkers*. These groups had little connection with industrial or commercial society, whose values they held in very low regard. Consequently they rarely invested in industry.

Even among the European middle classes, the same type of competitive entrepreneurial spirit that was exhibited by men like Matthew Boulton seems to have been in large part lacking. Capitalism was by no means absent in European countries, but the conduct of business was characterized by

greater caution and less willingness to obtain new capital from loans or the sale of stock to investors. This went hand in hand with a reluctance to innovate as well as a distaste for competition and the maximizing of profits. Consequently continental European countries failed to produce many counterparts to the captains of industry who had contributed much of the capital, technology, and entrepreneurial spirit to the Industrial Revolution in Britain.

A final reason for the slow industrialization of continental European countries was that they lacked the abundant raw materials that were readily accessible in Britain. The natural resources that Britain had in greatest quantities were coal and iron ore, both of which were indispensable to industrialization. At the same time British farms provided ample supplies of raw materials for the wool and leather industries. The French and the Germans had some coal deposits, but they were more difficult to mine, and they were not located near ocean ports. Continental countries also lacked the access to other raw materials that Britain could import through its vast trading network, and in particular from its overseas colonies. With a large empire on four continents and the world's largest merchant marine, Britain had abundant supplies of raw materials such as cotton as well as the capacity to import them cheaply and in large quantities. The greater difficulty European countries had in obtaining these raw materials did not prevent them from industrializing; it simply made the process slower.

Features of Continental Industrialization

During the first half of the nineteenth century, especially after 1830, Belgium, France, Switzerland, Germany, and Austria began to introduce machinery into the industrial process, use steam power in production, concentrate labor in large factories, and build railroads. This continental European version of the Industrial Revolution is usually described as an imitative process, one in which entrepreneurs or government officials simply tried to duplicate the economic success that Britain had achieved by following British example. Continental European nations did indeed rely to some extent on British industrial machinery. Some of them also relied on British skilled labor when they began to build their first factories and ironworks. In a few instances, in violation of British law, foreign agents actually smuggled blueprints, models, or machine parts out of Britain. British engineers, entrepreneurs, and managers were also occasionally hired to run British-style factories in France and Germany. But each European nation, responding to its own unique combination of political, economic, and social conditions, followed its own course of industrialization.

One distinctive feature of continental European industrialization was that once countries such as Belgium and Germany began to industrialize, their governments played a much more active role in encouraging and assisting in the process. In contrast to Britain, whose government allowed private industry to function with few economic controls, continental governments became active partners in the industrial process. They supplied capital for many economic ventures, especially the railroads and roads. In Prussia the state owned a number of manufacturing and mining enterprises. Many continental governments also imposed protective tariffs to prevent an influx of cheap British goods from underselling the products of their own fledgling industries. In a few cases continental European governments even provided financial support for investors in an effort to encourage capital formation. In some places, such as Austria, the state eliminated the regulations of urban guilds that had restricted industrial development in rural regions.

A second major feature of continental European industrialization was that banks, particularly in Germany and Belgium, played a central role in industrial development. This was necessitated by the low level of capital formation on the Continent and the reluctance of entrepreneurs to take risks by investing money themselves. Banks in Germany and Belgium played a particularly active role in stimulating industry. Drawing on the resources of both small and large investors, these corporate banks became in effect industrial banks, building railroads and factories themselves in addition to making capital available for a variety of industrial ventures.

A third distinct feature of continental European industrialization was that the railroads actually contributed to the beginning of industrial development. In Great Britain the railroads were introduced some sixty years after industrialization had begun and thus helped sustain a process of economic development that had been long afoot. By contrast the railroads on the Continent provided the basic infrastructure of its new economy and became a major stimulus to the development of all other industries. Railroads also gave continental European governments the ability to transport military troops quickly in time of war, which helps to explain why governments supported railroad construction with such enthusiasm. In Belgium, which was the first continental European nation to industrialize, the new government built a national railroad system during the 1830s and 1840s, not only to stimulate industry but also to unify the newly independent nation.

Of all the European countries that industrialized, only Belgium appears to have followed the British model closely by developing coal, iron, and textiles as the three main sectors of the new economy. Other countries tended to concentrate their activity in one specific area. France emphasized textiles, especially those such as worsted woolens that did not compete with British cottons. France's coal production and consumption never matched that of Great Britain or Belgium, and after 1850 it fell behind that of Germany as well. In 1860 France was importing 43 percent of its coal, and it was still relying on charcoal rather than coal to smelt pig iron. In Germany the main economic advances, which did not begin until 1850, occurred mainly in the area of heavy industry, that is, coal, iron, and engineering rather than

Medal Struck in 1835 to Commemorate the First German Railroad, from Nuremberg to Fürth

Industry is depicted as a female figure with her arm resting on a winged wheel. The first railroad in Europe had opened in England in 1825. German engineers had modeled their first locomotive on that of George Stephenson.

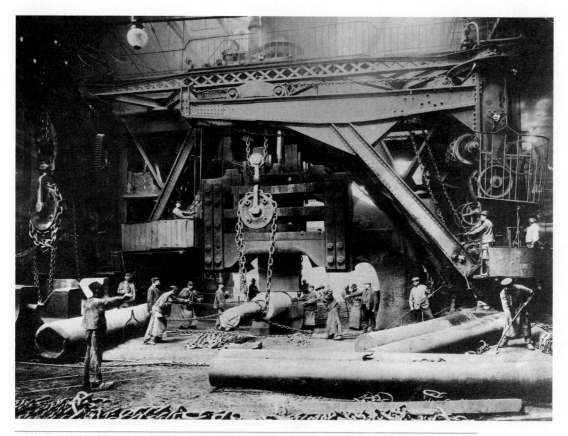

A Colossal Steam-Driven Hammer, Nicknamed "Fritz," Installed by Alfred Krupp at His Steelworks in Essen in 1861
Krupp's factory was located in the Ruhr region of Germany, the main center in that country for heavy industry.

textiles. Together with the United States, Germany began to offer the main economic competition to the British economy by the end of the nineteenth century.

Industrialization in the United States

Industrialization in the United States began during the 1820s, not long after Belgium and France had begun to experience their own industrial revolutions. It occurred first in the textile industry in New England, where factories using water power produced goods for largely rural markets. New England also began producing two domestic hardware products—clocks and guns—for the same market. Between 1850 and 1880 a second region between Pittsburgh and Cleveland became industrialized. This region specialized in heavy industry, especially steelmaking and the manufacture of large machinery, and it relied on coal for fuel.

American industrialization followed both British and continental European patterns. As in Britain and France, the development of cottage industry in the United States

preceded industrialization. Most of the industrial machinery used in the United States during the nineteenth century was modeled on imports from Britain. The most significant American technological innovation before 1900 was the sewing machine, which was patented by Elias Howe in 1846 and then developed and improved upon by Isaac Singer in the 1850s. This new machine was then introduced in Europe, where it was used in the production of ready-to-wear garments.

The state played an ambivalent role in early American industrialization. The U.S. federal government, whose powers were greatly limited, especially during the early nineteenth century, followed a policy of nonintervention in the economy, similar to the policy followed by the British government. The individual states in America, however, played a much more active role, especially in facilitating the growth of railroads. One of the ironies of early industrialization is that Prussia, with its tradition of strong state government and its control of the mines, did far less to promote the building of railroads than did the individual states in America.

After 1865, when American industrialization began to spread rapidly across the entire country, American entrepreneurs made a distinctive contribution to the industrial process in the area of business organization, especially the operation of international firms. Toward the beginning of the twentieth century, American manufacturers streamlined the production process by introducing the assembly line, a division of labor in which the product passes from one operation to the next until it is fully assembled. The assembly line required the production of interchangeable parts, another American innovation, first used in the manufacture of rifles for the U.S. government.

Like Great Britain, the United States possessed vast natural resources, including coal. It also resembled Britain in the absence of governmental involvement in the process of industrialization. The main difference between the industrializations of the two countries is that during the nineteenth century labor in America was in relatively short supply. This placed workers in a more advantageous situation in dealing with their employers and prevented some of the horrors of early British industrialization from recurring on the other side of the Atlantic. Only with the influx of European immigrants in the late nineteenth century did the condition of American workers deteriorate and begin to resemble the early-nineteenth-century British pattern.

Industrial Regionalism

Although we have discussed the industrialization of entire nations, the process usually took place within smaller geographical regions. There had always been regional specialization in agriculture, with some areas emphasizing crops and others livestock. During the Industrial Revolution, however, entire economies acquired a distinctly regional character. Regional economies began to take shape during the days of the domestic system, when merchants employed families in certain geographical areas, such as Lancashire in England, to produce textiles. In these regions there was a close relationship between agricultural and industrial production, in that members of the same household participated in both processes. Related industries, such as those for finishing or dyeing cloth, also sprang up close to where the cotton or wool yarn was spun and the cloth woven.

As industrialization spread outside Britain, this regional pattern became even more pronounced. In France the centers of the textile industry were situated near the northeastern border near Belgium and in the area surrounding Lyons in the east-central part of the country. Both of these areas had attracted rural household industry before the introduction of textile machinery. In Germany the iron industry was centered in the Ruhr region, where most of the country's coal was mined. In the city of Essen on the Ruhr River the industrialist Alfred

Krupp (1812–1887) established an enormous steelmaking complex that produced industrial machinery, railroad equipment, and guns for the Prussian army. Within the Habsburg Empire most industry was located in parts of Bohemia (now the Czech Republic).

The development of regional economies did not mean that markets were regional. The goods produced in one region almost always served the needs of people outside that particular area. Markets for most industrial goods were national and international, and even people in small agricultural villages created a demand for manufactured goods. The French iron industry, for example, was centered in the eastern part of the country, but it catered to the needs of the wealthier segments of its own and other European populations, as did the iron industry in the Ruhr region in Germany and the textile industry in the north of England.

The development of regional industrial economies helps to explain the striking contrast that persisted well into the twentieth century between the parts of countries that had become heavily industrialized and those that retained at least many of the appearances of a preindustrial life. In Britain and the rest of Europe industrial machinery and factories were not introduced into every village. Some areas remained exclusively agricultural, while others continued a tradition of rural industry. This pattern was particularly evident in France, where mechanized industry was concentrated in a limited number of centers in the northeastern half of the country. In 1870 more than two-thirds of the French population still lived in rural areas. As economic growth and industrial development continued, however, agricultural regions eventually began to lose their traditional character. Even if industry itself did not arrive, the larger industrial economy made its mark. Agriculture itself became mechanized, while railroads and other forms of mechanized transport integrated these areas in a national economy.

The Effects of Industrialization

■ What were the economic, social, and cultural effects of the Industrial Revolution?

The Industrial Revolution had a profound impact on virtually every aspect of human life. It encouraged the growth of the population and the economy, affected the conditions in which people lived, changed family life, created new divisions within society, and transformed the traditional rural landscape. The changes that it brought about were most evident in Britain, but in time they have occurred in every country that has industrialized, including the United States.

Population and Economic Growth

The most significant of these changes was the sustained expansion of both the population and the economy. As we have seen, the Industrial Revolution in Britain was facilitated by a significant population increase in the eighteenth century. That growth had created a plentiful supply of relatively cheap labor, which in turn had helped to bring about a marked increase in industrial output. As industry grew, population kept pace, and each provided a stimulus to the growth of the other.

Most contemporary observers in the late eighteenth century did not believe that this expansion of both the population and the economy could be sustained indefinitely. The most pessimistic of these commentators was Thomas Malthus (1766–1834), an English cleric who wrote *An Essay on the Principle of Population* in 1798.

Thomas Malthus, *Laws of Population Growth* (1798)

Malthus argued that population had a natural tendency to grow faster than the food supply. Thus, unless couples exercised restraint by marrying late and producing fewer children, the population would eventually outstrip the resources necessary to sustain it, resulting in poor nutrition, famine, and disease. These "positive checks" on population growth, which sometimes were initiated or aggravated by war, would drive population back to sustainable levels. These checks would also end periods of economic expansion, which generally accompany increases in population. For example, in the fourteenth century the Black Death, which killed about one-third of the European population, also ended a significant period of economic growth. A similar but less severe contraction of the European population and economy occurred in the second half of the seventeenth century, marking the end of the economic expansion that had begun in the sixteenth century. In both these instances the increase in population put pressure on the food supply, raised the price of food, reduced employment, and lowered wages. The scarcity of food and the reduced nutritional levels that followed had made the population vulnerable to disease. If these demographic and economic patterns were to recur, we might expect that the significant expansion of the population and the economy that took place in eighteenth-century England would likewise reach its limits, just around the time that Malthus was writing.

This predicted cyclical contraction of both the population and the economy did not take place. Europe for the first time in its history managed to escape the "Malthusian population trap." Instead of being sharply reduced after 1800, the population continued to expand at an ever-faster rate, doubling in Great Britain between 1800 and 1850 and following a similar pattern of rapid growth in all other countries that had industrialized. At the same time the economy, instead of contracting or collapsing, continued to grow and diversify.

It is not absolutely clear how Europe avoided the Malthusian trap in the nineteenth century. Part of the answer lies in the greater productivity of agriculture, which resulted from either private initiative, as in Britain, or governmental agrarian reforms, as in Austria. The importation of grain from central and eastern Europe also helped to feed the larger, more urbanized population. Improvements in medicine and public health reduced mortality during the nineteenth century, helping to maintain the size of the industrial population. But it was mainly developments in industry itself, especially the increased accumulation of capital, that kept Europe from succumbing to yet another cycle of depopulation and economic contraction. The accumulation of capital over a long period of time was so great that industry was able to employ large numbers of workers even during the 1790s and 1800s, when Europe was at war. Because they had income from wages, workers were willing to marry earlier and have larger families, and with lower food prices because of higher agricultural productivity they could afford to maintain a healthier diet and purchase more manufactured goods as well. Thus the Industrial Revolution itself, coupled with the changes in agriculture that accompanied it, proved Malthus wrong.

While the rapid growth of population in industrialized societies up until the late twentieth century is incontestable, the record of economic growth is not so clear. In order to claim that the Industrial Revolution has resulted in sustained economic growth, we have to take a broad view, looking at an overall pattern of growth and ignoring certain cyclical recessions and depressions. Nations that have industrialized, beginning with European countries in the nineteenth century, have all experienced a significant increase in both gross national product and per capita income over the long run. Although the contrast between the size of these industrial economies and those of preindustrial, agrarian countries is staggering, economic growth in industrialized countries was not always rapid or continuous. During the first six decades of industrialization in Britain, for example, economic growth was actually fairly slow, mainly because so much capital went into subsidizing the long war against France (1792–1802; 1804–1815). During this period Britain spent an average of 60 million English pounds, or 25 percent of its national income, on war. Nevertheless, there still was steady growth, and more important, the type of Malthusian economic contraction or collapse that had followed all previous periods of expansion did not occur. To that extent we can say that the Industrial Revolution has resulted in sustained economic growth in the West.

Standards of Living

Ever since the early years of the Industrial Revolution, a debate has raged over the effect of industrialization on the standard of living and the quality of life of the laboring population. The supporters of the two main schools of thought on this issue have been called the optimists and the

DOCUMENT

A French Geologist's Impressions of Birmingham, 1784

Barthélemy Faujas de Saint-Fond (1741–1819), a French scientist who rose to become professor of geology at the Muséum d'Histoire Naturelle in Paris, recorded the following impressions of the industrial city of Birmingham on a journey through England and Scotland in 1784. He was especially impressed by the variety of products made there, the number of workers in the various industries, and the dramatic increase in the city's population,

From the activity of its manufactures and its commerce, Birmingham is one of the most curious towns in England. If any one should wish to see in one comprehensive view the most numerous and varied industries, all combined in contributing to the arts of utility, of pleasure, and of luxury, it is hither that he must come. Here all the resources of industry, supported by the genius of invention and by mechanical skill of every kind are directed towards the arts and seem to be linked together to cooperate for their mutual perfection.

I know some travelers who have not given themselves the trouble to reflect on the importance and advantage of these kinds of manufactures in such a country as England have disapproved of most of these industrial establishments. I know that even an Englishman who has only taken a hasty, I would almost say an inconsiderate view of these magnificent establishments, William Gilpin, has said that it was difficult for the eye to be long pleased in the midst of so many frivolous arts, where a hundred men may be seen, whose labours are confined to the making of a tobacco box. But

besides that this statement is exaggerated and ill-considered, the author has not deigned to cast his eyes over the vast works where steam-pumps are made, these astonishing machines, the perfecting of which does so much honour to the talents and knowledge of Mr. Watt; over the manufactories in constant activity making sheet-copper for sheathing ships' bottoms; over those of plate-tin and plate-iron, which make France tributary to England, nor over that varied and extensive hardware manufacture which employs to so much advantage more than thirty thousand hands and compels all Europe, and a part of the New World, to supply themselves from England, because all ironmongery is made here in greater perfection, with more economy, and in greater abundance than anywhere else. Once more I say with pleasure, and it cannot be said too often to Frenchmen, that it is the abundance of coal which has performed this miracle and has created, in the midst of a barren desert, a town with forty thousand inhabitants, who live in comfort and enjoy all the conveniences of life. . . .

The population of Birmingham has made such an advance that during the war with the United States of America, a war which weakened the resources of England, at least three hundred new homes were added annually to the town, and this rate doubled as soon as peace was concluded. A well-informed person assured me that this was true, and he showed me, during my stay in the town, a whole street which was in process of erection with such rapidity that, all the houses being built on a given plan at the same time, one could believe that the street would be entirely completed in less than two months.

Source: From Faujas de Saint-Fond, *A Journey through England and Scotland to the Hebrides in 1784* (1907), pp. 345–50.

---

pessimists. The optimists have always emphasized the positive effects of both the process of mechanization and the system of industrial capitalism that arose during the revolution. They have focused on the success that industrialized nations have achieved in escaping the Malthusian trap and in achieving sustained economic growth. The Industrial Revolution, so they argue, has resulted in an unprecedented rise in individual income, which has made it possible for the mass of a country's population to avoid poverty for the first time in human history. In the second half of the twentieth century many optimists claimed that the industrialization of Western nations provided a blueprint for African, Asian, and Latin American countries that wished to escape from the poverty of a predominantly agrarian economy relying on organic sources of energy.

The main yardstick that the optimists have used to measure the improvement in living standards is per capita real income, that is, income measured in terms of its actual purchasing power. Real income in Great Britain rose about 50 percent between 1770 and 1850 and more than doubled during the entire nineteenth century. This increase in income allowed workers to improve their diets as well as to purchase more clothing and other basic commodities. These improvements, however, did not affect the lives of most workers for a long period of time—in Great Britain not until 1820, about sixty years after the beginning of industrialization. The increases that occurred after that date, moreover, were only averages, concealing disparities among workers with different levels of skill. Only in the late nineteenth and twentieth centuries did industrialization raise the real income of all workers to a level that made the benefits of industrialization apparent.

Even if the pessimists concede a long-term increase in real income, it has never been substantial enough to persuade them that industrialization was on balance a positive good, at least for the working class. The pessimists have always stressed the negative effects of industrial development on the life of the lower classes. In their way of thinking, industrialization was an unmitigated disaster. The cause of this disaster in their eyes was not the process of mechanization but the system of industrial capitalism°. This form of capitalism is characterized by the ownership of factories by private individuals and by the employment of wage labor. Like earlier forms of mercantile and agricultural capitalism, it involved a systematic effort to reduce costs and maximize profits. In the pursuit of this goal, employers tried to keep wages as low as possible and to increase production through labor-saving technology, thus preventing workers from improving their lot.

Pessimists regarding the Industrial Revolution over the past two centuries have usually claimed a moral basis for their position. In this respect they follow in a tradition begun by the poet William Blake (1757–1827), who referred to the new factories as "satanic mills," and the socialist Friedrich Engels, who in *The Condition of the Working Class in England in 1844* (1845) accused the factory owners in England of mass murder and robbery. Much pessimist writing has also been used to support a program of social or political reform. The German social philosopher Karl Marx (1818–1883), with whom Engels often collaborated and whose views we shall discuss more fully in Chapter 21, used his critique of industrial capitalism to call for a communist revolution in which the working class would seize political power and acquire ownership of the means of production.

Most of the evidence that social critics have used to support the pessimist position has come from the early period of industrialization in Britain, when incomes were either stagnant or declining and when conditions in factories and industrial and mining towns were most appalling. It

DOCUMENT

Chadwick's Report on Sanitary Conditions

is difficult to measure these living standards statistically, but the weight of qualitative evidence suggests that they deteriorated during the nineteenth century. Working-class housing was makeshift and crowded, and there were few sanitary facilities. A new word, *slum,* was coined to refer to these poverty-stricken working-class neighborhoods. Poor drainage and raw sewage gave rise to a host of new hygienic problems, especially outbreaks of typhus and cholera. Between 1831 and 1866 four epidemics of cholera killed at least 140,000 people in Britain, most of whom lived in poorer districts.

The impact of industrialization and urbanization on the environment was no less harrowing. The burning of coal and the use of industrial chemicals polluted the urban atmosphere. The famous London fogs, which were actually smogs caused by industrial pollutants, presented a serious public health problem throughout the nineteenth century and did not begin to disappear until the introduction of strict regulations on the burning of coal in the 1950s.

While life in the city was bleak and unhealthy, working conditions in the factory were monotonous and demeaning. Forced to submit to a regimen governed by the operation of the machine, workers lost their independence as well as any control whatsoever over the products of their labor.

They were required to work long hours, often fourteen hours a day, six days a week, with few breaks. Factory masters locked the doors during working hours, and they assessed fines for infractions such as opening a window when the temperature was unbearable, whistling while working, and having dirty hands while spinning yarn. Work in the mines was a little less monotonous, but it was physically more demanding and far more dangerous.

Women, Children, and Industry

During the early Industrial Revolution in Great Britain, large numbers of children and women were recruited into the workforce, especially the textile and mining industries. In the woolen industry in the western part of England, for example, female and child labor together accounted for 75 percent of the workforce. Children under age 13 made up 13 percent of the cotton factory workforce, and those under age 18 made up 51 percent. This pattern of employment reflects the demands of industrialists, who valued the hand skills and dexterity that children possessed as well as the greater amenability of both children and women to the discipline of factory labor. Some of the machines that were introduced into the textile industry in the late eighteenth century were specifically designed for women and children.

DOCUMENT

Industrial Society and Factory Conditions (early 1800s)

Female and child labor was both plentiful and cheap. Children received only one-sixth to one-third the wages of a grown man, while women generally took home only one-third to one-half of that adult male income. There was no lack of incentive for women and children to take one of these low-paying jobs. In a family dependent on wages, everyone needed to work, even when a large labor pool kept wages depressed.

The participation of both women and children in the workforce was not new. In an agricultural economy all members of the family contributed to the work, with parents and children, young and old, all being assigned specific roles. Rural industry also involved the labor of all members of the family. When people began working in the factories, however, they were physically separated from the home, making it impossible for workers to combine domestic and occupational labor.

As the workplace became distinct from the household, family life underwent a fundamental change, although this change did not occur immediately. During the early years of the Industrial Revolution, members of many families found employment together in the factories and mines. Factory owners also tried to perpetuate many aspects of family life in the new industrial setting, defining the entire factory community as an extended family, in which the factory owner played the paternalistic role. Gradually, however, mothers found it impossible to care for their youngest chil-

DOCUMENT

The Employment of Women

The German social philosopher Friedrich Engels (1820–1895) was one of the founders of modern socialism. He and Karl Marx collaborated in writing The Communist Manifesto *(1848), and he edited the final two volumes of Marx's* Capital *after Marx died. Having served as a manager in a factory in Manchester, Engels described these conditions throughout Britain in one of his earliest works,* The Condition of the Working Class in England in 1844 *(1845). He emphasized the exploitation and brutalization of the lower classes as they were turned into a wage-earning proletariat. In this passage Engels describes the negative effects of factory labor on women and the family.*

The employment of women at once breaks up the family; for when the wife spends twelve or thirteen hours every day in the mill, and the husband works the same length of time there or elsewhere, what becomes of the children? They grow up like weeds; they are put out to nurse for a shilling or eighteen pence a week, and how they are treated may be imagined. Hence the accidents to which little children fall victims in the factory districts multiply to a terrible extent. . . . Women often return to the mill three or four days after confinement, leaving the baby of course; in the dinner hour they must hurry home to feed the children and eat something, and what kind of suckling that can be is also evident. Lord Ashley repeats the testimony of sev-

eral work women: "M.H., twenty years old, has two children, the youngest a baby, that is tended by the other, a little older. The mother goes to the mill shortly after five o'clock in the morning, and comes home at eight at night; all day the milk pours from her breasts so that her clothing drips with it". . . . The use of narcotics to keep the children still is fostered by this infamous system and has reached a great extent in the factory districts. Dr. Johns, Registrar in Chief for Manchester, is of opinion that this custom is the chief source of the many deaths from convulsions. The employment of the wife dissolves the family utterly and of necessity, and this dissolution in our present society, which is based upon the family, brings the most demoralising consequences for parents and children. A mother who has no time to trouble herself about her child, to perform the most ordinary loving services for it during its first year, who scarcely indeed sees it, can be no real mother to the child, must inevitably grow indifferent to it, treat it unlovingly like a stranger. The children who grow up under such conditions are utterly ruined for later family life, can never feel at home in the family which they themselves found, because they have always been accustomed to isolation, and they contribute therefore to the already general undermining of the family in the working-class.

Source: From Friedrich Engels, *The Condition of the Working Class in England in 1844,* translated by F. K. Wischnewtzky (London: S. Sonnenschein, 1892).

dren on the job, and most of them dropped out of the full-time workforce. The restriction of child labor by the British Factory Act of 1833 reinforced this trend and led to the establishment of a fairly common situation in which the male wage earner worked outside the home while his wife stayed home with the children. As one young girl who worked in the mines testified before a parliamentary commission investigation of child labor in 1842, "Mother takes care of the children."

As more and more mothers left the factories, the female workforce became increasingly dominated by those who were unmarried. The few female workers who were married with children either came from the very poorest segments of society or took jobs only because their husbands were ill or unemployed. Neither the pay these women received nor the jobs they performed gave them financial autonomy or social prestige. Becoming an independent wage earner meant little when women's wages were on average one-third to one-half those of men. The jobs assigned to women within industry, such as operating textile machinery, generally required the least skill. When men and women were employed in the same workplace, the women were invari-

ably subordinated to the authority of male workers or foremen, thereby perpetuating the patriarchal patterns that prevailed in preindustrial society. The Industrial Revolution did nothing to improve the status of women, and even their exclusion from certain occupations, such as mining by an act of Parliament in 1842, only reinforced a new sexual division of labor that was even more rigid than that which had prevailed in preindustrial society.

Class and Class Consciousness

As Europe became more industrialized and urbanized, and as the system of industrial capitalism became more entrenched, writers began to use a new terminology to describe the structure of society. Instead of claiming that society consisted of a finely graded hierarchy of ranks to which individuals belonged by virtue of their occupations or their legal status, they divided society into three classes that could be distinguished by the type of property people owned and the manner in which they acquired it. At the top of this new social hierarchy was the aristocracy, consisting

The Sadler Committee on Child Labor

The widespread use of child labor in Britain during the early decades of the Industrial Revolution led to efforts by social reformers and members of Parliament to regulate the conditions under which children worked. Parliament passed legislation restricting the number of hours that all children could work in textile mills in 1819 and 1829, but neither of these laws was enforced effectively, and they did not apply to all industries. Complaints of inhumane treatment, moral degradation, and exploitation of child workers continued to surface. In 1831 Michael Sadler (1780–1835), a Tory member of the British Parliament, introduced a bill in Parliament to limit the number of hours that all children could work to ten hours per day. Like many social reformers, Sadler was inspired by what he considered his Christian duty to protect dependent members of the community.

Sadler chaired the committee to which his bill was referred. In order to muster support for the bill, Sadler held hearings in which child workers themselves came before the committee to report on the conditions under which they lived and worked. The success of his bill was by no means guaranteed. Many members of Parliament were deeply committed to the policy of *laissez-faire,* according to which the government should not intervene in the operation of the economy, treating it instead as a self-regulating machine. Sadler had to convince his colleagues that they should modify that policy in the case of children, on the grounds that the state was obliged to provide for the welfare of children when their parents were unable to do so. He also needed to make the members of Parliament and the broader

public aware of the brutality of the conditions under which the children worked.

The hearings that took place were not a trial in the strict sense of the word, but they possessed many of the features of a judicial investigation, not unlike those conducted by grand juries in criminal cases. The committee's proceedings were intended to expose, condemn, and ultimately remedy misconduct by the factory owners. Procedurally the committee members had more latitude than did courts of law. Because these parliamentary committees were designed to extract information rather than to bring offenders to trial, they did not need to adhere to any established judicial guidelines. There was no cross-examination of witnesses, nor could factory owners present a defense. The witnesses in this investigation were chosen because Sadler knew they would reveal the evils of the factory system.

The testimony presented to the Sadler Committee produced abundant evidence of the exploitation and physical abuse of child workers. Some of the most harrowing testimony came from the examination of a 17-year-old boy, Joseph Hebergam, on July 1, 1832. Hebergam revealed that he had begun the work of worsted spinning at age 7, that he worked at the factory from five A.M. until eight P.M., and that he had only thirty minutes for lunch at noon, leaving him to eat his other meals while standing on the job. In the factory there were three overlookers, one

of whom was responsible for greasing the machinery and another for whipping the workers. The latter overlooker walked continually up and down the factory with whip in hand.

When asked where his brother John was working, Joseph replied that he had died three years before at age 16. Sadler then inquired into the cause of his brother's death. The boy responded, "It was attributed to this, that he died from working such long hours and that it had been brought on by the factory. They have to stop the flies [part of the textile machinery] with their knees, because they go so swift they cannot stop them with their hands; he got a bruise on the shin by a spindle-board, and it went on to that degree that it burst; the surgeon cured that, then he was better; then he went to work again; but when he had worked about two months more his spine

Child Workers
These children are on their way to work in the Yorkshire textile mills.

Child Labor in the Textile Industry
Factory girls operate machinery in a textile mill under the tight supervision of the factory owner.

became affected, and he died." The witness went on to explain that his own severe labor had damaged his knees and ankles so much so that he found it painful to walk. His brother and sister would help carry him to the factory, but when they arrived late, even by as little as five minutes, the overlooker beat all three of them "till we were black and blue."[3] At the request of the committee, Joseph then stood up to show the condition of his limbs. He reported the death of another boy who had sustained massive injuries when he was caught in the shaft of the machinery he was running. Joseph concluded his testimony by recounting how the factory owners had threatened him and his younger brothers

with losing their jobs if they testified before the committee.

The hearings of the Sadler Committee were widely publicized, but they fell short of realizing their original objective. The bill, which eventually was approved by Parliament as the Factory Regulations Act of 1833, prohibited the employment of children under age 9 in all factories. Boys and girls were allowed to work up to nine hours a day from age 9 until their thirteenth birthday, and up to twelve hours a day from age 13 until their eighteenth birthday. The long-term effect of this legislation was to establish in Western industrialized countries the principle that early childhood was a period of life set aside for education rather than work.

Questions of Justice

1. This investigation was concerned with the achievement of social justice rather than the determination of criminal culpability. What were the advantages of using legislative committees in such an undertaking?
2. Child labor was not a new phenomenon in the early eighteenth century. Why did the Industrial Revolution draw attention to this age-old practice?

Taking It Further

Horn, Pamela. *Children's Work and Welfare, 1780–1890.* 1996. An examination of the scale and nature of child employment in Britain and changing attitudes toward the practice.

of those who owned land and received their income in the form of rent. The middle class or bourgeoisie, which included the new factory owners, possessed capital and derived their income from profits, whereas the working class owned nothing but their own labor and received their income from wages.

This new model of society served a number of different purposes. Marx and Engels used it to construct a comprehensive theory of historical development. According to this theory, the middle class had struggled for centuries to seize power from the aristocracy, while the working class would eventually take power from the middle class. For Marx and Engels, conflicts over control of the means of production created a state of continuous class conflict. David Ricardo (1772–1823), an English social philosopher whose political and social allegiances were very different from those of Marx, used a similar model of society to illustrate the crucial role that the middle class played in the economy. Ricardo compared society to a coach in which the middle class was the driver guiding the vehicle, the working class was the horse that provided the labor, and the aristocracy was the nonpaying passenger.

Historians and social scientists disagree over the extent to which men and women in the nineteenth century were actually conscious of their membership in these classes. Marxist historians have claimed that the growth of wage labor, the exploitation of the working class, and conflicts between capital and labor encouraged workers to think of themselves not so much as individuals who claimed a certain social status but as members of a large class of workers who shared the same relationship to the means of production. These historians have pointed to the growth of trade unions, political campaigns for universal male suffrage, and other forms of working-class organization and communication as evidence of this awakening of class consciousness.

Other historians have claimed that people were less conscious of their class position. True, at certain times in the early nineteenth century some workers thought of themselves as members of a class whose interests conflicted with those of factory owners and financiers. It was much more common, however, for them to think of themselves primarily as practitioners of a particular craft, as members of a local community, or as part of a distinct ethnic minority, such as the Irish. When they demanded the right to vote, workers based their claim on their historic constitutional rights, not on the interests of all wage earners. When they demonstrated in favor of the ten-hour working day, they did so to improve the conditions in which they worked, not to advance the struggle of all workers against the middle class. The work experiences of laborers were too varied to sustain an awareness among most of them that they belonged to one homogeneous group.

The various capitalists, shopkeepers, and factory owners who belonged to the bourgeoisie also lacked a clear sense of their membership in a single middle class. These people were capable of achieving solidarity on certain occasions, such as when they feared that workers threatened their interests. As we discussed in Chapter 18, the bourgeoisie often criticized the lifestyle and values of the landed aristocracy in print. But like the working class, the bourgeoisie was too diverse to allow for the development of a unifying class consciousness inspired by an identity of economic interest

Capital and Labor
This cartoon, drawn by the illustrator Gustave Doré, depicts wealthy industrialists gambling with workers tied together as chips.

The Industrial City of Birmingham in 1829
Factories dominated the landscape of the city of Birmingham in this watercolor attributed to Frederick Calvert. By this time contemporaries were already complaining about the poor quality of air caused by the smelting of iron.

against those who occupied social positions either above or below them.

Working men and women showed a marked reluctance to engage in militant or violent action against their employers. Appeals for working-class solidarity to a large extent fell on deaf ears. It is true that on certain occasions workers took violent action against their employers. In 1812 groups of hand loom weavers in the highly industrialized Midland region of England engaged in a determined campaign to destroy the new power looms that they blamed for rising unemployment and low wages. Often disguised and operating at night, these "Luddites," who took their name from their mythical leader Ned Ludd, smashed the new textile machinery that factory owners had introduced. (Even today people who object to the introduction of new technology are referred to as Luddites.) The government sent an army of 12,000 men to suppress the Luddites, a task made difficult by the protection given them by their communities.

The Luddites did not, however, represent the majority of the English working class. Factory workers in particular seemed reluctant to join working-class organizations. Most of the workers who participated in these associations and who campaigned for the rights of the workers were independent artisans who had little interest in the struggle that Marx and Engels had predicted would result in the victory of the working class.

Nevertheless, the growing tensions between industrial capitalists and labor, coupled with the recognition that those who had political power were reluctant to give workers the right to vote, led to the gradual emergence of class consciousness in England. A violent encounter between workers demonstrating for the right to vote and better working conditions in Manchester in 1819, described in detail in the Encounters & Transformations feature in this chapter, contributed to a growing awareness among workers and the members of the bourgeoisie alike that British society was divided into classes that were engaged in continual conflict with each other.

The Industrial Landscape

As industry spread throughout Europe and reached into areas that previously had been untouched by mechanization, urban and rural areas underwent dramatic changes. The most striking of these changes took place in the new industrial towns and cities, some of which had been little more than country towns before the factories were built. Manchester, for example, grew from a modest population of 23,000 people in 1773 to a burgeoning metropolis of 105,000 by 1820. Large factories with their smokestacks and warehouses, ringed by long rows of houses built to accommodate the armies of new industrial workers, gave these cities an entirely new and for the most part a grim appearance.

Cities experienced the most noticeable changes in physical appearance, but the countryside also began to take on a new look, mainly as a result of the transport revolution. The tunnels, bridges, and viaducts that were constructed to accommodate the railroad lines and the canals that were built to improve inland water transportation made an indelible imprint on the traditional terrain. In many ways this alteration of the landscape served as a statement of the mastery over nature that human beings had achieved at the time of the Scientific Revolution. The Industrial Revolution finally fulfilled the technological promise of that earlier revolution, and one of its effects was the actual transformation of the physical world.

The Peterloo Massacre, 1819

The most dramatic encounter between the middle class and the working class in early nineteenth-century Britain took place in the northern industrial city of Manchester. During the first fifty years of the Industrial Revolution Manchester had grown into a major textile-producing metropolis—known to some as "Cottonopolis"—with a population of some 120,000 people. With thousands of workers finding employment in the mills, the city provided an environment in which demands for a wide suffrage and an improvement in working-class conditions attracted widespread support. In August 1819 some 60,000 people, most of them workers and their families, gathered at St. Peter's Field to demonstrate support for universal male suffrage, annual parliaments, and relief from low wages, high prices, and long working hours. The fact that many of the workers had served in the Napoleonic wars and had been preparing for the demonstration by marching in military style had raised the fears of the middle-class establishment. Shortly after the meeting began, a violent confrontation took place between the demonstrators and the volunteer cavalry (known as yeomen), who belonged to the city's bourgeoisie. Frightened by the size of the demonstration and determined to prevent concessions that would reduce their profits, the yeomen decided to disperse the meeting by force. In the confrontation that ensued, the yeomen trampled hundreds of demonstrators and slashed many others with their swords, killing eleven people and wounding more than 400. "Over the whole field," wrote one observer, "were strewed caps, bonnets, hats, shawls, and shoes, and other parts of male and female dress, trampled, torn and bloody."

The violence that erupted at St. Peter's Field may have occurred too spontaneously to claim that the middle class deliberately attacked the workers who had assembled, but there is little doubt that the demonstration and the brutal response to it contributed to the growth of class solidarity, especially among the workers. The massacre inspired a number of calls for working class revolution. The young poet Percy Shelley (1792–1822), who was in Italy at the time, upon hearing of what had occurred in Manchester, called the working class to action:

> Rise like lions after slumber
> In unvanquishable numbers
> Shake your chains to earth
>   like dew
> Which in sleep had fallen on
>   you.
> You are many—they are few.

The British working class did not respond to Shelley's summons. The Peterloo Massacre did not lead to a working-class revolution in Britain. It did, however, lead to the transformation of Britain into a society that was increasingly divided along class lines. It led directly to the organization of British labor in unions as well as to the birth of the Chartist movement, which staged a number of demonstrations in favor of parliamentary reform and the improvement of working conditions in the 1830s and 1840s. The Peterloo Massacre also contributed to the growth of class consciousness. British workers did not always identify themselves as members of a single class, but incidents such as this violent clash encouraged them to think in such terms. Consequently Britain, the first country in the West to industrialize, gained a reputation, which it has not completely lost today, of being a society in which one's identity is based more on class than the place of one's origins.

For Discussion

The historian E. P. Thompson has referred to the Peterloo Massacre as class warfare. Is this an appropriate characterization of the events that transpired at St. Peter's Field?

The Peterloo Massacre, 1819
This drawing of the Peterloo Massacre shows the mounted yeomen with drawn swords attacking the demonstrators, who had gathered to hear the speeches by the reformers on the platform above.

Joseph M. W. Turner,
Rain, Steam and Speed:
The Great Western
***Railway* (1844)**
This was one of the first oil
paintings that had the railroad
locomotive as its theme.

The advent of modern industry also brought about a change in attitudes toward the landscape. The destruction of natural beauty in the interest of economic progress stimulated an appreciation of nature that had not been widespread during the medieval and early modern periods. Before the Industrial Revolution many features of the countryside, especially mountains, were viewed as obstacles to either travel or human habitation, not as sources of aesthetic appreciation. Urbanization and industrialization changed those perceptions, triggering a nostalgic reaction that became one of the sources of the romantic movement, which we shall consider in greater detail in the next chapter. Some of the idyllic landscapes of the English romantic painter John Constable (1776–1837), for example, represented an imaginative recreation of a countryside that had already been transformed by the advent of industry by the time he painted them.

Industry did not always form a blight on the landscape or offend artistic sensibilities. Some of the new industrial architecture, especially the viaducts and aqueducts that traversed valleys in the mountainous regions of the country, were masterpieces of modern engineering and architecture. Sir Walter Scott (1771–1832), the Scottish romantic novelist, claimed that the cast-iron Pont Cysyllte aqueduct in Wales, which carried the waters of the Caledonian Canal 127 feet above the River Dee, was the most beautiful work of art he had ever seen. The railroads also had the ability to inspire the artistic imagination, as they did in Joseph Turner's (1775–1851) romantic painting *Rain, Steam and Speed,* which captured the railroad's speed and beauty.

Industry, Trade, and Empire

■ **What was the relationship between the growth of industry and Britain's dominance in trade and imperial strength during the middle years of the nineteenth century?**

As the middle of the nineteenth century approached, Britain towered above all other nations in the volume of its industrial output, the extent of its international trade, and the size of its empire. In industrial production it easily outpaced all its competitors, producing two-thirds of the world's coal, about half of its cotton cloth, half of its iron, and 40 percent of its hardware. Little wonder that Britain became known as "the workshop of the world." Britain controlled about one-third of the world's trade, and London had emerged as the undisputed financial center of the global economy. Britain's overseas empire, which included colonies in Canada, the Caribbean, South America, India, Southeast Asia, and Australia, eclipsed that of all other European powers and would continue to grow during the second half of the century.

These three great British strengths—industry, trade, and empire—were closely linked. Britain's colonies in both Asia and the Americas served as trading depots, while the promotion of trade led directly to the acquisition of new imperial possessions. Even when Britain did not formally acquire territory, it often established exclusive trading relationships with those countries, thereby creating an informal "empire of trade." Trade and empire in turn served the purposes of industry. Many of the raw materials used in industrial production, especially cotton, came from Britain's imperial possessions. At the same time, those possessions provided markets for Britain's mass-produced manufactured goods. Such imperial markets proved immensely valuable when France blockaded its ports during the Napoleonic wars and thereby cut into British trade with the entire European continent (see Chapter 19).

The great challenge for Britain during the nineteenth century was to find new markets for its industrial products. Domestic demand had been strong at the beginning of the Industrial Revolution, but by the 1840s British workers did not possess sufficient wealth to purchase the increasingly large volume of hardwares and textiles manufactured in the mills and factories. Britain had to look overseas to find markets in which to sell the bulk of its industrial products. One possibility was to market them in other European countries, such as France and Germany, where demand for manufactured goods was high. These countries, however, were in the midst of their own industrial revolutions, and their governments had often legislated high protective tariffs against British goods to encourage the growth of their own industries. Britain therefore chose instead to market its goods in the less economically developed parts of the world, including its own colonies. We can see this trading pattern in the relationships that Britain had with three different regions: East Asia, India, and Latin America. In all three areas, moreover, British military power and diplomatic influence were enlisted in the cause of industry, trade, and empire.

East Asia: The Opium War, 1839–1842

British conflict with China provides the best illustration of the way in which the British desire to promote trade led to the acquisition of new colonies. For three centuries the Chinese had tightly controlled their trade with European powers. By 1842, however, British merchants, supported by the British government, managed to break down these barriers and give Britain a foothold in China, allowing it to exploit the East Asian market.

The conflict arose over the importation of opium, a narcotic made from poppy seeds and produced in great quantities in India. This drug, which numbed pain but also had hallucinogenic effects and could cause profound lethargy, was in widespread use in Europe and had an even larger market in Asia. In China opium had become a national addiction by the middle of the eighteenth century, and the situation became much worse when British merchants increased the volume of illegal imports from India to China in the early nineteenth century. The Chinese government prohibited the use of opium, but because it had difficulty

enforcing its own edicts, it decided to put an end to the opium trade.

Chinese efforts to stop British merchants from importing opium led to an increase in tensions between China and Britain. The situation reached a climax in 1839, when the Chinese seized 20,000 chests of opium in the holds of British ships and spilled them into the China Sea. It is unknown what effect the opium had on the fish, but the incident led to a British attack on Chinese ports. In this conflict, the first Opium War (1839–1842), the British had the advantage of superior naval technology, itself a product of the Industrial Revolution. The first iron-clad, steam-driven gunboat used in combat, the *Nemesis*, destroyed Chinese batteries along the coast, and an assault by seventy-five British ships on Chinkiang forced the Chinese to come to terms. In a treaty signed in 1842 China ceded the island of Hong Kong to the British, reimbursed British merchants for the opium it had destroyed, and opened five Chinese ports to international trade. As part of this settlement, each of these ports was to be governed by a British consul who was not subject to Chinese law. In this way Britain expanded its empire, increased its already large share of world trade, and found new markets for British manufactured goods in East Asia.

India: Annexation and Trade

The interrelationship of industry, trade, and empire became even clearer in India, which became known as the jewel in Britain's imperial crown. As we have seen in Chapter 17, Britain gained control of the Indian province of Bengal in the eighteenth century and subsequently acquired a number of other Indian states. After the Sepoy Mutiny of 1857 the British government brought all of India under its direct control.

Political control of India during the nineteenth century served the interests of British trade in two ways. First, it gave British merchants control of the trade between India and other Asian countries. Second, Britain developed a favorable balance of trade with India, exporting more goods to that country than it imported. Taxes paid to the British government by India for administering the country and interest payments on British loans to India increased the flow of capital from Calcutta to London. The influx of capital from India was in large part responsible for the favorable balance of payments that Britain enjoyed with the rest of the world until World War I. The capital that Britain received from these sources as well as from trade with China was funneled into the British economy or invested in British economic ventures throughout the world.

Control of India also served British interests by supplying British industries with raw materials while giving them access to the foreign markets they needed to make a profit. This promotion of British industry was done at the expense of the local Indian economy. The transportation of cotton grown in India to British textile mills only to be returned to India in the form of finished cloth certainly retarded, if it did not destroy, the existing Indian textile industry. Resentment of this economic exploitation of India became one of the main sources of Indian nationalism in the late nineteenth century.

Latin America: An Empire of Trade

British policy in Latin America developed differently from the way it had in China and India, but it had the same effect of opening up new markets for British goods. Great Britain was a consistent supporter of the movements for independence that erupted in South America between 1810 and 1824 (see Chapter 17). Britain supported these movements not simply because it wished to undermine Spanish and Portuguese imperialism, but because it needed to acquire new markets for its industrial products. Britain did not need to use military force to open these areas to British trade, as it did in China. Once the countries became independent, they attracted large volumes of British exports. In 1840 the British cotton industry shipped 35 percent of all its exports to Latin American countries, especially to Argentina, Brazil, Uruguay, Mexico, and Chile. Britain also exported large amounts of capital to these Latin American countries by investing vast sums of money in their economies. Britain thus established an informal "empire of trade" in Latin America. These countries were not controlled by Britain, but they had the same economic relationship with Britain as other parts of the British Empire.

British investment and trade brought the newly independent nations of Latin America into the industrial world economy. In so doing, however, Britain assigned these countries to a dependent position in that economy, not unlike the position that India occupied in Asia about the same time. One effect of this dependence was to transform the small, self-sufficient village economies that had developed alongside the large plantations in Central and South America. Instead of producing goods themselves and selling them within their own markets, these villages now became suppliers of raw materials for British industry. At the same time the Latin American population became more dependent upon British manufactured goods. This transformation not only retarded or destroyed native Latin American industry but also created huge trade deficits for Latin American countries by the middle of the nineteenth century.

Ireland: The Internal Colony

Of all the imperial possessions with which Britain engaged in trade, the position of Ireland was the most anomalous. Despite its proximity to England, Ireland had always been treated as a colony. In 1801, after the unsuccessful Irish rebellion of 1798 discussed in Chapter 17, Ireland was incorporated into the United Kingdom, the Irish parliament was abolished, and Irishmen elected representatives to sit in the British Parliament at Westminster. Even though Ireland thus became formally a part of the British state, Britain nonetheless continued to treat the country as an imperial possession, especially with respect to its economy.

Throughout the nineteenth century Ireland remained almost entirely agricultural; only in the north, in the province of Ulster, which produced ready-to-wear undergarments for women and shirts for men, did industrialization take place, and that usually took the form of cottage industry. At the same time, large agricultural estates in Ireland, many of them owned by absentee British landlords, provided Britain with large imports of grain. Unable to afford the high cost of grain, which British protectionist legislation kept artificially high, and without the opportunity to find employment in industry, Irish tenants eked out an existence on the land, relying on a diet consisting almost entirely of potatoes. When a blight destroyed the potato crop in 1845, the country experienced a devastating famine that killed more than one million Irish people and forced another million to emigrate—many of them to the United States and Canada—between 1845 and 1848. The famine occurred despite the fact that Irish lands produced enough grain to feed the entire population. As the Lord Mayor of Dublin complained in 1845, British commercial policy inflicted on the Irish "the abject misery of having their own provisions carried away to feed others, while they themselves are left contemptuously to starve."[4] Thus, even in this internal colony, the British government's policy of promoting industry at home while importing resources from its imperial possessions promoted British economic interests at the expense of the countries under its control.

Conclusion

Industrialization and the West

By 1850 the Industrial Revolution had begun to bring about some of the most dramatic changes in human life recorded in historical documents. Not since the Neolithic Age, when people began to live in settled villages, cultivate grains, and domesticate animals, did the organization of society, the patterns of work, and the landscape undergo such profound changes. In many ways the Industrial Revolution marked the watershed between the old way of life and the new. It gave human beings unprecedented technological control over nature, made employment in the home the exception rather than the rule, and submitted industrial workers to a regimentation unknown in the past. It changed family life, gave cities an entirely new appearance, and unleashed new and highly potent political forces, including the ideologies of liberalism and socialism, which shall be discussed in depth in the next chapter.

Industrialization changed the very definition of the West. In the Middle Ages the predominant cultural values of Western countries were those of Christianity, while in the eighteenth century those values were more often associated with the rational, scientific culture of the Enlightenment. Now, in the nineteenth century, the West was increasingly becoming identified with industrialization and the system of industrial capitalism it had spawned. In discussing the prospects of industrialization in the Ottoman Empire in 1856, a British diplomat wrote that "Europe is at hand, with its science, its labor, and its capital," but that the Qur'an and other elements of traditional Turkish culture "are so many obstacles to advancement in a Western sense."[5] The Industrial Revolution was creating new divisions between the West and the non-Western world.

Until the late nineteenth century, industrialization took place only in nations that have traditionally formed a part of the West. Beginning in the 1890s, however, countries that lay outside the West or on its margins began to introduce industrial technology and methods. Between 1890 and 1910 Russia and Japan underwent a period of rapid industrialization, and in the second half of the twentieth century a number of countries in Asia and Latin America, as well as Turkey, followed suit. This process of industrialization and economic development is often described as one of westernization, and it has usually led to conflicts within those countries between Western and non-Western values. The industrialization of these nations has not always been fully successful, and even when it has, doubt remains as to whether those nations should now be included within the West. Industrialization outside Europe and the United States reveals once again that the composition of the West changes from time to time and that its boundaries are often difficult to define.

Suggestions for Further Reading

For a comprehensive listing of suggested readings, please go to www.ablongman.com/levack2e/chapter20

Ashton, T. A. *The Industrial Revolution,* reprint edition with preface by P. Hudson. 1992. The classic statement of the optimist position, identifying the benefits of the revolution.

Berg, Maxine. *The Age of Manufactures, 1700–1820: Industry, Innovation and Work in Britain.* 1994. A study of the process and character of specific industries, especially those employing women.

Brinley, Thomas. *The Industrial Revolution and the Atlantic Economy: Selected Essays.* 1993. Essays challenging the view that Britain's Industrial Revolution was a gradual process.

Deane, Phyllis. *The First Industrial Revolution.* 1967. The best study of technological innovation in Britain.

Gutmann, Myron. *Toward the Modern Economy: Early Industry in Europe, 1500–1800.* 1988. A study of cottage industry, especially in France.

Hobsbawm, E. J. *Industry and Empire.* 1968. A general economic history of Britain from 1750 to 1970 that analyzes the position of Britain in the world economy.

Jacob, Margaret. *Scientific Culture and the Making of the Industrial West.* 1997. An exploration of the spread of scientific knowledge and its connection with industrialization.

Morris, R. J. *Class and Class Consciousness in the Industrial Revolution, 1780–1850.* 1979. A balanced treatment of the link between industrialization and class formation.

Pollard, Sidney. *Peaceful Conquest: The Industrialization of Europe, 1760–1970.* 1981. A linking of coal supplies to economic development.

Rule, John. *The Vital Century, England's Developing Economy, 1714–1815.* 1992. A general economic history establishing the importance of early eighteenth-century developments.

Stearns, Peter. *The Industrial Revolution in World History.* 2nd ed. 1998. The best study of industrialization in a global context.

Teich, Mikulas, and Roy Porter, eds. *The Industrial Revolution in National Context: Europe and the USA.* 1981. Essays illustrating similarities as well as national differences in the process of industrialization.

Wrigley, E. A. *Continuity, Chance and Change: The Character of the Industrial Revolution in Britain.* 1988. Includes the best discussion of the transition from an advanced organic economy to one based on minerals.

Notes

1. Lord Ashley's Commission on Mines, *Parliamentary Papers,* Vols. 15–17 (1842), Appendix 1, Note 26.

2. Sir James Kay-Shuttleworth (1832), quoted in John Rule, *The Labouring Classes in Early Industrial England* (1986).

3. "Report of the Select Committee on the Factories Bill," *Parliamentary Papers,* Vol. 20 (1833).

4. John O'Rourke, *The History of the Great Irish Famine of 1847* (1902).

5. David Gillard, ed., *British Documents on Foreign Affairs,* Vol. 1: *The Ottoman Empire in the Balkans, 1856–1875* (1984–1985), 20.

Ideological Conflict and National Unification, 1815–1871

21

O N MARCH 18, 1871, THE PRESIDENT OF THE FRENCH GOVERNMENT, Adolphe Thiers, sent a small unit of troops to Paris to seize cannons that had been used against Prussian forces during their siege of the city a few months before. The artillery was in the possession of the National Guard, the citizen militia of Paris. The members of the National Guard felt that the government had abandoned them by recently concluding an armistice with the Prussians, who were still camped outside the city. They also believed that the government was determined to gain control of the city, which had refused to comply with the orders of the national government. When the troops reached the city, they encountered a hostile crowd of Parisians, many of whom were armed. The crowd surrounded the two generals who led the detachment, placed them up against a wall, and executed them.

This action led to a full-scale siege of Paris by government troops. In the city a committed group of radicals formed a new municipal government, the Paris Commune, which was a revival of the commune established during the French Revolution in 1792. The Commune took steps to defend the city against the government troops, and during its short life it implemented several social reforms. The Communards, as the members were known, set up a central employment bureau, established nurseries for working mothers, and recognized women's labor unions. For many decades the Commune served as a model of working-class government.

The Paris Commune lasted only a few weeks. On May 21 the troops of the provisional government poured through the gates of the city, and during the "bloody week" that followed they took the city street by street, demolishing the barricades and executing the Communards. The Communards retaliated by executing a number of hostages, including the archbishop of Paris. They also burned down the Tuileries Palace, the hall of justice, and the city

Eugene Delacroix, *Liberty Leading the People* (1830) The romantic representation of Liberty carrying the French tricolor during the Paris revolution of 1830 conveys the ideological inspiration as well as the violence of that armed uprising.

hall. During this one week at least 25,000 Communards were killed, and because many bodies were burned in the fires that consumed the city, the numbers were probably much higher.

The short life of the Paris Commune marks the climax of a tumultuous period of European history. Between 1815 and 1871 Europe witnessed numerous movements for reform, periodic uprisings, and several revolutions. The people who participated in these momentous developments were inspired in large part by ideologies°, theories of society and government that lay at the basis of political programs. The ideologies that developed during this period—liberalism, conservatism, socialism, and nationalism—were the product of historical developments that had arisen in the West, and they endowed the West with a distinctive political culture. These four ideologies also provide a framework for understanding the complex and often confusing political and social history of the West from 1815 until 1871.

The main question that this chapter will address is how the ideological encounters of this period influenced the course of Western political development. More specifically, the individual sections of the chapter will address the following questions:

■ What were the main features of the ideologies that inspired people to political action during the period from 1815 to 1871?
■ How did the encounters among the people who espoused these ideologies shape the political history of Europe between 1815 and 1848?
■ How did liberal and conservative leaders use the ideology of nationalism as a tool to unite the people of various territories into nation-states between 1848 and 1871?
■ What role did ideology play in international warfare and diplomacy, especially in efforts to maintain the balance of power during this period?

New Ideologies in the Early Nineteenth Century

■ What were the main features of the ideologies that inspired people to political action during the period from 1815 to 1871?

In the wake of the French Revolution, four new ideologies—liberalism, conservatism, socialism, and nationalism—led thousands of Europeans to call for profound changes in the established political order. These ideologies had their roots in the works of eighteenth-century writers, but they developed into integrated systems of thought and inspired political programs in the first half of the nineteenth century. All four were influenced by the two great transformations of the West that we have discussed in the last two chapters: the French Revolution and the Industrial Revolution.

Liberalism: The Protection of Individual Freedom

Liberalism° is anchored in the beliefs that political, social, and economic freedoms are of supreme importance and that the main function of government is to protect those freedoms. The political agendas of nineteenth-century liberals varied from one country to another, but they all pursued three main objectives. The first objective was to establish and protect individual rights, such as the freedom of the press, freedom of religion, and freedom from arbitrary arrest and imprisonment. Liberals sought to guarantee these rights by having them enumerated in written constitutions. Opposed to aristocratic privilege, liberals supported the principle of equality before the law. They also tended to be anticlerical, a position that led to frequent tension between them and the Roman Catholic Church. As defenders of individual freedom they often campaigned to end slavery and serfdom.

The second objective of liberals was the extension of the franchise (the right to vote) to all property owners, especially those in the middle class. For the most part liberals were opposed to giving the vote to the lower classes, on the grounds that poor people, with little property of their own, could not be trusted to elect representatives who would protect property rights. Liberals also were opposed to giving the vote or any other form of political power to women. They justified the exclusion on the grounds that the proper arena for female activity was the home, where women occupied their natural domain. In this way liberals subscribed to the theory of separate spheres, which assigned men and women different gender roles. As we know from Chapter 18, this theory was based on the belief that women were different in nature from men and that they should be confined to an exclusively domestic role as chaste wives and mothers. Liberals believed that only male property holders should be allowed to participate in public affairs.

The third objective of liberals was to promote free trade with other nations and to resist government regulation of the domestic economy. This economic dimension of liberal ideology, which is grounded in the writings of the Scottish economist Adam Smith and other advocates of free-market capitalism, is usually referred to as laissez-faire°, a phrase that means "let (people) do (as they choose)." Advocates of *laissez-faire* held that the government should intervene in the economy only if it is necessary to maintain public order and protect property rights. As merchants and manufacturers, liberals favored a policy of *laissez-faire* because it offered them the freedom to pursue their own self-interest without governmental interference and thereby realize greater profits.

Some of the earliest expressions of liberal ideology appear in the works of John Locke and his fellow Whigs in England during the late seventeenth century (see Chapter 15). In arguing against the absolutist policies of Charles II and James II, the Whigs emphasized the inviolability of private property rights, freedom from state economic control, and the rights of those who held property to participate in government. In the eighteenth century these ideas were developed by Enlightenment thinkers who defended natural rights, and they found eloquent expression at the time of the American Revolution and the early years of the French Revolution. Liberal ideas were also embodied in the constitutions implemented in France, Germany, and Spain at the end of the Napoleonic period. When those constitutions and their principles came under attack after 1815, liberals sought to restore the freedoms they had lost without destroying public order. At that time liberalism became a distinct ideology.

Some liberals sought to realize their goals through the establishment of a republic, but the ideal form of government for most early nineteenth-century liberals was a limited monarchy—one in which the ruler did not act arbitrarily and suppress representative assemblies. As we shall see, liberal reformers in Britain during the 1830s wished to preserve the monarchy, and in France Louis-Philippe, the bourgeois citizen king installed during the Revolution of 1830, sought to implement liberal programs. In Germany, Belgium, and Greece, liberal revolts ended in the establishment of a constitutional monarchy.

DOCUMENT

John Stuart Mill Argues for the Sovereignty of the Individual in the Liberal State

John Stuart Mill (1806–1873) belonged to a group of British utilitarian social philosophers who gave liberalism its classic definition. In his most famous work, On Liberty *(1859), Mill discusses the nature and limits of the power that can be legitimately exercised over the individual. Mill recognized that this issue, the balance between freedom and authority, "has divided mankind almost from the remotest ages." His solution, which lies at the core of nineteenth-century liberalism, is that while the state can restrict one's liberty for the benefit of society, such as by compelling a person to pay taxes or to testify in court, in all undertakings that do not affect others, the individual has complete freedom over his actions and his opinions.*

The object of this essay is to assert one very simple principle, as entitled to govern absolutely the dealings of society with the individual in the way of compulsion and control, whether the means used be physical force in the form of legal penalties or the moral coercion of public opinion. That principle is that the sole end for which mankind are warranted, individually or collectively, in interfering with the liberty of action of any of their number, is self-protection. That the only purpose for which power can be rightfully exercised over any member of a civilized community, against his will, is to prevent harm to others. His own good, either physical or moral, is not a sufficient warrant. He cannot rightfully be compelled to do or forbear because it will be better for him to do so, because it will make him happier, because in the opinion of others to do so would be wise or even right.... The only part of the conduct of any one, for which he is amenable to society, is that which concerns others. In the part which merely concerns himself, his independence is, of right, absolute. Over himself, over his own body and mind, the individual is sovereign....

But there is a sphere of action in which society, as distinguished from the individual, has, if any, only an indirect interest; comprehending all that portion of a person's life and conduct which affects only himself, or, if it also affects others, only with their free, voluntary, and undeceived consent and participation.... This, then, is the appropriate region of human liberty. It comprises, first, the inward domain of consciousness; demanding liberty of conscience, in the most comprehensive sense; liberty of thought and feeling; absolute freedom of opinion and sentient on all subjects, practical or speculative, scientific, moral or theological. The liberty of expressing and publishing opinions may seem to fall under a different principle, since it belongs to that part of the conduct of an individual which concerns other people; but, being almost of as much importance as the liberty of thought itself, and resting in great part on the same reasons, is practically inseparable from it. Secondly, the principle requires liberty of tastes and pursuits; of framing the plan of our life to suit our own character; of doing as we like, subject to such consequences as may follow; without impediment from our fellow creatures, so long as what we do does not harm them, even though they should think our conduct foolish, perverse, or wrong. Thirdly, from this liberty of each individual follows the liberty, within the same limits, of combination among individuals; freedom to unite for any purpose not involving harm to others: the persons combining being supposed to be of full age, and not forced or deceived.

Source: John Stuart Mill, *On Liberty* (1901).

Liberalism found its greatest strength among the urban middle class: merchants, manufacturers, and members of the professions. These people formed the group that felt most aggrieved by their exclusion from political life during the eighteenth and early nineteenth centuries and most eager to have government protect their property. Their substantial wealth provided the basis for their claim to acquire a share of political power, and as manufacturers and merchants they had the most to gain from an economy unfettered by government regulations.

Liberal economic theory found its most articulate proponents in England, where industrial capitalism achieved its earliest and most significant successes. Two of the most prominent liberals in early nineteenth-century Britain were the utilitarians Jeremy Bentham and David Ricardo. Utilitarians° advocated economic and social policies that in their view would provide the greatest good to the greatest number of people. In pursuit of that goal, Bentham (1748–1832), a legal scholar and political philosopher, proposed that a government should give its people as much freedom as possible and impose only those laws that were socially useful. The economist Ricardo (1772–1823), the son of a Dutch Jewish banker, argued that the absence of government intervention would spur economic growth and thus contribute to the benefit of all people. This *laissez-faire* argument was far more persuasive to manufacturers than to workers. In *Principles of Political Economy and Taxation* (1819), Ricardo argued that if wages were left to the law of supply and demand, they would fall to near subsistence levels. This "iron law of wages" made it clear that *laissez-faire* liberalism would not benefit the working class.

Conservatism: Preserving the Established Order

Throughout human history people have demonstrated a desire to maintain the established order and to resist change. In the early nineteenth century, however, the ideals of the Enlightenment and the radical changes ushered in by the French Revolution led to the formulation of a new ideology of conservatism°, a set of ideas intended to prevent a recurrence of the revolutionary changes of the 1790s. The main goal of conservatives after 1815 was to preserve the monarchies and aristocracies of Europe against liberal and national movements.

The new conservatism justified the existing political order as the product of gradual change. This defense was most clearly expressed in the writings of the fiery, Irish-born parliamentary orator Edmund Burke (1729–1797). Burke was no reactionary; he advocated a number of changes in British public life, including electoral reform and a reorganization of the British Empire. But Burke, who is regarded as the founder of modern conservatism, had enormous respect for the existing social order, which he

considered the handiwork of God. Society according to Burke was a partnership between the living, the dead, and those who had yet to be born. Only within this historical partnership could change take place, and all changes would have to be gradual.

On the basis of this view of the social order, Burke attacked the liberal and radical ideas that had inspired the French Revolution. In *Reflections on the Revolution in France* (1790), he asserted that equality was a dangerous myth; its effect would be to allow those at the bottom to plunder those at the top and thus destroy the hierarchical order of society. Unlike the French revolutionaries, Burke had no faith in the people, whom he referred to as the "swinish multitude." In Burke's view rights did not derive from human nature, as they did for the philosophes of the Enlightenment; rights were privileges that had been passed down through the ages and could be preserved only by a hereditary monarchy. By claiming abstract rights for all men, the French had rejected their inheritance.

Conservative ideology justified the institution of monarchy on the basis of religion. The French writer Louis de Bonald (1754–1840) argued that Christian monarchies were the final creation in the development of both religious and political society. Only monarchies of this sort could preserve public order and prevent society from degenerating into the savagery witnessed during the French Revolution. De Bonald and his fellow French writer, Joseph de Maistre (1754–1821), rejected the entire concept of natural rights and reiterated the traditional doctrine of divine right, by which all political power came from God. De Maistre also reinforced the alliance between the throne and the altar by considering the monarchy and the Church as the foundations of the social order. In the nineteenth century, conservatives throughout Europe thought of religion as the basis of society. This view was especially strong in Catholic countries such as France and Austria, but Burke had put forth the same argument in Protestant England.

A fine line separates conservatism, which allows for gradual change, and reaction, which is the effort to reject any changes that have taken place and return to the old order. Early nineteenth-century conservatism provided an ideological foundation for the reactionary movements that arose throughout Europe after 1815. These movements had both national and international dimensions. In all western European countries, groups of influential and powerful individuals, usually nobles and churchmen, were determined to return to the days when they had more power. Internationally, the rulers of Europe, under the leadership of the Austrian foreign minister Clemens von Metternich, established a mechanism known as the Concert of Europe° to preserve the map of Europe as it was drawn at the Congress of Vienna (see Chapter 19). To do so meant taking concerted action against liberals and nationalists who attempted to unseat dynastic rulers.

In keeping with the identification of conservatism with religion, three of the four original powers in the Concert of Europe—Prussia, Russia, and Austria—gave their alliance a religious mission. At the Congress of Vienna Tsar Alexander I drafted a document in which the cooperation among European monarchs, whom he referred to as "the delegates of Providence," would be based "upon the sublime truths which the holy religion of Our Savior teaches." The British refused to subscribe to this document, claiming that it was "sublime mysticism and nonsense." So too did the future Louis XVIII of France (which was only a probationary member of the Concert of Europe until 1818) and even the pope. But Alexander's commitment to defend Christian values in what he called the Holy Alliance provided a religious foundation for the reactionary and repressive policies that Russia, Prussia, and Austria took steps to implement.

Socialism: The Demand for Equality

Socialism, the third new ideology of the early nineteenth century, arose in response to the development of industrial capitalism and the liberal ideas that justified it. Socialism calls for the ownership of the means of production (such as factories, machines, and railroads) by the community, with the purpose of reducing inequalities of income, wealth, opportunity, and economic power. In small communities, such as some early nineteenth-century socialist settlements, ownership could be genuinely collective. In a large country, however, the only practical way to introduce socialism would be to give the ownership of property to the state, which represents the people.

The main appeal of socialism was the prospect of remedying the deplorable social and economic effects of the Industrial Revolution. As we have seen in Chapter 20, the short-term effects of industrialization included wretched working conditions, low wages, a regimentation of the labor force, and a declining standard of living. Socialists did not object to the mechanization of industry as such. Like liberals, they wanted society to be as productive as possible. They did, however, object to the system of industrial capitalism that accompanied industrialization and the liberal economic theory that justified it.

The earliest socialists were known as Utopian socialists, a name given to them because they envisioned the creation of ideal communities in which perfect social harmony and cooperation would prevail. One of these Utopian socialists, the British industrialist and philanthropist Robert Owen (1771–1858), actually turned his mill in New Lanark, Scotland, into a model socialist community in which the principles of cooperation prevailed and where the workers were housed and their children were educated. In 1825 he established a similar community in New Harmony, Indiana. Utopian socialism was not particularly concerned with the

granting of political rights to workers, nor did it encourage class consciousness or class tensions.

A second generation of socialists became more concerned with using the power of the state to improve their lot. The most influential of these socialists was the French democrat Louis Blanc (1811–1882), who proposed that the state guarantee workers' wages as well as employment in times of economic depression. He also wanted the state to support the creation of workshops in which workers would sell the product of their labor directly without an intermediary. The principle underlying Blanc's concept of the social order was, "From each according to his abilities; to each according to his needs." Blanc's brand of socialism began a long tradition in which workers tried to improve their lot by influencing government. This initiative was closely related to the radical democratic goal of universal male suffrage, which became one of the main objectives of many socialists after 1840.

The most radical form of nineteenth-century socialism was formulated by the German social philosopher Karl Marx (1818–1883). Marx was much more preoccupied than

Karl Marx
Karl Marx, the German social philosopher who developed the revolutionary socialist doctrine of communism.

DOCUMENT

Karl Marx and Friedrich Engels, *The Communist Manifesto* (1848)

These excerpts from the final pages of The Communist Manifesto *summarize the communist plan for establishing a socialist society by means of revolution. They reveal Marx's view of history as a succession of class conflicts and his prediction that the proletariat will become the ruling class. The appeal for working-class solidarity and revolution illustrates the power of socialist ideology to inspire people to action.*

The history of all past society has consisted in the development of class antagonisms, antagonisms that have assumed different forms at different epochs. But whatever form they may have taken, one fact is common to all past ages, viz., the exploitation of one part of society by the other. . . .

We have seen above that the first step in the revolution by the working class is to raise the proletariat to the position of ruling class, to win the battle of democracy. The proletariat will use its political supremacy to wrest, by degrees, all capital from the bourgeoisie, to centralize all means of production in the hands of the state, i.e., of the proletariat organized as the ruling class, and to increase the total of productive forces as rapidly as possible.

If the proletariat during its contest with the bourgeoisie is compelled by the force of circumstances, to organize itself as a class, if by means of a revolution it makes itself the ruling class, and as such sweeps away by force the old conditions of production, then it will, along with these conditions, have swept away the conditions for the existence of class antagonisms and of classes generally, and will thereby have abolished its own supremacy as a class. . . .

Communists disdain to conceal their views and aims. They openly declare that their ends can be attained only by the violent overthrow of all existing social conditions. Let the ruling classes tremble at a Communist revolution. The proletarians have nothing to lose but their chains. They have a world to win. WORKING MEN OF ALL COUNTRIES UNITE!

Source: From Karl Marx and Friedrich Engels, *The Communist Manifesto*, 1848, translated in English by Friedrich Engels in 1888.

---

other socialists with the collective identity and political activities of the working class. Reading about working conditions in France during the early 1840s, he became convinced that workers in industrial society were the ultimate example of human alienation and degradation. In 1844 he began a lifetime association with another German-born philosopher, Friedrich Engels (1820–1895), who as we have seen in the preceding chapter exposed the wretchedness of working-class life in Manchester. Marx and Engels began to think of workers as part of a capitalist system, in which they owned nothing but their labor, which they sold to capitalist producers for wages.

Marx and Engels worked these ideas into a broad account of historical change in which society moved inevitably and progressively from one stage to another. They referred to the process by which history advanced as the dialectic°. Marx acquired the idea of the dialectic from the German philosopher Georg Wilhelm Friedrich Hegel (1770–1831), who believed that history advanced in stages as the result of the conflict between one idea and another. Marx disagreed with Hegel on the source of historical change, arguing that material or economic factors rather than ideas determined the course of history. Hence Marx's socialist philosophy became known as dialectical materialism°.

According to Marx and Engels, the first stage of the dialectic had taken place when the bourgeoisie, who received their income from capital, seized political power from the aristocracy, who received their income from land, during the English and French revolutions. Marx and Engels predicted that the next stage of the dialectic would be a conflict between the bourgeoisie and the working class or proletariat°, which received its income from wages. This conflict, according to Marx and Engels, would result in the triumph of the working class. Led by a committed band of revolutionaries, the proletariat would take control of the state, establish a dictatorship so that they could implement their program without opposition, and usher in a classless society.

Marx and Engels issued this call to action in *The Communist Manifesto* (1848), which ended with the famous words, "Working men of all countries unite!" Marx's brand of socialism, communism°, takes its name from this book. Communism is a revolutionary ideology that advocates the overthrow of "bourgeois" or capitalist institutions and the transfer of political power to the proletariat. Communism differs from other forms of socialism in its call for revolution, its emphasis on class conflict, and its insistence on complete economic equality. Communism belongs to a tradition that originated among members of the extreme wing of the democratic movement at the height of the French Revolution. One of those radicals, François-Noël Babeuf (1760–1797), demanded economic as well as political equality, called for the common ownership of land, and

DOCUMENT

Karl Marx, On the Question of Free Trade (1848)

spoke in terms of class warfare. Marx's achievement was to place Babeuf's radical ideas in a new philosophical and historical framework. That framework, dialectical materialism, was explained in great detail in Marx's monumental three-volume work, *Das Kapital,* or *Capital* (1867–1894).

Nationalism: The Unity of the People

Nationalism, the fourth new ideology of the early nineteenth century, also took shape during and after the French Revolution. A nation° in the nineteenth-century sense of the word refers to a large community of people who possess a sense of unity based on a belief that they have a common homeland and share a similar culture. The ideology of nationalism° is the belief that the people who form this nation should have their own political institutions and that the interests of the nation should be defended and promoted at all costs.

The geographical boundaries of nations do not often correspond to the geographical boundaries of states, which are administrative and legal units of political organization. For example, in the early nineteenth century Germans often referred to their nation as comprising all people who spoke German. At that time, however, there were several German states, such as Prussia, Bavaria, and Baden, and there were also many German speakers living in non-German lands, such as Bohemia. A primary goal of nationalists is to create a nation-state°, a single political entity that governs all the members of a particular nation. The doctrine that justifies this goal is national self-determination°, the claim that any group that considers itself a nation has the right to be ruled only by members of its own nation and to have all the members of the nation included in this state.

The ideology of nationalism had roots in the French Revolution. Most of the revolutionary steps taken in France during the 1790s were undertaken in the name of a united French people. Article 3 of the *Declaration of the Rights of Man and Citizen* (1789) declared that "the principle of all authority rests essentially in the nation." The French Republic was constructed as the embodiment of the French nation. It gave an administrative unity to the French people and encouraged them to think of themselves as sharing a common cultural bond. Instead of a collection of regions, France had become *la patrie,* or the people's native land.

Nationalists emphasized the antiquity of nations, arguing that there had always been a distinct German, French, English, Swiss, or Italian people living in their respective homelands. This claim involved a certain amount of fiction, because in the past the people living in those lands possessed little cultural unity. There was little uniformity, for example, in the languages spoken by people who were identified as German, French, or Italian. Until the eighteenth century most educated Germans wrote in French, not German. Only a small percentage of Italians spoke Italian, and the main language of many Italian nationalists of the nineteenth century was French. Even after nation-states were formed, a large measure of linguistic, religious, and ethnic diversity has persisted within those states and has made true cultural unity impossible. The nation is therefore something of a myth—an imagined community to which nationalists believe they belong, but which in reality has never existed.

The ideal of the nation-state has proved almost impossible to realize. The boundaries of nations and states have never fully coincided. Patterns of human settlement are too fluid to prevent some members of a particular cultural group from living as a minority in a neighboring state. Germans, for example, have always lived in Poland, Spaniards in Portugal, and Italians in Switzerland. France at the time of the French Revolution probably came closest to realizing the ideal of a nation-state, claiming jurisdiction over most French people. Nevertheless, different regional identities and languages, such as that of the people of the southern province of Languedoc who spoke their own dialect, prevented the emergence of a powerful sense of national identity in all parts of France until the late nineteenth or early twentieth century.

In Britain the creation of a nation-state has been a complicated process. National consciousness, which is a people's belief that they belong to a nation, developed earlier in England than in any other country in Europe. In the sixteenth century almost all English people spoke the same language, and they were also subject to the same common law. In 1536, however, Wales was united to the kingdom of England, thereby including two nations, the English and the Welsh, in the same state. In 1707 England and Scotland were united in a new state, the United Kingdom of Great Britain, and in 1801 Ireland was brought into the United Kingdom as well. Thus the United Kingdom now included four nations: the English, the Welsh, the Scots, and the Irish. The task of building a British, as opposed to an English or a Scottish, nation in this multinational state has taken time, and to this day Britons are more accustomed to think of themselves as primarily English or Scottish than as British.

Other peoples have faced even more daunting obstacles than the British in constructing nation-states. Many nations have been subsumed within large empires, such as Hungarians and Croatians in the Habsburg Empire and Greeks and Serbs in the Ottoman Empire. In those empires, nationalist movements have often taken the form of separatist revolts or wars of independence, in which a nationalist group attempted to break off and form a nation-state of its own. A very different situation prevailed in Germany and Italy, where people who shared some linguistic and cultural traditions lived under the control of many different sovereign states of varying size. In these cases nationalist movements have sought to unite the smaller states into a larger nation-state.

One of the great paradoxes of nationalism is that the acquisition of colonies overseas often strengthened nationalist sentiment at home. The military conquest of these lands became a source of pride for the people in the metropolis, and also gave them a sense of cultural superiority. The main source of British national pride was the rapid spread of British control over one-quarter of the world's surface during the eighteenth and nineteenth centuries. Nationalism could also promote the supremacy of one's own nation over others. The French revolutionaries who conquered a large part of the European continent in the early nineteenth century justified their expansion on the grounds that they were superior to the rest of the human race. In 1848 a fervent German nationalist declared his support for "the preponderance of the German race over most Slav races." The Italian national leader Giuseppe Mazzini (1805–1872), whom we shall discuss in detail shortly, preferred to be called a patriot rather than a nationalist on the grounds that nationalists were imperialists who sought to encroach on the rights of other peoples.

Nationalism was often linked to liberalism during the early nineteenth century, when both movements supported revolutionary programs to realize the goal of national self-determination. Liberals believed that representative government and a limited expansion of the franchise would provide a firm foundation for the establishment of the nation-state, both in nations like Spain with a long tradition of self-rule and in countries like Greece that were seeking their independence from autocratic rulers. In Germany and Italy, where there was no central state, nationalists and liberals joined together to create one. There was, however, a difference of emphasis between the two ideologies, even in the early years of the nineteenth century. Liberalism stressed individual freedom, whereas nationalism was more concerned with political unity. At times those different ideals came into conflict with each other. The liberal doctrine of free trade, for example, ran into conflict with the doctrine of economic nationalism, which encouraged the protection of national industries. The nationalist German economist Friedrich List (1780–1846) claimed that free trade benefited only the wealthy and the powerful; he advocated instead protective tariffs to benefit German businesses.

Nationalism was just as capable of supporting conservatism as liberalism in the early nineteenth century. Because the nation was often viewed as having deep roots in the distant past, some nationalists glorified the monarchical and hierarchical political arrangements that prevailed in the Middle Ages. In 1848 conservative Prussian landlords rallied around the cause of "God, King, and Fatherland." Later in the nineteenth century, nationalism became identified almost exclusively with conservatism when the lower middle classes began to prefer the achievement of national glory, either in warfare or in imperialistic pursuits, to the establishment of individual freedom.

Culture and Ideology

As the four great ideologies of the Western world were developing during the nineteenth century, they were influenced by two powerful cultural traditions: scientific rationalism and romanticism. These two traditions represented two sharply divergent sides of modern Western culture.

Scientific Rationalism

Scientific rationalism is a manner of thinking that traces its origins to the Scientific Revolution and reached its full flowering in the Enlightenment. This tradition has provided a major source of Western identity ever since the late eighteenth century. It has stressed the powers of human reason and considered science superior to all other forms of knowledge. Scientific rationalism is essentially a secular tradition, in that it does not rely on theology or Christian revelation for its legitimacy. The effort to construct a science of human nature, which was central to Enlightenment thought, belongs to this tradition, while the Industrial Revolution, which involved the application of scientific knowledge to production, was one of its products.

During the nineteenth century, scientific rationalism continued to have a powerful influence on Western thought and action. As scientific knowledge continued to grow, and as more people received a scientific education, the values of science and reason were proclaimed more boldly. Scientific knowledge and an emphasis on the importance of empirical data (that which can be tested) became essential components of much social thought. The clearest statement that science was the highest form of knowledge and would lead inevitably to human progress was the secular philosophy of positivism°.

The main elements of positivism were set forth by the French philosopher Auguste Comte (1798–1857). Like many thinkers in the Enlightenment tradition, Comte argued that human society passed through a succession of historical stages, each leading to a higher level. It had already passed through two stages, the theological and the metaphysical, and it was now in the third, the positive or scientific stage. The word *positive* in this context means that which has substance or concrete reality, as opposed to that which is abstract or speculative. Comte predicted that in the final positive stage of history the accumulation of factual or scientific knowledge would enable thinkers, whom we now call sociologists, to discover the laws of human behavior and thus make possible the improvement of society. This prediction of human progress, and Comte's celebration of the liberation of knowledge from its theological shackles, had particular appeal to liberals, especially those who harbored hostility to the Roman Catholic Church.

The values of science and the belief in its inevitable advance also influenced the social thought of Karl Marx. His ideology of communism has been referred to as scientific socialism, in that it too is based on a vision of history determined solely by positive, in this case material or economic, developments. Marxism rejects the metaphysical, idealistic world of Hegel and the theology of all Christian religion and thus fits into the same scientific tradition to which positivism and earlier Enlightenment thought belongs.

Romanticism

The cultural tradition that posed the greatest challenge to scientific rationalism was romanticism°. This tradition originated as an artistic and literary movement in the late eighteenth century, but it soon developed into a more general worldview. The artists and writers who identified themselves as romantics recognized the limits of human reason in comprehending reality. Unlike scientific rationalists, they used intuition and imagination to penetrate deeper levels of being and to comprehend the entire cosmos. Romantic art, music, and literature therefore appealed to the passions rather than the intellect.

Romantics did not think of reality as being simply material, as did the positivists. For them it was also spiritual and emotional, and their purpose as writers and artists was to communicate that nonempirical dimension of reality to their audiences. Romantics also had a different view of the relationship between human beings and nature. Instead of standing outside nature and viewing it objectively, in the manner of a scientist analyzing data derived from experiments, they considered themselves a part of nature and emphasized its beauty and power.

As an art form, romanticism was a protest against classicism and in particular the classicism that prevailed in the late eighteenth century. As we discussed in Chapter 18, classicism reflects a worldview in which the principles of orderliness and rationality prevail. Classicism is a disciplined style that demands adherence to formal rules that governed the structure as well as the content of literature, art, architecture, and music. By contrast, romanticism allows the artist much greater freedom. In literature the romantic protest against classicism led to the introduction of a new poetic style involving the use of imagery, symbols, and myth. One example of this new approach is "Rime of the Ancient Mariner" (1798) by the English romantic poet Samuel Taylor Coleridge (1772–1834), which uses the sun and moon as powerful symbols in describing a nightmarish sea voyage.

Many romantic works of literature, such as the novels of the Scottish author Sir Walter Scott (1771–1832), were set in the Middle Ages, a period often associated with superstition rather than science and enlightenment. Other romantic prose works explore the exotic, the weird, the mysterious, and even the satanic elements in human nature. Mary Shelley's introspective novel *Frankenstein* (1818), an early example of science fiction that embodies a critique of scientific rationalism, incorporates many of these themes.

Within the visual arts, romanticism also marked a rebellion against the classicism that had dominated eighteenth-century culture. Classicism emphasized formality and symmetry in art, and it celebrated the culture of an ideal Greek

F. G. Lardy, *Entrance to Chamonix Valley*
This painting reflects the romantic concern with the majesty and power of nature.

Mary Shelley's *Frankenstein:* The Body in Romantic Literature

In 1818, Mary Shelley, the 20-year-old daughter of the feminist Mary Wollstonecraft and the wife of the poet Percy Shelley, published a novel, *Frankenstein: or, The Modern Prometheus,* that became a literary sensation in contemporary England and has inspired books and films down to the present day. The depiction of the human body in the novel reflects the attitude of romantic writers toward nineteenth-century science.

The novel tells the story of an idealistic Swiss scientist, Victor Frankenstein, who discovers the secret of giving life to inanimate matter. Using his knowledge of chemistry, anatomy, and physiology, Frankenstein pieces together bones and flesh from corpses to construct the frame of a human being, which he then infuses with life. The creature turns out to be a freak of nature: a gigantic, ugly, and deformed monster with watery eyes, yellow shriveled skin, and straight black lips. Frankenstein is horrified by what he has wrought, and his rejection leads the monster to turn on his creator, eventually killing his brother, his friend, and his wife on their wedding night. Frankenstein pursues the creature to the Arctic region, but the monster brings about Frankenstein's death. Filled with self-loathing for having murdered "the lovely and the helpless," the monster declares that Frankenstein will be his last victim and sets off to throw himself on his own funeral pyre.

The body of the monster created by Frankenstein is unnatural in the manner of creation, its size, its features, and its preternatural strength. The depiction of monstrous creatures in literature was common during the early modern period, as a way of indicating supernatural intervention in the world. Shelley's depiction of this monster, which reflects the preoccupation of romantic literature with the exotic and the mysterious, differs from that older tradition in that it identifies modern science, not supernatural forces, as the source of the monster's abnormality. In trying to unite the body and the soul, Frankenstein produced a creature he called a daemon, a body inhabited by an evil spirit who commits multiple murders. Science had produced a moral and a physical aberration.

One of the important theological questions in the history of Christianity has been whether an evil spirit or demon can inhabit or possess a human body. Shelley was preoccupied by this issue, as evidenced by Victor Frankenstein's deep interest in the figure of Satan in the novel. Frankenstein's monster was a demonic figure, but unlike the Satan of the Bible, he was the product of science and its attempt to control nature. The real monster becomes science itself, whose power nineteenth-century intellectuals desired but at the same time feared.

Mary Shelley, like many romantic writers, thought of nature as a life force with which human beings should be in harmony. The novel reinforces this theme by showing how a human being's attempt to control nature leads to nature's revenge. Frankenstein's loss of physical and mental health, the thwarting of his ability to have children with his wife, and his eventual death are all penalties for his violation of nature.

For Discussion

How does *Frankenstein* reflect the themes of romanticism and in particular its critique of scientific rationalism?

Depiction of the Monster Created by Victor Frankenstein
The creation of the monster in Mary Shelley's novel embodied a critique of scientific rationalism.

and Roman past. By contrast, romantic painters depicted landscapes that evoked a mood and an emotion rather than an objective pictorial account of the surroundings. Romantic paintings were intended to evoke feeling rather than to help the viewer achieve intellectual comprehension. Some of them conveyed the power of nature while others depicted its majesty and grandeur.

Romantic music, which also appealed to the emotions, marked a similar but more gradual departure from the formal classicism that was triumphant during the eighteenth century. The inspirational music of Ludwig van Beethoven (1770–1827), the son of a German court musician from Bonn, marked the transition from classical to romantic forms. Beethoven's early work conformed to the conventions of classical music, but his later compositions, which were completed as he became progressively deaf and which defied traditional classical harmonies, were intended to evoke an emotional response. His famous "Ode to Joy," in his ninth and final symphony, remains unequaled in its ability to rouse the passions. In the view of one critic, Beethoven's music "opens the floodgates of fear, of terror, of horror, of pain, and arouses that longing for the eternal which is the essence of romanticism."

Another early romantic composer, Franz Schubert (1797–1828), who was born in Vienna, blended classical forms with romantic themes by incorporating Hungarian and gypsy folk music into his compositions. The emotionally powerful operas of the German composer Richard Wagner (1813–1883), which were set in the mythical German past, marked the height of the romantic movement in music. That style attained its greatest popularity during the second half of the nineteenth century with the lyrical symphonies and concertos of Johannes Brahms (1833–1897) in Germany and the symphonies, ballets, and operas of Peter Tchaikovsky (1840–1893) in Russia.

Romanticism, like the rational and scientific culture it rejected, had powerful political implications, leaving its mark on the ideologies of the modern world. In the early nineteenth century, romanticism appealed to many liberals because it involved a protest against the established order and emphasized the freedom of the individual. Romantic writers were themselves often outsiders, and therefore their protests took many different forms. The French romantic author Victor Hugo (1802–1885), whose epic novels *The Hunchback of Notre Dame* (1831) and *Les Misérables* (1862) depicted human suffering with great compassion, identified romanticism as "liberalism in literature." For Hugo a relationship existed between liberty in art and liberty in society. In France wealthy liberal bourgeoisie generally patronized romantic music and literature, while nobles and clerics denounced them. Romanticism could, however, support conservatism by idealizing the traditional social and political order of the Middle Ages and the central importance of religion in society. The hostility of romantics to the culture of the Enlightenment could also lead to political conser-

vatism. Sir Walter Scott and Samuel Taylor Coleridge were both conservatives, while the German writer Johann Wolfgang von Goethe (1749–1832), whose poems reflected many of the themes of romantic literature, opposed all liberal and republican movements in Germany.

Romanticism has a closer association with nationalism than with any other ideology. In the most general sense romanticism invested the idea of "the nation" with mystical qualities, thus inspiring devotion to it. Romantics also had an obsessive interest in the cultural, literary, and historical roots of national identity. This connection between romanticism and nationalism can be seen in the work of the German philosopher and literary critic Johann Gottfried von Herder (1744–1803), who was one of the leaders of the *Sturm und Drang* (storm and stress) literary movement. This movement, which developed in the 1770s and 1780s and included works by Goethe and Friedrich von Schiller (1759–1805), encouraged subjectivity and the youthful revolt of genius against accepted classical standards. Herder promoted the study of German language, literature, and history with the explicit purpose of giving the German people a common sense of national unity. He claimed that "a people may lose its independence, but it will survive as long as its language survives." Like many romantics, Herder idealized the Middle Ages and cultivated many of the myths that surrounded that epoch in Germany's history.

In other parts of Europe, especially in Poland and the Balkans, romantic writers and artists gave nationalists the tools necessary to construct a common culture and history of their nations. The Polish romantic composer Frédéric Chopin (1810–1849), who emigrated to Paris in 1831, inspired Polish nationalists by drawing on native Polish dances in his works for the piano. At the same time the romantic poet Adam Mickiewicz (1798–1855), another Polish exile in Paris, wrote *The Books of the Polish Nation* (1832), exalting his country as the embodiment of freedom and predicting that by its long suffering it would eventually liberate the human race.

Ideological Encounters in Europe, 1815–1848

■ How did the encounters among the people who espoused these ideologies shape the political history of Europe between 1815 and 1848?

The four new ideologies of the nineteenth century—liberalism, conservatism, socialism, and nationalism—interacted in a variety of ways, sometimes reinforcing each other and at other times leading to direct and violent political conflict. During the years between 1815 and 1831 the main ideological encounters occurred between liberalism, sometimes infused with nationalism, and conservatism. In 1815, at the time of the Congress of Vienna, it appeared that conservatism would carry the day. The determination of Metternich, the Austrian minister, to employ all the resources of the Holy Alliance to suppress any signs of revolutionary activity made the future of liberalism and nationalism appear bleak. The power of the new ideologies, however, could not be completely contained. Liberal and nationalist revolts took place in three distinct periods: the early 1820s, 1830, and 1848. During the latter two periods the demands of workers, sometimes expressed in socialist terms, added to the ideological mixture. In all these encounters conservatives had their say, and in most cases they emerged victorious.

Liberal and Nationalist Revolts, 1820–1825

Between 1820 and 1825 a sequence of revolts in Europe revealed the explosive potential of liberalism and nationalism and the determination of conservatives to crush those ideologies. These revolts also reflected the strength of movements for national self-determination. The three most significant revolts took place in Spain, Greece, and Russia.

The Liberal Revolts of 1820 in Spain and Portugal

The earliest clash between liberalism and conservatism occurred in Spain, where liberals ran into determined opposition from their king, Ferdinand VII (r. 1808–1833). Ferdinand had been restored to power in 1814 after his forced abdication in 1808. In 1812, during the rule of Joseph Bonaparte, the Spanish *cortes*—the representative assembly in that kingdom—had approved a liberal constitution. This constitution provided a foundation for a limited monarchy and the protection of Spanish civil liberties. In keeping with the ideas of the French Revolution, it also declared that the Spanish nation, not the king, possessed sovereignty. The tension began when King Ferdinand declared that he would not recognize this constitution. Even worse for the disheartened liberals was Ferdinand's decision to reestablish the Spanish Inquisition, invite exiled Jesuits to return, and refuse to summon the *cortes*. In 1820, when the Spanish Empire in the New World had already begun to collapse (see Chapter 17), liberals in Madrid, in alliance with some military officers, seized power.

This liberal revolt proved to be a test for the Concert of Europe. Metternich urged intervention, and although the British refused because they wanted to protect their trading interests with the Spanish colonies, the members of the Holy Alliance supported the invasion of Spain by a French army of 200,000 men. Ferdinand was restored once again to the throne, and once again he renounced the liberal constitution of 1812. The liberals not only lost this struggle, but they also suffered bitter reprisals from the government, which tortured and executed their leaders. The situation became only marginally better in 1833, when Ferdinand died and the liberal ministers of his young daughter, Queen Isabella II (r. 1833–1868), drew up another constitution. Her reign was marked by civil war, instability, and factional strife in which liberals made few substantial gains.

Shortly after the Spanish revolt of 1820, a similar rebellion based on liberal ideas took place in Portugal. The royal family had fled to Brazil during the Napoleonic wars, leaving Portugal to be governed by a regent. A group of army officers removed the regent and installed a liberal government, which proceeded to suppress the Portuguese Inquisition, confiscate church lands, and invite King John (r. 1816–1826) to return to his native land as a constitutional monarch. After the king returned in 1822, his enthusiasm for liberal government waned. His granddaughter, Maria II (r. 1826–1853), kept the liberal cause alive, relying on support from Portugal's traditional ally, Britain, but she struggled against the forces of conservatism and had only limited success.

The Nationalist Revolt of 1821 in Greece

A revolt in Greece in 1821, inspired more by nationalism than liberalism, achieved greater success than did the rebellions of 1820 in Spain and Portugal. It succeeded because other members of the Concert of Europe, not just Britain, lent their support to the revolt. Greece had long been a province in the sprawling Ottoman Empire, but a nationalist movement, organized by Prince Alexander Ypsilantis (1792–1828), created a distinct Greek national identity and inspired the demand for a separate Greek state. In 1821 a series of revolts against Ottoman rule took place on the mainland of Greece and on some of the surrounding islands. These rebellions received widespread support in Europe from scholars who considered Greece the cradle of Western civilization and from religiously inspired individuals who saw this as a struggle of Christianity against Islam. Hundreds of European volunteers joined the Greek rebel forces. Thus the insurrection became not only a liberal and national revolt but a broad cultural encounter between East and West. The English romantic poets George Lord Byron (1788–1824) and Percy Shelley (1792–1822) became active and passionate advocates for Greek independence, while the romantic painter Eugène Delacroix (1798–1863) depicted the horror of the Turkish massacre of the entire population at the island of Chios in 1822. The link between nationalism and romanticism could not have been made more explicit.

The Greek revolt placed the powers allied in the Concert of Europe in a quandary. On the one hand they were committed to intervene on behalf of the established order to crush any nationalist or liberal revolts, and they condemned the insurrection on those grounds when it

Eugène Delacroix, *The Massacre at Chios* (1824)

In 1821 the Greeks on the Aegean Islands rebelled against their Turkish rulers, and in April 1822 Turkish reprisals reached their peak in the massacre of the inhabitants of Chios. Romantic paintings were intended to evoke feelings, in this case horror, at the genocide perpetrated by the Turks against the Greek rebels. The painting reveals the close association of romantic art with the causes of liberalism and nationalism.

crush nationalist and liberal revolts, the Concert had in this case helped one succeed.

The Decembrist Revolt of 1825 in Russia

The least successful of the early liberal revolts took place in Russia, where a number of army officers, influenced by liberal ideas while serving in western Europe during the Napoleonic wars, staged a rebellion against the government of Tsar Nicholas I (r. 1825–1855) on the first day of his reign. The officers, together with other members of the nobility, had been meeting for almost a decade in political clubs, such as the Society of True and Faithful Sons of the Fatherland in St. Petersburg. In these societies they articulated their goals of establishing a constitutional monarchy and emancipating the serfs.

The rebels, known as Decembrists° for the month in which their rebellion took place, could not agree on the precise form of government they wished to institute. That disagreement, coupled with a reluctance to take action at the critical moment, led to their failure. When Tsar Alexander I died suddenly in 1825, the Decembrists hoped to persuade his brother Constantine to assume the throne and establish a representative form of government. Their hopes were dashed when Constantine refused to tamper with the succession and accepted the reign of his brother Nicholas. The reactionary Nicholas had no difficulty suppressing the revolt, executing its leaders, and leaving Russian liberals to struggle against police repression for the remainder of the nineteenth century.

first erupted. On the other hand they were Western rulers who identified the Ottoman Turks with everything that was alien to Christian civilization. Moreover, Russia wanted to use this opportunity to dismember its ancient enemy, the Ottoman Empire. The European powers eventually took the side of the Greek rebels. In 1827 Britain, France, and Russia threatened the Turks with military intervention if they did not agree to an armistice and grant the Greeks their independence. When the Turks refused, the combined naval forces of those three countries destroyed the fleet of the Turks' main ally, Egypt, at Navarino off the Greek coast. This naval action turned the tide in favor of the Greeks, who in 1833 finally won their independence and placed a Bavarian prince, Otto I (r. 1833–1862), on the throne. Thus the Greek war of independence effectively ended the Concert of Europe. Originally intended to

Liberal and Nationalist Revolts, 1830

A second cluster of early-nineteenth-century liberal and national revolts in 1830 achieved a greater measure of success than the revolts of the early 1820s. These revolutions took place in France, the kingdom of the Netherlands, and the kingdom of Poland.

The French Revolution: The Success of Liberalism

The most striking triumph of liberalism in Europe during the early nineteenth century occurred in France, where a revolution took place fifteen years after the final defeat of Napoleon at Waterloo. This liberal success did not come easily. During the first few years of the restored monarchy conservatives had their way, as they did elsewhere in Europe. Louis XVIII had approved a Charter of Liberties in 1814, but he was hardly receptive to any further liberal reforms.

Between 1815 and 1828 French politics was dominated by the ultraroyalists, who sponsored a "white terror" (so called because they displayed the white flag of the Bourbon monarchy) against liberals and Protestants. The terror was led by two men nicknamed Three Slices and Four Slices, indicating the number of pieces into which they butchered their Protestant enemies.

In 1824, when the conservative Charles X (r. 1824–1830) ascended the throne and took steps to strengthen the Church and the nobility, there appeared to be little hope for liberalism. Nevertheless liberal opposition to the monarchy gained support from merchants and manufacturers, as well as from soldiers who still kept the memory of Napoleon alive. When liberals feared that Charles would claim absolute power, and when a serious economic crisis afflicted the country in 1829, liberals at last gained a majority in the Chamber of Deputies, the French legislature.

Charles then embarked upon a perilous course. In what became known as the July Ordinances he effectively undermined the principles of the Charter of 1814. These ordinances dissolved the new Chamber of Deputies, ordered new elections under a highly restrictive franchise, and censored the press. The public reaction to this maneuver caught the king by surprise. Thousands of students and workers, liberals and republicans alike, poured onto the streets of Paris to demonstrate. Skirmishes with the king's troops only made the situation worse, and when the tricolor flag of the French Revolution appeared on top of Notre Dame Cathedral, protesters blocked the streets with barricades. Unable to restore order, the king abdicated in favor of his grandson, but the liberals offered the crown instead to the Duke of Orléans, who was crowned as Louis-Philippe I (r. 1830–1848).

Louis-Philippe accepted a revised version of the Charter of 1814 and doubled the franchise, giving the vote to middle-class merchants and industrialists. The king catered to this bourgeois constituency by encouraging economic growth and restricting noble privilege. His reign, which is often referred to as the "bourgeois monarchy," also achieved a measure of secularization when the Chamber of Deputies declared that Roman Catholicism was no longer the state religion. In keeping with mainstream liberal ideals, however, he did nothing to encourage republicanism or radical democracy, much less socialism. Efforts to depict him as the heir to the French Revolution did not persuade the bulk of the population. When the government brought the ashes of Napoleon from St. Helena to Paris, thousands of French men and women turned out to pay homage to the former emperor. Much to his disappointment, Louis-Philippe gained little political benefit from the move. France had acquired a liberal monarchy, but it stood on a precarious foundation.

The Belgian Revolution: The Success of Nationalism

The French Revolution of 1830 triggered the outbreak of a liberal and nationalist revolution in the neighboring country of Belgium. At the Congress of Vienna the Austrian Netherlands were united with the Dutch Republic in a new kingdom of the Netherlands. This union of the Low Countries did not work out, and soon after the formation of the new kingdom the Belgians began pressing for their independence as a nation. With a Dutchman, William I, as king and with the seat of government in Holland, the Dutch were the dominant partner in this union, a situation that caused considerable resentment in Belgium. Belgians spoke Flemish or French rather than Dutch, which had become the kingdom's official language. Moreover, most Belgians were Catholics, whereas the majority of Dutch people were Protestants. With their own language, religion, and culture, as well as their own history, Belgians thought of themselves as a separate nation. They also were more liberal than their Dutch neighbors, advocating free trade and the promotion of industry, while resenting the high tariffs imposed by the Dutch government.

The two main political parties in Belgium, the Liberals and the Clericals, joined forces to achieve autonomy. When the news of the Revolution in Paris reached Brussels, fighting broke out between workers and government troops. A national congress gathered to write a new constitution, and when the Dutch tried to thwart the rebellion by bombarding the Belgian city of Antwerp, Britain assembled a conference of European powers to devise a settlement. The powers agreed to recognize Belgium's independence, and they arranged for a German prince,

Scene from the French Revolution of 1830 in Paris
Demonstrations by students and workers led to the abdication of King Charles X and the establishment of a liberal government. Tricolor flags of the French Revolution hang from the windows.

Leopold of Saxe-Coburg, uncle of the future British Queen Victoria, to become king. The Dutch, however, refused to recognize the new government, and they renewed their military attacks on Belgium. Only in 1839 did all sides accept the new political arrangement.

The Polish Rebellion: The Failure of Nationalism

The French Revolution of 1830 triggered a second uprising, this one unsuccessful, in the kingdom of Poland (see Map 21.1). Poland had suffered many partitions at the hands of European powers during the eighteenth century, and in 1815 the Congress of Vienna had redefined its borders once again. After incorporating much of the eastern portion of the country into the Russian Empire, the Congress established a separate Polish kingdom, with Warsaw as its capital and the Russian tsar, Alexander I (r. 1815–1825), as its king.

With a Russian king the independence of Poland was a mere fiction, but Alexander had approved a liberal Polish constitution in 1815. He grew to regret this decision, and his rule as king of Poland gradually alienated Polish liberals

within the national legislature, the *sejm*. The accession of Nicholas in 1825 only aggravated those tensions. An uncompromising conservative, Nicholas accused the Polish opposition of complicity with the Russian Decembrist rebels, and he brought them to the brink of rebellion when he made plans to send the Polish army, together with Russian troops, to suppress the French Revolution of 1830 and to prevent the Belgians from receiving their independence.

The revolt began within the school of army cadets, who attacked the residence of the Grand Duke Constantine, but it quickly gained the support of the entire army and the urban populace. The revolt appealed to both liberals and nationalists, and it drew inspiration from a group of romantic poets who celebrated the achievements of the Polish past. A provisional government was established at Warsaw, but the liberal members of the elected national assembly were unwilling to enlist the peasantry in the conflict, fearful that they would rise against Polish landlords rather than the Russians. When the powers of western Europe refused to intervene on behalf of this liberal cause, Nicholas was able to crush the rebellion, abolish the *sejm,* and deprive the

DOCUMENT

Adam Mickiewicz, Excerpts from *The Books of the Polish Nation*

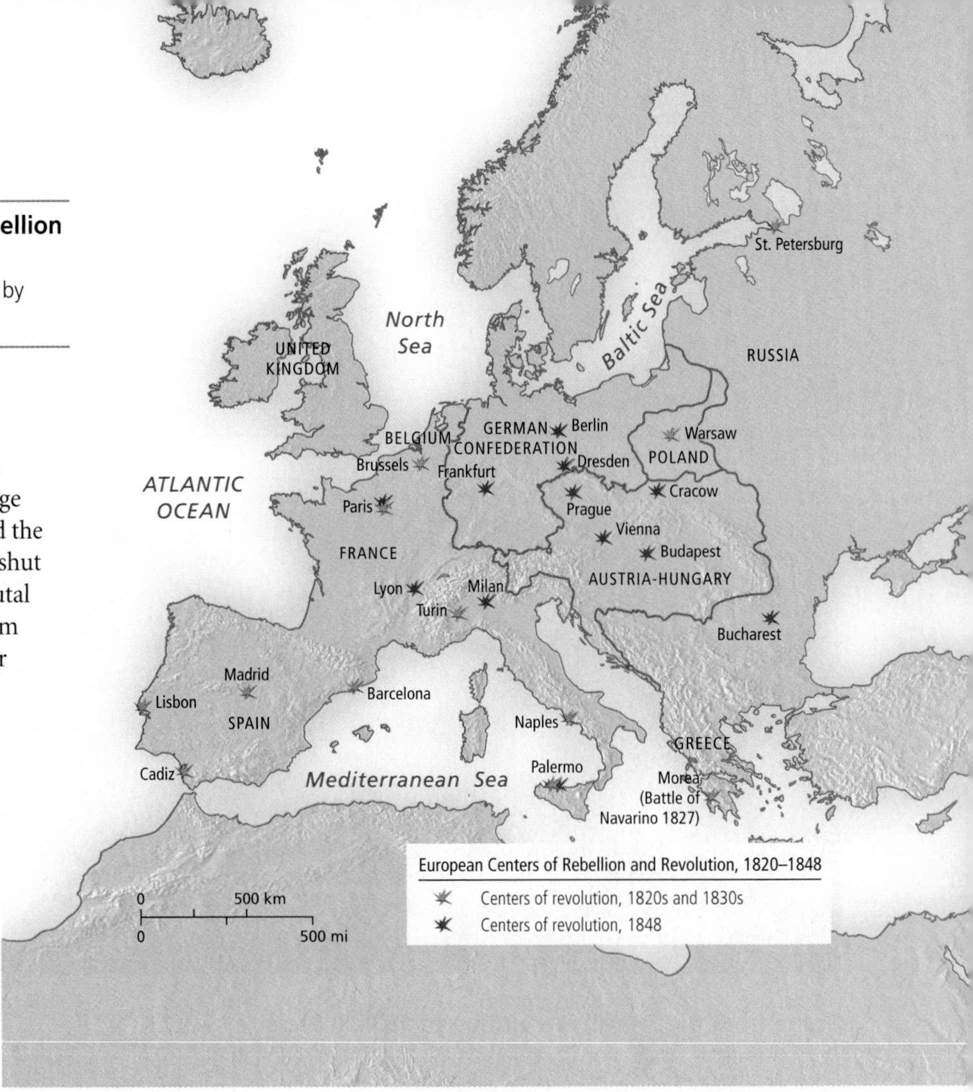

Map 21.1 European Centers of Rebellion and Revolution, 1820–1848

All these political disturbances were inspired by ideology.

European Centers of Rebellion and Revolution, 1820–1848
- ✳ Centers of revolution, 1820s and 1830s
- ✳ Centers of revolution, 1848

kingdom of Poland of its autonomous status. Nicholas visited a terrible revenge upon the leaders of the revolt, confiscated the lands of those who had emigrated, and shut down the University of Warsaw. His brutal repression set back the cause of liberalism and nationalism in Poland for another two generations.

Liberal Reform in Britain, 1815–1848

The challenges that liberals faced in Britain were somewhat different from those they confronted in most other European countries. Having maintained the status quo during the era of the French Revolution, the forces of British conservatism, which bore the ideological stamp of Edmund Burke, remained formidable. At the same time, however, Britons already enjoyed many of the rights that liberals on the European continent demanded, such as freedom of the press and protection from arbitrary imprisonment. The power of the British monarchy was more limited than in almost any other European country. The ideology of liberalism, which originated in England and had deep roots in British political and social philosophy, defined the political creed of many Whigs, who formed the main opposition to the ruling Conservative or Tory party after 1815.

In this relatively favorable political climate, British liberals pursued three major goals, which amounted to a program for reform rather than revolution. The first was parliamentary reform and the expansion of the franchise. The British had a long tradition of representative government, which had been secured by the Glorious Revolution of 1688, but the titled nobility in the House of Lords effectively controlled elections to the House of Commons, while the members of the gentry or lesser aristocracy held most of the seats in the House of Commons. In some boroughs real representation was a sham; the electorate consisted entirely of the borough councils, who elected the nominees of the noblemen who controlled them. Very few people lived in some of these "rotten boroughs"—one was nothing but a

pasture—whereas large segments of the population in the recently industrialized north had no representation at all in Parliament.

The Great Reform Bill of 1832, which was pushed through Parliament by the Whig prime minister, Lord Grey, marked a victory for British liberalism. The bill expanded the franchise to include most of the urban middle class. It eliminated the rotten boroughs and created a number of new ones in heavily populated areas. It also established a uniform standard for the right to vote in all parliamentary boroughs. In keeping with the principles of liberalism, however, the bill restricted the vote, and hence active citizenship, to property owners. It rejected the demands of radicals for universal male suffrage, and by using the phrase "male person" to identify eligible voters, the bill denied all women the vote.

Reform Bill of 1832 Cartoon

The second liberal cause was the repeal of legislation that denied political power to Catholics and also to Protestants who did not attend the services of the Anglican Church. In the seventeenth century a body of legislation had denied both of these religious minorities the right to hold national or local political office. Catholics suffered the additional liability of being denied the right to sit in Parliament. Liberals provided the basis of support for the political "emancipation" of Catholics and Protestant nonconformists. Liberals were opposed on principle to religious discrimination, and many of them belonged to Protestant nonconformist congregations. Conservatives opposed the repeal of this legislation, but they feared a civil war in Ireland if Catholics were not allowed to sit in the British Parliament. The Tory prime minister, the Duke of Wellington, who had defeated Napoleon at Waterloo, eventually agreed to liberal demands. The Protestant nonconformists were emancipated in 1828, while the Catholics had to wait until one year later. One of the first Catholics elected to Parliament in 1830 was Daniel O'Connell (1775–1847), an Irishman who worked tirelessly to improve the lot of his countrymen within the limits of the Irish union with Britain.

The third liberal cause was free trade. The target of this campaign was a series of protective tariffs on the import or export of hundreds of commodities, including raw materials used in production. The most hated protective tariff was on grain (known in Britain as corn), which kept the price of basic food commodities high in order to protect the interests of landlords and farmers. In this respect the determination of liberals for free trade conflicted with the determination of Parliament to defend the economic interests of its largely aristocratic membership. In 1837 a group of industrialists and radical reformers formed the Anti-Corn Law League with the purpose of bringing about the repeal of the Corn Law of 1815, which greatly restricted the importation of foreign grain into Britain. This campaign against protectionism did not succeed until 1845, when the Conservative prime minister, Sir Robert Peel, brought about repeal by securing

the votes of some of his own party and combining them with those of the Whigs, all of whom favored free trade. Peel took this action only after the potato famine in Ireland, which was discussed in Chapter 20, had begun to cause widespread starvation. The repeal of the corn laws allowed the importation of foreign grain into Ireland, but this change in government policy occurred too late to alleviate the suffering of the Irish people.

Unlike the liberals, socialists and radical democrats achieved little success in Britain during the first half of the nineteenth century. In 1834 the Utopian socialist Robert Owen established the Grand National Consolidated Trades Union, the purpose of which was to unite all workers in a peaceful struggle to realize his idealist goals. One of Owen's supporters hoped that the union would give "the productive classes a complete dominion over the fruits of their own industry." The refusal of many unions to join this association, coupled with opposition from the government, led to its disintegration. In its wake workers and radicals decided that economic improvement could come only through political means. In 1837 the newly formed London Workingman's Association, in collaboration with a few radical Members of Parliament, drew up a People's Charter, calling for the implementation of a program of radical democracy. Their demands included universal male suffrage, annual parliaments, voting by secret ballot, equal electoral districts, the elimination of property qualifications for Members of Parliament, and the payment of salaries to those same members. The workers who supported this cause became known as Chartists.

The Last Great Chartist Rally in Britain, April 10, 1848

Government precautions, including the appointment of special constables to handle the crowd, and rain kept the number of demonstrators in London lower than anticipated. The government ordered the leader of the movement, Feargus O'Connor, to stop the planned march to Parliament.

The strength of the Chartist movement fluctuated between 1837 and 1848, gaining the greatest popular participation when economic conditions deteriorated. Most Chartists restricted their activities to meetings to support candidates for Parliament and petitioning Parliament. A few of the more militant, such as the Irish immigrant Feargus O'Connor, called for "a holy and irresistible crusade" against the government. The British government and the upper classes became most frightened in 1848, when revolution broke out in France, Italy, and Germany, and when the Chartists decided to draft a new charter and threatened to form a revolutionary national assembly like that of France if Parliament were to reject the new document.

Within the next few years the Chartist movement died. British workers revealed, as they would throughout the remainder of the nineteenth century, that they had little inclination to take to the streets, especially after good economic times returned. The government's reduction of indirect taxes during the 1840s, coupled with the effective use of the police force and the strict enforcement of the criminal law, also helped prevent Britain from experiencing revolution in 1848. The price of this failure was that further liberal reforms, such as the extension of the franchise, did not take place in Britain for another two decades.

The Revolutions of 1848

Unlike Britain, almost every country in Europe experienced revolution in 1848. A wave of revolutionary activity spread rapidly throughout the Continent. The revolutions took place during a period of widespread economic discontent. European countries had suffered bad harvests in 1845 and 1846 and an economic recession in 1847, leading to a temporary decline in the standard of living among industrial as well as agricultural workers. Discontent took the form of mass protests and demonstrations, which increased the likelihood of violent confrontation. The revolutions of 1848 were more widespread than the revolts of the 1820s and 1830, and they involved greater popular participation. These revolutions also gave greater attention to both nationalist and socialist issues.

The French Revolutions of 1848

The first of the revolutions of 1848 took place in France, where the liberal government of Louis-Philippe faced mounting criticism. Declining economic conditions, which prevailed throughout Europe during the 1840s, provided an environment that brought the country to a crisis point. A series of demonstrations in Paris in favor of the right of workers to vote and to receive state assistance for their trades was the final precipitant. When troops from the Paris National Guard fired on the demonstrators and killed forty people, the barricades once again appeared in the streets and the rebels seized government buildings. France was experiencing its third revolution in sixty years. In an effort to save his regime, Louis-Philippe abdicated in favor of his grandson, but the revolutionaries abolished the monarchy and declared the Second French Republic.

A provisional government selected by the Chamber of Deputies was headed by nine republicans, but it included liberals and radical democrats. Most significantly it also included two socialists, Louis Blanc and a worker who preferred to be called by

---

CHRONOLOGY

The Revolutions of 1848

1848

February	Revolution in Paris
March	Insurrection in Berlin, peasant unrest in the countryside, formation of liberal governments in Prussia and other German states; revolutions in Milan and Venice, Ferdinand II issues a new constitution in Naples
April	Elections for a new National Assembly in France
May	Meeting of the Frankfurt Parliament; meeting of the Prussian Assembly
June	Suppression of working-class resistance in Paris; Pan-Slav Congress in Prague; suppression of the rebellion in Prague
October	Suppression of revolution in Vienna
December	Election of Louis-Napoleon as president of the Second French Republic; Frankfurt Parliament issues *Declaration of the Basic Rights of the German People;* Frederick William dissolves Prussian Assembly

1849

March	King Frederick William rejects the German crown offered by the Frankfurt Parliament
April	Frankfurt Parliament promulgates a new constitution; Hungarian Diet proclaims Magyar independence
May–June	Fall of the liberal ministries in German states
August	Venetian Republic surrenders to Austrian forces; suppression of the Hungarian movement for independence

the single name of Albert. The French Revolution of 1848 offered the socialists the first opportunity to realize their goal of a democratic and socialist republic. Many of the 200 clubs formed in Paris at this time, some of which were exclusively female, were either republican or socialist in their orientation. The socialist agenda included not only universal male suffrage, which was granted immediately by the government, but also active support for the masses of unemployed workers. Louis Blanc secured the establishment of national workshops to give the unemployed jobs on public projects. Ordinances reduced the length of the workday to ten hours in the city and twelve hours in rural areas, and the government authorized a commission to study working conditions.

These bold socialist initiatives did not last long. By the summer the euphoria of the revolution had dissipated and the aspirations of workers had been crushed. The elections held in April 1848 to constitute a new National Assembly and write a new constitution seated an overwhelming majority of conservative monarchists and only a small minority of republicans and socialists. Resentment of the provisional government's assistance to urban workers and anger at the levying of a surtax to pay for government programs revealed the lack of broad popular support for radical political programs. Tension between the new conservative assembly and the forces of the left mounted when the government closed the workshops and Parisian workers were either drafted into the army or sent to the provinces.

These newly adopted policies led to further working-class violence in Paris in June 1848. When General Louis Cavaignac, known as "the butcher," was called in to suppress this insurgency with regular army troops, there was a devastating loss of life. No fewer than 1,500 insurgents were killed in the streets or in summary executions, while another 4,000 were sent into exile in French colonies. These confrontations appeared to Karl Marx to constitute class warfare, a prelude to the proletarian revolution he predicted for the future. Louis Blanc, who was implicated in these uprisings, fled to England, where Marx himself would soon arrive and spend the rest of his life.

The revolution ended with the election of Napoleon's nephew, Louis-Napoleon Bonaparte (1808–1873), as the president of the Second French Republic in December 1848. Until the February Revolution it seemed highly unlikely that Louis-Napoleon, an impetuous adventurer and conspirator, would ever come to power. After staging two unsuccessful coups against the government of Louis-Philippe in 1836 and 1840, he was sentenced to life imprisonment. He managed to escape to England, however, and the events of February 1848 gave him the opportunity to return to France. He became a member of the new National Assembly, and then easily defeated Cavaignac in the presidential election.

Louis-Napoleon v. General Cavaignac— British Cartoon, 1848

As president, Louis-Napoleon drew support from conservatives, liberals, and moderate republicans. He also benefited from the legend that his uncle had created and the nationalist sentiment it inspired. Because the first Napoleon had become emperor, even those who preferred an empire to a republic could vote for his nephew. The younger Napoleon followed in his uncle's footsteps, dissolving the National Assembly in December 1851 and proclaiming himself emperor of the French one year later. This step brought the Second Republic to an end and established the Second Empire. The new emperor called himself Napoleon III, in deference to the dynastic rights of the uncrowned Napoleon II, the son of Napoleon I who had died in 1823.

The Revolutions of 1848 in Germany, Austria, Hungary, and Bohemia

Until French revolutionaries built barricades in the streets of Paris in 1848, liberalism and nationalism had achieved little success in Germany. German university students, inspired by the slogan "Honor, Freedom, Fatherland," had staged a number of large rallies during the early years of the nineteenth century, but the forces of conservatism had kept them in check. The Carlsbad Decrees of 1819, intended to suppress university radicalism, inaugurated a period of severe repression throughout Germany. The only success achieved by German liberals and nationalists prior to 1848 was the establishment of the *Zollverein*, a customs union of the various German states, in 1834. Even that project, which promoted free trade within German lands, did not attract support from all liberals.

A major opportunity for the liberal cause in Germany came in 1848 in the immediate wake of the February Revolution in France. As in France, however, this opportunity was complicated by the more radical demands of democrats and socialists for universal suffrage, including equal rights for women. German radicals also demanded government assistance for artisans and workers who had suffered economic hardship as a result of industrialization. In Berlin, the capital of Prussia, these discontents led radicals to barricade the streets. The situation became more serious after troops fired into the crowd, killing some 250 people. The violence spread to the countryside, where peasants demanded that landlords renounce their privileges and grant them free use of their lands. In response to these pressures, King Frederick William IV summoned an assembly, elected by universal male suffrage, to write a new Prussian constitution. Other German states also yielded to liberal pressure, establishing liberal governments known as the "March ministries."

As these events were unfolding, the contagion of revolution spread to Austria, the other major German kingdom, which formed the nucleus of the sprawling Habsburg Empire. News of the revolution in Paris led to demonstrations by students and workers in Vienna. An assortment of

DOCUMENT

The Carlsbad Decrees, 1819

The main source of liberal and national ideas in Germany after 1815 were university students, who often belonged to secret societies or fraternities. Conservatives considered these students dangerous revolutionaries and tried to expel them from the universities. When a student assassinated a conservative writer in 1819, the princes of the German Confederation issued a set of decrees that called for the monitoring of the lectures given at the universities, the removal of liberal professors, the expulsion of students, and the censorship of the press.

2. The confederated governments mutually pledge themselves to remove from the universities or other public educational institutions all teachers who, by obvious deviation from their duty, or by exceeding the limits of their functions, or by the abuse of their legitimate influence over youthful minds, or by propagating harmful doctrines hostile to public order or subversive to existing governmental institutions, shall have unmistakably proven their unfitness for the important office entrusted to them. No teacher who shall have been removed in this manner shall be again appointed to a position in any public institution of learning in another state of the Confederation.

3. Those laws which have for a long period been directed against secret and unauthorized societies in the universities shall be strictly enforced. The governments mutually agree that such persons as shall hereafter be shown to have remained in secret or unauthorized associations, or shall have entered such associations, shall not be admitted to any public office.

4. No student who shall be expelled from a university by a decision of the university senate which was ratified or prompted by the agent of the government, or shall have left the institution in order to escape expulsion, shall be received in any other university.

So long as this decree shall remain in force no publication which appears in the form of daily issues, or as a serial not exceeding twenty sheets of printed matter, shall go to press in any state of the union without the previous knowledge and approval of the state officials.

Source: From Readings in European History: 1789 to the Present, 2nd Edition by John L. Heineman. Copyright © 1994 by Kendall/Hunt Publishing Company. Used with permission.

Austrian liberal aristocrats, middle-class professionals, and discontented workers demanded an end to the long rule of the conservative minister, Clemens von Metternich. In response to the demands of these groups, Emperor Ferdinand I (r. 1835–1848) summoned a constitutional assembly and installed a moderate government. A conservative Prussian observer feared that these concessions had broken "the most secure dam against the revolutionary tide."

The main difference between the revolutions of 1848 in Austria and the other German lands was that events in Vienna awakened demands of Hungarians and Czechs for national autonomy within the empire. In Hungary the nationalist leader Lajos Kossuth (1802–1894) pushed for a program of liberal reform and national autonomy. This initiative created further tensions between the Magyars and the various national minorities within the kingdom of Hungary. Similar problems arose in Bohemia, where a revolution in Prague led to demands from the Czechs for autonomy within the Habsburg Empire. In June 1848 the Czech rebels hosted a Pan-Slav Congress in Prague to advance a nationalist plan for achieving unity of all Slavic people within the empire. This idealistic proposal could not be realized, for there were many distinct Slavic nationalities, each of which had a desire to preserve its autonomy. In addition, there was a large German-speaking population within Bohemia that identified with other German territories in the Confederation.

The most idealistic and ambitious undertaking of the revolution in central Europe was the meeting of the Frankfurt Parliament in May 1848. Some 800 middle-class liberals, many of whom were lawyers, officials, and university professors, came from all the German states to draft a constitution for a united Germany. The parliament produced powerful speeches in support of both liberal and nationalist ideals, and in December 1848 it promulgated a *Declaration of the Basic Rights of the German People.* This document recognized the equality of all German people before the law; freedom of speech, assembly, and religion; and the right to private property. Like so many liberal assemblies, however, the Frankfurt Parliament failed to address the needs of the workers and peasants. The delegates rejected universal male suffrage as a "dangerous experiment" and refused to provide protection for artisans who were being squeezed out of work by industrialization. For these reasons the parliament failed to win broad popular support.

In April 1849 the Frankfurt Parliament drafted a new constitution for a united Germany, which would have a hereditary "emperor of the Germans" and two houses of parliament, one of which would be elected by universal male suffrage. Austria, however, voted against the new plan, and without Austrian support the new constitution had little hope of success. The final blow to German liberal hopes came when King Frederick William of Prussia refused the Frankfurt Parliament's offer of the crown, which he referred to as coming from the gutter and "reeking of the stench of revolution." At that point the Frankfurt Parliament disbanded and the efforts of German liberals to unite their country and give it a new constitution came to an inglorious end.

By the middle of 1849, conservative forces had triumphed in the various German territories and the Habsburg Empire. In Prussia the efforts of the newly elected assembly to restrict noble privilege triggered a reaction from the conservative nobles known as Junkers. Frederick William dismissed his liberal appointees, sent troops to Berlin, and disbanded the assembly. A similar fate befell the other German states, such as Saxony, Baden, and Hanover, all of which had installed liberal governments in the early months of the revolution. In Austria Prince Alfred Windischgrätz, who had crushed the Czech rebels in June, dispersed the rebels in Vienna in October. When Hungary proclaimed its independence from the empire in April 1849, Austrian and Russian forces marched on the country and crushed the movement.

The Revolutions of 1848 in Italy

The revolutions of 1848 also spread to Austrian possessions in the northern Italian territories of Lombardy and Venetia. In Milan, the main city in Lombardy, revolutionary developments followed the same pattern as those in Paris, Berlin, and Vienna. When the barricades went up,

some of the Milanese insurgents used medieval pikes stolen from the opera house to fight off Austrian troops. Their success triggered rebellions in other towns in Lombardy, in Venice, and in the southern Kingdom of the Two Sicilies. In that kingdom the Spanish Bourbon king, Ferdinand II (r. 1830–1859), after suppressing a republican revolt in January, was forced to grant a liberal constitution. The spread of these revolts inspired the hope of bringing about the unification of all Italian people in one state.

This Italian nationalist dream had originated among some liberals and republicans during the first half of the nineteenth century. Its most articulate proponent was Giuseppe Mazzini, a revolutionary from Genoa who envisioned the establishment of a united Italian republic through direct popular action. In his youth Mazzini had been a member of the *Carbonari*, a secret conspiratorial society pledged to drive foreigners out of the Italian states, to secure constitutional liberties, and to bring about some form of Italian unity. His arrest led to one of many periods of exile in London, where he continued to pursue the cause of republicanism and democracy. In 1831 Mazzini founded Italy's first organized political party, Young Italy, which was pledged to realize national unification, democracy, and greater social equality. Mazzini combined a passionate commitment to the ideals of liberalism, republicanism, and nationalism. For him the nation was the highest ideal to which one could pledge devotion, one possessing almost

The German National Assembly Gathered in St. Paul's Church in Frankfurt, 1848
The parliament ultimately failed in its goal to give a liberal constitution to a united Germany.

Prostitution, Corporal Punishment, and Liberalism in Germany

In March 1822 Gesche Rudolph, a poor, uneducated 25-year-old woman from the northern German city of Bremen, was arrested by municipal authorities for engaging in prostitution without registering with the police. Ever since the days when troops from five different European nations had occupied her neighborhood, Rudolph had been selling her sexual services as her only form of livelihood. After her arrest she was not given a formal trial but was summarily expelled from the city and banned from ever returning. Unable to earn a living through prostitution in a village outside the city, where she resided with a brother who physically abused her, Rudolph returned to the city, where she was arrested once again for prostitution. This time she was sentenced to fifty strokes of the cane and six weeks in jail, after which she was once again expelled from the city. Returning again to Bremen, she was arrested in a drunken stupor in a whorehouse and subjected to a harsher sentence of three months' imprisonment and 150 strokes before another expulsion. This pattern of arrest, punishment, expulsion, and return occurred repeatedly during the next two decades, with the number of strokes rising to 275 and the period of imprisonment to six years. During a portion of her prison sentence she was given only bread and water for nourishment.

Rudolph's arrest in 1845 at the end of a six-year imprisonment and her subsequent expulsion and return to Bremen led to the appointment of a liberal lawyer, Georg Wilhelm Gröning, to represent her. After reviewing her case and calculating that she had been whipped a total of 893 times and imprisoned for a cumulative period of eighteen years, Gröning

appealed her sentence to the senate of Bremen on the grounds that her treatment was not only futile but immoral. His appeal addressed an issue that went far beyond this particular case or even the prosecution of the crime of prostitution. Gröning's action raised the highly controversial issue of the legitimacy and value of corporal punishment, an issue that divided liberals and conservatives, who had different notions of justice.

Until the eighteenth century the penal systems of Europe had prescribed corporal punishments, administered publicly, for most crimes. These punishments ranged from whippings and placement in the stocks for minor offenses to mutilation, hanging, and decapitation for felonies. They were justified mainly on the grounds that they provided retribution for the crime and deterred the criminal and those who witnessed the punishment from committing further crimes. These two main functions of retribution and deterrence are the same functions that capital punishment allegedly serves today. Corporal punishments were also intended to humiliate the criminal both by violating the integrity of the body and by subjecting the prisoner to the mockery and sometimes the maltreatment of the crowd. The torture of suspects to obtain evidence also served some of these functions, although judicial torture took place during the trial, not as part of the sentence.

The entire system of corporal punishment, as well as that of torture, came under attack during the eighteenth century. In Prussia torture was abolished in 1754, and the General Law Code of 1794 eliminated many forms of corporal punishment. The General Law Code reflected the concern of Enlightenment thinkers that all

such assaults on the body were inhumane and a denial of the moral dignity of the individual. Because corporal punishments in Prussia and elsewhere were administered mainly against people from the lower classes, they also were a violation of the liberal principle of equality before the law.

Despite these efforts at reform, the illegal administration of corporal punishment by public and private authorities continued in Prussia and the other German states. Conservatives, who had a different notion of justice from that of the liberals, defended these sentences on the grounds that all punishment, including imprisonment, was intended to deny the criminal freedom and hence his or her dignity. For them any reference to natural rights and human dignity were "axioms derived from abstract philanthropic speculation." The president of the Prussian police, Julius Baron von Minutoli, expressing the conservative position on the issue, claimed that corporal punishment was more effective than imprisonment in preventing crime, as it alone could instill terror in the criminal.

It was apparent that in the case of Gesche Rudolph, 893 strokes had not instilled terror in her or brought about any transformation of her spirit. The Senate made the young woman Gröning's ward and suspended her sentence. Gröning arranged for Rudolph to live in the countryside under the strict supervision of a competent countryman. This compromise solution at least broke the cycle of expulsion, return, and punishment that had failed to reform her. We do not know whether she gave up her life of prostitution.

Soon after Gesche Rudolph became Gröning's ward, the liberal critics of corporal punishment in

Germany celebrated a victory. King Frederick William IV of Prussia formally abolished the practice in his kingdom in May 1848. Shortly thereafter the Frankfurt Parliament included freedom from physical punishment by the state in its *Declaration of the Basic Rights of the German People*. Most German states and municipalities, including Bremen, wrote this right into law in 1849. The failure of the Frankfurt Parliament, however, and the more general failure of liberalism in Germany after 1849 led to a strong conservative campaign to reinstate corporal punishment in the 1850s. They succeeded only in maintaining corporal punishment within the family, on manorial estates, and in the prisons. Liberalism had not succeeded in completely establishing its standard of justice, but it did end exposure to public shame as a punishment for crime.

Questions of Justice

1. What elements of liberalism led those who adhered to this ideology in the nineteenth century to object to corporal punishment?
2. In addition to inflicting physical pain, corporal punishment produces social shame. What is the difference between social shame and legal guilt? In what ways does shame still play a role in punishments today?

Taking It Further

Evans, Richard. *Tales from the German Underworld: Crime and Punishment in the Nineteenth Century.* 1998. Provides a full account of the prosecution of Gesche Rudolph.

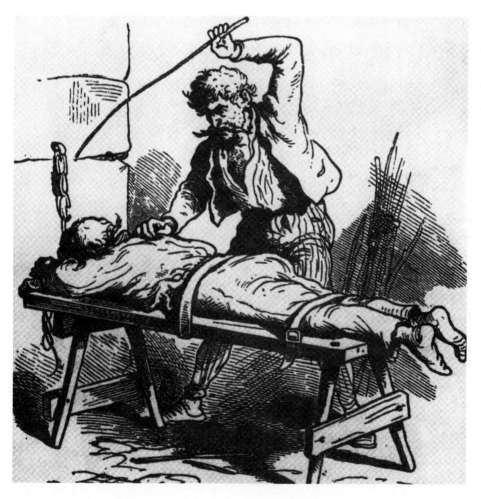

Corporal Punishment in Nineteenth-Century Germany
Whipping in prisons continued long after public corporal punishment was abolished in the middle of the nineteenth century.

mystical qualities. "We have beheld in Italy," he wrote, "the purpose, the soul, the consolidation of our thoughts, the country chosen of God and oppressed by men."

The ruler who assumed the nationalist mantle in 1848 was Charles Albert of Piedmont-Sardinia, the most economically advanced of the Italian states. This initiative began successfully, as Charles Albert's army, which included volunteers from various parts of Italy, marched into Lombardy and defeated Austrian forces. Instead of moving forward against Austria, however, Charles Albert decided to consolidate his gains, hoping to annex Lombardy to his own kingdom. This decision alienated republicans in Lombardy and in other parts of Italy as well as the rulers of the other Italian states, who feared that Charles Albert's main goal was to expand the limits of his own kingdom at their expense. By August 1848 the military tide had turned. Fresh Austrian troops defeated the Italian nationalists outside Milan. The people of that city turned against Charles Albert, forcing him to return to his own capital of Turin. The Italian revolutions of 1848 had suffered a complete defeat.

The Failure of the Revolutions of 1848

The revolutions of 1848 in France, Germany, the Habsburg Empire, and Italy resulted in victory for conservatives and defeat for liberals, nationalists, and socialists. All the liberal constitutions passed during the early phase of the revolutions were eventually repealed or withdrawn. The high hopes of national unity in Germany, Italy, and Hungary were dashed. Workers who built the barricades in the hope of achieving improvements in their working conditions gained little from their efforts.

Divisions among the different groups that began the revolutions were in large part responsible for their failure. The most serious division—in fact, one that was fatal—was the split between the liberals who formulated the original goals of the revolution and the lower-class participants who took to the streets. Liberals used the support of the masses to bring down the governments they opposed, but their ideological opposition to broad-based political movements and their fear of further disorder sapped their revolutionary fervor. Divisions also emerged between liberals and nationalists, whose goals of national self-determination required different strategies from those of the liberals who supported individual freedom.

The failure of the revolutions of 1848 did not, however, portend the death of the ideologies of liberalism, nationalism, and socialism. They all continued to manifest strength during the following two decades, and they often influenced the policies of the conservative governments that returned to power after the revolutions. In Germany, for example, the goal of nationalists was realized under conservative auspices and even mustered a measure of liberal support, while in France liberalism made some inroads

into the conservative and nationalist government of the Second French Empire after 1860.

National Unification in Europe and America, 1848–1871

■ How did liberal and conservative leaders use the ideology of nationalism as a tool to unite the people of various territories into nation-states between 1848 and 1871?

Prior to 1848 the forces of nationalism, especially when combined with those of liberalism, had little to show for their efforts. Besides the Greek rebellion of 1821, which succeeded largely because of international opposition to the Turks, the only successful nationalist revolution in Europe took place in Belgium. Both of these nationalist movements were secessionist in that they involved the separation of smaller states from larger empires. Efforts in 1848 to form nations by combining smaller states and territories, as in Italy and Germany, or by uniting all Slavic people, as proposed at the Pan-Slav Congress, had failed. Between 1848 and 1871, however, movements for national unification succeeded in Italy, Germany, and the United States, each in a different way. In the vast Habsburg Empire a different type of unity was achieved, but it did little to promote the cause of nationalism.

Italian Unification: Building a Fragile Nation-State

The great project of Italian nationalists, the unification of Italy, faced formidable obstacles. Austrian military control over the northern territories, which in the end had thwarted the nationalist movement of 1848, meant that national unification would not be achieved peacefully. The dramatic economic disparities between the prosperous north and the much poorer south posed a challenge to any plan for economic integration. A long tradition of local autonomy within the kingdoms, states, and principalities made submission to a strong central government unappealing. The unique status of the papacy, which controlled its own territory and which influenced the decisions of many other states, served as another challenge. Despite these obstacles, the dream of a resurgence of Italian power, reviving the achievements of ancient Rome, had great emotive appeal. Hatred of foreigners who controlled Italian territory, which dates back to the fifteenth century, gave further impetus to the nationalist movement.

The main question for Italian nationalism after the failure of 1848 was who could provide effective leadership of the movement. It stood to reason that Piedmont-Sardinia, the strongest and most prosperous Italian kingdom, would be central to that undertaking. Unfortunately the king, Victor Emmanuel II (r. 1849–1861), was more known for his hunting, his carousing, and his affair with a teenage mistress than his statesmanship. Victor Emmanuel did, however, appoint as his prime minister a nobleman with liberal leanings, Count Camillio di Cavour (1810–1861). Cavour displayed many of the characteristics of nineteenth-century liberalism. He favored a constitutional monarchy, the restriction of clerical privilege and influence, and the development of a capitalist and industrial economy. He was deeply committed to the unification of the Italian peninsula, but only under Piedmontese leadership, and preferably as a federation of states. In many ways he was the antithesis of the republican Mazzini, the other central figure in Italian unification. Mazzini's idealism and romanticism led him to think of national unification as a moral force that would lead to the establishment of a democratic republic, which would then undertake an extensive program of social reform. Mazzini often wore black, claiming that he was in mourning for the unrealized cause of unification.

Mazzini's strategy for national unification involved a succession of uprisings and invasions. Cavour, however, adopted a diplomatic course of action intended to gain the military assistance of France against Austria. In 1859 French and Piedmontese forces defeated the Austrians at Magenta and Solferino and drove them out of Lombardy. One year later Napoleon III signed the Treaty of Turin with Cavour, allowing Piedmont-Sardinia to annex Tuscany, Parma, Modena, and the Romagna, while ceding to France the Italian territories of Savoy and Nice. This treaty resulted in the unification of all of northern and central Italy except Venetia in the northeast and the Papal States in the center of the peninsula (see Map 21.2).

The main focus of unification efforts now turned to the Kingdom of the Two Sicilies in the south. A rebellion against the Bourbon monarch Francis II, protesting new taxes and the high price of bread, had taken place there in 1860. At that point the militant republican adventurer Giuseppe Garibaldi (1807–1882) intervened with decisive force. Garibaldi, who was born in Nice and spoke French rather than Italian as his main language, was determined no less than Cavour and Mazzini to drive all foreigners out of Italy and achieve its unification. Originally a supporter of Mazzini's republican goals, Garibaldi gave his support in the 1860s for Italian unification within the framework of a monarchy. A charismatic military leader, Garibaldi put together an army of volunteers, known as the Red Shirts for their colorful makeshift uniforms. In 1860 he landed in Sicily with an army of 1,000 men, took the main Sicilian

Garibaldi Surrendering Power—British Cartoon, 1860

city of Palermo, and established a dictatorship on behalf of King Victor Emmanuel. He then landed on the mainland and took Naples. Shortly thereafter the people of Naples, Sicily, and most of the Papal States voted their support for union with Piedmont-Sardinia. In March 1861 the king of Sardinia assumed the title of King Victor Emmanuel of Italy (r. 1861–1878). Complete unification was achieved when Austria ceded Venetia to Italy in 1866 and when French troops, which had been protecting a portion of the Papal States, withdrew from Rome in 1870.

The unification of Italy owed more to the statecraft of Cavour than the passion of Mazzini and Garibaldi. Their achievement did not fully realize the lofty nationalist goals of creating a culturally unified people or a powerful central state. Economic differences between northern and southern Italy became even greater after unification than before. The overwhelming majority of the people continued to speak their local dialects or even French rather than Italian. Traditions of local political autonomy and resentment

Giuseppe Garibaldi
The uniform he is wearing was derived from his days as a guerilla fighting in the civil war in Uruguay (1842–1846). Garibaldi also spent two years in asylum in the United States.

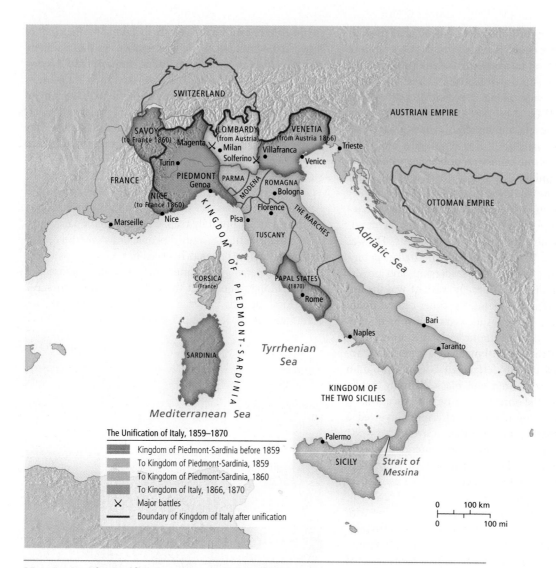

Map 21.2 The Unification of Italy, 1859–1870
The main steps to unification took place in 1860, when Piedmont-Sardinia acquired Tuscany, Parma, Modena, and the Romagna and when Garibaldi seized control of the Kingdom of the Two Sicilies in the name of King Victor Emmanuel of Piedmont-Sardinia.

against the concentration of wealth in the north retarded the development of loyalty to the new Italian state and inspired a series of bloody rebellions in the former Kingdom of the Two Sicilies during the 1870s and 1880s.

This instability was aggravated by the widespread practice of banditry in the southern mainland. Bandits were peasants who, in the hope of maintaining a world that appeared to be vanishing, swept through towns, opened jails, stole from the wealthy, and sacked their houses. Closely related to banditry was the growth in Sicily of the Mafia°, organizations of armed men who took control of local politics and the economy. The Mafia originated during the struggle for unification in the 1860s and strengthened their position in Sicily once the country had been unified.

Their power, the prevalence of banditry, and the enduring strength of Italian loyalty to the local community all made it difficult for the new Italian state to flourish. The movement for national unification had driven the French and the Austrians out of the peninsula, but it had failed to create a model nation-state.

German Unification: Conservative Nation-Building

Like Italy, Germany experienced a successful movement for national unification after the disappointments of 1848. The German movement, like the Italian, benefited from the actions of crafty statesmen and from the decisions made by other states. Unlike Italy, however, Germany achieved unification under the direction of highly conservative rather than liberal forces. One reason for this was that the severity of the reaction to the Revolution of 1848 had forced the emigration of many German liberals and nationalists to Great Britain and the Netherlands and as far west as the hill country of central Texas. Nevertheless a number of liberals, such as those who belonged to a Pan-German association known as the National Union, still kept alive the hopes of the Frankfurt Parliament for a German constitutional republic.

The main dilemma regarding German unification was whether Prussia or Austria would form the nucleus of any new political structure. In the end, Prussia, with its almost entirely German-speaking population, its wealth, and its strong army, assumed leadership of the movement. The key figure in this process was Count Otto von Bismarck (1815–1898), a lawyer and bureaucrat from an old Junker family whom King William I of Prussia appointed as his prime minister in 1862. By birth, training, and instinct Bismarck was an inflexible conservative, determined to preserve and strengthen the Prussian nobility and monarchy and to make the Prussian state strong and powerful. In the words of the liberal British ambassador to Berlin, Robert Morier, "not one mustard seed of faith in liberal principles exists in Count Bismarck's nature." Bismarck did not hesitate, however, to make alliances with any political party, including the liberals, to achieve his goals. This subordination of political means to their ends, and Bismarck's willingness to use whatever tactics were necessary, regardless of any moral considerations, made him a proponent of *Realpolitik*, the adoption of political tactics solely on the basis of their realistic chances of success.

Bismarck pursued the goal of national unification through the exercise of raw military and political power. "The great questions of the day," he said in 1862, "will not be settled by speeches and majority decisions—that was the error of 1848 and 1849—but by iron and blood." Bismarck did not share the romantic devotion of other German nationalists to the Fatherland or their desire to have a state that embodied the spirit of the German people. His determination to achieve German national unification became synonymous with his goal of strengthening the Prussian state. This commitment to the supremacy of Prussia within a united Germany explains his steadfast exclusion of the other great German power, Austria, from his plans for national unification.

Bismarck's achievement of German unification was based mainly on Prussian success in two wars (see Map 21.3). The first, the Austro-Prussian War of 1866, resulted

The Proclamation of the German Empire in the Hall of Mirrors at Versailles, January 21, 1871

King William I of Prussia, standing on the dais, is being crowned emperor of Germany. At the center of the picture, dressed in a white uniform jacket, is Otto von Bismarck, the person most responsible for the unification of all German territory in one empire.

in the formation of a new union of twenty-two states, the North German Confederation. This new structure replaced the old German Confederation, the loose association of thirty-nine states, including Austria, that had been established in 1815 by the Congress of Vienna. The North German Confederation had a centralized political structure with its own legislature, the *Reichstag;* the king of Prussia became its president and Bismarck its chancellor. The foundation of the North German Confederation was, however, only one step toward the unification of all Germany. Bismarck laid the foundation for the realization of this larger goal by strengthening the *Zollverein*, which included the southern German states. By encouraging free trade among all the German states he also won support for unification from German liberals.

The second war, which completed the unification of Germany, was the Franco-Prussian War of 1870–1871. This

Map 21.3 The Unification of Germany, 1866–1871

Prussia assumed leadership in uniting all German territories except Austria. Prussia was responsible for the formation of the North German Confederation in 1866 and the German Empire in 1871.

conflict began when Napoleon III, the French emperor, challenged Prussian efforts to place a member of the Prussian royal family on the vacant Spanish throne. Bismarck welcomed this opportunity to take on the French, who controlled German-speaking territories on their eastern frontier and who had cultivated alliances with the southern German states. Bismarck played his diplomatic cards brilliantly, guaranteeing that the Russians, Austrians, and British would not support France. He then used the army that he had modernized to invade France and seize the towns of Metz and Sedan. The capture of Napoleon III

during this military offensive precipitated the end of France's Second Empire and the establishment of the Third French Republic in September 1870.

As a result of the war Prussia annexed the predominantly German-speaking territories of Alsace and Lorraine. Much more important, it led to the proclamation of the German Empire with William I of Prussia as emperor. Officially the structure of the new empire, a term used to indicate that it embraced many separate states, was that of a federation, just like that of the North German Confederation that preceded it. In fact the government of the empire, like that of

Prussia, was highly centralized as well as autocratic, and the liberal middle classes did not participate in it, as they did in the governments of Britain, France, and Italy. The German imperial government won the support of the middle class by adopting policies supporting free trade, but the ideologies that underpinned the new German Empire were those of conservatism and nationalism, which encouraged devotion to "God, King, and Fatherland."

Unification in the United States: Creating a Nation of Nations

At the same time that Italy and Germany were achieving national unification, the United States of America engaged in a bitter process that preserved and strengthened the federal union it had instituted in 1787. The thirteen colonies that proclaimed their independence from Great Britain in 1776 shared common constitutional grievances against the mother country or metropolis, but each colony had its own identity. The U.S. Constitution, drawn up in 1787, sought to preserve this balance between the states and the federal government by dividing sovereignty between them, leaving to the states control over all matters it had not specifically given to the federal government. This arrangement generated friction and debate between the Federalists, who wished to strengthen the central government, and the Anti-Federalists, who feared that a strong central government would lead to corrupt, arbitrary rule. The Federalists won some early victories, including the establishment of a national bank, but they were unable to create a truly united people. The great victory of the Anti-Federalists was the Bill of Rights, the first ten amendments to the U.S. constitution, which was ratified by the states in 1791. By enumerating the rights of the citizens in a formal constitution, including freedom of speech and freedom of assembly, the Bill of Rights embodied one of the main elements of liberal ideology.

Throughout the early years of the republic Americans continued to think of themselves as citizens of particular states more than as members of a single national community. In the early nineteenth century, President Thomas Jefferson (1801–1809) imagined a new American nation, a people "with one heart and one mind," but nationalist sentiment, such as had developed in European countries on the basis of a common language and culture, had difficulty materializing in the United States. The American republic was originally the product of English-speaking colonists who shared the same language and culture as the British against whom they had rebelled. After the revolution, efforts were made to build a new nation on the basis of a distinctly American culture. *The American Dictionary of the English Language,* compiled by Noah Webster (1758–1843) in 1812, made one contribution to this endeavor by listing hundreds of American words that had never been included in English dictionaries. Patriotic sentiment, especially after the defeat

of British forces at the Battle of New Orleans in 1815, also helped give Americans a sense of common purpose and destiny.

These efforts at building an American nation became more challenging as the young republic began to incorporate Western territories into the federal union. Lands acquired by purchase or conquest were formed into territories and then gradually admitted into the union as states. This process of unification, which proceeded in a piecemeal fashion, took much longer than the unifications of Italy and Germany in the 1860s. It was marked by sustained military action against the Native American population and a war against Mexico between 1846 and 1848. Florida was annexed in 1819, while Texas, an independent republic for nine years, was admitted in 1845 and California in 1850. This process of gradual unification did not end until 1912, when New Mexico and Arizona, the last territories in the contiguous forty-eight states, were admitted to the union.

As the United States expanded westward into the Spanish-speaking Southwest, and as immigrants from various European nations swelled the population of the eastern as well as the western states, the country became more rather than less culturally diverse. Assimilation to a dominant Protestant English-speaking culture, even one that was gradually becoming distinct from that of Great Britain, could not provide the same commitment to the homeland that inspired Italians and Germans to support national unification. Americans might be patriotic, in that they proclaimed their allegiance to the federal republic, but they had more difficulty thinking that they shared a common culture with the people from different parts of the country. Building a nation-state in America was a task fraught with obstacles.

The great test of American national unity came during the 1860s, when eleven southern states, committed to the preservation of the economic system of slavery, and determined that it should be extended into new territories acquired by the federal government, seceded from the union and formed a confederation of their own. The issue of slavery had helped to polarize North and South, creating deep cultural and ideological divisions that made the goal of national unity appear even more distant. America had its own ideological and cultural encounters that paralleled those that prevailed in European countries.

The constitutional issue underlying the civil war was the preservation of the union. In a famous speech President Abraham Lincoln (1861–1865) declared that "a house divided against itself cannot stand . . . this government cannot endure permanently half slave and half free." When the war ended and slavery was abolished, that union was not only preserved but strengthened. Amendments to the U.S. Constitution provided for equal protection of all citizens under the law. The South, which had its own regional economy, was integrated into the increasingly commercial and industrial North. The whole process of national unification, both economic and social, was greatly facilitated by the building of railways. In the United States, even more than in Europe, railroads linked otherwise isolated communities and facilitated the spread of products and ideas across vast distances. Gradually the people of the United States began to think of themselves as a united people, drawn from many different nations of the world. The United States became "a nation of nations."

Nationalism in Eastern Europe: Preserving Multinational Empires

The national unifications that took place in Germany, Italy, and the United States formed part of a *western* European pattern in which the main units of political organization would be nation-states. Ethnic minorities would of course always live within the boundaries of these states, but the state itself would encourage the growth of a national identity among all its citizens. We can observe this process at work in France, Britain, and Spain, all of which had undergone a process of national unification before the nineteenth century. Minority populations within these large western European states have occasionally threatened to establish a separate political identity as nations, but with the one notable exception of Ireland, the southern portion of which became independent of Britain in the twentieth century, the

large states of western Europe have maintained their unity and promoted nationalist sentiment to sustain it.

In *eastern* Europe a very different pattern prevailed, especially in the Habsburg and Russian Empires. Instead of becoming unified nation-states, these two empires remained large, multinational political formations, embracing many different nationalities. This pattern was most obvious in the large, sprawling Habsburg Empire, which encompassed no fewer than twenty different ethnic groups, each of which thought of itself as a nation (see Map 21.4). The largest of these nationalities were the Germans in Austria and Bohemia and the Magyars in Hungary, but the Czechs, Slovaks, Poles, Slovenes, Croats, Rumanians, Bulgarians, and Italians (before 1866) all formed sizable minority populations. Map 21.4 only begins to reveal the full complexity of this diversity. The various nationalities within the empire had little in common except loyalty to the Habsburg emperor, who defended the Catholic faith and the privileges of the nobility. National unification of the empire would have presented a much more formidable task than the ones that confronted Cavour and Bismarck.

During the era of national unification the ideology of nationalism threatened to tear apart this precariously unified empire. It awakened demands of Hungarians, Czechs, and others for national autonomy and also spawned a movement for the national unity of all Slavs. The emperor,

Map 21.4 Nationalities Within the Habsburg Empire

The large number of different nationalities within the Habsburg Empire made it impossible to accommodate the demands of all nationalities for their own state.

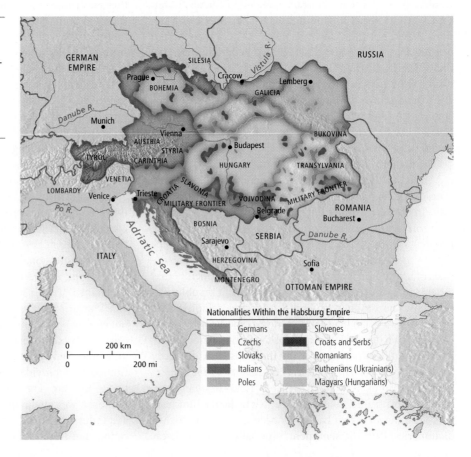

Nationalities Within the Habsburg Empire

- Germans
- Czechs
- Slovaks
- Italians
- Poles
- Slovenes
- Croats and Serbs
- Romanians
- Ruthenians (Ukrainians)
- Magyars (Hungarians)

Francis Joseph (r. 1848–1916), recognized the danger of nationalist ideology. He also feared that liberalism, which was often linked to nationalism, would at the same time undermine his authority, which he had reasserted with a vengeance after the failure of the revolutions of 1848. He therefore repressed these nationalist aspirations at every turn. This policy had disastrous consequences for the future history of Europe, as Slavic nationalism and separatism have remained a source of political instability of southeastern Europe until the present day.

The one concession that Francis Joseph did make during this volatile period was to establish the Dual Monarchy of Austria-Hungary in 1867. This significant increase of Hungarian power within the empire came in the wake of the disastrous defeats of Austrian forces by the French and Piedmontese in 1859 and the Prussians in 1866. Austrian liberals took this opportunity to call for the introduction of constitutional government, while the second-largest ethnic group within the empire, the Magyars, demanded more autonomy for Hungary. The *Ausgleich* (Settlement) of 1867, which was proposed by the wealthy Hungarian nobleman and lawyer Ferenc Deák (1803–1876), created a dual monarchy in which Francis Joseph would be both king of Hungary and emperor of Austria. Each monarchy would have its own parliament and bureaucracy, although matters of foreign policy and finance would be handled in Vienna. This arrangement represented a concession to Magyar nationalism but gave very little to all the other nationalities within both kingdoms. The *Ausgleich* officially recognized the equality of all nationalities within the empire and allowed schooling to be conducted in the local language, but it permitted only Germans in Austria and Magyars in Hungary to acquire their own political identity. Instead of a unified nation-state the emperor now presided over two multinational monarchies.

Ideology, Empire, and the Balance of Power

■ What role did ideology play in international warfare and diplomacy, especially in efforts to maintain the balance of power during this period?

The new ideologies of the early nineteenth century, and the movements for national unification to which they gave rise, had a disruptive impact on the conduct of international affairs. The original framework for international action after 1815 was the Concert of Europe, which was intended to prevent the recurrence of revolution and preserve the balance of power. It achieved much greater success in pursuing the second goal than it did the first. The five European powers in the Concert—Britain, Austria, Russia, Prussia, and France—could never contain the liberal and national forces that the French Revolution had unleashed, but as a group the five powers prevented any one of them from establishing a dominant position in Europe.

Challenges to the balance of power during this period came mainly from governments engaged in a process of imperial expansion. The first of these challenges arose in the Western Hemisphere during the 1820s, the second occurred in the 1850s in the Balkans, and the third took place after the Franco-Prussian War of 1870–1871.

Britain, the United States, and the Monroe Doctrine of 1823

In North America a clash of empires threatened to engulf European powers in a new round of imperial expansion and warfare during the early 1820s. As Spanish power in the Western Hemisphere began to collapse, the young republic of the United States feared that Austria or France might intervene in the new Latin American nations. The United States was also alarmed about Russian expansion down the western coast of North America, as we have discussed in Chapter 17. In order to prevent imperial expansion by any of these European powers, the United Sates found an ally in Britain, which even after the loss of the thirteen North American colonies still ruled a large empire of its own in Canada, the Caribbean, and South America. Britain did not wish to compromise the dominant influence it exercised in this area.

British and U.S. resistance to continental European imperialism in the Western Hemisphere had a foundation in liberal ideology. The United States, with its constitutional protection of individual liberty and its success in achieving national self-determination in the American Revolution, had become the very embodiment of European liberalism. No wonder it supported the independence of Latin American nations on ideological as well as diplomatic grounds. In Britain, as we have already seen, the liberal tradition was stronger than in other parts of Europe. Britain's liberal heritage also helps to explain its refusal to join the Holy Alliance of 1815. The British government viewed the Concert of Europe as a mechanism for preserving the balance of power, not for supporting autocratic regimes.

In 1823, President James Monroe (1817–1825) declared that the United States would consider any future attempts by European powers to colonize the Americas as hostile acts. The enforcement of this policy, which became known as the Monroe Doctrine, depended mainly on the support of the British navy, because the United States was not yet capable of taking on the powers of Europe by itself. During the next ten years Britain provided that naval support.

The main effect of the Monroe Doctrine, and Britain's enforcement of it, was to preserve the balance of power in the Western Hemisphere. The doctrine also created the concept of two hemispheres, one old and one new, each refraining from interference in each other's affairs. The broader ideological significance of the Monroe Doctrine was that it provided support for liberalism and nationalism both in Europe and in the Americas. Monroe's speech made explicit reference to the opposition of the United States to the repressive political systems of the allied powers, support for the liberal revolutions that had taken place in Spain and Portugal in 1820, and approval of the revolutions against Spanish rule in Latin America.

Russia, the Ottoman Empire, and the Crimean War, 1853–1856

The second major challenge to the balance of power occurred as a result of Russian imperial ambitions in the Balkans, resulting in the first major war among European powers since the defeat of Napoleon at Waterloo in 1815. The Crimean War (1853–1856), which claimed almost a million casualties on all sides, was the direct result of Russian imperial expansion. It began when Russia occupied the principalities of Moldavia and Wallachia (present-day Romania) in the Ottoman Empire in order to gain access to

the Straits of Constantinople and thus to the Aegean and Mediterranean seas. The weakness of the Ottoman Empire had invited Russian expansion into this area, which Russians justified by claiming they were protecting the Orthodox Christianity of people in the Balkans from their Turkish Muslim oppressors. They also claimed that they were promoting the national unity of all Slavic people under Russian auspices. This Russian version of Pan-Slavism differed from that developed by Czech Slavs at the Pan-Slav Congress of 1848. In effect it was an extreme form of Russian imperialism that rivaled the nationalism of individual Slavic nationalities.

Britain resisted the Russian occupation of Moldavia and Wallachia, ostensibly to protect its trade with the Turks but more urgently to prevent Russia from becoming too powerful. In this respect it was adhering to the principles of the Concert of Europe by trying to preserve the balance of power in Europe. The underlying British fear was that Russia might invade India, Britain's most important colony. When the Turks declared war on the Russians, therefore, the British followed suit and were joined by the French. Both powers sent large armies to begin a siege of the port of Sebastopol on the Black Sea.

The poorly trained British forces, commanded by officers who had purchased their commissions and who had no sound knowledge of military tactics, suffered staggering losses, more of them from disease than from battle. The most senseless episode of the war occurred when a British cavalry unit, the Light Brigade, rode into a deep valley, only to be cut down by Russian artillery perched on the surrounding hills. The slaughter was memorialized in a poem by the British poet Alfred Lord Tennyson (1850–1892), "The Charge of the Light Brigade."

Nevertheless, the British, French, and Turks prevailed, handing Russia its most humiliating defeat of the nineteenth century. The defeat led to a curtailment of Russian expansion for the next twenty years and preserved the balance of power in Europe. Within Russia the defeat contributed to a crisis that led to a series of liberal reforms during the rule of Tsar Alexander II (1855–1881). Alexander, an indecisive man who had inherited the throne in the middle of the Crimean War, was hardly a liberal (he once referred to the French system of government as "vile"), but he did yield to mounting liberal pressure to emancipate the serfs in 1861, a step that occurred two years before the emancipation of slaves in the United States.

CHRONOLOGY

French Politics, 1848–1871

1848

February 25	Establishment of the Second Republic
December	Election of Louis-Napoleon as president of the Second Republic

1851

December 2	Louis Napoleon dissolves the National Assembly

1852

November	Establishment of the Second Empire under Napoleon III

1870

July 19	Beginning of the Franco-Prussian War
September 2	Surrender of Napoleon III to Prussia at Sedan
September 4	End of the Second Empire and proclamation of the Third Republic

1871

February	National Assembly meets at Bordeaux
March	Rising of the Paris Commune
May 10	End of the Franco-Prussian War
May 21–27	"Bloody Week"; suppression of the Paris Commune

The German Empire and the Paris Commune, 1870–1871

A third, and in the long run the most serious, challenge to the balance of power in Europe came from Prussia. As we have seen, Prussian victories over

Execution of Paris Communards, May 1871
Troops of the provisional French government killed at least 25,000 Parisians during the uprising.

Austria in 1866 and France in 1871 allowed Bismarck to complete the unification of Germany. The newly created German Empire, which now possessed the strongest army in Europe, replaced Austria as the predominant power in central Europe. The growth of German military power, coupled with its expansionist territorial ambitions, soon made it a formidable rival to other European countries and threatened to upset the delicate balance of power. In the twentieth century Germany's territorial ambitions led ultimately to two world wars.

German military success in the Franco-Prussian War of 1870–1871 played a crucial role in French politics, exposing the complex ideological contradictions of the Second French Empire and laying the groundwork for the Third French Republic. After Napoleon III had established the Second Empire in 1852, he tried to mask his usurpation of power by preserving the tradition of universal male suffrage and by submitting his rule to popular ratification, just as his uncle had done. During the 1860s his government became known as "the Liberal Empire," a strange mixture of conservatism, liberalism, and nationalism. Although "the little Napoleon" ruled as an emperor, he gradually allowed a semblance of real parliamentary government to return, relaxed the censorship of the press, and encouraged industrial development. To this mixture he added a strong dose of nationalist sentiment by evoking the memory of Napoleon I.

These efforts failed to save Napoleon III's regime. His moderate liberal policies angered conservatives on the one hand and failed to satisfy the demands of republicans and socialists on the other. These complex ideological encounters came to a head in 1870 during the Franco-Prussian War, which Napoleon himself was in large part responsible for starting. Napoleon took the field at the Battle of Sedan and was captured. The Prussians allowed him to go into exile in England, where he lived until his death in 1873. On September 4, 1870, a large crowd invaded the Legislative Assembly in Paris and forced the deputies who still remained to join them in declaring the end of the Second Empire and the beginning of the Third Republic. Shortly thereafter Prussian troops surrounded Paris and began a long siege of the city, forcing hungry city dwellers to eat cats and dogs roaming the streets and an elephant seized from the Paris zoo.

In January 1871 Adolphe Thiers (1797–1877), a veteran statesman who had served as prime minister during the liberal government of the 1830s, negotiated an armistice with Bismarck. Thiers hoped to establish a conservative republican regime or possibly a restoration of the monarchy at the conclusion of the war. This prospect gained strength when elections to the new National Assembly, which Bismarck permitted so that the French legislature could conclude a formal peace treaty, returned a majority of monarchists.

The National Assembly then elected Thiers as president of the provisional government.

The National Assembly, which sat at Bordeaux, and the provisional government, which took up residence at Versailles, were determined to assert their authority over the entire French nation. In particular, they wanted to curb the independence of the city of Paris, which was determined to carry on the struggle against Prussia and to keep alive the French radical tradition that had flourished in the city in 1792 and again in 1848. The radicalism of the Paris Commune drew its strength from the large working-class population in the industrialized districts on the northern, eastern, and southern edges of the city. The socialist and republican ideals of the Commune's leaders, coupled with their determination to preserve the independence of the city, culminated in the bloodshed described at the beginning of this chapter. The crushing of the Commune marked a bitter defeat for the forces of French socialism and radicalism. The Third French Republic that was established in September 1870 endured, but its ideological foundation was conservative nationalism, not liberalism or socialism.

Conclusion

The Ideological Transformation of the West

The ideological encounters that took place between 1815 and 1871 resulted in significant changes in the political culture of the West. As the early nineteenth-century ideologies of liberalism, conservatism, socialism, and nationalism played out in political movements and revolutions, the people who subscribed to these ideologies often redefined their political objectives. Many British and French socialists, for example, recognizing the necessity of assistance from liberals, abandoned their call for creating a classless society and sought instead to increase wages and improve working conditions of the lower classes. The demands of socialists for greater economic equality pressured liberals to accept the need for more state intervention in the economy. The realities of conservative politics led liberal nationalists in Germany and Italy to accept newly formed nation-states that were more authoritarian than they had originally hoped to establish. Recognizing the strength of the ideologies to which they were opposed, conservative rulers such as Emperor Napoleon III and Tsar Alexander II agreed to adopt liberal reforms. Liberals, conservatives, socialists, and nationalists would continue to modify and adjust their political and ideological positions during the period of mass politics, which began in 1870 and which will be the subject of the next chapter.

The Western ideologies that underwent this process of adaptation and modification had a broad influence on world history. In the twentieth century, three of the four ideologies discussed in this chapter have inspired political change in parts of the world that lie outside the geographical and cultural boundaries of the West. Liberalism has provided the language for movements seeking to establish fundamental civil liberties in India, Japan, and several African countries. In its radical communist form, socialism inspired revolutions in Russia, a country that for many centuries had straddled the boundary between East and West, and in China. Nationalism has revealed its explosive potential in countries as diverse as Nepal, Thailand, and Zaire. Ever since the nineteenth century, Western ideologies have demonstrated a capacity both to shape and to adapt to a variety of political and social circumstances.

Suggestions for Further Reading

For a comprehensive listing of suggested readings, please go to www.ablongman.com/levack2e/chapter21

Anderson, Benedict. *Imagined Communities: Reflections on the Origin and Spread of Nationalism.* 1991. A discussion of the ways in which people conceptualize the nation.

Clark, Martin. *The Italian Risorgimento.* 1999. A comprehensive study of the social, economic, and religious context of Italian unification as well as its political and diplomatic dimensions.

Gellner, Ernest. *Nations and Nationalism.* 1983. An interpretive study that emphasizes the social roots of nationalism.

Hamerow, Theodore S. *Restoration, Revolution, Reaction: Economics and Politics in Germany, 1815–1871.* 1966. An investigation of the social basis of ideological encounters in Germany.

Honour, Hugh. *Romanticism.* 1979. A comprehensive study of romantic painting.

Hunczak, Tara, ed. *Russian Imperialism from Ivan the Great to the Revolution.* 1974. A collection of essays that illuminate Russian nationalism as well as imperialism over a long period of time.

Lichtheim, George. *A Short History of Socialism.* 1970. A good general treatment of the subject.

Nipperdey, Thomas. *Germany from Napoleon to Bismarck, 1800–1866.* 1996. An exploration of the creation of German nationalism as well as the failure of liberalism.

Onuf, Peter S. *Jefferson's Empire: The Language of American Nationhood.* 2000. A study of Jefferson's expansionary nationalism.

Pflanze, Otto. *Bismarck and the Development of Germany: The Period of Unification, 1815–1871.* 1963. The classic study of both Bismarck and the unification movement.

Pinckney, David. *The French Revolution of 1830.* 1972. The best treatment of this revolution.

Seton-Watson, Hugh. *Nations and States.* 1977. A clearly written study of the nation-state.

Sperber, Jonathan. *The European Revolutions, 1848–1851.* 1994. The best study of the revolutions of 1848.

Tombs, Robert. *The War Against Paris, 1871.* 1981. A narrative history of the Paris Commune.

The Coming of Mass Politics: Industrialization, Emancipation, and Instability, 1870–1914

22

I N THE SPRING OF 1881, A HARROWING SCENE TOOK PLACE IN ST. PETERSBURG, capital of the vast Russian Empire. A 28-year-old woman, Sofiia Perovskaia, was scheduled to be executed for her part in the assassination of Tsar Alexander II. Born into the ranks of wealth and privilege, Perovskaia had rejected her traditional role in order to join the revolutionary socialist movement. She became a leader of the People's Will, a small revolutionary group that sought to undermine the tsarist regime through a program of sabotage and assassination. These revolutionaries dared to set their sights on assassinating the tsar himself, and on March 1, 1881, they achieved this goal. Led by Perovskaia, six People's Will members (all under age 30) stationed themselves at prearranged points along the streets of St. Petersburg. At Perovskaia's signal, they released their bombs and assassinated one of the most powerful men in Europe.

Despite the death of the tsar and the audacity of the crime, however, the tsarist regime did not crumble. The six assassins were quickly arrested and sentenced to death by hanging. (One of the six was pregnant and therefore allowed to live.) On the day of Perovskaia's execution, she mounted the scaffold calmly, but when the noose was placed around her neck, she grabbed hold of the platform below with her feet. It took the strength of two men to pry her feet loose so that she could hang.

The image of Sofiia Perovskaia clinging to the platform with her bare feet while her two executioners strained to push her to her death captures the ferocity of political struggle not only in Russia but throughout Europe at the end of the nineteenth century. As Chapter 21 explained, the ideological

Mass Society at Play Pierre Auguste Renoir, *Le Moulin de la Galette* (1876). The growing cities offered both middle- and working-class men and women new opportunities for leisure and relaxation.

competition among liberals, conservatives, socialists, and nationalists shaped the political culture of the West in the nineteenth century. Economic developments after 1870 both intensified and widened this competition. Individuals and groups that had traditionally been excluded from power demanded a voice in political affairs. Even in authoritarian Russia, the political nation could not long remain the preserve of the titled and wealthy. Neither economic modernization nor the coming of mass politics ensured the victory of democracy, however. Like Sofiia Perovskaia's executioners, the governing classes often struggled hard to pry newcomers off the platform of political power—and they often won.

How did the new mass politics reshape definitions of the West by the beginning of the twentieth century? Four questions will structure our exploration of mass politics and its impact:

- How did the economic transformation of Europe after 1870 help shape the encounters between established political elites and newcomers to the political process?
- How did the ruling classes of the Western powers respond to the new threats and opportunities provided by mass political participation?
- What forms did mass politics assume during this time of industrial expansion and the spread of modern nationalist ideology?
- In what ways did the emergence of feminism in this period demonstrate the potential as well as the limits of political change?

Economic Transformation

- How did the economic transformation of Europe after 1870 help shape the encounters between established political elites and newcomers to the political process?

Europe's political development between 1870 and 1914 is inextricably linked to its economic transformation. Four important economic developments helped shape European actions and attitudes during these years: the onset of economic depression in 1873, the expansion of the Industrial Revolution into new geographic regions and economic sectors, the emergence of new patterns in the production and consumption of industrial goods, and accelerated urbanization and immigration. Together, these developments not only altered the daily life of the ordinary European, they also exacerbated social tensions and accelerated political change. The resulting series of often violent encounters within societies helped transform the political structures and ideologies of the West.

Economic Depression

In 1873, Europe's economy tilted sharply downward—prices, interest rates, and profits all fell, and remained low in many regions until the mid-1890s. Contemporaries referred to this as the Great Depression in Trade and Agriculture°. In hindsight, "Great Depression" may seem an inaccurate label for a period that saw a continuing rise in world production and growing levels of foreign investment in new industrial economies, but to many Europeans living in these decades, this Great Depression seemed depressing indeed. Agriculture was hardest hit of all economic sectors. By the 1890s, the price of wheat had fallen to only one-third of what it had been in the 1860s. Farm owners and laborers across Europe found it difficult to remain on the land and make a living. Business, too, faced hard times after 1873. Profit margins were squeezed as the prices of finished products fell, often by as much as 50 percent, while labor and production costs tended to remain much more static.

What caused this depression? Ironically, it was rooted in the very success of the Industrial Revolution. The development of the steamship and the expansion of railway lines across Europe and the United States sharply reduced the cost of transporting both agricultural and industrial goods. Cheaper transportation costs opened the breadbaskets of the American Midwest and Ukraine to European consumption. With wheat and other agricultural goods now flooding the market, farmers were forced to accept increasingly lower prices for their products. More generally, as regions and nations industrialized, they of course produced more goods. Yet many industrial workers, agricultural laborers, and landowning peasants still stood on the very edge of subsistence, with little money to spend on industrial products. In other words, by the 1870s, a mass consumer society had not yet emerged. Thus in many regions of Europe production exceeded consumption, and the result was a long-term agricultural and industrial depression.

Industrial Expansion

The onset and impact of economic depression is, then, closely linked to the second important economic development of this period—the continued expansion of the Industrial Revolution. As Chapter 20 detailed, the period between 1760 and 1860 saw gradual, spotty, but still dramatic changes in economic production, first in Britain, then in portions of western Europe. But throughout much of the nineteenth century many of the inhabitants of central, eastern, and southern Europe continued to live and work in ways not far removed from those of their great-grandparents. They used simple horse- or oxen-drawn plows, they harvested with scythes fueled by their own arms and backs, they celebrated births and mourned deaths with

Pre-Industrial Continuities

This photograph of French peasant women taking time off for a meal highlights the patchy nature of industrialization even in western Europe. Not until the 1880s and 1890s did many rural regions come within the embrace of the modern industrial economy.

rituals embedded in centuries-old peasant cultures. And they had little contact with unsettling ideas as high rates of illiteracy continued—almost 90 percent in some rural regions of the Austrian Empire, for example.

This cultural and economic isolation was breaking down by the time World War I erupted in 1914. Railways, which increasingly linked Europe's diverse regions into a single economic network, played a crucial role. Between 1870 and 1914 the world's rail network grew by 500 percent. In the 1880s, agriculture still employed the majority of Europe's population in all countries except Britain, Belgium, France, the Netherlands, and Switzerland, but even peasants still farming in traditional ways were caught up in the momentum of the industrial economy.

Imperial Russia serves as a good example of the breakdown of social and cultural isolation. By 1914 Russia had developed a significant industrial zone, one that tied it more closely than ever before to Western economic structures. In the 1890s, Russia underwent dramatic industrialization under the leadership of Sergei Witte (1849–1915), Alexander III's finance minister. Before serving the tsar in this capacity, Witte had a successful career in the railway industry. He used this experience to carry out a program of planned economic development. The state-owned railway network doubled in size. This impressive engineering achievement, which included the 5,000-mile trans-Siberian railway (begun in 1891), accelerated the movement of both goods and laborers across the vast expanse of Russian territory. Witte also placed Russia on the gold standard, making the Russian ruble easily convertible into other curren-

cies and so fostering international trade. High taxes and protective tariffs generated some of the capital to fuel industrial expansion, but foreign investment was also crucial. French, British, German, and Belgian capital poured into Russia, up from 98 million rubles in 1880 to 911 million by 1900. By the turn of the century, as a result of such policies, Russian steel production was ranked fourth worldwide—behind only Britain, Germany, and the United States—and Russia supplied 50 percent of the oil used by the industrialized world. Coal mines and steel mills dotted Ukraine, and huge state-run factories dominated Moscow and St. Petersburg.

The Second Industrial Revolution

The expansion of the Industrial Revolution coincided with a shift in the processes of industrialization itself. The decades after 1870 witnessed a new phase in the techniques and technologies of both production and consumption, a phase that some historians regard as so important that they call it the "Second Industrial Revolution°." Mechanical processes were altered with the development of more specialized lathes and the mechanization of tasks such as grinding that had previously been completed by hand. By the late 1870s, a series of technological innovations ensured that for the first time steel could be produced cheaply and in huge quantities. The availability of steel, more durable and more flexible than iron, expanded production in industries such as railroads, shipbuilding, and construction.

The Eiffel Tower Reaches to the Sky
Engineer Gustave Eiffel designed the Eiffel Tower for the Paris Universal Exposition of 1889. French politicians intended the exposition to highlight the "progress resulting from one hundred years of freedom," yet many of its displays featured artifacts from cultures France had conquered.

The construction industry itself was transformed. New technological advances in the production of not only steel but also iron, cement, and plate glass, combined with the inventions of the mechanical crane and stone cutter, allowed architects and builders to reach to the skies. Cityscapes changed dramatically as these spectacular new constructions thrust upward. In 1885, the engineering firm of Gustave Eiffel (1832–1923) proposed the construction of an iron and steel tower to celebrate the Paris World's Fair of 1889. Modeled on the structural supports of railway viaducts, the Eiffel Tower was ridiculed by critics as a "truly tragic street lamp" and a "half-built factory pipe," but it soon came to symbolize both Paris and the new age of modernity.

This same era saw the development of electric power. In 1866 the English scientist Michael Faraday (1791–1867) designed the first electromagnetic generator. Four years later the first commercially viable generator was produced. Once electricity could be cheaply generated and delivered to homes and shops, it then needed to be converted into usable forms. In 1879, the American Thomas Edison (1847–1931) invented the lightbulb and illuminated the practical possibilities of electric power. These developments created a huge new energy-producing industry. They also accelerated the production and distribution of other industrial goods as factories and shops, as well as the train and tram lines that serviced them, were linked to the city power grid.

One important characteristic that distinguished this new phase of industrialization was the role of the state in encouraging economic modernization. Governments implemented policies of economic regulation and intervention, such as the construction of state-owned and -operated railway networks and the provision of financial assistance to private business ventures. The challenge posed by the Great Depression hastened the retreat from the free-trade principles of economic liberalism. Faced with declining profits and increased competition, businessmen demanded that their governments act to protect domestic industries from foreign competition. In this period, only Britain, Denmark, and the Netherlands retained the liberal commitment to free trade and refused to construct tariff walls designed to overprice the goods of outside competitors.

The emergence of much larger and more complicated organizational structures also characterized this new industrial phase. As a result of the economic pressures of the Great Depression, businesses grew much bigger. Faced with the necessity of trimming production costs in a time of declining profits, business owners developed new organizational forms, including both *vertical integration*—buying up the companies that supplied their raw materials and those that bought their finished products—and *horizontal integration,* linking up with companies in the same industry to fix prices, control competition, and ensure a steady profit. The Standard Oil Company exemplifies both trends. Formed in 1870 by the American industrialist John D. Rockefeller (1839–1937), Standard Oil monopolized 75 percent of the petroleum business in the United States by the 1890s, and in addition controlled iron mines, timberland, and various manufacturing and transportation businesses.

Within these new, huge, often multinational companies, organization grew more complex and impersonal. The small family firm run by the owner who knew the name of every employee grew increasingly rare as an ever-expanding layer of managers and clerical staff separated worker from owner. Moreover, identifying "the owner" grew increasingly difficult. The need for capital to fuel these huge enterprises drove businesses to incorporation—the sale of "shares" in the business to numerous stockholders, each of whom now shared ownership in the company.

The development of more complicated organizational patterns at the production end of the economic process interacted with changes in the way goods were marketed.

DOCUMENT

The Ladies' Paradise

The French novelist Émile Zola recognized in the new department store a revolutionary force of modernization. His novel The Ladies' Paradise, *first published in 1883, explored the social and economic changes associated with this retail revolution. As this excerpt makes clear, Zola, through his fictional character Mouret, the fiercely competitive department store owner, saw women as playing a central role in the revolution.*

It was the cathedral of modern business, strong and yet light, built for vast crowds of customers. In the central gallery on the ground floor, after the bargains near the door, came the tie, glove, and silk departments; the Monsigny Gallery was occupied by the household linen and the printed cotton goods, the Michodiere Gallery by the haberdashery, hosiery, cloth, and woolen departments. Then, on the first floor, there were the ready-made clothes, lingerie, shawls, lace, and other new departments, while the bedding, carpets, and furnishing materials, all the bulky goods and those which were difficult to handle, had been relegated to the second floor. By this time there were thirty-nine departments and eighteen hundred employees, of whom two hundred were women. A whole world was springing up amidst the life echoing beneath the high metal naves.

Mouret's [the department store owner's] sole passion was the conquest of Woman. He wanted her to be the queen in his shop; he had built this temple for her in order to hold her at his mercy. His tactics were to intoxicate her with amorous attentions, to trade on her desires, and to exploit her excitement. He racked his brains night and day for new ideas. Already, to spare delicate ladies the trouble of climbing the stairs, he had installed two lifts lined with velvet. In addition, he had just opened a buffet, where fruit cordials and biscuits were served free of charge, and a reading-room, a colossal gallery decorated with excessive luxury, in which he even ventured to hold picture exhibitions. But his most inspired idea, which he deployed with women devoid of coquetry, was that of conquering the mother through the child; he exploited every kind of force, speculated on every kind of feeling, created departments for little boys and girls, stopped the mothers as they were walking past by offering pictures and balloons to their babies. Presenting a balloon as a free gift to each customer who bought something was a stroke of genius; they were red balloons, made of fine indiarubber and with the name of the shop written on them in big letters; when held on the end of a string they traveled through the air, parading a living advertisement through the streets!

Source: Émile Zola, *The Ladies' Paradise* (1883; NY: Oxford University Press, 1995), pp. 232–3. Translation by Brian Nelson.

During these decades, a revolution in retailing occurred, one that culminated in a new type of business aimed at middle-class customers—the department store. In a traditional shop, the retailer (who was often also the producer) offered a single product—gloves, for example—in limited quantity at a fairly high price. Often, this price was not set. The customer haggled with the tradesperson until they agreed on a price. "Browsing" was unheard of; an individual who entered a shop was expected to make a purchase. The department stores changed these practices. These new commercial establishments—Bon Marche in Paris, Macy's in New York, Marshall Field's in Chicago, Whiteley's in London—offered a vast array of products in huge quantities. They made their profits not from high prices, but from a quick turnover of a very large volume of low-priced goods. To stimulate sales, they sought to make shopping a pleasant experience. Thus, they provided huge, well-lighted expanses filled with appealing goods sold by courteous, well-trained clerks. In-store reading rooms and restaurants pampered the weary shopper. Another innovation, mail-order catalogs, offered the store's delights to potential customers stranded in distant rural regions and traditionally reliant for their goods on the itinerant peddler and the seasonal fair. Advertising became a crucial industry in its own right, as business sought to persuade potential customers of new needs and desires.

On the Move: Emigration and Urbanization

These three economic developments—the onset of the Great Depression, the expansion of industrialization, and the Second Industrial Revolution—accelerated already existing patterns of urbanization and immigration, and so helped widen the borders of local, regional, and national communities across Europe. The Great Depression hit agricultural regions particularly hard, at just the same time that continuing population growth exerted greater pressure on land and jobs. In addition, industrial expansion undercut rural manufacturing and handicraft production, crucial sources of income for rural populations. As a result, men and women from traditional villages sought new economic opportunities in the industrializing cities of Europe, or further abroad, in the United States, Canada, South America, and Australia.

European cities grew dramatically after 1870. In 1800, only 23 European cities had more than 100,000 inhabitants.

The Bicycle Revolution

The bicycle revolutionized daily life for ordinary Europeans. The introduction of equal-sized wheels in 1886 and of pneumatic tires in 1890 allowed for a far more comfortable ride than had been the case with the bone-breaking cycles built earlier. Mass industrial production made the bicycle affordable; for the first time, ordinary individuals, far too poor to afford a horse or motorcar, could dare to purchase their own private means of transportation that would get them where they wanted to go in one-quarter of the time that walking required. No longer confined to their village for work opportunities or social contacts, bicycle owners discovered that their daily world had widened fourfold. As this engraving shows, the bicycle also contributed to the expansion of the woman's sphere.

By 1900, 135 cities of such a size had sprung up. The European population as a whole continued to expand in this period, but the cities increased at a much faster pace. For example, in 1800 the city of Odessa in Ukraine held 6,000 inhabitants. By 1914, Odessa contained 480,000 people. In the same period, Hungary's Budapest expanded from 50,000 to 900,000 inhabitants.

The migration flow was not all one-way. Farm laborers moved to the cities when times were tough and then moved home again after they had earned some money. Most urban immigrants came to the cities from the surrounding countryside, and often stayed for less than a year. Duisberg, a steel- and tool-making center located in Germany's Ruhr Valley, grew in population from 8,900 to 106,700 between 1848 and 1904. Almost one-third of its newcomers in the 1890s came from villages less than fifteen miles away. No fewer than two-thirds of these immigrants eventually returned to their rural villages.

By 1910, however, one-sixth of Duisberg's immigrants came from other countries, particularly Italy and the Netherlands. The combined impact of agricultural crisis and urban industrial expansion broke down national boundaries to create an international industrial workforce by 1914. Inhabitants of industrially underdeveloped regions were drawn to more economically advanced areas. Italians headed to France and Switzerland, while the Irish poured across the Irish Sea into Liverpool and Glasgow.

Some immigrants headed not for the nearest city, but for an entirely different continent. Between 1860 and 1914, more than 52 million Europeans crossed the ocean in quest of a better life. Seventy-two percent of these transoceanic immigrants traveled to North America, 21 percent to South America, and the rest to Australia and New Zealand.[1] Irish and English immigration to the United States remained high throughout this period, but after the 1880s eastern Europeans accounted for an ever-larger share of those bound for America. One hundred thousand Poles moved to the United States over the course of the 1880s; in the first decades of the twentieth century, between 130,000 and 175,000 Poles were immigrating to the United States each year.

By the 1890s, a truly global labor market had developed. Both technological developments (primarily the shift from sailing to steam ships) and competition among shipping firms considerably reduced the cost of transoceanic travel. As a result, men from villages in southern Italy and Spain could cross the Atlantic in time for the fall harvest of wheat in Argentina, travel to Brazil to pick coffee beans, and then head back home in May. Clearly, in such societies, the borders between local villages and the rest of the world had become permeable.

Growing Social Unrest

Rapid economic change, combined with accelerated urbanization and immigration, heightened social tensions and destabilized political structures. The freefall in prices that characterized the Great Depression eroded capitalist profit margins, shattered business confidence, and increased middle-class resistance to workers' demands. Class hostilities

M. I. Pokzovskaya on Working Conditions of Women in the Factories (early 20th c.)

rose as workers responded angrily to businessmen's efforts to protect their profit margins by reducing the number of their employees and increasing labor productivity.

In rural regions such as Spain and Ireland, the devastating collapse in agricultural prices fostered serious social and economic crises. Increasingly desperate, agricultural laborers and peasants turned to violence to enforce their calls for a fairer distribution of land. The spread of industrialization into southern and eastern Europe also led to social unrest as handicraft producers and independent artisans fought to maintain their traditional livelihoods in the face of the industrial onslaught.

In regions such as Britain and parts of Germany, traditional producers had lost that battle against industrialization in the preceding generation, but the onset of the Second Industrial Revolution brought new social strains. The expansion of office and sales jobs widened the ranks of the lower middle class (or *petty bourgeoisie*). This increasingly important social group exhibited extreme class consciousness and an often fierce hostility toward the working class. With an income no higher than that of a skilled worker, the clerk had to fight hard to maintain middle-class status. The erosion of objective differences such as income levels accentuated the importance of subjective differences—wearing the correct clothing, speaking with the proper accent, living on the right street, keeping the children in school.

The flow of immigrants into Europe's cities also sent social and ethnic tensions soaring. Cities were often unable to cope with the sudden and dramatic increases in population, despite the spread of public health provisions such as water and sewer systems. Housing shortages and poor living conditions exacerbated social tensions as newcomers battled with established residents for jobs and apartments. The mixture of different nationalities and ethnic groups often proved particularly explosive.

Defining the Political Nation

■ How did the ruling classes of the Western powers respond to the new threats and opportunities provided by mass political participation?

The economic and social changes examined in the last section helped create mass politics—a new political culture characterized by the participation of men (but not yet women) outside the upper and middle classes. Mass politics was in many ways an industrial product. In general terms, industrial expansion broke down local and regional cultures, loyalties, and mindsets; it thus cleared the way for the development of national political identities and interests. More specifically, the new transportation and communication technologies introduced by industrializa-

tion made mass political participation possible. The railroads, telegraph, and telephone, for example, shattered the barriers of distance between province and capital, while new printing technologies made newspapers cheap and available to ordinary people. With access to information, they could now form opinions and participate in national and international debate as never before. At the same time, the dramatic growth of cities associated with industrialization created the environments in which mass political movements could grow.

Faced with the challenge of adapting to this new political culture, political leaders sought ways to quell social discontent and ensure the loyalty of their populations. They did so in the context of the turbulent international climate created not only by the spread of industrialization but also by the national unification of both Italy and Germany and the continuing decline of the Ottoman Empire (see Chapter 21). As the European balance of power shifted, governments scrambled to create policies that would strengthen their states both at home and abroad.

Nation Making

After 1870, all but the most authoritarian of European political leaders recognized the importance of "nation-making," of creating a sense of national identity powerful enough to overcome the conflicting regional, social, and political loyalties that divided their citizens and subjects. But while European political elites sought to make ordinary men feel a part of political life, they endeavored, through such nation-making policies, to retain their dominant social and political position. As socialism mounted an increasingly powerful challenge to both liberal and conservative regimes, those in power had to figure out how to stay there.

Franchise Expansion

One way to stay in power was by sharing power. The British political system proved the most flexible in this regard. In the first half of the nineteenth century, Britain's landed elite had accommodated middle-class demands for greater influence without relinquishing its own political dominance. Aristocrats and landed gentlemen played leading roles in both major political parties—the Liberals and the Conservatives (also called "Tories")—but both parties also pursued policies that encouraged industrial growth and benefited the middle classes. In the last third of the century, this system expanded to include working-class men. In 1867, many urban working men won the right to vote, and in 1884 this right was extended to rural male laborers. Although Britain did not achieve universal male suffrage until after World War I, these gradual measures of franchise expansion convinced many British working-class men that they could be a part of the political nation and that the political system did respond to demands for reform.

Across Europe in the last third of the nineteenth century and the opening decades of the twentieth century, we see similar patterns as both aristocratic and middle-class politicians enacted measures extending the vote to lower-class men. These political leaders regarded franchise reform as a preventive measure, a way to avoid socialist revolution by incorporating potential revolutionaries within the system. Even strongly conservative politicians came to realize that mass suffrage did not always mean radical political change, as the political structure of Germany attested. The new German state remained politically authoritarian, despite its democratic appearance. All adult males had the right to elect representatives to the German Reichstag (the lower house of parliament) but the Reichstag was fairly powerless. Real power lay in the hands of William I (r. 1861–1888), the first emperor (or *kaiser*) of the unified Germany, and his chancellor, the conservative aristocrat Otto von Bismarck.

Regardless of conservative or liberal intentions, however, the widened franchise was a key development in the creation of mass politics. New voters had to be wooed and wowed; they had to be persuaded to vote the way their leaders, or aspiring leaders, wished. Again, Germany provides a potent example. Even Bismarck could not entirely ignore the democratically elected Reichstag, because it possessed the power of the purse: It approved the budget and appropriated the funds necessary to run the government.

Social Reform

To attract workers' votes, but more important, to ensure working-class loyalty to the nation and its political leaders, political parties turned to social welfare legislation. In the

Map 22.1 Europe at the End of the Nineteenth Century

A comparison of this map with Map 19.2 ("Europe After the Congress of Vienna in 1815," page 638) shows the impact of modern nationalism on European political geography. The most striking change is the formation of the new states of Italy and Germany (the German Empire). In addition, nationalist movements succeeded in carving away large chunks of the Ottoman Empire's European territories. By the 1880s, Bosnia and Herzegovina were under Austrian administration, and Greece, Serbia, Montenegro, Rumania, and Bulgaria had all achieved independence.

1880s, for example, Bismarck introduced to Germany some of the most thoroughgoing social welfare measures yet seen in Europe. He initiated sickness benefits in 1883, coverage for industrial accidents in 1884, and old-age pensions and disability insurance in 1889. Bismarck, a fiercely conservative aristocrat, might seem an unlikely social welfare crusader, but his policies suited his overall goal of ensuring German stability, prosperity, and international power. Alarmed by the growing popularity of the German Social Democratic Party (SPD), Bismarck had outlawed it in 1878 and authorized the federal police to disband all socialist meetings and organizations. This attack on the SPD appealed to antisocialist groups such as conservative landowners, Roman Catholics, and liberal businessmen, but risked alienating the growing urban working class. To attract the support of this vital social segment and weaken the appeal of the SPD's call for violent revolution at the same time, Bismarck turned to social welfare legislation.

Bismarck was not the only or even the first conservative political leader to advocate social welfare as a means of winning the loyalty of the expanding industrial working classes. In Britain, the Conservative Party leader Benjamin Disraeli (1804–1881) argued that the traditional aristocratic policy of *noblesse oblige,* of the privileged caring for those below them, made the Conservatives the natural party of social reform. In the 1870s, his government strengthened trade union rights, established the beginnings of a public housing program, expanded the state's program of inspecting factories, and assumed some responsibility for the population's safety by beginning to monitor the sale of food and drugs.

The most substantial foundations of Britain's welfare state were, however, constructed in the early twentieth century by a Liberal government. Between 1906 and 1912, the Liberals enacted a series of welfare measures, including state-funded lunches for schoolchildren, pensions for the elderly, and sickness and unemployment benefits for some workers. This legislation, like Bismarck's two decades earlier, was a direct response to the political threat posed by working-class socialism. In 1906, British trade unionists and socialists allied together to form the Labour Party. Seeking to maintain their hold on working-class voters, the Liberals turned to social welfare measures.

A similar process occurred in Italy. Alarmed by the growing appeal of Italy's revolutionary socialist parties, the liberal leader Giovanni Giolitti (1842–1928) embarked on a conscious policy of improving workers' lives and so convincing their political leaders that real change did not require revolution. Giolitti legalized trade unions, nationalized the railroads, established public health and life insurance programs, cracked down on child labor, and established a six-day workweek.

Schooling the Nation

Social welfare was part of a broader nation-making agenda that sought to unite the masses with the elite in a strong national community. In this nation-making effort, schools also played an essential role. State elementary schools served as important tools in the effort to build internally united and externally competitive nation-states. During the last third of the nineteenth century, most of the nations of western and central Europe established free public elementary education systems. In Austria-Hungary, for example, free and compulsory education was decreed in 1869.

Of course, passing legislation is one thing, ensuring compliance another. Because children's wages contributed to the family income, many poor families deeply resented the laws that made school attendance mandatory. In poorer districts of Austria-Hungary such as Bukovina, only 36 percent of children attended school, despite the law. In Italy communities were required to provide free education to needy children as early as 1859, but as late as 1912 only 31 percent of the children in the southern region of Calabria were in school.

Despite these difficulties, the schools constituted an essential link in the chain of national identity. Schools broke the cultural barriers imposed by illiteracy. Individuals who could read had access to newspapers, magazines, and books that drew them far beyond the borders of their local village or neighborhood. Both political leaders and intellectuals recognized the power of education in creating a national community. In the 1880s, for example, French student teachers were instructed that "their first duty is to make [their pupils] love and understand the fatherland."[2]

Schools thus helped forge a national identity in very specific ways. First, they ensured the triumph of the national language. Required to abandon their regional dialect (and sometimes brutally punished if they did not), children learned to read and write in the national language. Second, history and geography lessons taught children particular versions of the past that buttressed their sense of belonging to a superior people and often served a specific political agenda. For example, French classrooms after 1870 displayed wall maps of France—maps that clearly included the provinces of Alsace and Lorraine, even though these regions belonged to Germany, which had seized them as the spoils of victory after the Franco-Prussian War. Finally, the schools, with their essentially captive populations, participated fully in newly designed nationalistic rituals, including singing aggressive patriotic songs such as "*Deutschland Über Alles*" ("Germany Over All") or "Rule Britannia," and observing special days to commemorate military victories or national heroes.

Inventing Traditions

Nationalistic ritual was not confined to the schoolroom and playground. Making nations often meant *inventing* traditions to captivate the imagination and capture the loyalty of the mass electorate. German policymakers, for example, developed "Sedan Day." This national holiday, which celebrated the battle that helped create the new German state, featured parades, flag raisings, and special services to foster a sense of German nationalism among its citizens. At the

**German Emperor
William II and
His Entourage**
William preferred to wear military regalia when he appeared in public. In this way, William himself symbolized the link between the German state and Germany's military might.

same time, the person of the emperor, or *kaiser*, became the center of nationalistic ceremony and loyalty, particularly after the accession of William II (r. 1888–1918), the first emperor to identify himself as truly German rather than Prussian. William used personal appearances, militaristic pageantry, and civic ritual to link together monarchy and subjects in a sturdy chain of nationalism.

The monarchy was even more central to British nationalism. Whereas Queen Victoria's coronation in 1837 had been a small, disorganized affair, by the final decades of the century the anniversaries of her accession to the throne (the Silver Jubilee of 1887 and the Diamond Jubilee of 1897) were dramatically different. Elaborately staged, beautifully costumed, and carefully orchestrated, these events were designed to make ordinary individuals feel part of a wider, powerful, meaningful national community. The new technologies of mass printing and mass production helped support this new mass politics of nationality. At the Jubilees, participants could purchase colorfully illustrated commemorative pamphlets, ceramic plates etched with the queen's silhouette, teapots in the shape of Victoria's head, or even an automated musical bustle that played "God Save the Queen" whenever the wearer sat down.

Crisis, Revolution, and Civil War: The Examples of France, Russia, and Ireland

In the climate of heightened international competition that followed Germany's unification and the spread of industrialization, political leaders recognized domestic unity as a vital ingredient of national strength as well as a strong bulwark against revolution. The very different examples of France, Russia, and Ireland demonstrate both the crucial importance and the complexity of creating a sense of national identity and fostering national unity in the years before World War I.

France: A Crisis of Legitimacy

A century of almost continuous political revolution ensured that in the final decades of the nineteenth century no consensus existed on who or what France actually was. After Napoleon III's capture by Prussian troops in 1871, his empire collapsed and the French returned to a republican form of government, based on universal manhood suffrage (see Chapter 21). Born in the humiliation of military defeat, the Third Republic faced a crisis of legitimacy. Key sectors of the population argued that the Republic had been foisted on the French by their Prussian conquerors, and that it was therefore not a legitimate state and not worthy of their loyalty or support.

This crisis of legitimacy was worsened by the failure of French politicians to generate much enthusiasm. A dozen different parties jostled for control of the legislature. Because no single party controlled a majority, the only way to form a government was through forging coalitions, and thus compromise, political wheeling and dealing, financial corruption, and constant reshuffling of office holders became the common tools of parliamentary politics.

The lackluster nature of French politics accentuated the appeal of those who wished to destroy the French Republic—monarchists who wanted a king back on the throne, Bonapartists longing for the glory days of Napoleonic empire, Roman Catholics disturbed by republican efforts to curb the political power of the Church, aristocrats opposed to democracy. To perceive the

The Mass Marketing of National Identity

Advertising and mass production allowed ordinary Britons to participate in the glamour of royalty by purchasing inexpensive trinkets, such as this 1902 coronation souvenir.

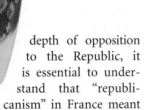

depth of opposition to the Republic, it is essential to understand that "republicanism" in France meant more than "no king, no emperor." Rooted in the radical Jacobin Republic of 1792, republicanism rested on a vision of an ideal France consisting of male equals—small shopkeepers and independent artisans, governed by reason rather than religion. Such a vision directly conflicted with the interests and ideals of monarchists, Bonapartists, and Roman Catholics, as well as of the growing number of working-class socialists. The encounter of these rival ideologies generated chaos in French politics throughout this era.

This fundamental lack of consensus about the nature or shape of France was strikingly revealed by the eruption of the Dreyfus Affair°. In 1894, on the basis of hearsay evidence and forged documentation, a French military court convicted Captain Alfred Dreyfus (1859–1935) of espionage. Prominent French intellectuals took up Dreyfus's case, and it became a full-fledged "affair," as supporters and opponents of Dreyfus battled in the streets and in the legislature. Support for Dreyfus, who was Jewish, became linked to support for the secular and egalitarian ideals of the Republic; the anti-Dreyfusards, in contrast, saw Dreyfus's Jewishness as a threat to France's Catholic identity and argued that to question the army hierarchy was to undermine France's military might. The Dreyfus Affair so dominated French politics that in 1899, when René Waldeck-Rousseau, a prominent politician, formed a governing coalition comprising members of a number of political parties, its unifying principle was support for Dreyfus.

Dreyfus was finally declared not guilty in 1906, but the consequences of the affair were far-reaching. The Dreyfus Affair revealed the strength of antirepublicanism in France, and so drove the Republic's supporters to seize the offensive. The government pushed through measures placing the army under civilian control, prohibiting members of Catholic religious orders from teaching in public *or private* schools, and removing the Catholic Church from its privileged position in French political life. With these measures politicians aimed to separate citizenship from religious affiliation and social rank and to redefine France in republican terms.

In 1914 on the eve of World War I, the success of this effort at redefinition remained unclear. National political life was dominated by the Radical Party, which represented the interests of small shopkeepers and independent artisans, not industrial workers, and drew its support from rural and small-town constituencies, not the growing cities. The Radicals' grip on power thwarted any significant efforts to address the grievances of the urban working class. Radicals opposed the high taxes necessary to establish social welfare programs and dragged their feet on social legislation such as the ten-hour workday (not passed until 1904) and old-age provisions (not established until 1910). As a result, workers increasingly turned to violent ideologies and actions, such as anarchism and sabotage. Although by 1914 the Third Republic was far stronger than it had been in the early 1870s, it clearly had not yet gained the approval of all segments of French society.

Russia: Revolution and Reaction

The success of French republican efforts to redefine the French nation may have remained unclear in 1914, but no one could have doubted the failure of the Russian imperial regime to construct any sense of national identity among the Russian masses at all. Convinced that God had appointed them to rule, Russia's tsars clung to absolutism. To catch up with the West, the tsarist regime adopted Western industrialization but it had no intention of accepting Western ideas of representative government. It could not, however, completely block the flow of these ideas into the Russian Empire. By the 1880s, many members of Russia's small but growing middle class espoused liberal political goals such as a written constitution and limited representational government. Other Russians went further and embraced socialism. Both liberalism and socialism constituted revolutionary ideological challenges to tsarist absolutism, and both liberals and socialists met with fierce repression.

As we saw at the opening of this chapter, some of these political dissenters turned to terrorism. In 1881, the revolutionary People's Will succeeded in assassinating Tsar Alexander II, but not in toppling the tsarist regime. With the use of repressive legislation and an ever-expanding

The Dreyfus Affair:
Defining National Identity in France

On September 27, 1894, the five officers who made up the counterespionage section of France's War Ministry examined a disturbing document—an unsigned, undated, torn piece of paper that had clearly served as a cover letter for a packet of documents containing information on French military equipment and training. The officers found no envelope, but they concluded that the letter was intended for Lieutenant Colonel Maximilian von Schwartzkoppen, the German military attaché in Paris. Thus, this torn piece of paper constituted evidence of treason. Someone in the French officer corps was selling military secrets to the Germans.

After a brief investigation and a cursory comparison of handwriting samples, the French investigators concluded that the traitor was Captain Alfred Dreyfus, a candidate officer on the General Staff. An unlikely traitor, Dreyfus had compiled a strong record during his military career and, by all accounts, was a staunch French patriot. Moreover, because of his marriage to a wealthy woman, he had no need to sell his country for money. He was, however, an aloof and arrogant man, disliked by most of his fellow officers and without a strong backer among his superiors. He was also a Jew.

Despite the lack of solid evidence, Dreyfus was convicted of treason. After a ceremony of military degradation, he was exiled in 1895 to a specially constructed prison hut on Devil's Island, a former leper colony twelve miles off the coast of French Guyana. Many French men and women believed he had gotten off too lightly. Both public and press clamored for his execution.

With Dreyfus safely imprisoned on his island, his case seemed closed. But in July 1895, Major

Marie-Georges Picquart was named chief of the Intelligence Bureau. An ambitious man determined to make a name for himself, Picquart soon discovered that the sale of military secrets to the Germans had continued even after Dreyfus's imprisonment. Ignoring his superiors' instructions to leave the Dreyfus case alone, Picquart set out to trap the man he first believed to be Dreyfus's accomplice. The evidence he uncovered, however, led him to conclude that Dreyfus was in fact innocent.

Picquart's investigations raised serious doubts about Dreyfus's conviction. These doubts were transformed into sensational charges on January 13, 1898, when one of France's most famous authors, Émile Zola, alleged in a Paris daily newspaper that the French military was engaged in a colossal cover-up. In an article headlined *"J'accuse!"* ("I accuse!"), Zola charged that the General Staff had knowingly convicted an innocent man. Zola's accusations aroused enormous public attention, and over the next six weeks, riots broke out in French cities.

Retried before a second military court in 1899, Dreyfus was again found guilty—although this time "with extenuating circumstances," a ridiculous verdict (there are no extenuating circumstances for the crime of treason) concocted to salvage the military's position despite Dreyfus's obvious innocence. In the subsequent riots that broke out in Paris, 100 people were wounded and 200 jailed. Ten days later, the French president pardoned Dreyfus in an effort to heal the divisions opened by the trial. Finally, in 1906, a French high court set aside the court-martial verdict and exonerated Dreyfus. Not until 1995, however, did the French military acknowledge the captain's innocence.

The Dreyfus Affair drew international attention, polarized French politics, and tore apart Parisian society. It sparked not only violent protests but also numerous duels and a series of related trials for assault, defamation, and libel. To uphold Dreyfus's conviction, high-ranking military officials falsified evidence, even to the point of forging entire documents. The question "Are you for or against Dreyfus?" divided families and destroyed friendships. During the height of the controversy, for example, the painter Edgar Degas spoke contemptuously of paintings by Camille Pisarro. When reminded that he had once admired these very same works, Degas said, "Yes, but that was before the Dreyfus Affair." Degas was a passionate anti-Dreyfusard; Pisarro believed Dreyfus was innocent.[3]

What about the Dreyfus Affair so aroused personal passion as to alter one painter's perception of another's work? What made this trial not simply a case, but an *affair,* a matter of public debate and personal upheaval, a cause of violent rioting and political turmoil?

To comprehend the Dreyfus Affair, we must understand that it was less about Captain Alfred Dreyfus than about the very existence of the French Third Republic, founded in 1871 in the wake of military defeat in the Franco-Prussian War and the collapse of Napoleon III's empire. The intellectuals and politicians who rallied in support of Dreyfus were defenders of the Republic, men and women who sought to limit the army's involvement in France's political life, who linked both monarchy and empire to national disaster rather than national glory, and who believed in a secular definition of the nation that would treat Roman Catholics no differently from Protestants, Jews, or atheists.

The Dreyfus Affair
Captain Alfred Dreyfus before his judges, 1899.

Dreyfus's opponents, in contrast, regarded the establishment of the Third Republic as a betrayal of the true France—a hierarchical, Roman Catholic, imperial state, steeped in military traditions. Defending the military conviction of Dreyfus became a way to express support not only for the army, but also for the authoritarian traditions that the Republic had jettisoned. The Dreyfus Affair was thus an encounter between competing versions of French national identity.

The question "What is France?," however, could not be answered without considering a second question: "Who belongs in France?"—or more specifically, "What about Jews?" France's small Jewish community (less than 1 percent of the total population) had enjoyed the rights of full citizenship since 1791—much longer than in most of Europe. Yet the Dreyfus Affair clearly demonstrated that even in France, the position of Jews in the national community was far from assured. Although anti-Semitism probably played little role in the initial charges against Dreyfus, it quickly became a dominating feature of the affair. More than seventy anti-Semitic riots ravaged France during this period. Anti-Semitic politicians and publications placed themselves in the vanguard of the anti-Dreyfus forces. For many anti-Dreyfusards,

Dreyfus's Jewishness explained everything. The highly acclaimed novelist and political theorist Maurice Barres insisted, "I have no need to be told why Dreyfus committed treason. . . . That Dreyfus is capable of treason I conclude from his race."[4]

Anti-Semites such as Barres regarded Jewishness as a kind of genetic disease that made Jews unfit for French citizenship. To the anti-Semitic nationalist, the Jew was a person without a country, unconnected by racial or religious ties to the French nation—the very opposite of a patriot. As a symbol of rootlessness, "the Jew" came to represent for many anti-Dreyfusards the forces of unsettling economic and political change that appeared to be weakening the French nation. Anti-Semites pointed to the successes of assimilated Jews such as Dreyfus—not only in the army but also in the universities, the professions, and business life—as evidence of what they perceived as the threat of Jewish "domination" of French culture.

Declared innocent in 1906, Dreyfus resumed his military career and served his country with distinction in the First World War. Like Dreyfus, the Third Republic survived the Dreyfus Affair. It was probably even strengthened by it. Outrage over the army's cover-up

led republican politicians to limit the powers of the military and so lessened the chances of an anti-republican military coup. Anti-Semitism, however, remained a pervasive force in French politics and cultural life well into the twentieth century.

Questions of Justice

1. What does the Dreyfus Affair reveal about definitions of national identity in late-nineteenth-century Europe?
2. Once Dreyfus was convicted, many French men and women believed that for the sake of the national interest, his conviction had to be upheld—whether he was actually guilty or not. In what situations, if any, should "national interest" override an individual's right to a fair trial?

Taking It Further

Cahm, Eric. *The Dreyfus Affair in French Society and Politics.* 1994. A wide-ranging history.

Kleeblatt, Norman, ed. *The Dreyfus Affair: Art, Truth, and Justice.* 1987. This richly illustrated collection of essays explores the cultural as well as political and legal impact of the case.

Lindemann, Albert S. *The Jew Accused: Three Anti-Semitic Affairs (Dreyfus, Beilis, Frank), 1894–1915.* 1991. An illuminating comparative study.

Snyder, Louis L. *The Dreyfus Case: A Documentary History.* 1973. An accessible collection of primary documents.

secret police force, both Alexander III (r. 1881–1894) and Nicholas II (r. 1894–1917) drove aspiring revolutionaries underground or into exile. They could not, however, quell the social unrest produced by economic change. By the turn of the century, rapid, state-sponsored industrialization had built an industrial structure in Russia, but it stood on a very faulty foundation. Russia remained a largely agricultural nation, with peasants still accounting for more than 75 percent of the population. Heavy taxation and rapid population growth, which increased competition for land, heightened social and economic anxiety among the peasant masses.

Within the industrial cities, social unrest also simmered. Factory workers labored more than twelve hours a day in wretched working conditions for very little pay. Any protest against these conditions was regarded as protest against the tsar and was quickly repressed. The workers themselves remained peasants in their loyalties and mindset. Separated from their families, who remained behind in the village, they lived in crowded state dormitories and traveled regularly back to their villages to plant and harvest. They had little sense of belonging to the Russian nation or of participating in the political structures that governed their lives.

In 1905, popular discontent flared into revolution. That year Japan trounced Russia in a war sparked by competition for territory in Asia. The military debacle of the Russo-Japanese War revealed the incompetence of the tsarist regime and provided an opening for reformers to demand political change. On a day that became known as "Bloody Sunday" (January 22, 1905), a group of 100,000 workers and their families attempted to present to the tsar a petition calling for higher wages, better working conditions, and the right to participate in political decision making. Government troops opened fire on the unarmed crowd; at least 70 people were killed and more than 240 were wounded.

The massacre horrified and radicalized much of Russian society. Across the Russian Empire, cities came to a standstill as workers went on strike and demanded both economic and political rights. In June, portions of the navy mutinied. By the fall, the empire was in chaos, with transportation, communications, energy, and water supplies all facing disruption. Taking advantage of this upheaval, states on the fringes of the empire, such as the Baltic regions, rose up in revolt against imperial rule, and middle-class liberals demanded limited representative government. In October, Tsar Nicholas II gave in and acceded to demands for the election of a legislative assembly. The Revolution of 1905 appeared to be a success.

The Revolution of 1905 in the Movies
On Bloody Sunday, January 22, 1905, Russian troops opened fire on more than 100,000 citizens who had gathered in St. Petersburg to present a petition to the tsar. Rather than subduing the revolt, the massacre sparked a revolution. This photograph, supposedly of the moment when the tsar's troops began to shoot the demonstrators, is one of the most familiar images of the twentieth century—yet it is *not* in fact a documentary record. Instead, it is a still taken from *The Ninth of January,* a Soviet film made in 1925.

By 1910, however, the tsar had regained much of his autocratic power. Revolutionary fervor dissipated as rival groups jostled for political influence. The tsar, with his army still loyal, refused to carry out many of the promised reforms. Tsarist autocracy remained intact, but so too did the causes of the discontent that had led to the revolution. Russia lacked an authentic national community, as Nicholas would discover during the First World War, when a new revolution would destroy the Russian imperial state.

The Irish Identity Conflict

In France, competing notions of "Frenchness" erupted into the Dreyfus Affair. In Russia, the lack of a widespread sense of Russian national identity increased the vulnerability of the tsarist state to revolutionary challenges. In Ireland, two very different forms of national identity took root during this era and led to the brink of civil war.

Theoretically, Ireland was not an imperial or conquered territory, but rather (since 1801) part of the United Kingdom, comprising England, Wales, Scotland, and Ireland. In reality, as we saw in Chapter 20, a chasm yawned between the first three overwhelmingly Protestant and industrialized nations, and the Roman Catholic, economically backward, peasant culture of Ireland. While the English, Scottish, and Welsh economies flourished under the impact of industrialization, the Irish economy stagnated. Peasant desperation fueled revolutionary Irish nationalism, as the economic grievances of Irish Catholics fused with their sense of political and religious repression, and convinced many of the need for independence from Britain. In the 1860s, the Irish Republican Brotherhood, or Fenian movement, endeavored to overthrow British rule by force. The Fenian "Rising" of 1867 failed dismally, but it planted a seed that took deep root in Irish soil—the belief that the British constituted an occupying force that must be violently resisted.

Faced with growing Irish Catholic nationalism, the British resorted to military rule, accompanied by attempts to alleviate peasant grievances through land reform. Such reform measures were always too little, too late. In 1898 Irish nationalists organized themselves as Sinn Fein (pronounced "shin fane"—Gaelic for "Ourselves Alone"), a political movement devoted to complete independence for Ireland by any means necessary. Sinn Fein grew rapidly, and by 1914 could call to arms a paramilitary force of 180,000 fighters. The success of Sinn Fein demonstrated that Irish Catholics had developed their own sense of nationhood, which refused to be subordinate to or absorbed by Britain.

But the refusal of Irish *Catholics* to accept British national identity was matched by the refusal of Irish *Protestants* to consider themselves as anything but British. The descendants of English and Scottish settlers in Ireland, these Protestants constituted a minority of the Irish population as a whole, but made up the majority in the northernmost province of Ulster. Frightened by the idea of belonging to a Catholic state, the Ulster Protestants opposed the British Liberal government's plans to grant Ireland "Home Rule," or limited autonomy, by 1914. The Ulstermen, or "Unionists," made it clear that they would fight to the death to preserve the union of Ireland with Britain. By 1914, they too were smuggling in arms and setting up clandestine paramilitary organizations. Only the outbreak of war in Europe postponed the coming civil war in Ireland.

Broadening the Political Nation

■ **What forms did mass politics assume during this time of industrial expansion and the spread of modern nationalist ideology?**

Through nation making, liberal and conservative political leaders sought both to strengthen their states and to ensure the loyalty of new political participants—industrial workers, peasants, the petty bourgeoisie. But in this era, mass support for socialist and racist-nationalist political parties challenged the political authority of traditional elites.

The Politics of the Working Class

The rise of working-class socialist political parties and the emergence of new, more radical forms of trade unionism reflected an escalation of class hostilities. Workers often rejected the political vision offered by their bosses and landlords, and instead fought hard to broaden the political nation on their own terms.

The Workers' City

In the decades after 1870, the combined impact of agricultural crisis and industrial expansion created large working-class communities in the rapidly growing industrial cities. These working-class communities tended to be increasingly isolated from the middle and upper class. Technological developments such as electrified tram lines, together with the expansion of the railway system, enabled Europe's middle classes to retreat from overcrowded, dirty, disease-ridden city centers to new and burgeoning suburbs. Workers knew members of the middle class only within the limited context of the "boss-employee" relationship— a relationship that was growing more hostile as economic depression drove middle-class employers to try to limit wages and raise productivity.

Within the sprawling industrial cities, industrial workers created a vibrant community life. They developed what sociologists call "urban villages," closely knit neighborhoods in which each family had a clear and publicly acknowledged

Urban Villages

Packed into slums, European workers developed a separate working-class culture. This painting by the Belgian painter Léon Frédérick (1856–1940) gives a sense of the crowded, tumultuous, community-oriented world of the urban worker. Painted in 1895, *The Stages of a Worker's Life* also illustrates the gender divisions in working-class culture: The left panel of the triptych shows the man's work world, while the right panel features the nurturing role of women as they care for their children in front of the market stalls where they buy their families' food. In the center panel workers of all ages commingle, with the funeral coach in the background reminding them of their inevitable end.

place. Sharply defined gender roles played an important part in ordering this world. The home became the woman's domain (although many working-class women continued to work outside the home as well). In many regions, the wife controlled the family income and made most of the decisions about family life. Men built up their own cultural and leisure institutions, free from middle-class (and from female) participation and control—the corner pub, the music hall, the football club, the choral society, the brass band. These institutions provided an escape from the physical and emotional confines of work and home; they also secured the bonds of male working-class identity, one that rested on a sharp distinction between "Us"—the ordinary men, the workers, the neighbors—and "Them," the bosses, the owners, the landlords, the people with privilege and power.

Working-Class Socialism and the Revolutionary Problem

This heightened class identity and hostility were embodied in the emergence of working-class socialist political parties. In the decades after 1870, socialism established itself as a powerful force in European parliamentary politics, the means by which workers sought to claim a place in the political nation. By 1914, socialist parties had been formed in twenty European countries.

Why socialism? As we saw in Chapter 21, by 1870 Karl Marx had published a series of books outlining his economic and political theory of revolutionary socialism. Not many workers had the time, education, or energy necessary for the study of Marx's complex ideas. But Marx's basic points, presented to workers by socialist party activists and organizers, resonated with many workers. Quite simply, most workers had already identified their boss as the enemy, and Marx assured them that they were right. His insistence that class conflict was inherent within the industrial system accorded with their own experience of social segregation and economic exploitation. In addition, the onset of economic depression in the 1870s appeared to confirm Marx's prediction that capitalism would produce ever more serious economic crises, until finally it collapsed under its own weight.

The most dramatic socialist success story was in Germany. Even after it was outlawed in 1878, the German Social Democratic Party (SPD) continued to attract supporters. In 1890, the SPD emerged from the underground as the largest political party in Germany. By 1914, it held 40 percent of the seats in the German Reichstag and served as the model for socialist parties founded in the Netherlands, Belgium, Austria, and Switzerland. Even more important, German socialists constructed a set of institutions that provided

DOCUMENT

Socialism: The Gotha Program

German workers with an alternative community. If they chose, they could send their children to socialist day care centers and bury their parents in socialist cemeteries. They could spend their leisure time in socialist bicycling clubs and gymnastic groups and choral societies and chess teams. They could read socialist newspapers, sing socialist songs, save their money in socialist savings banks, and shop at socialist co-operatives.

By the 1890s, the rapid growth of socialist parties such as the SPD persuaded many socialists that working-class revolution was just around the corner. In 1885 SPD leader August Bebel (1840–1913) told Marx's colleague Friedrich Engels, "Every night I go to sleep with the thought that the last hour of bourgeois society strikes soon."[5] Six years later in a speech before the SPD congress, Bebel told the gathered crowd, "I am convinced that the fulfillment of our aims is so close, that there are few in this hall who will not live to see the day."[6]

By the time Bebel made this promise, however, unexpected economic and political developments were creating serious problems for Marxist theory and practice. In 1890, the new German emperor, William II, fired Bismarck. Bismarck's antisocialist legislation was not renewed and the now-legal SPD faced a time of new opportunity, but also new challenges. To improve workers' wages and working conditions, the SPD worked in close connection with the rapidly growing German trade union movement—from 300,000 members in 1890 to 2.5 million in 1913. Such activity raised the fundamental question, what was the role of a socialist party within a nonsocialist state? To continue to attract voters, the SPD needed to push through legislation that would appeal to workers; yet the passage of such legislation, by improving workers' lives within a nonsocialist system, made the possibility of socialist revolution ever more remote. Why should workers resort to violent revolution when participation in parliamentary politics was clearly paying off?

The SPD's dilemma was shared by socialist parties across western Europe. According to Marx, capitalism would generate its own destruction—the growing misery of workers would fuel a social and political revolution. But in western European industrial nations in the last decades of the nineteenth century, working-class living standards were generally rising rather than deteriorating. In addition, the expansion of the franchise seemed to indicate that workers could gain political power without violent revolution. As socialist political parties grew in strength, then, they faced crucial and often divisive questions: Should they work for gradual reforms that would make life better for the worker—and risk making capitalism more acceptable? Could socialists participate in coalition governments with nonsocialists—and so lend legitimacy to parliamentary systems they condemned as oppressive and unequal?

The quest for answers to these questions led some socialists to socialist revisionism°, a set of political ideas most

DOCUMENT

The Socialist Culture

Songs played a vital role in the socialist culture developed in Germany at the end of the nineteenth century. Workers organized singing societies, which competed in local, regional, and national competitions. Rejecting the nationalist and religious songs of the middle-class choral society repertoire, workers often expressed their political ideals in their music. These overly didactic lyrics reveal not only the rage against economic injustice that fueled the socialist movement, but also its fundamental faith in human rationality and in parliamentary politics as an avenue of change.

"You Men, All of You" by Ernst Klaar

Already on all sides and throughout the world
The proletariat rises up together—
The fate of the poor is to be changed,
And to be changed through the state.
O, if we stand together firmly,
Who will be able to refuse us our right?
Upward, upward, you new generation,
Defiant let your banner wave!
    Put in the eight-hour day!
    Reduce the misery of toil!
    To our victorious march
    The drum now beats.
    Eight hours are enough!

Source: From "You Men, All of You" by Ernst Klaar, translated by Vernon L. Lidtke in *The Alternative Culture*, 1985. Reprinted by permission.

closely associated with the German socialist theorist Eduard Bernstein (1850–1932). Bernstein rejected the Marxist faith in inevitable violent revolution and argued instead for the gradual and peaceful evolution of socialism through parliamentary politics. Questioning Marx's insistence on the centrality of class struggle in modern politics, Bernstein called for German socialists to abandon their commitment to revolution, to form alliances with liberals, and to carry out immediate social and economic reforms.

In 1899, the German socialist party congress condemned Bernstein's revisionism and reaffirmed its faith in the inevitability of capitalism's collapse and working-class revolution. Bernstein had lost the battle—but he won the war. For regardless of what the congress affirmed as socialist theory, in practice the SPD acted like any other parliamentary party. It focused on improving the lot of its constituency through immediate and incremental legislative change. In the words of one socialist intellectual, the SPD was "a party which, while revolutionary, does not make a revolution."[7]

Its effect, although not its aim, was thus to make the existing political system more responsive to the needs of working-class constituents. Despite the almost hysterical fears of many middle- and upper-class Europeans, the successes of socialist political parties probably worked less to foment revolution than to strengthen parliamentary political systems.

Radical Trade Unions and the Anarchist Threat

To many at the end of the nineteenth century, however, revolution appeared a genuine possibility. The Great Depression, which shattered middle-class confidence and shrank capitalists' profit margins, led businesses to look for ways to cut costs. As management sought to reduce the number of laborers, to increase the rate of production, and to decrease wages, workers began to organize themselves in new and threatening ways.

The expansion and radicalization of trade unions highlighted growing working-class militancy. For example, in Britain between 1882 and 1913, union membership increased from 750,000 to 4,000,000. While size alone set apart the new unions from their midcentury predecessors, two additional differences marked them as much more subversive. First, the new unions were much more willing to resort to large-scale strikes and to violence. Second, the unions sought to better the lives of a wide range of workers, not just an elite of the highly skilled. In contrast to the unions of the 1850s and 1860s, which had tended to be small, craft-based groupings of skilled workers, the new unions aimed to organize all the male workers in an entire industry—for example, all male textile workers, rather than just the skilled weavers. (Unionists, fighting for higher pay, often resisted the unionization of female workers both because women earned much less than did men and because a central union aim was the "family wage"—a pay rate high enough for a man to support a family without his wife's second income.)

Political leaders reacted ferociously to the unionist challenge. In the coastal port of Hull in Britain, striking dockworkers in 1893 confronted Royal Navy gunboats. A little more than a decade later, the British government responded to a transport workers' strike in Liverpool by quartering 14,000 soldiers in the city and stationing two warships off the coast. Increasingly, "class war" seemed an appropriate label for interactions between workers and their middle-class employers. Even the simple act of getting a shave could prove dangerous for a member of the bourgeoisie: Unionized workers in barbershops were encouraged to "inflict nonfatal cuts on the clients of their capitalist masters."[8]

In the first decade of the twentieth century, the European labor movement became further radicalized by its encounter with the new ideology of syndicalism°. Syndicalists worked to overturn the existing social and political order by marshaling the economic might of the

The Unions' Challenge
In 1911 the British government deployed troops in the city of Liverpool to put down working-class labor unrest. In one confrontation, two people were killed.

laboring classes. They focused on the general strike as a means of change. In the syndicalist vision, if every worker in a nation went on strike, the resulting disruption of the capitalist economy would lead to working-class revolution. Thus they placed their revolutionary faith in economic rather than political action—in unions rather than parties, in the strike rather than the vote, and in compulsion rather than compromise. According to the French syndicalist theorist Georges Sorel (1847–1922), workers had to embrace violence to destroy the capitalist state. Sorel did not actually believe that a general strike was possible, but he believed that the idea of the general strike was crucial. In Sorel's view, the general strike served as an essential myth, an inspirational idea that would give workers the motivation and self-confidence they needed to overthrow the state.

In their rejection of parliamentary politics and in their willingness to utilize violent means to achieve their revolutionary ends, syndicalists were heavily influenced by anarchism°. In contrast to socialists who formed political parties to claim for workers a place in the political nation, anarchists shunned parliamentary politics. Opting for direct and violent action such as street fighting and assassination, anarchists aimed to destroy rather than control the state. The Russian anarchist Mikhail Bakunin (1814–1876) insisted that the great obstacle to achieving a just and egalitarian society was the state itself, not capitalism or the industrial middle class.

The combined impact of both syndicalism and anarchism created a climate of social unrest and political turmoil in much of Europe before 1914. In France, where a strong non-Marxist revolutionary tradition already existed, both syndicalism and anarchism possessed significant appeal. Impatient with parliamentary politics, anarchists resorted in the 1890s to a terrorist campaign in Paris, which began with a series of bombings and culminated in the fatal stabbing of President Sadi Carnot in 1894. Other prominent victims of assassination included Empress Elisabeth of Austria-Hungary in 1898, King Humbert of Italy in 1900, and U.S. president William McKinley in 1901.

The Politics of Race and Nation

The rise of socialist political parties and the spread of revolutionary ideologies such as anarchism and syndicalism fostered middle- and upper-class fears of a worker revolution. But the emergence of mass politics was not limited to left-wing ideologies. In the age of the masses, the right-wing ideas offered by nationalist, racist, and anti-Semitic parties also answered the demands of many ordinary people for a political voice. These parties possessed a special appeal in areas that industrialized late and so still contained a large peasant class profoundly threatened by the economic changes wrought by the continuing Industrial Revolution. Socialist politics also possessed little appeal for members of the petty bourgeoisie, who regarded the vision of working-class rule as a frightening nightmare. Instead, they turned to the new mass politics of nationalism.

Unlike the men who had dominated politics in the past, most newly enfranchised voters possessed only a basic education; they had little time for reading or sustained intellectual work; they worked long hours and therefore needed to be entertained. They needed a new style of politics—one based more on visual imagery and symbolism than on the written word, one that relied on emotional appeals rather than on intellectual debate. Nationalist politics fit the bill perfectly. Unlike socialists, who placed great faith in education and in rational persuasion, nationalist politicians did not recruit supporters with reasoned arguments. Instead, by waving flags, parading in historical costumes or military uniforms, and singing folk songs, they tapped into powerful personal and community memories to persuade voters of their common identity, one based not on shared political ideas or economic interests but rather on ethnic, religious, or linguistic ties. This

was as much a politics of exclusion as of inclusion—it defined the nation by identifying who was "not in" as well as who belonged.

Nationalism in the Ottoman Empire and Austria-Hungary: The Politics of Division

Nationalist mass politics proved very powerful in eastern Europe, particularly in the multiethnic, industrially underdeveloped Ottoman and Austrian-Hungarian Empires. These regions lacked a large, politically conscious urban working class. What they possessed was an abundant diversity of ethnic, linguistic and religious groups. Modern nationalist ideology taught these groups to identify themselves as nations, and to demand political statehood.

By the 1870s, nationalism had already diminished the Ottoman Empire's European territories. As we saw in Chapter 21, in 1833 Greece won its independence from the Ottomans. In the same period, the Ottomans granted autonomy, although not complete independence, to Serbia and the provinces that became Romania. Determined to hold on to what remained of his European empire, the Ottoman sultan in 1875 and 1876 suppressed nationalist uprisings in Bosnia-Herzegovina and Bulgaria with great ferocity. This repression backfired, however; it gave Russia the excuse it needed to declare war on the Ottoman Empire on behalf of its Slavic "little brothers" in the Balkans. In the aftermath of the Russo-Turkish War (1877–1878), Montenegro, Serbia, and Romania became independent states and Austria-Hungary received oversight of Bosnia-Herzegovina (see Map 22.2). Bulgaria received limited autonomy, which the Bulgars widened into full independence in 1908. The Ottomans had lost the bulk of their territory west of Istanbul.

Ottoman weakness appeared to make Austria-Hungary stronger. The Habsburg Empire not only gained territory—granted the administration of Bosnia-Herzegovina in 1878, Austria-Hungary annexed it outright in 1908—but it also benefited from the weakening of its once-formidable rival. The appearance of strength, however, was deceptive. Straining under the social and economic pressures of late industrialization, Austria-Hungary contained numerous ethnic and linguistic groups competing for power and privileges (see Map 21.4, page 704).

This competition intensified as the franchise was gradually widened in the 1880s and 1890s. (The Austrian half of the empire achieved universal manhood suffrage in 1907.) Various parties emerged that appealed to voters on the basis of ethnic identity and linguistic practice rather than economic interest. Language became a key battleground in this political competition. In a multilingual empire, which language would be taught in the schools? Which language would be required in official communications? Which language would guarantee career advancement? Not surprisingly, politicians tended to agitate for

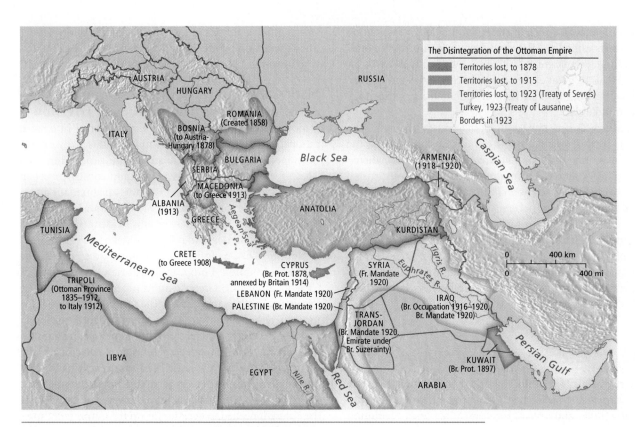

Map 22.2 The Disintegration of the Ottoman Empire

As Map 22.2 shows, the disintegration of the Ottoman Empire was a slow process that began at the end of the seventeenth century. By 1870, the Ottoman regime had already lost territory and political control over much of its once-mighty empire to both nationalist independence movements and to rival European powers. From the 1870s on, mass nationalism accelerated Ottoman disintegration. The Ottoman Empire would finally disappear as a consequence of the peace settlement of World War I.

the primacy of their own native language, and to jostle for the political power needed to ensure that primacy.

In Hungary, the ruling Magyar-speaking Hungarian landlords redrew constituency boundaries to give maximum influence to Magyar speakers and to undercut the power of other ethnic and linguistic groups. This policy of "Magyarization" in governmental offices and in the schools bred widespread resentment among non-Hungarians and fostered their own nationalist ambitions and their own political parties.

At the same time in the Austrian half of the empire, Czechs succeeded in gaining greater political power and official support for the Czech language. In response, German nationalist parties within Austria grew more aggressive in asserting German primacy. They called for closer ties with Germany and even a complete break of the link with Hungary. By 1900 the struggle over language laws in the Czech portion of the Austrian Empire had become so intense that no party could establish a majority in the

Reichsrat (the legislative assembly), and Emperor Francis Joseph (r. 1848–1916) resorted to ruling by decree.

In this context of nationalist divisions, anti-Semitic politics proved extremely powerful, particularly in the capital city of Vienna. In the last two decades of the nineteenth century, Vienna's Jewish population swelled, as Austrian Jews from the surrounding countryside came in search of jobs and Russian Jews fled the tsar's anti-Semitic regime.

The growing Jewish presence provided the opportunity for Karl Lueger (1844–1910), a lawyer, self-made man, and power-hungry politician. Lueger's Christian Social party demonstrates how hate-based politics could overcome social and economic divisions among members of a single ethnic or religious community. Lueger used both anti-Semitism and promises of social reform to unite artisans and workers with conservative aristocrats in a German nationalist party. His proposals to exclude Jews from political and economic life proved so popular that he was elected mayor of Vienna in 1897, despite the opposition of

Emperor Francis Joseph. Lueger was still the mayor in 1908, when 18-year-old Adolf Hitler, hoping to attend art school, moved to Vienna. Hitler's application to study art was denied, but he remained in Vienna for several years, soaking in the anti-Semitic political culture.

Anti-Semitism in Mass Politics

Anti-Semitism played a central role not only in Vienna but across Europe in the new nationalist mass politics. Across Europe, explicitly anti-Semitic parties emerged, while established conservative parties adopted anti-Semitic rhetoric to attract voters. In Germany, the widespread belief that Jews had conspired to cause the Great Depression fueled anti-Semitic politics; by the 1890s anti-Semitic parties had won seats in the Reichstag. In France, nationalists linked Jewish prosperity to French national decline and grew increasingly anti-Semitic in their ideology and rhetoric, until finally the Dreyfus Affair made explicit the connections between hatred of Jews and extremist French nationalism. Many of Dreyfus's opponents saw "Jewishness" and "Frenchness" as incompatible and regarded Dreyfus himself as part of a vast Jewish conspiracy to undermine France's religious, military, and national strength.

To explain the heightened anti-Semitism of this period, we need to understand three developments: the increased emphasis on racial identity, the upsurge in the numbers of Jewish immigrants into Western cities, and Jewish success in the new industrial economy. First, the triumph of nationalism meant a new concern with group boundaries and a greater focus on racial identity. Nationalism raised the question, "Who does *not* belong?" For many Europeans and Americans, race provided the answer. The new nationalism

meant new perceptions of common "racial roots." Ideas about "the English race" or of the shared racial heritage of the French had no scientific basis, but these perceptions of racial links nonetheless proved extremely powerful. In this new nationalistic climate, then, "Jewishness" was increasingly defined not only as a matter of religious belief but also as a racial identity. As a racial marker, Jewishness was not a matter of choice but of blood—something that could not be changed. A Jew who no longer ascribed to the Jewish faith or even a Jew who converted to Christianity remained a Jew. This shift to a more racial definition of Jewishness is one of the factors behind the upsurge in anti-Semitic actions and attitudes at the end of the nineteenth century. If national identity grew from supposedly racial roots, then in the eyes of many Europeans, Jews were a foreign plant. They were non-English, or non-French, or non-German—essentially outsiders whose very presence threatened national unity.

This perception of Jews as outsiders was also exacerbated by the growth in immigrant Jewish urban populations in the 1880s and 1890s. The Russian tsar Alexander III believed that a Jewish conspiracy was responsible for his father's assassination in 1881. He responded by reimposing restrictions on Jewish economic and social life with the May Laws of 1882. Pogroms—mass attacks on Jewish homes and businesses, sometimes organized by local government officials—also escalated. Fleeing this persecution, Jews from the Russian Empire settled in Paris, London, Vienna, and other European cities.

The encounter between these immigrant Jewish communities and their hosts was often hostile. Extremely poor, the immigrants spoke Yiddish rather than the language of their new home, dressed in distinctive clothing,

The Results of Anti-Semitism
In this 1905 painting by Samuel Hirszenberg, Hasidic Jews in Russian-governed Poland bury the victim of a pogrom. Hirszenberg called his painting *The Black Banner* in reference to both "The Black Hundreds," armed thugs who belonged to the anti-Semitic "Union of the Russian People," and *The Russian Banner*, the Union's newspaper that was partially funded by the tsar.

and sometimes practiced an ardently emotional style of Judaism that resisted assimilation. As the numbers of Jews escalated in Europe's cities, these new, impoverished, clearly identifiable immigrants received the blame for unemployment, the spread of disease, soaring crime rates, and any other difficulty for which desperate people sought easy explanations.

Many anti-Semites, however, associated Jews not with poverty but with wealth and power. A few Jewish families, such as the internationally connected Rothschild banking dynasty, did possess spectacular fortunes and corresponding political clout, but far more important in explaining the outburst of anti-Semitism in this era is what one historian has labeled the "rise of the Jews,"[9] or Jewish prominence in modern European societies. At the start of the nineteenth century, Jews were barred from political participation in most of Europe and often confined to certain economic roles and even certain territories or city districts. Jews in Russia, for example, could not live outside the area defined as the "Pale of Settlement." In the second half of the century, Jews throughout much of Europe gained civil and political rights. No longer barred from certain sectors of the economy, no longer required to live in certain territories, many Jews moved into new regions and into new economic and political roles. As newcomers, they often took up positions in the newest sectors of the industrial economy. They became department store owners or newspaper editors rather than farmers. At the same time, many Jews assimilated into European societies: They dropped distinctive dress styles and abandoned or modernized their practice of Judaism. They secularized the traditional Jewish emphasis on studying the Torah into an emphasis on education.

As a result of these developments, Jewish communities quickly assumed a significant presence in European economic and political life. In Budapest in 1900, for example, Jews formed 25 percent of the population, yet they accounted for 45 percent of the city's lawyers, more than 40 percent of its journalists, and more than 60 percent of its doctors. In Germany, almost all the large department stores were owned by Jewish businessmen, and in the cities of Frankfurt, Berlin, and Hamburg all the large daily newspapers were in the hands of Jewish proprietors.

The "rise of the Jews" meant that many Europeans linked Jewishness to economic modernity. For independent shopowners and traditional artisans with a great deal to lose from economic modernization, Jews became targets. Fearing the power of corporate capitalism as well as the revolutionary threat of socialism, they perceived both as somehow Jewish. Like Tsar Nicholas II, who blamed the Russian Revolution of 1905 on Jewish conspirators, ordinary men and women reacted to their own personal reversals of fortune by seeking a scapegoat. Jews became the embodiment of threatening change to many newly enfranchised European voters.

Zionism: Jewish Mass Politics

The heightened anti-Semitism of the last quarter of the nineteenth century convinced some Jews that the Jewish communities of Europe would be safe only when they gained a political state of their own. The ideology of Jewish nationalism was called Zionism°, as Jewish nationalists called for a return to Zion, the biblical land of Palestine. Most Jews in western nations such as France and Britain viewed Zionism with skepticism, but it had a potent appeal in eastern Europe, home to more than 70 percent of the world's Jewish community—and to the most vicious forms of anti-Semitism.

Zionism became a mass movement under the guidance of Theodor Herzl (1860–1904). An Austrian Jew born in Budapest, Herzl was living in Vienna when Karl Lueger was elected mayor. Confronted with the appeal of anti-Semitism to the mass electorate, Herzl began to doubt whether Jews could ever be fully accepted as Austrian citizens. His experience as a journalist reporting on the Dreyfus Affair from Paris confirmed these doubts. The vicious display of anti-Jewish hatred in a prosperous, industrialized, western European state convinced Herzl that Jews would always be outsiders within the existing European nations. In 1896, he published *The Jewish State*, a call for Jews to build a nation-state in Palestine. Herzl gained the financial support of wealthy Jewish businessmen such as Baron Edmund James de Rothschild, but he recognized that for Zionism to succeed, it must capture the imagination and loyalties of ordinary Jews. Through newspapers, popular publications, large rallies, and his own enthusiasm, Herzl made Zionism into an international mass movement.

As a mass movement, Zionism faced strong opposition. Many Jewish leaders argued that Zionism played into the hands of anti-Semites by insisting that Jews did not belong in Europe. In addition, by marking out Palestine as the Jewish "homeland," Zionists ran into a huge political obstacle: Arab nationalism. By the 1890s, Arab leaders had begun to dream of an Arab state, one that would be independent of the Ottoman Empire and that would include Palestine, home to 700,000 Arabs. Nevertheless, by 1914 some 90,000 Jews had settled in Palestine, where they hoped to build a Jewish state.

Outside the Political Nation? The Experience of Women

■ In what ways did the emergence of feminism in this period demonstrate the potential as well as the limits of political change?

Extending the suffrage to men outside the middle and upper classes also called attention to gender differences, as middle-class women demanded that they, too,

DOCUMENT

John Stuart Mill
on
Enfranchisement
of Women
(1869)

be made part of the political nation. The campaign for women's suffrage, however, was only part of a multifaceted international middle-class feminist movement° that, by the 1870s, demanded a reconsideration of women's roles. To the feminist movement, the vote was not an end in itself, but a means to an end, a way of achieving a radical alteration in cultural values and expectations. At the core of nineteenth-century feminism stood a rejection of the liberal ideology of separate spheres—the insistence that both God and biology destined middle-class men for the public sphere of paid economic employment and political participation, and women for the private sphere of the home. In seeking a place in the political nation, feminists sought not just to enter the public, masculine sphere, but in fact to obliterate many of the distinctions between the public and private spheres altogether and so to reconfigure political and social life.

During this period the feminist movement remained largely middle class in its membership and its concerns. Working-class and peasant women were occupied by the struggle for survival; obtaining the vote seemed fairly irrelevant to a woman listening to her children cry from hunger. Politically active working-class women tended to agree with Karl Marx that class, not gender, constituted the real dividing line in society. For help in bettering their lives, they turned to labor unions and to working-class political parties rather than middle-class feminist organizations. The British working-class feminist Selina Cooper (1868–1946), for example, fought hard for women's rights, but within the context of the British Labour movement. Cooper, who was sent to work in a textile mill at age 10, viewed the widening of women's opportunities and the achievement of working-class political power as two sides of the same coin. Similarly, in Germany, the SDP activist Clara Zetkin (1857–1933) argued that the fight against class oppression was inextricably linked to the fight against women's oppression.

Changes in the Position of Middle-Class Women

The middle-class women's movement operated within changing economic and social conditions that were pushing middle-class women into more public positions in European society. Married women moved into a new public role as consumers during this period. It was the woman who was the principal target of the new advertising industry, the woman whom the new department stores sought to entice with their lavish window displays and courteous shop clerks, the woman who rode the new tram lines and subways to take advantage of sale days.

The largest change for married middle-class women was much more basic, however. In the last third of the nineteenth century, middle-class men and women began to

limit the size of their families. In Britain in the 1890s, the average middle-class family had 2.8 children, a sharp reduction in family size from the middle of the century, when the typical middle-class family had 6 children. This enormous change, characteristic of all the advanced industrial nations, reflected both economic and social developments. As the Great Depression cut into business profits and made economic ventures ever more precarious, middle-class families looked for ways to cut expenses and yet maintain a middle-class lifestyle. At the same time, the growing tendency to keep both boys and girls in school longer meant added financial obligations for the middle-class family. Limiting births, through the use of already well-known methods such as abstinence, withdrawal, and abortion, provided the answer. In working-class families, in which children left school by age 11 or 12 and so began to contribute to the family income much earlier, family size continued to remain large, but in the middle class, married women no longer spent much of their adult life pregnant or nursing, and were thus free for other activities and interests, including feminist activism.

The expectations of unmarried middle-class women were also transformed during this period. In 1850, the unmarried middle-class woman who had to support herself had little choice but to become a governess or a paid companion to an elderly widow. By 1900 her options had widened. As we shall see, the women's movement played a crucial role in this expansion of opportunity, but so also did two more general economic and political developments: the expansion of the state and the Second Industrial Revolution.

The expansion of state responsibilities in this period significantly widened opportunities for women. By the final decade of the nineteenth century, local governments took over many tasks traditionally assigned to church volunteers and especially women charity workers, such as training the poor in proper hygiene and nutrition. Middle-class women quickly claimed both paying and elected positions in the new local bureaucracies, on the argument that women possessed an expertise in managing households and raising children that could be directly translated into managing poorhouses and running schools. Women served on school and welfare boards, staffed government inspectorates, voted in local elections, and were elected to local office. For example, in Britain between 1870 and 1914, approximately 3,000 women were elected to county and municipal governing bodies. In Germany, 18,000 women worked as local welfare officials by 1910. But the largest employers of middle-class women before 1914 were the new state-funded elementary schools. The implementation of compulsory mass education created a voracious demand for teachers and thus a new career path for unmarried women from the middle class as well as from the upper ranks of the working class.

The emergence of new technologies and the retail revolution also created new jobs for women, positions that did

Men in Black

Within a span of about fifty years, upper- and middle-class European and American men transformed the way they presented their bodies to the world. Before the late eighteenth century, social rank outweighed gender in determining clothing styles. Thus an aristocratic man dressed more like an aristocratic woman than like a male laborer. Aristocrats, both men and women, decorated themselves with expensive jewels, shaped their bodies with corsets and pads, powdered their faces and hair, sported huge hats decorated with ribbons, carried lacy fans, wore high heels, and dressed in brightly colored and elaborately ruffled silks and taffetas. By the middle of the nineteenth century, however, the man had lost his plumage, and decoration had become a distinctly female attribute. The aristocratic man of the 1850s looked like his middle-class counterpart. He dressed in darkly colored, loose-fitting trousers and jackets; wore sensible shoes; and put on a top hat when he went outside. Cosmetics, perfume, ruffles and lace, elaborate jewelry, hats, and fans all retreated to the woman's sphere.

Whether he was engaged actively in business or lived a life of leisure, the new man in black now presented a sharp contrast to his female companions. His clothing associated him with the world of practicality and production; her costume, however, was designed to reinforce the prevailing notions about women's incapacity for public or economic roles. Middle- and upper-class women's clothing not only remained brightly colored, decorative, and luxurious, it also became increasingly constrictive. The full crinolines and hoop skirts of the 1850s and 1860s, for example, made the simple task of sitting down a tricky endeavor, while tight corseting placed strenuous physical activity beyond reach of fashionable women.

Changes in clothing reflect new ideas about the relationships between a man's and a woman's identities and their physical bodies. After 1850 men's clothing styles de-emphasized their bodies. Whereas eighteenth-century aristocrats wore attention-grabbing colors, silk stockings that outlined their legs, short jackets that emphasized their waist, and tight-fitting breeches that highlighted the sexual aspects of the male body, the long loose jackets and trousers of the later nineteenth-century man masked rather than highlighted their wearer's physical characteristics. In contrast, women's fashions increasingly accentuated female sexuality. By shrinking the waist, tightly laced corsets made the bust and hips appear fuller. In the 1880s, the addition of the bustle emphasized the woman's bottom. Such clothing styles fortified the view that a woman's body in many ways determined her destiny, that women were designed to be wives and mothers.

Economic developments led to important changes in women's fashions in the 1890s. As middle-class women began to enter the workforce in large numbers, fashions adapted to fit their new roles. Dresses became more streamlined: Skirts moved slightly above the ankles and shrank in width, and bustles disappeared. But it took the demands of the First World War, when women assumed previously all-male positions in industry, agriculture, and transportation, to effect radical alterations in the way women presented their bodies and themselves to the world.

For Discussion

Changes in women's employment patterns clearly had an impact on women's dress styles. What other economic developments during this period may help explain changes in fashion?

Men in Black
Painting by James Tissot, *Cercle de la Rue Royale*, detail (1868). Although most are barons, marquises, or counts, the men whose portraits Tissot captured in this high-society painting dress like bankers or stockbrokers.

Loose-fitting jackets and trousers hide, rather than highlight, physical characteristics, and are more practical for a day of business.

Dark colors have replaced the bright colors of earlier times; lace, ribbons, and jewelry have disappeared.

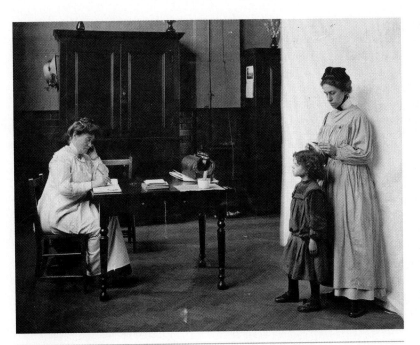

Women at Work

The expansion of local and central government interference in daily life created many opportunities for women's paid employment. Here government health inspectors check a schoolgirl for head lice.

not involve manual labor and so did not mean a descent into the working class. Middle-class women moved into the work world as typists, telephone and telegraph operators, sales clerks, and bank tellers. During the 1860s in England, the number of women working as commercial clerks and accountants increased tenfold.

Middle-class women thus found new ways to make a living; they did not, however, find the same opportunities as their male counterparts. A woman earned an average of between one-third and two-thirds less than a man working in the same job. The entry of large numbers of women into any job was certain to result in a recasting of that position as unskilled and low-paying. Unlike men, women lost their jobs when they married and found most supervisory positions closed to them.

By the 1880s, an international women's movement had emerged to challenge the legal, political, and economic disabilities facing European and American women. Consisting of a vast web of interconnected organizations, publications, and correspondence networks, the middle-class women's movement sought to challenge the ideology of separate spheres and to establish a new basis for both private and public relations. Its multifaceted campaigns focused on four fronts: the legal impediments facing married women, employment opportunities and higher education for girls and women, the double standard of sexual conduct enshrined in European laws, and national women's suffrage.

Women and the Law

European legal systems strongly reinforced the liberal ideology of separate spheres for men and women. Law codes often classified women with children, criminals, and the insane. Article 231 of the Napoleonic Code, the legal system of France and the basis of the legal codes of much of western and central Europe, declared that the wife was the dependent of the husband; hence, "the husband owes protection to his wife; the wife owes obedience to her husband." The Russian legal code agreed: "The woman must obey her husband, reside with him in love, respect, and unlimited obedience, and offer him every pleasantness and affection as the ruler of the household." In Russia a woman could not travel without her father's or husband's permission. The husband was also the legal guardian of all children; he alone had the authority to pick their schools, determine their punishments, and approve their marriage partners. Similarly, in Prussia the law declared that only the husband could decide when his baby should stop breastfeeding. English common law, based on tradition and precedent rather than on a single, systematized code, proclaimed much the same idea. As Sir William Blackstone explained in his famous *Commentaries on the Laws of England* (1765–1769), "the husband and wife are one person in law," and that person was the husband. A married woman simply disappeared in the eyes of the British common law. Most property brought into a marriage, or given to her or earned by her while married, became the property of her husband.

From the middle of the nineteenth century on, women's groups fought to improve the legal rights of married women. By the end of the 1880s, English married women had won rights to own their own property, control their own income, and keep their children. Two decades later, French women could claim similar rights. In contrast, the German women's movement suffered a sharp defeat with the promulgation of the Civil Code in 1900. The Civil Code, which formulated a single uniform legal system for Germany, proclaimed that "the husband takes the decisions in all matters affecting married life." It granted all parental authority to the husband—over his stepchildren as well as his own children. By German law, "if the parents disagree, the father's opinion takes precedence." While it allowed married women to keep money they earned while married, it declared that all property owned by the wife before marriage or given to her after marriage became the husband's.

Finding a Place: Employment and Education

In addition to their legal campaigns, feminists also worked to widen women's educational and employment opportunities as part of their effort to enter the public sphere. At the core of this aspect of the women's movement was a simple demographic reality—women outnumbered men in almost every region in Europe. In England by 1900, the higher rates of male emigration and infant mortality meant that there were 1,064 females for every 1,000 males. Clearly, not all women could marry. Thus, providing respectable jobs for middle-class single women was a high priority for early European and American feminists.

The problem of women's jobs quickly proved to be inseparable from the issue of women's education. Even girls from privileged families rarely received rigorous educations before 1850. The minority of girls who did go to school spent their time learning ladylike occupations such as fancy embroidery, flower arranging, and piano playing. Proper posture was more important than any literary or scientific attainments. Widening the world of women's education, then, became a crucial feminist aim and proved to be an area in which they achieved considerable, but still limited, success.

Feminists' educational campaigns in the second half of the nineteenth century had two main emphases: first, improving the quality as well as expanding the number of girls' secondary schools, and second, opening universities to women. The fight to upgrade the quality of girls' secondary education was often difficult. Many parents opposed an academic curriculum for girls, a position reinforced by medical professionals who argued that girls' brains simply could not withstand the strain of an intellectual education. Dorothea Beale (1831–1906), a pioneer in girls' education in England, established one of the first academically oriented high schools for girls in London in the 1850s, but she faced an uphill battle in persuading reluctant parents to allow her to teach their daughters mathematics. In France, feminists achieved their goal of a state-funded and state-run system of secondary schools for girls in the 1880s. They lost the battle for a university-preparatory curriculum, however, which made it difficult for girls to pass the exams necessary to enter the French university system.

Not surprisingly, the number of women in French universities remained very small throughout this period. Opportunities for university education for women varied enormously. In the United States, women accounted for one-third of all students in higher education as early as 1880, while in Germany, women were not admitted to full-time university study until 1901. In Russia, the development of women's higher education was particularly sporadic. Full-time university study became available to women in Moscow in 1872, and by 1880, women in Russia had some of the best opportunities for higher education in all of Europe. But the involvement of Sofiia Perovskaia—an educated woman—in the assassination of Tsar Alexander II in 1881 convinced the authorities that revolutionary politics and advanced female education went hand in hand. Most educational avenues for Russian women were blocked for more than two decades after the assassination.

Despite such limitations and reverses, the range of jobs open to women did broaden during this period. In 1900, French women won the right to practice law, and in 1903

On the Way to School
By the 1880s, the sight of middle-class girls in secondary and university education was not yet commonplace, but no longer rare.

in the French city of Toulouse, a woman lawyer presented a case in a European court for the first time. In 1906, the physicist and Nobel Prize winner Marie Curie became the first woman to hold a university faculty position in France. By the opening decades of the twentieth century, women doctors, although still unusual, were not unheard of. In Russia, women accounted for 10 percent of all physicians by 1914.

No More Angels

The campaigns for women's legal rights and an expansion of employment and educational opportunities helped women move out of the private and into the public sphere. But the third goal of feminist activity—to eradicate the double standard of sexual conduct—posed a more radical challenge to nineteenth-century middle-class culture and its ideology of separate spheres. By arguing that the same moral standards should apply to both men and women, feminists questioned whether two separate spheres should exist at all.

The ideology of separate spheres glorified women's moral purity and held that the more aggressive, more animal-like natures of men naturally resulted in such male pastimes as heavy drinking and sexual adventurism. The laws as well as the wider culture reflected these assumptions. For example, in France, a woman with an illegitimate child could not institute a paternity suit against the father: Premarital sex was a crime for the woman, but not for the man. Similarly, the English divorce legislation of 1857 declared that a woman's adultery was all that was necessary for a husband to sue for divorce, but a man's adultery was not a sufficient reason to end a marriage. For a wife to divorce her husband, she had to prove that he had committed additional crimes such as bigamy, incest, or bestiality.

To feminists, applying different moral standards to men and women degraded men and blocked women's efforts to better their own lives and society as a whole. As the French feminist leader Maria Desraismes explained, "To say that woman is an angel is to impose on her, in a sentimental and admiring fashion, all duties, and to reserve for oneself all rights. . . . I decline the honor of being an angel."[10]

In their effort to erase the moral distinctions between men and women, feminists fought on a variety of fronts. One key area of struggle was the regulation of prostitution. By the 1870s, many European countries, as well as the United States, had established procedures that made it safer for men to hire prostitutes, while still treating the women involved as criminals. In England, the Contagious Diseases Act, passed in 1870 to address the problem of venereal disease, declared that any woman suspected of being a prostitute could be stopped by the police and required to undergo a genital exam. Men, however, were subject to no such indignities. Feminists such as Josephine Butler (1857–1942)

contended that such legislation made it easier for men to indulge their sexual appetites, while punishing the impoverished women who were forced to sell their bodies to feed themselves and their children. For almost twenty years Butler led a concerted campaign both to repeal the legislation that regulated prostitution and to focus public attention on the lack of employment opportunities for women.

Abuse of alcohol was another key battleground for the women's movement. Arguing that the socially accepted practice of heavy male drinking had devastating consequences for women, in the form of both family poverty and domestic violence, feminist activists backed the temperance or prohibitionist cause. The movement triumphed in the United States in 1919 when decades of agitation from groups such as the Women's Christian Temperance Union led to the passage of the Eighteenth Amendment prohibiting the manufacture and sale of alcoholic beverages. "Prohibition," however, did little to transform gender relations; instead, it simply created new ways for organized crime syndicates to make money. The American prohibition experiment ended in 1933 with the repeal of the Eighteenth Amendment.

In general, feminist moral reform campaigns achieved only limited success. The regulation of prostitution did end in England in 1886 and in the United States, France, and the Scandinavian countries by 1914, but remained in effect in Germany. By 1884 in France, a husband's adultery, like a wife's, could end a marriage, but in England, the grounds for divorce remained differentiated by gender until 1923. In all European countries and in the United States, the sexual double standard remained embedded in both middle- and working-class culture far into the twentieth century.

The Fight for Women's Suffrage

The slow pace and uneven progress on both the legal and moral fronts convinced many feminists that they would achieve their goals only if they possessed the political clout of the *national* suffrage. In 1867 the National Society for Women's Suffrage was founded in Britain; over the next three decades suffrage societies emerged on the Continent. The French suffragist Hubertine Auclert (1848–1914) described the vote as "the keystone that will give [women] all other rights." As the editor of *La Citoyenne* ("The Citizeness"), Auclert agitated for full citizenship rights for adult women. In an imaginative move, she refused to pay taxes, on the grounds of "no taxation without representation." Auclert was also the first woman to describe herself as a "feminist," a word that entered the English language from the French around 1890.

Auclert and other American and European suffragists had little success. Only in Finland (1906) and Norway (1913) did women gain the national franchise in this period. (By 1913, women also possessed the vote in twelve American

DOCUMENT

In Favor of the Vote for Women

Many supporters of women's suffrage believed that education, reason, and persuasion would achieve the vote. If suffragists made their case in logical, reasonable terms, they would be able to convince a majority of male voters of the rightness of their cause. This excerpt from a French suffragist pamphlet, published in 1913, is very typical both in its effort to persuade its reader through a careful marshaling of factual evidence and in its belief that the women's vote would transform political life. French women did not win the vote for another thirty years.

We are going to try to prove that the vote for women is a just, possible and desirable reform. . . .

A woman has responsibility in the family; she ought to be consulted about the laws establishing her rights and duties with respect to her husband, her children, her parents.

Women work—and in ever greater numbers; a statistic of 1896 established that . . . the number of women workers was 35 per cent of the total number of workers, both male and female.

If she is in business, she, like any businessman, has interests to protect. . . .

If a woman is a worker or a domestic, she ought to participate as a man does in voting on unionization laws, laws covering workers' retirement, social security, the limitation and regulation of work hours, weekly days off, labor contracts, etc.

. . .

Finally, her special characteristics of order, economy, patience and resourcefulness will be as useful to society as the characteristics of man and will favor the establishment of laws too often overlooked until now.

The woman's vote will assure the establishment of important social laws.

All women will want:

To fight against alcoholism, from which they suffer much more than men;

To establish laws of health and welfare;

To obtain the regulation of female and child labor;

To defend young women against prostitution;

Finally, to prevent wars and to submit conflicts among nations to courts of arbitration.

Source: From a report presented to Besancon Municipal Council by the Franc-Comtois Group of the Union Française pour le Suffrage des Femmes. Besancon, March 1913, pp. 6–9.

states.) The social upheaval of World War I brought women the vote in Russia (1917), Britain (1918), Germany (1919), Austria (1919), the Netherlands (1919), and the United States (1920). Women in Italy had to wait until 1945; French women did not gain the vote until 1946, Greek women not until 1949. Women in Switzerland did not vote until 1971.

Feminists faced a number of significant obstacles in their battle for the national franchise. In Catholic countries such as France and Italy, the women's suffrage movement failed to become a political force not only because the Church remained fiercely opposed to the women's vote, but also because in Catholicism—in its veneration of the Virgin Mary and other female saints, in its exaltation of family life, in the opportunity for religious vocation as a nun—women found a great many avenues for emotional expression and intellectual satisfaction. Feminism had a much harder time taking root in these countries.

In central and eastern Europe the obstacles were even greater. In much of this region, economic development was far behind that of the western areas of Europe, and thus middle-class culture—the social base of feminism—was also underdeveloped. In the Russian Empire, the middle class was small and any political organization independent of the tsar was seen as a form of treason. No women's suffrage movement existed there until the Revolution of 1905 dramatically changed the political equation. After the revolution won the vote for men but failed to extend it to

women, an organized and vocal women's suffrage campaign emerged.

In contrast to Russia, in England the middle class was both large and politically powerful, and the political structure had shown itself capable of adaptation and evolution. Yet even in England, the site of the first and the strongest European female suffrage movement, women failed to win the vote in the nineteenth century. As a result, a small group of activists resorted to more radical tactics. Led by the imposing mother-and-daughters team of Emmeline (1858–1928), Christabel (1880–1958), and Sylvia Pankhurst (1882–1960), the suffragettes° formed a breakaway women's suffrage group in 1903. Convinced that the mainstream suffragists' tactics such as signing petitions, publishing reasoned arguments, and lobbying politicians would never win the vote, the suffragettes threw respectability to the winds. They adopted as their motto the slogan "Deeds, Not Words," and declared that women would never earn the vote through rational persuasion. Instead, they had to grab it by force. The suffragettes broke up political meetings with the cry "Votes for Women!," chained themselves to the steps of the Houses of Parliament, shattered shop windows, burned churches, destroyed mailboxes, and even, in a direct attack on a cherished citadel of male middle-class culture, vandalized golf courses.

In opting for violence, the suffragettes staged a full frontal assault on a central fortification of middle-class culture—the ideal of the passive, homebound woman. The fortress they were attacking proved well-defended, however. Their opponents reacted with fury. Police broke up suffragette rallies with sexually focused brutality: They dragged suffragettes by their hair, stomped on their crotches, punched their breasts, and tore off their blouses. Once in jail, hunger-striking suffragettes endured the horror of forced feedings. Several jailers pinned the woman to her bed while the doctor thrust a plastic tube down her throat, often lacerating her larynx in the process, and pumped in food until she gagged.

Conclusion

The West in an Age of Mass Politics

The clash between the suffragettes and their jailers was only one of a multitude of encounters, many of them violent, among those seeking access to political power and those seeking to limit that access, in the era from 1870 to the start of World War I in 1914. At the same time, changing patterns of industrialization and accelerated urbanization gave rise to other sorts of encounters—between the manager seeking to cut production costs and the employee aiming to protect his wages, for example, or among the newly arrived immigrants in the city, struggling to survive in an unfamiliar culture, and the long-established residents who spoke a different language.

Out of such encounters emerged key questions about the definition of "the West." Where, for example, did the West end? Did it include Russia? "Yes," replied the small revolutionary groups who embraced Karl Marx's socialist theories and argued that Russia would follow Western patterns of economic and political development. Other Russian revolutionaries, however, rejected Western models and sought a revolutionary path unique to Russia. The expansion of the franchise and the processes of making nations raised even more fundamental questions. Was the West defined by democracy? Should it be? Was it synonymous with white, western European men or could people with olive-colored or black skin—or women of any color—participate fully in Western culture and politics? Was "the West" defined by its rationality? In the eighteenth century, Enlightenment thinkers had praised the power of human rationality and looked to reason as the path to social improvement. The rise of a new style of politics, based on emotional appeal and often irrational racist hatred, challenged this faith in reason. But at the same time, developments in industrial organization and technologies, which helped expand European national incomes, seemed to point to the benefits of rational processes.

As we will see in the next chapter, the expansion of Western control over vast areas of Asia and Africa in this period led an increasing number of Europeans and Americans to highlight economic prosperity and technological superiority as the defining characteristics of the West. Confidence, however, was accompanied by anxiety as these years also witnessed a far-reaching cultural and intellectual crisis. Closely connected to the development of mass politics and changes in social and gender relations, this crisis slowly eroded many of the pillars of middle- and upper-class society and raised searching questions about Western assumptions and values.

Suggestions for Further Reading

For a comprehensive listing of suggested readings, please go to www.ablongman.com/levack2e/chapter22

Evans, Richard. *The Feminists: Women's Emancipation Movements in Europe, America, and Australasia, 1840–1920.* 1977. A helpful comparative overview.

Kern, Stephen. *The Culture of Time and Space, 1880–1918.* 1983. An innovative work that explores the cultural impact of technological change.

Lidtke, Vernon. *The Alternative Culture: Socialist Labor in Imperial Germany.* 1985. Looks beyond the world of parliamentary politics to assess the meaning and impact of working-class socialism.

Lindemann, Albert. *Esau's Tears: Modern Anti-Semitism and the Rise of the Jews.* 1997. A comprehensive and detailed survey that challenges many assumptions about the roots and nature of modern anti-Semitism.

Mayer, Arno. *The Persistence of the Old Regime: Europe to the Great War.* 1981. Argues that landed elites maintained a considerable amount of economic and political power throughout the nineteenth century.

Milward, A. S., and S. B. Saul. *The Development of the Economies of Continental Europe, 1850–1914.* 1977. A helpful survey.

Moch, Leslie. *Moving Europeans: Migration in Western Europe Since 1650.* 1992. Filled with maps and packed with information, Moch's work explodes many easy assumptions about the movement of Europeans in the nineteenth century.

Nord, Philip. *The Republican Moment: Struggles for Democracy in Nineteenth-Century France.* 1996. Illuminates the struggle to define and redefine France.

Pilbeam, Pamela. *The Middle Classes in Europe, 1789–1914: France, Germany, Italy, and Russia.* 1990. A comparative approach that helps clarify the patterns of social change.

Richards, Thomas. *The Commodity Culture of Victorian England: Advertising and Spectacle, 1851–1914.* 1990. Fascinating study of the manufacturing of desire.

Stearns, Peter N. *Lives of Labor: Work in a Maturing Industrial Society.* 1975. Explores changing economic and social patterns.

Steenson, Gary P. *After Marx, Before Lenin: Marxism and Socialist Working-Class Parties in Europe, 1884–1914.* 1991. Examines both ideology and political practice within Europe's socialist parties.

Weber, Eugen. *Peasants into Frenchmen: The Modernization of Rural France, 1870–1914.* 1976. A very important work that helped shape the way historians think about "nation making."

Notes

1. Leslie Moch, *Moving Europeans: Migration in Western Europe Since 1650* (1992), 147.

2. Quoted in Eugen Weber, *Peasants into Frenchmen: The Modernization of Rural France, 1870–1914* (1976), 332–333.

3. Norman Kleeblatt, *The Dreyfus Affair: Art, Truth, and Justice* (1987), 96.

4. Quoted in Eric Cahm, *The Dreyfus Affair in French Society and Politics* (1994), 167.

5. Quoted in Robert Gildea, *Barricades and Borders: Europe, 1800–1914* (1987), 317.

6. Quoted in Leslie Derfler, *Socialism Since Marx: A Century of the European Left* (1973), 58.

7. Karl Kautsky, quoted in Eric Hobsbawm, *The Age of Empire, 1875–1914* (1987), 133.

8. Eugen Weber, *France, Fin-de-Siècle* (1986), 126.

9. Albert Lindemann, *Esau's Tears: Modern Anti-Semitism and the Rise of the Jews* (1997).

10. Maria Desraismes, "La Femme et Le Droit," *Eve dans l'humanite* (1891), 16–17.

The West and the World: Cultural Crisis and the New Imperialism, 1870–1914

23

I N THE AUTUMN OF 1898, BRITISH TROOPS MOVED INTO THE SUDAN IN NORTH-east Africa to claim the region for the British Empire. On September 2, the British Camel Corps faced an army of 40,000 fighters. The Sudanese soldiers, Islamic believers known as dervishes who possessed a reputation for military fierceness, were fighting on their home ground against an invading force. Nevertheless, after only five hours of fighting, 11,000 dervishes lay dead. Their opponents lost just forty men. While the dervishes, armed with swords and spears, surged forward in a full-scale frontal assault, the British troops sat safely behind fortified defenses, and, using repeating rifles and Maxim guns (a type of early machine gun), simply mowed down their attackers. According to one participant on the British side, the future prime minister Winston Churchill, the biggest danger to the British soldiers during the battle of Omdurman was boredom: "The mere physical act [of loading, firing, and reloading] became tedious." The dervishes had little chance of boredom. Churchill recalled, "And all the time out on the plain on the other side bullets were shearing through flesh, smashing and splintering bone; blood spouted from terrible wounds; valiant men were struggling through a hell of whistling metal, exploding shells, and spurting dust—suffering, despairing, dying."[1]

The slaughter of 11,000 Sudanese in just over five hours formed but one episode in what many historians call the age of new imperialism, a period that witnessed both the culmination of, and a new phase in, Europe's conquest of the globe. This often-violent encounter between Europe and the regions that Europeans emphatically defined as non-Western was closely connected to the political and economic upheavals examined in Chapter 22. An understanding of the new imperialism, however, demands a close look not

Paul Gauguin, *Matamoe* ("Peacocks in the Country"), 1892 The Fauvist painter Paul Gauguin fled Europe for Tahiti in an effort to restore to his art the strong colors and emotions that he believed characterized non-Western cultures. The sights, sensibilities, and symbolism of Tahitian society profoundly affected his painting—and helped shape modernist art.

only at political rivalries and economic structures, but also at scientific, intellectual, and cultural developments in the last third of the nineteenth century. At the same time that European and American adventurers risked life and limb to chart Africa's rivers, exploit its resources, and subjugate its peoples, Western artists and scientists embarked on explorations into worlds of thought and perception far deeper than the surface reality accessible to the senses, and in so doing challenged the social order and even the meaning of reality itself. The final decades of the nineteenth century and the opening years of the twentieth thus comprised an era of internal fragmentation and external expansion.

This chapter examines the scientific, artistic, and physical explorations that characterized the period between 1870 and 1914 to answer a key question: In what ways did these explorations redefine the West and its relationship with the rest of the world? Three more specific questions guide this examination:

- **How did scientific developments during this period lead to not only greater intellectual and cultural optimism but also deepened anxiety?**
- **What factors led many Europeans in this period to believe they were living in a time of cultural crisis?**
- **What were the causes and consequences of the new imperialist ideology for both the West and non-Western societies?**

Scientific Transformations

- **How did scientific developments during this period lead to not only greater intellectual and cultural optimism but also deepened anxiety?**

During the final third of the nineteenth century, Europeans encountered in new ways both the human body and the wider physical universe. Forced by urbanization to cram more bodies into limited space, men and women grew increasingly aware of the human body, and of the way it interacted with other bodies, both human and microscopic. At the same time, the work of geologists and biologists highlighted the way the body itself had evolved to meet the challenges of survival, while the experiments of chemists and physicists revealed the inadequacies of accepted models for understanding the physical world.

These developments affirmed a central assumption of the dominant middle-class worldview—that human reason and endeavor can guarantee social, intellectual, and moral progress. Scientific advances in the final third of the nineteenth century helped improve the health and hygiene of the Western world. Yet these changes in scientific understandings of both the body and the cosmos also threatened

to destabilize Western society and therefore deepened the cultural anxiety of Europeans and Americans in this period.

Medicine and Microbes

In the second half of the nineteenth century, and particularly after 1870, a series of developments transformed the practice of Western medicine. Before this time, Western physicians assumed that illness was caused by bad blood and so relied on practices such as leeching (attaching leeches to the skin) and bloodletting (slicing open a vein). These procedures drained large amounts of blood, further weakening already ill patients. Admission into a hospital was sometimes a death sentence. Ignorant of the existence of bacteria and viruses, doctors commonly attended one patient after another without bothering to wash their hands or surgical instruments. The only anesthetic available was alcohol; pain was regarded as inevitable, something to be endured rather than eased.

Urbanization posed a fundamental challenge to such traditional medical practice and helped transform Western medicine. Expanding urban populations served as fertile seedbeds for contagious diseases. Cholera outbreaks, such as the epidemics that ravaged British cities in 1831 and 1848, forced doctors and public officials to pay attention to the relationship between overcrowding, polluted water, and epidemic disease. Hamburg was one of the first cities to undertake the construction of a modern water and sewer system in 1842; in 1848 the London cholera epidemic persuaded public officials to build a vast sewer system (most of which is still in use today).

It was not until the 1860s, however, that germ theory was developed. By exploring the transmission of disease among plants and animals in the French agricultural industry, the chemist Louis Pasteur (1822–1895) discovered the source of contagion to be microscopic living organisms—bacteria. Astonishingly productive, Pasteur developed vaccines against anthrax, hog fever, sheep pox, various poultry and cattle diseases, and rabies. (His process of purifying milk and fermented products is still known as pasteurization.) Following Pasteur, Robert Koch (1843–1910), professor of public health in Berlin, isolated the tuberculosis bacillus in 1882 and the bacteria that cause cholera in 1883.

The work of Pasteur, Koch, and other scientists in tracing the transmission of disease was crucial in improving Western medical practice. Between 1872 and 1900, the number of European deaths from infectious diseases dropped by 60 percent. Once physicians and surgeons accepted that microscopic organisms caused disease, they began to develop techniques to control their spread. The development of antiseptic surgery in the later 1860s improved the patient's odds of surviving the operating table.

The increasing use of anesthetics in the second half of the nineteenth century also improved those odds. In 1847 a

Scottish physician performed the first delivery of a baby using chloroform to dull the mother's pain. Although condemned by many Christian theologians (who regarded pain as both ennobling and a necessary part of sinful human existence), the use of anesthetics spread fairly quickly. Britain's Queen Victoria, who gave birth to nine children, probably articulated the feelings of many patients when she greeted the use of anesthetics in the delivery room with unfettered delight: "Oh blessed chloroform!"

Medical advances such as anesthetic techniques and an understanding of how diseases are spread gave Europeans genuine confidence that the conquest of nature through science would create a healthier environment. But the widespread awareness of germs also heightened anxiety. Isolation of the bacilli that caused an illness did not immediately translate into its cure, and viral infections remained often lethal. Measles, for example, continued to kill at least 7,000 people per year in Britain throughout the nineteenth century. After the 1870s, Europeans were aware that they lived in a world populated by potentially deadly but invisible organisms, carried on the bodies of their servants, their employees, their neighbors, and their family members. Those who could afford to isolate themselves from the danger often did so. As a result, this era witnessed striking growth in the number of seaside resorts as middle- and upper-class Europeans fled from urban centers of contagion.

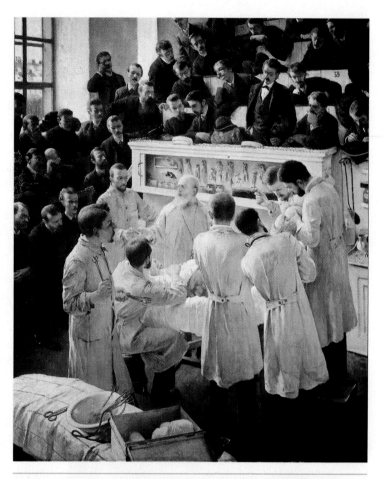

Adelbert Seligmann, *German Surgeon Theodor Billroth at Work in Vienna* (1890)

Modern surgery in the making: The patient has been anesthetized, but the modern operating room does not yet exist, nor are the doctors wearing gloves or masks. Billroth, the director of the Second Surgical Clinic in Vienna, pioneered surgical techniques for gastrointestinal illnesses and cancer.

The Triumph of Evolutionary Science

Developments in geology and biology also led to both confidence and anxiety. Evolutionary science provided a scientific framework in which educated Europeans could understand and justify their own superior social and economic positions. It also, however, challenged basic religious assumptions and depicted the natural world in new and unsettling ways.

Traditionally, Europeans had relied on the opening chapters of the Bible to understand the origins of both nature and humanity. By the 1830s, however, the work of geologists challenged the biblical account. Although a literal reading of the Bible dated the Earth at only 6,000 years old, geologists such as Charles Lyell (1797–1875) argued on the basis of the fossil record and existing geological formations that the Earth had formed over millions of years. Lyell's most famous work was the *Principles of Geology,* first published in 1830 and a nineteenth-century best-seller that

went through eleven editions. In three volumes of very readable prose, packed with illustrative examples, Lyell gently but rigorously refuted the orthodox Christian position that geological change and the extinction of species could be explained by the biblical account of the flood or other such supernatural interventions. Instead, he and others argued that the material world must be seen as the product of natural forces still at work, still observable today.

But how could one explain the tremendous variety of plant and animal species in the world on the basis of natural processes? In 1859, the British scientist Charles Darwin (1809–1882) answered this question in a way that proved quite satisfying to large numbers of educated Europeans—and quite horrifying to others. Darwin had spent two decades thinking about the data he collected during a five-year expedition to the South Pacific in the 1830s. Serving as an unpaid naturalist on the H.M.S. *Beagle* between 1831

Darwin's Disturbing Mirror
Simplified and often ridiculous versions of Darwin's ideas almost immediately entered popular culture. Here a monkey version of Darwin holds up a mirror to his fellow creature, who seems surprised by his reflection.

Darwin concluded that life is a struggle for survival, and that even quite small biological variations might help an individual member of a species win out in this struggle. From this understanding came the Darwinian theory° of the evolution of species.

Darwin's evolutionary hypothesis rested on two basic ideas: *variation* and *natural selection.* Variation refers to the small but crucial biological advantages that assist in the struggle for survival: A bird with a slightly longer beak, for example, might gain easier access to scarce food supplies. Over generations, the individuals more adapted for survival displace those without the positive variation. Variation, then, provides the means of natural selection, the process by which new species evolve.

Darwin provided a persuasive explanation for evolutionary change, but the fact that the laws of genetic heredity were not yet understood resulted in two key weaknesses in his formulation—first, its extreme gradualness, in that the process of variation required many, many generations; and second, the lack of a precise explanation of how variations first emerge and how they are inherited. Answers to both problems lay embedded in the research of an Austrian monk, Gregor Mendel (1822–1884). Experimenting in his vegetable garden with what we now call selective breeding, Mendel developed the laws of genetic heredity. Mendel's work was ignored almost completely until the end of the century, when the Dutch botanist Hugo DeVries (1848–1935) used his data to hypothesize that evolution occurred through radical mutations in the reproductive cells of an organism. These mutations are passed on to offspring at the moment of reproduction and, if they offer an advantage in the struggle for existence, enable the offspring to survive and to produce more mutant offspring. Thus evolution can proceed by leaps, rather than gradually over a very long period of time.

Long before these genetic underpinnings of evolution were understood, however, Darwin's theories proved extraordinarily influential. Published in 1859, *The Origin of Species* aroused immediate interest and controversy. This controversy intensified when, in 1871, Darwin published *The Descent of Man,* in which he firmly placed humanity itself within the evolutionary process. Many Christians reacted with horror to a theory that they believed challenged the biblical narrative of Creation and denied a special place for humankind within the physical universe. But the most troubling aspect of Darwin's theory was its view of nature. According to orthodox Christian theology, nature, like the Bible, reveals God to the believer. In the Darwinian universe, however, nature was not a harmonious, well-ordered system that revealed the hand of God. Instead, it was the arena of brutal and bloody competition for survival—"nature red in tooth and claw," as the British poet Alfred Lord Tennyson put it. In such a universe, ideas of purpose and

DOCUMENT

On Darwin
(1860s)

and 1836, Darwin observed that certain species of animal and plant life, isolated on islands, had developed differently from related species on the coast. After returning to Britain, Darwin read the population theory of Thomas Malthus (1766–1834). Malthus argued that population growth would outstrip food supply, and that in all species, more offspring are produced than can actually survive. Putting together Malthus's theory with his own observations,

DOCUMENT

The Descent of Man

First published in 1871, The Descent of Man *continued and completed Charles Darwin's theory of the evolution of species first introduced in his* Origin of Species *(1859). Darwin's work in many ways affirmed central prejudices and assumptions of his middle-class readers, as the following excerpts demonstrate.*

We have now seen that man is variable in body and mind; and that the variations are induced, either directly or indirectly, by the same general causes, and obey the same general laws, as with the lower animals. Man has spread widely over the face of the earth, and must have been exposed, during his incessant migration, to the most diversified conditions. . . . The early progenitors of man must also have tended, like all other animals, to have increased beyond their means of subsistence; they must, therefore, occasionally have been exposed to a struggle for existence, and consequently, to the rigid law of natural selection. Beneficial variations of all kinds will thus, either occasionally or habitually, have been preserved and injurious ones eliminated. . . .

Man in the rudest state in which he now exists is the most dominant animal that has ever appeared on this earth. He has spread more widely than any other highly organised form, and all others have yielded before him. He manifestly owes this immense superiority to his intellectual faculties, to his social habits, which lead him to aid and defend his fellows, and to his corporeal structure. . . .

The belief that there exists in man some close relation between the size of the brain and the development of the intellectual faculties is supported by the comparison of the skulls of savage and civilized races, of ancient and modern people, and by the analogy of the whole vertebrate series . . . the mean internal capacity of the skull in Europeans is 92.3 cubic inches; in Americans 87.5; in Asiatics 87.1; and in Australians only 81.9 inches. . . . Nevertheless, it must be admitted that some skulls of very high antiquity, such as the famous one of the Neanderthal, are well developed and capacious.

Source: From *The Descent of Man,* 2nd edition, by Charles Darwin, 1874.

---

meaning seemed to disappear. Faced with this disturbing vision, many Christians opposed Darwinian science.

Many other Christians, however, welcomed Darwin's evolutionary theory. They argued that evolution did not banish divine purpose from the universe but instead showed God's hand at work in the gradual development of more perfect species. Enthusiastically applying the idea of evolution to the ethical universe, they contended that the history of humanity showed that the morally fittest proved victorious in the ethical sphere, just as the strongest triumphed in the natural world.

By 1870, three-quarters of British scientists surveyed accepted evolutionary theory. More important, many middle-class Europeans and Americans welcomed Darwin's ideas as providing a coherent explanation of change that accorded with their worldview. They saw Darwin's work as a scientific confirmation of their faith in the virtues of competition and in the inevitability of progress. As Darwin himself wrote in *The Origin of Species,* because "natural selection works solely by and for the good of each being, all corporeal [bodily] and mental development will tend to progress toward perfection."

Social Darwinism and Racial Hierarchies

Darwin's explanation of evolution contributed to a new understanding of biological relationships and of the connections between humanity and the natural world. In the last quarter of the nineteenth century, however, a growing number of writers and social theorists insisted that evolutionary theory could and should be applied more broadly. One of the most influential of this group was the British writer Herbert Spencer (1820–1902). Trained as a civil engineer, Spencer became convinced that evolution held the key to engineering a better human society. A self-confident, eminently practical thinker, Spencer coined the phrase "the survival of the fittest" to describe what he viewed as the most basic explanation of development in both nature and human society. He believed that human societies evolve like plant and animal species. Only the fittest, those able to adapt to changing conditions, survive. A great champion of *laissez-faire* economics (see Chapter 21), Spencer contended that government interference in economic and social affairs interfered with the natural evolutionary process and so hindered rather than assured progress.

Spencer's essentially biological vision of society proved influential in shaping the theories of Social Darwinism°. Arguing that racial hierarchy was the product of natural evolution, the Social Darwinists applied Spencer's ideas about the importance of individual competition and the survival of the fittest to entire races. In their view, the non-white races in Africa and Asia had lost the game. Their so-called backward way of life showed they had failed to compete successfully with white Europeans and thus displayed their biological inferiority. The very popular British novelist Rider Haggard, in his best-selling thriller *She* (1887), summed up the Social Darwinist worldview: "Those who are weak must perish; the earth is to the strong . . . We run to place and power over the dead bodies of those who fail and fall; ay, we win the food we eat from out the mouths of starving babes. It is the scheme of things."

In their effort to construct a scientifically based racial hierarchy, Social Darwinists made use not only of Darwin's idea of natural selection but also of the theory of "recapitulation," first proposed by the German zoologist Ernst Haeckel (1834–1919). According to Haeckel, as an individual matures, he or she moves through the same stages as did the human race during the course of its evolution. For example, the gill slits of a human embryo "recapitulate" the fish stage through which the human race had evolved. The idea of recapitulation enabled scientists to fill in the gaps left by the fossil record. By observing the development of children into adults, they argued, we can witness the evolutionary maturation of the human race.

Social Darwinists used the theory of recapitulation to argue that only white European males had reached the pinnacle of evolutionary development. They contended that nonwhite men, as well as all women, embodied the more primitive stages of evolution through which the white European male had already passed. In other words, the nonwhite races and white women were suffering from arrested development. Their bodies and brains bore witness to their low-ranking position on the evolutionary ladder. Such ideas permeated much of Western culture in the late nineteenth century. Sigmund Freud, for example, argued that "the female genitalia are more primitive than those of the male," while Gustave LeBon compared the average female brain to that of a gorilla. G. A. Henty, a best-selling British novelist, insisted that the "intelligence of the average negro is about equal to that of a European [male] child of ten years old."[2]

Firmly convinced that the inferiority of women and nonwhites was a biological fact, nineteenth-century scientists and large sections of the European public welcomed evolutionary theory as scientific proof of deeply embedded cultural assumptions, such as the benefits of competition, the rightness of white rule and male dominance, and the superiority of Western civilization. Yet evolutionary science also worked to undermine European confidence because with the idea of evolution came the possibility of regression: Was the traffic on the evolutionary ladder all one-way, or could species descend to a lower evolutionary level? Could humanity regress to its animal origins?

The concept of the "inheritance of acquired characteristics," associated with the work of the French scientist Jean-Baptiste Lamarck (1744–1829), played a crucial role in fostering these fears of regression. More than fifty years before Darwin published his *Origin of Species,* Lamarck theorized that acquired characteristics—traits that an individual develops in response to experience or the environment, such as

the stooped back of a miner, the poor vision of a lace maker, or the deep tan of an agricultural laborer—could be passed on to the individual's offspring. Because the process of genetic reproduction was not understood until the twentieth century, Lamarck's theories remained very influential throughout the nineteenth century and possessed deeply disturbing implications. Middle-class Europeans began to speculate that the conditions of urban industrial life were producing undesirable characteristics among urban workers. In their view, characteristics such as physical weakness, sexual promiscuity, and violent criminality were being passed from one generation to the next and were threatening to reverse the evolutionary ascent of Western civilization.

The Revolution in Physics

Darwin's work revolutionized the field of biology. Between 1880 and 1910 a revolution in physics occurred as well. Although the most dramatic consequences of this revolution—atomic weapons and nuclear energy—would not be realized for another half century, this transformation in scientific understanding contributed to both the exhilaration and the uncertainty that characterized the intellectual and cultural history of Europe in the decades before World War I.

At the core of the revolution in physics lay the question, "What is matter?" For most of the nineteenth century, the answer was simple: Matter was what close observation and measurement, as well as common sense, showed it to be. Material bodies, made up of the building blocks called atoms, rested and moved against a fixed backdrop of space and time. Matter was three-dimensional, defined by height, width, and depth. Accessible to reason, observation, and common sense, the material world could be understood and controlled. The triumph of the theories of Isaac Newton had ensured that for 200 years, educated Westerners regarded the natural world as a precise and predictable machine (see Chapter 16).

As the new century opened, this picture of the universe began to crumble. A series of discoveries and experiments challenged this commonsense view of the universe and offered in its place a much more mysterious and unsettling vista. The discovery of the X-ray in 1895 had already disrupted prevailing assumptions about the solidity and predictability of matter. They were shaken even further in 1898 when the Polish-French chemist Marie Curie (1867–1934) discovered a new element, radium, which did not behave the way matter was supposed to behave. Because it continually emitted subatomic particles, radium did not possess a constant atomic weight. Two years later, the German scientist Max Planck (1858–1947) theorized that a heated body radiates energy not in the continuous, steady, predictable stream most scientists envisaged, but rather in irregular clumps, which he called *quanta.* Although at first dismissed by most scientists as contrary to common sense, Planck's quantum theory accorded with the emerging picture of a changeable universe.

These scientific discoveries provide the context for the work of Albert Einstein (1879–1955), certainly the most famous and readily recognizable scientist of the twentieth century. Bored by his job as a patent clerk, Einstein passed the time speculating on the nature of the cosmos. In 1905, he rang the death knell for the Newtonian universe by publishing an article that introduced to the world the theory of relativity. Einstein rejected the nineteenth-century assumption of the absolute nature of time and space. Instead, he argued, time and space shift relative to the position of the observer. Similarly, matter itself shifts. Mass depends on motion, and thus time, space, and matter intermingle in a universe of relative flux. The result of Einstein's vision was a revolution in perspective. The universe is not three- but four-dimensional: To height, width, and depth, Einstein added *time*.

This new understanding was much harder to grasp than that offered by Newtonian science. With the revolution in physics, much of science became incomprehensible to ordinary men and women, even educated ones. The new science also challenged the basic assumptions that governed nineteenth-century thought by offering a vision of the universe in which what you see is *not* what you get, in which objective reality might well be the product of subjective perception.

Social Thought: The Revolt Against Positivism

Just as the revolution in physics presented a new and more disturbing picture of the physical universe, so social thinkers in the last third of the nineteenth century began to formulate troubling theories about the nature of human society. As Chapter 21 explained, the mainstream of nineteenth-century thought was positivist: It placed great faith in human reason and therefore in the validity of applying methods drawn from the natural sciences to the study of human affairs. Positivism viewed the world as eminently knowable and progress as ultimately guaranteed, given the capacity of rational human beings to understand and therefore control both physical and human nature. This faith in human reason, however, came under attack in the last decades of the century. In this era, social thinkers (writers and scientists whose work would lay the foundations for new academic disciplines such as sociology, psychology, and anthropology) began to emphasize the role of nonrational forces in determining human conduct.

Social thinkers confronted the power of the nonrational first in the new mass politics of this era. The rise of racist and nationalist political parties demonstrated that individuals were often swayed more by emotion than by rational argument. In an effort to understand and therefore to manipulate political demonstrations, the French theorist Gustave LeBon (1841–1931) developed the discipline of crowd or collective psychology. He showed how appeals to emotion, particularly in the form of symbols and myths, can influence crowd behavior. In LeBon's view, democracy relinquished political control to the easily swayed masses and so would lead only to disaster.

Unlike LeBon, the German social theorist Max Weber (1864–1920) believed in democracy, but he, too, recognized the role of the nonrational in influencing the mass electorate. Weber was both fascinated and frightened by the development of modern industrial society. His studies focused on the "bureaucratization" of modern life—the tendency of both political and economic institutions to become increasingly standardized and to grow ever larger and more impersonal. Weber judged the triumph of bureaucracy as the victory of reason and science over individual prejudice and interest-group politics, and so as a generally progressive force. But at the same time he recognized that because growing bureaucracies could crush both ideals and individuals, they posed a real threat to personal and political freedom. Troubled by the vision of individuals trapped within "the iron cage of modern life," Weber in 1898 suffered a nervous breakdown. After four years Weber was able to free himself from the grip of debilitating depression, but he remained profoundly pessimistic about the future, which he described as "a polar night of icy darkness and hardness."[3]

According to his wife, when Weber fell into depression, "an evil something out of the subterranean unconscious . . . grasped him by its claws."[4] This view of the individual as a captive of the unconscious was central to the revolt against positivism and reached its fullest development in the highly influential work of the Viennese scientist and physician Sigmund Freud (1856–1939). Freud argued that the conscious mind plays only a very limited role in shaping the actions of each individual. His effort to treat patients suffering from nervous disorders led him to hypnosis and dream analysis, and to the conviction that behind the conscious exterior existed a deeper, far more significant reality—the unconscious. In *The Interpretation of Dreams* (1900), Freud argued that beneath the rational surface of each human being surge all kinds of hidden desires, including such irrational drives as the longing for death and destruction.

Freud thought of himself as a scientist. He believed that he could understand human behavior (and treat mental illness) by diving below the rational surface and exploring the submerged terrain of unconscious desire. Yet the emergence of Freudian psychology convinced many educated Western individuals not that the irrational could be uncovered and controlled, but rather that the irrational was *in* control.

Cultural Crisis: The Fin-de-Siècle and the Birth of Modernism

■ What factors led many Europeans in this period to believe they were living in a time of cultural crisis?

The growing recognition of the power of irrational forces in shaping human society contributed to a growing cultural crisis. The sense of crisis, and more specifically the fear that Western civilization was declining, that degeneration and decay characterized the contemporary experience, was summed up in a single French phrase: fin-de-siècle°. Literally translated as "end of the century," fin-de-siècle served as a shorthand term for the mood of cultural uneasiness, and even despair, that characterized much of European society in the final decades of the nineteenth century and the opening years of the twentieth. Uncertainty colored many aspects of European thought and culture. Fast-moving economic and social change, coupled with the new scientific ideas, convinced many Europeans that old solutions were no longer sufficient. The quest for new answers fostered the birth of what would become known as *modernism*, a broad label for a series of unsettling developments in thought, literature, and art. Many Europeans celebrated modernism as a release from the restraints imposed by middle-class cultural codes. Others, however, responded fearfully. Both exhilaration and anxiety, then, characterize this time of cultural crisis.

Edgar Degas, *Absinthe* (1876–1877)
Parisian café-goers often indulged in absinthe, a strong alcoholic drink flavored with anise. Degas's portrait of one such absinthe drinker is a picture of deterioration: This woman's lined face and weary posture, as well as her sense of isolation, provide an evocative image of the fin-de-siècle.

The Fin-de-Siècle

A series of social problems common to increasingly urbanized nations reinforced Europeans' fear of degeneration. As cities spread, so too did the perception of a rising crime rate. This perception of a more criminal society went hand-in-hand with the reality of increasing drug and alcohol use. Diners in high society finished their sumptuous meals with a dessert course consisting of strawberries soaked in ether; respectable bourgeois men offered each other cocaine as a quick "pick-me-up" at the end of the working day; middle-class mothers fed restless babies opium-laced syrups; workers bought enough opium-derived laudanum on Saturday afternoon to render them unconscious until work on Monday morning. Using Lamarck's theory of the inheritance of acquired characteristics, scientists contended that addictions could be passed on from generation to generation, thus contributing to national decline and a culture of decadence.

Popular novels of the fin-de-siècle also contributed to the fear of degeneration by depicting Western culture as diseased or barbaric. In a twenty-volume work, the French novelist Émile Zola (1840–1902) traced the decline of a once-proud family to symbolize the decay of all of France. As alcoholism and sexual promiscuity pollute succeeding generations, the family disintegrates. In *Nana* (1880), Zola used the title character, a prostitute, to embody his country. Watching as French soldiers march off to defeat in the Franco-Prussian War, Nana is dying of smallpox, her face "a charnel-house, a heap of pus and blood, a shovelful of putrid flesh."[5] Novels such as *Dr. Jekyll and Mr. Hyde* (1886) and *Dracula* (1897) showed that beneath the cultured exterior of a civilized man lurked a primitive, bloodthirsty beast and so revealed a deep sense of anxiety.

The most influential advocate of the idea that Western culture had degenerated was the German philosopher and poet Friedrich Nietzsche (1844–1900). In Nietzsche's view, most people were little more than sheep, penned in by outdated customs and conventions. Bourgeois morality, rooted in Christianity, helped sap Western culture of its vitality. "Christianity has taken the side of everything weak," Nietzsche claimed. He traced the weakness of Western culture beyond Christianity, however, and back to ancient Greece, to Socrates' exaltation of rationality. In Nietzsche's view, an overemphasis on rational thought had deprived Western culture of the power of more primal urges, such as the irrational, emotional, and instinctive aspects of human nature.

Even more fundamentally, Nietzsche argued that the belief that human reason has direct access to scientific fact is an illusion. Trained as a classical philologist, Nietzsche's study of language convinced him that everything we know must be filtered through a symbolic system—through language or some other means of artistic or mathematic representation. We can know only the representation, not the thing itself. Not even science can uncover "reality." Even the style of Nietzsche's publications worked to expose the limits of reason. Rather than write carefully constructed essays that proceeded in a logical, linear fashion from fact to fact, Nietzsche adopted an elusive, poetic style characterized by disconnected fragments, more accessible to intuitive understanding than to rational analysis.

Nietzsche's writings attracted little attention until the 1890s, when his ideas first exploded in Germany and Austria, and then spread throughout Europe. Nietzsche's call to "become what you are" attracted young enthusiasts, who embraced his conviction that the confining assumptions and aspirations of bourgeois society held back the individual from personal liberation. "God is dead," Nietzsche proclaimed, "and we have killed him." If God is dead, then "there is nobody who commands, nobody who obeys, nobody who trespasses."

Tightening Gender Boundaries

The fear of degeneration evident throughout European culture and society in the last decades of the nineteenth century also expressed itself in a multifaceted effort to draw more tightly the boundaries around accepted definitions of "maleness" and "femaleness." Both the feminist and the homosexual joined the alcoholic, the drug addict, the prostitute, and the criminal in the list of dangerous and degenerate beings.

As discussed in Chapter 22, the years after 1850 and particularly after 1880 witnessed the birth of modern feminism. The emergence of legal, educational, and political reform campaigns challenged nineteenth-century middle-class domestic ideology. Antifeminists viewed these campaigns with alarm. They insisted that a woman's physiology demanded that she remain in the home. In the view of antifeminists, a woman who chose political activism or paid employment not only risked her own physical and mental breakdown, she also tended to produce physically and morally degenerate children.

Like feminists, homosexuals were also singled out as threats to the social order. Before 1869, *homosexual* was not a word: Coined by a Hungarian scientist seeking a new label for a new concept, it entered the English language in 1890. Traditionally, Europeans and Americans had viewed same-sex sexual practice as a form of immoral behavior, indulged in by morally lax—but otherwise normal—men. (Few considered the possibility of female homosexual behavior.) In the last third of the nineteenth century, however, the emphasis shifted from *actions* to *identity*, from condemning a specific type of sexual behavior to denouncing a certain group of people now considered abnormal and dangerous. Scientists argued that "the homosexual" was diseased—and that he could communicate this disease to others.

These ideas gained in force as homosexual subcultures increased in number in European and American cities. The anonymity and mobility of urban life offered homosexuals the possibility of creating a space for themselves in which a new, more confident and assertive homosexual identity could be expressed. But these subcultures soon encountered fierce repression as the moral and medical condemnation of male homosexuality became enshrined in legislation. The Penal Code of the new Germany stipulated severe punishment for homosexuality, while the British government in 1885 made illegal all homosexual acts, even those between consenting adults in the privacy of their own home.

The new concern about homosexuality was nurtured by a wider anxiety about the man's role in society, an anxiety provoked not only by the challenge of feminism, but also by the economic changes associated with the rise of corporate capitalism (see Chapter 22). Required by liberal ideology to be aggressive, independent, self-reliant initiators, middle-class males increasingly found themselves bound to desks, demoted from being those who delivered orders to those who received them. No longer masters of their own fates, they were now bit players in the drama of corporate capitalism. Thus the fear of both feminism and homosexuality arose in part from the compelling need to shore up masculine identity.

The new science of sexuality also heightened this concern about the definition of the "normal" man and woman. During the final decades of the nineteenth century, scientists invaded the most intimate areas of human behavior and made important breakthroughs in the understanding of human reproduction and sexual physiology. In 1875, for example, a German physiologist discovered the basic process of fertilization—the union of male and female sex cells. Four years later, scientists for the first time witnessed, with the aid of the microscope, a sperm cell penetrating an egg. In the following decade, scientific research uncovered the link between hormonal secretions and sexual potency, affirmed the existence of erogenous zones, and began to explore the role of chromosomes in reproduction.

The Trial of Oscar Wilde

In March 1895 the Marquis of Queensberry left a message with the porter of a gentleman's club in London. The message, written on Queensberry's calling card, read "To Oscar Wilde, posing as a *somdomite*." What Queensberry meant to write was *sodomite,* a common term for a man who engaged in sexual relations with other men. By handing the card to the porter, Queensberry openly accused Wilde, a celebrated novelist and playwright, of homosexual—and therefore criminal—activity. Ten years earlier the British Parliament had declared illegal all homosexual activity, even consensual relations between adults in a private home. Queensberry's accusation, then, was extremely serious. Oscar Wilde responded by suing Queensberry for libel—and set in motion a legal process that led to Wilde's imprisonment, and indirectly, to his early death.

Wilde made a reckless mistake when he chose to sue for libel, for in fact Queensberry had not libeled him. Wilde was a homosexual, and he and Queensberry's son, Lord Alfred Douglas, were lovers. Why, then, did Wilde dare to challenge Queensberry? Perhaps the fact that he was married, with two children, seemed to provide a certain shield against the charge of homosexuality. Or perhaps Wilde's successes as a novelist and playwright gave him a misguided sense of invulnerability. With

two of his plays currently appearing on the London stage to favorable reviews, Wilde stood at the pinnacle of his career in the spring of 1895.

Wilde had built that career on a deliberate flouting of middle-class codes of morality. He saw himself as an artist, and insisted that art should be freed from social convention and moral restraint. His "High Society" comedies about privileged elites living scandalous lives and exchanging witty epigrams were far from the morally uplifting drama expected by middle-class audiences.

He also used his public persona to attack the conventional, the respectable, and the orthodox. Widely recognized for his outrageous clothing and conversation, Wilde had consciously adopted the mannerisms of what nineteenth-

century Britons called a "dandy"— a well-dressed, irreverent, artistic, leisured, and most of all, effeminate man. Before the Oscar Wilde trial, such effeminacy did not serve as a sign of, or a code for, homosexual inclinations, but it did signal to many observers a lavish—and loose—lifestyle. Oscar Wilde, then, was a man many British men and women loved to hate.

Even so, when his trial opened Wilde appeared to be in a strong position, the prosecutor rather than the defendant. Because Wilde had Queensberry's card with the "sodomite" charge written right on it, Queensberry faced certain conviction unless he could show that Wilde had engaged in homosexual activity. Wilde knew, of course, that Queensberry would not risk bringing the legal spotlight to bear on his own son's homosexuality.

At first, Queensberry's attorney, Edward Carson, focused on Wilde's published works, trying to use Wilde's own words against him. It proved an ineffective strategy. On the witness stand, Wilde reveled in the attention and ran circles around Carson.

On the second day of the libel trial, however, Wilde's witticisms proved insufficient as Carson began to question him about

Oscar Wilde and Lord Alfred Douglas
Although the British government pursued its case against Wilde, it made no effort to put together a case against Douglas.

his frequent visits to a male brothel and his associations with a number of young, working-class men who worked as male prostitutes. Suddenly the issue was no longer the literary merit or moral worth of Wilde's published writings, but rather his sexual exploitation of working-class boys. At this point, Wilde withdrew his libel charge against Queensberry, and the court declared the marquis not guilty.

If Queensberry was not guilty of libel in calling Wilde a sodomite, then by clear implication, Wilde was guilty of homosexual activity and therefore a criminal. Within days he was charged with "gross indecency" with another male. The jury in that case failed to reach a verdict, but the state was determined to obtain a conviction and brought the charges again. Wilde was refused bail, and on May 20 he was back in court.

On May 25, 1895—just three months after Queensberry had left his misspelled message with the club porter—Wilde's promising literary career ended. He was found guilty of seven counts of gross indecency with other men. The presiding judge, Sir Alfred Wills, characterized the trial as "the worst case I have ever tried," and declared, "I shall under the circumstances be expected to pass the severest sentence the law allows. In my judgment it is totally inadequate for such a case." He sentenced Wilde to two years at hard labor. The physical punishment took its toll. Wilde died in 1900 at age 46.

In sentencing Wilde, Wills described him as "the centre of a circle of extensive corruption of the most hideous kind." How do we account for the intensity of Wills's language, as well as the severity of Wilde's sentence? Homosexual activity had long been condemned on religious grounds, but this condemnation grew much more fierce in the closing decades of the nineteenth century. In a time of rapid and threatening change, the marking of gender boundaries became a way to create and enforce social order. Wilde crossed those boundaries, and so had to be punished.

Moreover, by the end of the nineteenth century, the state had assumed new responsibilities. Desperate to enhance national strength in a period of heightened international competition, governments intervened in areas previously considered to be the domain of the private citizen. By the turn of the century, western European governments were compelling working-class parents to send their children to school, regulating the hours adults could work, supervising the sale of food and drugs, providing limited forms of old-age pensions and medical insurance—and policing sexual boundaries.

The policing of sexual boundaries became easier after the Wilde trial because it provided a homosexual personality profile, a "Wanted" poster to hang on the walls of Western culture. For many observers of his very well-publicized trial, Wilde became the embodiment of "the homosexual," a particular and peculiar type of person, and a menace to cultural stability. The Wilde trial linked "dandyism" to the new image of the homosexual. Outward stylistic choices such as effeminacy, artistic sensibilities, and flamboyant clothing and conversation became, for many observers, the telltale signs of substantial inner corruption. Thus the Wilde case marked an important turning point in the construction, as well as the condemnation, of a homosexual identity.

Questions of Justice

1. How does this trial illustrate the role of medical, legal, and cultural assumptions in shaping sexual identity in the late nineteenth century?
2. Did the trial of Oscar Wilde achieve justice? If so, of what kind and for whom?

Taking It Further

An Ideal Husband. 1999. A film adaptation of Oscar Wilde's very funny play, which exemplifies his lighthearted but devastating critique of conventional manners and morals.

Ellman, Richard. *Oscar Wilde.* 1988. An important biography of Wilde.

Hyde, H. Montgomery. *The Trials of Oscar Wilde.* 1962. Includes extensive quotations from the trial transcripts as well as photographs of some of the documentary evidence.

McLaren, Angus. *The Trials of Masculinity: Policing Sexual Boundaries, 1870–1930.* 1997. Places the Wilde trial within a wider cultural context.

This greater understanding of sexual *physiology* went hand in hand with the effort to apply the scientific method to sexual *practice*. With data drawn from biology, anthropology, and human physiology, scientists in Europe and the United States sought to define "normal" sexual behavior. In seven weighty volumes, the British scientist Havelock Ellis (1859–1939) explored the range of child and adult sexuality. Ellis used his data to argue for sex education, legalization of contraception and nudism, and tolerance of homosexuality. Other sex researchers, however, turned to science to buttress middle-class moral codes. The German scientist Richard von Krafft-Ebing labeled homosexuality a pathology in 1886, while many publications condemned masturbation and frequent sexual intercourse. Other works offered support for antifeminism by arguing that female physiology incapacitated women for public life.

Heightened concern about gender boundaries also pervaded the visual art of late-nineteenth-century Europe. Women often appeared as elemental forces, creatures of nature rather than civilization, who threatened to trap, emasculate, engulf, suffocate, or destroy the unwary man. In *Medicine*, by the Austrian painter Gustav Klimt (1862–1918), the liquid portraits of women flow between and into images of sex and death in a disturbing and powerful painting. Such images recur even more graphically in the work of Klimt's student, Egon Schiele (1890–1918). In his very short life Schiele created more than 3,000 works on paper and 300 paintings, many of these depictions of the dangerous female. In works such as *Black-Haired Girl with Raised Skirt* (1911), harsh colors and brazen postures present an unsettling vision of female sexuality. A series of Schiele's paintings with titles such as *Dead Mother* place children in the arms of dead or expressionless women—a direct challenge to the middle-class glorification of motherhood.

The Birth of Modernism

Schiele's disturbing paintings exemplify the new modernist movement. Although the term modernism° was not commonly used until the 1920s, the main developments it embraced were well underway by 1914. It is a difficult term to define, in part because it refers to a variety of artistic, literary, and intellectual styles. Despite this variety, however, modernist art and literature expressed a set of common attitudes and assumptions that centered on a rejection of established authority. In the final decades of the nineteenth century, many artists tossed aside accepted standards and rules and embarked on a series of bold experiments. Oscar Wilde (1854–1900), the British playwright whose dramas mocked Victorian conventions and outraged middle-class sensibilities, wrote, "It is enough that our fathers believed. They have exhausted the faith-faculty of the species. Their legacy to us is the skepticism of which they were afraid."[6]

Gustav Klimt, *Medicine* (1901)
Klimt was commissioned by the University of Vienna to create a work that would celebrate medicine's great achievements. Not surprisingly, the painting he produced provoked great controversy. The woman in the forefront is Hygeia, the Greek goddess of health, but behind her swim images of female sexuality and death. Klimt's paintings often featured women as alluring but engulfing elemental forces.

At the core of modernism was a questioning of all accepted standards and truths, particularly those that shaped the middle-class liberal worldview.

In that liberal worldview, the arts served a useful purpose and were a vital part of civilized society. Going to art galleries, for example, was a popular activity, rather like going to the movies today. Respectable workers and middle-class men and women crowded into exhibitions where they viewed paintings that told an entertaining story and had a clear moral message. Modernism shattered this community between artist and audience. It rejected the idea of art as an instrument of moral or emotional uplift. Modernists argued that art is autonomous—it stands alone, of value in and of itself rather than for any impact it may have on society. Modernist painters, for example, did not seek to tell a story or to preach a sermon, but rather to experiment with line, color, and composition.

In addition to rejecting the idea that art must be useful, modernists also challenged middle-class liberalism by insisting that history is irrelevant. Nineteenth-century culture was "historicist." Fascinated with the process of change over time—with the evolution not only of species but also of ideas and societies—the middle-class mindset viewed history as the orderly forward march of progress. In contrast, modernists argued that fast-moving industrial and technological change had shattered the lines connecting history and modernity. Painters such as the Futurists in Italy and the Vorticists in Britain (two of the many artistic movements that clustered under the modernist umbrella) reveled in the new machine age, a world cut off from anything that had gone before. In their paintings they depicted human beings as machines in motion, moving too fast to be tied down to history.

New musical styles emerging in both popular and high culture in these decades also demonstrated the modernist sense of discontinuity. Ragtime, for example, combined syncopation with unexpected rhythms and sudden stops, while jazz, which developed around the turn of the century in black urban neighborhoods in the United States, created a musical universe of constant change. At the same time, symphonic musicians such as Russian composer Igor Stravinsky (1882–1971) and his Austrian counterpart Arnold Schoenberg (1874–1951) shocked their audiences by tossing aside the convention that a piece should state a central theme, which is then repeated in a sequence of variations. In Stravinsky's ballet *The Rite of Spring* (1913), the meter changes no fewer than twenty-eight times in the final thirty-four bars of the central dance. Similarly, Schoenberg eliminated repetition from his works and used rapid tempo changes.

Modernism also rejected the dominant nineteenth-century faith in the power of human reason and observation, and instead emphasized the role of individual emotion and experience in shaping human understanding. In Paris, for example, a group of artists centered on the Spaniard Pablo Picasso (1881–1973) dared to juxtapose different perspectives and points of view on a single canvas. They called themselves Cubists°. Just as Albert Einstein revolutionized physics by arguing that time and space shift as the position of the observer changes, so Cubism transformed Western visual culture by revealing the incompleteness and even incoherence of individual perception. In one cultural historian's apt description, "Cubists cracked the mirror of art."[7] Their fragmented, jagged, energetic works no longer reflected the world "out there," but instead revealed the artist's fluid and contradictory vision (see page 762).

Léon Bakst, *Nijinsky in The Afternoon of a Faun* (1912)
The Russian dancer Vaslav Nijinksy (1890–1950) brought modernism to the ballet, with startling, awkward poses and sudden, jerky moves. In this painting, however, the Russian artist Bakst uses the flowing lines of the Art Nouveau style to evoke Nijinsky in movement.

This emphasis on art as a form of personal expression is also seen in the Expressionist° movement, centered not in France as was Cubism, but in central and eastern Europe. Expressionists such as Egon Schiele argued that art should express the artist's interior vision, not the exterior world. In nude self-portraits, Schiele depicted himself as ugly and emaciated, a graphic expression of his tormented internal universe. His fellow Expressionist, the Russian painter Wassily Kandinsky (1866–1944), went even further in shattering artistic boundaries and splashing his emotions all over the canvas. Kandinsky sought to remove all form from his painting, to create a universe of pure color that would express a fundamental spiritual

DOCUMENT

Cubist Painters

Born in 1880, the Frenchman Guillaume Apollinaire became part of the modernist circle of artists and poets that dominated Parisian cultural life at the turn of the century. His Cubist Painters, *written in 1911 and published two years later, is both a study and an example of modernism. In its fragmentary style it resembles a Cubist painting; it rejects a point-by-point reasoned narrative for the use of juxtaposition, contrast, and poetic analogies.*

The rainbow is bent, the seasons quiver, the crowds push on to death, science undoes and remakes what already exists, whole worlds disappear forever from our understanding, our mobile images repeat themselves, or revive their vagueness, and the colors, the odors, and the sounds to which we are sensitive astonish us, then disappear from nature—all to no purpose.

The monster, beauty, is not eternal . . .

You cannot carry around on your back the corpse of your father. You leave him with the other dead. You remember him, miss him, speak of him with admiration. And if you become a father yourself, you cannot expect one of your children to be willing to split in two for the sake of your corpse.

. . .

Many new painters limit themselves to pictures which have no real subjects. . . . These painters, while they still look at nature, no longer imitate it, and carefully avoid any representation of natural scenes which they may have observed, and then reconstructed from preliminary studies.

Real resemblance no longer has any importance, since everything is sacrificed by the artist to truth, to the necessities of a higher nature, whose existence he assumes, but does not lay bare. The subject has little or no importance any more.

Generally speaking, modern art repudiates most of the techniques of pleasing devised by the great artists of the past.

. . .

Cubism differs from the old schools of painting in that it aims, not at an art of imitation, but an an art of conception, which tends to rise to the height of creation . . . .

I love the art of today because above all else I love the light, for man loves light more than anything; it was he who invented fire.

Source: Guillaume Apollinaire. *The Cubist Painters: Aesthetic Meditations,* trans. Lionel Abel (1913; New York: Wittenborn and Company, 1944), pp. 9, 10–11, 14, 15.

Wassily Kandinsky, *Composition VII* **(1913)**
Kandinsky's experiments in color and form led him to pure abstraction.

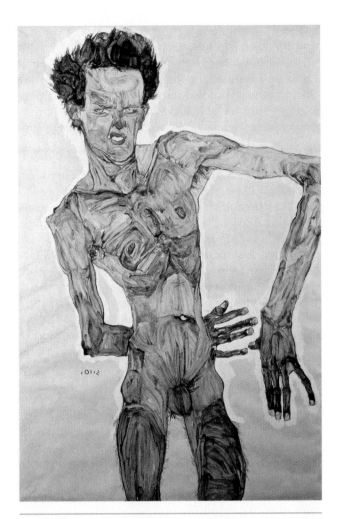

Egon Schiele, *Nude Self-Portrait with Open Mouth* (1910)
Schiele's paintings exemplify the Expressionist movement with their bold use of color and their no-holds-barred exploration of human emotion and sexuality.

scenes, novels told a moral tale, and music offered harmonious charm. At the same time that Picasso was shattering perspective, one of the most popular pieces of art in the English-speaking world was *The Light of the World* by William Holman Hunt (1827–1910). This moralistic piece with its easy-to-understand and uplifting story, completely at odds with every modernist principle, triumphantly toured the British Empire from 1905 to 1907. In cities throughout Australia, South Africa, Canada, and Britain, enthusiastic crowds jostled for tickets and hailed the painting as both a religious and an artistic masterpiece.

William Holman Hunt, *The Light of the World* (1903)
This devotional painting is rich in Christian symbolism. Jesus, the light of the world, stands knocking at the closed door of a lost soul. The overgrown weeds and fallen fruit symbolize sin; the lantern stands for Christ's illuminating power, while the stars and crescents on it represent Christ's appeal to Jews and Muslims.

reality. In the process, he produced the first purely abstract paintings in Western art.

Because they so radically challenged middle-class and liberal standards and assumptions, modernist works were greeted with incomprehension and outrage. At the first performance of Schoenberg's *Five Orchestral Pieces* (1909) in London in 1912, one listener reported that "the audience laughed audibly all through . . . and hissed vigorously at the end." The next year in Vienna, the performance of a different Schoenberg piece had to be abandoned after the audience rioted. Modernist painting was routinely condemned as sick, pornographic, anarchic, and simply insane. One London reviewer dismissed the painter Paul Cézanne (1869–1954) as "an artist with diseased retinas." Most middle-class men and women remained firmly within a cultural milieu in which paintings revealed pretty

Popular Religion and Secularization

As the response to Holman Hunt's depiction of Jesus shows, religious belief remained a powerful force in the decades after 1870. In Britain, regular Sunday worship continued to be a central aspect of middle-class culture, and the still-strong Sunday School movement as well as religious instruction in state schools ensured that working-class children were taught the fundamentals of the Christian faith. On the Continent, many Europeans connected revolutionary anarchy with unbelief after revolutionaries executed the Archbishop of Paris in 1871 (see Chapter 21). The excesses of the Paris Commune thus contributed to a religious revival. Much of this popular Catholic religiosity focused on the cult of the Virgin Mary: By the 1870s, the shrine at Lourdes, site of Mary's miraculous appearance in 1858, was attracting hundreds of thousands of Catholic pilgrims.

Three additional factors contributed to the religiosity of late-nineteenth-century Europe. First, the high rate of immigration, which meant that large groups of people often found themselves searching for something familiar in foreign cities, fostered attachments to the religious cultures of the homeland. In English cities, for example, Irish immigrants looked to the local Roman Catholic Church for spiritual solace, material support, and social contacts. Second, in many regions nationalism also shored up religious belief and practice. Hence, for Polish nationalists dreaming of independence from Russian rule, Roman Catholicism was a key part of a separate national identity. Finally, as we shall see in the next section, imperialism became interwoven with Western Christianity. Missionary publications and societies not only lobbied intensely for continued Western expansion abroad, but also served to inspire and unite Western Christians at home. Foreign mission work gave Western Christians a sense of both purpose and power as imperial expansion appeared to provide clear evidence of the ongoing triumph of Christianity.

Yet this triumphalism met growing anxiety as Christians faced a series of challenges, most obviously those posed by science. As we saw in our discussion of Darwin, developments in geology and biology undermined the orthodox Christian view of a harmonious, divinely directed, natural world. Medical advances also worked to narrow the appeal of traditional religion. Tragedies once accepted as "acts of God," such as epidemic disease, now appeared to be curable and controllable. Increasingly, scientists seemed able to answer questions once thought the province of the theologians.

At the same time, the emergence of the social sciences posed a direct challenge to Christian belief by simply dismissing the question of religious truth and asking instead, what is the function of religious belief in a society? Emile Durkheim (1858–1917), one of the founders of French sociology, dared to lump Christianity with "even the most barbarous and the most fantastic rites and the strangest myths." Durkheim insisted that no religion is more true than any other; each fills a social need.[8]

The Christian response to these challenges varied. Some Christians embraced the scientific method as a gift from God, and argued that the Christian faith must adapt to the ongoing expansion of human knowledge. To many theologians as well as ordinary believers, the study of the Bible as a historical and literary document—as a collection of divinely inspired texts produced by all-too-human writers—promised to free Christians *from* antiquated beliefs impossible to sustain in the new scientific age, and *for* a more worldly, reform-oriented religious life. Other Christians, however, resisted any accommodation to the scientific age. Protestant fundamentalists insisted on retaining a belief in the literal, historical, and scientific accuracy of the Christian scriptures, a stance that led them to oppose science as the enemy of religion.

Similarly, the Roman Catholic papacy adopted a defiant pose in the face of the scientific challenge. In 1864, Pope Pius IX (r. 1846–1878) issued a *Syllabus of Errors,* which condemned not only materialism but also the idea that the pope should "harmonize himself with progress, with liberalism, and with modern civilization." Five years later, a church council—the first called since the sixteenth-century Catholic Reformation—proclaimed the doctrine of papal infallibility. According to this doctrine, any decrees issued by the pope with regard to faith and morals were free from error and good for all time and all places. The proclamation of the doctrine of papal infallibility was a sharp rebuff to those Catholic theologians who argued that Christianity must adapt to the modern world.

The Roman Catholic Church also faced a crucial political challenge from both liberal and socialist movements. In Roman Catholic countries, the Church's alliance with conservatism pushed anticlericalism° to a dominant position on the liberal agenda. In France, for example, Roman Catholics were in the forefront of the conservative forces seeking to overturn the Republic established in 1871 and to return to monarchical or authoritarian rule. As a result, Frenchmen who wanted the Republic to survive fought to reduce the Church's influence over French politics and culture. At the same time, the spread of socialism provided European workers with an alternative belief system and source of communal life. The result was to widen the secular sphere and limit the influence of traditional Christianity.

The most significant challenge faced by Christianity after 1870, however, emerged not from scientific laboratories, parliamentary assemblies, or socialist rallies but rather from the department stores and playing fields. In the growing industrial cities, both working- and middle-class individuals enjoyed new, secular sources of entertainment, inspiration, and desire. Energies once focused on Christian devotion were now increasingly displaced onto the activities of consumption and recreation. Whereas shared religious worship had once cemented community life, the increasingly elaborate rituals of spectator sports now forged new bonds of loyalty and identity. At the same time, the delectable array of colorful products displayed in shop windows promised fulfillment and satisfaction in the here and now, an earthly paradise rather than a heavenly reward.

The New Imperialism

■ What were the causes and consequences of the new imperialist ideology for both the West and non-Western societies?

Many of those items on display behind the new plate-glass shop windows were the products of imperial conquest. After 1870, Europe entered not only a new age of mass consumption but also a new era of imperialist expansion. Imperialism intertwined with many of the economic, scientific, and cultural developments already examined in this chapter. Telegraphs ensured rapid communication from far-flung empires while mass printing technologies guaranteed that illustrated tales of imperial achievement made their way into homes and schools; Social Darwinism supplied a supposedly scientific justification for the conquest of peoples deemed biologically inferior; swift and decisive victories over other lands and societies helped quell anxiety about European degeneration. For many Europeans—particularly the British, who presided over the largest empire in the world—imperialist domination served as reassuring, even incontrovertible, evidence of the superiority of Western civilization.

Understanding the New Imperialism

Imperialism was not, of course, new to Europe. In the fifteenth century, Europeans had embarked on the first phase of imperialism, with the extension of European control across coastal ports of Africa and India, and into the New World of the Americas. In the second phase, which began in the late seventeenth century, European colonial empires in both Asia and the Western Hemisphere expanded as governments sought to augment their profits from international trade. Trade motivated much of the imperial activity after 1870 as well, with the need to protect existing imperial possessions often impelling further imperialist conquests. The desire to protect India—the "Jewel in the Crown" of the British Empire—explains much of British imperial acquisition throughout the nineteenth century. Britain's annexation of Burma and Kashmir, its establishment of spheres of influence in the Middle East, and its interests along the coast of Africa were all vitally linked to its concerns in India.

Neither defense of existing empires nor commercial considerations, however, fully explain the headlong rush into empire in the later nineteenth century. After 1870 and particularly after 1880, Europe's expansion into non-European territories became so much more aggressive that historians label this third phase the age of new imperialism°. A few figures illustrate the contrast: Between 1800 and 1880, European colonial empires grew by 6,500,000 square miles, but between 1880 and 1910, these empires increased by an astonishing 8,655,000. In just thirty years, European control of the globe's land surface swelled from 65 to 85 percent. In addition, new players joined the expansionist game. Recently formed nation-states such as Germany and Italy jostled for colonial territory in Africa, the United States began to extend its control over the Western Hemisphere, and Japan initiated its imperialist march into China and Korea. What factors lay behind this new imperialism?

Technology, Economics, and Politics

Part of the answer lies in the economic developments examined in Chapter 22. The new technologies characteristic of the Second Industrial Revolution meant that industrial Europe increasingly depended on raw materials available only in non-Western regions such as Asia, Africa, and South America. Rubber, for example, was essential not only for tires on the new automobiles, but also for insulating the electrical and telegraph wires now encircling the globe. Palm oil from Africa provided the lubricant needed for industrial machinery. Africa's once-plentiful elephant herds were slaughtered to provide the ivory for many of the new consumer goods now displayed prominently in department store windows and middle-class parlors—piano keys, billiard balls, knife handles. Increasingly dependent on these primary resources, European states were quick to respond to perceived threats to their economic interests. The Germans even coined a word to describe this fear of losing access to essential raw materials: *Torschlusspanik,* or "fear of the closing door."

Competition for markets also accelerated imperial acquisition. With the onset of economic depression in 1873 (discussed in Chapter 22), industrialists were faced with declining demand for their products in Europe. Imperial expansion seemed to provide a solution, with annexed territories seen as captive markets. As an editorial in the largest French mass-circulation newspaper explained in 1891, "every gunshot opens another outlet for French industry."[9]

By the mid-1890s, however, the depression had ended in most regions, and Europe embarked on the longest investment boom it had yet experienced. Western European capital spread across the globe, underwriting railway lines, digging mines, and erecting public utilities in the United States, Latin America, Russia, Asia, and Africa. This global investment boom also contributed to new imperialism. With each railroad or coal mine or dam, European interests in non-European regions expanded, and so did the pressure on European governments to assume formal political control should those interests be threatened, whether by the arrival of other European competitors or by local political instability.

Britain provides an important example of the link between empire and economics. By the end of the nineteenth century, the British Empire covered one-quarter of the globe and contained one-quarter of the world's population. This empire reflected Britain's position at the center of the world's economy, as the chief agent of global economic exchange. Despite the emergence of Germany and the United States as industrial powerhouses, Britain remained the world's largest trading nation. Even more important, British stockbrokers, currency traders, and banks managed the global exchange system that emerged in the last third of the nineteenth century. In this era British loans abroad were larger than the combined investments of Britain's five largest competitors—France, Germany, the Netherlands, the United States, and Belgium.

Imperialism was motivated by more than economic concerns. Political pressures also contributed to imperialist acquisition. First, in the age of mass politics, political leaders needed to find issues that would both appeal to new voters and strengthen the status quo. Imperialism was one such issue. It assured ordinary men that they were part of a superior, conquering people. Tales of dangerous explorations and decisive military victories engaged the emotions and prodded the ordinary individual to identify more closely with the national group.

A second political factor motivating new imperialism was nationalist competition. Newly formed nations such as Italy and Germany sought empires outside Europe as a way to gain both power and prestige within Europe. The nineteenth-century German historian Heinrich von Treitschke explained, "All great nations in the fullness of their strength have desired to set their mark on barbarian lands and those who fail to participate in this great rivalry will play a pitiable role in time to come." Similar concerns about status and strategic advantages motivated nations such as Britain and France both to defend and expand their existing empires.

The Imperial Idea

New imperialism was not simply a policy embraced by elites for economic, political, and strategic advantage. One of its most distinctive features was the way it functioned as a belief system, as an idea that permeated middle-class and mass culture in the decades after 1870. Images of empire proliferated, appearing in boys' adventure stories, glossy ads for soap and chocolates, picture postcards, cookie tins, and cheap commemorative china plates and mugs. In the music halls and theaters, imperialist songs and dramas received popular applause. At exhibitions and world's fairs, both goods and peoples from conquered regions were put on display to educate the crowds of viewers in the "imperial idea."

Imperialism from the European Perspective

France here brings the peoples of Morocco the wealth of Western education, technology, and military discipline.

At the center of this idea stood the assumption of the *rightness* of white European dominance over the world. Europeans would not have sought to remake the world in the European image had they not been convinced of the superiority of that image. What led white Europeans to believe they had both the right and the responsibility to take charge of other cultures and continents?

One key factor was the perceived link between Western Christianity and "civilization." Christian missionaries served as a vanguard of Western culture throughout the nineteenth century. The celebrated Scottish explorer David Livingstone (1813–1873), who mapped out much of central and southern Africa, was a Protestant missionary (although not a very successful one—his only convert eventually renounced the Christian faith). Moreover, missionary society publications introduced their readers to exotic territories, while the societies themselves served as powerful political interest groups that often lobbied for Western territorial expansion to promote the spread of Christian missionary activity.

Europeans also pointed to their advanced technologies as evidence of their material and moral superiority, and as a justification for their imperial rule. Before the nineteenth century, the technological gap between European and non-European societies had not loomed large; in some cases, such as China, non-European societies had held the technological advantage. Industrialization, however, gave Europe the technological edge. Thus Mary Kingsley (1862–1900), a British adventurer who was actually unusually admiring of African culture and customs, wrote, "when I come back from a spell in Africa, the thing that makes me proud of being one of the English is . . . a great railway engine . . . [I]t is the manifestation of the superiority of my race."[10]

DOCUMENT

Mary Kingsley and the Bubi of Fernando Po (1890s)

Although many European Christians regarded the West's technological advantages as a sign that God intended Europe to Christianize (that is, westernize) the globe, a growing number of prominent thinkers, writers, and policy-makers viewed the force that conferred this civilizing duty upon Europeans as natural rather than supernatural—biology rather than God. Social Darwinism lent a seemingly scientific authority to the imperial idea by supposedly proving the mental and moral superiority of white Europeans over all peoples of color. Thus the British Lord Milner (1854–1925) explained in a speech in South Africa in 1903: "The white man must rule, because he is elevated by many, many steps above the black man; steps which it will take the latter centuries to climb, and which it is quite possible that the vast bulk of the black population may never be able to climb at all."

DOCUMENT

Imperialism and the White Man's Burden (1899)

Often white Europeans presented the idea of a biologically ordained imperial destiny in somber terms. They saw imperial rule as a heavy responsibility that must be shouldered by the civilized. Men and women in the West had a moral duty to bring the benefits of their civilization to the rest of the world. This idea of the burden of imperialism was dramatically expressed by Rudyard Kipling (1865–1936), the preeminent British poet of new imperialism. In 1899, Kipling urged American policymakers to complete their conquest of the Philippines with these words:

> *Take up the White Man's burden—*
> *Send forth the best ye breed—*
> *Go bind your sons to exile,*
> *To serve your captives' need;*
> *To wait in heavy harness*
> *On fluttered folk and wild—*
> *Your new-caught sullen peoples,*
> *Half devil and half child.*

Not all Europeans embraced the idea of the "White Man's burden," and many rejected the imperialist assump-tion of Western superiority. Some modernist artists, for example, looked to non-Western cultures for artistic inspiration and argued that these societies had much to teach the West. The Fauves ("wild beasts"), a Paris-based circle of artists that included Henri Matisse (1869–1954) and Paul Gauguin (1848–1903), condemned most Western art as overrefined and artificial, and sought in their own brilliantly colored works to rediscover the vitality that they found in non-Western cultures (see page 742).

Critics of empire often focused on its domestic political and economic implications. The British economist J. A. Hobson (1858–1940) charged that overseas empires benefited only wealthy capitalists while distracting public attention from the need for domestic political and economic reform. Hobson argued that unregulated capitalism led almost inevitably to imperialist expansion. While impoverishing the masses, the capitalist system generates huge surpluses in capital for a very small elite, who must then find somewhere to invest these surpluses. Hobson's ideas proved very influential among European socialists, who condemned imperialism along with capitalism.

Many liberals also condemned imperialism. The British prime minister William Gladstone (1809–1898) clung fast to the liberal belief that free trade between independent nations fostered international peace. Gladstone and other liberals were uneasy about the expense of empire and acutely aware of the contradictions between liberal ideals and imperialist practice. It was difficult, for example, to reconcile the liberal commitment to individual freedom with the widespread use of forced labor in colonial Africa.

Yet between 1880 and 1885—while Gladstone was prime minister—the British Empire expanded at the rate of 87,000 square miles per year, with Gladstone himself ordering the bombardment of Alexandria and the military occupation of Egypt. When Gladstone did hold firm to his anti-imperialist ideals and ordered British troops to withdraw from the Sudan in 1885, he outraged the British public. Critics of empire were in the minority, not only in Britain but throughout Europe. The imperial idea permeated European and much of American culture in the final decades of the nineteenth century.

The Scramble for Africa

New imperialism reached its zenith in Africa. In 1875 European powers controlled only 11 percent of the African continent. By 1905, 90 percent of Africa was under European control. In just thirty years, between 1875 and 1905, Europeans established thirty new colonies and protectorates encompassing ten million square miles of territory and controlling 110 million Africans (see Map 23.1). The conquest of the African continent was so rapid and

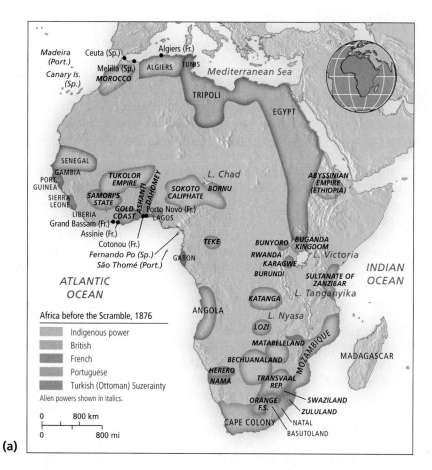

(a)

Map 23.1 (a) Africa Before the Scramble, 1876 and (b) Africa After the Scramble, 1914

A comparison of these two maps reveals the dramatic impact of the new imperialism on African societies. Indigenous empires such as the Sokoto Caliphate in West Africa came under Western rule, as did tribal societies such as the Herero. Even indigenous states ruled by whites of European descent came under European rule, as the examples of the Transvaal and the Orange Free State in South Africa illustrate. Only Ethiopia preserved its independence.

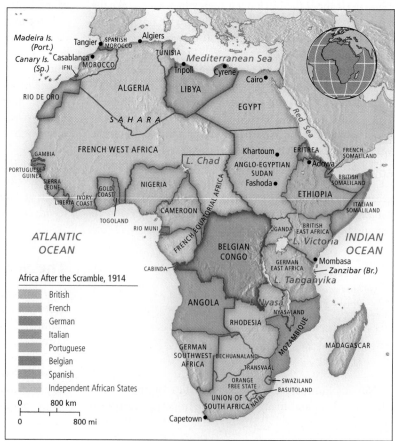

(b)

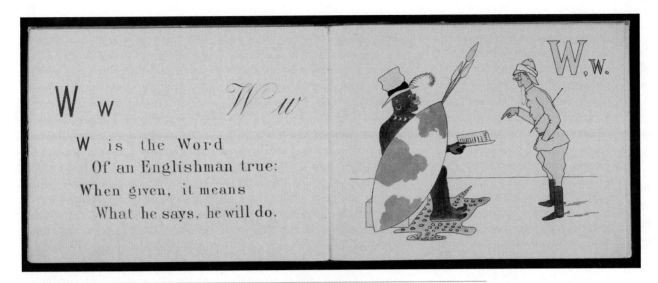

A Lesson in the Imperial Idea
As this alphabet reader makes clear, education in imperial ideology began early.

dramatic that as early as 1884 mystified Europeans began to talk about the Scramble for Africa°.

Overcoming the Obstacles

When the nineteenth century began, Europeans knew little more about the continent of Africa than the ancient Greeks had known. A vast and profitable trading network between European merchants and Africa's coastal regions had developed, centering on the exchange of European goods for African gold and slaves. European efforts to establish settlements in the interior, however, faced three key obstacles—the climate, disease, and African resistance.

Africa was known as "the white man's grave," deservedly so. Seventy-seven percent of the white soldiers sent to West Africa in the early nineteenth century died there, and another 21 percent became invalids. Temperatures of more than 100 degrees Fahrenheit in some regions and constant rainfall in others made travel extremely difficult. The mosquito and the tsetse fly made it deadly. Mosquito bites brought malaria, while the tsetse fly carried trypanosomiasis, or sleeping sickness, an infectious illness that began with a fever and ended in a deadly paralysis. Sleeping sickness also posed a grave danger to livestock and so aggravated the problem of transportation within the African interior. In regions with endemic trypanosomiasis, such as equatorial, southern, and eastern Africa, the use of horses and oxen was impossible. Despite the dangers posed by the climate and disease, Europeans did endeavor to establish inland settlements in Africa but then faced the obstacle of African resistance. In the seventeenth century, for example, the Portuguese set up forts and trading centers in modern Zimbabwe but were driven out by local African populations.

Beginning around 1830, a series of developments altered the relationship between Europe and Africa and prepared the groundwork for European conquest. First, the efforts of European explorers changed the Western vision of Africa. Between 1830 and 1870, adventurers mapped out the chief geographical features of Africa's interior and so illuminated the "Dark Continent" for Europeans. They discovered that central Africa was not the vast, empty desert that Europeans had assumed, but rather a territory with abundant agricultural and mineral resources—and lots of people, all of them potential consumers of European goods.

The shift in the European vision of Africa—from empty desert to potential treasure house—coincided with important changes within Africa itself. In the first half of the nineteenth century, various forces destabilized African political structures and so weakened the African ability to withstand conquest in later decades. Although the precise nature of the destabilizing forces varied by region, one common denominator prevailed—the unsettling impact of early encounters with the West. In the 1830s, for example, Britain and other European powers, pressured by humanitarian and missionary lobby groups, embarked on an effort to stamp out the West African slave trade. They succeeded but only in West Africa. The slave trade shifted to the central and eastern regions of the continent and wreaked havoc with political arrangements there. African slaving nations relied on frequent military raids to obtain their human merchandise. These raids—carried out by Africans against Africans—disrupted agricultural production, shattered trade networks, and undermined the authority of existing political rulers. With political systems in disarray, many African regions were vulnerable to European encroachment.

Picasso Goes to the Museum

After months of work and more than 800 preparatory sketches, Picasso judged the painting finished at last. But when he showed *Les Demoiselles d'Avignon* to his friend and rival Matisse, the Frenchman thought the work a joke. Another friend and fellow painter, Georges Braques, found it appalling. Picasso did not exhibit the painting for several years; it remained largely unknown until 1939 when it went on display at the Museum of Modern Art in New York City. Today, *Demoiselles* is one of the most well-known modernist works of art in the western world, "the amazing act on which all the art of our century is built."[11] It helped transform the history of Western art and even, perhaps, the history of perception itself.

With its in-your-face sexuality, *Demoiselles* retains its ability to shock. Five naked whores (*demoiselles* means "prostitutes") advertise for trade, twisting their bodies into erotic, even pornographic poses. The painting's eroticism alone, however, does not explain its impact.

The painting as we now know it resulted from a very specific encounter that occurred when Picasso went to a museum in Paris. Some time in 1906 or 1907, when he was already deeply involved in this painting, Picasso viewed African tribal masks on exhibit at the Ethnographic Museum in the Trocadero. This museum visit profoundly excited and upset the Spanish painter. His girl-friend Fernande Olivier reported, "Picasso is going crazy over Negro works and statues."[12] In Picasso's view, these "Negro works and statues" possessed the vitality and authenticity missing from Western art.

Picasso and many modernists believed that Western civilization, with its urbanization and industrialism, its organizations and academies, its codes and regulations, had stifled artistic expression. They saw most modern art as weak and lifeless—the tired-out product of a worn-out society. In contrast, they argued, African art resembled the pictures drawn by children: energetic, playful, creative, colored outside the lines.

This notion of African culture as childlike, of course, reflected the imperialist idea of "backward peoples." Picasso and other modernists rejected the imperialist notion of Western superiority and often sharply criticized Western empires, yet clearly they could not escape imperialist stereotypes. Within the limits of these stereotypes, however, modernists turned the cultural relationship of the West and Africa upside down. Picasso went to African art to learn, not to conquer.

Picasso's encounter with the African masks transformed both this specific painting and modern art itself. After his Trocadero visit, Picasso reconfigured the faces of the two women on the right so

that their masklike appearances now clash awkwardly with those of the three other prostitutes. This step destroyed any unity of narrative or composition in the painting: The five figures are no longer part of a single story or share a single point of view. At the same time that Picasso fragmented the painting, he fragmented each of the bodies, flattening them and reducing them to jutting geometric forms. Thus *Demoiselles* pushed Picasso toward Cubism, one of the most influential artistic styles of the twentieth century (see page 755). As the art historian John Golding has written, "In the *Demoiselles* Picasso began to shatter the human figure. . . . He spent the rest of his artistic life dissecting, reassembling, and reinventing it."[13] After Picasso, Western artists spent the rest of the twentieth century dissecting, reassembling, and reinventing the way we see and depict our world.

For Discussion

Clearly Picasso's encounter with the African sculptures on display at the Trocadero transformed this specific painting. But why is this single work of art so important?

**Pablo Picasso,
*Les Demoiselles
d'Avignon* (1907)**

The mask-like features of the prostitutes reflect the influence of African tribal art on Picasso.

The edge of the table engages the viewer as a participant in the painting: the viewer's perspective is that of a customer sitting at a table in a brothel.

Finally, three specific developments shifted the balance of power in the West's favor—the steamship, the "quinine prophylaxis," and the repeating, breech-loading rifle. The steam revolution was inaugurated in 1807 when the *Clermont,* a ship powered by a steam engine invented by the American Robert Fulton, chugged its way along the Hudson River between Albany and New York City. By the 1820s, steamships were widely in use on European lakes and rivers. Steam proved crucial in enabling Western imperialists to overcome the obstacles to traveling through Africa by allowing them to use the continent's extensive but shallow river system.

But until the 1850s and the development of the "quinine prophylaxis," such journeys almost guaranteed death sentences because of the risk of malaria. Steam enabled Westerners to penetrate the African interior; quinine helped them survive once they got there. Produced commercially from 1827 on, quinine was prescribed by doctors for malaria. Death and disability rates from the disease remained high, however, until a series of chance discoveries revealed the importance of taking quinine prophylactically—of saturating the system with quinine before any risk of infection. By the 1860s, Westerners were routinely ingesting quinine in preparation for postings in Africa—and their death rates dropped dramatically.

African death rates, however, soared because of the third crucial technology of imperialism—the repeating, breech-loading rifles carried by Europeans from the 1870s on. Before the invention of these rifles, Europeans used muskets or muzzle-loading rifles that had to be loaded one ball or cartridge at a time while standing up, and were prone to foul easily, particularly in damp weather. Such weapons did not provide Europeans with much of a military advantage, even over spears. With the repeating rifle, however, "any European infantryman could now fire lying down, undetected, in any weather, fifteen rounds of ammunition in as many seconds at targets up to half a mile away." As we saw at the beginning of this chapter, in regions such as the Sudan, where armor-clad cavalrymen fought with spears, swords, and arrows like medieval knights, the repeating breech-loader and its descendant the machine gun made the European conquest "more like hunting than war."[14]

Slicing the Cake: The Conquest of Africa

In the decades after 1870, convinced that the conquest of African territories would guarantee commercial prosperity and strengthen national power, European states moved quickly to beat out their rivals and grab a piece of the continent. As King Leopold II of Belgium (1865–1909) explained in a letter to his ambassador in London in 1876, "I do not want to miss a good chance of getting us a slice of this magnificent African cake."[15]

Leopold's slice proved to be enormous. Presenting himself as a humanitarian whose chief concern was the abolition of the slave trade, he called on the other European

Congo Atrocities

Harsh punishments were used by Leopold's forces to subdue the Congolese people and increase his personal profits.

leaders to back his claim to the Congo, a huge region of central Africa comprising territory more than twice as large as central Europe. After a decade of controversy and quarreling, representatives of the European powers met in Berlin in 1884 and agreed to Leopold's demands. At the same time, they used the Berlin Conference to regulate the Scramble for Africa. According to the terms established in Berlin, any state claiming a territory in Africa had to establish "effective occupation" and to plan for the economic development of that region.

But as the history of the Congo Free State demonstrated, colonialism in Africa was far from a humanitarian endeavor. Leopold's personal mercenary army turned the Congo into a hellhole of slavery and death. By claiming all so-called vacant land, Leopold deprived villagers of the grazing, foraging, and hunting grounds they needed to survive. He levied impossibly high rubber quotas for each village, forcing villagers to harvest wild rubber for up to twenty-five days each month while their families starved. Brutal punishments ensured compliance: Soldiers chopped off the hands of villagers who failed to meet their rubber quota. In other cases, babies were chained in sweltering huts until

Belgian King Crushing the Congo Free State— Cartoon

their mothers delivered their quota. At the same time, the Belgians forced black Africans to serve as human mules. This practice spread sleeping sickness from the western coast into the interior. Between 1895 and 1908, an epidemic of sleeping sickness decimated the already weakened population. As an estimated three million people died from the combined effects of forced labor, brutal punishments, starvation, and disease, the enormous profits from the Congo enabled Leopold II to indulge his hobby of building elaborate tourist resorts on the Riviera.

King Leopold's personal brand of imperialism proved so scandalous that in 1908 the Belgian government replaced Leopold's personal rule with state control over the Congo. Yet the king's exploitation of the Congo differed only in degree, not in kind, from the nature of European conquest elsewhere in Africa. Forced labor was common throughout European-controlled areas, as were brutal punishments for any Africans who dared resist. Faced with tribal revolt in Southwest Africa, the German colonial army commander in 1904 ordered that the entire Herero tribe be exterminated. Twenty thousand Africans, including children, were forcibly driven from their villages into the desert to die of thirst.

African Resistance

As the Herero rebellion demonstrates, Africans frequently resisted the imposition of these often-brutal imperial regimes, but to no avail. The only successful episode of African resistance to European conquest occurred in northern Africa, in the kingdom of Ethiopia (also called Abyssinia). After four centuries of isolation, Ethiopia modernized in the 1850s. By the time of the European Scramble for Africa, Ethiopia had developed not only a modern standing army but also an advanced infrastructure and communications system. These factors enabled the Ethiopian nation, in 1896, to defeat the Italian army at the battle of Adowa.

Adowa, however, was the exception. Most African resistance was doomed by the technological gap that yawned between the indigenous peoples and their European conquerors. A booming arms trade developed between European rifle manufacturers and African states desperate to obtain guns. Frequently, however, the arms shipped to Africa were inferior models—muskets or single-firing muzzle-loaders rather than the up-to-date and deadly efficient repeating rifles and early machine guns possessed by the European invaders.

African military leaders who did obtain advanced weaponry often did not make the strategic leap necessary to adapt their military tactics to new technologies. (As we will see in Chapter 24, European military leaders made similar mistakes in World War I.) In the 1890s, for example, the West African state of Dahomey imported repeating rifles to enable it to resist French annexation. A prosperous, highly centralized state, Dahomey possessed a 4,000-soldier stand-

ing army with a deservedly fierce reputation. Dahomey's military command, however, failed to change the attack drill devised for a musket-based regiment. The troops advanced forward at a run, fired from the hip, and withdrew—a strategy that worked well with muskets because they did not have to be aimed, but that proved disastrous with more advanced weapons. In 1892, French forces, outnumbered six to one, annihilated the Dahomian army. By 1900, Dahomey had become part of the French empire.

Yet even African resistance leaders who did adapt military strategy as well as adopt modern military weapons could not stand for long against the industrial might of Western powers. The most famous African resistance leader, Samori Ture (1830–1900), built a vast West African empire of 115,000 square miles and held off the forces of French imperialism for fifteen years, but he, too, was conquered in the end. Utilizing information obtained by spies sent to infiltrate the French military, Samori trained his massive infantry in modern military maneuvers and armed his elite cavalry troops with 6,000 repeating rifles, used with deadly effect against the French in a series of battles in the 1880s. Even more important, Samori was one of the first military commanders to conceive of the tactics of modern guerilla warfare—hit-and-run attacks, night battles, the crucial advantage of knowing the land. These measures enabled him to elude French capture for more than seven years after the French in 1891 sent a massive force to destroy the Samorian state. Yet 6,000 repeating rifles and guerilla tactics could not hold off the vast weight of French imperialism. Ambushed in 1898, Samori died in exile two years later, with his empire in European control.

The Scramble for Africa provides the most dramatic illustration of new imperialism but certainly not the only one. The same era witnessed the extension of European empires throughout Asia. Moreover, it was in Asia that non-European powers—the United States and Japan—entered the imperial game, and that Russia made its bid for empire.

Asian Encounters

Unlike most of Africa, many of the diverse states of Asia had already been woven into the web of the Western economy well before 1870. Pacific states such as Java and Malaysia formed a part of the eighteenth-century mercantilist empires established by Dutch, British, Portuguese, and French trading companies. (See Chapter 17.) Throughout the nineteenth century, European governments formalized their control over many of these island states, primarily to protect trade routes or to ensure access to profitable commodities such as rubber, tin, tobacco, and sugar. The Dutch, for example, gradually expanded their East Indies empire, moving from control of the island of Java in 1815 to domination over almost the entire archipelago several decades later. Similarly, Britain steadily expanded its control over India throughout the nineteenth century (see Map 23.2).

A number of factors accelerated the pace of imperialist acquisition in Asia beginning in the 1870s. In the age of steam, the Pacific islands took on strategic significance because European powers and the United States needed coaling stations for their commercial and naval fleets. At the same time, new industrial processes often heightened the economic value of many of these regions. The development of a process for producing dried coconut, for example, made Samoa so valuable that Germany, Britain, and the United States competed for control over the tiny islands.

As in Africa, however, the most important factor in imperialist expansion after 1870 was a phenomenon we can call the *scramble effect:* Imperialist gains by one power led to anxiety and a quicker pace of expansion by its rivals. The steady erosion of Chinese political stability—itself a result of encounters with the West—intensified this Asian scramble. Competition for access to Chinese markets was an important factor in determining the course of Western imperialism throughout much of Asia. The quest for a protected trade route to China, for example, impelled the French to extend their control over neighboring Indochina. By 1893, the Union of French

Map 23.2   Imperialism in Asia, 1914

The impact of the new imperialism on Asia was not as dramatic as in Africa, but the spread of Western rule is significant nonetheless. This map shows a key development: the entry of non-European powers—Japan and the United States—into the imperialist game. What it does not show is the extent of Western and Japanese influence in China. Profoundly destabilized by foreign intervention, China in 1914 was in the midst of revolution.

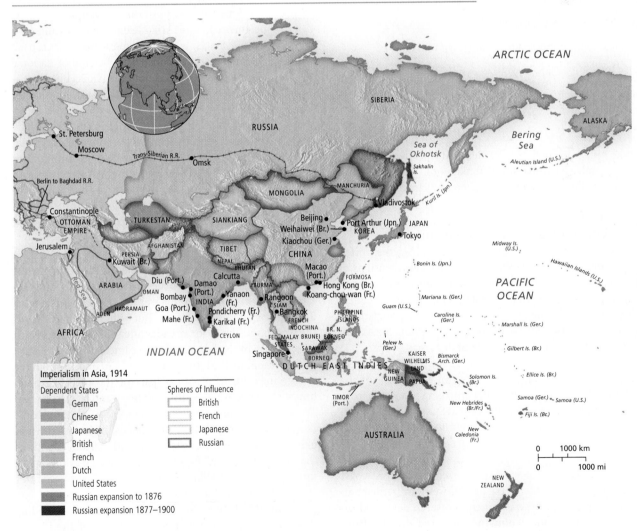

Indochina included the formerly independent states of Laos, Cambodia, Annam, and Tonkin—the latter two better known by their contemporary name of Vietnam.

Expanding the West: The United States and Australia

In the latter half of the nineteenth century, both the United States and Australia established themselves as extensions of the West. In both of these regions, the nineteenth century was a period of internal consolidation, territorial expansion, and the subjugation of the indigenous populations. Both regions also witnessed a determined effort to create a national identity that explicitly excluded Asian peoples.

For the United States, the acquisition of an empire in Asia followed consolidation of control over much of the North American continent. After emerging victorious from a war with Mexico in 1846, the United States gained the territory of California (which included today's New Mexico and part of Arizona) and so extended its reach to the Pacific. The completion of the transcontinental Union Pacific railroad in 1869 both symbolized this coast-to-coast dominion and accelerated the pace of westward settlement.

The conquest of the continent, however, depended on the defeat of its indigenous peoples. The decades from

1860 through 1890 were punctuated by a series of Indian wars throughout the American West. As in Africa, even those Indians who acquired repeating rifles, such as Crazy Horse's troops who wiped out General George Armstrong Custer (1839–1876) at Little Big Horn in 1876, could not hold out for long against the industrial might of the United States.

With its borders now touching the Pacific Ocean, the United States quickly emerged as an imperialist power in Asia. In 1853, Commodore Matthew Perry used the potent threat of his squadron of four warships to force the opening of Japan to American commerce, and during the 1860s and 1870s the United States participated with the European powers in chipping away at China's national sovereignty to ensure favorable terms of trade there. By the end of the century, the United States had annexed Hawaii and part of Samoa, and as a result of the Spanish-American War had acquired Guam, the Philippines, Cuba, and Puerto Rico.

American acquisition of empire in Asia heightened anti-Asian sentiment within the United States, as many Americans of European descent sought to construct a version of national identity that excluded not only Asians but all peoples of color. The Chinese Exclusion Act, passed in 1882 and renewed in 1902, prohibited Chinese immigration. In 1913, the Alien Land Law, which outlawed land ownership by noncitizens, sought to restrict the property rights of Japanese immigrants. During this same period, legislators in the American South deprived blacks of their right to vote through literacy tests, poll taxes, and violent intimidation, while Jim Crow° or segregation laws defined blacks as second-class citizens, in but not really of the West.

Australia's conquest and consolidation as a Western zone paralleled many of the American developments. Discovered and claimed for the British Crown by Captain James Cook in 1770, Australia was first used by Britain as a dumping ground for convicts. But with the expansion of the wool industry in the decades after 1830, the six British colonies established in Australia became a center of British immigration. In 1901, these colonies joined together in the Commonwealth of Australia, part of the British Empire but a self-governing political entity—and a self-defined "Western" nation, despite its geographical location in the Eastern Hemisphere. Many Australians, including the new nation's first prime minister, Edmund Barton, identified the "West" as "white." Barton, who campaigned on a platform calling for a "White Australia," regarded his country as an outpost of Western civilization.

As in the United States, the process of extending Western civilization demanded the defeat of the indigenous population. At the very start of Britain's occupation of Australia in 1787, King George III had forbidden anyone to "wantonly destroy [the Aboriginal peoples] or give them any unnecessary interruption in the exercise of their several occupations."[16] But the landing of whites intent on building cities, planting farms, and fencing in land for pastures clearly interrupted the nomadic way of life for the estimated 500,000 inhabitants of Australia, living in scattered tribal groupings. In 1795, the first major clash between Aborigines and British settlers occurred. Over the next hundred years, these clashes were frequent—and disastrous for the Aboriginal populations.

The British divided over how to treat the Aborigines. To many British settlers, and as the decades passed, to many in the growing group of Australia-born whites, the Aborigines constituted a clear and violent threat that had to be eradicated. Massacres of Aborigines resulted. Christian and humanitarian groups, as well as the British government in London, opposed this sort of violence and insisted that the Aborigines should be westernized and Christianized. From the 1820s on, mission stations housed and educated Aboriginal children. Forcibly removed from their homes, these children were schooled in British ways and then at age 15 placed in employment as apprentices and domestic servants. Despite these missions, few Aborigines assimilated to the Western way of life. Thus the final decades of the nineteenth century saw a shift in official policy from assimilation to "protection." Aborigines and mixed-race individuals were declared legal wards of the state and required to live on reserves. Aborigines did not receive Australian citizenship until 1967.

White Australians perceived not only the Aborigines but also Asian immigrants as threats to their Western identity. By the 1850s, tens of thousands of Chinese had emigrated to Australia. Arriving as indentured servants, they worked under brutal conditions. Many, for example, labored in the gold mines, where they received one-twelfth of the wages paid to a European. As the numbers of Chinese immigrants grew, so, too, did anti-Chinese sentiment. Most British immigrants and white native Australians, often fiercely divided in their vision of what sort of nation Australia should be, agreed that it should be colored white. One newspaper editor noted, "The Chinese question never fails. At every meeting, somebody in the hall has a word to say in regard to it, and visions of millions of the barbarians swooping upon the colony in a solid body rise in the mental horizons of every man present."[17] In 1888, the Australian government turned back ships containing Chinese immigrants; restrictive immigration legislation soon followed.

The Continued Expansion of the Russian Empire

As in the United States and Britain, in nineteenth-century Russia, imperial expansion took the form of territorial consolidation across a continent. During this era, Russia continued the colonization of Siberia that had begun in the sixteenth century, when Russian serfs had first fled to Siberia in search of land and freedom. The end of serfdom actually accelerated the Siberian exodus, because peasants now needed to escape the debts imposed on them by the emancipation legislation of 1861 (see Chapter 21). The completion of the trans-Siberian railway in the 1890s made this journey even more appealing. Between 1800 and 1914, seven million Russians settled in or were deported to Siberia.

Just as American expansion westward and the British conquest of Australia dramatically depleted Indian and Aboriginal numbers, so Russian migration into Siberia displaced much of that region's original population. Until 1826 Russians could trade Siberians as slaves; many died because of brutal treatment. Two additional factors were even more devastating to the indigenous Siberians. First, the immigrants brought with them new epidemic diseases. And second, the booming fur trade depleted the animal herds that served as the aborigines' main food source. Disease and famine decimated the Siberian population.

Russia also expanded southward into central Asia, primarily as a preemptive response to the growth of British power in India. Fearing that the British might push northward, the Russians pushed south. By 1885, the Black Sea region, the Caucasus, and Turkestan had all fallen to Russian imperial control, and Muslims now constituted a significant minority of the tsar's subjects. Over the next three decades the oil fields of the Caucasus would become a crucial part of the Russian industrial economy.

By 1914, the Russian Empire stretched from Warsaw in central Europe to Vladivostok on the Sea of Japan—8,660,000 square miles, or one-seventh of the global land surface. Ethnic Russians composed only 45 percent of the population of this vast empire.

As the tsarist regime expanded its Asian empire, it increasingly encroached upon Chinese territory, a move that contributed to the destabilization of China and to growing hostilities between Russia and Japan. By 1860, Russia had gained from China a sizable chunk of land along the Pacific coast and began pressing into Manchuria. Manchuria, however, was a region also coveted by Japanese imperialists. The growing antagonism between Russia and Japan led to the outbreak of the Russo-Japanese War in 1904 and, as we noted in Chapter 22, to a dramatic Japanese victory. Military defeat by a people regarded as racially inferior shocked Russians and led to demands for radical political change. With Tsar Nicholas II's regime clearly weakened and his troops tied up in Manchuria, this domestic discontent exploded in the Russian Revolution of 1905. The return of his soldiers from the Manchurian front enabled Nicholas to withstand this challenge to his authoritarian rule. His regime, however, was fundamentally weakened: Imperialism could be a risky business.

Japanese Industrial and Imperial Expansion

Japan's victory over Russia in 1905 vividly illustrated its remarkable rise to global power and its emergence as an imperialist player. Until 1853, Japan had remained sealed off from the West, a result of a decision made by the Japanese emperor in the 1630s to close Japanese ports to all foreigners except a small contingent of Dutch and Chinese traders confined to the city of Nagasaki. The Japanese government rebuffed all Western overtures until 1853, when Commodore Perry used warships to force Japan to open two of its ports to American ships. Over the next fifteen tumultuous years, Western powers pushed to expand their economic influence in Japan and Japanese elites fought over the question of how to respond to the West. Anti-Western terrorism became endemic, civil war broke out, and a political revolution ensued.

In 1868, Japan emerged from this turbulent time with a new government. For more than 200 years effective political control had rested in the hands not of the Japanese emperor, but rather of the "Shogun," the military governor of Japan. When the Shogun adopted pro-Western policies, Japan's warrior nobility tossed him from power and restored the young Emperor Mutsuhito (1867–1912) to effective rule—the Meiji Restoration.

The Meiji Constitution, 1889

Even more dramatically, these anti-Western elites determined that the only way to resist Western domination was to adopt Western industrial and military technologies and techniques. The next four decades witnessed a thoroughgoing revolution from the top as a modern centralized state, modeled on France, replaced Japan's feudalist political system. Young Japanese men traveled to Europe and the United States to learn Western ways. Western technologies and techniques helped modernize the Japanese economy.

Modernization was not an end in itself, however. The purpose of opening Japan to the West was to build up its

---

DOCUMENT

"A Dream of the Future"

In 1878, Tachibana Mitsuomi published his "Dream of the Future" in Hochi Shimbun, *the newspaper that he edited. Tachibana's dream is a nightmare. It reveals the anxiety prevalent in Japan during its time of rapid modernization and increasing contact with Western economies and ideas. In this excerpt, Tachibana projects the consequences of an imaginary decision to lift regulations on the importation of Western capital. In actual fact, no such decision was made. The Japanese government borrowed technology, techniques, and institutions from the West, but restrained the inflow of Western capital, thus retaining control over the Japanese economy.*

Tachibana's story opens with his bewilderment at suddenly finding himself on a busy street in Tokyo in 1967:

The houses in the surrounding streets were splendidly built and some of them three, and others five stories high; flags from every merchant's house were waving in the air; all kinds of precious articles were displayed in the shops and carriages and horses were incessantly passing to and fro. Indeed, a most flourishing trade was actually before my eyes. Greatly puzzled at this, I went into a shop and found that the master of the shop was a White man with blue eyes and red hair, wearing handsome clean clothes and sitting in an easy position by a desk; and that those wearing scanty and torn apparel and in the employment of the master of the house, were none but the yellow-coloured and high-cheek-boned brethren of ours. . . . I was informed that . . . all the large houses in the main streets [were] occupied by the Whites. . . .

. . . I then passed into the [side] streets and on looking at the state of the houses, I saw none but immense numbers of my countrymen flocking together like sheep or pigs, in a few poorly-built houses . . . their scanty dress leaving portions of their body uncovered . . . their wives were weeping from the cold, and the children crying from hunger, the husbands being employed by the Western people, and were earning scarcely sufficient wages to fill the mouths of their families. . . .

I, seeing this, could hardly keep from weeping and was sorely puzzled why my countrymen should have fallen to such misery . . . I saw a respectable looking gray-haired old man standing on the bridge . . . I approached him and after bowing to him, I asked, "Is this country Japan? Is this the capital, Tokei [Tokyo]? How is it that the Western people alone are enjoying such great wealth, whilst the Japanese are in such a miserable state? . . . "

The old man explains to Tochibana that the Japanese "were outdone by the superior strength of capital and intellect" from the West. As a result of lifting regulations on Western investment and ownership within Japan, "those who have control over the wealth of Japan . . . are none but the Western people." Tochibana concludes, "At this, I was very sad and deeply affected, and I was on the point of bursting into tears, when I suddenly awoke and found that it was all a dream."

Source: From Tachibana Mitsuomi, "A Dream of the Future," *Hochi Shimbun,* October 17, 1878. For the full version and a commentary, refer to Ian Inkster, *Japanese Industrialisation: Historical and Cultural Perspectives* (Routledge: London and New York, 2001), pp. 1–6.

Japanese Sailors Waiting for Battle Against Russia, 1904
The Japanese began the war with a surprise attack on Russian ships in Port Arthur. Many in Britain and the United States admired the Japanese for the audacity of their offensive—rather ironically, given the moral outrage that greeted a similar surprise attack carried out by the Japanese against American forces at Pearl Harbor in 1941.

national wealth, and with this wealth, to remake Japan as a global military power. Thus funds poured into building a modern navy, modeled on Britain's, and a powerful conscript-based army, modeled on Germany's. Beginning in the 1890s, Japan used its now formidable military force to push its way into the imperialist game. War with China in 1894 and Russia in 1904 led to the Japanese seizure of Taiwan and Korea, and to expanded Japanese economic influence in Manchuria. One Japanese writer, Tokutomi Soho (1863–1957) proclaimed that Japan's imperial conquests showed that "civilization is not a monopoly of the white man."[18] Certainly imperialist violence was not a white man's monopoly: The Japanese brutally punished Koreans and Taiwanese who dared to protest against their new rulers.

Scrambling in China

While Japan used its encounter with the West to modernize and militarize its society, China proved far less successful in withstanding Western hegemony. Throughout the nineteenth century, Chinese national sovereignty slowly eroded,

as European powers, soon joined by Russia, the United States, and Japan, jostled for access to China's markets and resources.

We saw in Chapter 20 that Britain's victory over China in the First Opium War in 1842 marked the beginnings of Western encroachment on Chinese territory. During the 1890s, Western influence expanded rapidly. Following China's defeat in the Sino-Japanese War of 1894–1895, Western powers scrambled to claim spheres of influence throughout China. The European powers and the United States did agree in 1899 to back the American "open door" policy, which opposed the formal partitioning of China (as had just occurred in Africa), but this policy increased rather than blocked Western interference in Chinese economic and political affairs.

Chinese opposition to intensified Western encroachment provoked even greater outside interference—and the collapse of the Manchu dynasty that had governed China since the seventeenth century. In 1900, a secret society devoted to purging China of Western influence began attacking foreigners. The Boxer Rebellion (a rough translation of "Harmonious Fists," a name that refers to the society's commitment to the discipline of martial arts) received the covert support of the Chinese government. With more than 200 missionaries and several thousand Chinese Christians killed, and European diplomatic headquarters under attack in Beijing, the West responded in fury. A combined military force, drawing 16,000 soldiers from Russia, Germany, Austria-Hungary, France, Britain, Japan and the United States, crushed the rebellion and sacked Beijing. Required to pay a large indemnity to the West and to grant further trade and territorial concessions to its invaders, the Chinese central government was fatally weakened. In 1911, revolution engulfed China and propelled it into four decades of political and social tumult.

A Glimpse of Things to Come: The Boer War

Writing at the time of the Opium War (1840–1842), a British journalist in China urged the Chinese to accept what he regarded as the crucial lesson of history: "Ever since the dispersion of man, the richest stream of human blessings has, in the will of Providence, followed a western course." To many Europeans, Australians, and Americans, the rapid expansion of Western imperial control over much of the world after 1870 confirmed this lesson. At the very end of the nineteenth century, however, the British found themselves embroiled in a bloody imperial conflict that challenged this complacent view. The Boer War of 1899–1902 shook British self-confidence and in many ways foreshadowed both the total warfare and the crumbling of empires that

Concentration Camps

This illustration, which appeared in the French magazine *Le Petit Journal* in 1901, attempts to depict the anxiety and suffering of both the Boer families and their black servants who were imprisoned in English camps during the Boer War, yet it cannot convey the lack of sanitation that led to rampant disease.

CHRONOLOGY

The Struggle for Control in South Africa

1806	Britain takes control of the Cape Colony from the Dutch
1837	Boers establish independent republics of Transvaal and Orange Free State
1884	German annexation of Southwest Africa
1886	Gold discovered in the Transvaal
1899	Anglo-Boer War begins
1910	Self-government granted to South Africa

would mark the experience of the West in the twentieth century.

The Boer War was the culmination of a century of hostility among British imperialists, Dutch settlers (called Boers, the Dutch word for "farmer"), and indigenous Africans in the southern triangle of Africa. Germany's move into Southwest Africa in 1884 worsened this conflict: The British in the Cape Colony feared that the Boers would work with Germany to limit British expansion in the region. But even more important was the discovery in 1886 of diamonds and gold in the Transvaal, an independent Boer republic. British investors in the profitable diamond and gold mines resented Boer taxation and labor policies, and

Map 23.3   South Africa
After the defeat of the Boer states—the Transvaal and the Orange Free State—in the Boer War, the Union of South Africa comprised the Cape Colony and the two Boer republics.

pressed the British government to use military force to place the Boer republics under British rule.

In 1899, these imperialists got the war they had demanded, but it turned out to be rather different from what they expected. Skilled riflemen who were fighting for their very homes, the Boers proved to be fierce enemies who successfully adopted guerilla tactics against their numerically superior foe. By the spring of 1901, the war had reached a stalemate. The British military command in South Africa then decided to smoke out the Boer fighters through a scorched-earth policy: British troops burned more than 30,000 farms to the ground and confined the Boer women and children, and their black African servants, in poorly provisioned concentration camps. Diseases such as diphtheria and typhus soon took their toll. Almost 20,000 Boer women and children, and at least 14,000 blacks, died in these camps. The British finally defeated the Boers in April 1902, but this victory was limited. The Boer states were brought under British control but the Boers (or Afrikaners, as they were increasingly called) outnumbered other whites in the newly created Union of South Africa (see Map 23.3). After South Africa received self-government in 1910, the Afrikaners dominated the political system and created a nation founded on segregation and racist oppression.

More immediately, Britain emerged from the war with both its military and its humanitarian reputation severely tarnished. The war aroused strong opposition inside Britain and made clear that popular support for imperialism could be rapidly eroded if the costs of imperial conquest proved too high. The conflict between the war's opponents and supporters inside Britain was one that would be repeated within imperialist countries many times over the course of the next several decades as nationalist challenges against imperial rule multiplied and as the imperial idea grew less

IMAGE

The Boer War and Queen Victoria— Dutch Caricature

and less persuasive. More ominously, the sight of noncombatants confined—and dying—in concentration camps would soon become all too familiar. The Boer War thus served as a fitting opening to the twentieth century.

Conclusion

Reshaping the West: Expansion and Fragmentation

Africans and Asians who saw their political and social structures topple under the imperialist onslaught would probably have agreed with the Austrian poet Hugo von Hoffmansthal (1874–1929) when he wrote in 1905 that "what other generations believed to be firm is in fact sliding." Hoffmansthal, however, was commenting not on Africa or Asia or any other region of imperialist conquest, but rather on the Western cultural and intellectual landscape, which, like colonial political boundaries, underwent enormous and disturbing change in the period between 1870 and the outbreak of World War I in 1914. In this era, matter itself began to slide, as the Newtonian conception of the world gave way to a new, much more unsettling picture of the physical universe. At the same time, changes in medical practice, the revolt against positivism, and the triumph of Darwin's evolutionary theory helped undermine established assumptions and contributed to the sense that the foundations of Western culture were shifting; so, too, did the birth of modernism as well as broader cultural changes such as the move of middle-class women into the public sphere and the redefinition of sexual boundaries.

In the decades after 1870, then, a series of encounters reshaped the West. Its geographic boundaries expanded as non-European regions such as the United States emerged as significant economic and imperial powers. With Australians claiming Western identity, "the West" even spilled over into the Eastern Hemisphere. Yet fragmentation as well as expansion characterized the Western experience after 1870. At the same time that some social thinkers were proclaiming white cultural superiority, European artists such as Gauguin and Picasso were embracing the visual forms of non-European, nonwhite societies in an effort to push open the boundaries of Western culture. While scientific and technological achievements convinced many Europeans and Americans that the West was destined to conquer the globe, others regarded these scientific and technological changes with profound uneasiness.

The next chapter will show that the sense that old certainties were slipping led some Europeans to welcome the outbreak of war in 1914 as a way to restore heroic values and clear purpose to Western society. The trenches of World War I, however, provided little solidity. Many nineteenth-century political, economic, and cultural structures slid into ruin under the impact of total war.

Suggestions for Further Reading

For a comprehensive listing of suggested readings, please go to
www.ablongman.com/levack2e/chapter23

Adas, Michael. *Machines as the Measure of Men: Science, Technology, and Ideologies of Western Dominance.* 1989. A superb study of the way in which the ideology of empire was inextricably connected with cultural and intellectual developments within the West.

Betts, Raymond F. *The False Dawn: European Imperialism in the Nineteenth Century.* 1975. A general survey that looks at the ideas that underlay imperialism as well as the events that shaped it.

Bowler, Peter. *Evolution: The History of an Idea.* 1989. Looks at the development of evolutionary theory both before and after Darwin.

Butler, Christopher. *Early Modernism: Literature, Music, and Painting in Europe, 1900–1916.* 1994. Wide-ranging and nicely illustrated.

Dijkstra, Bram. *Idols of Perversity: Fantasies of Feminine Evil in Fin-de-Siècle Culture.* 1986. This richly illustrated work shows how anxiety over the changing role of women permeated artistic production at the end of the nineteenth century.

Dodge, Ernest. *Islands and Empires: The Western Impact on the Pacific and East Asia.* 1976. A useful study of Asian imperialism.

Ellis, John. *The Social History of the Machine Gun.* 1975. Lively, nicely illustrated, and informative.

Gould, Stephen Jay. *The Mismeasure of Man.* 1996. A compelling look at the manipulation of scientific data and statistics to provide "proof" for racist and elitist assumptions.

Headrick, Daniel R. *The Tools of Empire: Technology and European Imperialism in the Nineteenth Century.* 1981. Highlights the important role played by technology in determining both the timing and success of Western imperialism.

Hochschild, Adam. *King Leopold's Ghost.* 1998. Blistering account of Leopold's imperialist rule in the Congo.

Pick, Daniel.*Faces of Degeneration: A European Disorder, c. 1848–1918.* 1993. Argues that concern over degeneration formed a central theme in European culture in the second half of the nineteenth century.

Showalter, Elaine. *Sexual Anarchy: Gender and Culture at the Fin de Siècle.* 1990. An illuminating look at the turbulence that characterized gender relations in the fin de siècle.

Sperber, Jonathan. *Popular Catholicism in Nineteenth-Century Germany.* 1984. A look at the religious dimensions of popular culture.

Thornton, A. P. *The Imperial Idea and Its Enemies: A Study in British Power.* 1959; reprinted 1985. An older but still-important look at imperialist ideology and opposition.

Vandervort, Bruce. *Wars of Imperial Conquest in Africa, 1830–1914.* 1998. An up-to-date study by a military historian.

Wesseling, H. L. *Divide and Rule: The Partition of Africa, 1880–1914.* 1996. A solid survey of complex developments.

Notes

1. Winston Churchill, *The River War: An Account of the Re-Conquest of the Sudan* (1933); quoted in Daniel Headrick, *The Tools of Empire: Technology and European Imperialism in the Nineteenth Century* (1981), 118.

2. Quoted in Anne McClintock, *Imperial Leather: Race, Gender, and Sexuality in the Colonial Contest* (1995), 50.

3. Quoted in H. Stuart Hughes, *Consciousness and Society: The Reorientation of European Social Thought, 1890–1930* (1958), 332.

4. Quoted in Hughes, *Consciousness and Society,* 296.

5. Quoted in Shearer West, *Fin de Siècle* (1993), 24.

6. Quoted in Christopher Butler, *Early Modernism: Literature, Music, and Painting in Europe, 1900–1916* (1994), 2.

7. Stephen Kern, *The Culture of Time and Space, 1880–1918* (1983), 195.

8. From *Elementary Forms.* Quoted in Hughes, *Consciousness and Society,* 284–285.

9. Quoted in William Schneider, *An Empire for the Masses: The French Popular Image of Africa, 1870–1900* (1982), 72.

10. Mary Kingsley, in *West African Studies* (1901), 329–330.

11. Yve-Alain Bois, "Painting as Trauma," in Christopher Green, *Picasso's* Les Demoiselles d'Avignon (2001), 49.

12. Brassaï, *Conversations with Picasso,* trans. Jane Marie Todd (1999), 32.

13. John Golding, "*Les Demoiselles D'Avignon* and the Exhibition of 1988," in Green, *Picasso's* Les Demoiselles, 29.

14. Headrick, *The Tools of Empire,* 101. Headrick is the historian who identified the crucial role of the steamship, the quinine prophylaxis, and the breech-loading, repeating rifle in the conquest of Africa.

15. Quoted in Thomas Pakenham, *The Scramble for Africa, 1876–1912* (1991), 22.

16. Quoted in F. K. Crowley (ed.), *A New History of Australia* (1974), 6.

17. Ibid., 207.

18. Quoted in W. G. Beasley, *Japanese Imperialism, 1894–1945* (1987), 31–33.

The First World War

24

O N THE MORNING OF JULY 1, 1916, IN THE FIELDS OF NORTHERN France near the Somme River, tens of thousands of young British soldiers crawled out of ditches and began to walk across a muddy expanse filled with shards of metal and decomposing human bodies. Encumbered with backpacks weighing more than sixty pounds, the men trudged forward. For the past week their heavy artillery had pummeled the Germans who lay on the other side of the mud. Thus they expected little opposition. In less than sixty seconds, expectations and reality horribly diverged. The German troops, who had waited out the bombardment in the safety of "dugouts"—fortified bunkers scooped from the earth beneath the trenches—raced to their gunnery positions and raked the evenly spaced lines of British soldiers with machine-gun fire. The slowly walking men made easy targets. Those who were lucky enough to make it to the enemy lines found their way blocked by barbed-wire fences—still intact, despite the bombardment. Standing in front of the wire, they were quickly mown down. More than 20,000 British soldiers died that day, thousands within the first minutes of the attack. Another 40,000 were wounded. Yet the attack went on. Between July 1 and November 18, 1916, when the Battle of the Somme finally ended, almost 420,000 British soldiers were killed or wounded. Their French allies lost 200,000 men to death or injury. German casualties are estimated at 450,000.

Such carnage became commonplace during the First World War. At the Battle of Verdun, which began before the Somme conflict and continued after, the French and Germans suffered total casualties of at least 750,000, while in the disastrous Gallipoli offensive of 1915, ANZAC (Australia and New Zealand) troops experienced a casualty rate of 65 percent. Between 1914 and 1918, European commanders sent more than eight million men to their deaths in a series of often futile attacks. The total number of casualties—killed, wounded, and missing—reached more than 37 million.

Death on the Western Front This movie still comes from *The Battle of the Somme,* a documentary filmed during the battle and the first "war movie" shown in Britain.

These casualty figures were in part the products of the Industrial Revolution. Between 1914 and 1918 the nations of the West used their factories to churn out ever more efficient tools of killing. The need for machine guns, artillery shells, poison gas canisters, and other implements of modern warfare meant that World War I was the first total war°, a war that demanded that combatant nations mobilize their industrial economies as well as their armies, and thus a war that erased the distinction between civilian and soldier. In total war, victory depended on the woman in the munitions factory as well as the man on the front lines.

The First World War helped redefine the West. By shattering the authoritarian empires of eastern and central Europe and integrating the United States more fully in European affairs, the war ensured that commitment to democratic values became central to one dominant twentieth-century definition of "the West." But the war also strengthened antidemocratic forces: It catapulted into power a communist regime in Russia, intensified eastern Europe's ethnic and nationalist conflicts, and undermined many of the economic structures on which Western stability and prosperity rested. The years after the war, then, would see an acceleration of the fragmentation of Western cultural and social life already underway in the prewar period.

How did the encounter with total war transform Western cultures? Four questions inform this chapter's examination of the origins and experience of the First World War:

- **What factors led Europe into war in 1914?**
- **When, where, and how did the Allies defeat the Central Powers?**

- **How did total war structure the home fronts?**
- **What were the consequences of this war for the European and the global political and international order?**

The Origins of the First World War

- **What factors led Europe into war in 1914?**

On June 28, 1914, the heir to the throne of the Austrian-Hungarian Empire, Archduke Franz Ferdinand (1863–1914), was assassinated by ethnic Serbian terrorists. Austrian officials accused the Serbian government of involvement with the assassination. One month after the archduke's death, Austria declared war on Serbia. One week later, Europe was at war. Germany entered the war on Austria's side. These two Central Powers°, as they were known, squared off against not only small Serbia but also the colossal weight of Russia, France, and Britain, called the Allies°. By the time the war ended in late 1918, the conflict had embraced not only most of Europe, but also nations from around the globe.

Why did the murder of one man on the streets of a Balkan city lead to the deaths of millions in theaters of war ranging from muddy ditches in northern France to beaches along the Mediterranean, from the mountains of Italy to the deserts of northern Africa and the depths of the Atlantic? To understand the war's origins, we need to exam-

Arrest of Gavrilo Princip
Princip was only 18 years old when he assassinated Archduke Franz Ferdinand and set into motion the sequence of events that led to the First World War. Because of his young age, he did not receive the death penalty but instead was sentenced to twenty years in prison. He did not serve out his term; he died at age 22 of tuberculosis.

ine four interlocking factors: first, eastern European nationalism; second, the creation of rival alliance systems; third, the requirements of an industrialized military; and finally, the "will to war," the conviction among both policymakers and ordinary people that war would provide a resolution to social and cultural crisis.

Nationalism in Eastern Europe: Austria-Hungary and the Problem of Serbia

The roots of the First World War extend deep into the soil of nationalist conflict in eastern Europe. Western European national identities coalesced in accordance with existing political boundaries; in eastern Europe, however, the "nation" was defined by ethnic, religious, or linguistic identities rather than political citizenship. More than 27 million subjects of the Habsburg monarchy, for example, did not identify themselves with the Austrian-Hungarian Empire's dominant German or Magyar (Hungarian) peoples.[1] For the Czechs or Slovenians or Serbs, translating national into political identity—creating a "nation-state"—demanded the breakup of empires and a radical redrawing of political boundaries. Unlike in much of western Europe, then, in the East nationalism served as an explosive rather than a unifying force.

The divisive impact of nationalism explains why officials within the vast Austrian-Hungarian Empire regarded the small state of Serbia as a major threat. As a multiethnic, multilinguistic empire, Austria-Hungary's very survival depended on damping down the fires of nationalism wherever they flamed up. Yet much of Serbian politics centered on fanning the nationalist flame. In 1903, a group of Serbian army officers had shot Serbia's despised king and queen, chopped their bodies into little bits, and threw the pieces out the window. The new king, a member of a rival Serbian royal dynasty, recognized that his position on the throne was precarious, to say the least. To remain in power he catered to the demands of radical nationalists, who sought the unification of all Serbs into a Greater Serbian state. Given the fact that more than seven million Serbs lived not in Serbia but in Austria-Hungary, it is not surprising that the Austrian monarchy regarded the call for Serbian unification as a direct threat to its existence.

The hostile relations between Serbia and Austria-Hungary led directly to the outbreak of World War I. In 1908 Austria annexed Bosnia, a region with a large Serbian population. The Serbian government, which viewed Bosnia as an integral part of what it hoped would become Greater Serbia, responded to the Austrian annexation by encouraging Bosnian Serb separatist and terrorist groups. After one such group, the Black Hand, succeeded in assassinating Archduke Franz Ferdinand in the summer of 1914, Austrian officials decided to crush Serbia once and

for all. On July 23 a representative of the Austrian-Hungarian Empire presented the Serbs with an ultimatum, a set of demands that would have given Austria-Hungary the right to an unprecedented degree of involvement in Serbian internal affairs. Austrian diplomats informed the Serbian government that anything short of unconditional acceptance of the impossible ultimatum within just forty-eight hours would be taken as a declaration of war. Serbian officials agreed to comply with every demand except one. On July 28 Austria-Hungary declared war on Serbia.

DOCUMENT

Borijove Jevtic: The Murder of Archduke Franz Ferdinand

International Competition and Rival Alliance Systems

But why did war between Austria-Hungary and Serbia mean war across Europe? To understand what transformed this Austro-Serbian conflict into a continental war, we need to look beyond the unsettling impact of nationalism in eastern Europe to the heightened international competition that divided Europe into rival alliance systems. Concerned with protecting and enhancing the economic and military might of their states in an increasingly unsettled international climate, diplomats wove a web of alliances across Europe. As we will see, these alliances helped escalate a regional conflict into a European and then a global war.

One crucial factor in the growing intensity of international competition in the prewar years was Germany's unification as a state in 1871. By creating a military and economic powerhouse in the middle of Europe, the unification of the German states upset the balance of power on the Continent. Until 1890, however, the diplomatic maneuvers of Otto von Bismarck (1815–1898), the chancellor of the new nation, ensured a certain degree of stability. Bismarck recognized that Germany's position in the center of Europe made it vulnerable to encirclement by hostile powers. To avoid such an encirclement, Bismarck patched up relations with Austria in the aftermath of the Austrian-Prussian War, an effort that resulted in the signing of the Dual Alliance between Germany and the Austrian Empire in 1879. In 1882, the Dual Alliance became the Triple Alliance° when Italy joined the two Central Powers in a defensive treaty. At the same time, Bismarck was careful to maintain an alliance with Russia. By the terms of the Reinsurance Treaty of 1887, Russia and Germany agreed to remain neutral if either was attacked. Bismarck thus ensured that if Germany were to go to war against its old enemy, France, it would not face battle on two fronts.

But in 1888, a new emperor, Kaiser William II (r. 1888–1918), ascended the German throne. William, an ambitious and impatient young man, dismissed Bismarck in 1890 and launched Germany down a more dangerous path. The new kaiser made a fatal break with Bismarck's policies in two areas. First, William let the Reinsurance Treaty with Russia lapse, thus allowing fiercely anti-German France to form a partnership with Russia, formalized as the Franco-Russian Alliance of 1894. Germany now faced exactly the sort of encirclement by hostile powers, and the resulting threat of a two-front war, that Bismarck had sought to avoid.

Second, William favored a new "world policy" (*Weltpolitik*) for Germany that pushed Britain toward allying with Russia and France. Whereas Bismarck had insisted that Germany's interests were confined to Europe, William

and many prominent Germans wanted to see Germany claim its "place in the sun" as a global imperial and naval power. In 1898 Germany passed a naval law mandating the construction of nineteen battleships; a second law passed in 1900 doubled the number of ships. At the same time Germany adopted a more aggressive stance in Africa.

Such policies were guaranteed to aggravate and alienate Britain. As an island nation with a vast overseas empire, Britain based its military defense system on its naval su-

Map 24.1   Europe, August 1914

In August 1914 each of the Central Powers faced the challenge of war on two fronts, but the entry of the Ottoman Empire into the war on the side of the Central Powers in November 1914 blocked Allied supply lines to Russia through the Mediterranean.

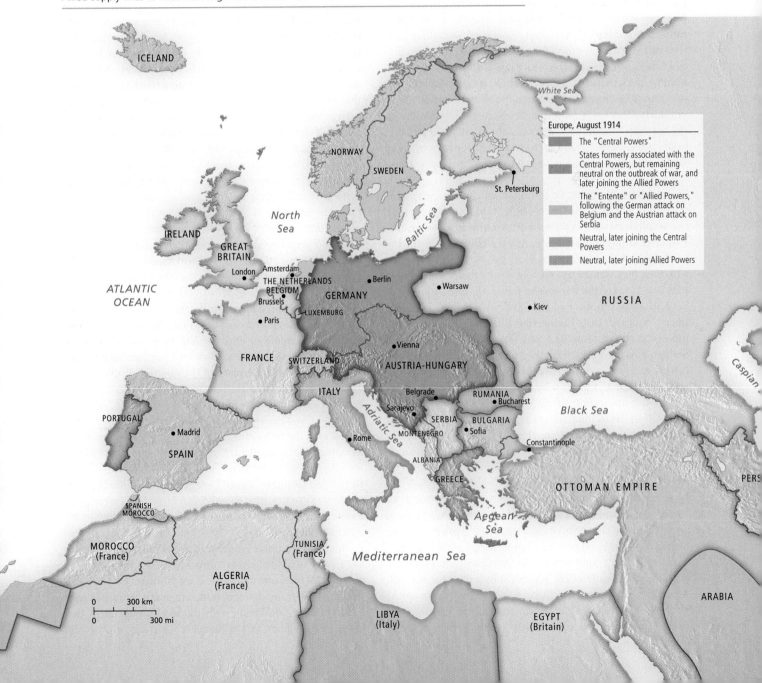

premacy. From the British point of view, a strong German navy was nothing less than a direct challenge to British national security, just as an expanding German empire was bound to conflict with British imperial interests.

Hostility toward German ambitions overcame Britain's long tradition of "splendid isolation" from continental entanglements. In the first decade of the twentieth century, a series of military, imperial, and economic arrangements formed ever-tighter links between Britain and both Russia and France. These arrangements cleared the way for the formation of the Triple Entente° among France, Russia, and Britain. An informal association rather than a formal alliance, the Triple Entente did not *require* Britain to join in a war against Germany. There is no doubt, however, that British officials increasingly viewed Germany as the major threat to British interests.

By the first decade of the twentieth century, then, Europe had split into two opposing camps: the Triple Alliance versus the Triple Entente. To German policymakers, it appeared that Germany stood surrounded by hostile powers. With Italy regarded as unreliable, Germany's alliance with Austria-Hungary took on greater and greater importance. Strengthening this crucial ally became paramount.

These considerations guided German policymaking in July 1914. When Austrian officials debated their response to the assassination of Franz Ferdinand, Kaiser William and his chancellor Theobold von Bethmann-Hollweg (1856–1921) urged a quick and decisive blow against Serbia. According to the Austrian ambassador, the kaiser told him "he would regret if we did not make use of the present moment, which is all in our favour."[2] In what some historians have described as an act akin to issuing a "blank check," the kaiser assured the ambassador that Germany would stand by Austria, even at the risk of a war with Russia.

Why would an Austrian move against Serbia heighten the risk of a wider war with Russia? The basic answer is that such a move threatened Russian interests. Eager to expand its influence in the Balkan region (and so gain access to the Mediterranean Sea), the Russian Empire had for decades positioned itself as the champion of Slavic nationalism in the Balkans and as the protector of small independent Slavic states such as Serbia. Thus both German and Austrian policymakers recognized that if Austria attacked Serbia, Russia might well mobilize against Austria and its ally, Germany (see Map 24.1).

German officials gambled, however, that Russia was not strong enough to wage war on Serbia's behalf. After all, in 1905, Russia had exposed its military shortcomings to the world with its loss in the Russo-Japanese War of 1905 (discussed in Chapter 23). And if they were wrong and Russia did mobilize for war? Then, as Bethmann-Hollweg explained, Germany's chances of winning were "better now than in one or two years' time."[3] German officials were well aware that the tsarist government, in response to its humiliating defeat in 1905, had implemented a military reform

and rearmament program. Given a few more years, the Russian Empire would constitute a formidable foe.

Mobilization Plans and the Industrialized Military

Germany's alliance with Austria emboldened Austrian policymakers to embark on an aggressive attack on Serbia. In addition, the links between Serbia and Russia made it very likely that this attack against Serbia would pull in the Russian Empire, which of course did not stand alone but was allied with France. Alliances alone do not explain the transformation of the Austro-Serbian conflict into a European war, however. Consider the case of Italy. Although a member of the Triple Alliance, Italy did not join Germany and Austria in August 1914. In fact, when Italy did enter the war in 1915, it did so on the opposing side. Even more significantly, no alliance *required* either Russia or Britain to enter the fray. We need to look at a third factor in the origins of World War I—the widening gap between the expectations of traditional diplomacy and the requirements of an increasingly industrialized military. This growing gap ensured that when preparations for war were underway in the summer of 1914, control of the situation slipped out of the hands of the diplomats and their political superiors and into the grasp of the generals. The generals had planned for a European war. Once set in motion, their plans began to dictate events.

In the decades before 1914 military planning was dominated by a new reality, the railroad. The criss-crossing of the European continent with train tracks gave military planners a new and powerful weapon: the ability to move large numbers of men quickly to precise locations. The speed with which nations could now throw armies into battle almost obliterated the distinction between mobilization and actual war. *Mobilization* refers to the transformation of a standing army into a fighting force—calling up reserves, requisitioning supplies, enlisting volunteers or draftees, moving troops to battle stations. Traditionally, mobilization meant preparation for a possible fight, a process that took months and could be halted if the diplomats succeeded in avoiding war. But the railroads accelerated the mobilization process and thereby changed the very nature of military plans. Aware that the enemy could also mobilize quickly, military planners stressed the importance of preventive attacks, of striking before being struck. Once a nation mobilized, the momentum toward war became almost irresistible.

These factors help explain the origins and impact of the Schlieffen Plan°, the military blueprint that structured German actions—and Allied reactions—in the summer of 1914. The Franco-Russian Alliance, signed in 1894, meant that German military planners had to prepare for the possibility of a two-front war. They devised the Schlieffen Plan for just that eventuality. The plan called for a quick knockout blow against France, which would then allow the German army to concentrate on defeating the much larger force of Russia. The key assumption here was that Russia's mobilization would take time: The vastness of its territory and its underdeveloped industrial infrastructure would slow its military mobilization and so guarantee that Russian troops would not pose an immediate threat to German borders. According to the Schlieffen Plan, the smaller Austrian army would hold off the slowly mobilizing Russians while the German army moved with lightning speed against France (see Map 24.2).

The need for speed dictated the next step in the plan—an attack against France via Belgium. German planners knew that the French expected any German attack to come from the northeast, through Alsace and Lorraine (the provinces taken from France by the victorious Germans after the Franco-Prussian War in 1870). The Schlieffen Plan called for the bulk of the German army to avoid France's heavily fortified northeastern border and instead swing to the west. Moving rapidly in a wide arc, the German army would flood into France through Belgium, encircle Paris, and scoop up the French forces before their generals knew

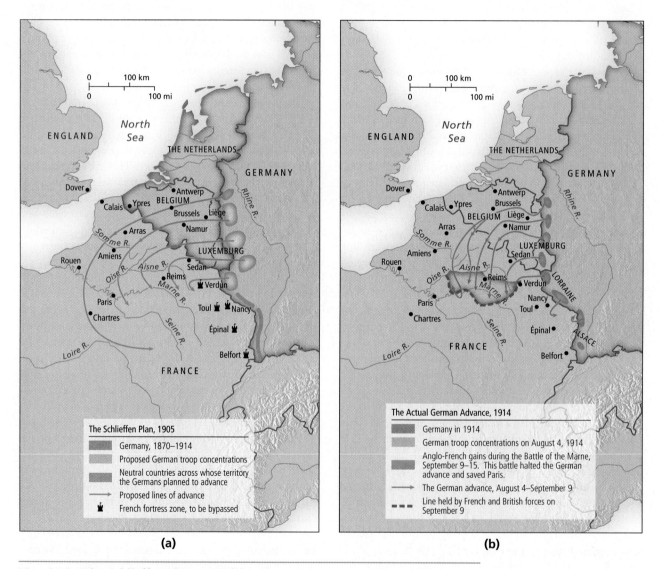

(a)   (b)

**Map 24.2   The Schlieffen Plan, 1905 (a) and
The Actual German Advance, 1914 (b)**
Count Alfred von Schlieffen's original plan of 1905 called for the sleeves of the German soldiers on the right flank to brush the English Channel—in a daring move, the German army would sweep in a huge arching movement west. In the fall of 1914 Helmut von Moltke modified Schlieffen's plan: The crucial right flank was only three times as strong as the left, rather than eight times as strong as Schlieffen stipulated, and Moltke moved his troops north and east of Paris instead of south and west. Military historians today still argue over whether Schlieffen's original plan could have succeeded.

what had hit them. With France out of the fight, the German troops would then board trains and speed back to the Eastern Front to join their Austrian allies in defeating the Russians.

The need for speed—the key factor in the Schlieffen Plan—placed enormous pressure on German politicians to treat a Russian declaration of mobilization as a declaration of war itself. And that is what happened. Only two days elapsed between Russia's order of mobilization and the German declaration of war. As soon as Russia began to mobilize, German military leaders pressured their political counterparts to break off diplomatic negotiations so that the troop-laden trains could set off.

Moreover, the plan for a speedy thrust into France meant that Germany went ahead with its invasion of Belgium—a decision that brought Britain into the war. Belgium was a neutral nation, with its neutrality protected by Britain under a long-standing treaty. German policymakers gambled that Britain would stay out of the conflict, but their gamble failed. Germany's unprovoked and brutal invasion of Belgium provided the British government with the public-pleasing moral justification it needed to enter the war with mass support. Thus, just six weeks after a Bosnian terrorist shot an Austrian archduke in Sarajevo, British and German soldiers were killing each other in the mud of northern France.

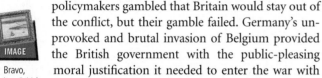

Bravo, Belgium-British Cartoon, WWI

The Will to War

The events that pushed those soldiers into that mud were dictated not by diplomatic maneuvers but by the needs of an industrialized military. Unable to rein in the new forces of industrial warfare, diplomats also faced new pressures from public opinion. This public pressure, or the "will to war," constitutes the fourth factor that helps explain the outbreak of World War I in 1914.

Still drawn largely from the aristocracy, diplomats moved from elaborate hall to exclusive dinner, secure in their belief that with their secret agreements and coded dispatches they could manipulate international affairs. Mired in traditional protocol, they also remained enmeshed in traditional assumptions. Prominent among these assumptions was the notion of balancing power among the principal European states. But they sought to maintain a balance of power in a world increasingly unbalanced by the forces of nationalism, mass politics, and industrial change. To these men, the traditions of secret diplomacy made perfect sense. They believed that only a small elite possessed the education, temperament, and background to understand and control international affairs. Increasingly, however, foreign affairs interested and excited the mass public, whose assumptions about the course of international events clashed strongly with those of the career diplomats.

CHRONOLOGY

The Outbreak of the First World War, 1914

June 28	Assassination of Archduke Franz Ferdinand
July 28	Austrian-Hungarian declaration of war against Serbia
July 30	Russian mobilization
July 31	French, Austrian, and German mobilization
August 1	German declaration of war on Russia
August 3	German declaration of war on France
August 4	German invasion of Belgium; British declaration of war against Germany

A number of developments accounted for this mass interest in foreign affairs. First, new technologies such as the telegraph, telephone, and camera collapsed distances and made international news much more immediate and accessible. Second, the rise of the popular press—cheap newspapers marketed to a semiliterate public—changed the coverage of foreign affairs. The competition to attract readers increased the pressure on editors and reporters to simplify and color their coverage, to make the often dull, dense, gray complexities of foreign relations into a compelling drama of Good Guys versus Bad Guys. Finally, the emergence of mass nationalism played an important role in shaping public opinion. Well-schooled in national identity, the European masses by 1914 viewed international relations as a vast nationalistic competition. They wanted evidence that "we" were ahead of "them."

Public opinion, therefore, constituted a new ingredient in international affairs in the years before the outbreak of World War I. Public opinion also constituted a real although impossible-to-measure factor in the war's outbreak. In the last weeks of July, pro-war crowds gathered in large cities. In Berlin, for example, a crowd of 30,000 young men and women paraded through the streets on the evening of July 25, singing patriotic songs and massing around statues of German heroes. Not all Europeans greeted the prospect of war with enthusiasm. Middle-class men and women, particularly students, predominated in the cheering crowds. In the countryside, farmers and villagers were more fearful, while in working-class neighborhoods anti-war demonstrations received solid support in July. The declaration of war, however, silenced these demonstrations. Opposition to the war was very much a minority movement after August 1914, even among working-class socialists. The German Social Democratic Party (SPD), for example, sponsored anti-war parades in July, but when war was declared in August, voted overwhelmingly to approve war appropriations. Socialist parties throughout Europe did likewise; national loyalties proved far stronger than class solidarity. In Britain, a total of 2.5 million men

DOCUMENT

War as a Unifying Force

Many Europeans welcomed the outbreak of war because it offered a chance to step aside from peacetime quarrels and factions. This excerpt from The Diary of a French Army Chaplain, first published in 1915, illustrates the way political party competition was forgotten as French society mobilized for war. The author, Felix Klein, contrasts the prewar political infighting of the French legislature with the spirit of unity expressed in the declaration of war on August 4, 1914.

Where, but a few weeks ago, could be found a more grievous spectacle than the first sittings of the new Chamber? And where, even in turning over the annals of many Parliaments, could be found a more admirable scene than that it offered on the 4th August. . . . And in this hot-bed of dissensions, quarrels, selfish desires, boundless ambitions, what trace remained of groups, of rivalries, of hates? Unanimous the respect with which the Presidential message was received; unanimous the adhesion to the Chief of the Government and his noble declaration: "It is the liberties of Europe that are being attacked of which France and her allies and friends are proud to be the defenders. . . . " And without debate, with no dissentient voice, all the laws of national defense, with the heavy sacrifices they imply, are at once voted. . . .

The fact is that we know ourselves no longer; barriers are falling on every side which, both in public and private life, divided us into hostile clans. . . . The relations between citizens are transformed. In the squares, in the streets, in the trains, outside the stations, on the thresholds of houses, each accosts the other, talks, gives news, exchanges impressions; each feels the same anxiety, the same hopes, the same wish to be useful, the same acceptance of the hardest sacrifices.

Source: From *Diary of a French Army Chaplain* by Felix Klein. London: Melrose, 1915.

volunteered to fight in the war, with 300,000 enlisting in the first month.

What made the idea of war so appealing to so many men and women in 1914? For some Europeans, war constituted a purging force, a powerful cleanser that would scour the impurities and corruptions from European society. As Chapter 23 explained, the years before 1914 witnessed a widespread cultural crisis in Europe, marked by fears of racial degeneration and gender confusion. War seemed to provide an opportunity for men to reassert their virility and their superiority. It also offered them the chance to be part of something bigger than themselves—to move be-

yond the boundaries of their often-restricted lives and join in what was presented as a great national crusade. As Carl Zuckmayer, a German playwright and novelist and a volunteer in the conflict, explained later, men like him welcomed the war as bringing "liberation . . . from . . . the saturation, the stuffy air, the petrifaction of our world."[4]

For political leaders, war provided the opportunity to mask social conflicts, to displace domestic hostilities onto the battlefield. We saw in Chapter 22 that the decades before 1914 were characterized by the rise of aggressive and often violent trade union movements and the increasing strength of socialist political parties, as well as anarchist-inspired

The Will to War

In western Europe, much of the public welcomed the news that war had begun. Here the crowds cheer as a French regiment embarks for the front. Enthusiasm for the war was less marked in working-class and peasant communities than in middle-class areas.

assassinations, ethnic terrorism, and feminist protests. To many European elites, their society seemed on the verge of disintegration. But, as the future British prime minister Winston Churchill explained, war united societies with "a higher principle of hatred."

The war for which university students cheered and for which the politicians and generals had planned was not anything like the war that actually happened, however. Most anticipated a short war. Theorists argued that in the new industrial age, the cost of waging war was so high that no nation would be able to sustain a conflict for very long. Everything depended on throwing as many men and as much materiel as possible into the battlefield at the very beginning. The men who marched off in August 1914 expected that they would be home by Christmas. Instead, if they survived, which few of them did, they would spend not only that Christmas, but the next three, in the midst of unspeakable and unprecedented horror.

The Experience of Total War

■ When, where, and how did the Allies defeat the Central Powers?

Expecting a German attack through Alsace and Lorraine, French military commanders in August 1914 poured their troops into these provinces. Counting on élan, the French military spirit, to see them to victory, the French troops swung into battle sporting bright red pants and flashy blue tunics. At their head rode the cream of the French military education system, the graduates of the elite Saint-Cyr military academy, who charged forward wearing their parade dress of white gloves and plumed hats. All that color and dash made easy targets for the German machine guns. As one military historian has written, "Never have machine-gunners had such a heyday. The French stubble-fields became transformed into gay carpets of red and blue."[5] Those "gay carpets," colored with the blood and broken bodies of young French men, signaled that this would be a war that shattered expectations, a war of revolutionary possibilities and devastating slaughter.

The Western Front: Stalemate in the Trenches

Implementing a modified version of the Schlieffen Plan (see Map 24.2), the German troops swept into Belgium in August 1914. By the first week of September the German troops had swung into France and seemed poised to take Paris. The Germans had overstretched their supply lines, however, and French and British forces turned back the

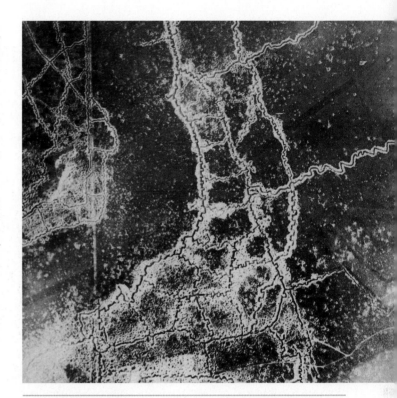

The Trench System
In this British reconnaissance photo, we can see the three lines of German trenches on the right, no-man's-land in the center, and the British trenches partly visible on the left. A trench system consisted of three parallel lines: the front or fire trenches, the support trenches, and the reserve trenches, all connected by intersecting communications trenches. If the enemy succeeded in gaining the front trenches, the defending forces could withdraw to the support or even the reserve trenches and still hold the line.

German offensive at the Marne River. In an episode that provided a glimpse of how important the internal combustion engine—and the oil that fueled it—was to become to modern warfare, an ingenious French commander was able to exploit a gap in the German lines by moving troops rapidly from the city of Paris to the front in the only vehicles available: taxicabs. (The army paid the drivers full fare for the trip.)

The taxicabs had saved Paris, but the French and British forces were unable to push the German army out of France. By the middle of October, the German, British, and French forces were huddling in trenches that eventually extended more than 300 miles from the Belgian coast to the borders of Switzerland. There they stayed for the next four years.

The Troglodyte War
Literary scholar Paul Fussell has used the phrase "the troglodyte war" to sum up what the soldiers experienced on the Western Front.[6] Like prehistoric cavemen, the men on

both sides of the conflict found themselves confined to underground dwellings. As British poet and World War I veteran Siegfried Sassoon explained, "when all is said and done, this war was a matter of holes and ditches."[7]

A Typical British Trench System

From the strategic point of view, these holes and ditches—the trenches—were defensive fortifications, and the long stalemate on the Western Front shows that they worked well. The defensive advantages of the trench system are easy to comprehend. Attacking infantry units faced the dreadful task of walking forward against troops armed with machine guns and sheltered behind wide barbed-wire fences and a thick wall of dirt and sandbags. Despite numerous attempts between the fall of 1914 and the spring of 1918, neither side was able to break through the enemy line.

A discussion of trench strategy, however, conveys nothing of the appalling misery summed up by the term "trench warfare." Imagine standing in a ditch that is about seven or eight feet deep and about three or four feet wide. The walls of the ditches are packed mud, propped up with sandbags. Wooden boards cover the floor, but the mud squelches between them. The top side of the ditch facing the enemy is reinforced with piled sandbags and barbed-wire barricades, thus deepening your sense of being underground. Moreover, the trenches do not run in tidy straight lines. Instead, the trenches zigzag at sharp angles, restricting the range of fire for enemy snipers and limiting the impact of explosives, but also ensuring that everywhere you look you see a wall of mud. Because you are in northern France, it is probably raining. Thus you are standing not on but *in* mud—if you are lucky. In some parts of the line, soldiers stand in muddy water up to a foot deep. On the other side of your sandbag defenses stretches no-man's-land°, the territory dividing the British and French trench systems from the German. Pocked with deep craters from heavy shelling, often a sea of mud churned up by the artillery, no-man's-land is littered with stinking corpses in various states of decomposition—all that is left of the soldiers who died during previous attacks. Your constant companions are lice (the term *lousy* was coined on the Western Front) and rats. For the rats, the war is an endless feast as they grow enormously fat, nibbling their way through the piles of dead.

From 1915 on, the horror of the Western Front escalated with the introduction of a new killing tool—poison gas, first deployed against enemy troops by the Germans in the spring of 1915. The Allies condemned the use of poison gas as inhumane, but within a matter of months the British and French, too, were firing poison gas canisters across the lines. The consequences were appalling: blinded eyes, blistered skin, seared lungs, death by asphyxiation. Gas proved to be an unreliable weapon, however. With a sudden wind shift, artillery units found they had asphyxiated their own troops. By 1916, with the gas mask a standard part of every soldier's uniform, military companies

Life and Death in the Trenches
The dead, the dying, and the surviving jostle one another in a French trench.

resembled hordes of insects. And, like insects, they were easily squashed. In the summer of 1915 an average of 300 British men became casualties on the Western Front every day, not because they were wounded in an attack but because they were picked off by snipers, felled by an exploding shell, or wasted by disease brought on by living in the mud amid putrefying corpses.[8]

The Offensives

The offensives, the attacks launched by both sides on the Western Front, sent the numbers of dead and wounded soaring. None of the elderly commanders—the Germans Helmut von Moltke and Erich von Falkenhayn, the French Joseph Joffre and Ferdinand Foch, and the British Douglas Haig and John French—knew what to make of trench warfare. Schooled to believe that war is about attacking, they sought vainly to move this conflict out of the ditches by throwing vast masses of both artillery and men against the enemy lines. But time and time again these mass attacks were foiled by the machine gun.

DOCUMENT

Expectations vs. Reality

Written by two young upper-middle-class British writers, the following poems illustrate the shift from the initial enthusiasm for the war to later disillusionment and despair. In the first poem, written just as the war began, Rupert Brooke welcomes the war as an ennobling and purifying force that will bring genuine peace. In contrast, Wilfred Owen's later piece flatly describes a soldier asphyxiated by poison gas. Brooke died of blood-poisoning on his way to Gallipoli in 1915; Owen was killed in battle in 1918, just days before the war ended.

1914. *Peace* by Rupert Brooke

Now, God be thanked Who has matched us with His hour,
And caught our youth, and wakened us from sleeping,
With hand made sure, clear eye, and sharpened power,
To turn, as swimmers into cleanness leaping,
Glad from a world grown old and cold and weary
Leave the sick hearts that honor could not move,
And half-men, and their dirty songs and dreary,
And all the little emptiness of love.

Dulce et Decorum Est by Wilfred Owen

Bent double, like old beggars under sacks,
Knock-kneed, coughing like hags,
we cursed through sludge,
Till on the haunting flares we turned our backs
And towards our distant rest began to trudge.
Men marched asleep. Many had lost their boots

But limped on, blood-shod. All went lame; all blind;
Drunk with fatigue; deaf even to the hoots
Of tired, outstripped Five-Nines that dropped behind.
Gas! Gas! Quick, boys!—An ecstasy of fumbling,
Fitting the clumsy helmets just in time;
But someone still was yelling out and stumbling
And flound'ring like a man in fire or lime . . .
Dim, through the misty panes and thick green light,
As under a green sea, I saw him drowning.
In all my dreams, before my helpless sight,
He plunges at me, guttering, choking, drowning.
If in some smothering dreams you too could pace
Behind the wagon that we flung him in,
And watch the white eyes writhing in his face,
His hanging face, like a devil's sick of sin;
If you could hear, at every jolt, the blood
Come gargling from the froth-corrupted lungs,
Obscene as cancer, bitter as the cud
Of vile, incurable sores on innocent tongues,—
My friend, you would not tell with such high zest
To children ardent for some desperate glory,
The old Lie: "Dulce et decorum est
Pro patria mori."*

---

*"It is good and right to die for one's country."

Sources: From "Peace" from *"1914" Five Sonnets* by Rupert Brooke. London: Sidgwick & Jackson, 1915; "Dulce et Decorum Est" from *Poems* by Wilfred Owen, with an Introduction by Siegfried Sassoon. London: Chatto and Windus, 1920.

A New Kind of War

From 1915 on, nerve gas became a part of the soldier's experience. Here tradition meets modernity as horses as well as soldiers are equipped with gas masks.

The Battle of the Somme, described in the opening of this chapter, provides a classic illustration of a failed offensive. The Somme, however, was only one of a number of fruitless attacks launched by both sides on the Western Front. By the end of 1917, the death tolls on the Western Front were astonishing, yet neither side had gained much ground. Soldiers, who enlisted not for a specific term or tour of duty but "for the duration"—until the war ended—became convinced that only the dead escaped from the trenches.

A Modernist War

To the artists and intellectuals who took up arms and found themselves in the trenches, the war often seemed like a modernist painting that had escaped its frame. The characteristics of modernist art—fragmentation, an emphasis on the isolation and the incommunicability of each individual's perception, surprising juxtaposition—also described the soldier's experience on the Western Front. Confined on all sides by mud walls, he glimpses only a bit of sky. When sent "over the top" in an attack, he knows only his own little part; he is unable to see the battlefield, or comprehend the battle plan, in its entirety. In letters home he finds he cannot communicate to his parents or to his lover the reality in which he is living and expects to die. Yet the front is often close enough to home to receive food packages sent just a few days earlier, so that he might find himself sitting in the mud, a few yards from the skeletal remains of other soldiers, eating a piece of his mother's best lemon tart.

Like modernist artists, soldiers quickly learned to question accepted truths, to mistrust the past, and to doubt the power of human reason. Recruited with promises of glory, they watched rats eat the bodies of their friends. While the generals clung to their history books, which taught that offensives won wars, soldiers died in great numbers. Not surprisingly, the modernist rejection of history resonated in the trenches. The past seemed to offer little of value in this new kind of war. Similarly, the war revealed the absurdity of the nineteenth-century faith in rationality. As the weeks, months, and years wore on, and the death tolls climbed higher and higher, many soldiers were struck by the senselessness, the sheer irrationality, of the conflict. The war often seemed to be governed not by reasoning men but rather by unthinking machines.

The mechanical nature of this war became a dominant theme in soldiers' accounts, just as machines dominated prewar modernist art. Seeking the chance to be heroes, men volunteered to fight and found themselves reduced to interchangeable parts in a colossal war machine. Like mechanical gears, army companies moved in circles: from the firing trenches to the reserve trenches to the support trenches to behind the lines and back to the firing trenches. Thus in works such as *Returning to the Trenches,* British artist Christopher Nevinson (1889–1946) used modernist techniques to represent the reality of mechanized war. In Nevinson's work, the men cease to be individuals. Welded into a single machine, they are propelled into the trenches by a force beyond their control, components of a purely mechanized landscape. French war veteran and writer Georges Duhamel (1884–1966) even likened the front-line ambulances to factory repair shops. The function of the ambulances was to repair the broken-down parts (the soldiers) of the war machine and get them back into production.

We saw in Chapter 23 that in the decades before 1914 members of the press and the general public often condemned modernist styles and idioms as outrageous,

***Returning to the Trenches* by Christopher Nevinson (1914–1915)**
Nevinson's work demonstrates the close parallels between wartime reality and modernist representation.

degenerate, and removed from reality. By 1918, however, as Nevinson's painting shows, these forms seemed to offer an accurate, even realistic means of conveying the horror of the war experience. Thus the British cultural historian Samuel Hynes has argued, "modernism had not changed, but reality had."[9]

Yet the realities of this war did change modernism. Horrified by the mass slaughter, many modernist artists abandoned the modernist principle of "art for art's sake," the idea that art has no moral purpose or social responsibility, that it conveys no message. Instead, they used modernist techniques to communicate their outrage. Paul Nash (1889–1940), a British landscape painter and army volunteer, explained in 1918, "I am no longer an artist, interested and curious, I am a messenger who will bring back word from the men who are fighting to those who want the war to go on forever. . . . may it burn their lousy souls."[10] Nash's depiction of the Western Front, *We Are Making a New World* (1918), transformed the landscape genre from an evocation of pastoral tranquility into a cry of pain.

The War in Eastern Europe

The Western Front was only one in a number of theaters of war. Floundering in the snows of the Italian Alps, the Italian and Austrian armies fought each other along a stationary front for two brutal years after Italy, enticed by the promise of territorial gain, joined the war on the Allies' side. Characterized by futile offensives and essential immobility,

the war in Italy mirrored the conflict on the Western Front. In eastern Europe, however, a different plot unfolded. For three years, massive armies surged back and forth, as the plains and mountains of eastern Europe echoed with the tumult of spectacular advances, headlong retreats, and finally political revolution.

The Eastern Front: A War of Movement

Much of the movement in eastern Europe consisted of Russians running—running forward in surprising advances, running back in terrifying retreats. When the war began in August 1914, Russia shocked its enemies by fielding a much stronger army much more quickly than German and Austrian military planners had expected. In a two-pronged onslaught, Russian troops headed against the Germans in East Prussia and against the Austrians in Galicia, the northeastern region of the Austrian Empire. Surprised by the speed of the Russian advance, German troops in East Prussia at first fell back, but skillful maneuvering by the German commanders Paul von Hindenburg (1847–1934) and Erich von Ludendorff (1865–1937) turned the Russian tide at the Battle of Tannenberg at the end of August. Within two weeks the Germans had shoved the Russian troops back across the border. In the subsequent months, the Germans advanced steadily into Russian imperial territory. At the same time, a combined German and Austrian assault forced the Russian army to retreat from Austrian Galicia—and more than 300 miles into its own territory. Russian casualties in the offensive stood at 2.5 million.

Over the next two years the pattern of Russian advances and retreats continued. Russian soldiers pushed into Austria-Hungary in June 1916, but could not sustain the attack. The summer of 1917 saw another initially successful Russian advance, but it too soon disintegrated into a retreat (see Map 24.3).

These retreats revealed that Russia's economic and political structures could not withstand the pressures of total war. Russian supply lines were so overextended that the poorly fed and inadequately clothed Russian troops found themselves without ammunition and unable to press ahead. Demoralized by defeat and by the daily grind of life without adequate rations or uniforms or weapons, Russian soldiers began to desert in ever-larger numbers. On the home front Russian workers and peasants grew ever more impatient with wartime deprivations and demands. This disaffection

led to revolution. As we will explore in detail later in this chapter, revolution forced the tsar to abdicate in March 1917. In November, the Bolsheviks, a small group of socialist revolutionaries, seized control and moved quickly to pull Russia out of the war.

The Bolshevik military withdrawal finally freed Germany from the burden of waging a two-front war. Signed in March 1918, the Treaty of Brest-Litovsk° ceded to Germany all of Russia's western territories, containing a full one-third of the population of the prewar Russian Empire. Germany now controlled the imperial Russian territories in Poland, the Baltic states, and part of Byelorussia. But because it had to commit large numbers of troops to controlling this new territory, Germany reaped less advantage from this victory than might have been expected.

Map 24.3 The Eastern and Middle Eastern Fronts, 1915–1918

Unlike the Western Front, the Eastern Front was far from stationary. By 1918, the Central Powers occupied Serbia, Romania, and much of European Russia. The entry of the Ottoman Empire on the side of the Central Powers in November 1914 extended the conflict into the Middle East. In 1915 Ottoman forces not only repelled an initial British advance toward Baghdad but also threatened Egypt. By the end of 1917, however, Arab nationalists helped the British defeat the Central Powers in the Middle East.

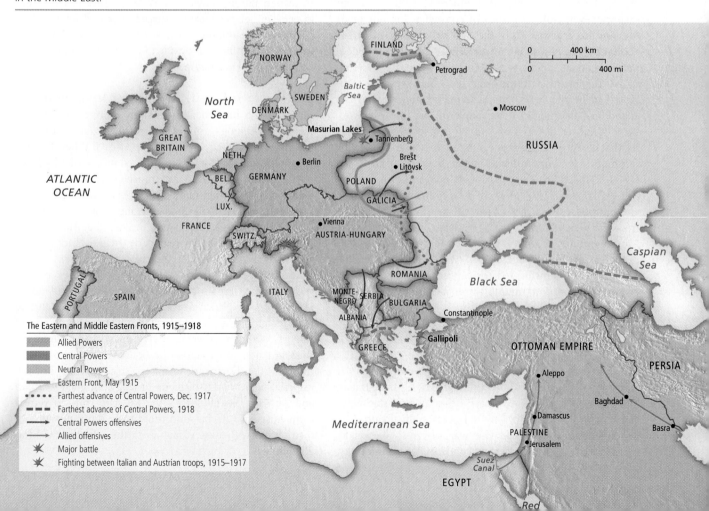

The Eastern and Middle Eastern Fronts, 1915–1918

- Allied Powers
- Central Powers
- Neutral Powers
- Eastern Front, May 1915
- Farthest advance of Central Powers, Dec. 1917
- Farthest advance of Central Powers, 1918
- Central Powers offensives
- Allied offensives
- Major battle
- Fighting between Italian and Austrian troops, 1915–1917

The Forgotten Front: The Balkans

The new Balkan states were no strangers to war by 1914. After shrugging off Ottoman control, Greece, Bulgaria, Romania, and Serbia fought each other in the First and Second Balkan Wars of 1912 and 1913. In southeastern Europe, World War I was thus in many ways the "Third Balkan War," yet another installment in an ongoing competition for territory and power. Bulgaria joined the Central Powers in 1915, hoping to gain back the territory it had lost in the Second Balkan War. To protect its hold on this territory, Romania entered the war on the Allies' side in August 1916 and quickly found itself crushed between invading Bulgarian, German, and Austrian-Hungarian troops.

The Serbian experience was even more bleak. In the first year of the war Austrian and Serbian troops jostled back and forth for control of the country, but in October 1915 Bulgarian, German, and Austrian forces advanced into Serbia from three different directions. By November, the Serbian army had been pushed to the Albanian border. Two hundred thousand Serbian soldiers fled over the snow-swept mountains of Albania to the Adriatic Sea, in a disastrous "Winter March." Austrian troops occupied Serbia and placed the country under military rule. Like most military occupations, this one was brutal. By the war's end, approximately 25 percent of Serbian citizens lay dead.

The Winter March
Of the 200,000 Serbian soldiers who attempted the "Winter March" in 1915, at least 40,000 died and another 60,000 were wounded.

The World at War

The imperialist expansion of the later nineteenth century ensured that as soon as the war began, it jumped outside European borders. The British and French Empires supplied the Allies with invaluable military and manpower resources. Australia, New Zealand, Canada, India, South Africa, and Ireland supplied no less than 40 percent of Britain's military manpower during the war. More than 650,000 men from Indochina, Algeria, and French West Africa assisted the French war effort. (One of these men was

A World at War: Sikh Cavalry Officers
Sikh cavalry officers from India patrol the Western Front. India provided 1.3 million men to assist the British war effort. Indian troops fought—and more than 49,000 Indian soldiers died—in battles in the Middle East, in East Africa, and on the Western Front. Similarly, black Senagalese soldiers fought for France on various fronts; 30,000 Senagalese died during the war.

Ho Chi Minh, who would later lead the Vietnamese struggle against France and then the United States.)

Fighting fronts multiplied around the globe as the major combatants struggled for imperial as well as European supremacy (see Map 24.4). Portugal joined the Allies largely because it hoped to expand its colonial possessions in Africa. Japan, too, entered the war for colonial gain. When the war began in August 1914, Japan seized the opportunity to snatch German colonial possessions in China. In return, Japan contributed to the Allied war effort by using its navy to protect Allied troop and supply ships in both the Pacific and the Mediterranean. By the end of 1914, most of Germany's colonies in the Far East had been occupied by Japanese and ANZAC troops.

The Middle East also became a key theater. When the Ottoman Empire joined the war on the side of Germany and Austria-Hungary in 1914, it posed a serious threat to Britain's economic and military interests in the Mediterranean and Middle East. Britain was desperate to protect Allied access both to the Suez Canal—a vital link to the soldiers and supplies of India, Australia, and New Zealand—and to Persian oil fields, an important source of fuel for the British navy. In a move that would have far-reaching consequences for twentieth-century geopolitics, the British joined forces with Arab nationalists. Led by a British soldier named T. E. Lawrence (1888–1935)—better known as "Lawrence of Arabia"—and inspired by promises of postwar national independence, Arab nationalists used guerilla

Map 24.4   The World at War

Imperialist relationships and global economics ensured that a European conflict became a world war. In Africa both Portuguese and South African troops fought a bush war against German and native soldiers. Japan, the first non-European power to enter the war, occupied German colonial territories in Asia and the Pacific region. When the United States joined the Allies in April 1917, a number of Latin American countries also declared war on Germany.

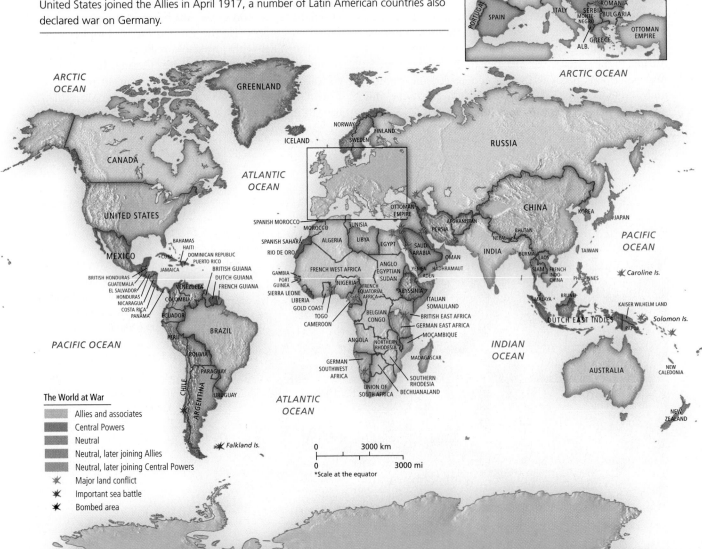

warfare to destroy what remained of Ottoman rule in the Middle East. By 1917 the Ottomans had lost control of almost the entire coastal region of the Arabian peninsula bordering the Red Sea, and Lawrence and his Arab allies had captured Jerusalem.

The War at Sea and the Entry of the United States

Despite the losses of its ally in the Middle East, at the beginning of 1918 Germany looked to be in a winning position. Engulfed in revolution, Russia had dropped out of the war and relieved Germany of the burden of fighting on two fronts. With Serbia and Romania both occupied by their forces, the Central Powers could claim to have won the war in eastern Europe. Yet Germany was far weaker than any map of its eastern conquests in 1917 could indicate. Germany was being strangled from the sea.

While infantrymen rotted in trenches and froze in mountain passes, the German and British navies fought a critical war at sea. German submarines sought to cut Britain's imperial lifeline and starve out its civilian population by sinking ships before they could reach British ports. Almost 14,000 British sailors and civilians died in these submarine attacks. In turn, British destroyers stretched a blockade across all ocean and sea passageways to Germany and its allies.

The Allied blockade proved effective in preventing food and other essential raw materials from reaching Germany, Austria-Hungary, and their associates. Food shortages sparked riots in more than thirty German cities in 1916. When the potato crop that year failed and eliminated one of the only sources of nutrition left, children's rations were limited to *one-tenth* of their actual needs.

Desperate to win the war quickly, German policymakers in 1917 took a huge gamble when they decided to up the tempo of their submarine war against Britain. Suspecting that supposedly neutral American passenger ships were delivering essential war materiel to Britain, they ordered their submarines to sink without warning any ship heading for British shores. The Germans were well aware that this policy of unrestricted submarine warfare would very likely pull the United States into the war. In May 1915, a German submarine had torpedoed the British passenger liner *Lusitania* and killed almost 1,200 people, including 128 Americans. The furious response from the United States had forced Germany to restrict its submarine attacks. By 1917, however, Germany stood on the brink of economic collapse, and German policymakers decided they had no choice but to resume unrestricted attacks on ships heading for British ports. They gambled they could defeat Britain in a last-ditch effort before the addition of the United States to the Allies could make much of a difference. Over

CHRONOLOGY

The End of the War, 1917–1918

1917	Stalemate continues on the Western Front
March	Collapse of the Russian imperial government
April	U.S. declaration of war on Germany
November	Bolshevik Revolution in Russia
December	Bolsheviks sign armistice with Germany; capture of Jerusalem by British troops
1918	
March	Treaty of Brest-Litovsk
March–July	German offensive on Western Front, rapid gains
July–November	Allied counteroffensive begins
September	Bulgaria and Allies sign armistice
November 3	Austria-Hungary sues for peace with Allies
November 9	Kaiser William abdicates
November 11	Fighting ends on Western Front at 11:00 A.M.

the next eight months German submarines sank 500 British merchant ships.

The United States declared war on Germany in April 1917. Outrage over American deaths at sea served as the most immediate cause of American entry into the war. Four other factors, however, also played a role. First, Franco-British news stories about German atrocities during the invasion of Belgium had persuaded many Americans that right rested on the Allied side. Second, the Russian Revolution of March 1917 removed an important obstacle to American cooperation with the Allies—the tsarist regime. Americans had balked at the idea of allying with the repressive government of Tsar Nicholas II, but the March Revolution, which overthrew Nicholas, reminded many in the United States of the American Revolution and offered American policymakers a more ideologically acceptable wartime partner. Third, by the time President Woodrow Wilson asked the U.S. Congress for a declaration of war, the American economy was thoroughly intertwined with that of the Allies. Trade between the United States and the Allied nations had grown from $825 million in 1914 to more than $3 billion in 1916, and American bankers had loaned more than $2 billion to the Allied governments. Finally, the German government committed a serious blunder in the spring of 1917 when it offered to back Mexico in recovering New Mexico, Arizona, and Texas in exchange for Mexican support should war break out between Germany and the United States. The interception of a telegram sent by the German foreign minister Arthur Zimmermann exposed this offer and inflamed anti-German sentiment in the

United States. The German resumption of unrestricted submarine warfare, then, simply put flame to kindling that was already in place.

The U.S. declaration of war (followed by those of Brazil, Costa Rica, Cuba, Guatemala, Haiti, Honduras, Nicaragua, and Panama) provided an immediate psychological boost for the Allies, but several months passed before American troops arrived on the battlefield in significant numbers. By July 1918, however, the United States was sending 300,000 fresh soldiers to Europe each month. The Allies now had access to an almost unlimited supply of materiel and men. Eventually nearly two million American soldiers were sent to Europe and almost 49,000 American soldiers died in battle.

Back in Motion:
The Western Front in 1918

Faced with the prospect of having to fight fresh American forces, German policymakers decided to gamble one more time. On March 2, 1918—before the bulk of the U.S. army had been deployed—the German army launched a massive ground assault against British and French lines. The gamble almost succeeded. In just thirty minutes the German troops broke through the British front line; in seven days, German soldiers advanced forty miles; by April the German army stood just fifty miles from Paris.

What explains this sudden shift on the Western Front from a conflict characterized by stalemate and deadlock to a war of rapid and decisive movement? The answer is that after three and a half years of relentless, pointless slaughter, the German High Command in 1918 finally developed strategies that matched offensive techniques with industrialized killing technology. As we have seen, in the first years of the war commanders remained committed to offensive techniques suited to an age of preindustrial warfare—the mass charge, the cavalry attack. What they failed to realize was that industrial technologies such as the machine gun had transformed the power of defensive war. Certainly Western commanders were well-acquainted with the power of the machine gun. In the imperial conflicts discussed in Chapter 23, the machine gun enabled small European forces to mow down enormous indigenous armies. But on the Western Front, both sides possessed the machine gun. In other words, both sides were good on defense but poor on offense.

In 1918, however, the Germans came up with a new offensive strategy. They did not simply throw masses of men against machine guns. Instead of a frontal assault dictated by commanders sitting well behind the lines, Germany's offensive of 1918 consisted of a series of small group attacks aiming to cut behind British and French positions rather than straight on against them. In addition, the Germans in 1918 scrapped the massive preliminary artillery barrage that signaled when and where an attack was about to begin. In place of the barrage they employed sudden gas and artillery bursts throughout the offensive. The rapid German advance in the spring of 1918 showed that technique had caught up with technology.

In July, however, the Allies stopped the German advance; in August they broke through the German lines and began to push the German army backward. Throughout the summer the push continued. By September the Western Front, which had stood so stationary for so long, was being rolled eastward at a rapid clip.

The final German gamble failed for three reasons: First, the German advance was so rapid that it overstrained German manpower and supply lines; second, the Allies learned from their enemies and adopted the same new offensive strategies; and third, the Allies figured out how to make effective use of a new offensive technology—the tank. Developed in Britain, the tank obliterated the defensive advantages of machine-gun-fortified trenches. A twentieth-century offense met a twentieth-century defense, and the war turned mobile.

1916 Debut of the British Tank

Reinforced with fresh American troops and the promise of more to come, the Allied forces surged forward against the hungry and demoralized Germans. When the Bulgarian, Ottoman, and Austrian armies collapsed in September and October, Germany stood alone. On November 11, 1918, German leaders signed an armistice and the war ended.

The Home Fronts

■ How did total war structure the home fronts?

The term *home front* was coined during World War I to highlight the fact that this conflict was fought not only by soldiers on the front lines, but also by civilians at home. Created by industrialization, total war demanded the wholehearted mobilization of a combatant nation's productive capacity. Total war recast and in some cases revolutionized not only the economic but also the political, social, and gender relations of the nations involved.

Industrial War

World War I was the first industrial war. Poison gas, the machine gun, barbed wire, canned foods, mass-produced uniforms and boots, and of course shovels all poured out of Europe's factories and helped shape this war. Even more important, industrialization made it possible for governments to deploy the vast masses of men mobilized in this conflict. Consider this comparison: The Battle of Waterloo, which ended the Napoleonic Wars in 1815, involved 170,000 men; the Battle of Sedan, which ended the Franco-Prussian War in 1870, involved 300,000 soldiers. The first Battle of the Marne, however, fought between the Germans and the

French in September 1914, involved one million combatants. By the war's end, more than 70 million men had been mobilized; in France and Germany, approximately 80 percent of the men of draft age were called up. Only industrialized production could keep these huge armies supplied with weapons, ammunition, and other necessities.

It thus became clear that this war would be won in the factories as much as on the front lines. Those nations that collapsed did so at least in part because they lost the war at home. In Austria-Hungary, factories could not produce enough uniforms to clothe the empire's soldiers. Similarly, Russia's underdeveloped industrial sector and infrastructure meant that its soldiers failed to receive needed supplies. In the end, the Allies (minus Russia) won the war in large part because of their greater economic power.

The Expansion of the State

At first, no government realized the crucial role that industrial labor would play in this war. Both military and political leaders believed that the war would end quickly, and that success depended on throwing as many men as possible into the front lines. In France, even munitions factories were shut down and their workers sent to the front. Governments practiced "business as usual"—letting the free market decide wages, prices, and supply—with disastrous results. Soaring rates of inflation, the rapid expansion of the black market, growing public resentment over war profiteering (the practice of private businessmen making huge profits off the war), and, most crucially, shortages of essential military supplies, including shells, proved that a total war economy needed total regulation.

Beginning in 1915, both the Allied and Central Powers' governments gradually assumed the power to requisition supplies, dictate wages, limit profits, and forbid workers to change jobs. In Germany, the increasing regulation of the economy was called "war socialism," a misleading term because it was big business rather than ordinary workers who benefited. The German army worked in partnership with large industrial firms to ensure the supply of war materiel to the front lines, while the Auxiliary Service Law of 1916 drafted all men age 17 to 60 for war work. Measures such as these greatly expanded the size and power of the central governments in the combatant states. For example, in 1914 the British office in charge of military purchases employed twenty clerks. By 1918, it had become the Department of Munitions, an enormous bureaucratic empire with 65,000 employees overseeing more than three million men and women working in government-owned and -operated munitions plants.

This expansion of governmental power was one of the most striking aspects of the war experience on the home front. Even in Britain, bastion of liberalism, the demands of total war seriously restricted individual freedom. Flying in the face of tradition, in 1916 Britain's government imposed the draft—a clear example of the requirements of the state overriding the desires of the individual. By the war's end, governments had moved further, not only dictating all aspects of economic life but also controlling many areas of social and intellectual choice. The British government restricted the hours that pubs could be open, as a way of encouraging workers to show up for work sober. It also tampered with time itself, introducing Daylight Saving Time as a means of maximizing war production.

The Politics of Total War

The war's reliance on industrial production greatly empowered industrial producers—the workers. In 1915 both France and Britain abandoned political party competition and formed coalition governments, which included socialist and working-class representatives. At the same time, political leaders welcomed labor unionists as partners in shaping the wartime economy. In return, French and British union leaders agreed to a ban on labor strikes and the "deskilling" of certain jobs—a measure that allowed unskilled laborers, particularly women, to take the place of skilled workers at much lower rates of pay.

Despite these "no strike" agreements, both Britain and France witnessed a sharp rise in the number of labor strikes in 1916 and in 1917. Faced with the potential of disintegration on the home front, political leaders in Britain and France reacted similarly. Both countries witnessed the emergence of war governments committed to total victory. In Britain, David Lloyd George (1863–1945) became prime minister at the end of 1916. A Welsh artisan's son who had fought hard to reach the top of Britain's class-bound, English-dominated political system, Lloyd George was not a man to settle for a compromise peace. One year later, Georges Clemenceau (1841–1929) became prime minister of France. Nicknamed the "Tiger," Clemenceau demanded victory. When asked to detail his government's program, he replied simply, "*Je fais la guerre!*" ("I make war!").

Making war, however, was not possible without public support, as officials in both France and Britain realized. They cultivated this support in two ways. First, they sought to depict the war as a struggle between democracy and authoritarianism—a crusade not simply for national power or economic gain but for a better world. Second, they recognized that if civilian morale were to be sustained, the basic needs of ordinary citizens had to be met. Both governments intervened regularly in the economy to ensure that workers received higher wages, better working conditions, and a fair distribution of food stocks. In state-owned munitions factories, workers for the first time received benefits such as communal kitchens and day care. Food rationing (although not implemented until quite late in the war) actually improved the diets of many poor families.

The situation in Germany differed significantly. The parliamentary political voice of the German working class, the Social Democratic Party (SPD), was not invited to participate in a coalition government. Instead, until the very last weeks of the war German political leadership remained in the hands of the conservative aristocracy. Increasingly, the aristocratic generals Hindenburg and Ludendorff—the heroes of the Battle of Tannenberg—called the political shots. The army and big industrial firms seized control of German economic life. Given the power to set prices and profit margins, industrialists—not surprisingly—made a killing. Their incomes soared, while ordinary workers were ground down by escalating inflation and chronic food shortages. By 1917, industrial unrest had slowed German war production, and civilian discontent had reached dangerous levels. Unlike the British and the French, the German government proved unable to control the unrest. The success of the Allied blockade meant Germans were starving. In contrast, living standards among employed workers in France and in Britain rose during the war.

The World Turned Upside Down

By the war's end, changes in the relations among classes and between men and women caused many Europeans to feel as if their world had turned upside down. European workers grew more radical as they realized the possibilities of their own collective power, as well as the potential of the state as an instrument of social change. The fact that by 1917 many of these workers were women also had revolutionary implications. In the work world and in society at large, gender roles, like class relations, underwent a marked shift.

The War's Impact on Social Relations

In the trenches and on the battlefields, World War I had a leveling effect. For many young middle- and upper-class soldiers, the war provided their first sustained contact with both manual labor and manual laborers. In letters home, they testified to a newfound respect for both, as the horrors of the war experience broke down rigid class barriers.

On the home front, however, social relations grew more rather than less hostile. During the war years, inflation eroded the savings of the middle class and left bourgeois men and women desperately seeking ways to maintain their social and economic status. In Germany and throughout eastern Europe, drastic food shortages and falling real wages produced a revolutionary situation. By contrast, in both Britain and France, a rising standard of living demonstrated to workers the benefits of an active and interventionist state. Yet class hostilities rose in western Europe, too. Workers, having finally tasted the economic pie, fought for a bigger piece, while the middle class fought to defend its shrinking share. Working-class activists demanded that the state continue to regulate the economy in peacetime as it did in waging total war, to improve the standard of living of ordinary workers.

The War's Impact on Gender Relations

By 1916, labor shortages in key military industries, combined with the need to free up as many men as possible for fighting, meant that governments on both sides actively recruited women for the paid workforce. Women were suddenly everywhere in very visible roles: as bus drivers, eleva-

Women in the War
Women often served at the front in extremely dangerous conditions. The two women in this photograph set up a dressing station to treat the wounded just five yards behind the trenches.

tor operators, train conductors, and sales clerks. In eastern Europe, the agricultural labor force came to consist almost entirely of women. In western Europe, women joined labor unions in unprecedented numbers. They took on extremely dangerous positions in munitions factories; they worked just behind the front lines as ambulance drivers and nurses; in 1917 and 1918, they often led the way in walking off the job to demand better conditions.

The impact of the war on women's roles should not be exaggerated, however. Throughout the war, more women continued to work in domestic service—as cooks, maids, nannies—than in any other sector of the economy. The great majority of the women who did move into skilled industrial employment were not new to the world of paid employment. Before 1914 they had worked in different, lower-paying jobs. And they certainly were not treated as men's equals. In government-run factories in Britain, women received as little as 50 percent of men's wages for the same job.

Nevertheless, for many women, the war constituted a profoundly liberating experience. With their husbands away, many wives made decisions on their own for the first time. The average wages of female munitions workers in Britain were three times their prewar earnings. But just as crucially, the war validated women's claims to citizenship. Total war made the female civilian into a combatant. For example, the *Win the War Cookery Book* (1917) urged British housewives to view the preparation of meals in a time of food shortages as part of the war effort: "The British fighting line shifts and extends now *you* are in it. The struggle is not only on land and sea; it is in *your* larder, *your* kitchen and *your* dining room. Every meal you serve is now literally a battle."[11] With "women's work" as central to national survival as men's work, women came to see themselves as an integral part of the national community.

Middle-class women, especially, testified to the freedom the war brought. Before 1914, the position of middle-class women in Europe had undergone important changes, as Chapter 22 detailed. From 1870 on, the numbers of women in higher education and paid employment expanded, women increasingly served in local government, and a European-wide women's suffrage campaign emerged. Despite the rise of these strong challenges to the ideology of separate spheres, however, the predominant idea remained that women were biologically suited for the private confines of home and family and men for the public arena of work and politics. Many middle-class girls continued to live lives marked by immobility and passivity—sheltered within the family home, subject to paternal authority, waiting for a marriage proposal. The war, however, threw women into the public space. The middle-class girl who before 1914 was forbidden to travel without a chaperone might be driving an ambulance, splashing through the mud and blood, or washing the bodies of naked working-class soldiers.

At the same time that the war smashed many of the boundaries to which women had been confined, it sharply narrowed the world of the middle-class male soldier. While women were in charge and on the move—driving buses, flying transport planes, ferrying the wounded—men were stuck in the mud, confined to narrow ditches, waiting for orders. Expecting to be heroes, men of action, they found themselves instead living the sort of immobile, passive lives that had characterized the prewar middle-class women's experience. Ironically, then, at the same time the war gave women new power, it introduced many men, particularly middle-class men, to new levels of powerlessness. In total war, even gender roles turned upside down.

Yet when the war ended, some of these radical changes proved to be very temporary indeed. The much-heralded wartime movement of women into skilled factory jobs and public positions such as bus drivers and train conductors was rapidly reversed. For example, by the terms of the British Restoration of Pre-War Practices Act (1919), women who had taken up skilled factory jobs received two weeks' pay and a train ticket home.

Other changes appeared more permanent. France in 1919 possessed ten times as many female law students and three times as many female medical students as it had in 1914. British women over age 30 received the vote on a limited basis while in the United States, Germany, and most of the new states in eastern Europe, the achievement of female suffrage was more complete. (Women in France, Italy, Switzerland, and Greece remained unenfranchised.) Cultural changes also seemed to signal a gender revolution. Women began to smoke in public; trousers became acceptable female attire; hemlines rose dramatically; the corset and bustle disappeared for good.

Identifying the Enemy: From Propaganda to Genocide

We have seen that total war demanded an unprecedented expansion of state control over economic affairs. To ensure that their citizens remained committed to the war effort, governments also regulated the production and distribution of ideas. First, they eliminated ideas they viewed as dangerous. Pacifists and war objectors faced prison sentences and even execution. French prime minister Clemenceau adopted a particularly harsh stance toward all dissenting opinion. Journalists and rival politicians—even the former prime minister—who dared suggest that France negotiate with Germany rather than fight on for total victory were thrown in prison.

At the same time, governments worked to create ideas that would encourage a total war mentality. Propaganda now emerged as a crucial political tool. The careful censorship of newspapers and doctoring of photographs ensured that the public received a positive image of the war. In

Shell Shock: From Woman's Malady to Soldier's Affliction

Broken in mind as well as body, the casualties of World War I forced medical practitioners to think anew about the connections among emotional anguish, physical disabilities, and gender roles. Doctors discovered to their horror and surprise that in the trenches of total war, men's bodies began to act like women's. Pouring into hospital units came thousands of men with the symptoms of a malady that before the war was considered a woman's disease—hysteria.

The word *hysteria* comes from the Greek word *hystera,* for "womb" or "uterus," and for much of Western history doctors believed that women were doomed to suffer from hysteria because of their physical makeup—because they were afflicted with wombs. Physicians long considered the uterus to be an inherently weak and unstable organ, prone even to detach itself from its proper place and wander about the body causing havoc. By the end of the nineteenth century, however, the diagnosis had changed. Doctors continued to regard hysteria as primarily a woman's disease but they were more inclined to view it as a neurosis, a mental and emotional disorder. The symptoms varied enormously but included bouts of shrieking, emotional problems such as depression or breakdown, and physical ailments without any clear physical cause—ranging from abnormal fatigue or insomnia to the inability to walk.

With war came thousands of soldiers with the symptoms of hysteria—men who could not stop shaking, men with healthy limbs who could not move, men certain that rats were nibbling at their bodies. At first, doctors dismissed such symptoms as signs of cowardice: These were men faking illness to avoid doing their duty. But by 1916, with such men accounting for 40 percent of the casualties in British combat zones alone, doctors realized they were dealing with an epidemic of male hysteria.

The war illustrated that hysteria was linked not to the uterus or the weak female nervous system but rather to an environment of immobility and passivity. Neither the length of time a soldier had served nor the intensity or horror of his combat experience were significant in producing breakdowns. Instead, the most important factor was his level of immobility. Men on the Western Front suddenly found themselves in positions of passivity and confinement. Deprived of the ability to make decisions, to determine their future, to act, many men broke down.

Yet the reincarnation of what had been considered a woman's malady as a soldier's affliction did not lead doctors to reexamine their understanding of the woman's body or the woman's role. Instead, they reconfigured the disease. Hysteria became "shell shock." The treatment differed as well. Convinced that female hysteria was a result of the overstimulation of the nervous system, doctors prescribed total rest cures for their female patients. Women found themselves confined to rooms with bare walls and shuttered windows, forbidden to read or to receive visitors. In contrast, doctors ordered male soldiers with shell shock to engage in intense physical and mental activity. Thus, despite the upheaval in gender roles caused by total war, doctors continued to view women's bodies as inherently passive and men's as naturally active. The findings of medical science remained linked to cultural conventions.

Red Cross Christmas Roll Call Dec. 16-23ʳᵈ

The GREATEST MOTHER *in the* WORLD

Role Reversal
In this British Red Cross poster, the soldier is infantilized in the arms of the nurse. Many men found their forced confinement and passivity profoundly unsettling.

For Discussion

Why does the contrast between the medical treatment of hysteria and that of shell shock indicate that the war had a limited impact on gender roles? What evidence in this chapter points to the opposite conclusion?

Never Forget!

This French poster uses the image of a raped woman and her murdered child to arouse anti-German passions. The image recalls the German invasion of neutral Belgium, which soon came to be called "the rape of Belgium." All combatant states produced similar propaganda pieces.

Germany, giant wooden statues of the war hero Hindenburg were paraded to rally war enthusiasm, while in all the combatant nations, poster campaigns used the techniques developed in the new mass advertising industry to arouse patriotic fervor.

Fostering a total war mentality meant not only cultivating love for the Father- or Motherland, but also stirring up hatred for those labeled as the Enemy. In words that were soon set to music and became a popular wartime song, the poet (and army private) Ernst Lissauer (1882–1937) urged Germans to "hate [England] with a lasting hate . . . Hate of seventy millions, choking down."[12] In Britain, anti-German sentiment was so strong that the royal family changed its name from Hanover to Windsor in an effort to erase its German lineage.

In the ethnic cauldron of eastern Europe, this hatred was often directed at minority groups who were perceived as the enemy within: In Austria-Hungary, for example, more than 500 Bosnian Serbs and hundreds of Ukrainians were shot without trial because they were seen as Russian sympathizers.

The most horrific result of the tendency to look for the enemy at home occurred not in Austria-Hungary but in the Ottoman Empire, where suspicion of the Armenian minority resulted in mass murder. Massacres of Armenians under Ottoman rule had punctuated the decades before 1914. The war accentuated the Turkish-Armenian conflict. Recognizing that Armenian loyalty to imperial rule was shaky, to say the least, the Ottoman government decided to eliminate the Armenian population from Turkey. This brutal "solution" to what was described as the "Armenian question" began in April 1915. After arresting Armenian elites (and thus removing potential resistance leaders from Armenian communities) Turkish troops rounded up and killed Armenian men. In some cases, special

DOCUMENT

A Turkish Officer Describes the Armenian Massacres

The Harvest of War

The Turkish massacre of more than one million Armenians illustrates the destructive consequences of combining nationalist hatred with total war. This criminal horror is often seen as foreshadowing the Jewish Holocaust during World War II.

forces marched the men outside their town or village and then shot them; in other instances, they were pushed into caves and asphyxiated by fires blocking the entrances. The Ottoman government then ordered the women, children, and the elderly deported to Syria. Driven from their homes on short notice, they marched through mountain and desert terrain without food or water. Rapes and executions were commonplace. Between 1915 and 1918, more than one million Armenian men, women, and children died in this attempt at genocide, the murder of an entire people.

War and Revolution

■ What were the consequences of this war for the European and the global political and international order?

The machinery of total war tore at the social and political fabric of European societies. As seams began to fray and gaping holes appeared, many welcomed what they saw as the opportunity to tear apart the old cloth and create something entirely new. Some of these revolutionaries were Marxists aiming to build a socialist world order. Others were nationalists, determined to assert the rights of their ethnic or linguistic group, or to overthrow their colonial rulers. Not all revolutionaries belonged to underground or terrorist groups. One individual who dared to demand a new world order was the president of the United States, Woodrow Wilson. The peace settlement, however, fell far short of creating a new world. In Europe, many of the conflicts that had caused the war remained unresolved, with disastrous consequences for the next generation. Outside Europe, redesigned imperialist regimes encountered anti-Western forces that emerged from the war stronger than ever before.

The Russian Revolutions

Tsarist Russia began the war already sharply divided, its 125 million inhabitants splintered into more than one hundred different national groups—from Inuits in the north to Kazakhs in the southeast to Germans in the west. Ethnic hostilities sapped Russia's defenses from the very start. In Poland, for example, many of the four million Jews under Russian imperial rule welcomed the German army as liberators from tsarist violence and repression. In the regions of Latvia and Lithuania, anti-Russian sentiment flared high, and nationalists saw the war as opening the door to national independence.

The war brought political chaos to Russia. Nicholas II (r. 1894–1917), a man of limited intelligence and a remarkable capacity for self-delusion, insisted on going to the front and commanding his army. He left political affairs in the hands of his wife Alexandra (1872–1918) and her spiritual mentor Grigorii Rasputin (1869–1916). Rasputin is one of the more intriguing characters in twentieth-century history. An illiterate, unwashed faith healer from a peasant background, he possessed a well-documented and still-unexplained ability to stop the bleeding of Alexei, the young hemophiliac heir to the throne. To many high-ranking Russians, however, Rasputin was not a miracle worker but a traitor. Because Rasputin opposed the war against Germany, they perceived him as a voice of treason whispering in the German-born tsarina's ear. In 1916 Russian noblemen murdered Rasputin, in hopes of restoring authority and stability to the tsarist government.

The March Revolution

Rasputin's removal was not enough to stop the forces of revolution stirred up by total war. The political disarray he observed at the highest levels of government dumbfounded the French ambassador, who wrote in January 1917, "I am obliged to report that, at the present moment, the Russian Empire is run by lunatics."[13] The lack of effective political leadership, combined with Russian losses on the battlefield, brought to a boil the simmering disaffection with the tsarist government. Almost two million Russian soldiers had died and many more had been wounded or taken prisoner. Economic and communications networks had broken down, bread prices were rising, and people were hungry. Even members of the tsarist government began to ask not *if* revolution would occur, but *when*.

The answer came on March 8, 1917. A group of women workers in Petrograd staged a demonstration to protest inadequate food supplies. Over the course of the next few days, similar demonstrations flickered across the city; on March 11, they coalesced into a major revolutionary fire when the troops who were ordered to put down the protest joined it instead. Governmental orders lost all authority, and on March 15 Tsar Nicholas was forced to abdicate. The Russian Revolution had begun.

Who now controlled Russia? Two competing centers of power soon emerged: the Provisional Government and the Petrograd Soviet. On March 12, the Duma, or Russian parliament, created a Provisional Government from among its members. Like the Duma, the new Provisional Government was dominated by members of the gentry and middle classes: professionals, businessmen, intellectuals, bureaucrats. These men tended to be liberals who believed that Russia was now moving along the path toward a parliamentary democracy. They quickly enacted important reforms such as universal suffrage, the eight-hour workday, and civic equality for all citizens.

But at the same time that the Provisional Government was struggling to bring order to the chaos of revolutionary Russia, across the empire industrial workers and soldiers formed soviets°, or councils, to articulate their grievances and hopes. As Russian revolutionary socialists in exile

DOCUMENT

Revolution in the Front Lines

At age 25, Maria Botchkareva, a poor Russian woman who had been forced to work as a prostitute, volunteered for service as a soldier. Women served as nurses, ambulance drivers, and transport plane pilots on both sides of the war, but only in Russia did women serve in combat, and even there the presence of a woman on the front lines was quite exceptional. Botchkareva earned a well-deserved reputation as a fierce fighter, and was honored for her bravery. In 1917, she was serving at the front with her company when she heard startling news from the capital.

The first swallow to warn us of the approaching storm was a soldier from our Company who had returned from a leave of absence at Petrograd: "Oh my! If you but knew, boys, what is going on in the rear! Revolution! Everywhere they talk of overthrowing the Tsar. The capital is aflame with revolution." . . . Finally, the joyous news arrived. The Commander gathered the entire Regiment to read to us the glorious words. . . . The miracle had happened! Tsarism, which enslaved us and thrived on the blood and marrow of the toiler, had fallen. Freedom, Equality and

Brotherhood! How sweet were these words to our ears! We were transported. There were tears of joy, embraces, dancing. It all seemed a dream, a wonderful dream. Who ever believed that the hated regime would be destroyed so easily and in our own time?

The Commander read to us the manifesto, which concluded with a fervent appeal to us to hold the line with greater vigilance than ever, now that we were free citizens, to defend our newly won liberty from the attacks of the Kaiser and his slaves. . . . Then came Order No. 1, signed by the Petrograd Soviet of Workmen and Soldiers. Soldiers and officers were now equal, it declared. All the citizens of Free Russia were equal henceforth. . . .

We were dazzled by this shower of brilliant phrases. The men went about as if intoxicated. For four days the festival continued unabated. . . . There were meetings, meetings, and meetings. . . . All duty was abandoned. . . . The front became a veritable insane asylum.

One day, in the first week of the revolution, I ordered a soldier to take up duty at the listening-post. He refused.

Source: From Maria Botchkareva, *Yashka: My Life as Peasant, Officer and Exile* (New York: Frederick A. Stokes Company, 1919), 139–145.

across Europe returned to their homeland in the weeks after the March Revolution began, they assumed leading roles in the Petrograd Soviet, which soon became a powerful political rival to the less radical Provisional Government.

The revolution, however, did not originate with nor was it controlled by either the liberals in the Provisional Government or the socialists in the Petrograd Soviet. Nicholas II was overthrown by a popular revolution, and at the core of this popular revolution stood a simply stated demand: "Peace, Land, Bread." Soldiers—and most Russians—wanted an immediate end to a war that had long ceased to make any sense to them. Peasants, as always, wanted land, their guarantee of survival in a chaotic world. And city dwellers wanted bread—food in sufficient quantities and at affordable prices.

The Provisional Government could not satisfy these demands. It did promise the gradual redistribution of royal and monastic lands, but peasants, inspired by the revolution and unconstrained by the liberal regard for law and the rights of private property, wanted land immediately. More important, by the summer of 1917 no Russian government could have provided bread without providing peace. Russia no longer had the resources both to continue its war effort and to reconstruct its economy. The population of the cities began to dwindle as food disappeared from the shops, factories ceased operation because of shortages of raw materials, and currency had little value. Peace appeared impossi-

ble, however. Not only did Russia have commitments to its allies, but German armies stood deep within Russian territory. A separate peace with Germany would mean huge territorial losses. And so the war continued.

But so, too, did the revolution. Peasants effected their own land reform by simply seizing the land they wanted. Soldiers declared their own peace by deserting in huge numbers. (Of every 1,000-man troop sent to the front, fewer than 250 men actually made it into combat. The rest deserted.) The Provisional Government grew increasingly unpopular. Not even the appointment of the popular socialist and Petrograd Soviet member Alexander Kerensky (1881–1970) as prime minister could stabilize the government's position.

The November Revolution

This tumultuous situation created the opportunity for the Bolsheviks°, one of the socialist factions in the Petrograd Soviet, to emerge as a powerful revolutionary force. In April 1917, the Bolshevik leader, Vladimir Lenin (1870–1924), returned from almost twenty years in exile. While still in his teens, Lenin had committed himself to revolution after his older brother was executed for trying to assassinate Tsar Alexander III. Iron-willed and ruthlessly pragmatic, Lenin argued that a committed group of professional revolutionaries could force a working-class revolution on Russia immediately.

The Revolution's Hero

In this heroic portrait by Gemalde von A. M. Gerassimow, Lenin pushes the revolution and the Russian people forward.

By the fall of 1917, Bolshevik membership had grown from 10,000 to 250,000, and the party had achieved a majority in the Petrograd Soviet. Lenin now demanded the immediate overthrow of the Provisional Government. "Insurrection is an art," he declared, something to be made, not something that happens spontaneously. By promising "Peace, Land, Bread," Lenin would take control. On November 9, Bolshevik fighters captured the Winter Palace in Petrograd, where the Provisional Government had been sitting.

The *second* Russian Revolution was underway. The Bolsheviks declared a policy of land and peace—land partition with no payment of compensation to estate owners and an immediate peace with Germany, regardless of the cost. (And as we have seen, the cost was high: According to the terms of the Treaty of Brest-Litovsk, signed with Germany in 1918, Russia lost its western territories.) Not everyone in Russia was won over by promises of peace and land, however. Confronted with a diverse array of opponents, the Bolsheviks turned to the methods of terror. After an assassination attempt against Lenin in August 1918, the

Bolshevik secret police received the power to execute without trial. More than 500 individuals were shot in a single day in Petrograd.

During the next two years, the Bolsheviks waged a brutal war against domestic and international opponents of their Communist Revolution. This civil war proved Lenin's promises of "Peace, Land, Bread" to be hollow. Peasant farms were transformed into battlefields as five years of civil war killed off more combatants than had World War I. In the resulting famine, death tolls reached as high as five million. Yet, as the next chapter shows, the Bolsheviks emerged victorious. The Russian Empire was remade as the Soviet Union, a communist state.

The Spreading Revolution

The victory of the Bolsheviks in Russia inspired socialists across Europe and around the world. In January 1919, communists in Buenos Aires, Argentina, led by Russian immigrants, controlled the city for three days until they were crushed by the Argentine army. British dockworkers struck in support of the Bolshevik Revolution, and in French cities general strikes caused chaos. In Austria, revolutionaries attempted to take control of government buildings in Vienna but were quickly defeated by the Austrian army. In Hungary, Bela Kun, a journalist who had come to admire the Bolsheviks while a prisoner of war in Russia, established a short-lived soviet regime in the spring of 1919.

Revolution also swept through defeated Germany. Disillusion with the kaiser's regime had set in long before Germany had lost the war. Defeat simply accentuated the desire for radical political change. But the first revolutionary step in Germany was a response not to popular desire but to American demands. In October 1918, Germany's military commanders recommended that the German government enter into peace negotiations. U.S. president Woodrow Wilson, however, saw the war as a democratic crusade and so refused to allow the Allies to negotiate with representatives of the kaiser's authoritarian regime. To placate Wilson, the kaiser was forced to overhaul Germany's political system. For the first time, representatives of left-wing and centrist parties—including the SPD, the largest socialist party in Europe—were invited to join the government.

This "revolution from above" coincided with and was challenged by a "revolution from below." Inspired by the success of the Bolshevik Revolution, many German workers rejected the SPD's vision of socialism as too moderate. The members of the SPD believed in working for gradual social reform through parliamentary action and debate. A much more radical alternative was offered by a breakaway socialist faction called the Spartacists (after Spartacus, the gladiator who led a slave revolt against Rome in the first century B.C.E.). Directed by Karl Liebknecht (1871–1919) and Rosa Luxemburg (1870–1919), the Spartacists wanted Germany to follow Russia down the path to communist revolution.

The Spartacist Revolution in Germany
The effort to establish a soviet government in Berlin took the form of street fighting. This photograph shows one street skirmish that occurred in the city's newspaper district.

In Berlin, thousands rallied behind Liebknecht and Luxemburg. By November 8, communists had declared the establishment of a Soviet republic in the province of Bavaria; the Red Flag—symbol of communism—was flying over eleven German cities; and revolutionaries had seized control of all the main railroad junctions.

On November 9, the head of the SPD, Friedrich Ebert (1871–1925), became chancellor of Germany and the kaiser abdicated. One of Ebert's colleagues in the SPD triumphantly proclaimed from the window of the Reichstag building in Berlin that Germany was now a parliamentary democracy. Almost at that very moment, Karl Liebknecht stood at another window (in the occupied royal palace) and announced that Germany was now a revolutionary communist state. With two opposing versions of revolution on offer, civil war raged until the spring of 1919, when the SPD defeated the communists for control of the new Germany.

The Failure of Wilson's Revolution

At the beginning of 1919, the representatives of the victorious Allied nations gathered in Paris to draw up the treaties that would wrap up the war. Yet their aims were far higher than simply ending the war; they wished to construct a new Europe and to reconfigure the conduct of international affairs. At the center of this high endeavor was the American college-professor-turned-president Woodrow Wilson. Like the Bolsheviks, Wilson offered a vision of a radical new future. He based *his* version of revolutionary change on the ideal of national self-determination—a world in which "every people should be left free to determine its own polity, its own way of development, unhindered, unthreat-

ened, unafraid, the little along with the great and powerful." The map of Europe would be redrawn, the old empires replaced with independent, ethnically homogenous, democratic nation-states.

These new nation-states would interact differently from the empires of the past. In what he called his Fourteen Points, Wilson demanded a revolution in international affairs. He argued that "Points" such as freedom of the seas, freedom of trade, and open diplomacy (an end to secret treaties) would break down barriers and guarantee peace and prosperity for all peoples. The cornerstone of this new world order would be an international organization, the League of Nations°, which would oversee the implementation of these new measures and would have the power to resolve disputes between nations. Wilson and other planners

CHRONOLOGY

Revolution in Russia, 1917–1921

1917	
March 8	St. Petersburg/Petrograd women's protest; revolution begins
March 12	Establishment of Provisional Government
March 15	Abdication of Tsar Nicholas II
November 9	Bolshevik overthrow of the Provisional Government
1918–1921	Civil war

Revolutionary Justice:
The Nontrial of Nicholas and Alexandra

On July 16, 1918, Bolshevik revolutionaries shot and killed Nicholas II, tsar of Russia; his wife, the tsarina Alexandra; his heir, 14-year-old Alexei; their four daughters—Olga (age 23), Tatiana (age 21), Maria (age 19), and Anastasia (age 17); their three servants; and their physician. When news of the deaths reached other countries, the killings were condemned as murders. The Bolsheviks, however, termed them executions, acts of revolutionary justice.

When Nicholas II abdicated on March 15, 1917, after twenty-three years on the throne, he expected to embark on a life of exile in Britain. Instead, the Provisional Government placed the tsar and his family under house arrest and appointed a Commission of Inquiry to investigate the persistent rumors that the tsar's German-born wife had conspired with Germany to destroy Russia. The commission found no evidence to convict the tsar or his wife of treason, but by the autumn of 1917, its findings were irrelevant. The war with Germany was effectively over, whereas the war against all that the tsar had stood for had just begun.

The civil war that followed the Bolshevik Revolution proved fatal for the royal family. Faced with counterrevolutionary challenges on all sides, the Bolsheviks feared that if Nicholas escaped, he would serve as a symbolic center for these antirevolutionary forces. They decided to move him to a region firmly under Bolshevik control. In April 1918, a special train transported the tsar and his family to Ekaterinburg (about 900 miles east of Moscow), where they were placed in the hands of the Bolshevik-dominated Ural Regional Soviet. Meanwhile, the revolutionary Bolshevik government prepared to try Nicholas publicly for his crimes against the Russian peo-

ple. The charge was no longer secret contacts with Germany—the Bolsheviks themselves had negotiated with Germany and ended Russia's participation in the war—but rather the tsar's both real and symbolic leadership of a politically repressive regime. Leon Trotsky, the head of the Petrograd Soviet, planned to present the case against Nicholas.

But the case was never made. By July, an anti-Bolshevik army was approaching Ekaterinburg from the east. If these troops freed the imperial family, they would score a crucial victory. Told that Ekaterinburg might fall to the enemy within days, the Ural Soviet decided to execute the tsar and his family immediately, most likely with Lenin's approval.

Pavel Medvedev, one of the tsar's guards, later offered a detailed account of the events of the evening of July 16. His interviewer recorded what Medvedev had told him:

> [He said,] The Tsar, the Tsaritsa [Tsarina], the Tsar's four daughters, the doctor, the cook and the lackey came out of their rooms. The Tsar was carrying the heir [Alexei] in his arms. . . . In my presence there were no tears, no sobs and no questions. . . .

Medvedev then testified that he was ordered out of the room. When he returned a few minutes later:

> . . . he saw all the members of the Tsar's family lying on the floor with numerous wounds to their bodies. The blood was gushing. The heir was still alive—and moaning. [The commander] walked over to him and shot him two or three times at point blank range. The heir fell still.[14]

What Medvedev's understated account did not relate were the more gruesome details of the execution. In an effort to preserve

part of the family fortune, the tsar's daughters were wearing corsets into which had been sewn diamonds. When they were shot, the bullets, in the words of one eyewitness, "ricocheted, jumping around the room like hail."[15] Even after several pistols were emptied, one of the girls remained alive. The guards resorted to bayonets.

The killing of not only the tsar but also his wife and children was a startling act, as the Bolsheviks themselves recognized. The Ural Regional Soviet announced the tsar's execution, but said nothing about his family, while the official statement from Moscow reported that "the wife and son of Nicholas Romanov were sent to a safe place."[16]

These omissions and lies reveal the Bolsheviks' own uneasiness with the killings. Why, then, was the entire family shot? The Bolsheviks' determination to win the civil war regardless of the cost provides part of the answer. According to Trotsky, Lenin "believed we shouldn't leave the Whites [the anti-Bolshevik forces] a live banner to rally around."[17] Any of the tsar's children could have served as such a banner. The rapid approach of the White army meant the royal family had to be disposed of quickly. But Trotsky also viewed the killings as an essential and absolute break with the past. In his words, "the execution of the Tsar's family was needed not only to frighten, horrify, and to dishearten the enemy, but also in order to shake up our own ranks, to show them that there was no turning back, that ahead lay either complete victory or complete ruin."[18] For the Bolsheviks, there was no middle ground.

The killing of Tsar Nicholas and his family thus forms part of the pattern of escalating violence that characterized the First World War's

Tsar Nicholas II and Family
Tsar Nicholas II, the Tsarina Alexandra, and their family.

revolutionary aftermath. But in the blood of these killings we can also see reflected two ideas that had a powerful impact on postwar political life—first, the subordination of law to the revolutionary state; second, the concept of collective guilt.

The Bolsheviks offered a different idea of justice. As a Bolshevik publication explained in a discussion of the tsar's killing:

> *Many formal aspects of bourgeois justice may have been violated. . . . However, worker-peasant power was manifested in the process, making no exception for the All-Russian murderer, shooting as if he were an ordinary brigand. . . . Nicholas the Bloody is no more.*[19]

In the Bolshevik model, the law was not separate from but rather subordinate to the state. Legal rights and requirements—the "formal aspects of bourgeois justice"—could be suspended in the service of "worker peasant power," as embodied in the revolutionary state.

This concept of the law subordinate to the state helps us understand the tsar's execution without trial; the concept of collective guilt provides a context for the killing of his children. The Bolshevik model of socialism assumed that *class* constituted objective reality. Simply by belonging to a certain social class, an individual could be—and was—designated an enemy of the revolution. The Bolshevik constitution equated citizenship with social class. Workers and peasants received the vote, but seven categories of people, such as those who lived off investment interest,

were disenfranchised. For the next two decades, aristocratic and middle-class origins served as an indelible ink, marking a person permanently as an enemy of the revolutionary state—regardless of that person's own actions or inclinations. Thus, from the Bolshevik perspective, the tsar's children bore the taint of their royal origins. When their continuing existence threatened the revolution, they were shot. Over the next four decades, the concept of collective guilt would result in the deaths of millions in the new Soviet Union.

When World War I ended and representatives of the Allied victors met in Paris in 1919 to build the new postwar world, they sought to establish nationalist-based democracies, in which the rule of law would guarantee the rights of individuals. These two interlinked concepts of law and human rights became for many the defining features of "the West," of democracy, and of civilization itself. The Bolsheviks challenged this definition. They offered instead a definition of democracy based on class and an understanding of the law resting on the demands of continuing revolution.

Questions of Justice

1. In what ways was the murder of the Russian royal family the by-product of total war rather than the result of any revolutionary ideals?
2. In what ways, if any, were the Bolsheviks correct in arguing that "justice" is never blind, that legal systems always reflect the interests of a society's dominant groups? Is there such a thing as impartial justice?

Taking It Further

Kozlov, Vladimir, and Vladimir Khrustalëv. *The Last Diary of Tsaritsa Alexandra.* 1997. A translation of the tsarina's diary from 1918.

Rosenberg, William, ed. *Bolshevik Visions: First Phase of the Cultural Revolution in Soviet Russia.* 1990. The section on "Proletarian Legality" explores the Bolsheviks' effort to develop a legal system that embodied their revolutionary ideals.

Steinberg, Mark, and Vladimir Khrustalëv. *The Fall of the Romanovs.* 1999. A detailed account of the last two years of the tsar and his family, based on recently opened archives.

806 **Chapter 24** The First World War

Wilson and the Peace
Setting sail for the Paris Peace Conference on December 4, 1918, Wilson believed he was also embarking on a journey in which he would lead Europe into political democracy and international peace.

of the postwar era envisioned the league as a truly revolutionary organization, one that would guarantee that World War I was "the war to end all wars." To replace the system of secret diplomacy and Great Power alliances that had led to the horrors of total war, the league offered an international forum in which all states, big and small, European and non-European, would have a voice and in which negotiations would be conducted openly and democratically. War would become outmoded.

These soaring social and political expectations went largely unrealized. In Paris in 1919 and 1920, the Allies and their defeated enemies signed a series of treaties.* In drawing up these agreements, the treaty writers sought to create a new international order based on three features: a

*These treaties were named after the French palaces in which they were signed—the Treaty of Versailles, with Germany; the Treaty of St. Germain, with Austria; the Treaty of Neuilly, with Bulgaria; the Treaty of Trianon, with Hungary; and the Treaty of Sèvres, with Turkey.

democratic Germany, national self-determination in eastern Europe, and a viable system of international arbitration headed by the League of Nations. They failed in all three.

The Treaty of Versailles and German Democracy

At the center of the new Europe envisioned by Woodrow Wilson was to be a new democratic Germany. French leader Georges Clemenceau did not share this vision. He had lived through two German invasions of his homeland and wished to ensure that Germany could never again threaten France. Clemenceau proposed the creation of a Rhineland state out of Germany's industrialized western region, both as a neutral buffer zone between France and Germany and as a way to reduce Germany's economic power. The British leader, David Lloyd George, who had just won an election on the campaign slogan "Hang the Kaiser" and who had promised his people that he would squeeze Germany "until the pips squeak," publicly supported Clemenceau's hardline approach to the peace settlement with Germany. In private, however, he expressed fear that such an approach would backfire by feeding the flames of German resentment and undermining the structures of German democracy.

Lloyd George's fears proved well-grounded. The German people bitterly resented the Versailles Treaty°, which they perceived as unjustly punitive. By the terms of the treaty, Germany lost all of its overseas colonies, 13 percent of its European territory, 10 percent of its population, and its ability to wage war. The German army was limited to a defensive force of 100,000 men and allowed no aircraft or tanks. Clemenceau failed in his effort to create a separate Rhineland state, but the Rhineland was demilitarized, emptied of German soldiers and fortifications. In addition, the coalfields of the Saar region were ceded to France for fifteen years (see Map 24.5).

Even more significantly, the Versailles Treaty declared that German aggression had caused the war, and therefore that Germany must recompense the Allies for its cost. In 1921, the Allies presented Germany with a bill for reparations° of 132 billion marks ($31.5 billion). As we will see in the next chapter, this reparations clause helped set up an economic cycle that was to prove devastating for both global prosperity and German democratic politics.

The Failure of National Self-Determination

The map of Europe drawn by the peace treaties appeared to signal the establishment of a new international order. The old authoritarian empires of eastern and central Europe disappeared, replaced with independent nation-states. In keeping with the principle of national self-determination, Poland once again became an independent nation, with pieces carved out of the German, Austrian, and Russian Empires. One entirely new state was formed out of the rubble of the Austrian-Hungarian Empire—Czechoslovakia. Romania, Greece, and Italy all expanded as a result of serv-

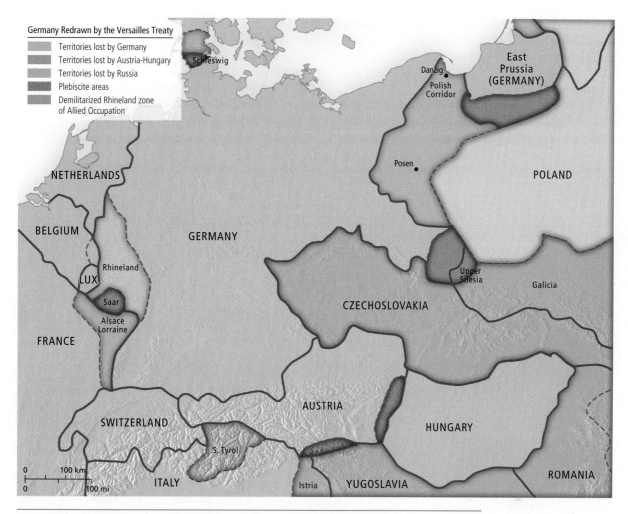

Germany Redrawn by the Versailles Treaty
- Territories lost by Germany
- Territories lost by Austria-Hungary
- Territories lost by Russia
- Plebiscite areas
- Demilitarized Rhineland zone of Allied Occupation

Map 24.5   Germany Redrawn by the Versailles Treaty

By the terms of the Versailles Treaty, Germany lost 13 percent of its prewar territory and 10 percent of its prewar population. France regained Alsace and Lorraine; reconstructed Poland was given a corridor to the sea; and the industrialized Rhineland became a demilitarized zone.

ing on the winners' side, while Serbia became the heart of the new Yugoslavia. The defeated nations shrank, some dramatically. Austria, for example, became a mere rump of what had been the mighty Habsburg Empire, while Hungary was reduced to one-third of its prewar size. All that remained of the Ottoman Empire was Turkey.

These changes were heralded as the victory of "national self-determination." But as Woodrow Wilson's own secretary of state, Robert Lansing, complained, "This phrase is simply loaded with dynamite. It will raise hopes which can never be realized." Wilson had called for "every people" to be left free to determine its political destiny—but who constituted "a people"? Did the Macedonians? Should there be an independent Macedonia? Macedonians said yes, but the Paris peace negotiators answered no. Macedonia was enveloped by Yugoslavia and Greece, and in consequence,

throughout the 1920s and 1930s Macedonians waged a terrorist campaign in the Balkans. Wilson's peaceful new world seemed far, far away when in 1923, a Macedonian nationalist group kidnapped the Bulgarian prime minister, chopped off his head, and sliced off his limbs.

The Macedonians were not the only dissatisfied ethnic group in eastern Europe. Even after the peace settlements redrew the map, no fewer than 30 million eastern Europeans remained members of minority groups. Less than 70 percent of Hungarians, for example, lived in Hungary—more than three million were scattered in other states. Over nine million Germans resided outside the borders of Germany. In the newly created Czechoslovakia, one-third of the population was neither Czech nor Slovak. The new state of Yugoslavia contained an uneasy mixture of several ethnic groups, most resentful of the dominant Serbs.

Rather than satisfying nationalist ambitions, then, the peace settlements served to inflame them, thus creating a volatile situation for the post–World War I world.

The Limits of the League

True to Wilson's vision of a new international order, the treaty makers included the Covenant of the League of Nations in each of the treaties. The league, however, never realized Wilson's high hopes of making war obsolete. One crucial weakness was that it did not represent every state.

When the league met for the first time in 1920, three significant world powers had no representative present: Germany and the Soviet Union were excluded, and, in a stunning defeat for President Wilson, the U.S. Senate rejected membership. The failure of these three states to participate in the league at its beginning stripped the organization of much of its potential influence.

Two additional factors explain the league's failure. First, the league had no military power. Although it could levy economic sanctions against states that flouted its decisions,

Map 24.6 Europe and the Middle East After World War I

A comparison of this map with Map 24.1 on page 780 illustrates the vital role played by the war in shaping eastern Europe and the Middle East.

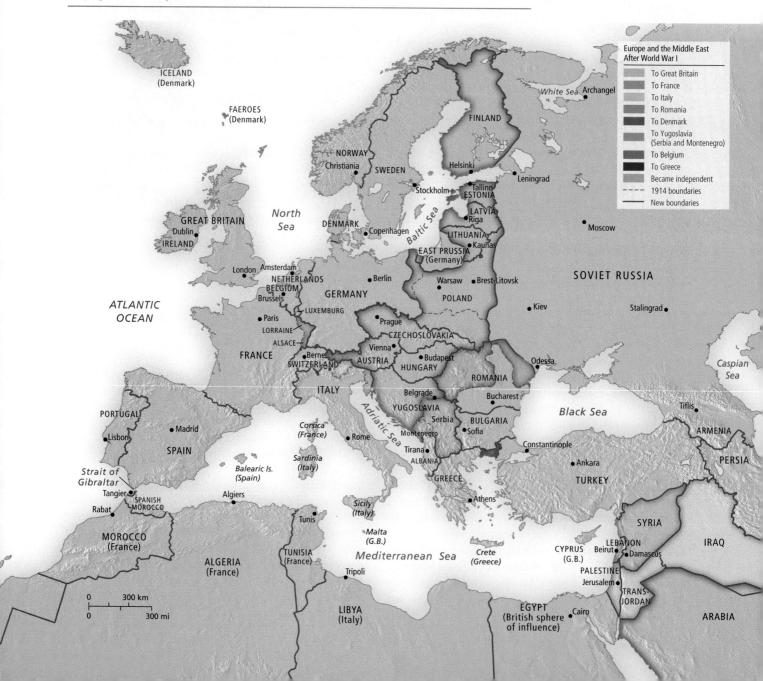

it could do nothing more. And perhaps most important, the will to make the league work was lacking. With Wilson removed from the picture, European leaders were free to pursue their own rather more traditional visions of what the league should be. French politicians, for example, believed that the league's primary reason for existence was to enforce the provisions of the Versailles Treaty—in other words, to punish Germany rather than to restructure international relations.

The Making of the Modern Middle East

The high hopes that accompanied the end of the war extended beyond the borders of Europe and invigorated nationalist movements throughout Europe's empires. In the Middle East, the war's end meant an entirely new map, but not the end of European dominance. Under terms set by the new League of Nations, the Allies carved Ottoman territory in the Middle East into separate and nominally independent states. These states, however, were judged "not yet able to stand by themselves under the strenuous conditions of the modern world" and so were placed under French or British control (or "Mandate"). Syria and Lebanon fell to the French, while Britain claimed Iraq (Mesopotamia), Palestine, and Transjordan (later called simply Jordan). Britain also continued to exercise its influence over Egypt, Iran (Persia), and what would become Saudi Arabia.

This remaking of the Middle East failed to effect a lasting settlement in the region. First, the new map clashed with promises made to indigenous groups during the war, and so created a long-lasting legacy of mistrust and resentment against the West. Second, the new states imposed on the region were artificial, the creation of the Allied victors rather than a product of historical evolution or of the wishes of the inhabitants themselves. And finally, Western mandatory supervision (which in actual practice differed little from old-fashioned imperial rule) brought with it Western practices and concepts that destabilized regional social and economic structures.

The early history of Iraq exemplifies these three developments. First, the drawing of Iraq, together with Syria, Lebanon, Palestine, and Jordan, betrayed promises made by the British to their Arab allies during the war. In 1915, the British High Commissioner in Egypt, Sir Henry McMahon, wrote to Sharif Husayn (Hussein) ibn Ali, head of the Hashemite dynasty that acted as traditional guardian of Islamic holy sites, and agreed to grant him control over Arab areas liberated from Ottoman rule in exchange for his military support against the Central Powers. This "McMahon-Husayn Correspondence" did not establish precisely the actual boundaries under discussion, but the Hashemites and their supporters believed that they had been promised an independent Arab kingdom centered on Damascus—the same

area that the Allies carved up into the five mandatory states. The British argued they had kept their promise when they placed Husayn's son Faisal on the throne of Iraq and his other son Abdullah on the throne of Jordan, but many Arabs felt betrayed.

The artificiality of Iraq, as well as the other new states, also created a revolutionary situation. In creating Iraq, the Allies glued together three Ottoman provinces—Basra, Baghdad, and Mosul—that had never been treated as a single political or economic unit by the Ottomans, nor regarded as in any way united by the inhabitants themselves. The population of this new state consisted of a volatile mixture of both ethnicities (including Arab, Kurd, and Assyrian) and religions (including not only the majority Shia Muslim community but also Sunni Muslims, Christians, Jews, and Zorastrians). None of these diverse groups identified themselves as "Iraqi." Many of the inhabitants of the new state also lacked a sense of allegiance to their new ruler; they regarded Faisal (along with his brother Abdullah in Jordan) as an imperialist puppet, jumping as British "advisers" pulled the strings.

Finally, the British inadvertently destabilized Iraq's social structures when they set out to make the new state into a friendly regime that would protect British access to both air bases and oil resources. The introduction of British legal and economic concepts destroyed indigenous traditions. For example, by applying the concept of private land ownership to Iraqi customary relations, the British transformed the traditional tie between tribal sheikh and tribesmen into an economic arrangement between landowner and tenants—an arrangement that tended to enrich the landowner while impoverishing the tenants.

Iraq erupted into full-scale rebellion in 1920, a revolt the British quelled with mustard gas bombs. Similar rebellions—and similar use of brutal force, often airborne, to crush such rebellions—occurred throughout much of the Middle East immediately after World War I.

The settlement of the region labeled Palestine destabilized the region even further. As we noted, the Hashemites and their supporters believed that the British had promised that Palestine would be included in an independent Arab kingdom after the war ended. Yet at the same time, British officials pledged support for a Jewish state in Palestine. In making this pledge, British policymakers were influenced by the anti-Semitic myth of a powerful Jewish elite wielding influence over world affairs: More specifically, they believed that Jewish influence could determine whether the U.S. would enter and Russia would remain in the war. Desperate to ensure both, the British government in 1917 issued the Balfour Declaration°. This declaration announced that Britain favored the Zionist goal of a Jewish national homeland in Palestine (the biblical land of Israel).

Palestine in 1920 passed into British hands in the form of a United Nations mandate formally committed to the Balfour Declaration. Ninety percent of the inhabitants of

Palestine in 1920 were Arabs (both Christians and Muslims) who viewed the Zionist dream of a Jewish Palestine as a form of European imperialism that threatened to dispossess them of their land. But as Arthur Balfour (the Conservative politician who gave the Balfour Declaration its name) explained, "in Palestine we do not propose even to go through the form of consulting the wishes of the present inhabitants of the country."[20] Arab protests and riots in Palestine erupted and by 1922, the British government decided to slow the pace of Jewish immigration into the region to alleviate Arab fears. This decision was only a stopgap solution, however; over the next two decades the British faced continuous pressure from both Arab and Jewish nationalist forces. Like the remaking of eastern Europe, the remaking of the Middle East ushered in decades of political turmoil and violence.

Conclusion

The War and the West

Sparked by nationalist fervor, international competition, and a widespread will to believe that in war lay the solution to political divisions and cultural fears, World War I quickly slipped out of the control of both the diplomats and the generals. Industrialization changed the face of combat. Total war smashed the boundaries of the battlefield, eroded the distinction between soldier and civilian, and demanded an overhaul of each combatant nation's political, economic, and social structures.

The idea of "the West" also changed as a result of the impact of this war. The entry of American forces in the final year of the war signaled that in the twentieth century, the United States would have to be factored into any definition of "Western culture" or "Western civilization." At the same time, the spread of the war to the Middle East and Africa and the significant role played by soldiers from imperial territories such as Tunisia, India, and Australia demonstrated the global framework that complicated and constrained Western affairs. The war's revolutionary aftermath also had profound consequences for formulations of "Western identity." With the triumph of the Bolshevik Revolution, two versions of modernity now presented themselves—one associated with the United States and capitalism, and the other represented by the new Soviet Union and its communist ideology. Soviet communism's intellectual roots lay in Marxism, a quintessentially Western ideology, one shaped by Western ideals of evolutionary progress and the triumph of human reason. But after the Russian Revolution, communism was increasingly viewed in the West as something foreign, essentially Eastern, the Other against which the West identified itself.

The carnage of World War I also challenged the faith of many Europeans that through industrial development the West was progressing morally as well as materially. In the final decades of the nineteenth century, European and American soldiers had used repeating rifles and machine guns to conquer huge sections of the globe in the name of Western civilization. In 1914, European and American soldiers turned their machine guns on each other. The world the war had created was one of unprecedented destruction. Millions lay dead, with millions more maimed for life. Vast sections of northern France and eastern Europe had been turned into giant cemeteries filled with rotting men and rusting metal. Across central and eastern Europe, starvation continued to claim thousands of victims, while a worldwide influenza epidemic, spread in part by the marching armies, ratcheted up the death tolls even higher. In the new world shaped by relentless conflicts such as the Battle of the Somme, the pessimism and sense of despair that had already invaded much of the arts in the decade before the war became more characteristic of the wider culture. For many Europeans, the optimism and confidence of nineteenth-century liberalism died in the trenches.

Yet, paradoxically, the war also fostered high hopes. Wilson declared that this had been the war to end all wars. The fires of revolution burned high and many in the West believed that on top of the ashes of empire they would now build a better world. The task of reconstruction, however, proved immense; as we shall see in Chapter 25, in many areas, retrenchment replaced revolution. Seeking stability in an increasingly unsettled world, many Europeans and Americans did their best to return to prewar patterns. The failure of the peace settlement ensured that the "war to end all wars" set the stage for the next, far more destructive total war.

Suggestions for Further Reading

For a comprehensive listing of suggested readings, please go to www.ablongman.com/levack2e/chapter24

Cork, Richard. *A Bitter Truth: Avant-Garde Art and the Great War*. 1994. A beautifully illustrated work that looks at the cultural impact of the war.

Eksteins, Modris. *Rites of Spring: The Great War and the Birth of the Modern Age*. 1989. Explores the links among modernism, the war experience, and modernity.

Ferguson, Niall. *The Pity of War*. 1999. A bold reconsideration of many accepted interpretations of the origins and experience of the war.

Fitzpatrick, Sheila. *The Russian Revolution, 1917–1932*. 1994. As the title indicates, Fitzpatrick sees the revolutions of 1917 as the opening battle in a more than ten-year struggle to shape the new Russia.

Gilbert, Martin. *The First World War: A Complete History*. 1994. A comprehensive account, packed with illuminating detail.

Gilbert, Martin. *The Routledge Atlas of the First World War.* 1994. Much more than a set of maps, Gilbert's atlas provides a very clear and useful survey of both the causes and results of the war.

Higonnet, Margaret. *Lines of Fire: Women's Visions of World War I.* 1998. An important study of women's experiences.

Joll, James. *The Origins of the First World War.* 1984. One of the best and most carefully balanced studies of this complicated question.

Read, Christopher. *From Tsar to Soviets: The Russian People and Their Revolution, 1917–1921.* 1996. An up-to-date study of the popular revolution and its fate.

Winter, J. M. *The Experience of World War I.* 1989. Despite the title, this richly illustrated work not only covers the war itself but also explores the factors that led to its outbreak and outlines its chief consequences.

Winter, J. M., and R. M. Wall, eds. *The Upheaval of War: Family, Work and Welfare in Europe, 1914–1918.* 1988. A series of essays examining the home front experiences.

Notes

1. Figures from Alan Sharp, "The Genie That Would Not Go Back into the Bottle: National Self-Determination and the Legacy of the First World War and the Peace Settlement," in Seamus Dunn and T. G. Fraser, eds., *Europe and Ethnicity,* (1996), 10.

2. Quotation from Karl Kautsky et al., eds., *The Outbreak of the World War: German Documents* (1924), 76.

3. Quoted in Niall Ferguson, *The Pity of War* (1999), 152.

4. Quoted in Eric Leeds, *No Man's Land: Combat and Identity in World War I* (1979), 17.

5. Allister Horne, *The Price of Glory: Verdun, 1916* (1967), 27.

6. Paul Fussell, *The Great War and Modern Memory* (1975), ch. 2.

7. Siegfried Sassoon, *Memoirs of an Infantry Officer* (1937), 228.

8. Figure from Tony Ashworth, *Trench Warfare, 1914–1918* (1980), 15–16.

9. Samuel Hynes, *A War Imagined: The First World War and English Culture* (1991), 195.

10. Quoted in Richard Cork, *A Bitter Truth* (1994), 198.

11. Quoted in Sheila Rowbotham, *A Century of Women* (1997), 72.

12. Ernst Lessauer, "Hymn of Hate" (1914), in *Jugend* (1914). Translated by Barbara Henderson, *New York Times,* October 15, 1914.

13. Quoted in W. Bruce Lincoln, *Red Victory: A History of the Russian Civil War* (1989), 32.

14. Quoted in Edvard Radzinsky, *The Last Tsar,* trans. Marian Schwartz (1993), 336.

15. From the written account of Yakov Yurovsky, quoted in Radzinsky, *The Last Tsar,* 355.

16. Quoted in William Henry Chamberlin, *The Russian Revolution, 1917–1921,* Vol. 2: *From the Civil War to the Consolidation of Power* (1987), 91.

17. Quoted in Lincoln, *Red Victory,* 151.

18. Ibid., 155.

19. Quoted in Radzinsky, *The Last Tsar,* 326.

20. Quoted in Walid Khalidi (ed.), *From Haven to Conquest: Readings in Zionism and the Palestine Problem Until 1948* (1987), 208.

Reconstruction, Reaction, and Continuing Revolution: The 1920s and 1930s

25

O N SEPTEMBER 14, 1927, AN OPEN CAR ACCELERATED DOWN A STREET in Nice in southern France. In its passenger seat sat a woman, who let her long silk shawl whip in the wind. This woman in free-flowing clothing, speeding down the streets in a convertible, provides a fitting image for Western culture in the decade after World War I. Entranced by the automobile, Americans and Europeans embraced its promise of mobility and freedom. They perceived themselves as moving ahead, breaking through traditional barriers and heading off into new directions. Even more fitting was the identity of that female passenger: Isadora Duncan, by 1927 one of the most famous artists in Europe. In the years before World War I, the American-born Duncan had rejected classical ballet as an artificial form that restricted and deformed the female body. She cast aside ballet's confining toe shoes and tutus, and opted for bare feet and simple tunics. For Duncan, dance was not a force imposed on the body from outside; instead, dance flowed from the body itself. In her break with the highly regulated system of classical ballet, her quest for more natural forms, and her desire to liberate women, both physically and artistically, Duncan serves as an apt symbol for modernity. Moreover, as an American, Duncan appeared to personify the new culture that for many Europeans represented the world of the future. Even her clothing—loose tunics, free-flowing scarves, fluid shawls—symbolized a love of freedom and movement.

Yet freedom is sometimes dangerous and movement can be violent. On that autumn day in 1927 Duncan's long scarf became entangled in the wheel of her car and strangled the dancer. Gruesome as it is, the image of Duncan's sudden death serves as an appropriate introduction to the history of the West in the 1920s and 1930s, the turbulent interlude between two tragic

CHAPTER OUTLINE

■ Cultural Despair and Desire

■ Out of the Trenches: Reconstructing National and Gender Politics in the 1920s

■ The Rise of the Radical Right

■ The Polarization of Politics in the 1930s

■ The West and the World: Imperialism in the Interwar Era

"The World Will Soon Be Yours" This Soviet propaganda poster promises workers around the world a global communist revolution. In *The Communist Manifesto*, Karl Marx had addressed the working classes in these famous words: "Workers of the world, unite! You have nothing to lose but your chains!" Adapting this call, the poster's banner declares, "You have nothing to lose but your chains, but the world will soon be yours."

world wars. The American president Woodrow Wilson had hailed World War I as the "final war for human liberty." Many Europeans agreed; they thought that the war would propel their society down a new road, yet in much of Europe the drive toward freedom ended quickly. The interwar period saw the strangulation of democracy in eastern and southern Europe and the rise of political and cultural ideologies that viewed human liberty as an illusion and mass murder as a tool of the state.

These developments had profound implications for the idea of the West. In the Wilsonian vision, "the West" stood as a culture that promoted individual freedom through democratic politics and capitalist economics. But the success of antidemocratic and anticapitalist ideologies in capturing the hopes and allegiances of large numbers of Europeans illustrated that Wilson's definition of the West was only one among many.

Why was the link between "Western" and "democratic" so fragile? To answer this question, we will look closely at diverse responses to the revolutionary aftermath of World War I. Five more specific questions will guide our examination:

- What was the impact of the war on European cultural life?
- In what ways did reconstruction rather than revolution characterize the postwar period?
- What circumstances explain the emergence of the Radical Right?
- What factors led to the polarization of European politics in the 1930s?
- How did the interaction between the West and the world outside change after World War I?

Cultural Despair and Desire

- What was the impact of the war on European cultural life?

To many Europeans in the 1920s and 1930s, World War I seemed to have torn a huge and irreparable gash in the fabric of culture and society. It appeared as the sudden and horrifying end to an age of science and progress, an era of technological improvement and social optimism. Yet this perception of a radical cultural break masked fundamental continuities. As we observed in Chapter 23, beginning in the 1870s, anxiety intermingled with optimism in European culture, and widespread fear of degeneration and decay marked Western society. Well before World War I, modernist painters, musicians, and poets pushed beyond the limits of nineteenth-century art and articulated disturbing visions of a world in purposeless flux. The real

change in the years after the war was that modernism's fragmented canvases and dissonant choruses no longer seemed alien; they echoed the sensibilities of societies shattered by total war. But the war had also injected art with an often passionate political intensity. Excitement as well as anxiety thus marked the art and the age. The interwar era was a time of contradictions, one in which many Europeans despaired at the future of their society but many others dreamed of building a new and better world.

The Waste Land

Within just a few years of the war's end, war memorials were erected in cities, towns, and villages throughout France and Britain. Significantly, these memorials rarely celebrated the Allies' victory; instead, they focused on dead soldiers. Slaughter, not success, was the dominant theme. At Verdun, for example, the memorial was an ossuary, a gigantic receptacle for the skulls and bones of 130,000 men. In some ways, European culture after the war took on the form of an ossuary, as intellectuals and artists looked at the death tolls from the war and concluded that the end product of human reason and scientific endeavor was mass destruction.

In the English-speaking world, the American expatriate poet T. S. Eliot (1888–1965) supplied the most evocative portrait of postwar disillusion. In 1922, Eliot published a lengthy poem called "The Waste Land," which became a metaphor used by many Europeans to express their own sense of the waste wrought by the war. Arising out of Eliot's own personal anguish, "The Waste Land" contains no straightforward narrative. Instead, like a Cubist collage painting, it comprises fragments of conversation, literary allusions, disjointed quotations, mythological references, all clashing and combining in a modernist cry of despair.

The heightened anxiety and loss of certainty that characterized much of Western literature after the war is also clear in the realms of theology and philosophy. In the nineteenth century, theologians emphasized the harmony of religion and science. Their argument that God is present in the world, guiding its rational and progressive evolution, was difficult to sustain in a society that had experienced the absurd slaughter of World War I. In his postwar writings, the Swiss theologian Karl Barth (1886–1968) emphasized human sinfulness and argued that an immense gulf separated humanity from God. Neither scientific analysis nor historical inquiry could bridge the gap. Reaching God demanded a radical leap of faith.

Barth's German colleague Rudolf Bultmann (1884–1976) made the leap of faith even more radical. Bultmann argued that the Jesus Christ depicted in the New Testament—the foundation of Christianity—was largely fictional. In Bultmann's view, the Gospels were something like Eliot's "Waste Land" poem, a collection of fragments originating from myth and folk tale, layered on one another and capable of multiple interpretations. Rational inquiry and scientific methods cannot deliver a certain image of the historical Jesus, who remains essentially unknowable, obscured by the myths built up over centuries. Yet Bultmann, a Lutheran pastor, did not discard his Christian beliefs. Instead, he argued that within and through the Christian mythology rests ultimate spiritual—although not scientific or historical—truth.

Bultmann's form of Christianity is often called Christian existentialism° because Bultmann put a Christian twist on the existentialist philosophy taught by his friend, the philosopher Martin Heidegger (1889–1976). At the core of existentialism was a profound despair. The human condition is one of anxiety and alienation, even *Nausea,* as Heidegger's student Jean-Paul Sartre (1905–1980) entitled one of his most famous works. For Barth and Bultmann, the way out from this anxiety was through submission to God. As an atheist, Heidegger found this route blocked. Instead, he taught that the individual must struggle to rise above mere existence to a consciousness of the genuine and authentic. Sartre's version of existentialism was more pessimistic. At a time when, as we will see, dictatorships were rising across Europe, Sartre insisted that the fundamental fact of human existence is that "man is condemned to be free" in a universe devoid of meaning or reason. Yet Sartre, too, offered a way out from this prison of freedom: Individuals must recognize that they are free to make choices, and then must do so. During World War II, Sartre's own heroic acts in the French Resistance against the Nazis exemplified his insistence on the necessity of making moral choices in an absurd world.

A sense of absurdity and waste dominates much of the visual art of the period. War veteran Otto Dix (1891–1969) filled his canvases with crippled ex-soldiers. The vivid colors and distorted figures of the Expressionist style enabled Dix to articulate his outrage at the world he saw about him. In *Flanders,* painted in 1934, Dix depicted a nightmare of trench soldiers, rotting like blasted trees. Here there is no heroism, only horror.

Building Something Better

Stuck in the mud, the soldiers in Dix's *Flanders* provide a haunting image of European culture in the interwar years. A very different image takes shape when we examine the work of Dix's contemporaries in the *Bauhaus.* Established in Berlin in 1919 as a school for architects, craftsmen, and designers, the Bauhaus epitomized not the despair but rather the near-utopianism of much of European society after the war. The Bauhaus sought to eliminate the barriers between "art" (what we put on our walls or see in museums) and "craft" (what we actually use in daily life: furniture, textiles, dishes, and the like), and so to enhance daily

---

DOCUMENT

The Waste Land

T. S. Eliot's "The Waste Land" comprises 434 lines; the excerpt given here is thus just one small piece of a much larger and complex poetic work that provides an evocative portrait of a despairing age. One of its central images, drawn from the English legends of King Arthur, is of an impotent and sickly king, reigning over a dried-up land.

April is the cruellest month, breeding
Lilacs out of the dead land, mixing
Memory and desire, stirring
Dull roots with spring rain.
Winter kept us warm, covering
Earth in forgetful snow, feeding
A little life with dried tubers.
. . .
But at my back in a cold blast I hear
The rattle of the bones, and chuckle spread from ear to ear.
A rat crept softly through the vegetation
Dragging its slimy belly on the bank
While I was fishing in the dull canal
On a winter evening round behind the gashouse
Musing upon the king my brother's wreck
And on the king my father's death before him.
White bodies naked on the low damp ground
And bones cast in a little low dry garret,
Rattled by the rat's foot only, year to year.

Source: From "The Waste Land" by T. S. Eliot. First published in 1922. Reprinted by permission of Faber and Faber Ltd.

---

living by making it more effective, efficient, and beautiful. Its founder, Walter Gropius (1883–1969), hoped his students would become nothing less than "the architects of a new civilization."[1]

Gropius's belief that the arts could serve a social purpose was commonly shared in the interwar years. As the British poet W. H. Auden (1907–1973) explained, although good poetry is "not concerned with telling people what to do," it should "[lead] us to the point where it is possible for us to make a rational and moral choice."[2] Many artists abandoned the prewar modernist ideal of "art for art's sake" and produced work steeped in political passion and a desire for a better world.

Machinery and Movement

Much of the near-utopianism of European culture focused on the transforming power of technology. The "machine aesthetic" triumphed most completely in the Soviet Union, where the Bolsheviks encouraged artistic experiment and

Otto Dix, *Flanders* (1934–1935)
In this painting, the Flanders landscape is literally shaped by the bodies of soldiers. Like these soldiers—and much of postwar European culture—Dix could not escape the war. His paintings reveal a man permanently wounded.

innovation as part of their revolution. The engineer became the image of a communist hero, and industrial motifs permeated Soviet culture in the 1920s. In the revolutionary theater of Vsevelod Meyerhold, mechanical gestures replaced naturalistic expressions and sets consisted of scaffolding. Similarly, a factory whistle opens the chorus of Dmitri Shostakovich's *Second Symphony* (1927), written to praise industrial labor.

Postwar architecture in the West also provides a vivid illustration of this mechanical faith. A house, explained the Swiss architect Le Corbusier (1887–1965), was "a machine for living in." Le Corbusier and his fellow modernist architects stripped their buildings of all ornament and frequently exposed the essential machinery—the supporting beams, the heating ducts, the elevator shafts. Concrete, steel, and glass became the building materials of choice as modernist skyscrapers—glittering rectangles—transformed urban skylines and testified to the triumph of the human-made.

Closely related to the worship of the machine in the interwar period was a celebration of movement and speed. The automobile evolved from a rich man's toy to a middle-class necessity, made possible by the assembly-line techniques developed in Henry Ford's Detroit factories. The assembly line, which reduced the entire industrial workforce of a factory to a single efficient machine, was imported from the United States into Europe in the later 1920s. The airline industry also took off in this era. In 1919 the first air passenger service between London and Paris began; the next decade saw Europe's major cities linked by air net-

works. The car and the plane became potent symbols of a new age of possibility and opportunity. In 1927, when the American Charles Lindbergh (1902–1974) became the first person to fly across the Atlantic alone, he was hailed not only as a national but as an international hero, an icon of human resourcefulness and technological mastery.

The idea that Western society was moving rapidly and that anything was possible in a world of change shaped much of the culture of the interwar era. Take the popular dance craze of the 1920s—the Charleston. Arms outstretched and legs firing like pistons, the entire body becomes a fast-moving machine. Another American import, Hollywood's "moving pictures," even more clearly represented and stimulated the ideal of a society in motion. The Italians and the French had dominated the movie industry before 1914, but during the war film production in Europe halted. American filmmakers quickly filled the void. After the war, moviegoing became a truly popular pastime—and most of the movies on the screen were made in America. Hollywood presented European audiences with an appealing, if unrealistic, picture of the United States as a land of fabulous wealth, technological modernity, and unlimited mobility.

Scientific Possibilities

While the United States dominated the fantasy land of popular films in the interwar years, Germany and Britain still clung to their leadership positions in the ongoing scientific revolution. At its most basic level, this revolution overthrew

Building Something Better
Built between 1929 and 1930, the Villa Savoye exemplified Le Corbusier's goal to build "a machine for living (in)." The villa's ribbon windows echo industrial architecture but provide openness and light. True to modernist principles, the house has no historical or traditional ornamentation and uses ramps, spiral staircases, and built-in furniture to create a sense of fluidity.

the mechanistic explanation of the universe that had held sway since the first scientific revolution in the seventeenth century. From the 1890s on, scientists began to replace Isaac Newton's now-discredited universe with a new, more complicated model based on Albert Einstein's theory of relativity. As Chapter 23 explained, Einstein's model replaced Newton's static universe with a world in which space, time, matter, and energy are all interchangeable.

In the 1920s and 1930s, this effort to construct an entirely new understanding of the cosmos electrified the discipline of physics and attracted some of the most brilliant young thinkers of the twentieth century. Students from all over the world traveled to Germany and Britain in pursuit of the best teachers and in hopes of joining research teams in both university and state-funded laboratories.

Much of the excitement in physics stemmed from Einstein's concept of matter as "frozen energy." In theory, if the energy could be "thawed out," then this energy could be released. But could this theory become reality? In 1936, the distinguished British scientist Ernest Rutherford (1871–1937), head of one of the most important research laboratories in the Western world, answered that question with a resounding "no." He dismissed the idea of unlocking the atom to release energy as "moonshine." Yet four years earlier, a scientist working in Rutherford's own laboratory had in fact found the key to unlocking the atom. In 1932, James Chadwick (1891–1974) discovered that atoms contain not only positively charged protons and negatively charged electrons, but also neutrons. Because neutrons possess no electrical charge, they are not repelled by either an atom's protons or its electrons. In theory, then, a bombardment of heavy neutrons could split open an atom's nucleus—a process called nuclear fission. The split nucleus would itself emit neutrons, which would then burst open other atoms, which in turn would emit further neutrons . . . and on and on in a nuclear chain reaction. The result: a colossal burst of energy, energy so abundant that it could perhaps satisfy industrial society's insatiable appetite for energy resources—or produce an atom bomb.

Such possibilities remained purely theoretical—pure "moonshine," in Rutherford's words—until 1938, when two scientists working in Berlin proved Rutherford wrong. Otto Hahn (1879–1968) and Fritz Strassmann (1902–1980) bombarded uranium with a stream of neutrons and broke open the uranium atom. Matter had been unlocked. Within a year, more than 100 articles on the implications of this discovery were published in scientific journals around the world. As one historian has noted, "Physicists viewed the discovery of nuclear fission like the finding of a lost treasure map."[3]

Out of the Trenches: Reconstructing National and Gender Politics in the 1920s

■ In what ways did reconstruction rather than revolution characterize the postwar period?

As we saw at the end of Chapter 24, in the years immediately following World War I Europe stood on the brink of revolutionary change. The war toppled empires and redrew the map of eastern and central Europe. Gender roles turned upside down, imperial patterns shattered, and social expectations were raised. The American president Woodrow Wilson promised a radically new world of peace and democracy. In Russia, the Bolshevik revolution offered an even more radical vision of communist free-

dom. Despite these expectations and fears, however, retrenchment rather than revolution characterized much of the immediate postwar period. In many areas, World War I was the turning point that failed to turn, as Europeans sought to reconstruct the structures toppled by total war.

The Reconstruction of Russia: From Tsar to Commissar

Even in the newly formed Soviet Union, the nation that epitomized revolution, important aspects of prewar society reemerged in the postwar period. By 1922 and against all odds, the Bolsheviks had won the civil war and established their authority over most of the regions of the old tsarist empire. The Bolsheviks also reestablished many features of the tsarist regime: authoritarian rule built on violent coer-

---

Map 25.1   Europe in the 1920s and 1930s

The map shows the consequences of not only World War I but also such successor conflicts as 1. the Irish-English struggles, which resulted in the partition of Ireland: Northern Ireland remained a part of Britain while the rest of the island became the independent nation-state of Eire (see p. 840); 2. the war between Bolshevik Russia and its enemies, which widened the western frontiers of the Soviet state (see p. 819); and 3. the Turkish uprising, which kept Turkey intact and independent (see pp. 842–843).

cion, a highly centralized state, a large bureaucratic elite living in conditions of privilege that cut it off from ordinary people, and a peasant economy.

How do we explain the continuity of authoritarian rule in Russia? The first crucial factor was the impact of civil and international war. Across Russia in 1919 the Bolsheviks faced fierce opposition from rival bands of socialists, middle-class liberals, and aristocratic supporters of the tsar. These opponents of the Bolshevik revolution—called the "Whites" to distinguish them from the "Red" Bolsheviks—were supported by foreign troops. Fearing the spread of communist revolution, fourteen different countries (including the United States, Britain, France, and Japan) sent more than 100,000 soldiers to fight in Russia. In addition to these forces, the new Bolshevik state confronted numerous attempts by non-Russian nationalists to throw off the yoke of Russian rule. This was warfare at its most savage. When Ukrainian peasants resisted Russian control, the Bolsheviks resorted to methods of mass reprisal. Entire villages were burned, the men executed, the women and children sent to slower deaths in prison camps. The Bolsheviks did not have a monopoly on murder, however. White forces in the Ukraine massacred more than 100,000 Jews.

As the scale of savagery escalated, so too did Russia's economic disintegration. In the cities, residents faced anarchic conditions. Transportation systems shut down, the water supply ceased to run, and furniture became the only source of fuel. When the furniture ran out, entire families froze to death inside apartment blocks. The urban areas emptied as their inhabitants fled to the countryside. By 1921, Moscow had lost half its residents and Petrograd (formerly St. Petersburg) had lost two-thirds. Yet conditions in the countryside were also brutal. To feed the cities,

the Bolsheviks adopted the policy of "War Communism": requisitioning (stealing) food and seed stores from the peasants. The peasants resisted, both actively, in violent revolt, and passively, by reducing the amount they planted. Food shortages and other war-related hardships increased the population's vulnerability to epidemic disease. Between 1918 and 1921, the number of deaths from the combined impact of the civil war, starvation, and typhus surpassed the number of those who died in World War I.

The need to impose order on this chaotic situation led the Bolsheviks to adopt increasingly authoritarian measures. Like the Jacobins in 1792 during the French Revolutionary Wars, the Bolsheviks turned to terror to defeat their enemies, both domestic and foreign. In the first six years of Bolshevik rule, the Cheka (Lenin's secret police force) executed at least 200,000 people. In contrast, in the fifty years before the Bolsheviks came to power, 14,000 Russians had died at the hands of the tsarist secret police.

But the antidemocratic nature of the Bolshevik regime was not solely a response to the pressures of war. Ideology also helps explain the continuity of authoritarian rule in post-tsarist Russia. Faced with the task of building a communist state in an isolated, economically backward, peasant society, the Bolshevik leader Vladimir Lenin modified Marxist theory. In a peasant society, Lenin argued, the agent of revolutionary change could not be the working class alone: There simply were not enough industrial workers in Russia. Instead, the Bolshevik or Communist Party, an elite of highly disciplined, politically aware and committed individuals, would be the "vanguard" of revolution. Because the masses could not be trusted to make their own decisions, government officials, strictly controlled by the party, would make these decisions for them. The number of

The High Costs of Civil War

Civil War raged in Russia between 1918 and 1922 as the Bolsheviks fought not only tsarist supporters but also other revolutionary groups and ethnic nationalists. The chaos in the countryside, exacerbated by the Bolshevik policy of seizing peasant produce, resulted in famine.

bureaucrats multiplied and by 1925 had become a privileged elite, with access to the best jobs, food, clothing, and apartments. The rule of the tsar had been replaced not with democracy but with the rule of the commissar, the Communist Party functionary.

In the economic sphere, as in the political system, important continuities shaped the Russian experience. Famine and widespread peasant unrest forced Lenin to revise his program. In 1921 Lenin announced a New Economic Policy (NEP)°. Under NEP, peasants were allowed to sell their produce for profit. Although the state continued to control heavy industry, transport, and banking, NEP encouraged the proliferation of small private businesses and farms—just as the tsar's economic policymakers had done before the war.

The Reconstruction of National Politics in Eastern and Central Europe

U.S. president Woodrow Wilson's vision of a new international order based on democratic politics offered the war-torn states of Europe a sharp alternative to Bolshevik one-party rule. But in the new states of eastern Europe, democracy proved to be fragile, and in most cases short-lived. Much of old Europe survived the war intact.

The Defeat of Democracy in Eastern Europe

After the peace negotiations concluded in 1922, postwar eastern Europe certainly looked markedly different from its prewar counterpart (see Map 25.1). The Russian, Austrian-

Hungarian, and Ottoman Empires had all disappeared, replaced by a jigsaw puzzle of small independent nations. But lines on the map did not change key political and economic realities. Three important threads tied these new states to their prewar past: ethnic disputes, economic underdevelopment, and antidemocratic politics.

As we saw at the end of Chapter 24, the Allies paid lip service to the ideal of national self-determination but found it impossible to create ethnically homogenous nation-states in eastern Europe. As a result, nationalist-ethnic divisions continued to haunt postwar political structures. In the new Yugoslavia, for example, Croats and Slovenes had expected a federalist system that would grant them local autonomy. Instead, they found themselves in a centralized state under Serbian control. As a result, Croat representatives refused even to sit in the new parliament, and ethnic struggles dominated Yugoslav politics.

Economic difficulties also threatened eastern European stability. In many regions, eastern Europe remained a world of peasants and aristocratic landlords. In Romania, Poland, and Hungary, at least 60 percent of the population worked the land; in Bulgaria and Yugoslavia the figure was 80 percent—versus 20 percent in industrialized Britain. With little industrial growth in these regions and few cities to absorb labor, unemployment rates and land hunger were both high.

Thus ethnic divisions and economic underdevelopment helped destabilize eastern Europe's new democratic political systems. The result was the collapse of democracy across eastern Europe. As the chronology (left) shows, with the exception of Czechoslovakia, every eastern European nation returned to authoritarian politics during the 1920s or early 1930s. In Poland, for example, democracy crumbled in 1926 when the World War I hero Marshal Josef Pilsudski (1867–1935) seized power in a military coup, after parliamentary representatives proved unable to overcome class and ethnic divisions. Pilsudski told the squabbling legislators, "The time has come to treat you like children, because you behave like children."[4] In Yugoslavia, the death of democracy was even more dramatic. Years of escalating ethnic violence peaked in 1928 when a popular Croatian political leader was shot to death on the floor of the legislature. The ensuing ethnic unrest gave King Alexander (a Serb) the excuse he needed to abolish the constitution and replace parliamentary democracy with a royal dictatorship. A brutal repression of Alexander's opponents followed. In Bulgaria, Albania, Hungary, and Romania, too, continuing ethnic conflicts and economic underdevelopment ensured the destruction of democracy.

The Weakness of the Weimar Republic

In Germany, as in the new states of eastern Europe, the appearance of radical change masked crucial continuities between the pre- and postwar eras. The kaiser's empire

CHRONOLOGY

The Return of Authoritarian Rule to Eastern Europe

1923	Boris III establishes a royalist dictatorship in Bulgaria
1926	Marshal Josef Pilsudski establishes a military dictatorship in Poland
1928	A new constitution gives King Zog in Albania almost unlimited powers
1929	Alexander I establishes a royal dictatorship in Yugoslavia
1932	Fascist leader Gyula Gombos appointed prime minister in Hungary
1938	King Carol establishes a royal dictatorship in Romania

gave way to the Weimar Republic°, led by a democratically elected parliamentary government. This democratic political structure, however, sat uneasily atop fundamentally antidemocratic social and political foundations.

The survival of authoritarian attitudes and institutions resulted in part from the civil war that raged throughout Germany in the fall of 1918 and the first months of 1919. In this struggle, communists, inspired by the Bolshevik revolution, fought their one-time colleagues in the more moderate socialist party (the SPD) for control of the new Germany. Anxious to impose order on a potentially anarchic situation, the SPD leaders who now controlled the German government chose not to replace the existing state bureaucracy—the elite corps of aristocratic civil servants that had served the kaiser—but to work with it. To put down the communist threat, they also abandoned their longstanding loathing of the German military and deployed both regular army units and the "Free Corps" (volunteer paramilitary units, often comprising demobilized soldiers addicted to violence). By the spring of 1919, this strange alliance of moderate socialists, traditional aristocrats, soldiers, and thugs had triumphed. In January 1919, Free Corps officers murdered the communist leaders Karl Liebknecht and Rosa Luxemburg in Berlin. Three months later, an equally savage repression crushed the communist soviet in Munich, with the Free Corps killing more than 600 people.

The SPD had won. Yet it lost. By allying with the aristocratic civil service, the army, and the Free Corps, the SPD crushed more than the communist revolution; it also crushed its own chances of achieving significant social change. The officers in the army and the bureaucrats in the civil service were representatives of the old Germany, vehemently opposed to not only communism but also parliamentary democracy. Continuing in positions of authority and influence, they constituted a formidable antidemocratic force at the very heart of the new Germany. The approximately 400,000 men who made up the Free Corps also regarded democratic ideals and the new German republic with contempt—"an attempt of the slime to govern."[5] The attitude of the Free Corps men is summed up in their slogan: "Everything would still have been all right if we had shot more people."[6]

The antidemocratic nature of the Free Corps became clear in 1920, after the Allies imposed restrictions on the size of Germany's military force and most Free Corps units were officially dissolved. Disaffected corpsmen joined the right-wing politician Wolfgang Kapp (1858–1922) and the World War I hero Erich von Ludendorff in an effort to overthrow the Weimar regime. This "Kapp Putsch" quickly fizzled out, defeated by both divisions in the ranks of the rebels and a general strike, but the threat posed by the Free Corps did not disappear. Disguising themselves as athletic societies, haulage companies, and even circuses,

many corps units continued their violent anti-Weimar activities. In 1923, some of these corpsmen tried once again to overthrow the Weimar government by force, with another "putsch," this time originating in a beer hall in Munich and led by a former army corporal named Adolf Hitler. Like the Kapp Putsch, Hitler's "Beer Hall Putsch°" did not succeed. The laughably light sentences imposed on its participants, however, made clear the strength of antirepublican sentiments not only among disgruntled Free Corps men but also far up the ranks of the Weimar judicial system.

Antidemocratic forces in the Weimar Republic fed on the widespread resentment among Germans aroused by the severity of the Versailles Treaty. Many Germans could not separate the birth of the republic from the national humiliation imposed by Versailles. They blamed the moderate socialist government that signed the treaty for this humiliation. Army officers encouraged the idea that Germany could have kept on fighting had it not been "stabbed in the back" by the socialists. This "stab-in-the-back" legend helped undermine support not only for the SPD's moderate socialism but even for democracy itself.

The shaky foundations of democracy in Weimar Germany were eroded further by the dramatic events of 1923. In that year, the German mark collapsed completely and paper money ceased to have any value. This hyperinflation was the unintended by-product of the Weimar government's effort to force the Allies to reconsider reparations. In 1922, the Weimar government halted payments and demanded a new economic settlement. The French retaliated by sending troops into Germany's Ruhr Valley to seize coal as a form of reparations payment. German laborers in the Ruhr Valley resisted the invasion by going on strike. Already relying on a policy of inflationary spending to meet its budget deficit, the German government began printing money with abandon to pay the striking Ruhr workers. The inflation rate surged upward. By January 1923, the mark, which in 1914 could be traded for the American dollar at a rate of 4:1, had plummeted to an exchange rate of 22,400:1. By October, the exchange rate from mark to dollar was at 440,000,000:1. Families who had scrimped for years found they had only enough savings to buy a loaf of bread.

As a result of this disaster, the French army pulled out of the Ruhr Valley and in 1924 Allied and German representatives drew up the Dawes Plan, which renegotiated reparations. By the end of 1924, the German economy had stabilized; the later 1920s were years of relative prosperity. Yet for many Germans, the memory of hyperinflation tainted the Weimar Republic. Many Germans concluded that democracy meant disorder and degradation. They looked with longing back to the prewar period, an era of supposed social stability and national power.

France Demands War Reparations from Germany— *L. A. Times* Cartoon

The Trial of Adolf Hitler

On February 24, 1924, Adolf Hitler appeared in court in Munich to confront a charge of high treason following his pathetic attempt three months earlier to overthrow the Weimar government by armed rebellion. The trial marked a crucial point in Hitler's career. It gave him a national platform and, even more important, convinced him of the futility of an armed offensive against the state. From 1925 on, Hitler would work through the parliamentary system in order to destroy it. But the trial of Adolf Hitler is also significant in what it reveals about the power of antidemocratic forces in the new Germany. The trial made clear that many in positions of authority and responsibility in the Weimar Republic shared Hitler's contempt for the democratic state. By treating Hitler not as a traitorous thug but rather as an honorable patriot, his prosecutors helped weaken the already fragile structures of German democracy.

Hitler's attempt to overthrow the Weimar Republic by force occurred at the height of hyperinflation and the ensuing political chaos. By November 8, 1923, when Hitler took up arms, the German mark was worth only one-trillionth of its prewar value. As its currency eroded, the Weimar Republic saw its political legitimacy seeping away as well. Separatist movements in several states threatened the sovereignty of the central government in Berlin. Separatist politics attracted the support of many men from aristocratic backgrounds, members of the traditional conservative elite who viewed Weimar democracy as a foreign and unwelcome import.

Hitler had little interest in the separatist movement, but he believed he could channel its antidemocratic sentiments into a national revolution. He attracted a number of supporters, including one of the most important men in Germany, the World War I hero General Erich von Ludendorff. Seeking to avoid the blame for Germany's defeat in 1918, Ludendorff insisted that his army could have won the war had it not been stabbed in the back by the Social Democratic politicians who now ran the government. Like many German conservatives—and like Hitler—he viewed the Weimar Republic as illegitimate.

On November 8 Hitler made his move. His men surrounded a Munich beer hall where 2,000 supporters of Bavarian separatism had gathered. Hitler declared that both the Bavarian and the national governments had been overthrown and that he was now the head of a new German state, with Ludendorff as his commander-in-chief. Around noon the next day, Hitler, Ludendorff, and several thousand of their followers marched toward the regional government buildings located on one of Munich's main squares. Armed police blocked their passage. In the ensuing firefight, seventeen men were killed. Despite the bullets whizzing through the air, Ludendorff marched through the police cordon and stood in the square awaiting arrest. Hitler ran away. Police found him two days later, cowering in a supporter's country house about thirty-five miles outside Munich.

The Beer Hall Putsch had clearly, utterly, completely failed. In jail awaiting trial, Hitler contemplated suicide. Yet later he described his defeat as "perhaps the greatest stroke of luck in my life." The defeat meant a trial; the trial meant a national audience— and an opportunity for Hitler to present his case against the Weimar Republic. He admitted that he had conspired to overthrow the democratically elected Republican government, but he insisted he was not therefore guilty of treason. The real treason had occurred in November 1918, when the Social Democratic government had surrendered to the Allies: "I confess to the deed, but I do not confess to the crime of high treason. There can be no question of treason in an action which aims to undo the betrayal of this country in 1918. . . . I consider myself not a traitor but a German." He argued that he was not aiming for personal power: "In what small terms small minds think! . . . What I had in mind from the very first day was a thousand times more important than becoming a [Cabinet] minister. I wanted to become the destroyer of Marxism." Thus Hitler depicted himself as a patriot, a nationalist motivated by love of Germany and hatred of communists and socialists. "The eternal court of history," according to Hitler, would judge him and his fellow defendants "as Germans who wanted the best for their people and their Fatherland, who were willing to fight and to die."[7]

Despite Hitler's own admission of conspiring against the government, the presiding judge could persuade the three lay judges (who took the place of a jury) to render a guilty verdict only by arguing that Hitler would most likely be pardoned soon. The reluctance of the judges to convict Hitler highlights the extraordinary sympathy shown to him and his political ideas throughout the trial and during his imprisonment. The chief prosecutor offered a rather surprising description of an accused traitor: "Hitler is a highly gifted man, who has risen from humble beginnings to achieve a respected position in public life, the result of much hard work and dedication. . . . As a soldier he did his duty to the utmost. He cannot

Hitler in Landsberg Prison, 1924
This photo of Hitler during his short imprisonment was made into a postcard, to be purchased by his supporters.

be accused of having used the position he created for himself in any self-serving way." In delivering the verdict, the judge emphasized Hitler's "pure patriotic motives and honorable intentions." Rather than being deported as a foreign national convicted of a serious crime (Hitler was still an Austrian citizen), Hitler was given a slight sentence of five years, which made him eligible for parole in just six months. In prison he was treated like a visiting dignitary—exempted from work and exercise requirements, provided with prisoners to clean his rooms, even given a special table decorated with a swastika banner in the dining hall. When he was released in September, his parole report described him favorably as "a man of order."[8]

Hitler's gentle treatment reveals the precarious state of democratic institutions in Germany after World War I. Many high-ranking Germans in positions of power and influence (such as judges and prosecutors) viewed parliamentary democracy with loathing. The trial also reveals the willingness of conservative aristocrats to ally with Radical Right groups such as the Nazis. Still not very strong, the Nazis in 1923 were easily reined in. A decade later, however, the conservatives who thought they could ride Hitler to power suddenly found that they were no longer in control.

Questions of Justice

1. Imagine you are a German war veteran reading about this case in the newspaper in 1924. Why might you be attracted to the party of Adolf Hitler?
2. Hitler appealed to the "eternal court of history." What do you think he meant? How would Hitler have defined "justice"?

Taking It Further

Gordon, Harold, Jr. *Hitler and the Beer Hall Putsch*. 1972. This lengthy study (more than 600 pages) provides a detailed account of the putsch and its aftermath.

The Hitler Trial Before the People's Court in Munich, trans. H. Francis Freniece, Lucie Karcic, and Philip Fandek (3 vols.). 1976. An English translation of the court transcripts.

George Grosz, "The Pillars of Society" (1926)

The Expressionist artist George Grosz was, like Otto Dix (see page 816), a World War I veteran and a sharp critic of Weimar Germany. In Grosz's scathing critique, the Weimar state had failed to carry out essential social reforms and thus the old order still survived. In this painting, a drunken military chaplain continues to preach while soldiers slaughter behind his back. In the foreground sits a lawyer, supposedly a modern professional, but out of his head bursts a cavalry officer bent on destruction. To the lawyer's right, a press baron, his limited intelligence indicated by the chamber pot on his head, clutches the newspapers that guarantee his fortune and that delude the masses. To the lawyer's left totters an SPD politician. Both his pudgy, drink-reddened cheeks and the pamphlet he presses to his chest (headlined "Socialism is Work") indicate Grosz's contempt for the gradual reformism of the SPD.

The Reconstruction of Gender

Many of the patterns that shaped interwar national politics also characterized the politics of gender in these years. World War I wrought a profound upheaval in gender roles in European society. The demands of total war had meant that women moved into economic areas previously designated as "men only." The war, therefore, seemed an important turning point in the history of women in the West. But here again the turning point failed to turn. Important changes in women's expectations did occur, but nineteenth-century gender roles were quickly reconstructed after the war.

The New Woman

At first sight, the postwar period seems an era of profound change in the roles of women. In the films, magazines, novels, and popular music of the 1920s, the "New Woman" took center stage. Living, working, and traveling on her own, sexually active, she stepped out of the confines of home and family. Women's dress reinforced this idea of a new woman. Whereas nineteenth-century women's clothing had accentuated the womanly body while restricting the woman's movement, the clothing of the 1920s ignored a woman's curves and became much less confining. Complementing this revolution in clothing came a revolution in hairstyle. Women chopped off the long locks regarded for generations as a sign of femaleness and sported fashionable new bobs.

This perception of the New Woman rested on important changes in women's political and economic expectations. By 1920 women in the United States and many European countries had received the right to vote in na-

tional elections and to hold national office. In all the industrialized countries, the expansion of both the health care and service sectors meant new jobs for women as nurses, social workers, secretaries, telephone exchange operators, and clerks. Women's higher-education opportunities also widened in this period.

The biggest change affecting the lives of ordinary women was the spreading practice of limiting family size. We saw in Chapter 22 that by the 1870s middle-class women in Western nations were practicing forms of birth control. In the 1920s and 1930s, an increasing number of working-class women began to do so as well. In Britain, for example, between 1911 and 1931 the average number of

The "New Woman"

Almost every aspect of the "New Woman" captured in this 1928 French photograph offended traditionalists: short skirts and bobbed hair, smoking in public, the association with a car and therefore with mobility and illicit sex—all crossing the border into masculine terrain.

DOCUMENT

The Threat of the New Woman

The perceived movement of women into less traditional roles was profoundly upsetting to many Europeans after the war. Much of this distress focused on a clearly visible target: the dramatically different dress and hairstyles sported by fashionable women, as is evident in this description of the New Woman by a French law student in 1925:

Can one define *la jeune fille moderne* [the young modern woman]? No, no more than the waist on the dresses she wears. Young girls of today are difficult to locate precisely. If you want to be true to French tradition, it would be barbaric, in my opinion, to call our pretty young *parisiennes* young girls.

These beings—without breasts, without hips, without "underwear," who smoke, work, argue, and fight exactly like boys, and who, during the night at the Bois de Boulogne, with their heads swimming under several cocktails, seek out savory and acrobatic pleasures on the plush seats of 5 horse-power Citroens—these aren't young girls!

There aren't any more young girls! No more women either!

Source: Quoted in Mary Louise Roberts, *Civilization Without Sexes: Reconstructing Gender in Postwar France, 1917–1927* (1994), p. 20.

---

children per family fell from 3.4 to 2.2, with most of this decrease resulting from changes in working-class family size. Fewer pregnancies and fewer mouths to feed meant a significant improvement in women's health and living standards.

The Reconstruction of Traditional Roles

Despite these important changes, however, women's roles actually altered little in the two decades after World War I. These years witnessed a strong reaction against the wartime gender upheaval and a concerted effort to reconstruct nineteenth-century masculine and feminine ideals.

Both the war's lengthy casualty lists and the drop in the average family size provoked widespread fear about declining populations—and thus declining national strength. Governments, religious leaders, and commercial entrepreneurs joined together to convince women that their destiny lay in motherhood. Sale and purchase of birth control devices became illegal during the 1920s in France, Belgium, Italy, and Spain. France outlawed abortions in 1920. In

Britain after 1929, a woman who had an abortion could be sentenced to life imprisonment.

To encourage population growth, governments also turned to more positive incentives ranging from the symbolic to the economic. Mother's Day, an American invention, crossed into Europe during the 1920s. In France from 1920 on, women who gave birth to at least five children received a bronze medal; those who bore seven or more children earned the silver; and mothers who produced ten offspring brought home the gold. German women had an easier time: They needed only seven children to get the gold. Of more lasting importance was the expansion of welfare services—family allowances, subsidized or state-provided housing, school lunches, health insurance, prenatal and well-baby clinics—with the express aim of strengthening the family, encouraging women to stay at home, and raising the birth rate. Eugenics played an important role in this legislation. National leaders wanted to increase not only the quantity but the quality of the population. On the positive side, this meant improving the health of babies and mothers. More ominously, much of the rhetoric focused on separating the "fit" from the "unfit," with both class and race among the factors that determined who was "fit" to produce children for the nation.

Despite the calls for women to remain at home, many women had to work in paid employment. In the work world, just as in the family, traditional roles were strengthened after World War I. Most working women returned to jobs in domestic service or to factory positions labeled unskilled and therefore low-paying. Women tended to be barred from management positions, assigned to the most repetitive tasks, and paid by piecework, with the result that the wage gap between male and female laborers remained wide. In both Germany and Britain, unemployment benefits were frequently denied to married women workers, even though they had regularly paid into the insurance system while they were working. The numbers of women employed in the clerical and service sectors did rise in this era, but the movement of women into these positions meant such jobs were reclassified as "women's work," a guarantee of low pay and little power.

Women and the Bolshevik Revolution

In sharp contrast to these efforts to buttress the traditional family structures, in Russia the Bolsheviks promised to revolutionize gender roles. Lenin believed that the family was a middle-class institution doomed to "wither away." In the ideal communist society, marriage would be a mutually beneficial—and in many cases temporary—arrangement between two equally educated and equally waged partners, and both housework and child care would move from the private domestic household into the public sphere of paid employment. To create such a society, the Bolsheviks turned to legislation. One month after seizing power, they legalized divorce and civil marriages. In October 1918, a new family legal code declared women and men equal under the law, made divorce readily available, and abolished the distinction between legitimate and illegitimate children. To free women from housework—described by Lenin as "barbarously unproductive, petty, nervewracking, and stultifying drudgery"[9]—the Bolsheviks established communal child care centers, laundries, and dining rooms. In 1920, just as other nations were outlawing abortion, the practice became legal in Bolshevik Russia.

By 1922, however, the newly created Soviet Union seemed about to self-destruct, and as we have already seen, Lenin retreated from rigorous communist economic ideology to institute the New Economic Policy. NEP also meant significant reversals in the gender revolution. By 1923, the dining halls had been closed and more than half of the day care centers had shut down. The decade of the 1920s was a time of high unemployment for Soviet women. Those who did find jobs received wages that averaged only 65 percent that of men's. An increasing number turned to prostitution. In addition, the traditional patriarchal peasant household—with women in a clearly subordinate role—remained firmly intact. Even in revolutionary Russia, therefore, certain continuities linked the pre- and postwar experience of women.

The Rise of the Radical Right

■ **What circumstances explain the emergence of the Radical Right?**

As the revolution in gender roles was reversed, as Lenin's communist revolution shifted into a lower gear, and as Wilson's democratic revolution ran out of gas, a very different sort of revolution was occurring in Italy, a region long on the periphery of European power. The fascist revolution introduced Europe to a new sort of politics, the politics of the Radical Right. Like conservatism, the new Radical Right ideologies—fascism° and its younger cousin, Nazism—dismissed equality as a socialist myth and emphasized the importance of authority. But neither fascism nor Nazism was conservative. These radical political systems sought to use the new technologies of the mass media to mobilize their societies for a program of violent nationalism.

The Fascist Alternative

Conceived in the coupling of wartime exhilaration and postwar despair, fascism offered an alternative to the existing political ideologies. Fascism was more than a set of political ideas, however. As presented by its creator, Benito Mussolini (1883–1945), fascism was an ongoing performance, a spectacular sound-and-lights show with a cast of millions.

Mussolini's Rise to Power

Fascism originated in Italy. In 1915 after a fierce internal debate that widened the already huge gaps in Italian society, Italy entered the war on the side of the Allies. Many pro-war Italians viewed the war as a cleansing force, a powerful disinfectant that would leave Italian society stronger and more powerful. Mussolini, a socialist journalist, shared these views. Because the Socialist Party opposed Italy's entry into the war, Mussolini broke with the socialists, joined the army in 1915, and fought until he was wounded in 1917. When the war ended, he sought to create a new form of politics that would translate the military camaraderie and the exhilaration of violent action that he had experienced during the war. The result was fascism.

In March 1919, Mussolini and a little more than 100 men and some women gathered in Milan and declared themselves the fascist movement. Like Mussolini, many of these "fascists of the first hour" were war veterans; a number had served in the *arditi*, elite commando units that fought behind enemy lines. The arditi uniform, a severe black shirt, became the fascist badge of identity. The arditi slogan, *"me ne frego"* ("I don't give a damn") became the blackshirts' creed, a fitting summary of their willingness to throw aside conventional standards and politics.

The March on Rome, October 28, 1922
The fascist march on Rome was a carefully orchestrated show of power, not an armed rebellion. Mussolini had already been offered the premiership of Italy, as is clear from his clothing: He has changed his black shirt for a proper suit.

Just three and a half years after the first fascist meeting in Milan, Mussolini became prime minister of Italy. His astonishing rise to power occurred against a backdrop of social turmoil. In 1919 and 1920, more than one million workers were on strike, factory occupations became commonplace, and a wave of land seizures spread across the countryside. Increasingly frightened that revolution would engulf Italy just as it had destroyed tsarist Russia, large landowners and industrialists, as well as the professional and commercial middle classes, looked to Mussolini's fascists for help. Fascist squads disrupted Socialist Party meetings, vandalized the offices of socialist newspapers, broke up strikes, beat up trade unionists, and protected aristocratic estates from attack. By 1922, the fascists were a formidable political force and Mussolini was engaged in negotiations aimed at bringing the fascists into a coalition government. In October 1922, King Victor Emmanuel III (r. 1900–1946) asked Mussolini to become not only a member of the government but its prime minister. Mussolini agreed. In a carefully orchestrated display of muscle, fascists from all over Italy converged in the "March on Rome," a piece of street theater designed to demonstrate Mussolini's mass support, as well as the disciplined might of his followers.

The Fascist Revolution in Italy

Over the next four years Mussolini used both legal and illegal methods, including murder, to eliminate his political rivals and remake Italy as a one-party state. By 1926, he had succeeded. Party politics, an independent press, and the trade union movement ceased to exist. Victor Emmanuel

CHRONOLOGY

Mussolini's Rise to Power

1915–1917	Serves in the Italian army
1919	Participates in the creation of the fascist movement
1921	Fascist Party wins thirty-five seats in parliament
1922	Becomes prime minister
1925–1926	Abolishes party politics and establishes himself as dictator
1929	Signs Lateran Accords with the Roman Catholic Church

remained on the throne, the official head of state, but power lay in Mussolini's hands. The restored death penalty and a strong police apparatus stood ready to enforce Mussolini's will and to remake Italy into a fascist society.

But what was fascism? Mussolini conceived of fascism as the politics of modernity. He condemned the existing political ideologies as outdated. Socialism exalted the working class; liberalism viewed the individual as the core of society; conservatism clung to social hierarchy. Fascism, however, identified the *nation* as the dominant social reality. With a strong leader at the wheel, with violent action as its fuel, the fascist nation would crash through social and economic barriers and transport its people into a new and more powerful age.

Yet Mussolini's supposedly radical revolution reinforced traditional elite interests. Early fascist promises of land redistribution were quickly forgotten, and the end of democracy meant that the control of local government rested not with elected officials but rather with Mussolini's appointees—usually drawn from the ranks of the traditional agrarian elite. Fascist economic theory, such as it was, promised to replace capitalist competition and the profit motive with corporatism: Committees (or "corporations") made up of representatives of workers, employers, and the state were to direct the economy for the good of the nation. In actuality, workers' rights disappeared while industrialists' profits remained untouched.

Mussolini's revolution, then, was not about leveling society. Mussolini had no intention of giving *actual* political power to ordinary people; he did, however, recognize the importance of giving them the *illusion* of power. The fascist revolution offered individuals a sense of power by making them feel a part of the nation. A series of "after-work" occupational and recreational groups served as a channel for fascist propaganda and connected ordinary people more closely to the fascist state, while at the same time occupying their leisure hours. By 1939, four million Italians were participating in fascist sporting clubs, holiday camps, and cultural outings.

The "Cult of the Duce" also provided an important means of fostering a sense of participation in the life of the nation. Mussolini insisted, "I am Fascism." Carefully choreographed public appearances gave ordinary Italians the chance to see, hear, and adore their Duce ("Leader"), and through contact with his person, to feel a part of the new Italy. To stimulate public adoration of himself, Mussolini paid careful attention to his public image. He ordered that the press ignore his birthdays and the births of his grandchildren: The Duce could not be seen to age. Instead, in photograph after photograph, Mussolini appeared as a man of action. Depicted in planes, in trains, and in racing cars, he was always on the move, always pressing forward.

At the same time, Mussolini combined up-to-date advertising and the latest mass media technologies with age-old rituals inspired largely by the Catholic Church.

Huge public rallies set in massive arenas, carefully staged with lighting and music, inspired his followers. A popular fascist slogan summed up the leadership cult: "Believe, Obey, Fight." Italians were not to think or question; they were to *believe*. What were they to believe? Another slogan provides the answer: "Mussolini is always right."

The Great Depression and the Spread of Fascism After 1929

The simple certainty offered by a slogan such as Mussolini's proved highly appealing throughout much of Europe after 1929. During the 1930s, fascist movements emerged in almost every European state. The key factor in the spread of fascism was the Great Depression°. On October 24, 1929, the American stock market collapsed. Over the next two years, the American economic crisis evolved into a global depression. Banks closed, businesses collapsed, and unemployment rates rose to devastating levels. Even by the end of the 1930s, the production rates of many nations remained low. Desperate people looked for desperate answers. Fascism provided some of these.

Why did the Depression spread so quickly and last so long? The explanation lies with the changing role of the United States in Europe. World War I accelerated the shift of the world's economic center away from Europe and toward America. New York's stock market emerged to rival London's, and U.S. businesses increasingly displaced European competitors as the chief suppliers of industrial goods to regions such as Latin America. While European nations sold off their domestic and foreign assets and borrowed heavily to pay for the war, the United States moved from the position of debtor to creditor nation. By the end of 1918 Allied nations owed the United States more than $9 billion—and American officials made it clear that they expected this money to be repaid in full, with interest.

The problem of wartime indebtedness quickly became entangled with the issue of German reparations. Britain, France, and Italy could pay off their debts to the United States only if Germany paid reparations to them. Hyperinflation and the near-collapse of the German economy in 1923, however, forced the revision of the reparations schedule established by the Versailles Treaty. In 1924 and again in 1928 American and European financial representatives met to reconfigure (and in 1928 to reduce) the payments. American credit became the fuel that kept the European economy burning. From 1925 on, American investors loaned money to Germany, which used the money to pay reparations to the Allies, which in turn used the money to pay back the United States. The system worked for a short time. Fueled by loans, the German economy kicked into gear. Currencies stabilized, production rose, and American money flowed not only into Germany but into all of Europe. If these loans dried up, however, Europe faced disaster.

In 1929 that disaster struck. With the collapse of the U.S. stock market, savings portfolios lost between 60 and 75 percent of their value almost overnight. Scrambling to scrape up any assets, American creditors liquidated their European investments, and European economies tumbled. Germany, the country whose economy was most directly linked to the United States, saw its industrial output fall by 46 percent, while its number of jobless grew to more than six million.

The political and social disarray that accompanied the Great Depression enhanced the appeal of fascist promises of stability, order, and national strength. In the 1930s, fascist movements emerged across Europe. Few succeeded in seizing the reins of government, but existing authoritarian regimes adopted many fascist trappings in order to stay in power. For example, Romania's King Carol II (r. 1930–1940) faced a strong challenge to his rule from the Iron Guard, the first mass fascist movement in the Balkans. To compete with the guard, Carol embraced its language of national renewal, as well as typically fascist features such as uniformed paramilitaries, a youth group, and mass rallies. In 1938 he abolished all political parties, placed the judicial system under military control, and declared himself a royal dictator. He then dissolved the Iron Guard and garroted its leader.

The Nazi Revolution

In Germany, the Nazi Party offered a different version of Radical Right ideology. Just as the emergence of fascism was inextricably linked to the career of one man, Benito Mussolini, so Nazism° cannot be separated from Adolf Hitler (1889–1945). To understand the Nazi revolution in Germany, we need first to explore Hitler's rise to power and then to examine the impact of Nazi rule on ordinary people.

Hitler's Rise to Power

Hitler, an ardent German nationalist, was not a citizen of Germany for most of his life. Born in Austria, Hitler came of age in Vienna, where he made a meager living as a painter while absorbing the anti-Semitic German nationalism that permeated the capital city of the Habsburg Empire. When World War I broke out, Hitler grabbed at the chance to fight the war in a German rather than an Austrian uniform. He regarded army life as "the greatest of all experiences." Hitler served as a German soldier for almost the entire length of the war until he was temporarily blinded by poison gas in 1918. After the war he settled in Munich, home to large bands of unemployed war veterans and a breeding ground for nationalist and racist groups.

The Nazi Party began as one of these small fringe groups, with Hitler quickly emerging as its leader. *Nazi* is shorthand for *National Socialist German Workers' Party,* but this title, like all of Nazi ideology, was a lie. Nazism fiercely opposed socialism, communism, trade unionism, and any political analysis that emphasized class conflict or workers'

CHRONOLOGY	
Hitler's Rise to Power	
1914–1918	Serves in the German army
1919–1923	Establishes himself as a right-wing activist in Munich
1923	Fails to overthrow the government with the Beer Hall Putsch
1929	Collapse of the U.S. stock market; onset of Great Depression
1930	Nazis win 107 seats in German parliament
1932	Nazis win 230 seats; become largest party in German parliament
1933	
January	Becomes chancellor
February	Uses Reichstag fire as pretext to gain emergency powers
March	Uses the Enabling Act to destroy democracy in Germany

rights. For the Nazis, race, not class, constituted the key social reality. To Hitler, all history was the history of racial struggle, and in that racial struggle, the Jews were always the principal enemy. Hitler regarded Jewishness as a biological rather than a religious identity, as a sort of toxic infection that could be passed on to future generations and that posed a threat to the racially pure "Aryans"—white northern Europeans.*

Like Mussolini, Hitler exalted the nation. He believed Germany was destined to become a powerful empire controlling central and eastern Europe. This new age would dawn, however, only after a mighty battle between the racially superior Germans and their numerically superior enemy: the forces of "Judeo-Bolshevism." In Hitler's distorted vision, Jewishness and communism formed two parts of the same evil whole. He saw the Bolshevik victory in Russia and the call for communist world revolution as part of a much larger struggle for Jewish world domination.

In its early days Nazism appealed to men like Hitler, individuals without much power or, apparently, much chance of getting it—demobilized and now unemployed soldiers, small shopkeepers wiped out by postwar inflation, lower-middle-class office clerks anxious to preserve their shaky social status, and workers who had lost their jobs. Nazism

Aryan is actually a linguistic term referring to the Indo-Aryan or Indo-European language groups. Anti-Semites such as Hitler misapplied the term to racial groups to lend a supposedly scientific authority to their racism.

offered a simple explanation of history, a promise of future glory, and a clear and identifiable scapegoat for both personal and national woes. By the time of the Beer Hall Putsch in November 1923, party membership stood at about 55,000.

As we saw earlier in the discussion of postwar Germany, the Beer Hall Putsch failed in its aim to overthrow the Weimar Republic, but it did bring Hitler a national audience. Both his speeches during the ensuing trial for treason and *Mein Kampf* ("My Struggle"), the book he wrote while in prison, publicized his racialized view of German political history. After Hitler emerged from prison, he concentrated on transforming the Nazis into a persuasive political force. To infiltrate German society at all levels, Nazis formed university and professional groups, labor unions, and agrarian organizations, while the Nazi paramilitary organization, the SA (*Sturmabteilung*), terrorized opponents. The party held meetings and rallies incessantly, not just during election periods, and so ensured that Germany was saturated with its message. Even so, in the elections of 1928, Nazi candidates won only 2.6 percent of the vote.

It was the Great Depression that gave the Nazis their chance at power. After 1929, unemployment rates skyrocketed and the Weimar political system began to collapse. No German political leader could put together a viable governing coalition. Parliamentary power dwindled; in all of 1932 the federal parliament met for only thirteen days. As the mechanisms of parliamentary democracy faltered, the German chancellor Heinrich Bruning increasingly relied on a stopgap measure in the German constitution—the presidential emergency decree. The constitution declared that in emergency situations, decrees signed by the German president could become law without parliamentary consent. But this practice meant that power shifted from the parliament to the president, the World War I hero General Paul von Hindenburg. Already in his eighties, Hindenburg was a weak man easily manipulated by a small circle of aristocratic advisors and cronies.

In this unstable climate, political polarization accelerated as Germans looked for extreme solutions to extreme problems. By July 1932, the Nazis had become the largest party in the parliament, winning the support of 37 percent of the German voters. Support for their communist rivals also continued to grow.

Terrified of the threat posed by communism and convinced that Hitler could be easily controlled, a small group of conservative politicians persuaded Hindenburg to offer Hitler the position of chancellor in January 1933. One of the group, Baron Franz von Papen, reassured a friend that Hitler posed "no danger at all. We have hired him for our act. In two months' time we'll have pushed Hitler so far into the corner, he'll be squeaking."[10] But von Papen was wrong.

Within six months Hitler had destroyed what remained of democracy in Germany and established a Nazi dictator-

ship. Almost as soon as he took office he persuaded Hindenburg to pass an emergency decree mandating the seizure of all Communist Party presses and buildings. Then in February a fire destroyed the German parliament building. Declaring (wrongly) that the fire was part of a communist plot against the state, Hitler demanded the power to imprison without warrant or trial. Mass arrests of more than 25,000 of his political opponents followed—not only communists but also social democrats and anyone who dared oppose him openly. At the end of March, German politicians, cowed by Nazi threats of imprisonment, passed the Enabling Act. This key act gave Hitler the power to suspend the constitution and pass legislation without a parliamentary majority. By the summer of 1933, parliamentary political life had ceased to exist in Germany and a dictatorship had destroyed democracy.

Often presented as a model of authoritarian efficiency, the Nazi dictatorship was actually a confusing mass of overlapping bureaucracies, in which ambitious officials competed with each other for power and influence. This planned chaos ensured that none of Hitler's deputies acquired too much authority. It also enhanced the mystery of the state. The individual citizen attempting to make a complaint or resolve a problem would soon feel as if he were engaged in a battle with a multilimbed monster.

This multilimbed monster, however, had only one head: Adolf Hitler. The entire system was designed to make clear that there was only one man in charge, one leader—the *Führer*. Like Mussolini, Hitler realized the importance of personalizing his rule. During election campaigns before 1933 and in the early years of power after, Hitler was constantly on the move, using cars and planes to hit city after city, to deliver speech after speech, to touch person after person. In 1932 and 1933, he conducted election campaigns from the sky, often visiting four or five cities in a single night. He always arrived late, so that his plane could fly above the packed stadium, the focus of every upturned face. Leaders of the Hitler Youth were required to take this oath: "Adolf Hitler is Germany and Germany is Adolf Hitler. He who pledges himself to Hitler pledges himself to Germany."[11]

National Recovery

Jews, communists, socialists, and other groups defined as enemies of the state faced the constant threat of persecution and imprisonment under the Nazi regime during the 1930s. But for many Germans not in these groups, life got better. Nazi rule brought full employment, restoration of national pride, and a cultural revolution that linked the power of nostalgia to the dynamism of modernity.

Economic depression gave the Nazis the chance at power; economic prosperity (or the appearance of it) enabled them to hold on to this power. Because Hitler perceived himself as a revolutionary, bound by no existing rules, he was able to intensify and accelerate unorthodox economic programs put in place by the preceding government. The rules of economic orthodoxy dictated that in times of depression, a government should cut spending and maintain a balanced budget. Struggling to cope with the broken economy, Hitler's predecessors had set aside the rules and instead began devising a program of deficit spending on things such as a national network of highways (the *Autobahnen*). Hitler took up these plans and ran with them. He made the autobahn a reality, invested heavily in other public works, and after 1936 poured marks into rearmament. These programs created thousands of jobs. By 1938, unemployment in Germany had been defeated, dropping from 44 percent in 1932 to 14.1 percent in 1934 to less than 1 percent in 1938. In contrast, double-digit unemployment rates persisted in much of western Europe.

Germans and non-Germans alike hailed Nazi Germany as an economic success. In many ways, they were wrong. Under Nazi rule, real wages fell and the concentration on rearmament led to shortages in food supplies and in consumer goods. In 1938, meat consumption remained below the level of 1929. Yet many Germans *believed*

"Heil (Hail) Hitler!"
An enthusiastic crowd salutes Hitler at a Nazi party rally. The women in the traditional costumes illustrate a key aspect of the Nazis' appeal: their promise to restore women to their traditional domestic roles. The men in military uniform indicate a second source of Nazi popularity: the restoration of military strength and national pride.

themselves to be much better off. The expansion of social welfare assistance (for those considered "Aryan") helps explain this perception, as does the establishment of the "Strength through Joy" program (directly inspired by Mussolini's "after-work" organizations), which provided workers with cheap vacations, theater and concert tickets, and weekend outings. But most important, under the Nazis, Germans were working. The abundance of jobs—despite the low wages, despite the disappearance of workers' rights, despite the food shortages—made Hitler an economic savior to many Germans.

Many also viewed him as a national savior, a leader who restored Germany's pride and power. Payment of war reparations, demanded by the humiliating Versailles Treaty, halted in 1930 because of the global economic crisis. Hitler never resumed payment. He also ignored the treaty's military restrictions and rebuilt Germany's armed forces. By 1938, parades featuring row after row of smartly uniformed troops, impressive displays of tanks, and flybys of military aircraft all signaled the revitalization of German military might.

For many ordinary Germans, traumatized and shamed by the sequence of national disasters—military defeat, loss of territory, hyperinflation, political and fiscal crises, unemployment—the sight of troops goose-stepping under the German flag meant a personal as well as a na-

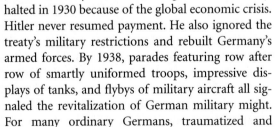

IMAGE

German Painting Idolizing Hitler

tional renaissance. As one Nazi song proclaimed, "And now the me is part of the great We."[12]

To create the "great We," Hitler utilized modern techniques and technology. The Nazis published a glossy illustrated magazine, produced their own films, and littered cities with propaganda posters. Impressed by Mussolini's use of the radio to popularize fascism, Hitler subsidized the production of radios in Germany so that by the end of the 1930s most Germans had access to a radio—and to Hitler's radio talks. He also recognized the power of the cinema, and hired the brilliant filmmaker Leni Riefenstahl (1902–2003) to film Nazi rallies. These still-astonishing films show an overwhelming mass spectacle in which an entire nation appears to be marching in step behind Hitler.

But Hitler also perceived the power of nostalgia for many Germans, and so used modern techniques and technologies to establish the Nazis as bulwarks of tradition. In speeches, posters, and films, the Nazis painted a picture of a mythic Germany, an idyllic community peopled by sturdy blond peasants, small shopkeepers, and independent craftsmen. The Nazis promised that under their leadership, individual Germans would regain meaning and purpose as part of a single national community. Nazi ideology condemned international corporations, large department stores, and supermarket chains as elements of a vast Jewish-controlled conspiracy to deprive ordinary people of their livelihoods.

Campaigns of Repression and Terror

Part of the appeal of the "great We" that Hitler was creating relied on the demonization and violent repression of the "not Us," those defined as outside or opposed to the nation. Hitler used the existing German police force as well as his own paramilitary troops—the brownshirted SA and the blackshirted SS (*Schutzstaffeln*)—to terrorize those he defined as enemies of the nation. The Nazis first targeted political opponents. By 1934 half of the 300,000 German Communist Party members were in prison or dead; most of the rest had fled the country. The Nazis also persecuted specific religious groups on the basis of their actual or presumed opposition to the Nazi state. Roman Catholics could no longer work in the civil service and faced constant harassment, and about half of Germany's 20,000 Jehovah's Witnesses were sent to concentration camps.

The groups that the Nazis deemed biologically inferior suffered most severely. Beginning in 1933, the Nazi regime forced the sterilization of the Roma (Gypsies), the mentally and physically handicapped, and mixed-race children (in most cases, the offspring of German women and black African soldiers serving in the French occupation force in the Rhineland). By 1939, 370,000 men and women had been sterilized.

The Jewish community—less than 1 percent of the German population—bore the brunt of Nazi racial attacks. To Nazi anti-Semites, Hitler's accession to the German chancellorship was like the opening of hunting season. They beat up Jews in the streets, vandalized Jewish shops and homes, threatened German Christians who associated with Jews, and violently enforced boycotts of Jewish businesses. Anti-Jewish legislation piled up in an effort to convince Germans of the separateness, the "non-Germanness," of Jewish cultural and racial identity. In 1933, "non-Aryans" (Jews) were dismissed from the civil service and the legal profession, and the number of Jewish students in high schools and universities was restricted. Every organization in Germany—youth clubs, sports teams, labor unions, charitable societies—underwent "Nazification," which meant the dismissal of all Jewish members and the appointment of Nazis to leadership roles. In 1935, the "Nuremberg Laws" labeled as Jewish anyone with three or more Jewish grandparents. Marriage or sexual relations between German Jews and non-Jews now became a serious crime.

Women and the Radical Right

Much of the appeal of both fascism and Nazism lay in the promise to restore order to societies on the verge of disintegration. Restoration of order meant, among other things, the return of women to their proper place. According to Nazi propaganda, "the soil provides the food, the woman supplies the population, and the men make the action."[13] Hitler proclaimed, "the Nazi Revolution will be an entirely male event." Mussolini agreed: "Woman must obey. . . . In our State, she must not count."[14]

In Nazi Germany, the restoration of order translated into a series of financial and cultural incentives to encourage women to stay at home and produce babies. These measures ranged from marriage loans (available only if the wife quit her job) and income tax deductions for families to the establishment of discussion, welfare, and leisure groups for housewives. Not surprisingly, the Nazis also used disincentives. One of the first actions of the new Nazi government was to dismiss women from the civil service and to rule that female physicians could work only in their husbands' practices. By 1937, both women physicians and women Ph.D.s had lost the right to be addressed as "Doctor" or "Professor." Women could no longer work as school principals. Coeducational schools were abolished. Birth control became illegal and penalties for abortion increased while prosecutions doubled.

In fascist Italy, Mussolini's government focused its legislation on both men and women. Unmarried men over age 30 had to pay double income tax (priests were exempt), homosexual relations between men were outlawed, and fatherhood became a prerequisite for men in high-ranking public office. A wide-ranging social welfare program that included family allowances, maternity leaves, and marriage loans sought to strengthen the traditional family. Quotas limited the number of women employed in both the civil service and in private business, while women found themselves excluded entirely from jobs defined as "virile," a varied list that included boat captains, diplomats, high school principals, and history teachers.

The Polarization of Politics in the 1930s

■ **What factors led to the polarization of European politics in the 1930s?**

The apparent successes of fascist Italy and Nazi Germany appealed to many Europeans and Americans disenchanted with democracy in the era of the Great Depression. During this period, the Soviet Union also seemed a success story. While the capitalist nations struggled with high unemployment rates and falling industrial output, the Soviet Union appeared to be performing economic miracles. Politics in the West thus became polarized between communism on the radical left and fascism and Nazism on the radical right. In both the United States and Europe, however, politicians and policymakers sought to maintain the middle ground, to retain democratic values in a time of extremist ideologies.

The Soviet Union Under Stalin: Revolution Reconstructed, Terror Extended

Many Europeans looked with envy at the Soviet Union in the 1930s. Unemployment had disappeared; huge industrial cities transformed the landscape; the development of new industries such as chemicals and automobiles, together with a full-scale exploitation of the Soviet Union's massive natural resources, sent production indices soaring. But this economic transformation rested on dead bodies, millions of dead bodies. During the 1930s, mass murder became an integral part of the Soviet regime under Joseph Stalin (1879–1953).

Stalin's Rise to Power

By 1928, Stalin was the uncontested head of the party. At the time of Lenin's death in 1924, however, few observers would have predicted Stalin's success. Although a stalwart Bolshevik, he stood in the shadow of more charismatic, intellectually able colleagues. How, then, did Stalin seize control of the Communist Party and the Soviet state?

One key factor in Stalin's rise to power was the changing nature of the Communist Party. The party that made the revolution in 1917 comprised only 24,000 members. Following a massive recruitment campaign to honor Lenin's memory, party membership in 1929 stood at more than one and a half million—and only 8,000 of these had been members in 1917. In other words, the vast majority of communists in 1929 had not fought in the revolution. For them, communism was not a revolutionary ideology challenging the tsarist political order; it was itself the political order. Party membership was not a revolutionary act; it was a guarantee of privileged status and career opportunities. Moreover, unlike the original Bolshevik revolutionaries, most of the new members were not well educated or well versed in communist ideology. In fact, 25 percent of the party membership was functionally illiterate.

As party secretary from 1922 on, Stalin led the recruitment drive that enlisted many of these new party members. Other party leaders dismissed Stalin as the "card-index Bolshevik"—the paper-pusher, the gray guy with the boring job. But Stalin, an astute politician, recognized that his card index held enormous power. Not only did he determine the fate of party membership applications, he also decided who got promoted to what and where. Thus, throughout the 1920s Stalin slowly built up a broad base of support within the party. Vast numbers of ordinary communists owed their party membership, and in many cases their livelihoods, to Stalin.

CHRONOLOGY	
Stalin's Rise to Power	
1917	
March	Popular Russian Revolution
November	Bolshevik revolution
1918–1921	Russian civil war
1921	New Economic Policy (NEP) begins
1922	Stalin appointed general secretary of the Central Committee of the Communist Party
1924	Death of Lenin
1925–1928	Leadership disputes; Stalin emerges as the head of the Communist Party
1929	NEP ended; collectivization begins
1934	The Congress of Victors
1934–1938	The Great Purge

While Stalin expanded his support at the grassroots, a fierce ideological struggle at the highest levels of the Communist Party distracted his rivals for the party leadership. By the time of Lenin's death, the New Economic Policy (NEP) had restored economic stability to the Soviet Union. The nation, however, remained far behind its capitalist competitors in both agricultural and industrial productivity. All communists agreed on the need to launch the Soviet economy into industrialization. The problem was, how could this backward nation obtain the capital it needed for industrial development? One faction of the party, led by Leon Trotsky (1879–1940), argued that the answer was to squeeze the necessary capital out of the peasantry through high taxation and even, if necessary, the confiscation of crops. Trotsky wanted to abandon NEP and its encouragement of small private farming initiatives. The opposing faction, led by Nikolai Bukharin (1888–1938), pointed to the lessons taught by western European industrialization. In the West, industrial capital came from agricultural profits. Bukharin insisted on the need for gradualism: Agricultural development must precede industrialization. "Enrich the peasant," Bukharin argued.

Stalin at first backed Bukharin and those who wished to continue on the NEP course, because he perceived the charismatic Trotsky as the more immediate threat to his ambitions. Once Trotsky had been expelled from the party, however, Stalin reversed course and turned on Bukharin. In 1928, Stalin emerged as the sole leader of the party and as a fierce advocate of the abandonment of NEP, the total socialization of the Soviet economy, and a fast march forward into full-scale industrialization.

The "Revolution from Above": Collectivization and Industrialization, 1928–1934

As party leader, Stalin placed the Soviet Union firmly back on a revolutionary course, with the aim of catapulting the Soviet Union into the ranks of the industrialized nations.

DOCUMENT

Stalin Demands Rapid Industrialization of the USSR (1931)

The first step in what was called "the revolution from above" was collectivization°, the replacement of private and village farms with large cooperative agricultural enterprises run by communist managers according to directives received from the central government. Collectivization had both economic and political aims. Regarded as more modern and efficient, collective farms were expected to produce an agricultural surplus and thereby raise the capital needed for industrialization. But in addition, collectivization would realize communist ideals by eradicating the profit motive, abolishing private property, and transforming the peasants into modern state employees.

The peasants resisted this transformation, however. They burned their crops and slaughtered their livestock. Famine followed. The numbers of deaths resulting from collectivization and the famine of 1931–1932 remain the subject of intense controversy; the available quantitative evidence points to death figures between five million and seven million. Ukraine and Kazakhstan were hardest hit. Almost 40 percent of the Kazakh population died from starvation or typhus; the number of dead in Ukraine alone may have reached four million.[15] Perhaps as many as ten million peasants were deported in these years; many of these died either on the way to or in forced labor camps.

While class war raged in the countryside, city dwellers embarked on the second stage of the "revolution from above"—industrialization. In 1931 Stalin articulated the task facing the Soviet Union: "We are fifty or a hundred years behind the advanced countries. We must catch up this distance in ten years. Either we do it or we go under."[16] Doing it demanded, first, unprecedented levels of labor output. Despite the massive investment in heavy industry, the Soviet Union throughout the 1930s remained undermechanized. What it lacked in technology, however, it possessed in population. Thus Soviet industry was highly labor intensive. To ensure that workers produced at the levels needed, the Soviet state under Stalin imposed fierce labor discipline. Only productive workers received ration cards. Internal passports restricted workers' freedom of movement. If fired, a worker was automatically evicted from his or her apartment and deprived of a ration card.

Catching up with the West also demanded reducing already low levels of personal consumption. Eighty percent of all investment went into heavy industry, while domestic construction and light industry—clothing, for example, and furniture—were ignored. Scarcity became the norm, long lines and constant shortages part of every urban resident's existence. Economists estimate that Soviet citizens endured a 40 percent fall in their already low standard of living between 1929 and 1932.

While millions starved in the countryside, young communists acclaimed these years of hardship and horror as an era of heroism. They volunteered to organize collective farms, to work in conditions of extreme brutality at construction sites, to labor long hours in factories and mines. Babies born in this decade received names like "Little Five Years" (for girls) and "Plan" (for boys), reflecting their parents' enthusiasm for the series of Five-Year-Plans issued by the central government as outlines for the new world order. Much of this enthusiasm was stirred up by propaganda campaigns aimed at persuading laborers to work ever harder and sacrifice ever more. Ordinary workers who achieved record-breaking feats of production earned medals, special ceremonies, and material gifts. Immense publicity focused on the gargantuan engineering achievements of the era—the cities built atop swampland, the hydroelectric projects with their enormous dams and power plants, the Moscow subway system. Such publicity made party members feel part of a huge and powerful endeavor. A popular song announced, "We were born to make fairy tales come true."[17]

Just as important as the propaganda campaigns was the reality of unprecedented opportunity. The Soviet Union in the 1930s has been called "the quicksand society," one in which traditional structures and relations (and people too) were swallowed up at a breathtaking pace. As these traditional structures disappeared, new ones emerged, bringing tremendous geographic and social mobility to Soviet society. For example, Nikita Khrushchev (1894–1971), who would succeed Stalin as the head of the party and state in the 1950s, was the son of a poor peasant.

No propaganda campaign and no amount of effort from enthusiastic young communists, however, could provide the Soviet Union with the labor it needed to catch up with the West in ten years. Forced labor was crucial. Throughout the 1930s, as many as five million men, women, and children—peasants, political opponents of Stalin, religious dissenters, ethnic minorities—labored in prison camps.[18] By some estimates, forced labor accounted for no less than 25 percent of all construction work in the Soviet Union in the 1930s. Many of the huge engineering triumphs of the decade rested on the backs of prisoners and deportees.

By the end of the 1930s, Stalin's "revolution from above" had achieved its aim. The pouring of resources into heavy industry and the wringing of every ounce of labor out of an exhausted, cold, and hungry populace succeeded in building the foundations of an industrial society. This society would stand the test of total war in the 1940s.

But Stalin's revolution failed to convert Soviet agriculture into a modern, prosperous sector of the economy. Rural regions remained backward. Peasant villages, for example, were not electrified until the later 1950s. Most peasants regarded the collective farm as belonging not to them or to the community but to the state, just another in a long line of harsh landlords. Under Stalin, peasants were second-class citizens, ineligible for internal passports, with little access to the benefits of Soviet industrialization. Like their ancestors under serfdom, peasants at the end of the 1930s found themselves tied to a particular village, saddled with forced labor obligations, and compelled to spend the bulk of their time farming for someone else's profit. Most peasants viewed the communist state as the enemy, to be ignored when possible, tricked if necessary, and endured no matter what.

Stalin's Consolidation of Power: The Great Purge and Soviet Society, 1934–1939

By the mid-1930s, the worst seemed to be over. Most villages were collectivized and the mass violence had ended. The 17th Party Congress in 1934 was known as the "Congress of Victors," as the party celebrated its industrial successes and the achievement of collectivization. But for many of the men and women at this congress, the worst was yet to come. Within five years, half of the 2,000 delegates had been arrested; of the 149 elected members of the congress's Central Committee, 98 were shot dead. These Congress delegates, and hundreds of thousands of other Soviet citizens, were victims of the "Great Purge°." In the purge, Stalin's effort to eliminate any possible rival to his power converged with widespread paranoia and economic crisis to produce a nationwide witch-hunt and mass executions.

The early victims of the purge tended to be top-ranking Communist Party officials, many of whom had opposed Stalin on various issues during the 1920s. By charging these powerful men with conspiring against the communist state, Stalin reduced the chances that any competitor might oust him. In a series of three spectacular show trials attended by journalists from all over the world, leading Bolsheviks—some of the Soviet Union's most respected men, such as Nikolai Bukharin—pleaded guilty to charges of conspiracy and sabotage, and were immediately executed. Numerous smaller trials replicated the process throughout the Soviet Union. Non-Russians suffered heavily. By the end of the 1930s, for example, 260 of the 300 party secretaries in Georgia had been killed. The purge also swept the armed forces. Those executed included three of the five Soviet marshals, thirteen of fifteen army commanders, and fifty-seven of eighty corps commanders.

The purge quickly spread beyond the top ranks of the party and military. With the show trials indicating that even the highest-level Bolsheviks were not to be trusted, people began to suspect that traitors lurked within every factory

"Pictures Can't Lie . . . "

Stalin was not Lenin's closest associate, nor did Lenin select him as his successor. To claim and consolidate his position as sole leader of the Communist Party and of the Soviet Union, Stalin had to falsify history and present himself as Lenin's chosen heir. Murder and mass executions could remove competitors from the present, but to erase them from the past, Stalin turned to the airbrush and the scissors rather than the gun. Pictures showing other Bolsheviks standing next to Lenin were cropped, leaving him with Stalin, or if such a pairing could not be achieved, standing alone. Compare these two photos, taken by the same photographer, within five seconds of each other. In the first, Lev Kamenev and Leon Trotsky—leading Bolsheviks and rivals with Stalin for the party leadership after Lenin's death—stand on the steps to Lenin's left. But in the second, Kamenev and Trotsky have been cut out and some steps have been drawn in. Stalin sought to airbrush Trotsky and Kamenev out of Soviet history, just as he eliminated them from Soviet politics. Trotsky was forced into exile in 1929 and murdered in 1940; Kamenev was executed in 1936.

and local party gathering. At the same time the shortcomings of an overly centralized and poorly run economy were multiplying: Subject to an endless stream of ever-changing and often irrational program and policy directives, managers falsified key economic statistics, while poorly trained workers misused machines and cut all available corners.

People were anxious and hungry, and eager to find someone to blame for breakdowns and failures. The purge made it easy to point the finger, to charge this manager with deliberately failing to order tractors or that engineer with implementing the wrong system of crop rotation to sabotage production. Thus the Great Purge quickly spun out of control to embrace low-level party members, managers in state agencies, factory directors, and engineers. Many were killed without trial, others executed after a legal show, and still others deported to slave labor camps to be worked to death on Stalin's vast construction projects. Death estimates vary widely; at least 750,000 people died, with the numbers of those arrested, imprisoned, or deported running into the millions.[19]

The Great Purge consolidated Stalin's hold on the Soviet Union. It not only eliminated all potential competitors, it also tied huge numbers of people more tightly to Stalin and his version of revolution. The shocking thing about the Great Purge was its popularity. The purge hit primarily urban managers. For the most part, ordinary workers and peasants were safe from its onslaught. These ordinary citizens, who had been ordered about, reprimanded, fined, insulted, and assaulted by these self-same managers, tended to believe that the purge's victims got what they deserved. Moreover, the purge can also be seen as a huge job creation program. Individuals who moved into the positions left vacant by the purge's victims had an enormous material as well as psychological stake in viewing the purge as an act of justice.

Stalin and the Nation

The popularity of the purge was also closely linked with the emergence of a Stalin-centered personality cult. By the time the purge began, the cult was an omnipresent part of Soviet urban life. Huge posters and statues ensured that Stalin's figure remained constantly in front of Soviet citizens. Textbooks rewrote the history of the Bolshevik revolution to highlight Stalin's contribution and linked every scientific, technological, or economic advance in the Soviet Union to the person and power of Stalin. The scores of letters personally addressed to Stalin that poured into central government offices testify to the success of this cult. To many Soviet citizens, Stalin personified the nation.

Increasingly the *nation*—not the worker, not socialism, not the revolution—assumed the central role in Soviet propaganda. Lenin had condemned Russian nationalism as a middle-class ideology to be eradicated along with capitalism. The working class, not the nation, mattered. But Stalin reversed this aspect of Lenin's revolution. In the 1930s, "Russia" and "the motherland/fatherland" both reappeared in political discourse. The tsarist past, which Lenin had condemned or ignored, was resurrected to emphasize Russian greatness. The imperial anthem resounded once again, while films and books praised strong Russian leaders such as Peter the Great. While this resurgence of Russian nationalism was popular in Russia itself, it spelled real difficulties for the 50 percent of the Soviet population who lived outside Russia and who found it necessary to repress their own sense of national identity—or face deportation.

Exalting the motherland went hand in hand with exalting the mother. Just as Stalin resurrected Russian nationalism in the 1930s, so he sought to resurrect the Russian family. He promoted the family as a vital prop of the national order, an institution to be strengthened rather than encouraged to wither away (as Lenin had insisted). In 1936, Stalin's regime outlawed abortion and made divorce more difficult.

СБЫЛИСЬ МЕЧТЫ НАРОДНЫЕ!

"People's Dreams Have Come True!"
In this typical example of "Socialist Realism," an older Soviet citizen points proudly to the achievements of Stalinist industrialization while the young boy, in the uniform of the Pioneers, the Stalinist youth organization, listens eagerly.

DOCUMENT

The Cult of the Leader

The personality cult characterized not only the Radical Right ideologies of Italian fascism and German Nazism, but also the ideological system that stood at the opposite end of the political spectrum: Stalinist communism. Searching for a way to mobilize the masses without granting to them actual political power, Mussolini, Hitler, and Stalin erected around themselves leadership cults. Their own images came to embody the nation. As the following set of excerpts shows, the cults of Mussolini, Hitler, and Stalin took on religious dimensions, with all three men adored as secular saviors.

I. Description of Mussolini's Visit to Trieste in 1938

Finally we have seen and heard Him! . . . These first reactions, expressed with indescribable joy, eyes moved to tears and an ineffable, agonizing joy. . . . It is not easy to describe the expression on most faces, on those of the little people as on those of the educated, of the mass as a whole. Expressions of wonderful contentment and pride among those who saw Him pass close by—especially among the dockworkers He visited yesterday—and those whose eyes He met, those who caught His eye. "Never such eyes! The way he looks at you is irresistible! He smiled at me . . . I was close, I could almost touch him. . . . When I saw him my legs trembled" . . . and a thousand other similar statements show and confirm the enormous fascination exercised by his person.

II. Description of an Early Nazi Rally by Louise Solmitz, Schoolteacher

The April sun shone hot like summer and turned everything into a picture of gay expectation. There was immaculate order and discipline . . . the hours passed. . . .

Expectations rose. There stood Hitler in a simple black coat and looked over the crowd. Waiting. A forest of swastika pennants swished up, the jubilation of this moment was given vent in a roaring salute. . . . How many look up to him with a touching faith! As their helper, their savior, their deliverer from unbearable distress—to him who rescues the Prussian prince, the scholar, the clergyman, the farmer, the worker, the unemployed, who leads them from the parties back into the nation.

III. Speech by a Woman Delegate at a Workers' Conference in the Soviet Union

Thank you comrade Stalin, our leader, our father, for a happy, merry kolkhoz life!

He, our Stalin, put the steering-wheel of the tractor in our hand. . . . He, the great Stalin, carefully listens to all of us in this meeting, loves us with a great Stalinist love (*tumultuous applause*), day and night thinks of our prosperity, of our culture, of our work. . . .

Long live our friend, our teacher, the beloved leader of the world proletariat, comrade Stalin! (*Tumultuous applause, rising to an ovation. Shouts of "Hurrah!"*)

Sources: "I. Description of Mussolini's Visit to Trieste in 1938," reprinted by permission of the publisher from *The Sacralization of Politics in Fascist Italy* by Emilio Gentile, translated by Keith Botsford, p. 147, Cambridge, Mass.: Harvard University Press. Copyright © 1996 by the President and Fellows of Harvard College. "II. Description of an Early Nazi Rally by Louise Solmitz, Schoolteacher," copyright © 1988 by Claudia Koonz. From *Mothers in the Fatherland: Women, the Family, and Nazi Politics* by Claudia Koonz. Reprinted by permission of St. Martin's Press, LLC. "III. Speech by a Woman Delegate at a Worker's Conference in the Soviet Union," from *Stalin's Peasants: Resistance and Survival in the Russian Village After Collectivization* by Sheila Fitzpatrick. Copyright © 1996 by Oxford University Press, Inc. Published by Oxford University Press, Inc.

Like Western leaders, Stalin also sought to increase the national birth rate by granting pregnant women maternity stipends and increasing the number of prenatal health clinics. There was no effort to pull women out of the workforce, however. Of the more than four million new workers entering the labor force between 1932 and 1937, 82 percent were women. The Soviet Union continued to provide women with access to higher education and professional jobs— women worked as doctors, engineers, scientists, and high-ranking public officials. (And women were deported and executed in huge numbers—one could argue that Stalin was an equal-opportunity killer.)

In the arts, too, Stalinism meant a retreat from the radicalism of Lenin's revolution. Whereas Soviet artists under Lenin had been in the vanguard of modernism,

under Stalin art came firmly under state control. Artists knew that their literal survival depended on their conforming to the principles of "Socialist Realism": *Partinost* (loyalty to the state), *Ideinost* (correct ideology and content), and *Narodnost* (easy accessibility to ordinary viewers). The abstract experiments of the early Soviet period gave way to pretty pictures of happily collectivized peasants and portraits of Stalin in heroic poses.

The Response of the Democracies

The apparent economic successes of fascism and Nazism on the right, and Stalinism on the left, polarized European politics. For many Europeans in the 1930s, it seemed that the middle ground was collapsing beneath their feet, that democracy had failed and that they had no choice but to scramble to one extreme or the other. Yet in both western Europe and in the United States, important steps were taken to ensure not only that democracy survived but that it eventually delivered a decent standard of living to the great mass of ordinary people.

A Third Way? The Social Democratic Alternative

The effort to meet the challenge of the depression without embracing either Nazism or Stalinism accelerated the development of the political model that would dominate western Europe after World War II: social democracy°. In a social democracy, a democratically elected parliamentary government accepts the responsibility of ensuring a decent standard of living for its citizens. To achieve this goal, the government assumes two important functions—first, regulating an economy containing both private enterprise and nationalized or state-controlled corporations; second, overseeing a welfare state, which guarantees the citizen access to unemployment and sickness benefits, pensions, family allowances, and health services. Although social democracy did not triumph in western Europe until after the massive bloodletting of another total war, the interwar years witnessed important steps toward this third path, an alternative to the extremes of both the Radical Right (fascism and Nazism) and the Radical Left (Stalinism).

One of the most striking experiments in changing the relationship between democratic governments and the economy occurred in the United States. Franklin Delano Roosevelt (1882–1945) became president in 1932 at the height of the Great Depression, when unemployment stood at 24 percent (15 million workers were without jobs) and Washington, D.C., witnessed federal troops called out to quell rioting among unemployed veterans. Promising a "New Deal" of "Relief, Recovery, Reform," Roosevelt tackled the depression with an activist governmental policy that included agricultural subsidies, public works programs, and the Social Security Act of 1935, which set the foundations of the U.S. welfare program.

Yet even with this sharp upswing in government activity, unemployment remained high—ten million workers were without jobs in 1939—and the gross national product (GNP) did not recover to 1929 levels until 1941. In the view of some economists, Roosevelt failed to solve the problem of unemployment because he remained committed to the ideal of a balanced budget. In contrast, the British economist John Maynard Keynes (1883–1946) insisted that in times of depression, the state should not reduce spending and endeavor to live within its budget, but instead should adopt a program of deficit spending to stimulate economic growth. Only when prosperity returned, Keynes advised, should governments increase taxes and cut expenditures to recover the deficits.

The experience of Sweden appeared to confirm Keynes's theory. The Swedish Social Democratic Party took office in 1932 with the intention of using the powers of central government to revive the depressed economy. The government allowed its budget deficit to climb while it financed a massive public works campaign, as well as an increase in welfare benefits ranging from unemployment insurance to maternity allowances to subsidized housing. By 1937 unemployment was shrinking rapidly as the manufacturing sector boomed.

Throughout most of western Europe, however, governments proved far more reluctant to advocate radically new policies, despite an expansion of the state's role in economic affairs. For example, Britain's limited economic recovery in the later 1930s was based largely on private initiatives such as an expansion in housing construction and the emergence of new industries aimed at domestic consumption (radios and other small electronics, household goods, automobiles). In the areas hardest hit by depression—the heavy export industries such as coal, shipbuilding, textiles, and steel, located primarily in northern Britain—the lack of government intervention meant continuing high unemployment rates and widespread poverty and deprivation throughout the 1930s.

Taking a Stand

British women demonstrate against legislation that tightened requirements for receiving unemployment benefits and caused widespread suffering.

The Popular Front in France

The limited success of democratic governments in addressing the problems of the Great Depression meant that many experienced the 1930s as a hard, hungry decade when democracy failed to deliver a decent standard of living. The example of France illustrates both the political polarization occurring in Europe in the 1930s and the sharp limits on governments seeking both to maintain democratic politics and to improve the living conditions of their citizens. France lacked such basic welfare benefits as old-age pensions and unemployment insurance. As the economy plummeted, therefore, social unrest rose, and so, too, did the appeal of the fascist movement. In 1934, fascist riots left 17 dead and more than 2,000 injured.

The increasing strength of fascism, combined with the deepening national emergency, led to the formation of the Popular Front, a coalition comprising the centrist Radical Party, the moderate leftist Socialist Party, and the far-left Stalinist Communist Party. In 1936, the Popular Front won the national elections. The Socialist leader Leon Blum (1872–1950) took office as prime minister in the midst of a general strike involving two million workers. He settled the strike to the workers' benefit by granting them a 15 percent pay raise and the right to collective bargaining. Over the next year, Blum nationalized the key war industries and gave workers further pay increases, paid holidays, and a forty-hour workweek.

Many conservative French voters saw Blum's policies of social reform as the first step on the road to Stalinism. Thus they cried, "Better Hitler than Blum!"—in other words, better the Radical Right than the Stalinist Left. The global business community pulled capital out of France, resulting in a major financial crisis and the devaluation of the French franc. Dependent on foreign loans, Blum's government faced sharp pressure to pull back from its program of social and economic reforms. When it tried to do so, its working-class constituency rose in revolt. In May 1937 the suppression of a left-wing demonstration left 7 dead and 200 injured. Blum resigned the next month. The Popular Front in France quickly disintegrated.

The Spanish Civil War

Spain became the arena in which the struggle of Europe's polarized political forces turned into outright war. In 1931, a democratically elected republican government replaced the Spanish monarchy and in 1936, a Popular Front government, comprising both socialists and communists, took office. In July, army officers led a right-wing rebellion against this government.

The struggle between the left-wing Republican government and the right-wing rebels quickly became an international issue. Both fascist Italy and Nazi Germany supported the rebellion, enabling General Francisco Franco

The Spanish Civil War
The Spanish Civil War mobilized women as well as men. These soldiers, fighting in the uniform of the anarchist militia, are defending the barricades of Barcelona against rebel attack.

(1892–1975) and his crack Moroccan troops to cross into Spain from their station in North Africa and launch an all-out offensive against the republic. The Republican government appealed to the democracies for aid, but the only government that came to its assistance was that of the Soviet Union. Soviet tanks and aircraft enabled the besieged city of Madrid to hold out against Franco's forces but at the same time the Soviet intervention split the Republican movement, with anarchists and socialists resisting Stalinist control. Unnerved by the Soviet involvement, the governments of France, Britain, and the United States remained neutral. Appalled by this official inaction, many citizens of these countries served in the International Brigade, which fought for the cause of democracy in Spain.

The Spanish Civil War raged until March 1939, when the last remnants of the Republican forces finally surrendered to Franco. Four hundred thousand men and women died in the war; in the following four years, another 200,000 were executed. Franco established an authoritarian government that crushed Spanish democracy. Spain became a potent symbol for all of Europe. To both fascists and their democratic opponents, Franco's victory illustrated how easily democracy could be destroyed.

The West and the World: Imperialism in the Interwar Era

■ How did the interaction between the West and the world outside change after World War I?

In the interwar struggle between authoritarian and democratic forms of politics, we can see contrasting definitions of "the West" competing for dominance. In this same period, the clash between advocates and enemies of Western imperialism revealed multiple notions of "Western culture" as well. The Allies claimed to have fought during World War I for national self-determination, but they had no intention of allowing their overseas empires the right to determine their own national selves. Britain and France emerged from the war with not only their imperialist ideologies intact but their empires greatly expanded. They divided up Germany's overseas colonies in Africa and Asia, and as we saw in Chapter 24, became the dominant powers in the Middle East.

During the 1920s and 1930s, popular imperialism reached its zenith in Europe. Filmmakers and novelists found that imperial settings formed the perfect backdrop for stirring tales of individual heroism and limitless adventure. Governments also played a role in strengthening the culture of empire. In both Britain and France, imperial history became a required part of school curricula. British children learned to identify the pink-colored sections of the world map as "ours," while a series of colonial exhibitions impressed on the British public the importance of the empire to Britain's economic prosperity. In Belgium, the government promoted the Congo as a "model colony." The economic ties between European states and their imperial territories grew tighter. For example, by 1940 more than 45 percent of French overseas investment went to regions within its empire (see Map 25.2).

The Irish Revolution

This period, however, also witnessed the emergence of important challenges to the imperial idea. The most successful of these occurred in Ireland. Many Irish men, both Catholic and Protestant, fought for Britain during World War I, but a small group of revolutionary nationalists saw the war as an opportunity for revolt. They mounted an armed rebellion on Easter Monday in 1916. Although quickly and brutally suppressed, the "Easter Rising" became for Irish nationalists

a key moment in the fight for an independent Ireland. The executed leaders of the rising became martyrs for the sacred cause of nationhood, while the ease with which the British crushed the revolt convinced Irish nationalist leaders of the necessity of employing guerilla tactics rather than open military assault to defeat their much more powerful foe.

In 1921, ground down by more than two years of guerilla warfare waged with consummate skill by the Irish Republican Army (IRA), the British government offered Ireland independence. The offer, however, came with strings attached. The new state would remain within the British Empire and Ireland itself would be partitioned. Its six northern counties, dominated by Protestants who opposed Irish independence, were to remain part of Britain. A delegation led by the charismatic IRA chief Michael Collins (the "Big Fella") accepted this offer. It took two years of civil war—a war that cost Collins his life—to persuade many Irish nationalists to do the same. Ireland continued as an uneasy member of the British Empire until the end of the 1930s, when it cut all constitutional ties to Britain. Northern Ireland remains a part of Britain to this day.

Changing Power Equations: Ideology and Economics

Ireland's revolt against British imperial rule, while unusual in its success, revealed the growing power of anti-imperialist forces across the world. The triumph of communism in Russia helped strengthen these forces. In his publications, Lenin argued that imperialism was the logical consequence of capitalism and its quest for markets, and thus that anti-capitalism and anti-imperialism went hand in hand. Under Lenin, the Soviet Union declared itself the defender of oppressed nationalities everywhere, and provided ideological and material assistance to nationalist independence movements in Indonesia, Indochina, Burma, and most significantly, China, where Soviet advisers helped form the Communist Party in 1921.

Communism alone, however, does not account for the spread of anti-imperialist nationalist movements in the interwar years. Changing economic relationships were crucial. During World War I, the demands of industrial warfare forced Europe's imperial powers to utilize fully their colonial resources, a strategy that brought with it unintended but far-reaching social change. Throughout Europe's empires, wartime economic demands escalated labor migration rates, expanded urban populations, and enveloped once-isolated villages in the global economic web. These changes were not often welcomed by the peoples involved. In Africa, for example, the Allies tailored their colonial economies to meet wartime demands for commodities such as rubber. This policy benefited multinational companies such as Unilever, which pocketed increasing profits, but had a negative impact on local populations: Native merchants

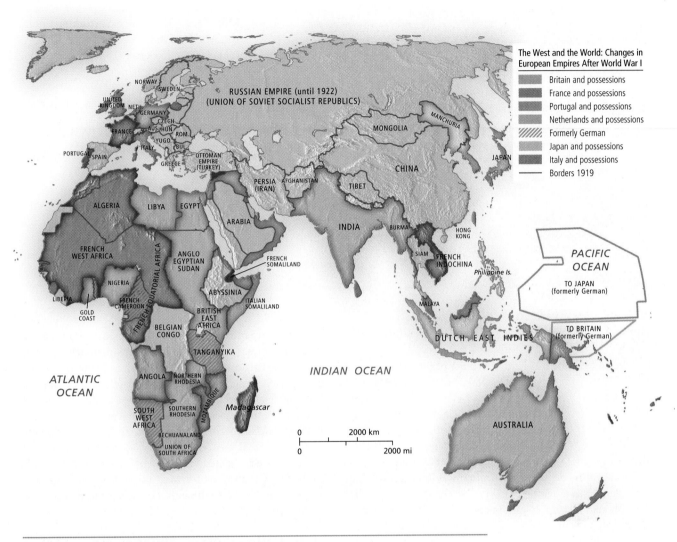

**Map 25.2 The West and the World:
Changes in European Empires After World War I**

Britain, France, and Japan were the principal beneficiaries of Germany's loss of empire after World War I.

saw their independence and their incomes disappearing; African peasants lost their land and became waged laborers; the concentration on cash crops reduced food production at a time when the population was growing steadily.

In the 1930s, economic conditions grew worse in the wake of the Great Depression. The sharp fall in the prices of primary products spelled disaster for regions of the world that had shifted their agricultural economies to the production of cash crops for export. At the same time, the benefits of imperial governance diminished. Looking for ways to reduce expenditures, European governments cut funds to colonial schools, public services, and health care. Direct taxation rates rose while unemployment rates soared. So, too, did the numbers attracted to nationalist movements.

Postwar Nationalism, Westernization, and the Islamic Challenge

These economic and social developments not only helped subvert the legitimacy of imperialist rule but also fostered the growth of anti-Western movements, often in religious form. In Africa, for example, a revival of animist religion expressed both an explicit rejection of the Christian teachings brought by European and American missionaries and an implicit refusal of Western cultural and political styles. Throughout many African regions, however, Islam possessed the most potent appeal. In the growing cities, immigrants cut off from their village and its religious practices found that Islam provided an alternative

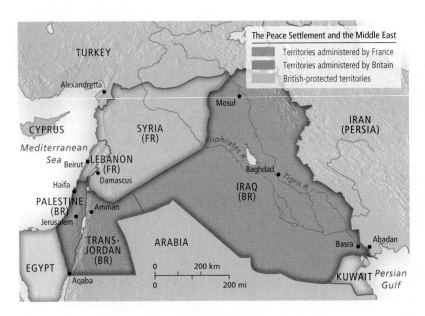

Map 25.3 The Peace Settlement and the Middle East

For many Arab nationalists, the division of the Middle East into Western-controlled "Mandates" was a source of deep discontent. After widespread anti-British riots in Iraq in 1920, the British ceded nominal independence to King Faisal's government. The British, however, retained control over financial, military and diplomatic matters.

cultural identity to that one offered by their European rulers.

The end of World War I marked the beginning of a new era in Islamic history. Feeble though it was by 1914, the Ottoman Empire had nevertheless symbolized a unified Islam: As caliph, the Ottoman sultan claimed religious authority over all Muslims, even those not under Ottoman political rule. The sultan's role as caliph helps explain why the vast majority of Arabs in the Middle East did not join the Hashemites in their alliance with Britain against the Ottomans (see Chapter 24). Most Arabs did not see the Turkish sultan as a foreign oppressor; instead, as Muslims, they regarded him as their rightful leader. For similar reasons, Muslims in British India experienced a profound conflict of loyalties during the war.

The collapse of the Ottoman Empire and the abolition of the Ottoman caliphate in the wake of World War I created a new religious and political environment for Muslims. Many followed Western secular models and turned to ethnic nationalism. Others, however, found both spiritual solace and political identity in Islamic revival movements that sought to unify Muslims under an Islamic ruler and Islamic law once again.

The Emergence of Pan-Arabism

In the Middle East, pan-Arabism° emerged in the interwar era as a powerful form of nationalism. Just as pan-Slavism promoted the ideal of a single Slavic state, so pan-Arabism insisted that all Arabs—including the minority who were not Muslim—should unite in an Arab state. Three postwar developments nourished pan-Arabism. First, as already noted, the collapse of the Ottoman regime shattered traditional loyalties. But second, the new map of the Middle East drawn by the postwar peace settlement placed Arabs in states they regarded as artificial, unrelated to dynastic or tribal identities. (See Chapter 24.) Thus nationalist movements centering on these new states—Iraqi nationalism, for example, or Syrian, or Lebanese—possessed little appeal. And finally, as we saw in Chapter 24, the system of "Mandates" created in the wake of the war actually continued imperial rule in a new form (see Map 25.3). As it quickly became clear that Western interests shaped policy in the new Middle Eastern states, resentment grew toward both Western imperialism and toward the state system imposed by the West. These sentiments nourished the pan-Arabist movement.

State Nationalism on the Western Model

Not all Arab nationalists, however, embraced pan-Arabism. In states such as Egypt, with a national identity not imposed by Western imperialists or the peace settlement, nationalism tended to coalesce around the state itself. Hence in Egypt, the nationalist political party, Wafd, called not for Arabic unity but for Egyptian national freedom. Wafd, whose full name translates as "Egyptian delegation," originated as precisely that, a delegation of Egyptian representatives to the Paris peace conferences after World War I. When the Allies refused to let the delegation participate in the peace process, Wafd organized into a political movement fighting against not only the British but also the British-backed Egyptian monarchy for full Egyptian independence. Although Wafd opposed the monarchical government as too subservient to Western economic and political interests, it sought social and economic reforms that would Westernize and modernize Egypt.

For nationalists such as those in Wafd, the successful nationalist revolution in Turkey provided an important source of inspiration. After World War I, the Allies forced the defeated Ottoman government to sign a humiliating treaty: The Treaty of Sèvres not only dispossessed the Ottoman government of its Middle Eastern empire, it also gave territories in the Anatolian heartland (modern Turkey) to Greece, Italy, an autonomous Kurdistan, and an independent Armenia. In addition, Sèvres stripped the Ottoman government of national sovereignty by ceding to the Allies the right of intervention in economic, military, and foreign affairs. Turkish nationalists, led by Mustafa Kemal Pasha, rejected the Treaty of Sèvres and rose up against the government that dared sign such a document. Kemal's nationalist rebellion overthrew the sultan, defeated a Greek invasion, and forced the Allies to draw up a new settlement. In 1923, the Treaty of Lausanne restored to Turkey much of its territory and its full national sovereignty.

But while Kemal had no intentions of letting Western powers govern in Turkey, he was not anti-Western. He

VIDEO
Ataturk
(Mustafa
Kemal)

viewed the West as modern; to modernize Turkey, he believed he had to reconfigure its culture as Western. Thus Kemal declared Turkey a secular republic, outlawed polygamy, granted women civil and legal rights, and required all Turks to take surnames—he became known as Kemal "Ataturk" ("Father of the Turks"). A mass literacy program aimed not only to teach Turks how to read and write, but how to do so using the Latin alphabet. Schoolmasters who dared use Arabic lettering were arrested. Ataturk even condemned the traditional form of Turkish headwear, the fez, as "an emblem of ignorance, negligence, fanaticism, hatred of progress and civilization."[20] To represent Turkey's new Western orientation, Turkish men were ordered to wear bowler hats and Western suits. But while he favored the English bowler hat, Ataturk was less enthusiastic about English political freedom. Despite setting up a parliament elected by universal suffrage, he made full use of emergency executive powers to govern with an iron grip over a one-party state. He also continued the Ottoman policies of repression toward Turkey's Armenian minority.

Kemal Ataturk's secularist, Westernized model of nationalism proved powerful. During the 1920s and 1930s nationalists in the Middle East, Africa, and Asia tended to embrace Western models, even as they rejected Western (or Western-imposed) rulers. They formed parliamentary political parties, advocated Western political ideologies such as liberalism and communism, regarded the state as essentially secular, and saw political independence as a crucial step toward industrial modernization and economic prosperity.

The Islamic Challenge

Beneath the surface of political life, however, different styles of movements, with very different aims, were coalescing. Throughout the new states of the Middle East, for example, the soaring sales of popular biographies of the Prophet Muhammad and other caliphs, as well as the proliferation

of Islamic leagues and clubs, hinted that many inhabitants of these new states found the secularism of the nationalists as alien as the faces of their Western-imposed rulers or the boundaries on the new European-drawn map.

These sentiments would not harden into explicitly political movements until the 1940s, but both the Wahhabi religious revival in central Arabia during the 1920s and 1930s and the foundation of the Muslim Brotherhood in Egypt in 1928 proved crucial in shaping the relationship of Islam and the West in the later twentieth century.

Founded by Muhammad Abd al-Wahhab (1703–1787) in the eighteenth century, Wahhabism demanded the purification of Islam by ridding it of centuries of heretical accretions such as saint worship and other forms of mysticism, and by returning to a strict interpretation of the *Sharia,* or Islamic law. Over the next century, this militant form of religious revival inspired a number of popular revolts—on the Arabian peninsula (against the Ottomans), in India (against the British), in Algeria (against the French), and in Daghistan (against the Russians). Although all of these revolts were defeated, Wahhabism's call to return to fundamental truths and practices continued to appeal to Muslims, particularly in times of unsettling political change. It is not surprising, then, that Wahhabism revived in the tumultuous period after World War I. The Wahhabi revival in Arabia had a powerful patron: Abd al-Aziz Ibn Saud (ca. 1888–1953), the head of the Saudi dynasty whose conquests on the Arabian peninsula became the basis for the kingdom of Saudi Arabia.

Like Wahhabism, the Islamic Brotherhood (or *Ikhwan*) rejected modernizing interpretations of Islam and sought to reassert the universal jurisdiction of Islamic law. For the Brotherhood, Islam governed not just religious belief but all areas of life. The Brotherhood rejected Western practices and political institutions less because they were foreign than because they were associated with infidels. Working through youth groups, educational institutes, and business enterprises, the Brotherhood spread from its Egyptian base throughout the Middle East during the 1930s.

Moral Revolution in India

During this same era, a very different sort of anti-Western protest movement took shape in India. In 1916 a British-educated lawyer returned from South Africa, where he had spent twenty years fighting to improve the lot of indentured Indian laborers and developing a revolutionary approach to the fight for national independence. Mohandas Gandhi (1869–1948) called on his followers to fight British rule in India not with armed weapons but with moral force—with nonviolent protest and civil disobedience. As the war ended, Gandhi led a mass protest movement in India against British rule. In this *Satyagraha* ("hold fast to

From Mohandas to Mahatma: Gandhi's Transformation

In April 1893, a young, well-dressed Indian lawyer purchased a first-class train ticket from Durban to Pretoria (South Africa). The first part of the journey proceeded uneventfully, but then another traveler, a white man, entered the first-class compartment. He turned around and returned with two guards, who demanded that the Indian man sit in third class, with the other "colored" passengers. The young lawyer refused, and so was thrown off the train at the next stop.

Mohandas Gandhi's experience on the train to Pretoria was not unusual. The Indian immigrant community in South Africa had long endured legal discrimination, economic exploitation, and frequent violence; the black African community suffered far worse. But the 24-year-old Gandhi knew little about such things. Growing up as the spoiled youngest son in an upper-caste family in India, he had known privilege rather than prejudice. Even the three years he spent in London studying law did not expose him to racial discrimination. Gandhi, in fact, felt that when he left Britain he was leaving "home." He returned to India in 1891 convinced of the superiority of British law and culture. He banned Indian-style clothing from his household, insisted that his illiterate young wife learn English, and decreed that oat porridge and cocoa be served at breakfast. He saw himself as a successful British lawyer.

But others did not see him that way. When Gandhi asked a British official for a favor for his brother, he was humiliated, actually pushed out the door by a servant. "This shock changed the course of my life," Gandhi later noted.[21] Offered a job in South Africa, he went— and on that train to Pretoria encountered further humiliation. By the time Gandhi finally reached Pretoria, he had decided to fight. He became the leader of the Indian civil rights movement in South Africa.

Gandhi lived in South Africa for 21 years. During these decades, the westernized, Britain-loving lawyer became a Hindu holy man; Mohandas became Mahatma, the "great-souled one." This transformation occurred in part because of Gandhi's sense of betrayal as he encountered the racial discrimination embedded in British imperialism. From his London experience, Gandhi had concluded that Britain epitomized the Western ideals of impartial justice and individual rights. But the British colonial regime he encountered in South Africa violated those ideals. Disillusioned, Gandhi turned back to his Hindu roots.

Western culture also, however, played a positive role in Gandhi's transformation. During his time in South Africa, Gandhi read widely in Christian and Western texts, including Jesus' Sermon on the Mount in the New Testament, and books by nineteenth-century European social and cultural critics that exposed the spiritual and material failures of industrial society. Gandhi's intellectual encounter with these texts helped him formulate the idea of *Satyagraha* ("Truth-Force"). In its most specific sense, Satyagraha is a political tool. Through nonviolent mass civil disobedience, the powerless persuade the powerful to effect political change. But Satyagraha is also a spiritual act, the victory of goodness over violence and evil.

Gandhi's specific encounters with the injustice of imperial rule, first in the home of a British official in India and then on his South African train ride, forced him to embark on a different sort of spiritual and political journey, an exploration of both Western and Hindu thought. This journey transformed Gandhi from Mohandas into Mahatma and led him to Satyagraha—and the transformation of Indian nationalism into a mass movement. By 1948, this movement had made it impossible for the British to govern India.

For Discussion

Both negative and positive encounters with Western ideas and Western people contributed to Gandhi's transformation "from Mohandas to Mahatma." In what ways have Gandhi's ideas transformed Western culture and politics?

The Mahatma
Gandhi drew on both Hindu and Western traditions in formulating his ideal of moral protest.

the truth") campaign, Indians refused to cooperate with the imperial system in any way, including wearing British-made cloth.

Before Gandhi's arrival, the cause of Indian independence belonged to the educated, westernized elite. Gandhi transformed the Indian National Congress into a mass movement by appealing to traditional Indian customs and religious identities. He did not oppose modernization, but he argued that modernization did not necessarily mean westernization, that India could follow its own path. Thus Gandhi rejected Western dress and presented himself in the role of the religious ascetic, a familiar and deeply honored figure in Indian culture. In his insistence that the nationalist struggle be one of "moral force" rather than a physical fight, Gandhi drew on the Hindu tradition of nonviolence. He was careful, however, not to equate "Indian" with "Hindu." He worked hard to incorporate the minority Muslim community into the nationalist movement, and he broke with the traditional Hindu caste system by campaigning for the rights of those deemed "untouchable." Ordinary Indians surged into the movement, calling Gandhi "Mahatma," or "great-souled," a term of great respect.

Unable to decide whether to arrest Gandhi as a dangerous revolutionary or to negotiate with him as a representative of the Indian people, the British did both. In 1931, Gandhi and the viceroy of India (literally the "vice-king," the highest British official in India) met on equal terms for a series of eight meetings. A few months later Gandhi was in prison, along with 66,000 of his nationalist colleagues. Successive British governments did pass a series of measures granting Indians increasing degrees of self-government, but Gandhi and the Indian National Congress demanded full and immediate national independence. The resulting impasse led to escalating unrest and terrorist activity, despite Gandhi's personal commitment to nonviolence. India remained the jewel in Britain's imperial crown, but the glue holding it in place was deteriorating rapidly by the end of the 1930s.

The Power of the Primitive

When asked what he thought of "Western civilization," Gandhi replied, "I think it would be a very good idea." Just as nationalists outside of the West such as Gandhi began to challenge the equation of the West with civilization, so too did Westerners themselves. For nineteenth-century European culture, "civilization" was what gave the West the right to rule the rest of the world. In the latter decades of the nineteenth century, ideologues had described inhabitants of Asia, Africa, and South America as barbarians who needed the guidance and discipline of the more advanced European white races. But by 1918, in the wake of the war, at least some Europeans were asking, "Who is the barbarian now?"

Developments in psychology further undermined the idea of Western superiority by eroding the boundaries between so-called primitive and modern cultures. In his post-war writings, Sigmund Freud (1856–1939) emphasized that human nature was fundamentally aggressive, even bestial. Freud's three-part theory of personality, developed in the 1920s, argued that within each individual the *id*, the unconscious force of primitive instinct, battles against the controls of the *ego*, or conscious rationality, and the *superego*, the moral values imposed by society. Although Freud taught that the continuity of civilization depended on the repression of the id, many Freudian popularizers insisted that the individual should allow his or her primitive self to run free.

The work of Freud's onetime disciple Carl Jung (1875–1961) also stressed the links between the primitive and the modern. Jung contended that careful study of an individual's dreams will show that they share common images and forms—"archetypes"—with ancient mythologies and world religions. These archetypes point to the existence of the "collective unconscious," shared by all human beings, regardless of when or where they lived. Thus, in Jung's analysis the boundary between "civilized" and "primitive," "West" and "not West," disappeared.

In the work of other thinkers and artists, that boundary remained intact, but Western notions of cultural superiority were turned upside down. The belief that white Western culture was anemic, washed out, and washed up led to a new openness to alternative intellectual and artistic traditions. This era saw a lasting transformation of popular music as the energetic rhythms of African-American jazz worked their way into white musical traditions. Many writers argued that the West needed to look to outside its borders for vibrancy and vitality. The German novelist Herman Hesse (1877–1962) condemned modern industrial society as spiritually barren and celebrated Eastern mysticism as a source of power and wisdom.

Similarly, the *Négritude* movement stressed the history and intrinsic value of black African culture. Founded in Paris in 1935 by French colonial students from Africa and the West Indies, Négritude condemned European culture as weak and corrupted and called for blacks to recreate a separate cultural and political identity. The movement's leading figures, such as Leopold Senghor (1906–2001), who later became the first president of independent Senegal, vehemently opposed the continuation of European empires and demanded African self-rule. Drawing together Africans, Afro-Caribbeans, and black Americans, Négritude assumed the existence of a common black culture that transcended national and colonial boundaries. The movement stole the white racists' stereotype of the "happy dancing savage" and refigured it as positive: Black culture fostered the emotion, creativity, and human connections that white Western industrial society destroyed.

The Power of the Primitive

When the American dancer Josephine Baker first hit the stage in Paris in 1925, her audience embraced her as the image of African savagery, even though Baker was a city kid from Philadelphia. A Parisian sensation from the moment she arrived, Baker's frenetic and passionate style of dancing, as well as her willingness to appear on stage wearing nothing but a belt of bananas, seemed to epitomize for many Europeans the essential freedom they believed their urbanized culture had lost, and that both the United States and Africa retained. As Baker's belt of bananas, designed by her white French employer, makes clear, much of this idealization of the primitive was deeply embedded in racist stereotypes. But it is also clear that both Baker's blackness and her Americanness represented a positive image of liberation to many Parisians.

Conclusion

The Kingdom of Corpses

In 1921, the Goncourt Prize, the most prestigious award in French literature, was awarded not to a native French writer but to a colonial: René Maran, born in the French colony of Martinique. Even more striking than Maran's receiving the prize was the content of the novel for which he was honored. In *Batouala*, Maran mounted a fierce onslaught against Western culture: "Civilization, civilization, pride of the Europeans and charnel house of innocents. . . . You build your kingdom on corpses."[22]

For many in the West, Maran's description of Europe as a kingdom of corpses seemed apt in the aftermath of total war. The 1920s and 1930s witnessed a dramatic reevaluation of Western cultural and political assumptions. Both Soviet communism on the left and Nazism and fascism on the right rejected such key Western ideals as individual rights and the rule of law. Such extremist ideologies seemed persuasive in the climate of despair produced not only by the war, but by the postwar failure of democracy in eastern Europe and the collapse of the global economy after 1929. As a result, the kingdom of corpses grew: in Nazi Germany, in Spain, and most dramatically in the Soviet Union. The kingdom of corpses was, however, a particularly expansionist domain. As the 1930s ended, the West and the world stood on the brink of another total war, one in which the numbers of dead would spiral to nearly incomprehensible levels.

Suggestions for Further Reading

For a comprehensive listing of suggested readings, please go to www.ablongman.com/levack2e/chapter25

Bookbinder, Paul. *Weimar Germany: The Republic of the Reasonable.* 1996. An innovative interpretation.

Brendon, Piers. *The Dark Valley: A Panorama of the 1930s.* 2000. Fast-paced but carefully researched and comprehensive overview of the histories of the United States, Germany, Italy, France, Britain, Japan, Russia, and Spain.

Carrère D'Encausse, Hélène. *Stalin: Order Through Terror*, Vol. 2: *A History of the Soviet Union, 1917–1953.* 1981. A brief but convincing account of the way Stalin seized and held power in the Soviet Union.

Fischer, Conan. *The Rise of the Nazis.* 1995. Summarizes recent research and includes a section of primary documents.

Fitzpatrick, Sheila. *Everyday Stalinism. Ordinary Life in Extraordinary Times: Soviet Russia in the 1930s.* 1999. Explores the daily life of the ordinary urban worker in Stalinist Russia.

Fitzpatrick, Sheila. *Stalin's Peasants: Resistance and Survival in the Russian Village After Collectivization.* 1995. A superb history from the bottom up.

Getty, J. Arch, and Oleg V. Naumov. *The Road to Terror: Stalin and the Self-Destruction of the Bolsheviks, 1932–1939.* 1999. Interweaves recently discovered documents with an up-to-date interpretation of the Great Purge.

Gilbert, Bentley Brinkerhoff. *Britain 1914–1945: The Aftermath of Power.* 1996. Short, readable overview, designed for beginning students.

Jackson, Julian. *The Popular Front in France: Defending Democracy, 1934–1938.* 1988. A political and cultural history.

Kershaw, Ian. *Hitler.* 1991. A highly acclaimed recent biography.

Kitchen, Martin. *Nazi Germany: A Critical Introduction.* 2004. Short, clearly written, up-to-date. An excellent introduction and overview.

Lewis, Bernard. *The Shaping of the Modern Middle East.* 1994. Concise but comprehensive analysis.

Mack Smith, Denis. *Mussolini: A Biography.* 1983. An engaging read.

Pedersen, Susan. *Family, Dependence, and the Origins of the Welfare State: Britain and France, 1914–1945.* 1993. Shows how welfare policy was inextricably linked to demographic and eugenic concerns.

Rothschild, Joseph. *East Central Europe Between the Wars.* 1974. An older source, but still one of the best accounts of this tumultuous region in this tumultuous time.

Thomas, Hugh. *The Spanish Civil War.* 1977. An authoritative account.

Whittam, John. *Fascist Italy.* 1995. A short synthesis of recent research. Includes a section of primary documents and an excellent bibliographic essay.

Wolpert, Stanley. *Gandhi's Passion: The Life and Legacy of Mahatma Gandhi.* 2001. An intellectual and spiritual biography by one of the foremost historians of modern India.

Notes

1. Quoted in Peter Gay, *Weimar Culture* (1970), 99.

2. Quoted in T. W. Heyck, *The Peoples of the British Isles from 1870 to the Present* (1992), 200.

3. Martin J. Sherwin, *A World Destroyed: Hiroshima and the Origins of the Arms Race* (1987), 17.

4. Quoted in Martin Gilbert, *A History of the Twentieth Century, Vol. I* (1997), 700.

5. Quoted in Michael Burleigh, *The Third Reich: A New History* (2000), 36.

6. Quoted in Burleigh, *The Third Reich,* 52.

7. Quoted in Joachim Fest, *Hitler* (1973), 190–193.

8. Ibid., 192, 218.

9. Quoted in Wendy Goldman, *Women, the State, and Revolution: Soviet Family Policy and Social Life, 1917–1936* (1993), 5.

10. Quoted in Claudia Koonz, *Mothers in the Fatherland* (1987), 130.

11. Quoted in Fest, *Hitler,* 445.

12. Quoted in Koonz, *Mothers in the Fatherland,* 194.

13. Ibid., 178.

14. Ibid., 56; Victoria DeGrazia, *How Fascism Ruled Women: Italy, 1922–1945* (1992), 234.

15. See J. Arch Getty and Roberta Manning, *Stalinist Terror: New Perspectives* (1993), 11, 265, 268, 280, 290.

16. Quoted in Mark Mazower, *Dark Continent: Europe's Twentieth Century* (1998), 123.

17. Quoted in Sheila Fitzpatrick, *Everyday Stalinism* (1999), 68.

18. See Stephen G. Wheatcroft, "More Light on the Scale of Repression and Excess Mortality in the Soviet Union in the 1930s," in Getty and Manning, *Stalinist Terror,* 275–290.

19. "Appendix 1: Numbers of Victims of the Terror," in J. Arch Getty and Oleg V. Naumov, *The Road to Terror: Stalin and the Self-Destruction of the Bolsheviks, 1932–1939* (1999), 587–594.

20. Quoted in Felix Gilbert, *The End of the European Era* (1991), 162.

21. Mohandas K. Gandhi, *An Autobiography: The Story of My Experiments with Truth* (1957), 120.

22. Quoted in Tyler Stovall, *Paris Noir: African Americans in the City of Light* (1996), 32.

World War II

26

N THE WEEKS IMMEDIATELY PRECEDING THE END OF THE SECOND WORLD WAR in Europe, many Allied soldiers faced their most difficult assignment yet. Hardened combat veterans, accustomed to scenes of slaughter and destruction, broke down and wept as they encountered a landscape of horror beyond their wildest nightmares: the world of the Nazi concentration and death camps. As one American war correspondent put it, "we had penetrated at last to the center of the black heart, to the very crawling inside of the vicious heart."[1] The American soldiers who opened the gates of the camp in Mauthausen, Austria, never forgot their first sight of the prisoners there: "By the thousands they came streaming . . . Hollow, pallid ghosts from graves and tombs, terrifying, rot-colored figures of misery marked by disease, deeply ingrained filth, inner decay. . . . squat skeletons in rags and crazy grins."[2]

Similarly, the British troops who liberated Bergen-Belsen in Germany were marked indelibly by what they encountered within the camp's walls. Bergen-Belsen had become the dumping ground for tens of thousands of prisoners evacuated from camps in eastern Europe, as the Nazi SS desperately retreated in front of the advancing Soviet army. Already sick and starving, these prisoners were jammed, 1,200 at a time, into barracks built to accommodate a few hundred. By March 1945, both drinking water and food had disappeared, human excrement dripped from bunk beds until it coated the floors of the barracks, and dead bodies piled up everywhere. In these conditions, the only living beings to flourish were the microorganisms that cause typhus. Floundering in this sea of human want, British soldiers, doctors, and nurses did what they could; even so, 28,000 of Bergen-Belsen's 60,000 inmates died in the weeks following liberation.

In Mauthausen and Bergen-Belsen, in the piles of putrefying bodies and among the crowds of skeletal survivors, American and British soldiers encountered the results of Adolf Hitler's effort to redefine the West. In Hitler's vision, Western civilization comprised ranks of white, northern Europeans, led by Germans, marching in step to a cadence dictated by the antidemocratic

Wilhelm Becker, *Bombing Raid in Berlin* (1943) The intentional and intensive bombing of civilian centers was one of the defining characteristics of the Second World War.

state. To realize this vision, he turned to total war and to mass murder. This quest to reconfigure the West as a race-based German empire also led Hitler to join hands with an ally outside the West: Japan. The German-Japanese alliance between transformed a European war into a global conflict. Thus, understanding World War II demands that we look not only at the results of Nazi racial ideology but also at global power relations and patterns of economic dependency. Like Hitler, Japan's governing elites longed for empire—in their case, an Asian empire to ensure both Japanese access to the resources and Japanese domination over the peoples of the Pacific region. With such access and such domination, they hoped to insulate Japan's economic and political structures from Western influence or control. The Pacific war thus constituted the most brutal in a long series of encounters between Japanese elites and the West. As we examine both the European and the Pacific theaters of war, we will need, then, to ask how competing definitions of "the West" helped shape this conflict. We will also confront the question of results: How did the cataclysm known as World War II re-define the West?

To organize its exploration of the many facets of World War II, this chapter focuses on five questions:

- What were the expectations concerning war in the 1920s and 1930s, and how did these hopes and fears lead to armed conflict in both Europe and Asia?
- How did Nazi Germany conquer the continent of Europe by 1941?
- Why did the Allies win in 1945?
- How and why did the war against the Jews take place, and what were its consequences?
- What did total war mean on the home front?

The Coming of War

- What were the expectations concerning war in the 1920s and 1930s, and how did these hopes and fears lead to armed conflict in both Europe and Asia?

The 1914–1918 war had been proclaimed the "war to end all wars." Instead, a little more than twenty years later, total war once again engulfed Europe and then the world. Adolf Hitler's ambitions for a German empire in eastern Europe account for the immediate outbreak of war in September 1939. But other, longer-term factors also contributed and help explain the origins of World War II. During the 1930s, the uneasy peace was broken by a series of military conflicts. These confrontations underlined the fragility of the post–World War I international settlement and foreshadowed the horrors to come in World War II.

An Uneasy Peace

The origins of the Second World War are closely tied to the settlement of the First. Rather than ending war for all time, the treaties negotiated after 1918 created an uneasy peace, one that could not be sustained. As we have already seen, much of Hitler's appeal to his German followers lay in his openly displayed contempt for the economic and military terms of the Versailles Treaty. But the peace settlement of World War I led to World War II in other, less direct ways as well. First, the redrawing of the map of eastern and central Europe fostered political instability in these regions. The mapmakers failed to fulfill the nationalist ambitions of many groups—the Macedonians, the Croats, the Ukrainians, and a host of others—and created as many territorial resentments as they resolved. For example, Germans could not forget that parts of Silesia now belonged to Poland, and Hungarians mourned the loss of traditionally Hungarian lands to Czechoslovakia, Romania, and Yugoslavia. Demands for boundary revisions, as well as ethnic hostilities and economic weaknesses, debilitated the new central and eastern European states carved out of the prewar Austrian-Hungarian, Russian, and German Empires.

Second, the League of Nations, created to replace the competitive alliance systems that many blamed for starting World War I, could not realize the high hopes of its planners. Poorly organized, lacking military power, boycotted by the United States and at various times excluding the key nations of Germany and the Soviet Union, the league proved too weak to serve as the basis of a new international order. Instead, alliances, such as that between the French and Polish governments or the "Little Entente" of Czechoslovakia, Yugoslavia, and Romania, formed the framework of a more traditional and very precarious international system.

Finally, the peace settlements created resentments among the war's winners as well as its losers. Italian nationalists argued that their nation's contribution to the Allies' victory should have been more fully compensated and looked longingly at territories granted to Yugoslavia, Austria, and Albania. Japanese nationalists, too, felt betrayed by the peace. Japan had cooperated fully with Britain and the United States during the First World War and expected this cooperation to be rewarded in the postwar era. Instead, many Japanese contended that the peace settlement disregarded Japan's economic needs and international ambitions. The results of the postwar Washington Conference particularly enraged Japanese nationalists. The conference, convened in Washington, D.C., in 1921, assembled representatives of the war's nine victorious powers—Britain, France, Italy, the United States, Belgium, the Netherlands, Portugal, China, and Japan—who pledged themselves to uphold China's territorial integrity and political independence as a means of restoring stability to the region. European and especially American capital poured into China during the

1920s while Western advisers assisted in the reform of the Chinese tax and currency systems. Japanese nationalists, however, viewed a united, Western-oriented China not as a guarantor of regional stability but rather as a threat to Japanese political power and economic development.

The 1930s: Prelude to World War II

The onset of the Great Depression in 1929 heightened international instability. Throughout Europe economic nationalism intensified as nations responded to economic collapse by throwing up tariff walls in an effort to protect their own industries. In addition, leaders sought escape from economic difficulties through territorial expansion. In Japan, the collapse of export markets for Japanese raw silk and cotton cloth made it difficult for the Japanese to pay for their vital imports of oil and other industrial resources. Anti-Western Japanese nationalists contended that Western capitalism was terminally ill and that the time had come for Japan to embark on a course of aggressive imperialist expansion to ensure its access to vital resources. In 1931, Japanese forces seized Manchuria.

Similarly, Mussolini proclaimed empire as the answer to Italy's economic woes, as well as a way to recreate the glories of ancient Rome. Seeking

CHRONOLOGY

On the Road to World War II

1919	Versailles Treaty
1921–1922	Washington Conference
1929	Onset of the Great Depression
1931	Japan invades Manchuria
1933	Hitler becomes chancellor of Germany
1935	Hitler announces a German air force and military conscription; Italy invades Ethiopia
1936	German troops occupy the Rhineland; civil war breaks out in Spain; Hitler and Mussolini form the Rome-Berlin Axis
1937	Japan advances against China; Rape of Nanking
1938	
March	Germany annexes Austria (the *Anschluss*)
September	Munich Conference: Germany occupies the Sudetenland
1939	
March 15	Germany invades Czechoslovakia
August 23	German-Soviet Non-Aggression Pact
September 1	Germany invades Poland
September 3	Great Britain and France declare war on Germany

The Prelude to World War II
The Japanese resumption of their war in China in 1937 added to the horrors of the 1930s. Here a photographer captured the agony of a baby separated from its parents in the railway station in Shanghai.

to expand Italy's North African empire and to avenge Italy's humiliating defeat at the Battle of Adowa in 1896, when Ethiopian troops had beaten back an Italian invasion, Mussolini ordered his army into Ethiopia in 1935. The Italian forces inflicted on the Ethiopian people many of the horrors soon to come to the European continent, including the saturation bombing of civilians, the use of poison gas, and the establishment of concentration camps. At the end of June 1936, Ethiopia's now-exiled Emperor Haile Selassie (1892–1975) addressed the Assembly of the League of Nations and warned, "It is us today. It will be you tomorrow."[3]

One year after Italian troops invaded Ethiopia, civil war broke out in Spain. As Chapter 25 explained, the war between the elected republican government and General Franco's rebels quickly became an international conflict. Hitler and Mussolini sent troops and equipment to assist Franco, and Stalin responded by sending aid to communists fighting on the republican side. Reluctant to ally with Stalin, the governments of France, Britain, and the United States remained neutral, and seemed, therefore, to signal that aggressors could act with impunity.

While the Spanish Civil War raged, the Japanese resumed their advance in China. The Japanese conquest was brutal. In what became known as the Rape of Nanking (Nanjing), soldiers used babies for bayonet practice, gang-raped as many as 20,000 young girls and women, and left the bodies of the dead to rot in the street. The League of Nations had condemned Japan's seizure of Manchuria in 1931 but could do little else.

Map 26.1   The Expansion of Germany in the 1930s

Beginning with the remilitarization of the Rhineland in 1936, Hitler embarked on a program of German territorial expansion. This map also indicates the expansion of the Soviet Union into Poland as a result of the secret terms of the German-Soviet Non-Aggression Pact.

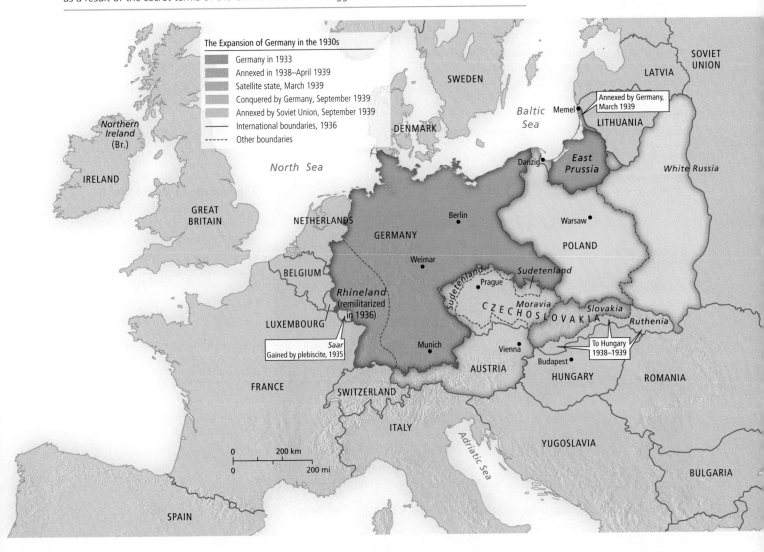

Against this backdrop of military aggression and the democracies' inaction, Hitler made his first moves to establish a German empire in Europe (see Map 26.1). In 1933, he withdrew Germany from the League of Nations and two years later announced the creation of a German air force and the return of mass conscription—in deliberate violation of the terms of the Versailles Treaty. In 1936, Hitler allied with Mussolini in the Rome-Berlin Axis° and again violated his treaty obligations when he sent German troops into the Rhineland, the industrially rich region on Germany's western border. Yet France and Britain did not respond. Two years later, in March 1938, Germany broke the Versailles Treaty once more by annexing Austria after an intense Austrian Nazi propaganda campaign punctuated by violence.

After the successful *Anschluss* ("joining") of Germany and Austria, Hitler demanded that the Sudetenland, the western portion of Czechoslovakia inhabited by a German-speaking majority, be joined to Germany as well. He seemed finally to have gone too far. France and the Soviet Union had pledged to protect the territorial integrity of Czechoslovakia. In September 1938, Europe stood on the brink of war. The urgency of the situation impelled Britain's prime minister Neville Chamberlain (1869–1940) to board an airplane for the first time in his life and fly to Munich to negotiate with Hitler. After intense negotiations that excluded the Czech government, Chamberlain and French prime minister Edouard Daladier agreed to grant Hitler the right to occupy the Sudetenland immediately. Assured by Hitler that this "Munich Agreement" satisfied all his territorial demands, Chamberlain flew home to a rapturous welcome. Crowds cheered and church bells rang when he claimed to have achieved "peace in our time."

"Peace in our time" lasted for six months. In March 1939, German troops occupied the rest of Czechoslovakia and Hitler's promises proved to be worthless. On August 23, Hitler took out an insurance policy against fighting a two-front war by persuading Stalin to sign the German-Soviet Non-Aggression Pact°. The pact publicly pledged the two powers not to attack each other; it also secretly divided Poland between them and promised Stalin substantial territorial gains—much of eastern Poland and the Baltic regions of Latvia, Estonia, and parts of Lithuania. On September 1, 1939, German troops invaded Poland. The British and French declared war against Germany on September 3. Two weeks after German troops crossed Poland's borders in the west, the Soviets pushed in from the east and imposed a regime of murderous brutality. The Second World War had begun.

Evaluating Appeasement

Could Hitler have been stopped before he catapulted Europe into World War II? The debate over this question has centered on British policy during the 1930s. France advocated an aggressive policy toward Germany in the 1920s, even to the point of sending troops into the Rhineland in 1923 to seize reparations. But during the 1930s, debilitating economic and political crises left France too weak to respond strongly to Hitler. With the United States remaining aloof from European affairs and the now-communist Soviet Union regarded as a pariah state, Britain assumed the initiative in responding to Hitler's rise to power and his increasingly aggressive actions.

After World War II broke out, one term came to be equated with passivity and cowardice in the face of aggression. That term was appeasement°—the policy of conciliation and negotiation that British policymakers,

"Peace in Our Time"
In September 1938, British prime minister Neville Chamberlain announced his diplomatic triumph: With the German annexation of the Sudetenland, Hitler declared himself satisfied and Chamberlain announced "peace in our time."

particularly Neville Chamberlain, pursued in their dealings with Hitler in the 1930s. Chamberlain, however, was not a coward and was far from passive. Convinced he had a mission to save Europe from war, he actively sought to accommodate Hitler. Chamberlain thought like the businessmen who voted for him. He believed that through negotiation a suitable agreement—the "best price"—can always be found. His fundamental failure was not passivity or cowardice but rather his insistence that Hitler was a man like himself. Chamberlain could not believe that Hitler would find a war worth the price Germany would need to pay.

For Chamberlain, and many other Europeans, the alternative to appeasement was a total war that would surely destroy Western civilization. They remembered the last war with horror and agreed that the next war would be even worse, for it would be an air war. The years after 1918 saw the aviation industry come into its own in Europe and the United States, and both military experts and ordinary people recognized the disastrous potential of airborne bombs. Stanley Baldwin (1867–1947), Chamberlain's predecessor as prime minister, told the British public that there was no defense against a bomber force: "The bomber will always get through." The horrendous civilian casualties inflicted by the Italian air force in Ethiopia and by the bombing of Spanish cities in the Spanish Civil War convinced many Europeans that Baldwin was right, and that war was completely unacceptable. Just two years after the British Peace Pledge Union was founded in 1934, it had 100,000 supporters pledged not to fight in a war.

Motivated by the desire to avoid another horrible war, appeasement also rested on two additional pillars—first, the assumption that many of Germany's grievances were legitimate; second, the belief that only a strong Germany could neutralize the threat posed by Soviet communism. During the 1920s, many historians, political scientists, and policymakers studied the diplomatic records concerning the outbreak of World War I and concluded that the treaty makers at Versailles were wrong in blaming Germany for starting the war. During the 1920s, then, British leaders sought to renegotiate reparations, to press the French into softening their anti-German policies, and to draw Germany back into the network of international diplomatic relations. Hitler's rise to power gave added impetus to a policy already in place. British leaders argued that they could rob Hitler of much of his appeal by rectifying legitimate German grievances.

British policymakers' fear of communism reinforced their desire to stabilize Germany. Many politicians applauded Hitler's moves against German communists and welcomed the military resurgence of Germany as a strong bulwark against the threat posed by Soviet Russia. The startling announcement of the German-Soviet Non-Aggression Pact in the summer of 1939 revealed the hollowness of this bulwark, just as the German invasion of Czechoslovakia in March had exposed Hitler's promises of peace as worthless.

Europe at War, 1939–1941

■ How did Nazi Germany conquer the continent of Europe by 1941?

German soldiers crossed the Polish border on September 1, 1939; just two years later, Hitler appeared to have achieved his goal of establishing a Nazi empire in Europe. By the autumn of 1941, almost all of continental Europe was either allied to or occupied by Nazi Germany.

A New Kind of Warfare

During these two years, the German army moved from triumph to triumph as a result of its mastery of the new technology of offensive warfare. Executing a strategy of attack that fully utilized the products of modern industry, the German military demonstrated the power of a mobile, mechanized offensive force. Germany's only defeat during these years came in the Battle of Britain, when Germany confronted a mobile, mechanized defense. Like Germany's victories, this defeat highlighted the central role of industrial production in modern warfare.

The Conquest of Poland

In its attack on Poland, the German army made use of a new kind of warfare. As Chapter 24 explained, in World War I a full frontal infantry assault proved no match for a deeply entrenched defensive force armed with machine guns. In the 1920s and 1930s, military strategists theorized that the way to avoid the stalemate of trench warfare was to use both the airplane and the tank to construct an "armored fist" strong and swift enough to break through even the most well-fortified enemy defenses. The bomber plane provided a mobile bombardment, one that shattered enemy defenses, broke vital communication links, and clogged key transport routes. Simultaneously, motorized infantry and tank formations punched through enemy lines.

Germany's swift conquest of Poland provided the world with a stunning demonstration of this new offensive strategy. Most of the German army, like all of the Polish, moved on foot or by horseback, as soldiers had done for centuries. Fast-moving motorized divisions, however, bludgeoned through the Polish defenses, penetrated deep into enemy territory, and secured key positions. While these units wreaked havoc on the ground, the Luftwaffe—the German air force—rained ruin from the air. Thirteen hundred planes shrieked across the Polish skies and in just one day destroyed the far smaller, less modern Polish air force, most of whose planes never left the ground. Warsaw surrendered after just ten days.

Blitzkrieg in Western Europe

Western newspaper reporters christened this new style of warfare blitzkrieg°—lightning war. Western Europeans experienced blitzkrieg firsthand in the spring of 1940. The German army invaded Denmark and Norway in early April, routed the French and British troops sent to aid the Norwegians, and moved into western Europe in May. The Netherlands fell in just four days; Belgium, supported by French and British units as in World War I, held out for two weeks.

On May 27, 1940, the British army and several divisions of the French force found themselves trapped in a small pocket on the northern French coast called Dunkirk. Their destruction seemed certain. But over the next week, the

Blitzkrieg

In blitzkrieg, the tank and bomber plane worked together to punch openings in the enemy's defenses. Motorized infantry divisions then poured through the holes.

only Allied success in the campaign unfolded. The British Royal Air Force (RAF) succeeded in holding off the Luftwaffe and enabling the British navy and a flotilla of fishing and recreational boats manned by British civilians to evacuate these troops. By June 4, 110,000 French and almost 240,000 British soldiers had been brought safely back to Britain. But, as the newly appointed British prime minister Winston Churchill (1874–1965) reminded his cheering people, "wars are not won by evacuation."

Over the next two weeks the Germans steadily advanced through northern France, and on June 14, German soldiers marched into Paris. The French Assembly voted to disband and to hand over power to the World War I war hero Marshal Philippe Pétain (1856–1951), who established an authoritarian government. On June 22 this new Vichy regime° (named after the city Pétain chose for his capital) signed an armistice with Germany that pledged French collaboration with the Nazi regime. Theoretically, Pétain's authority extended over all of France, but in actuality the Vichy regime was confined to the south, with Germany occupying France's western and northern regions, including Paris, as well as the Atlantic seaboard. One million French soldiers became prisoners of war. Germany, with its allies and satellites, held most of the continent.

The Battle of Britain

After the fall of France, Hitler hoped that Britain would accept Germany's domination of the continent and agree to a negotiated peace. But his hopes went unrealized. Military disaster in Norway had thoroughly discredited Prime Minister Chamberlain and his halfhearted approach to war making. A member of Chamberlain's own party, Leo Amery, spoke for the nation when he shouted at Chamberlain, "In the name of God, go!" Chamberlain went. Party politics were suspended for the duration of the war, and the British government passed to an all-party coalition headed by Winston Churchill, a vocal critic of Britain's appeasement policy since 1933. Never a humble man, Churchill wrote that when he accepted the position of prime minister, "I felt as if I were walking with Destiny, and that all my past life had been but a preparation for this hour and this trial . . . I was sure I should not fail." In his first speech as prime minister, Churchill promised, "Victory—victory at all costs."

Faced with the British refusal to negotiate, Hitler ordered his General Staff to prepare for a land invasion of Britain. But placing German troops in the English Channel while Britain's Royal Air Force still flew the skies would be a certain military disaster. Thus, a precondition of invasion was the destruction of the RAF. On July 10, German bomber raids on English southern coastal cities opened the Battle of Britain, a battle waged in the air—and in the factories. Fortunately for Britain, from 1935 on the government's defense policy had accorded priority to the RAF. In the summer of 1940, British factories each month produced twice the number of fighter aircraft coming out of German plants in the same period. Preparing for air attack, the British had constructed a shield comprising fighter planes, anti-aircraft gun installations, and a chain of radar stations. These preparations, its higher production rates of aircraft, and the fact that RAF pilots were fighting in the skies above their homes gave the British the advantage. On September 17, 1940, Hitler announced that the invasion of Britain was postponed indefinitely.

The Invasion of the Soviet Union

War against Britain had never been one of Hitler's central goals, however. His dreams of the "Third Reich," a renewed Germanic European empire that was to last a thousand years, centered on conquest of the Soviet Union. Hitler believed that the rich agricultural and industrial resources of the vast Russian empire rightly belonged to the superior German race. He also believed that Soviet communism was an evil force and a potential threat to German stability and prosperity. Moreover, one of Hitler's aims in invading the Soviet Union was to realize his dream of a new racial order

DOCUMENT

In the Tanks

If World War I was the war of the trenches, then World War II was the war of the tanks. In the Battle of Kursk on the eastern front, for example, the Russians and Germans sent a thousand tanks into combat on a single day (July 12, 1943). In the first two years of the war, just the sight of these armored monsters crashing through barriers could demoralize an entire infantry regiment. By 1942, however, both sides had developed effective antitank defensive systems. For the men in the tanks, the experience of combat was harrowing.

Alan Gilmour, 48th Royal Tank Regiment (Britain), Tunisia, 1943

In the low padded compartment . . . we crouch, the two of us shapeless figures engulfed in a miasma of smoke and dust through which the facia lights barely penetrate. Behind us in the turret the crew are choking with the fumes of cordite which the fans are powerless to dissipate. Cut off from visible contact with the outside world, the wireless operator, wedged in his seat, cannot possibly know in which direction the vehicle is moving. To all five of us, the intercom, our lifeline, relays a bedlam of orders, distortions, and cries from another world.

Nat Frankel, American Private, France, 1944

It takes twenty minutes for a medium tank to incinerate; and the flames burn slowly, so figure it takes ten minutes for a hearty man within to perish. You wouldn't even be able to struggle for chances are both exits would be sheeted with flame and smoke. You would sit, read *Good Housekeeping,* and die like a dog. Steel coffins indeed!

Anonymous British Tank Company Commander, Italian Front, 1944

We were ordered to make the attack in the face of an anti-tank screen firing down the line of advance. We knew that we should not get far. . . . armour-piercing shot seemed to come from all directions. . . . the tanks were knocked out one by one. Most of them burst into flames immediately. A few were disabled, the turrets jammed or the tank made immobile. As the survivors jumped out, some of them made a dash across the open. . . . but they were almost all mown down by German machine gun fire.

Sources: From Bryan Perrett, *Through Mud and Blood: Infantry.* Published by Robert Hale, 1975. Reprinted by permission of Watson, Little, Ltd., licensing agents; from Nat Frankel and Larry Smith, *Patton's Best: An Informal History of the 4th Armored Division.* Hawthorne Books, New York, 1978; and from Douglas Orgill, *The Gothic Line,* Heinemann, 1967. Reprinted by permission of John Johnson Limited.

in Europe. This dream demanded a war against the Jews, the majority of whom lived in Poland and the Soviet Union.

A Crucial Postponement

In July 1940, at the very start of the Battle of Britain, Hitler ordered his military advisers to begin planning a Soviet invasion. By December the plan was set: German troops were to invade the Soviet Union in April 1941. But they did not. Hitler postponed the invasion for two crucial months because the ambitions of an incompetent ally—Mussolini—threatened to undermine the economic base of the Nazi war machine.

Italy was ill-equipped to fight a broad-based war. Its military budget was only one-tenth the size of Germany's, its tanks and aircraft were outdated, it had no aircraft carriers or anti-aircraft defenses, and most crucially, it lacked an adequate industrial base. Yet in 1940 Mussolini's hopes of rebuilding the Roman Empire drove him to launch just such a war. In July 1940, Italian troops invaded British imperial territories in North Africa, and in October Mussolini's soldiers marched into Greece. By the spring of 1941, the Italian advance was in trouble. The British army in North Africa pushed the Italians back into Libya while the Greeks mounted a fierce resistance against the invaders.

Hitler feared the consolidation of British power in Africa and was even more terrified that Mussolini's adventurism would pull the British into eastern Europe. If Britain were able to build air bases in Greece, the Balkans

Map 26.2   The Nazi Empire in 1942

By 1942, Nazi Germany occupied or was allied to not only most European countries but also much of North Africa and the Middle East. Spain, Portugal, Ireland, Iceland, Sweden, and Switzerland remained neutral. Great Britain and the Soviet Union east of Moscow remained unconquered.

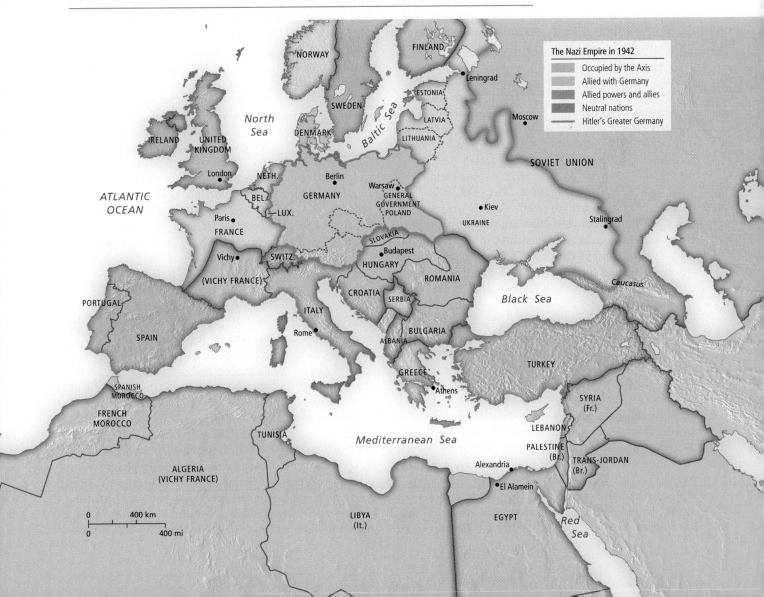

would lie open to British bombing runs. The British could then cripple the German war effort. Germany received 50 percent of its cereal and livestock from the Balkan region, 45 percent of its aluminum ore from Greece, and 90 percent of its tin from Yugoslavia. Most crucially, the oil fields of Romania constituted Germany's chief source of this vital war-making resource. Without oil, there would be no *blitz* in *blitzkrieg*.

These economic considerations led Hitler to delay the invasion of the Soviet Union while the German army mopped up Mussolini's mess in the Balkans and North Africa. In April 1941, German armored units punched through Yugoslavian defenses and encircled the hapless Yugoslav army. Greece came next. The British sent troops as well as state-of-the-art tanks and airplanes to aid the Greeks, but by the end of April Greece was in German hands. Meanwhile, in North Africa German field marshal Erwin Rommel's (1891–1944) Afrika Korps recaptured all the territory taken by the British the previous year.

In the summer of 1941, then, Germany stood triumphant, with dramatic victories in North Africa and the Balkans (see Map 26.2). But these victories came at a high price. They had postponed the German invasion of the Soviet Union. By the winter of 1941, the delay in beginning the Soviet invasion would imperil the German army.

Early Success

On June 22, 1941, the largest invading force the world had yet seen began to cross the Soviet borders. Three million German soldiers, equipped with 2,770 modern aircraft and 3,350 tanks, went into battle. In a matter of days, most of the Soviet air force was destroyed. By October 1941, only four months after the invasion began, German tanks were within eighty miles of Moscow, Kiev had fallen, and Leningrad was besieged. An astonishing 45 percent of the Soviet population was under German occupation, and the Germans controlled access to much of the Soviet Union's natural and industrial resources, including more than 45 percent of its grain and 65 percent of its coal, iron, and steel.

The early German victories in the Soviet campaign illustrated the power of blitzkrieg. Although the bulk of the German army traveled on foot or horseback (the Germans went into the Soviet Union with 700,000 horses), its spearhead force consisted of tank and motorized infantry divisions. This force shattered the Soviet defensive line and then moved quickly to seize key targets. Two additional factors contributed to the initial German success. First, Stalin's stubborn refusal to believe that Hitler would violate the Non-Aggression Pact and attack the Soviet Union weakened Russian resistance. Soviet intelligence sources sent in more than eighty warnings of an imminent German attack; all, however, were classified as "doubtful" and a number of the messengers were punished, some even executed. Even as German troops poured over the border and German bombs fell on Soviet cities, Stalin distrusted the news of a German invasion and ignored his generals' pleas for a counterassault.

A second factor that contributed to the early German victories was the popularity of the invasion among many of the peoples being invaded. The initial German advance occurred in territories where Stalin's rule had brought enormous suffering. In areas that had come under Soviet rule in the previous two years—eastern Poland and the Baltic states—anti-Soviet sentiment was especially high. Ceded to the Soviets by the German-Soviet Non-Aggression Pact, these regions were still bleeding from the imposition of Stalinist terror after 1939. Over two million ethnic Poles had been thrown into cattle cars and sent to Siberian labor camps. Thousands had been shot, including 10,000 Polish army officers who were marched to the Katyn forest and gunned down in front of mass graves. To many in these regions, then, the Germans at first seemed like liberators.

The Fatal Winter

On October 10, Hitler's spokesman announced to the foreign press corps that the destruction of the Soviet Union was assured. German newspapers proclaimed, "CAMPAIGN IN THE EAST DECIDED!"[4] But within just a few months, the German advance had stalled. Leningrad resisted its besiegers and Moscow remained beyond the Germans' reach.

Three obstacles halted the German invasion: stiffening Soviet resistance, the difficulty of supplying the Germans' overstretched lines, and the Russian weather. German troops rapidly squandered the huge reserves of anti-Stalinist sentiment in occupied Soviet territory by treating the local populations with fierce cruelty. Both SS and German army units moved through Soviet territories like a plague of locusts, stripping the regions of livestock, grain, and fuel. The Nazi governor of Ukraine insisted, "I will pump every last thing out of this country."[5] By 1941, both Ukraine and Galicia were devastated by human-made famine. German atrocities in the occupied territories strengthened the will to resist among the Soviets still in the Germans' path. Anti-German partisan units worked behind the German lines, sabotaging their transportation routes, hijacking their supplies, and murdering their patrols. They found the Germans especially vulnerable to this sort of attack because of their overstretched supply lines. Ironically, the Germans had succeeded too well: Since June they had advanced so far so fast that they overstrained their supply and communication lines.

The weather worsened these logistical problems. An early October snowfall, which then melted, turned Russia's dirt roads to impassable mud. By the time the ground froze several weeks later, the German forces, like Napoleon's army 130 years earlier, found themselves fighting the Russian winter. Subzero temperatures wreaked havoc with transportation lines. Horses froze to death, and machinery refused to start. Men fared just as badly. Dressed in light-weight spring uniforms and forced to camp out in the cold, German soldiers fell victim to frostbite. By the end of the winter, the casualty list numbered more than 30 percent of the German East Army.

At the close of the winter of 1941–1942, the German army still occupied huge sections of the Soviet Union and controlled the vast majority of its agricultural and industrial resources. More than three million Soviet soldiers had been killed and another three million captured. But the failure to deal the Soviets a quick death blow in 1941 gave Stalin and his military high command a crucial advantage—*time*. In the zones soon to be occupied by the German army, Soviet laborers dismantled entire factories and shipped them eastward to areas out of German bombing range. Between August and October 1941, 80 percent of the Soviet war industry was in pieces, scattered among railway cars, heading to safety in Siberia. With time, these factories could be rebuilt and the colossal productive power of the Soviet Union geared for the war effort. And that is what happened. By 1943, Russia was outproducing Germany: 24,000 tanks versus 17,000; 130,000 artillery pieces versus 27,000; 35,000 combat aircraft versus 25,000. In a total war, in which victory occurs on the assembly line as well as on the front line, these were ominous statistics for Hitler and his dreams of a German empire.

The World at War, 1941–1945

■ Why did the Allies win in 1945?

In December 1941, as the German advance slowed in the Soviet Union, Japanese expansionism in the Pacific fused with the war in Europe and drew the United States into the conflict. Neither Japan nor Germany could compete with the United States on the factory floor. Over the next four years, as millions of soldiers, sailors, and civilians lost their lives in a gargantuan and complicated conflict, industrial production continued to supply a crucial advantage to the Allies.

The Globalization of the War

Even before 1941, Europe's imperialist legacy ensured that World War II was not confined to Europe. As we have seen, Mussolini's desire to expand his North African empire pushed the fighting almost immediately outside European borders. In addition, Britain would never have been able to stand alone against the German-occupied continent without access to the manpower and materials of its colonies and Commonwealth. German efforts to block British access to these resources spread the war into the Atlantic, where

British merchant marines battled desperately against German submarines to keep open the sea lanes into Britain.

Britain also drew heavily on the resources of the United States. Throughout 1941 the United States maintained a precarious balance between neutrality and support for the British war effort, as American naval escorts accompanied supply ships loaded with goods for Britain across the Atlantic. In March, the U.S. Congress passed the Lend-Lease Act°, which guaranteed to supply Britain all needed military supplies, with payment postponed until after the war ended. The passage of Lend-Lease was one of the most important decisions in all of World War II. It gave first Britain and then the Soviets access to the incredible might of American industry.

At the same time that the United States was drawing closer to Britain, its relations with Japan were growing increasingly hostile. In 1941 the Japanese occupied Indochina, and the United States responded by placing an embargo on trade in oil with Japan. Threatened with the loss of a key resource, Japanese policymakers viewed this boycott as tantamount to an act of war. Japan's imperial ambitions demanded that it move decisively before its oil ran out. The South Pacific, a treasure house of mineral and other resources, beckoned.

Between December 7 and 10, 1941, Japanese forces attacked American, British, and Dutch territories in the Pacific—Hong Kong, Wake and Guam Islands, the Philippines, Malaya, Molucca in the Dutch East Indies, and most dramatically, the U.S. Pacific fleet base at Pearl Harbor. After an attack that lasted only a few hours, the American Pacific fleet in Hawaii lay gutted. Guam fell immediately; Wake held out until December 23; Hong Kong surrendered on Christmas Day; by February, Malaya had been defeated. On February 15, 1942, the garrison of 130,000 British, Indian, Australian, and local troops surrendered Singapore to a Japanese force less than half its size. By May, this astounding success had been cemented with the conquest of Indonesia, Burma, and the Philippines. In just a few months, the Japanese had established themselves as imperial overlords of the South Pacific, with its wealth of raw materials (see Map 26.3).

The audacity of the Japanese attack impressed Hitler. Although he had long feared American industrial power, he declared war on the United States on December 11, 1941. In Europe Germany now faced the alliance of Britain, the Soviet Union, and the United States. Even against such an alliance, Germany appeared to occupy a strong position. By January a spectacular offensive in North Africa had brought Rommel's forces within two hundred miles of the strategically vital Suez Canal. And in June the German army resumed its advance in the Soviet Union. Within a few months German troops stood at the borders of Russia's oil fields in the southern Caucasus. With Germany on the offensive in the east and Japan controlling the Pacific, the Allies looked poised to lose the war.

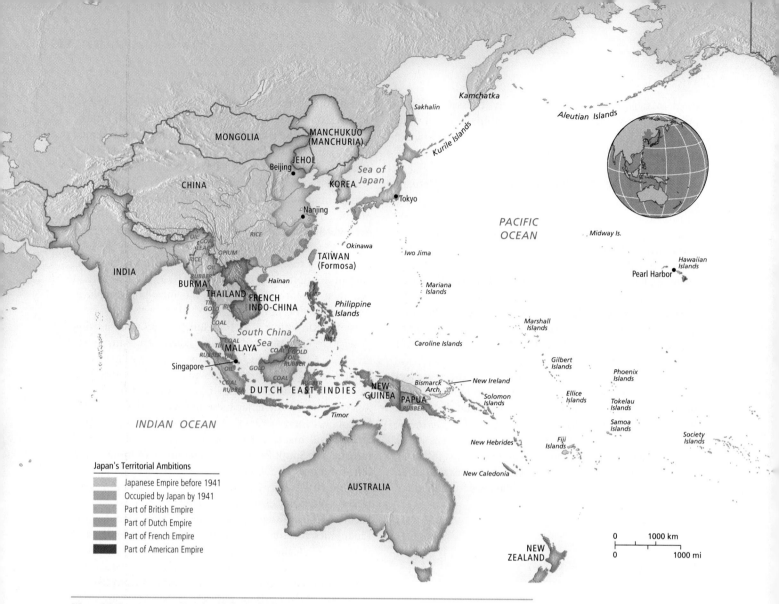

Map 26.3 Japan's Territorial Ambitions

Lacking its own supply of natural resources, Japan embarked on imperial conquest.

Japan's Territorial Ambitions

- Japanese Empire before 1941
- Occupied by Japan by 1941
- Part of British Empire
- Part of Dutch Empire
- Part of French Empire
- Part of American Empire

From Allied Defeat to Allied Victory

Twelve months later the situation had changed, and the Allies were on the road to eventual victory. This road, however, proved long and arduous. The period from 1943 through 1945 was marked by horrendous human suffering, unprecedented attacks on civilians, and cataclysmic military battles. Yet in the end American and Soviet industrial supremacy, allied with a superior military strategy, pushed the balance in the Allies' favor.

VIDEO

FDR on Winning the War

The Turning Point: Midway, El Alamein, and Stalingrad

The second half of 1942 proved the turning point as three very different battles helped transform the course of the war. In the Pacific, victory at the Battle of Midway gave the

U.S. forces a decisive advantage. In North Africa, British forces experienced their first battlefield victory at El Alamein. And in Europe, the Battle of Stalingrad dealt Germany a blow from which it never recovered.

The Battle of Midway resulted from the Japanese effort to ensure its air supremacy by drawing the U.S. Pacific fleet's aircraft carriers into battle. To do so, the Japanese attacked Midway Island, a U.S. outpost, on June 4, 1942. By midmorning the Japanese had shot down two-thirds of the American planes. But then an American dive-bomber group, which had gotten lost, suddenly found itself above the main Japanese carriers. Caught in the act of refueling and rearming the strike force, their decks cluttered with gas lines and bombs, the carriers made remarkably combustible targets. In five minutes, three of Japan's four carriers were destroyed; the fourth was sunk later in the day. Japan's First

The Surrender of Singapore

In one of the most humiliating moments in British military history, General Arthur Percival surrenders the Union Jack, and Singapore, to the Japanese in February 1942. More than 130,000 troops were taken prisoner by a Japanese force containing half that number. The Japanese had captured the island's water reservoirs and so had placed Percival in a helpless situation.

Air Fleet was decimated. The destruction of the Japanese fleet dealt Japan a blow from which it could not recover. The United States possessed the industrial resources to rebuild its lost ships and airplanes. Japan did not. In five explosive minutes at Midway the course of the Pacific war changed.

In contrast, the battle of El Alamein marked the culmination of over two years of fighting in North Africa. In September 1940, Mussolini had ordered his troops to advance from Libya (an Italian colony) into Egypt, as part of his effort to establish an Italian empire in the Mediterranean. That winter British and Australian troops not only pushed the Italians back but drove far into Libya itself. The stakes were too high for Hitler to let his Italian ally lose: Control over North Africa and the Middle East meant control over both the strategically and economically vital Suez Canal and the southern shipping lanes of the Mediterranean, as well as access to key oil fields. The Germans entered the conflict and by June 1941, the German Afrika Korps, led by Field Marshal Erwin Rommel, had muscled the British back into Egypt. For more than a year the two armies pushed each other back and forth across the desert. But finally British field marshal Bernard Montgomery, an abrasive, arrogant man whose meticulous battle strategy included the leaking of false plans, caught the Germans by surprise at El Alamein in October 1942. One month later combined British and American forces landed in Morocco and Algeria, and over the next six months

CHRONOLOGY

1942: The Turning Point

1941

December 7	Japan bombs Pearl Harbor
December 11	Germany declares war on United States

1942

January 21	Rommel's Second Offensive begins in North Africa
February 15	Surrender of British forces to Japan at Singapore
April 22	British retreat from Burma
May 6	Japan completes conquest of the Philippines
June 4	Battle of Midway
August 7	First U.S. Marine landing on Guadalcanal
August 23	German Sixth Army reaches Stalingrad
October 23	Battle of El Alamein begins
November 8	Anglo-American landing in North Africa begins
November 23	German Sixth Army cut off at Stalingrad

pushed Germany out of North Africa. The following year North Africa served as the Allies' jumping-off point for their invasion of southern Italy in July 1943. El Alamein thus marked a crucial turning point in the war. Churchill said of it, "It is not the beginning of the end, but it may be the end of the beginning."[6]

Churchill's apt description fits the third turning point of 1942, the battle of Stalingrad, as well. In July the German army was sweeping southward toward the oil-rich Caucasus. Hitler ordered the southern offensive split into two, with one arm reaching up to conquer Stalingrad on the Volga River. The conquest of Stalingrad would give the Germans control over the main waterway for the transport of oil and food from the Caucasus to the rest of the Soviet Union: The Soviet lifeline would be cut. But by dividing his offensive, Hitler widened his front from 500 to 2,500 miles. By the time the German Sixth Army reached Stalingrad on August 23, German resources were fatally overstretched.

Recognizing Germany's vulnerability, Stalin's generals assured him they could attack the exposed German lines and then encircle the German Sixth Army—but only if Stalingrad's defenders could hold on for almost two months while they assembled the necessary men and machinery. An epic urban battle ensued, with the Russian and German soldiers fighting street by street, house by house, room by room. By November, the Russians had surrounded the Germans. When the German commander, General Friedrich von Paulus (d. 1953), requested permission to surrender, Hitler replied, "The army will hold its position to the last soldier and the last cartridge."[7] Paulus finally disobeyed orders and surrendered on January 30, 1943, but by then his army had almost ceased to exist. The Germans were never able to make up the losses in manpower, material, or morale they suffered at Stalingrad.

The Allies on the Offensive

The Allies were now on the offensive. In 1942 British bomber command ordered the intensive bombing of German civilian centers. Soon joined by the American air force, the RAF bombers brought the war home to the German people.

The Allies followed their victory in North Africa with an invasion of Italy. This campaign was a response, first, to Stalin's pleas that his Allies open a "Second Front" in Europe and so relieve the pressure on Russian troops and, second, to Churchill's desire to protect British economic and imperial interests in the Mediterranean. The Italian offensive began on July 10, 1943, when Anglo-American forces landed in Sicily, prepared to push up into what Churchill called the "soft underbelly" of German-controlled Europe. Within just fifteen days, Mussolini had been overthrown in a high-level coup and his successor opened peace negotiations with the Allies. But then German muscle hardened the "soft underbelly": The German army occupied Italy. British and American soldiers faced a long, brutal, slow-moving push up the peninsula. Ridged with mountains and laced with rivers, Italy formed a natural defensive fortress. In an eight-month period, the Allied forces advanced only seventy miles.

The European war was decided, then, not in the mountains of Italy but on the eastern front. Beginning in the summer of 1943, the Russians steadily pushed back the Germans. By the spring of 1944 the Red Army had reached the borders of Poland. In August Soviet troops turned south into Romania and Hungary. By February 1945 they were within 100 miles of Berlin (see Map 26.4).

Two interconnected factors proved vital in the Soviet victory over the Germans in the east. The first was the evolution of Soviet military strategy. By 1943, the Red Army had learned important lessons from being on the receiving end of blitzkrieg. It had not only increased its tank units, but it had concentrated these into armies in which motorized infantry regiments accompanied massive numbers of tanks, antitank battalions, and mobile anti-aircraft artillery. In addition, a vast expansion in the number of radios and field telephones overcame the organizational chaos that had greeted the German invasion in 1941.

These changes in technique and technology were closely connected to achievements in industrial production, the second key factor in the Soviet victory. Mobile armored forces depended on factories churning out steel, rubber, oil, and all the various machine parts needed by a modern army. Access to the industrial wealth of the United States pro-

---

Stalingrad: Turning Point on the Eastern Front

The battle for Stalingrad proved to be not only the turning point in the European war, but also a conflict that tested human endurance to the utmost. German and Russian soldiers fought street by street, house by house, room by room in the bitter Russian winter.

vided the Soviet Union with assistance in this task. By 1943, Lend-Lease deliveries of aircraft and tanks were pouring into Soviet ports. Lend-Lease supplied the Soviet Union with the basics needed to keep its army moving: rails and locomotives, jeeps, trucks and gasoline, and 15 million pairs of boots. Yet the Soviets did not rely only on imports. The Soviet industrial effort was enormous. In 1943, Russia manufactured four times as many tanks as it imported, and Soviet production of tanks and antitank guns was double that of Germany.

The Fall of Germany

As the Red Army closed in on Germany from the east, the British and Americans pushed in from the west. On June 6, 1944, the Allies carried out the largest amphibious operation the world had ever seen. Five seaborne divisions (two American, two British, and one Canadian) and three airborne divisions (two American and one British) crossed the English Channel and landed on a sixty-mile stretch of coastline in northern France. The "D-Day" landings illustrated the Allied advantage in manpower and material. Against the Allies' eight divisions, the Germans had four; against the Allies' 5,000 fighter planes, the Germans could send up 169.

Yet the strength of the German resistance—particularly on Omaha Beach, where the U.S. landing encountered more than 4,000 casualties—signaled that the road to Berlin would not be easy. The Allies faced the formidable task of uprooting the Germans from territory where they had planted themselves five years earlier. For ten long months, the British, American, Canadian, and imperial troops fought a series of hard-won battles. By March 1945, as the Russian army approached Berlin from the east, the British and American armies reached Germany's Rhine border and by mid-April stood within fifty miles of Berlin.

The Allies agreed, however, to leave the conquest of Berlin to the Soviet Army. In this climactic battle of the European war, 320,000 Germans, many of them young

Map 26.4 Allied Victory in Europe, 1942–1945
Beginning in late 1942, Allied forces moved onto the offensive.

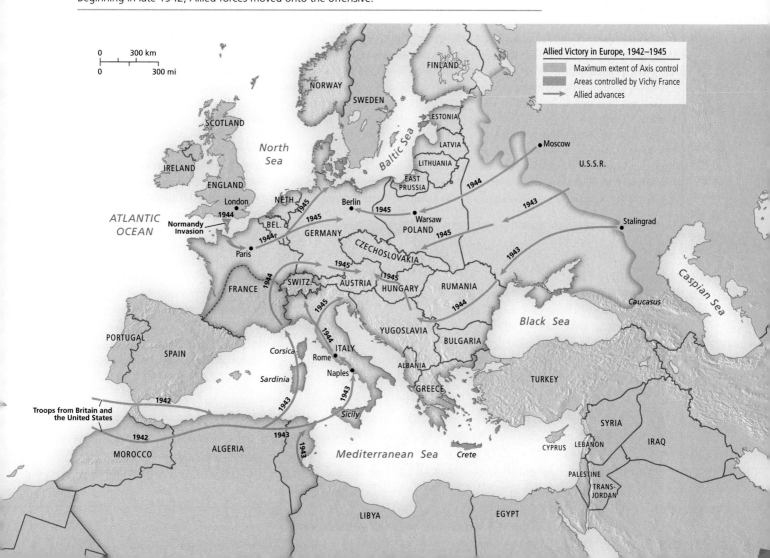

The GI

On January 26, 1942, the first soldiers from the United States arrived in Britain to prepare for the invasion of Nazi-controlled Europe. By the spring of 1944, Britain was host to a million and a half American soldiers, sailors, and airmen, awaiting the opening of the Second Front in Europe. The coming of the "Yanks" to war-weary, bomb-blasted Britain was an event of more than military significance. For the majority of individuals on both sides, it was their first prolonged encounter with another culture, another way of life. Cultural clashes were commonplace. Forgetting that most essential items were strictly rationed, the GIs (slang that comes from the military label "government issue") at times infuriated their hosts with insensitive complaints about cold rooms, inadequate food, and the shabby style of British dress. The British found the Americans naive, supremely self-confident, alarmingly friendly, and most of all, BIG.

The bigness of the GI is a constant theme in British descriptions and recollections. One British man, urging greater toleration for the GIs, explained to his countrymen, "An American is like a large dog trying to be friendly with everyone in the room, whilst wrecking everything with its tail wagging." A Lancashire nurse recalled her first sight of GIs: "They all seemed to be handsome six-footers with friendly grins and toothpaste advert teeth." But we know that not every GI stationed in Britain was tall and husky; the average height of American servicemen in this era was 5'10". How do we explain this focus on the bigness of the GI body?

A number of factors helped shape British perceptions. First, the bigness of America in general was a constant obsession of both the GIs and their British hosts. *Meet the U.S. Army,* a publication distributed in British schools, told the children, "In the USA, you can get in a car—a high-powered car at that—and drive for a week or more in a comparatively straight line without running into the sea." Second, the Americans *looked better.* The GI's uniform was of a higher-quality fabric and a closer fit than that of the average British soldier's: American privates often found that their flashy uniforms led not only British civilians but even British soldiers to mistake them for officers. Third, compared to the British, the Americans were big eaters and big spenders. An American private earned five times as much as his British counterpart—and spent it with abandon. British pubgoers were sometimes dismayed to find that American soldiers had already consumed the pub's entire stock of beer. Undisciplined by rationing, American appetites seemed huge to the British. One soldier enjoyed his dinner in a British home: "Only afterwards did I discover that I had eaten the family's special rations for a *month.*" GIs also had access to items such as chocolate and canned fruit that had long been unobtainable in Britain. And finally, different cultural norms magnified the impact of the GI's presence. Americans spoke more loudly. They used exaggerated expressions that struck the more understated British as boastful. They tended to lounge, to slouch, to lean against walls, to throw their bodies around in ways that startled many British, schooled in more restrained patterns of public behavior. All of these factors combined to ensure that the GI made an indelible impression on British culture.

Embraced with enthusiasm by many British citizens (particularly women), derided by others (particularly men) as "overfed, overpaid, oversexed, and over here," the GI's body became a symbol, a shorthand reference to American power, influence, and plenty. As World War II ended and the Cold War began, and as the United States took on a new role as the undisputed leader of the "West," the American soldier became a familiar figure throughout western Europe, the visible reminder of the reconfiguration of military and economic dominance.[8]

For Discussion

What other bodies became symbols or shorthand references during World War II? What did these bodies symbolize?

Wartime Encounters
British women entertain GIs headed for the front in France.

boys, fought three million Soviet troops. Even so, it took eleven days before the city's commander surrendered on May 2. Two days earlier, Hitler had taken a cyanide capsule and then shot himself with his service pistol. On May 7, 1945, General Alfred Jodl (1890–1946) signed the unconditional surrender of German forces.

The Air War, the Atom Bomb, and the Fall of Japan

When Germany surrendered, the war in the Pacific was still raging. After the Midway battle of 1942, the United States steadily, but slowly, agonizingly, pushed the Japanese back island by island. Japanese industry could not make up for the weapons and ammunition expended in these brutal battles. In contrast, American factories were just gearing up. Whereas in 1940 American assembly lines produced only a little more than 2,000 aircraft, by 1944 they had manufactured over 96,000 bombers and fighters. American productivity per worker hour was five times that of Japan.

While U.S. troops moved closer to the Japanese mainland, British and Indian troops rebuffed a Japanese attempt to invade India and pushed the Japanese out of Burma. Australian forces, with American assistance, held the line at New Guinea and forestalled a Japanese invasion of Australia. By February 1945, then, when U.S. Marines landed on the small island of Iwo Jima, just 380 miles from

CHRONOLOGY		
The Long March Toward Allied Victory		
1943		
February	German surrender at Stalingrad; Red Army goes on the offensive; Allied round-the-clock bombing of Germany begins; Japanese surrender at Guadalcanal	
May	German surrender in North Africa	
July 10	Allied invasion of Italy begins	
1944		
January	Lifting of the siege of Leningrad	
June 4	Allies liberate Rome	
June 6	D-Day landings; Allied offensive in France begins	
August 24–26	Allied liberation of Paris	
September	Allies liberate the Netherlands, Belgium, and Luxembourg	
October	U.S. invasion of Philippines	

Japan's home islands, the Japanese war effort was in tatters and an Allied victory was ensured.

Obtaining this final victory, however, proved far from easy. In the month of fighting for the island of Iwo Jima, one-third of the American landing force died or suffered injury. The April conquest of Okinawa was even more hard-won. Outnumbered two to one, the Japanese endured

The Battle for Berlin
On April 20, 1945, Hitler celebrated his fifty-sixth birthday and made a rare visit out of his Berlin bunker to visit with the troops defending his city. As this photograph shows, these "soldiers" were just children. Ten days later, Hitler committed suicide.

unbelievable losses—110,000 of the 120,000 soldiers on the island died. Yet they still inflicted serious damage on the attacking force, killing or wounding 50,000 Americans before the fight was over. (Nobody bothered to count how many Okinawans died in a battle they had done nothing to provoke; estimates range as high as 160,000.)

The Air War

Despite the high price exacted to win them, the battles of Iwo Jima and Okinawa were significant victories: The United States now had the bases it needed to bomb Japanese cities. This air war utilized tactics and technologies developed over the previous five years in Europe. For many European civilians, World War II was the war of the bomber. In Britain, until late 1941, civilian deaths outnumbered military, and most civilians died in bombing raids. During autumn 1940, Londoners endured the "Blitz"—seventy-six consecutive nights of mass bombing. By May 1941, almost every main industrial city in Britain had been bombed, and 43,000 noncombatants lay dead. British bombers, joined in 1943 by the American air force, retaliated in kind, and as the war wore on, developed new techniques of airborne destruction. In May 1942, British planes destroyed Cologne with the world's first 1,000-bomber raid, and one year later, introduced the world to the horror of the firestorm with the bombing of Hamburg. In this human-made catastrophe, fires caused by incendiary bombs combine with winds to suck the oxygen out of the air and raise temperatures to combustible levels. As one survivor recalled, "The smallest children lay like fried eels on the pavement."[9] In a single night, 45,000 of Hamburg's residents were killed. In total, more than 500,000 German civilians died in bombing attacks. Twenty percent of the dead were children.

In 1945 the conquests of Iwo Jima and Okinawa enabled the U.S. air command to adopt the British tactics perfected in the skies over Germany as a key strategy to defeat Japan. On one March evening, American bombs and the ensuing firestorm killed 85,000 residents of Tokyo. Over the next five months, American bombers hit sixty-six Japanese cities, burned 180 square miles, and killed approximately 330,000 Japanese. At the same time, a U.S. naval blockade cut Japan off from its supply lines.

The Manhattan Project

While American bombers pulverized Japanese cities during the spring and summer of 1945, a multinational group of scientists fought a very different sort of battle in a secret military installation in New Mexico. The Manhattan Project°, the code name for the joint British-American-Canadian effort to construct an atom bomb, was an extraordinary endeavor, the biggest and most expensive weapons research and development project up to that point in history. Comprising thirty-seven installations in nineteen

---

DOCUMENT

Living Under the Bombs

During the 1930s, European statesmen and politicians condemned the aerial bombing of civilian populations as an act of barbarity and criminality. Once World War II began, the targeting of civilians in order to break home front morale and impede industrial production became commonplace. Analysts disagree about the military effectiveness of urban bombing, but no one can dispute the human horror.

In this first excerpt, an elderly air warden from Hull, one of Britain's northern port cities, is speaking. One night, when he returned from his post, he found that his street:

Was as flat as this 'ere wharfside—there was just my 'ouse like—well, part of my 'ouse. My missus were just making me a cup of tea for when I come 'ome. She were in the passage between the kitchen and the wash'ouse, where it blowed 'er. She were burnt right up to 'er waist. 'Er legs were just two cinders. And 'er face— The only thing I could recognize 'er by was one of 'er boots—I'd 'ave lost fifteen 'omes if I could 'ave kept my missus. We used to read together. I can't read mesen [myself]. She used to read to me like. We'd 'ave our armchairs on either side o' the fire, and she read me bits out o' the paper. We 'ad a paper every evening. Every evening.

In the following excerpt, a German woman, 19 years old on July 28, 1943, recalls the bombing of Hamburg and the firestorm it induced:

We came to a door which was burning just like a ring in a circus through which a lion has to jump. . . . I struggled to run against the wind in the middle of the street but could only reach a house on the corner. . . . We got to the Loschplatz [park] all right but I couldn't go across the Eiffestrasse [street] because the asphalt had melted. There were people on the roadway, some already dead, some still lying alive but stuck in the asphalt. They must have rushed on to the roadway without thinking. Their feet had got stuck and then they put out their hands to try to get out again. They were on their hands and knees screaming.

Sources: Excerpt from a Mass-Observation typescript report, filed at Mass-Observations offices, no. 844, August 23, 1941. Copyright © by the Trustees of the Mass-Observation Archive. Reprinted by permission; and from Martin Middlebrook, *The Battle of Hamburg*, Allen Lane, 1980. Reprinted by permission of the author.

American states and in Canada, it employed 120,000 individuals. Yet this gargantuan effort was top-secret, unknown even to American vice president Harry Truman, who first learned of the project only after President Roosevelt died.

The Manhattan Project originated as part of the war against Germany, not Japan. When the European war began, a number of scientists—many of them eastern and central European émigrés who had fled the Nazis, many of them Jewish—feared that Germany, with its stellar tradition of scientific research and state-of-the-art laboratories, possessed the potential for developing an atom bomb. They pressured the British and American governments to build the Bomb before Hitler did so. Britain took the initial lead by creating a committee to oversee atomic research in spring 1940. By the following summer, British research had persuaded the Americans that an atom bomb could be constructed. In October 1941—two months before Japan bombed Pearl Harbor—Roosevelt and Churchill agreed to create an atomic partnership.

For three years the Manhattan Project scientists labored to unlock the atom's power. They finally succeeded on July 16, 1945, when the world's first atomic explosion—the Trinity test—detonated over the desert of New Mexico. The date of the Trinity test is crucial because by the time of the test, Nazi Germany had already fallen to the Allies, and Japan was staggering under the combined effects of the American naval blockade and nightly bombing raids (see Map 26.5). Given this situation, the decision to use atom bombs against Japan generated controversy from the very start. Many of the scientists on the Manhattan Project opposed the decision, as did important American military officials such as General Dwight Eisenhower (1890–1969), supreme commander of the Allied forces in Europe; General Douglas MacArthur (1880–1964), supreme commander of the Allied forces in the Pacific; and Admiral William Leahy (1875–1959), chairman of the U.S. Joint Chiefs of Staff.

Advocates of dropping the atom bomb on Japan argued that the fierce Japanese resistance encountered by Americans at Iwo Jima and Okinawa and by the British in Burma signaled that an invasion of Japan's home islands would result in horrifying casualties. Leahy noted to Truman that if casualty rates were as high as those on Okinawa, then the numbers of Americans killed in the first phase of the invasion could reach 50,000.

An invasion of Japan was, however, not a foregone conclusion in the spring and summer of 1945. Leahy and others argued that the naval blockade would end the war *without* an invasion, and in 1946, the U.S. Strategic Bombing Survey concluded that "in all probability prior to 1 November 1945, Japan would have surrendered . . . even if no invasion had been planned or contemplated." Survey officials, of course, had the benefit of hindsight, an advantage denied to Truman and his advisers in the summer of 1945. But more important, from Truman's perspective, continuing to blockade and to drop conventional bombs on Japan

The Mushroom Cloud
The detonation of the atomic bomb over Hiroshima on August 6, 1945, produced what would become one of the most familiar images of the post–World War II age.

meant continuing to put American soldiers in harm's way, a cost he was unwilling to pay. The atom bomb's appeal was not in its potential to kill tens of thousands in a single night; conventional bombs were already doing that, and doing it rather effectively. But the idea of massive casualties, caused by a single atomic bomb, dropped by a single plane, promised to have an enormous psychological impact on the Japanese, and so to end the war more quickly and to bring Allied servicemen home.

A Light Brighter Than a Thousand Suns
As a result, at 8:15 A.M. on August 6, 1945, an American plane named the *Enola Gay* (after the pilot's mother) dropped an atom bomb above the city of Hiroshima. A

Map 26.5   Japan in 1945
By the summer of 1945, American bombing raids had decimated many Japanese cities, including Tokyo. Hiroshima escaped unscathed until August 6, 1945. Nagasaki received the
second atom bomb on August 9 only because clouds obscured
the primary target of Kokura.

CHRONOLOGY

The End of World War II

1945

March 16	American victory on Iwo Jima
April	Berlin encircled by Red Army
April 11	American troops reach Elbe River in Germany
April 30	Hitler commits suicide
May 7	Official German surrender
June 22	American victory at Okinawa
August 6	U.S. drops atomic bomb on Hiroshima
August 8	Soviet Union enters war against Japan
August 9	United States drops atomic bomb on Nagasaki
September 2	Official Japanese surrender

light "brighter than a thousand suns" flashed in the sky. Temperatures at the site of the atomic explosion reached 5,400 degrees Fahrenheit. All those exposed within two miles of the center suffered primary thermal burns—their blood literally boiled and their skin peeled off in strips. Scientists calculated that the atom bomb produced casualties 6,500 times more efficiently than an ordinary bomb. Of Hiroshima's wartime population of 400,000, 140,000 died by the end of 1945, with another 60,000 dying in the next five years.

An Eyewitness to Hiroshima (1945)

The Japanese reacted to the atomic bombing of Hiroshima with incomprehension and confusion. They literally did not know what had hit them. Within the high levels of the Japanese government, gradual realization of the atomic bomb's power strengthened the position of those officials who recognized that Japan must now give up. A hardline faction of the military, however, wished to fight on.

Then, on August 8, the Soviet Union declared war on Japan. The next day American forces dropped an atom bomb on the city of Nagasaki and killed 70,000 outright, with another 70,000 dying over the next five years. On August 10, Emperor Hirohito (1901–1989) told his military leaders to surrender. Viewed in the West as an implacable warlord, Hirohito was actually a man with fairly limited political power who had been pressing for peace since June. Negotiations between the Allies and the Japanese continued until August 15, when the war officially ended.

In Hiroshima and Nagasaki, however, another war was raging, this time against an unseen and at first unrecognized enemy—radiation. The lingering horror of radiation sickness, accounts of which were at first dismissed by many Americans as Japanese propaganda, signaled that the atom bomb was not just a bigger weapon, not simply more bang for the buck. In the months after the war's end, Europeans and Americans came to recognize that the revolutionary new force of atomic power had introduced the world to new possibilities—and new horrors.

The War Against the Jews

■ How and why did the war against the Jews take place, and what were its consequences?

In the months following the war's end, the world also confronted a very different sort of horror, as people began to piece together the story of Hitler's war against the Jews. For European Jews, World War II brought unprecedented terror and, for millions, death. Chapter 25 explained that hatred of the Jewish people stood at the heart of Hitler's world view and Nazi ideology. Yet anti-Semitism alone cannot explain the mass murder that we now call the

Holocaust°, nor was the Holocaust the product of a detailed plan carefully plotted by Hitler long before he came to power. The decision to murder Europe's Jews evolved over time, in the context of total war.

From Emigration to Extermination: The Evolution of Genocide

During the 1930s, Nazi policies focused on forcing German Jews to emigrate. By 1938, these policies had driven out about 25 percent of Germany's Jewish population. At the same time, however, the unification of Germany and Austria, followed by the seizure first of the Sudetenland and then all of Czechoslovakia, meant 300,000 more Jews in the expanded Germany. These numbers skyrocketed with the outbreak of the war. The invasion of Poland brought almost two million more Jews under German control. Pushing Jews to emigrate no longer seemed a workable solution to what the Nazis defined as the "Jewish Problem." But even more important, the fact of war itself made a radicalization of policy and a turn toward murderous violence much more acceptable.

The German occupation of Poland marked the first step toward the Nazi construction of a new racial order in Europe. Hitler intended the Slavic populations, defined in his racist hierarchy as biologically inferior, to serve as a vast labor pool for their German superiors. To reduce the Polish people to slaves, the Nazis embarked on a wholesale destruction of Polish society and culture. They seized businesses and bank accounts, replaced Polish place names with German, closed universities and high schools, and murdered Polish intellectuals and professionals. By the time the war ended in 1945, more than 20 percent of Poland's population had died.

Within the context of their larger plan of racial reordering, Nazi officials talked about "eliminating" Jews from Poland. At this point, however, "elimination" did not yet mean total extermination but instead referred to vaguely articulated plans for mass deportations. German policy toward the Jews in Poland initially focused on "ghettoization." The Nazis forcibly expelled Jews from their homes and confined them in ghettos sealed off from their non-Jewish neighbors. Packed into overcrowded apartments, with inadequate food rations and appalling sanitary conditions, the ghetto populations lived in a nightmare of disease, starvation, and death.

In the almost two-year period between the invasion of Poland and the invasion of the Soviet Union, an estimated

The Holocaust Underway in Lithuania, July 1941
Nazi soldiers adopt a supervisory role while citizens in the Lithuanian city of Kovno murder their Jewish neighbors.

30,000 Jews died, killed outright by German soldiers or dying a more lingering death from starvation and disease as a result of deportation and ghettoization. Yet the suffering had only begun. In the summer or fall of 1941, the Nazis decided on what they termed the Final Solution° to the "Jewish problem": genocide.

The German invasion of the Soviet Union helped shape the "Final Solution." Marching with the forces of the regular army were special mobile units of the SS called Einsatzgruppen° ("strike forces"). With the army providing logistical support, these small motorized units (about 3,000 men in all) took on the task of liquidating those designated as enemies of the Nazi Reich—which meant killing communists and Jews.

Most of these murders followed the same general pattern: SS soldiers rounded up all of the Jewish men, women, and children in a town or village and marched them in batches to a field or woods. They ordered the first batch to dig a large ditch. They then stripped their victims of their clothing, lined them up on the edge of the ditch, and shot them at point-blank range. Subsequent batches were lined up and shot as well, so that by the end of a day's worth of killing, dead and dying bodies filled the ditch. A thin layer of soil was then thrown on top, transforming the ditch into a mass grave. Estimates of the final death count of the Einsatzgruppen actions range from 1.5 to 2 million.

In their war against the Jews, the Einsatzgruppen found ready allies among large sectors of the occupied population. Recall that the earliest stages of the German invasion of the

Einsatzgruppen Action
A soldier shoots the last remaining Jew in a Ukrainian village.

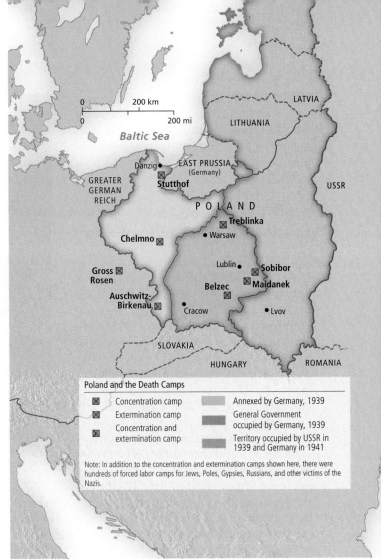

Map 26.6   Poland and the Death Camps
The Nazis set up a vast network of concentration and labor camps across Europe, but built death camps only in Poland.

Soviet Union took place in the territories that had been seized by the Soviets in 1939 as a result of the German-Soviet Non-Aggression Pact. Hence the local populations often welcomed the German troops as liberators and aided the SS in hunting down and killing Jews. In Lvov in eastern Galicia, for example, anti-Soviet Ukrainian fighters turned on the large Jewish community and in two days of violence killed at least 7,000 Jews—*before* the Einsatzgruppen had even arrived.

The Death Camps: Murder by Assembly Line

On January 20, 1942, senior German officials met in a villa in Wannsee, outside Berlin, to finalize plans for killing every Jew in Europe. SS lieutenant colonel Adolf Eichmann

(1906–1962) listed the number of Jews in every country; even the Jewish populations in neutral countries such as Sweden and Ireland showed up on the target list. The Wannsee Conference marked the beginning of a more systematic approach to murdering European Jews, one that built on the experience gained by the Einsatzgruppen in the Soviet war.

To accomplish mass murder, the Einsatzgruppen had become killing machines. By trial and error, they discovered the most efficient ways of identifying and rounding up Jews, shooting them quickly, and burying the bodies. But the Einsatzgruppen actions also revealed the limits of conventional methods of killing. Shooting took time, used up valuable ammunition, and required large numbers of men. Moreover, even the best-trained and carefully indoctrinated soldiers eventually cracked under the strain of shooting unarmed women and children at close range. A systematic approach was needed, one that would utilize advanced killing technology and provide a comfortable distance between the killers and the killed. This perceived need resulted in a key Nazi innovation: the death camp.

The death camp was a specialized form of a concentration camp. From 1933 on, Hitler's government had sentenced communists, Jehovah's Witnesses, the Roma, and anyone else defined as an enemy of the regime to forced labor in concentration camps. After the war began, the concentration camp system expanded dramatically. Scattered throughout Nazi-controlled Europe, concentration camps became an essential part of the Nazi war economy. Some firms, such as the huge chemical conglomerate I. G. Farben,

IMAGE

Emaciated Woman at Bergen-Belsen

established factories inside or right next to camps, which provided vital supplies of forced labor. All across Europe during the war, concentration camp inmates died in huge numbers from the brutal physical labor, torture, and diseases brought on by malnutrition and inadequate housing and sanitary facilities. But it was only in Poland that the Nazis constructed death camps, specialized concentration camps with only one purpose—murder, primarily the murder of Jews (see Map 26.6).

The death camps marked the final stage in a vast assembly line of murder. In early 1942 the trains conveying Jewish victims to the death camps began to rumble across Europe. Jewish ghettos across Nazi-occupied Europe emptied as their inhabitants moved in batches to their deaths. Individuals selected for extermination followed orders to gather at the railway station for deportation to "work camps" farther east. They were then packed into cattle cars, more than 100 people per car, all standing up for the entire journey. Deprived of food and water, with hardly any air, and no sanitary facilities, often for several days, many Jews died en route. The survivors stumbled off the trains into a nightmare world. At some camps, SS guards culled stronger Jews from each transport to be worked to death as slave laborers. Most, however, walked straight from the transport trains into a reception room, where they were told to undress, and then herded into a "shower room"—actually a gas chamber. Carbon monoxide gas or a pesticide called Zyklon-B killed the victims. After the poison had done its work, Jewish slaves emptied the chamber and burned the bodies in vast crematoria, modeled after industrial bake ovens.

DOCUMENT

The Holocaust: Memoirs from the Commandant of Auschwitz (1940s)

The Nazis thus constructed a vast machine of death. In this machine, slave laborers constituted key components, each with identification numbers tattooed onto their

---

DOCUMENT

The "Jager Report"

Karl Jager was a German businessman who joined the SS in 1932. In 1941 he was appointed Commander of Einsatzkommando 3 of Einsatzgruppe A, which was given the task of ridding Lithuania of Jews. The following is an excerpt from his nine-page report on his squad's activities in the summer and fall of 1941. The first six pages contain a day-by-day tally of the number of "executions" (murders) carried out. The final total: 137,346 Jews killed. Jager became a farm laborer after the war, but in 1959 he was arrested; he hanged himself before he could be tried for war crimes.

Kauen [Kaunas], 1 December 1941. Secret Reich Business!
. . .

Today I can confirm that our objective, to solve the Jewish problem for Lithuania, has been achieved by EK 3. In Lithuania there are no more Jews. . . . It was only possible to achieve our objective . . . by forming a raiding squad consisting of specially selected men led by SS-Obersturmfuhrer Hamann, who grasped my aims completely and understood the importance of ensuring cooperation with the Lithuanian partisans and the relevant civilian authorities.

The execution of such actions is first and foremost a matter of organization. The decision to clear each district of Jews systematically required a thorough preparation of each individual action and a reconnaissance of the prevailing conditions in the district concerned. The Jews had to be assembled at one or several places. Depending on the number of Jews a place for the graves had to be found and then the graves dug. . . .

In Rokiskis 3,208 people had to be transported 4½ km before they could be liquidated. In order to get this work done within 24 hours, over sixty of the eighty available Lithuanian partisans had to be detailed for cordon duty. The rest, who had to be relieved constantly, carried out the work together with my men. . . . It was only through the efficient use of time that it was possible to carry out up to five actions of week, while still coping with any work that arose in Kauen, so that no backlog was allowed to build up.

The actions in Kauen itself, where there was an adequate number of reasonably well-trained partisans available, were like parade-ground shootings in comparison with the often enormous difficulties which had to be faced elsewhere.

All the officers and men in my Kommando took an active part in the major actions in Kauen. . . . I consider the Jewish action more or less terminated as far as Einsatzkommando 3 is concerned.

Source: *"The Good Old Days": The Holocaust as Seen by Its Perpetrators and Bystanders.* Eds. Ernst Klee et al. (1991), pp. 46–58.

forearms, a type of human "bar coding." Along a murderous assembly line the human raw material moved from arrival through selection to the undressing rooms to the gas chamber to the crematoria. Approximately three million Jews died in these factories of death. The death camp victims joined the millions who starved or died of disease in the ghettoes, suffocated in the cattle cars, were shot in mass graves, or worked to death in the labor camps. Children were especially vulnerable. Of the Jewish children living in 1939 in the regions already or soon to be under German control, only 11 percent survived.

In total, the Holocaust claimed the lives of approximately six million Jews. The numbers of Roma victims remains unclear. Somewhere between 200,000 and 600,000 died in what the Roma call the *Porajmos*—the Devouring. Jews and Gypsies were the only groups singled out for total extermination based on their supposed biological identity. But Hitler's drive to create his new Germany claimed three to five million other victims as well. Five to fifteen thousand homosexuals perished. So, too, did at least three million Polish Christians.

The Allies' Response

Allied leaders had access to surprisingly accurate information about the Holocaust from very early on. British code breakers translated German military radio transmissions throughout the summer of 1941 so that as the German army—and the Einsatzgruppen—moved into the Soviet Union, British officials confronted intercepted messages such as this one from August 27: "Regiment South shot 914 Jews; the special action staff with police battalion 320 shot 4,200 Jews." By June 1942, Allied leaders knew that death camps existed.

Such information quickly became accessible to ordinary people. British and American newspaper readers and radio listeners received numerous reports about Jewish massacres; after 1942, these reports told about the death camps. But this information had to compete with other war news and many of these articles were written in a skeptical tone, as both reporters and editors had a difficult time believing that such atrocities could be taking place. Pressure from Jewish and non-Jewish public-interest groups did succeed in pushing the British and American governments to issue an inter-Allied declaration in December 1942 that in no uncertain terms announced and condemned Hitler's effort to exterminate European Jewry. This declaration was broadcast all over the world.

Despite this official acknowledgment of the mass murder of Jews, the Allies did not act directly to stop the killings. Should the Allies then be considered bystanders in the crime of the Holocaust? Some historians contend that anti-Semitism in both British and American society structured the Allies' military priorities and prevented leaders from exploring strategies such as sending in commando units, bombing the rail lines into the death camps, or even bombing the camps themselves. Other historians argue these alternatives were not militarily feasible, and that the Allies did the only thing they could do on the Jews' behalf—win the war as quickly as possible.

In the months after the war ended, Allied leaders struggled to bring Nazi leaders to trial to account for their crimes. What one participant called "the greatest trial in history" opened on November 14, 1945. For eleven months, a tribunal of four judges—American, British, French, and Soviet—sat in a courtroom in the German city of Nuremberg to judge nineteen prominent German military, political, and industrial leaders. The Nuremberg trials°, broadcast by the crowds of journalists packed into the courtroom, offered the world its first encounter with the Holocaust. The trials highlighted the Nazi onslaught against European Jewry as one of the most horrendous of the Nazis' many "crimes against humanity," a category first introduced into international law at Nuremberg.

IMAGE

Liberating the Concentration Camps

The Home Front: The Other Wars

■ **What did total war mean on the home front?**

As the Holocaust made vividly clear, for many Europeans during World War II the home front was not a place of safety or normalcy but a place where other wars were fought. The spreading resistance against the Nazi regime, as well as bombing raids and forced labor obligations, obliterated the distinction between combatant and noncombatant, blurred gender roles, and provoked calls for radical social change.

The Limits of Resistance

Throughout the war individuals and groups in occupied Europe performed heroically, hiding Jews and others on the run, sabotaging equipment, disrupting transportation systems, and relaying secret information to the Allies. In the Soviet Union and in mountainous regions of Yugoslavia, Italy, and southern France, where the terrain offered shelter for guerillas, anti-Nazi fighters formed partisan groups that attacked German army units. In one of the best-known cases of resistance, the Jews in the Warsaw ghetto rose up in the spring of 1943. Armed with only one or two submachine guns and a scattering of pistols, rifles, hand grenades, and gasoline bombs, Jewish fighters held off the far superior German military force for more than a month. In the

Mass Grave at Bergen-Belsen

British soldiers liberated the camp of Bergen-Belsen on April 15, 1945. For many prisoners, however, death provided their only "liberation." The Allies forced German civilians living in the regions around camps such as these to view the mass graves, in an effort to compel them to face up to their passive participation in the Holocaust. Few Germans accepted responsibility.

end, however, the ghetto was leveled, and all its survivors deported to Nazi death camps.

Both men and women participated in the Resistance, the struggle against Nazi rule. In Yugoslavia, 100,000 women fought as soldiers in the partisan ranks: 25,000 were killed and 40,000 injured. Most women in the Resistance were not in combat units. Instead, they played gender stereotypes to great advantage: They hid bombs in baby carriages, tucked vital messages under their shopping, disarmed Germans with feminine charm. One Italian partisan used to catch rides on German trucks to deliver her illegal communications: "What was there to fear? You only had to give them a few smiles."[10] With men at risk of being rounded up for forced labor in Germany, women often shouldered the burden of distributing clandestine publications, delivering supplies and arms, and finding safe houses.

But only a minority of Europeans, men or women, fought in the Resistance. As the Dutch historian Louis de Jong has noted of European actions and attitudes under Nazi occupation, "Unwilling adjustment was the rule, intentional resistance the exception."[11] Why did so few Europeans join the Resistance? Important factors include the Germans' military might, their success at infiltrating Resistance organizations, and their willingness to use brutal force to crush any threat. The German network of concentration camps throughout occupied Europe possessed enormous deterrent value. Concerned for their own and their families' safety, most Europeans hoped simply to keep their heads down and survive the war.

The German practice of exacting collective retribution for Resistance actions particularly undercut mass support for anti-German efforts. In 1942, for example, British intelligence forces parachuted Czech agents into German-held Czechoslovakia. The agents assassinated the chief SS official in the region, Reinhard Heydrich (1904–1942), but they were immediately betrayed by one of their own. In retaliation, the Germans massacred the entire population of the village of Lidice. Similarly, an assassination attempt against Hitler in 1944 led to mass arrests and the executions of an estimated 5,000 Germans.

In Germany itself and in countries allied to rather than conquered by the Germans, potential resisters had to convince themselves that patriotism demanded working against their own government. In France until 1943, resistance meant opposing the lawfully instituted but collaborationist Vichy government of Marshal Pétain. As a World War I hero, Pétain had an almost godlike reputation in France and was popular even with those who did not share his authoritarian conservatism. As a result, in the early years of the war many French men and women viewed the members of the Resistance as traitors against France, rather than as heroes fighting against the Nazis. By 1943, however, an alternative focus of national loyalty had emerged: the Free French headed by General Charles De Gaulle (1890–1970), a career military man who had gone into exile rather than accept the armistice with Nazi Germany. After the Anglo-American landing in North Africa in November 1942, De Gaulle claimed Algeria as a power base and declared himself

The Trial of Adolf Eichmann

On May 23, 1960, David Ben-Gurion (1886–1973), the prime minister of Israel, made a spectacular announcement: Israeli secret service agents had kidnapped Adolf Eichmann, a wanted Nazi war criminal, and smuggled him into Israel to await trial. Eichmann, the head of the Gestapo's Jewish Affairs unit, had implemented Nazi policies on Jewish emigration and deportation. His office sorted through the complicated bureaucratic procedures to ensure that the trains laden with Jews kept to their schedules and delivered their human cargo to the gas chambers on time. It was to Eichmann that Jewish leaders came to plead for emigration visas and for work permits. It was with Eichmann that Jewish leaders negotiated about the timing, size, and composition of deportations. For many Jews, then, Eichmann represented German power and came to personify Nazi evil. He had disappeared in the chaotic final days of World War II and eventually made his way to Argentina, where, as "Ricardo Klement," he lived a quiet, respectable life with his wife and children—until 1960.

From the moment of Ben-Gurion's sensational announcement, the Eichmann case occupied the attention of the world. Six hundred foreign correspondents attended the trial, which was one of the first to be filmed by television cameras. More than 1,500 documents were submitted and 120 witnesses testified in the 114 sessions held between April 11 and August 14, 1961. Three judges, each of whom had been born in Germany and had emigrated to Palestine in 1933, heard the evidence. On December 15, they sentenced Eichmann to death. He died by hanging on May 31, 1962, the first execution in Israel, which had abolished capital punishment for all crimes except genocide.

The Eichmann trial told the story of Jewish suffering during World War II to the widest possible audience. Both Ben-Gurion and the chief prosecutor, Gideon Hausner, stated publicly that the trial aimed to construct "a living record of a gigantic human and national disaster," and so educate both young Israelis and the entire world in the causes and consequences of the Holocaust.[12] As Hausner explained in his emotional opening statement, he saw himself as the spokesman for "six million accusers . . . [whose] ashes were piled up in the hills of Auschwitz and in the fields of Treblinka, or washed away by the rivers of Poland."[13] Hausner (who, like many Israelis, had lost most of his relatives in the Nazi death camps) called more than 100 witnesses, many of them death camp survivors. Their testimony, published or broadcast throughout the world, painted an unforgettable and detailed picture of the horror of genocide.

By the time the prosecution rested its case, no one could doubt that Eichmann was a guilty man, one who had played an essential role in the murder of millions. Yet the Eichmann trial attracted an enormous amount of criticism and continues to arouse great controversy. Critics charged that to achieve moral justice for Holocaust victims and survivors, the Israeli court committed a legal injustice against Eichmann. The trial was not only made possible by a violation of international law (Eichmann's kidnapping), it also was filled with irregularities, including the introduction of testimony that did not pertain to the specific crimes charged. Critics also disputed Israel's legal right to try Eichmann: The crimes had not occurred in Israeli territory, nor were Eichmann's victims Israeli citizens. (Israel did not exist until 1948.)

In reply to these critics, Hausner and other supporters of the prosecution insisted that justice demanded that Eichmann be brought to trial, and that the Israeli government had pursued the only course of action open to it. In the Eichmann trial, then, we confront a case in which what was legal on the one hand and what was just on the other appeared very much at odds. There is no doubt that Eichmann was guilty of horrendous crimes; there is also no doubt that the Israeli government stepped beyond the boundaries of international law in kidnapping Eichmann.

The Eichmann trial also raised important questions about the nature of the Holocaust. Was it a crime perpetrated by a few very evil men, or did the evil penetrate deep into German, and European, society? The prosecution's case sought to depict Eichmann as a monster, a brilliant and demonic mastermind responsible for the deaths of millions of Jews. As Hausner contended, "it was [Eichmann's] word that put gas chambers into action; he lifted the telephone, and railway trains left for the extermination centers; his signature it was that sealed the doom of tens of thousands."[14] Such a depiction provided a comforting explanation for the Holocaust—it was perpetrated not by ordinary human beings but by monstrous devils.

Yet many trial observers and subsequent historians argued that such a depiction was simply wrong. This argument appeared in forceful terms in the most well-known critique of the prosecution—Hannah Arendt's *Eichmann in Jerusalem: A Report on the Banality of Evil,* published in 1963. Arendt (1906–1975), a Jewish philosopher who had fled Nazi Europe in 1941, argued that the evidence provided in the trial

Eichmann sits on the left in a cage of bulletproof glass.

The three judges hear the case from the high table on the right.

Eichmann on Trial

showed Eichmann to be a fairly commonplace man, motivated by ambition as much as by ideology, a rather plodding bureaucrat obsessed with trivial details—in other words, an ordinary man, capable of extraordinary evil.

Must ordinary men be held responsible for following evil orders? This is the final question raised by the Eichmann trial. Defense attorney Robert Servatius insisted that the Holocaust was an "act of state," a crime carried out by a political regime, for which no civil servant could bear the blame. Eichmann only followed orders. Servatius concluded his arguments by asking Eichmann how he viewed "this question of guilt." Eichmann replied,

Where there is no responsibility, there can be no guilt. . . .

The questions of responsibility and conscience are for the leadership of the state. . . . I condemn and regret the act of extermination of the Jews which the leadership of the German state ordered. But I myself could not jump over my own shadow. I was a tool in the hands of superior powers and authorities.[15]

Eichmann's judges disagreed. In declaring Eichmann guilty of genocide, they argued,

We reject absolutely the accused's version that he was nothing more than a "small cog" in the extermination machine. . . . He was not a puppet in the hands of others. His place was among those who pulled the strings.[16]

Questions of Justice

1. Even if Eichmann's assertion that he was simply "a tool in the hands of superior powers and authorities" could be proven correct, to what degree was he culpable for his actions?

2. In the Eichmann case, the letter of the law and justice appeared to be at odds. In what situations—if any—must the law be broken to ensure that justice prevails? Who has the authority to make such a judgment?

Taking It Further

Laqueur, Walter. "Hannah Arendt in Jerusalem: The Controversy Revisited," in Lyman H. Legters, ed., *Western Society After the Holocaust.* 1983. Examines the impact of Arendt's critique of the trial.

The Trial of Adolf Eichmann: Record of Proceedings in the District Court of Jerusalem. Vols. 1–9. 1993–1995. The basic primary source.

the head of a Free French provisional government. French patriots could declare themselves loyal to this alternative government and fight in the Resistance against both Nazi rule and Vichy collaboration.

In many areas—for example, much of Italy after the German army occupied the country in 1943—a genuine spirit of unity characterized the Resistance struggle, with socialists, communists, and Catholics working together not only to defeat the Nazis but also to create the foundations of a better society. In other areas, divisions within the Resistance limited its impact. Conservative army officers fighting to preserve the prewar status quo clashed with guerilla groups that espoused radical political goals. Fighting among Resistance factions shaded into civil war. In Ukraine, nationalists fought against communist partisans as well as the Germans. In Greece, the communist-dominated National Liberation Front battled not only the Nazis but also a rival Resistance group, the royalist National Greek Democratic Union.

Civil War in Yugoslavia

The fiercest struggle occurred in Yugoslavia, where political and ethnic divisions split both the country and the Resistance. Wartime Yugoslavia experienced a bloodletting unmatched anywhere in Europe except in the German-occupied regions of Poland and the Soviet Union. Parts of the country such as Slovenia and Macedonia were occupied by German or German-allied armies and endured brutal repression. The scale of violence peaked in the fascist state of Croatia, created after the German invasion of 1941. This Nazi-sponsored regime immediately embarked on a savage program of ethnic homogenization, with a ferocious campaign of terror against Jews, Bosnian Muslims, and Serbs.

In Yugoslavia, therefore, the Resistance was not simply or even primarily aimed at the Germans. Guerilla bands of Serbian soldiers called *Chetniks* supported the now-exiled Yugoslav monarchy and regarded the Croatian regime as their main enemy, although, like the Croatian fascists, the Chetniks also slaughtered both Muslims and Jews. In the midst of this bloody free-for-all, a second Resistance group emerged, one based not on ethnicity but on political ideology. Led by communist Josip Broz (1892–1980), alias "Tito," these partisans saw the war as a chance for social revolution and promised equality for all in a reunited Yugoslavia. Tito's partisans focused on fighting Germans (diverting ten German divisions from the eastern front), but they also fought their fellow Yugoslavs, with the royalist Chetniks fiercely opposing Tito's aim of a communist state.

Tito's partisans won the civil war. In 1944 they fought alongside the Soviet army and liberated Yugoslavia from German control. With 90 percent of the vote in the first postwar election, Tito assumed control of the new communist state of Yugoslavia, a position he held for the next thirty-five years. Beneath the uniform surface created by communist ideology, however, the jagged edges of ethnic division remained sharp.

Under Occupation

In occupied Europe, Nazi racial ideology shaped the experience of both soldiers and civilians. The Nazis drew a sharp line between the peoples of western Europe—the Dutch, Norwegian, Danes, and Flemish, all considered of racially superior "Germanic stock"—and the Slavs of eastern Europe. The ferocity of Nazi brutality increased exponentially in the eastern occupied regions.

The German treatment of prisoners of war (POWs) illustrates the contrast between the western and eastern European experience during World War II. By the end of 1941, 2.5 million Soviet soldiers had been captured. By February 1942, two million of these had died, both from starvation and from epidemic diseases nurtured by the poor conditions in the camps. In contrast, of the more than one million French soldiers captured by the Germans in 1940, nineteen out of twenty returned home at the end of the war. When dealing with western European POWs, the Germans abided by international rules; in eastern Europe, World War II was a game without rules and without limits.

The German occupation of western Europe was less heavy-handed than in the east, particularly during the first half of the war. The Nazis believed that "Germanic" peoples such as the Dutch could be taught to become good Nazis and therefore spared them the extreme violence and mindless brutality that characterized the German occupation in the east. Moreover, in western Europe the Germans sought to work with rather than to annihilate political and economic elites. For example, in both Belgium and the Netherlands civil servants continued to do their prewar jobs. Nonetheless, the German occupation in the west, even in the first two years of the war, was far from lenient. The Nazis forced occupied countries to pay exorbitant sums to cover the costs of their own occupation. In addition, they were required to sell both manufactured products and raw materials to Germany at artificially low prices. Anyone who spoke out against the Nazis faced imprisonment or death. The occupation grew even more harsh after 1943 as German military losses piled up, stocks of food and essential supplies dwindled, and German demands for civilian labor increased.

For millions of European men and women, the war meant forced labor in Germany. With the need to free up German men for the front lines, the Nazis faced crucial labor shortages in almost every sector of the economy. Placing the economy on an all-out war footing would have meant imposing unpopular measures such as the conscrip-

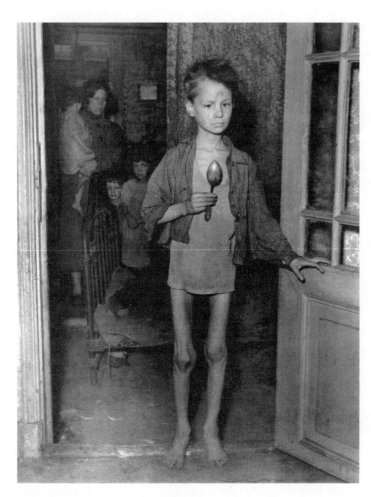

The *Hongerwinter*
By the fall of 1944, the southern provinces of the Netherlands were liberated, but the north remained under German occupation. After Dutch railway employees refused to transport any more German troops, the Germans retaliated by blocking all food shipments to the north. Twenty thousand Dutch civilians died in the resulting "Hunger Winter."

tion of women for industrial labor, lengthening working hours, and prohibiting holidays. The Nazis chose instead to recruit labor from conquered territories. Within days of the invasion of Poland, Polish POWs were working in German fields. By August 1944, German farmers and factory owners employed over 5.7 million foreign civilian laborers (one-third of whom were women) and almost two million POWs. These foreign workers accounted for more than half the labor in German agriculture and in German munitions plants and one-third of the labor force in key war industries such as mining, chemicals, and metals.

Hostile, hungry, and often untrained for the jobs in which they were placed, foreign workers proved to be less productive than German laborers. Nevertheless, foreign labor played a crucial role in wartime Germany, not only in fueling the German war machine but also in maintaining German civilian morale. Foreign labor cushioned German civilians from the impact of total war and reassured them that they belonged to a superior race. Many German factory owners were relieved to find they now had a labor force with few political rights. The director of one aircraft manufacturing firm explained, "The great advantage of employing foreigners . . . is that we only have to give orders. There

is no refusal, no need to negotiate."[17] The labor of foreigners also benefited the German working class. Nazi regulations stipulated that German workers were to regard themselves as the masters of the foreign laborers working alongside them. Thus ordinary Germans held positions of privilege and power. Some families even found themselves able to afford new luxuries. Beginning in 1942, the Nazi regime brought Russian women into Germany to serve as maids in German households. As a result, according to a report in January 1943, "even those households with many children, whose financial situation previously did not permit them to hire domestic help, can now afford to maintain a worker."[18]

The Women's War

As we have seen, women joined the ranks of the Resistance and were forced to labor in German industries. Women also tended to bear the brunt of home front deprivation, as they were the ones who had to get a meal on the table and clothe their children in the face of severe rationing. Basic household goods such as frying pans, toothbrushes, bicycle tires,

Some Women's War
British women did not have to endure the hell of Nazi occupation or forced labor. They did, however, participate fully in the war effort. Only the Soviet Union mobilized its women more completely.

baby bottles, and batteries almost disappeared; food was in short supply; clothing had to be recycled. It was Europe's women who became experts at "make do and mend," as British government pamphlets advised.

British women were fully mobilized. They did not serve in combat, but they were drafted for service in civilian defense, war-related industry, or the armed forces. Women accounted for 25 percent of the civilians who worked in Britain's Air Raid Protection services as wardens, rescuers, and telephone operators. All citizens—male or female—working less than 55 hours per week had to perform compulsory fire-watching duties from 1941 on. The numbers of women employed in male-dominated industries such as metals and chemicals rose dramatically.

Only the Soviet Union mobilized women more fully than Britain. Soviet women constituted 80 percent of the agricultural and 50 percent of the industrial labor force. All Soviet adult men and women under age 45 who were not engaged in essential war work were required to work eleven hours a day constructing defenses. Unlike in Britain,

Russian women also served in combat. By 1944, 246,000 women were in front-line units. For all Soviet citizens, male and female, life on the home front meant endless labor, inadequate food supplies, and constant surveillance under martial law. Stalin demanded an all-out war against not only the German invaders but also anyone at home who undermined the war effort in any way. The Soviet government established a compulsory sixty-hour workweek and issued ration cards only to those who worked.

Until 1943, the German home front contrasted sharply with that of Britain and the Soviet Union. The Nazi policy toward female employment rested on Hitler's conviction that Germany had lost World War I in part because of the collapse of morale on the home front. As a result, Hitler placed a high priority on maintaining civilian morale. Generous allowances for soldiers meant that their wives, unlike in Britain, did not have to work to feed their families. In the first years of the war, the Nazi government rationed clothing and food supplies but did not dramatically cut consumption levels. Moreover, Hitler hesitated to conscript middle-class German women for industrial labor. For Hitler, ideology came before economics. He believed that the future of the "German race" depended on middle-class women being protected from the strains of paid labor so that they could bear healthy Aryan babies.

In Germany the use of foreign labor took the place of the full-scale mobilization of women. Top-ranking Nazis explicitly linked the use of foreign workers to gender considerations. At the end of 1941, for example, Hermann Göring (1893–1946) announced that Soviet workers would be brought into Germany to guarantee "that in future, the German women should not be so much in evidence in the work process."[19] The number of women in the German workforce actually fell by 500,000 between 1939 and 1941. German women who did work were prohibited from working long hours or at night, and from performing heavy physical labor. Instead, eastern European workers (many of them women) were given the tough jobs and the poor hours. At the Krupp metalworks factory, for example, German women worked for six hours at light jobs during the day; Russian women did the heavy labor during the twelve-hour night shift.

Military necessity eventually undercut Nazi gender ideology. The fall of Stalingrad marked a turning point in Nazi policy toward German women at work. With losses on the eastern front averaging 150,000 men per month, the German army desperately needed more men. At the same time, the German war economy demanded more workers. In response, Hitler's deputy Joseph Goebbels (1897–1945) declared that Germany must fight a total war, which meant total mobilization of the home front. The final, desperate year of the war saw a concentrated use of female labor in Nazi Germany.

Of all the combatant states, the United States stands out as unique with regard to the home front. The United States never fully mobilized its economy, and more than 70 percent of its adult women remained outside the paid workforce. Rationing was comparatively minimal and consumption levels in the United States high. In fact, for many families, the war years brought prosperity after years of economic depression. But most important, American cities were never bombed, and thus the United States was able to maintain a clear distinction between soldier and civilian, man and woman—a distinction that was blurred in other combatant nations.

What Are We Fighting For?

To mobilize their populations for total war, governments had to convince their citizens of the importance of the war effort. Maintaining morale and motivating both civilians and soldiers to endure deprivation and danger demanded that leaders supply a persuasive answer to the question: What are we fighting for?

Myth Making and Morale Building

All nations—democratic or authoritarian—rely on myths, on stories of national origins and identity, to unify disparate individuals, classes, and groups. In times of total war, such myths become crucial. During World War II, the process of myth making was institutionalized by government agencies responsible for propaganda. In Britain, the newly formed Ministry of Information (democracies tend to shy away from using the word *propaganda*) took on the task of propping up civilian morale. Staffed by upper-class men, the MOI's efforts often betrayed its class composition: Many of its posters and leaflets adopted a hectoring tone, subjecting ordinary citizens to a barrage of do's and don'ts. Far more effective were the speeches of Prime Minister Winston Churchill, whose romantic vision of Britain as a still-great power destined to triumph was exactly the myth that the beleaguered British needed. In Germany, strict censorship had already subordinated the arts and entertainment industries to the demands of the state. The war heightened this control as censorship tightened even further, paper shortages limited the production of books and periodicals, and the threat of being drafted for the eastern front kept artists in line.

In all the combatant nations, governments enlisted artists, entertainers, and the technologies of the mass media for myth making and morale building. The British artist Henry Moore's (1898–1986) drawings of ordinary people in air raid shelters (completed under an official

commission) evoke the survival of civilized values in the midst of unspeakable degradation. Perhaps the most famous musical work from the war is Dmitri Shostakovich's (1906–1975) *Seventh Symphony*—now universally known as the *Leningrad Symphony* and a symbol of human resilience. Shostakovich composed the early drafts of this work in Leningrad while German shells were falling, and it was actually performed in Leningrad in August 1942, while the city was still under siege.

During the war, film came into its own as an artistic form capable of creating important myths of national unity. Laurence Olivier's version of Shakespeare's *Henry V* (1944) comforted British moviegoers with its classic story of a stirring English military victory against huge odds. In Italy, a group of filmmakers known as the Neo-Realists created a set of films that dramatized the Resistance spirit of national unity. Shot on location, with amateur actors and realistic sets, films such as Roberto Rossellini's *Open City* (1945) depicted lower-class life with honesty and respect and called for the creation of a better society from the rubble of the old.

Planning for Reconstruction

Rossellini's call for the creation of a new society was echoed throughout Europe during the war. Across Europe a consensus emerged on the need for *social democracy*, a society in which the state intervenes in economic life to ensure both public welfare and social justice. As early as December 1942, a government committee set out a radical plan for a new Britain. In rather unusual language for an official document, the committee's report identified "five giants on the road to reconstruction": Want, Disease, Ignorance, Squalor, and Idleness. To slay these giants, the committee recommended that the state assume responsibility for ensuring full employment and a minimum standard of living for all through the provision of family allowances, social welfare programs, and a national health service. The Beveridge Report (named after the committee's chairman) became a bestseller in Britain and the basis for a number of postwar European social welfare plans. Churchill, however, reacted lukewarmly to its proposals—a major reason for his defeat in the election of June 1945. The Labour Party, which enthusiastically endorsed the Beveridge Report and campaigned with slogans such as "Fair Shares for All," won by a landslide. Similarly, Charles De Gaulle found that in order for his Free French Committee to be recognized as the provisional government of France, he had to display a commitment to democracy and radical social reform. Thus he espoused women's suffrage, and his government promised not only free medical services and expanded family allowances, but also the nationalization of key industries and economic planning.

Four factors explain this radical reorientation of European politics. First, and most important, as the war dragged on and the death tolls mounted, European men

Wartime Gains

British children began enjoying free school milk during the war, as part of the state's efforts both to ensure equitable distribution of resources and to shore up the health of the population. Popular sentiment demanded that such communal efforts be continued in peacetime as well.

and women demanded that their suffering be worthwhile. They wanted to know that they were fighting not to rebuild the depressed and divided societies of the 1930s, but to construct a new Europe. Second, the war (and the ongoing revelations of Nazi atrocities) completely discredited the politics of the far right. This sort of politics, whether fascist, Nazi, or conservative-authoritarian, disappeared from legitimate political discussion. But in Europe (although not in the United States) the liberal ideal of the free and self-interested individual competing in an unregulated economy also lay in ruins, the victim of the prewar Great Depression. The new Europe, then, had to be built along different lines. The third factor that explains the radical reorientation of European politics was the combatant nations' success in mobilizing their economies for total war. If governments could regulate economies to fight wars, why could they not regulate economies for peacetime prosperity? Finally, the important role of socialists and communists in the Resistance enhanced the respectability of radical political ideas. Out of the Resistance came a determination to break the mold of prewar politics and create a new Europe. In France, for example, the Resistance Charter of 1944 demanded the construction of a "more just social order" through the nationalization of key industries, the establishment of a comprehensive social security system, and the recognition of the rights of workers to participate in management.

More generally, the Resistance raised key questions about the role of the individual in modern society. In the 1930s, many Europeans had been persuaded by Hitler, Mussolini, and other far-right theorists that the individual was not important, that only the state mattered. But what the Resistance revealed is the power of human choice and the need for individual action in a world run amok. Despite—even because of—the horrors of the war, Europeans such as the French writer Albert Camus (1913–1960) emerged convinced of the power of human action: "A pessimist with respect to the human condition, I am an optimist with respect to man." Thus democracy reclaimed the activist state from fascism and Nazism on the one hand, and Stalinism on the other. Europeans saw that the power of the state could be used to improve the well-being of its citizens without at the same time trampling on the rights of the individual.

Conclusion

The New West: After Auschwitz and the Atom Bomb

The wartime encounter with the Nazi vision of the West as a race-based authoritarian order was crucial; from it emerged a sharpened commitment within the West to the processes and values of democracy. But to present the Second World War as a conflict between democracy and Nazism is to oversimplify. To defeat Nazi Germany, the democracies of Britain and the United States allied with Stalin's Soviet Union, a dictatorial regime that matched Hitler's Germany in its contempt for democratic values and human rights and that surpassed it in state-sanctioned mass murder.

The Soviet Union emerged from the war as the dominant power in eastern Europe; as we will see in the next chapter, the presence of the Red Army obliterated any chance to establish democratic governments in this region. The tensions inherent in the Anglo-American alliance with the Soviets led directly to the Cold War, the ideological and political conflict that dominated the post-World War II world and that once again forced a redefinition of the West. From 1949 until 1989, it was easy to draw the West on any map: One simply shaded in the United States and the countries allied to it—and against the Soviet Union. At the same time, however, a new division emerged. World War II marked the beginning of the end of European imperial control over the non-European world. The postwar era would thus see growing tensions between "North" and "South"—between the industrially developed nations and the underdeveloped regions seeking to shrug off their colonial past.

Much of the impetus for imperial control over non-European regions had come from the conviction of Western supremacy. During World War II, however, Japanese victories had exposed the illusion of Western military invincibility. And after the war, the gradual realization of the full horror of the Holocaust demolished any lingering claim to Western cultural superiority. What sort of superior position could be claimed by a culture in which educated, supposedly civilized men sent children into gas chambers disguised as showers? The atomic bombings of Hiroshima and Nagasaki added more questions to the ongoing debate about the meaning of the West. With the best of intentions, some of the greatest minds in the Western world had produced weapons designed to kill and maim tens of thousands of civilians within seconds. Had Western technology outdistanced Western ethics? And what about the implications of such technologies in a democratic society? For example, would the need to control such weapons lead to measures that eroded individual freedoms? Thus the assembly-line techniques of mass murder developed by the Nazis and, in very different ways, the sheer efficiency of the atom bomb in obliterating urban populations forced both individuals and their political leaders to confront the destructive potential of Western industrialism. For centuries, the use of the methods of scientific inquiry to uncover truth and achieve both material and moral progress had supported Westerners' self-identification and their sense of cultural superiority. But World War II demonstrated that the best of science could produce the worst of weapons, that technology and technique could combine in the death factory. The task of accepting this knowledge, and facing up to its implications, helped shape Western culture after 1945.

Suggestions for Further Reading

For a comprehensive listing of suggested readings, please go to www.ablongman.com/levack2e/chapter26

Alperovitz, Gar. *Atomic Diplomacy: Hiroshima and Potsdam. The Use of the Atomic Bomb and the American Confrontation with Soviet Power.* 1994. The first edition of this book, published in 1965, sparked an ongoing scholarly debate about the role of Cold War concerns in shaping U.S. decision making at the end of World War II.

Browning, Christopher. *Ordinary Men: Reserve Police Battalion 101 and the Final Solution in Poland.* 1992. A powerful account of the participation of a group of "ordinary men" in mass murder.

Calder, Angus. *The People's War: Britain, 1939–1945.* 1969. Lengthy—but worth the effort for students wishing to explore the war's impact on British society. (Those who want a shorter account can turn to Robert Mackay, *The Test of War: Inside Britain 1939–45* [1999].)

Frayn, Michael. *Copenhagen.* 1998. A remarkable play in which Frayn dramatizes a meeting (that actually did occur) between the German atomic physicist Werner Heisenberg and his Danish anti-Nazi colleague Niels Bohr. Contains both extremely clear explanations of the workings of atomic physics and a provocative exploration of the moral issues involved in the making of the atom bomb.

Friedlander, Saul. *Nazi Germany and the Jews, 1933–1939.* 1998. An important study of the evolution of Nazi anti-Semitic policy before the war.

Hilberg, Raul. *Perpetrators, Victims, Bystanders: The Jewish Catastrophe, 1933–1945.* 1992. As his title indicates, Hilberg looks at the three principal sets of participants in the Holocaust.

Iriye, Akira. *The Origins of the Second World War in Asia and the Pacific.* 1987. Part of Longman's "Origins of Modern Wars" series aimed at university students, this short and readable study highlights the major issues and events.

Keegan, John. *The Second World War.* 1989. Provides clear explanations of military technologies and techniques; packed with useful maps and vivid illustrations.

Kitchen, Martin. *Nazi Germany at War.* 1995. A short and nicely organized survey of the German home front.

Marrus, Michael R. *The Holocaust in History.* 1987. A clearly written, concise account of historians' efforts to understand the Holocaust. Highly recommended.

Moore, Bob, ed. *Resistance in Western Europe.* 2000. A collection of essays that explores recent research on this controversial topic.

Overy, Richard. *Russia's War: A History of the Soviet War Effort, 1941–1945.* 1997. A compelling account, written to accompany the television documentary *Russia's War.*

Paxton, Robert. *Vichy France: Old Guard and New Order, 1940–1944.* 1972. A now-classic study of the aims and evolution of France's collaborationist government.

Rhodes, Richard. *The Making of the Atomic Bomb.* 1986. A lengthy but very readable account; very good at explaining the complicated science involved.

Rhodes, Richard. *Masters of Death: The SS-Einsatzgruppen and the Invention of the Holocaust.* 2002. Compelling account of the Einsatzgruppen actions during the German invasion of the Soviet Union.

Rock, William R. *British Appeasement in the 1930s.* 1977. A balanced and concise appraisal.

Weinberg, Gerhard. *A World at Arms: A Global History of World War II.* 1994. Places the war within a global rather than simply a European context.

Notes

1. Quoted in Robert H. Abzug, *Inside the Vicious Heart: Americans and the Liberation of Nazi Concentration Camps* (1985), 19.

2. Quoted in Gordon Horwitz, *In the Shadow of Death: Living Outside the Gates of Mauthausen* (1991), 167.

3. Quoted in Piers Brendon, *The Dark Valley: A Panorama of the 1930s* (2000), 282.

4. Quoted in Richard Overy, *Russia's War* (1998), 95.

5. Quoted in Mark Mazower, *Dark Continent: Europe's Twentieth Century* (1999), 157.

6. Quoted in Peter Clarke, *Hope and Glory: Britain, 1900–1990* (1996), 204.

7. Quoted in Joachim Fest, *Hitler* (1973), 665.

8. Quotations from Juliet Gardiner, *"Over Here"—The GIs in Wartime Britain* (1992), 62, 53, 132.

9. Quoted in Richard Rhodes, *The Making of the Atomic Bomb* (1988), 474.

10. Quoted in Jane Slaughter, *Women in the Italian Resistance 1943–1945* (1997), 63.

11. Quoted in Bob Moore, ed., *Resistance in Western Europe* (2000), 210.

12. Gideon Hausner, *Justice in Jerusalem* (1966), 291.

13. Ibid., 323–324.

14. From Hausner's opening statement; quoted in Moshe Pearlman, *The Capture and Trial of Adolf Eichmann* (1963), 149.

15. Ibid., 463–465.

16. Ibid., 603; Hausner, *Justice in Jerusalem,* 422.

17. Quoted in Ulrich Herbert, *Hitler's Foreign Workers* (1997), 306.

18. Ibid., 149, 189.

19. Ibid., 149.

Redefining the West After World War II

27

ON ONE APPARENTLY ORDINARY DAY IN AUGUST 1961, WESTERN European television viewers witnessed an extraordinary sight. While the news cameras rolled, policemen from East Berlin—the section of Berlin controlled by East Germany's communist government—played tug-of-war with firemen from West Berlin, the half of the city that belonged to the democratic state of West Germany. Between them was not a length of rope, but rather a middle-aged German woman. This horrifying contest had been set in motion by the construction of the Berlin Wall. Appalled by the growing numbers of East German citizens who were fleeing communist rule through the gateway of West Berlin, the East German and Soviet authorities decided to shut the gate. In the early morning hours of August 13, East German workers erected a barbed-wire fence along Berlin's east-west dividing line. In some cases, this line ran right through apartment buildings. For the next few weeks, these apartments provided literal "windows to the west." West Berlin firemen waited with blankets ready to catch anyone willing to jump out of a window—and out of communist eastern Europe. The woman caught on camera was one of a number of Berliners who sought to jump out a window in search of freedom.

These windows closed quickly. The communist authorities bricked them up; later they leveled entire apartment buildings to create a moat in front of what was now the armed fortress of East Berlin. The barbed-wire fence became a concrete wall buttressed by gun towers, lit by searchlights, and patrolled by armed guards with "shoot to kill" orders.

The unidentified woman literally caught between West and East serves as an appropriate symbol for Europe during the 1950s and 1960s. In these decades, the Cold War between the United States and the Soviet Union influenced European politics, culture, and society. European governments and their populations found their freedom of maneuver checked by Cold War constraints. The woman's desperation to reach the West reminds us that American influence in western Europe should not be equated with Soviet

No! The fear of nuclear war colored the post–World War II decades, as this 1958 poster from the Soviet Union attests.

Tug-of-War at the Berlin Wall
Caught by the television cameras, this woman sought to escape through her window into West Berlin. She succeeded.

Significantly, the Cold War turned "hot" not in Europe but in places such as Korea, Cuba, and Vietnam. The developing world served as the site of crucial Cold War conflicts in this era. The postwar years witnessed the widening of the economic gap between "North" and "South"—between the industrialized nations, largely located in the Northern Hemisphere, and the economically underdeveloped regions (many but certainly not all of which were situated south of the equator), now shrugging off colonial rule and seeking both political independence and economic prosperity. Thus, as Europeans encountered each other across the Cold War divide, they also encountered non-Europeans across a huge economic gulf. Two very different contests—North versus South and West versus East—quickly became entangled with each other as the Cold War moved beyond Europe's borders to the developing regions.

To explore the impact of these encounters on the postwar West, this chapter addresses four questions:

- Why and how did the world step from World War II to the Cold War?
- What was the impact of decolonization and the Cold War on the global balance of power?
- What patterns characterized the history of the Soviet Union and eastern Europe after the death of Stalin?
- What patterns characterized the history of western Europe in the 1950s and 1960s?

A Dubious Peace, 1945–1949

- Why and how did the world step from World War II to the Cold War?

World War II ended in the spring of 1945, but the killing did not. Postwar purges and deportations ensured that the death totals continued to mount, while in many regions, world war gave way to civil war. Most significantly, as the "hot" war waned, the Cold War between the Soviet Union and the countries it controlled, and the United States and its Western allies, began.

Devastation, Death, and Continuing War

If there was peace in Europe and Asia in 1945, it was the "peace of a graveyard," with an estimated 55 million people dead. In the immediate postwar period, the death statistics continued to rise as the victors turned with vengeful fury against the vanquished. In Czechoslovakia, purges killed 30,000 collaborators between 1945 and 1948. In Yugoslavia, Tito ordered the massacre of anticommunists. No one

control of eastern Europe: Cultural and economic dominance are not the same as political tyranny. Nevertheless, many Europeans in the West as well as the East felt that they no longer controlled their own societies.

The Cold War was in part an encounter of two clashing ideologies, as much a battle of ideas and values as weapons and warriors. Both sides laid claim to universal cultures—to have achieved a way of life that would benefit *all* human societies. This ideological encounter forced a redefinition of "the West." Previous chapters have described the way in which this cultural construct shifted over time. By the late nineteenth century, Christianity, although still important, played a less central role in defining "the West" than did a mix of other factors, including the possession of industrial technology, the illusion of white superiority based on pseudoscientific racist theorizing, and faith in both capitalist economics and liberal political values. The Cold War added an anti-Soviet stance and a fear of communist ideology to the mix. These additions at times eroded the Western commitment to democracy, particularly within the developing world.

knows how many died; some estimates range as high as 60,000.

Those left alive faced the overwhelming task of reconstruction. Throughout Europe, the bombers had rendered most highways, rail tracks, and waterways unusable. With laborers, seed, fertilizer, and basic equipment all in short supply, agricultural production in 1945 stood below 50 percent of prewar levels. Less visible, but just as devastating, was the destruction of the financial system. Few European currencies were worth much. In occupied Germany, cigarettes replaced marks as the unit of exchange.

One of the most serious problems facing Europe was that of the refugees or displaced persons (DPs). The war, and Hitler's attempt at racial reordering, had uprooted millions from their homes. The DP problem grew even larger as a result of the peace settlement. The Soviet Union kept the Polish territories it had claimed in 1939 and Poland received a large chunk of what had been prewar Germany. The new Polish government then expelled the German inhabitants from this region. In Czechoslovakia, Romania, Yugoslavia, and Hungary, too, ethnic Germans were forced out. More than 11 million Germans suffered from these

Map 27.1 Europe in the Cold War

As this map shows, during the Cold War the "West" was defined culturally and politically, rather than in geographic terms. Greece and Turkey stand far to the east in Europe, yet their membership in NATO placed both within the "West."

deportations. As many as two million died en route to Germany. In addition, between 1945 and 1948, eastern European governments forcibly transferred seven million non-German refugees, in a brutal solution to the ethnic divisions that had destabilized prewar political structures.

Forced deportation can be understood as a continuation of war—a war carried out by governments against groups marked as dangerous because of their ethnic makeup. Other forms of war also continued after 1945. Ukrainian nationalists kept up a guerilla war against the Soviets until the early 1950s. In Greece civil war between communist and anticommunist forces raged until 1949, while in Trieste (along the Italian-Yugoslav border) civil war continued until 1954. In the forests and marshes of Poland, anticommunist guerilla groups fought against the new communist regime until 1956.

The Cold War
Military
Stand-off

From Hot to Cold War

The conflict that aroused the most alarm and posed the greatest threat to the dubious peace after 1945 was the Cold War°, the struggle for global supremacy between the United States and the Soviet Union.

Within just a few years of the defeat of Germany and Japan, the allies became enemies, and what Winston Churchill called an "Iron Curtain" dropped between eastern and western Europe. The divisions of the Cold War were rooted in World War II, nurtured by the fears and hopes it aroused.

Fraying Seams, 1943–1945

Each of the Allied leaders had different aims and interests. To ensure his own and the Soviet Union's security, Stalin demanded communist-controlled governments along the Soviet borders. In contrast, U.S. president Franklin D. Roosevelt believed that global international security and economic prosperity depended on the establishment of European democracies, committed to capitalist economic principles and practices. British prime minister Winston Churchill possessed a third set of aims. Concerned about the postwar balance of power in Europe and the maintenance of the British Empire, Churchill recognized that once Germany was defeated, a power vacuum would exist in central and eastern Europe. He feared that the Soviets might prove too eager to fill that vacuum. A permanent Soviet presence in the Balkans particularly threatened British military and economic interests throughout the Mediterranean. The "Big Three°," then, came to the negotiating table with

The Big Three I (Yalta, February 1945)
From 1941 until April 1945, the Big Three meant Churchill, Roosevelt, and Stalin. At the very end of the war, however, the composition of the Big Three suddenly changed, as Harry Truman replaced Roosevelt and Clement Attlee replaced Churchill.

clashing interests and aims; even before the war ended, the fabric of the alliance was under strain.

Reluctant to place too much pressure on the alliance's fraying seams, Roosevelt opted for postponing the hard decisions. He was not seeking simply to sidestep controversy. Rather, he hoped that the controversial questions would be settled after the war by a new international body, the United Nations (UN). In Roosevelt's vision, such a body could succeed where the now-discredited League of Nations had failed: It could guarantee that conciliation and negotiation would replace armed conflict in settling disputes between countries. Roosevelt recognized that if the Soviet Union refused to participate in the United Nations, the UN, like the league, would be a failure. Therefore he sought to avoid confrontations that might give Stalin a reason to block Soviet membership in the UN.

Roosevelt also hoped that new international economic structures would provide a framework for settling the disputes that divided the Allies. In 1944 leading American and European economists gathered in New Hampshire to construct a system for postwar economic revival. Well aware of the economic chaos that had followed World War I, and desperate to avoid a repeat of the Great Depression of the 1930s, they drew up the Bretton Woods Agreement°, which became the basic framework for the Western postwar economic order. To keep the global economy running smoothly, Bretton Woods established the American dollar as the world's reserve currency and fixed the currency exchange rates of its forty-four participating nations. It also established two new international economic institutions—the International Monetary Fund (IMF), to maintain the stability of member currencies, and the World Bank, to encourage global economic development.

Through the establishment of such international organizations as the IMF and the UN, Roosevelt sought "the end of the system of unilateral action, the exclusive alliances, the spheres of influence, the balances of power, and all the expedients that have been tried for centuries and have always failed." Yet neither Stalin nor Churchill shared Roosevelt's vision. Standing on opposite ends of the political spectrum, the Russian communist and the English aristocrat both continued to believe in precisely those "spheres of influence, the balances of power" that Roosevelt proclaimed outmoded. In the worldview of both Stalin and Churchill, armed force, not a new international organization, would determine the shape of the postwar world. As Stalin pointed out to Tito, the Yugoslav communist leader, "Everyone imposes his own system as far as his armies can reach. It cannot be otherwise."

By 1945, Stalin's army had a long reach. When the Big Three met in Yalta in February 1945, the communist partisans controlled Yugoslavia, and the Soviet Army had occupied Romania, Bulgaria, Hungary, and much of Czechoslovakia. This situation was in part the result of earlier Big Three negotiations. Throughout 1942 and 1943,

Stalin had pressed his Allies to open a Second Front in Europe and so relieve the pressure on Soviet forces. Churchill, concerned about the prospect of Soviet armies moving into eastern Europe, wanted to push into German-dominated Europe through the Balkans—and thus ensure that British and American forces were on the ground in eastern Europe when the war ended. But at the first Big Three summit in Tehran in 1943, Stalin and Roosevelt overruled Churchill and agreed that the Anglo-American invasion would be a single, concentrated attack across the English Channel into France (the D-Day invasion of June 1944). This decision left eastern Europe open to the Red Army.

The presence of the Red Army in eastern Europe weakened the negotiating positions of Churchill and Roosevelt at Yalta. Roosevelt's desire to obtain Stalin's commitment to enter the war against Japan also reduced his bargaining power. A series of problematic compromises resulted. Stalin signed a declaration promising free elections in eastern Europe; at the same time, Roosevelt and Churchill agreed that such freely elected governments should be pro-Soviet. Germany's future remained undecided although the Big Three agreed to share the postwar occupation by dividing Germany, as well as the symbolically and strategically vital city of Berlin, into occupation zones controlled by the United States, the Soviet Union, France, and Britain.

The final Big Three summit in the German city of Potsdam in July 1945 did not bridge the gap between the Soviet Union and its allies. At this summit, Stalin faced two unfamiliar negotiating partners. The new U.S. president Harry Truman (1884–1972) replaced Roosevelt, who had died in April, and midway through the summit, the new British prime minister, Labour Party leader Clement Attlee, arrived to take Churchill's place. The change of personnel made little difference, however. Stalin was determined to maintain control over the territories occupied by his armies, while the British and Americans increasingly saw Stalin's demands as a threat to both democratic ideals and the European balance of power. Moreover, during the summit Truman received a telegraph informing him of the successful Trinity test of the atomic bomb in New Mexico (see Chapter 26). This news meant that the war against Japan would soon be over—and that the Americans and British no longer needed or wanted Stalin to join the war in the Pacific. With Western incentives for placating Stalin now removed, the tone of the negotiations became more hostile.

Yet the wartime alliance had not yet completely torn apart. Throughout the rest of 1945 and 1946 Truman hoped to resolve the allies' differences and resisted the idea of a permanent American military presence in Europe. Stalin, too, was unwilling to push too far. He not only feared American military might, but also wished to retain access to Western economic assistance and expertise. In addition, to get his economy moving again, Stalin needed to scale back military expenditures. Thus he proceeded with rapid demilitarization: Soviet army strength went from 12 million men in 1945 to 3 million by 1948. He also adopted a policy of passivity for communist parties operating in regions that he viewed as part of the Western sphere of influence. He refused to assist Greek communists seeking to overthrow the British-backed monarchical regime, and he ordered communist parties in western Europe to participate with noncommunists in coalition governments.

During this period, however, the British pushed Truman to adopt a hard line toward Stalin and his demands. British foreign policy was in the hands of the foreign secretary, Ernest Bevin (1881–1951). A labor leader with a history of fighting against communist efforts to control British unions, Bevin was a fierce anti-Stalinist. He was also an ardent British nationalist who regarded the maintenance of the British Empire, particularly in the Mediterranean and the Middle East, as crucial to preserving Britain's Great Power status in the postwar world. Bevin thus urged the United States to stand tough when the Soviets demanded a stake in what had been Italy's North African empire and he urged a strong response when Stalin delayed pulling Russian troops out of Iran. (Soviet and British troops had occupied Iran during the war to keep its oil supplies out of German hands.)

Torn in Two, 1946–1949

Within just a few years of the war's end, clashing aims and interests had shredded the wartime alliance. Three key developments—the breakdown of cooperation over Germany, the Truman Doctrine°, and the Marshall Plan°—tore apart the former allies.

Allied cooperation in the occupation of defeated Germany quickly broke down over economic issues. At Potsdam, Truman and Attlee had agreed to Stalin's demand for German reparations. By 1946, however, British and American authorities became convinced that Germany faced mass starvation. To feed the Germans in the British zone, Attlee's government imposed bread rationing on the British public—a drastic step never taken during the war itself. The British and Americans decided that the immediate priority must be German economic recovery. To stabilize Germany's economy, they combined their zones into a single economic unit and, much to Stalin's fury, stopped reparations deliveries to Soviet territory.

The announcement of the Truman Doctrine the following year intensified the hostilities between Stalin and the West. In February 1947 Attlee's government informed Truman's administration that it could not afford to continue its fight against communist rebels in Greece. The United States immediately assumed Britain's role in Greece, but more importantly, Truman used this development to issue the Truman Doctrine, which committed the U.S. to the policy of containment°, resisting communist expansion wherever in the world it occurred.

President Harry Truman: The Truman Doctrine (1947)

DOCUMENT

Curtains and Camps

The Cold War gave rise to a new set of metaphors, as politicians, diplomats, and journalists struggled to find ways to explain the new world order. Two of the most compelling metaphors arose very early: the "Iron Curtain," coined by Winston Churchill in 1946, and "the two camps," used in a speech by Stalin's spokesman Andrei Zhdanov in 1947.

In 1946, Churchill was still the leader of Britain's Conservative Party but was no longer prime minister. On a visit to the United States, he gave a pivotal speech that warned of a divided Europe.

From Stettin in the Baltic to Trieste in the Adriatic, an iron curtain has descended across the Continent. Behind that line lie all the capitals of the ancient states of Central and Eastern Europe. Warsaw, Berlin, Prague, Vienna, Budapest, Belgrade, Bucharest and Sofia, all these famous cities and the populations around them lie in what I must call the Soviet sphere, and all are subject in one form or another, not only to Soviet influence but to a very high and, in many cases, increasing measure of control from Moscow. . . .

At the founding meeting of the Cominform in September 1947, Zhdanov delivered a speech that clearly articulated the postwar division of the world into two hostile blocs.

In the post-war period sharp changes have taken place in the international situation. . . . Two opposite political lines took shape: at one pole, the policy of the USSR and the democratic countries, aimed at undermining imperialism and strengthening democracy; at the other pole the policy of the USA and Britain, aimed at strengthening imperialism and strangling democracy. . . .

Thus two camps have come into being. . . .

The Truman-Marshall Plan is only one component part . . . of a general plan of worldwide expansionist policy that is being carried out by the USA in all parts of the world. . . . Yesterday's aggressors, the capitalist magnates of Germany and Japan, are being groomed by America for a new role, that of serving as an instrument of the USA's imperialist policy in Europe and Asia. . . . Under these conditions it is essential for the anti-imperialist and democratic camp to close ranks, work out a common programme of actions and develop its own tactics against the main forces of the imperialist camp. . . .

Sources: From a speech by Winston Churchill, delivered to Westminster College, Fulton, Missouri, March 5, 1946; and from G. Procacci (ed.), *The Cominform: Minutes of the Three Conferences 1947, 1948, 1949*, Milan, 1994.

A War of Words
The poster on the left demonstrates the official Soviet view of NATO: an American device to dominate Europe. The poster on the right warns Italian voters that if they vote for the Italian Communist Party, the Soviet Union will be their boss.

The Marshall Plan further divided Europe into two hostile camps. In 1947, U.S. secretary of state General George Marshall (1880–1959) toured Europe and grew alarmed at the devastation and despair that he witnessed across the Continent. Fearing that hungry Europeans might turn to communism, Marshall proposed that the United States underwrite Europe's economic recovery. Initially, Marshall's proposal received little attention in the United States, but in Britain, Foreign Secretary Ernest Bevin heard a report of it on the radio. Believing that British interests demanded a firm American commitment to Europe, Bevin perceived the Marshall Plan as the first step toward establishing this ongoing U.S. presence. He called the plan "a lifeline to sinking men." Bevin's French counterpart, Foreign Minister Georges Bidault (1899–1983), shared his enthusiasm, and together they helped make the Marshall Plan a reality. With representatives from twelve other European states, Bevin and Bidault drew up a list of European resources and requirements and devised a four-year plan for European economic reconstruction. In 1948, the first food shipments from the United States reached European ports. Eventually $17 billion in aid poured into Europe, while a new international body, the Organization for European Economic Cooperation (OEEC), worked to coordinate aid, eliminate trade barriers, and stabilize currencies.

The Marshall Plan helped integrate the economies of western Europe and accelerated Europe's leap into postwar prosperity. Stalin's response to the plan, however, cemented the division of East and West. The United States offered aid to any country that chose to accept it, including the Soviet Union and the states of eastern Europe, but required participating governments to join the OEEC. Stalin viewed the OEEC as an instrument of American economic domination and so refused to allow eastern European governments to accept Marshall aid. When the Czechs tried to do so, he engineered a communist coup that destroyed what remained of democracy in Czechoslovakia.

In 1949, the basic Cold War pattern that would hold for forty years took shape. The British and American zones of occupied Germany, joined with the French zone, became the Western-allied state of West Germany. The Soviet zone became communist East Germany. In April 1949 nine western European nations[1] allied with the United States and Canada in the North Atlantic Treaty Organization (NATO)°, a military alliance specifically aimed at repelling a Soviet invasion of western Europe. Months later, on August 29, 1949, the Soviet Union tested its own atomic bomb. Over the next few years, Stalin forced his eastern European satellites into an anti-Western military alliance (finalized as the Warsaw Pact° in 1955) and both the United States and the Soviet Union developed hydrogen

bombs. Europe stood divided into two hostile military blocs, each dominated by a superpower in possession of a nuclear arsenal.

The West and the World: Decolonization and the Cold War

■ **What was the impact of decolonization and the Cold War on the global balance of power?**

While the conflict between East and West dominated much of the postwar period, it soon blended with a very different struggle, that between the peoples of the developing nations and European imperialism. By the end of the 1960s, the age of the vast European overseas empires had finally ended. As decolonization became entangled with Cold War rivalries, superpower influence replaced European imperial control in many areas of the world. The Soviet Union and the United States used economic and military aid, as well as covert action, to cajole and coerce newly independent nations into choosing sides in the global Cold War conflict. The superpowers served as magnetic poles, drawing competing nationalist forces toward themselves and so entangling Cold War concerns with nationalist independence struggles throughout the world.

The End to the Age of European Empires

In the economic hard times following World War II, European governments regarded their empires as more crucial than ever. Faced with the reality of superpower domination in Europe, nations such as Britain and France looked to their imperial possessions to give them international power and prestige. The war, however, had aroused nationalists' demands for independence from European rule to a fever pitch. They pointed to the inherent contradiction between the Allies' claim to be fighting for democracy and the fact that many Allied states denied democratic rights to their imperial subjects. In the Pacific region, many colonial nationalists had sided with the Japanese against the British, Dutch, and French, whom they regarded not as defenders of democracy but as imperial overlords. The Japanese internment of the Dutch population in Indonesia in 1942 allowed nationalists to assume positions in the country's government. In Burma, the student-based nationalist movement, led by Aung San (1915–1947), supported the Japanese invasion. Similarly, the Indian nationalist Subhas Chandra Bose

(1897–1945) formed a National Army that fought alongside the Japanese and against the British. Of the 45,000 Indian troops captured by the Japanese in the conquests of Malaya and Singapore, 40,000 chose to join Bose's army.

When the war ended, these nationalists resisted European efforts to reimpose imperial rule, and a series of bloody colonial conflicts resulted. In Indonesia, for example, war raged from 1945 to 1949, as the Dutch fought bitterly to keep hold of a region they viewed as vital to their economic survival. They lost the fight, however, and in 1949 the nationalist Ahmed Sukarno led his country into independence.

Like the Dutch, the British found their empire in revolt in the postwar period. Throughout the war Churchill had placed a high priority on preserving the British Empire, but the economic and military demands of total war significantly weakened Britain's ability to control its far-flung possessions. Clement Attlee, who succeeded Churchill as prime minister in July 1945, sought to retain Britain's hold on its essential imperial interests by jettisoning those that Britain no longer needed—or could no longer afford.

CHRONOLOGY

The End to European Empire

1946 French colonial war in Indochina begins

1947 India, Pakistan, and Burma achieve independence

1948 State of Israel established; apartheid regime in South Africa comes into power

1949 Indonesia achieves independence from Dutch rule

1954 Defeat of French forces in Indochina; partition Vietnam; beginning of Franco-Algerian War

1955 Bandung Conference: the "Third World" is born

1957 Kwame Nkrumah becomes first prime minister of Ghana

1960 Congo, Nigeria, and most French colonies in Africa become independent

1962 Algeria achieves independence from French rule

1963 Jomo Kenyatta becomes first prime minister of Kenya

1965 U.S. bombing of North Vietnam begins

1967 Suharto ousts Sukarno as leader of Indonesia

Map 27.2   After Empire: Independent Asia

Dates of national formation often give no indication of the continuing political upheaval and violence that afflicted the countries of Asia in the postwar period. The formation of the nations of Vietnam, Laos, and Cambodia in 1953–1954, for example, did not mean an end to warfare in Indochina.

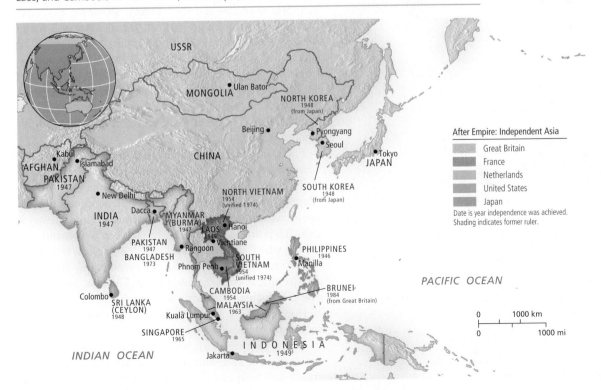

The British first jettisoned the Indian subcontinent. During World War II, the refusal of Indian nationalists to cooperate with the war effort made clear that Britain could no longer rule India. After the war, therefore, Attlee's government opened negotiations with nationalist leaders. Muslim nationalists led by Muhammad Ali Jinnah (1876–1948) refused to accept citizenship in an independent state dominated by Hindus, and won from the British the creation of a separate Muslim state—Pakistan. India and Pakistan, as well as Burma, received independence in August 1947 (see Map 27.2). The partition of the Indian subcontinent sparked widespread devastation, just as the redrawing of boundary lines in eastern Europe had resulted in brutal deportations and mass death. More than ten million people fled their homes and became refugees—Muslims fearing Hindu rule, Hindus fearing Muslim rule, Sikhs fear-

The Tandon Family at Partition (1947)

ing both. Mahatma Gandhi traveled from village to village in some of the most afflicted areas and begged for an end to the killing, but the death tolls reached 250,000—and included Gandhi himself, who was shot by an assassin just six months after India achieved independence.

In Palestine, too, British retreat led to bloodshed. After the war in Europe ended, European Jewish refugees, persuaded by Hitler that a Jew could be safe only in a Jewish state, poured into British-controlled Palestine. Many soon found themselves waging guerilla warfare against the British, who sought to maintain regional political stability by limiting Jewish immigration. Faced with mounting violence as well as growing international pressure to grant Jewish demands for statehood, the British turned the problem over to the new United Nations. At the end of 1947, the UN adopted a plan calling for the partition of Palestine into a Jewish and Arab state. Arab leaders rejected the plan, however, and the British pulled out their troops in May 1948 without transferring authority to either party. Jewish leaders immediately proclaimed the new state of Israel, and the region erupted into all-out war. After nine months of fighting, an uneasy peace descended, based on a partition of Palestine among Israel, Jordan, and Egypt (see Map 27.3). Approximately 750,000 Palestinian Arabs became stateless refugees.

By withdrawing from hot spots such as India and Palestine, the British hoped to preserve and stabilize what remained of the British Empire. During the 1950s, successive British governments sought to diminish the force of nationalism throughout their colonial territories by diverting it down channels of constitutional reform and systems of power sharing—and then fiercely stomping down on nationalists who broke out of these channels. Many African leaders, such as Kwame Nkrumah (1957–1966) in Ghana and Jomo Kenyatta (1963–1978) in Kenya, moved from British prison cells to prime ministerial or presidential offices. Neither compromise nor coercion could stem the tide of nationalism, and by the end of the 1960s, the British Empire had been reduced to an assortment of island territories.

France, too, saw its empire disintegrate in the postwar decades despite efforts to resist nationalist movements. In Indochina, the nationalist leader Ho Chi Minh (1890–1969) adopted the U.S. Declaration of Independence for his model when he proclaimed independence in September 1945. The stirring rhetoric, however, failed to convince the French, who fought for almost a decade to retain their hold in southeast Asia. But in 1954, the French army suffered a decisive defeat at Dien Bien Phu in Vietnam, and French rule in Indochina ended.

Humiliated by this defeat, French army officers responded ferociously to the outbreak of a nationalist revolt in Algeria that same year. Many prominent politicians and ordinary men and women shared the army's view that France had been pushed too far and must now stand fast.

Map 27.3 Israel and Its Neighbors, 1949

The map inset outlines the United Nations' plan to partition Palestine into Jewish and Arab states, with Jerusalem as an international zone. This plan was not implemented.

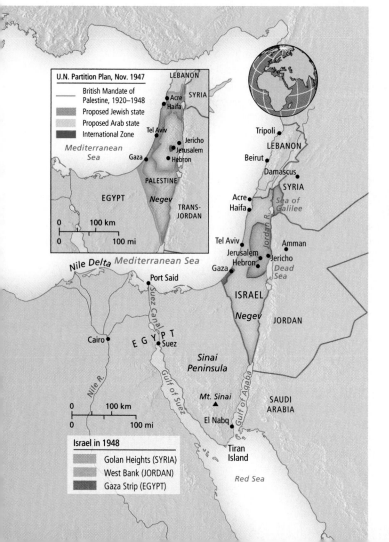

France teetered on the brink of civil war, with French army officers preparing for an assault on Paris. The World War II hero Charles De Gaulle forced through a new constitution, which sharply tilted the balance of power in French domestic politics toward the president (conveniently De Gaulle himself).

The Imperialist Legacy

As the Algerian crisis showed, decolonization was not something that just happened "out there" in the world beyond the West; rather it had an often profound impact on Western politics. In the United States, for example, the burgeoning African-American civil rights movement directly linked its struggle to the colonial independence movements happening at the same time. As the civil rights leader Martin Luther King Jr. (1929–1968) asserted, "the determination of Negro Americans to win freedom from all forms of oppression springs from the same deep longing that motivates oppressed peoples all over the world."[2] Organizations such as the National Association for the Advancement of Colored People (NAACP), founded in 1910, had long fought against racial discrimination in the United States, but in the 1950s, in part inspired by nationalists' battles around the globe, the civil-rights struggle became a mass movement with an innovative program of "freedom rides," lunch counter sit-ins, boycotts, and voter registration campaigns.

The legacy of imperialist rule lingered long, particularly in areas with large white European settlements such as Rhodesia and South Africa. Despite UN sanctions and a violent black nationalist movement, white settlers in Rhodesia (present-day Zimbabwe) retained a lock on political and economic power until 1980. In South Africa, the white supremacist Afrikaner Nationalist Party assumed control in 1948 and implemented the policies of apartheid°, the rigid segregation of communities based on race. To break down any chance of resistance, the apartheid regime deliberately accentuated tribal divisions among black South Africans and denied them basic human rights. The "No Trial Act" of 1963, for example, gave the government the right to detain anyone, without charge or trial, for as long as it chose.

VIDEO
Creating Apartheid in South Africa

Imperialism also left a long-lasting economic legacy. European states lost their monopoly on the raw materials and markets of their one-time colonies, yet in the postcolonial era, African states grew more economically dependent than ever on the West, a development that anti-Western

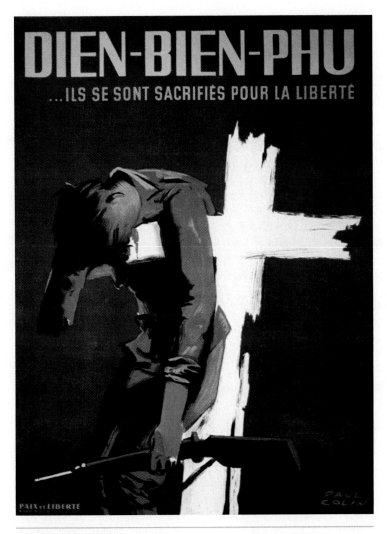

Imperial Sacrifice

This poster reminds French men and women of the sacrifice made by their army at the Battle of Dien Bien Phu in Vietnam: "They sacrificed themselves for your liberty." The memory of the army's defeat at Dien Bien Phu helped strengthen French determination to hold on to Algeria.

The result was the Franco-Algerian War, a brutal fight that raged from 1954 until the early 1960s. By the time Algeria claimed independence in 1962 (see Map 27.4), approximately 200,000 Algerian nationalist fighters had been killed or imprisoned. Fifteen thousand French soldiers and auxiliary forces were dead, as were almost 23,000 civilians in both France and Algeria.

The Franco-Algerian War seriously divided French society, called into question the meaning of French democracy, and transformed France's political structure. Supporters of the French army in Algeria saw it as a force fighting on behalf of Western civilization against barbarism (both Muslim and communist). Critics, pointing to the evidence that the French army used torture against its enemies, argued that the war threatened to corrupt French society. By 1958

DOCUMENT

Rejecting the West

Born in Martinique, Frantz Fanon became a champion of Algerian independence. He died of leukemia in 1961, shortly before an independent Algeria came into being. His writings, published posthumously, articulated clearly the discontent of the colonized. Riveting dissections of the relations of power in Western capitalism, they also helped inspire the protests of 1968.

"The last shall be first and the first last."* Decolonization is the putting into practice of this sentence. . . . The naked truth of decolonization evokes for us the searing bullets and bloodstained knives which emanate from it. For if the last shall be first, this will only come to pass after a murderous and decisive struggle between the two protagonists.

. . . As soon as the native begins to pull on his moorings, and to cause anxiety to the settler, he is handed over to well-meaning souls who in cultural congresses point out to him the specificity and wealth of Western values. But . . . it so happens that when the native hears a speech about Western culture he pulls out his knife—or at least he makes sure it is within reach. The violence with which the supremacy of white values is affirmed and the aggressiveness which has permeated the victory of these values over the ways of life and thought of the native mean that, in revenge, the native laughs in mockery when Western values are mentioned in front of him.

. . . For centuries the capitalists have behaved in the under-developed world like nothing more than war criminals. Deportations, massacres, forced labour and slavery have been the main methods used by capitalism to increase its wealth, its gold or diamond reserves, and to establish its power. . . . So when we hear the head of a European state declare with his hand on his heart that he must come to the help of the poor under-developed peoples, we do not tremble with gratitude. Quite the contrary; we say to ourselves: "It's a just reparation which will be paid to us."

---

* Fanon is quoting Jesus' words in Matthew 19:30. But as the rest of the excerpt makes clear, Fanon's interpretation of this verse contrasts with the usual Christian emphasis on submission.

Source: From Frantz Fanon, *The Wretched of the Earth*, translated by Constance Farrington. Copyright © 1963 by Présence Africaine. Used by permission.

African nationalists labeled "neo-colonialism." Desperate for cash, newly independent African governments increased production of cash crops for export—cotton, coffee, nuts, sugar—and also expanded their mining industries, producing uranium, lithium, copper, tin, gold, diamonds, and zinc for Western markets. Such exports were extremely vulnerable to fluctuations in demand and prices. At the same time, African nations became ever more dependent on importing manufactured goods from the industrialized West, with aid from Western nations often contingent on trading deals requiring such imports.

For many of the newly independent nations of Africa and Asia, political stability proved as elusive as economic prosperity. To be solid, democratic political structures must rest on a foundation of popular participation, yet almost a century of imperialist rule made such participation very problematic. For example, when the Congo became independent in 1960, it possessed only sixteen university graduates out of a population of 13 million—the result of the Belgian policy of restricting Congolese children to a basic education. In Africa as a whole, 80 percent of the African people could not read or write. Not surprisingly, then, by 1966 military regimes had replaced elected governments in the former colonial territories of Nigeria, Congo Brazzaville, Burkina Faso, Algeria, the Benin Republic, and the Central African Republic. In many newly independent states, competition between rival groups for power led to civil war. Nigeria, which gained independence from Britain in 1960, was overcome by political corruption and regional secession. In its civil war, which began in 1966, at least one million people died, either in battle or from starvation. The Congo stepped directly from Belgian rule in 1960 into a protracted civil war.

The Globalization of the Cold War

The process of decolonization often became entangled with Cold War rivalries, and in many regions, superpower influence replaced imperial control. In the Congo, for example, both overt and covert superpower involvement prolonged the civil war and destabilized the post-independence political structure. Despite fears of World War III and a Europe devastated by nuclear weapons, the Cold War actually turned hot only in places like the Congo—in the developing nations, at the intersection of superpower rivalries and nationalist conflicts.

The Korean War, 1950–1953

The first such intersection occurred in Korea. Once part of the Japanese Empire, Korea, like Germany, was divided after World War II. A Soviet-linked communist regime as-

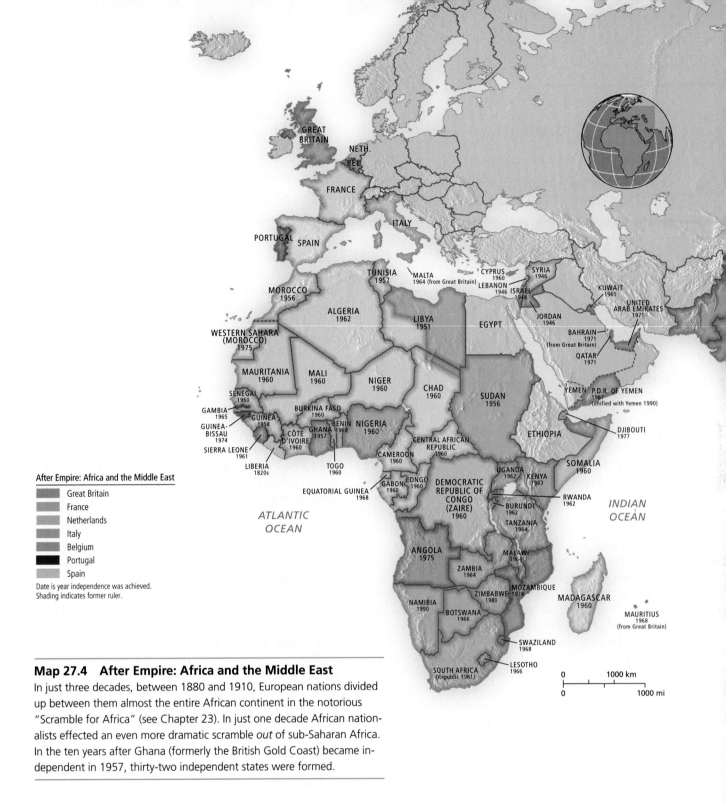

Map 27.4 After Empire: Africa and the Middle East

After Empire: Africa and the Middle East

- Great Britain
- France
- Netherlands
- Italy
- Belgium
- Portugal
- Spain

Date is year independence was achieved.
Shading indicates former ruler.

In just three decades, between 1880 and 1910, European nations divided up between them almost the entire African continent in the notorious "Scramble for Africa" (see Chapter 23). In just one decade African nationalists effected an even more dramatic scramble *out* of sub-Saharan Africa. In the ten years after Ghana (formerly the British Gold Coast) became independent in 1957, thirty-two independent states were formed.

sumed power in North Korea, and an anticommunist state propped up by the United States controlled the south. In 1950, North Korean troops invaded South Korea in an attempt to unite the country under communist rule. This civil war, a struggle between rival groups of Korean nationalists, was quickly swallowed up by the Cold War. A UN-sponsored, largely American army fought alongside South Korean troops, while the Soviet Union supplied arms and Communist China provided soldiers to support North Korea.

The Korean War accelerated the globalization of the Cold War. As a result of the Korean conflict, the French government was able to persuade Truman's administration to support its struggle against Ho Chi Minh and the communist nationalists in Indochina, thus drawing the United States onto the path that would lead to its war in Vietnam.

The conflict in Korea also welded Japan firmly into the Western alliance. As the U.S. army turned to the Japanese for vital military supplies, more than $3.5 billion poured into and rejuvenated the Japanese economy. (American military orders for trucks guaranteed the success of a struggling new Japanese firm called Toyota.) Transformed from an occupied enemy to a staunch ally and an economic powerhouse, Japan became the dam holding back "the red tide that threatens to engulf the world."[3] Thus, in a curious way, Japan—geographically as far "East" as one can get—became a part of the "West."

The Korean War also solidified the Cold War and U.S. interests within Europe. Fearing that the war's outbreak signaled a more aggressive Soviet policy in Europe as well as Asia, western European leaders pushed for the transformation of NATO from a loose defensive alliance to a coordinated fighting force. This transformation, however, came at a price. As the U.S. military budget exploded from $13.5 billion to $50 billion per year, Truman's administration demanded that its European allies strengthen their own military forces and permit the rearmament of West Germany. With the trauma of German conquest and occupation so recently behind them, many Europeans were horrified by the prospect. Britain's prime minister Clement Attlee warned, "The policy of using Satan to defeat Sin is very dangerous." Even within West Germany the proposal aroused strong opposition, although Konrad Adenauer (1876–1967), the new state's first chancellor, argued that only a rearmed West Germany could prevent the forcible reunification of Germany on Soviet terms. After four years of controversy and a failed effort to create a western European army (the European Defense Community, or EDC), West Germany rearmed, as the United States had initially demanded, under the NATO umbrella.

Changing Temperatures in the Cold War, 1953–1960

In 1953, both sides in the Cold War changed leaders. Stalin died in March, just a few months after a new Republican administration headed by President Dwight Eisenhower (1890–1969) took office in the United States. This change of leadership heralded a new phase in the Cold War. When Eisenhower took office, he condemned Truman's policy of *containing* communism as defeatist, a "negative, futile and immoral policy . . . which abandons countless human beings to a despotism and Godless terrorism."[4] Instead, he committed the United States to *roll back* communism and insisted that communist aggression would be met with massive nuclear retaliation. This newly aggressive American stance was matched on the other side of the Cold War divide. After a period of uncertainty following Stalin's death in 1953, Nikita Khrushchev (1955–1964) emerged in 1955 as the new Soviet leader. Loud and boisterous, given to off-the-cuff remarks and spontaneous displays of emotion, Khrushchev contrasted sharply with the disciplined, reserved Stalin. (It is hard to imagine Stalin taking off his shoe and beating it on a table, as Khrushchev did in front of the television cameras at an assembly of the United Nations.) Khrushchev played a dangerous game of nuclear bluff, in which he persistently and often quite successfully convinced allies and foes alike that the Soviet Union possessed a far stronger nuclear force than it actually did.

Both Khrushchev and Eisenhower recognized, however, that nuclear weapons made total war unwinnable and both sought ways to break out of the positions into which they were frozen by Cold War hostilities. Thus the period from 1953 until 1964 was characterized by thawing superpower relations followed by the icy blasts of renewed hostilities. In 1955, for example, representatives of Britain, France, the United States, and the Soviet Union met in Geneva for the first summit of the Cold War. This initial thaw ended one year later when Khrushchev sent tanks into Hungary to crush a nationalist rebellion—a clear demonstration that he would permit no challenge to Soviet authority in eastern Europe.

The Soviets' successful launch of the first human-made satellite, *Sputnik*, in 1957 was even more chilling. Khrushchev claimed—falsely—that the Soviets possessed an advanced intercontinental ballistic missile (ICBM) force and that Soviet factories were producing rockets "like sausages from a machine."[5] To western Europeans, *Sputnik* had especially ominous implications. The development of ICBMs meant that American cities were now vulnerable to a Soviet nuclear strike. Europeans began to ask themselves whether the United States would actually risk Chicago to save Paris: If the Soviets invaded western Europe with conventional forces, would the Americans respond with nuclear weapons and so open their own cities to nuclear retaliation?

Yet in the late 1950s, the Cold War ice seemed to be breaking once again. In 1958 the Soviet Union announced a voluntary suspension on nuclear testing. The United States and Britain followed suit and nuclear test ban talks opened in Geneva. The next year Khrushchev spent twelve days touring the United States—much to his regret, security concerns kept him from visiting Disneyland. The communist leader impressed Americans as a down-to-earth, ordinary sort of guy, a man rather than a monster. Khrushchev ended his U.S. visit with the promise of another four-power summit in 1960.

On the Brink: The Berlin Wall and the Cuban Missile Crisis

These warming relations, however, turned frosty in 1960 after the Soviet Union announced it had shot down an American spy plane and captured its pilot. This announcement aborted the planned summit and initiated one of the most dangerous periods in the post–World War II era, during which the construction of Berlin Wall° provided a concrete symbol of the Cold War divide. As we saw at the beginning of this chapter, the continuing outflow of East Germans to the West through Berlin led the East German communist leader Walter Ulbricht (1893–1973) and Khrushchev to take dramatic action in 1961. Two weeks after the wall went up, the Soviet Union ended a three-year moratorium on nuclear testing. The new American president John F. Kennedy (1961–1963) increased military spending and called for an expanded civil defense program to prepare for nuclear war. Across Europe men and women feared that their countries would become a nuclear wasteland.

Such a war was narrowly avoided in the fall of 1962 as once again the Cold War intersected with a nationalist struggle. In 1959, a nationalist revolutionary movement led by Fidel Castro (b. 1926) toppled Cuba's pro-U.S. dictator. Castro quickly aligned Cuba with the Soviet Union. In 1962, Kennedy learned that the Soviets were building nuclear missile bases in Cuba. What Kennedy did not know was that the Soviet forces in Cuba were armed with nuclear weapons—and with the discretionary power to use these weapons if U.S. forces attacked. Some of Kennedy's advisers urged just such an attack, but instead the president used secret diplomatic channels to broker a compromise. Khrushchev removed the missiles and in exchange, Kennedy withdrew NATO's nuclear missiles from Turkey and guaranteed that the United States would not invade Cuba.

In the aftermath of the crisis, both the United States and the Soviet Union backed off from brinkmanship. In 1963, the superpowers agreed to stop aboveground nuclear testing with the Nuclear Test Ban treaty and set up between them the "hotline," a direct communications link (at first not a telephone but a system of telegraph lines and teleprinters) to encourage immediate personal consultation in the event of a future crisis.

Cold War Arenas: Vietnam and the Middle East

Yet relations between the superpowers remained tense throughout the 1960s, and the globalization of the Cold War accelerated. In both Southeast Asia and the Middle East, as the superpowers replaced European empires as regional powerbrokers, nationalist conflicts and regional power struggles escalated.

The transformation of the Vietnam War from a nationalist struggle against European imperial rule into a Cold War conflict illustrates this process clearly. After the defeat of French imperial forces at Dien Bien Phu in 1954, rival Vietnamese nationalists fought to control the Indochinese peninsula. Ho Chi Minh and his communist regime in North Vietnam relied on the Soviet Union and China for support, while American military and economic aid propped up an anticommunist government in South Vietnam. Under the Kennedy presidency (1961–1963), the number of military advisers in Vietnam expanded rapidly, as did American involvement in South Vietnamese politics.

When Kennedy's successor, Lyndon Johnson (1908–1973), took office, he issued a clear order, "Win the war!" In 1964, the American Congress granted Johnson the authority to take "all necessary measures" to do so. By 1968, more than 500,000 American soldiers were fighting in Vietnam. Fifty-eight thousand GIs died during the war—as did well over one million Vietnamese.

Like Vietnam, the Middle East also became a Cold War arena as the superpowers replaced the French and British in the region. During the 1950s, Gamel Abdel Nasser, a vehemently anti-Western Arab nationalist who took control of Egypt after the overthrow of the monarchy in 1952, proved adept at playing the superpowers against each other. When the United States withdrew its promised funding for the Aswan High Dam power plant, a massive project intended to harness the energy of the Nile River to fuel Egypt's economic development, Nasser simply turned to the Soviet Union for military and economic assistance.

The Six-Day War of June 1967 escalated the tendency of Middle Eastern states to pick sides in the Cold War. After a decade of heightened Arab nationalist rhetoric calling for the destruction of Israel, the Israeli government moved in a preemptive strike. Facing a surprise attack on three fronts, Arab forces quickly crumbled. In just six days of fighting, Israel gained possession of the Sinai peninsula from Egypt, the West Bank from Jordan, the Golan Heights from Syria—and one million stateless Palestinian refugees. (See Map 27.5.) In the wake of the war, U.S. foreign policy shifted to decisive support for Israel. In turn, Egypt, Syria, Iraq, Sudan, and Libya aligned with the Soviet Union.

The Third World

Many newly independent nations sought to resist being pulled into the orbit of either superpower. In 1955, Ahmed Sukarno (1949–1966), the nationalist leader who had led Indonesia out from under Dutch rule six years before, hosted the Bandung Conference of "nonaligned" nations. Bandung signaled the desire of many national leaders to find a place for their nations between or apart from the United States or the Soviet Union. French jour-nalists at the conference gave these nations a collective label—neither the first (Western, capitalist) nor the second (Eastern, communist) but rather the Third World°. Few of these nonaligned nations had much power on their own, but the General Assembly of the United Nations provided them with an important forum for making their voice heard. As the pace of decolonization acceler-ated, the number of independent nations voting in the UN grew.

Map 27.5 The Results of the Six-Day War

A comparison of this map with Map 27.3 ("Israel and Its Neighbors, 1949," p. 894) reveals the startling results of the war of 1967. Israel's conquest of the Sinai peninsula, the Golan Heights, and the Gaza Strip vastly increased its territorial holdings—and the resentment of Palestinians. Israel withdrew from western Sinai in 1975 and from the whole of the peninsula in 1981. The West Bank and the Gaza Strip were placed under Palestinian self-rule in 1994.

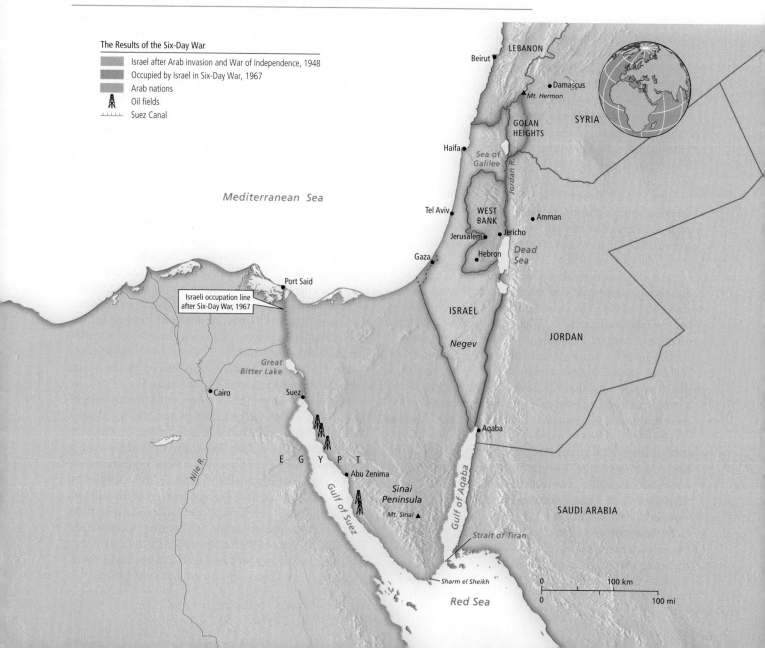

Genuine independence, however, proved difficult to retain as even Sukarno, the nonaligned movement's founder, discovered. Sukarno's quest for material and military assistance led him into the Soviet sphere of influence by the mid-1960s. In 1967, General Mohamed Suharto (b. 1921) overthrew Sukarno in a bloody coup. With his country's rivers clogged with the headless corpses of 100,000 victims, Suharto aligned Indonesia with the West.

The Soviet Union and Eastern Europe in the 1950s and 1960s

▓ What patterns characterized the history of the Soviet Union and eastern Europe after the death of Stalin?

Divided by the Cold War, the peoples of western and eastern Europe in the 1950s and 1960s followed separate paths. For the citizens of eastern Europe and the Soviet Union, the end of World War II brought renewed terror. Stalin's death in 1953 inaugurated a period of political reform and the seeming promise of prosperity, but by the end of the 1960s, economic stagnation and political discontent characterized life in the Soviet bloc.

From Stalinist Terror to De-Stalinization

As the Red Army slowly pushed the Germans out of Soviet territory and then back through eastern Europe in the final years of World War II, many of the inhabitants of these regions found that liberation from German occupation did not mean freedom, and that the end of the war did not mean peace. Stalin accused entire ethnic groups, such as the Chechens, of collaborating with the Germans. Soviet soldiers loaded hundreds of thousands of men, women, and children onto freezing freight cars without adequate supplies of food, water, or warm clothing, and shipped them eastward. An estimated 25 percent of these people died on the journey or in the first few years of barren existence in their new homes. These deportations continued into the early 1950s.

Terror also marked the daily lives of eastern Europeans in the late 1940s and early 1950s, as Stalin imposed his control over the Soviet satellite states. Developments in Yugoslavia played a crucial role in shaping the terror in eastern Europe. In 1948, Yugoslavia's communist leader, Tito, broke with Stalin and refused to let the Soviets dictate Yugoslavia's foreign and domestic policies. Alarmed by his loss of control over Yugoslavia, Stalin strove frantically to tighten his grip on the rest of eastern Europe by eliminating

CHRONOLOGY

The Soviet Bloc in the Postwar Era

1948 Yugoslav leader Tito breaks with Stalin; terror underway in Eastern Europe

1953 Death of Stalin; relaxation of terror in eastern Europe and Soviet Union

1955 Khrushchev emerges as new Soviet leader

1956 Khrushchev's "Secret Speech," de-Stalinization accelerates; unrest in Poland results in new regime under Gomułka; Hungarian Revolution crushed by Soviet forces

1964 Khrushchev ousted; Brezhnev era begins

1968 Prague Spring crushed

any potential Tito imitators from these societies. The Cold War provided Stalin with additional incentives to battle against any possible threat to his personal power. Stalin insisted that a Western conspiracy to divide and conquer the Soviet bloc could be defeated only by a thoroughgoing purge of communist ranks.

The citizens of eastern Europe thus experienced a replay of the Soviet terror of the 1930s. Labor and prison camps soon dotted eastern European maps. Between 1948 and 1953, many more communists were killed by their own party members than had died at the hands of the Nazis during World War II. Arrested, charged with sabotage or espionage, and savagely tortured, prominent communists were convicted in public show trials at which they recited the confessions that had been prepared for them. As in the Soviet Union a decade earlier, the terror quickly spread beyond the communist ranks. Factory supervisors were assigned quotas; they knew if they did not come up with a required number of names of "criminals," they would be imprisoned. In Budapest, frightened citizens watched the police vans that slid through the street every Monday, Wednesday, and Friday night at two A.M., picking up the next allotment of victims. The security forces targeted anyone remotely connected to "the West," including veterans of the Spanish Civil War and members of international organizations such as the Boy Scouts. Jews, considered "cosmopolitan" and therefore potentially pro-Western, were particularly suspect. Only Stalin's death in 1953 caused the wave of persecution to recede.

Soviet leaders jostled for power after Stalin's death but by 1955 Nikita Khrushchev had triumphed over his rivals and claimed control. A true communist success story, Khrushchev was born to illiterate peasants, began work as a coal miner at age 14, and rose to the top of the Soviet system.

Show Time:
The Trial of Rudolf Slánský

On the night of July 31, 1951, Rudolf Slánský—general secretary of the Communist Party of Czechoslovakia (CPC) and the second most powerful man in Prague—left his 50th birthday party and headed home, a frightened man. Outwardly, nothing was wrong. The CPC had celebrated the day in style. The communist president, Klement Gottwald, presented to Slánský the medal of the Order of Socialism, the highest honor awarded in Czechoslovakia. Telegrams of congratulations poured in from all over the country. But the huge stack of congratulatory telegrams contained no greeting from Stalin. Slánský knew he was in trouble.

At another place and in another time, Slánský's fear could be dismissed as mere paranoia. But in the upper ranks of the Communist Party in Czechoslovakia in 1951, signs of Stalin's approval or disapproval were literally a matter of life or death. The Stalinist purge of eastern Europe was well underway, with thousands arrested, tortured, imprisoned, or killed.

Slánský knew he was vulnerable on three counts. First, he held a rank high enough to ensure a spectacular show trial. As the Soviet Great Purge of the 1930s had demonstrated, trials and executions of leading communists worked both to terrorize Stalin's potential rivals and, by rousing ordinary citizens to perpetual vigilance, to cement mass loyalty to the regime. But for a trial to be a genuine show, the defendant had to be worth showing. Slánský, as the CPC general secretary, was the perfect defendant.

Slánský was a target for Stalin's purge, second, because he was a Czech, and Stalin viewed his Czech colleagues with particular suspicion. Czechoslovakia was the only state in eastern Europe with a history of successful democracy and without Soviet troops in occupation after 1945. Moreover, the CPC had participated with noncommunists in a coalition government longer than any other eastern European communist party.

Such differences linked the CPC to the ideology of "national communism," which taught that the Soviet path to communism was not the only one, that each nation must find its own route. "National communism" became a heresy in Stalin's eyes after his break with the Yugoslav communist leader Tito in 1948. Tito had dared to lead Yugoslavia down a different path and had dared to defy Stalin's leadership. Determined to prevent any additional defections from his eastern European empire, Stalin embarked on a quest for real or potential "titoists." To save his own skin, CPC leader Klement Gottwald needed to demonstrate his willingness to uproot titoism from his party and his government. Slánský became that demonstration.

Finally, Slánský was vulnerable because he was a Jew. When the purges in eastern Europe began in 1948, anti-Semitism played no prominent role, but by 1950 the intersection of Middle Eastern power plays, Cold War hostilities, Stalin's paranoia, and the still-powerful tradition of Jew-hating in eastern European culture made Jewish communists particularly suspect. Aiming to establish a Soviet presence in the Middle East after the war, Stalin had tried to persuade the new state of Israel to align with the Soviet Union by offering the new Israeli government diplomatic recognition and arms deals. But Stalin's efforts failed. By 1950, Israel had become an ally of the United States. Stalin responded with fury. All Jews came under suspicion of "Zionist" (that is, pro-Israel and therefore pro-Western) tendencies.

Stalin's failure to send Slánský a birthday telegram signaled that Slánský was now on the list of suspects. Over the following months Soviet advisers and home-grown Czech torturers pressured prisoners already caught in the net of the purge to confess that they were part of a Slánský-led conspiracy to overthrow the communist government and to turn Czechoslovakia against the Soviet Union. These torture-induced confessions were then used to prepare a flimsy case against Slánský and thirteen other men (eleven of them Jews).

Shortly before midnight on November 24, 1951, security agents arrested Slánský at his home. A lifelong atheist, Slánský could say nothing except "Jesus Maria." He knew what was coming. Instrumental in initiating the Stalinist purge in Czechoslovakia, Slánský had approved the arrests and torture of many of his colleagues. Ironically, he had drafted the telegram asking Stalin to send Soviet advisers to assist in the Czech purge—the very same advisers who decided to target Slánský.

For the next year, Slánský endured mental and physical torture, directed by these advisers. Common torture tactics included beatings and kickings; prolonged periods without sleep, food, or water; all-night interrogation sessions; and being forced to stand in one place or march in circles for days on end. One interrogator recalled, "Instead of getting evidence, we were told that they were villains and that we had to break them."[6] Breaking Slánský took six months; the remaining months were spent defining and refining the details of his imaginary crimes against the communist regime, and rehearsing for the all-important show trial.

Slánský's trial, which began on November 20, 1952, was in every sense a show. Before the trial began, party officials had already determined the verdict and the sentences. Prosecutors, defense attorneys, judges, and the accused spoke the lines of a script written by security agents. Thus, one year after his arrest, Slánský stood up in court and pleaded guilty to the crimes of high treason, espionage, and sabotage. A founding member of the CPC, he said he had conspired to overthrow the communist government. A resistance fighter during World War II, he confessed to working with the Nazis against the communists. A zealous Stalinist, he announced that he was a titoist-Zionist who had plotted to hand Czechoslovakia to the Americans.

Why did Slánský make such a ludicrous confession? Fear of further torture is clearly one motive, but other factors also came into play. Communists such as Slánský believed that the interests of the party always came first, ahead of individual rights, ahead of abstractions such as "truth." Slánský may have believed that his confession, false though it was, served the party. As one experienced interrogator noted about a different defendant, "He'll confess; he's got a good attitude toward the party."[7] In addition, Slánský may have been promised, as were other show trial defendants, that his life would be spared and his family protected if he confessed.

In his closing statement Slánský said, "I deserve no other end to my criminal life than that proposed by the state prosecutor."[8] The prosecutor demanded the death penalty. Slánský was executed on December 3, 1952. Ten of his co-accused also hanged. Their families were stripped of their party memberships and privileges, deported with only the barest essentials to designated districts, and assigned to manual labor.

Questions of Justice

1. In what ways did Cold War concerns shape Slánský's trial?
2. What sort of justice was served in the trial of Rudolf Slánský?

Taking It Further

Lukes, Igor. "The Rudolf Slánský Affair: New Evidence." *Slavic Review* 58, 1 (Spring 1999): 160–187. Illuminating study of the role of Cold War intrigue in determining Slánský's fate.

Kaplan, Karel. *Report on the Murder of the General Secretary.* 1990. Kaplan emigrated from Czechoslovakia to West Germany in the late 1970s, with a stack of hidden documents, and wrote this report.

Rudolf Slánský on Trial
Slánský, already a broken man, bows his head as he hears his death sentence on November 27, 1952.

Recognized as a man with talent by the Communist Party, he trained as an engineer and helped build the Moscow subway system. Khrushchev owed everything to the Communist Party, and he never forgot it. Confident in the moral and material superiority of communism, Khrushchev believed that the Soviet Union would win the Cold War on the economic battlefield. But this ultimate victory would take place only if Soviet living standards substantially improved, and only if the Stalinist systems of terror and rigid centralized control were dismantled.

Nikita Khrushchev Challenges the West to Disarm

Khrushchev's determination to set communism on a new course became clear in February 1956 when, in a lengthy speech before the Twentieth Congress of the Communist Party, he shocked his listeners by detailing and condemning Stalin's crimes. This "Secret Speech" marked the beginning of de-Stalinization, a time of greater openness in the Communist bloc as governments dismantled many of the controls on speech and publication, and for the first time in years dissent and debate reappeared in public life.

The most dramatic sign of de-Stalinization was the release of at least four and a half million prisoners from slave labor camps. As one Soviet citizen recalled, their return was disturbing: "in railway trains and stations, there appeared survivors of the camps, with leaden grey hair, sunken eyes, and a faded look; they choked and dragged their feet like old men."[9] These survivors often returned to find their spouses remarried, their children embarrassed by their presence, their world destroyed. Some, such as Alexander Solzhenitsyn, wrote horrifying accounts of their experiences. Solzhenitsyn's books narrated the daily degradation of prison life and provided a detailed map of the network of slave labor camps that he christened "The Gulag Archipelago."

De-Stalinization certainly did not mean an end to all cultural controls in the Soviet Union, as artists discovered in the early 1960s. At first, Khrushchev's ascendancy seemed to promise that Soviet artists could finally break out of the prison of Socialist Realism to which Stalinist doctrine had confined them (see Chapter 25). In 1956, works by Picasso that had lain unseen in state museums for decades were finally put on exhibit. Inspired by what was to them truly revolutionary work, Soviet artists turned to producing their own nonfigurative, abstract art. But the display of some of this work in Moscow in 1962 made clear the limits of de-Stalinization. Khrushchev thundered, "What's hung here is simply anti-Soviet. It's immoral."[10] Within days, the artists who had dared to experiment found themselves censured, expelled, and unemployed.

De-Stalinization also did not mean an end to all political and religious repression. In 1959 the Gulag still held at least a million prisoners. As part of his effort to revitalize communist culture, Khrushchev embarked on a massive offensive against religious practice, which included the razing of churches, the arrest of clergy, the closure of seminaries and monasteries, and even in some cases the forcible removal of children from Christian homes. At the same time, anti-Semitism continued to mark communist policy and practice, with Soviet Jews targeted for harassment and repression.

Most ominously for the future of the Soviet Union itself, de-Stalinization failed to remedy long-term economic weaknesses. In 1962, per capita consumption of consumer goods stood at only 40 to 60 percent that of France, West Germany, and Britain. In agriculture, the economic sector where the Soviet Union lagged the furthest behind the West, Khrushchev embarked on an ambitious reform program, which included rapid mechanization, a massive chemical fertilizer program, and the plowing of virgin lands. He refused to retreat from collectivization, however. As a result, the fundamental productivity problem remained unsolved—and in fact worsened in the long term as immense ecological damage was inflicted on the Soviet countryside. Soil erosion increased exponentially, nitrogen runoff from fertilized fields contaminated water supplies, and over-irrigation led to salinization and a decline in soil fertility. The full force of these problems would not be felt until the 1980s, but as early as 1963 the Soviet Union had to import Western grain, a humiliating admission of failure for Khrushchev's regime.

Re-Stalinization and Stagnation: The Brezhnev Era

Khrushchev's reforms unsettled many high-ranking communists; as a result, he was forced out of office in 1964. After a short period of collective leadership, Leonid Brezhnev (1906–1982) emerged as the new Soviet leader, a position he held until his death in 1982. A polite man with no interest in literature, art, or original ideas, Brezhnev was far more reassuring to Soviet bureaucrats than the flamboyant Khrushchev, whose boisterous embrace of new ideas and ambitious schemes had proven so destabilizing. Fifty-eight years old and already physically ailing when he assumed the party leadership, the increasingly decrepit Brezhnev matched his era.

Under Brezhnev the Soviet economy stagnated. Growth rates in both industrial production and labor productivity slowed during the second half of the 1960s. In the 1970s, growth virtually ceased. This economic stagnation was, however, masked by improving living standards. Brezhnev continued Khrushchev's policies of free higher education and rising wages, while accelerating the expansion of consumer goods. State subsidies ensured that the cost of utilities, public transport, and rents remained far lower than in the West (although apartments were in short supply), and an extensive welfare system eased pressures on ordinary people.

By the middle of the 1960s, the Soviet Union appeared to have achieved a sort of stability. It was, however, a stability built on repression as well as stagnation. Judging de-Stalinization to be a risky business, Brezhnev and his colleagues embarked on a rehabilitation of Stalin's reputation. As statues of the dictator began to reappear, the limited cultural and intellectual freedoms introduced under Khrushchev vanished. Never subtle, state officials took to bulldozing outdoor art shows as rigid censorship and repression once again characterized Soviet society. Those who expressed dissident views soon found themselves denied employment and educational opportunities, imprisoned, sent to the Gulag, or confined indefinitely in a psychiatric ward.

Yet dissent did not disappear. Soviet society may have resembled a stagnant pond by the 1970s, but beneath the surface churned dangerous currents that, in the late 1980s, would engulf the entire communist system. Reviving a practice employed by reformers under the tsarist regime, dissidents evaded the censors by *samizdat* or "self-publishing." Novels, plays, poetry, political treatises, and historical studies were circulated privately, copied by hand or duplicated on treasured (and often confiscated) typewriters and photocopiers and distributed more widely. Nonconformist artists, banned from official exhibitions, used private apartments to show their work.

Nationalism among the non-Russian populations served as the source of much discontent within the Soviet Union during this era. As the Soviet economy grew, Russian managers and technicians were sent to places such as oil-rich Kazakhstan. Russian immigration to the Baltic states was particularly dramatic: In 1970, native Latvians made up only 59 percent of the Latvian population. Resentment of these Russian immigrants, perceived as the privileged representatives of a colonialist power, escalated. By the mid-1960s, clandestine nationalist political organizations had emerged in almost every non-Russian republic of the Soviet Union.

Diversity and Dissent in Eastern Europe

Despite the uniformity imposed by Soviet-style communist systems during these decades, the nations of eastern Europe developed in different ways. De-Stalinization contributed to this diversification. In his "Secret Speech" of 1956, Khrushchev declared, "it is ridiculous to think that revolu-

De-Stalinization

On October 31, 1956, Hungarian demonstrators pulled down a huge statue of Joseph Stalin and then dragged it two miles through the city center. Stalin's head still sits at an intersection in Budapest.

tions are made to order"[11] and so indicated that communist nations could follow paths diverging from the road traveled by the Soviet Union.

1956 and After

But just how far from the Soviet road could those paths go? The contrasting fates of Poland and Hungary in 1956 provide the answer. In Poland, popular protests against rigid Stalinist controls proved strong enough in 1956 to bring back into power Władisław Gomułka (1905–1982). An influential Polish communist who had been purged in the Stalinist terror of 1951, Gomułka succeeded in establishing a uniquely Polish brand of communism, one that abandoned collective farming and efforts to control Polish Catholicism and yet remained loyal to the Warsaw Pact.

During these same years, Hungary also pursued a de-Stalinizing "New Course" under the leadership of a reformist communist. Unlike Gomułka, however, Imre Nagy (1896–1958) proved unable to resist demands for a break with the Soviet Union. On October 31, Hungary withdrew from the Warsaw Pact—or tried to. Four days later, Khrushchev sent in the tanks. As many as 20,000 Hungarians may have died as the Red Army crushed all resistance.[12] Nagy was executed in 1958.

The repression of the Hungarian revolt defined the limits of de-Stalinization in eastern Europe: The Soviet

Union's satellite states could not follow paths that led out of the Warsaw Pact. Within the confines of this structure and of the one-party state, however, the governments of eastern Europe continued to pursue different courses. East Germany became the most industrially advanced and urbanized country in eastern Europe, while Poland's countryside was dotted with family farms. Perhaps most surprisingly, post-1956 Hungary became the most liberal country in the Eastern bloc under Nagy's successor, János Kádár (1912–1989), a reformist communist who, like Gomułka, had survived torture and imprisonment during the Stalinist terror of the early 1950s. Kádár encouraged debate within the Communist Party, loosened censorship on film studios and publishers, and permitted private business ventures. In sharp contrast, Romanians endured the reign of the "mini-Stalins." Gheorghe Gheorghiu-Dej (1901–1965) and Nicolai Ceauşescu (1918–1989) imposed not only one-party but one-man control over the country through Stalinist methods of terror.

Within the diverse experiences of eastern Europeans, certain commonalities characterized the post-1956 era. Except in Romania and even more oppressive Albania, living standards improved. Educational opportunities expanded, the supply of consumer goods increased, and political repression became less overt. Even so, overcentralization, bureaucratic mismanagement, and political corruption ensured that living standards remained below those of the West. Moreover, the very consumer goods that were supposed to persuade eastern European citizens of the superiority of the communist system instead demonstrated its deficiencies. With a radio, a Hungarian teenager could tune into Radio Free Europe and hear of a livelier, more abundant society in the West. In East Germany, television watchers could view West German networks and catch a glimpse of Western prosperity.

The Prague Spring

Discontent and dissent simmered throughout the eastern bloc during the 1960s and then, in 1968, boiled over in Czechoslovakia. During the 1960s, a reform movement emerged in the ranks of the Czechoslovakian Communist Party. It included both Slovaks, who believed that the regime's highly centralized policies favored Czechs, and the new elite of highly educated technocrats who resented the power of poorly educated party superiors. At the beginning of 1968, this resentment fueled an intraparty revolution which brought to power the reformist Communist (and Slovak) Alexander Dubček (1921–1992). Dubček embarked on a program of radical reform, aimed at achieving "socialism with a human face." This more humane socialism included freedom of speech, press, assembly, and travel; the removal of Communist Party controls from social and cultural life; and decentralization of the economy.

Dubček's effort to reform the system from the top quickly merged with a wider popular protest movement that had arisen among intellectuals, artists, students, and workers. The result was the "Prague Spring"°—the blossoming of political and social freedoms throughout Czechoslovakia, but especially in the capital city of Prague.

Well aware of the fate of Hungary in 1956, Dubček reassured Brezhnev and the other Soviet leaders that these reforms would not lead Czechoslovakia out of the Warsaw Pact. But by the summer of 1968, many of the ideas of the Prague activists were filtering through to other eastern European countries and to the Soviet Union itself. In Ukraine, nationalist protesters looked to Prague for inspiration, while in Poland, student riots, which broke out in all the major cities, featured placards reading "Poland is awaiting its own Dubček." Frightened communist leaders throughout the eastern bloc demanded that Brezhnev act to stifle the Prague Spring.

On the night of August 20–21, 80,000 troops—drawn from not only the Soviet Union but also Poland, Hungary, and East Germany—crossed the Czech border. They were immediately confused: Czechs had removed road signs and painted over street numbers in order to confound the invaders. Thirty Czechs died on the first day of the invasion, and hundreds more were injured. The resistance spread. Workers went on strike, 20,000 Czechs marched in Prague to protest the invasion, and children ran in front of the tanks, shaking their fists. But over the next several weeks, the Prague Spring was crushed. The scientists, artists, and intellectuals who had supported the movement found themselves either in prison or unemployed. As one Communist Party journal explained, the new regime "will not permit all flowers to blossom. We will cultivate, water, and protect only one flower, the red rose of Marxism."

But that rose needed an army to hold it up. In the fall of 1968, Brezhnev acknowledged that Soviet domination in eastern Europe rested on force alone when he articulated what came to be known as the "Brezhnev Doctrine." Formally a commitment to support global socialism, the Brezhnev Doctrine was essentially a promise to use the Red Army to stomp on any eastern European effort to achieve fundamental change.

Even more important, after 1968 eastern Europeans recognized the futility of attempting to reform a system that had now been revealed as beyond reform. Many, perhaps most, eastern Europeans retreated to private worlds of friendship and family life (or to the easy escape provided by alcohol). Others, however, refused to give up or to give in to a system they now viewed as utterly corrupt. They sought, in the words of the Czech playwright and dissident Václav Havel (b. 1936), to "live in truth" in the midst of a society based on lies. As the Polish author Konstanty Gebert explained, living in truth raised "a small, portable barricade between me and silence, submission, humiliation, shame. Impregnable for tanks, uncircumventable. As long as I man it, there is, around me, a small area of freedom."

The West: Consensus, Consumption, and Culture

■ **What patterns characterized the history of western Europe in the 1950s and 1960s?**

As in eastern Europe, in western Europe both the experience of total war and Cold War concerns helped shape postwar societies. The desire to make the suffering of the war years worthwhile, as well as fear of communism, furthered the integration of Europe's economies and helped define the political centrism characteristic of western Europe in the 1950s and 1960s. The dominant fact of the postwar years was, however, material prosperity as western European economies embarked on two decades of dramatic economic growth and consumer spending.

The Triumph of Democracy

In sharp contrast to the interwar years, the parties in power in western Europe in the 1950s and 1960s, and the voters who put them there, agreed on the viability and virtues of parliamentary democracy. The new constitutions of France, West Germany, and Italy guaranteed the protection of individual rights, and French and Italian women achieved suffrage. The democratic ideal of the universal franchise had finally been realized in most of western Europe.

Citizenship, though, meant more than the right to vote after 1945. As the social democratic vision triumphed in western Europe after World War II, the meaning of citizenship broadened to include the right to a decent standard of living. Through the nationalization of key industries, the establishment of public agencies to oversee and encourage investment and trade, and the manipulation of interest rates and currency supplies, governments assumed the task of ensuring full employment and material well-being for their citizens. A slogan of the German Social Democratic Party—"as much competition as possible, as much planning as necessary"—sums up an approach common to much of western Europe at this time.

This commitment, however, embraced a variety of national styles. The British stressed the nationalization of heavy industry, while the French emphasized the role of centralized planning. Led by the pragmatic visionary Jean Monnet (1888–1979), France's postwar Planning Commission set economic targets and directed investment. In contrast, in West Germany, where centralized direction of the economy was linked to Nazism, politicians chose a more free-market path to industrial success.

Yet even in West Germany, citizens had access to an extensive welfare system. With the construction of comprehensive welfare states, postwar governments undertook to guarantee their citizens adequate incomes and medical care. By the end of the 1950s, the average western European working-class family received 63 percent of its income from wages. The substantial remaining income came from welfare benefits such as family allowances, national health services, sickness and disability insurance, and old-age pensions. In addition, state-run vaccination and inoculation programs, stricter sanitation regulation, and the development of policies to control communicable diseases all meant an improvement in the health of Europe's populations.

As we saw in Chapter 26, this triumph of social democracy was rooted in the suffering of World War II, when Europeans grew determined to create a better world out of the rubble of total war. This determination remained, but much of the radicalism of the wartime spirit quickly receded as the Cold War constricted the parameters of political debate. The mainstream political parties—Christian Democrats or Conservatives on the right, Social Democrats or Socialists on the left—agreed in refusing to allow Communist Party members to participate in governing coalitions. In France and Italy, communist parties consistently drew 20 to 30 percent of the vote but were effectively marginalized by their exclusion from office after 1948.

With the communists isolated, and with the ideologies of the extremist Right such as fascism and Nazism discredited by the horrors of the war, western European politics took on a new and marked stability during the 1950s and early 1960s. Christian Democratic° parties—which have no American or British counterpart—flourished on the Continent during the postwar era. Drawing on a Roman Catholic base for their support and espousing a largely conservative social ideology combined with a progressive commitment to the welfare state, Christian Democratic parties dominated much of European politics in the 1950s and 1960s. Christian Democrats played significant roles in the political life of France and Belgium, governed West Germany between 1949 and 1969, and provided every prime minister except two in Italy between 1945 and 1993.

Three factors account for Christian Democracy's success. First, as anticommunists and advocates of the free market, Christian Democrats benefited from Cold War anxieties and more directly from American aid and support. Second, because they were based on religion (Roman Catholicism) rather than class, Christian Democratic parties were able to appeal to both middle-class and working-class voters, and particularly to women, who tended to be more religious and to vote more conservatively than men. But finally and most important, the triumph of Christian Democracy rested on its dramatic transformation from a right-wing to a centrist political movement. In the interwar period, Christian Democracy, rooted in a religious and political tradition based on hierarchy and authoritarianism, had veered close to fascism. But during World War II, many Catholics served in the resistance movement, where they absorbed progressive political ideas. This war-inspired desire to use the power of the state to improve the lives of ordinary people blended with more traditional Catholic paternalism. After the war the Christian Democrats not only jettisoned their authoritarianism and embraced democracy, they also supported the construction of comprehensive welfare states.

Prosperity in the West

These political developments unfolded against an economic backdrop of increasing prosperity. In the first half of the 1950s, Europeans moved rapidly from the austerity of the immediate postwar years to an age of unprecedented affluence.

Economic Integration

One important factor in this new prosperity was the greater coordination of western European economies. World War II provided the impetus for this economic integration. Fighting in conditions of unprecedented horror, Europeans looked for ways to guarantee a lasting peace. In 1943, Jean Monnet (1888–1979), who would oversee French economic planning in the postwar era, declared, "there will be no peace in Europe, if the states are reconstituted on the basis of national sovereignty." In July 1944, Resistance leaders from France, Italy, the Netherlands, and a number of other countries met in Geneva to embrace Monnet's vision and declare their support for a federal, democratic Europe.

No such radical restructuring of Europe occurred, but the push toward greater European union moved forward in the years after 1945, impelled by Cold War concerns. Opposition to Stalin helped western Europeans see themselves as part of a single region with common interests. At the same time, American postwar planners—anxious to restore economic prosperity to Europe in order to lessen the appeal of communism—urged their European colleagues to dismantle trade barriers and coordinate national economic plans, and required recipients of Marshall aid to develop transnational economic institutions. Looking back on this early stage of European integration, the Belgian prime minister (and ardent proponent of European union) Paul-Henri Spaak (1899–1972) wrote in the later 1960s, "Europeans, let us be modest. It is the fear of Stalin and the daring views of Marshall which led us into the right path."[13]

A Common Market and European Integration (1960)

Spaak was a socialist, but many Christian Democrats also promoted European economic union, including Konrad Adenauer, the first chancellor of West Germany; Alcide de Gaspari, the postwar prime minister of Italy; and the French foreign minister Robert Schuman (1886–1963). Schuman's upbringing opened him to an internationalist perspective: Reared in Alsace under both German and French rule, Schuman had served as a German army officer before he entered French politics.

Desperate to break down the nationalist and economic rivalries that had led to World War II, Schuman in 1950 proposed the merger of the German and French coal and steel industries. The resulting European Coal and Steel Community (ECSC), established in 1952, comprised not only Germany and France, but also Italy, Belgium, the Netherlands, and Luxembourg. It proved to be an economic success, stimulating economic growth throughout the member economies.

Heartened by the success of the ECSC, the six member nations in 1957 formed the European Economic Community° (EEC) or Common Market°. The EEC sought not only to establish an enormous free trade zone across member boundaries, but also to coordinate policies on wages, prices, immigration, and social security. Between 1958 and 1970, trade among its six member states increased fivefold. The rapid movement of goods, services, and even workers ensured that the economies of member states flourished. In contrast, Britain, which had chosen to remain outside the EEC in order to preserve its preferential trading relationships with its former and current colonies, struggled to compete, with growth rates below those of its continental competitors.

The Age of Affluence

If a European living in 1930 had been transported by a time machine to the Europe of 1965, he or she would probably have been most astonished, however, not by European economic integration but by the cornucopia of consumer goods spilling over the lives of ordinary Europeans. After years of wartime rationing, Europeans went on a spending spree and did not stop. A swift and unprecedented climb in real wages—by 80 percent in England, for example, between 1950 and 1970—helps explain why. So too does the construction of the welfare state. With full employment and comprehensive welfare services offering unprecedented financial security, Europeans shrugged off habits of thrift.

This spending spree transformed both the interiors of European homes and their exterior environment. The postwar period witnessed a boom in housing construction. The annual volume of construction rose by 80 percent between 1950 and 1957. With new houses came new household goods. Items such as refrigerators and washing machines, once unaffordable luxuries, now became increasingly common in ordinary homes. In France, for example, the stock of home appliances rose by 400 percent between 1949 and 1957.

At the same time, the automobile revolutionized much of both the rural and urban landscape. Highways, few and far between in 1950, cut across the countryside, and parking meters, unknown in Europe before 1959, dotted city streets. In 1964, the archbishop of Florence presided over a

DOCUMENT

The Age of Affluence

Full employment and rising real wages meant that the European working class joined the mass consumer society in the postwar era. In Alan Sillitoe's novel Saturday Night and Sunday Morning, *20-year-old Arthur Seaton seethes with unarticulated anger over continuing class divisions and his own powerlessness, yet he is well aware of the stark material contrast between the 1930s and the 1950s. Seaton credits the war, not the welfare state, with the material improvements he observes around him. He confronts his father on Monday morning before heading to work:*

"You'll go blind one day, dad," he said, for nothing, taking the words out of the air for sport, ready to play with the consequences of whatever he might cause.

Seaton turned to him uncomprehendingly, his older head still fuddled. It took ten cups of tea and as many Woodbines [cigarettes] to set his temper right after the weekend. "What do you mean?" he demanded, intractable at any time before ten in the morning.

"Sittin' in front of the TV. You stick to it like glue from six to eleven every night. It can't be good for yer. You'll go blind one day. You're bound to. I read it in the *Post* last week that a lad from the Medders went blind . . . "

"Ye're barmy," Seaton said. "Go an tell yer stories somewhere else . . . "

The subject was dropped. His father cut several slices of bread and made sandwiches with cold meat left from Sunday dinner. Arthur teased him a lot, but in a way he was glad to see the TV standing in a corner of the living-room, a glossy panelled box looking, he thought, like something plundered from a spaceship. The old man was happy at last, anyway, and he deserved to be happy, after all the years before the war on the dole [on unemployment benefit], five kids and the miserying that went with no money and no way of getting any. And now he had a sit-down job at the factory, all the Woodbines he could smoke, money for a pint [of beer] if he wanted one, though he didn't as a rule drink, a holiday somewhere, a jaunt on the firm's trip to Blackpool [a seaside resort], and a television-set to look into at home. The difference between before the war and after the war didn't bear thinking about. War was a marvellous thing in many ways, when you thought about how happy it had made so many people in England.

. . . Once out of doors they were aware of the factory rumbling a hundred yards away. . . . The thousands that worked there took home good wages. . . . With the wages you got you could save up for a motor-bike or even an old car, or you could go on a ten-day binge and get rid of all you'd saved. Because it was no use saving your money year after year. A mug's game, since the value of it got less and less and in any case you never knew when the Yanks were going to do something daft like dropping the H-bomb on Moscow.

Source: From *Saturday Night and Sunday Morning* by Alan Sillitoe, copyright © 1958 by Alan Sillitoe. Used by permission of Alfred A. Knopf, a division of Random House, Inc.

---

thanksgiving service in a gas station to celebrate the completion of a highway linking Milan and Naples. Out-of-town shopping centers, geared to the convenience of car owners, proliferated while city centers decayed.

Spending begot more spending. Credit buying (what the British called "buying on the never-never") became commonplace and made possible even more consumption. Television commercials (first seen in the mid-1950s), the Yellow Pages (first distributed in Europe in the early 1960s), and color advertising supplements in the Sunday newspapers (an innovation, again, of the early 1960s) all encouraged a culture of consumption.

Western Culture and Thought in the Age of Consumption

Cultural developments in Western society highlight the shift from an era structured by the memories of World War II to a period shaped by prosperity. Existentialism and modernism retained their dominant cultural position in the later 1940s and 1950s. By the beginning of the 1960s, however, artists began to retreat from engagement with the horrors of World War II and the overwhelming challenges of the Cold War. Instead, they produced works that reflected, commented on, and reveled in the cascade of consumer abundance that was transforming Western culture.

Finding Meaning in the Age of Auschwitz and the Atom Bomb

Forged in the despair of the 1930s (see Chapter 25), existentialism remained a powerful cultural force in the early postwar era. Jean-Paul Sartre's conviction that existence has no intrinsic meaning, and yet that the individual retains the freedom to act and therefore make meaning, resounded loudly in a world that had experienced both the Holocaust and the Resistance. The existentialist emphasis on individual action as the source of meaning could lead to a life of political activism—Sartre, for example, worked with the French Resistance and became a prominent participant in left-wing political causes in the 1950s and 1960s. On the other hand, existentialism also justified political disengagement. In the Irish-French playwright Samuel Beckett's (1906–1989) existentialist masterpiece *Waiting for Godot* (1952), two tramps sit in an empty universe, waiting for someone who never comes. In this absurd void, politics has no relevance or resonance.

Existentialist themes echo throughout the visual arts in the 1950s. The sculptures of the Swiss artist Alberto Giacometti (1901–1966) are the embodiments of existentialist anguish—fragile, insubstantial, they appear ready to crack under the strain of being. While Giacometti's sculptures embody existentialist terror, the works of the preeminent British painter of the 1950s, Francis Bacon (1909–1992), evoke outright nausea. Bacon's disturbing canvases are case studies in the power of the subconscious. He painted the people he saw around him, but his perceptions were of a society disfigured by slaughter. Slabs of meat, dripping in blood, figure prominently. Bacon explained, "When you go into a butcher's shop . . . you can think of the whole horror of life, of one thing living off another."[14] By the end of the decade, solitary figures, secluded in claustrophobic settings and embodying Sartre's description of human existence as essentially isolated, recurred frequently in Bacon's work.

In this period, the terrors of the nuclear age also helped shape cultural consciousness. Because figurative painting seemed utterly incapable of capturing the power and terror of the atomic age, the Bomb reinforced the hold of abstract art over the avant-garde. But abstract art itself changed. Formal geometric abstractions had characterized much of prewar art; after the war, a new modernist movement, Abstract Expressionism, displayed more spontaneous styles. The Abstract Expressionist Jackson Pollock

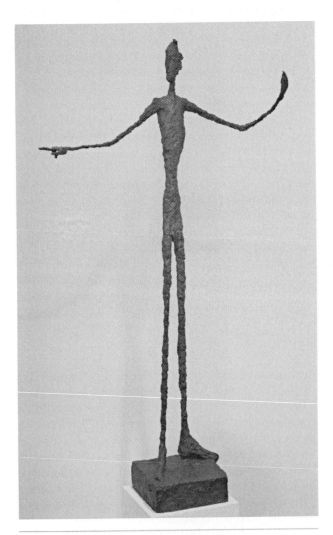

Alberto Giacometti, *Man Pointing* (1947)
Giacometti's sculptures embodied existentialist anguish. His account of this piece's creation seems to be lifted from a Samuel Beckett play or one of Jean-Paul Sartre's novels: "Wanting to create from memory [the figures] I had seen, to my terror the sculptures became smaller and smaller, they had a likeness only when they were small, yet their dimensions revolted me, and tirelessly I began again, only to end several months later at the same point."

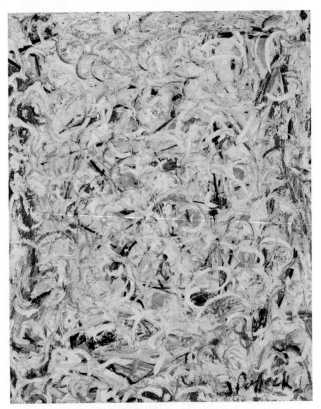

Jackson Pollock, *Shimmering Substance* (1946)
Many of Pollock's postwar works—huge paintings that pulse with power—show an obsession with heat and light, surely no coincidence in the dawn of the nuclear age.

(1912–1956), for example, invented an entirely new way of painting. Placing the canvas on the ground, he moved around and in it, dripping or pouring paint. In Pollock's works, the canvas has no clear center, no focal point. Instead, it disintegrates, like matter itself. As Pollock explained, "New needs need new techniques . . . The modern painter cannot express his age, the airplane, the atom bomb . . . in the old forms."[15]

Most people confronted their nuclear fears not in art galleries, but rather in movie theaters and popular fiction. In the movies, various nuclear-spawned horrors, including giant spiders, ants, and turtles, wreaked weekly havoc on the Western world. Fittingly enough, many of these films were produced in Japan. Throughout the 1950s, nuclear war and the postnuclear struggle for survival also filled the pages of popular fiction. Probably the most important "nuclear" novel, however, confined mention of atomic bombs to a single sentence. In *Lord of the Flies* (1954), British author William Golding (1911–1993) told the simple but brutal story of a group of schoolboys stranded on an island after they flee atomic attack. Their moral deterioration poses basic questions about the meaning of civilization, a question brought to the forefront of Western society by its use of advanced science and technology to obliterate civilian populations during World War II.

Culture and Ideas in the World of Plenty

By the early 1960s, however, artists began to turn away from such big questions and to focus instead on the material stuff of everyday existence. In works such as the British artist Richard Hamilton's *Just What Is It That Makes Today's Homes So Different, So Appealing?* (1956), artists satirized and yet celebrated postwar materialism and revealed their fascination with the plethora of material objects pouring off assembly lines. Hamilton was a leading force in the Independent Group, a loose association of British artists, designers, and architects that sought in their work to embody the "aesthetics of plenty"—the idea that consumer affluence had smashed the barriers between fine art and popular culture. The Independent Group, along with other movements such as "New Realism" in France and "Capitalist Realism" in West Germany, helped shape what became known as pop art°.

Pop artists dismissed the anguish of Bacon and Giacometti as the concerns of an older generation still mired in World War II. Pop art looked outward rather than inward, and focused on the material rather than the spiritual. Pop artists spoke in the vocabulary of mass material culture, and even relied on mass production and mass marketing.

By doing so, they challenged accepted ideas about the role of both art and the artist in Western society. When Gerhard Richter (b. 1932) placed himself in the furniture display of a West German department store and called the resulting "piece" *Living with Pop* (1963) he turned the artist, as well as art, into a commodity, something to be bought and sold just like anything else. In the age of consumption, pop advocates declared, the individual artist's intentions were unimportant, and concepts such as artistic genius were irrelevant.

Similar themes also characterized developments in social thought. Existentialism had elevated the individual as the only source of meaning in an absurd universe. In the late 1950s, however, a new social theory, structuralism°, pushed the individual off center stage. Structuralism, which French anthropologist Claude Levi-Strauss (b. 1908) first introduced to a wide audience, transformed a number of

Richard Hamilton, *Just What Is It That Makes Today's Homes So Different, So Appealing?* (1956)
British artist Richard Hamilton was one of the leading figures in the pop art of the 1950s.

academic disciplines, including literary criticism, political theory, sociology, and even history. Levi-Strauss argued that the myths told in all cultures, whether that of Brazilian Indian tribes still using Stone Age tools or medieval French peasants or contemporary Londoners, shared certain "deep structures," repeated patterns such as pairings and oppositions that help give order to the cultural world. The actual stories are unimportant. To use a newspaper metaphor offered by the intellectual historian Roland Stromberg, the structuralist is interested not in the content of the articles but in the layout of the page—the arrangement of articles, the juxtaposition of images, the shape of headlines. By analyzing the "layout" of cultures, the structuralist can uncover the basic structures of human thought. In structuralism, then, as in pop art, the individual matters little. Human beings exist within a ready-built structure that shapes and dictates the way they perceive the world.

Science and Religion in an Age of Mass Consumption

At the same time that structuralists depicted the individual as stuck within a cultural and linguistic web, his or her choices firmly constrained by the sticky fibers of that web, radical breakthroughs in the biological sciences posited that perhaps the web lay inside the individual, its fibers comprising chemicals and chromosomes that determined individual capabilities. In 1953, the British biologist Francis Crick (1916–2004) and his American colleague James Watson (b. 1928) discovered the structure of DNA, the basic building block of genetic material. Crick and Watson's model of the "double helix," the intertwined spirals of chemical units that, in a sense, issue the instructions for an individual's development, caught the attention of the world. As biologists and geneticists furthered their investigations into human genetic inheritance, they raised exciting yet potentially disturbing possibilities, such as the cloning of living organisms and genetic manipulation, and added a new dimension to the perennial debate about individual freedom.

Other scientific developments assured human beings more freedom from their physical environment than ever

CHRONOLOGY

Medical Breakthroughs

1950	First kidney transplant
1952	First sex-change operation
1952	Polio vaccine first produced
1953	Discovery of DNA
1957	CAT scan developed
1967	First heart transplant

before. Motivated by the Cold War, the space race launched humanity beyond the confines of Earth, culminating in 1969 with the American astronaut Neil Armstrong's moon walk. Medical breakthroughs in this era seemed to promise that infectious diseases could be eradicated. Large-scale production of penicillin transformed ordinary medical care, as did rapid development of vaccines against many childhood killers such as measles. In 1953, the American Jonas Salk announced the first successful clinical trial of a polio vaccine. In this era, blood transfusions become more commonplace, along with the development of organ transplants, following the first successful kidney transplant in Chicago in 1950. Like washing machines and television sets, a long and healthy life suddenly appeared accessible to many people in the West.

While scientists were claiming more control over the physical environment, the organized churches continued to offer spiritual authority and sustenance. Church attendance, which had declined in most Western countries in the interwar period, rose during the 1950s. In the United States between 1942 and 1960, church membership per capita grew faster than at any time since the 1890s. No European nation shared this dramatic religious upsurge; nevertheless, except in Scandinavia, western Europe experienced a gentle religious revival. In Britain during the 1950s, church membership, Sunday school enrollment, and the numbers of baptisms and religious marriages all increased. In West Germany, the rate of churchgoing rose among Protestants from 1952 until 1967. Throughout Catholic Europe, the vibrancy of Christian Democratic politics reflected the vital position of the Catholic Church in society.

In the 1960s, however, the situation changed dramatically. Europeans abandoned the church sanctuary in favor of the department store, the sports stadium, and the sofa in front of the television set. Declining rates of church attendance, a growing number of civil rather than religious marriage ceremonies, and an increased reluctance to obey Church teaching on issues such as premarital sexual relations all pointed to the secularization of European society. By the 1970s, churchgoing rates in both Protestant and Catholic countries were in freefall. In what had once been called "Christendom," the fastest-growing religious community was Islam.

The churches did not remain stagnant during this time of change. A number of Protestant theologians argued that Christianity could maintain its relevance in this more secular society only by adapting the biblical message to a modern context. The British theologian (and Anglican bishop) John Robinson achieved great notoriety in 1963 when he proclaimed the "death of God." Most of those who jeered at or cheered for Robinson's statement missed his point: The language in which Christians articulate their faith must be updated to make sense in the modern world.

The biggest change occurred in Roman Catholicism. In 1963 the Second Vatican Council—widely known as Vatican II°—convened in Rome, the first catholic council to meet since 1870. In calling the council, Pope John XXIII (r. 1958–1963) sought to modernize and rejuvenate the Church, a process that, he recognized, would demand "a change in mentalities, ways of thinking and prejudices, all of which have a long history."[16] John did not live to see this change in mentalities take place, but his successor Paul VI (r. 1963–1978) presided over a quiet revolution.

The Church emerged from Vatican II less hierarchical and more open, with local and regional councils sharing more power with the papacy. For ordinary Catholics, the most striking changes occurred in the worship service, where a number of reforms narrowed the gap between priest and people. The priest moved from in front of to behind the altar, so that he could face the congregation; he spoke in the vernacular rather than in Latin; and all worshipers, not only the priest, received the wine at communion.

Vatican II was less revolutionary in its approach to sexual issues and gender roles. The council said nothing about homosexuality, reaffirmed the traditional doctrine of clerical celibacy, and insisted that only men could be ordained as priests. The council left open the question of birth control but three years later, the pope declared contraceptive use to be contrary to Church teaching. The issues of clerical celibacy, women's ordination, and contraceptive use would bedevil the Church for the rest of the century.

McDonald's on the Champs-Elysées in Paris
In the postwar era, the United States functioned as a symbol of modernity. The McDonald's hamburger franchise represented the United States to many Europeans because it typified modernity's standardization and mass consumerism. Assembly-line production lowered costs and made dining out affordable to the masses.

Social Encounters in the Age of Affluence

With the unprecedented prosperity of the postwar years came a series of encounters between different cultural and social groups. As trade and production increased in Europe, so, too, did the volume and variety of goods imported from elsewhere. The demand for laborers rose as well, bringing with it a rising tide of immigration and of women's employment. Affluence also permitted more young people than ever before to attend colleges and universities. The encounters that resulted from these developments both shaped and were shaped by western Europeans' efforts to make sense of the new material world.

Americanization, Coca-Colonization, and the Gaullist Protest

For many Europeans, this new world seemed overwhelmingly American, as U.S.-based corporations scattered branch offices throughout western Europe, and U.S.-produced goods filled the shelves of European shops. The U.S. presence in science and technology was also formidable. The United States invested more in scientific research and development, produced more graduates in the sciences and engineering than all other Western countries combined, and came out on top in terms of numbers of papers published and patents registered.

American domination of popular culture was even more striking. Immediately after World War II, the U.S. government forced European states to dismantle quotas on American film imports by threatening to withhold much-needed loans. By 1951, American productions accounted for more than 60 percent of film showings in western Europe. American television, too, quickly established a central position in European mass culture. In the mid-1950s, few European households had a television, while the average American family was watching more than five hours of programming every day. In the second half of the decade, then, as the number of television owners in Europe began to expand rapidly (more than doubling between 1955 and 1956), American television networks were well-situated to take advantage of this new market. By 1960, CBS, ABC, and NBC were selling their programs to the world. The popular *Lone Ranger* series, for example, appeared in twenty-four countries. Language itself seemed subject to American takeover. Words such as *babysitter* and *comics* entered directly into German, while French children coveted *les jeans* and *le chewing-gum*.

Europeans differed in their response to the new American presence. Many enthusiastically embraced American culture, equating it with greater openness and freedom. Others, however, feared that American products such as Coca-Cola would not only conquer European markets but degrade European tastes. Europeans spoke with alarm about the "brain drain" as scientists and academics headed across the Atlantic to the richer universities of the United States. They argued that even as Europe was losing its colonial possessions, it was itself undergoing colonization, or at least "coca-colonization."[17]

One of the most powerful voices protesting "coca-colonization" belonged to Charles De Gaulle, France's president throughout the 1960s. De Gaulle is usually classified as politically conservative, but the politics of "Gaullism"° are not easy to place on any simple left-right political spectrum. De Gaulle combined a fierce anticommunism and an ardent defense of traditional social values with a firm commitment to a strong state and centralized direction of the economy. Perhaps most centrally, Gaullism championed France and Frenchness. In De Gaulle's imagination, France was "like the princess in the fairy stories or the Madonna in the frescoes, as dedicated to an exalted and exceptional destiny . . . France cannot be France without greatness."[18]

De Gaulle did not sympathize in any way with the Soviet Union, but he believed that the more immediate threat to the French way of life came from American culture. Taken in 1960 to view a new highway in California, De Gaulle gazed somberly at the sight of cars weaving in and out on a traffic cloverleaf and commented, "I have the impression that all this will end very badly."[19] To reduce American influence in Europe, and thus to restore France to its rightful position of grandeur and glory, De Gaulle pursued independent foreign and military policies. He extended diplomatic recognition to China, made a state visit to Moscow, and withdrew French forces from NATO command (although France remained formally a part of the NATO alliance). In 1960 France exploded its own atomic bomb.

Like De Gaulle, Europeans across the political spectrum feared their countries' becoming secondhand versions of the United States, yet the cultural history of this era was one of reciprocal encounters rather than one-way Americanization. Europeans consumed American products with great gusto, but in the process they adapted these products to suit their own needs. In the late 1950s, for example, four young

working-class men from the northern British seaport of Liverpool latched on to the new American rock and roll, mixed in their own regional musical styles, and transformed popular music not only in Europe but also in the United States. The impact of the Beatles testified to the power of European culture to remake American cultural products. Even McDonald's, when it arrived in European cities in the 1960s, made subtle changes to the composition of its fast food to appeal to the differing tastes of the new markets.

Immigration and Ethnic Diversity

A second set of encounters that transformed European societies during this era resulted from the presence of rising numbers of immigrants, who brought with them new and in many cases non-Western cultural traditions. Immigration was the by-product of both decolonization and economic prosperity. As European imperial control collapsed, white settlers retreated to their country of origin, and colonial "losers"—indigenous groups that had allied with the now-defeated colonial powers—fled because they feared discrimination, retribution, or perhaps simply a loss of status. In France, for example, Algerian independence led to the influx not only of Algeria's white French population but also of 80,000 Algerian Harkis whose loyalty to the

Immigrants Arriving in Britain, 1956
Many immigrants from regions within the British Empire had been taught that Britain was the "mother country" or "home." They were shocked to discover that once in Britain, they were regarded as foreign and as inferior.

colonial administration jeopardized their place in the new Algeria.

At the same time, as northern and western European states experienced both soaring economic growth figures and a slowing rate of population increase, governments undertook to recruit foreign labor. Beginning in 1955, the West German government negotiated a series of immigration contracts with Italy, Greece, Turkey, Yugoslavia, and the North African states. In Britain, both public and private agencies turned for workers to the West Indies, India, and Pakistan. France recruited workers from Spain and Italy, as well as its colonial territories such as Algeria, Morocco, Tunisia, Senegal, Mali, and Guadeloupe. By the beginning of the 1970s, the nations of northern and western Europe were home to approximately nine million immigrants, half of these from the less prosperous Mediterranean states of Portugal, Spain, Italy, and Greece. The other half came from Turkey, Yugoslavia, and countries in Asia, Africa, and the Caribbean.

These workers did the dirtiest, most dangerous, least desirable jobs. They worked the night shifts, emptied the bedpans, dug the ditches, and cleaned the toilets. They lived in substandard housing, often confined to isolated dormitories or inner-city slums, and accepted low, often illegally low, pay rates. The reason they did so is starkly presented in the table below. Despite racial discrimination and economic exploitation, western Europe offered greater economic opportunities than were available in the immigrants' homelands.

The majority of the early immigrants were single men. They tended to see themselves, and were seen by their host countries, as "guestworkers," temporary laborers who would earn money and then return home to their native lands. By the mid-1960s, however, families were beginning to join these men, and a second generation of "immigrants" was being born. This generation changed the face of Europe. By the 1980s European societies had become multiethnic.

The Appeal of Immigration—Annual Per Capita Gross National Product in the Mid-1960s

Pakistan	$125
Turkey	$353
Jamaica	$520
Spain	$822
Italy	$1,272
Britain	$1,977
France	$2,324

Source: Leslie Page Moch, *Moving Europeans: Migration in Western Europe Since 1650* (1992), 177.

The emergence of urban ethnic subcultures immeasurably enlivened European cultures and economies (and diets); it also complicated domestic politics and raised challenging questions about the relationship between national and ethnic identity. Racism became more overt as the white settler groups who returned "home" in the wake of decolonization often brought with them hardened racist attitudes, and the presence of nonwhite minority groups, clustered in certain cities, sparked resentment in societies unused to cultural diversity.

The Second Sex?

In 1949, the French writer Simone de Beauvoir (1908–1986) published *The Second Sex*. In this influential critique of gender divisions in Western industrial society, de Beauvoir argued that women remained the "second sex"— that despite changes in their political and legal status, women were still defined by their relationship to men rather than by their own actions or achievements. Over the next two decades, the new prosperity pushed women into higher education and the labor force and so, in the long run, worked to undermine the traditional gender roles that de Beauvoir described. In the short run, however, affluence accentuated women's domestic identity.

A number of changes both reflected and reinforced postwar domesticity. The most important were demographic. Marriage rates rose and the marriage age dropped in the postwar years. In the United States between 1940 and 1957, the fertility rate rose by 50 percent. Europe experienced a baby "boomlet" rather than a baby boom. European birth rates rose in the late 1940s but dropped again in the 1950s (whereas U.S. fertility rates remained high into the 1960s). Nevertheless, although family sizes were small, a higher percentage of western European women than ever before had children.

By exalting women's maternal identity, both religion and popular culture provided a potent ideology for these demographic changes. The Roman Catholic Church of the 1950s placed renewed emphasis on Mary, the paragon of motherhood. Pope Pius XII (r. 1939–1958) particularly encouraged the growth of devotion to Mary. He proclaimed in 1950 that Mary had ascended bodily into heaven (the Doctrine of the Assumption) and designated 1954 as the Year of Mary. This Marian devotion encouraged women to regard motherhood as a holy calling, the very core of female identity. Popular culture reinforced this religious message, with its glossy images of what families should look like and how they should interact. In television programs and in the articles and advertisements of women's magazines, the woman stayed at home, presiding over an expanding array of household machines that, in theory, reduced her housework burden and freed her to focus on the satisfactions of motherhood.

At the same time, a number of cultural, economic, and technological changes transformed the Western home into a much more private place. Because of the boom in house

The Kitchen Debate

The kitchen—stocked with an abundance of attractively packaged foods and a glittering array of time-saving appliances—symbolized not only material plenty but also moral stability. In the Western domestic ideal, the kitchen represented the center of family life and the woman's proper domain. When Vice President Richard Nixon traveled to Moscow in 1959 to open an American exhibition, he pointed to the display model of a suburban kitchen as evidence of Western superiority. Khrushchev refused to be impressed. Nixon and Khrushchev's argument became known as the "Kitchen Debate."

building, by the mid-1950s couples forced by wartime deprivation to live with their parents could now move into their own apartment or house. Accelerated suburbanization, made possible by the expansion of private car ownership and the spread of highway networks, meant that relatives now lived farther apart. "Family" increasingly meant the nuclear family.

Prosperity accentuated the family's isolation. Economic growth translated into a rapid drop in the number of domestic servants as workers turned to better-paying jobs and household appliances took their place. Because the new houses and apartment buildings possessed modern conveniences such as indoor plumbing, communal baths, toilets, and washhouses gradually disappeared. Television moved the social center away from cinemas, cafés, and pubs to the family living room.

Cold War concerns also accentuated the Western woman's domestic role in two very different ways. First, anticommunist propaganda hailed domesticity as a sign of Western superiority, by contrasting the favorable lot of Western women to their Soviet counterparts, who led lives of almost endless labor. The vast majority of Soviet women combined their domestic duties with full-time outside employment, often in jobs involving heavy manual labor, and they spent a substantial portion of each day lining up to purchase scarce goods. Second, the nuclear age made the nuclear family seem all the more important. Feeling increasingly helpless in a superpower-dominated world on the brink of nuclear annihilation, Europeans tended to withdraw for shelter to family life.

For some women, this shelter was more like a prison. In *The Captive Wife,* published in 1966, the British sociologist Hannah Gavron (b. 1944) asked, "Have all the great changes in the position of women in the last one hundred and fifty years come to nothing?" In *The Feminine Mystique* (1963), the American journalist Betty Friedan (b. 1921) identified what she called "the problem that had no name," a crisis of identity and purpose among middle-class, educated women confined in the role of housewife and mother.

Whether a nightmare or a dream, the domestic ideal remained removed from the reality of many women's lives in the postwar era. In the poorer social classes, women by necessity continued to work outside the home, as they always had. At the same time, the new culture of consumption demanded that many women, clinging precariously to the middle rungs of the social ladder, take on paid employment to pay for the ever-expanding list of household necessities.

A new pattern of employment emerged that reconciled the new domesticity with the needs of expanding economies. Increasingly, single women, including those in the middle class, worked until they married. Many continued to do so until the first child arrived and resumed paid employment after the last child had left home or at least started school. This work was regarded, however, as secondary to their main job—the making of a home and the rearing of children. Part-time employment, with lower wages and few or no benefits, expanded accordingly. Everywhere pay rates remained unequal.

Inequalities in legal status continued as well. Until 1964 and the passage of the Matrimonial Act, for example, a married French woman could not open her own bank account, run a shop, or apply for a passport without her husband's permission. Traditional gender roles remained firmly intact, despite the material and political changes of the postwar era.

DOCUMENT

Rock and Revolution

In 1967, the Beatles, already global superstars, released Sgt. Pepper's Lonely Hearts Club Band. *Called the "most influential rock album ever produced,"* Sgt. Pepper's *revolutionized rock music. The complexity of its compositions impressed serious music critics, who for the first time acknowledged that rock music was worth listening to. The album's lyrics, too, received unprecedented praise, with one reviewer comparing the last song on the album ("A Day in the Life") to T. S. Eliot's modernist masterpiece, "The Waste Land" (see Chapter 24). Although not overtly political,* Sgt. Pepper's *illustrates many of the themes of the protests that marked the era in which it was produced. Infused with a sense of playfulness and celebration, the album called its listeners to burst out of the confines of order, authority, and rationality, and embrace instead the values of human community and emotional liberation.*

She's Leaving Home

Wednesday morning at five o'clock as the day begins
Silently closing her bedroom door
Leaving the note that she hoped would say more
She goes downstairs to the kitchen clutching her
    handkerchief
Quietly turning the backdoor key
Stepping outside she is free.
She (We gave her most of our lives)
is leaving (Sacrificed most of our lives)
home (We gave her everything money could buy)

She's leaving home after living alone
For so many years. Bye, bye
Father snores as his wife gets into her dressing gown
Picks up the letter that's lying there
Standing alone at the top of the stairs
She breaks down and cries to her husband
Daddy our baby's gone.
Why would she treat us so thoughtlessly
How could she do this to me.
She (We never thought of ourselves)
is leaving (Never a thought for ourselves)
home (We struggled hard all our lives to get by)
She's leaving home after living alone
For so many years. Bye, bye
Friday morning at nine o'clock she is far away
Waiting to keep the appointment she made
Meeting a man from the motor trade.
She (What did we do that was wrong)
is having (We didn't know it was wrong) fun
Fun is the one thing that money can't buy
Something inside that was always denied
For so many years. Bye, bye
She's leaving home bye bye

The Protest Era

The unprecedented prosperity of the West in this era permitted a dramatic expansion of higher-education systems. By the later 1960s, the expanding university campuses became the center of powerful protests as political demonstrations exploded in almost every Western country and in the developing nations well. In France, a student demonstration blossomed into a full-scale social revolt. Within a few days, eight million French men and women were on strike. "Paris '68" came to symbolize the political and social discontent of many in the West, particularly the youth, during these years.

Much of this discontent focused on the New Left° argument that ordinary people, even in democratic societies, possessed little power. Appalled by the excesses of Stalinism and concerned about the growth of large corporations and of the state itself in the West, New Left thinkers such as the German philosopher Herbert

The Protests of 1968

French students battle police in Paris during the tumultuous spring of 1968.

The Pill: Controlling the Female Body

In the postwar period, all sorts of pills appeared on the shelves of American and European pharmacies. Offered in a myriad of colors and sizes, they promised all sorts of remedies for all sorts of ailments. But only one earned the designation "*the* Pill"—the oral contraceptive, first marketed in the United States in 1960. In 1993, the *Economist* (a respected British weekly news magazine) listed the Pill as one of the seven wonders of the modern world. A revolutionary contraceptive, the Pill helped alter the place of the female body in Western culture.

The Pill's entry into the mass market coincided with two other developments. First, sexual practices and attitudes changed significantly among some sectors of the population—particularly middle-class men and women with university educations. Second, the birth rate slowed throughout the United States and western Europe. Thus it is often assumed that the Pill caused both a sexual and demographic revolution.

This assumption is incorrect. Although by 1965 the Pill was the most popular form of birth control in the United States (used by 80 percent of white, non-Catholic, college graduates between ages 20 and 24), in Europe it became a part of women's lives much more slowly. Introduced to Britain in 1961, the Pill was not mass-marketed there until the late 1960s. In France and Czechoslovakia, withdrawal remained the most popular form of birth control until well into the 1970s, when the Pill began to be distributed widely. In Italy, contraceptives of all types, including the Pill, were illegal until 1971. In Ireland, they remain illegal for unmarried men and women. In the Soviet Union, the Pill was never widely accessible. Most Soviet women relied on withdrawal, rhythm, and abortion—on the average, four to six abortions during the childbearing years. Moreover, throughout Europe and the United States, the Pill always remained more popular with the wealthier sectors of society. Because women who wanted to use it were required to visit their doctor every six months, many poor women viewed the Pill as prohibitively expensive (and many single women simply could not obtain a prescription).

The Pill, then, did not cause the sexual revolution. It did, however, have a radical impact. The Pill offered a new, yet ambivalent way of viewing the female body. Other methods of birth control dealt with the consequences of sexual intercourse (the barrier methods, withdrawal, and abortion) or sought to limit its practice (rhythm). The Pill, however, was not an external object to be inserted or applied or fitted. By manipulating the female reproductive cycle, it actually altered the body itself, permitting women to experience what had been defined as an exclusively male prerogative—the detachment of sexual intercourse from pregnancy. At the same time, the Pill allowed women to distance themselves from their bodies. One of the problems with other forms of female contraceptives was that they required women to touch their genitals, a requirement that many European and American women found distasteful.

The Pill also raised important questions about controlling the female body. During the course of the twentieth century, childbirth had altered radically in the Western world. No longer occurring at home and presided over by women, childbirth now occurred in the hospital, where doctors—usually male—were in charge. It had become "medicalized": The birthing woman had become a patient, a medical problem, in need of drugs and other scientific devices. The Pill fit with this process. Although many women hailed it as a liberator that allowed them to control their own bodies, the Pill was initially marketed to doctors very differently. In its advertising, the Searle pharmaceutical company assured doctors that the Pill would allow them to supervise and regulate their patients' birth control practices. The Pill, then, offered the promise of controlling the female body; the question was, who was in charge?

For Discussion

Why has the Pill become a powerful symbol of changes in women's roles in the contemporary era?

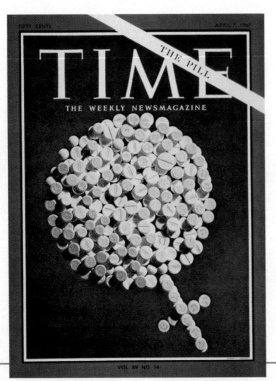

One Little Pill
In 1967, *Time* magazine's cover story on the Pill was titled "Freedom from Fear."

Marcuse (1898–1979) warned that expanding corporate and state power threatened the individuality and independence of the ordinary citizen. They argued that debate might seem open, but that experts and elites, not ordinary people, made the actual choices. Hence the protesters demanded "participatory" rather than parliamentary democracy, the revitalization of citizenship through active participation in decision making.

Discarding orthodox political solutions went hand in hand with overturning traditional social rules. In their demand for "liberation," the students focused as much on cultural as on economic and political issues. Commentators began to talk about a sexual revolution as practices became commonplace that in the 1950s were labeled immoral or bohemian—couples living together before marriage or individuals engaging in sexual relationships with a variety of partners.

The protests of the later 1960s were also linked to the wider context of decolonization and the Cold War. Protesters identified their struggle for a more open politics with colonial independence movements. Rejecting both Soviet-style communism and free-market capitalism, they turned for inspiration to the newly emerging nations of Latin America and Asia. Seeking to break free from the confines of the Cold War, they fiercely criticized American involvement in Vietnam, in which they believed the United States served not as "the leader of the free world" but rather as an imperialist oppressor.

Wolf Vostell, *Miss America*, 1968
By juxtaposing Miss America, a symbol of American luxury and even decadence, with one of the most notorious photographs to come out of the Vietnam War, the German artist Wolf Vostell articulated a powerful protest. Associated Press photographer Eddie Adams won the Pulitzer Prize for the photograph of General Nguyen Ngoc Loan, the chief of the U.S.-backed South Vietnamese National Police, caught in the act of executing a Vietcong suspect (a supporter of the communist North Vietnam) on the streets of Saigon in 1968. Broadcast to 20 million viewers on the American television network channel NBC, this photograph was reproduced in countless newspapers, magazines, and books published across the world. For many, it became a symbol of a war gone wrong.

Conclusion

New Definitions, New Divisions

The Cold War was in part an ideological encounter, with both sides laying claim to the title "democratic." When Soviet tanks rolled through the streets of Budapest in 1956, they flattened not only the Hungarian Revolution but also any illusions about the democratic nature of Soviet-style communism. Yet the hope that the communist system could be reformed, that Marx's original concern for social justice and political equality could be reclaimed, remained—until twelve years later when the tanks rolled again in an eastern European city. The crushing of the Prague Spring destroyed any hope of a democratic eastern Europe within the confines of the Cold War.

In contrast, democracy took firm root in western Europe during the postwar era, even in nations with antidemocratic cultural traditions such as West Germany and Italy. Yet in 1968, protesters in Paris and in cities throughout the world challenged the easy linkage of "the West" with democracy. They pointed out that the increasing scale and complexity of industrial society deprived ordinary people of opportunities for genuine participation in political decision making. And they pointed to the way that Cold War divisions superseded democratic commitments. Despite its abandonment of democratic practices to reinforce racial apartheid, for example, South Africa considered itself, and was considered by other powers, as part of "the West." Within the Cold War context, "the West" sometimes seemed to mean simply "anti-Soviet."

By the early 1970s, the sharp bipolarities of West versus East had begun to break down. Over the next three decades, economic crisis, combined with revolutionary changes in eastern European and Soviet affairs, would reshape the contemporary world. By the early 1990s, the Cold War was over and nationalist conflicts, often fueled by vicious ethnic and religious hatreds, once again played front and center, after twenty years of being upstaged by superpower hostilities.

Suggestions for Further Reading

For a comprehensive listing of suggested readings, please go to www.ablongman.com/levack2e/chapter27

Ansprenger, Franz. *The Dissolution of Colonial Empires*. 1989. A clear and comprehensive account (that unfortunately includes no maps).

Castles, Stephen, et al. *Here for Good: Western Europe's New Ethnic Minorities*. 1984. A useful exploration of the impact of postwar immigration, despite the rather rigid Marxist analysis.

Crampton, R. J. *Eastern Europe in the Twentieth Century—And After*. 1997. Detailed chapters on the 1950s and 1960s, including a substantial discussion of the Prague Spring.

Cronin, James. *The World the Cold War Made: Order, Chaos, and the Return of History*. 1996. An intelligent and thought-provoking overview of the impact of the Cold War.

Fineberg, Jonathan. *Art Since 1940: Strategies of Being*. 1995. A big, bold, lavishly illustrated volume that makes the unfashionable argument that individuals matter.

Fink, Carole, et al. *1968: The World Transformed*. 1998. A collection of essays that explores both the international and the domestic political context for the turmoil of 1968.

Gaddis, John Lewis. *The Cold War: A New History*. 2005. A comprehensive overview by a prominent Cold war historian.

Gross, Jan T., ed. *The Politics of Retribution in Europe: World War II and Its Aftermath*. 2000. This series of essays makes clear that war did not end in Europe in May 1945.

Isaacs, Jeremy, and Taylor Downing. *Cold War: An Illustrated History*. 1998. The companion book to the CNN television series. Filled with memorable photographs.

Judge, Edward, and John Langdon. *A Hard and Bitter Peace: A Global History of the Cold War*. 1999. An extremely useful survey for students. Excellent maps.

Keep, John. *Last of the Empires: A History of the Soviet Union, 1945–1991*. 1995. Looks beyond the Kremlin to explore social, cultural, and economic developments.

Mazrui, Ali, and Michael Tidy. *Nationalism and New States in Africa*. 1984. Offers a thematic rather than chronological account of African state building.

Poiger, Uta. *Jazz, Rock, and Rebels: Cold War Politics and American Culture in a Divided Germany*. 2000. Explores the interplay among youth culture, Americanization, and political protest.

de Senarclens, P. *From Yalta to the Iron Curtain: The Great Powers and the Origins of the Cold War*. 1995. A look at the diplomatic, political and military concerns that created the Cold War.

Stromberg, Roland. *After Everything: Western Intellectual History Since 1945*. 1975. A swiftly moving tour through the major intellectual developments.

Urwin, Derek. *A Political History of Western Europe Since 1945*. 1997. Readable, reasonably up-to-date, and comprehensive.

Wyman, Mark. *DPs: Europe's Displaced Persons, 1945–1951*. 1989. An important study of an often-neglected topic.

Zubok, Vladislav, and Constantine Pleshakov. *Inside the Kremlin's Cold War: From Stalin to Khrushchev*. 1996. A close examination of the Cold War on the Soviet side.

Notes

1. The original signatories of the NATO treaty were Iceland, Norway, Great Britain, Belgium, the Netherlands, Luxembourg, France, Italy, and Portugal. Greece and Turkey joined the alliance in 1951, West Germany in 1954, and Spain in 1982. Sweden, Finland, Switzerland, Austria, Yugoslavia, and Albania remained nonaligned with either the United States or the Soviet Union.

2. Quoted in Donald W. White, *The American Century* (1996), 328.

3. Quotation from *Time* magazine, 1950; quoted in Martin Walker, *The Cold War and the Making of the Modern World* (1993), 66–67.

4. Quoted in Walker, *The Cold War,* 83.

5. Quoted in White, *The American Century,* 286.

6. Quoted in Karel Kaplan, *Report on the Murder of the General Secretary* (1990), 159.

7. Ibid., 242.

8. Ibid., 231.

9. Quoted in John L. H. Keep, *Last of the Empires: A History of the Soviet Union, 1945–1991* (1995), 79.

10. Quoted in Michael Scammell, *From Gulag to Glasnost: Nonconformist Art in the Soviet Union,* eds. Alla Rosenfeld and Norton T. Dodge (1995), 61.

11. Quoted in Walker, *The Cold War,* 105.

12. Official Hungarian statistics reported 3,000 dead. John Lewis Gaddis places the number at 20,000 in *We Now Know: Rethinking Cold War Evidence* (1997).

13. Quoted in Robert Paxton, *Europe in the Twentieth Century* (1997), 578.

14. Quoted in Jonathan Fineberg, *Art Since 1940: Strategies of Being* (1995), 144.

15. Ibid., 89.

16. Quoted in Adrian Hastings, *Modern Catholicism: Vatican II and After* (1991), 29.

17. Reinhold Wagnleitner, *Coca-Colonization and the Cold War: The Cultural Mission of the United States in Austria After the Second World War* (1994).

18. Quoted in Felix Gilbert, *The End of the European Era, 1890 to the Present* (1991), 429.

19. Quoted in Richard Kuisel, *Seducing the French: The Dilemma of Americanization* (1993), 147.

The West in the Contemporary Era: New Encounters and Transformations

28

O N THE EVENING OF NOVEMBER 9, 1989, EAST GERMAN BORDER guards stationed at the wall that divided East and West Berlin gazed out nervously at an unprecedented sight. Thousands of their fellow citizens had gathered in front of the gates and were demanding to be let through into the western half of the city. This demand was extraordinary; in the twenty-eight years that the Berlin Wall had stood, more than 200 people had been shot trying to cross it. But the autumn of 1989 was no ordinary time. A radically reformist regime had emerged in the Soviet Union and publicly proclaimed that its eastern European allies could no longer rely on the Soviet army to assist them in putting down domestic dissent. Poland and Hungary were in the process of replacing communist governments with pluralist parliamentary systems. And in East Germany, 200,000 disaffected citizens had taken advantage of relaxed border controls in Hungary and Czechoslovakia to flee to the West in just a few weeks, while more than one million had joined illegal protest demonstrations.

On November 9, in response to overwhelming public pressure, the East German government announced that it would drastically relax the requirements for obtaining an exit visa to visit or emigrate to the West. In a press conference to announce the upcoming changes, the East Berlin Communist Party boss Gunter Schabowski gave a carelessly worded reply to a reporter's question about the new travel policy—and sparked a revolution. Schabowski indicated, wrongly, that as of the next morning, anyone who wanted to head to the West could obtain an automatic exit visa at the border. The news spread quickly, and huge crowds gathered at the checkpoints that dotted the Berlin Wall. The nervous border guards had no idea what to do. Neither did their superiors, who refused to issue the guards any clear instructions. As the crowds pressed forward, the guards gave in and

And the Wall Came Tumbling Down Berliners celebrate the fall of the Berlin Wall in November 1989.

opened the gates. While television cameras broadcast the scene to an astonished world, tens of thousands of East Germans walked, ran, and danced across the border that had for so long literally and symbolically divided West from East. Elated with their new freedom and energized with a sense of power and possibility, they then turned on the wall itself. Jumping on top of it, they transformed it from an instrument of coercion and division into a platform for partying. Caught, the East German government saw no way to close the gates. Within a few days, and again without any official approval, ordinary Germans, equipped with hammers and chisels, began to dismantle the wall that the politicians had erected almost three decades earlier.

As extraordinary as the fall of the wall was, the events that followed over the next two years proved even more dramatic—the collapse of communist regimes throughout eastern Europe, the end of the Cold War, the disintegration of the Soviet Union, and the onset of civil war in Yugoslavia and in many formerly Soviet regions. Over the next two decades, both governments and ordinary people—not only throughout Europe but across the globe—struggled to build new structures to suit the vastly changed geopolitical landscape.

How did the meaning of "the West" change with the collapse of communism and the sundering of the Iron Curtain that had once divided Europe? This chapter will look at four key questions as it seeks to understand the causes and consequences of these dramatic developments and their implications for Western identity:

- How did economic and political developments in the 1970s and 1980s undermine the international structures of the postwar era?
- What factors explain not only the outbreak but also the success of the revolutions of 1989–1991?
- What were the consequences of these revolutions for the societies of eastern Europe?
- What were the implications of these developments for the meaning of "the West" itself?

Economic Stagnation and Political Change: The 1970s and 1980s

- How did economic and political developments in the 1970s and 1980s undermine international structures of the postwar era?

As the 1960s drew to a close, the risk of nuclear war seemed to recede with the onset of detente°, the effort to stabilize superpower relations through negotiations and arms control. But stability remained elusive.

Economic crisis heightened political and social polarization, while the renewal of the Cold War at the end of the 1970s destabilized both international and domestic relations.

The 1970s: A More Uncertain Era

In the early 1970s, the United States and Europe—both East and West—entered a new era. Detente signaled a relaxing of the Cold War tensions that had structured so much of international relations since the end of World War II. But at the same time, economic developments warned that the easy affluence of the postwar era had ended.

The Era of Detente

Changes in the Cold War climate were first felt in West Germany. In 1969 the West Berlin mayor and Social Democratic Party (SPD) leader Willy Brandt (1913–1992) became chancellor. For the first time in its history, West Germany had a government that was not led by a Christian Democrat. Brandt proceeded to implement a new *Ostpolitik* or "Eastern policy"—the opening of diplomatic and economic relations between West Germany and the Soviet Union and its satellite states. In the triumphant climax of Ostpolitik, East and West Germany recognized the legitimacy of each other's existence in 1972 and in the next year, both Germanys entered the United Nations.

During this era, the leaders of the superpowers also acted to break down the bipolarities of the Cold War. By the end of the 1960s, both the Soviet Union and the United States faced stagnating economies, and both were spending $50 million per day on nuclear weapons. These economic pressures led Soviet and American leaders to embrace detente. In November 1969 Soviet and American negotiators began the Strategic Arms Limitation Talks (SALT). Signed in 1972, the agreement froze the existing weapons balance. With both superpowers possessing sufficient nuclear weaponry to destroy the globe several times over, SALT may seem to have been inconsequential, but it helped arrest the armaments spiral and, more important, revealed a shift in Cold War power relations.

Important changes within the communist world also contributed to detente. Throughout the 1930s and 1940s, the Chinese communist leader Mao Zedong was an obedient disciple of Stalin. In the 1950s, however, relations cooled when Mao challenged Khrushchev's aim of "peaceful coexistence" with the West. Khrushchev, in turn, opposed Mao's "Great Leap Forward." This effort to transform a peasant society into an industrial powerhouse in one single year led to the deaths of an estimated 30 million Chinese, victims of starvation and Mao's fantasies. Horrified, Khrushchev suspended economic aid to China in 1960. By the time the first Chinese atomic bomb exploded in 1964, the split between China and the Soviet Union was open and irrevocable. U.S. president Richard

Detente

U.S. president Richard Nixon and Soviet leader Leonid Brezhnev joke before signing the SALT I treaty in 1972.

Nixon (1913–1994) and his national security adviser Henry Kissinger (b. 1923) decided to take advantage of this Sino-Soviet split. In 1971, Nixon announced the lifting of travel and trade restrictions with China and then sent shock waves through the world by visiting China himself. Nixon's reconciliation with communist China was a turning point: In the 1950s and 1960s, "East versus West" had formed a basic building block of international relations. In the 1970s, the shape of international politics looked much less clear.

Economic Crisis in the West

The economic outlook also blurred in this era as the 1970s brought an unprecedented combination of high inflation and high unemployment rates. Commentators labeled this new reality stagflation°—the escalating prices of a boom economy combined with the joblessness of an economy going bust. Between 1974 and 1976 the average annual growth rate within western European nations dropped to zero.

War and oil played important roles in creating this economic crisis. In October 1973, Egyptian and Syrian armies attacked Israel. When Soviet forces began airlifting supplies to the invading troops, Israel appealed to the U.S. for military aid. In retaliation for American assistance to Israel, the oil-producing states, or OPEC (Organization of Petroleum Exporting Countries), imposed an embargo on sales to the U.S. and more than quintupled the price of a barrel of oil. In 1979 political revolution in Iran doubled the price again. These price increases vastly accelerated the inflationary spiral.

Inflation and Economic Performance in the West

	France	Great Britain	Italy	United States	West Germany
Inflation over Previous Year (percent)					
1970	5.2%	6.4%	5.0%	5.9%	3.4%
1975	11.8	24.2	17.0	9.1	6.0
1979	9.1	13.4	14.8	11.3	4.1
Gross Domestic Product (Percentage Growth/Decline over Previous Year)					
1970	+5.7%	+2.3%	+5.3%	−0.3%	+5.1%
1975	+0.2	−20.6	−23.6	−0.1	−1.6
1979	+3.3	+2.4	+2.7	+2.4	+4.2

Source: Martin Walker, *Cold War: A History* (1993), 234.

Yet rising oil prices were not the sole cause of the economic crisis of the 1970s and 1980s. Two other factors also contributed. First, in 1973 U.S. president Richard Nixon took drastic action to defend the weakening dollar. He decided to let the dollar "float," to let market forces rather than fixed currency exchange rates determine the dollar's value against other currencies. This decision gutted the Bretton Woods Agreement, which had governed international economic affairs since World War II (see Chapter 27), and introduced a more volatile economic era. Whereas the Bretton Woods system had worked to direct the flow of capital to countries in need of investment, the new unregulated system allowed capital to surge into markets in which investors could reap immediate gains. National economies lay vulnerable to speculative attacks. No fewer than sixty-nine countries experienced serious banking crises, and the annual economic growth rates of the developed nations fell by one-third in the decades that followed the collapse of Bretton Woods.

A second factor in the economic crisis of the 1970s was international competition. Both western Europe and the United States struggled to compete with the emerging Asian and South/Latin American economies. Western societies possessed a politicized workforce that demanded relatively high wages and extensive social services. Increasingly, manufacturing concerns moved south and east, to take advantage of the lack of labor regulation and protection in the developing world.

Consequences of the Crisis

The economic crisis had stark social consequences. As the economic pie grew smaller, competition for slices grew fierce. The 1970s saw a resurgence of industrial unrest in western Europe. In Britain, conflict with the unions brought down three successive governments in a decade. In both Italy and West Germany, workers became increasingly militant and succeeded in winning large wage increases. These industrial settlements only worsened the problem of inflation. Workers demanded large pay increases to meet the rising cost of living, but employers, faced with having to pay higher wages, raised the prices of their goods and services. And so the cost of living continued to climb.

The new economic climate of austerity also led to heightened racial conflict throughout much of western Europe. We saw in Chapter 27 that postwar governments struggling to cope with labor shortages had encouraged immigration, both from the poorer countries of southern and eastern Europe and from colonial or former colonial regions such as Algeria, India, and Jamaica. By 1971, nine million immigrants were living in northern and western Europe.

With the onset of economic crisis, these immigrant communities soon found themselves under attack. European governments reacted to rising unemployment rates by halting labor immigration. By 1975 West Germany, France, the Netherlands, Britain, Belgium, Sweden, and Switzerland had all banned further immigration. Because it explicitly (although incorrectly) linked the presence of immigrants to unemployment, anti-immigration legislation helped solidify racist attitudes among many sectors of the European population. Violence against immigrants began to escalate.

Ironically, anti-immigration legislation actually increased the size of immigrant communities. West Germany saw its number of foreign residents rise by 13 percent between 1974 and 1982; in the same period, France witnessed a 33 percent increase. Foreign workers scrambled to get into western Europe before the doors shut, and once they were in, were reluctant to leave because of the well-grounded fear that they would not be able to return. Family members came too—only Switzerland banned the entry of dependents.

In the 1980s, then, what sociologists call "migration streams" solidified into ethnic minority communities—not "guestworkers," but rather a permanent part of western European societies. By 1991, 25 percent of the inhabitants of France were either immigrants or the children or grandchildren of immigrants. For both economic and social reasons, minority groups clustered in certain areas in certain cities. In West Germany in the early 1980s, ethnic minorities constituted 6 percent of the population as a whole, but 24 percent of the population of Frankfurt—and in the city's central district, 80 percent.

The resulting encounters among peoples of different religious and ethnic traditions reshaped European culture. In Britain, for example, Afro-Caribbean styles of dress and music had a profound influence on white working-class youth culture. These encounters also posed a potent challenge to ideas of national identity. By the 1980s, British journalists were writing about "third-generation immigrants," as if someone born in Britain to British citizenship were somehow less British than other British citizens. Such terminology indicated a deep reluctance to classify individuals with brown or black skin as British, an inability to conceive of national identity as anything but white. In France, the highly centralized education system became the site of hostile encounters, as Islamic parents fought for the rights of their daughters to attend school in traditional Muslim headdress, a practice resisted by some French authorities who feared that "Frenchness" would be diluted if immigrants failed to accept the traditions of the host society.

In both France and Britain, immigrants could become or already were legal citizens. In West Germany, Switzerland, and the Scandinavian countries, however, foreign workers remained foreign, with no chance of obtaining citizenship. Thus by the 1980s, a dangerous situation had emerged in these countries, with the children of foreign workers growing up in a society in which they had no political rights.

DOCUMENT

"Young, British, and White"

During the 1980s, racist violence increased in Britain, as throughout much of Europe. Overtly racist political parties such as the National Front capitalized on anti-immigrant sentiment to recruit new members for their movements. In this document, the American journalist Bill Buford describes a birthday party held in a pub for one young member of the National Front. The excerpt begins with a dangerous moment: football (soccer) rivalries are threatening to divide the partygoers.

On the far side, some of the new members had started in on their football chants, just as Neil had feared. These appeared to be West Ham supporters. They were then answered, from the other side of the room, by Chelsea supporters.* A contrapuntal chorus of West Ham and Chelsea songs followed, one that sent Neil scurrying through his record collection. It was time to change the music. . . . It was time to play the White Power music.

None of the songs was played on any of the established radio stations or sold in any of the conventional shops. It was a mail-order or cash-in-hand music trade, and from the titles you could see why: "Young, British, and White"; "England Belongs to Me"; "Shove the Dove"; "England" and "British Justice." These were the lyrics of "The Voice of Britain":

Our old people cannot walk the streets alone.
They fought for this nation and this is what they get back.
They risked their lives for Britain, and now Britain belongs
   to aliens.
It's about time Britain went and took it back.

This is the voice of Britain.
You'd better believe it.
This is the voice of Britain
C'mon and fly the flag now.
. . .

The music was delivered with the same numbing, crushing percussion that had characterized everything else that had been played that evening. . . . There was one refrain I could follow, and that was because it was played repeatedly, and because, each time, everyone joined in. It seemed to be the theme song.

Two pints of lager[†] and a packet of crisps.[‡]
Wogs[§] out! White power!
Wogs out! White power!
Wogs out! White power!

It was interesting to contemplate that the high-point of the evening was organized around this simple declaration of needs: a lad needed his lager; a lad needed his packet of crisps; a lad needed his wog.

---

[*] *West Ham and Chelsea = rival English soccer teams.*
[†] *"Lager" = beer.*
[‡] *"Packet of crisps" = bag of potato chips.*
[§] *"Wog" = racially derogatory term for Southeast Asians.*

Source: From *Among the Thugs: The Experience, and the Seduction, of Crowd Violence* by Bill Buford. Copyright © 1991, 1990 by William Buford. Used by permission of W. W. Norton & Company, Inc. and The Random House Group Limited.

These "foreigners" experienced widespread discrimination in education, housing, and employment. In West Germany in the late 1970s, more than 40 percent of "foreign" workers lived in housing without a bath or shower. (Only 6 percent of German citizens did so.) Forced to live in such substandard accommodation by poverty, immigrants were often then stereotyped as dirty and uncivilized.

Explicitly racist political parties capitalized on the new anti-immigration sentiment. In France, for example, Jean-Marie Le Pen (b. 1928), a veteran of the Algerian war, created the *Front National* in 1974 as an anti-immigration party. In Le Pen's view, "Everything comes from immigration. Everything goes back to immigration." Unemployment, rising crime rates, an increase in illegitimate births, crowded schools, AIDS—Le Pen blamed it all on nonwhite immigrants. Appealing particularly to young, male working-class voters, Le Pen's party remained a threatening political presence for the next three decades.

The 1980s: The End of Political Consensus in the West

The economic crisis of the 1970s called into question the social democratic assumptions that had governed political life since World War II. Western Europeans had emerged from the horror of total war in 1945 determined to build better societies. Rejecting the extremes of communism on the left and fascism on the right, they took the centrist social democratic path. Two features characterized social democracies—first, mixed economies that combined nationalization of key industries with private enterprise, and second, an interventionist state that took responsibility for maintaining full employment and providing extensive welfare services. The stagflation of the 1970s, however, seemed to indicate that these social democratic solutions no longer worked. Discontented voters looked for radically new answers. In Spain, Portugal, and Greece, they turned to socialist parties. Throughout most of western Europe and in the United States, however, New Conservatism° dominated political society.

The New Conservatives

Three leaders epitomized the New Conservatism: the Republican Ronald Reagan in the United States (1911–2004), the Christian Democrat Helmut Kohl in West Germany (b. 1930), and the Conservative Margaret Thatcher in Britain (b. 1925). On the most fundamental level, the New Conservatives rejected the postwar emphasis on social improvement in favor of policies intended to create more opportunities for individual achievement. Thatcher even insisted, "There is no such thing as society." In the New Conservative worldview, there was instead the individual, freely competing in a world governed by market forces rather than governmental regulations or state planning. As Kohl demanded during his 1983 campaign, "Less state, more market; fewer collective burdens, more personal performance; fewer encrusted structures, more mobility, self-initiative, and competition." Privatization of nationalized or state-owned industries constituted a key part of the New Conservative agenda—removing the state from the economy and allowing private enterprises to compete. In Britain under Thatcher, the coal industry, transport, and utilities were all shifted to private ownership.

New Conservatives also mounted an attack on the welfare state, insisting that rising social expenditures, funded by rising taxes, lay at the heart of the economic crisis that had afflicted the West since the early 1970s. They pointed to the fact that the years between 1960 and 1981 had seen a dramatic rise in social spending (for programs such as health, disability, and unemployment insurance; pensions; and family allowances). Minimizing the successes of these social programs in reducing poverty, New Conservatives instead linked rising social expenditures to surging inflation and declining economic growth rates.

Yet New Conservative fiscal policies did not actually break sharply from their social democratic predecessors. Reagan, for example, used deficit spending to finance skyrocketing military budgets (up by 40 percent during his administration). The real break lay in the New Conservatives' willingness to tolerate high unemployment rates. By imposing high interest rates on their economies, Thatcher and Reagan brought inflation under control. High interest rates, however, overvalued the British pound and the American dollar. As a result, manufacturers found it hard to sell their products abroad and many went under. In Britain, 13 percent of the workforce was unemployed by 1984. In West Germany, too, Kohl's policies of holding down taxes and government expenditures were accompanied by unemployment rates of more than 9 percent in the mid-1980s.

By the end of the 1980s, as a result of falling global oil prices and the Reagan military spending spree that primed the pump of the global economy, Western economies re-

Spending on Social Services as a Percentage of the Gross Domestic Product

	France	West Germany	Sweden	United Kingdom
1960	13.2	15.5	11.0	10.8
1965	15.6	16.5	13.8	11.8
1970	15.1	17.1	18.6	13.1
1975	23.9	23.7	25.0	17.1
1980	26.3	24.0	31.9	18.1
1985	28.7	23.8	30.7	20.3

Source: Susan Pedersen, *Family, Dependence, and the Origins of the Welfare State: Britain and France, 1914–1945*, 1993, p. 416. Reprinted with the permission of Cambridge University Press.

turned to growth. But the average late-1980s growth rates of 2 to 3 percent per year were lower than those of 5 to 6 percent that had characterized Western economies in the 1950s and 1960s. At the same time, unemployment rates tended to hover between 5 and 7 percent—levels that would have been regarded as unacceptably high in the earlier period. A new political culture, based on lowered expectations, had come into being.

Even Europe's leftist parties had to adapt to this new political culture. Socialist and social democratic governments in Sweden, Italy, Greece, Spain, and France followed New Conservatives along the path of reduced health and social security expenditures, as well as wage cuts. The most dramatic example of this adaptation of the left occurred in France. In 1981, French voters elected Socialist Party leader François Mitterrand (1916–1996) to the presidency. In his first year in office, Mitterrand implemented a series of radical social democratic measures, including a rise in the minimum wage, a reduction in the workweek, expanded social welfare, and higher taxes for the wealthy. But in 1982, Mitterrand was forced by a series of economic catastrophes—falling exports, rising trade and budget deficits, soaring inflation rates—to cut social spending and to let unemployment rates rise.

New Challenges and New Identities: New Feminism

The triumph of New Conservatism demonstrated that economic crisis had shattered the post–World War II social democratic consensus. The protests of the 1960s also helped break apart this consensus, and in the 1970s, two offshoots of these protests—new feminism and environmentalism—offered new cultural and political alternatives. New feminism° emerged directly out of the student protest movement of the 1960s. Female activists grew frustrated at being

The Greenham Common Protests

In the spring of 1983, protesters formed a fourteen-mile human chain across Greenham Common in England to protest against NATO's deployment of cruise missiles. The protest was part of a much wider movement in western Europe and the United States, which articulated wide-spread public discontent with the renewal of the Cold War. It also played a pivotal role in British feminism, as female activists established a women-only camp at the Greenham Common military base.

denied a voice in the movement—"we cook while the men talk of revolution."[1] At the same time, they were increasingly eager to connect analyses of political subordination to experiences of sexual repression. Their efforts to liberate women from political and cultural limits and expectations gave birth to what was, by the 1980s, an international feminist movement.

Economic and demographic changes buttressed the new feminism. The numbers of women working outside the home rose in these decades—up by 50 percent in Italy between 1970 and 1985, for example. By the late 1970s, women in France accounted for more than 34 percent of the labor force; in Britain, 31 percent; in West Germany, 37 percent. During the same decade, the age at which men and women first married began to climb and birth rates continued to fall.

Western politics gradually responded to the changes in women's roles. By the mid-1980s, women averaged about one-third of the members of parliament in Sweden, and women members accounted for approximately half of Norway's cabinets. In the British general elections of 1992, twice as many women stood as parliamentary candidates compared to 1979.

The movement, however, refused to confine its focus to the world of party politics, arguing instead that "the personal is political." Much of the new feminist critique focused on the female body—its image, its oppression, its control. Feminists challenged feminine stereotypes through attacks on beauty pageants and critiques of the fashion industry and sought the reform of legal codes to outlaw spousal rape and to legalize abortion. Legalization of abortion occurred first in northern Europe: in Britain in 1967, in Denmark in 1970. Catholic Europe followed: In Italy abortions became legally available in 1978, in France in 1979.

In the economic and educational spheres, feminists demanded equal pay for equal work and greater access to educational and professional opportunities. They pressed for more generous parental leave policies, family allowances, and child care provisions. In addition, with women accounting for approximately half of the university students in many Western countries, feminists began to alter the content of the curriculum. Challenging the male biases that had regarded women's contributions as irrelevant and women's lives as insignificant, for example, feminist historians brought to light the "hidden history" of women.

New Challenges and New Identities: Environmentalism

DOCUMENT

Chico Mendes on the Rain Forest

Environmentalists added their voice to the political cacophony of the 1970s and 1980s. They challenged the fundamental structures of industrial economies (whether capitalist or communist), particularly their inherent emphasis on "more, bigger, faster, now." The movement embraced the ideas of unorthodox economists such as Britain's E. F. Schumacher (1911–1977), who insisted that quantitative measures of economic growth (such as the GNP) failed to factor in environmental destruction and social dislocation, and that in many contexts, "small is beautiful." At the heart of radical environmentalism was the concept of natural limits, of "Spaceship Earth"—the vision of the planet as a "single spaceship, without unlimited reservoirs of anything."[2]

New media-savvy organizations such as Greenpeace publicized the environmentalist cause with colorful protests, such as sailing in small rubber dinghies to challenge whaling fleets. The most popular of radical environmentalist targets was nuclear power. From the mid-1970s on, protests against the construction of nuclear power plants in western Europe drew tens of thousands of supporters. The movement's slogan, "Nuclear Power? No Thanks," was translated into more than forty languages.

The environmental movement helped create a new sort of political party. Green politics° drew its ideas not only from environmentalism but also from feminism. The Greens contended that the degradation of the natural environment stemmed from the same root as discrimination against women—an obsession with physical power and an unwillingness to tear down hierarchical structures. By the late 1980s Green Parties had sprouted in fifteen western European countries. The Greens were the most successful in West Germany, where they sat in the legislature from 1983 and formed an important voting bloc.

From Detente to Renewed Cold War

At the same time that economic crisis, feminist protest, and the new environmental awareness undermined political consensus, rising superpower tensions put an end to the era of detente and caused greater rifts within western European societies. In the first half of the 1970s, detente had appeared to be flourishing. In 1975 representatives of 32 European states, Canada, the United States, and the Soviet Union signed the Helsinki Accords. They declared their acceptance of all existing European borders, agreed to a policy of joint notification of all major military exercises (thus reducing the chances of accidental nuclear war), and promised to safeguard the human rights of their citizens.

Yet the Helsinki Accords marked not only the culmination but also the beginning of the end of the detente era. First, eastern European and Soviet dissidents used the Helsinki human rights clauses to publicize the human rights abuses committed by their governments and to

demand fundamental reforms. Second, U.S. president Jimmy Carter, who took office in 1976, chose to place human rights at the center of his foreign policy. Carter's approach infuriated Soviet leaders, who resented what they regarded as his meddling in their internal affairs. As detente crumbled, the arms race accelerated, with both the Warsaw Pact and NATO increasing their defense budgets and deploying intermediate-range nuclear missiles. Detente finally died in December 1979, when Soviet troops invaded Afghanistan. Calling the invasion "the most serious threat to peace since the Second World War," Carter warned that if the Soviets moved toward the Middle East, he would not hesitate to use nuclear weapons.

With the election of New Conservatives such as Thatcher in 1979 and Reagan in 1980, the renewal of the Cold War took on a greater intensity. Reagan labeled the Soviet Union the "Evil Empire"—a reference to the popular *Star Wars* film series that was first released in the 1970s— and revived the anticommunist attitudes and rhetoric of the 1950s. Thatcher strongly supported Reagan's decision to accelerate the arms buildup begun by Carter. Her hard-line anticommunism won her the nickname "Iron Lady" from Soviet policymakers.

The renewal of the Cold War, like the end of economic prosperity, opened up large rifts within western European societies. NATO's decision to deploy its new generation of nuclear missiles drew hundreds of thousands of protesters into the streets of London, Bonn, Amsterdam, and other cities. Many of these protesters demanded not only the cancellation of the cruise missiles but also a withdrawal from NATO's nuclear umbrella.

War in Afghanistan

The Soviet invasion of Afghanistan in 1979 helped end the era of detente. It also catapulted the Soviet army into a winless war, one that many commentators labeled "the Soviet Vietnam."

Revolution in the East

■ **What factors explain not only the outbreak but also the success of the revolutions of 1989–1991?**

Between 1989 and 1991, revolution engulfed eastern Europe and the Soviet Union. The appointment of Mikhail Gorbachev (1985–1991) as Soviet Communist Party secretary in 1985 proved pivotal. Gorbachev's efforts to reform the Soviet system led to a series of breathtaking changes: Soviet control over eastern Europe ended, the Cold War came to an abrupt halt, the Soviet Union itself ceased to exist. Ironically, Gorbachev set in motion the first two of these developments precisely to avoid the third.

The Crisis of Legitimacy in the East

While Western countries in the 1970s struggled with stagflation and disappearing economic growth rates, the Soviet Union posted record-breaking production figures. By 1984, for example, the Soviet Union was producing 80 percent more steel and six times as much iron ore than the United States. But Soviet prosperity was an illusion. Published growth and productivity statistics had little to do with actual economic performance. The Soviet economy continued to be hampered by overcentralization. The state planning commission, GOSPLAN, had the impossible task of coordinating the production of over four million different products in at least 50,000 factories. "Success" in Soviet industry meant fulfilling arbitrary quotas, regardless of the quality of goods produced, the actual demand for the product, or the cost of producing it.

The Soviet command economy also proved far too rigid to keep pace with global economic change. While triumphantly proclaiming its fulfillment of the heavy industrial expansion planned by Khrushchev in the early 1960s, Soviet leaders in the 1970s failed to recognize that increasingly, microchips counted for far more than iron ore—that fiber optics, not steel, would buttress the new modernity. When the first Soviet home computer reached the market in the 1980s, it cost ten times as much as the comparable Western model.

By the 1980s, the only growth sectors in the Soviet economy were oil and vodka—and then the bottom dropped out of the oil market. After peaking at $35 per barrel in 1981, oil prices began a steady decade-long fall. For the Soviet economy, the results were catastrophic.

The Soviet leadership proved incapable of responding to the economic crisis. Throughout the 1970s, Soviet leader Leonid Brezhnev's increasing physical frailty mirrored that of the country at large. Like many of his colleagues, Brezhnev had been a child at the time of the Russian Revolution; he knew only Soviet rule and had risen into major office very young because of the employment oppor-

tunities created by Stalin's Great Purge. In 1982, the average age of members of the Politburo was 68. These men had a vested interest in maintaining the status quo, not in carrying out fundamental reform.

The Soviet Union's satellite states in eastern Europe also lurched from apparent prosperity into economic crisis during this period. During the 1970s, the Soviets provided oil to their eastern European allies at prices far below the market value and so shielded these economies from some of the tensions afflicting their western European rivals. At the same time, eastern European governments borrowed heavily from Western banks. Western loans did not, however, solve fundamental problems such as overcentralization and the divorce of prices from production costs.

In the 1980s, the debt-laden economic structures of eastern Europe began to collapse. Governments found that they had to borrow simply to service their existing debt. And, as oil prices fell, the Soviet Union responded by charging market value for oil sales to their satellites, thus depriving these economies of a crucial support. Ordinary people soon felt the impact of this economic crisis, as governments restricted the flow of consumer goods and imposed higher prices.

The Moment of Solidarity, the Moment of Punk

Events in Poland at the end of the decade illustrated how economic discontent and political dissent could create a revolutionary situation. Faced with negative economic growth rates, the Polish government announced price increases for meat and other essentials in July 1980. Poles hit the streets in angry protest. This protest gave birth to Solidarity°. Led by a charismatic and politically savvy electrician named Lech Wałęsa (b. 1943), Solidarity was both a trade union and a political movement. It demanded not only the right to unionize and strike, but also the liberation of political prisoners, an end to censorship, and a rollback of the state's power. Within just a few months, ten million Poles had joined Solidarity's ranks.

Fearing Soviet military intervention, the Polish communist government cracked down. In December 1981 Prime Minister Wojciech Jaruzelski declared martial law and arrested more than 10,000 Solidarity members (including Wałęsa). Like the Hungarian Revolution in 1956 and the Prague Spring of 1968, Solidarity seemed to be one more futile and defeated protest in eastern Europe.

But Solidarity refused to be defeated. Both in prison and out, its members resolved to act as if they were free. They met in small groups, published newspapers and ran a radio station, and organized election boycotts. Solidarity remained a political presence and a moral force in Polish society throughout the 1980s, and in 1989 it emerged to lead Poland into democracy.

Before 1989 no other eastern European country experienced a protest movement as dramatic as Solidarity, yet

Rock and the Velvet Revolution

In September 1968, less than one month after the armies of the Soviet Union and its satellite states had crushed the Prague Spring, a Czech bass player named Milan Hlavsa formed a rock band. The military invasion and the subsequent political crackdown throughout Czechoslovakia appalled Hlavsa, but it never occurred to him that he could do anything to change the harsh reality of life in the communist bloc. He certainly did not see forming a rock band as a political act; he and the other members of the band liked Western rock music (particularly the "psychedelic" music of Frank Zappa, the Velvet Underground, and the Doors), and they wanted to play in a rock band. Yet the encounter between the communist state and the anarchic energy of psychedelic rock helped undermine communist rule and so contributed to the transformation of eastern Europe.

Hlavsa and his friends called their band "The Plastic People of the Universe" (PPU), after a Frank Zappa song, and PPU quickly became the most popular psychedelic group in Prague. But almost as quickly the band ran into trouble. As part of the post-1968 crackdown, the communist government insisted that rock bands conform to a set of official guidelines governing how, what, and where they performed. PPU refused and, in

January 1970, lost its professional license. In the communist system, the state not only controlled broadcasting and recording, but even owned the distribution of musical instruments and electrical equipment. Without a license, PPU lost access to rehearsal and recording space, and their instruments as well. But the band played on by repairing cast-off instruments and constructing homemade amplifiers from old transistor radios. Banned in 1972 from performing in Prague, PPU moved to the countryside and when it was banned in 1974 from playing anywhere, it dove underground. Fans alerted other fans when the band would be playing at some remote farm or within some woods, while recordings made in houses and garages circulated illegally. During this period PPU became more than just a rock band; it became the center of what artistic director and manager Ivan Jirous labeled the "Second Culture." An alternative to the official communist "First Culture," the "Second Culture" comprised musicians, fans, artists, writers, and anyone else who sought to carve out a space of individuality and integrity in a society based on conformity and lies.

On March 17, 1976, the Secret Police arrested twenty-seven musicians, including every member of PPU. Six months later rock music went on trial. In response to inter-

national protests, the Czech government released most of the twenty-seven rockers. But Jirous and the band's saxophonist, Vratislav Brabenec, as well as two musicians from other groups, were found guilty of "organized disturbance of the peace" and sentenced to between eight and eighteen months in prison.

In the courtroom the day of the sentencing sat Václav Havel, an ardent Frank Zappa fan as well as a playwright who used his art to mount veiled attacks on the communist system. The imprisonment of Jirous and Brabenec infuriated Havel. For the next several years, he opened his farmhouse to PPU for illegal concerts and recording sessions. More important, Havel walked out of the courtroom convinced that the time had come to challenge communism openly. On January 1, 1977, Havel and other artists and intellectuals announced the formation of "Charter 77" to publicize human rights abuses under communism. Over the next decade many Charter members, including Havel, spent time in prison. Yet, calling the state to account for its crimes, Charter 77 helped weaken the communist regime. When revolution came in 1989, that regime toppled with astounding ease. PPU had split up two years before and so did not sing in the new era, but fittingly, one of the first individuals that President Václav Havel invited to the new free Czechoslovakia was an aging psychedelic rocker named Frank Zappa.

For Discussion

Imagine that the post-1968 Communist government in Czechoslovakia simply ignored the PPU. Would events have unfolded any differently? Why or why not?

Rocking the Bloc
In 1977, the Plastic People of the Universe play an illegal concert in Václav Havel's farmhouse.

The Moment of Solidarity
Lech Wałęsa addresses workers in the Gdansk shipyard in 1980. Note the pictures of the pope and the Virgin Mary—Roman Catholicism served as a vital source of national unity and identity, one opposed to communism.

throughout the region economic hardship fed widespread political alienation and a deepening longing for radical change. One sign of the widening gap between the communist authorities and the people they governed was the emergence of punk music as a cultural force among eastern European youth.

Punk had first appeared in Britain in the mid-1970s, the product of economic decline and social division. Dressed in clothes that deliberately mocked the consumerism and respectability of mainstream middle-class society—ripped trousers held together with safety pins, dog collars, spiked and outrageously colored hair—punks promoted a do-it-yourself style of rock music that also spat on middle-class standards. Punk rockers rarely had any musical training or expertise; even talent was not actually necessary. All that was needed was rage, which was readily available.

The nihilistic message of bands such as Britain's Sex Pistols—"no future for you, no future for me"—resonated in eastern Europe. With names like Doom, Crisis, Shortage, Paralysis, Sewage, and Dead Organism, Eastern punk bands, like their Western models, often expressed utter despair: "No goal, no future, no hope, no joy!" But this nihilism butted against explicit political protest. At punk

concerts in Poland, bands and their audiences stood in silent homage to Solidarity. In Hungary, the members of one punk group received prison sentences for a performance in which they mocked their government as a "rotten, stinking communist gang" while tearing up a live chicken.[3]

Nature and the Nation

The dissatisfaction expressed by punk bands permeated eastern European society, and increasingly took political form. Just as the emergence of radical environmentalism demonstrated a strong current of dissatisfaction with the political order in the West, so similar movements in the East pushed for radical change.

For decades, the conquest of nature had been a key part of Soviet ideology: "We cannot wait for favors from nature; our task is to take from her."[4] Beginning in the 1930s, Soviet engineers sought to fill what they regarded as nature's "empty spaces" with exotic plant and animal life, thus wreaking havoc with the ecological balance of much of the Soviet environment. In the early 1960s, Khrushchev's "Virgin Lands" scheme introduced intensive chemical fertilization and irrigation across huge swathes of Soviet territory, resulting in the fall of lake water levels, the destruction of wetlands, and the salinization of extensive stretches of land.

The situation worsened in the 1970s. The rapid expansion of heavy industry focused on churning out products, not on human safety or environmental sustainability. Communist governments throughout the Soviet bloc ignored the most basic environmental precautions, dumping both untreated sewage and nuclear waste directly into lakes and rivers. By 1977, Soviet scientists concluded that Lake Baikal—the most voluminous and deepest freshwater lake in the world, home to more than 800 plant and 1,500 animal species—had experienced irreversible environmental degradation.

As a result of this wholesale destruction, environmentalist protest groups emerged in the Soviet Union and throughout eastern Europe. Because Soviet officials regarded the environment as insignificant, they tended to view environmentalist protest as unimportant, as a "safe" outlet for popular frustration. Thus environmentalism became one of the few areas in communist society that permitted ordinary people free expression and in which public opinion was allowed a voice. Environmental activism worked like a termite infestation, nibbling away from within at the structures of Soviet communism.

Environmentalism also proved crucial in underlining nationalist identity and fueling nationalist protest. The various national and ethnic groups within the vast Soviet empire watched their forests disappear, their lakes dry up, and their ancient cities bulldozed, as a result of decisions made in faraway Moscow by men they regarded as foreigners—as *Russians* rather than as *comrades*. By the 1980s, schools in Latvia issued gas masks as a routine safety precaution because of the dangers of chemical spills. Many Latvians concluded that they would be better off independent of Soviet control.

Gorbachev and Radical Reform

In 1982, the decrepit Leonid Brezhnev died—and so, in rapid succession, did his two successors, Yuri Andropov (1982–1984) and Konstantin Chernenko (1984–1985). The time had come for a generational change. When Mikhail Gorbachev succeeded Chernenko, he was 54 years old. Compared to his elderly colleagues on the Politburo, he looked like a teenager.

Gorbachev's biography encompassed the drama of Soviet history. He was born, in 1931, into the turmoil of collectivization. One-third of the inhabitants of his native village in Stavropol were executed or imprisoned or died from famine or disease in the upheavals of the early 1930s. Both of his grandfathers were arrested on trumped-up charges. Yet Gorbachev's family continued to believe in the Communist dream. During World War II his father served in the Red Army (and was twice wounded), and in 1948 Gorbachev and his father together won the Order of Red Banner of Labor for harvesting almost six times the average crop. Because of this award and his academic abilities, Gorbachev won entry to Moscow University. After earning degrees in economics and law, he rose through the

ranks of the provincial Communist Party. In 1978, at age 47, he became the youngest member of the Communist Party Central Committee, the key leadership body in the Soviet Union.

Glasnost and Perestroika

Gorbachev came to power in 1985, convinced that the Soviet system was ailing, and that the only way to restore it to health was through radical surgery. What he did not anticipate was that such surgery would in fact kill the patient. His surgical tools were glasnost and perestroika, two Russian terms without direct English equivalents.

Glasnost°, sometimes translated as "openness," "publicity," or "transparency," meant abandoning the deception and censorship that had always characterized the Soviet system, for a policy based on open admission of failures and problems. To Gorbachev, "Broad, timely, and frank information is testimony of faith in people . . . and for their capacity to work things out themselves."[5]

Not surprisingly, Soviet citizens remained wary of Gorbachev's talk of glasnost—until April 1986 and the Chernobyl nuclear power plant disaster. Operator error at the Ukrainian power plant led to the most serious nuclear accident in history. In the days following the accident, thirty-five plant workers died; over the next five years the cleanup effort would claim at least 7,000 lives. The accident placed more than four million inhabitants of Ukraine and Belarus at risk from excess radiation and spread a radioactive cloud that extended all the way to Scotland. When news of the accident first reached Moscow, party officials acted as they had always done: They denied that anything had happened. But monitors in Western countries quickly

Glasnost
Mikhail Gorbachev meets with workers in Moscow in 1985.

picked up on the excess radiation spewing into the atmosphere. Gorbachev initiated an about-face and insisted that accurate information about the disaster be released to the public. Chernobyl became the first Soviet media event. In 1986, 93 percent of the Soviet population had access to a television set and what they saw on their screens convinced them that glasnost was real. A powerful change had occurred in Soviet political culture.

DOCUMENT

Mikhail Gorbachev on the Need for Economic Reform (1987)

Through glasnost Gorbachev aimed to overcome the alienation and apathy that he perceived as endemic in Soviet culture, to convince citizens of the importance of participating in the structures of political and economic life. At the same time, he sought to change those structures through perestroika°, often translated as "restructuring" or "reconstruction." Gorbachev believed he could reverse his nation's economic decline only through a series of reforms focusing on modernization, decentralization, and the introduction of a limited market.

Gorbachev knew, however, that even limited economic reforms threatened the vested interests of communist bureaucrats. Thus the success of economic perestroika depended on political perestroika. The culmination of political restructuring came in May 1989, when Soviet voters entered the voting booths to elect the Congress of People's Deputies, and for the first time in Soviet history they had a choice of candidates. True, all of these candidates were members of the Communist Party, but just one year later, Gorbachev ended the Communist Party's monopoly on parliamentary power, and the Soviet Union entered the brave new world of multiparty politics.

Ending the Cold War

Restructuring Soviet economics and politics led almost inevitably to restructuring international relations—and to ending the Cold War. By the 1980s, at least 18 percent of the Soviet GNP was absorbed by the arms race; Gorbachev concluded that the Soviet Union simply could not afford the Cold War. As soon as Gorbachev took office, he signaled to the West his desire to resume arms control negotiations. The results of these negotiations were startling. In December 1987, Gorbachev and U.S. president Ronald Reagan signed the INF (Intermediate Nuclear Forces) Treaty, agreeing to the total elimination of land-based intermediate-range nuclear missiles. In 1991, the Soviets and Americans signed the Strategic Arms Reduction Treaty (START I), pledging themselves to a mutual reduction of intercontinental ballistic missiles (ICBMs). The nuclear arms race had ended.

At the same time, Gorbachev signaled an end to Soviet global intervention by reducing Soviet military commitments abroad. In 1989, he brought the Red Army home from both Afghanistan and Mongolia and removed Soviet-sponsored Cuban forces from Angola.

The Revolutions of 1989 in Eastern Europe

Even more remarkably, by the end of 1990, the Red Army had pulled out of every state in eastern Europe except East Germany and Poland (and would soon withdraw from these countries as well). The Soviet Union could not afford to wage the Cold War, nor could it afford to maintain the eastern European empire that was both a cause and a consequence of that conflict.

In his first informal meetings with eastern European communist leaders in 1985, Gorbachev told them they should no longer expect Soviet tanks to enforce their will on rebellious populations. By the time Gorbachev addressed the UN General Assembly at the end of 1988 and declared that the nations of eastern Europe were free to choose their own paths, dramatic changes were already underway.

Hungary and Poland were the first to jettison communist rule. Even before Gorbachev took power, economic crisis had driven both of these states to embrace fundamental reforms. In the early 1980s Hungary moved toward a Western-oriented, market-driven economy by joining the World Bank and the International Monetary Fund (IMF) and establishing a stock market. Political reforms accompanied these economic changes. In 1983, Hungarian voters

CHRONOLOGY

Revolution in Eastern Europe

1989	
January	Noncommunist parties and unions legalized in Hungary
February	Roundtable talks between Polish government and Solidarity
June	Free elections in Poland
September	Solidarity forms government in Poland
November	Fall of Berlin Wall; reformist communists overthrow Zhivkov in Bulgaria
December	Collapse of communist government in Czechoslovakia and East Germany; execution of Ceaușescu in Romania
1990	
March	Free elections in East Germany and Hungary
October	Reunification of Germany
December	Wałęsa elected president of Poland

for the first time had a choice of candidates (all still Communist Party members); eighteen months later, independent candidates were allowed to run—and many were elected. In Poland, Jaruzelski's government also experimented with restoring some measures of a market economy and with political liberalization. Once martial law ended in 1983, censorship loosened considerably. Newspapers published criticisms of governmental policy that would never have been permitted before 1980.

With Gorbachev in power, the pace of reform in both Poland and Hungary accelerated rapidly. In January 1989, Hungary took the leap into political pluralism by legalizing noncommunist political parties and trade unions. In February, Solidarity and Polish communist officials began "roundtable talks" aimed at restructuring Poland's political system. In June, Poland held the first free elections in the Soviet bloc. Solidarity swept the contest and formed the first noncommunist government in eastern Europe since 1948.

A bewildered world waited to see if Gorbachev would send in the tanks. Only one day before the Polish elections, the Chinese communist government, oblivious to the television cameras that broadcast the horrible scenes around the globe, had used brutal force to crush a student pro-democracy uprising centered in Beijing's Tiananmen Square. Hundreds died. Horrified by the carnage, Gorbachev insisted that "the very possibility of the use or threat of force [in Poland] . . . is totally unacceptable."[6]

With the prop of the Red Army removed, the communist states of eastern Europe toppled easily. In November 1989, the Berlin Wall fell. The collapse of the wall echoed to the sound of communist governments crashing throughout eastern Europe. In December, after a year of ever-widening protest demonstrations, the communist government in Czechoslovakia resigned. Alexander Dubček, the hero of the Prague Spring of 1968, returned in triumph to assume the leadership of parliament, and the playwright and leading dissident Václav Havel (b. 1936) became the Czech president. In March 1990, the Christian Democrats took over the government from the communists in East Germany; seven months later the states of East and West Germany ceased to exist, and a single Germany was reborn. At the end of the year, reform-minded Communist Party members in Bulgaria overthrew the government of Todor Zhivkov, who had been in power for thirty-five years.

All of these revolutions occurred with very little bloodshed. The pace of change in Czechoslovakia was so smooth, in fact, that the events earned the nickname "the Velvet Revolution." But in Romania, the revolutionary cloth came soaked in blood. In December 1989, Romania's dictator Nikolai Ceauşescu ordered the army to fire on a peaceful protest; hundreds died. In a matter of days, however, the soldiers turned against Ceauşescu. Fighting spread across the nation as the dictator's security forces battled with both the demonstrators and the army. Ceauşescu and his wife

"Comrades, It's Over!"
This Hungarian political poster sums up the revolutions of 1989.

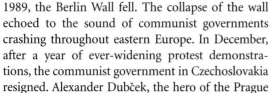
Escaping the Berlin Wall

went into hiding, but on Christmas Day they were caught and executed by a firing squad. The televised pictures of their dead bodies were broadcast around the world. A new government was formed under Ion Iliescu (b. 1930), a reformist communist who had attended Moscow University with Gorbachev.

The Disintegration of the Soviet Union

By 1990, Gorbachev was one of the best-known leaders in the Western world. Both Western political leaders and ordinary people praised Gorbachev for ending the Cold War and loosening the Soviet hold on eastern Europe. But for Gorbachev, these changes in the international structure were means to an end—freeing the Soviet economy for prosperity and thereby saving the communist system. But prosperity eluded his grasp, and the system he sought to save disintegrated.

Between 1985 and 1991, Gorbachev's administration started and stopped twelve different national economic plans, in ever-more-desperate attempts to prop up the Soviet economy. These reforms seemed only to worsen the economic crisis. By 1990, food and other essential goods were scarce, prices had risen by 20 percent since the year before, and both productivity figures and incomes were falling. Dramatic increases in the number of prostitutes (accompanied by a tripling of the rate of venereal disease in Moscow), abandoned babies, and the homeless population all signaled a society in the midst of economic breakdown.

By the early 1990s Gorbachev faced fierce opposition not only from hard-line communists who opposed his reforms, but also from more liberal reformers who viewed the communist system as utterly broken, and who wanted to accelerate the shift to a capitalist economy. These reformers found a spokesman in Boris Yeltsin (b. 1931), a charismatic, boisterous politician who became the president of Russia (as distinct from the Soviet Union) in 1991. As Gorbachev increasingly began to tack toward the right, Yeltsin emerged as the leader who would keep the revolution on course. When communist hard-liners attempted to overthrow Gorbachev in August 1991, it was Yeltsin who led the popular resistance movement that defeated the coup attempt.

Gorbachev was finally ousted not by a political coup but by the power of nationalism. Glasnost had allowed separatist nationalist movements within the Soviet Union to surface from the underground, but Gorbachev, despite his commitment to freedom of choice for eastern Europe, firmly opposed the breakup of the Soviet Union. In 1990, he deployed troops to quell nationalist rioting in both Azerbaijan and Georgia and to counter independence movements in the Baltic states of Latvia, Estonia, and Lithuania. Short of an all-out civil war, however, there was little Gorbachev could do to hold the union together. By December 1991, the Soviet Union had broken apart (see Map 28.1). On December 25, Gorbachev resigned his office as president of a state that no longer existed.

IMAGE

Statue of Lenin Toppled During the Soviet Collapse

Map 28.1 The Former Soviet Union

In December 1991, the Soviet empire disintegrated. In its place stood fifteen independent and very diverse republics, ranging from tiny and impoverished Moldova to relatively affluent and European-ized Latvia to Russia itself, still the dominant power in the region but economically stagnant.

The Disintegration of the Soviet Union

Gorbachev attempted to halt the disintegration of the Soviet Union by sending in crack Soviet troops to wrest back control of public buildings in Vilnius, Lithuania. Fourteen protesters died, and Lithuania asserted its independence.

In the Wake of Revolution

■ **What were the consequences of these revolutions for the societies of eastern Europe?**

With the Cold War over and the long struggle between communism and capitalism clearly won by the latter, one best-selling author talked of the "end of history," by which he meant the end of the ideological struggles that had so defined the last two centuries of historical development.[7] But such talk was premature. "History" returned with a vengeance in the 1990s. As nationalism replaced the capitalist-communist struggle, many of the divisive issues that had led to world war in 1914 and 1939 moved back to center stage. The former Soviet Union and all the former Soviet satellite states in eastern Europe experienced high inflation rates, high unemployment, and economic instability in the wake of the revolution. Many faced nationalist hostilities from minority groups; some confronted the ultimate challenge of civil war.

Crisis Throughout the Former Soviet Union

For many ordinary Russians, the ending of the Soviet regime meant freedom of the worst kind—freedom to be hungry, freedom to be homeless, freedom to be afraid. In January 1992, Yeltsin applied "shock therapy" to the ailing Russian economy. He lifted price controls, abolished subsidies, and privatized state industries. By mid-1994, the state sector of the Russian economy had shrunk to under 40 percent. But the economy did not prosper. Prices climbed dra-matically and the closure of unproductive businesses sent unemployment rates upward, while at the same time cuts in government spending severed welfare lifelines. By 1995, 80 percent of Russians were no longer earning a living wage. Food consumption fell to the same level as the early 1950s, with meat almost disappearing from the diets of many.

The economic situation worsened in 1998, when Russia effectively went bankrupt. The value of the ruble collapsed and the state defaulted on its loans. Even Russians with jobs found it difficult to make ends meet. Workers at the Moscow McDonald's, for example, had regarded themselves as privileged: They were paid regularly and well. But overnight in 1998, the value of their paycheck dropped by 70 percent. Workers in state jobs simply were not paid at all.

For many Russians, capitalism meant lawlessness. Managers of state industries were often able to manipulate privatization for their own private enrichment, so they grew fabulously wealthy, while ordinary employees experienced sharp pay cuts or the loss of their jobs. By the mid-1990s, a new force had appeared in Russian life—the "Russian Mafia," crime syndicates with international links that used extortion and intimidation to seize control of large sectors of the economy.

In the non-Russian republics, often the situation was even worse. The end of the Soviet Union meant the end of Soviet subsidies for these impoverished regions. Tajikistan, for example, had depended on Soviet financial aid to prop up the extensive irrigation system that allowed its farmers to grow cotton for export. The collapse of the Soviet Union meant the collapse of the Tajikistan economy. By the end of the 1990s, almost half of Tajikistan's 6.2 million inhabitants were struggling to survive in the face of severe food shortages. In Moldova, the economy shrank by 60 percent between 1991 and 2001, while life expectancy rates fell by five years. One Moldovan elementary school principal admitted she was "hungry for Soviet days," which she recalled as a time when salaries were steady and health care universally available.[8] In the post-Soviet era, Moldovans resorted to marketing their body organs to Western entrepreneurs for $3,000 each.

The economic and social collapse that followed the end of the Soviet Union fostered a climate of desperation in which extremist nationalism flourished. Independence did not mean stability in the republics of Georgia, Armenia, and Azerbaijan, all of which experienced civil war in the 1990s. In Russia itself, Yeltsin faced strong opposition from nationalist groups who viewed the breakup of the Soviet Union as a humiliation for Mother Russia.

The sharpest nationalist challenge to Yeltsin came from Chechnya, one of twenty-one autonomous republics within the larger Russian Federation. When the Soviet Union broke up, Chechnya became part of independent Russia. But the Chechens demanded their own state, and in 1991 declared Chechnya independent. The Chechen-Russian dispute simmered until 1994 when Yeltsin committed 30,000 troops to forcing Chechnya back within Russia's embrace. In the ensuing twenty-month conflict, 80,000 died and 240,000 were wounded—80 percent of these Chechen civilians. Yeltsin negotiated a truce in the summer of 1996, but four years later his successor, Vladimir Putin (b. 1952), renewed the war.

While Putin continued Yeltsin's battle against Chechen independence, his assumption of the presidency signaled a change in Russia's direction—but just where Russia was heading was not very clear. On the one hand, the well-manicured, tightly controlled, even austere Putin promised a more competent, stable style of government than Russia had experienced under the hard-drinking, jovial, often erratic Yeltsin. Yet Putin soon displayed authoritarian instincts. He moved quickly to centralize power under his own control and ran roughshod over such key democratic touchstones as freedom of the press and the right to a fair trial. Western governments struggled with the question of how to encourage Russia's economic stabilization without sacrificing its still fledgling democracy.

Eastern Europe: Stumbling Toward Democracy

Like the former Soviet Union, the states of Eastern Europe found the path from communist rule to democracy far from easy. The dissolution of the Soviet bloc meant that economic networks established over the last four decades suddenly disintegrated. In addition, Western advisers and the International Monetary Fund, which controlled access to much-needed loans, insisted that the new governments follow programs of "austerity" aimed at cutting government spending and curbing inflation. The result was economic

hardship far beyond what any Western electorate would have endured. In Poland, for example, the new Solidarity-led government instituted the "Big Bang" on New Year's Day 1990. Controls disappeared and prices jumped between 30 and 600 percent overnight. The inflation rate for 1990 in Poland was a remarkable 550 percent. Even in 1995, when the economy had stabilized, inflation remained at 20 percent, while joblessness stood at 15 percent.

But by the second half of the 1990s, it was clear that Poland was succeeding in moving from communism to capitalism. With some measures of market reform already in place before 1988, both Poland and Hungary were the best prepared for the transition from a command to a capitalist economy. The Czech Republic and the Baltic nations also moved fairly rapidly through the most difficult stages of this transition. In countries such as Romania, Bulgaria, and Albania, economic instability continued, with the majority of their populations experiencing severe poverty.

Political stability was also hard-won during this decade. The revolutionary coalitions that had led the charge against communist rule in 1989–1990 quickly fragmented as their members moved from the heady idealism of challenging authoritarianism to the nitty-gritty of parliamentary politics. In addition, voters who were fed up with economic hardship turned to the people who represented a more stable past. Between 1993 and 1995, ex-communists returned to power in Lithuania, Hungary, Bulgaria, and Poland. In Romania, they had never left. Yet the revolutions of 1989 were not reversed. Ex-communists continued with the economic liberalization programs of their opponents, although in many cases opting for a more gradual transition. No former communist regime returned to authoritarian rule or a centralized state-run economy.

A far greater threat to eastern European democracy was posed by the revival of pre–World War II political ideas and styles. For example, the claim of Josef Antall, Hungary's prime minister in the early 1990s, to be the leader of "all Hungarians" (two million of whom lived in Romania and another 600,000 in Slovakia) recalled the vehement Hungarian nationalism of the 1920s and 1930s. Much of eastern Europe witnessed a resurgence of ethnic hostilities in the 1990s. In Czechoslovakia, Hável's government could not bridge the regional-ethnic divide that opened up between the Czech half of the country and Slovakia. In 1993, Czechoslovakia ceased to exist, replaced by the separate nations of the Czech Republic and Slovakia. The breakup of Czechoslovakia occurred peacefully, but ethnic divisions turned violent in much of eastern Europe. In Romania escalating discrimination against the Hungarian and Roma minority populations stirred up memories of interwar racist violence. Throughout eastern Europe, anti-Semitic rhetoric returned to political discourse. In 1990, Lech Wałęsa's election campaign was tainted by anti-Jewish references; graffiti appeared on the walls of Warsaw buildings: "Jews to the ovens."

The "German Problem"?

The problems that engulfed Germany after its eastern and western halves reunited in October 1990 illustrated the difficulties faced by eastern Europeans as they struggled to adjust to a post–Cold War, post-Soviet world. Almost half the population of East Germany crossed the border into West Germany in the first week after the fall of the Berlin Wall. They returned home dazzled by the consumer delights they saw in store windows and eager for a chance to grab a piece of the capitalist pie. West German chancellor Helmut Kohl recognized the power of these desires, and skillfully forced the pace of reunification. When the two Germanys united at the end of 1990, Kohl became the first chancellor of the new German state.

Kohl trusted that West Germany's economy was strong enough to pull its bankrupt new partner into prosperity, but he proved overly optimistic. The residents of the former East Germany soon found their factories closing and their livelihoods gone. These economic troubles quickly leached over into the western regions of Germany. By 1997, unemployment in Germany stood at 12.8 percent—the highest since World War II. In the eastern regions, over 20 percent of the population was out of work.

For the women of the former East Germany, life in the new Germany meant an especially intense culture clash. The concept of the male breadwinner/head of household was enshrined in the West German legal code until the end of the 1970s and prominent in West German culture for a long time after. Many women from the former East Germany found this concept alien. In East Germany, women had expected to work full time and to have access to state-provided day care, abortion, and contraceptives. In the new united Germany, which adhered to West German legal and cultural traditions, more conventional gender roles and conceptions of sexual morality dominated. For at least some East German women, then, the end of communist rule was not unambiguously liberating.

At the same time, economic despair throughout much of the former East Germany resulted in racial violence. Looking for scapegoats, eastern German youths targeted the foreign workers in their cities. Violent attacks against Turkish workers escalated in the 1990s, as did support for neo-Nazi organizations.

In 1998, these economic and social problems led German voters to reject Kohl and the Christian Democrats. The Social Democrats, out of office since 1982, took charge under the leadership of Gerhard Schroeder (b. 1944). Schroeder, however, was unable to reverse the economic slide. By 2001, the German economy was standing still, with a GDP growth rate of little more than zero. The gap between the former West and East Germanys remained wide, with easterners enduring the worst of the German economic crisis. In a hugely controversial effort to resolve the crisis, Schroeder in 2004 forced through legislation that scaled back German welfare benefits. Many Germans, however, saw this move as a repudiation of the social democratic promise of guaranteeing a decent standard of living to all Germans. In September 2005, Shroeder's Social Democrats lost their majority in the German parliament. The Christian Democrats, however, also failed to gain a majority. The inconclusive results of the election revealed a worrying lack of consensus among voters about Germany's direction in the twenty-first century.

The Breakup of Yugoslavia

In Yugoslavia the "return of history" proved most marked and, given the nature of that history, most horrific. When the communist guerilla leader Tito seized control of the Yugoslav state after World War II, he sought to free Yugoslavia from the divisive and bloody battles of its recent past. But in the 1980s and 1990s, the revival of nationalist hostilities within Yugoslavia led to civil war and

DOCUMENT

"How's the Family?"

The conflict in Yugoslavia was a civil war, which meant that frequently the fighters knew their enemy personally. Victims of ethnic cleansing testified that it was their neighbors, colleagues, or schoolmates who had thrust them out of their homes, killed their fathers and brothers, and raped their mothers and sisters. The men at the top also knew each other. In this excerpt, a transcript of a telephone conversation made in Croatia in 1991, the Serb military commander Ratko Mladic is speaking to his Croat counterpart:

"Is that you, Mladic?"

"Yes it is, you old devil, what do you want?"

"Three of my boys went missing near . . . and I want to find out what happened to them."

"I think they're all dead."

"I've got one of their parents on to me about it, so I can tell them for certain that they're gone?"

"Yep, certain. You have my word. By the way, how's the family?"

"Oh not so bad, thanks. How about yours?"

"They're doing just fine, we're managing pretty well."

"Glad to hear it. By the way, now I've got you on the line, we've got about twenty bodies of yours near the front and they've been stripped bare. We slung them into a mass grave and they're now stinking to high heaven. Any chance of you coming to pick them up because they really are becoming unbearable. . . ?"

Source: From Misha Glenny, *The Fall of Yugoslavia* (1994), p. 28.

state-sanctioned mass murder, to scenes of carnage and to mass atrocities not seen in Europe since the 1940s.

Although Yugoslavia had appeared on European maps since the end of World War I, one could argue it did not really exist until after World War II. During the 1920s and 1930s, the subjects of the Serbian monarchy did not regard themselves as "Yugoslavs"; they were Serbs or Croats, Muslims or Montenegrins, Albanians or Slovenians. And during World War II, as we saw in Chapter 26, Serbs and Croats fought each other with a savage intensity—a bitter reminder of the lack of a single national Yugoslav identity.

To construct a united nation out of Yugoslavia's diverse and often hostile cultures, Tito utilized two tools—federalism and communism. A federal political structure consisting of six equal republics prevented Serbia, or any other of the republics, from dominating Yugoslavia. Communism served as a unifying ideology, a cluster of ideas that transcended the divisions of race, religion, and language. Ethnic identities and rivalries were declared unacceptable, part of the bourgeois past that had supposedly been left behind.

Yugoslavs often said, however, that their nation consisted of "six nationalities, five languages, four religions, . . . and one Tito." According to this folk wisdom, Tito—not communism, not federalism—was the glue that held together this diverse state. In 1980, Tito died. Ominously, the year after his death saw the outbreak of riots between ethnic Albanians and Serbs in the province of Kosovo. Even more ominously, Tito's death coincided with the onset of serious economic crisis. The drastic rise in oil prices in 1979 undercut the Yugoslav economy, as did its rising debt load. Between 1979 and 1985 real wages fell in Yugoslavia by almost 25 percent. By 1987, inflation was raging at 200 percent per year; two years later it had burst through into hyperinflation— 200 percent *per month.*

Under pressure from this economic crisis, the federal structure built by Tito began to collapse, as the wealthier Yugoslav republics such as Croatia sought to loosen the ties that bound them to the poorer republics such as Serbia. Then, in 1989, the revolutions that swept through the Soviet satellite states shattered the hold of communism on Yugoslavia as well. Ethnic nationalism, long simmering under the surface of Yugoslavian political life, poured into the resulting ideological void. New leaders emerged with new agendas.

In Serbia, the former communist functionary Slobodan Milošević (b. 1941) transformed himself into a popular spokesman for aggressive Serbian nationalism. Milošević used rallies and the mass media, which he controlled, to

CHRONOLOGY
The Shattering of Yugoslavia

1989	Slobodan Milošević becomes president of Yugoslavian Republic of Serbia
1991	
July	Civil war in Croatia begins
1992	
April	Civil war in Bosnia begins
1994	
April	NATO air strikes against Bosnian Serb positions begin
1995	
December	Dayton Accords
1998	Large-scale fighting in Kosovo between Albanians and Serbs
1999	
March	NATO air strikes against Serbia
June	Cease-fire in Kosovo
2000	
October	Milošević defeated in Serbian elections
2001	
June	Milošević extradited to the Hague to be tried for genocide

convince Serbs that their culture was under attack and to paint himself as the defender of that culture. To enhance Serbia's power—and his own—Milošević fiercely opposed any talk of destroying the Yugoslav federation. Moreover, Milošević possessed a powerful weapon to enforce his will: the Yugoslav army, the fourth-largest fighting force in Europe, dominated by Serbs.

Thus, when Croatia declared independence in June 1991, the result was civil war. Milošević mobilized the Yugoslav army against the Croatian separatists. In 1992 the war spread to Bosnia-Herzegovina after its government, too, declared independence. The war quickly degenerated into an ethnic bloodbath, with memories of World War II shaping the conflict. Serbs viewed Croats as the direct heirs of the murderous Nazi-backed Croatian fascists, responsible for the mass slaughter of Serbs (and Jews) in World War II. In turn, Croats called all Serbs "Chetniks," linking them to the anti-Croat Serbian guerilla bands of the war years. (See Chapter 26.) The presence of paramilitary forces also heightened the brutality of the war. With no military discipline and often possessing criminal records, the

Map 28.2 The Former Yugoslavia

The breakup of Yugoslavia began in June 1991 with the Slovenian and Croatian declarations of independence. Bosnia and Macedonia soon followed.

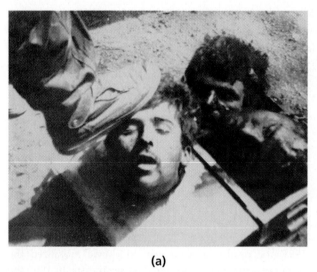

(a)

(b)

Bosnian War Atrocities

(a) Serbian heads, found after Serb fighters raided a Muslim base in northern Bosnia in 1993. (b) A mass grave of Muslim civilians in Pilica, northwest of Srebrenica, in the spring of 1996. Twelve thousand of the men and boys of Srebrenica tried to flee to safety—about half made it; many of those that didn't were forced by Serb fighters to dig their own graves and then shot in front of them. The citizens of Srebenica who did not flee were told by Bosnian Serbian general Ratko Mladic, "No one will harm you." Mladic then ordered his soldiers to shoot all Muslim men between ages 17 and 60. Reviewing the evidence against Mladic, the UN tribunal noted, "These are truly scenes from hell, written on the darkest pages of human history."

volunteers in these units plunged into a fury of plunder, murder, and rape.

This war introduced the world to the horrors of ethnic cleansing° and rape camps. By 1994, all sides within the Bosnian war were practicing ethnic cleansing, although it is clear that Serbs initiated the practice and used it most extensively. To create all-Serb zones within Croatia and Bosnia, Serb paramilitary units embarked on a campaign of terror designed to force Muslims and Croats to abandon their homes and villages. They burned mosques, closed schools, and vandalized houses. Most villagers fled; the paramilitaries tortured and often killed those who stayed. Women were sometimes rounded up and placed in special camps where they were subjected to regular, systematic rape. An estimated 20,000 women, most of them Muslim, endured this vicious effort to subjugate and humiliate a people.

With Serbia assisting the Bosnian Serbs and Croatia assisting the Bosnian Croats, the Muslim community within Bosnia suffered the most intensely, and begged western governments to abandon their positions of neutrality and to stop the atrocities. Finally, in 1994, NATO planes began bombing Serb positions, the first time in its history that NATO had gone into combat. One year later, the Dayton Accords, signed in Dayton, Ohio, brought an uneasy peace to Bosnia (see Map 28.2).

Peace eluded Serbia during this period, however. The sort of vicious nationalism embodied by Milošević demanded a constant supply of enemies and a continuous cycle of violence. In 1998, large-scale fighting between Serbs and Albanians erupted in the province of Kosovo. Ethnic cleansing, mass rape, and a huge exodus of refugees began once again. After a NATO bombing campaign in Serbia, NATO and Russian troops moved into Kosovo, and in 2001, a police helicopter transported Milošević to the Netherlands to be tried for genocide before the International War Crimes Tribunal.

Rethinking the West

■ **What were the implications of these developments for the meaning of "the West" itself?**

At the start of the 1990s, a sense of triumphalism characterized much of Western culture—at its simplest, expressed as "we won the Cold War." But who was "we"? For forty years, the Cold War had provided a clear enemy and thus a clear identity: The West was anticommunist, anti-Soviet, anti–Warsaw Pact. Communism's loss of credibility, the disintegration of the Soviet Union, and the dismantling of the Warsaw Pact all demanded that the West revise itself. But so, too, did other important social, political, and cultural changes that occurred in the wake of the tumultuous events of the later 1960s and the economic downturn of the 1970s.

The European Union

With the ending of the Cold War, the nations of western Europe, united under the umbrella of the European Union° (EU), moved to take on a much more important role in global affairs. We saw in Chapter 27 that the EU began in the 1950s as the Common Market or EEC (European Economic Community), an economic free-trade organization of six western European nations. By the end of the millennium, this organization had become a powerful entity possessing not only economic but also political clout, a potential counterweight to the United States.

During the 1970s and 1980s, the EEC widened both its membership and its areas of cooperation. Britain, Denmark, and Ireland joined in 1973, Greece in 1981, Spain and Portugal in 1986. (Austria, Finland, and Sweden joined in the 1990s.) In 1979, a European Parliament chosen directly by European voters met for the first time. Throughout these decades, the European Court of Justice gradually began to assert the primacy of the European Community over national law, thus pushing western Europe down the road toward political integration. The EEC—the European Economic Community—became the EC, or the European Community, a political and cultural as well as economic organization.

The pace of change accelerated in the 1980s and 1990s as the Single European Act of 1985 and the Maastricht Agreements of 1991 replaced the European *Community* (EC) with the European *Union* (EU), defined by France's President Mitterrand as "one currency, one culture, one social area, one environment." The establishment of the EU meant visible changes for ordinary Europeans. They saw their national passports replaced by a common EU document, and border controls eliminated. The creation of a single EU currency— the euro, which replaced national currencies in 2002—tore down one of the most significant economic barriers between European countries. At the same time, the powers of the European Parliament expanded and member states moved toward establishing common social policies (such as labor rights).

While these developments occurred, Europeans also faced the unexpected challenge posed by the ending of the Cold War. Should the European Union (often called simply "Europe") now include East as well as West? Attracted by the undoubted prosperity of the EU, the nations of the former Soviet bloc answered that question with a resounding "yes." The leaders of western Europe, however, looked with trepidation at the prospect of joining their countries to

IMAGE

European Union Flag

eastern Europe's shattered economies and divided societies and drew up a list of rigorous qualifications for applicant nations. To be recognized as belonging to "Europe," nations applying for EU membership had to meet a set of complex financial requirements that demonstrated both the essential stability of their economies and their commitment to market capitalism. Thus "Europe" was defined, first of all, as capitalist. But a set of political requirements made clear that "Europe" also meant a commitment to democratic politics. Applicants' voting processes, treatment of minority groups, policing methods, and judicial systems were all scrutinized, as the EU used its considerable economic clout to nurture fledgling democratic structures in eastern Europe. In 2004, Estonia, Latvia, Lithuania, Poland, the Czech Republic, Slovakia, Slovenia, and Hungary, as well as Cyprus and Malta, all joined the EU (see Map 28.3).

Many Europeans greeted both the launch of the euro in 2002 and the dramatic expansion of the EU in 2004 as signs

that the dream of a united Europe was being realized. Other Europeans, however, perceived this dream as a nightmare. "Euro-skeptics" questioned the economic value of unification. They pointed out that throughout the 1990s, the U.S. economy continued to outperform that of the EU, and European unemployment rates were often high. Britain, Denmark, and Sweden all refused to join the conversion to the euro, fearing that their economies would be dragged down by their slower-performing EU partners. Small traders and independent producers opposed the seemingly endless stream of orders and regulations issued by EU bureaucrats and the way in which economic integration privileged large, international firms over small, local shops. Many Europeans feared the growing political power of the EU and saw it as a threat to national sovereignty. Still others predicted that the expansion of the EU would mean the loss of jobs as western European firms moved eastward to take advantage of the lower wage rates and lax standard of work-

Map 28.3 Contemporary Europe
The revolutions of 1989 and their aftermath mark a clear turning point in European history, as a comparison of this map and that of "Europe in the Cold War" (p. 887) will show. Significant changes include the breakup of the Soviet Union and Yugoslavia, the replacement of Czechoslovakia by the Czech Republic and Slovakia, and the unification of Germany.

ers' protections in eastern Europe. All of these fears came into the open in the spring of 2005 when voters in both France and the Netherlands rejected a proposed EU constitution. These "no" votes from traditionally pro-EU states forced the shelving of the constitution and raised serious doubts about both the process and the pace of Europe's political and economic unification.

Islam, Terrorism, and European Identity

Significantly, the expansion of the EU in 2004 did not include Turkey. A member of NATO since 1952, Turkey first applied for associate membership in the EU (then the EEC) in 1959 but did not succeed in becoming an associate until 1991. In 2004 EU officials announced that talks on Turkey's entry as a full member would begin in 2005, but denied to the Turkish government any guarantees. A number of issues had frustrated Turkey's efforts to join the EU, including its refusal to recognize the independence of Cyprus, the clash between Turkey's repressive penal system and EU human rights legislation, and its poverty. If Turkey joined the EU, it would immediately become the most populous and the poorest member of the union. Opponents to Turkey's bid for membership feared that the European economy could not absorb the expected massive influx of impoverished Turkish migrant workers. They also, however, opposed full membership in "Europe" for Turkey because most Turks are Muslim, and for many Europeans, "European" and "Islamic" described clashing cultures.

Muslim Communities in Europe

The struggle over Turkish membership in the EU was just one of many controversies in contemporary Europe resulting from an ongoing battle to reconcile European identity with a growing Islamic cultural and political presence. By 2004, the number of European Muslims stood at 20 million—5 percent of the EU's population. Because the European Muslim birth rate is three times the non-Muslim birth rate, the percentage of Muslims within Europe is likely to continue to expand.

There is, of course, no single "Muslim Europe." In eastern European countries such as Bulgaria, Albania, and Bosnia, Muslims were part of the indigenous nation, the descendants of those who converted to Islam centuries earlier during the era of Ottoman rule. In western Europe, by contrast, most Muslims were immigrants or the children or grandchildren of immigrants, drawn to the West by greater economic and educational opportunities.

Even in western Europe, the Muslim experience varied. The majority of Britain's two million Muslims had roots in India or Pakistan, and thus received citizenship because of their Commonwealth inheritance; in contrast, until the passage of new citizenship laws in 2004, few of the three

million Muslims living in Germany—most of them Turks or of Turkish descent—could claim the rights of citizenship. Many Muslims were highly educated and prosperous, but overall, the Muslim standard of living throughout Europe lagged behind that of non-Muslims: Muslims were far more likely to be unemployed; to work in low-paying, dead-end jobs; to live in substandard housing; and to possess fewer educational qualifications than their non-Muslim neighbors. Many of these "neighbors," however, lived far away, as Muslims, responding both to poverty and discrimination as well as their own desire to retain their distinct communities, tended to cluster in certain areas and cities, part of a subculture largely separate from and, in some cases, increasingly hostile to the majority culture. As minarets began to rival church steeples in the skylines of European cities, an increasing number of non-Muslim Europeans argued that Western culture itself was under threat. The decision of Iran's Ayatollah Khomeini to issue a death sentence against the British writer Salman Rushdie in 1989 forced many of these tensions and hostilities into the open but provided no easy answers to questions about Islamic, European, and Western identity.

Terrorism, the West, and the Middle East

Terrorism both deepened hostilities between Muslims and non-Muslims in the West and made the resolution of these hostilities even more urgent. This textbook has traced the way in which "the West" changed meaning, often in response to places and peoples defined as "not West." With the ending of the Cold War, the West lost its main enemy, but a replacement stood readily at hand. In 1996, the American president Bill Clinton (b. 1946) identified terrorism as "the enemy of our generation." In the post–Cold War world, terrorism in many ways replaced communism as the new foe against which the West defined itself. Many Europeans and Americans, however, not only viewed terrorism as "not West," they also linked "terrorism" with "Islam."

Terrorism directly opposes what many now regard as the bedrock of Western culture—a commitment to democracy and the rule of the law. Because terrorists seek to achieve political ends through violence and intimidation, terrorism short-circuits the democratic process: Decision-making shifts from the ballot box to the bomb. Yet the equation of the West with law and democracy conveniently ignores the history of the West and of terrorism itself. Together with fascism and Nazism, terrorism is one of the less savory products of Western political culture. Terrorism grew out of late nineteenth-century anarchism, which advocated violence as a means of political change (see Chapter 22). Like the assassins who killed Tsar Alexander II in 1881, contemporary terrorists belonged to groups lacking access to political power. Unable to achieve their goals through political persuasion (lobbying, campaigning, winning votes), they endeavored to destabilize the societies they opposed through acts of terror. In the twentieth century, thwarted

The Sentencing of Salman Rushdie

In February 1989, the Ayatollah Khomeini, political leader of Iran and spiritual head of the Shi'a Muslim community, issued a death sentence against the novelist Salman Rushdie and offered an award of $2.5 million to any faithful Muslim who killed him. Rushdie, a British citizen who had never been tried in any Iranian or Islamic court, immediately went into hiding, where he remained for several years. His death sentence ignited the "Satanic Verses Affair," a tumultuous international crisis caused by a resounding clash of cultural assumptions and expectations.

The crisis centered on a book. In the early autumn of 1988 Viking Penguin published Rushdie's *The Satanic Verses,* a difficult novel about the complexities and contradictions of the modern immigrant experience. Born in India and raised in an Islamic home, Rushdie wrote *The Satanic Verses* to describe "migration, metamorphosis, divided selves, love, death, London, and Bombay."[9] The novel received immediate critical acclaim, with reviewers praising it as an astonishing work of postmodernist fiction.

Other readers judged it differently. Many Muslims around the world regarded the book as a direct attack on the foundations of their religious faith. One scene in the novel particularly horrified devout Muslims. In this episode, the central character has a psychotic breakdown and falls into a dream: Muhammad appears as a corrupt businessman, and prostitutes in a brothel take on the names of the Prophet's wives.

The novel aroused intense controversy from the moment of its publication. The government of India banned it almost immediately; within a matter of weeks, several other states followed suit. Anti-Rushdie demonstrations in both India and Pakistan turned violent, resulting in fifteen deaths. Bookstores selling the novel received bombing and death threats. In western Europe, hostilities between Muslims and non-Muslims intensified. Then, on February 14, 1989, an announcer on Radio Tehran read aloud the text of a *fatwa,* or decree, issued by the Ayatollah Khomeini:

> *I would like to inform all the intrepid Muslims of the world that the author of the book entitled* The Satanic Verses, *which has been compiled, printed and published in opposition to Islam, the Prophet and the Koran, as well as those publishers who were aware of its contents, have been sentenced to death. I call on all zealous Muslims to execute them quickly, wherever they find them. . . . Whoever is killed on this path will be regarded as a martyr, God willing.*

Western governments reacted quickly against Khomeini's call for Rushdie's death. The twelve nations of the European Community, the United States, Sweden, Norway, Canada, Australia, and Brazil all condemned Khomeini's judgment, recalled their ambassadors from Tehran, and cancelled high-level diplomatic contacts with Iran. British prime minister Margaret Thatcher provided police protection for Rushdie and dismissed British Muslim demands to ban the book: "It is an essential part of our democratic system that people who act within the law should be able to express their opinions freely."[10]

Large numbers of Muslims, including many who spoke out against Rushdie's book, also condemned Khomeini's fatwa. Some Muslim scholars contended that the Ayatollah's fatwa was a scholarly opinion, not a legally binding judgment; others argued that Rushdie could not be condemned without a trial, or that because Rushdie lived in a society without an Islamic government, he was not bound by Islamic law.

But many ordinary Muslims ignored these high-level theological and legal disputes and greeted the Ayatollah's fatwa with delight. The news of the Ayatollah's fatwa brought crowds of cheering Muslims into the city streets. In Manchester and Bradford, young British Muslim men insisted they would kill Rushdie if given the chance. In Paris, demonstrators marched to cries of "We are all Khomeinists!"

Why did Khomeini's fatwa arouse such popular enthusiasm within Western Muslim communities? A partial answer to this question is that many Muslims were frustrated with what they regarded as the unequal application of the laws of censorship. Faced with what they saw as a hate-filled, pornographic caricature of Islam, they demanded that Western governments use the laws censoring pornography and banning hate crimes to block the publication of Rushdie's book. In Britain, Muslims were particularly outraged that the existing law against blasphemy protected only Christianity, the official state religion.

But the controversy was not simply a dispute about censorship. For some Muslims, Rushdie's *Satanic Verses* epitomized Western secular society, with its scant regard for tradition or religious values. As Dr. Kalim Siddiqui of the pro-Iranian Muslim Institute in Britain proclaimed, "western civilization is fundamentally an immoral civilization. Its 'values' are free of moral constraints."[11] From this perspective, Khomeini's fatwa condemned not just one book or one author, but an entire culture that seemed inherently opposed to Islam. Khomeini had already proven himself a forceful leader in the Iranian hostage crisis of 1979–1980, when he successfully thumbed his nose at American power. Now once again he seemed willing to take on the West to defend Islam.

The anti-Western stance of some radical Muslims was mirrored by the anti-Islam position soon occupied by some Rushdie supporters. In one of the most ironic twists in the entire Satanic Verses Affair, Rushdie's books, which condemned the endemic racism in British society and exposed the falsehood of Western claims to cultural superiority, were championed by individuals who articulated precisely the sort of Western cultural chauvinism against which Rushdie had written so passionately. For example, Robert Maxwell, a multimillionaire communications tycoon, offered $10 million to any individual "who will, not kill, but civilise the barbarian Ayatollah" by forcing him to recite publicly the Ten Commandments.[12] Many western Europeans agreed with the conclusion drawn in this letter to a British daily newspaper: "The lesson of the Rushdie affair is that it was unwise to let Muslim communities establish themselves in our midst."[13] The lines were drawn, with Islam standing for irrationalism, barbarity, intolerance, and ignorance, while the "West" was linked to democracy, reason, freedom, and civilization. At precisely the moment when the crumbling of communism and the ending of the Cold War deprived the West of one of its defining attributes, the Satanic Verses Affair offered up a new Other against which the West could define itself.

Questions of Justice

1. On what grounds are publications censored in secular, Western societies? Given the existence of this censorship, should Rushdie's book have been banned?
2. In what ways does the Satanic Verses Affair illuminate the tensions within many European societies from the 1970s on, as communities struggled to adapt to the challenges of ethnic and religious diversity?

Taking It Further

Bowen, David G., ed. *The Satanic Verses: Bradford Responds.* 1996. This collection of essays and documents helps explains why many British Muslims viewed the British government's failure to censor Rushdie's book as an act of injustice.

A Clash of Cultures?
In London, a policeman chases a demonstrator during a protest against the publication of *The Satanic Verses.*

nationalism provided especially fertile soil for the growth of terrorism. In Northern Ireland, assassinations and bombings became commonplace after the Irish Republican Army (IRA) turned to terror to pressure the British government to relinquish its control over the province. In Spain, the Basque separatist group Eta has for three decades waged a campaign of terror to achieve its aim of an independent Basque state. Terrorism is thus one of the negative aspects of "Western civilization." Yet by the 1990s, terrorism was often perceived as the antithesis of the West, as an outside threat, usually bearing an Arabic face and carrying a copy of the Qur'an.

Terrorist activity sparked by the Palestinian-Israeli conflict helped create this perception. Frustrated by the failure of the United Nations to implement its 1947 resolution promising a Palestinian state, Palestinian nationalists (most but not all of whom were Muslim) in 1964 formed the Palestine Liberation Organization (PLO). Like the IRA in Northern Ireland or Eta in Spain, the PLO saw violence as the only means to its nationalist ends. The PLO's commitment to terrorism deepened after the Six-Day War of 1967, which (as we saw in Chapter 27) led to Israel occupying East Jerusalem, the West Bank, and the Golan Heights. During subsequent decades the PLO took its campaign of terror around the world, bombing airports, targeting tourists, and persuading many in the West that "Arab," "Muslim," and "terrorist" were interchangeable terms.

At the same time, U.S. support for Israel convinced many Muslims that "the West" (often equated simply with the United States) was an enemy. Between 1949 and 1998, Israel received more American aid than any other country. As Israel went on the offensive against not only Palestinian terrorism but also popular Palestinian uprisings in the 1980s and 1990s (the first and second "intifadahs"), Palestinians and their supporters argued that the United States was bankrolling a repressive regime, and that Israel was a Western colonialist outpost (see Map 28.4).

Islamism and the West

Western perceptions of a link between Islam and terrorism were further strengthened by the development of Islamism°. Also called Islamic fundamentalism or *jihadism* (after the Islamic idea of "jihad," or holy war), Islamism is explicitly anti-Western—and is rejected by most Muslims as a corruption or negation of Islamic values. Islamism views Western culture as a threat to Islamic identity; regards the United States as the standard-bearer of the West and thus as a particular enemy of Muslim interests; and accepts violence, including the murder of civilians, as an acceptable means to its ends.

A confluence of developments helped swell the Islamist tide. Modernity itself created in its wake a fundamentalist surge, not only within Islam but within other religious traditions such as Christianity and Hinduism. In times of often confusing change and growing secularization, men and

women sought clear answers and the guarantee of order through rigid religious systems. This guarantee of order particularly appealed to the children of Muslim immigrants in western Europe. Many in this generation, young men in particular, felt betrayed by the cultures in which they lived. Their ongoing struggle against poverty, discrimination, and disempowerment turned many European Muslims toward Islamism.

A series of international developments also nourished Islamism. First, the West's willingness during the Cold War to prop up unpopular and corrupt governments turned the Western promise of democracy into a sham for many Muslims. In Iran, for example, the United States supported the autocratic regime of the Shah. In 1979 a popular revolution vaulted into power the Ayatollah Khomeini (1901–1989), who rapidly reversed the westernizing and modernizing policies of the Shah and decried the United States as the "Great Satan."

DOCUMENT

Ayatollah Khomeini's Vision of Islamic Government

The Gulf War of 1991 sharpened these hostilities. In this conflict American and British forces led a twenty-eight-country coalition in a military intervention to drive invading Iraqi forces out of tiny but oil-rich Kuwait. The war itself could not be construed as "the West versus Islam" or "the West versus the East": One Arab and Islamic country had invaded another. But in the aftermath of the war, U.S. forces remained in American-controlled bases in Saudi Arabia, home of some of the most holy sites in Islam. For Islamists, the presence of the United States in this region both sullied Islamic purity and insulted Arabic political independence.

Finally, the wars in both Bosnia and Chechnya fed Islamist hatred of the West. The initial passivity of both western Europe and the United States while Muslim men and boys were slaughtered and Muslim women and girls raped during the Bosnian war of 1992–1995 convinced many European Muslims that Western governments had an anti-Muslim agenda. This perception grew stronger when western states refused to back the Chechens (who are Muslim) in what many view as the Chechen war of independence against Russian oppression, ongoing from 1994.

Significantly, many Islamists viewed Russia as part of the West against which they were fighting. The predominantly Muslim states of the Caucasus had a long history of fighting against Russian rule, and Soviet communism had been no more tolerant of Islam than it had been of Judaism or Christianity. Most important, however, was yet another recent war: the Soviet-Afghan War of 1979–1989. To Islamists, the Afghan guerillas fighting both the pro-Soviet Afghan regime and the Soviet army came to represent the wider struggle to free Islam from Western control and purify it from Western corruption. More practically, many Islamists received military training in this conflict.

Ironically, many of these Islamist rebels in Afghanistan were supported by the United States. Soviet troops withdrew from Afghanistan in defeat in 1989. The pro-Soviet Afghan government collapsed, and after a period of turmoil, the Taliban, a revolutionary Islamist group, seized control.

Events in Afghanistan seemed a long way away from Europe and the United States—until September 11, 2001, when Islamists declared open war on the West in one of the most deadly episodes of terrorism yet seen. Three jets hijacked by Islamist terrorists (most of them Saudi) smashed into the World Trade Center in New York City and the Pentagon (the U.S. military headquarters in Washington, D.C.), while a fourth crashed in Pennsylvania. Almost 3,000 people died. U.S. and European intelligence officers quickly linked the suicide pilots to Al Qaeda, an Islamist terrorist organization run by Osama bin Laden, a wealthy Saudi exile. Evidence of ideological and financial links between bin Laden and the Taliban led the United States to begin air attacks against Afghanistan in October 2001. The Taliban regime fell within weeks, but bin Laden remained at large and the "war against terror" continued.

In March 2003, this widely ranging war took a new turn when U.S. and British forces attacked Iraq. No direct connection linked Osama bin Laden to Iraq's government,

Map 28.4 The Middle East in the Contemporary Era

Although placed under Palestinian self-rule in 1994, the West Bank and Gaza Strip remain contested areas, sites of frequent confrontations between Palestinians and Israelis.

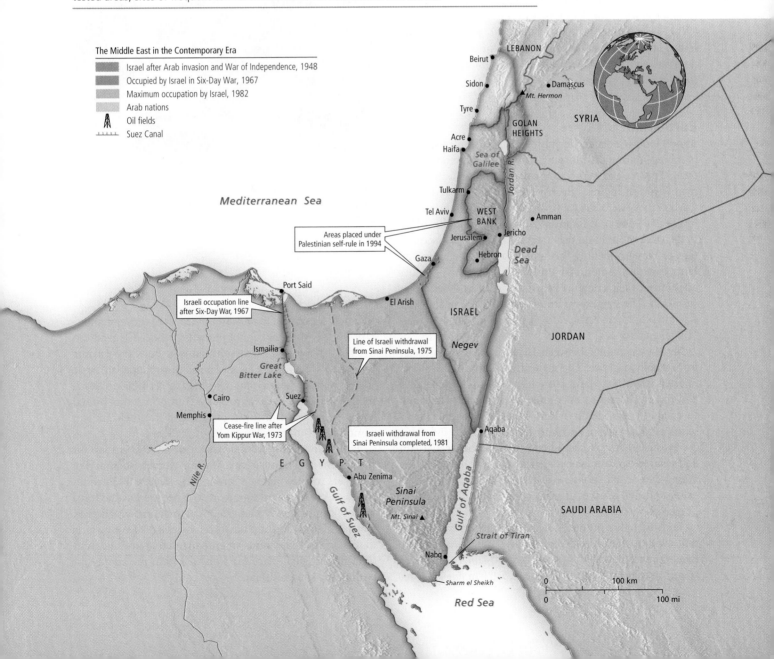

which was firmly controlled by Saddam Hussein, a secular dictator with a long history of torturing and killing Islamists like bin Laden who threatened his personal power. But in the world after "9/11," Saddam Hussein's refusal to allow UN inspections of his weapons factories convinced both the American and British governments that Iraq possessed the ability to launch a terrorist strike, in the form of biological or chemical weapons, against Western targets. The result was the first preemptive war ever waged by U.S. forces and, after a three-week conflict involving both air strikes and land battles, the toppling of Saddam Hussein's dictatorial regime. Many Iraqis cheered the dictator's overthrow, but other Iraqis—and many Arabs in the surrounding states—condemned the Anglo-American intervention as yet another episode in a long history of Western imperial intrusions on Arab territory.

The war in Iraq proved controversial, especially after Al Qaeda demonstrated its continuing ability to carry out lethal terrorist attacks. On the third anniversary of "9/11"—September 11, 2004—almost 200 people died after four bombs exploded on commuter trains during the rush hour in Madrid. Al Qaeda linked the bombing to Spain's support of the Iraq war.

Euro-Islam

Almost one year later, on July 7, 2005, a similar spate of bombings during the morning rush hour in London killed over 50 people and injured more than 700. Significantly, the men involved in this attack were not only linked to Al Qaeda, they were also British. The London bombings revealed the power of Islamism within the West itself. Thus, in the wake of 9/11 and the attacks that followed, the question of Western identity was more troublesome than ever. European and American Muslims found their loyalties questioned, their religious beliefs regarded as grounds for suspicion. The long, complex history of Islam in the West was often ignored, replaced by a simplistic "Them" versus "Us" mentality.

Yet the encounter between Islam and Europe was far from wholly negative. The majority of European Muslims rejected Islamism. Many, particularly those of the second and third generations of immigrant families, endeavored to create a new identity: Euro-Islam°. Regarding themselves as fully Muslim and fully European, these individuals insisted that no contradiction existed between Islam and what many Westerners view as the core values of the West—democratic politics, respect for individual differences, and civil liberties guaranteed by law to all, regardless of race and gender.

Euro-Islam has produced significant theological innovations within the Islamic community. Traditional Islamic theology cuts the world into two: *dar al-Islam*, or "house of Islam," and *dar al-harb*, or "house of war." In *dar-al-Islam*,

The Terrorist Age: Madrid, March 11, 2004
On March 11, 2004, a series of bombs ripped through four commuter trains in the Spanish capital city. Al Qaeda claimed responsibility for the attack, which killed 191 people and injured more than 1,500.

Islamic law prevails. In *dar-al-harb* (most of the contemporary world), Muslims cannot properly practice Islam and so live in a state of constant spiritual war. But Euro-Islamic proponents such as the Swiss scholar Tariq Ramadan argue there is a third "house": *dar ash-shahada*, or "house of testimony," regions—such as western Europe or the United States—where Muslims can profess and live their faith in community with non-Muslims.

European Muslim women have also played an important role in shaping Euro-Islam. Muslim women such as the members of the French group *Ni Putes Ni Soumises* (Neither Whores Nor Submissives) have been at the forefront of campaigns to eradicate such traditional practices as female circumcision and the forced marriage of young girls to men from their parents' or grandparents' homelands and to claim an equal place for women within the context of both Europe and of Islam.

An Identity Struggle
In the wake of 9/11, European Muslims fought to assert their Western identity. Symbols became particularly important; this teacher won her battle in German courts to wear her Islamic head scarf in the classroom of a state school. In France, however, Islamic girls in head scarves were not permitted in schoolrooms.

Into the Postmodern Era

The end of the Cold War, the formation of the European Union, and the growth of significant Muslim communities within western Europe all demanded a reevaluation and re-definition of West. So, too, did a number of intellectual, artistic, and technological developments that together helped created the postmodern era. A grab-bag term covering a huge array of styles and stances, postmodernism° at its core constitutes the rejection of Western cultural supremacy and, more particularly, a challenge to the idea that Western science and rationality had constructed a single, universally applicable form of "modernity."

The Making of the Postmodern

Postmodernism resulted from the joining of three specific intellectual and cultural streams: postmodernist architecture, postmodernist art, and the literary theories of poststructuralism.

Postmodernism first clearly took form in architecture, perhaps because the failures of modernist architecture were so obvious by the early 1970s. Motivated by an intense faith in both human rationality and modern technology, modernist architects had sought to build new forms of housing that they believed would enable people to live better, more beautiful lives. But the concrete high-rises they constructed failed to connect with the needs and emotions of their inhabitants, and many became derelict, crime-ridden, graffiti-scarred tenements.

Faced with this sense of failure, a new generation—the postmodernists—insisted that architects needed to start communicating with ordinary people. The American architect Charles Jencks (b. 1939) argued that because people tend to rely on the familiar to make sense of their world, modernism was wrong to reject traditional forms. For example, most Europeans and Americans connect domestic housing with gabled roofs (ask a child to draw a picture of a house and see if he or she draws a flat roof). Was it surprising, Jencks asked, that the concrete rectangles used by modernists for housing proved profoundly alienating to many people? Postmodernist *anti-elitism* thus led to *eclecticism*, to re-creating and combining forms and styles from past eras (such as gabled roofs), and to efforts to revive local and regional styles. Why should the streets of Tokyo look like the center of London or downtown Chicago? Instead, postmodernists embraced an architecture rooted in the specifics of time and place. In addition to being anti-elitist and eclectic, then, postmodernist architecture was also *anti-universalist*: It condemned modernism for its assumption that the same modern (and Western) ideals and forms fit all individuals and all societies.

The same sorts of criticism of modernism surfaced in the art world, as the wider political context of the late 1960s and early 1970s transformed the visual arts in three ways. First, in the wake of the protests of 1968, artists—many coming out of left-wing activist environments—rejected ideologies based on hierarchy and authority. This rejection led to an attack on the modernist idea of the "avant-garde," a small elite of artistic geniuses fighting to advance the frontiers of aesthetic excellence. Even more than their modernist predecessors, postmodernist artists celebrated the possibilities of the mass media and condemned distinctions between "high" and popular culture. Second, the experience of political protest led many artists to reject the modernist ideal of "art for art's sake," insisting instead that art had to say something to the world around it. To communicate with a wider public, they plundered both the past and popular culture for familiar forms and material. As the art critic

Postmodernism at Play
Designed by the American architect Frank Gehry and his Czech collaborator Vlado Mulunić, the "Dancing Building" fills a bomb site left vacant in central Prague since World War II. Also called "Fred and Ginger" (after the famous Hollywood dancing duo Fred Astaire and Ginger Rogers), this postmodernist piece both delighted and enraged the people of Prague.

Edit DeAk explained, postmodernist art relied on "the shock of recognition instead of the shock of the new."[14] Finally, feminism proved crucial in shaping the new art. Women began to challenge the dominance of men in the art world not only by highlighting the systematic exclusion of women from gallery and museum exhibitions, but also by questioning the aesthetic hierarchy that relegated to the lower status of "craft" traditionally female art forms such as weaving.

By the end of the 1970s, postmodernist practices in art and architecture both were reinforced by and in turn strengthened a growing body of literary and cultural theory often called *poststructuralism*. The theory of poststructuralism centered on the work of an assorted group of French thinkers whose ideas were taken up in American universities and then filtered back into European intellectual circles. These thinkers included Jacques Derrida (1930–2004) and Roland Barthes (1915–1980) in literary studies, Michel Foucault (1926–1984) in history, and Jacques Lacan (1901–1981) in psychoanalytic theory.

Like postmodernist theories in architecture and art, poststructuralism began as an exploration into the problems of communication. Jacques Derrida argued that the world we see and experience is a world structured by language—we cannot even understand or express our very selves apart from language. But because there is no inherent match between a word (what Derrida called a "signifier") and the thing or idea to which that word refers (the "signified"), communication is never straightforward. An endless variety of meanings and interpretations results, and thus, Derrida argued, we must abandon the idea of a fixed or single truth, of ultimate or universal meaning. In a related argument, Roland Barthes declared the "Death of the Author," by which he meant that the purpose of literary study is not to ask, "What does the author mean?" but instead to explore the way in which the reader creates his or her own meanings.

This effort to challenge any center of authority (sometimes called "decentering") linked the poststructuralist concern with communication to its analysis of power. Michel Foucault and Jacques Lacan dissected hierarchies of authority (not only in the political sphere but also in academic disciplines, for example, or in the medical world), and the way these authorities created and manipulated seemingly objective bodies of knowledge to retain their hold on power.

Postmodernism in its most general form emerged by the later 1980s out of the blending of these poststructuralist theories of communication and power with the critique of modernism already flourishing in architecture and the arts. Thinkers, writers, and artists argued that Western elites had shaped global culture and had ignored or distorted the cultures of non-Western and minority groups. This view of culture as bound up in a global contest for power disturbed many more traditional thinkers (with "modernist" now increasingly perceived as traditional) who continued to insist that criteria of aesthetic excellence ("Beauty") and objective standards of knowledge ("Truth") did exist. These critics warned that cultural "decentering" would destroy the social cohesion and political stability of the West.

Postmodern Cultures and Postindustrial Technologies

In many ways popular culture confirmed postmodern theories. In Britain, for example, the "Big Beat" songs that dominated the club scene in the late 1990s were produced not by vocalists or instrumentalists but by disc jockeys who lifted snatches from old records, played them at different speeds, and combined them with contrasting styles. Like postmodernist paintings, Big Beat contained chunks of the past, recycled in startling new ways. More generally, a series of technological developments meant that popular culture was clearly "decentered," that at the very least a multitude of popular cultures coexisted and that the individual consumer of culture, like Barthes's reader, was free to make meaning as he or she chose. The videocassette recorder (VCR), first marketed in 1975, not only transported film viewing from the public to the private sphere, it also provided the film viewer with the possibility to tailor the film to his or her own preferences—to adjust the volume or choose another soundtrack entirely, to omit or fast-forward through certain scenes, to replay others endlessly. Similarly, the proliferation of cable and satellite television stations during the 1980s and 1990s fragmented the viewing audience and made it impossible to speak of popular culture in the singular.

Postmodernist concerns with communication and codes, with the way in which interpretations can be endlessly modified, and with the abolition of a single center of authority certainly seemed appropriate for an era that many called "the Information Age" and others called the postindustrial society°. The industrial phase of economic development had been characterized by an emphasis on production. But in the postindustrial phase, the *making* of things becomes less important than the *marketing* of them. A postindustrial society, in fact, is characterized less by *things* in general than by *images, ideas, and information.*

If the factory symbolized industrial society, then the epitome of the postindustrial era is the home computer, with its capacity to disperse information, market products, and endlessly duplicate yet constantly alter visual and verbal images. By the end of the 1990s, relatively inexpensively priced home computers gave their users access to libraries, art galleries, and retail outlets from across the world, and provided, for entrepreneurs, the opportunity to make (and lose) enormous fortunes by exploiting this new image-oriented means of marketing products and information—all without any central regulating authority. Governments scrambled desperately to impose control on the proliferating technologies of the postindustrial age, but in true postmodern fashion the centers of authority broke down. Existing laws that regulated pornography, for example, proved difficult to apply to the Internet, the vast global communications web.

Similarly, developments in medical technologies raised important questions about authority and ownership. In 1978, Louise Brown was born in Britain, the world's first "test-tube baby." Over the next twenty years, assisted fertility treatment resulted in the births of more than a million babies. As the technology grew more sophisticated, so too did the ethical and political questions. Societies strug-

CHRONOLOGY

Medical Challenges and Achievements

1977	First diagnosed case of AIDS
1978	First test-tube baby
1980	Worldwide eradication of smallpox
1982	First use of genetic engineering (insulin manufactured from bacteria)
1983	First artificially created chromosome
1984	HIV identified
1985	First use of laser surgery to clear blocked arteries
1997	Successful cloning of sheep
2001	Human genome decoded

gled to determine the legality of practices such as commercial surrogate motherhood, in which a woman rents her womb to a couple, and postmenopausal motherhood, in which a woman past childbearing age is implanted with a fertilized egg.

Genetic research provoked even more debate about which authorities or what principles should guide scientific research. In 1997, British scientists introduced the world to Dolly the sheep, the first mammal cloned from an adult. Many scientists declared that the cloning of human beings, long part of science fiction and horror stories, was inevitable, even if declared immoral by religious leaders and illegal by political authorities. The announcement in February 2001 that the human genome had been decoded—that scientists had mapped the sequencing of the human genome, or set of instructions in every cell in the human body—immediately raised such questions as, Who owns this information? Who has the authority to decide how it is to be used?

Postmodern Patterns in Religious Life

Postmodern patterns—the fragmentation of cultures, the collapse of centers of authority, the supremacy of image—also characterized Western religious faith and practice after the 1970s. Christianity no longer served as a common cultural bond. In a time of increasing immigration and cultural diversity, Islam was the fastest-growing religious community in western Europe. In Britain, Muslims outnumbered Methodists by two to one. By the end of the twentieth century, established Protestant churches in western Europe faced a serious crisis, with regular churchgoers now a small minority of the population—less than 5 percent in most countries. The decline of the mainline churches in the United States was also dramatic, although a greater percentage of Americans—25 to 30 percent—attended church regularly. Religious faith became a private matter, the mark of subcultures (often defined by an "Us versus Them" mentality), rather than a bond tying together individuals and groups into a cohesive national culture.

At the same time, however, the long-reigning Pope John Paul II (r. 1978–2005) experienced unprecedented popularity. The most well-traveled and populist-oriented of twentieth-century popes, John Paul II became a media star, met with the same sort of cheering crowds and tee-shirt vendors that accompanied famous rock bands. Much of his popularity rested on his intimate connection with Poland's Solidarity, and therefore with an image of liberation. Born Karol Wojtyla, John Paul was the first non-Italian pope since 1523 and the first-ever Polish pope. Twelve million people—one-third of the Polish population—greeted him in Warsaw in 1979 when he made the first visit by any pope to a communist country. Many Solidarity members testified to the importance of this visit in empowering them to challenge the political order fourteen months later. But the pope's support for Solidarity did not mean he supported other forms of rebellion against authority. Opposing the promise of continuing change inherent in Vatican II (see Chapter 27), John Paul II adopted a thoroughly authoritarian approach to church government and took an uncompromising stand against birth control, married clergy, and the ordination of women. Confronted with the postmodernist message that authority had fragmented and that no universal truth existed, many Christians found the pope's uncompromising stand a source of great comfort.

Yet the papacy of John Paul II confirmed as well as contradicted postmodernist ideas; much of the pope's popularity was based on image rather than authority. Despite censoring liberal Catholic theologians, the pope was unable to bring into line an increasingly rebellious flock throughout Europe and the United States. In the United States, millions turned out to cheer the pope waving from an open car (the "popemobile"), yet the percentage of American Catholics using birth control—in direct violation of papal teachings—mirrored that of the population at large. By the 1980s, Catholic Italy boasted the second-lowest birth rate in the world (after China), with the one-child family becoming the norm. It was hard to avoid the conclusion that in much of Western Roman Catholicism, as in much of postmodern society, image ruled while authority dissipated.

The Global Challenge

At the same time that postmodern artists and theorists were questioning the validity of Western cultural forms, economic and environmental developments called into doubt other key assumptions of Western societies. Both the globalization of market capitalism and a worldwide environmental crisis crashed down national borders, limited the

scope of action open to individual governments, and raised significant questions about the ecological sustainability of Western habits of consumption.

The Global Economy

In the 1990s, a number of technological and economic developments helped make national borders even more permeable and accelerated the globalization of economic production. Personal computers, fax machines, and wireless telephones all ensured that "the office" could be anywhere. Fiber-optic cables that transmitted signals 4,000 times faster than their copper predecessors made instant communication across national boundaries a reality.

Technological innovations demanded organizational change. In the postindustrial economy, firms had to be more flexible, able to respond immediately to rapidly changing markets and technologies. They did not want too much capital investment in one way of doing things, in one kind of machinery, in one labor force, in one stock of supplies. Rather than economies of scale, they looked for other economies, such as subcontracting, outsourcing, and downsizing. The worker became more vulnerable. Concepts such as "a job for life" or "loyalty to the firm" had little relevance as companies merged and fragmented, shedding large number of workers in the endless pursuit of efficiency and the competitive edge. In this global economy, multinational corporations, with quick access to cheap Third World labor and raw materials, possessed significant economic power. In 2000, corporations such as ExxonMobil and DaimlerChrysler had annual revenues that exceeded the GDP of Norway or Singapore.

Increasingly, however, it was the far more nebulous "markets" that dictated the course of economic and political affairs across the world. In the 1990s, the volatility that had characterized the global economy since the collapse of the Bretton Woods Agreement in 1973 (see Chapter 27) became even more intense as currency speculators moved their money in and out of currency markets with astonishing rapidity, and with often devastating consequences for the countries involved. In 1997, for example, Thailand was forced to devalue its currency, and the economic catastrophe of collapsing currencies and stock markets quickly spread to Indonesia, Malaysia, the Philippines, and South Korea. By 1998, the Japanese economy had slid into serious recession.

As the Asian economic crisis of the later 1990s revealed, "the markets," rather than elected leaders, played an increasingly important role in determining a country's path. So, too, did the dictates of the World Bank and the IMF, the institutions that directed the flow of aid and loans throughout much of the world. The IMF, for example, insisted that governments receiving loans follow the orthodoxy of "austerity"—cutting government spending on social and welfare programs and restricting the flow of money supply to reduce inflation. Thus economists in offices far away, not

DOCUMENT

The West and the Rest

In 1998, economic historian David Landes published The Wealth and Poverty of Nations: Why Some Are So Rich and Some So Poor. *Landes, a professor at Harvard University, had been writing on the history of industrial and technological change since the 1950s. Now he turned his attention to the present and endeavored to answer one of the most pressing problems of the contemporary era. His introduction laid out the key issues.*

The old division of the world into two power blocs, East and West, has subsided. Now the big challenge and threat is the gap in wealth and health that separates the rich and poor. These are often styled North and South, because the division is geographic; but a more accurate signifier would be the West and the Rest, because the division is also historic. Here is the greatest single problem and danger facing the world of the Third Millennium. The only other worry that comes close is environmental deterioration, and the two are intimately connected, indeed are one. They are one because wealth entails not only consumption but also waste, not only production but also destruction. It is this waste and destruction, which has increased enormously with output and income, that threatens the space we live and move in.

How big is the gap between rich and poor and what is happening to it? Very roughly and briefly: the difference in income per head between the richest industrial nation, say Switzerland, and the poorest nonindustrial country, Mozambique, is about 400 to 1. Two hundred and fifty years ago, this gap between richest and poorest was perhaps 5 to 1, and the difference between Europe and, say, East or South Asia (China or India) was around 1.5 or 2 to 1.

. . . Our task (the rich countries), in our own interest as well as theirs, is to help the poor become healthier and wealthier. If we do not, they will seek to take what they cannot make; and if they cannot earn by exporting commodities, they will export people. In short, wealth is an irresistible magnet; and poverty is a potentially raging contaminant: it cannot be segregated, and our peace and prosperity depend in the long run on the well-being of others.

. . . the best way to understand a problem is to ask: How and why did we get where we are? How did the rich countries get so rich? Why are the poor countries so poor? Why did Europe ("the West") take the lead in changing the world?

A historical approach does not ensure an answer. Others have thought about these matters and come up with diverse explanations. Most of these fall into two schools. Some see Western wealth and dominion as the triumph of good over bad. The Europeans, they say, were smarter, better organized, harder working; the others were ignorant, arrogant, lazy, backward, superstitious. Others invert the categories. The Europeans, they say, were aggressive, ruthless, greedy, unscrupulous, hypocritical; their victims were happy, innocent, weak—waiting victims and hence thoroughly victimized. . . . both of these manichean visions have elements of truth, as well as of ideological fantasy. Things are always more complicated than we would have them.

Source: From *The Wealth and Poverty of Nations: Why Some Are So Rich and Some So Poor* by David S. Landes. Copyright © 1998 by David S. Landes. Used by permission of W. W. Norton & Company, Inc.

elected leaders, called the shots. Moreover, both the World Bank and the IMF embodied the characteristic Western confidence of the postwar era. Local traditions and leaders were ignored, replaced instead by outside economists and agronomists who believed that an infusion of Western economic and technological expertise would set the rest of the world on the path to economic growth.

By the 1990s, the widening gap between "North" and "South," the rich and poor nations of the world, called into question these easy assumptions. Meetings of the World Bank, the IMF, and the "G8" (Japan, the United States, Britain, Canada, France, Germany, Italy, and Russia) were disrupted by "antiglobalization" campaigners who highlighted the social costs of global capitalism, particularly the devastation wrought by what was called the "debt crisis." More than fifty of the world's poorest countries (thirty-six in Africa) were paying off their debts to Western banks and governments by withdrawing money from sanitation, health, and education programs. Relief organizations estimated that as many as seven million children died each year during the 1990s because of the debt crisis.

The Environmental Crisis

The urgency of the environmental crisis also revealed the limitations of Western expertise. By 1985, 257 multilateral treaties mandated some form of environmental protection—restrictions on trade in endangered species, wetlands preservation, forest conservation, regulation of industrial emissions. Almost half of these had been signed since 1970. Yet the degradation of the planet proceeded apace. At the end of the millennium, half of the world's rivers were polluted or running dry, and the number of people displaced by water crises stood at 25 million (versus 21 million war-related refugees). In the 1980s, almost half of the world's tropical forests were cleared, posing a serious threat to the planet's biodiversity.

The destruction of the rain forests contributed to what is perhaps the largest threat facing not only Western but global civilization at the beginning of the third millennium—global warming. Global warming is linked to industrial development. The burning of fossil fuels such as oil and coal (which releases carbon dioxide into the atmosphere) and deforestation (which reduces the "natural sinks" that absorb the gas) together produce the "greenhouse effect"—the trapping of solar radiation in the Earth's atmosphere, with rising temperatures as a result. Faced with predictions of widespread climate change (and resulting economic devastation on a colossal scale), representatives from 160 countries met in Kyoto in 1997 and agreed to cut "greenhouse gas emissions" by 10 percent. In 2001, however, U.S. president George W. Bush rejected the Kyoto Agreements. Without the cooperation of the world's largest producer of greenhouse gases, the Kyoto Agreements' impact would be minimal.

Europeans, both political leaders and ordinary citizens, reacted with fury to the American withdrawal from the Kyoto Agreements. They condemned the unilateral American action as that of a superpower out of control, no longer constrained by the Cold War to march in step with its allies. This perception of the United States as a bullying "hyperpower" was strengthened in 2003 by the Anglo-American invasion of Iraq. Across Europe, anti-war rallies drew huge crowds as Europeans protested against what they perceived to be an unwarranted use of American military force. As new divisions and alliances emerged both within and outside Europe, the meaning of "the West" remained a subject of intense debate.

North versus South
An Ethiopian farmer wages a losing war against drought and famine.

would Melbourne—or Budapest or Warsaw. Nevertheless, the economic and social trauma that afflicted Russia and the poorer nations of the former Soviet bloc such as Romania and Bulgaria in the 1990s and after demonstrates that the "West" retains its distinct identity, for clearly the gap between it and the "East" remains wide. The admittedly hesitant, still incomplete spread of the Western ideal of democracy has thrown a fragile bridge across that gap. But perhaps the real divide for the twenty-first century stretches between "North" and "South"—the huge and growing difference between the global Haves and the Have-Nots. Whether any bridge can stretch across that span remains to be seen.

Conclusion

Where Is the West Now?

In England, the most popular fast food is not fish and chips, long the quintessential English national supper, nor is it the Big Mac, as opponents of economic globalization might predict. Instead it is curry, the gift of the minority South Asian immigrant community. In the new millennium, "the West" may no longer serve as an important conceptual border marker. By many of the criteria explored in this textbook—economic, technological, political, and cultural—Tokyo would be defined as a Western city. So, too,

Suggestions for Further Reading

For a comprehensive listing of suggested readings, please go to
www.ablongman.com/levack2e/chapter28

Ardagh, John. *Germany and the Germans: The United Germany in the Mid-1990s.* 1996. A snapshot of a society in the midst of social and economic change.

Hughes, H. Stuart. *Sophisticated Rebels: The Political Culture of European Dissent, 1968–1987.* 1988. A perceptive and imaginative exploration of "dissenters," ranging from Solidarity and Soviet dissidents to German Greens, Welsh nationalists, and an assortment of novelists and philosophers.

Kavanagh, Dennis. *Thatcherism and British Politics: The End of Consensus?* 1987. Kavanagh answers the question posed in his title with a convincing "yes."

Lewis, Jane, ed. *Women and Social Policies in Europe: Work, Family and the State.* 1993. A series of essays exploring the position of women in western Europe. Packed with statistics and useful tables.

McNeill, John. *Something New Under the Sun: An Environmental History of the Twentieth Century.* 2000. Argues that twentieth-century human economic activity has transformed the ecology of the globe—an ongoing experiment with a potentially devastating outcome.

Ost, David. *Solidarity and the Politics of Anti-Politics: Opposition and Reform in Poland Since 1968.* 1990. Although the bulk of this account was written before the Revolution of 1989, it provides a compelling study of Solidarity's emergence, impact, and ideology.

Rogel, Carole. *The Breakup of Yugoslavia and the War in Bosnia.* 1998. Designed for undergraduates, this work includes a short but detailed historical narrative, biographies of the main personalities, and a set of primary documents.

Rosenberg, Tina. *The Haunted Land: Facing Europe's Ghosts After Communism.* 1995. Winner of the Pulitzer Prize, this disturbing account focuses on the fundamental moral issues facing postcommunist political cultures.

Sandler, Irving. *Art of the Postmodern Era: From the Late 1960s to the Early 1980s.* 1996. Much more broad-ranging than the title suggests, this well-written, blessedly jargon-free work sets both contemporary art and the theories of the postmodern within the wider historical context.

Stokes, Gale. *The Walls Came Tumbling Down: The Collapse of Communism in Eastern Europe.* 1993. A superb account, firmly embedded in history.

Young, John W. *Cold War Europe, 1945–1991: A Political History.* 1996. A solid survey.

See also the works by Crampton, Cronin, Gaddis, Isaacs and Downing, Judge and Langdon, Keep, and Urwin listed at the end of Chapter 27.

Notes

1. Quoted in Robert Paxton, *Europe in the Twentieth Century* (1997), 613.

2. Kenneth Boulding, "The Economics of the Coming Spaceship Earth," first published in 1966, reprinted in *Toward a Steady-State Economy,* ed. Herman Daly (1973).

3. Quotations from Timothy W. Ryback, *Rock Around the Bloc: A History of Rock Music in Eastern Europe and the Soviet Union* (1990), 184–185, 176.

4. Quoted in D. J. Peterson, *Troubled Lands: The Legacy of Soviet Environmental Destruction* (1993), 12.

5. Quoted in Archie Brown, *The Gorbachev Factor* (1996), 125.

6. Quoted in R. J. Crampton, *Eastern Europe in the Twentieth Century—And After* (1997), 408.

7. Francis Fukuyama, *The End of History and the Last Man* (1992).

8. Quoted in *The Observer* (London), (April 8, 2001), 20.

9. Salman Rushdie, "Please, Read *Satanic Verses* Before Condemning It," *Illustrated Weekly of India* (October 1988). Reprinted in M. M. Ahsan and A. R. Kidwai, *Sacrilege Versus Civility: Muslim Perspectives on The Satanic Verses Affair* (1991), 63.

10. Quoted in Malise Ruthven, *A Satanic Affair: Salman Rushdie and the Wrath of Islam* (1991). 562.

11. Quoted in Ruthven, *A Satanic Affair,* 100.

12. *Bookseller,* London (February 24, 1989). Quoted in Lisa Appignanesi and Sara Maitland, *The Rushdie File* (1990), 103–104.

13. *The Sunday Telegraph* (June 24, 1990). Quoted in Ahsan and Kidwai, *Sacrilege Versus Civility,* 80.

14. Quoted in Irving Sandler, *Art of the Postmodern Era* (1996), 4.

Glossary

absolutism (p. 478) A form of government in the seventeenth and eighteenth centuries in which the ruler possessed complete and unrivalled power.

acropolis (p. 70) The defensible hilltop around which a polis grew. In classical Athens, the Acropolis was the site of the Parthenon (Temple of Athena).

Aeneid (p. 157) Written by Virgil (70–19 B.C.E.), this magnificent epic poem celebrates the emperor Augustus by linking him to his mythical ancestor, Aeneas, the Trojan refugee who founded the Roman people. Considered by many to be the greatest work of Latin literature, the poem has had enormous influence in the West.

agrarian capitalism (p. 404) A form of economic organization characteristic of European colonialism in which Europeans organized the production of certain kinds of commercial crops (such as sugar, tobacco, and indigo) on land expropriated from native peoples and with slave labor.

agricultural revolution (p. 273) Refers to technological innovations that began to appear during the eleventh century, making possible a dramatic growth in population. The agricultural revolution came about through harnessing new sources of power with water and wind mills, improving the pulling power of animals with better collars, using heavy plows to better exploit the soils of northern Europe, and employing a three-field crop rotation system that increased the amount and quality of food available.

agricultural societies (p. 14) Settled communities in which people depend on farming and raising livestock as their sources of food.

alchemy (p. 518) A form of learned magic that was intended to turn base metals into precious ones.

aldeias (p. 396) Settlements for natives who had converted to Christianity in Brazil. In these settlements the Jesuit fathers protected the natives from enslavement.

Allies (p. 778) During World War I, the states allied against the Central Powers of Germany and Austria-Hungary. During World War II, the states allied against the regimes of Nazi Germany, fascist Italy and imperial Japan.

Anabaptism (p. 425) Meaning "to rebaptize"; refers to those Protestant radicals of the sixteenth century who rejected infant baptism and adopted adult baptism. Anabaptists treated the Bible as a blueprint for reforming not just the church but all of society, a tendency that led them to reject the authority of the state, to live in self-governing "holy communities," and in some cases to practice a primitive form of communism.

anarchism (p. 728) Ideology that views the state as unnecessary and repressive, and rejects participation in parliamentary politics in favor of direct, usually violent, action.

anticlericalism (p. 758) Opposition to the political influence of the Roman Catholic Church.

Antonine Decree (p. 149) In 212 C.E. the emperor Aurelius Antoninus, called Caracalla, issued a decree that granted citizenship to all the free inhabitants of the Roman Empire. The decree enabled Roman law to embrace the entire population of the empire.

apartheid (p. 895) System of racial segregation and discrimination put into place in South Africa in 1948.

Apologists (p. 164) Christian writers in the second and third centuries C.E. who explained their religion to learned non-Christians. In the process they helped Christianity absorb much of Hellenistic culture.

appeasement (p. 853) British diplomatic and financial efforts to stabilize Germany in the 1920s and 1930s and so avoid a second world war.

Arians (p. 183) Christians who believe that God the Father is superior to Jesus Christ his Son. Most of the Germanic settlers in western Europe in the fifth century were Arians.

aristocracy (p. 576) A term that originally applied to those who were considered the most fit to rule and later identified the wealthiest members of society, especially those who owned land.

Asceticism (p. 183) The Christian practice of severely suppressing physical needs and daily desires in an effort to achieve a spiritual union with God. Asceticism is the practice that underlies the monastic movement.

Auschwitz (p. 869) Technically Auschwitz-Birkenau; death camp in Poland that has become the symbol of the Holocaust.

auto-da-fé (p. 451) Meaning literally a "theater of faith," an *auto* was practiced by the Catholic Church in early modern Spain and Portugal as an extended public ritual of penance designed to cause physical pain among the sinful and promote fear of God's judgment among those who witnessed it.

Babylonian Captivity of the Church (p. 329) Between 1305 and 1378 seven consecutive popes voluntarily chose to reside in Avignon, France, in order to escape anarchy in the streets of Rome. During this period the popes became subservient to the kings of France.

Babylonian Exile (p. 64) The period of Jewish history between the destruction of Solomon's temple in Jerusalem by Babylonian armies in 587 B.C.E., and 538 B.C.E., when Cyrus of Persia permitted Jews to return to Palestine and rebuild the temple.

balance of power (p. 487) An arrangement in which various countries form alliances to prevent any one state from dominating the others.

Balfour Declaration (p. 809) Declaration of 1917 that affirmed British support of a Jewish state in Palestine.

baroque (p. 483) A dynamic style in art, architecture, and music intended to elicit an emotional response. It was closely associated with royal absolutism in the seventeenth century.

Battle of Kadesh (p. 42) The battle between Egyptian and Hittite armies in Syria in 1274 B.C.E. that set the territorial limits of both empires in Canaan and the Middle East for a century during the International Bronze Age.

Beer Hall Putsch (p. 821) Failed Nazi effort to overthrow the German government by force in 1923.

Berlin Wall (p. 899) Constructed by the East German government, the wall physically cut the city of Berlin in two and prevented East German citizens from access to West Germany; stood from 1961 to 1989.

Big Three (p. 888) Term applied to the British, Soviet, and U.S. leaders during World War II: until 1945, Churchill, Stalin, and Roosevelt; by the summer of 1945, Attlee, Stalin, and Truman.

blitzkrieg (p. 855) "Lightning war;" offensive military tactic making use of airplanes, tanks, and motorized infantry to punch through enemy defenses and secure key territory. First demonstrated by the German army in World War II.

boers (p. 548) Dutch farmers in the colony established by the Dutch Republic in South Africa.

Bolsheviks (p. 801) Minority group of Russian socialists, headed by Lenin, who espoused an immediate transition to a socialist state. It became the Communist Party in the Soviet Union.

bourgeoisie (p. 583) A social group, technically consisting of those who were burghers in the towns, that included prosperous merchants and financiers, members of the professions, and some skilled craftsmen known as "petty bourgeoisie."

Bretton Woods Agreement (p. 889) Agreement signed in 1944 that established the post–World War II economic framework in which the U.S. dollar served as the world's reserve currency.

brinkmanship (p. 899) Style of Cold War confrontation in which each superpower endeavored to convince the other that it was willing to wage nuclear war.

bronze (p. 33) An alloy of tin and copper that produces a hard metal suitable for weapons, tools, ornaments, and household objects. Bronze production began about 3200 B.C.E.

bubonic plague (p. 310) An epidemic disease spread from rats to humans via flea bites. The infection enters the bloodstream, causing inflamed swellings called buboes (hence, "bubonic" plague) in the glands of the groin or armpit, internal bleeding, and discoloration. Although disputed by some, most experts consider bubonic plague the cause of the Black Death, which killed at least one-third of the population of Europe between 1348 and the early 1350s. Bubonic plague reappeared recurrently in the West between 1348 and 1721.

caliph (p. 226) After Muhammad's death in 632, the ruler of the Islamic state was called the caliph. The sectarian division within Islam between the Shi'ites and Sunni derived from a disagreement over how to determine the hereditary succession from Muhammad to the caliphate, which combined governmental and some religious responsibilities.

caliphate (p. 223) The Islamic imperial government that evolved under the leadership of Abu Bakr (r. 632–634), the successor of the prophet Muhammad.

calling (p. 423) The Calvinist doctrine that God calls the Elect to perform his will on earth. God's calling gave Calvinists a powerful sense of personal direction.

canon law (p. 282) The collected laws of the Roman Catholic Church. Canon law applied to cases involving the clergy, disputes about church property, and donations to the Church. It also applied to the laity for annulling marriages, legitimating bastards, prosecuting bigamy, protecting widows and orphans, and resolving inheritance disputes.

capital (p. 652) All the physical assets used in production, including fixed capital, such as machinery, and circulating capital, such as raw materials; more generally the cost of these physical assets.

caravels (p. 381) Hybrid three-masted ships developed about 1450 in the Iberian peninsula by combining the rigging of square with triangular lateen sails. These ships could be sailed in a variety of winds, carry large cargoes, be managed by a small crew, and be defended by guns mounted in the castle superstructure.

Carnival (p. 455) The most popular annual festival in much of Europe before modern times. Also known as Mardi Gras, the festival took place for several days or even weeks before the beginning of Lent and included all kinds of fun and games.

Carolingian Renaissance (p. 250) The "rebirth" of interest in ancient Greek and Latin literature and language during the reign of the Frankish emperor Charlemagne (r. 768–814). Charlemagne promoted the intensive study of Latin to promote governmental efficiency and to propagate the Christian faith.

Catholic Reformation (p. 430) A series of efforts during the sixteenth century to purify the Church that evolved out of late medieval spirituality and that included the creation of new religious orders, especially the Society of Jesus.

Central Powers (p. 778) Germany and Austria-Hungary in World War I.

Chalcedonians (p. 181) Christians who follow the doctrinal decisions and definitions of the Council of Chalcedon in 451 C.E. stating that Christ's human and divine natures were equal, but entirely distinct and united in one person "without confusion, division, separation, or change." Chalcedonian Christianity came to be associated with the Byzantine Empire and is called Greek Orthodoxy. In western Europe it is known as Roman Catholicism.

chinoiserie (p. 564) A French word for an eighteenth-century decorative art that combined Chinese and European motifs.

Christian Democracy, Christian Democratic parties (p. 907) Conservative and confessionally based (Roman Catholic) political parties that dominated much of western European politics after World War II.

Christian humanists (p. 413) During the fifteenth and sixteenth centuries these experts in Greek, Latin, and Hebrew subjected the Bible to philological study in an attempt to understand the precise meaning of the founding text of Christianity.

circuit court (p. 296) Established by King Henry II (r. 1154–1189) to make royal justice available to virtually anyone in England. Circuit court judges visited every shire in England four times a year.

civic humanism (p. 356) A branch of humanism introduced by the Florentine chancellor Leonardo Bruni who defended the republican institutions and values of the city. Civic humanism promoted the ethic of responsible citizenship.

civilization (p. 12) The term used by archaeologists to describe a society differentiated by levels of wealth and power, and in which religious, economic, and political control are based in cities.

civitas (p. 143) The Roman term for a city. A city included the town itself, all the surrounding territory that it controlled, and all the people who lived in the town and the countryside.

clans or kin groups (p. 243) The basic social and political unit of Germanic society consisting of blood relatives obliged to defend one another and take vengeance for crimes against the group and its members.

class (p. 578) A large and often cohesive social group that was conscious of its shared economic and political interests.

classicism (p. 580) A style in art, architecture, music, and literature that emphasizes proportion, adherence to traditional forms, and a rejection of emotion and enthusiasm.

Cluny (p. 280) A monastery founded in Burgundy in 910 that became the center of a far-reaching movement to reform the Church that was sustained in more than 1,500 Cluniac monasteries, modeled after the original in Cluny.

Cold War (p. 888) Struggle for global supremacy between the United States and the Soviet Union, waged from the end of World War II until 1990.

collectivization (p. 834) The replacement of private and village farms with large cooperative agricultural enterprises run by state-employed managers. Collectivization was a key part of Joseph Stalin's plans for modernizing the Soviet economy and destroying peasant opposition to communist rule.

colons (p. 568) White planters in the French Caribbean colony of Saint Domingue (Haiti).

Columbian exchange (p. 400) The trade of peoples, plants, animals, microbes, and ideas between the Old and New Worlds that began with Columbus.

Columbian question (p. 402) The debate among historians and epidemiologists about whether syphilis or its ancestor disease originated in the Americas and was brought to the Old World after Columbus's voyages.

Common Market (p. 908) Originally comprising West Germany, France, Italy, Belgium, Luxembourg, and the Netherlands, the Common Market was formed in 1957 to integrate its members' economic structures and so foster both economic prosperity and international peace. Also called the European Economic Community (EEC). Evolved into the European Union (EU).

communes (p. 277) Sworn defensive associations of merchants and workers that appeared in north-central Italy after 1070 and that became the effective government of more than a hundred cities. The communes evolved into city-states by seizing control of the surrounding countryside.

communism (p. 680) The revolutionary form of socialism developed by Karl Marx and Friedrich Engels that promoted the overthrow of bourgeois or capitalist institutions and the establishment of a dictatorship of the proletariat.

Concert of Europe (p. 678) The joint efforts made by Austria, Prussia, Russia, Britain, and France during the years following the Congress of Vienna to suppress liberal and nationalist movements throughout Europe.

Conciliar Movement (p. 330) A fifteenth-century movement that advocated ending the Great Schism and reforming church government by calling a general meeting or council of the bishops, who would exercise authority over the rival popes.

Confessions (p. 450) The formal sixteenth-century statements of religious doctrine: the Confession of Augsburg for Lutherans, the Helvetic Confessions for Calvinists, the Thirty-Nine Articles for Anglicans, and the decrees of the Council of Trent for Catholics.

Congress of Vienna (p. 638) A conference of the major powers of Europe in 1814–1815 to establish a new balance of power at the end of the Napoleonic Wars.

conquistadores (p. 388) Spanish adventurers in the Americas who explored and conquered the lands of indigenous peoples, sometimes without legal authority but usually with a legal privilege granted by the king of Spain who required that one-fifth of all things of value be turned over to the crown. The conquistadores extended Spanish sovereignty over new lands.

conservatism (p. 678) A nineteenth-century ideology intended to prevent a recurrence of the revolutionary changes of the 1790s and the implementation of liberal policies.

containment (p. 890) Cold War policy of blocking communist expansion; inaugurated by the Truman Doctrine in 1947.

Corpus of Civil Law (p. 197) The body of Roman law compiled by the emperor Justinian in Constantinople in 534. The Corpus became a pillar of Latin-speaking European civilization.

cosmology (p. 514) A theory concerning the structure and nature of the universe such as those proposed by Aristotle in the fourth century B.C.E. and Copernicus in the sixteenth century.

counties (p. 250) Territorial units devised by the Carolingian dynasty during the eighth and ninth centuries for the administration of the empire. Each county was administered by a count who was rewarded with lands and sent to areas where he had no family ties to serve as a combined provincial governor, judge, military commander, and representative of the king.

courtly love (p. 302) An ethic first found in the poems of the late twelfth- and thirteenth-century troubadours that portrayed the ennobling possibilities of the love between a man and a woman. Courtly love formed the basis for the modern idea of romantic love.

creoles (p. 548) People of Spanish descent who had been born in Spanish America.

Crusades (p. 263) Between 1095 and 1291, Latin Christians heeding the call of the pope launched eight major expeditions and many smaller ones against Muslim armies in an attempt to gain control of and hold Jerusalem.

Cubism (p. 755) Modernist artistic movement of the early twentieth century that emphasized the fragmentation of human perception through visual experiments with geometric forms.

cultural relativism (p. 404) A mode of thought first explored during the sixteenth century to explain why the peoples of the New World did not appear in the Bible. Cultural relativism recognized that many (but not necessarily all) standards of judgment are specific to particular cultures rather than the fixed truths established by natural or divine law.

culture (p. 12) The knowledge and adaptive behavior created by communities that helps them to mediate between themselves and the natural world through time.

cuneiform (p. 17) A kind of writing in which wedge-shaped symbols are pressed into clay tablets to indicate words and ideas. Cuneiform writing originated in ancient Sumer.

Curia (p. 283) The administrative bureaucracy of the Roman Catholic Church.

Cynics (p. 105) Cynics followed the teachings of Antisthenes (ca. 445–360 B.C.E.) by rejecting pleasures, possessions, and social conventions in order to find peace of mind.

Darwinian theory of evolution (p. 746) Scientific theory associated with nineteenth-century scientist Charles Darwin that highlights the role of variation and natural selection in the evolution of species.

Decembrists (p. 687) Russian liberals who staged a revolt against Tsar Nicholas I on the first day of his reign in December 1825.

de-Christianization (p. 625) A program inaugurated in France in 1793 by the radical Jacobin and former priest Joseph Fouché that closed churches, eliminated religious symbols, and attempted to establish a purely civic religion.

deduction (p. 521) The logical process by which ideas and laws are derived from basic truths or principles.

deists (p. 529) Seventeenth- and eighteenth-century thinkers who believed that God created the universe and established immutable laws of nature but did not subsequently intervene in the operation of nature or in human affairs.

Delian League (p. 76) The alliance among many Greek cities organized by Athens in 478 B.C.E. in order to fight Persian forces in the eastern Aegean Sea. The Athenians gradually turned the Delian League into the Athenian Empire.

demand (p. 653) The desire of consumers to acquire goods and the need of producers to acquire raw materials and machinery.

democracy (p. 58) A form of government in which citizens devise their own governing institutions and choose their leaders; began in Athens, Greece, in the fifth century B.C.E.

demonic magic (p. 531) The invocation of evil spirits with the goal of utilizing their supernatural powers to change the course of nature or to alter human behavior.

de-Stalinization (p. 904) Khrushchev's effort to decentralize political and economic control in the Soviet Union after 1956.

detente (p. 924) During the 1970s, a period of lessened Cold War hostilities and greater reliance on negotiation and compromise.

dialectic (p. 680) The theory that history advanced in stages as the result of the conflict between different ideas or social groups.

dialectical materialism (p. 680) The socialist philosophy of Karl Marx according to which history advanced as the result of material or economic forces and would lead to the creation of a classless society.

Diaspora (p. 160) Literally "dispersion of population;" usually used to refer to the dispersion of the Jewish population after the Roman destruction of the Temple in Jerusalem in 70 C.E.

division of labor (p. 649) The assignment of one stage of production to a single worker or group of workers to increase efficiency and productive output.

domestication (p. 13) Manipulating the breeding of animals over many generations in order to make them more useful to humans as sources of food, wool, and other byproducts. Domestication of animals began about 10,000 years ago.

Dreyfus Affair (p. 721) The trials of Captain Alfred Dreyfus on treason charges dominated French political life in the decade after 1894 and revealed fundamental divisions in French society.

dualistic (p. 522) A term used to describe a philosophy, such as that of René Descartes, in which a rigid distinction is made between body and mind or between the material and the immaterial world.

Dutch Revolt (p. 466) The rebellion against Spanish rule of the seven northern provinces of the Netherlands between 1579 and 1648, which resulted in the independence of the Republic of the United Provinces.

Edict of Nantes (p. 463) Promulgated by King Henry IV in 1598, the edict allowed the Huguenots to build a quasi-independent state within the kingdom of France, giving them the right to have their own troops, church organization, and political autonomy within their walled towns, but banning them from the royal court and the city of Paris. King Louis XIV revoked the edict in 1685.

Einsatzgruppen (p. 869) Loosely translated as strike force or task force; SS units given the task of murdering Jews and Communist Party members in the areas of the Soviet Union occupied by Germany during World War II.

empires (p. 542) Large political formations consisting of different kingdoms or territories outside the boundaries of the states that control them.

enclosure (p. 652) The consolidation of scattered agricultural holdings into large, compact fields which were then closed off by hedges, bushes, or walls, giving farmers complete control over the uses of their land.

encomienda (p. 391) The basic form of economic and social organization in early Spanish America, based on a royal grant awarded to a Spaniard for military or other services that gave the grantee and his successors the right to gather tribute from the Indians in a defined area.

enlightened despots (p. 600) The term assigned to absolute monarchs who initiated a series of legal and political reforms in an effort to realize the goals of the Enlightenment.

Enlightenment (p. 585) An international intellectual movement of the eighteenth century that emphasized the use of reason and the application of the laws of nature to human society.

Epicureans (p. 104) Followers of the teachings of the philosopher Epicurus (341–271 B.C.E.). Epicureans tried to gain peace of mind by choosing pleasures rationally.

ethnic cleansing (p. 943) A term introduced during the wars in Yugoslavia in the 1990s; the systematic use of murder, rape, and violence by one ethnic group against members of other ethnic groups in order to establish control over a territory.

Etruscans (p. 111) A people native to Italy, the Etruscans established a league of militaristic cities in central Italy that grew rich from war and trade. Etruscans had a great influence on the formation of the Roman state.

Eucharist (p. 289) Also known as Holy Communion or the Lord's Supper, the Eucharistic rite of the Mass celebrates Jesus' last meal with his apostles when the priest-celebrant consecrates wafers of bread and a chalice of wine as the body and blood of Christ. In the Middle Ages the wafers of bread were distributed for the congregation to eat, but drinking from the chalice was a special privilege of the priesthood. Protestants in the sixteenth century and Catholics in the late twentieth century began to allow the laity to drink from the chalice.

Euro-Islam (p. 950) The identity and belief system being forged by European Muslims who argue that Islam does not contradict or reject European values.

European Economic Community (EEC) (p. 908) Originally comprising West Germany, France, Italy, Belgium, Luxembourg, and the Netherlands, the EEC was formed in 1957 to integrate its members' economic structures and so foster both economic prosperity and international peace. Also called the Common Market.

European Union (EU) (p. 943) A successor organization to the EEC; the effort to integrate European political, economic, cultural, and military structures and policies.

excommunication (p. 282) A decree by the pope or a bishop prohibiting a sinner from participating in the sacraments of the Church and forbidding any social contact whatsoever with the surrounding community.

existentialism (p. 815) Twentieth-century philosophy that emerged in the interwar era and influenced many thinkers and artists after World War II. Existentialism emphasizes individual freedom in a world devoid of meaning or coherence.

Expressionism (p. 755) Modernist artistic movement of the early twentieth century that used bold colors and experimental forms to express emotional realities.

factories (p. 544) Trading posts established by European powers in foreign lands.

fanatic (p. 460) Originally referring to someone possessed by a demon, a fanatic came during the sixteenth century to mean a person who expressed immoderate enthusiasm in religious matters or who pursued a supposedly divine mission, often to violent ends.

fascism (p. 826) Twentieth-century political ideology that rejected the existing alternatives of conservatism, communism, socialism, and liberalism. Fascists stressed the authoritarian power of the state, the efficacy of violent action, the need to build a national community, and the use of new technologies of influence and control.

federalists (p. 617) The name assigned by radical Jacobins to provincial rebels who opposed the centralization of the state during the French Revolution.

feminism, feminist movement (p. 733) International movement that emerged in the second half of the nineteenth century and demanded broader political, legal, and economic rights for women.

Fertile Crescent (p. 14) Also known as the Levantine Corridor, this twenty-five mile wide arc of land stretching from the Jordan River to the Euphrates River was the place where food production and settled communities first appeared in Southwest Asia (the Middle East).

feudalism (p. 255) A term historians use to describe a social system common during the Middle Ages in which lords granted fiefs (tracts of land or some other form of income) to dependents, known as vassals, who owed their lords personal services in exchange. Feudalism refers to a society governed through personal ties of dependency rather than public political institutions.

fief (p. 255) During the Middle Ages a fief was a grant of land or some other form of income that a lord gave to a vassal in exchange for loyalty and certain services (usually military assistance).

Final Solution (p. 869) Nazi term for the effort to murder every Jew in Europe during World War II.

fin-de-siecle (p. 750) French term for the "turn of the century"; used to refer to the cultural crisis of the late nineteenth century.

First Triumvirate (p. 125) The informal political alliance made by Julius Caesar, Pompey, and Crassus in 60 B.C.E. to share power in the Roman Republic. It led directly to the collapse of the Republic.

Forms (p. 85) In the philosophical teachings of Plato, these are eternal, unchanging absolutes such as Truth, Justice, and Beauty that represent true reality, as opposed to the approximations of reality that humans encounter in everyday life.

Forum (p. 111) The political and religious center of the city of Rome throughout antiquity. All cities in the empire had a forum in imitation of the capital city.

franchise (p. 602) The right to vote; also called suffrage.

freemasons (p. 598) Members of secret societies of men and women that flourished during the Enlightenment, dedicated to the creation of a society based on reason and virtue and committed to the principles of liberty and equality.

French Wars of Religion (p. 461) A series of political assassinations, massacres, and military engagements between French Catholics and Calvinists from 1560 to 1598.

Gaullism (p. 914) The political ideology associated with twentieth-century French political leader Charles DeGaulle. Gaullism combined the advocacy of a strong, centralized state with social conservatism.

German-Soviet Non-Aggression Pact (p. 853) Signed by Stalin and Hitler in 1939, the agreement publicly pledged Germany and the Soviet Union not to attack each other, and secretly divided up Poland and the Baltic states between the two powers.

Girondins (p. 616) The more conservative members of the Jacobin party who favored greater economic freedom and opposed further centralization of state power during the French Revolution.

glasnost (p. 943) Loosely translated as openness or honesty; Gorbachev's effort after 1985 to break with the secrecy that had characterized Soviet political life.

Gothic (p. 303) A style in architecture in western Europe from the late twelfth and thirteenth centuries, characterized by ribbed vaults and pointed arches, which drew the eyes of worshipers upward toward God. Flying buttresses, which redistributed the weight of the roof, made possible thin walls pierced by large expanses of stained glass.

grand jury (p. 296) In medieval England after the judicial reforms of King Henry II (r. 1154–1189), grand juries were called when the circuit court judge arrived in a shire. The sheriff assembled a group of men familiar with local affairs who constituted the grand jury and who reported to the judge the major crimes that had been committed since the judge's last visit.

Great Depression in Trade and Agriculture (p. 712) Downturn in prices and profits, particularly in the agricultural sector, in Europe from 1873 through the 1880s.

Great Depression (p. 828) Calamitous drop in prices, reduction in trade, and rise in unemployment that devastated the global economy in 1929.

Great Persecution (p. 174) An attack on Christians in the Roman empire begun by the emperor Galerius in 303 C.E. on the grounds that their worship was endangering the empire. Several thousand Christians were executed.

Great Purge (p. 835) Period of mass arrests and executions particularly aimed at Communist Party members. Lasting from 1934 to 1939, the Great Purge enabled Stalin to consolidate his one-man rule over the Soviet Union.

Great Schism (p. 329) The division of the Catholic Church (1378–1417) between rival Italian and French claimants to the papal throne.

Green movement, Green politics (p. 930) A new style of politics and set of political ideas resulting from the confluence of environmentalism, feminism, and anti-nuclear protests of the 1970s.

guilds (p. 319) Professional associations devoted to protecting the special interests of a particular trade or craft and to monopolizing production and trade in the goods the guild produced.

haciendas (p. 391) Large landed estates that began to be established in the seventeenth century replaced encomiendas throughout much of Spanish America.

Hallstatt (p. 109) The first Celtic civilization in central Europe is called Halstatt. From about 750 to about 450 B.C.E., Hallstatt Celts spread throughout Europe.

helots (p. 73) The brutally oppressed subject peoples of the Spartans. Tied to the land they farmed for Spartan masters, they were treated little better than beasts of burden.

heresies (p. 181) Forms of Christian belief that are not considered Orthodox.

hetairai (p. 80) Elite courtesans in ancient Greece who provided intellectual as well as sexual companionship.

Holocaust (p. 869) Adolf Hitler's effort to murder all the Jews in Europe during World War II.

Homo sapiens sapiens (p. 13) Scientific term meaning "most intelligent people" applied to physically and intellectually modern human beings that first appeared between 200,000 and 100,000 years ago in Africa.

hoplites (p. 72) Greek soldiers in the Archaic Age who could afford their own weapons. Hoplite tactics made soldiers fighting as a group dependent on one another. This contributed to the internal cohesion of the polis and eventually to the rise of democracy.

Huguenots (p. 461) The term for French Calvinists, who constituted some 10 percent of the population by 1560.

humanists (p. 365) During the Renaissance humanists were writers and orators who studied Latin and sometimes Greek texts on grammar, rhetoric, poetry, history, and ethics.

Hundred Years' War (p. 321) Refers to a series of engagements (1337–1453) between England and France over England's attempts to assert its claims to territories in France.

hyperinflation (p. 821) Catastrophic price increases and currency devaluation, such as that which occurred in Germany in 1923.

Iconoclasm (p. 216) The destruction of religious images in the Byzantine empire in the eighth century.

icons (p. 215) The Christian images of God and saints found in Byzantine art.

ideologies (p. 676) Theories of society and government that form the basis of political programs.

Ideologues (p. 631) A group of liberal writers and philosophers in France who objected to Napoleon's religious policy on the grounds that it would inaugurate a return of religious superstition.

induction (p. 521) The mental process by which theories are established only after the systematic accumulation of large amounts of data.

indulgences (p. 329) Certificates that allowed penitents to atone for their sins and reduce their time in purgatory. Usually these were issued for going on a pilgrimage or performing a pious act, but during the Babylonian Captivity of the Church (1305–1378) popes began to sell them, a practice Martin Luther protested in 1517 in an act that brought on the Protestant Reformation.

industrial capitalism (p. 662) A form of capitalism characterized by the ownership of factories by private individuals and the employment of wage labor.

intendants (p. 481) French royal officials who became the main agents of French provincial administration in the seventeenth century.

interdict (p. 283) A papal decree prohibiting the celebration of the sacraments in an entire city or kingdom.

Investiture Controversy (p. 282) A dispute that began in 1076 between the popes and the German emperors over the right to invest bishops with their offices. The most famous episode was the conflict between Pope Gregory VII and Emperor Henry IV. The controversy was resolved by the Concordat of Worms in 1122.

Islamism (p. 948) Islamic radicalism or *jihadism*. The ideology that insists that Islam demands a rejection of Western values and that violence in this struggle against the West is justified.

Jacobins (p. 614) A French political party supporting a democratic republic that found support in political clubs throughout the country and dominated the National Convention from 1792 until 1794.

Jim Crow (p. 768) Series of laws mandating racial segregation throughout the American South.

Junkers (p. 493) The traditional nobility of Prussia.

justification by faith alone (p. 415) Refers to Martin Luther's insight that humanity is incapable of performing enough religious good works to earn eternal salvation. Salvation is an unmerited gift from God called grace. Those who receive grace are called the Elect.

knight (p. 255) During the Middle Ages a knight was a soldier who fought on horseback. A knight was a vassal or dependent of a lord, who usually financed the knight's expenses of armor and weapons and of raising and feeding horses with a grant of land known as a fief.

Koine (p. 101) The standard version of the Greek language spoken throughout the Hellenistic world.

La Tène (p. 109) A phase of Celtic civilization that lasted from about 450 to 200 B.C.E. La Tène culture became strong especially in the regions of the Rhine and Danube Rivers.

laissez-faire (p. 676) The principle that governments should not regulate or otherwise intervene in the economy unless it is necessary to protect property rights and public order.

lapis lazuli (p. 45) A precious, deep-blue gemstone found in the Middle East that was traded widely for jewelry during the International Bronze Age.

latifundia (p. 155) These huge agricultural estates owned by wealthy Romans, including the emperor, often used large slave-gangs as labor.

Latin Christendom (pp. 181, 238) The parts of medieval Europe, including all of western Europe, united by Christianity and the use of Latin in worship and intellectual life. Latin served as an international language among the ruling elites in western Europe, even though they spoke different languages in their daily lives.

lay investiture (p. 281) The practice of nobles, kings, or emperors installing churchmen and giving them the symbols of office.

League of Nations (p. 803) Association of states set up after World War I to resolve international conflicts through open and peaceful negotiation.

Lend-Lease Act (p. 859) Passed in March 1941, the act gave Britain access to American industrial products during World War II, with payment postponed for the duration of the war.

Levantine Corridor (p. 14) Also known as the Fertile Crescent, this twenty-five mile wide arc of land stretching from the Jordan River to the Euphrates River was the place where food production and settled communities first appeared in Southwest Asia (the Middle East).

liberalism (p. 676) An ideology based on the conviction that individual freedom is of supreme importance and the main responsibility of government is to protect that freedom.

linear perspective (p. 361) In the arts the use of geometrical principles to depict a three-dimensional space on a flat, two-dimensional surface.

liturgy (p. 238) The forms of Christian worship, including the prayers, chants, and rituals to be said, sung, or performed throughout the year.

lord (p. 255) During the Middle Ages a lord was someone who offered protection to dependents, known as vassals, who took an oath of loyalty to him. Most lords demanded military services from their vassals and sometimes granted them tracts of land known as fiefs.

Macedonian Renaissance (p. 217) During the Macedonian dynasty's rule of Byzantium (867–1056), aristocratic families, the Church, and monasteries devoted their immense riches to embellishing Constantinople with new buildings, mosaics, and icons. The emperors sponsored historical, philosophical, and religious writing.

Mafia (p. 700) Organizations of armed men who took control of local politics and the economy in late nineteenth-century Sicily.

magic (p. 457) Learned opinion described two kinds of magic: natural magic, which involved the manipulation of occult forces believed to exist in nature, and demonic magic, which called upon evil spirits to gain access to power. Widely accepted as a reality until the middle of the seventeenth century.

Magisterial Reformation (p. 421) Refers to Protestant churches that received official government sanction.

Magna Carta (p. 296) In 1215 some English barons forced King John to sign the "great charter," in which the king pledged to respect the traditional feudal privileges of the nobility, towns, and clergy. Subsequent kings swore to uphold it, thereby accepting the fundamental principle that even the king was obliged to respect the law.

Manhattan Project (p. 866) Code name given to the secret Anglo-American project that resulted in the construction of the atom bomb during World War II.

marches (p. 250) Territorial units of the Carolingian empire for the administration of frontier regions. Each march was ruled by a margrave who had special powers necessary to defend vulnerable borders.

Marshall Plan (p. 890) The use of U.S. economic aid to restore stability to Europe after World War II and so undercut the appeal of communist ideology.

mechanical philosophy (p. 522) The seventeenth-century philosophy of nature, championed by René Descartes, holding that nature operated in a mechanical way, just like a machine made by a human being.

mendicant friars (p. 288) Members of a religious order, such as the Dominicans or Franciscans, who wandered from city to city and throughout the countryside begging for alms rather than residing in a monastery. Mendicant friars tended to help ordinary laypeople by preaching and administering to the sick and poor.

mercantilism (p. 484) The theory that the wealth of a state depended on its ability to import fewer commodities than it exported and thus acquire the largest possible share of the world's monetary supply. The theory encouraged state intervention in the economy and the regulation of trade.

mesmerism (p. 599) A pseudoscience developed by Franz Anton Mesmer in the eighteenth century that treated sickness by massaging or hypnotizing the patient to produce a crisis that restored health.

metropolis (p. 542) The parent country of a colony or imperial possession.

Mishnah (p. 186) The final organization and transcription of Jewish oral law, completed by the end of the third century C.E.

Modern Devotion (p. 331) A fifteenth-century religious movement that stressed individual piety, ethical behavior, and intense religious education. The Modern Devotion was promoted by the Brothers of the Common Life, a religious order whose influence was broadly felt through its extensive network of schools.

modernism (p. 754) Term applied to artistic and literary movements from the late nineteenth century through the 1950s. Modernists sought to create new aesthetic forms and values.

monastic movement (p. 183) In Late Antiquity, Christian ascetics organized communities where men and women could pursue a life of spirituality through work, prayer, and asceticism. Called the monastic movement, this spiritual quest spread quickly throughout Christian lands.

Monophysites (p. 181) Christians who do not accept the Council of Chalcedon (see Chalcedonians). Monophysites believe that Jesus Christ has only one nature, equally divine and human.

monotheism (p. 39) The belief in only one god, first attributed to the ancient Hebrews. Monotheism is the foundation of Judaism, Christianity, Islam, and Zoroastrianism.

Montagnards (p. 616) Members of the radical faction within the Jacobin party who advocated the centralization of state power during the French Revolution and instituted the Reign of Terror.

mosque (p. 222) A place of Muslim worship.

nabobs (p. 564) Members of the British East India Company who made fortunes in India and returned to Britain, flaunting their wealth.

Napoleonic Code (p. 631) The name given to the Civil Code of 1804, promulgated by Napoleon, which gave France a uniform and authoritative code of law.

nation (p. 681) A large community of people who possess a sense of unity based on a belief that they have a common homeland and share a similar culture.

nationalism (p. 681) The belief that the people who form a nation should have their own political institutions and that the interests of the nation should be defended and promoted at all costs.

national self-determination (p. 681) The doctrine advanced by nationalists that any group that considers itself a nation has the right to be ruled only by the members of their own nation and to have all members of the nation included in that state.

nation-state (p. 681) A political structure sought by nationalists in which the boundaries of the state and the nation are identical, so that all the members of a nation are governed by the same political authorities.

NATO (North Atlantic Treaty Organization) (p. 892) Defensive anti-Soviet alliance of the United States, Canada, and the nations of western Europe established in 1949.

natural magic (p. 525) The use of magical words and drawings to manipulate the occult forces that exist in nature without calling on supernatural beings for assistance.

nawabs (p. 561) Native provincial governors in eighteenth-century India.

Nazism (p. 829) Twentieth-century political ideology associated with Adolf Hitler that adopted many fascist ideas but with a central focus on racism and particularly anti-Semitism.

neoclassicism (p. 580) The revival of the classical art and architecture of ancient Greece and Rome in the eighteenth century.

Neoplatonism (pp. 189, 522) A philosophy based on the teachings of Plato and his successors that flourished in Late Antiquity, especially in the teachings of Plotinus. Neoplatonism influenced Christianity in Late Antiquity. During the Renaissance Neoplatonism was linked to the belief that the natural world was charged with occult forces that could be used in the practice of magic.

NEP (New Economic Policy) (p. 820) Lenin's economic turnaround in 1921 that allowed and even encouraged small private businesses and farms in the Soviet Union.

New Conservatism (p. 928) Political ideology that emerged at the end of the 1970s combining the free market approach of nineteenth-century liberalism with social conservatism.

new feminism (p. 928) Re-emergence of the feminist movement in the 1970s.

new imperialism (p. 759) The third phase of modern European imperialism, that occurred in the late nineteenth and early twentieth centuries and extended Western control over almost all of Africa and much of Asia.

New Left (p. 917) Leftwing political and cultural movement that emerged in the late 1950s and early 1960s; sought to develop a form of socialism that rejected the over-centralization, authoritarianism, and inhumanity of Stalinism.

nobility (p. 570) Members of the aristocracy who received official recognition of their hereditary status, including their titles of honor and legal privileges.

no-man's-land (p. 786) The area between the combatants' trenches on the Western Front during World War I.

North Atlantic Treaty Organization (NATO) (p. 892) Defensive anti-Soviet alliance of the United States, Canada, and the nations of western Europe established in 1949.

Nuremberg trials (p. 872) Post-World War II trials of members of the Nazi Party and German military; conducted by an international tribunal.

Old Regime (p. 600) The political order of eighteenth-century France, dominated by an absolute monarch and a privileged nobility and clergy.

oligarchy (p. 78) A government consisting of only a few people rather than the entire community.

opera (p. 366) A musical form invented in the final decades of the sixteenth century by a group of humanist-musicians who thought the power of ancient Greek music could be recovered by writing continuous music to accompany a full drama. The drama was performed as a kind of speech-song with the range of pitch and rhythms closely following those of natural speech.

orthodox (p. 181) In Christianity, the term indicates doctrinally correct belief. Definitions of Orthodoxy changed numerous times.

ostracism (p. 77) Developed in democratic Athens, this practice enabled citizens in the assembly to vote to expel any Athenian citizen from the city for ten years for any reason.

Ottonian Renaissance (p. 260) Under the patronage of the Saxon Emperor Otto I (936–973) and his brother Bruno, learned monks, Greek philosophers from Byzantium, and Italian scholars gathered at the imperial court, stimulating a cultural revival in literature and the arts. The writers and artists enhanced the reputation of Otto.

paganism (p. 178) The Christian term for polytheist worship (worshiping more than one god). In the course of Late Antiquity, the Christian church suppressed paganism, the traditional religions of the Roman empire.

palimpsests (p. 246) Because parchment sheets used for copying were expensive, monks often scrubbed off an old text and copied another in its place. These reused sheets of parchment often contain layers of valuable texts that can be retrieved by scientists.

pan-Arabism (p. 842) Nationalist ideology that called for the political unification of all Arabs, regardless of religious affiliation.

panhellenic (p. 72) This word means covering all Greek communities. It applies, for example, to the Olympic Games, in which competitors came from all over the Greek world.

papacy (p. 177) The bishop of the city of Rome is called the Pope, or Father. The papacy refers to the administrative and political institutions controlled by the Pope. The papacy began to gain strength in the sixth century in the absence of Roman imperial government in Italy.

paradigm (p. 525) A conceptual model or intellectual framework within which scientists conduct their research and experimentation.

parlements (p. 481) The highest provincial courts in France, the most important of which was the Parlement of Paris.

pastoralist societies (p. 14) Nomadic communities that move from place to place to find pastures for their herds of domesticated animals.

patricians (p. 113) In ancient Rome, patricians were aristocratic clans with the highest status and the most political influence.

patrons and clients (p. 119) In ancient Roman society, a powerful man (the patron) would exercise influence on behalf of a social subordinate (the client) in anticipation of future support or assistance.

Pax Romana (p. 132) Latin for "Roman Peace", this term refers to the Roman Empire established by Augustus that lasted until the early third century C.E.

perestroika (p. 935) Loosely translated as "restructuring;" Gorbachev's effort to decentralize, reform, and thereby strengthen Soviet economic and political structures.

personal rule (p. 500) The period from 1629 to 1640 in England when King Charles I ruled without Parliament.

phalanx (p. 72) The military formation favored by hoplite soldiers. Standing shoulder to shoulder in ranks often eight men deep, hoplites moved in unison and depended on one another for protection.

philology (p. 355) A method reintroduced by the humanists during the Italian Renaissance devoted to the comparative study of language, especially to understanding the meaning of a word in a particular historical context.

philosophes (p. 581) The writers and thinkers of the Enlightenment, especially in France.

pilgrimage (p. 186) Religious journeys made to holy sites in order to encounter relics.

Pillars of Islam (p. 222) The five basic principles of Islam as taught by Muhammad.

plainchant (p. 304) A medieval form of singing based on a straightforward melody sung with simple harmony by a choir to accompany the recitation of the text of the liturgy.

plantation colony (p. 382) First appearing in the Cape Verde Islands and later in the tropical parts of the Americas, these colonies were established by Europeans who used African slave labor to cultivate cash crops such as sugar, indigo, cotton, coffee, and tobacco.

plebeians (p. 113) The poorest Roman citizens.

polis (p. 70) Or city-state, developed by Greeks in the Archaic Age. A polis was a self-governing community consisting of a defensible hilltop, the town itself, and all the surrounding fields farmed by the citizens of the polis. Poleis (plural) shared similar institutions: an assembly place for men to gather and discuss community affairs, a council of elders, and an open agora, which served as a market and a place for informal discussions.

polyphony (p. 304) A form for singing the Christian liturgy developed around 1170 in which two or more independent melodies were sung at the same time.

polytheistic (p. 21) Refers to polytheism, the belief in many gods.

pop art (p. 911) Effort by artists in the 1950s and 1960s both to utilize and to critique the material plenty of post-World War II popular culture.

popular sovereignty (p. 625) The claim that political power came from the people and that the people constituted the highest political power in the state.

portolanos (p. 381) Books of sailing directions that included charts and descriptions of ports. Portolanos appeared in the Mediterranean in the Late Middle Ages.

positivism (p. 682) The philosophy developed by August Comte in the nineteenth century according to which human society passed through a series of stages, leading to the final positive stage in which the accumulation of scientific data would enable thinkers to discover the laws of human behavior and bring about the improvement of society.

postindustrialism, postindustrial society (p. 953) A service- rather than manufacturing-based economy characterized by an emphasis on marketing and information and by a proliferation of communications technologies.

postmodernism (p. 951) Umbrella term covering a variety of artistic styles and intellectual theories and practices; in general, a rejection of a single, universal, Western style of modernity.

Prague Spring (p. 906) Short-lived popular effort in 1968 to re- form Czechoslovakia's political structures; associated with the phrase "socialism with a human face."

predestination (p. 423) The doctrine promoted by John Calvin that since God, the all-knowing and all-powerful being, knew everything in advance and caused everything to happen, then the salvation of any individual was predetermined.

prerogative (p. 499) The set of powers exercised by the English monarch alone, rather than in conjunction with Parliament.

Price Revolution (p. 448) After a long period of falling or stable prices that stretched back to the fourteenth century, Europe expe- rienced sustained price increases between about 1540 and 1640, causing widespread social and economic turmoil.

priesthood of all believers (p. 417) Martin Luther's doctrine that all those of pure faith were themselves priests, a doctrine that undermined the authority of the Catholic clergy over the laity.

proletariat (p. 680) The word used by Karl Marx and Friedrich Engels to identify the class of workers who received their income from wages.

protectionism (p. 550) The policy of shielding domestic indus- tries from foreign competition through a policy of levying tariffs on imported goods.

Radical Reformation (p. 421) Refers to Protestant movements that failed to gain official government recognition and were at best tolerated, at worst persecuted, during the sixteenth century.

Raiders of the Land and Sea (p. 49) The name given by Egyptians to the diverse groups of peoples whose combined naval and land forces destroyed many cities and kingdoms in the eastern Mediterranean and Anatolia, thereby bringing the International Bronze Age to an end.

Reign of Terror (p. 620) A purging of alleged enemies of the French state between 1793 and 1794, superintended by the Committee of Public Safety, that resulted in the execution of 17,000 people.

relics (p. 186) In Christian belief, relics are sacred objects that have miraculous powers. They are associated with saints, biblical figures, or some object associated with them. They served as con- tacts between Earth and Heaven and were verified by miracles.

Religious Peace of Augsburg (p. 420) In 1555 this peace between Lutherans and Catholics within the Holy Roman Empire estab- lished the principle of *cuius regio, eius religio*, which means "he who rules determines the religion of the land." Protestant princes in the Empire were permitted to retain all church lands seized be-

fore 1552 and to enforce Protestant worship, but Catholic princes were also allowed to enforce Catholic worship in their territories.

Renaissance (p. 344) A term meaning "rebirth" used by histori- ans to describe a movement that sought to imitate and under- stand the culture of antiquity. The Renaissance generally refers to a movement that began in Italy and then spread throughout Europe from about 1350 to 1550.

reparations (p. 806) Payments imposed upon Germany after World War I by the Versailles Treaty to cover the costs of the war.

republicanism (p. 345) A political theory first developed by the ancient Greeks, especially the philosopher Plato, but elaborated by the ancient Romans and rediscovered during the Italian Renaissance. The fundamental principle of republicanism as de- veloped during the Italian Renaissance was that government offi- cials should be elected by the people or a portion of the people.

requerimiento (p. 388) A document read by conquistadores to the natives of the Americas before making war on them. The doc- ument briefly explained the principles of Christianity and com- manded the natives to accept them immediately along with the authority of the pope and the sovereignty of the king of Spain. If the natives refused, they were warned they would be forced to ac- cept Christian conversion and subjected to Spain anyway.

revisionism, socialist revisionism (p. 727) The belief that an equal society can be built through participation in parliamentary politics rather than through violent revolution.

rhetoric (p. 356) The art of persuasive or emotive speaking and writing, which was especially valued by the Renaissance humanists.

Roman Republic (p. 110) The name given to the Roman state from about 500 B.C.E., when the last king of Rome was expelled, to 31 B.C.E., when Augustus established the Roman Empire. The Roman Republic was a militaristic oligarchy.

Romanesque (p. 302) A style in architecture that spread through- out western Europe during the eleventh and the first half of the twelfth centuries and characterized by arched stone roofs sup- ported by rounded arches, massive stone pillars, and thick walls.

romanization (p. 149) The process by which conquered peoples absorbed aspects of Roman culture, especially the Latin language, city-life, and religion.

romanticism (p. 683) An artistic and literary movement of the late eighteenth and nineteenth centuries that involved a protest against classicism, appealed to the passions rather than the intel- lect, and emphasized the beauty and power of nature.

Rome-Berlin Axis (p. 853) Alliance between Mussolini's Italy and Hitler's Germany formed in 1936.

Schlieffen Plan (p. 781) German military plan devised in 1905 that called for a sweeping attack on France through Belgium and the Netherlands.

scholasticism (p. 299) A term referring to a broad philosophical and theological movement that dominated medieval thought and university training. Scholasticism used logic learned from Aristotle to interpret the meaning of the Bible and the writings of the Church Fathers, who created Christian theology in its first centuries.

Scramble for Africa (p. 763) The frenzied imposition of European control over most of Africa that occurred between 1870 and 1914.

scriptorium (p. 246) The room in a monastery where monks copied books and manuscripts.

Second Industrial Revolution (p. 713) A new phase in the industrialization of the processes of production and consumption, underway in Europe in the 1870s.

Second Triumvirate (p. 126) In 43 B.C.E. Octavian (later called Augustus), Mark Antony, and Lepidus made an informal alliance to share power in Rome while they jockeyed for control. Octavian emerged as the sole ruler of Rome in 31 B.C.E.

seigneur (p. 582) The lord of a French estate who received payments from the peasants who lived on his land.

separate spheres (p. 595) The theory that men and women should conduct their lives in different social and political environments, confining women to the domestic sphere and excluding them from the public sphere of political involvement.

sepoys (p. 562) Indian troops serving in the armed forces of the British East India Company.

Septuagint (p. 103) The Greek translation of the Hebrew Bible (Old Testament).

serfs (p. 275) During the Middle Ages serfs were agricultural laborers who worked and lived on a plot of land granted them by a lord to whom they owed a certain portion of their crops. They could not leave the land, but they had certain legal rights that were denied to slaves.

settler colony (p. 382) A colony authorized when a private person obtained a license from a king to seize an island or parcel of land and occupied it with settlers from Europe who exported their own culture to the new lands. Settler colonies first appeared among the islands of the eastern Atlantic and portions of the Americas.

simony (p. 281) The practice of buying and selling church offices.

Social Darwinism (p. 747) The later-nineteenth-century application of the theory of evolution to entire human societies.

social democracy (p. 838) Political system in which a democratically elected parliamentary government endeavors to ensure a decent standard of living for its citizens through both economic regulation and the maintenance of a welfare state.

Solidarity (p. 931) Trade union and political party in Poland that led an unsuccessful effort to reform the Polish communist state in 1981; survived to lead Poland's first non-communist government since World War II in 1989.

Sophists (p. 85) Professional educators who traveled throughout the ancient Greek world, teaching many subjects. Their goal was to teach people the best ways to lead better lives.

soviets (p. 800) Workers' and soldiers' councils formed in Russia during the Revolution of 1917.

Spanish Armada (p. 465) A fleet of 132 ships, which sailed from Portugal to rendezvous with the Spanish army stationed in the Netherlands and launch an invasion of England in 1588. The English defeated the Armada as it passed through the English Channel.

Spanish Reconquest (p. 233) Refers to the numerous military campaigns by the Christian kingdoms of northern Spain to capture the Muslim-controlled cities and kingdoms of southern Spain. This long, intermittent struggle began with the capture of Toledo in 1085 and lasted until Granada fell to Christian armies in 1492.

spiritualists (p. 428) A tendency within Protestantism, especially Lutheranism, to emphasize the power of personal spiritual illumination, called the "inner Word," a living form of the Scriptures written directly on the believer's soul by the hand of God.

stagflation (p. 925) Term coined in the 1970s to describe an economy troubled by both high inflation and high unemployment rates.

states (p. 542) Consolidated territorial areas that have their own political institutions and recognize no higher political authority.

Stoicism (p. 104) The philosophy developed by Zeno of Citium (ca. 335–ca. 263 B.C.E.) that urged acceptance of fate while participating fully in everyday life.

structuralism (p. 911) Influential post-World War II social theory that explored the common structures of language and thought.

Struggle of the Orders (p. 113) The political strife between patrician and plebeian Romans beginning in the fifth century B.C.E. The plebeians gradually won political rights and influence as a result of the struggle.

suffragettes (p. 738) Feminist movement that emerged in Britain in the early twentieth century. Unlike the suffragists, who sought to achieve the vote for women through rational persuasion, the suffragettes adopted the tactics of violent protest.

supply (p. 653) The amounts of capital, labor, and food that are needed to produce goods for the market as well as the quantities of those goods themselves.

Syncretism (p. 158) The practice of equating two gods and fusing their cults was common throughout the Roman Empire and helped to unify the diverse peoples and religions under Roman rule.

syndicalism (p. 728) Ideology of the late nineteenth and early twentieth century that sought to achieve a working-class revolution through economic action, particularly through mass labor strikes.

Talmuds (p. 186) Commentaries on Jewish law. Rabbis completed the Babylonian Talmud and the Jerusalem Talmud by the end of the fifth century C.E.

Tetrarchy (p. 172) The government by four rulers established by the Roman emperor Diocletian in 293 C.E. that lasted until 312. During the Tetrarchy many administrative and military reforms altered the fabric of Roman society.

Third World (p. 900) Term coined in 1955 to describe nations that did not align with either the Soviet Union or the United States; commonly used to describe the industrially underdeveloped nations.

Thomism (p. 301) A branch of medieval philosophy associated with the work of the Dominican thinker, Thomas Aquinas (1225–1274), who wrote encyclopedic summaries of human knowledge that confirmed Christian faith.

Time of Troubles (p. 474) The period from 1604 to 1613 when Russia fell into chaos, which ended when the national assembly elected Tsar Michael Romanov, whose descendants ruled Russia until they were deposed in 1917.

total war (p. 778) A war that demands extensive state regulation of economic production, distribution, and consumption; and that blurs (or erases entirely) the distinction between civilian and soldier.

trading posts (p. 388) Built by European traders along the coasts of Africa and Asia as a base for trade with the interior. Trading posts or factories were islands of European law and sovereignty, but European authority seldom extended very far beyond the fortified post.

transubstantiation (p. 289) A doctrine promulgated at the Fourth Lateran Council in 1215 that explained by distinguishing between the outward appearances and the inner substance how the Eucharistic bread and wine changed into the body and blood of Christ.

Treaty of Brest-Litovsk (p. 790) Treaty between Germany and Bolshevik-controlled Russia, signed in March, 1918, that ceded to Germany all of Russia's western territories.

trial by jury (p. 296) When disputes about the possession of land arose after the late twelfth century in England, sheriffs assembled a group of twelve local men who testified under oath about the claims of the plaintiffs, and the circuit court judge made his decision on the basis of their testimony. The system was later extended to criminal cases.

Triple Alliance (p. 779) Defensive alliance of Germany, Austria-Hungary, and Italy, signed in 1882.

Triple Entente (p. 781) Informal defensive agreement linking France, Great Britain, and Russia before World War I.

triremes (p. 75) Greek warships with three banks of oars. Triremes manned by the poorest people of Athenian society became the backbone of the Athenian empire.

troubadours (p. 302) Poets from the late twelfth and thirteenth centuries who wrote love poems, meant to be sung to music, which reflected a new sensibility, called courtly love, about the ennobling possibilities of the love between a man and a woman.

Truman Doctrine (p. 890) Named after U.S. president Harry Truman, the doctrine that in 1947 inaugurated the Cold War policy of resisting the expansion of communist control.

Twelfth-Century Renaissance (p. 300) An intellectual revival of interest in ancient Greek philosophy and science and in Roman law in western Europe during the twelfth and early thirteenth centuries. The term also refers to a flowering of vernacular literature and the Romanesque and Gothic styles in architecture.

tyrants (p. 72) Political leaders from the upper classes who championed the cause of hoplites in Greek city-states during the Archaic Age. The word "tyrant" gained its negative connotation when democracies developed in Greece that gave more political voice to male citizens than permitted by tyrants.

Unitarians (p. 429) A religious reform movement that began in the sixteenth century and rejected the Christian doctrine of the Trinity. Unitarians (also called Arians, Socinians, and Anti-Trinitarians) taught a rationalist interpretation of the Scriptures and argued that Jesus was a divinely inspired man, not God-become-man as did other Christians.

universal law of gravitation (p. 518) A law of nature established by Isaac Newton in 1687 holding that any two bodies attract each other with a force that is directly proportional to the product of their masses and indirectly proportional to the square of the distance between them. The law was presented in mathematical terms.

universal male suffrage (p. 615) The granting of the right to vote to all adult males.

Utilitarians (p. 678) Nineteenth-century British liberals who promoted social and economic policies that in their view would provide the greatest good for the greatest number of people.

vassals (p. 255) During the Middle Ages men voluntarily submitted themselves to a lord by taking an oath of loyalty. Vassals owed the lord certain services—usually military assistance—and sometimes received in exchange a grant of land known as a fief.

Vatican II (p. 912) Popular term for the Second Vatican Council that convened in 1963 and introduced a series of changes within the Roman Catholic Church.

Versailles Treaty (p. 806) Treaty between Germany and the victorious Allies after World War I.

Vichy, Vichy regime, Vichy government (p. 855) Authoritarian state established in France after defeat by the German army in 1940.

Warsaw Pact (p. 892) Military alliance of the Soviet Union and its eastern European satellite states in the Cold War era.

Weimar Republic (p. 821) The democratic German state constructed after defeat in World War I and destroyed by the Nazis in 1933.

wergild (p. 243) In Germanic societies the term referred to what an individual was worth in case he or she suffered an injury. It was the amount of compensation in gold that the wrongdoer's family had to pay to the victim's family.

witch-hunt (p. 457) Refers to the dramatic increase in the judicial prosecution of alleged witches in either church or secular courts from the middle of the sixteenth to the middle of the seventeenth centuries.

Zionism (p. 732) Nationalist movement that emerged in the late nineteenth century and sought to establish a Jewish political state in Palestine (the Biblical Zion).

Zoroastrianism (p. 59) The monotheistic religion of Persia founded by Zoroaster that became the official religion of the Persian Empire.

Credits

Unless otherwise acknowledged, all photographs are the property of Pearson Education, Inc.
Page abbreviations are as follows: **(T)** Top, **(B)** Bottom, **(L)** Left, **(R)** Right, **(C)** Center.

What Is the West?
2 Canali Photobank **4** European Space Agency/Photo Researchers, Inc. **5** Courtesy of Adler Planetarium & Astronomy Museum, Chicago, Illinois (W-264). **8** American Museum of Natural History Library (AMNH#314372)

Chapter 1
10 Giraudon/Art Resource, NY **12** Augustin Ochsenreiter/ South Tyrol Museum of Archaeology **17** Courtesy of the Trustees of the British Museum **19** Robert Harding Picture Library **21** Scala/Art Resource, NY **23** Erich Lessing/Art Resource, NY **29** Roger Ressmeyer/Corbis

Chapter 2
33 The Art Archive/National Archaeological Museum Athens/Dagli Ort **36** Dagli Orti/The Art Archive **38** The Art Archive/ Egyptian Museum Cairo/Dagli Orti (A) **39** Osiride Head of Hatshepsut, originally from a statue. Provenance: Thebes, Deir el Bahri. Limestone, painted. H. 64 cm. H. with crown 124.5 cm. The Metropolitan Museum of Art, Rogers Fund, 1931, (31.3.157) Photograph © 1983 The Metropolitan Museum of Art **41** British Museum, London/Bridgeman Art Library **44** Nimatallah/Art Resource, NY **48** Hirmer Fotoarchiv **53** Erich Lessing/Art Resource, NY

Chapter 3
56 Erich Lessing/Art Resource, NY **61** SEF/Art Resource, NY **66** Israel Museum **71 (BR)** The American Numismatic Society **71 (BL)** The American Numismatic Society **71 (TR)** The American Numismatic Society **71 (TL)** The American Numismatic Society **75** Erich Lessing/Art Resource, NY **79 (T)** Foto Marburg/Art Resource, NY **79 (BR)** Pedicini/Index s.a.s. **79 (BL)** Louvre, Paris, France/Bridgeman Art Library **80** Staatliche Antikensammlungen und Glyptothek, Munich **81** Robert Harding Picture Library **84** Column krater (missing bowl) (detail), Greek, Archaic Period (Late Corinthian), about 550 B.C., Place of manufacture: Greece, Corinthia, Corinth, Ceramic, Black Figure, Height 33 cm (13 in); diameter: 41cm (16⅛ in.), Museum of Fine Arts, Boston, Helen and Alice Colburn Fund (63.420) Photograph © 2003 Museum of Fine Arts, Boston **85** British Museum, London, Great Britain/HIP/Art Resource, NY **87** Scala/Art Resource, NY **88** Scala/Art Resource, NY

Chapter 4
92 Scala/Art Resource, NY **96** Bildarchiv Prüßischer Kulturbesitz/ Art Resource, NY **100** Réunion des Musées Nationaux/Art Resource, NY **101** Bildarchiv Prüßischer Kulturbesitz/Art Resource, NY **102** Réunion des Musées Nationaux/Art Resource, NY **105** Erich Lessing/Art Resource, NY **110 (T)** Erich Lessing/ Art Resource, NY **110 (B)** Bildarchiv Prüßischer Kulturbesitz/Art Resource, NY **112** Robert Harding Picture Library **119** Vanni/ Art Resource, NY **121** Alinari/Art Resource, NY

Chapter 5
130 Erich Lessing/Art Resource, NY **134** Erich Lessing/Art Resource, NY **137** SEF/Art Resource, NY **139** Leo C. Curran **141** Erich Lessing/Art Resource, NY **144** Yann Arthus-Bertrand/ Corbis **148** Vasari/Index s.a.s. **150** Robert Harding Picture Library **152** akg-images **156** Scala/Art Resource, NY **159** Scala/Art Resource, NY **160** Scala/Art Resource, NY **161** Jewish Museum, London **162** Courtesy of the Trustees of the British Museum

Chapter 6
168 Österreichische Nationalbibliothek, Vienna **170** Scala/Art Resource, NY **171** SEF/Art Resource, NY **172** Erich Lessing/Art Resource, NY **177** Scala/Art Resource, NY **179** Victoria & Albert Museum, London/Art Resource, NY **182** Réunion des Musées Nationaux/Art Resource, NY **186** The Jewish Museum, New York, NY/Art Resource, NY **191** Alinari/Art Resource, NY **197** Réunion des Musées Nationaux/Art Resource, NY **199** Scala/ Art Resource, NY **202 (T)** Courtesy of the Trustees of the British Museum **202 (B)** Courtesy of the Trustees of the British Museum

Chapter 7
204 Erich Lessing/Art Resource, NY **209 (T)** Balatoni Museum, Keszthely, Hungary **209 (B)** Balatoni Museum, Keszthely, Hungary **213** David and Goliath, Byzantine, Made in Constantinople, 629–630; Early Byzantine, Silver, D. 1½ in. (3.8 cm); Diam. 19½ in (49.4 cm); The Metropolitan Museum of Art, Gift of J. Pierpont Morgan, 1917 (17.190.396) Photograph © 2000 The Metropolitan Museum of Art **215** British Museum/The Art Archive **216** State Historical Museum, Moscow **217** Courtesy of His Eminence Archbishop Damianos and the Holy Council of the Fathers, Saint Catherine's Monastery. Photograph © Idryma Orous Sina, Mt. Sinai Foundation **218** Pushkin Museum, Moscow, Russia/Bridgeman Art Library **220** Werner Forman/ Art Resource, NY **223** Associate Press/AP **225** Freer Gallery of Art, Smithsonian Institution, Washington, D.C.: Purchase, F1930.60a **228** Robert Harding Picture Library **230 (TR)** The Nasser D. Khalili Collection of Islamic Art **230 (TL)** The Nasser D. Khalili Collection of Islamic Art **230 (BR)** Bibliothèque Nationale de France (2001 A 83708) **230 (BL)** Bibliothèque Nationale de France (2001 A 83707) **233** Vanni/Art Resource, NY

Chapter 8
236 Art Resource, NY **251** Vanni/Art Resource, NY **252** Eric Lessing/Art Resource, NY **254** Werner Forman/Art Resource, NY **255** Werner Forman/Art Resource, NY **257** Scala/Art Resource, NY **259** akg-images **261** Werner Forman/Art Resource, NY **264** HIP/Scala/Art Resource, NY **265** Dagli Orti/The Art Archive **266** Bildarchiv Preussischer Kulturbesitz/ Art Resource, NY **274** Réunion des Musées Nationaux/Art Resource, NY

Index

moral standards by gender and, 737; as threat, 751; in 1980s, 928–929; post-modernist art and, 952. *See also* Women; specific rights

Fenian "Rising" (1867), 725

Ferdinand I (Holy Roman Empire), 470

Ferdinand II (Aragon), 368; Isabella of Castile and, 369, 369 (map), 488; Loyola and, 431

Ferdinand II (Bohemia, Hungary, Holy Roman Empire), 493, 496

Ferdinand II (Kingdom of the Two Sicilies), 695

Ferdinand VII (Spain), 635, 686

Ferguson, Adam: on human development, 589

Ferrara, 345 (map), 348; Duke of, 360

Fertile Crescent. *See* Levantine Corridor

Fertility rate: rise in, 651, 915

Fertilization: scientific understanding of human, 751

Fertilizers, 652; in Soviet Union, 904, 933

Festivals: Christian, 178

Feudal dues, 578, 611

Feudalism, 255–258; vassalage under, 284; in England, 296; armies and, 367

Fez: in Turkey, 843

Fiber-optic cables, 954

Fichte, Johann Gottlieb, 636

Ficino, Marsilio, 347

Fiefs, 255, 258; in England, 296; in Russia, 473

Fiji: England and, 544

Film. *See* Movies

Final Solution, 869

Finances: Athenian power and, 78; of Christian communities, 177; in France, 323, 367, 484, 609; sale of indulgences and, 416; in Spain, 490; slavery and, 558; in postwar Europe, 887; New Conservatism and, 928. *See also* Taxation

Financing: of military, 480–481; of railroads, 650–651

Fin-de-siècle (end of the century) culture, 750–759

Finland: women's suffrage in, 737

Firestorm: in Second World War, 866

First and Second Book of Maccabees, 108, 109

First Balkan War, 791

First Coalition: against France, 617

First Consul: Napoleon as, 622–623, 622 (illus.)

First Crusade, 264–265

First Intermediate Period (Egypt), 25

First Macedonian War, 117

First Opium War, 771

First Punic War, 115

First Triumvirate (Rome), 125

First World War, 776 (illus.), 777–778; battles in, 777; casualties in, 777, 786, 789, 794, 798; assassination of Franz Ferdinand and, 778, 778 (illus.), 779, 781; origins of, 778–785; Europe before, 780 (map); mobilization for, 781–783; strategy in, 781–783, 782 (map), 794; public pressure ("will to war") and, 783–785; trench warfare in, 785–786, 785 (illus.), 786 (illus.); offensives in, 786–788, 794; modernism and, 788–789, 788 (illus.), 789 (illus.); Russia in, 789–790; in eastern Europe, 789–791, 790 (map); Balkan region in, 791; as world war, 791–794, 792 (map); U.S. entry into, 793–794; end of, 794; home fronts in,

794–800; women in, 795, 796–797, 796 (illus.); Paris Peace Conference after, 803–806; peace after, 803–809, 850; mandate system after, 809–810, 842; cultural impact of, 814; nationalism after, 841–843; empires after, 841 (map); events leading to Second World War after, 850–851

Fisher, John, 424

Fishing industry, 396, 545

Fission. *See* Nuclear fission

Five Orchestral Pieces (Schoenberg), 757

Five Pillars of Islam, 222

Fixed exchange rates, 926

Flagellation, 311 (illus.); in Spanish America, 392, 392 (illus.)

Flamininus, Titus Quinctius, 118

Flanders: trade in, 279; market cities in, 279 (map); worker rebellions in, 320; painting in, 364–365

Flanders (Dix), 815, 816 (illus.)

Flavian dynasty (Rome), 134; Agricola and, 142

Flemish language, 465, 688

Flemish painting, 364–365

Flood: tales of, 69

Flooding: in Sumer, 15

Florence, 345 (map); coins of, 279; growth of, 279; Black Death in, 311; banking in, 319; guilds in, 319; Ciompi revolt in, 319–320; Machiavelli in, 343; Italian Renaissance in, 345–347; Medici family in, 346–347; vendettas in, 352; Baptistery in, 360 (illus.), 361, 361 (illus.); sculpture in, 363; cathedral of, 363 (illus.)

Florida, 550; colonization of, 396, 543

Florin (coin), 319

"Flowery war": by Aztecs, 384–385

Flying buttresses, 303, 304 (illus.)

Fontenelle, Bernard de, 535–536

Food: revolution in production of, 13–14, 13 (map); production in communities, 14–15, 27; medieval agricultural revolution and, 275; costs of, 307; insufficiency of, 308–309; rationing in First World War, 795; shortages in First World War, 796; U.S. shipments to postwar Europe, 891

Foot soldiers: in Hundred Years' War, 328

Forced labor: in Africa, 766; in Soviet Union, 834; from concentration camps, 871; in Nazi-occupied Europe, 876–877

Ford, Henry, 816

Foreign affairs: mass interest in, 783

Foreigners: Greek contacts with, 106–110

Foreign labor: for Nazi Germany, 877–878

Foreign policy: after Second World War, 890

Foreign workers, 926; rights for, 926–927

Forests: destruction for farming, 308; energy from, 646–647

Forms (absolutes): Plato on, 85–88, 189; Aristotle on, 88

Fortescue, John, 499

Forts. *See* Trading posts

Fortune: temple of, 119

Fort William, India, 562

Forum. *See* Roman Forum

Fossil(s), 745

Fossil fuel: environment and, 956

Foucault, Michel, 952

Fouché, Joseph, 620, 625

Four Books on the Family (Alberti), 351

Fournier, Jacques. *See* Benedict XII (Pope)

Fourteen Points (Wilson), 803

Fourth Crusade, 265, 283, 315

Fourth Lateran Council, 284, 289; on trial by ordeal, 257; Jews and, 290, 291

Fox, George, 543

France: Greek settlement in, 70; Franks in, 239; feudalism in, 258; use of term, 260; papacy and, 284, 329; Cathars (Albigensians) in, 290; Jews and, 290, 731; modern state in, 294–296; in late 12th century, 295 (map); Hundred Years' War and, 308, 321–328, 323 (illus.), 324 (map); Black Death in, 311; England and, 319, 325, 545, 551; worker rebellions in, 320; jurisdiction of kings in, 322–323; Aquitaine and, 323; Edward III (England) and, 323; Italian Wars and, 366; Church in, 367; state (nation) in, 367–368; Estates General in, 368; dynastic marriage encircling, 369–370, 369 (map); Holy Roman Empire and, 370; Italy invaded by, 370; Verrazano and, 396; popes in, 410; after wars of religion, 445; Huguenots in, 460–461; literature in, 467–468; absolutism in, 481–488; economy in, 484, 655, 908; territorial acquisitions of, 486–487, 486 (map); Spain and, 488 (map), 686; Dutch Republic and, 508; overseas empire of, 543; trading companies of, 543; War of the Austrian Succession and, 551; Anglo-French wars and, 551–554; slave trade and, 559; civil law in, 561; Haitian Revolution and, 568–569; nobility in, 577, 656; aristocracy in, 579; peasants in, 582; bourgeoisie in, 583; philosophes in, 585; criminal justice in, 590; Voltaire and, 592; women in, 595, 735, 736, 737, 738, 916, 929; republic in (1792–1799), 613–623; Consuls in, 622 (illus.); academies in, 623–624; cultural change in, 623–627; political culture in, 625–627; revolutionary calendar in, 627; under Napoleon, 627–639; administration of, 631–632; boundaries of, 638–639, 638 (map); after Congress of Vienna, 639; after Revolution, 639–640; science and technology in, 653; industrialization in, 654, 657; textile industry in, 659; Paris Commune in, 675–676; liberalism in, 677, 687–688; nationalism in, 681, 682; nation-state in, 681; Revolution of 1848 in, 692–693; Second Empire in, 693, 702, 707; Third Republic in, 702, 707, 708, 720–721; Austrian defeat by, 705; Concert of Europe and, 705; national identity in, 719; Dreyfus Affair in, 720–721, 722–723, 723 (illus.); political crises in, 720–721; syndicalism and anarchism in, 729; Roman Catholicism in, 758; Dahomey and, 766; First World War and, 778, 785; Schlieffen Plan and, 782–783; soldiers in, 785, 786 (illus.); after First World War, 806; Alsace and Lorraine and, 807 (map); in Middle East, 809, 840; Resistance in, 815, 873; Popular Front in, 839; in Second World War, 855, 872; De Gaulle in, 873–876, 895; Marshall Plan and, 891; Algeria and, 894–895, 914–915; Indochina and, 897, 899; central planning in, 907;

Grand vizier, 496

Granicus River, Battle of the, 97

Gravitation: Newton on, 518; Descartes on, 521

Great Britain. *See* England (Britain)

Great Depression: of 1873, 712, 714, 716–717; of 1930s, 828–829, 830; in United States, 838; colonies and, 841; international relations and, 851

Greater Serbia, 779

Great Famine, 308–309

"Great Fear" (France), 611

Great Khan (Mongolia), 288–289, 315

Great Kings: Egyptian, 38; Hittite, 42; Persian, 59, 60; Alexander as, 98

"Great Leap Forward" (China), 924

Great Northern War, 497

Great Persecution (Rome), 174

Great Plague (London, 1665), 311, 651

Great Power: Britain as, 890

Great Purge (Soviet Union), 835–836

Great Pyramid (Giza), 24

Great Schism, 308, 325, 329–330, 339, 350, 410

Greece, 718 (map), 791; in Byzantine Empire, 208 (map); Byzantine control of, 239 (map); Venice and, 347; table fork in, 456; liberalism in, 677; in Ottoman Empire, 681; nationalist revolt (1821) in, 686–687; independence of, 729; women's suffrage in, 738; after First World War, 806–807; Anatolian territory to, 843; Mussolini and, 857; Nazis in, 858; U.S. and Truman Doctrine in, 890; socialist party in, 927–928

Greece (ancient): culture of, 3 (illus.), 4; International Bronze Age and, 34; Minoan Crete and, 44–45; Mycenaean, 45–46; Classical Age in, 58, 67 (map), 76–89; democratic traditions from, 58; Ionia and, 59; Persia and, 60–62, 75; Dark Age in, 66–67; rebuilding of (1100–479 B.C.E.), 66–76; Archaic Age in, 67–74, 67 (map); alphabet in, 68–69; myth of Flood in, 69; polis in, 70; colonization and settlements by, 70–72; coins from, 71, 71 (illus.); hoplites in, 72–73; barbarians and, 73; Sparta and, 73; Athens and, 73–74; slavery in, 80–81; intellectual thought in, 82–89; philosophy in, 85–88; arts in, 88–89; Hellenistic culture and, 93–94; Macedon and, 95; Philip II (Macedon) and, 96; Persians and, 98; settlement of Alexander's conquests by, 98; Etruscan trade with, 112; Rome and, 114, 118–119; Carthage and, 115; Macedonian Wars and, 117–118; revival of learning from, 298, 300–301; Italian Renaissance thinkers and, 354–355. *See also* Hellenistic Age

"Greek Fire," 214

Greek language, 146 (map), 180, 183; Linear B and, 45; in Hellenistic world, 94, 99, 103; Koine and, 101; Romans and, 118; in eastern Roman Empire, 181, 190; in Western Christianity, 181; in Christian writing, 188; Justinian and, 197

Greek literature: Arabic translations of, 231

Greek Orthodox, 238

Greek people: in Venice, 348

Greenham Common Protests, 929 (illus.)

Greenhouse emissions: cutbacks in, 956

Greenland, 255, 276, 311, 378

Greenpeace, 930

Green politics, 930

Gregory I (the Great, Pope), 187, 245, 246, 280; on relics, 187; Jewish conversions and, 247

Gregory VII (Pope), 281–282

Gregory of Nyssa, 190; Neoplatonism and, 190

Grey, Charles (Lord), 690

Grimmelshausen, H. J. C., 492

Gritti, Andrea, 348

Gropius, Walter, 815

Grosz, George, 824 (illus.)

Grotius, Hugo, 508

Guam, 768, 859

Guanche people, 382

Guarani people, 393

Guelfs, 284

Guerilla warfare: in Africa, 766; in Boer War, 773

Guestworkers, 915. *See also* Immigrants and immigration

Guiana: Dutch in, 545

Guicciardini, Francesco, 371, 372

Guide for the Perplexed, The (Maimonides), 301

Guido of Arezzo: musical notation system of, 304

Guilds: universities as, 300; economic role of, 319–320; "German Paragraph" in statutes of, 338; art commissioned by, 359; in cities, 448; industrialization and, 648

Guillotin, Joseph-Ignace, 617

Guillotine (France), 617, 620

Guinea, 379, 380

Guion, François, 443, 460

Guise family, 462; Henry of, 462

Gula (goddess), 43

Gulag Archipelago, 904, 905

Gulf War (1991): Islamism and, 948

Gunpowder, 317, 328, 480

Guns: introduction of, 328

Gutenberg, Johannes, 359, 412, 412 (illus.)

Gymnasium Greek, 101 (illus.)

Gypsies. *See* Roma (Gypsies)

Habsburg Empire: Treaty of Utrecht and, 487; German and Spanish territory in, 493; Ottoman Turks and, 497, 729; industry in, 659; nations in, 681; Czech autonomy from, 694; nationalities in, 704–705, 704 (map); after First World War, 807. *See also* Austria; Austrian Habsburg Monarchy; Habsburg Monarchy; Holy Roman Empire; specific rulers

Habsburg Monarchy, 551; Philip II (Spain) and, 464; Enlightenment and, 600. *See also* Austria; Austrian Habsburg Monarchy

Haciendas, 391

Hadrian (Pope), 252 (illus.)

Hadrian (Rome), 134; mausoleum of, 138; Pantheon and, 139; Jews and, 148; jurists and, 149; frontier boundaries and, 150; Plotina and, 156

Hadrian's Wall, 150, 150 (illus.)

Haeckel, Ernst, 748

Haggard, Rider, 747–748

Haghia Sophia (Constantinople), 198, 204 (illus.)

Hahn, Otto, 817

Haig, Douglas, 786

Haile Selassie (Ethiopia), 852

Haiti: abolition of slavery in, 559; revolution in, 568–569. *See also* Saint Domingue

Hakon III (Norway), 256

Hall of Mirrors, Versailles: German Empire proclaimed at, 701 (illus.)

Hallstatt culture, 109

Hals, Franz, 508

Hamburg: water and sewer system in, 744; bombing of, 866

Hamilcar Barca (Carthage), 115

Hamilton, Richard, 911, 911 (illus.)

Hamlet (Shakespeare), 469

Hammer of Witches, The, 339, 458

Hammurabi (Babylon), 19

Hammurabi's Code, 19–20, 22–23, 23 (illus.)

Handbook for the Militant Christian (Erasmus), 413–414

Handicraft workshops, 649–650

Handwriting: Carolingian minuscule as, 251

Hanging Gardens of Babylon, 52–53

Hannibal (Carthage), 93, 115–117

Hanseatic League, 279

Hansen's disease. *See* Lepers

Hapiru people, 62. *See also* Hebrews

Hargreaves, James, 645

Harkis people (Algeria), 914–915

Harold (Anglo-Saxon, England), 260

Harquebus, 328

Harun al-Rashid (caliph), 231

Harvey, William, 106, 519, 520, 521, 525

Hasdai ibn Shaprut, 233

Hashemites, 809, 842

Hashimite clan: of Quraysh tribe, 226

Hastings, Warren, 562 (illus.)

Hatshepsut (Egypt), 38, 39 (illus.)

Hattushas (Hittite capital), 49

Hausmännin, Walpurga, 458

Hausner, Gideon, 874

Havana, 550

Havel, Václav, 906, 932, 932 (illus.), 939

"Haves": and "Have-Nots," 956

Hawaii: Russia and, 549; U.S. annexation of, 768; Japanese attack on, 859

Haydn, Franz Joseph, 580

Heavy plow, 273 (illus.), 274, 274 (illus.)

Hebergam, Joseph, 664

Hebrews, 58; history of, 4; Hammurabi's Code and, 20; civilization of, 62–65; prophets of, 63–64; calendar of, 64; Babylonian exile of, 64–65. *See also* Bible (Hebrew); Jews and Judaism

Hegel, Georg Wilhelm Friedrich, 680

Heidegger, Martin, 815

Helena (mother of Constantine): pilgrimages and, 186

Heliocentric theory. *See* Sun-centered theory

Helios (god), 159

Hell: in Dante's *The Divine Comedy*, 334, 335

Hellenes, 94

Hellenism: Jews and, 108

Hellenistic Age, 93–94; religion in, 59, 158; Alexander the Great and, 94, 96–98; cultural areas in, 95 (map); worship of monarchs in, 100; cities in, 100–103; society in, 100–103; women in, 103; culture in, 103–110; philosophy in, 104–105; contacts

thought on, 286; veneration of, 287; cult of Virgin Mary and, 758

Mary I (England), 423, 424; Philip II (Spain) and, 464

Mary II (England), 505. *See also* William and Mary (England)

Mary, Duchess of Richmond (Reynolds), 583 (illus.)

Maryland, 545

Mary Magdalen, 286, 286 (illus.)

Mary of Burgundy, 368, 370

Mary of Modena, 505

Mary Stuart (Scotland), 425

Masaccio, 363; fresco by, 363 (illus.), 364 (illus.)

Masolino, 363 (illus.)

Masons. *See* Freemasons

Mass (Catholic), 289

Massachusetts Bay: English settlement in, 397

Massacres: at Vassy, France, 462; St. Bartholomew's Day, 462–463, 463 (illus.); in Novgorod, 473; Peterloo, 668, 668 (illus.); Russia's "Bloody Sunday" and, 724; of Australian Aborigines, 769; of Armenians, 799–800, 799 (illus.)

Mass consumption: culture, ideas, and, 911–912; science, religion, and, 912–913

Mass media: postmodernists and, 951

Mass movement: Zionism as, 732

Mass murder: in former Yugoslavia, 941

Mass politics, 717; franchise and, 718; anti-Semitism in, 731–732; Zionism and, 732; women and, 732–739; nonrational thought and, 749; new imperialism and, 760; First World War and, 783

Mass society, 710 (illus.)

Matamoe (Gauguin), 742 (illus.)

Material identity, 915

Mathematical Principles of Natural Philosophy (Newton), 518, 518 (illus.), 522

Mathematics: Sumerian, 17; Neo-Babylonian, 54; Euclid and, 105; Newton and, 518; deductive reasoning and, 521; nature and, 521–522; industrialization and, 653

Matilda of Tuscany, 282 (illus.)

Matisse, Henri, 761, 762

Matriarchies: in Renaissance families, 354

Matrimonial Act (France, 1964), 916

Matter: Descartes on, 523; ancient philosophers on, 524; defined, 748; Einstein on, 817

Matthew (Evangelist), 236 (illus.)

Matthew, Gospel of, 177

Maurice of Nassau (United Provinces), 466

Mauthausen, Austria: concentration camp in, 849

Maxentius (Rome), 175

Maximian (Rome), 172, 175

Maximilian I (Holy Roman Empire), 368, 370

Maximus (prefect), 198

Maxwell, Robert, 947

Mayans, 384, 392; chocolate and, 556

May Laws (Russia, 1882), 731

"Mayor of the Palace," 241

Mazarin, Jules, 482, 484

Mazzini, Giuseppe, 682, 695, 699

McDonald's, 913 (illus.), 914

McKinley, William: assassination of, 729

McMahon, Henry, 809

McMahon-Husayn Correspondence, 809

Measles, 402, 745

Measurement: metric, 623, 627

Mecca, 222, 223; Kaaba in, 223 (illus.)

Mechanical philosophy, 522–523, 530–531

Mechanics: Aristotle on, 88, 523; Archimedes on, 524

Mechanization, 713; mining improvements from, 527; Industrial Revolution and, 536; in France, 659; in warfare, 788; Soviet, 904

Medes, 58

Medicean Age (Florence), 346

Medici family: Cosimo de', 346, 350; in Florence, 346–347; Lorenzo the Magnificent, 346 (illus.), 347, 351; as Magi, 346 (illus.); Giuliano, 347; as art patrons, 365; Catherine de Médicis, 460, 461–462, 463; Marie de', 463, 481; Cosimo II de', 526

Medicine, 518, 744–745, 745 (illus.), 912; Babylonian, 43; Hippocrates and, 73; Hellenistic, 106; Galen and, 158; blood circulation and, 519; dissection and, 520; bathing and, 584; population growth and, 660; Christianity and, 758

Medicine (Klimt), 754, 754 (illus.)

Medina, 221, 222

Mediterranean region: West and, 5; Egypt and, 20, 26; Minoan civilization of, 44–45; Mycenaeans in, 45–46, 46 (map); port cities in, 49; Raiders of the Land and Sea in, 49; Greece and, 70, 76; Celts and, 109; Roman conquest of, 116 (map); Muslims in, 226; Ottoman Turks in, 377–378; demographic shift from, 445; First World War and, 792

Medvedev, Pavel, 804

Megaliths: in Linear Pottery culture, 28

Megara, 70

Megiddo: battle at, 38–39

Mehmed II (The Conqueror, Ottomans), 316–317, 496

Mein Kampf ("My Struggle") (Hitler), 830

Melania the Younger (Saint), 184

Melkie church, 229

Memoirs of a Woman of Pleasure (Cleland), 597

Memphis, Egypt, 21, 35

Men: in food-producing communities, 14; as European warriors, 29; in Greece, 79–80, 79 (illus.); homosexuality and, 80 (illus.), 751; as mystics, 289; male sodomy and, 291–294; marriage, sexuality, and, 451–455; nature and, 536–538; voting rights for, 717–718; clothing for, 734; role in society, 751; in Italy, 832; in Resistance, 873. *See also* Husbands

Menander of Athens, 103–104

Mendel, Gregor, 746

Mendicant friars, 288

Mennonites, 428

Mental disorder: of Holy Roman emperors, 470

Mentuhotep II (Egypt), 25

Mercantilism: in France, 484; Dutch, 508–509; protectionism and, 550; warfare over, 550; in Asia, 766. *See also* Colonies and colonization; Empire(s); specific empires

Mercenaries: in England, 370; from Switzerland, 421

Merchant fleet: in France, 484

Merchant guilds, 319

Merchant marine: British, 656

Merchants, 448; wealth of, 277; business tools, capitalism, and, 279; Dutch, 507, 508; in bourgeoisie, 583. *See also* Commerce; Trade

Mercia, 240

Mercury (god), 158

Meritocracy: in France, 632

Merovingian dynasty, 247; Childeric and, 240–241; Clovis and, 241; Mayors of the Palace and, 241; Roman traditions and, 243; division of kingdom under, 247–248; decentralization in, 250

Mesmer, Franz Anton, 599

Mesmerism, 599

Mesoamerica: before European arrival, 384–386

Mesopotamia, 14; flood control in, 15; Sumer in, 15–17; civilization in, 15–20; Akkadians in, 17–18; Amorites in, 19; justice in, 22–23; International Bronze Age and, 34; Egypt and, 37; Kassites in, 43; empires of, 43–44; decline of kingdoms in, 49; Assyria and, 51–52; Persian conquest of, 59; conquest by Romans, 150; Jews in, 229

Messenia, 73

Messiah, 162; Babylonian concept of, 108; Persian concept of, 108

Mestizos, 560; in Spanish America, 393

Metallurgy: in Linear Pottery culture, 28

Metals: Phoenician commerce and, 50. *See also* specific metals

Metalworking: railroads and, 650

Metamorphoses (Ovid), 156–157

Methodism: cleanliness and, 584

Methodius (missionary), 209

Methodius (Saint), 261

Metric system: in France, 623, 627

Metropoleis (city-states), 71

Metropolitan (Eastern Church), 176

Metternich, Clemens von, 638–639, 694; conservatism of, 678

Metz: Bismarck and, 702

Mexico: Aztecs in, 384–385; Cortés in, 389, 389 (illus.); religion in, 392; native population of, 401; Russia and, 549; revolution in (1810), 570; independence of, 571; U.S. war with, 703; United States and, 768; Germany and, 793–794

Mexico City: viceroy in, 393

Meyerhold, Vsevelod, 816

Mézières, Philippe de, 333

Michael VIII Palaeologus (Byzantine Empire), 315

Michelangelo Buonarroti, 359–360, 362, 362 (illus.), 363; frescoes of, 437–438, 437 (illus.)

Mickiewicz, Adam, 685

Microbes, 744–745

Microscope, 359, 519

Middle Ages: empires during, 205–206; defined, 206; civilizations during, 238; trials by ordeal in, 256–257; women in, 258, 286, 287; rise of Western Europe in, 270–305; agriculture in, 273–275, 307, 308–309, 652; manors in, 275–276; serfs in, 275–276; migrations and land hunger in, 276–277; cities and towns in, 277–280; education in, 279, 288, 299–300; Roman Catholicism during, 280–294; papacy in, 281–284; governmental forms in, 294; culture in, 298–305;

Plato (Athens), 85–88, 104, 164, 190, 521; Academy of, 85, 104; on human soul, 182; Augustine and, 188; Neoplatonism and, 189–190; Renaissance interest in, 346–347

Platonic thought, 85–88; Copernicus and, 521–522

Plautus (Roman playwright), 118

Plays. *See* Drama

Plebeian Assembly (Rome), 113, 124; Gracchi and reforms through, 123, 124

Plebeians (Rome), 113, 122, 154; Sulla and, 125

Pliny the Elder (Rome), 153, 246

PLO. *See* Palestine Liberation Organization (PLO)

Plotina (Rome), 156

Plotinus (philosopher), 189, 522

Plows, 273 (illus.), 274

Pneumonic plague, 310

Poem of My Cid, The, 266

Poets and poetry: Homer and, 70; Tyrtaeus and, 72; Hellenistic, 104; Roman, 119; Horace and, 157; Virgil and, 157; *Digenes Akritas* as, 212–213; Latin, 246; Viking, 255; epic poems, 266; medieval, 298; troubadours and, 302; *The Divine Comedy* (Dante), 334–336; Petrarch and, 355; in Iberia, 468; romantic, 683; after First World War, 814

Poggio Bracciolini, 357

Pogroms: against Jews, 338, 731, 731 (illus.)

Poison gas: in First World War, 778, 786, 787, 787 (illus.); in death camps, 871

Poitiers: nunnery in, 212; battle at (732), 226, 241; battle at (1356), 323

Poland: Celts and, 110; Latin Christianity in, 261–262; Germanic invasion of, 276; Russia and, 549; classes in, 577; nobility in, 577–578, 579; constitution in (1791), 613; Napoleon and, 633; nationalist rebellion in (1830), 689–690; immigrants from, 716; pogroms in, 731 (illus.); First World War and, 790; after First World War, 806, 807 (map), 820; Silesia and, 850; German-Soviet division of, 853; Nazi invasion of, 853, 854–855; Soviets and, 858; Jews in, 869; death camps in, 870 (map), 871; Second World War and, 877, 887; communism in, 905; protests in, 906; Solidarity in, 931–933, 939; market economy in, 936; anti-Semitism in, 939; in EU, 944

Poland-Lithuania, 471–473, 472 (map); religious toleration in, 429, 430; Russian wars with, 473

Polio vaccine, 912

Polis (Greek city-state), 70; athletic competitions in, 72; Sparta and, 73; Athens as, 73–74; Macedon and, 96; Hellenistic, 101

Polish people: Catholicism of, 260; Christians in Holocaust, 872

Politburo (Soviet Union), 931

Political culture: in France, 625–627, 640; after 1870, 717–725; in 1980s, 928

Political institutions: in Ur, 19; in Europe, 477; Western views of Eastern, 563

Political parties: in England, 717; socialist, 726–727; in First World War, 795; in 1950s and 1960s, 907; after Second World War, 907. *See also* specific parties

Political system: revolutions and, 609

Political theory: in Enlightenment, 592–595

Politics: in Athens, 76–77; Aristotle on, 88; Roman Senate and, 139; iconoclasm controversy and, 216; papacy and, 284; in Renaissance, 344; modern thought about, 372–373; ideologies and, 561; admiration of Chinese and Indian, 564; bourgeoisie and, 583–585; after French Revolution, 640; industrialization and, 655; romanticism and, 685; in France, 720–721; revolutionary, 720–725; working-class, 725–729; race and nationalism in, 729–732; anti-Semitism in, 731–732; Zionism and, 732; women and, 732–739; new imperialism and, 759–760; of total war, 795–796; in 1920s, 818–826; in eastern Europe, 820, 939; Nazis in, 830; polarization in 1930s, 832–840; in Second World War, 856, 879–880; in newly independent nations, 896; in 1950s, 907; after Second World War, 907–908; De Gaulle and, 914; in 1970s, 924–927; in 1980s, 927–930; Green, 930; in Hungary, 935–936

Pollock, Jackson, 910–911, 910 (illus.)

Poll Tax controversy (England), 321

Pollution: in Soviet Union, 933; global, 955

Polo, 565

Polo family: Marco, 278, 315

Polybius (Rome), 117, 118, 153

Polyclitus: Spear-Carrier by, 88 (illus.)

Polygamy: Christian marriage and, 261

Polyphony, 304

Polytheism and polytheists, 4, 176, 178; in Rome, 158–160, 176, 178–179; Christianity and, 170; attacks on, 179; decline of Roman Empire and, 190; Justinian and, 197, 198–199; icons and, 215–216; Arabs and, 222; Islam and, 223; Muslims and, 228; at end of 11th century, 238; Lombards and, 242; in Germanic kingdoms, 244; invasions of West by, 253–255, 253 (map); conversion of, 260–262

Pombal, Marquis of (Portugal), 549

Pompeii: riots in, 141 (illus.)

Pompey (Gnaeus Pompeius, Rome), 125, 126

Pont du Gard (aqueduct), 137 (illus.)

Pontifex Maximus (High Priest, Rome), 136

Poor. *See* Poverty

Poor Clares, 288

Poorhouses, 448

Pop art, 911, 911 (illus.)

Pope(s), 177; authority of, 177, 356–357, 410, 413; as bishop of Rome, 177; Theodoric and, 196; Leo III (Byzantium) and, 216; Frankish protection of, 249–250; administration of, 280; obedience to, 281; as monarch, 281–284; German Empire and, 297; Great Schism and, 308; in Renaissance, 350–351; Conciliar Movement and, 410; Protestant Reformation and, 410; divorce of Henry VIII and, 424; Catholic Reformation and, 430; Jesuits and, 431; in Counter Reformation, 434; Napoleon and, 630–631; papal infallibility and, 758; popularity of, 954. *See also* Papacy; Roman Catholicism; specific popes

Popery: in England, 500

Popular and Republican Society of the Arts (France), 623

Popular culture, 951; after Reformation, 444; suppression of, 455–457; table manners and, 456; French political culture as, 625; Americanization of, 913–914, 913 (illus.); postmodernist, 951–952, 952 (illus.)

Popular Front: in France, 839

Popular music, 914

Popular press, 599

Popular sovereignty, 603; Charles I (England) and, 502; in France, 625; after French Revolution, 640

Population: of Rome, 113; of slaves in Rome, 154; plague (542) and, 200; of medieval Europe, 273; agricultural revolution and growth in, 276; in cities, 277; of 14th-century Europe, 307, 308; deaths from Black Death, 311; of Africans in Americas, 401; epidemic disease and, 401–402; of Early Modern Europe, 444–450; growth of, 445, 660; distribution in 16th century, 447 (map); Price Revolution and, 449; European, 651; on Continent, 655; Malthus on, 660; after 1870, 716; of Russian Empire, 769; Muslims in European, 945

Porajmos (Devouring): Holocaust as, 872

Pornography, 597; regulation of, 953

Poros (India), 98

Port Arthur, 771 (illus.)

Portobelo, 550

Portolanos, 381

Portrait of the Prince Baltasar Carlos. . . . (Velázquez), 490

Portraits: in Renaissance painting, 363 (illus.); of Protestant reformers, 436

Ports: Crusades and, 277; Black Death in, 311

Portugal, 368; Roman control of, 117; Mali and, 379; Ethiopia and, 380; West Africa and, 381 (illus.); colonies of, 382; Africa and, 383–384, 449; Columbus and, 386–387; exploration by, 387, 527; Treaty of Tordesillas and, 387; Asia and, 388; Brazil and, 393–396; slave trade and, 393–396, 559; Nova Scotia and, 396; trading post empire of, 398–399; Spain and, 464, 488 (map); kingdom of, 489; overseas empire of, 543; British imperialism and, 544; Dutch and, 545; Napoleon and, 634; liberal revolt in, 686; First World War and, 792 (map); socialist party in, 927–928

Portuguese Empire, 548–549

Portuguese language, 126, 196

Positivism, 682, 749

Postal system: in Persia, 60

Postmodernism, 951–954; cultures, technologies, and, 952–953; in religion, 953–954

Poststructuralism, 952; in intellectual thought, 952

Potatoes, 402, 403; in Ireland, 671

Potosí, 391, 449

Potsdam meeting (1945), 889, 890

Pottery: in Sumer, 15; in Linear Pottery culture, 27

Poverty: Benedict of Nursia and, 184; in Middle Ages, 272; of religious orders, 288; Black Death and, 312; in cities, 447; assistance from religious institutions, 448

Power (energy): revolution in, 273–274; water, 645; steam, 646; mineral and organic sources of, 646–647; thermodynamics and, 653; for industrialization, 657; nuclear fission and, 817

Power (political): in Rome, 122; of papacy, 245; of medieval lords, 258; absolutism and, 477–499; of aristocracy, 578–580; sharing of, 717–718; during interwar years, 840–841

Power loom, 645, 646

POWs (prisoners of war): Nazi treatment of, 876

Poznan: bishopric at, 261

Praetorian Guard, 140

Praetorian prefects (Rome), 175

Pragmatic Sanction of Bourges, 367

Prague: Rudolf II in, 470–471; Defenestration of, 492 (illus.), 493

Prague Spring, 906, 932

Praise of Folly, The (Erasmus), 414

Praxagoras of Cos, 106

Prayers: Muslim, 223

Preachers: women as, 419

Predestination, 508

Predynastic period (Egypt), 20

Prefects (France), 632

Presbyterianism: in Scotland, 425; in England, 502; Scots-Irish and, 569

Press: in France, 625; after French Revolution, 640

Preternatural: science and, 530

Prez, Josquin de, 365–366

Price, Richard, 603, 612–613

Price Revolution, 445, 448–450; human suffering in, 449–450

Prices: 14th-century rise in, 307

Pride: sin of, 332–333

"Priesthood of all believers" doctrine (Luther), 417

Priestley, Joseph, 602

Priests and priestesses: in Egypt, 21, 35, 37; in Greece, 80; Christian, 176; female, 179 (illus.); sacrificing to gods, 179 (illus.); role in trials by ordeal, 256–257; sexual purity of, 281

"Primitivism," 845, 846 (illus.)

Primogeniture: land availability and, 264; abolition in France, 611–612

Prince, The (Machiavelli), 372

Princeps (First Citizen): Octavian (Augustus) as, 132–133

Princes: in Italy, 345, 348–349, 360; papal, 350–351; in Germany, 370, 420–421; Fronde of (France), 482–493

Princip, Gavrilo, 778 (illus.)

Principalities: in Italy, 348

Principe (island), 545

Principles of Geology (Lyell), 745

Principles of Political Economy and Taxation (Ricardo), 678

Printing: revolution in, 411–412; Erasmus and, 413; spread of Enlightenment ideas and, 597–598

Printing press, 359, 412 (illus.); Scientific Revolution and, 527

Prison camps: Soviet, 834, 901

Prisoners of war: French, 855–856

Privateers, 396

Private property: Anabaptists on, 425

Privatization: in 1980s, 928; in Russia, 938

Procession of the Catholic League, 442 (illus.)

Producers: demand by, 653–654

Production: food, 13–14, 13 (map); in United States, 659; control of means of, 666; depression of 1873 and, 712; business growth and, 714; in First World War, 795. *See also* Factories; Industrialization; Productivity

Productivity: agricultural, 652; Soviet, 904

Products: American, 914

Professions: in Middle Ages, 280; Jews in, 732; women in Nazi Germany and, 832

Professors: in medieval universities, 300

Profits: industrial, 643

Progress: Enlightenment and, 536, 589; evolutionary theory and, 747

Prohibitionism, 737

Proletariat: Marx and Engels on, 680

Propaganda: in France, 625; in First World War, 797–799, 799 (illus.); in Russia, 812 (illus.), 836; in Nazi Germany, 831; in Russia, 834; in Second World War, 879

Property: women and, 244, 258; of Catholic Church, 280; Jewish, 290; class hierarchy by, 663–666; socialism and, 679

Property rights: in France, 611–612; for women, 735

Prophets: Hebrew, 63–64, 222; Muhammad as, 222

Proselytizing: by Christians, 165. *See also* Conversion (to Christianity)

Prosperity: after Second World War, 908–909; family and, 916

Prostitution: sacred, 51; in Greece, 80; Mary Magdalen and, 286; in Germany, 696–697; regulation of, 737; in Russia, 826

Protagoras, 85

Protectionism: mercantilism and, 550; industrialization and, 655; continental industrialization and, 657

Protective tariffs: industrial markets and, 670; in England, 691

Protectorate (England), 504

Protest(s): by Cathars, 290; by French peasants, 582; by Irish peasants, 582; bourgeoisie and, 583–585; against Stalin, 905; in 1960s, 917–919; against nuclear missiles, 929, 929 (illus.), 930; Solidarity as, 931–933; environmental, 933–934

Protestant Reformation, 409–410; Brothers of the Common Life and, 331; causes of, 410–415; print revolution and, 412; Lutheran, 415–421; spread of, 417–421; women and, 418–420; Charles V and, 420–421; in England, 423–425. *See also* Protestants and Protestantism

Protestants and Protestantism: diversity of, 421–430; in England, 424–425, 500; as Baptists, 428; in Hungary, 430; in Poland-Lithuania, 430; Council of Trent and, 435; iconoclasm of, 435–436; church music of, 439; religious extremism and, 443–444; marriage and, 454; St. Bartholomew's Day Massacre and, 462–463, 463 (illus.); Dutch Revolt and, 465–466, 466 (map); in Poland, 472; in France, 481–482, 484, 631; in Austrian Habsburg lands, 496; science and,

525–526, 531; in Ireland, 569, 725; cleanliness and, 584; in Prussia, 600; French Revolution and, 611; in Belgium, 688; English nonconformists as, 691; church attendance and, 912; postmodernism and, 953. *See also* Huguenots; Puritans; St. Bartholomew's Day Massacre; specific countries

Provençal language, 302

Provence, 117, 241

Provinces: Byzantine, 213–214; Muslim, 227

Provinces (Rome), 125, 132; revolts in, 134, 141, 145–148; Romanization of, 140–141, 142, 144; government of, 142, 145; citizenship rights and, 149; prosperity in eastern, 170, 175; political power shifting to, 171, 175; imperial capitals in, 171–172; in late antiquity, 175, 189; in Western Europe, 189, 190, 192; Britain and, 192; defense of, 192; Germanic tribes in, 192; loss of, 192, 202

Provisional Government (Russia), 800–801, 802

Prussia, 311, 491, 493, 494–495, 581; absolutism in, 486; Hohenzollerns in, 494; War of the Austrian Succession and, 551; England and, 552; enlightened despotism in, 600; religious toleration in, 600; French Revolution and, 613; war with France and, 615; in First Coalition against France, 617; Napoleon and, 633, 638; after Congress of Vienna, 639; industrialization in, 657; in Concert of Europe, 679, 705; nationalism in, 682–683; revolution in (1848), 693–694; Junkers in, 695; German unification and, 700–703, 701; Austrian defeat by, 705; women in, 735

Psalter: education and, 189

Psalter of Dagulf, 252 (illus.)

Psychology, 845; collective (crowd), 749; Freud and, 749; "primitivism" and, 845

Ptolemaic universe, 514, 515, 515 (illus.), 517, 525

Ptolemies (Egypt), 98, 100 (illus.); Ptolemy II, 100, 103; Ptolemy VI, 100 (illus.); Arisinoë and, 103; resentment of, 108

Ptolemy, Claudius (astronomer), 157–158, 358, 386, 514, 515 (illus.), 527

Public: entertainment for, 366

Public health: population growth and, 660; smog and, 662

Public libraries, 597

Public opinion: First World War and, 783–784

Public servants: Athenian, 77

Public service: in Italian Renaissance, 349

Public sphere: bourgeoisie in, 583–585; women in, 737

Puerto Rico: Spain and, 571; U.S. acquisition of, 768

Pugachev, Emelian, 582–583

Pumpkins, 402

Punic Wars, 115–117

Punishment: in Roman imperial army, 140; in Roman Empire, 149; crucifixion as, 163; for sins, 415; in cities, 447–448; in England, 580; Enlightenment thinkers on, 589

Punk rock, 933

Punt (Somalia), 24 (map), 26

Purges: in Czechoslovakia, 886; Jews and, 902. *See also* Great Purge (Soviet Union)

948–950; postmodernism in, 953–954. *See also* Bible (Christian); Bible (Hebrew); Catholic Reformation; Gods and goddesses; Protestant Reformation; Secular culture; Toleration; specific religions

Religious art, 435–436

Religious doctrine: disputes over, 450

Religious liberty: in Poland, 472

Religious orders, 284, 287–289; in Spanish America, 393; in Catholic Reformation, 431–434; of women, 433–434; in France, 623. *See also* specific orders

Religious Peace of Augsburg (1555), 420–421, 460, 465, 471

Religious wars, 460; French, 460–463; Philip II and, 464–465; Dutch Revolt and, 465–466

Rembrandt van Rijn, 508, 508 (illus.)

Reminder of Death (religious theme), 332–333

Rémusta, Countess de, 630

Renaissance, 340; culture in, 4; religion in, 4; Macedonian, 216–219; Carolingian, 250, 344; Ottonian, 260; Twelfth-Century, 300–302; Machiavelli and, 343–344; in Italy, 343–367; nature studied in, 358–359; arts in, 359–364; music in, 365–366; Northern, 413–415; Elizabethan, 468–469; of Poland-Lithuania, 471–473; science in, 523–525

Renaissance Man: ideal of, 357

René of Anjou (France), 368

Renoir, Pierre Auguste, 710 (illus.)

Rents, 578

Reparations: German, 806, 821, 828; after Second World War, 890

Repeating rifles: in Africa, 765, 766

Representative government: absolutism and, 480; in France, 637; in England, 690

Reproduction, 536–537; understanding of, 751

Republic(s), 560; Montesquieu on, 593; in France, 608, 613–623; American, 703; Russian, 905; in former Soviet Union, 938–939; in former Yugoslavia, 941

Republic, The (Plato), 88

Republican clubs (France), 693

Republicanism: liberalism and, 677

Republicans: Italian, 345; in Spain, 839, 852

Republic of the United Provinces, 466

Requerimiento (document), 388–389

Research: practical applications of, 535–536. *See also* Scientific Revolution

Reserves: for Australian Aborigines, 769

Resistance: to French king, 482; by peasants, 582; in Africa, 766; in Second World War, 872–876. *See also* Revolts and rebellions

Resistance movement (Second World War): German retribution against, 873; in Yugoslavia, 876; radical ideas and, 880; Catholics in, 908

Resources: in United States, 659; new imperialism and, 759; Japan and, 860 (map)

Responsible citizenship: Bruni on, 356

Re-Stalinization: in Soviet Union, 904–905

Restoration: in France, 637, 640

Retailing, 715; stores and, 715

Returning to the Trenches (Nevinson), 788, 788 (illus.)

Reunification: of Germany, 898, 940

Revenge (Liutprand of Cremona), 260

Revenue: Akkadian, 18

Revisionism: socialist, 727

Revolts and rebellions: in Hittite Empire, 49; against Athens, 76; by Roman slaves, 122; against Roman Empire, 134, 141, 145–148, 151–152, 172; by Jews, 185; Ciompi, 319–320; Jacquerie, 320; *Maillotins* and, 320; peasant revolts in England, 320–321; by German peasants, 420; Dutch Revolt against Spain, 465–466, 466 (map); in Holy Roman Empire, 471; in Spain, 477, 686; in France, 482–483, 617; in Spanish territories, 490; Sepoy Mutiny as, 562–563; in Ireland, 569–570, 671; by peasants, 582–583; between 1815 and 1871, 676; liberal, 686, 687–690; in Portugal, 686; in Greece (1821), 686–687; in Poland (1830), 689–690; in 1820–1848, 690 (map); in Africa, 766; Boxer Rebellion as, 772; in Iraq, 809; after First World War, 843; in Hungary (1956), 905–906; in Tiananmen Square, China, 936

Revolution(s): in Rome, 123–127; in power, 273–274; agricultural, 273–277; military, 328; in England (1689), 499, 505–506; in Caribbean region, 561; against empires, 566–571; in Spanish America, 570–571; use of term, 589; Enlightenment and, 601–603; in France, 607–640, 692–693; in Belgium (1830), 688–689; in Poland, 689–690; of 1820–1848, 690 (map); of 1848, 692–698; in Austria, 693–694; in Hungary, 694; in Germany (1848), 694–695; in Italy (1848), 695–698; Russian execution of revolutionaries and, 711–712; in Russia (1905), 724, 724 (illus.); working-class, 728; Chinese (1911), 772; after Bolshevik Revolution, 802–803; after First World War, 805; communist, 819–820; in Ireland, 840; in India, 843–845; in Cuba, 899; in eastern Europe (1989), 935–936. *See also* American Revolution; French Revolution; Russian Revolutions

Revolutionary socialism: in Russia, 711; working class and, 726–728

"Revolution from above" (Soviet Union), 834–835

Revolutions of the Heavenly Spheres, The (Copernicus), 515, 522

Reynolds, Joshua, 583 (illus.)

Rheims, 325

Rhetoric: in Rome, 157; Petrarch and, 356; humanists and, 371

Rhineland: Prussia and, 639; after First World War, 806; remilitarization of, 852 (map)

Rhine River: Roman Empire and, 191

Rhodesia, 895

Ricardo, David, 666, 678

Rice, 402

Rich. *See* Wealth

Richard I (the Lion-Hearted, England), 265

Richard II (England), 321

Richard III (England), 370

Richelieu, Cardinal (Armand Jean du Plessis de Richelieu), 481–482, 482 (illus.)

Richter, Gerhard, 911

Riefenstahl, Leni, 831

Rifles: repeating, 765, 766

Right (political). *See* Conservatives and conservatism; Reaction; Right wing

Right of Magistrates (Bèze), 463

Rights: Jews on, 160; in Rome, 165; of serfs, 275; of workers, 320; American Revolution and, 567–568; of women, 595, 639, 916; in Declaration of Independence, 603; in France, 611; liberalism and, 676; Mill on, 677; conservatives on, 678; socialism and, 679; in England, 690; in U.S. Constitution, 703; of married women, 735; in Turkey, 843; for foreign workers, 926–927

Rights of Man, The (Paine), 595, 599

Rights of Women, The (De Gouges), 596, 639

Right wing: after First World War, 826–832; Second World War and, 880. *See also* Radical Right

"Rime of the Ancient Mariner" (Coleridge), 683

Riots: in Pompeii, 141 (illus.); against English Poll Tax, 321; in France, 610–611; by Luddites, 667

Rite of Spring, The (Stravinsky), 755

Rituals: Catholic, 281, 284, 330; Protestant and Catholic, 450

Rivers and river regions: Sumerian control of, 15; as industrial power sources, 645; transportation and, 650. *See also* specific rivers and river regions

Roads and highways: in Persia, 59, 60; of Roman Empire, 142, 144, 173; in western Europe, 278; in Nazi Germany, 831

Roanoke, 397; English settlement at, 543

Robert II, the Pious (France), 260

Robert the Monk, 262

Robespierre, Maximilien, 617, 620; Rousseau and, 594; Cult of the Supreme Being and, 626

Robin Hood: legends of, 296

Robinson, John, 564, 912

Rock and roll, 914; Beatles and, 917

Rockefeller, John D., 714

Roma (Gypsies), 939; in Nazi Germany, 832; in concentration camps, 871; deaths in Holocaust, 872

Roman Catholicism, 181; Latin language of, 181; vs. Orthodox Christianity, 208; Photian Schism and, 218; Latin Christianity and, 238; in Ireland, 245, 423, 569; Carolingian rule and, 250; of Árpád dynasty, 254; trial by ordeal and, 256–257; conversions to, 260–262; arts, intellectual thought, and, 273; reform in, 280–281; consolidation of, 280–294; obedience to pope in, 281; uniform rites of, 281; canon law in, 282–283; Eucharist and, 289; heresy and, 290; in England, 296, 424, 425, 500, 690–691; in France, 296, 484, 630–631, 637, 688, 721; Greek philosophy and, 301; in Later Middle Ages, 328–331; Babylonian Captivity of the Church and, 329–330; Great Schism and, 329–330; last rites of, 333; witchcraft and, 339, 534; Renaissance and, 344; causes of Protestant Reformation and, 410–415; on penance and punishment, 415; of Mary I (England), 424; Catholic Reformation and, 430–435; anti-Catholic propaganda and, 436 (illus.); religious extremism and, 443–444; state and, 450;

1905 in, 724, 724 (illus.); women in, 735, 736, 737, 738, 826; Japan and, 769; First World War and, 778, 789–790; Germany and, 779; Franco-Russian Alliance and, 780; Serbia and, 781; civil war in, 818–819, 819 (illus.); after First World War, 818–820; Yeltsin in, 937, 939; under Putin, 939; Islamist view of, 948. *See also* Russian Revolutions; Soviet Union

Russian: origins of term, 210

Russian-American Company, 549

Russian Empire, 399, 542, 704; capital of, 499; in Pacific region, 549; expansion of, 601, 769

Russian Mafia, 938

Russian Revolutions: of 1905, 769; of 1917, 790, 793, 800–802, 804–805

Russo-Japanese War (1905), 769, 771, 771 (illus.), 781

Rutherford, Ernest, 817

Ryswick, Treaty of, 487

SA (Nazi Germany), 830

Saar region: after First World War, 806

Sabaea (Sheba), 63

Sabbaths: of Devil, 534

Sable Island: French in, 396

Sacks: of Rome, 109, 114, 169, 188, 192, 424; of Antioch, 201; of Beijing, 772

Sacraments (Catholic), 284, 289, 330; Reformation and, 410; Luther on, 416

Sacred Band: in Greece, 80

Sacrifice: Carthaginian, 50; in Rome, 112, 158–159; in mythology, 159; Jews and, 160; Jesus Christ as, 161, 164; Eucharist as, 164; Christian end to, 178; by Aztecs, 385, 385 (illus.); Christian missionaries and, 392

Saddam Hussein, 950

Sadism, 597

Sadler, Michael, 664

Sadler Committee: on child labor (Britain), 664–665

Safavid Empire, 543

Sagredo, Giovanfrancesco, 526

Sailing and sailors: Phoenician, 49–50; in absolutist age, 480; navigational improvements and, 527. *See also* Navigation; Ships and shipping

St. Augustine, Florida, 396

St. Bartholomew's Day Massacre, 462–463, 463 (illus.)

St. Denis: Gothic church at, 303, 304 (illus.)

Saint Domingue, 545, 566; slaves in, 559; revolution in, 568–569; independence of, 633

Saint-Fond, Barthélemy Faujas de, 661

St. Germain, Treaty of, 806n

St. Helena: Napoleon on, 638

St. John's, Newfoundland, 396

St. Lawrence River: exploration of, 396

Saint Mark (basilica, Venice), 285, 285 (illus.)

St. Martin at Tours: Alcuin at, 251

Saint Paul Outside the Walls (Rome), 177–178

St. Peter's Basilica (Rome), 178, 351

St. Petersburg, Russia, 498, 499; West and, 498, 498 (illus.); execution of revolutionaries in, 711–712; March Revolution in, 800–801; November Revolution in, 802; in Second World War, 858

Saints: relics of, 215; belief in, 285–287; women as, 287

Saladin (Egypt and Syria), 265

Salamis, battle at, 75

Salerno: medical faculty at, 300

Salian Franks, 240, 247

Salic Law, 244

Salinization: Soviet, 904, 933

Salk, Jonas, 912

Salons, 574 (illus.), 598–599, 598 (illus.), 640

Salt March: by Gandhi, 844 (illus.)

SALT Talks. *See* Strategic Arms Limitation Talks

Salvation, 410; in religion, 159, 160; in Jewish thought, 160; of humanity by Jesus Christ, 164; Augustine on, 189; Luther on, 409, 415–416, 417; Calvin on, 423

Salvian of Marseilles, 189, 195

Samarkand, 226

Samizdat (self-publishing): Soviet, 905

Samoa, 767; U.S. annexation of, 768

Samuel ibn Nagrela, 233

Sanbenitos (tunic), 452, 453 (illus.)

Sancho I (Navarre), 233

Sanhedrin, 162, 163

Sans-culottes: in French Revolution, 614, 614 (illus.), 616, 620, 625

Sansovino, Jacopo, 348

"Sans Souci" (palace), 600

Santa Maria (ship), 387

Santa Maria Maggiore (Rome), 177 (illus.)

São Paulo, 396

São Tomé, 545, 558

Saqqara: pyramids at, 24

Saramakas, 401

Sardinia: Rome and, 115; in First Coalition against France, 617; king of, 700

Sardis (Persian city), 74

Sargon (Akkad), 17; legend of, 18; empire of, 18 (map)

Sartre, Jean-Paul, 815, 909–910, 910 (illus.)

Sasanian dynasty (Iran), 151, 200, 201 (map), 202, 211

Sasson, Siegfried, 786

Satan. *See* Devil

Satanic Verses (Rushdie), 946–947

Satellite states (Soviet), 905–906; in 1970s and 1980s, 931. *See also* Eastern Europe; specific countries

Satellite television, 953

Satrapies: in Persia, 61

Satraps (Persian noblemen), 61

Satyagraha (India), 843–845, 844 (illus.)

Saudi Arabia, 948; England and, 809; after First World War, 843

Saul (Hebrews), 62

Savior. *See* Messiah

Savorgnan family (Italy), 352

Savorgnan lords, 446

Sawi Chemi Shanidar (settlement), 14

Saxons, 192; invading Britain, 195; language of, 196; Charlemagne and, 248

Saxony: dukes of, 259

Scandinavia: Vikings from, 253 (map), 254–255; bishoprics in, 260; conversion of polytheistic tribes from, 260–261; migrations in, 276; foreign workers in, 926

Scapegoats: minority groups as, 332

Scarlet fever, 402

Schabowski, Gunter, 923

Schembartlauf (Nuremberg), 457

Schiele, Egon, 754, 755, 757 (illus.)

Schiller, Friedrich von, 685

Schlieffen, Alfred von, 782 (map)

Schlieffen Plan, 781–783, 782 (map)

Schliemann, Heinrich, 45, 48 (illus.)

Schmalkaldic League, 420

Schmarcher, E. F., 930

Schoenberg, Arnold, 755, 757

Scholarship: by women, 103; from Ireland, 245; in Enlightenment, 587. *See also* Intellectual thought

Scholasticism, 299, 301; religion, science, and, 531

Schools: disappearance of, 189; monastic, 247, 288, 299; at Aachen, 251; in Italy, 279; cathedral, 299; of Brothers of the Common Life, 331; French Revolution and, 623, 627; social reforms and, 719; women workers in, 733; in France, 926; Latvian pollution and, 934. *See also* Education

Schroeder, Gerhard, 940

Schubert, Franz, 685

Schuman, Robert, 908

Schwartzkoppen, Maximilian von, 722

Schwenckfeld, Caspar, 428–429

Science, 105–106; Babylonian, 43, 52, 54; in Ionia, 83–84; in Roman Empire, 157–158; in Islamic world, 158; Arab traders and, 230; monasteries and, 246; in Renaissance, 358–359, 523–525; printing press and, 359; in France, 485–486; in late medieval period, 523; collapse of paradigms in, 525; Protestantism and, 525–526; intellectual developments outside, 525–527; coming of millennium and, 526; patronage and, 526–527; and religion, 529–531; preternatural and, 530; demonic magic and, 534; applied, 536; male control of women and, 538; Voltaire and, 589–592; popular books on, 599; industrialization and, 653; medicine, microbes, and, 744–745; evolution and, 745–747; physics and, 748–749; after First World War, 816–817; weapons from, 881; mass consumption and, 912–913. *See also* Scientific Revolution; Technology

Scientific academies, 526–527

Scientific method, 521; Christianity and, 758

Scientific rationalism, 682–683

Scientific Revolution, 512 (illus.), 513–538; Renaissance and, 358–359; forerunners of, 470; in astronomy, 514–517; in physics, 517–518; chemistry and, 518–519; in biology, 519; search for scientific knowledge in, 519–523; causes of, 523–527; intellectual effects of, 528–534; natural law and, 586; after First World War, 816–817

Scientific societies, 598

Scientific writing: in Rome, 157–158

Scipio Aemilianus, Publius Cornelius (Scipio the Younger), 118, 153

Scipio Africanus, Publius Cornelius (Scipio the Elder), 93, 117

Scorched-earth policy: in Boer War, 773

Sieyès, Emmanuel-Joseph, 610, 622
Siffin, battle at, 224–225
Sikhs, 894; in First World War, 791 (illus.)
Silesia, 495, 551, 552, 552 (map), 600, 850
Silk: trade in, 152, 278; demand for, 564
Silk Road, 152, 153 (map)
Silver: Viking use of, 254, 255 (illus.); trade in North Africa, 380; Price Revolution and, 449
Simon de Montfort, 292
Simons, Menno, 428
Simony, 281
Sin: in Middle Ages, 332–333; Luther on penance and, 415; Schwenckfeld on, 429; Calvinist treatment of, 451; Catholic treatment of, 451, 452–453, 453 (illus.)
Sinai peninsula, 899
Singapore, 859, 861 (illus.)
Singer, Isaac, 658
Single European Act (1985), 943
Sinn Fein (Ireland), 725
Sino-Japanese War, 771
Sino-Soviet split, 924–925
"Sin taxes," 556
Siraj-ud-Daulah (nawab of Bengal), 561–562
Sistine Chapel: Michelangelo and, 360, 437–438, 437 (illus.)
Six Books of a Commonweal (Bodin), 479
Six-Day War (1967), 899; results of, 900 (map); PLO after, 948
Skepticism: of Spinoza, 529; about demons and magic, 534; of Hume, 589
Sketch for a Historical Picture of the Progress of the Human Mind, A (Condorcet), 589
Skilled workers, 649, 728
Skin color: racism and, 565
Slánský, Rudolf, 902–903, 903 (illus.)
Slave labor: in death camps, 871–872; Soviet, 904
Slaves and slavery, 541; Nubian, 26; in Greece, 79, 80–81; freedom for, 81; Rome and, 113–114, 122, 123, 132, 145, 149, 154–155; manumission of, 155; in Germanic society, 243; on medieval farms, 275; in Americas, 377; plantation labor and, 382–383, 402; in Spanish America, 393; in colonies, 543, 545; historical, 557–558; abolition of, 559, 612; Atlantic culture and, 560; Haitian Revolution and, 568–569
Slave Ship, The (Turner), 559 (illus.)
Slave trade, 400–401, 554–557; in Roman Empire, 155; Portugal and, 393–396, 549; factory in, 400 (illus.); Equiano on, 541; in Atlantic region, 557–559; end of, 559
Slavic language, 209
Slavic liturgy, 209
Slavic peoples, 238; Celts and, 109–110; migration into Balkans, 207; Rus and, 209–210; conversion to Christianity, 217, 261–262; Russia and, 497, 706; Pan-Slav Congress (1848) and, 694; national unity for, 704–705; Ottomans and, 729
Sleeping sickness, 763, 766
Slovakia, 109; in EU, 944
Slovaks, 807, 906, 939
Slovenia, 876; in EU, 944
Slovenians, 779, 941; in Yugoslavia, 820
Slums, 662, 726 (illus.)
Sluys, Battle of, 323

Smallpox, 402; in Seven Years' War, 552
Smelting: Phoenician, 50
Smith, Adam, 587, 676; on human development, 589; on division of labor, 648, 649
Smog, 662
Smoking: in Russia, 497; by women, 825. See also Tobacco
Snake Goddess (Minoan), 44, 44 (illus.)
Social Contract, The (Rousseau), 594, 595, 611
Social Darwinism, 747–748; new imperialism and, 759, 761
Social democracy, 838
Social Democratic Party (SPD, Germany), 719, 726–727, 783, 821, 907, 924, 940; First World War and, 795, 802, 803
Social Democratic Party (Sweden), 838
Social Democrats, 907
Socialist clubs (France), 693
Socialist parties, 727; in France, 839. See also Socialists and socialism; specific parties
Socialist Realism, 904; in Soviet Union, 836 (illus.), 837
Socialists and socialism, 679–681, 907; Utopian, 679; radical, 679–681; French Revolution of 1848 and, 692–693; revolutionary, 711; in Russia, 721; working-class, 726–728; culture of, 727; Christianity and, 758; imperialism and, 761; First World War and, 783; Bolshevik model of, 805; Mussolini on, 828. See also specific parties
Social relations: First World War and, 796
Social sciences: in Enlightenment, 587; Christianity and, 758
Social thought: positivism and, 749
Social War (Rome), 124
Social welfare: in England, 719; in Germany, 719, 831; in Italy, 719, 832; women workers and, 733; after First World War, 825; in France, 839; Soviet, 905; New Conservatism and, 928
Society: hierarchy in, 5, 560; civilization and, 12–13; in European New Stone Age, 28–29; Babylonian, 43; in Israelite kingdoms, 63–64; in Classical Greece, 79–82; Hellenistic, 99, 100–103; Hallstatt, 109; in Roman Republic, 113–114, 119–123; in Roman Empire, 174–175; Byzantine, 213–216; Germanic, 242–244; Scandinavian (Viking), 254; medieval, 255–258, 275–276; agricultural revolution and, 275; urban, 279–280; in Later Middle Ages, 318–321; guilds in, 319–320; in Venice, 348; Aztec, 384–385; Inca, 385–386; after Reformation, 444; class structure in, 575–576; natural law and, 587; Voltaire on, 592; Rousseau on, 594; French Revolution and, 611, 639; under French Directorate, 621; industrialization and, 659–669; conservatism in, 678; socialism and, 679; mass, 710 (illus.); unrest in, 716–717; reforms of, 718; radicalism and, 729; Jews in, 732; evolution of, 747; First World War and, 784–785; after First World War, 814–817; Soviet, 835–836, 905, 937; after Second World War, 880, 911–912; affluence in, 913–914; economic crisis of 1970s and, 926–927; in 1980s, 927–930. See also Classes; specific groups

Society of Friends. See Quakers
Society of Jesus. See Jesuits
Society of United Irishmen, 569
Socinians, 429
Socinus, Faustus, 429
Sociology: Durkheim and, 758
Socrates, 80, 85, 87 (illus.), 164; trial and execution of, 86–87
Sodom: sin in, 291
Soil: crops and, 274–275; improvement of, 652
Soil erosion: Soviet, 904
Sokoto caliphate, West Africa, 764 (map)
Solar system, 513
Soldiers: in Sparta, 73; Greek, 78; in Rome, 113–114; Byzantine, 218–219; in Hundred Years' War, 328; infantry, 480; in First World War, 777, 788, 790, 801; in trenches, 786, 786 (illus.); shell shock and, 798; Soviet in Second World War, 858; GIs in Britain, 864, 864 (illus.)
Solidarity movement, 931–933, 933 (illus.), 936
Solidus (Roman coin), 175
Solomon (Hebrews), 63–64
Solon (Athens), 74
Solzhenitsyn, Alexander, 904
Somalia: as Punt, 24 (map), 26; Greek trade with, 107
Somme, Battle of the, 776 (illus.), 777, 788
Somnium (Lunar Astronomy) (Kepler), 535
"Song of Brother Sun, The" (Francis of Assisi), 288
Song of Roland, The, 266
"Son of a god" (Augustus), 136
Sophists, 85
Sophocles, 83
Sorbonne (Paris), 412
Sorel, Georges, 728
Soul: Plato on, 182; Neoplatonists on, 189–190
South (global), 881, 886; wealth gap and, 955, 956
South (U.S.): slavery in, 543
South Africa, 773 (map), 895; Boer War in, 772–773; First World War and, 791, 792 (map). See also Africa
South America, 388, 543; Magellan and, 388; Spain and, 393; Portugal and, 548; immigration to, 716; economic competition in, 926
South Asia: English control of, 544
Southeast Asia: British influence in, 544; European conquests in, 561; superpowers in, 899
Southern Europe: marriage in, 451
South Korea, 896–897; economic collapse in, 954. See also Korean War
South Pacific region: England and, 544; Japanese conquests in, 859. See also Pacific Ocean region
South Vietnam, 899
Southwest Africa: resistance in, 766
Southwest Asia: Western civilization and, 5, 14; civilizations in, 15–20; Hammurabi's Code and, 19–20, 22–23; Egypt and, 26, 37. See also Middle East
Sovereignty: principle of, 294; in Spain, 686; of Ottoman Empire, 843
Soviet(s): defined, 800; in Petrograd, 800, 801, 802
Soviet-Afghan War: Islamists and, 948–949

160°W 140°W 120°W 100°W 80°W 60°W 40°W 20°W

80°N

Arctic Cir

GREENLAND
(KALAALLIT NUNAAT)
(Den.)

ICELAND

ALASKA
(U.S.)

60°N

CANADA

UNIT
KINGD

IRELAND

FRA

40°N

UNITED STATES

AZORES (Port.)

ATLANTIC
OCEAN

PORTUGAL

SI

MOROC

Tropic of Cancer

HAWAII (U.S.)

CANARY IS. (Sp.)

WESTERN SAHARA
(Mor.)

20°N

MEXICO

BAHAMAS
DOMINICAN
REPUBLIC
HAITI
PUERTO RICO (U.S.)
ST. KITTS AND NEVIS
ANTIGUA AND BARBUDA
DOMINICA
ST. VINCENT AND THE GRENADINES
BARBADOS
GRENADA
TRINIDAD AND TOBAGO
GUYANA
SURINAME
FRENCH GUIANA (Fr.)

CUBA
JAMAICA
BELIZE
GUADELOUPE (Fr.)
MARTINIQUE (Fr.)
ST. LUCIA

GUATEMALA
HONDURAS
EL SALVADOR
NICARAGUA

COSTA RICA

PANAMA

VENEZUELA

COLOMBIA

MAURITANIA

CAPE
VERDE

SENEGAL
THE GAMBIA
GUINEA-BISSAU
GUINEA
SIERRA LEONE
LIBERIA
CÔTE D'IVOIRE

MA

PACIFIC OCEAN

0° Equator

GALÁPAGOS IS.
(Ec.)

ECUADOR

PERU

BRAZIL

BURKINA FAS
GHAN

WESTERN
SAMOA
AMERICAN
SAMOA (U.S.)

TONGA

FRENCH
POLYNESIA (Fr.)

BOLIVIA

20°S

Tropic of Capricorn

PARAGUAY

CHILE

ATLANTIC
OCEAN

URUGUAY

0   1,500   3,000 Miles

0   1,500   3,000 Kilometers

ARGENTINA

40°S

**Contemporary
Political Map
of the World**

FALKLAND IS. (U.K.)

60°S

Antarctic Circle

80°S